D1757721

The SCIENCE of BIOLOGY

Fifth Edition

The SCIENCE of BIOLOGY

Paul B. Weisz and Richard N. Keogh

Professor of Biology
Brown University

Professor of Biology
Rhode Island College

McGraw-Hill Book Company
New York St. Louis San Francisco Auckland Bogotá
Hamburg Johannesburg London Madrid Mexico Montreal
New Delhi Panama Paris São Paulo Singapore Sydney
Tokyo Toronto

THE SCIENCE OF BIOLOGY

1234567890 KPKP 898765432

ISBN 0-07-069145-2

See Illustration Credits not already found in legends on pages 977–982.
Copyrights included on this page by reference.

This book was set in Primer by York Graphic Services, Inc.
The editors were Jay Ricci, Anne T. Vinnicombe, and James W. Bradley;
the designer was Merrill Haber;
the production supervisor was Dominick Petrellese.
New drawings were done by J & R Services, Inc.
Kingsport Press, Inc., was printer and binder.

Cover Photograph
Water lily pads trail along the surface of the Concord River.
(*Photograph by Farrell Grehan.*)

Library of Congress Cataloging in Publication Data

Weisz, Paul B., date
The science of biology.

Includes bibliographies and index.
1. Biology. I. Keogh, Richard N. II. Title.
QH308.2.W45 1982 574 81-14254
ISBN 0-07-069145-2 AACR2

Contents

PART 3 The Operations of Life: Metabolism

Preface

Scientific knowledge continues to accumulate in exponential fashion. This in part explains the increased scope of this fifth edition of *The Science of Biology*, which includes several new or expanded topics. Among these are the biology of aging, the regulation of eukaryotic gene expression, photosynthetic pathways in C_4 plants, the structure and function of biological membranes, hormonal control in plants, immunobiology, population dynamics, sociobiology, and the evolution of hominids.

Nevertheless, the proliferation of biological knowledge is only one aspect of the increased scope of this edition. A second concerns the equally rapid increase in both the actual and potential uses of this knowledge. A glance at the table of contents reveals that this book not only provides an up-to-date integration of basic biological principles but also documents numerous applications of these principles to technological, medical, and human social concerns. As a result, such topics as the impact of people on the organization of living systems, cancer, food production, contraceptive physiology, recombinant DNA technology, drug-induced behavior modification, cardiovascular disease, and agricultural uses of plant hormones are discussed far more extensively than in previous editions.

Such presentations punctuate both the main body of the text and several of the Biology Highlight essays, another innovation in this edition. For example, the Highlight in Chapter 12 illustrates the application of fermentation to the commercial production of beer and wine; the Highlight in Chapter 11 applies principles of ecology and soil formation to human malnutrition. However, the Biology Highlights do more than illustrate applications of biological principles. They also provide insights into the history, procedures, and personalities of the science. The Highlight in Chapter 27, for example, focuses on an experimental approach that paved the way for a new subdiscipline of biology. The experiment that revealed the causative agent of one of this century's most publicized epidemics is described in the Highlight in Chapter 30. Several other examples of experimental methodology have been incorporated throughout other sections of the book.

This new emphasis on the procedures and applications of the science has in no way replaced the "principles approach" to biology that has been a hallmark of earlier editions. The structural framework of this edition continues to be based on fundamental interrelations between biological principles. Discussions of these principles are not aimed at simple establishment of data. Instead the discussions seek to explain the foundations and consequences of the principles themselves. Such presentations are based on the premise that comprehension emerges not through rote memorization but through conceptual analysis and synthesis. By showing how applications of science stem from basic principles, this edition extends the holistic approach to biological science. It shows how principles of biology are interrelated not only with themselves but also with human concerns of all kinds.

The book is again divided into seven parts. Following the introductory chapters on the scientific and biological study of living systems, Part 2 illustrates the organizational structure of the living world. These chapters represent a step-by-step examination of all levels of organization from the molecule to the biosphere. The principles of chemistry and biochemistry have not been deemphasized, but the presentation of molecular concepts in Chapters 3 and 4 has been simplified. Further, the basic organizational patterns of plants and animals, presented in two different parts of previous editions, are now presented wholly in Part 2. Discussion of ecological concepts and their relations to current environmental problems has undergone considerable expansion. These topics, previously introduced in two chapters, are now presented in the final three chapters of Part 2.

Parts 3 to 6 form a unit concerned mainly with the functional, operational properties of living matter. They serve to show how the structural components of the living world are maintained. Part 3 concentrates on metabolism, and Part 4 on steady-state controls, the processes by which the individual organism is maintained. Parts 5 and 6 deal with reproduction and adaptation, the processes by which life is perpetuated.

All chapters in Parts 3 to 6 have undergone substantial revision, and in a few instances the topic sequence differs from that in the fourth edition. Thus, the discussion of hormones now appears in two chapters of Part 4, one devoted to plants and the other to animals. A new chapter on human reproduction and another on aging and death have been added to Part 5. A discussion of methods by which the genetic constitution of organisms can be manipulated and controlled has been incorporated into a new chapter in Part 6.

Part 7 concentrates on the specific organisms that embody and exhibit the organizational hierarchy of life. These chapters, which composed Part 3 of earlier editions, have been reorganized, moved to the end of the book, and tightly integrated with the concepts of evolution and adaptation presented in Part 6. As a result, Part 7 introduces both the adaptive characteristics and probable evolutionary linkages of all major groups of organisms.

A corresponding degree of change characterizes the nontextual components. The most significant change is the incorporation of performance-based learning objectives at the beginning of each chapter. These provide valuable information about the organization of topics within each chapter and, more important, detail exactly what learning accomplishments are expected of the student once the chapter has been read. Essay-type review questions have been retained at the end of each chapter, and the reader is encouraged to use both these and the corresponding learning objectives as mutually reinforcing instructional tools. The learning objectives are designed to help students master individual concepts and recognize the components of basic principles. Many of the review questions are more general and force the reader to integrate basic principles into larger conceptual wholes.

A large number of new diagrams and photographs have been included, and this revision is even more heavily illustrated than the fourth edition. In addition, many diagrams have been redesigned and redrawn. Four full-color photo essays augment the numerous black-and-white photographs. Moreover, the collateral readings have been brought up to date, and each title of the readings is accompanied by a brief description of the contents. There are also available for supplementary use with the new edition a Study Guide, a Laboratory Manual, and an Instructor's Manual.

We would like to thank those colleagues who reviewed all or parts of this revision, at various stages of preparation, for their criticisms and suggestions: Albert A. Benedict, University of Hawaii, Honolulu; Miriam F. Bennett, Colby College; S. Robert Bradley, Iowa State University; Robert M. Brenner, Oregon Regional Primate Research Center; Edmund D. Brodie, Jr., Adelphi University; Stephen C. Bromley, Michigan State University; Barbara Burkett, Gardner Webb College; Peggy Jo Korty Dobry, The Upjohn Company, Michigan; Warren D. Dolphin, Iowa State College; Charles V. Foltz, Rhode Island College; Sister Colman Gayer, Ursuline College; Elizabeth Godrick, Boston University; Jonathan J. Goldthwaite, Boston College; Joseph L. Hindman, Washington State University; Martin D. Hollingsworth, Tallahasse Community College; Russell L. Jones, University of California, Berkeley; Georgia E. Lesh-Laurie, Cleveland State University; Dorothy S. Luciano; James P. Mack, Monmouth College; Joseph E. McDade, Center for Disease Control, Atlanta; John E. Niederhuber, University of Michigan Medical Center; Barbara M. Reed, Oregon State University; David Smith, San Antonio College; B. L. Strehler, University of Southern California; Ralph E. Thorson, University of Notre Dame; and Warren H. Wagner, Jr., University of Michigan.

Paul B. Weisz
Richard N. Keogh

The SCIENCE *of* BIOLOGY

Part 1
The Study of Life

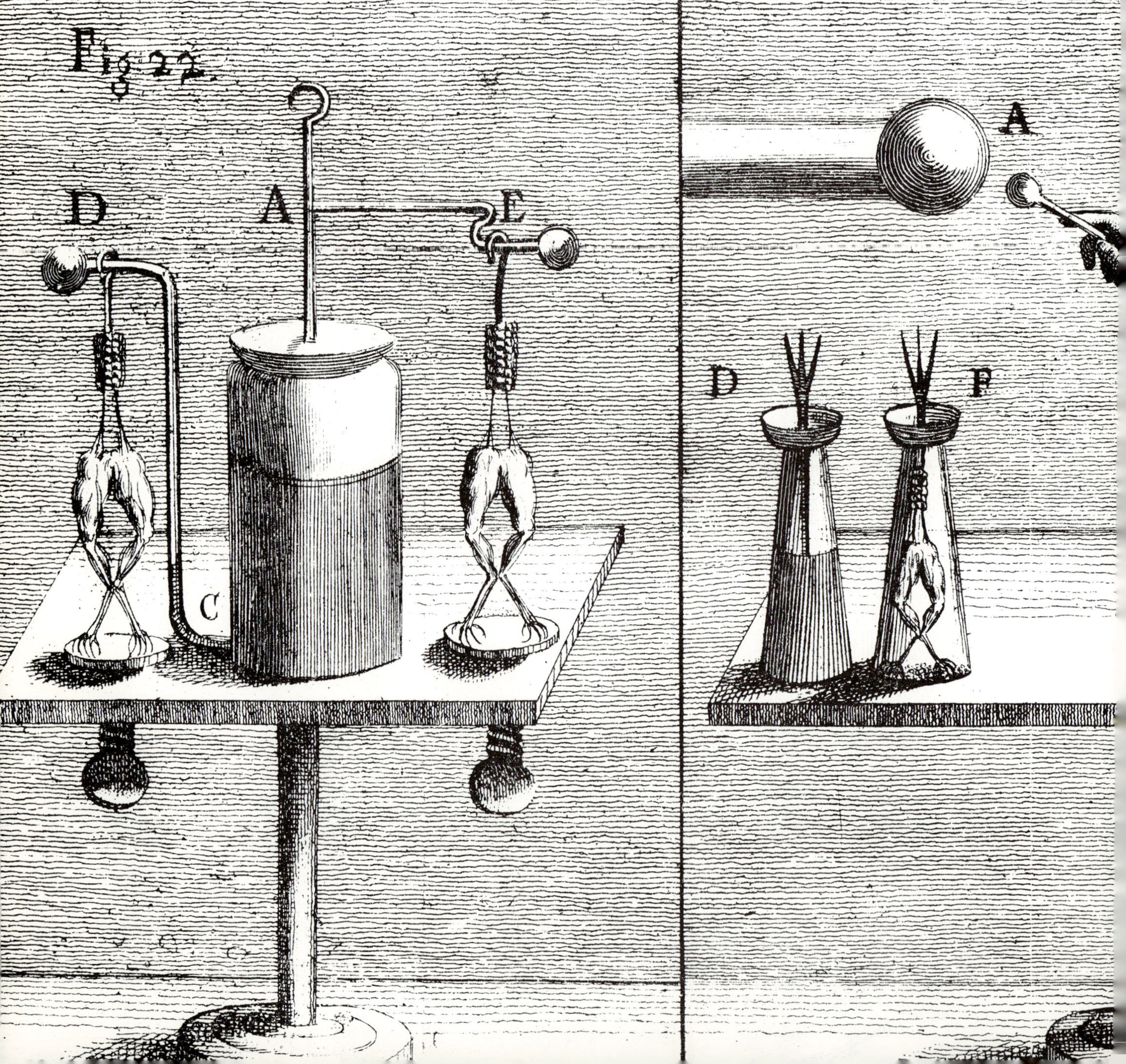

The investigation of living things is the concern of the science of biology. Therefore, a study of biology may begin with two questions. First, what is science? Second, what do we mean by "living?" Answers to these questions are outlined in the chapters of this first part.

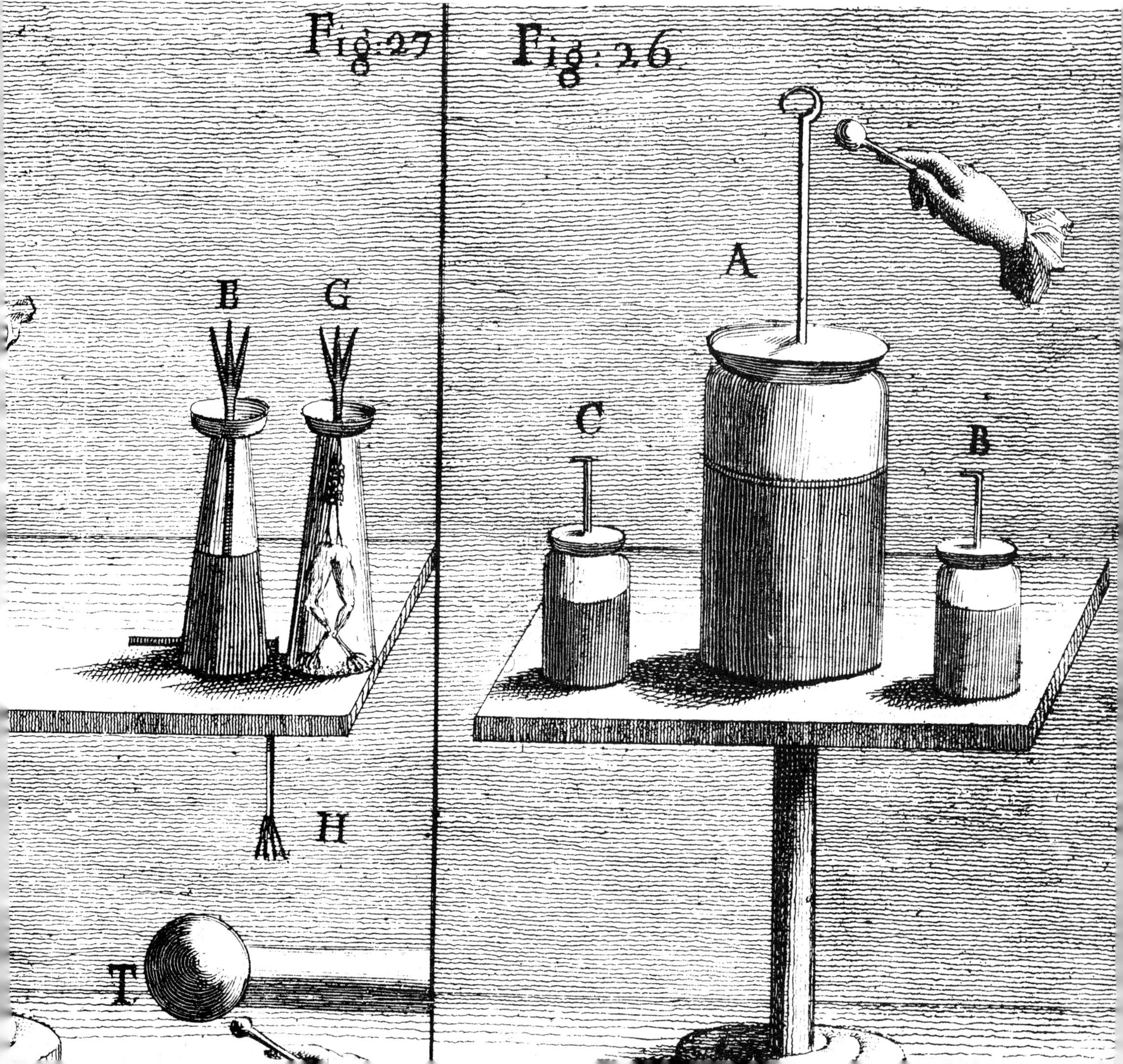

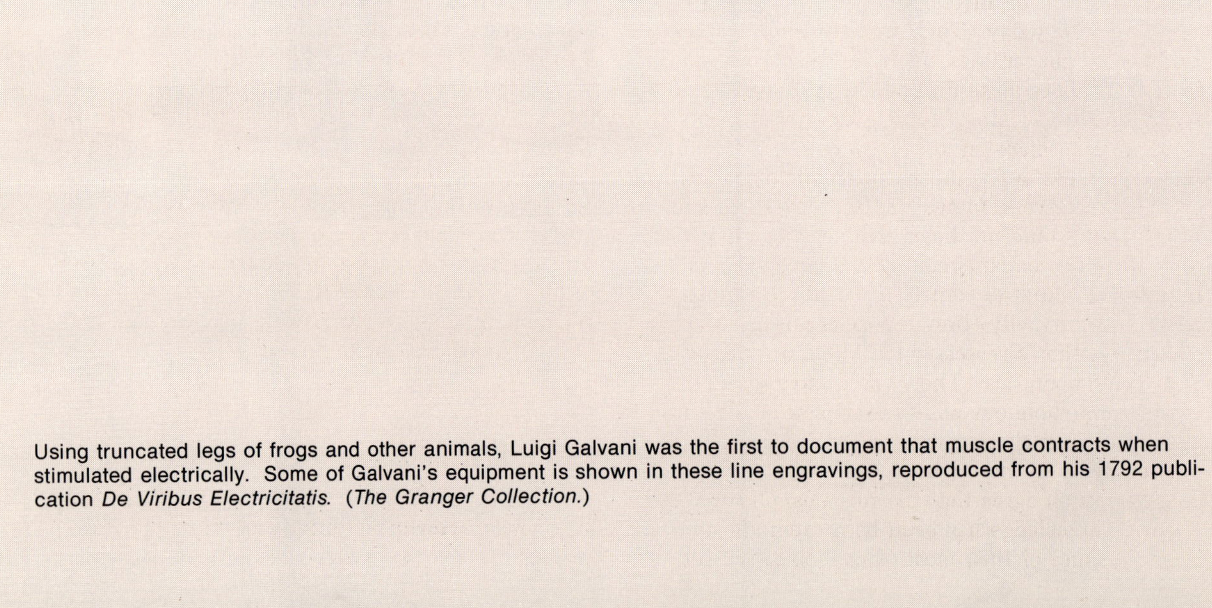

Using truncated legs of frogs and other animals, Luigi Galvani was the first to document that muscle contracts when stimulated electrically. Some of Galvani's equipment is shown in these line engravings, reproduced from his 1792 publication *De Viribus Electricitatis.* (*The Granger Collection.*)

Chapter 1 The Scientific Background

Learning Objectives

After reading this chapter you should be able to:

1. Identify the roles played by supernatural rituals, early Greek philosophers, and Galileo in the historical development of modern science; list at least one difference between modern scientific methodology and the *philosophia* of early Greek intellectuals.
2. Differentiate between vitalism and mechanism, and specify how causalism and teleology are related to these two contrasting systems of thought.
3. Define and state at least one relationship between each of the following subprocesses of scientific methodology:
   - **a.** observation
   - **b.** definition of a problem
   - **c.** hypothesis
   - **d.** experiment
   - **e.** experimental results
4. Differentiate between deductive and inductive logic; state an example of these contrasting kinds of logic and illustrate how they can be used to develop hypotheses and design experiments.
5. Distinguish between hypothesis, theory, and scientific law; differentiate between generalizing and explanatory hypotheses.
6. Differentiate between basic and applied research, and list at least one example of each; write a paragraph illustrating how pure and applied research are interdependent.
7. List at least:
   - **a.** one reason why science cannot be considered antireligious
   - **b.** three limitations of science
   - **c.** one reason why science cannot decide moral issues
8. Evaluate the roles of scientists and nonscientists in determining how scientific knowledge shall be discovered and used.

Ninety per cent of all scientists who have ever lived are alive today. Their accomplishments have made our daily routines, attitudes, perspectives, fears, and hopes quite different from those of our recent ancestors. Most of our great-grandparents would look in disbelief at our computerized credit cards, journeys to the moon, automatic dishwashers, polluted rivers, fouled air, and developed suburbs. They would not have dreamed that their immediate descendants could have developed so rapidly the ability to control the birth of a human being or to virtually eliminate tuberculosis, polio, and many other diseases which killed or crippled their contemporaries. They would have found equally incredible our ability to deplete world supplies of fossil fuels so quickly or to destroy natural environments so thoroughly.

We can all agree that the recent application of scientific knowledge has been both rapid and uneven. Because of this, most of us look to the future with a mixed sense of hope and fear. Will future applications of science lead to utopia or Aldous Huxley's "Brave New World"?

Science will surely continue to have a major impact on our lives. It is useless to think that inhumane applications of science can be avoided simply by doing away with science. People will continue to explore and apply knowledge in spite of risks. Our trademark is our curious nature. To quote Philip Handler, a well-known American scientist, "Man is doomed to live with his brain and its achievements. That is both his glory and his curse, and there can be no escape."

HISTORY AND PHILOSOPHY OF SCIENCE

We begin our study of science by asking: What is science? How did it originate? How did it develop?

Fig. 1.1 Rites and rituals. Most human societies, even so-called civilized ones, are laden with a variety of practices aimed at quelling malevolent spirits. In some cultures, for example, the wearing of a beaded necklace is considered vital to future good fortune.

You may be surprised to learn that the origin of science lies in the supernatural. Several thousand years ago people lacked the knowledge necessary to explain the universe and its workings in "scientific" terms. To early man, the forces of nature were both powerful and inexplainable. Yet their origin and control must exist somewhere, perhaps in some being or beings more powerful than man himself. Undoubtedly, such reasoning led to the establishment of primitive religions and the belief that the world and all happenings on it were under the controlling influence of spirits and gods.

Many primitive cultures believed that events beneficial to human welfare were controlled by benevolent spirits. Other spirits, such as those bringing sickness and death, were evil and malicious. Still others appeared exceedingly unpredictable, friendly one moment and hostile the next. The impulsive character of these beings explained why a gentle rain might eventually develop into a disastrous flood. Such is the origin of myths.

Early man never held out hope of understanding such gods. These people did attempt, however, to appease and influence them through creation of various rites and rituals (Fig. 1.1). For instance, the earliest farmers believed that the phenomenon of rainfall was similar to a sexual act; sex and rainfall were both associated with fertilization, reproduction, and growth. Indeed, many early cultures believed that sex and rainfall were under the control of identical or similar gods. Farmers thereby could not only "explain" the phenomenon of rainfall but also had "discovered" the god with the appropriate rite. Thus, in many cultures, attempts to bring rain were accompanied by rituals involving intense sexual activity.

On many occasions the ritual appeared to succeed. Rains often did come a few days following the ritual. Such results reinforced the idea that sex and rainfall were indeed related and that unseen spirits could be influenced. Rituals, however, did not produce desired results in all cases. In time, more perceptive individuals realized that rituals played no role in controlling the forces of nature. This was a momentous discovery and a scientific one.

The first to make and record this discovery were the ancient Greek philosophers. Most of these men became convinced that the universe was a great machine governed by inflexible laws. They began the exciting intellectual exercise of attempting to discover the nature of those laws. They established an orderly system of logic essential to anyone trying to determine underlying laws of nature from observed data.

The rules of this system, or *philosophia* ("philosophy") as it came to be called, were threefold: observation, categorizing, and deduction. First, the "philosopher" must collect observations about some aspect of nature. For example, a stone sinks in water, wood floats, an iron bar sinks, a drop of salad oil floats, a drop of mercury sinks. Next, the observations must be organized in an ordered fashion. All objects that sink in water are listed in a column; all objects that float are placed in an adjacent column. Finally, an underlying principle of nature is obtained by examining relationships between the ordered items. Thus, heavy objects sink in water and light objects float.

Such sets of "philosophical rules" constitute what later came to be called *inductive* and *deductive logic.* The significance of the establishment of these contrasting kinds of logic cannot be overstated. As you will find later in this chapter, inductive logic is used in formulating most scientific theories. Deductive logic provides the basis for the design of virtually all experiments in modern science.

Mechanism versus Vitalism

The second major Greek contribution to what was to become science was the philosophy of *mechanism,* which officially marks the initial divergence of "science" from its supernatural heritage. In the mechanistic view of nature, the universe is governed by a set of natural laws, namely, the laws of physics and chemistry. The mechanistic philosophy holds that if all physical and chemical events in the universe can be accounted for, no other events will remain. Therefore, life, too, must be a result of physical and chemical processes *only*, and the course of life must be determined automatically by the physical and chemical occurrences within living matter.

This mechanistic philosophy stands in opposition to *vitalism,* which maintains that the universe, and particularly its living components, are controlled by supernatural powers. Such powers are held to guide the behavior of atoms, planets, stars, living things, and indeed all components of the universe. Most religious philosophies are inherently vitalistic.

Clearly, these differences between vitalism and mechanism point up a conceptual conflict between religion and science. However, this conflict is not necessarily irreconcilable. To bridge the conceptual gap, one might ask how the natural laws of the universe came into being to begin with. A possible answer is that they were created by God. On this view, it could be argued that the universe ran vitalistically up to the time that natural laws were created and mechanistically thereafter. The mechanist would then have to admit the existence of a supernatural Creator at the beginning of time (even though he has no *scientific* basis for either affirming or denying this; mechanism cannot, by definition, tell anything about a time at which natural laws might not have been in operation). Correspondingly, the vitalist would have to admit that, so long as the natural laws continue to operate without change, supernatural control would not be demonstrable.

Thus it is not necessarily illogical to accept both scientific and religious philosophies at the same time. However, it is decidedly illogical to try to use religious ideas as explanations of scientific problems or scientific ideas as explanations of religious problems.

Yet many people, some scientists included, still find it exceedingly difficult to keep vitalism out of science. Biological events, undoubtedly the most complex of all known events in the universe, have been particularly subject to attempts at vitalistic interpretation.

Teleology versus Causalism

Even a casual observer must be impressed by the apparent nonrandomness of natural events. Every part of nature seems to follow a plan, and there is a definite directedness to any given process. In living processes, for example, developing eggs behave *as if* they knew exactly what the plan of the adult is to be. A chicken soon produces two wings and two legs, *as if* it knew that these appendages were to be part of the adult. All known natural processes, living or otherwise, similarly start at given beginnings and proceed to particular endpoints. This observation poses a philosophical problem: How is a starting condition directed toward a specific terminal condition? How does a starting point appear to "know" what the endpoint is to be?

Such questions have to do with a detailed aspect of the more general problem of the controlling forces of the universe. We should expect, therefore, that two sets of answers would be available, one vitalistic and the other mechanistic. This is the case. According to vitalistic doctrines, natural events *appear* to be planned because they actually are planned. A supernatural "divine plan" is held to fix the fate of every part of the universe, and all events in nature, past, present, and future, are programmed in this plan. All nature is therefore directed toward a preordained goal, the fulfillment of the divine plan. As a consequence, nothing happens by chance but everything happens on purpose.

Being a vitalistic, experimentally untestable concept, the notion of purpose in natural events has no place in science. Does the universe exist for a purpose? Do people live for a purpose? Science is not designed to tackle such questions. Moreover, if you already hold certain beliefs in these areas, you cannot expect science either to prove or to disprove them for you.

Yet many arguments have been attempted to show purpose from science. For example, it has been maintained by some that the whole purpose of the evolution of living things was to produce people—the predetermined goal from the very beginning. This conceit implied not only that people are the finest product of creation but also that nothing could ever come after human beings, for we are supposed to be the last word in living magnificence. As a matter of record, people are sometimes plagued by parasites that cannot live anywhere except inside human beings. And it is clear that you cannot have a person-requiring parasite before you have a person.

The form of argumentation that has recourse to purposes and supernatural planning is generally called *teleology.* In one system of teleology, the preordained plan exists outside natural objects, in an external Deity, for example. In another system, the plan resides within objects themselves. According to this view, a starting condition of an event proceeds toward a particular end condition because the starting object has built into it supernatural foreknowledge of the end condition. For example, an egg develops toward the goal of the adult because the egg is endowed with information about the precise nature of the adult state. Clearly, this and all other forms of teleology "explain" an end state by simply asserting it to be already mapped out at the beginning. And in thereby putting the future in the past, the effect before the cause, teleology negates time.

The scientifically useful alternative to teleology is *causalism,* a form of thought based on mechanistic philosophy. Causalism denies foreknowledge of terminal states, preordination, purposes, goals, and fixed fates. It holds instead that natural events take place stepwise, each one conditioned by, and dependent on, earlier ones. Events occur only as previous events *permit* them to occur, not as preordained goals or purposes make them occur. End states are consequences, not foregone conclusions, of beginning states. A headless earthworm regenerates a new head because conditions in the headless worm are such that only a head—*one* head—can develop. It becomes the task of the biologist to find out what these conditions are and to see if, by changing the conditions, two heads or another tail could be produced. Because scientists actually can obtain different end states by changing the conditions of initial states, the idea of predetermined goals loses all validity in scientific thought.

Care must therefore be taken in scientific endeavors not to fall unwittingly into the teleological trap. Consider often-heard statements such as: "the *purpose* of the heart is to pump blood"; "the ancestors of birds evolved wings *so that* they could fly"; "eggs have yolk *in order to* provide food for development." The last statement, for example, implies that eggs can "foresee" that food will be required in development and they therefore store up some. In effect, eggs are given human mentality. Teleologists are always anthropocentric, that is, they imply that the natural events they discuss are governed by minds like theirs. In making biological statements some of the teleological implications can be avoided by replacing every "purpose" with "function," every "so that" or "in order to" with "and."

Clearly then, science in its present state of development must operate within carefully specified, self-imposed limits. The basic philosophic attitude must be mechanistic and causalistic, and we note that the results obtained through science are inherently without truth, without value, and without purpose. But it is precisely because science is limited in this fashion that it advances. Truth is as subjective as ever, values change with time and place, and purposes basically express little more than our desire to make the universe behave according to our own very primitive understanding. It has therefore proved difficult to build a knowledge of nature on the shifting foundations of values and truths or on the dogma of purpose. What little of nature we really know and are likely to know in the foreseeable future stands on the bedrock of science.

METHODS OF SCIENCE

Although many roots of modern science can be traced to the early Greeks, their "natural philosophy" was marred by one highly significant defect: they regarded experimental testing of their conclusions as unnecessary. To a Greek philosopher, arrival at "absolute truths" through deductive reasoning was the height of intellectual excellence. It was absurd and degrading to suggest that conclusions resulting from such a perfect system of logic required confirmation through direct testing.

Indeed, many of their original conclusions about the operations of the universe are consistent with those derived through more recent experimental testing. There is no doubt that Aristotle and many of his colleagues were extraordinarily gifted in their use of deductive logic. But use of deductive logic is not infallible. As you will note presently, some of Aristotle's absolute truths later were found to be neither absolute nor valid.

Natural philosophy became less popular during the rise of the Roman Empire, and following the collapse of Roman rule and the rise of Christianity, moral philosophy, based on vitalistic arguments, was the chief intellectual pursuit. Natural philosophy was virtually forgotten until the beginning of the Renaissance in the fourteenth century.

At that time, the works of Aristotle, Plato, and other Greek philosophers were "rediscovered." At first, experimental testing of absolute truths was as unfashionable as it had been during Aristotle's time, but experimentation gradually became philosophically respectable. The experimental foundation of modern science, however, was not fully established until the mid-seventeenth century.

Primarily it was Galileo, who delivered the death blow to the ancient Greek practice of establishing conclusions without experimental evidence (Fig. 1.2). For example, Galileo provided a direct test of Aristotle's idea that objects would fall at a rate directly proportional to their weight, an "absolute truth" that had gone unchallenged for nearly 2000 years. Galileo is reported to have climbed to the top of the leaning tower of Pisa and dropped two balls of unequal weight. Aristotelian science died the instant the two balls struck the ground simultaneously.

In view of the significance of this result, it is ironic that Galileo probably never actually performed the experiment as reported. It was so typical of his dramatic exploits, however, that this legend has survived for centuries. Undoubtedly, Galileo conducted equally valid experiments disproving Aristotle's theory by rolling balls down inclined planes. From Galileo's day to the present time, everything that is properly called science has been based on experiments designed in accordance with scientific methods.

Modern scientists often solve problems and make discoveries through use of a sequence of interrelated steps outlined below. Such steps sometimes are erroneously termed *the* scientific method, but it soon will become apparent that scientists do not always follow the order of steps listed, nor are all of these steps always included in the solution of every problem. There is no single, uniform, or absolute scientific method, and no research scientist follows a formalized ritual in performing experiments. Indeed, there is wide disagreement among scientists about the nature of scientific methodology. Nevertheless, *observations* of natural phenomena often set in motion a series of subsequent mental and physical activities among scientists that eventually lead to the uncovering of new facts and the refining of old principles.

Fig. 1.2 Galileo. The "father" of modern science. (*Courtesy of Yeshiva University.*)

Observation, Definition of a Problem

Observation immediately puts a boundary around the scientific domain; something that cannot be observed cannot be investigated by science.

Everybody observes, with eyes, ears, touch, and all other senses, and therefore everyone has the potential to be a scientist. It is important to observe correctly, however. Unsuspected bias can seriously impede good observation. People often see only what they *want* to see or what they think they *ought* to see. It is extremely hard to rid oneself of such unconscious prejudice and to see just what is actually there, no more and no less. Past experience, "common knowledge," and often teachers can be subtle obstacles to correct observation, and even experienced scientists may not always avoid them. That is why a scientific observation is not fully accepted until several scientists have repeated it independently and have reported the same thing. That is also a major reason why one-time, unrepeatable events generally cannot be investigated scientifically.

After an observation has been made, a second usual step of scientific procedure is to define a *problem;* one asks a question about the observation. Again, most people already possess the basic skills to define problems. Having a curious and inquisitive nature is really the most important element for this step. If you have wondered why leaves turn color in fall, or why sap flows in trees, or how homing pigeons navigate, you are implicitly asking a question about a natural process.

Postulating a Hypothesis

Once a proper question has been asked, the common third step of scientific methodology usually involves the seemingly quite unscientific procedure of guessing what the answer to the question might conceivably be. Scientists refer to this as postulating a *hypothesis.* To have scientific value, hypotheses must be both logical and testable. It must be possible to evaluate the validity of a hypothesis; otherwise it is impossible to determine whether a proposed explanation is right or wrong.

Scientists generally use *inductive logic* in the formulation of hypotheses. Inductive logic involves coming to a general premise on the basis of many individual observations. For example, a person might notice that water in a nearby stream flows downhill. The person might then observe that water in a sink, in a river, and in a drainpipe also flows downhill. From these several observations, the person might use inductive logic to conclude that water always flows downhill. Knowingly or unknowingly, this person has established a testable hypothesis: "Water always flows downhill."

A further example will illustrate how inductive reasoning can be used to establish hypotheses that relate to biological processes. Consider the phenomenon of seasonal changes in coat coloration of snowshoe hares, animals found in Canada and the northern United States (Fig. 1.3). The fur of these animals appears white in winter and brown in summer. This trait provides considerable survival potential, for their coats blend with the background coloration of the environment at any season. This observation has been made repeatedly by trappers, hunters, and others living in the northern latitudes, and many of these people undoubtedly have marveled as snowshoe hares change coat color in concert with the changing seasons.

A

B

Fig. 1.3 Snowshoe hares. (A) The winter coat of snowshoe hares is white, effectively camouflaging the animals against a snowy background. (B) In spring, the white coat is shed and replaced by a brown coat. (*Courtesy of Leonard Lee Rue III.*)

An obvious question about this phenomenon arises in the mind of an inquisitive observer: What is responsible for the seasonal change in coat color among snowshoe hares? There are several possible answers to this question. We might note that steadily decreasing temperatures in fall and increasing temperatures in spring are responsible for many environmental changes. Ice forms as winter approaches, and it melts in spring. The ground freezes in winter, thaws in spring. Using inductive reasoning, we might hypothesize that seasonal changes in temperature are also responsible for observed changes in the coat color of snowshoe hares.

The tentative conclusions about the flow of water and coat-coloration changes in snowshoe hares are examples of the two kinds of hypotheses usually formulated by scientists. The first, called *generalizing hypotheses,* simply summarize a group of specific observations and permit logical, summary conclusions to be tested. The conclusion "water always flows downhill" is a generalizing hypothesis. The second kind of hypothesis, *explanatory hypotheses,* generally have greater scientific importance. They do more than generalize from a group of similar observations. Explanatory hypotheses are tentative explanations of *causes* of natural phenomena. The suggestion that "changes in temperature trigger seasonal coat-color changes in snowshoe hares" can be categorized as an explanatory hypothesis.

As scientists, we have no way of knowing whether our hypotheses are correct or incorrect. A given question can have thousands of logical answers but often only a single right one. Thus, chances are excellent that a random guess will be wrong. To distinguish between wrong hypotheses and right ones, we must establish *tests* of individual hypotheses. Testing hypotheses often is the most tedious part of science. Yet in science there is no other way. Science proceeds solely by postulating hypotheses and testing their predictions, and it is this quality which distinguishes science from most other disciplines.

There are two general ways of testing hypotheses. The first is by looking for naturally occurring observations that either support or invalidate a hypothesis. Many generalizing hypotheses lend themselves to such testing. For example, the hypothesis "water always flows downhill" can be tested simply by looking at large numbers of naturally flowing bodies of water. All bodies of water that flow downhill provide additional support for the hypothesis. However, bodies of water occasionally do flow uphill, as when incoming tides force water upstream in tributaries emptying into oceans along coastal shores. The hypothesis as stated is therefore false, disproved by a single contradictory observation.

Some hypotheses, explanatory ones in particular, often cannot be tested by naturally occurring observations. For these, observations must be generated by *experimentation.*

Experiment, Theory

Guesses that are correct explanations of natural phenomena can be termed true hypotheses. The major principle underlying the experimentation step of scientific inquiry is that *true hypotheses can never give rise to a prediction that can be proved false.*

This principle can be illustrated through our hypothesis that temperature is the environmental factor responsible for triggering seasonal color changes in snowshoe hares. A testable prediction of this hypothesis can be obtained through *deductive logic.* This kind of reasoning proceeds from a general premise to specific conclusions that are based on the premise and therefore is the opposite of inductive logic (Table 1.1). Sometimes called "if . . . then . . ." reasoning, deductive logic is used extensively by scientists to obtain predictions from hypotheses. For example: *If* temperature is the environmental factor responsible for triggering seasonal color changes of snowshoe hares, *then* hares kept at winter temperatures in spring and

TABLE 1.1
Comparison of Inductive and Deductive Logic

Inductive	Deductive
begins with observations; leads to hypothesis	begins with hypothesis; leads to predictions
proceeds from specific to general	proceeds from general to specific
a method of discovery	a method of verification

SOURCE: J. Baker and G. Allen, "The Study of Biology," 3d ed., table 1.1, p. 15, Addison-Wesley, Reading, Mass., 1977.

summer will retain their white coat and will not change to brown. The portion of the preceding sentence following the word "then" is a logical conclusion of the portion stated before the word "then." All that a scientist need do now is test the validity of the conclusion (prediction) to ascertain the validity of the accompanying hypothesis.

Usually, predictions from hypotheses can be obtained easily through application of the "if . . . then . . ." deductive format. Most scientists are so accustomed to deductive reasoning that formal construction of "if . . . then . . ." statements is unnecessary in setting up experiments. However, formal construction of "if . . . then . . ." statements is helpful in gaining an appreciation of how scientists design experiments.

Use the following procedure to accustom yourself to this format. First, write down a testable hypothesis. Place the word "if" before the hypothesis, and follow it with the word "then." Complete the now unfinished sentence with a logical conclusion. As a scientist, your next task would be to construct an experiment to provide a "yes" or "no" answer to your prediction.

Our hypothesis regarding coat-coloration changes in snowshoe hares can be used to illustrate this next step of scientific inquiry. Assume that an experimenter takes a white snowshoe hare from the field in December and places it in a refrigerated room where "winter" temperatures can be maintained indefinitely. The hare is retained in this room until late the following summer. Suppose the hare's coat color remains white. Would this prove that change in temperature is the environmental factor responsible for triggering the seasonal color changes? Certainly not.

Temperature is only one of several environmental changes that could have accounted for the hare keeping its white coat. Perhaps some factor in the hare's natural diet is responsible for changes in coat color. This factor may not have been present in the laboratory food after the hare was moved to the refrigerated room. Or perhaps the longer daylight hours in spring are responsible for triggering the coat-coloration changes. Lack of change might have been a result of illumination patterns in the refrigerated room that differed from those in nature.

What is clearly needed here is *experimental control:* for every snowshoe hare maintained in the refrigerated room, a precisely equal group must be maintained in another room where all environmental conditions are identical *except* for temperature. If the two groups respond differently, the responsible factor must be temperature because all other factors are identical for both groups.

Thus, every experiment requires at least two parallel tests identical in all respects except one. One set of tests is the *control series,* to provide a standard of reference for assessing the results of the *experimental series.* Such procedures are often laborious, expensive, and time-consuming. In drug experiments on people, for example, up to 100,000 to 200,000 tests, half of them controls and half of them experimentals, must sometimes be performed. And despite a most ingenious design and a most careful execution, the result may still not be a clear "yes" or "no." In a drug testing experiment, for example, it is virtually certain that some of the ill test subjects in the experimental group will not respond to the drug treatment, while some of the control subjects will get better even without the drug.

The result of any experiment represents *evidence.* As with legal evidence, scientific evidence can be strong and convincing, or merely suggestive, or poor. With regard to snowshoe hares, the evidence is strong that temperature is not the main environmental factor responsible for triggering seasonal coat-color changes. Hares maintained at "winter" temperatures in greenhouse environments undergo a spring change to brown coats at the same time as hares maintained in the same greenhouse at outside temperatures. Evidence obtained through other experiments supports the hypothesis that seasonal change in day length is the environmental factor responsible for triggering coat-color changes. This hypothesis has been endorsed by most scientists because of the strength and consistency of the experimental evidence. It is incorrect to conclude, however, that the hypothesis has been "proved." *No scientific evidence, regardless of strength, can ever prove the absolute validity of any hypothesis. This inability is inherent in the nature of scientific methodology.*

Recall that science proceeds by testing predictions deduced from hypotheses and that true hypotheses can never give rise to false predictions. However, false hypotheses can give rise to predictions that will be supported by the results of valid experiments. This principle can be illustrated through another of Aristotle's erroneous absolute truths. The Greek philosophers believed that the earth was the center of the universe and that the sun circled the earth daily. Apply deductive reasoning to this hypothesis to obtain a testable prediction: *If* the earth is the center of the universe, *then* the sun should rise on one horizon in the morning, move across the sky, and set on the opposite horizon. So it does. Thus, predictions that are verified by the results of experiments do not prove hypotheses. At best, we can only state that experimental evidence "supports" or "is consistent with" specific hypotheses. There is always room for more and better evidence or for new contradictory evidence or for better hypotheses.

Experimental evidence is the basis for the final step in scientific procedure, the formulation of a theory, a broadly based hypothesis supported by many tests that usually have been conducted over several years. Theories that withstand the test of thousands of individual experiments are sometimes called scientific laws. The *law of gravity* and the *second law of thermodynamics* are common examples.

Most theories, however, have brief life-spans. For example, consider the simple theory: "Day length is the environmental factor responsible for triggering seasonal coat-coloration changes in *all* mammals that are white in winter and brown in summer." This theory requires immediate modification since the coat colors of many mammals are influenced by factors other than day length. Such exceptions to theories become new observations, which often lead to new hypotheses, new experiments, and new or revised theories.

As mentioned earlier, however, it is incorrect to conclude that scientists usually follow an ordered list of steps in solving problems. How testable hypotheses are formulated and experiments designed varies considerably from one scientist to another and from one situation to another. This is because hypothesis formation and experimental design are activities that are essentially creative, not prescribed.

To be sure, good scientists usually are expert at formulating generalizing and explanatory hypotheses. They often are quick to develop ways of testing hypotheses that are both reliable and effective. In addition, good scientists generally take immediate advantage of situations that provide unique opportunities for making new observations about natural processes, and they recognize that scientific inquiry is not restricted to bright, modern laboratories filled with complex and expensive equipment (see accompanying Biology Highlights section). But why some scientists are more perceptive than others is not well understood.

It should now be clear that scientists cannot be the cold, inhuman automatons they are so often pictured to be. Scientists are essentially artists who require a sensitivity of eye and of mind as great as that of any master painter, and an imagination and keen inventiveness as powerful as that of any master poet.

The following is the first in a series of short, often anecdotal essays collectively called Biology Highlights. Each essay highlights events, topics, procedures, or personalities introduced in the accompanying chapter. The Highlights attempt to provide added insight into the true nature of science in general and biology in particular. The essays will not increase your factual knowledge substantially but should influence and improve your perception of science. This first Highlight, for example, illustrates how an American Army physician used the methodology of science to further our understanding of a basic biological process during the first half of the nineteenth century.

Biology Highlight

The Window in St. Martin's Stomach

In 1822 Alexis St. Martin was a young, tough, shiftless, hard-drinking French-Canadian canoeman who earned his livelihood as a fur trapper along the shores of Lake Michigan. One day, while he was drinking with several fellow fur trappers at John Jacob Astor's store on Mackinac Island, a shotgun discharged accidently, leaving a huge wound in St. Martin's side.

Bystanders quickly summoned the only physician within 300 miles, Dr. William Beaumont, an American Army doctor stationed at a nearby military post. Dr. Beaumont sighed despairingly after looking at St. Martin's wound (Fig. 1). The hole in his side was as big as a man' hand. Part of St. Martin's stomach, which was also punctured, protruded through the hole. Beaumont was certain that his patient would die within 20 minutes.

Whether his cantankerous nature contributed to his survival is not certain, but St. Martin did not die from the gunshot wound, nor would he submit to an operation that would have closed it. Within a few months of the accident, healthy scar tissue formed, adhering the rim of St. Martin's stomach puncture to the body surface. The fusion of stomach and surface tissues produced a narrow canal, called a *gastric fistula,* that led into his stomach (Fig. 2).

The lining of St. Martin's stomach eventually grew across the opening of the fistula, forming a leakproof valve, but the "window" in St. Martin's stomach did not close completely. A small hole remained, large enough for Beaumont to open with his forefinger and look directly into the stomach cavity. As a scientist, Dr. Beaumont could not pass up the opportunity to observe the process of digestion directly. Here was a unique chance to gain insight into how digestive organs break food down into the basic nutrients required by the body. Beaumont succeeded in convincing the stubborn French-Canadian to become his servant and to submit to an occasional examination of his stomach cavity.

Fig. 1 William Beaumont's skill as a physician saved the life of Alexis St. Martin. The surgery later afforded a unique opportunity to view the digestion of food in a human stomach. (*Courtesy Reader's Digest Assoc., Inc., copyright* © 1951.)

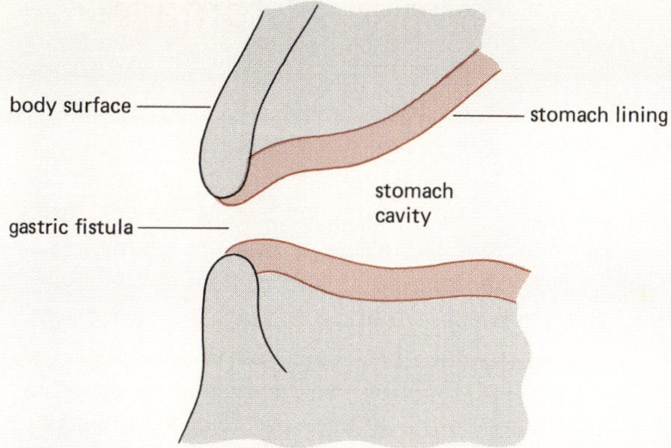

Fig. 2 The "window" in St. Martin's stomach actually was the opening of a gastric fistula, a short canal produced by the adherence of stomach lining to body wall.

Beaumont observed that the walls of St. Martin's stomach were velvety, coated with a mucous fluid, and rippled with many surface folds. When the physician inserted bread crumbs through the "window," the pale color of the walls turned bright pink. In addition, many droplets of mucus formed along the stomach lining and trickled down the surface folds. After a while, the bread crumbs disappeared.

Using a rubber tube, Dr. Beaumont removed some of the stomach fluid. It had the pronounced odor of hydrochloric acid. He then placed some of the fluid in a glass vial and dropped in a chunk of boiled beef. Beaumont later wrote: "In 40 minutes digestion had commenced over the surface of the meat." After 2 hours, "the cellular texture seemed to be entirely destroyed, leaving the muscular fibers loose and unconnected, floating about in fine small shreds." In 10 hours "every part of the meat was completely digested."

Beaumont collected his observations and concluded that the stomach has an inherent capacity to respond to swallowed food by secreting an acidic gastric juice that "is the most general solvent of food in nature." Whether Beaumont realized it or not, he had constructed a generalizing hypothesis based on a number of similar observations.

Dr. Beaumont then tested his hypothesis by feeding St. Martin an "endless variety of food" and observing the reactions of his stomach. St. Martin proved to be a willing accomplice, consuming "crude food in abundant quantities." All observations supported Beaumont's generalizing hypothesis. He concluded, "even the hardest bone cannot withstand the action of gastric juice."

Several of Beaumont's observations triggered additional questions and hypotheses. This is both a perplexing and satisfying consequence of testing hypotheses. Subsequent observations and experimental results commonly raise more questions than they answer. For example, one morning St. Martin became annoyed at not receiving his breakfast at the usual hour. Beaumont noted that St. Martin's anger seemed to affect the digestive process, slowing it noticeably. An explanatory hypothesis immediately popped into Beaumont's mind. Perhaps anger and emotional excitement generally "check the secretion of gastric juice."

To determine the validity of this hypothesis, Beaumont designed a crude but effective experiment. When St. Martin became angry, Beaumont fed him a piece of meat, usually roast beef. Considering his obstinate temperament, getting St. Martin to eat at such times tested Beaumont's ability to persuade, cajole, and occasionally even bribe. But Beaumont succeeded more often than not, and he noted that roast beef eaten in anger frequently took twice as long to reach a given state of digestion than when St. Martin was calm. Thus, the experimental results supported Beaumont's hypothesis that emotion can have a significant and measurable influence on digestion. Subsequent experiments provided further documentation of this relationship.

Beaumont used St. Martin's stomach as a vehicle for testing hypotheses about human digestion for more than a decade. In 1833, the physician published "Experiments and Observations on Gastric Juice and the Physiology of Digestion," now regarded as an original classic of American medicine. In it, Beaumont provides quantitative support for several hypotheses, such as "fatty foods are more difficult to digest than lean foods," and "hot, humid weather depresses gastric secretion."

William Beaumont exhibited many traits of an excellent scientist. He was inventive and innovative, undismayed by the limitations of his "laboratory equipment," which often consisted of kitchen utensils and the few tools within his black physician's bag. He also displayed considerable ability in developing highly perceptive generalizing and explanatory hypotheses and in testing each of them thoroughly and effectively. Finally, like all responsible scientists, Beaumont published his findings for others to criticize, repeat, validate, and build upon.

Beaumont and St. Martin parted company about 3 years after the physician's work was first published. The parting was to have been temporary, but the doctor and his former patient never saw each other again. Apparently, St. Martin had experienced enough of science. Beaumont tried to convince him to return for further experimentation, but the attempt was fruitless. Beaumont died 20 years later.

St. Martin, tough, durable, and cantankerous, outlived Beaumont by more than 25 years. He was nearly 80 years old when death came in 1880. He spent his last months chopping firewood for a living, apparently unaffected by the 58-year-old "window" in his stomach.

LIMITATIONS OF SCIENCE

Science and Religion

Because of the enormous impact of science on modern society, there exists a tendency among many people to regard science as potentially unlimited in its capacity to solve problems. Others look on science as an all-powerful force whose capacity to destroy and corrupt is infinite. Our examination of scientific methodology has revealed several limitations that nullify both of these views.

First, science cannot answer all categories of questions. Thus, questions that do not lead to testable hypotheses are outside the domain of science. How often have you heard that "science argues against the existence of God" or that "science is antireligious?" Such statements assume that science can prove or disprove the existence of God. Consider how science would attempt to answer this question. A hypothesis is needed. Suppose we "guess" that God does not exist. Being untested, this hypothesis might be right or wrong. Regardless of any prediction obtained through deductive logic, an experiment about God would require experimental control, that is, two situations, one with God and one without, but otherwise identical.

If our hypothesis is correct, God would not exist anywhere. Hence He would not be present in any test we might conduct. Yet for a controlled experiment, we would need a test in which God was present. On the other hand, if our hypothesis is wrong, He would exist everywhere and would be present in every control situation we might devise. Yet for a controlled experiment, we would need to construct a situation in which God was not present. Clearly, the question of God's existence is untestable scientifically.

Science is useless as a tool to discover or evaluate any truth that cannot be tested experimentally. Moreover, we have already learned that scientific truths are rarely absolute. Theories are being modified continually in the light of new evidence. Frustration awaits all who look to science for absolute truths.

Pure and Applied Science

Second, science cannot guarantee quick solutions to troublesome problems. No scientist, for example, can guarantee that the results of an experiment will support a hypothesis. Often there are hundreds of wrong hypotheses for every correct one, and experiments that prove hypotheses incorrect usually take as much time to carry out as those that provide supporting evidence. Proving hypotheses incorrect, however, usually does little to increase our ability to solve practical problems.

It is equally impossible for scientists to predict the potential usefulness of their experimental results. Many nonscientists fail to recognize this limitation and sometimes complain about their tax dollars being spent on research having no direct, practical "relevance." They frequently argue that most of their tax dollars should be spent on *applied* science, which concerns itself with immediate human needs; correspondingly little should be expended on *basic* or *pure* science, which seeks to develop knowledge about the operation of the universe and its parts, without regard to practical application. Why support studies of coat-color changes in snowshoe hares or the behavior patterns of fish when a much more pressing concern is to find cures for cancer and other diseases?

Such arguments reflect two basic misconceptions about the interdependence between pure and applied science. One is the assumption that knowledge having direct human application derives exclusively from applied research. Very often the results of basic research prove this assumption false.

For example, much applied research has been carried out to discover an effective and safe shark repellent. Such a chemical would have obvious practical value in ensuring the safety of swimmers in shark-inhabited waters. However, most chemicals that have been tested have proved ineffective or unreliable. Recently, an extremely potent shark repellent was found in the secretions of a small flounderlike fish inhabiting the Red Sea. This secretion apparently protects the fish from attacks by sharks and probably from other predators as well. The scientists who made this discovery were engaged in basic research and were not attempting to isolate a shark repellent. Their discovery was accidental and could not have been predicted in advance. Yet their findings could lead to the eventual development of a highly effective agent against sharks. The point is clear; if support is given exclusively to research dealing with "practical" problems, society will deprive itself of many unpredictable applications of knowledge derived from basic research.

The argument that applied science is "more important" than basic science contains a second and more serious flaw. Study of seasonal coat-color changes in snowshoe hares, for example, may not provide any information of immediate usefulness to human beings. However, it does provide a small piece of information about the way living systems react to their environment. Coupled with countless other pieces of information, gathered through years of painstaking efforts, a more complete understanding of the general principles governing the operation of living systems—living human systems included—are bound to emerge. Entirely new and different applications can then result from this more complete understanding, perhaps generating solutions to many different human problems. A scientific "breakthrough" will have been achieved—as in fact such breakthroughs have been achieved many times in the past, almost invariably with diverse "practical" benefits for humanity.

Contrary to popular opinion, such breakthroughs do not develop suddenly. They almost always rest upon a bedrock of fundamental knowledge developed slowly through years of basic research. Discovery of the Salk vaccine against polio, for example, depended on a fundamental understanding of the nature and life cycle of viruses. Development of this understanding took years and hundreds of experiments.

The moral of this lesson is not that society must support all experiments of all scientists. As human beings, some scientists are more gifted and productive than others. Certain experimental approaches are more likely to succeed than others. But we must always recognize the interdependence of applied and basic science. Neither can exist without the other. Every basic scientist depends on equipment and techniques developed by applied science, and every applied scientist depends on ideas, insights, and knowledge generated by basic research. Starve either form of science and both will suffer. Failure to recognize this fundamental interdependence will frustrate all long-term attempts to speed application of science to human problems by increasing support of applied research at the expense of basic research.

Application of science to human needs is also slowed by the collaborative nature of the discipline. As applied and basic research are interdependent, so are scientists themselves interdependent. No experimental result is ever accepted by the scientific community at large unless and until it has been repeated by a second, independent scientist. This practice helps to ensure that the body of facts composing scientific knowledge is accurate and unbiased. In effect, the ability of science to solve problems quickly is sacrificed deliberately to ensure orderly, steady, and reliable progress and to avoid the wastefulness and chaos that otherwise would result.

Science and Society

Finally, science is limited by its inability to make moral or value judgments. Scientific results by themselves do not contain any built-in values, and nowhere in scientific inquiry is there a value-revealing step. As a tool, like a hammer or a paintbrush, science is inherently neither good nor evil, responsible or irresponsible, powerful or impotent. Those who perceive such values or purposes in science are, in reality, merely viewing a reflection of human values and purposes. Thus, the science that produces weapons for destroying and killing and weapons for healing and creating cannot, of itself, determine whether such tools are good or bad. The decision in each case must rest on the moral opinions of people.

If human beings must determine the uses of science, how should such decisions be made? It might be possible, for example, to give scientists the exclusive right to make all decisions related to social applications of scientific theory. But most people, most scientists included, do not believe that such decisions should be left to any one segment of society. Scientists are no better suited to make decisions involving the justice or injustice of, say, abortion than lawyers, plumbers, or bricklayers. Science and technology have made the abortion of human fetuses relatively safe and practicable, but science does not and cannot establish moral and societal standards for the practice itself.

Nevertheless, some scientists argue that they have a special responsibility to influence public decisions that relate to uses of scientific knowledge. Such scientists believe that this responsibility grows out of their special training and their ability to perceive social implications of developing technologies before they are recognized by the general public. Others question the motivation of these often outspoken individuals and believe that scientists should merely present unbiased information and leave all final decisions concerning the uses of scientific knowledge to the public.

There are similar disagreements concerning the role of the lay citizen in science. Some scientists insist that nonscientists should have little input into decisions relating to scientific experimentation. These scientists argue, for example, that issues relating to the dangers of specific experimental techniques are too complex for people who lack formal scientific training. Others reply that nonscientists can make rational policy judgments regarding scientific procedures and issues if they have an opportunity to hear articulate advocates present their case and respond to opposing arguments. Indeed, many who support an increased role for the nonscientist in decisions involving scientific matters favor creation of special adversary forums where significant questions of science and technology can be debated in front of panels of impartial judges. Such panels might issue judgments that pertain to disputed technical issues, and these opinions could then be used in the drafting of local, state, or national laws.

Proposals for the establishment of such forums stem in part from the demands of increasing numbers of nonscientists who want greater participation in decisions involving the use of certain kinds of experimental procedures in research laboratories. Other lay citizens have witnessed the environmental and human devastation that can result from misuse of scientific knowledge and now wish a formal role in directing science toward more "responsible" goals.

Despite protestations by some and misinformed views of science by others, this recent trend toward a "democratization" of science is likely to become more pronounced in the years to come. In the United States and many other countries, relationships between the discovery and use of scientific knowledge probably will be defined increasingly by "science courts," boards of review, legislative committees, and city councils.

Although such "democratization" can do much to increase public respect and support of science, it cannot be accomplished unless scientists remain attentive to the views and fears of the lay citizen concerning the discovery and use of scientific knowledge, and scientists must do more to educate the public about the nature of science and specific scientific issues. For their part, nonscientists must obtain at least a rudimentary knowledge of scientific principles, understand the relationships between basic and applied science, and be aware of both the potentials and limitations of science. Only then will scientists and nonscientists be able to work cooperatively and intelligently criticize, question, and evaluate future applications of scientific theory.

Review Questions

1 What are the aims and limitations of science? Review fully.

2 Consider the following statement: Scientists should be required to obtain approval for certain kinds of experiments. Do you agree or disagree with this statement? Give reasons for your opinion. If you agree, who should approve or disapprove proposals for scientific investigations, and on what grounds?

3 Review the procedures commonly employed in scientific inquiries, and discuss the nature of each such procedure. Define controlled experiment.

4 How would you show by controlled experiment whether or not:

- **a.** temperature affects the rate of growth of living things?
- **b.** houseflies can perceive differently colored objects?
- **c.** plants use up some of the soil they grow in?

5 Suppose it were found in the experiment described in question 4a that, at an environmental temperature of 28°C, fertilized frog eggs develop into tadpoles roughly twice as fast as at 18°C. What kinds of hypotheses could such evidence suggest?

6 Review the contributions of the ancient Greek philosophers to modern science. Which of the ideas you have previously held about science should you now, after studying this chapter, regard as popular misconceptions? Review your responsibilities as a citizen in determining how science should be applied to specific social and human concerns.

7 Can you think of observations or problems that have so far not been investigated scientifically? Try to determine in each case whether or not such investigation is inherently possible.

8 Define mechanism and causalism, and contrast these systems of thought with those of vitalism and teleology. Can conceptual conflicts between science and religion be reconciled?

9 Consider the legal questions: "Do you swear to tell the truth, the whole truth, and nothing but the truth?" and "Is it not a fact that on the night of . . .?" If questions of this sort were to be used in a strictly scientific context, how should they be properly formulated?

10 What distinguishes good scientists from poor ones? Was William Beaumont a good scientist? Why or why not?

Collateral Readings

Ayala, F. J., and **T. Dobzhansky** (eds.): "Studies in the Philosophy of Biology," University of California Press, Berkeley, 1975. This excellent collection of essays describes the methods of modern biology and discusses the impact of this science on society.

Baker, J. J. W., and **G. E. Allen:** "Hypothesis, Prediction, and Implication in Biology," Addison-Wesley, Reading, Mass., 1971. A book that illustrates the functioning of biology both as an investigative science and as a discipline whose hypotheses often possess far-reaching philosophical and sociological significance.

Beaumont, W.: Experiments and Observations on the Gastric Juice and the Physiology of Digestion, in J. J. W. Baker and G. Allen (eds.), "The Process of Biology: Primary Sources," Addison-Wesley, Reading, Mass., 1970. Beaumont's comments on what he observed looking through the window in St. Martin's stomach.

Bronowski, J.: "The Ascent of Man," Little, Brown, Boston, 1973. Originally prepared as a television series, this illuminating history of the sciences also discusses the impact of science and technology on human culture.

———: "Science and Human Values," Harper & Row, New York, 1959. A well-known paperback, containing a stimulating discussion of the role of science in modern society.

Dethier, V. C.: "To Know a Fly," Holden-Day, San Francisco, 1962. A popularly written and often amusing discussion of scientific research. This paperback contains several good examples of how controlled experiments are designed.

Fischer, R. B.: "Science, Man and Society," 2d ed., Saunders, Philadelphia, 1975. This paperback discusses the nature of science and its relationship to human values, government, and technology.

Gardner, M.: "Fads and Fallacies in the Name of Science," Dover, New York, 1957. A very interesting description of several pseudo-scientific theories. The book explains how Bridey Murphy, Atlantis, and other myths gained adherents and how most of them can be shown invalid.

Stent, G. S.: Prematurity and Uniqueness in Scientific Discovery, *Scientific American,* September 1972. Contrasts scientific discoveries with artistic creations. A good comparison of the similarities and differences between art and science.

Terman, L. M.: Are Scientists Different?, *Scientific American,* January 1955. A psychologist examines the traits generally characteristic of scientists and compares them with those of nonscientists.

Van Norman, R. W.: "Experimental Biology," 2d ed., Prentice-Hall, Englewood Cliffs, N.J., 1971. Questions concerning use of the biological literature, setting up experiments, making measurements, statistics in biology, and writing scientific papers are answered in this useful book.

Wilson, E. B., Jr.: "An Introduction to Scientific Research," McGraw-Hill, New York, 1952. A good discussion of the nature of the scientific method and its application in scientific investigations.

Chapter 2 The Biological Background

Learning Objectives

After reading this chapter you should be able to:

1. Distinguish between living, dead, and inanimate objects.
2. Identify and define each of the interdependent subfunctions that constitute metabolism and self-perpetuation; identify the functional roles played by each of the subfunctions in the maintenance of life.
3. List two major ways in which organisms obtain foods.
4. Construct a diagram that illustrates how living matter is organized at successively higher levels of organization; generally compare the amounts of energy required to support each of these levels.
5. Write a structural and functional definition of a cell; define and provide at least one example of a unicellular organism, cellular colony, tissue, organ, organ system, and multicellular organism; define organelle and differentiate among family, society, population, species, and community.
6. List at least:
   - **a.** one general characteristic that usually distinguishes a cell of a single-celled organism from a cell of a multicellular organism.
   - **b.** two functional advantages of cellular specialization in multicellular organisms.
7. Define taxonomy and list the general characteristics of the Linnean taxonomic system; list the principal ranks of the Linnean system; state why structural characteristics have been used almost exclusively to establish taxonomic distinctions between organisms.
8. Differentiate between "natural" and "unnatural" taxonomic classifications, and list an example of each; state why the classification of all organisms as plants or as animals is no longer justifiable.
9. Name the characteristics of Fungi, Plantae, and Animalia, and list characteristics that distinguish these categories from Monera and Protista; construct a diagram depicting the probable evolutionary relationships between these taxonomic categories.
10. List the rules that govern the classification of species; classify human beings according to at least 10 taxonomic ranks; define each of the taxonomic rank categories you identify.

The properties of life are exhibited by individual living creatures, or *organisms.* What does "being alive" actually signify, and what is an "organism?"

Surely the most obvious difference between something living and something nonliving is that the first *does* certain things the second does not do. The essence of "living" evidently lies in particular activities, or processes, or *functions.*

"Nonliving" could mean either "dead" or "inanimate," terms that are not equivalent. If a chicken does not perform its living functions it is dead, but it is still distinguishable readily from an inanimate object such as a stone. Chickens, living or dead, are organisms; stones are not. All organisms are put together in such a way that the functions of life are or once were actually possible. Accordingly, the essence of "organism" lies in the way in which particular building materials are organized as *structures.*

A "living organism," therefore, is what it is by virtue of its functions and structures; the functions endow it with the property of life, and the structures permit execution of the life-sustaining functions. What are these functions and structures?

LIFE AND FUNCTION

Metabolism

Embracing all chemical reactions involved in running the machinery of living organisms, *metabolism* is largely made up of three subcomponent processes, *nutrition, respiration,* and *synthesis.*

Nutrition

Nutrition provides raw materials for maintenance of life. All living matter depends unceasingly on such raw materials, for the very act of living continuously uses up two basic commodities, energy and matter. In this respect a living organism is like a mechanical engine or indeed like any other action-performing system in the universe. Energy is needed to power the system, to make the parts operate, to keep activity going—in short, to maintain function. And matter is needed to replace parts, to repair breakdowns, to continue the system intact and able to function—in short, to maintain structure. Therefore, by its very nature as an action-performing unit, a "living" organism can remain alive only if it continuously uses up energy and matter. Both must be replenished from the outside through nutrition.

The external raw materials used in this function are *nutrients.* One general class of nutrients includes water, salts, and other materials obtainable directly from the physical environment of the earth. Another class comprises *foods,* which are available in the biological environment.

Foods are obtained in two main ways. One group of organisms, the *autotrophic* ("self-feeding") types, manufactures its foods from the raw materials present in the physical world—the soil, water, and air in which organisms live. In most autotrophs sunlight is used as an energy source in the production of food. The process through which these organisms manufacture food is termed *photosynthesis.* Such organisms include plants, algae, and others that contain the green pigment *chlorophyll,* an essential component in photosynthesis (Fig. 2.1).

The second group of organisms, comprising the *heterotrophic* ("other-feeding") types, is unable to manufacture its own foods and must therefore depend on already existing supplies of them. In this category are animals, fungi, most bacteria, and generally all those organisms which must make use of ready-made foods available in other organisms, living or dead. Eating by animals is one familiar method of obtaining preexisting foods. Thus, whereas autotrophs can survive in a strictly physical, nonbiological environment, heterotrophs, which cannot make their own food, require a biological as well as a physical environment (Fig. 2.2).

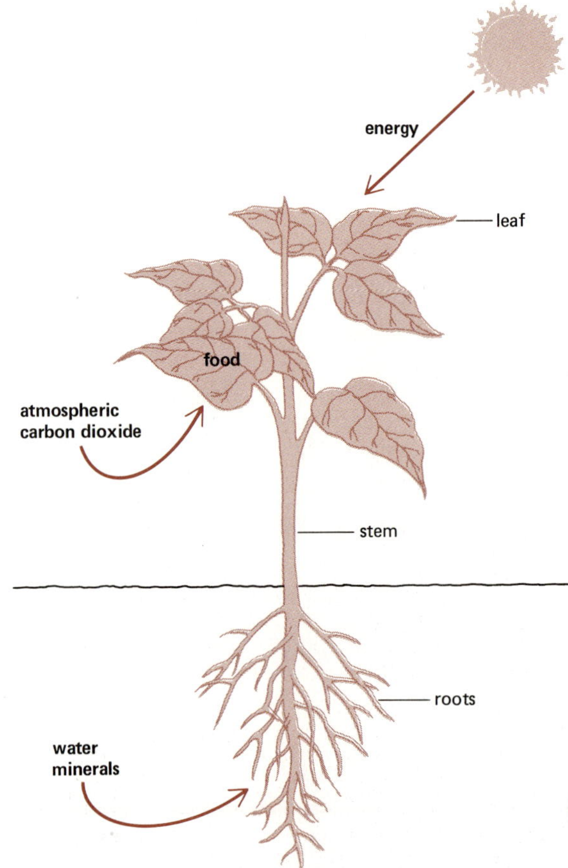

Fig. 2.1 Nutrition: autotrophism. Most autotrophic organisms manufacture food through photosynthesis, a process in which sunlight is used as an energy source. Water, dissolved minerals, and carbon dioxide are the chief nutrients for photosynthesis. Most terrestrial plants absorb water and minerals through underground roots; atmospheric carbon dioxide enters leaves directly through small pores.

Fig 2.2 Nutrition: heterotrophism. Animals and all other heterotrophs obtain food directly or indirectly from autotrophic organisms such as grasses.

Respiration

Nutrients of all kinds, foods included, are chemicals, and as such they contain chemical energy. All living matter is maintained on the chemical energy obtained from nutrients. Certain nutrients become decomposed inside an organism, through a series of energy-yielding chemical reactions; and the energy made available by these reactions sustains living activities. In this respect living systems are in principle quite similar to many familiar machines. In a gasoline or steam engine, for example, fuel is decomposed by burning, and this process releases energy that drives the motor. In the living "motor," nutrients likewise function as fuels; indeed, foods and engine fuels belong to the same families of chemical substances. Moreover, foods are decomposed in a way that is actually a form of burning, and the energy so obtained then drives the living "machine."

In living organisms the process of obtaining

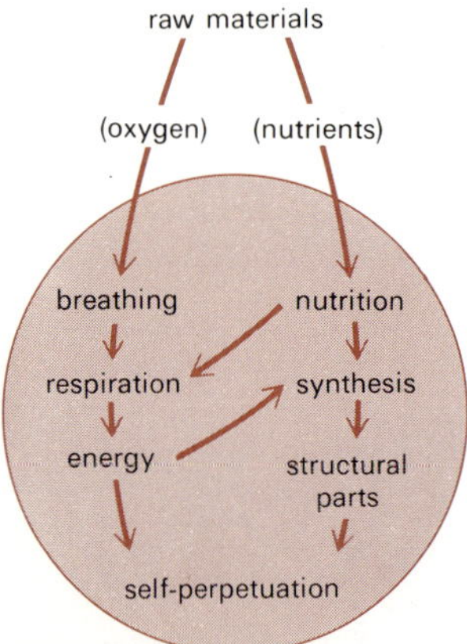

Fig. 2.3 Metabolism. The main processes of metabolism and their interrelations. Note that nutrients provide the raw materials for both respiration and synthesis. Respiration provides immediately useable supplies of energy for synthesis and self-perpetuation; synthesis provides most of the structural materials required for self-perpetuation.

energy through decomposition of foods is called respiration. This function is a second major activity of living matter; it is the basic power source that maintains *all* living processes—including nutrition and even respiration itself. Energy made available through previous nutrition and respiration is needed to make possible continued nutrition and respiration.

SYNTHESIS

Nutrients also serve as construction materials. The whole structure of the living organism must be built from, and kept intact with, nutrient "bricks." Thus, the chemical stuff of living matter—the substance of your skin or your heart, for example—is fundamentally the same as that of nutrients. Clearly, the expression "you are what you eat" is literally true.

The reverse is equally true. Since nutrients and the structural components of organisms are basically equivalent and nutrients are also respiratory fuels, organisms are able to use themselves as fuel. When people on diets restrict their nutrient intake, their bodies use some of their own matter to fuel respiration. The result is a loss in total weight. All living matter is inherently self-decomposing and self-consuming. The living motor cannot tell the difference between external fuel and internal structural parts, because both are fundamentally the same. Organisms are therefore unstable structurally, but they counteract this instability with the aid of nutrients. Some of these substances are fashioned continually into new structural parts, and such new parts replace those that burn away.

Living matter thus changes from moment to moment. As wear and tear and reconstruction occur side by side, the substance of living matter always "turns over"; the structural pattern remains the same, but almost every bit of the building material is replaced sooner or later. Moreover, if new building materials are incorporated faster than old ones wear away, the living organism will grow. Growth is a characteristic outcome of the use of nutrients in the construction of living matter. The processes by which nutrients are formed into new structural parts can collectively be called synthesis

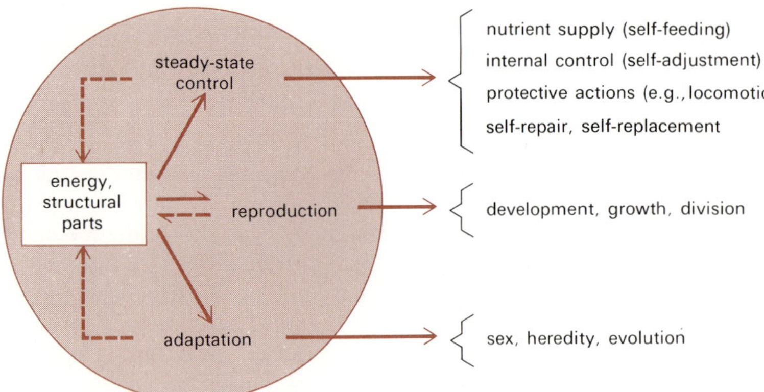

Fig. 2.4 Self-perpetuation. The main processes of self-perpetuation and their interrelations. As noted in the previous figure, metabolism provides the energy and structural parts for the three subprocesses of self-perpetuation, whose major functions are shown in brackets. However, metabolism cannot continue for an extended period of time in the absence of steady-state controls, reproduction, and adaptation. This complementary relationship is symbolized by arrows attached to broken lines.

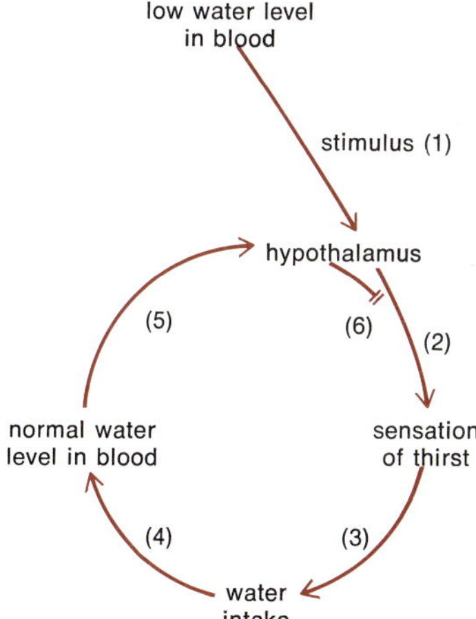

Fig. 2.5 Steady-state control. Water balance in human beings and many animals is regulated by the hypothalamus. This part of the brain reacts to the stimulus of low water levels in blood (1) by transmitting nerve impulses to other parts of the brain that create the sensation of thirst (2). This sensation causes animals to drink water (3), thereby returning the concentration of water in blood to normal levels (4). The hypothalamus senses this return to normal levels (5) and responds by abolishing (double bar = inhibition) nerve transmissions that create the sensation of thirst (6).

activities. They represent a third basic function of all living things. Like other functions of life, synthesis requires energy, and respiration must provide it (Fig. 2.3).

Self-Perpetuation

Metabolism, by itself, is not equivalent to "life." To be sure, a system that nourishes, respires, and synthesizes is *capable* of undertaking more nutrition, more respiration, and more synthesis. But metabolism will not continue for long without *control.* In this respect living matter is again like an engine. Continuous engine operation demands that the different parts of the engine act in harmony and that they become adjusted and readjusted in response to internal or external events that might change engine performance. In the same manner, continuation of metabolism in living matter depends on harmonized activity.

The necessary control for metabolism is provided by *self-perpetuation,* a broadly inclusive set of processes. Self-perpetuation ensures that the metabolizing machinery continues to run indefinitely, despite internal and external happenings that might otherwise alter or stop its operation (Fig. 2.4).

Steady-State Control

The most direct regulation of metabolism is brought about by the self-perpetuative function of *steady-state control,* often also called *homeostasis.* Such control permits a living organism to receive *information* from within itself and from the external environment and to act on this information in a usually self-preserving manner. The information is generally received in the form of *stimuli,* and the ensuing actions are *responses.*

For example, metabolism functions most efficiently when the water content of our bodies is maintained at an optimum level. We become thirsty when the water level in our tissues drops below this optimum—the drop in water content is a stimulus. Response to this stimulus is initiated by a portion of our brain called the *hypothalamus* (Fig. 2.5). If the hypothalamus detects a lower-than-optimum water content in the blood, it transmits nerve impulses to other portions of the brain and to the body, creating the sensation of thirst. This sensation is diminished as we respond to the stimulus by drinking water, thereby returning the water content of our tissues to its optimum level. Numerous other internal controls preserve adequate operating conditions throughout living matter, and while it is in such a steady state, a living organism can remain intact and functioning.

But the span of existence of an organism is invariably limited. Death is a built-in attribute of living matter because the parts of the organism that maintain steady states are themselves subject to breakdown or destruction. When some of its controls become inoperative, the organism suffers *disease.* Diseases can be regarded generally as failures of steady-state controls, or as temporary *unsteady* states. Other, still intact controls may initiate self-repair, but in time so many controls break down simultaneously that too few remain intact to effect repairs. The organism is then in an irreversibly unsteady state and must die.

Fig. 2.6 Reproduction. This subcomponent of self-perpetuation extends the operation of living units in space and in time. The photograph shows a newly born baboon being groomed by its mother. Compared with other animals, monkeys, apes, and human beings mature to adulthood very slowly. This infant will be nursed by its mother for almost a year. (*Irven DeVore, Anthro-Photo.*)

A

B

Fig. 2.7 Adaptation: change with the environment. The upper figure (A) is a drawing of a placoderm, a type of fish long extinct but very common some 300 million years ago. Fishes of this group were the ancestors of modern fish, of which one, a speckled brook trout, is shown in the lower figure (B). Most of the differences between ancestor and descendant, here as in other cases, appear to be a result of adaptation to changes in the physical and biological environment.

Reproduction

However, before an organism dies it may have brought into play a second major self-perpetuative function, *reproduction*. With the help of energy and raw materials the living organism has enlarged, and such growth in size prepares the way for later growth in numbers. Reproduction in a sense anticipates and compensates for unavoidable individual death. By means of reproduction successive generations are produced and in this manner life can be carried on indefinitely (Fig. 2.6).

Adaptation

As generation succeeds generation, long-term environmental changes are likely to have their effect on the living succession. In the course of thousands and millions of years, for example, climates may change profoundly; ice ages may come and go; mountains, oceans, vast tracts of land may appear and disappear. Moreover, living organisms themselves in time alter the nature of a locality in major ways. Consequently, two related organisms many generations apart could find themselves in greatly different environments. And whereas the steady-state controls of the ancestor may have coped effectively with the early environment, such controls could be overpowered rapidly by the new environment. In the course of many generations, therefore, organisms must change *with* the environment if they are to continue in existence. They actually do change, through *adaptation*. As will become apparent later, this self-perpetuative function itself consists of three subfunctions: *sex, heredity,* and *evolution* (Fig. 2.7 and see Fig. 2.4).

Life: The Harmonic Integration of Metabolism and Self-Perpetuation

Self-perpetuation as a whole therefore comprises three basic kinds of activities. Steady-state controls maintain appropriate operating conditions in individual organisms. Reproduction ensures a continuing succession of individual organisms. And adaptation molds and alters the members of this succession in step with the slowly changing nature of the environment. In effect, self-perpetuation adds the dimension of time to metabolism; regardless of how the environment might change in time, self-perpetuation virtually guarantees the continuation of metabolism. Metabolism in turn makes possible uninterrupted self-perpetuation, and the system so able to metabolize and to perpetuate itself can persist indefinitely; it becomes a "living" system.

Living Matter

Based on the preceding discussion, the fundamental meaning of "living" can now be defined: *any structure that metabolizes and perpetuates itself is alive.*

A first implication of this definition is that, by their very nature, living systems collectively are highly permanent kinds of matter, perhaps the most permanent in the universe. They are certainly the most enduring on earth. Every inanimate or dead object on earth sooner or later decomposes and crumbles to dust under the impact of the environment. But every living object metabolizes and perpetuates itself and consequently can avoid such a fate. Oceans, mountains, even whole continents have come and gone several times during the last 2 or 3 billion years, but living matter has continued indestructibly during that time and, indeed, has become progressively more abundant.

A second implication is that any structure that does not satisfy the above definition in every particular is either inanimate or dead. Life must cease if even one of the functions of metabolism or self-perpetuation ceases. This criterion of life offers an instructive contrast to the operation of modern machines, many of which perform some of the functions that also occur in living organisms. As noted, for example, a machine can take on "nourishment" in the form of fuel and raw materials. The fuel can be "respired" to provide operating energy, and, with it, the raw materials can then be "synthesized" into nuts, bolts, and other structural components out of which such a machine might be built. Evidently, machines can carry out activities fully equivalent to those of metabolism. Like living systems, moreover, many automated machines have ingenious steady-state controls built into them. For example, such controls could make a machine automatically self-feeding and self-adjusting.

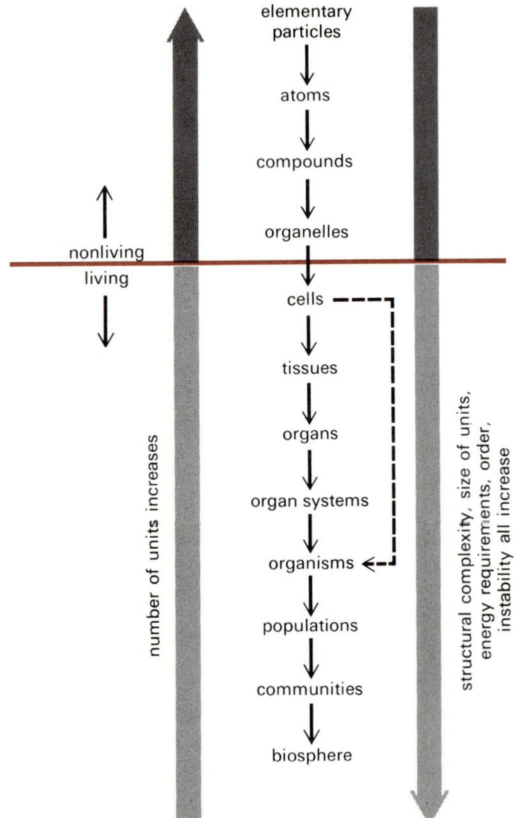

Fig. 2.8 Hierarchy of levels in the organization of matter. The biosphere represents the sum total of all living things on earth.

But no machine is as yet self-protecting, self-repairing, or self-healing to any major extent, and no machine certainly is capable of growing. Furthermore, whereas living matter can reproduce before death, machines cannot. It is in this capacity of reproduction that living systems differ most critically from inanimate systems. However, the theoretical knowledge of how to build a self-reproducing machine now exists. A device of this kind would metabolize, maintain steady states, and eventually "die" but, before that, would produce "offspring." It would be almost living. If it had the additional capacity of adaptation, it would be fully living. Here too the theoretical know-how is already available. On paper, machines have been designed that could carry out "sexual" processes of a sort, that could pass on heredity characteristics to their "progeny," and that could "evolve" and change their properties in the course of many "generations." If such machines should actually be built some day, then the essential distinction between "living" and "machine" will have disappeared.

This consideration points up a third implication of the definition above: the property of life basically does not depend on a particular substance. Any substance of whatever composition will be "living" provided that it metabolizes and perpetuates itself. It happens that only one type of such a substance is now known. We call it "living matter," or often also *protoplasm,* and it exists in the form of organisms. But if some day we should be able to build a fully metabolizing and self-perpetuating system out of nuts, bolts, and wires, then it too will have to be regarded as being truly alive. Similarly, if some day out in space we should encounter a metabolizing and self-perpetuating being made up in a hitherto completely unknown way, it too will have to be considered living. It will not be "life as we know it," or life based on the earthly variety of protoplasm, but in any case it will be truly living if it metabolizes and self-perpetuates.

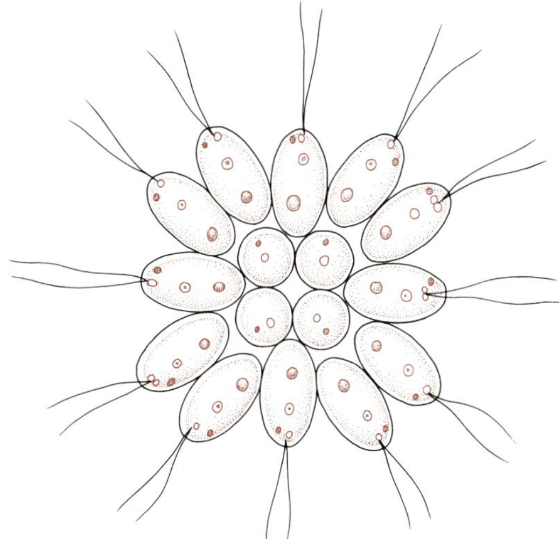

Fig. 2.9 ***Gonium pectorale.*** A motile, colonial green alga. This colony consists of 12 outer and 4 central cells. (*After T. Delevoryas, "Plant Diversification," Holt, New York, 1966.*)

ORGANISM AND STRUCTURE

Levels of Organization

Structural Levels

The smallest structural units of matter, living matter included, are *subatomic particles*—mainly electrons, protons, and neutrons. The next larger units are *atoms,* each of which consists of subatomic particles. Atoms in turn form still more complex combinations called *chemical compounds;* and these are variously joined together as even more elaborate units, or *complexes of compounds.*

These units can be regarded as representing successively higher *levels of organization* of matter. They form a pyramid, or hierarchy, in which any given level contains all lower levels as components and is itself a component of all higher levels. For example, atoms contain subatomic particles as components, and atoms are themselves components of chemical compounds (Fig. 2.8).

All structural levels up to and including those of complexes of compounds are encountered in both the nonliving and the living world. For example, two familiar chemical compounds found in living as well as nonliving matter are water and table salt. Examples of complexes of compounds in the nonliving world are rocks, which are composed of several types of compounds (water and table salt among them). In living matter, complexes of compounds often occur as microscopic and submicroscopic bodies called *organelles.* But even in their most elaborate and complicated forms, organelles or complexes of compounds of any kind cannot qualify as living units. To reach the level of life, we must go to the next higher structure level, that of *cells.*

A cell is a specific combination of organelles, a usually microscopic bit of matter organized just complexly enough to contain all the necessary apparatus for the performance of metabolism and self-perpetuation. A cell in effect represents the least elaborate known structure that can be fully alive. It follows that a living organism must consist of at least one cell. Indeed, *unicellular* organisms probably constitute the majority of living creatures on earth. All other organisms are *multicellular,* each composed of up to hundreds of trillions of joined cells.

Several distinct levels of organization can be distinguished within multicellular organisms. The simplest multicellular types contain comparatively small numbers of cells. If all such cells are more or less alike, the organism is often referred to as a cellular *colony*. For example, the microscopic organism *Gonium pectorale* consists of 16 photosynthetic cells (Fig. 2.9). A *tissue* consists of many cells that usually are similar in structure and function (see Color Fig. 4). Muscles, nerves, and the lining of the intestine are examples of tissues. Complex organisms not only contain several tissues, but some of the tissues may also be joined further as one or more units called *organs* (Fig. 2.10). The heart is an example of an organ; it includes muscle tissues, nerve tissue, and tissues which interconnect and hold together its various parts. The most complex organisms not only contain many tissues and organs, but also groups of organs united as one or more *organ systems* (see Color Fig. 5). The alimentary system, for example, is made up of several organs, among them the stomach, the liver, the pancreas, and the intestine (see Fig. 2.10). Thus, living organisms exhibit one of at least five levels of structural complexity: single-celled form, colonial form, organism with tissues, type with organs, and type with organ systems.

Beyond organisms of all kinds, several still higher levels of life can be distinguished. A few individual organisms of one kind together may make up a *family*. Groups of families of one kind may form a *society* (Fig. 2.11). Groups of families, societies, or simply large numbers of organisms of a particular kind make up a geographically localized *population*. All populations of the same kind together form a *species*. Several different species are represented in a local *community*. And the sum of all local communities represents the whole living world.

This hierarchical organization of matter as levels permits us to formulate a structural definition of life and nonlife. Up to and including the level of complexes of compounds, matter is nonliving. At all higher levels matter is living, provided that, at each such level, metabolic and self-perpetuative functions are carried out. To be living, a society, for example, must metabolize and perpetuate itself on its own level, as well as on every lower level down to the cell.

This hierarchy of levels provides a rough outline of the past history of matter. The universe as a whole is now believed to have begun in the form of subatomic particles. These then became joined as atoms and formed galaxies, stars, and planets. The atoms of planets later gave rise to chemical compounds and complexes of compounds. On earth, some of the complexes of compounds eventually produced living matter in the form of cells, and unicellular types were the ancestors of multicellular types. Among the latter, colonial types arose first, forms with organ systems last (see also Chap. 29). Considered historically, therefore, matter appears to have become organized progressively, level by level, and the presently existing hierarchy is the direct result.

Each level of organization includes fewer units than any lower level. There are fewer communities than species, fewer cells than organelles; and there is only one living world, but there are uncountable numbers of subatomic particles. Also, each level is structurally more complex than lower ones; a particular level combines the complexities of all lower levels and has an additional complexity of its own. For example, social complexity results from the characteristics of each member organism as *well as* from numerous special characteristics that arise out of the ways in which the members are organized as a society.

Energy

In any hierarchy of levels, a jump from one level to the next can often be achieved only at the expense of energy. It takes energy to build atoms into chemical compounds, and it took energy to create cells out of chemical complexes. Similarly, energy is needed to produce tissues out of cells or societies out of separate families. Indeed, once a higher living level has been created, energy expenditures must usually continue thereafter to maintain that level. For example, if the energy supply to the cell, the organ, or the organism is stopped, death and decomposition soon follow and reversion to lower levels occurs. Similarly, maintenance of a family or a society requires work over and above that needed to maintain the organization of subordinate units.

This requirement is an expression of the *second law of thermodynamics*, about which more will be said in the next chapter: if left to itself, any system tends toward a state of greatest stability. "Randomness," "disorder," and "probability" are

A

Fig. 2.10 Tissues, organs, and organ systems. (A) Section of snowshoe hare skin, showing epidermal and dermal tissues. A dark band of tightly packed epidermal cells overlies the thicker, less heavily stained dermis. The two tissues function together as a surface organ, protecting deeper body tissues of the hare from dessication, overheating, invasion of microbes, etc. (B) The human alimentary system. Several organs make up the human alimentary tract. They include the mouth, tongue, esophagus, stomach, small intestine, and large intestine. Other organs produce secretions that empty into the alimentary tract. They include salivary glands, liver, and pancreas.

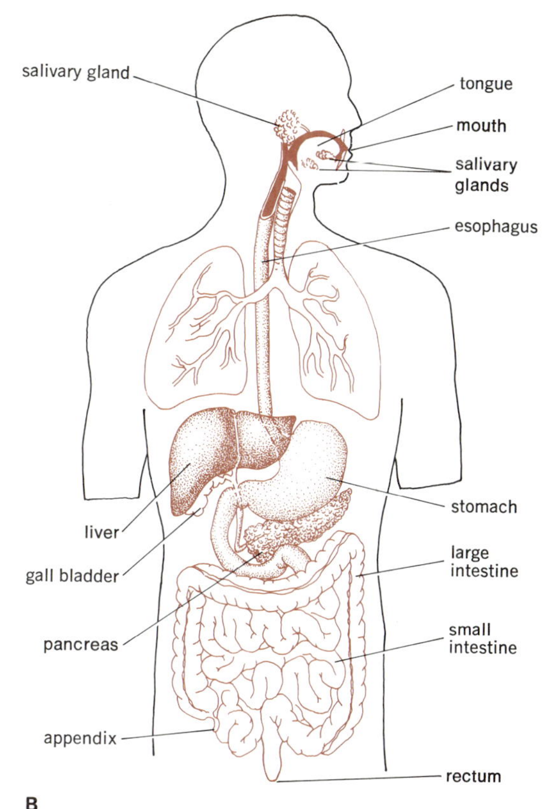

B

Fig. 2.11 Families and societies. (A) A family of scarlet tanagers. Individual members of a family or society often interact in ways that increase the survival potential of the larger unit. For example, incubation of eggs is left almost entirely to the duller-colored female tanager (perched at the right of the nest). But both parents cooperate in gathering food for the young. (B) Aggressive displays between rival individuals in societies prevents overcrowding and contributes to the dispersal of families over a wider area.

A

B

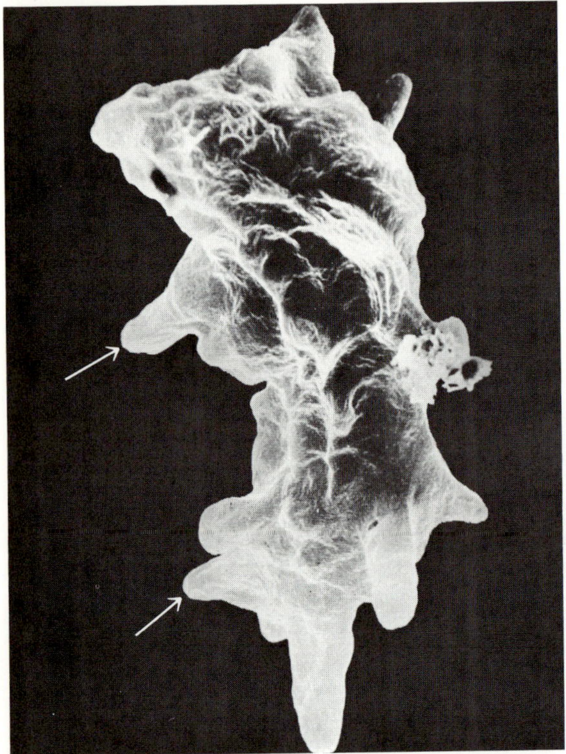

Fig. 2.12 ***Amoeba proteus*** (approx. 700X). Like all other unicellular organisms, this freshwater protozoan carries out all metabolic and self-perpetuative functions in a single cell. Often one of these functions—locomotion, for example—precludes a simultaneous execution of another—feeding, for example. Arrows indicate pseudopodia, fingerlike extensions that serve in locomotion and feeding.

equivalent to this meaning of stability. When a system includes high levels of organization, it also exhibits a high degree of order and it is correspondingly nonrandom and improbable. The second law tells us that such a system is unstable and that if we leave it to itself it will eventually become disordered, more random, more probable, and therefore more stable. Living systems are the most ordered, unstable, and improbable systems known. If they are to avoid the fate predicted by the second law, a price must be paid. That price is external energy—energy to maintain the order despite the continuous tendency toward disorder.

Such energy expenditures represent the price that must be paid for the new properties obtained at the higher level. One of these new properties is united, integrated function, arising out of cooperation between functional parts. For example, once atoms unite and form compounds, they function jointly as a single "cooperative" unit. Similarly, cells forming a multicellular unit surrender their independence and become a cooperative, integrated system. The fundamental advantage of such higher-level cooperative arrangements is *operational efficiency;* the cooperating whole is more efficient in performing the functions of life than its lower-level components acting separately and competitively.

Specialization

Duplication of effort can be avoided whenever parts of a whole become specialized to perform different functions. In a set of separate cells, for example, every cell is exposed to the environment on all sides and must therefore expend energy and materials on all sides to cope with the impact of the environment. However, if the same cells are grouped together as a compact tissue, only the outermost cells are in direct contact with the environment, and inner cells then need not channel their resources into protective activities.

Also, in addition to avoiding duplication of effort, cooperative groupings make possible continuity of effort. The general principle can be illustrated by contrasting unicellular and multicellular organisms, for example. A unicellular organism must necessarily carry out all survival functions within its one cell. In many instances, however, the performance of even one of these functions requires most or all of the capacities of the cell. Thus, the *entire* cell surface must often serve as gateway for entering nutrients and departing wastes. And *all* parts of the cell may be required directly in locomotion or in feeding, for example. Very often, therefore, two such functions cannot be performed at the same time, for one function may preclude the simultaneous performance of the other. Mutual exclusion of some functions by others is a common occurrence in all unicellular forms (Fig. 2.12).

In multicellular types, by contrast, continuity of a given effort becomes possible through *division of labor* among the cells. The total task of survival can be divided up into several subtasks, and each of these can become the continuous responsibility of particular cells only. Some cells might function in feeding, continuously so, and others in locomotion, again continuously. Frequently division of labor is actually so pronounced that many or most cells are permanently limited in functional capacity; they can perform only certain jobs and no others. For example, mature nerve cells can conduct nerve impulses only and are quite unable to reproduce or move. Mature muscle cells can move by contracting but they normally do not reproduce. Indeed, the majority of the cells of a multicellular organism is generally restricted in some ways in functional versatility. Such cells exhibit greater or lesser degrees of *specialization*.

An individual *specialized* cell therefore cannot perform all the functions necessary for survival. This is why, when some cells are removed from the whole organism, as in injury, for example, such cells usually die; the specialized cell has lost independence. The whole task of survival can be carried out only by the entire multicellular system with its many *differently* specialized cells.

Specialization makes possible not only division of labor but also increased effectiveness of labor. For example, all unicellular organisms are sensitive to environmental stimuli, but the degree of this relatively unspecialized sensitivity is quite modest. By contrast, many multicellular organisms have highly specialized sensory cells that are exceedingly sensitive and respond to even very weak stimuli. Moreover, several kinds of sensory cells are often present, some specialized specifically for light stimuli, others for sound stimuli, still others for mechanical stimuli, and so on. Thus both the degree and the range of sensitivity can become enormously greater in multicellular forms, in which the cells can become specialized. This is true for all other functions as well.

We can now understand the fundamental advantage of higher organizational levels generally and of multicellular levels specifically:

1. A multicellular structure permits division of labor, through which duplication of effort can be avoided and several efforts can continue simultaneously and uninterruptedly.

2. Division of labor leads to specialization, which permits any given effort to become highly effective.

The overall result is an enormous saving of energy and materials, hence cheaper operation, and an enormous gain in efficiency. This is one reason why living history has produced multicellular organisms, equipped successively with tissues, organs, and organ systems, rather than only bigger and better unicellular organisms.

LIVING ORGANISMS: THE MAIN GROUPS

The classification of organisms on the basis of their specializations is the concern of the biological subscience of *taxonomy* (or *systematics*). The present method of classifying organisms was originated by Carolus Linnaeus, a Swedish naturalist of the early eighteenth century. This Linnean system of taxonomy has since become greatly elaborated and is now in universal use. It is based on the proposition that if certain organisms can be shown to have similar body construction, they can be regarded as members of the same classification group. Moreover, an evolutionary inference is also made: the more closely two organisms resemble each other, the more closely they are likely to be related. Thus, taxonomy deals with the structural makeup of organisms directly and with their evolutionary histories indirectly (see also Chap. 29).

In a given classification group it is often possible to distinguish several subgroups, each containing organisms having even greater similarity of body structure and, by inference, evolutionary history. Such a subgroup can often be subdivided still further, and a whole hierarchy of classification groups can be established in this fashion. The progressively lower levels in this hierarchy represent *taxonomic ranks*, or *categories*. The main categories, from highest, or most inclusive, to lowest, or least inclusive, are: *kingdom, phylum, class, order, family, genus*, and *species*. Intermediate ranks sometimes interpolated between two main levels are identified by the prefixes *sub-* or *super-;* for example, *subphylum, superclass, subgenus*. The actual organisms included in a given rank-category are referred to technically as *taxa*. For example, moss plants form a taxon of phylum rank; mammals are a taxon at the class rank.

In the hierarchy as a whole, progressively

A

B

C

Fig. 2.13 Resemblance of related taxonomic groups. The three members of the vertebrate class of mammals shown here are alike in, for example, having fur and nursing their young with milk. However, the copperhead squirrel belongs to the order Rodentia (rodents), whereas both the Bengal tiger and the North American wolf belong to the order Carnivora (carnivores). The two orders resemble each other greatly, and they also have similar evolutionary histories. But they differ in, for example, tooth structure, eating habits, and locomotion. Of the two carnivores shown, the tiger belongs to the cat family Felidae and the wolf to the dog family Canidae. The two resemble each other more in anatomy and evolutionary history than either resembles the squirrel.

lower ranks consist of progressively more but smaller groups. The living world contains only some three dozen phyla but as many as $1\frac{1}{2}$ to 2 million or more species. Also, the groups at successively lower ranks have increasingly similar body forms and evolutionary histories. Thus the members of a class resemble each other to a great extent, but the members in one of the orders of that class resemble each other to an even greater extent. A corresponding relation holds for evolutionary histories (Fig. 2.13).

Taxonomy provides direct and inferential information about two kinds of data: body structure and evolutionary history. Organisms have other characteristics as well, notably functions and ways of life, but they play only a limited role in defining taxonomic types. Because metabolism and self-perpetuation are broadly the same in all organisms, such functions are not very useful as distinguishing traits. Moreover, both the ways of life and the detailed ways of performing functions can become modified greatly. Such characteristics therefore are usually less permanent than body architecture and evolutionary history.

Structural resemblances of presently living organisms can be studied readily, and indeed they are well known for the most part. But studies of evolutionary histories—through fossils, for example—represent an independent line of investigation, and the amount of information available here varies greatly. In general, evolutionary knowledge is less precise the higher the taxonomic rank. For many high rank-groups evolutionary information actually is quite incomplete or lacking altogether, and in such cases classification must be based almost wholly on studies of body structure. Conclusions regarding evolutionary histories are then correspondingly uncertain. In instances of this sort, classification is said to be artificial, or "unnatural," to greater or lesser degree.

The most unnatural grouping in the taxonomic hierarchy in effect is the kingdom. By tradition that goes back to Linnaeus and even to earlier times, all organisms have been classified into two kingdoms, the plant kingdom and the animal kingdom (Table 2.1). It is highly questionable whether this familiar, simple, and 250-year-old way of subdividing the living world is still justifiable or adequate today. For it is now clear that, in this Linnean sense, plant and animals are ultimately indistinguishable by biological criteria. Every trait usually regarded as characteristic of one kingdom occurs also in the other. For example, plants are defined traditionally as organisms that photosynthesize and do not exhibit locomotion, and animals as organisms that exhibit heterotrophic nutrition as well as locomotion. On such a basis, however, many algae and all fungi and slime molds would have to be animals, for all these organisms are nongreen heterotrophs and a good many of them exhibit locomotion as well. Yet sponges, corals, barnacles, tunicates, and other groups could not be strictly labeled as animals since the adult forms are attached and without locomotion. Moreover, certain primitive algal types would be both plant and animal at once, since, as will be shown in Chap. 31, such organisms can be alternately photosynthetic and nonlocomotor or heterotrophic and locomotor. Traits other than nutrition or locomotion fail similarly as distinguishing criteria.

TABLE 2.1
The Traditional Classification of Organisms: Plant and Animal Kingdoms

kingdom Plantae	subkingdom Thallophyta	algae, fungi, bacteria, slime molds
	subkingdom Embryophyta.	moss plants, vascular plants
kingdom Animalia	subkingdom Protozoa	largely unicellular types
	subkingdom Metazoa	multicellular types

In effect, some organisms fit in neither the plant nor the animal category, and several other groups fit in both. Traditional views notwithstanding, for example, bacteria really have very little in common with either plants or animals, and quite a number of unicellular algae and other types can be regarded equally well as plants *or* animals. To be sure, no one has much difficulty in deciding whether advanced organisms like cabbages and cats are plants or animals. But such a difficulty does exist with many organisms now known to be primitive, that is, organisms closely related to the ancestral types that gave rise to both cabbages and cats. As will be shown in Chap. 31 such ancestral types exhibited both plantlike and animal-like traits *simultaneously*, as is still true of some of their primitive descendants today. And if we go even farther back in time, the very first organisms on earth appear to have had neither plantlike nor animal-like traits at all.

The point is that plants and animals, clearly so recognizable, were not in existence right from the beginning. Instead, some of the early organisms *evolved* in plantlike or animal-like directions, slowly and gradually; and a definite "plant" status or "animal" status was attained only relatively late in evolutionary history. Therefore, a division of the living world merely into plant and animal kingdoms is too simple. It does not take into account the *gradual* evolution of distinct plant and animal groups, and it allows no place for those primitive organisms that even now are neither "plant" nor "animal" or that are both.

In view of this taxonomic difficulty, attempts have been made to establish alternative classifications that do reflect our present knowledge of evo-

TABLE 2.2
The Main Categories of Living Organisms

Kingdom	Representative phyla or classes*	Representative membership
Monera	Schizophyta	bacteria
	Cyanophyta	blue-green algae
Protista	Euglenophyta	*Euglena*
	Pyrrophyta	dinoflagellates
	Chrysophyta	golden algae, diatoms, yellow-green algae
	Gymnomycota	slime molds
	Protozoa	protozoans
Fungi	Chytridiomycetes	chytrids
	Oomycetes	water molds, white rusts, downy mildews
	Zygomycetes	bread mold
	Ascomycetes	yeasts, morels, truffles
	Basidiomycetes	mushrooms, toadstools
	Deuteromycetes (Fungi Imperfecti)	athlete's foot fungus, *Penicillium,* a number of fungi used in making cheeses
Plantae (Metaphyta)	Rhodophyta	red algae
	Phaeophyta	brown algae
	Chlorophyta	green algae
	Bryophyta	moss plants; mosses liverworts, hornworts
	Tracheophyta	vascular plants; ferns, coniferous seed plants, flowering seed plants
Animalia (Metazoa)	Porifera	sponges
	Cnidaria (Coelenterata)	hydras, jellyfishes, corals, sea anemones
	Ctenophora	comb-jellies or sea walnuts
	Platyhelminthes	flatworms: planarians, flukes, tapeworms
	Rhyncocoela (Nemertea)	proboscis worms
	Nematoda	roundworms
	Acanthocephala	spiny-headed worms
	Chaetognatha	arrow worms
	Nematomorpha	horsehair worms
	Rotifera	rotifers
	Bryozoa	"moss" animals
	Brachiopoda	lamp shells
	Annelida	segmented worms: earthworms, leeches
	Arthopoda	arthopods: crustaceans, insects, scorpions, spiders, ticks, millipedes, centipedes
	Mollusca	mollusks: snails, clams, squids, octopuses
	Echinodermata	spiny-skinned animals: starfishes, sea urchins, sea cucumbers, brittle stars, sea lilies
	Chordata	notochord-possessing animals (tunicates, amphioxus, and vertebrates): among vertebrates; jawless fishes (lampreys), bony fishes (herring, tuna, etc.), cartilage fishes (sharks), amphibia (salamanders, newts, toads, frogs), reptiles (turtles, lizards, snakes, alligators), birds, mammals

*The subgroups of fungi are classes; all others are phyla.

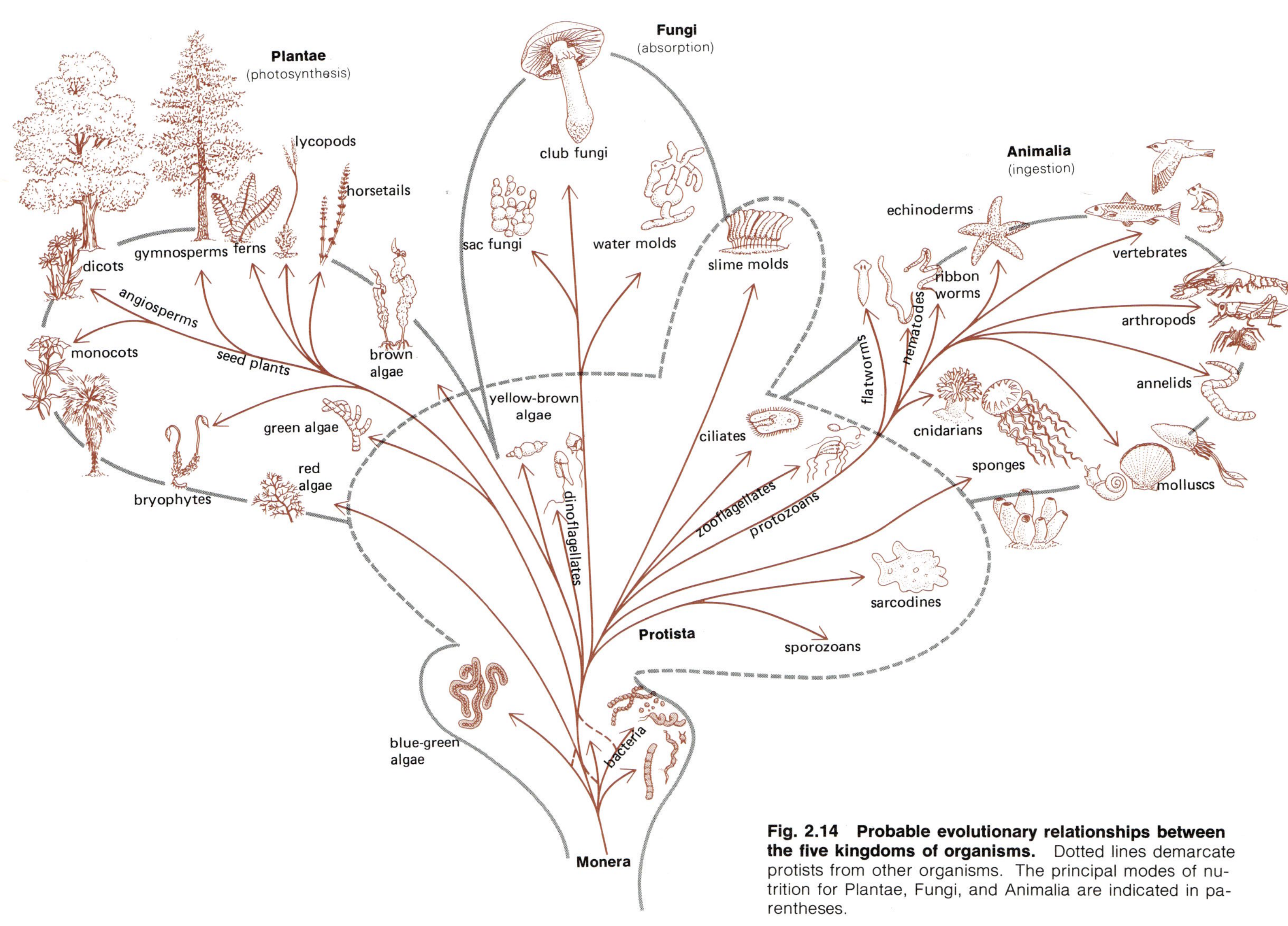

Fig. 2.14 Probable evolutionary relationships between the five kingdoms of organisms. Dotted lines demarcate protists from other organisms. The principal modes of nutrition for Plantae, Fungi, and Animalia are indicated in parentheses.

TABLE 2.3
A Partial Classification of Corn Plants and Human Beings

Taxonomic rank	Corn plant	Human being
phylum	Tracheophyta: plants with vascular tissues	Chordata: animals with notochords
subphylum	Pteropsida: types with large leaves	Vertebrata: types with vertebral columns
superclass	Spermatophyta: seed producers	Tetrapoda: terrestrial; four limbs; bony skeletons
class	Angiospermae: flowering plants; seeds inside fruits	Mammalia: types with hair and milk glands
subclass	Monocotyledonae: parallel-veined leaves; single seed leaf; flower parts in threes or multiples of threes	Eutheria: offspring develop in female parent, nourished by placenta
order	Graminales: grasses	Primates: fingers; flat nails
family	Graminaceae: leaves in two rows on round or flattened stem	Hominidae: upright posture; flat face; stereoscopic vision; large brain; hands and feet
genus	Zea: corn plants	Homo: double curved spine; long life-span and long youth
species	Zea mays: cultivated, domesticated corn plants	Homo sapiens: with chin and high forehead; thin skull bones

lution. For example, several variants of three-kingdom and four-kingdom classification schemes recently have been proposed. In the taxonomic scheme used in this book, five kingdoms of organisms are recognized, namely, *Monera, Protista, Fungi, Plantae* (*Metaphyta*), and *Animalia* (*Metazoa*). The kinds of organisms included in each of the kingdoms are listed in Table 2.2 and the probable evolutionary interrelations of the five are sketched in Fig. 2.14.

In this five-part classification, every living creature has a proper place. Monera are variously plantlike, animal-like, both, or neither. Among Protista, some algae are again both plantlike and animal-like simultaneously, but most have lost heterotrophic capacities and now have more or less plantlike traits. Conversely, slime molds and protozoa have lost the plantlike modes of nutrition. Yet in other respects these protistan groups again display certain plantlike and animal-like traits in combination. Many slime molds are rather more plantlike, protozoa, more nearly animal-like. However, all protists share more characteristics in common with each other than with any other group of organisms. Moreover, all categories of protists are primarily unicellular or consist of small colonies of unicellular organisms.

Because of several unique characteristics, fungi are segregated as a separate kingdom. Like animals, fungi are nonphotosynthetic, but in most other respects these organisms more closely resemble plants. Although a few fungi, such as yeasts, are unicellular, most are composed of weblike threads that absorb nutrients from the surrounding environment.

Fungi, Plantae, and Animalia all are believed to have evolved from ancient protists, independently and at different times. The last two groups are almost exclusively multicellular, and their structural complexity reaches the level of complicated organs and organ systems. Plantae are photosynthetic and except for certain algae without locomotion; virtually all these organisms are unmistakably "plants." Animalia are exclusively nonphotosynthetic and largely (but not always) capable of locomotion: they are unmistakably "animals."

The five major categories above can be defined more sharply than the two Linnean kingdoms. Moreover, the five-part scheme has the important advantage of being more nearly in line with the known evolutionary and structural characteristics of existing organisms. Throughout this book, therefore, any unqualified reference to plants or animals is restricted to mean Plantae and Animalia, respectively. Also, a golden alga is not regarded as a plant nor a protozoan as an animal, but both organisms are identified as protists

In passing from the highest level to lower taxonomic ranks, classification tends to become progressively more "natural": evolutionary knowledge is more complete, and structural and evolutionary data come to dovetail more and more. At the lower levels taxonomy thus tends to indicate an actual, real interrelation of organisms. For example, some notable exceptions notwithstanding, a phylum generally can be defined as the largest group of organisms for which a common ancestry has been demonstrated reasonably well and which is characterized by a common, basically unique body construction.

Table 2.3 indicates that most phyla represent more or less familiar categories of organisms, often named for one of their most distinctive anatomic features. For example, the phylum *Chordata* includes all animals possessing an internal skeletal support, the *notochord*, at least as embryos. This phylum contains a subphylum of *vertebrates*, characterized by the presence of a vertebral column. Within the vertebrate subphylum, one of the classes is represented by the *mammals*. These animals share the possession of a vertebral column with all other vertebrate classes, namely, birds, reptiles, amphibia, and several classes of fishes. But mammals are set off from other vertebrate classes by their possession of hair and by their nursing young with milk. Every other class has its own distinguishing traits.

In many cases the subgroups within a phylum differ greatly in their ways of life and their methods of executing functions, and a common body structure then may not be readily apparent. Consider, for example, the different appearance of a desert plant like a cactus, an aquatic plant like a water lily, and an underground plant like an onion bulb. Or consider the different appearance of a fish and a person. Nevertheless, most organisms within a phylum use the same kinds of structures in solving the different problems of their different environments. Thus, the spines of a cactus, the surface float of a water lily, and the white, tear-producing layers inside an onion bulb, all are basically the same kind of structures, namely, leaves. They all have evolved along different paths from one ancestral type of foliation. Similarly, the fins of a fish and the arms of a person are basically the same kind of structures, having evolved from one common ancestral type of body appendage.

Using such criteria of structural and evolutionary correspondence between and within groups, one can recognize orders within a class, families within an order, genera within a family, and species within a genus. The species, normally the lowest unit, is the most natural of all taxonomic categories. As pointed out in Chap. 8, it is defined as an *interbreeding* group: the members of a species normally interbreed only with one another, and not with members of a different species. In this instance, therefore, classification is based on a characteristic that undoubtedly results from a very close structural and evolutionary similarity of the organisms in question. For example, all human beings now in existence are members of the same single species.

According to Linnean tradition and internationally accepted rules, a species is always identified by *two* technical names. These names are in Latin or are latinized and are used uniformly all over the world. For example, the species of grass frogs is known technically as *Rana pipiens;* the species to which we belong is *Homo sapiens.* Such species names are always underlined or printed in italics, and the first name is capitalized. This first name always identifies the genus to which the species belongs. Thus, the human species belongs to the genus *Homo* and the grass-frog species to the genus *Rana. Homo sapiens* happens to be the only presently living species within the genus *Homo,* but the genus *Rana* contains *Rana pipiens* as well as many other frog species.

A complete classification of an organism tells a great deal about the nature of that organism. For example, if we knew nothing else about corn plants and people except their taxonomic classifications, we would know that the characteristics of these organisms are as listed in Table 2.3. Such data already represent a substantial detailing of the body structure. We would also know by implication that the evolutionary history of corn plants traces back to the common ancestry of flowering plants, and that the history of human beings goes back to a common chordate ancestry.

The taxonomic ranks assigned today to a number of particular groups of organisms are far from final, and in some cases a given group is actually placed at different rank levels by different authorities. In general, taxonomic agreement among biologists increases with the lower, more natural rank categories and decreases with the higher, less natural ones. Indeed, the higher categories are being reshuffled more or less continually. But this is probably as it should be, for as our knowledge of the evolution of organisms improves, the rankings of the organisms must be adjusted accordingly.

Review Questions

1 What is metabolism? Self-perpetuation? What are the main subfunctions of each and what specific roles do these subfunctions play in the maintenance of life?

2 What are the fundamental differences between inanimate, dead, and living systems? Discuss carefully and fully. Define living.

3 Review the hierarchy of levels in the organization of matter, and discuss how living matter is characterized in terms of levels.

4 Review the relationship of levels of organization to energy, to numbers of units, to complexity, to competition and cooperation, and to operational efficiency.

5 Define cell structurally and functionally. Define organelle, tissue, organ, organ system, organism, family, society.

6 In terms of cellular specializations, how does a cell of a single-celled organism differ from a cell of a multicellular organism? What are the functional advantages of specialization?

7 Review the structure of the Linnean taxonomic system. What are the main ranks? Name and define them, and cite groups of organisms of each. How is this system related to the size and the members of groups at each rank?

8 On what characteristics of organisms is the taxonomic system based? Why are other possible characteristics not used? Why are organisms not simply classified alphabetically or by some system equivalent to book cataloging in libraries?

9 What is meant by natural and unnatural taxonomic classifications? Give examples. Review the taxonomic classification of human beings, with attention to the definition of each rank category.

Collateral Readings

Grobstein, C.: "The Strategy of Life," 2d ed., Freeman, San Francisco, 1974. A thoughtful and stimulating paperback containing a section on levels of organization as well as discussions of other general phenomena of life.

Margulis, L., and **K. Schwartz:** "Phyla of the Five Kingdoms: An Illustrated Guide to the Kinds of Life on Earth," Freeman, San Francisco, 1980. Representing a catalogue of the world's living diversity, this book lists and illustrates the nearly 100 phyla of the five kingdoms. The book provides a good survey of the five-kingdom system of classification.

Minsky, M. L.: Artificial Intelligence, *Scientific American*, September 1966. On the "thinking" processes of which a computer is capable.

Penrose, L. S.: Self-Reproducing Machines, *Scientific American*, July 1959. Models of self-duplicating mechanical systems are described, paralleling the action of self-duplicating biological systems.

Schrödinger, E.: "What Is Life?," Cambridge University Press, New York, 1944. A stimulating essay by a noted physicist, discussing some of the basic characteristics of life.

Part 2
The Organization of Life

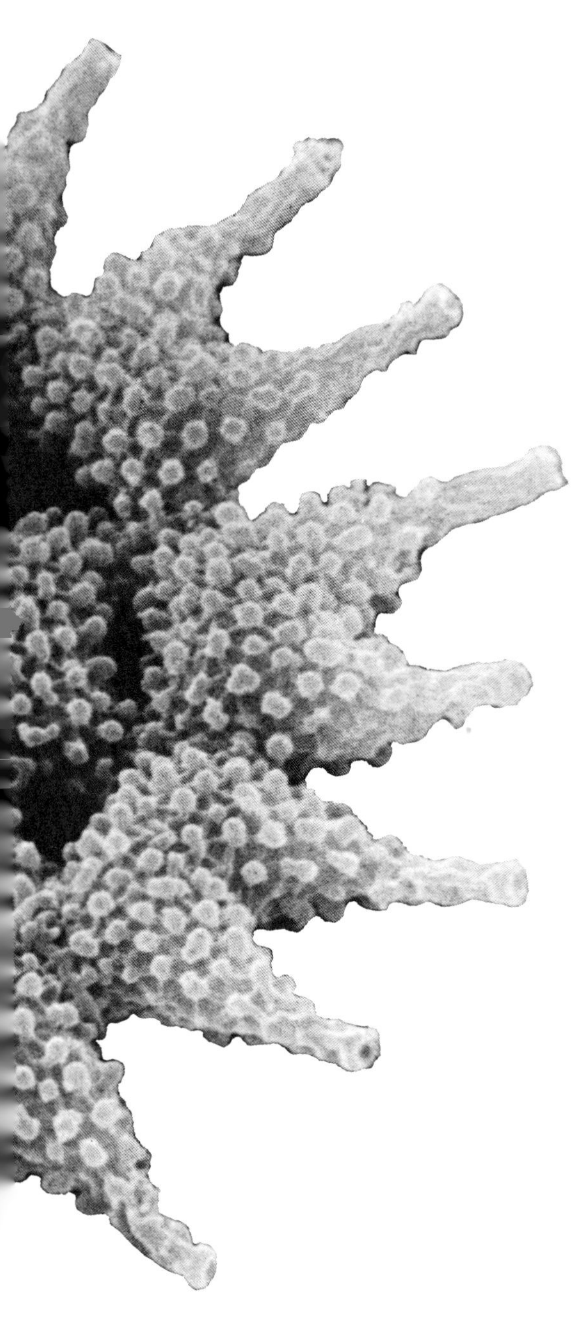

In this part we examine the structure of the living hierarchy in some detail. Our first concerns are the chemical makeup of living matter and the specific ways in which living matter forms organisms composed of cells, tissues, organs, and organ systems. Whole organisms in their turn are components of higher living levels—populations, species, communities, and ecosystems. The organization of these larger units is our second subject of discussion. Groups of this kind live in, and indeed are greatly influenced by, the geographic localities that serve as their homes. These most inclusive levels thus encompass all living matter on earth, as well as the total physical environment of the globe. The often deleterious impact of human beings on the organization of the living hierarchy is the final topic in this series of chapters.

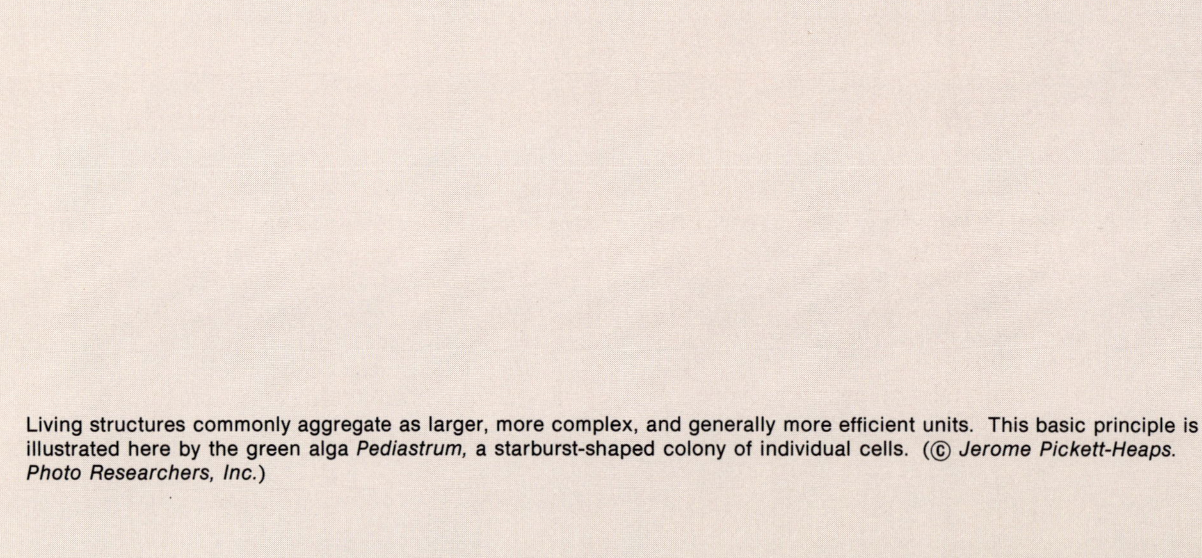

Living structures commonly aggregate as larger, more complex, and generally more efficient units. This basic principle is illustrated here by the green alga *Pediastrum*, a starburst-shaped colony of individual cells. (© *Jerome Pickett-Heaps. Photo Researchers, Inc.*)

Chapter 3

Cells: Chemical Foundations

Learning Objectives

After reading this chapter you should be able to:

1. Define element, atom, compound, molecule; write a structural formula for a compound that contains 6 carbon atoms, 12 hydrogen atoms, and 6 oxygen atoms.
2. Differentiate between ionic, covalent, and hydrogen bonds; list at least one example of each.
3. Construct a diagram that depicts the relative positions and electric charges of protons, electrons, and neutrons in a molecule.
4. Name the four elements that constitute 95 per cent of your body.
5. Illustrate how the polarity of water molecules creates resistance to rapid changes of temperature and makes this substance an almost universal solvent; list at least two reasons why each of these properties of water are important to living systems.
6. Distinguish between metals and nonmetals, and state an example of each.
7. Define dissociation and differentiate between acids, bases, and salts.
8. Define buffer and list at least one reason why buffers are important to living systems; using chemical reactions, write a paragraph explaining how sodium bicarbonate can relieve "acid indigestion."
9. Define chemical reaction; name three general types of chemical reactions and write an example of each; list at least one way in which each of these types of reactions contributes to cellular metabolism.
10. Define the relation between chemical energy and chemical bonds; state the first and second laws of thermodynamics, differentiate between endergonic and exergonic reactions and between enthalpy and entropy; write a paragraph explaining the relationship between enthalpy and the generalized chemical reaction:

$$\mathrm{A + B \longrightarrow C + D + energy\ (to\ environment)}$$

11. Write a paragraph explaining the relationship between entropy and the generalized chemical reaction:

$$\mathrm{A + B + C \longrightarrow D}$$

assuming that the total energy content is the same before and after the reaction.

12. List four factors capable of influencing the rates of chemical reactions.
13. Define the law of mass action and state an example of it.

Can anything alive be composed of the same chemical elements which compose nonliving matter? Can the vital functions of living systems be explained in terms of the same types of chemical reactions occurring in inanimate objects? Such questions were central in the debate between *vitalists* and *mechanists* during the eighteenth and early nineteenth centuries. Vitalists held that organisms were immune to the natural laws of chemistry and physics; mechanists held the opposite view. In an attempt to answer such questions, certain biologists began to "dismantle" cells experimentally, to determine how the pieces fit together to form life's basic units. From their experiments, and those of modern biologists, a substantial body of evidence has been amassed supporting the mechanistic viewpoint.

TABLE 3.1
Some Common Chemical Elements

Element	Symbol	Common valences
hydrogen	H	+1
sodium	Na	+1
potassium	K	+1
chlorine	Cl	−1
iodine	I	−1
calcium	Ca	+2
magnesium	Mg	+2
sulfur	S	−2
oxygen	O	−2
copper	Cu	+1, +2
iron	Fe	+2, +3
carbon	C	+2, +4
silicon	Si	+4
aluminum	Al	+3
nitrogen	N	−3, +5
phosphorus	P	−3, +5

The chemical elements and chemical reactions of living systems are fundamentally no different from those found in any other objects. Cells and organisms are not alive by virtue of the matter composing them but by virtue of the way their common matter is uncommonly organized.

A basic understanding of the nature of common matter is essential to an appreciation of its uncommon organization in living things. We therefore begin at the lowest levels of the structural hierarchy—the levels at which subatomic particles, atoms, and molecules interact.

CHEMICALS

Atoms

The universe is made up of roughly 100 fundamental kinds of materials called chemical *elements.* Iron, carbon, gold, oxygen, and aluminum are some familiar examples. Some others, most of them present also in living matter, are listed in Table 3.1. Each element exists in the form of exceedingly small units called *atoms.* Thus, a gold atom is the fundamental unit of the element gold.

Each element has a chemical symbol, often the first or the first two letters of its English or Latin name. For example, the symbol for hydrogen is H, that for carbon is C, and that for silicon is Si (see also Table 3.1). To represent a single atom of an element, one simply writes the appropriate symbol. For example, the letter H stands for one atom of hydrogen. If more than one atom is to be indicated, the appropriate number is put before the atomic symbol. For example, five separate hydrogen atoms are written as 5 H.

An atom is made up of *subatomic particles.* Two kinds of these, *neutrons* and *protons,* occur in varying numbers in the center of an atom, where they form an *atomic nucleus.* Neutrons are electrically neutral; protons carry one unit of positive charge. The atomic nucleus as a whole is therefore electrically positive. Orbiting around the nucleus are certain numbers of a third type of particle, *electrons.* Each of these carries one unit of negative electric charge, and an atom normally contains exactly as many electrons as there are protons in its nucleus. The electrons are maintained in orbit because they are attracted by the positively charged nucleus. Since the total positive charge equals the total negative charge, an atom as a whole is electrically neutral (Fig. 3.1).

Just as planetary orbits lie at various distances from the sun, so electron orbits are spaced out from the atomic nucleus at a number of fixed distances. The orbital paths at these distances form so-called electron "shells," one outside the other. The first shell, closest to the atomic nucleus, can hold a maximum of two electrons; the second shell, a maximum of eight. Known maximums also characterize all other shells. Electrons usually fill these shells from the innermost outward. Thus depending on the number of electrons in an atom, the outermost shell will be either complete and filled to capacity or incomplete to greater or lesser degree. Hydrogen, for example, has an incomplete outer shell since the single electron present does not fill the first shell to capacity. But helium, with two electrons, does fill this shell completely. In an oxygen atom, similarly, two of the total of eight electrons fill the first shell and the remaining six occupy the second. Since this second shell can hold as many as eight electrons, oxygen has an incomplete outer shell (Fig. 3.2).

An atom is most stable when its electron shells

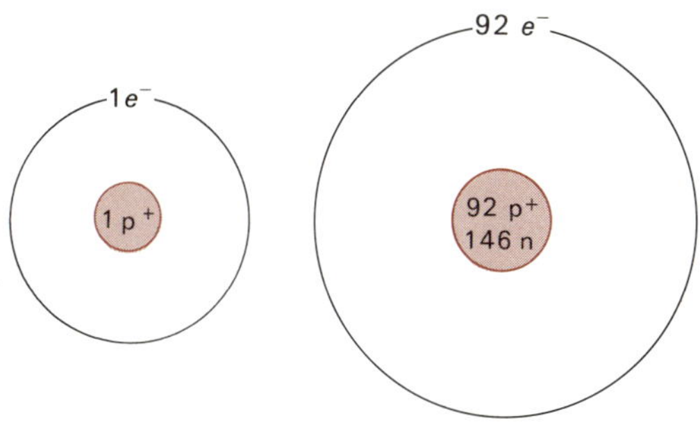

Fig. 3.1 Atomic structure: hydrogen and uranium. The atomic nucleus of hydrogen contains a single proton (p^+); that of uranium, 92 protons and 146 neutrons (*n*). The number of electrons (e^-) orbiting around the nucleus equals the number of protons.

are complete. Helium, for example, with a complete first shell, is stable and it is therefore usually also quite inert chemically; normally it does not react with other atoms. Similarly stable and chemically inactive are neon, with two complete shells, argon with three, krypton with four, xenon with five, and radon with six. These elements are the *inert gases.* In all other elements the outermost electron shells of the atoms are incomplete, and such atoms are more or less unstable. They reveal this comparative instability by their chemical reactivity; when two or more atoms come into contact, their incomplete outer shells can make them undergo chemical reactions. More specifically, atoms can become attached to one another through electric bonding forces, or *chemical bonds,* and the resulting atomic combinations are *compounds.* In effect, the chemical properties of atoms are determined by their outermost electron shells.

Each compound has a chemical name and a formula, both reflecting the kinds and numbers of atoms present. For example, table salt is technically the compound "sodium chloride," the name indicating the presence of sodium and chlorine. The formula NaCl also shows the quantitative ratio of these components: one sodium atom is linked to one chlorine atom. Water is technically the compound "hydrogen oxide," and the formula H_2O indicates the presence of two hydrogen atoms for every one of oxygen. The number of like atoms in a compound is customarily shown as a subscript. For example, iron oxide, Fe_2O_3, contains two iron atoms for every three oxygen atoms. A more complex compound is calcium phosphate $Ca_3(PO_4)_2$. The formula here is a shorthand notation for the following combination of atoms: three calcium atoms are bonded to two subcombinations, each of which consists of one phosphorus and four oxygen atoms. Thus, thirteen atoms together form one unit of the compound calcium phosphate. If more than one unit of a compound is to be written in symbols, the appropriate number is put before the formula. For example, H_2O stands for one unit of the compound water and 5 H_2O stands for five such units.

Different kinds of atoms form bonds and compounds in different ways.

Ions

Every atom has a tendency to complete its outer electron shell and thereby to become as stable

Fig. 3.2 Atomic electron shells. Helium has a complete (first) shell of two electrons. In oxygen the first shell is complete, but the second shell is incomplete by two electrons. Chlorine has complete first and second shells and a nearly complete third shell. And sodium has a nearly empty third shell.

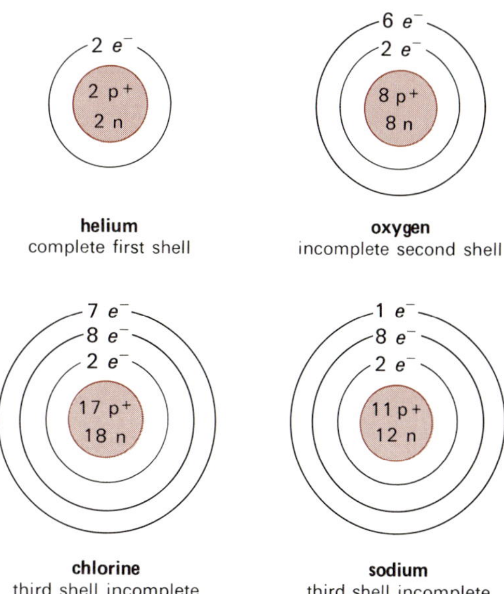

as possible. How can an originally incomplete electron shell become complete? Consider an atom of chlorine. Of its 17 orbital electrons, 2 form a complete first shell, 8 a complete second shell, and the remaining 7 an incomplete third shell (see Fig. 3.2). Like the second shell, the third similarly can hold a maximum of 8 electrons. Evidently, the chlorine atom is just one electron short of having a complete outer shell. If the atom could in some way *gain* one more electron, it would satisfy its strong tendency for electronic completeness and greatest stability. Chlorine is said to have a bonding capacity, or *valence,* of -1 (see Table 3.1), an indication that the gain of one electron can establish stability.

Consider now an atom of sodium. Of its 11 electrons, 2 form a complete first shell, 8 a complete second shell, and the remaining 1 a highly incomplete third shell (see Fig. 3.2). If this atom were to *lose* the single electron in the third shell, its second shell would then become the outermost shell. Since this second shell is already complete, the atom would have satisfied its tendency for completeness and would be stable. Sodium, therefore has a valence of $+1$, an indication that loss of one electron can establish stability. Chlorine and sodium can become stable simultaneously if an electron is transferred from sodium to chlorine. Such *electron transfers* actually occur, and they represent one major class of chemical reactions (Fig. 3.3).

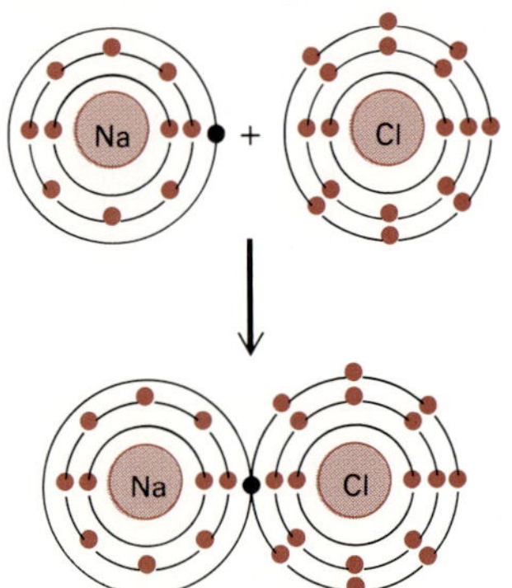

Fig. 3.3 Electron transfer and ionic compounds. In a reaction between one atom of sodium and one of chlorine, the single electron in the third shell of sodium (black) is transferred to the third shell of chlorine. Sodium thereby acquires a complete outer (second) shell of eight electrons and chlorine a complete outer (third) shell of eight electrons. In this form sodium and chlorine are ions, and both together represent the ionic compound sodium chloride. (Black electrons here and in Fig. 3.4 designate which electrons are being transferred or shared.)

Since electrons carry negative charges, their transfer has important electric consequences. In the sodium-chlorine reaction, for example, neither atom is electrically neutral after the transfer. Sodium has lost a negative charge and has therefore become electropositive; and since chlorine has gained a negative charge, it has become electronegative. Atoms or groups of atoms that have lost or gained electrons are called *ions;* electron transfer produces an *ionization* of the participating atoms. One of the ions formed is always electropositive, the other electronegative. And since positively and negatively charged particles attract each other, a positive and a negative ion will similarly exert mutual attraction. It is this attraction that forms a chemical bond between the ions, and it is this bond that unites the ions as a compound. Atoms that tend to lose electrons and thereby become positively charged ions are otherwise known as *metals;* and atoms that gain electrons and become negatively charged ions are *nonmetals.* Sodium is a metal, chlorine, a nonmetal.

Compounds formed by electron transfers and mutual attraction of the resulting ions are *ionic compounds.* They represent a major category of chemical substances, and they are abundant in living matter. The chemical bonds in an ionic compound are *ionic,* or *electrovalent, bonds.* The number of such bonds in a compound generally equals the number of electrons transferred. For example, the ionic compound sodium chloride contains a single bond; the attracting force between the sodium and chloride ion results from transfer of a single electron:

$$\left.\begin{array}{l} \mathrm{Na} \longrightarrow \mathrm{Na}^+ \\ \quad\quad e^- \\ \mathrm{Cl} \longrightarrow \mathrm{Cl}^- \end{array}\right\} \longrightarrow \mathrm{Na}^+\mathrm{Cl}^-$$

Molecules

Atoms can become stable not only by transferring but also by *sharing* electrons. For example, suppose that chlorine atoms are prevented from gaining electrons from other kinds of atoms because no other atoms are present. A chlorine atom can then complete its outer shell of seven electrons by interacting with another chlorine atom. We already know that a chlorine atom can attract one additional electron quite strongly. If two such atoms

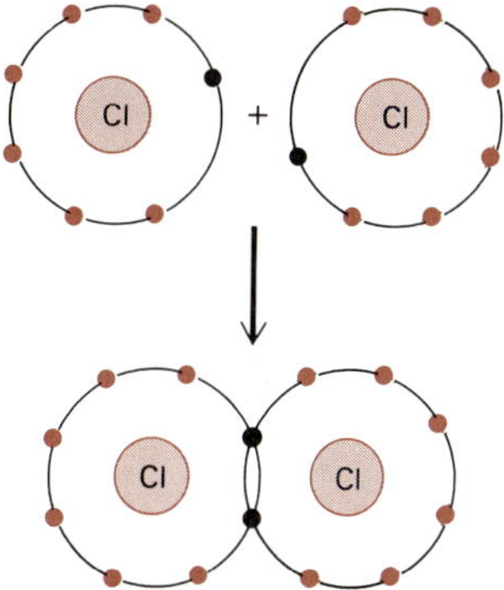

Fig. 3.4 Electron sharing and molecular compounds. Two chlorine atoms with their seven outer electrons are shown at top. If the two atoms share one pair of electrons (black) as at bottom, each atom acquires a complete outer shell of eight electrons. The result is a molecule of chlorine, Cl_2.

come into contact, each will therefore attract an electron of the other with equal force. But each atom holds on to its own electrons, and an electronic "tug of war" will take place that neither atom can "win"; and without a decision, the mutual tugging will continue indefinitely. As a result the atoms will remain linked together, just as equally matched opponents of a real tug of war remain linked by the mutual pull they exert on each other. In this case electrons are not transferred and ions are not formed. Instead, as each atom pulls on an electron of the other, a pair of electrons is shared: each atom has its own seven outer electrons plus one that it attracts from the other. Both atoms then behave as if they actually contained eight outer electrons each, and this establishes their stability (Fig. 3.4).

Hydrogen atoms too can share electrons:

$$\mathrm{H}\cdot + \mathrm{H}\cdot \longrightarrow \mathrm{H}:\mathrm{H}$$

The two electrons then "belong" to both atoms equally, and each atom has a sphere of attracting influence over the two electrons it requires for a complete orbital shell. In many cases more than one pair of electrons can be shared. For example, an oxygen atom with six outer electrons can share two pairs with another oxygen atom:

$$\underset{\cdot\cdot}{\overset{\cdot\cdot}{\mathrm{O}}}: + :\underset{\cdot\cdot}{\overset{\cdot\cdot}{\mathrm{O}}} \longrightarrow \underset{\cdot\cdot}{\overset{\cdot\cdot}{\mathrm{O}}}::\underset{\cdot\cdot}{\overset{\cdot\cdot}{\mathrm{O}}}$$

Each oxygen atom now has a sphere of attracting influence over eight electrons, the required number for a complete outer shell. Oxygen can also share two pairs of electrons with, for example, hydrogen:

$$\mathrm{H}\cdot + \cdot\mathrm{H} + \cdot\underset{\cdot\cdot}{\overset{\cdot\cdot}{\mathrm{O}}}\cdot \longrightarrow \mathrm{H}:\underset{\cdot\cdot}{\overset{\cdot\cdot}{\mathrm{O}}}:\mathrm{H}$$

Here each of the three participating atoms attracts just enough electrons for a complete outer shell—oxygen a shell of eight electrons and each hydrogen a shell of two.

Atoms such as chlorine or hydrogen either transfer or share electrons, depending on what other kinds of atoms are available for reaction. Another group of atoms (including sodium, magnesium, and many other metals) reacts almost exclusively by electron transfer. And in a third group (represented by oxygen, nitrogen, carbon, and others), electrons are almost always shared. Carbon, for example, can share its four outer electrons with four hydrogen atoms:

$$\cdot\underset{\cdot}{\overset{\cdot}{\mathrm{C}}}\cdot + 4\,\mathrm{H}\cdot \longrightarrow \begin{array}{c}\mathrm{H}\\ \mathrm{H}:\underset{\cdot\cdot}{\overset{\cdot\cdot}{\mathrm{C}}}:\mathrm{H}\\ \mathrm{H}\end{array}$$

Or carbon can also react with two oxygen atoms:

$$:\mathrm{C}: + 2\,\underset{\cdot\cdot}{\overset{\cdot\cdot}{\mathrm{O}}}: \longrightarrow \underset{\cdot\cdot}{\overset{\cdot\cdot}{\mathrm{O}}}::\mathrm{C}::\underset{\cdot\cdot}{\overset{\cdot\cdot}{\mathrm{O}}}$$

As the electron distributions here indicate, each of the participating atoms again attracts just the number of electrons required for a complete outer shell.

Electron sharing represents a second major way in which compounds are formed. Compounds of this type are *molecular compounds,* or simply *molecules.* The chemical bonds in molecules are *covalent bonds,* each represented by a shared electron pair. In present contexts it will usually not be necessary to distinguish between electrovalent and covalent bonds, but the position of bonds will need to be shown fairly often. A compound can then be symbolized by means of a *structural* formula, in which the location of bonds (either electrovalent or covalent) is indicated by short dashes between appropriate atoms. For example,

NaCl	or	Na—Cl	sodium chloride
Cl_2	or	Cl—Cl	chlorine molecule
H_2O	or	H—O—H	water molecule
O_2	or	O═O	oxygen molecule
N_2	or	N≡N	nitrogen molecule
CH_4	or	$\begin{array}{c}\mathrm{H}\\ \vert\\ \mathrm{H—C—H}\\ \vert\\ \mathrm{H}\end{array}$	methane molecule
CO_2	or	O═C═O	carbon dioxide molecule

Note that more than one dash exists between the C and O atoms of CO_2 and between the N atoms of N_2. Here more than a single pair of electrons is being shared between atoms. Two pair are shared between C and each of the O atoms of CO_2, hence the two *double bonds.* Three pair of electrons are shared between the nitrogen atoms of a nitrogen molecule, hence the *triple bond.* Under some circumstances, even *quadruple bonds* can exist between atoms.

The chemical properties of a compound are determined by the *arrangement,* the *numbers,* and the *types* of atoms present. Two molecules might contain the same set of atoms, but if they are arranged differently the molecules will have different properties. For example, the molecules

```
    H   H   H   H
    |   |   |   |
H — C — C — C — C — H
    |   |   |   |
    H   H   H   H
```

and

```
    H         H         H
    |         |         |
H — C ——————— C ——————— C — H
    |         |         |
    H     H — C — H     H
              |
              H
```

contain identical atoms, and both molecules can be symbolized as C_4H_{10}. But since their atoms are bonded in different patterns, they are actually different molecules with different properties. Variations in the bonding patterns of otherwise similar molecules are particularly significant in the chemistry of living matter.

Importance of Water

If all the elements making up your body were accumulated and weighed, approximately 95 per cent of the total would consist of oxygen, carbon, hydrogen, and nitrogen (Table 3.2). Most of the hydrogen and oxygen atoms in your body are present as water, perhaps the most common molecule on earth. Water makes up 50 to 95 per cent of the weight of most organisms. But water, although common, is far from ordinary. In fact, very few

TABLE 3.2
Atomic Composition of Human Beings

Element	Percentage of total composition
oxygen	62.81
carbon	19.37
hydrogen	9.31
nitrogen	5.14
phosphorus	0.63
sulfur	0.64
all others	2.10
total	100.00

cell functions can be carried out in the absence of water.

Properties of Water

Most of the unique properties of water are due to the physical relation between its oxygen and hydrogen atoms. Both hydrogen atoms are bound covalently to oxygen and, because of chemical restraints, both are bound toward one side of the oxygen atom (Fig. 3.5). The relatively larger size of the positively charged oxygen nucleus attracts hydrogen electrons more strongly than either hydrogen nucleus. This fact, together with the asymmetric shape of the water molecule, causes the "oxygen end" of the molecule to carry a slight negative charge relative to its "hydrogen end." Because of this slight charge differential, or *polarity,* a water molecule will tend to become positioned with each of its more positively charged hydrogen atoms directed toward the more negatively charged oxygen poles of two adjacent water molecules. This type of electrostatic attraction between hydrogen atoms and other negatively charged atoms is called *hydrogen bonding.* The movement of electrons about the entire water molecule is such that a negatively charged oxygen pole of one molecule can bond with two hydrogen atoms, one from each of two adjacent water molecules. Consequently, each water molecule tends to hydrogen-bond with four neighboring water molecules (see Fig. 3.5).

Because of the relative weakness of hydrogen bonds, this precise latticework arrangement of water molecules becomes rigidly established only at lower temperatures when liquid water freezes as ice. However, the tendency of water molecules to

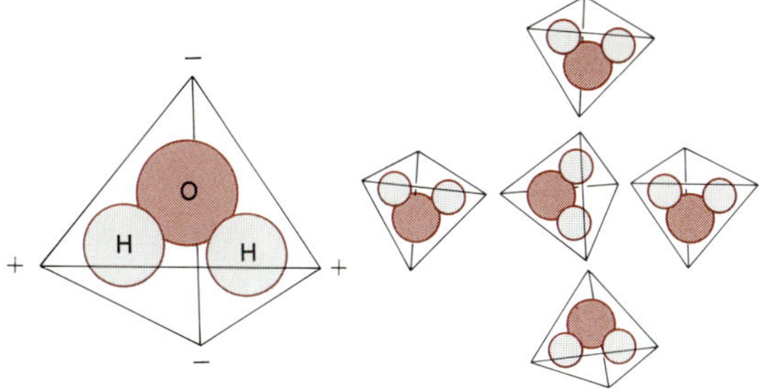

Fig. 3.5 Polarity of water. (A) Orientation of hydrogen and oxygen atoms in a single molecule of water. Note the two positive and two negative "corners" of the molecule. (B) Because of its polar "corners," each water molecule can form hydrogen bonds with four other water molecules.

bond momentarily with one another at higher temperatures is the major factor responsible for the considerable cohesiveness and stability of liquid water.

For example, hydrogen bonding between water molecules explains why water resists changes in temperature far more than a metal frying pan does. The temperature of an object is related directly to the speed at which its molecules or atoms are vibrating—the faster the vibratory motion, the higher the temperature. Hydrogen bonding between water molecules creates resistance to increased molecular movement, hence to an increase in temperature. The resistance of water to abrupt temperature changes has enormous significance in living systems. Most chemical reactions in cells occur only in restricted temperature ranges. If cell temperature ranges beyond these limits, cell function ceases. In addition to its many other functions, the high water content of cells serves to protect them from rapid temperature fluctuations.

The polarity of its molecules also explains why water is an almost universal solvent. Relatively few materials resist dissolution in water. Its polar charges tug and pull on similarly charged portions of immersed compounds, separating them from one another. This occurs, for example, when sugar dissolves in water.

Other compounds are broken apart when mixed with water, or *dissociated* as free ions. For example,

$$\underset{\textit{acetic acid}}{CH_3COOH} \xrightarrow{H_2O} \underset{\textit{acetate ion}}{CH_3COO^-} + \underset{\textit{hydrogen ion}}{H^+}$$

$$\underset{\textit{ammonium hydroxide}}{NH_4OH} \xrightarrow{H_2O} \underset{\textit{ammonium ion}}{NH_4^+} + \underset{\textit{hydroxyl ion}}{OH^-}$$

Several ions are critical to maintenance of normal cell function. Sodium and potassium ions play a vital role in transmission of nerve impulses, and calcium ions are equally important to muscle contraction. Such ions cannot be produced in cells in the absence of water.

Acids, Bases and Salts

Substances that release hydrogen (H^+) ions when dissolved in water are called *acids;* substances that release hydroxyl (OH^-) ions are *bases,* or *alkalies.* When an acid and base are mixed, the hydrogen ion of the acid unites with the hydroxyl ion of the base, forming water. The remainder of the acid, or *anion,* combines with the rest of the base, or *cation,* forming a *salt.* Strong acids or bases such as hydrochloric acid (HCl) or sodium hydroxide (NaOH) dissociate in water almost completely. But the ionic compound acetic acid (CH_3COOH) is a *weak* acid, for in water only a few ion pairs are formed; most of the compound remains whole and undissociated.

It is often important to determine the acid or alkaline strength of a solution, that is, the degree to which the compounds in the solution are dissociated. This can be done with an electrical apparatus that measures the relative number of H^+ ions (actually H^+ bound to water in the form of H_3^+O) and OH^- ions in the solution; for the more of these ions are found, the more the acids and bases present are dissociated (Fig. 3.6). The result is expressed as a number, called the *pH* of the solution. In living material, the numbers that indicate pH range from 0 to 14. A pH of 7 indicates chemical *neutrality;* the solution is neither acidic nor basic because the number of H^+ ions *equals* the number of OH^- ions. Below 7, the *lower* the pH of a solution, the *more acid* it is; it contains more H^+ ions than OH^- ions. Conversely, above 7, the *higher* the pH, the *more*

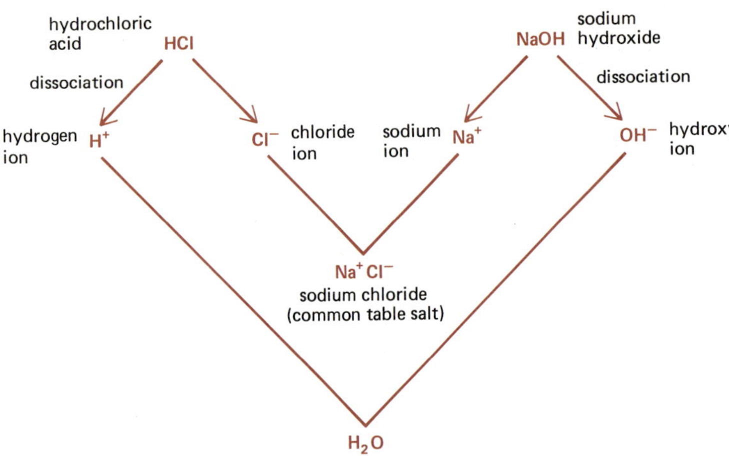

Fig. 3.6 Acids, bases, and salts. Acids dissociate in water yielding hydrogen ions and negatively charged anions. Bases dissociate producing hydroxyl ions and positively charged cations. Salts result from union of anions and cations. This illustration depicts the dissociation of hydrochloric acid and sodium hydroxide, an acid and base, respectively. The resulting hydrogen and hydroxyl ions unite, forming water; common table salt, sodium chloride, is produced when sodium and chloride ions bond ionically.

alkaline a solution is. Thus, a strong acidity is indicated by pH 0, a strong alkalinity, by pH 14 (Fig. 3.7).

Although sufficient numbers of ions are important to cell function, inadequate or excessive ion concentrations can produce major chemical and physical disturbances (see also the Biology Highlight, "Acid Rain: Unpremeditated Chemical Warfare," in Chap. 10). Too many H^+ or OH^- ions, for example, can cause dissolution of many important cellular chemicals, including those making up the structural fabric of cells themselves. Living matter actually has a pH usually very near neutrality. For example, the pH of human blood is generally 7.3. Distinctly higher or lower pH levels do occur, however, but usually in restricted regions only. For example, lemons and stomach cavities are characteristically quite acid. Living matter does not tolerate significant variations in its normal acid-base balance, and its pH must remain within fairly narrow limits.

Fig. 3.7 The pH scale.

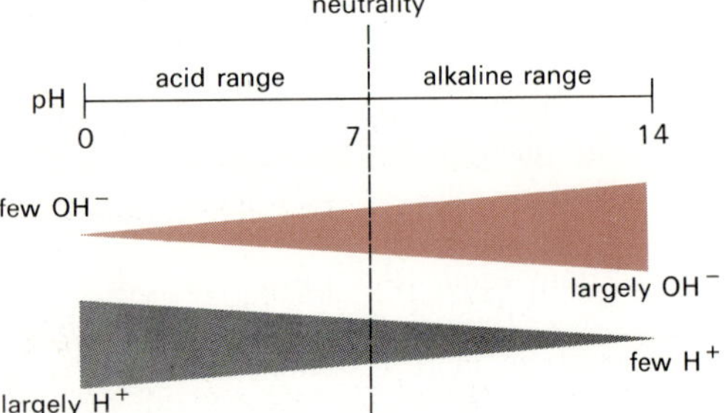

Optimal pH levels for cell function are maintained largely by substances called *buffers.* These compounds function by removing excess H^+ or OH^- ions from tissues and cells. When buffered aspirin or a seltzered product is used to prevent or relieve "acid indigestion," an external source of buffers is ingested to supplement those naturally occurring in the digestive system. Sodium bicarbonate ($NaHCO_3$) often is one of the principal buffers in these products. This compound dissociates as sodium (Na^+) and bicarbonate (HCO_3^-) ions in water. Excess H^+ ions in the digestive system can unite with HCO_3^- ions, producing carbonic acid (H_2CO_3):

$$NaHCO_3 \longrightarrow Na^+ + HCO_3^-$$
$$H^+ + HCO_3^- \longrightarrow H_2CO_3$$

Like acetic acid, carbonic acid is a weak acid and does not dissociate readily. Some of it does decompose as H_2O and CO_2, however; the latter being the "gas" released by burping. In effect, supplementing HCO_3^- ions in water removes excess H^+ ions from the digestive tract and relieves the symptoms of acid indigestion. Phosphate ions have a similar buffering effect against added acids, and several positively charged ions in living matter protect against added bases. To be sure, if living material or any buffered system is flooded with large quantities of additional acids or bases, pH protection will be inadequate.

CHEMICAL CHANGES

Reactions

Chemical reactions occur whenever one or more chemical bonds between atoms are formed or broken. Such processes generally occur as a result of *collisions* between molecules or ions; direct contact is necessary if compounds are to be close enough together for bond breaking or bond formation.

Inasmuch as reactions always imply changes in chemical bonding, the invariable outcome of any reaction is a *rearrangement* of atoms and bonding patterns. For example:

$$\begin{array}{ccccccccccc} & & H & & H & & H & & H & & \\ & & | & & | & & | & & | & & \\ H & — & C & — & C & — & C & — & C & — & H \;\longrightarrow \\ & & | & & | & & | & & | & & \\ & & H & & H & & H & & H & & \end{array}$$

$$\begin{array}{ccccccccc} & & H & & & H & & & H & \\ & & | & & & | & & & | & \\ H & — & C & — & — & C & — & — & C & — H \\ & & | & & & | & & & | & \\ & & H & & H — & C & — H & & H & \\ & & & & & | & & & & \\ & & & & & H & & & & \end{array}$$

Or generally,

$$A \longrightarrow B$$

If reactions take place between two or more types of compounds, the atomic rearrangements are usually accompanied by three kinds of broader results.

Synthesis

First, two or more molecules or ions can come together and form a single larger unit; a *synthesis* can occur. For example:

$$\underset{\text{bicarbonate ion}}{HCO_3^-} + \underset{\text{hydrogen ion}}{H^+} \longrightarrow \underset{\text{carbonic acid}}{H_2CO_3}$$

Or generally,

$$A + B \longrightarrow AB$$

Reactions of this general type include the processes of synthesis which, as noted in the preceding chapter, represent a major metabolic activity of living matter.

Decomposition

Second, a single molecule or ion can become fragmented into two or more smaller units; a chemical *decomposition* can take place, the reverse of synthesis. For example:

$$H_2CO_3 \longrightarrow H^+ + HCO_3^-$$

Or generally,

$$AB \longrightarrow A + B$$

Reactions of this general type include the decomposition reactions of respiration, another metabolic activity referred to in Chap. 2.

Exchange

Third, synthesis and decomposition can occur simultaneously; the decomposition products of one set of compounds can become the building blocks for the synthesis of another set. In such a process, one or more of the atoms or ions of one compound trades places with one or more of the atoms or ions of another compound. This is an *exchange* reaction. For example:

$$\underset{\text{hydrochloric acid}}{\mathbf{H}\text{—Cl}} + \underset{\text{sodium hydroxide}}{\text{Na—}\mathbf{OH}} \longrightarrow \underset{\text{water}}{\mathbf{H\text{—}OH}} + \underset{\text{sodium chloride}}{\text{Na—Cl}}$$

Or generally,

$$AB + CD \longrightarrow AD + BC$$

Note that each of these reaction types actually does include a rearrangement of atoms and bonding patterns. In every case one or more bonds are broken and one or more new ones are formed. However, the total numbers and types of atoms are exactly the same before and after the reaction; atoms *are neither gained nor lost.* In symbolic representations of reactions, therefore, it is important to make sure that equations balance; the total numbers and types of atoms to the left of the reaction arrow must equal exactly those on the right.

Apart from belonging to one of the reaction types just described, any chemical process has two fundamental characteristics. The first is *direction.* In the examples above, the directions of the reactions have been indicated by arrows, but this has been possible only because of knowledge gained from earlier experience. If such experience were lacking, it would not necessarily be clear whether a given reaction would proceed to the right or to the left. What determines the actual direction? The second characteristic is reaction *rate,* a measure of how fast and for how long a reaction proceeds. Reactions result from collisions of chemical units, as noted, and the generalization can be made that reaction rate is directly proportional to collision rate. Any factor or condition promoting collisions will also promote rates. What are these rate determinants?

The direction of a reaction is governed by the *energetics* of the reacting chemicals; and the rate is determined by *temperatures,* by *pressures* and *concentrations,* and by *catalysts.*

Energetics

Laws of Thermodynamics

Like all other kinds of changes in the universe, chemical changes obey certain laws of *thermodynamics* and are governed by them. These most fundamental rules of nature deal with the *energy* relations of a system and its surroundings. The general concept of energy is roughly equivalent in meaning to work potential, or the capacity to do work. A "system" can be regarded as any set of materials on which attention is focused at the moment, such as a group of chemicals undergoing reactions. The surroundings then are all other parts of the universe, the total environment in which the system exists.

A *first law of thermodynamics,* also called the *law of conservation of energy,* states that, in any process, the sum of all energy changes must be zero. Expressed differently, energy can be neither created nor destroyed. Thus if a chemical system gains energy, that amount of energy must be lost by the surroundings of the system. Or if a chemical system loses energy, that amount must be gained by the environment. The first law therefore implies that energy can only be redistributed, changed in form, or both.

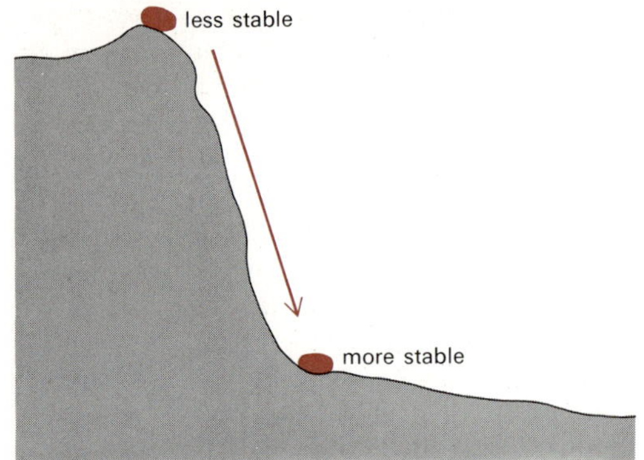

Fig. 3.8 Thermodynamics and stability. A stone on a hillside can be regarded as a closed thermodynamic system. If the stone is left to itself, a unidirectional process can occur; the stone can fall to the valley and thereby assume a more stable state.

A *second law of thermodynamics,* already referred to in Chap. 2, states that, if left to itself, any system tends toward a state of greatest stability. A stone near the top of a hillside represents a less stable (and also a more ordered and less probable) system than a stone at the bottom of the slope. The second law indicates that, whereas such a stone might roll downhill to a more stable state, by itself it can never roll uphill. To be sure, a stone can be *brought* uphill if an environmental agent expends energy and pushes the stone up; but in that case the system is no longer "left to itself." Evidently, natural processes tend to be *unidirectional,* even though they are inherently reversible. Correspondingly, all chemical processes are theoretically reversible, but in actuality they proceed either in one direction or the other, according to which one of these leads to a more stable (less energetic) state (Fig. 3.8).

Accordingly, living systems require continuous inputs of externally supplied energy to support the millions of energy-requiring synthesis reactions so vital to the maintenance of their extremely organized, highly unstable states. Plants and other photosynthetic organisms use light as their external energy source; animals, and heterotrophic organisms generally, depend on the bond energy of nutrient molecules produced in other organisms—plants or other animals. If external energy supplies are insufficient to maintain their high degree of organization, organisms die; and in the process they disintegrate into chemical compounds that contain far less energy but much greater stability.

Enthalpy

The actual stability of chemical systems depends mainly on two factors, both involving the energy of compounds. One factor is *enthalpy,* the *total energy content* of a chemical system. As already pointed out, a compound is held together by chemical bonds resulting from mutual electric attraction between atoms or ions. These bonding forces represent *chemical energy,* or *bond energy.* The greater the attraction between two atoms or ions, the greater the bond energy. Two bonded atoms or ions will become disunited only if some external force pushes them apart and thereby breaks the bond. Such forcible separation requires work, or energy, and the amount of energy needed clearly must be at least great enough to overcome the attraction between the two atoms or ions. In other words, the energy required to break a bond equals, and defines, the bond energy. Accordingly, the enthalpy, or total chemical energy, of a compound can be defined as the energy needed to break all the bonds in the compound.

If now two or more compounds are close together, such a chemical system will be most stable if and when its total chemical energy is at a *minimum.* The second law of thermodynamics shows that, for any system, a state of minimum available energy is the most likely; and it is because of this greatest likelihood that minimum energy states are the most stable. Chemical reactions will therefore tend to proceed in such a way that, at the end, the total energy content of all participants will be least. For example, assume that in the generalized reaction

$$A + B \longrightarrow C + D$$

the total energy of all the bonds in A and B together is greater than the total energy of all the bonds in C and D together. In other words, more potential energy is available in the bonds of the starting materials than is needed to form the bonds of the end products. If all other conditions are suitable, such a reaction can occur readily because C + D, containing less total energy, is more stable than A + B. The energy difference will be lost from the reaction system to the surrounding environment:

$$A + B \longrightarrow C + D + \text{energy (to environment)}$$

Such a liberation of energy can become evident, for example, through a spontaneous rise of temperature in the reaction mixture. Reactions that yield energy as above are said to be *exergonic* (or *exothermic,* if the energy is liberated in the form of heat). Decomposition reactions, including respiratory decompositions in living matter, tend to be this type (Fig. 3.9).

Conversely, assume that the total energy of A + B is less than that of C + D. In this case A +B is more stable, and the second law stipulates

Fig. 3.9 Energy and reactions. Left, exergonic reaction. The mixture A + B contains more total energy than C + D, and the energy difference escapes the reacting system. Right, endergonic reaction. The mixture A + B contains less energy than C + D. Hence if a reaction is to take place the energy difference must be supplied to the reacting system from an external source.

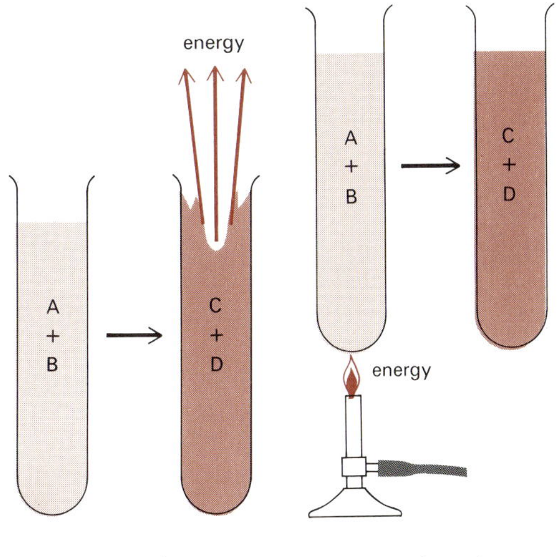

that no process can proceed by itself from a more stable to a less stable state. However, the reaction could be made to occur if energy were supplied *from* the environment *to* the reaction system. For example, the starting materials could be heated over a flame. Then, so long as external energy continues to be supplied, the reaction can proceed:

$$A + B + \text{energy (from environment)} \longrightarrow C + D$$

Reactions that *require* external energy, as above, are said to be *endergonic* (or *endothermic*, if the energy is required in the form of heat). Synthesis reactions generally, including those in living matter, are of this type. Evidently, chemical (or any other) synthesis tends to be expensive in terms of energy.

Energy-yielding and energy-requiring reactions are often *coupled*, some of the released energy of exergonic reactions being used to drive endergonic reactions:

exergonic reaction: $A + B \longrightarrow C + D + \text{energy}$

endergonic reaction: $E + F \longrightarrow G + H$

For example, the released energy of exergonic reactions can power an engine, as in the decomposition of fuels by burning. Metabolically coupled reactions are exceedingly common in living systems. Indeed, energy required for the synthesis of virtually all components of organisms is derived from the decomposition reactions of respiration (see Chap. 12).

Entropy

The second factor that determines the relative stability of a chemical system is its *entropy*, or *energy distribution*. A system is most stable when entropy is at a maximum, with energy distributed as uniformly or randomly as possible. It can be shown that, of all possible energy distributions in a system, the most random or unordered is the most likely; it is because of this greatest likelihood that maximum entropy states are the most stable.

For example, consider again the reaction $A + B \longrightarrow C + D$, and assume that the total energy content is the same before and after the reaction. Assume however that A is energy-rich and B energy-poor and that C and D each contain intermediate amounts of energy. The energy distribution in A + B is therefore more uneven or less random than in C + D, and C + D will be more stable. The reaction to the right thus can occur, and it will increase the entropy of the system.

Consider now the reaction

$$A + B + C \longrightarrow D$$

and again assume that the total energy content is the same before and after the reaction. On the left side the total energy is distributed among three particles, but on the right all the energy is concentrated in one. With everything else being equal, the A + B + C state thus has a more scattered, more random energy distribution, and this state will be more stable and have a greater entropy than the D state. The reaction will therefore not be possible if the system is left to itself. However, energy supplied from the environment could conceivably lower the entropy of A + B + C sufficiently to make the reaction to D possible.

The energetics of a chemical system thus determine one basic attribute of reactions, their direction. The second attribute, rate, is specified by factors that influence the frequency of collision between chemical units.

Reaction Rates

Pressure and Temperature

The effect of pressure on reacting systems varies greatly, depending on whether the chemicals participating in the reaction are in a gaseous, liquid, or solid state. Reaction rates among gases are the higher the greater the environmental pressure; increasing pressure forces gases into progressively smaller volumes, and the possibility of direct contact among gas ions or molecules is thereby enhanced. Thus, potentially combustible gases, such as hydrogen, are more dangerous when confined under relatively high pressures. Pressure has far less effect on liquids, which are virtually incompressible, and on solids, which may or may not be compressible.

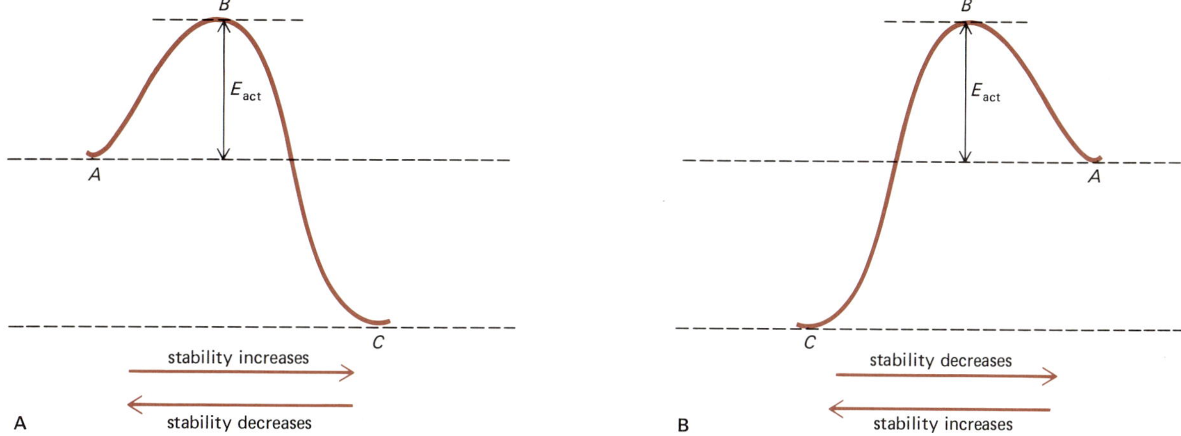

Fig. 3.10 Activation energy. (A) If *A* represents a less stable chemical system than *C*, an energy-yielding reaction from *A* to *C* can occur when activation energy E_{act} is first applied to *A*. E_{act} brings the reacting system over an energy barrier (symbolized by *B*), and as *A* then becomes *C*, energy is released. This energy release "pays back" the E_{act} expended earlier, and it also yields additional energy. (B) Conversely, in an energy-requiring reaction from *C* to *A*, *C* must not only be activated (E_{act}) but must also be supplied with external energy. The only energy gain then is E_{act}; hence the net energy expenditure is the amount required to raise *C* to *A*.

More significant than pressure is the environmental temperature. Reactions depend on contact between chemical units, and the usual agency that brings chemical units into contact is *heat* motion. All atoms, ions, and molecules, regardless of whether they are in a gas, a liquid, or a solid, vibrate uninterruptedly in random back-and-forth movements, and in gases and liquids they also move from place to place over relatively greater distances. We feel these movements as heat and we measure them as temperature. At a high temperature chemical units are in violent motion. Conversely, at −273°C, the theoretical absolute zero temperature, heat is by definition entirely absent and all chemical units are stationary. But every known natural or experimentally produced material always contains at least some heat, and the chemical units undergo more or less intense motions. Such thermal movements produce collisions between the chemical units. At a given temperature, chemical units therefore have a characteristic collision rate, and the collision rate in turn is a major determinant of the reaction rate between the units.

Ordinary room temperature often provides enough heat to agitate chemical units adequately for chemical reaction. But for many reactions room heat is insufficient. For example, a mixture of fat and water reacts so slowly at room temperature that the result is quite unnoticeable. However, molecular collisions and thus the speed of reaction can be increased by heating the mixture, for example.

The external energy needed to produce significant reaction rates is called *activation energy*. Most materials in the physical world, as in the living world, actually require activation energies far greater than those provided by ordinary temperatures. That is why, for example, the oxygen molecules in air and the molecules of wood or coal do not interact spontaneously, despite the numerous collisions between these substances. As is well known, combustible fuels must be heated substantially, or activated effectively, before they will react with aerial oxygen and thus burn. To start any reaction, therefore, enough activation energy must first be supplied from the outside. Interaction of the chemical units can then begin.

The significance of activation energies in chemical reactions can be illustrated by considering a stone lying near the edge of a cliff. If the stone fell over the edge, its descent to the valley would yield energy that could be used to perform work. But some external force must first move the stone over the cliff edge, and this force is equivalent to the activation energy. Assume that, in Fig. 3.10A, point *A* represents the degree of stability of a chemical system before a reaction has started, and position *C*, the degree of stability at the end of the reaction. The lower position of *C* signifies that, as with a falling stone, stability is greater at the end of the reaction. But note that the stability curve from *A* to *C* passes through point *B*, located at a higher level than either *A* or *C*. This means that the stability of the system first decreases from *A* to *B* before it increases from *B* to *C*. The amount of this decrease from *A* to *B* represents the activation energy E_{act} which must be supplied from the outside to bring the reaction system "over the cliff." Thereafter, just as a stone falls on its own, the reaction proceeds by itself; and in the process it not only "pays back" the energy expended for activation but also yields net free energy usable for work.

In the reverse reaction from *C* to *A*, adequate activation requires external energy in an amount sufficient to raise *C* through point *B* (see Fig. 3.10B). Here only E_{act} is paid back when the reaction later "falls" from *B* to *A*. The net energy expenditure therefore is far greater than in the reaction from *A* to *C*; more work must be done to move a stone up from a valley onto a cliff than in the opposite direction.

After having been activated, a reaction will proceed the faster the more heat is supplied to it. It has been found that every temperature rise of 10°C increases the speed of reactions approximately 2 to 3 times. The implications for reactions in living systems are important. Plants and most animals lack internal temperature controls, and the temperatures in their bodies largely match those of the external environment. As a result the life-maintaining chemical processes in a housefly, for example, will occur 2 to 3 times as fast on a day that is 10°C warmer than another. By contrast, temperature controls are present in birds and mammals, and these animals maintain constant internal temperatures. In these "warm-blooded" types, therefore, the rates of chemical reactions do not fluctuate directly with changes in environmental temperature.

Concentration

Apart from pressure and temperature, reaction rates also depend on the amount per volume, or *concentration*, of the reacting compounds present; for the greater the concentration of the starting materials, the more frequently collisions can occur and the faster the reaction will proceed. Other factors being equal, therefore, the rate of a reaction is proportional to the concentrations of the participating compounds. This generalization is sometimes referred to as the *law of mass action.*

Assume that the reversible reaction

$$\text{1 glycerol} + \text{3 fatty acids} \rightleftharpoons \text{1 fat} + \text{3 water}$$

is in *equilibrium;* concentrations are constant, and all other conditions are such that the reaction to the right occurs at the same rate as the reaction to the left. A *net* change will not occur so long as the equilibrium conditions are maintained. However, the equilibrium will be disturbed when some fat or water is removed from the system. The glycerol and fatty acids then in effect will have a relatively higher concentration, and according to the principle of mass action the reaction to the right will now take place at a greater rate than the reaction to the left. If we keep on removing the end products as fast as they form, the reaction to the right will proceed to completion and the yield of fat and water will become maximal.

Catalysis

Some substances lower activation energies of reactions without participating either as raw materials or end products. Such substances, called *catalysts,* often produce reactions at temperatures far lower than otherwise required. Almost all reactions occurring in living systems are catalyzed by *enzymes.* Since all enzymes are *proteins,* the ways in which enzymes govern the speed and direction of reactions are introduced in the next chapter in conjunction with a discussion of protein structure and function.

Review Questions

1 Define element, atom, compound, ion, molecule, chemical energy, chemical bond.

2 What is an ionic bond? How is such a bond formed? Explain in terms of ionic structure. What is a covalent bond? Describe how such a bond can be formed. Again explain in terms of atomic structure.

3 Review the properties of water and explain

how these properties contribute to normal cell functions.

4 Consider the following equation:

$$Ca(OH)_2 + 2HCl \longrightarrow CaCl_2 + 2H_2O$$

a. Identify the different atoms by name.
b. Rewrite the equation to show bonds in each compound.
c. Is the equation balanced?
c. Is this an exchange, synthesis, or decomposition reaction?

5 Define dissociation, metal, acid, base, salt. Is H_2SO_4 an acid, a base, or a salt? How does sodium sulfate (Na_2SO_4) dissociate? The magnesium ion is Mg^{2+} and the nitrate ion is NO_3^-; write the formulas for magnesium hydroxide, nitric acid, and magnesium nitrate.

6 What does the pH of a solution indicate? What would you expect the pH of a solution of NaCl to be? Of HCl? Of NaOH?

7 What is a chemical reaction and what kind of event produces it? What general types of reactions are known? What factors determine the directions and rates of reactions?

8 State the first and second laws of thermodynamics and describe their general implications. Describe also their specific implications for chemical processes. Why are most natural processes unidirectional in practice?

9 Define enthalpy and entropy. How does each of these concepts apply to a reacting system? How do energy changes differ for exergonic and endergonic reactions?

10 How do pressure and concentration affect a reaction? Review the effect of environmental heat on reactions. What is activation energy? How is this energy related to total energy changes during reactions?

Collateral Readings

Baker, J. J. W., and **G. E. Allen:** "Matter, Energy, and Life," 3d ed., Addison-Wesley, Reading, Mass., 1975. This paperback contains accounts of reaction energetics, catalysis, reaction rates and equilibria, and thermodynamics. Recommended.

Hill, J. W.: "Chemistry for Changing Times," 2d ed., Burgess, Minneapolis, 1975. A good, very basic introduction to chemistry.

King, E. L.: "How Chemical Reactions Occur," Benjamin, New York, 1963. A paperback especially relevant to the contents of this chapter. Highly recommended.

Speakman, J. C.: "Molecules," McGraw-Hill, New York, 1966. This book, which is available in paperback, contains a helpful summary of basic chemistry.

White, E. H.: "Chemical Background for the Biological Sciences," 2d ed., Prentice-Hall, Englewood Cliffs, N.J., 1970. A chapter on chemical reactions is included in this paperback.

Chapter 4 Molecule to Cell

Learning Objectives

After reading this chapter you should be able to:

1. List at least two characteristics of organic compounds that distinguish them from inorganic compounds.
2. Name the four classes of organic compounds found in all cells and list at least one example of each.
3. Define polymer.
4. Define and list at least one relationship between the following combinations of terms:
    - **a.** monosaccharide, disaccharide, polysaccharide.
    - **b.** pentose, hexose, simple sugar.
    - **c.** glucose, fructose, sucrose.
    - **d.** cellulose, glycogen, starch.
5. Define and list the principal relationship between dehydration synthesis and hydrolysis.
6. Using specific examples, illustrate at least two different functions of carbohydrates in living systems.
7. List the characteristics of fatty acids and illustrate the dehydration synthesis of a fat; differentiate between saturated and unsaturated fatty acids; list one relationship between the formation of plaque in blood vessels and elevated levels of cholesterol in blood; name at least three functions of fats and fatty acids in living systems; list at least four classes of compounds that are closely related to fats and state at least one function of each class.
8. Write the general formula for an amino acid and state the chief relationship between amino acids and proteins; list at least three reasons why an almost infinite number of proteins can be synthesized from only 20 amino acids.
9. Define protein specificity and list at least two examples of the consequences that can occur when proteins are transferred between organisms.
10. Distinguish between primary, secondary, tertiary, and quaternary structures of proteins; name three functions of proteins in living systems.
11. Construct a diagram to illustrate how enzymes speed up chemical reactions; differentiate between substrates and activation sites of enzymes.
12. State how changes in temperature or pH can affect enzyme-catalyzed reactions.
13. Name the chemical components of nucleotides and state the principal relationship between nucleotides and nucleic acids; name the pentose sugars found in DNA and RNA; list the nitrogen bases found in DNA and do the same for RNA.
14. Differentiate between purines and pyrimidines; list three general functions of nucleotides in cells; distinguish between AMP, ADP, and ATP; write a short paragraph explaining why ADP, ATP, and certain other nucleotide derivatives are often called energy carriers.
15. Distinguish between cofactors and coenzymes and state at least one functional relationship of each to enzymes; state at least one relationship between coenzymes and nucleotides.
16. Using symbols for the various components of nucleotides, diagram a single strand of DNA that contains the following nitrogen base sequence—adenine, thymine, guanine, cytosine, adenine; then diagram a second strand of DNA that would parallel the first; next state how the three-dimensional structure of this segment of double-stranded DNA would differ from the straight double chain you have drawn.
17. Differentiate between glycoproteins, lipoproteins, and glycolipids, and state at least one function of each.

It may seem strange that living systems, the most complex of all systems, are composed almost entirely of the simplest chemical elements. Of the more than 100 elements known, the entire mass of living organisms consists largely of six—oxygen, carbon, hydrogen, nitrogen, phosphorus, and sulfur (see Table 3.2). In living organisms these elements are found almost exclusively as parts of compounds. Yet, as seen in the previous chapter, most compounds making up living systems are themselves simple and relatively common.

INORGANIC COMPOUNDS

One major class of such compounds comprises water, minerals, metallic and nonmetallic materials, and in general those substances that make up the bulk of the physical, nonliving universe. A good many of such substances occur also in living matter. This class represents the so-called *inorganic compounds.* Directly or indirectly, all inorganic compounds in cells are of mineral origin and are ultimately derived as finished nutrients from the external physical environment. As already noted, the most abundant substance in cells is *water,* accounting for 50 to 90 per cent of the total weight of most organisms (see Chap. 3).

The other inorganic components of cells are *mineral solids.* Such substances are present in amounts averaging about 1 to 5 per cent. A considerable fraction of the minerals often forms hard deposits such as crystals inside cells or secreted precipitates on the outside of cells. Silicon- or calcium-containing deposits are common. For example, diatoms, certain protozoa, and the surface cells of certain grasses are protected externally with layers of glasslike silica; the hard part of bone is largely calcium phosphate, secreted in layers around bone-forming cells; clamshells consist of secreted calcium carbonate.

Other cellular minerals are in solution, either as free ions or combined with other compounds. The most abundant positively charged inorganic ions are H^+, hydrogen ions; Ca^{2+}, calcium ions; Na^+, sodium ions; K^+, potassium ions; and Mg^{2+}, magnesium ions. Abundant negatively charged mineral constituents include OH^-, hydroxyl ions; CO_3^{2-}, carbonate ions; HCO_3^-, bicarbonate ions; PO_4^{3-}, phosphate ions; Cl^-, chloride ions; and SO_4^{2-}, sulfate ions. In general, the kinds of minerals found in cells occur also in the ocean and in rocks. This is not a coincidence, for rocks are dissolved by water, water finds its way to the ocean and into soil, and living organisms ultimately draw their mineral supplies from these sources.

Although exceedingly important to cell function, inorganic compounds by themselves do not account for the special chemical attributes of living matter. The compounds that do are the so-called organic compounds.

ORGANIC COMPOUNDS

Unlike inorganic substances, organic ones are often exceedingly complex, and they in particular are responsible for the "living" properties of cells. Indeed, they are so named because they occur almost exclusively in living or once-living matter. Moreover, organic compounds represent the *foods* required by all organisms; inorganic compounds too serve as nutrients, but they are not foods. Chemically, organic substances are compounds of *carbon,* or more specifically, compounds in which the main chemical bonds join two or more carbon atoms or carbon and hydrogen atoms. Thus, carbon dioxide (CO_2), carbonate ions (CO_3^{2-}), and materials derived from them are not organic, since the carbon here is bonded to oxygen. But methane, CH_4, with its carbon-hydrogen bonds, is an organic compound. Most of the organic compounds of biological interest contain not only carbon-hydrogen but also numerous carbon-carbon bonds.

In this respect carbon is a rather unusual element. The atoms of most other elements link to atoms of like kind too, but the number of atoms so bondable is usually quite limited. For example, a hydrogen atom can join with one other hydrogen atom (H—H, H_2); sulfur can form molecules of eight atoms, S_8. But a carbon atom is far more versatile. It can form as many as four (covalent) bonds with other atoms, including other carbon atoms. Long *chains* of carbon atoms can form in this way:

```
  |   |   |   |
—C—C—C—C—
  |   |   |   |
```

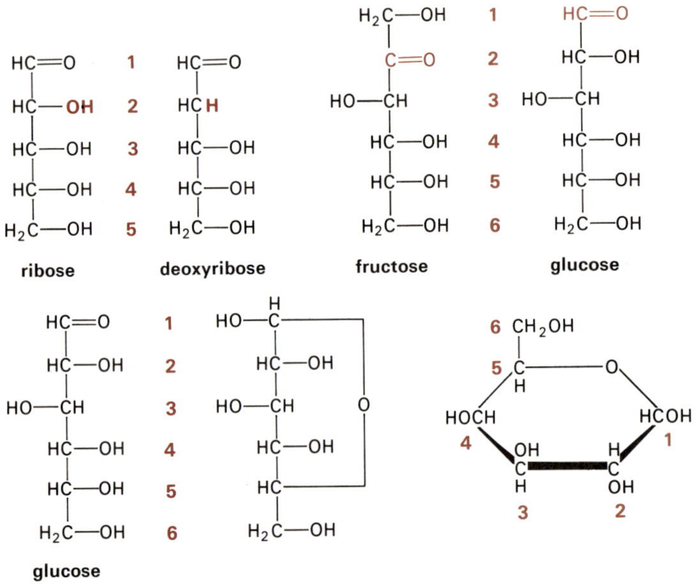

	ribose		deoxyribose		fructose		glucose
1	HC═O	1	HC═O	1	H₂C—OH	1	HC═O
2	HC—OH	2	HCH	2	C═O	2	HC—OH
3	HC—OH	3	HC—OH	3	HO—CH	3	HO—CH
4	HC—OH	4	HC—OH	4	HC—OH	4	HC—OH
5	H₂C—OH	5	H₂C—OH	5	HC—OH	5	HC—OH
				6	H₂C—OH	6	H₂C—OH

	glucose	
1	HC═O	H / HO—C—
2	HC—OH	HC—OH
3	HO—CH	HO—CH O
4	HC—OH	HC—OH
5	HC—OH	HC—
6	H₂C—OH	H₂C—OH

6 CH₂OH
5 C O
H
HOCH HCOH
4 OH H 1
C C
H OH
3 2

Fig. 4.1 Pentoses and hexoses. In the pentose sugars ribose and deoxyribose, the structural difference is one oxygen atom in ribose (color). In the hexose sugars glucose and fructose, a —C═O group is terminal in glucose, subterminal in fructose; both are $C_6H_{12}O_6$. The structure of glucose (as of other sugars) can be depicted in several ways, either as a chain or as a ring, as illustrated in the bottom row. Colored numerals identify carbon positions.

Such chains represent parts of organic molecules in which various other atoms are attached to the carbons. Further, carbon atoms can be joined in ringlike fashion, as in *benzene,* for example:

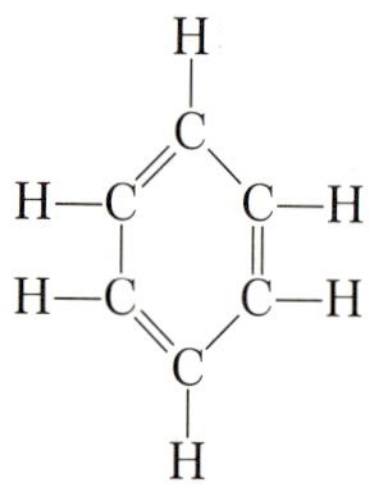

H
C
H—C C—H
H—C C—H
C
H

Many other types of configuration exist. Thus, carbon chains can be branched, rings and chains can become joined to each other, and any of these carbon structures can also be three-dimensional. Carbon combinations can therefore be exceedingly complex and varied. Organic substances actually display more complexity and more variety than all other chemicals put together.

Cells contain hundreds of different classes of organic compounds. Of these, four classes in particular are found in all cells and form the organic basis of living matter:

1. Carbohydrates
2. Lipids
3. Proteins
4. Nucleotides

Carbohydrates

Carbohydrates are molecules that usually conform to the general formula $C_x(H_2O)_y$, where x and y are whole numbers. Carbohydrates derive their name from the typical 2:1 ratio of the hydrogen and oxygen they contain, as in water. Thus, most carbohydrates are literally *hydrates,* or water-containing substances, of carbon.

If x and y are low numbers, from 3 to about 7, the formula describes the composition of the most common carbohydrates, the simple sugars, or *monosaccharides.* In these the carbon atoms form a chain to which H and O atoms are attached. Several classes of monosaccharides are distinguished on the basis of the numbers of carbons present. For example, C_3 sugars are *trioses,* and C_4 sugars are *tetroses.* The suffix *-ose* always identifies a sugar. Frequent reference will be made to *pentose* sugars, which contain five carbon atoms per molecule, and to *hexose* sugars, each of which contains six carbon atoms per molecule. Thus, if x and y in the formula above are 5, the resulting sugar may be the pentose *ribose,* $C_5H_{10}O_5$; and if x and y are 6, hexoses such as *glucose, fructose,* or *galactose* result, all with the formula $C_6H_{12}O_6$. Note that such sugars differ not in the numbers and types of atoms present but in the patterns in which the atoms are bonded together (Fig. 4.1).

Two or more monosaccharides of similar or identical type can become joined together end to end, forming chainlike larger molecules. If two monosaccharides become so joined, a double sugar, or *disaccharide,* results. For example, a combination of two glucose units forms the disaccharide *maltose,* malt sugar; a combination of glucose and fructose forms *sucrose,* the familiar cane or beet sugar used as a sweetening agent; and a combination of glucose and galactose forms *lactose,* milk sugar. All three of these disaccharides have the formula $C_{12}H_{22}O_{11}$, and their formation is described by the same equation:

$$2C_6H_{12}O_6 \longrightarrow H_2O + C_{12}H_{22}O_{11}$$

Note that the atoms of a disaccharide equal the sum of all atoms contained in the two reacting monosaccharides *minus* one molecule of water. Water often is a by-product produced from two or more similar subunits during the synthesis of larger molecules. Reactions of this type are known as *dehydration syntheses* (Fig. 4.2). For example, carbohydrates larger than disaccharides, or *polysaccharides,* are formed by dehydration synthesis from many monosaccharides.

All molecules composed of many similar subunits are termed *polymers,* and the general chemical process through which large molecules are built up from smaller units of like type is known as *polymerization.* Polysaccharides are said to be *polymers* of simple sugars. A polymer consisting of some hundreds or thousands of glucose units forms *glycogen,* an animal polysaccharide of considerable importance. Another polysaccharide is *cellulose,* a polymer of up to 2000 glucose units, rare among animals but very common in plants. Also common in plants is *amylose,* a polysaccharide of 300 to 1000 joined glucose units and a main component of starch (Fig. 4.3).

As a group, carbohydrates function in cells in two general capacities: they are structural building blocks of the cellular substance, and they are energy-rich molecules suitable as fuels in respiration. Cellulose is a particularly important building block, forming much of the structural surface of plant cells. It gives considerable rigidity to these surface structures and possesses substantial economic value in some plants, particularly cotton.

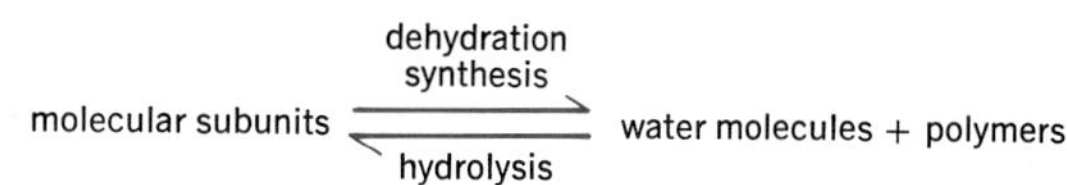

Fig. 4.2 Dehydration synthesis and hydrolysis. Molecular subunits are linked together in the formation of polymers during dehydration synthesis. Two hydrogen and one oxygen atom are removed from the reacting molecules as each subunit is added to the polymer. These atoms unite as molecules of water. Hydrolysis is the reverse of dehydration synthesis. Here hydrogen and oxygen atoms of water molecules are reinserted as each subunit is split from the polymer. See Figs. 4.5 and 4.8 for specific examples of dehydration synthesis.

As respiratory fuels, certain carbohydrates are important foods. Glucose, for example, is a common fuel for respiration, and starch and glycogen are prime sources of this monosaccharide. Starch often is housed in specialized storage tissues of plants. Such tissues are found in various structures, but roots commonly are principal sites for starch storage. Starch plays an important part in breaking the winter dormancy of plants that lose their leaves annually. In spring, this polysaccharide is decomposed into its glucose subunits through *hydrolysis,* the reverse of dehydration synthesis (see Fig. 4.2). Water molecules, removed previously through dehydration synthesis, are reinserted during hydrolysis to permit separation of whole glucose molecules from the large starch polymer. Glucose so formed becomes dissolved in sap and rises through the stems of such plants, nourishing and stimulating the growth of dormant buds. Certain types of maple trees are tapped in early spring to obtain the sugary sap, which is drained off to make maple sugar and maple syrup.

Glycogen is found in small amounts in most animal tissues, and it occurs abundantly in muscle and liver. Like starch, it can be hydrolyzed to free glucose, which happens whenever concentrations of glucose become reduced. For example, the liver converts glycogen to glucose when blood sugar levels become low. Glycogen in muscle provides the chief source of energy for contraction. Muscle glycogen actually represents the largest carbohydrate store of most animals; up to a third of the body weight of an animal can be muscle weight, and the greatest amount of energy is expended on muscular contraction.

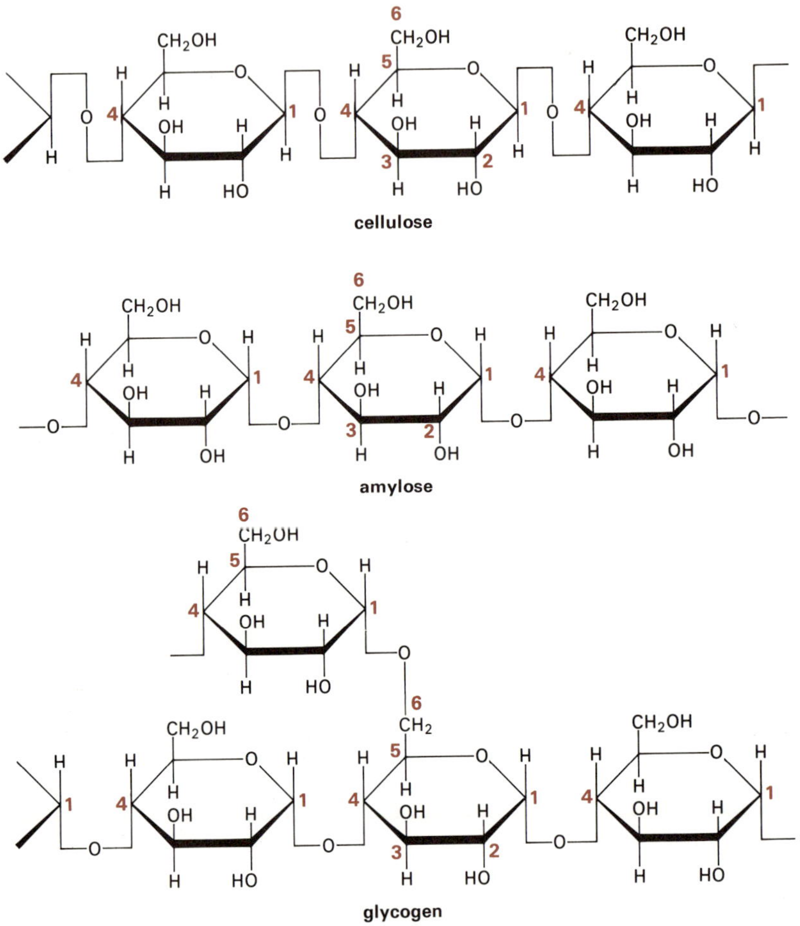

cellulose

amylose

glycogen

Fig. 4.3 Polysaccharides. All three shown here are composed entirely of glucose units. In cellulose and amylose two adjacent glucose units are joined by a 1,4 link (the difference being the alignment of the atoms in such links). Both these polysaccharides are straight-chain compounds. In glycogen the straight-chain portions have 1,4 links (as in amylose) and branch-chain portions are joined by 1,6 links (carbon 6 of one glucose unit joins carbon 1 of another glucose unit).

Lipids

Lipids consist of a diverse array of compounds that are generally insoluble in water. Fats and waxes are two particular kinds of lipids. The principal lipids in living systems are the *fatty acids.* Like the sugars, these acids are composed of C, H, and O, the carbon atoms being arranged as chains of various lengths. At one end each such chain carries a *carboxyl* group, —COOH, which confers acid properties on a fatty acid; hydrogen ions can dissociate from carboxyl groups, leaving $—COO^-$.

$$—COOH \longrightarrow —COO^- + H^+$$

The simplest fatty acid is *formic acid* (HCOOH). A series of increasingly complex fatty acids is formed by successive addition of $—CH_2—$ groups to HCOOH. For example, addition of one such group produces *acetic acid* (CH_3COOH), the active ingredient of vinegar. Fatty acids larger than acetic acid, have the general formula

$$CH_3(CH_2)_nCOOH$$

where n is an integer other than zero (Fig. 4.4).

In most naturally occurring fatty acids, n is an even number; cells synthesize fatty acids from acetic acid (2-carbon, or even-numbered) building units. Common fatty acids in most plant and animal matter include, for example, *palmitic acid,*

$$CH_3(CH_2)_{14}COOH \quad (\text{or } C_{16}H_{32}O_2)$$

and *stearic acid,*

$$CH_3(CH_2)_{16}COOH \quad (\text{or } C_{18}H_{36}O_2)$$

Structure	Composition	Name
H—COOH	CH_2O_2	formic
α CH_3—COOH	$C_2H_4O_2$	acetic
β α CH_3—CH_2—COOH	$C_3H_6O_2$	propionic
γ β α CH_3—CH_2—CH_2—COOH	$C_4H_8O_2$	butyric
$CH_3(CH_2)_4COOH$	$C_6H_{12}O_2$	caproic
$CH_3(CH_2)_6COOH$	$C_8H_{16}O_2$	caprylic
$CH_3(CH_2)_{14}COOH$	$C_{16}H_{32}O_2$	palmitic
$CH_3(CH_2)_{16}COOH$	$C_{18}H_{36}O_2$	stearic

Fig. 4.4 Fatty acids. The (incomplete) series is arranged according to increasing molecular complexity. Carbon positions are identified by Greek letters, starting at the carbon next to the carboxyl group.

Fatty acids like these are said to be *saturated;* all available bonds of the carbon chains are filled with hydrogen atoms. By contrast, *unsaturated* fatty acids have one or more double bonds in the carbon chains. For example, the widely occurring *oleic acid,* $CH_3(CH_2)_7CH{=}CH(CH_2)_7COOH$ (or $C_{18}H_{34}O_2$), contains one double bond. Fatty acids having more than one double bond are said to be *polyunsaturated.*

Animal fat generally contains higher concentrations of saturated fatty acids than the fat of plants. Ingestion of foods high in saturated fatty acids appears to be linked in some people with the presence of excessive amounts of *cholesterol,* a derivative of fat (see Fig. 4.6). In some individuals high cholesterol levels can be associated with the production of fatty accumulations called *plaque,* which can cause blockage of blood vessels and, in turn, heart attack and other cardiovascular diseases. For people with high blood cholesterol, many physicians prescribe diets containing few saturated fatty acids. The fats present in such diets are derived almost exclusively from plants.

A fat molecule is formed when three molecules of fatty acids are joined to one molecule of glycerol by the process of dehydration synthesis (Fig. 4.5). Related to carbohydrates, glycerol is a chainlike C_3 compound that serves as a carrier for the fatty acids. The properties of a fat are determined by the chain lengths and the degrees of saturation of the fatty acids present. Fats containing fatty acids that are short-chained, unsaturated, or both tend to be volatile or oily liquids. For example, oleic acid is oily, and fats containing oleic acid tend to be oily too. By contrast, fats with long-chained and saturated fatty acids tend to be hard tallow.

Fats and fatty acids are important energy-storage compounds in most organisms. As such, they are even richer sources of respiratory energy than carbohydrates. Mixtures of fat molecules form the "marble" of steak, and in birds and mammals constitute the layers of fatty tissue underlying the skin. These subcutaneous layers of fat not only serve as depots of stored nutrient but also insulate internal tissues against fluctuations in temperature. Like carbohydrates, lipids also play significant roles as structural components of cells. For example, the surface membranes of cells typically are composed of 40 per cent lipid, but this figure may vary from 25 to 75 per cent depending on cell type (see also Chap. 5). Most of the lipids in such membranes are *phosphoglycerides,* a family of fat-related com-

Fig. 4.5 Fat formation. Three molecules of fatty acid combine with one molecule of glycerol, resulting in three water molecules and one fat molecule.

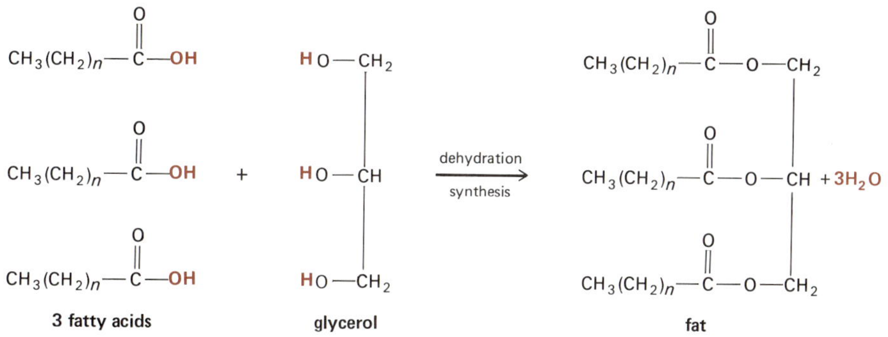

carotene, a carotenoid

vitamin D, a steroid

estradiol, a steroid

steroid ring structure

cholesterol, a steroid

testosterone, a steroid

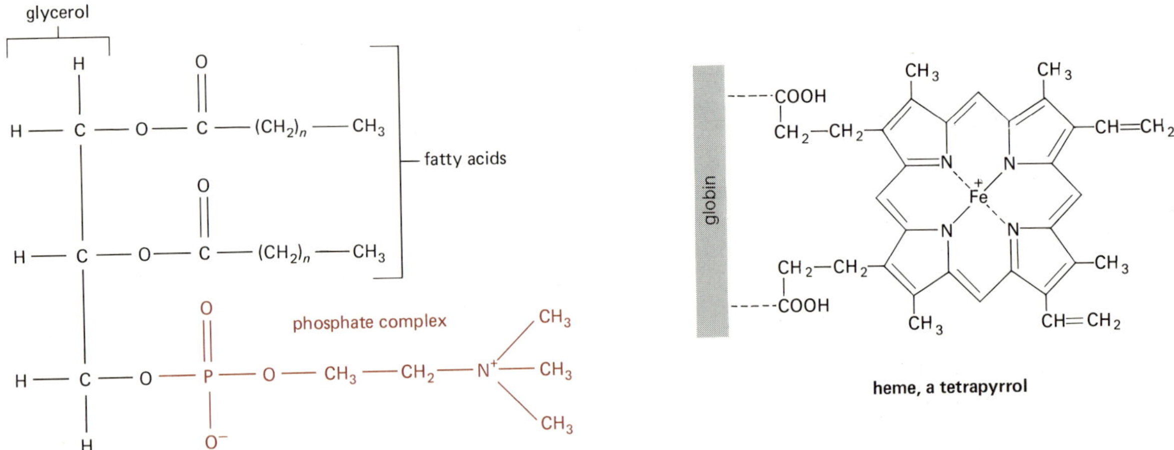

Fig. 4.6 Lipid derivatives. Top, molecular structure of the carotenoid pigment carotene. Middle, four steroids. The common ring structure of this class of compounds is depicted at right. Note the structural similarity of testosterone and estradiol, the most potent of the male and female sex hormones, respectively. Bottom left, structure of a phosphoglyceride, showing the glycerol portion of the molecule attached to two fatty acids and a phosphate complex (color). Bottom right, hemoglobin. Like all tetrapyrrols in cells, the ringlike heme group is bonded to a protein, globin. Hemoglobin transports oxygen in vertebrate blood (see also Fig. 4.10). See Fig. 13.3 for the structure of chlorophyll, another ringlike tetrapyrrol.

pounds containing only two fatty acids bound to glycerol. A phosphorus-containing atomic grouping is attached to the third position on the glycerol molecule (Fig. 4.6). Phosphoglycerides are sometimes loosely referred to as *phospholipids,* although some phosphorus-containing lipids belong to other classes of fat-related compounds.

Several other biologically important compounds are related to fats. *Carotenoids,* for example, are fatty acid–like carbon chains carrying carbon rings at each end (see Fig. 4.6). These compounds are pigments, producing red, orange, yellow, cream, and brown colors in both plant and animal matter. Carotenoids include the *carotenes* and the *xanthophylls.* Carotenes occur widely in all leaves and are also responsible for the colors of, for example, tomatoes, pumpkins, egg yolk, butter, milk, and other plant and animal products. Vitamin A is a derivative of carotene. Xanthophylls are as widely distributed as the carotenes. For example, *lutein* is a common xanthophyll of leaves, responsible for the yellow colors in autumn foliage, and *fucoxanthin* is an important pigment in brown and other algae.

Also related to lipids are *steroids,* complex ring structures that form the molecular framework of vitamin D and of several animal hormones, including the sex hormones and adrenal hormones of vertebrates (see Fig. 4.6).

As explained in geater detail in Chaps. 16 and 17, hormones are chemical secretions of specialized tissues that regulate and integrate processes in diverse parts of an organism. *Prostaglandins,* for example, can act as hormones in influencing several functions in animals. Derived from 20-carbon unsaturated fatty acids, all natural prostaglandins have at least some effect on lowering blood pressure and inducing contraction of smooth muscle. These compounds were first discovered in human semen but have since been found in many tissues. Some prostaglandins antagonize the actions of certain hormones, and others eventually may be used to induce labor in pregnant women or to induce therapeutic abortions.

More distantly related to lipids are the *tetrapyrrols,* a group of pigmented compounds serving a wide variety of functions in plants and animals. Among these compounds are red, blue, yellow, and other pigments found, for example, in several algal groups, in the shells of robin and other bird eggs, and in mammalian feces and urine. Some of the tetrapyrrols are complex ringlike molecules that contain a single atom of a metal in the center of such rings (see Fig. 4.6). Two important tetrapyrrols of this type are *cytochrome* and *heme,* red pigments in which the metal atom is iron. Cytochrome is an electron-transporting compound required in the respiration of all cells and in the photosynthesis of green cells; and heme is the oxygen-transporting component of hemoglobin present in the blood of many animals. The green pigment of photosynthetic organisms, *chlorophyll,* similarly is a ringlike tetrapyrrol, the central metal atom here being magnesium (see Fig. 13.3).

Proteins

Structure

These compounds are polymers of molecular units called *amino acids.* The general structure of an amino acid is

$$\begin{array}{c} \quad\;\; H \\ \quad\;\; | \\ H_2N—C—COOH \\ \quad\;\; | \\ \quad\;\; R \end{array}$$

where $—NH_2$ is an amino group, —COOH a carboxyl group, and R— an atomic grouping that can vary in composition considerably. For example, the simplest amino acid is *glycine,* where R = H; if $R = CH_3$, the amino acid is called *alanine.* Many other amino acids are characterized by comparatively more complex R— groups. Cells typically contain 20 different types of amino acids.

Hundreds and even thousands of amino acid units can be joined together in a single protein molecule (Fig. 4.7). Whenever molecules attain exceedingly large sizes, they are referred to as *macromolecules.* Proteins are very often macromolecules, and some of them are among the largest chemical structures known.

Adjacent amino acids in a protein are united in such a way that the amino group of one acid links to the carboxyl group of its neighbor; the bond is formed through dehydration synthesis (Fig. 4.8). The resulting grouping —NH—CO— represents a *peptide bond,* and two amino acids so joined form a *dipeptide.* If many amino acids are polymerized by means of peptide bonds, the whole chainlike complex is a *polypeptide.*

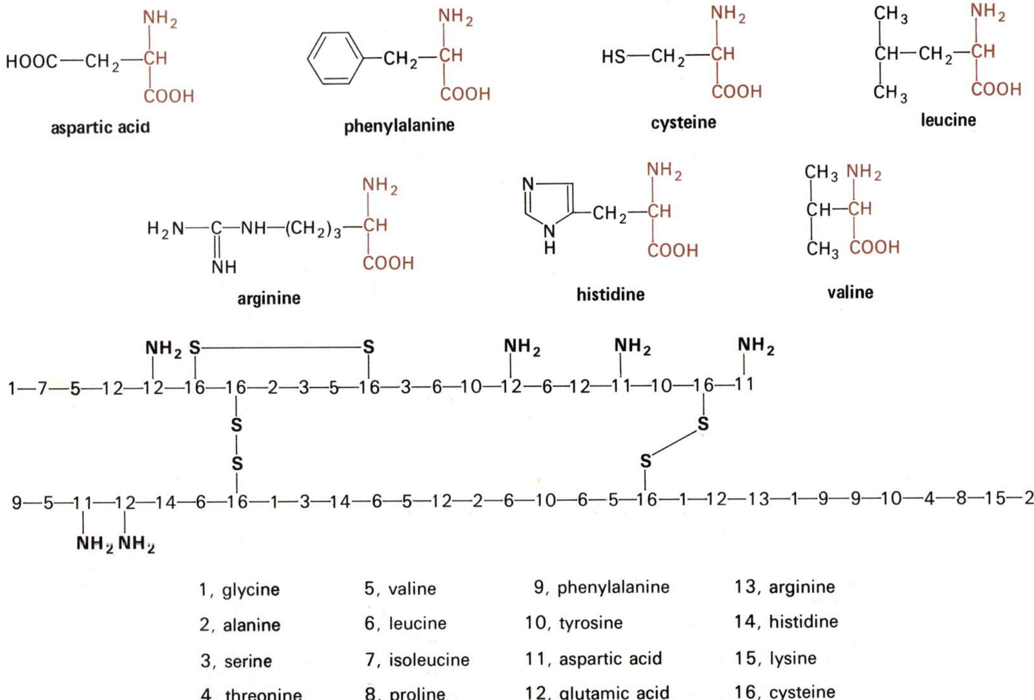

Fig. 4.7 Amino acids and proteins. Top, the structure of seven representative amino acids. The common atomic grouping that characterizes all of these compounds as amino acids is shown in color. Bottom, the structure of the insulin molecule, a protein consisting of 51 amino acid units. One chain consists of 21 units, another of 30 units, and the two are held together by sulfur-containing cysteine units. Insulin is one of the smallest proteins known.

Chemically, proteins can vary in practically unlimited fashion:

1. A protein can contain any or all of the 20 different *types* of amino acids.

2. A protein can contain virtually any *number* of each of these types of amino acids.

3. The specific *sequence* in which given numbers and types of amino acids are joined as a chain can vary almost without restriction.

4. The chains can be folded two- and three-dimensionally in a very large variety of patterns.

Forming a protein is comparable to forming words and sentences from an alphabet of letters. In the English language, 26 different letter symbols can be ordered almost at will to form an infinite variety of word combinations. In proteins, the "letter symbols" are 20 different types of amino acids. And unlike real words, the protein "words" need not remain strung out in straight lines but can be branched and folded in practically any direction and form. The number of theoretically possible proteins is therefore astronomical.

A polypeptide chain with its particular sequence of amino acids and peptide bonds represents the so-called *primary* structure of a protein. Such a chain has the physical form of a twisted ribbon. If a line were drawn through all the R— portions of the consecutive amino acids present, the line would mark out a spiral (Fig. 4.9). Such spirals are in some cases "right-handed" (*α helix*), in others "left-handed" (*β helix*). In either configuration the backbone of the spiral is a bonded sequence of

—N—C—C—N—C—C—N—

atoms, each —N—C—C— portion representing the skeleton of one amino acid unit. Projecting out

Fig. 4.8 Amino acid bonding. Two amino acids combine with loss of water. The result is a peptide bond, as indicated in the tinted area at right.

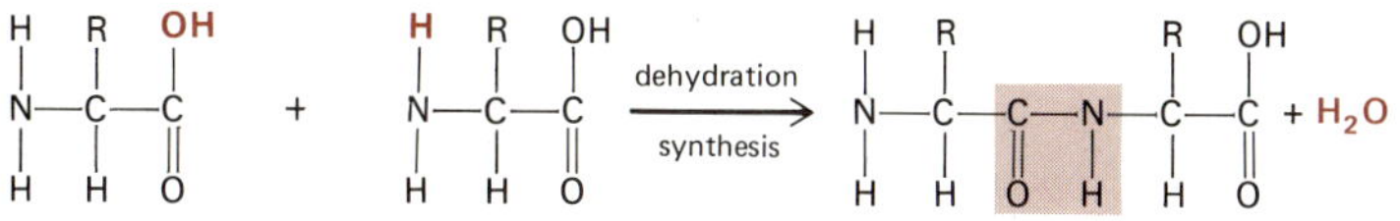

from this ribbon are the H—, O═, and R— groups of the amino acid unit. In most proteins the polypeptide spirals have fairly similar geometric properties.

This spiral configuration is held together by *hydrogen bonds* (see also Chap. 3). Such a bond is formed when a H atom is shared between the nitrogen of one amino acid unit and an oxygen of a nearby unit. More precisely, the H of the —NH of one unit is bonded to the O of —C═O three amino acid units away (see Fig. 4.9). All —NH and —C═O groups of a polypeptide chain are hydrogen-bonded in this fashion, each such bond linking amino acids three units apart. The resulting spiral configuration is relatively stable, and it represents a common *secondary structure* of proteins.

If long coils of this sort remain extended and threadlike, the protein molecule is said to be *fibrous*. In many cases, however, the coils are looped and twisted and folded back on themselves, in an almost infinite variety of ways. Protein molecules then are *globular*, balled together somewhat like entangled twine. Such loops and bends give a protein a *tertiary structure* (Fig. 4.10).

Some proteins consist of not one but several separate polypeptide chains bonded to each other, often in the form of a bundle. Proteins of this type are said to possess a *quaternary structure* (see Fig. 4.10). The polypeptides here are held together largely by the bond types already referred to above.

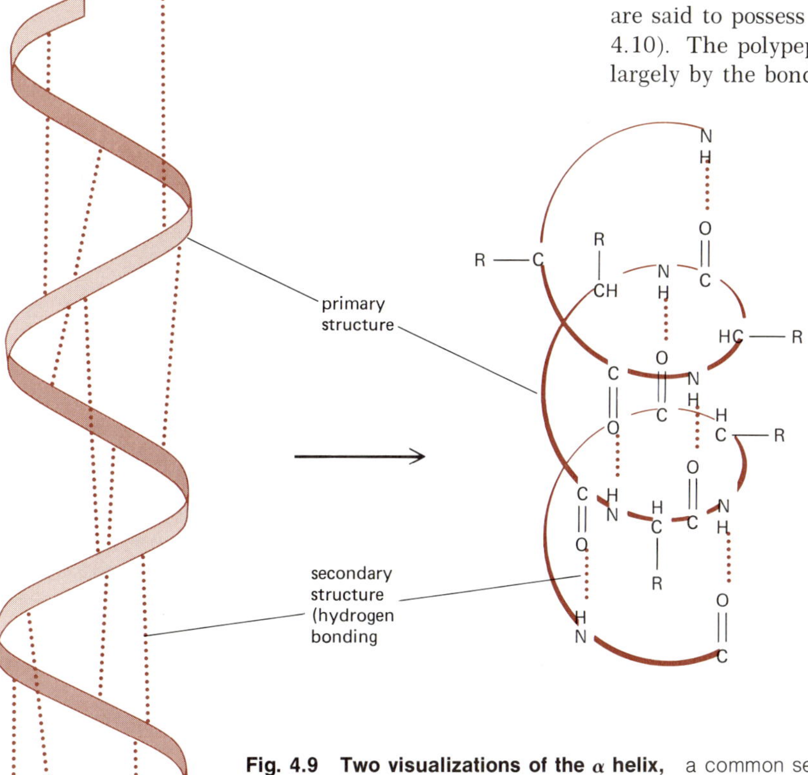

Fig. 4.9 Two visualizations of the α helix, a common secondary structure of proteins. On the left, the polypeptide is depicted as a simple helical ribbon. On the right, some of the atoms and bonds of the polypeptide backbone are shown. In both cases, the dotted lines represent the hydrogen bonds that stabilize the helix. The chemical properties of a polypeptide such as this would be determined by the nature of the R groups projecting outward from the helix.

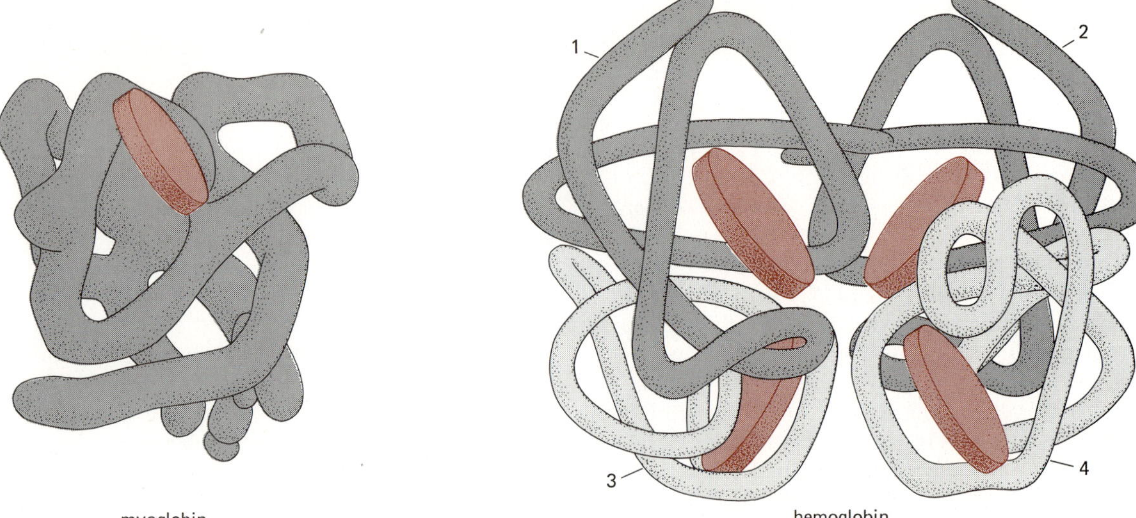

Fig. 4.10 Tertiary and quaternary structures of proteins. Myoglobin (left), a protein that binds to oxygen in muscle, shows tertiary structure. The helical coils of myoglobin are folded and twisted at specific points, giving the molecule its unique three-dimensional configuration. Hemoglobin (right) consists of four folded polypeptide chains (numbered). The quaternary structure of this molecule is maintained by bonds that interconnect the four units. Each of the flat colored disks represents a heme group (see Fig. 4.6).

For example, one of the hormones of the pancreas, *insulin,* is a protein made up of two parallel polypeptide chains, held together by two covalent bonds, one between each of two pairs of sulfur atoms (Fig. 4.11 and see Fig. 4.7). Such bonds, called *disulfide bonds,* commonly link portions of proteins and, together with hydrogen and ionic bonds, maintain the tertiary and quaternary structures of these molecules. Thus, differences in the properties of proteins can arise from differences in as many as four aspects of structure.

Of all the bonds that maintain a globular protein configuration, hydrogen bonds are the weakest. Such bonds are disrupted readily by physical or chemical changes in the environment of a protein—for example, by excessive heat, pressure, pH, electricity, heavy metals, and other agents that create suboptimal conditions. When some or many of its hydrogen bonds are broken, a protein cannot retain its globular configuration, and its quaternary, tertiary, or even secondary structure will be lost. An originally highly folded molecule will then become a straight, fibrous one. Also, in the original globular state the protein might have been soluble in water, for ball-like particles disperse readily; but long fibrous molecules pile together like a log jam and generally become insoluble in water.

Such changes in protein configuration are called *denaturation.* If the disruptive effect is mild and of brief duration, denaturation is often temporary and the protein can later revert to its original *native* state. But if the environmental change is drastic and lasting, denaturation becomes permanent and irreversible and the protein will be *coagulated.* For example, the protein of egg white, *albumen,* is globular (and water-soluble) in the raw native state but becomes fibrous (and water-insoluble) in the cooked, coagulated state (like boiled egg white). Denaturation usually destroys the biological properties a protein has in the native state—a major reason why excessive heat or other excessive environmental changes kill cells.

Proteins differ considerably from carbohydrates or fats in their nearly unlimited structural variations. Even a highly complex carbohydrate, for example, is structurally the same whether we obtain it from mushrooms or mangoes, from mice or from men. A given lipid, similarly, is the same

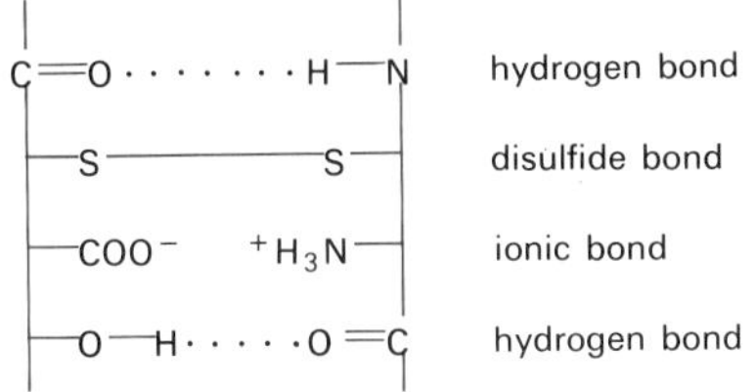

Fig. 4.11 Bonds in protein. Separate polypeptide chains on different segments of a single chain (vertical lines) can be held together by bonds such as shown. In a hydrogen bond, a H atom is held in common by two side groups on the polypeptides (top and bottom). Disulfide bridges are formed by S-containing amino acid units, mainly cysteine. Ionic links between charged side groups on polypeptide chains hold together by electric attraction.

lipid regardless of where we find it. Not so for proteins, however; these compounds vary so much that, as noted, no two organisms contain precisely the same types. Even twin organisms have slightly different proteins, and the differences are the greater the less closely two organisms are related. Proteins evidently have a high degree of *specificity:* the proteins of an organism are unique for that organism.

Protein specificity has well-known consequences. For example, transfer of a given protein from one organism into the cells of another amounts to the introduction of foreign bodies, and disease can result. Thus, the proteins of plant pollen can produce allergy in man and other animals. When blood from a donor animal is mixed with a noncompatible blood of a recipient, death of the recipient may follow. Infective bacteria produce many diseases partly because their proteins differ from those of host organisms. And when portions of one organism are grafted to another, the grafts normally do not heal into place but are rejected because the two sets of proteins differ.

Function

Nonenzymatic functions To some extent, normally far less than carbohydrates or fats, proteins are used in cells as foodstuffs. But proteins serve mainly in two far more important cellular roles. First, they represent vital construction materials out of which much of the basic framework of cells is built. Carbohydrates, fats, minerals, and other cellular components are organized around such *structural proteins* that form the molecular "scaffolding" of living material. Second, many proteins serve as reaction-catalyzing *enzymes*, a function examined next.

Enzymes Most chemical reactions of biological interest require fairly high activation energies—so high, indeed, that environments far hotter than room temperature would be needed. For example, a fat-water mixture at room temperature (or even at body temperature) remains virtually unchanged for days. In the body, however, fat and water react appreciably within an hour or so, yet body temperature remains comparatively low. In living matter generally, sufficiently high rates of molecular collisions are produced without additional heat through *catalysis*, or acceleration of reactions by means of *catalysts* instead of heat.

Catalysts of various kinds are well known and widely used by chemists dealing with nonliving processes. The special catalysts that occur in living matter are proteins called *enzymes.* Virtually every one of the thousands of chemical reactions in living matter is speeded up enormously by a particular enzyme. Without enzymes the reactions could not occur fast enough at ordinary temperatures to sustain life. Enzymes therefore represent a supplement to thermal motion, a means by which reactions requiring high temperatures in test tubes can occur at low temperatures in living organisms. The effect of enzymes is to lower the activation-energy requirements (see Chap. 3). These catalysts thereby promote appreciable reaction rates at lower temperatures than would be possible otherwise. Note, however, that enzymes only influence reaction rates, not the direction in which reactions proceed (see Chap. 3 for a discussion of factors influencing the direction of chemical reactions).

An enzyme produces such an effect by combining temporarily with the reacting compounds. Mutual contact of these compounds is then no longer a matter of chance collision but a matter of certainty; hence reactions are faster. This rate-accelerating action results directly from the unique surface properties of enzymes. Consider the dehydration synthesis of sucrose:

$$\text{UDP-glucose} + \text{fructose} \xrightarrow[\text{synthetase}]{\text{sucrose}} \text{sucrose} + H_2O$$

In many plants, sucrose results from the union of two hexoses—fructose and a modified form of glu-

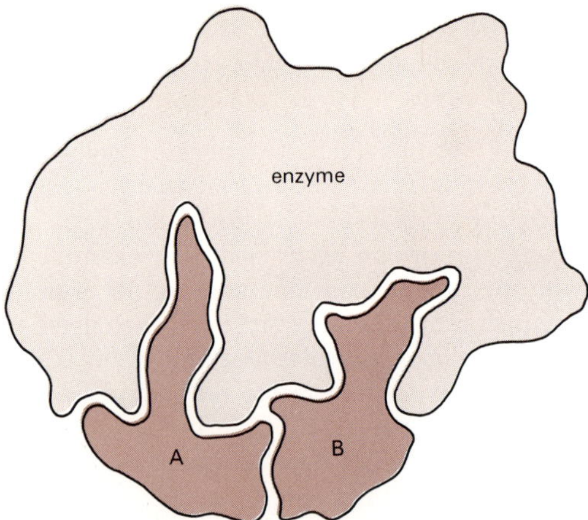

Fig. 4.12 Enzyme action. The surfaces of molecules A and B fit into the surface of the enzyme. Reaction between A and B can thereby be speeded up, for contact between A and B now does not depend on chance collision.

cose called UDP-glucose. Random collisions usually will not produce the disaccharide at appreciable rates. By ensuring an effective collision, the enzyme sucrose synthetase accelerates the rate of sucrose synthesis. Sucrose synthetase has a unique surface configuration that facilitates its physical union with a molecule of UDP-glucose and fructose. The enzyme "holds" the two sugars in a juxtaposition that ensures a reaction-producing collision. Other enzymes similarly affect the speed of reactions by physically interlocking with reactant molecules (Fig. 4.12).

In describing enzyme-accelerated reactions, it is customary to speak of reacting molecules such as UDP-glucose and fructose as the *substrates.* When substrate molecules are attached to an enzyme, the whole is referred to as an *enzyme-substrate complex.* Formation of such complexes may be thought of as "lock-and-key" processes. Only particularly shaped keys fit into particularly shaped locks. Similarly, only molecules of certain shapes will establish a close fit with a given type of enzyme protein (Fig. 4.13). Because enzyme proteins are huge molecules compared with most substrates, the whole surface of an enzyme is probably not required to promote a given reaction; in many cases it has been shown that only one or at most a few limited surface regions, called *active sites,* are involved. Hence even if other parts of enzyme molecules become altered chemically or physically, the enzymes may still be effective so long as their active sites remain intact.

Until recently enzymes were generally believed to be rigid molecular structures, templates of fixed shapes, and enzyme activity was thought to depend on this permanence of the geometry. Newer research indicates, however, that enzyme molecules actually are flexible in a physical sense and that the structure of a particular substrate can *induce* the enzyme to bend or mold itself over the substrate. Such an "induced fit" facilitates better integration between enzyme and substrate, and ultimately makes the whole complex more reactive.

The activity of some enzymes results solely from their structures. Many enzymes, however, operate adequately only in the presence of certain *cofactors* (Fig. 4.14). These substances may be as simple as single metal ions, such as Na^+, bound to a critical site on an enzyme. Ionic cofactors of this kind often serve in binding substrate and enzyme together. Or cofactors may be complex molecules called *coenzymes.* These often cooperate with enzymes in reactions where a portion of one substrate molecule is removed and transferred to another compound. In such cases, the enzyme itself usually catalyzes removal of the group of atoms, but a specific coenzyme carries out the transfer. Some coenzymes are chemical derivatives of vitamins, and many are manufactured from *nucleotides,* a category of compounds discussed below.

Fig. 4.13 Enzyme specificity. Reactants B and C fit partially into the surface of the enzyme, but reactant A does not. Hence the enzyme can speed up the reactions involving B and C but not those involving A.

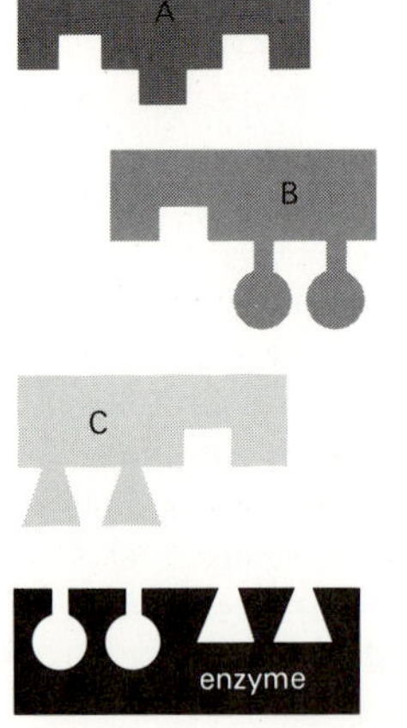

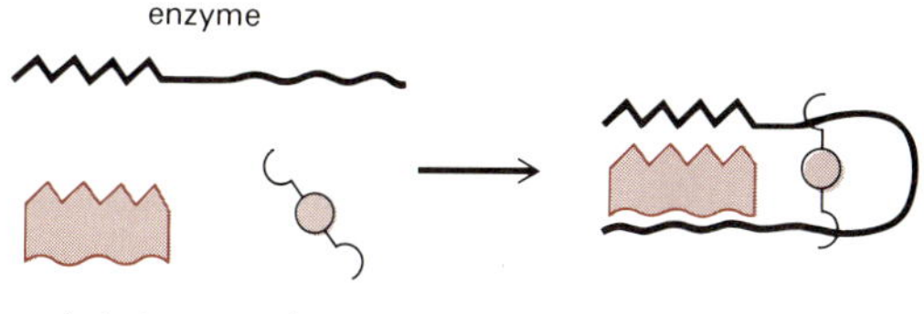

Fig. 4.14 Cofactors. The enzyme diagramed here is assumed to have an active site at each end. A cofactor can aid in producing a fit between the substrate and the active sites of the enzyme. Cofactors include various mineral ions and a variety of coenzymes.

The effectiveness of enzymes varies greatly with changes of temperature, pH, and environmental conditions in general, just as all proteins are affected by such changes. More specifically, as either temperature or pH rises, the effectiveness of enzymes increases up to a certain optimum but decreases thereafter. Most enzymes operate optimally in a temperature range of about 25 to 40°C (human body temperature is 37°C) and in a pH range of about 6.0 to 7.5. At lower temperatures reactions of all kinds decrease in rate, as noted in Chap. 3, and at higher temperatures the thermal motion of the atoms in an enzyme becomes intense enough to disrupt the physical structure of the enzyme protein. Similarly, pH changes to either side of the optimum range produce structural changes that result in enzyme inactivation. These are basic reasons why excessive temperature or pH changes can be lethal to living matter.

Enzymes are usually named according to the kinds of compounds they affect. Thus enzymes that accelerate reactions of carbohydrates are *carbohydrases.* Similarly, *proteinases* and *lipases* are enzymes catalyzing certain reactions of, respectively, proteins and lipids. The suffix *-ase* always identifies a name as one of an enzyme (although not all enzyme names have this suffix). In writing an enzymatic reaction symbolically, the enzyme is conventionally indicated just above the reaction arrow (see the sucrose synthetase–catalyzed reaction above).

For both structural and functional reasons life probably would be impossible without molecular agents such as proteins. But even with proteins and all the other cellular compounds already described, a cell could not yet be alive; the chemicals discussed thus far only endow a cell with the *potential* of having a structure (proteins and other constituents), the *potential* of accumulating usable foods (carbohydrates and fats). The cell has not yet been equipped chemically to make these potentials actual: *how* to use the foods, *what* actual structure to develop, and *which* functions to carry out. These all-important capacities emerge from the organic compounds considered next.

Nucleotides

A nucleotide is a molecular complex of three units: a *phosphate group,* a *pentose sugar,* and a *nitrogen base.* Phosphate groups are derivatives of phosphoric acid (H_3PO_4), an inorganic mineral substance. At the relatively neutral pH of living systems, phosphate groups are ions with a double negative charge, HPO_4^{2-}, symbolized more simply as *P.*

The pentose sugar in a nucleotide is one of two kinds, *ribose* or *deoxyribose* (see Fig. 4.1). Therefore, according to the kind of sugar present, two types of nucleotides can be distinguished: *ribose nucleotides* (or *ribonucleotides*) and *deoxyribose nucleotides* (or *deoxyribonucleotides*).

The nitrogen base of a nucleotide is one of a series of ring compounds that contain nitrogen as well as carbon. A single ring occurs in *pyrimidines,* and a double ring characterizes *purines* (Fig. 4.15). Pyrimidines include three variants of significance, *thymine, cytosine,* and *uracil.* Among purines are two important types, *adenine* and *guanine.*

The nitrogen base in a ribose nucleotide usually is either uracil or cytosine or adenine or guanine. Similarly, a deoxyribose nucleotide typically contains either thymine or cytosine or adenine or guanine. Thus, nucleotides occur in the following two series:

ribonucleotides	*deoxyribonucleotides*
adenine-ribose-P	adenine-deoxyribose-P
guanine-ribose-P	guanine-deoxyribose-P
cytosine-ribose-P	cytosine-deoxyribose-P
uracil-ribose-P	thymine-deoxyribose-P

Uracil occurs only in the ribose series; thymine only in the deoxyribose series; adenine, guanine, and cytosine occur in both. Each nucleotide has a name indicative of its component parts. For exam-

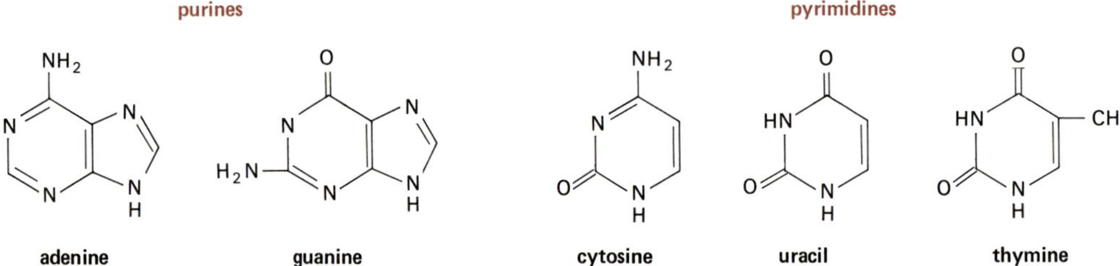

Fig. 4.15 Nitrogen bases.

ple, adenine-ribose-P is called adenosine monophosphate (AMP for short). The other nucleotides have similarly constructed designations (as well as letter symbolizations such as GMP, CMP, UMP, and TMP).

Nucleotides are building blocks of larger molecules that serve three crucial functions in cells: some are *energy carriers;* others are *coenzymes;* and still others form *genetic systems.*

Energy Carriers

A nucleotide is able to link up in serial fashion with one or two additional phosphate groups. For example, if an additional phosphate is added to adenosine monophosphate (AMP), then *adenosine diphosphate,* or ADP is formed; and if a third phosphate is added to ADP, then *adenosine triphosphate,* or ATP results:

adenine-ribose-P	AMP
adenine-ribose-P∼P	ADP
adenine-ribose-P∼P∼P	ATP

The wavy symbol (∼) between phosphate groups indicates the presence of a so-called high-energy bond. Although commonly used and accepted by biologists, this term is somewhat misleading, since many chemical bonds in living systems contain far more energy. A special designation for these bonds is appropriate, however, considering their great significance in living systems. More specific reference to the functional role of these bonds will be made in Chap. 12. Here it need be noted only that formation of chemical bonds between phosphate groups requires substantially more energy than formation of bonds elsewhere in a nucleotide. Correspondingly, larger amounts of energy are released from such bonds when they are broken, and this energy can be used to drive a variety of cell functions. Indeed, energy so liberated drives virtually *all* cell functions in *all* organisms.

Thus, conversion of AMP to ADP and ADP to ATP requires not only additional phosphate groups but also relatively large energy inputs. Such energy is derived in cells from respiratory fuels, and, as we shall see, the primary function of respiration actually is to create the high-energy bonds of ATP. This compound is the significant energy-rich end product of respiration. In effect ATP is an *energy carrier,* the most widespread of such carriers in cells. Derivatives of some of the other nucleotides play a more limited energy-carrying role. For example, by addition of phosphate groups and energy, UMP can become UDP and UTP.

Coenzymes

As noted earlier in this chapter, a coenzyme is a carrier molecule that functions in conjunction with a particular enzyme. It happens often in a metabolic process that a group of atoms is removed from one compound and transferred to another. In such cases a specific enzyme accelerates the decomposition reaction that brings about the removal, but a specific coenzyme must also be present to carry out the transfer. The coenzyme temporarily joins with, or accepts, the removed group of atoms and later transfers it to another compound. The majority of coenzymes happen to be chemical derivatives of nucleotides.

More specifically, in many coenzymes the nitrogen base of a nucleotide is replaced by another chemical unit, usually a derivative of a particular vitamin. For example, one of the B vitamins is *riboflavin* (B_2). This compound consists of a ribose portion and, attached to it, a complex *flavin* portion. In cells a phosphate group becomes linked to riboflavin, and the result is the nucleotidelike com-

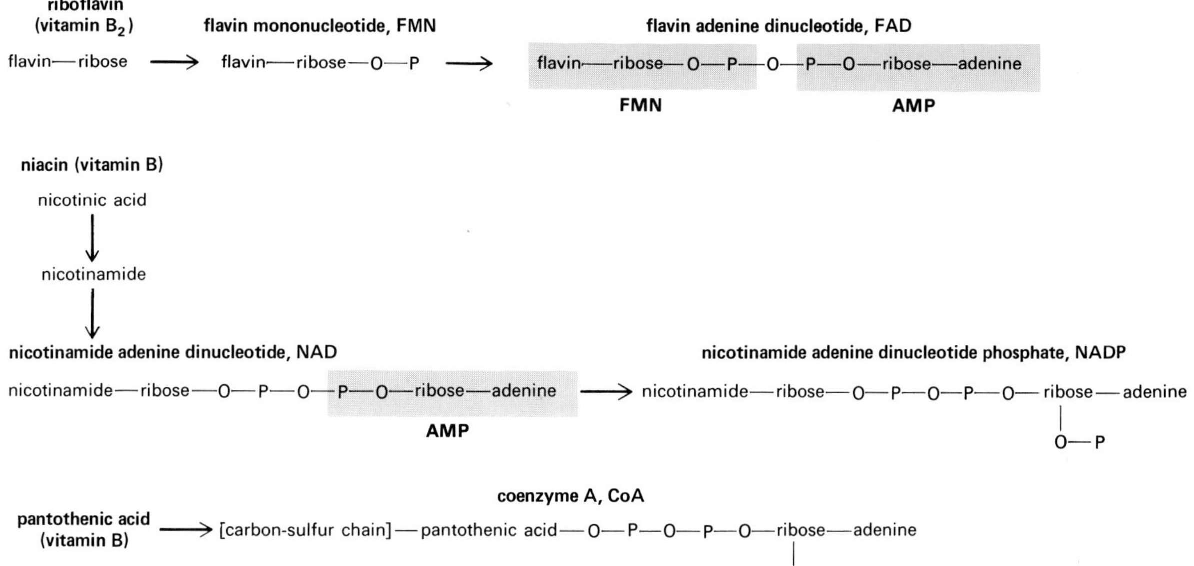

Fig. 4.16 Coenzymes. In the examples shown here, coenzymes are derived in part from vitamins, in part from nucleotides. Top, from the B vitamin riboflavin cells manufacture the coenzyme FMN by addition of a phosphate group, and the coenzyme FAD by the further addition of adenosine monophosphate (AMP). Center, the B vitamin niacin is the cellular source for the formation of nicotinamide, a compound used in the syntheses of the coenzymes NAD and NADP. Bottom, the B vitamin pantothenic acid is a component in the construction of coenzyme A in cells.

plex flavin-ribose-P. Called *flavin mononucleotide* (FMN), this complex can then become joined to the nucleotide AMP, resulting in a double nucleotide known as *flavin adenine dinucleotide* (FAD, Fig. 4.16). Both FMN and FAD are cellular coenzymes that serve as carriers in many processes in which electrons are transferred from one compound to another.

Two other electron-carrying coenzymes, called NAD and NADP, are constructed from adenine-containing nucleotides and from nicotinamide, a derivative of the B vitamin nicotinic acid (niacin). Nucleotides and still another B vitamin, pantothenic acid, contribute to the structure of *coenzyme A* (CoA), a compound that carries a specific group of atoms. In later contexts we shall encounter not only the coenzymes mentioned here but also some others that are not nucleotide derivatives.

Genetic Systems

If any single group of chemicals could qualify as the "secret" of life, that group would unquestionably have to be the *nucleic acids.* (But since we can actually make such an identification today, it is really no longer possible to speak of any secret.) Nucleic acids are *polynucleotides,* extended chains of up to thousands of joined nucleotide units.

Such chains are of two types, depending on whether the nucleotides composing them belong to the ribose series or the deoxyribose series. A chain consisting of ribose nucleotides is a *ribose nucleic acid* (RNA), and a chain of deoxyribose nucleotides is *deoxyribose nucleic acid* (DNA). In either type, the sugar component of one nucleotide unit bonds to the phosphate component of the next. Thus, the sugar (S) and phosphate (P) components form an extended "backbone" from which nitrogen bases (N) project as side chains:

```
—P—S—P—S—P—S—P—S—
   |   |   |   |
   N   N   N   N
```

In RNA the particular types, numbers, and sequences of the four possible kinds of nitrogen

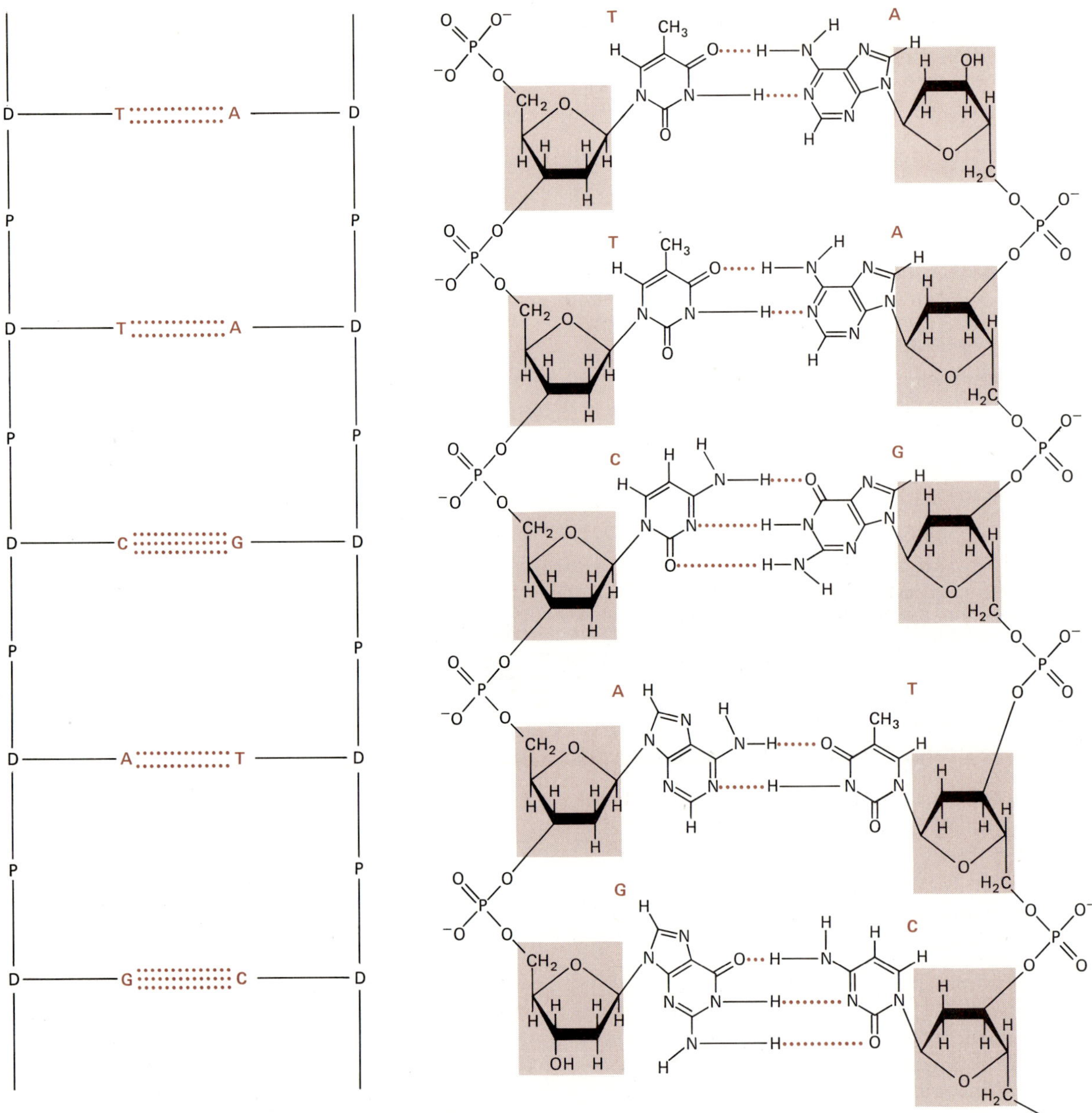

Fig. 4.17 The Watson-Crick model of DNA structure. (A) Schematic representation (P, phosphate; D, deoxyribose; A, T, G, C, purines and pyrimidines. A P—D—A unit represents one of the nucleotides). Dotted lines between nitrogen bases represent hydrogen bonds. Two such bonds join adenine and thymine; three join cytosine and guanine. In the —P—D—P—D— double chain, four kinds of purine-pyrimidine pairs are possible: A•T, T•A, G•C, and C•G. Each of the four can occur many times, and the sequence of the pairs can vary in unlimited fashion. (B) Molecular structure of nucleotide sequence presented in A. Colored dots indicate positions of hydrogen bonds between nitrogen bases. Shaded areas indicate positions of deoxyribose. Phosphate groups are specified by the clusters of phosphorus and oxygen atoms.

bases can vary almost infinitely. A given segment of a long RNA molecule, for example, might read

$$-\mathrm{P}-\underset{\substack{|\\ \mathrm{A}}}{\mathrm{R}}-\mathrm{P}-\underset{\substack{|\\ \mathrm{U}}}{\mathrm{R}}-\mathrm{P}-\underset{\substack{|\\ \mathrm{G}}}{\mathrm{R}}-\mathrm{P}-\underset{\substack{|\\ \mathrm{G}}}{\mathrm{R}}-\mathrm{P}-\underset{\substack{|\\ \mathrm{C}}}{\mathrm{R}}-$$

where R stands for ribose and A, U, G, C, for adenine, uracil, guanine, and cytosine, respectively. Evidently, RNA molecules differ according to their different nitrogen-base sequences, and that is actually the key to their importance. The four possible nitrogen bases can be regarded as a four-letter alphabet out of which, just as with amino acids in proteins, any number of words and sentences can be constructed. As will become apparent later, the protein sentences precisely correspond to, and indeed are determined by, the RNA sentences.

Except for certain types of viruses, the original source of the sentences is not RNA itself but DNA. This type of nucleic acid is a long *double* chain of nucleotides; two parallel single chains are held together by hydrogen bonds between pairs of nitrogen bases (Fig. 4.17). By virtue of their particular structure these bases can be paired only in four different ways: adenine with thymine or the reverse, and guanine with cytosine or the reverse. But there is apparently no limit to the number of times each of these combinations can occur in a long double chain. Nor do there appear to be restrictions as to their sequence. Thus A · T, T · A, G · C, and C · G can be regarded as an original four-symbol alphabet, and sequences of any length can be constructed by using these symbols as often as desired and in any order. The possible number of different DNAs is therefore practically unlimited. A final structural characteristic of DNA is that the double chain of the molecule is spiraled, not straight (Fig. 4.18). The molecular structure outlined here is referred to as the *Watson-Crick model,* after the investigators who proposed it on the basis of x-ray diffraction studies of DNA.

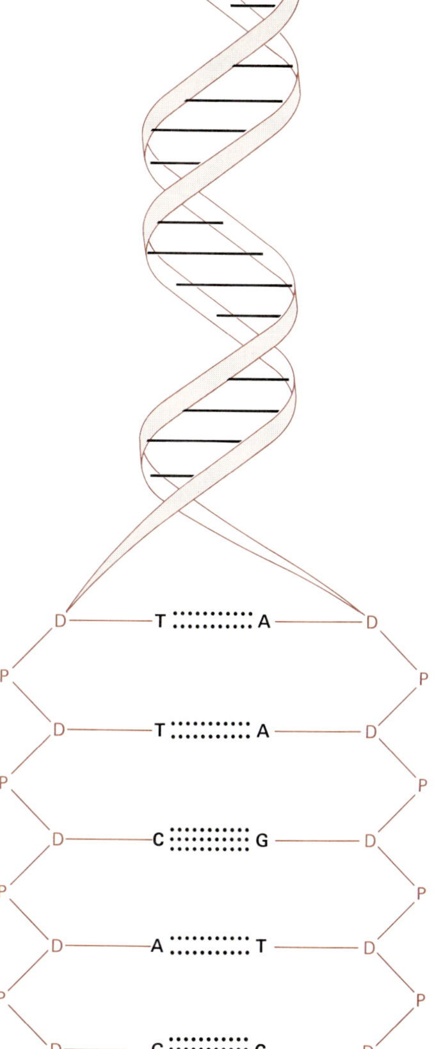

Fig. 4.18 The DNA spiral. The two complementary chains of the DNA "ladder" are twisted in cells and form a double helix. Nitrogen bases and the hydrogen bonds between them are in color.

Functionally, DNA exhibits three properties that make it the universal key to life. (1) As will be shown in Chap. 14, DNA provides the cell with instructions on how to manufacture specific proteins. And through this control of protein manufacture, DNA ultimately controls the entire structural and functional makeup of every cell. (2) Cellular DNA, functioning in cooperation with many enzymes, ions, and other substances, has the property of being self-duplicating; DNA is a reproducing molecule. That a chemical should be able to direct its own duplication under certain conditions may perhaps be astounding, but this capacity is nevertheless a known, unique property of DNA. Reproduction of DNA is at the root of all reproduction, and in a fundamental sense even the reproduction of a whole plant or animal is, after all, a reproduction of "chemicals." (3) Under certain conditions DNA can undergo *mutations,* or become slightly but permanently altered in its nitrogen-base content. When such changes occur, the structural and functional traits of a cell can become changed correspondingly. Through changes in its cells a whole organism and its progeny can then become changed in the course of successive generations, a process equivalent to *evolution.*

In short, DNA is the material that forms *genes,* cellular components long recognized as the carriers of heredity but now known to be even more crucial as the ultimate controllers of all metabolism and all self-perpetuation. DNA molecules, or genes, thus are the basis of life. The discussion of Chap. 14 will show how the structure of the nucleic acids actually permits genes to function in such fundamental ways.

Other Compounds

Carbohydrates, lipids, proteins, and various nucleotide derivatives form the organic bulk of living matter. However, hundreds of other kinds of organic substances exist in cells. Some of these compounds are derivatives of one of the four groups; others are combinations of two or more of the basic four. Some proteins, for example, are almost always bound to a carbohydrate unit. Such *glycoproteins* serve a variety of functions. Some project from the outer surfaces of cells and function as chemical receptors (see Fig. 5.12). Other glycoproteins are responsible for the slippery quality of fluids that lubricate the joints of vertebrates.

Similarly, certain proteins usually are joined to lipids. Some of these *lipoproteins* function in the transport of fats and other lipids in the bloodstream. Combinations of carbohydrates and lipids, called *glycolipids,* are important components of cell membranes (see Chap. 5). Like glycoproteins, such molecules can act as chemical receptors at the cell surface. For example, one class of glycolipid appears to mediate the response of cells to certain hormones.

Many other classes and subtypes of biologically important molecules could be listed, but such a listing would only make the following general conclusion even more apparent. Almost the whole vast array of organic substances in cells is related to, or derived from, only a half dozen or so fundamental classes of compounds; and among these the main types are carbohydrates, fatty acids, amino acids, and nucleotides. Nature apparently builds with but a limited number of fundamental construction units, yet the possible combinations and variations among them are practically unlimited.

It should be kept in mind also that the diverse chemical components of a cell are not "just there," randomly and passively dissolved or suspended in water like the ingredients of a soup. Cells consist of highly organized systems of macromolecular and micromolecular substances, some dissolved in the aqueous intracellular environment and some incorporated within the cellular ultrastructure. None of the molecular components—not DNA, or even the sum total of all organic and inorganic components of a cell is alive. Instead, it is the *organization* of that sum total which provides new qualities and attributes, those which in fact we call life.

Review Questions

1 What are inorganic compounds? Organic compounds? What principal classes of each occur in living matter and in what relative amounts?

2 What are polymers? What is the functional relationship between dehydration synthesis and hydrolysis?

3 Review the chemical composition and molecular structure of carbohydrates. What are monosaccharides, disaccharides, and polysaccharides? Give examples of each. What are pentoses and hexoses?

4 Review the composition and structure of fatty acids. Distinguish between saturated and unsaturated kinds and give examples. How is a fat formed? What general functions do carbohydrates and fats have in living matter?

5 Discuss the functions of fat-related compounds, such as phosphoglycerides, carotenoids, prostaglandins, and tetrapyrrols.

6 Review the structure of amino acids, and show how these compounds differ among themselves.

Write out the formation of a peptide bond. What is a polypeptide, and in what ways can polypeptides differ in composition?

7 What is the primary, secondary, tertiary, and quaternary structure of a protein, and what kinds of bonds produce such structures? What is an α helix? What are globular and fibrous proteins? Review the general role of proteins in cells.

8 What is a catalyst? What is an enzyme and how does it work? What is an active site of an enzyme? A cofactor? How does enzyme activity relate to the activation energy of a reaction?

9 Show how enzyme activity varies with temperature and pH. What are the usual optimal conditions for enzyme activity? Review the general characteristics of enzymes.

10 Why is a carbohydrase ineffective in accelerating the reaction glycerol + fatty acids $\rightarrow$ fat + water? What kind of enzyme does such a reaction actually require?

11 Distinguish between nitrogen bases, nucleotides, ribonucleotides, and deoxyribonucleotides. Give examples of each. What are adenosine phosphates? Review the structure and function of coenzymes, and give the names of some of them.

12 What is the chemical composition and molecular structure of nucleic acids? In chemical terms, what are DNA and RNA? What different kinds of nucleotides occur in nucleic acids?

13 What makes nucleic acids specific, and what are the general functions of such acids? How are they related to genes?

Collateral Readings

Baker, J. J. W., and **G. E. Allen:** "Matter, Energy, and Life," 3d ed., Addison-Wesley, Reading, Mass., 1975. This paperback contains a good general discussion of all classes of cellular chemicals. Recommended for further reading.

Hanawalt, P. C.: "Molecules to Living Cells," Freeman, San Francisco, 1980. A compilation of *Scientific American* articles that describes the functional role of a large variety of molecules in living systems.

Hoffman, K. B.: "Chemistry of Life," National Science Teachers' Association, Washington, 1964. A very readable introduction to the principles of biochemistry. Well illustrated.

Kendrew, J. C.: The Three-Dimensional Structure of a Protein Molecule, *Scientific American,* December 1961. Historically important, this article describes how the three-dimensional structure of myoglobin was deduced. This molecule was the first protein whose folding pattern was determined.

Koshland, D. E.: Protein Shape and Biological Control, *Scientific American,* October 1973. A description of how enzymes catalyze biochemical reactions.

Lehninger, A. L.: "Biochemistry," 2d ed., Worth, New York, 1975. Unquestionably one of the best biochemistry textbooks available. For the advanced student. A superior reference source.

Nass, G.: "The Molecules of Life," McGraw-Hill, New York, 1970. An excellent discussion of the role molecules play in cells.

Sharon, N.: Carbohydrates, *Scientific American,* November 1980. An illuminating account of the structural and functional roles played by these important components of living systems.

Thompson, E. O. P.: The Insulin Molecule, *Scientific American,* May 1955. The first successful effort to determine the primary structure of a protein is described.

Chapter 5

Cells: Structure and Function

Learning Objectives

After reading this chapter you should be able to:

1. List the three principles that compose the modern cell theory; identify the two scientists who founded this theory.
2. Specify the diameter of an average cell in micrometers and millimeters.
3. List one reason why electron microscopes have greater magnification potentials than light microscopes.
4. Distinguish between prokaryotic and eukaryotic cells and give an example of each.
5. Construct a diagram depicting a single cell of *Acetabularia;* illustrate the structural relationships between stalk, rhizoid, cap, and nucleus of an *Acetabularia* cell.
6. Design experiments to show that:
   - **a.** nuclei of *Acetabularia* cells are essential for continued regeneration of lost cell parts.
   - **b.** RNA is the nucleus-produced substance which promotes regeneration of lost cell parts in *Acetabularia*.
   - **c.** the cytoplasm contains factors which influence development of *Acetabularia* nuclei.
7. Construct a diagram depicting the fluid-mosaic model of membrane structure; state how freeze-etching techniques have clarified structural relationships between the molecular components of cell membranes; differentiate between hydrophobic, hydrophilic, polar, and nonpolar substances.
8. Define absorption, secretion, diffusion, osmosis, and membrane transport; state how each of these processes contributes to the procurement of raw materials by cells; define and list one example of a selectively permeable membrane; state how molecular polarity and lipid solubility influence membrane permeability.
9. State at least one example of the effects of osmotic pressure on cells; differentiate between isotonic, hypotonic, and hypertonic solutions.
10. Differentiate between facilitated diffusion and active transport.
11. Differentiate between pinocytosis, phagocytosis, and exocytosis.
12. Draw a composite cell that illustrates the structural relations between the following components:
    - **a.** nucleus
    - **b.** nucleolus
    - **c.** chromosomes
    - **d.** chromatin
    - **e.** nuclear envelope
    - **f.** nuclear pores
    - **g.** rough endoplasmic reticulum
    - **h.** smooth endoplasmic reticulum
    - **i.** ribosomes
    - **j.** vacuoles
    - **k.** mitochondria
    - **l.** chloroplasts
    - **m.** flagellum
    - **n.** cilium
    - **o.** pseudopodia
    - **p.** microtubules
    - **q.** microfilaments
    - **r.** Golgi apparatus
    - **s.** lysosomes
    - **t.** microbodies
    - **u.** centrioles
    - **v.** kinetosomes
    - **w.** plasma membrane
    - **x.** cell wall
13. Identify at least one function for each of the cellular components listed in Objective 12.
14. Distinguish between primary cell wall, secondary cell wall, and middle lamella.
15. Identify at least two junctional structures that interlock cells.
16. Identify at least two extracellular coatings of cells and list at least three functions for such substances.
17. Differentiate between leucoplasts, chromoplasts, and chloroplasts.
18. Distinguish between grana, stroma, and thylakoids of a chloroplast and between the matrix and cristae of a mitochondrion.
19. State the broad functional relationships between the nucleus and cytoplasm of cells.
20. List at least two ways in which plant and animal cells differ structurally.

Every living organism is, or at some time has been, a cell.

Like most fundamental principles of science, this cornerstone theory of biology developed slowly. Cells were viewed, described, and illustrated for 200 years before their fundamental significance was recognized. Once established, however, the cell theory formed the basis of modern biology, a springboard for the development of modern medicine and, indeed, for most applications of biology to our daily lives.

THE CELL THEORY

Cells were described first by the English scientist Robert Hooke. In 1665, Hooke was examining several objects with a primitive microscope. Among them was a piece of cork which, when magnified, appeared to consist of thousands of small cubicles each surrounded by a rigid wall. The cubicles were arranged much like the cells of a honeycomb. In fact, Hooke used the term *cell* to describe his observations in a publication printed later that year.

Although Hooke introduced the term, he failed to recognize the true nature of cells. He believed that cork cells were similar in function to veins and arteries of animals, transporting "vital juices" from one region of a plant to another. Actually, cork is composed of dead walls of cells and is derived from the bark of trees, where it serves in waterproofing and protecting underlying plant tissues. Students examining pieces of cork with modern laboratory microscopes often express amazement that such a gifted scientist as Hooke could have misinterpreted so completely the true relationships between these cell remains. Hooke's inaccurate perceptions, however, were due largely to the distorted images produced by his primitive microscope.

As the technology of microscopy improved, scientists obtained more accurate views of cell structure. By 1824, sufficient observations had been made to prompt the French biologist Dutrochet to establish the first of three major principles composing the modern cell theory, namely, that all living things are composed of one or more units called cells. The other two principles were not established fully until 1858, when, in a widely read publication, Rudolf Virchow argued forcefully, first, that cells were capable of independent existence and, second, that new cells can arise only from preexisting cells (Fig. 5.1).

The Modern Cell Theory

1. All living organisms are composed of cells.
2. Cells are the smallest living units.
3. All living organisms are derived from cells.

Fig. 5.1 Cornerstone principles of the cell theory.

Most of the evidence for these two generalizations had been gathered earlier in 1838 and 1839 by the German biologists M. J. Schleiden and Theodor Schwann. Schleiden was the first to publish his arguments. He was a revolutionary botanist for his time, dissatisfied with the practice of simply identifying, naming, and describing new species of plants. In the face of a growing mass of information detailing differences between species, Schleiden sought a unifying principle common to all plants. His persistence was rewarded. In 1838 he wrote: "Each cell leads a double life; one independent, pertaining to its own development; the other incidental, as an integral part of a plant." In 1839 Schwann capitalized on the work of Schleiden, by demonstrating that the botanist's major conclusions applied equally to animals. Because of the significance of their contributions, Schleiden and Schwann are credited by most biologists as the major founders of the modern cell theory.

GENERAL STRUCTURE OF CELLS

The development of the cell theory was accompanied by the discovery that most cells contain particular kinds of *organelles* ("little organs"). The rigid walls surrounding Hooke's cork cells were found in most plant cells and were named *cell walls* (Figs. 5.2 and 5.3). A thinner, more pliable *plasma membrane* was discovered lying just inside the cell wall of plant cells. In animal cells, cell walls are largely absent and plasma membranes form their only boundaries (Fig. 5.4 and see Color Fig. 1). In 1831 the English scientist Robert Brown reported the existence of small spherical structures in cells, which he termed *nuclei* (Fig. 5.5). Subsequently, *nuclear membranes* (*nuclear envelopes*)

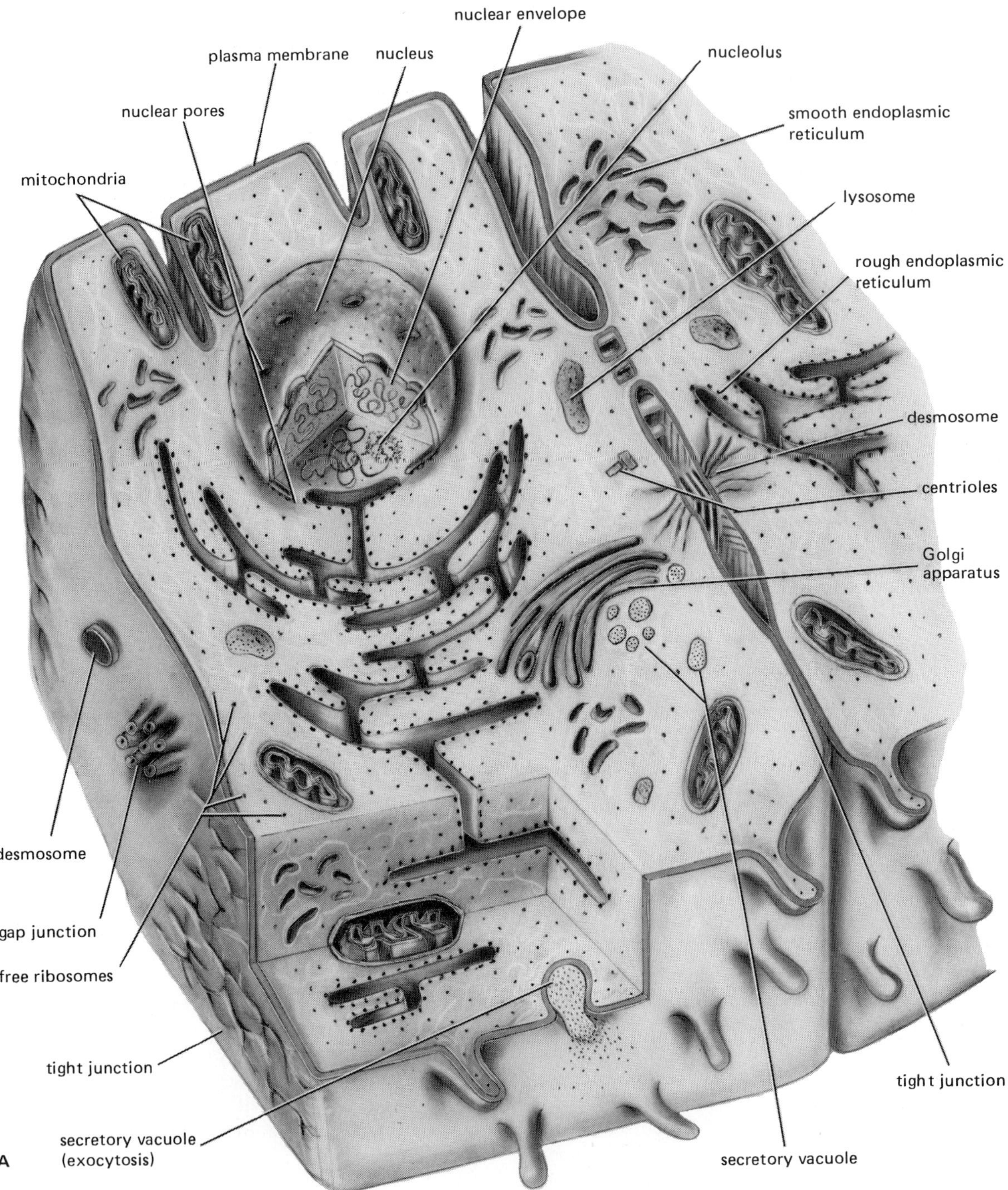

Fig. 5.2 Cell structure. Diagram of a "typical" animal (A) and plant (B) cell. These diagrams illustrate structural relationships between many of the organelles frequently found in animal and plant cells. The organelles shown here do not occur in all cells. Moreover, some cells contain organelles not shown in these diagrams.

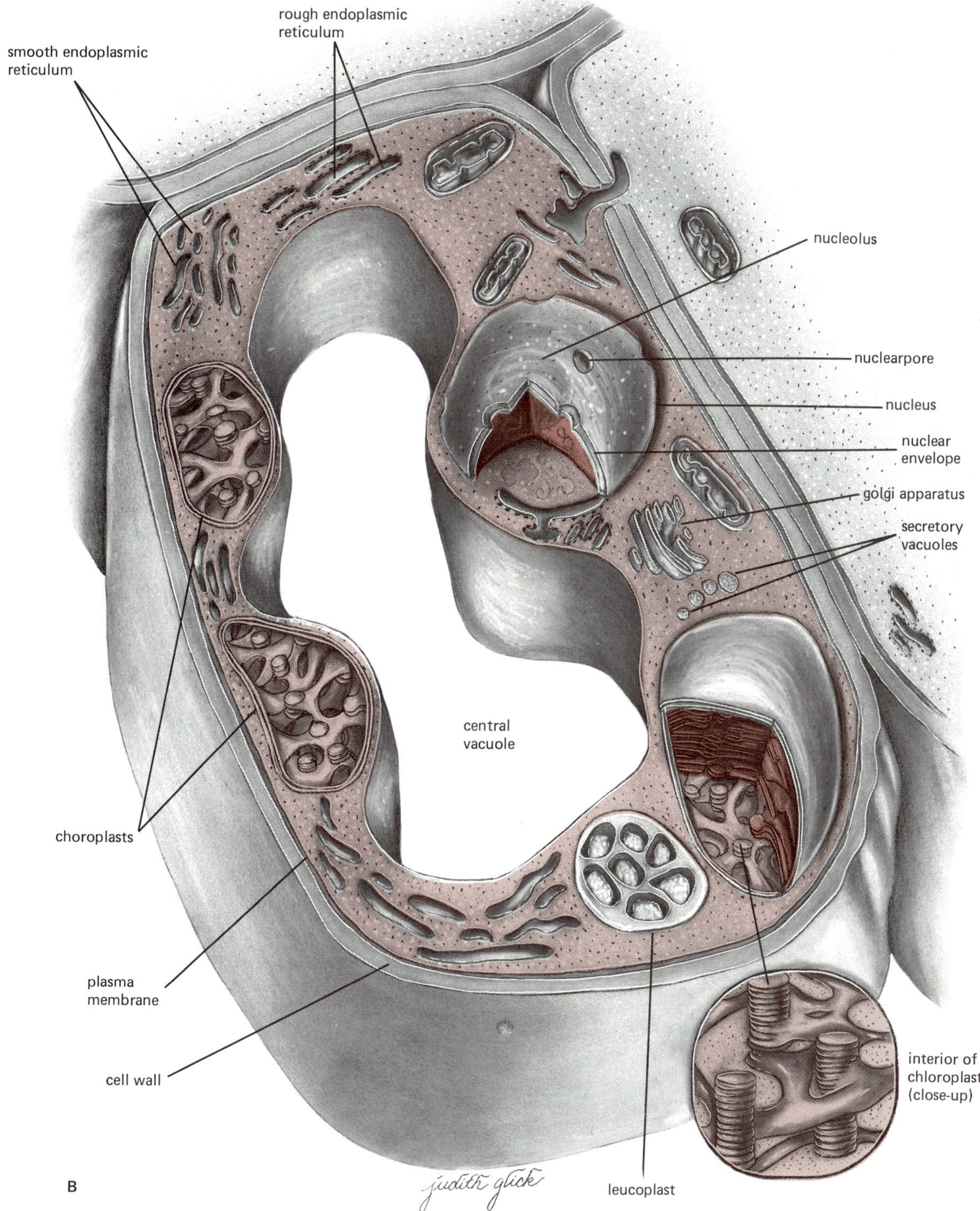
rough endoplasmic
reticulum
smooth endoplasmic
reticulum
nucleolus
nuclearpore
nucleus
nuclear
envelope
golgi apparatus
secretory
vacuoles
central
vacuole
choroplasts
plasma
membrane
cell wall
interior of
chloroplast
(close-up)
leucoplast
B
judith glick

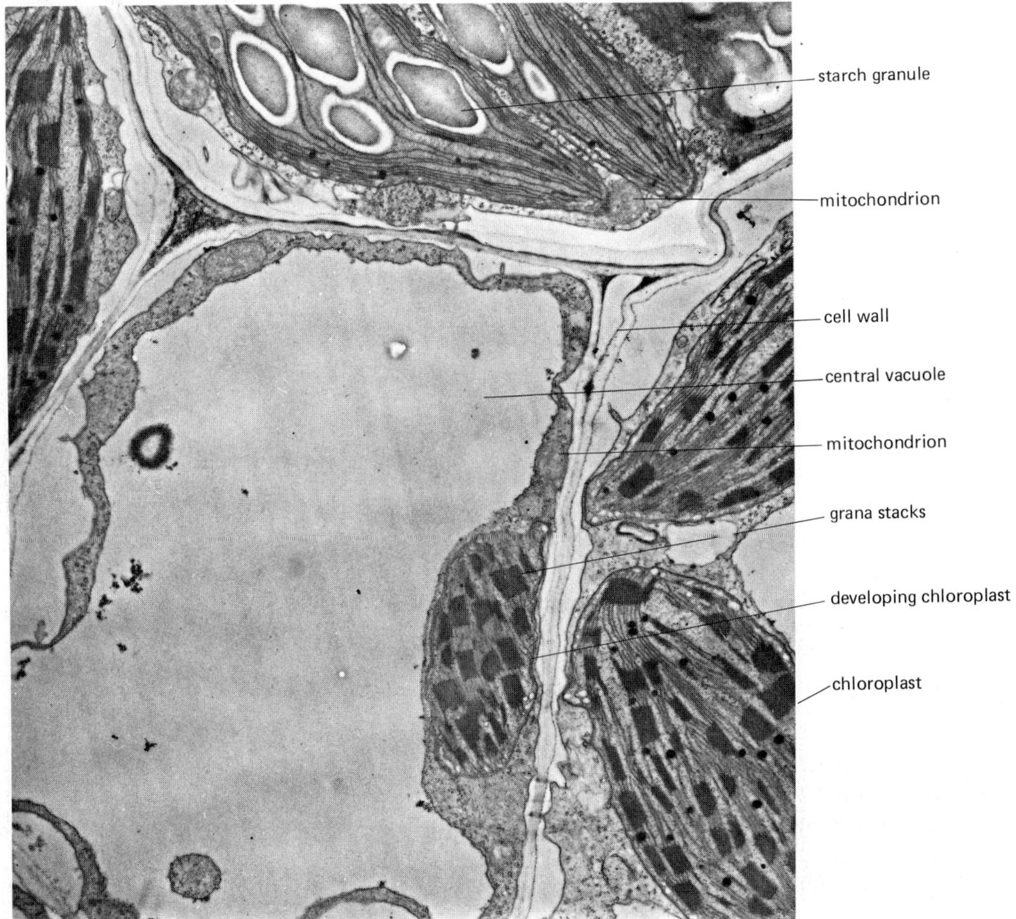

Fig. 5.3 Plant cells. Some of the organelles commonly found in plant cells are shown in this electron micrograph of tissue prepared from a leaf of a corn plant. The functions of each of these are introduced later in this and other chapters (approx. 11,250×).

were discovered, which separate the contents of nuclei from other parts of cells. These other parts, lying between nuclear and plasma membranes, were collectively termed *cytoplasm.*

Some cells, especially bacteria and blue-green algae, do not contain nuclei. These two largely unicellular groups probably resemble the first cells that evolved on earth. It is presumed that these earliest cells also lacked nuclei. Consequently, modern bacteria and blue-green algae are called *prokaryotes* (*pro-*, "before"; *karyon*, "nucleus"; see Section A of Glossary). All other organisms, whose cells do contain nuclei, are termed *eukaryotes* (*eu-*, "true"; *karyon*, "nucleus").

Most eukaryotic cells contain a single nucleus, although several cell types, such as the unicellular protozoan *Paramecium*, have more than one (see Fig. 31.14). Eukaryotic cells degenerate quickly if nucleus and cytoplasm become separated. Considerable experimental evidence supports the premise that nucleus and cytoplasm are interdependent parts of a whole, and only a whole cell can remain alive for an extended period and reproduce other cells (see accompanying Biology Highlight). Attempts to isolate self-maintaining parts of cells that would exhibit and retain all attributes of life have failed consistently. The almost universal minimum for life among eukaryotic cells is one complete nucleus, the surrounding cytoplasm, and the bordering cell membrane.

Several additional types of organelles were discovered in the century following Brown's description of nuclei, but most attempts to obtain accurate views of cellular fine structure were frustrated by the limited resolving capacity of the light microscope. A microscope using light as a source of illumination cannot distinguish two points lying closer together than 0.17 μm [1 micrometer (μm) = $\frac{1}{1000}$ mm; see also Appendix A]. Objects lying closer than that appear as single, not separate entities.

Although some cell types are exceptionally large, with diameters of several millimeters or more, the vast majority have diameters between 0.5 and 15 μm, and a few are as small as 0.2 μm. Thus, light microscopes are useful for distinguishing entire cells or for locating large organelles such as nuclei, but they are useless for examining smaller structures that may lie as close together as a few thousandths of a micrometer.

Much of this problem was resolved by the development of an entirely new type of microscope, which uses a concentrated beam of electrons in-

Fig. 5.4 Animal cell. An electron micrograph of a plasma cell. The functions of the mitochondrion and endoplasmic reticulum are discussed starting on page 101.

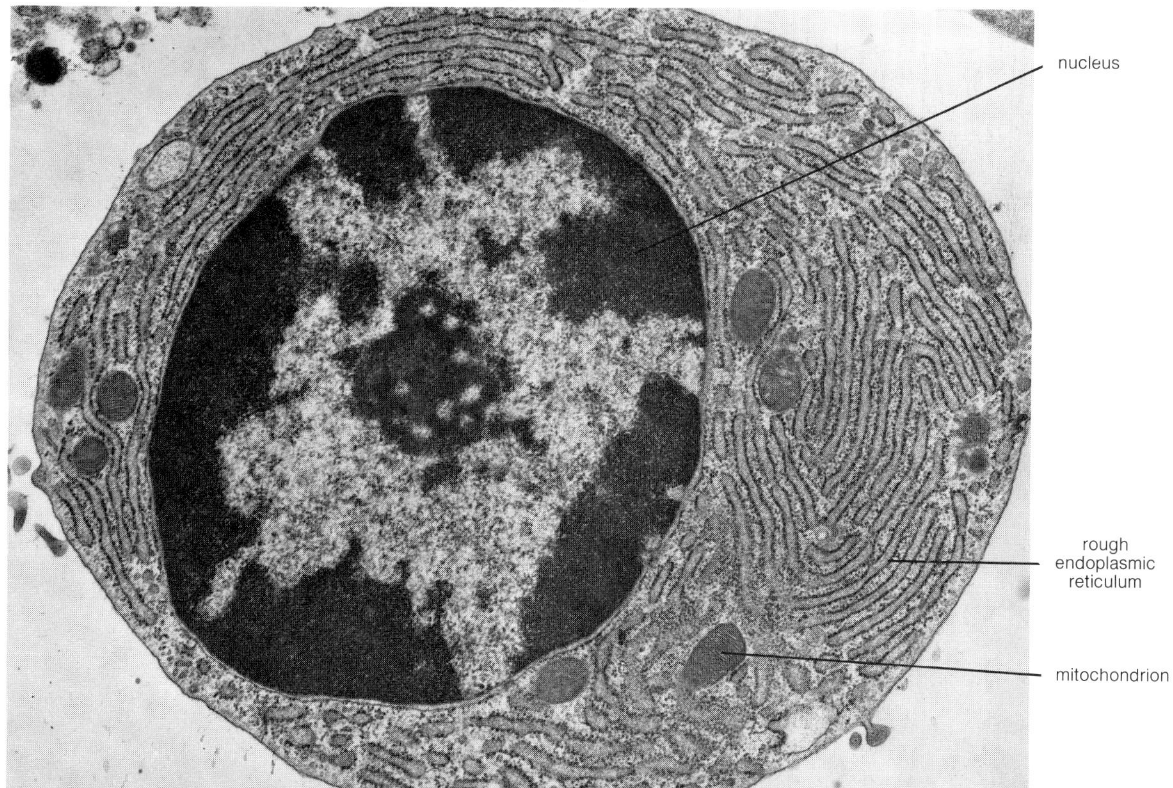

Biology Highlight

Hämmerling's Giant Sea Cells

For many years, early microscopists marveled at the delicate nature of cell nuclei, wondering what functions such organelles served. Were nuclei essential to the life of cells? Were they special storehouses of some vital substance? Perhaps cytoplasmic organelles were produced or controlled by nuclei. Or perhaps nuclei were products of the cytoplasm. If it were only possible to separate nucleus and cytoplasm or to transplant nuclei from one cell type to another, such procedures might provide at least some answers to these fundamental questions.

Today, nuclei are removed from cells more or less routinely, transplanted to enucleated cells, that is, cells whose nuclei have been extracted or destroyed, and even fused with two, three, or more nuclei in a common cytoplasm (see Chap. 28). But in the early 1930s, when Joachim Hämmerling became interested in studying the relationships between nucleus and cytoplasm, such techniques were mere pipe dreams. Nuclei and even whole cells seemed far too small for such manipulations. But if a suitable species of resilient, giant cells could be found, perhaps experimental separation of nucleus and cytoplasm might prove feasible.

Hämmerling learned of the existence of such cells from his colleagues at the Max Planck Institute of Marine Biology in Wilhelmshaven, Germany. Several species of giant cells, all belonging to the genus *Acetabularia,* were being studied at the institute. Sometimes called the mermaid's wineglass because of its graceful shape, *Acetabularia* is a tropical unicellular seaweed that can grow to a length of several centimeters. Each cell consists of an umbrellalike *cap,* a slender *stalk,* and a basal *rhizoid* that attaches the cell to a solid object, usually a rock on the sea floor. The rhizoid contains the cell nucleus (Fig. 1).

Fig. 1 ***Acetabularia mediterranea.*** (A) Each umbrella-stem combination constitutes a single cell. (B) Diagrammatic representation of an individual *A, mediterranea* cell, showing cap, stalk, and nucleus-containing rhizoid.

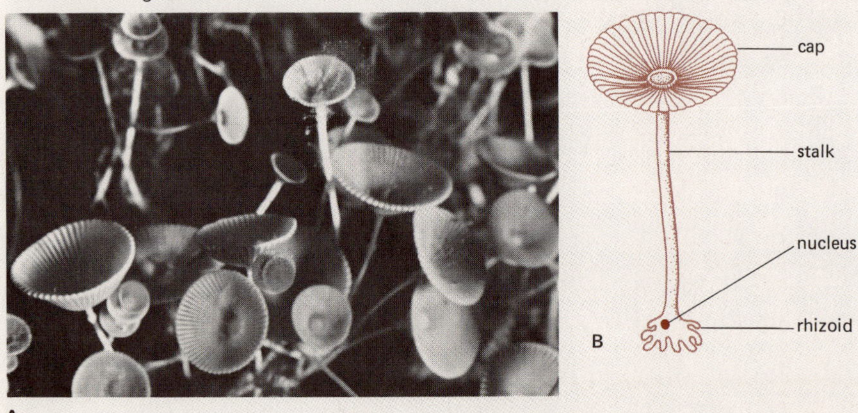

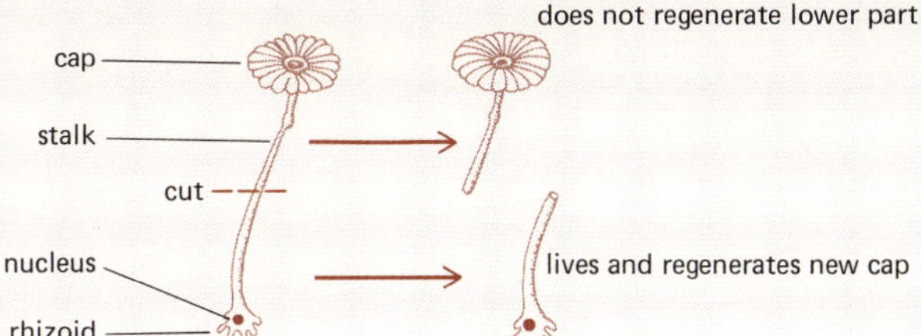

Fig. 2 ***Acetabularia.*** One of Hämmerling's first experiments demonstrated the importance of the nucleus for regeneration. When the stalk of *Acetabularia* is cut, the upper enucleated portion soon degenerates. The nucleus-containing bottom segment lives and grows a new umbrellalike cap.

Most of Hämmerling's first experiments with *Acetabularia* evaluated the functional role of the nucleus. Could an enucleated segment of *Acetabularia* survive and propagate without a nucleus? To test this question, Hämmerling cut a stalk of a cell just above the rhizoid (Fig. 2). The damaged ends of the stalk healed rapidly, and both the rhizoid and the enucleated portion of the cell lived for some time. But after a while, the upper enucleated portion died. By contrast, the truncated rhizoid regenerated a new upper portion complete with umbrella.

Hämmerling pondered the meaning of these results. Perhaps the nucleus is essential for the long-term survival of *Acetabularia* cells and for the regeneration of lost parts. If this hypothesis is true, enucleated portions of *Acetabularia* should not be able to regenerate lost parts. To test the hypothesis, Hämmerling cut a segment of stalk from a cell, leaving umbrella and nucleus-containing rhizoid behind. The stalk regenerated a new umbrella, seemingly refuting the hypothesis (Fig. 3A).

But perhaps this result is not a total refutation. Testing the hypothesis further, Hämmerling recut the *same* stem that had regenerated an umbrella in the previous experiment. This time the cut stem did not regenerate an umbrella (Fig. 3B).

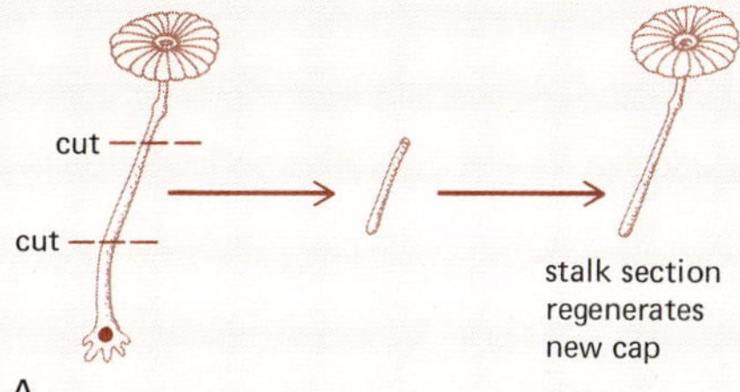

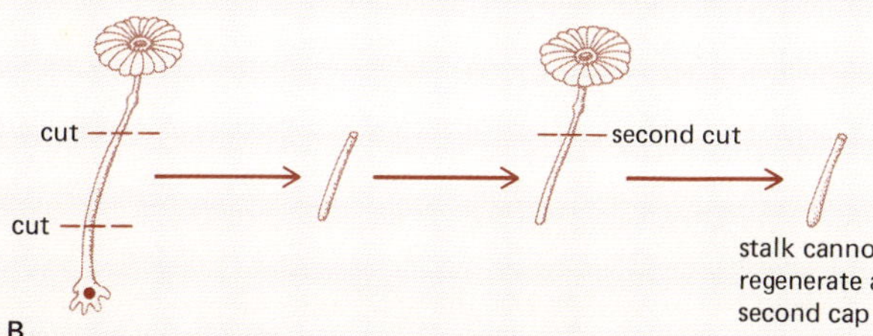

Fig. 3 ***Acetabularia*** **regeneration.** Isolated *Acetabularia* stalks can regenerate a new cap once, as in (A), but not twice, as in (B).

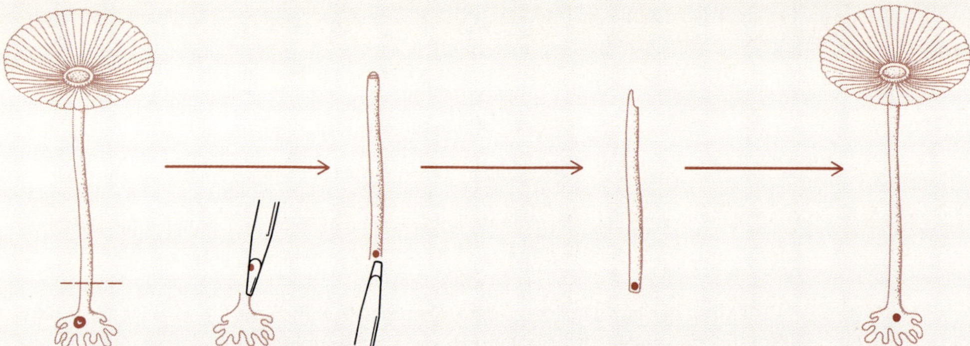

Fig. 4 Nuclear transplantation. Hämmerling removed the nucleus from a rhizoid of *Acetabularia*. He then transplanted the nucleus to an excised stalk. The nucleated stalk grew both a cap and a rhizoid, further documenting the importance of the nucleus for regeneration.

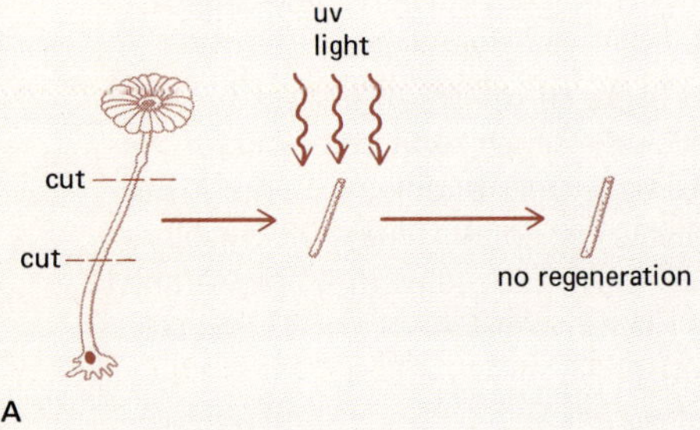

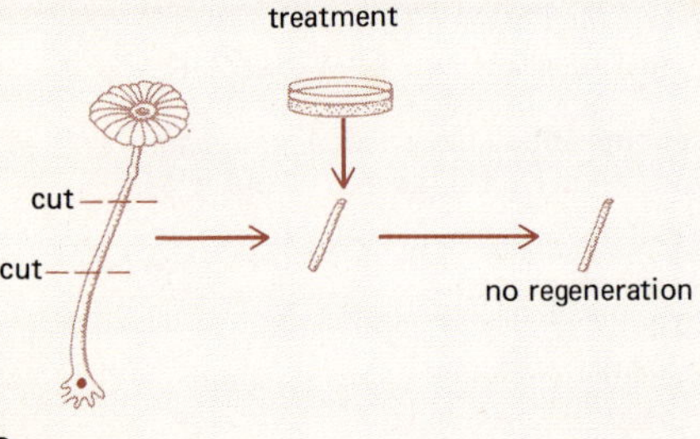

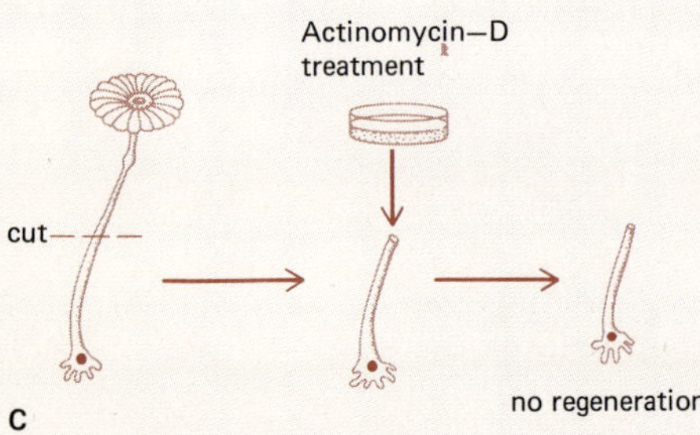

Experimental results often raise more questions than they answer, as is the case here. Why did the cut stalk lose its ability to regenerate an umbrella? Was the ability to promote the first regeneration inherent in stalk cytoplasm, or was it acquired from the nucleus? Perhaps some regeneration-promoting substance emanated from the nucleus to the cytoplasm of the isolated stalk. And perhaps this substance disappeared or was used up during the first regeneration and was not available for a second.

This last possibility was confirmed by another of Hämmerling's experiments. A nucleus was first squeezed out of an *Acetabularia* cell, washed to remove most of the adhering cytoplasm, and then transplanted into an isolated stalk that had lost the ability to regenerate another cap. The nucleated stalk not only regenerated a new umbrella but a new rhizoid as well (Fig. 4). Thus, the original hypothesis that *Acetabularia* nuclei are essential for regeneration of lost cell parts is not incorrect, only incomplete. *Acetabularia* nuclei are essential for the *continued* regeneration of lost cell parts.

More recently, other biologists have identified the chemical substance that moves from *Acetabularia* nuclei to the cytoplasm and promotes regeneration of lost cell parts. It is RNA, one of the nucleic acids introduced in Chap. 4. Several kinds of evidence support this conclusion. For example, nucleic acids are damaged by ultraviolet light. Stalks isolated from *Acetabularia* rhizoids are unable to regenerate umbrellas when treated with ultraviolet light.

In addition, treatment of cut stalks with *ribonuclease,* an enzyme that specifically breaks down RNA, also prevents regeneration. Moreover, chemicals that inhibit the synthesis of RNA prevent regeneration of decapitated cells that still retain nuclei in basal rhizoids (Fig. 5). That the regeneration-promoting substance should be RNA is not surprising, for it is now

Fig. 5 Evidence that RNA is a chemical mediator between nucleus and cytoplasm. (A), (B) Treatment of isolated stalks with ultraviolet light or ribonuclease, an enzyme that specifically degrades RNA, prevents regeneration of caps. (C) Treatment of truncated rhizoids with actinomycin D, a chemical that inhibits RNA synthesis, also prevents regeneration.

known that RNA is intimately involved in regulating cytoplasmic function through protein synthesis (see Chaps. 14 and 15).

This evidence, together with the results of many other experiments, demonstrates that nuclei are the chief control centers for virtually all cellular processes. Enucleated cells often remain alive for a while, but they cannot grow or reproduce and generally have very limited life spans.

It is incorrect to conclude, however, that information transfer between nucleus and cytoplasm is unidirectional. Several of Hämmerling's experiments show that nuclei can be greatly influenced by cytoplasmic factors. For example, Hämmerling's colleagues at the Max Planck Institute had earlier demonstrated that mature, umbrella-containing *Acetabularia* develop from smaller, more or less spherical cells. During cap production, the nuclei of developing *Acetabularia* are larger than at other times. When Hämmerling decapitated a cell producing a cap, the nucleus shrank considerably (Fig. 6).

Hämmerling also noticed that once a cap had fully matured, the nucleus of the cell began to divide repeatedly, an event that signaled the onset of *Acetabularia* reproduction. When he fixed a mature cap atop the truncated base of a young, developing cell, Hämmerling observed that the nucleus of the hybrid organism always divided much earlier than if the young cell had produced its own cap (see Fig. 6).

Both these experiments strongly suggest that cytoplasmic factors influence the developmental state of nuclei. Results of experiments with cells of other organisms support this generalization. Thus, although nuclei exert primary control over cell function, this organelle is responsive to changing conditions in the cytoplasm. Neither nucleus nor cytoplasm is independent, and neither exhibits the properties of life by itself. Such properties can develop only when nucleus and cytoplasm enter into a dynamic, interdependent relationship. This is an important subcomponent principle of the modern cell theory, one revealed in large part through an elegant series of experiments on a graceful marine alga.

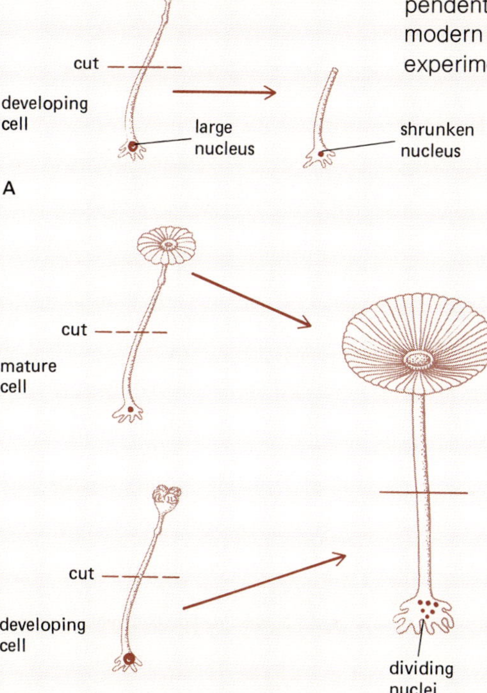

Fig. 6 Evidence that cytoplasmic factors can influence development of nuclei. (A) *Acetabularia* that are developing caps normally have large nuclei. Decapitating developing *Acetabularia* cells causes shrinkage of nuclei. (B) Transplanting mature caps to young rhizoids causes early division of nuclei.

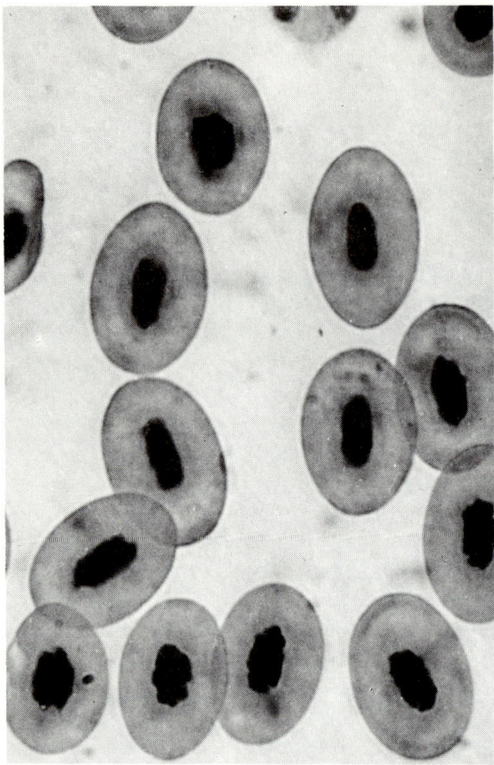

A

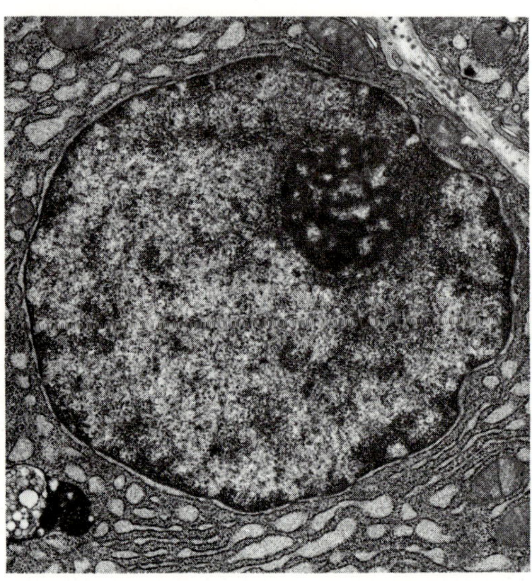

B

Fig. 5.5 The cell nucleus. (A) Blood cells of a frog (approx. ×2000). Note the darkly stained cell nuclei. (B) Electron micrograph of a whole nucleus, covering most of the photo. Inside the nucleus the dark patch is a nucleolus and the dark speckle elsewhere is chromatin (approx. ×40,000). *(A, Courtesy of Eric V. Gravé; B, Courtesy of Keith R. Porter.)*

stead of light as the source of "illumination." Although far more complex and expensive, modern *electron microscopes* have a resolving power 200 times that of the finest light microscopes and by now have been so improved that structures composed of only a few molecules can be distinguished. Through use of electron microscopes, it has been learned that cells are highly organized, complicated bodies, with an intricate internal fine structure.

FINE STRUCTURE OF CELLS

The Cell Surface

Every cell is bounded by a plasma membrane. This exceedingly thin structure, often less than 0.01 μm thick, plays a critical role in all cell functions, since, directly or indirectly, every cell function depends on *absorption* of materials from the exterior, *excretion* of materials from the interior, or both.

Plasma membranes largely determine which substances enter or leave cells and in what amounts. Some substances pass across plasma membranes readily; others move across slowly or only under certain circumstances; and still others normally cannot enter cells at all. Thus, plasma membranes are *selectively permeable;* they differentiate between the substances to be transported. Such differences in permeability result chiefly from how potentially transportable substances interact with the molecular components of plasma membranes. We therefore begin our study of the surface properties of cells with an examination of membrane structure.

Membrane Structure

Up to this point, our discussion of membranes has dealt with the plasma membrane only. However, many intracellular organelles are largely composed of membranes, and the nucleus of eukaryotic cells is separated from the cytoplasm by a double membrane. These important organelles are described later in this chapter, but it is important to note here that the membranous components of these intracellular structures are similar in overall construction to the plasma membrane. For example, virtually all cell membranes are composed chiefly of proteins and lipids. Of these, proteins usually constitute the major portion (Fig. 5.6). In addition, most cell membranes also contain variable amounts of glycoproteins and glycolipids (see Chap. 4).

Some membranes contain considerable quantities of cholesterol, but most of the lipids in membranes are phosphoglycerides (see Chap. 4). The "heads" of such molecules become ionized under the pH conditions commonly found in cells. By contrast, the "tail" ends of phosphoglycerides usually remain uncharged (Fig. 5.7). The polar and nonpolar regions of these molecules react quite differently when placed in water. The polar "heads" tend to form hydrogen bonds with water molecules. Consequently, the charged regions of phosphoglycerides are said to be *hydrophilic* ("water-loving"). The nonpolar regions of such lipids tend to aggregate so that contact with water is minimized. The uncharged tails are therefore said to be *hydrophobic* ("water-hating"). Several studies have confirmed that phosphoglycerides in membranes are arranged as molecular double layers, or bilayers. The polar heads of phosphoglycerides and other closely related lipids are in contact with intra- and extracellular aqueous fluids, while the nonpolar tails are directed toward the center of the bilayer, isolated from water molecules (Fig. 5.8).

Whereas much is known about the structural configurations of membrane lipids, comparatively little is known about the types, structural relationships, or functions of the protein components. The structure of proteins cannot be determined easily unless they are extracted from membranes and isolated in a purified state. But most membrane proteins cannot be extracted unless drastic chemical procedures are used, and such procedures often disrupt both the structural and functional integrity of these molecules. Moreover, many of the proteins function only when they are integral parts of membranes.

Of the several hypotheses proposed to explain the structural arrangement of proteins and lipids in cell membranes, the most widely accepted is the *fluid-mosaic model* of membrane structure. First proposed in 1971 by S. J. Singer, this model depicts cell membranes as mosaics of lipids and proteins. The lipids are envisioned as a bilayer in which proteins are embedded to varying depths (Fig. 5.9). Singer has metaphorically compared the basic structure of membranes to icebergs (proteins) floating in a sea (lipid). Thus, proteins are envisioned as being able to move laterally in the plane of the membrane, and the structural association of proteins and lipids is viewed as dynamic rather than fixed.

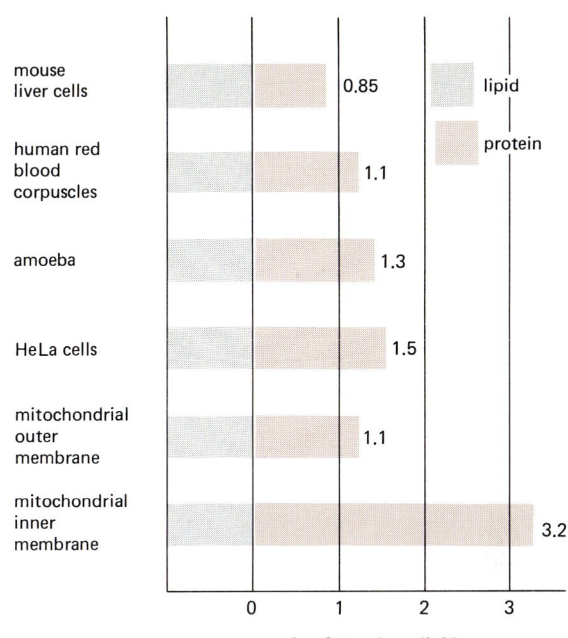

Fig. 5.6 Protein-lipid ratios in cell membranes. Except for a few cells, such as those of mouse liver, proteins either equal or exceed the quantities of lipids in nearly all cell membranes. HeLa cells are a variety of human cancer cell (see also Chap. 22).

The fluid-mosaic model classifies proteins as integral or peripheral, depending on how deeply they penetrate into the lipid bilayer. Integral proteins go deep. Indeed, some are believed to be large enough to extend from the outer to the inner surface of membranes (see Fig. 5.9). Peripheral proteins are pictured as being embedded to shallow depths or loosely attached to the membrane surface. Some peripheral proteins appear to be interlocked end to end along the membrane surface,

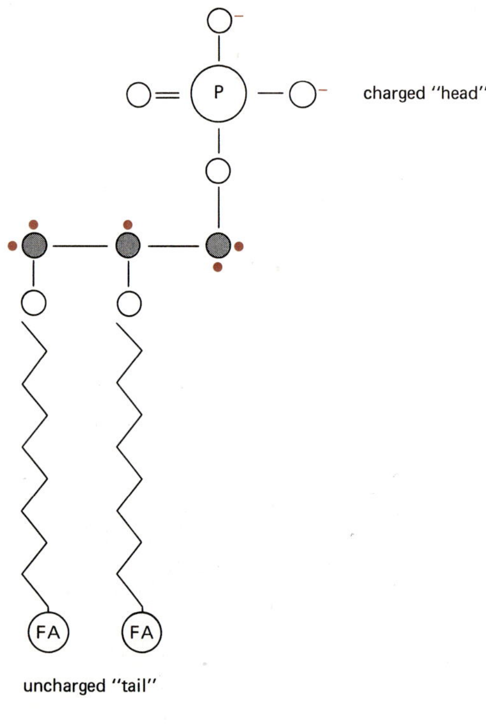

Fig. 5.7 General structure of phosphoglycerides. Phosphoglycerides are similar to triglycerides except that one fatty acid of the triglyceride has been replaced by a phosphate group. Such groups generally become ionized (and therefore charged) under the pH conditions usually found in cells. The phosphate groups of some phosphoglycerides are bonded to additional aggregations of charged atoms. Fatty acids usually remain uncharged at the opposite, or "tail," end of phosphoglycerides.

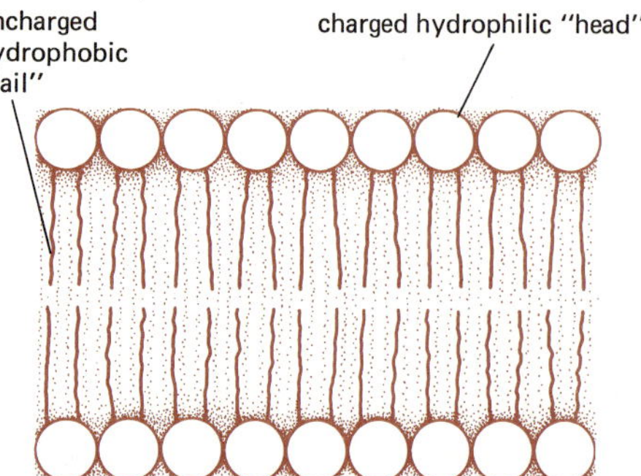

Fig. 5.8 Lipid bilayers. Most membrane lipids exist in bilayers. The ionized head of each lipid molecule is positioned toward the aqueous exterior. The uncharged hydrophobic tails of each molecular lipid layer are positioned toward the center of membranes, away from aqueous surfaces.

each molecule of the chain attached to an integral protein protruding from the lipid bilayer. By tying integral proteins together in this manner such surface chains probably add considerable mechanical strength to membranes (Fig. 5.10).

Evidence in support of the fluid-mosaic model has been obtained through diverse experimental procedures. The *freeze-etching* technique, for example, has provided direct visual evidence. The procedure involves freezing cells in liquid nitrogen. The frozen cell membranes are then fractured so that the two layers of lipid separate, exposing the interior region of the membrane. Electron microscopy reveals many particles protruding above the lipid layer on these fractured internal surfaces (Fig. 5.11). Examined in this way, the particles look very much as icebergs would appear if viewed from below. More recent experiments have confirmed that such particles are membrane proteins and that some of them extend through the entire thickness of the membrane.

The structural relationships between glycoproteins, glycolipids, and other membrane components is not clearly understood, but it is known that carbohydrate portions of many glycoproteins project into the extracellular environment at the cell surface (Fig. 5.12). Several glycoproteins appear to function as molecular receptors for various substances that attach to the cell surface.

Membrane Permeability

Membranes are permeable to a wide variety of substances, but not all membranes are permeable to the same substances. Inter- and intracellular specialization of functions depend largely on differences in permeability between the membranous components of cells.

Nevertheless, it is possible to make a few generalizations about membrane permeability. (1) Substances that are soluble in lipids usually traverse cell membranes faster than lipid-insoluble substances. Many fat-soluble substances can penetrate directly through the lipid bilayer of cell membranes. Lipid-insoluble substances, such as water,

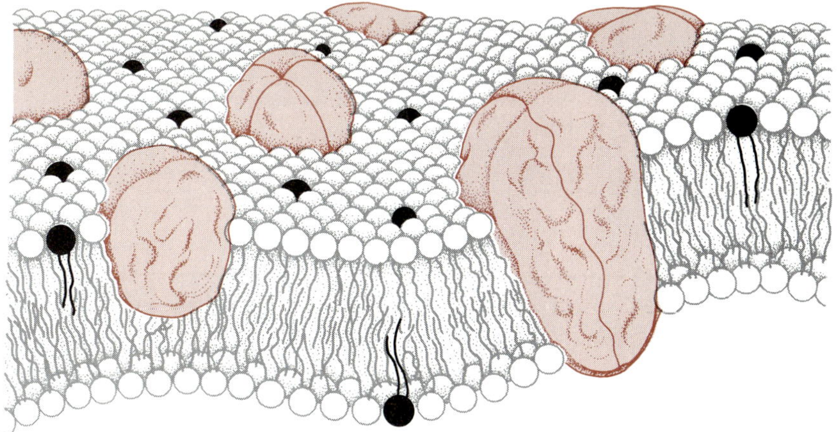

Fig. 5.9 The fluid-mosaic model of membrane structure. Proteins (color) protrude into the lipid bilayer (gray) to varying depths. Peripheral proteins are distributed along the hydrophilic surfaces of the bilayer or embedded to shallow depths. Integral proteins protrude deeply, and some pass entirely through the bilayer. The latter may contain pores through which certain substances pass into and out of cells. Molecules of cholesterol (black) are important structural components of many membranes.

cannot penetrate the internal hydrophobic region of the bilayer easily. (2) Nonpolar substances, which do not contain electrically charged groups of atoms, often pass through cell membranes more easily than polar substances, perhaps because nonpolar substances generally are more soluble in lipids than ionic compounds. (3) Small molecules pass through membranes more readily than large ones. For example, plasma membranes are essentially impermeable to proteins. However, lipid solubility often is a more important determiner of permeability than molecular size. Thus, molecules having high lipid solubility usually will cross plasma membranes faster than molecules having low lipid solubility.

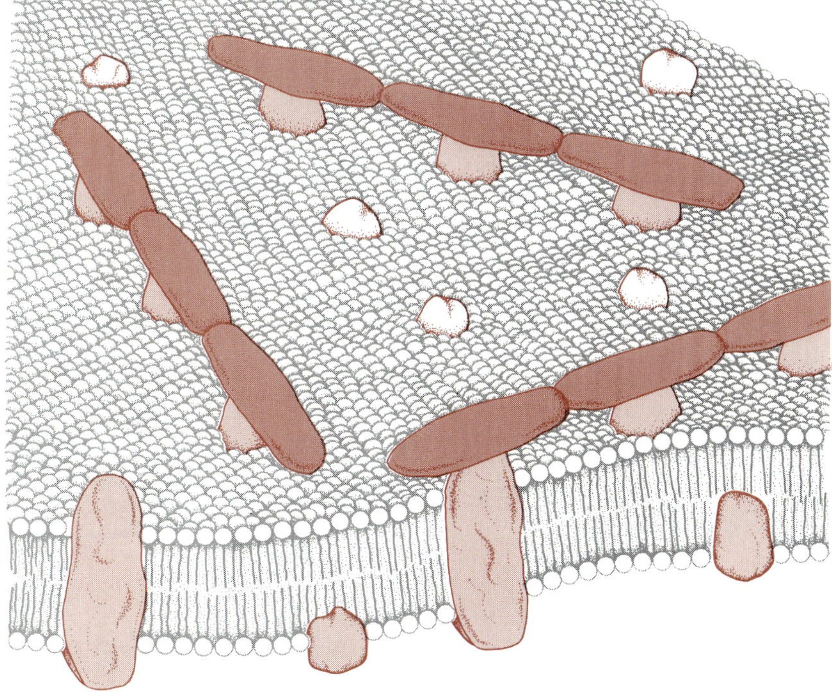

Fig. 5.10 Peripheral and integral proteins. Schematized view of the inner face of a cell membrane. Rodlike assemblages of certain peripheral proteins (color) probably increase membrane rigidity by interlocking with several integral proteins.

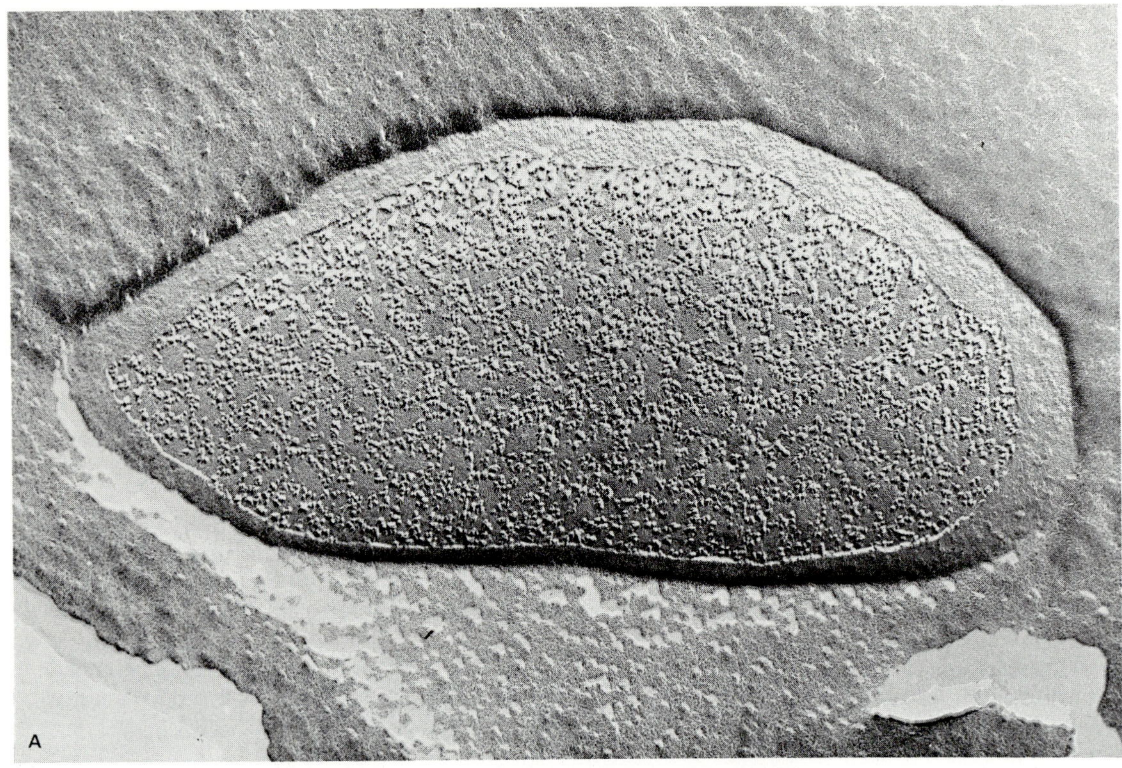

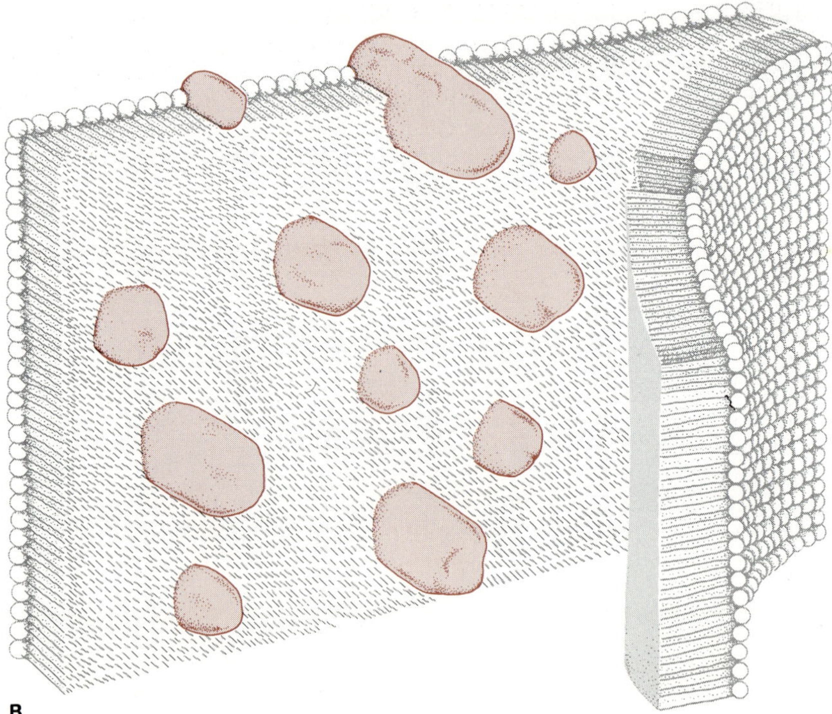

Fig. 5.11 Internal structure of cell membranes. (A) Freeze-etching of a red blood cell. One of the two bilayers of lipid has been stripped away from the plasma membrane of this red blood cell (oblong structure) in a manner illustrated in (B). Proteins formerly embedded in the bilayer (color in B) are now exposed and give a "pebbled" appearance to the etched surface of the cell.

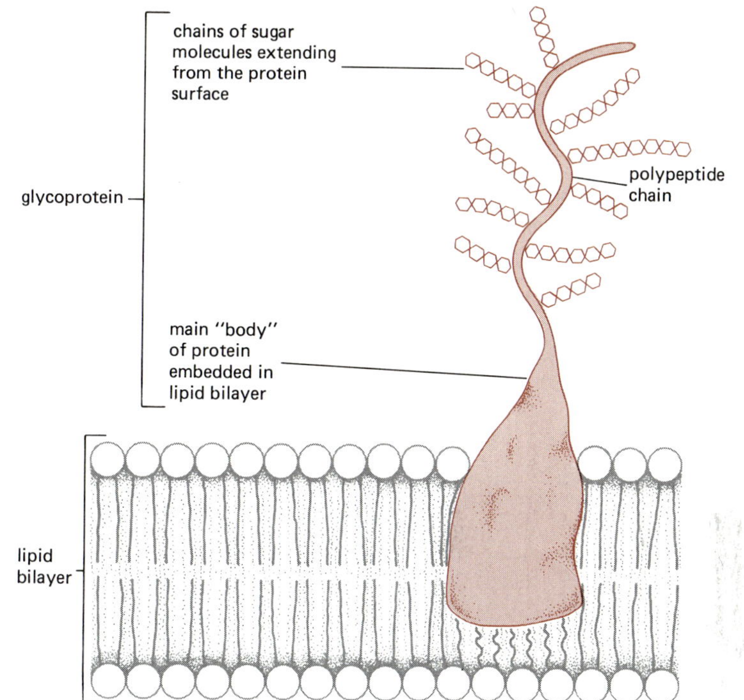

Fig. 5.12 Glycoproteins. Most glycoproteins are found on the outer surfaces of plasma membranes. Glycoproteins consist of protein and carbohydrate components. The main body of the protein component, embedded in the lipid bilayer of the plasma membrane, often contains a polypeptide extension. Polymers of simple sugars branch away from such extensions. Some glycoproteins function as receptors for specific hormones.

Diffusion A few substances, such as water, oxygen, and carbon dioxide, pass easily across nearly all cell membranes via *diffusion.* This process involves the net migration of particles from a more concentrated to a less concentrated region. Carbon dioxide, for example, accumulates in cells as a by-product of cellular respiration and readily diffuses from the inside of cells to the outside, where the concentration of CO_2 is less. Diffusion also plays an important role in the intracellular movement of materials, for it often happens that particles inside a cell are distributed unevenly. Diffusion will then tend to equalize the distribution.

Diffusion is a familiar phenomenon. If a bottle of perfume is opened at one corner of a room, the scent eventually permeates the entire room even if the air is still. If a colored dye is released at the surface of a test tube filled with water, the dye eventually becomes dispersed throughout the water.

Diffusion occurs as a direct result of thermal motion of particles (see Chap. 3). The mechanics of this process are illustrated in Fig. 5.13, which depicts the arrangement of 30 molecules of sucrose dissolved in a U-shaped tube of water. Note that all the sugar molecules initially are located on the left-hand side of the tube. The concentration of a substance in solution varies in direct proportion to the number of particles dissolved per unit volume. Therefore, the concentration of sucrose in Fig. 5.13 is more highly concentrated on the left side of the tube than on the right.

The thermal motion of sugar and water molecules brings them into random collisions, and individual molecules bounce away from each other in any direction with equal probability. Since the concentration of sugar molecules is higher on the left side of the tube, it is more likely that random collisions between molecules will result in more sugar molecules moving from left to right than from right to left. Random collisions between molecules also will cause a net flow of water molecules from right to left because the concentration of water is higher on the right side of the tube. Diffusion will cease when the two populations of molecules become more or less uniformly mixed. At such points of *equilibrium,* movement of molecules from one side

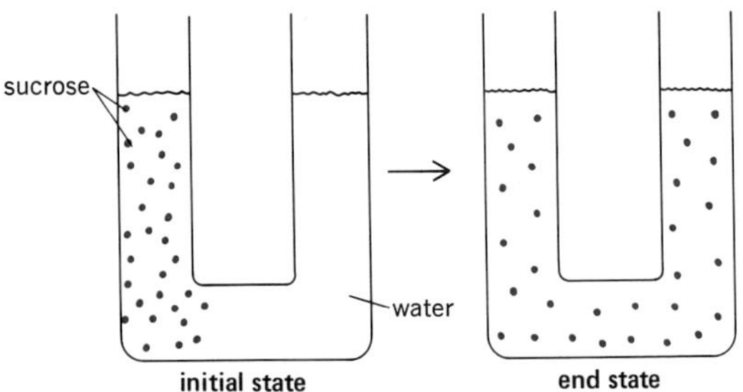

Fig. 5.13 Diffusion. In the initial state at left, sucrose molecules are distributed unevenly. A given molecule of sucrose will therefore have more freedom to move in the direction of lower concentrations. This eventually leads to an even distribution of sucrose, as in the end state at right.

of the tube is counterbalanced by the movement of the same kind and number of molecules in the opposite direction.

Osmosis The diffusion of *water* across a selectively permeable membrane from regions of higher to lower concentrations is called *osmosis.* The general features of this process are illustrated in Fig. 5.14. Except for the selectively permeable membrane separating the right and left halves of the tube, Fig. 5.14 is identical to Fig. 5.13. Like cell membranes, the selectively permeable membrane of Fig. 5.14 is impermeable to sucrose but permeable to water. Although water diffuses unimpeded from the right side of the tube to the left, the selectively permeable membrane prevents diffusion of sucrose in the opposite direction. Consequently, the concentrations of the two substances cannot reach equilibrium. The force exerted by the right-to-left flow of water molecules is called *osmotic pressure.* The amount of osmotic pressure exerted is directly proportional to the difference in the "concentration of water" on either side of the membrane. Water will continue to flow from right to left until the weight of accumulating molecules on the left side of the tube equals the osmotic pressure.

Fig. 5.14 Osmosis. In the initial state, the "concentration of water" is greater on side B, and water will therefore move from B to A. The flow of water continues until the weight of molecules on side A counterbalances the osmotic pressure. From this point on, further net migration of water does not occur (just as much water moves from A to B as from B to A). The line (X) represents a selectively permeable membrane.

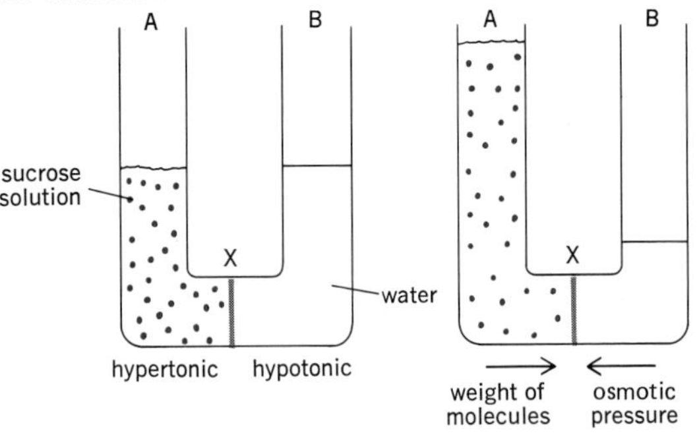

Thus, differences in osmotic pressure largely account for differences in the amount of water transferred between cells and their environments. Osmotic pressure does not exist when the concentration of dissolved particles is equal on both sides of a selectively permeable membrane. Such solutions are said to be *isotonic.* Osmotic pressure is generated only when the concentration of dissolved particles is unequal. The side that contains the lesser concentration of particles is called *hypotonic,* and the side containing the greater concentration is termed *hypertonic.* Water moves from hypotonic solutions to hypertonic solutions during osmosis.

If the osmotic pressure is great enough, cells can dehydrate and collapse. For example, plant cells placed in hypertonic solutions can lose so much water that their plasma membranes shrink away from their cell walls, a phenomenon known as *plasmolysis* (Fig. 5.15). This process can be reversed by transferring the cells to a hypotonic solution. As water moves into cells in such solutions, their plasma membranes return to their original state. In similar situations, an animal cell could absorb so much water that it would burst unless it had some mechanism for expelling the excess fluid (see Chap. 18). But as plant cells absorb more water in hypotonic solutions, their rigid cell walls limit expansion of plasma membranes and prevent bursting.

The mechanism by which water passes through living membranes remains an enigma. As mentioned earlier, most polar, lipid-insoluble compounds cross membranes slowly, if at all. Water has both these characteristics, yet it easily penetrates most plasma membranes. Some evidence indi-

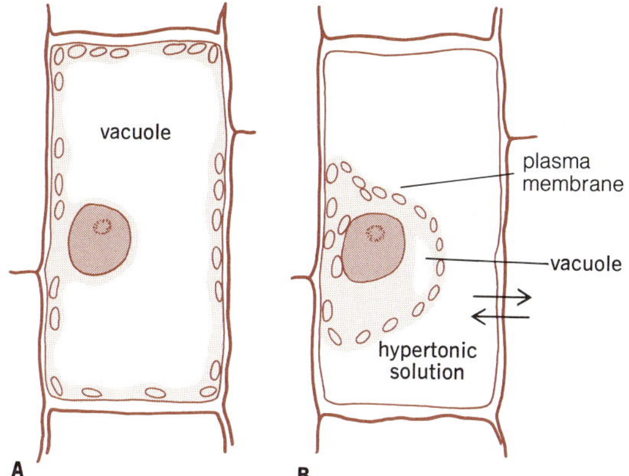

Fig. 5.15 Plasmolysis. (A) Normal cell. (B) Plasmolyzed cell. Water has moved through the plasma membrane into the hypertonic solution, which has penetrated the cell wall but not the plasma membrane.

cates that water may pass through special membranous channels or pores. Such channels could be formed by groups of integral proteins that extend from one side of a membrane to the other. Because they would not come in contact with the hydrophobic interior of the lipid bilayer, water molecules probably could readily pass through such protein-lined channels. Despite the attractiveness of this hypothesis, much more supporting evidence must be obtained before it can be accepted. In any event, osmosis is one process by which water can be redistributed across plasma membranes. Since water is a basic metabolite in all cells, the importance of osmosis in metabolism cannot be overstated.

Membrane transport Although water, oxygen, CO_2, some minerals, and some foods commonly enter or leave cells by simple diffusion, most substances must be "carried" across by special transport mechanisms. For example, sugars, amino acids, nucleotides, and many ions cannot diffuse across cell membranes even when their concentration on one side greatly exceeds that on the other. To be transported, such compounds must first bind with a *carrier molecule* at the surface of the membrane. Thus, the permeability characteristics of a cell membrane are determined at least partly by the types and numbers of carrier molecules present in the membrane. A few nonprotein carrier molecules have been isolated and identified, but most carriers are enzymelike proteins called *permeases.*

Certain substances are transported by carrier molecules only from regions of higher concentration to regions of lower concentration, a form of transport called *facilitated diffusion.* As the name implies, carrier molecules facilitate diffusion of substances into or out of cells without altering the direction in which the substances would tend to move on their own.

In other cases, carrier molecules transport substances "uphill," i.e., from regions of lower concentration to regions of greater concentration. In contrast to facilitated diffusion, this process requires expenditure of energy by cells and therefore is called *active transport.* The source of this energy often is ATP. For example, root-hair cells of many plants can absorb dissolved inorganic nutrients when the concentration of such materials is higher inside the cells than in the soil. Such "pumping" of materials across cell membranes by active transport usually ceases if cells are prevented from using the energy stored in ATP. Several substances can be transported across membranes in more than one way. For example, glucose and certain amino acids enter cells by facilitated diffusion in some circumstances and by active transport in others.

Biologists are only beginning to understand the mechanics of membrane transport. Several hypotheses have been proposed to explain how carrier molecules move substances across cell membranes. One model (Fig. 5.16) suggests that the three-dimensional shapes of carriers become changed when they attach to transportable substances. The changed configuration of the carrier shifts the attached substance from one side of the membrane to the other, where it is then released. As for all other hypotheses of membrane transport, acceptance or rejection of this model awaits results of further experimentation.

Specialized Surface Structures

Cell surfaces are specialized in diverse ways; some of these specializations augment the intercellular transport capacities of particular cell types. For example, the exposed surface of cells lining the small intestine consists of many folded projections of the cell membrane called *microvilli* (Fig. 5.17). These convolutions greatly increase the surface area of cells and thus provide tremendous absorptive area.

Other cells absorb or excrete materials in mem-

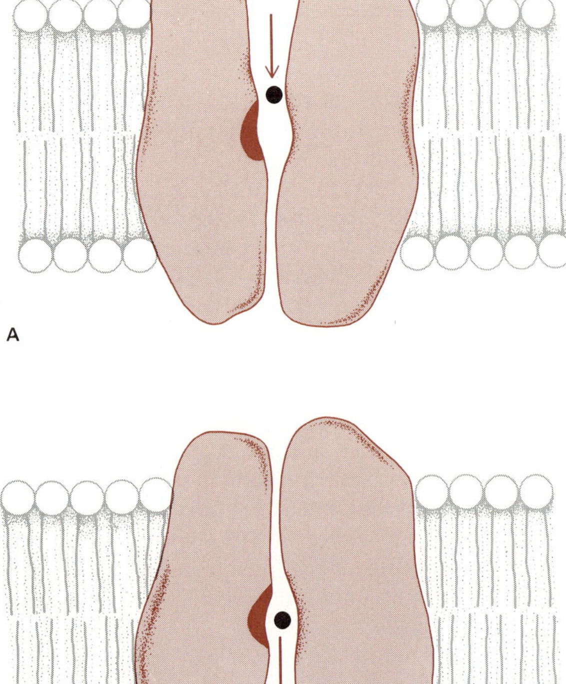

Fig. 5.16 Membrane transport. Some aggregates of integral proteins form pores through membranes. It is likely that some substances pass through certain of these pores by attaching to an active site (color) on an integral protein, as in (A). Such "pore" proteins are permeases. Attachment probably triggers a shift in the configuration of the protein subunits, an event that "squeezes" the transport substance through the membrane, as in (B). Membrane transport is highly specific; the only substances that can pass through such channels are those capable of inserting into active sites on permeases. In facilitated diffusion, the concentration of substances to be transported is higher outside the cell than inside. In active transport such substances are "pumped uphill" against a concentration gradient (see model of sodium-potassium pump in Chap. 19).

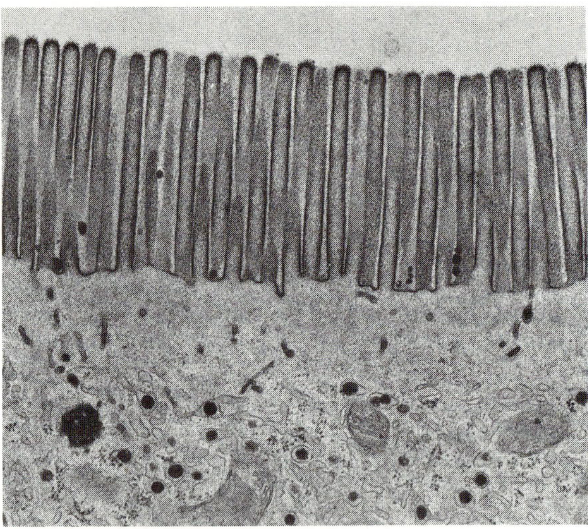

Fig. 5.17 Microvilli. The long fingerlike structures at the top of this electron micrograph are microvilli, surface projections that substantially increase the absorptive capacity of this rat intestinal cell.

brane-bound capsules called *vacuoles.* For example, some cells absorb fluid or solid particles by forming blunt protrusions of their plasma membranes. Any liquids or solids that lie betwen a pair of such membranous folds become trapped in a vacuole that forms when the tips of the protrusions fuse. All such engulfments of materials are various forms of the general phenomenon of *amoeboid* movement, in which fingerlike extensions, or *pseudopodia,* are formed anywhere on the cell surface (Fig. 5.18). Some algae and protozoa, including amoebas, move and feed by means of pseudopodia. Many kinds of animal cells are similarly capable of amoeboid movement. For example, many types of eggs engulf sperm cells in fertilization, and several categories of blood cells engulf foreign bodies, bacteria, and other potentially harmful bodies. When one cell "swallows" particles in amoeboid fashion, the process is called *phagocytosis;* when fluid is engulfed, the process is termed *pinocytosis* (Fig. 5.19). These two processes sometimes are collectively termed *endocytosis.* Many cells secrete or excrete substances through a reverse process called *exocytosis.* In this case, vacuoles containing substances for export fuse with the plasma membrane from the inside and expel their contents to the outside.

The surfaces of cells are specialized in many other ways. For example, most plasma membranes usually are not naked but enveloped partially or wholly by extracellular substances. These outer boundaries are easier to see in plant cells, which have a cell wall around the plasma membrane.

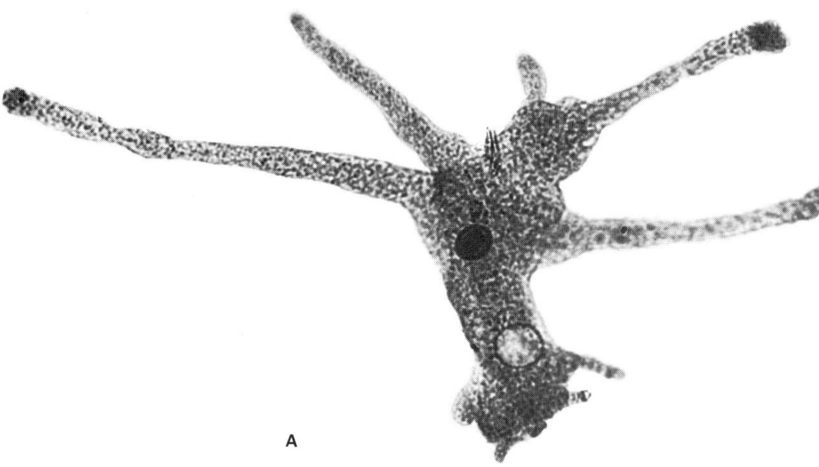

Fig. 5.18 Amoeboid movement. (A) *Amoeba* (approx. ×5000). Like all other unicellular organisms, this protozoan carries out all metabolic and self-perpetuative functions in a single cell. Note nucleus (dark central body), excretory vacuole (light spherical body), and the pseudopodia, fingerlike extensions that serve in locomotion and feeding. (B) A slipper-shaped paramecium, another kind of unicellular protozoan, is being captured between two pseudopodia of a larger amoeba. The pseudopodia will join, engulfing the paramecium in a membrane-bound food vacuole.

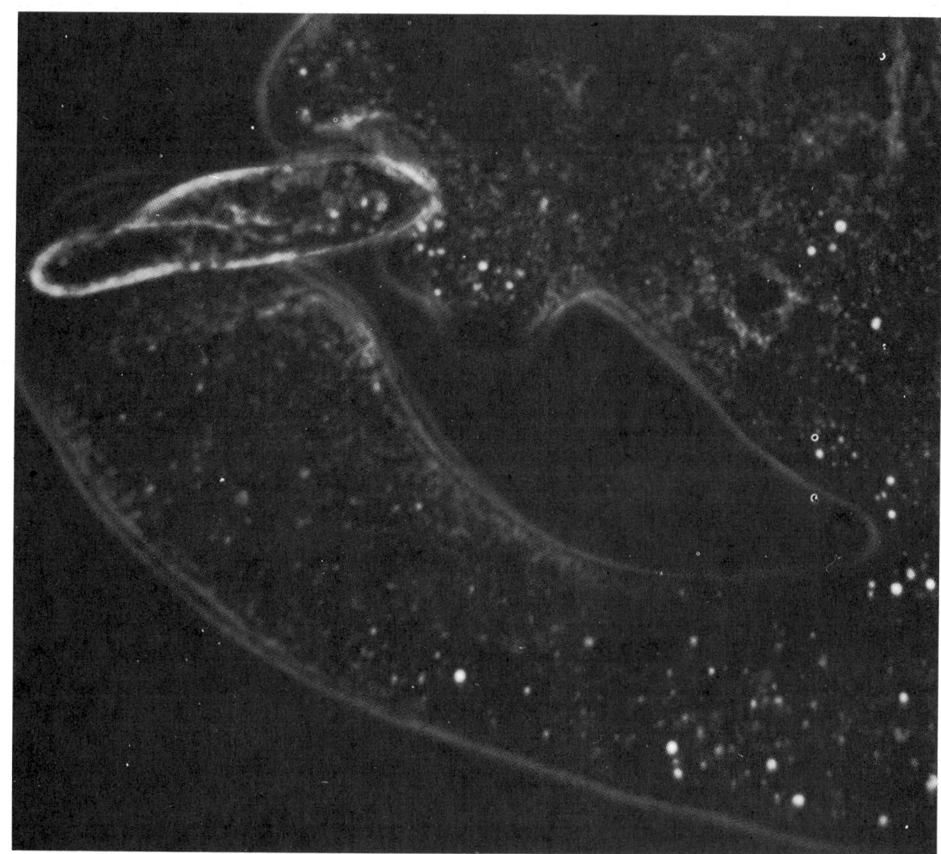

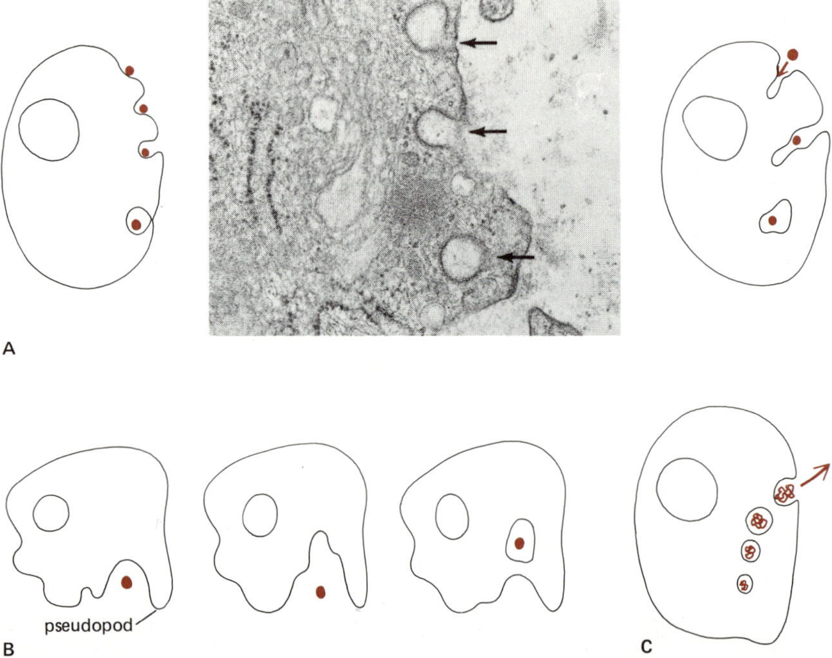

Fig. 5.19 Endocytosis and exocytosis. (A) Pinocytosis. The drawings illustrate two ways in which pinocytotic vacuoles form in cells. Such vacuoles are also termed vesicles. In the left diagram, fluid (color) becomes trapped within shallow depressions in the plasma membrane. The marginal protrusions of the plasma membrane then fuse, sealing the fluid within a pinocytotic vacuole. This process is also illustrated by the electron micrograph (middle). Arrows indicate three stages of pinocytotic vacuole formation in a fibroblast cell. The diagram at the right illustrates how pinocytotic vacuoles form in *Amoeba* and certain other cells. Fluid (color) enters long channels, formed by extensive involutions of the plasma membrane. Vacuoles are pinched off at the base of the channels (see also Color Fig. 1). (B) Phagocytosis. The diagrams illustrate phagocytosis in amoeboid cells. Fingerlike extensions, called pseudopodia, wrap around solid particles (left and middle). Phagocytotic vacuoles form when the tips of pseudopodia fuse (right). (C) Exocytosis. Some cells export substances through exocytosis, a process in which vacuoles first migrate to the plasma membrane and then fuse with it. During fusion, the contents of a vacuole are released to the extracellular environment.

Very much thicker and more rigid than plasma membranes, cell walls are responsible for the hardness of plant tissues compared with those of animals.

A *primary cell wall* is formed while a cell grows and develops (Fig. 5.20). Mature, nongrowing cells often deposit additional materials on the inner surfaces of their primary walls, and such additions form a *secondary cell wall.* Adjacent plant cells are held together by a thin layer of cementing material, called a *middle lamella.* In many cases such cells are interconnected further by *plasmodesmata,* fine strands of cytoplasm that pass through the cell walls and the middle lamella. Plant cells exposed directly to the external air also secrete *cuticles* on their exposed surfaces, in addition to cell walls. Composed of waxy and fatty materials, cuticles make the exposed cells relatively impermeable to water (see Fig. 5.20).

Unlike plant cells, most animal cells and many algal and protozoan cells lack exterior walls. But the plasma membranes of these cells usually are covered by less rigid coatings. In some cells these outer coverings have a protective function. For example, the skin cells of most vertebrates, including people, secrete coats of the protein *keratin,* a substance that also covers surface structures such as hair, nails, and feathers (see Fig. 7.16). A similarly hard substance, *chitin,* is the principal ingredient in the protective shells of lobsters, crayfish, and insects.

The coatings of some plasma membranes are far more flexible and exceedingly thin. The slimy coverings surrounding the cell membranes of many algae, for example, prevent excessive evaporation of water from the cytoplasm. As already noted, glycoproteins and glycolipids extend into the extracellular environment from the plasma membranes of many animal cells. Such molecules often form a cell coat, or *glycocalyx,* visible in many electron micrographs (Fig. 5.21). At least some molecules of the glycocalyx contain chemical receptors that enable cells to recognize and react to changes in the extracellular environment (see above).

Junctional structures Several varieties of specialized structures join or interconnect neighboring cells in plant and animal tissues. Already mentioned are *plasmodesmata,* cytoplasmic strands that interconnect certain kinds of cells in plants. Compact animal tissues often possess more substantial junctional structures that interlock cells tightly. The *desmosome* is the most complex of these various structures (Fig. 5.22). It consists of short lengths of thickened, adjacent membranes running strictly parallel to one another and separated by an enlarged intercellular space. Bundles of fine filaments exist in the intercellular space, and these may serve to bind the adjacent membranes.

Similar specialized regions of cell surface membranes include *tight junctions,* where adjacent plasma membranes are fused in such a way that intercellular spaces do not occur between them, and *gap junctions,* where two closely apposed plasma membranes are separated by small dense particles (see Fig. 5.22). Some intercellular movement of materials appears to occur at tight and gap junctions, and small cytoplasmic bridges have been observed crossing these structures.

Locomotor structures Many cell types are capable of locomotion. Those not moving in amoeboid fashion are usually equipped with specialized locomotor organelles on the cell surface. Among these are *flagella,* long, slender, threadlike projections from cells (Fig. 5.23). The base of a flagellum is anchored in the cell cytoplasm on a motion-controlling *kinetosome* granule. In some cases a threadlike fibril, or *rhizoplast,* connects the kinetosome with the centriole in the cell interior (see below for a discussion of kinetosomes and centrioles). A cell usually bears one flagellum, but often many more are present, all anchored in the same kinetosome region.

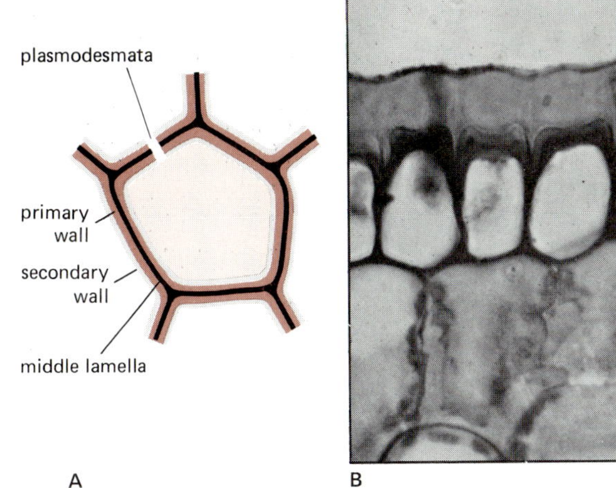

Fig. 5.20 Cell surfaces in plants. (A) Primary and secondary cell walls and plasmodesmata between adjacent cells. (B) Portion of a leaf showing epidermal cells with thick walls (dark) and a waxy cuticle along the exposed side at top. (*B, Courtesy of Melvin S. Fuller.*)

Fig. 5.21 Glycocalyx. The microvilli (fingerlike projections) of these intestinal cells are covered by a thin outer coating (arrow), the glycocalyx, which contains numerous glycoproteins and glycolipids (see also Fig. 5.22).

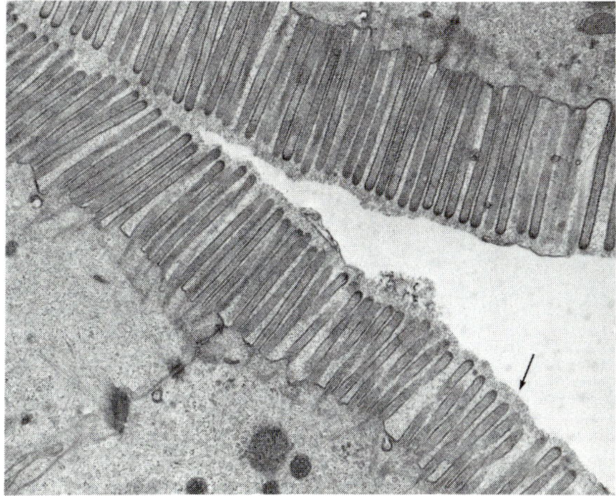

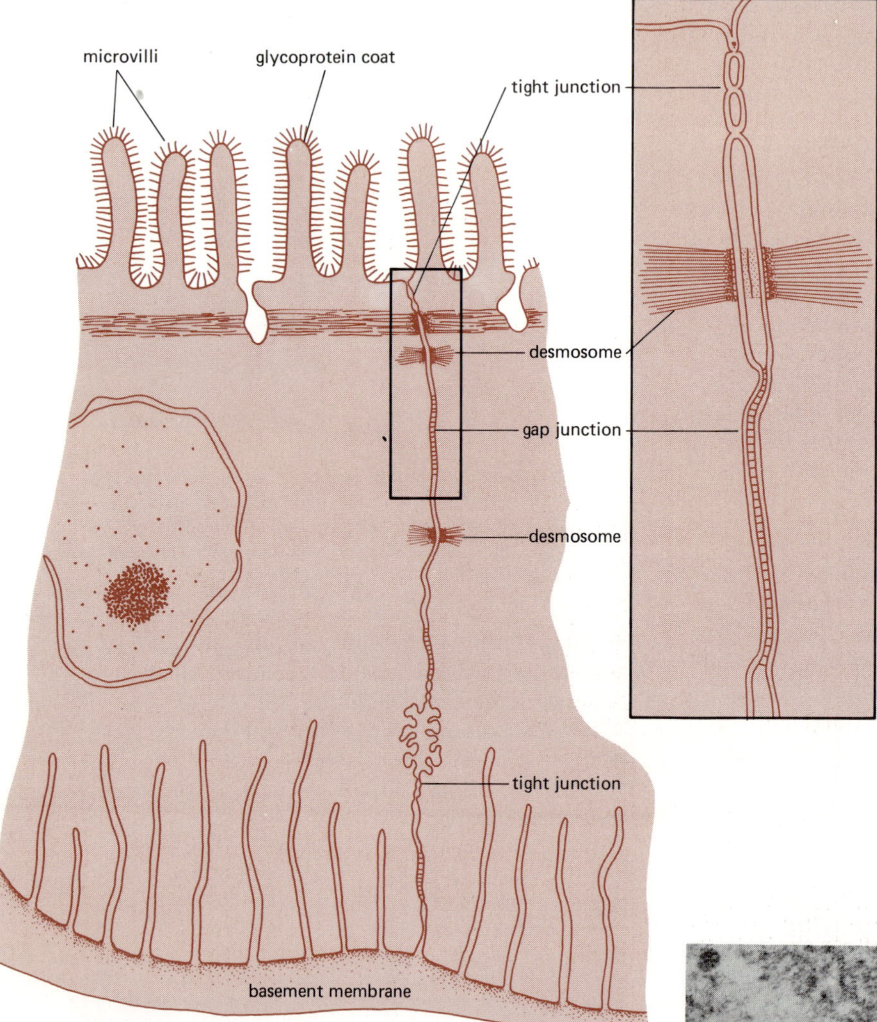

Fig. 5.22 Intercellular junctions. (A) Diagram of a tight junction, desmosome, and gap junction between two epithelial cells. These junctional structures are shown in higher magnification at the right. Note the many folded projections of the cell membrane (microvilli) along the free border of the cells. (B) Desmosome. Note the thickened cell membranes of the darkly stained desmosome that joins a part of two cells. The cytoplasms of the two cells extend beyond the right and left edges of the photograph (×95,000). (C) Arrow points to a tight junction between two closely aligned epithelial cells of a chicken.

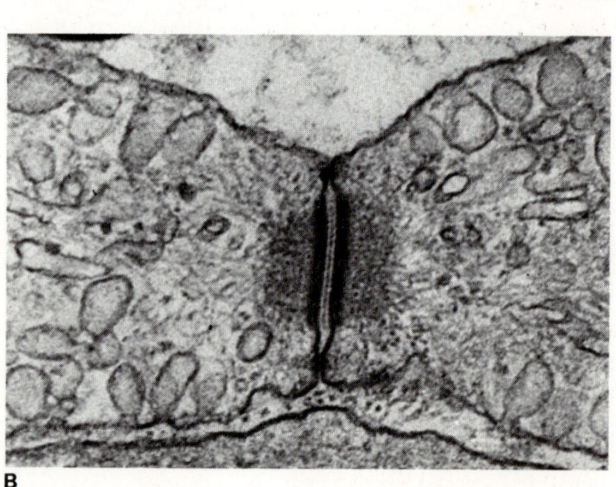

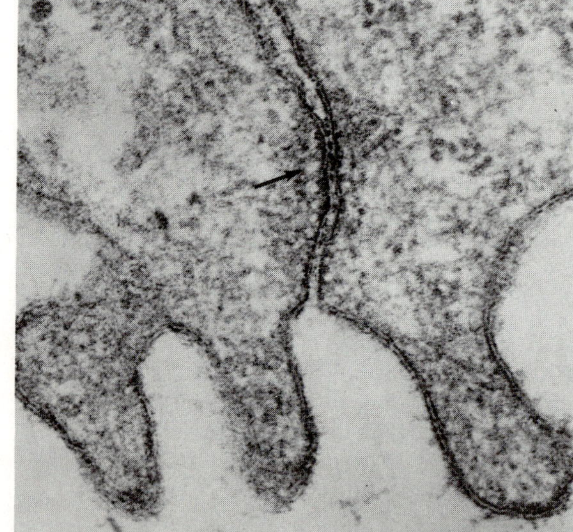

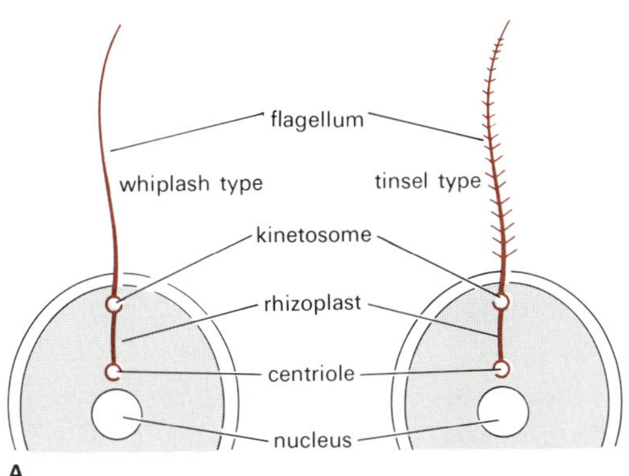

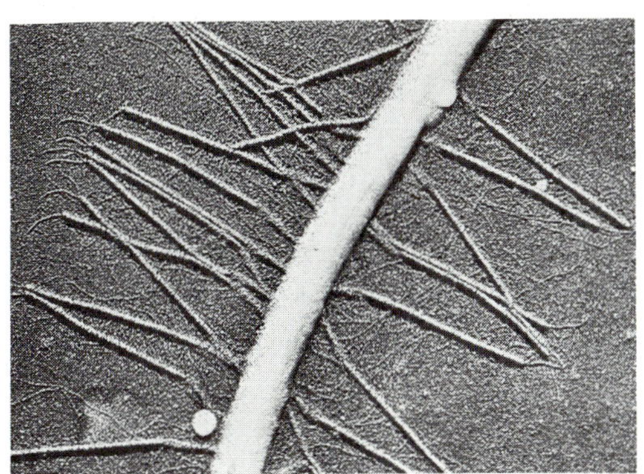

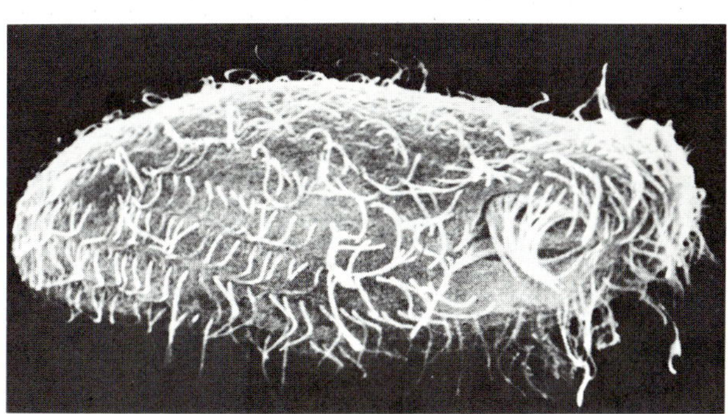

Fig. 5.23 Flagella and cilia. (A) Types of flagella (color) and their insertion in cells. (B) Electron micrograph of a portion of a tinsel-type flagellum, showing the fine lateral filaments (×35,000). (C) A scanning electron micrograph of the freshwater protozoan *Tetrahymena,* showing the rows of cilia covering the body surface.

Numerous types of cells have shorter variants of flagella called *cilia.* They are usually present in large numbers and cover all or major portions of a cell like tiny bristles (see Fig. 5.23C). Each cilium has its own separate kinetosome at its base.

Flagella are the locomotor structures in numerous algae and protozoa and in most sperm cells of plants and animals. Generally the flagellum is at the anterior end of a cell, and its whiplike beat pulls the cell behind it. By contrast, in many sperms and in some fungal cells the flagellum is at the posterior end, and its beat pushes the cell forward. Flagella or cilia also occur in many embryos, larvae, and small adult animals, which have flagellate or ciliated skins that serve in locomotion, in creating food-bearing water currents, or both. Moreover, most animals have flagellate or ciliated cells inside the body. For example, such cells occur in certain sense organs; in the lining tissues of breathing, alimentary, and reproductive channels; and generally in any location where air, water, or solid materials must be moved over a surface or through a duct. Thus, cell surfaces, like the cells of which they are a part, are specialized in many ways; they transport, regulate transport, protect, and play an important role in cell movement.

CYTOPLASM

Cytoplasm consists of a semifluid *ground substance* in which large numbers of several kinds of organelles are suspended. The following types of organelles are widespread among many or all cell types.

Endoplasmic Reticulum

This structure is a network of exceedingly fine double membranes that often traverses all regions of the cytoplasm and is continuous with the plasma membrane and the nuclear envelope (Fig. 5.24). In some cases the endoplasmic reticulum also passes

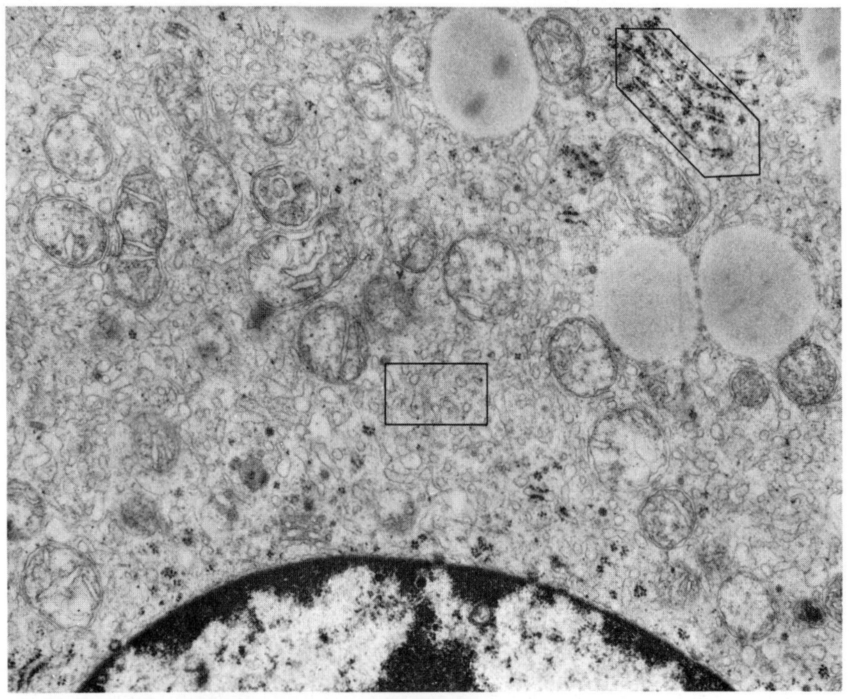

A

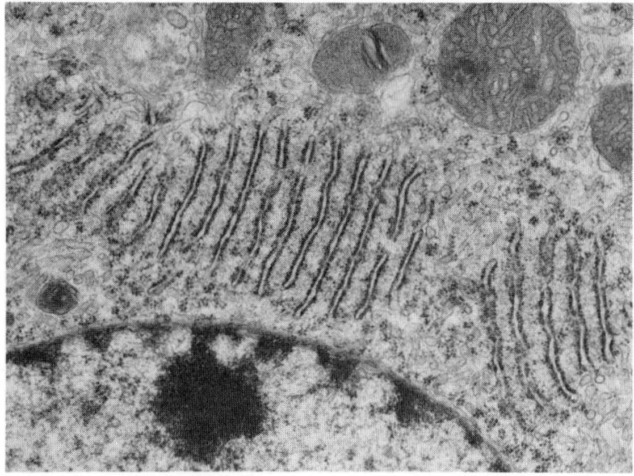

B

Fig. 5.24 Endoplasmic reticulum. (A) Portion of a cell of an adrenal gland. The box in the middle of the electron micrograph surrounds membranous channels of the smooth endoplasmic reticulum. The box at the upper right of the photograph surrounds rough endoplasmic reticulum, also shown at higher magnification in (B). Note the denser appearance of the rough ER, caused by the heavily stained, attached ribosomes.

from one cell to adjacent ones. Attached to this membrane system are many of the other cytoplasmic organelles.

The endoplasmic reticulum appears to function broadly in two ways: (1) It can serve as a network of traffic pathways and conducting channels. Materials in transit from one cell region to another, or from the cell to the outside and vice versa, can migrate along the narrow spaces between the membranes. (2) By interconnecting other organelles, the endoplasmic reticulum forms an ultrastructural framework that keeps the nonfluid components of cytoplasm in certain relative positions. The membranes of the endoplasmic reticulum can form, dissolve, and form again rapidly, often in conjunction with the frequent shifts of position and streaming movements of the other cell contents. Thus although the cell as a whole is readily deformable and the interior contents flow and intermix unceasingly, the endoplasmic reticulum still keeps other organelles properly stationed and distributed in relation to each other. As a result little is really "loose" in a cell, and an orderly organization is maintained.

Ribosomes

Production of these small granules begins in a specialized region of the nucleus called the *nucleolus* (little nucleus) (see Fig. 5.5B). Their manufacture is completed once they leave the nucleus and enter the cytoplasm. There they lie free, or they become attached to portions of the endoplasmic reticulum, giving them a pebbled appearance. Such regions are termed *rough endoplasmic reticulum* (*rough ER*), in contrast to ribosome-free regions, called *smooth endoplasmic reticulum* (*smooth ER*). Ribosomes and the rough endoplasmic reticulum are the principal "factories" for the manufacture and transport of proteins. As noted in Chap. 4, proteins serve a wide variety of cellular functions. Some, for example, are enzymes; others are structural components of cell organelles.

Ribosomes attached to rough ER often produce proteins that are transported to other regions of the cell or secreted to the extracellular environment. Some secreted proteins influence metabolic processes elsewhere in an organism. They appear to pass from attached ribosomes across the membrane of the ER and into the intermembranous cavity, where they are transported to other locations in the cell or secreted to the outside. However, proteins produced on attached ribosomes do not always pass into the cavity of the ER, and attachment of ribosomes to ER membranes may be associated with functions other than protein secretion. Furthermore, many proteins are also produced by unattached ribosomes that lie free in the cytoplasm. Such proteins usually function in the cell where they are produced and generally are not secreted.

The smooth endoplasmic reticulum is associated with a wide range of functions, including the synthesis of fats and certain kinds of hormones (see Chaps. 4, 13, and 17). At least some portions of the smooth ER appear to be derivatives of rough ER from which ribosomes have become detached. Thus, rough and smooth ER can be contiguous components of a single intracellular system of membranes subdivided into structurally and functionally distinct regions.

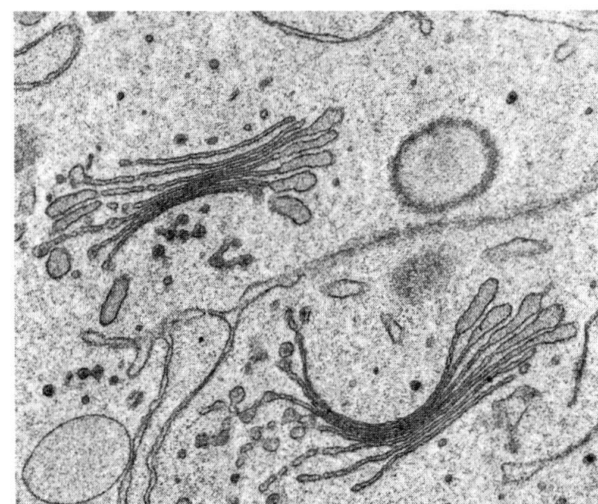

Fig. 5.25 Golgi apparatus. An electron micrograph of cytoplasm with a Golgi apparatus at the upper left and lower right. Each Golgi apparatus is composed of a double stack of parallel double membranes (×50,000). (*Courtesy of W. G. Whaley.*)

Golgi Apparatus

This type of organelle, named after Camillo Golgi who discovered it in 1898, consists of stacks of thin membranes (Fig. 5.25). In some cells the Golgi apparatus functions in "packaging" and exporting substances produced along the rough ER and transported to the Golgi apparatus through the intermembranous channels of the endoplasmic reticulum (Fig. 5.26). However, the Golgi apparatus can receive materials produced elsewhere in cells, and synthesis of certain substances occurs along the membranes of this organelle. For example, the protein and carbohydrate segments of certain glycoproteins are chemically united here.

The Golgi apparatus is particularly conspicuous in actively secreting gland cells where small, fluid-filled vacuoles can be seen "pinching" away from the membranous stacks. Such vacuoles move to the cell membrane and eliminate their contents by exocytosis (see Figs. 5.19C and 5.26). The formation of cell walls in plant cells depends on materials contained in vacuoles produced by the Golgi apparatus. Moreover, the membranes of some of

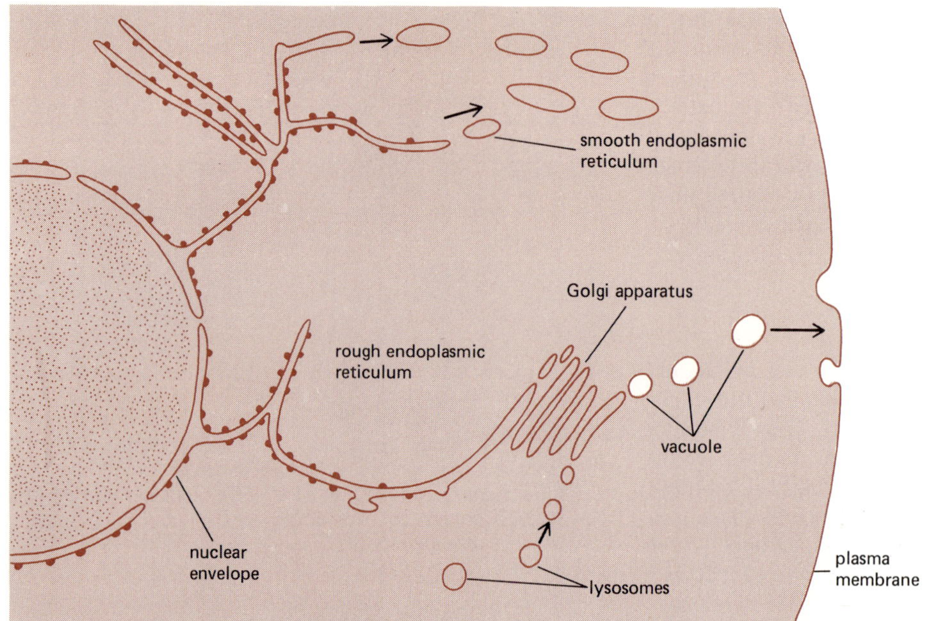

Fig. 5.26 Interrelationships between membranous components of cells. Several structurally distinct organelles actually are localized modifications of a single intermembranous system, each subdivision specialized for particular functions. Thus, the rough ER often appears as an extension of the outer membrane of the nuclear envelope. Similarly, at least some components of the smooth ER are derived from rough ER, and most lysosomes probably originate from the Golgi apparatus. Moreover, substances produced by the rough ER of some cells have been observed passing through intermembranous channels to the Golgi apparatus. The substances sometimes become compartmentalized in vacuoles that originate as pinched-off extensions of the Golgi complex. Such vacuoles can unite with the plasma membrane, extruding their contents to the extracellular environment (see also Fig. 5.19C).

these vacuoles also contribute to formation of new cell membranes following division of plant cells (see Fig. 22.8).

Vacuoles

As stated previously, these comprise a wide variety of membrane-bound sacs found in many different cell types. They include pinocytotic, phagocytotic, digestive, and secretory vacuoles (see Fig. 5.19). These, and other varieties as well, often function as temporary storage depots. Many plant cells contain a large central water vacuole occupying as much as 80 to 90 per cent of the total cell volume (see Fig. 5.3).

Mitochondria

These are the chief chemical "factories" in which cellular respiration is carried out. Under the light microscope mitochondria appear as short rods or thin filaments averaging 0.5 to 2 μm long. The electron microscope shows that the surface of a mitochondrion consists of two fine membranes (Fig. 5.27). The inner one has folds, called *cristae,* that project into the interior, or *matrix,* of the mitochondrion. Cristae are known to be the specific locations where respiratory reactions take place. These reactions are discussed in Chap. 12.

Mitochondria display greater autonomy than most cell organelles. For example, new mitochondria are not the products of other structures but originate solely through growth and division of preexisting mitochondria. They contain an internal complement of ribosomes, and some mitochondrial proteins are synthesized in the mitochondrial matrix. Moreover, mitochondria contain DNA, which directs the synthesis of some mitochondrial pro-

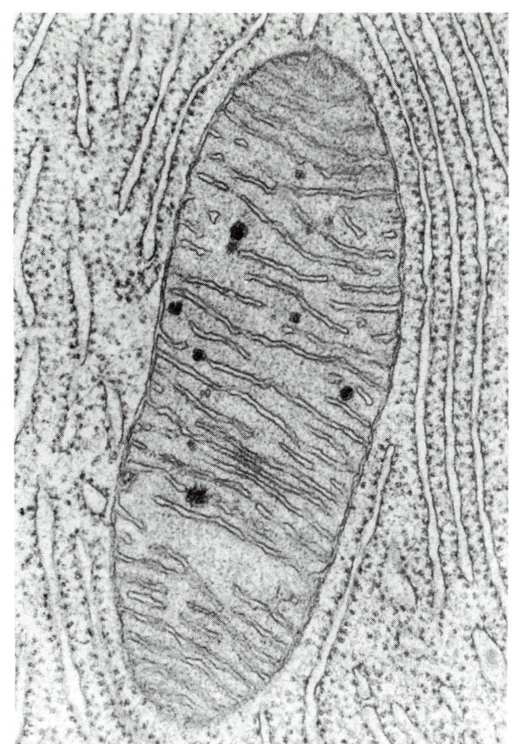

Fig. 5.27 Mitochondria. Electron-micrographic section through a mitochondrion of a mammalian pancreatic cell (×45,000). Note the double-layered exterior boundary and the many infoldings of the inner membrane (mitochondrial cristae). The dark spots in the interior of the mitochondrion are calcium-rich granules. Outside the mitochondrion are parts of the rough endoplasmic reticulum (double membranes with clear channels inside) and numerous ribosomes (small dark granules). *(Courtesy of Keith R. Porter.)*

teins. However, most proteins used in mitochondria are manufactured from genetic information housed in nuclear DNA.

Plastids

These round, oval, or disk-shaped bodies occur in the cells of most algae and all green plants. Three kinds of plastids can be distinguished on the basis of their pigment content. One kind, the *leucoplasts*, lacks pigments and often serves as starch-storing organelles, as in the cells of potatoes (Fig. 5.28). A second kind, called *chromoplasts*, contains a variety of carotenoid pigments. For example, carrots and tomatoes owe their colors to carotenoids localized in chromoplasts. The third type of plastid usually contains carotenoid pigments too, but their colors are masked by large quantities of the green pigment *chlorophyll.* Plastids with chlorophyll are *chloroplasts*, and they endow leaves and other plant parts with their characteristic green color.

Structurally, chloroplasts are bounded by two membranes that enclose an internal framework of stacked membranes (Fig. 5.29). Looking like a pile of coins, each of these stacks is called a *granum* (pl. *grana*). Channels of enclosed membranes interconnect individual grana, and all such membranous components are suspended in the liquid matrix, or *stroma*, of the chloroplast. The internal membranes of a granum are arranged as flattened sacs called *thylakoids* (see Fig. 13.2). Chlorophyll and other pigments are embedded in the thylakoids of a granum; all phases of photosynthesis that require direct participation of chlorophyll occur at these

Fig. 5.28 Starch grains. (A) Two starch grains of a potato. (B) Single grain of a garden bean. (C) Banana (several grains in a single cell, and one grain enlarged). The structure of starch grains varies greatly among different plants, so much so that specific varieties can often be identified by microscopic examination of these organelles. *(After C. L. Wilson, W. E. Loomis, and T. A. Steeves, "Botany," 5th ed., Holt, New York, 1971.)*

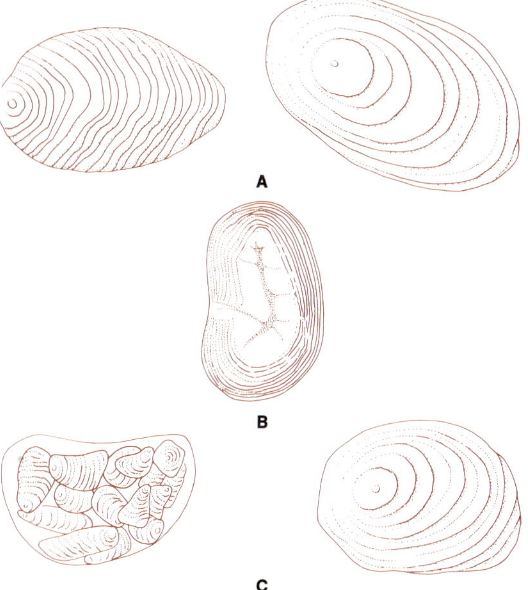

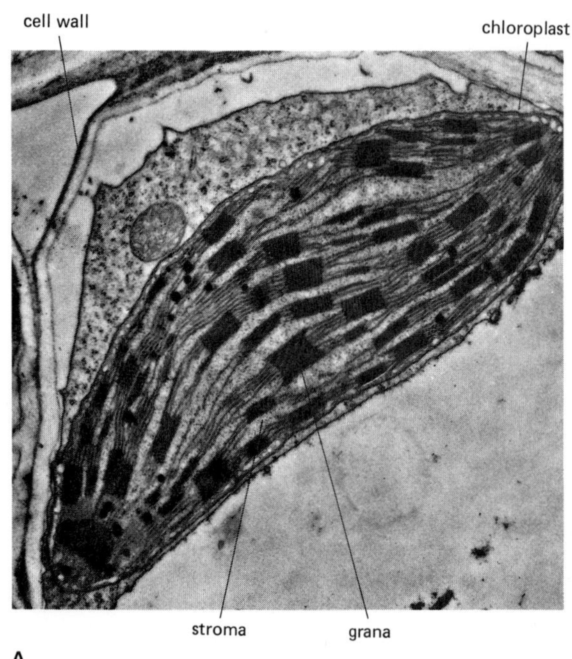

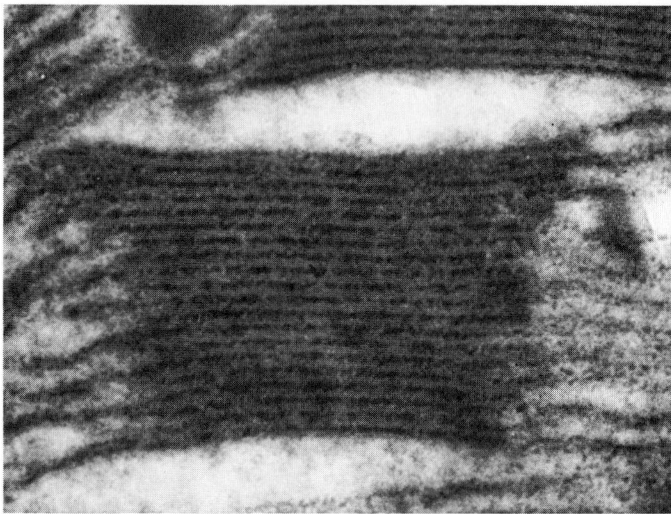

Fig. 5.29 Chloroplasts and grana. (A) This section through a cell in a leaf of a corn plant shows a chloroplast located near a portion of the cell wall. Note the numerous darkly staining grana and the intermembranous stroma (approx. ×12,500). (B) Higher magnification of a single granum (×200,000).

sites. Like mitochondria, chloroplasts contain DNA. Many of the proteins produced from information contained in chloroplast DNA are required for photosynthesis.

Lysosomes

Lysosomes, discovered in 1952 by the French biologist Christian DeDuve, appear to originate from the Golgi apparatus or the smooth endoplasmic reticulum of animal cells (Fig. 5.30; see also Fig. 5.26). These membrane-bound sacs contain enzymes capable of decomposing a wide variety of substances. Lysosomes often function in the digestion of materials brought into cells through phagocytosis or pinocytosis. Vacuoles containing such substances become fused with lysosomes, forming a single digestive vacuole. The fusion ensures decomposition of ingested matter without exposing the remainder of the cell to the destructive chemicals of lysosomes. Bacteria and other foreign substances entering animal cells are often destroyed by lysosomes in a similar fashion. Lysosomes also destroy other cellular components such as mitochondria that may have malfunctioned or become too numerous. Simultaneous disruption of many or all lysosomes brings about a self-destruction of old or malfunctioning cells. Thus, lysosomes play a direct role in the elimination of worn cellular components and in normal replacement of old cells by new ones generated by cell reproduction.

Microbodies (Peroxisomes and Glyoxysomes)

Like lysosomes, microbodies are membrane-bound sacs that contain highly specialized substances, but microbodies do not bring about cell destruction. Instead, they serve as "isolation booths" for specific metabolic processes within the cytoplasm. Certain microbodies, called *peroxisomes*, are found in both plant and animal cells. These organelles effectively isolate the manufacture and subsequent destruction of hydrogen peroxide, a highly toxic substance (see the discussion of photorespiration in Chap. 13 for a specific example of peroxisome function).

Glyoxysomes, a second variety of microbody, are found most prominently in plant seedlings (Fig. 5.31). Stored fatty acids supply much of the nutrient for seedling growth. Many of these acids are converted to carbohydrates, which are then metabolized further by mitochondria and other organelles. Much of the conversion of fatty acids to carbohydrates in plant seedlings takes place in glyoxysomes.

Centrioles and Kinetosomes

A centriole is a small granule located near (and in some cases inside) the nucleus (Fig. 5.32). Centrioles occur in some algae, some fungi, and all animals (but not in most of the cells of plants). As will be shown later, these granules play some role in cell reproduction. Another type of granule, called a basal body or kinetosome, is found in cells that have surface flagella or cilia (see above). Kinetosomes anchor and control the development of such surface structures. Centrioles and kinetosomes appear to have arisen from a common evolutionary source, a single type of granule that served simultaneously as a centriole and a kinetosome. Many primitive cell types today still contain such granules with joint dual functions. In later cell types the originally single granule evidently evolved as two separate ones, one retaining the centriole function only, the other, the kinetosome function only. Moreover, ancestral cells that evolved as plants largely lost both centrioles and kinetosomes.

Fig. 5.30 Lysosomes. A portion of a rat liver cell, showing six spherical membrane-covered lysosomes. Note the darkly stained material in some of the lysosomes, and portions of the rough endoplasmic reticulum at the top of the photo. (*Courtesy of Luis Biempica, Albert Einstein College of Medicine, New York.*)

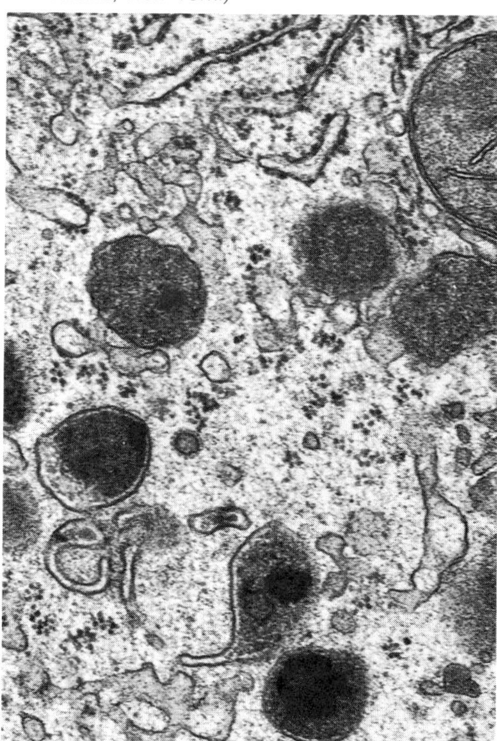

The Cytoskeleton: Microtrabeculae, Microfilaments, Intermediate Filaments, Microtubules

Most cells contain complex networks of threadlike and tubelike strands. Some elements of this network provide internal structural support for cells; other components appear to be responsible for the motion of cytoplasm in cells and for locomotion of whole cells. Collectively, this aggregation of diverse rods makes up the *cytoskeleton* of a cell.

The thinnest components of the cytoskeleton are called *microtrabeculae.* Little is known about the function of these strands, but they may coordinate movements of at least some organelles. They also may provide a structural framework upon which functionally related aggregations of molecules are organized.

Somewhat thicker than microtrabeculae are the threadlike *microfilaments.* Composed of *actin,* a principal protein of muscle (see Chap. 19), microfilaments are found frequently in dense bundles just under the plasma membrane. Through contraction they appear to cause depressions, foldings, ruffling movements, and other motions of plasma membranes (see Color Fig. 1). They also are at least partly responsible for the eddying and streaming of cytoplasm in cells, movements that help ensure a thorough mixing of nutrients, oxygen, and other substances.

Microtubules constitute the thickest elements of the cytoskeleton. Unlike microfilaments, which are solid, microtubules are hollow, fluid-filled cylinders. In some cells these elongated tubes form an internal "skeleton," providing rigidity and structural reinforcement. Microtubules often are organized in complex parallel arrays. In some instances such arrays channel the movement of cytoplasm, directing the flow toward certain areas of a cell and away from other regions.

Microtubules are arranged in a similarly nonrandom fashion within cilia and flagella. Two central microtubules are surrounded by 18 others arranged as 9 pairs (Fig. 5.33). This 9 + 2 arrangement of microtubules is embedded in a matrix enclosed by an extension of the plasma mem-

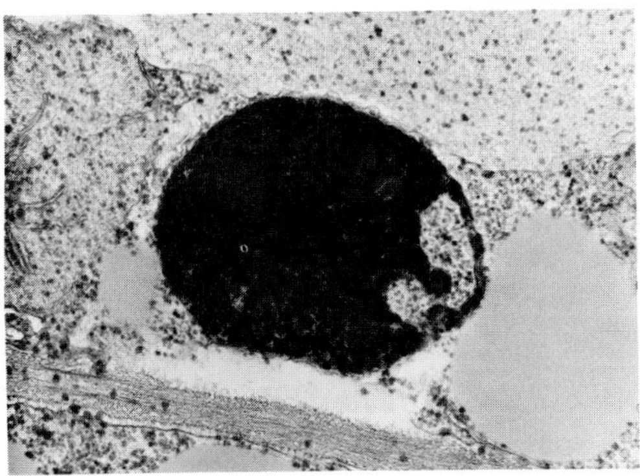

Fig. 5.31 Microbodies. (A) Peroxisomes. Portions of a leaf cell of a tobacco plant showing a peroxisome positioned between two larger chloroplasts (left and below) and a smaller mitochondrion (right). Peroxisomes typically have an enzyme-containing crystalline core (dark square). (B) Glyoxysomes. Electron micrograph of a glyoxysome (dark sphere) in a cell of a cucumber seed.

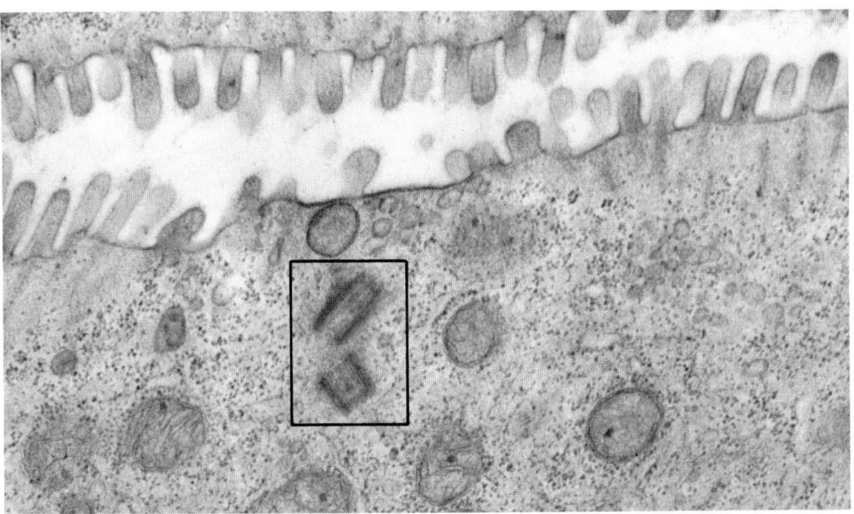

Fig. 5.32 Centrioles. Electron micrograph showing part of an intestinal cell of a chicken embryo. The centrioles are the two dark, cylindrical structures within the rectangular box. Note their usual perpendicular orientation (×41,000). The tooth-shaped structures along the top edge are microvilli, foldings of the cell membrane that increase the absorptive surface area of these cells. (*Courtesy of Sergei Sorokin.*)

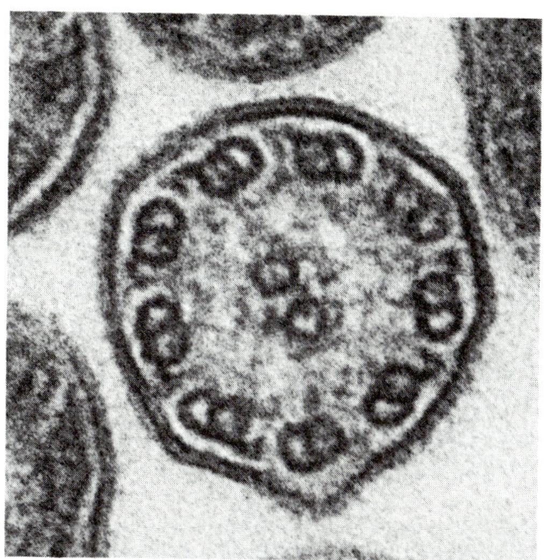

Fig. 5.33 Internal structure of flagella and cilia. Electron-micrographic cross section through a cilium (from a cell in a monkey oviduct), showing the central two and nine peripheral microtubules. The peripheral microtubules are continuous with the microtubules of the kinetosome (×100,000). (*Courtesy Robert M. Brenner, Oregon Primate Research Center.*)

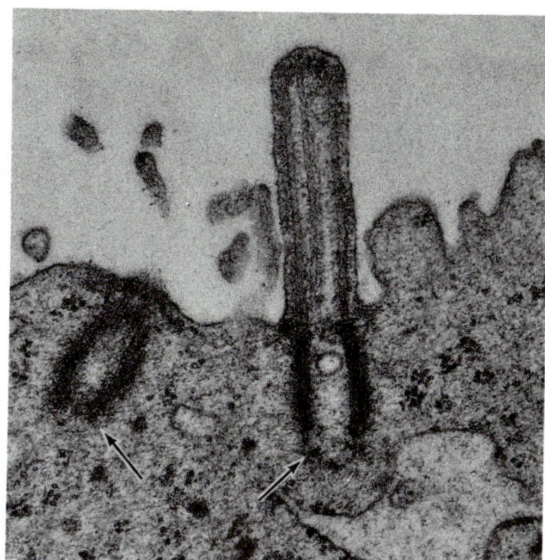

Fig. 5.34 Kinetosomes. Electron-micrographic section through two kinetosomes (arrows) of a cell in a monkey oviduct, with a cilium growing out from the kinetosome at the right. Note that the ciliary microtubules are continuous with those of the kinetosome. Also note the small vacuole inside this kinetosome (×40,000). (*Courtesy of Robert M. Brenner, Oregon Primate Research Center, and Journal of Fertility and Sterility, vol. 20, pp. 599–611, 1969.*)

brane. Sliding of microtubules past each other brings about movement of a cilium or flagellum.

As stated earlier, a kinetosome anchors the base of individual cilia and flagella. Each kinetosome is made up of a ringlike array of nine sets of parallel microtubules, with a fine layer of boundary material around the ring (Fig. 5.34). Centrioles have a nearly identical structure. Cilia and flagella appear to develop from kinetosomes. Indeed, two-thirds of the microtubules in kinetosomes are continuous with the nine outer pairs of microtubules in cilia and flagella. Aggregates of microtubules also form the *spindle fibers* and *asters* of dividing cells (see Chap. 22). Such fibers, apparently in conjunction with microfilaments, play a role in the movements of *chromosomes* during cell division (see Chap. 22).

The function of *intermediate filaments,* the fourth component of the cytoskeleton, is obscure. As implied by their name, the average diameter of these cellular rods is larger than that of microfilaments but smaller than that of microtubules. In some respects intermediate filaments resemble microtubules. For example, both structures are hollow, elongated cylinders, and both are produced via polymerization of protein subunits. Moreover, some cell biologists have reported seeing cross bridges interconnecting microtubules and intermediate filaments. Nevertheless, the molecular components of these two tubular structures are quite distinct. Their functions, although probably interrelated, may also be distinct in several ways. Unfortunately, few definitive statements can be made about the cellular role of intermediate filaments. Only further research will elucidate the degree to which subcomponents of the cytoskeleton are structurally and functionally intertwined.

NUCLEUS

Most of the information ultimately controlling cellular processes resides in *chromosomes,* the main nuclear organelles (Fig. 5.35). In fact, the nucleus as a whole can be regarded primarily as a protective housing for these slender, threadlike bodies.

In stained cells examined under a light microscope, chromosomes become distinct only during

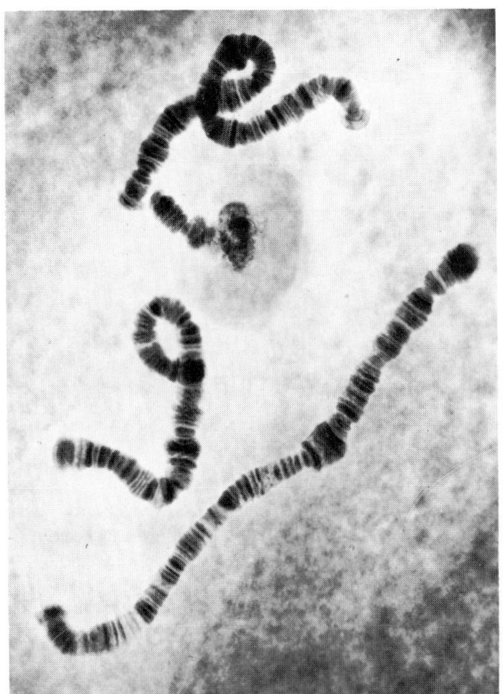

Fig. 5.35 Chromosomes. A stained preparation of insect chromosomes (×3000). Note the characteristic cross-bands. *(From D. F. Poulson and C. W. Metz, Journal of Morphology, vol. 63, p. 366.)*

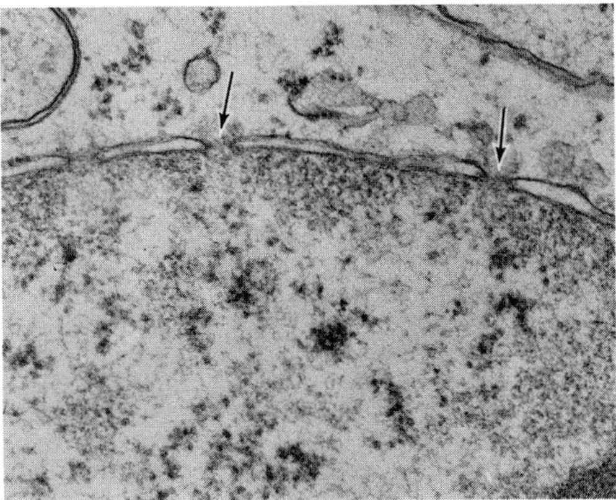

Fig. 5.36 The nuclear envelope. In this electron-micrographic closeup of a cell in the spinal cord of a bat, the nuclear substance is at bottom, cytoplasmic substances at top. Note that the nuclear envelope is a double layer with pores (×40,000). *(Courtesy of Keith R. Porter.)*

cell reproduction. At other times, the chromosomal material appears dispersed throughout the nucleus in darkly staining *chromatin* clusters (see Fig. 5.5B). Since they are interconvertible, it is not surprising that chromatin and chromosomes are composed largely of the same materials, mostly nucleic acids and proteins. Most of the DNA in a cell is housed in chromosomes, which therefore constitute the chief repository of genetic information. The exact number of chromosomes that emerges from diffuse chromatin during cell reproduction is an important species-specific trait. For example, cells of human beings contain 46 chromosomes each. The cells of every other type of organism have their own characteristic chromosome number.

In a stained nucleus one or more *nucleoli* are usually clearly visible (see Fig. 5.5B). Long considered a structurally independent organelle, a nucleolus is now recognized as a distinct region of chromatin specialized for the production of small particles which subsequently join together to form ribosomes. The number of nucleoli per nucleus varies for different cell types, often in direct relation to the number of ribosomes required for normal cell function.

Chromosomes and nucleoli are immersed in granular fluid called *nucleoplasm.* Electron microscopy has revealed that the *nuclear membrane,* which separates the nucleoplasm from the cytoplasm, actually is a double membrane. For this reason, this membrane system is often termed the *nuclear envelope.* The two membranes, each similar to the plasma membrane, are fused to each other in numerous places forming openings, or *nuclear pores* (Fig. 5.36). These probably play a role in the selective passage of materials into and out of a nucleus. Chromatin is anchored to the inner nuclear membrane, usually at the edges of nuclear pores. The outer membrane is continuous in the cytoplasm with the endoplasmic reticulum.

Thus, the overall picture that emerges from microscopic examination of cellular fine structure is one of relatively fixed interconnections between organelles. Most structures do not float freely. Like precise arrangements of assembly-line equipment in factories, the structural relations between cellular organelles are vital to efficient functional integration; see Table 5.1 for a summary of these relationships. By virtue of its chomosomes, the nucleus is the control center of cellular activities.

TABLE 5.1
Some Structural Components of Cells and Their Main Functions

Cell part	Structure	Function
Nucleus	chromosomes	gene carriers, ultimate control of cell activities
	nucleolus	auxiliary to protein synthesis
	nuclear envelope	traffic control to and from cytoplasm
Cytoplasm	endoplasmic reticulum	secretion channels, connection between cell parts, attachment surfaces
	mitochondria	site of respiration
	ribosomes	site of protein synthesis
	Golgi apparatus	site of specific secretion synthesis
	lysosomes	stores of hydrolytic enzymes
	microbodies	"isolation booths" for specific metabolic processes
	chloroplasts	site of photosynthesis
	centrioles	auxiliary to cell division
	kinetosomes	anchor and control flagella, cilia
	microfilaments	contraction
	microtubules	skeletal support, movement of flagella and cilia
	granules, vacuoles	transport, storage, processing centers
Surface	plasma membrane	traffic control to and from cell
	cell wall	support, protection, cell shape
	cuticles, pellicles	support, protection, waterproofing
	cilia, flagella	locomotion, current creation, feeding
	pseudopodia	locomotion, feeding, phagocytosis

The cytoplasm functions largely as the executive center in which the directives of the nucleus are carried out. But just as management and labor are functionally interdependent in industry, so are nucleus and cytoplasm in the maintenance of life; the existence of one is bound reciprocally to the other.

Review Questions

1 Review the contributions of Hooke, Dutrochet, Schleiden, and Schwann to the modern cell theory.

2 Define cell structurally and functionally.

3 What are the structural subdivisions of cells? What are the main components of each of these subdivisions, where are they found, and what functions do they carry out?

4 Discuss the significance of Hämmerling's experiments with *Acetabularia*. How did his experiments contribute to our understanding of the relationships between the cytoplasmic and nuclear components of cells?

5 Describe the fluid-mosaic model of membrane structure. What structural relationships does this model postulate between proteins, carbohydrates, and lipids? How does it account for the passage of substances into and out of cells?

6 What coatings and structures are found on or between the surfaces of various cell types? What are the functions of these coatings and structures? How do the surfaces of plant and animal cells differ?

7 Review and identify the functions of cytoplasmic organelles found in all cell types. Do the same for organelles found only in certain cell types. How do plant and animal cells differ structurally?

Collateral Readings

Albersheim, P.: The Walls of Growing Plant Cells, *Scientific American,* April 1975. Studies of how polysaccharides are arranged in cell walls provide insight into the special properties of plant surfaces.

Albrecht-Buehler, G.: The Tracks of Moving Cells, *Scientific American,* April 1978. Some of the functions of microfilaments are described in this fascinating article.

Allison, A.: Lysosomes and Disease, *Scientific American,* November 1967. On the role of these organelles in normal and abnormal cellular processes.

Berns, M. W.: "Cells," Holt, New York, 1977. A well-illustrated introduction to cells and their activities.

Capaldi, R. A.: A Dynamic Model of Cell Membranes, *Scientific American,* March 1974. An instructive description of the structure and functions of cell membranes.

Dustin, P.: Microtubules, *Scientific American,* July 1980. The structure and function of these cytoskeletal elements are discussed.

Dyson, R. D.: "Cell Biology: A Molecular Approach," 2d ed., Allyn and Bacon, Boston, 1978. One of the best and most comprehensive accounts of cell structure and function. For the advanced student.

Gibor, A.: Acetabularia. A Useful Giant Cell, *Scientific American,* November 1966. Further information about Hämmerling's giant cells.

Karp, G.: "Cell Biology," McGraw-Hill, New York, 1979. An excellent, well-illustrated textbook. A good reference for the advanced student.

Ledbetter, M. C., and **K. Porter:** "Introduction to the Fine Structure of Plant Cells," Springer, New York, 1970. An outstanding atlas of electron micrographs of plant cells.

Loewy, A. G., and **P. Siekevitz:** "Cell Structure and Function," 3d ed., Holt, New York, 1979. A good introductory textbook on cell structure and function.

Luria, S. E.: Collicins and the Energetics of Cell Membranes, *Scientific American,* December 1975. Experiments related to a study of active transport are discussed.

Porter, K. R., and **M. Bonneville:** "An Introduction to the Fine Structure of Cells and Tissues," 4th ed., Lea & Febiger, Philadelphia, 1973. An excellent atlas of electron micrographs of animal cells. Detailed commentaries accompany the photographs.

——— and **J. B. Tucker:** The Ground Substance of the Living Cell, *Scientific American,* March 1981. Speculations on the structure and function of microtrabeculae.

Satir, B.: The Final Steps in Secretion, *Scientific American,* October 1975. Discusses how a variety of cellular organelles interact in the production and export of substances.

Satir, P.: How Cilia Move, *Scientific American,* October 1974. A good account of structural and functional components of cilia.

Sharon, N.: Glycoproteins, *Scientific American,* May 1974. A good summary of some of the functions of these important substances.

Singer, S. J., and **G. Nicolson:** The Fluid Mosaic Model of the Structure of Cell Membranes, *Science,* vol. 175, pp. 720–731, Feb. 18, 1972. The original publication of Singer's model. A good introduction to professional scientific literature.

Staehelin, L. A., and **B. E. Hull:** Junctions between Living Cells, *Scientific American,* May 1978. The structure and function of intercellular junctions is described.

Thomas, L.: "The Lives of a Cell: Notes of a Biology Watcher," Viking, New York, 1974. A series of short essays that broaden our appreciation of cells and all living things. Strongly recommended.

Weissmann, G., and **R. Claiborne** (eds.), "Cell Membranes: Biochemistry, Cell Biology and Pathology," H. P. Publishing Co., New York, 1975. A collection of well-illustrated articles introducing a diversity of subtopics related to cell membranes.

Chapter 6

Cell to Organism: The Plant Pattern

Learning Objectives

After reading this chapter you should be able to:

1. List at least three common characteristics of Plantae; name at least two kinds of plants that do not share these general characteristics.
2. Name at least five terrestrial adaptations of plants.
3. Define radial symmetry and illustrate how it is adaptively advantageous for plants.
4. List at least four categories of tissues found in all plants and state the adaptive value of each.
5. State the three classes of bryophytes and name at least one representative of each.
6. Construct a diagram of a moss plant; label the following structures and list at least one function for each:
   - **a.** protonema
   - **b.** rhizoids
   - **c.** stem
   - **d.** leaves
   - **e.** leaf epidermis
   - **f.** leaf cortex
7. Construct a diagram of a liverwort thallus that depicts the location of the epidermis, the spongy mass of photosynthetic cells, and the nongreen cortex; state at least one function for each of these tissues.
8. Name at least three tracheophytes and at least two characteristics that distinguish tracheophytes from bryophytes.
9. Name the two principal classes of tracheophytes; state at least one common and two distinguishing characteristics of these classes; list at least four differences between monocots and dicots, and name at least two representatives of each.
10. Define and state the functions of xylem and phloem; define meristem and differentiation.
11. Construct a diagram of a longitudinal section of a root that depicts the root cap, zone of elongation, zone of maturation, and root hairs. Label each of these structures and zones and state a function for root cap cells and root hairs.
12. Define stele; construct a diagram of a cross section through a root that depicts each of the following tissue layers:
    - **a.** cortex
    - **b.** epidermis
    - **c.** endodermis
    - **d.** pericycle
    - **e.** primary and secondary xylem
    - **f.** primary and secondary phloem
    - **g.** vascular cambium

    Label each of these tissues and list at least one function for each.
13. List at least one function for each of the following types of cells; then state at least one tissue in which each of these cells types is found:
    - **a.** parenchyma
    - **b.** sclerenchyma
    - **c.** sieve tubes
    - **d.** companion cells
    - **e.** tracheids
    - **f.** vessels
    - **g.** collenchyma
14. Differentiate between pit membranes and sieve plates.
15. List at least three anatomical differences between roots and stems; construct a diagram of a cross section through a typical herbaceous monocot and dicot stem that depicts the position of epidermis, vascular bundles, cortex, and pith.
16. Construct a diagram of a stem that includes the following structures and regions:
    - **a.** leaf primordia
    - **b.** terminal bud
    - **c.** branch bud
    - **d.** leaf scar
    - **e.** internode
    - **f.** petiole
    - **g.** stipules
    - **h.** leaf blade

17. Construct a diagram of a cross section through a leaf that depicts the following structures:

- **a.** lower and upper epidermis
- **b.** palisade layer
- **c.** spongy layer
- **d.** guard cells
- **e.** stomata
- **f.** leaf vein

Label these structures and list at least one function for each; state the functional relation between the structure of guard cells and the size of stomata.

18. Differentiate between simple and compound leaves, and between pinnately and palmately compound leaves; construct a diagram that depicts alternate, opposite, and whorled patterns of leaf attachment to stems; differentiate between primary and secondary growth and between herbaceous and woody plants.

19. Construct a diagram of a woody dicot stem that depicts the anatomical relations among the following tissue layers:

- **a.** cork
- **b.** cork cambium
- **c.** phelloderm
- **d.** vascular cambium
- **e.** primary and secondary xylem
- **f.** primary and secondary phloem
- **g.** pith

Label each tissue layer and list at least one function for each; define annual ring, lenticel, heartwood, sapwood, and bark.

In spite of their subordinate position in the structural hierarchy of life, unicellular organisms continue to exist and thrive as they have since their origin some 3.5 billion years ago. Biological success is correlated directly with environmental adaptations of organisms and is unrelated to relative position in the structural hierarchy. Nevertheless, one multicellular organism usually is far more efficient in its use of energy and materials than an equal mass of unicellular organisms.

Increased operational efficiency in multicellular organisms has been achieved through cooperation, integration, and specialization of the component cells. Several cells functioning as independent units are analogous to several men each attempting to build a house by himself. All houses may be built eventually, but they could be built faster and more efficiently if the men all joined together as a cooperative unit and accepted mutually integrated, specialized roles. In fact, many barn raisings were carried out in just this manner during the westward migration of American settlers in the eighteenth and nineteenth centuries.

The discovery that several types of multicellular organisms evolved following the initial establishment of unicellular forms is therefore not surprising. Modern plants and animals are among their most complex descendants. Our examination of intercellular relations in organisms begins with plants—abundant, commonplace, often ignored, yet vital to our existence and that of all animal life.

GENERAL CHARACTERISTICS

Plants, collectively classified as *Plantae* (*Metaphyta*), are primarily multicellular, nonmotile, exclusively photosynthetic organisms adapted largely for life on land.

A few plants do not fit within this generalization. For example, Plantae include some algae, most of which are adapted to aquatic life. Moreover, some of these algae are motile, unicellular organisms. Furthermore, some parasitic plants, such as Indian pipe, are unable to produce food through photosynthesis (see Color Fig. 31).

The distinguishing characteristics of all major taxa of plants are introduced in Chap. 32. The primary function of this chapter is to introduce the general structural features of the most successful groups of Plantae, the comparatively large terrestrial plants. Such information will serve as a basic reference for subsequent discussion of plant metabolism and self-perpetuation, introduced in the next four parts of this book.

Body Organization

Most distinguishing characteristics of land plants are a consequence of their nonmotile nature, their mode of nutrition, and their evolution as terrestrial organisms from aquatic protistan ancestors. Most plants, for example, have a radially symmetrical body organization. Like pies, all radially symmetrical organisms have mirror-image right and left halves relative to any plane passing through the center (Fig. 6.1). This basic body plan provides considerable advantages for plants (and also for sessile animals). Radial symmetry accommodates the extension of roots in all directions from the main vertical axis of a plant and thus permits efficient nutrient absorption from all sides. Moreover, the more or less radial extension of branches and leaves around the stem permits maximum exposure to air and sunlight (Fig. 6.2).

The radial symmetry of plants also provides a mechanically balanced body. Roots anchor plants on all sides, and the radial arrangement of branches distributes weight equally around the vertical axis. Also, the typical upward tapering of plants allows the greatest weight to rest on the broadest foundation.

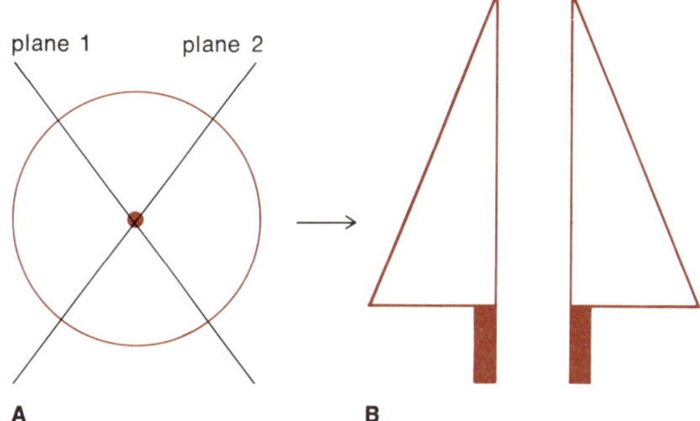

Fig. 6.1 Radial symmetry. (A) Any downward-slicing plane through the center of a radially symmetrical object (such as plane 1 or plane 2 through a spruce tree) will produce (B) halves that are mirror images of each other.

Common Tissues

The protistan ancestors of plants lived in aquatic environments, and much of their weight was supported by the buoyancy of water. Air is far less bouyant than water, however, and most modern terrestrial plants contain substantial quantities of antigravity *skeletal tissues* (see Fig. 6.2). Such support tissues reach their most advanced form in the wood of trees.

In the absence of open water around all surfaces, terrestrial plants also have specialized *absorbing tissues* that project into soil. Since such structures occur only in localized body regions, most plants also contain nutrient-distributing or *conducting tissues.* The most highly developed conducting tissues occur in the vessel-bearing or *vascular plants.* Here water is conducted through specialized *xylem* tissues; food is transported via *phloem* tissues.

Plants usually have very large surface areas relative to their volumes, due in part to their radially symmetrical architecture. Many of these surfaces are covered by leaves. Located near or at the ends of radially arranged branches and exposed directly to light and air, leaves contain abundant *photosynthesizing tissues.* Skeletal and conducting tissues usually do not contain chlorophyll and make up much of the internal structure of plants. Thus, the typical root-stem-leaf organization of most plants is a specific adaptation to terrestrial environments. Roots absorb nutrients from the ground, leaves photosynthesize, and stems interconnect, conduct, and support.

Exposed to air, terrestrial plants minimize the danger of drying out through waxy *cuticles* on leaves and other free surfaces (see Fig. 6.2). Such coverings let light pass but not water or atmospheric gases. However, gases must be exchanged with the environment, and plants actually contain surface pores, or *stomata,* which permit diffusion of gases into and out of internal tissues (see also Figs. 6.32 to 6.34).

The structures and processes of reproduction likewise represent adaptations to life in an aerial environment. Reproductive organs of plants contain at least two tissues: an exterior nonreproductive tissue that protects against drying and an interior tissue that produces reproductive cells. Such cells are encapsulated by protective tissues or they are released only during wet or rainy periods. Moreover, the life cycle of plants always includes an embryonic phase, which provides the developmental time necessary for the elaboration of the many specialized tissues of the mature plant. Since this internal elaboration is an adaptation to terrestrial conditions, the plant embryo too can be regarded as an evolutionary response to the requirements of land life.

LAND PLANTS

Bryophytes

Sometimes called nonvascular plants because they contain neither xylem nor phloem, and also

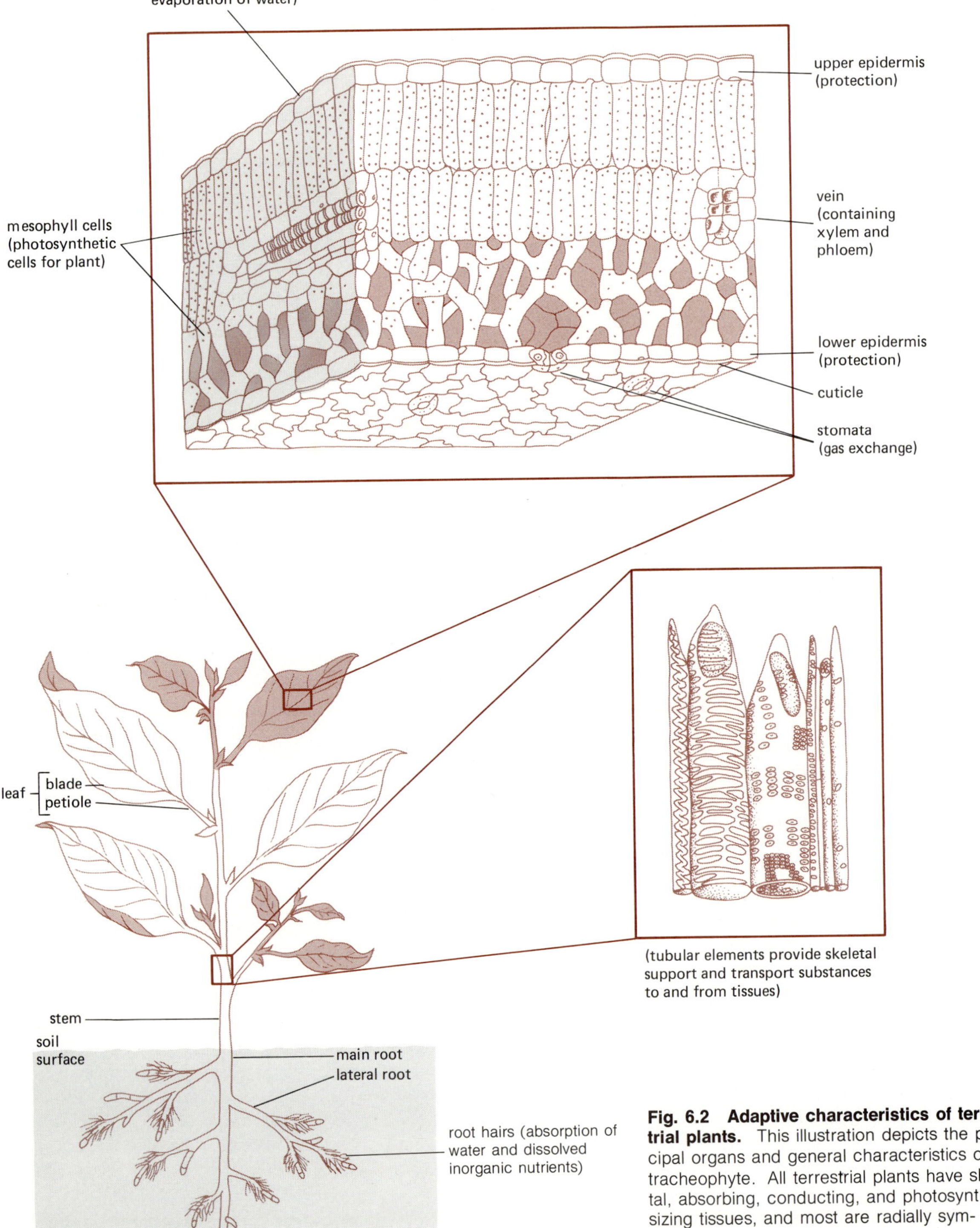

Fig. 6.2 Adaptive characteristics of terrestrial plants. This illustration depicts the principal organs and general characteristics of a tracheophyte. All terrestrial plants have skeletal, absorbing, conducting, and photosynthesizing tissues, and most are radially symmetrical.

called moss plants, *bryophytes* constitute one of the five phyla of Plantae. The phylum includes three classes of plants: the Bryopsida, or *mosses;* the Hepaticopsida, or *liverworts;* and the Anthoceropsida, or *hornworts* (Fig. 6.3 and see also Chaps. 23 and 32). Bryophytes are highly cosmopolitan, some species growing in the cold regions of the world, in the tundra, and high on mountains; others growing in deserts, near hot springs, and in the tropics. Mosses and liverworts are particularly conspicuous in tropical rain forests where clouds hang low at night and where mist and rain are of frequent occurrence. In such "mossy forests," bryophytes are found abundantly on leaves, hanging in festoons, and often covering completely the surface of branches and the trunks of trees.

Bryophytes frequently serve as important soil formers and protectors. They may settle where lichens (see Chaps. 9 and 31) have degraded the bare surfaces of rock to particles of coarse sand, and bryophyes then contribute to a further transformation of the rock surface to soil (Fig. 6.4). Moreover, many bryophytes form dense, soil-covering carpets that minimize soil erosion and retain water between the closely spaced plants.

Sphagnum and similar types of mosses often accumulate in swamps and bogs in the form of deep deposits called *peat* (Fig. 6.5). Such deposits are of considerable biological and economic importance. The deeper regions of many peat bogs were formed several thousand years ago and usually contain large numbers of preserved pollen grains and other ancestral forms of plant and animal life. Comparative environmental histories and life histories can be deduced from such bogs by studying changes in the numbers and types of organisms found in successive strata. Peat is added routinely to garden soils to enhance their water-holding capacity and, in some countries, is dried and burned as fuel. In addition, the flavor of Scotch whisky is enhanced by peat smoke.

Mosses

Mosses are the most common bryophytes. The body of a moss typically consists of a branched network of green filaments spread flat over the ground (Fig. 6.6). Each green filament, called a *protonema,* supports many small nongreen extensions, which grow down into soil. These *rhizoids* anchor the plant and, in some species, absorb water and

A

B

C

Fig. 6.3 Bryophytes. (A) *Polytrichum,* a common moss. (B) A bed of *Marchantia,* a liverwort. Note the broad, flattened thalli of these plants. The starlike structures that project above some of the thalli are female sex organs. (C) *Anthoceros,* a hornwort. The common name of these plants derives from the spikelike structures (sporophytes) that project above the flattened thalli. See Chap. 23 for a discussion of the life cycle of bryophytes. (*Carolina Biological Supply Company.*)

Fig. 6.4 Soil formation. Lichens have contributed to the crumbling of rock and the formation of coarse gravel in the lower right of the figure. Mosses (upper portions of figure and lower left) then become established and gradually enrich the organic content and water-holding capacity of the soil. Note the few clumps of grasses that eventually will spread and replace the mosses once sufficient organic matter has built up in the soil. (*Courtesy of Hans-Erik Wennberg, Rhode Island College Audio Visual Department.*)

minerals. A protonema also gives rise to one or more green shoots that project into the air. Each shoot consists of an upright *stem* to which are attached radially arranged *leaves.* At maturity, a shoot also bears terminal *sex organs* (see Chap. 23).

Fig. 6.5 Harvesting peat in an Irish bog. Blocks of dried peat were used as a principal source of fuel in Ireland for many centuries. (*Courtesy of Irish Tourist Board.*)

The tissue composition of mosses is simpler than that of vascular plants. The moss stem typically consists of three regions. The outermost layer of cells constitutes the *epidermis,* which is specialized to protect internal tissues from desiccation, disease, and damage. A *cortex,* composed of cells specialized for storage of starch and other nutrients, underlies the epidermis. The innermost core of cells, absent or degenerate in some species, functions in the transport of water and dissolved nutrients to all parts of the plant body. The leaves of some mosses are formed from a single layer of chloroplast-containing green cells, but in other cases several different specialized layers are present.

Liverworts

Whereas mosses typically have vertical, radially symmetrical parts, liverworts are horizontal plants. Their curious name is due to the lobed nature of the flattened *thallus,* a term reserved for plant bodies that are not subdivided structurally as roots, stems, and leaves (Fig. 6.7 and see Fig. 6.3). The thalli of many liverworts are reminiscent of the rounded lobes of an animal liver. Most liverworts grow prostrate, close to the ground, on the bark of trees, on rotted wood, or on moist rocks along woodland streams.

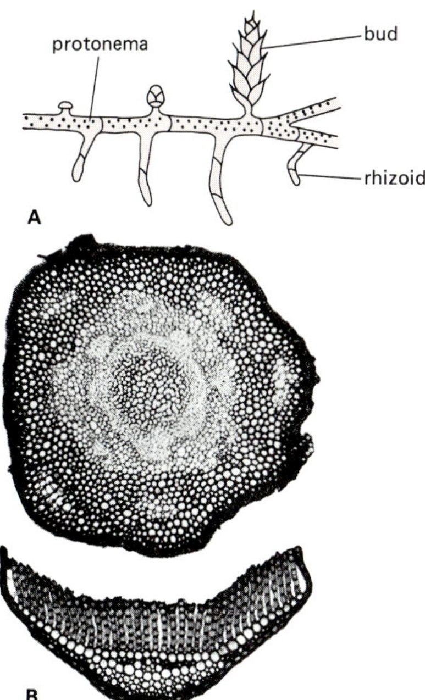

Fig. 6.6 Moss structure. (A) A horizontal protonema, with rhizoids growing into the ground and buds and young shoots growing upward. (B) Cross section through the stem and a leaf of a shoot. In stem (top) note thick-walled cortex cells and thin-walled core cells. In leaf (bottom) note columns of cells along the upper surface and air spaces between the columns. (*B, Courtesy of Melvin S. Fuller.*)

The liverwort thallus usually consists of an upper and lower epidermis lining the upper and lower surfaces, respectively. A loosely arranged mass of photosynthetic cells underlies the upper epidermis. Its spongy nature is highly adaptive, facilitating movement of water vapor, carbon dioxide, oxygen, and other gases. A nongreen layer of cortical cells, specialized for nutrient storage and conduction, underlies the photosynthetic zone and rests just above the lower epidermis.

Hornworts

Like liverworts, hornworts possess simpler rhizoids than mosses and generally require moister conditions; a thallus constitutes the major portion of the total body. In other ways, hornworts are distinct from both mosses and liverworts. A photosynthetic cell of the hornwort thallus usually contains a single large chloroplast. Photosynthetic cells of other bryophytes typically contain numerous chloroplasts. Also, internal air chambers often are absent between photosynthetic cells of the hornwort thallus. Such chambers commonly exist in the corresponding tissues of mosses and liverworts.

Fig. 6.7 Liverwort structure. (A) Thalli of *Marchantia*. In each thallus note the pair of lobes at the forward margin (well seen at upper left, for example). The growing point is located in the notch between the two lobes. (B) The internal structure of the *Marchantia* thallus. (*Courtesy of C. J. Hillson.*)

A

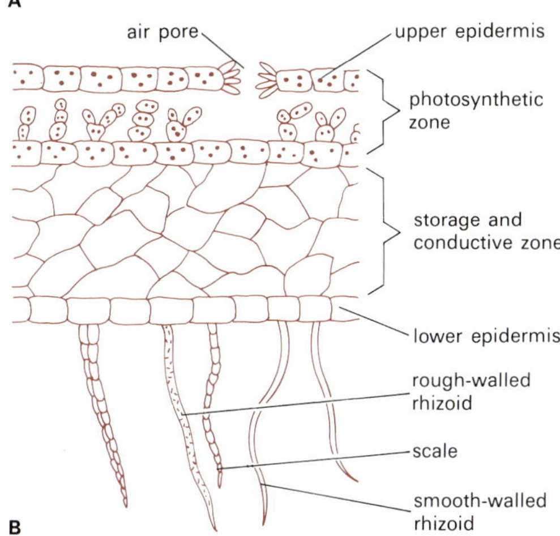

Fig. 6.8 Tracheophytes (A) *Lycopodium,* a club moss. Note the spore-forming cones at the top of this plant (see Chap. 23 for a discussion of plant reproduction). (B) *Equisetum,* a horsetail. This plant is also called a scouring rush. (C) *Cycas,* one of a small group of gymnosperms called cycads. This organism is also known as Sago palm. Only a few cycads survive today, but 200 million years ago these plants were widespread. (D) *Osmunda,* commonly called cinnamon fern. The central stalks contain spore-producing structures called sporangia (see Chap. 23). (E) *Picea,* an oriental spruce. Pines, firs, and spruces, are the most common modern gymnosperms. (F) Angiosperms. Shown here is a lily commonly called adder's tongue.

Fig. 6.9 Pine-seed germination, two stages.

Tracheophytes

The larger and more successful of the two phyla of land plants are the vascular plants, or *tracheophytes.* Included in this phylum are the club mosses, horsetails, ferns, the cone-bearing (coniferous) evergreens, and the flowering plants (Fig. 6.8 and also Chaps. 23 and 32). All cone-bearing and flowering species are *seed plants.* Such organisms produce encapsulated structures called seeds that contain *embryos* and stored nutrients. During *germination,* the protective outer coat breaks open, and the stored nutrients of a seed support development of the embryo to a young seedling (Fig. 6.9 and see Chap. 23).

The cone-bearing and other nonflowering seed plants are known collectively as the class *gymnosperms* ("naked seeds"). Flowering plants form the class *angiosperms,* which literally means "hidden seeds." The term is quite appropriate, since the seeds of flowering plants are enclosed by many more protective encasements than those of gymnosperms. Of the two classes, flowering plants are the more abundant and familiar. They inhabit nearly all environments except the open ocean, and they enrich the world with color and scent. Terrestrial animals owe their continued existence largely to the angiosperms, for they are the essential food producers for most life on land. Angiosperms are unique among seed plants in their formation of fruits and other reproductive features, discussed in Chap. 23.

The two subclasses of angiosperms are named and distinguished on the basis of the number of food-storing leaflike structures in the seeds, called *cotyledons.* Each member of the *monocot* subclass has one such seed leaf; each member of the *dicot* subclass usually has two. Monocots characteristically have leaves with parallel veins and flower parts in threes or multiples of three. By contrast, dicots have leaves that usually are net-veined and flowers in which the petals and other structures typically occur in fours or fives or in multiples of these (Fig. 6.10).

The dicots are the more abundant and more primitive group. They include both *woody* and nonwoody, or *herbaceous,* types. In this subclass are all the flowering trees and shrubs, including apple, peach, cherry, oak, chestnut, walnut, elm, and rubber trees, and many others; as well as strawberry, bean, cabbage, turnip, cotton, cocoa, coffee, avocado, celery, carrot, parsley, spinach, citrus, lilac, blueberry, cranberry, potato, tomato, to-

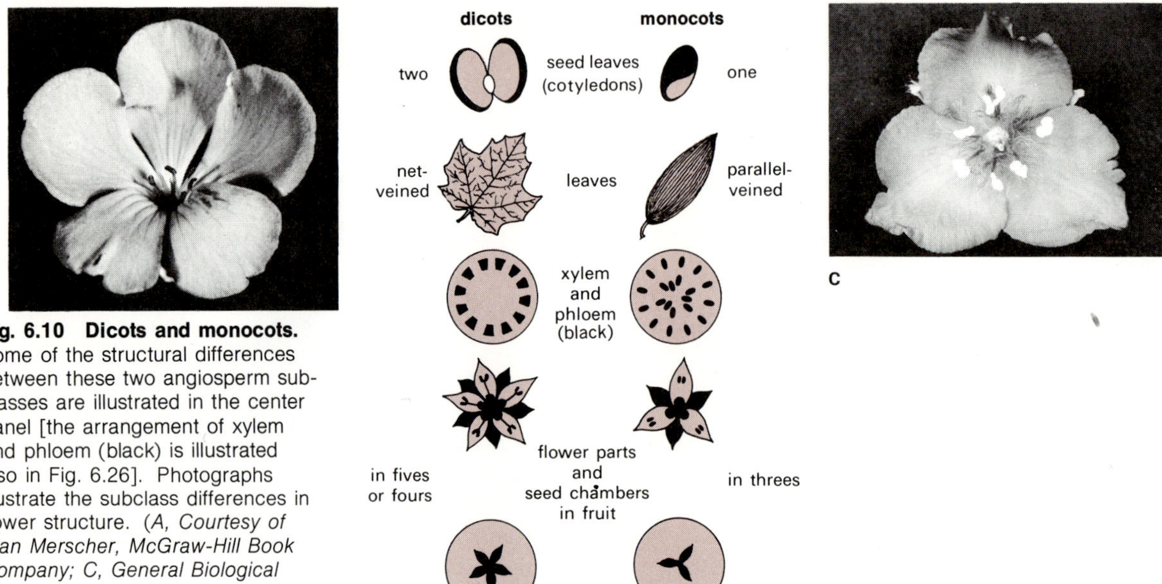

Fig. 6.10 Dicots and monocots. Some of the structural differences between these two angiosperm subclasses are illustrated in the center panel [the arrangement of xylem and phloem (black) is illustrated also in Fig. 6.26]. Photographs illustrate the subclass differences in flower structure. (*A, Courtesy of Stan Merscher, McGraw-Hill Book Company; C, General Biological Supply House, Inc.*)

bacco, pepper, melon, cucumber, lettuce, goldenrod, rhubarb, and artichoke plants, and thousands more. Monocots probably evolved from ancestral dicots very early during the history of angiosperms. Monocots have at least equal or even greater economic importance, for in this subclass are wheat, corn, rye, rice, oat, barley, bamboo, sugar cane, and all other grasses; as well as palms, lilies, irises, pineapples, bananas, and orchids. With a few exceptions, such as palms and bamboos, all monocots are nonwoody, herbaceous plants.

All tracheophytes possess (and derive their name from) two highly specialized vascular tissues, xylem and phloem, the nutrient-conducting vessels mentioned earlier. These tubular elements, which are not present in bryophytes, interconnect all parts of vascular plants and, in a sense, are analogous to our blood vessels. Unlike our circulatory system, however, vascular tissue also provides structural support, permitting the leaves and branches of many vascular plants to grow several feet or more above the ground. An additional characteristic of all vascular plants is their subdivision into *roots, stems,* and *leaves,* each body part representing a true organ.

TRACHEOPHYTE STRUCTURE

Primary Growth

Unlike most animals, vascular plants continue to grow in length throughout life; roots continue to grow downward and laterally, and branches upward and outward. Such growth in length, called *primary growth,* results from the continuous reproduction of cells at two regions, the tips of roots and stems. Specific tissues, called *apical meristems,* remain permanently embryonic at these tips. They continue to divide, producing cellular offspring which mature, or *differentiate,* into the various tissue layers of the elongating adult plant.

Roots

Root tips The apical meristem of roots is covered externally by a conical group of cells called the *root cap* (Fig. 6.11). Usually formed by the apical root meristem, a root cap is an important adaptive device. As the root tip advances, hard soil particles would soon crush unprotected meristem tissue. But the presence of a root cap means that

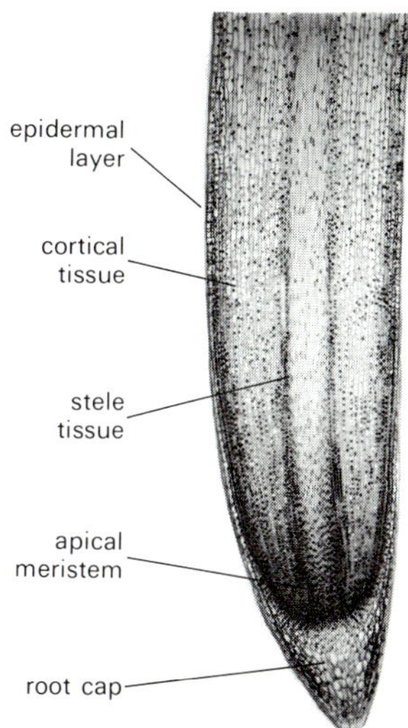

Fig. 6.11 Root structure. Longitudinal section through a root tip, showing the cells of the root cap and, immediately behind them, the dense small cells of the apical root meristem. The tissues that will later become the stele form a central column, and around it is the developing cortex. Both stele and cortex are defined below. The epidermis covers the exterior. *(Courtesy of Melvin S. Fuller.)*

the cap cells wear off instead, and the growing tip is shielded effectively. New cap cells continue to be formed by root meristem.

Cells that become positioned behind the apical root meristem first elongate in a *zone of elongation* and then differentiate in a more extensive *zone of maturation* (Fig. 6.12). Differentiating root cells form concentric tissue layers. On the outside is the *epidermis,* a covering tissue one cell layer thick. In the zone of maturation only, many epidermal cells develop elongated fingerlike projections of the cytoplasm on the side exposed to the soil (Fig. 6.13). These *root hairs* greatly increase the surface area of the root in this region, an important factor in nutrient absorption.

Cortex Underlying the epidermis is the *cortex,* the primary storage area for starch and other nutrients in many plants (Fig. 6.14). This region is extensive, particularly in the large *tap roots* such as carrots, beets, or turnips (see also Fig. 32.27). The most abundant cortical components are *parenchyma* cells, which store food and water (Fig. 6.15). Under certain conditions, parenchyma cells can specialize further and develop into a large variety of other cell types. Groups of such cells may even develop into whole roots or stems or into complete new plants.

Parenchyma cells usually have large intercellular spaces and only relatively thin primary walls. If such cells develop into other cell types, thicker secondary walls may be laid down inside the primary ones. Given points along these walls then usually remain thin *pits,* and opposing pits of two neighboring cells may come to form *pit pairs* (Fig. 6.16). The two pits of a pair are separated by a *pit membrane,* consisting of the middle lamella and the primary wall on both sides. These structures apparently facilitate intercellular transport; plasmodesmata are frequently found traversing pit pairs (see also Chap. 5).

The cortex often also contains very highly specialized *sclerenchyma cells,* which function mainly in providing mechanical support (Fig. 6.17). Such cells have thick primary walls and very thick secondary walls; they are strong and quite inelastic.

Fig. 6.12 Root development. The condition depicted on the right changes to that on the left after a period of growth. Note how any given zone transforms to the more mature condition of the zone above it. Through continued cell divisions, the apical meristem perpetuates itself and maintains a root cap.

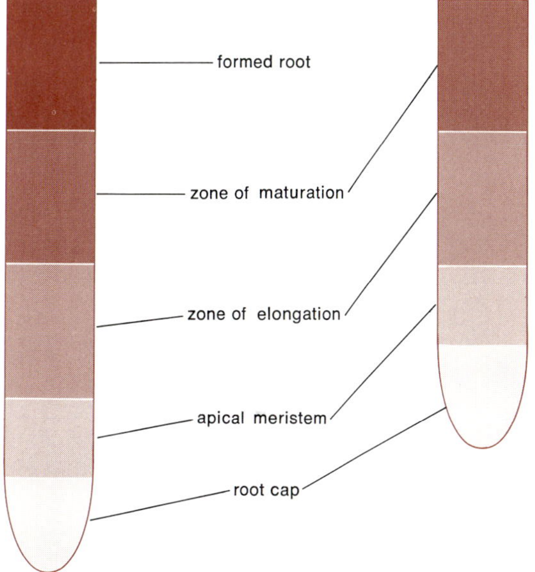

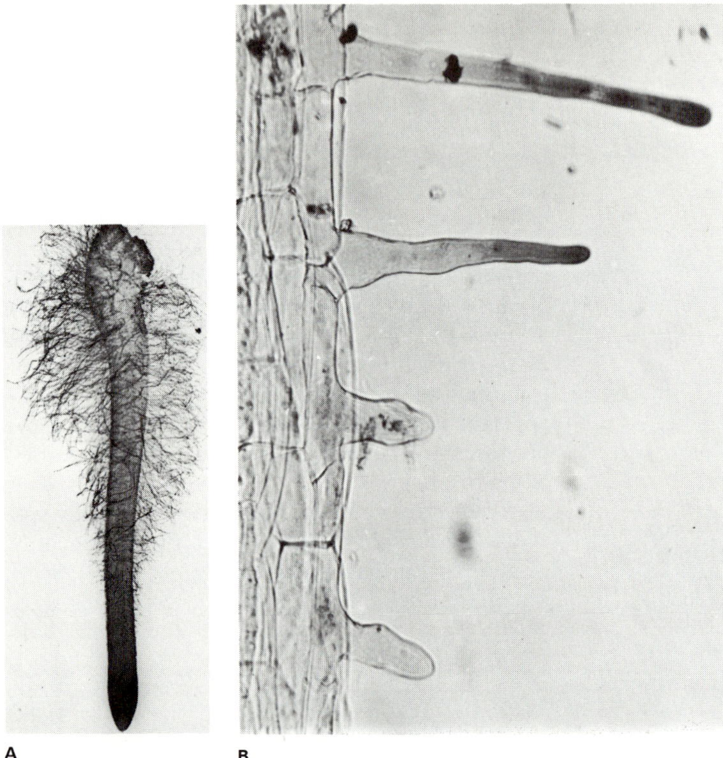

Fig. 6.13 Root hairs. (A) Terminal part of a root, showing the root-hair zone and the thickened root-cap region at the tip. (B) Root epidermis with root hairs at various stages of growth (×400). *(A, General Biological Supply House, Inc.; B, Courtesy of Melvin S. Fuller.)*

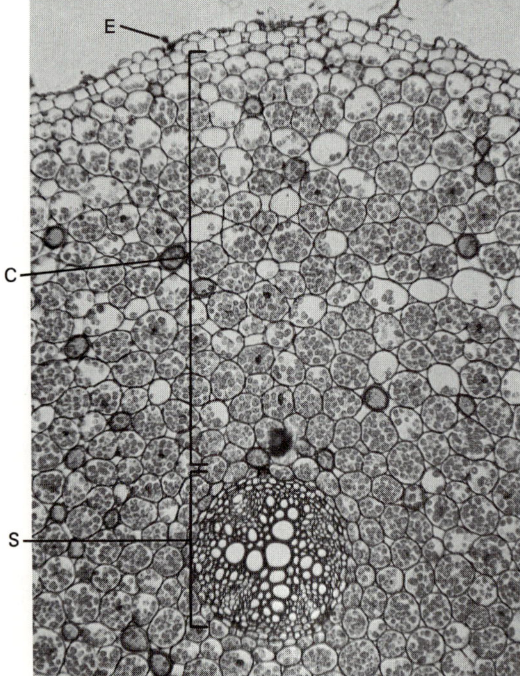

Fig. 6.14 Root tissue. Part of a section through a buttercup root. The epidermis (E) consists of a thin layer of protective cells at the root surface. Most of the root consists of cortical tissue (C), whose cells are shown at higher magnification in Fig. 6.15. Dark structures in the cortical cells are starch-storing amyloplast granules. The cylindrical core of cells in the lower portion of the photo is the stele (S), discussed in the next section of this chapter (×85).

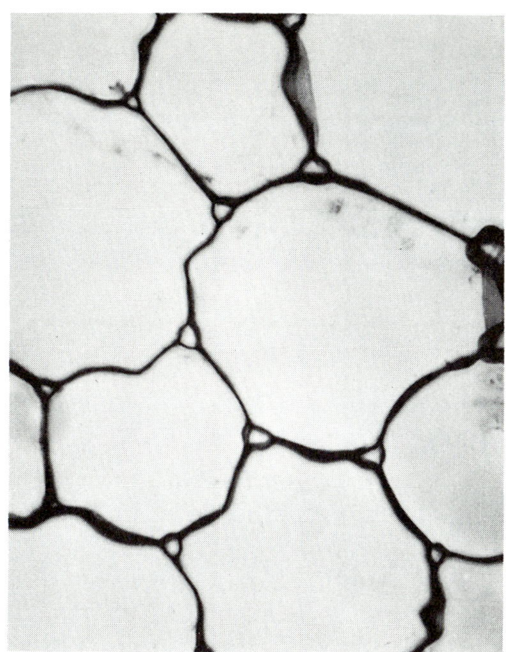

Fig. 6.15 Parenchyma cells. (*Courtesy of Melvin S. Fuller.*)

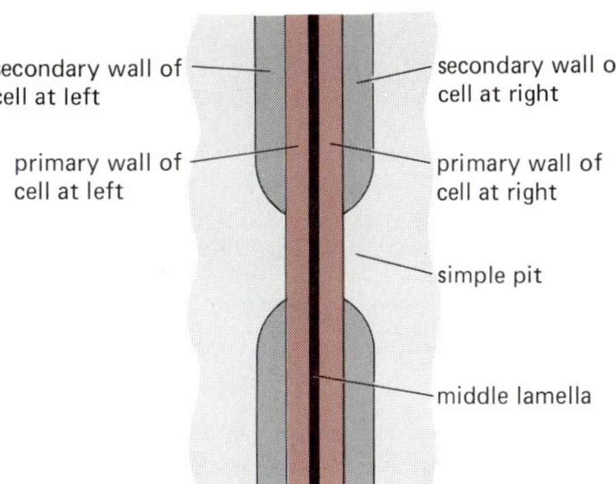

Fig. 6.16 Parenchyma pits. A simple pit pair in two adjacent parenchyma cells is shown. The pit membrane is formed by the middle lamella and the primary wall on each side of it.

After sclerenchyma cells have developed fully, their nuclei and cytoplasms usually disintegrate. Only the thick walls are left, and mature sclerenchyma may therefore be wholly nonliving and no longer "cellular."

Of two cell types classified as sclerenchyma, *fibers* are greatly elongated and usually have tapered ends. Such cells lend support to roots and other elongated plant parts. The second variant of sclerenchyma comprises the *sclereids,* which have varied and irregular shapes. Their main function is to provide rigidity or hardness. For example, sclereids known as *stone cells* are present in the flesh of pears, where they give this fruit its characteristic gritty texture.

The innermost layer of the cortex is the *endodermis,* prominent usually only in roots (Fig. 6.18). This tissue is composed of a single layer of fairly large cells, which play an important role in lateral water transport through the root (see Chap. 11).

Stele The endodermis surrounds a group of tissues known collectively as the *stele* (see Fig. 6.14). The outermost tissue layer of the stele, directly adjacent to the endodermis, is the *pericycle,* which consists of one or more layers of parenchyma cells. This tissue often becomes meristematic, producing lateral growths of cells that break through the surface of the root and develop into *branch roots* (Fig. 6.19).

Along the inner boundary of the pericycle, a second tissue of the stele is the *primary phloem.* This is a complex tissue composed of parenchyma cells, sclerenchyma fibers and sclereids, and cellular complexes called *sieve tubes* (Fig. 6.20). A sieve tube usually develops from a vertical column of adjacent embryonic cells. Each of these cells divides, and one of the two resulting cells is a *sieve-tube cell.* Remaining joined to it, the other cell forms one or more smaller *companion* cells. Fully developed sieve-tube cells are without nuclei, and the activities of such cells appear to be controlled by the companion cells, which do retain their nuclei. During the maturation of a sieve-tube cell, a specialized perforated area known as a *sieve plate* develops at each end of the cell. Passing through the perforations of such sieve plates are strands of cytoplasm that connect with adjacent sieve-tube cells. These cytoplasmic bridges play an important role in food conduction through a long sieve tube. The long-distance transportation of organic materials is actually the chief function of sieve tubes and of phloem tissue as a whole.

A third tissue of the stele is the complex *primary xylem,* located typically along the inner boundary of the primary phloem. It contains parenchyma cells and sclerenchyma fibers, as well as *tracheids* and *vessels.* Tracheids are elongated, spin-

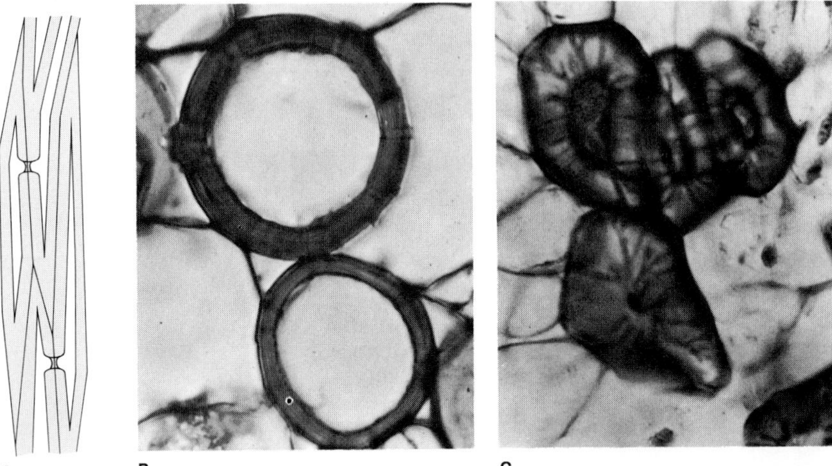

Fig. 6.17 Sclerenchyma. (A) Fibers in longitudinal view. (B) Fibers in cross-sectional view. (C) Stone cells in cross-sectional view. Note the exceedingly thick walls. (*B, C, Courtesy of C. J. Hillson.*)

Fig. 6.18 Root tissues. Magnified view of buttercup stele, consisting of pericycle, phloem and xylem, and surrounding endodermis and cortex (approx. ×85).

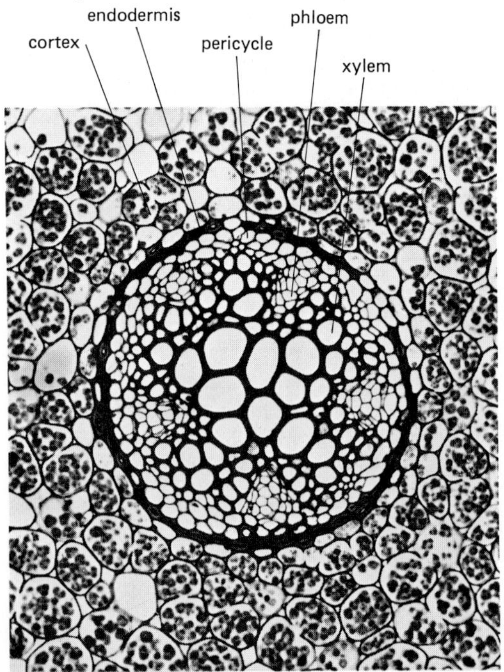

Fig. 6.19 Lateral roots. This cross section through a primary root shows a lateral branch root growing out from the pericycle region. (*Courtesy of J. Limbach, Ripon Microslides, Inc.*)

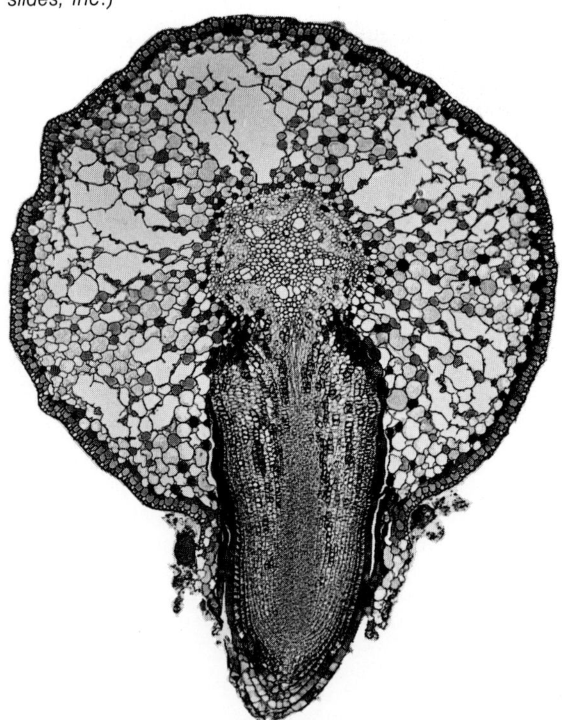

dle-shaped cells that form vertical columns extending from root to leaf (Fig. 6.21 and see Color Fig. 4). Like a sclerenchyma cell, a tracheid loses its nucleus and cytoplasm during development, and the remaining walls then enclose only water. These walls contain primary as well as secondary layers, both rigid and impregnated with *lignin*, a chemically complex strengthening material.

Also present in the walls of tracheids are elaborate *bordered pits*, specialized regions similar in some respects to the pits of parenchyma cells. In a bordered pit primary cell wall material forms a *torus*, a small round or oval plug attached to the pit membrane (see Fig. 6.21). The secondary wall overhangs the pit around its rim and is absent in the region of the torus. Thus, if water pressure in an adjoining cell pushes the pit membrane and the torus into the tracheid, the torus is prevented from

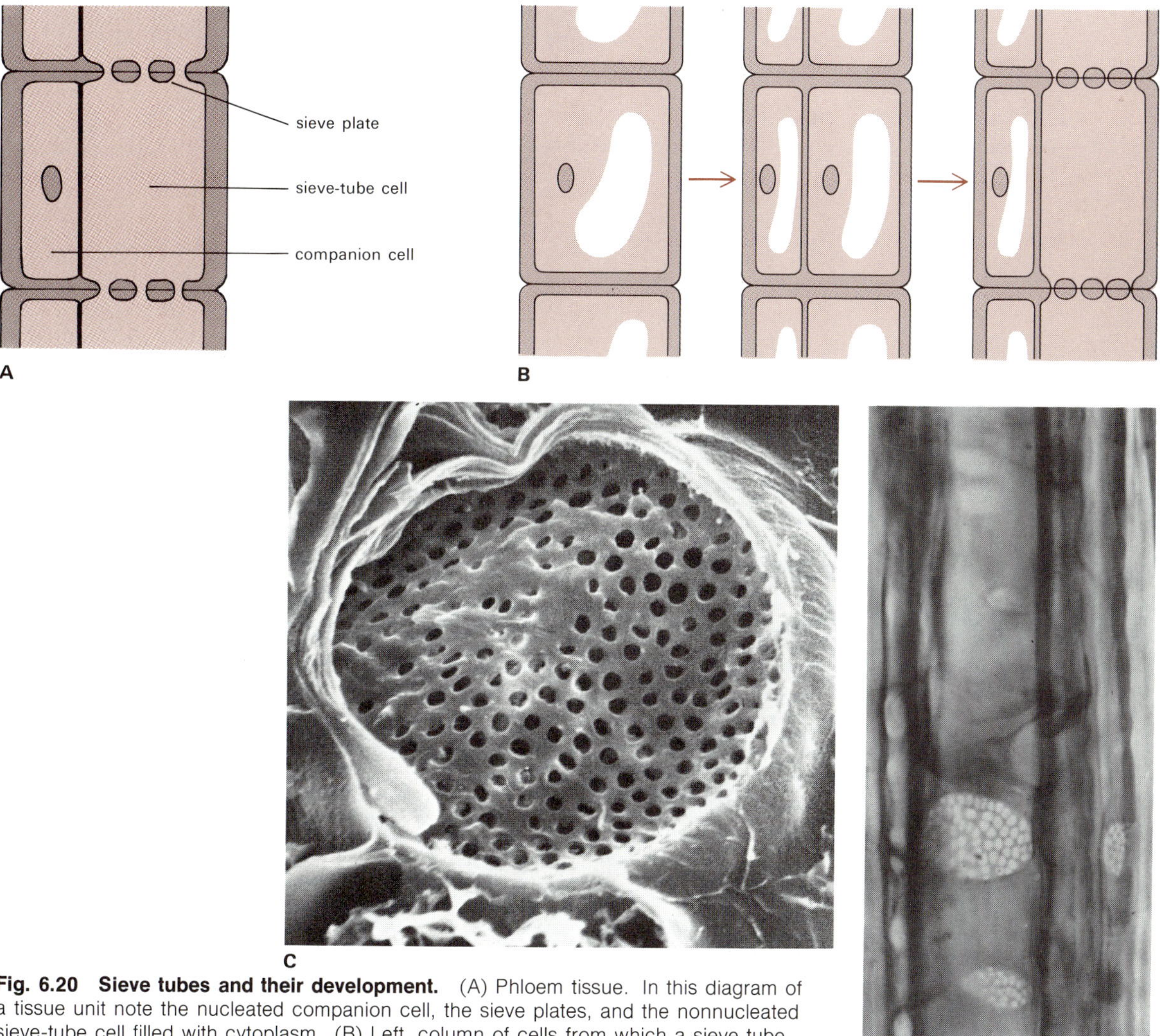

Fig. 6.20 Sieve tubes and their development. (A) Phloem tissue. In this diagram of a tissue unit note the nucleated companion cell, the sieve plates, and the nonnucleated sieve-tube cell filled with cytoplasm. (B) Left, column of cells from which a sieve tube will form. Middle, division gives rise to a smaller companion cell (at left). Right, the companion cell remains as before, but in the other cell, sieve plates develop and the nucleus disintegrates. A column of such specialized cells forms a sieve tube. (C) Scanning electron micrograph of a sieve plate in top view (approx. ×4000). (D) Sieve tube, with sieve plates along the side walls (facilitating lateral transport between sieve tubes).

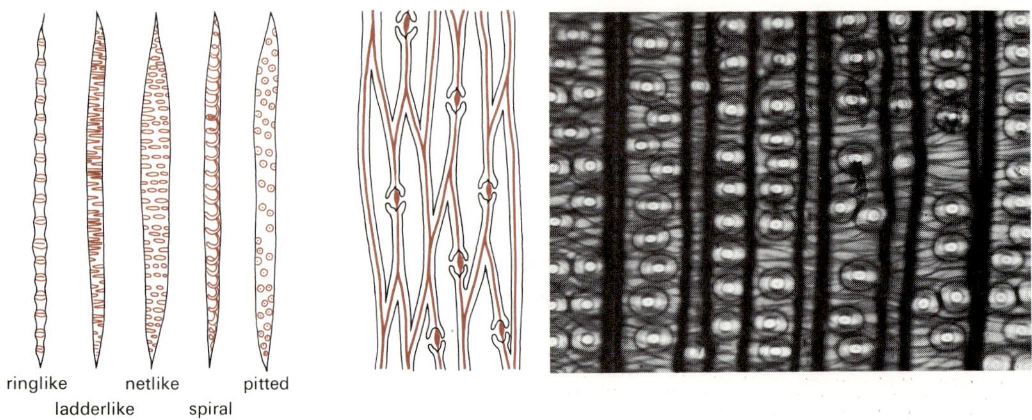

Fig. 6.21 Tracheids. (A) Tracheids with various kinds of secondary thickenings. (B) Tracheids with pits in longitudinal section. The thin pit membranes provide lateral pathways from one cell to an adjacent one. The thickening in the middle of the pit membranes (torus) serves as a stopper that prevents the membrane from ballooning out too far to either side. (C) Section through tracheids of a fir showing pits in surface view (approx. ×1000).

moving too far by the rim of the secondary wall. The torus in effect functions like a valve.

The vessels of primary xylem develop from vertical columns of adjacent embryonic cells (Fig. 6.22). As each such cell matures, it produces primary walls and lignin-impregnated secondary walls with bordered pits, just like tracheids. Eventually the nucleus and the cytoplasm disintegrate, and the transverse end walls, where one cell of the column abuts against the next, develop one or more openings or often dissolve altogether. In effect, the column becomes a hollow water-filled tube, with remnants of transverse cross walls still present in places. Such a nonliving structure is a vessel.

By virtue of its tracheids and vessels, primary xylem is both a vascular and a supporting tissue; it functions in long-distance conduction of water and supports a plant against gravity. Plants having these two vascular tissues, primary phloem and xylem, are appropriately called *vascular plants.* Note that another name for xylem is *wood.* However, if only a little xylem is present, as is usually the case in primary xylem, the tissue is not bulky enough to make a plant distinctly woody in external appearance. For example, although a green bean stem technically contains wood, or primary xylem, the stem of such a plant is not "woody."

In plants that do become woody, a thin meristematic layer of *vascular cambium* differentiates from the parenchyma cells lying between primary xylem and phloem tissues (Fig. 6.23). This cambium subsequently produces additional layers of *secondary* vascular tissue. All substantial growth in the width of woody plants is due to the presence of such additional vascular tissue (see below).

Stems

Like root growth, stem growth also occurs through cell reproduction of the apical meristem. Cells produced behind this meristem first elongate, pushing the growing stem tip upward, and then differentiate into the concentrically arranged tissues of the mature stem (Fig. 6.24). Apical stem meristem is not covered by a protective cap of cells, but in many other respects the tissues of roots and stems are similar. Young stems have an outer epidermis which covers an inner cortex of parenchyma, sclerenchyma, and other types of cells. Also, the phloem, vascular cambium, and xylem of stems are composed of the same general cell types as in the corresponding tissues of roots.

There are three principal anatomical differences between the stems and roots. (1) Most stems function as the chief supporting structures of plants and usually are reinforced more substantially by greater numbers of sclerenchyma and other sup-

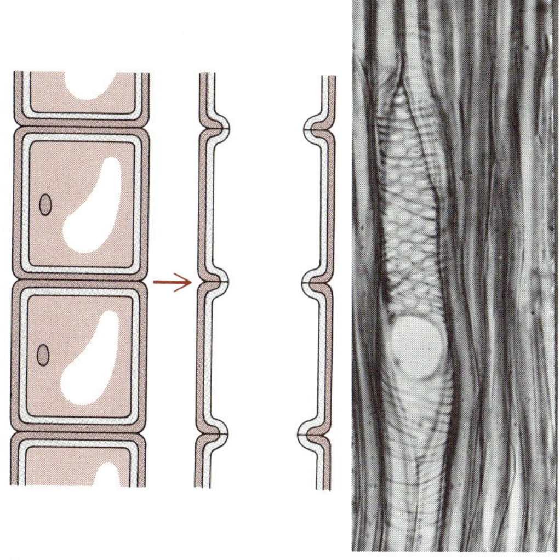

Fig. 6.22 Xylem vessels and their development. (A) Left, column of cells from which a vessel will form. Right, primary and secondary walls at top and bottom have degenerated, leaving a continuous vertical vessel. (B) Longitudinal section of xylem vessels. One of the vessels has a conspicuous simple pit (the white opening) and spiral thickenings along the wall.

porting types of cells. For example, parenchyma cells lying near the epidermis of stems often differentiate as thick-walled elastic *collenchyma* cells, rarely found in roots (Fig. 6.25). Collenchyma cells are also abundant in developing leaves, where they function as the chief supporting tissue. (2) A few tissues common to roots are found only infrequently in stems. For example, stems usually lack an endodermis and often contain a poorly defined pericycle. (3) Tissues are arranged differently in stems and in roots. Moreover, there are major differences in arrangement of the tissues that constitute dicot and monocot stems. Unlike roots, herbaceous dicot stems have their vascular tissue arranged as a circular array of *vascular bundles,* which lie between the outer cortex and an inner core of parenchyma cells called the *pith* (Fig. 6.26 and see Fig. 6.10). Parenchyma cells of both cortex and pith function in water and nutrient storage. Within each vascular bundle, phloem lies to the outside, xylem to the inside, with a layer of vascular cambium in between.

Monocot stems differ from those of herbaceous dicots in two main ways: (1) Vascular bundles are scattered throughout the stem (see Fig. 6.26), and a distinction between pith and cortex cannot be made; (2) vascular cambium usually does not develop in the vascular bundles, and most monocot stems are consequently incapable of continued growth in width.

Leaves

Leaf development Leaves originate through reproduction of cells localized along the sides of the apical shoot meristem. Cells in these areas divide more rapidly than surrounding cells and form small, fingerlike projections called *leaf primordia* (Fig. 6.27). These embryonic structures gradually develop as mature leaves.

Fig. 6.23 Root cambium. Stages in development of cambium and of cambium-derived secondary tissues are shown.

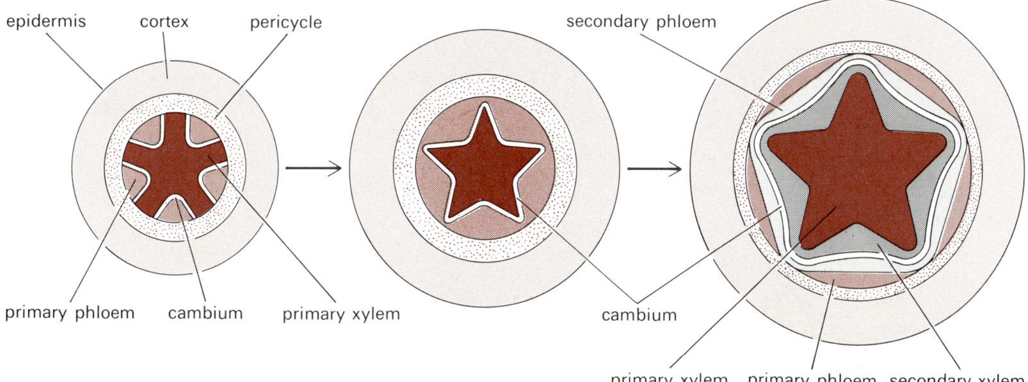

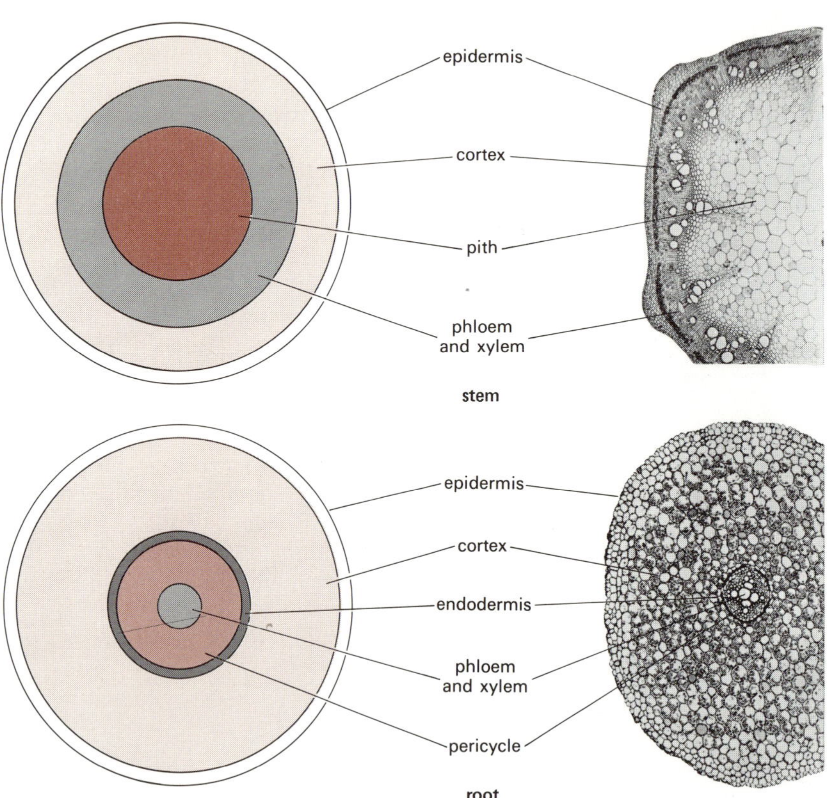

Fig. 6.24 Tissue arrangements in dicot plants. Top, stem tissues at left and bean-stem section at right. Bottom, root tissues at left and buttercup-root section at right. (*Carolina Biological Supply Company.*)

Fig. 6.25 Collenchyma cells. Note the strengthening wall material at the corners of the cells (×5000). (*Courtesy of Melvin S. Fuller.*)

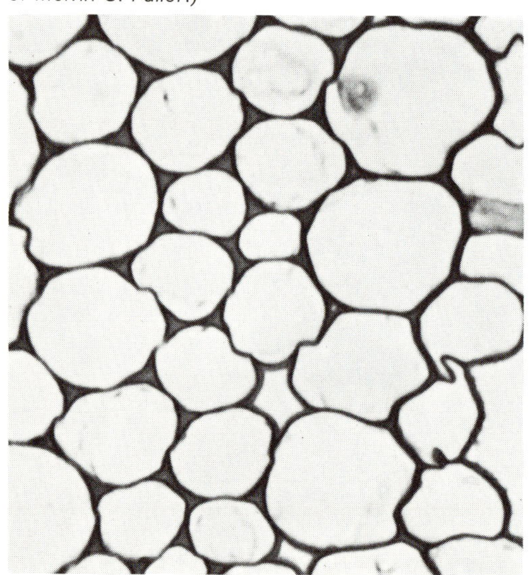

The points at which leaf primordia arise on stems are called *nodes,* and the stem regions between successive nodes are called *internodes* (Fig. 6.28). Stem tips usually contain a series of leaf primordia separated by very short internodes. Most of the increase in stem length results from elongation of cells that make up these short internodes. Before their elongation, leaf primordia separating the short internodes at the stem tip are cupped around the apical meristem, producing a compound structure called a *terminal bud.* In plants that lose their leaves in the fall, the surfaces of buds are protected by overlapping *bud scales* throughout the winter months (Fig. 6.29). When the buds of such *deciduous* plants open in spring, the bud scales curve away and become detached, and cells rapidly elongate in the internode regions, producing an increase in stem length. Thus, in a sense, a bud is an embryonic twig.

As a leaf primordium develops, cells at its base form a leaf stalk, or *petiole* (Fig. 6.30). Other cells

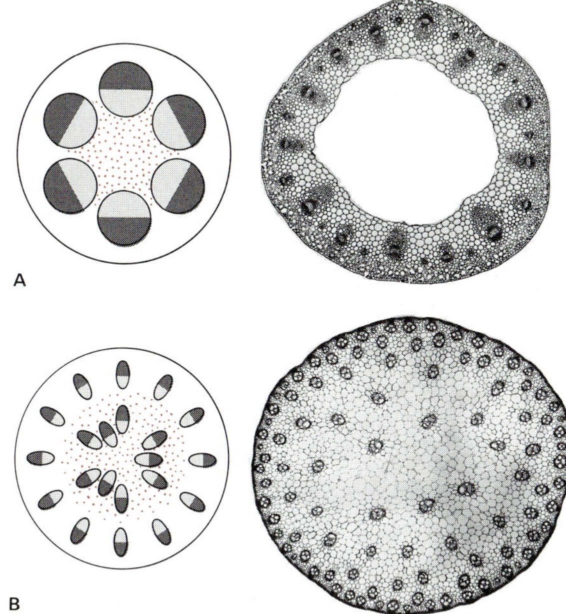

Fig. 6.26 Stem structure: steles. (A) Characteristic arrangement of vascular bundles in stems of gymnosperms and dicot angiosperms. Left, schematic representation of photograph at right (cross section through a buttercup stem): phloem, dark; xylem, light gray; pith, stippled. Phloem and xylem form vascular bundles in which phloem is toward the outside. (B) Characteristic arrangement of vascular bundles in stems of monocot angiosperms. The photograph shows a cross section through a corn stem. Color key for tissues is the same as in A.

Fig. 6.27 Leaf and branch growth. Longitudinal section through a shoot tip, showing apical meristem and various stages of leaf and branch development. (*Courtesy of Melvin S. Fuller.*)

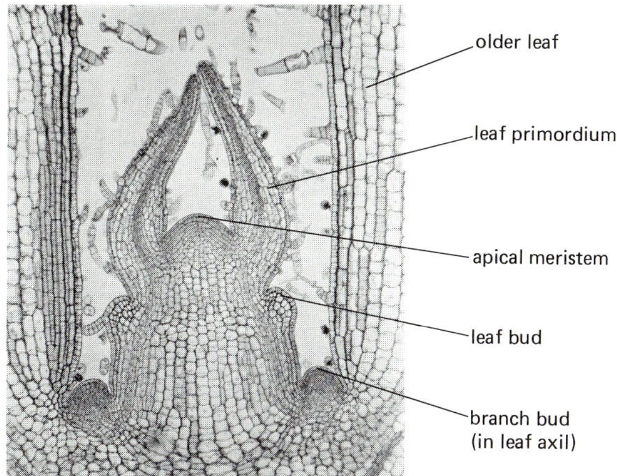

differentiate into two *stipules,* small appendages growing out near the base of the petiole in many species, and into the *leaf blade* itself. A second type of bud usually develops in the angle between the stem axis and the petiole before leaf differentiation is completed. These *branch buds* contain the same structures as terminal buds and have the potential of developing into branch stems (see Figs. 6.29 and 6.30). Branch buds often do not mature immediately. Some remain dormant for many years, and others may not develop at all. In wintering stems, dormant branch buds usually are clearly visible just above small, roughly circular areas where leaves have been attached during previous growing seasons. Such areas are called *leaf scars* (Fig. 6.31).

Leaf tissues When fully formed, a leaf consists of four major tissue layers: an epidermal layer at the upper and lower leaf surfaces, and two internal layers of photosynthetic cells (Fig. 6.32). Epidermal cells usually lack chloroplasts and are covered by a layer of waxy secretion, the *cuticle,* which retards movement of water and gases into and out of leaves. Water loss and gas exchange through leaves are regulated by pairs of crescent-

Fig. 6.28 Stem elongation. Cell elongation in terminal buds establishes spaces, or nodes, between the points at which leaves originate. Individual branch buds develop in the angle made by the stem and the leaf stalk. Such angles are called leaf axils (see also Fig. 6.27). Because they develop at these sites, branch buds are also called axillary buds.

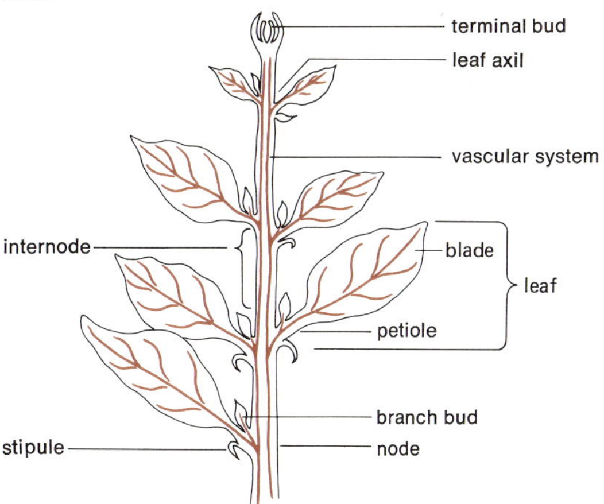

Fig. 6.29 Stem buds. A terminal and two branch buds in dormant condition. (*Courtesy of Melvin S. Fuller.*)

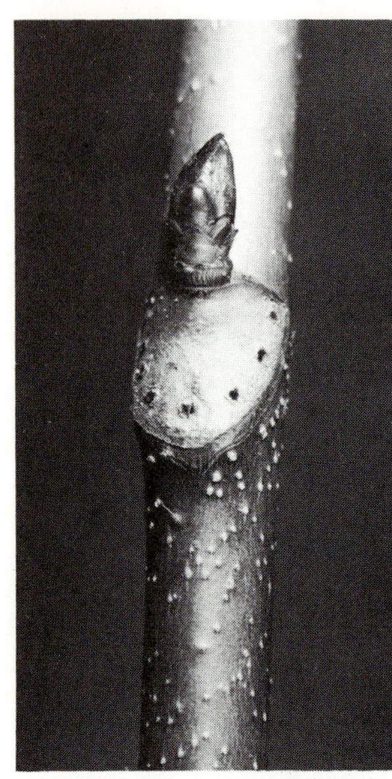

Fig. 6.31 Leaf scars. A dormant branch bud just above a leaf scar. (*Courtesy of Melvin S. Fuller.*)

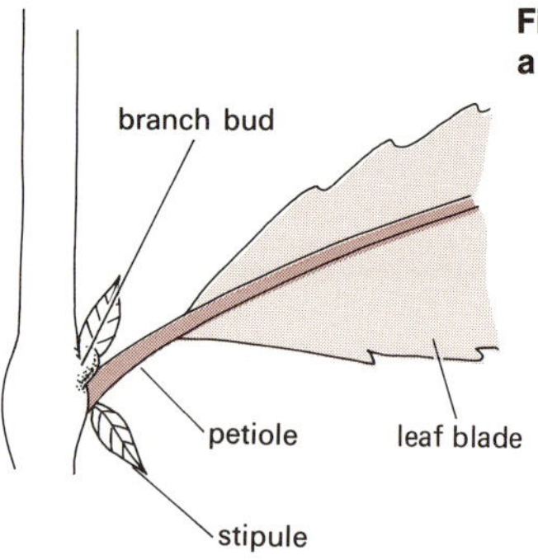

Fig. 6.30 Basal parts of a mature leaf.

shaped *guard cells,* positioned so that the concave side of one cell of a pair faces the concave side of the other (Fig. 6.33). The open space left between such a pair of cells is a *stoma* (pl. *stomata*). The inner walls of guard cells are much thicker than their outer walls and this, together with their crescent shape, causes the inner walls to draw toward or away from each other as changes occur in the water content of guard cells. When water is plentiful throughout the plant, guard cells become swollen with water, or *turgid,* and their inner walls pull away from each other, causing the stomatal opening to enlarge (Fig. 6.34). Considerable evaporation of water and exchange of gases occur under such conditions.

Conversely, when water is scarce, as during droughts, guard cells contain less water and become *flaccid.* At these times the inner walls of guard cells draw closer together, and the size of the stomatal opening is reduced as well. Stomata may be present in both epidermal layers, but they are usually more abundant in the lower epidermis, away from the sun where the evaporating effect of solar heat is somewhat reduced.

In many plants the epidermis of leaves carries hairlike projections of various kinds that form as outgrowths from single cells or cell clusters (Fig. 6.35). The epidermal hairs of some plants are stiff, thick-walled structures that protect against the foraging of leaf-eating insects. Even more formidable are the stinging hairs of plants such as nettles, which can penetrate the skin of animals and inject irritating poisons.

Except for guard cells, all other photosynthetic cells of leaves are found in the two *mesophyll* layers lying between the upper and lower epidermis. The layer adjacent to the upper epidermis, called the *palisade* mesophyll layer, consists of densely packed, elongated cells. Below these lies a contrasting layer of loosely arranged cells honeycombed extensively with *air spaces.* Appropriately, this has been named the *spongy* mesophyll layer. The large and numerous air spaces in it connect with each

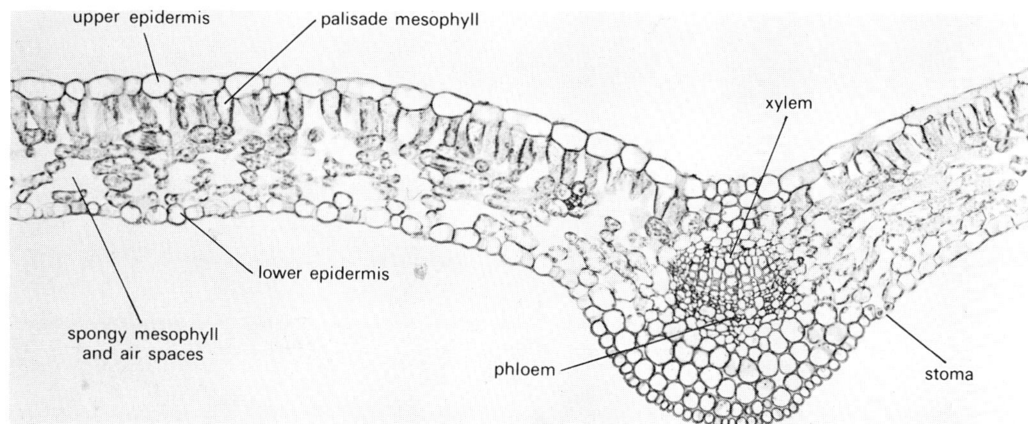

Fig. 6.32 Leaf structure. In this cross section the xylem and phloem (and usually also surrounding fiber tissue) form a vein. Note stomata in the lower epidermis. (*General Biological Supply House, Inc.*)

other and lead to the exterior of the leaf through open passages in the palisade tissue and the stomata. Such a structural arrangement permits the greater part of most photosynthetic cells to come into direct contact with fresh external air.

The cells of both inner layers of a leaf usually contain large numbers of chloroplasts, and each cell has a large central water vacuole. These mesophyll cells, named for their middle, or "meso," position in leaves, account for the bulk of the leaf and for most of the photosynthetic activity of a plant (see Fig. 6.32).

Embedded in mesophyll tissue are leaf *veins*, bundles of xylem, phloem, and fiber tissue that are continuous with the vascular tissues of the stem. Such veins give mechanical support and carry nu-

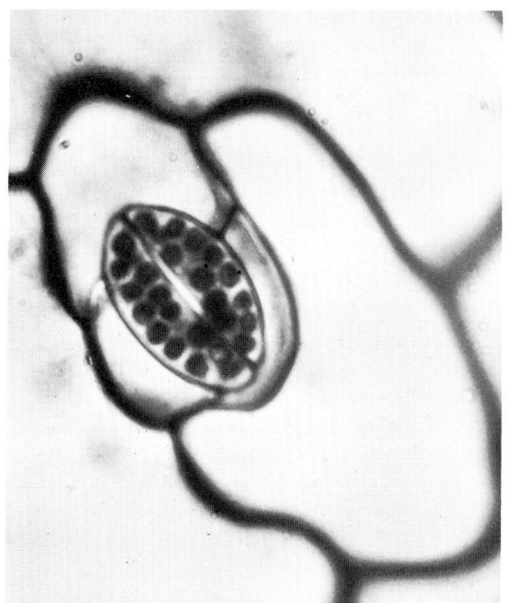

Fig. 6.33 Stomata. (A) Surface view (light microscopy) of leaf epidermis showing a pair of guard cells (×4800). Note the chloroplasts in them and the stoma between them. (B) Scanning electron micrograph of leaf epidermis showing five stomata (×1100). Guard cells rise from the epidermal surface, one pair of cells flanking each stoma.

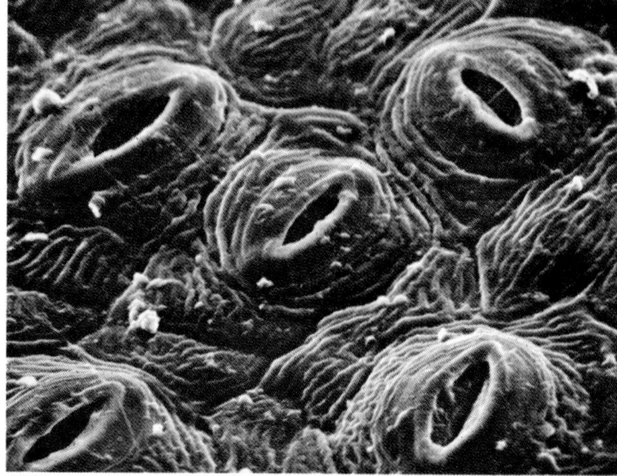

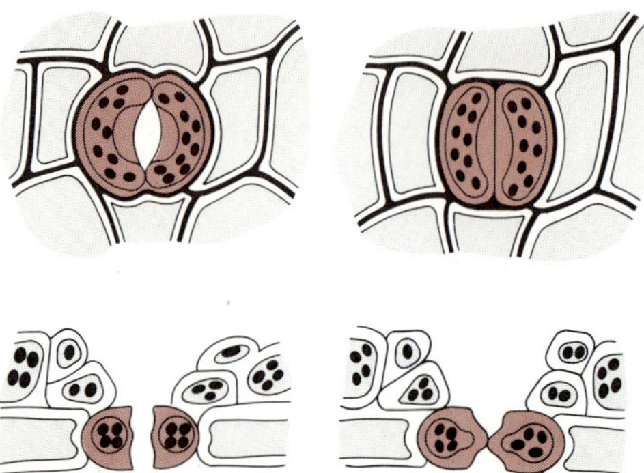

Fig. 6.34 Stomatal action. A pair of guard cells in a leaf. Top, surface view. Lower, cross-sectional view. Left, stoma open. Right, stoma closed.

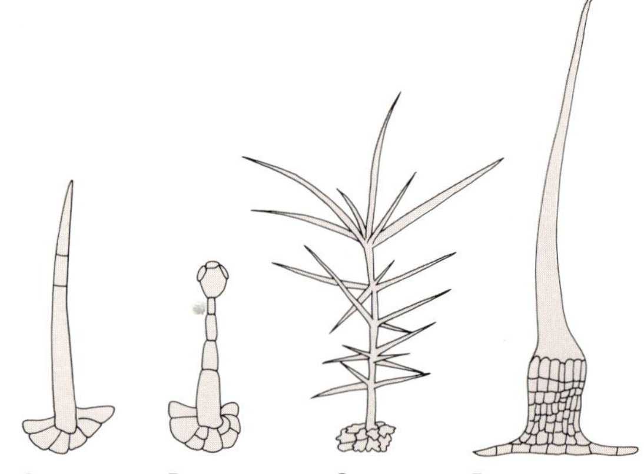

Fig. 6.35 Plant "hairs." (A) Simple hair of geranium (*Pelargonium domesticum*). (B) Glandular hair of geranium. (C) Branched hair of mullein (*Verbascum thapsus*). (D) Stinging hair of nettle (*Urtica dioica* var. *procera*). (*After C. L. Wilson, W. E. Loomis, and T. A. Steeves, "Botany," 5th ed., Holt, New York, 1971.*)

trients to and from all parts of the leaf. As stated previously, the veins of dicots branch repeatedly and form increasingly smaller strands that extend to all parts of a leaf; the veins of monocots usually are arranged as parallel strands (see Fig. 6.10B).

In external form, the leaves of dicots are either *simple* or *compound*. The blade of a simple leaf is one continuous piece; familiar examples are the leaves of oak or poplar trees (Fig. 6.36). By contrast, the blade of a compound leaf is subdivided as a number of small leaflike parts called *leaflets*. When the leaflets each arise from a small stalk, as do those of roses and beans, the whole leaf is said to be *pinnately* compound. All leaflets of a *palmately* compound leaf arise from a common point, as occurs in the horsechestnut, for example.

Dicot leaves also exhibit different patterns of growth from plant stems. In an *alternate* pattern, single leaves are attached at successive stem levels, and the leaf bases then mark out a spiral winding up along a stem. The geometric characteristics of such spirals are quite distinct for given species. Leaves are *opposite* if two leaves grow out at the same stem level, and they are *whorled* if more than two arise at the same level (Fig. 6.37).

Secondary Growth

The whole organization of the tracheophyte body described up to this point represents the product of primary growth: all body parts are direct derivatives of the apical meristems. As stated earlier, primary growth permits extension in *length*, and any increase in the thickness of stems and roots is due mainly to enlargement of cells in a lateral direction. In many tracheophytes, such as ferns, grasses, snapdragons, petunias, and most "vegetable" plants, primary growth is the only means of increasing body size. However, numerous tracheophytes are capable of growing not only in length but also in thickness, through lateral increase of cell *number*. These plants undergo processes of *secondary growth* superimposed on a continuing primary growth. Apart from comparatively enormous increases in stem and root girth, the large-scale result of secondary growth is the development of *bark* and *wood*.

Wood tends to be formed in relatively large quantities, and new layers are added each year to those accumulated previously. Plants of this type develop into shrubs and trees and become recognizably *woody* in appearance. As stated earlier, primary growth gives rise to wood too, namely primary xylem. But in the vast majority of cases, primary xylem is formed in such small amounts that the plant is left in a *herbaceous* condition; and if a distinctly woody plant is to develop, abundant wood must be formed by secondary growth. Thus, the phrase "woody plants" refers largely to plants in which secondary growth occurs, that is, gymnosperms and many of the dicot angiosperms.

Fig. 6.36 Dicot leaf types. (A) Simple leaves. (B) The two kinds of compound leaves.

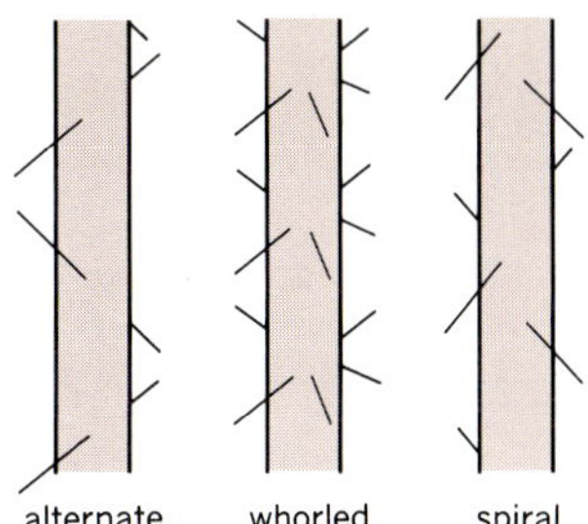

Fig. 6.37 Leaf arrangements on stems. Leaf stalks are arranged on a stem in various geometric patterns, as shown.

In such woody plants, young shoots and roots develop as in all other cases through primary growth. The plant also continues to elongate through primary growth at each tip, and the regions immediately behind the tips maintain the characteristic primary structure of nonwoody roots and stems. In older regions well behind each tip, these primary patterns later become transformed into secondary ones. Thus, the early shoots and later growing tips remain "green" even in woody plants. Since leaves bud off near the shoot apex and have no growing tips of their own, they do not participate in secondary development at all.

The transformation of roots and stems from primary to secondary states is brought about by *secondary meristems,* or *cambia.* Two kinds of cambia develop, a *vascular cambium* and a *cork cambium.* Each arises from different primary tissues, and the process of formation differs somewhat in root and stem.

Vascular Cambium

In a root, the vascular cambium forms between the primary xylem and phloem in the stele (see Fig. 6.23). A layer of cells here remains permanently embryonic and relatively unspecialized. This layer becomes the vascular root cambium, which ultimately surrounds the primary root xylem completely.

In a stem, part of the vascular cambium again forms from a cell layer between primary xylem and phloem (Fig. 6.38). Since these tissues in most dicot stems form a ring of vascular bundles, the cambium layer between the xylem and phloem is interrupted between neighboring bundles. Such interruptions soon disappear, however, for a layer of parenchyma cells between the bundles acquires the properties of a cambium. The vascular stem cambium thereby becomes a complete tube, continuous with the corresponding tube in the root; and in the course of the further elongation of the stem-root axis through primary growth at the apical tips, the open-ended cambial tube lengthens as progressively more cambium develops behind the shoot and root tips.

In both the root and the stem, the cells of the vascular cambium continue to divide and produce new cells toward both the inside and the outside. In this manner whole *layers* of cells continue to be deposited at both sides of the cambium. Some of these cells form lengthening strands of parenchymatous tissue extending toward the center and toward the surface of the stem and root. These are *xylem rays* and *phloem rays,* respectively, and they function in lateral transport of nutrients within stem and root. All other cells budded off toward the inside of the cambial layer soon mature into the various components of xylem tissue; and cells budded off toward the outside become components of

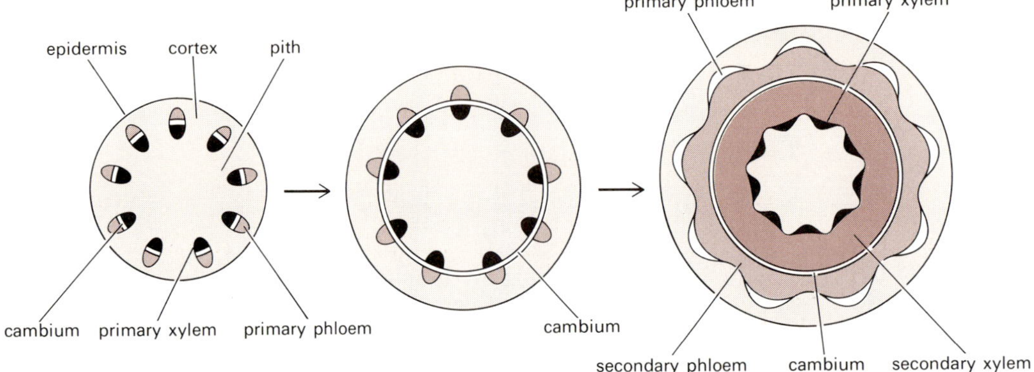

Fig. 6.38 Stem cambium. Stages in development of cambium and of cambium-derived secondary tissues are shown. The development of corresponding tissues in a root is depicted in Fig. 6.23.

phloem tissue. Vascular tissue so generated by cambium represents *secondary xylem* (or *wood* proper) and *secondary phloem.* These tissues are traversed in places by the xylem and phloem rays (Fig. 6.39).

As secondary xylem continues to be formed in successive concentric layers within the cambial tube, it cannot grow too far inward, for this space is already occupied by the primary xylem and the pith. An outward expansion will therefore take place, and the thickness of the stem or the root will increase. Similarly, as secondary phloem develops outward, it increases the thickness of stem or root still more. Indeed, as secondary phloem presses increasingly against primary phloem, cortex, and epidermis, these primary tissues become highly compressed and they eventually rupture.

The smallest amounts of secondary tissue are always near the apical tips, where cambial activity is just beginning; the largest amounts have accumulated at the stem-root juncture, the region that has grown for the longest period and is the oldest. This is therefore the region of greatest girth, and from here the stem *tapers* up and the root tapers down (Fig. 6.40).

Cork Cambium

The second of the cambial tissues is the cork cambium. This single layer of cells develops from the pericycle in roots and from the cortex or the phloem in stems. Like the vascular cambium, the cork cambium produces new cell layers toward the inside and the outside (Fig. 6.41). Layers formed toward the inside constitute *phelloderm,* a tissue largely composed of parenchymal cells. Layers generated toward the outside form *cork.* During their

Fig. 6.39 The woody stem. This is a cross section through a portion of a 3-year-old (basswood) stem. Production of cork, the outermost tissue of a woody plant, is discussed in the next section of this chapter. (*General Biological Supply House, Inc.*)

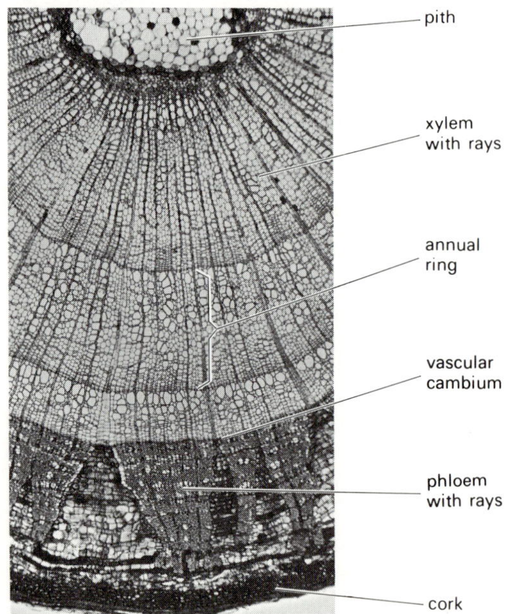

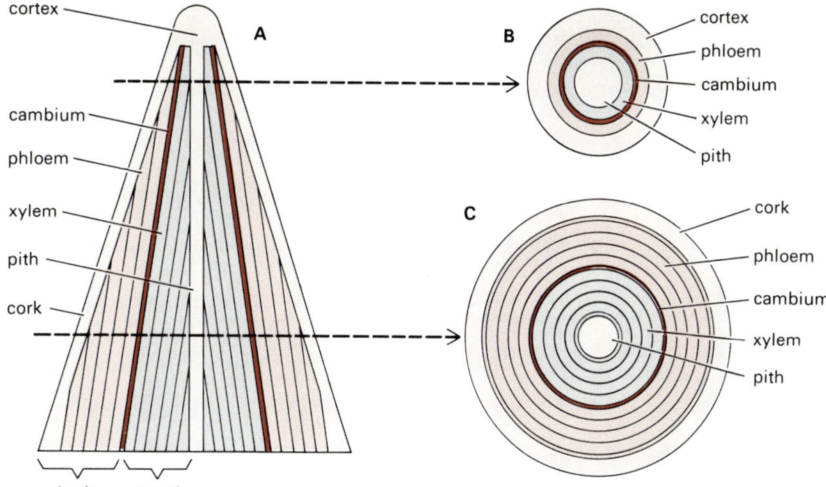

Fig. 6.40 Tissue arrangements in a woody shoot. (A) Diagrammatic longitudinal view, showing the formation of successive tissue layers to the outside and inside of the cambium. A cross section at the level of the upper broken line would appear as in (B) and at the level of the lower broken line, as in (C).

maturation cork cells deposit heavy coats of *suberin,* a waterproofing substance, on their walls. After the walls have been coated, the cell interiors disintegrate. Mature cork is thus wholly nonliving.

Cork cells usually are packed close together, an arrangement that makes the outer covering of a woody plant quite impervious to water and air. At various places, however, the cork cambium produces loosely arranged cork cells separated by intercellular spaces. Such spongy regions, or *lenticels,* permit gas exchange between the atmosphere and the interior living tissues of root or stem (Fig. 6.42).

Cork first develops where the epidermis and the cortex have ruptured as a result of the outward expansion of xylem and phloem. Later, after epidermis and cortex have torn away completely, a continuous layer of cork comes to surround the entire outside surface of stem and root. Further increases in stem and root diameter then cause a rupturing and flaking off of the original cork, and

Fig. 6.41 Cork cambium and its products in a woody stem. Cork is formed toward the outside of cork cambium, phelloderm toward the inside. Cork, cork cambium, and phelloderm are shown in the photo. Bark is made up of all tissues outside the vascular cambium.

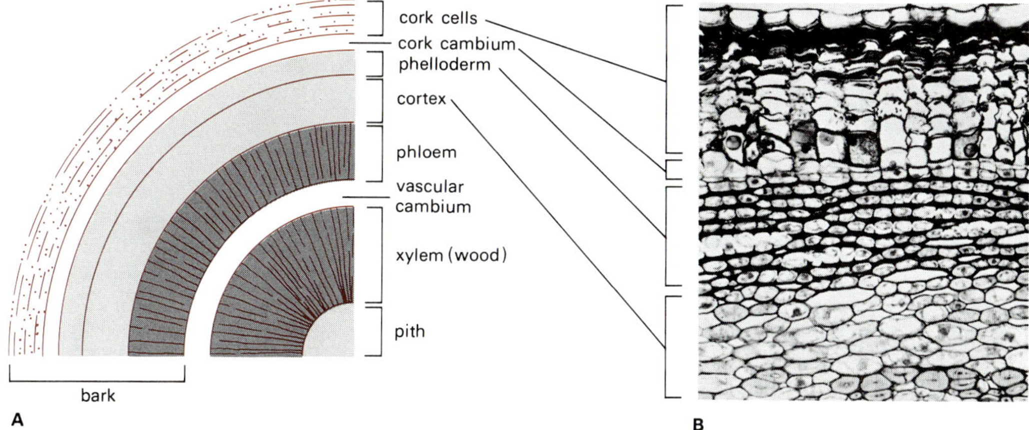

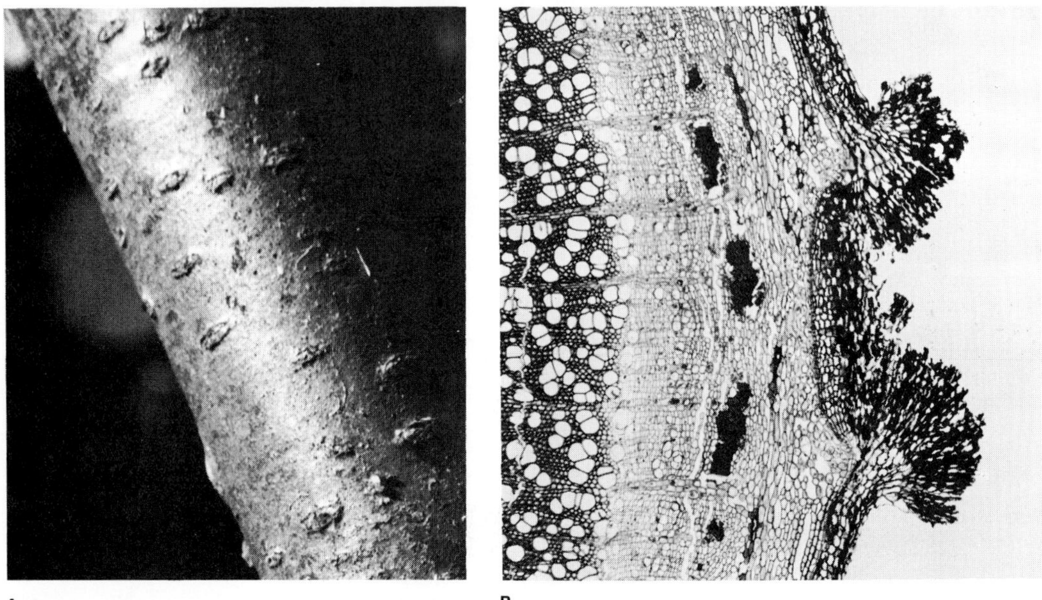

Fig. 6.42 Lenticels. (A) External view. (B) Cross-sectional view. *(A, Courtesy of Melvin S. Fuller; B, J. Limbach, Ripon Microslides, Inc.)*

Fig. 6.43 Wood and annual rings. Portion of a tree trunk showing 12 rings. *(U.S. Forest Service.)*

new cork is produced in its place. This new tissue in turn ruptures and flakes off, and the cycle of new formation and flaking off repeats indefinitely.

All tissues outside the vascular cambium are collectively called *bark.* In a cut section of a tree the main tissues then are (concentrically from the outside inward) cork; the microscopically thin layer of cork cambium; phelloderm; phloem; the microscopic layer of vascular cambium; and wood, which fills the space within the ring of vascular cambium. In a stem section, a microscopic accumulation of pith is in the very center (see Fig. 6.39). Older phloem, right below the surface of a tree trunk, continually flakes off as the trunk thickens. At any given time, therefore, only a thin rind of young phloem is present inside the bark. Only young xylem transports water. Older xylem, near the center of a trunk, in time gradually blocks up with resins and gums, and water conduction through these channels becomes impossible. Such central regions are called *heartwood.* The core of a tree can therefore be hollowed out without interfering with xylem conduction. But the outer, young wood of a tree, called the *sapwood,* must remain intact if a tree is to remain alive.

In an older tree growing in the temperate zone, the xylem vessels laid down during spring generally have a larger diameter than those formed in summer. In spring, melting snow provides the tree with much water, and wider conducting channels formed at that season accommodate the greater flow. This alternation of narrow summer xylem and wider spring xylem is recognizable by the naked eye as a concentric series of dark and light bands, or *annual rings* (Fig. 6.43 and see Fig. 6.39). The number of rings indicates the age of a tree. Moreover, from the comparative widths of spring and summer rings, it is often possible to estimate the amount of rainfall, hence general climatic conditions, during the past seasons as far back in time as the tree has lived.

Review Questions

1 Review the identifying characteristics of *Plantae.*

2 What are some of the basic characteristics shared by all plants? Which of these characteristics are adaptations to:

- **a.** A nonmotile existence?
- **b.** Autotrophism?
- **c.** Terrestrial environments?

3 Describe the group characteristics and basic structure of bryophytes. Name the classes of bryophytes and their identifying features. Define thallus, rhizoid, protonema.

4 State the identifying characteristics of tracheophytes. What are seed plants? Angiosperms? State the identifying characteristics of each subclass of angiosperms?

5 How does a root or a stem grow in length? Review the characteristics of various cell types among plants. Which cell types function primarily in conduction? In mechanical support? What cell types are unique to roots? To stems?

6 Describe the development and structure of xylem vessels and of sieve tubes. What is a stele? What justifies the designation of a stem or a root as an organ?

7 Describe the structure of a leaf. How does a leaf develop? In what tissues does photosynthesis occur? How do branches of plants develop?

8 What is secondary growth? Show how a vascular cambium forms secondary xylem and phloem. Describe the activities of a cork cambium.

9 Define lenticel, annual ring, heartwood, bark, and wood.

10 Describe the complete structural organization of a mature woody plant in:

- **a.** The woody part of the stem
- **b.** The nonwoody apical part of the stem
- **c.** The woody part of the root
- **d.** The nonwoody part of the root

11 Contrast the internal structure of a woody and a herbaceous angiosperm.

Collateral Readings

Baker, H. G.: "Plants and Civilization," 3d ed., Wadsworth, Belmont, Calif., 1976. This paperback illustrates the profound influence of plants on our economic, cultural, and political history.

Epstein, E.: Roots, *Scientific American,* May 1973. The author describes the variety of root systems in plants and illustrates how roots absorb water and dissolved minerals from soil.

Esau, K.: "Plant Anatomy," 2d ed., Wiley, New York, 1965. An outstanding reference on plant structure; contains many drawings and photomicrographs.

Fritts, H. C.: Tree Rings and Climate, *Scientific American,* May 1972. Describes how tree ring patterns can be used to deduce the climate of bygone times.

Galston, A. W.: "The Green Plant," Prentice-Hall, Englewood Cliffs, N.J., 1968. This paperback contains a concise summary of plant growth and development.

Greulach, V.: "Plant Structure and Function," Macmillan, New York, 1973. A short text that provides a concise introduction to the organization and physiology of plants.

Ledbetter, M. C., and **K. Porter:** "Introduction to the Fine Structure of Plant Cells," Springer, New York, 1970. An excellent atlas of electron micrographs of plant cells.

McMahon, T. A.: The Mechanical Design of Trees, *Scientific American,* July 1975. This article describes a search for the fundamental mechanisms that govern the shape of trees.

Raven, P., R. Evert, and **H. Curtis:** "Biology of Plants," 2d ed., Worth, New York, 1975. A good introductory botany text.

Ray, P. M.: "The Living Plant," 2d ed., Holt, New York, 1972. An outstanding paperback describing the basic nature of plants and plant cells.

Weier, T. E., C. R. Stocking, and **M. G. Barbour:** "Botany: An Introduction to Plant Biology," 5th ed., Wiley, New York, 1974. An especially well illustrated introductory botany textbook.

Chapter 7

Cell to Organism: The Animal Pattern

Learning Objectives

After reading this chapter you should be able to:

1. Identify the two different patterns in which motile and sessile animals obtain food; write a paragraph explaining how holotrophic nutrition and the requirement for locomotion determine and influence the characteristics of all other aspects of animal nature.
2. List at least one function for each of the following organ systems of animals:
   a. nervous system
   b. alimentary system
   c. endocrine system
   d. skeletal system
   e. integumentary system
   f. circulatory system
   g. breathing system
   h. excretory system
   i. reproductive system
   j. muscular system
3. List at least one way in which bilateral symmetry is of adaptive value for motile organisms.
4. Define endoskeleton and exoskeleton; name an animal with an endoskeleton and one with an exoskeleton.
5. Differentiate between larva and embryo; state how these terms relate to hatching and metamorphosis.
6. List the three primary germ layers of embryos, and name at least one organ system derived from each of these layers.
7. List at least two characteristics and two functions of connective tissues; name the most fundamental variant of these tissues in your body; name at least three types of cells found in connective tissues, and list one function for each.
8. Distinguish between cartilage and bone and between dermal and replacement bone; construct a diagram that illustrates the formation and growth of replacement bone.
9. Distinguish between simple and stratified epithelia and list one example of each; name and list an example of the three types of simple epithelia; list at least two ways in which epithelia usually differ from connective tissues; using the liver, skin, or gut as an example, illustrate the structural and functional roles of epithelia and connective tissues.
10. Name the three types of animal tissue that cannot be classified strictly as epithelia or connective tissues; list at least one characteristic of each of these three types of tissue.
11. Differentiate between smooth, striated, and cardiac muscle; list at least one organ in which each of these muscle tissues is found; define motor unit.
12. Construct a diagram of a cross section through the human intestine that depicts the structural relations between mucosa, submucosa, muscularis, and serosa; label and list a function for each of these tissues.

The gradual increase in complexity accompanying the evolution of plants has occurred also in animals. In this respect plants and animals are similar, but in many other ways they are very different. One of the most fundamental differences is nutritional.

Plants are autotrophic, dependent on light energy and relatively simple inorganic raw materials; animals are heterotrophic, dependent on complex organic nutrients produced, directly or indirectly, by autotrophs. Animals must break down these complex organic nutrients before the subunits of these molecules can be used in the synthesis of new cellular components.

Most animals obtain nutrients through *holotrophism*, a form of heterotrophism in which bulk food is ingested and then processed in a series of organs constituting the *alimentary tract.* Indeed, *alimentation* can be viewed as the animal counterpart of photosynthesis in plants. More than any other process, alimentation influences the whole nature of animals.

This chapter describes for animals what the preceding one establishes for plants; it introduces the structural pattern of animals organization, including the fundamental arrangements of all basic categories of animal tissues and organs. Information in this chapter paves the way for an examination of the functional attributes for living things, presented in Parts 3 to 6. The distinguishing characteristics of all major taxa of Animalia are introduced in Part 7.

GENERAL CHARACTERISTICS

Locomotion

One immediate consequence of alimentation is the necessity of active motion, since in most cases movement by passive means—such as random dispersion by water and wind—would not carry animals to appropriate kinds of food.

Flagella, cilia, and particularly a *muscular system* are the means of animal motion, and this motor capacity is used in two major ways to obtain food. In the more common case, an animal carries out some form of *locomotion;* it propels its whole body toward the location of a likely food source. In the second case, the animal remains stationary and *sessile* and lets the food source move toward it. All sessile animals are aquatic. They use their motion-producing equipment to create water currents that carry food organisms to them or to trap food organisms that happen to pass close by.

Once the capacity of motion has developed, it may function not only in feeding but also secondarily in other vital activities. As is well known, for example, locomotion helps animals significantly in protecting them from potential environmental dangers. Locomotion also plays an important role in mate selection and in reproduction generally. Yet in virtually all cases, the most frequent locomotor effort made by animals probably comes in the search for food.

Before an animal can effectively move toward food or vice versa, it is clearly essential for the animal to recognize an object as a potential source of food. Moreover, after food has been located, it is equally essential to *control* the ensuing motion—to set and adjust course and speed, and to determine when movement is to begin and to terminate. What is evidently needed is a complete guidance apparatus, and most animals possess it in the form of a *nervous system.* In it, sense organs of various kinds permit recognition of environmental detail, impulses in nerves produce control over motion, and a brain or brainlike organ correlates, coordinates, and fits a given set of recognitions to an appropriate set of motions.

Control is actually essential not only in motion but also in performing any other function. Indeed, most animals possess *chemical* coordinating systems in addition to the neural ones. In many instances, chemical control is exercised by components of other organ systems (for example, blood, kidneys, gills), and in some groups chemical regulation is also achieved by hormone-producing *endocrine systems.*

Symmetry

The requirement of motion influences the architecture of animals in major ways. Movement is most efficient when the external medium offers the least possible resistance. Unlike a plant, therefore, which is constructed in a branching shape for maximum exposure to light, air, and soil, an animal is built as compactly as possible, for minimum surface exposure. Most motile animals also tend to be *bilaterally symmetrical* and *elongated* in the direction of motion, a shape that aids in further reducing resistance to movement. Moreover, since one end of an elongated animal necessarily enters new environments first, that end will serve best as the place for the chief sense organs and nerve centers and for the food-catching apparatus. The leading part of the body so becomes a *head.* At the same time elimination products of all kinds are best released at the hind end, where they do not impede forward progression. A general build of this sort is actually standard and nearly universal among moving animals (Fig. 7.1).

By contrast, sessile animals and also many of the slow and sluggish types face their environment more or less equally from all sides, as plants do, and this circumstance is reflected in their architec-

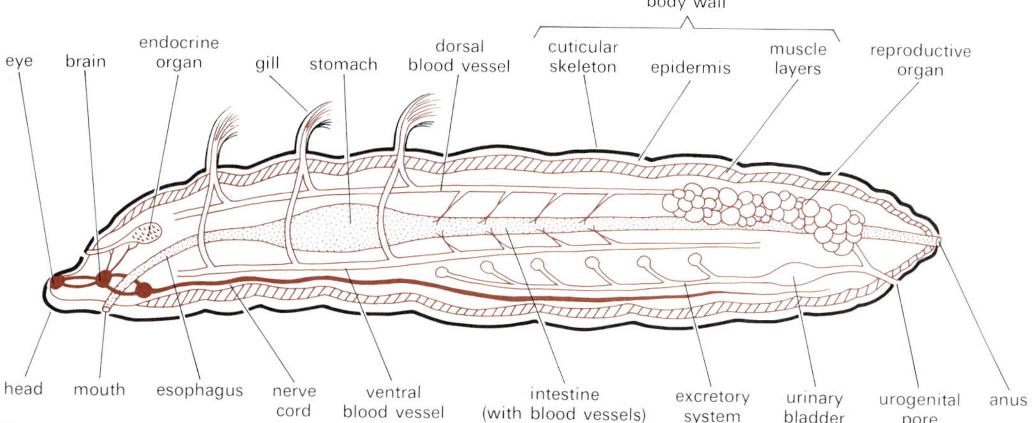

Fig. 7.1 Structure in motile animals. A hypothetical animal and the general position of organ systems. The integumentary and nervous systems are at or near the surface; the alimentary, breathing, excretory, and reproductive systems communicate with the surface; and the circulatory and muscular systems extend throughout the body. Endocrine and skeletal systems if present often range throughout the body as well, and a skeletal system can be on the outside or the inside (see Fig. 7.3).

ture. They are or tend to be *radially symmetrical,* and a distinct head is usually not present. Also, with locomotion absent or limited, nervous systems and sense organs tend to be greatly reduced (Fig. 7.2).

Structural Support

Numerous important characteristics of animals result from the bulkiness and compactness of the body. Since animal cells have comparatively little inherent rigidity, a large collection of such cells is likely to sag to a formless mass under the influence of gravity. Animals therefore require antigravity supports, and they have them in the form of muscular systems and particularly *skeletal systems.* That muscles function not only in motion but also in support is well illustrated in animals such as earthworms, which lack a skeleton. The same muscles that move such animals also hold them together and maintain their shapes. Moreover, even an animal with a skeleton would sag out of shape if muscles did not maintain a firm organization. Conversely, that skeletons function in support as well as locomotion is also clear. A large, heavy animal without rigid supports could neither hold its shape nor propel itself forward by muscles alone.

Fig. 7.2 Symmetry of sessile animals. Related distantly to earthworms, sessile feather-duster worms live in attached tubular housings and project feathery food-trapping crowns from the open end of the tube. Note the radial symmetry of the crowns. (*Courtesy of D. P. Wilson.*)

A

B

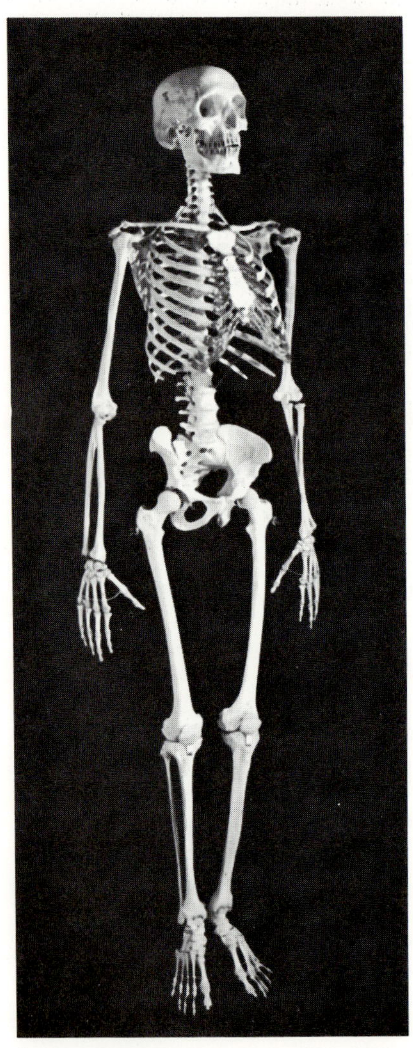

C

Fig. 7.3 Skeletal types. (A) The calcareous exoskeleton of a snail. (B) The horny exoskeleton of an insect. (C) The calcareous endoskeleton of a human female.

Animal skeletons are calcium-containing *calcareous* supports or silicon-containing *silicaceous* supports or variously composed *horny* supports. The skeletons are organized as *exoskeletons* or as *endoskeletons* (Fig. 7.3). In an exoskeleton, exemplified by the shells of clams or snails, the supporting material is on the outside of the animal and envelops the body partly or wholly. In an endoskeleton, as in the cartilage- and bone-possessing vertebrates, the supports are internal, and soft tissues are draped over them. With increasing body size an exterior skeleton rapidly becomes inadequate for the support of deep-lying tissues. Interior supports, however, can buttress all parts of even a large animal. It is not surprising, therefore, that the largest animals are those whose spinal cords are encased in a series of *vertebrae* composed of cartilage or bone (Fig. 7.4). The soft tissues of such *vertebrate* animals, are draped over the vertebrae and the other internal supports, which are similarly composed of cartilage or bone.

Nutrient Acquisition, Internal Transport, Excretion

The bulky construction of animals also creates problems of internal logistics. For example, after food is eaten and digested, the usable nutrients must be distributed to all parts of the animal body. If the distances between the alimentary system and the farthest body parts are appreciable, as in most animals, then some sort of internal transport system becomes essential. The *circulatory systems* of animals meet this requirement (Fig. 7.5). In such networks of vessels, the transport vehicle of food is blood, and one or more muscular pumping organs, or hearts, maintain a circulation of blood throughout the body. Blood is not pigmented in all animals. Where it is, the pigments function specially in transport of oxygen, not food, a circumstance pointing up another problem of internal logistics.

Because of the compact construction of an animal, most of the cells are not in immediate contact with the external environment. Yet all cells require environmental oxygen for respiration, and every cell also must release waste substances to the environment. In the majority of animals, blood in the circulatory system again serves as the main traffic vehicle between the environment and the interior of the body. In animals such as earthworms and frogs, exchange of materials between blood and the external environment can occur through the whole skin, which is thin and permeable. In many animals, however, the *integumentary system* is elaborated more complexly and is relatively impermeable. Animals so covered can exchange materials with the environment only at restricted areas, where surface thinness and permeability are preserved and the blood supply is particularly abundant. For protection, such thin and sensitive areas are frequently tucked well into the body. These areas represent parts of the *breathing* and the *excretory systems.* Gills and lungs are the main types of oxygen collectors, but these organs also contribute importantly to waste excretion. Serving primarily in excretion are kidneys and other functionally equivalent types of organs (see Fig. 7.5).

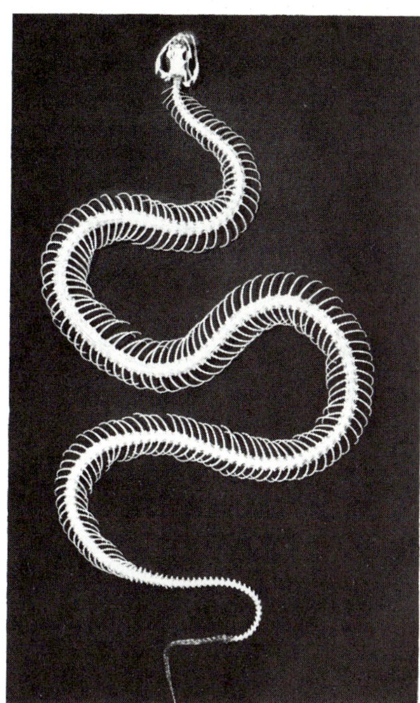

Fig. 7.4 Vertebrae. The backbone, or vertebral column, of vertebrates consists of many interlocking vertebrae. Note the elongated vertebral column of the snake skeleton and the absence of limbs. (*Ward's Natural Science Establishment, Inc.*)

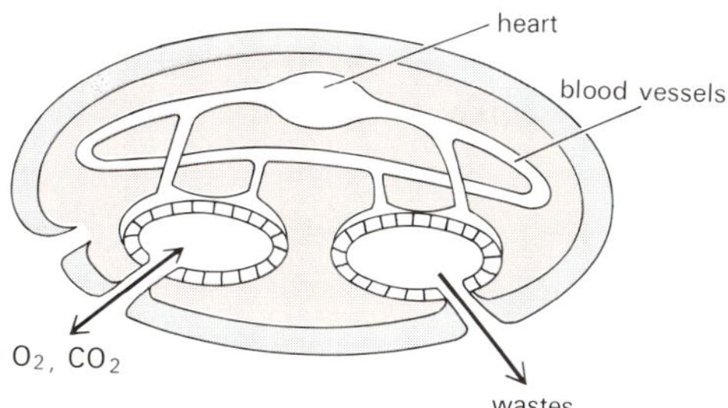

Fig. 7.5 Surface structure and animal complexity. In complexly structured animals, as symbolized here, the surface layers are generally thick and impermeable, and the breathing and excretory surfaces usually are parts of specialized, interiorized organ systems. Internal transport of materials is accomplished by distinct circulatory systems.

Reproduction

Bulk and complex organization affect yet another aspect of animal nature, namely, the pattern and process of reproduction. Like plants, animals too possess *reproductive systems* that manufacture sperms and eggs and thereby contribute to the formation of fertilized eggs. Yet the development of such eggs must be considerably more complex than in plants, for animal development must produce elaborate body parts that plants do not possess: nervous systems, muscular systems, skeletal supports with jointed components, alimentary structures—all those, in short, which are required in a way of life based on heterotrophism and locomotion.

Fig. 7.6 Animal development. Stages in the life cycle of Amphibia symbolize the main stages in the sexual development of animals generally. (A) Egg; (B) embryo; (C) larva; (D) adult. The transition from embryo to larva is achieved by hatching; that from larva to adult, by metamorphosis. The photographs are not reproduced on the same scale. (*Courtesy of R. H. Noailles.*)

Animal development actually does occur in a uniquely characteristic manner. Two major distinguishing features are the *embryo* and, typically, the *larva*. The embryonic phase starts with the fertilized egg and usually terminates in a process of *hatching*. The following larval phase then continues up to *metamorphosis*, or transformation to the adult (Fig. 7.6). Some animals, including birds, human beings, and all other mammals, develop without metamorphosis. Here individuals are transformed gradually during development from embryos to adults.

Heterotrophism and Structural Complexity

All major aspects of animal nature evidently can be considered consequences of the basic conditions of heterotrophism and great structural complexity. As noted, these two conditions at once necessitate the presence of nervous, muscular, skeletal, alimentary, circulatory, excretory, breathing, and integumentary systems. And if to these we add a reproductive system and in some cases also an endocrine system, we have a complete list of all the architectural ingredients that compose an animal. Implied also is a good deal about how an animal moves, behaves, feeds, develops, copes with its environment—in short, pursues life. Moreover, we know in broad outline how the structural ingredients must be put together to form a sensibly functioning whole. As suggested in Fig. 7.1, some of the organ systems must be in surface positions in whole or in part (integumentary, nervous); others can lie deep but must at least communicate with the surface (alimentary, breathing, excretory, and also reproductive); and still others must extend through all portions of the body (skeletal, circulatory, nervous, endocrine).

On the basis of such a preliminary sketch, the fundamental anatomy of a motile, elongated animal can be visualized as a complex tube that has a triple-layered construction. The outermost layer of the tube is the body wall, which includes mainly the integumentary system and parts of the nervous system. The innermost layer, which encloses the open channel through the tube, is represented chiefly by the alimentary system. And the bulky middle layer contains all other organs and systems. Such a triple-layered picture of animal architecture actually is more than a rough analogy; for at an early stage of development most animal embryos do consist of just three layers, one inside the other and each originally not more than one cell thick. From the outside inward these *primary germ layers* are the *ectoderm,* the *mesoderm,* and the *endoderm* (Fig. 7.7). Later they each proliferate greatly and give rise to the triple-layered adult. Ectoderm forms, for example, the integumentary and nervous systems. Mesoderm develops in part into the muscular, circulatory, and reproductive systems. And endoderm produces the alimentary system. Other systems arise from different germ layers in different animal groups.

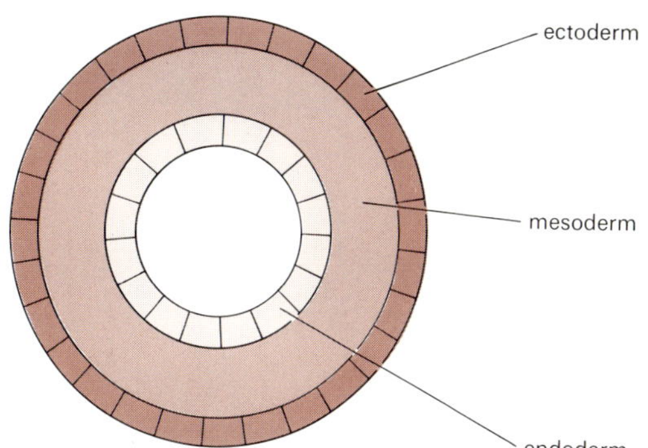

Fig. 7.7 Primary germ layers. These embryonic layers will give rise to the triple-layered "tube" of the adult body (as in Fig. 7.1). Ectoderm generally forms epidermis and nervous system; endoderm forms the alimentary system; and mesoderm develops into muscular, circulatory, and reproductive systems. The other systems arise from different germ layers in different animal groups.

ANIMAL TISSUE

As in plants, the cells that form animal tissues and organs are specialized and often arranged in discrete layers. In contrast to plant cells, those of animals typically possess centrioles and, except for those in direct contact with the external environment, lack substantial protective coverings outside their cell membranes.

Most animals are structurally more complex than plants and usually have a much greater diversity of specialized cells. Nevertheless, most tissues of most animals can be classified either as *connective tissues* or as *epithelia.* Not normally included in this classification are three specific tissues, nerve, muscle, and blood.

Connective Tissues

Connective tissues are identified by comparatively widely separated cells, the spaces between the cells being filled with various fluid or solid materials. Another identifying characteristic is the relatively unspecialized nature of the cells. With appropriate stimulation, they can transform from one connective-tissue cell type to another. In this respect the cells are roughly equivalent to the parenchyma cells of plants.

The most fundamental variant of the connective tissues is *fibroelastic tissue* (Fig. 7.8), containing large numbers of threadlike fibers, some tough and strong, others elastic. These fibers are suspended in fluid and form an irregular, loosely arranged meshwork. The cells of the tissue are dispersed throughout the mesh, and they secrete materials that give rise to the fibers outside them.

The cells are of various types. Many are *fibrocytes,* generally spindle-shaped and believed to be

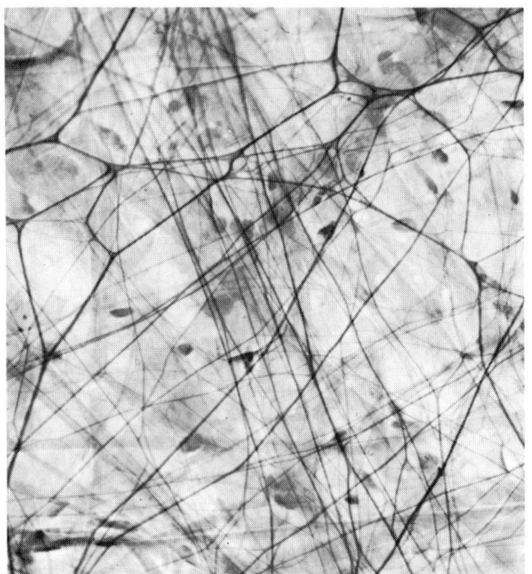

Fig. 7.8 Fibroelastic connective tissue. Fibers form a network, and the cells (small dark dots) secrete the fibers and are embedded in the network (×500). (*General Biological Supply House, Inc.*)

the chief fiber-forming cells. Others, the *histiocytes,* are capable of amoeboid motion and of engulfing foreign bodies (such as bacteria in infected regions). Also present are *fat cells* and, above all, *mesenchyme cells.* The latter are undeveloped and relatively quite unspecialized. They form all the connective tissues of an embryo and later give rise to the various cell types present in adult connective tissues. Thus it is possible to define connective tissues as all those that have a mesenchymal origin in the embryo (Fig. 7.9).

In many animals, mesenchyme cells "left over" from embryonic stages play an important role in healing and regeneration. The cells can migrate to injured body regions and contribute to the redevelopment of lost body parts and to scar-tissue formation. Actually, most fibroelastic tissues can likewise transform one into the others. For example, a fibrocyte might become a fat cell, then perhaps a histiocyte, then a fibrocyte again. The specializations of any of these cells evidently are not fixed.

By virtue of its cellular components, fibroelastic tissue functions in food storage and in body defense against infection and injury; and by virtue of its fibers, the tissue is a major binding agent that holds one body part to another. For example, fibroelastic tissue connects skin to underlying muscle. The tough fibers provide connecting strength, yet the elastic fibers still permit the skin to slide over the muscle to some extent.

The relative quantities of cellular and fibrous components can vary greatly, and on the basis of such variations one can distinguish other types of connective tissues. For example, *tendons* are dense

Fig. 7.9 Connective-tissue cell types. (A) Mesenchyme cells in tissue culture (×5000). (B) Histiocyte from the skin of a monkey. Note the large, irregularly shaped nucleus containing darkly stained chromatin.

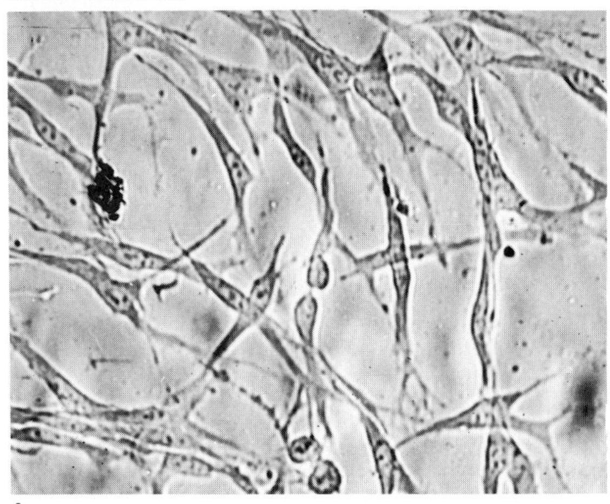

A

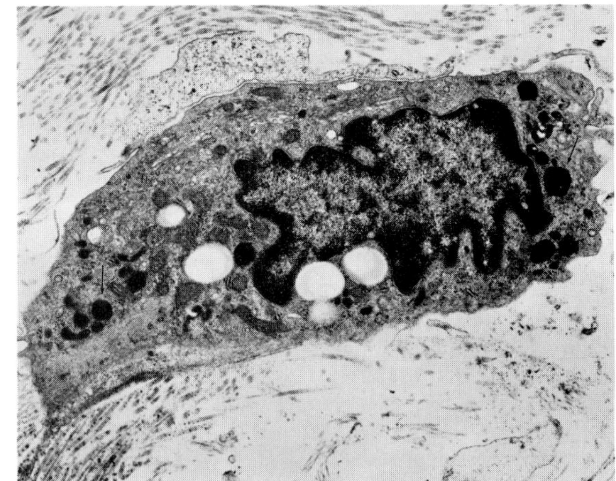

B

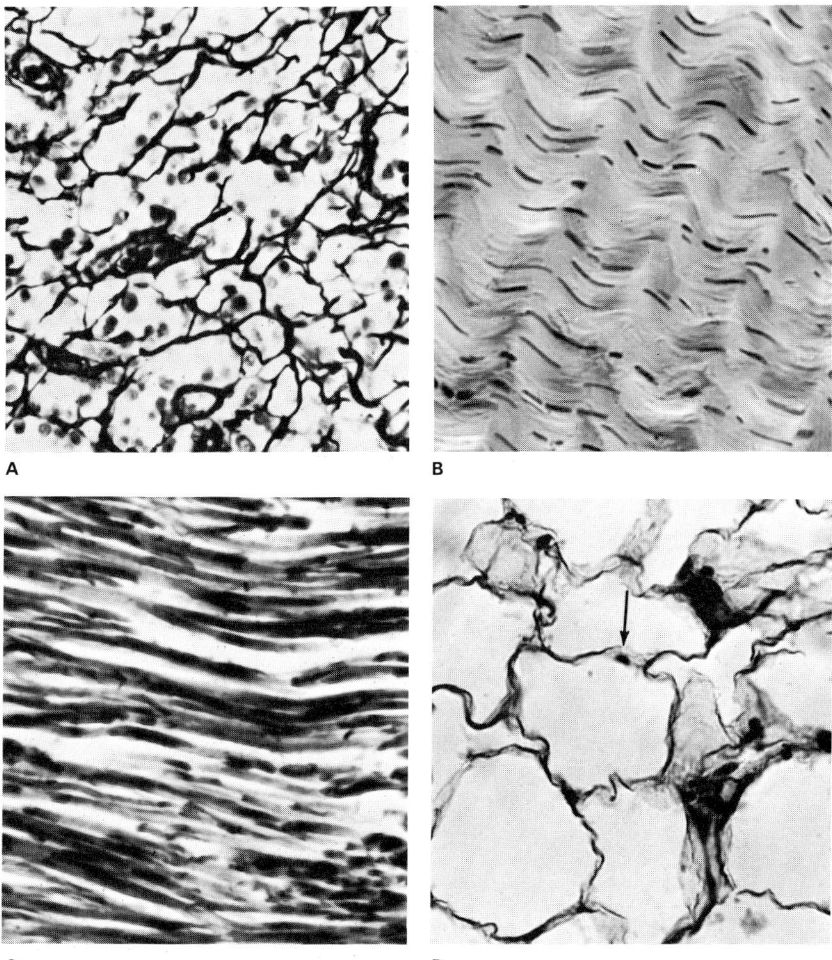

Fig. 7.10 Variants of fibroelastic connective tissue. (A) Reticular tissue, composed of fibrous and cellular components. This type of tissue is found in lymph nodes and lungs, and in preadult stages is also a forerunner of mature fibroelastic tissue. (B) Tendon. (C) Ligament. (D) Adipose cells. The whitish, transparent material filling most of these cells is fat. Arrow points to the darkly stained nucleus of a cell.

tissues containing only fibrocytes and tough fibers, the latter being arranged as closely packed parallel bundles (Fig. 7.10). Tendons typically connect muscles to parts of the skeleton. A *ligament* is similar to a tendon, except that both tough and elastic fibers are present and are arranged in more or less irregular manner. Another variant of fibroelastic tissue is *adipose tissue,* of which fat cells are the most abundant components. Each fat cell contains a large fat droplet that fills almost the entire cellular space. A collection of such cells has the external appearance of a continuous mass of fat. Still other variants of fibroelastic tissue are known.

Many animals possess *jelly-secreting* connective tissues. The cells in such cases are mesenchymal and as these secrete gelatinous substances, they become separated from each other more and more. Mesenchymal jelly tissue can become quite bulky, as in jellyfishes, for example. Such tissues also occur abundantly in numerous other animals (for example, around and in human eyes).

In some connective tissues, the cells secrete organic and especially inorganic materials that form solid precipitates around the cells. The cells thus appear as islands embedded in hard intercellular deposits. The chief variants of this tissue type are *cartilage,* encountered in several invertebrate groups and in all vertebrates, and *bone,* characteristic of vertebrates (Fig. 7.11). Both cartilage and bone arise from mesenchymal cells, and both func-

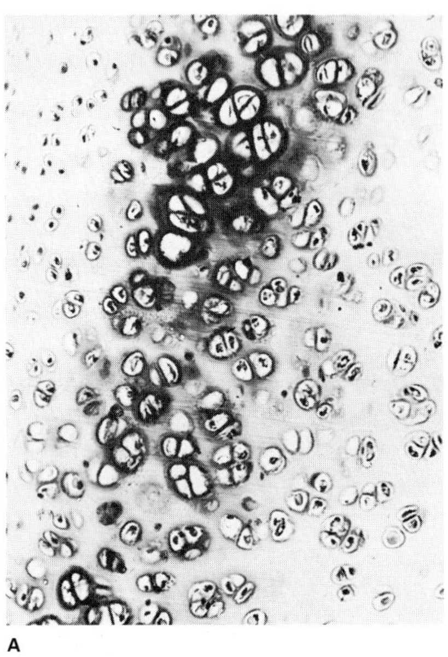

A

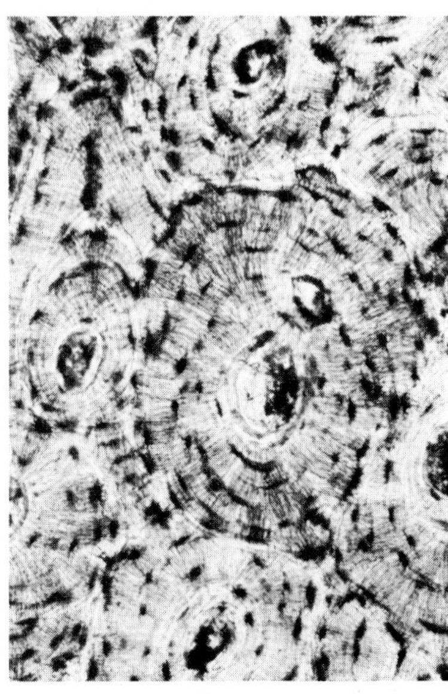

B

Fig. 7.11 Cartilage and bone. (A) The many cartilage-forming cells are surrounded by their own secretions. (B) Bone-forming cells are in the dark patches, arranged in concentric patterns. Hard bone substance appears light. (*A, General Biological Supply House, Inc.; B, Ward's Natural Science Establishment, Inc.*)

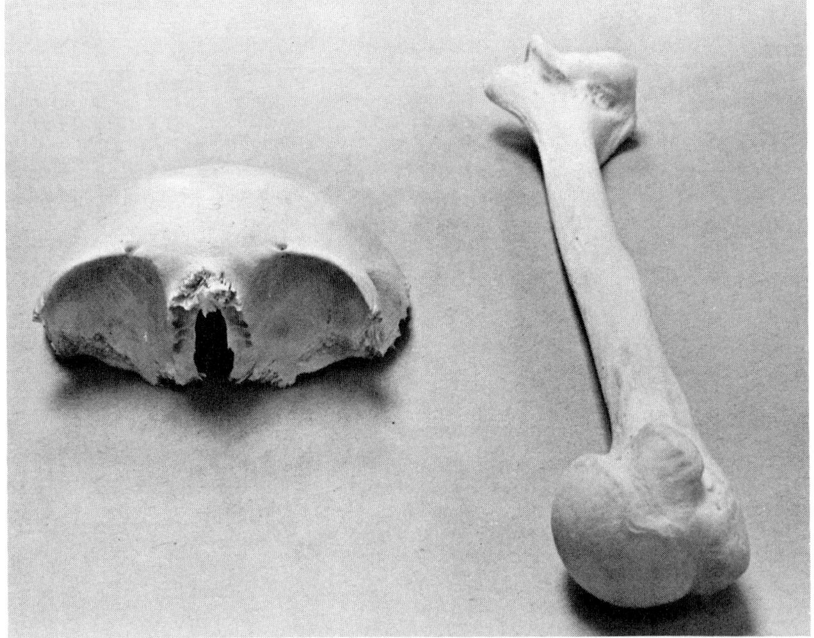

Fig. 7.12 Dermal and replacement bone. Left, temporal bone of a human skull. Like most bones of the skull, the temporal is a dermal bone. Right, humerus of a human skeleton. This replacement bone extends from the shoulder to the elbow. (*Len West, Rhode Island College Art Department.*)

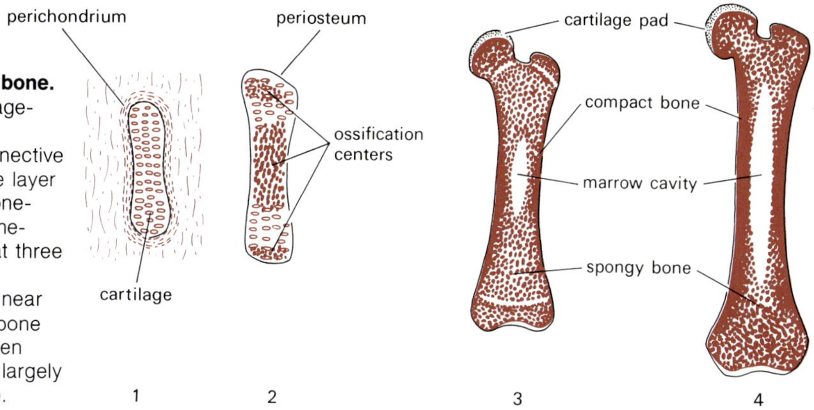

Fig. 7.13 Formation of replacement bone. A cartilage rod is first shaped by cartilage-forming and cartilage-destroying cells produced from the perichondrium (connective tissue) (1). This then becomes a tissue layer called the periosteum that produces bone-forming and bone-destroying cells. Bone-forming cells secrete bone substance at three ossification centers (2). Spongy bone replaces all cartilage except in regions near joints (white bands of 3). In a mature bone (4), cartilage layers near joints have been replaced by bone, and spongy bone is largely replaced by compact bone (solid color).

tion in support and in protection. For example, the long bony rods of the appendages support other tissues around them, and the flat bony plates of the skull cover and protect the underlying brain.

Among vertebrates, cartilage is the only skeletal tissue in types such as lampreys and sharks. In other vertebrates, people included, the skeleton is largely bony, bone developing in two ways. Most of the skull and part of the pectoral girdle—skeletal parts that consist of flat plates and lie close to the body surface—arise as *dermal bones,* directly from the connective tissue in the inner layers of the skin (Fig. 7.12). All other skeletal parts—those that form deep-lying and predominantly elongated supports—develop as *replacement bones;* they are first laid down as cartilage, which is replaced later by bone substance (Fig. 7.13). In people, such replacement of cartilage by bone is usually not complete until approximately the twentieth year of life. A few regions do not become bony at all, for example, the cartilages of the nose and the outer ears.

Epithelia

As a group, the connective tissues serve largely as a structural framework of the animal body. By contrast, the primarily functional parts of an animal are formed chiefly by the epithelial tissues. An epithelium is a tissue in which the cells adhere directly to one another and form single-layered sheets, multilayered sheets, or irregular, compact, three-dimensional masses.

Epithelia that form sheets generally rest on *basement membranes,* flat networks of tough fibers secreted as supporting fabrics (Fig. 7.14). Sheets consisting of single layers of cells are called *simple* epithelia (Fig. 7.15). Distinctions between them are made mainly on the basis of cell shape. If the cells are flat and joined along their edges, the tissue is a "pavement" or *squamous* epithelium. Many tissue membranes and the surface layer of the skin of

Fig. 7.14 Basement membranes. The wavy, dark line (indicated by the arrow) is the basement membrane underlying epidermal cells of monkey skin. The epidermis of skin is an example of a stratified epithelium (see Fig. 7.16).

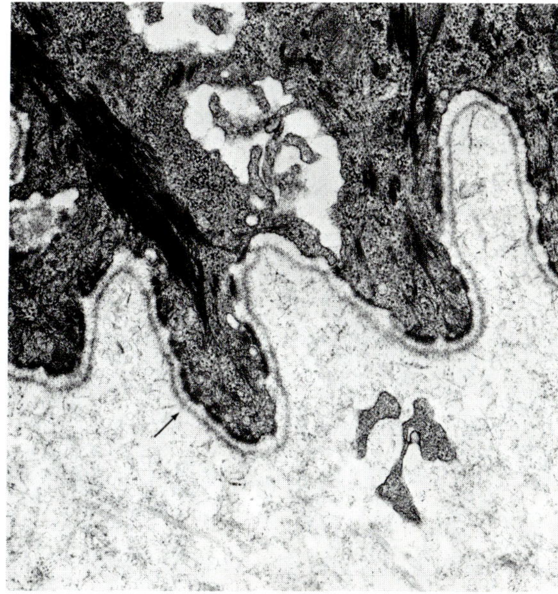

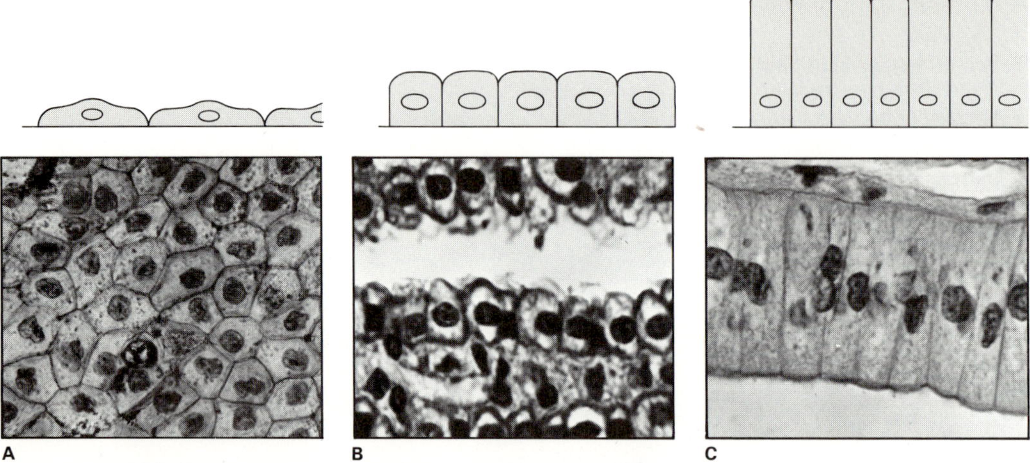

Fig. 7.15 Epithelia. (A) Squamous epithelium, diagram of cross section and photograph of surface view of frog epidermis. Note close packing of cells, flat shapes, and angular outlines produced by mutual pressure of cells (×1000). (B) Cuboidal epithelium, diagram and photo of cross section of lining of tubule in kidney (×1400). (C) Columnar epithelium, diagram and photo of intestinal tissue.

many animals are of this type. If the cells have the shape of cubes, the tissue is a *cuboidal* epithelium. The walls of ducts and glands frequently consist of such tissues. If the cells are prismatic and are joined along their long sides, a *columnar* epithelium is formed. In many animals, this type occurs in, for example, the innermost (digestive-juice-secreting) layer of the intestine.

If several epithelial layers of a given type are stacked as a multilayered sheet, the term *stratified epithelium* is often applied. The mammalian epidermis, the outermost tissue of the skin, is a good ex-

Fig. 7.16 Stratified epithelia and skin. (A) Section of skin of frog tadpole, showing stratified epidermis (dark tissue) and connective tissue dermis under it. Note progressive flattening of epidermal cells toward skin surface (×1500). (B) Section through lining of human uterus. This lining tissue resembles the epidermis of skin. Again note flattening of cells toward surface (×50). (C) Mammalian skin. Note the thick protective layer of dead, keratinized cells at the top. This layer has been produced by living epidermal cells (the dark tissue layer that runs diagonally through the center of the photo). Keratin is a tough, fibrous protein. The dermis underlies the epidermis at the bottom of the photo. Parts of the duct of a sweat gland can be seen meandering from the dermis through the epidermis to the skin surface (×50).

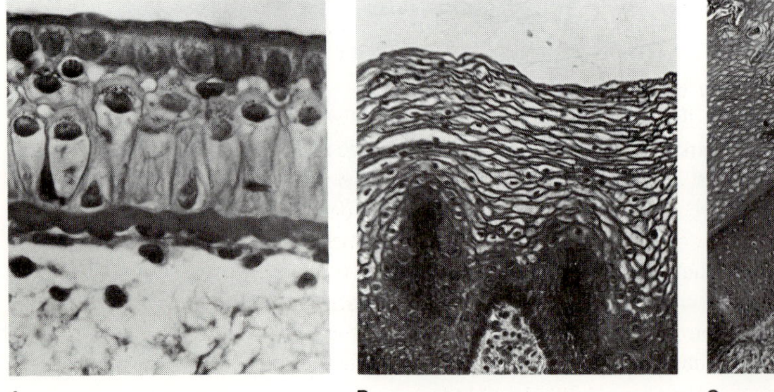

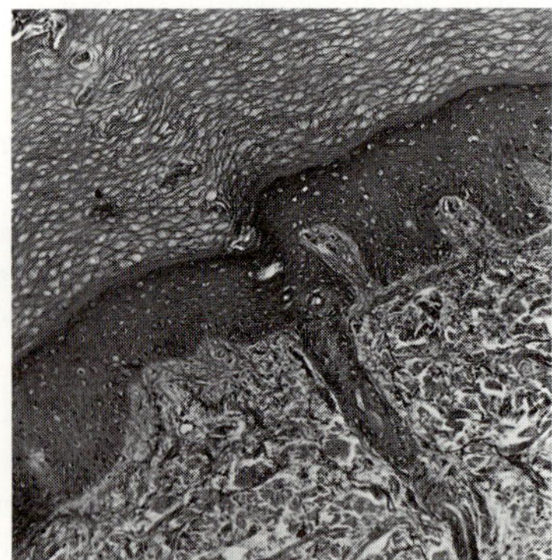

A B C

ample of a mixed stratified epithelium; the cells are squamous along the outer surface and become increasingly cuboidal with greater distance from the surface (Fig. 7.16).

In contrast to the connective tissues, the epithelia are all fairly highly specialized. Once their cells are mature, they do not change in their basic structural characteristics. Also, by the time maturity is reached, the cells have acquired given fixed functions that they then perform throughout the life of the animal.

Blood, Nerve, Muscle

As already noted, blood, nerve, and muscle cannot be classified strictly as either connective or epithelial tissue. Actually they share certain characteristics of both. Blood is generally like a connective tissue in that it contains cells and extensive intercellular deposits, fluid in this case (see also Chap. 18). But although some of the blood cells have a mesenchymal origin, some do not. Nerve tissue, on the contrary, has an epithelial origin, and it resembles an epithelium in some respects. But in others—for example, its frequent netlike arrangement—it does not (Fig. 7.17 and see Chap. 18). Muscle tissue has a mesenchymal origin, yet adult muscle resembles epithelium more than connective tissue. Muscle is usually the most abundant tissue in animals. In people, for example, as much as two-thirds of the total body weight is muscle weight.

Muscle tissues occur as *smooth, striated,* and *cardiac* types (Fig. 7.18). In the smooth variety, the cells are elongated and spindle-shaped, and groups of such cells may be oriented in parallel, forming a layer. In vertebrates, smooth muscle is generally not connected to the skeleton and is not under voluntary nervous control.

Striated, "skeletal," or "voluntary" muscle is made up of units called *syncytia.* A syncytium is a multinucleate structure in which individual cells are unseparated by plasma membranes. Each syncytial unit of skeletal muscle is a *muscle fiber,* which develops through repeated divisions of a single cell. Boundaries between daughter muscle cells disappear during development of the fiber. Groups of muscle fibers are enveloped by fibroelastic connective tissue and form a *muscle bundle.* Several of these bundles in turn form a *muscle,* enclosed within a connective tissue sheath of its own. At either end, a muscle may merge gradually with a tendon and connect to a part of the skeleton.

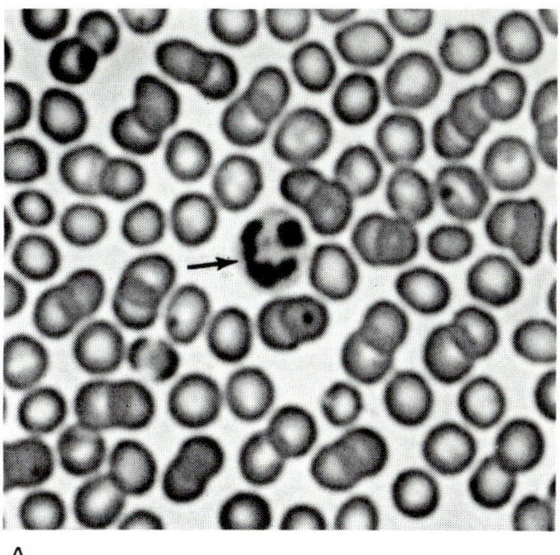

A

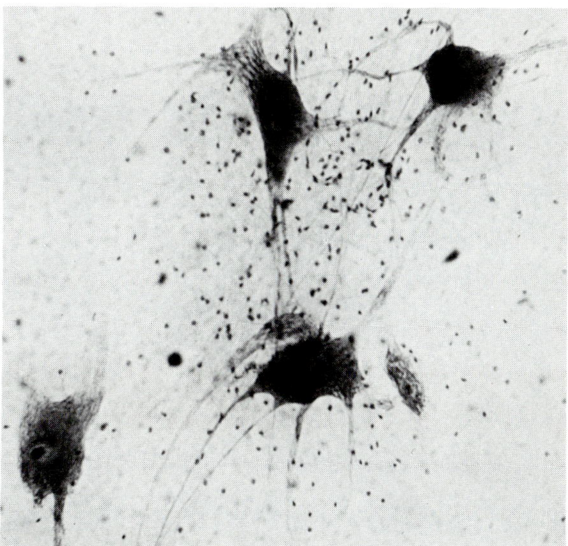

B

Fig. 7.17 Blood and nerve tissue. (A) Human blood. Most of the cells in this light micrograph are erythrocytes, or red blood cells. Their red color is due to hemoglobin, an oxygen-carrying pigment. The arrow indicates a white blood cell. (B) Nerve cells. Note the numerous branches that extend from the main body of these cells.

In vertebrates, all muscle fibers innervated by a single nerve fiber form a *motor unit* (Fig. 7.19). Hundreds of such units can be present in a whole muscle. Each motor unit operates in an all-or-none manner: either it contracts fully or it does not contract at all. The motor units within a whole muscle work in relays, different ones contracting at any given moment.

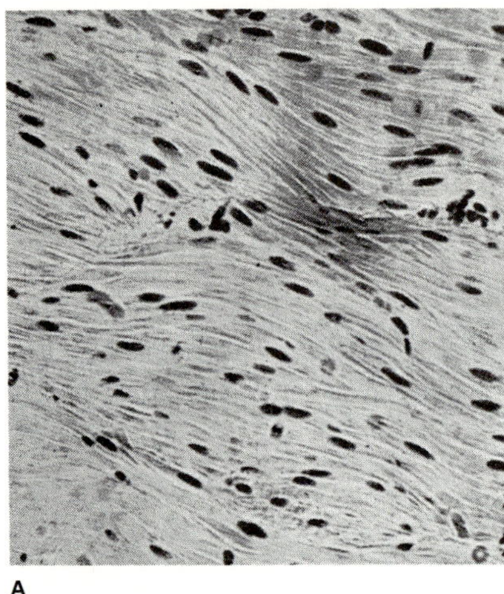

A

Fig. 7.18 Muscle types. (A) Smooth muscle. Note the spindle-shaped cells. (B) A few fibers of skeletal muscle. Note the cross-striations and the nuclei in each fiber. (C) Cardiac muscle. Note the branching fibers, the nuclei, the faint longitudinal fibrils in each fiber, and the cross-striations. (*A, C, Carolina Biological Supply Company; B, Courtesy of M. C. Noailles.*)

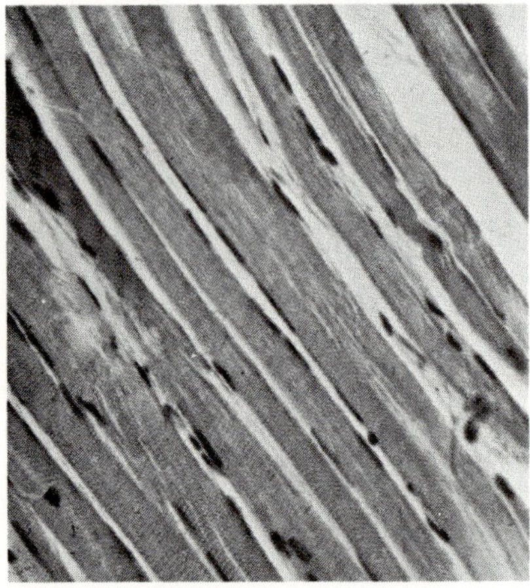

B

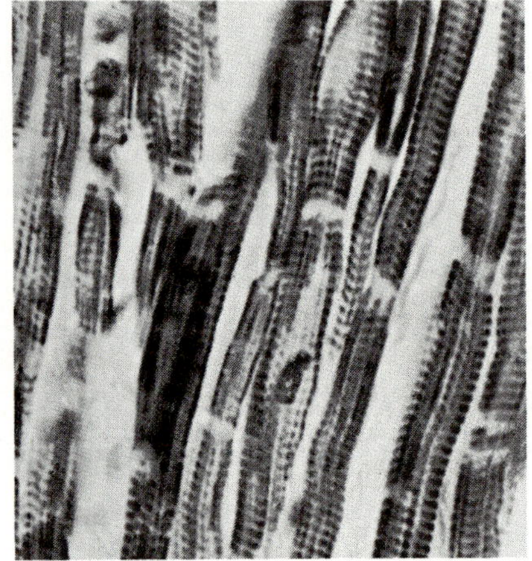

C

Striated muscles operate far more rapidly than smooth muscles. Consequently the striated musculature can produce faster, more abruptly alterable, and more finely adjustable motions. On the other hand, the smooth musculature requires comparatively less energy, and its slower, more sustained motions are well suited in steady, continuing activities—maintenance of digestion through gut-wall contractions, for example.

Cardiac muscle composes the bulk of the heart. Like smooth muscle, it is not normally under voluntary control. Individual cardiac muscle cells are separated by thickened plasma membranes, called *intercalated disks,* which provide added structural support to a muscle that contracts rhythmically and continuously throughout life.

ORGANS AND SYSTEMS

An animal organ typically consists of one or more epithelia and one or more connective tissues. Many organs also contain variable amounts of muscular, nervous, and blood tissues. Epithelia carry out the characteristic specialized functions of organs, and connective tissues provide the necessary structural support. Thus the connective tissues maintain the shape and the position of the organ as a whole, and they carry the nerves, blood vessels, and other ducts that pass to and from the epithelia.

For example, in a compact organ like the liver, connective tissues form an external enveloping layer and also extend into the interior as partitions. The connective tissues thereby make up a

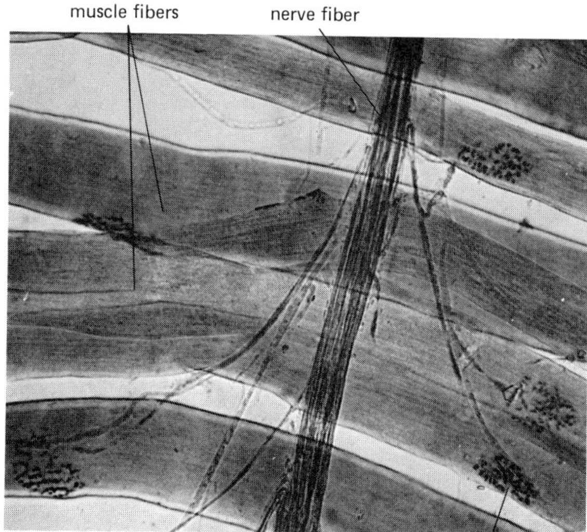

Fig. 7.19 Motor end plates. Note the knobbed terminals of nerve branches on individual muscle fibers. The group of muscle fibers so innervated by a single nerve fiber and its terminal branches makes up a motor unit, a set of muscle fibers that functions together (×2000). (*Ward's Natural Science Establishment, Inc.*)

stroma, a supporting framework that subdivides the liver into islands of epithelial cells (Fig. 7.20). These islands usually represent complete functional units of the organ, and the traffic of materials to and from the units is carried by the surrounding stroma. Groups of such islands often form anatomically recognizable *lobules* or *lobes.*

In sheetlike organs such as skin, epithelia and connective tissues usually are arranged in adjacent layers. For example, vertebrate skin consists of two main layers, an outer *epidermis,* which is a multilayered stratified epithelium, and an inner *dermis,* a multilayered fibroelastic connective tissue (see Fig. 7.16). Each of these layers also gives rise to other tissues and organs in various body regions. Thus the epidermis produces series of glandular ingrowths into the dermis (for example, excretory *sweat glands,* oil-secreting *sebaceous glands*), as well as numerous outgrowths such as beaks, claws, hoofs, nails, scales, feathers, and hair. The dermis produces dermal bones, as noted earlier (the scales of fishes are included here), as well as teeth, combs, and wattles in birds. In effect, the skin as a whole, or *integument,* is not merely a single organ but an integrated group of numerous organs; it is an organ system.

In tubular organs such as the gut, epithelia and connective tissues are again arranged in alternating layers. For example, the wall of the mammalian small intestine consists of four main layers formed by at least six or seven different tissues (Fig. 7.21). The innermost layer is the *mucosa,* which contains a surface layer of simple columnar epithe-

Fig. 7.20 Mammalian liver. In this section of a pig liver are seen a few of the epithelial lobules, separated from each other by layers of the connective tissue stroma. Branches of the hepatic portal vein in the stroma carry blood to a lobule. Blood then passes freely through the canal-like spaces between the strands of lobule cells and it is eventually carried off by a branch of the hepatic vein, seen as a large, clear space in the center of a lobule (×200). (*Courtesy of M. C. Noailles.*)

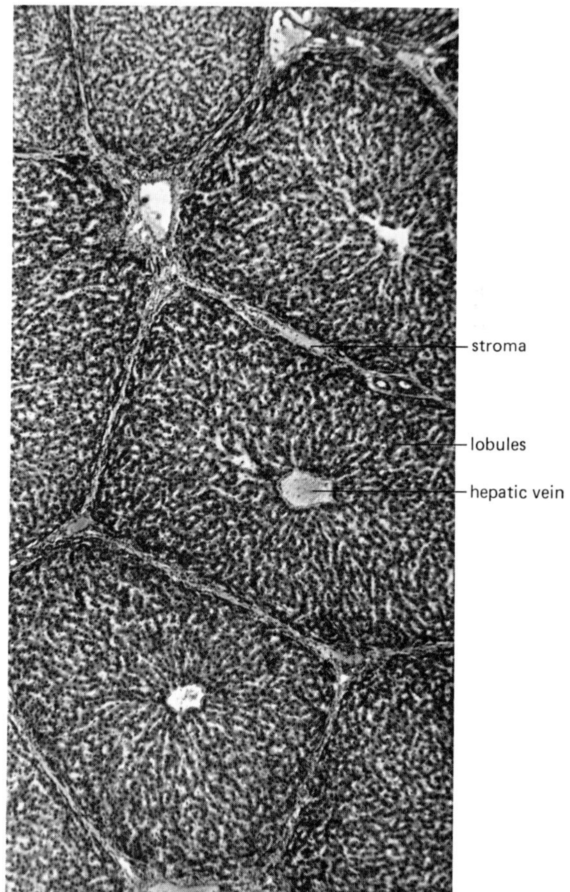

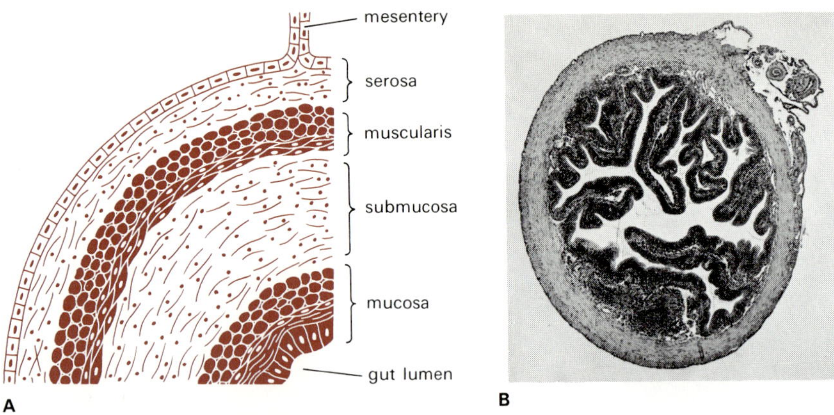

Fig. 7.21 Mammalian intestine. (A) A cross section through a portion of the intestinal wall. The mucosa, adjacent to the lumen (gut cavity), consists of columnar epithelium, connective tissue, and thin layers of muscles; the submucosa is made up of connective tissue, nerves, and blood vessels; the muscularis has thick layers of inner circular and outer longitudinal muscles; and the serosa is composed of connective tissue and squamous epithelium, the latter continuous with a membrane (mesentery) that holds the whole intestine in place. (B) Section through the intestine, showing the highly folded condition of the mucosa. (*B, Ward's Natural Science Establishment, Inc.*)

lium and a sublayer of fibroelastic connective tissue. Its chief function is to complete the digestion of foods and to absorb the digested nutrients from the cavity of the gut. Adjoining the mucosa is the *submucosa*, a substantial layer of fibroelastic connective tissue that contains numerous blood vessels, lymph vessels, and nerve fibers. The function of the submucosa is to transfer nutrients from the mucosa to the blood and lymph circulations for further distribution to other body parts. Surrounding the submucosa is the *muscularis*, the chief muscle tissue of the gut wall. This tissue, composed of smooth muscle, contains an inner circular and an outer longitudinal sublayer. More nerve tissue is present between these two muscle layers. The muscularis maintains the tubular shape of the gut and produces a series of gut movements that play an important role in digestion. The outermost layer of the intestinal wall is the *serosa*, composed of an inner sublayer of fibroelastic tissue and an outer sublayer of squamous epithelium. The serosa as a whole is the limiting membrane of the gut, and it is continuous with the membranes that keep the entire intestine in place in the body.

All these tissues of the small intestine cooperate in performing the single group function of food processing. A series of other organs, each similarly constructed from two or more tissues, carries out other functions of food processing. Included here are, for example, mouth, stomach, liver, pancreas, salivary glands, large intestine, and others. Together these organs form the alimentary system (see Fig. 2.10). Similar structural and functional integration exists between organs constituting all other organ systems.

Most animals are structurally simpler than we are and lack one or more of the 10 organ systems described earlier. For example, worms have no skeletal systems; many animals lack circulatory, breathing, and excretory systems; and many animals lack endocrine systems. In such structurally simpler animals, as indeed also in plants, the functions performed elsewhere by systems are performed by individual cells, tissues, or organs. As structurally complex animals, we are no better or worse off biologically than the most simply constructed organisms. By themselves, biological complexity or simplicity do not have adaptive value. What is important is how well an organism can survive with the structures it has inherited.

All well-adapted organisms, simple or complex, are self-maintaining, distinct units. As such, individual organisms are the most readily identifiable units of the living world. Regardless of its complexity, however, no individual organism can be entirely self-sufficient. Although they often are not apparent, very real and powerful bonds unite organisms with each other. Such bonds are predominantly biological, not physical, and they create larger living units at higher organizational levels. This consideration leads to our next topic.

Review Questions

1 Show in some detail how holotrophic nutrition and the requirement of locomotion determine and influence the characteristics of all other aspects of animal nature. As far as you can, contrast such typically animal attributes with those generally considered to be characteristic of plants.

2 In what architectural respects are moving animals generally different from sessile ones?

3 Name the various organ systems of human beings and identify familiar organs that belong to each of these systems. Show how each system contributes specifically to metabolism and self-perpetuation.

4 What is a connective tissue? Describe the makeup of several types of connective tissue, and state their general function.

5 What is an epithelium? List several variants of this type of tissue. Give specific examples of each. How are tissues joined as organs?

6 Describe the development and structure of dermal and of replacement bone. What types of muscle tissue are there, and how are they distinguished? What makes a muscle or a bone an organ?

Collateral Readings

Bloom, W., and **D. W. Fawcett:** "Textbook of Histology," 10th ed., Saunders, Philadelphia, 1975. This or any similar standard text can be consulted for further information on animal *histology,* the subscience that deals with the tissue and organ structure of animals.

Griffen, D. R., and **A. Novick:** "Animal Structure and Function," 2d ed., Holt, New York, 1970. One of the best summaries of these topics.

Gross, J.: Collagen, *Scientific American,* May 1961. A good review of this important component of connective tissue.

Kessel, R. G., and **R. H. Kardon:** "Tissues and Organs: A Text-Atlas of Scanning Electron Microscopy," Freeman, San Francisco, 1979. Containing hundreds of remarkable scanning electron micrographs, this book illustrates and describes many animal tissues. The book also includes diagrams, light micrographs, and transmission electron micrographs.

Luciano, D. S., A. J. Vander, and **J. H. Sherman:** "Human Structure and Function," McGraw-Hill, New York, 1978. This text introduces all major tissues making up the human body.

Montagna, W.: The Skin, *Scientific American,* February 1965. A good review of the structure and function of this organ system in human beings.

Porter, K. R., and **M. A. Bonneville:** "An Introduction to the Fine Structure of Cells and Tissues," 3d ed., Lea & Febiger, Philadelphia, 1968. An excellent atlas of electron micrographs of animal cells. Detailed commentaries accompany the photographs.

Ross, R., and **P. Bornstein:** Elastic Fibers in the Body, *Scientific American,* June 1971. This article describes the composition and function of fibers in connective tissues.

Chapter 8 Organism to Ecosystem

Learning Objectives

After reading this chapter you should be able to:

1. Define species in a reproductive, evolutionary, and ecological context.
2. Define and state at least one example of a:
   a. syngen
   b. cline
   c. subspecies
   d. species-population
   e. community
3. Define and illustrate polymorphism, dimorphism, and ecological niche.
4. Define and list at least two examples of ecosystems; distinguish between producer, herbivore, carnivore, and omnivore.
5. Construct a diagram that illustrates the cyclic flow of matter between specific producers, herbivores, carnivores, and decomposers; differentiate between trophic level and food chain; construct a diagram that illustrates how an organism can feed at more than one trophic level.
6. Define saprotrophism.
7. Beginning and ending with a molecule of CO_2, construct a diagram that traces the cyclic flow of a single atom of carbon through at least four organisms; do the same for an atom of atmospheric nitrogen.
8. State the functional roles of nitrogen-fixing, nitrate, nitrite, and denitrifying bacteria in the global nitrogen cycle; state the symbiotic relation between legumes and nitrogen-fixing bacteria.
9. Identify the ultimate source of energy for all ecosystems; construct a diagram that depicts the noncyclic flow of energy through at least three trophic levels of a food chain; list at least three ways in which energy is lost to the environment between trophic levels; state one way this loss of energy is reflected in the comparative cost of specific food items in supermarkets.
10. Differentiate between biotic potential and environmental resistance, and state how they interact in determining the growth rates of populations; list and exemplify three kinds of factors that can contribute to environmental resistance.
11. Outline an experiment demonstrating that two species cannot occupy indefinitely the same ecological niche; distinguish between interspecific and intraspecific competition.
12. Differentiate between facultative and obligatory symbiosis; define and illustrate mutualism, commensalism, and parasitism.
13. Define predator and prey; illustrate how the population size of a predator can be influenced by the population size of prey; list at least one example each of an interspecific, an intraspecific, and an abiotic factor that can affect the relative population balance between predator and prey.
14. Define and illustrate territoriality and dominance hierarchies; write a paragraph that explains how these two factors can influence the size of populations.
15. State at least one detrimental and one beneficial effect of emigrations on ecosystems.
16. Write a verbal and a mathematical definition of exponential growth.
17. Differentiate between J- and S-shaped population growth patterns, state an example of each, and distinguish between factors responsible for these two patterns.
18. Define carrying capacity; illustrate how changes in the physical environment can alter the carrying capacity of ecosystems.
19. State and exemplify at least one relationship between population density and optimum yield of biological resources.
20. State and illustrate at least three relationships between species diversity and geography.
21. Write a paragraph describing how living organisms influence nutrient cycling, energy flow, and species diversity in ecosystems.

Every organism invariably depends on the environment, and particularly on other organisms, for some essential product or process; survival requires group association. Such associations are the special concern of the biological subscience of *ecology.*

This chapter deals with two major ecological associations above the level of the organism, the *species* and the *ecosystem.* A species consists of like individuals that live together in *populations.* Groups of populations belonging to several different species form the next higher level, that of the *community.* And a community together with the physical space in which it exists represents an ecosystem.

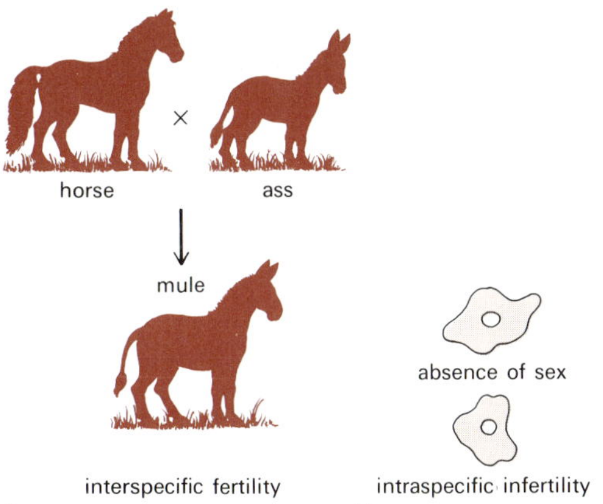

Fig. 8.1 Species definition: exceptions. (A) Horses and asses are distinct species, yet matings between them can occur. (B) Organisms such as *Amoeba proteus* are sexless and thus by definition infertile; nevertheless all individuals belong to the same taxonomic species.

SPECIES

Reproductive Units

The classification of organisms is based primarily on the concept of species. It therefore may seem surprising that biologists have yet to devise a single, all-inclusive, or even wholly satisfying definition of this most important taxonomic unit.

When natural historians began classifying organisms, species were distinguished on purely structural grounds. If, for example, the beaks or feathers of two birds were somehow different, the birds might be classified as distinct species. This practice quickly proved unsatisfactory. Arguments developed over which characteristics should be used as the principal means of species determination. Moreover, almost all individual organisms, even most identical twins, are structurally unique in some respect. When do such differences become sufficiently great to warrant separate species designations? All too often, biologists were unable to come up with a mutually agreeable answer.

A newer definition of species, based primarily on reproductive compatibility, not only has proved more workable than that based on structural criteria but is also more consistent with the results of modern ecological and evolutionary studies. According to the newer definition, a species is a taxonomic unit encompassing all organisms that interbreed in natural environments. The expression *natural environments* is particularly important. Representatives of different species sometimes can be interbred successfully under experimental conditions (Fig. 8.1). The offspring of such crosses are usually sterile. Matings between horses and donkeys, for example, produce infertile *mules.* Similarly, lions and tigers have been interbred in zoos to produce sterile *tiglons* (a tiger is the father) and *ligers* (a lion is the father). Experimental matings between members of different species occasionally yield fertile offspring, as occurs when cabbages and radishes are crossbred.

Nevertheless, the probability that a new species will result from interspecific matings is virtually zero, for such matings almost never occur under natural conditions. Lions and tigers coexisted in much of India until the nineteenth century (Fig. 8.2). They were reproductively isolated, however, largely because of great differences in behavior. Lions roam in groups called *prides,* are more social, and hunt in open plains. Tigers are solitary and frequently remain secluded in forests. Thus, lions and tigers rarely associated under natural conditions. Matings occur only when these organisms are brought together in confined environments. Many other barriers to interspecific breeding exist and will be discussed in Chap. 29.

Despite its general acceptance and unquestioned value, this newer definition of species has a few glaring weaknesses. For example, *asexual* species, such as the unicellular protozoan *Amoeba pro-*

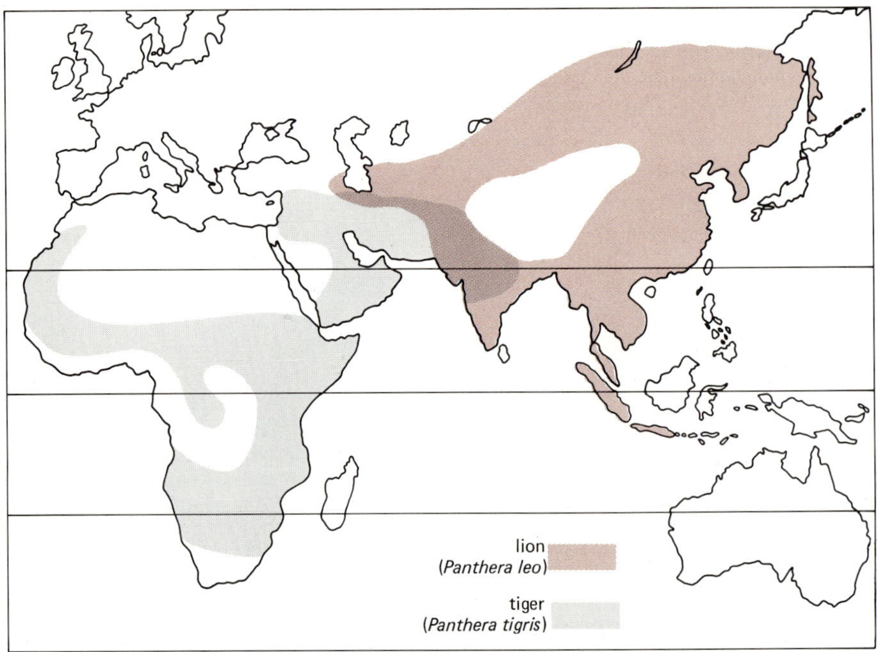

Fig. 8.2 Eighteenth century ranges of lions and tigers. Ranges of lion and tiger overlapped (darkest shading) throughout much of India until the nineteenth century. These two species no longer coexist in natural environments.

teus, do not interbreed at all (see Fig. 8.1). Here biologists continue to distinguish between species almost entirely on the basis of structural differences. Also, some species, certain plants in particular, occasionally interbreed with other species that are structurally quite distinct. Botanists studying breeding interrelationships between oak trees of the Pacific Coast of North America have identified at least six species of the genus *Quercus* that interbreed occasionally with one or more other species of the same genus. Such organisms, which sometimes are termed *semispecies,* have proved exceedingly difficult for taxonomists to classify. Nevertheless, for the vast majority of organisms the newer definition of species holds up well, and reproduction does represent an important unifying link.

Evolutionary Units

Because it is a reproductive unit, each species is also an *evolutionary* unit; since interbreeding has taken place in a species throughout its history, the member organisms are more closely related to each other than to members of any other species. As a result, the members of a species have in common a basic set of structural and functional traits. However, no two organisms are exactly alike, and the members of a species actually differ from each other quite considerably; superimposed on the common traits, *variations* of structure, function, or both, occur in each species (Fig. 8.3).

Variations can be *inheritable* or *noninheritable.* The first are controlled genetically and can be transmitted to offspring. Noninheritable variations are the result of developmental or environmental influences, and they therefore disappear with the death of the individuals that exhibit them. Thus only inheritable variations are significant in determining the lasting traits of a species. An athlete's muscular system is likely to be developed much more than that of the average person. This is a noninheritable variation; the degree of muscular development depends primarily on exercise, not on heredity. By contrast, blood type or skin color are

A

B

Fig. 8.3 Individual variation. A and B are umbrella birds that belong to the same species, *Cephalopterus ornatus,* but are members of different populations. Their structural differences are quite pronounced. Technically these birds are said to belong to different subspecies of the same species.

examples of hereditary variations. They are part of the genetic inheritance from parents and earlier forebears and will in turn influence the traits of future generations (Fig. 8.4).

Some variations appear to be associated with climates and geography. In warm areas, for example, individuals of many animal species tend to have smaller body sizes, darker colors, and longer ears, tails, and other protrusions than fellow members of the same species living in cold climates (Fig. 8.5). Indeed, gradual changes in structural characteristics, called *clines,* sometimes can be observed among members of a species whose range extends from warmer to cooler climates. For example, birds of the Australian species *Seisura inquieta* are 22 per cent larger in cooler southern portions of the continent than in warmer northern regions, and a gradual increase in body size can be observed along a north-to-south gradient (Fig. 8.6).

Such structural variations are usually adaptive

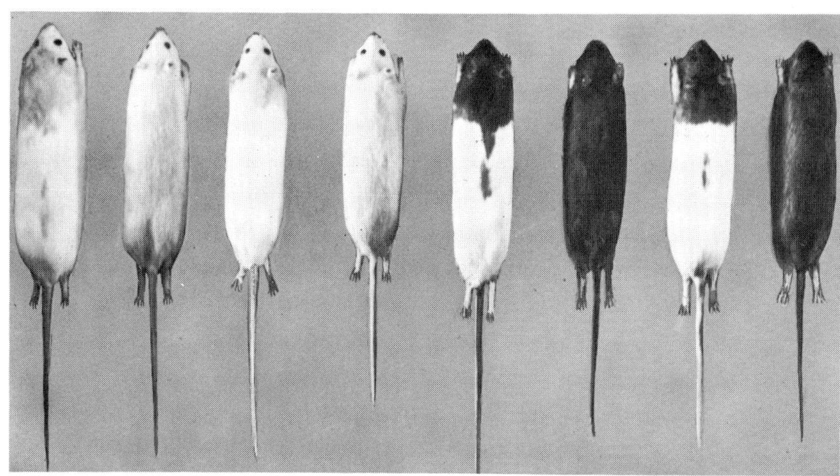

Fig. 8.4 Inheritable variations. These are litter-mate rats produced by the same two parents. Considerable variation in coat color is evident. Such differences are controlled genetically and are superimposed on common basic traits. For example, despite the color differences, all the litter mates are distinctly rats and share not only the traits common to the species but also those specifically characteristic of their breeding line.

A

B

Fig. 8.5 Variations and climate. Evaporation surfaces tend to be larger in warm-climate animals than in corresponding cool-climate ones. For example, the Arabian desert goat shown here (A) has external ears very much larger than those of related types in temperate regions (B).

or advantageous in the different environments. Thus, smaller bodies and longer ears give animals larger skin surfaces relative to body volumes. Surface evaporation is then comparatively rapid, and the resulting cooling effect is of considerable benefit. The converse holds in a cool climate. However, it is often difficult to recognize the adaptive value of a variation, and some variations well may be nonadaptive, without inherent advantage to the possessors.

Most geographic variations in species characteristics are far too irregular for classifications as clines. *Crotalus viridis,* for example, is a species of rattlesnake that exists throughout most of the western United States. However, the body proportions, arrangement of scales, and coloration of these animals vary in a nonclinal pattern in nine different regions (Fig. 8.7). Individuals taken from any of these regions can interbreed, but mating usually occurs only along the boundaries of adjacent zones. Offspring exhibiting mixed characteristics are frequently found along such boundaries.

Taxonomists usually classify such structurally distinct populations as *subspecies* (or *varieties*) and identify them by adding a third name to their genus and species designation. Thus the subspecies of rattlesnake commonly found in the southernmost parts of California is called *Crotalus viridis helleri,* the last name designating the subspecies. Distinguishing characteristics of subspecies usually

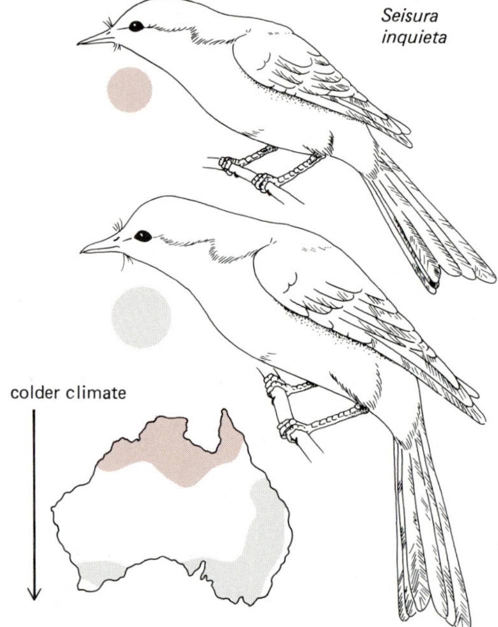

Fig. 8.6 Clines. Three populations of *Seisura inquieta* inhabit Australia. Larger members of the cline are found in cooler southern regions of the continent. Size differences between members of the cline are adaptive. Because they have a lower ratio of exposed body surface to total weight, larger birds conserve heat more efficiently than smaller birds.

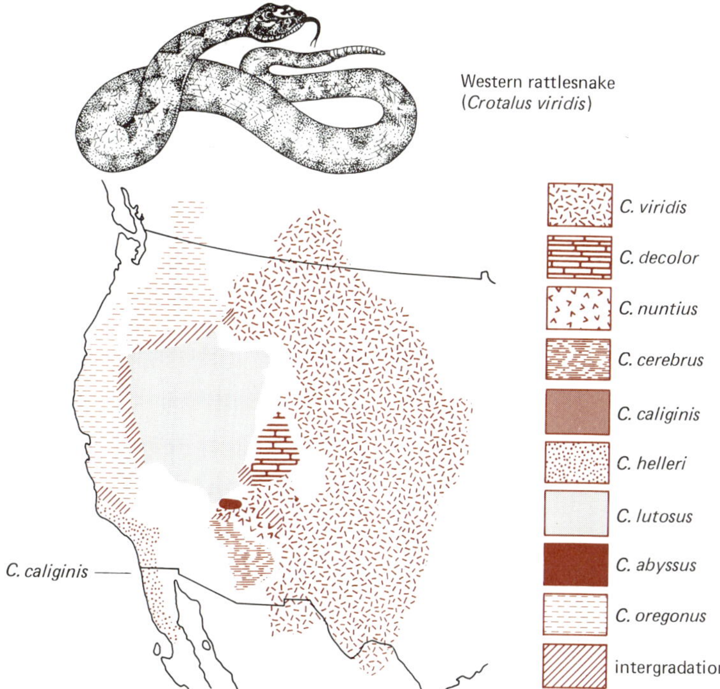

Fig. 8.7 Subspecies. Geographic variation in the western rattlesnake, *Crotalus viridis.*

represent adaptations to unique environmental conditions of a region.

Even within subspecies, individual organisms never are structurally identical. The members of all species and subspecies exhibit a greater or lesser degree of *polymorphism;* they have "many shapes" (Fig. 8.8). For example, a species always includes variant individuals in the form of immature and mature organisms. Often also males and females differ in appearance, a form of polymorphism called *sexual dimorphism.* Polymorphism can be so pronounced that the close relation of two individuals of the same species becomes evident only through careful study. Among social insects, for example, a species can include queens, drones, soldiers, workers, and others, all quite dissimilar in structure. Such instances of polymorphism are expressions of structural *specialization.* And where organisms exhibit great polymorphic diversity, a high degree of functional interdependence usually follows as well. In a colony of social insects, for example, only the whole colony, with representatives of all types of polymorphic variants, is functionally self-sufficient.

Ecological Units

By virtue of being evolutionary units all species are also *ecological* units. Each is defined by its *ecological niche,* its place in nature: it inhabits a certain geographic region, it uses up particular raw materials in that region, and it produces particular by-products and end products. For example, the environment offers numerous opportunities for carnivorous modes of animal existence, all differing from each other in hundreds of fine details. Thus a carnivorous species can subsist by being terrestrial, aquatic, or aerial; sessile or motile; a cold-, temperate, or warm-climate type; a type that hunts in daytime or nighttime; a form that specializes in small prey or large prey. And each such coarse category contains innumerable finer categories of possible carnivorous ways of life. All such different opportunities represent ecological niches, and given species occupy them. Therefore, just as each species is identified by a particular set of structural, functional, and evolutionary characteristics, so it is also identified uniquely by its ecological niche. No two species have precisely identical niches, and

Fig. 8.8 Polymorphism. (A) The Portuguese man-of-war *Physalia*. This coelenterate is a floating colony of numerous individuals of various structural types—feeding, reproductive, protective, and float-forming polymorphs. See also Chap. 33. (B) Ants (as well as bees and other social insects) exhibit polymorphism in that queens (shown here) are winged, whereas all other individuals of a species are wingless. See also Chap. 21. (C) Sexual dimorphism, a special form of polymorphism, is illustrated by the fur seals shown here. The male at right is far larger and more colorful than the female at left. (*A, New York Zoological Society; B, Ward's Natural Science Establishment, Inc,; C, U.S. Fish and Wildlife Service.*)

a given niche cannot be occupied indefinitely by more than one species (Fig. 8.9).

Such niches are associated intimately with geography; in similar kinds of environments, even if widely separated, species with similar ways of life will be found. For example, widely different localities offering similar conditions of soil and climate will support prairies composed of grass species having similar requirements. Prairies in turn offer opportunities for grazing animals, and each prairie region of the world actually has its own animal species filling available grazing niches—antelopes in Africa, bisons in North America, kangaroos in Australia. In like manner, plant and animal species on high mountains occupy similar ecological niches. Several similar niches may also be available in a single territory. For example, the central African plains support not only one but several species of grasses, and not only numerous types of antelopes but also zebras, giraffes, and other grazing species. The ways of life of such species overlap in many respects, but they are not identical in all details; each species normally fills a unique niche.

ECOSYSTEMS

Every species consists of one or more populations, or *species-populations*. Examples of such relatively stable, geographically localized groups are the dandelions in a field, the minnows in a pond, the earthworms in a plot of ground, or the people in a village. Individual organisms multiply and die, emigrate or immigrate, but collectively a population persists. It may split into subpopulations or fuse with adjacent sister populations, yet the basic characteristics of the group as a whole do not thereby change. All members of a population share the

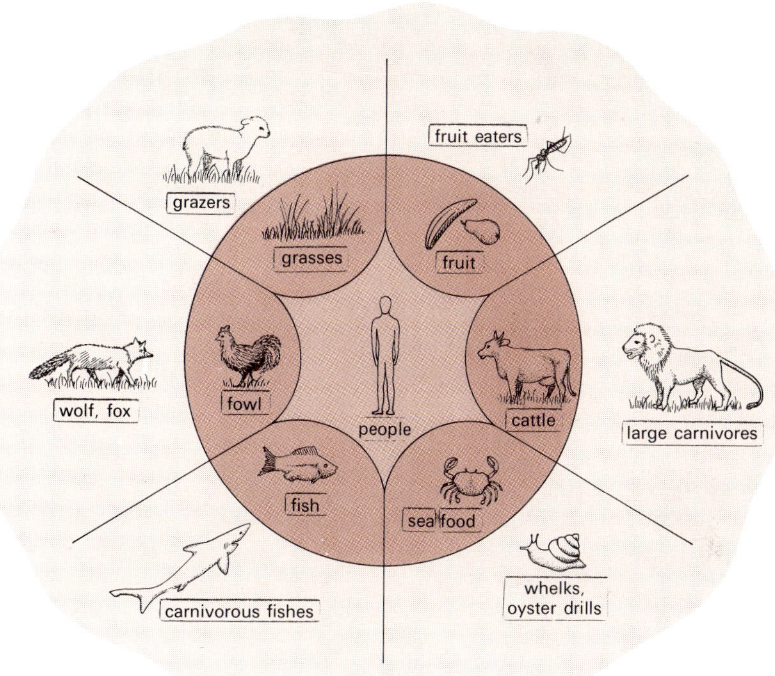

Fig. 8.9 The ecological niche of human beings. It is characterized in part by nutritional requirements shown inside the circle. These food organisms also happen to form parts of the ecological niches of other animals, as indicated outside the circle, but such animals also use foods not used by people. Thus although these niches partly overlap ours, each is nevertheless distinct and characteristic of a particular species. Ecological niches are defined not only by food organisms but also by geographic territory, waste products, structures, and other attributes of species.

same food sources and the same local territory, and the members also interbreed more or less preferentially with one another. Also, interbreeding with members of sister populations occurs fairly often. A population thus is a reproductive cohesive unit, integrated more loosely with other such units.

Localized associations of several populations of different species constitute *communities,* groupings of organisms at the next higher organizational level. Almost always, a community includes an interdependent association of plants, animals, and microorganisms. Communities, together with the physical environments in which they live, represent *ecosystems.* Examples are a pond, a forest, a meadow, a section of ocean shore, a portion of the open sea, a coral reef, or a village with its soil, grasses, trees, people, bacteria, cats, dogs, and other living and nonliving components.

Just as cells, tissues, and organs are specialized in organisms, so populations are specialized in ecosystems. Like the pieces of a jigsaw puzzle, each population has specific structural and functional roles that are interlocked with those of all other populations in an ecosystem.

Structure

Autotrophic organisms compose the structural foundation supporting all other living components of ecosystems. Except for small populations of *chemosynthetic bacteria,* which extract energy from simple inorganic compounds, all autotrophs are photosynthetic; they use the energy of sunlight to combine hydrogen from water and carbon dioxide from air as organic nutrients. Because these nutrients support all other forms of life on earth, autotrophs are termed *producers* (Fig. 8.10).

The total weight, or *biomass,* of the producers in an ecosystem supports heterotrophic *consumers.* Those which feed directly on producers are termed primary consumers, or *herbivores.* These include algae-eating fish in aquatic ecosystems, or elephants, deer, giraffes, zebras, and field mice in terrestrial ecosystems. Most farm livestock, including cattle, chickens, turkeys, and hogs, are descendants of wild herbivores domesticated by our ancestors to serve their nutritional needs.

Other animal populations subsist at secondary, tertiary, and even more distant consumer levels.

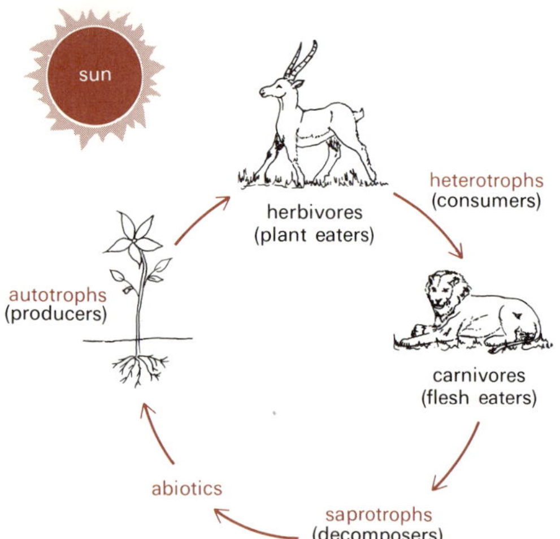

Fig. 8.10 Nutritional structure of an ecosystem. Abiotics represent the physical, nonbiological components of the system. Arrows indicate flow of energy and materials.

All feed on other animals and these are termed *carnivores.* Spiders, sea anemones, praying mantises, sharks, lions, centipedes, and hawks are carnivores of various sizes and types that exist in a variety of ecosystems.

The specific positions that organisms occupy in the producer-consumer structure of ecosystems are called *trophic (feeding) levels,* and the sequences in which nutrients are transferred between these levels are known as *food chains.* For example, organic nutrients are manufactured by grasses, passed on to cattle, and subsequently eaten by people; this sequence forms a relatively simple and short food chain. Grasses, as producers, exist at the base trophic level in the chain; cattle and people are at the second and third trophic levels, respectively.

Some animals feed exclusively at one trophic level on only one or two species. Many animals are less selective and feed simultaneously at more than one trophic level. These make food chains highly complex and variable. For example, an aquatic insect larva may eat algae and in turn be eaten by a small fish. This fish subsequently might be eaten by a larger fish, which in turn might be eaten by a predator bird. In this example, the carnivorous bird exists at the fifth trophic level. However, the bird might also eat another fish that had been subsisting only on algae. In that case the bird would be feeding at the third trophic level (Fig. 8.11). Other animals, human beings included, exist both as herbivores and carnivores and are called *omnivores.*

The ability to feed at more than one trophic level is an important adaptive feature of many organisms. Such organisms can withstand minor changes in the structure of ecosystems and are not forced into immediate extinction if one of their food sources is unavailable for extended periods. Through such adaptability, these populations provide stability to ecosystems and to an extent safeguard such systems against structural collapse.

Matter

Very little new matter comes to the earth from outer space. Meteorites and smaller objects from space, including atomic particles, add to the mass of the earth, but in quantities that are much too insignificant to aid in the support of the total biomass of all living systems. Atoms used in the construction of living organisms today are recycled and used repeatedly in the biomass of subsequent generations.

Fig. 8.11 Possible food chains in a pond. Assume that algae (1) growing on a submerged rock are eaten by an insect larva (2). Further assume that the larva becomes food for a small fish (3), which is then eaten by a larger fish (4). In this example, the algae, larva, small fish, and large fish exist at trophic levels 1 to 4, respectively, and the predator bird (5) exists at the fifth trophic level if it eats the larger fish. However, if the smaller fish subsists only on algae suspended in the pond (6) and the bird eats the smaller fish, the bird will feed at the third trophic level.

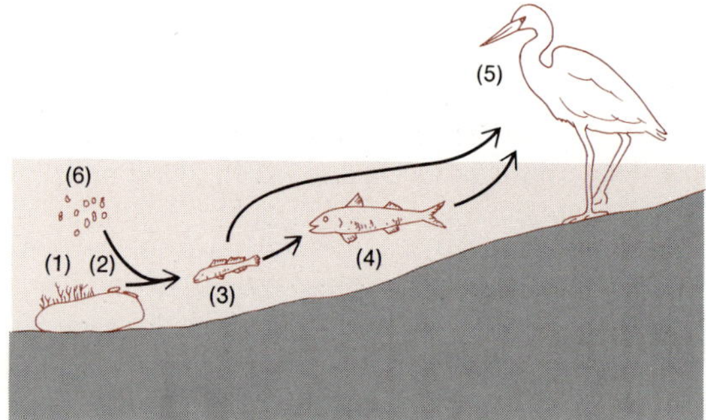

Fig. 8.12 Nutrient cycles and population balance. A large plant population reduces the soil nutrients available (1, 2). This eventually leads to starvation of plants and reduction of their numbers (3). But decomposers break down the dead bodies of plants and other organisms (4), and an increase in the number of living plants therefore can occur again. Through continued repetition of such a cycle the size of the plant population is maintained relatively constant over the long term. Quite similar cycles occur in animal populations.

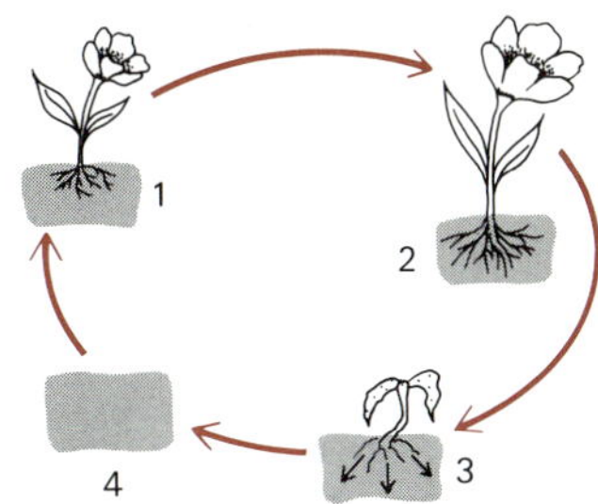

The flow of matter through an ecosystem becomes cyclic largely through another major group of heterotrophs, the *decomposers*, which comprise chiefly the fungi and bacteria (see Fig. 8.10). Most decomposers consume nutrients through a form of heterotrophism called *saprotrophism,* in which hydrolytic enzymes are released into dead organisms or their wastes. Some of the digested products are then absorbed and used by decomposers as nutrients. Among the by-products generated by decomposers are inorganic molecules such as water, carbon dioxide, nitrates, and phosphates. These in turn are used again by producers for the synthesis of most of their cellular components (Fig. 8.12).

The cycle of matter is thereby completed. In obtaining nutrients to support their own existence, decomposers produce inorganic nutrient pools which serve as fertilizers for plants and, in turn, support the existence of all heterotrophs. Two specific examples will provide a better appreciation of how the cyclic flow of matter molds and binds the structural components of ecosystems.

Carbon Cycle

Through their ability to bond together in long chains, carbon atoms form the "backbone" of virtually all organic molecules in living systems. Thus, the availability of carbon is a crucial factor in the maintenance of all populations. Carbon is transferred between organisms of all trophic levels through the *carbon cycle* (Fig. 8.13). Atmospheric carbon dioxide enters plants largely through stomata and is used by chloroplasts in the photosynthetic production of carbohydrates. These molecules then serve as primary fuels in respiration and as the raw materials in the synthesis of other molecular components of plant cells.

Plants serve as sources of carbon-containing compounds for herbivores, and then by becoming food themselves, herbivores constitute sources of organic substances for carnivores. Decomposers obtain carbon-containing nutrients from animal waste or from the bodies of dead plants and animals.

Organisms at each trophic level also break up organic nutrients during respiration, and carbon dioxide is thereby released to the external environment. The methods of CO_2 release vary considerably. In unicellular and other small organisms, CO_2 reaches the exterior directly from the surface of cells. In plants, the gas is expelled through surface cells, stomata, lenticels, and other porous openings. In large animals CO_2 is eliminated chiefly from specialized breathing structures such as gills or lungs. The replenished environmental supply of CO_2 now can be used once again by plants in photosynthesis.

This recycling of carbon dioxide through photosynthesis and respiration is the main but not the only way by which carbon atoms move through ecosystems. Approximately 280 million years ago, the earth entered a period of higher mean temperatures

Fig. 8.13 The carbon cycle.

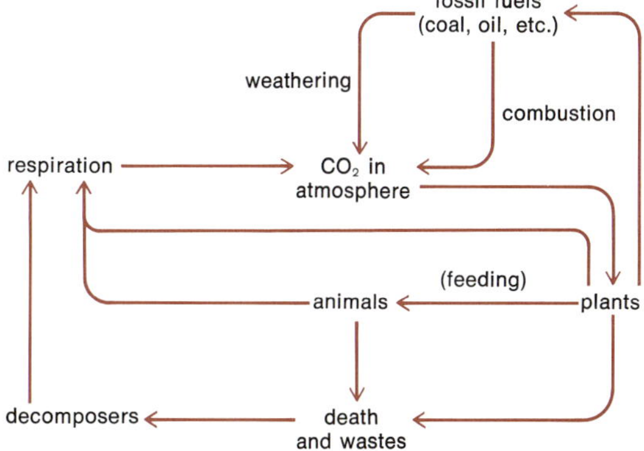

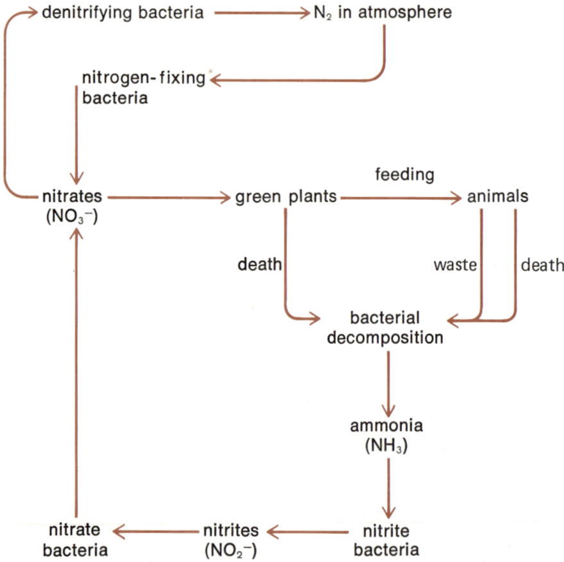

Fig. 8.14 The nitrogen cycle.

and steamy atmospheric conditions, which led to a luxuriant growth of vegetation in many areas. Great masses of decaying plants piled up in swampy bogs and gradually became covered in some regions with inorganic material. In time, such inorganic matter hardened and formed sedimentary rock, including shale and sandstone. The pressure of these overlying rocks, together with continued plant decay, created increasingly higher temperatures that hastened the conversion of the plant residue to coal.

Small amounts of carbon-containing compounds in coal degenerate through erosion and weathering, processes that liberate CO_2 molecules to the atmosphere. Far greater quantities of carbon dioxide are released when coal and other fossil fuels are burned by people as a source of energy. Carbon dioxide released in this manner adds to the environmental supply of CO_2 and forms an additional "loop" in the carbon cycle. Moreover, excess CO_2 formed by burning may be altering the composition and characteristics of the atmosphere. The level of atmospheric CO_2 has increased about 12 per cent since 1880, and a portion of this increase appears linked to the coincident increase in the burning of fossil fuels. Scientists have become concerned over this increase, since changes in the concentration of atmospheric CO_2 could conceivably trigger substantial changes in climate (see Chap. 10).

Alternate "loops" frequently exist in the cyclic regeneration of all other forms of matter in ecosystems. Each so-called cycle actually is a composite of many smaller interrelated cycles. This feature, like the ability of many organisms to feed at several trophic levels, is highly adaptive affording considerable flexibility and stability to ecosystems. If one cyclic path temporarily becomes blocked or overloaded, the cyclic flow of chemical elements often can continue uninterrupted through alternate paths.

Nitrogen Cycle

Highly specialized organisms often are essential in maintaining the cyclic flow of matter through ecosystems. For example, four different types of bacteria play vital roles in the *nitrogen cycle* (Fig. 8.14). Nitrogen is abundant in ecosystems and constitutes 80 per cent of the atmosphere. But atmospheric nitrogen is rather inert chemically, and it cannot be used as such by the majority of organisms. The most common usable nitrogen source is the *nitrate* ion, NO_3^-. Virtually all plants can absorb this ion directly from the environment and employ it in the manufacture of proteins and nucleic acids.

A few organisms can convert atmospheric nitrogen directly to sources of usable nitrogen. One group of these organisms are the *nitrogen-fixing bacteria,* found free in soil and inside special nodules on the roots of *legumes,* that is, certain members of the pea family (Fig. 8.15). These bacteria are unique in that their nitrogen-fixing action depends on living inside the root tissues of leguminous hosts. The microorganisms obtain energy by extracting nutrients from the host legume, and then can convert atmospheric nitrogen to nitrogen-containing compounds. The plant subsequently can use the compounds for its own existence. Such reciprocal relationships between two or more types of organisms living in intimate contact are examples of *symbiosis,* a widespread phenomenon occurring in every ecosystem and in every major group of organisms. Additional examples of symbiosis are introduced later in this chapter.

Sources of usable nitrogen also are added to soil by the decomposition of organic matter. Decomposers break down organic nitrogen to ammo-

Fig. 8.15 Root nodules. These growths consist of large masses of nitrogen-fixing bacteria living in root tissue. The nodules of pea plants are shown here. (*Courtesy of R. H. Noailles.*)

nia, NH_3, which then becomes a nutrient for *nitrite* bacteria. These organisms extract energy from ammonia and release nitrite ions, NO_2^-, as a waste product. Nitrites are exceedingly toxic to many organisms, people included. But most NO_2^- becomes converted quickly to nitrate ions by *nitrate bacteria* that use nitrites as nutrients. Nitrates can be absorbed through plant roots where they are used as nutrients, or they can be converted to atmospheric nitrogen through the action of yet another group of microorganisms, the *denitrifying* bacteria.

The nitrogen "cycle," evidently, consists of two main cycles, which maintain a continuous turnover of nitrogen between the physical and the living components of ecosystems. Note that the four different sets of bacteria act as they do, not because they are aware of the grand plan of the global nitrogen cycle, but because they derive immediate metabolic benefit from their action. Note also that the concept of "waste" is not relevant in natural ecosystems. Compounds toxic to one group of organisms become the nutrients of another group. Indeed, in ecosystems "one man's food is another man's poison." Thus, if the existence of any of the four groups of bacteria were jeopardized, so would the continuation of the nitrogen cycle and therefore the existence of all ecosystems. Picture, for example, what would happen if one of the synthetic chemicals we are adding to our environment were lethal to nitrite bacteria. The death of these microbes would lead not only to a substantial decline in soil fertility, but also to a steady increase in the concentration of atmospheric ammonia.

Similar interconnections between the living and the nonliving components of ecosystems govern the flow of water, oxygen, phosphorus, calcium,

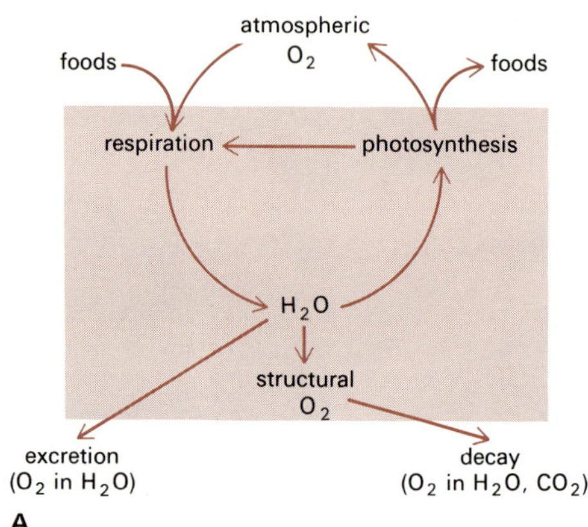

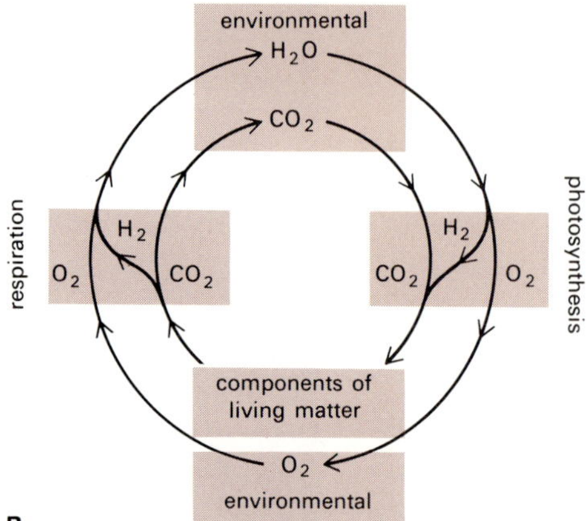

Fig. 8.16 Oxygen, water, and mineral cycles. (A) Oxygen cycle. The parts of the cycle that occur inside organisms are shown in the colored rectangle. Atmospheric oxygen enters the living world as a respiratory gas, and in the course of respiration it combines with hydrogen and forms water (see Chap. 12). This water becomes part of the general water content of living matter, and as such it undergoes three possible fates. (1) It can be excreted immediately to the physical environment. (2) It can be used in the construction of more living matter as a source of the elements hydrogen and oxygen. Structural oxygen of this sort remains in an organism until decay after death converts most of it into H_2O or CO_2, which return to the environment. (3) Water is a raw material in photosynthesis, where the hydrogen participates in food manufacture and the oxygen returns to the environment as a by-product. (B) Interrelations of oxygen, water, and carbon cycles. (C) The global mineral cycle. Minerals absorbed by terrestrial plants and animals return to soil by excretion and death. Rivers carry soil minerals to the ocean, where some of them are deposited at the bottom. Portions of sea bottom then are occasionally uplifted by geologic forces, which reintroduce minerals to a global cycle.

and other inorganic materials (Fig. 8.16). Moreover, no cycle operates independently. The same bacteria that convert nitrites to nitrates also require water, oxygen, phosphorus, calcium, and other inorganic materials. The cellular components of these bacteria are disassembled at death by the same types of decomposers that disassemble all other dead organisms. Nothing is or can be independent in ecosystems: everything is connected to everything else.

Energy

The structure of ecosystems also is influenced by the availability and flow of energy between trophic levels. Whereas the flow of matter is cyclic, the flow of energy is not. For reasons stated in Chap. 3, all organisms require a continuous input of externally supplied energy. The ultimate source of energy for ecosystems is sunlight. During photosynthesis, plants use light energy in the manufacture of sugars, starches, and all other organic molecules making up plants. In this way, light energy becomes "fixed" in the bodies of plants.

Such photosynthetically fixed energy supports virtually all living members of ecosystems. For example, some of the energy fixed in plants is transferred tc herbivores when these animals forage on the plants. However, only a portion of the total nutrient energy available in the plants can be transferred to herbivores; the remainder is lost to the environment as heat. Similar loss of energy results when herbivores are eaten by carnivores, and when, in their turn, carnivores are eaten by other carnivores. Thus the total energy content of

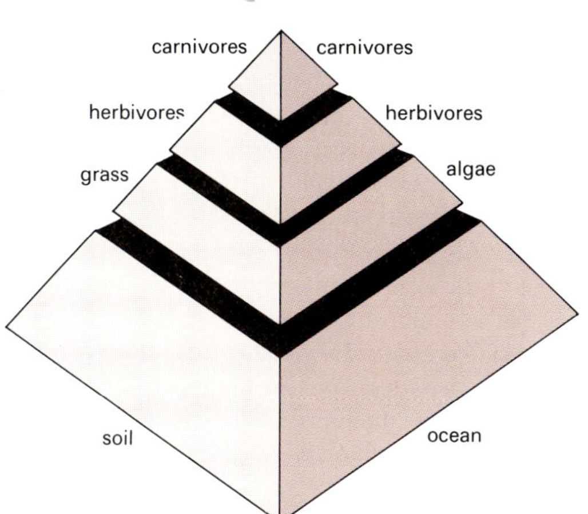

Fig. 8.17 Food pyramids. Soil and ocean support plant life; plant-eating animals (herbivores) subsist on the plants; and flesh-eating (carnivores) subsist on the herbivores.

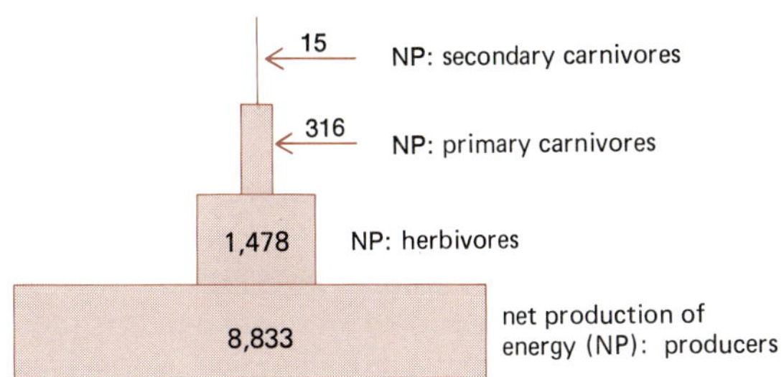

Fig. 8.18 Reduction of fixed energy in food chains. Energy pyramid of Silver Springs, Florida, showing typical reductions in fixed energy at successive trophic levels (units of energy are kilocalories per square meter per year).

herbivores in an ecosystem always is less than the total energy content of producers, and there is a corresponding decrease in the total fixed energy of carnivores at each succeeding trophic level.

Organisms use some of the energy of nutrients in increasing or maintaining their weight, or *biomass.* Because less energy is available at succeeding trophic levels, there is a corresponding decrease in the total biomass. For example, the total weight of plants in a field or forest typically exceeds the total weight of field mice, skunks, squirrels, and all other herbivores. Similarly, a forest usually contains a much smaller number of hawks than rabbits.

The energy relations between trophic levels of an ecosystem resemble a pyramid (Fig. 8.17). Producers form the broad base of an energy pyramid, herbivores make up a second tier, and carnivores at successive trophic levels form progressively smaller tiers. The energy pyramid of Silver Springs, Florida, is presented in Fig. 8.18. Note the dramatic decrease in fixed energy at each step upward in trophic levels. Of 8833 units of energy available in producer biomass, only 15 units become fixed as the biomass of secondary carnivores. All of the

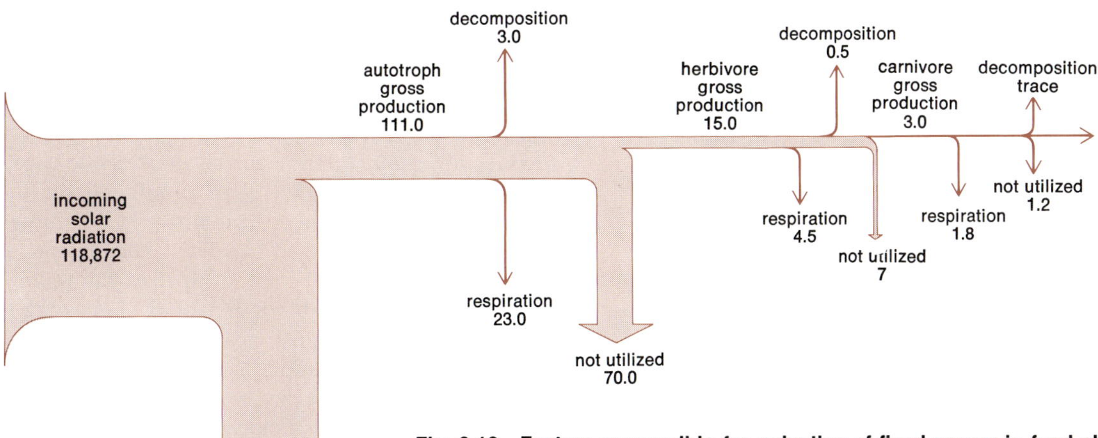

Fig. 8.19 Factors responsible for reduction of fixed energy in food chains. Fate of energy incorporated at producer, herbivore, and carnivore trophic levels in Cedar Bog Lake, Minnesota (units of energy are gram calories per square centimeter per year).

remainder dissipates to the physical components of the ecosystem and subsequently is radiated from the earth to outer space as heat.

Some of the factors responsible for the substantial decrease in fixed energy between trophic levels are presented in Fig. 8.19, a diagram depicting the flow of energy between trophic levels in Cedar Bog Lake, Minnesota. These data were obtained in the early 1940s by Raymond Lindeman, one of the first ecologists to recognize the principles of energy dynamics in ecosystems. Following months of painstaking effort, Lindeman determined that, of 118,872 units of radiant energy striking the lake, only 111 units could be incorporated by producers, representing an efficiency of energy capture of only 0.10 per cent. Of the remaining 118,761 units, most were either lost through reflection or absorbed as heat by the water molecules of the lake.

Moreover, of the 111 units captured by producers, only 15 energy units became incorporated at the herbivore level. The 96-unit difference was lost to the environment in three major ways. First, 23 units were respired by the producers. Second, much of the total producer biomass was not eaten by herbivores. The dead remains of such plants fell to the lake bottom and became part of the accumulating sediments; 3 of the original 111 units were used by decomposers that feed on such sediments. Third, some of the producer biomass eaten by herbivores was not digested and was returned to the ecosystem as animal waste. Of the 15 units of energy captured by herbivores, only 3 units were incorporated into the biomass of primary carnivores; and even less energy became available for the necessarily smaller populations of secondary carnivores. This figure illustrates the overall noncyclic movement of energy through ecosystems. Note, first, that energy captured by producers does not recycle back to the sun, and second, that the smaller amounts of energy fixed at successive trophic levels cannot support any preceding trophic level. Without sunlight, ecosystems collapse.

It is not surprising, therefore, that a pound of steak always has been and will continue to be more expensive than a pound of lettuce. The growth of consumers is more expensive biologically than the growth of producers. The economy of mankind is influenced and indeed governed by the same principles that operate in ecosystems. And, as will be stressed in Chap. 10, attempts by people to thwart or override these principles can lead to catastrophe.

POPULATION DYNAMICS

Anyone who has been frustrated in an attempt to create a "balanced" aquarium of fish, snails, plants, and other organisms is well aware that ecosystems can degenerate rapidly. Usually, such degenerations are due to subtle imbalances between populations and their physical environments. Imbalanced relations between any two populations generally lead to chain reactions of imbalances. For example, excessive foraging of herbivores results in reduced populations of plants which, in turn, opens the way to soil erosion, flooding, and other environmental changes of direct and significant consequence for people (Fig. 8.20).

Fortunately, stable relations between populations often are reinforced by a number of agents that usually are sufficient to counterbalance most natural or man-made disruptions. Chief among these are factors that determine both the growth pattern of individual populations and the number of species that can coexist in an ecosystem. These determinants contribute to either of two categories of opposing forces, *biotic potential* and *environmental resistance.*

Biotic Potential

Biotic potential is the inherent capacity of a species to increase its numbers under ideal conditions. This capacity varies considerably for different species. For example, some bacteria can reproduce once every 20 min in optimum environments and give rise to over 1 million times as many individuals in less than $7\frac{1}{2}$ hours. The biotic potential of larger organisms is more limited. Under optimum conditions (not necessarily the most ideal, depending on your viewpoint) one woman could produce up to 40 children during her reproductive lifetime, provided she gave birth to only one individual at a time. However, it is unlikely that anyone ever has accomplished this feat. For reasons that will become clear below, no species can reproduce indefinitely at its biotic potential. Following introduction of the English sparrow into the United States in 1899, for example, it was estimated that the biotic potential of a single pair of sparrows was 275,716,983,698 descendants over a 10-year period, and that by 1920 there would be about 515 birds per 100 acres. Yet when 1920 arrived, there were approximately 22 birds per 100 acres, less than 5 per cent of the number estimated.

A

B

Fig. 8.20 Erosion. (A) Eroded land with sandy gullies. These would normally erode further and enlarge. (B) Same landscape after planting and about 3 years of growth. Erosion has been halted. Plants evidently protect land against wind and water erosion. (*Soil Conservation Service.*)

Factors that prevent populations from growing indefinitely at their biotic potentials constitute environmental resistance, which usually increases in direct proportion to population size. For example, if a small population is introduced into a new and favorable environment, as the English sparrow was in 1899, its initial reproduction typically begins at a low rate, and then becomes higher, with individuals eventually reproducing at rates close to their biotic potential. However, population growth always slows sooner or later and either levels off or drops precipitously as a result of environmental resistance.

Environmental Resistance

Environmental resistance results from three kinds of factors: (1) purely physical, or *abiotic,* factors; (2) restrictions imposed by interaction of two or more populations of different species, or *interspecific* factors; and (3) restrictions resulting from interactions between individuals in a single population, or *intraspecifc* factors.

Abiotic Factors

Weather is among the important abiotic factors that control population sizes. For example, populations of muskrats can be affected seriously by seasonal fluctuations of water levels. Muskrats dig burrows near water for protection and housing, and in fall plug the entrance of these burrows with mud. In winter, frozen mud prevents foxes, minks, and other predators from entering the burrows. However, fall droughts can reduce the availability of mud substantially, thereby increasing the vulnerability of muskrats to predators and reducing their populations. Alternatively, higher than normal water levels in spring flood the burrows, drowning the young and forcing adult muskrats to live in open shore areas, where they again become easy prey. As will be noted shortly, geography of the physical environment is another abiotic factor that influences population density and balance.

Interspecific Factors

Among the important interspecific factors controlling population size are competition, various forms of symbiotic relations, and predation.

Competition Interspecific competition results from dependence of two or more populations on the same limited resources. Experiments have demonstrated that an ecological niche cannot be occupied indefinitely by more than one species. Closely related species often compete for the same space, or *habitat*, or for the same food. Eventually, one of the competing species displaces all others.

One of the first demonstrations of this phenomenon, called *interspecific exclusion*, involved two related species of unicellular organisms, *Paramecium caudatum* and *Paramecium aurelia*. Each species can thrive independently in an aquatic culture medium with bacteria as a source of food. But when cultured together, *P. aurelia* always displaces *P. caudatum* in approximately 24 days (Fig. 8.21).

In natural ecosystems, competition usually is far more complex. Species, niches, and mechanisms that lead to interspecific exclusion vary greatly. Species rarely compete for precisely the same resources, and habitats are considerably more complex and varied than experimental culture media. Closely related species eat at different times of day or reproduce at different times of year, and in general they do not compete for exactly identical niches. Although the sizes of their populations may

Fig. 8.21 Interspecific exclusion. These graphs depict the population growth rates of *Paramecium aurelia* and *Paramecium caudatum* when these two species are grown in separate cultures and when mixed in the same culture. Note the gradual exclusion of *P. caudatum* when this species is mixed with *P. aurelia*.

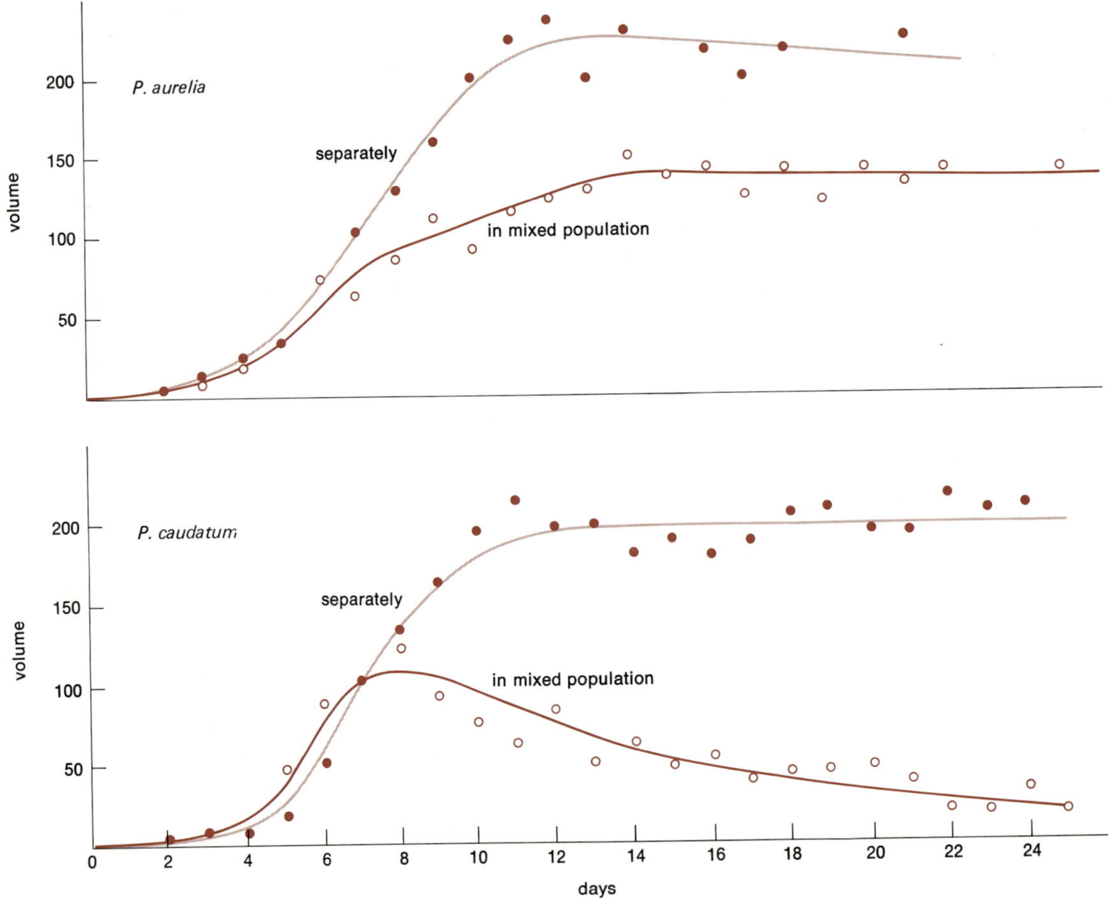

be restricted by competition, such closely related species can coexist indefinitely.

For example, *Paramecium bursaria* feeds on the same bacteria as *P. aurelia* and *P. caudatum*. Yet *P. bursaria* and *P. caudatum* can coexist in the same culture medium; they occupy different regions of the medium. Thus, competition for niches often serves as a population-regulating mechanism that enables several species to occupy a single habitat. The resulting increase in species diversity contributes greatly to the stability of ecosystems, a principle treated more extensively in the next chapter.

Symbiosis The size and distribution of populations often is influenced by symbiosis, a second type of regulatory factor between species. As stated earlier, a symbiotic relation is a special form of communal life in which two organisms of different species live together in intimate, more or less lasting physical contact.

Symbiosis occurs in two basic patterns. In *facultative* associations, two different organisms "have the faculty" of entering a more or less intimate symbiotic relationship. But they need not necessarily do so, being able to survive as free-living forms. In *obligatory* associations, one organism *must* unite symbiotically with another, usually a specific one, if it is to survive. The ancestors of obligatory symbionts have invariably been free-living organisms that in the course of history have lost the power of living on their own. Before becoming obligatory symbionts, they formed facultative associations with organisms on which they came to depend more and more.

A symbiont affects its host in different ways. In *mutualism*, both associated partners derive some benefit from living together. The relation between legumes and nitrogen-fixing bacteria, mentioned earlier, is an example of mutualism. Another is the interesting association of aphids and certain kinds of ants. Aphids are small insects that obtain nutrients by sucking juices from the leaves and branches of plants. Some species of ants "milk" aphids by gently stroking them (Fig. 8.22). The aphids respond to this stroking by excreting droplets of partly digested plant juices, which are then consumed by the ants. In return for this nutrient-rich fluid, the ants protect the aphids from carnivorous beetles, parasitic wasps, and other predators.

A second type of symbiosis, *commensalism*, benefits one of the partners, and the other is neither helped nor harmed by the association. Commensalism is illustrated by the so-called shark sucker, or *remora*. In this fish a dorsal fin is modified as a holdfast device, by means of which the fish attaches to the underside of sharks, thereby securing scraps of food, wide geographic dispersal, and protection. The shark neither benefits nor suffers (Fig. 8.23). In another example, barnacles can attach to the skin of whales and can thereby secure geographic distribution and wider feeding opportunities. In this instance a trend toward parasitism is in evidence; in some cases the barnacles send rootlike outgrowths into the whale that eat away bits of host tissue.

Parasitism, a third type of symbiosis, is of ad-

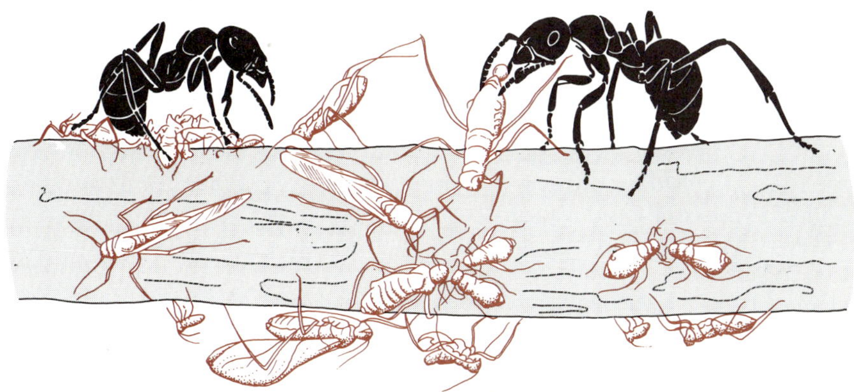

Fig. 8.22 Mutualism. Aphids excrete a sugar-rich "honeydew" from their abdomens (top center) when stroked by certain kinds of ants. In return for this food, the ants protect aphids from predators (see also Color Fig. 7).

Fig. 8.23 Commensalism. Shark with three suckerfish (remoras) attached to it. (*American Museum of Natural History.*)

vantage to the parasite but is detrimental to the host to a greater or lesser extent (Fig. 8.24). Many parasites are relatively harmless and have little impact on the population size or distribution of their hosts. These are the most successful parasites and, like the barnacles of whales, often become distributed in great numbers. In a minority of cases, however, parasitic infections can reduce significantly the population sizes of hosts. For example, lungworm infections are a chief cause of illness and mortality in bighorn sheep in Wyoming and Colorado; heartworm infections have reached epidemic proportions among certain populations of dogs and wolves. Early in this century hookworm was a widespread and debilitating disease among Americans, particularly those living in southern states (Fig. 8.25). Malaria, caused by a protozoan, remains a significant health hazard in many parts of the world (see also Chap. 31).

Thus, symbiotic interactions between species assume a variety of forms, ranging from mutually beneficial relations that contribute to the maintenance or increase of population size, to detrimental relations by which one population debilitates or even excludes another.

Predation In some respects the relation between predator and prey is similar to that of parasite and host. How energy is obtained is quite different in the two cases, however. The British ecologist Charles Elton put the difference in economic terms when he noted that "predators live on capital, whereas parasites live on interest." Killing of prey is essential for successful predation; survival of hosts is essential for successful parasitism.

Fluctuations in sizes of snowshoe hare and lynx populations in Canada between 1846 and 1937 illustrate a typical predator-prey interaction. Snowshoe hares are small, prolific herbivores, characterized chiefly by their seasonal changes of coat color; they constitute the major food of lynx, a smaller, distant cousin of the mountain lion.

Because of the dissipation of energy between the trophic levels of herbivores and carnivores, the peak populations of hares always are larger than the corresponding peak populations of lynx (Fig. 8.26). This figure also shows that a decline in the population of lynx usually follows a decline in the population of hares, a pattern typical of most predator-prey relations. The population sizes of predators usually fluctuates in direct proportion to changes in population sizes of prey, particularly when the prey is an exclusive food source for a predator. Thus, food supply and predation also can stabilize and restrict interdependent populations.

Intraspecific Factors

Interspecific and abiotic factors alone probably do not explain the cyclic fluctuations in the population sizes of snowshoe hares. For example, the precipitous plunge of the extraordinarily large population of hares in 1864 begins long before a significant rise in the population of the lynx. Although predators other than lynx may have contributed to this decline, it is possible that intraspecific factors were involved as well.

Examination of Fig. 8.26 reveals that peak populations of snowshoe hares occurred every 9 to 10 years. Hares became both more abundant and more crowded as their population approached such peaks; in other words, population *size* and *density* were increasing jointly. Several other animal populations also undergo concurrent cyclic fluctuations of population size and density. For example, the Norway lemming, a small hamsterlike rodent, exhibits peak population densities every 3 to 4 years.

Some experimental evidence suggests that intraspecific factors may contribute to the recurrence of such cycles. For example, in 1864 and in other years that coincided with peak populations of snowshoe hares, trappers frequently reported hares behaving oddly. Many would be found "in shock," dead or dying for no outwardly apparent reason. Subsequent experiments on hares and on other mammals that reacted similarly to increased population densities revealed significant hormonal changes when the animals were maintained under crowded conditions. Hormones influencing reproductive behavior and the metabolism of carbohydrates often were found at abnormal concentrations in the tissues of dying animals.

These experiments have led some biologists to propose a hypothesis of population limitation by intraspecific *social stress,* which states that increases in population density produce increased behavioral interactions between members of the population. The hypothesis further suggests that, in some species, such intensified interactions stress hormonal control systems and that the consequent malfunctioning of these systems results in death or

A

B

Fig. 8.24 Parasites. (A) A blood-sucking wood tick attached to the fur of a deer. (B) Mistletoe extracting nutrients from a branch of a pine tree. (*A, Courtesy of Leonard L. Rue; B, U.S. Department of Agriculture.*)

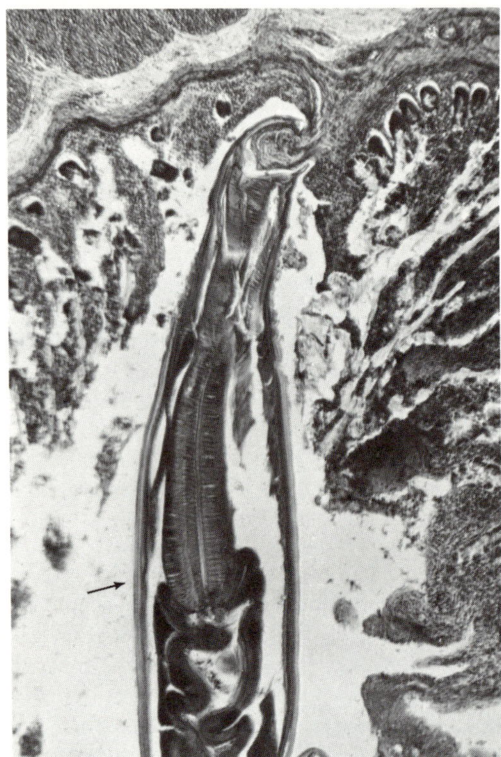

Fig. 8.25 Hookworm. Section through the anterior part of a hookworm (arrow) clamped to the mucosal lining in the gut of a host. (*Armed Forces Institute of Pathology.*)

in an inability to reproduce. Other biologists question the general applicability of this hypothesis. They point out that evidence of hormonal imbalance has been obtained only in laboratories and has not been corroborated by similar experiments conducted in natural ecosystems.

There is no doubt, however, that many species do exhibit abnormal behavior under unusually crowded conditions and that deviations from normal behavior often reduce population density. For example, when albino rats are raised in densities higher than normal, many behavioral aberrations result, including increased incidence of homosexuality, frigidity, cannibalism, spontaneous abortion, and breakdowns of premating rituals.

Another type of intraspecific behavior, *territoriality,* is characteristic of many animals and also influences population density. Animals exhibiting territorial behavior "stake out" and defend a specific area of their habitat against invasion by other members of the species (Fig. 8.27). In some cases the territory is defended through extremely aggressive behavior. Actual bloodshed occurs infrequently, however; territorial confrontations usually are highly ritualistic and involve only the threat of attack. Indeed, confrontation often is avoided, particularly among animals that "warn" neighboring individuals of their presence by "marking" their territorial limits. Dogs, for example, mark an area by urinating on strategic places along the boundary. Despite the stories you may have read as a child, birds do not "sing" because they are 'happy"; their songs usually warn other members of their population of territorial boundaries.

Thus, territoriality acts to partition the space occupied by a population into discrete subdivisions and ensures a more or less uniform population density over a wide area. Individuals that can main-

Fig. 8.26 Predator-prey interactions. Oscillations in populations of snowshoe hares and lynx.

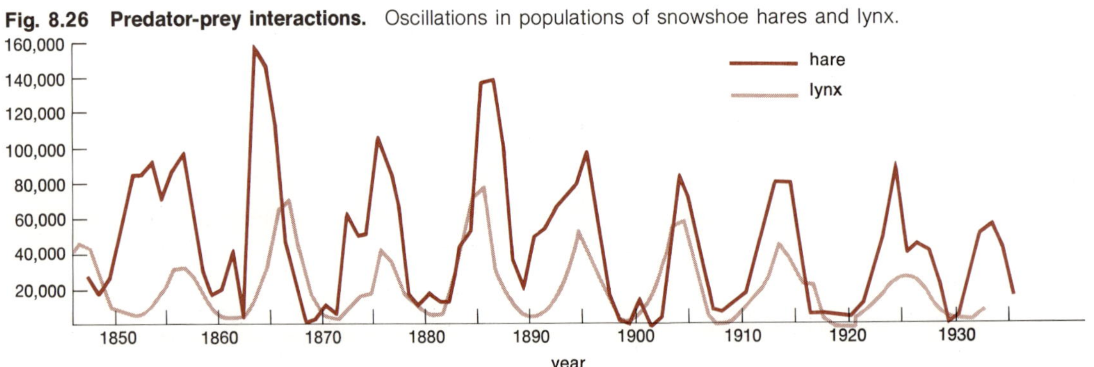

Fig. 8.27 Territoriality. A territorial confrontation between two hamadryas baboons.

tain territories have an excellent chance of extracting food for themselves and their offspring. Those which cannot are eliminated effectively from the population. Accordingly, populations comprising individuals exhibiting well-defined territorial behaviors usually are maintained at a reasonable optimum, both with respect to the total amount of reproduction in the population as a whole and the density of individuals feeding on available sources of food.

Dominancy hierarchies are a third intraspecific factor that influences population dynamics. Whereas territoriality subdivides resources on a spatial basis, dominance hierarchies establish priorities of resource use among individuals of a population. Hierarchical systems have been observed in most vertebrates and in many invertebrates.

A dominance hierarchy to some extent resembles a caste system in that the members of a group are ranked according to a scale of relative status or superiority. However, whereas in a caste system an individual inherits a fixed rank, in a dominance hierarchy he must seek status on his own. Moreover, this status can become higher or lower in the course of time. The most widespread basis of superiority scales is physical size and strength, or at least display features that suggest size and strength.

Thus, large vertebrates usually dominate without contest over smaller ones, older individuals dominate over younger ones, and males largely dominate over females. Among individuals of more or less equal apparent status, the actual status is determined by sham or actual contests. Losers then usually indicate their acceptance of subordinate status by various forms of submissive behavior. Once the relative status of two individuals has become determined, it tends to have a measure of permanence; in a subsequent encounter the two individuals are not likely to recontest their comparative rank.

Between more than two individuals, hierarchic *peck orders* become established through whole series of pair contests, carried out in round-robin fashion (Fig. 8.28). Among chickens, for example, the females of a flock become ranked by pecking contests. A given hen may then peck without danger of reprisal all lower-ranking birds, and she in turn may be pecked by any higher-ranking bird. If a new hen is introduced, she is subjected to a pecking contest with each of the others. Winning here and losing there, she soon acquires a particular rank.

Individuals of high status generally are favored in almost all respects. They can claim the largest amounts of the choicest food and the preferential services of members of the opposite sex. Indeed, if food is scarce, the lowest-ranking members often starve while the dominant ones eat all the available

A

walk of dominant male

B walk of low-ranking male

Fig. 8.28 Dominance hierarchies. (A) Peck orders are characteristic in social groups such as flocks of hens. (B) Differences in posture indicate social status of rhesus monkeys. High-ranking males walk with heads held high and tail hooked upward. Low-ranking males slouch and walk with tail lowered.

food. In addition, low-ranking individuals often exhibit "psychological castration," or inability to mate in the presence of dominant animals.

Dominance hierarchies apparently limit the population densities of some species. Proportionately fewer individuals are able to achieve high rank as population density increases. Consequently, population density is restricted as proportionately larger numbers of low-ranking individuals are unable to obtain food or acquire a mate.

Emigration is still another intraspecific factor that can limit population density. The departure of large numbers of individuals from a population usually is not accidental. It often represents a distinct form of behavior that results in the dispersal of a crowded population.

One of the most dramatic and often devastating emigrations of organisms is illustrated by plague locusts. These insects normally feed within relatively fixed geographic boundaries whenever population densities are not high. At such times they look very much like other species of grasshoppers. However, many individuals of the plague species have an altered physical appearance when population densities are high. Generations of grasshoppers that develop under crowded conditions often have longer wings, a darker color, and more slender bodies. These transformed grasshoppers, now called locusts, begin to band together and fly beyond the usual feeding range. If they aggregate in sufficient numbers, usually in a mass of millions, the locusts form a plague swarm. Such swarms can travel up to 200 miles or more. The swarm occasionally sweeps down on grass and farmland, destroying crops over thousands of acres and leaving large areas barren of vegetation (Fig. 8.29).

Plague locusts are most common in drier regions of the world, such as Egypt, where for many centuries they have destroyed crops periodically. Despite modern advances in pest control, plague swarms continue to destroy cropland in more arid parts of Africa and the Middle East. Orbiting satellites recently have been used to monitor these regions visually, by photographing changes in terrestrial conditions often associated with the early rapid growth of grasshopper populations. Such information can prove useful in checking the population growth of these insects.

Emigrations commonly have at least two effects on populations; they reduce crowding in home territories, and they provide for the start of new populations elsewhere. Individuals remaining behind in home territories benefit by obtaining proportionally greater amounts of food and other life-sustaining resources. Emigrants may find new territories favorable for other cycles of rapid population growth.

Population Growth

Whether a population grows, declines, or remains constant in size depends entirely on interactions between factors contributing to biotic potential and environmental resistance. Both the factors and the nature of these interactions must be known if the growth patterns of specific populations are to be predicted. Ecologists often have too little information to predict future population densities precisely, but the population-growth histories of individual species often are useful in evaluating the effects of natural or man-made changes on population balances in ecosystems.

All species grow at rates near their biotic potentials when environmental resistance is low. This often occurs, for example, at the beginning of a growing season, when a few individuals enter a new territory, or when unused resources become available. At such times the rate of population growth is proportional to the number of individuals in the population; the larger the population, the faster it grows. Populations grow in an accelerating fashion under these conditions, or at "compound interest." This form of increase, called *exponential growth,* can be expressed mathematically as

$$\text{rate of increase in number of individuals} = \begin{bmatrix} \text{average birth rate} - \text{average death rate} \end{bmatrix} \times \text{number of individuals}$$

Because of environmental resistance, populations do not grow in exponential fashion indefinitely. Resources, space, or some combination of factors becomes limiting, and sooner or later popu-

Fig. 8.29 Plague locusts. (A) An adult desert locust. (B) Part of a plague swarm, showing locusts covering the doorstep of an Iranian home.

A

B

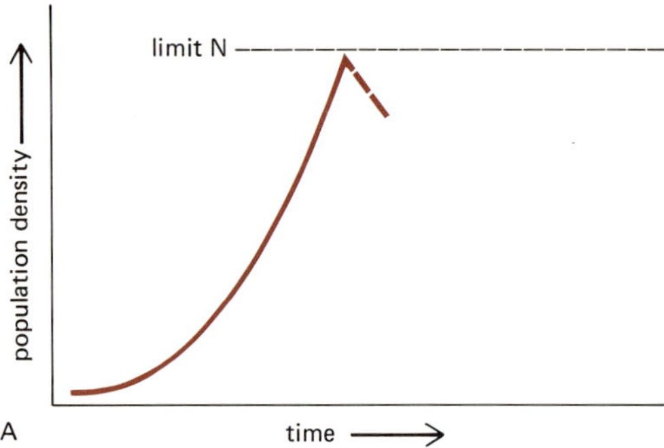

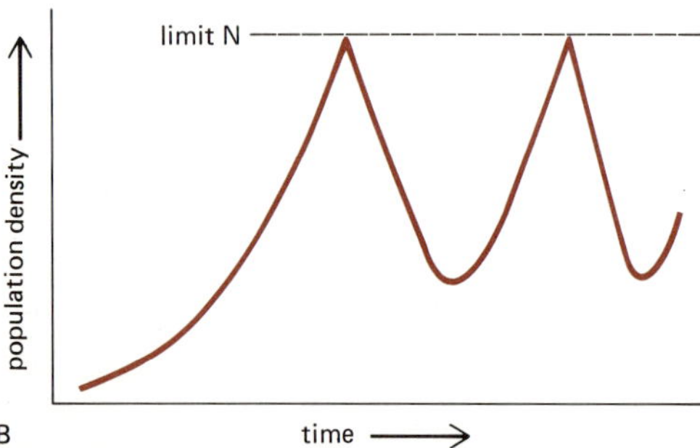

Fig. 8.30. J-shaped pattern of population growth. (A) Basic pattern. Populations increase exponentially until density-independent factors (N) force a rapid decline in population size. (B) "Boom and bust" cycles of exponential growth, a common variant of the J-shaped growth pattern.

Fig. 8.31 Needle-eating caterpillars. Organisms such as the gypsy moth, shown here eating the needles of a pine tree, often exhibit J-shaped growth patterns. At peak densities, such populations can cause extensive defoliation of forests.

lation growth slows or declines. The growth of some populations comes to an abrupt halt, and their densities then decline rapidly until conditions again become favorable for another cycle of rapid growth. This *J-shaped growth pattern* is characteristic of such populations, which typically follow "boom and bust" cycles of exponential growth (Fig. 8.30).

Well-documented examples of the J-shaped pattern are the outbreaks from 1880 to 1940 of needle-eating caterpillars in the pure pine forest of Germany (Fig. 8.31). Populations of caterpillars grew exponentially every 5 to 10 years during this period. At peak densities, as many as 10,000 organisms per 1000 m^2 of forest were counted. This contrasts with a "normal" density of less than 1 per 1000 m^2. Each of these outbreaks was followed by a rapid decline in population density. The declines were due in part to starvation (caused by the defoliation of trees by the caterpillars) and in part by increased populations of caterpillar-eating predators. Both are interspecific factors. Intraspecific factors, which are almost always density-dependent, usually do not play a role in regulating populations characterized by J-shaped growth curves. For this reason, population growth characterized by J-shaped curves is said to be *density-independent.*

Population growth rates of other species are *density-dependent,* and intraspecific factors often are important regulators of population size. Such populations tend to be self-limited in that their rates of growth usually are inversely proportional to density. The growth curves of these species follow a sigmoid, or *S-shaped growth pattern* (Fig. 8.32).

Growth of such populations levels off as organisms become increasingly crowded and their numbers approach the maximum sustainable density in the ecosystem. This maximum level is called the *carrying capacity* of the ecosystems for a given species at a given time.

Biotic potential and environmental resistance reach equilibrium at carrying capacity. Birth and death rates are equal at such times, and the rate of increase in the number of individuals equals zero (see equation above). Thus, species are said to have reached *zero population growth* at carrying capacity. Birth rates usually are higher than death rates below carrying capacity and lower above this level. However, birth rates often temporarily re-

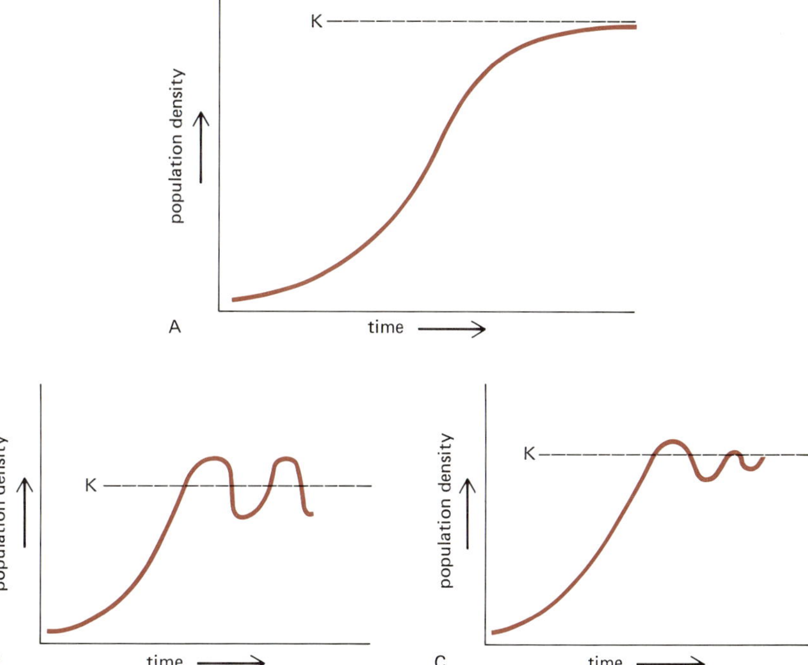

Fig. 8.32 S-shaped pattern of population growth. (A) Basic pattern. Exponential growth slows as populations approach carrying capacity (K). Intraspecific factors usually are chiefly responsible for the gradual slowdown of population growth. (B), (C) Common variants of the S-shaped pattern. These two graphs shown undamped (B) and damped (C) oscillations that occur when sigmoid growth overshoots carrying capacity.

main higher than death rates after populations have reached carrying capacity, particularly after a long period of exponential growth. This causes populations to overshoot carrying capacity for a short period. But death rates eventually become higher than birth rates and population crashes then follow.

The severity of such crashes depends on many factors, including the biotic potential of a species and the kinds of factors that contribute to environmental resistance. Many Norway lemmings, for example, react to overcrowded conditions by jumping from nearby cliffs into the ocean and drowning. This kind of intraspecific behavior produces large-scale oscillations in population density (see Fig. 8.32B). The amplitude of such oscillations is far less in other species and actually can dampen in time. The densities of these more stable populations often remain constant at carrying capacity until natural or man-made imbalances occur in an ecosystem (see Fig. 8.32C).

Certain imbalances, such as those affecting the size of a habitat or the availability of a food resource, can dramatically alter the carrying capacity of an ecosystem either upward or downward. This can be illustrated by the following experiment (Fig. 8.33). If a pair of flour beetles, *Tribolium confusum,* is placed in a large jar containing 64 grams of flour, the resulting population growth will level off at approximately 1750 beetles. If another pair of beetles is placed in a jar of equal size containing only 16 grams of flour, the population will reach zero population growth at about 650 beetles. The different carrying capacities of the two ecosystems, 1750 versus 650, are almost entirely due to differences in the amount of flour available. The flour serves both as food and physical environment. People can change the size of natural habitats by actions such as polluting a portion of a bay or partial drainage of a swamp. Other examples are included in Chap. 10. The S-shaped growth pattern provides other valuable insights into relationships between density and growth of populations. For most species displaying density-dependent growth patterns, maximum rates of population expansion occur along the linear, midportion of the S-shaped curve (Fig. 8.34). Undercrowding and overcrowding both restrict population growth.

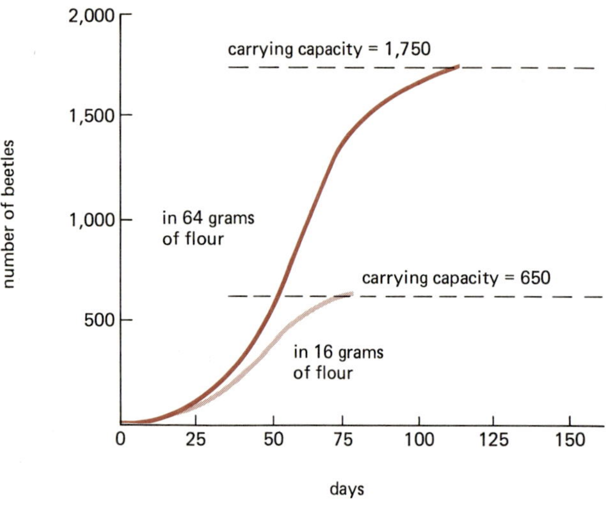

Fig. 8.33 Carrying capacity and population growth. Population growth curves for two populations of the flour beetle *Tribolium confusum*. Carrying capacity was altered by varying the amount of flour in which the beetles lived.

The population growth rates of oysters illustrate this principle. Like many other invertebrates, oysters pass through an immature *larval stage* of development before becoming adults (see also Chap. 24). Oyster larvae swim free for a time, but they must settle on a hard surface if they are to undergo transformation to shelled adults. The shells of previous generations of oysters provide excellent surfaces for this transformation. Too many shells of old oysters limit the space available for the growth of new generations, but too few shells reduce the number of surfaces suitable for the attachment of larvae. Population growth rates therefore are greatest at intermediate densities.

Fig. 8.34 Optimum yields. Maximum rates of population growth usually occur at intermediate densities, or along the linear segments (between points *A* and *B*) of sigmoid growth curves.

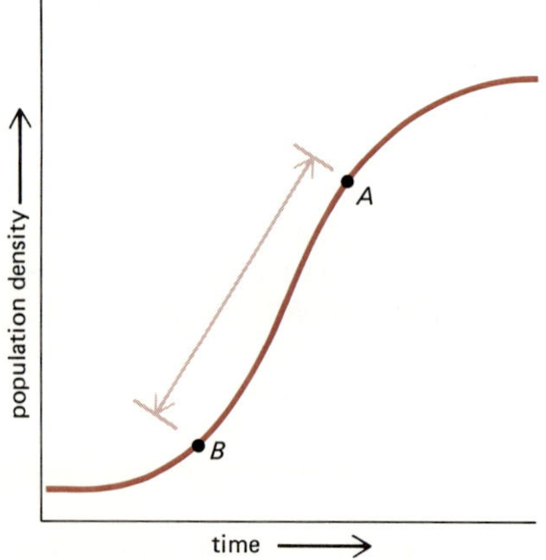

Production of timber, food, and other goods derived from living organisms usually can be increased by maintaining resource populations at points along the linear portion of the S-shaped growth curve. Such maintenance often produces the greatest harvests, or *optimum yields* (see Fig. 8.34). Thus, forests must occasionally be "cropped" to reduce overcrowding of trees, and populations of commercial fishes should not be reduced below critical levels. Unfortunately, people often have ignored this basic relationship between population density and growth in pursuit of short-term profits. Populations of cod, haddock, halibut, and other commercial fishes have been driven substantially below optimum yield in many parts of the world. Because of overharvesting, some oyster beds are no longer economically productive even though oyster larvae swim in the water.

Such practices reflect either an ignorance or intolerance of basic principles of ecology. It is now clear that these principles must guide the interests of all people, but especially those whose actions directly influence population growth rates.

Population Balance

Factors contributing to environmental resistance limit not only the number of individuals in a population, but also the number of different species-populations in an ecosystem. For example, the number of species that occupy a region is greatly influenced by geography. The relationship between area and species diversity is illustrated in Fig. 8.35A, which compares the sizes of several islands in the East Indies with the number of different land and freshwater birds inhabiting each. Such a graph constitutes the *species-area curve* for the birds on the Sunda Islands as well as the Philippines and New Guinea. The straight line through this graph approximates the gradient of average species per area values for these islands.

Note that as the area of the islands increases by a factor of 10, the number of species approximately doubles. Thus, Bawean Island, having an area of about 100 square miles, supports about 40 species of birds, and Simalur Island, occupying an area of almost 1000 square miles, supports about 80 species. Larger ecosystems usually provide greater numbers of habitats and ecological niches than smaller ones, and this appears to be partly responsible for the relationship between area and species number. The relationship not only applies to islands but also to any isolated biological community. It holds for lakes, ponds, streams, and patches of land habitats, such as a pine grove in a forest of oak and hickory.

The number of species inhabiting an ecosystem is influenced by other geographic factors as well. For virtually all phyla, the number of species per unit area increases markedly in the direction of the equator. For example, Greenland has 56 species of breeding birds, New York State has 105 species, Guatemala has 469, and Colombia has 1395. Species diversity in marine environments follows a similar trend. Most ecologists suggest that this pattern probably is related to some combination of climatic factors that change gradually with latitude, but a firm basis for this claim has not been established.

Geographically isolated ecosystems also tend to have fewer numbers of species than less remote regions of equal size. Isolated ecosystems usually receive few immigrants from other habitats. Because fewer new species arrive, smaller numbers of species occupy remote ecosystems.

For example, the islands of Melanesia, Micronesia, and Polynesia, which are located far to the east of New Guinea and many miles from other land masses, contain fewer species than any similarly sized island of the Sunda chain (Fig. 8.35B). As mentioned earlier, the larger Sunda Islands support greater numbers of species than the smaller ones, in accordance with the principle that species number in a given latitude generally doubles as the area of ecosystems increases tenfold. The Sunda Islands form a closely spaced chain, and individuals from one island often are able to emigrate to the next without great difficulty. But the more distant islands east of New Guinea receive few immigrants from any land mass. Consequently, the position of these islands on the species-area curve for land and freshwater birds lies below the gradient of average values for the Sunda Islands (straight line in Fig. 8.35B). Moreover, islands nearest New Guinea, which have a greater chance of receiving immigrants than more distant islands, lie proportionately closer to the gradient. Geographic barriers to immigration also influence the rates at which new species come into existence and old species become extinct. These relationships are illustrated in Chap. 29.

Population balance in ecosystems is affected not only by purely physical variables. The kinds of organisms that exist in a community can greatly influence nutrient cycling, energy flow, and species diversity. For example, the ribbed mussel *Modiolus demissus* plays a vital role in maintaining the structure of salt marshes in the southeastern United States. This mollusk is about the size of an oyster and lives in small colonies at the bottom of marshes. Populations are never very large; densities average about 8 mussels per square meter.

Like many other mollusks, mussels obtain food by filtering small organisms from tidal waters that move into and out of marshes twice daily. These animals collectively transport thousands of gallons of seawater through their filtering organs each day. While filtering organisms as food, the mollusks also strain large quantities of particles suspended in the water. The particles, which are rich in phosphorus and other minerals, are excreted along with undigested food as sediments in mud at the marsh bottom (Fig. 8.36). The feeding behavior of mussels thus retains in marshes considerable amounts of inorganic nutrients that otherwise would be swept out to sea by tides. The amount of phosphorus removed from seawater by mussels is particularly large. Every $2\frac{1}{2}$ days these organisms remove a quantity of phosphorus equal to the average amount present in all particles suspended in the water (approximately 14 mg/m^2).

By retaining large amounts of phosphorus and

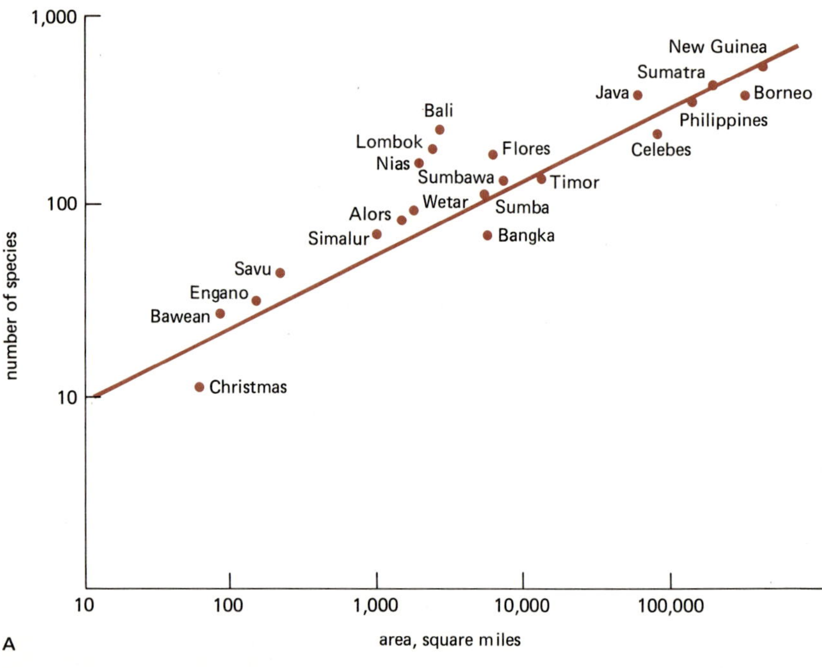

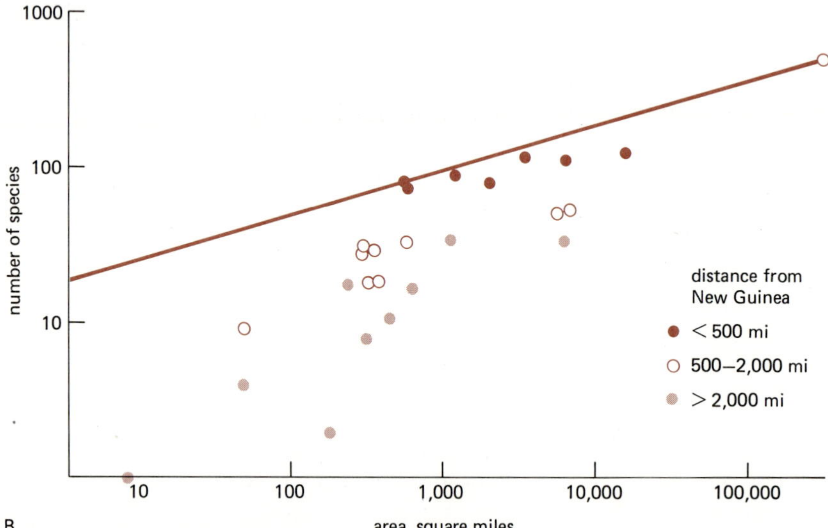

Fig. 8.35 Species diversity and area. (A) Species-area curve for freshwater and land birds of the East Indies. (B) Relationships between species diversity and distance from principal sources of colonization. In general, remote islands, which in this example are those farthest away from New Guinea, contain fewer species than similarly sized islands located near sources of colonization. The straight line is the Sunda Islands' species-area curve for freshwater and land birds.

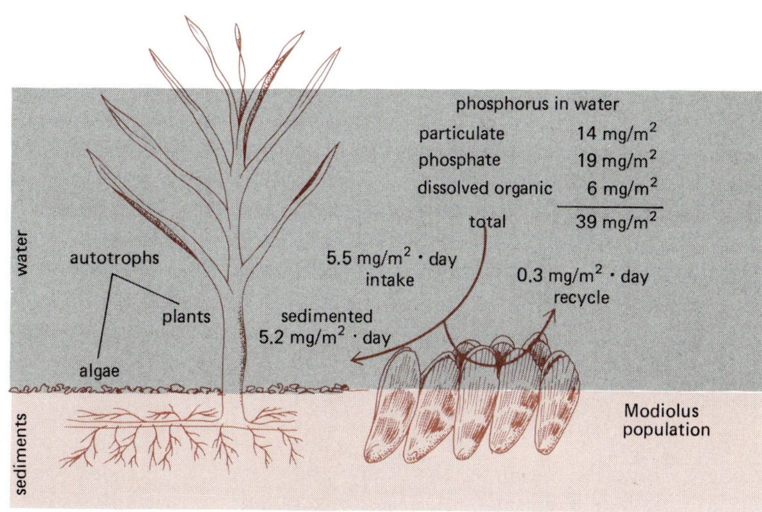

Fig. 8.36 Community composition and population balance. The ribbed mussel, *Modiolus demissus,* extracts large quantities of phosphorus and other minerals from ocean water that passes through its filtering organs. In a salt marsh in the southeastern United States, for example, ribbed mussels extracted phosphorus at an average rate of 5.5 mg/m²·day. Of this amount, only 0.3 mg/m²·day was recycled back to seawater. The remaining 5.2 mg/m²·day was deposited as sediment in mud at the marsh bottom. Without this continued replenishment of sedimented phosphorus, several species of algae and plants would disappear from the marsh.

other inorganic nutrients, mussels play a major role in creating and maintaining the rich fertility of salt marshes. If their populations should decline, the accompanying drop in available phosphorus would greatly reduce populations of autotrophs, perhaps eliminating species that depend on relatively high concentrations of this inorganic nutrient. The resulting decline in producer biomass would have a dramatic impact on the numbers and kinds of consumers in the marsh. Clearly, despite their relatively small population size, the mussels have a major impact on the cycling and retention of phosphorus in this ecosystem. As a result, they also play a major role in determining and maintaining population balance in the marsh.

Many factors therefore control the size, structure, boundaries, balance, and all other characteristics of populations of ecosystems. Some of these factors are purely physical, some purely biological, but most result from interactions between organisms and their habitats. Organisms both change and are changed by environments. Like organisms, ecosystems consist of many interdependent parts organized as integrated wholes. And, also like organisms, ecosystems develop, mature, die, are replaced by new ecosystems, and are functional units of an even larger whole. These last features are the subjects of the next chapter.

Review Questions

1 What characteristics does a species have as an evolutionary unit, a reproductive unit, and an ecological unit? What is an ecological niche?

2 What are individual variations? Distinguish between inheritable and noninheritable variations and give examples of each. Is the usual definition of "species" applicable to all organisms? Why or why not?

3 What is a subspecies? How is this taxonomic rank related to variations between members of a species? Give examples of such variations and discuss their biological significance.

4 Describe the functional relationships among producer, herbivore, and carnivore trophic levels of ecosystems. How is the ability to feed at more than one trophic level an important adaptation of many species?

5 How do organisms contribute to the cycling of matter through ecosystems? What is the role of decay in the cycling process? Outline the carbon and nitrogen cycles. What groups of bacteria maintain the nitrogen cycle? How are these cycles dependent on each other?

6 What factors are responsible for the substantial decreases in fixed energy between trophic levels? What is the ultimate source of energy for all ecosystems?

7 Describe reproductive and protective links that make the populations of a community interdependent. Describe how abiotic, interspecific, and intraspecific factors help maintain stable relations among populations in an ecosystem. How do symbiosis, territoriality, dominance hierarchies, and emigration contribute to stable relations?

8 Suppose you are given an aquarium and a supply of fresh water. You wish to create an aquatic ecosystem that will remain "balanced" indefinitely at room temperature when placed near a source of sunlight. Describe the materials (if any) and the relative numbers and kinds of organisms that you would put in the aquarium.

9 What are the various forms of symbiosis and how are they defined? Give specific examples of each.

10 What makes some populations exhibit a J-shaped growth pattern and others an S-shaped pattern? What is exponential growth? Under what conditions do populations grow exponentially? What population densities usually produce optimum yields of biological resources?

11 What is carrying capacity? How is carrying capacity related to biotic potential and environmental resistance?

12 Describe how species diversity is influenced by geography. Use several examples to illustrate your discussion.

13 Suppose all ribbed mussels of the genus *Modiolus demissus* were killed in a salt marsh in the southeastern United States. Describe how the loss of this species might affect population balance in the marsh.

Collateral Readings

Bormann, F. H., and **A. E. Likens:** Nutrient Cycles of an Ecosystem, *Scientific American,* October 1970. A summary of an extensive study conducted at the Hubbard Brook Experimental Forest in the White Mountains of New Hampshire.

Brill, W. J.: Biological Nitrogen Fixation, *Scientific American,* March 1977. An excellent review of this vital process.

Cheng, T. C.: "Symbiosis," Pegasus, New York, 1970. A popularly written review of the many kinds of symbiosis.

Emmel, T. C.: "An Introduction to Ecology and Populations," Norton, New York, 1973. A short paperback for the layman.

Flanagan, D.: "The Biosphere," Freeman, San Francisco, 1970. A compilation of *Scientific American* articles that deals with energy flow, nutrient cycles, and the impact of people on ecosystems.

Gates, D. M.: The Flow of Energy in the Biosphere, *Scientific American,* September 1971. An excellent discussion of how energy flows through trophic levels of ecosystems.

Gosz, J. R., R. T. Holmes, G. E. Likens, and **F. H. Bormann:** The Flow of Energy in a Forest Ecosystem, *Scientific American,* March 1978. This article illustrates how the partitioning of energy in a forest is regulated.

Janick, J., C. H. Noller, and **C. L. Rhykerd:** The Cycles of Plant and Animal Nutrition, *Scientific American,* September 1976. Some of the most fundamental ecological relationships between plants and animals are clearly documented.

Kormondy, E. J.: "Concepts of Ecology," 2d ed., Prentice-Hall, Englewood Cliffs, N. J., 1976. A good, concise introductory text. Available in paperback.

Krebs, C. J.: "Ecology: The Experimental Analysis of Distribution and Abundance," 2d ed., Harper & Row, New York, 1978. An excellent, clearly written textbook that focuses on the ecology of populations.

Lack, D.: "Population Studies of Birds," Clarendon, New York, 1966. An interesting, readable book about population regulation. Written by a famous student of birds, the book contains informative anecdotes on the natural history of these fascinating animals.

Lamb, I. M.: Lichens, *Scientific American,* October 1959. The symbiotic relationships between the algal and fungal components of these organisms is described.

Langer, W.: Checks on Population Growth: 1750–1850, *Scientific American,* February 1972. Describes factors regulating human populations in Europe before the advent of modern medicine.

Odum, E.: "Ecology," 2d ed., Holt, New York, 1975. An excellent introductory text. Available in paperback.

Young, C. M.: Giant Clams, *Scientific American,* April 1975. Describes the symbiotic relations between giant clams and algae that live in their tissues.

Chapter 9 Ecosystem to Biosphere

Learning Objectives

After reading this chapter you should be able to:

1. Define ecological succession and climax community; illustrate the process of ecological succession by identifying and characterizing the sequence of stages that oligotrophic lakes pass through as they become swamps.
2. Construct a diagram that illustrates the relation between thermoclines and seasonal changes in the cycling and decomposition of organic matter in lakes; state how thermoclines affect the abundance of fish in aquatic environments; distinguish between epi- and hypolimnion, and between phyto- and zooplankton.
3. Write a short essay that describes the successional transformation of barren rock to land supporting a climax community. As part of your essay:
    - **a.** define humus, loam, topsoil, and subsoil
    - **b.** describe the formation of soil from rock and identify the roles played by at least two organisms in the formation of topsoil
    - **c.** identify, illustrate, and list reasons for changes in species diversity and biomass that usually accompany ecological succession in terrestrial environments
4. State at least two soil-forming processes; distinguish between gravel and clay and state why neither provides favorable environments for rapid succession of terrestrial communities.
5. Differentiate between primary and secondary succession and give an example of each.
6. List and exemplify at least five basic characteristics of terrestrial succession.
7. Define sere and state at least one reason why ecological succession does not always lead to the establishment of climax communities; show why there usually is no absolute climax community that develops and extends over a broad geographical area; list at least one example of slightly different climax communities in a relatively small geographical area; define and give an example of a pulse-stabilized community.
8. Illustrate the principle that different seres in similar environments tend to succeed toward similar climax communities.
9. Write an essay describing how the distribution, physical characteristics, and abundance of marine life are influenced by light intensity, salinity, thermoclines, water pressure, and tides.
10. List three horizontal and two vertical habitats of oceans; state the relationships of these habitats to plankton, nekton, and benthos.
11. Construct a diagram depicting relationships between continental shelf, continental slope, abyssal plain, midocean ridges, and deepsea rifts.
12. Define estuary and show why these habitats are among the most productive in the biosphere.
13. Define biome; list the principal characteristics of the following North American biomes and identify at least three organisms that inhabit each of these areas:
    - **a.** tundra
    - **b.** northern coniferous forest
    - **c.** temperate deciduous forest
    - **d.** grassland
    - **e.** desert
14. Define the geographical boundaries of each biome listed in Objective 13; illustrate the relation between latitude and altitude in the establishment of similar biomes.
15. Define permafrost; state the principal reason why deserts sometimes develop near mountain ranges; list at least three specific adaptations of organisms to tundra and desert environments.
16. Identify the geographical boundaries and at least one characteristic each of the eastern pine-oak, subtropical, and broad-sclerophyll biomes of the United States.

The sum of all ecosystems on earth represents the *biosphere*, and the physical portion of this largest ecological unit is the global environment. This physical portion consists of three interdependent subdivisions: the aquatic components, or *hydrosphere;* the terrestrial components, or *lithosphere;* and the gaseous components, or *atmosphere.*

Because few species reside permanently in the atmosphere, the two main categories of habitats are the *aquatic* and the *terrestrial.* Both range from equator to pole and from a few thousand feet below to a few thousand feet above sea level. Aquatic ecosystems are classified as *freshwater* or *marine.* Terrestrial ecosystems are distinguished generally on the basis of dominant types of vegetation, such as grasses, shrubs, or trees. Major terrestrial ecosystems often are called *biomes.* Whether aquatic or terrestrial, all major ecosystems contain communities in various stages of development, each progressing through a more or less orderly series of changes leading toward a terminal, self-perpetuating *climax community.* Such progressive developmental stages form an *ecological succession.*

ECOLOGICAL SUCCESSION

We are surrounded by evidence of ecological succession. Crabgrass, dandelions, and plantain infiltrate lawns; weeds collect in window boxes and gardens; lichen and mosses cover exposed surfaces of rocks; sumac, huckleberry, wild blueberry, and other shrubs encroach on open pastures.

In each case, new species displace or compete with previously established populations. This process alters the composition of communities and usually also increases their stability and complexity. As the population sizes of newly established species increase, the by-products and activities of these species further modify the environment of the ecosystem. Other species that possess the necessary adaptations for survival in this modified environment now become established, modifying the environment still further. This process of modification continues through a series of successional stages, until a dynamic equilibrium is achieved between all components of the ecosystem. Such stable, self-perpetuating climax communities persist indefinitely, unless events (whether natural or the result of human intervention) disrupt their structure. A more specific understanding of this process can be obtained from an examination of a few examples of aquatic and terrestrial succession.

Aquatic Succession

Ten thousand years ago, many depressions were carved in the surface of North America as glaciers advanced southward across Canada and into the United States. Most of the lakes of Minnesota, Wisconsin, Michigan, New England, and other northern states were formed when worldwide increases in temperature released meltwaters from receding glaciers into the larger depressions.

At first, the newly formed lakes contained only small populations of bacteria and other small organisms. Such nutrient-poor, or *oligotrophic*, lakes contained little organic matter and bottom sediment. The concentration of inorganic nutrients increased slowly, however, as rain and erosion washed nitrates, phosphates, and similar compounds from the surrounding land into the lakes. This increased concentration of inorganic nutrients in a lake triggered the gradual development of diversified food chains. But it also triggered the eventual death of the lake, for all lake ecosystems pass through a series of stages that terminate with the establishment of a complex terrestrial ecosystem in place of the lake (Fig. 9.1).

Increasing concentrations of dissolved inorganic nutrients in oligotrophic lakes make possible the establishment of new and expanding populations of autotrophs. Some of these populations consist of aquatic plants, but most are small photosynthetic protists collectively called *phytoplankton.* These microscopic organisms live within a few meters of the lake surface, where sufficient amounts of light penetrate the water for photosynthesis. This upper portion of a lake is the *photic zone,* in contrast to the deeper, perpetually dark *aphotic zone.* The gradual increase in numbers of autotrophs within oligotrophic lakes supports new and expanding populations of consumers. The first to increase are populations of microscopic consumers of phytoplankton, called *zooplankton.* Older lakes contain large populations of plankton as well as abundant organic and inorganic nutrients. Such lakes are termed *eutrophic.*

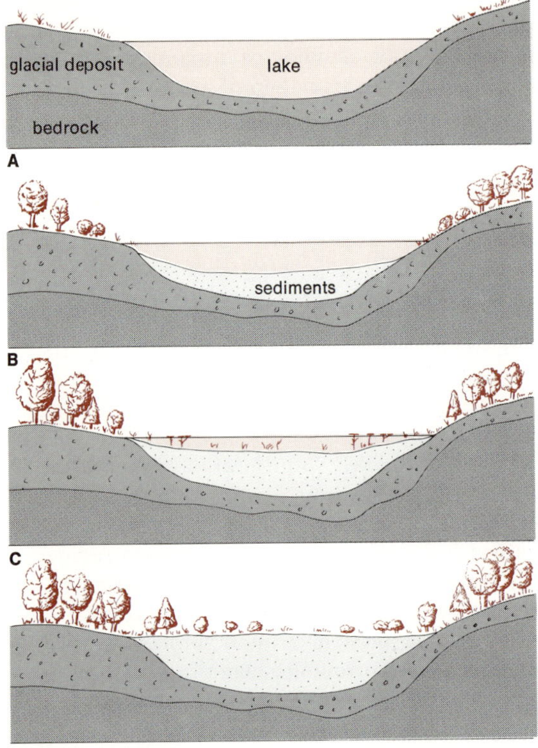

Fig. 9.1 Lake succession. (A) Newly formed lake as it would have looked shortly after retreat of a glacier, some 10,000 years ago. At this time the lake is highly oligotrophic. A layer of granular glacial deposits covers the underlying bedrock. Some vegetation has reappeared on the land surrounding the lake. (B) The lake as it would look now, 10,000 years later than stage A. The lake bottom is about half filled with mud sediments, and the surrounding land is reforested. (C) The lake a few thousand years later than stage B. Accumulating bottom sediments have produced a shallow lake. The shore of the lake supports marshes, and growth of aquatic plants is extensive. (D) The lake aged to a terrestrial form. Marsh occupies what was the center of the lake, and forest occupies the once muddy shore. Given additional centuries, the full area of the lake may become occupied by forest. (*Adapted from R. H. Whittaker, "Communities and Ecosystems," 2d ed., Macmillan, New York, 1975.*)

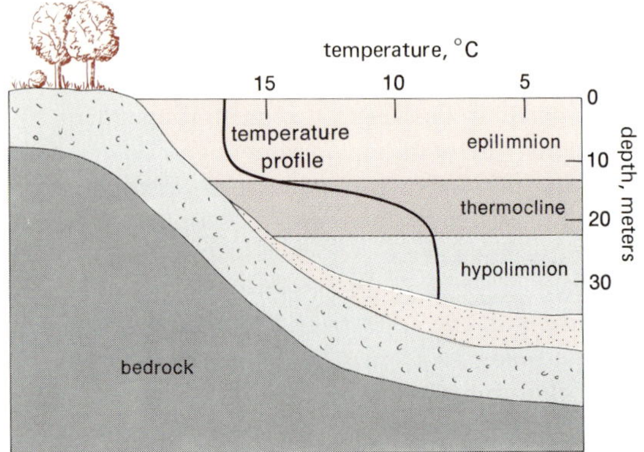

Fig. 9.2 Thermal stratification of lakes. In summer, deep lakes stratify into three layers; a warm epilimnion (penetrating to about the same depth as the lower boundary of the photic zone), a zone of rapid temperature change or thermocline, and a cold hypolimnion. (*Modified from R. H. Wagner, "Environment and Man," 2d ed., Norton, New York, 1971.*)

Most populations of organisms in lakes undergo seasonal cycles of growth and decline. Such cycles contribute to an increased fertility and shallowness of eutrophic lakes. In summer the photic zone is warmed by the sun and becomes less dense than water at the lake bottom. This difference in density causes the warmer upper layer, or *epilimnion*, to become isolated temporarily from the lower colder layer, or *hypolimnion*. The epilimnion "floats" on the hypolimnion, and little mixing occurs between the two. Separating the two layers is a thin middle layer, called the *thermocline*, across which occurs a sharp temperature gradient (Fig. 9.2).

This relatively stable thermal stratification produces several important differences between the upper and lower regions of a lake. Through photosynthesis, oxygen remains abundant in the epilimnion during the summer. However, since mixing normally does not occur between upper and lower layers, water below the thermocline contains very little oxygen. This low oxygen concentration restricts the activities of the decomposers at the lake bottom and, as a result, the dead bodies of organisms that fall from above are decomposed only partly. Most inorganic nutrients that are produced by the activities of decomposers at the lake bottom remain dissolved in the hypolimnion. Consequently, the reproductive and growth rates of organisms in the epilimnion decline steadily throughout the summer as these organisms use up the available supplies of dissolved inorganic nutrients.

As the temperature of surface water decreases in fall and its density increases, the thermocline disappears and upwellings mix the nutrient-rich

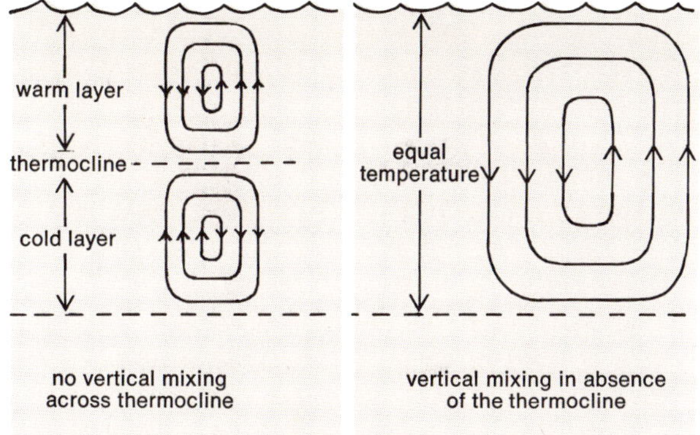

Fig. 9.3 Thermoclines and vertical mixing of water in lakes. Thermoclines prevent significant vertical mixing of water in summer (left). In early spring and late fall, surface waters do acquire the same temperature as deeper layers; the thermocline then disappears, and vertical mixing does become possible (right).

water of the hypolimnion with the oxygen-rich water of the epilimnion (Fig. 9.3). A similar turnover of water occurs in the spring, causing rapid growth of organisms at the lake surface and of decomposers at the lake bottom.

In spite of such semiannual "turnovers," decomposers do not break down all the organic debris that falls from surface waters. Consequently, eutrophic lakes become increasingly shallow as they age, and eventually they transform to swamps. Later, after additional layers of sediment accumulate, swamps become dry land, undergo additional succession, and eventually support dense ground covers or forests (Fig. 9.4).

The increased productivity that accompanies eutrophication not only renders lakes progressively shallower but also increases species diversity and brings about changes in the kinds of organisms that inhabit these aquatic ecosystems. Trout, for example, require cool, clear, oxygen-rich water. They thrive in lakes that are young and deep. In aged lakes, which contain little oxygen below the thermocline during summer months, trout are replaced by bass, sunfish, and pickerel. Similarly, lily pads and other rooted vegetation usually are found only in older and thus shallower lakes and ponds.

Terrestrial Succession

Soil Formation

Succession does not occur exclusively in aquatic environments. For example, succession can begin on rock formed from a volcanic outpouring of lava. Lichens often are the first organisms to in-

Fig. 9.4 Swamps. (A) A swamp region. Note the greater density of vegetation at the edges of the swamp. (B) Several species of plants, such as these cattails, stabilize the shores of swamps and hasten their succession to dry land. Cattails reduce wave action and trap sediments that erode from land surrounding swamps. (C) Desmids, unicellular phytoplankton that form pond scum on stagnant fresh water. Organic debris, generated in part from the decay of such scums, eventually adds to bottom sediments, furthering transformation of the swamps to dry land.

A

B

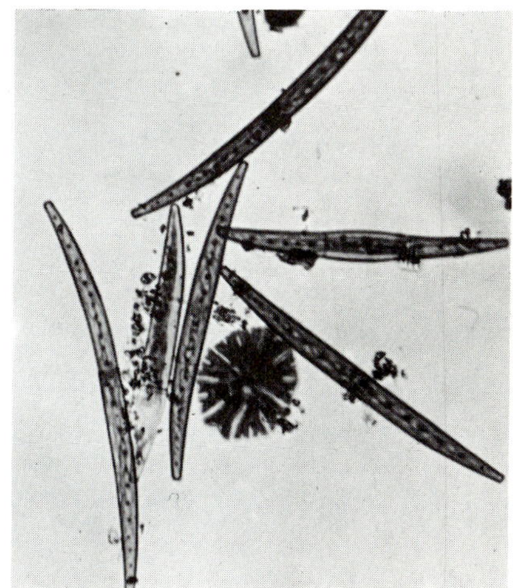
C

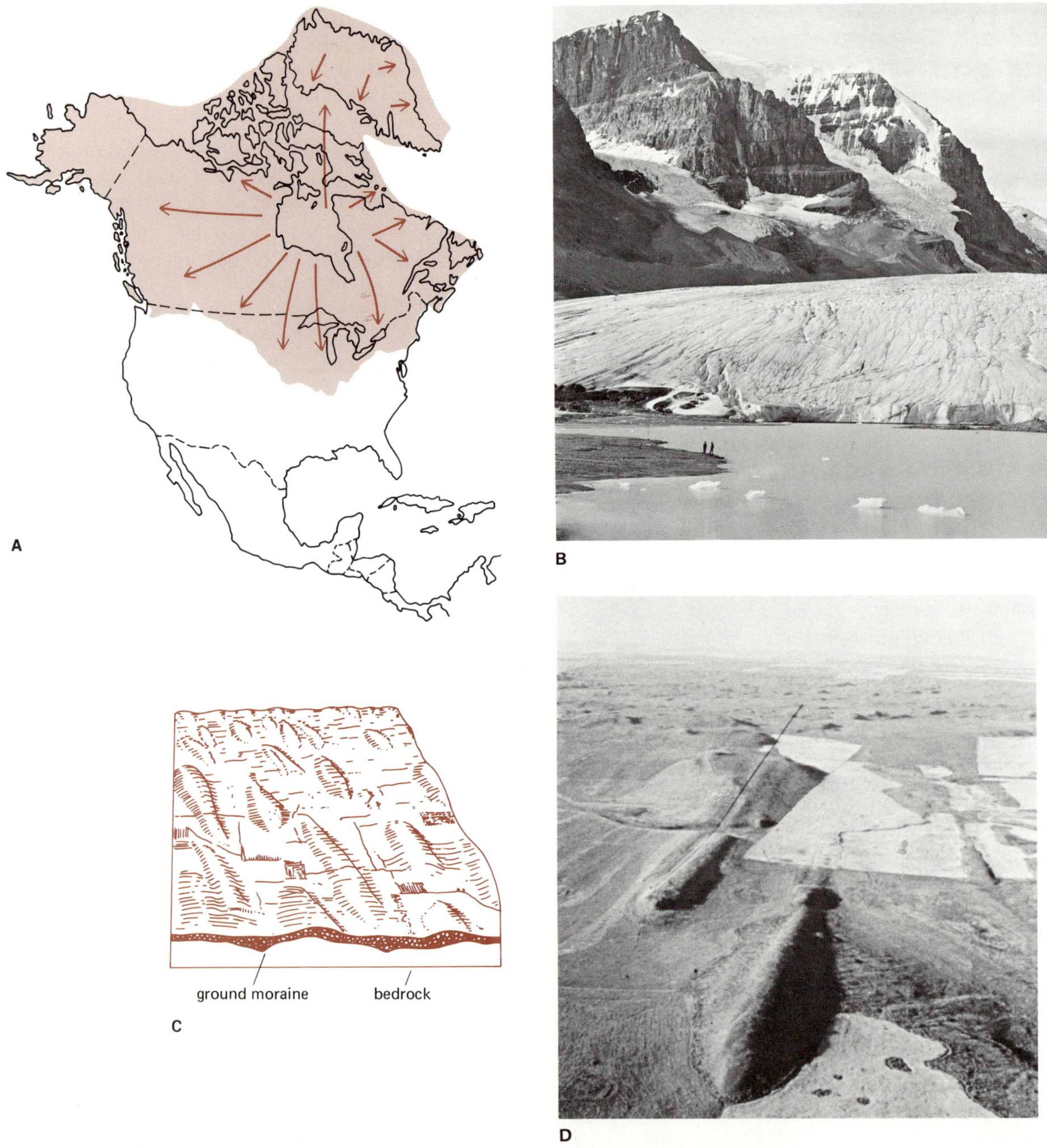

Fig. 9.5 Glaciers and soil formation. (A) Extent of glaciation during the last great ice age. Color denotes regions in the Northern Hemisphere that were covered by a glacier at some point during the last ice age, some 10,000 years ago. Arrows indicate direction of ice flow. (B) Tongue of the Athabasca Glacier, part of the Columbia Icefield, Jasper National park, Alberta, Canada. Note the lake in the foreground, maintained by meltwater from the glacier. (C) Cross section of land formed by the advance and subsequent retreat of a glacier. Ground moraine consists of rock fragments, clay, and other surface debris released by a melting glacier. In some places the debris forms streamlined hills, called drumlins, as shown in (D). Over the past 10,000 years, organisms have transformed much of the surface of such land from barren debris to fertile loams.

habit such environments, beginning the process of soil formation from rock as described in Chap. 6. Once lichens have modified the environment of the rock surface, they often are joined and eventually displaced by mosses and short grasses (see Fig. 6.4). The activities of these early successional communities transform the rock surface into a thin, granular soil capable of supporting more complex communities of taller grasses and weeds.

Organisms almost always play a major role in determining the qualities and rates of formation of soils, but these attributes also are influenced by many physical factors, including the origin of the land, climate, and topography. Some soils develop in place from underlying parent rock. Others are derived at least in part from matter carried by wind, water, glaciers, and other physical agents. Soils across most of the northern United States have developed from rock fragments produced by the southward advance of glaciers thousands of years ago. Ground from rocks by thick sheets of ice, the fragments were carried hundreds of miles and deposited where the glaciers finally melted (Fig. 9.5). Much of the soil in the central United States is derived from *loess*, deposits formed by the accumulation of dust particles carried long distances by wind.

Such diverse origins of land greatly influence early stages of soil formation and community succession. For example, glacial deposits usually contain large amounts of coarse *gravel*. Conversely, *clay* is formed from aggregation of large numbers of very small particles. For very different reasons, neither gravel nor clay provides a favorable environment for rapid development of terrestrial communities. Water and dissolved nutrients leach quickly through gravel, and insufficient amounts of these substances are retained for substantial plant growth. Heavy clay is so compact that it absorbs little water, contains few air pockets, and often cannot be penetrated by roots.

Most plants thrive best in *loams*, soils that contain a mixture of coarse and fine particles. Loams have large numbers of channels through which water can drain, but they are sufficiently compact for retention of moisture and air. The rate at which a forest, prairie, or other complex terrestrial community becomes established on a barren surface is determined largely by the rates at which early successional communities interact with physical factors in transforming land surfaces to loams.

Fig. 9.6 Topsoil. The soil on the right is darker because it contains much more humus than the impoverished soil on the left.

Because they support large populations of many different organisms, loams contain large amounts of decomposing organic matter, or *humus*. This complex organic material binds together granular particles and adds to the water-retaining characteristics of soil (Fig. 9.6). Two main layers gradually develop in succession in young soils as increasing amounts of organic matter collect at the surface: an upper, darker *topsoil* composed of humus, minerals, and small granular deposits, and a lighter *subsoil* composed mostly of inorganic parent material. These layers become distinguishable at about the time short grasses appear on newly formed soil (Fig. 9.7). At this point, the topsoil is enriched sufficiently to support shrubs that are displaced by large trees in some environments. Thus, as a result of hundreds of years of ecological succession, dense forests can stand on sites once occupied by barren rock (Fig. 9.8).

Species Diversity

As succession advances toward establishment of climax communities in terrestrial environments, the number of different species making up communities usually increases. This trend also accompanies eutrophication of aquatic ecosystems, and it can be illustrated by examining the successional development of land in southern Canada (Table 9.1). Note that only 13 species of male birds were sighted in wet bogs, but 28 species inhabited land that had succeeded to a black spruce and hemlock forest.

Ecological niches usually increase in number as communities become successionally more advanced, and this accounts for most of the increase in species diversity. At early stages of succession, communities are composed almost exclusively of plants and decomposer organisms. Immigration of herbivores usually follows, and they, in turn, provide food for carnivores. Thus, older communities usually provide a greater variety of resources that can be used by an increased number of species.

Increases in species diversity usually enhance the stability of ecosystems. Accordingly, species diversity and stability often are greatest in climax communities. This important principle is illustrated by the following example. Suppose a lawn is composed of only one species of grass. The entire lawn may be destroyed if the species becomes diseased. But suppose this species is one of five different types of plants in a lawn. The lawn may be damaged if one species becomes diseased, but it is less likely to be destroyed. Although a lawn composed of different grasses and many weeds may seem less attractive than one composed of a few selected species, it is more stable because of its increased species diversity. Thus, the practice of maintaining lawns in a more artificial and therefore less stable state always will remain a frustration to homeowners and a boon to manufacturers of lawn products.

◀ **Fig. 9.7 Soil profile.** In this grass-covered Alaskan soil, topsoil extends to a depth of about 10 inches. Approximately 3 inches of clay underlies the topsoil. The subsoil consists largely of mixed sand and gravel.

Fig. 9.8 Stages in the succession of a climax terrestrial community. The sequence of communities depicted typifies terrestrial succession in the Piedmont region of the southeastern United States. The predominant types of plants in each successional community are illustrated in the lower portion of the figure. (*From E. P. Odum, "Fundamentals of Ecology," Saunders, Philadelphia, 1959.*)

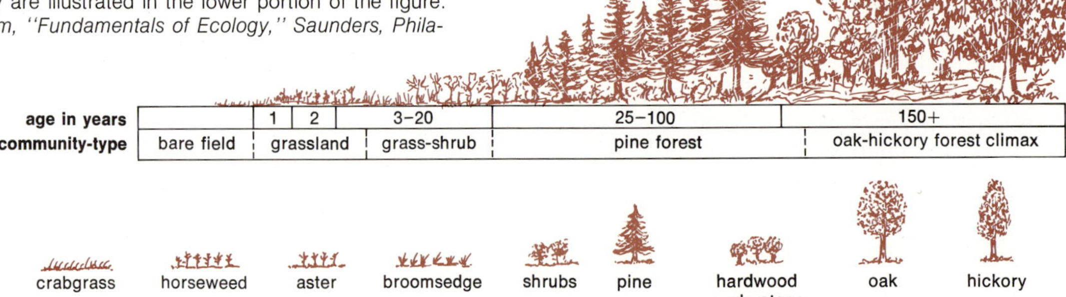

TABLE 9.1

Changing Compositions of Male Birds Based on Sightings in 100 Acres of Land in Southern Canada

Species	State of succession		
	Wet bog	Black spruce	Black spruce and hemlock
barn swallow	×		
black duck	×		
alder-flycatcher	×		
bronzed grackle	×		
red-winged blackbird	×		
kingbird	×		
tree swallow	×		
swamp sparrow	×		
purple finch	×	×	×
yellow-shafted flicker	×	×	×
cedar waxwing	×	×	×
yellowthroat	×	×	×
blue jay		×	
ruffed grouse		×	
yellow-bellied sapsucker		×	
hermit thrush		×	
Canada jay		×	×
brown creeper		×	×
black and white warbler		×	×
Blackburnian warbler		×	×
slate-colored junco		×	×
white-throated sparrow		×	×
black-capped chickadee		×	×
northern water thrush		×	×
olive-backed thrush		×	×
Nashville warbler		×	×
Canada warbler		×	×
myrtle warbler		×	×
winter wren		×	×
golden-crowned kinglet		×	×
magnolia warbler		×	×
yellow-bellied flycatcher		×	×
arctic three-toed woodpecker			×
scarlet tanager			×
ruby-crowned kinglet			×
chestnut-sided warbler			×
red-breasted nuthatch			×
spruce grouse			×
veery			×
American olive-sided flycatcher			×
total number of species	12	24	28

SOURCE: Modified from N. D. Martin, *Ecology*, vol. 41, pp. 126–140, 1960.

A B

Fig. 9.9 Succession on abandoned farmland. (A) A recently abandoned field near Philadelphia, dominated by Queen Anne's lace during later summer. (B) After 10 to 15 years, small trees begin to grow up. Unless succession is disrupted, a low forest will occupy this site in 25 to 50 years, and a climax forest community will develop in 100 to 200 years. *(From R. E. Ricklefs, "Ecology," Chiron Press, Newton, Mass., 1973.)*

Species Composition of Communities

Examination of Table 9.1 illustrates another general characteristic of ecological succession. Note that only four species of birds sighted in wet bogs were also found in forested land; the remaining eight were displaced by new populations. Few species have the adaptive tolerance for the many environmental changes that occur during succession, and few therefore persist long in preclimax communities. During early stages of succession ecosystems typically provide many resources for rapid population growth. Thus, species that become established in immature ecosystems tend to have high biotic potentials and are well adapted for exploitation of unused resources. But these species usually are not well adapted to the more crowded conditions and limited resources that characterize climax communities. The increased number of niches in well-developed communities favors species that have slower rates of growth and are well adapted to living at, or near, carrying capacity. And, as might be expected, the number of species displaying close symbiotic interactions often increases greatly as ecosystems mature.

Biomass

As succession advances toward the climax stage, the total biomass of communities generally increases. During the early stages of ecological succession, the amount of energy fixed as producer biomass from photosynthesis exceeds the amount of energy respired by all organisms of a community. At such times, the total biomass of communities usually grows rapidly. In terrestrial ecosystems, for example, small plants like mosses and short grasses are replaced by taller grasses and shrubs. In their turn, these species are replaced by still larger and taller plants such as maples, oaks, or pines (Fig. 9.9 and see Fig. 9.8).

Growth in total biomass gradually slows down, however, as the climax condition is approached. This reduced growth rate results largely from a steady increase in community respiration, compared with the total amount of energy fixed by producers. For example, a forest contains a proportionately greater biomass of consumers than a meadow. A disproportionate increase in the number of niches available for consumers has accompanied the vertical increase in living matter from meadow to forest. Animal populations inhabiting the tops of trees are able to coexist with populations occupying ground-level habitats. In tropical environments, several different vertically distributed populations of insects and birds can be studied by climbing a single tree.

Moreover, a proportionately greater amount of energy from respiration is required to produce and support the greatly increased amounts of nonphotosynthetic tissues of woody forest plants, compared with the predominately herbaceous plants of a meadow. Consequently, correspondingly smaller amounts of energy are available to support further increases in total biomass. This trend can be seen in Table 9.2, which compares the production and consumption of fixed energy in three communities at different stages of development. Net production is highest in the least advanced community and zero at the climax stage. Moreover, the ratio of total production P to total respiration R is greater than 1 for both preclimax communities but equal to 1 for the climax rain forest. These data illustrate the gradual decline in the rate of biomass accumulation that accompanies development of ecosystems. Net production of biomass ceases in climax communities, and a dynamic equilibrium between production and consumption of fixed energy is achieved. Barring man-made or natural disruptions, this self-perpetuating equilibrium will be maintained indefinitely.

Succession and Environment

Although all instances of succession are consistent with the general pattern described thus far, the exact sequence of communities in a specific succession depends on the nature of the environment in which the succession occurs. Thus, the sequence of communities, or *sere,* that begins on bare rock and succeeds to an oak-hickory forest in Missouri will differ substantially from the sere that begins on lava and leads to a dense jungle in the South Pacific. Seres that originate from areas devoid of soil and organic matter are examples of *primary succession;* communities have not existed previously on these sites. Examples are lake successions that begin following glaciation or terrestrial successions that begin on bare rock. A recent example of primary succession on a large scale began in 1883, when islands of the Krakatoa group in Indonesia were devastated by volcanic activity (see Fig. 10.15). The center of one lava-covered area was 25 miles from the nearest source of life. Yet after only 50 years, this locale supported a complex ecosystem containing 271 species of plants.

In other cases, the previous existence of destroyed communities continues to influence the character of the physical environment. This effect occurs, for example, when a forest is destroyed completely by fire. Succession begins anew on such sites but on soil modified by the activities of previous communities. Seres that originate from areas

TABLE 9.2

Annual Production and Consumption of Fixed Energy during Terrestrial Succession, kcal/m²

	Early pine plantation (England)	**Medium oak-pine forest (New York)**	**Climax rain forest (Puerto Rico)**
gross production	12,200	11,500	45,000
plant respiration	4,700	6,400	32,000
net production	7,500	5,000	13,000
animal respiration	4,600	3,000	13,000
net community production	2,900	2,000	0
gross production converted to biomass (net community production/gross production)	23.77%	17.40%	0%
accumulation of biomass	yes	yes	no
P/R value (gross production/community respiration)	1.31	1.22	1

SOURCE: Modified from Eugene P. Odum, "Fundamentals of Ecology," 3d ed., p. 46, Saunders, Philadelphia, 1971.

Fig. 9.10 Secondary succession. Succession can be disrupted by numerous factors such as fire. This area, once the site of a dense forest, was destroyed by fire and now supports populations of grasses and low shrubs. A forest may eventually reoccupy this site if succession is not disrupted again.

Fig. 9.11 Pulse-stabilized communities. This aerial photograph of the Florida Everglades shows marsh and mangrove islands (light) interspersed with shallow bays (dark). The land and water components of this complex habitat constitute interdependent units. Together, they make up one of the most fragile, yet most productive, ecosystems in the world.

of previously existing communities are examples of *secondary succession* (Fig. 9.10).

Although both types of succession progress toward a climax state, both are influenced by factors that often result in the establishment of several climax communities in a region. In Missouri, for example, small communities dominated by sugar maples are found within more extensive climax communities characterized by oak and hickory. These pockets of sugar maple, however, are self-perpetuating communities that show little evidence of succeeding to the more typical oak-hickory state.

Such localized climax communities exist in all major ecosystems and are found wherever soil, climate, terrain, and other environmental conditions differ significantly from those characterizing the region generally. For example, the microclimate of areas dominated by sugar maple is somewhat cooler and more humid than most regions of Missouri. Sugar maples are better adapted to these cooler and more humid regions than oaks or hickories, and consequently they dominate the localized climax communities of these regions.

Hence there usually is no absolute climax community that develops and extends over a broad geographical area. Although certain types of vegetation are found frequently throughout such areas, climax communities that develop on specific sites vary with different localized environments.

Some agents, such as fires, floods, and earthquakes, can cause successively older communities to revert to simpler states. Such factors frequently are induced by people, whose activities often destroy the natural stability that usually accompanies ecological succession. Several examples of the destructive impact of people on ecosystems and community succession are presented in the next chapter.

Other factors impede or halt succession before climax, and some communities remain indefinitely at intermediate stages of development between youth and maturity. Salt marshes are a good example. As described in Chap. 8, these ecosystems are extremely fertile and productive. In view of their great net production of organic matter, they might be expected to succeed rapidly to terrestrial environments. Yet most salt marshes persist as swampy ecosystems because most of their daily net increase in biomass is swept away by tides.

Ecosystems such as salt marshes, rice paddies, and the Florida Everglades are said to be *pulse-stabilized* in a preclimax state by the flushing action of tides (Fig. 9.11). Pulse-stabilized communities are extremely important components of the total environment because of the surplus production of organic matter that passes into surrounding ecosystems and partly nourishes them. This is one reason why ecologists usually recommend that marshes be preserved in their natural states.

Succession, therefore, is a dynamic process determined by the interactions of organisms between themselves and with their physical environments. The process always progresses toward establishment of an equilibrium between living and nonliving components, except when influenced by factors that halt or interfere with this natural progression. Thus, seres beginning from dissimilar starting points in similar environments typically succeed toward similar climax communities or pulse-stabilized ecosystems.

These principles are illustrated by Fig. 9.12, which depicts several seres coexisting in central Missouri. Note that seres beginning either on bare rock or in a lake can succeed to similar climax forests dominated by oak and hickory. But also note that either of these seres can be arrested short of the climax state by various disruptive factors. For example, a sere beginning in open water will terminate as a swampy flood plain if people or climate maintain wetter than average conditions. Alternatively, a strictly terrestrial sere will terminate as grassland if soil conditions, fire, or cultivation prevents the growth of shrubs and small trees.

In summary, the most significant characteristics of ecological succession can be grouped under five headings:

1. Species diversity tends to increase during succession.

2. The species composition of communities changes continually during succession.

3. Species found in more developed communities tend to have slower rates of population growth and are better adapted for interspecific cooperation than species occupying less advanced ecosystems.

4. The total amount of living matter and decomposing organic materials tends to increase during succession.

5. Succession progresses toward establishment of equilibria between production and consumption of fixed energy in communities, except when influenced by factors that cause P/R values to increase or stay higher than 1.

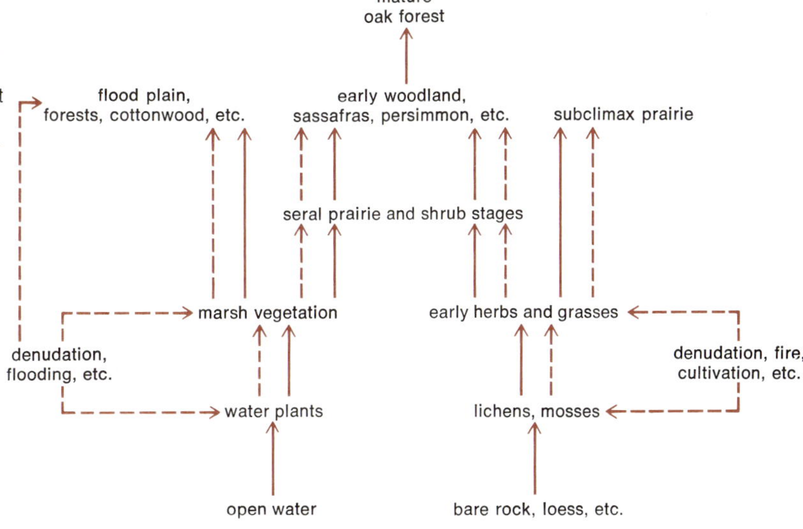

Fig. 9.12 Successional pathways. Schematic diagram of successional pathways from dissimilar starting points toward a terminal (climax) community in central Missouri. Convergence is not inevitable, since one or more of the seres may be arrested short of the theoretical climax. Both primary successional (solid lines) and secondary successional (broken lines) seres are included. *(From C. L. Kucera, "The Challenge of Ecology," Mosby, St. Louis, 1973.)*

MAJOR ECOSYSTEMS OF THE BIOSPHERE

Major Aquatic Ecosystems: Oceans and Seas

Physical Characteristics

Oceans constitute the largest and most stable ecosystem. Approximately 70 per cent of the earth's surface is covered by salt water. Food chains begin with the smallest known autotrophs and end with the largest animals.

Marine life is greatly influenced by many physical factors—currents, tides, waves, temperature, pressure, and light intensity. But the most familiar physical attribute of seawater is its high mineral content. The proportions of the different types of salt are almost the same all over the globe, as a result of thorough mixing of all waters by currents. Since sodium and chlorine make up a large proportion of ions in seawater, about three-fifths of the mineral content of oceans consists of table salt.

However, the total salt concentration, or *salinity,* varies considerably from region to region. The highest salinities occur in tropic water, where high temperatures and extensive evaporation concentrate the oceanic salts. In the Red Sea the salt concentration is 4 per cent, one of the highest known. At higher latitudes, by contrast, seawater evaporates less and is therefore less salty. Moreover, salinities are lower for often several hundred miles around the mouths of great rivers. The lowest known salinity is that of the Baltic Sea, where it is 0.7 per cent (that of human blood is 0.9 per cent). Salinity determines the density, or buoyancy, of ocean water, being the greater the higher the salinity. Both salinity and buoyancy are of considerable significance to all marine life; salinity affects, for example, the mineral balances of living matter, and buoyancy helps organisms counteract the pull of gravity.

An ocean basin has the general form of an inverted hat (Fig. 9.13). A gently sloping *continental shelf* stretches away from the coastline for about 100 miles (discounting often extreme deviations from this average). Located under and along the shelf are the bulk of undersea oil and mineral deposits. The angle of descent then changes fairly abruptly, and the shelf grades over to a steep *continental slope.* This slope eventually levels off and becomes the ocean floor, a more or less horizontal expanse called the *abyssal plain.*

The plain is scarred by rifts, the deepest being the approximately 7-mi-deep Japan and Philippine trenches along the western edge of the Pacific. Elsewhere the plain gives rise to mountains, with peaks sometimes so high that they rear up above sea level as islands. Chains of underwater mountains commonly rise from the abyssal plain at midocean. Volcanic activity occurs frequently along these ridges, and the lava that pours forth adds to the sea floor. These accumulating deposits are slowly forcing some continents apart and others together. The mid-Atlantic ridge, for example, is the former line of contact between North America and Europe. Most of the sea floor of the Atlantic has been produced by laval outpourings on each side of this midocean ridge. Production of new sea floor continues to spread the continents apart at an annual rate of about 1 inch. The effects of such *continental drift* on the evolution of species will be discussed in Chap. 29.

Fig. 9.13 The structure of an ocean basin.

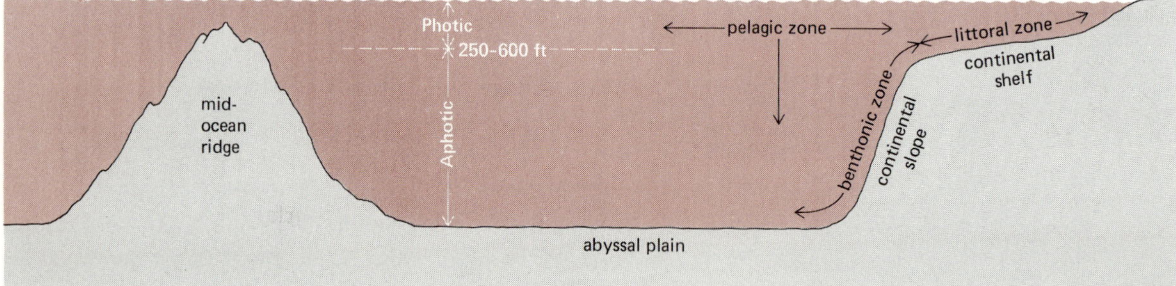

Major Habitats

Ocean basins provide five major habitats for marine life, three stratified horizontally and two vertically. The sea floor from the shore out to the edge of the continental shelf forms a *littoral zone* (see Fig. 9.13). Beyond it, the sea floor along the continental slope and the abyssal plain represents the *benthonic zone.* And the water that fills the ocean basin is the *pelagic zone.* Sunlight penetrates water only to an average depth of about 250 ft, and to at most 600 ft in certain seas. Thus, with respect to sunlight, oceans are stratified vertically into the same two zones found in deep lakes. Photosynthesizing organisms can exist only in the sunlit *photic zone.* Animal life directly dependent on these organisms must therefore remain near the surface as well. In sharp contrast, the dark *aphotic zone* is totally free of photosynthetic organisms and contains only animals, bacteria, and possibly fungi.

On the basis of its relationship to these habitats, marine life can be classified generally as *plankton, nekton,* and *benthos.* Plankton, a collective term for phyto- and zooplankton, includes all drifting and floating organisms. As in lakes, most of them are microscopic and are found largely in the photic zone. Although many of these forms have locomotor structures, they are nevertheless too weak or too small to counteract water currents (Fig. 9.14). Nekton comprises the strong swimmers, capable of changing stations at will. All nektonic types thus are animals, and they are found along the surface as well as in the sea depths. The benthos consists of crawling, creeping, and attached organisms; they are found along the sides and the bottom of the ocean basin.

Phytoplankton at the surface of oceans includes teeming trillions of algae that as a group probably synthesize more than twice as much food as all land plants combined. This vegetation represents the richest pasture on earth; directly or indirectly it forms the nutritional basis of all marine life. Most of the algal types in this "grass of the sea" are microscopic, and among them the single-celled, yellowish- and brownish-green *diatoms* are probably the most abundant (Fig. 9.15 and see Fig. 9.14).

Zooplankton lives side by side with the phytoplankton in open surface water. These organisms include bacteria, protozoa, eggs, larvae, tiny shrimp, and other small animals carried along by surface drift. They feed directly on the microscopic vegetation. Most of the nekton, largely fishes and marine mammals, comes to these waters and feeds either on zooplankton or on phytoplankton directly.

Through its influence on water temperature the sun has important effects on the distribution and abundance of plankton, hence on marine life in general. Thermoclines become established in most northern and southern seas in summer and are present all year long in tropical waters. Organisms above a thermocline deplete the water of mineral raw materials, and after the organisms die these materials sink down without being returned to the surface by vertical mixing. As a result, the amount of surface life is limited, and warm seas actually are relatively barren. In cold seas, by contrast, surface and deeper waters have roughly the same low temperature, thermoclines tend to be less pronounced or even absent, and vertical mixing of water can occur more readily. Minerals are then recirculated more rapidly and surface life can be correspondingly more abundant. The perennially cold arctic, antarctic, and subpolar waters actually support huge permanent plankton populations. And as is well known, the best commerical fishing grounds are in the high north and south, not in the tropics, and the best fishing seasons are spring and fall, not summer.

Warm and cold seas differ not only in the total amount but also in the diversity of life: warm oceans typically sustain small populations of many species, and cold oceans harbor large populations of comparatively few species. The reason is that higher temperatures promote all reactions, including those leading to evolution. Warm-climate life will therefore tend to become more diverse than cold-climate life. However, the limited mineral content of warm seas will keep the numbers of individuals low.

The sun also stimulates *diurnal migrations* of most planktonic organisms. During the night the organisms are distributed vertically throughout the surface waters, but during the day most of the plankton shuns the bright light and moves down to the dim layers of the photic zone. Larger animals feeding on plankton migrate up and down correspondingly. As a result even richly populated seas are quite barren on the surface during the daytime, and it is well known that surface fishing is more successful at night (Fig. 9.16).

Nearer to shore, in the water above the conti-

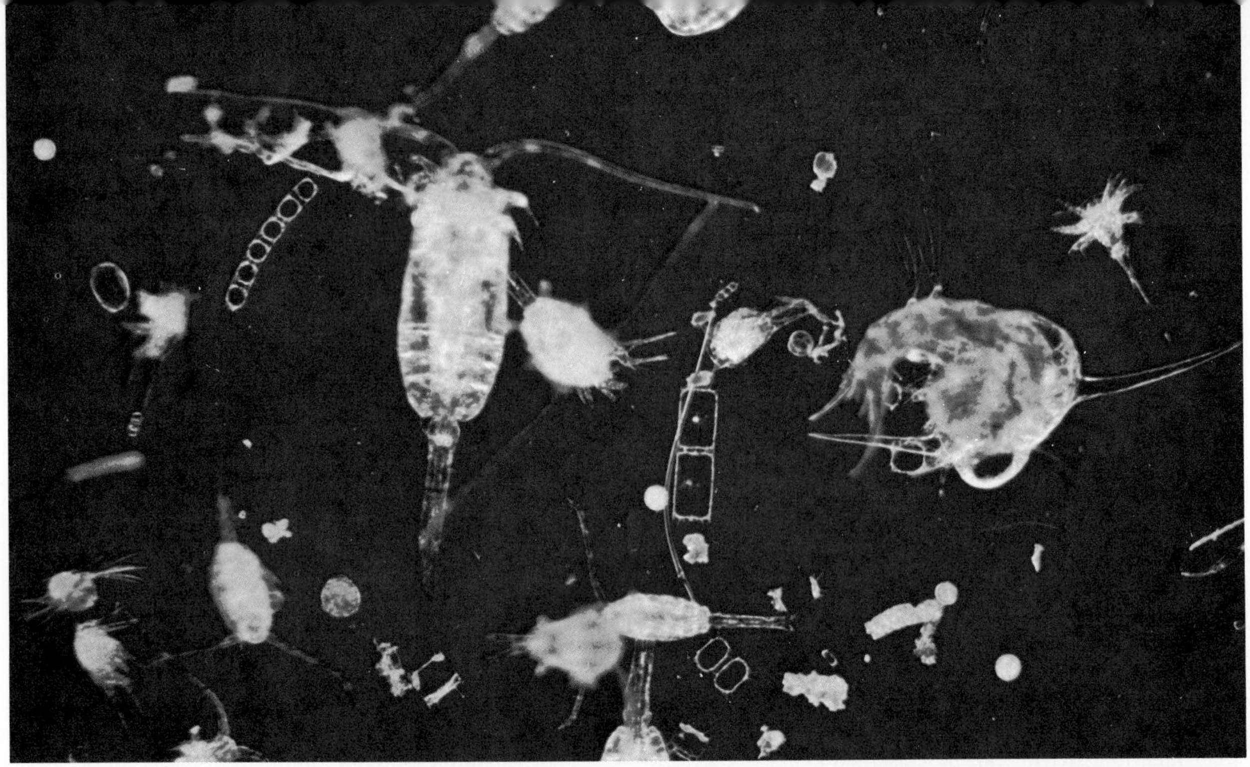

A

Fig. 9.14 Marine plankton. (A) Diatoms, copepods, crustacean larvae, protozoa, animal eggs, and other organisms. (B) Diatoms.

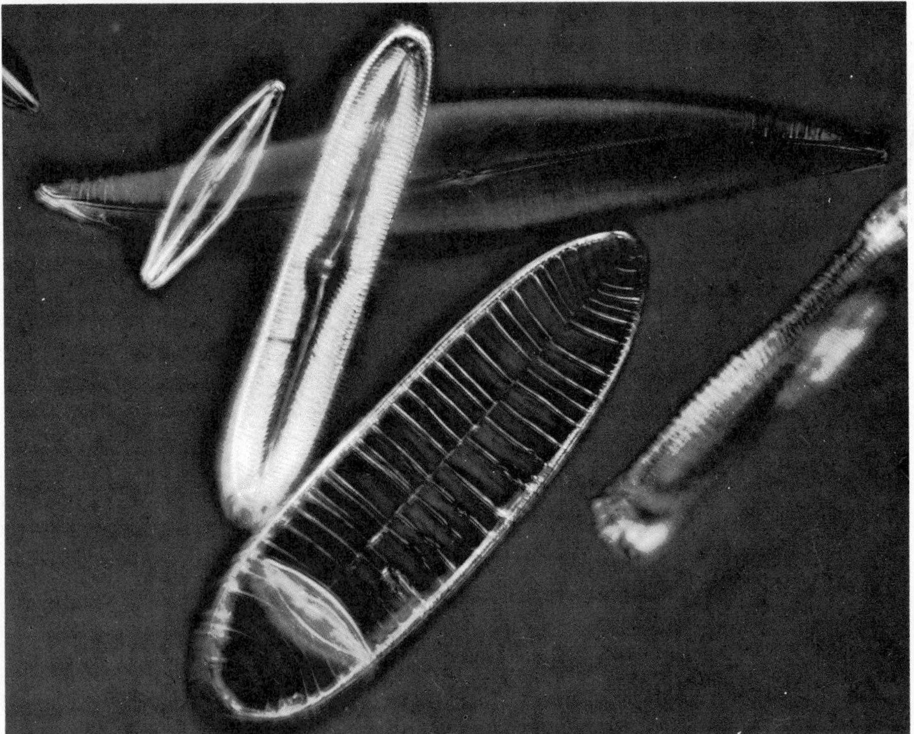

B

Fig. 9.15 Macroplankton. Not all phytoplankton is microscopic. The photo shows Sargassum weed, a brown alga. A related species forms the main seaweed that floats in the Sargasso Sea (see Figs. 32.1 and 32.2). The bulbous structures on the algae are air bladders.

nental shelf, even a bottom dweller is likely to be within the range of sunlight. The main problem here is to remain attached to solid ground, for the force of waves and ground swells is considerable. In the tidal zone, moreover, a still greater problem is the rhythmic alternation between aquatic and essentially terrestrial conditions twice every 24 h. As the meeting ground of water, land, and air, the tidal region actually is among the most violently changing habitats on earth.

Vegetation in this coastal region again is largely algal. In addition to the single-celled and small planktonic types, multicellular algae abound. Most of these seaweeds are equipped with specialized holdfasts that anchor the organisms to underlying ground. Green, brown, and red algae are particularly common. For example, the soft, slippery mats of vegetation that encrust rocks along the shore are familiar to many, as is *Fucus*, a common leathery brown alga found in dense populations on coastal rock. Animals in these waters include representatives of almost all major groups. In addition to planktonic types the region contains numerous nektonic animals, largely fish, as well as attached, burrowing, and creeping forms adapted to rocky, muddy, or sandy bottoms (Fig. 9.17).

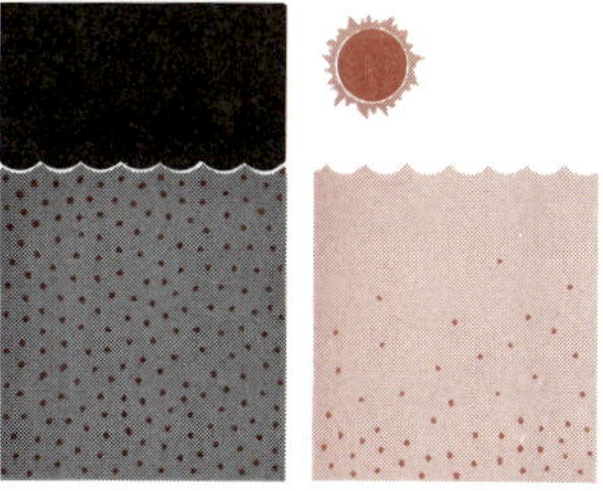

Fig. 9.16 Diurnal migrations of plankton. At night (left) plankton is distributed throughout the dark surface water. In daytime (right) plankton migrates away from the surface to darker, deeper waters.

The contrast between the surface habitat within reach of the sun and the aphotic zone below it is dramatic. As the one is forever fluctuating, so the other is perennially steady and relatively unchanging. Several unique physical conditions characterize this world of the sea depths.

First, in the total absence of sunlight, the region is pervaded with an eternal blackness of a kind found nowhere else on earth. Second, seasons and changing weather are practically absent. Localized climatic changes do occur, either as a result of occasional submarine volcanic activity, or, more regularly, through deepsea currents. These produce large-scale shifts of water masses and, incidentally, bring oxygen to even the deepest parts of the ocean. The deep waters are also perpetually cold. Temperatures range from about 10°C at the top of the dark zone to about 1°C along the abyssal plain.

Third, water pressure increases steadily from the surface down, 1 atmosphere (atm) for every 33 ft of descent. In the deepest trenches of the ocean the pressure is therefore about a thousand times as great as at sea level. And last, a continuous slow rain of the remains of dead surface organisms drifts down toward the sea bottom. A good deal of this material dissolves completely during the descent, but much microscopic mineral matter reaches the abyssal plain, where it forms ever-thickening layers of ooze. Accumulating over the millennia, the older layers are eventually compressed to rock. Vertical bore samples of such rock have revealed a great deal about the past history of the oceans and their former surface inhabitants.

Contrary to early beliefs that life should be impossible in such an environment, a surprisingly

Fig. 9.17 Coastal life. (A) *Laminaria,* a common brown alga attached to rocks in shallow water. (B) *Fucus,* another, even more common brown algal seaweed on coastal rocks. (C) *Caryophyllia,* a coral-forming coelenterate of warm shallow water. (D) *Eudistylia,* a feather-duster worm (distantly related to clamworms and earthworms) that forms and lives in secreted tubes attached along shallow coastal bottoms. The feathery tentacles trap minute food organisms.

rich diversity of organisms has been found in deep ocean habitats (see also Biology Highlight in Chap. 35). Apart from bacteria and perhaps fungi, the community is characteristically animal; photosynthetic organisms cannot live in perpetual darkness. Nearly all animal groups are represented, many by strange and bizarre types uniquely adapted to the locale (Fig. 9.18). Except for animals such as toothed whales, which can traverse the whole ocean from bottom to surface, most of the nektonic deepsea forms are adapted to particular water pressures. Such animals are therefore rigidly confined to limited pressure zones at fixed depths. Food normally must be obtained either from the dead matter

Fig. 9.18 **Deepsea life.** (A) An angler fish with a stalked, luminescent "lantern" over the mouth. Note the vertical position of the mouth, which facilitates catching prey lured to the light of the lantern. (B) The angler fish shown here is a female. The structure above the eye is a parasitic male, which is carried about permanently attached. This neatly solves the problem of finding a mating partner in the dark. Many of these large-mouthed, dagger-toothed fishes are surprisingly small; for example, the fish shown here fits comfortably in one's palm. (C) Another "lantern" fish, in which not only the organ above the mouth but also the "beard" is probably bioluminescent. (D) A school of luminescent deepsea squids.

A

B

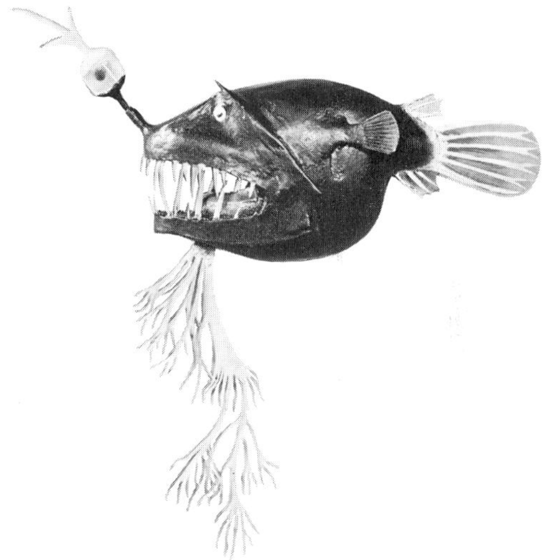

C

D

drifting down from the surface—a meager source, particularly in deeper water—or from other nektonic types.

This last condition makes the deep sea one of the most fiercely competitive habitats on earth. The very structure of the animals underscores their violently carnivorous, "eat-or-be-eaten" mode of existence. For example, most of the fishes have enormous mouths equipped with long, razor-sharp teeth, and many can swallow fish larger than themselves. Since the environment is pitchblack, one of the critical problems for these animals is, to begin with, *finding* food. A highly developed pressure sense provides one solution. Turbulence in the water created by nearby animals can be recognized and, depending on the nature of the disturbance, can be responded to by flight or approach.

Another important adaptation to the dark is *bioluminescence.* Many deep sea animals have light-producing organs of different shapes, sizes, and distributions. The light patterns emitted probably serve partly in species recognition. Identification of a suitable mate, for example, must be a serious problem in an environment where everything appears equally black. Another function of the light undoubtedly is to warn or to lure; certain fish carry a "lantern" on a stalk protruding from the snout. An inquisitive animal attracted to the light of the lantern will discover too late that is has headed straight into powerful jaws (see Fig. 9.18).

The boundary between land and sea is filled with a band of diverse and unique habitats, including rocky shores, sand beaches, intertidal mud flats, and *estuaries.* The last are semienclosed bodies of water where salinity is intermediate between fresh and salt water and where tidal currents are important physical regulators of biological activities. Examples of estuaries include the mouths of rivers and coastal bays (Fig. 9.19).

Fig. 9.19 Estuaries. The point of land projecting into the ocean in the foreground is Prouts Neck, Maine. Note the estuary, the semienclosed body of water in the center of the photograph. Fresh water enters the estuary from several surrounding tributaries; tidal currents force considerable amounts of salt water into the estuary from the ocean. As a result, the water of estuaries is brackish, intermediate in salinity between salt and fresh water.

Estuaries receive organic matter from ocean currents flowing landward along the bottom of the littoral zone. These currents mix with fresh water that carries an often richer supply of organic matter leached from the surrounding land. Consequently, estuaries are highly productive ecosystems that support varied and abundant communities. Moreover, estuaries are the nursery grounds for many mollusks, fish, and other species that spend most of their adult lives offshore. Because of their physical and biological interdependence, despoilment of estuaries, marshes, and other boundary ecosystems can greatly disrupt population balance in the littoral zone and vice versa.

Major Terrestrial Ecosystems: Biomes

Because ecological succession on land is greatly influenced by climate, it is not surprising that similar terrestrial ecosystems exist at similar latitudes and altitudes throughout the world. Aggregations of such similar ecosystems are called *biomes.*

For example, the *northern coniferous forest biome* extends over both the Old and New Worlds at approximately the same latitude (Fig. 9.20). Latitudinal divisions of biomes are also evident in eastern North and South America (but not in the high mountain regions that form the western "backbone" of the two continents, where the influence of latitude is modified greatly by altitude). A general appreciation of the nature of the biomes can be gained by a brief examination of the major biomes of North America.

Tundra

Arctic tundra is the northernmost biome of North America, extending generally north of latitude 57°N. The cold climate and frozen soil preclude growth of trees (Fig. 9.21). Grasses and sedges typically are found in marshes and poorly drained areas; various heath plants, such as bilberry and dwarf huckleberry, and low flowering herbs extend over large areas. The most abundant autotroph is a lichen known as "reindeer moss," a favorite food of the Alaskan caribou. Other mammals inhabiting the tundra include the muskox, grizzly bear, polar bear, arctic hare, gray wolf, arctic fox, and lemming.

Most plant life is dormant during the long, dark winter. Animals such as the caribou survive by migrating south to a more favorable climate; others, such as the lemming, remain in burrows beneath the ice and snow. Most animals become more active during the summer, when plants undergo a brief growing season. At that time num-

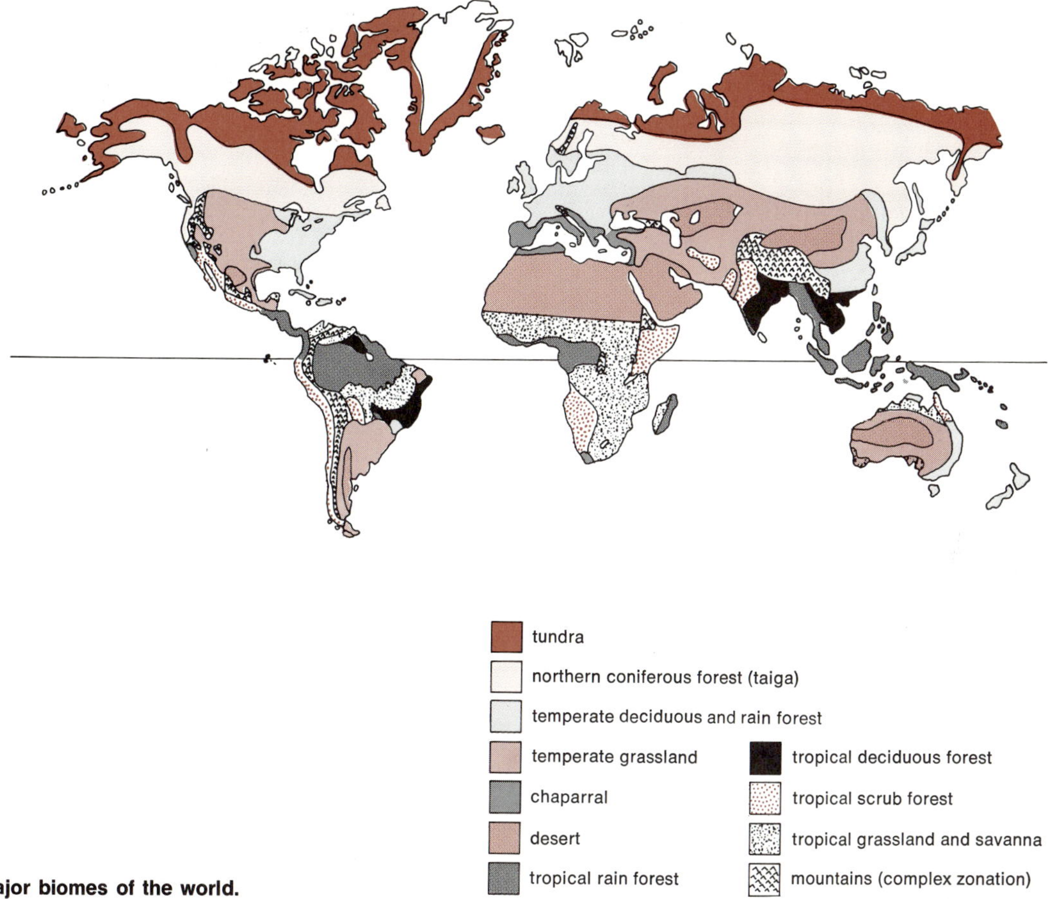

Fig. 9.20 Major biomes of the world.

bers of migratory waterfowl such as ducks, geese, and swans arrive to breed and establish nesting areas. Even in summer, however, the spongy, uneven ground often remains permanently frozen a few inches below the surface. Such perpetually frozen surface terrain is called *permafrost.*

Because of the relative simplicity of its community structure, the tundra is fragile and especially vulnerable to disruption. Any large-scale development or misuse of the region could upset the equilibrium between vegetation and soil and thus threaten dependent food chains. For this reason, ecologists are watching the effects of the Alaska oil pipeline project closely. For at least the first few years of operation, the pipeline appears not to have seriously jeopardized the stability of tundra soil.

Tundra also exists in more southerly regions at high mountainous altitudes (Fig. 9.22). However, greater numbers of flowering plants are found in alpine tundra compared with arctic tundra—a condition brought about largely by the absence of permafrost, better soil drainage, and a generally longer growing season.

Northern Coniferous Forest

This biome, sometimes called the "great north woods," exists largely between latitudes 45 and 57°N in Alaska, Canada, and the northern portions of the continental United States (see Fig. 9.20). It has counterparts in mountainous regions as far south as Costa Rica. The climate is warmer and more humid than in the tundra, most precipitation

Fig. 9.21 The habitat of the tundra. (A) Alaskan tundra landscape. Note complete absence of trees. (B) Muskox, a mammal characteristic of the tundra. (*A, U.S. Fish and Wildlife Service; B, courtesy of W. Suschitzky.*)

Fig. 9.22 Mountain habitats. The sequence of habitat zones between equator and pole is repeated altitudinally between the base and the top of a mountain.

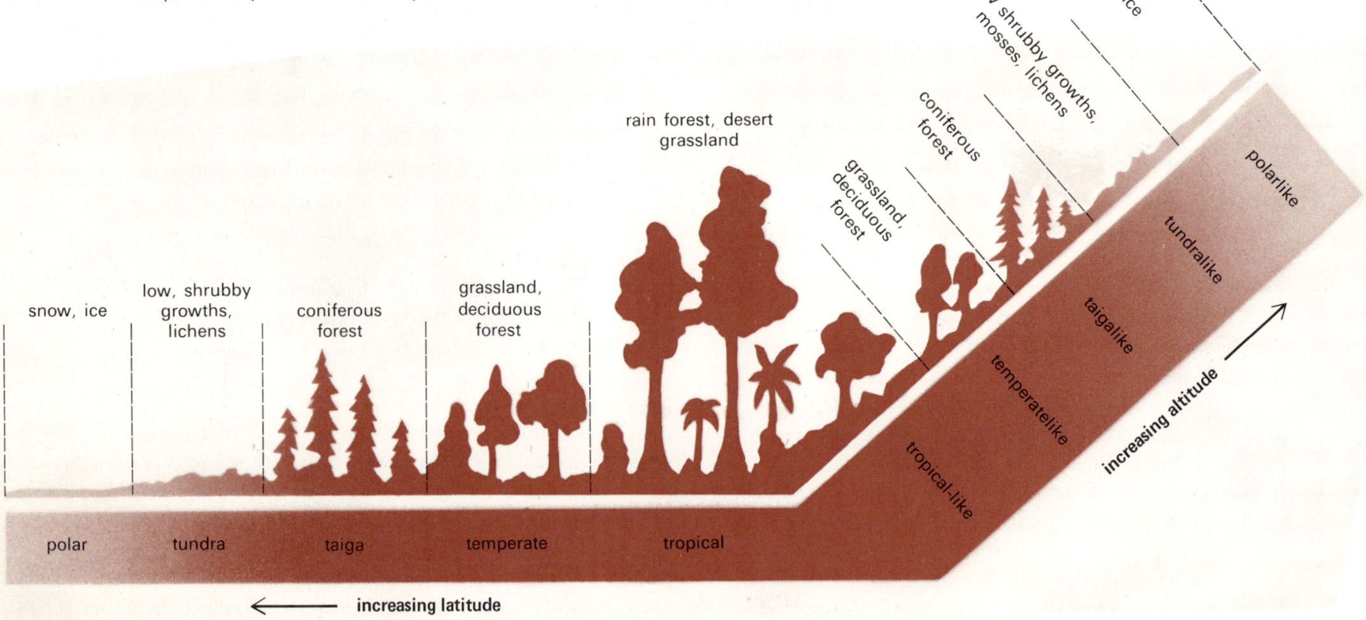

snow, ice
low, shrubby growths, lichens
coniferous forest
grassland, deciduous forest
rain forest, desert grassland
grassland, deciduous forest
coniferous forest
low shrubby growths, mosses, lichens
snow, ice
polar
tundra
taiga
temperate
tropical
tropical-like
temperatelike
taigalike
tundralike
polarlike
increasing latitude
increasing altitude

PHOTO ESSAY 1: LEVELS OF LIFE

The properties of life occur at all levels of organization within the living hierarchy. This sequence of photographs illustrates some of these properties and levels.

Cells and Organelles

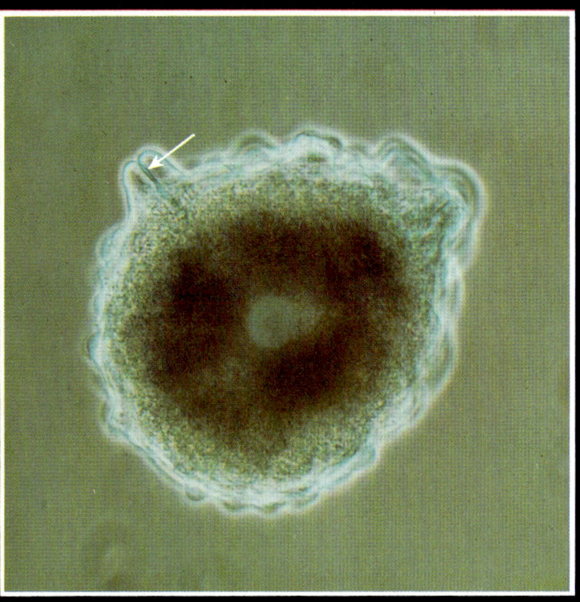

A

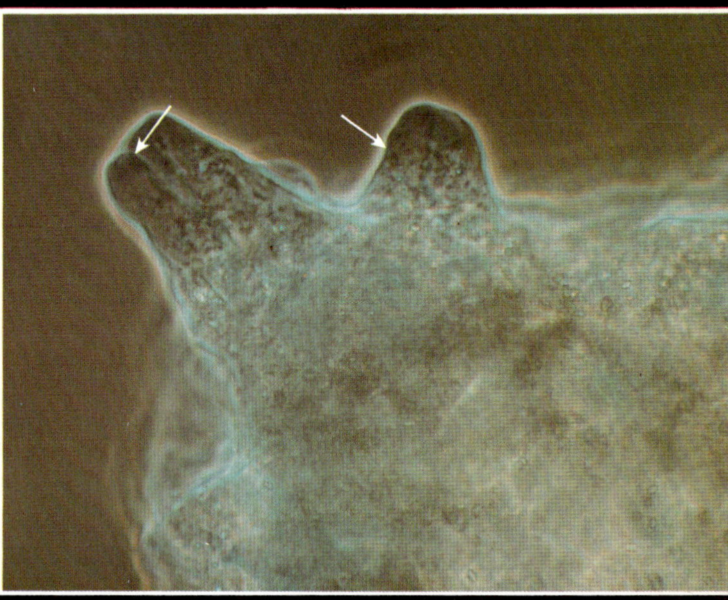

B

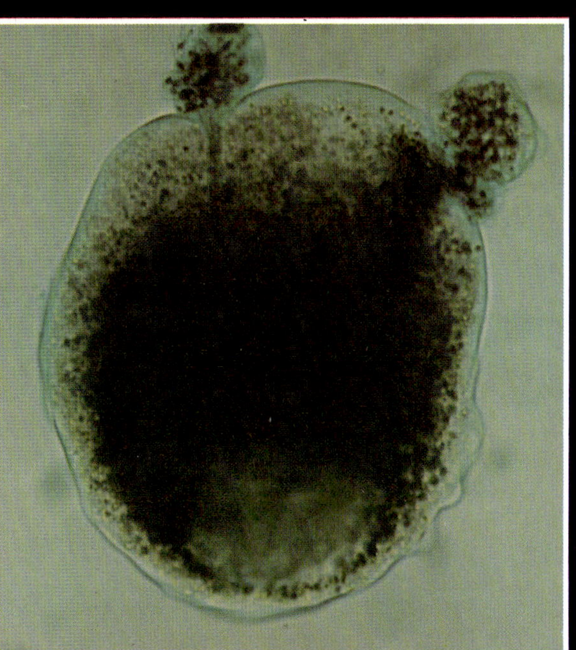

C

Color Fig. 1. Plasma membranes. Whole cells constitute the least elaborate living units, but the functional properties of life can be observed among subcellular components. For example, the plasma membrane of the *Amoeba* in (A) is undergoing repeated undulating movements, a process sometimes called "ruffling." In some cells, such movements always accompany certain specialized activities. In most cases, the functional significance of "ruffling" is unknown. The amoebas in these three photographs have been immersed in a solution containing alcian blue, a dye that induces pinocytosis ("cell drinking"). Pinocytotic channels (arrows), formed from involutions of the plasma membrane, can be seen in (A) and (B). The blue dye is transported into the cells along such channels and incorporated within tiny, membrane-bound vacuoles (vesicles) that "pinch off" from the involuted plasma membrane at the base of each channel. Unlike other fluids, which can serve as nutrients, alcian blue is poisonous. The dye is excreted via exocytosis (C). Note the two balloonlike masses of fluid at the top of this cell. The fluid, which consists largely of alcian blue, has been excreted through channels formed from involutions of the plasma membrane. Thus, plasma membranes can form channels for a flow of substances either into or out of cells. *(Courtesy Dr. Robert Prusch, Dept. of Biology, Gonzaga University, Spokane, Wash.)*

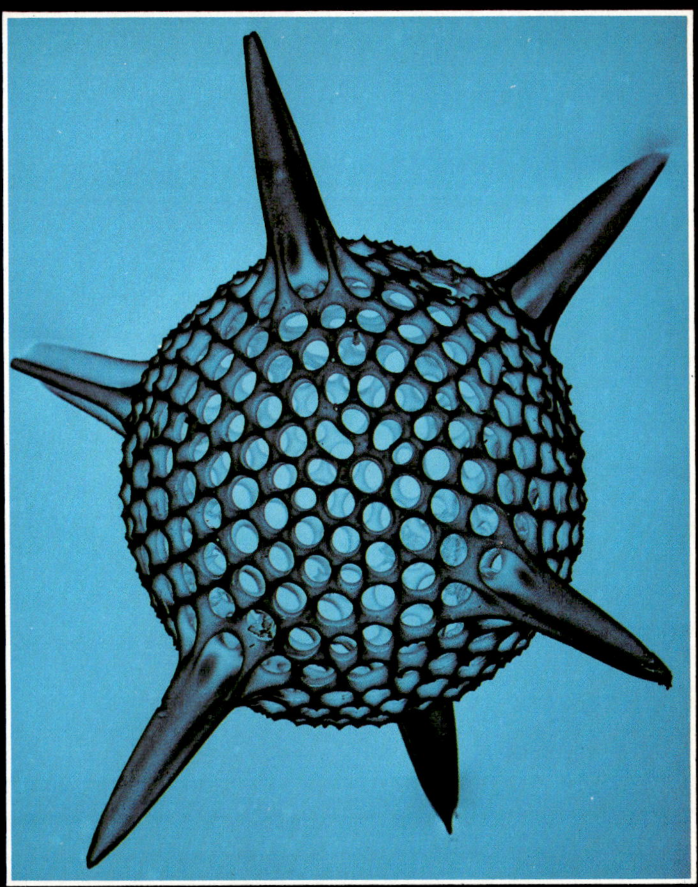

Color Fig. 2. Single cells. This beautifully sculptured shell, constructed mostly of silica secretions, once housed a unicellular amoeboid radiolarian. The many openings in the shell form passageways through which pseudopodia were projected. *(Manfred Kage, © Peter Arnold, Inc.)*

Color Fig. 3. Colonies of cells. *Volvox*, a colonial green alga composed of many flagellate cells. The cells are arranged as a single-layered sphere, each cell in direct contact with the water environment. In the interior are several offspring colonies, which develop there and eventually burst through the parent. *(M. C. Noailles.)*

Color Fig. 4. Tissues. (A) Plant tissue. Vascular plants typically contain elongated xylem elements called tracheids. The spotted appearance of the tracheids in this ash stem is due to an interspersion of pits and secondary thickenings in cell walls. (B) Animal tissue. The orange-colored areas in this thyroid tissue are regions where thyroid hormone accumulates before being transported away by blood. *(A, William J. Dederick, DPI; B, M. C. Noailles.)*

A

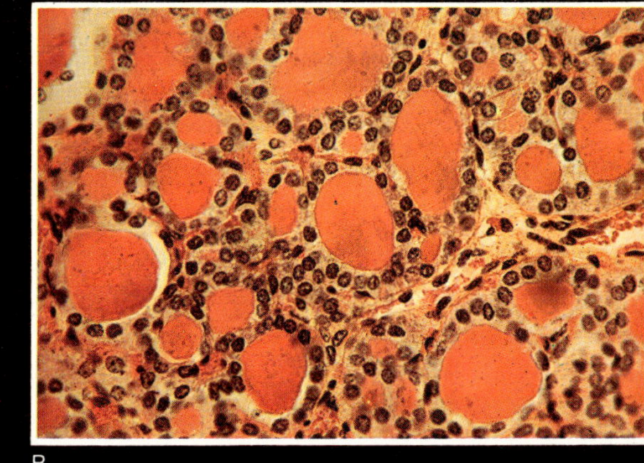

B

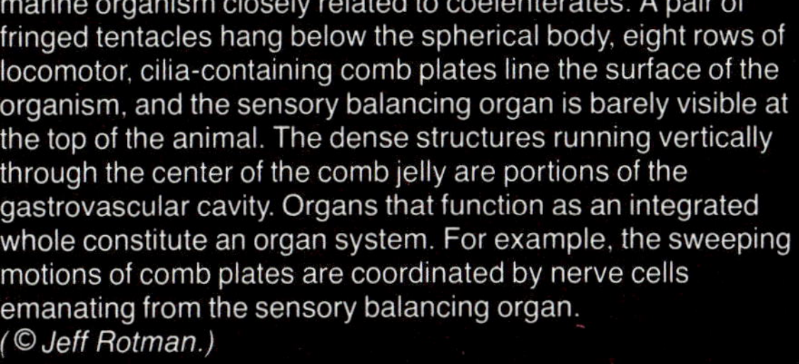

Color Fig. 5. Organs and organ systems. Several organs can be seen in this transparent ctenophore (comb jelly), a marine organism closely related to coelenterates. A pair of fringed tentacles hang below the spherical body, eight rows of locomotor, cilia-containing comb plates line the surface of the organism, and the sensory balancing organ is barely visible at the top of the animal. The dense structures running vertically through the center of the comb jelly are portions of the gastrovascular cavity. Organs that function as an integrated whole constitute an organ system. For example, the sweeping motions of comb plates are coordinated by nerve cells emanating from the sensory balancing organ. *(© Jeff Rotman.)*

A

B

Color Fig. 6. Predator-prey interactions. Organisms are interdependent in many ways. Some, for example, represent sources of nutrients for others. (A) A water beetle (*Dytiscus marginalis*) preys on an amphibian larva. (B) The larger ant on the right will soon supply nutrients for the smaller carnivore. *(A, B, © Hans Pfletschinger, Peter Arnold, Inc.)*

Color Fig. 7. Symbiosis. (A) Commensalism. In this form of symbiosis ("living together"), one species clearly benefits from the association while the other is largely unaffected. The tentacles of this sea anemone contain "stinging cells" that can quickly paralyze fish. Yet this clownfish swims among the tentacles without being harmed. The sea anemone is neither benefited nor harmed by the clownfish, which is protected from predators when surrounded by the tentacles. (B) Parasitism. Caterpillar of a moth, carrying the pupal cocoons of a parasitic wasp. *(A, © Jeff Rotman; B, Carolina Biological Supply Company.)*

A

B

Color Fig. 8. Ecosystems and Biomes. Local associations of organisms and the nonliving components of their environments constitute ecosystems. Aggregations of similar terrestrial ecosystems are biomes. The diversity of these large and most elaborate units of the living hierarchy is illustrated by the following sequence of photographs. (A) A cheetah peers across the flat, tropical grassland of Kenya, Africa. Mount Kilimanjaro rises

(B) Deserts are filled with beauty, as evidenced by the flowering plants of Oregon Pipe National Monument in

(C) Terrestrial and aquatic organisms form complex interdependent associations in marshes and swamps.

(D) A portion of a West German deciduous forest biome in autumn. Note the successionally less-advanced field adjacent to the near-climax forest.

(E) Part of a coniferous forest biome along the Northwestern coast of the United States. The firs, redwoods, and other conifers shown here are well-adapted to the cool climate of this region. The comparatively moist soil beneath the forest canopy supports a dense growth of mosses and shrubs. Most people reside in grassland, deciduous forest, or coniferous forest biomes, because they best support human life. *(A, J. Alex Langley, DPI; B, Stephen J. Kraseman, © Peter Arnold, Inc.; C, M. P. Kahl, Bruce Coleman, Inc.; D, Karales, © Peter Arnold, Inc.; E, Werner H. Müller, © Peter Arnold, Inc.)*

occurring during the summer. Plant and animal populations are much more varied than in the tundra. Spruce, fir, pine, and hemlock are the principal trees of this biome; mosses, grasses, sedges, and cold-adapted herbs form most of the ground cover. Mammals typically include snowshoe hares, lynx, squirrels, marten, mink, fisher, wolf, deer, moose, and black bear (Fig. 9.23). A number of birds migrate to this biome for summer breeding, including ruffed grouse, crossbills, and siskins.

The forests of this great region differ from others in that they usually consist of a single species of tree. For example, spruce may be the only kind of tree present over a very large area. At the northernmost boundary of this biome, the forest is scrublike, dominated by stands of relatively short spruce and fir. Toward the southern boundary, however, the forests contain great timber resources, including the populations of magnificient Douglas fir and redwoods in the northern United States.

Some regions of southern coniferous forest have been exploited severely and reduced to scarred and eroded landscapes. Fortunately, research in methods of forest management has led to the development of highly effective reforestation techniques, and many areas have been replanted on a sustained yield basis. If such techniques are used and developed further, continuous yields of timber can be produced without destroying the substantial beauty of these regions.

Temperate Deciduous Forest

As its name implies, this biome is characterized by a moderate climate and deciduous trees. The biome occupies most of the eastern half of the United States from the Atlantic seaboard to the mid-Mississippi Valley and from Canada to central Florida. On its northern boundary the deciduous and coniferous forests merge, and there is a gradual shift in dominant species along the north–south climatic gradient. Several coniferous species remain prominent south of this boundary, including northern hemlock, cedar, jack pine, red pine, and white pine. All these conifers are important successional species in New England and other transitional zones and are followed by climax forests dominated by oak, hickory, and other deciduous trees (Fig. 9.24).

Fig. 9.23 The habitat of the northern coniferous forest. (A) A typical landscape, with single (coniferous) tree species covering a large area. (B) Moose, a mammal characteristic of this biome. *(A, U.S. Forest Service; B, courtesy of Leonard L. Rue.)*

A

B

A

B

Fig. 9.24 The habitat of the deciduous forest. (A) A typical deciduous forest, with maples the predominant trees. (B) Mountain lion, a mammal characteristic of many deciduous forests. *(A, U.S. Forest Service; B, © Walt Disney Productions.)*

The basic climatic conditions of this biome are cold winters, warm summers, and well-spaced rains bringing some 30 to 40 inches of precipitation per year. Day and night temperatures tend to differ less than the average summer and winter temperatures. Winter makes the growing season discontinuous, and plants are adapted to this.

At its southern boundary, the biome merges with a complex of forest types, including those of the broadleaf evergreen in which magnolia and swamp bay are dominant species. Rainfall decreases steadily toward the western boundary. Accordingly, species requiring higher amounts of precipitation disappear, and only oak, hickory, and ash are found at the western edge of the forest, forming a transition with tall grasses at the eastern boundary of the grassland biome.

Grassland

The grassland community covers vast stretches of land throughout central North America. Rainfall is generally less than in forested regions, averaging 10 to 30 inches/year. Taller grasses such as bluestem and Indian grass typify the moister eastern regions of the biome, and shorter species such as buffalo grass and bluegrass characterize the drier western plains (Fig. 9.25). These shorter grasses were the mainstay of the large bison herds that once roamed the plains. Before the western migration of settlers, the bison population numbered several million animals, but human exploitation reduced the population to the point of extinction. Laws now protect bison, and several herds have been reestablished. Trees in general are limited to stream valleys, where cottonwood dominates, and to the tops of low mountains such as the Black Hills of South Dakota.

The rapid decomposition of organic matter in grassland soils makes this biome one of the richest agricultural regions of the world. However, as discussed in Chap. 10, overgrazing and extensive cultivation have reduced the complexity of this major ecosystem tremendously: the approximately 120 species of native plants have been replaced in many areas by two domestic varieties, wheat and corn. We cannot return the prairie to its virgin condition. Even if this were possible, all the grain from these crops and more is needed to feed our expanding population. But the cost of maintaining simplified ecosystems is expensive, for they lack the stability of more complex ones. Moreover, there are limits to the amount of simplification an ecosystem can withstand before community structure collapses completely.

Deserts

Deserts consist of bush-covered land in which widely dispersed plants are separated by stretches of bare, sandy soil (Fig. 9.26). They are arid biomes receiving less than 10 inches of rain per

Fig. 9.25 The habitat of the grassland. (A) A typical grassy plain. (B) Black-tailed prairie dogs, a mammal characteristic of the western plains.

year. Many deserts occur adjacent to mountain ranges that force air upward to higher altitudes, where cooler temperatures frequently cause moisture to condense as rain. The moisture-depleted air then moves across adjacent regions, thereby maintaining the arid environment of deserts (Fig. 9.27). For example, air masses from the Pacific Ocean that reach the west coast of the United States often contain considerable amounts of water vapor. Much of this water is lost as rain when these air masses are driven upward by the Sierra–Cascade mountain range. Many areas west of these ranges receive 60 to 80 inches of rain per year. However, extensive areas of desert extend east of these two ranges, including much of Idaho, Nevada, Arizona, and Utah. Under unusual conditions, moisture-laden air occasionally reaches these arid areas, but usually in amounts sufficient to produce only brief showers.

Desert organisms show many adaptations to the scarcity of water. For example, many animals seek food only at night, resting by day in underground burrows away from direct exposure to the sun. The intestines and kidneys of many desert animals reabsorb considerable quantities of water. As a result, the feces and urine of such animals are released in a highly dehydrated state (see also Chap. 18). Animals such as the kangaroo rat, a rodent found in the southwestern deserts of the United States, can exist indefinitely without any open supply of water. Its water-absorbing and water-retaining capabilities are so highly developed that it can obtain sufficient water from the seeds that constitute its principal source of food.

Similar adaptations to arid conditions occur in desert plants (see also Chaps. 13 and 32). Many, such as cacti, absorb and store large amounts of water during infrequent rains. Others have extensive root systems that absorb water trapped deep below the surface of the soil. Some have very small leaves or are covered with thick, waxy cuticles that prevent excessive water loss. Still others undergo rapid growth and development following periods of rain, often completing their life cycle in a few days. Although such plants die quickly once the rainy period has ended, their seeds remain dormant and will germinate only when conditions again become favorable for a brief burst of rapid growth.

Desert soils often contain excessive amounts of minerals and salts but little organic matter. Thus, attempts to make deserts agriculturally productive by simply adding water to the soil often fail. For example, the United States spent millions of dollars in the 1950s irrigating an Afghanistan desert in an attempt to increase food production in the region. The desert did "bloom" for a 2-year period, but plants quickly exhausted the scant supply of nutrients, salt accumulated at the surface of the soil, and further plant growth was inhibited. Deserts can be made productive, as has been demonstrated in Israel and in the western United States, where desert farms are dependent totally on specialized soil-maintenance techniques and on water piped from wells or rivers many miles away. Nevertheless, the cost of ecosystem modification is high and potentially dangerous and requires rigorous scientific scrutiny.

Lesser Biomes

In addition to major biomes, several others occupy more restricted regions of the United States. One of these, the *eastern pine-oak*, occupies the coastal plain from Long Island and New Jersey to the border of Texas; the region is dominated by extensive pine forests (Fig. 9.28). Another is the *subtropical* biome at the southern tip of Florida. It is a region characterized by uniformly warm temperatures and abundant precipitation. The Everglades in this biome is dominated by tall sawgrass in freshwater marshes and dense swamps of red mangrove in tidal areas. On the southern coast of California, is the *broad-sclerophyll* biome, a subtropical, semiarid region dominated by various evergreen plants with thick, hard leaves (Fig. 9.29). Drier

A

B

Fig. 9.26 The habitat of the desert. (A) A desert landscape with tall saguaro cacti, barrel cacti (center foregound), cholla cacti (foreground), and palo verde trees (see also Color Fig. 8). (B) Bobcat, a mammal characteristic of many deserts. (*A, U.S. Department of Agriculture; B, © Walt Disney Productions.*)

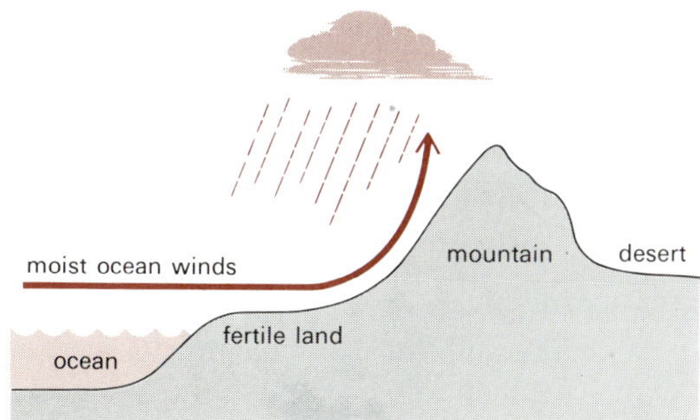

Fig. 9.27 Mountains and climate. A mountain deflects moisture-rich ocean winds upward and causes rain to remain confined to the slope facing the ocean. That slope will therefore be fertile, but the far slope will become a desert.

Fig. 9.28 Eastern pine-oak biome. Pine barrens of Ocean County, New Jersey, showing a young stand of pitch pine. The lower deciduous trees are small oaks and sassafras. (*U.S. Forest Service.*)

Fig. 9.29 Broad-sclerophyll biome. Chaparral dominated by redshank, ceanothus, and sage in Cleveland National Forest, California. (*U.S. Forest Service.*)

areas of this biome contain low, dense thickets of evergreen shrubs such as chamise and manzanita; such formations are called *chapparal.*

Other major biomes, such as *tropical rain forests* and *savannas,* exist outside North America (see Fig. 9.20). They are not described here, but interested students will find them treated extensively in the Collateral Readings at the end of this chapter. Like those of the North American continent, each of these major ecosystems is determined by climate and a few other physical variables. Similar factors also influence the characteristics of aquatic ecosystems and some, like solar light, solar heat, precipitation, and wind are global. Together they add up to the large-scale "environment" that determines and modifies all ecosystems regardless of location. With this we reach the apex of the structural organization of living matter, the *biosphere,* in which a thin surface layer of the planet maintains a carpet of life.

Like cells, organisms, and communities, the biosphere is a dynamic, ever-changing system. Continents become modified in shape and location; ice ages come and go; species become extinct, their niches occupied by new ones. Seemingly, life thrives on change and remains stable by not being static. But such stability is deceptive and is based almost wholly on relatively slow rates of change. Abrupt changes in the physical components of the biosphere can produce large-scale disruptions in the organizational hierarchy of living matter at all levels. Human beings are the chief protagonists of environmental change. Our impact on the organization of life is examined next.

Review Questions

1 What are ecological succession, climax communities, seres? How does primary succession differ from secondary succession? Describe the developmental stages that occur in the succession of a lake to dry land, of an open field to a forest.

2 What are thermoclines and how do they influence the abundance of populations in aquatic ecosystems?

3 Describe how rock is converted to soil. What organisms contribute to soil formation? What are the main components of soil? In what ways does soil serve in maintaining plant life?

4 Describe the physical differences that characterize clay, gravel, and loams. What processes contribute to the formation of such soils? Why do loams provide a more favorable environment for rapid terrestrial succession than clay or gravel?

5 Describe the principal characteristics of terrestrial succession. Discuss how species diversity, species composition, total biomass, and P/R values change as ecosystems mature. What properties usually distinguish climax communities from successionally less mature communities? Give examples.

6 Name factors that can prevent establishment of climax communities. What are the distinguishing characteristics of pulse-stabilized communities? Why do such communities not develop to a climax stage?

7 What is the structure of an ocean basin? What are the major habitats of such a basin? What role does the sun play in creating subdivisions in these habitats? What physical conditions characterize the various subdivisions?

8 Define plankton, nekton, and benthos. Give specific examples of each. Where in the ocean are each of these types of organisms found?

9 Describe how marine life is greatly influenced by physical factors. Discuss several kinds of factors and give specific examples. What factors make life in tropic waters generally less abundant but more diverse than in temperate or subpolar waters?

10 What are the principal biomes of North America, and what physical and biological conditions characterize each of them? In what ways are the terrestrial ecosystems at different latitudes related to those at different altitudes?

Collateral Readings

"The American Wilderness Library," Time-Life, New York, 1972. A series of books describing the natural habitats of North America.

Cooper, C. F.: The Ecology of Fire, *Scientific American,* April 1961. This still-relevant article describes how some communities depend on periodic burning for their perpetuation.

Farb, P.: "Face of North America," Harper & Row, New York, 1963. This interesting book describes the natural history of North America. Interactions between climate, geologic change, plants, and animals are discussed at a level appropriate for lay readers.

Good, R.: "The Geography of Flowering Plants," 4th ed., Longmans, London, 1974. A classic account of the geographic distribution of the earth's vegetation. Factors governing the distribution of plants are highlighted.

Horn, H.: Forest Succession, *Scientific American,* May 1975. This article describes principles that govern succession of temperate deciduous forests.

Isaacs, J. D.: The Nature of Oceanic Life, *Scientific American,* September 1969. The ecology of marine habitats is described.

Krutch, J. W.: "The Desert Year," Viking, New York, 1960. This paperback, written by one of America's best-known authors, describes the plants and animals that inhabit the deserts of the United States.

MacArthur, R. H.: "Geographical Ecology," Harper & Row, New York, 1972. An introduction to several concepts regarding species diversity and distribution. For the advanced student with a background in mathematics.

Marples, M. J.: Life on the Human Skin, *Scientific American,* January 1969. The surface of skin contains an abundance of microorganisms. This article examines the interrelationships between them from an ecological perspective.

Smith, R. L.: "Ecology and Field Biology," 3d ed., Harper & Row, 1980. Sections of this text provide excellent descriptions of the biomes of North America. Especially appropriate for the amateur naturalist.

Tinbergen, N.: "Curious Naturalists," Doubleday, Garden City, N. Y., 1968. This book, available in paperback, contains many interesting accounts of the activities and discoveries of field biologists.

Walter, H.: "Vegetation of the Earth in Relation to Climate and the Eco-Physiological Conditions," trans. from the German by J. Wieser, English Universities Press, London, 1973. Although its title has the sound of a Ph.D. thesis, this is a short, highly readable book about the world's biomes and the environmental conditions responsible for their perpetuation.

Went, F.: The Plants of Krakatoa, *Scientific American,* September 1949. Life on this island was virtually eradicated by a massive volcanic eruption on Aug. 27, 1883. The gradual reemergence of living organisms on the island afforded biologists a first-hand opportunity to study primary succession. This article describes some of the results of that study.

Whittaker, R. H.: "Communities and Ecosystems," 2d ed., Macmillan, New York, 1975. This moderately advanced textbook has a first-class section on biomes.

Chapter 10

People and the Organization of Life

Learning Objectives

After reading this chapter you should be able to:

1. List at least five ways in which human modification of the environment has had a detrimental effect on human health.
2. List two reasons for the substantial increase in lead pollution that has occurred in the Northern Hemisphere since 1940; name two ways in which lead can disrupt cell function.
3. State at least one way in which nitrate ions can accumulate excessively in drinking water and illustrate how nitrate pollution can cause methemoglobinemia in infants.
4. List the principal sources of carbon monoxide, hydrocarbons, oxides of nitrogen, and sulfur oxide pollutants in air; state at least one way in which each of these pollutants can affect human health; define photochemical smog.
5. Illustrate how pollutants can affect human health through synergistic interactions.
6. List at least two factors that prevent some pollutants from becoming distributed uniformly in ecosystems; illustrate how certain kinds of pollutants become concentrated in organisms that usually feed at high trophic levels and list three general characteristics of these kinds of pollutants; state how chlorinated hydrocarbons can cause the extinction of entire species of predator birds; state why, in attempts to increase crop yields, persistent use of chlorinated hydrocarbons often has the opposite effect; define genetic resistance to pesticides.
7. List at least three substances that could trigger significant changes in the average temperature of the earth and the possible consequences of such changes; illustrate how each substance could trigger a change in the annual mean temperature of the earth and list the principal sources of each substance; define "greenhouse effect."
8. State at least two examples of how human activities have influenced ecological succession on a large scale.
9. List at least three kinds of agricultural practices that have contributed to soil erosion; state why such practices have accelerated loss of topsoil; identify at least two ways in which soil erosion affects crop productivity.
10. Name the two most important physical forces responsible for soil erosion and state an example of each.
11. State how a long-term reduction in United States farm production could have serious international repercussions; list at least three reasons why little has been done to conserve topsoil in the United States; state at least three reasons why crop productivity has been increased over the past 40 years despite an accompanying loss of topsoil.
12. State the three chief factors that have contributed to the disruptive impact of people on the organization of living systems.
13. Illustrate statistically the exponential population growth of human beings; list at least three ways in which human beings have eliminated or reduced the impact of factors that usually restrict exponential growth of populations.
14. Illustrate how affluence and exponential population growth interact synergistically in substantially increasing the total amount of matter and energy needed to support mankind.
15. Differentiate between cyclic and noncyclic economies; illustrate how urbanization and human population growth have combined to disrupt a specific ecosystem; state at least two ways in which the type of waste being discarded into the environment by people of the United States has changed since 1940 and illustrate how these changes have disrupted the organization of living systems.
16. State why societies cannot expect "science" to devise a specific plan to solve environmental problems.
17. List at least four methods of conserving soil and state why each reduces loss of topsoil.
18. List at least three species-specific methods of pest control and illustrate why such methods are likely to be slower-acting and initially more

expensive than use of broad-spectrum pesticides; define integrated control and illustrate how this practice can increase crop yields.

19. Define acid precipitation; state how nitrogen- and sulfur-containing compounds released in one part of the world can result in acid precipitation in a region hundreds or even thousands of miles from the emission source; list at least two ways in which acid precipitation can cause a decline in populations of fish; list at least three deleterious effects of acid precipitation on terrestrial ecosystems; describe what is being done to study and reduce the damaging effects of acid precipitation.

Throughout the thousands of centuries of their existence, human beings have become increasingly adept at modifying and exploiting the environment to suit their needs. In this century particularly, human influence over the complex organization of living systems at all levels has increased enormously. We have constructed great dams to increase our supply of drinking water and to obtain hydroelectric power, developed new "wonder drugs" to increase our life expectancy, and bred new varieties of plants and animals to increase our food supply. Our power to influence nature is now without precedent. But power is not control.

Until recently, we neither understood nor examined the impact of our environmental exploitation on the organization of living systems. This omission is more than unfortunate; indeed it already has proved tragic and may prove fatal, for our increasing capacity to modify the environment has led to increased simplicity and randomness among components of the biosphere. Complexity and nonrandomness are attributes common to all living systems, from cells to ecosystems, and increasing simplicity and randomness always accompany their death and decay.

NATURE OF THE IMPACT

Lower Levels of Organization: Cells and Organisms

Our modification of the environment has produced unexpected and undesired effects on many types of cells and organisms. Some affect people directly and constitute serious health hazards. For example, the concentration of lead in the environment has increased dramatically since World War II. Studies have documented a fivefold increase in the lead content of the Greenland ice cap between 1750 and 1940, and a twentyfold increase between 1940 and 1967. Most of this increase appears linked, first, to the development of lead smelting in the Northern Hemisphere and, more recently, to the combustion of gasoline containing tetraethyllead. Although automobile engines recently have been redesigned to operate efficiently on unleaded gasoline, most cars manufactured before 1970 "knock" excessively if run on unleaded gas.

Each of us is exposed to lead pollution in a variety of ways—most frequently from automobile exhausts, but also from lead-containing ceramics, paints, pesticides, solder used to seal food cans, pipes, and numerous other sources (Fig. 10.1). It is estimated that the average American ingests lead at an approximate rate of 400 μg/day. This amount may seem small, but lead is a cumulative poison that can disrupt the function of many different cells and organs. Malfunctions appear most frequently in the nervous, muscular, and circulatory systems. Many of these malfunctions are caused by the binding of lead to various cellular enzymes. This binding can alter the three-dimensional structure of active sites and thus bring about a loss of catalytic activity. Lead also causes groups of proteins to coagulate in semisolid clusters. As lead accumulates in cells, more enzymes become inhibited and greater numbers of proteins coagulate. The symptoms of lead poisoning increase correspondingly. Other heavy metals such as mercury and cadmium also can disrupt cell function and constitute equally serious health hazards whenever they accumulate excessively in the environment (Fig. 10.2).

These and most other pollutants usually enter organisms through the respiratory and digestive systems. For example, since many communities lack sewage-treatment facilities designed to eliminate heavy metals, viruses, detergents, sulfuric acid, and ammonia, these and other potentially harmful substances are often common in drinking water. Many cities draw their drinking water from rivers at

A

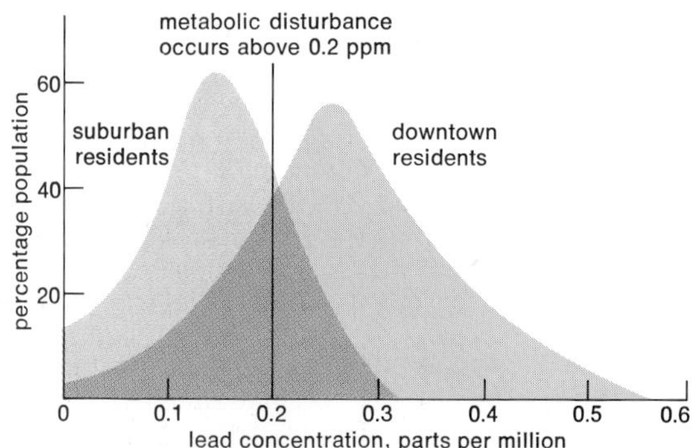

B

Fig. 10.1 Lead pollution. (A) Chips of peeling paint sometimes are eaten by children. If the paint contains lead, such children can suffer acute lead poisoning. (B) Lead pollution usually is greater in urban areas, where automotive exhausts and industrial wastes are more highly concentrated. Consequently, there are differences between the concentrations of lead that accumulate in the tissues of downtown and suburban inhabitants. Increasing use of lead-free gasolines in the U.S. should reduce concentrations of lead in the tissues of Americans. (*A, Courtesy of Charles Gatewood; B, from John T. Hardy, "Science, Technology, and the Environment," Saunders, Philadelphia, 1975.*)

points below the sewage and industrial discharges of other communities located upstream (Fig. 10.3). Although chlorination does destroy many potentially harmful microorganisms, an increasing amount of evidence indicates that some viruses are "protected" from the effects of chlorine by high concentrations of organic matter in water. Some scientists have hypothesized that this phenomenon may be related to recent increases in the incidence of infectious hepatitis, a virus-induced disruption of liver function.

A particularly hazardous type of pollutant contaminating the drinking water of an increasing number of communities is the nitrate ion, the principal source of inorganic nitrogen used by plants. The contamination often is caused by inorganic fertilizers that have been spread on nearby crops. Only a portion of the nitrates present in these fertilizers is taken up by plants; most of the remainder either leaches through the soil into underground water supplies or is washed by rain into surrounding lakes and streams (Fig. 10.4). Although the nitrate themselves are not hazardous to our health, certain bacteria, abundant in the digestive tracts of infants and many farm animals, convert nitrates to highly toxic nitrite ions.

Nitrites combine readily with the hemoglobin of red blood corpuscles. Hemoglobin produces the red color of blood and functions chiefly in the acquisition and transport of oxygen from the lungs of all cells of the body. Hemoglobin, however, combines preferentially with nitrite ions, thus reducing the amount of oxygen supplied to cells. As concentrations of nitrite rise in blood, lesser amounts of oxygen are transported, resulting in an occasionally fatal type of anemia called *methemoglobinemia*. Nitrate pollution has become a serious public health problem in some parts of Illinois, Wisconsin, Missouri, and particularly in the Central Valley of California, where doctors often recommend that infants be given only pure bottled water to drink.

Many other pollutants contaminate the air we breathe. Some exist in smog suspended above the tops of buildings in all major cities (Fig. 10.5). Many burn our eyes, irritate our lungs, mask sunlight, damage crops, corrode paint and steel, rot

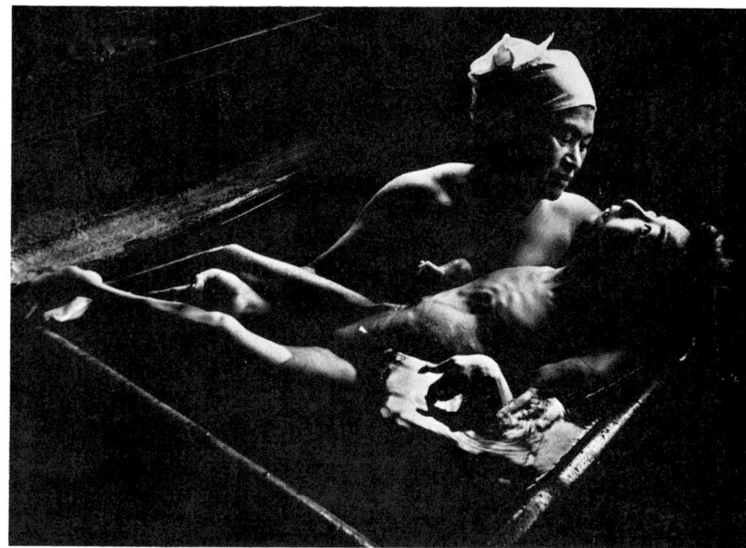

Fig. 10.2 Mercury poisoning. Organic compounds that contain mercury can be extremely toxic. Such compounds can impair nerve function and cause coma and death. *(Courtesy of W. Eugene Smith, Magnum Photos, Inc.)*

clothing, and crack rubber. Most are detrimental to our health. Estimates of the annual American financial loss resulting from the effects of air pollution on health run as high as 14 to 29 billion dollars. The major sources of air pollution in the United States are presented in Table 10.1.

Most of the carbon monoxide (CO) and hydrocarbons in our atmosphere result from the incomplete combustion of gasoline in automobiles. Like nitrite ions, carbon monoxide combines readily with hemoglobin, reducing the amount of oxygen supplied to cells. Steady-state controls of the body respond to reduced oxygen supplies by stimulating the heart to beat faster and the respiratory system to increase its inhalation-exhalation cycle. This response can produce a critical strain in people with heart or lung disease. An extensive study in 1971 linked high concentrations of atmospheric carbon monoxide with higher mortality rates in Los Angeles County, California, for the years 1962 to 1965.

Hydrocarbon pollutants comprise a diversity of molecules composed exclusively of carbon and hydrogen atoms, and some of them have been shown to trigger development of lung cancer in experimental animals. Similarly, many suspended particles in the air, or *particulates*, have been linked to cancer; evidence that airborne particles of asbestos can cause lung cancer is unequivocal (Fig. 10.6).

Oxides of nitrogen, such as nitrogen dioxide (NO_2), are formed whenever fossil fuels are burned at high temperatures. Like carbon monoxide, they reduce the oxygen-carrying capacity of blood, but they also produce a variety of toxic effects on lung tissues. Atmospheric nitrogen oxides and hydrocarbons interact chemically in the presence of sunlight to produce a variety of air pollutants collectively

Fig. 10.3 Water pollution. Detergent foam on the Mississippi River near Alton. *(Courtesy of John H. Gerard, from National Audubon Society.)*

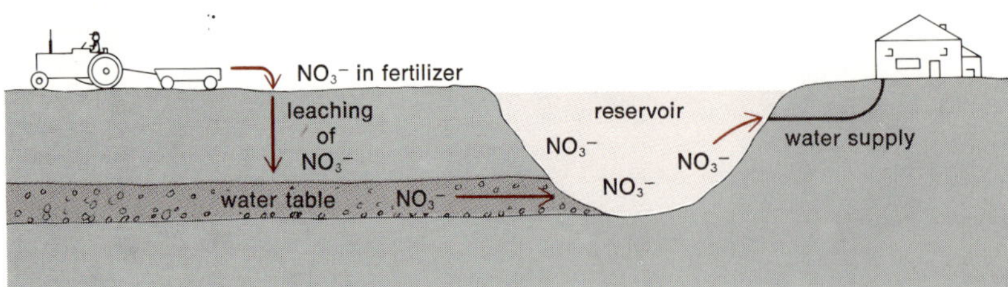

Fig. 10.4 Nitrate (NO_3^-) pollution. Nitrates are highly concentrated in most inorganic fertilizers. These ions can enter reservoirs and then be carried to homes through municipal water systems. High concentrations of nitrates can result in nitrite poisoning and methemoglobinemia in infants.

called *photochemical smog*. Some of these, such as ozone (O_3), are particularly irritating to tissues of the eye and the breathing passages.

Sulfur oxides result chiefly from the combustion of coal and fuel oil. Sulfur dioxide (SO_2) debilitates lung tissue and has been implicated in recent increased incidences of asthma, bronchitis, and emphysema (Fig. 10.7). Each of these diseases reduces the supply of oxygen in blood, thereby producing a strain on the heart.

Thus, air pollution not only damages property but also kills. Since it kills slowly and results in heart attacks, lung cancer, and other diseases also caused by factors unrelated to air pollution, its role as a killer is unobtrusive. Indeed, some of the effects of air pollution remain controversial. Like most pollutants, those contaminating air are numerous, varied, and often difficult to detect.

Fig. 10.5 Smog over New York City. *(Courtesy of Maurice E. Lándre, from National Audubon Society.)*

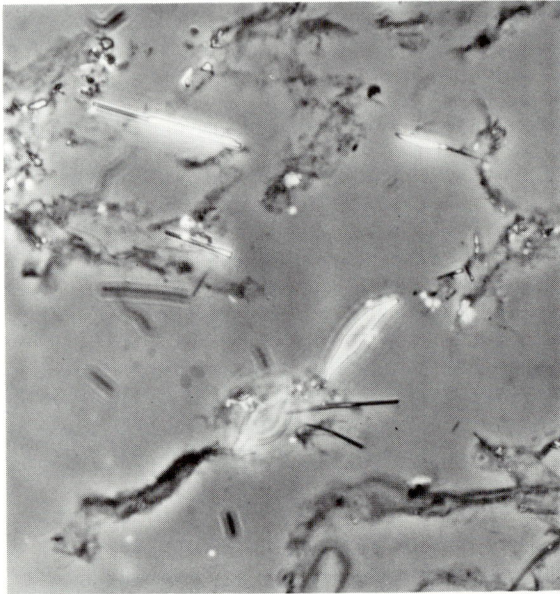

Fig. 10.6 Asbestos pollution. The rod-shaped structures are asbestos particles in human lung tissue. *(Courtesy of Mt. Sinai School of Medicine.)*

Moreover, living tissue reacts differently to pollutants, depending on whether they exist alone or in combination. For example, most cancer-inducing particles of asbestos are expelled from our lungs by the action of ciliated cells that line the breathing passages. The beating cilia force these and all other foreign particles back toward the mouth, where they are either expelled through exhalation or swallowed. Inhalation of air containing sulfur dioxide or cigarette smoke interferes with this cleansing action, and particles such as asbestos remain in contact with lung tissue longer. The result can be increased probability of lung cancer. This relationship between sulfur dioxide and asbestos is an example of a *synergistic* interaction,

TABLE 10.1
Major Sources of Air-Pollution Emissions in the United States

Source	Carbon monoxide, %	Particles, %	Nitrogen oxides, %	Sulfur oxides, %	Hydrocarbons, %
transportation	77.7	6.7	47.6	2.6	42.1
stationary fuel combustion	1.0	30.2	48.9	77.4	5.6
industrial processes	13.4	56.4	2.7	19.7	10.2
solid-waste disposal	2.5	2.6	0.4	0.0	2.0
miscellaneous*	5.4	4.1	0.4	0.3	40.1
total	100.0	100.0	100.0	100.0	100.0

*Includes oil and gasoline production.
SOURCE: Environmental Protection Agency, in Council on Environmental Quality, "Environmental Quality," 1975, p. 440.

which occurs whenever two agents or conditions interact and produce an effect greater than the sum of their individual effects. Such interactions occur frequently in living systems and often increase the difficulty of predicting and treating pollution-induced disease.

Higher Levels of Organization: Communities and Ecosystems

Although the disruptive effects of pollutants on cells, tissues, and organs are both costly and detrimental to our health, they eventually may prove less significant than pollution-induced damage to communities and ecosystems. Several factors limit the capacity of the biosphere to absorb pollutants without detriment. All contradict the once accepted and seemingly irrefutable adage: "The solution to pollution is dilution." This adage erroneously assumes the following: If 1 gallon of poison is added to 1 billion gallons of water, the highest concentration of poison that could exist in aquatic organisms will be approximately 1 part poison per billion parts water. If this were the case, the maximum concentration of the insecticide DDT that could be present in the tissues of oysters should be approximately 1.2 parts per billion; this is the maximum concentration of DDT in seawater. However, oysters have been found to contain DDT concentrations 700 times as high.

Many factors prevent DDT and other pollutants from becoming distributed uniformly throughout the biosphere. For example, cycling regional currents of wind and water occasionally restrict the movement of pollutants (see the accompanying Biology Highlight). Prevailing wind patterns in the Northern Hemisphere prevent most of the lead dispersed in the atmosphere over North America and Europe from mixing with air cycling throughout the Southern Hemisphere (Fig. 10.8).

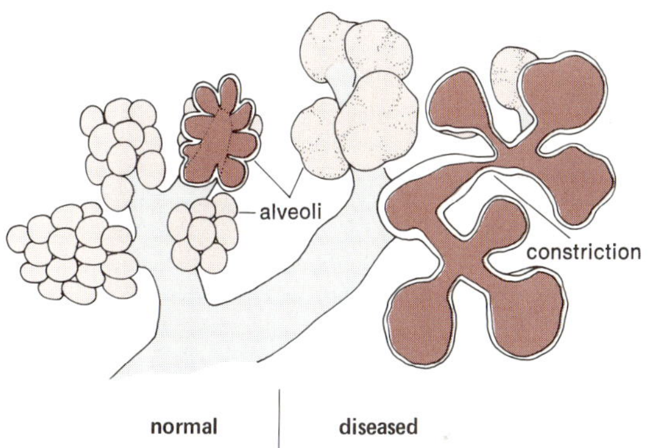

Fig. 10.7 Air pollution and lung disease. Bronchial tubes of lungs branch into millions of tiny saclike chambers called alveoli, where oxygen is transferred to blood. Sulfur dioxide and other air pollutants can cause alveoli to coalesce, reducing the amount of surface area available for the transfer of oxygen. Moreover, some air pollutants cause constrictions in the branches of bronchial tubes, thereby reducing the rate at which air is exchanged between alveoli and the external environment.

More significant, however, are factors that cause certain types of pollutants to become concentrated at higher trophic levels in ecosystems. Such pollutants usually have the following characteristics:

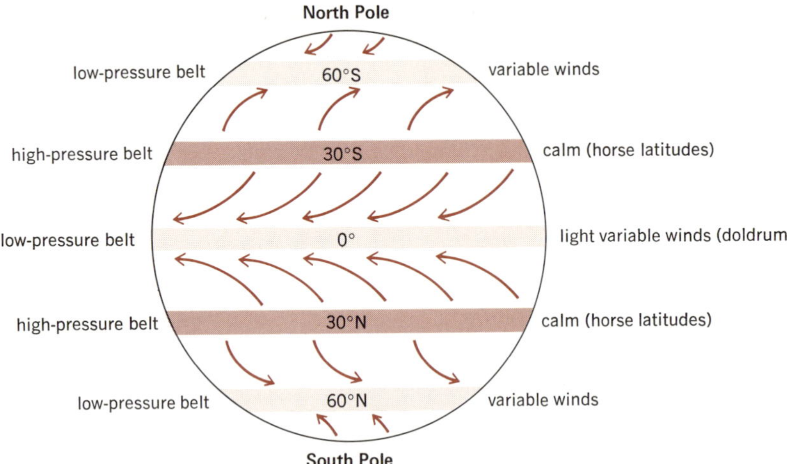

Fig. 10.8 Wind systems of the lower atmosphere. Winds tend to circulate in restricted zones above the surface of the earth. Each zone is separated by belts of relatively calm air currents. As a result, pollutants released into one zone are not dispersed quickly to other zones.

1. They are not broken down rapidly by purely physical environmental factors.

2. They are not metabolized rapidly by cells and transformed to other chemicals; in other words, they are not biodegradable.

3. They become incorporated by living tissue.

Chlorinated Hydrocarbons: Persistent Pesticides

Of all substances having the characteristics listed above, the chlorinated hydrocarbon insecticides have received the most intense study. These include DDT, toxaphene, chlordane, dieldrin, aldrin, endrin, lindane, and several other related compounds. They are broad-spectrum poisons, toxic to most animals, including many vertebrates. They are relatively inexpensive to produce and have been used routinely in many parts of the world to reduce crop damage by insects. Dichlorodiphenyltrichloroethane (DDT) has been used more extensively than any other insecticide. It is the oldest of the chlorinated hydrocarbon family of insecticides and was used first during World War II

Fig. 10.9 Chlorinated hydrocarbons. Direct application of DDT in a village of Afghanistan. This method was used frequently in World War II to prevent epidemics of diseases transmitted by insects. ▶

to prevent the spread of insect-transmitted diseases, such as malaria and typhus (Fig. 10.9). However, chlorinated hydrocarbons become concentrated in organisms that feed at high trophic levels, (the higher the level, the greater the concentration), and they have contributed significantly to the simplification of ecosystems (Fig. 10.10).

The principles causing such "biological amplifications" in ecosystems were presented in Chap. 8. Recall that the total biomass of populations is reduced at each transer of energy between trophic levels. Because chlorinated hydrocarbons are not biodegraded and thus are not lost when nutrients are transferred between trophic levels, the concentration of the insecticides becomes magnified correspondingly. For example, 10 grams or more of producer biomass must be eaten to support 1 gram of herbivore biomass. If each gram of producer bio-

Fig. 10.10 DDT accumulation in food chains. A portion of a tidal marsh food chain on Long Island, New York. Note the increasing concentrations of DDT in organisms that feed at higher trophic levels. The DDT values are given in parts per million. (*Adapted from J. M. Moran, M. D. Morgan, and J. H. Wiersma, "An Introduction to Environmental Sciences," Little, Brown, Boston, 1973.*)

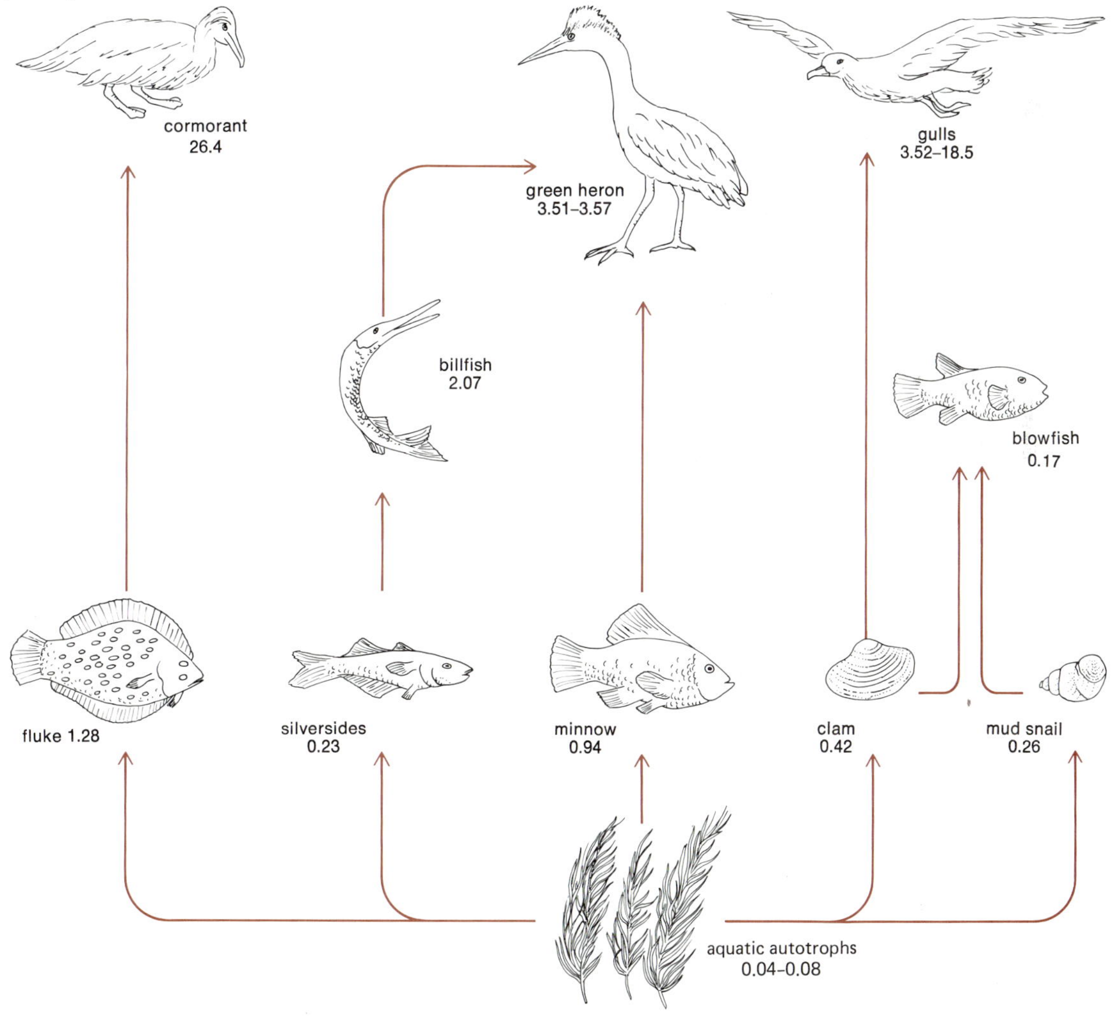

Biology Highlight

Acid Precipitation: Unpremeditated Chemical Warfare

"Silence—that's the first indication of something gone wrong. No frogs croak. Nothing moves along the shore. The water is clear, like crystal, yet nothing breaks the surface. The fish are all gone."

These are the words of a young ecologist describing her first visit to Brooktrout Lake, one of more than 2000 lakes and ponds in New York's Adirondack Park. "The fish are all gone." How could this be? No sewers empty into the lake. There are no nearby cities, no visible human activity of any kind. Just getting to the lake requires hiking over 9 miles from the nearest road.

The decline of trout, pike, and other game fish that once made Brooktrout Lake a fisherman's paradise was first noticed in the 1950s. Wildlife managers almost immediately blamed logging operations. Some scientists later suggested that the problem stemmed from an overabundance of decaying vegetation produced by a great windstorm in 1950. Others blamed several recently constructed beaver dams. But the cause of the declining populations of fish was nothing so visible.

It was the steadily increasing acidity of Brooktrout Lake and other nearby mountain lakes (above 1900 ft) that finally led scientists to the root cause of the problem. As the pH of lakes and ponds declines (becomes more acidic), so does the number of fish contained within these aquatic ecosystems (Fig. 1). Between 1929 and 1937, only 4 per cent of all mountain lakes in the Adirondacks had a pH under 5.0. Over 51 per cent of them have an average pH below 5.0 today, and 90 per cent of these acidic lakes are devoid of fish (see Chap. 3 for a discussion of acids, bases, and pH).

Fig. 1 Fish and acid precipitation. Relative status of fish populations in 1679 lakes located in southwestern Norway. Data for construction of this graph were collected in the mid-1970s. Note that populations of fish decline as the acidity of lakes increases.

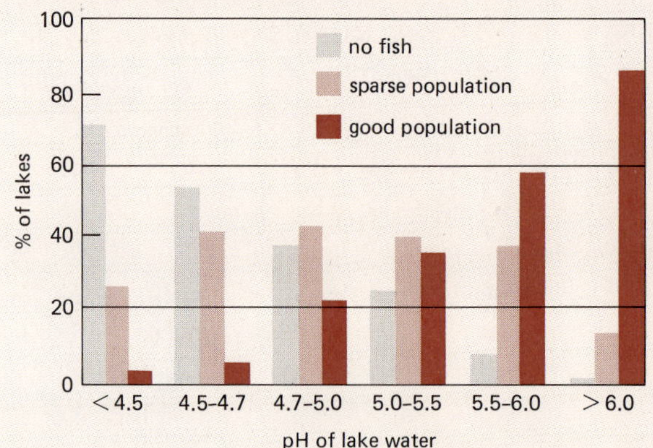

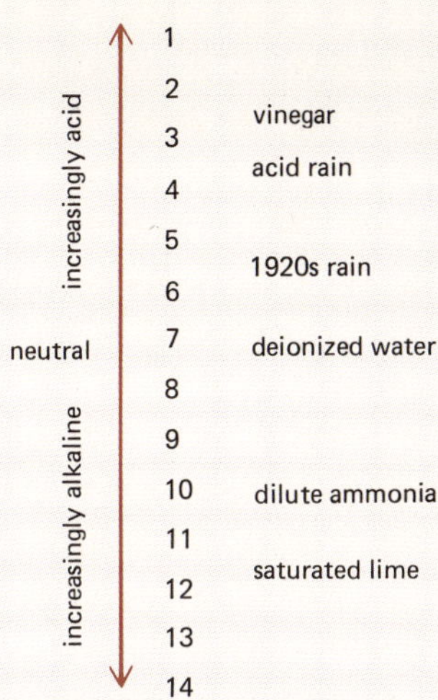

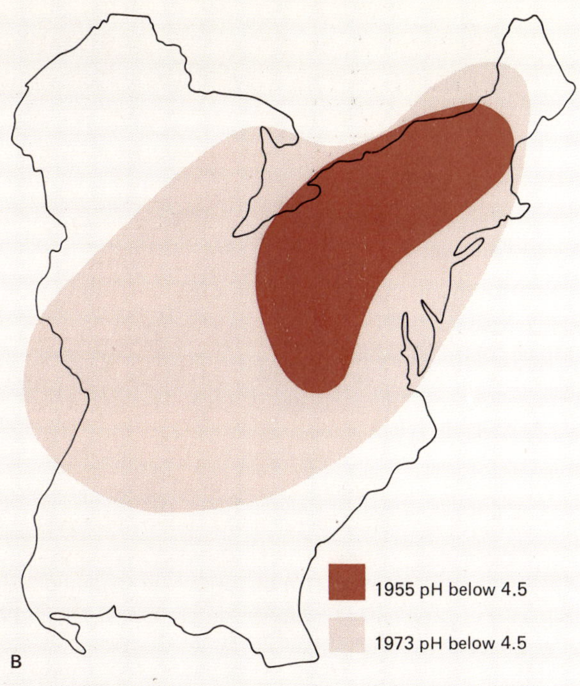

Fig. 2 Acid precipitation and pH. (A) The pH scale. The pH of some common acids and bases is indicated. Precipitation is considered acid when its pH falls below approximately 5.5. Because the pH scale is logarithmic, each 1-unit change, from 5 to 4, for example, represents a tenfold change in the concentration of hydrogen ions. (B) The spread of increasingly acidic precipitation. This map shows the spread of acid precipitation in the eastern United States between 1955 and 1973. In 1955, only the darker-colored portion of the eastern United States received precipitation having a pH below 4.5. By 1973, the entire lighter-colored region received such precipitation.

The ability of fish to store and metabolize calcium decreases as lakes become increasingly acidic. Eventually, the calcium levels in fish become so low that females cannot produce eggs. Even if eggs do develop, both the eggs and the newly hatched fish are vulnerable to comparatively high concentrations of hydrogen ions. Adult fish, too, are stressed by acidic environments. Individuals become weak and debilitated and often die in large numbers. Thus, within a few generations a sufficiently low pH can wipe out whole populations of fish.

What acids are getting into these lakes and ponds? How do acids enter aquatic environments, and where do they come from? The acids are contained in rain and snow, which have become increasingly acidic in many parts of the world over the past few decades. The pH of rain in the northeastern United States 25 to 30 years ago was about 5.6, the normal pH of "pure" rainwater. Because of natural acids in the atmosphere and the tendency of CO_2 to dissolve in water, forming weak carbonic acid, rainwater usually has a pH somewhat less than 6. Today, the average pH of rainwater in the northeast is about 4.1, representing a fortyfold increase in acidity (Fig. 2).

Most of the acids contained in precipitation that falls on Adirondack lakes are not produced in New York or even in the Northeast. Acids enter the atmosphere from smokestacks of industries located hundreds of miles away. Factories in the midwestern United States, for example, discharge over 33 million tons of nitrogen and sulfur compounds into the sky each year. As these compounds are carried eastward by prevailing winds, they become transformed into nitric and sulfuric acids. By the time these chemi-

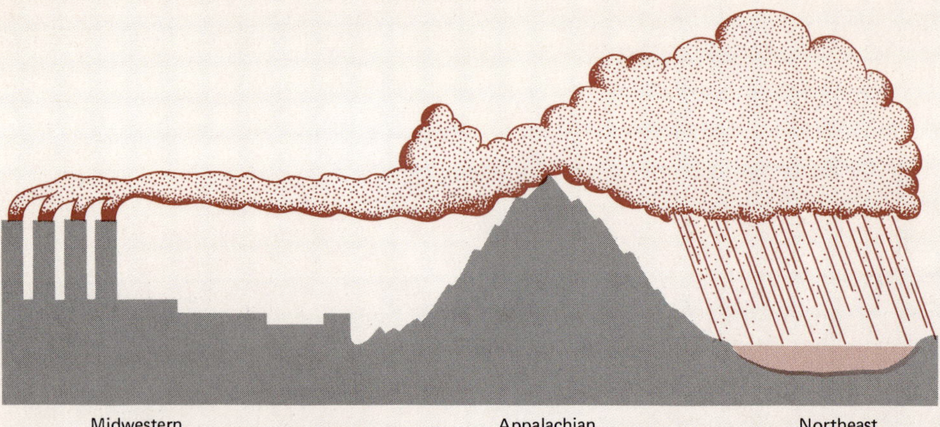

Fig. 3 Fossil fuels and acid precipitation. Most of the pollutants contributing to acid precipitation in the northeastern United States are produced by the combustion of fossil fuels in midwestern states. Mountains in the Northeast cause an upward flow of moisture-laden air, thereby cooling it and triggering precipitation of acid rain or snow.

cal changes have occurred, the nitrogen- and sulfur-containing substances may have drifted 100 to 1000 miles. The acid-laden air cools as it rises over mountainous sections of New York, Vermont, and New Hampshire, and the cooling often triggers precipitation. As a result, many of the acids produced by pollutants released over extensive areas fall to earth over comparatively small regions (Fig. 3).

Acid precipitation sometimes falls on ecosystems that can accommodate modest changes of pH. For example, many large lakes and most fertile soils contain an abundance of buffers (see Chap. 3), such as calcium carbonate, that can neutralize the acids. But in areas where the underlying rock is granite or lava, as in most mountainous regions, there are relatively few buffering chemicals. Lakes in these environments are extremely vulnerable to acids.

The damaging effects of acid precipitation are not confined to the northeastern United States. Over the past two decades, the most rapid increase in the acidity of precipitation falling in America has been in the Southeast. Coincidentally, this region has experienced a significant increase in industrial development over the same period.

A similar drop in the pH of rain and snow has been noted in Scandinavia. The hydrogen-ion concentration of precipitation in some parts of Norway and Sweden has increased more than 200-fold during the past 20 years. More than 70 per cent of the sulfur in air over these countries appears to stem directly from human activities, and over 75 per cent of this amount is thought to originate outside of Scandinavia. Densely populated industrialized areas in England, Germany, and other western European countries are frequently cited as sources of this sulfur.

As in America, the most obvious deleterious effects of acid precipitation in Scandinavia and other parts of the world are on freshwater ecosystems, but there is a growing realization that acid precipitation also damages terrestrial environments. Biologists have reported a broad spectrum of acid-rain-induced plant disorders, including diminished germination of seeds, less efficient photosynthesis, reduced resistance to plant diseases, increased numbers of lesions on leaves and needles, erosion of protective cuticles (see Chap. 6) from plant surfaces, and decreased uptake of soil nutrients (Fig. 4).

Fig. 4 Acid precipitation: biological effects. The lesions and "burn" spots on this spinach leaf were caused by acids in rain water.

Acid rain and meltwater from acid snow can also promote increased leaching of certain kinds of metals from soils. Elevated concentrations of dissolved metals can produce many disruptive effects when they enter aquatic ecosystems. Carl Schofield of Cornell University describes a potentially lethal effect.

"We found that acid rain has substantially increased leaching of aluminum from soils around many of the lakes in the Adirondack region. Aluminum in this situation is very toxic to fish. In fact, the acid runoff with aluminum added is more poisonous to trout than the acid rain alone."

Schofield and his colleagues suspect that the higher than normal concentrations of mercury and other metals recently found in several remote Canadian lakes and rivers are also due in part to the leaching effects of acid precipitation. Research further indicates that above normal amounts of dissolved acids can increase the concentration of metals in lakes and streams by promoting extraction of these substances from bottom sediments.

Other effects of acid precipitation are less clear, but some studies show that these pollutants can reduce nitrogen fixation by soil and aquatic microbes, slow the growth of timber in forests, and lower yields of agricultural crops. Not in dispute are the effects of acid rain on many human artifacts. The acids clearly accelerate erosion of metal, painted wood, and various kinds of stone. Geologist K. Lal Gauri, an expert on the restoration of stone, warns that structures like the Parthenon, the Colosseum, and the Taj Mahal may be ruined unless something is done to reduce levels of atmospheric pollution (Fig. 5).

The acid-precipitation forecast for the future is not promising. In the face of diminishing supplies of oil and natural gas, some nations, the United States in particular, plan to rely on coal as a prime source of energy. Be-

Fig. 5 Acid precipitation: physical effects. The Egyptian stone obelisk "Cleopatra's Needle" clearly shows the destructive effects of acid precipitation. The photo on the left was taken several years ago when the obelisk was placed in Central Park in New York City. The photo on the right, taken during the late 1970s, shows that most of the obelisk's hieroglyphics have been severely eroded. Scientists have determined that much of this erosion has been caused by acids contained both in city smog and in precipitation falling on the city.

A

B

cause much of the world's coal reserves are of the high-sulfur variety, the acid-precipitation problem could become much worse. Resolving the dilemma will not be easy. Smokestack scrubbers, which can remove most sulfur emitted from the burning of fossil fuels, are effective but very expensive. Most other attempts to alleviate the impact of acid precipitation on lakes and other ecosystems have produced marginal or only temporary benefits.

Much of the difficulty in developing workable solutions to the problem of acid precipitation lies in the paucity of information about the phenomenon itself. One of the people most concerned about the lack of knowledge is Ellis Cowling, a biologist in the School of Forestry at North Carolina State University. Cowling maintains that much more must be known about the whole process of how airborne substances are produced and deposited before we can attempt to alter any part of it. He argues that a simplistic view of acid precipitation can lead to oversimplified and dangerous attempts to deal with it.

"One solution that has been suggested," Cowling states, "is to inject ammonia into stack gases to produce ammonium sulfate instead of sulfuric acid. But when plants take up ammonium sulfate, they produce still more acid, which is more harmful than the acid precipitation alone."

Together with other scientists, Cowling has taken meaningful action to generate the information needed for development of safe and workable solutions to the acid precipitation problem. This group of scientists helped set up a cooperative network of experiment stations in 26 states. Established in 1978, the network receives primary support from the U.S. Department of Agriculture, with additional assistance from the U.S. Forest Service, the U.S. Geological Survey, the Department of Energy, and several other state and federal agencies. The alliance, now called the National Atmospheric Deposition Program (NADP), is building an expanding bank of data on the acid-precipitation problem and on the deposition of atmospheric substances generally. Cowling has high hopes for the program.

"We are beginning to determine the relative importance of various forms of atmospheric deposition," he says, "and we are now coordinating research on the effects of various airborne substances on agricultural lands, forests, rangeland, and surface waters."

The research and data-collecting capabilities of the NADP may continue to expand. Cowling was one of four scientists who produced a national plan for research on atmospheric deposition for the President's Council on Environmental Quality, an administrative agency associated with the Executive Branch. Because atmospheric pollutants drift across national boundaries, it is important that nations work together in a coordinated attempt to study and limit the detrimental impact of acid precipitation. With the help of scientists like Ellis Cowling we may yet learn how to solve international environmental problems in a cooperative manner.

mass contains 1 unit of DDT, as many as 10 units could become associated with each gram of herbivore biomass. Similarly, 10 grams or more of herbivore biomass is required to support 1 gram of carnivore biomass. Since in our example that is equivalent to 100 grams of producer biomass, each containing 1 unit of DDT, primary carnivores could contain as many as 100 units of DDT per gram of biomass.

Chlorinated hydrocarbons concentrate largely in the fat deposits of most vertebrates, human beings included. Although DDT has not been proved a health hazard in people, high concentrations of the insecticide have induced higher than normal incidences of cancer in mice, and its impact on populations of predator birds has been overwhelming.

Predator birds such as bald eagles, peregrine falcons, and brown pelicans feed exclusively at high trophic levels. Consequently, concentrations of chlorinated hydrocarbons become magnified thousands of times in these species. For example, the concentration of DDT in herring gull eggs found recently in Wisconsin was 200 parts per million, 40,000 times higher than that in the surrounding environment. Such concentrations interfere with the process of eggshell formation by restricting the transfer of calcium from bone to the eggshell-producing tissues of female birds. Calcium is a major component of eggshells, and its diminished supply frequently results in eggs whose shells are so thin that they are crushed by the weight of nesting parent birds (Fig. 10.11). The net effect is to threaten entire species with extinction in just a few generations. Examination of peregrine falcon and sparrowhawk eggs laid between 1900 and 1970 in Britain revealed a sharp decline in eggshell thickness beginning in 1945, coinciding with the first widespread use of DDT in the area (Fig. 10.12).

DDT can therefore disrupt biological systems at low and high organizational levels simultaneously. It not only interferes with normal integration of tissue function in predator birds but also simplifies entire ecosystems by reducing the size of populations. Although many of us value the beauty and grace of these birds, their reduced numbers constitute far more than an esthetic loss. Their diminished population size already has generated a small decrease in the stability of many ecosystems.

The impact of DDT on nonpest populations also explains why, in attempts to increase crop yields, persistent use of the insecticide often has the opposite effect. For example, use of DDT in the control of cotton-foraging insects on a large

A

B

Fig. 10.11 DDT and predator birds. (A) DDT interferes with the metabolism of calcium in many birds. High concentrations of DDT in the tissues of predator birds results in thin eggshells that break easily. Pictured here is a broken pelican egg. (B) DDT has played a major role in greatly reducing the numbers of peregrine falcons in the United States. *(A, © Gordon Menzie, Photophile, San Diego; B, Luther C. Goldman, Bureau of Sport Fisheries & Wildlife.)*

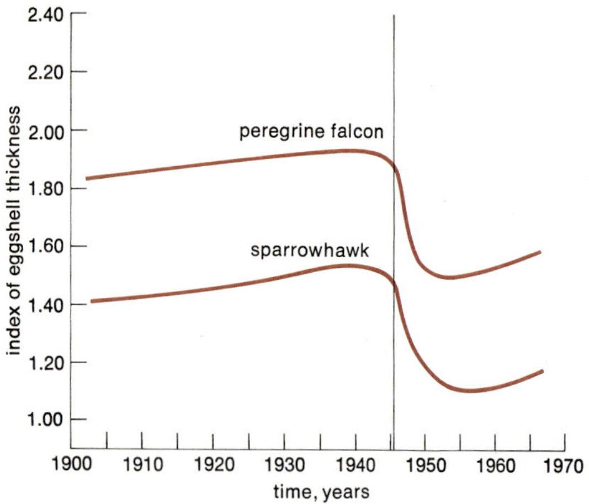

Fig. 10.12 Eggshell thickness. Changes in thickness of eggshells of peregrine falcon and sparrowhawk in Britain. Vertical line indicates the first widespread use of DDT. *(From P. Ehrlich, A. Ehrlich, and J. Holden, "Population, Resources, and Environment: Issues in Human Ecology," Freeman, San Francisco, 1973.)*

farm in Peru increased cotton production from 440 to 650 lb/acre over the first 4 years; but the harvest dropped to 350 lb/acre in the fifth year, almost 100 lb/acre less than before the insecticide was used. Thus, the effect of DDT was only temporary.

During the first 4 years, DDT reduced the population of insect pests to low levels, but the insecticide also reduce populations of birds and other carnivores that prey on the insects. Moreover, the herbivorous insects existed at a lower trophic level than their predators. Consequently, the insects were far more abundant than the predators. The number of individuals exhibiting a natural immunity to a pesticide increases in direct proportion to population size. The large population of cotton-foraging insects contained a few DDT-resistant individuals, and they soon gave rise to a rapidly expanding population of DDT-resistant offspring. Because of their higher biotic potential, the DDT-tolerant insects repopulated the farmland faster than the predators. Thus, after DDT had been used for 4 years, the number of insects immune to this insecticide was much greater than before. Yet the number of insect predators immune to this insecticide was much lower. The meager cotton yield in the fifth year was a direct consequence of this DDT-induced population imbalance (Fig. 10.13).

Genetic resistance to insecticides severely limits the long-term effectiveness of any chemical poison. At least a dozen species of insects had exhibited some resistance to DDT by 1945, less than 5 years after the first widespread use of this compound. By 1967 the number had increased to 165 species. About 30 of these carry diseases and another 75 are serious agricultural pests. Indeed, at least one species can no longer thrive in a DDT-free environment.

Climate

The limited capacity of the biosphere to absorb pollutants without detriment also can be illustrated by examining the theoretical impact of people on climate. As we have seen, climate is the principal factor determining the characteristics of biomes. This relation between climate and biome is not unidirectional, however, for biomes also influence climate. The humidity of a region, regional air currents, and fluctuations of ground temperatures all vary in response to the dominant type of vegetation present in biomes. Thus, climatic changes could be triggered by pollutants such as sulfur dioxide, which influence ecological succession by damaging the photosynthetic tissues of different species of terrestrial plants in varying intensities.

Human beings could be promoting changes in climate by altering the flux of energy absorbed and reflected by the global earth-atmosphere system. The amount of energy absorbed and reflected back to space by this system is influenced greatly by the composition of the atmosphere. Principles governing this energy flux are not understood sufficiently for scientists to predict accurately the consequences of altering the composition of the atmosphere. Theoretically, however, any modification that causes the earth to absorb more energy than it reflects back to space will result in a global increase in temperature. Fresh water locked in polar ice caps would be released in amounts directly proportional to the temperature increase, lowering the salinity of oceans and causing them to rise over coastal plains. The characteristics of biomes would change dramatically in response to rising temperatures, shifting patterns of rainfall, and changes in many other conditions that affect climate.

Conversely, any modification of the atmosphere that causes an opposite change in the energy balance of the earth will produce a global decrease in temperature. Increasing amounts of water will

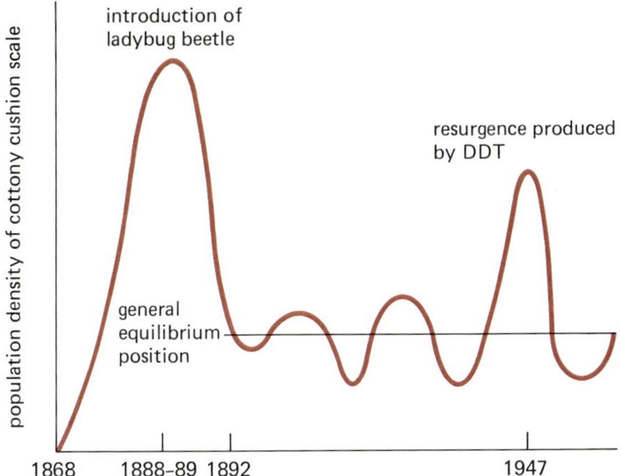

Fig. 10.13 Pesticides and predatory-prey interactions. Indiscriminate use of pesticides can affect crop yields adversely by disrupting population balances between predators and prey. For example, the cottony cushion scale, an insect that punctures plants and feeds on sap, was accidently introduced into California in 1868. Because the insect had few natural enemies in the United States, it spread rapidly and caused great damage to citrus trees. Two species of predatory ladybird beetles were introduced into California in 1888 in an attempt to combat the scale. The predators quickly reduced the scale population to a level of low economic damage (general equilibrium position), but later use of DDT disrupted the population balance between predators and prey. The rapid growth of scale populations that resulted from the reduced numbers of beetles led to renewed infestations of citrus trees.

freeze, glaciers will form and increase in size, and a new ice age will have begun.

People already have altered the composition and characteristics of the atmosphere on a global scale. Although insufficient evidence exists to prove a correlation, some of these alterations may be influencing energy absorption and dissipation. Since the 1940s, there has been a small but steady decline in the temperature of the earth's Northern Hemisphere (Fig. 10.14). This trend has been accompanied by a steady increase in the concentration of atmospheric particulates. Some of these particles have been produced from volcanic eruptions or the effects of wind blowing across deserts, but many have been produced by human activities. Automobiles, aircraft, power plants, incineration of trash, dust blown from farmland, all contribute to the turbidity of the atmosphere. Increases in airborne particulates usually bring about a corresponding increase in the total amount of sunlight reflected back to space by the atmosphere. The effects of such increases on climate can be enormous.

In 1815, for example, the eruption of Mount Tambora in Indonesia ejected approximately 80 km^3 of volcanic ash and other particles into the atmosphere. By contrast, only about 1 km^3 of particulates was released to the atmosphere during the May 18, 1980, eruption of Mount St. Helens in the state of Washington (Fig. 10.15). Despite causing numerous deaths and millions of dollars worth of damage, the effects of the volcanic discharge of Mount St. Helens are miniscule compared with the Mount Tambora eruption. 1816 was the year of "no summer" in the northern United States, and snow fell in many areas during July and August. The average temperature during July in England was 56°F, 5° colder than the usual average for the month.

There is little doubt that the dramatic increase in atmospheric particulates caused the reduced temperatures. The three coldest decades on record in England were 1781–1790, 1811-1820, and 1881-1890. These coincided with the 1783 eruptions of Mount Asama in Japan and Mount Skaptar in Ice-

Fig. 10.14 Temperature changes. Changes of the mean annual temperature of the Northern Hemisphere: 1875 to 1970. (*D. M. Gates, "Man and His Environment: Climate," Harper & Row, New York, 1972.*)

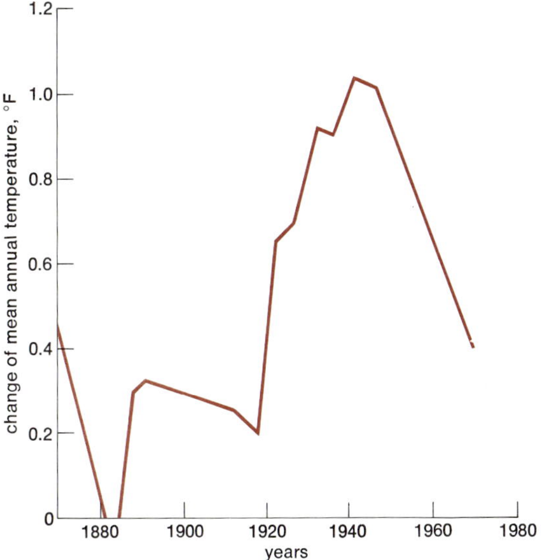

A

land, the 1815 eruption of Mount Tambora, and the 1883 eruption of Krakatoa. A cause-effect relationship between the increased concentrations of atmospheric particulates due to air pollution and the recent decline in temperature of the Northern Hemisphere has not been proved. Nevertheless, the dramatic impact of volcanic eruptions on climate warns of the potential conseqences that could result from changes in the composition of the atmosphere resulting from human activities. It is sobering to consider the effect of a Tambora-scale eruption on the severely limited world food supply of today.

The temperature-depressing effects of particulates are counterbalanced by numerous other factors, among them the relative concentration of atmospheric carbon dioxide. The concentration of CO_2 in air is determined and maintained by the carbon cycle described in Chap. 8. Plants remove CO_2 from the air and use it as a raw material for photosynthesis. Carbon dioxide is returned to the

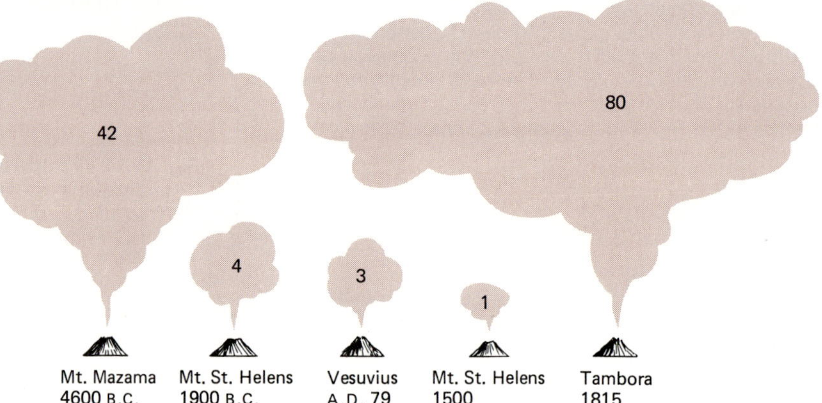

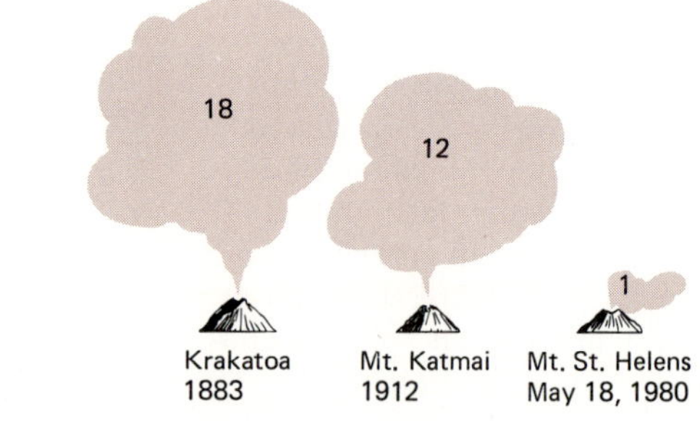

B

Fig. 10.15 Volcanoes and climate. (A) The May 1980 eruption of Mount St. Helens. (B) The amount of debris released to the atmosphere by several historic volcanic eruptions is compared. Numbers indicate cubic kilometers of ash and other particulates ejected. The amount of ash released by the 1980 eruption of Mount St. Helens had little, if any, effect on climate.

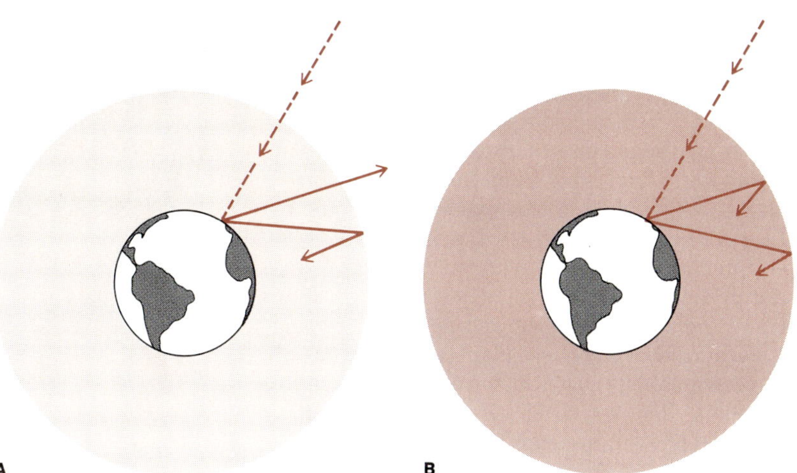

Fig. 10.16 Greenhouse effect. (A) The earth surrounded by an atmosphere that contains a "normal" concentration of CO_2. Shorter wavelengths of light from the sun (dashed line) penetrate the atmosphere and strike the earth's surface. Some of the energy of these shorter wavelengths is reflected back to outer space as heat (solid lines), but some is "trapped" by molecules of CO_2 and reradiated back to the surface of the earth. (B) If the CO_2 content of the atmosphere increases (darker color), more heat will be trapped and the average surface temperature of the earth will increase.

atmosphere through cell respiration, weathering, and the combustion of fossil fuels. The CO_2 content of the atmosphere has increased by approximately 12 per cent since 1880, attributable partly to the burning of agricultural products and fossil fuels. Not unexpectedly, this rate of increase appears to be rising.

Carbon dioxide influences the temperature of the earth through a *greenhouse effect.* Although widely used, this expression is partly a misnomer. Scientists once believed that the internal warmth of a greenhouse resulted chiefly from special heat-retaining properties of glass. When visible light passes through glass and strikes the ground, some of its energy is converted to heat in the form of longer wavelengths of infrared radiation. Glass does not transmit infrared radiation as efficiently as shorter wavelengths, and many scientists believed that this property prevented heat from escaping to the outside of a glass-enclosed greenhouse. It has been shown, however, that heat is retained largely because the closed environment of the greenhouse prevents mixing of warmer air inside with colder air outside.

Carbon dioxide also is transparent to sunlight and resists transmission of heat to space from the earth's surface (Fig. 10.16). Increased concentrations of atmospheric CO_2, should therefore produce a corresponding rise in the temperature of the earth. Except for a decade beginning in the early 1950s, average annual temperatures appear to have been rising in most of the Southern Hemisphere, and a similar trend occurred in the Northern Hemisphere between 1880 and 1940. As noted earlier, annual temperatures have been declining in the Northern Hemisphere since then. It is possible that the recent sharp increase in airborne particles in the more heavily populated and industrialized Northern Hemisphere has negated the effect of the coincident rise in the concentration of CO_2, but this is only one of several explanations. The average temperature of the earth underwent many variations before the appearance of mankind. Other factors, unrelated to human activities, may be responsible for the different temperature fluctuations in the Northern and Southern Hemispheres. That our activities have altered the composition of the atmosphere is certain; only the effects of these alterations remain unclear.

Soil Degradation

Human beings also have altered the characteristics of terrestrial ecosystems, including those of entire biomes. Many of these changes are the result of agricultural practices. We continue to depend on fertile soil for most of our nutrients; about three-quarters of all human food comes from the world's croplands. Only 11 per cent of the land surface is naturally suitable for crop production, and conservation techniques must be used if these soils are to remain productive.

Yet farmers never have been required or even encouraged to conserve cropland. In earlier times nomadic farmers could simply abandon land that had become unproductive and move to unspoiled regions that offered virgin soils. Failure to conserve farmland has led to permanent and large-scale alterations of ecosystems, including replacement of fertile grasslands with deserts. Extensive cutting of forests and overplowing of land by the ancient Carthaginians greatly accelerated evaporation of water from soils along the coast of North Africa. Today much of this region has become part of the still-expanding Sahara Desert.

Similar practices have severely damaged cropland in the western and midwestern United States. One of the most significant and devastating examples occurred in the Great Plains at the height of the economic depression in the 1930s and again in the 1950s. The hot, dry areas of the southern Great Plains often undergo long periods of below-average rainfall. However, the short, sod-forming grasses that dominate this region normally protect the underlying topsoil from drought-induced damage and erosion.

During the westward migration of settlers, much of this area was cultivated as farmland. Considerable more acreage was plowed and planted with wheat in 1914, when the grain belt of Europe was ravaged by war. Above-average rainfall in this region of the Great Plains prompted even more agricultural exploitation between 1914 and 1931. In spite of records showing periodic drought in the area, all the land judged suitable for farming was plowed.

Like fire and many forms of pollution, farming reduces the complexity of ecosystems. Instead of a more mature ecosystem consisting of several populations of microorganisms, animals, and a mixture of grasses, much of the Great Plains had been stripped of its natural vegetation by the plow. As stated earlier, simpler ecosystems usually lack the stability of older ecosystems and are more susceptible to factors that disrupt normal relations between the community and the physical environment.

In 1931, drought returned to the Great Plains. So much soil was unprotected by natural grass cover that a series of storms, beginning in 1933, blew great waves of dust across Oklahoma, Kansas, and parts of Texas, darkening the skies and making much of this area virtually uninhabitable for livestock or people (Fig. 10.17). As much as 12 inches of topsoil was lost from farmland throughout the region as drifting dunes buried farmland, roads, fences, and even houses. Appropriately, the area was nicknamed the Great Dust Bowl.

A

B

Fig. 10.17 The dust bowl. (A) A dust storm in Kansas. (B) Wind-blown sand covering farm lands in Kansas. Scenes like these were common in the Great Plains during the early 1930s. *(A, USDA-Soil Conservation Service. B, by R. C. McLean, USDA-Soil Conservation Service.)*

An effort to repair the damage was begun in 1935 with creation of the Soil Conservation Service. Federal aid and technical knowledge were given to farmers, and grass was replanted across much of the region. Cultivation continued only on land best suited for agriculture.

The long drought finally ended in the early 1940s, and many farms were restored to productivity. But much of the European grain belt was destroyed again by war, and much of the restored ecosystem of the Great Plains was simplified again to produce wheat for the allied armies. As World War II ended, the lessons of the Great Dust Bowl had been forgotten, and no attempt was made to rebuild the fragile ecosystem of the plains. In 1950 drought returned, and dust storms again swept across eroded farms and overgrazed ranges. Once again, federal aid and technical advice were required to reestablish grass in many areas.

Fig. 10.18 Soil erosion. Water eroding soil from a plowed field.

Although scientists now understand the causes of farm and rangeland destruction, soil-conservation practices still remain inadequate, as evidenced by the periodic reappearance of dust clouds throughout midwestern America. In 1976, the average annual loss of topsoil from United States farmland was approximately 12 tons/acre. This is equivalent to 2 bushels of topsoil lost for each bushel of corn harvested. Crop yields cannot be maintained indefinitely under these conditions. New topsoil is produced during terrestrial succession, but only at a rate of 1 inch in 300 to 1000 years. Under normal farming conditions, topsoil forms at a rate of about 1 inch every 100 years, or about 1.5 tons/acre annually. And even under ideal conditions of soil management the rate is only 1 inch every 30 years.

Soil erosion affects crop productivity in many adverse ways. Most of the nutrients required for plant growth are located in topsoil, and a large fraction of them are lost when topsoil is blown or washed away. More than 50 million tons of nitrogen, phosphorus, potassium, and other inorganic nutrients are lost from America's agricultural lands each year. In 1977 the cost of replacing these nutrients with fertilizers was estimated at between 7 and 8 billion dollars.

Loss of humus from the land surface leads to compaction of the soil left behind. As a result, eroded soil often contains fewer air pockets than necessary for rapid plant growth. Because of compaction, eroded land absorbs less water than fertile soils. Water runoff increases as soil erodes, often flooding adjacent land.

Most of the soil eroded from agricultural land is carried away by water (Fig. 10.18). Over 3 billion tons of sediment wash into American waterways each year. Another billion tons of waterborne sediments comes from nonagricultural sources, such as construction or logging. About 1 billion tons of the 4 billion total ends up in the ocean; the remainder settles in lakes, rivers, and reservoirs. The sediments often have a detrimental impact on aquatic organisms; they interfere with salmon and trout spawning, for example, and reduce egg survival. Sediments can also cover crevices and other hiding places of young fish, thus increasing the likelihood that the fish will be eaten by predators. Wind accounts for about one-quarter of the total erosion of soil that occurs in North America. Although less serious than water runoff, wind erosion can be severe in semiarid environments. About 800 tons of topsoil is eroded each year from farmland in the drier western regions of the United States.

North America contains some of the richest farmland in the world. By contrast, poor agricultural practices coupled with centuries of continuous cultivation have greatly impoverished farmland in many other parts of the world. Today several Asian, South American, and European countries depend heavily on grain exported from the United States. Many nations are now so dependent on imported grain that a long-term reduction in United States production could have serious international repercussions. Yet little has been done to conserve topsoil on American farms.

There are several reasons for this apparent lack of concern. One is related to the urban orientation of American society. Most people give little thought to the relationships between soil fertility and the availability of fruits, vegetables, and meats in supermarkets. In addition, farmers have been burdened with greatly increased costs for tractor fuel, pesticides, labor, and equipment. Many farmers cannot institute soil-conservation practices because sufficient capital is lacking. Moreover, the short-term costs of maintaining soil-conservation techniques are sometimes greater than the short-term returns.

Also, crop yields have been maintained and often increased in eroded soils through use of newly developed strains of plants that grow rapidly in response to heavy applications of inorganic fertilizers (Fig. 10.19). Greater use of pesticides also has increased crop yields. Nevertheless, the costs of boosting crop production on eroding soils has been high and is increasing rapidly. The greater quantities of fossil fuels in the form of inorganic fertilizers, pesticides, and other materials needed to offset the decline in soil quality equaled 5 gallons of oil per acre in 1976. This is equivalent to 50 million barrels of oil annually, or about 4 per cent of America's total oil imports in 1970.

Degradation of land outside the United States is even greater. Largely because of poorer maintenance of farmland and the increased need for housing and highways, soil erosion in developing countries is estimated to be almost twice as severe as in the United States. The erosion problem is expected to intensify as demand for food increases. The world is rapidly reaching a point where additional amounts of fertilizers and pesticides will not be able to compensate for additional losses of topsoil. Millions of acres of grassland already have been degraded to deserts. The loss of additional millions could be devastating.

Fig. 10.19 Miracle rice. Shorter strains of rice (left), first produced in the 1960s, generate more grain per acre than the taller conventional variety on the right. The shorter strain can support heavier heads of grain and use fertilizer more efficiently. Higher-yielding varieties of wheat and other food plants also have been produced over the past two decades.

These examples clearly illustrate the capacity of people to disrupt the organizational hierarchy of living matter at all levels, from cell to biosphere. This potential has grown enormously in recent years, and some have placed the blame entirely on "science and technology." As discussed in Chap. 1, however, such a view is both simplistic and inaccurate. Our impact on the organization of life stems from the size of our populations, our values, and our institutions. Perhaps the comic strip character Pogo said it more succinctly: "We have found the enemy—and he is us."

CAUSES OF THE IMPACT

Three principal factors have contributed to our disruptive impact on the organization of living systems: our exponential population growth, our desire for affluence, and the "linear" nature of our economy.

Population Size and Affluence

The first populations of human beings appeared between 3 and 4 million years ago, probably on the continent of Africa. Since then, human beings have spread to all continents of the earth. Our population, which now numbers over 4.5 billion people, has been growing exponentially for at least 500,000 years (Fig. 10.20). As explained in Chap. 8, each addition to the population becomes a contributor to new additions during exponential growth. Thus, the *rate* of population growth increases as population size increases.

The effect of exponential growth on human population size can be seen in Table 10.2. Approximately 5 million people inhabited the earth in 8000 B.C., and about 1500 years were required for the population to double. Because of exponential growth, the next doubling, from 500 million to 1 billion, took only 200 years, and the doubling from 1 to 2 billion was achieved in 80 years. The rate of growth continued to increase, and approximately 4 billion people inhabited the earth in 1975, only 45 years later. If the growth rate of 1972 were to continue there would be 8 billion people by the year 2010.

As stated in Chap. 8, such rapid population growth usually occurs whenever species are reproducing close to their biotic potentials. Also, note again that exponential growth never continues indefinitely. Eventually environmental resistance forces population size to level off or to drop precipitously. Our ability to eliminate or reduce the impact of environmental factors that tend to restrict our population growth also has grown exponentially. In 1870, when the population of human beings was approximately one-fourth its present size, people had little knowledge of the relation between pathogenic bacteria and infectious disease. By 1970, only 100 years later, scientists had discovered penicillin and developed many other wonder drugs that increased human life expectancy dramatically. During the same period, development of insecticides, synthetic fertilizers, and new varieties of plants increased the annual production of food immensely. Although the birthrate of mankind has decreased significantly since the mid-1950s in many industrialized countries, factors such as those above have produced an even faster decline in the death rate of human beings, thus preventing a substantial reduction in the overall rate of population growth (see also Chap. 11).

Moreover, the rapid development of new technology that also occurred during this period permit-

Fig. 10.20 Human population growth. *(Adapted from How Many People Have Lived on Earth, Population Bulletin, vol. 18, 1962.)*

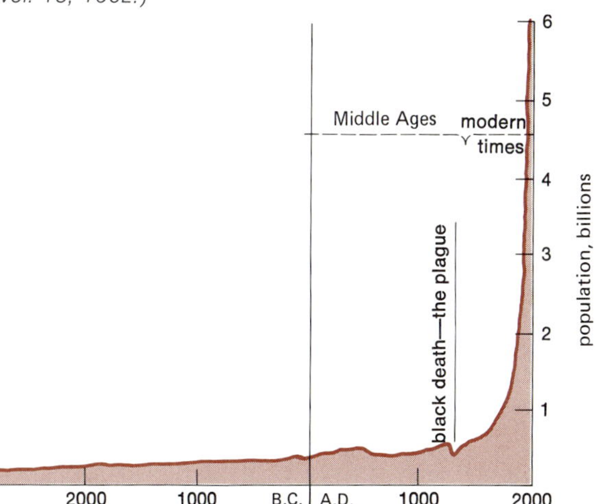

TABLE 10.2
Time Required for the Human Population to Double in Size: 8000 B.C.–1975

Date	Estimated world population: Millions	Billions	Time required for population to double, years
8000 B.C.	5		1500
1650 A.D.	500		200
1850 A.D.	1000	1	80
1930 A.D.	2000	2	45
1975 A.D.	4000	4	35

SOURCE: Table 6, Elements, 4E, p. 152.

ted exploitation of natural resources such as oil, water, timber, and minerals at higher rates. This in turn has led to increased affluence, particularly in industrialized countries like the United States (Table 10.3). An important relationship exists between affluence and exponential population growth. These two factors usually interact synergistically, increasing substantially the total amount of matter and energy needed to support people (Table 10.4).

For example, the amount of food that must be obtained increases as the population does. If each new individual added to the population consumes the minimum amount of food required for survival, the total increase, however substantial, is far less than that required to support the same number of new individuals at the average rate of food consumption in the United States. Similarly, the total amount of matter and energy required to provide each new household with a clothesline is much less than that required to equip each with an electric clothes dryer.

As we have seen, matter and energy cannot be extracted from the environment without cost. In nature, as in economics, "there is no such thing as a free lunch." Refusal to "pay" our "environmental debt" has resulted in disruptions of living systems at all levels, and additional disruptions could jeopardize the functional integrity of the biosphere.

Two important questions now face mankind: Can we accelerate the extraction of matter and energy from the environment to maintain affluence and exponential population growth? And if we can, *should* we? Diminishing natural resources and the increasing shortage of world food supplies may make the second question academic. But perhaps people can continue to use science to push aside factors that limit the growth of the population and wealth. Should new technology designed to accomplish this objective be rushed into application? Hasty application of new technology often breeds mistakes. Are the risks worth the effort?

TABLE 10.3
Stock of Consumer Durables in the United States

Item	1940s: Number	Year	1973
automobiles use per capita	0.21	1940	0.59
refrigerators use per capita	0.15	1946	0.27
clothes dryers use per capita	0.001	1949	0.16
households with air conditioners, %	0.2	1948	48.6

SOURCE: P. R. Ehrlich, A. H. Ehrlich, and J. P. Holdren, "Ecoscience: Population, Resources, Environment," table 12-4, p. 722, Freeman, San Francisco, 1977.

Noncyclic versus Cyclic Economics

Population and affluence are not the only factors contributing to our detrimental impact on the organization of life. If our rate of population in-

TABLE 10.4
Per Capita Consumption of Basic Resources in the United States

Year	Annual steel production, lb	Annual energy consumption, million Btu	Daily water use, gal
1900	300	96	
1910	635	154	875
1940	1020	181	1030
1946	941	205	1170
1970	1285	328	1600
1975	1092	333	1800

SOURCE: P. R. Ehrlich, A. H. Ehrlich, and J. P. Holdren, "Ecoscience: Population, Resources, Environment," fig. 12-3, p. 721, Freeman, San Francisco, 1977.

crease suddenly fell to zero and our present level of affluence remained constant or even declined somewhat, the "noncyclic" nature of our economic system would continue to erode the stability of ecosystems and threaten our survival.

Our economy and its supporting technology are the principal means by which sufficient energy and matter have been extracted from the environment to support both population growth and affluence. Except for people, all organisms extract matter and energy from the biosphere and eliminate wastes into it purely by biological means. Wastes rarely are produced in quantities sufficient to disrupt the cyclic flow of matter through ecosystems. Indeed, the activities and wastes of organisms are vital to the perpetuation of this cyclic economy (see Chap. 8). But the economy we have developed is basically noncyclic and has not been designed to interlock efficiently with the cyclic economy of matter in the biosphere. The linear noncyclic nature of our economy can be illustrated by the following example.

Oil, obtained from wells drilled into the surface of the earth, supplies fuel for almost all internal combustion engines operating today. All fossil fuels, including oil, are nonrenewable natural resources, since their rate of production in the earth is insignificant compared with their rate of depletion. Once obtained, oil is refined, and some of it is converted to gasoline. When burned, the chemical energy of gasoline can be transformed to mechanical energy, moving most of the vehicles so important to the economy and affluence of all industrialized nations. But fossil fuels also serve as raw materials for the synthesis of fertilizers, plastics, insecticides, and many other agricultural products. Crude oil, therefore, also has become vital to the maintenance of our population growth.

However, the technology that obtains and uses oil usually is not coupled with other technologies designed to reconvert the waste products of oil to new supplies of crude oil. Instead, these wastes usually are simply discarded into the environment. In this instance, therefore, our economy is noncyclic (Fig. 10.21). Crude oil is extracted from the environment but not replenished.

Until recently, most people were unaware that anything of significance would happen after the waste products of gasoline combustion entered the atmosphere. Since exhaust fumes usually are almost invisible, many assumed that they just disappeared. As we have learned, however, matter cannot disappear in the biosphere. It is a closed system, and everything is connected to everything else. There is no "away" place; everything must go somewhere. Toxic substances, discarded into the environment by noncyclic economies, often reenter our bodies and those of all organisms because each is a functional link in the cyclic movement of matter through ecosystems. We are part of nature, and there can be no escape.

Most of the damage caused by noncyclic economies has occurred since the end of World War II. There are two principal reasons for this recent damage, one quantitative, the other qualitative. The first relates to urbanization. In industrialized and nonindustrialized countries alike, the greatest population growth has occurred in and around cities. In the United States, for example, approximately 6 per cent of the population lived in urban

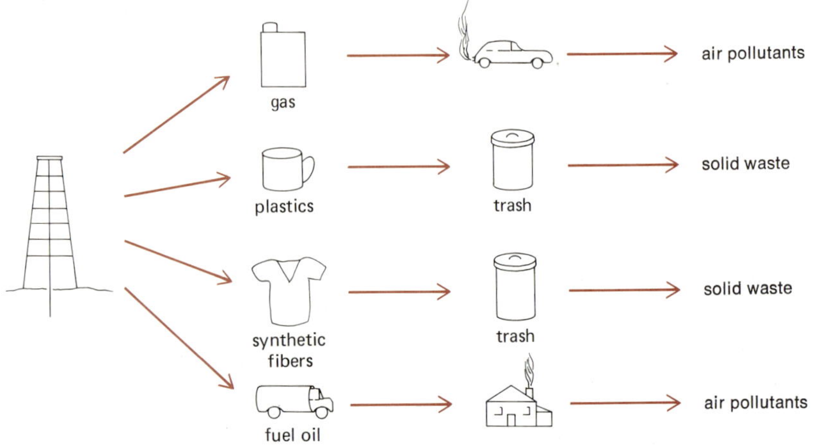

Fig. 10.21 Noncyclic economies. Crude oil, taken from deep deposits in the ground, is used in the manufacture of many products. Too often, these products or their derivatives enter the environment as toxic wastes.

areas in 1800, 15 per cent in 1850, 40 per cent in 1900; today, nearly 75 per cent live in cities or their suburbs. Consequently, the volume of waste produced in urban areas has increased tremendously, even faster than the rate of urbanization in some cases.

The increased concentration of waste deposited into restricted environments can greatly disrupt the stability of ecosystems. For example, the effluent of several large cities, including Cleveland, Detroit, Toledo, and Buffalo, are deposited into Lake Erie. During the 1960s nearly all of the beaches surrounding this lake were closed because of pollution, and each summer huge mounds of decaying fish and algae accumulated on the shore (Fig. 10.22). So much oil floated on the surface of rivers leading to the lake that two were declared fire hazards, and one of these, the Cuyahoga, which flows into the lake at Cleveland, actually burned (Fig. 10.23).

Fig. 10.22 Overfertilization of aquatic ecosystems. Excessive amounts of sewage and other organic wastes frequently produce oxygen deficits in aquatic ecosystems Many species of fish cannot survive such deficits.

Overfertilization of Lake Erie has produced a dramatic change in the populations of organisms that inhabit the lake. Most of this overfertilization has been caused by sewage dumped directly into the lake and the leaching of agricultural fertilizers from surrounding farmland. Usually, producers and decomposers are first affected by such increases in lake fertility. The size of both populations increases rapidly in response to increased supplies of dissolved inorganic nutrients and organic wastes. As the amount of suspended organic waste becomes excessive, the respiratory activities of correspondingly larger populations of decomposers remove large quantities of dissolved oxygen from aquatic ecosystems. *Oxygen deficits* occur in such ecosystems whenever this removal produces below-normal concentrations of dissolved oxygen. These deficits can become sufficiently large to kill fish and other aquatic organisms in great numbers.

In Lake Erie, the oxygen deficit in the bottom waters of the central basin was 270 million pounds of oxygen during the summer of 1964. The concentration of dissolved oxygen had become too low to support the once abundant and commercially profitable populations of whitefish, lake herring, and blue pike. These and other species had been replaced by expanded populations of perch, sheepshead, catfish, carp, and other "rough" fish of less

Fig. 10.23 The oil-laden Cuyahoga River on fire in Cleveland, Ohio. *(Cleveland Plain Dealer.)*

commercial value that were better adapted to the reduced concentrations of oxygen (Fig. 10.24). The lake, however, was not only dying commercially but biologically as well, for the greatly increased fertility of the lake was accelerating its rate of eutrophication.

Since 1964 the Federal Environmental Protection Agency, environmental groups, civic leaders, and others have taken steps to decrease the rate of eutrophication of Lake Erie and to improve its quality generally. Considerable progress has been made. Whether viewed from a biological, economic, or recreational standpoint, Lake Erie is far healthier today than at any time during the 1960s. Nevertheless, the 1964 deficit of 270 million pounds of oxygen indicates how the structural and

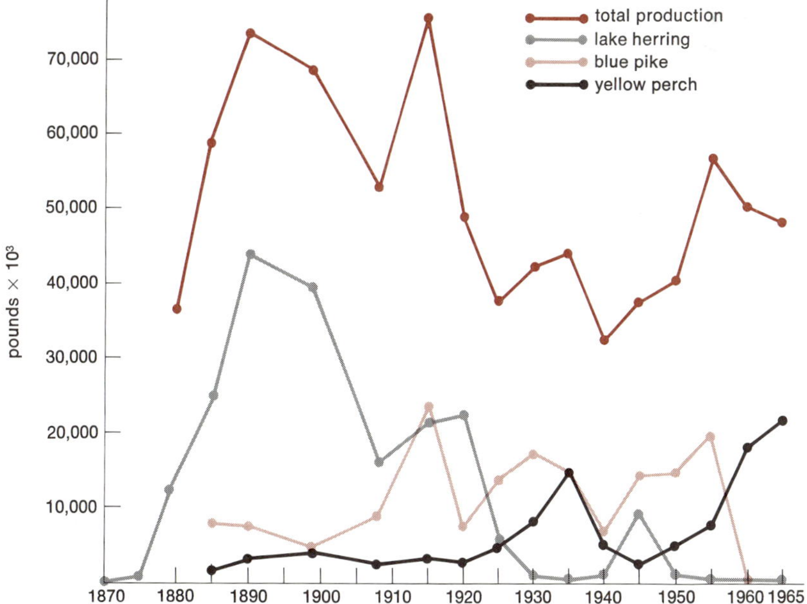

Fig. 10.24 Changes in the yearly catch of selected fish in Lake Erie: 1870 to 1965.

TABLE 10.5
Average Percentage Change in United States Manufacture of Selected Products: 1946–1971

Product	Change, %
nonreturnable soda bottles	+53,000
synthetic fibers	+5,980
mercury (mildew-resistant paints)	+3,120
plastics	+1,960
electric housewares	+1,040
synthetic organic chemicals	+950
aluminum	+680
chlorine gas	+600
electric power	+530
pesticides	+390
consumer electronics	+217
food	+42
lumber	−1
cotton fiber	−7
returnable beer bottles	−36
wool	−42

SOURCE: Barry Commoner, "The Closing Circle," Knopf, New York, 1971.

functional integrity of entire ecosystems can be disrupted by the sheer volume of human waste.

Quantities of waste do not account for the whole impact of our noncyclic economy on the organization of living systems. Often the type of waste being discarded is just as significant. Average percentage changes in the United States production of several commodities between 1946 and 1971 appears in Table 10.5. Note that many of the products showing the greatest postwar growth are composed of man-made compounds, or *synthetics*, and many that show the greatest decline are composed of natural compounds. For example, much of the clothing worn today is composed of synthetic fibers. The manufacture of such fibers has increased almost 6000 per cent since World War II. Conversely, the manufacture of cotton fabric, largely composed of cellulose, has decreased 7 per cent, and wool production has decreased 42 per cent during the same period.

Many synthetic compounds cannot be broken down by decomposers but remain intact for years until they disintegrate through weathering. Some of these synthetics, such as DDT, interfere with chemical reactions vital to normal cell functions. Moreover, waste by-products often are produced during the manufacture of most modern commodities, and some of these by-products, such as certain mercury-, lead-, and sulfur-containing compounds, are extremely toxic to living organisms.

One of the most troublesome problems facing industrialized countries is finding safe disposal sites for toxic wastes and cleaning up the billions of tons of potentially dangerous substances already dumped into terrestrial and aquatic ecosystems. Until recently, burial was both a cheap and acceptable method of refuse disposal, regardless of the substance being buried. Many abandoned disposal sites were covered over and converted to residential areas. Houses, schools, and playgrounds often were developed on the filled land. In the meantime, chemicals that had been dumped there diffused steadily into groundwater. People living on or near former disposal sites breathed, ingested or otherwise came in contact with the toxic wastes whenever contaminated groundwater pooled at the soil surface or seeped through home basement walls.

The effects of improper toxic-waste disposal can be tragic, as illustrated by the poisoning of the Love Canal area near Niagara Falls, New York. The canal, built as part of an aborted nineteenth-century industrial project financed by the flamboyant entrepreneur William T. Love, had been used by the Hooker Chemical Company as a disposal site for at least 20,000 tons of toxic industrial wastes. People living in houses constructed on filled land near the canal began experiencing an unusually high number of seemingly unrelated health problems throughout the 1960s and 1970s. Studies have shown that many of these problems probably stem, directly or indirectly, from the pool of more than 80 hazardous chemicals found in groundwater throughout the Love Canal area. At least 10 of these compounds probably cause cancer, and at least 14 are damaging to the brain and central nervous system. When a state-employed biologist analyzed the air content of a basement in one of the Love Canal homes, he found that the "safe exposure" time there was less than 2.4 min. The probability that the inhabitants of this house would contract cancer or some other disabling disease was significantly greater than that for people living in a less toxic environment.

Love Canal is not the only hazardous chemical dump site in the United States. During 1979, the

Environmental Protection Agency identified 32,254 sites where hazardous wastes are stored or buried, and a subsequent study suggested that the number may be as high as 51,000. Many of these sites are in or near urban areas. Other federal figures estimate that approximately 35 million tons of toxic wastes is produced each year and that over 90 per cent of this amount receives inadequate disposal.

Clearly, we must continually limit our impact on the organization of living systems to prevent future damage to the biosphere of possibly far more tragic consequences than those that already have occurred at Love Canal. The next section examines some of the ways we may be able to reduce this impact.

SOLUTIONS

Those who describe serious problems often are expected to offer solutions. Yet it is difficult to devise a specific plan to eliminate our own deleterious impact on the organization of living systems. It is not that solutions do not exist but that any possible solutions will precipitate significant social and cultural changes. The desirability of such changes involves value judgments. As pointed out in Chap. 1, all issues involving value judgments lie outside the realm of science. Decisions relating to such issues should involve the participation of all people.

Whatever decisions are made relative to solving the problems of pollution and human population growth, these problems are global in scope, and all people are suffering the consequences of permitting them to go untreated. We are bound to each other not simply through common biological ancestry or through philosophic dreams of oneness but, far more directly, through the same atmosphere, the same water, the same food-producing soil. The ancient query, "Am I my brother's keeper?" demands a very practical answer today.

In view of the lack of any meaningful response to the 1978 recommendations of the United Nations World Food Council or to the 1979 report of the U.S. Presidential Commission on World Hunger, one has reason to doubt rapid future progress toward a global solution to this problem. Yet without it, only two other solutions appear to remain: reduction of our numbers through nuclear catastrophe, conventional wars no longer being sufficiently destructive to affect global population growth; and the "natural" solution, through which the ecosystem always balances itself on its own accord—large-scale periodic waves of famine and death whenever the food supply falls below minimum sustenance levels.

Avoidance of these latter two solutions calls for treatment of all three causes of the present impact: population growth, affluence, and our noncyclic economy. Since they are interdependent, all must be treated simultaneously. If all people are to achieve a reasonable level of affluence, increased efforts will be required to reverse the population growth of mankind and reduce the amount of toxic waste that emanates from our noncyclic economy. Our plight is not hopeless, for we know how to limit births and how to begin interlocking our economy more efficiently with the cyclic economy of nature. As discussed more thoroughly in Chap. 25, birth control has become easy, safe, effective, and relatively inexpensive. Widely regarded as a more hopeful and more effective procedure than attempts to increase the food supply, birth control has indeed been successful in technically advanced nations. In the United States, for example, increased use of birth-control methods appears to be chiefly responsible for a 50 per cent reduction in unwanted pregnancies between 1960 and 1970. But success has been far less impressive in countries where the population and food crises are at their worst. In many places large populations still are considered evidence of national strength, and in others various religious beliefs and economic requirements continue to foster excessively large families. The combined and renewed efforts of scientists, economists, politicians, social workers, clergy, and others will be required to reduce the effects of famines that are virtually inevitable in some of these areas.

Substantial advances have been made in creating technology designed to reduce the deposition of waste into the environment. Metal, glass, paper, and other valuable resources, previously incinerated or dumped into sanitary landfills, are now being recovered by new forms of technology tested in several cities throughout the United States. Other scientists are attempting to convert garbage to fuel, and still others are designing new and cleaner-burning automobile engines.

Science and technology can also be used to reduce erosion of farmland. Indeed, several soil-con-

Fig. 10.25 Contour plowing. Plow lines are run at right angles to the slope of the land to reduce wind and water erosion.

servation techniques are now available. Crops planted in parallel rows are particularly susceptible to soil erosion, especially when placed on sloping land. Topsoil losses often can be reduced by planting crops in furrows that follow the natural contour of fields. Each furrow acts as a small dam that keeps soil from washing downhill (see Fig. 10.25). Such *contour planting* can be extremely effective. For example, the annual erosion rate for potatoes planted in up and down hill rows near Ithaca, New York, was 14.4 tons of topsoil per acre, whereas potatoes planted along the contour of the hill lost only 0.1 ton/acre annually.

Alternating soil-conserving crops, such as grasses or legumes, with other crops is another effective method of erosion control (Table 10.6). Called *crop rotation,* this practice can not only reduce loss of topsoil but also improve soil fertility. The highly branched roots of grasses hold soil in place far better than corn or other cereal grains. Legumes also protect soil from erosion and, like grasses, provide a valuable source of humus when they are plowed in. In addition, legumes house large populations of nitrogen-fixing bacteria, and thus add substantial quantities of nitrates to the soil.

One of the most effective new soil-conservation techniques is *minimum tillage* (Fig. 10.26). Machinery has been developed that deposits seeds in narrow furrows or small holes. This kind of planting disturbs soil only slightly and leaves strips of sod and plant residue between crop rows. The sod and residues from previous crops break the fall of raindrops and slow down water runoff. A marked reduction in erosion can result. A study in Nebraska, for example, has demonstrated that minimum tillage can lead to a threefold reduction in soil erosion compared with traditional plowing methods. Minimum tillage also requires less labor and conserves soil moisture better than traditional methods.

Other soil-conservation techniques include periodic applications of livestock manure, planting cover crops during periods when food grains are not on fields (see Table 10.6), and interseeding legumes with certain crops such as corn. Moreover, research is being conducted that eventually may provide methods of injecting special strains of ni-

TABLE 10.6
Cropping Systems and Soil Erosion*

Cropping system	Average annual loss of soil per acre, tons	Percentage of total rainfall running off land
bare, cultivated, no crop	41.0	30
continuous corn	19.7	29
continuous wheat	10.1	23
crop rotation (corn, wheat, clover)	2.7	14
continuous bluegrass	0.3	12

*Average of 14 years measurements of runoff and erosion at Missouri Experiment Station, Columbia, Missouri. Soil type: Shelby loam; length of slope 90.75 ft; degree of slope 3.68%.
SOURCE: R. Dasmann, "Environmental Conservation," 2d ed., table 5, p. 118, Wiley, New York, 1968.

trogen-fixing bacteria into the roots of nonleguminous plants such as corn, wheat, and other grain crops. For example, it may be possible to mass-produce such strains through use of genetic engineering techniques discussed in Chap. 28. The man-made bacteria would produce an immediately usable source of nitrogen for agricultural plants, thereby reducing the need for inorganic fertilizers. Such research deserves financial support, but scientists must proceed cautiously. Overproduction of ammonia and nitrates by laboratory-modified bacteria could alter the pH of soils substantially and otherwise disrupt natural population balances in ecosystems.

Scientists are also attempting to reduce the dependence of farmers on chemical pesticides by developing alternate methods of pest control. Unlike broad-spectrum pesticides, which kill both harmful and beneficial species, most of the newer methods attempt to reduce population densities of specific pests without significantly affecting other organisms.

For example, it is both possible and advisable in some cases to import predators of pest organisms (see Fig. 10.13). Scientists have successfully imported into the United States a species of oriental wasp that preys on the destructive Japanese beetle (Fig. 10.27). An adult wasp provides food for its young by paralyzing a beetle larva and attaching an egg to it. When the young wasp hatches, it eats the larva as its first food. Since the wasp is not a predator of other insects, this type of control is *species-specific* and does not disrupt population balances between other organisms.

However, a potentially beneficial species can become a pest itself if the density of its population becomes too great. The practice of importing exotic organisms into the United States from other countries was a fad during the late nineteenth century. Several organizations and societies sprang up at this time, all devoted to diversifying the kinds of organisms found in America, particularly in the urban environments. The starling, a bird found in many parts of Europe, Asia, and North Africa but not in North America, was one of the imported exotics. In 1890, 60 birds were released in Central Park in New York City. Approximately 40 more starlings were brought to the United States and released the following year. The starling population grew far faster than anyone had anticipated; the birds now inhabit virtually all parts of the United States. Because they eat fruits as well as insects

Fig. 10.26 Minimum tillage. These corn plants were planted by a machine that deposited seeds in unplowed ground. Stubble from an earlier crop of wheat surrounds the growing corn plants. The ability to grow new crops on unplowed fields has greatly reduced erosion of topsoil.

Fig. 10.27 Biological control of pests. (A) Adult Japanese beetle. (B) Wasp depositing eggs into the pupal case of a developing insect. When the eggs hatch, the young wasps will consume their host. A related species of wasp preys upon Japanese beetles in similar fashion.

and often roost in buildings, starlings have become a nuisance to farmer and city-dweller alike. Scientists, therefore, must carefully study the life cycles of foreign organisms before they are imported into new environments.

Sterilization of adult male insects is another species-specific method of controlling insect pests. The technique has been used to eradicate most of the screwworm flies inhabiting the southeastern United States. Many cattle ranches have incurred large financial losses because of screwworm infestations. Larvae of these insects parasitize cattle, producing ugly sores that weaken and sometimes kill the host (Fig. 10.28).

Several years ago, the U.S. Department of Agriculture raised millions of male screwworm flies, sterilized them with x-rays, and then released them in their natural breeding grounds. Matings between female flies and sterile males produced infertile eggs. The sterilization program gradually reduced the population density of screwworms, and within 2 years the insects were virtually eradicated from the target area (see Fig. 10.28). Other pest-control techniques involve spraying synthetic hormones that interfere with normal growth of insects, use of species-specific sex-attractants to lure insects into electrocution chambers, and breeding pest-resistant strains of crops.

It is unlikely that any of these techniques will prove useful in maintaining all species of insects at nondestructive levels. Screwworms, for example, were particularly susceptible to the sterilization program because the flies concentrate in small, well-defined southern regions of the United States during winter months and female screwworms copulate only once in their lifetime. Female insects that copulate with many males are less susceptible to the irradiation technique because of the much higher probability that they will mate with at least one fertile male.

A similar x-ray program aimed at the codling moth met with limited success. This insect, a serious pest of apple and pear orchards, is distributed over a much wider area than the screwworm. Millions of male moths were sterilized and released to target regions, but migration of fertile males to these regions from surrounding areas reduced the density of sterile males to noneffective levels. It is unlikely, therefore, that sterilization methods alone will control the codling moth successfully, but a multilateral program of sterilization, chemical spray, and predator importation might. Indeed, many biologists believe that such *integrated control* programs provide the only realistic hope of significantly reducing use of broad-spectum chemical pesticides.

Integrated control will never be conceptually or technically as simple as chemical control alone. It probably will be slower-acting and more expensive, at least initially, and it will require greater planning and more cooperation between biologists, farmers, and government officials. However, there

Fig. 10.28 Sterilization of insect pests. (A) Adult screwworm fly. (B) Screwworm infestation in the skin of a steer. (C) Number of fertile and sterile screwworm egg masses found among 11 groups of penned goats for each of the first 16 weeks following start of a screwworm sterilization program in Curaçao, off the coast of Venezuela. Almost no fertile egg masses were found after 7 weeks of the first release of sterile males, and screwworms were eradicated from the target area within the next few weeks.

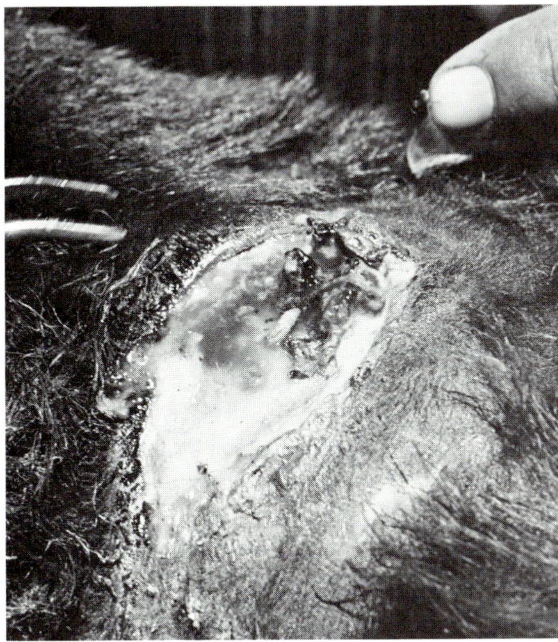

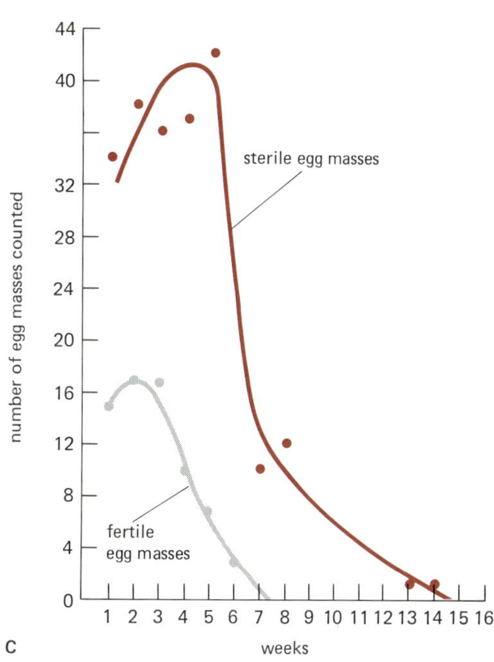

are indications that integrated control measures can be cheaper and more effective over the long run.

Mention was made earlier of reduced cotton yields that accompanied several years use of DDT in Peru. Following the crop failure, the following integrated control program was established. (1) Predacious and parasitic insects were imported from nearby valleys. (2) Cultivation of marginal land was halted in an attempt to eliminate many weaker plants, which provide better breeding grounds for pests than healthy plants. (3) Planting and irrigation schedules were modified in an effort to interfere with the life cycles of pests. (4) Spraying of chemical pesticides was permitted only with the permission and supervision of a panel of scientists. Despite less cultivation of land and little use of chemical insecticides, cotton yields for the area grew steadily and eventually reached record levels.

Implementation of soil-conservation practices often is similarly expensive and time-consuming. Contour planting, for example, results in a 5 to 7 per cent increase in both farming time and fuel use when compared with up and down hill row planting. Nevertheless, soil-conservation practices can sometimes increase net revenues immediately. In Texas, for example, yields of cotton grown on contour were 25 per cent greater than those grown on the slope. Under certain circumstances, production of corn, soybeans, and wheat also can be increased significantly through contour planting. Moreover, the economic benefits of soil conservation probably will increase markedly as the price of fuels, fertilizers, and pesticides continues to climb. In the meantime, greater consideration should be given to expanding support of research aimed at developing cheaper and more effective soil-conservation techniques that simultaneously increase crop yields.

Thus, the science and technology that have been used to pollute the environment can be used differently to reduce pollution and halt the human population growth. Our basic problem is not science and technology as such but in agreeing on what they should be used for. If pollution, affluence, and human population growth continue to threaten our survival, it will not be the result of an inherent defect in science. Indeed, science can now be used to solve most of the problems discussed in this chapter, but only if mankind *wishes* to apply science to these problems, agrees to pay the price of that application, and agrees to limit consumption and destruction of natural resources.

Review Questions

1 Describe how pollutants can disrupt the functions of cells, organs, and organ systems. Illustrate how the synergistic interaction of two or more pollutants can impair human health.

2 What factors limit the capacity of the biosphere to absorb pollutants without detriment? Describe the amplification effects of pollutants.

3 How are we affecting the composition and characteristics of the atmosphere? Describe the possible consequences of these effects. What is the greenhouse effect, and how does it affect the average temperature of the earth?

4 Describe how people have influenced aquatic and terrestrial succession on a large scale.

5 What are the principal causes of soil erosion? How have agricultural practices accelerated the rates of such erosion? How does soil erosion affect crop productivity? What factors are responsible for increased crop yields over the past 40 years? What can be done to decrease loss of topsoil from cropland?

6 Assess the worldwide political and social ramifications of a long-term decline in United States farm production.

7 It often becomes necessary to spray increasing amounts of a chemical insecticide to kill the same number of insect pests. Can you explain the decreased susceptibility of insects to chemical poisons?

8 One indiscriminate spraying of DDT could destroy the effectiveness of an integrated control program. Why?

9 What are the chief causes of our disruptive influence on the organization of life? Discuss the ecological consequences of human overpopulation and illustrate environmentally harmful synergistic interactions between human population growth and affluence.

10 Distinguish between cyclic and noncyclic economies. What factors are responsible for the greatly increased detrimental impact of people on the environment since World War II? Illustrate the impact of each factor you identify?

11 How have science and technology been used to alleviate the detrimental environmental impact of human populations? Outline your own solutions to our various environmental crises and systematically examine the ecological consequences of these suggestions.

12 What is acid precipitation? Why are certain lakes more vulnerable to the deleterious effects of acid precipitation than others? Describe some of these effects. How can acid precipitation affect terrestrial ecosystems? What is being done to reduce the damaging effects of acid precipitation? How can scientists contribute to the resolution of environmental problems?

Collateral Readings

Carson, R.: "The Silent Spring," Houghton Mifflin, Boston, 1962. This book (which caused considerable controversy when it first appeared) examines the disruptive effect of our use of chemicals and other agents on the ecological balance of nature.

Chisolm, J. J.: Lead Poisoning, *Scientific American,* February 1971. Describes the effects of lead in human beings.

Commoner, B.: "The Closing Circle," Knopf, New York, 1971. An excellent book that deals with the legal, economic, and practical aspects of environmental degradation. Recommended.

Ehrlich, P. R., A. H. Ehrlich, and **J. P. Holdren:** "Ecoscience: Population, Resources and Environment," Freeman, San Francisco, 1977. This textbook contains many statistical data on human ecology.

Goldwater, L. J.: Mercury in the Environment, *Scientific American,* May 1971. A discussion of the causes and effects of mercury poisoning.

Hardin, G.: The Tragedy of the Commons, *Science,* vol. 162, pp. 1243–1248, December 1968. A sobering appraisal of our misuse of common resources.

———**:** "Exploring New Ethics for Survival: The Voyage of the Spaceship Beagle," Viking, New York, 1972. Outstanding treatment of interrelations between natural resources, population, and pollution from an evolutionary perspective.

LaBastille, A.: The Deadly Toll of Acid Rain: All of Nature Is Suffering, *Science Digest,* October 1979. A short, readable introduction to the problem.

Likens, G. E., R. F. Wright, J. N. Galloway, and **T. J. Butler:** Acid Rain, *Scientific American,* October 1979. A good, factual account of the acid-precipitation phenomenon; well illustrated.

Moran, J. M., M. D. Morgan, and **J. H. Wiersma:** "Introduction to Environmental Science," Freeman, San Francisco, 1980. A good comprehensive textbook that presents environmental issues in a straightforward, nonemotional manner.

Peakall, D. B.: Pesticides and the Reproduction of Birds, *Scientific American,* April 1970. Describes how chlorinated hydrocarbons accumulate in food chains and how high concentrations of these compounds can interfere with egg production.

Scientific American, September 1974. A collection of 11 articles dealing with the human population.

Wagner, R. H.: "Environment and Man," 3d ed., Norton, New York, 1978. A good treatment of the major ecological problems of the day.

Woodwell, G. M.: The Carbon Dioxide Question, *Scientific American,* January 1978. This article describes the causes and possible climatic effects of the increasing CO_2 content of the earth's atmosphere.

Part 3
The Functions of Life: Metabolism

Up to this point our main concern has been the "what" of living matter: what are the characteristics and forms of the living material and what kinds and groupings of living units are known? We shall continue to heed the what, but for the next four parts of this book our main concern will be the "how": how is the living world maintained, how are its structures developed, and how are its functions carried out? In short, the emphasis will be less on the *organizational* and more on the *operational* nature of living material. All operations of living matter can be considered under the two general headings of metabolism and self-perpetuation. Metabolism, examined in this next group of chapters, comprises those processes that permit an otherwise inactive system to remain active and living. Such metabolic processes include chiefly *nutrition,* which supplies raw materials; *respiration,* which liberates energy in usable form from some of the raw materials; and *utilization* of both raw materials and energy in chemical activities such as synthesis.

Directly or indirectly, virtually all metabolic reactions are controlled by genes. This high-magnification electron micrograph shows a tandemly arranged series of identical ribosomal RNA genes from the newt *Triturus viridescens.* The filamentous projections emanating at right angles from the central, pencil-thin line are molecules of ribosomal RNA; the central line is DNA. Note the short segments of DNA from which ribosomal RNA is not being produced. Such segments, called spacer DNA, separate the active genes. (*Courtesy of O. L. Miller, Jr.*)

Chapter 11 Nutrition

Learning Objectives

After reading this chapter you should be able to:

1. Differentiate between autotrophic, heterotrophic, photosynthetic, chemoautotrophic, holotrophic, saprotrophic, and symbiotic modes of nutrition.
2. List in order the sequence of tissues a molecule of water would pass through during its transport from a root-hair cell to a chloroplast in a mesophyll cell of a leaf; define root pressure and transpirational pull and state the role played by each of these processes in the transport of water and dissolved minerals from roots to leaves; state how osmosis and the secretion, evaporation, and cohesion of water molecules contribute to root pressure and transpiration pull; define guttation and relate its adaptive significance.
3. State the mass-flow hypothesis; outline how this hypothesis relates to the two-way transport of sap in sieve tubes.
4. List the seven types of nutrients that are essential for the survival of an animal; list five kinds of nutrients that animals cannot synthesize and must obtain from plants.
5. Show how concentrations of glucose influence the hunger and satiety centers of the brain; describe how these centers control food consumption by animals.
6. State the overall function of digestion; differentiate between mechanical and chemical digestion; list the major organs of the mammalian digestive system that secrete digestive juices; list the three general kinds of enzymes present in digestive juices and give the function of each; list the sources of hydrochloric acid and bile and name a function for each of these substances in digestion.
7. State at least one role of peristalsis and intestinal villi in digestion; list at least two functions of the large intestine and at least two activities of saprotrophic bacteria that live in the colon.
8. Construct a diagram that depicts the transport of nutrients to the capillaries and the lacteal of an intestinal villus; differentiate between blood, interstitial fluid, and lymph, and list at least one functional relation between them, trace two routes through which nutrients enter the body circulation after being absorbed by an intestinal villus; list at least three general functions of the liver that relate to nutrient processing.
9. State the principal reason for the steadily increasing number of malnourished people in the world; draw a graph that generally compares the birth and death rates of affluent countries with those of developing countries; show how different patterns of birth and death rates relate to differences in the human population growth rates of affluent and developing nations.
10. Differentiate between starvation and protein malnutrition; list at least four foods that contain all essential amino acids and outline the symptoms and consequences of protein malnutrition; state at least one physical defect that can result from vitamin malnutrition; illustrate how cultural practices sometimes can thwart attempts to improve poor diets.
11. Indicate why vegetarians can be sustained more economically than people who eat meat.
12. List at least five new methods of increasing food production and evaluate the advantages and disadvantages of each; list at least two examples of recent advances in food technology that have resulted in substitution of plant nutrients for animal nutrients; state a common relationship between a nation's standard of living and the growth rate of its human population.

TABLE 11.1
The Basic Forms of Nutrition: Distinguishing Characteristics and Representative Organisms

Basic category	Subcategory	Distinguishing characteristics	Representative organisms
autotrophism: all required foods manufactured from inorganic nutrients	photosynthesis	light is primary energy source for food synthesis; light energy (trapped by chlorophyll), CO_2, and water or H_2S constitute raw materials for carbohydrate synthesis	virtually all plants and algae; purple and green sulfur bacteria
	chemoautotrophism (chemosynthesis)	inorganic chemicals are primary energy source for synthesis of carbohydrates	sulfur bacteria; nitrifying bacteria
heterotrophism: survival impossible in an exclusively inorganic environment; foods constitute primary energy source for these organisms	holotrophism	bulk feeders	animals with alimentary tracts; *Paramecium, Amoeba*
	saprotrophism	nutrients obtained from dead organisms	bracket fungi, mushrooms, toadstools, many other fungi; putrefying bacteria
mixed forms		most are symbiotic associations in which two partner organisms support the nutrition of each other, or in which one partner subsists on nutrients provided by the other	algal-fungus partnerships in lichens; beef tapeworms, leeches, other parasites

In all organisms, nutrition includes both *intake* of raw materials and internal *distribution* of such raw materials; every cell must be nourished if the organism as a whole is to be nourished. Substances functioning as raw materials for nutrition are termed *nutrients.* As noted in Chap. 2, the term *food* is customarily restricted to *organic* metabolites or nutrients; inorganic nutrients do not have a special collective name.

PATTERNS

Forms of Nutrition

All organisms obtain inorganic nutrients directly from the physical environment. Such nutrients are water, mineral ions, and some atmospheric gases. With respect to organic nutrients, an organism is either an *autotroph* or a *heterotroph* (Table 11.1).

Autotrophs manufacture all required foods from inorganic nutrients. The basic food produced from such inorganic nutrients is a carbohydrate, usually a sugar or sugar derivative, and from it all other required organic substances are then manufactured. The specific inorganic raw materials for sugar synthesis are environmental carbon dioxide and water. Carbon dioxide constitutes the source of both carbon and oxygen for the carbohydrate end product of photosynthesis; water is the hydrogen source. The oxygen of water becomes a by-product

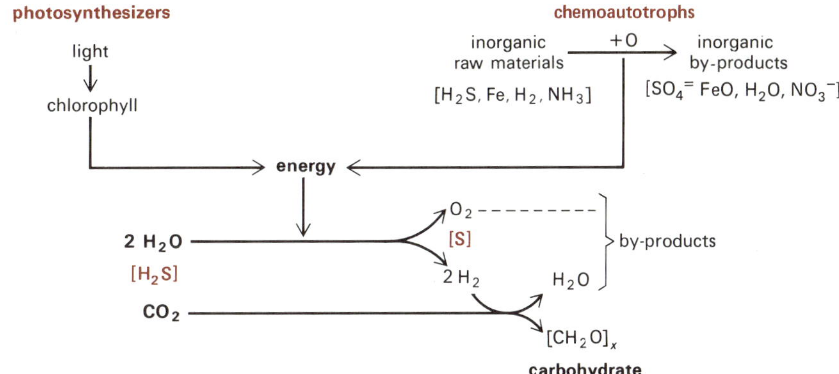

Fig. 11.1 The autotrophic pattern. Photosynthesizers and chemoautotrophs obtain energy in different ways, but most autotrophs use this energy in similar fashion in producing carbohydrate foods from water and CO_2 raw materials.

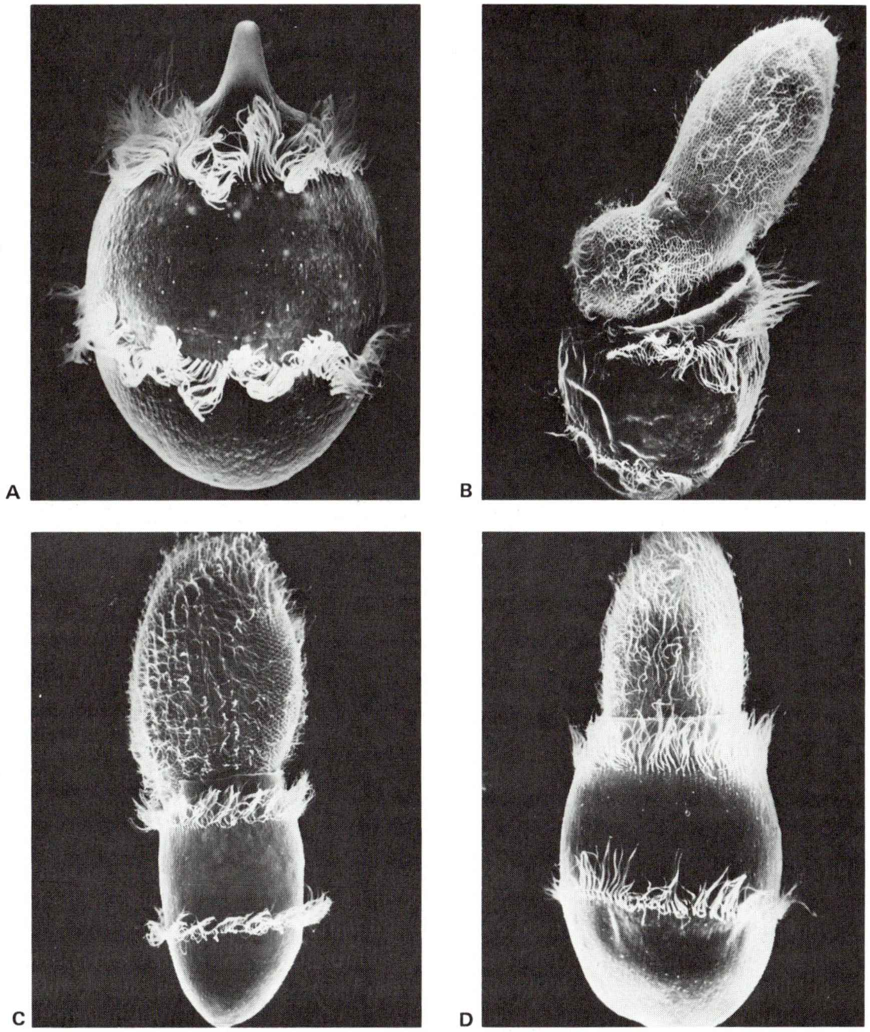

Fig. 11.2 Holotrophism. This kind of heterotrophic nutrition is illustrated by the carnivorous protozoan *Didinium nasatum.* (A) Scanning electron micrograph of *Didinium.* Note the two circular bands of cilia, which function in locomotion. *Didinium* is a voracious feeder of other protozoa. Prey are ingested through an opening at the top of the organism. (B)–(D) show three successive stages in the engulfment of a *Paramecium* by *Didinium.* (A, approx. 2250X; B–D approx. 1500X.)

Fig. 11.3 Saprotrophism. This bracket fungus, *Polyporus applanatus,* is subsisting on the bark and wood of a decaying tree stump.

that returns to the environment:

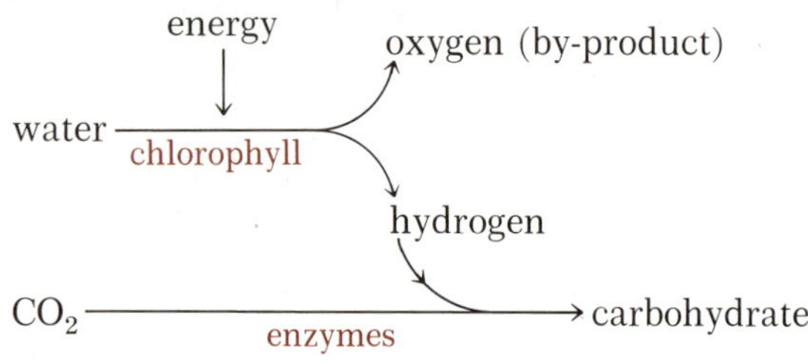

This process of carbohydrate manufacture requires energy. In most autotrophs the primary energy source is light, and one or more varieties of chlorophyll serve in trapping the energy of light. Such organisms are *photosynthesizers* (Fig. 11.1). They include virtually all plants, algae, and two groups of bacteria (purple and green sulfur bacteria, in which the hydrogen source is not water but H_2S; the by-product then is sulfur, not oxygen—see color brackets in Fig. 11.1).

In a second group of autotrophs, the primary energy source for carbohydrate synthesis is certain environmental chemicals the organisms absorb as inorganic nutrients. Inside the organisms these chemicals are combined with oxygen, yielding inorganic by-products and energy, and the energy is then used to synthesize carbohydrates. Organisms of this type are called *chemoautotrophs* or *chemosynthesizers* (see Fig. 11.1). All are bacteria, such as the chemoautotrophic *sulfur bacteria* and the *nitrifying bacteria.* They are named according to the chemicals they use as energy sources, and they usually live in restricted environments where such chemicals abound (see Biology Highlight in Chap. 35). However, the nitrifying bacteria are cosmopolitan and are important participants in the global nitrogen cycle. For them the starting chemical is ammonia (NH_3), and they gain energy by converting it to nitrites and nitrates (NO_2^- and NO_3^-). Nitrates then serve as essential nitrogen sources for other organisms (see Chap. 8).

Heterotrophs cannot survive in an exclusively inorganic environment. Food chemicals, not light, constitute the primary energy sources for virtually all such organisms. Heterotrophs include *holotrophic, saprotrophic,* and *symbiotic* types. Holotrophs are bulk feeders, largely animals with alimentary systems, but also unicellular protists that ingest food in amoeboid fashion or through specialized ingestive structures (Fig. 11.2). Saprotrophs, which include many fungi and bacteria, subsist on anything nonliving that contains organic materials (Fig. 11.3). Saprotrophs thereby bring about *decay,* which makes them vital components in the global water, oxygen, and carbon cycles (see Chap. 8). Among the symbiotic organisms a few are holotrophic, but most, especially parasites, absorb molecular nutrients directly from their living hosts.

Processes of Nutrition

The basic function of nutrition is the funneling of nutrients to every cell of an organism. At the level of the cell, the chief process of nutrition is *absorption,* the transfer of compounds from the exterior to the interior of a cell through the cell surface. As noted in Chap. 5, cells absorb materials in several ways. Water, for example, is absorbed by *osmosis.* Compounds dissolved in water are absorbed in part by *diffusion.* In addition, dissolved materials can be absorbed by energy-consuming *pinocytosis* and *active transport.* Solid particles are sometimes taken into cells by *phagocytosis* (see Chap. 5).

In unicellular and simply constructed multicellular organisms, these five kinds of absorption constitute the primary or sole means of acquiring nutrients. Absorption often can occur all along the surfaces of these organisms. However, in complex multicellular species, nutrient intake occurs only at limited specialized regions: through root and leaf surfaces in plants and through alimentary systems in animals. Internal distribution of nutrients then follows, in part by direct short-distance transfer from one cell to immediately adjacent cells, in part by long-distance transfer through the vascular tissues—xylem and phloem in plants, blood and lymph vessels in animals.

How these procurement and transport functions take place in multicellular organisms is outlined next.

PLANTS: ABSORPTION AND CONDUCTION

All divisions of the plant body participate in nutritional activities. Leaves and green stems acquire atmospheric gases and manufacture foods; roots absorb water and dissolved minerals and gases; and stems conduct nutrients of all kinds from leaves to roots and vice versa. Xylem and phloem serve as the long-distance vertical conductors and to some extent as short-distance lateral conductors as well. The chief lateral conductors are the mesophyll tissues in leaves and the parenchyma cells in the cortex of roots and stems, in the pith of stems, and in the xylem and phloem rays of woody plants.

Roots, Leaves, and Xylem Transport

Soil nutrients are absorbed largely into the epidermal root-hair cells, which provide most of the surface available for absorption. After being absorbed, the inorganic supplies are transported to the xylem at the root core. The vertical tracheids and vessels present there reach uninterruptedly from root tip to leaf tip and serve as channels for upward conduction (see also Chap. 6).

Passage of water from root-hair cells to the endodermis is a relatively straightforward process. The cellulose walls of plant cells are permeable to water, and large spaces surround most cortical cells. Therefore, water and dissolved substances can diffuse freely through the cell walls and intercellular spaces of the cortex without necessarily passing across plasma membranes. This is no longer possible when water reaches the endodermis. As noted in Chap. 6, the endodermis constitutes the innermost layer of the cortex. The walls of these cells are thin except for a bandlike thickening, the *Casparian strip,* running around each cell. This thickened band contains appreciable amounts of *suberin,* a waterproofing substance. Because the cells of the endodermis are tightly packed and are encircled by the Casparian strip, water cannot move inward to vascular tissue without passing through the plasma membranes of endodermal cells. The plasma membranes and cytoplasm of these cells function as a living filter, influencing which dissolved substances will reach vascular tissues and, consequently, which will be transported by xylem to tissues in leaves (Fig. 11.4).

Passage of water from root-hair cells to xylem is continuous and uninterrupted. It is maintained by *root pressure,* an active push generated by the combined absorptive forces of all root cells. This absorption is caused chiefly by the accumulation of ions and other solutes in root cells. Solute concentrations generally are higher in root tissues than in soil, producing a more or less continuous movement of water into the root. The rate at which water moves into xylem elements depends largely on the relative difference between solute concentrations inside and outside the root. The root pressure that derives from this osmotic flow of water can be considerable. If the shoot of a plant is cut a few inches above soil level, root pressure often will force fluid out of the cut ends of xylem vessels and tracheids, a phenomenon known as *bleeding.*

Accompanying and reinforcing this upward "push" of water by root pressure, a second force generates "pull" from above. This force is *transpiration,* or evaporation of water from leaves (Fig. 11.5). As water vaporizes from a mesophyll cell, the concentration of cellular particles tends to increase. As a result of this osmotic change, water will move in from neighboring cells, and *these* cells now tend to develop a water deficit. An osmotic pull is propagated back in this manner, along cell paths leading to xylem terminals. Water is then pulled up osmotically through xylem, and in quantities equivalent to the amount transpired through leaves. The effectiveness of this *transpiration pull* from above is quite familiar. An isolated leaf or a flower with a stub of stem and a few leaves survives for a considerable time when put into a glass

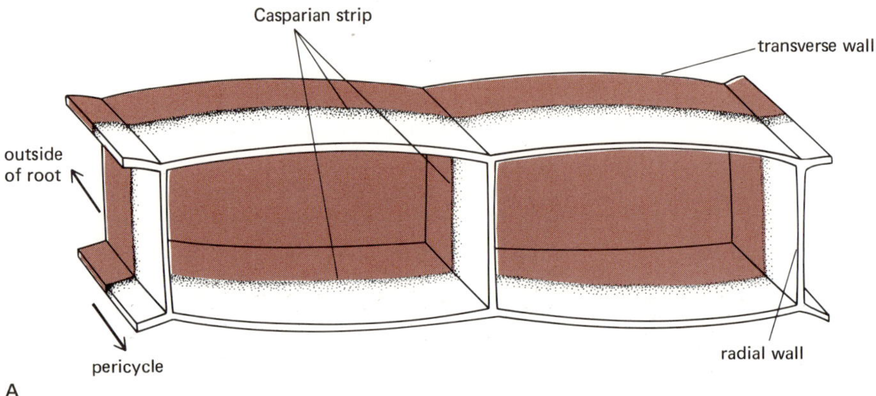

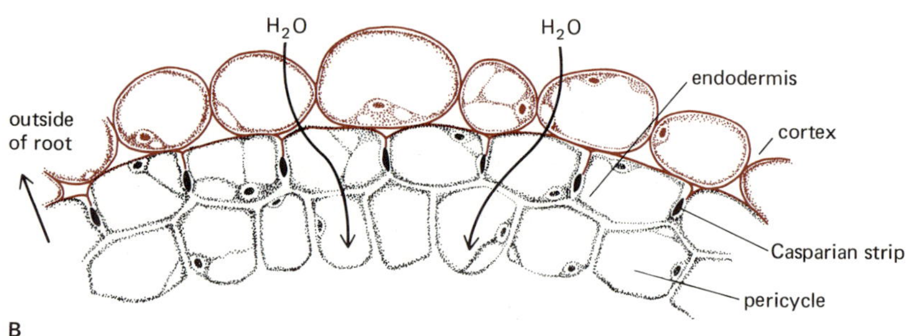

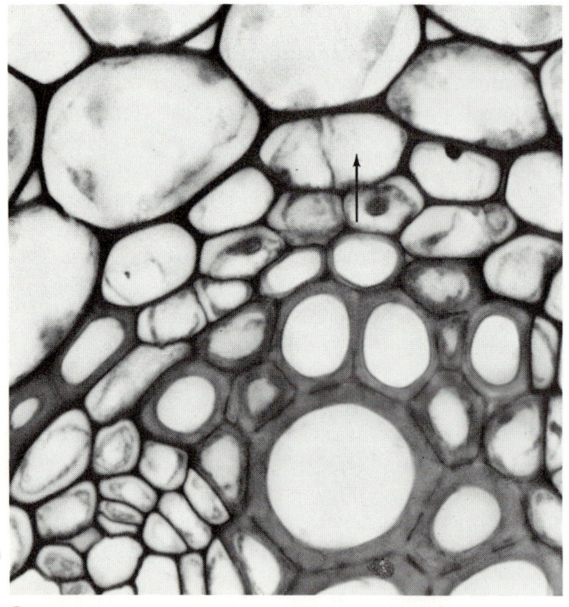

Fig. 11.4 Lateral transport of water and dissolved substances in roots. (A) Three-dimensional view of two endodermal cells. The stippled band indicates position of the circular Casparian strip. Water can diffuse through the cellulose walls of endodermal cells up to the suberized Casparian strip. Water and dissolved substances emerging on the inner side of the strip must be processed through the plasma membrane, which is selectively permeable. (B) Relationship between outer cortical cells, endodermis, and pericycle. Cell walls shown in color contain water that has not necessarily passed through the plasma membranes of cortical cells. Cell walls on the inner side of the Casparian strip contain water that has been filtered by endodermal cells. (C) Cross section through the root of a dicot plant. Arrow points to an endodermal cell. The thick-walled cells in the lower portion of the photograph are xylem vessels. Phloem tissue can be seen in the lower left corner. Large cortical cells (top of photo) are located along the outer boundary of the endodermis.

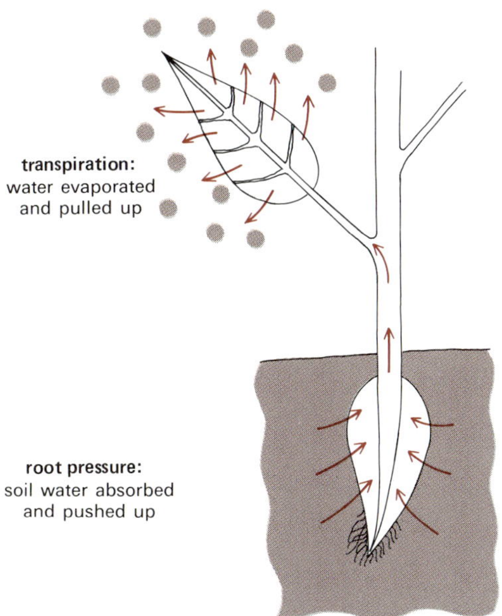

Fig. 11.5 Xylem transport. Xylem vessels contain continuous columns of water. Root pressure adds more water at the bottom, and transpiration removes water at the top through evaporation. Water in xylem is transported upward in this fashion.

of water; as water transpires from exposed plant tissues, fluid is pulled up from below.

Osmosis is not the only factor contributing to the transpiration pull of water through xylem; the *cohesion* of water molecules is also significant. Individual molecules attract one another rather strongly (see Chap. 3), and a column of water therefore "hangs together" with appropriate tenacity. As water molecules evaporate through the stomata of leaves, they tend to pull adjacent water molecules with them (Fig. 11.6). Thus, as the rate of leaf transpiration increases, so does the upward pull on columns of water in xylem.

On occasion water droplets are exuded from leaf surfaces in a process known as *guttation*. The water appears at so-called *hydathodes*, which in many cases are modified stomata incapable of closing (Fig. 11.7). Root pressure then can force water from xylem through mesophyll cells and out at hydathodes. In other cases hydathodes are distinct glands that actively secrete water from the interior of a leaf. Through guttation plants can eliminate water when the roots absorb more than the leaves can transpire, as under conditions of high environmental humidity, for example.

The important point about xylem transport is that the power source lies in living roots and leaves. The nonliving xylem channels are passive, in roughly the same way that a pipeline between two pumping stations is passive. Conduction through phloem is different in this respect, for here the transportation system is composed almost entirely of living cells.

Fig. 11.6 Transpiration pull. The hydrogen atoms of every water molecule (smaller circles) are bonded to a single atom of oxygen (larger circles). Hydrogen atoms also bond weakly to the oxygen atom of the nearest water molecule. These weak bonds are indicated by three dots and are responsible for the cohesive nature of water molecules (see also Chap. 3). Thus, as each molecule of water evaporates through a stoma, it pulls the next molecule along behind it.

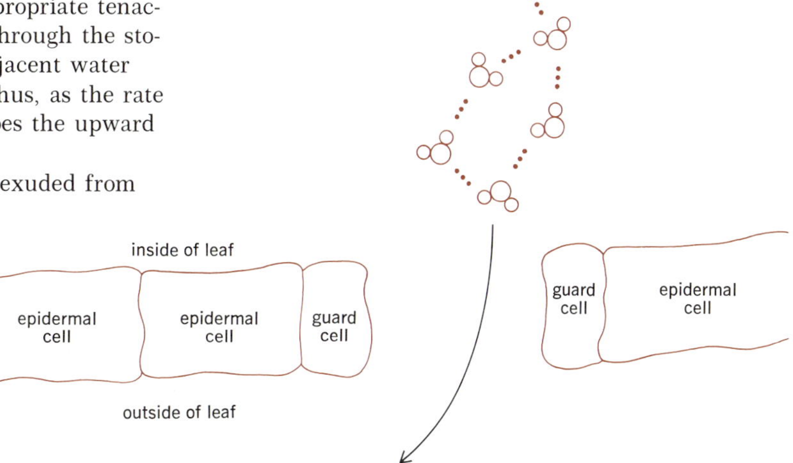

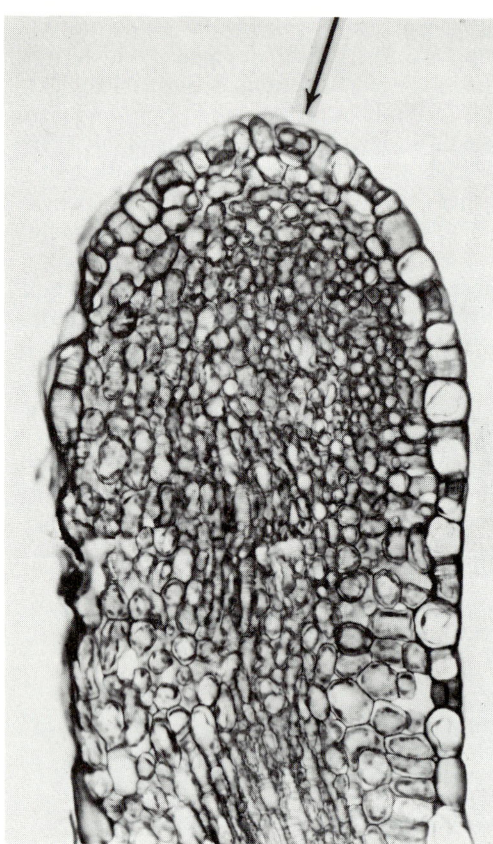

Fig. 11.7 Hydathodes. Column of cells forms a water-conducting channel. Arrow points to permanently open stoma of hydathode.

Fig. 11.8 Phloem transport. Experiments show that tobacco leaves grafted to tomato roots will not contain nicotine (left). This indicates that nicotine is formed in the roots but not in the leaves of tobacco plants. If tomato leaves are grafted to tobacco roots, the leaves will eventually contain nicotine (right). This experiment shows that nicotine is transported upward by the phloem. The phloem channels evidently carry organic materials up as well as down.

Leaves, Stems, and Phloem Transport

Plants are so constructed that most living cells are in direct or nearly direct contact with the external environment. Gas exchange thus can take place in correspondingly direct fashion.

Most of the atmospheric oxygen and carbon dioxide used by a plant enter via the stomata in leaves and green stems. Such gases then diffuse through the cell surfaces and dissolve in cellular water. As they are transported in water through phloem channels, the gases eventually reach stem and root tissues. Gases dissolved in soil water also enter the plant through the roots. Since some of these supplies reach xylem vessels, stem and leaf tissues can therefore obtain gases by that path as well. If the stem is woody, lenticels and any crack in the bark provide additional entry points for air (see Chap. 6). Finally, inasmuch as green tissues produce oxygen during photosynthesis and all tissues produce CO_2 during respiration, plants also have their own internal sources of these gases.

Conversely, excess gases in a plant can diffuse to the environment either directly from exposed cells or via phloem, xylem, and stomata. In effect, exchange of gases in plants can be accomplished without specialized breathing systems; gas diffusion to and from individual cells and a certain amount of transport by xylem and phloem suffice. Since most of the deep tissues of a woody vascular plant form nonliving supporting and conducting material, the gas requirement in such regions is virtually zero.

Food transport is a more specialized activity, and the sieve tubes of phloem are the specific conducting channels of organic nutrients: photosynthesis-derived foods migrate from leaves and green stems downward, and stored foods travel from roots and stem upward. Lateral conduction of organic nutrients may take place by cell-to-cell transfer all along sieve tubes.

Unlike the xylem channels, sieve tubes are two-way paths. Downward conduction in sieve tubes has long been known to occur: many roots store foods photosynthesized only in leaf or stem. The occurrence of upward conduction has come to light through grafting experiments. For example, a stem of a tobacco plant grafted to a root of a tomato plant develops normal tobacco leaves, but they are entirely free of nicotine. Conversely, a tomato stem transplanted to a tobacco root produces tomato leaves, but they are full of nicotine. The first graft indicates that only the roots of a tobacco plant synthesize nicotine; the second graft indicates that the chemical is transported upward. And since xylem channels are virtually free of nicotine, upward conduction must occur largely via phloem (Fig. 11.8).

The forces that move organic nutrients through phloem are not well understood, but many botanists believe that this phenomenon can best be explained by the *mass-flow hypothesis* (Fig. 11.9). It proposes that excess sugars produced by mesophyll cells are pumped into the terminal sieve-tube elements of leaf veins by active transport. The hypothesis also proposes that the resulting increased concentration of intracellular sugars causes corresponding increases in the osmotic flow of water into these elements from nearby xylem. Because sieve-tube elements have rigid walls, this accumulation of water produces substantial intracellular pressures.

According to the hypothesis, lower pressures normally would exist in sieve-tube elements located in roots and other nonphotosynthetic parts of a plant. Such lower pressures would result from the transfer of sugars from these sieve-tube elements to all surrounding nonphotosynthetic cells that require organic nutrients. As the concentration of sugars drops in such sieve-tube elements, water would tend to diffuse from the elements to the surrounding cells. Thus, a difference in pressure should exist between sieve-tube elements located in photosynthetic parts of a plant and elements situated in nonphotosynthetic parts. Such pressure gradients actually have been measured and may be responsible, at least in part, for the conduction, or *translocation,* of sugars through sieve tubes.

In summer, sugars generally are translocated downward to nonphotosynthetic regions of plants. Sugars and other organic materials also can be translocated upward if pressure gradients are reversed. This is the case, for example, in winter and early spring, when leaves are absent and photo-

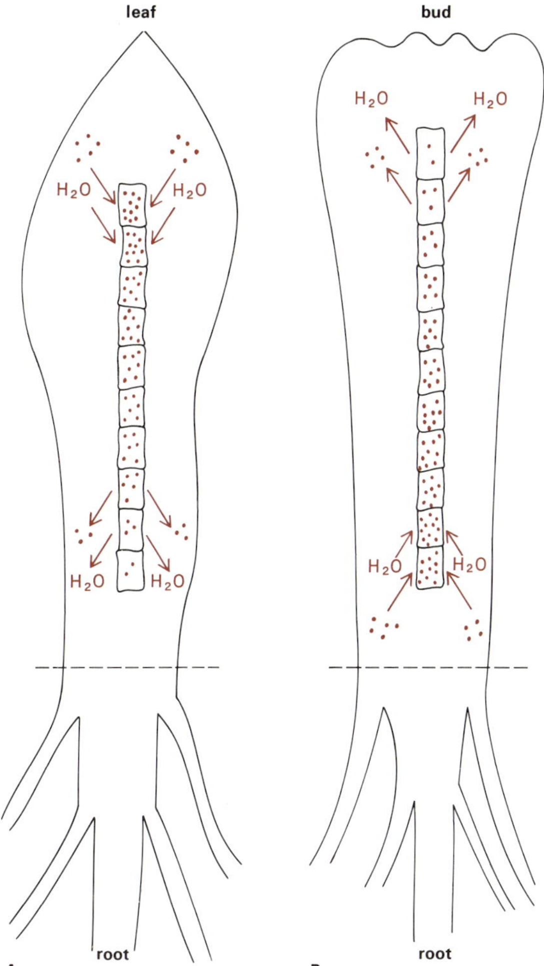

Fig. 11.9 Mass-flow hypothesis. (A) During periods of active photosynthesis, sugars (dots) are pumped into terminal sieve-tube elements of leaves by active transport. The high concentrations of sugars draw water into these elements, producing substantial intracellular pressures. As sugars are removed by nonphotosynthetic cells in the stem and roots, water flows out from sieve-tube elements, and intracellular pressures are reduced. As a result of these pressure differences, sap tends to flow downward from leaves toward roots. (B) In early spring, intracellular pressures are greatest in sieve-tube elements located near nutrient storage sites in roots. Consequently, sap flows upward and provides nutrients for the growth of tissues in buds. *(Modified from P. McRay, "The Living Plant," 2d ed., Holt, New York, 1972.)*

synthesis does not take place. Foods stored in the roots during the preceding summer then travel upward to the food-requiring regions of the stem and the crown.

All absorptive and transporting activities in plants not only contribute to but indirectly also depend on photosynthesis. For it is this most essential nutritional activity that permits formation of the whole plant to begin with, including roots, leaves, and transport tissues. The molecular and cellular aspects of photosynthesis are discussed in Chap. 13, in the specific context of synthesis.

ANIMALS: ALIMENTATION AND CIRCULATION

In most animals, nutrients are obtained by ingestion through a mouth, digestion in stomach and intestine, and egestion of unusable remains through an anus. In many simply constructed animals, usable supplies resulting from digestion are absorbed through the wall of the alimentary system into surrounding tissues. However, in more complex animals, including people and all vertebrates, nutrients are absorbed through intestinal walls into circulatory vessels, which then transport the supplies to virtually all body tissues.

Nutrients and Ingestion

Essential Nutrients: Plants versus Animals

Green plant cells require only CO_2, water, light, and minerals for survival. Through photosynthesis, such cells are able to manufacture all life-supporting organic compounds. Nongreen plant cells, such as those of roots, require a few simple carbohydrates in addition to water, oxygen, and minerals. But if an animal is given only carbohydrates, oxygen, and inorganic nutrients, it soon dies, for it requires four additional types of materials that, unlike the plant cell, it cannot manufacture on its own.

First, animal cells require usable organic nitrogen for the construction of proteins and nucleic acids, among other compounds. Plants can use mineral nitrates in the manufacture of these compounds (see Chap. 8), but animals cannot and require nitrogen-containing organic compounds that have been produced directly or indirectly by plants.

Second, plants can convert organic materials to all the vitamins they require. Animals cannot. Most animals manufacture at least some of their own vitamins, although often only in inadequate quantities. Specific abilities here vary with the species, but no species is as self-sufficient in this regard as a green plant. Missing vitamins consequently must be supplied in prefabricated form, and plants are again the ultimate source of supply.

Third, unlike plants, animals are unable to convert organic starting materials to all 20 kinds of amino acids needed for protein synthesis. Depending on the species, 8 or 10 kinds, so-called *essential amino acids* (even though all amino acids are "essential"), must be supplied in prefabricated form, and plants are the ultimate suppliers here as well.

Lastly, again unlike plants, many animals are unable to convert organic starting materials to all necessary kinds of fatty acids. Accordingly, various *essential fatty acids* must be obtained ready-made from plants.

The minimum nutrient supplies to an animal cell must therefore include at least seven types of materials: *water, minerals, organic carbon, organic nitrogen, vitamins, essential amino acids,* and *essential fatty acids.* Consequently, animals cannot survive without autotrophs, which provide five of these seven items (Fig. 11.10).

In most cases nutrients are available to animals only in more or less bulky masses of plant or animal matter, living or dead. The basic function of the alimentary system is to break down bulk nutrients to individual ions and molecules directly usable by cells. The first step of this process is ingestion.

Ingestion Control

Most animals eat whenever food is obtainable; hunger is virtually permanent. In a few animals, human beings among them, hunger and food intake usually tend to be intermittent. The brain here plays an important role in controlling the rate and amount of food consumption. According to an early popular hypothesis, the stomach was believed to regulate the quantities of food eaten. Muscular contractions of an empty stomach were thought to control the sensations of hunger, and a hungry animal was assumed to eat until its stomach was

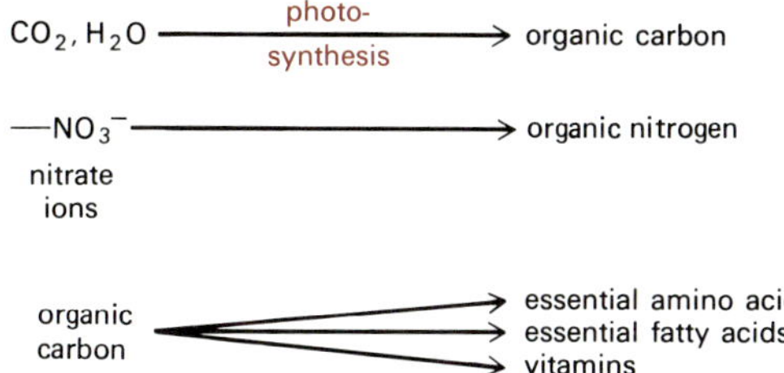

Fig. 11.10 Animal dependence on plants. Five classes of compounds that green plants can synthesize and that the cells of most animals cannot synthesize. Animals depend on green plants for these products.

filled. Such filling was believed to stop hunger pangs and food intake. But this hypothesis turned out to be untenable long ago, for even after surgical removal of the entire stomach, hunger sensations nevertheless continue to come and go as before. Moreover, a "stomach hypothesis" of hunger control does not account for chronic overeating or undereating.

A better explanation emerged after experiments had indicated that the mammalian brain contains two special eating-control centers. One is a *hunger center.* When this center is stimulated, it sends out nerve impulses to various parts of the body prompting the animal to eat. The other is a *satiety center,* which, when stimulated, prompts the animal to refuse food. In test rats, tiny electrodes can be used to stimulate one or the other of these centers. Animals so treated either overeat and become extremely obese, or undereat and starve despite a plentiful food supply. Evidently, the amount of food a mammal normally eats is determined primarily by the commands the hunger and satiety centers send to the body.

How do these centers determine whether to send a command "eat" or a command "do not eat"? Experiments show *blood glucose* to be the critical agent that stimulates one or the other of the two centers. Glucose circulating in the blood is a sensitive indicator of the hour-by-hour nutritional state of the body. Shortly after a meal, the glucose concentration in blood tends to rise. Long after a meal, this concentration tends to fall. If blood reaching the brain contains a high glucose level, the satiety center probably responds selectively to this level and issues the command "do not eat." Conversely, low glucose levels probably stimulate the hunger center selectively, resulting in the command "eat" (Fig. 11.11).

Thus, any condition that directly or indirectly influences glucose delivery to the brain or affects the operation of the brain centers is bound to affect food intake. Dozens of such conditions may actually do so. Proper glucose delivery depends, for example, on normal digestive processes, normal liver function, normal blood circulation, normal hormone balances, and normal nervous activities. All these factors affect glucose metabolism profoundly. And if through disturbances in any of these functions the brain receives consistently inappropriate information about the actual glucose supplies in the body, consistent overeating or undereating may result. Evidently, the seemingly simple decision whether or not to eat actually is determined by a multitude of interconnected processes. It is therefore not surprising that, as we all know from experience, practically *any* disturbance of *any* body function has an effect on food intake.

Digestion and Egestion

After food is ingested, digestion in different parts of an alimentary tract is achieved by *mechanical* and *chemical* means. Mechanical digestion, carried out for example through chewing by teeth

Fig. 11.11 Control of food intake. Desire or lack of desire for food is governed by the satiety (S) and hunger (H) centers of the brain, which in turn respond to the glucose concentration in blood.

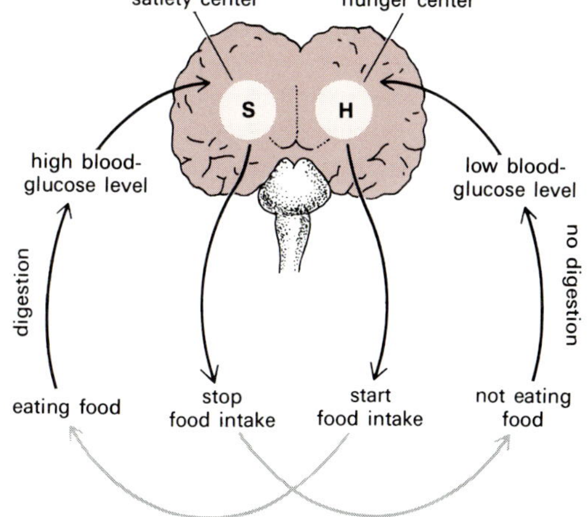

and muscular grinding by a stomach, breaks down ingested materials to fine particles suspended in water. Chemical digestion then reduces these particles to molecular dimensions. In the process, usable ions and molecules become separated out and more complex molecules are broken up into smaller, usable ones. In this chemical dissolution of foods, *digestive enzymes* secreted by *digestive glands* play important roles.

No matter where it occurs or what food is involved, every reaction of chemical digestion is an *enzymatic hydrolysis,* a decomposition reaction in which *water* is one of the reactant molecules (see also Chap. 4). A generalized digestive reaction can be written

$$\text{food} + H_2O \xrightarrow{\text{enzyme}} \text{food components}$$

In most animals digestive enzymes are *extracellular;* they are produced inside cells, but they are secreted and function outside. This puts them into a special category, for virtually all other enzymes in organisms are intracellular and function within cells. Moreover, digestive enzymes are unusual also in that many of them can act on entire categories of chemicals. For example, digestive *lipase* promotes the decomposition of fat to fatty acids and glycerol:

$$\text{fat} + H_2O \xrightarrow{\text{lipase}} \text{fatty acids} + \text{glycerol}$$

The lipase here can be effective with any kind of fat, regardless of what specific types of fatty acids a fat is composed of. Similarly, certain protein- and carbohydrate-digesting enzymes decompose many *different* kinds of proteins and carbohydrates, respectively. By contrast, intracellular enzymes are highly specific, and each is effective only in reactions of one particular type of molecule. Like all enzymes, however, digestive enzymes operate best at particular temperatures and pH. Appropriately acid, alkaline, or neutral conditions are actually maintained in the digestive juices and the alimentary organs where enzymes occur.

Animals with specialized feeding habits are correspondingly specialized in their digestive enzymes. For example, blood feeders among worms and insects secrete large amounts of digestive *proteinase* but only little *carbohydrase.* Clothes moths, which eat nothing but the protein of sheep hair (wool), likewise produce digestive proteinases almost exclusively. By contrast, flour beetles and boll weevils secrete an abundance of carbohydrases. Similar specializations occur in silk-, glue-, or wood-eating animals. Also, numerous parasitic animals are fairly narrowly specialized in their digestive capacities. The broadest assortment of digestive enzymes is usually found in free-living omnivores, which can survive on nearly any kinds of food. Many mammals, people included, are in this category.

In a mammal, digestion occurs mainly in the *mouth, stomach,* and *small intestine.* At each of these sites specialized digestive glands secrete one or more digestive juices into the alimentary channel (Fig. 11.12 and Table 11.2). The salivary glands produce *saliva,* which acts in the mouth and, carried along by food, in the stomach. Contact of food with the tissues in the mouth stimulates nerve endings that transmit impulses to the brain; impulses from there to the salivary glands then bring about secretion of saliva. It is well known that the smell, sight, or mere thought of food can start the flow of saliva; pleasant past experiences with food have the same effect as actual food in the mouth (conditioned reflexes; see Chap.19).

From the mouth food passes through the *pharynx,* where the food channel crosses the air channel leading from the nasal passages to the windpipe (Fig. 11.13). During swallowing the upper end of the windpipe (larynx) is raised against a flap of tissue, the *epiglottis.* The air channel is thereby closed off, and food is forced to pass from the pharynx to the *esophagus* that leads to the stomach. Wavelike muscular contractions in the wall of the esophagus (*peristalsis*) push a ball of food along. (The direction of peristalsis is reversed in vomiting.)

The stomach completes mechanical digestion by its muscular grinding action, and it continues chemical digestion through *gastric juice* secreted from the stomach lining. Sight, smell, and thought of food, which can start salivary secretion, can at the same time initiate gastric secretion. Moreover, stomach cells in contact with food release *gastrin,* a hormone, which is distributed by blood throughout the body. When some of this hormone returns to the stomach and reaches the specialized cells capa-

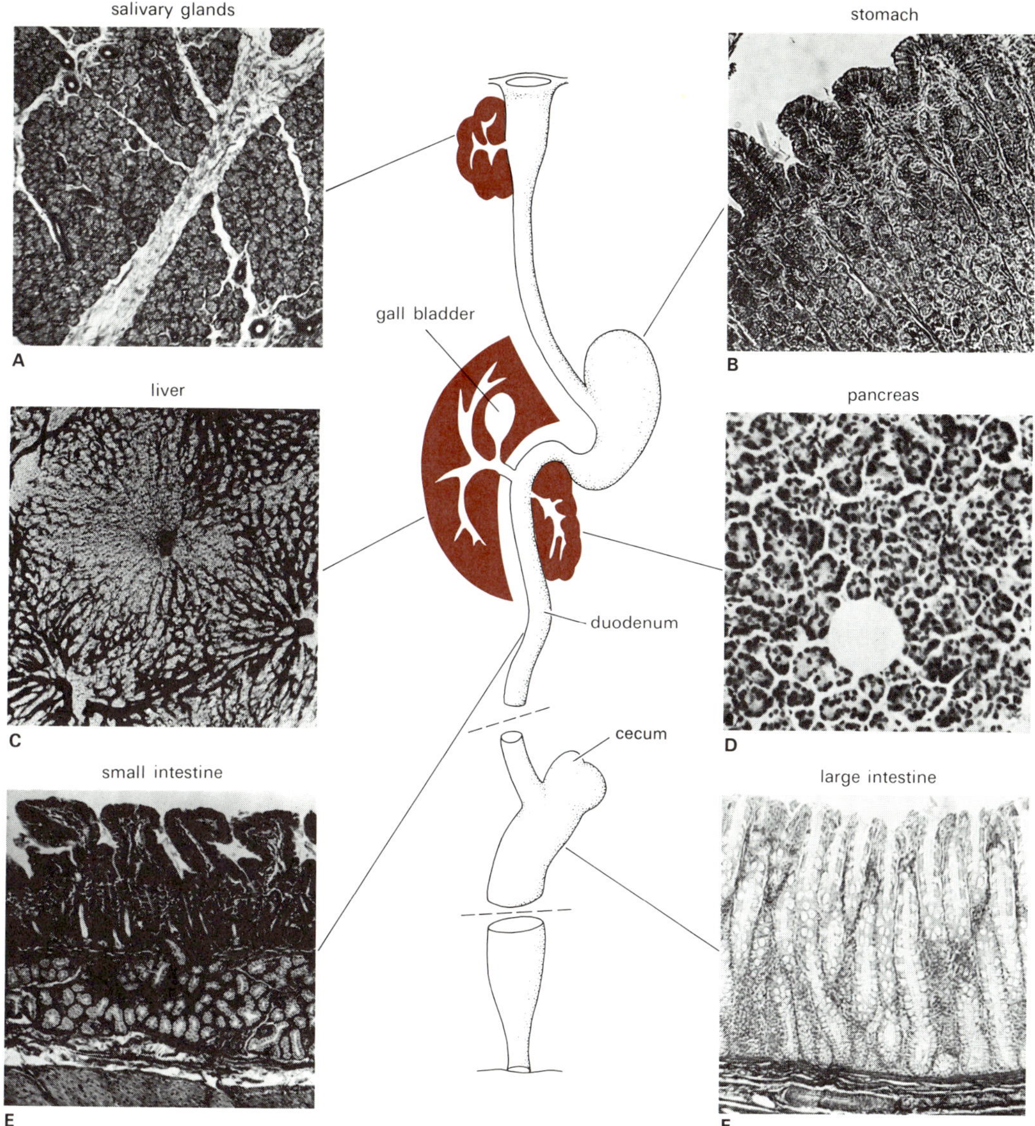

Fig. 11.12 The mammalian alimentary tract. (A) Section through a salivary gland. Note the connective tissue stroma (light areas in photo) traversing the gland and binding groups of gland cells together. Note also the several small salivary ducts (dark rings). (B) Section through a portion of stomach wall. Note folded mucosa near the top. (C) Section through liver, showing parts of a few lobules injected to reveal the blood channels (dark). Blood brought by the hepatic portal vein to a lobule passes to the hepatic vein in the center of the lobule (see also Fig. 7.20). (D) Section through pancreas. The large round space is a branch of the pancreatic duct. (E) Section through the wall of the duodenum. The cavity of the gut is toward the top. Underneath the folded inner surface tissues note the glandular layer. Its secretion is discharged to the gut cavity and contributes to the composition of intestinal juice. (F) Section through a mucosal fold of the large intestine. Note the many mucous-secreting goblet cells in the mucosal lining. *(A, D, Courtesy of B. J. Serber; B, C, courtesy of M. C. Noailles; E, General Biological Supply House, Inc.; F, Carolina Biological Supply Company.)*

TABLE 11.2
Composition and Action of Digestive Juices

	Saliva	**Gastric juice**	**Intestinal juice**	**Pancreatic juice**	**Bile**
source	salivary glands	stomach wall	duodenal wall	pancreas	liver, gallbladder stored in
pH	neutral	highly acid	alkaline	alkaline	alkaline
secretion started by	food in mouth reflex; thought of food	food in mouth; emotions; food in stomach → gastrin hormone, stimulates stomach wall	food contact in duodenum	secretin hormone from intestinal juice	secretin hormone from intestinal juice
carbohydrases	amylase, for polysaccharides; maltase, for maltose		amylase, for polysaccharides; disaccharases (maltase, sucrase, lactase), for disaccharides	amylase, for polysaccharides	
lipases		lipase (brought in from duodenum)	lipase	lipase	
proteinases		prorennin $\xrightarrow{HCl}$ rennin → curdles milk protein (present only in ruminant mammals) pepsinogen → pepsin, for proteins	amino-peptidases, for products of partial protein breakdown (polypeptides)	trypsinogen → trypsin,* for proteins chymotrypsinogen → chymotrypsin,* for proteins carboxy-peptidases, for products of partial protein breakdown (polypeptides)	
other components (all contain water, mucus, mineral ions)		HCl, macerates food, activates gastric proteinases	enterokinase, activates trypsinogen, chymotrypsinogen* secretin hormone, stimulates pancreas and liver secretions		bile salts, emulsify fats to colloidal drops bile pigments, excretion products from hemoglobin breakdown in liver

*The pancreatic proteinases are secreted in inactive form, which protects pancreatic tissues from being digested. Enterokinase from intestinal juice converts trypsinogen to active trypsin and chymotrypsinogen to active chymotrypsin.

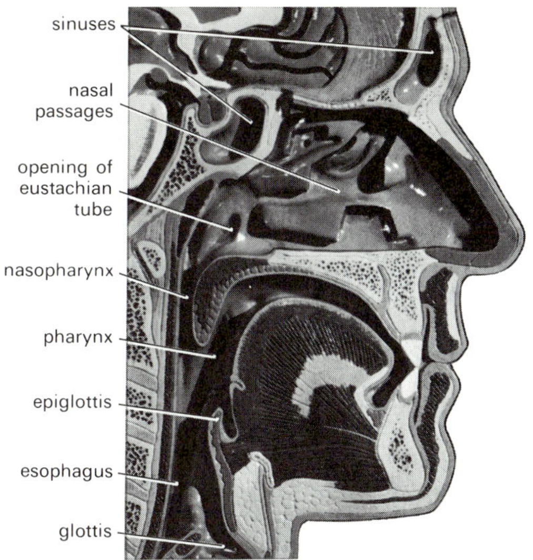

Fig. 11.13 Food and air channels. In the pharynx the air path (from nasopharynx to glottis) crosses the food path (from mouth cavity to esophagus).

ble of manufacturing gastric juice, these cells are activated (see Table 11.2).

Gastric juice contains strong *hydrochloric acid*, which through its decomposing action contributes to the physical subdivision of food. Also present is *pepsinogen*, an inactive molecule that in the presence of hydrogen ions from HCl becomes the active proteinase *pepsin*. This enzyme catalyzes the breakdown of proteins to free amino acids. The gastric juice of cattle and certain other mammals (but not people) contains *rennin*, another digestive enzyme. This catalyst is similarly secreted as *prorennin* and becomes activated by hydrogen ions (see Table 11.2). Rennin acts specifically on milk proteins, clumping them together. For some time after birth, milk is the sole nutrient received by the young of some mammals. The rennin mechanism is highly adaptive for these animals; in curdled, solidified form milk stays in the stomach longer than it would as a liquid, and pepsin digestion can therefore proceed for a longer period.

Carbohydrate and fat digestion occurs in the stomach only to the extent that saliva is carried in from the mouth and lipase regurgitates from the intestine. It is in the small intestine, particularly the section next to the stomach (*duodenum*), where the most thorough chemical digestion of all foods takes place. Here *intestinal juice* is liberated from the gut wall, and ducts carry in *pancreatic juice* from the pancreas and *bile* from the liver. The composition and action of these fluids are indicated in Table 11.2.

In the course of intestinal digestion, carbohydrates not yet fully acted on become decomposed to monosaccharides such as glucose and fructose. Proteins are broken up into individual amino acids. Fats are subdivided physically to colloidal fat droplets through the emulsifying action of the bile salts, and substantial numbers of such droplets are then also decomposed chemically to fatty acids and glycerol (Fig. 11.14).

Therefore, when digestion is completed, the intestine contains water and dissolved mineral ions, monosaccharides, amino acids, fatty acids, glycerol, and vitamins (unaffected by digestion). Also present are colloidal fat droplets, as well as undigested or indigestible materials (including cellulose, for example, or any other compounds that cannot be decomposed by the enzymes present). Such unprocessed substances will be egested, and most other materials will be absorbed.

The food solution in the intestine is continuously agitated by peristaltic contractions of the gut

Fig. 11.14 Digestion summary. Polypeptides are products of partial protein breakdown. Bile salts act physically, not chemically; they emulsify fats and thereby reduce large fatty masses to tiny droplets.

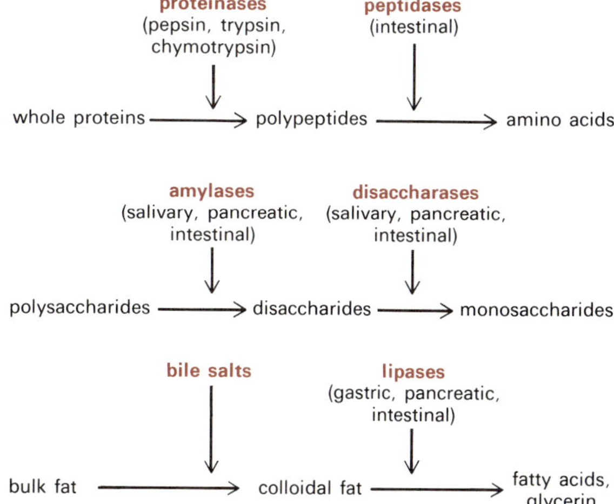

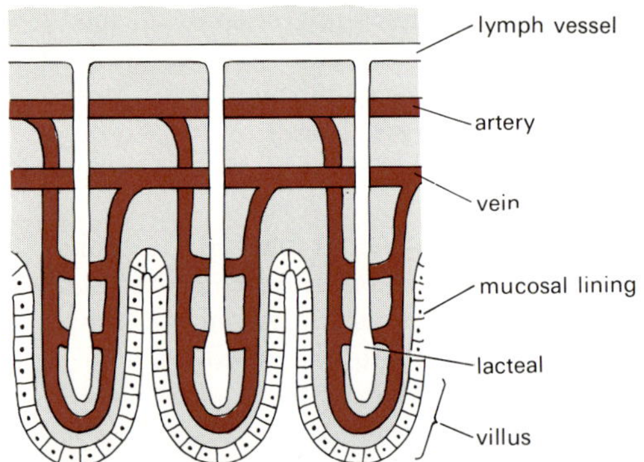

Fig. 11.15 Intestinal villi. Colloidal whole fat enters the blind-ended lymphatic lacteals, passes from there to the lymph circulation of the body, and bypasses the liver. All other organic nutrients from the intestine are absorbed directly into the blood circulation of the villi and are transported from there to the liver.

wall, a process that mixes and remixes food with the digestive juices. Churning also brings the food solution into thorough contact with the mucosa, the tissue layer along the interior surface of the gut (see Fig. 7.21). This layer is highly folded and in addition is studded with millions of near-microscopic *villi.* These fingerlike projections give the mucosa a velvety, carpetlike texture and an exceedingly large surface area (see Fig. 11.12). Moving back and forth continuously, the villi also help stir the food solution and circulate it thoroughly over the mucosal lining.

In human beings, food stays in the small intestine from 4 to 8 hours. During this time the organ absorbs most of the minerals and organic nutrients but comparatively little water. In fact, by pouring digestive juices into the alimentary canal the small intestine actually *adds* water to food. Water is absorbed mainly in the *large intestine,* or *colon.* The first portion of the large intestine is the *cecum,* a blind pouch that in people and a number of other mammals carries a terminal fingerlike extension, the *appendix* (see Fig. 11.12). At its far end the large intestine joins the *rectum,* a short tube opening at the *anus.*

So called because of its greater diameter, the large intestine has a dual function. First, it is an *absorbing* and *excreting* organ. During the 10- to 12-hour stay of materials in the large intestine, most of the water and the remaining inorganic nutrients are absorbed. At the same time, certain metabolic wastes and excess inorganic substances present in the body are excreted from blood to the cavity of the large intestine. Thus, by absorbing from, and adding to, the materials in the alimentary canal, the large intestine helps maintain a properly balanced internal composition of the body. That the large intestine actually does contribute to the regulation of, for example, the internal water balance is indicated by the familiar upset conditions of diarrhea and constipation.

Second, the indigestible and unabsorbable materials undergo decay in the large intestine. This action is brought about by dense, permanent populations of saprotrophic bacteria that live in the alimentary canal as symbionts. The microorganisms obtain food from many of the materials the host cannot digest or absorb, and as a result of such bacterial activity the substances in the large intestine undergo rapid decay. Frequently the bacteria release by-products of their own metabolism; some of these can be nutrients usable by the host, vitamins among them. Mammals actually obtain an appreciable fraction of their vitamin supply from intestinal bacteria.

After food has passed through the large intestine, chiefly *roughage* is left: tough fibers, gristle, pieces of cellulose, unmacerated plant tissue, all suspended in more or less reduced quantities of water. Mixed with this are bile pigments, colon excretions, bacteria and bacterial products, and whatever else may have been added or left over in the passage of food through the alimentary canal. These *feces* are in a more or less advanced state of decay, and they are ultimately egested as semisolid masses.

Absorption and Distribution

Transfer of usable nutrients into the circulating blood and lymph is achieved by absorption. A few substances—alcohol, for example—can be taken up through the stomach wall, but most foods are absorbed through the intestine. Nutrients here pass through the mucosa to the deeper tissues of the intestinal wall, where blood and lymph vessels are situated.

Absorption into the mucosa is brought about by osmosis of water, diffusion of materials dissolved in water, and active transport by mucosal cells. The selective action of the mucosa is illustrated well by the different rates with which nutrients are absorbed. For example, the sugars glucose, galactose, and fructose all have the same molecular size and atomic composition, namely, $C_6H_{12}O_6$. Yet galactose is absorbed most rapidly, fructose least rapidly. Moreover, sugar molecules containing only 3, 4, or 5 carbon atoms, though smaller than the three 6-carbon sugars just referred to, are generally absorbed much more slowly, if at all. Mucosal cells evidently "recognize" and select among the substances present in digested food.

Water, minerals, amino acids, and vitamins diffuse through the mucosa unchanged. Similarly, colloidal fat droplets, as well as fatty acids and glycerol are passed without change through the mucosa and reappear on the other side. Here some of the fatty acids and glycerol recombine immediately as whole fats.

Each villus of the intestinal wall contains capillaries of the circulatory system (Fig. 11.15). Blood is pumped to the intestine through a few large arteries, which then branch out as extensive networks of microscopic capillary vessels. These capillaries pick up most of the nutrients absorbed through the intestinal mucosa—water, minerals, vitamins, monosaccharides, amino acids, and fatty acids and glycerol.

Nutrient-laden blood now leaves the intestine. The capillaries in the gut collect into larger vessels, these join and rejoin, and a single very large channel eventually emerges from the whole intestine. This vessel, the *hepatic portal vein,* leads directly to the *liver* (Fig. 11.16). Nutrients not transported to the liver in this fashion are collected by vessels of the *lymph system.* They are mainly the colloidal droplets of whole fat, which are enormously larger than molecules, but the lymph system also receives water, minerals, and variable quantities of other substances that may have escaped transport by blood.

The lymph system (Fig. 11.17) returns to the blood any fluid lost from the blood circulation. As blood flows in its closed network of vessels, a certain amount of fluid normally passes through the thin walls of the blood capillaries. This escaped liquid, or *interstitial fluid,* is responsible for the moist condition of all body tissues, and it is through interstitial fluid that the cells of the body are ultimately supplied with water and other necessary supplies (see also Chap. 18). Interstitial fluid eventually enters microscopic lymph capillaries (see Fig. 11.17). The fluid together with other materials transported by lymph vessels is termed *lymph.* Capillaries of the lymph system originate in all parts of the body, intestine included. The capillaries then join into progressively larger and fewer ducts until a single large channel is formed. This channel empties into a vein in the left shoulder region and so returns lost fluid to the blood circulation.

The lymph capillaries originating in the intestine are called *lacteals* (see Fig. 11.15). One lacteal is situated in each villus, and it is here that colloidal fat droplets and some other nutrients enter the lymph system. After reaching the blood circulation, the fat droplets are transported to the fat-storing

Fig. 11.16 The liver. (A) Abdominal dissection of a mouse showing the position and gross external appearance of the liver (large dark organ). Internal liver structure is illustrated in Figs. 7.20 and 11.12. Upper and lower arrows on the right indicate stomach and large intestine, respectively. Arrow on the left indicates the highly coiled small intestine. (B) Generalized summary of the food-distributing role of the liver.

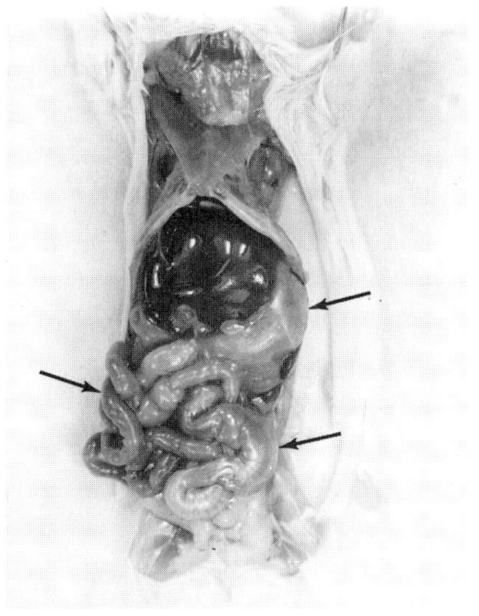

A

nutrient supply from intestine ⟶ liver ⇄ (blood) body tissues ⟶ nutrient utilization in cells

B

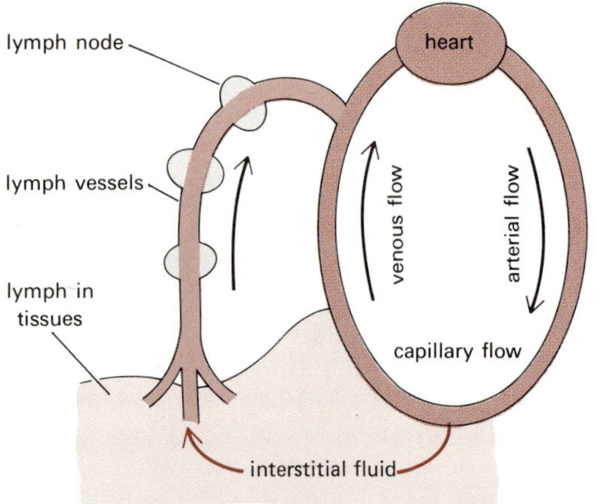

Fig. 11.17 Lymph circulation. Fluid escapes from the blood capillaries to the tissues of the body (colored arrow) and returns via lymph vessels to the venous part of the blood circulation. Along the path of larger lymph vessels are lymph nodes, which produce some types of blood cells and purify lymph.

regions of the body and in effect bypass the liver. But other nutrients conducted by the lymph system eventually do circulate via blood to the liver, where they join those already carried in by the hepatic portal vein.

In the liver, the hepatic portal vein breaks up into a very extensive network of small blood channels (see Figs. 11.12 and 7.20). Cells lining these channels are more loosely attached to each other than cells lining blood vessels of other organs. Gaps between the loosely attached cells facilitate transfer of bloodborne substances to liver cells, which process the absorbed materials and return finished products to the blood. All such blood ultimately leaves the liver through a single large *hepatic vein*, which carries liver-processed foods into the general body circulation. In this manner, nutrient supplies reach all parts of the body.

Representing the largest gland of the vertebrate body, the liver has been estimated to carry out some 200 separate functions. The most important will be discussed in the course of later chapters. Although many liver functions are not concerned directly with nutrient transport, the many that are make the liver the main receiving station, processing plant, warehouse, distributing organ, and traffic control center, all rolled into one.

For example, liver cells carry out numerous chemical transformations of incoming materials and serve as storage depots for others. Moreover, by regulating both the kinds and quantities of nutrients sent out to body tissues, the liver greatly influences the overall rate of metabolism in vertebrates. In fact, it is largely because of the quarter-mastering activities of this organ that the metabolism of vertebrates with livers can remain at a continuously steady level, regardless of the daily pattern of eating.

The liver may be regarded as one side of a nutritional balance. The other side is the remainder of the body, and blood serves as carrier, signal mechanism, and general connecting link between the two (see Fig. 11.16B). Nutrients coming or not coming from the gut to the liver may shift the balance one way; nutrients used up or not used up by the body tissues may shift it the opposite way. As will become clear in later contexts, these balancing processes operate through chemical equilibria. They normally adjust in such a manner that the original balance is maintained or, if upset, reestablished.

Among the nutrients delivered from the liver to individual animal cells are glucose, amino acids, fats, fatty acids, glycerol, water, mineral ions, vitamins, and various special organic compounds. Many people, however, receive neither adequate amounts nor types of these essential nutrients. This sorry state of nutrition exists in spite of unprecedented advances in agricultural technology over the past several decades (see accompanying Biology Highlight).

Biology Highlight

Malnutrition: The Deepening Crisis

CAUSES AND EFFECTS

In 1967 President Johnson's Science Advisory Committee Panel on the World Food Supply estimated that 20 per cent of the people in less developed countries were receiving inadequate amounts of food energy and that 60 per cent were *malnourished*. The latter were judged to be receiving inadequate amounts of one or more basic nutrients, usually protein. About two-thirds of the world's population live in less developed nations, and thus at least 1.5 billion people were either undernourished or malnourished in 1967. Data gathered by the panel also indicated that approximately 0.5 billion people would die directly or indirectly from starvation in 1967.

Conditions have not improved since this study was first published. Its conclusions remain generally valid, and still ignored. To be sure, human malnutrition and starvation are not new phenomena; they have been common among the poor of the world for centuries. Nevertheless, the total number of malnourished people has increased sharply over the past several decades. Chief among the factors responsible is the continuing human population growth, greatest in countries where food shortages are most pronounced (Fig. 1).

The spread of modern medicine has reduced the death rates of rich and poor nations alike, but the declining birthrates that have accompanied this reduction in most affluent countries have not occurred in most of the less developed nations (Fig. 2). Consequently, the population growth of most poorer nations greatly exceeds that of most industrialized countries. The annual population growth rates of many industrialized countries is now

Fig. 1 Overpopulation. Human population growth rates generally are higher among the less affluent countries of the world, where malnutrition already is a serious problem. (*World Health Organization, United Nations.*)

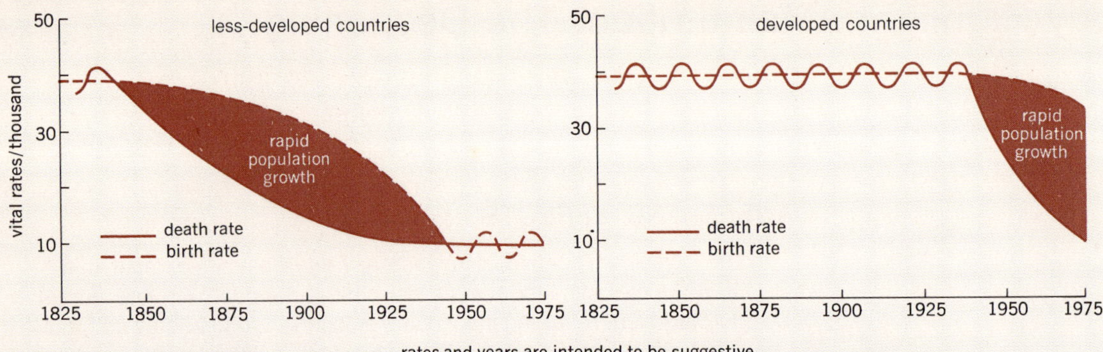

Fig. 2 Population growth. Public health programs have greatly reduced the human death rate in many less developed countries, but since birthrates have not declined as rapidly, the population growth of these countries generally is much higher than in developed countries, where birth- and death rates now are nearly equal. (*From T. T. Poleman, World Food: A Perspective, Science, vol. 188, May 1975.*)

below 0.5 per cent; that of many poorer nations exceeds 3 per cent. Populations growing at this greater rate more than double in a single generation.

Thus, a 20 per cent average increase in food production during the 1960s in rich and poor countries did not result in a per capita increase in food consumption in most nonindustrialized nations. In 1970, for example, most African nations were producing less food per person than they had in the mid-1950s. By contrast, per capita food consumption in the United States, Europe, Russia, and other developed countries increased between 1950 and 1975. In terms of food, the rich have become richer over the past 30 years and the poor have become poorer. Because of rapid population growth and gross inequities in the worldwide distribution of food, the number of malnourished and starving people has reached unprecedented levels (Fig. 3).

Despite their increasing numbers, most of the world's malnourished obtain the daily minimum average of 1700 kilocalories for survival (a calorie is a unit of energy, measuring 4.184 joules; 1 kilocalorie equals 1000 calories). But most of these people are not obtaining sufficient amounts of proteins and vitamins to maintain good health (Fig. 4).

Protein malnutrition is most common among people whose diets are derived mainly from plants. Few vegetables contain all the essential amino acids necessary to sustain life, whereas meat, fish, milk, and eggs do. People who subsist strictly as vegetarians must eat a variety of specific types of vegetables to avoid protein malnutrition.

The consequences of not obtaining sufficient amounts of amino acids are most serious for children between the ages of 1 and 6, for these compounds are vital to normal physical and mental development. The human body grows less than 20 per cent of its adult size during the first 3 years, but during the same time the brain can grow to 80 per cent of its adult size. Most of the nerve cells of the brain are present in a human embryo after only

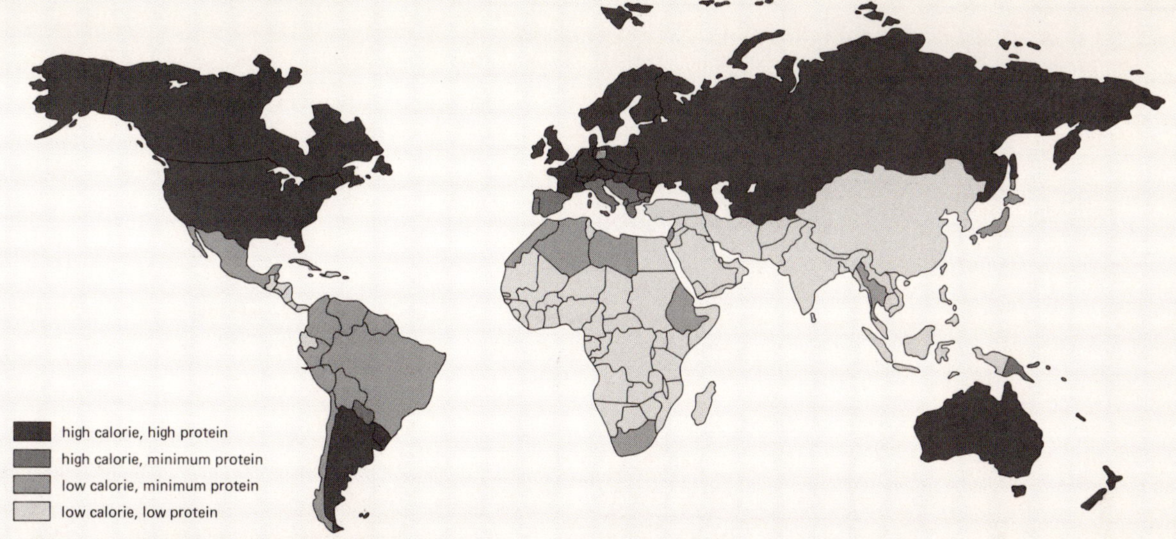

Fig. 3 The geography of world hunger. *(Modified from P. Ehrlich and A. Ehrlich, "Population, Resources, Environment: Issues in Human Ecology," Freeman, San Francisco, 1970.)*

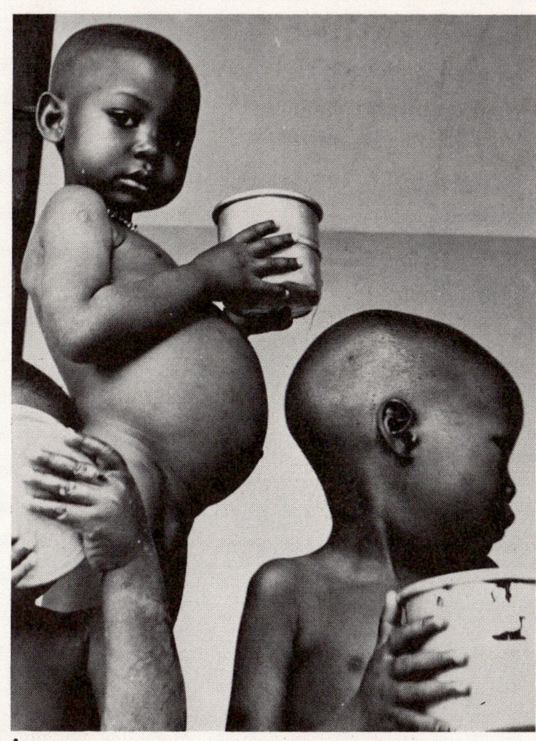

A

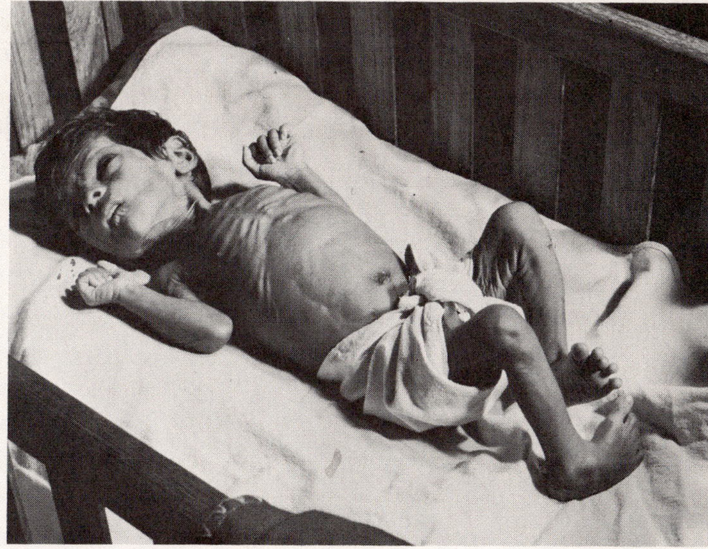

B

Fig. 4 Malnutrition. (A) Children suffering from kwashiorkor. This type of malnutrition syndrome is caused by diets that contain carbohydrates but little protein. (B) This child is afflicted with marasmus. This form of malnutrition occurs when individuals are truly starving and receiving insufficient amounts of protein, carbohydrates, and fats. Note the wasting of both muscle and subcutaneous fat.

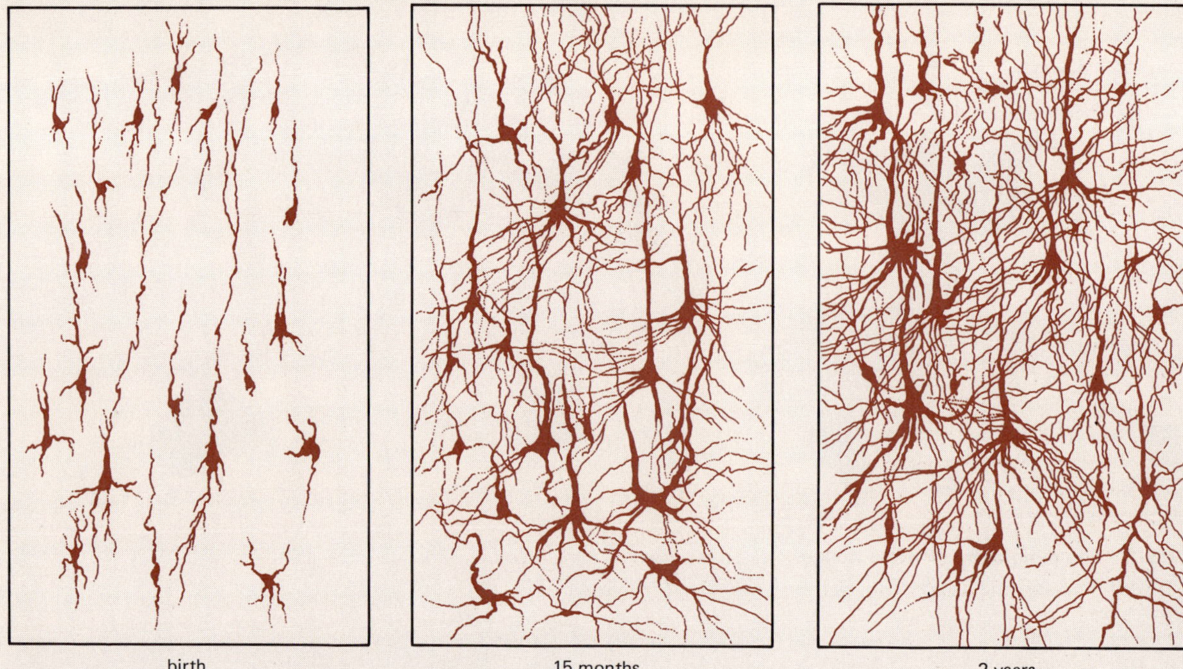

Fig. 5 Development of nerve cells (neurons) in the cerebrum of a young child. Almost all nerve cells are present at birth, but they are immature. Fibrous extensions of neurons develop gradually during the first 3 years of life. The drawings depict normal development of such extensions at birth, and in a 15-month- and 2-year-old child. Development is retarded if children receive inadequate amounts or kinds of nutrients. See Chap. 19 for additional information on nerve-cell function.

18 weeks of development. However, maturation of these cells takes place largely after birth, as does development of the brain tissue that provides functional support for nerve cells (Fig. 5). This extremely rapid growth of the brain cannot occur without adequate amounts and types of nutrients. Below-normal head and brain size is frequent among people who were severely malnourished during the first 3 years of life.

Such underdevelopment can affect reasoning ability, memory, and other human functions in many adverse ways. A study conducted recently in Mexico indicated that children who had been undernourished before the age of 5 had an average IQ 13 points lower than a control group that had not experienced severe protein malnutrition. Abnormally poor manual dexterity and clumsiness have also been observed among undernourished children. Furthermore, the damage to tissues of the brain and central nervous system caused by inadequate amounts of dietary protein is sometimes irreversible. People living in poverty often cannot afford or obtain the variety of vegetables or meat necessary to ensure adequate intake of all essential amino acids. Their diets often consist entirely of inexpensive, starchy foods such as cassava, cereal, and bananas. They and their children therefore remain malnourished regardless of the amount of such foods they consume. Moreover, poor parents often cannot provide the kinds of stimulating environments children need for normal social and intellectual development. Results of recent studies indicate that environmental and nutritional deprivation often interact synergistically in restricting mental development.

Vitamins constitute other quality nutrients frequently deficient in poor diets, and the deficiency diseases that result are particularly tragic. Vitamins are required in small amounts, can be manufactured synthetically, and can be added to food at a low cost. Milk, breakfast cereals, and many other foods produced in developed countries are now routinely *fortified* with vitamins. Yet vitamin-deficiency diseases are common in many less developed countries. Vitamin A deficiency, for example, which often accompanies protein malnutrition, can produce a variety of eye abnormalities. Symptoms of severe vitamin A inadequacy include drying of eye membranes and softening of the *cornea,* a protective layer of nonliving cells that covers the exposed surface of eyes (see Chap. 19). Containers of nonfat dry milk shipped to poorer nations from the United States have been fortified with vitamin A since 1965. Even so, the United Nations estimates that up to 100,000 children become blind each year in the Far East alone because of vitamin A deficiency.

Insufficient production and inadequate distribution of food are the chief causes of malnutrition in the world today, but cultural differences between people also can increase the difficulty of upgrading diets. In southern China, for example, people refused to eat unmilled rice that could have prevented a vitamin B deficiency disease. They objected to the flavor of the new rice and complained about the additional cooking time required. New varieties of food plants often have characteristics different from traditional strains, and even minor differences can make a food unacceptable to people of a particular culture.

Conversely, some cultural practices of developed countries have been widely adopted by people in less wealthy nations. Acceptance of these customs has often improved the health and nutrition of poor people, but not always. Until recently, almost all infants born in less developed countries have been breast-fed. Many poor mothers in these nations now have adopted the practice of bottle feeding and early weaning, habits learned from wealthier urban classes of their own countries and from people living in industrialized nations.

There are several reasons for this shift away from breast feeding, including the idea that bottle feeding must be better because the rich do it. Unfortunately, a basic knowledge of sanitation and nutrition, essential to good bottle feeding, is generally lacking among the poor of the world. Bottles prepared for infants of low-income families often contain powdered or condensed milk that has been "stretched" with extra water. Moreover, formulas are frequently prepared with polluted water or used hours after standing unrefrigerated.

Out of ignorance, some mothers substitute barley flour or cornstarch for milk. Such substances contain little protein and few vitamins, and are far less nutritious than milk produced by lactating mothers. Mother's milk also contains substances that protect infants from infectious diseases and diarrhea, and it does not transmit parasites. Breast feeding also delays reestablishment of fertility in women an average of 6 months longer than when babies are bottle-fed (see Chap. 25). The delay increases the spacing be-

Fig. 6 Meat and grain consumption. (A) Per capita consumption of beef and poultry in the United States, 1910–1973. Note the dramatic rise in United States meat consumption since 1950. (B) Direct and indirect consumption of grain as related to per capita income in selected countries. In general, only affluent countries can afford the large amounts of grain used in livestock production.

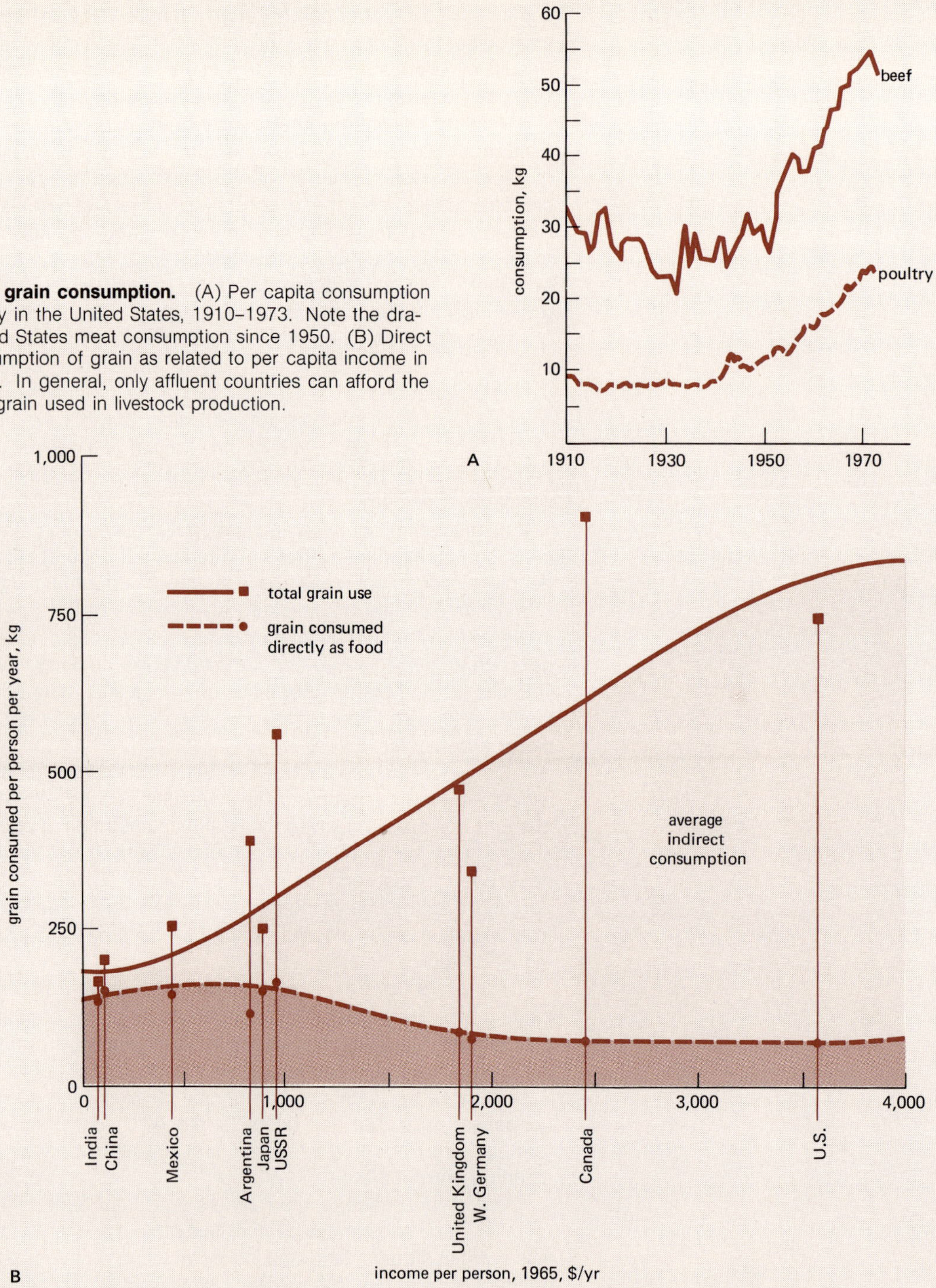

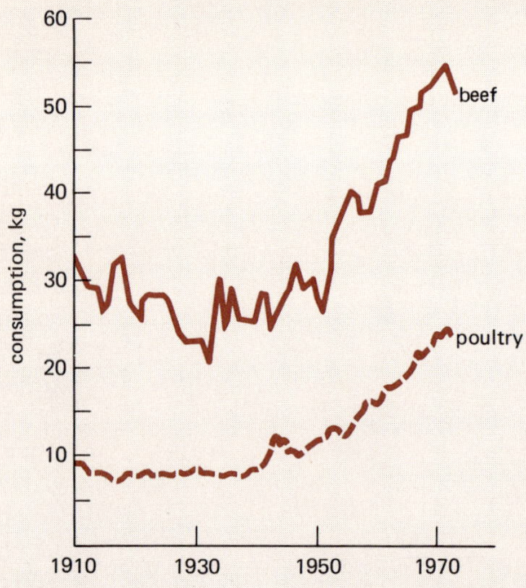

tween pregnancies among women who do not practice birth control, and this contributes to lower birthrates and to better health among both women and children in poorer nations.

There are disadvantages to prolonged nursing of infants. Mother's milk alone provides adequate nourishment for only the first 4 to 6 months after birth, and breast feeding can drain nutritional reserves of mothers who are not adequately fed. Nevertheless, the additional nutrients required by lactating women can be provided far more cheaply than substitutes for mother's milk.

The switch from breast to bottle feeding has been studied extensively in Chile, where the practice of breast feeding declined from 95 per cent in the 1950s to 6 per cent in 1970. Less dramatic reductions have occurred in many other less developed nations. Infant mortality has been rising in some of these countries, and this increase appears to have been caused partly by the shift to bottle feeding. In Chile, for example, deaths among bottle-feeding infants were 3 times higher than among breast-fed babies.

Malnutrition is not an exclusive problem of less developed nations. A U.S. Government Public Health Survey in 1969 revealed that between 10 and 15 million Americans were "chronically hungry" and that an equal number had incomes too low to provide a well-balanced diet. More recent surveys suggest that the proliferation of government food programs since 1968 has improved the nutritional status of many poor Americans but that millions still do not receive adequate amounts of food.

Most Americans, however, have more than enough to eat, and many eat too much of some kinds of food and not enough of others. People in affluent countries consume far more grain than people in poorer nations, but most of it is consumed indirectly as meat. Per capita consumption of poultry more than doubled in the United States between 1952 and 1972, and that of beef nearly doubled. Similar increases occurred in other developed countries, but few people eat more meat than Americans (Fig. 6).

About three-quarters of the food energy contained in the typical Asian diet comes directly from grain; Asians eat about 300 to 400 pounds of grain per person annually. By contrast, the American per capita consumption is almost 2000 pounds of grain per year, but 80 per cent of this total is fed to livestock. Because meat eaters feed at higher trophic levels than vegetarians, most of the food energy of livestock grain is lost: 10 pounds or more of grain is needed to produce 1 pound of beef when feedlot methods are used to fatten livestock (Fig. 7). Livestock were fed one-third of the world's annual production of grain in 1974, and this proportion has increased slowly over the past few years.

The amount of grain consumed by livestock could be reduced if cattle and sheep were fed greater quantities of forage plants. Although greater numbers of animals can be raised more rapidly when supplied with grain in feedlots that when range-fed, the meat of feedlot cattle is "marbled" with an excessive amount of fat. Moreover, the fat of grain-fed beef contains far greater amounts of saturated fatty acids than that of range-fed cattle. As noted in Chaps. 4 and 18, consumption of large amounts of saturated fats appears to promote a variety of cardiovascular diseases in some individuals. In addition, diets containing high concentrations of proteins and fats have been linked to certain kinds of cancer that are more prevalent in developed countries than in less developed nations.

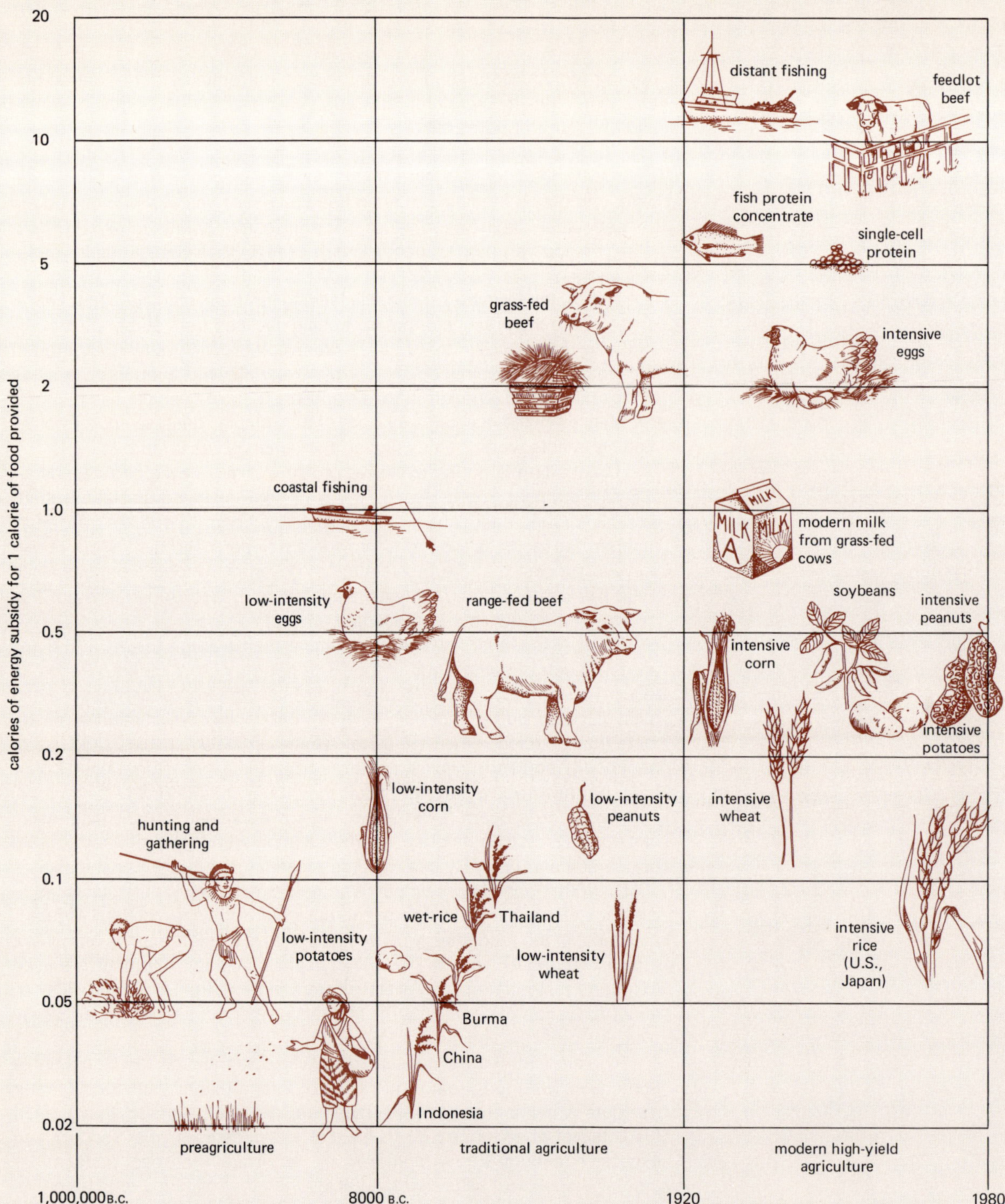

Fig. 7 Energy subsidies for various food crops. Considerably more energy must be expended to produce beef by feedlot or grass-feeding methods than by range feeding. Also, modern agricultural methods, which usually depend on technological innovation, generally require higher expenditures of energy than traditional methods. High-intensity crops yield more food per unit area than low-intensity crops.

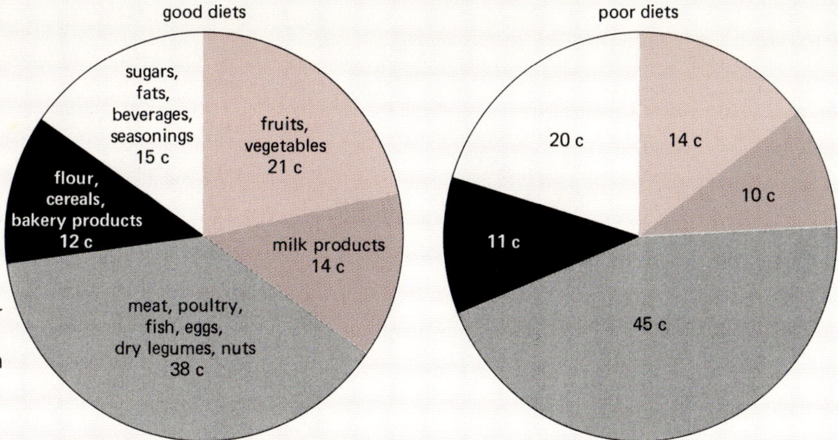

Fig. 8 Quality of diets reflected in percentage of items bought by one "food dollar." Good diets generally contain greater quantities of fruits, vegetables, and milk products than poor diets, which often contain too much carbohydrate and saturated fats.

The diets of many Americans also contain too much sugar and salt. The worldwide average annual consumption of sugar is less than 50 pounds per person. For Americans the equivalent figure exceeds 100 pounds. Excessive consumption of sugar seems to contribute to the development of diabetes in some people. Other studies suggest that people who sprinkle liberal amounts of salt on their food are more likely to develop chronic high blood pressure than people who restrict consumption of salt.

To make matters worse, many Americans literally have been taking this nutritional abuse sitting down. Habits of affluent people have become increasingly sedentary over the past several decades. As a result, 10 to 20 per cent of all American children and one-third to one-half of their parents are overweight, a condition that further promotes heart attack, stroke, diverticulitis, and several other diseases. Thus, the health and life expectancy of people who subsist on hamburgers, salted french fries, and soda pop could be improved if they exercised more and incorporated a greater proportion of fruits, vegetables, cereal grains, and defatted dairy products into their diets (Fig. 8). All the latter are important sources of vitamins and minerals, and food plants contain cellulose. This polysaccharide does not have nutritional value for human beings, but it does provide the bulk and "fiber" required for normal functioning of the large intestine. People who obtain too little cellulose from the diet develop a higher than average number of intestinal disorders, including cancer of the large intestine.

SOLUTIONS

The world's population of human beings recently has been growing at an annual rate close to 2 per cent and, barring a catastrophic rise in the death rate, is expected to continue growing rapidly for the next several decades. Even if the distribution of food were made more equitable during the next few years, unpredecented famines will almost certainly occur unless substantial increases in food production accompany growth of the world's population.

According to United Nations estimates, food production must be raised at least one-third above 1975 levels to provide the same amount of food for each person projected to be living in 1990. Similar conclusions have been reached by other study groups, including the U.S. Department of Agriculture and the University of California Food Task Force. These sources estimate that developed countries will require only a 15 to 30 per cent increase in food production between 1975 and 1990 to maintain per capita consumption. Most poorer nations, however, will require almost a 100 per cent increase. Because of its slower population growth, China probably will require less than an 80 per cent increase. Countries growing at faster rates, such as Iran, Iraq, Nigeria, and Thailand, will require more than twice as much food. Can this increased demand for food be met? If so, how and for how long?

area	percent of ocean	average production
open ocean	92.0	57
continental shelf	7.3	162
upwelling zones	0.1	225
estuaries	0.4	810
algal bed and reef	0.2	900

Fig. 9 Productivity of oceans and estuaries. Units of annual average productivity are grams of carbon per square meter.

Several new methods of producing food have been proposed as partial solutions to the worsening food crisis. Some of these may eventually increase the availability of food; others will not. One approach that appears both too costly and too unproductive is the harvesting of substantially greater amounts of food from the open sea. Marine biologists have measured the productivity of various regions of the ocean environment (Fig. 9). The open sea, which makes up 90 per cent of the total surface area of marine habitats, is essentially a biological desert. Photosynthesis occurs only in the comparatively shallow photic zone, and thermoclines often prevent the upwelling of large amounts of photosynthesis-supporting nutrients (see Chap. 9). Proposals have been made to increase the productivity of phytoplankton by pumping nutrients to the surface of open seas from bottom sediments, but the costs of such schemes are prohibitive even if rich harvests of marine life could be guaranteed. Closer to shore, where currents bring nutrients to the surface without the help of human technology, productivity is 2 to 6 times higher than in open seas (see Fig. 9). It is in these far less expansive areas that most seafood is now obtained and some increase might be feasible.

For example, it may be possible to augment the food supply of some countries through *aquaculture,* raising and harvesting relatively dense populations of organisms grown in ponds, marshes, estuaries, and similar aquatic environments. Aquaculture is a centuries-old practice in the Far East, where farmers stock flooded rice fields with small fishes, which eat mosquito larvae and other insect pests, thereby reducing the need for pesticides. The fishes also fertilize the rice plants by excreting wastes into the water. Fishes and rice are harvested together when the paddies are drained, and some of the fishes are used to restock the rice fields during the next growing season.

Aquaculture already supplies about 20 to 40 per cent of the fish and shellfish consumed in Indonesia and China. These organisms are rich sources of protein, making plans to expand aquaculture in Asia even more significant. Fish farming probably will also make a larger contribution to future American diets than it does today. Some companies are now raising fish in small ponds in Canada and the United States, and marine biologists are experimenting with raising shellfish on algae grown on sewage sludge. Some businessmen expect the American consumption of fish produced by aquaculture to more than double between 1978 and 1985.

Some of the most unusual and novel proposals for combating malnutrition involve production of protein supplements. If they could be produced cheaply and in large quantities, such supplements might be used to enrich the protein-deficient diets of many poor people throughout the world. Biologists have proposed growing dense populations of bacteria or algae on petroleum by-products, sewage sludge, and other organic wastes. The populations could be harvested periodically, ground to a protein-rich powder, and then added to milk or other foods. Such powders already have been produced and have been used to alleviate symptoms of protein-deficiency diseases in malnourished children.

Another promising method of producing dietary supplements involves the extraction of proteins from the leaves of alfalfa or other forage crops. Alfalfa can yield up to 2500 pounds of protein per acre, far more than most plants. Morever, forage plants can be grown on soils and terrains unsuitable for cereal grains. Proteins extracted from forage plants could be fed to pigs or poultry in attempts to boost the meat supplies of less developed nations, used as fertilizer, or made into a powder for human consumption. The extraction process also produces a fibrous residue that can be used as feed for cattle and other ruminant livestock. Unfortunately, the process of producing leaf extracts and other protein supplements involves use of sophisticated, energy-consuming technology (see Fig. 7). Many people believe that the manufacture of protein supplements will not reduce malnutrition significantly unless less expensive production techniques can be found.

Other advances in food technology have made a greater impact. Most notable are those offsetting some of the increased cost of producing animal nutrient by substituting similar products of vegetable origin. This change has been most pronounced in the replacement of animal fats with vegetable oils. Oleomargarine is a prime example of successful livestock-product imitation. Americans consumed, on the average, 14 pounds of butter and 2 pounds of margarine in 1940. By 1970 the annual consumption was 6 pounds for butter and 10 pounds for margarine.

Lard has been replaced almost entirely by vegetable shortenings, almost 70 per cent of all whipped toppings now are derived from vegetable products, and "meat" that looks and tastes like bacon has been produced from soybeans. Indeed, Americans now eat small amounts of soybean meats along with real meat in soup mixes, canned stews and chili, frozen ravioli, and frozen hamburger patties. If the substitution of vegetable products for those traditionally derived from animals continues, the amount of land, water, and other resources needed to feed and maintain livestock will continue to be reduced.

Despite such advances, most techniques of producing new sources and kinds of food must be viewed as hopes for the future, not ready-made panaceas. Some of these methods may eventually make modest contributions to the human diet, but most scientists agree that the best means of combating starvation and malnutrition involve increasing the production and quality of traditional foods. People are used to eating such foods and are therefore less likely to reject them. Furthermore, production of traditional foods often does not require new or expensive manufacturing techniques.

Among the goals of modern agricultural research programs is the production of new varieties of grain containing a greater abundance of proteins, especially proteins rich in lysine, tryptophan, and other essential amino acids. Such strains have been produced, but most suffer from the disadvantages of yielding relatively small amounts of grain and requiring very large applications of fertilizer. However, other researchers are attempting to breed plants that photosynthesize more efficiently than existing species. Thus, it may be possible to increase the food-producing capacity of high-protein cereal grains, thereby raising their yields.

Other biologists are attempting to improve the efficiency of nitrogen-fixing bacteria. Such improvements could reduce the need for inorganic fertilizers and increase the growth rates of new varieties of plants. Similar research is aimed at increasing the rates at which plants absorb and utilize inorganic nutrients. Several scientists are developing technologies that may reduce losses of food supplies in fields, during transport, and in storage. About 30 per cent of such supplies are lost each year to pests, diseases, and spoilage in many countries, and the loss may be even higher in a few less developed nations. Techniques to reduce this loss could greatly improve the world food supply.

Evidently, science and technology can provide a vast and increasing array of tools to reduce world hunger substantially. However, these tools can do little to bring about an actual reduction unless they are supported by a coordinated international strategy aimed at increasing the quality and quantity of food throughout the world and simultaneously decreasing rates of population growth. Where standards of living are high, population growth and malnutrition often are low. In effect, efforts to satisfy our nutritional needs and to slow the rate of population growth often reinforce each other positively. Progress made on one front can enhance the prospects for progress on the other–but not without coordinated political, social, and economic commitment toward these goals. Indeed, no large-scale application of science and technology can succeed where such coordination or commitment is lacking.

Review Questions

1 Define nutrition. What are the major nutritional processes of organisms? Define autotroph and heterotroph and review the general patterns of food procurement in the various types of autotrophs and heterotrophs.

2 Through what processes do different groups of organisms obtain:

- **a.** Water?
- **b.** Other mineral substances?
- **c.** Molecular foods?

3 Describe the mechanism of xylem conduction. What kinds of nutrients are transported in xylem and in what direction? What are root pressure and transpiration pull? How are these forces generated, and what roles do they play in xylem conduction? What is the importance of cohesion of water in xylem conduction?

4 What is the mass-flow hypothesis; how does it explain phloem conduction? What kinds of nutrients are carried in phloem and in which direction?

5 If a cut length of stem bearing some leaves is submerged upside down in a glass of nutrient-rich water, how will xylem conduction and phloem conduction be affected? How has it been proved that phloem can transport in both directions?

6 Contrast the nutrient requirements of plants and animals. For which materials are animals dependent on plants and why? What role does the brain play in hunger control in mammals?

7 What is the composition of saliva, and how is salivary secretion initiated? What mechanical and chemical digestive processes occur in the mouth? Through what processes is food transferred to the stomach?

8 What is the composition of gastric juice, and by what processes is secretion of this fluid controlled? Review the mechanical and chemical events of gastric digestion. What are the specific functions of HCl, pepsin, and rennin? What are the results of gastric digestion?

9 Which digestive fluids are added to food in the duodenum, and what is the composition of these fluids? Where are the fluids manufactured, and what processes stimulate their secretion?

10 Review the specific course of protein, carbohydrate, and fat digestion in the intestine. What enzymes are involved in each case? What are the results of these digestive processes What are intestinal villi, and what are their functions? How and in what form are different categories of food absorbed by the intestinal wall?

11 What are the functions of the large intestine? What is the role of the intestinal bacteria? Do these symbionts live mutualistically, commensalistically, or parasitically? If pure glucose were eaten, where would it be digested? Why are orally administered medicines not digested in the alimentary tract?

12 Describe the blood circulation through the intestine. Which food materials are carried away from the intestine by blood? Describe the pattern of the lymph circulation in the body as a whole. What is the arrangement of the lymph vessels in the intestine?

13 By what pathways do foods reach the liver? What are the pathway and destination of colloidal fat?

14 What is the general function of the liver, and what is the adaptive advantage of such an organ?

15 What factor is chiefly responsible for the steadily increasing numbers of malnourished people? Distinguish between starvation and protein malnutrition. What are the symptoms and consequences of protein malnutrition? Suggest actions that could be taken to reduce world hunger. Evaluate the consequences of these actions.

Collateral Readings

Benarde, M. A.: "The Chemicals We Eat," McGraw-Hill, New York, 1975. This short, highly readable paperback is a good primer on food additives.

Bowling, D. J. F.: "Uptake of Ions by Plant Roots," Chapman & Hall, London, 1976. This book reviews experimental evidence on how roots obtain water and dissolved nutrients.

Braidwood, R. J.: The Agricultural Revolution, *Scientific American,* September 1960. A discussion of the early use and development of agriculture.

Brink, R. A., J. W. Densmore, and **G. A. Hill:** Soil Deterioration and the Growing World Demand for Food, *Science,* vol. 197, pp. 625–630, Aug. 12, 1977. An excellent discussion of soil deterioration based in part on a study of five watersheds in Wisconsin.

Cox, G. W., and **M. D. Atkins:** "Agricultural Ecology: An Analysis of World Food Production Systems," Freeman, San Francisco, 1979. A good, thorough treatment of how people manipulate ecosystems to produce food.

Davenport, H. W.: Why the Stomach Does Not Digest Itself, *Scientific American,* January 1972. Mechanisms and secretions that protect the stomach wall from hydrochloric acid and digestive enzymes are described.

Epstein, E.: Roots, *Scientific American,* May 1973. A review of how plants procure and transport nutrients through roots.

Fernstrom, J. D., and **R. J. Wurtman:** Nutrition and the Brain, *Scientific American,* February 1974. This article discusses the steady-state control mechanisms that regulate food consumption.

Harlan, J. R.: "Crops and Man," American Society of Agronomy, Crop Science Society of America, Madison, Wis., 1975. A good review of plants that have been important to human societies.

Harpstead, D. D.: High-Lysine Corn, *Scientific American,* August 1971. Lysine is an essential amino acid present only in small quantities in traditional varieties of this grain plant. Harpstead's article describes how higher levels of this substance were bred into corn.

Heisner, C. B.: "Seed to Civilization: The Story of Man's Food," Freeman, San Francisco, 1975. The origins and development of agriculture are the focus of this interesting book.

Hodgson, H. J.: Forage Crops, *Scientific American,* February 1976. The importance of grasses and legumes as the mainstay of United States agriculture is stressed.

Hulse, J. H., and **D. Spurgeon:** Triticale, *Scientific American,* August 1974. This article reviews experiments that led to the development of a new and highly productive cereal grain.

Kappas, A., and **A. P. Alvares:** How the Liver Metabolizes Foreign Substances, *Scientific American,* June 1975. A description of how the liver inactivates alcohol and other potentially harmful substances that are absorbed through the walls of the alimentary tract.

Loomis, W. F.: Rickets, *Scientific American,* December 1970. The relationship between this vitamin-deficiency disease and sunlight is examined.

Mayerson, H. S.: The Lymphatic System, *Scientific American,* June 1963. The functions of this system are described.

Moore, A. M. T.: A Pre-Neolithic Farmers' Village on the Euphrates, *Scientific American,* August 1979. The beginnings of the Neolithic Period, some 10,500 years ago, traditionally has been associated with the emergence of agriculture. This article describes recent evidence suggesting an earlier origin of farming by people living in pre-neolithic Syria.

Morton, J.: "Guts: The Form and Function of the Digestive System," St. Martin's, New York, 1967. A short book summarizing the comparative anatomy and functioning of the alimentary tracts of several animals.

Ray, P.: "The Living Plant," 2d ed., Holt, New York, 1972. A short section on the mass-flow hypothesis is included in this paperback.

Roberts, W. O.: "The Climate Mandate," Freeman, San Francisco, 1979. The interplay between climatic variation, food production, and human population growth is analyzed.

Salisbury, F. B., and **C. W. Ross:** "Plant Physiology," 2d ed., Wadsworth, Belmont, Calif., 1978. This textbook contains an updated account of translocation.

Scientific American, Food and Agriculture, September 1967. The entire issue concerns various aspects of this topic.

Scrimshaw, N. S., and **V. R. Young:** The Requirements of Human Nutrition, *Scientific American,* September 1976. An interesting and readable discussion of human nutritional requirements.

Vander, A. J., J. H. Sherman, and **D. S. Luciano.:** "Human Physiology," 3d ed., McGraw-Hill, New York, 1980. This exceptional book contains an excellent discussion of digestion.

Ware, G. W.: "The Pesticide Book," Freeman, San Francisco, 1978. An encyclopedia of pesticides for the nonspecialist.

Watt, B. K., and **A. L. Merrill:** "Handbook of the Nutritional Contents of Foods," Dover, New York, 1975. A compendium of data on the nutritional value of a wide variety of foods.

Young, V. R., and **N. S. Scrimshaw:** The Physiology of Starvation, *Scientific American,* October 1971. This article examines how the human body adopts to prolonged starvation and how best to use food when it is scarce.

Chapter 12 Respiration

Learning Objectives

After reading this chapter you should be able to:

1. Name the two principal functions served by nutrients in living systems.
2. Define respiration and give two reasons why it does not produce the high temperatures that usually accompany most forms of combustion.
3. Define phosphorylation and differentiate between low-energy and high-energy bonds; state the role of respiration in the formation of high-energy bonds; identify the principal product of respiration and list at least two ways in which this product is used in living systems.
4. Differentiate between catabolism and anabolism and between the energy content of hydrogen-rich organic molecules and anhydrides; use the equation $C_6H_{12}O_6 + 6O_2 \rightarrow 6H_2O + 6CO_2$ to illustrate how differences in energy content relate to the chemical conversions that occur during respiration.
5. Distinguish between oxidations and reductions; identify and illustrate the most common type of redox reaction in respiration; describe the relationship between redox reactions and the release of energy from fuel molecules.
6. Identify and list at least one example of the two general ways in which the energy of fuel molecules is transferred to ATP and identify the method that yields the greater amounts of ATP.
7. Give evidence demonstrating that the carriers of the electron-transport system are integral components of the inner mitochondrial membrane; construct a diagram illustrating the structural relationships between the M and O compartments of mitochondria and the inner and outer mitochondrial membranes.
8. Outline the chemiosmotic hypothesis and list at least three kinds of experimental evidence that support it; differentiate between F_0 and F_1 particles and state a functional relationship between them; describe the function of oxygen in electron transport and identify the final product of this process; list in order the actual electron carriers of the electron-transport system and at least one functional relationship between each pair of carriers in the chain.
9. Distinguish between fuel decomposition and energy transfer, and state how these two subcomponent processes of cellular respiration are functionally interrelated.
10. Differentiate between aerobic and anaerobic respiration; show how specialized breathing and circulatory systems support aerobic respiration in animals; identify the principal products formed when pyruvic acid reacts with hydrogen under anaerobic conditions in yeast and human beings; list at least three examples of how fermentation is used to produce a commercial product.
11. Construct a diagram that depicts the central roles of pyruvic acid and acetyl CoA in the fuel decomposition of carbohydrates, fats, and proteins; list in order the sequence of steps that produce two molecules of CO_2 from one molecule of acetyl CoA; describe the fate of hydrogen atoms that are removed from compounds of the citric acid cycle.
12. List the major products of glycolysis, the citric acid cycle, electron transport, and oxidative phosphorylation in the respiration of carbohydrates; outline the functional relationships between these processes.
13. Differentiate between deamination and transamination and illustrate how they provide respiratory fuels; list at least three compounds common to the fuel decomposition of amino acids and glucose.
14. Define and illustrate β-oxidation of a fatty acid; show why fats constitute a richer source of usable energy than equivalent amounts of protein or carbohydrate.

Adequate supplies of nutrients are required by all cells for two reasons: (1) they provide energy for the maintenance of all living processes, and (2) they serve as raw materials for the synthesis of new living substance. The role of nutrients as fuels will be considered in this chapter.

THE PATTERN

The process whereby chemical energy of organic nutrients is converted to energy usable in living cells is called *respiration.* It is a *cellular* process, an activity performed by each cell of an organism.

Apart from depending on nutrients, respiration also is associated with an exchange of atmospheric gases; oxygen usually is a required raw material, and carbon dioxide normally is always a by-product. Plants and many animals are so constructed that their living cells are in direct or nearly direct contact with the external environment. Gas exchange here takes place largely via diffusion. Specialized *breathing systems,* such as lungs and gills, generally occur only in complexly structured animals. Such systems usually operate in conjunction with *circulatory systems;* oxygen is obtained from the environment by a breathing system, transferred to oxygen-carrying pigments in blood, and then distributed by the circulatory system to all cells (see Chap. 18). Oxygen passes across cell membranes and moves to the inner membranes of mitochondria, where it becomes reduced to H_2O.

Most respiration occurs in mitochondria, cytoplasmic organelles often located near structures that require a substantial or continuous input of energy. For example, mitochondria exist in arrays along contractile filaments in muscle. Also, mitochondria frequently are found near sources of fuel molecules such as cytoplasmic droplets of fat.

Respiration consists of a series of energy-yielding decomposition reactions: respiration is a form of burning, or *combustion,* in which chemical bonds in nutrient molecules are broken and the bond energy becomes available for metabolic work. But unlike a fire and most forms of combustion, respiration does not produce high temperatures, for two principal reasons. First, a fire is *uncontrolled* combustion, in the sense that all the bonds in a fuel molecule may be broken simultaneously. A maximum amount of energy can then be released all at once. Such a sudden, explosive release generates the high temperatures of a fire. But respiration is *controlled* combustion; energy is obtained from breaking one or a few bonds at a time. If a nutrient fuel is respired completely, the total energy yield is the same as if it had been burned in a furnace, but in respiration the energy is removed bit by bit, bond by bond. Temperatures therefore stay low.

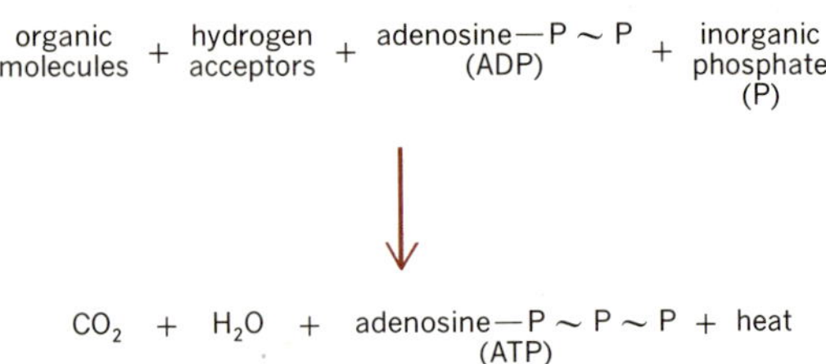

Fig. 12.1 High-energy bonds. As a result of respiration, some of the energy of organic molecules is concentrated in high-energy phosphate bonds (symbolized as ~P). Most of the remaining energy released during respiration is dissipated as heat.

Second, the energy produced in a fire is dissipated largely as heat and to some extent as light. But in respiration only some of the available energy escapes as heat and practically none as light. Instead, much of it is "packaged" directly as new *chemical* energy. This energy-packaging process, already referred to in Chap. 4, is represented by the reaction that converts adenosine diphosphate (ADP) to adenosine triphosphate (ATP). The principal reactants and products of this reaction are presented in Fig. 12.1.

Although the energy of chemical bonds covers a wide range of values, from very low to very high, it is often convenient to group all such bonds into two categories, *high-energy bonds* and *low-energy bonds.* In cells, high-energy bonds generally are associated with atomic groupings called phosphate groups ($—PO_3^{2-}$). If we symbolize such a group as P, as in Fig. 12.1, then the bond that joins P to adenosine or to another P is a *phosphate bond.* High-energy bonds are distinguished from low-energy bonds by the symbol ~. Thus, a low-energy phosphate bond is symbolized as —P, and a high-energy phosphate bond as ~P.

Phosphate bonds are produced by a process called *phosphorylation.* A relatively large amount of energy is expended in phosphorylations that produce high-energy bonds. A correspondingly large amount then becomes available when such bonds are broken. During respiration, much of the energy released from breaking bonds in nutrient fuels is used in the formation of high-energy phosphate bonds of ATP. Respiration therefore accomplishes more than the mere making of new bonds with the energy released from old bonds; it uses phosphorylation reactions in the transfer of energy from the bonds of fuel molecules to high-energy phosphate bonds.

ATP then is the main product of respiration. Once produced, ATP can be used as the energy source for the movement of contractile filaments in muscle, the synthesis of new living substance, or for virtually any energy-requiring process in cells.

Fuel Decomposition

The actual fuels in cells are organic compounds that contain bond energies—in effect, *any* organic constituent of cells: carbohydrates, fats, proteins, nucleotides, their various derivatives, vitamins, other special compounds, and indeed all the innumerable substances that together make up a cell. Like a fire, respiration is no respecter of materials; but under normal conditions, a cell receives a steady enough supply of external foods to make *them* the primary respiratory fuels rather than the structural parts of a cell. Nevertheless, the formed parts of a cell *are* decomposed gradually. A cell therefore can remain intact and functioning only by continuous construction of new living components. Destructive metabolism (*catabolism*) and constructive synthesis metabolism (*anabolism*) are normally in balance, and nutrients serve as both fuel for the one and building materials for the other. The components of a cell in effect are continuously "turned over," existing parts being replaced by new ones, and the living substance consequently is never quite the same from instant to instant.

Just how is energy released from a fuel molecule? Since respiration involves energy-yielding decomposition reactions, the end products will contain less energy and will therefore be more stable than the nutrient fuels. As noted in Chap. 3, reactions tend to proceed in such a way that the least energetic, most stable states are attained. It is this basic thermodynamic circumstance that ultimately "drives" all respiratory processes. The energy liberated in respiration comes from the carbon bonds in nutrients, and different carbon bonds have different stabilities. The least stable, hence most energy-rich carbon bonds generally occur in *hydrocarbon* groups, atomic groupings that contain only carbon and hydrogen. These exist in organic molecules in forms such as CH_4, $—CH_3$, $—CH_2—$, $=CH—$. On the other hand, the most stable, least energy-rich carbon combination is CO_2, a so-called *anhydride*, or hydrogen-free grouping. In general, therefore, usable respiratory energy will result from conversions of hydrocarbons into anhydrides or from the replacement of H atoms bonded to carbon by O atoms.

This principle is illustrated by the following equation:

$$C_6H_{12}O_6 + 6O_2 \longrightarrow 6CO_2 + 6H_2O$$

Glucose ($C_6H_{12}O_6$) is the main organic fuel molecule for many cells. During its respiration, all 12 hydrogen atoms are removed by *dehydrogenation* and replaced by oxygen. As glucose is being dehydrogenated, it also becomes fragmented, and the six carbon atoms in glucose then are released in the form of six molecules of CO_2.

Dehydrogenation is one type of a general class of reactions called *oxidation-reduction*, or *redox*, reactions. Every redox reaction consists of two subreactions, an oxidation and a reduction (Fig. 12.2). Oxidations occur when one or more electrons are removed from a compound. In dehydrogenations whole hydrogen atoms are removed, i.e., electrons together with protons. Reductions occur when the removed electrons or hydrogen atoms are attached to another compound.

Dehydrogenations are the most common kind of redox reactions in respiration and represent the critical energy-yielding events. As in all redox reactions, the end products of dehydrogenations are thermodynamically more stable than the starting materials. In the above reaction, for example, the end products, CO_2 and water, are thermodynamically more stable than the starting materials, glucose and oxygen; the reaction yields energy. Glucose is the hydrogen donor, and the carbon of glucose is oxidized to CO_2. At the same time, oxygen becomes reduced to H_2O.

oxidation: yields energy	**reduction:** requires energy
electron loss: $Na \longrightarrow Na^{+} + e^{-}$	electron gain: $Cl + e^{-} \longrightarrow Cl^{-}$
or	or
hydrogen loss: $CH_4 \longrightarrow CO_2$	hydrogen gain: $CO_2 \longrightarrow CH_4$

Fig. 12.2 Oxidation and reduction. The properties of these two types of reaction are summarized.

For convenience, we may refer to the whole process simply as an "oxidation." This actually is common practice in discussions of respiration reactions, which are often called "biological oxidations." Notwithstanding the incomplete name, however, every oxidation implies and is accompanied by a reduction.

As already noted, a respiratory decomposition does not take place in a single large step but in several small ones; a *series* of consecutive redox reactions occurs, in which hydrogen is removed from fuel molecules bit by bit and energy is released bit by bit.

Energy Transfer

An appreciable fraction of the energy released during the dehydrogenation of fuel molecules dissipates free into the environment, largely in the form of heat, and respiration actually is the most important source of internal heat in all organisms. But not all of the energy from respiratory oxidations is radiated to the external environment as heat; a valuable fraction is transferred to high-energy phosphate bonds of ATP, in two general ways.

Transfer of High-Energy Phosphate Bonds from Fuel Molecules

During respiration, high-energy phosphate bonds sometimes are produced directly on a fuel molecule. ATP is produced when such high-energy phosphate bonds subsequently are transferred to ADP. The process often begins with the dehydrogenation of a fuel molecule. In some cases, part of the energy released by the dehydrogenation is used to attach a phosphate group to the fuel molecule via a high-energy bond. In other cases, fuel molecules containing low-energy phosphate bonds undergo internal rearrangements of atoms with the result that energy becomes concentrated in the vicinity of the phosphate group, forming a high-energy bond. In both instances, the resulting high-energy bonds subsequently are transferred to ADP, forming ATP (Fig. 12.3). Relatively small amounts of ATP are generated by this process.

Electron Transport and Oxidative Phosphorylation

Substantially greater amounts of ATP can be produced through *electron transport* and *oxidative phosphorylation,* two separate but closely integrated processes that occur in mitochondria.[1] During electron transport, the electrons of hydrogen atoms (derived from the dehydrogenation of fuel molecules) are separated from their protons and passed along a succession of molecules called *electron carriers.* The last of these carriers releases electrons to oxygen (Fig. 12.4). Water is produced as a final product of electron transport when an oxygen atom unites with two electrons and a pair of hydrogen ions. Some of the latter are generated when electrons of hydrogen atoms are separated from their protons following the dehydrogenation of fuel molecules.

Each step in this serial electron transfer is a complete redox process. A given electron carrier becomes oxidized when it passes on electrons to the next carrier in the series, and it becomes reduced when it accepts electrons from the preceding carrier. Some of the energy released during each of these redox reactions is used to attach a high-energy phosphate to ADP. Because oxygen is required for these phosphorylations of ADP, this pattern of ATP production is called *oxidative phosphorylation.*

The great precision with which electrons are passed along the chain of electron carriers strongly suggests that the carriers are arranged spatially in an ordered pattern. Experiments conducted over several years have confirmed such ordering and have demonstrated that the carriers are located within the inner of the two mitochondrial membranes.

Since mitochondria break apart when suspended in various solutions, preparations can be made that contain selected subcomponents of whole

[1]Many prokaryotes, which lack mitochondria, also can generate ATP through electron transport and oxidative phosphorylation. However, these processes may differ in several respects from those described here. Unless otherwise stated, all references to electron transport and oxidative phosphorylation in this book refer specifically to processes occurring in mitochondria of eukaryotic cells.

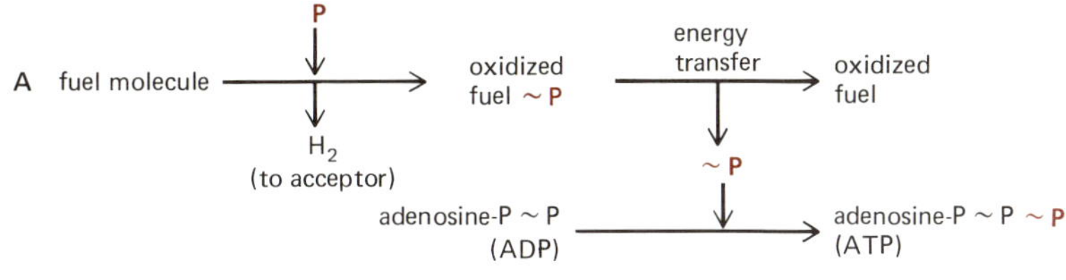

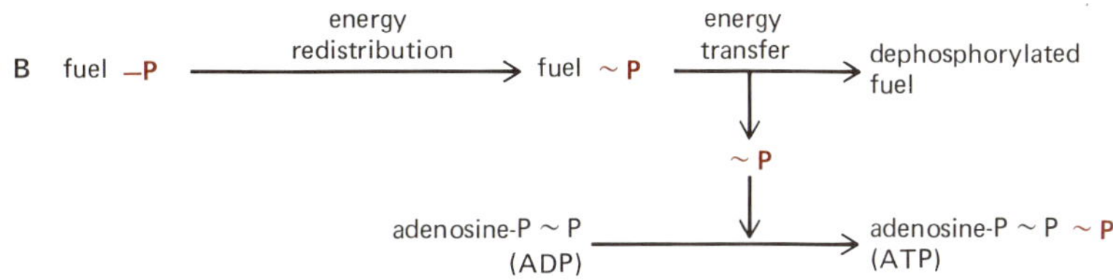

Fig. 12.3 ATP production. Two ways in which ATP is produced through transfer of high-energy phosphate bonds from fuel molecules. (A) Some ATP of cells is generated by the combined dehydrogenation and phosphorylation of a fuel molecule. A portion of the energy released by the dehydrogenation is used in forming a high-energy phosphate, which is transferred to ADP, forming ATP. (B) Shifts in the internal energy distribution of some fuel molecules transform low-energy phosphate bonds into the high-energy variety. The resulting high-energy phosphates are then transferred to ADP.

mitochondria. For example, some suspensions contain only fragments of outer mitochondrial membranes and fluid derived from the space between the inner and outer membranes, the so-called *O compartment* (Fig. 12.5). Such suspensions do not show any sign of electron transport. Suspensions containing only inner mitochondrial membranes can transport electrons, however, and the carriers cannot readily be washed from the membranes. These observations strongly suggest that the electron carriers are structural components of the inner membrane and are not found in the mitochondrial matrix (*M compartment*).

Results of subsequent experiments have shown how specific electron carriers are sequenced in repeated clusters inside the inner membranes of mitochondria. Such clusters are termed *respiratory assemblies.* The experiments also have established how most of the carriers are positioned in the plane of the inner membrane; in each respiratory assembly, the carriers are organized in a more or less zigzag pattern. As will become apparent, this structural organization plays an important role in providing the energy required for manufacturing ATP.

The Chemiosmotic (Mitchell) Hypothesis

During electron transport, how is the released energy actually transferred to high-energy phosphate bonds of ATP? Of the several hypotheses proposed to explain the coupling of electron transport and oxidative phosphorylation, the best experimental support has been provided for the *chemiosmotic hypothesis,* proposed in 1961 by Peter Mitchell of the Glynn Research Laboratories in England. For this contribution to science, Mitchell was awarded a Nobel Prize in 1978.

According to the chemiosmotic hypothesis, electrons derived from the decomposition of nutrient fuels are transferred first to an electron acceptor called *nicotinamide adenine dinucleotide* (NAD), a coenzyme derived at least in part from one of the B vitamins. The reduced molecule of NAD (NAD_{red}) then moves into the mitochondrial matrix. Here it contacts flavoprotein (FP), mentioned above, the first electron acceptor built into the inner mitochondrial membrane (Fig. 12.6). FP accepts two electrons from NAD_{red}. FP simultaneously binds two hydrogen ions (H^+) from the mitochondrial matrix. As a result, reduced FP (FPH_2) contains two whole hydrogen atoms more than when it was oxidized.

The next carrier in the respiratory assembly is a protein called Fe•S. It can accept electrons from the two hydrogen atoms of FPH_2, but it does not accept the protons of these atoms (proton and hydrogen ion are synonymous). Instead, the protons are pumped against a concentration gradient through the inner membrane of the mitochondrion into the O compartment. Electrons of reduced Fe•S then are passed to *coenzyme Q,* a complex ring-shaped molecule embedded entirely inside the inner

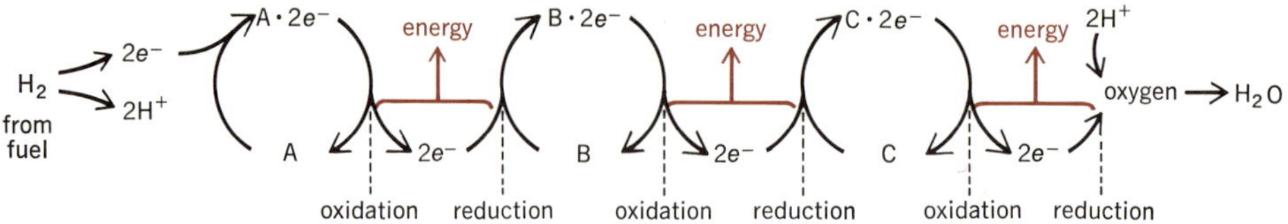

Fig. 12.4 ATP production. Production of ATP through electron transport and oxidative phosphorylation. During electron transport, electrons from hydrogen atoms of fuel molecules are passed along a chain of electron carriers (symbolized as A, B, and C). Electron carriers operate cyclically and are alternately reduced and oxidized; and C · $2e^-$ is more stable than B · $2e^-$, which in turn is more stable than A · $2e^-$. The most stable compound appears at the last transfer, when hydrogen combines with oxygen and forms water. Electron transfer by carriers yields energy at each transfer step. Much of this energy is converted into high-energy phosphate bonds of ATP through oxidative phosphorylation.

membrane. Coenzyme Q also picks up two hydrogen ions from the mitochondrial matrix. Consequently, reduced coenzyme Q contains two whole hydrogen atoms more than when it was oxidized.

The next electron acceptor is the first of five *cytochrome* carriers, each slightly different from the others. Cytochromes are red iron-containing coenzymes, structurally similar to the iron-containing portion of hemoglobin in red blood corpuscles. Like Fe·S, all the cytochromes can accept electrons, but none become bound to protons transferred from the preceding carrier. Thus, *cytochrome b,* the first of the five cytochrome carriers, only accepts two electrons from coenzyme Q. The protons of the transferred hydrogen atoms are pumped through the inner membrane to the O compartment.

Fig. 12.5 Mitochondria. Structural relationships between outer and inner mitochondrial membranes, O and M compartments, and F_1 particles are shown. As discussed more fully in the text, submitochondrial vesicles have yielded considerable information about the function of respiratory assemblies. Note that the M side of the inner membrane, distinguished by F_1 particles, is exposed on the outer surface of the vesicle.

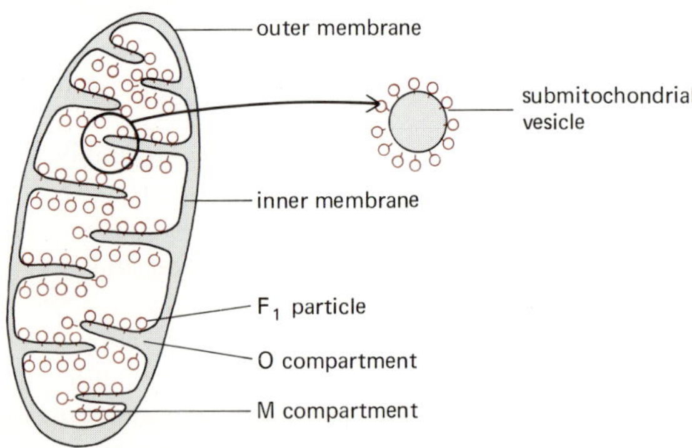

As presumed by Mitchell's hypothesis, electrons zigzag across the inner membrane 3 times as they pass along the entire chain of electron carriers in a respiratory assembly. Each time, proton-binding carriers pick up hydrogen ions from the M compartment of the mitochondrion and release them into the O compartment. This pumping of protons against a concentration gradient clearly requires energy. Such energy is generated by the redox reactions that occur as electrons are passed successively along the chain of carriers.

Since most of the inner mitochondrial membrane is not permeable to protons, these positively charged particles thus accumulate in the O compartment. The proton gradient existing between the O and M compartments now constitutes a reservoir of potential energy. If the protons could be made to flow "downhill" (from a higher to lower energy level; see Chap. 3 for a discussion of chemical energetics) through the inner membrane from the O to the M compartment, energy would be released. This energy could be "captured" by the cell and used to carry out a wide variety of cellular functions. That is precisely what the Mitchell hypothesis assumes.

Narrow corridors have been found in the inner mitochondrial membrane that are permeable to protons. Such channels are formed by proteins that extend from one side of the inner membrane to the other (*F_o particles* in Fig. 12.6). Globular structures, called *F_1 particles* (F for "factor"), normally protrude from F_o particles into the M compartment. Because of their comparatively large size, individual F_1 particles can be discerned with the electron microscope (Fig. 12.7).

Under certain experimental conditions it is possible to remove F_1 particles from the inner mito-

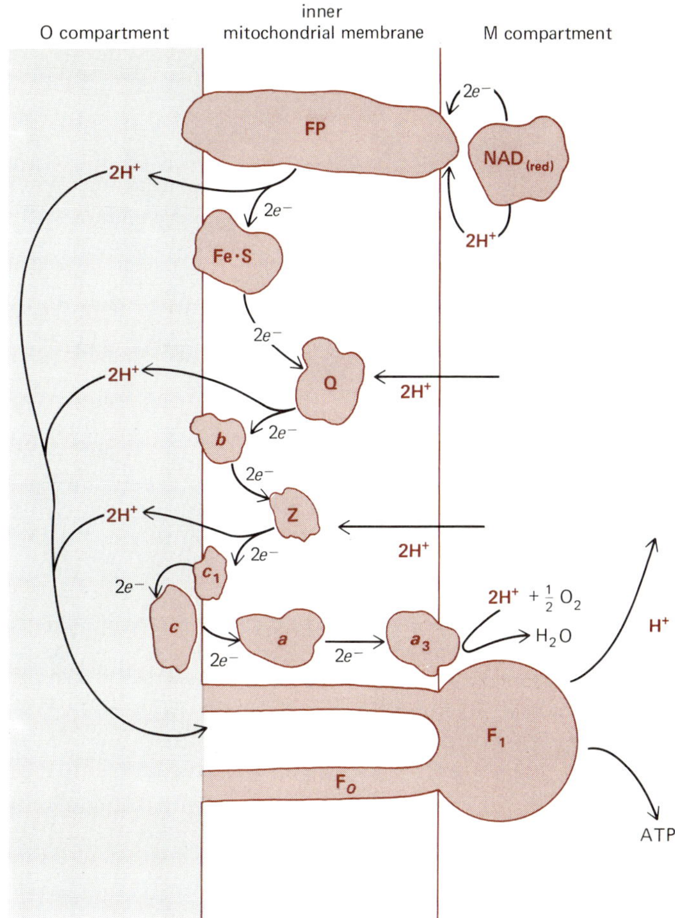

Fig. 12.6 Chemiosmotic hypothesis: pathway of proton and electron transfer. This incomplete and partly hypothetical model shows the arrangement of some electron carriers in a respiratory assembly. Fe · S is an iron-containing protein; Q is coenzyme Q; *b, c,* c_1, *a,* and a_3 are cytochromes; Z is a hypothetical carrier that binds protons from the mitochondrial matrix; F_O and F_1 denote position of an F_O and F_1 particle, respectively. Flavoprotein (FP) becomes reduced when it accepts a pair of electrons from reduced NAD (NAD_{red}). FP also accepts a pair of protons. Reduced FP transfers two hydrogen atoms, but Fe · S, the next carrier, accepts only the electrons. The two protons are pumped into the O compartment. Reduced Fe · S passes the electron pair to coenzyme Q, which also accepts a pair of protons from the mitochondrial matrix. Coenzyme Q transfers the electrons to cytochrome *b,* two protons being pumped to the outside. Electrons are then passed to Z, which simultaneously binds to two protons from the M compartment. Z then passes the electrons to cytochrome *c.* The two protons that were accepted by Z are pumped to the outside. The electrons are then passed through the remaining cytochromes to cytochrome a_3. Electrons are finally transferred to oxygen, which unites with two protons, forming water. Protons pumped into the O compartment can return to the M compartment only through channels provided by F_O particles. Energy released by the "downhill" flow of protons through F_O particles is used to drive ATP synthesis. Production of ATP is catalyzed by ATPase, an enzyme making up F_1 particles. Theoretically, three molecules of ATP can be made by the transfer of a pair of electrons along the entire chain of carriers.

chondrial membrane. Cell biologists have determined that inner membranes denuded of F_1 particles still can transport electrons but cannot manufacture ATP. On the other hand, isolated F_1 particles can split high-energy phosphate bonds of ATP but cannot produce these bonds. When F_1 particles are reunited with denuded inner membrane, coupling of electron transport and oxidative phosphorylation is reestablished. Observations of this kind have prompted the conclusion that F_1 particles are composed of *ATPase,* an enzyme that catalyzes both the formation and splitting of high-energy phosphate bonds of ATP. The chemiosmotic hypothesis postulates that the energy required for formation of the high-energy bonds is generated by the downhill flow of protons through F_o particles.

A substantial amount of evidence supports the chemiosmotic hypothesis. Some of the most convincing has been derived from experiments with *submitochondrial vesicles* (see Fig. 12.5), structures which are produced when mitochondria are fragmented by treatment with certain detergents or by exposure to high-frequency sonic irradiation. Fragmented sections of inner membranes turn inside out and coalesce, forming small vesicles. The inside-out eversion causes F_1 particles to project to the *outside* of submitochondrial vesicles. Because of the reversed organization of inner membranes, the chemiosmotic hypothesis predicts that protons should be pumped into the interior of these spherical structures. This prediction has been verified experimentally.

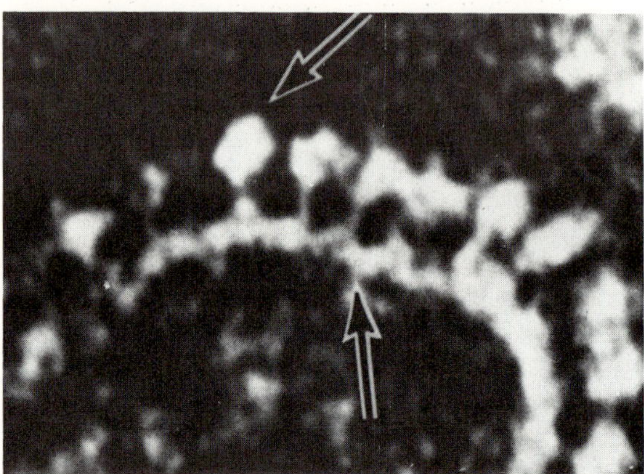

Fig. 12.7 F_1 particles. Highly enlarged portion of a crista (in beef heart muscle), showing array of stalked F_1 particles. Upper arrow points to head piece of a particle, which projects into the M compartment of the mitochondrion. The knoblike heads are attached by a thin stalk to the inner surface of the cristae membranes (lower arrow). F_1 particles contain ATPase, the ATP-forming enzyme.

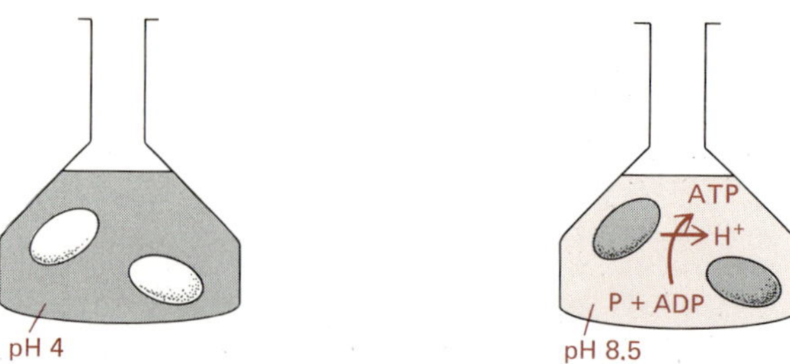

Fig. 12.8 Proton gradients and ATP synthesis. Left, chloroplasts are suspended in an acid bath until their internal hydrogen-ion concentration comes into equilibrium with that of the external environment. Right, the chloroplasts are then transferred to a basic medium. The hydrogen-ion concentration in the chloroplasts initially is greater than in the surrounding medium. Consequently, a proton gradient exists between the inside and outside of the chloroplasts. Energy released by the flow of protons out of chloroplasts is used in the attachment of phosphate units (P) to ADP, forming ATP.

Mitchell's hypothesis also states that the inner membranes of mitochondria must be impermeable to protons except where F_0 particles reside, and this too has been documented experimentally. A leakage of protons through other segments of the membrane would dissipate the reservoir of potential energy established by a proton gradient. Some chemicals do increase the proton permeability of the inner membrane and, as predicted by the chemiosmotic hypothesis, such chemicals greatly reduce or eliminate ATP production through oxidative phosphorylation.

Other experiments have demonstrated that the "downhill" flow of protons across a living membrane can drive ATP synthesis. One of these experiments uses chloroplasts, as the chemiosmotic hypothesis also purports to explain how ATP is generated by electron transport during photosynthesis (see Chap. 13). Chloroplasts are first suspended in an acidic solution having a pH of 4 (Fig. 12.8). After a few minutes, the concentration of hydrogen ions (protons) in the interior of the suspended chloroplasts comes into equilibrium with the solution. The chloroplasts are then moved to a basic medium having a pH of 8.5. Initially, the interior of a transferred chloroplast contains a higher concentration of protons than the external alkaline environment. Thus, a proton gradient will have been established between the inside and outside of the organelles. Biologists have shown that protons move out of chloroplasts under such conditions. The experimenters also have demonstrated that the downhill flow of protons across the membranes of chloroplasts drives the synthesis of ATP.

Biologists are now discovering that the "downhill" flow of protons across gradients energize far more cellular work than was once supposed. For example, energy supplied by the "downhill" flow of protons often is essential for movement of ions and certain other substances across living membranes. This flow even provides energy for certain mechanical processes, such as the rotation of bacterial flagella (see Chaps. 5 and 30).

Respiration: Two Interrelated Processes

In summary, respiration as a whole can be said to consist of two interrelated processes, *fuel decomposition* and *energy transfer*. The first occurs when a nutrient is decomposed by a series of redox reactions. Fuel molecules are degraded completely to CO_2, and hydrogen is released as a result of fuel decomposition.

Energy transfer occurs in two general ways. The first, and least important in terms of total ATP harvested, takes place when high-energy phosphate bonds are produced on fuel molecules and subsequently transferred to ADP. The second occurs when the electrons of hydrogen atoms removed from nutrient fuels are passed along a chain of electron carriers. Such chains are positioned in a highly ordered fashion along the inner membranes of mitochondria.

This second energy transfer takes place only if oxygen is available in mitochondria; oxygen acts as the final acceptor of transferred electrons. Energy, produced by the redox reactions of electron transport, is used to pump protons through the inner membrane of mitochondria, from the M to the O compartment, establishing a proton gradient across the inner membrane. Protons evidently can flow back to the M compartment only through special channels in the inner membrane. Energy released from the downhill flow of these protons is then used to drive ATP synthesis.

Aerobic and Anaerobic Respiration

Any pattern of electron transport in which oxygen is the final electron acceptor constitutes an *aerobic* (with air) form of respiration. It is the standard, universal form of respiration in the vast majority of organisms.

In aerobes, if any one of the aerobic electron-transport reactions were stopped, the whole electron-transport sequence would become inoperative and the energy it normally supplies to produce ATP would remain unavailable. Reaction blocks actually can occur in a number of ways. For example, *inhibitor* substances of various kinds can interfere specifically with particular transport reactions. Thus, cyanides specifically inhibit the cytochromes, and this is why cyanides are poisons. Another form of reaction block occurs if one of the hydrogen carriers is in deficient supply. For example, inasmuch as niacin (a vitamin of the B group) is a structural part of the NAD molecule (see Fig. 4.16), a consistently niacin-deficient diet would soon impair the reactions in which NAD participates.

Although cyanide poisoning and vitamin B deficiencies are not particularly common hazards, all organisms frequently must contend with inadequate supplies of atmospheric oxygen. Lack of oxygen is a reaction block of the same sort as cyanide poisoning or vitamin deficiencies, with the consequence that aerobic respiration as a whole stops. Whenever electron transport to oxygen is blocked, organisms can respire in a way that does not require oxygen. This *anaerobic* (without air) respiration

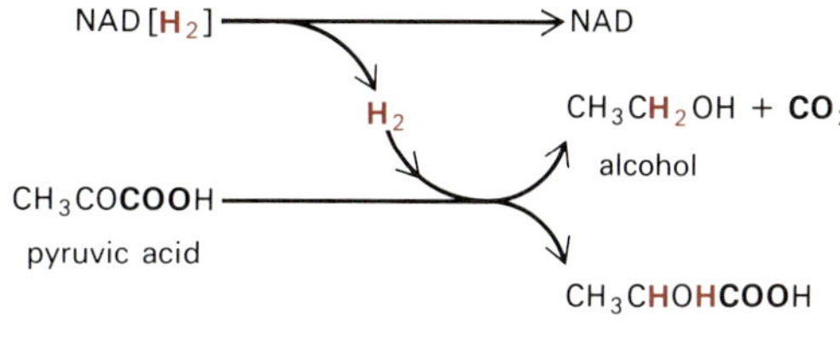

Fig. 12.9 Anaerobic respiration. Pyruvic acid accepts hydrogen from NAD and becomes either alcohol and CO_2 in plants and most microorganisms or lactic acid in animals and certain bacteria. Different enzymes in these two sets of organisms account for the different results.

functions as an auxilliary source of energy for most aerobes, people included; but—as will become apparent shortly—anaerobic respiration by itself generates far too little ATP to maintain life in all but the most simply constructed organisms.

Several forms of anaerobic respiration, or *fermentation,* have been discovered in a wide variety of organisms. Among aerobes, fermentation reactions constitute a preparatory step for further decomposition reactions that are oxygen-dependent. The principle underlying all fermentations is relatively simple. With the path from NAD to oxygen blocked, another path must be used. Such an alternative path is provided by *pyruvic acid,* one of the compounds normally formed in the course of carbohydrate respiration (see below). If enough oxygen is available, pyruvic acid is merely one of the intermediate steps in the decomposition of carbohydrates to CO_2. But pyruvic acid has the property of reacting readily with hydrogen atoms, including those derived from the dehydrogenation of fuel molecules. In circumstances where electron transport and oxidative phosphorylation do not function, pyruvic acid ceases to be a fuel and becomes an acceptor of hydrogen.

When pyruvic acid reacts with hydrogen, the result is the formation of alcohol and CO_2 in plants and most microorganisms, and the formation of lactic acid in animals and certain bacteria (Fig. 12.9). This reaction completes anaerobic respiration; alcohol or lactic acid accumulates in a cell and eventually diffuses to the outside.

The relatively small amounts of ATP that are generated during anaerobic respiration suffice to maintain the life of yeast, bacteria, and other relatively small organisms that can or must survive

Biology Highlight

Wine and Beer: Case Studies in the Commercial Exploitation of Yeasts

Human exploitation of yeasts has been going on now for several thousand years. So long, in fact, that no one can remember when it all began. Of course, yeasts have long been used in baking and, more recently, in making home-made root beer, but to many many people the use of yeasts in the development of alcoholic beverages is a matter of far greater import.

The discovery of the first fermented brew is obscured by myths and legends. According to people of the Cyclades, a group of islands north of Crete, the first wine was produced and consumed by St. Dionysius. In one story this legendary saint describes a journey he took from Mount Olympus, in northern Greece, to Naxos, the largest island of the Cyclades. During the journey, he supposedly discovered a beautiful plant growing by the roadside. Captivated by its beauty, he picked it and then placed it in the hollowed-out bone of a bird to protect it from the sun. Before St. Dionysius had traveled much farther, the plant grew larger. To protect it better he placed it, bone and all, in the bone of a lion. The plant still grew, so St. Dionysius placed his treasure into the legbone of an ass.

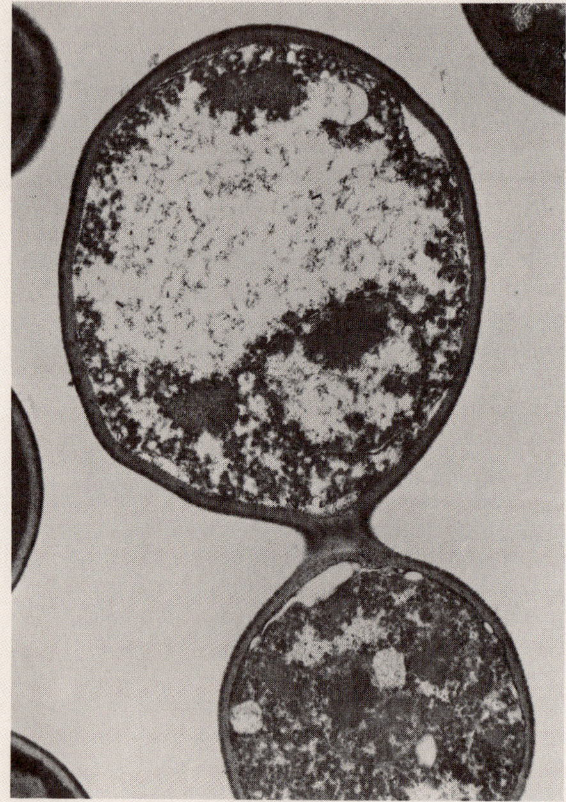

Fig. 1 Brewer's yeast. These cells are *Saccharomyces carlsbergensis*. In the right hands, this strain can produce a delectable brew. Note the connection between the two cells. The smaller cell at the bottom has been produced from the top cell by a form of reproduction called budding (see Chap. 22).

On reaching Naxos, St. Dionysius discovered that his plant had rooted so firmly in the bones that he had no choice but to plant everything in the ground. After a short while, the plant sprouted a vine and produced fruit, from which St. Dionysius made the first wine. Legend says that when he had consumed a little of his freshly fermented liquid, St. Dionysius sang like a bird; when he drank a little more, he felt as strong as a lion; but when he consumed too much, he became as foolish as an ass.

The inebriating effects of alcohol probably were discovered by someone who left the juice of crushed fruit exposed to air. The lower atmosphere carries many wild yeast spores, which quickly reproduce in any open vessel containing fermentable sugars. Such uncontrolled fermentations generally yield harsh, sour beverages. We would turn our noses up at most of the alcoholic liquids relished by our distant forebears. Gradually people became more adept at culturing yeasts that produce good-tasting wines and beers (Fig. 1). Maintaining stocks of such yeasts is a major concern of modern wine makers and brewers. Just the thought of losing a prime strain of yeasts is enough to give a wine maker or brewer nightmares. Moreover, the fermentation and aging of many wines and beers is now monitored by some of the most sophisticated technology ever developed.

The basic raw material for wines is *must,* the slightly acid, sugar-containing juices of grapes. Must is first sterilized to kill populations of undesirable yeasts and other microorganisms present in the raw juice. Following sterilization, the must is innoculated with special strains of wine yeasts and placed in vats to ferment (Fig. 2).

The type of wine produced depends not only on the variety of grape and the strain of yeast but also on the procedures carried out during and following fermentation. For example, fermentation is halted earlier in the production of "sweet" wines compared with "dry" wines. Since yeast has more time to convert sugar to alcohol, dry wines characteristically are more pungent and contain less sugar than sweet varieties. Like all organisms, yeasts have limited tolerance to alcohol, and most strains are killed when the concentration of alcohol in the fermentation keg reaches approximately 12 per cent. Wines, such as sherry or port, that contain substantially higher concentrations of alcohol are called *fortified* wines. Alcohol is added to such wines to obtain these higher concentrations.

Some champagnes and sparkling wines are carbonated naturally by the CO_2 that results from fermentation. However, most inexpensive sparkling wines sold today are carbonated artificially. The CO_2 of fermentation is permitted to escape from most wines, which are called *still wines*.

Following fermentation, wine is aged, red wines generally longer than white wines. Many of the subtle differences between wines result from chemical reactions that occur during the aging process. Since some of these reactions require oxygen, a small amount of air is permitted to mix with wine during aging. Too much oxygen, however, can spoil wines. All aging wines contain small populations of *acetic acid bacteria* capable of oxidizing ethyl alcohol to acetic acid and water.

$$\underset{\text{ethyl alcohol}}{C_2H_5OH} + O_2 \longrightarrow \underset{\text{acetic acid}}{CH_3COOH} + H_2O$$

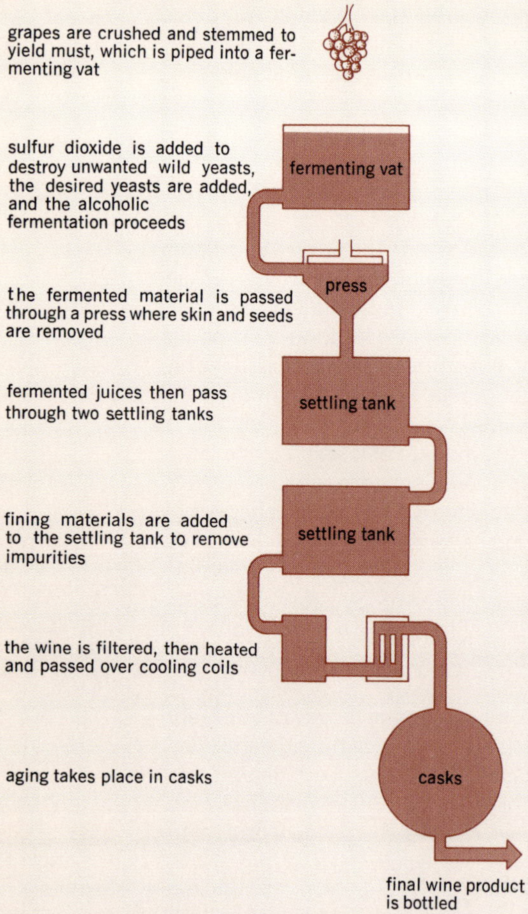

grapes are crushed and stemmed to yield must, which is piped into a fermenting vat

sulfur dioxide is added to destroy unwanted wild yeasts, the desired yeasts are added, and the alcoholic fermentation proceeds

fermenting vat

press

the fermented material is passed through a press where skin and seeds are removed

fermented juices then pass through two settling tanks

settling tank

settling tank

fining materials are added to the settling tank to remove impurities

the wine is filtered, then heated and passed over cooling coils

aging takes place in casks

casks

final wine product is bottled

Fig. 2 The production of red wine. Commercial wine production in the United States follows this general scheme.

Acetic acid is the principal component of vinegar. If the concentration of oxygen in an aging wine becomes too great, its population of acetic acid bacteria grows rapidly and produces sour wine. Although detrimental to wine production, this process has been exploited in the production of many types of vinegar.

The sugar-rich counterpart of must in the production of beers and ales is a liquid called *wort,* made chiefly from barley seeds. The seeds typically are spread out in a large, specially designed room and then moistened and warmed to induce germination. During the initial stages of germination, carbohydrases and proteases are produced. These enzymes convert carbohydrates and proteins, respectively, to sugars and amino acids (see Chap. 4), smaller molecules normally used as respiratory fuels and as building blocks for the development of the barley seedlings. However, brewers raise temperatures sharply shortly after germination begins, thus stopping the process before many sugars and amino acids have been produced.

Because maltose is one of the principal sugars produced from starch in germinating barley, this first step in the production of wort is called *malting.* The main purpose of malting is to generate carbohydrases and proteases, which catalyze most of the chemical reactions that occur during *mashing,* the second step of wort production.

Mashing begins when the partly germinated barley seeds, or *malt,* are ground to a predetermined particle size and mixed with water in a large vessel called a *mash tun* (Fig. 3). The ion content, pH, and temperature of the mixture are carefully adjusted during mashing. Ion concentrations typically are altered through addition of calcium salts, such as calcium chloride or calcium sulfate; pH often is adjusted by adding sulfuric acid, phosphoric acid, or lactic acid to the mash.

Such adjustments not only ensure the constant taste of a particular brand of beer but also facilitate enzymatic reactions. Different enzymes function best at different temperatures, pH levels, and ion concentrations. Temperatures of 100 to 120°F, for example, are optimum for many proteases, but temperatures of 145 to 160°F are optimum for most *amylases,* enzymes that degrade starches. Many brewers also add corn grits, rice, or millet during mashing, ingredients that mainly increase the concentration of starches and sugars in the mashing tun.

Mashing concludes when the temperature of the mash is raised to approximately 170 to 175°F. Such temperatures denature enzymes, halting most of the chemical reactions in the mashing tun. Before mashing, the amount of protein and carbohydrate in malt is about 13 and 78 per cent respectively. Most of the carbohydrates are starches. After mashing, about two-fifths of the original protein has been converted to amino acids and small polypeptides; about 95 per cent of the starches have been degraded to small carbohydrate polymers and simple sugars.

During *lautering,* the final step in the production of wort, mash is pumped into a vessel called a *lauter tun.* Here dissolved sugars, proteins, polypeptides, amino acids, and other valuable substances are separated from husks of barley seeds and other by-products. The sugar-rich liquid portion, wort, is then boiled in a large *brew kettle* for about $1\frac{1}{2}$ to 2 hours (Fig. 4).

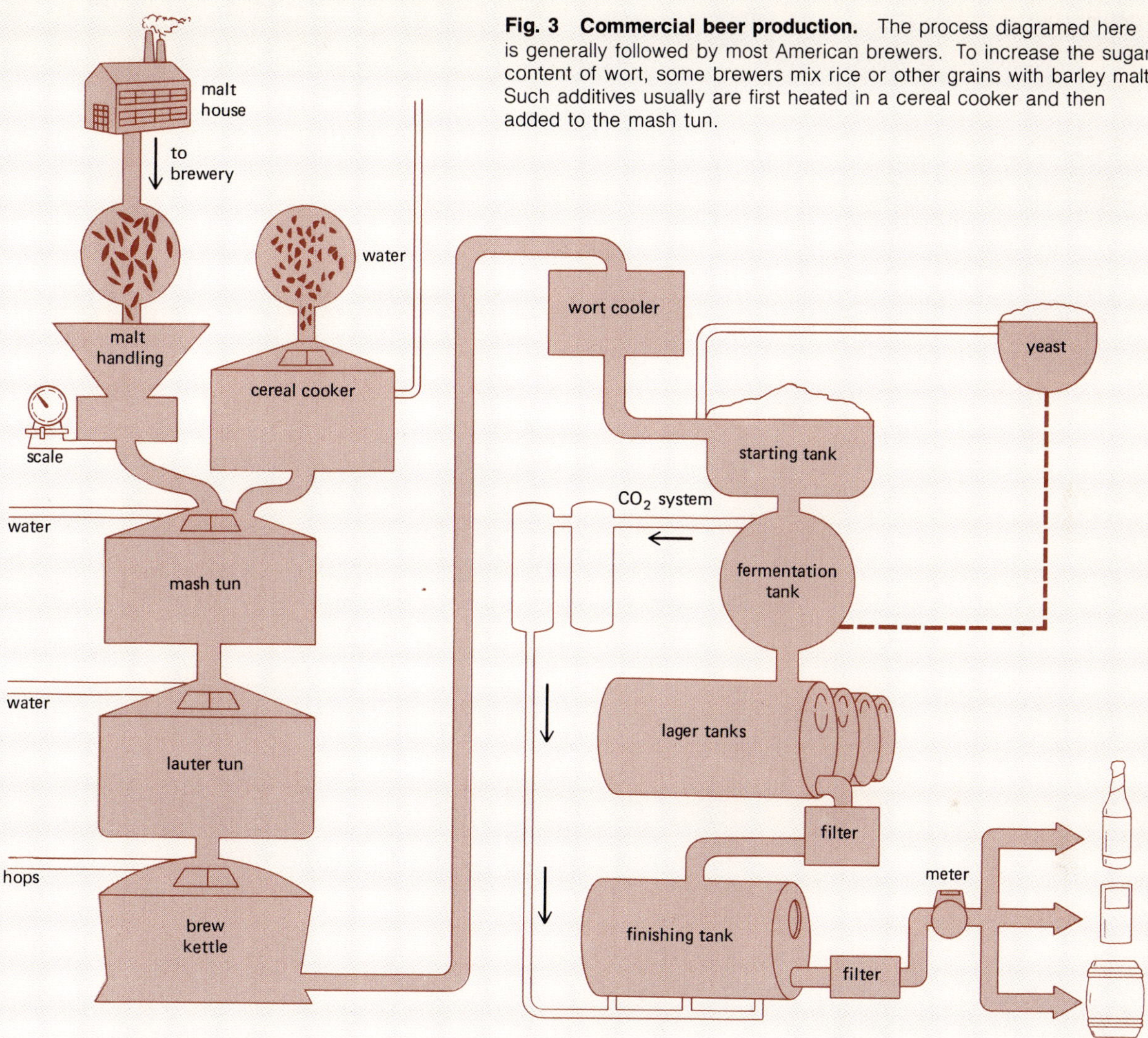

Fig. 3 Commercial beer production. The process diagramed here is generally followed by most American brewers. To increase the sugar content of wort, some brewers mix rice or other grains with barley malt. Such additives usually are first heated in a cereal cooker and then added to the mash tun.

Hops, which are flowers of the plant *Humulus lupulus,* are added to wort during kettle boiling. A resinous substance, *lupulin,* occurs in concentrated form at the junction of the flower petals and stems. During kettle boiling, acids present in lupulin are transformed to substances that impart the characteristic bitter flavor of beer. Many brewers no longer use whole, fresh hops; hop extracts are used instead.

The hopped wort is then cooled and transferred to a fermentation tank (see Fig. 3). A carefully maintained strain of brewer's yeast is added, and fermentation begins. Fermentation time and temperature are strictly controlled. In some of the largest breweries, fermentation and other aspects of the brewing process are regulated and monitored by computer. After fermentation, most beers are stored in large *lager tanks* at tempera-

Fig. 4 Brew kettles. Richard Yuengling, president of D. G. Yuengling and Sons Inc., checks one of his company's brew kettles at the Pottsville, Pennsylvania, brewery. Yuengling claims that his is the oldest brewery in America.

tures near 32°F, almost 20 degrees colder than normal fermenting temperatures (Fig. 5). The term *lager* is derived from a German verb meaning "to store," and all true lager beers are stored and aged for about 14 days to 3 months or more.

During storage, some of the larger proteins settle out, clarifying the beer. The aging process also yields a generally better-tasting beer. Aged beer is further clarified to remove any remaining suspended ingredients that might make it hazy. Clarifying procedures vary. Some breweries, for example, add substances that bond with proteins and other suspended materials chemically, forming large complexes that settle out of the beer. Other clarifying procedures involve filtering or centrifuging beer to remove suspended proteins.

Clarifying processes do not remove all proteins from beer. In fact, complete removal of proteins would harm the beer. A certain percentage of suspended proteins is essential if a beer is to have good heading properties when poured. Some beers consistently fail to produce and maintain a rich, creamy head because of an insufficient concentration of suspended proteins.

Fig. 5 Lagering. A worker at an Anheuser-Busch brewery places beechwood chips into a "torpedo," which then will be inserted into one of the huge stainless steel lager tanks shown in the background. The surfaces of the beechwood chips support large populations of yeasts during lagering.

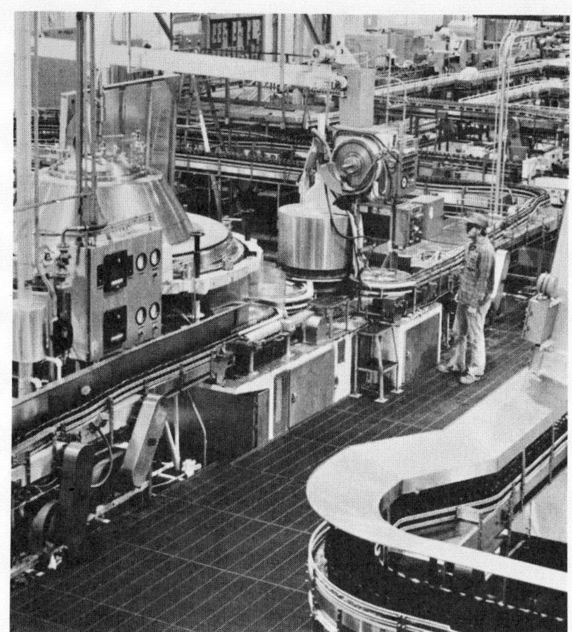

Fig. 6 Bottling and packaging. Bottles and cans of beer are filled and sealed in efficient assembly-line fashion at all modern breweries. Shown here is part of the bottling process at an Anheuser-Busch plant.

Fig. 7 Draught beer. Some 360 kegs of beer are filled and bunged (sealed) hourly on this draught line of an Anheuser-Busch brewery.

Beer is carbonated before being put in bottles, cans, or kegs. Some brewers generate this CO_2 by adding wort to the lager tanks. Sugars in the wort trigger a vigorous secondary fermentation. The CO_2 of these beers is a by-product of this secondary fermentation. Most brewers, however, inject CO_2 into beer much as soft-drink manufacturers carbonate their beverages.

Finished beer to be marketed in cans or bottles is *pasteurized* before packaging (Fig. 6). This treatment, which involves heating beer to about 140°F, kills any microorganisms that might spoil the beer. Draught beer is not pasteurized but put in kegs, which must be refrigerated to prevent spoilage (Fig. 7).

Production of fermented beverages has come a long way since St. Dionysius set out for Naxos from the monastery on Mount Olympus. Without modern technology, brewers and wine makers could not begin to satisfy the current demand for good, moderately priced beers and wines. But in some respects, things have not changed much. Yeasts remain, as always, the essential ingredient.

without oxygen. The ability of yeast to decompose nutrient fuels to ethyl alcohol (C_2H_5OH) and CO_2 has been exploited in the production of vinegar and all alcoholic beverages (see accompanying Biology Highlight), but the energy yield of anaerobic respiration by itself is insufficient to sustain life in most aerobes. As is well known, such organisms die within minutes if oxygen is unavailable. Even so, fermentation nevertheless can *supplement* the aerobic energy gains. Whenever energy demands are high, as during intensive muscular activity in animals, the oxygen supply to the cells may become insufficient despite faster breathing. Under such conditions of *oxygen debt,* fermentation can proceed in parallel with aerobic respiration and provide a little extra energy. During a later rest period, faster breathing at first continues. The oxygen debt is thereby repaid, the extra oxygen permitting a complete oxidation of the accumulated lactic acid.

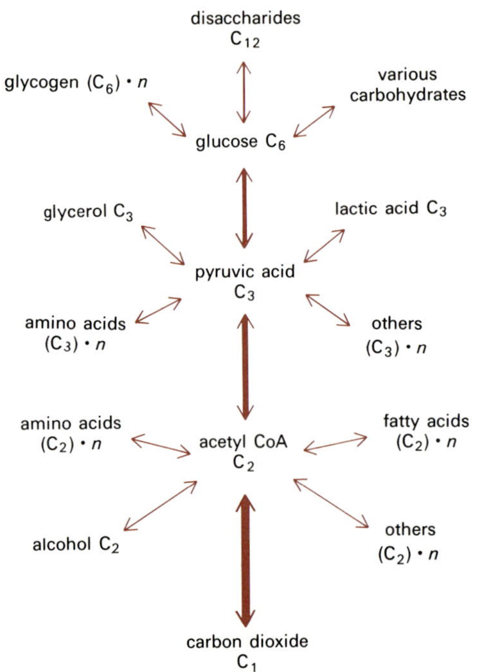

Fig. 12.10 Pathways in respiration. Pyruvic acid, acetyl CoA, and carbon dioxide form a main sequence that other pathways join, like branches of a tree. (*n* stands for a large, undesignated number of units.)

THE PROCESS

In the course of being decomposed progressively, nutrient molecules lose their carbons one at a time, until sooner or later the entire molecule is converted to 1-carbon (C_1) fragments, or CO_2. If we follow the decomposition sequence backward, the next-to-last stage in fuel breakdown should be a C_2 fragment. This is the case; every fuel molecule sooner or later appears as a 2-carbon fragment, namely, as an *acetyl* group ($CH_3C{=}O$), a derivative of acetic acid. Acetyl groups do not exist by themselves but are attached to a carrier coenzyme called *coenzyme A* or CoA. An acetyl group joined to CoA is *acetyl CoA* (CH_3CO—CoA).

How the acetyl CoA stage is reached differs for different types of fuels. For example, many carbohydrates are first broken up into 3-carbon compounds. Complex carbohydrates often are built up from 3-carbon units, and their carbon numbers then are whole multiples of 3. This holds, for example, for glucose and all other 6-carbon sugars, for 12-carbon disaccharides, and for polysaccharides such as starch and glycogen. When any of these are used as respiratory fuels, the original 3-carbon units reappear in the course of breakdown. All such C_3 units eventually are converted to *pyruvic acid,* the common 3-carbon stage in respiration. Pyruvic acid then loses one carbon in the form of CO_2 and becomes acetyl CoA. Fatty acids and related molecules do not break up into 3-carbon units but become 2-carbon units directly, and these eventually appear as acetyl CoA. Amino acids break down partly to pyruvic acid (which subsequently becomes acetyl CoA) and partly to acetyl CoA directly. This holds also for many other substances used as fuel.

Thus, the overall pattern of aerobic fuel combustion may be likened to a tree with branches or to a river with tributaries (Fig. 12.10). A broad main channel is represented by the sequence pyruvic acid → acetyl CoA → carbon dioxide. Numerous side channels lead into this sequence, some funneling into the C_3 pyruvic acid step, others into the C_2 acetyl CoA step. In the end, the flow from the entire system drains out as C_1 carbon dioxide. It is best to discuss this common last step first, namely, the decomposition of acetyl CoA (2 carbons) to carbon dioxide (1 carbon).

Formation of CO_2

The breakdown of the C_2 acetyl fragment in the mitochondria of cells takes the form of a *cycle* of enzymatic reactions. Acetyl CoA is funneled in at one point of the cycle, two carbons emerge at other points as CO_2, and the starting condition is eventually regenerated. The whole sequence is known as the *citric acid cycle,* after one of the participating compounds, or as the *Krebs cycle,* after its discoverer. Most of the enzymes that catalyze reactions of the citric acid cycle are located in the matrix (M compartment) of mitochondria.

A simple, condensed representation of the cycle (Fig. 12.11) shows that acetyl CoA first interacts with water and with *oxaloacetic acid,* a C_4 molecule normally present in the mitochondria of a cell (step 1 in Fig. 12.11). The result is the formation of free CoA and the C_6 compound *citric acid.* In a following series of reactions (step 2), this acid loses 1 H_2 and 1 CO_2 and becomes *ketoglutaric acid,* a C_5 compound. In a further series of reactions (step 3), ketoglutaric acid loses CO_2 in its turn, yielding the C_4 compound *succinic acid.* Through a final sequence (step 4), succinic acid eventually becomes rearranged to oxaloacetic acid, the same C_4 compound that started the cycle.

In the whole sequence, the raw materials are one molecule of acetyl CoA and three molecules of water. The end products are two CO_2 (which represent the two carbons fed into the cycle at the start as acetyl), free CoA, and four H_2. The electrons of the eight hydrogen atoms are passed along the chain of electron carriers inside the inner mitochondrial membrane. The energy thereby released is used to generate ATP by oxidative phosphorylation. Altogether, a total of 12 molecules of ATP are generated for every acetyl processed through the citric acid cycle. In summary

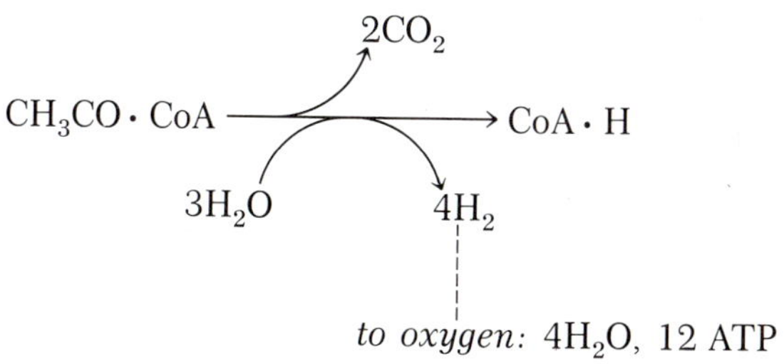

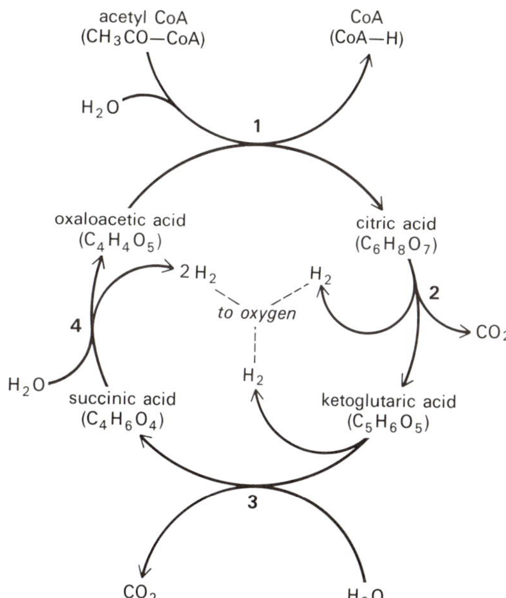

Fig. 12.11 The citric acid cycle, greatly simplified.

As pointed out earlier, acetyl groups generally form by respiratory decomposition of various nutrients. How do such foods become acetyl, and how are they thereby funneled to the citric acid cycle;

Carbohydrate Respiration

Glycolysis

Carbohydrate fuels are first converted to pyruvic acid, a common C_3 stage, as already noted. In this conversion, called *glycolysis,* polysaccharides, such as starch or glycogen, are initially split up and phosphorylated to glucose phosphate. If free glucose is used as fuel, it too becomes glucose phosphate through phosphorylation by ATP. Glucose phosphate is therefore a common early stage of glycolysis. Its further transformation to pyruvic acid is outlined in Fig. 12.12.

This figure shows that the reaction sequence includes, first, a series of additional phosphorylations; —P groups become attached at *each* end of the C_6 chain of glucose-phosphate. Then the chain splits into two C_3 chains, and two more —P groups become attached, one to each free end of these C_3 compounds. Next, in successive oxidations, all —P groups now present are transformed to ~P

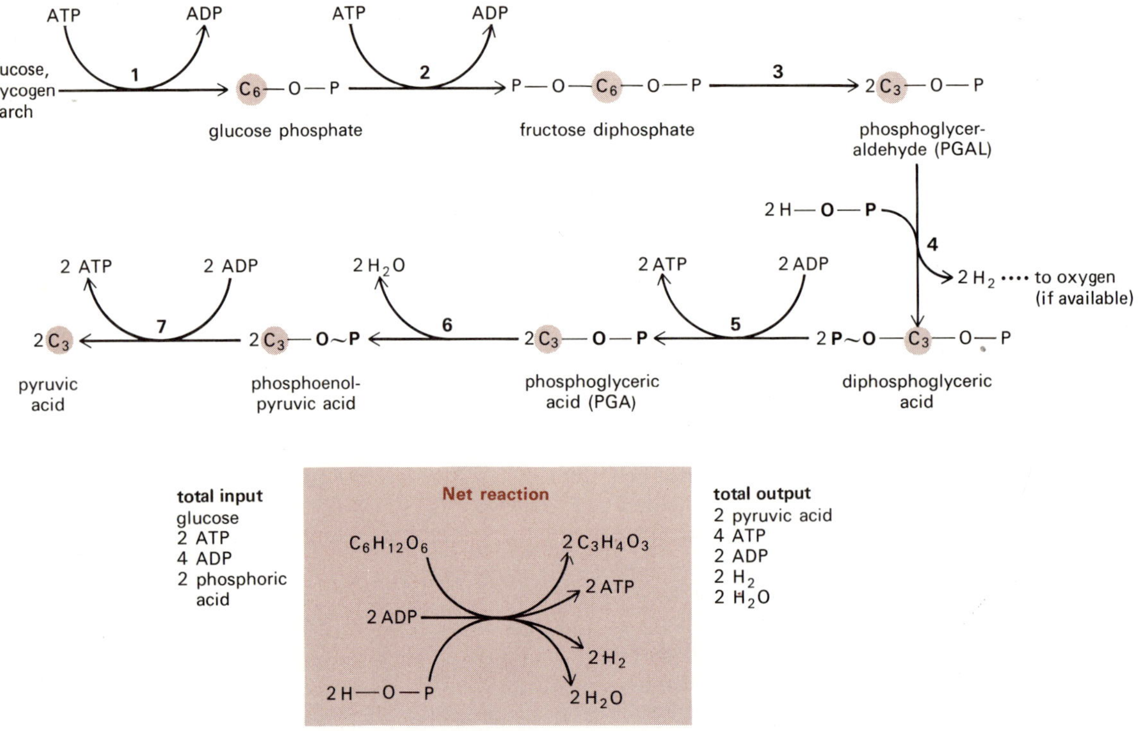

Fig. 12.12 Glycolysis. The nine actual steps are shown here simplified and abbreviated as seven, and the structure of the participating compounds is indicated only in the form of carbon numbers. In step 4, the —P added by phosphoric acid becomes a high-energy phosphate, which is then transferred to ATP (step 5). Step 4 also yields 2 H_2. The electrons of these atoms are transported by carriers to oxygen. Through steps 4 and 5, phosphoglyceraldehyde (PGAL) becomes an acid (PGA). In step 6 oxidative removal of water produces another high-energy phosphate, transferred again to ATP (step 7). The summary below the reaction sequence assumes that free glucose is the starting fuel and that 2 ATP must therefore be expended in the preliminary phosphorylations (steps 1 and 2) for every 4 ATP gained at the end.

groups. And lastly, these high-energy phosphates are transferred to ADP. What is then left of the original fuel is a C_3 compound, pyruvic acid.

If free glucose is considered to be the original raw material, glycolysis includes four phosphorylations, two by ATP and two by the "pool" of phosphate ions dissolved in the cytoplasm. Each of the four added phosphates eventually becomes a high-energy phosphate. Of the four ATP then formed, two "pay back" for the two expended at the start of glycolysis, while two represent the net gain. The fate of the atoms in glucose can be described by the equation

$$C_6H_{12}O_6 \longrightarrow 2C_3H_4O_3 + 2H_2$$

The net loss of atoms from glucose therefore amounts to $2H_2$.

If respiration occurs under anaerobic conditions, the pyruvic acid formed must serve directly as the final hydrogen acceptor. Carbohydrate oxidation in this case stops with the formation of alcohol or lactic acid, and the 2 ATP gained represent the net energy yield of the entire process. But if conditions are aerobic, two desirable consequences follow.

First, the electrons of the four hydrogen atoms released during glycolysis can be transported to oxygen through electron transport, a transfer that yields three additional ATP molecules per H_2, or 6 ATP total. Second, since pyruvic acid need not

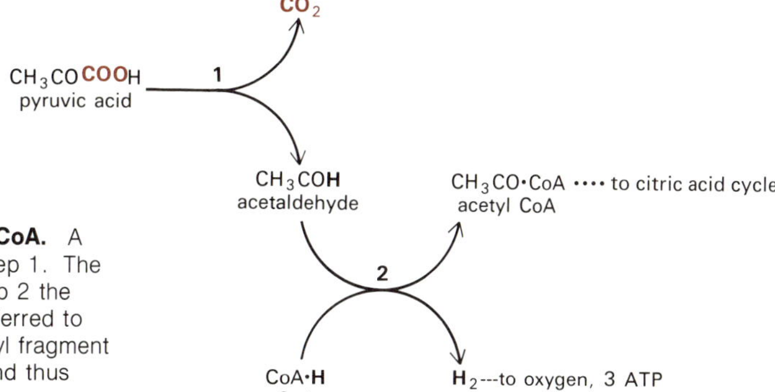

Fig. 12.13 Conversion of pyruvic acid to acetyl CoA. A molecule of CO_2 is removed from pyruvic acid in step 1. The resulting 2-carbon fragment is acetaldehyde. In step 2 the electrons of the released hydrogen atoms are transferred to oxygen via the electron-transport system. The acetyl fragment left after H_2 removal is accepted by coenzyme A, and thus acetyl CoA is formed.

serve as a hydrogen acceptor, it can be oxidized further and more of its chemical energy can become usable.

Pyruvic acid is transformed to acetyl CoA through a series of reactions in which two hydrogen atoms and CO_2 are removed from pyruvic acid (Fig. 12.13). In these reactions oxygen must be present to accept the electrons of the hydrogen atoms (transfer of these electrons through electron transport yields 3 ATP). Another required participant is CoA, which is the carrier of what is left of pyruvic acid after H_2 and CO_2 have been removed. This remnant is an acetyl group, and acetyl CoA arises in this manner.

Acetyl CoA can then be respired via the citric acid cycle, and we already know that 12 ATP are gained from one acetyl group. If it is therefore assumed that the original starting fuel is free glucose and that it is respired completely to CO_2, the aerobic energy yield can be shown to be 38 ATP, as outlined in Fig. 12.14. This represents an energy-trapping efficiency of 40 per cent, which is comparable to the best fuel-using engines. Such a net total contrasts sharply with an anaerobic yield of only 2 ATP, or about 5 per cent of the aerobic yield.

The Hexose Shunt

Many plant and animal cells have another pathway of glucose degradation involving neither glycolysis nor the citric acid cycle. Known as the *hexose shunt,* this oxidation process occurs in the free cytoplasm, and it too has the form of a complex cycle of reactions. Although it is not the main pathway by which energy is obtained from nutrients in most organisms, the hexose shunt does produce NADP[H_2], a molecule required for the synthesis of fatty acids and steroids. NADP[H_2] is

Fig. 12.14 Glucose respiration summary.

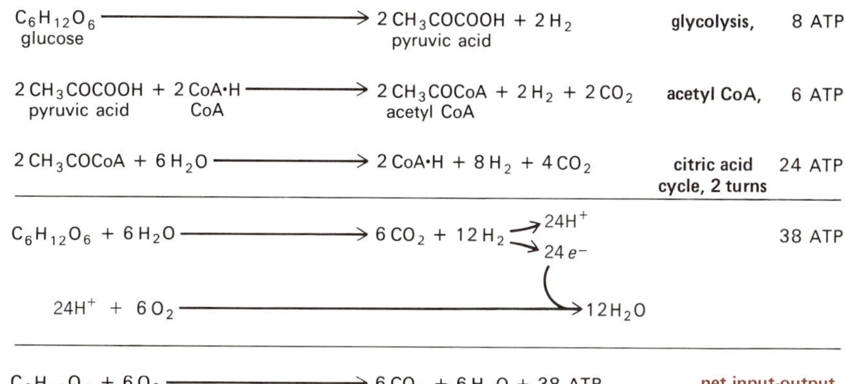

$$6\ \text{glucose—P} + 12\ \text{NADP} + 6\ H_2O \longrightarrow 5\ \text{glucose—P} + 12\ \text{NADP}[H_2] + 6\ CO_2 + P$$

$$6\ O_2 \longrightarrow 12\ \text{NADP} + 12\ H_2O$$

$$1\ \text{glucose—P} + 6\ O_2 \longrightarrow 6\ CO_2 + 6\ H_2O + P + 35\ \text{ATP} \quad \textbf{net input-output}$$

Fig. 12.15 The hexose shunt, summary. In a cyclical reaction sequence one out of six glucose-phosphate molecules is oxidized to CO_2 and H_2O.

reduced NADP, the latter being a phosphorylated form of NAD. The hexose shunt also converts hexoses to pentoses, and one of these 5-carbon sugars is required for the synthesis of nucleic acids. Consequently, this alternate respiratory pathway is more commonly used in tissues that synthesize large amounts of lipids, such as the liver, mammary gland, and adipose tissues, or in tissues where certain pentose sugars are in short supply. By contrast, the hexose shunt functions infrequently in skeletal muscle, which synthesizes only small amounts of fatty acids.

The hexose shunt is summarized in a highly condensed manner in Fig. 12.15. Pentose sugars and other intermediate products of the reaction sequence are not shown. The raw materials are water, NADP, and glucose phosphate, the latter representing the starting fuel. The end products are CO_2, free phosphate, H_2 held by NADP, and one less molecule of glucose phosphate than the number present at the start. In effect, one glucose phosphate has been decomposed to CO_2 and H_2, and the 12 hydrogen pairs are passed on to oxygen via NADP. This hydrogen transfer yields 36 ATP, of which one must pay back for the ATP used up in the conversion of free glucose to glucose phosphate. Thus the net energy yield is 35 ATP per molecule of glucose, only slightly less than the 38 ATP obtainable via glycolysis.

Protein Respiration

As noted previously, cells are capable of using any organic nutrient as a respiratory fuel. Thus, nucleic acids are used infrequently by cells as fuel molecules. Proteins are respired more often, but usually only when stores of carbohydrates and lipids have been exhausted. Under these conditions, proteins are broken down into their component amino acids, which can enter respiratory pathways in two general ways.

Deamination

One way is made possible by *deamination,* a reaction in which an amino group (—NH_2) is removed from an amino acid (Fig. 12.16). In vertebrates this process takes place largely in liver cells. In other animals and in plants deaminations can occur in a variety of cell types. The resulting free ammonia, being highly alkaline, is toxic and it is ultimately excreted. The excreted substance often is unchanged ammonia, as in most aquatic types. Or ammonia can undergo various chemical transformations and be excreted in the form of *uric acid,* as in insects and birds, or in the form of *urea,* as in mammals (see Chap. 18).

What remains of an amino acid after deamination is a *keto acid,* characterized by a *ketone* group ($>$C=), where the amino group of the original amino acid had been attached (see Fig. 12.16).

Some keto acids, such as ketoglutaric and oxaloacetic acids, are normal components of the citric acid cycle (see Fig. 12.11). Production of these keto acids via deamination thus provides nutrient fuels that can be respired readily. Deamination does not always generate such keto acids, but they can also be produced by *transamination,* a process in which amino and keto groups are exchanged (see Fig. 12.16).

Transamination

Through transamination reactions, many keto acids can be transformed to other keto acids provided the appropriate amino acid is available. Under such conditions, one or more of the keto acids of the citric acid cycle often can be produced. For example, if the amino acid glutamic acid participates in a transamination, it becomes ketoglutaric acid (Fig. 12.17). Similarly, when the amino acid aspartic acid is transaminated, the corresponding keto acid formed is oxaloacetic acid. Moreover, if alanine transaminates with some other keto acid, alanine becomes pyruvic acid.

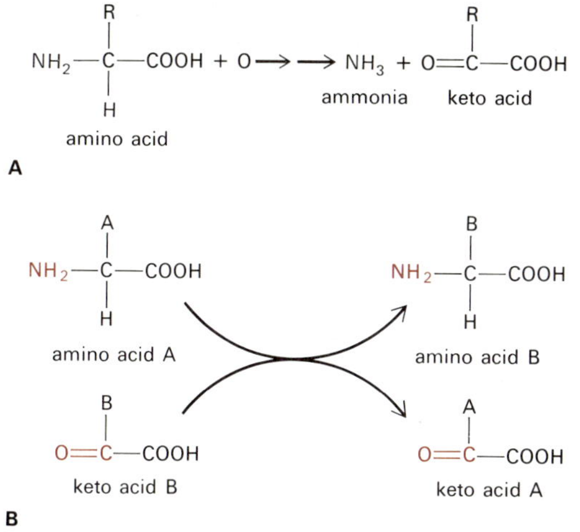

$$NH_2\text{—}\overset{\displaystyle R}{\underset{\displaystyle H}{C}}\text{—}COOH + O \longrightarrow NH_3 + O\text{=}\overset{\displaystyle R}{C}\text{—}COOH$$

amino acid — ammonia — keto acid

A

$$NH_2\text{—}\overset{\displaystyle A}{\underset{\displaystyle H}{C}}\text{—}COOH \;\;\; (\text{amino acid A}) \qquad NH_2\text{—}\overset{\displaystyle B}{\underset{\displaystyle H}{C}}\text{—}COOH \;\;\; (\text{amino acid B})$$

$$O\text{=}\overset{\displaystyle B}{C}\text{—}COOH \;\;\; (\text{keto acid B}) \qquad O\text{=}\overset{\displaystyle A}{C}\text{—}COOH \;\;\; (\text{keto acid A})$$

B

Fig. 12.16 Deamination and transamination. (A) Oxidation of an amino acid yields a free ammonia molecule, which is excreted, and a keto acid, so named for its ketone ($>C{=}O$) in place of amino group. (B) Interaction of an amino acid A and a keto acid B can result in a substitution of the amino group by a ketone group in A and by a reverse substitution in B.

Transamination also allows for interconvertibility between amino acids; many amino acids can be converted to other amino acids provided the appropriate keto acid is available. Therefore, many amino acids can become glutamic acid or aspartic acid or alanine. Because these three amino acids can become ketoglutaric or oxaloacetic or pyruvic acid by further transamination, several different amino acids can be converted to components of the citric acid cycle.

The ATP yields of protein and amino acid respiration vary according to the specific reaction pathways followed, but the energy-trapping efficiency is similar to that of carbohydrates, roughly 40 per cent.

Lipid Respiration

Like many carbohydrates, lipids generally are prime nutrient fuels for cells. In vertebrates, fats supply at least half of the energy for liver and kidney function. Moreover, fat virtually is the sole source of energy for fasting or hibernating animals. Fats first are converted to glycerol and fatty acids.

Fig. 12.17 Three transamination reactions important in amino acid respiration. The keto acids resulting from transamination happen to be participants in glycolysis and the citric acid cycle. Therefore, through the reactions shown, amino acids can enter the same final respiratory pathways as carbohydrates and fatty acids.

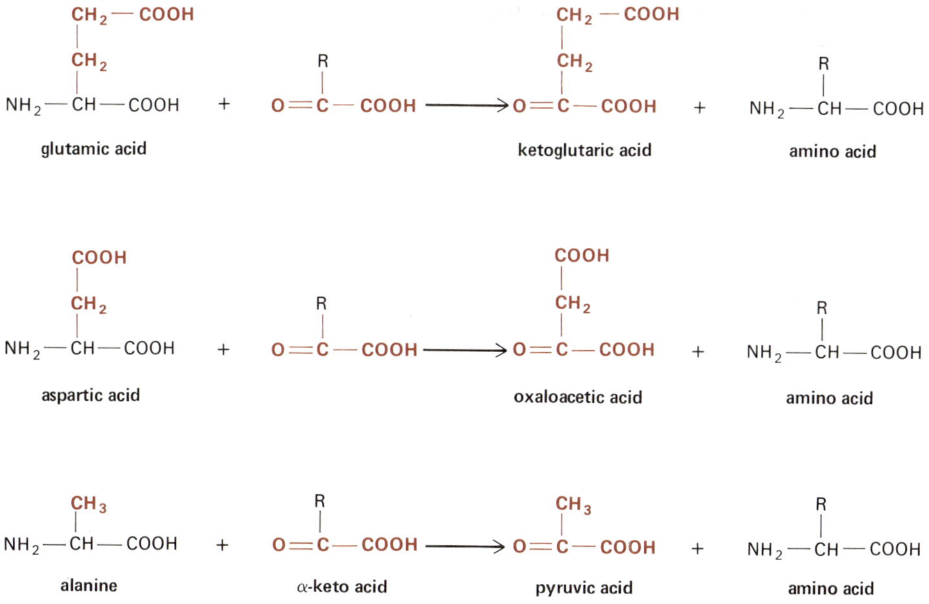

$$NH_2\text{—}\overset{\displaystyle CH_2\text{—}COOH \atop \displaystyle |\atop \displaystyle CH_2}{CH}\text{—}COOH + O\text{=}\overset{\displaystyle R}{C}\text{—}COOH \longrightarrow O\text{=}\overset{\displaystyle CH_2\text{—}COOH \atop \displaystyle |\atop \displaystyle CH_2}{C}\text{—}COOH + NH_2\text{—}\overset{\displaystyle R}{CH}\text{—}COOH$$

glutamic acid — ketoglutaric acid — amino acid

$$NH_2\text{—}\overset{\displaystyle COOH \atop \displaystyle |\atop \displaystyle CH_2}{CH}\text{—}COOH + O\text{=}\overset{\displaystyle R}{C}\text{—}COOH \longrightarrow O\text{=}\overset{\displaystyle COOH \atop \displaystyle |\atop \displaystyle CH_2}{C}\text{—}COOH + NH_2\text{—}\overset{\displaystyle R}{CH}\text{—}COOH$$

aspartic acid — oxaloacetic acid — amino acid

$$NH_2\text{—}\overset{\displaystyle CH_3}{CH}\text{—}COOH + O\text{=}\overset{\displaystyle R}{C}\text{—}COOH \longrightarrow O\text{=}\overset{\displaystyle CH_3}{C}\text{—}COOH + NH_2\text{—}\overset{\displaystyle R}{CH}\text{—}COOH$$

alanine — α-keto acid — pyruvic acid — amino acid

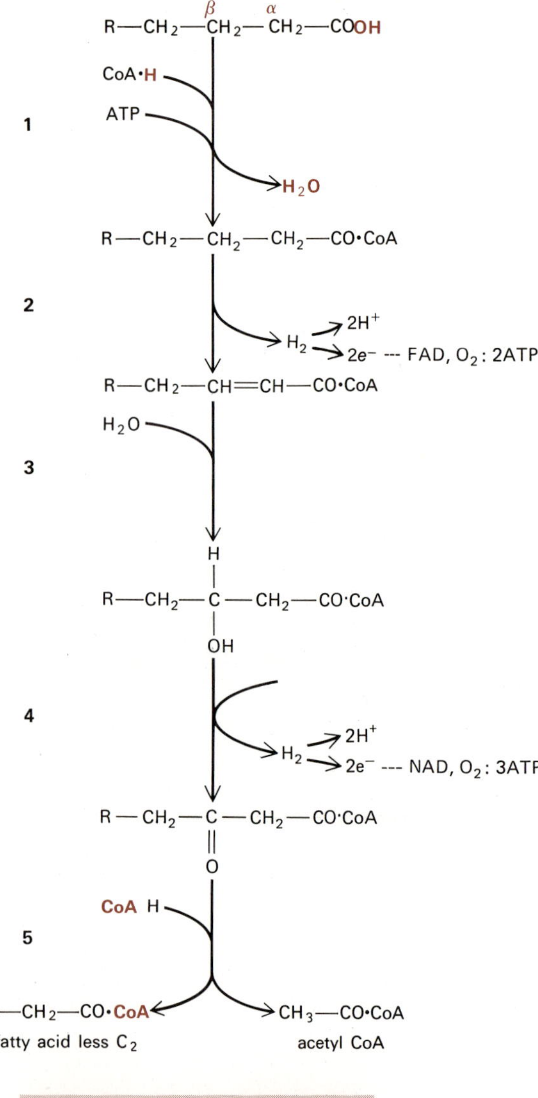

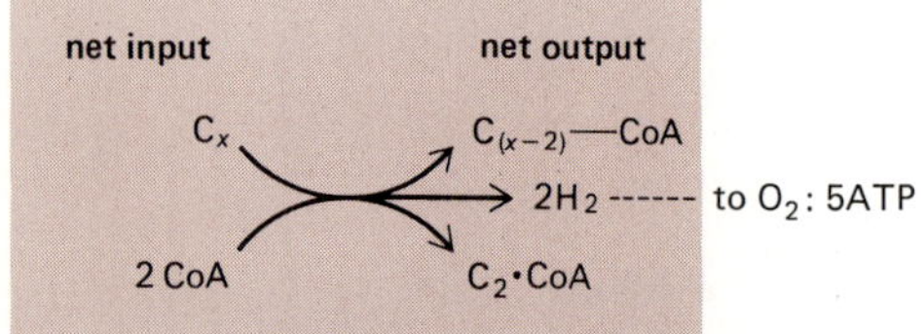

Fig. 12.18 β-oxidation of fatty acids. In step 1 a fatty acid is activated by combination with CoA and concurrent removal of water. Step 2 is dehydrogenation, FAD being the electron acceptor. Step 3 is an addition of water and represents the actual β-oxidation. The oxidized molecule is then dehydrogenated (step 4). In step 5 the 2-carbon fragment acetyl is split off, resulting in acetyl CoA and a fatty acid shorter by two carbons than the original one. The summary shows that 5 ATP are gained through electron transport to oxygen. C_x here stands for a fatty acid with x number of C atoms.

Glycerol, a compound containing three carbon atoms, is then converted to phosphoglyceraldehyde (PGAL) and respired as if this compound had originated from glucose (see Figs. 12.12 and 12.13).

Fatty acids are decomposed by a process known as *β-oxidation;* the second, or β, carbon of the acid (counted after the —COOH group) undergoes oxidation. Figure 12.18 summarizes the main steps. In a first step, CoA becomes linked to the acid end of the fatty acid, with the help of energy from 1 ATP. A dehydrogenation occurs next, one H atom being removed from each of the α and β carbons. The electrons of the two hydrogen atoms are accepted by *flavin adenine dinucleotide* (FAD), a coenzyme derived in part from *riboflavin,* vitamin B_2 (see Fig. 4.16). These electrons are transferred to oxygen along the electron-transport chain, yielding 2 ATP in the process (not three since the NAD step is omitted; Fig. 12.19).

Next, a molecule of water is added to the dehydrogenated fatty acid. The rehydrogenated molecule is then dehydrogenated once again as two hydrogen atoms are removed from the β carbon. Both electrons of the removed hydrogen atoms are transferred to NAD. Subsequent electron transport here yields 3 ATP.

Finally, another molecule of CoA is added at the β carbon. Two fragments are thereby produced. One is acetyl CoA, and the other is a CoA-carrying fatty acid two carbons shorter than the original acid. This shorter acid may now undergo β-oxidation in turn, and consecutive acetyl CoA units are cut off in this way.

Consequently, 5 ATP are gained for every acetyl CoA unit formed. If, for example, an actual starting fuel is assumed to be stearic acid, a C_{18} fatty acid very common in animal fats, then β-oxidation of this acid can occur successively 8 times, yielding acetyl CoA each time and leaving a ninth acetyl CoA as a remainder. At 5 ATP per β-oxidation, the yield is therefore $5 \times 8 = 40$ ATP, minus 1 ATP expended in the first reaction of the stearic acid starting molecule. Therefore, one C_{18} fatty acid yields a net of 39 ATP and 9 acetyl CoA. The latter generate 9 × 12 = 108 ATP in the citric acid cycle, so that the total energy gained from the complete respiration of stearic acid is 147 ATP.

As a comparison, we already know that one glucose molecule yields 38 ATP. Since stearic acid is a C_{18} compound whereas glucose is a C_6 compound, the fatty acid might be expected to yield 3 times as much ATP. However, three glucose molecules yield only 114 ATP, which means that an 18-carbon fatty acid actually produces *more* than 3 times as much (almost 4 times as much) ATP as a 6-carbon carbohydrate.

Fatty acids generally constitute a richer source of usable energy than equivalent amounts of protein or carbohydrate. The reason is that carbon atoms of fatty acids usually are bound to a greater total number of hydrogen atoms than equal weights of the other two types of compounds.

An overall summary of respiratory reactions is outlined in Fig. 12.19. All these reactions take place exceedingly rapidly in cells. In vertebrates, moreover, respiratory rates are influenced greatly by the thyroid hormone *thyroxine,* which accelerates respiration in proportion to its concentration.

Most organisms are not vertebrates, however, and their respiration is not under thyroxine control. Nevertheless, respiratory decompositions still occur extremely rapidly; a glucose molecule can be respired in less than 1 second. Very efficient enzyme action is probably one condition that makes such speed possible. Another undoubtedly is the close, ordered arrangement of all required participants in the submicroscopic spaces of the mitochondria. Just as a well-arranged industrial assembly line turns out products at a great rate, so do the even better arranged molecular components of mitochondria.

The fate and function of the chief product of respiration, ATP, are subjects of the next chapter.

Fig. 12.19 Respiration: overall summary. The center panel outlines the main pathways of the respiratory breakdown of carbohydrates, fats, and proteins. The left-hand panel indicates that some ATP produced during respiration is formed via the production of high-energy phosphate bonds on fuel molecules. Such high-energy phosphates subsequently are transferred to ADP. The right-hand panel summarizes electron transport and oxidative phosphorylation. Note that some hydrogen atoms pass to FAD. This coenzyme inserts electrons at a midpoint in the transport chain. Consequently, only two molecules of ATP are generated when hydrogen is shunted via FAD. Three molecules of ATP can be produced if the electrons of hydrogen are passed via NAD down the entire chain of carriers.

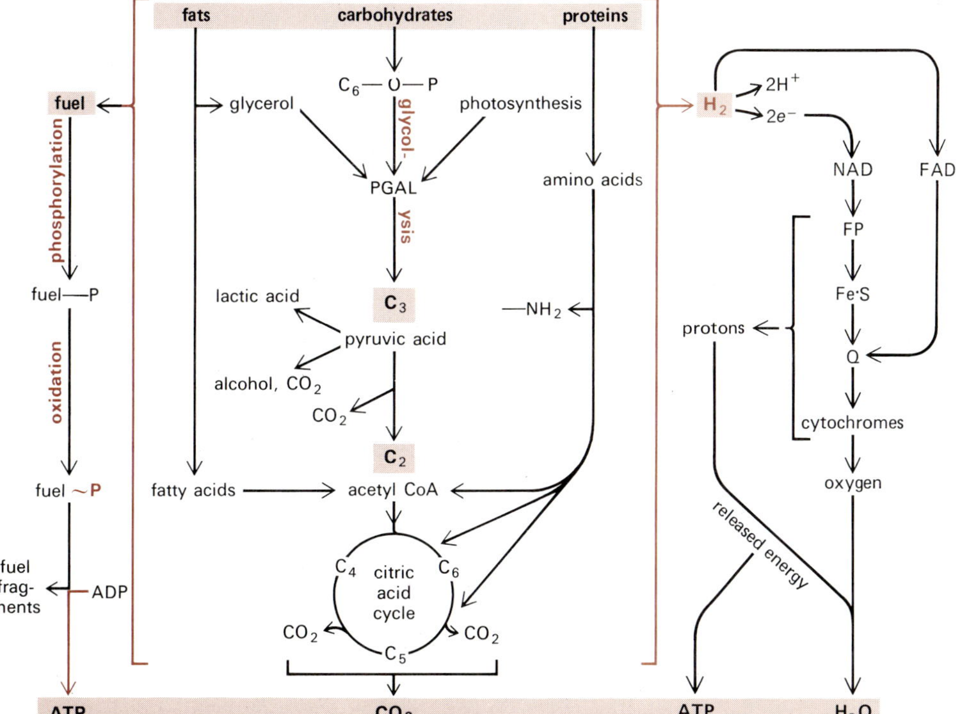

Review Questions

1 Compare and contrast a fire with respiration. What do they have in common? What is different? What materials are fuels in respiration? What general types of events occur in respiration? Where in cells does respiration occur?

2 What are redox reactions? What is dehydrogenation? Where does it occur, and what role does it play in respiration? Under what conditions does it take place?

3 Describe the chemiosmotic hypothesis. What evidence supports this hypothesis? Where are the carriers of the electron-transport system located? The term "charge separation" has been used to underscore a fundamental attribute of the chemiosmotic hypothesis. Is this an appropriate expression? Give reasons for your answer. Where are the enzymes of the Krebs cycle?

4 Describe the sequence of electron carriers and the specific role of each during aerobic and anaerobic respiration. Under what conditions does either take place? How and where can aerobic respiration become blocked? How is alcohol or lactic acid formed? How can anaerobic respiration be used in the production of wine, beer, and vinegar?

5 Describe the role of adenosine phosphates in respiration. What is a high-energy bond? How and where are such bonds produced in fuels? How and where are such bonds produced during electron transport?

6 Describe the general sequence of events in the citric acid cycle. What is the total input and output of the cycle?

7 Review the sequence of events in glycolysis. How much energy is obtained? Which classes of nutrients pass through a pyruvic acid stage in respiration?

8 Review the conversion of pyruvic acid to acetyl CoA. How much energy is gained and where? What classes of nutrients pass through an acetyl CoA stage in respiration?

9 Review and summarize the overall fate of one molecule of glucose during compete respiratory combustion. What is the total net input and total net output? What happens to the individual atoms of glucose? What is the total ATP gain, and how much is gained during each of the main steps of decomposition?

10 Summarize the events of the hexose shunt. What respiratory role does this process play and where does it occur? How does the energy gain compare with that of glycolysis?

11 Describe the process of β oxidation. How much energy is gained and where? Generally show how amino acids are respired.

Collateral Readings

Amerine, M. A.: Wine, *Scientific American,* August 1964. An interesting discussion of some of the interacting substances in wine and a description of procedures followed by modern wine makers.

Anderson, S. F.: "The Art of Making Beer," Longman, Don Mills, Ont., 1971. A short, entertaining paperback containing procedures and recipes for those interested in brewing their own.

Dyson, R. D.: "Cell Biology: A Molecular Approach," 2d ed., Allyn and Bacon, Boston, 1978. This outstanding textbook contains an excellent account of cell respiration; for the advanced student.

Hinkle, P. C., and **R. E. McCarty:** How Cells Make ATP, *Scientific American,* March 1978. Presents an updated account of how this important substance is manufactured in bacteria, mitochondria, and chloroplasts.

Karp, G.: "Cell Biology," McGraw-Hill, New York, 1979. A good treatment of respiration is included in this fine text.

Krebs, H. A.: "The History of the Tricarboxylic Acid Cycle," *Perspectives in Biology and Medicine,* vol. 14, p. 154, 1970. An informative description of how the citric acid cycle was worked out, written by the scientist who received a Nobel Prize for accomplishing the feat.

Loewy, A. C., and **P. Siekevitz:** "Cell Structure and Function," 3d ed., Holt, New York, 1979. Another text providing a good summary of cell respiration. A somewhat less detailed account than Dyson's or Karp's.

Stryer, L.: "Biochemistry," Freeman, San Francisco, 1975. An excellent, well-illustrated biochemistry text with a good discussion of cell respiration.

Wagner, P.: Wines, Grape Vines and Climate, *Scientific American,* June 1974. Explores relationships between climate and the many different kinds of wine.

Chapter 13 Synthesis

Learning Objectives

After reading this chapter you should be able to:

1. Write the overall chemical equation for photosynthesis and illustrate its importance in supporting all forms of life on earth.
2. Construct a diagram that depicts the structural relationships between thylakoids, grana, and the stroma of a chloroplast; define and state at least one functional relationship between photolysis and CO_2 fixation; state where each of these processes occurs in chloroplasts.
3. List the colors of the visible spectrum that are absorbed most strongly and least strongly by chlorophyll; show how these differences in absorption relate to the green appearance of leaves; outline a functional relationship between accessory pigments and chlorophyll.
4. Define fluorescence and show how this phenomenon relates to the oxidation and reduction of chlorophyll.
5. List at least one functional relationship between all possible pairs of the following during noncyclic electron transfer:
   - **a.** light
   - **b.** water
   - **c.** photosystem I
   - **d.** photosystem II
   - **e.** electron carriers
   - **f.** ferredoxin
   - **g.** oxidized NADP
6. Give the locations of photosystems I and II in chloroplasts; differentiate between cyclic and noncyclic electron transfer and name the principal products of each.
7. Distinguish between the C_3 and C_4 photosynthetic pathways; show how they are integrated in C_4 plants; describe how the C_4 cycle offers an adaptive advantage for plants living in hot, dry habitats.
8. State at least one functional relationship between CO_2, phosphoenolpyruvate (PEP), and phosphoglyceraldehyde (PGAL) in C_4 plants.
9. Describe how mesophyll and bundle-sheath cells are arranged in the leaves of C_4 plants; indicate at least one functional relationship between these two kinds of cells.
10. Define photorespiration; identify the circumstances under which photorespiration occurs in plants; outline the metabolic consequences of photorespiration and show how this process "short-circuits" the Calvin cycle.
11. Identify at least one functional relationship between each of the following paired subcomponents of the Calvin cycle:
    - **a.** reduced NADP and CO_2
    - **b.** CO_2 and ribulose diphosphate (RuDP)
    - **c.** phosphoglyceric acid (PGA) and RuDP
    - **d.** PGA and ATP
    - **e.** reduced NADP and the hexose shunt
12. List three principal fates of PGAL in plants.
13. Describe and illustrate an important functional relationship between PGAL, glucose phosphate, and UDP-glucose in the synthesis of polysaccharides; illustrate how the vertebrate liver influences concentrations of blood glucose after a meal and during fasting; outline an important functional relationship between acetyl CoA, fatty acids, and glycerol in the synthesis of lipids; state why certain amino and fatty acids are termed "essential"; construct a diagram depicting the synthesis of amino acids by transamination; construct a second diagram illustrating how the synthesis and respiration of proteins, carbohydrates, nucleic acids, and fats each depend on the production of PGAL.

Once nutrients and ATP are available, a cell can carry out metabolic *synthesis* activities. Of these, *photosynthesis* is unquestionably the most fundamental; this process, which occurs exclusively in the green cells of plants and many other autotrophs, produces both ATP and basic foods and thus ultimately makes possible other synthesis activities of plant or animal cells. Photosynthesis is therefore considered first.

PHOTOSYNTHESIS

The Pattern

It is hardly possible to overestimate the importance of the photosynthetic reactions through which *inorganic* CO_2 and H_2O are transformed to *organic* compounds, specifically carbohydrates. These compounds are the primary substances from which virtually the whole living world is constructed and on which virtually all organisms depend for their food. The only organisms not dependent on photosynthesis are the chemoautotrophic bacteria, which together constitute probably less than 0.0001 per cent of all the living matter on earth (see Chap. 11 and the Biology Highlight in Chap. 35).

It has been estimated that some 200 billion tons of carbon go through the photosynthetic process every year. This makes photosynthesis the most massive chemical event and (after the global water cycle) the second most massive event of all kinds on earth. Carbon dioxide is used up in photosynthesis in such large amounts that, without replenishment through plant and animal respiration and other combustion processes, the CO_2 content of the entire atmosphere would be exhausted in a few months and that of the ocean in about 300 years. Oxygen is released through photosynthesis so voluminously that all the O_2 of the present atmosphere could be generated in about 2000 years, an incredibly short time from a geologic standpoint. Finally, the solar energy harvested annually through photosynthesis in the form of carbohydrates amounts to fully one-fourth the total energy now available from all sources.

Because CO_2 and water are the known raw materials and carbohydrates and oxygen the known end products, an overall chemical description of photosynthesis is the equation

$$6CO_2 + 6H_2O \xrightarrow[\text{chlorophyll}]{\text{light}} C_6H_{12}O_6 + 6O_2$$

But this equation does not describe the details of the photosynthetic process. For example, CO_2 does *not* react directly with water; if it did, the result would be nothing but carbonated water. Research has shown that in photosynthesis CO_2 reacts with the *hydrogen* of water, and the oxygen of water becomes a by-product. Evidently, a first step in photosynthesis is the decomposition of water molecules into separate hydrogen and oxygen components. This decomposition is associated with processes involving the green pigment chlorophyll and the energy of light. This first phase of photosynthesis is therefore called *photolysis,* that is, light-associated water decomposition. In a second phase, hydrogen resulting from photolysis reacts with CO_2 and a carbohydrate is formed. This phase is called *CO_2 fixation,* implying a combination of CO_2 and hydrogen. Unlike photolysis, CO_2 fixation does not require light and can occur in the dark (Fig. 13.1). Because photolysis is light-dependent, chemical processes constituting this first phase of photosynthesis often are collectively termed *light reactions.*

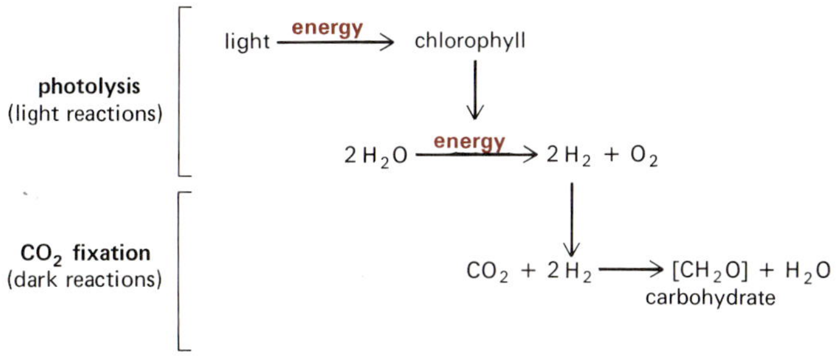

Fig. 13.1 Photolysis and CO_2 fixation. During photolysis water is split into its hydrogen and oxygen components, the latter being released as a gas. Sunlight provides energy for the fragmentation. The actual splitting of water involves chlorophyll which has been energized by sunlight. Carbohydrate is formed when CO_2 is united with photolysis-produced hydrogen. This second subprocess of photosynthesis is called CO_2 fixation. Unlike photolysis, which depends on sunlight, CO_2 fixation can occur either in light or darkness. Consequently, the chemical steps of photolysis are collectively termed light reactions; the chemical reactions of CO_2 fixation are known as the dark reactions.

photolysis (light reactions)

light $\xrightarrow{\text{energy}}$ chlorophyll

$$2\,H_2O \xrightarrow{\text{energy}} 2\,H_2 + O_2$$

CO_2 fixation (dark reactions)

$$CO_2 + 2\,H_2 \longrightarrow [CH_2O] + H_2O$$

carbohydrate

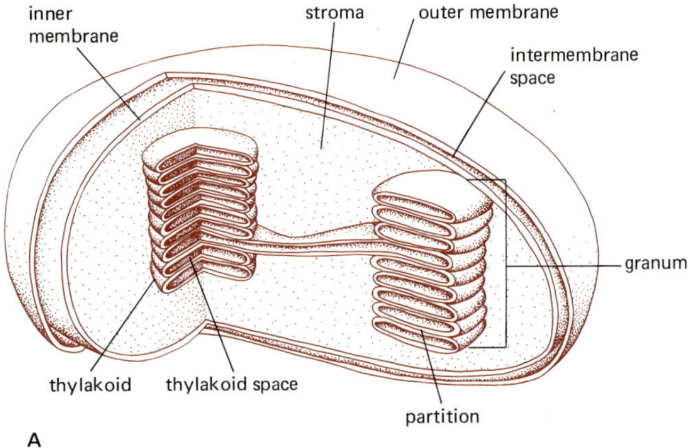

Fig. 13.2 Chloroplast structure. (A) Cutaway view of a chloroplast showing the inner and outer membranes that form its "hull." Convolutions of the inner membrane make up a complex network of membranous disks. Individual disks, or thylakoids, are arranged in stacks called grana. Stroma is the internal ground substance of the chloroplast in which grana are dispersed. (B) Three grana showing tubular interconnections between thylakoids of different grana.

Conversely, processes making up CO_2 fixation are often called *dark reactions.*

Both photolysis and CO_2 fixation take place in the chloroplasts of green cells. In angiosperms, most chloroplasts are located in the mesophyll cells of leaves. Each mesophyll cell usually contains about 40 chloroplasts, and the total surface area available for light absorption of all chloroplasts in a mature tree can amount to some 150 square miles.

Chloroplasts are bounded by two membranes, and the inner membrane is folded into the internal matrix, or *stroma,* of the chloroplast. These infoldings are organized in parallel arrays of flattened, disk-shaped sacs. Looking like a stack of coins, each such array constitutes a *granum;* each of the sacs making up a granum is called a *thylakoid* (Fig. 13.2).

The inner surfaces of thylakoids are studded with many small particles, which contain most of the chemical "machinery" of photolysis. Compounds making up a thylakoid particle appear to be positioned in an orderly array and include various enzymes, electron carriers, one or more types of chlorophyll, and certain *accessory pigments.* The latter include the carrot-red to butter-yellow *carotenoids* and the bright yellow to brownish *xanthophylls.* Almost all enzymes required for CO_2 fixation are localized in the stroma.

In many plants, production and maintenance of chlorophyll ordinarily depend on exposure to light. A young shoot, for example, does not turn green until it is well above the soil surface; and in a plant grown in a dark chamber chlorophyll soon breaks down and the plant loses its green color. In the fall, the chlorophyll of many plants disintegrates. As a result, the more stable accessory pigments become unmasked and give rise to the brilliant colors of autumn foliage.

Photolysis (Light Reactions)

Chlorophyll and Light

Light energy is absorbed by chlorophyll in photosynthetic cells. A molecule of chlorophyll consists of a "head" and a "tail" (Fig. 13.3). The head contains four carbon-nitrogen rings joined as a larger ring. At the center of this larger ring is a single atom of magnesium. The tail is a chain of linked carbons attached to the head. Different

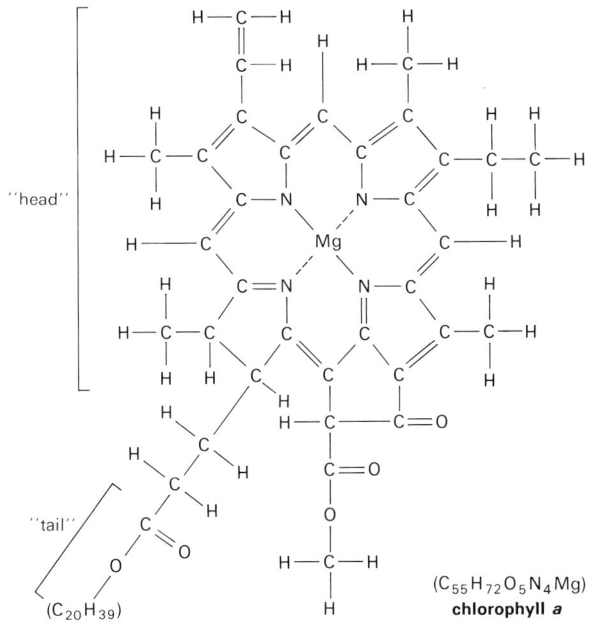

"head"

"tail"

$(C_{20}H_{39})$

$(C_{55}H_{72}O_5N_4Mg)$
chlorophyll *a*

Fig. 13.3 Chlorophyll, molecular structure.

groups of photosynthetic organisms are distinguished by various structural forms of chlorophyll. Such chemical variants differ mainly in the kinds and arrangements of other atoms attached to the basic head-tail structure. Except for photosynthetic bacteria, which contain distinct forms of chlorophyll not found elsewhere, all photosynthesizers possess *chlorophyll a*. The almost universal presence of chlorophyll *a* in photosynthetic organisms suggests, and experimental data actually confirm, that this pigment is most directly involved in the transformation of light energy to chemical energy.

Ordinary visible light consists of a mixture of different wavelengths which, when unmixed, are seen in the colors of a rainbow—red, orange, yellow, green, blue, and violet. These light waves contain variable amounts of energy; red light is the longest wavelength we can see and contains the least energy; violet is the shortest we can see and contains the most energy.

When a mixture of wavelengths as in ordinary "white" light falls on a chlorophyll molecule, the molecule absorbs red and violet wavelengths strongly, and orange, yellow, and blue wavelengths somewhat less strongly. By contrast, green wavelengths are hardly absorbed at all and are for the most part transmitted through the chloroplast or reflected. This is why an illuminated leaf appears green; chlorophyll has absorbed all *but* the green wavelengths in light. Accessory pigments of thylakoids absorb light energy at wavelengths other than those absorbed by chlorophyll and then transfer this energy directly to chlorophyll. In effect, such pigments serve as supplementary light receptors and extend the range of light available for use in photosynthesis.

The absorption of light by chlorophyll causes certain of its electrons to become so highly energized that they are dislodged from the molecule, much as a spaceship traveling fast enough can be dislodged from earth orbit to outer space. The loss of electrons from chlorophyll causes these molecules to become ions. Ionized chlorophyll will readily accept any electron it can "capture." When chlorophyll is isolated in solution and illuminated, most of the dislodged electrons are recaptured by molecules of ionized chlorophyll. During the recapture process, electrons give up their extra energy, largely in the form of red (low-energy) light (Fig. 13.4). This phenomenon, called *fluorescence,* can be demonstrated easily. Chlorophyll can be extracted from green leaves and dissolved in solution, which becomes green because of the dissolved chlorophyll. If the solution is illuminated by bright light, the color changes to red.

However, as integral parts of thylakoids, most dislodged high-energy electrons are not directly or immediately recaptured by chlorophyll itself but by other electron carriers present in chloroplasts, and these electrons come to play a critical role in photosynthesis.

Photosystems

Thylakoids of green leaves contain two different pigment systems that absorb light energy. Although the types and distributions of pigments in these systems are different, both contain chlorophyll *a* and accessory pigments. The functional relationship between these systems is illustrated by Fig. 13.5 Light energy is first absorbed by chlorophyll molecules of photosystem I (PS I). Electrons of these molecules are energized, dislodged, and transferred to a yet unidentified electron acceptor

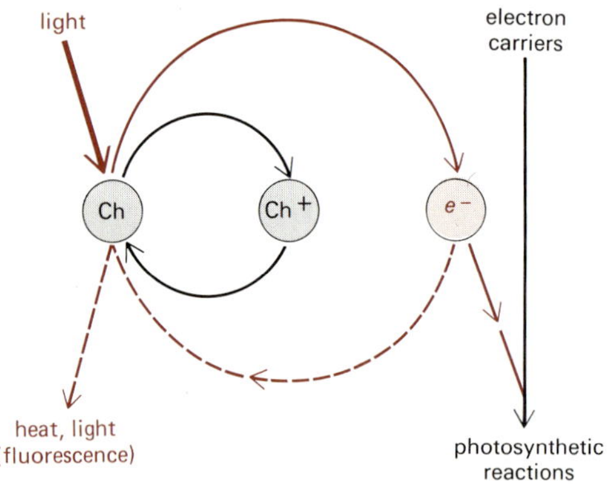

Fig. 13.4 Photoionization. When light "excites" chlorophyll molecules (Ch), high-energy electrons (e^-) become dislodged, and chlorophyll thereby acquires a positive charge (Ch^+). Some of the high-energy electrons return to chlorophyll immediately, and the extra energy dissipates as heat or as light (in which case chlorophyll is weakly fluorescent). High-energy electrons are also captured by specific carrier molecules present in chloroplasts, and such electrons participate in photosynthetic processes.

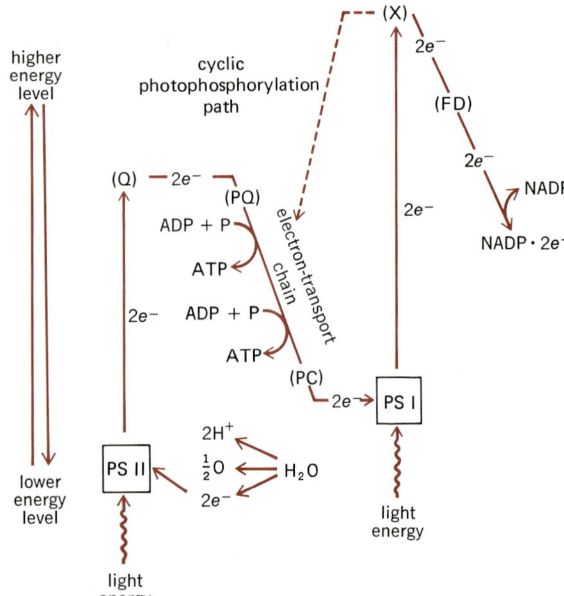

Fig. 13.5 Cyclic and noncyclic photophosphorylation. High-energy electrons ($2e^-$) are dislodged from chlorophyll when light is absorbed by pigment system I (PS I). The electrons are captured by electron acceptors (X) and ferredoxin (FD), and used in the reduction of NADP (NADP · $2e^-$). Ionized chlorophyll of PS I is reduced by electrons derived from chlorophyll of pigment system II (PS II). These electrons are dislodged and captured by electron acceptor (Q) when chlorophyll of PS II is ionized by light. The electrons then are passed from (Q) down a series of electron carriers to ionized chlorophyll of PS I. In the course of being transported, the electrons yield energy for ATP formation. Ionized chlorophyll of PS II is reduced by electrons derived from hydrogen atoms of water molecules. The principal products of this series of reactions, called noncyclic electron transfer, are oxygen, ATP, and reduced NADP. The latter two products constitute raw materials for CO_2 fixation. In certain circumstances, the high-energy electrons of (X) are returned to chlorophyll of PS I via electron carriers. The net output of this series of reactions, called cyclic photophosphorylation, is ATP.

(X). This acceptor passes electrons to ferredoxin (FD), a carrier protein containing iron and sulfur atoms. Electrons next are transferred from ferredoxin to NADP, an electron acceptor identical to NAD of the respiratory electron-transport system except for an additional phosphate group. This now reduced NADP is a raw material for CO_2 fixation and represents one of the three principal products of photolysis. As will become evident shortly, the other two main products are ATP and oxygen.

Once electrons have been transferred to NADP, they cannot be returned to ionized chlorophyll. But unless ionized chlorophyll is itself reduced, no additional electrons can be transferred to reduce more NADP. What is needed here is another source of electrons to resupply those dislodged from chlorophyll of PS I. Water is this other source, and the transfer of its electrons involves photosystem II (PS II).

PS II resembles PS I in containing chlorophyll, which becomes ionized when it absorbs energy, but it differs in that the high-energy electrons dislodged cannot be transferred to NADP. Instead, they are first transferred to another unidentified electron acceptor (Q). Electrons then pass from this compound through a series of electron carriers, which function like those of the electron-transport system in mitochondria. Some of these carriers are cytochromes; others include a fat-soluble ring-shaped compound called *plastoquinone* (PQ) and a copper-containing protein, *plastocyanin* (PC). Energy is extracted from electrons as they are passed along this chain of carriers, and ATP is produced by a process resembling oxidative phosphorylation.

In fact, it is now generally believed that the

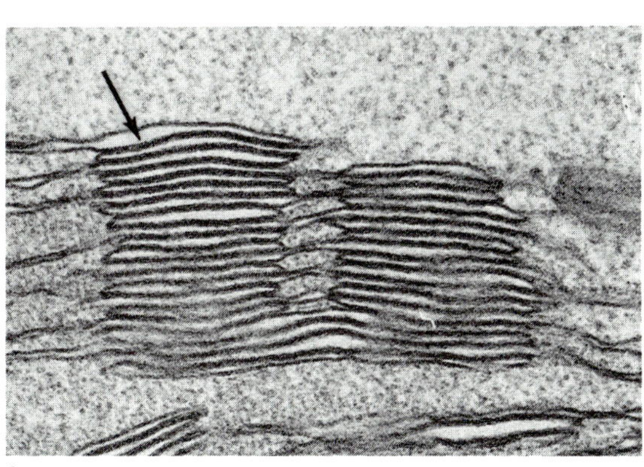

A

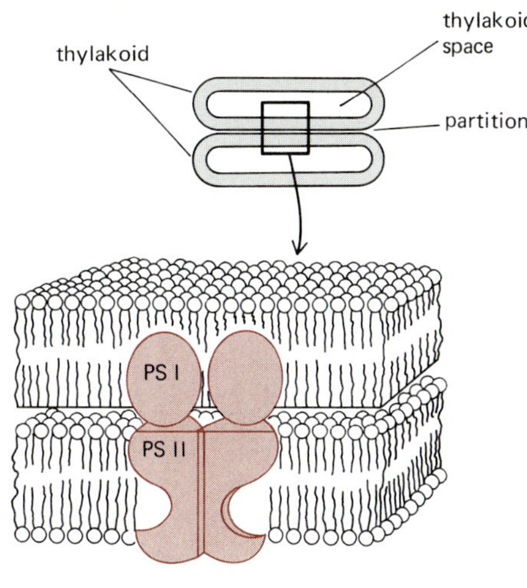

B

Fig. 13.6 Photosystems and thylakoids. (A) Arrangement of thylakoids in grana. Arrow points to the thylakoid space of a thylakoid. This internal space is depicted diagrammatically in (B) and in Fig. 13.2 A narrower space [the "partition" in (B) and in Fig. 13.2], which separates adjacent thylakoids, is not readily visible in this electron micrograph. (B) This diagram shows the probable organization of photosystems I and II in thylakoid membranes. The two photosystems appear to interact across the partition separating adjacent thylakoids. A portion of photosystem I evidently projects into the partition. Photosystem II probably spans thylakoid membranes, projecting partially into the thylakoid space.

chemiosmotic hypothesis, described in Chap. 12 in relation to mitochondrial ATP production, probably is equally applicable to ATP production in chloroplasts. Even so, the coupled processes of electron transport and ATP production are not identical in the two organelles. For example, the final electron acceptor in thylakoids is not oxygen but ionized chlorophyll of PS I. Once reduced, these molecules of chlorophyll can be reionized to reduce additional molecules of NADP.

Transfer of electrons between photosystems cannot continue unless a source of electrons is available to reduce the ionized chlorophyll of PS II. This source of electrons is hydrogen atoms of water molecules. As a result of the transfer of these electrons to PS II, water molecules are fragmented, yielding hydrogen ions and oxygen atoms. The latter combine in pairs and form molecular oxygen.

Unlike the electrons of organic nutrients used as respiratory fuels, the electrons of water contain little energy at the start of photolysis. But when they become components of chlorophyll, these electrons are energized twice by light during their successive transfer through PS II and PS I. Energy obtained in PS II is extracted from these electrons as they are passed through an electron-transport chain to PS I. Electrons again are energized by light in PS I and are used in the production of reduced NADP.

All oxygen-producing photosynthetic cells contain photosystems I and II. Photosynthetic bacteria, which do not produce oxygen, contain a single photosystem that is similar to photosystem I. Because such bacteria are among the most primitive autotrophs, many biologists postulate that photosystem I evolved before photosystem II. Thus release of oxygen during photolysis and use of water as a source of electrons probably represents a later elaboration of a more primitive photosynthetic process.

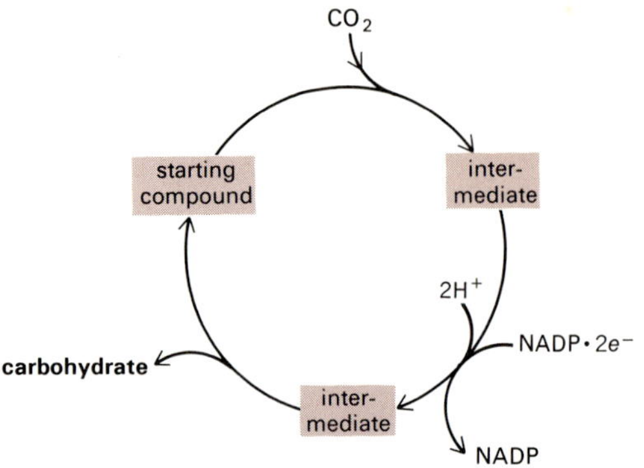

Fig. 13.7 CO_2 fixation: the C_3 cycle. In step 1 (top), CO_2 enters the cycle as a raw material, and in step 2 (lower right) electrons from reduced NADP enter as a raw material and combine with hydrogen ions. Step 3 (lower left) yields the carbohydrate end product and regenerates the starting compound.

The molecular components of photosystems I and II are located at different sites in thylakoids. At least part of photosystem I is contained within small particles that project mainly from stroma-facing sides of thylakoid membranes. The components of photosystem II appear to be associated with an array of larger particles that project mainly from inward-facing sides of thylakoid membranes, i.e., toward the thylakoid space (Fig. 13.6 and see Fig. 13.2).

Under certain circumstances, PS I can operate without input of electrons from PS II (see Fig. 13.5). At such times, electrons energized in PS I are not transported to NADP but are transferred to the electron-transport chain linking the two pigment systems. The electrons then are transported back to ionized chlorophyll of PS I, and their extra energy is used to produce ATP. These molecules of reduced chlorophyll then can be reionized and their dislodged electrons used repeatedly to produce more ATP. This circular pattern of electron transfer, which results only in the phosphorylation of ADP, is appropriately called *cyclic photophosphorylation;* it has been observed in isolated chloroplasts under experimental conditions, but it is not known whether the process normally occurs in living plants.

The main, noncircular pattern of transport, whereby electrons are transferred from water through both photosystems to NADP, is *noncyclic photophosphorylation.* The principal products of this process are oxygen, ATP, and reduced NADP. Because CO_2 fixation depends directly on input of reduced NADP from photolysis, noncyclic photophosphorylation is more significant in food production than cyclic photophosphorylation. However, ATP also is a necessary raw material for CO_2 fixation, and cyclic photophosphorylation may provide a means of quickly replenishing depleted supplies of ATP in chloroplasts of green plant cells.

CO_2 Fixation (Dark Reactions)

The C_3 (Calvin) Cycle

Carbon dioxide becomes fixed as carbohydrate in plants through one of two reaction sequences. The most common of these is the *C_3 cycle.* The C_3 designation refers to the 3-carbon compounds that constitute most of the intermediate participants in the reaction sequence. The C_3 cycle is also called the *Calvin cycle,* named for one of the discoverers of the process.

During the C_3 cycle electrons from reduced NADP are united with CO_2 through a cyclic reaction sequence consisting of three basic steps, each with several substeps (Fig. 13.7). As in the citric acid cycle, each substep is regulated by a specific enzyme. In the first series of reactions, CO_2 enters the cycle as a raw material. In the second series, electrons from reduced NADP enter as a raw material. And in a last series, the carbohydrate end product emerges, while at the same time the starting point of the cycle is regenerated.

This starting point is *ribulose diphosphate* (RuDP), a 5-carbon sugar carrying a phosphate group at each end of the carbon chain. It can be shown that the cycle must run completely through three consecutive turns before a single molecule of carbohydrate end product is obtained. To condense the description, it is convenient to add the three turns together; and instead of starting with one molecule of RuDP and running the cycle three times, we can start with three molecules of RuDP and run the cycle just once. Although such an artificial summation does not correspond to the actual reaction pattern, it portrays the sequence of steps adequately and is also correct arithmetically.

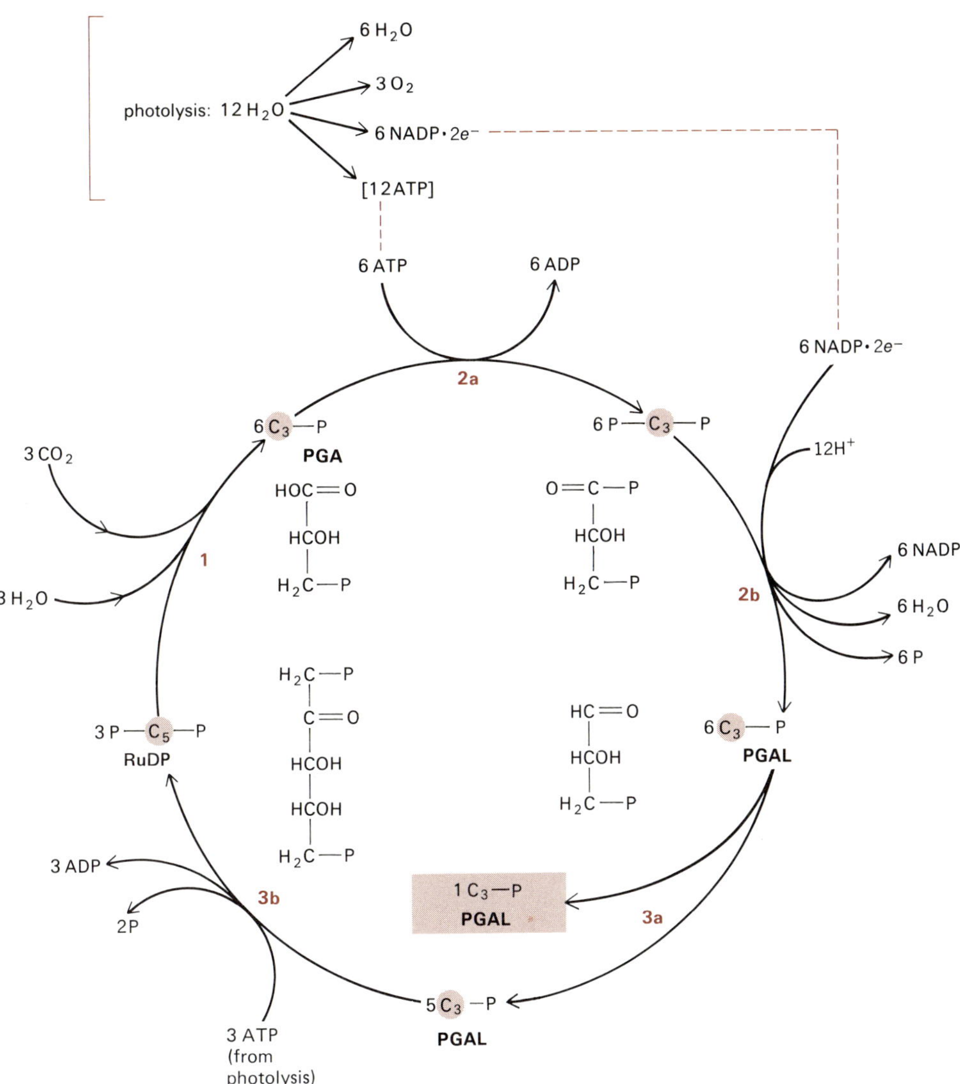

Fig. 13.8 The Calvin cycle. The compounds along the main path of the cycle are shown as carbon numbers with phosphate groups; complete structural formulas are alongside. In step 1, addition of CO_2 lengthens the 5-carbon chain of RuDP to a 6-carbon chain; an extra carbon is interposed between the second and third carbons of RuDP. The result is unstable and breaks into two identical PGA chains. The reactions of step 2, in which hydrogen ions and electrons from NADP · $2e^-$ are added to PGA, results in PGAL. The amount of photolysis necessary to provide NADP · $2e^-$ and the ATP for step 2 is indicated at top. One PGAL molecule is the net end product, and the remaining five PGAL are reconverted into three RuDP with the aid of more ATP from photolysis. An input-output summary is given in Fig. 13.9.

If, then, 3 RuDP are taken as the starting point, the first reaction series involves an addition of three molecules of CO_2 and three molecules of H_2O (Fig. 13.8). As a result of this addition, together with an accompanying rearrangement of atoms, six molecules of phosphoglyceric acid (PGA) are produced. This is the same 3-carbon compound as in the discussion of glycolysis during glucose res-

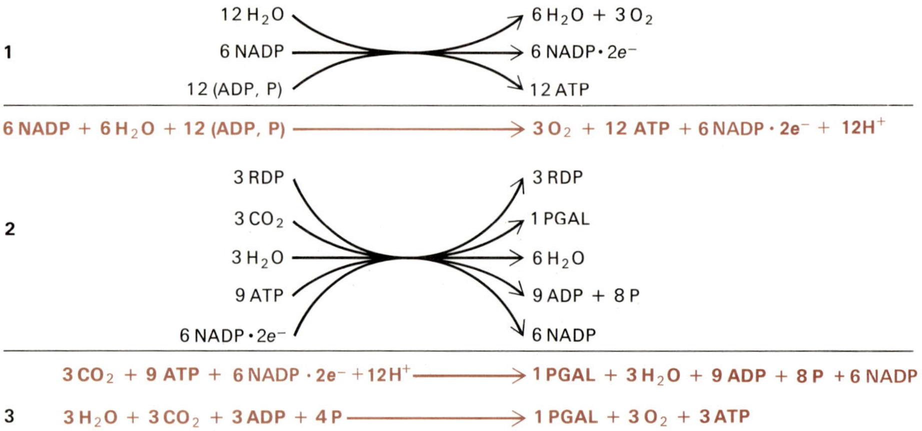

Fig. 13.9 Chemical summaries of photosynthesis. (P symbolizes phosphate). (1) Total and (color) net inputs and outputs of photolysis to create 6NADP · $2e^-$ for the Calvin cycle. (2) Total and (color) net inputs and outputs of the Calvin cycle to create an end product of 1 PGAL. Of the nine phosphate groups supplied by ATP, one is used in PGAL formation and eight thus appear as free by-product. (3) Net input and output of photosynthesis as a whole, obtained by adding the net inputs and outputs of reactions 1 and 2; this equation summarizes the formation of one PGAL molecule, the net end product.

piration (see Chap. 12). Note that the total number of carbon atoms in 3 RuDP and 3 CO_2 equals the total number of carbons in 6 PGA.

In the second step, these 6 PGA first are phosphorylated by 6 ATP produced during photolysis, and they then interact with six molecules of reduced NADP also formed during photolysis. The main end product of this series of reactions is six molecules of phosphoglyceraldehyde, PGAL, again already familiar as an intermediate in glycolysis.

Note, incidentally, that reduced NADP is generated not only through photolysis but also through carbohydrate respiration via the hexose shunt (see Fig. 12.15). This shunt can therefore keep the Calvin cycle going—but only temporarily: the shunt produces reduced NADP by using up already existing carbohydrates; yet if such carbohydrates are to be available, the Calvin cycle must first have produced them. Ultimately, therefore, the Calvin cycle depends on photolysis, the only process that creates reduced NADP independently of preexisting carbohydrates.

Of the 6 PGAL formed, 1 represents the main carbohydrate end product of photosynthesis as a whole. Solar energy, grana, chlorophyll, photolysis, CO_2 fixation—all cooperate to yield this final result. The five remaining PGAL undergo a set of final transformations through which RuDP, the starting compound of the cycle, is regenerated. Again note that the total number of carbon atoms in 5 PGAL equals the total number of carbons in 3 RuDP. In this process more photolysis-derived ATP molecules provide energy and required phosphate groups.

An input-output summary of the Calvin cycle and of photosynthesis as a whole is given in Fig. 13.9. The three *inorganic* carbons supplied by separate CO_2 molecules are now "fixed," that is, joined together as *organic* carbon in a single molecule of PGAL.

The C_4 (Hatch-Slack) Cycle

For many years, the C_3 cycle, discovered in the early 1940s, was thought to be the only reaction sequence leading to formation of carbohydrate in plants. Then, in 1954, Hugo Kortschak conducted an experiment which led to the discovery of an alternate method. Kortschak was treating sugar cane with radioactive carbon dioxide. He was surprised to find that the radioactive compound did not incorporate immediately into compounds containing three carbon atoms. Instead, the radioactive CO_2 first appeared in *4-carbon* compounds, usually either *malic* or *aspartic acid* (Fig. 13.10). Further analysis revealed that these acids resulted from the

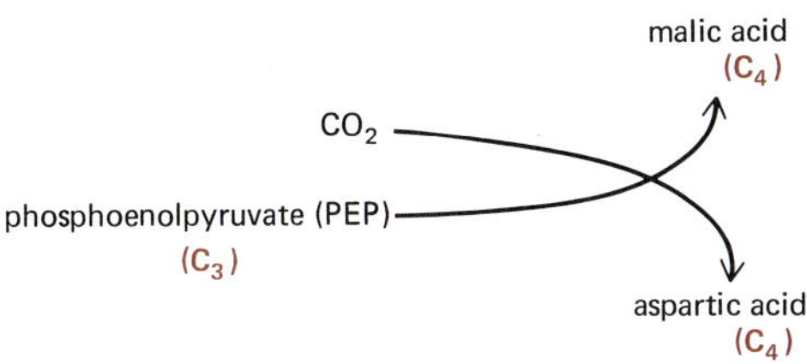

Fig. 13.10 CO_2 fixation in C_4 plants. CO_2 becomes bound to the 3-carbon compound phosphoenolpyruvate in C_4 plants. The product of this carboxylation usually is either malic or aspartic acid, both 4-carbon compounds.

union of CO_2 with the 3-carbon compound *phosphoenolpyruvate* (PEP).

At first, fixation of CO_2 via this 4-carbon (C_4) pathway seemed illogical. Compared with the C_3 cycle, use of PEP requires additional expenditure of ATP and thus is less energy-efficient. Moreover, a direct biochemical route leading from malic or aspartic acid to carbohydrate does not exist in plants.

The adaptive value of the C_4 pathway becomes apparent when the habitat of sugar cane and most other C_4 plants is considered: most of them grow in hot, dry environments where desiccation is an almost continual threat to life. Because of the arid conditions, the stomata of many C_4 plants often remain closed for extended periods during daylight hours. Photosynthesis greatly reduces concentrations of CO_2 in leaf tissues at such times. In fact, levels of CO_2 often become so low that photosynthesis cannot occur in plants able to fix CO_2 solely by the Calvin cycle (C_3 plants).

This stoppage of photosynthesis in C_3 plants stems from a peculiarity of the enzyme that catalyzes the carboxylation (addition of CO_2) of RuDP. When concentrations of CO_2 are sufficiently high (greater than 50 parts per million), the enzyme catalyzes the carboxylation of RuDP, forming two molecules of PGA. But when concentrations of CO_2 are insufficient, the enzyme brings about the oxidation of RuDP, a phenomenon called *photorespiration*. Apparently, oxygen can bind to the enzyme at the very same site that also binds CO_2. The binding of oxygen is favored when CO_2 concentrations are low, bringing about a corresponding increase in the oxidation of RuDP. The oxidation causes a breakdown of RuDP, some of its carbon atoms being released in molecules of CO_2 (Fig. 13.11).

Photorespiration also is favored by high temperatures, which occur commonly in habitats occupied by many C_4 plants. Unlike other kinds of respiration, photorespiration does not result in the production of ATP, and because it also short-circuits the Calvin cycle, this oxidation appears to be an extremely wasteful process. The adaptive value of photorespiration, if any, remains unknown.

The destructive consequences of photorespiration are thwarted by two distinctive features of C_4 plants. The first is the specialized anatomy of their leaves. Unlike C_3 plants, whose leaf anatomy is described in Chap. 6, most of the chloroplast-containing cells of C_4 plants are arranged in cylinders. Each cylinder contains two concentric rings of cells wrapped about a leaf vein. The outer ring is made up of mesophyll cells; the inner ring is composed of closely packed *bundle-sheath* cells (Fig. 13.12). Leaf veins of C_3 plants also are enveloped by a bundle sheath, but the cells of this tissue usually lack chloroplasts. By contrast, bundle-sheath cells of C_4 plants contain many large chloroplasts.

The second distinctive feature of C_4 plants is their ability to fix CO_2 via the *C_4 cycle*, the reaction sequence discovered by Hugo Kortschak. Because the subcomponent events of the cycle were worked out in the late 1960s by two Australian biologists, M. D. Hatch and C. R. Slack, the C_4 cycle is also known as the *Hatch-Slack pathway* (Fig. 13.13).

As anticipated from Kortschak's earlier study, Hatch and Slack found that in C_4 plants CO_2 becomes fixed to PEP, forming a 4-carbon compound.

Fig. 13.11 Photorespiration. CO_2 is fixed to RuDP in chloroplasts when concentrations of the gas are sufficiently high. Some molecules of PGA that result from the carboxylation eventually are converted into carbohydrate. Photorespiration occurs when concentrations of CO_2 in chloroplasts drop to low levels. RuDP is oxidized under such circumstances, forming CO_2 and a variety of other compounds. Some of the latter are produced in peroxisomes, cellular organelles described in Chap. 5.

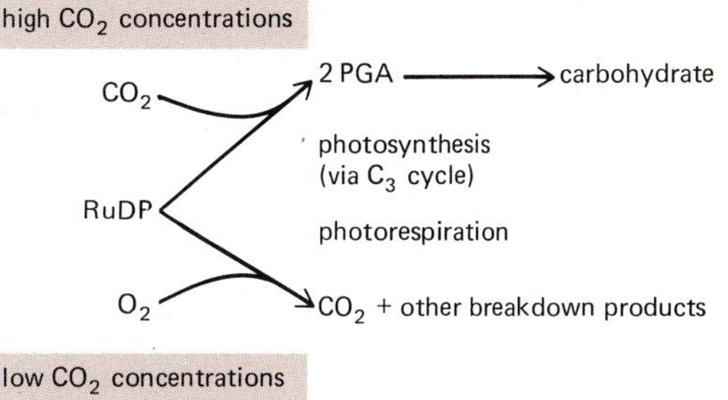

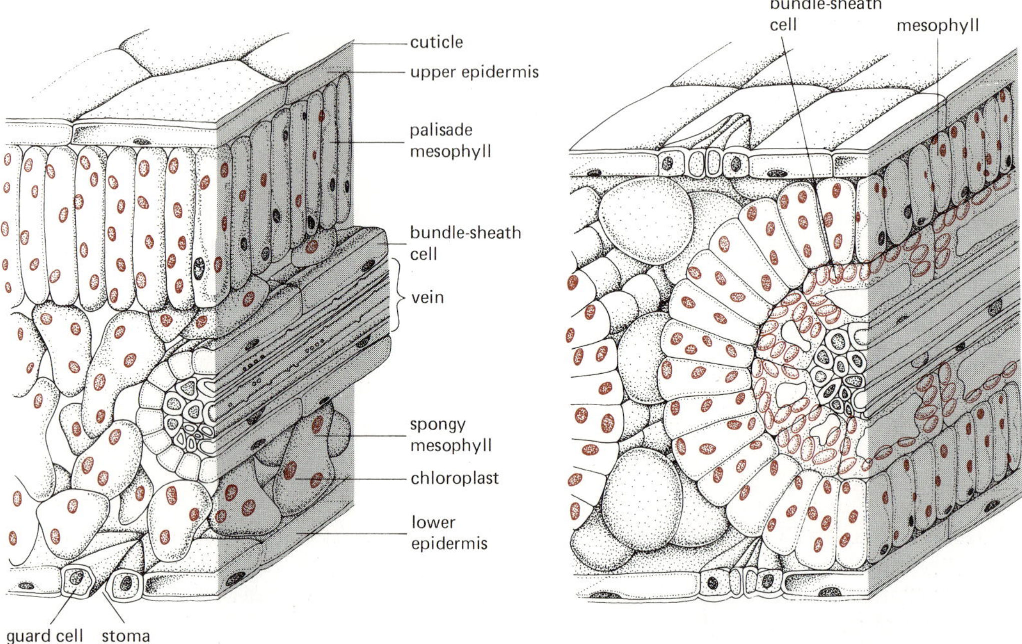

Fig. 13.12 Leaf anatomy of C_3 and C_4 plants. (A) Anatomy of a C_3 leaf. Note that mesophyll cells are arranged in a palisade (upper) layer and a spongy (lower) layer. Bundle-sheath cells usually lack chloroplasts (see also Fig. 6.32). (B) Anatomy of a C_4 leaf. Most chloroplast-containing mesophyll cells surround an inner cylinder of bundle-sheath cells. The latter contain numerous large chloroplasts. This distinctive arrangement of leaf tissues facilitates transport of CO_2-carrying compounds from mesophyll cells into the bundle sheath.

The carboxylation occurs in the mesophyll cells that surround the bundle sheath. The adaptive advantage of fixing CO_2 to PEP stems from the properties of the enzyme catalyzing the carboxylation; this enzyme is *not* inhibited by low concentrations of CO_2. Thus, CO_2 fixation can occur in C_4 plants even when CO_2 concentrations in mesophyll cells are as low as 1 or 2 parts per million. The PEP carboxylation continues unabated under conditions where photorespiration would halt CO_2 fixation in C_3 plants.

The 4-carbon components produced by the C_4 cycle are not used as nutrients. Instead, they are passed inward to the tightly packed bundle-sheath cells. There, CO_2 is split from the 4-carbon compounds. The resulting 3-carbon fragment is transported back to the surrounding mesophyll cells, where it is transformed to PEP, completing the cycle. The CO_2 fragment remains in the cells of the bundle sheath.

Unlike most leaf tissues, the bundle sheath is relatively impermeable to atmospheric gases. As a result, concentrations of CO_2 continue to rise in bundle-sheath cells as molecules of CO_2 continue to be split from the 4-carbon carrier compounds. CO_2 levels in bundle-sheath cells can be as much as 100 times higher than in the outer mesophyll cells. Such concentrations are more than sufficient for CO_2 fixation via the C_3 cycle, and this is precisely what happens.

Thus, C_3 plants, which are far more widespread than C_4 plants, have only one method of fixing CO_2 as carbohydrate. C_3 plants are best adapted to habitats where stomata normally can remain at least partly open most of the day. Because concentrations of CO_2 usually remain higher than 50 parts per million (average atmospheric concentrations of CO_2 are about 330 parts per million), photorespiration normally does not block CO_2 fixation. The C_3 cycle also exists in the chloroplasts of

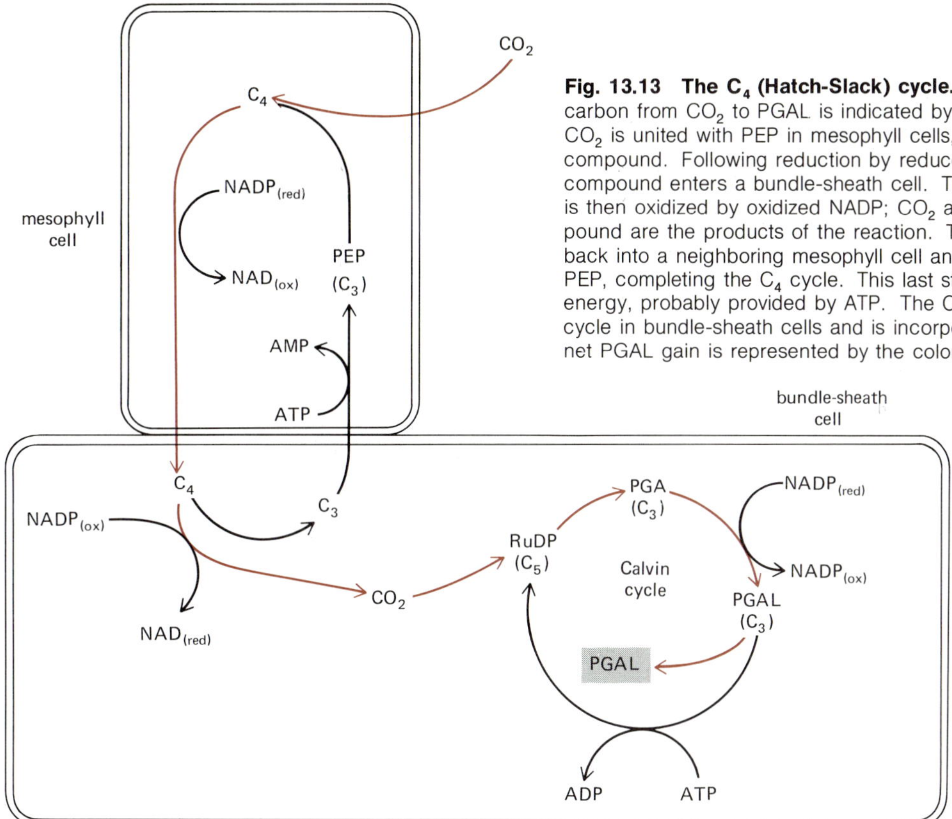

Fig. 13.13 The C_4 (Hatch-Slack) cycle. The path followed by carbon from CO_2 to PGAL is indicated by the colored arrows. CO_2 is united with PEP in mesophyll cells, forming a 4-carbon compound. Following reduction by reduced NADP, the 4-carbon compound enters a bundle-sheath cell. The 4-carbon compound is then oxidized by oxidized NADP; CO_2 and a 3-carbon compound are the products of the reaction. The C_3 compound moves back into a neighboring mesophyll cell and is transformed into PEP, completing the C_4 cycle. This last step requires metabolic energy, probably provided by ATP. The CO_2 enters the Calvin cycle in bundle-sheath cells and is incorporated into PGAL. The net PGAL gain is represented by the colored box, as in Fig. 13.8.

C_4 plants, but these organisms have a preliminary fixation pathway, the C_4 cycle. Coupled with a specialized leaf anatomy, the C_4 cycle provides a means of maintaining metabolically elevated concentrations of CO_2 in bundle-sheath cells, which produce carbohydrate via the C_3 pathway.

C_4 plants apparently have evolved independently in different evolutionary lines. The C_4 cycle is being observed in a growing list of unrelated plants that includes both monocots (e.g., corn, sorghum, and crabgrass) and dicots (e.g., saltbush and *Portulaca*).

The End Product

Whether produced by C_3 or C_4 plants, the primary end product of photosynthesis is PGAL, a *food.* A plant nourished artificially with prefabricated PGAL can survive without photosynthesis and without any other organic nutrients.

As PGAL forms it does not accumulate to any great extent, for it is soon used in one of three main ways: it can be used directly as a *nutrient* in the cell that produced it; it can be "packaged" for *export* to other cells; or it can be packaged for *storage* (Fig. 13.14).

As a nutrient, PGAL is usable immediately in respiration. It can happen, therefore, that some of the PGAL just manufactured is respired at once to pyruvic acid and through the citric acid cycle. PGAL is also usable directly as a building material; it can contribute to the synthesis of any of the innumerable structural components of plant cells, including some of the chemical machinery required for PGAL production itself.

But a green cell generally manufactures much more PGAL than it requires for its own mainte-

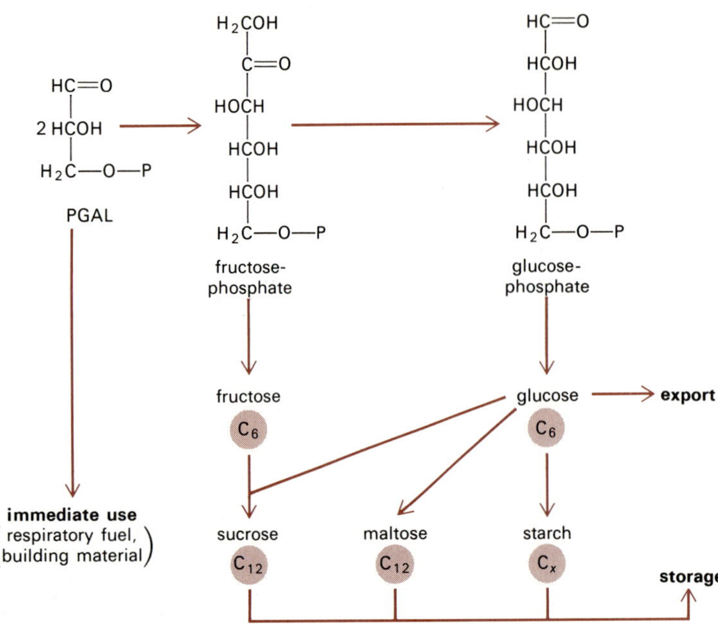

Fig. 13.14 Possible fates of PGAL. PGAL can be used immediately as a building material or processed through respiratory pathways as a nutrient fuel. Alternatively, PGAL molecules can be converted to monosaccharides or disaccharides and exported. These sugars can then be used as building materials or respiratory fuels in other cells or converted into starch for long-term storage.

nance. The bulk of the photosynthesis product then becomes available for export to nongreen cells of the organism. PGAL is not exported as such; it is probably too reactive. In transit from leaf to root, for example, it would react with other substances long before it could reach its destination. The green cell converts PGAL to less reactive compounds, particularly sugars such as glucose, fructose, and sucrose.

In these conversions two PGAL molecules are joined, forming one monosaccharide molecule. Since production of sugars (particularly sucrose) and export to other cells is the fate of most of the photosynthesized carbohydrate, sugar is often, though not quite correctly, regarded as the primary end product of photosynthesis.

The green cells of a plant normally produce enough PGAL not only to meet all current food requirements of the nongreen cells but also to provide appreciable amounts for longer-term storage. Green cells themselves store foods to some extent, but roots and stems are particularly specialized for this function (for example, taproots and tubers). Like export, storage does not involve PGAL as such. In any efficient storage, the stored material should take up as little space as possible and should also be out of circulation, i.e., relatively unavailable for rapid utilization. Since PGAL reacts readily with cellular components in its vicinity, it would not remain out of circulation for long. Even glucose, though less reactive, would enter metabolic processes fairly rapidly.

Plants actually condense PGAL molecules into more compact and relatively unreactive packets. For example, sugar cane, sugar beets, and many kinds of fruits owe their sweetness to stored fructose and sucrose. Numerous other plants accumulate carbohydrates in the form of starches. Still other plants manufacture storage fats instead of, or in addition to, carbohydrate reserves (for example, olive oil, castor oil, peanut oil, coconut oil). Such storage syntheses occur in both green and nongreen cells, and sugars are the usual starting materials (see Fig. 13.14 and also the following sections). In most cases storage molecules are more compact physically than the separate starting units. For example, disaccharides such as sucrose or maltose consist of two C_6 units but contain one fewer water molecule than two separate monosaccharides. Similarly, a polysaccharide in starch composed of, say, 500 C_6 units contains 499 fewer water molecules than 500 separate glucose molecules. It is this physical condensation that makes storage synthesis of adaptive value.

Photosynthesis as a whole is a very efficient process. It has been estimated that under ideal conditions up to 50 per cent of all the light energy absorbed by chloroplasts can be recovered as energy built into carbohydrates. However, a field of wheat absorbs only about 2 per cent of the total light energy it receives from the sun; chloroplasts are spread rather thinly over the whole field. Yet this 2 per cent of sunlight, produced by thermonuclear reactions 93 million miles away, represents the whole power source that keeps living organisms alive through photosynthesis.

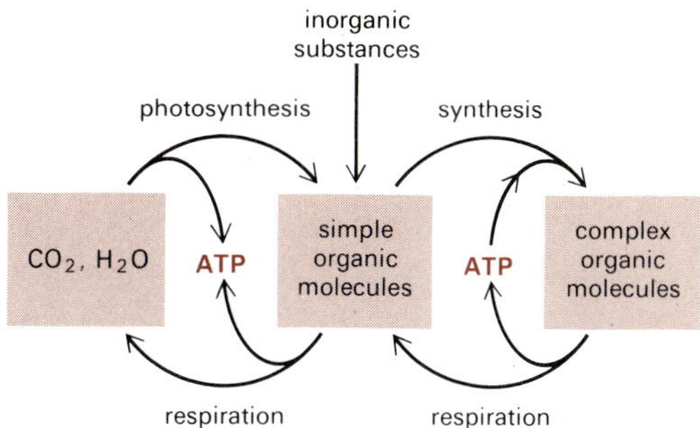

Fig. 13.15 Metabolic balance. All synthetic and other creative processes of metabolism are sometimes collectively referred to as *anabolism*, and all respiratory and other destructive processes, as *catabolism*.

SYNTHESIS METABOLISM

The metabolic link between photosynthesis and finished living matter is a large variety of synthesis reactions. These produce the chemicals a cell does not obtain directly as preexisting nutrients or as secretions from other cells. Such missing ingredients include most of the critically necessary compounds for cellular survival: nucleic acids, structural and enzymatic proteins, polysaccharides, fats, and numerous other groups of complex organic substances. In most cases, such synthesis reactions are ATP-requiring. A cyclical interrelationship is therefore in evidence. On the one hand, breakdown of organic compounds leads to a net buildup of ATP through respiration. On the other, breakdown of ATP leads to a net buildup of organic compounds through chemical synthesis (Fig. 13.15).

Synthesis of cellular components and breakdown occur simultaneously all the time. But even when the two processes are balanced exactly, they cannot sustain each other in a self-contained self-sufficient cycle. Energy dissipates irretrievably through physical activities and through heat losses in chemical reaction, and materials are lost through elimination, evaporation, and friction. Just to maintain a steady state, therefore, a cell must be supplied continuously with energy and raw materials. Moreover, the rate of supply in many cases must exceed the rate required for mere maintenance, for net synthesis often exceeds net breakdown, as in growth or repair after injury.

In a general sense, synthesis reverses the result of respiratory decomposition; the products formed at successive steps of respiration can be the starting materials in synthesis. However, only green cells and autotrophic cells generally can reverse the final step of respiration. Only they can "fix" the respiratory end product CO_2 and create original PGAL from this inorganic source. But once organic compounds are available, *all* cells, including nongreen plant cells and the cells of animals, can add CO_2 to these compounds and thereby increase the lengths of carbon chains.

Carbohydrates

Most carbohydrates in any organism usually are synthesized from glucose. This sugar can itself be formed from C_3 units such as PGAL, as noted (essentially by the reverse of part of the reaction sequence of glycolysis). Alternatively a cell obtains glucose as a prefabricated nutrient, in plants by transport in phloem from storage regions, in animals by transport in blood from gut or liver.

Glucose usually is phosphorylated as it enters cells. The products of this phosphorylation, in which ATP serves as the phosphate donor, are ADP and *glucose phosphate.* The latter normally interacts almost immediately with *uridine triphosphate* (UTP), a nucleotide derivative functionally equivalent to ATP. The result of this interaction is a *uridine diphosphate–glucose* complex (Fig. 13.16A). UDP-glucose is the actual starting material in many glucose-requiring syntheses. For example, UDP-glucose participates in the manufacture of monosac-

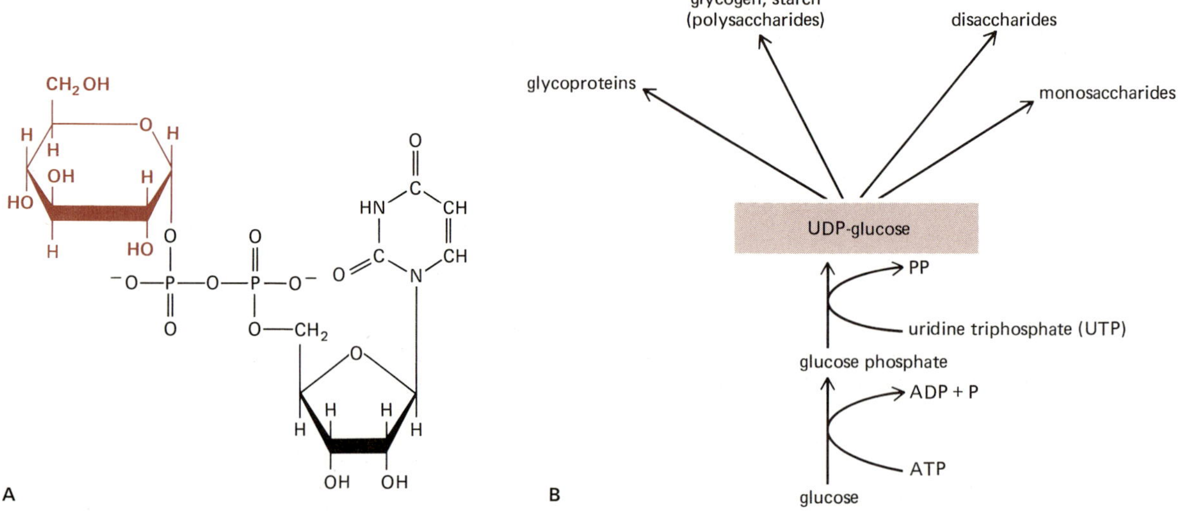

Fig. 13.16 UDP-glucose. (A) Structure. The glucose portion of the molecule is in color. (B) Manufacture of UDP-glucose begins when glucose is phosphorylated by ATP, forming glucose phosphate. The latter compound then combines with uridine and one additional phosphate, both derived from uridine triphosphate (UTP). Two phosphates are released as by-product. UDP-glucose is a prime raw material for synthesis of many disaccharides, polysaccharides, and glycoproteins.

charides such as galactose, disaccharides such as sucrose, polysaccharides such as starch, cellulose, and glycogen, and the carbohydrate portions of glycoproteins (Fig. 13.16B).

Starches stored in plant cells and glycogen in animal cells are normally the most abundant carbohydrates. They are also the usual starting carbohydrates both in respiration and in other syntheses. When used as fuel, starch or glycogen is phosphorylated by ATP and converted directly to glucose phosphate; and when used as building materials, these polysaccharides are reconverted to UDP-glucose. Glucose phosphate and UDP-glucose are themselves interconvertible, and glucose phosphate can also be exported from a cell in the form of free glucose. In most organisms a chemical balance is probably maintained between carbohydrates inside cells and free glucose outside them. Such balances are particularly precise in vertebrates, where the liver performs an important carbohydrate-regulating function (Fig. 13.17).

The liver stores incoming carbohydrates as glycogen and releases carbohydrates to the blood as glucose. Moreover, small-scale fluctuations notwithstanding, the liver maintains a fairly *constant* glucose concentration in blood. Whenever the glucose level in blood tends to rise, as after a meal, when large quantities of carbohydrates pass from the gut to the circulation, liver cells withdraw the excess from blood, produce UDP-glucose, and convert the latter to storage glycogen. Conversely, when blood-glucose levels tend to fall, as during intense body activity, when muscles and other tissues use up carbohydrates rapidly, liver cells convert stored glycogen to glucose phosphate and then to free glucose and release that sugar to the blood. If blood glucose decreases in concentration, the reaction equilibrium shifts in such a way that liver glycogen is transformed to free glucose; and if blood glucose increases in concentration, the equilibrium shifts in such a way that glucose will be converted to glycogen.

The amount of glycogen the liver can store is not particularly large. When sugars supplied by food exceed the storage capacity, the excess carbohydrates are converted to *fats.* These are stored partly in the liver, partly in other parts of the body. Such fat production explains why even a nonfatty diet can lead to obesity, particularly if for long periods more food is eaten than the body requires.

Conversely, when so few carbohydrates are

consumed that glycogen stores are severely reduced, the fat stores of the body can be converted to carbohydrates. Indeed the liver can maintain normal blood-glucose levels even when the diet is carbohydrate-free, provided food contains compensating amounts of fat (see Fig. 13.17).

One major role of the vertebrate liver thus emerges. The organ ensures that all cells of the body receive an adequate carbohydrate supply regardless of when or how often food is eaten. In invertebrates and all other organisms, which do not have organs functioning in exactly the same way, carbohydrate balances are far less regulated.

Lipids

As discussed in Chap. 4, lipids constitute a category of diverse organic molecules insoluble in water. Lipids include triglycerides (fats), oils, waxes, phospholipids, and steroids. Triglycerides, phospholipids, and steroids play especially important roles in living systems. Triglycerides are important nutrient-storage compounds, phospholipids are essential components of biological membranes, and many hormones are steroids.

Fatty acids are important starting materials for the synthesis of all triglycerides and many other lipids (see Chap. 4). The simplest starting material for fatty acid synthesis is the 2-carbon acetyl group (Fig. 13.18). Fatty acids of any length can be synthesized from acetyl CoA. This process is almost exactly the reverse of β-oxidation: successive C_2 groups in the form of acetyl CoA are added to acetyl CoA itself or to already existing longer carbon chains. The main steps can be traced by reading Fig. 12.18 in reverse. Recall here that animal cells are unable to synthesize certain essential fatty acids, which must be supplied fully formed in the diet.

Glycerol is a second kind of building material required for the synthesis of triglycerides, phospholipids, and certain other kinds of lipids. Glycerol is usually formed from C_3 compounds such as PGA or PGAL (see Fig. 13.18). In triglyceride synthesis, one molecule of glycerol is joined enzymatically to three molecules of fatty acids (see Fig. 4.5). Fatty

Fig. 13.17 Carbohydrate balance in vertebrates. (A) The pathways of interconversion between liver glycogen, blood glucose, and tissue glycogen. The hormones promoting given reactions are indicated in smaller type. Any excess liver glycogen can be converted into fat. Tissue glycogen is a main respiratory fuel as well as a starting compound in synthesis. (B) The maintenance of blood-glucose balance by the liver. If much sugar is supplied to blood from food and little is used, the blood-glucose concentration will tend to be high (left). Under such conditions the liver withdraws glucose and stores it as glycogen, thus establishing a normal glucose level (top). But if much glucose is used up and little is supplied, the blood-glucose concentration will tend to be low (right). The liver then adds glucose to blood from its glycogen stores and so reestablishes the normal glucose level (bottom). By these means the liver maintains a constant blood-glucose concentration.

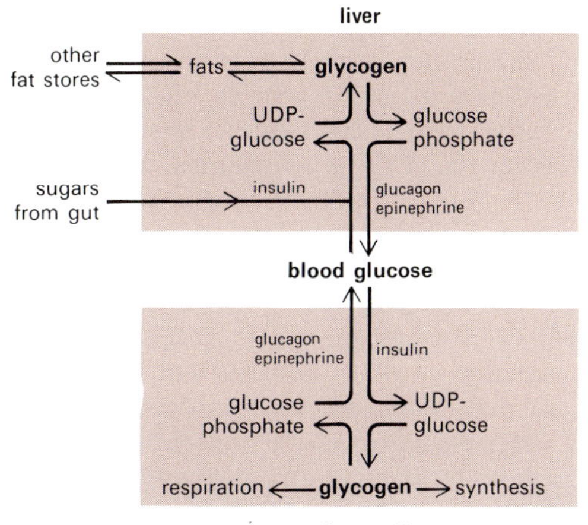

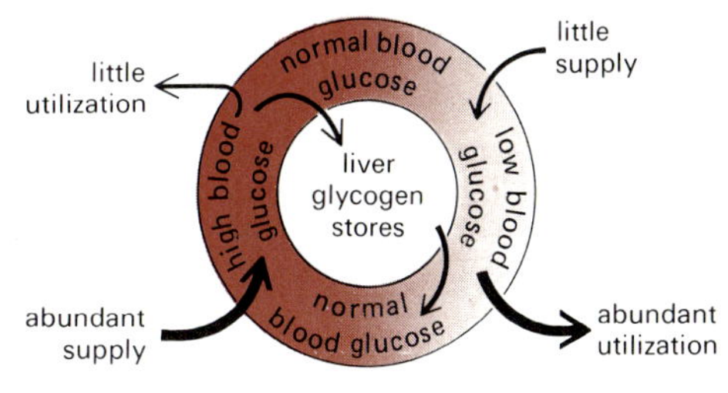

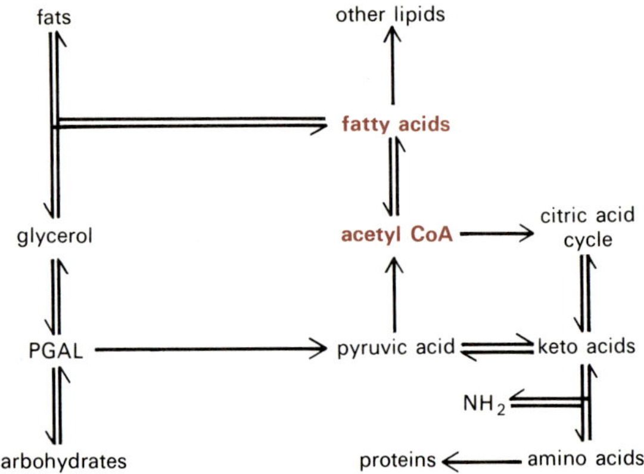

Fig. 13.18 Main pathways in lipid synthesis. The key compounds acetyl CoA and fatty acids are interconverted by β-oxidation or its reverse. Note that lipid metabolism is interconnected with carbohydrate and protein metabolism.

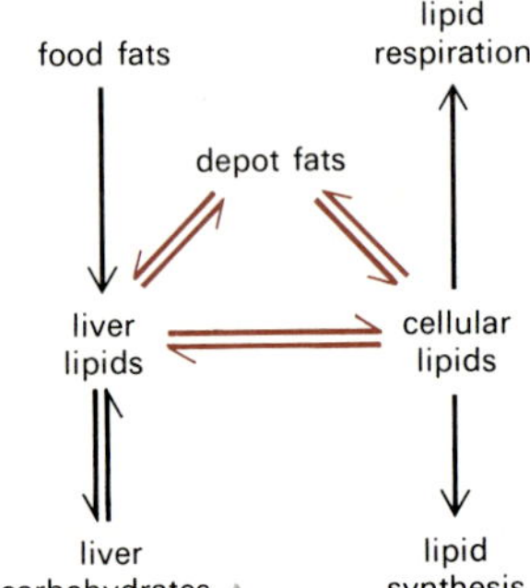

Fig. 13.19 Lipid balance in vertebrates.

acids and triglycerides also can arise from carbohydrate starting materials via the citric acid cycle, and from amino acids as well (see Fig. 13.18).

As already noted, fats (triglycerides) are the basic lipid reserves of organisms. Plants frequently store fats as oils in fruits and seeds, and animals contain fat bodies or other specialized regions for fat storage. In vertebrates, for example, fats are deposited under the skin, around the heart and the kidneys, and particularly along the mesenteries, the peritoneal membranes that envelop the intestine.

The liver, too, is an important fat depot, as noted above. Its total fat store is in balance with the reserves in other body regions. If liver fat increases too much, the excess is exported through the circulation to the other depots. Conversely, the other depots make up any deficiency in liver fat. In these redistributions fat is transported largely in the form of fatty acids and glycerol. The nonstoring tissues of the body are supplied either by the liver or by the other fat depots. Fat balance in a vertebrate is therefore maintained by an equilibrium between three groups of compounds, as shown in Fig. 13.19.

Amino Acids

Amino acid synthesis in cells ordinarily takes place by transamination (see Figs. 12.16 and 12.17). Thus, any amino acid can be formed if an amino group ($—NH_2$) interacts with an appropriate keto acid derived from lipids or carbohydrates:

$$\underset{\textit{amino donor}}{NH_2—\underset{|}{X}\!-\!H} + \underset{\textit{keto acid}}{O{=}\overset{R}{\overset{|}{C}}—COOH} \longrightarrow \underset{\textit{amino acid}}{NH_2—\overset{R}{\overset{|}{\underset{H}{\underset{|}{C}}}}—COOH} + O{=}X$$

Amino groups can be supplied by other available amino acids, but, as noted in Chap. 8, the ultimate source is mineral nitrate, NO_3^-. Microorganisms and plants can convert these ions to $—NH_2$. Animals cannot, and they depend on each other and ultimately on plants for their supply of amino groups. Recall also that plants must supply animals with essential amino acids, or, more specifically, those keto acid portions of amino acids which animal cells cannot synthesize on their own.

Plant cells usually synthesize amino acids only in amounts actually required for current construction processes; hence little if any excess or deficiency of amino acids is likely to exist. Animal cells are different in this respect, for their supply of amino acids, particularly essential ones, depends on the food intake of the whole animal, a factor not under direct control of an individual cell. Moreover, unlike carbohydrates or fats, amino acids are not stored. If the supply from the gut is inadequate, an amino acid deficiency will develop. Breakdown of proteins already in a cell or transamination can alleviate such shortages temporarily, but the cell and indeed the whole animal eventually will suffer disease or death if essential amino acids remain unavailable. Animals therefore must consume daily doses of essential amino acids (or the corresponding keto acids).

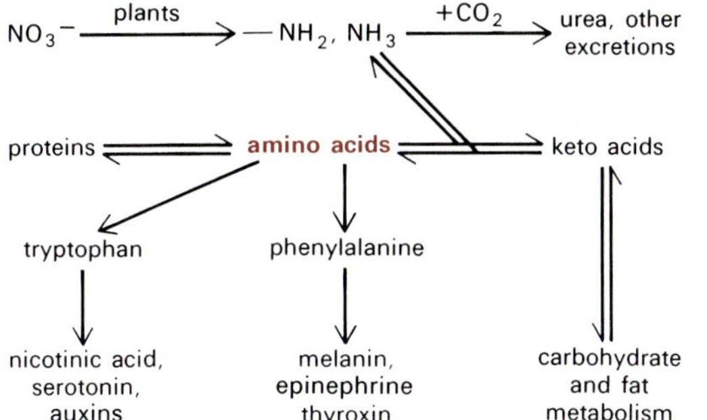

Fig. 13.20 Main pathways in amino acid synthesis. Arrows do not necessarily imply single reaction steps. In animals, keto acids for the essential amino acids must be obtained from the diet. Tryptophan and phenylalanine are amino acids themselves. Serotonin, auxins, adrenalin, and thyroxin function as hormones, and melanin is a black pigment.

Normally, however, animal diets actually supply more than immediately needed amounts of amino acids. Requirements are greatest in young, growing animals, in pregnant females, and in animals with extensively damaged or diseased parts undergoing healing. In all such cases large amounts of amino acids are used in protein synthesis. But even then more amino acids are usually eaten than required. In healthy adults growth and structural replacement occur at a much reduced rate, and amino acid requirements are correspondingly lower. Any excess of amino acids is then degraded, in vertebrates mainly in the liver and in other animals probably in all cells. This degradation takes the form of deamination, as already outlined in Chap. 12 (see Fig. 12.16). The resulting keto acids later participate in carbohydrate or lipid metabolism (see Fig. 13.18), and the ammonia, a toxic alkaline waste product, is excreted (see Chap. 18).

Apart from amino acids that are deaminated, all others, either synthesized directly in a cell or supplied to a cell as nutrients, serve as raw materials in a wide variety of manufacturing processes (Fig. 13.20). For example, the amino acid tryptophan is converted to the B vitamin *nicotinic acid,* which in turn contributes to the formation of NAD and NADP. Tryptophan also is a precursor of *serotonin,* a hormonelike substance of the vertebrate nervous system, and of *auxins,* the chief growth hormones of plants. The amino acid phenylalanine is the starting compound in the synthesis of the common black pigment *melanin* and the animal hormones *epinephrine* and *thyroxin.* But amino acids play their most important role by far as raw materials in protein synthesis, a process associated intimately with nucleic acid synthesis. This topic will occupy our attention in the next chapter.

A comprehensive summary of the main synthesis pathways in cells generally is given in Fig. 13.21. Note that all these relationships depend on the production of PGAL. Thus, all these chemical reactions, and therefore all organisms, are totally dependent on the green cells that can reverse the final step in respiration. Only they can fix the respiratory end product CO_2 and produce original PGAL from this inorganic source.

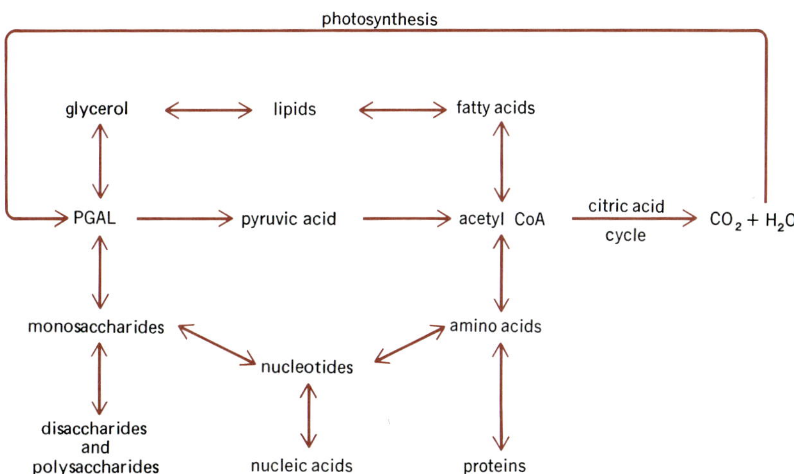

Fig. 13.21 Synthesis metabolism: overall summary. Many of the reaction pathways shown here are reversible and can lead either to synthesis or to respiratory degradation.

Review Questions

1 What physical processes are implied by the statement "chlorophyll is green"? What is the internal architecture of chloroplasts? State the general chemical nature and function of photosynthesis as a whole. Distinguish between photolysis and CO_2 fixation and state where each process occurs in chloroplasts. Review the sources of the carbon, hydrogen, and oxygen atoms that compose photosynthetic carbohydrates.

2 What is fluorescence, and how does this phenomenon demonstrate the ability of chlorophyll to absorb and transmit energy?

3 Describe the functional relationships between water, light, chlorophyll, electron carriers, and NADP in photolysis. Distinguish between cyclic and noncyclic electron flow, and show how such transfers contribute to ATP formation and food manufacture. What carrier compounds participate in electron transfers? Write a net input-output statement of photolysis.

4 What is photorespiration, and why can it be considered a wasteful process? Describe how the destructive effects of photorespiration are thwarted by the leaf anatomy of C_4 plants and by the C_4 cycle. Show how the C_3 and C_4 photosynthetic pathways are integrated in C_4 plants.

5 Describe the main steps of the Calvin cycle. Write a net input-output statement of this cycle and of photosynthesis as a whole.

6 What is the main end product of photosynthesis? Review the possible fates of this end product. What are the chief transportation and storage forms of carbohydrates in plants?

7 Show how these interconversions can occur:

a. Carbohydrate to fat
b. Fat to carbohydrate
c. Carbohydrate to amino acid or vice versa
d. Fat to amino acid or vice versa

Review patterns of carbohydrate synthesis. How can carbon chains be lengthened in cells? Shortened? What is the role of UDP-glucose, and what compounds can be formed from it?

8 By what processes does the vertebrate liver maintain a constant glucose concentration in blood? Describe several specific situations in which the blood-glucose level tends to change and show how such tendencies are counteracted by the liver.

9 Suppose that an animal is not given any food for a long time. What changes will occur in the bodywide balance of carbohydrates, fats, and amino acids?

10 Can an animal survive if its food consists of:

a. Only carbohydrates?
b. Only fats?
c. Only proteins?
d. Carbohydrates and fats only?
e. Carbohydrates and amino acids only?
f. Fats and amino acids only?

Collateral Readings

Bassham, J. A.: The path of Carbon in Photosynthesis, *Scientific American,* June 1962. A good, well-illustrated presentation of CO_2 fixation.

Dyson, R. D.: "Cell Biology: A Molecular Approach," Allyn and Bacon, Boston, 1978. Contains an excellent discussion of photosynthesis and synthesis metabolism generally.

Govindjee, G., and **R. Govindjee:** The Primary Events of Photosynthesis, *Scientific American,* December 1974. A lucid discussion of the biochemical aspects of photolysis.

Lehninger, A. L.: "Biochemistry," 2d ed., Worth, New York, 1975. This exceptional text contains discussions of the molecular aspects of biological energy transformations, including those of respiration and photosynthesis. More advanced than the presentation in this chapter. Recommended for those interested in greater detail.

Rabinowitch, E. I., and **G. Govindjee:** "Photosynthesis," Wiley, New York, 1969. Available in paperback, this excellent book describes the experimental results that underlie our present understanding of photosynthesis.

Stoeckenius, W.: The Purple Membrane of Salt-Loving Bacteria, *Scientific American,* June 1976. A unique kind of photosynthesis is described. Instead of chlorophyll these bacteria contain a photosynthetic pigment similar to visual pigment of animals.

Chapter 14 Genetic Codes, Proteins

Learning Objectives

After reading this chapter you should be able to:

1. Write a paragraph that defines the primary function of genes, and show how this function relates to the processes of replication, transcription, and translation.
2. Construct a diagram that depicts a segment of DNA and illustrate how each strand of this segment can serve as a template for the production of new complementary strands.
3. Define genetic code.
4. State how DNA polymerase, unwinding proteins, and DNA ligase function in the replication of moneran genes; define and state the functional significance of replicons.
5. List at least one functional role played by each of the following in the synthesis of a protein:
   - **a.** DNA
   - **b.** RNA polymerase
   - **c.** sigma factor
   - **d.** promotor regions
   - **e.** messenger RNA
   - **f.** ribosomal RNA
   - **g.** transfer RNA
   - **h.** ribosomes
   - **i.** amino acids
   - **j.** ATP
   - **k.** initiation codons
   - **l.** initiation factors
   - **m.** termination codons
6. Illustrate the functional relationship between tRNA, amino acids, and aminoacyl-tRNA synthetase in the manufacture of aminoacyl-tRNA.
7. Differentiate between A and P sites on ribosomes and illustrate how these sites function during the translocation of ribosomes; construct a diagram that illustrates the structural relationships among each of the following components of a polyribosome:
   - **a.** large and small subunits of ribosomes
   - **b.** messenger RNA
   - **c.** polypeptide chains
8. Explain how all structures and functions of living things ultimately are determined by DNA.

Apart from photosynthesis in green cells, protein and nucleic acid synthesis are the most basic synthesis processes in cells. The production of these polymers differs in several respects from the manufacture of all other cellular components. In fact, the behavior of the macromolecules described in this chapter often appears both amazing and spectacular. Biological processes discussed in earlier chapters largely involve stationary or semimobile arrays of molecules occupying different positions in mitochondria, chloroplasts, and other organelles. In this chapter, we become acquainted with a extraordinarily dynamic group of molecules that unzip, proofread, decode, repair or cut away segments of other molecules, block or turn on precise sequences of chemical reactions, travel at startingly high rates of speed, and perform a host of equally surprising functions (see also Chap. 28).

Nucleic acids and proteins are unique not only behaviorally but often structurally as well. Cells of different tissues and organisms, which frequently produce identical carbohydrates and fats, synthesize identical proteins and nucleic acids only under special circumstances.

The diversity of species, individual organisms, and cells is a direct consequence of protein and nucleic acid specificity. For example, human characteristics differ from those of chimpanzees and maple trees. Yet we share more characteristics with apes than with trees. Such similarities and differences are the products of chemical reactions that occur in different species; the more diverse the nature and timing of such reactions, the more diverse the species, and vice versa. Similarly, cells of different tissues are different because the chemical reactions occurring in each are not identical. As noted in Chap. 4, chemical reactions in cells are almost entirely determined and maintained by enzymes. Since all enzymes are proteins, the unique characteristics of cells, individual organisms, and species derive largely from protein specificity. Protein synthesis therefore requires *specificity control;* a "blueprint" must provide instructions about the precise sequence in which given numbers and types of amino acids are to be joined in a particular protein.

Ultimately, such specificity control is exercised by *genes,* the DNA of a cell. *The primary function of genes is to control specificities in protein synthesis.*

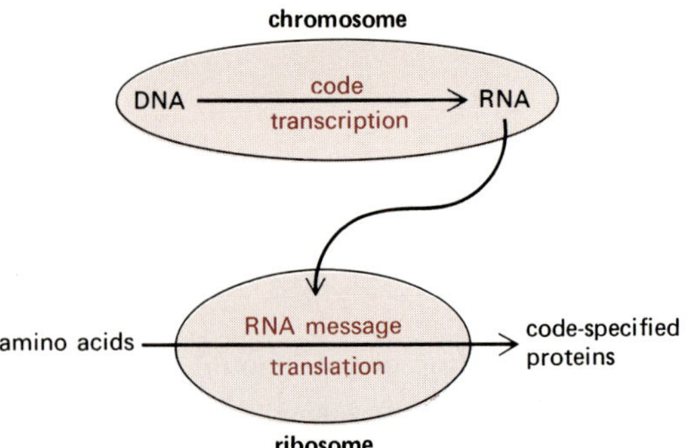

Fig. 14.1 The pattern of protein synthesis. The genetic "message" in the chromosomal DNA of a cell is transcribed to RNA and translated from RNA to specific amino acid sequences in proteins manufactured on ribosomes.

GENES AND PROTEIN SYNTHESIS

The Pattern

Sequences of nitrogen bases in DNA, or genes, represent coded chemical instructions. Many of these sequences specify the order in which amino acids are to be joined in proteins. In other words, different genes in a cell carry different instructions, and a cell can manufacture proteins only as these genetic instructions dictate.

Although mitochondria and chloroplasts contain DNA that directs the synthesis of some of their proteins, most genes are housed in chromosomes inside the nucleus. The "factories" where proteins are actually put together are the ribosomes and the cytoplasm, and genetic instructions are transmitted to the ribosomes by RNA.

Chromosomes produce RNA, and in the process the chemical message of DNA becomes incorporated, or *transcribed,* in the structure of RNA. The new RNA molecules then leave the chromosomes and diffuse into the cytoplasm, and they eventually reach the ribosomes. Here amino acids are joined together as proteins in accordance with the genetic instruction supplied by the RNA molecules (Fig. 14.1).

Thus, genes are essentially passive information carriers that can be likened to important original "texts" carefully stored and preserved in the "library" of the nucleus. There they are available as permanent, authoritative "master documents," from which expendable duplicate copies—RNA—can be prepared. RNA passing to the cytoplasm actually is expendable and usually short-lived; soon after it has exercised its function as a code carrier, most RNA is degraded by respiration. New copies of such RNA must be produced in the nucleus if continued protein synthesis is to occur.

Inasmuch as the RNA formed by the chromosomes carries chemical messages to the ribosomes, it is called *messenger* RNA (mRNA). The process whereby the coded information of mRNA is used to determine the sequence of amino acid in proteins is called *translation.* Two additional types of RNA are required for translation. One is *ribosomal* RNA (rRNA), a normal structural component of ribosomes. Ribosomal RNA is produced in the nucleoli of a cell nucleus and is joined with proteins in the manufacture of two structurally distinct subunits of whole ribosomes. These two types of subunits differ in size, and a whole ribosome consists of one larger and one smaller subunit. Both types of subunits are transferred independently through nuclear pores to the cytoplasm, where they ultimately join as whole ribosomes.

The third type of RNA is *transfer* RNA (tRNA), which functions as an amino acid carrier. A cell has 61 different kinds of tRNA, roughly three times as many as there are different kinds of amino acids. When a particular kind of amino acid is used in protein synthesis, a corresponding kind of tRNA becomes attached to the amino acid and carries it to the ribosomes. Here the tRNA "delivers" its amino acid at a particular place along a mRNA chain. Other tRNA carriers similarly deliver their amino acids at other specific locations along the mRNA chain. In this manner, large

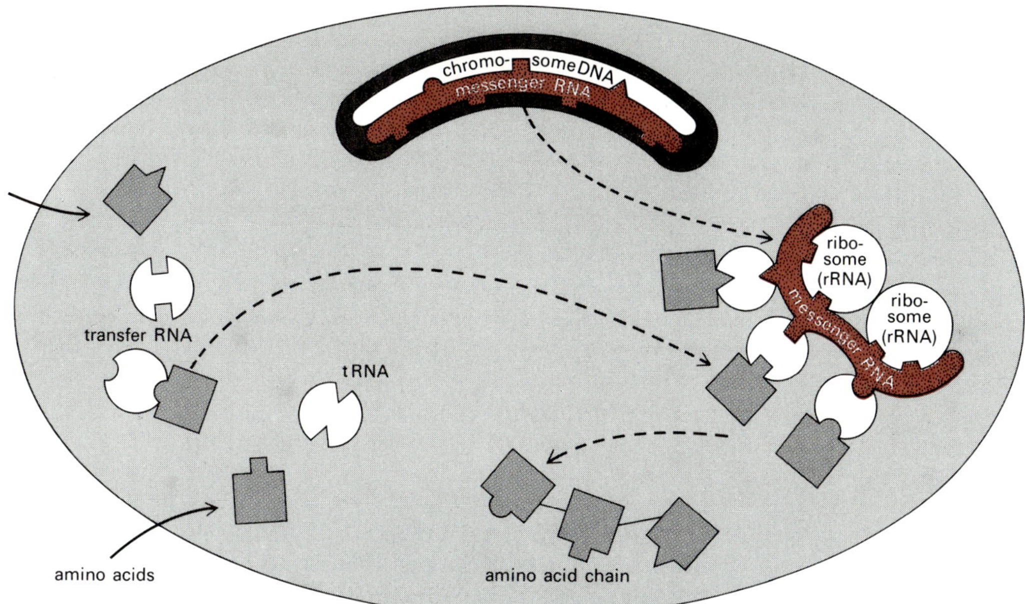

Fig. 14.2 The pattern of protein synthesis. Specific messenger RNA (mRNA) manufactured in chromosomes becomes attached at ribosomes. Amino acids entering a cell as food become joined to specific transfer RNA molecules, and the tRNA–amino acid complexes attach at specific, code-determined sites along the messenger RNA. The amino acids there link together through formation of successive peptide bonds (as in Fig. 4.8). The completed, code-specific amino acid chains then become free.

numbers of amino acids become lined up along mRNA in a particular sequence. As will become apparent presently, the nature of this sequence has been determined by the chemical message in mRNA. The "correctly" stationed amino acids then become joined to each other, and a protein with a gene-determined specificity results (Fig. 14.2).

The Process

DNA Replication

Since the unique characteristics of all cells are determined ultimately by DNA, new cells produced by cell reproduction must inherit the genes of the parent cell. If this were not the case, the specific characteristics of parent cells could not be maintained in the descendants. But how do parent cells transmit identical genes to their descendants? The most direct method would be to duplicate the original genes and then transmit one copy to each "daughter" cell. Indeed, this is what actually happens. The process whereby DNA is duplicated, or *replicated,* prior to cell reproduction requires a brief reexamination of the chemical composition of DNA.

As stated previously, DNA is a spiraled double chain of nucleotides (see Figs. 4.17 and 4.18). In it, the genetic formation is represented by a four-letter "alphabet" of nitrogen bases, and in the double chain these bases occur in four pair-combinations, A · T, T · A, G · C, and C · G. A gene then consists of a specific succession of such pairs. The scientists primarily responsible for deducing the structure and genetic significance of DNA were James Watson and Francis Crick. Their discovery is one of the milestones in the history of science.

If the genes of a given segment of a DNA chain are to be replicated, the first requirement is an unspiraling and "unzipping" of this segment of the double chain into two separate single chains. Assume that, as in Fig. 14.3, the nitrogen-base sequence of one of these single chains is AGCT.

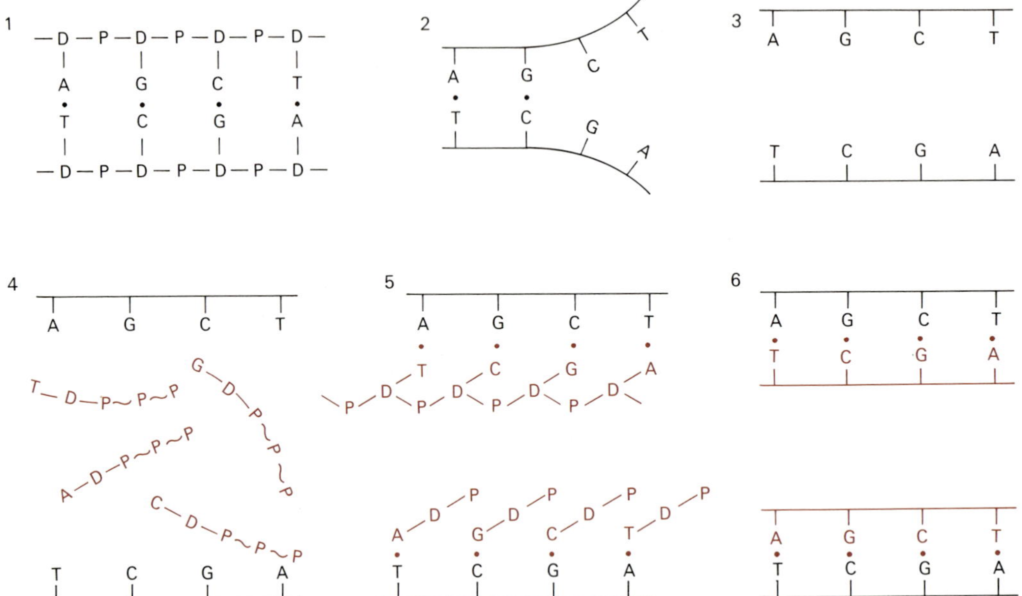

Fig. 14.3 DNA replication. (A, G, C, T, nitrogen bases; D, deoxyribose; P, phosphate.) If a double DNA chain (1) is to be replicated, it separates progressively (2) into two single chains (3). Nucleotide-triphosphate raw materials (4) then become attached to each free nitrogen base, and the two terminal phosphates of each of these raw materials split off in the process (5, bottom). The deoxyribose and phosphate parts of adjacent nucleotides then become joined with the aid of DNA polymerase (5, top). Two DNA double chains thus result (6), identical to each other as well as to the original parent chain. Note that in each newly formed double chain one single chain served as the code-specific template in the manufacture of the (colored) new single chain.

Thus, the complementary sequence in the other single chain must be TCGA. During DNA replication, each of these single strands becomes the foundation, or *template,* for the production of a new complementary strand. As templates, each single strand of DNA provides information about the order in which nucleotides are to be assembled in each new complementary strand.

For example, the first nitrogen base in the upper template of DNA in Fig. 14.3 is A, adenine. We know that such a base can join only to the nitrogen base T, thymine, and form an A · T pair. If therefore the available raw materials in a chromosome include a thymine-containing nucleotide, then such a molecule can bind to the A of DNA. The raw material actually required is *deoxythymidine triphosphate* (dTTP), a molecular complex containing thymine, deoxyribose, and three phosphate units (T—D—P∼P∼P in part 4 of Fig. 14.3). In the process of bonding enzymatically to the DNA chain, the two terminal phosphates split off as by-products; the split high-energy phosphates provide bonding energy, and the molecule that remains attached to DNA is *deoxythymidine monophosphate* (dTMP, symbolized as T—D—P in part 5 of Fig. 14.3).

Quite similarly, a T of DNA can bond to *deoxyadenosine monophosphate* (dAMP); a C can bond to *deoxyguanosine monophosphate* (dGMP); and a G can bond to *deoxycytidine monophosphate* (dCMP). All such monophosphates are derived from their respective triphosphates (Table 14.1).

The first nitrogen base in the lower template in Fig. 14.3 is T, thymine, and its complementary base is A, adenine. Formation of a strand of DNA complementary to the lower template first requires bonding of dAMP to T. The production of complementary strands continues progressively as the nitrogen bases of both templates become linked successively to complementary nucleotides. Thus,

TABLE 14.1
Nomenclature of the Nucleosides and Nucleotides

Base	Sugar	Nucleoside (base plus sugar)	Nucleotide (base plus sugar plus phosphate)
		DNA	
adenine	deoxyribose	deoxyadenosine	deoxyadenosine monophosphate (dAMP), deoxyadenylic acid
guanine	deoxyribose	deoxyguanosine	deoxyguanosine monophosphate (dGMP), deoxyguanylic acid
cytosine	deoxyribose	deoxycytidine	deoxycytidine monophosphate (dCMP), deoxycytidylic acid
thymine	deoxyribose	deoxythymidine	deoxythymidine monophosphate (dTMP), deoxythymidylic acid
		RNA	
adenine	ribose	adenosine	adenosine monophosphate (AMP), adenylic acid
guanine	ribose	guanosine	guanosine monophosphate (GMP), guanylic acid
cytosine	ribose	cytidine	cytidine monophosphate (CMP), cytidylic acid
uracil	ribose	uridine	uridine monophosphate (UMP), uridylic acid

SOURCE: W. DeWitt, "Biology of The Cell: An Evolutionary Approach," table 7.1, Saunders, Philadelphia, 1977.

DNA replication is equivalent to DNA *reproduction;* one double chain gives rise to two identical double chains. One of the two single chains in each daughter DNA existed originally in the parent DNA, the other single chain has been newly manufactured. In this manner, genetic information is duplicated, and each copy now can be transmitted to a new generation of cells.

Unwinding the DNA during replication is a complex process that involves several enzymes and other proteins. DNA in most Monera (bacteria and blue-green algae) is a ring-shaped molecule. Replication begins when such a ring is broken enzymatically at a specific point and continues as DNA is unwound from this point in clockwise and counterclockwise directions (Fig. 14.4). Thus, the circular shape of moneran DNA is maintained during replication. The unzipping of DNA is promoted by a group of *unwinding proteins,* which bind to the two strands of the double helix and separate them. As the strands separate, complementary nucleotides are linked in place by the enzyme *DNA polymerase.* Three forms of this enzyme have been discovered, each appearing to promote formation of complementary strands under different circumstances.

All three forms of DNA polymerase can remove nucleotides from elongating strands of DNA as well as add them. The enzymes normally remove only improperly placed nucleotides that have been inserted mistakenly into an elongating strand. This "proofreading" ability provides great fidelity of replication, and ensures that almost all improperly placed nucleotides will be removed before the next nitrogen base is added. Following replication, the ends of each new double helix are joined by *DNA ligase,* an enzyme that fuses broken segments of DNA molecules.

The nuclear DNA of plants, animals, and virtually all other nonmoneran cells is linear, not circular, and is replicated bidirectionally from many sites (Fig. 14.5). The points where enzymes and unwinding proteins begin to separate and replicate linear DNA are called *sites of origin* (*O* in Fig. 14.5A). The two lateral points at which replication ceases are called *sites of termination.* Thus, on each side of a site of origin is a site of termination (*T* in Fig. 14.5A). Regions between adjoining sites of termination are called *replicons.* Two complete double-stranded molecules of DNA result when all replicons of the original molecule have been replicated.

Cells of plants, animals, and other eukaryotes have much more DNA (and thus many more genes) than cells of prokaryotes; replication from many origins speeds up the duplication process. It has been calculated, for example, that 16 days would be needed to replicate the DNA contained in the largest chromosome of a fruit fly if replication pro-

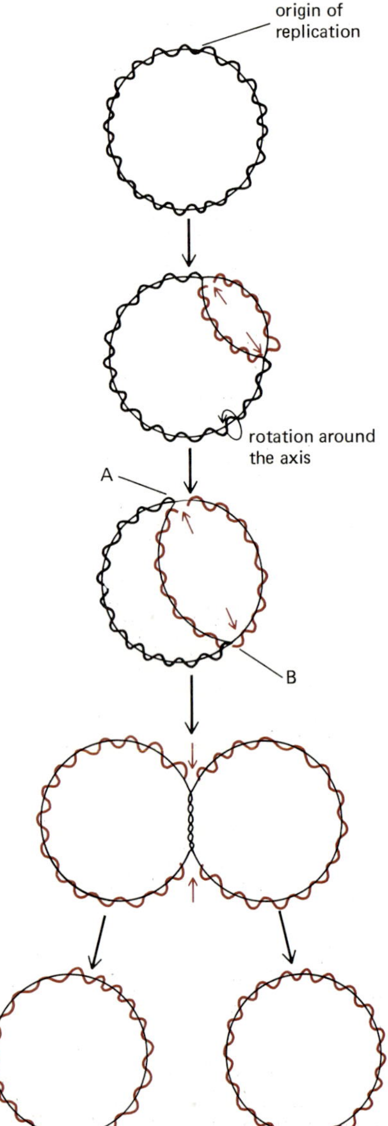

Fig. 14.4 Bidirectional replication of circular DNA. Replication of ring-shaped molecules of DNA begins at one point and progresses simultaneously in clockwise and counterclockwise directions (arrows). Template strands are shown in black, newly replicated strands in color.

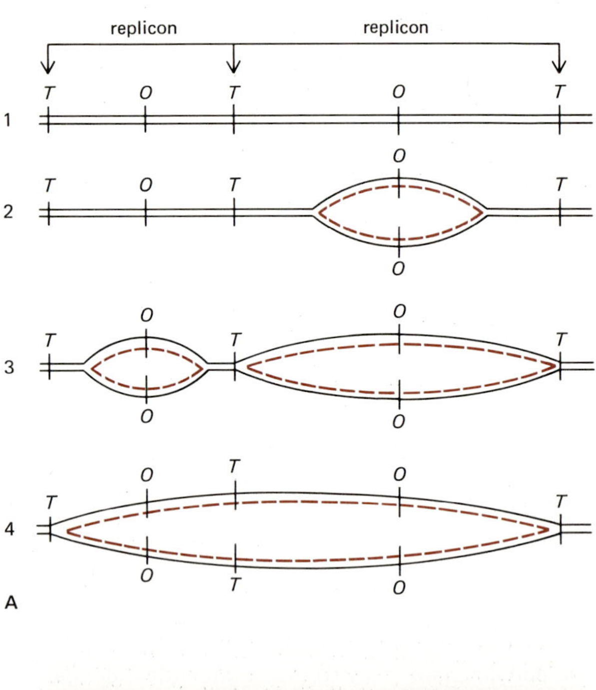

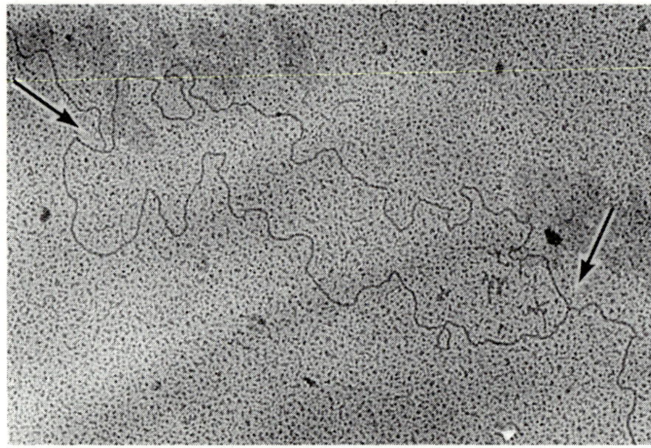

Fig. 14.5 Bidirectional replication of linear DNA. (A) Replication of eukaryotic DNA, which is linear, begins at many points of origin (*O*) and progresses bidirectionally to points of termination (*T*). In this illustration, replication begins first in the right replicon (2) and then in the left replicon (3). Template strands are shown in black, newly replicated strands in color. (B) Replication of yeast DNA, revealing a configuration similar to those shown in (A). Replication is progressing laterally from the growing points (arrows).

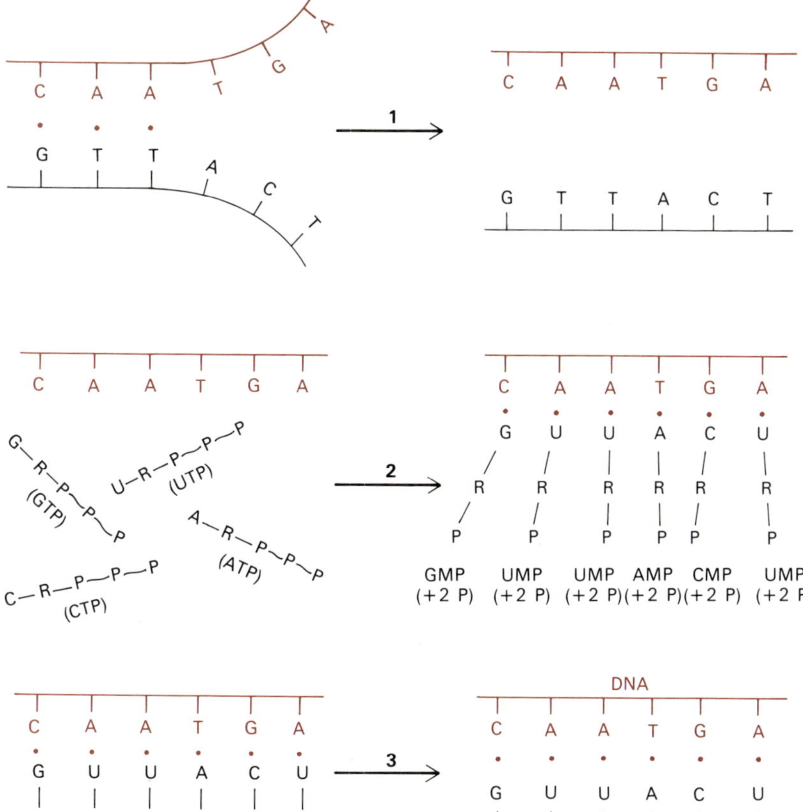

Fig. 14.6 Code transcription from DNA to mRNA. (A, T, G, C, U, purine and pyrimidine bases; R, ribose; P, phosphate.) In a first step part of the DNA double chain unzips. In a second step the nucleotide-triphosphate raw materials ATP, GTP, CTP, and UTP become bonded as monophosphates to appropriate nitrogen bases along a single DNA chain (color). In the third step a linked ribose-phosphate chain is formed under the influence of RNA polymerase. The finished mRNA then has a nitrogen base sequence specifically determined by that of DNA. After mRNA becomes detached from DNA, the spiraled double chain of DNA is reformed. In certain respects this message transcription from DNA to mRNA resembles that of transcription from DNA to DNA (compare with Fig. 14.3).

ceeded from only one point of origin. The DNA of this chromosome actually is replicated from many points of origin in about 3 min.

RNA Transcription

DNA serves not only as a template for its own synthesis but also for the transcription of all types of RNA. Production of RNA has many features in common with DNA replication. A DNA double strand first separates into single strands. Nucleotides then are incorporated in RNA using one of the DNA strands as a template.

For example, assume that the nitrogen base sequence CAATGA of one strand of DNA is to be transcribed to RNA (Fig. 14.6). Since the first nitrogen base of the DNA strand is C, the first nucleotide bonded to the template is GMP, *guanosine monophosphate* (G—R—P in part 2 of Fig. 14.6). GMP is identical to dGMP used in DNA replication except that GMP contains ribose instead of deoxyribose (see Table 14.1). The next nucleotide incorporated into RNA is UMP, *uridine monophosphate* (recall that RNA contains uracil where DNA contains thymine). Ribose-containing nucleotides complementary to the sequence of nitrogen bases of the DNA strand are inserted progressively until a finished molecule of RNA has been produced.

The enzyme primarily responsible for this synthesis is RNA *polymerase.* This molecule is attached to a protein subunit, called the *sigma factor,* capable of "recognizing" specific nitrogen base sequences of DNA that function as "start" signals for RNA transcription (Fig. 14.7). Such initiation signals are called *promotors.* Binding of sigma fac-

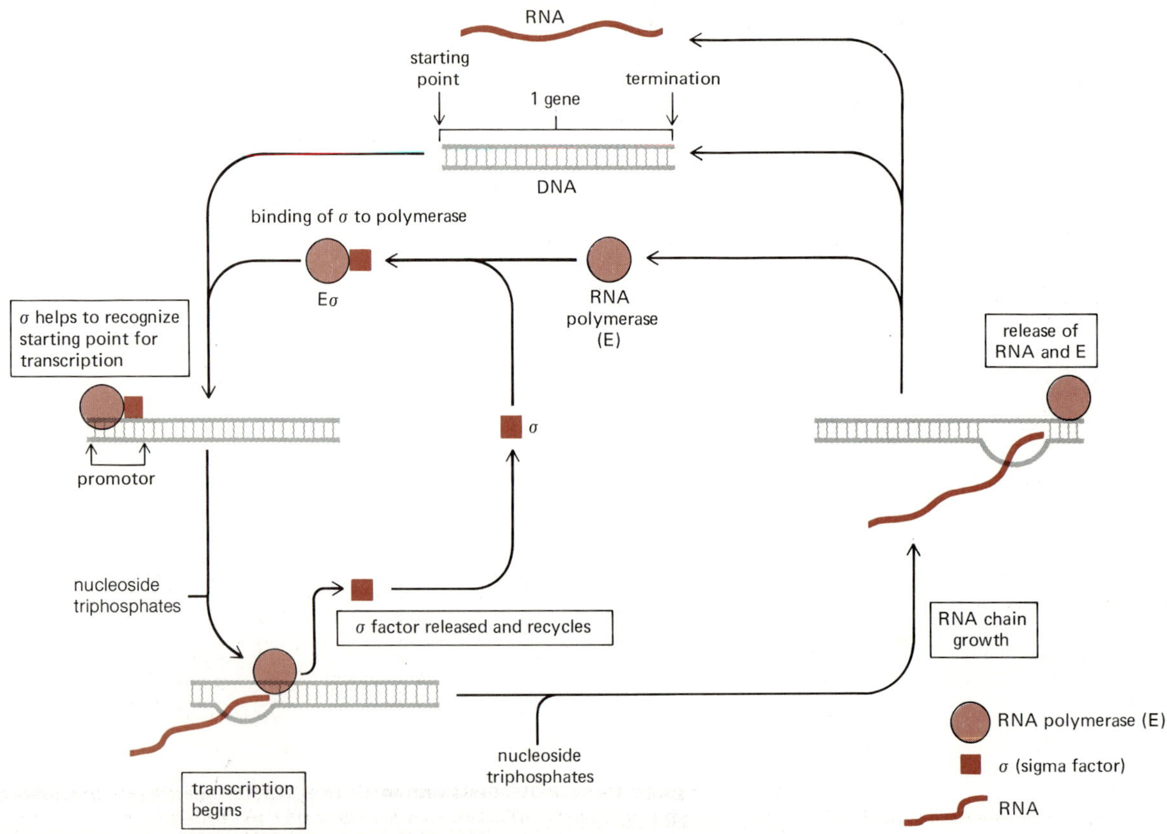

Fig. 14.7 RNA synthesis. Synthesis under conditions where RNA polymerase can "read" the terminating signal by itself. In other cases another molecule, called a *rho factor*, participates in the release of RNA and from DNA.

tor to the promoter results in a local unwinding of the DNA helix. One of the two unwound strands (not always the same one) serves as a template for RNA transcription.

The sigma factor detaches from the remainder of the RNA polymerase after transcription begins. The portion of the RNA polymerase now free of sigma factor continues catalysis of RNA synthesis until the enzyme reaches a sequence of nitrogen bases on DNA that signal termination of RNA transcription. Completed molecules of RNA then are released from the DNA template and enter the cytoplasm. Ribosomal RNA moves out of the nucleus within subunits of ribosomes. Transfer RNA and messenger RNA enter the cytoplasm as independent units. Many molecules of RNA can be transcribed simultaneously along individual segments of DNA, a process that can now be observed directly (Fig. 14.8). Segments of DNA unwound during transcription are rewound as the last molecule of RNA is produced.

The net result of RNA transcription is a polynucleotide strand whose nitrogen base sequence is complementary to that of the DNA template. The *genetic code* of DNA is imprinted in its RNA transcript rather in the way a photographic negative shows light objects as dark areas or that a plaster cast shows elevated objects as depressions. We also know that such inverted negative codes in mRNA must somehow "spell out" in chemical terms an identification of the 20 different amino acids, and that it must do so with a four-letter alphabet. Assuming that nature is as concise as it can be, how are 20 different identifying "words" constructed out of four letters so that each word contains as few letters as possible?

If the code consisted of one-letter words, a four-letter alphabet A-B-C-D would allow only four different identifications: A, B, C, D. If the code were made up of two-letter words, there could be 4^2, or 16, different letter combinations: AA, AB, AC, AD, BB, BA, BC, etc. Yet 16 combinations are still too few to specify 20 amino acid "words." However, if the code contained three-letter words, there could be 4^3, or 64 different letter combinations, more than enough to spell out 20 words (and roughly as many as there are different kinds of transfer RNA).

On the basis of such reasoning, it was hypothesized and later confirmed that the genetic code "names" each amino acid by a sequence of three "letters," i.e., three adjacent nitrogen bases. In such a *triplet code*, at least 20 triplets would be "meaningful" and would spell out amino acid identities.

Which nitrogen base triplets, or *codons*, identify which amino acids? The answer has been obtained through ingenious experiments. It is possible to produce in the test tube artificial RNA molecules that contain known sequences of nitrogen bases. To such RNA can be added a mixture of known amino acids and other materials necessary for protein synthesis, and in this fashion chains of linked amino acids can be synthesized in the test tube. Analysis of these chains show which amino acids are present and in what sequence. In the first experiments of this kind, for example, the synthetic RNA consisted entirely of a sequence of ura-

Fig. 14.8 Genes in action. Electron micrograph showing one segment of DNA from the nucleolus of an amphibian egg. The fine filaments are molecules of RNA being formed along the DNA strands. (*Courtesy of O. L. Miller, Jr.*)

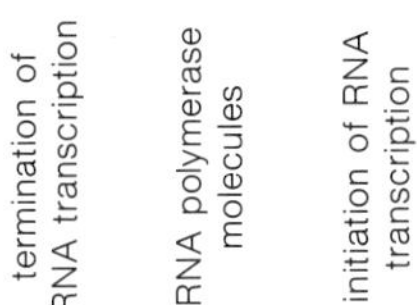

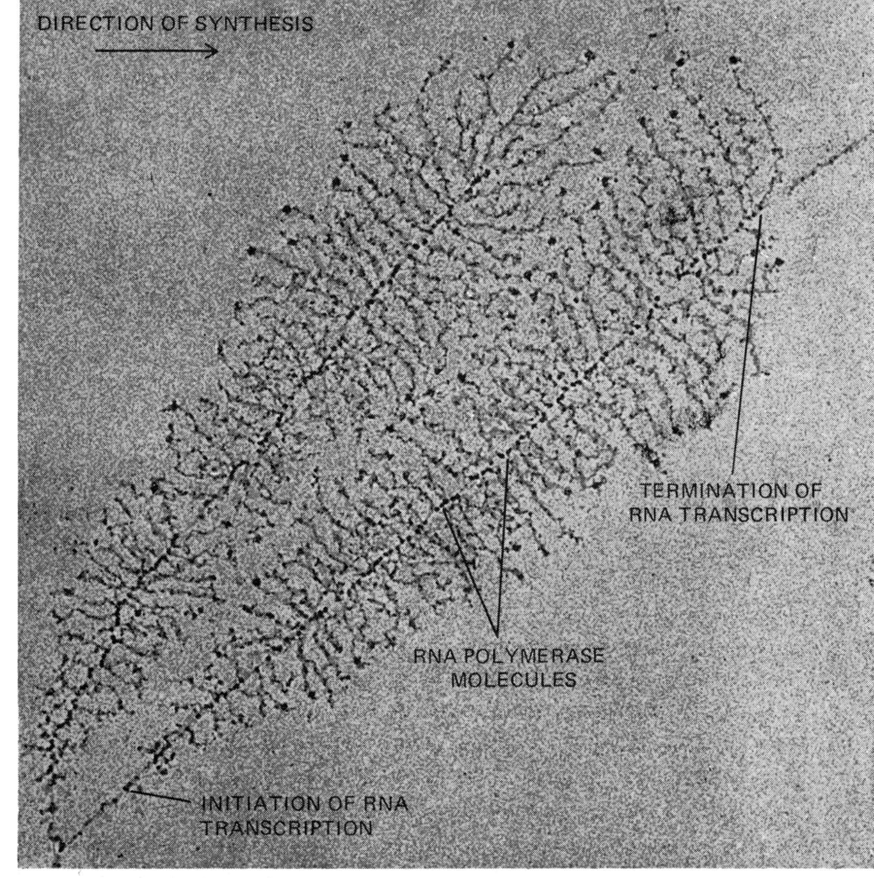

first letter	second letter: U	second letter: C	second letter: A	second letter: G	third letter
U	UUU, UUC: phe UUA, UUG: leu	UCU, UCC, UCA, UCG: ser	UAU, UAC: tyr UAA: End UAG: End	UGU, UGC: cys UGA: End UGG: tryp	U C A G
C	CUU, CUC, CUA, CUG: leu	CCU, CCC, CCA, CCG: pro	CAU, CAC: his CAA, CAG: glun	CGU, CGC, CGA, CGG: arg	U C A G
A	AUU, AUC, AUA: ileu AUG: met	ACU, ACC, ACA, ACG: thr	AAU, AAC: aspn AAA, AAG: lys	AGU, AGC: ser AGA, AGG: arg	U C A G
G	GUU, GUC, GUA, GUG: val	GCU, GCC, GCA, GCG: ala	GAU, GAC: asp GAA, GAG: glu	GGU, GGC, GGA, GGG: gly	U C A G

abbreviation	amino acid
ala	alanine
arg	arginine
aspn	asparagine
asp	aspartic acid
cys	cysteine
glu	glutamic acid
glun	glutamine
gly	glycine
his	histidine
ileu	isoleucine
leu	leucine
lys	lysine
met	methionine
phe	phenylalanine
pro	proline
ser	serine
thr	threonine
tryp	tryptophan
tyr	tyrosine
val	valine

Fig. 14.9 The genetic code. The 64 mRNA triplet codes and their corresponding amino acids (A, adenine; U, uracil; G, guanine; C, cytosine). Identification of amino acid abbreviations appears at the right. Three triplets, UAA, UAG, and UGA, have been identified as termination codons. *(Modified from a table originally developed by F. H. C. Crick.)*

cil-containing nucleotides. After mixed amino acids were added, it was found that the amino acid chain formed in the test tube consisted only of *phenylalanine.* From this it could be concluded that the codon for the amino acid phenylalanine must be UUU.

Later work along related lines has led to the identification of the code triplets for all amino acids (Fig. 14.9). It has also been found that certain amino acids are coded by more than a single triplet. Leucine, for example, is coded as UUA, UUG, CUU, CUC, CUA, and CUG. Because of such multiple codings, the genetic code is said to be *degenerate.* A limited degree of degeneracy is of considerable adaptive advantage, for despite a change of one code letter—by mutation, for example—the meaning of the whole triplet sometimes can still be preserved. Moreover, the genetic code is *universal;* it is the same in all organisms.

Translation

To explain how the genetic code is translated to a finished polypeptide, we must first turn our attention to tRNA. At least one tRNA exists for each of the 20 amino acids found in proteins. Each tRNA is a comparatively short nucleic acid, which can be depicted as having a cloverleaf configuration (Fig. 14.10). Appropriate amino acids always are attached to the "stem" end of this cloverleaf. Several hydrogen bonds interlock the "arms" of the cloverleaf, bending the molecule into a three-dimensional configuration that is roughly L-shaped. The stem of the cloverleaf forms one end of the L (see Fig. 14.10).

The linking of an amino acid to this "stem" requires ATP as an energy donor and occurs in a two-step reaction sequence catalyzed by the enzyme *aminoacyl-tRNA synthetase* (Fig. 14.11). This enzyme exists in several forms, at least one for each different amino acid. In a first step, a molecule of synthetase catalyzes the addition of an amino acid to AMP. This reaction requires energy, which is supplied by the conversion of ATP to AMP and two phosphate units. The principal product of the reaction is the molecular complex *aminoacyl-AMP,* also called an *activated amino acid.* Aminoacyl-AMP actually remains attached to the synthetase. In the second step of the reaction sequence, the enzyme catalyzes transfer of the aminoacyl portion of the complex to the amino acid attachment site of a tRNA. The net result of the two reactions is formation of an *aminoacyl-tRNA* (see Fig. 14.11).

Once bonded to its amino acid, tRNA in its turn bonds to mRNA. Three nitrogen bases, called

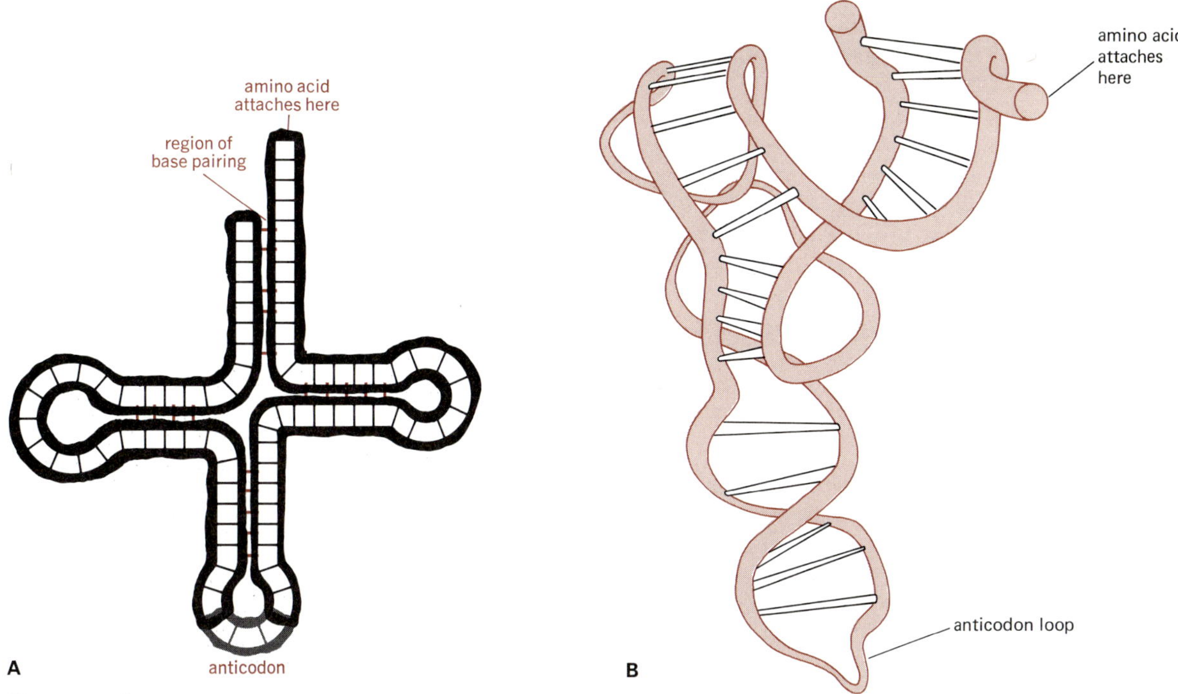

Fig. 14.10 Transfer RNA. (A) Two-dimensional cloverleaf structure of tRNA. The dark cross-bridges represent bonds between some of the nucleotides of tRNA. The locations of these bonds causes the molecule to fold in the general shape of a cloverleaf. Amino acids attach to the "stem" of the molecule opposite the triplet of nitrogen bases that constitutes the anticodon. (B) Three-dimensional L shape of tRNA.

an *anticodon,* are located in the loop of tRNA opposite the stem (see Fig. 14.10A). The anticodon of each type of tRNA specifically "recognizes" and bonds to a complementary codon on mRNA. This cannot occur, however, until one of the smaller ribosomal subunits becomes attached to the end of a mRNA molecule containing the first portion of the transcribed code for protein synthesis. Special codons, called *initiation codons,* are always positioned at this end of mRNA molecules. The most common initiation codon is AUG (methionine). In bacteria, initiation codons designate a special form of methionine called *formyl methionine.* This amino acid is identical to methionine except that it contains a formyl group, $\overset{O}{\underset{H}{\gg}}C-$, attached to its nitrogen atom (Fig. 14.12).

Initiation codons are "recognized" by at least three protein *initiation factors* associated with a smaller ribosomal subunit during its initial attachment to mRNA. The larger ribosomal subunit then joins the complex so that mRNA becomes positioned in a groove between the two subunits (Fig. 14.13). The initial contact of aminoacyl-tRNA molecules with mRNA occurs at the so-called P (peptidyl) site on the ribosome. Methionine-tRNA (or in prokaryotes, formyl methionine) usually is the first such molecule to bind to this site since its anticodon UAC is complementary to the initiation codon AUG (Fig. 14.14).

A second site on the ribosome, the A (aminoacyl) site, lies next to the P site and is positioned over the second codon of mRNA. The A site can accept a tRNA with the appropriate anticodon. The second codon of mRNA pictured in Fig. 14.14 is GUU, which codes for the amino acid valine. Only valine-tRNA has the anticodon CAA and, as depicted in Fig. 14.14, one of these molecules becomes attached to the A site next to methionine-tRNA. A peptide bond (see Chap. 4) then forms

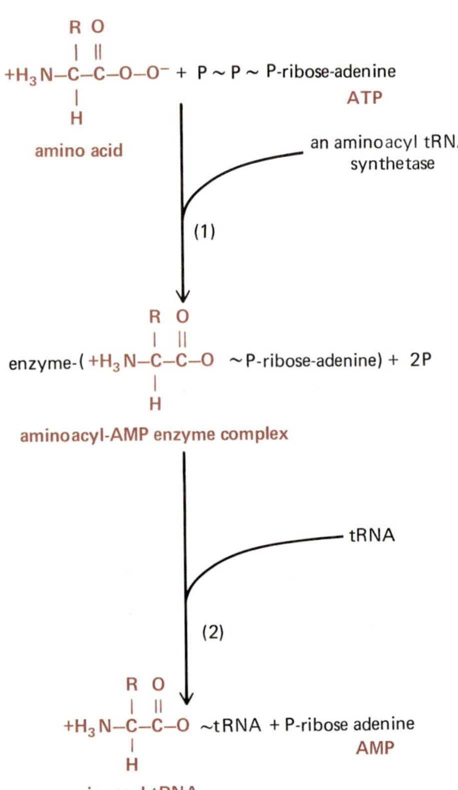

Fig. 14.11 Amino acid activation. See the text for a description of the two-step process.

between the amino acids. Formation of the bond is catalyzed by an enzyme attached to the larger ribosomal subunit.

Methionine becomes detached from its tRNA during peptide bond formation and becomes the first amino acid of a dipeptide attached to valine-tRNA (see Fig. 14.14). The tRNA at the P site now leaves the ribosome and moves to the cytoplasm, where is can become attached to another molecule of methionine. The tRNA carrying the dipeptide is then moved, or *translocated,* to the empty P site, and the ribosome moves along the mRNA a distance of three nucleotides. Such translocations and almost all other movements of molecules and ribosomes require enzyme catalysts, and most require expenditures of energy.

The process is repeated as additional amino acids are added to the growing polypeptide chain, in a sequence determined originally by a coded series

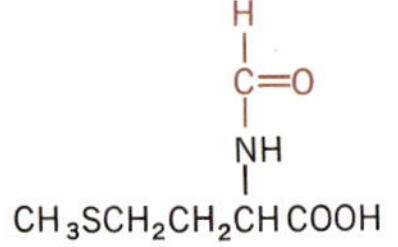

Fig. 14.12 Formyl methionine. Atoms in color designate the formyl group.

of nitrogen bases in DNA. Polypeptides gradually fold in three-dimensional configurations as they are produced and finally drop away as finished proteins.

How does the "machinery" of protein synthesis "know" where to terminate the manufacture of a protein and release it into the cytoplasm? If the genetic code contains initiation codons, does it also contain *termination codons*? Indeed it does. In all organisms studied, three codons (UGA, UAG, and UAA) play important roles in terminating the synthesis of proteins. In effect, they function as "periods" at ends of "sentences." Since these codons do not identify amino acids, protein synthesis stops whenever one of these codons is "read" by the protein synthesizing machinery.

Messenger RNA molecules usually are read by a number of ribosomes simultaneously. Like an automobile assembly line, a new ribosome joins mRNA as soon as a preceding ribosome has moved from the AUG initiation signal. Fully loaded, a mRNA molecule can be bound to as many as 100 ribosomes, each making a copy of the same protein. Such linear aggregations of ribosomes attached to individual molecules of mRNA are called *polyribosomes,* or *polysomes* (Fig. 14.15). Since sev-

Fig. 14.13 Initiation of protein synthesis. (A) Special binding factors associated with the smaller ribosomal subunit recognize the initiation codon AUG of mRNA. (B) Code translation begins after the larger subunit has locked into position. The mRNA lies in a groove between the two subunits.

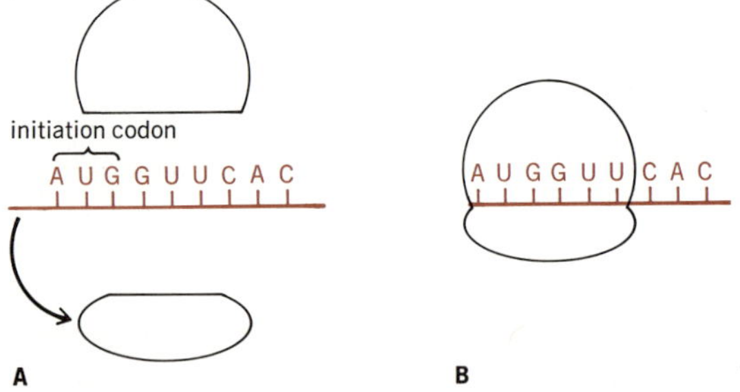

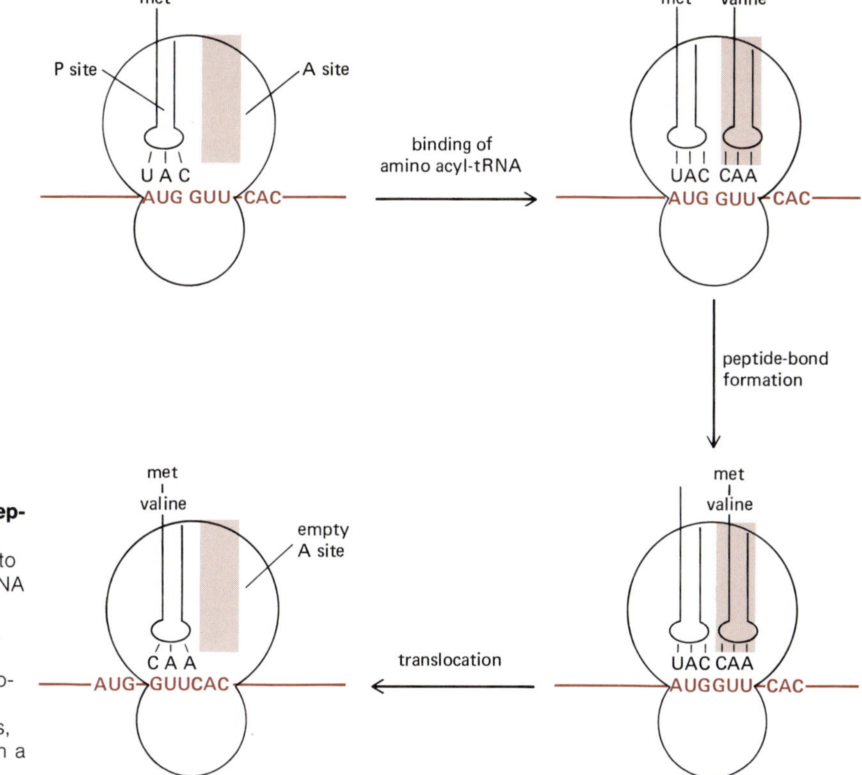

Fig. 14.14 Elongation of polypeptides during translation. Molecules of tRNA carry amino acids to ribosomes. The anticodons of tRNA molecules attach specifically to complementary codons of mRNA. As ribosomes move along mRNA, molecules of tRNA disjoin from codons and leave their amino acids behind. As the process continues, amino acids are joined together in a code-directed sequence.

eral proteins are made simultaneously, polyribosomes greatly increase the efficiency of protein synthesis.

Newly formed proteins become part of the structural and functional makeup of a cell. Some proteins might be incorporated in various fibrils, membranes, mitochondria, chromosomes, ribosomes, or indeed any other cellular organelle. Other proteins might, by virtue of their particular specificities, come to function as specific enzymes and thus determine at what rates the reactions in a cell can take place. Each of the many genes present in a cell controls the manufacture of a different kind of protein, and the totality of the proteins

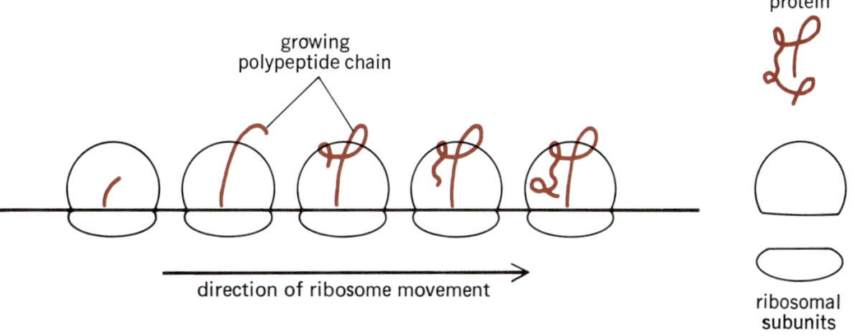

Fig. 14.15 Polyribosomes. Many ribosomes can read individual molecules of mRNA simultaneously. Polypeptide chains increase in length as ribosomes approach a termination codon. Completed proteins are released when ribosomes separate as subunits at termination codons. The subunits can rejoin again as whole ribosomes at the initiation site.

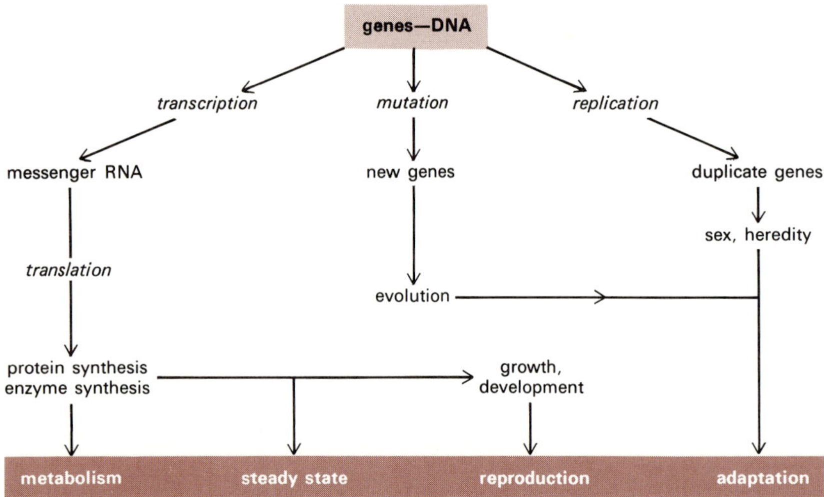

Fig. 14.16 The pattern of gene action. Through the fundamental action of transferring their coded specificities, genes control cellular metabolism and all phases of cellular self-perpetuation.

formed then determines and maintains the nature of that cell.

DNA: An Overview

Genetic DNA is among the most stable of all organic compounds. Indeed, unless it were relatively stable, it would be useless as a dependable code carrier. Yet despite this inherent stability, DNA still is subject to structural change, like any other material on earth. As shown later, a variety of physical and chemical agents can affect and alter gene structure and therefore gene specificity. Often the change need not involve more than a substitution or switching of nitrogen bases at a single position in a code triplet. Such a *mutation* will be stable and will be transmitted to all duplicates of the affected DNA molecule. Protein synthesis will then be affected correspondingly, and cell traits will become altered as a result. If such cellular changes also influence the larger-scale traits of a whole organism and its progeny, as is sometimes the case, the final result after numerous generations can be a stable evolutionary change.

In effect, therefore, by governing the synthesis of new genes and of specific proteins, DNA plays so strategic a role that it ultimately controls the whole nature and the very life of every cell in every organism (Fig. 14.16). First, since proteins make up the basic organic framework of cells, DNA determines the fundamental *structure* of every cell. Second, genes determine what kinds of *metabolic processes* are possible in a cell, for virtually all such processes are enzyme-dependent, hence protein-dependent, hence DNA-dependent. Third, DNA is the ultimate maintainer of *steady states,* for through its control over metabolism, it also governs all control agents within cells, including itself (see Chap. 15). Fourth, by governing synthesis generally and production of new DNA specifically, DNA directs growth, development, and the *reproduction* of cells (see Chap. 22). By being exchanged among cells and pooled within cells, DNA becomes the basis of sex. By duplicating itself and being inherited by offspring cells, DNA becomes the basis of *heredity* (see Chap. 27). And through its property of undergoing occasional mutations, DNA becomes the key to *evolution* (see Chap. 29).

By so controlling all of metabolism and all of self-perpetuation, DNA governs cell structure, cell function, and cell development. And by governing the life of cells, DNA governs the life of all organisms, hence the survival of the whole living world.

Review Questions

1 Review the chemical structure of DNA. Review the structure of RNA, and distinguish between mRNA, rRNA, and tRNA. Where in a cell do each of these occur, and what are their functions?

2 How does DNA replication take place? What is the role of DNA polymerase? Unwinding proteins? How is the stability of genes safeguarded? What is the importance of gene stability? Show how replication begins from many points of origin along molecules of eukaryotic DNA.

3 What is the genetic code, what are code triplets, and on the basis of what reasoning has a triplet code been postulated for amino acid specification?

4 In what sense is the genetic code degenerate, and what are the functional consequences of this degeneracy?

5 Review the entire pattern of genetically controlled protein synthesis. Describe the functional relationships between DNA, RNA polymerase, sigma factor, promotor regions, mRNA, ribosomal subunits, tRNA, and amino acids. Describe the mechanism of amino acid activation. How do amino acids become polypeptides along mRNA? Describe the importance of nucleic acid and protein synthesis in the life of a cell.

6 What are mutations, and what are their general effects in a cell? What is the importance of gene stability? Review the pattern of gene function as a whole, and show in what way DNA controls all aspects of metabolism and self-perpetuation.

Collateral Readings

Avery, O. T., C. M. MacLeod, and **M. McCarty:** Studies on the Chemical Nature of the Substance Inducing Transformation of Pneumococcal Types, *Journal of Experimental Medicine,* vol. 79, p. 137, 1944. The paper that convinced most scientists that DNA and genes were synonymous.

Brown, D. D.: The Isolation of Genes, *Scientific American,* August 1973. A good description of the first successful attempts to isolate individual genes.

Crick, F. H. C.: The Structure of the Hereditary Material, *Scientific American,* October 1954. Writing just two years after the first publication of the Watson-Crick model, Crick describes the discovery of the structure of DNA.

———: The Genetic Code, *Scientific American,* October 1962. Crick describes experiments confirming that each amino acid in a protein is coded by a triplet of nucleotides.

Goodenough, U.: "Genetics," 2d ed., Holt, New York, 1978. This introductory text in genetics has a good section on nucleic acid transcription and translation. Recommended for those who wish greater detail.

Miller, O.: The Visualization of Genes in Action, *Scientific American,* March 1973. The author illustrates how the electron microscope can be used to photograph molecules of RNA being transcribed from DNA.

Rich, A., and **S. H. Kim.:** The Three-Dimensional Structure of Transfer RNA, *Scientific American,* January 1978. The authors describe and illustrate how the three-dimensional configuration of tRNA was worked out.

Watson, J. D.: "The Double Helix," New American Library, New York, 1968. The personalities and events that led to the discovery of the genetic significance of DNA are described. An enjoyable book that reveals much about the nature of scientific research. Recommended.

———:"Molecular Biology of the Gene," 3d ed., Benjamin, Menlo Park, Calif., 1976. An outstanding treatment of molecular genetics. Strongly recommended for the serious student.

Yanofsky, C.: Gene Structure and Protein Structure, *Scientific American,* May 1967. An interesting review of how the correspondence between the genetic code and the amino acid sequence in polypeptides was demonstrated.

Part 4
The Operations of Life: Steady States

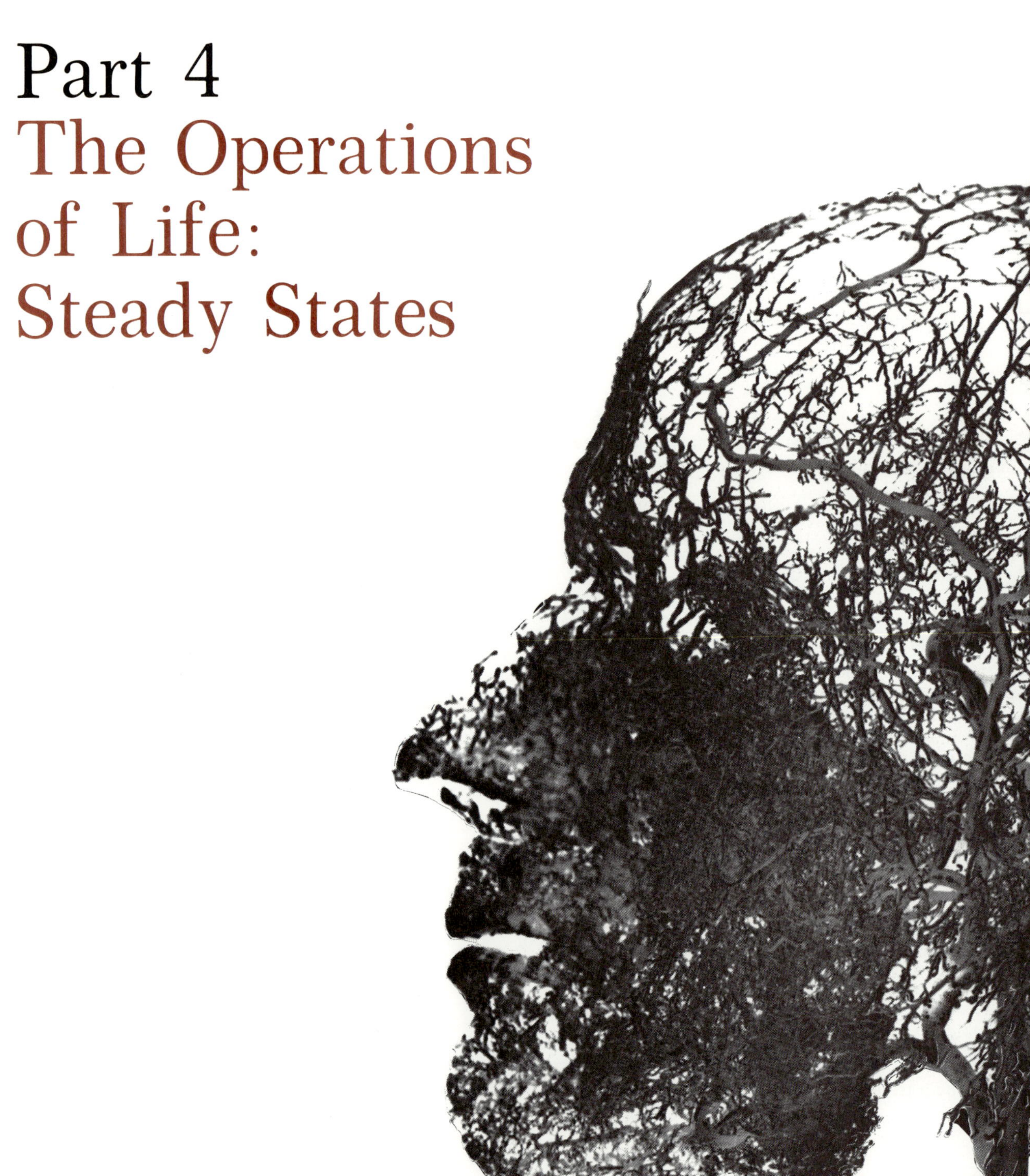

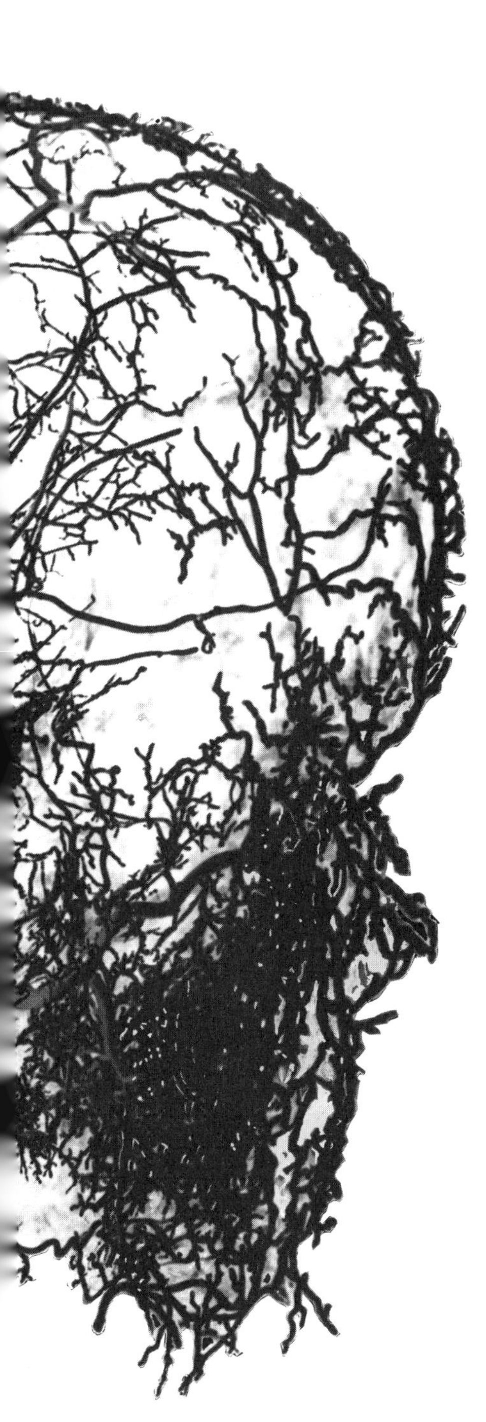

Recall that self-perpetuation comprises, first, processes that maintain the *steady state* of living units and adjust and coordinate their internal operations; second, processes of *reproduction*, which extend the operations of living units in space and in time; and third, processes of *adaptation*, which mold and fit the long-term characteristics of living units to the characteristics of specific environments. All three functions are carried out at all levels of the living hierarchy. However, the maintenance of *cellular* steady states is the foundation of all steady states and indeed also of self-perpetuation as a whole. Accordingly, this part begins with an examination of the nature of control functions generally and of cellular controls specifically. The steady-state controls of higher organizational levels are considered thereafter.

Circulatory systems contribute heavily to the maintenance of steady states in many animals. The intricate network of blood vessels in the head of a human being is shown here. To obtain this photograph, a human head was drained of blood and a polymer liquid was injected into the blood vessels and allowed to solidify. Subsequent treatment of the head with nitric acid left only the blood vessels intact. (*Manfred Kage. © Peter Arnold, Inc.*)

Chapter 15 Cellular Control

Learning Objectives

After reading this chapter you should be able to:

1. Identify and state the function of each structural component of every steady-state control system in living organisms; outline the role of information flow in the maintenance of steady states.
2. Differentiate between sensory and motor pathways and describe the role of each in steady-state control.
3. List at least four general features common to all steady-state control systems; state the significance of feedback in the operation of control systems; list at least two consequences of overloading steady-state control systems of living organisms.
4. List at least two organelles usually present in cells and name a cellular activity in which each organelle functions as:
   - **a.** receptor
   - **b.** modulator
   - **c.** effector
   - **d.** sensory or motor pathway

   Give an example of a steady-state control system in your body that involves at least three different organs or organ systems.
5. Show how cellular steady states are influenced by mechanisms that adjust both the activity and abundance of enzymes; identify six levels of control in cells at which regulatory mechanisms influence the production or activity of enzymes; list at least two reasons why more is known about the regulation of gene expression in prokaryotes than in eukaryotes; list at least three ways in which the genetic systems of prokaryotes differ from those of eukaryotes.
6. Illustrate how the expression of prokaryotic genes is regulated at the transcriptional, translational, and posttranslational levels of control; differentiate between enzyme induction and enzyme repression; define operon and state the functional relations between regulatory genes, structural genes, promotor and operator regions, repressor proteins, and RNA polymerase; show how operons increase the functional efficiency of cells; define corepressor substance and illustrate how such substances can affect operon function; identify at least one example of an enzyme system in bacteria that does not appear to be influenced by the external environment.
7. Illustrate how gene expression in eukaryotes is affected by control mechanisms that alter the structural organization of genes; show how eukaryotic gene expression either is or could be influenced by regulatory mechanisms operating at the transcriptional, posttranscriptional, translational, and posttranslational levels of control.
8. Differentiate between histone and nonhistone proteins and name at least one probable function for each kind of protein; describe an experiment whose results suggest that nonhistones probably contribute to the regulation of genes in eukaryotic cells; define polytene chromosome and show how study of these chromosomes has contributed to an understanding of gene transcription.
9. Define "split gene" and state at least three ways in which a molecule of eukaryotic mRNA is altered before its transport from the nucleus to the cytoplasm.
10. Illustrate at least one way in which cellular metabolism could be altered by mechanisms that influence translation of mRNA.
11. Show how chemical reactions can constitute steady-state control systems in cells; define allosteric site and illustrate how such sites can influence rates of metabolic reactions; indicate how enzyme function can be affected by changes of pH.
12. List the three major kinds of growth factors in living organisms and show generally how such factors contribute to steady-state control.

13. Differentiate between biological and clinical effects of vitamin deficiency; name the principal food sources and cellular functions of at least one vitamin from the A, B, C, D, E, and K groups; list the clinical effects of dietary deficiencies of each vitamin you identify; show why vitamin deficiencies often develop when fats are rigidly excluded from the diet.

The general function of all control activities in an organism is the maintenance of adequate, and as far as possible *optimal,* operating conditions despite changes in the internal and external environment (see also Chap. 2). The net result of control is *steady state,* or *homeostasis,* and, through this, maintenance of life for the longest possible time.

All control devices of living matter operate according to the same fundamental principles. This common *pattern of control* is the subject of the first part of the chapter. The following parts deal with the specific control operations on the cellular level, particularly those performed by *genes, enzymes,* and *vitamins.*

THE PATTERN

Any condition that tends to upset the smooth operations of a system can be regarded as a *stress.* In a living organism stresses often are produced by the environment—enemies, injurious agents, lack of food, change of temperature, and innumerable other physical, chemical, and biological conditions. Internally, stresses arise continuously as a result of life processes—nutrients are used up, concentrations change, parts age and wear out, waste products accumulate (see also Chap. 2). Consequently, living systems are being stressed to a greater or lesser extent amost all the time.

The problem of maintaining a steady state therefore is to counteract or to relieve stress. Doing so requires, first, ability to *recognize* stress, and second, ability to *react* to stress in a self-preserving fashion. Thus if a system can recognize a stressful *stimulus* and can carry out an appropriate *response* to that stimulus, it exercises *control.* And it can then remain intact and functioning despite stresses that would otherwise upset its operations.

Control Operations

To achieve control, a first fundamental requirement is continuous flow of *information* between the parts of a system. Each part must receive signals about the action of other parts, and if a stimulus affects one part, other parts must receive appropriate information about it. Moreover, if the system is capable of responding to a stimulus in more than one way, a second requirement is the ability to make *selections.* A simple system that always gives the same response is not required to select. But where several response possibilities exist ability to choose between them is crucial, for choice of inappropriate responses leads to unsteady, not steady, states (Fig. 15.1).

The terms "information" and "selection" imply messages or signals of some sort, message carriers, senders, receivers, transmission pathways, relays, switches, channel selectors—in short, all the components of a communications system. Indeed, in one form or another communications systems are found wherever biological steady states are maintained; we find them in cells and between cells, in organisms and between organisms, on all levels of organization. Such systems are *control systems.*

Living control systems largely operate on a common pattern. An initial stimulus irritates, or *excites,* a receiving device, called a *receptor.* Excitation of this receptor causes the emission of a signal, which is transmitted over a *sensory pathway* to an "interpreting" and response-selecting device. Such a device can be referred to generally as a *modulator.* This component sends out an appropriately chosen command signal over an appropriately chosen *motor pathway.* The signal leads to an *effector,* a unit that executes the commands and thereby produces a response to the original stimulus (Fig. 15.2).

The operation of such a system can be illustrated by means of a physical model. Suppose that the water level of a flow tank, as in Fig. 15.3, is to be maintained in steady state; despite possible variations of inflow or outflow the water level is to stay at a predetermined height. This objective can be fulfilled through an automatic regulating device such as that sketched in Fig. 15.3. An air-filled float R here is comparable to a receptor; as it

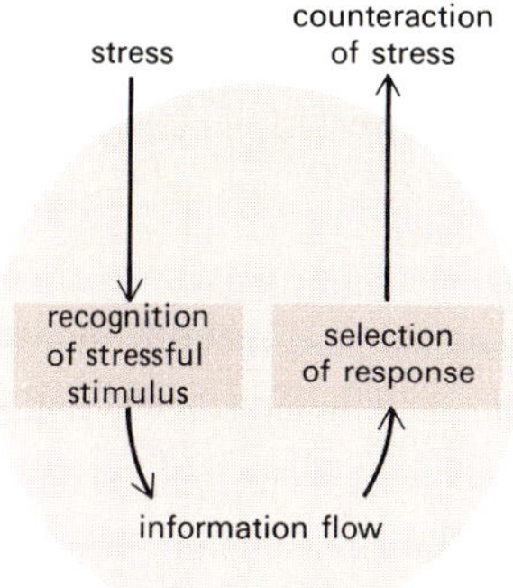

Fig. 15.1 **Steady state.** The general pattern of maintenance and control.

moves up or down with the water, it "senses" changes of water level. Any up or down motion of R is communicated by a rod sp, the "sensory pathway," to the modulator M. Here the up or down motion of sp is "interpreted," and appropriate commands for response are sent out. Imagine M to be so built that any change in the position of sp trips electric switches and that each switch causes the flow of an electric current of different characteristics. These electrical impulses are the command signals transmitted over the motor pathways mp to the two effectors E. The effectors are engines that operate the valves at the inflow and the outflow; at each command signal the valves are moved to a particular position.

Imagine now that for some external reason the water flow decreases. The water level will begin to drop, but at once the modulator M will be informed of this change through R and sp. Appropriate electric signals will therefore go to the effectors and the inflow valve will open more, the outflow valve close more. As a result, before the water level can drop very far, the net inflow will increase and the water will rise back to normal. This new change of level will again be communicated to the modulator; new signals will go out to the effectors; and the valves will be returned to their original positions. If at this point the inflow is still reduced, the control device will go into action once more, precisely as above. Clearly, by readjusting as often as necessary the device is capable of maintaining a steady state despite changes in the "environment."

This model illustrates a number of general features common to control systems, living ones included. First, internal *operating energy* is needed to make the system work. In the model energy is

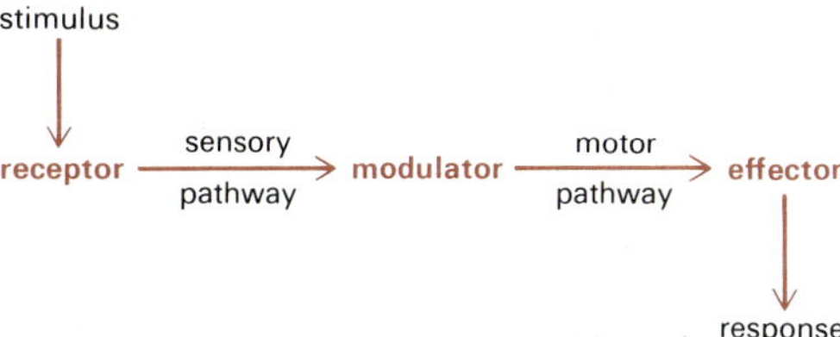

Fig. 15.2 Control components in living systems.

required for the transmission of electric signals and for the motors that move the valves. In living control systems, similarly, small amounts of energy are needed for the transmission of information and comparatively large amounts of energy are required to operate the effectors. All this energy must be supplied by ATP produced through respiration.

A second common feature of many control devices is that response to a stimulus often is not a sudden, single event but a stepwise, repeated one. In the model, a small initial change in valve position produces a small initial change in water level. The receptor immediately signals to the modulator that a certain adjustment has been carried out. Accordingly, the modulator then cues the effectors to continue, to stop, or to reverse operations. The resulting effector action is essentially a new stimu-

Fig. 15.3 Steady-state maintenance. (R, receptor; M, modulator; E, effector; sp, sensory pathway; mp, motor pathway.) If this model is adjusted as described in the text, any change of inflow or outflow will bring about signals through R $\longrightarrow$ sp $\longrightarrow$ M $\longrightarrow$ mp $\longrightarrow$ E. Valve positions will then be adjusted so that the valves will counteract the change of inflow or outflow and reestablish the original water level in the tank.

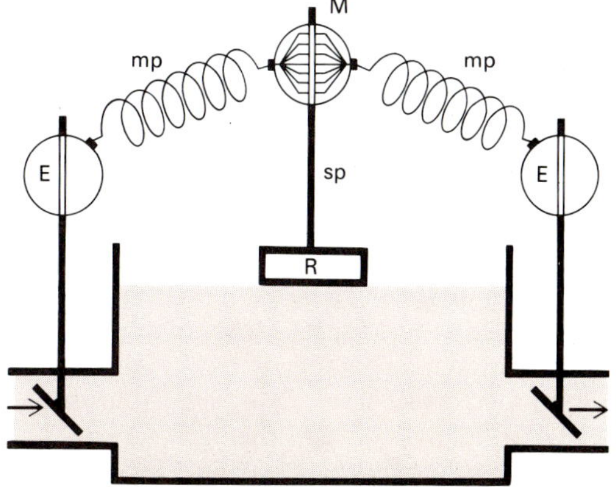

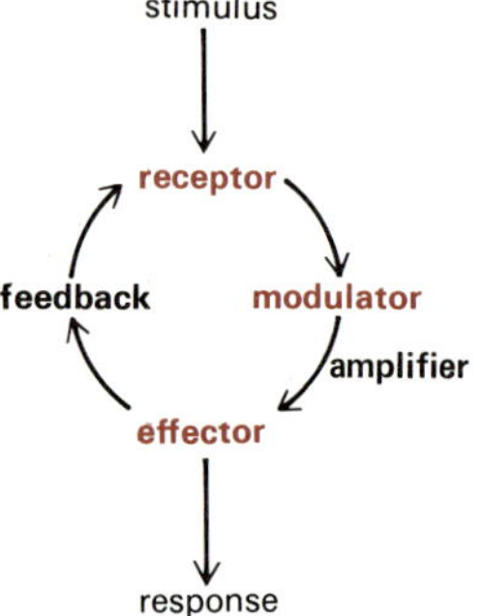

Fig. 15.4 Feedback. The role of feedback in a control cycle is shown. An amplifier provides energy for powerful effector action. Modulators typically integrate the actions of amplifiers and effectors. ATP produced in effectors usually serves as the amplifier in living control systems.

lus, which again is communicated back through the receptor to the modulator. In this manner continuous information passes from sensory to motor component and from motor back to sensory component. Many such cyclical passages of information, each contributing a small effector action, usually are required before a total response to a stimulus can be achieved. Indeed the regulating device is not at rest even then. For in the absence of environmental stimuli the receptor is stationary, and this absence of motion in effect is equivalent to the signal "no change." The modulator then sends "no adjustment required" to the effector, and the effector in turn informs the receptor of "no operation."

In such unceasing cyclical passages of information, each response is "fed back" to the sensory end of the regulating device as a new stimulus (Fig. 15.4). *Feedback* is an important element in the operation of a control system; for without feedback the modulator would not become informed about the action of the effector and it would not be able to send out "correct" new commands.

Feedbacks and continuous cycles of information account for a third property of many control systems; they function essentially by *trial and error,* by "hunting" for the correct equilibrium (balanced) condition. Refer again to the model. If the water level begins to drop, a few seconds might elapse before the valves are brought to corrective positions. By that time the water level could already be below the correct level. The water then begins to rise, but again there will be a time lag before the effectors return the valves to normal. By that time the water could already have risen somewhat above the correct level. New signals to reverse valve positions a bit will therefore go out, and by the time that action is executed the water could again be below the appropriate level.

Many controls *overshoot* in this fashion, and they undergo hunting oscillations to either side of an equilibrium state. Poorly adjusted controls often produce hunting oscillations that do not subside but increase, in which case "steady" states of course will not be maintained. Good examples are the often erratic paths of organisms that move from dark to light regions or vice versa, or in general from unsuitable to more suitable environments. Such organisms tend to "tack" first to one side, then to the other, in irregular paths. Their internal controls make these organisms "hunt" for regions of progressively greater suitability, in trial-and-error fashion.

A fourth general property of control systems is that they have inherent limits of efficiency. If they are overloaded they must work too fast or too hard, and they then can make *errors* in sensing stimuli or in "interpreting" signals or in selecting and executing responses. Extreme overloading also can cause structural breakdowns. In living organisms such functional or structural failures of control systems can result in *disease.* Irreversible failures of control systems in living organisms often result in death.

Control Systems

The regulating devices of living systems form a hierarchy paralleling that of the organizational levels of living matter. Molecules and organelles make up the control systems of cells, whole cells are the control systems of tissues, tissues in turn form the control systems of organs, and so on.

Within cells, organelles serve as control components by virtue of their other functions. For example, pigment-containing bodies such as chloroplasts absorb light, and thus their function is comparable to that of receptors of light stimuli. The nucleus with its genes directs protein synthesis and thus serves in a sense as a modulator. Kinetosomes and flagella bring about cell movement, and in this sense they are effectors. Most organelles actually have *multiple* regulating functions. For example, the cell surface can be regarded as a receptor when it distinguishes between two or more different molecules but as an effector when it allows some of these molecules to pass through. The nucleus, apart from being a modulator, also is a receptor, for it receives numerous chemical stimuli from the cytoplasm; and it is an effector as well, for it executes many responses. In short, any given organelle can serve as a receptor in one instance, as a modulator in another, and as an effector in yet a third. Its role as a control component is as varied as its functioning.

The cellular level is the lowest on which modulators are capable of *selecting* between various possible responses. For example, the cell surface is *selectively* permeable. Functioning as a modulator, it may "interpret" the chemical nature of different kinds of molecules in contact with it, and it may "decide" how fast and to what extent each such molecule is to be passed through. Similar selectivity is displayed by other complex control components in a cell (and also by all control systems above the cell level). This crucial capacity of "making decisions" can result from the circumstance that every organelle contains many different *molecular* control systems, each capable of a single response. Therefore, the number of decisions a complex modulator can make is perhaps related to the number of different molecular control systems of which it is composed.

The control activities in a cell collectively form important elements of control on higher levels. Thus if a cell as a whole functions as receptor, its response can represent a sensory signal on the tissue level. Or the cell could serve as modulator, which makes its response a motor signal on the tissue level. Or the cell might act as effector, and its response then could serve as a feedback signal on the tissue level. The response of a cell is propagated to other cells by direct contact or by the internal transport systems—xylem and phloem in plants, blood circulation in animals. If one cell stimulates others in a chain reaction, a whole tissue or organ or organism can eventually be drawn into a larger response. Steady-state regulation of this kind is still essentially cellular. Although more than one cell is involved, receptors, modulators, and effectors beyond those present in individual cells do not exist.

This form of functional control predominates in plants and also in animals such as sponges. The tissues and organs of these organisms are not specialized mainly or exclusively just for control functions. They carry out many functions, and, to a greater or lesser degree, control generally is one of them. In this respect most animals are different; they have body parts that are specialized more or less exclusively for control functions—nervous systems, for example. In nervous control, sense organs are receptors, brains or brain ganglia are the chief modulators, muscles and glands are common effectors, and nerves serve as sensory and motor paths. Transmission of information through such a sequence of structures constitutes a *reflex*, a key form of nervous steady-state control (Fig. 15.5).

Fig. 15.5 Steady-state control: reflex action. The components of any kind of steady-state-maintaining device are indicated along the top row and those of a nervous reflex immediately underneath. A stimulus (such as light) will produce a response such as muscle contraction and/or glandular secretion. The response itself then becomes a feedback, or a new stimulus, through which the modulator is "informed" whether the response has produced an adequate reaction to the original stimulus. The feedback stimulus then may or may not initiate a new reflex.

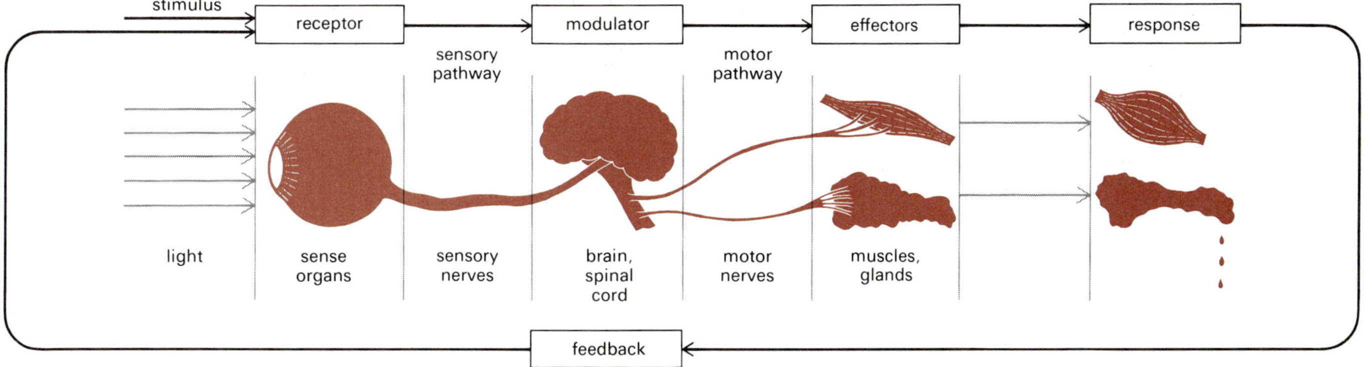

Where present, endocrine systems likewise exercise important control through their hormones. But *every* other organ system actually contributes to regulation as well. For example, the vertebrate liver is not only a digestive gland but also a major regulator in nutrient distribution (see Chap. 11). The circulatory system is not only a series of transport channels but also an important contributor to body defense, to internal chemical regulation, and to other control functions (see Chap. 18). Similarly, the excretory and breathing systems, and indeed most organs and systems of the animal body, participate in many ways in internal regulation.

In effect, every part of living matter is regulated *by* all other parts and at the same time contributes *to* the regulation of all other parts. As a result, "regulating" becomes a major component of "living," and without such control, life becomes nonlife. Conversely, nonlife became life when the first regulating mechanism came into existence. That probably was the nucleic acid molecule, the gene. How do genes, and cellular regulating agents in general, actually exercise their governing functions?

CONTROL IN CELLS

Regardless of how a cell is stressed, the stress stimulus usually affects one or more *metabolic* reactions—processes of respiration or synthesis or physical activities such as movement are likely to be speeded up or slowed down. Similarly, regardless of how a cell responds, the response ultimately is produced by metabolic reactions—acceleration back to normal of those which had been slowed down or deceleration of those which had been speeded up.

In short, steady states can be maintained if a cell can adjust and readjust the pattern of its metabolic reactions in response to particular stimuli. Since reaction patterns are determined by enzymes, cellular steady states are maintained largely by mechanisms that adjust both the activity and abundance of enzymes. Hypothetically, such mechanisms could operate at several different levels of control. The following are among the most apparent:

Structural alterations in the organization of genes. Such modifications could radically alter the patterns of RNA transcription and the abundance of specific gene products.

RNA transcriptional controls. Individual genes could be "turned on" under certain circumstances, triggering RNA transcription. Other conditions might block transcription, thereby turning genes off.

Posttranscriptional controls. Modification of mRNA immediately after transcription might increase or decrease its availability for translation. As will be shown, such mechanisms most likely occur in eukaryotic cells, whose molecules of mRNA often are substantially altered before they move out of the nucleus.

Translational controls. A variety of mechanisms could extend or shorten the life of mRNA, increasing or decreasing the number of proteins produced. Other mechanisms could alter the rates at which ribosomes attach to mRNA.

Posttranslational controls. Several factors could influence the catalytic properties of enzymes.

Processes affecting the activity and abundance of enzymes have been found at each of these levels of control, but comparatively little is known about specific mechanisms governing control of gene expression among eukaryotes; most well-documented mechanisms stem from research on prokaryotes.

The reasons for this disparity are relatively simple. Biologists usually look to the simplest experimental systems with which to conduct their research. Such systems afford the greatest probability of success. Thus, many of the first scientists investigating the regulation of gene expression began experimenting with prokaryotes, which are easier to grow and maintain than most eukaryotes. Biologists investigating gene regulation in eukaryotes not only must deal with organisms and cells that are physically more difficult to work with than most prokaryotes, but also with genetic systems that are far more elaborate than those of bacteria and viruses.

That eukaryotic genes should be regulated in a more complex fashion than the DNA of prokaryotes is not surprising. Both pro- and eukaryotic cells must be capable of responding to fluctuations in environmental conditions, as would occur, for example, if nutrient supplies became temporarily exhausted. The response to such a stressful circumstance usually involves control mechanisms that generate new or augmented supplies of enzymes capable of converting intracellular materials to products that can be respired rapidly. Most adult eukaryotes, however, are composed of many specialized cells that usually develop either from a fertilized egg or from a group of comparatively unspecialized cells (see Part 5). As the specialized cells of such eukaryotes develop, many different sets of genes undoubtedly are turned on and off in many different sequences in many different cells. Integration of these genetic activities obviously requires more elaborate regulatory mechanisms than are needed in prokaryotes, which do not undergo such complex patterns of development.

In addition to being more elaborate, the genetic systems of eukaryotes often behave very differently from those of prokaryotes. For example, many genes of specialized eukaryotic cells usually are turned off more or less permanently. Genes coding for highly specialized enzymes of liver cells probably are never active in kidney cells, and vice versa. Such virtually permanent inactivation of genes almost never occurs in prokaryotic cells. Indeed, rendering even rarely used genes inactive could prove highly disadvantageous to bacteria and most other prokaryotes, which frequently encounter sudden, dramatic changes in environmental conditions. Almost any gene product might prove essential for life at almost any moment.

Eukaryotic genes also appear to be organized differently from the genes of prokaryotes. Genes which have related functions or which jointly coordinate production of a single trait generally are grouped closely together on strands of prokaryotic DNA. Such structurally allied genes often are transcribed together as a single unit. By contrast, functionally related eukaryotic genes usually are noncontiguous, frequently scattered in several different chromosomes.

Of all known mechanisms controlling gene expression in pro- and eukaryotes, those showing the greatest dissimilarity operate largely at the first four levels of control listed above. They are exemplified in the two sections that follow. Many of the mechanisms controlling the catalytic properties of enzymes operate in a similar fashion in both kinds of cells. Such posttranslational mechanisms are illustrated in a later section.

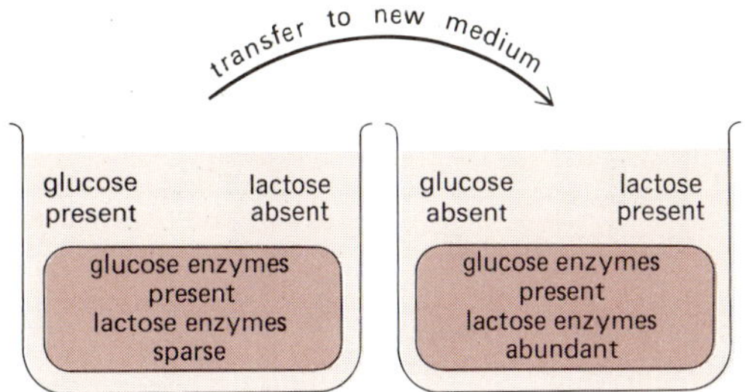

Fig. 15.6 Enzyme induction. The dark colored boxes inside the beakers represent populations of *E. coli*. As the available supplies of lactose vary in abundance, so the internal bacterial enzymes capable of acting on lactose come to vary in abundance too. Enzymes participating in the metabolism of glucose are produced more or less continuously.

Higher Levels of Gene Control in Prokaryotes

RNA transcription and translation are influenced by a large number of different control mechanisms. Those operating at the transcriptional level have received the greatest study and are the most thoroughly documented.

Transcriptional Control

The best-understood mechanisms controlling prokaryotic RNA transcription are those initiating synthesis of enzymes only under certain conditions; transcription of RNA is blocked at other times. Not all prokaryotic genes are controlled in this manner. For example, molecules of mRNA that produce enzymes participating in the breakdown of glucose in bacteria are transcribed more or less continuously.

Control mechanisms that activate and deactivate RNA transcription in prokaryotes typically respond to specific *inducer* and *inhibitor* substances. For example, the bacterium *Escherichia coli*, which inhabits a diversity of environments, including the human alimentary tract, contains genes coding for three enzymes that metabolize lactose, a 12-carbon sugar (see Chap. 4). Lactose is uncommon in habi-

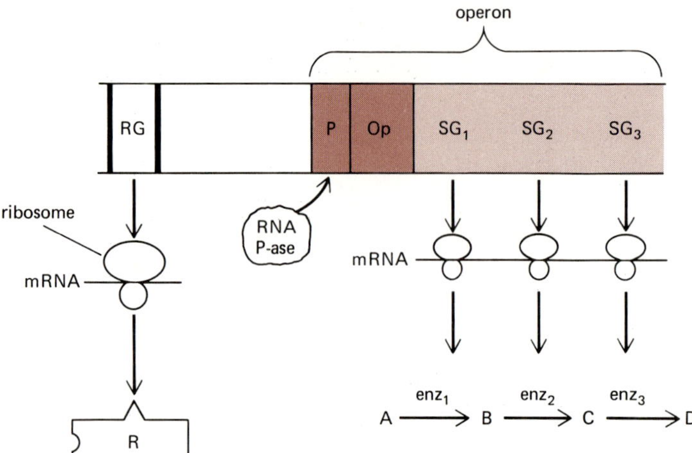

Fig. 15.7 Operon structure. SG, structural gene; P, promotor; Op, operator gene; RG, regulator gene; all three of these gene types are located along segments of prokaryotic DNA. R, protein product formed by RG and influencing P and Op in ways to be shown in Figs. 15.8 and 15.10. The three structural genes are transcribed successively, producing a single molecule of mRNA that contains the codon sequences for all three enzymes (enz). RNA polymerase (RNA P-ase) catalyzes the transcription after first binding to P. Once produced, the three enzymes participate in a reaction sequence in which compound A is converted to compound D.

tats normally occupied by *E. coli,* and the bacterium produces substantial copies of the three lactose-metabolizing enzymes only when the sugar is present in the extracellular environment.

This phenomenon, called *enzyme induction,* involves two kinds of bacterial genes, *regulatory genes* and *structural genes* (Fig. 15.6). Regulatory genes control the manufacture of repressor proteins, which in turn specifically affect the activity of structural genes. The latter code for enzymes and other proteins required for cell function.

As is common in prokaryotes, the three structural genes that code for the three lactose-metabolizing enzymes are aligned successively along a segment of DNA. Transcription of the three-gene unit is regulated by a "genetic switch" called an *operator* (Op), a short sequence of nucleotides located next to the structural genes. Another sequence of nucleotides, the *promotor* (P), is located next to the operator. The promotor functions as a site of attachment for a molecule of RNA polymerase, the enzyme that catalyzes production of RNA. The promotor, operator, and adjacent structural genes collectively are called an *operon* (Fig. 15.7).

Once a molecule of RNA polymerase becomes attached to the promotor, it slides past the operator and along the three structural genes, producing one molecule of mRNA. This molecule then enters the cytoplasm, and after translation the three enzymes are released independently.

A regulatory gene (RG), located a short distance away from the operon, produces a repressor protein (R). When lactose is not present in the surrounding environment, R binds to Op and physically blocks attachment of RNA polymerase to P (Fig. 15.8). At such times, transcription of structural genes is inhibited. But if lactose is present in the environment, the sugar (actually a metabolically altered form of lactose) combines with R and produces a molecular complex that can no longer bind to Op. RNA polymerase then attaches to P and transcribes the associated structural genes (see Fig. 15.8).

Most control of RNA transcription in prokaryotes involves operons, but not all operons function in the same way. Some, like the so-called *lac* (lactose) *operon,* just described, are inactive until induced. Consequently, they are termed *inducible operons.* Others, called *repressible operons,* function in an almost opposite manner.

Control of repressible operons is well illustrated by the response of *Salmonella,* another bacterium, to the amino acid histidine. When this amino acid is *not* present in its environment, a *Salmonella* cell will produce a group of nine enzymes that synthesize histidine from other starting compounds. But if an external source of histidine becomes available, synthesis of the nine enzymes ceases abruptly (Fig. 15.9).

The structural genes for the nine enzymes are positioned next to each other in the *his* (histidine) *operon.* An associated regulatory gene codes for a repressor protein, but the repressor by itself cannot bind to the operator of the *his* operon. If, however,

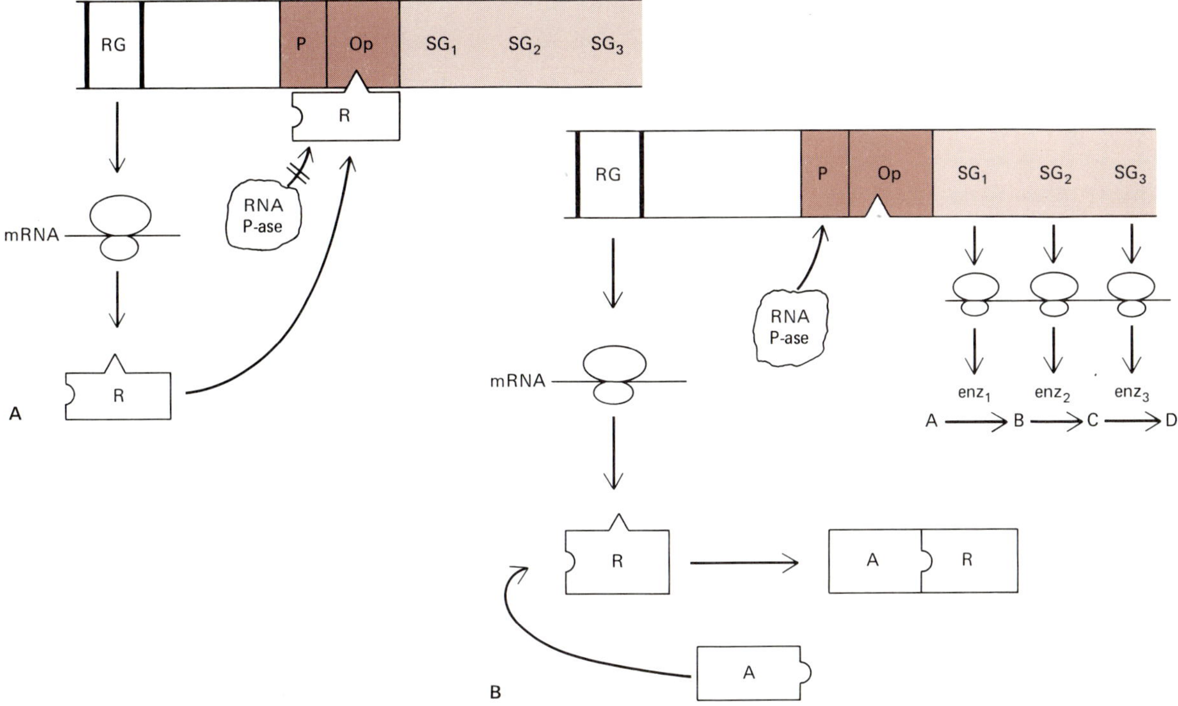

Fig. 15.8 Inducible operons. (A) Operon repressed. R binds to Op and blocks attachment of RNA polymerase to P (double crossbar denotes inhibition). Thus, the SGs are not transcribed and the reaction end product D (see Fig. 15.7) is not formed. (B) Operon induced. If starting material A (see Fig. 15.7) is introduced into the cellular environment, R combines with A (or a derivative of A). The complex AR cannot bind to Op, thereby permitting attachment of RNA polymerase to P. The SGs are then transcribed. When the resulting single molecule of mRNA is translated, the three enzymes convert A to D. Operons functioning in this manner are inactive until induced and consequently are called inducible operons.

the repressor first binds to histidine, the amino acid-protein complex does bind to the operator, stopping transcription of the nine structural genes. Histidine thus functions as a *corepressor.* When histidine is absent, Op is not repressed and the histidine-generating enzymes are produced. But when the corepressor is present, the *his* operon is repressed and the nine enzymes are not produced (Fig. 15.10).

Inducible operons typically (but not always) code for proteins not usually required for survival, and such operons are normally inactive. By contrast, repressible operons typically carry genes for more "vital" proteins and are normally "switched on." Although most operons in prokaryotes can be categorized as inducible or repressible, several are

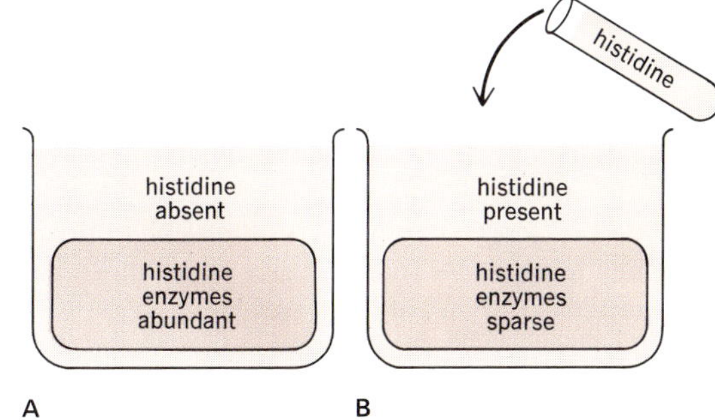

Fig. 15.9 Enzyme repression. The abundance of some bacterial enzymes is limited by substances that act as repressors. (A) Enzymes responsible for the synthesis of histidine are produced in large amounts by *E. coli* when environmental supplies of the amino acid are unavailable. (B) When added to the medium, histidine inactivates genes that code for histidine-synthesizing enzymes. In this way, energy is not wasted in the synthesis of products that can be obtained readily from the environment.

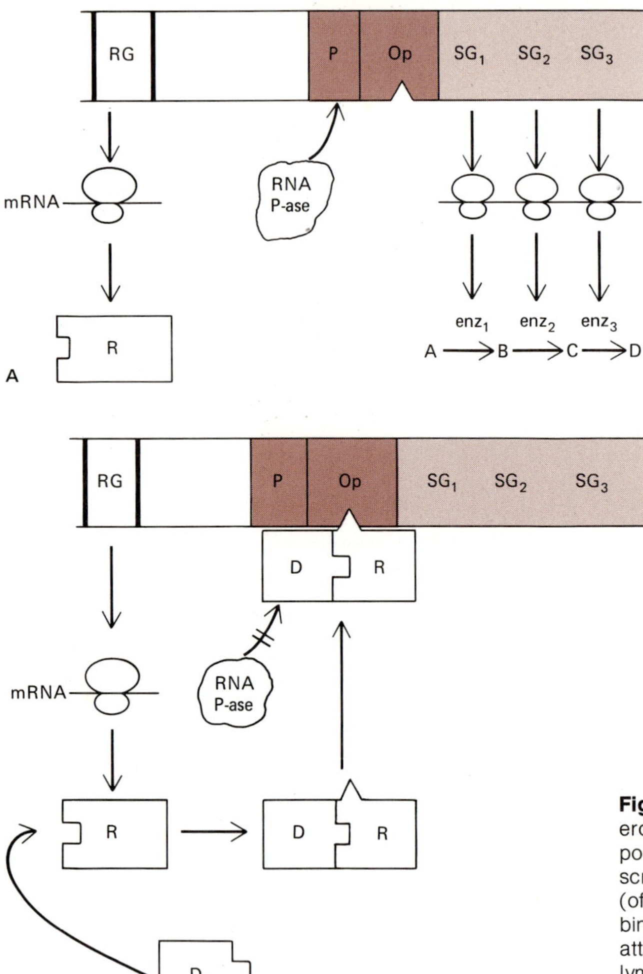

Fig. 15.10 Repressible operons. (A) Active operon. Because R by itself does not affect Op, RNA polymerase can bind to P and the SGs are transcribed. (B) Operon repressed. If a corepressor (often the end product of a reaction sequence) binds to R, the repressor-corepressor complex (DR) attaches to Op and blocks attachment of RNA polymerase to P. Operons functioning in this manner are termed repressible operons.

regulated in more than one way (see Collateral Readings for sources that describe these more complex patterns of control).

Clearly, control through operons saves a cell considerable amounts of energy and materials. Enzymes are synthesized only when they are actually needed. Quite as important, operon control permits a cell to be responsive to its environment. Compounds entering a cell as food can be the specific stimuli for their own utilization, by enzyme induction; and compounds accumulating as finished products can be the specific stimuli halting their own manufacture. Adjusting its metabolic activities in this manner, the cell can exercise steady-state control.

Translational Control

Cellular metabolism also can be regulated by mechanisms that alter the rates at which proteins are manufactured from RNA templates. In *E. coli*, for example, the three lactose-metabolizing enzymes generated through RNA transcription of the *lac* operon normally are not synthesized in equal numbers; usually they are produced in a ratio of 10:5:2. Several hypotheses have been proposed to explain such differential rates of RNA translation.

Perhaps ribosomes attach to different starting points along a given mRNA molecule at different rates, or perhaps ribosomes detach at different endpoints along mRNA at different frequencies. Further experimental testing is necessary to determine whether either of these hypotheses provides a valid explanation of how individual molecules of bacterial mRNA can be translated at different rates.

Steady-state controls that influence the rate at which molecules of mRNA are destroyed provide still another way of regulating biochemical reactions. The average lifetime of mRNA in *E. coli* is about 2 min. The molecules are then broken down enzymatically, and the free nucleotides are phosphorylated and can be reused in the synthesis of new mRNA. Thus, the templates for many enzymes must be replaced every few minutes if the concentrations of these enzymes are to remain at constant levels. The quick degradation of mRNA assures rapid reductions in the rates of specific biochemical reactions shortly after corresponding operons become inactive.

However, some molecules of mRNA in *E. coli* are degraded more rapidly than others. Some, for example, are destroyed within a few seconds of their formation; others remain intact for a few minutes. The enzymatic mechanisms that degrade mRNA are not well understood, but it is clear that such mechanisms can influence the number of enzymes produced by a single template.

Higher Levels of Gene Control in Eukaryotes

As has already been noted, much less is known about mechanisms that regulate gene expression in eukaryotes. What little is known suggests that many of the control mechanisms are very different from those of prokaryotes and that a great diversity of control mechanisms probably exists in eukaryotes, perhaps at every possible level of control.

Structural Alterations in the Organization of Genes

The following two examples illustrate one of the most direct ways in which gene expression is regulated, i.e., through changes in the organization of genes themselves. The first example illustrates how the abundance of rRNA is increased rapidly in certain cells; the second shows how some genes are activated through positional rearrangements.

Gene amplification In a 24-hour period, more than 25,000 copies of mRNA often can be produced from one copy of a eukaryotic gene. Translation of these molecules of mRNA can generate more than 2.5 billion copies of a specific protein per day. This rate of production yields sufficient amounts of gene products for most cell functions but not for all. In some instances, one or even two copies of a gene cannot be transcribed fast enough to meet the demand for a specific product.

Fig. 15.11 Multiple-copy rRNA genes. Tandem nucleolar rRNA genes from the salamander *Triturus viridenscens*. Arrows point to short segments of spacer DNA that are not being transcribed. The spacers separate identical rRNA genes. Developing molecules of rRNA project from the genes.

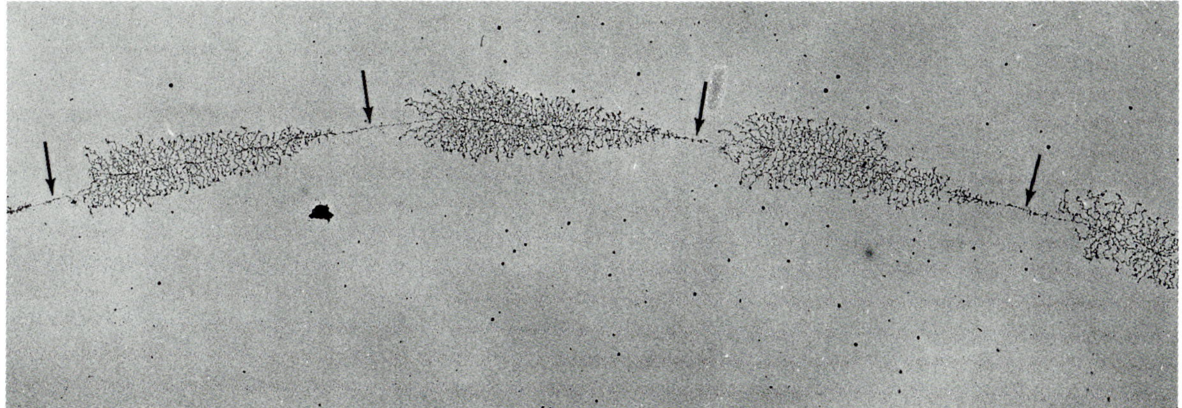

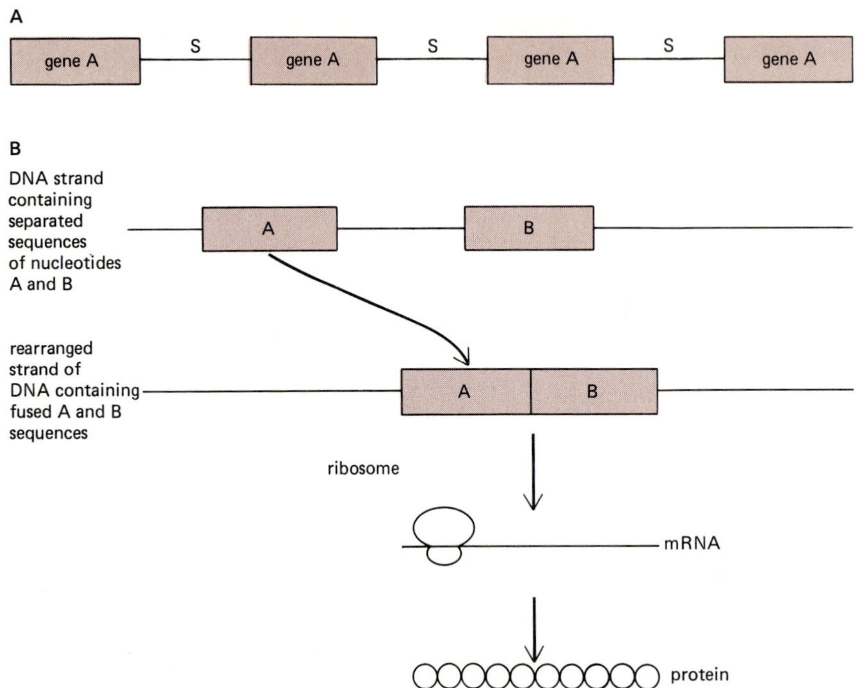

Fig. 15.12 Control of gene expression through alterations in gene organization. (A) Gene amplification. Synthesis of certain substances in eukaryotes is increased through duplication of specific genes. In this example, many copies of the same gene (gene A) are repeated in tandem arrangement along a strand of DNA. Such serially arranged duplicate genes usually are separated by spacer DNA (S), which is not transcribed. (B) Gene rearrangement. Production of immunoglobins (and probably several other eukaryotic proteins) involves fusion of two separate sequences of nucleotides. RNA transcription does not occur until a whole functional gene is generated through fusion of the two sequences.

For example, the amount of rRNA required for the production of ribosomes often requires up to 1500 times the amount of rRNA that can be transcribed from a single gene. Biologists therefore were not surprised to find between 100 and 20,000 serially arranged copies of genes coding for rRNA in most eukaryotic cells (Fig. 15.11). Most of these genes are found in nucleoli, where the synthesis of ribosomes begins. Multiple copies of eukaryotic genes also exist for transfer RNA and for *histones,* a class of proteins discussed later in this chapter. By contrast, nearly all genes of prokaryotic cells are represented only once.

In some eukaryotic cells, even a normal complement of extra genes for rRNA is insufficient to meet cell demand. For example, the egg-producing cells of some vertebrates and insects must make all the ribosomes necessary for the early development of an embryo. Moreover, production of this extraordinarily huge number of ribosomes must occur within a comparatively short period of time. The temporarily higher rate of ribosome synthesis is accomplished in these cells through *gene amplification,* a process whereby up to 2 million additional copies of genes coding for rRNA are produced (Fig. 15.12). The extra copies are organized inside a large number of new nucleoli, which become scattered throughout the nucleus. After enough ribosomes have been produced, the extra nucleoli disappear and the number of rRNA genes return to preamplification levels.

Amplification of genes coding for mRNA seemingly could provide a way of substantially increasing the abundance of specific kinds of enzymes and structural proteins in cells. Yet biologists have searched in vain for examples of such gene amplifications. For some reason, gene amplification seems to be used only for heightened production of rRNA.

Gene rearrangement Some segments of DNA periodically shift positions in eukaryotic cells, moving to new locations in the same chromosome or even to other chromosomes. The functional significance of most of these *gene rearrangements,* which also occur in prokaryotes, is unknown, but production of *immunoglobulin* clearly involves systematic gene rearrangements that are prerequisite to RNA transcription (see Fig. 15.12). Immunoglobulins are an important class of *antibodies,* proteins partly responsible for the immune response of vertebrates. As discussed more extensively in Chap. 18, immunoglobulins, like all antibodies, are produced by specialized white blood cells called *lymphocytes.*

The genetic code for the production of a specific immunoglobulin is contained in two (or more) separate sequences of nucleotides in DNA. The coding sequences for the immunoglobulin are not transcribed until the two segments of DNA are first excised and then spliced together as a single functional gene. The excision and fusion involve enzymes capable of recognizing specific "splicing sequences" of nucleotides. Biologists speculate that similar kinds of rearrangements occur before RNA transcription of many other eukaryotic genes.

RNA Transcriptional Controls

Nowhere do differences in the regulation of gene expression in pro- and eukaryotic cells appear more pronounced than at the transcriptional and posttranscriptional levels of control. Some of these differences undoubtedly stem from the fundamentally different ways in which transcription and translation are integrated in the two kinds of cells. In prokaryotes mRNA is translated as it is transcribed on ring-shaped molecules of DNA (Fig. 15.13). In eukaryotes, transcription and translation are distinctly separate processes, the first occurring in the nucleus and the second in the cytoplasm. Because these processes occur in different locations in pro- and eukaryotic cells, it is not surprising that corresponding differences also exist between steady-state controls that regulate and integrate the transcriptional and posttranscriptional processing of mRNA.

Other differences in the regulation of gene expression appear to stem from dissimilarities in the way DNA is complexed to proteins in pro- and eukaryotic cells. The ring-shaped "chromosomes" of prokaryotes consist largely of pure DNA loosely bound to small amounts of basic proteins. By contrast, most eukaryotic DNA is tightly bound to proteins inside masses of intranuclear *chromatin* fibers (Fig. 15.14, and see Chaps. 5 and 22). In addition to nucleic acids, chromatin consists of five kinds of basic proteins, called *histones,* and a greater number of largely acidic, *nonhistone* proteins. The basic or acidic qualities of proteins result from differences in their amino acid composition. Histones are positively charged (and therefore basic) molecules because they contain large amounts of lysine, arginine, and other positively charged amino acids. Many nonhistones contain large numbers of negatively charged (and therefore acidic) amino acids.

Histones obtained from cells of different species are remarkably similar. For example, the amino acid sequence of one kind of histone in cells of pea seedlings differs from the corresponding histone in cells of calf thymus at only 2 out of 102 amino acid positions. Because of such similarities, it is unlikely that histones trigger the expression of different genes in different eukaryotic cells. Instead, most evidence suggests that histones are important structural components of chromatin. At least one kind of histone plays an important role in the shortening and thickening of chromosomes during cell division (see Fig. 15.14 and Chap. 22). This does not mean that histones are uninvolved in gene expression. On the contrary, results of several experiments suggest that these basic proteins probably play a role in preventing RNA transcription by masking DNA in some undetermined manner.

Unlike histones, nonhistone proteins do exhibit a great deal of structural variation according to the species of eukaryote. Several experiments, conducted in the late 1960s and early 1970s, provided circumstantial evidence implicating these proteins as regulators of gene expression. For example, nonhistones were shown to be concentrated in regions of chromatin where RNA was being transcribed. In addition, certain hormones and other substances known to induce or inhibit RNA transcription seemed to alter the binding of nonhistones to DNA.

Then, in 1973, J. Paul and his colleagues provided the first clear demonstration that nonhistones actually can regulate genes. They conducted experiments with brain cells and *erythrocyte* precursor cells, relatively unspecialized cells that develop as mature erythrocytes (red blood cells). The precursor cells actively synthesize large quantities of *hemoglobin,* a red oxygen-carrying pigment (see Chap.18). Brain cells do not normally produce

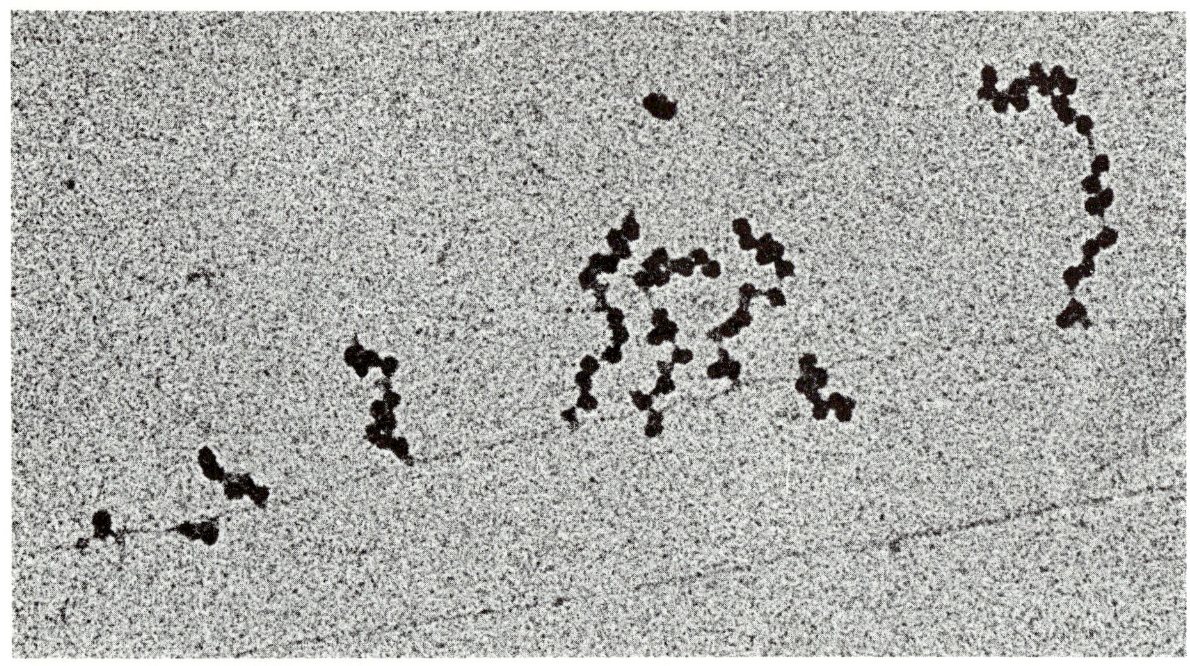

A

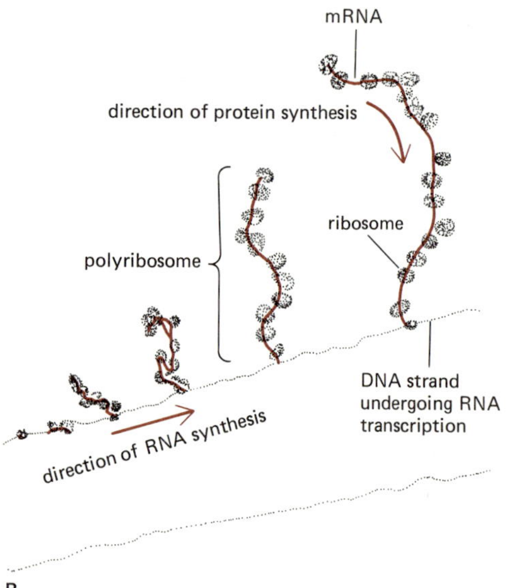

B

Fig. 15.13 Transcription and translation of mRNA in prokaryotes. (A) Electron micrograph showing the almost simultaneous transcription and translation of bacterial mRNA. (B) Schematic interpretation of the electron micrograph. Note that ribosomes (dark particles in photograph) attach to molecules of mRNA as they are being transcribed.

mRNA for *globin,* the protein component of hemoglobin, presumably because the genes for this protein are inactive in such cells.

Paul and his associates were able to remove nonhistone proteins from chromatin extracted from both brain and erythrocyte precursor cells. When brain chromatin was reassembled using nonhistones of erythrocyte precursor cells, the reconstituted chromatin produced globin mRNA. When erythrocyte chromatin was reconstituted using nonhistones from brain chromatin, globin mRNA was not made (Fig. 15.15). Evidently, the normally inactive globin genes in brain chromatin were turned on by one or more nonhistone proteins present in the chromatin of erythrocyte precursor cells. How nonhistones interact with other components of chromatin in triggering RNA transcription is not known. Available evidence merely suggests that this important class of nuclear proteins, which contributes little to the structural architecture of chromatin, may function by somehow "unmasking" histone-repressed segments of DNA.

Cell biologists have noted a second correlation between the DNA and proteins of chromatin that also is related to the transcription of eukaryotic DNA. Apparently, the nucleoprotein fibers of chro-

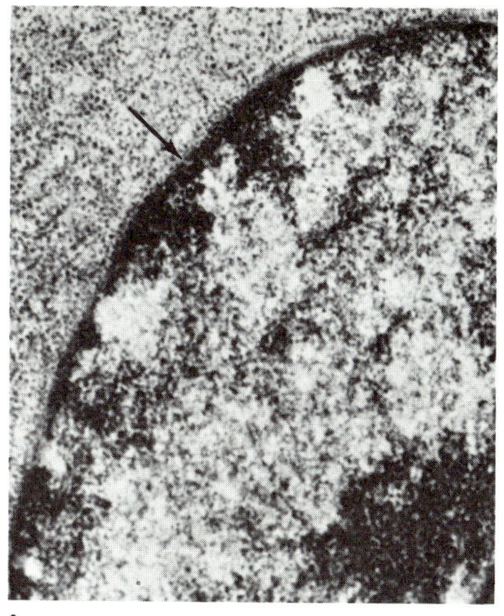
A

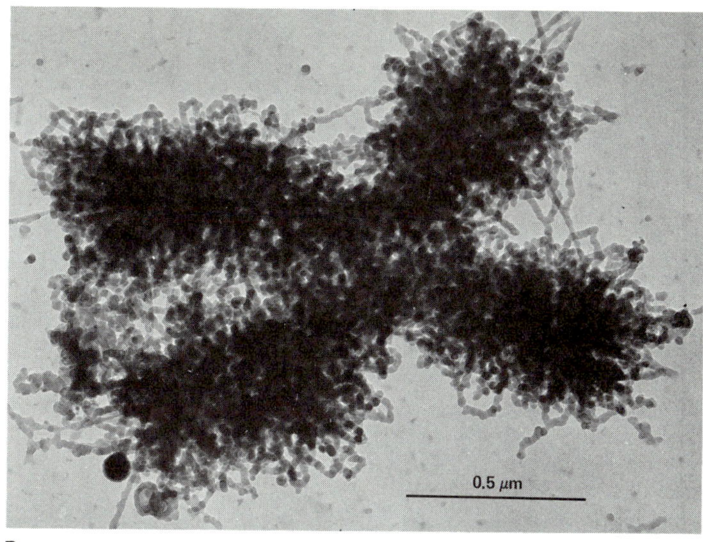

B

Fig. 15.14 Chromatin and chromosomes. (A) Portion of a nucleus, containing darkly stained chromatin. Arrow points to the boundary of the nucleus. The lightly stained area at the upper left is cytoplasm. During cell division (see Chap. 22), dispersed chromatin condenses as chromosomes. (B) Electron micrograph of a highly condensed (metaphase) chromosome.

matin must unwind before RNA transcription can occur; genes located in tightly coiled regions of chromatin are not expressed.

Separation and uncoiling of chromatin can be observed microscopically in certain instances. For example, the salivary gland cells in various insects contain thick giant (*polytene*) chromosomes consisting of an extraordinarily large number of tightly coiled chromatin fibers joined together in bundles. Messenger RNA synthesis in polytene chromosomes occurs specifically in regions where the chromosomes exhibit conspicuous enlargements, or *puffs* (Fig. 15.16). The puffed regions give the impression that the chromatin fibers there have become

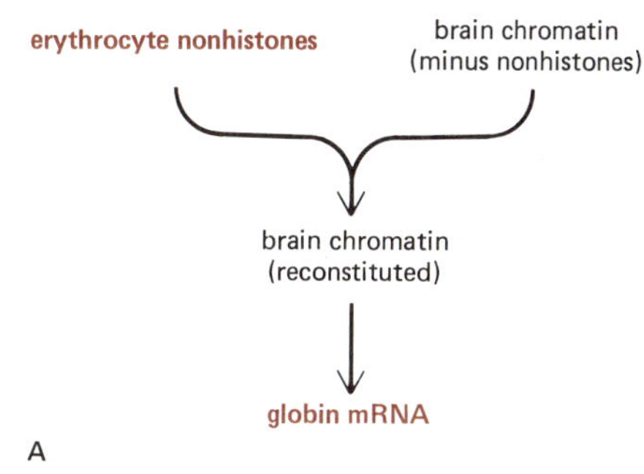

A

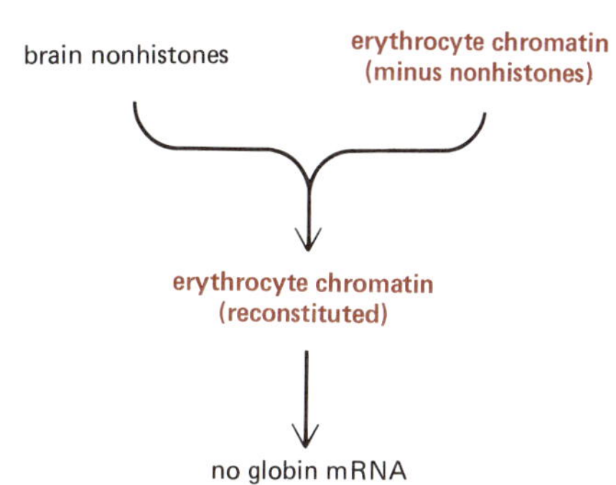

B

Fig. 15.15 Nonhistones and gene expression. (A) Brain chromatin normally does not produce globin mRNA, but erythrocyte chromatin normally does. Globin mRNA transcription can be induced from brain chromatin if the latter is first depleted of its own nonhistones and reconstituted with nonhistones extracted from erythrocyte chromatin. Evidently, the globin genes of brain chromatin, which are normally inactive, have been turned on by erythrocyte nonhistones. (B) Globin mRNA cannot be transcribed from erythrocyte chromatin when the latter is depleted of its nonhistones and complexed with nonhistones of brain chromatin. Globin genes, normally active in erythrocyte chromatin, apparently have been turned off by interaction with brain nonhistones.

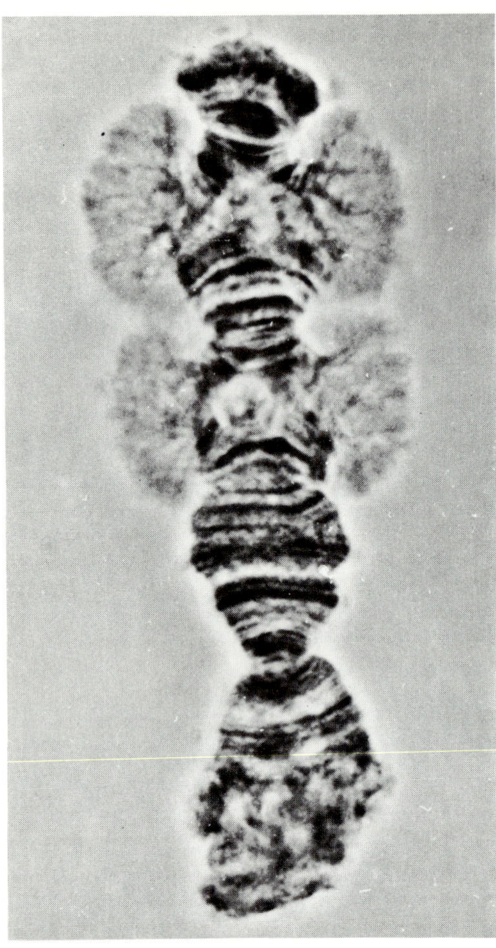

A

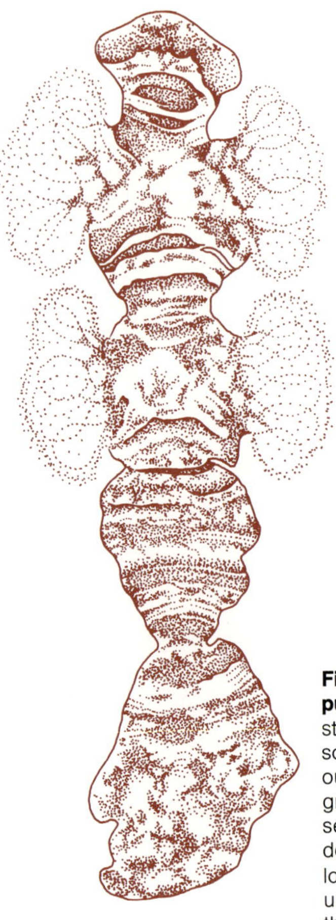

B

Fig. 15.16 Chromosome puffs. (A) High-power view of a stained salivary gland chromosome of a midge, with conspicuous puffs in upper part of photograph. (B) Schematized representation of midge chromosome depicted in (A). The puffs are loops of nucleoprotein that have uncoiled from the main axis of the chromosome.

separated and loosened like the strands of a frayed string, as if the chains exposed themselves as fully as possible to surrounding raw materials. Puffs wax and wane at any one region, and they appear at different chromosome regions at different times and at different developmental stages of the organism. These observations suggest that not all genes of a cell are active simultaneously in mRNA synthesis, as indeed would be expected from what is known about gene function.

That chromosome puffs actually do represent regions of active mRNA synthesis is indicated fairly conclusively by various experiments. For example, the antibiotic *actinomycin D* is known to be a specific inhibitor of RNA synthesis, and it also has been found to inhibit the formation of puffs. Similarly, uracil is a nitrogen base that occurs specifically in RNA and is required in RNA synthesis. If radioactive uracil is introduced into a cell, the compound accumulates exclusively in the chromosome puffs, indicating that RNA synthesis occurs only there. Interactions between histones, nonhistones, and DNA undoubtedly occur during the coiling and uncoiling of chromatin, but just how all these aspects of eukaryotic gene expression are regulated is not yet clear.

Still other differences in the control of gene expression between pro- and eukaryotes probably stem from the dissimilar organization of their genes. Although biologists know comparatively lit-

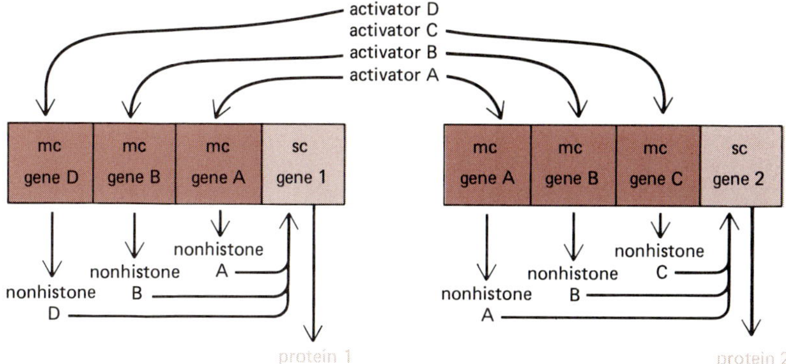

Fig. 15.17 Hypothetical explanation of gene regulation in eukaryotic cells. This hypothesis assumes that sequences of multiple-copy (mc) genes regulate mRNA transcription of single-copy (sc) genes, and that each mc gene codes for a specific nonhistone. The model further assumes that a given single-copy gene is activated only through interaction with the entire complement of nonhistones produced by the associated regulatory sequence of mc genes. RNA transcription of each mc gene is presumed to be triggered by a specific activator substance. Such substances might be products of specific intracellular reaction sequences (recall the role of histidine in the regulation of a repressible operon), or they might be secretory products of other cells. In this illustration, transcription of sc gene 1 occurs only if nonhistones A, B, and D are present in the nucleus. Transcription of sc gene 2 requires production of nonhistones A, B, and C. Thus, single-copy genes are assumed to be regulated by an overlapping but not identical set of nonhistones. In this way, a large combination of single-copy genes could be activated by a much smaller number of different control (multiple-copy) genes.

tle about the location and integration of eukaryotic genes, it now seems certain that none of these genes are organized as operons.

In addition, almost all genes of prokaryotic cells are represented only once, as noted earlier. By contrast, virtually all eukaryotic cells contain multiple copies of certain genes. One example has already been discussed: genes coding for rRNA are present side by side in sequences that are repeated in tandem within nucleoli (see Fig. 15.11). Histones also are produced by multiple-copy genes. Codes for the five histones of sea urchin eggs are clustered together as a unit along a segment of DNA. Each unit is repeated at least 400 times in the chromatin of an unfertilized egg. The adaptive value of such multiple-copy genes is clear. Cells require extremely large amounts of certain gene products, and multiple copies of rRNA and histone genes assure volume production.

The adaptive value of another kind of multiple-copy gene is less clear. Shorter in length than most tandem rRNA and histone genes, these sequences of nucleotides are interspersed between single-copy genes, unrepeated segments of DNA that probably code for most of the enzymes, secretory proteins, and structural proteins of a cell. A growing body of evidence suggests that single-copy genes are regulated by adjacent batteries of these shorter multiple-copy genes, some of which appear in a large number of batteries. How such multiple-copy genes might exert such control remains a matter of active speculation and research (Fig. 15.17).

Posttranscriptional Controls

Processing of mRNA following transcription differs greatly in pro- and eukaryotic cells. In prokaryotes, mRNA undergoes little modification following transcription. Most prokaryotic mRNA is translated as soon as it is produced (see Fig. 15.13). By contrast, eukaryotic mRNA normally undergoes substantial modification in the nucleus before being transported to the cytoplasm.

One of these modifications involves attachment of a derivative of guanosine triphosphate (GTP) to one end of mRNA. As pointed out in Chaps. 4 and 14, GTP is one of four energy carriers required for

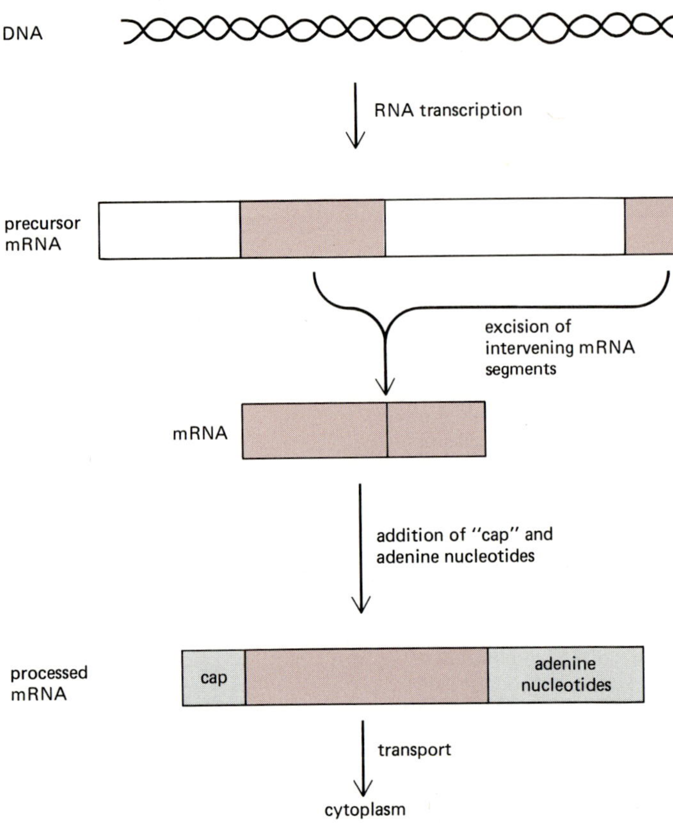

Fig. 15.18 Posttranscriptional processing of eukaryotic mRNA. Many (but not all) molecules of eukaryotic mRNA undergo all the processing steps shown. Each of the steps occurs in the nucleus before transport to the cytoplasm. In the first step, a nonfunctional precursor molecule of mRNA is transcribed from DNA. Segments of the precursor molecule that code for sequences of amino acids in a protein are excised and spliced together as a shorter molecule of mRNA. A derivative of guanosine triphosphate is attached (capped) to one end of the molecule; a long strand of adenine nucleotides is attached to the opposite end. The finished molecule then enters the cytoplasm, where it is translated. As noted in the text, control of gene expression could occur at any of these steps.

the synthesis of nucleic acids. The end of an mRNA that has been altered in this fashion is said to be *capped.* The opposite end of an mRNA also is modified by the addition of a long chain of adenine nucleotides (Fig. 15.18). Recent studies suggest that the capping and addition of adenine nucleotides both appear to increase the stability and life of mRNA. If so, controls influencing these modifications could affect the number of proteins translated from a molecule of mRNA.

Discovery of another posttranscriptional modification of mRNA grew out of studies that compared the number of DNA nucleotides coding for a molecule of mRNA with the number of nucleotides present in the mRNA during translation. In most instances, the molecules being translated did not contain the full sequence of nucleotides of the corresponding gene. To account for the missing nucleotides, several biologists hypothesized that portions of newly produced mRNA are cut from either end of the molecule shortly after transcription. Segments cut away presumably do not contain codons essential for translation of a finished protein.

This hypothesis appears to explain how some molecules of mRNA are reduced in size before translation, but it does not account for most mRNA shortening. Of the many molecules of mRNA that undergo shortening before transport from the nucleus, *the majority have sequences of nucleotides cut from nonterminal regions.* This totally unexpected finding means that many eukaryotic genes are arranged piecemeal, interspersed between segments of DNA that are not translated as proteins (see Fig. 15.18).

Examples of such "split" genes include those coding for globin, insulin, and antibodies. RNA transcription of split genes proceeds somewhat differently from that for unfragmented ones, which include those coding for histones. First, a molecule of mRNA is transcribed from the entire length of DNA that contains fragments of the gene. Often there is so much extra DNA that the mRNA copy of the fragmented gene and its intervening sequences is up to 10 times longer than the combined length of all gene fragments. Next, the mRNA copies of the extra DNA are snipped out of the long mRNA by enzymes. Messenger RNA copies of DNA segments that code for amino acid sequences in a protein are then spliced together as a shortened strand of mRNA. The shortened transcript then moves to the cytoplasm, where it is translated.

Biologists are uncertain why some genes of animals are arranged in pieces. Moreover, almost nothing is known about the signals that so precisely define splice sites in long molecules of mRNA or whether the efficiency of splicing at particular sites may contribute to the regulation of gene expression. At the moment, there are far more questions about how mRNA is processed in eukaryotes than there are answers.

Translational Controls

The life span of most eukaryotic mRNA is much longer than that of prokaryotes. As noted earlier, most prokaryotic mRNA is translated almost immediately after its production and is broken down only minutes later. Translation of eukaryotic mRNA often continues for many hours, and some animal cells produce mRNA that remains untranslated for many days. For example, molecules of mRNA used for protein synthesis during the early development of most vertebrate embryos is manufactured in eggs before fertilization. Such long-lived mRNA is stored in the cytoplasm of unfertilized eggs in an inactive, or masked, form, and becomes unmasked as a consequence of fertilization. Mechanisms responsible for this unmasking largely operate in the cytoplasm and coordinate early embryonic development by regulating the timing and rates of mRNA translation.

Similar kinds of masked mRNA have been found in the green alga *Chlorella.* These cells sometimes contain large quantities of mRNA templates for a particular photosynthesis-regulating enzyme. The templates often remain untranslated for long periods. Moreover, translation of the mRNA is interrupted when glucose is added to the medium in which the cells are grown. Results of several experiments demonstrate that glucose does not prevent enzyme production by inhibiting RNA transcription; glucose somehow blocks translation of mRNA.

Posttranslational Controls

Whether produced by pro- or eukaryotic cells, enzymes themselves can function as modulators of metabolic reactions. In fact, enzymes constitute the simplest and most basic kinds of regulating devices in cells. Consider, for example, the reversible reaction

$$\text{glucose} \xrightleftharpoons{\text{enz}} \text{polysaccharide}$$

In this case, the totality of glucose molecules in a cell, or *glucose pool,* can function as a receptor. If additional glucose arrives in the cell as food, this excess can represent a stimulus. By mass action, the reaction to the right will then occur at a higher rate than that to the left, and more polysaccharide will be formed. The polysaccharide pool here is equivalent to an effector, and increase of polysaccharide concentration is the response. For as polysaccharide accumulates at the expense of glucose, the glucose pool decreases to normal levels, and the original stimulus is thereby removed. The extra polysaccharide in turn can be a new stimulus in the cell, initiating other reactions and new responses.

But the designations "receptor" and "effector" are not fixed. If a cell were to acquire additional polysaccharide rather than glucose, the polysaccharide pool would function as a receptor and the glucose pool as an effector. In either case the function of modulator is performed by the enzyme; it takes a specific enzyme to act on a specific molecular stimulus and to promote a specific molecular response.

The rates and directions of metabolic reactions also can be affected by several factors that alter the catalytic activities of enzymes. For example, the rates of some reactions are increased or decreased when certain substances bind with enzymes. In some cases an inhibitor binds to an active site of an enzyme, thereby blocking formation of an enzyme-substrate complex. Several poisons, such as certain insecticides, function in this way.

In other cases, small molecules alter the shapes of enzymes by binding to them at locations other than their active sites. Such locations are called *allosteric sites,* and the resulting change in enzyme configuration is called an *allosteric effect* (Fig. 15.19). Substances that promote allosteric effects are common in cells and frequently prevent uncon-

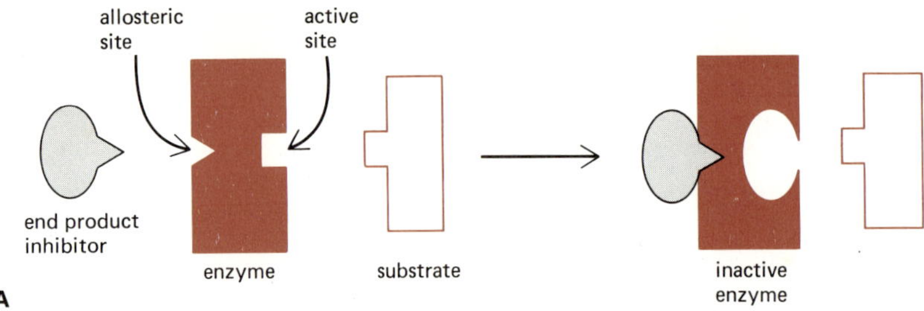

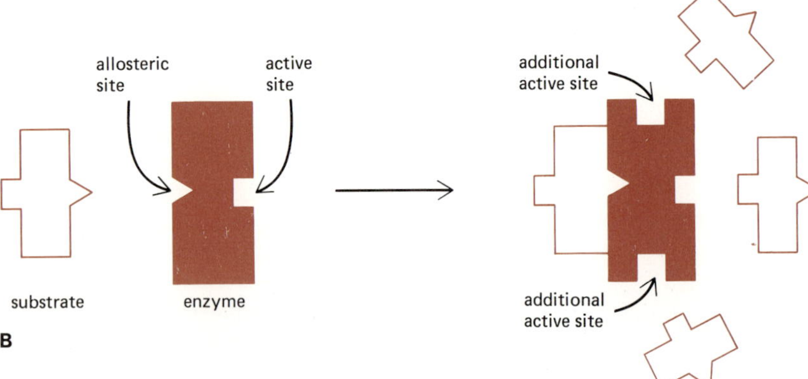

Fig. 15.19 Allosteric effects. These two examples show how the bonding of substances to allosteric sites can inhibit or accelerate chemical reactions in cells. (A) End-product inhibition. By bonding to allosteric sites, some end products of reaction sequences change the three-dimensional structure of enzyme active sites. Such changes prevent formation of enzyme-substrate complexes. (B) Under certain conditions, the binding of a substrate to an allosteric site increases the number of active sites on enzymes, thereby increasing the rate at which enzyme-substrate complexes form.

trolled depletion of substrates as well as excessive accumulation of reaction products. It has long been known that in certain reaction sequences in cells the end product of the sequence often tends to inhibit some earlier point of the sequence. For example, in a serial transformation of compound A to compound Z, the end product Z, once formed in given amounts, might inhibit some earlier step, such as B $\longrightarrow$ C, by binding to an allosteric site on an enzyme:

$$A \xrightarrow{enz_1} B \xrightarrow{enz_2} C \xrightarrow{enz_3} \cdots \xrightarrow{enz_x} Z$$

Such feedback inhibitions prevent more end product from being formed.

Conversely, for some reaction sequences in cells, it has been found that addition of excess amounts of reactants leads to a rapid formation of excess amounts of specific enzymes. For example, in a transformation of A to B, an excess of A can lead to an increase in the number of available active sites on the enzyme that converts A to B. The increase can be caused by the binding of A to an allosteric site on the enzyme. The resulting change in enzyme shape exposes additional active sites on the catalyst and increases the rate at which substrate A is converted to product B (see Fig. 15.19).

Enzyme shape also is affected by changes in pH, which can alter the ionization of charged groups on amino acids. Such alterations can cause adjacent amino acids to twist slightly, thereby changing the tertiary structure of enzymes and other proteins. Deformation of enzyme shape can destroy the catalytic properties of enzymes, but changes of pH sometimes are essential for establishment of active sites. The protease pepsin, for example, is manufactured as the inactive molecule pepsinogen in secretory cells of the stomach lining (see also Chap. 11). Intracellular activation of the enzyme would result in destruction of these cells. This does not occur because the pH of the secretory cells is nearly neutral. But when pepsinogen is exposed to the low pH of the stomach cavity, the inhibiting portion of the enzyme is removed and active pepsin is produced:

$$\text{pepsinogen} \xrightarrow{H^+} \text{pepsin} + \text{fragment}$$

Cells often produce potentially destructive enzymes; these too exist in an inactive form or are housed in lysosomes or similar enclosures and thus are isolated from the rest of the cell. Upon activation or release, such enzymes often destroy cells, tissues, and even whole organs. The timing of tissue breakdown is very important in the development of many organisms, e.g., when the tails of frog tadpoles regress during metamorphosis (see Fig. 17.11).

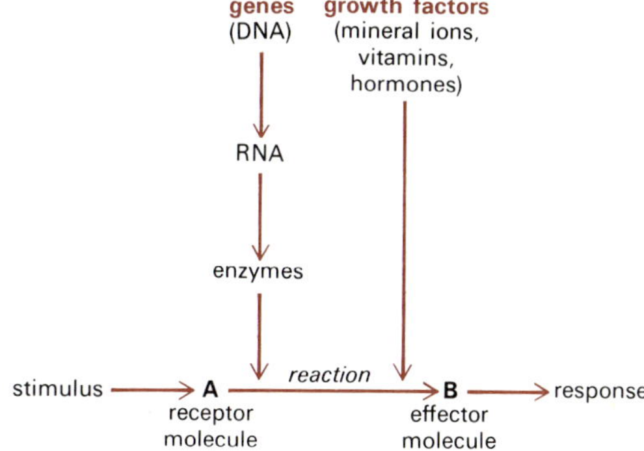

Fig. 15.20 Molecular modulators and their control over steady-state-maintaining metabolic reactions in a cell. Through RNA, genes control production of enzymes. Availability and activity of growth factors in cells also is controlled by genes and their products. In this way, genes constitute the ultimate modulators of cellular steady states.

Growth Factors

In addition to enzymes, which often function as primary modulators of metabolic reactions, cells also contain a variety of *growth factors* that function as secondary modulators (Fig. 15.20). A growth factor is any controlling agent a cell requires but cannot manufacture on its own. Included in this category are chiefly *minerals, hormones,* and *vitamins.* Minerals and vitamins influence the metabolism of virtually all cells; hormones are the almost exclusive products of multicellular eukaryotes. These three kinds of substances are named "growth" factors because they often reveal their action most obviously through particular effects on growth. In this sense genes and enzymes qualify as growth factors, too, but they are produced directly in the cell in which they act.

In some cases, growth factors influence metabolic reactions by affecting the expression of genes at the higher levels of control described earlier. For example, certain *steroid* hormones appear to regulate RNA transcription of certain genes in some animal cells (see Chap. 17). But most growth factors function at the posttranscriptional level of control.

Minerals

Mineral substances are required by all organisms as growth factors. Minerals serve in two general capacities: in part they are nutrients used as structural components of cells, and in part they function as ionic *cofactors,* essential for binding enzymes to their substrates (see also Chap. 4). In some cases the same mineral contributes to both functions. For example, magnesium is both a structural component (in chlorophyll) and a cofactor for enzymes participating in respiratory and other reactions. By and large, most organisms require roughly the same kinds of mineral substances.

Hormones

More complex than minerals, these organic molecules regulate cell metabolism at almost all levels of control. As already mentioned, some hormones probably function by activating or inhibiting RNA transcription of specific batteries of genes in target cells. Other hormones apparently affect the rates at which proteins are manufactured on mRNA templates. Still others interact with receptor molecules at cell surfaces and influence absorption and secretion of specific substances. *Insulin,* for example, accelerates uptake of glucose by many cells. Other hormones inhibit absorption of glucose and accelerate its release from cells. Hormones frequently interact in this manner as brakes or accelerators of reactions. A more extensive discussion of hormone function is presented in Chaps. 16 and 17.

Vitamins

Except for animals, most organisms synthesize their own vitamins, usually directly in the cells

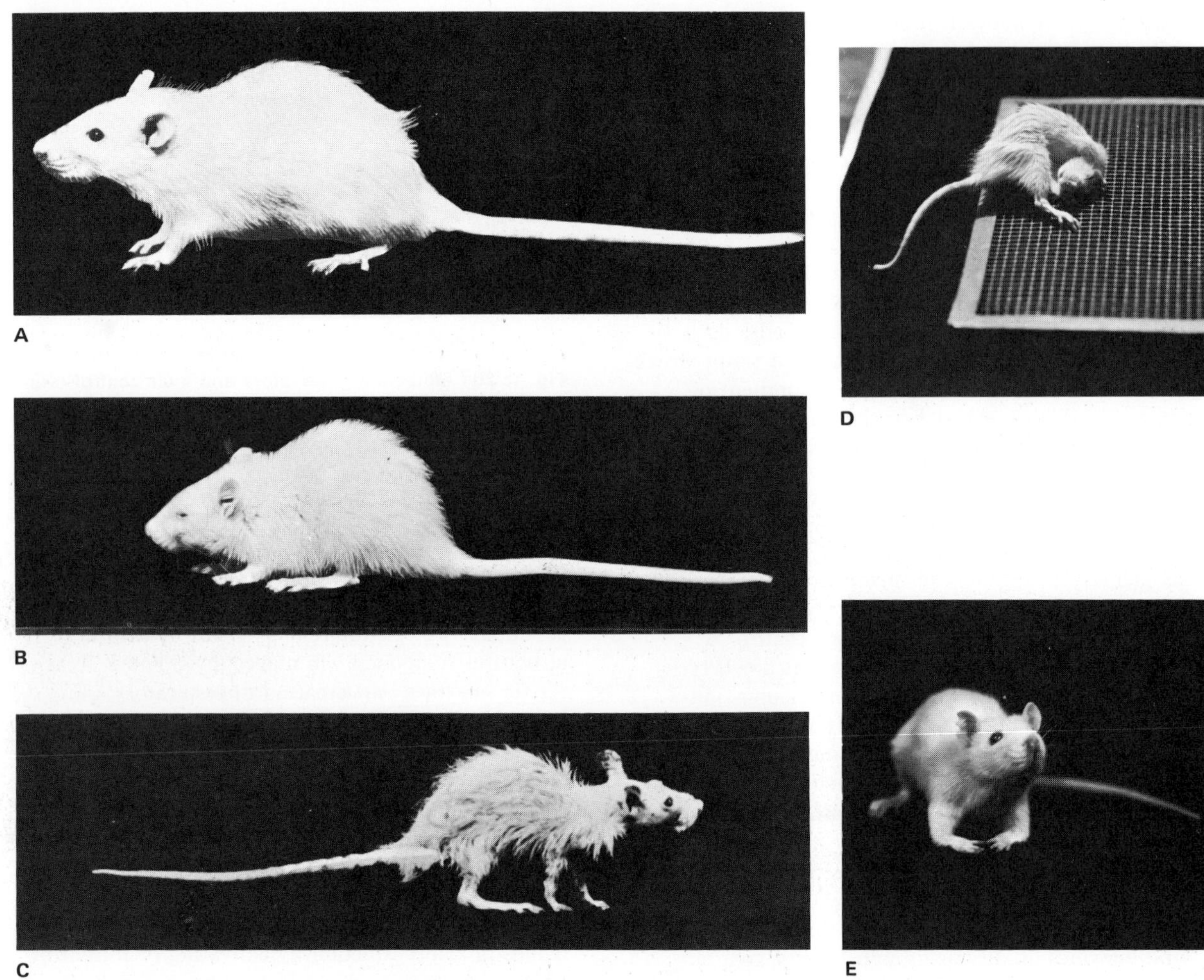

Fig. 15.21 Vitamins. All rats shown have the same age. (A) Normal rat, weight about 170 grams (g). (B) Vitamin A deficiency: eyes infected, fur rough, weight about 60 g. (C) Riboflavin deficiency: hair loss, sickly, weight about 60 g. (D) Thiamine deficiency: lack of muscle coordination. (E) Vitamin D deficiency: abnormal bone development.

where they act. In such organisms vitamins belong to the same self-manufactured group of control agents as cyclic AMP (see Chap. 17) and enzymes. Vitamins cannot be considered growth factors in these organisms. However, few animals synthesize all the vitamins necessary for survival; at least some vitamins are obtained solely from ingested foods, and such vitamins do qualify as growth factors.

Moreover, the vitamin-synthesizing capacity of animals can vary greatly. Insects, for example, can synthesize all except the B vitamins. Apes, human beings, and a few rodents cannot manufacture their own vitamin C, but other animals can. People happen to be particularly poor vitamin synthesizers, being unable to produce sufficient quantities of any except the D vitamins. Such differences in synthesizing ability between different species probably result from the loss or alteration of genes coding for vitamins. Once an organism loses the capacity of synthesizing a particular vitamin, that vitamin becomes a required growth factor for that species.

TABLE 15.1
The Main Vitamins and Their Functions

Name	Food source	Chief cell function	Effect of deficiency
vitamin A	leaves, yellow foods, liver	chemistry of vision; membrane integrity	night blindness; infectious diseases; bone, nerve abnormalities
thiamine (B_1)	grain products, yeast, beans, nuts, liver, eggs, meat	cocarboxylase precursor	beriberi
riboflavin (B_2)		FMN and FAD precursor	hair loss; growth failure
nicotinic acid		NAD and NADP precursor	pellagra
pantothenic acid		coenzyme A precursor	anemia; growth failure; hemorrhages; bone disorders; nerve, skin disorders; infectious diseases
biotin (H)		CO_2-carrying coenzyme precursor	
choline		$—CH_3$-carrying coenzyme	
pyridoxine (B_6)		$—NH_2$-carrying coenzyme	
folic acid		nucleic acid metabolism	
vitamin B_{12}		nucleic acid metabolism	
vitamin C	citrus fruits, tomatoes, cabbage	aerobic H transfer; synthesis of cell cement	scurvy
vitamin D	liver, fish oils	calcium and phosphorus regulation	rickets
vitamin E	most foods	aerobic hydrogen transfer	sterility; eye abnormalities; nerve, muscle disorders
vitamin K	–		failure of blood clotting

More than 30 compounds are known to have the properties of vitamins. They are needed in very small amounts. Vitamins are raw materials for the production of a large number of *coenzymes*, substances vitally important to the function of many enzymes (see Chap. 4). Consequently, the prolonged absence of vitamins from a cell impairs metabolic processes and produces unsteady or diseased states. In this connection, careful distinction should be made between the *biological* and the *clinical* effects of a deficiency. Most, and possibly all, cells of an organism require most or all vitamins; if a vitamin deficiency exists, some metabolic process in cells will be impaired. This is a biological effect. The B vitamin riboflavin, for example, is a precursor of a coenzyme that functions during respiration. If riboflavin is in deficient supply, respiratory reactions in cells will be affected.

Superimposed on such biological effects are clinical ones. These become evident when the cells of given tissues or organs are more sensitive to a deficiency than other cells. Such sensitive cells will then exhibit symptoms of disease sooner or more pronouncedly than others. For example, riboflavin deficiency in mammals has long been known to lead to loss of hair, to growth failure, and to eye disorders (Fig. 15.21). By themselves, clinical data alone would imply that riboflavin is required specifically in hair, bones, and eyes. Actually, however, clinical results represent only the large-scale secondary consequences of the deeper biological effects of deficiency, which influence most or all cells.

When they were first investigated, vitamins were given letter designations. Later virtually every vitamin so labeled was found to consist of not one but several often related substances. Letters with subscripts then came into use. Today the tendency is to refer to a new vitamin by its chemical name only. Many vitamins therefore do not have a letter designation, and some have both letter and chemical names (Table 15.1). Some vitamins are fat-soluble; others are water-soluble. The first group includes vitamins A, D, E, and K; the latter, vitamins B and C. In vertebrates, fat-soluble vitamins require bile for proper absorption from the gut. Therefore, whenever secretion of bile from the gallbladder is impaired or when fats are rigidly excluded from the diet, a deficiency of fat-soluble vitamins can develop readily. Water-soluble vitamins are normally present in the fluids in and around cells and tissues; hence such fluids are nutritionally valuable.

Vitamin A Group

The several closely related substances in this group are derivatives of the *carotene* pigments synthesized in plastids. Carotenes therefore can be found in leaves, and other rich sources are red-orange-yellow plant parts such as carrots, tomatoes, squash, and sweet potatoes. Spinach, egg yolk, butter, and cream are among other products rich in carotene. Spinach contains more carotene than an equal weight of egg yolk. In yellow foods, depth of color is an index of comparative carotene content.

When a molecule of carotene is split enzymatically in the presence of water, two molecules of vitamin A are formed (see also Fig. 4.6):

$$\underset{\textit{carotene}}{C_{40}H_{56}} + 2H_2O \longrightarrow \underset{\textit{vitamin A}}{2C_{20}H_{30}O}$$

The vitamin is stored in the vertebrate liver (fish livers and their oils contain particularly large amounts; hence the nutritive value of, for example, cod-liver oil). Fish obtain carotene through food chains originating with algae.

Among the nutritional disorders affecting infants and children, vitamin A deficiency ranks second in importance to protein and caloric malnutrition (see also Biology Highlight in Chap. 11). Very often the two occur together, with serious consequences. Of the effects caused by vitamin A deficiency, those involving the eye are the most pronounced and widespread. Several thousand children become blind each year because of this dietary deficiency, which is most prevalent in poor, nonindustrialized countries. As a preventive measure, several foods such as milk are now fortified with vitamin A.

Among its other cellular functions, vitamin A controls proper growth of bones, tooth enamel, and nerve tissue. It also prevents drying and cracking of exposed, normally moist membranes, like those in the eyes, the breathing system, and the alimentary and urogenital tracts. Because pathogenic bacteria and other disease-causing microbes could easily penetrate such tissues if they became cracked or abraded, vitamin A probably reduces the incidence of infectious diseases (vitamin A actually is sometimes called the "anti-infection vitamin," but such a designation applies equally well to many other vitamins).

Vitamin B Group

These water-soluble vitamins include *thiamine* (B_1), *riboflavin* (B_2), *nicotinic acid* ("niacin"), *pyridoxine* (B_6), *biotin* (H), *vitamin* B_{12}, *pantothenic acid, folic acid,* and *choline.* The substances are not particularly related in chemical structure or biological function. They are grouped together largely because they tend to occur together in plant and animal foods. Most of the vitamins have been identified chemically, and many can be synthesized in the laboratory. The B vitamins occur in natural foods of all types; rich sources are whole-grain products, yeast, peas, beans, and nuts among plant foods, and liver, egg yolk, and meat among animal foods. Intestinal bacteria synthesize many of the B vitamins. Most of these vitamins are raw materials in the synthesis of cellular coenzymes.

A more or less well-defined clinical disease is associated with lack of each of the B vitamins. Thus, mild thiamine deficiency produces fatigue, weakness, and lassitude. More severe thiamine starvation over a period of weeks can result in *beriberi,* a disease characterized by muscular paralysis. Riboflavin deficiency leads to hair loss, eye disorders, and stunted growth, as noted; niacin deficiency, to *pellagra,* a disease of the skin and the nervous system; vitamin B_{12} and folic acid deficiencies, to anemia; choline deficiency, to bone deformities (in chickens) and internal hemorrhages; and pyridoxine and pantothenic acid deficiencies, to growth failure, anemia, lowered resistance to infections, and nerve and skin disorders. In all these cases administration of the appropriate vitamin usually relieves the disease.

Vitamin C

This compound is *ascorbic acid,* a derivative of monosaccharide sugars. It is widely synthesized in plants, particularly in citrus fruit, cabbage, and tomatoes. As pointed out, most animals—but not people—manufacture it. Ascorbic acid is one of the least stable vitamins. Cooking destroys it, and in fresh and canned foods much of this water-soluble vitamin diffuses out to the food juices. Vitamin C participates in electron transport in mitochondria. Vitamin C also takes part in a phase of synthesis metabolism; it plays a role in the production of the cementing substance that binds tissue cells together. When this function is impaired, *scurvy* results. Blood vessels become abnormally permeable, and hemorrhages can occur in any part of the body. Connective tissues no longer bind efficiently, and teeth loosen from their sockets. In more advanced stages bones weaken, muscles degenerate, and death ultimately supervenes. Mild deficiencies need not lead to an outright scorbutic condition, but they can impair energy metabolism enough to produce lassitude and to cause fleeting, rheumatismlike pains in limb joints.

Vitamin D Group

Some ten related compounds are included in this group. Two of them, D_2 and D_3, are particularly potent. In people, precursors of the D vitamins are present in skin. Such precursors are converted to active vitamins by irradiation with ultraviolet light, hence the designation of the D vitamins as "sunshine vitamins." The active vitamins are stored in the liver along with vitamin A in the lipid reserves. Good external sources of D vitamins are fish-liver oils, dairy foods, and, in general, foods rich also in vitamin A.

The D vitamins participate in reactions involving calcium and phosphorus, particularly in the complex processes of bone formation and bone maintenance. In the cells of the gut the vitamins probably balance calcium and phosphorus absorption against excretion to the gut cavity. Through this the vitamins play a part in maintaining an optimum supply of calcium and phosphorus in the body, and then they regulate the deposition of these raw materials as bone and tooth substance.

Deficiency of the D vitamins leads to *rickets,* a disease marked by softening and bending of bones, beading of ribs, erosion of teeth, and elimination of calcium and phosphorus in urine. Conversely, continued overdoses of vitamin D can lead to abnormal thickening of bones and some calcification of soft tissues.

Vitamin E Group

Several closely related compounds are in this category. These vitamins are relatively unstable, but they are so widely distributed in both plant and animal fats that a deficiency is not likely to arise on any normal diet. These substances are often called "antisterility vitamins"; deficiency can be shown to lead to permanent infertility in male rats and to death of embryos or to premature births in pregnant female rats. In people, embryos deficient in vitamin E often undergo abnormal eye development. As to its cellular function, vitamin E is known to participate in the electron-transport systems of mitochondria (see Chap. 12).

Vitamin K Group

These vitamins are known best for their role in blood clotting; deficiency leads to failure of the clotting mechanism (see Chap. 18). For this reason vitamin K often is administered before surgery, particularly surgery on bile ducts blocked by gallstones. Since vitamin K is dissolved in the fatty portions of food, bile is required for its proper absorption from the gut cavity. If the bile duct is blocked, a person is likely to be vitamin K–deficient and to have an impaired blood-clotting mechanism.

Like vitamin E, vitamin K contributes to electron transport in mitochondria. These two groups of vitamins also resemble each other in chemical structure, in their wide occurrence among foods, and in being synthesized by intestinal bacteria.

Review Questions

1 What general kinds of processes take place in the execution of control activities? What general function do such controls serve in the maintenance of life?

2 Interpret the temperature-regulating action of a home thermostat in terms of a control system and indicate the specific roles of feedback and of trial and error.

3 In what sense does a molecular reaction constitute a control system? What kinds of substances and organelles can serve as modulators? Review the general pattern of steady-state control on supracellular levels.

4 Briefly describe how the genetic systems of prokaryotes differ from those of eukaryotes. Why were biologists not surprised when they discovered that the genes of eukaryotes are regulated in a more complex fashion than the genes of prokaryotes?

5 Illustrate how gene expression of prokaryotes is regulated at the transcriptional, translational, and posttranslational levels of cellular control.

6 Show how eukaryotic gene expression either is or could be regulated at each of the six levels of control described in this chapter.

7 How can structural alterations in the organization of genes affect gene expression? Give specific examples.

8 Explain the role of growth factors in steady-state control. Discuss the general cellular functions of enzymes.

9 Review the general cellular functions of vitamins. How do autotrophs and heterotrophs differ in their vitamin requirements? How and why do different heterotrophs differ in their vitamin requirements? Review the food sources and chemical nature of the principal vitamins. What are the clinical effects of deficiencies of these vitamins?

Collateral Readings

Brown, D. B.: Gene Expression in Eukaryotes, *Science,* vol. 211, p. 667, Feb. 13, 1981. A good review of this topic. For the advanced student.

Chambon, P.: Split Genes, *Scientific American,* May 1981. The author describes how the split gene for the protein ovoalbumin was discovered.

Changeaux, J.: The Control of Biochemical Reactions, *Scientific American,* April 1965. A description of cellular feedback controls governing enzyme synthesis on the one hand and enzyme activity on the other. Very pertinent to the topics of this chapter.

Davidson, E. H., and **R. J. Britten:** Regulation of Gene Expression: Possible Role of Repetitive Sequences, *Science,* vol. 204, pp. 1052–1059, June 8, 1979. This article not only reviews much of the recent literature relating to the control of gene expression in animals but also illustrates how scientists use experimental data to generate new hypotheses.

Dyson, R. D.: "Cell Biology: A Molecular Approach," Allyn and Bacon, Boston, 1978. This text contains a good treatment of gene regulation in pro- and eukaryotes.

Gabriel, M. L., and **S. Fogel:** "Great Experiments in Biology," Prentice-Hall, Englewood Cliffs, N.J., 1955. Included in this paperback is a section on vitamins in which some of the original classic studies on these growth factors are reprinted. Recommended.

Goodenough, U.: "Genetics," 2d ed., Holt, New York, 1978. This text contains a good review of the structure and function of operons.

Jacob, F., and **J. Monod:** Genetic Regulatory Mechanisms in the Synthesis of Proteins, *Journal of Molecular Biology,* vol. 3, p. 318, 1961. The classic paper on the functioning of operons in *E. coli.*

Karp, G.: "Cell Biology," McGraw-Hill, New York 1979. Several good sections on control operations in cells.

Maniatis, T., and **M. Ptashne:** A DNA Operator-Repressor System, *Scientific American,* January 1976. The interactions between operators and repressor proteins in a virus are described.

Ptashne, M., and **W. Gilbert:** Genetic Repressors, *Scientific American,* June 1970. The first isolation of inhibitor substances produced by regulator genes is described.

Stern, G. S., J. S. Stein, and **L. J. Kleinsmith:** Chromosomal Proteins and Gene Regulation, *Scientific American,* February 1975. The roles of histone and nonhistone proteins are discussed.

Watson, J. D.: "The Molecular Biology of the Gene," 3d ed., W. A. Benjamin, Menlo Park, Calif., 1976. Several sections of this textbook are pertinent to the topics of this chapter.

Chapter 16 Hormonal Control in Plants

Learning Objectives

After reading this chapter you should be able to:

1. Define hormone; show how hormones are transported to target structures in plants, simple animals, and complex animals.
2. Differentiate between the functional properties of hormones and enzymes; name at least three ways in which hormones initiate or integrate cellular activities.
3. List at least one function for each of the following hormones or groups of hormones:
   - **a.** auxins
   - **b.** gibberellins
   - **c.** cytokinins
   - **d.** ethylene
   - **e.** abscisic acid
4. Describe at least one response of plants that results from the antagonistic effects of two or more of the hormones listed in Objective 3.
5. Outline an experiment that demonstrates a growth-controlling effect of auxins.
6. Show how the growth-controlling effects of gibberellins were discovered; identify at least one mechanism by which auxins, gibberellins, and cytokinins influence plant growth and development.
7. Exemplify and define:
   - **a.** secondary growth substance
   - **b.** allelopathy
8. Indicate how hormones influence each of the following activities of plants:
   - **a.** phototropic responses of stems
   - **b.** geotropic responses of stems and roots
   - **c.** transpiration
   - **d.** bud development
   - **e.** leaf senescence, leaf fall, and fruit drop
9. Identify, define, and illustrate two kinds of growth movements and two kinds of turgor movements in plants.
10. Define apical dominance and bud dormancy; describe the functional relationships between temperature, photoperiod, and hormones in controlling the induction and reactivation of dormant buds; identify the principal relationships between temperature and hormones in stimulating seed germination; outline the adaptive value of enforced dormancy in certain plants.
11. Differentiate between flowers, flower buds, and flower primordia; show how temperature and photoperiod can influence flowering; list the distinguishing characteristics of short-day, long-day, and day-neutral plants and list an example of each; outline experiments to
    - **a.** distinguish between short-day, long-day, and day-neutral plants
    - **b.** demonstrate the role of leaves in controlling flower development in short-day plants
    - **c.** demonstrate the importance of dark periods in regulating flowering in short- and long-day plants
12. Define phytochrome, show how phytochrome regulates flowering in short- and long-day plants, and indicate how phytochrome is affected by orange-red and far-red light.
13. Define florigen and state why it is improbable that a single unique florigen is produced by all plants; list evidence demonstrating the existence of a flowering stimulus in plant tissues; outline a functional relationship between photoperiod and the flowering stimulus.
14. List at least five practical applications that have resulted from basic research on the hormonal controls of plant growth and development.

PATTERNS OF CONTROL

Maintenance of steady states in large and complex organisms usually requires coordination of several processes occurring simultaneously in different body parts. For example, if a mouse is to be successful in escaping pursuit of an onrushing cat, energy-rich compounds must be made available immediately in the muscles of the mouse. Thus, chemical reactions that promote release of glucose from the liver would have to be initiated or accelerated, the heart should increase its beat to pump nutrient-rich blood to muscles, and blood vessels supplying tissues not directly involved in the escape activity should be constricted to divert more blood to muscles.

Also, entirely new processes often begin simultaneously or occur in sequence within variously located cells. Such events occur frequently during embryonic development. For example, many structures of a caterpillar must be altered simultaneously or in sequence during its transformation into a flying adult. Such alterations require integration of many gene repressions, gene activations, and enzyme-catalyzed reactions.

Regulation of metabolic rates and integration of processes in diverse parts of organisms are controlled primarily by hormones in plants and by hormones and nerves in animals. Produced by specialized cells in localized areas, hormones are chemical messengers that exert their control on target cells, tissues, or organs located elsewhere in an organism. The target structures often are quite distant from the hormone-producing cells. In plants, hormones are transported directly between cells or through vascular tissue. In simple animals, hormones also are transported directly between cells. But in complex animals such as vertebrates, hormones usually are produced by specialized tissues or organs, released into the blood, and transported by the circulatory system. Although they are transported to all cells of an organism, hormones affect only cells that are "programmed" to respond to specific hormonal stimuli.

How hormones exert control on cells generally is not well understood and appears to vary for different hormones. It is known, however, that hormones do not function in the same manner as enzymes. Whereas enzymes catalyze specific chemical reactions directly, hormones appear to "trigger" specific "preprogrammed" processes in target cells. In a sense, target cells can be likened to enormously complex computers, genetically programmed to regulate or initiate a particular process or chain of processes. The arrival of a particular hormone then can be compared to pressing a "start button," which directs the cell to carry out its "program."

Although the location and nature of start buttons in most target cells are not resolved, it has become increasingly apparent that different hormones operate by different mechanisms in initiating and coordinating cellular activities. This circumstance is not particularly surprising, since plant and animal hormones comprise a highly varied group of compounds, ranging from relatively simple modified amino acids to complex steroids (lipid derivatives) and whole proteins. Some hormones appear to attach themselves to receptor sites on the surfaces of cells. Such attachments in turn stimulate release of a "second messenger," which travels from the cell membrane into the cytoplasm or nucleoplasm and there influences the action of particular enzymes or genes. Other hormones appear to alter the permeability of cell membranes, thus influencing the rate at which certain molecules enter or leave the cytoplasm. In still other cases, hormones enter the interior of cells and directly activate or suppress particular genes which, in their turn, influence cell function. Still other modes of hormone action are likely to be discovered.

Whatever their exact mechanism of action, hormones are exceedingly potent molecules. Concentrations of only a few parts per million in target structures usually are sufficient to produce demonstrable changes in the internal functioning or observable behavior of an organism. How hormones bring about such changes in plants is the chief concern of this chapter. Hormonal integration of animal functions is discussed separately in the next chapter.

PLANT HORMONES: GENERAL CHARACTERISTICS

The normal growth and development of an adult plant are regulated largely by the antagonistic actions of promoting and inhibiting hormones. Certain plant hormones accelerate existing growth

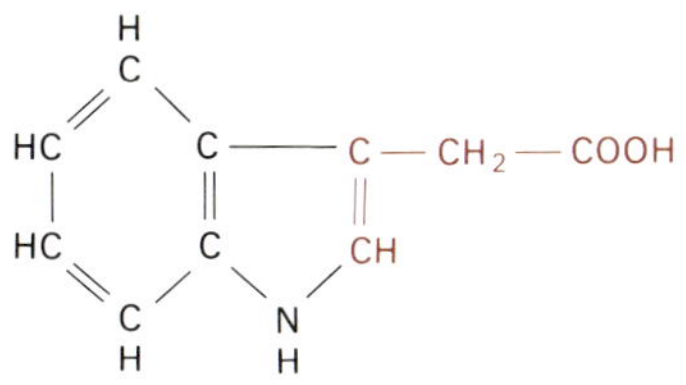

indole acetic acid
(IAA)

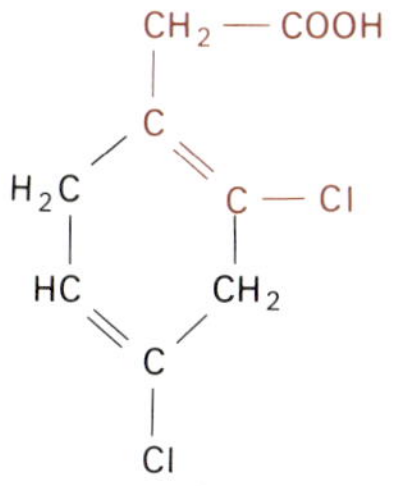

2,4-dichlorophenoxyacetic
acid (2,4-D)

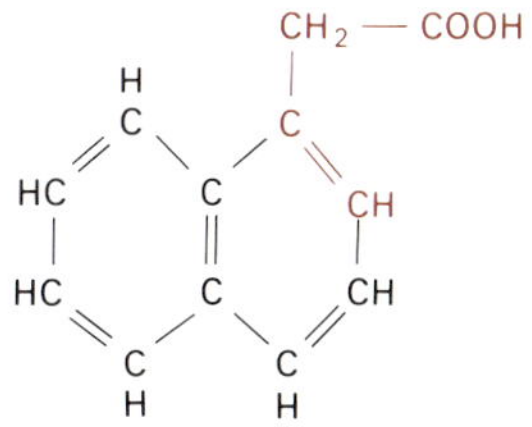

α–naphthalene acetic
acid (NAA)

Fig. 16.1 Auxins. Structure of three auxin compounds. Portions of formulas in color emphasize the similar atomic groupings often present in auxins.

processes or initiate new ones, and other hormones decelerate or retard these same processes. In many plants, for example, a stimulating effect of one set of hormones on nucleic acid synthesis and cell division is counterbalanced by an inhibitory effect of another set. Through checks and balances of this kind, an orderly, controlled pattern of growth is achieved.

In the details of their operation, such systems of checks and balances are exceedingly complex. For example, the specific effect of individual hormones depends greatly on concentration, on environmental conditions that have conditioned plant growth previously, on the presence or absence of particular nutrients, and on the type of tissue or the developmental stage that is affected. Thus, whereas certain concentrations of a particular hormone can cause cells to elongate, other concentrations of the same hormone can inhibit elongation. Whereas one hormone promotes flowering in certain plants, a completely different hormone promotes flowering in another group of plants.

Such marked differences demonstrate not only the exceedingly delicate control exerted by plant hormones, but also their exceedingly complex modes of action. These differences also underscore the principle that hormones themselves do not execute given responses but trigger a variety of preprogrammed responses in a variety of cell types.

The chief hormones known to regulate plant growth and development are abscisic acid, ethylene, and three groups of chemicals: auxins, gibberellins, and cytokinins. Of these, *auxins* have received the greatest amount of study. The most abundant and widespread naturally occurring auxin is an amino acid derivative of tryptophan called *indole acetic acid* (IAA) (Fig. 16.1). Actively growing and developing regions of a plant usually produce the largest amounts of auxins. Thus, particularly auxin-rich regions are meristems of all kinds, including shoot tips, root tips, and cambia.

One of the first demonstrations of the growth-controlling effects of auxins occurred in 1928 as a result of experiments conducted by the Dutch plant physiologist Fritz Went. He worked with oat seedlings, organisms well suited to studies of plant growth and development. As in other grasses, the tip of a young oat seedling is covered by a hollow, cylindrical structure, the *coleoptile,* which protects the tip from damage (see Fig. 23.24).

Apices of coleoptiles previously had been shown to be production sites for a substance that stimulated growth of stems. Went extracted this substance, later named auxin, by removing the apices of several oat coleoptiles and placing them on a block of agar for several hours (Fig. 16.2). Many chemicals diffuse through agar, a relatively inert gelatinous material made from seaweed. Such

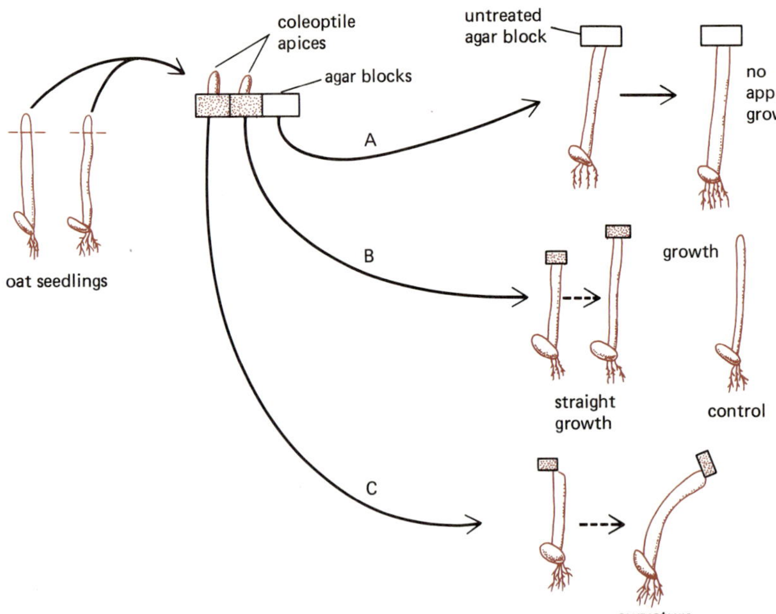

Fig. 16.2 Oat seedling experiments of Fritz Went. Two coleoptile apices are cut from oat seedlings and placed on agar blocks. A third block is left untreated. (A) Decapitated oat seedlings do not grow appreciably when "capped" with untreated blocks. (B) Auxins diffuse from treated blocks, stimulating growth in decapitated seedlings. The amount of growth here is about equal to that of nondecapitated control seedlings. (C) Treatment of one-half of a decapitated seedling produces differential growth. Auxins diffuse only into the left side of a decapitated seedling, producing greater elongation of cells on that side. Consequently, the treated stem bends to the right.

agar blocks were then placed on decapitated oat seedlings. After some time, the seedlings began to elongate. By contrast, decapitated control seedlings exposed to untreated agar blocks did not show appreciable growth. Thus, Went's experiment had demonstrated clearly that a chemical stimulator of stem growth had diffused from coleoptile tissues into agar blocks.

In addition to their effects on cell elongation, auxins also participate in controlling the seasonal fall of leaves and fruits, in inhibiting growth of branch buds, and in stimulating development of adventitious roots, flowers, and fruits in many plants. How auxins produce such a variety of effects in different plant tissues is not yet known with certainty, but these chemicals appear to exert at least some of their control by influencing RNA transcription. For example, the stimulatory effect of auxins on stem elongation in some plants has been shown to be inhibited by actinomycin D. As pointed out in the previous chapter, this antibiotic binds to DNA and prevents RNA transcription. Treatment of plant nuclei with IAA normally brings about a significant increase in RNA synthesis. This increase can be prevented by addition of actinomycin D.

IAA probably does not stimulate RNA transcription by binding directly to DNA. Instead, the hormone appears to bind to a special protein produced in the cytoplasm of plant cells. This complex then moves to the nucleus, where it binds to chromatin and stimulates transcription of certain genes. Auxins undoubtedly influence metabolic processes in other, unidentified ways, for some of the effects of IAA occur too rapidly to be the result of gene activation.

Apart from auxins, the best-known hormones of plants are the *gibberellins,* discovered by Japanese scientists investigating a fungal disease of rice characterized by an abnormal elongation of rice seedlings. In 1926, E. Kurosawa demonstrated that the fungus responsible for the elongation, *Gibberella fujikuroi,* secretes a substance that induces symptoms of the disease when sprayed on healthy rice plants. The substance, named *gibberellin A,* also induced stem elongation when it was sprayed on plants of several other species.

The Japanese discovery of gibberellin A remained unpublicized in Europe and the United States until after World War II, when teams of English and American biologists began an active exchange of scientific information with their Japanese counterparts. Following intensive investigations by biologists in all three countries, it was found that gibberellin A actually is a mixture of six chemically distinct substances. The most common and most extensively studied of these is *gibberellic acid.*

Subsequent studies showed that green plants also contain gibberellins, some identical to those isolated from *G. fujikuroi* and others having different structures. About 55 different gibberellins are now known to occur naturally in plants, and more are likely to be found.

In view of the circumstances surrounding their discovery, it is not surprising that the most dramatic effects of gibberellins are on stem elongation. In young stems, particularly, the hormones increase the length of all the internodes without affecting the number of nodes. The results can be striking. For example, by applying gibberellins to cabbage, normally a low head with closely packed leaves, the plant can be induced to become tall and vinelike (Fig. 16.3). Gibberellins generally lengthen plant structures by promoting cell elongation, but these hormones also can greatly increase the rates of cell reproduction in meristems.

In addition, gibberellins also induce enzyme formation in certain seeds and stimulate flowering of some plants. Moreover, they increase leaf size of several plants when applied in a spray. The size of flower blossoms similarly is increased in camellias, geraniums, and a number of other plants. Just how these hormones produce such varied responses in diverse targets is not known, although some of the effects of gibberellins on enzyme production in seeds can be blocked by actinomycin D.

Cell reproduction and elongation in young fruits, developing seeds, and several other tissues of vascular plants are stimulated by another group of growth-promoting hormones, the *cytokinins.* These hormones also appear to inhibit the aging and breakdown, or senescence, of certain tissues. When cytokinins are applied to leaf tissue, for example, the breakdown of chlorophyll and protein that normally occurs during aging is slowed significantly (Fig. 16.4). Moreover, these hormones have been shown to increase resistance of plant tissues to such harmful influences as virus infections, herbicides, and low temperatures.

Cytokinins are derivatives of purines such as adenine or guanine, and at least some of them are produced in root tips and translocated through xylem to the shoots. Like auxins and gibberellins, cytokinins involve selective gene activation in some of their actions. A substantial increase in RNA synthesis occurs in many plant cells treated with cytokinins, and this increase can be blocked by addition of actinomycin D.

Fig. 16.3 Effects of gibberellins. (Left) Untreated cabbage. (Right) Cabbage after gibberellin treatment. Internodes have elongated enormously. *(Courtesy of S. H. Wittwer and M. J. Bukovac; and from Economic Botany, vol. 12, 1958, p. 213.)*

The growth-promoting effects of auxins, gibberellins, and cytokinins generally are counterbalanced by the opposing actions of *abscisic acid,* a plant hormone chemically related to the carotenoid pigments. Abscisic acid plays an important role in inducing bud dormancy in many woody plants. In autumn, developing leaves growing above the stem

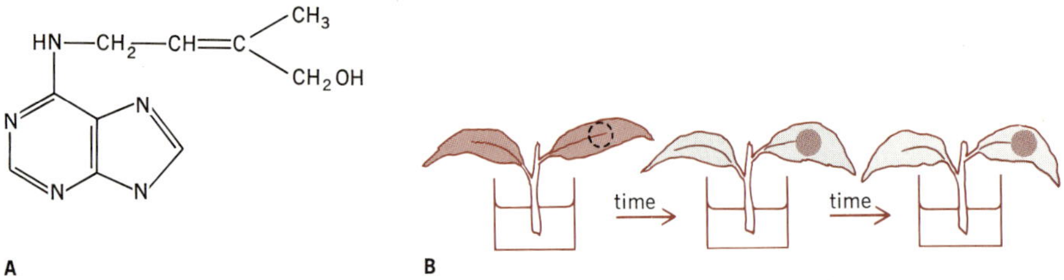

A B

Fig. 16.4 Cytokinins. (A) Zeatin, a naturally occurring cytokinin. (B) Surface application of cytokinins to a circular area of a detached leaf retards breakdown of tissue in the treated area. (*From D. Rayle and L. Wedberg, "Botany: A Human Concern," Houghton Mifflin, Boston, 1975.*)

Fig. 16.5 Allelopathy. A thicket of the short shrub *Salvia leucophylla* is located in the center of the photo. Smaller clusters of the plant can be seen above the larger thicket. *Salvia* releases volatile compounds (terpenes) into the atmosphere, which inhibit growth of nearby plants. Note the almost total absence of plants in circular zones surrounding each thicket.

apices of such plants become converted to stiff bud scales. The scales enclose the meristem and protect it during winter months (see Fig. 6.29). Abscisic acid accumulates in meristems in the fall and promotes conversion of immature leaves to bud scales. The hormone is not actually produced in meristems but is synthesized in mature leaves and passes to the apical meristems via phloem.

Abscisic acid also promotes abscission (cutting off) of leaves, fruits, and other plant parts through its interactions with other hormones (the name "abscisic" acid is derived from this effect). In addition to its growth-inhibiting actions, abscisic acid accumulates rapidly in leaves whenever plants receive inadequate amounts of moisture. The hormone accelerates closing of stomata, thereby inhibiting transpiration.

Ethylene ($H_2C{=}CH_2$) similarly counteracts the growth-promoting effects of other hormones. Released from tissues as a gas, ethylene inhibits stem and root growth, promotes aging and abscission of leaves, and retards elongation and development of lateral buds. This gaseous hormone also stimulates ripening of many fruits and promotes destruction of chlorophyll.

In addition to the five kinds of hormones already mentioned, many plants secrete other hormonelike substances that play important roles in determining and maintaining population balances between species. Such secretory products often are categorized under the general heading of *secondary growth substances.*

Some plants secrete secondary growth substances that inhibit growth of other plants, a phenomenon called *allelopathy* (Fig. 16.5). The inhibitory secretions sometimes are released in an active form, but many are released as nontoxic compounds that become activated when they enter the soil or atmosphere. In some areas of southern California, for example, the shrub *Salvia leucophylla,* a member of the mint family, is commonly found in grass-covered fields. The shrub secretes camphor and other substances that inhibit germination and growth of grasses. Thus, when grass seeds germinate following a rain, the toxic growth substances inhibit seedling development and prevent establishment of a grass cover around the base of *Salvia* plants.

The inhibitory effects of secondary growth substances are not always interspecific. Soil-decomposition products of certain plants often tend to be toxic to later individuals of the same species, resulting in a gradual decline of vigor over successive generations. Crop rotation is beneficial partly for this reason.

Through their regulatory actions, plant hormones and secondary growth substances affect the behavior of plants in many ways. Such behavior is expressed by movement and by development.

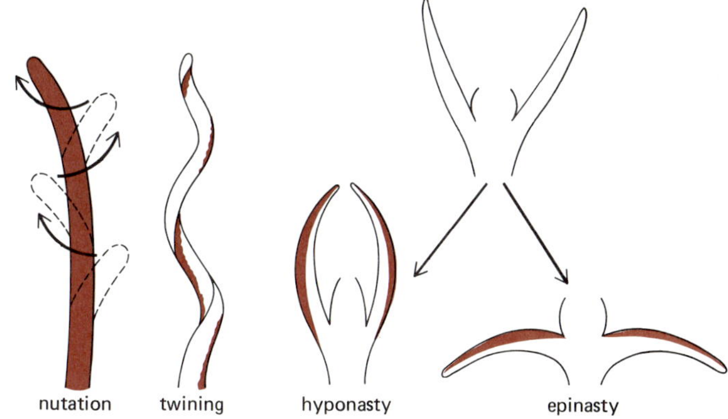

Fig. 16.6 Nastic movements. The plants carry out the movements shown largely in response to externally generated stimuli. The opening and folding inward of plant body parts are termed epinasty and hyponasty, respectively.

MOTION RESPONSES

In response to particular stimuli, given body parts of a fixed plant can undergo *growth* movements or *turgor* movements.

Growth Movements

Leaves generally project outward from the stems of a mature plant, roots tend to grow downward, and stems usually grow upward. These and other growth movements of plants involve responses to external stimuli.

At least two kinds of growth movements can be distinguished in plants. *Nastic movements* are responses independent of the direction from which the stimulus strikes a plant. One such movement is *nutation,* a back-and-forth rocking or nodding motion of apical shoot tips of certain species (Fig. 16.6). It is caused by alternately changing growth rates on opposite sides of the apical tip. Another motion response is *spiral movement,* a rotational growth of an elongating shoot around its long axis. A common form of spiral motion is *twining,* in which rotational growth of the shoot tip produces a spirally curving stem. Although many nastic responses are the result of permanent differential patterns of growth, some, e.g., the opening of certain flowers at sunrise, are reversible turgor movements. For most of these responses, the actual regulating functions of hormones is not clearly understood.

Much more is known about how hormones control *tropisms,* growth movements whose direction is either toward or away from a stimulus. Several kinds of tropisms can be distinguished on the basis of various growth-inducing stimuli: light-induced *phototropism,* gravity-induced *geotropism,* contact-induced *thigmotropism,* chemical-induced *chemotropism,* and others. A given tropic response is said to be positive or negative according to whether a plant part grows toward or away from the stimulus. For example, leaves and stems are positively phototropic and negatively geotropic: they grow toward light and away from the gravitational center of the earth (Fig. 16.7). Roots, on the other hand, are positively geotropic and negatively phototropic.

These phototropic and geotropic responses in particular are known to be under the control of auxins. As already noted, the apical meristem of the shoot produces IAA, which then promotes elongation of cells behind the apical meristem. If the shoot is illuminated predominantly from one side, auxins on that side diffuse away from the light and the opposite, shaded side therefore elongates more. The shoot then curves toward the light source as it lengthens. Thus, the stem is positively phototropic and behaves as if it were "aware" of the position of the light source (Fig. 16.8). How light produces such lateral movements of auxins is not well understood.

Lateral movements of auxins also appear to regulate the negative geotropism of stems. Auxins are influenced by gravity in these structures and will diffuse toward downward surfaces of stem tissues. For example, it can be shown that if a plant is placed horizontally, as much as two-thirds of all auxins in a shoot tip will accumulate on the lower side of the tip. As the auxins then move back to

Fig. 16.7 Tropic movements. Left, the effect of gravity: geotropic response. Right, the effect of light: phototropic response. The plant is illuminated from the left, and it grows in the direction of the light.

cells capable of elongating, most of the hormones reach cells located on the lower side of the stem. These cells therefore elongate more than cells on the upper side, and the stem tip curves upward as a result (Fig. 16.9).

The positive geotropism of roots is regulated somewhat differently, since auxins apparently do not become distributed unequally across horizontally placed roots. The downward growth of roots probably is controlled by growth inhibitors that diffuse from their sites of production in root caps to cells of elongating root tissues (see Fig. 16.9). The existence of such inhibitors has been demonstrated by several experiments. Removal of root caps, for example, causes a brief *increase* in root growth, not a decrease as would be expected if root caps were producing only growth-promoting substances.

Some biologists speculate that abscisic acid is the chief growth inhibitor produced by root caps. They hypothesize further that this hormone accumulates on lower surfaces of a horizontally placed root, restricting growth of cells there. As a result, cells toward the upper surface of such a root elongate more rapidly, causing the root to bend downward. Additional experimental confirmation is needed for general acceptance of this hypothesis.

Fig. 16.8 Phototropism. Light and auxin interact in the control of stem growth.

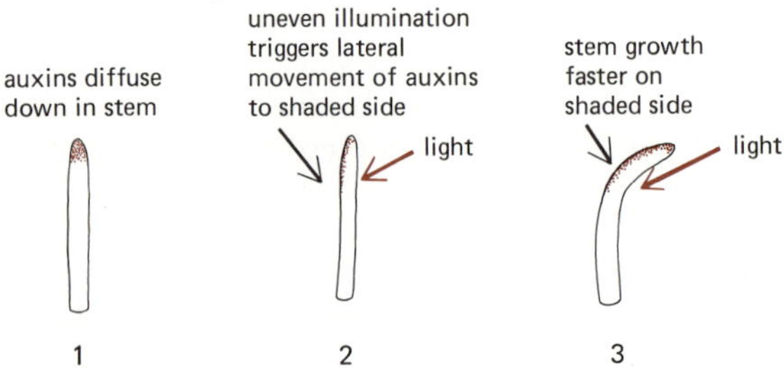

Turgor Movements

Changes in hormone distribution and concentration may play a role in other growth movements as well, and indeed also in at least some turgor movements, the second type of motion response of plants. In most of these cases, however, it is still not quite clear how the external stimulus actually brings about particular hormone activities. Turgor movements result from changes in water pressure within given cells or cell groups. Unlike growth movements, which are slow and produce more or less permanent results, turgor movements are rapid and reversible.

The most widespread type of turgor movements is the opening and closing of the epidermal *guard cells* in leaves and stems. The walls of these crescent-shaped cells are thickest and stiffest on the inner sides, where they form the stomatal pore (see Figs. 6.33 and 6.34). This construction permits a stoma to open or close when turgor changes in the guard cells.

Turgor increases when guard cells photosynthesize (Fig. 16.10). Mechanisms responsible for such increases are not completely understood. According to one hypothesis, for example, stomata open and

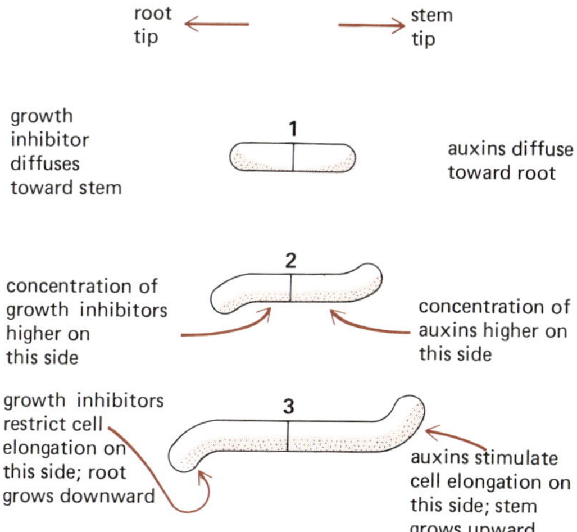

Fig. 16.9 Geotropism. Gravity and auxins interact in the control of stem growth. Gravity and growth inhibitors regulate the positive geotropism of roots. These processes are independent of light and occur also in the dark.

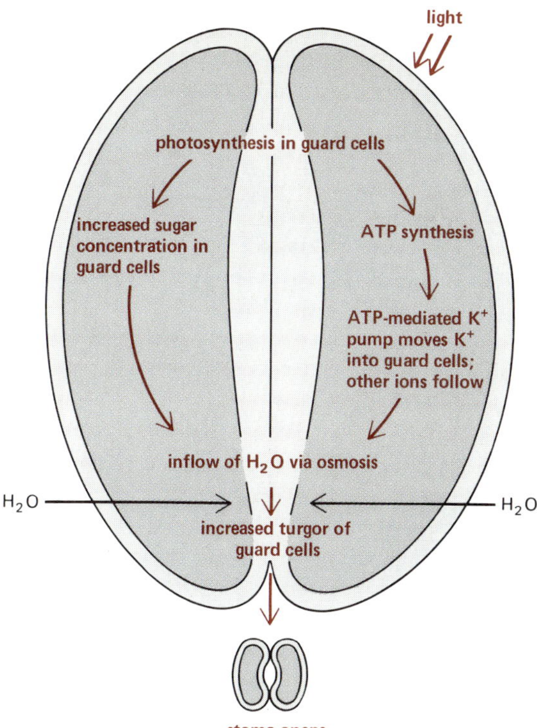

Fig. 16.10 Two hypothetical mechanisms regulating guard-cell movements. Increased intracellular concentrations of ions or sugars could cause water to enter guard cells via osmosis, thereby increasing turgor. These two mechanisms are not mutually exclusive. Moreover, stomata size can be influenced by several other factors.

close as a direct consequence of shifting concentrations of sugars in guard cells. Sugars are presumed to accumulate in these cells during photosynthesis, and this accumulation could draw water osmotically into the cells from the surrounding epidermis, which is nonphotosynthetic. The extra water would cause guard cells to swell and the thin outer portions of their walls to curve out farther under the increasing water pressure. The inner, thicker portions of the walls would curve more too, opening the stomata. Thus, when plants are illuminated and actively producing sugars, stomata should open, permitting CO_2 to enter a leaf and O_2 to escape. This hypothesis is consistent with the observation that the stomata of light-exposed plants normally are open.

Conversely, the sugar concentration of guard cells is presumed to decrease when plants are in darkness. Water then should leave guard cells, causing their elastic walls to revert to the original positions, thereby closing the stomata. These pores in fact are closed, or nearly so, in unilluminated plants.

This "fluctuating sugar" hypothesis, once widely accepted, has recently fallen into disfavor. Apparently, the sugar content of at least some guard cells is not significantly different under day and night conditions. Moreover, results of several experiments support a different explanation of how stomatal size is regulated. Illuminated guard cells of open stomata have been shown to contain much higher concentrations of potassium (K^+) ions than those of closed, unilluminated stomata, suggesting that potassium ions are being pumped into guard cells by active transport when leaves are illuminated. The molecular components of the "potassium pump" undoubtedly are located chiefly in the plasma membranes of guard cells. The source of energy for the transport appears to be ATP, produced during photosynthesis (see Chap. 13). The "pump" presumably is turned off at night, resulting in an outward diffusion of potassium ions to the extracellular environment. Because water molecules accompany this outward flow of potassium ions, the turgor of guard cells decreases and stomata close.

A

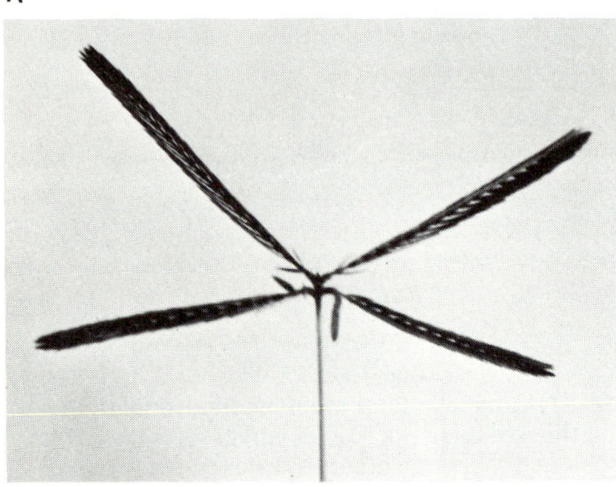

B

Fig. 16.11 Contact movements. *Mimosa,* the sensitive plant, is shown (A) before and (B) after stimulation of leaflets and leaves.

It is possible, of course, that the size of stomata is regulated by fluctuations in both the ion and sugar concentrations of guard cells (see Fig. 16.10); but even so, it is likely that other factors also participate in controlling stomatal size. For example, low concentrations of CO_2 around guard cells promote the opening of stomata, whereas high concentrations cause rapid closing in light or in darkness. And, as mentioned earlier, abscisic acid can trigger rapid closure of stomata; its production by leaf tissue increases significantly during wilting. Indeed it is in responding to combinations of various stimuli that guard cells display perhaps their most important adaptive function. For example, on a very dry, hot summer day the stomata may be almost fully closed, despite the ample illumination. The rate of photosynthesis in a leaf is then reduced, inasmuch as not enough CO_2 can enter, but the evaporation of internal water, a problem of more immediate concern, is held down at the same time.

A second type of turgor movements comprises *contact movements,* produced when external agents touch parts of certain plants. For example, the leaves of *Mimosa,* the "sensitive plant," drop down from an erect position almost instantaneously when touched (Fig. 16.11). Leaves are normally kept erect by large, turgid cells at the base of the petioles. A touch stimulus quickly leads to the transmission of a chemical signal from the point of contact to the leaf base, and the cells there lose water rapidly. As a result the whole leaf drops down. A turgid, erect condition is reestablished after some 10 min.

Reversible contact movements also produce the insect-trapping action of the leaves of carnivorous plants such as Venus's-flytrap (Fig. 16.12). The trapping mechanism in this plant is triggered by touch-sensitive hairs on the inner leaf surfaces. Other types of contact movements occur in the flowers of certain plants. In some, for example, certain flower parts snap to altered positions when an insect touches them, thereby powdering the insects with pollen. Turgor changes and signal transmission by diffusible chemical agents appear to be involved in all such plants, but the details of action are still unknown.

Changes in light intensity are the specific stimuli for so-called *sleep movements* in many plants, legumes in particular. In this third type of turgor movements, the leaves assume one position during the day and another during the night. The day position usually is horizontal, the night position usually vertical, either upright or hanging. Here again the mechanism of action is not understood as yet, nor is the possible functional significance of these particular movements.

DEVELOPMENTAL RESPONSES

Vegetative Structures

The growth and development of many vegetative (nonflowering) structures of plants are regulated by hormones. Auxins and ethylene, for example, both participate in the regulation of bud development (Fig. 16.13). As noted in Chap. 6, lat-

A

B

C

Fig. 16.12 Contact movements: Venus's-flytrap. (A) Whole plant with traps in various states of closure. Hairs on the inner surfaces of the traps are sensitive to contact with external objects. (B), (C) One of the traps in action. *(A, courtesy Carolina Biological Supply Company.)*

eral stem buds form in the axil of leaves. Buds near the stem tip usually remain dormant, but those farther back along the stem may break dormancy and develop as branch stems. This pattern of growth is caused by an inhibiting effect of terminal buds on branch buds closest to the stem tip. This inhibition, called *apical dominance,* is produced indirectly by auxins.

Because auxins are manufactured by apical shoot meristems, these hormones are most highly concentrated at the tips of stems. As auxins move back toward lateral buds, their concentration gradually decreases. At high concentrations, auxins stimulate production of ethylene. As noted earlier, ethylene is a potent inhibitor of lateral bud growth in many plants. Therefore, as high concentrations of auxins reach buds near the stem tip, ethylene is formed, inhibiting bud growth there. As auxins move progressively farther away from the stem tip, the concentration of the hormones eventually decreases so much that ethylene is no longer produced. At these regions the combined growth-promoting effects of auxins and cytokinins stimulate lateral bud growth. The visible result is the usual tapering growth pattern of the branch system of a plant.

Auxins also exert developmental control over meristematic tissues such as *cambia.* It has been suggested that in woody plants auxins produced in the spring by actively growing shoots diffuse to the cambia, where the hormones activate the cambial tissues and stimulate them to form that season's wood and bark.

Another important developmental function of hormones is their control of *leaf senescence, leaf fall,* and *fruit drop.* Leaf senescence is triggered by specific environmental cues such as decreasing day length. The metabolic rates of leaf cells decrease steadily as leaves begin to die in autumn. Chlorophyll is among the first pigments to degenerate. As a consequence, previously masked yellow-orange carotenoids and red anthocyanins become visible. Later, the dead leaves separate from a plant at an *abscission layer,* a region of specialized cells formed where a leaf petiole joins the stem (Fig. 16.14). Fruit drop also results from the formation of such layers at the base of fruit stalks. The cement between adjacent cells eventually dissolves in abscission layers, the cells die, and the leaf or the fruit then drops off.

The control of leaf senescence and abscission is not understood completely, but it is clear that many hormones play a role. During the life of a leaf, auxins are produced and transported continuously through the petiole into the stem. As winter approaches, this production of auxins diminishes. Reduced concentrations of auxins in leaf tissue,

Fig. 16.13 Effects of auxins on bud development. Auxins (dark color) released from a terminal bud are concentrated enough to stimulate production of ethylene. The latter inhibits development of the first three buds that produce branches behind the terminal bud. Lateral buds farther back receive less than the necessary concentration of auxins to stimulate production of ethylene and thus can break dormancy.

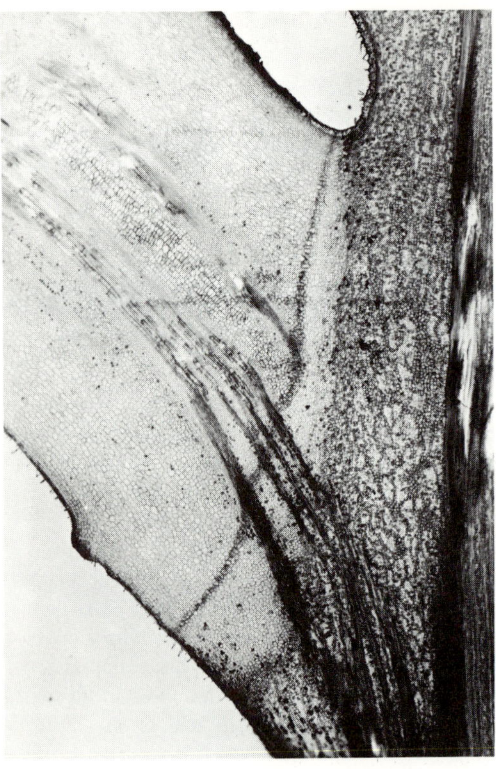

A

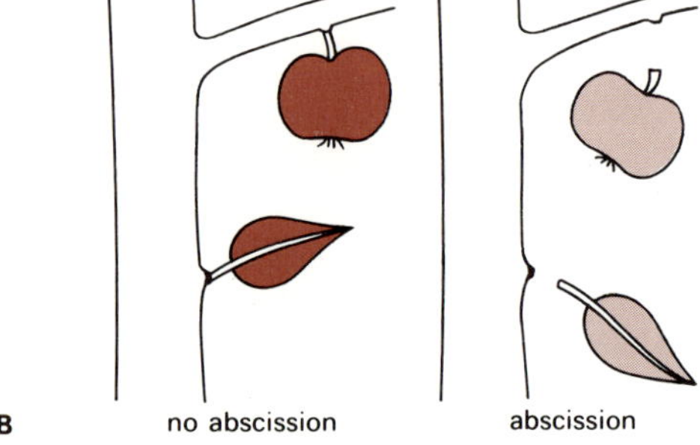

Fig. 16.14 Abscission. (A) Section through junction of leaf and stem, showing abscission layer (dark transverse cell layer) across leaf base. (B) If auxin concentrations (suggested by depth of color) in leaves or fruits are higher than in the stem, abscission will not occur (left); in the converse situation the abscission cells die and leaves or fruits then drop off (right).

together with decreased transport of cytokinins from roots to leaves, are thought to bring about onset of leaf senescence.

Induction and reactivation of dormant buds is still another developmental process regulated by the opposing actions of hormones. As noted earlier, abscisic acid is an important inducer of bud dormancy in many woody plants. Indeed, dormancy often can be artificially induced by spraying the hormone on the surface of plants. Day length decreases as winter approaches, and shortened light durations (photoperiods) appear to be the principal trigger for the increased concentrations of abscisic acid accumulating in the leaves of many plants in autumn.

Cold does not appear to be necessary for induction of dormancy, but exposure of plants to prolonged periods of low temperatures is usually necessary before dormancy can be broken. Dormant trees moved into greenhouses often will not resume growth until they have been exposed to at least 250 hours (h) of cold temperatures, and some trees require at least 1000 h. Moreover, prolonged exposure to cold is not the only requirement for breaking dormancy. In many plants, warm temperatures and increasing photoperiods also are prerequisites for bud reactivation.

Most newly formed seeds similarly must undergo a period of enforced dormancy before they can germinate. Concentrations of abscisic acid are often high in such seeds, and this hormone appears to be an important inhibitor of germination. Ethylene and other growth inhibitors probably also contribute to seed dormancy in some plants. Like bud reactivation, the breaking of seed dormancy usually requires exposure to low temperatures. Cold appears to promote loss of inhibitors from the seeds of several plants.

Gibberellic acid has been shown to be a potent inducer of bud reactivation and seed germination. Substantial amounts of gibberellins accumulate in seeds just before seed germination. Moreover, the artificial induction of bud dormancy by sprayings of abscisic acid often can be prevented by simultaneous applications of gibberellic acid. It is likely that cytokinins and other growth-promoting hormones also contribute to breaking bud and seed dormancy.

The adaptive value of extended periods of enforced dormancy are clear. If development of dormant buds and seeds could be activated by short periods of favorable temperatures, then an unexpected warm spell in early or late winter might stimulate bud sprouting or seed germination. But a subsequent return to low temperatures would then kill newly formed tissues.

Flowering

Flowering is the most colorful and spectacular developmental process of plants. Flower formation usually marks a major transition in the life cycle of angiosperms: the period of rapid vegetative growth is over, and production of seeds and fruits becomes the chief energy-consuming process.

Cells produced by apical meristems of young and rapidly growing shoots become specialized as new stem or leaf tissue. But sooner or later some of these cells begin a very different course of development, in which they first aggregate as small clusters at shoot apices. Such clusters, called *flower primordia,* later become *flower buds,* which then mature as flowers. Because they house the sex organs of angiosperms, flowers are vital to the perpetuation of this class of vascular plants (see also Chap. 23).

Several processes trigger development of flower primordia, and most of them must occur in sequence if flowering is to take place (Fig. 16.15). Flower primordia usually do not develop in young plants; most angiosperms first must produce a sufficient number of leaves before flowering can begin. In some cereal grains, for example, a minimum of seven leaves usually is required. Flowering in some varieties of tomato plants does not begin until the growing stem has 13 nodes. When such a minimum size has been reached, the plant is said to be *ripe to flower.*

Temperature

Certain environmental stimuli must be present to trigger the next step of flower development. The effect of temperature on flowering, a phenomenon

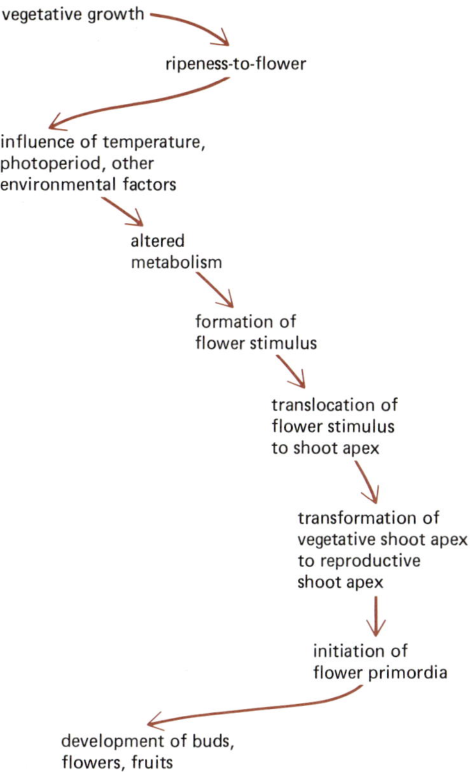

Fig. 16.15 Flower development. Some processes involved in the initiation of flower primordia. A flowering stimulus, discussed later in this chapter, induces floral development in shoot tips.

called *vernalization,* was discovered in 1918 (Fig. 16.16). Temperature stimulates flower development in most biennials, i.e., angiosperms that flower only in the second year of their 2-year life cycle (see also Chap. 32). Examples of biennials are carrots, beets, and cabbages. These plants will not flower unless they are exposed to prolonged cold, such as occurs during winter months.

Flowering of several other kinds of plants has been shown to depend on the temperature to which the germinating seeds of such plants had been exposed. For example, seeds of temperate-zone annuals like winter wheat must be exposed to low temperatures if flowering is to occur later in the mature plants. Such seeds are normally sown in the fall and the subsequent winter provides the required low temperature. If the seeds are not exposed to winter temperatures, flowering does not occur. By contrast, seeds of certain tropical plants

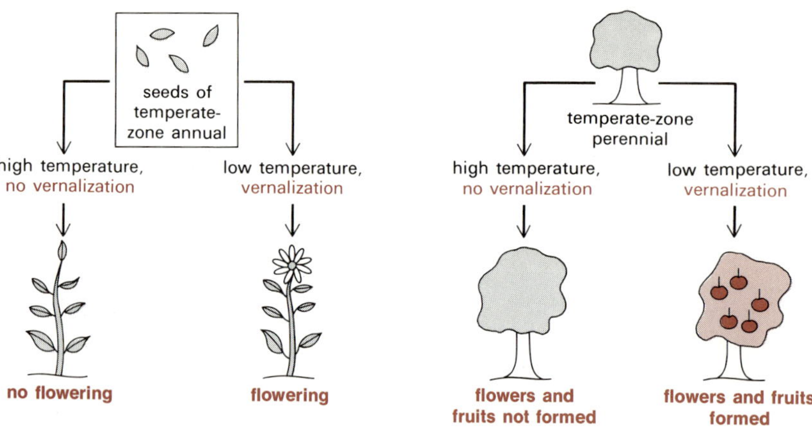

Fig. 16.16 Vernalization. (A) Some temperate-zone annuals will flower only when the seeds from which they develop have been exposed to low temperatures. (B) Some temperate-zone perennials, such as apple and peach trees, will flower only when the mature plant has been exposed to a period of prolonged cold.

must be exposed to high temperatures (80°F or more) if later flowering is to take place.

Photoperiod

At about the same time biologists first observed the effects of temperature on the development of flower primordia. W. W. Garner and H. A. Allard, of the U.S. Department of Agriculture, discovered that day length plays a major role as well. They found that a new strain of tobacco called Maryland Mammoth would flower only when exposed to short periods of light, and they therefore called it a *short-day plant.* By subjecting plants to light of varying durations (photoperiods) Garner and Allard discovered several other short-day plants, including soybeans, cosmos, and ragweed. These plants usually flower only if their photoperiods are shorter than about $15\frac{1}{2}$ h. If such plants are exposed to longer light periods, their flowering is greatly retarded or they fail to flower altogether. Violets, asters, strawberries, and chrysanthemums are other examples of short-day plants.

Garner and Allard also discovered several plants that flower only when exposed to long photoperiods. These *long-day plants* include spinach, radishes, lettuce, henbane, clover, beets, and traditional varieties of wheat. Many of these plants require day lengths of 15 to 16 h for initiation of flowering. If long-day plants growing in the vicinity of Boston or Chicago, for example, are moved toward the equator, where day length is close to 12 h/day throughout the year, the plants remain vegetative and do not flower. Knowledge of plant photoperiodism has been exploited by florists, who bring large numbers of poinsettias, chrysanthemums, and other kinds of plants into bloom for particular holidays by growing them in greenhouses where photoperiods can be regulated artificially.

Plants which flower without regard to photoperiods are called *day-neutral plants.* Examples include tomatoes, cucumbers, cotton, sunflowers, and dandelions.

The global distribution of flowering plants tends to reflect their photoperiodic nature to some degree. Thus, most plants native to equatorial regions are short-day species. The temperate zone supports both short-day and long-day types. The former flower mainly during the short-day seasons of spring and fall, the latter during the long-day season of summer. In higher latitudes above the temperate zone most plants are long-day species, adapted to the long days and short nights that characterize most of the growing season. Day-neutral plants are distributed widely over all climatic zones.

Some factors involved in producing photoperiodic responses of plants are known. It has been determined, for example, that leaves are the receptors specifically sensitive to light durations. This contrasts with the vernalization response, in which the apical meristems of shoots function as receptors of the low-temperature stimulus. Two experiments demonstrating the role of leaves in photoperiodism are illustrated in Fig. 16.17. Both involve the short-day cocklebur plant *Xanthium.*

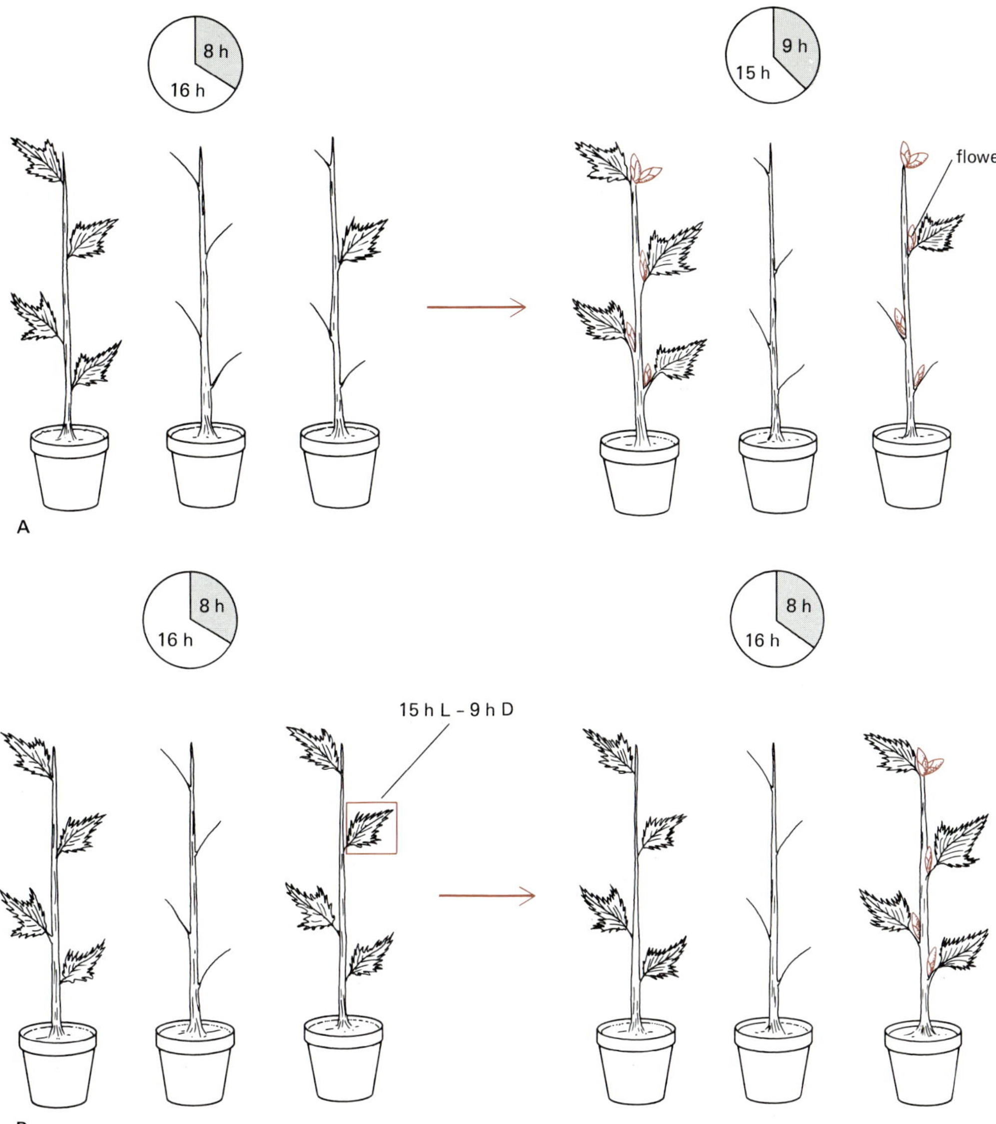

Fig. 16.17 Effects of shortened photoperiods on cockleburs. (A) Cockleburs having at least one leaf flower when photoperiod is reduced to 15 hours light/9 hours darkness. (B) Flowering can be induced in cockleburs when only a single leaf is subjected to an appropriately reduced photoperiod.

In the first experiment, three cocklebur plants are treated with an artificial photoperiod of 16 h light and 8 h darkness. Vegetative growth continues under these conditions, but flowering does not occur. One of these plants is then stripped of its leaves, and a second is stripped of all but one leaf. The remaining plant is not defoliated. The three plants are next treated with a shortened photoperiod of 15 h light and 9 h darkness. This reduced photoperiod triggers flowering in the two plants that have at least one leaf. The completely defoliated plant does not flower.

In the second experiment, another set of three cocklebur plants is given the same treatment as the

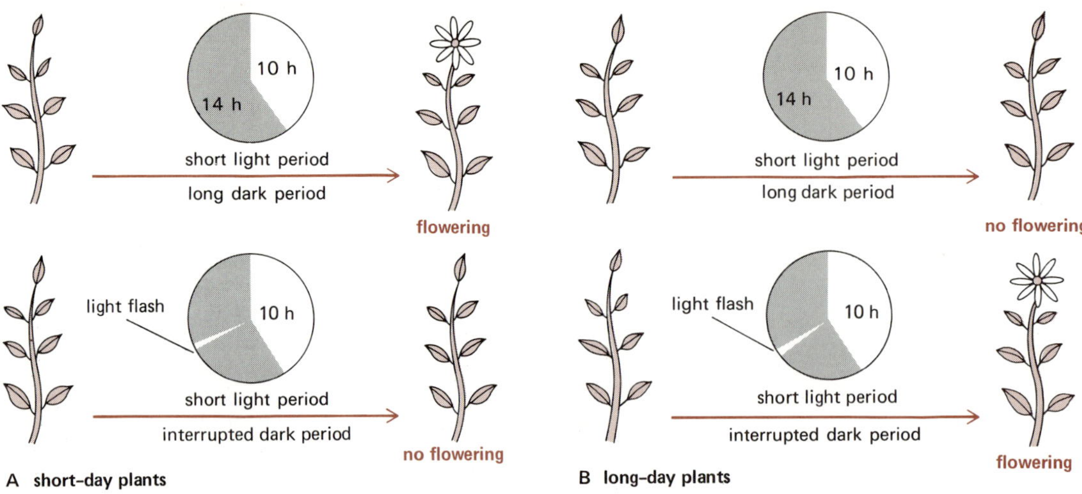

Fig. 16.18 Photoperiodism. (A) Exposing short-day (long-night) plants to a single flash of light during a long dark period usually prevents flowering. (B) Long-day (short-night) plants flower in response to the same treatment.

first set, but they are maintained at the long-day photoperiod of 16 h light and 8 h darkness. A single leaf of the intact plant then is subjected to a short day of 15 h light and 9 h darkness. This plant subsequently flowers; the other two do not.

These results demonstrate that photoperiods shorter than 16 h of light can trigger flowering in cockleburs and that leaves are the receptors of the light stimulus. The experiments also illustrate the sensitivity of the photoreceptor system; flowering of cockleburs can be induced by exposure of a single leaf to an appropriately shortened photoperiod.

Additional experiments have shown that the important photoperiodic factor actually is the length of *night,* not the length of day. Interrupting the daylight period with short intervals of darkness does not have any effect on the induction of flowering, but interrupting the dark period with artificial illumination can prevent flowering in many short-day plants. For example, flowering of cockleburs exposed to a photoperiod of 15 h light and 9 h darkness can be prevented by exposing these short-day plants to a single flash of light during the dark period. Conversely, flowering of long-day plants is inhibited by long periods of uninterrupted darkness. If the long dark period is interrupted by a flash of light, spinach and other long-day plants initiate flower primordia (Fig. 16.18). Thus, short-day plants can justifiably be called *long-night plants,* and long-day plants similarly can be termed *short-night plants.*

Biologists also have discovered that different wavelengths of light inhibit or promote flowering to varying degrees. The most effective light rays for inhibiting flowering of cockleburs and other short-day plants are in the orange-red (660-nm) portion of the visible spectrum (see Chap. 13 and Appendix C). These wavelengths also are the most effective for triggering flowering of long-day plants. The photoperiodic effects of orange-red light can be reversed by far-red (infrared) light, a band of wavelengths at about 770 nm, just beyond the red portion of the visible spectrum. Accordingly, the flower-inhibiting effects of orange-red light on cockleburs can be reversed by exposing the plants to far-red light.

These antagonistic effects of orange-red and far-red are completely reversible. For example, cockleburs can be exposed to alternate flashes of 660- and 770-nm wavelengths during the "night" phase of a 15-h light and 9-h dark cycle. Whether the plants then flower or not depends on the wavelength of the last flash (Fig. 16.19). This reversible effect prompted several biologists to propose that flowering is influenced by a leaf pigment which becomes converted to one form when exposed to

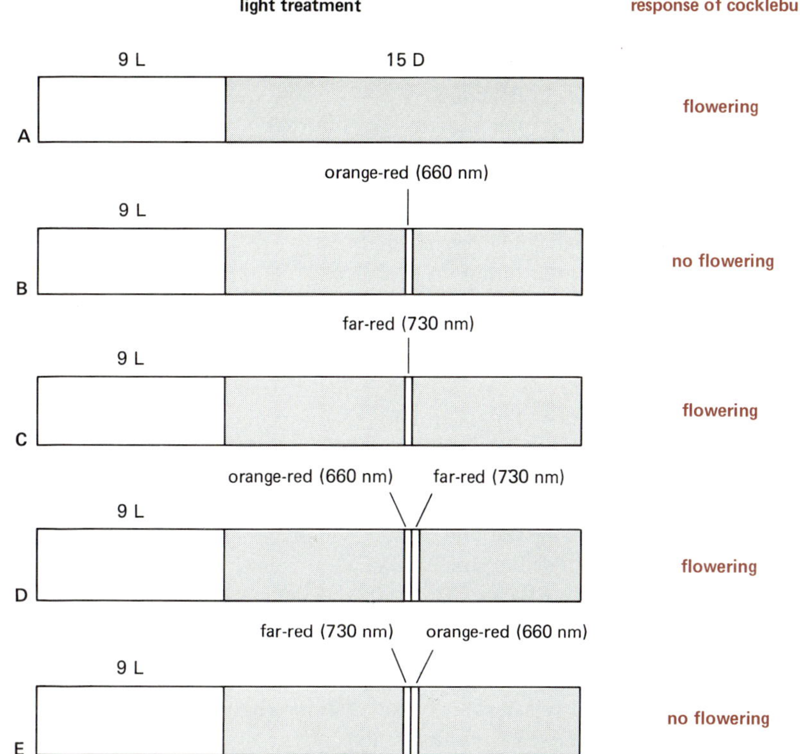

Fig. 16.19 Responses of cockleburs to orange-red and far-red light. Sufficiently long periods of darkness can induce flowering in cockleburs, a short-day plant (A). Flashes of orange-red light (660 nm) during the long dark period prevent flowering (B), (E). This effect can be reversed by exposing cockleburs to a flash of far-red light (730 nm), as in (C), (D). Long-day plants respond to such treatments in an opposite fashion.

orange-red light and to an alternate form when exposed to far-red light. The reversible pigment has now been isolated and is called *phytochrome.* It is a blue pigment and consists of a protein linked to a series of complex ring-shaped molecular subunits.

The forms of phytochrome that absorb orange-red and far-red wavelengths have been designated P_r and P_{fr}, respectively. P_r is converted to P_{fr} by orange-red light; P_{fr} converts to P_r when exposed to far-red light. Furthermore, P_{fr} interacts with a yet unidentified substance (X), forming a $P_{fr} \cdot X$ complex, which triggers most photoperiodic responses of plants (Fig. 16.20).

The amount of P_f and P_{fr} present in leaves depends on two principal factors. (1) The amount of far-red light striking the earth is greatest during fall and winter months, when the sun is low on the horizon. Conversely, the amount of orange-red light striking the earth is greatest during spring and summer months, when natural photoperiods are longest. Consequently, leaves contain proportionately greater amounts of P_{fr} after exposure to sunlight in spring than in fall or winter. Compara-

Fig. 16.20 Phytochromes. P_r and P_{fr} are interconvertible forms of phytochrome. The concentrations of each in leaves depends on the relative amounts of orange-red and far-red light striking a plant. P_{fr} slowly converts to P_r in the dark, and it is less stable than P_r. $P_{fr} \cdot X$ appears to be the substance responsible for flower induction in long-day plants and for the inhibition of flowering in short-day varieties.

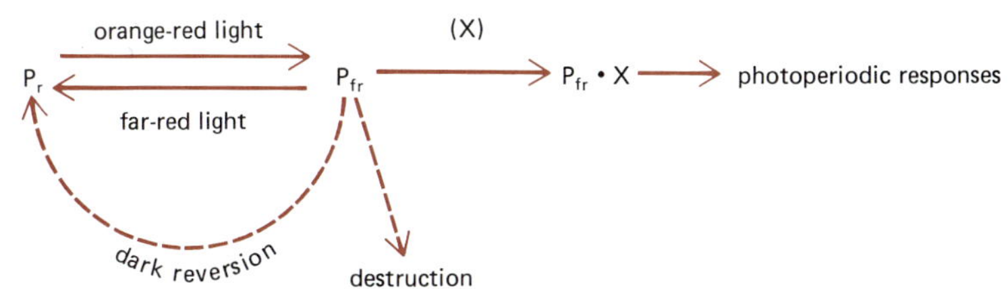

tively little P_{fr} is present in the leaves of plants exposed to winter sunlight. (2) P_{fr} is less stable than P_r, and the far-red form of phytochrome slowly converts to P_r in darkness.

These two factors help explain the different flowering responses of short- and long-day plants. Substantial amounts of P_{fr} are present in the leaves of both kinds of plants after exposure to spring or early summer sunlight. Correspondingly large amounts of $P_{fr} \cdot X$ accumulate in such leaves, and this complex prevents development of flower primordia in short-day plants. The same complex triggers the opposite response in long-day plants, which react by flowering. P_{fr} converts to P_r at night, leading to reduced levels of $P_{fr} \cdot X$ in leaves. In spring, when nights are comparatively short, levels of $P_{fr} \cdot X$ remain sufficiently high to prevent flowering in short-day plants and to induce flowering in long-day plants. But in fall and winter, when nights are long and smaller amounts of P_{fr} are produced in leaves after exposure to sunlight, concentrations of P_{fr} are insufficient to inhibit flowering in short-day plants or to stimulate flowering in long-day plants.

Such reciprocal relationships also explain why flowering can be affected so dramatically by exposing plants to intense flashes of light during the dark phase of photoperiodic cycles. In the case of short-day plants, a flash of light during the dark period reverses the slow conversion of P_{fr} to P_r and thus maintains high concentrations of $P_{fr} \cdot X$, which inhibits flowering (see Fig. 16.20). And in long-day plants nighttime flashes of light stimulate flowering by inhibiting conversion of P_{fr} to P_r. Phytochrome has been shown to participate in the regulation of several other developmental processes in some plants, including stem elongation, fruit ripening, seed germination, and seedling development.

The Flowering Stimulus

Despite its importance in regulating flowering, $P_{fr} \cdot X$ does not stimulate development of flower buds directly. As stated earlier, flower primordia are produced at shoot tips. Interconversions of P_r and P_{fr} take place in leaves. How can changes occurring in leaves trigger production of flower primordia in the tips of shoots?

Results of many experiments indicate that a flowering stimulus is produced in leaves and translocated to shoot tips, where it stimulates floral development (see Fig. 16.15). One such experiment (Fig. 16.21) involves grafting a long-day plant onto a short-day plant. Since grafting interconnects the vascular systems of both plants, substances produced in the leaves of one plant are translocated to the shoots of the other via the graft. When the grafted plants are exposed to short- or long-day light conditions, both partners flower. In experiments where grafts do not take, flowering occurs only in the partner exposed to the appropriate photoperiod. These results are interpreted as demonstrating (1) that a flowering stimulus is transferred from the leaves on one plant to the shoots of both and (2) that living cells are essential for translocation of a flowering stimulus.

All attempts to isolate a flowering hormone, or *florigen*, so far have been without success. Gibberellins induce flowering in many plants, but indole acetic acid, cytokinins, abscisic acid, and ethylene all have been shown to participate in the induction of flowering under different circumstances in different plants. Indeed, interactions between these and other substances appear necessary for floral induction in some plants. It is therefore improbable that a single unique florigen is produced by all plants.

It is not known how the flowering stimulus triggers the shift from leaf to flower development at the tips of shoots. Several studies report increased rates of cell reproduction in shoot apices within 24 hours after plants have been exposed to a flower-inducing photoperiod. Shifts in patterns of RNA and histone synthesis accompany such bursts of cell reproduction. Thus it appears likely that the flowering stimulus somehow activates previously repressed genes, which respond by synthesizing new proteins. Several of these proteins are undoubtedly enzymes, and these catalysts probably establish reaction sequences in shoot apices that lead to the formation of flowers (see Fig. 16.15).

Temperature and photoperiods are the major but not the only environmental factors responsible for flower initiation. For example, the degree of flowering often varies with the total amount of light energy received by the leaves. If two plants are illuminated for the same appropriate period but one receives light of greater intensity, that plant is likely to flower faster or more extensively. Moreover, atmospheric CO_2 normally is required for flower induction. The role of the gas here does not

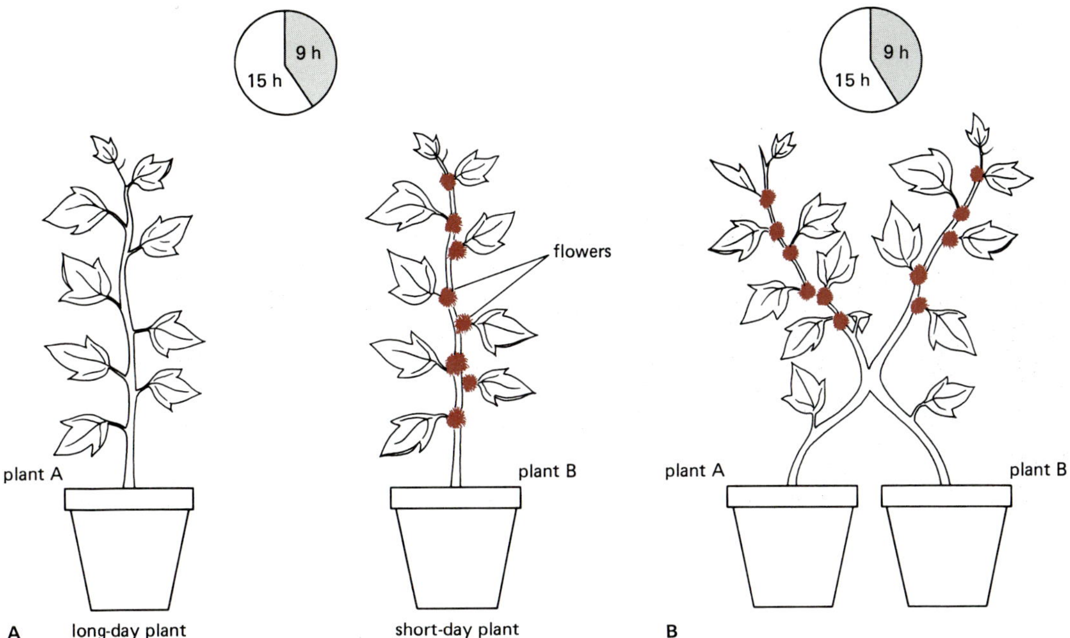

Fig. 16.21 Experimental evidence demonstrating translocation of a flowering stimulus in plants. (A) Long-day plants normally do not flower when subjected to a photoperiod of 9 h light and 15 h darkness; short-day plants usually flower under these conditions. (B) A flowering stimulus, produced only in plant B under the short photoperiod, is translocated to both plants via a graft, triggering flower production in the long- and short-day plants.

appear to be nutritional, for even a well-nourished plant often cannot be induced to flower if CO_2 is not present.

Thus, the importance of flowering in the life of plants is fully matched by the complexity of its control. Temperature, light, hormones, and presumably other agents as well, all must exercise their separate effects; the total result then is the development or nondevelopment of a flower. The adaptive value of this complex control probably lies in a saving of energy and materials; a flower is normally formed only under the best possible environmental conditions, when the reproductive effort is most likely to succeed.

ECONOMIC AND AGRICULTURAL APPLICATIONS

Basic research on the hormonal controls of plant growth and development has yielded much information that has been turned to economic, horticultural, and agricultural advantage. Not surprisingly, the extensive research on auxins has produced the greatest number of practical applications.

Several synthetic auxins have been manufactured that promote even greater development of roots than naturally occurring auxins. Indeed, weak solutions of such auxins frequently are used to promote root formation in stem *cuttings,* a common means of propagating mature plants (Fig. 16.22).

Other synthetic auxins are potent herbicides. One of these, 2,4-dichlorophenoxyacetic acid (2,4-D), is probably the most widely used synthetic auxin (see Fig. 16.1). This substance drastically interferes with the metabolism and development of plants. Dicot weeds are particularly sensitive to 2,4-D, and many of these plants can be killed by topical applications of the compound. By contrast, monocots such as grasses, corn, wheat, and rice are hardly affected by concentrations of 2,4-D that kill

Fig. 16.22 Auxins and roots. After auxin application the cut stem at left develops as at right.

dicot weeds. Not surprisingly, this compound is now used routinely by many farmers of cereal grains to kill weeds that compete with grain plants and reduce crop yields (Fig. 16.23). 2,4-D also is the active ingredient in many commercial "weed and feed" lawn fertilizers. The synthetic auxin exerts its weeding effect by killing dandelions, plantain, and other sun-loving dicots that often compete with grasses.

Still other synthetic auxins are sprayed on fruit trees by operators of commercial orchards. In spring, the addition of synthetic auxins to natural ones produces an exceedingly high total concentration of these hormones. Such concentrations promote premature abscission of many young fruits. This effect probably is due to ethylene, which results from the response of stem tissue to high concentrations of auxins. Thus, some young fruits drop from the trees in spring, and the remaining ones become larger than they would have if the trees had not been thinned of fruit. Conversely, spraying auxins on fruit trees in late summer augments the decreasing concentrations of natural auxins in stems and retards abscission. Fruits remain on trees longer and consequently grow larger.

Fruit growers also have been served by the knowledge that ethylene exerts substantial control over fruit ripening. Producers of oranges and bananas frequently use ethylene gas to regulate the ripening process. For example, holds of banana boats are fumigated routinely with ethylene at a suitable time before docking. Retailers thus are assured that fruit picked green will have started ripening.

The growth-promoting effects of gibberellins likewise have been put to use in agriculture and horticulture. For example, the stems of grape plants elongate dramatically if gibberellins are ap-

Fig. 16.23 Weed killers. Portion of a cultivated field showing the effect of weed-killing hormones on left side. An untreated section is on the right side.

plied at the appropriate time and in the proper concentration. As a result, bunches of grapes are less tightly packed, the quality of grapes is increased, and the fruits are less prone to fungal infections. Gibberellins also can be used to increase the size of individual grapes. Today, all seedless grapes produced commercially in California are gibberellin-treated to increase yield. These hormones also have been used on many plants to promote early flowering and fruiting and to break dormancy of seeds artificially.

Research on more recently discovered hormones, such as cytokinins and abscisic acid, already has led to several agricultural innovations. The antisenescent properties of a synthetic cytokinin called *benzyladenine* have been used commercially to prolong the usable life of crops such as broccoli. Also, synthetic growth inhibitors similar to abscisic acid have been used to accelerate the onset of fruit production by young apple trees.

Knowledge of photoperiodic responses has been turned to horticultural advantage, too. As stated earlier, artificially created photoperiods are routinely used by florists to induce or inhibit flowering of commercially important plants at virtually any season of the year. Plant growth also can be influenced by regulating light intensity. Many plants respond to low light intensities by producing larger leaves, thereby increasing the photosynthetic surface area. Where leaf size is of commercial importance, as in lettuce or tobacco, plants can be shielded by light screens or nets to promote development of larger leaves.

Basic research on the hormonal control of plant growth and development will probably lead to many additional useful applications in the future. Derivatives of secondary growth substances, for example, eventually may be used to eliminate undesirable weeds or to control insect and other plant pests. But the desire to apply knowledge hurriedly to generate immediate benefits always must be tempered with caution; as seen in Chap. 10, unexpected damage to living systems can result whenever synthetic molecules are routinely spread into ecosystems.

Review Questions

1 Review the functional properties of hormones and describe how these substances are transported to target structures. Show how hormones contribute to maintenance of steady states in organisms.

2 Name the principal hormones produced by plants and describe the functions of each. Show how plant hormones interact in accelerating or decelerating specific processes.

3 Describe the experiments of Fritz Went and discuss how they have implicated auxins as growth-controlling substances.

4 Describe the various motion responses of plants and review the role of hormones in producing such responses. Discuss the mechanism of the opening and closing movements of guard cells and describe the nature of the responses of sensitive plants to touch.

5 What physical and chemical agents are responsible for induction of bud dormancy? For reactivation of dormant buds? For seed germination?

6 Review the role of hormones in controlling developmental responses of plants. What is an abscission layer? Suggest a procedure for artificially promoting or inhibiting fruit drop.

7 Describe the developmental responses of plants to:

- **a.** Light intensity
- **b.** Light quality
- **c.** Light duration

8 What evidence suggests that phytochrome and flowering stimuli exist? Suppose a short-day plant were continuously exposed to orange-red light only. Would the plant flower? Why or why not? Can a defoliated plant flower?

9 How are the photoperiodic characteristics of given plants reflected in the global distribution of the plants? What are secondary growth substances? Can you account for the evolution of allelopathy?

10 How could you counter the statements of someone who argues that money spent on research dealing with basic properties of plant hormones could be better spent on projects that directly support human needs?

Collateral Readings

Bidwell, R. G. S.: "Plant Physiology," 2d ed., Macmillan, New York, 1979. An up-to-date account of the regulatory effects of plant hormones.

Cleland, C. F.: The Flowering Enigma, *Bioscience,* April 1978. A review of what is known about the flowering stimulus.

Galston, A. W., and **P. J. Davies:** "Control Mechanisms in Plant Development," Prentice-Hall, Englewood Cliffs, N.J., 1970. Although somewhat dated, this short text contains well-written sections on plant growth and plant hormones. Available in paperback.

Leopold, A. C., and **P. E. Kriedemann:** "Plant Growth and Development," 2d ed., McGraw-Hill, New York, 1975. A good reference source for these topics.

Raven, P., R. Evert, and **H. Curtis:** "Biology of Plants," 2d ed., Worth, New York, 1975. A handsomely illustrated introductory botany text with a good treatment of plant hormones.

Salisbury, F. B., and **C. W. Ross:** "Plant Physiology," 2d ed., Wadsworth, Belmont, Calif., 1978. Another good reference source for topics discussed in this chapter.

Wareing, P. F., and **I. D. J. Phillips:** "The Control of Growth and Differentiation in Plants," Pergamon, New York, 1978. A somewhat more advanced treatment than the other sources listed here.

Chapter 17 Hormonal Control in Animals

Learning Objectives

After reading this chapter you should be able to:

1. Differentiate between endocrine glands and neurosecretory cells; name a chief functional relationship between the nervous and endocrine elements of neuroendocrine systems.
2. Identify the mechanism by which most hormones are transported in blood; list at least two general mechanisms by which hormones trigger intracellular effects; construct a diagram illustrating how certain hormones trigger formation of cyclic AMP; define kinase and state a probable relationship between this class of enzymes and cyclic AMP; list at least three responses of cells that are mediated by cyclic AMP; define steroid and show how most steroid hormones produce responses in target cells.
3. List three ways in which parathormone and calcitonin regulate the calcium content of body fluids; outline the clinical effects of a parathormone-calcitonin imbalance; indicate why the pituitary should not be termed the "master endocrine gland."
4. Draw a diagram that illustrates the anatomical and functional relations among the hypothalamus, posterior pituitary, and anterior pituitary; list and identify at least one function for each of the hormones released by the pituitary.
5. Distinguish between releasing factors and tropic hormones and illustrate how production of such hormones is regulated; name a function for each of the hormones synthesized by the hypothalamus.
6. Define thyroxine, state its principal functions, and list the effects of abnormally high and low concentrations of thyroxine in human beings.
7. Define photoperiodism and state at least one way in which hormones regulate a photoperiodic response of an animal.
8. Define and name at least one symptom of diabetes mellitus; list at least one way in which each of the following contributes to the metabolism and intercellular transport of glucose in vertebrates:
    - **a.** pancreas
    - **b.** insulin
    - **c.** glucagon
    - **d.** epinephrine
    - **e.** adrenal gland
    - **f.** cyclic AMP
    - **g.** STH
    - **h.** cortisol
9. Illustrate how hormones can act synergistically in controlling the metabolism of carbohydrates.
10. Show how hormones contribute to the "fight or flight" response of vertebrates.

ANIMAL HORMONES: GENERAL CHARACTERISTICS

Unlike plants, virtually all animals have nervous systems that integrate the actions of different body parts. In addition, most animals probably contain chemical agents that are produced in one body part and have specific regulatory or coordinating effects in other parts. Such substances generally are referred to as *humoral* agents. For example, CO_2 qualifies as a simple humoral agent in mammals; among other effects it exerts a controlling function over breathing (see Chap. 18).

In certain instances humoral agents are distinct hormones, produced by specialized *endocrine* cells and discharged not through ducts but directly into body fluids.

Some endocrine structures are functional extensions of nervous systems. Indeed, the endocrine systems of insects, annelid worms, mollusks, and other complex invertebrates are composed almost exclusively of nerve cells that release their secretions directly into body fluids (Fig. 17.1). The hormones of such *neurosecretory cells* then coordinate the responses of target cells located in diverse parts of an animal. In developing insects, for example,

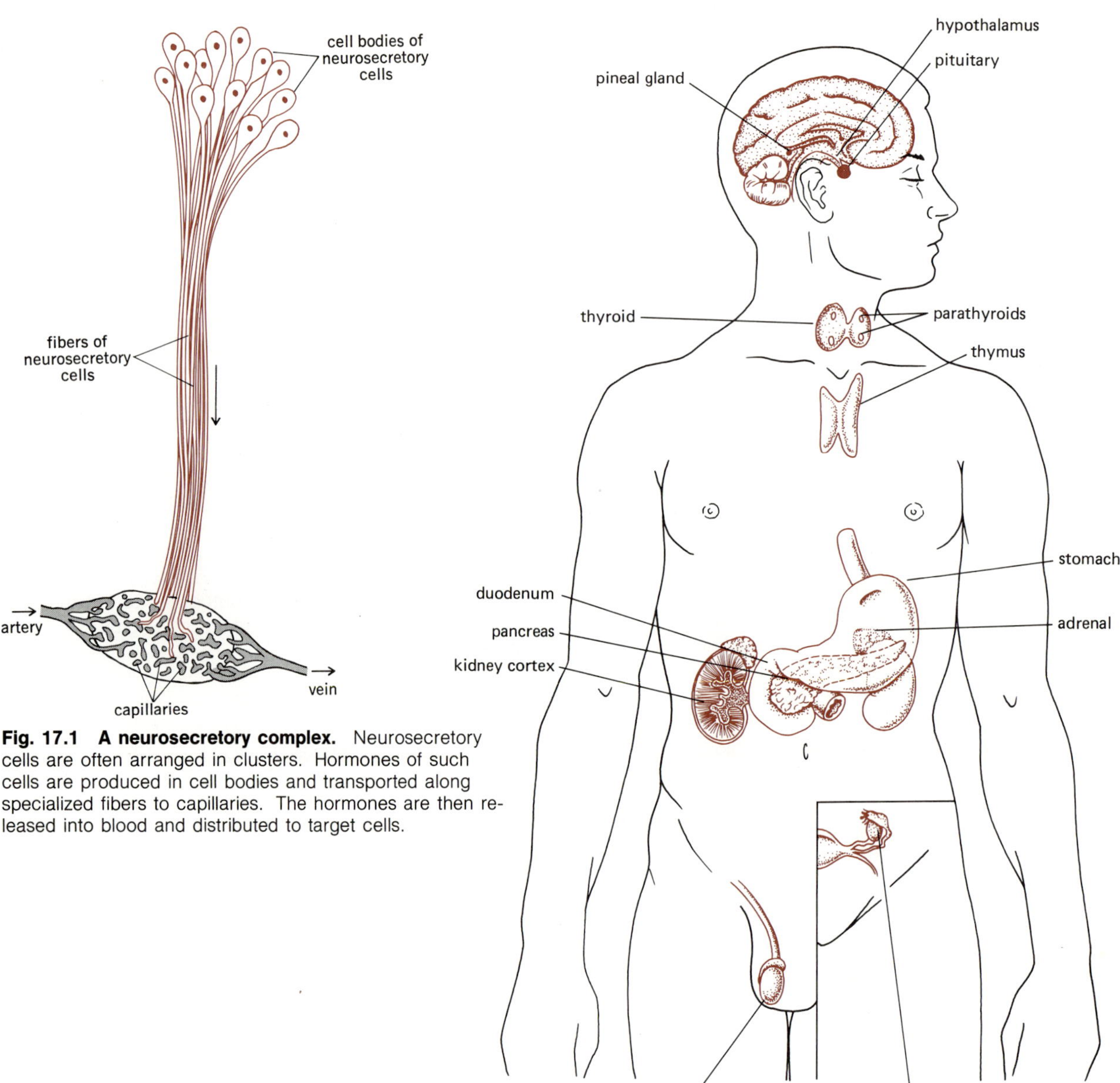

Fig. 17.1 A neurosecretory complex. Neurosecretory cells are often arranged in clusters. Hormones of such cells are produced in cell bodies and transported along specialized fibers to capillaries. The hormones are then released into blood and distributed to target cells.

Fig. 17.2 Principal endocrine organs of human beings.

the rigid armorlike shells, or *exoskeletons,* are shed periodically and are replaced by new and larger ones. Such *molting* is regulated in part by the hormone *ecdysone,* liberated from neurosecretory cells in the brain. In squids and octopuses, neurosecretory hormones appear to control mainly the movements of pigment granules contained in specialized skin cells. By such means, the animal can change its coloration and blend with environmental backgrounds.

In vertebrates hardly any function occurs that is not influenced at least in part by hormones. Unlike most other animals, vertebrates usually have specialized *endocrine glands* that discharge hormones directly into the circulatory system (Fig. 17.2). But many functions of vertebrates also are coordinated by neurosecretory cells. Indeed, the integration between nervous and endocrine structures often is so extensive that biologists refer to them jointly as the *neuroendocrine systems.* In many instances, the nervous elements of these systems supply information about the external environment while the endocrine components regulate the internal response to this information.

Through hormonal messengers, the various components of neuroendocrine systems remain integrated with each other even as they integrate other functions of the body. Thus, nerves and neurosecretory cells respond to hormonal signals as well as transmit chemical messengers of their own. Moreover, neuroendocrine control of body functions almost always involves balances between hormones acting together or in sequence. For example, milk production and secretion by human breasts (mammary glands) requires interactions between at least 12 hormones released from at least 5 different endocrine organs.

Like vitamins, most animal hormones are required by most or all cells of the body. Accordingly, labels such as "sex hormones," for example, are somewhat misleading. To be sure, sex hormones are manufactured in sex organs, and the hormones contribute to the proper functioning of these organs; but sex hormones often contribute to the functioning of virtually every other organ of an animal. It happens that the effect of deficiency or excess of a given hormone reveals itself first or most obviously in a particular body part. For convenience we may then name the hormone according to this body part, but we cannot conclude that the hormone functions only there. *Prolactin,* for example, bears a name indicative of its stimulatory effect on milk production in mammary glands. However, prolactin now is known to have numerous other effects as well, including a general growth-stimulating function in young vertebrates.

Animal hormones vary greatly in chemical composition. Some are proteins, others are complex lipid derivatives called *steroids,* a few are amino acids, and the rest are various other simple or complex compounds. The chemical structures of several hormones are now known, and some of them can be synthesized in the laboratory. On the other hand, many hormones are known only through the abnormal effects produced by their deficiency or excess.

MECHANISMS OF HORMONE ACTION

Some hormones exert a large number of different effects on several different organs in many different species. The vertebrate hormone *thyroxine,* for example, influences metabolic rates, the metamorphosis of tadpoles into adult frogs, maze learning in rats, water retention in mammals, production of pigment in bird feathers, development of teeth in human beings, and growth of antlers in deer. Because of such myriad effects and because hormones comprise many different kinds, shapes, and sizes of molecules, it seems unlikely that all hormones have the same mode of action. Results of many experiments actually confirm this suspicion. Nevertheless, some general statements can be made about the ways hormones trigger responses in target cells.

Many hormones are transported in blood as components of molecular complexes. The nonhormonal units of such couplings are almost always proteins that circulate in blood in minute amounts. Such carrier molecules are highly specific; they unite only with a particular hormone or group of hormones. Moreover, they appear to serve as more than transport vehicles. Hormones that remain unbound to carriers usually are destroyed quickly as they circulate through organs such as the liver or kidneys. Carrier-bound hormones generally are destroyed or inactivated far less rapidly. Thus, the number of carriers available at least partly determines the number of hormone molecules present in body fluids, and this in turn may protect organisms from excessive concentrations of bloodborne hormones.

Hormones exert their effects by attaching to receptor molecules located on or in target cells. The identification and characterization of such receptors has become one of the most intensively studied aspects of hormone research. Most receptor molecules appear to be wholly or partly composed of proteins. Two major kinds of cellular receptor sites so far have been identified. Some receptors, located on the outer surfaces of cells, commonly bind to protein or peptide hormones, which usually

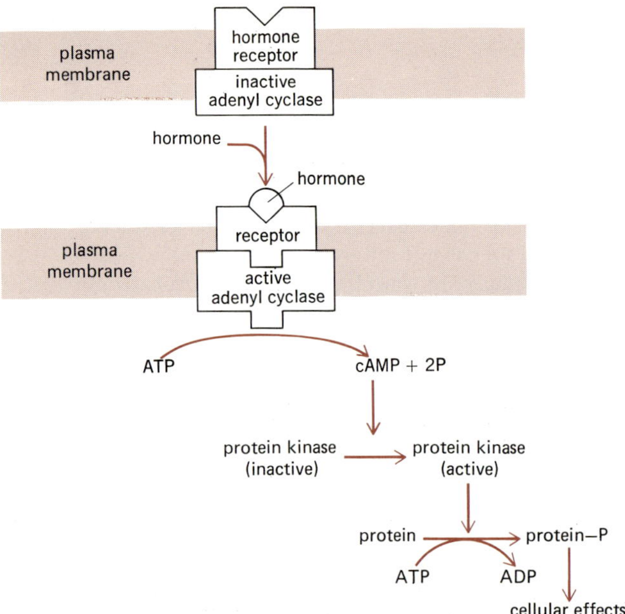

Fig. 17.3 Cyclic AMP. Some hormones influence cell functions by triggering production of a second messenger called cyclic AMP. These hormones induce changes in the shape of receptor molecules located in plasma membranes. The change in shape activates adenyl cyclase, an enzyme that catalyzes conversion of ATP to cyclic AMP. The latter activates one or more protein kinases, which in turn phosphorylate certain proteins. Most of the intracellular effects of the hormonal first messenger appear to be mediated directly by the phosphorylated proteins.

cannot penetrate plasma membranes. Other receptors exist inside cells, either on the inner surface of the plasma membrane or in the cytoplasm. Such receptors usually are specific for steroid hormones. Because they are relatively small, lipid-soluble molecules, steroids often pass easily through plasma membranes.

Hormones that interact with cell surface receptors exert most of their intracellular effects indirectly. Many of these hormones trigger release of a *second messenger* from the inner surface of the plasma membrane. Such second messengers then establish specific responses to hormonal first messengers by influencing intracellular controls. The second messenger for many hormone-mediated responses of cells has been identified as a breakdown product of ATP, called *cyclic adenosine monophosphate,* or *cyclic AMP.* A similar breakdown product of GTP, *cyclic guanosine monophosphate* (GMP), has been implicated as a second messenger in a number of cells. As will be illustrated shortly, the effects of cyclic GMP have been shown to oppose those of cyclic AMP in several instances. However, intracellular concentrations of cyclic GMP are much lower than those of cyclic AMP, and much less is known about its regulatory effects.

Production of cyclic AMP can result from the binding of certain hormones to their receptors at the cell surface. Such bindings appear to produce changes in the three-dimensional structures of receptor molecules, which in turn lead to activation of the enzyme *adenyl cyclase.* Located on the inner surface of plasma membranes, this enzyme catalyzes conversion of ATP to cyclic AMP (Fig. 17.3).

Cyclic AMP produces a variety of strikingly different effects in cells of different tissues. In some cells the compound affects the rates at which certain substances are synthesized or degraded, while in others it affects transport or secretory processes. Like certain other substances that act as second messengers, cyclic AMP appears to promote selected intracellular responses by activating a class of enzymes called *protein kinases.* All such enzymes catalyze the attachment of one or more phosphate groups to proteins. The phosphorylated proteins seem to be the direct mediators of cellular responses, the nature of the response depending on which proteins are phosphorylated (see Fig. 17.3).

Other hormones, most notably steroids, exert their effects by passing through the plasma membrane and binding to intracellular receptors. Produced from cholesterol, all steroids have a common central structure of four interconnected rings of carbon atoms. Differences between steroids result from varying patterns of chemical bonds in the rings and from different orientations of side groups attached to the rings (Fig. 17.4). Steroid hormones include the various male and female sex hormones and the hormones secreted by the outer layer, or *cortex,* of the adrenal gland.

Apparently most steroid hormones elicit their effects by activating particular genes. Upon entering the cytoplasm of target cells, these hormones unite with specific protein receptors (Fig. 17.5). Such receptors are present only in specific cells, and this explains why hormones do not have a discernible effect on nontarget tissues. Receptors undergo structural changes following their binding to hormones. Such changes enable a hormone-receptor complex to enter the cell nucleus and attach to one or more nonhistone proteins of chromatin. The

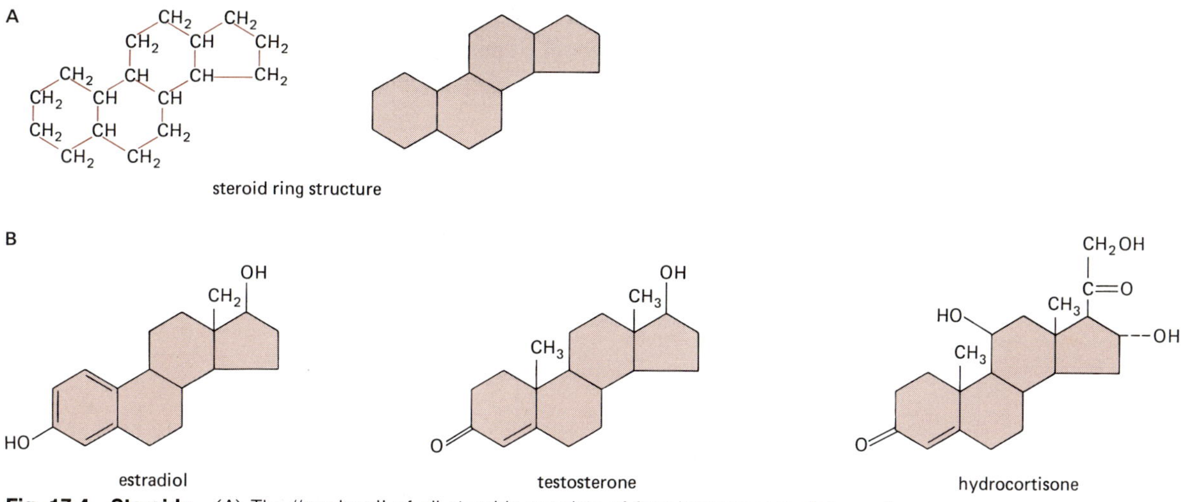

A

steroid ring structure

B

estradiol

testosterone

hydrocortisone

Fig. 17.4 Steroids. (A) The "nucleus" of all steroids consists of four interconnected rings of carbon atoms. (B) Differences in side groups attached to the four-ring nucleus account for the specific actions of different steroids. See Table 17.1 for the sources and principal functions of these hormones.

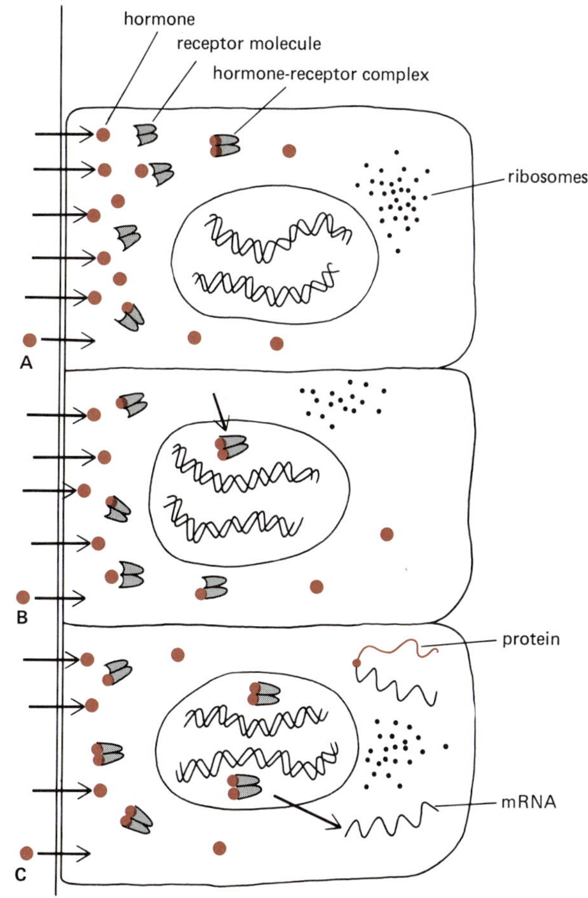

Fig. 17.5 Probable mechanisms of steroid hormone action. (A) Steroid hormones diffuse into and out of all cells, but they become bound to specific protein receptors in the cytoplasm of target cells. (B) The steroid-hormone complexes accumulate in the nucleus, where they bind to certain nonhistone proteins in chromatin. This binding probably exposes a segment of DNA for mRNA transcription. (C) The newly manufactured mRNA moves to the cytoplasm, where it is translated.

attachment somehow alters chromatin structure such that RNA polymerase becomes bound to DNA. The subsequent transcription of specific segments of DNA leads to the synthesis of specific proteins, which in their turn coordinate the hormonal response of the target cell.

Examples of how these two kinds of hormone receptor systems operate in vertebrates are presented later in this chapter. In preparation for this discussion we first examine some of the structural and functional relations between major components of the vertebrate neuroendocrine system.

THE VERTEBRATE NEUROENDOCRINE SYSTEM

As seen from Table 17.1, the *pituitary gland,* a small endocrine organ located at the base of the brain, plays a central role in regulating many other

TABLE 17.1

The Main Vertebrate Endocrine Glands and Their Principal Hormones

Gland	Hormones	Chief function	Effects of deficiency or excess
pituitary: anterior lobe	TSH (thyrotropic; also called thyroid-stimulating hormone)	stimulates thyroid	
	ACTH (adrenocorticotropic)	stimulates adrenal cortex	
	FSH (follicle-stimulating)	stimulates ovary (follicle)	
	LH (luteinizing)	stimulates testes in male, corpus luteum in female	
	prolactin (lactogenic)	stimulates milk secretion, parental behavior	
	STH (somatotropic hormone; also called growth hormone)	promotes cell metabolism	dwarfism, gigantism
posterior lobe			
pars intermedia	MSH (melanophore-stimulating hormone)	controls adjustable skin-pigment cells, e.g., in frogs	
pars nervosa	oxytocin	smooth-muscle response of uterus	
	ADH (vasopressin)	promotes reabsorption of water by kidney	increased or reduced water excretion
thyroid	thyroxine	stimulates respiration; inhibits TSH secretion	goiter; cretinism; myxedema
	calcitonin	reduces Ca^{2+} release from bone; generally opposes action of parathormone	nerve, muscle abnormalities; bone thickening or weakening
parathyroid	parathormone	promotes Ca^{2+} release from bone; generally opposes action of calcitonin	nerve, muscle abnormalities; bone thickening or weakening; similar to those of calcitonin
adrenal cortex	cortisone, other corticoid hormones	controls metabolism of water, minerals, carbohydrates; controls kidney function; inhibits ACTH secretion; duplicates sex-hormone functions	Addison's disease
adrenal medulla	epinephrine, norepinephrine	"fight or flight" reaction; for example, raises blood pressure, heart rate, blood-sugar level	inability to cope with stress
pancreas	insulin	glucose → glycogen conversion	diabetes
	glucagon	glycogen → glucose conversion	
stomach	gastrin	stimulates gastric juice secretion	
small intestine	secretin	stimulates bile and pancreatic juice secretion	
	cholecystokinin	contraction of gallbladder; enzyme secretion by pancreas	

TABLE 17.1 (*Continued*)

Gland	Hormones	Chief function	Effects of deficiency or excess
kidney	renin erythropoietin	decreases blood volume and pressure increases production of red blood cells	
pineal gland	melatonin	opposes action of MSH in ectothermic (cold-blooded) vertebrates; may regulate secretion of gonadotropins in some endothermic (warm-blooded) vertebrates	
testis	testosterone, other androgens	promote cell respiration, blood circulation; maintain primary and secondary sex characteristics, sex urge; inhibit FSH secretions	atrophy of reproductive system; decline of secondary sex characteristics
ovary; follicle	estradiol, other estrogens		
ovary: corpus luteum	progesterone	promotes secretions of oviduct, uterus growth in pregnancy; inhibits LH secretions	spontaneous abortion
ovary, uterus, placenta	relaxin	enlargement of birth canal by relaxation of uterine cervix and pelvic ligaments	

endocrine glands of vertebrates. For example, secretions of the pituitary control the release of hormones produced by the ovaries and testes, the thyroid gland, and those hormones produced in the cortex of the adrenal gland. Because of this "tropic" nature, i.e., its ability to stimulate other endocrine organs, the pituitary was once called the "master gland." However, this nickname is inappropriate. Some endocrine glands operate in a relatively independent manner; their secretions are not controlled significantly by pituitary hormones. Among these are the *parathyroid glands,* located near or in the *thyroid gland,* and the *pancreas* (Fig. 17.6 and see Fig. 17.2). The secretion of hormones produced by these glands is governed largely by the relative concentration of specific substances in blood.

For example, release of *parathormone* and *calcitonin* by the parathyroid and thyroid glands, respectively, is regulated chiefly by the concentration of calcium in blood. Low concentrations of calcium trigger increased secretion of parathormone; high concentrations stimulate secretion of calcitonin. Parathormone increases the calcium content of body fluids in three main ways: by promoting absorption of calcium from nutrients being digested in the intestine; by accelerating calcium reabsorption in the kidney; and by stimulating the release of calcium into blood from bones.

Calcitonin generally opposes these actions. Optimal concentrations of calcium in blood are largely maintained by the antagonistic effects of these hormones.

The amount of parathormone and calcitonin released to the bloodstream must be regulated precisely. Too much parathormone and too little calcitonin can lead to destruction of bones and the formation of hard calcium deposits in the stomach, intestine, and kidneys. An opposite imbalance can result in malfunctions of several tissues, muscles and nerves particularly. Spasms of facial and throat muscles can impair speech, choking can occur, and malfunctions of rib muscles can prevent normal breathing. Death inevitably results from a severe imbalance of these two calcium-regulating hormones. Because the pituitary has little influence on the production and secretion of parathormone, calcitonin, and other hormones equally essential for life, it clearly cannot be viewed as the sole "concert master" of the "endocrine orchestra."

Moreover, research has demonstrated that most secretions of the pituitary are themselves either produced or regulated by neurosecretory cells of the brain. An examination of the structural relation between the pituitary and brain will help to reveal the nature of this control. As seen in Fig. 17.2, the pituitary is suspended from the *hypothalamus,* a midbasal region of the brain. The gland is about

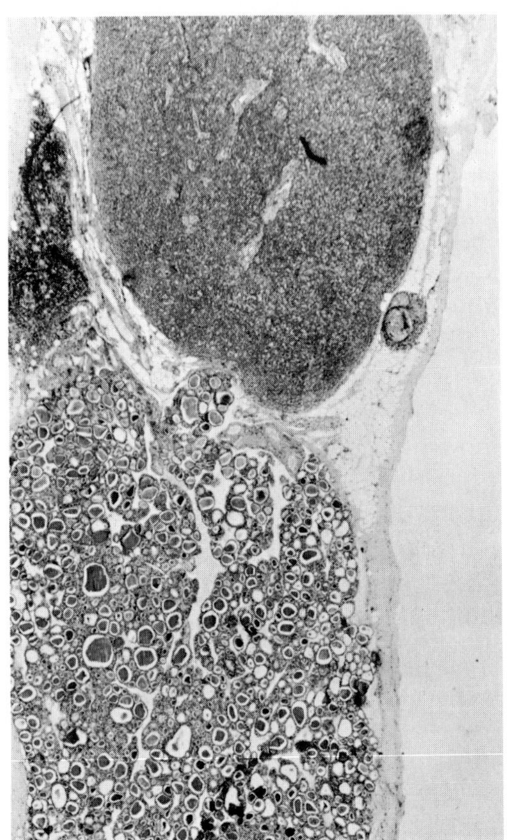

Fig. 17.6 Thyroid and parathyroid. A portion of the parathyroid gland is seen at top (darker, denser tissue). In the thyroid section at bottom, the round spaces largely filled with dark material are the regions where thyroxine accumulates before being carried off in blood. (*Ward's Natural Science Establishment, Inc.*)

the size of a pea in an adult man and slightly larger in a woman. The pituitary consists of two main parts, each having a different embryonic origin. The posterior portion of the gland is formed by a downgrowth from the base of the embryonic brain (Fig. 17.7). Indeed, this *posterior pituitary* is little more than an extension of the hypothalamus.

In young human beings, and in most other vertebrates, a narrow portion of the posterior lobe, the *pars intermedia,* borders the forward *anterior lobe* of the gland. The pars intermedia merges with the remainder of the posterior lobe as people age, and gradually becomes obscure. This narrow, midportion of the pituitary is not present in the pituitary glands of whales, armadillos, birds, and a few other vertebrates. The pars intermedia secretes *melanophore-stimulating hormone* (MSH), which regulates skin pigmentation in several vertebrate animals. In a frog, for example, the hormone brings about dispersion of pigment granules in melanophores, one of the major pigment cells in frog skin (Fig. 17.8). In the absence of MSH, frog melanophores have the appearance of small black dots, and are said to be in the *punctate* configuration. At such times pigment granules are concentrated about the nucleus of a melanophore. Treating punctate melanophores with MSH causes pigment granules to disperse widely throughout the cytoplasm. Because a greater surface area is covered by pigment granules following dispersion, frog skin appears darker than when melanophores are punctate. Such skin-coloration changes have obvious adaptive value. The color of frog skin can be adjusted to approximate the hue of the background environment, providing camouflage protection.

The remainder of the posterior pituitary, called the *pars nervosa,* releases two principal hormones, *oxytocin* and *vasopressin*. These are produced by neurosecretory cells located in the hypothalamus, some distance away from the pituitary. The hormones then are transported along fingerlike extensions of the neurosecretory cells and stored in the posterior pituitary before release. Oxytocin produces contractions of the smooth uterine muscles that result in the birth of offspring, and it causes milk to be released from mammary glands. Vasopressin is named for its ability to constrict blood vessels and thereby to increase blood pressure. The hormone also promotes water reabsorption by nephrons of the kidney and therefore is known also as *antidiuretic hormone* (ADH). The release of both oxytocin and vasopressin is triggered largely by nerve cells of the brain.

The anterior lobe of the pituitary is formed by an upgrowth of tissue lining the roof of the embryonic mouth (see Fig. 19.4). When this tissue fuses with the posterior pituitary, the connection to the underlying tissue of the mouth cavity is severed. The whole pituitary then becomes positioned in a pocket of bone at the base of the hypothalamus. Six hormones are produced by cells of the anterior pituitary, and their release into the bloodstream is

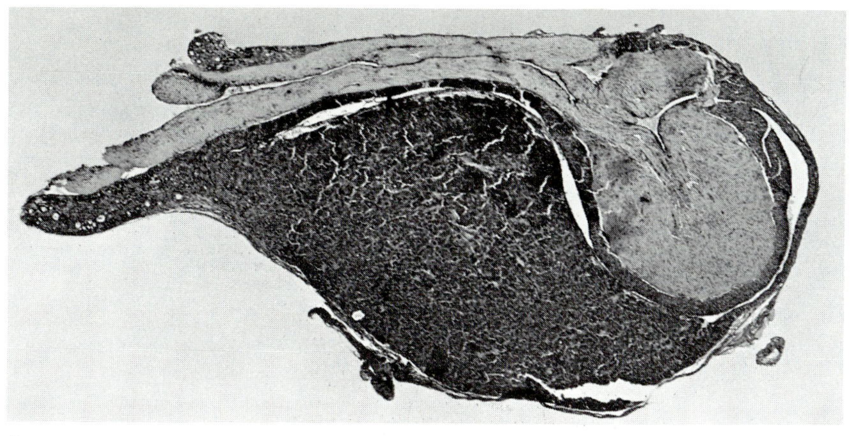

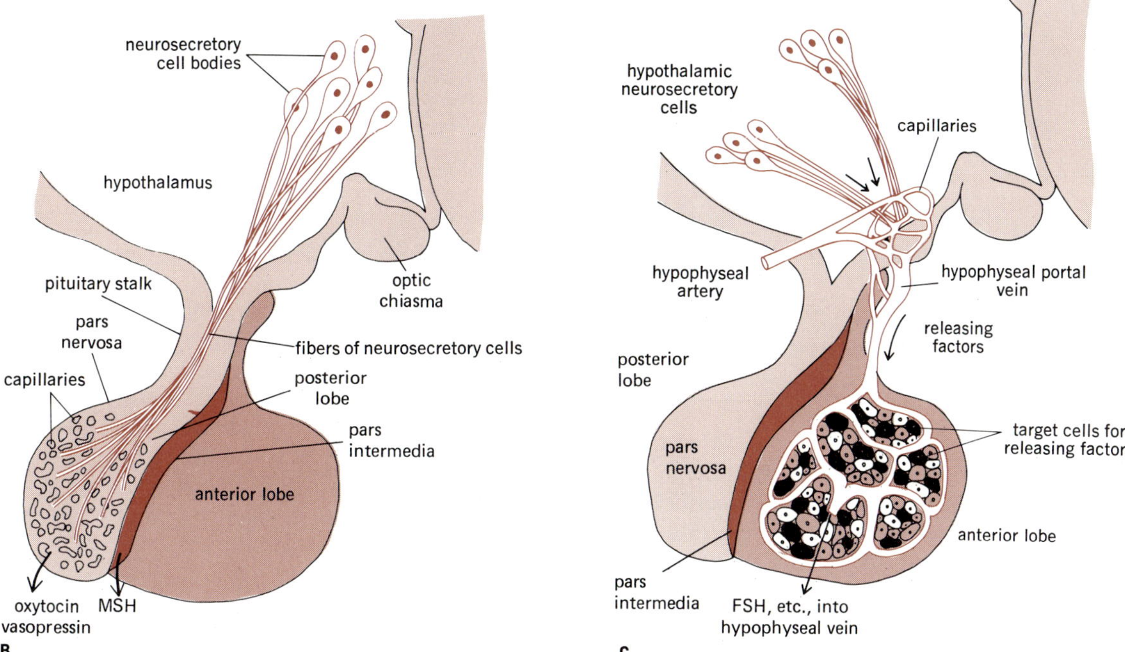

Fig. 17.7 Pituitary and hypothalamus. (A) Section through a pituitary gland. The larger and darker anterior lobe is the left part of the gland; the lighter posterior lobe is on the right. The posterior lobe continues dorsally as a stalk that joins the whole gland to the hypothalamus. (B) Posterior lobe. The hormones oxytocin and vasopressin are produced in a bundle of neurosecretory cells located in the hypothalamus. The hormones are transported down the fibers of the neurosecretory cells and released into capillaries of the pars nervosa of the posterior lobe. The pars intermedia portion of the posterior lobe, present in most but not all vertebrates, produces and secretes MSH. (C) Anterior lobe. Releasing factors, produced by groups of hypothalamic neurosecretory cells, are transported to capillaries at the base of the hypothalamus. The releasing factors are transported to the anterior lobe of the pituitary by the hypophyseal portal vein, where they regulate the secretions of target endocrine cells. The hypophyseal vein carries away hormones produced in the anterior lobe. (*A, Ward's Natural Science Establishment, Inc.*)

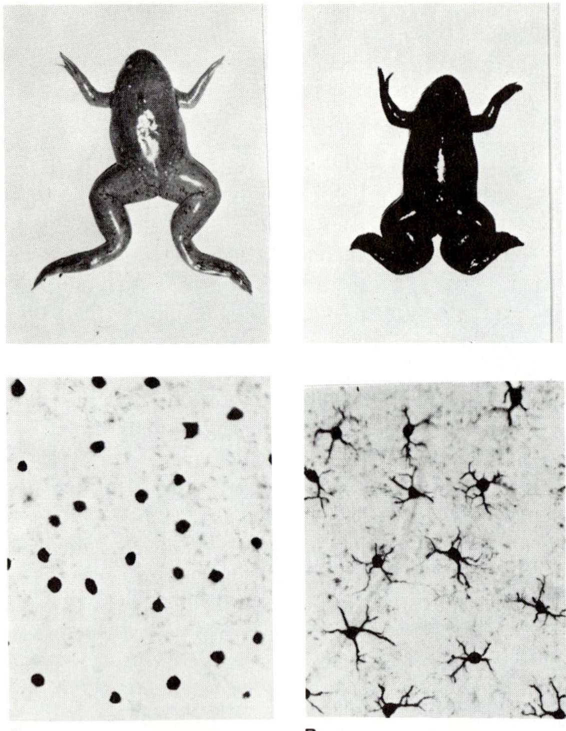

Fig. 17.8 Frog melanophores. (A) Punctate state. Pigment granules are clustered around the nucleus (not visible) of each melanophore, giving a frog a light appearance (above). (B) Dispersed state. Granules are dispersed through the highly branched melanophores, darkening the skin of a frog (above).

TABLE 17.2
Principal hormones of the hypothalamus

Hormone	Abbreviation	Chief function
corticotropin releasing factor	CRF	stimulates release of ACTH
thyrotropin releasing factor	TRF	stimulates release of TSH
luteinizing-hormone releasing factor	LRF	stimulates release of LH
follicle-stimulating hormone releasing factor	FSH-RF	stimulates release of FSH
growth-hormone releasing factor	GRF	stimulates release of STH
growth-hormone inhibiting factor (somatostatin)	GIF	inhibits release of STH
prolactin inhibiting factor	PIF	inhibits release of prolactin
melanophore-stimulating hormone inhibiting factor	MIF	inhibits release of MSH

controlled largely by neurosecretions of the hypothalamus (Table 17.2). In contrast to the posterior pituitary, these neurosecretions, called *releasing factors,* are transported to the anterior pituitary by a network of small blood vessels. Most of the blood supply to the anterior pituitary first passes through the hypothalamus where it picks up releasing factors. When these neurosecretions reach the anterior pituitary, they regulate release of its hormones.

For example, *corticotropin-releasing factor* (CRF) stimulates the anterior pituitary to release *adrenocorticotropic hormone* (ACTH) (Table 17.1, Fig. 17.9, and see accompanying Biology Highlight). Like the other tropic hormones of the anterior pituitary, ACTH regulates the release of hormones from another endocrine gland. The target structure of ACTH is the cortex of the adrenal gland, which produces a group of steroids called *corticoid hormones.* Some of these steroids promote the synthesis of carbohydrates and the breakdown of proteins. The relative concentration of corticoids in blood has a direct effect on the release of ACTH by the pituitary and an even greater effect on the release of CRF by the hypothalamus. High concentrations of corticoids inhibit release of both of these hormones, particularly CRF. Consequently, corticoids reduce their own production by inhibiting release of ACTH from the pituitary.

Fig. 17.9 Regulation of tropic hormones. Corticotropin releasing factor (CRF), produced by neurosecretory cells of the hypothalamus, promotes release of ACTH from the pituitary. The latter is a tropic hormone that regulates release of corticoid hormones from the adrenal cortex. High concentrations of corticoids inhibit release of both CRF and ACTH. Other tropic hormones of the pituitary similarly influence their own production.

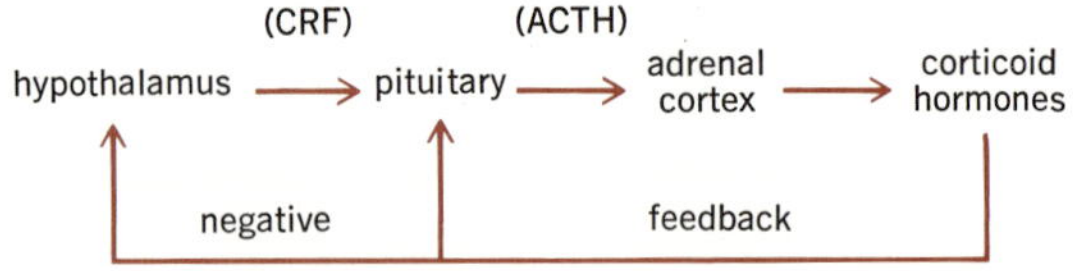

Biology Highlight

The Quest for Hypothalamic Hormones: The Saga of Roger Guillemin and Andrew Schally

A

B

Fig. 1 Guillemin and Schally. (A) Roger Guillemin at work. (B) Andrew Schally.

Beginning students of science sometimes perceive scientists as brilliant but often austere people whose professional lives, although interesting, are devoid of much emotion. Examination of science journals appears to lend credence to this view. Most research publications are highly structured, scholarly reports that intentionally avoid conveying any emotion of excitement experienced by scientists who conducted the research. But scientists are real people, not automatons, and science is a human invention practiced by human beings who display both noble and ignoble traits. Feelings of frustrations, jealousy, pride, despair, ecstasy, and even rage are as common among scientists as among thespians, musicians, business executives, or lawyers.

The story of the search and eventual isolation of hypothalamic hormones illustrates particularly well how scientific research is a human and often highly competitive activity. Two scientists, Andrew Schally and Roger Guillemin, led the controversial effort to extract and identify the hypothalamic secretions that regulate release of hormones from the anterior pituitary (see Table 17.2). The first hypothalamic hormone to be isolated was TSH. Its identification culminated a 14-year-long search characterized by an intense and often bitter rivalry between two research teams, one headed by Schally and the other by Guillemin (Fig. 1). The two scientists subjected each other to a barrage of criticism for most of the 14-year period, and they in turn were subjected to skepticism and mockery by many of their colleagues.

The search began in 1955, when Guillemin and Schally discovered independently that anterior pituitary tissue placed in a test tube will produce hormones only when cultured jointly with hypothalamic tissue. The discovery provided evidence in support of a hypothesis first proposed by the English biologist Geoffrey Harris, who suggested that the hypothalamus controls secretion of at least some pituitary hormones, by releasing chemical messengers into a network of interconnecting blood vessels. Schally and Guillemin published the results of their experiments separately, and then both began a search for CRF, the hypothalamic secretion that stimulates production of ACTH. The choice was unfortunate, for CRF proved exceedingly difficult to extract; indeed, it has yet to be isolated and analyzed chemically. Nevertheless, the initial search for CRF led to the development of several innovative techniques that were instrumental in the later identification of TSH, and other less elusive hypothalamic secretions.

One of the first problems Guillemin and Schally encountered was procurement of sufficient hypothalamic tissue for chemical extraction of CRF. Hypothalamic secretions are produced in exceedingly small amounts, and hundreds of thousands of hypothalami are required for extraction of even a few milligrams of these brain hormones. The two scientists obtained the necessary quantities of tissue from meat-processing companies that killed large numbers of animals in slaughterhouses. Guillemin began working with sheep hypothalami and Schally with those of pigs.

The laboratories of the two scientists were converted into small factories for processing brain tissue. Chemical isolation of CRF demanded all the time and resources each research team could muster, as well as thousands of dollars of government research funds. The futile effort lasted until the early 1960s, when both research teams abandoned the attempt to isolate CRF and independently began a search for TRF.

The early search for TRF proved just as difficult and disappointing as the attempt to isolate CRF. By the mid-1960s, an increasing number of endocrinologists became openly critical of the investigations being conducted by Schally and Guillemin. Some wondered aloud why the research teams had been so unsuccessful for so long. Did Guillemin and Schally lack the skills necessary to isolate the hormones? Other scientists questioned the existence of such substances. Criticism gradually became more intense. The two biologists were subjected to sarcasm, skepticism, ridicule, and even contempt from their fellow scientists.

The criticism came to a head in the Endocrinology Study Section, the committee of scientists that advised the National Institutes of Health on which projects in the field of endocrinology should be funded. Should grant money awarded to Guillemin and Schally be diverted to other scientists? The committee decided to convene a conference to evaluate attempts to isolate hypothalamic releasing factors and, indirectly, to evaluate the competence of Guillemin and Schally. The meeting was scheduled for January 1969 in Tucson, Arizona.

Fortunately, after 14 years of effort, Guillemin's team made an important breakthrough just 3 weeks before the Tucson conference was to begin. After processing more than 270,000 sheep hypothalami, Guillemin had extracted 1 mg of TRF. The sample was found to consist of just three amino acids, proline, glutamine, and histidine. Actually Schally had determined in 1966 that pig TRF contains these three amino acids, but he had detected an additional segment of the molecule; he assumed it to be the portion of TRF responsible for promoting release of TSH from cells of the anterior pituitary. Guillemin's sample of sheep TRF was large enough and sufficiently pure for him to deduce correctly that the apparent additional segment of the molecule was an *impurity*: TRF was a tripeptide.

Guillemin's announcement of the discovery triggered a frantic race between the two research teams to determine how the three amino acids were joined as a biologically active molecule. Schally's team won the race to publish the correct sequence (glutamine-histidine-proline) by a margin of 5 weeks. In a broader sense, however, the race was a draw. Had it not been for Guillemin's discovery that TRF is a tripeptide, identification of the exact sequence of amino acids undoubtedly would have required more time.

Guillemin and Schally went on to discover other regulatory secretions of the hypothalamus. By March 1971, Schally had deduced the structure of luteinizing-hormone releasing factor (LRF), which regulates release of luteinizing hormone (LH), one of the pituitary gonadotropins (see Table 17.2 and Chap. 24). He was not absolutely certain of his conclusion, however. Schally became concerned that Guillemin or one of three other rival research teams attempting to extract and analyze LRF might announce the molecular structure at a conference to be held in New York in May. Schally sent one member of his team to the meeting with instructions to announce the structure of LRF only if one of the other teams did so. But none of the teams had progressed as far as Schally's, and his representative held back information regarding the nature of LRF. Schally personally announced the identity of LRF at a scientific meeting held in San Francisco a few weeks later.

Guillemin, although disappointed by his loss to Schally in the race to identify LRF, immediately began searching for other hypothalamic hormones. So did Schally and several other scientists. The intended prize this time was GRF, the hormone that presumably regulates secretion of growth hormone (STH) from the anterior pituitary.

Schally actually published a structure for GRF in 1971, but he was incorrect, a mistake that Guillemin has pointed out in his writings. The real GRF has not yet been isolated. For his part, Guillemin avenged his earlier defeat by being the first to isolate a hypothalamic hormone that *inhibits* release of STH from the pituitary. Called *somatostatin*, the molecule is a Q-shaped chain of 14 amino acids.

The often controversial and highly competitive effort to extract and isolate hypothalamic hormones has special significance in a number of respects. Unquestionably, it laid the foundation for the newest branch of neuroendocrine research. Because of the significance and extraordinary nature of their contributions, Guillemin and Schally were both honored by a Nobel Prize in 1977.

Chemical identification of the brain's regulatory substances also has great practical significance. It may eventually be possible, for example, to place chemically altered molecules of LRF in contraceptive pills that need be taken only once a month by a woman to prevent pregnancy. Moreover, LRF also participates in the normal development of sperms, and thus knowledge of its chemical structure may lead to development of contraceptive pills for men. Further, the hormone has been shown to influence mating behavior in vertebrates, a discovery that could eventually be applied to the production of synthetic aphrodisiacs.

Identification of somatostatin is similarly significant. The hormone is manufactured not only by the pituitary but also by specialized cells of the pancreas, where it participates in controlling the production of insulin and glucagon. Thus it may be possible to employ somatostatin in the treatment of diabetes.

The struggle to isolate brain hormones also provides insight into the character of many research scientists. The most successful of them are often exceedingly dedicated, meticulous, strong-willed people. Guillemin and Schally each made the isolation of hypothalamic hormones his prime goal. Both refused to be swayed by the harsh criticism and public skepticism of their peers. Many people seem to work best when under pressure or when competing, and scientists are no exception.

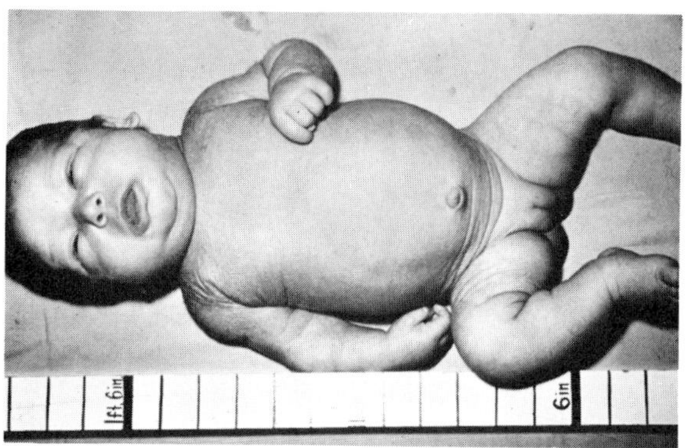

A

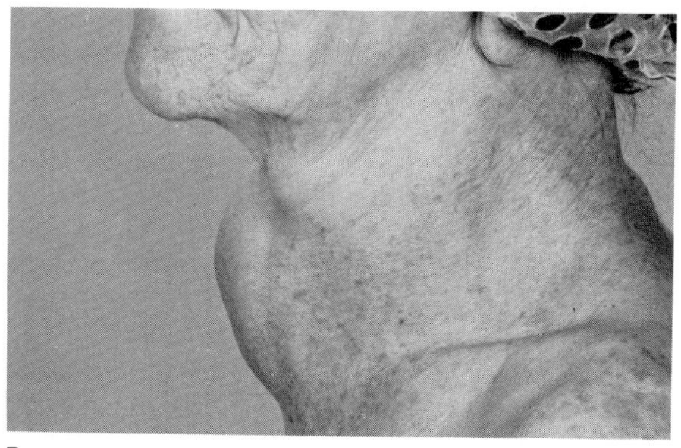

B

Fig. 17.10 Thyroid malfunctions. (A) Cretinism. Note the stunted growth of this child, caused by a deficiency of thyroxine. (B) The pronounced swelling of this woman's neck is caused by a goiter, an enlarged, defective thyroid.

Thyroxine, a hormone produced by the thyroid gland, similarly influences its own rate of production by affecting hypothalamic and pituitary function. The hypothalamus produces *thyrotropin releasing factor* (TRF), which stimulates release of *thyrotropic hormone* (TSH) from the anterior pituitary. The principal function of TSH is to stimulate the thyroid gland, which lies along the trachea below the larynx. Without TSH the thyroid is inactive, and thyroxine is not produced.

Thyroxine functions chiefly in accelerating rates of cellular respiration. If a thyroxine deficiency develops in early youth, the clinical result can be *cretinism* (Fig. 17.10). In this disease growth is stunted, mental development is retarded, sexual development is delayed or does not take place, and body weight increases unduly since little food is respired but much is stored as fat. In the adult, thyroxine deficiency leads to *myxedema*, marked by reduction of mental and bodily vigor, loss of sex drive, loss of hair, and abnormal water accumulation in the skin.

In many cases thyroxine deficiency is counteracted by enlargement of the thyroid gland and secretion of more hormone. Body functions then can become normal, but a *goiter* will be in evidence. Hormone deficiencies (and goiter) can be relieved by administration of thyroxine from an external source. Under conditions of thyroxine excess, so much heat is generated through respiration that the affected individual feels hot all the time. Despite abundant food intake so much is burned that body weight can decrease. The hyperthyroid individual also is tense and highly irritable and is unable to do sustained work because of lack of fuel reserves.

Release of appropriate amounts of thyroxine to body tissues is therefore essential for maintenance of metabolic steady states. Higher than optimum concentrations of thyroxine in blood normally inhibit release of TRF from the hypothalamus and TSH from the pituitary. Lower than optimum concentrations of thyroxine have the opposite effect. Thus, like corticoid hormones, thyroxine normally regulates its own concentrations in the body by influencing release of a tropic pituitary hormone.

Other hormones, including STH and the sex hormones, likewise influence their own production by similar feedback circuits. In addition, the neurosecretory activities of the hypothalamus also are controlled by nerve cells located in other regions of the brain. Thus, neither the pituitary nor indeed any single structure functions as a master gland in controlling secretions of the endocrine system. Although different structures and hormones affect some reactions more than others, the balance of hormones in a vertebrate at any given moment results from integrated sets of responses produced by diverse structures located in diverse parts of an organism. Such structures respond to each other by manufacturing chemical products that are transported to all other structures either by the circulatory system alone or, more often, by a communications network involving both nervous and circulatory systems.

HORMONES AND STEADY STATES

As already noted, hormones function as modulators of steady-state control in many organisms, and they also serve as chief regulators of embryonic development. Thyroxine, for example, plays a critical role in the development of frogs and other amphibians. If thyroid function in a tadpole is inhibited in some way (by excising the thyroid gland, for example), the animal remains a tadpole permanently (Fig. 17.11). Conversely, if a frog tadpole is given an excess of thyroxine, the embryo develops prematurely into a tiny froglet. The role played by other hormones in animal development will be discussed in Chap. 24.

Here, two examples will illustrate the mechanics of steady-state control between various components of vertebrate neuroendocrine systems. The first, photoperiodism, exemplifies the capacity of these systems to respond to external stimuli; the second, hormonal control of glucose metabolism, illustrates how these systems respond to an internal stress.

Photoperiodism

We have already noted the effects of photoperiods on flowering in plants. Gradual changes in day lengths also influence other seasonal events in many organisms, animals as well as plants, vertebrates included. Reproductive cycles, changes in pelage and plumage, and the migratory behavior of animals often are synchronized to seasonal fluctuations of climate. Such synchronizations usually are adaptively advantageous, because they ensure that diverse functions will occur primarily at the most appropriate times of a year. Changes in photoperiod are among the most important stimuli that initiate such functional changes, and the control for most of these changes in vertebrates is provided by the neurosecretory system.

For example, most vertebrates (as well as other animals and also plants) become sexually active only during a limited *breeding season*, most often in spring. At other times of the year their reproductive organs remain inactive, and sexual behavior does not occur. Day lengths gradually increase during late winter and early spring. The changing photoperiods are detected by nerve centers in the brain that connect to the eyes (Fig. 17.12). Through nervous connections to the hypothalamus, these centers stimulate production of releasing factors. In their turn, the neurosecretions

Fig. 17.11 Frog development. In these photographs of a developing frog, some parts of the animal degenerate (e.g., tail), some parts proliferate (e.g., legs), and some parts undergo relatively little change (e.g., skin). Many of these transformations are triggered by thyroxine. (A) Tadpole, hind legs developing. (B) Hind legs at advanced stage, forelegs already visible underneath skin. (C) Forelegs have broken through, tail is degenerating. (D) Limbs well developed, tail resorbed almost completely.

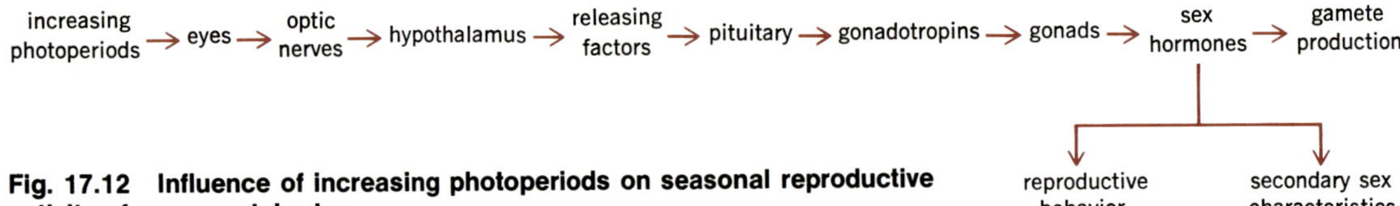

Fig. 17.12 Influence of increasing photoperiods on seasonal reproductive activity of many vertebrates.

of the hypothalamus bring about the release of pituitary hormones called *gonadotropins.* These control the functioning of the sex organs, ovaries and testes, collectively called *gonads.* The principal gonadotropins of vertebrates are *follicle-stimulating hormone* (FSH) and *luteinizing hormone* (LH).

Results of recent experiments suggest that *melatonin,* a hormone of the *pineal gland,* may also participate in regulating the reproductive cycles of some vertebrates. The pineal gland is a small, pea-shaped structure located in the midportion of the brain above the hypothalamus (see Fig. 17.2). Melatonin causes a marked lightening of skin when injected into frogs and several other cold-blooded vertebrates. The hormone therefore appears to oppose the effects of MSH in these animals. But when injected into rats, hamsters, and certain birds, melatonin inhibits production of sex cells and sex hormones by ovaries and testes. Moreover, secretion of melatonin increases sharply when these birds and mammals are subjected to short photoperiods, and it decreases with treatment by long photoperiods. It is not yet clear how melatonin inhibits the function of gonads in these animals, but some experimental evidence indicates that high concentrations of the hormone may reduce secretion of gonadotropin releasing factors from the hypothalamus. Thus, through its secretion of melatonin, the pineal gland may serve as a connecting link between the eyes and hypothalamus in regulating the photoperiodic reproductive cycles of vertebrates.

Once sufficient amounts of gonadotropins have been released from the pituitary, the gonads of a vertebrate enlarge and produce sex hormones. The latter secretions promote overt sexual behavior and the development of secondary sex characteristics. Such characteristics include all nonreproductive sex distinctions between males and females; many of them help bring potential mates together in courtship and help provide protection and nutrition of the young. Examples of secondary sex characteristics are the different patterns and colors of male and female birds. Such differences are influenced directly by sex hormones and often serve as mating signals between members of a species.

As day length reaches a maximum in early summer and then begins to shorten, a reduced hypothalamic stimulation brings about a correspondingly reduced output of gonadotropins. As a result, reproductive systems become increasingly quiescent, sexual behavior diminishes, and secondary sex characteristics often disappear.

Hormones and Carbohydrate Metabolism

Neuroendocrine systems not only respond to external stimuli but also control changes in the internal functions of an organism. Optimum concentrations of glucose in blood, for example, are maintained largely by hormones, and severe metabolic malfunctions occur if these concentrations are not maintained within narrow limits. The brain is particularly sensitive to prolonged excesses or deficiencies in the availability of glucose. Consequently, serious brain damage can result if the concentration of blood glucose fluctuates widely.

Diabetes mellitus, often simply called diabetes, is the most prevalent disease affecting the metabolism of glucose in people (see also Chap. 18). Diabetes is a rapidly increasing health problem. The number of diabetics in the United States, for example, has increased more than 300 per cent since 1950, while the population has grown only 50 per cent. This affliction results from malfunctions of the hormonal controls that regulate the uptake and use of glucose by many different cells. Glucose, either ingested or mobilized from nutrient storage sites of the body, cannot be absorbed by most tissues of diabetics. If such individuals are not treated, glucose accumulates excessively in their blood and urine. The high concentrations of blood glucose can lead to many serious consequences, including dangerous changes in the pH of blood, atherosclerosis, and other diseases of blood vessels, eye capillaries most

TABLE 17.3
Principal hormones regulating glucose metabolism

Hormone	Tissue of origin	Target tissue	Primary action
insulin	pancreas (β cells)	all tissues	increases uptake of glucose and amino acids by cells
glucagon	pancreas (α cells)	liver	stimulates breakdown of glycogen and promotes release of glucose from liver cells
thyroxine	thyroid	most tissues, especially muscle, liver, and kidney	increases metabolic rate
epinephrine and norepinephrine	adrenal medulla	most tissues	increases respiration of glucose, promotes release of glucose from cells to blood, and stimulates breakdown of fats
STH	anterior pituitary and pancreas	all tissues	increases glucose in blood; promotes uptake of amino acids by cells; increases breakdown of fats
corticoid hormones	adrenal cortex	most tissues	influences interconversions of carbohydrates, fats, and proteins

SOURCE: Modified from R. Eckert and D. Randall, "Animal Physiology," table 11.7, p. 353, Freeman, San Francisco, 1978.

particularly. Furthermore, a chemical called *sorbitol* accumulates rapidly in the lenses of eyes whenever the concentration of glucose in blood becomes excessive. This accumulation often leads to the formation of cataracts.

Although many cases of diabetes can be treated effectively, this disease remains the fifth leading cause of death and the second leading cause of blindness in the United States. Thus, study of the hormonal control of glucose metabolism is not simply academic.

As can be seen from Table 17.3, the concentration of glucose in body tissues is regulated by several interacting hormones, among them *insulin* and *glucagon,* hormones produced by the pancreas; *epinephrine* and *norepinephrine* (also called *adrenaline* and *noradrenaline,* respectively), hormones produced by the core region, or *medulla,* of the adrenal gland; several *corticoid* hormones, produced by cells of the adrenal cortex; and STH, produced by the anterior pituitary. In addition, thyroxine influences glucose metabolism generally

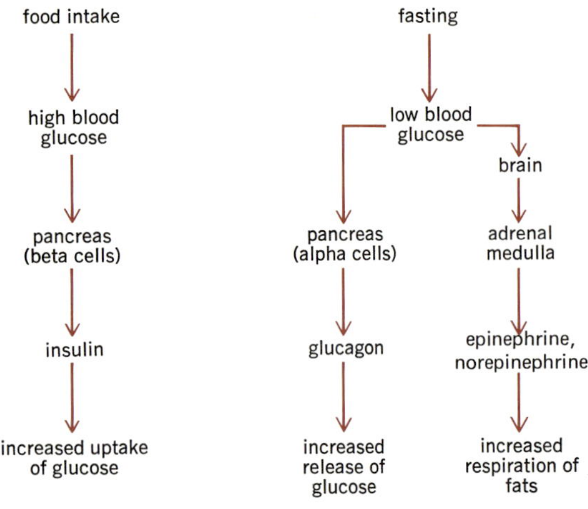

Fig. 17.13 Hormonal control of glucose concentrations in blood. (A) Eating increases the concentration of glucose in blood. Pancreatic beta cells respond to such high concentrations by releasing insulin into the bloodstream. Insulin promotes glucose uptake by the liver, adipose tissue, muscle, and several other tissues. (B) Fasting results in decreased concentrations of glucose in blood. Pancreatic alpha cells respond to such low concentrations by releasing glucagon, a hormone that promotes release of glucose from tissue to blood. Low concentrations of glucose in blood also result in increased secretion of epinephrine and norepinephrine from the adrenal medulla. The latter two hormones stimulate increased respiration of fats and promote decreased glucose uptake from blood (see also Table 17.3.)

by its overall control of the rates at which most molecules are metabolized in cells.

Directly or indirectly, the production and release of certain of these hormones is influenced greatly by the relative concentration of glucose in blood (Fig. 17.13). Following a meal, for example, glucose is absorbed by intestinal villi and transported through capillaries into the bloodstream (see Chap. 11). The increased concentration of blood glucose resulting from this uptake has two effects on certain specialized cells of the pancreas. These cells are located in clusters, called *islets of Langerhans,* scattered throughout the pancreas. Surrounding each islet are the more numerous nonendocrine cells of the pancreas that secrete digestive enzymes. Each islet contains two cell types, *alpha cells* and *beta cells.* The latter, which secrete insulin, are stimulated by increased concentration of blood glucose. The cells respond by releasing insulin into blood. The alpha cells, which produce glucagon, are inhibited by a rising concentration of insulin. Thus, the relative concentrations of insulin and glucagon in blood normally are related inversely.

Insulin stimulates uptake of glucose by most cells of a vertebrate, especially those of the liver, muscle, and fat-storing (*adipose*) tissue. Glucose is converted primarily to glycogen by liver and muscle, and to fat by adipose cells. In addition, insulin greatly increases the rate of glycolysis in muscle. The overall effect of an increased concentration of insulin, therefore, is a rapid clearance of glucose from the blood and a change to carbohydrates and fats, which are stored by body tissues. The beta cells of the pancreas respond to such decreased concentrations of glucose in blood by reducing their output of insulin. Accordingly, body tissues become progressively less permeable to glucose, and the synthesis of glycogen and fat slows down.

When the concentration of insulin falls sufficiently, alpha cells of the pancreas respond by releasing glucagon (see Fig. 17.13). In addition, nerve centers in the brain respond to low concentrations of blood glucose by transmitting nervous impulses to specialized nerve cells and to the adrenal medulla (see also Chap. 11). In their turn, these structures respond by secreting epinephrine and norepinephrine into body fluids. Glucagon, epinephrine, and norepinephrine all function as antagonists of insulin. For example, the three hormones stimulate breakdown of glycogen to glucose by the liver, and they also promote conversion of the amino acids to carbohydrates.

Unlike glucagon, epinephrine and norepinephrine also greatly stimulate breakdown of fats to fatty acids and glycerol. This action has two general effects. First, it increases the quantity of nutrient fuels that can be respired directly by most cells. Second, it increases the availability of raw materials that can be converted rapidly to glucose. In diabetics, steady-state controls that regulate the release of epinephrine and norepinephrine usually function normally, but those regulating the balance between insulin and glucagon apparently do not. Subnormal amounts of insulin usually are released from the pancreas of diabetics, while the output of glucagon is almost always excessive.

Substantial amounts of epinephrine and norepinephrine are secreted whenever a vertebrate becomes frightened. As a result, the concentrations of glucose and fatty acids in blood undergo an equally rapid rise and thus supply large quantities of nutrient fuels for "fight or flight" responses. If the stimuli provoking such responses continue unabated for an extended period, the sustained high concentrations of hormones from the adrenal medulla trigger still another hormonal response. In such situations, the hypothalamus induces an increased release of ACTH from the anterior pituitary. As state earlier, this tropic hormone stimulates release of several corticoid hormones from the adrenal cortex. One of these is *hydrocortisone.* This hormone greatly increases the rate at which proteins are broken down and converted to glucose by many tissues, especially the liver. Other corticoid hormones shift metabolic balances such that the concentrations of fatty acids increase in cells.

STH also plays an important role in regulating carbohydrate metabolism. Like glucagon and epinephrine, STH promotes increased concentrations of glucose in blood; the hormone also accelerates conversion of glucose to glycogen in muscle. Further STH increases the rates at which stored fat is broken down to fatty acids. Regulation of glucose metabolism therefore involves many independent but closely integrated steady-state controls; some purely endocrine, others strictly neural, and still others consisting of a mixture of both.

Biologists gradually are increasing our knowledge of how hormones regulate carbohydrate metabolism and other cellular processes. It is now known, for example, that STH, ACTH, glucagon, and epinephrine all exert their effects by triggering release of cyclic AMP at the surface of target cells. Insulin probably opposes the effects of glucagon by stimulating release of cyclic GMP from the inner surface of the cell membrane. Indeed, cyclic AMP and cyclic GMP appear to be intracellular mediators for several sets of regulatory substances that produce opposing effects in target cells.

Like most steroids, corticoid hormones produce many of their effects by forming complexes with intracellular receptors. The complexes then bind to chromatin and regulate RNA transcription. One corticoid hormone, *cortisol,* triggers production of a specific set of carbohydrate-regulating enzymes in liver cells. Manufacture of these enzymes can be blocked completely when the cells are treated with actinomycin D and other inhibitors of protein synthesis.

But despite considerable progress, much remains to be discovered about the mechanics of hormone action. For example, some of the effects of cortisol on carbohydrate metabolism are not blocked by inhibitors of protein synthesis. Thus, cortisol probably exerts its effects on cells in more than one way. Other hormones also appear to influence different cell functions through different modes of action. Moreover, STH influences many cell processes by enhancing the effectiveness of other hormones. It appears to do so by producing in target tissues the kinds of environments that facilitate the actions of other hormones. Just how STH and other regulatory substances produce synergistic effects is not clear, but much research is now aimed at discovering how such substances interact to yield different net effects. Results of this research will further increase our knowledge of how cells are controlled normally, and this in turn will increase our ability to manipulate these controls when they malfunction.

In most animals steady-state regulation is achieved not only by hormones and growth factors in general, but also by various tissue- and organ-level control systems without counterparts in plants. These unique animal controls are examined in the following chapters.

Review Questions

1 Review the functional relations between endocrine and neurosecretory structures. The pituitary gland is sometimes called "the concert master of the endocrine orchestra." Is this an appropriate analogy? Why or why not?

2 How are hormones transported in blood to target structures? Review the principal ways in which hormones trigger intracellular responses. What are second messengers, and how are they produced? How do second messengers contribute to steady-state control? Can you account for the evolution of second messengers? (*Hint:* Compare the biochemical properties of hormones usually employing second messengers with the permeability characteristics of most cell membranes; see Chap. 5.)

3 Review the structural and functional relations between the hypothalamus and pituitary. How do releasing factors contribute to the functional integration of these two structures? Make a diagram showing how the hypothalamus and pituitary are influenced by the hormones of other endocrine glands and vice versa.

4 What are the specific hormones produced by the various endocrine glands of vertebrates? As far as is known, what are the primary cellular functions of each of these hormones? In each case, what are the clinical effects of hormone deficiency and hormone excess?

5 Review how neuroendocrine structures contribute to seasonal photoperiodic responses of vertebrates.

6 Describe the neuroendocrine mechanisms that regulate the metabolism and intercellular transport of glucose in vertebrates. What is the "fight or flight" response of vertebrates? How do hormones contribute to this response?

7 Has your reading of the Biology Highlight in this chapter changed your view of how scientific research is conducted? If so, how?

8 In what respects are the actions of hormones, vitamins, and minerals similar, and in what respects are they different? (Review Chap. 15.)

Collateral Readings

Eckert, R., and **D. Randall:** "Animal Physiology," Freeman, San Francisco, 1978. This well-illustrated text contains a good treatment of animal hormones.

Gardner, L. I.: Deprivation Dwarfism, *Scientific American,* July 1972. This article describes how environmental factors can influence the secretion of growth hormone.

Guillemin, R.: Peptides in the Brain: The New Endocrinology of the Neuron, *Science,* vol. 202, pp. 390–402, Oct. 27, 1978. This article gives background for the Biology Highlight of this chapter and that of Chapter 19.

——— and **R. Burgus:** The Hormones of the Hypothalamus, *Scientific American,* November 1972. Reviews relation between hypothalamus and pituitary.

LeBaron, R.: "Hormones: A Delicate Balance," Pegasus, New York, 1972. A highly readable book on the structure and functions of vertebrate endocrine organs that requires little technical background.

Levine, S.: Stress and Behavior, *Scientific American,* January 1971. The relations between hormones, stress, and learning are discussed.

Notkins, G. L.: The Causes of Diabetes, *Scientific American,* November 1979. Describes and contrasts the two principal types of diabetes mellitus, the maturity- and juvenile-onset forms.

O'Malley, B. W., and **W. T. Schrader:** The Receptors of Steroid Hormones, *Scientific American,* February 1976. This article describes how steroids influence gene transcription by interacting with protein receptors of cells.

Pastan, I.: Cyclic AMP, *Scientific Amercian,* August 1972. The discovery and functions of this ubiquitous substance are described.

Schally, A. V.: Aspects of Hypothalamic Regulation of the Pituitary Gland, *Science,* vol. 202, pp. 18–28, Oct. 6, 1978. The author gives his account of the search for hypothalamic regulatory hormones.

Turner, C. D., and **J. T. Bagnara:** "General Endocrinology," Saunders, Philadelphia, 1976. Perhaps the most comprehensive of the introductory textbooks in this field.

Vander, A. J., J. H. Sherman, and **D. S. Luciano:** "Human Physiology," 3d ed., McGraw-Hill, New York, 1980. Good sections on how hormones integrate functions of the human body.

Chapter 18 Intercellular Control

Learning Objectives

After reading this chapter you should be able to:

1. List the functional relations among the circulatory, breathing, and excretory systems of animals.
2. Differentiate between blood, lymph, and interstitial fluid, and list the principal function of each; distinguish between open and closed circulatory systems; define blood sinus.
3. Differentiate between blood plasma and blood serum; list at least five components of blood plasma, and state a function for each component you identify.
4. List at least three cellular components of blood and name at least one function for each; identify the principal relationships between hemoglobin, bilirubin, jaundice, and the liver; name the source and role of erythropoietin in maintaining optimum concentrations of oxygen in blood; list in sequence the reactions that lead to blood clotting and state the role of blood platelets in this process; differentiate between phagocyte, leukocyte, and lymphocyte, and give the principal functions of each.
5. List at least two changes that occur in tissues during inflammation; define gamma globulin.
6. Indicate the functional relations between each of the following:
   - **a.** antibodies and antigens
   - **b.** antibodies and complement proteins
   - **c.** B cells and antibodies
   - **d.** B cells and plasma cells
   - **e.** B cells and memory cells
   - **f.** B cells and T cells
7. Differentiate between humoral and cellular immune responses; between primary and secondary immune responses; between immune agglutinates and immune lysis; show how the spleen and lymph nodes contribute to the immune response.
8. Construct a diagram that depicts the structural relations between the two light and two heavy chains of an antibody; identify the antigen-attachment sites, the variable regions, and the constant regions of an antibody.
9. Show why the first exposure of a person to an antigen usually is counteracted more slowly than a second exposure to the same antigen.
10. Indicate one way in which B cells are influenced by a cooperative interaction with T cells; distinguish between natural and induced tolerance; list at least two diseases that are now thought to result from a breakdown of steady-state controls governing natural tolerance.
11. Identify a principal cause and effect of histamine release by mast cells; name at least two remedies that relieve the discomforting symptoms of hay fever.
12. Outline the structural and functional relations between the principal organs of vertebrate circulatory systems; specify at least one structural and one functional difference between arteries and veins, between arteries and capillaries, between veins and lymphatics; state the chief function of lymphatic systems.
13. List the structural and functional relations between the main parts of the mammalian heart; list in order the events that occur during a complete heartbeat; list the functional relations between the medulla oblongata, vagus nerves, pacemaker, AV node, and bundle of His in the control of heartbeat; illustrate how at least two nonnervous factors control heartbeat; differentiate between the heart-rate center and the vasomotor center of the medulla oblongata, list factors that influence each of these centers, and show how these centers regulate heartbeat and blood pressure.
14. Define atherosclerosis, plaque, coronary arteries, coronary thrombosis, and stroke; list five factors that are related statistically to an increased risk of heart attack; outline at least three steps that can be taken to reduce the risk of heart attack.
15. Describe the anatomical and functional relations between the following components of the mammalian breathing system:
    - **a.** pharynx
    - **b.** trachea

   c. larynx
   d. glottis
   e. epiglottis
   f. bronchioles
   g. alveoli

16. List the functional relations between the following structures in an inhalation-exhalation cycle of the mammalian breathing system:
   a. intrathoracic cavity
   b. diaphragm
   c. rib muscles
   d. stretch receptors of lungs
   e. medulla oblongata

17. State the chief causes and effects of the hyperventilated condition and the "bends"; specify the functional role of hemoglobin and list the conditions that trigger interconversions of hemoglobin and oxyhemoglobin; list two ways in which CO_2 is transported by blood and show how concentrations of CO_2 in blood influence breathing rates; show why carbon monoxide is a poison.

18. List and give examples of the three kinds of processes performed by excretory systems; differentiate between initial urine and final urine; list at least three organs of human beings that perform excretory functions.

19. State the structural and functional relations between the glomerulus and the nephric (Bowman's) capsule of a nephron.

20. Describe where and how urine becomes concentrated as it passes through a nephron; show how the hairpin design of Henle's loop contributes to water reabsorption in the mammalian kidney; name two hormones that influence reabsorption of substances from initial urine.

21. List the anatomical and functional relations between the ureters, bladder, and urethra.

22. Construct a table that shows how final urine differs from initial urine with respect to the kinds and concentrations of substances present in each.

Cells are in steady state relative to their immediate surroundings. In an animal these surroundings are other cells and, in vertebrates, three body fluids, *blood, lymph,* and *interstitial fluid.* The first two are contained in specialized vessels that transport the fluids throughout the body. The third, interstitial fluid, fills all the spaces between cells. A diffuse group of specialized cells exists in body fluids and, through their *immune response,* some of these cells destroy pathogenic organisms and other potentially harmful substances. In effect, the body fluids are not only the general transport vehicle in the body but also major controllers of steady states within and between cells; cells and tissues reflect the conditions prevailing in body fluids and vice versa.

The attributes of the body fluids are controlled primarily by three systems. The *circulatory* system regulates the physical properties of the fluids it carries, such as pressure, distribution, and rate of flow. And the *breathing* and *excretory* systems govern the chemical properites of the body fluids. Both systems continuously monitor and adjust the composition of the body fluids, and they control the exchange of materials between body fluids and the external environment. In the process they also determine what is or is not a waste product.

BLOOD AND INTERSTITIAL FLUID

Blood is a tissue confined either partly or wholly within a set of specialized tubes called *blood vessels.* Blood and blood vessels together constitute the *circulatory system.* Two kinds of circulatory systems exist in animals, *open* and *closed* (Fig. 18.1). In the latter, blood vessels form a complete, self-contained circuit, and the only access to and exit from such a system is *through* the vessel walls. Closed circulatory systems are found in all vertebrates and in some invertebrates. Blood vessels of open circulatory systems have open ends, and blood therefore flows partly through vessels, partly through free spaces in the body. Such spaces usually are termed *blood sinuses* (see Fig. 18.1). Open systems of this type occur in clams, insects, spiders, and many other invertebrates. Open circulatory systems are described in greater detail in other chapters; most of this chapter deals with the closed systems of humans and other vertebrates.

Plasma

Blood consists of two components: liquid *plasma,* and *cellular elements* suspended in plasma.

The main ingredient of plasma is water. Its source is food and metabolic water exported from cells to the body fluids. The supply of water is carefully adjusted by elimination of excess amounts through the breathing and excretory systems. In this fashion the total water content of the body, hence blood volume, is maintained constant. The water of plasma also influences blood pressure, and it is the transport vehicle of cellular elements, of dissolved nutrients, and numerous other substances. Except for proteins and other very large molecules, most materials in plasma readily pass through the walls of the smallest blood vessels to the surrounding tissues. This intercellular liquid, or *interstitial fluid*, provides an aqueous environment for all parts of the body.

Materials dissolved in plasma are of two general types (Table 18.1). One comprises substances that fluctuate more or less widely in concentration, depending on body activity. In this category are a number of foods, hormones, certain waste products (urea, for example), and many other compounds. In the second group are components normally maintained at constant concentrations. Included here are water itself, mineral ions, nutrients such as glucose, and numerous other compounds that are either nutrients in transit to tissue cells or waste products in transit to the excretory organs.

Constancy in the concentration of these substances is achieved by a balance between supply and removal. Supplies are obtained by tissue cells from interstitial fluid via the alimentary system, particularly the gut and the liver. Removal of materials from tissue cells usually involves diffusion to interstitial fluid and transfer to the circulatory system. Waste products then are processed and eliminated through the excretory system. In each case too high or too low a concentration of a given substance in blood is the critical stimulus for its own removal or replenishment. For example, a moderately high blood-glucose level stimulates release of hormones that promote uptake of glucose by liver cells (see Chap. 17). Such cells convert the excess glucose to glycogen. A higher blood-glucose level stimulates carbohydrate storage not only in liver but also in muscle and skin; a very high concentration leads to glucose excretion from the kidneys.

The mineral ions in plasma are of the same types as those in interstitial fluid and in the interior of cells generally. These ions contribute to

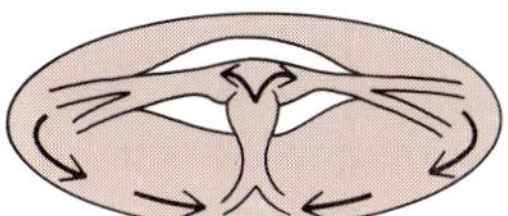
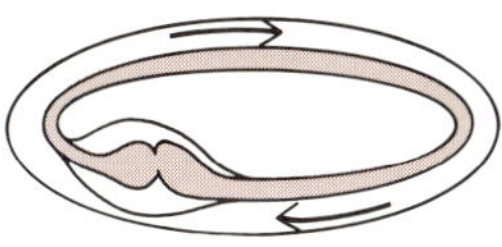

A B

Fig. 18.1 Open and closed circulatory systems. (A) In animals with open systems, such as a snail or clam, blood flows out of vessels into blood sinuses (open colored area). Movement of blood to and from blood vessels is through open ends of the blood vessels themselves. Clams and other mollusks have a small body cavity (white) that surrounds the heart. (B) Animals such as vertebrates have closed systems. The vertebrate heart is located toward the ventral (belly) side. Blood is almost always retained in vessels, and exchange of gases and other substances occurs almost entirely through the vessel walls. A portion of the body cavity is partitioned off about the heart.

TABLE 18.1

The Main Components of Blood Plasma and Their Functions*

Component	Function
1. water	maintains blood volume and pressure; constitutes principal component of interstitial fluid and lymph
2. mineral ions	maintain osmotic balance, pH balance; buffer capacity; varied effects on tissue cells
3. plasma proteins	all maintain osmotic and pH balance
a. fibrinogen	participates in blood clotting
b. prothrombin	participates in blood clotting
c. albumins, enzymes	functions obscure
d. globulins	basis of some blood types; act as antibodies
4. glucose, other organic metabolites	in transit to and from cells
5. urea, CO_2, O_2, various foods, hormones, vitamins, and others	in transit to and from cells

*Categories 1 to 4 are maintained at constant concentrations; materials in category 5 occur in variable concentrations.

salt, pH, and *osmotic balance* between plasma, interstitial fluid, and tissue cells. For example, if intake of excess salt should cause the mineral concentration of blood to rise, the tissues would lose water osmotically and would become dehydrated. Conversely, if intake of too much plain water should cause the ion concentration in blood to fall, the tissues would gain water. Temporary fluctuations of this sort (and accompanying pH changes) can occur frequently; but fairly narrow limits are imposed by the excretory organs, which eliminate any excess material. From hour to hour, therefore, blood has constant osmotic pressure and pH; in human blood the pH normally is 7.3 or 7.4.

Plasma differs importantly from interstitial fluid in that it contains an appreciable concentration of *blood proteins,* another group of components kept at constant concentrations. In vertebrates these proteins are manufactured largely in the liver, they normally leave the circulation only in very limited amounts, and they function in a variety of nonnutritional roles. First, like the mineral ions, all these proteins contribute to maintaining the osmotic pressure and pH of blood. Particularly important in osmotic regulation are the *albumins,* blood proteins named after their chemical resemblance to egg white. Second, some of the proteins are ingredients in the *clotting* reaction (see below). Third, many of the proteins are active enzymatically. One such enzyme, *prothrombin,* is a clotting factor. Fourth, blood proteins called globulins are the basis of differences in several blood types of animals, a consequence of the general phenomenon of protein specificity. And lastly, other proteins, including many globulins, participate in the immune response (see below).

Apart from its protein content, plasma in many animals differs from interstitial fluid also in another respect, the presence of oxygen-carrying pigments. However, in a good many vertebrates such pigments occur not in plasma but in certain of the cellular elements of blood.

Cellular Elements

The blood of many animals contains pigmented cells, and most bloods also contain nonpigmented cells of various kinds (Fig. 18.2). Pigmented blood cells in vertebrates are manufactured in the liver and spleen of embryos and the bone marrow of adults. These cells derive their color from oxygen-carrying pigments dissolved in their cytoplasms. As their name implies, such pigments chiefly transport oxygen, but CO_2 is carried to some extent too (see below). Hemoglobin (Hb) is by far the most widespread oxygen-carrying pigment; its presence has been demonstrated in most animals and even in some protists. This compound consists of a red iron-containing pigment *heme* (chemically similar to cytochromes) and of the protein *globin.*

In mammals the nuclei of pigmented blood cells disintegrate as they mature. Lacking nuclei, the life span of such *red blood cells* is relatively short, approximately 120 days in human beings. The numbers of red blood cells are maintained constant; the spleen and to some extent also the liver destroy such cells while bone marrow manufactures them. It has been estimated that, in human blood,

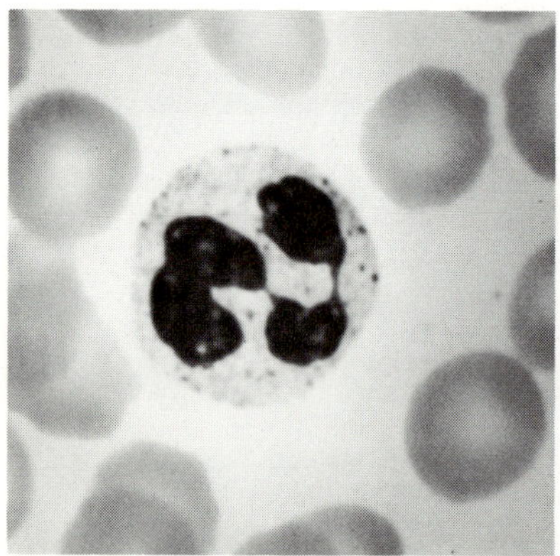

A

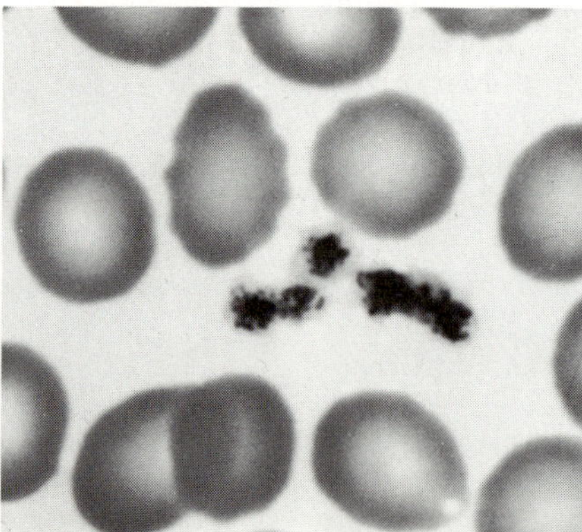

B

Fig. 18.2 Blood cells. Human red blood cells are shown in both photos. Note absence of nuclei. (A) White blood cell (nucleated) is shown in center. (B) A few blood platelets in center. See also Fig. 5.5. (*General Biological Supply House, Inc.*)

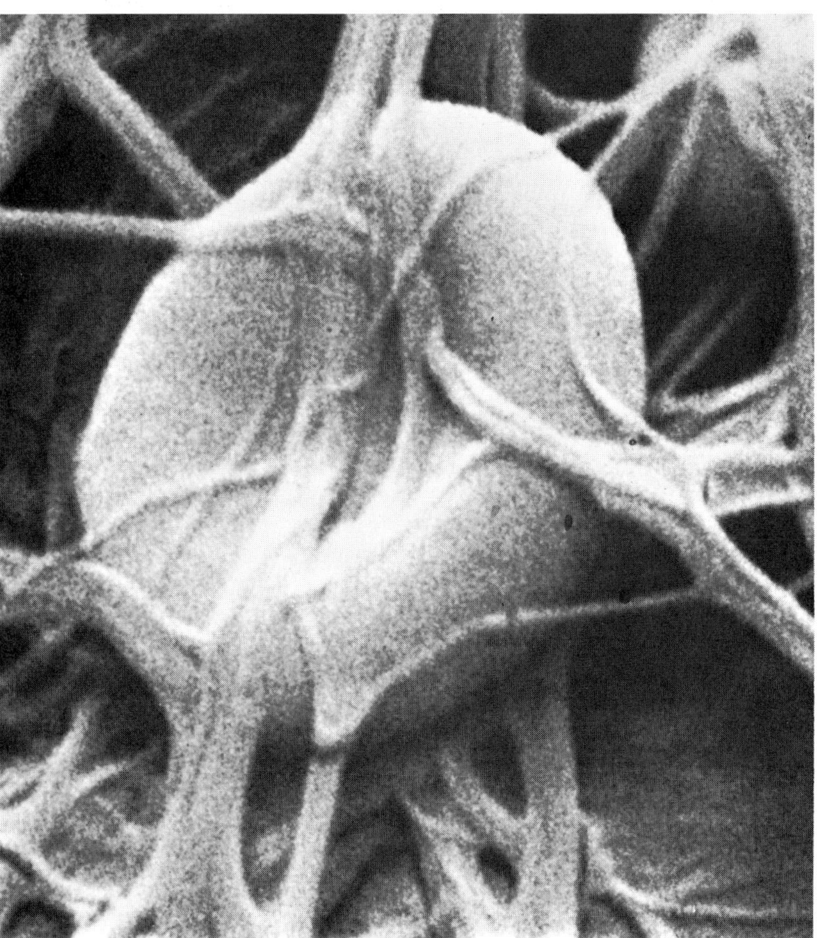

Fig. 18.3 Fibrin. Scanning electron micrograph of red blood cell trapped in a meshwork of fibrin (×10,000).

some 10 million red blood cells are destroyed every *second*. This amount may seem very large, but the total number of red blood cells in an average person is about 25 *trillion*, making them the most abundant cellular element in blood.

Hemoglobin is decomposed during the destruction of red blood cells and converted to a yellow-red compound called *bilirubin*, which is released to the blood. Bilirubin then is absorbed by the liver and becomes a component of bile. Only small amounts of bilirubin are absorbed by diseased or damaged livers, and its accumulation in blood can give a yellow color to skin. Such a condition is called *jaundice*.

The manufacture of red blood cells is controlled directly by *erythropoietin*, a complex molecule produced mainly by the kidneys, and influenced by the concentration of oxygen in blood. The rate of erythropoietin production is inversely proportional to the concentration of oxygen in blood. In turn, the rate of red blood cell manufacture by bone marrow is directly proportional to the amount of erythropoietin released into blood by the kidneys. In this example of steady-state control, the oxygen concentration of blood is a stimulus, the kidneys are receptors, bone marrow functions as a modulator, and oxygen-carrying red blood cells constitute effectors.

Bone marrow also generates the *platelets* of vertebrate blood (see Fig. 18.2B). Produced by the fragmentation of larger cells, these nonpigmented spherical bodies often lack nuclei. Like red blood

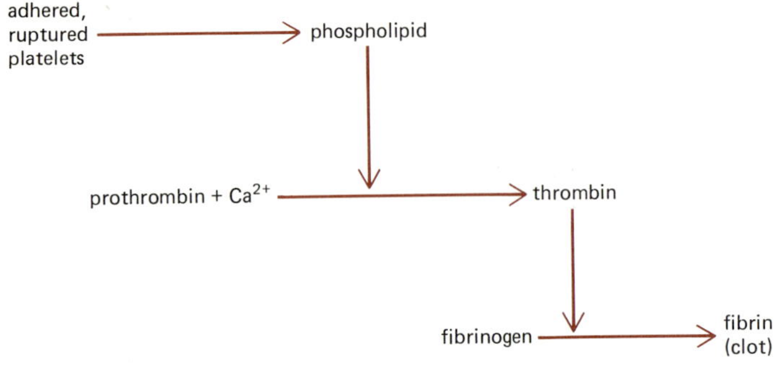

Fig. 18.4 Summary of blood-clotting mechanism.

cells, the number of platelets normally is constant; a cubic millimeter of human blood contains some 250,000 platelets, on the average.

Platelets play an important role in preventing excessive loss of blood from severed or damaged blood vessels. These cellular elements quickly adhere to the rough edges of torn vessels and often rupture as they adhere. The attachment and rupturing trigger release of several chemicals from platelets, including ADP (adenosine diphosphate). ADP causes the surfaces of adhered platelets to become very sticky, so that new platelets readily attach to those already there. As a result, a plug of ruptured platelets rapidly forms at the injured site. In addition, the aggregated platelets release *serotonin* and *epinephrine,* two hormones that stimulate contraction of muscles in the walls of blood vessels. The contraction significantly narrows damaged vessels, thereby minimizing loss of blood from an open wound.

Platelets also participate in the formation of blood clots, a process that further restricts loss of blood from torn vessels. Blood clots result from the enzymatic conversion of a soluble blood protein, *fibrinogen,* to an insoluble coagulated protein, *fibrin.* In this reaction several small polypeptides are split from fibrinogen. The remaining large molecule then readily forms side-to-side and end-to-end interconnections with others like it. The resulting end product, fibrin, forms as a yellowish-white meshwork of fibers. Since pigmented cellular elements quickly become trapped in this meshwork, the clot is usually red (Fig. 18.3).

The catalyst for the conversion of fibrinogen to fibrin is the protein *thrombin.* This enzyme, which is not normally present in blood in an active form, usually is produced only where blood vessels have been damaged. Such injuries trigger a complex series of reactions that result in the manufacture of thrombin from an inactive precursor molecule called *prothrombin,* normally present in blood (Fig. 18.4). The reaction sequence requires participation of calcium and other mineral ions, and also a phospholipid cofactor released from platelets that have ruptured at the edges of damaged blood vessels. Platelet phospholipid, thrombin, and all other active components of the clotting response are inactivated rapidly, and thus are not transported throughout the circulatory system. Quick inactivation of these substances is highly adaptive, for it prevents widespread clotting of blood in undamaged vessels.

Clotting cannot occur when any of the ingredients are missing or inoperative. For example, fibrinogen can be removed fairly easily from whole blood or plasma, a procedure often used in storing blood or plasma for transfusions. Plasma minus fibrinogen is *blood serum.* Clotting also is inhibited in the absence of calcium or when blood platelets are defective. In one type of human hereditary disease, platelets are not produced. In another, platelets have thickened membranes that do not rupture on contact with obstructions. In either of these *bleeder's diseases* the slightest wound can be fatal.

Most nonpigmented blood cells perform their functions in interstitial fluid or lymph, and many of them are capable of amoeboid movement. Called *white blood cells,* or *leukocytes,* such cells can squeeze themselves past adjacent cells of a capillary vessel and enter interstitial fluid (Fig. 18.5).

Most white blood cells contribute to body defense. *Phagocytic leukocytes,* for example, migrate

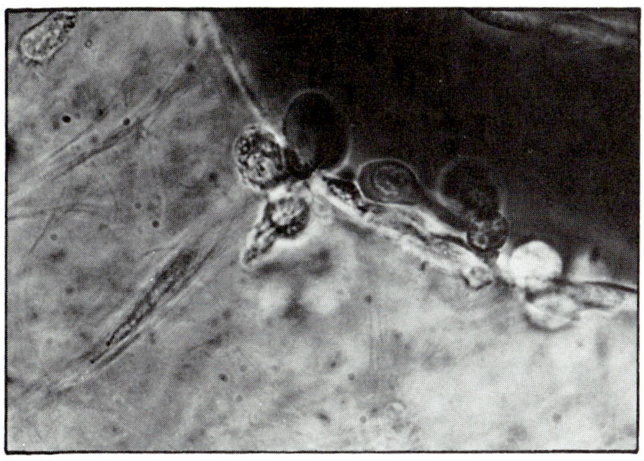
A

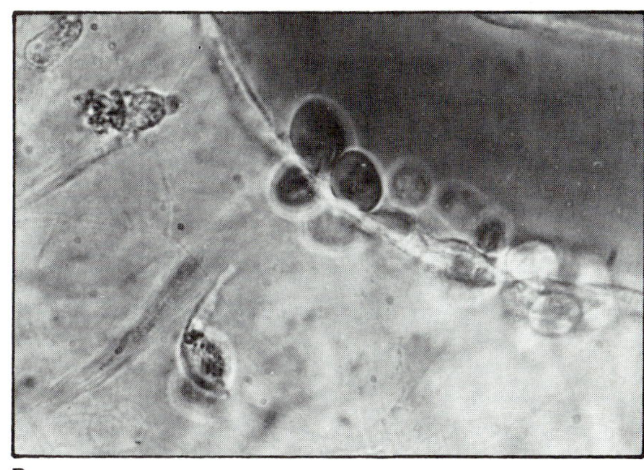
B

Fig. 18.5 Blood cell migration. A blood-filled capillary is in the upper right portion of each photograph. (A) Two white blood cells have just penetrated through the capillary wall into surrounding tissues. (B) The white blood cells have migrated farther into the tissues. (*Courtesy of Robert Brenner, Oregon Regional Primate Research Center.*)

in amoeboid fashion to sites of infection and engulf bacteria present there (Fig. 18.6). Others, called *lymphocytes*, attack foreign cells directly or secrete molecules that immobilize foreign substances. The various ways leukocytes and other blood cells protect vertebrates against pathogenic microorganisms, dust particles, and other "foreign" substances that enter body fluids are known collectively as the *immune response.*

THE IMMUNE RESPONSE

Suppose several populations of pathogenic bacteria and viruses enter your body through a cut in your skin. By reproducing and releasing toxic substances, these microorganisms can produce illness by infecting tissues and disrupting steady-state controls.

Inflammation

The first response of infected tissues to invading microbes is *inflammation*. Blood vessels enlarge in diameter, increasing blood flow to such tissues. In addition, the walls of these dilated vessels become highly permeable to plasma proteins, which accumulate in interstitial fluid. Large amounts of water and dissolved ions accompany this flow of plasma proteins, greatly increasing the volume of interstitial fluids and producing the characteristic swelling of inflamed tissues. All these responses to infection are highly adaptive. Larger supplies of blood increase the number of amoeboid leukocytes in infected tissues, promoting destruction of bacteria and other foreign particles. Increased permeability of blood vessels to large molecules ensures an adequate supply of proteins that participate in several other kinds of immune responses to be described below.

Most of the changes in blood-vessel diameter and permeability are triggered by the chemical *histamine* and by a group of polypeptides called *kinins.* Histamine is secreted by certain leukocytes and by certain connective tissue cells in response to injury or when such cells encounter foreign substances. In addition to its effects on blood vessels, histamine promotes contraction of many involuntary muscles, particularly those controlling the diameter of breathing passages in lungs (see accompanying Biology Highlight). Kinins are produced from proteins that circulate in blood plasma.

Lymphocytes

Lymphocytes constitute another "line of defense" against proliferation of microorganisms in vertebrate tissue. These cells are able to detect differences in the surface configurations of many molecules. The proteins, polysaccharides, and other

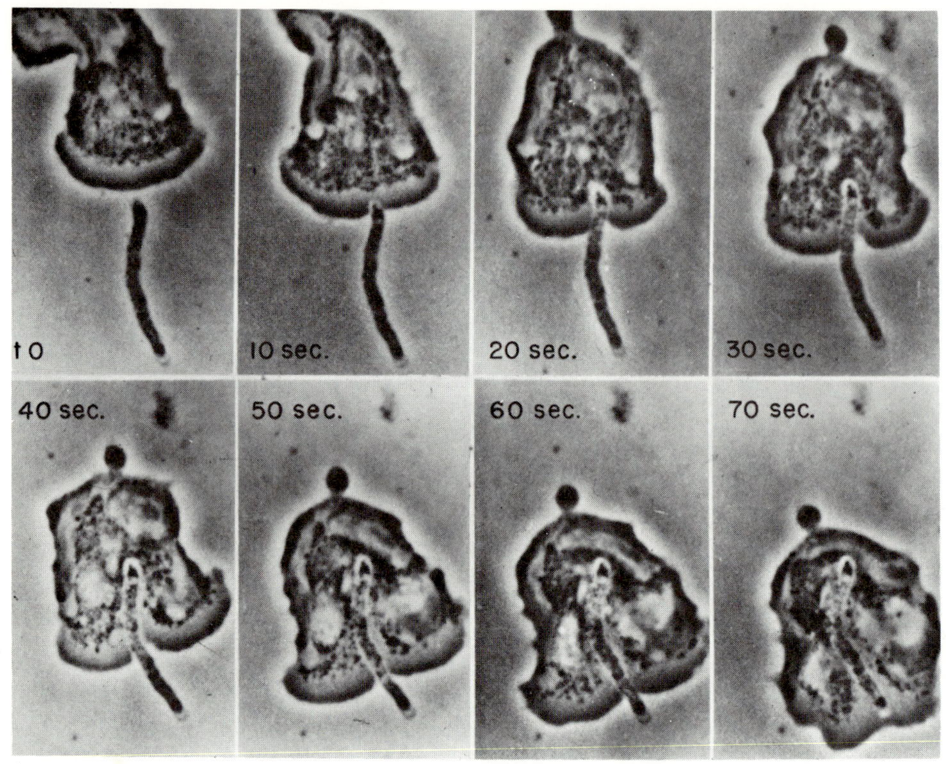

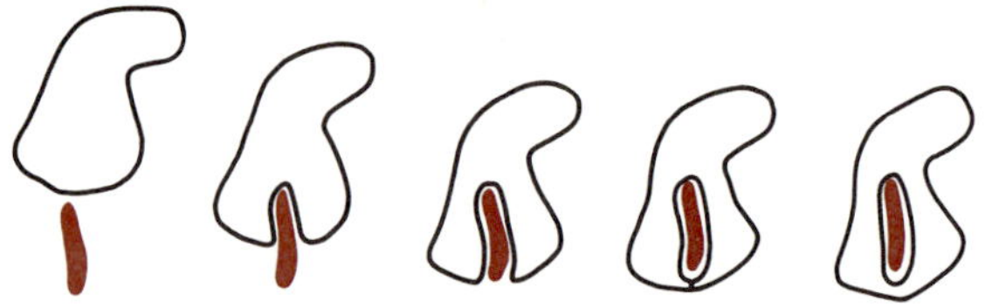

Fig. 18.6 Cellular engulfment. (A) Prints from a motion picture of a human leukocyte engulfing a bacterium. (B) The same engulfment depicted diagrammatically.

large molecules making up your cells have unique surface configurations that distinguish them from similar molecules making up bacteria, viruses, or even the cells of another human being. Such surface configurations are called *epitopes*, or *antigenic determinates*, and all molecules that have them are called *antigens*.

Humoral Immune Response

Certain lymphocytes, called *B cells*, originate in bone marrow (Fig. 18.7). When mature, these cells produce *antibodies*, a class of molecules belonging to the family of proteins known as *immunoglobulins*. These antibodies are subdivided into five categories, according to differences in chemical structure and biological function. The categories are designated by the letters G, A, M, D, and E affixed to the symbol Ig (for immunoglobulin); IgG, for example.

Like antigens, each antibody has a distinct shape that enables it to attach only to a complementary epitope of an antigen. Thus, union between individual antigens and antibodies is a highly specific process. Antibody production by B

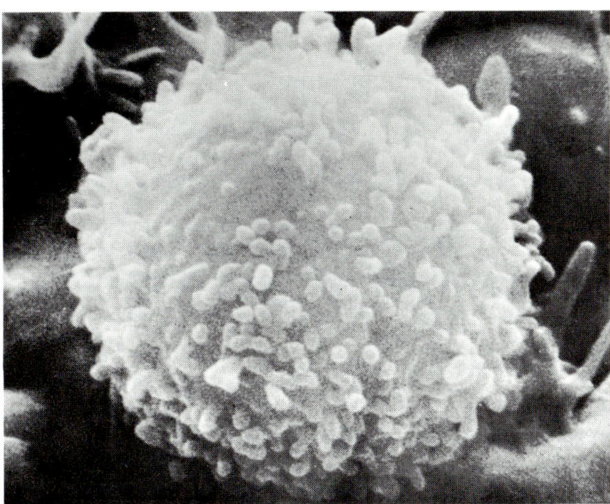

Fig. 18.7 Scanning electron micrograph of a lymphocyte. Note the abundant fingerlike projections of the cell membrane. (*Courtesy of Robert A. Good, Memorial Sloan-Kettering Cancer Center.*)

cells constitutes one of two general types of immune responses generated by lymphocytes. Because substances released into body fluids were once called "humors," the production and release of antibodies is termed the *humoral immune response.*

Fig. 18.8 Antibody structure. The structure of IgG, the most common type of antibody, is illustrated here. The two longer heavy chains and two shorter light chains of these antibodies are joined by pairs of linked sulfur atoms called disulfide bridges. Each chain contains a variable region (white) and a constant region (gray). Different IgG antibodies contain different sequences of amino acids in the variable regions.

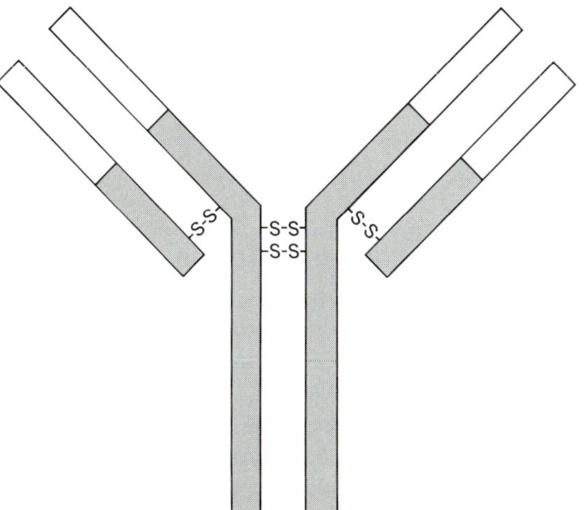

All antibodies basically consist of four joined polypeptide chains: two identical smaller polypeptides, called *light chains,* and two identical large polypeptides, called *heavy chains.* A light chain consists of about 220 amino acids; each heavy chain contains about twice as many. In the most common type of antibody, IgG, the four chains are bound together as a single Y-shaped molecule (Fig. 18.8). Moreover, all such antibodies are almost identical except for terminal sequences of amino acids located along the branches of the Y. This end of an antibody is the so-called *variable region,* and it is here that structural modifications at the end of each branch enable antibodies to interlock with complementary epitopes on antigens. The structural modifications at each end branch of an antibody are identical. One antibody, therefore, can attach to two antigens simultaneously, one to each branch of the Y. Also, because antigens usually have more than one epitope, individual antigens often become bonded to several antibodies simultaneously. Consequently, a complex lattice is formed in which each antibody is attached to two antigens, and each antigen is attached to two or more antibodies (Fig. 18.9). Such lattices then are engulfed and destroyed by amoeboid white cells.

Fig. 18.9 Antigen-antibody lattices. In this example, each antigen bears four epitopes, and each antibody can interlock with two adjacent antigens.

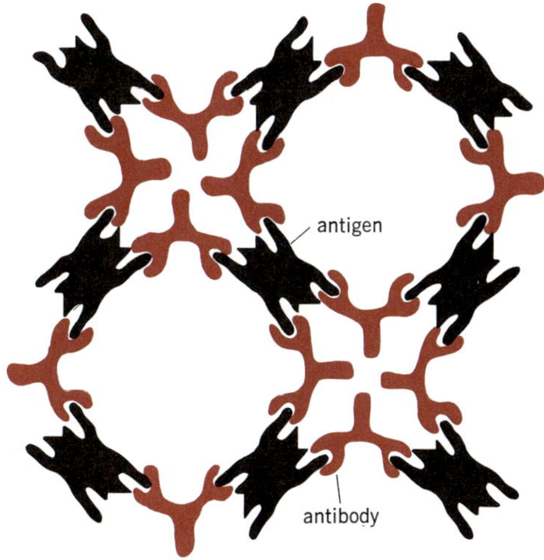

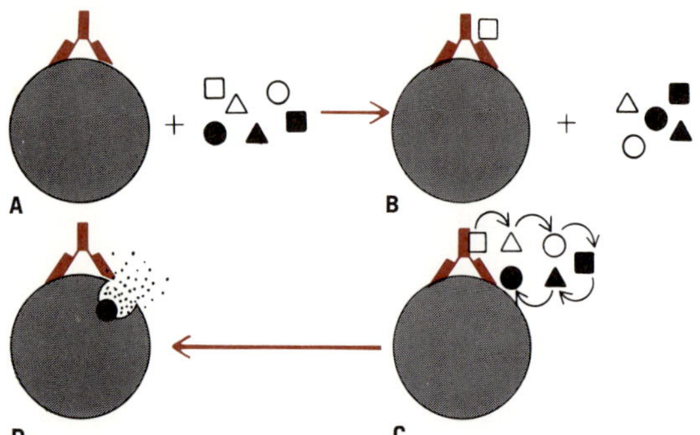

Fig. 18.10 Immune lysis. (A) Binding to antigen probably produces a small change in the shape of an antibody, thereby exposing a site for attachment of a complement protein. (B) One of the complement proteins attaches to the antibody. (C) A sequence of chemical reactions follows, involving several complement proteins. (D) The last complement protein in the reaction sequence digests the cell membrane, and the cell bursts.

In this way, antibodies can neutralize poisonous substances, or *toxins,* secreted by many pathogenic bacteria. They also can interlock with viruses, thereby preventing their attachment to cells (see also Chap. 30). If antigens are components of a cell surface, such as a bacterial cell wall, these cells become trapped and immobilized by the meshlike lattice. Such *immune agglutinates* likewise are engulfed and destroyed by amoeboid white blood cells. An accumulation of white blood cells, immune agglutinates, and cellular debris in wounded areas is called *pus.*

Fig. 18.11 Lymph nodes. A section through a node is shown. The position of such nodes in the lymph system is illustrated in Fig. 11.17. (*Courtesy of Boris Gueft.*)

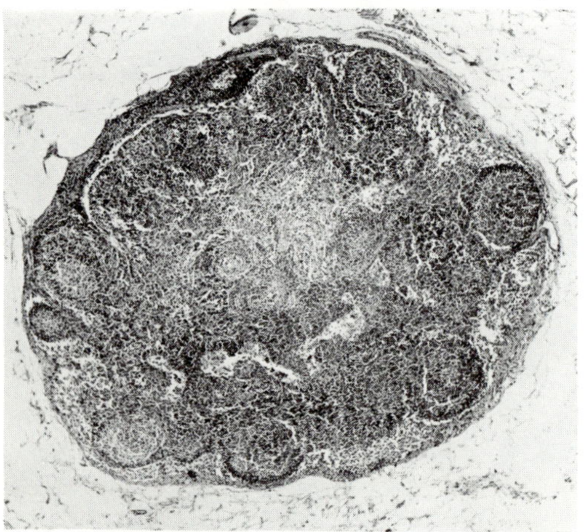

Antibodies also initiate a second process that destroys foreign cells. This process, called *immune lysis,* begins when antibodies attach to antigens at the surfaces of cells. The attachment produces a change in the configuration of the antibodies, enabling them to react with a set of *complement proteins* present in body fluids. These proteins are enzymes that remain inactive until they join with an antibody. The union of antibody with complement produces an enzymatically active complex that digests through the cell surface. As cells are thereby punctured, their contents spill out and the cells perish. The surfaces of dead bacteria that have been attacked in this manner resemble crater-scarred battlefields (Fig. 18.10). Some complement proteins function as attractors for amoeboid white blood cells, which then "home in" on the site of infection in increased numbers.

Thus, antibodies are exceedingly efficient molecules that act against antigens in a highly selective fashion. How does the selection process work? More basic research is needed to establish a definitive answer to this question, but a few general conclusions can be drawn.

As stated, antibodies are produced exclusively by lymphocytes called B cells. Following their production in bone marrow, B cells migrate to several sites within the bodies of vertebrates. The most important of these are the *spleen,* an organ located posteriorly to the liver and stomach of most vertebrates and *lymph nodes* (Fig. 18.11). The latter are ovoid or bean-shaped meshworks of cells and fibers that filter lymph as it is channeled back to the general circulation. Once stationed at such diverse locations, each B cell produces multiple copies of a specific antibody. In an animal not exposed to a particular antigen previously, the number of B cells able to produce antibodies complementary to its epitopes is relatively small. Moreover, none of these B cells actually secretes antibodies. Instead, each produces about 75,000 copies of its specific antibody that become attached to the outer surface of its cell membrane. If one of these "sample" antibodies binds to a complementary epitope, the B cell responds first by reproducing a large colony, or *clone,* of daughter B cells. Most of these daughter cells, called *plasma cells,* then produce large quantities of antibodies that are identical to those displayed on the surface of the parent cell. Unlike their parent, however, plasma cells release their antibodies into body fluids. The antibodies then are transported by body fluids from lymph nodes and other antibody-producing sites to all tissues of the body.

Overall, the process of antibody selection operates much like a factory containing millions of machines, each capable of producing a unique pair of shoes. None of these machines operates until a buyer comes into the factory requesting shoes of a specific shape, style, and size. Since the factory contains millions of slightly different machines, the chances are excellent that one of them will be capable of producing shoes with the desired characteristics.

In general, this is how specific antibodies are produced and selected. By a more or less random replacement of amino acids in the variable regions of heavy and light chains, millions of different antibodies are produced. Although any one B cell produces only one type of antibody, there is a sufficient total number of different kinds of antibody-producing B cells to virtually guarantee an effective response to practically any type of antigen.

The first encounter between antigens and antibodies constitutes the *primary immune response.* Immunity usually also implies increased resistance to subsequent invasions of pathogenic organisms. Indeed, resistance to a second occurrence of a disease often continues for many months or even years. For example, people who have had chicken pox usually are immune to the disease permanently; B cells capable of producing antibodies against chicken pox antigens respond more rapidly and efficiently to a second invasion of these antigens. Consequently, pathogenic organisms carrying such antigens are destroyed before they can multiply in great numbers.

This faster reaction to a subsequent invasion of antigen, called the *secondary immune response,* is accomplished by a specialized group of daughter cells produced during the first invasion of the antigen. This group, called *memory cells,* does not produce antibodies against a first invasion of antigens. Instead, these cells are programmed to produce antibody only during a later invasion of the same antigen (Fig. 18.12). Unlike their antibody-producing counterparts, memory cells persist long after a first invasion of the antigen and in numbers far greater than the original population of parent B cells. Moreover, memory cells generate large numbers of plasma B cells more quickly than the original parent cells. Thus, both the total number of antibodies and the rate of antibody production is increased in response to a second invasion of antigens.

Cellular Immune Response

Foreign cells are attacked and destroyed also by a second major type of lymphocyte, the *T cell.* Like

Fig. 18.12 Primary and secondary immune responses. B cells produce both plasma and memory cells in response to a first encounter with an antigen. Memory cells circulate in body fluids and rapidly produce large numbers of plasma cells in response to a second exposure to the antigen.

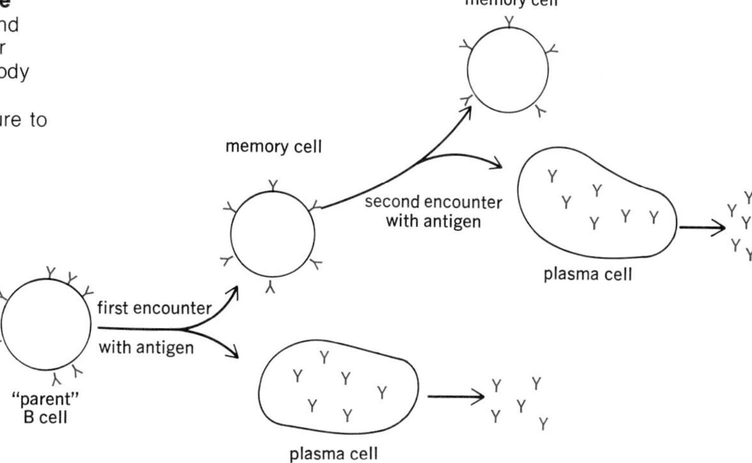

B cells, these white blood cells originate in bone marrow, but then they migrate to the *thymus gland* before their final release to the spleen and lymph nodes. The thymus, located in the chest of most mammals just above the heart, plays an important role in regulating maturation of T cells. For example, the thymus produces a hormone required for normal functioning of T cells. In addition, other aspects of T cell development are controlled by certain epithelial cells of the gland; still others appear to be influenced by a group of leukocytes that normally reside in the thymus.

T cells possess antibodylike receptor molecules along their surfaces. These receptors bind to epitopes of antigens like the surface antibodies of B cells. Unlike B cells, however, T cells do not produce antibody against the antigen. Instead, T cells travel from the spleen and lymph nodes to sites of infection where, upon combination with antigens, they release chemicals that either kill foreign cells directly, or attract other white blood cells, including more T cells. Such "sensitized" cells join the attack in large numbers and thus are able to destroy even considerable quantities of foreign cells relatively quickly. This reaction, called the *cellular immune response,* is the other general type of immune response generated by lymphocytes, and the one that frustrates most attempts to transplant tissues or organs between people.

To reduce this response, recipients of transplanted organs are treated with various drugs and procedures that reduce the population of active lymphocytes, particularly T cells. Such treatment, called *immune suppression,* decreases chances of organ rejection, but it also reduces the immune response to infection. Many patients who have died after receiving a transplanted organ have succumbed to infectious disease and not to failure of the transplanted organ. Undoubtedly, more sophisticated and reliable methods of combining immunologically different tissues will be developed when the cellular immune response is understood in greater detail.

Integration and Control

Lymphocyte interaction Recently it has been determined that T cells perform a second general function closely related to antibody production by B cells. This function can be illustrated by the following experiments. The immune response of an animal can be destroyed completely if its thymus gland is removed surgically and if the animal then is treated with a dose of x-irradiation sufficient to destroy its ability to produce lymphocytes. If T cells are injected into such a treated animal, its cellular immune response is restored but not its ability to manufacture antibodies. Alternatively, if lymphocytes derived exclusively from bone marrow are injected into a treated animal, its cellular immune response is not restored, *and its ability to produce antibody is restored only partially.* Since T cells cannot develop from bone marrow precursor cells in an animal whose thymus gland has been removed, the absence of a cellular immune response following injection is not surprising. But if B cells produce antibody independently, the injection of bone marrow should restore the humoral response almost completely.

Perhaps cooperation between B and T cells is necessary for total restoration of the humoral response. This hypothesis can be tested by injecting a treated animal with T cells *and* bone marrow cells. When this is done, both immune responses are restored completely. We conclude, therefore, that production of many antibodies by B cells is triggered directly or indirectly by T cells. Many other experiments have provided additional evidence supporting this conclusion. T cells that assist B cells in the secretion of antibodies are termed *helper cells* to distinguish them from *killer cells,* the variety of T cell that destroys foreign cells on contact. Other kinds of T cells also exist; some, for example, suppress antibody production by B cells, and still others suppress the cellular immune response of killer cells. Just how lymphocytes communicate with each other is not known, but much of this interaction appears to occur in lymph nodes (see Fig. 18.11).

Thus, the immune response cannot be viewed simply as the product of individual responses by independent cells. Instead, immune responses stem from dynamic interactions of several populations of cells, some cooperating, some producing antibody, some producing complement proteins, some stimulating, and some inhibiting. Successful interplay between parts of this diffuse combination of cells often eliminates all invading microorganisms from infected regions and paves the way for the final stage of the inflammatory process, *tissue repair.*

Biology Highlight

Wheezing In September: Causes and Effects

Do your eyes itch after passing a field of flowering ragweed? Do you sneeze after petting your neighbor's cat? Do your sinuses fill whenever you cut your lawn or dust the house? If so, you probably suffer from hay fever, a respiratory allergy afflicting about 20 per cent of the world's population.

Hay fever is caused by antigens located on the surfaces of pollen, dust, and other airborne particles. In allergic individuals, the antigens stimulate secretion of abnormally large amounts of IgE antibodies by plasma cells. These antibodies can trigger immune responses, some of them poorly understood, among several kinds of cells. One of the most important of these responses is produced by *mast cells,* a variety of secretory cell derived from precursor cells in bone marrow. Many circulating IgE antibodies become attached to specialized receptors on the plasma membranes of mast cells. The cytoplasm of these cells contains secretory vesicles (vacuoles) with high concentrations of *histamine* (Fig. 1). This molecule is identical to the amino acid histidine minus the carboxyl group.

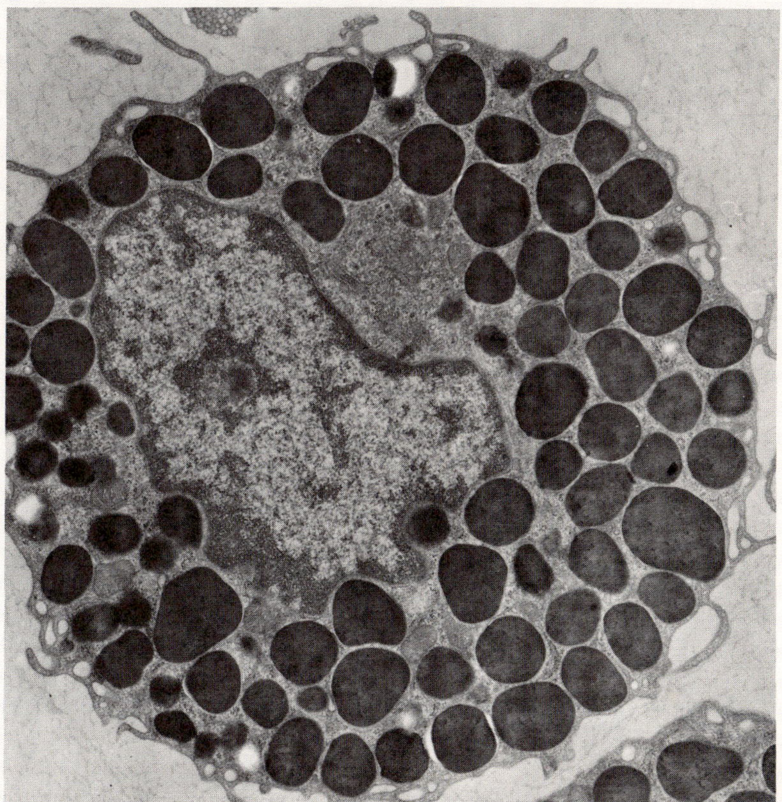

Fig. 1 Mast cells. The many darkly stained vacuoles of this mast cell are histamine-filled secretory vesicles. The more lightly stained, irregularly shaped structure in the left-center of the cell is the nucleus.

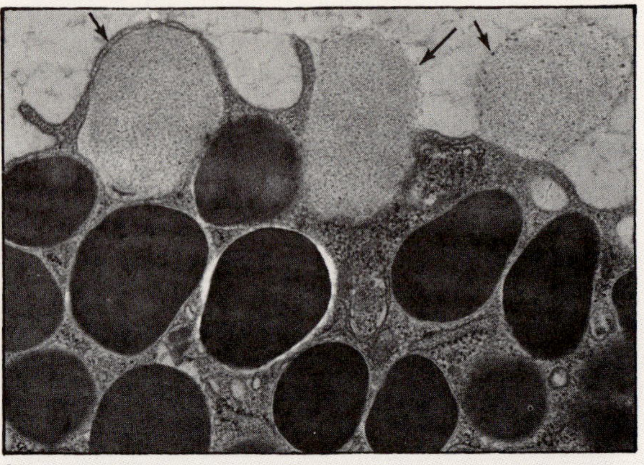

A

Fig. 2 Mast cell exocytosis. (A) Arrow at left points to a histamine-filled secretory vesicle fusing with the plasma membrane of a mast cell. Following fusion, the contents of the vesicle will be released to the extracellular environment, a process indicated by the arrows at right. (B) Mast cells become sensitized for exocytosis by the attachment of IgE antibodies at the cell surface. Exocytosis occurs if the cell encounters an antigen capable of cross-linking IgE antibodies.

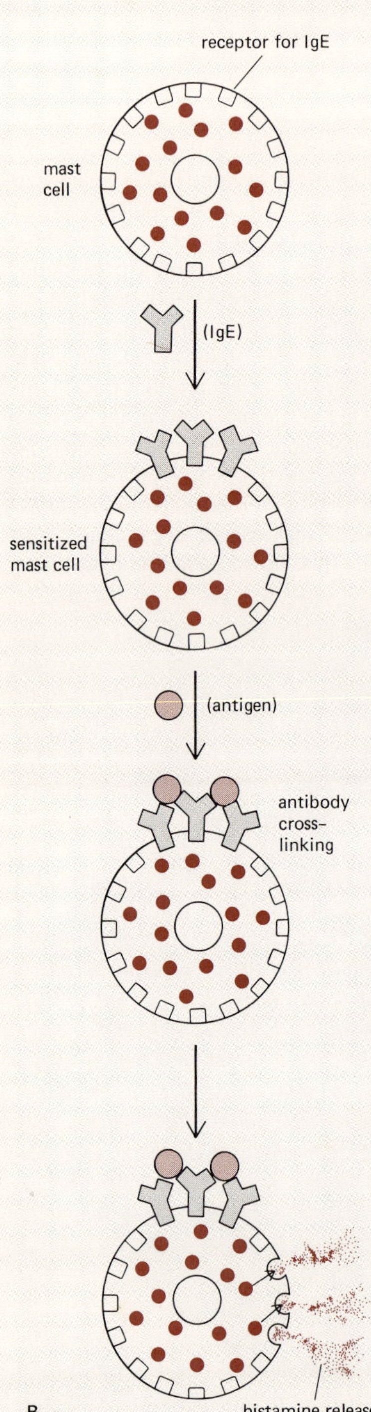

Histamine is secreted when antigens of pollen, dust, or other extraneous agents become linked to IgE antibodies positioned along the surface of mast cells. Binding of antigens and antibodies changes the permeability of mast cell membranes, permitting influx of calcium ions from the extracellular environment. By some unknown mechanism, the influx of calcium triggers exocytosis (see also Chap. 5); histamine vesicles migrate to the cell surface, unite with the plasma membrane, and release their contents to the extracellular environment (Fig. 2).

The importance of calcium ions to exocytosis of histamine vesicles has been demonstrated by several experiments. It is possible, for example, to place sensitized mast cells (cells with IgE antibodies attached to surface receptors) in a calcium-free liquid medium. Under such conditions, exocytosis does not occur when the cells are mixed with histamine-releasing antigens.

Many symptoms of hay fever are caused by released histamine. In association with other molecules, histamine produces local inflammation when it attaches to specialized receptors located on the surface membranes of various cells. The inflammatory response of lung tissue to histamine can be intense. Histamine not only dilates blood vessels in tissues lining the breathing passages but also stimulates secretion of mucus into these passages. In addition, it promotes contraction of the muscles controlling the diameter of bronchioles and other air channels. Consequently, people suffering from hay fever often complain of running noses, sneezing, and difficulty in breathing.

Certain kinds of molecules, collectively called *antihistamines,* can relieve some of the discomfort experienced by hay fever sufferers. A chief ingredient of hay fever pills, antihistamines compete with histamine for receptor sites on plasma membranes. Antihistamines do not trigger inflammatory responses; and they limit the annoying effects of histamine by blocking its receptors.

Another remedy for hay fever victims involves successive injections of progressively larger amounts of the offending antigens. This technique, which has been used for about 70 years, gradually reduces the allergic response of individuals. Mechanisms underlying both the immune and inflammatory responses are understood far better today than just a few years ago, and this knowledge has led to increasingly effective allergy "shots." The injections now reduce the symptoms of hay fever for about 70 per cent of allergic people who begin receiving shots a few weeks before the hay fever season begins and receive a sufficient number of injections.

Nevertheless, most physicians agree that the best (and usually least expensive) remedy for hay fever is simple avoidance of the troublesome antigens. Antihistamines and allergy shots sometimes produce side effects that can be almost as annoying as those of hay fever. Some people, for example, become very drowsy after taking certain kinds of antihistamines.

Despite recent improvements in our understanding of the mechanisms responsible for respiratory allergies, one puzzling question remaining concerns the evolutionary significance of hay fever. Because they usually are far more damaging to the body than the antigens themselves, these allergic reactions appear to be highly maladaptive. In some people the reactions can lead to respiratory arrest and death. Why should maladaptive responses persist? Doesn't evolution always eliminate such responses from populations of organisms? Chapters 27 and 29 contain some possible answers to these questions.

Cells reproduce rapidly in many organs at such times, regenerating tissue that has been damaged or destroyed. New fibers of connective tissues are laid down, reestablishing boundaries between adjacent cell layers.

Tolerance Thus far we have been concerned with the response of lymphocytes to foreign antigens. We now turn to a more difficult problem. How do lymphocytes of an animal distinguish between foreign antigens and those produced by other cells of the same animal? Lymphocytes normally are prevented from initiating an immune response against "self-antigens," a phenomenon called *natural tolerance.* How is this tolerance established?

One hypothesis proposes that lymphocytes capable of producing antibodies against self-antigens are killed or inactivated permanently when they first encounter these antigens during embryonic development. A testable prediction of this hypothesis can be obtained using deductive reasoning (see Chap. 1). *If* lymphocytes capable of producing antibodies against self-antigens are inactivated permanently during embryonic development, *then* a foreign, or "nonself-antigen" injected into an embryo should be tolerated as a self-antigen when the embryo becomes an adult. Indeed, such *induced tolerance* can be established in just this way.

The results of more recent experiments, however, have undermined previous support for this hypothesis. For example, it has become possible to couple self-antigens with nonself-antigens. When such an artificially produced molecular complex is injected into the donor of the self-antigen, the animal frequently responds by producing antibody against its own antigen. Clearly, this could not occur if the population of B cells capable of producing the antibody had been inactivated permanently. Furthermore, tolerance to nonself-antigens has been induced in adult animals by injecting antigens in very low or very high concentrations. These results imply that there is nothing special about young lymphocytes as far as tolerance induction is concerned. Apparently, lymphocytes are neither permanently activated nor inactivated. Instead, like light bulbs, they can be turned on or off by one or more control switches.

Although the nature of these "switches" is not resolved, the results of several experiments suggest that establishment of tolerance probably involves interaction between B and T cells. Regardless of their nature, these control mechanisms undoubtedly are more complex than we now realize. But that is to our advantage. Once they are understood, complex control systems can be regulated more precisely than simpler systems. Many practical applications await the results of basic research in immunology. Potential applications to transplantation surgery already have been mentioned. In addition, several chronic diseases of mankind now are thought to result from a breakdown of control mechanisms governing tolerance. These include some forms of cancer, rheumatic heart disease, rheumatoid arthritis, and many other debilitating diseases. A better understanding of the interactions between parts of this diffuse and complex association of cells will not only enhance our appreciation of living systems but also further reduce human afflictions.

CIRCULATION

Vessels and Heartbeat

By virtue of its various constituents, blood as a whole plays a vital role in steady-state maintenance. In addition to its many transport functions, blood also is comparable to a receptor that receives stimuli from all body regions; to a sensory and motor path that interconnects all cells; to a modulator that contributes to optimum operating conditions in all body parts; and, through antibodies, white blood cells, and clotting capacity, to an effector that serves as the first line of internal defense. All these control functions can be exercised, however, only if blood circulates.

The organs of a circulatory system usually are *hearts, arteries, veins,* and, in many animals, also *capillaries* (Fig. 18.13). Blood is carried away from a heart by arteries, toward a heart by veins. Capillaries are vessels of microscopic diameter interconnecting the narrowest arteries and veins. A capillary consists of a single layer of flat epithelial cells, and it is through them that the all-important material exchanges occur between blood and tissue cells (Fig. 18.14).

Vessels with larger diameters have additional tissues on the outside, mainly layers of connective tissue and muscle. Arteries, which carry blood under the greatest pressure, have thicker walls than veins. At frequent intervals along the larger

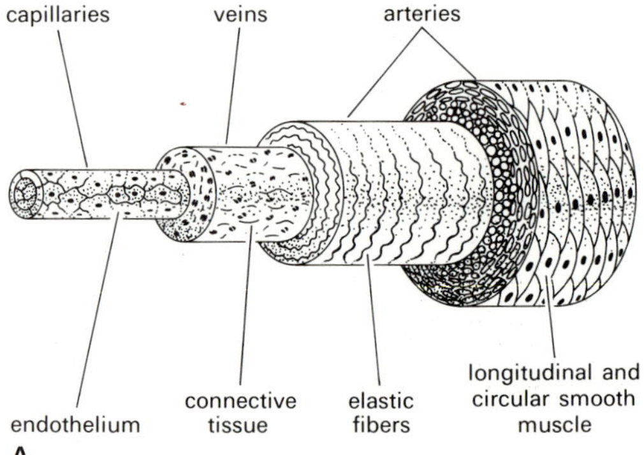

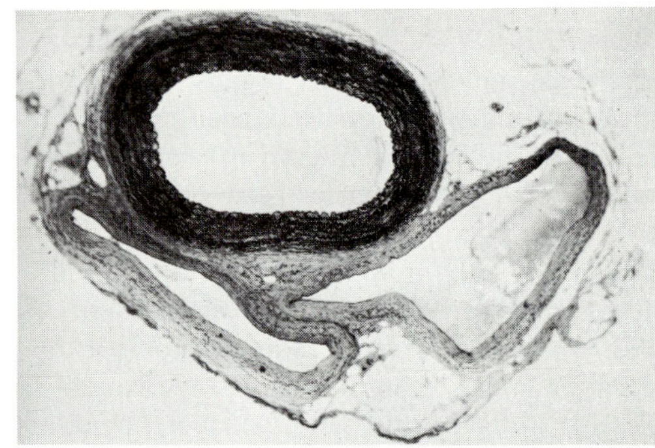

Fig. 18.13 Blood vessels. (A) Diagram illustrating the progressively greater thickness and tissue complexity of capillaries, veins, and arteries. The single cell layer of squamous endothelium is continuous throughout a vessel system. Additional tissues do not necessarily occur in such neat layers as sketched here. (B) Section through an artery and two veins. Note the thicker wall of the artery and the many elastic fibers (dark wavy lines) in this wall.

veins there are internal *valves* that open toward the heart and prevent backflow of blood.

As already noted, lymph vessels are not integral components of vertebrate circulatory systems but instead constitute one-way drainage routes from intercellular spaces to blood. Lymph vessel systems arise as a group of blind-ended *lymph capillaries,* which are permeable to almost all components of interstitial fluid. The liquid contents of the capillaries, or *lymph,* flow into larger vessels that are collectively termed *lymphatics.* Such vessels are thinner than blood veins and contain more internal valves (Fig 18.15). Along the course of lymphatics are lymph nodes, mentioned earlier.

In most animals, hearts generally consist of two types of chambers, *atria,* which receive blood, and *ventricles,* which pump blood out. The mammalian heart contains two of each, a right and left atrium, and a right and left ventricle (Fig. 18.16). The atria are comparatively thin-walled, but in the ventricles the walls are quite thick. Oxygen-poor venous blood from all body regions enters the right atrium through a large vessel, the *vena cava.* Blood then passes from the right atrium to the right ventricle through the *tricuspid valve.* The three tissue flaps of this valve prevent blood from flowing in the opposite direction. From the right ventricle blood leaves through the *pulmonary artery,* a vessel that leads to the lungs. In the lungs blood is oxygenated, and oxygen-rich arterial blood then flows through the *pulmonary vein* to the left atrium.

A *biscuspid* (*mitral*) *valve,* equipped with two tissue flaps, separates the left atrium and ventricle. Like the tricuspid valve on the right side, the bicuspid valve opens to the ventricle only. Both valves are known as auriculoventricular (AV) valves. Blood leaves the left ventricle through the large, thick-walled *aorta,* a vessel that sends branches to all parts of the body. Valves are present where the aorta and the pulmonary artery leave the heart.

A heartbeat starts with the full distention of both atria by incoming blood. Atrial contraction then forces blood into the ventricles (Fig. 18.17). As the ventricles now distend, the atria relax and slowly distend again in preparation for the next beat. Fully distended ventricles contract in their turn. Blood is thereby forced against the AV valves, and their flaps snap together and prevent backflow to the atria. The impact of blood against the valve flaps produces a *first heart sound,* which can be heard as "the" heartbeat.

Blood can then leave the ventricles only through the aorta and the pulmonary artery. These vessels dilate as blood rushes through them, but their elastic walls snap back and add to the forward pressure of blood. Blood also tends to be

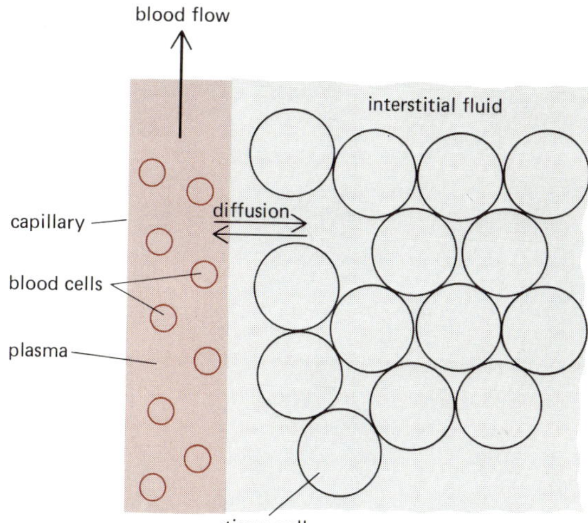

Fig. 18.14 Capillary function. Blood-tissue exchanges of dissolved gases, ions, and many other substances occur largely across capillary walls.

Fig. 18.15 Lymphatics. Longitudinal section through a lymph vessel showing an internal valve. Such valves prevent backflow. Valves very much like this are present also in the larger veins. (*General Biological Supply House, Inc.*)

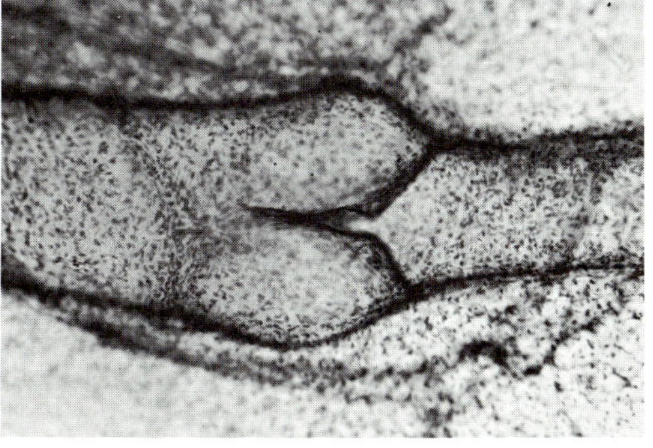

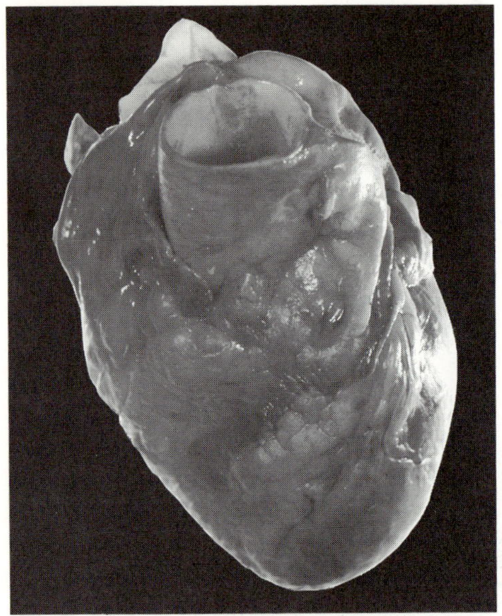

A

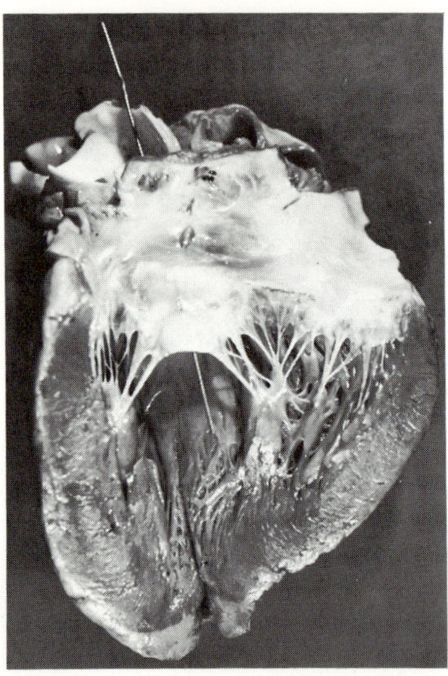

B

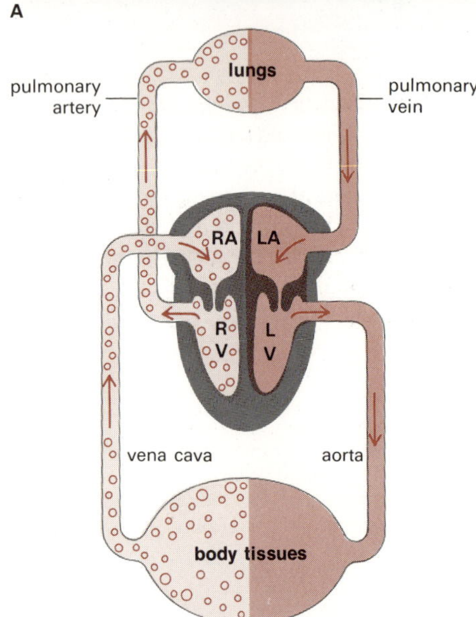

C

Fig. 18.16 Heart and circulation. (A) The human heart. The large blood-vessel stump is the aorta. The atria are partly hidden by the aorta. The size of your fist is very nearly the actual size of your heart. (B) The human heart cut open to show the interior of the left ventricle. Note the strands of tissue attached to the two flaps of the bicuspid valve. These strands prevent the valve from opening into the atrium (white area above the ventricle). (C) The mammalian blood circulation. Arterial blood is in the left side of the circulatory system (right side of diagram), venous blood in the right side of the system.

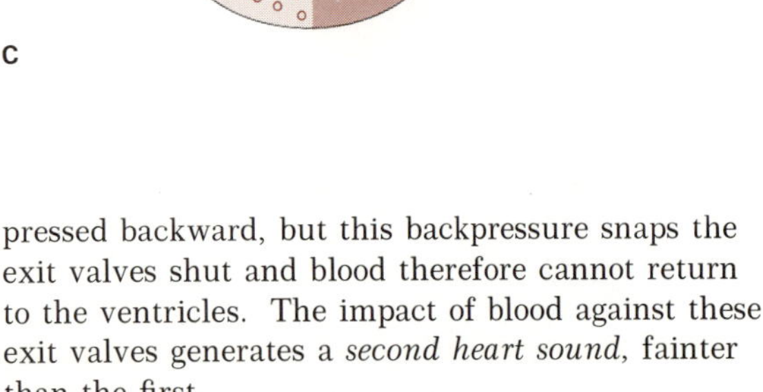

pressed backward, but this backpressure snaps the exit valves shut and blood therefore cannot return to the ventricles. The impact of blood against these exit valves generates a *second heart sound,* fainter than the first.

The whole beat lasts about 0.8 sec (Fig. 18.18). Atria contract during the first tenth, ventricles during the following three tenths. At all other periods the chambers are relaxed, and thus even the ventricles rest more than half the time. When contraction does occur, it is primarily the pressure generated by heart muscle that determines the position of the heart valves, hence the path that blood can take.

Arterial blood flows in rhythmic spurts according to the rhythm of the heart. As each spurt of fluid impinges on the walls of arteries, it gives rise to *pulse* vibrations. With increasing distance from the heart the arterial flow becomes more nearly continuous. By the time blood has passed through capillary vessels and has reached veins, it no longer spurts but flows in a continuous, even stream. The heart here produces very little push. Venous blood

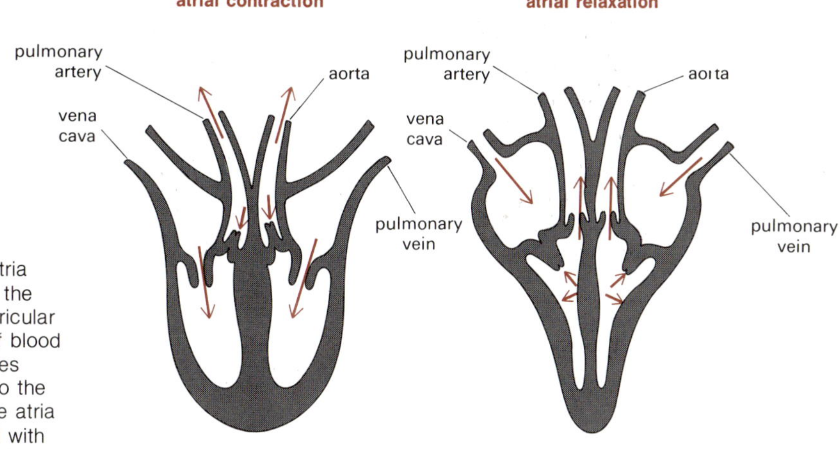

Fig. 18.17 Heart action. When atria contract (left), they force blood into the relaxed ventricles. The auriculoventricular valves are open, but the pressure of blood closes all other exits. When ventricles contract (right), they force blood into the pulmonary artery and the aorta. The atria are relaxed at the same time and fill with blood in preparation for the next beat.

keeps moving by the push of blood from behind and by contraction of skeletal muscles that squeeze the veins. In lymph vessels the pressure of lymph is even lower than that of blood. Here again pressure of lymph from behind and muscular activity provide the major forces that return lymph to the blood circulation.

Heart Rate and Blood Pressure

The mammalian heart contains a built-in signal-generating system that can initiate successive beats. In the wall of the right atrium lies a *pacemaker,* or *sinus node,* a specialized patch of modified heart muscle (Fig. 18.19). This structure emits periodic impulses, each of which produces a wave of contraction that spreads over both atria. Atrial contraction in turn stimulates a second patch of modified muscle, the *AV node,* located in the median partition of the heart. At this node originates a so-called *bundle of His,* a set of specialized muscle strands that conduct impulses through the walls of both ventricles. Such impulses lead to ventricular contraction. The time required for impulse transmission from pacemaker to AV node ensures that the ventricles will contract a fraction of a second *after* the atria.

By virtue of these nodes and conducting structures, the heart has an *intrinsic beat* that can be maintained even when the organ is separated from the body. But in the body the beat is under close nervous control; nerve impulses from the brain to the pacemaker override the intrinsic beat and impose a variable, adjustable heart rate.

A *heart-rate center* is located in the hindbrain, in a region called the *medulla oblongata* (see Fig. 18.19). Two pairs of nerves lead from there to the pacemaker. One pair travels part of the way through the spinal cord, and impulses through these nerves accelerate the heart. The second pair forms part of the large *vagus nerves,* the 10th cranials, which travel through the neck alongside the windpipe (see Chap. 19). Impulses through these decelerate or inhibit the heart. Variable degrees of inhibition have been shown to be more important in heart-rate control than acceleration. Thus the heart speeds up mainly when the impulse

Fig. 18.18 Heartbeat. The atria contract and generate pressure when the ventricles are relaxed, and vice versa. The whole heart is relaxed for half the time of a beat.

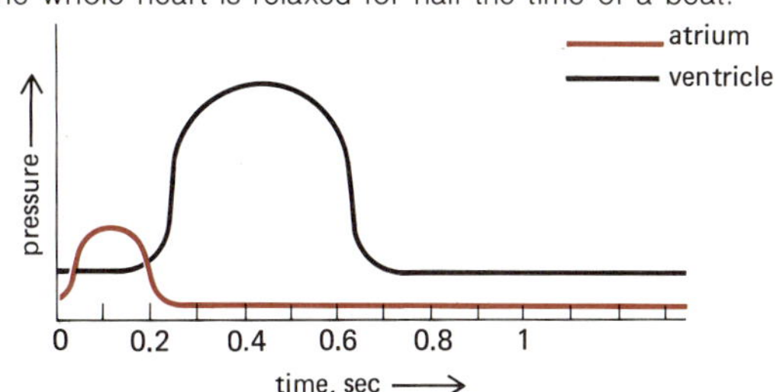

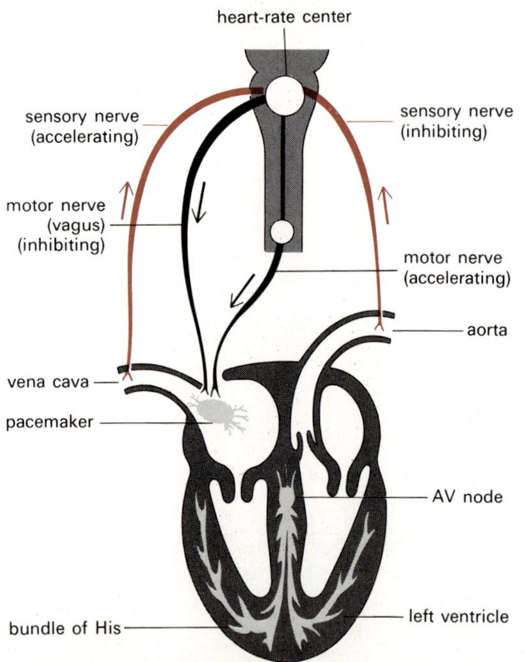

Fig. 18.19 Innervation of the heart. The heart-rate center receives messages through many sensory nerves. Some of them originate in the vena cava and the aorta. Such messages can initiate a stretch reflex: the center can send command signals to the pacemaker via motor nerves that either inhibit or accelerate the heart. Note that sensory impulses from the vena cava lead to accelerating motor signals, and impulses from the aorta lead to inhibiting motor signals. Impulses from the pacemaker then stimulate the atria (which contract as a result) and then the AV node, which in turn sends contraction signals to the ventricles through the bundle of His.

frequency through the vagus nerves decreases; a faster beat results more from reduced braking action than from stepped-up acceleration. Similarly, a slower beat is produced primarily by increased braking action through the vagus nerves.

The heart-rate center sends out brake or accelerator signals in response to sensory nerve impulses that affect it. Such impulses can reach it from anywhere in the body. As is well known, heart rate is influenced greatly by environmental changes communicated through vision, hearing, and other senses. Emotions, too, affect heart rate, and so do internal body activities. For example, suppose that strenuous work is started. Muscles become active and compress many veins vigorously, and much blood returns to the heart as a result. This more abundant flow distends the vena cava greatly and initiates a *stretch reflex* (see Fig. 18.19): sensory nerves in the walls of the vena cava are stimulated and impulses are conveyed to the heart-rate center. This center then sends impulses to the heart that increase the rate of beat. The heart thus will beat faster just when the tissues require more fuel and oxygen and when more incoming blood must be pumped out. This increased outflow now dilates the walls of the aorta. Stretch reflexes originate in this vessel, too, but they *slow* the heart; they prevent the heart from beating *too* rapidly. Through such controls the heart rate is automatically adjusted to the volume of blood the heart must handle. Moreover, any excessive speedup produces signals forcing a slowdown and vice versa.

Heart rate is regulated also by nonnervous means, through stimuli acting directly on the heart muscle or the pacemaker. For example, higher temperatures accelerate the heart, lower temperatures decelerate it. Heart rate also is increased by a lower pH, particularly when increased respiration during intensive body activity raises the CO_2 content of blood: CO_2 reacts with the water of blood and becomes carbonic acid, which lowers blood pH temporarily. Increased CO_2 concentrations also speed up breathing (see below), hence a fast heart and fast breathing usually go together. Hormones, too, have marked effects on heart rate; as already noted earlier, for example, epinephrine accelerates the heart during conditions of stress. At any given moment, therefore, the actual rate of the heart is a net response to numerous stimuli.

Adequate circulation requires not only an appropriately controlled rate of blood flow but also a properly regulated blood pressure. This pressure depends mainly on three factors: the *force* generated by heart-muscle contraction; the total *volume* of blood in the circulatory vessels; and the size of the blood *space* inside the vessel system. The first two of these conditions can change to some extent, but blood pressure is controlled chiefly by nervous regulation of the amount of space the blood vessels provide. Near the heart-rate center in the medulla oblongata is a *vasomotor center.* Nerves from it lead to the smooth muscles in the walls of arteries, and nerve impulses to different sets of arterial muscles initiate either *vasoconstriction,* a narrowing of vessels, or *vasodilation*, a widening of vessels (Fig. 18.20).

Simultaneous vasoconstriction in all parts of the body raises overall blood pressure, and vasodilation lowers it. Vasomotion also can occur in limited body regions and lead to a constriction of vessels in one region and a dilation in another. Less blood then will flow through regions with constricted vessels and more through regions with dilated ones. Vasomotion thus adjusts not only the pressure but also the *distribution* of blood in the body.

These adjustments are initiated by the vasomotor center, which, like the heart-rate center, acts in response to nervous and chemical cues from all parts of the body. Almost any sensory nerve impulse reaching the brain is likely to have an effect not only on the heart-rate center but on the vasomotor center as well. For example, pain, emotions, and stresses in general all tend to affect both heart rate and vasomotion, hence blood pressure. If an animal sustains a wound, the internal response normally includes increases in heart rate and overall blood pressure. The faster circulation will then provide improved capacity to cope with the external stress that produced the wound. At the same time the blood vessels in the wounded area will dilate, permitting more blood to flow to that region. More nutrients and oxygen become available there as a result, and more water becomes available to dilute and carry off any toxic substances.

Like the heart-rate center, the vasomotor center is sensitive to the CO_2 content of blood. Low CO_2 concentrations lead to vasodilator impulses throughout the body, hence to a fall in blood pressure. Conversely, high CO_2 concentrations initiate a general rise in blood pressure. Thus whenever CO_2 accumulates in blood, as during intense activity, the gas promotes its own rapid elimination: increased blood pressure and heart rate raise the rate of CO_2 collection and transport, and faster breathing raises the rate of exhalation through the lungs. At the same time these changes also bring more nutrients and oxygen to the tissues.

In body regions where much CO_2 is produced, the gas has a local vasodilator effect, distinct from its effect on the vasomotor center (see Fig. 18.20). After a meal, for example, the active alimentary tract produces large amounts of CO_2. Locally this gas brings about vasodilation, hence increased blood flow to the region. As noted above, however, the gas also acts on the vasomotor center, which initiates vasoconstriction elsewhere in the body. Blood flow will then decrease in, for example, the head and the skeletal muscles. This flow pattern is reversed when muscles are active and the alimentary system is empty. Such blood distributions explain why an animal is disinclined to undertake physical activity immediately after a heavy meal, or, conversely, why eating is best avoided just before strenuous muscular exertions.

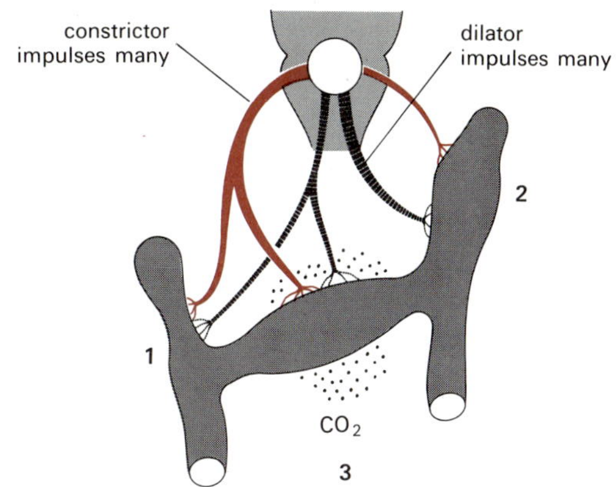

Fig. 18.20 Vasomotion. Vasoconstriction as at (1) occurs when a blood vessel receives many constrictor impulses (color) and few dilator impulses (black) from the vasomotor center. Vasodilation as at (2) occurs when constrictor impulses are few and dilator impulses are many. Locally produced CO_2 as at (3) can override the vasoconstriction ordered by the vasomotor center and can bring about a local vasodilation.

Cardiovascular Disease

Malfunctions of the heart or blood vessels account for more than half of all human deaths in the United States each year. Most of these malfunctions are caused by *atherosclerosis*, or "hardening of the arteries." The inner walls of atherosclerotic arteries are lined with an uneven layer of fatty substance called *plaque*. The chief component of plaque is *cholesterol*, an important and necessary metabolite in the synthesis of several hormones and in many other cell functions. But for reasons that are not understood completely, cholesterol accumulates excessively in the blood of some people and is incorporated readily in plaque.

The accumulation of plaque restricts blood flow to many parts of the body (Fig. 18.21). Moreover, blood clots form more frequently in atherosclerotic arteries than in normal blood vessels. Evidently, the unevenly distributed deposits of plaque produce a more turbulent blood flow, and this increased turbulence causes blood to clot more frequently. Such a clot, or *thrombus,* can block already reduced openings of an artery and produce serious complications (Fig. 18.22). *Strokes,* for example, can occur when a thrombus plugs an artery leading to cells of the brain. The resulting loss of oxygen and nutrients can damage or destroy brain cells and cause permanent afflictions. A frequent result of stroke is a paralysis of facial muscles, arms, and legs, usually on one side of the body.

Blood clots also can plug the *coronary arteries,* which supply blood to the heart itself (Fig. 18.23). This blockage, called a *coronary thrombosis,* can cause severe damage to heart tissue and produce a "heart attack." The danger of coronary thrombosis increases as plaque accumulates in a coronary artery. If the destruction of tissue that results from the blocked coronary artery is not too great, the heart continues functioning less efficiently until alternate blood vessels develop and restore blood supply to damaged tissue. Such alternate vessels, called *collateral arteries,* develop as branches from the coronary artery.

Heart attacks account for approximately 700,000 deaths in the United States annually. The majority of these occur in males. Women experience far fewer heart attacks than men up to age 65, when both sexes become equally susceptible. Although

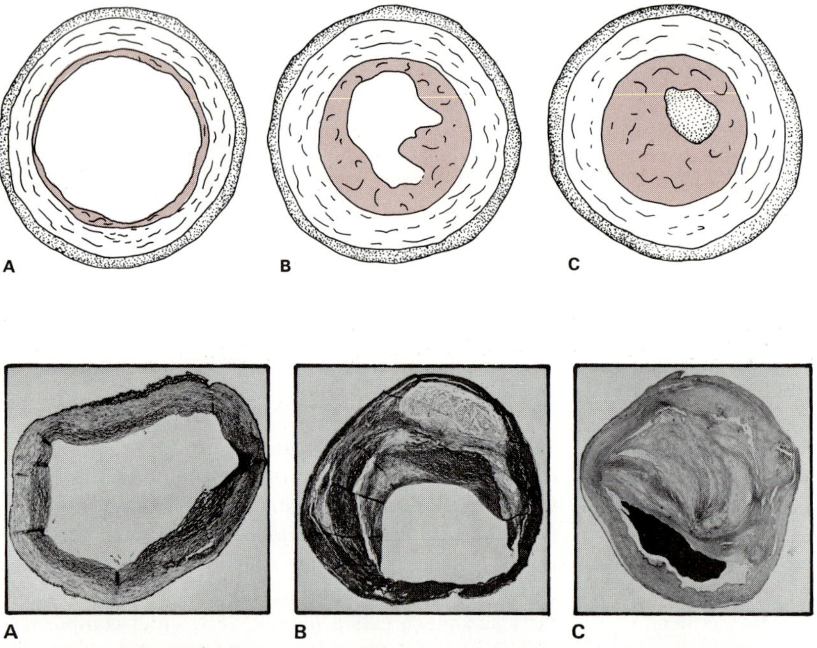

Fig. 18.21 Atherosclerosis. These corresponding sequences of diagrams and photographs show the gradual build up of plaque that occurs in atherosclerotic arteries. (A) Plaque (color in diagram, dark inner layer in photo) begins to build up on the inner walls of an artery. (B) The accumulation continues, and plaque now clogs much of the passageway. (C) A blood clot has formed, and the artery is now completely blocked (compare with Fig. 18.22). *(From P. W. Davis and E. Solomon, "The World of Biology," © 1974 by McGraw-Hill, Inc., New York.)*

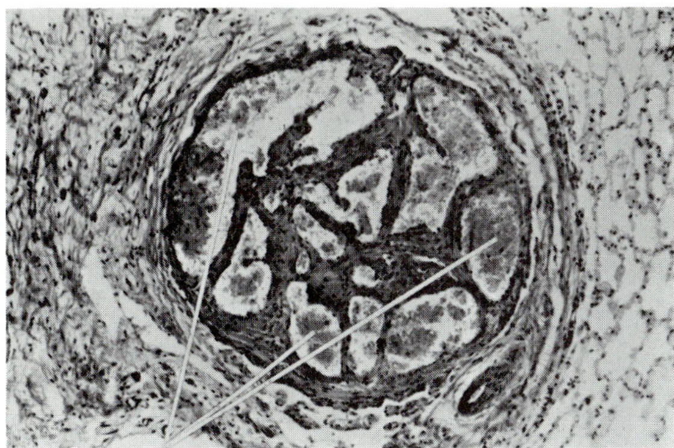

Fig. 18.22 Thrombus. Clotted blood completely obliterates this artery.

Fig. 18.23 Coronary arteries. A right and left coronary artery branch from the aorta and supply the heart with blood.

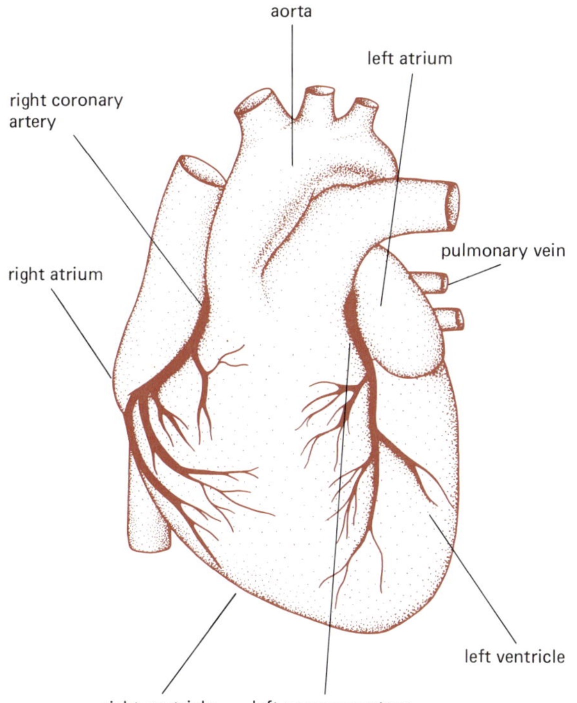

the causes of this difference in susceptibility have not been established, several factors have been linked statistically to increased incidences of heart attack in both men and women. These include the gradual breakdown of heart tissue that normally occurs during aging, high blood pressure, overweight, high concentrations of blood cholesterol, and cigarette smoking. Some of these "high-risk factors" may be causes of others, but all act synergistically to increase the probability of heart attack. For example, people who smoke cigarettes, have high blood pressure, and have a high concentration of cholesterol in their blood suffer almost 3 times as many heart attacks as people with only two of these characteristics, and over five times as many as those with only one.

Steps can be taken to reduce or eliminate many of these high-risk factors. Several drugs now can be prescribed to control blood pressure; modification of diet can reduce blood cholesterol concentrations and eliminate excessive body fat; regular exercise can reduce some causes of high blood pressure and stimulate proliferation of collaterals from the coronary artery; and smoking is a habit that often can be broken. Since atherosclerosis probably begins during the teenage years, these steps will be most effective if begun early in life.

BREATHING

The Apparatus

The basic component of any breathing system is a *breathing surface*, where O_2 can diffuse in and CO_2 can diffuse out. As shown in Chaps. 34 and 35, such surfaces are provided by skin, gills, tracheal tubes, lungs, or modifications of such organs. In each case the breathing surface permits exchange of respiratory gases between the external environment and either the circulating body fluids or the tissue cells directly.

In mammals the breathing apparatus contains an air channel that leads to and from the lungs through the nose and the mouth (Fig. 18.24). The air path between nose and lungs passes *across* the food path between mouth and esophagus, the region of intersection being the pharynx. The nasal channels connect through openings with a series of *head sinuses,* paired air-filled cavities in some of

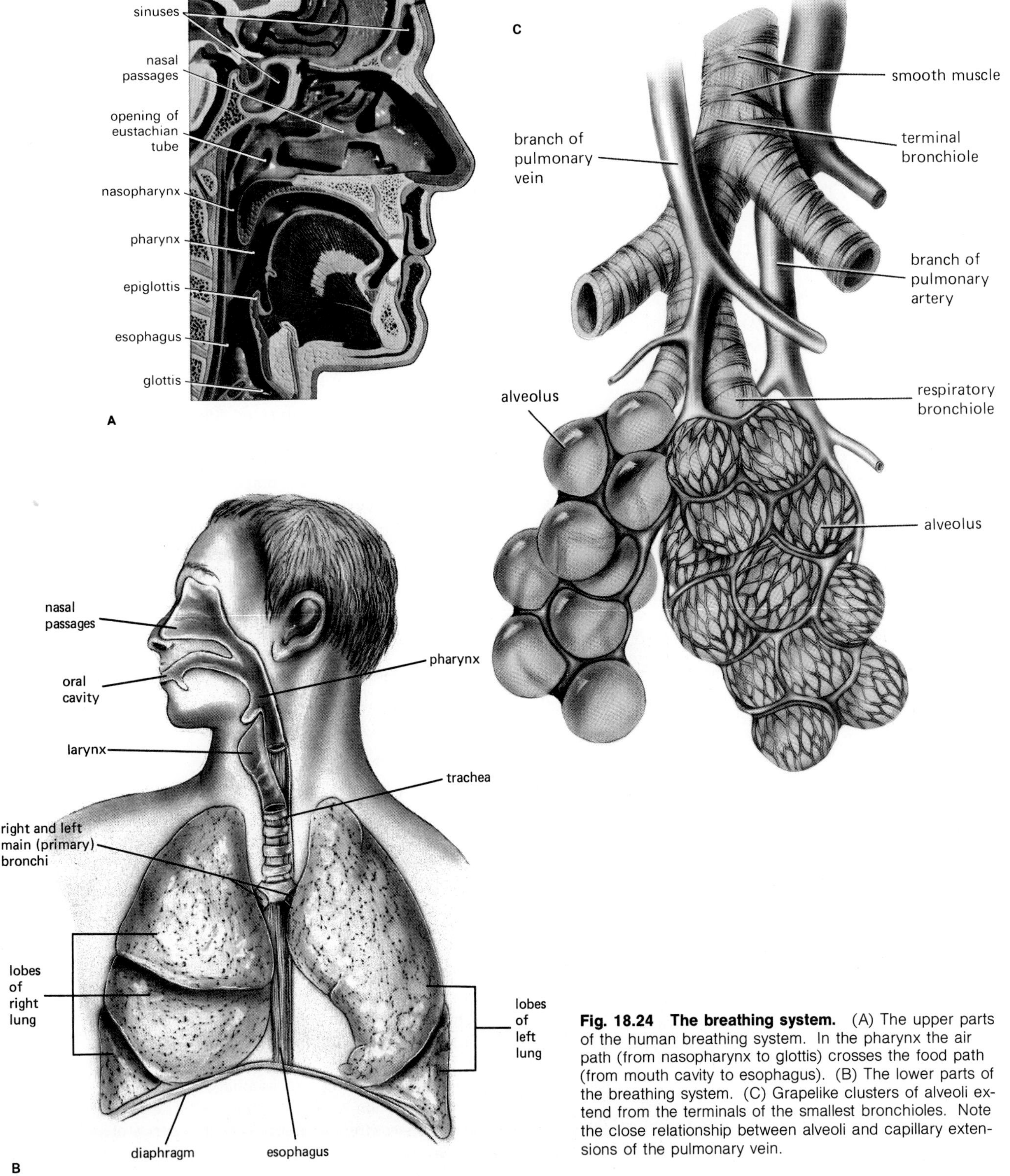

Fig. 18.24 The breathing system. (A) The upper parts of the human breathing system. In the pharynx the air path (from nasopharynx to glottis) crosses the food path (from mouth cavity to esophagus). (B) The lower parts of the breathing system. (C) Grapelike clusters of alveoli extend from the terminals of the smallest bronchioles. Note the close relationship between alveoli and capillary extensions of the pulmonary vein.

the skull bones. Also leading to the nasal passages are the *tear ducts*, which collect the lymphlike fluid secreted continuously by tear glands in the outer corners of the eyes. Near the connection of the nasal channels with the pharynx are the openings of the *eustachian tubes*, a pair of ducts leading to the middle-ear cavities (see Figs. 19.17 and 18.24). These tubes permit equilibration of air pressure between the external atmosphere and the middle ear. The eardrums prevent air from reaching the middle ears directly. In the nasal passages themselves, some of the ciliated lining cells are specialized as odor receptors. Nerves lead from them to the nearby brain, where impulses are interpreted as smell.

The pharynx connects with the lungs through the windpipe, or *trachea* (see Fig. 18.24). At the upper end of the trachea is the *larynx*, or voice box. It is formed from a number of cartilage plates that are held together by membranes and can be moved by muscles. After air enters the larynx through an upper slit, the *glottis*, it passes through the opening left between the *vocal cords*, two horizontal fibroelastic ligaments. The tension of these cords and the size of the opening between them can be changed by the muscles attached to the laryngeal cartilages. Sounds are produced when the cords are made to vibrate by exhaled air (Fig. 18.25).

The shape of the glottal opening and, as in a violin string, the tension of the vocal cords determine tone pitch. The volume of the sound produced depends on the force of the air blast and on the amplitude with which the cords vibrate. A third characteristic of voice, tone quality, is influenced by the size and shape of the resonating cavities: chest, pharynx, mouth, and nasal passages. That tone quality changes as the position of lips, tongue, jaws, and cheeks is changed is quite familiar. During puberty in males, the chest cavity and larynx enlarge and the vocal cords lengthen. The voice then "breaks" as the individual learns to control his modified sound equipment.

During swallowing the whole larynx moves upward and is pressed against the *epiglottis*, a cartilaginous flap that comes to lie over the glottis and thereby prevents food from entering the air channel (see Figs. 18.24 and 18.25). The larynx and trachea are lined with a ciliated, mucus-secreting epithelium. Also in the wall of the trachea are C-shaped cartilage rings that prevent this air channel from collapsing.

At its lower end the trachea divides into a left and right *bronchus*, and after some distance each of these subdivides into *bronchioles*. Each of them then branches repeatedly in turn. The diameters of these channels become progressively smaller and their walls become thinner. Only the ciliated lining layer and some connective tissue continue to the microscopic terminations of the branch system. Each such terminus is an *alveolus*, a raspberry-shaped sac. The sum of all alveoli represents a lung. A thin layer of connective tissue around the alveoli carries nerves and a dense network of blood capillaries (see Fig. 18.24).

The lung on each side lies in an *intrathoracic cavity* that is sealed off from the rest of the body

Fig. 18.25 Vocal cords. The view is from above, looking into the human larynx and trachea. From left to right, sequence of vocal-cord positions during the transition from quiet breathing to voicing.

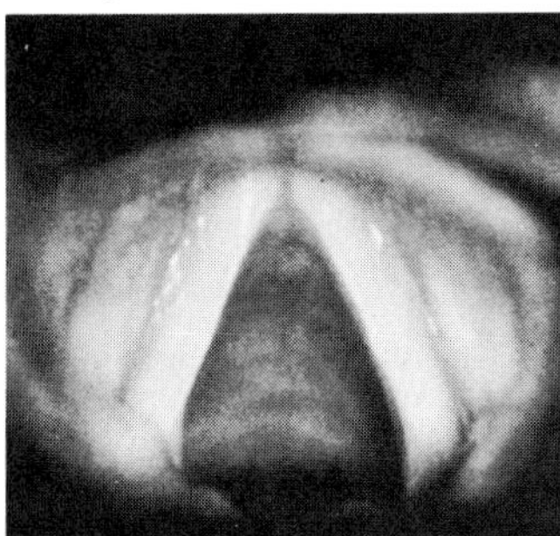

A

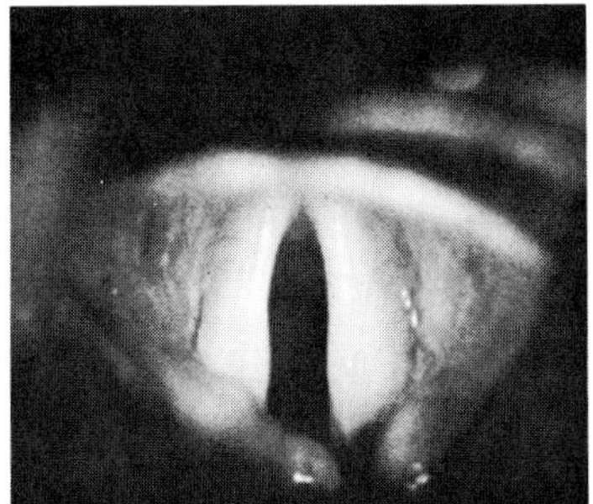

B

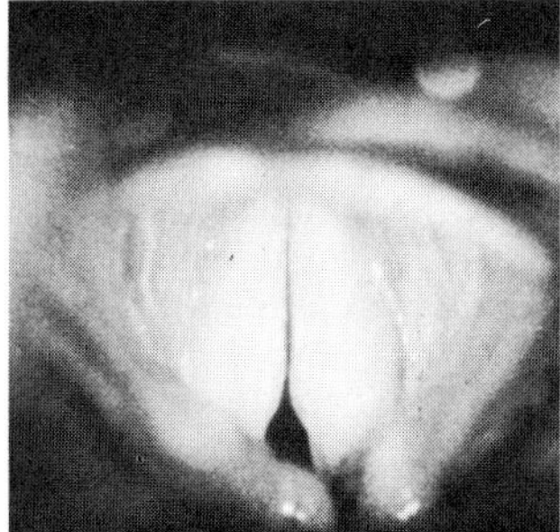

C

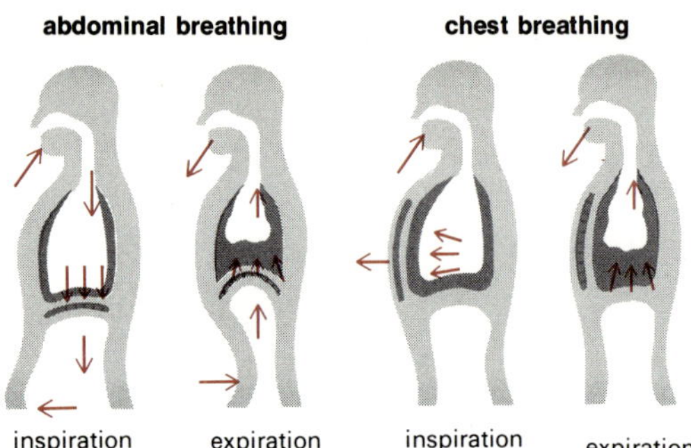

Fig. 18.26 Breathing movements.

cavity by a muscular partition, the *diaphragm* (see Fig. 18.24). Dome-shaped at rest, the diaphragm flattens out on contraction and enlarges the chest cavity. The suction thus generated enlarges the lung alveoli, and external air rushes into them. Relaxation of the diaphragm then permits elastic recoil of the lungs and expulsion of air (Fig. 18.26). Inhalation and exhalation also can be brought about by the *rib muscles* present between successive ribs. When these muscles raise the rib cage, the chest cavity enlarges and an inhalation occurs. Conversely, a lowering of the rib cage leads to exhalation. This principle is used in the various procedures of "artificial respiration" and in iron lungs, by means of which air is forced into and out of the lungs intermittently.

The Process

Breathing is under nervous and chemical control. A *breathing center* in the medulla oblongata, located near the heart-rate and vasomotor centers, sends motor impulses to the diaphragm and the rib muscles. This nerve center is spontaneously active; it generates rhythmic motor impulses with a basic frequency that is ultimately determined genetically. When an impulse arrives at the diaphragm or the rib muscles, these contract and produce an inhalation (Fig. 18.27). As a result the lungs become inflated and stretched, and this stretching in turn stimulates sets of sensory nerves in the walls of the lungs (stretch receptors). Impulses from there then temporarily *inhibit* the breathing center from sending more signals to the breathing muscles. These consequently relax and exhalation occurs. As the lungs now recoil, the stretch receptors there cease to be stimulated, and the breathing center therefore ceases to be inhibited. At this point the center sends out motor impulses again, and a new cycle starts.

As pointed out earlier, the rate of breathing tends to be higher the greater the CO_2 concentration in blood. Thus, breathing becomes faster during intense physical or emotional activity, when CO_2 levels in blood tend to be high. The gas here hastens its own removal through the lungs, and faster breathing at the same time increases the oxygen supply, just when the tissues require more oxygen. Recall also that CO_2 speeds up the heart, which aids further in accelerating gas exchange. If an animal holds its breath deliberately, the accumulating CO_2 soon stimulates the center so strongly that breathing *must* be resumed, even against the most intense will; the automatic controls ensure that breathing does not occur too slowly.

Conversely, breathing slows down during rest or sleep, when respiration and CO_2 production are minimal. The extreme is the *hyperventilated* condition, produced, for example, when breathing is intentionally made as deep and as rapid as possi-

Fig. 18.27 Breathing control. Sensory impulses (color, left diagram) from an inflated lung inhibit the breathing center, resulting in exhalation (right). Sensory impulses no longer emanate from stretch receptors of a deflated lung (right), releasing the breathing center from inhibition. The breathing center then responds by transmitting motor impulses (color, right diagram) to the diaphragm, bringing about inhalation (left).

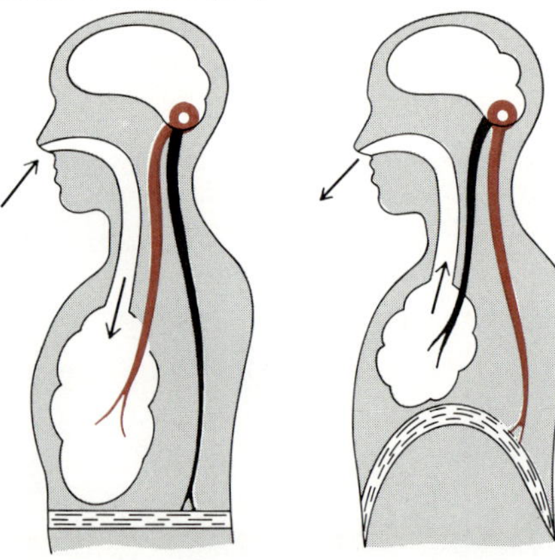

ble. Carbon dioxide then is exhaled so fast that its concentration in blood becomes abnormally low. In that case the breathing center usually ceases to operate temporarily, a "blackout" ensues, and breathing will remain stopped until the CO_2 concentration again has built up to a normal level.

Fresh inhaled air contains some 20 per cent oxygen and 0.03 per cent carbon dioxide. Exhaled air includes only 16 per cent oxygen but as much as 4 per cent carbon dioxide. A fifth of the available oxygen thus is retained in the body, and more than 100 times the amount of CO_2 is expelled. This exchange is governed by differences in gas pressures between blood and lung. Venous blood flowing to the lungs from the body is comparatively oxygen-poor, but air in the lungs is oxygen-rich. A pressure gradient therefore leads from the lungs *to* blood, and more oxygen diffuses into the blood capillaries than in the reverse direction (Fig. 18.28). At the same time, venous blood coming to the lungs is almost saturated with CO_2, whereas the air in the lungs contains a far lower concentration of this gas. A pressure gradient here leads *out* of the blood capillaries, and more CO_2 diffuses to the lungs than in the opposite direction. As a result blood ceases to be venous, and the incoming oxygen makes it arterial.

As in the lungs, gas exchange between blood and the body tissues likewise is governed by pressure gradients. Tissue cells use up oxygen, and the higher pressure of this gas in blood therefore drives oxygen into the cells. Blood then ceases to be arterial. At the same time respiration in cells builds up a higher CO_2 pressure than in blood, and CO_2 therefore diffuses out of the cells. Blood here becomes venous (see Fig. 18.28).

In blood itself, small amounts of the respiratory gases (and indeed of all aerial gases) are dissolved physically in plasma. Thus if the environmental pressure should drop suddenly, as in too rapid ascents from great depths or to high altitudes, then the dissolved gases can bubble out of blood like gases fizzing out from an opened bottle of soda. The results often are internal blood clots and dangerous "bends."

The bulk of the respiratory gases is carried in blood by chemical means. Oxygen combines reversibly with the respiratory pigments. If the pigment is hemoglobin, as in the red cells of vertebrates, *oxyhemoglobin* forms:

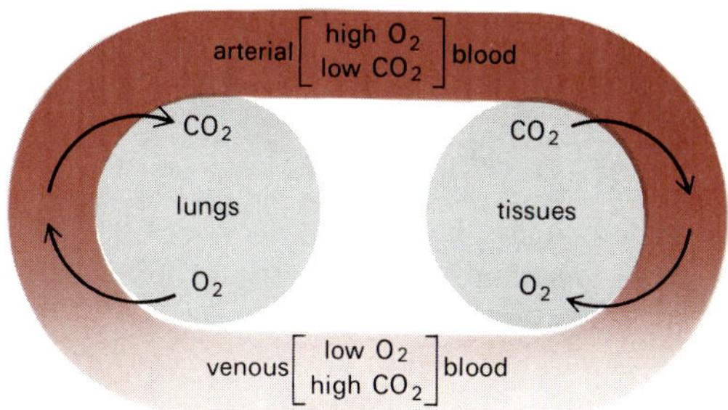

Fig. 18.28 Gas exchange between lungs and blood, and between body tissues and blood. Oxygen enters blood in the lungs and leaves in the tissues. Carbon dioxide enters in the tissues and leaves in the lungs.

$$Hb + O_2 \rightleftharpoons HbO_2$$

This reaction shifts to the right in the lungs, where oxygen enters the blood in quantity. HbO_2 then is transported to the body tissues. There the reaction proceeds to the left, liberating free O_2 to the oxygen-poor cells.

As pointed out in Chap. 10, hemoglobin can also combine with carbon monoxide (CO) and indeed this union takes place more easily than that with oxygen. Carbon monoxide therefore is a poison, for formation of HbCO in preference to HbO_2 prevents or severely impairs the transport of oxygen.

Hemoglobin normally transports also a small amount of CO_2, but most of this gas interacts with the water of plasma and is carried in the form of bicarbonate ions:

$$CO_2 + H_2O \underset{\text{in breathing system}}{\overset{\text{in body tissues}}{\rightleftharpoons}} H^+ + HCO_3^-$$

This reaction proceeds to the right in the tissues, where CO_2 enters the blood continuously, and to the left in the lungs, where CO_2 passes into the air.

The breathing system eliminates not only CO_2 but also water, which saturates expired air, and often vapors of other volatile compounds as well. Through these functions the system contributes significantly to the *excretory* activities of an animal.

EXCRETION

Excretory systems are not named very adequately, for elimination of wastes is only one of their functions; they also selectively adjust the internal concentrations of a large variety of substances in an organism. Indeed, what is or is not "waste" at any given moment is precisely what an excretory system must determine. The basic wastes are excess water, excess salts, ammonia and other nitrogenous by-products of metabolism, and CO_2. In most animals, ammonia and its derivatives are toxic wastes in almost any amounts, and CO_2, excreted mainly through breathing surfaces, is largely waste.

For water and salts, however, the difference between waste and nonwaste is a difference of amount, not kind. For example, in a paramecium, a unicellular organism adapted to freshwater habitats, relatively large amounts of water must be excreted. Concentrations of water are almost always higher outside than inside the organism. Consequently, water moves into the cell via osmosis. If the water accumulating inside the cell were not excreted, the paramecium would burst. Paramecia and many other unicellular organisms eliminate excess water through specialized excretory organelles called *contractile vacuoles* (Fig. 18.29). These often spherical or star-shaped structures go through pumping cycles in which they first fill with water and dissolved wastes and then contract, ejecting the contents of the vacuole to the extracellular environment. Water also tends to move osmotically into the cells of multicellular organisms adapted to freshwater environments, and they too excrete large amounts of water.

By contrast, the greatest threat to life of land-adapted organisms is desiccation. Among terrestrial vertebrates, for example, water is lost more or less continually through evaporation, egestion of feces, and excretion of urine. Water rarely constitutes waste in such organisms. Accordingly, the most successful land-adapted animals generally are those having excretory systems which remove comparatively little water from body fluids.

Complex excretory systems, such as those found in vertebrates, carry out their functions through three kinds of processes, *filtration, reabsorption,* and *secretion* (Fig. 18.30). Filtration takes place between the body fluids and the interior of an excretory structure. The pressure of the fluids—blood pressure in vertebrates, for example—supplies the force necessary for filtration. Cells and proteins in blood normally cannot pass through the filter, but most other components can. Thus, the filtrate collecting within the excretory structure is essentially interstitial fluid, here called *initial urine.* A separation of waste from nonwaste then occurs when initial urine flows through another region of the excretory system on its way to the outside. Reabsorption takes place there: excretory cells in contact with initial urine remove sub-

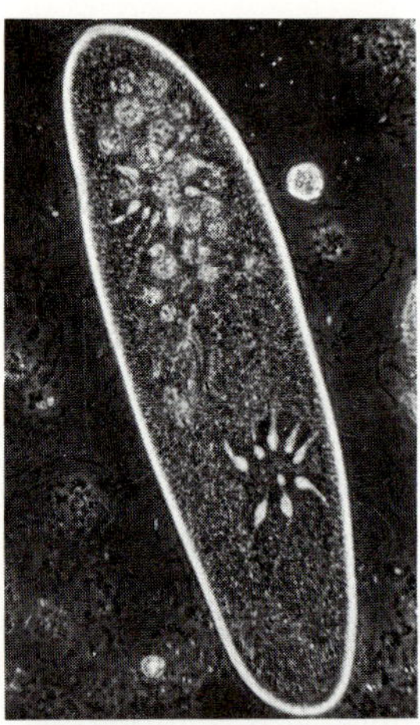

Fig. 18.29 Contractile vacuoles. The unicellular protozoan *Paramecium* normally contains two rosette-shaped contractile vacuoles, which pump excess water and dissolved wastes from the cytoplasm to the extracellular environment. One rosette is visible at each end of the organism.

Fig. 18.30 Excretory processes. In the vertebrate excretory system a filtrate of blood (or interstitial fluid) forms initial urine, from which some materials are reabsorbed and to which other materials are secreted. These functions are performed by the cells lining the system. Final urine is the ultimate product.

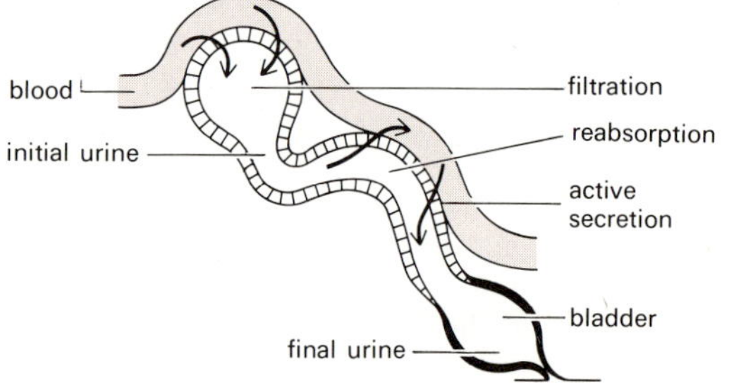

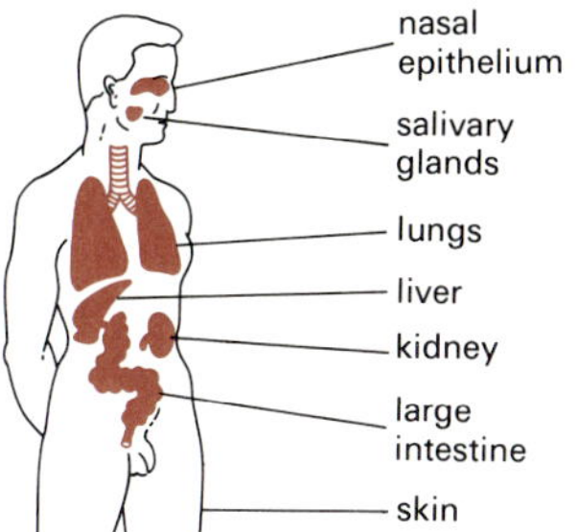

Fig. 18.31 Mammalian excretory organs.

stances "judged" to be valuable and return them to the body fluids.

The third process, secretion, may take place in the same general region of the excretory system or in another body part altogether (gills, for example). Secretion transfers materials from the body fluids to urine or the external environment directly. Secretion and reabsorption therefore operate in opposite directions, but the substances reabsorbed may differ greatly from those being secreted. The fluid then present, *final urine,* is ultimately discharged to the outside.

The organs contributing to excretion in mammals are shown in Fig. 18.31. Evidently, all organs with access to the outside of the body either directly or through the alimentary system play an excretory role. But the kidneys exercise the main excretory control; if they should become inoperative death would soon follow. Each kidney consists of an outer *renal cortex* and an inner *renal medulla* (Fig. 18.32). Located partly in the cortex and partly in the medulla are many thousands of *nephrons,* the functional units of a kidney.

A nephron is composed of a *glomerulus,* a tiny ball of capillaries; a double-layered, cup-shaped *nephric capsule* (also called *Bowman's capsule*) around the glomerulus; and a long *nephric tubule* leading away from the capsule. Such a tubule contains two highly coiled, or *convoluted* regions, interconnected by an extended, U-shaped *loop of Henle.* At its far end the nephric tubule leads into a *collecting duct* that receives the output of many other such tubules. The numerous collecting ducts in a kidney eventually join and form a wide vessel, the *ureter.* This channel carries urine to the *urinary bladder.* As urine accumulates, the bladder distends, and at a certain stage it contracts reflexly and discharges to the outside through the *urethra.*

Fig. 18.32 Kidney structure. (A) Section through rat kidney. Note outer renal cortex, inner renal medulla. (B) The kidneys, their ducts, and the bladder (kidney on right in section). (C) A nephron unit, showing a single nephron and its surrounding bed of capillaries. Henle's loop, which extends into the medulla of the kidney, is positioned between two convoluted tubules. The one nearest the nephric capsule is called the proximal convoluted tubule (proximal means "near"); the one farthest from the nephric capsule is called the distal convoluted tubule (distal means "far"). Both convoluted tubules are located in the cortex of the kidney.

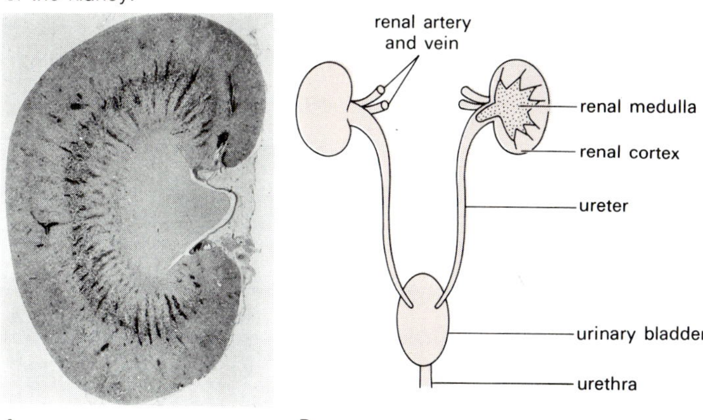

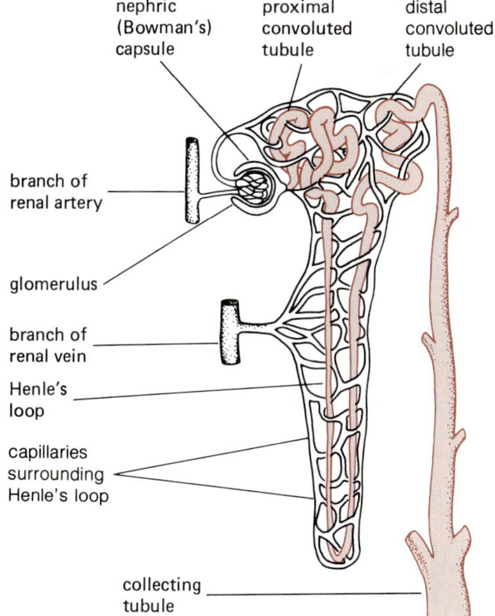

A large *renal artery* enters the kidney where the ureter leaves, and branches out repeatedly. One of the capillary branches forms the glomerulus in a nephron, and blood from there passes into a dense capillary bed that envelops all parts of a nephric tubule. Blood then drains through progressively larger and fewer veins and eventually leaves the kidney through a single large vessel, the *renal vein*.

In each nephron blood is filtered from the glomerulus into the interior space of the nephric capsule. Initial urine then flows through the nephric tubule, where reabsorption and secretion take place. Water is the most abundant of the substances filtered from blood and later returned to it. The two kidneys of a human being, for example, filter the equivalent of about 160 qt of blood plasma a day, but only about $1\frac{1}{2}$ qt of fluid actually is released as final urine; some 99 per cent of the water in the blood filtrate is reabsorbed.

The hairpin design of the loop of Henle plays an important role in water reabsorption. The nephric capsule, both convoluted tubules, and a small part of the collecting tubule are located in the cortex of the kidney; Henle's loop and most of the collecting tubule are located in the medulla. Cells in the ascending limb of Henle's loop actively secrete chloride (Cl^-) ions from initial urine into the tissue fluid of the medulla. Certain positively charged ions, such as sodium (Na^+) ions, also move out of initial urine into the tissue fluids. Although some of these ions diffuse back passively into initial urine through the descending limb of Henle's loop, most do not. As a result, the tissue fluid of the

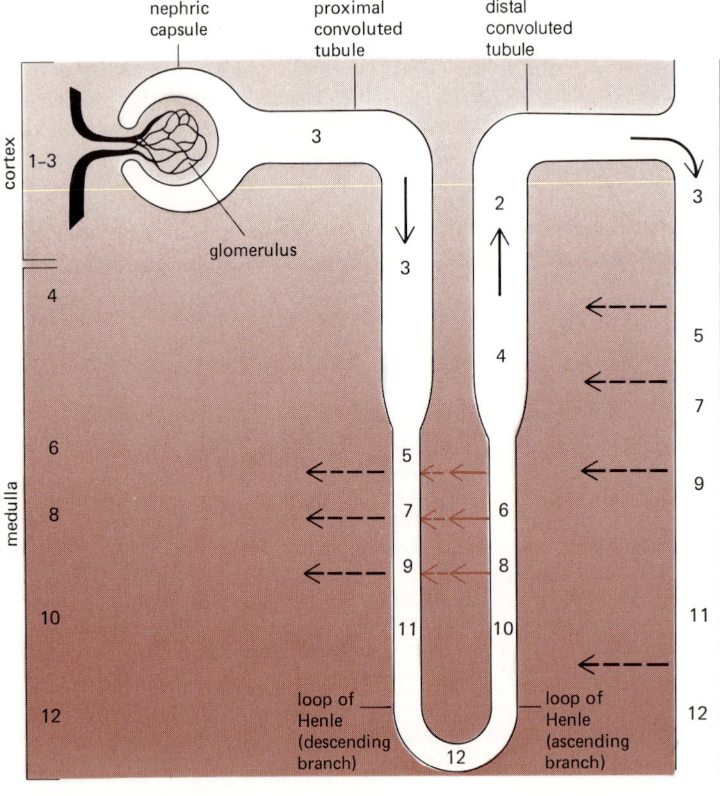

Fig. 18.33 Production of concentrated urine in mammals. Chloride ions (Cl^-) are actively pumped from initial urine during its transport along the ascending limb of Henle's loop. Sodium ions (Na^+) follow passively, maintaining a charge balance. Only a fraction of these ions diffuses back into initial urine through cells forming the descending branch of Henle's loop. Consequently, concentration of salt in tissue fluids bathing the nephron increases progressively from cortex (lighter color) to the inner regions of the medulla (darker color). The salty, hypertonic fluids of the medulla produce an osmotic flow of water from initial urine to the exterior of the nephron. However, cells of the ascending branch of Henle's loop are impermeable to water. Therefore, production of a concentrated final urine occurs in the collecting tubule, whose cells are permeable to water. Numbers indicate concentration of solute in hundreds of milliosmols per liter.

medulla is more "salty" than that of the cortex (Fig. 18.33).

To understand how this difference in tonicity promotes reabsorption of water, we must also understand that water cannot always diffuse freely through the walls of Henle's loop. As initial urine passes through the descending portion of the loop, some water does diffuse outward into the "salty" hypertonic fluid of the medulla; but the cells of the ascending limb of Henle's loop are impermeable to water. Consequently, urine which enters the collecting tubule still contains a large amount of water. So much, in fact, that a person would quickly succumb to desiccation if urine were excreted at this point.

Urine becomes increasingly concentrated as it passes along the collecting tubule. Unlike cells constituting the ascending limb of Henle's loops, those of the collecting tubule normally are permeable to water. The extent of their permeability is regulated by *vasopressin* (also called *antidiuretic hormone*), a hormone secreted by the posterior lobe of the pituitary gland (see Chap. 17). Receptors in the posterior lobe respond to changes in the water content of the body by promoting or inhibiting release of this hormone.

Increased secretion of vasopressin increases the permeability of the collecting tubule to water. Because most of the collecting tubule is surrounded by the hypertonic fluids of the medulla, large amounts of water diffuse from the comparatively hypotonic initial urine into the tissue fluids. The accumulating water is then transported back into the bloodstream through the walls of nearby capillaries. By the time urine reaches the terminal extension of a collecting tubule, it has lost almost all its water content. Decreased secretion of vasopressin reduces the permeability of collecting tubules to water. The increased flow of urine that accompanies the imbibing of alcohol is due in part to this decreased permeability; alcohol suppresses secretion of vasopressin from the pituitary.

Mammals are the only animals whose nephrons contain a loop of Henle and, because of this loop, mammals can produce a final urine that contains much less water than their blood. The extent to which final urine becomes concentrated varies considerably. Mammals adapted to arid environments generally excrete a urine that is far more concentrated than the urine produced by mammals living in aquatic environments. Desert rodents, such as the kangaroo rat, can produce urine that is 14 to 25 times as concentrated as their blood. Such animals often can live indefinitely without drinking, subsisting on the water contained in their food. A beaver, on the other hand, excretes urine that is only twice as concentrated as its blood.

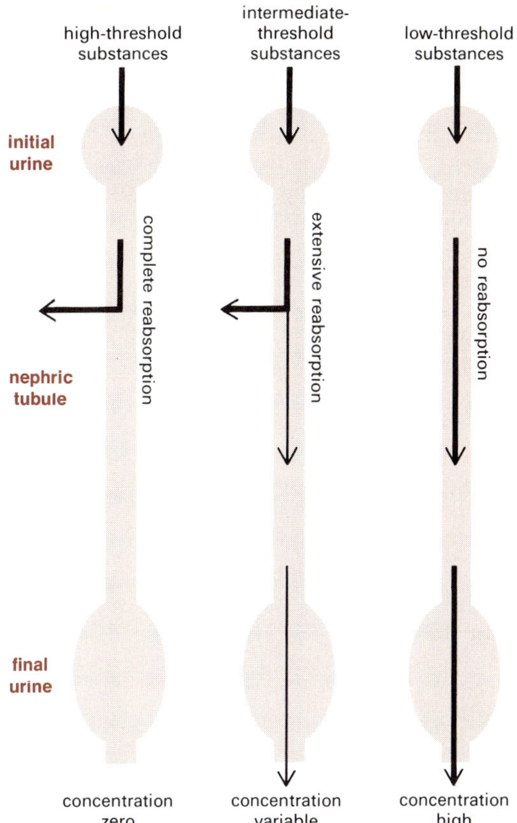

Fig. 18.34 Selective excretory action of the cells of a nephric tubule. The color areas symbolize nephric capsules, tubules, and bladders of excretory systems. (Left) High-threshold substances like glucose are reabsorbed more or less completely. (Right) Low-threshold substances like urea are not reabsorbed at all. (Center) Intermediate-threshold substances, like water and many mineral ions, are reabsorbed in part, depending on the amounts already present in blood.

Water is not the only substance reabsorbed into the blood from nephric tubules. Glucose, for example, is reabsorbed almost completely. Initial urine contains glucose in the same concentration as in blood. But all this glucose tends to be returned to the blood, and none normally escapes in final urine. Other materials undergoing more or less complete reabsorption include amino acids, lipids, vitamins, hormones—in short, all the essential nutrients and other usable supplies in transit to cells. Such materials are said to be *high-threshold* substances; they are reabsorbed entirely unless their concentrations in blood are excessively high (Fig. 18.34).

For example, the concentration of glucose becomes excessively high in the blood of people afflicted with *diabetes mellitus* (see also Chap. 17). Such abnormal concentrations result from an inadequate production of the pancreatic hormone *insulin.* This protein increases the rate of glucose uptake from blood into certain cells, particularly liver and muscle cells. A deficiency of insulin reduces this uptake and causes glucose to concentrate in blood. When this concentration rises above threshold, glucose appears in final urine. Thus, consistently high concentrations of glucose in final urine are symptomatic of diabetes mellitus.

Other substances usually are not reabsorbed into blood. Among these *low-threshold* substances are nitrogenous by-products such as urea, pigmented blood-breakdown products, and other materials the tubule cells determine to be outright wastes. They become highly concentrated as water is withdrawn from initial urine. For example, final urine contains some 70 times more urea than an equal volume of initial urine.

A third group of materials, which includes water, comprises the *intermediate-threshold* substances. They are or are not absorbed, depending on whether or not they are present in blood in proper amounts. Mineral ions belong to this category. For example, if blood already contains normal concentrations of sodium chloride, then additional salt intake through food will be followed by salt excretion. But if the internal supply is low, the tubule cells will reabsorb salt and thus will not reduce the concentration in blood any further.

The reabsorption of some ions is regulated by hormones. For example, the amount of sodium ions reabsorbed is influenced greatly by *aldosterone,* a steriod hormone produced by the cortex of the adrenal glands (see Chap. 17). Increased secretion of aldosterone increases reabsorption of sodium ions from initial urine into the bloodstream; decreased secretion has the opposite effect. The rate of aldosterone secretion by the adrenal glands is controlled by a complex feedback circuit which, as might be predicted, involves a response to the concentration of sodium in blood.

Thus, kidneys function not merely as excretory organs but as "retention" organs as well. This is why examination of urine can reveal not only how well the kidneys function but also how well chemical steady states are maintained in the body as a whole.

Review Questions

1 Review the basic functions of blood, lymph, and interstitial fluid. Describe the composition of blood plasma, and explain the functions of each group of components.

2 What cellular components occur in blood, and what are the functions of each? By what process is the number of red blood cells maintained relatively constant? Review the reaction pattern of blood clotting?

3 Why is a pronounced yellowing of skin sometimes symptomatic of liver disease? Why does the skin often take on a yellowish hue when the liver malfunctions?

4 Why does injured tissue become swollen? What is the adaptive value of such swelling?

5 Describe how antigens induce respiratory discomfort among people who suffer from hay fever. What can be done to relieve the symptoms of hay fever?

6 Suppose bacteria enter your body through a cut in your hand. Describe the immune response of your body to these bacteria. What cells and molecules would participate in this response? Suppose bacteria carrying the same antigens entered your body through a different cut a few weeks after the first group of invading bacteria has been destroyed.

Would the immune response of your body to the second invasion differ in any way from the first response? Explain fully. Does research into the mechanics of the immune response have any practical value?

7 Describe the structure and function of the main components of the vertebrate circulatory system. Name the main parts of the mammalian heart and the principal blood vessels. Review the general course of the blood circulation. What functions do lymph nodes have in internal steady-state regulation?

8 Review the events during a complete heartbeat, with attention to pressure patterns, valve positions, direction of blood flow, and heart sounds. How is blood moved through veins and lymph vessels?

9 Describe the nervous controls of the heart. How are control signals transmitted through the heart itself? Which motor signals accelerate the heart and which decelerate it? Describe stretch reflexes that accelerate and decelerate the heart.

10 Through what specific processes is the heart speeded up when physical exercise is begun? Slowed down during rest or sleep? What nonnervous agencies affect heart rate?

11 What three major factors control blood pressure, and what governs each of these factors? Describe the action of the vasomotor center. What nervous and chemical agencies affect this center and how?

12 Suppose that physical exercise is begun; describe the specific processes that lead simultaneously to:

a. Increased heart rate
b. Increased breathing rate
c. Increased blood pressure
d. Redistribution of blood in the body

13 Review the principal causes of cardiovascular disease. How can you change the way you live to reduce the risk of a heart attack or stroke?

14 Describe the anatomy of the human breathing system. How is sound produced, and how can sound be varied in pitch, volume, and quality? What is an alveolus, and what is its relation to the lung? What chest structures surround the lungs?

15 Describe the pressure changes in the body associated with inhalation and exhalation in abdominal breathing and in chest breathing. How are inhalation-exhalation cycles controlled and maintained automatically? Review here the roles of CO_2 and the brain.

16 How are the respiratory gases transported in blood? What reactions occur in the lungs and the tissues?

17 Describe the processes through which breathing rate increases when physical exercise is begun and decreases at the onset of sleep. What is hyperventilation, and what is its effect?

18 Interpret the automatic alternation of inhalation and exhalation in terms of control activity. What parts of the breathing system serve as receptors, modulators, effectors, and transmission paths, and what are the stimulus, the feedback, and the response?

19 What is the basic structure and function of an excretory system? What does it excrete? Distinguish between excretory filtration, secretion, and reabsorption.

20 What organs compose the mammalian excretory system, and what is the specific excretory role of each? Describe the general structure of the mammalian kidney and its associated ducts.

21 Describe the structure of a nephron, its ducts, and its blood circulation. Review in detail the process of urine formation in human beings. What are the roles of filtration and reabsorption; where and how does each occur? What are high-threshold substances? Give examples.

Collateral Readings

Avery, M. E., N-S Wang, and **H. W. Taeusch, Jr.:** The Lung of the Newborn Infant, *Scientific American,* April 1973. Functional changes occurring in the lung just before birth are described.

Benditt, E. P.: The Origin of Atherosclerosis, *Scientific American,* February 1977. Discusses theories relating to the cause of this affliction.

Comroe, J. H., Jr.: The Lung, *Scientific American,* February 1966. A recommended review of the biology of this organ.

Cooper, M. D., and **A. R. Lawton:** The Development of the Immune System, *Scientific American,* November 1974. A good account of the origins and interrelations of the diverse cells that defend the body against foreign antigens.

Cunningham, B. A.: The Structure and Function of Histocompatibility Antigens, *Scientific American,* October 1977. This article describes the antigens involved in the rejection of transplanted tissues.

Eckert, R.: "Animal Physiology," Freeman, San Francisco, 1978. One of the best references available for topics included in this chapter.

Kappas, A., and **A. Weber:** How the Liver Metabolizes Foreign Substances, *Scientific American,* June 1975. Describes one of the many important activities of this vital organ.

Koffler, D.: Systemic Lupus Erythematosus, *Scientific American,* July 1980. Describes malfunctions of the immune system that produce this rheumatic disease.

Kolata, G. B., and **J. L. Marx:** Epidemiology of Heart Disease: Searches for Causes, *Science,* vol. 194, pp. 509–512, Oct. 29, 1976. This article identifies factors associated with increased risk of developing heart disease, and describes the various forms of this disease.

Lewin, R.: "In Defense of the Body," Anchor Books, Garden City, N.Y., 1974. A good, readable paperback that describes the cellular and molecular mechanisms of the immune response.

Mayer, R.: The Complement System, *Scientific American,* November 1973. This article describes how foreign cells are attacked by an intricately linked set of proteins.

Mayerson, H.: The Lymphatic System, *Scientific American,* June 1963. A good account on the biology of this system.

Milstein, C.: Monoclonal Antibodies, *Scientific American,* October 1980. Describes how individual antibodies can be produced in great quantities for long periods of time. This revolutionary technique may lead to many therapeutic applications in the near future.

Naeye, R.: Sudden Infant Death, *Scientific American,* April 1980. Relates evidence suggesting that abnormalities in respiratory controls may account for these tragic deaths.

Nossal, G. J. V.: "Antibodies and Immunity," 2d ed., Basic Books, New York, 1978. Written for the layperson, this book reviews much of the important recent research in immunobiology.

Perutz, M. F.: Hemoglobin Structure and Respiratory Transport, *Scientific American,* December 1978. How hemoglobin transports both oxygen and CO_2 is the subject of this interesting article.

Rose, N.: Autoimmune Disease, *Scientific American,* February 1981. The author describes how several human diseases are caused by malfunctions in which the immune system loses its ability to distinguish foreign antigens from those produced by the body's own cells.

Ross, R., and **J. A. Glomset:** Atherosclerosis and the Arterial Smooth Muscle Cell, *Science,* vol. 180, pp. 1332–1339, June 1973. A good description of the changes in smooth muscles that accompany hardening of the arteries.

Schmeck, H. M.: "Immunology: The Many-Edged Sword," Braziller, New York, 1974. An excellent book on fundamental concepts of immunology. Several health-related topics are included.

Schmidt-Nielson, K.: How Animals Breathe, *Scientific American,* December 1971. An account of a breathing system very different from that of human beings and other mammals.

———: "How Animals Work," Cambridge University Press, New York, 1972. A very readable, short paperback, designed to introduce students to the field of animal physiology.

Smith, H.: The Kidney, *Scientific American,* January 1953. Well written and still relevant, this article examines kidney function and evolution of the vertebrate kidneys.

Wood, J. E.: The Venous System, *Scientific American,* January 1968. An excellent article on the structure and functions of these vessels.

Zucker, M.: The Functioning of Blood Platelets, *Scientific American,* June 1980. Describes normal and abnormal interactions between the content of platelets and other blood-borne substances.

Chapter 19 Nervous Control

Learning Objectives

After reading this chapter you should be able to:

1. Differentiate between neurons and neuroglia; specify the structural and functional relations between the dendrites, cell bodies, and axons of neurons; define reflex arc, and name the functional relationships between sensory neurons, motor neurons, and interneurons; show how neurons contribute to steady-state control; differentiate between Schwann cells and myelin sheaths.
2. Outline the anatomical relations between neurons, nerves, ganglia, and brains; distinguish between central and peripheral nervous systems.
3. List the three major divisions of the vertebrate brain and name the principal subdivisions of each; indicate the anatomical relations between the following components of a vertebrate brain:
   - **a.** olfactory lobes
   - **b.** cerebral hemispheres
   - **c.** thalamus
   - **d.** hypothalamus
   - **e.** optic lobes
   - **f.** cerebellum
   - **g.** pons
   - **h.** medulla oblongata
   - **i.** corpus callosum
   - **j.** pineal body
4. Name at least one function for each of the structures listed in Objective 3.
5. Distinguish between myelinated and nonmyelinated nerve fibers and explain how myelinated fibers can conduct nerve impulses faster than nonmyelinated ones; differentiate between cranial and spinal nerves.
6. Differentiate between the afferent and efferent divisions of peripheral nervous systems; distinguish between the two principal components of the efferent division; construct a diagram that illustrates the regulation of at least one specific function by the autonomic nervous system of vertebrates; distinguish between the sympathetic and parasympathetic subdivisions of the autonomic nervous system.
7. Define and state the anatomical relations between preganglionic and postganglionic nerve fibers.
8. Distinguish between nerve impulse and action potential and list at least three ways in which a nerve impulse can be triggered in a neuron; define threshold and all-or-none response; describe two mechanisms by which the central nervous system of animals can distinguish between different intensities of stimuli.
9. Show how nerve impulses are propagated along neurons; explain how the sodium-potassium pump establishes an electric potential across the plasma membrane of a neuron and show how at least two other factors contribute to the establishment and maintenance of such electric potentials.
10. List at least two ways in which nerve impulses are transmitted between neurons; distinguish between synapse and synaptic cleft and indicate the role of neurotransmitters in propagating nerve impulses between neurons; name at least three neurotransmitters; name and describe at least one human disease caused by inadequate production of a neurotransmitter; define and state the function of the blood-brain barrier.
11. Differentiate between excitatory and inhibitory neurons; show how behavioral responses of organisms are related to the structural organization of excitatory and inhibitory neurons.
12. Distinguish between programmed behavior, habituation, classical conditioning, and operant conditioning, and give an example of each; define and illustrate the function of the vertebrate reticular formation.
13. Define and list at least three examples of neural receptors; identify a location for each receptor you identify and indicate how neural receptors contribute to steady-state control.
14. Specify the structural and functional relations between each of the following components of the human ear:
    - **a.** outer ear

- **b.** eardrum
- **c.** hammer, anvil, and stirrup
- **d.** round and oval windows
- **e.** cochlea

15. Show how different frequencies of sound waves trigger different patterns of impulses in sensory neurons that lead from the ear to the brain.

16. Construct a diagram that depicts the structure and location of at least one type of chemoreceptor.

17. Name the structural and functional relations between each of the following components of the vertebrate eye:
- **a.** retina
- **b.** sclera
- **c.** choroid coat
- **d.** cornea
- **e.** iris
- **f.** lens
- **g.** ciliary ligaments and muscles
- **h.** aqueous humor and vitreous body

18. Define visual accommodation and explain how this process is regulated; distinguish between rods and cones of the human retina and state the principal functions of each; show how eye pigments and the transmission of nerve impulses from the eyes to the brain are related functionally.

19. Differentiate between skeletal, cardiac, and smooth muscle; outline the anatomical and functional relations between each of the following components of striated muscles:
- **a.** muscle fibers
- **b.** myofibrils
- **c.** myofilaments
- **d.** sacromeres

20. Construct a diagram that depicts the structural relations between the following subdivisions of a sarcomere:
- **a.** Z lines
- **b.** A bands
- **c.** I bands
- **d.** H zone

21. Show how the different densities of I bands, A bands, and H zones are related to the arrangement of actin and myosin filaments in sarcomeres; state the sliding-filament theory of muscle contraction and list evidence that supports this theory; explain how muscles contribute to steady-state control.

22. Describe the structural and functional relations between each of the following in the contraction of striated muscle:
- **a.** neurons
- **b.** neurotransmitters
- **c.** sarcoplasmic reticulum
- **d.** ATP
- **e.** calcium ions
- **f.** troponin, tropomyosin, actin, and myosin

23. Illustrate how muscle contraction can be inhibited chemically.

24. List at least two kinds of evidence indicating production of natural morphinelike substances by tissues of the central nervous system; describe evidence suggesting that endorphins regulate certain aspects of animal behavior; show why biologists now suspect that substance P is a transmitter of pain signals in vertebrates; list at least two kinds of evidence suggesting an antagonistic relationship between enkephalins and substance P; outline evidence suggesting a possible relationship between endorphins and acupuncture; identify at least two ways in which endorphins or endorphinlike substances may eventually be used to treat human disorders; indicate why the story behind our steadily increasing knowledge of pain transmission and suppression provides a good illustration of how science proceeds.

Most intercellular functions of animals are at least partly coordinated by nervous activity. Even routine operations usually involve exceedingly complex nervous controls. Consider, for example, simply grasping an object, something most of us accomplish repeatedly every day. Information concerning the location and position of such objects first must traverse thousands of nervous interconnections between the eyes and various parts of the nervous system that control muscle activity. Finger muscles then must be extended and contracted, the amount of extension and contraction varying with the size, shape, and weight of the object. The wrist, elbow, and shoulder also must be extended in a coordinated manner. Because the center of gravity of the body shifts during extension of the arm, patterns of contraction for many other muscles must be adjusted continuously if an upright posture is to be maintained.

Like many other activities of animals, such movements are controlled by an integrated set of nervous structures that function as receptors, sensory pathways, modulators, and motor pathways. The neural receptors are either specialized *sensory cells* or specialized parts of nerve cells. In many cases such cells or cell parts are structural components of sense organs, such as eyes.

Sensitive to environmental or internal stimuli, receptors initiate nerve impulses that convey information related to the stimuli. These impulses are transmitted over *sensory nerve fibers* to modulators such as ganglia, nerve cords, and brains. Modulators "integrate" sensory impulses, often store incoming information as memory, and send out motor impulses that usually are in some way associated with the incoming information. Such impulses pass through *motor nerve fibers* to effectors. The two most common effectors in animals are *muscles* and *glands.* They then carry out responses which normally bear some more or less direct relation to the original stimuli, and which in the long run usually tend to preserve steady states. Many of these responses contribute to recognizable forms of *behavior.*

NEURAL PATHWAYS

General Characteristics

Nerve impulses are generated and conducted by specialized cells called *neurons* (Fig. 19.1). Each neuron typically consists of a nucleus-containing *cell body* and one or more filamentous outgrowths, or *fibers,* that extend away from the cell

Fig. 19.1 Nerve tissue. (A) General structure of a neuron with a myelinated axon. Relative lengths of cell parts are not drawn to scale. Axons, for example, are often many times the combined length of all other parts. (B) Micrograph of a stained motor (multipolar) neuron. (C) Nonmyelinated and myelinated fibers. Left, cross-sectional view of a fiber without myelin, showing a Schwann cell surrounding an axon almost completely. Right, cross-sectional view of a developing myelinated fiber. A myelin sheath grows as an extension of the Schwann cells, each of which wraps around the axon several times (more often than shown) and forms an envelope of many layers. The inner layers collectively represent the myelin sheath. (D) High-power view of a single neuroglia cell. Note the elongated extensions from the main part of the cell (×1500).

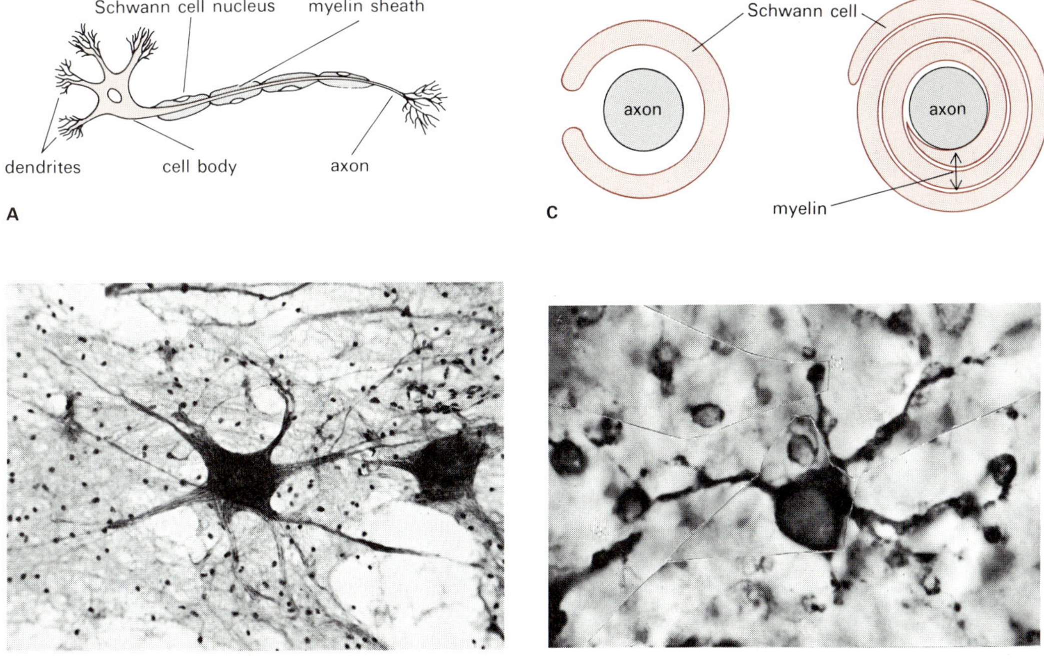

body. The neurons of vertebrates generally have two kinds of fibers, *dendrites* and *axons.* A nerve impulse usually originates at the terminals of a dendrite, which then conducts the impulse to the cell body. Impulses travel away from a cell body through axons. Vertebrate neurons can have one or more dendrites, but most of these cells have only one axon. Many dendrites and axons are short, but others are over a meter long, e.g., axons from the base of the human spinal cord to the toes.

The long axons and dendrites are enveloped by a cellular sheath. Among neurons in the vertebrate *central nervous system* (*brain* and *spinal cord*), such sheaths largely consist of cells called *neuroglia*, or *glial cells.* The functions of such cells, which vastly outnumber neurons, are largely unknown. Some evidence suggests that glial cells insulate individual fibers of neurons, preventing "cross jumping" of nerve impulses between them.

In the *peripheral nervous system,* outside the brain and spinal cord, the sheaths surrounding axons and dendrites usually are composed of *Schwann cells.* In certain cases these cells wind around a nerve fiber several times, and the fatty contents of these wrapping layers then form a *myelin sheath* (see Fig. 19.1). Such sheaths function in speeding up conduction of nerve impulses. Myelinated fibers conduct impulses at speeds up to 100 meters per second. By contrast, many nonmyelinated fibers conduct impulses at only a quarter of this rate. How myelin sheaths increase rates of nerve impulses is discussed below. Like sheaths composed of glial cells, myelin sheaths also may ensure that nerve impulses will pass between neurons only at a specialized junction called a *synapse.* The terminals of adjacent neurons usually do not touch at a synapse; with few exceptions the terminals are separated by a microscopic space, the *synaptic cleft.*

Transmission of nerve impulses across a synaptic cleft is mediated by chemical secretions called *neurotransmitters.* Until recently, most biologists believed that neurotransmitters emanated exclusively from axons, passed across a synaptic cleft, and triggered a nerve impulse in adjacent dendrites. This rule of thumb remains generally valid today, but in a few instances dendrites have been shown to form synapses with other dendrites. Moreover, some neurons secrete neurotransmitters that initiate nerve impulses in the *axons* of others.

In crude terms a whole nervous system can be envisaged as an intricate network of neurons, with fibers interconnecting functionally at numerous synapses. Many pathways in such a network form *reflex arcs,* composed of a sequence of neurons with specific functions. Thus, *sensory* (or *afferent*) neurons transmit impulses from a modulator to an ceptor to a modulator, and *motor* (or *efferent*) neurons transmit impulses from a modulator to an effector. Neurons in a modulator are *interneurons* (Fig. 19.2). Groups of nerve fibers frequently traverse a body region as a single collective fiber bundle, or *nerve.* Nerves are designated as sensory, motor, or mixed, depending on whether they contain sensory fibers, motor fibers, or both; most nerves are mixed.

The most primitive type of neuron arrangement known is a *nerve net* (Fig. 19.3). Consisting of a loosely organized mesh of neurons scattered throughout one or more tissues, nerve nets repre-

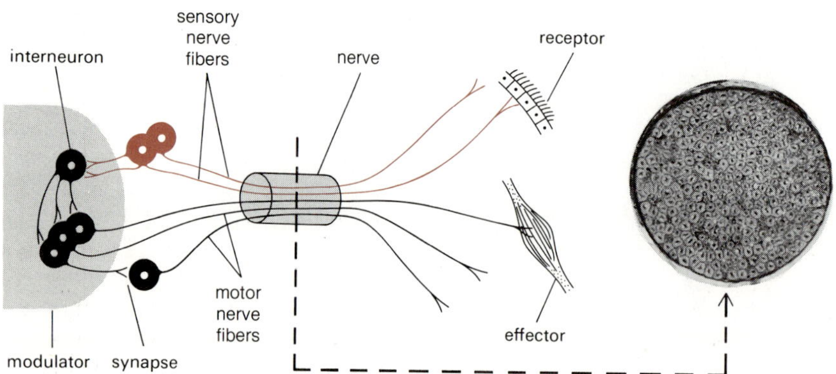

Fig. 19.2 Neural pathways. Sensory nerve fibers (color) conduct impulses from receptors to modulators, where interneurons transmit the impulses to motor nerve fibers. The latter send impulses to effectors. Neurons interconnect functionally across synapses. Collected bundles of neuron fibers form nerves. The photograph at right depicts a cross section through such a nerve. Note the many individual nerve fibers. (*General Biological Supply House, Inc.*)

sent the only neural structures in many animals such as jellyfish. But such nets also form at least part of the nervous systems of more complex animals. In vertebrates, for example, nerve nets occur in the wall of the alimentary tract. Nerve impulses initiated in any one neuron of a nerve net usually are transmitted through all neurons of the net to all effectors. Thus, although such primitive neural networks permit reaction to many stimuli, the responses that result generally are gross, unmodifiable, and relatively nonspecific.

Most animals also have *nerve cords,* condensed regions of nets, and *ganglia,* dense accumulations of neurons and fiber terminals (see Fig. 19.3). Ganglia may be sensory, motor, or mixed, according to the kinds of fibers they connect with. Large ganglia usually contain functional subdivisions called *nerve centers,* specialized groups of interneurons regulating specific activities. Very large ganglia also may store new information as memory and control intricate forms of behavior. Large ganglia or groups of ganglia that integrate the main sensory inputs and motor outputs of animals constitute *brains.*

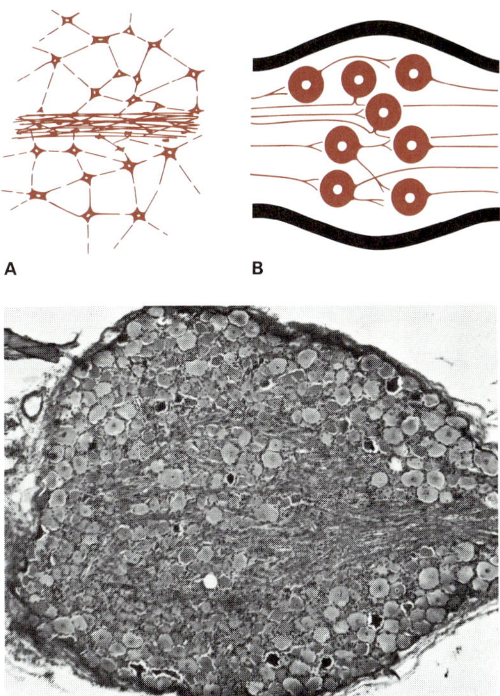

Fig. 19.3 Nerve nets, cords, and ganglia. (A) A dense concentration of parts of a nerve net, which forms a portion of a nerve cord. (B) Schematic representation of a ganglion; a mixed ganglion is indicated here, with sensory and motor neurons as well as interneurons. (C) Section through a spinal (sensory) ganglion of a mammal; note the many cell bodies and also the nerve fibers, some seen in cross section, some in longitudinal section. (*C, Ward's Natural Science Establishment, Inc.*)

Vertebrate Central Nervous Systems

By far the most complex central nervous systems are those of vertebrates. The main parts of the brain and spinal cord develop from a hollow dorsal *neural tube,* formed in the embryo as an ingrowth from the ectoderm (see Chap. 24). The anterior portion of the tube enlarges as the brain, the posterior portion becomes the spinal cord, and nerves grow out from both. Anteriorly, the fluid-filled space in the tube forms a series of cavities, or *ventricles,* in the brain. Posteriorly, the fluid-filled space forms the *spinal canal.*

A mature vertebrate brain is composed of three major divisions, *forebrain, midbrain,* and *hindbrain* (Table 19.1 and Fig. 19.4). Of the two main subdivisions of the forebrain, the more anterior one is the *telencephalon.* It contains paired *olfactory lobes,* the centers for the sense of smell. In birds and mammals the telencephalon is enlarged greatly as a pair of *cerebral hemispheres,* which cover virtually all the rest of the brain. These hemispheres, collectively termed the *cerebrum,* contain the centers for the most complex sensory integration and for voluntary motor activities, and they also play the key roles in the control of memory and intelligence. A conspicuous set of nerve tracts, the *corpus callosum,* interconnects the two hemispheres.

The second major subdivision of the forebrain is the *diencephalon.* The largest part of this unit is the *thalamus,* a structure that functions as a way station and integrating center for most sensory impulses being transmitted to the cerebrum. Lying just below the thalamus is the *hypothalamus.* This tiny component of the diencephalon appears to be the single most important control area for regulation of internal body functions. It also influences emotional states. In people undergoing brain surgery, electrical stimulation of certain regions of the hypothalamus produces rewarding or pleasurable sensations while stimulation of other hypothalamic

TABLE 19.1
Components of a Mature Vertebrate Brain

Primary divisions	Secondary divisions	Principal structures
forebrain	telencephalon	olfactory lobes
		cerebral hemispheres (cerebrum)
	diencephalon	thalamus
		hypothalamus
		epithalamus
midbrain (mesencephalon)		optic lobes
hindbrain	metencephalon	cerebellum
		pons
	myelencephalon (medulla oblongata)	most cranial nerves

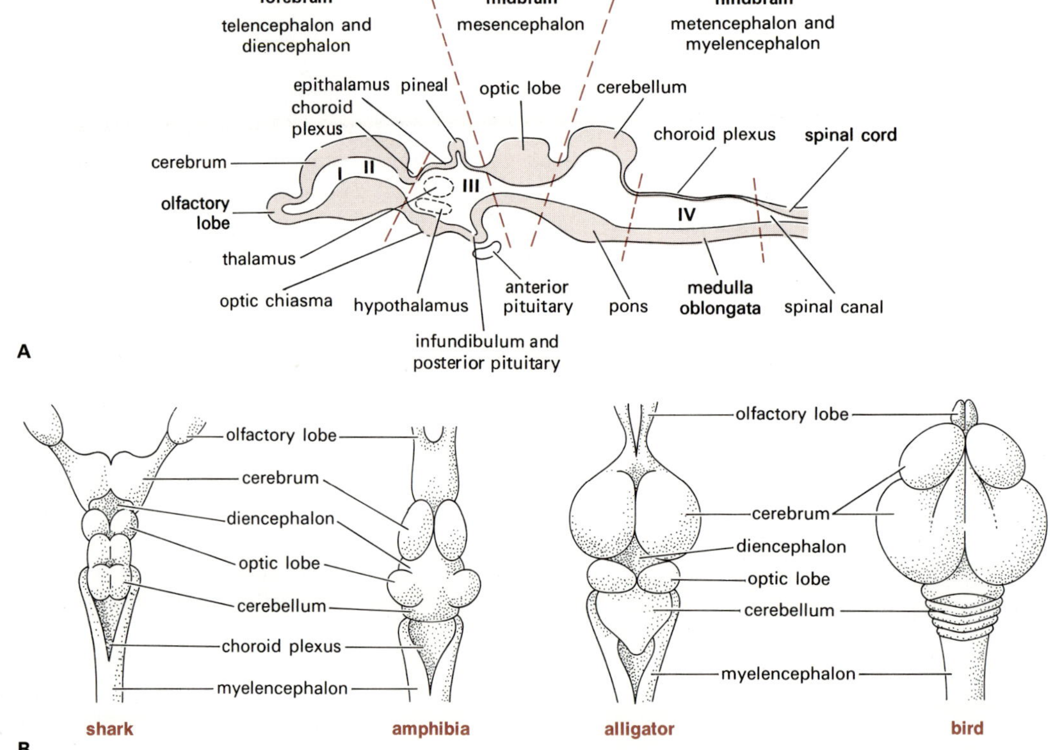

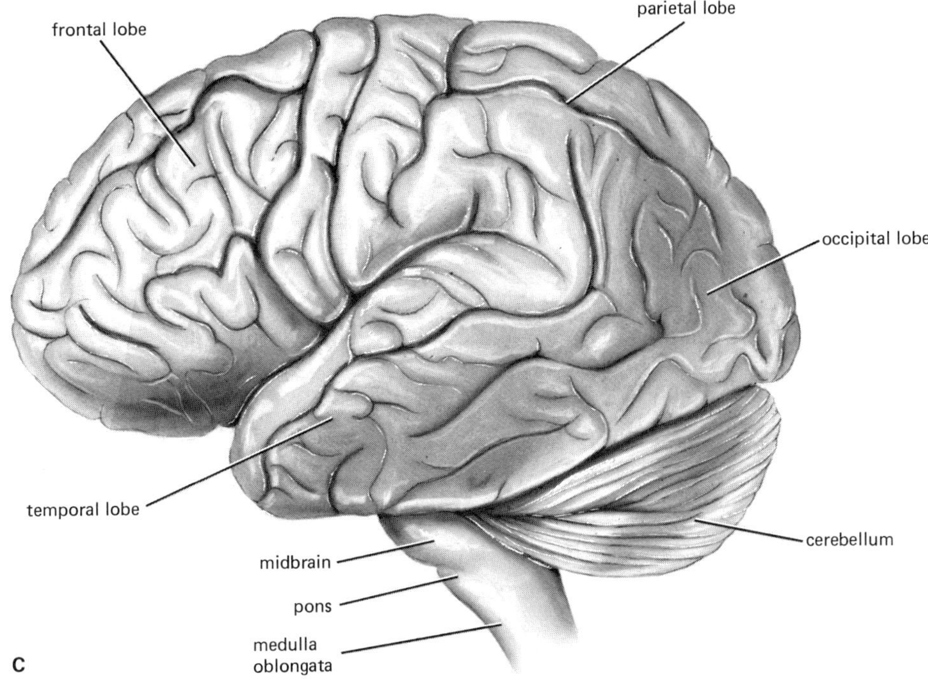

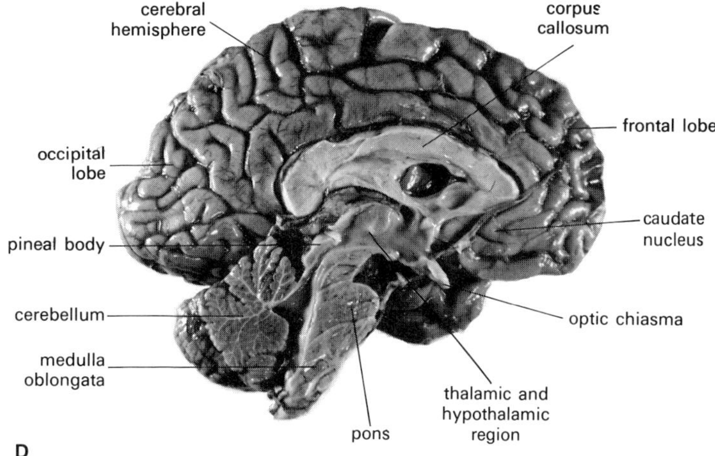

Fig. 19.4 The vertebrate brain. (A) Median section through primitive vertebrate brain (as in fishes), showing basic structural plan. Roman numerals refer to ventricles. Thalamus and hypothalamus regions are indicated in light broken lines, since these brain parts lie on each side of the median plane (as do ventricles I and II). The portion of the pituitary that becomes the anterior lobe forms as an outpouching from the roof of the mouth. The infundibulum, or pituitary stalk, and posterior lobe of the pituitary arise from the brain (see Chap. 17). The two choroid plexi are vascular membranous regions that form much of the cerebrospinal fluid filling the ventricles. (B) Dorsal views of brains in different vertebrate classes. Note the proportionate progressive enlargement of the cerebrum in the posterior direction (and the parallel reduction of the olfactory lobes). (C) Lateral view of human cerebrum (color). (D) Median section through the human brain. The cerebrum is so large that, in dorsal view, it covers the cerebellum posteriorly. The functions of the optic chiasma, caudate nucleus and occipital lobe of the brain are described below.

areas often generates unpleasant feelings. The hypothalamus also regulates endocrine secretions of the pituitary which, as noted in Chap. 17, projects ventrally from its base.

The thalamus is covered dorsally by the *epithalamus,* the third chief component of the diencephalon (see Table 19.1 and Fig. 19.4). This region contains the unpaired pineal body, a structure that forms a third eye on the top of the head of lampreys (see Chap. 35). Hidden under the cerebral hemispheres in birds and mammals, the pineal body secretes *melatonin.* This hormone inhibits reproductive functions in some vertebrates; its role in human beings remains unknown.

The midbrain, or *mesencephalon,* contains dorsally located *optic lobes.* In all vertebrates except the mammals, these lobes function as the center for vision, and the optic nerve tracts from the eyes terminate there. In mammals, these nerve tracts continue onto visual centers located posteriorly in the cerebral hemispheres. The original optic lobes here are little more than relay stations for visual nerve impulses.

The hindbrain consists of two subdivisions, an anterior *metencephalon* and a posterior *myelencephalon,* or *medulla oblongata.* Dorsally the metencephalon includes the *cerebellum,* a comparatively large lobe that coordinates muscle contractions as smoothly integrated movements. For example, locomotion and balancing activities are influenced by

Fig. 19.5 The main nerves. Underside of brain and part of human spinal cord, showing the origin of cranial and spinal nerves. The dorsal root ganglia are sensory, the ventral root, motor.

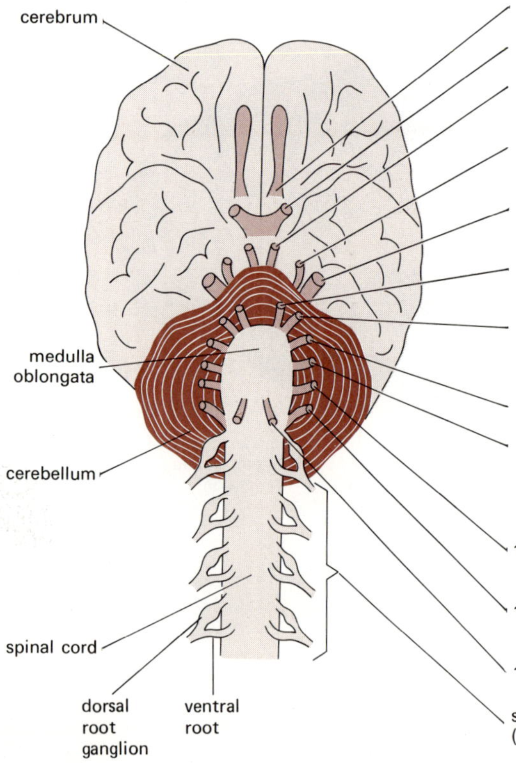

cerebrum
medulla oblongata
cerebellum
spinal cord
dorsal root ganglion
ventral root

cranial and spinal nerves in mammals

name	type	innervation
1 olfactory	sensory	from nose
2 optic	sensory	from eye
3 oculomotor	motor	to muscles of eyeball
4 trochlear	motor	to muscles of eyeball
5 trigeminal	mixed	from and to face, teeth
6 abducens	motor	to muscles of eyeball
7 facial	mixed	from taste buds to salivary glands and facial muscles
8 auditory	sensory	from ear
9 glossopharyngeal	mixed	from and to pharynx, from taste buds to salivary glands
10 vagus	mixed	from and to chest and abdomen
11 spinal accessory	motor	to shoulder muscles
12 hypoglossal	motor	to tongue
spinal nerves (31 pairs)	mixed	from and to muscles in arms, legs, and trunk

this lobe. Ventrally the metencephalon contains a conspicuous bulge, the *pons*, in which the nerve tracts between brain and spinal cord cross from one side to the other. Because of similar crossovers in various brain regions, the left side of the brain controls most of the activities on the right side of the body and vice versa.

The medulla oblongata, which contains the nerve centers controlling heartbeat, vasomotion, and breathing, continues posteriorly as the spinal cord. Ten pairs of *cranial nerves* (twelve pairs in reptiles, birds, and mammals) emerge from the brain, and most of them lead away from the medulla oblongata (Fig. 19.5). The spinal cord gives rise to paired, segmental *spinal nerves*, which pass to the trunk and the appendages. In each spinal nerve, sensory fibers enter the dorsal part of the spinal cord, and motor fibers leave from the ventral part. The cell bodies of the sensory fibers lie just outside the spinal cord, in *dorsal root ganglia* (Fig. 19.6).

Vertebrate Peripheral Nervous Systems

Vertebrates also have well-developed peripheral nervous systems, which are separated into *afferent* and *efferent* divisions (Table 19.2). As noted earlier, afferent neurons transmit information from receptors to the central nervous system, and efferent neurons pass impulses from the central nervous system to effectors.

TABLE 19.2
Divisions of the Peripheral Nervous System

I. afferent fibers
II. efferent fibers
  A. somatic
  B. autonomic
    1. sympathetic
    2. parasympathetic

SOURCE: D. S. Luciano, A. J. Vander, and J. H. Sherman, "Human Function and Structure," table 8-2, p. 258, McGraw Hill, New York, 1978.

The efferent division is more complex than the afferent and is subdivided further into *somatic* and *autonomic* components. Because they innervate muscles that move skeletal parts, somatic motor neurons control movements that generally are under voluntary control. The cell bodies of these neurons are arranged in groups within the brain and spinal cord, and their large, myelinated axons connect directly to skeletal muscle fibers. Controlling involuntary activities and containing only nonmyelinated nerve fibers, autonomic neurons emanate from nerve centers in the spinal cord and the

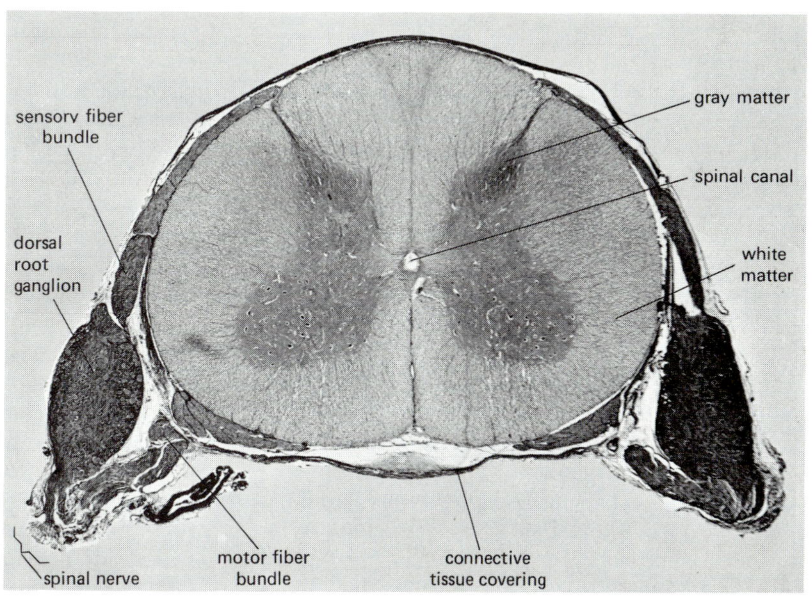

Fig. 19.6 The mammalian spinal cord, cross section. Note that each spinal nerve divides into two fiber bundles. The motor bundle connects with the cord ventrally, and the sensory bundle passes through a dorsal root ganglion and connects with the cord dorsally. The spinal cord itself is a dense mesh of neurons and fiber bundles. The cell bodies of the neurons are aggregated around the center and form so-called gray matter. The axons (fibers) of these neurons form the white matter around the gray matter. The central spinal canal is occluded or may contan lymphlike spinal fluid.

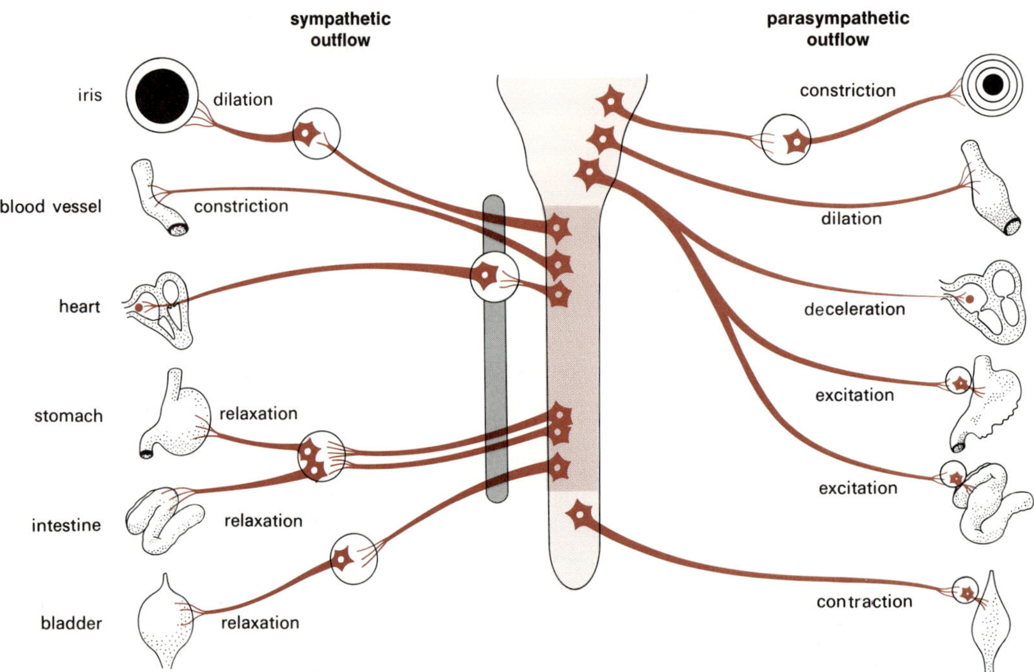

Fig. 19.7 Autonomic nervous system: some of the major motor pathways. In the spinal cord (center), parasympathetic centers are shown in light color; sympathetic centers are darker. The column to the left of the spinal cord represents the sympathetic trunk on that side. Each neural path shown occurs pairwise, one on each side of the body. For simplicity, only one side is indicated in each case, but most organs are innervated by both sympathetic and parasympathetic nerves.

brain, and they synapse with a second set of neurons in a series of small peripheral ganglia. The autonomic nervous system influences a wide variety of functions. Some, for example, involve regulation of heartbeat, control over smooth muscles in blood vessels, urinary bladder, and alimentary canal, and control of secretions from salivary, sweat, and intestinal glands.

From the autonomic centers lead away *two* functionally different sets of *autonomic motor fibers* (Fig. 19.7). Fibers from the brain and the most posterior part of the spinal cord represent a *parasympathetic outflow* of the autonomic system, and fibers from the midportion of the spinal cord form a *sympathetic outflow.* In general, each organ of the body controlled by autonomic nerves receives fibers from both outflows, and they usually have opposing effects. If parasympathetic fibers inhibit a particular organ, sympathetic fibers stimulate it; or vice versa. For example, the inhibitory fibers to the pacemaker of the heart (which travel in the cranial vagus nerves; see Chap. 18) are part of the parasympathetic outflow, and the accelerating fibers to the heart belong to the sympathetic outflow. Similarly, fibers that stimulate secretion of digestive glands in the stomach are parasympathetic, whereas those inhibiting secretion emanate from the sympathetic division. Most other organs that function involuntarily likewise are equipped with both braking and accelerating controls.

Each autonomic motor path to a given organ consists of at least two consecutive neurons, which synapse in a ganglion located somewhere along the path to the organ. The nerve fiber leading to this ganglion is said to be *preganglionic,* and the fiber from the ganglion to the organ is *postganglionic.* Many sympathetic ganglia lie on each side of the spinal cord; each column of ganglia are interconnected as a *sympathetic trunk,* or *chain ganglia* (Fig. 19.8). Parasympathetic ganglia are more dispersed and are not arranged as chains.

The involuntary functions of autonomic neu-

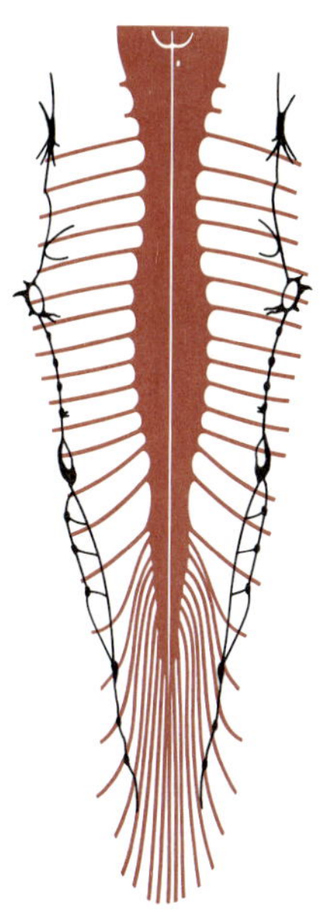

Fig. 19.8 Sympathetic trunks. Spinal cord and nerves in color, sympathetic trunks in black.

rons are interrelated closely with the voluntary operations of somatic nerve cells. During sobbing, for example, autonomic neurons control tear secretions, but somatic cells determine breathing patterns and regulate contraction of facial muscles.

NEURAL IMPULSES

General Characteristics

A nerve impulse occurs when a neuron is stimulated in some way—by an electric shock, a change of pH, touch, or a variety of other stimuli. Regardless of its nature, the stimulus must be of sufficient intensity to trigger an impulse. Stimuli below a certain intensity, or *threshold,* will not elicit a response. Conversely, increasing the intensity of a stimulus above threshold does not increase the intensity or speed of the impulse. Either individual neurons transmit impulses to a maximum potential or impulses are not transmitted at all. Appropriately, this kind of biological reaction is termed an *all-or-none response.*

The all-or-none response of neurons raises an immediate question. How does the central nervous system of an animal distinguish between different intensities of the same stimulus? People, for example, are able to distinguish between a soft caress and a forceful squeeze. Stimuli of different intensities are detected in more than one way. For example, the frequency with which nerve impulses travel along neurons can vary substantially. More intense stimuli usually trigger a higher frequency of impulses in a neuron. Also, different neurons have different thresholds. A low-intensity stimulus triggers impulses only in low-threshold neurons, while a high-intensity stimulus triggers impulses in both low- and high-threshold neurons. Thus, a high-intensity stimulus, like a forceful squeeze, triggers impulses in a greater number of neurons than a low-intensity stimulus and simultaneously triggers a greater frequency of nerve impulses in at least some of these neurons.

Transmission of Nerve Impulses along Neurons

The Action Potential

Biologists began studying the nature of nerve impulses over 100 years ago. Their early experiments demonstrated that a nerve impulse involves electrical events, but it soon became clear that neurons are not at all like wires, which conduct electrons along their length. Neurons transmit impulses far more slowly than wires conduct electricity. Moreover, the cytoplasm of a cell is highly resistant to the flow of an electric current.

Eventually, in the 1930s, the true nature of the nerve impulse became known. It was found to consist of a wavelike series of electrochemical events that involve changes in the distribution of ions inside and outside a neuron. To understand how the distribution of ions changes during the transmission of a nerve impulse, it is first necessary to understand how the ions normally are arranged in a resting, nonstimulated neuron.

The plasma membrane of a neuron is so constructed that, in the rest state, a higher concentration of positively charged ions is maintained outside the neuron than inside the cell. Thus, at rest, a neuron is electrically positive along the outside of its surface membrane and electrically negative along the inside (Fig. 19.9). Sodium (Na^+) ions are the most abundant positively charged substances

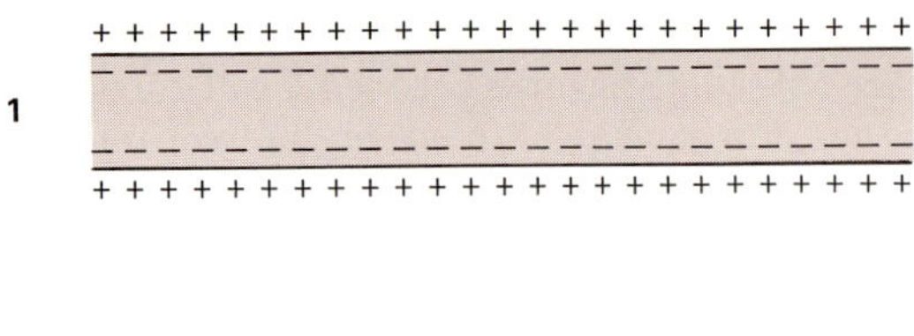

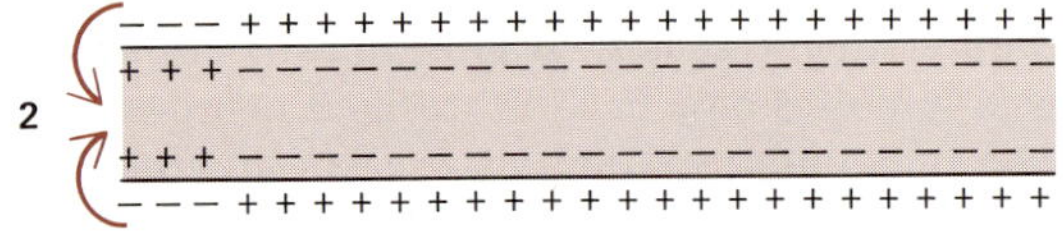

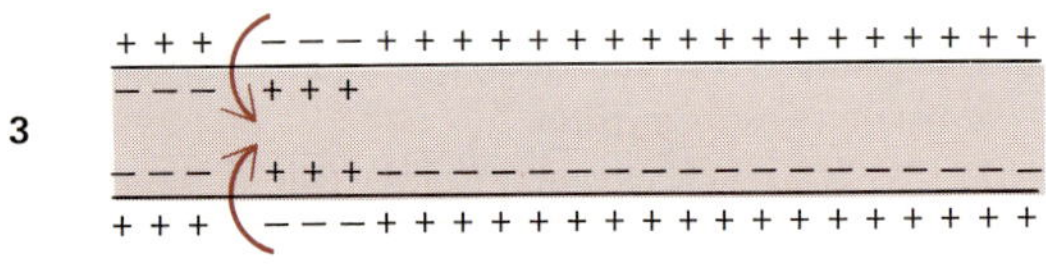

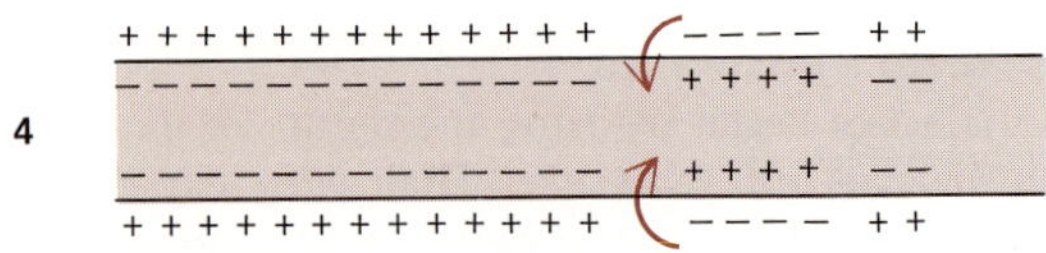

Fig. 19.9 The nerve impulse. Because of an unequal distribution of ions, a resting neuron (1) is electrically positive along the outside of its plasma membrane and electrically negative on the inside. The permeability of the membrane changes dramatically at a point where a neuron is stimulated, permitting large numbers of sodium (Na^+) ions to rush into the cell (arrows). The number of sodium ions entering at the point of stimulation is so rapid that the inside of the cell momentarily becomes electropositive to the outside (2). Within half a millisecond, channels permitting the outward flow of potassium (K^+) ions open in the plasma membrane. The movement of positively charged potassium to the outside of the cell reestablishes the net negative charge inside (3). The momentary reversal of charge triggers an identical change of permeability in an adjacent portion of the plasma membrane (3), which in turn triggers depolarization at a point farther along the neuron (4).

maintained outside a resting neuron. The extracellular fluid contains about 10 times as many sodium ions as are inside a neuron. This is not to say that positively charged ions do not exist inside resting neurons. On the contrary, the concentration of potassium (K^+) ions is much higher inside than outside. But the total positive charge generated by these ions is more than offset by an abundance of negatively charged ions inside the cell.

This unequal distribution of ions stems in part from the selective permeability of the plasma membrane of a resting neuron. The membrane normally is highly resistant to the movement of ions between the extra- and intracellular environments. However, the permeability characteristics of the membrane change radically when a neuron is stimulated. At such times the membrane initially becomes highly permeable to sodium ions at the point of stimulation. Sodium ions rush into the cell, moving through channels formed by alterations in the shape of paired proteins that extend from one side of the plasma membrane to the other (see Chap. 5).

The movement of sodium ions into the cell is extremely rapid, for two chief reasons: (1) differences in the concentration of sodium inside and outside the cell tend to produce a net inward movement of the ions, and (2) the higher concentration of negatively charged ions inside the cell attracts the positively charged sodium ions. The inward movement of sodium is so rapid that the net charge of the cytoplasm becomes positive with respect to the extracellular fluid, but only for a moment. Less than 0.5 millisecond after sodium begins to rush into the cell, potassium channels become established in the membrane, permitting a large outward flow of these positively charged ions. The outward movement of potassium quickly reestablishes the net negative charge inside the neuron (see Fig. 19.9).

The brief reversal of electric charge that occurs when sodium rushes into a neuron at the point of stimulation is called the *action potential.* This electrochemical change triggers an identical cycle of ionic changes at an adjacent point on the plasma membrane. The second depolarization triggers a third, and so on along the length of the neuron. In this way, a wavelike series of action potentials travels along the neuron surface. This wave of action potentials represents a *nerve impulse.*

As noted earlier, myelinated fibers conduct nerve impulses faster than nonmyelinated ones. Action potentials do not occur where fibers are wrapped with myelin. However, myelin sheaths are interrupted at regular intervals at points where one Schwann cell ends and another begins. Such points are called *nodes.* Action potentials jump from node to node along a myelinated fiber instead of passing along its entire surface. This jumping causes a nerve impulse to be propagated much faster than during an uninterrupted transmission.

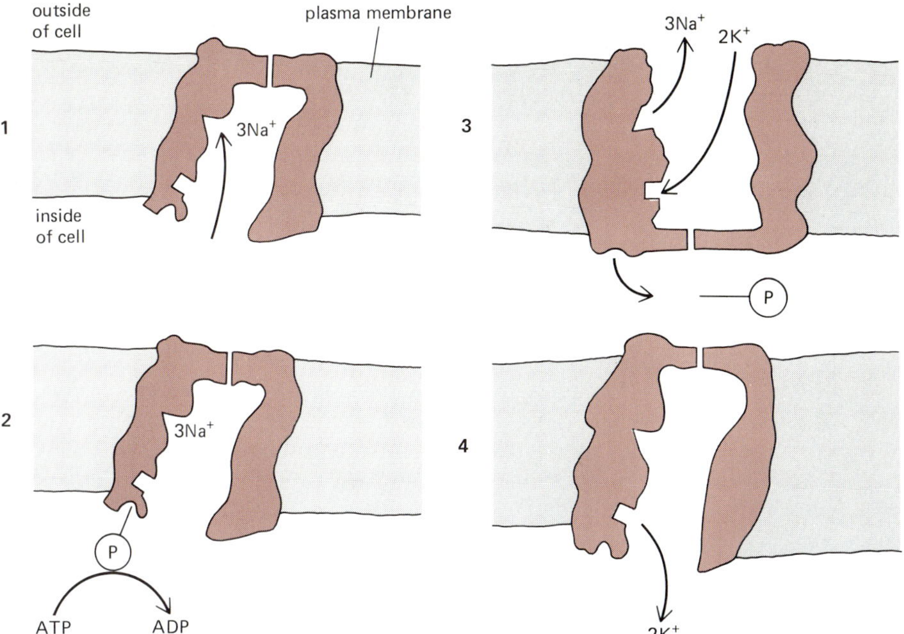

Fig. 19.10 The sodium-potassium pump. The plasma membrane of neurons contains many copies of a protein complex called the sodium-potassium pump. In this hypothetical model, the protein complex (color) is shown in its E_1 conformation (1, 2, and 4) and E_2 conformation (3). Sodium ions bind readily to the complex when it is in the E_1 state. At such times the binding site for sodium (triangle) is turned toward the cytoplasm. The binding of sodium (1) triggers phosphorylation of the complex by ATP (2). Attachment of the phosphate unit brings about a change in conformation to the E_2 state, whereupon sodium ions are released to the outside. Sodium does not attach readily to the complex when it is in the E_2 conformation, but potassium ions do. Binding potassium to its site (square) triggers dephosphorylation, which in turn causes the pump complex to revert to the E_1 conformation. Potassium ions have a low affinity for their binding site when the complex is in the E_1 state and therefore tend to be released to the cytoplasm. Experiments have shown that three sodium ions are transported outward for every two potassium ions brought into a cell.

The Sodium-Potassium Pump

Once a nerve impulse has passed a region along a nerve fiber, a large concentration of sodium ions exists inside the neuron and large numbers of potassium ions are contained in extracellular fluids. For a subsequent action potential to occur, the original distribution of ions must be reestablished. Many cells in addition to neurons are able to establish unequal distributions of ions across surface membranes, and biologists have long puzzled over the mechanisms responsible. Although much remains unknown, recent research has shown that the plasma membrane of neurons (and other cells) contains multiple copies of a protein complex that actively pumps sodium ions to the extracellular environment in exchange for potassium ions. The latter are transported into the cell.

Each protein complex, called a *sodium-potassium pump,* contains a separate binding site for sodium and potassium ions and probably spans the plasma membrane from its inner to its outer surface (Fig. 19.10). The complex apparently exists in two conformations, called E_1 and E_2. In the E_1 conformation, the binding sites for sodium and potassium ions are turned toward the cytoplasm of the cell. They are reversed in the E_2 conformation and turned toward the extracellular environment.

Sodium ions readily bind to the pump complex when it is in the E_1 conformation. Attachment of Na^+ triggers transfer of a phosphate group from ATP to the complex. The phosphorylation brings about a shift to the E_2 conformation. The attachment of sodium ions to their binding sites is very weak when the pump is in the E_2 conformation.

Biology Highlight

Tell Me Where It Hurts: The Neurobiology of Pain

Tell me where it hurts. The response to this simple statement often provides invaluable information in attempts to determine both the source and cause of human afflictions. Pain usually signals continuing damage to one or more body parts, and it frequently warns of potentially fatal consequences if the root cause of the pain cannot be counteracted or eliminated. As a penalty for failure to avoid danger, pain can also teach.

But why do we feel pain? Why are soldiers in battle sometimes oblivious to their wounds until hours after the fighting? Why do acupuncture and hypnosis sometimes reduce or eliminate sensations of pain? Why do some people tolerate pain more than others? Why do some people suffer chronic pain almost continuously and far in excess of any obvious physical cause? No one has complete answers to these questions. Scientists do not understand how the brain, the organ that perceives pain, receives sensory information from the body and the environment and integrates it into a ''picture'' of what is happening.

However, several recent discoveries coupled with two almost forgotten ones have provided considerable insight into how pain signals are transmitted and processed in the central nervous systems of vertebrates. The findings are exciting and highly significant. They may lead to more effective methods of treating certain kinds of mental illness, reduce the incidence of chronic pain, and provide better methods of anesthesia for patients undergoing surgery. Equally important, these new findings eventually may lead to a better understanding of how the brain integrates and responds to all sorts of neurosensory information.

One of the two almost forgotten discoveries now recognized as having special relevance to nervous transmission of pain signals was made in 1931, when Ulf S. von Euler and John Gaddum were looking for acetylcholine in extracts of brain and intestine. They injected one of the substances isolated from these tissues into test animals and found that it caused contraction of smooth muscles in the intestinal walls of vertebrates. The substance also lowered blood pressure by producing vessel dilation.

The substance was not acetylcholine; it appeared to be an unknown chemical. The two biologists named it *substance P* because it was found in a powder prepared from tissue extracts. Gaddum and von Euler determined that substance P was a peptide, but they soon abandoned study of the newfound chemical. The peptide attracted little additional interest for many years. In fact, the probable role of substance P in the neurotransmission of pain signals was not to be deduced until almost 50 years after its discovery.

A second, seemingly unrelated incident took place in 1964, when Choh Hao Li, an endocrinologist at the University of California at San Francisco, discovered a peptide hormone in the pituitary of mammals that accelerates the breakdown of lipids. He named the hormone *beta lipotropin* (''lipid-stimulating''). Li's discovery was not considered exceptionally significant.

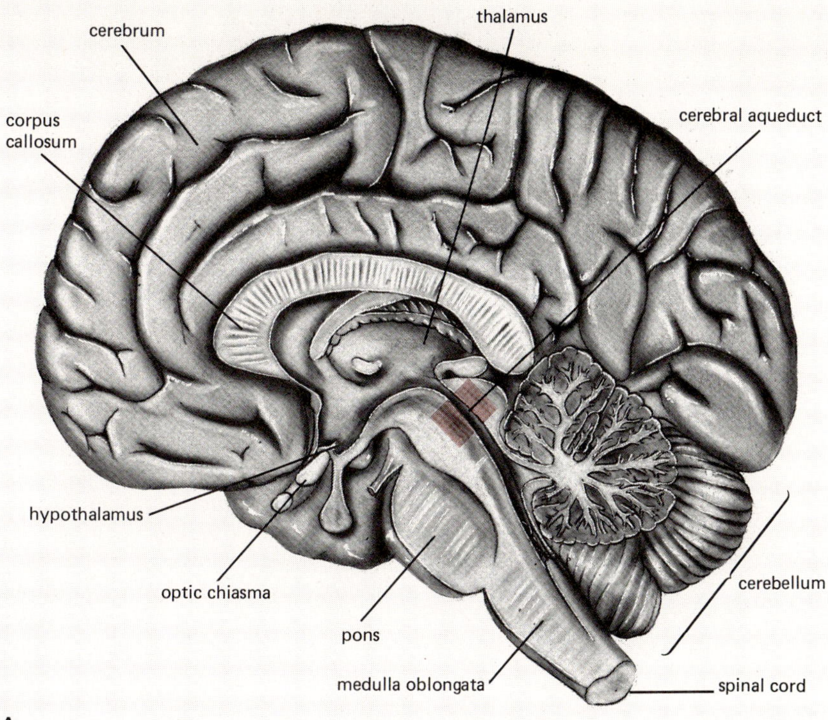

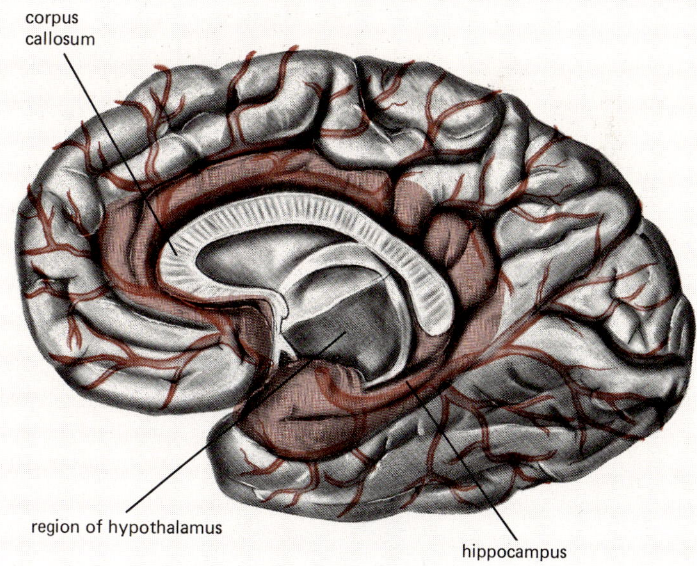

Fig. 1 Pain suppression. These diagrams depict two regions of the brain that appear to play a role in the suppression of pain. (A) The central gray matter (color) surrounds the cerebral aqueduct in the midbrain. (B) Neural receptors for opiates have been found in the limbic system (color) of the brain. The hippocampus, an important subdivision of the limbic system, also has been implicated in memory storage (see Chap. 20). Note that the limbic system is not an anatomically distinct structure, but rather a group of brain areas that borders much of the corpus callosum. The region of the hypothalamus and corpus callosum are included as reference points for comparison with Fig. 19.4D.

Other hormones appeared to exert a far greater influence on lipid metabolism. As the sixties waned, so did interest in beta lipotropin.

Beginning in 1971, a series of experiments began that eventually would trigger speculation that substance P and beta lipotropin play roles in mediating pain responses of vertebrates. One of the first of these experiments was conducted by David Mayer, Huda Akil, and John Liebeskind, three neurophysiologists working in the United States. They showed that electrical stimulation of the so-called *central gray matter*, a region in the midbrain, abolishes the pain response of rats (Fig. 1). Almost identical effects were later observed in cats and people.

The researchers noted a number of similarities between the analgesia (a state of not being able to feel pain) produced by brain stimulation and that produced by morphine, the addictive pain-killing opiate. Perhaps stimulation of the central gray matter triggered release of a natural morphinelike substance that somehow blocks transmission of pain signals.

To test this hypothesis, the neurosurgeons injected *naloxone* into experimental animals before electrical stimulation. This substance inhibits the pain-suppressive effects of morphine. If naloxone blocked the analgesia produced by electrical stimulation, researchers would have the first substantial evidence that the brain produces natural opiatelike pain suppressives. Results of the experiment were positive. Naloxone substantially reduced the analgesic effects of brain stimulation.

Intrigued by these results, several biologists began a systematic search for neurons containing postsynaptic receptors for pain-inhibiting opiates. Clusters of such neurons in the brain were discovered in 1973 by researchers in Eric Simon's laboratory at New York University, and almost simultaneously by scientists working with Solomon Snyder at Johns Hopkins University. Candace Pert, an associate of Snyder's recalls the discovery vividly.

"I had tried and tried and tried and gotten nothing," she states, "and then one day—there they were: I was looking at something in the brain no one had ever seen before" (Fig. 2).

Pert's plotting of receptor sites showed them to be situated largely in the central gray area and in the limbic system, a doughnut-shaped ring of

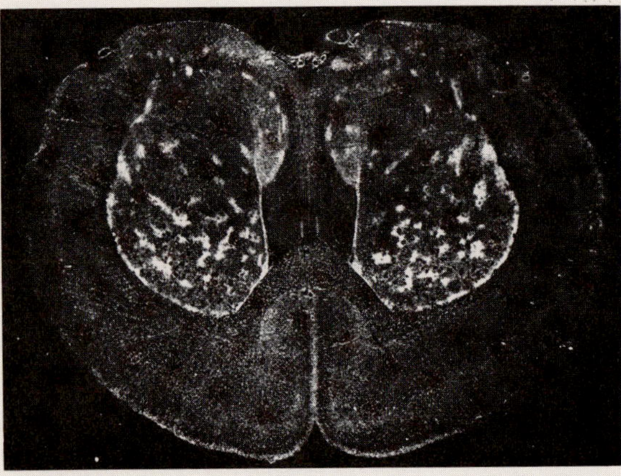

Fig. 2 Opiate receptors in the brain. Several opiate receptors (white splotches) are visible in this specially treated cross section through a portion of the limbic system of a rat.

cerebral tissue known to influence a broad spectrum of emotional responses (see Fig. 1). Further research demonstrated that similar receptors exist in the brains of hagfishes, one of the most primitive vertebrates (see Chap. 35). This finding surprised some biologists, for it indicated that neural opiates and their receptors were not new but had evolved in animals at least 350 million years ago.

Several natural opiatelike molecules were extracted from animal tissues and identified during the mid-1970s. All were peptides. The first two were found in preparations of pig brains by John Hughes and Hans Kosterlitz in Scotland. In announcing discovery of the small peptides, which were named *enkephalins* ("in the brain"), the scientists noted that a replica of one of them was contained in the sequence of amino acids making up beta lipotropin, Li's all-but-forgotten hormone.

Actually, Li already had the enkephalin replica on his laboratory shelf. In 1972, Li and an Iraqi graduate student had wondered whether beta lipotropin of camels was the same as that found in sheep, the original source of Li's hormone. When the graduate student went home to Iraq, he sent Li 200 camel pituitaries. Upon analyzing the glands, Li found not beta lipotropin, but a new, somewhat smaller hormone that proved to contain a replica of one of the enkephalins isolated by Hughes and Kosterlitz.

When Li learned of the amino acid sequences of the two enkephalins isolated in Scotland, he knew immediately that the larger hormone extracted from camel pituitaries probably was an important pain suppressive. Li supplied some of his hormone, later named *beta endorphin* ("the morphine within"), to Roger Guillemin, a scientist already well known for his work on interactions between the hypothalamus and pituitary (see Biology Highlight in Chap. 17).

When beta endorphin was injected into the brains of experimental animals, Guillemin found that it had an analgesic potency up to 100 times that of morphine, and was up to 40 times more effective as a pain killer than either of the smaller enkephalins. Moreover, Guillemin showed that injection of the hormone sometimes produces *catatonia* in animals, a state of extreme unresponsiveness accompanied by immobility and muscular rigidity. The symptoms are remarkably similar to those observed in people suffering from severe schizophrenia.

Since Hughes and Kosterlitz announced discovery of two enkephalins, others have been found in the brain, intestine, cerebrospinal fluid, and blood. In addition, two other peptides, named alpha and gamma endorphin, have been found in extracts of mixed pituitary and hypothalamic tissues. Where these enkephalins and endorphins are produced is not yet clear. They might be manufactured locally in different tissues, or exclusively in neurons, or all these peptides could be derived from a single "mother" molecule, beta lipotropin. There are other possibilities, and biologists are not sure whether all or even most of these natural opiates have yet been identified.

One puzzling question raised by the discovery of natural animal pain suppressives is: what do they suppress? Identification of these morphinelike chemicals tells us little about how pain signals are transmitted and processed, but a parallel line of investigation is beginning to provide answers, most of which appear to involve substance P. In fact, results of several

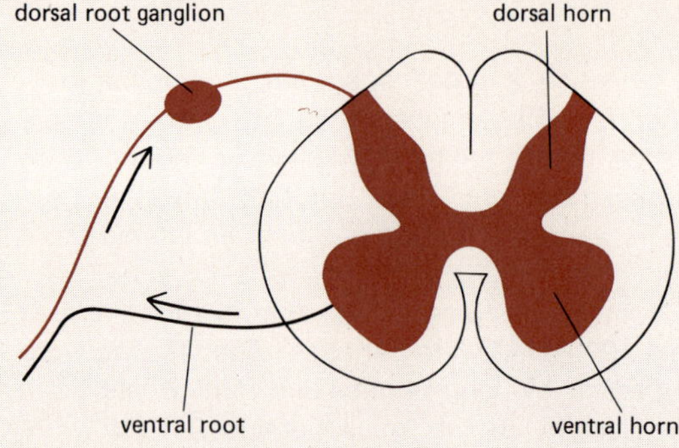

Fig. 3 Dorsal horns. Sensory nerve fibers extend from dorsal root ganglia to dorsal horns of vertebrate spinal cords. Some of these fibers form portions of neural relays that transmit pain signals to the brain (see also Fig. 19.6).

recent experiments suggest that substance P is a neurotransmitter of pain signals.

Some of these experiments have used *capsaicin*, a chemical isolated from Hungarian red peppers. Administration of capsaicin produces an immediate sensation of intense pain in people and most other vertebrates. Fred Lembeck of the University of Graz in Austria has shown that capsaicin causes release of substance P from the dorsal horn of vertebrate spinal cords. Dorsal horns are portions of the gray matter in spinal cords that mainly contain cell bodies receiving sensory nerve fibers (Fig. 3). Such fibers emanate from dorsal root ganglia. Prolonged capsaicin treatment eventually causes depletion of substance P from the dorsal horn. Coincidentally, animals become increasingly less sensitive to prolonged capsaicin treatments, presumably because of the gradual decrease of substance P from neurons transmitting pain signals in the spinal cord. Lembeck hypothesizes that substance P is a neurotransmitter through which incoming sensory nerve fibers communicate with neurons in the dorsal horn. Fibers of neurons in the spinal cord then carry the impulses to the brain. Further research is required before Lembeck's hypothesis can receive widespread support.

Investigation of substance P is providing some additional insight into how pain-suppressive chemicals of the body exert their effects. For example, biologists at Harvard and Cambridge have shown that a laboratory-synthesized enkephalin blocks release of substance P in brain tissue known to contain axon terminals of pain-transmitting neurons. The synthetic enkephalin does not prevent release of substance P in control animals treated with naloxone, the specific inhibitor of opiates mentioned earlier. Moreover, other experiments demonstrate the presence of specialized receptors for opiates on nerve fibers containing substance P. Taken together, these results suggest that opiatelike molecules in the central nervous system suppress pain perception by blocking release of substance P from pain-transmitting neurons.

Since knowledge gained from studies of pain transmitters and suppressors could have considerable medical and social impact, it is likely that interest in these substances will remain high over the next several years. Some benefits are being realized even now. Recently, for example, a group of people suffering from severe chronic pain agreed to receive injections of human beta endorphin into their brains. The pain experienced by most of these people decreased considerably. Routine administration of beta endorphin is not expected in the near future. Production of the hormone

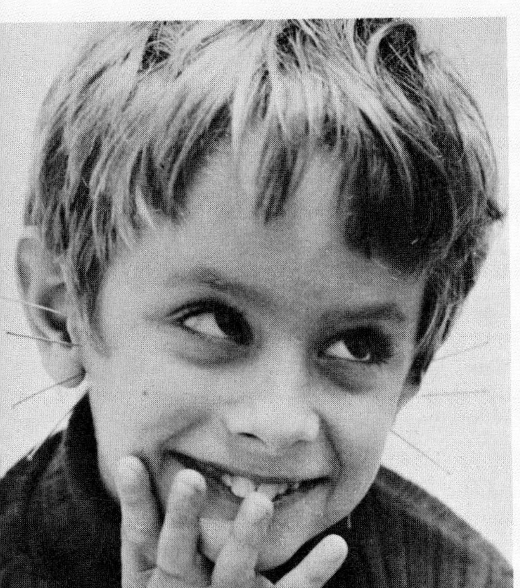

Fig. 4 Needles and pins. This 9-year-old boy is shown undergoing acupuncture treatment for deafness. The boy's hearing improved 10 decibels following 10 treatments.

remains very expensive; the first injections administered to people cost over $3000 each. Furthermore, the addictive potential of beta endorphin must be clarified. Studies indicate that animals can become physically dependent on beta endorphin, just as they can become addicted to heroin and morphine.

More information about the relationships between pain transmitters and suppressors also may increase our understanding of the beneficial effects of acupuncture. This technique, which involves inserting needles into the body at specific points, has been used for centuries by Chinese physicans to treat a wide range of human afflictions. Many acupuncture treatments produce analgesia in specific parts of the body. Results of several experiments suggest that insertion of needles at certain points triggers release of one or more endorphins from the pituitary. For example, the analgesic effects of acupuncture are much less in animals whose pituitaries have been surgically removed or in animals treated with naloxone. Some effects of acupuncture, however, appear unrelated to the release of pain suppressives (Fig. 4).

The observation that endorphins can sedate and even produce catatonia suggests that these molecules have an important role in regulating certain kinds of animal behavior. In 1977 a group of scientists received permission from the United States Food and Drug Administration (FDA) to test beta endorphin on human patients suffering from a variety of mental disorders. None of the patients had responded favorably to any other form of treatment. Seven of the fifteen patients who received intravenous injections of beta endorphin reported marked improvement in mood and self-perception immediately after the injection. The beneficial effects lasted for several hours, and in some cases for much longer periods. However, a more recent study showed beta endorphin to be ineffective in the treatment of patients suffering from schizophrenia.

Additional clinical studies are needed to evaluate the true potential of endorphins as antipsychotic drugs. Such studies also may provide much valuable information regarding the neurological causes of mental illness. If many of these afflictions are the result of imbalances among neurochemicals in the brain, it eventually should be possible to readjust the balance, thereby providing effective treatment for thousands of mentally ill people.

The story behind our steadily increasing knowledge of pain transmission and suppression not only demonstrates the practical potential of basic science but also provides a good illustration of how science proceeds. Different researchers often attack different aspects of related biological problems. Interrelations between bits of information produced by these scientists are not always clear. Scientists must look for possible relationships by constantly comparing and contrasting experimental results, much as a person compares the shapes of individual pieces of a complex jigsaw puzzle.

But jigsaw puzzles offer important advantages usually not afforded scientists. All jigsaw pieces are present from the beginning, and in one place. In science, data linking several bits of information into a conceptual whole may not be available all at once. In the early 1970s, for example, information suggesting a possible relationship between substance P and beta lipotropin had not yet been discovered, a fact that underscores how important it is for scientists to keep open both their minds and their lines of communication.

Thus, when the complex shifts to the E_2 state, sodium tends to detach from the pump and enter the extracellular fluids. Potassium ions, however, strongly attach to their binding site when the pump complex is in the E_2 state. The binding of K^+ appears to trigger dephosphorylation of the complex, causing it to revert to the E_1 state. The K^+ binding site has a low affinity for the ions in this conformation, and potassium tends to be released to the cytoplasm.

Note that the sodium-potassium pump requires an expenditure of energy; it cannot function without ATP. Biologists have determined that more than half the ATP used by a neuron is consumed in pumping sodium and potassium ions across the plasma membrane. Biologists also have discovered that the pump does not exchange sodium and potassium ions in equal numbers. For every two potassium ions transported into a cell, the pump transports three sodium ions to the outside. The net effect of the sodium-potassium pump, therefore, is to increase the number of positive charges outside a cell relative to the number inside. In other words, the pump builds up an *electric potential* across the plasma membrane.

As already noted, the selective permeability of the plasma membrane of a neuron also helps establish and maintain an electric potential. Except when stimulated, the membrane is highly impermeable to many substances. However, the resting membrane is not totally impermeable to all materials. Some substances move across resting membranes in small amounts and to varying degrees. Potassium ions are about 50 times more likely to pass through the plasma membrane of a resting neuron than sodium ions. Consequently, K^+ leaks out of a cell faster than Na^+ leaks in. Because hardly any of the negatively charged ions in the cytoplasm leak from the cell, this unequal diffusion of K^+ and Na^+ tends to increase the charge difference across a resting membrane still further. Thus, the electric potential of a resting neuron is established and maintained by three principal factors: the sodium-potassium pump, the unequal diffusion of K^+ and Na^+ across the plasma membrane, and the inability of negatively charged ions to leave the cell.

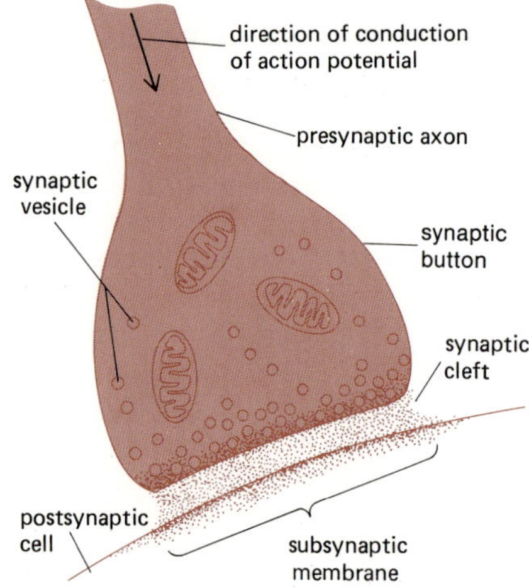

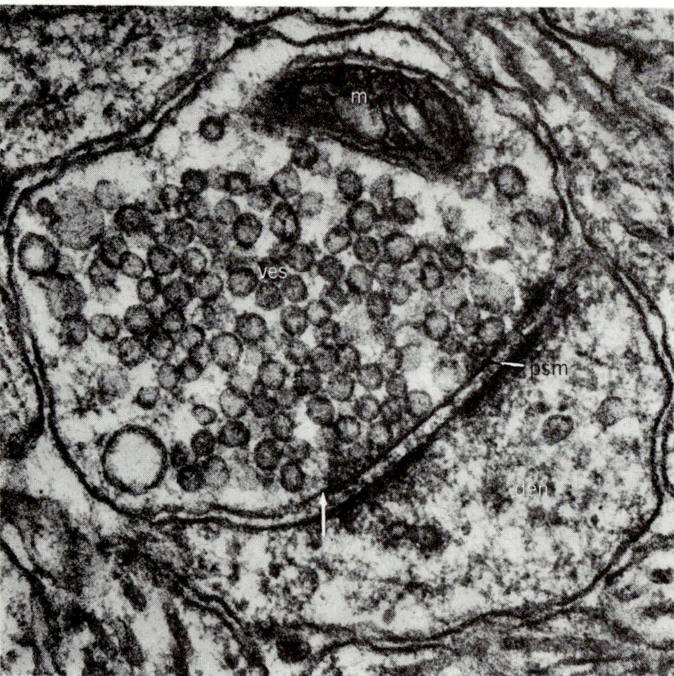

Fig. 19.11 Synapses. (A) Diagram of a synapse. (B) Electron micrograph of a synapse, showing a synaptic button containing synaptic vesicles (ves) and a mitochondrion (m). The dendrite (den) of the postsynaptic neuron shows a thick postsynaptic membrane (psm). The arrow indicates the presynaptic membrane. The narrow space between pre- and postsynaptic membranes is the synaptic cleft.

Transmission of Nerve Impulses between Neurons

As already noted, nerve impulses normally pass from one neuron to another at junctions called synapses. Such junctions usually are located where the end of an axon of one neuron comes close to the dendrite terminals of a second. Because axons and dendrites often are highly branched, an individual neuron can synapse with many others.

The terminals of an axon ordinarily are covered with many small button-shaped swellings called *synaptic buttons* (Fig. 19.11). At some synapses the membrane of a button is held close to the membrane of an adjacent dendrite by a gap junction (see Chap. 5). Such junctions facilitate direct and almost immediate transmission of action potentials between neurons. Physical contact between neurons at a synapse occurs largely in circumstances where speed of nerve-impulse transmission is of great importance.

In most synapses, however, a synaptic cleft separates synaptic buttons from dendrites. How, then, does an impulse get across a synaptic cleft? In almost all cases it can be shown that when an impulse reaches a synaptic button, the button acts as an endocrine structure and secretes minute amounts of a neurotransmitter. Such substances are produced by neurons and stored in vacuoles inside synaptic buttons. When a nerve impulse reaches a button, these vacuoles unite with the cell membrane of the neuron and release their contents into the synaptic cleft (see Fig. 19.11). The neurotransmitter then diffuses across the cleft and attaches to receptor molecules located on the surface of a postsynaptic neuron. If enough neurotransmitter molecules unite with these receptors, a new nerve impulse is generated in the postsynaptic neuron.

Once a neurotransmitter has interacted with a postsynaptic neuron, its actions must be terminated rapidly, or else the neurotransmitter would exert its effects for too long and precise control would be lost. Such loss of control is exactly what some insecticides bring about. Poisons known as organophosphates block destruction of the neurotransmitter *acetylcholine* by the enzyme *cholinesterase*. As a result, acetylcholine stimulates a large number of neurons indefinitely, causing uncontrolled spasms. Control among neural components usually becomes so disrupted that death ensues quickly. After they have triggered a nerve impulse in a postsynaptic neuron, neurotransmitters normally are inactivated either by enzymes such as cholinesterase or by being reabsorbed by the same presynaptic neurons that released them.

Acetylcholine is an extremely important neurotransmitter, being released from the axon terminals of all somatic motor neurons and all preganglionic fibers of autonomic neurons (Fig. 19.12). Acetylcholine also is released by all postganglionic parasympathetic fibers. Other such *cholinergic* fibers are located throughout the central nervous system.

Several other neurotransmitters function in vertebrates. *Norepinephrine,* for example, is secreted by some interneurons in the brain and spinal cord and by most postganglionic sympathetic fibers. Norepinephrine is related chemically to *epinephrine,* a hormone produced by the medulla of the adrenal gland (see Chap. 17). Epinephrine probably functions as a neurotransmitter too, although not to the same degree as norepinephrine.

Dopamine, another vertebrate neurotransmitter, was once thought to be simply an intermediate in the synthesis of norepinephrine and epinephrine. But this amino acid derivative now is known to function as a neurotransmitter in the brain, where it is released from neurons that influence movement and behavior. The axons of some dopamine-containing neurons terminate in an area of the cerebrum called the *caudate nucleus* (see Fig. 19.4D). This area, which plays a vital role in the integration of movement, is known to function abnormally in individuals who suffer from the crippling effects of Parkinson's disease, an affliction characterized by an uncontrollable tremor, weakness, and rigidity of muscles. Virtually no dopamine can be found in the caudate nuclei of patients afflicted with Parkinson's disease. This affliction is caused by a lack of sufficient dopamine to activate postsynaptic neurons in the caudate nucleus.

This finding has led to a major therapeutic breakthrough in the treatment of Parkinson's disease. It now is possible to make up the deficiency of dopamine in the caudate nuclei of afflicted people by injecting the amino acid dihydroxyphenylalanine, or *dopa,* into the bloodstream. Unlike dopamine, dopa passes readily from the bloodstream

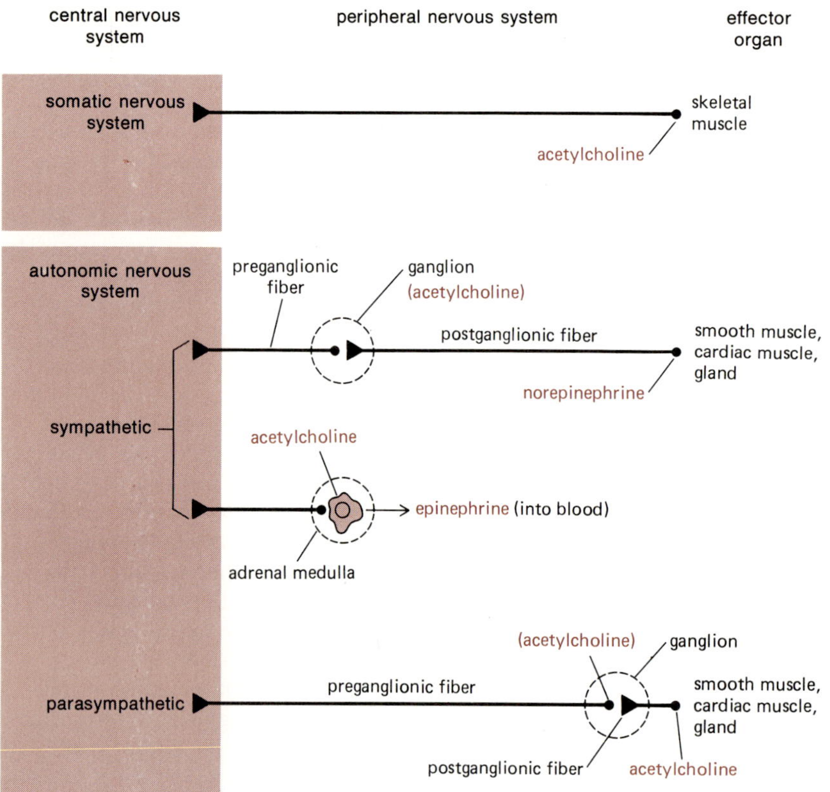

Fig. 19.12 Neurotransmitters and the efferent peripheral nervous system. The principal neurotransmitters secreted by each efferent subdivision are noted.

to neurons of the brain, and there it can be converted to dopamine. Such treatments are highly effective, relatively simple and inexpensive to administer, and they illustrate how basic research sometimes can lead rapidly to a new treatment for a disease.

Other neurotransmitters are likely to be isolated. Some already may have been identified. For example, many biologists now suspect that a substance isolated from vertebrate tissues about 50 years ago is a neurotransmitter specifically involved in the transmission of pain signals to the brain (see accompanying Biology Highlight).

NEURAL CENTERS

In general, the activity of all types of neural modulators is based on two kinds of information: genetically inherited information and newly acquired information obtained via the sensory system.

Heredity

Genes determine much of the gross and the fine organization of the nervous system of an animal, hence certain neural pathways and patterns of neural activity are already established once the animal has completed its embryonic development. Even in a just-formed nervous system, therefore, relatively simple sensory inputs to the modulators often can evoke fairly complex outputs to the effectors, and behavior can be correspondingly complex.

In some cases, sensory inputs may not be required at all: neural centers often are spontaneously active. This is particularly true for those that control the most vital rhythmic processes, such as breathing, for example. Thus, as already pointed out in Chap. 18, the breathing center in the medulla oblongata sends out rhythmic motor responses spontaneously. This rhythm can be shown to persist even if the center is isolated surgically. Similarly spontaneous activity takes place in the heart-rate center and in many—possibly most—other neural control centers as well. In effect, the genetic endowment ensures that, as soon as an animal is completely developed, it has fully functional neural controls for at least those motor activities which are basic to survival.

Experience

Excitation and Inhibition

To a greater or lesser degree, however, inherited neural activity usually is modified by sensory experience—information about the current status of the external and internal environment. Such information is acquired by receptors and transmitted to the neural centers in the form of nerve impulses. For example, a person may react intensely when confronted with a rubber rattlesnake, especially if its actual composition is not apparent. However, if the true nature of the snake is already known, the response will be more subdued. Such modifications result directly from the structural arrangement of excitatory and inhibitory neurons. As stated earlier, neurotransmitters released at synapses can trigger nerve impulses in adjacent neurons. But neurotransmitters also can hinder the triggering of such impulses. Excitatory neurons promote the triggering of nerve impulses in postsynaptic dendrites; inhibitory neurons prevent such triggerings.

Moreover, different axon terminals of a single neuron can be excitatory at one synapse and inhibitory at another. Since some neurons can secrete more than one kind of neurotransmitter, it is possible that for such cells these opposing actions result from release of different neurotransmitters at different axon terminals. Other neurons apparently produce only one kind of neurotransmitter, however, and these too can produce both inhibitory and stimulatory effects at different terminals. The variable actions of single neurotransmitter-releasing neurons may depend on the nature and response of receptor molecules located on the surface membranes of postsynaptic cells. For example, attachment of a neurotransmitter to one receptor might produce a change in the plasma membrane of a postsynaptic neuron that promotes depolarization. Conversely, attachment of the same neurotransmitter to a different receptor might inhibit depolarization.

An appreciation of how interactions between inhibitory and excitatory neurons can produce different responses in different circumstances can be gained by examining the "wiring diagram" of a simple neural circuit in Fig. 19.13. This circuit has three sensory neurons of the excitatory type, an interneuron of the inhibitory type, and two motor neurons. If we assume that a net release of neurotransmitter from at least two axonal terminals of excitatory neurons is necessary to stimulate a postsynaptic neuron, the six neurons of Fig. 19.13 can interact to produce either no response at all, or a response from either of the two motor neurons, or a response from both motor neurons. The nature of the response from this neural circuit depends on the pattern of excitatory stimuli being transmitted by the sensory neurons. Thus, a simple external

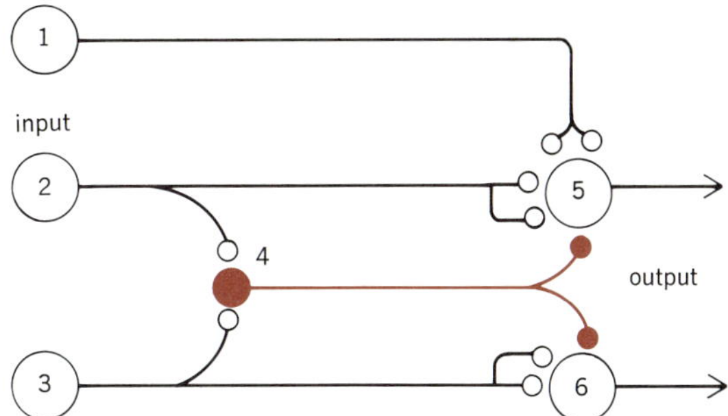

input neurons activated	output neurons activated			
	none	5 only	6 only	5 and 6
1		X		
2		X		
3			X	
1 and 2		X		
1 and 3				X
2 and 3	X			

Fig. 19.13 Information processing. Excitatory input neurons 1, 2, and 3 (open circles) synapse with output neurons 5 and 6. Excitatory neurons 2 and 3 also synapse with an inhibitory neuron (4). Assume that neurotransmitter from a *net* of at least two excitatory terminals must be released to trigger a nerve impulse in neurons 4, 5, or 6. Because two of three terminals of neuron 2 synapse with neuron 5, input from neuron 2 would trigger a nerve impulse in neuron 5. Neuron 4, however, will not depolarize unless neurons 2 and 3 are activated simultaneously. As indicated by the summary table, four output patterns can result from the different interactions of these six excitatory and inhibitory neurons. (*After W. R. Klemm, "Science, the Brain and Our Future," Pegasus, New York, 1972.*)

stimulus can lead to the completion of many simultaneous responses, all occurring as a single, integrated pattern of activity. Such patterns of activity are termed *programmed behavior.*

A good example of programmed behavior is one of the human *defense responses.* When an unexpected blow is directed at the head, the eyes close, the head is lowered, a crouching stance is assumed, the hands are raised to the face. These are some of the several dozen separate reflexes occurring simultaneously, as a unified "program."

Most programs of this type depend on how excitatory and inhibitory neurons are arranged structurally in an organism and thus are determined largely by heredity. In comparatively large-brained animals, the majority of neurons again probably form fixed inborn circuits, yet substantial numbers seem to remain available for the later development of new or modified circuits. Such animals are capable of *learning* and of storing learned experiences as *memory.*

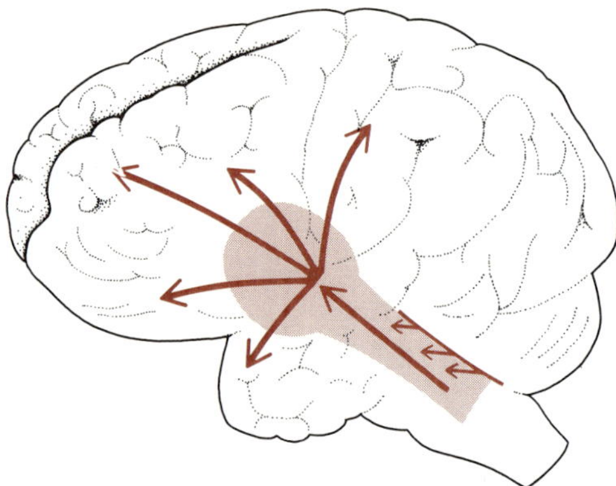

Fig. 19.14 Reticular formation. Incoming sensory information is "screened" by the reticular formation (shaded area). Selected stimuli are then transmitted from this neural center to various regions of the mid- and forebrain. The reticular formation plays an important role in arousing vertebrates from sleep.

Learning

The simplest form of learning probably involves *habituation,* or progressive loss of responsiveness to repeated stimulation. For example, rats, mice, and many other vertebrates typically give a *startle response* when they hear a loud bell rung for the first time. But this response becomes progressively less pronounced after several ringings and ultimately often disappears altogether. This kind of behavior is mediated in part by the vertebrate *reticular formation,* a diffuse collection of many-branched neurons that extend from the medulla oblongata through the midbrain (Fig. 19.14). Axons of these neurons interconnect with nerve cells in many parts of the brain, including the thalamus and cerebral cortex.

The reticular formation continuously receives sensory input concerning the status of the external environment, but much of this information is inhibited, i.e., "ignored," by areas of the brain directly concerned with conscious behavior. Thus, we usually remain unaware of the background hum of a motor while we read or the sound of a jet aircraft passing overhead while we talk. Yet we instantly become attentive to certain kinds of stimuli. The muffled whimper of her baby is often sufficient to awaken a mother who sleeps through the much louder noise of automobile traffic outside her window.

Neurons of the reticular formation somehow screen incoming sensory information and "arouse" conscious centers of the brain only when the information has particular significance. For example, most vertebrates become instantly attentive to the first sounding of a loud bell, because it represents a meaningful and unexpected change in the status of the external environment. But subsequent ringings of the bell do not produce the same interplay between reticular formation and cerebral cortex. The animals quickly learn that the ringings are inconsequential and therefore can be ignored. Habituation does not necessarily require complex nervous systems. Indeed, organisms without nervous systems can habituate, hence learning of this type probably occurs at an "intracellular," chemical level.

A more complex form of learning involves *conditioned reflexes.* In so-called *classical conditioning,* two or more stimuli are presented to an animal simultaneously and repeatedly, until the animal learns to execute the same response to either stimulus. For example, if bright light is directed into the eyes the pupils will contract reflexly. If the light stimulus is given repeatedly and is accompanied each time by food, sound, or some other stimulus, then pupillary contraction eventually can be made to occur by such a stimulus alone, without the bright light. Through learning, the animal now associates the second stimulus with light.

In people, pupillary retraining can occur even if the second stimulus is no more than a single spoken word and if this word is spoken by the person undergoing retraining. Indeed, it is not even necessary for the word to be spoken—merely thinking of the word often is sufficient. Such self-conditioned people then are able to contract their pupils at will. The occasionally recorded feats of human self-control over pain and other normally nonvolitional responses are undoubtedly based on self-conditioning of this sort.

Learning also can occur through *operant conditioning,* which differs from the classical type in that the animal participates actively and deliberately in the learning process. Thus if a certain activity at first happens to be carried out by chance and if this activity happens to have desirable consequences, then the animal can re-create these consequences by deliberately repeating the activity. Learning by this means becomes particularly effective if it is "reinforced," i.e., if repetition of an activity entails material or psychological rewards. Much of the learning of vertebrates—mammals and people in particular—is based on operant conditioning of this sort (see Chap. 20).

Undoubtedly the most complex modulator activities are those involved in intelligence, personality, ability to think abstractly, and capacity to manipulate and control the environment. Depending extensively on memory and learning, such functions are developed to any notable degree only in the most advanced mammals. But note again that, regardless of their relative complexities, all modulators depend on adequate *information;* apart from whatever built-in, inherited information they have available, modulators can act only on information that the neural receptors supply in the form of sensory impulses.

RECEPTORS: SENSE ORGANS

Receptor cells are either *epitheliosensory* or *neurosensory* (Fig. 19.15). The first type is a specialized, nonnervous epithelial cell that receives stimuli at one end and is innervated by a sensory nerve fiber at the other. The second type is a modified sensory neuron that carries a dendritelike stimulus-receiving extension at one end. At the other is an axon that synapses with other neurons. Both types of receptor cells can occur in clusters

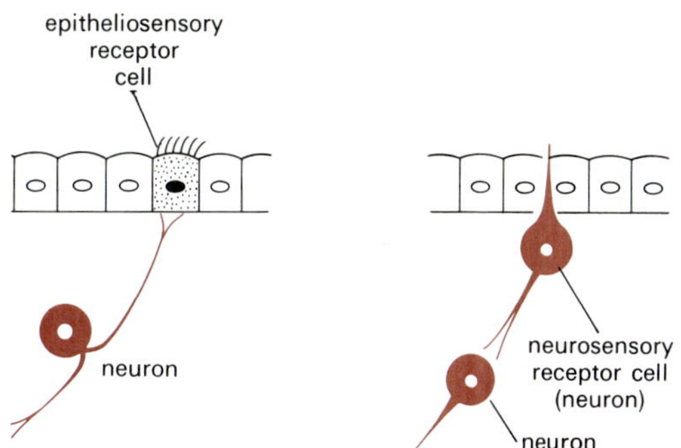

Fig. 19.15 Two kinds of receptor cells.

and together with accessory cells form *sense organs.* Most receptor cells of invertebrates are of the neurosensory type. Vertebrates contain both neurosensory and epitheliosensory receptors.

Nerve impulses generated by receptors become perceptions only in the neural centers. In effect, eyes do not see and ears do not hear; eye-brain complexes are required for seeing, ear-brain complexes for hearing. In some instances the perceptions become conscious, but more often they do not. When nerve impulses reach the brain from a blood vessel, for example, sensing takes place, but in this case the sensation does not become conscious.

Environmental change as such is known to be an important factor in the production of sensory impulses by receptor cells. For when a given stimulus persists unchanged for a time, a sense dulls, or "adapts." For example, we soon become relatively insensitive to the pressure of clothes, to a persistent odor, or to a taste. Pain is most difficult to adapt to, but odor perception dulls very easily. We cannot judge our own body odors, for example, since we live with them and adapt to them continuously.

Different kinds of sense perceptions depend in part on different connections of sensory fibers in the brain. For example, if a fiber from a heat receptor and a fiber from a cold receptor could be cut and the cut ends were allowed to reinnervate the sense organs in switched order, the animal would feel hot when the cold receptor was stimulated and cold when the heat receptor was stimulated. In other words, the quality of a perception depends on which of various brain centers receives signals.

Furthermore, correct *localization* of a stimulus similarly depends on the central connections. The anatomical distribution of receptors throughout the body is matched virtually point for point in the anatomical distribution of neural centers. So long as these structural relations are preserved, impulses will be correctly interpreted as coming from particular body regions and particular receptors. That this is actually so has been demonstrated through experimental rearrangements of neural pathways.

Sensory receptors are classified according to the stimuli that trigger their actions. Thus, there are *thermal receptors* that detect changes of temperature, *mechanoreceptors* that provide information about touch, balance, and hearing; *chemoreceptors* that mediate the senses of taste and smell; and *photoreceptors* for vision.

Thermal Receptors

The thermal receptors of most vertebrates, people included, consist of neurosensory cells with endings located mainly in the skin. The rate of nerve impulses transmitted by these cells varies in direct proportion to changes of environmental temperature. Neural centers in the brain interpret these impulses as temperature sensations.

Mechanoreceptors

Mechanoreceptors often are neurosecretory cells with free nerve endings that sometimes are highly branched or elaborated as meshworks. Such receptors occur abundantly in skin and in muscles, tendons, and most connective tissues (Fig. 19.16). Mechanoreceptors are stimulated by mechanical displacement or by changes in the mechanical stresses affecting surrounding parts. In mammals, for example, the base of each hair is surrounded by a meshlike terminal of a receptor fiber, and a nerve impulse is initiated if the hair is touched even lightly. Bending or stretching of a part of the skin or of an internal organ also is likely to result in receptor stimulation. Mechanoreceptors thereby provide information about contacts with external objects and about movements of any body part.

Some of the most complex mechanoreceptors in animals are those involved with hearing. A distinct sense of hearing is restricted to some arthropods (certain crustacea, spiders, and insects) and to vertebrates; by and large only animals that make sounds can also hear them. In arthropods the receptor organs are located in various body regions. For example, mosquitoes hear with their antennae, and a mature male mosquito can best hear the sounds of the same frequency produced by the wings of flying females.

The ear of terrestrial vertebrates contains innervated clusters of hair cells, each cluster most sensitive to a different frequency of sound waves. Sound is transmitted to these clusters through three cavities. The outermost cavity, called the *outer ear,* transmits sound from the external environment to a membrane, the *eardrum,* that separates the outer ear from the second cavity, or *middle ear* (Fig. 19.17). Three tiny bones, *hammer, anvil,* and *stirrup,* form an adjustable sound-transmitting bridge from the eardrum across the middle ear to a third and innermost cavity, the *inner ear.* Two membranes, the *round window* and the *oval window,* close off the middle-ear cavity from the inner ear. The stirrup bone is anchored on the oval window.

The inner ear is an intricate system of interconnected canals and spaces, all surrounded by bone and filled with lymphlike fluid. The *cochlea,* a coiled, very elaborate receptor organ for the sense of hearing, lies within the inner ear (Fig. 19.18). Extending throughout the length of the cochlea is a *basilar membrane,* and the innervated clusters of hair cells lie along this membrane. Sound waves transmitted into the cochlea produce fluid vibrations of given frequencies, and hair cells sensitive to such frequencies are moved up and down as a result. Vibrating hair cells then come into contact with an overhanging *tectorial membrane,* and it is presumably these contacts that initiate nerve impulses. Impulses from different clusters of hair cells are interpreted in the temporal lobes of the brain as sounds of different pitch. Basilar membrane, hair cells, and tectorial membrane together represent the *organ of Corti.*

Chemoreceptors

Chemoreceptors give information about environmental chemicals. They include receptors that mediate the senses of *smell* and of *taste.* In most animals the receptor structures are located in the skin, and they usually are free sensory nerve end-

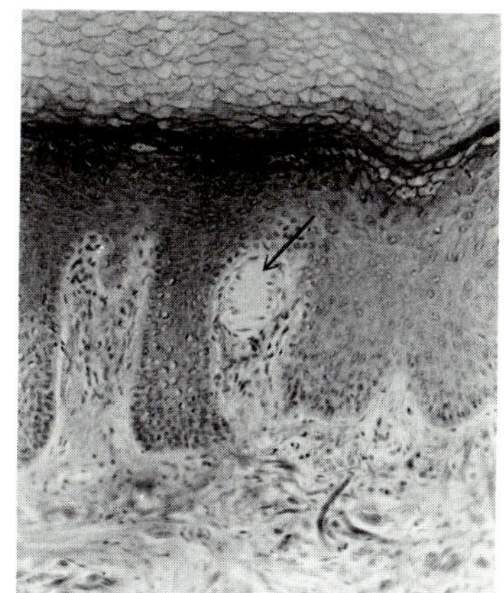

Fig. 19.16 Mechanoreceptors. (A) Section through a Pacinian corpuscle, a pressure receptor in mammalian skin. (B) The location of a Pacinian corpuscle in the skin.

ings that may be stimulated directly by certain chemicals. The ability to sense common environmental chemicals has particular significance for many invertebrates, especially aquatic ones. This sense permits an animal to detect the presence of irritants or poisons and the chemical exudates of enemies, prey, food, and mates.

Smell is mainly a distance sense. Aquatic animals smell traces of chemicals in solution, terrestrial types smell vaporized chemicals or traces of chemicals that adhere to the ground. In vertebrates, the smell receptors are parts of the ciliated epithelium lining the upper nasal passages. Sensory fibers from there lead to the olfactory lobes of the forebrain, relatively small in human beings but large in many other vertebrates.

The sense of taste conveys information mainly about the general chemical nature of potential food substances. Insects such as flies and moths taste with their legs and mouth parts, the receptors being in bristles on these appendages. In mammals the taste receptors are components of *taste buds,* clusters of elongated ciliated cells set into depressions in the tongue. Given chemicals stimulate buds in different regions of the tongue, and different taste sensations are then perceived. The four primary tastes are *sweet, sour, salty* and *bitter* (Fig. 19.19). Stimulation of buds near the tip of the tongue produce sweet tastes; those at the back, bitter tastes; and those along the tongue edges, sour and salty tastes.

Fig. 19.17 The mammalian ear. Note ear bones in the middle-ear cavity. The auditory (eustachian) tube interconnects the middle ear and pharynx. The semicircular canals, utricle, and saccule are a part of the inner ear that detects changes in head and body position.

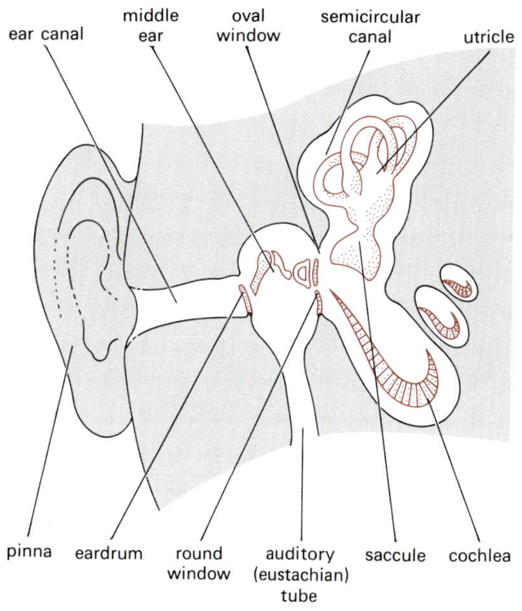

Photoreceptors

Light-sensitive animals have photoreceptor cells containing special *photopigments,* which are chemically similar in all animals. Each consists of two

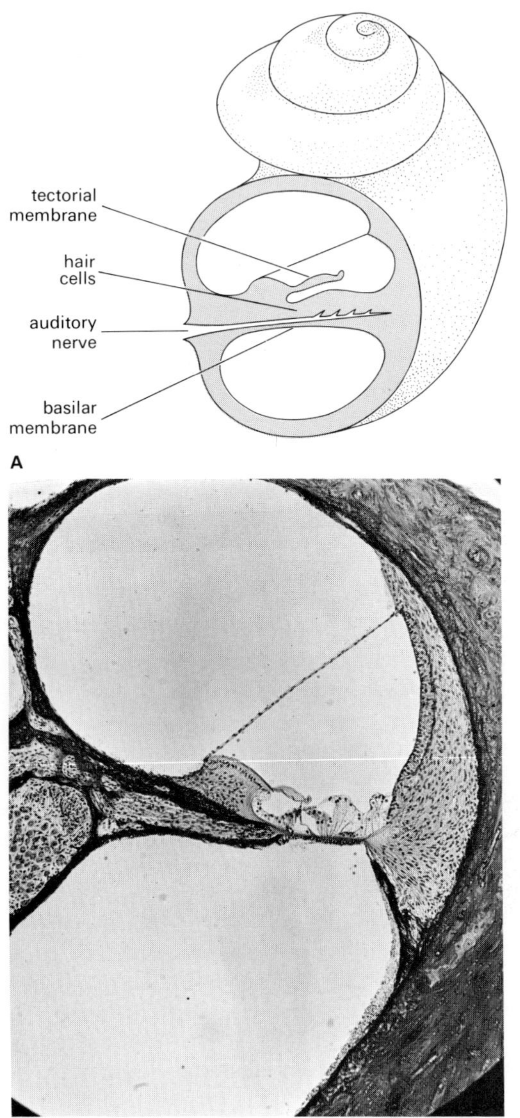

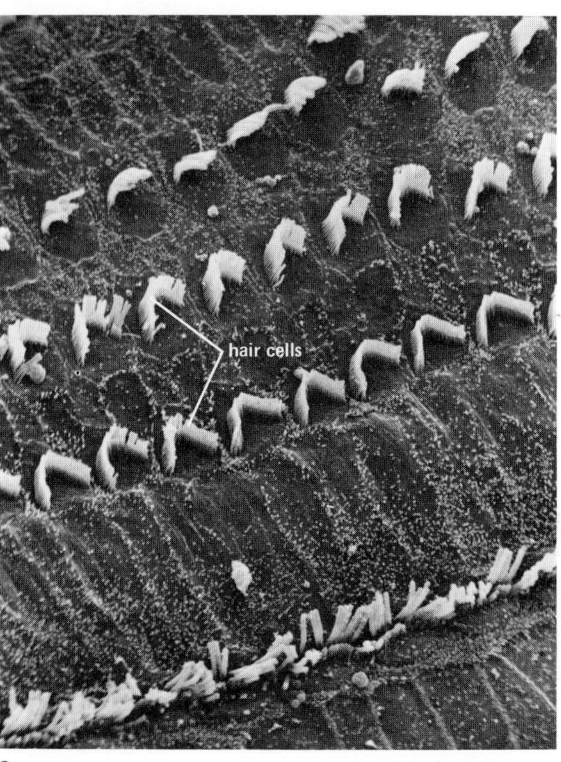

Fig. 19.18 The cochlea. (A) The coils of the cochlea and a cochlear cross section with the parts of the organ of Corti. (B) Section through the organ of Corti. (C) Scanning electron micrograph of an organ of Corti (guinea pig) showing rows of hair cells. Such cells are easily damaged by loud sounds, such as highly amplified music or the noise from low-flying jet aircraft.

joined molecular parts. One is a variant of *retinal,* a derivative of vitamin A; the other is a variant of *opsin,* a protein. Light splits retinal from opsin, and in the process light energy is converted to chemical energy. Further chemical and electrical reactions then produce nerve impulses in the nerve fibers. At the same time retinal is rejoined to opsin through a series of ATP- and enzyme-requiring reactions, and the photopigment is thereby regenerated (Fig. 19.20).

Numerous invertebrate groups and all vertebrates have photopigments in elongated receptor cells that enable the animals to perceive different black-white intensities of light. Such cells serve mainly as illumination and motion detectors. In vertebrates these cells are called *rods,* and their photopigment is "visual purple," or *rhodopsin.* In addition, a few animal groups, notably some insects, some reptiles, most birds, and monkeys, apes, and people, also have receptor cells that detect

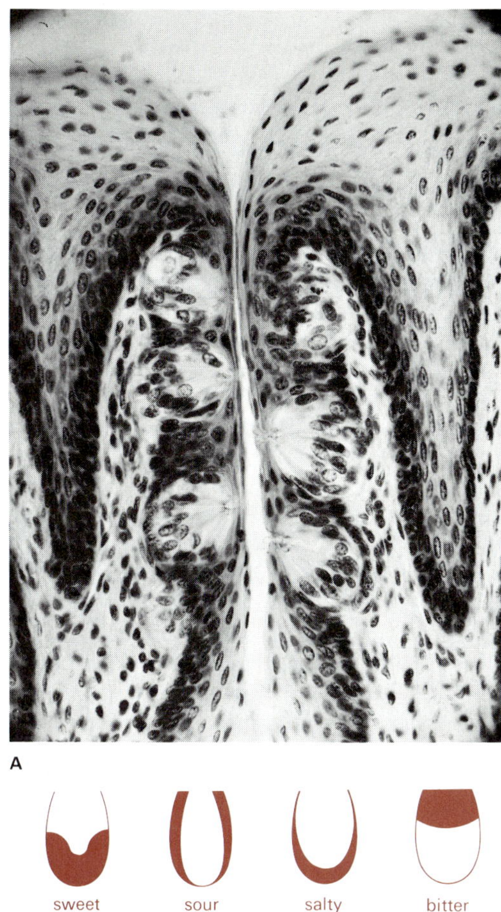

Fig. 19.19 Chemoreceptors. (A) Section through the tongue showing taste buds; the buds are located along the deep narrow channel leading into the tongue from the surface. (B) The distribution of taste buds for the four taste sensations.

color. In vertebrates with color vision, these cells, called *cones*, are structurally different from rods. Three kinds of cone cells are present in such eyes, each containing a variant of opsin sensitive to one of the three primary colors, red, green, and blue. Since all colors are produced from combinations of these three primary colors, the three kinds of cones together can detect and analyze light of any color.

Together with other associated cells, clusters or layers of photoreceptor cells form *retinas*, the main

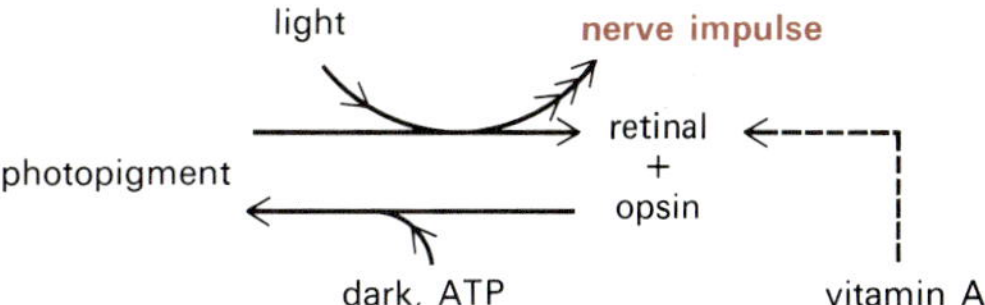

Fig. 19.20 Photoreception. The photopigment is rhodopsin in rod cells and iodopsin in one type of cone cell. Note that vitamin A can replenish the supply of retinal.

components of seeing organs. Some of these organs are relatively simple constructed *eyespots*, flush with the body surface. Others are *eyecups*, and the most complex are more or less spherical *eyes*. Most types of eyes usually are equipped with various accessory structures, including light-screening pigment layers and transparent, light-concentrating lenses.

In the vertebrate eye the retina is the innermost of three coats (Fig. 19.21). The outer coat is the *sclera*, fibrous in people, cartilaginous in many other mammals. The middle coat is the *choroid*, a black-pigmented light-screening layer that also carries blood vessels to and from the eye. (In many vertebrates a thin film of crystalline light-screening material coats the choroid, which makes the eyes of these animals shine in near darkness.) In the front of the eye these coats are modified structurally. The sclera merges with the transparent *cornea*.

Fig. 19.21 The structure of the mammalian eye.

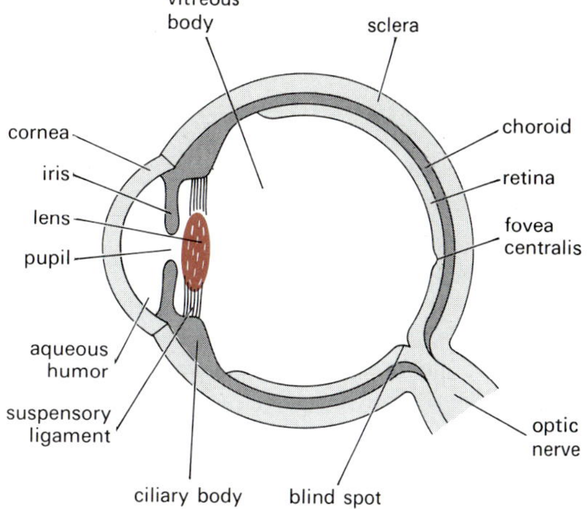

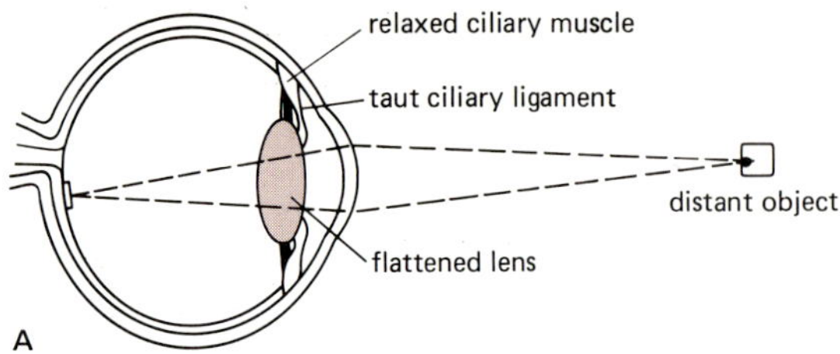

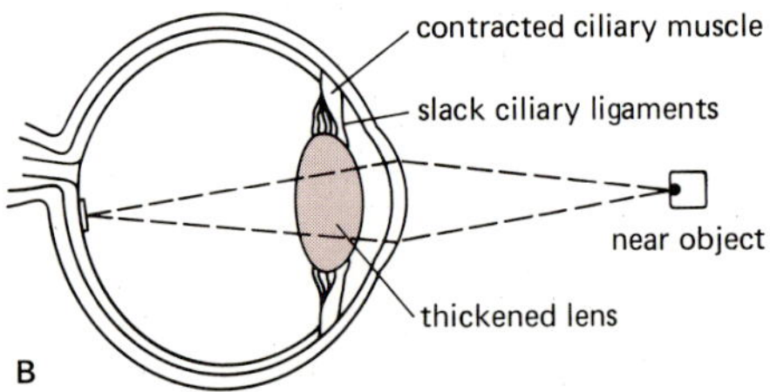

Fig. 19.22 Lens accommodation. (A) The lens is stretched (flattened) for focusing images of distant objects. (B) Focusing images of near objects requires a thickened lens.

The choroid coat continues as the pigmented *iris,* which encloses the *pupil.* Just behind the iris is a ring-shaped muscle, the *ciliary body,* to which the *lens* is attached by ligaments. The spaces between lens and cornea are filled with a lymphlike *aqueous humor;* and the space between lens and retina contains a jellylike *vitreous body.*

Functionally the eye resembles a photographic camera. The pupil, corresponding to the diaphragm of a camera, narrows or widens and thereby regulates the amount of light admitted to the eye. Intense light initiates a reflex through the retina, the autonomic nervous system, and a set of circularly arranged muscles in the iris (see Fig. 19.7). These muscles contract, the pupil narrows, and less light is admitted. Conversely, low light intensity results in reflex signals to a set of iris muscles arranged like the spokes of a wheel. When these contract the pupil enlarges and permits more light to enter.

The lens focuses the image of an object on the retina by changing shape according to the distance of the object, a process called *accommodation.* Lens shape is controlled by the *ciliary ligaments.* The outer surfaces of these ligaments are attached to *ciliary muscles;* their inner surfaces are attached to the lens (Fig. 19.22). Pressure exerted by fluids of the eye produces tension on these ligaments, which in turn produce tension on the elastic lens and cause it to flatten. Such a flattened lens focuses the eye for distant vision. Focusing on near objects required a lens to become more spherical. This is brought about by the contraction of ciliary muscles. By their contraction, these muscles relieve the tension of the ciliary ligament, which in turn permits the lens to bulge as a result of its own elasticity. Because the focusing of near objects requires contraction of ciliary muscles, close vision is more tiring than far vision.

Abnormally shaped lenses or eyes often prevent images from being focused on the retina (Fig. 19.23). People who have inherited overly short or elongated eyes, for example, usually cannot see both close and distant objects clearly without glasses or contact lenses. Because the distance between lens and retina is too great in elongated eyes, images of distant objects are focused slightly in front of photoreceptor cells. People who have such eyes are said to be *nearsighted* or *myopic.* Conversely, the ciliary muscles of abnormally short eyes cannot alter the shape of the lens sufficiently to permit focusing images of close objects. In these eyes, such images tend to be focused behind the retina. These individuals are *farsighted,* or *hyperopic.* Nearsightedness and farsightedness also can result from other causes. For example, the farsightedness that often develops in middle-aged people usually is due to loss of lens elasticity.

The retina consists of several layers of neurons that innervate one layer of rod and cone cells adjacent to the choroid coat (Fig. 19.24). Light therefore must pass through the neuron layers before it reaches the rods and cones. The fibers of the neuron layers collect as a thick optic nerve that leaves the hind part of the eye at one point, somewhat off-center. At this *blind spot* the layer of rods and cones, the choroid coat, and the sclera are interrupted (Fig. 19.25). The concentration of rod cells is greatest at the periphery of the retina and decreases toward the optical center of the eye. Thus the retinal periphery is particularly efficient in detecting movement and in black-and-white vision. Conversely, the concentration of cone cells increases toward the optical center of the retina, and this central area therefore is best adapted for reception of sharp, stationary images and for color vision. Indeed, only cones occur in the *fovea centralis,* a tiny depression at the very optical center of

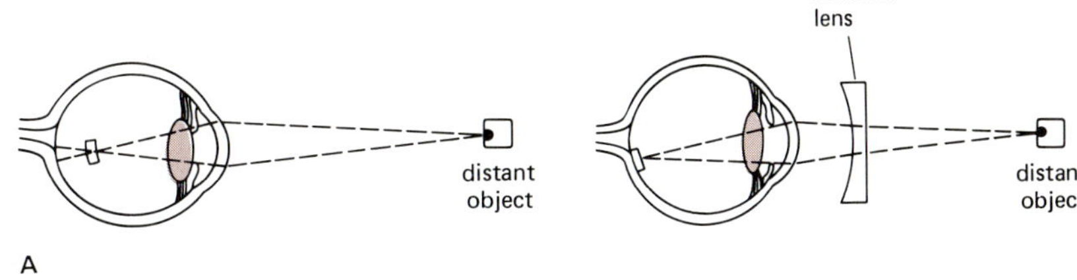

Fig. 19.23 Myopia and hyperopia. (A) Concave lenses must be worn by nearsighted people to facilitate focusing images of distant objects. (B) Farsighted people must wear convex lenses to accommodate focusing images of near objects.

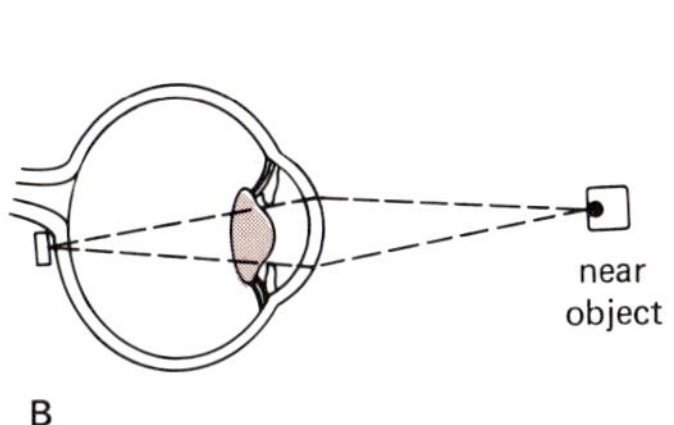

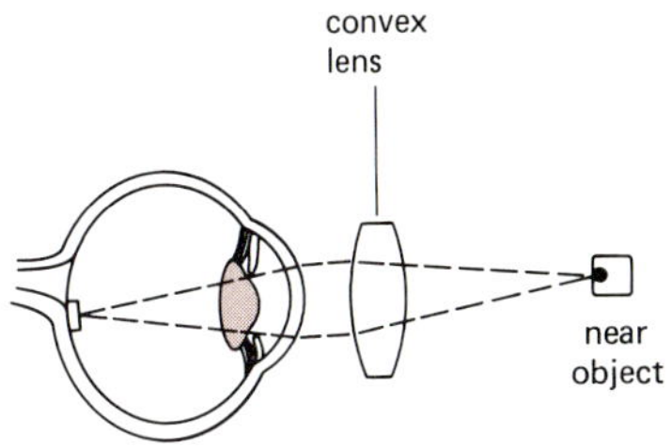

Fig. 19.24 The retina, greatly simplified section. Light passes through neuron layers before it reaches the photosensitive rods and cones.

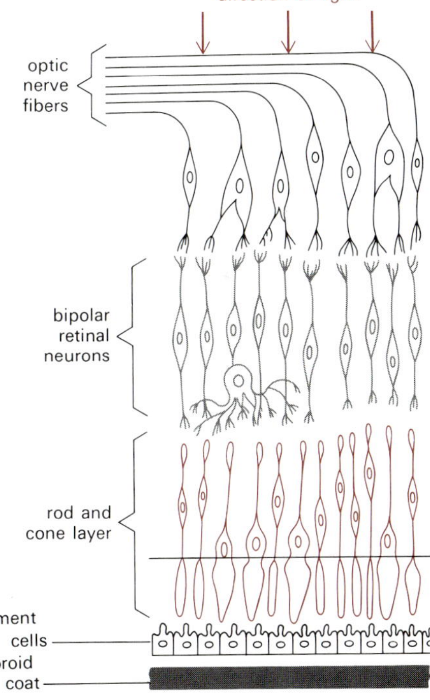

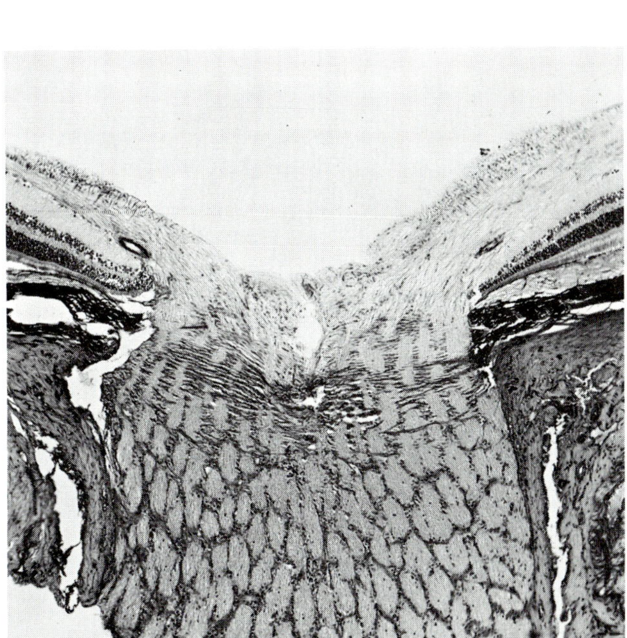

Fig. 19.25 Retina, blind spot, and optic nerve. Note the neuron layers at the surface of the retina (top of photo) and the merging of the neuron fibers at the depression of the blind spot, forming the optic nerve (leading down in the photograph).

the retina. Rods are absent here, as are overlying neurons: hence the cones are exposed to light directly. The fovea is the receptor region for the most acute vision.

An external object is "pictured" on the retina as a series of points, like the dots of a newspaper photograph. Each point corresponds to a rod or a cone. Impulses from these points are transmitted to the brain according to the pattern illustrated in Fig. 19.26. In nonmammalian vertebrates impulses from these points are transmitted to the optic lobes in the midbrain, where visual perception takes place. But in mammals, impulses from retinal neurons first travel to the thalamus. Partial processing of visual information occurs here, whereupon nervous stimuli are transmitted to the *visual cortex*, located along the posterior surface of the cerebrum (see Fig. 19.26). Additional processing of visual information takes place within this cluster of cortical interneurons.

Sorting of visual information actually begins in groups of retinal neurons, which carry out a considerable amount of "data processing" before impulses are sent to the brain. It has been found, for example, that the retina of a frog generates four distinct sets of impulses to the brain. One set provides the animal with a black-and-white "outline drawing" of the stationary content of the visible world. A second set similarly provides an outline drawing, but only of illuminated objects that move across the visual field. A third set informs of objects that blot out illumination in part of the visual field and that become rapidly larger—undoubtedly indicating the approach of potentially dangerous animals. And a fourth set informs of moving objects that blot out illumination but remain small—probably an insect-detecting device of special importance to a frog. These four sets of impulses are neatly superimposed in the brain, resulting in a single interpretation. The visual systems of animals do not form actual pictures. What the brain "sees" at any given moment is a specifically coded pattern of action potentials formed by the simultaneous activation of many sets of neurons.

In addition to these impulses, neural centers also receive thousands of other impulses simultaneously from other receptors of an organism. Neural centers thereby are provided with a continuous input of information about environmental conditions both inside and outside an animal. These centers then process the sensory information and often direct responses to stimuli through one or more effectors. The most visible effector responses of animals are those resulting in movement, either of whole organisms or their parts. Virtually all such movements result from the contraction of muscles.

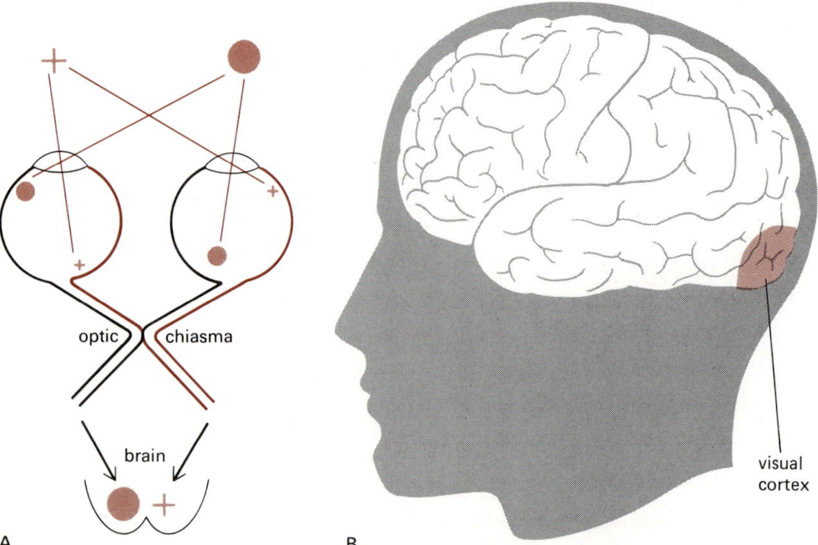

Fig. 19.26 Eye and brain. (A) Diagrammatic representation of the visual pathway between the eyes and visual cortex of mammals. An object in the left field of vision registers on the right halves of both retinas, and impulses are transmitted to the right half of the brain. (B) Location of visual cortex in the cerebrum of mammals.

EFFECTORS: MUSCLES

Animals carry out few functions that do not include muscular contraction. Moreover, muscles are often the most abundant tissue of an animal, particularly a vertebrate, and a proportionately large amount of energy must be expended to keep muscles operating. Even during "inactive" periods like sleep, for example, the muscular system maintains vital functions such as breathing, heartbeat, and blood pressure. Mainly because of muscular movement, the energy requirements of animals are far greater pound for pound than those of any other kind of organism.

Muscles consists of parallel arrays of elongated *muscle fibers.* Some muscles, called *striated muscles,* are composed of fibers that under the microscope appear striped with alternating light and dark bands (Fig. 19.27). Examples of striated muscles are those attached to bones (also called *skeletal muscles*). The heart (also termed *cardiac muscle*) consists of striated fibers too. The muscles of most internal organs, such as those lining the gut, do not have a microscopically striped appearance and are called *smooth muscles.* Skeletal muscles are controlled by the somatic nervous system and can be coordinated voluntarily by an organism, but cardiac and smooth muscle are under the involuntary control of the autonomic nervous system.

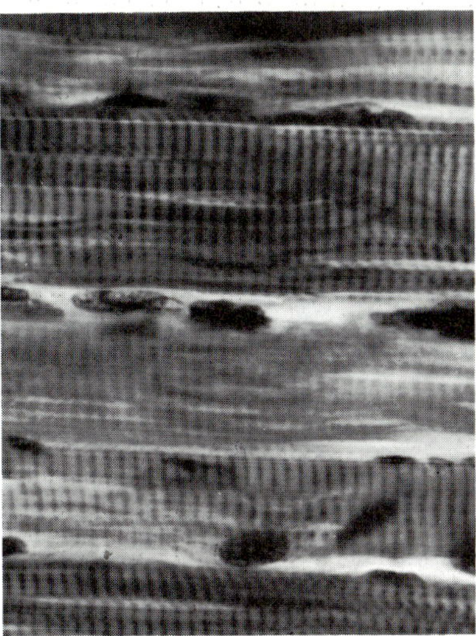

Fig. 19.27 Skeletal muscle fibers. Note the cross-striations, the faintly visible internal longitudinal myofibrils, and the nuclei, which appear as dark patches. (*Ward's Natural Science Establishment, Inc.*)

Structural Components

The functional units of skeletal and cardiac muscle fibers are long bundles of filaments called *myofibrils;* each filament in a myofibril is termed a *myofilament* (Fig. 19.28). The myofilaments of these muscles are arranged in regularly spaced parallel sets of identical units called *sarcomeres* (Fig. 19.29). Dark bands, called *Z lines,* form the outer boundaries of each sarcomere. Centrally positioned in each sarcomere is a dense region called the *A band.* This band is uniformly dense except at its center. This central region, called the *H zone,* is somewhat less dense than the remainder of the A band. The density of the A band is reduced greatly and abruptly on both its sides by I bands. Z lines extend through the center of these less compact bands.

The different densities of I and A bands are due to an overlapping of two types of myofilaments. The I bands contain thin filaments composed chiefly of a protein called *actin.* These filaments are attached to the Z lines and extend toward the center of the A band from both ends of the sarcomere. The A bands contain the ends of these thin filaments plus thicker filaments that stretch across the entire A band. These thicker filaments are composed of the protein *myosin.* Thus, I bands are the least dense regions of sarcomeres because they contain only thin filaments. A bands contain both thick and thin filaments except at the H zone. This zone consists exclusively of thick myosin filaments and therefore is slightly less dense than the remainder of the A band, but more dense than I bands. It is this pattern of alternating dark and light A and I bands that gives skeletal and cardiac muscle its striated appearance under the microscope.

Muscle Contraction

Study of these bands has provided considerable information about the mechanics of muscular contraction. It has been determined, for example, that the width of A bands remains unchanged during the contraction of striated muscle, but that I bands

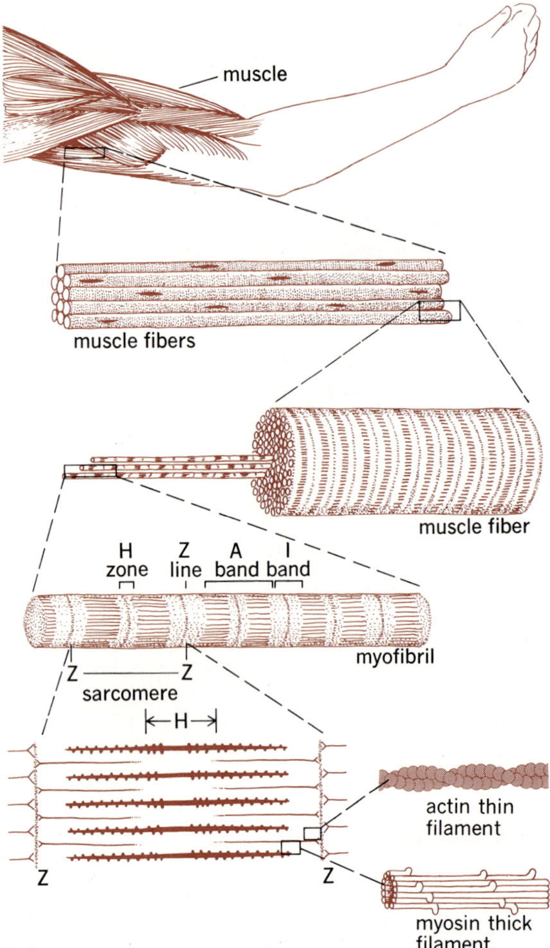

Fig. 19.28 Organization of the structural components of skeletal muscle. *(From A. J. Vander et al., "Human Physiology: The Mechanisms of Body Functions," 2d ed., © 1975 by McGraw-Hill, Inc., New York.)*

and H zones become narrower or disappear entirely. Other experiments have demonstrated that neither actin nor myosin is able to contract alone. Contraction of these proteins occurs only when both are present in solutions that contain water, ATP, and certain inorganic ions.

These observations are consistent with the *sliding-filament theory* of muscular contraction, which attributes muscle shortening to the movement of thick and thin myofilaments past each other (Fig. 19.30). Simply stated, this theory proposes that cross bridges interlink actin and myosin filaments and that contraction occurs when these cross bridges move. The formation of such bridges would not be surprising considering the nature of the two proteins. All myosin molecules, for example, have a large "head" that projects from thick filaments toward the thin filaments of a sarcomere. A cross bridge thus would consist of a union of an actin and a myosin molecule between a thin and thick filament. Contraction of myofibrils would occur if these cross bridges swiveled in an arc around their fixed positions on the surface of myosin filaments, much like the oars of a boat, and if the cross bridges subsequently broke their contacts and reattached one notch higher on the surface of actin molecules. If this cycle were repeated, thick and thin filaments would move past each other in a ratchetlike manner (Fig. 19.31).

According to this theory, muscles return to their original extended conditions by first relaxing. Relaxation would require the simultaneous breaking of all cross bridges in contracted myofibrils so that filaments would be free to slip past each other. A relaxed muscle then would be extended by the contraction of opposing muscles. Indeed, muscles usually are arranged in antagonistic pairs so that the contraction of one member of the pair extends the other. The action of muscles in flexing the arm or leg illustrates this principle (Fig. 19.32).

A considerable amount of evidence has been amassed in support of the sliding-filament theory. The theory explains satisfactorily why neither actin nor myosin can contract alone. Moreover, it explains why I bands and H zones of sarcomeres shorten during contraction. Because actin filaments are anchored to Z lines, the sliding of actin filaments toward each other draws Z lines and the ends of myosin filaments closer together. It is this same inward movement of actin filaments that causes H zones to shorten (see Fig. 19.30). H zones should disappear when all actin filaments of a myofibril meet in the center of sarcomeres. Both these predictions of the sliding-filament theory have been confirmed experimentally for striated muscle. Myofilaments also make up the bulk of smooth muscles, but the organization and contraction of these filaments is understood less well. Indeed, the lack of visible striations in smooth muscle indicates that its myofilaments are not organized as discrete myofibrils.

Directly or indirectly, the contraction of all

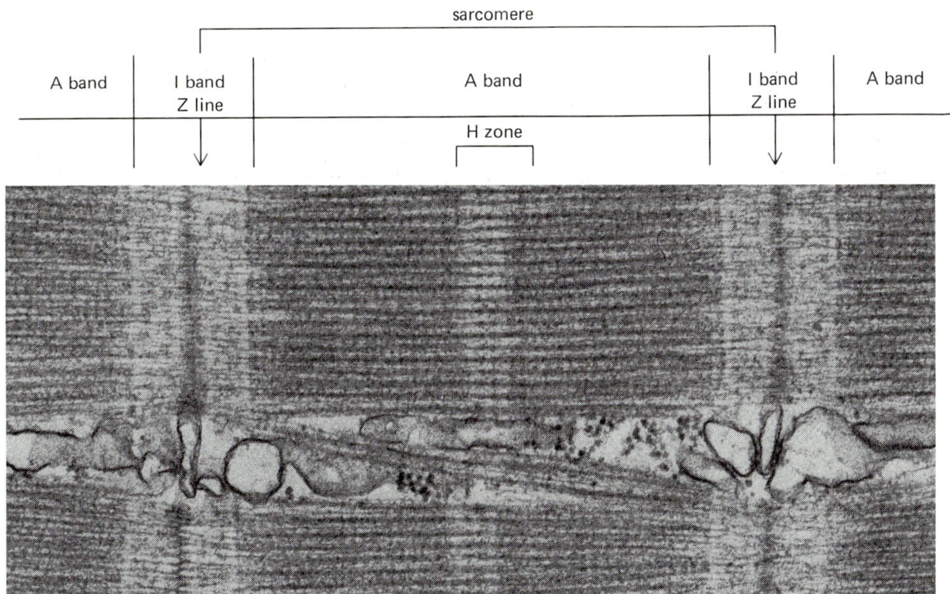

Fig. 19.29 Myofibrils. Electron micrograph of portions of two horizontal myofibrils (in tail muscles of a frog tadpole), separated by a layer of cytoplasmic material (sarcoplasmic reticulum). The cross-striations in Fig. 19.27 appear here as A and I bands. The portion of a myofibril between two Z lines constitutes a sarcomere. The distribution of myosin and actin in these bands is shown in Fig. 19.30. (*Courtesy of Keith R. Porter.*)

Fig. 19.30 Muscle activity. Myosin, thick horizontal bars; actin, black lines. (Top) Extended state. (Middle) Partly contracted state. (Bottom) Fully contracted state. "Heads" (not shown) project from myosin filaments and unite with actin filaments during contraction, forming cross bridges (see Fig. 19.31). The cross bridges then pull along the actin filaments in a ratchetlike manner and cause a shortening of the sarcomere. The A band and the portions of the adjacent I bands of a myofibril shown here are intended to represent a working unit repeated horizontally many times in a whole fiber. (*From A. J. Vander et al., "Human Physiology: The Mechanisms of Body Function," 2d ed., © 1975 by McGraw-Hill, Inc., New York.*)

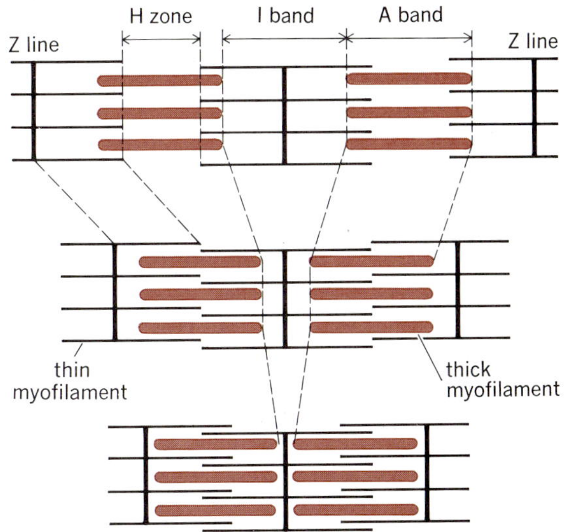

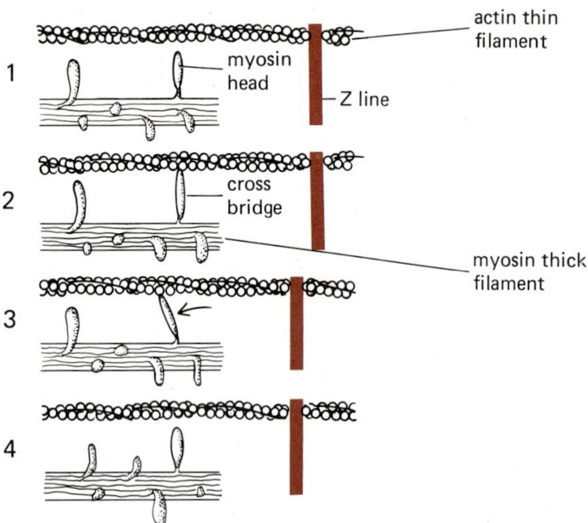

Fig. 19.31 Myosin cross bridges. Movements of cross bridges produce the sliding of thick and thin filaments shown in Fig. 19.30.

muscles is controlled by motor neurons. In striated muscle, for example, a group of muscle fibers usually is innervated collectively by one motor neuron. Acetylcholine, released from the terminals of the neurons, stimulates contraction by bonding to receptor molecules on the surface membranes of muscle fibers. These surface membranes interconnect with tubules that extend transversely across a fiber. The *transverse tubules* in turn connect with the *sarcoplasmic reticulum,* a system of longitudinally arranged tubules (Fig. 19.33 and see Fig. 19.29). The bonding of acetylcholine to receptors at the surface of muscle fibers produces changes in the permeability of this crisscrossing network of transverse and longitudinal tubules. Such changes result in a release of stored calcium ions from the sarcoplasmic reticulum to the sarcomeres. The ions selectively inhibit two regulator proteins, *troponin* and *tropomyosin,* which are attached to actin molecules and normally block attachment of myosin cross bridges to the thin filaments. Calcium deactivation of these regulators results in cross bridge attachment and the release of energy from ATP, prerequisites for muscle contraction. Indeed, it is difficult to overstate the importance of calcium as an intracellular regulator, either for muscle contraction or for a host of other processes. For example, calcium ions now are known to influence movements of chromosomes during cell division, the maturation of lymphocytes, the streaming of cytoplasm in cells, phagocytosis, exocytosis (including release of synaptic vesicles), and intercellular recognition and adhesion.

Fig. 19.32 Antagonistic muscle pairs. (A) Contraction of the triceps extends the forearm and lengthens the biceps. (B) Contraction of the biceps muscle flexes the forearm and lengthens the triceps. (*From A. J. Vander et al., "Human Physiology: The Mechanisms of Body Function," 2d ed., © 1975 by McGraw-Hill, Inc., New York.*)

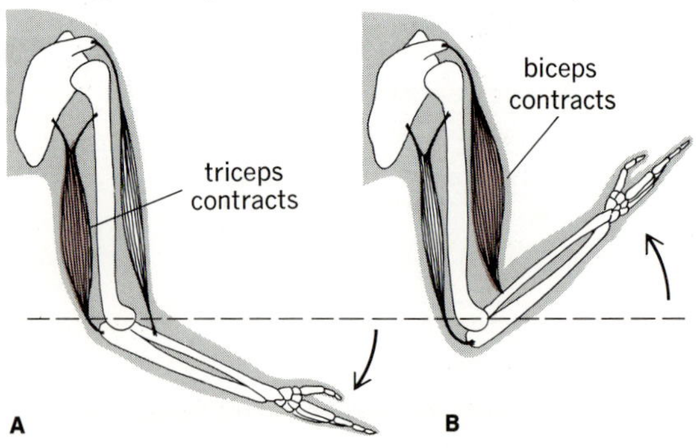

Certain drugs interfere with various aspects of the excitation-contraction phase of muscle function. *Curare,* for example, a poison used by South American Indians to kill wild game, blocks acetylcholine receptor sites in skeletal muscles. Unlike acetylcholine, curare does not trigger release of calcium ions from the sarcoplasmic reticulum. Thus, motor neurons in curare-poisoned animals release normal amounts of acetylcholine from axon terminals, but blockage of receptor sites prevents muscular contraction. Because breathing movements partly result from contraction of skeletal muscles, curare causes death through asphyxiation.

Other substances prevent release of acetylcholine from axon terminals of motor neurons. One of these, *botulinus toxin,* is produced by *Clostridium botulinum,* the species of bacteria responsible for an often deadly form of food poisoning called *botulism.* This species can reproduce rapidly in improperly processed canned foods. The toxin is extremely potent; less than 0.1 μg is sufficient to kill a person. Still other chemicals, such as the active ingredients of certain "muscle relaxant" drugs, interfere with the release of calcium ions from the sarcoplasmic reticulum. These drugs can prevent contraction of muscles even when normal amounts of acetylcholine are released from motor neurons.

Fig. 19.33 Sarcoplasmic reticulum. Three-dimensional arrangement of sarcoplasmic reticulum surrounding six myofibrils of a skeletal muscle fiber. Transverse tubules interconnect components of the sarcoplasmic reticulum with the surface membrane that surrounds the muscle fiber. These tubules play an important role in triggering changes in the permeability of the sarcoplasmic reticulum, which in turn produces muscle contraction.

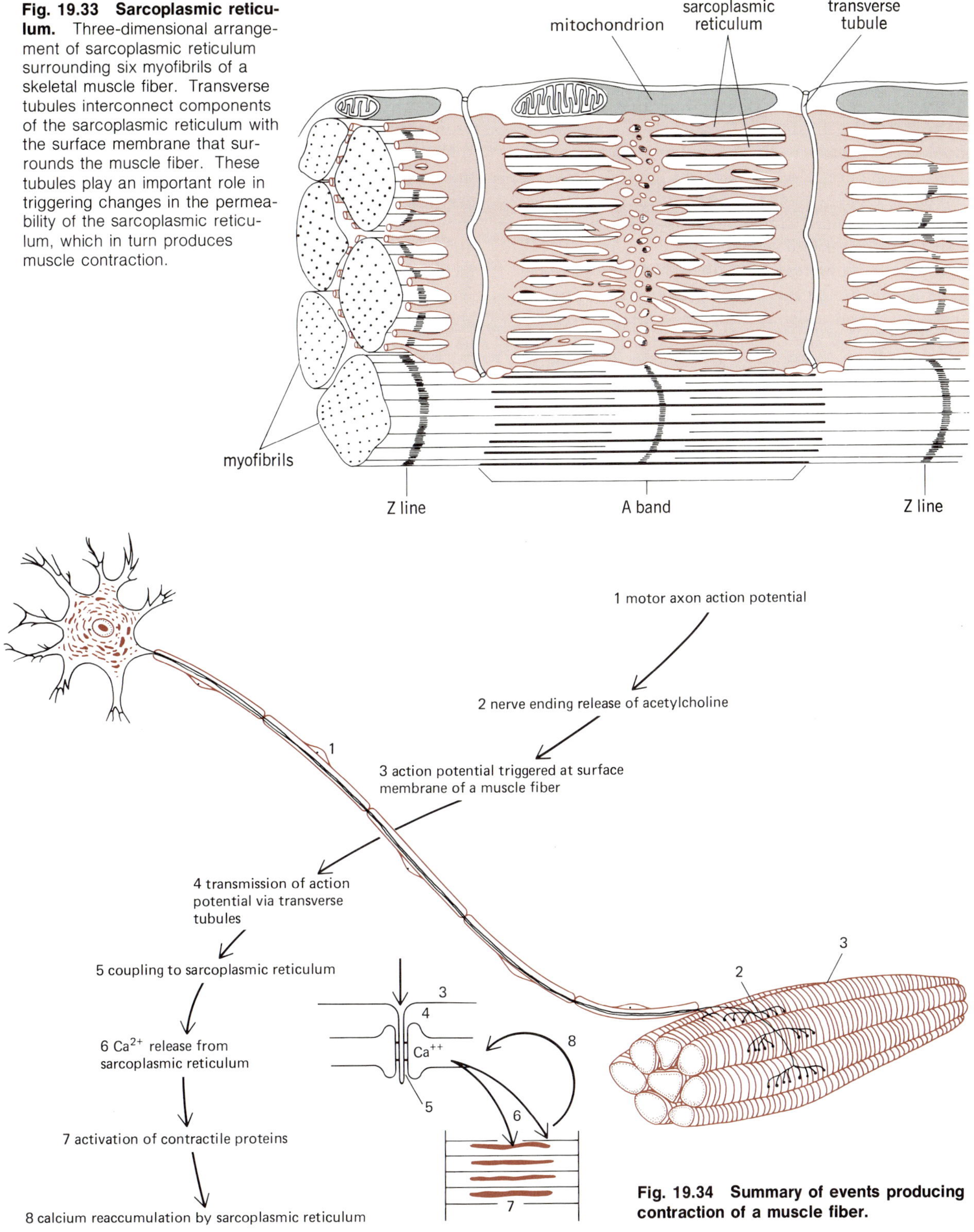

Fig. 19.34 Summary of events producing contraction of a muscle fiber.

The degree of tension produced by a striated muscle is determined largely by the frequency of impulses generated in motor neurons that innervate the muscle; the greater the frequency, the greater the degree of tension. Relatively large amounts of acetylcholine are released by motor neurons when impulses arrive at their terminals in rapid succession. Proportionately large amounts of calcium ions then are released into sarcomeres, which in their turn promote a correspondingly high degree of muscle tension. As the frequency of motor nerve impulses decreases, calcium ions are "pumped" back into the fluids of the sarcoplasmic reticulum by active transport, producing increased relaxation of muscle fibers (Fig. 19.34).

The integration between sensory receptors, neurons, glands, and muscles permit animals to respond effectively to the simultaneous input of many different stimuli. Although this integration is exceedingly complex in all animals, it is particularly so in animals with a well-developed brain. Yet in spite of the frustrations that await all who study this most complex organ, two groups of scientists are slowly increasing our understanding of brain function. Each group is studying the brain from a different perspective, with different tools and techniques.

Neuroscientists are examining the organization and chemical interactions between neurons and neural centers, while behaviorists are attempting to subdivide the complex overt responses of animals into their fundamental components. The results and social implications of their research are considered next.

Review Questions

1 Review the roles of neural receptors, neurons, and muscles in the maintenance of steady-state conditions.

2 Describe the structural components of the vertebrate nervous system. What are the structural and functional relations between neurons, nerves, nerve nets, nerve cords, ganglia, and brains? Describe the main structural components of the vertebrate brain and indicate the general functions of each component.

3 Review the structure and functioning of the autonomic nervous system. Distinguish structurally and functionally between the sympathetic and parasympathetic subdivisions of that system. What are preganglionic and postganglionic nerve fibers?

4 Review how a nerve impulse is propagated along a nerve fiber and between neurons. Describe how electric potentials are established and maintained in resting neurons. How does the distribution of ions on both sides of the plasma membrane of a neuron change during transmission of a nerve impulse? How do the central nervous systems of animals distinguish between different intensities of stimuli?

5 Describe the activities of neural centers. Discuss how the structural organization of excitatory and inhibitory neurons influences the behavioral responses of animals. Distinguish learning by habituation, by classical conditioning, and by operant conditioning.

6 What is the basic function of all sensory receptors? Describe the general functions of thermal receptors, mechanoreceptors, chemoreceptors, and photoreceptors.

7 Describe the structural and functional relations between the main components of the human ear. Do the same for the human eye. Review the chemistry of vision. What components form the focusing mechanism of the human eye, and how is the function of focusing carried out? What are the principal causes of farsightedness and nearsightedness?

8 Describe the components of striated muscles. Describe the subdivisions and the molecular components of sarcomeres. Review the events that occur during the contraction of a sarcomere. How do ATP and calcium ions contribute to the contraction of striated muscle?

9 Suppose you are walking along railroad tracks and suddenly become aware of a train approaching rapidly. Describe as fully as possible the anatomical and functional interrelations that must occur between sense organs, nervous system, and muscles if you are to avoid being struck by the train.

10 Describe how pain signals are transmitted from sensory structures in vertebrates to the brain. What substances appear to suppress pain? Where are these substances produced? What evidence supports the hypothesis that the central nervous system of vertebrates produces morphinelike pain suppressants? That substance P is a transmitter of pain signals? That endorphins and substance P interact antagonistically?

Collateral Readings

Axelrod, J.: Neurotransmitters, *Scientific American,* June 1974. The kinds, properties, and effects of neurotransmitters are discussed.

Camhi, J.: The Escape System of the Cockroach, *Scientific American,* December 1980. This article investigates the neural implications of a fascinating behavioral response.

Cohen, C.: The Protein Switch of Muscle Contraction, *Scientific American,* November 1975, The effects of calcium on muscle contraction are discussed.

DiCara, L. V.: Learning in the Autonomic Nervous System, *Scientific American,* January 1970. Describes experiments suggesting that some of the "involuntary" responses of animals can be modified through learning.

Eccles, J. C.: "The Understanding of the Brain," McGraw-Hill, New York, 1977. A short introduction to brain function by one of world's noted neurophysiologists. Written for the general public.

Evarts, E. V.: Brain Mechanisms in Movement, *Scientific American,* July 1973. This article describes the parts of the brain that control muscular movements.

Gazzaniga, M. S.: The Split Brain in Man, *Scientific American,* August 1967. Experiments on people who have undergone surgery to sever the corpus callosum have provided much information on how speech and language are coordinated in the brain.

Heimer, L.: Pathways in the Brain, *Scientific American,* July 1971. Connections between nerve cells of the brain are described in this article.

Heller, H. C., L. I. Crawshaw, and H. T. Hammel: The Thermostat of Vertebrate Animals, *Scientific American,* August 1978. The temperature-regulating effects of the hypothalamus are highlighted.

Horridge, G. A.: The Compound Eye of Insects, *Scientific American,* July 1977. An excellent discussion of this fascinating visual organ.

Keynes, R. D.: Ion Channels in the Nerve-Cell Membrane, *Scientific American,* March 1979. The operation of molecular channels in the plasma membranes of neurons is discussed.

Klemm, W. R.: "Science, the Brain, and Our Future," Bobbs-Merrill, Indianapolis, 1972. Written for the layman, this nontechnical paperback introduces the basic components of the nervous system and discusses the social signficance of brain research.

Krieger, D. T., and **A. S. Liotta:** Pituitary Hormones in Brain: Where, How, and Why? *Science,* vol. 205, pp. 366–372, July 27, 1979. A review of peptides recently discovered in the central nervous system. Some of these peptides appear to influence our perception of pain.

Lester, H. A.: The Response of Acetylcholine, *Scientific American,* February 1977. How muscle responds to acetylcholine is the focus of this article.

Llinás, R. R.: The Cortex of the Cerebellum, *Scientific American,* January 1975. The structure and function of this part of the brain are described.

Luria, A. R.: The Functional Organization of the Brain, *Scientific American,* March 1970. Describes experiments aimed at correlating functions of the body with specific structural components of the brain.

Marx, J.: Brain, Peptides: Is Substance P a Transmitter of Pain Signals? *Science,* vol. 205, pp. 886–889, August 1979. A good review of the effects of substance P and other peptides that may influence the perception of pain.

Merton, P. A.: How We Control the Contraction of Our Muscles, *Scientific American,* May

1972. The author describes the interaction of sensory neurons, motor neurons, and specialized muscles that allows us to move as we choose.

Morell, P., and **W. T. Norton:** Myelin, *Scientific American,* May 1980. This well-illustrated article describes how myelin becomes wrapped around nerve fibers, providing electrical insulation.

Murray, J. M., and **A. Weber:** The Cooperative Action of Muscle Proteins, *Scientific American,* February 1974. Describes interactions between four proteins during muscle contraction.

Nathanson, J. A., and **P. Greengard:** "Second Messengers" in the Brain, *Scientific American,* August 1977. This article shows how the chemical signals of neurotransmitters are translated by "second messengers" within cells.

Patterson, P. H., D. D. Potter, and **E. J. Furshpan:** The Chemical Differentiation of Nerve Cells, *Scientific American,* July 1978. This article reviews experiments attempting to determine how different neurons become programmed to produce different neurotransmitters.

Rushton, W. A. H.: Visual Pigments and Color Blindness, *Scientific American,* March 1975. The causes of color blindness are discussed in this article.

Schneider, D.: The Sex-Attractant Receptor of Moths, *Scientific American,* July 1974. How a specific pheromone triggers impulses in neural receptors of moths is discussed.

Schwartz, J. H.: The Transport of Substances in Nerve Cells, *Scientific American,* April 1980. Describes how molecules formed in the cell body of a neuron are transported to the terminal buttons of an axon.

Scientific American, September 1979. The entire issue is devoted to the structure and function of the brain.

Shepherd, G. M.: Microcircuits in the Nervous System, *Scientific American,* February 1978. Describes complex synapses that occur in sensory organs.

Chapter 20 Behavioral Control: The Individual

Learning Objectives

After reading this chapter you should be able to:

1. Define behavior; define kinesis, taxis, and tropism and list at least one example of each; differentiate between reactive, active, and cognitive forms of behavior and list at least one example of each; name the kinds and relative amounts of learning usually associated with each of these forms of behavior.
2. Cite at least one identifying feature, and list at least one example, of exploratory behavior, play, and manipulative behavior.
3. Distinguish between short-term memory and long-term memory; define and give an example of memory consolidation; outline the relationship between consolidation and short- and long-term memory; name one region of the human brain that is associated with consolidation; name at least two factors that can prevent consolidation of memories.
4. Describe at least two hypotheses that have been proposed to account for long-term memory storage; list evidence that supports each of the hypotheses.
5. Define schizophrenia and outline a hypothesis that explains the neural cause of this group of abnormal behavioral patterns; list evidence that supports this hypothesis.
6. Define motivation and illustrate the four phases that characterize most motivational activities.
7. Define releaser stimulus and sign-induced behavior and list at least two examples of each. Define pheromones and list at least two examples of pheromone-induced behavior; state at least one practical application of basic research on pheromones.
8. Define imprinting and outline an experiment that illustrates this kind of behavior; list at least one specific characteristic of imprinting and identify at least one way in which imprinting differs from other kinds of learning.
9. Define and state the general characteristics of behavioral rhythms; list at least four examples of such rhythms; define biological clock and list evidence in support of the hypothesis that organisms possess biological clocks; define and list at least one example of entrainment; name at least two kinds of factors that appear to regulate behavioral rhythms.
10. Define sun-compass orientation and name at least five kinds of animals that exhibit this type of behavior; give evidence in support of the hypothesis that some animals use the position of the sun as orienting cues; list at least three other kinds of orienting cues that are used by certain animals.

Behavior includes any externally observable activity of an organism—microorganism, plant, or animal. In most cases behavior involves some form of movement, either motion of body parts or outright locomotion. But secretions to the outside, color changes, or slow alterations brought about by growth similarly qualify as behavioral events. Moreover, absence or cessation of an overt activity is itself an expression of behavior.

In all its forms behavior is basically adaptive and has a self-perpetuative function; directly or indirectly it tends to promote survival. Moreover, behavioral acts are just as subject to evolutionary change as their functions; behavior and function evolve together.

FORMS OF BEHAVIOR

Inheritance and Learning

Like all other properties and activities of organisms, behavioral processes are ultimately under genetic control. The kind of behavior an animal can elicit is therefore constrained and at least partly determined by the genetic information it has inherited. For example, people can communicate with each other verbally partly because they have inherited genes that bring about development of muscles and other structures of the mouth and throat prerequisite for speech. Gorillas, however, have not inherited such genes and cannot speak, even though they can understand combinations of words and can communicate with people by sign language.

Although some forms of animal behavior appear to be "programmed" responses, determined solely by genes, virtually every behavioral process studied closely is now known to include *both* inherited and learned elements. Equivalent to "inherited" in this context are also terms such as "inborn," "innate," or "instinctive," all of which signify that given aspects of a behavior are based on the genetic endowment of an organism and are controlled by mechanisms that develop independently of learning. Terms equivalent to "learned" include "acquired," "experiential," or "environmental," and they signify that certain aspects of a behavior are based on experience and are controlled by nongenetic mechanisms. Because they are always influenced by genes *and* environment, behavioral (or other) processes can no longer be categorized—as they usually have been in the past—in sharp alternatives like "instinctive" or "learned."

But although both inherited and learned factors thus play a role in almost any behavior, the relative contributions of these two sets of determinants are known to vary considerably for different behaviors. Such relative contributions usually can be judged by the degree of modifiability of a behavioral process. A behavior can be largely unlearned and nearly unmodifiable, or partly learned and fairly modifiable, or largely learned and exceedingly modifiable. For present purposes we can arbitrarily refer to these three general categories respectively as *reactive, active,* and *cognitive* forms of behavior.

Reactive Behavior

Reactive behavior includes all largely automatic, stereotyped activities. As a group they probably represent the most primitive behavioral level. Reactive responses by and large are fully "programmed" as soon as an organism has completed its embryonic development, and thereafter they occur in relatively fixed all-or-none fashion. In this type of behavior are included *kineses* (singular: *kinesis*), *taxes* (singular: *taxis*) and *tropisms* (Fig. 20.1).

Kineses are comparatively primitive orientational responses that are not directed toward or away from external stimuli. Organisms exhibiting kinetic behavior react to stimuli by moving around to a greater or lesser extent. For example, the ciliate protozoan *Paramecium* changes course by a fixed angle whenever it encounters an obstruction or an unfavorable environment. The organism continues to alter its course until a more favorable environment is found.

Taxes, by contrast, are movements whose direction is determined by the spatial relationships between organisms and external stimuli (see Fig. 20.1). A moth, for example, tends to fly toward an electric light. Such behavior constitutes a *positive phototaxis.* Other organisms, such as cockroaches, move away from light and therefore are commonly found only in dark environments. Taxes are not always oriented directly at or away from an external stimulus, however. Honeybees, for example, maintain a straight course of flight by moving at a constant angle to the sun, 30° to the left, 15° to the right, or whatever angle leads back to the hive.

Tropisms are directed growth movements of organisms that are oriented to external stimuli. As noted in Chap. 16, for example, plants react to external stimuli such as light by growing toward or away from the stimulus source. The execution of such responses in plants has a strictly chemical basis, the internal reactions being regulated by hormonal substances and enzymes.

In this respect the reactive behavior of animals is generally more diverse than that of plants, for in addition to chemical controls, neural ones usually play an important role as well. Animal kineses and taxes include, for example, the fairly complex balancing, positioning, and orienting processes that are largely under the control of nervous reflexes. Apart from these comparatively simple orientational responses, the predominantly reactive behaviors of animals also comprise certain routine and recurrent "housekeeping" activities, such as breathing, circulation, pupillary responses, and in general most processes that in vertebrates are controlled primarily by the autonomic nervous system and that in people do not or need not become conscious.

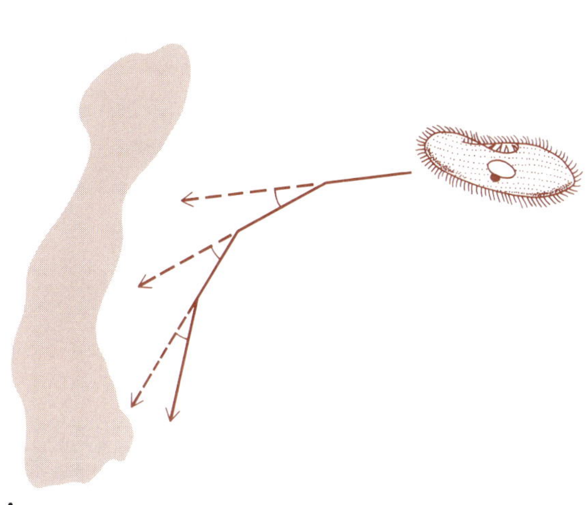

A

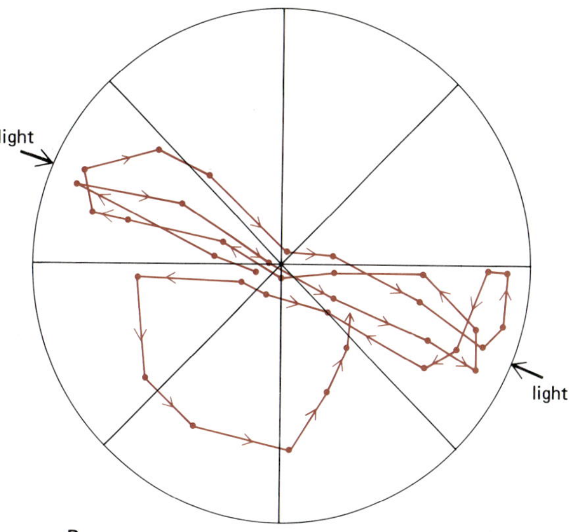

B

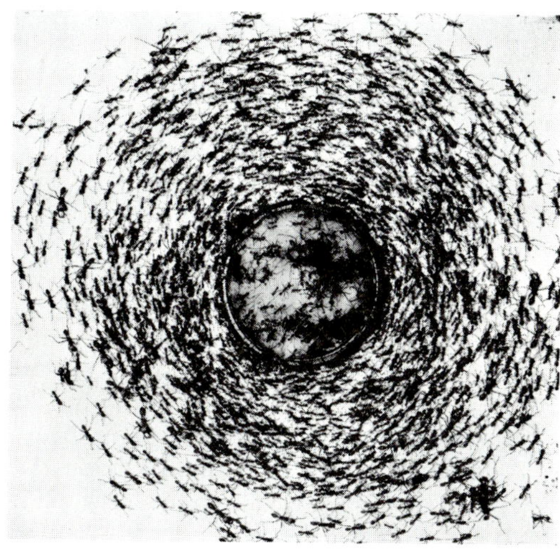

C

Fig. 20.1 Reactive behavior. (A) Kineses. When an unfavorable environment is encountered (shaded area), a *Paramecium* continues to alter its course by a fixed angle until a more favorable environment is found. (B) Taxes. Route of a starfish, as seen from above when the organism was placed in the center of an arena illuminated by two spotlights positioned 180° apart. This starfish displays positive phototaxis, tending to move toward light. (C) Taxes. The comparatively minor influence of learning in most kinds of reactive behavior is illustrated here. If a column of army ants is made to travel in a circle, as in the picture, they will continue to circle endlessly. Evidently this behavior is governed so completely by internal factors that the insects are incapable of modifying their response. Examples of tropisms are illustrated in Figs. 16.7, 16.8, and 16.9.

In all organisms reactive behavior evidently maintains some of the most basic vital functions. It is therefore a considerable adaptive advantage that such behavior is comparatively unmodifiable. It would be highly detrimental if, for example, a life-preserving balancing or heat-avoiding response were readily modifiable by external factors. Nevertheless, reactive behaviors actually can be modified, even if only to a minor degree in many cases. Most commonly such modifications occur through *habituation*—progressive loss of responsiveness to repeated stimulation as outlined in Chap. 19. In some instances more drastic modifications are possible through classical conditioning. For example, as also pointed out in Chap. 19, the pupillary response in human beings is amenable to considerable retraining.

Active Behavior

In the category of active behavior, genetic inheritance endows an organism with certain behavioral potentials, but the actual realization of these potentials depends to a substantial degree on learning and the directive influence of the environment.

Fig. 20.2 Active behavior based on learning. These circus elephants respond to stimuli selectively and display behavior made possible by earlier training and conditioning.

Thus, whereas an organism behaving reactively is comparable to a robot (a system that passively delivers preprogrammed responses on command), an organism behaving actively first "assesses" and "judges" stimuli and then "chooses" and adjusts its responses. It does so essentially by "comparing" a present situation with the memorized experiences of similar past situations and then behaving accordingly. The organism therefore is not merely automatically reactive, but selectively active (Fig. 20.2).

This form of behavior requires a fairly elaborate nervous system, and in effect it is limited largely to relatively advanced animals, most notably vertebrates. The specific behaviors in this category all must become perfected progressively, in part through parental training at immature stages and in part through later experience. Examples are searching for and handling food, grooming and sanitary behavior, communicating, courtship and mating, and most activities associated with offense and defense, family life, and sociality. Some elements of such responses are largely learned; others are largely programmed genetically. For example, food swallowing as such requires little or no training, but the preparatory actions leading up to swallowing generally do. Similarly, the activities preceding copulation in mammals are influenced greatly by experience, but copulation itself appears to be unlearned.

Cognitive Behavior

The most advanced forms of behavior are represented by cognitive activities. In these, genes provide only a very broad and general background for behavioral potentials, and the actual utilization of such potentials depends very largely on external influences. A cognitive activity in effect is an action pattern elaborated in more or less "deliberate" fashion by the animal itself. The animal here does not merely respond to stimuli actively, but it can search out new means of *how* to respond; it can *invent* its own actions. In the process the animal often also manipulates the environment—an important distinction from merely active behavior, in which such manipulation typically does not occur (Fig. 20.3).

Among the simplest cognitive behaviors, found in a few invertebrates and all vertebrates, are *exploratory* activities, through which an animal familiarizes itself with any new condition in its environment (Fig. 20.4). Strange objects are approached and inspected by sight, smell, and touch. Withdrawal usually follows quickly. Inspections are then undertaken repeatedly, but with gradually declining frequency. For any animal studied it has been found that the most complex novelties in the environment always tend to elicit the most exploration; a simple environmental change evidently is not as "interesting" or significant to the animal as an elaborate one. Exploration also is most likely when the stimuli are neither too weak nor too strong. Weak stimulation can fail to arouse curiosity, and strong stimulation can evoke withdrawal or escape rather than approach.

Animals placed in unvaryingly monotonous environments still exhibit exploratory behavior, though in greatly reduced fashion. Also, if mammals, people included, are prevented for extended periods from carrying out exploratory activities, their behavior can become highly abnormal. This is often the case with caged animals and with people suffering prolonged imprisonment. Similarly, if human infants are deprived of opportunities to accumulate experience through visual exploration, the later adults often have difficulty in distinguishing visual patterns such as triangles and circles and they can be handicapped in sight-associated activities in general.

Another type of cognitive behavior is *play*, particularly common in mammals but observed also in most other vertebrates. Play can involve activities more complex and diversified than those of exploration, and in some cases play and exploration can have the same adaptive result: increased familiarization with the environment, including most particularly the social environment. In this respect play among young animals often has an incidental (but nevertheless important) training function for later offensive and defensive behavior, for courtship activity, and for management of social conflicts.

In many animals, for example, play involves activities that are but slightly modified forms of aggression or courtship. Also, mammals raised to adulthood in isolation or with insufficient social play later tend to make poor parents and often will ignore or abandon their offspring. Similarly, rhesus

Fig. 20.3 Cognitive behavior. (A) A banana is placed out of reach of a chimpanzee near two unstacked boxes. (B) The chimp uses the boxes as a means of reaching the banana. Deliberate manipulation of some part of the environment is characteristic of most cognitive forms of behavior.

Fig. 20.4 Exploratory behavior. (*Wisconsin Regional Primate Research Center.*)

Fig. 20.5 Social behavior. Social interaction begins very early in people.

monkeys raised in isolation or by imitation mothers have been shown unable to mate properly. Indeed, when mammals mature without opportunity to play with littermates or to learn from social contacts in general, then not only their later reproductive behavior but *all* aspects of their behavior often tend to be abnormal.

Social behavior in people, for example, begins to be learned in the period between the sixth week and the sixth month of life. During this time an infant will generally smile at all strangers and can readily transfer affection from mother to other family members, nurse, foster mother, or others (Fig. 20.5). Thereafter, however, fear of strangers increases, and emotional attachments become more selective. Consequently, if infants are protected unduly from exposure to strangers up to their sixth month of life, the normal tendency of infants to play, learn, and practice social responses during this time will remain unexercised, and all later social behavior can be affected adversely.

Both exploration and play often contribute to the development of even more complex cognitive activities, including particulary manipulative, or *instrumental*, behavior. It is characterized by responses that require "insight" and "foresight" and a capacity to analyze and weigh alternative choices. Also, such behavior can include purposeful alterations of environmental conditions and an exercise of skills, creativity, and inventiveness. Behavior of this type is restricted very largely to advanced mammals, particularly to monkeys, apes, and human beings, the most advanced primates. Behavioral control here (in people, at any rate) is fully subject to conscious volition, and the result is conspicuously individual-specific; each individual must develop his or her own level of manipulative competence, and in this respect the members of the species can vary greatly.

Most manipulative behavior, and cognitive behavior as a whole, depends largely on learning through operant conditioning (see Chap. 19). In the human case the reinforcement generally associated with such learning can be exceedingly subtle and indeed need not be immediate. In many instances, for example, we regard the very execution of a particular activity as its own reward, and we often find sufficient incentive for certain behaviors in a mere expectation of potential rewards, even if they accrue to others after our own lifetimes.

In this context it should be pointed out that the amount or kind of learning possible in any animal depends only partly on the relative complexity of its nervous system; the adaptive function that learning has in the life of an animal is just as significant. It is not an accident, for example, that rats turn out to be good test subjects for maze-learning experiments. Their ability to search through complex terrains is a particularly important adaptation for survival. Many other mammals are just as intelligent but are poor maze learners; they have learning abilities specially significant to them. In short, learning ability tends to be specialized for particular survival requirements. People are specialized in this respect too, and we are not uniformly good in all kinds of learning. We excel in abstract and symbolic learning, capabilities that were of special adaptive importance during our early evolution (see Chap. 36). Yet we are readily outmatched by many fishes, birds, and mammals in navigational learning or even by rats in maze learning.

Learning and Memory: Role of the Brain

Since virtually all forms of behavior are at least partly influenced by past experiences, many scientists are attempting to determine the neural and chemical basis of memory storage. If mechanisms underlying such storage can be discovered, it may be possible to improve or otherwise control learning in many animals, human beings included.

Memory storage appears to be a two-stage process. Experiences are stored first as *short-term memory*. Depending on several factors, including the nature of the experience, short-term memory can be converted to *long-term memory* through a secondary process called *consolidation*. Some experiences are rarely consolidated. For example, infrequently used telephone numbers usually are remembered for only short periods; memories of such numbers must be "refreshed" by referring to the telephone directories. But we are far less dependent on such directories for numbers we use frequently. These numbers have been consolidated as long-term memories. The temporary nature of short-term memory appears to be adaptive, for it probably keeps our "memory banks" uncluttered by irrelevant data.

One region of the brain that seems particularly important for consolidation is a small area of the cerebrum called the *hippocampus* (see Fig. 1 of Biology Highlight in Chap. 19). Drug-induced suppression of neural transmission in the hippocampus often interferes with consolidation, although animals treated in this manner retain the ability to learn and recall long-term memories. Similarly, patients in mental hospitals who receive electric-shock therapy frequently cannot recall very recent experiences following treatment, but their ability to recall events that occurred more than a few days earlier usually is unaffected. Significantly, electric-shock therapy, coma, deep anaesthesia, and an insufficient supply of blood to the brain all disrupt normal patterns of neural depolarizations in the brain; they all also interfere with retention of recently acquired information. Results like these suggest that consolidation is a time-dependent process and that memories of recent experiences are "held" for a short period of time in regions of the brain that include the hippocampus. They also indicate that short-term memories may be stored as unique patterns of neural impulses established by temporary structural and chemical modifications of synapses in the brain. Accordingly, short-term memories should be lost when subsequent modifications of the synapses abolish previously established impulse patterns.

Even less is known about long-term memory storage. The eliciting of long-term memories appears to be controlled at least in part by the temporal lobes of the cerebral cortex (see Fig. 19.4C). Because pain receptors are not present in the brain, general anesthetics often are not administered to patients undergoing brain surgery. When neurons of their temporal lobes are stimulated artificially by electricity, such patients often report "seeing" or "hearing" various sights and sounds of past experiences. For example, some patients have been able to recite the lyrics of long "forgotten" songs, or describe in detail events that occurred during their childhood. However, removal of the part of the temporal lobes that had been stimulated does not prevent later recall of the memories. The results of these and other experiments thus indicate that long-term memories are not stored in localized "memory centers."

Several hypotheses have been proposed to account for long-term memory storage. One of these proposes that frequent use of a neural circuit established for a short-term memory structurally "reinforces" the circuit and facilitates later transmissions through it; whereas disuse of such a circuit promotes its abolition. The results of certain experiments support this idea. For example, it is possible to cut a sensory nerve leading to the spinal cord and thereby prevent impulses from reaching corresponding motor nerves. After a few weeks, the lack of sensory input often causes the motor nerves to shrink. This shrinkage can be prevented by electrically stimulating the portion of the truncated sensory nerve that remains attached to the spinal cord. Similarly, the number of neuronal projections between presynaptic and postsynaptic neurons can be shown to increase or decrease in response to corresponding changes in the rate of impulse transmission between the neurons. Such proliferations may reinforce and stabilize short-term memory circuits and thereby facilitate later transmissions. Although other experimental results suggest that similar structural alterations of nervous systems can result from learning, none of these alterations has yet been shown to be responsible for memory storage.

Other hypotheses are based on experimental evidence that not only appears to demonstrate the production of "memory molecules" by nervous systems, but also suggests that such molecules can affect learning when they are transferred between animals. Many of these hypotheses propose that long-term memory storage results either from the manufacture of new memory molecules or from modifications in the locations, concentrations, or availability of existing molecules.

Some of the evidence is derived from research on flatworms called *planarians* (see also Chap. 33). The nervous system of such a worm consists of a concentration of nervous tissue in the head, called the *brain ganglion*, and a pair of nerve cords that lead from this ganglion posteriorly. These organisms contract their bodies when stimulated by an electric shock. By flashing a light and providing an electric shock simultaneously, planarians can be conditioned to contract their bodies solely in response to a flash of light. If the trained worms are then ground up, RNA can be extracted from their tissues and injected into untrained worms. Some researchers who have done this report that the injected worms learned to contract their bodies in response to a light flash considerably sooner than uninjected control worms. Moreover, researchers conducting other types of experiments have reported finding proteins in the brain tissue of rats that accumulate in direct proportion to the quantity of new experiences to which the animals have been exposed.

Such results suggest that memory storage involves changes in the RNA and protein content of neurons. The data also imply that it may eventually be possible to affect learning and behavior simply by the injection of specific molecules. However, more recent research has led many biologists to question the validity of the "memory molecule hypothesis." For example, planarians have been reported to perform better at learning when injected with RNA derived from untrained worms or even from plants. Furthermore, subsequent tests of early "memory transfer" experiments have failed to provide consistent results, and other experiments repeatedly have failed to demonstrate a role either for RNA or for protein synthesis in memory storage. Although considerably more research is needed to resolve these inconsistencies, it is clear that the brain cannot be viewed simply as a static organ composed of functionally distinct parts. Indeed, the structure and chemistry of the brain well may be in continuous flux, molded in part by the experiences of a lifetime.

Research on the cellular and chemical basis of brain function during the past two decades also has increased our understanding of several types of abnormal behavior in people. Some of the knowledge so gained already has contributed to the treatment of several brain-related afflictions. Much of this research has stemmed directly from the discovery that certain drugs alleviate the symptoms of some forms of abnormal human behavior by affecting neurotransmitters in the brain. For example, many drugs used to relieve mental depression increase the amount of norepinephrine in certain groups of synapses in the brain. Conversely, drugs that sometimes induce depression often decrease the amount of norepinephrine in these synapses.

Moreover, drugs such as *chlorpromazine* have revolutionized the treatment of *schizophrenia,* a group of abnormal behavior patterns characterized by disorientation and loss of contact with reality. It has been discovered that most of the antischizophrenia drugs block dopamine receptors in the brain. These results suggest that many types of schizophrenia are caused by an excessive release of dopamine in certain regions of the brain. Support for this hypothesis has come from research on the neural effects of stimulatory drugs called *amphetamines.* Large doses of these drugs produce compulsive behavior and hallucinogenic delusions indistinguishable from the symptoms displayed by many schizophrenics. Amphetamines appear to produce these effects by stimulating a release of large quantities of dopamine in the brain. As predicted by the above hypothesis, the schizophrenialike symptoms produced by amphetamines usually can be relieved quickly by administration of antischizophrenia drugs. The social implications of this and other types of research on the brain are highly significant and potentially controversial, for this new knowledge increasingly provides the means of manipulating the mechanisms that both control and determine complex patterns of behavior (see also Biology Highlight in Chap. 19).

Fig. 20.6 Four components of behavioral sequences. These sequences are illustrated here by aggressive behavior in lesser black-backed gulls. (A) Elicitation phase: two males sight each other at boundary between their territories. (B) Appetitive phase: the animals approach each other warily and "examine the situation." (C) Consummation phase: a fight occurs. (D) Satiation phase: grooming after disengagement. (*Courtesy of N. Tinbergen*.)

SYSTEMS OF BEHAVIOR

Stimulus and Response

Most behavior is *goal-oriented.* Accordingly, responses of organisms generally are directed at *selected* stimuli only—food, a mate, an intruder, or some other stimulus that triggers a goal-oriented response. Animal tendencies to behave in this manner are often called *drives* or *motivations,* terms borrowed from (and most applicable in) the field of human psychology. In a general biological context, a drive may be regarded as an expression of internal control operations that are incomplete and still in progress; a drive will be manifested so long as particular stimuli have *not* yet elicited appropriate behavioral responses.

Many motivated activities consist of a sequence of four more or less distinct phases (Fig. 20.6). The first phase is an *elicitation,* a process of activation, triggering, or arousal. In feeding behavior, for example, elicitation includes sighting of food, orienting toward it, and fixing on it visually and posturally. Next follows an *appetitive* phase, in which specific "appetites" for certain end results become dominant, and in which various internal and external processes produce a state of readiness for the ensuing events. In the case of feeding, this phase includes motion toward food, inspection and testing of food, and reflex initiation of an internal flow of digestive juices. The third part of the sequence is a *consummatory* phase, in which the functional goal is realized—actual food consumption in our example. This activity leads to the terminal *satiation* phase, during which the original arousal stimuli cease to be effective. Thus, after a period of food intake an animal eventually turns away from food and for the time being becomes resistant to further stimulation by it. Feeding behavior has been the original model for naming these phases. The four-part sequence is also discernible in, for example, aggressive behavior and mating.

Goal-oriented responses are triggered by many kinds of stimuli. In some cases the nature of the response depends on the context in which stimuli are perceived, the whole configuration (or *Gestalt*) of an environmental situation. As is well known, for example, the same stimuli can elicit diametrically opposite responses in different environmental circumstances. The ability to assess the setting in which stimuli are perceived and to modulate responses accordingly is a function of cognitive behavior and depends on learning and experience.

Releasers

In many other cases, by contrast, the contexts of stimuli are quite unimportant; selected stimuli often evoke certain responses regardless of the environmental setting. Such stimuli are said to be *symbols,* behavioral *signs,* or *releasers;* they trigger, or "release," certain preprogrammed activities. Behavior in this case is active or even reactive; the most animals need learn is how to recognize given releaser stimuli. The response then follows in more or less stereotyped fashion.

Visual releasers In herring gulls, for example, young birds peck at the bill of a parent when they wish to receive regurgitated food from the parent. The pecking is directed particularly at a red spot located near the tip of the lower bill of the parent. Experiments with cardboard models show that this pecking behavior does not require an actual parent. Any pencil-shaped object with a red spot near its tip will elicit pecking. Indeed, if the colored area is designed in the shape of several short red stripes, the young gulls will peck more effectively and more vigorously at this substitute "bill" than at that of the natural parent (Fig. 20.7 and see Color Fig. 16).

Similarly, many birds flee when a flying predator bird comes into their field of vision. Tests with cardboard models show that this standardized escape response can be evoked by any overhead object having the general outline of a longstemmed cross—suggestive of the short neck, extended wings, and long fuselage typical of most predator birds. Many birds retrieve eggs that have rolled out of the nest. More vigorous retrieval can be induced by imitation eggs that, for example, have larger color speckles or larger sizes than the real eggs (Fig. 20.8).

Among animals other than birds, male sticklebacks are prompted to courtship activity by nearly any model having a pronouncedly swollen, silvery underside, suggestive of a female with eggs. A true fishlike shape is otherwise not required, and male attraction will be the greater the more the model bulges downward. In their home territory these

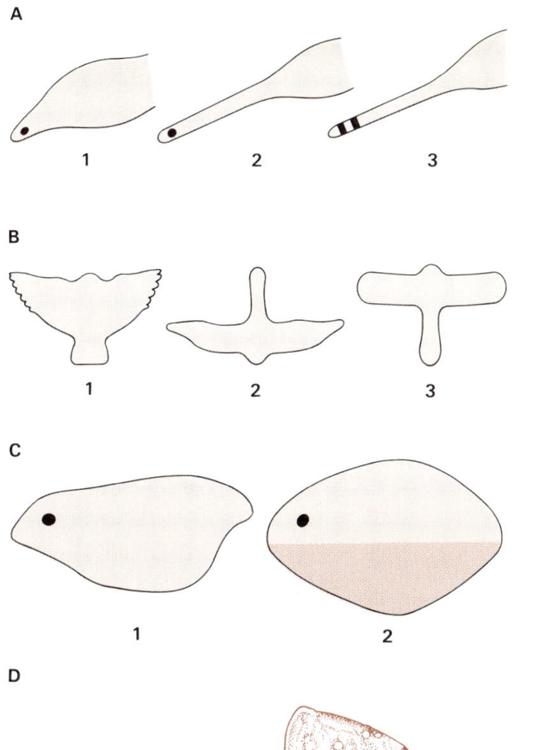

Fig. 20.7 Releasers. (A) Models of bills of herring gulls, effective in eliciting pecking by young birds. Long thin model bills [as in (2)] are more effective as symbols than short thick ones, and the models are more effective if the red pigmented areas near the tips have the form of several stripes [as in (3)]. (B) The hawk model (1) will elicit an escape response by birds, but the goose model (2) will not. Model 3 will provoke escape if it is moved in the direction of the top of the page but not if it is moved in the opposite direction. In the first case it suggests a hawk, in the second, a goose. (C) A male stickleback will court an inanimate model of a fish having a swollen underside (1) suggestive of a female with eggs. Also, a male will attack a model having a red underside (2), suggestive of another male in breeding condition. (D) When frightened, many animals suddenly present a pair of eyes of the type characterizing vertebrate predators. In this case, the caterpillar of the Malayan butterfly *Ophideres fullonica* raises part of its body to enhance the effect; a South American peacock butterfly, *Automeris memusae,* spreads its forewings to reveal its "eyes." Almost any threatening stimulus can function as a releaser and trigger such "eye" displays. The display response is highly adaptive; it too functions as a releaser stimulus, frightening many potential predators of these insects.

male fish also will attack virtually any round or ovoid model with a red underside, the specific sign of another male in breeding condition. Courtship in certain male butterflies has been shown to be elicited not so much by the presence of females as by the speed with which females flutter their wings. Cardboard models that do not resemble females to any great extent but have winglike parts with particularly high flutter rates can arouse males even more than real females.

These various examples not only reveal the effectiveness of visual signs as such but also show clearly that greatly exaggerated stimuli often tend to be more effective than normal ones. In people, too, supernormal stimulation is well known to be preferred in a wide variety of activities, and this phenomenon appears to be a general attribute of sign-induced behavior. Such stimulus preferences presumably can have evolutionary consequences, for individuals having traits that are preferred by

Fig. 20.8 Supernormal stimuli. (A) Most birds routinely retrieve eggs that have slid from the nest. (B) Many animals, however, react preferentially to supernormal stimuli. This herring gull, for example, has abandoned its own egg (lower right) and attempts to incubate a much larger artificial egg.

other members of the species are more likely to mate and produce numerous offspring.

Auditory releasers Signs need not necessarily be visual but can also involve auditory, tactile, or any other sensory modes. In sound-producing animals, for example, auditory symbols are well known to be specific releasers in courtship and mating, in offense and defense, and indeed in most social behavior.

The "song" of male crickets, for example, functions in attracting females of the same species. This auditory releaser is produced when a cricket rubs a "scraper" on one wing against a "file" on the other wing. Each species of cricket in a community produces a characteristic song that differs from the songs of all other species in pitch, rate of repetition, and other qualities. Although many slightly different cricket songs fill the air on warm summer evenings, female crickets are attracted only to the sound produced by a male of the same species.

Chemical releasers Numerous releasers are chemical, mediated by the senses of taste and smell. For example, certain clams will exhibit an escape response if placed in water in which starfish had been present. Pollinating insects undertake nectar searches in stimulus models smelling like certain flowers. And among mammals, aggressive or submissive behavior evoked by chemical signs are particularly well known and familiar. Thus, a cat is alerted to flight by dog smells but to attack by rodent smells.

Specially important are chemical signals used between members of the same species. The name *pheromones* has been given to such intraspecific chemical signals. For example, bees in a food-rich area secrete pheromones that attract other bees to the location. When wounded, minnows and other fishes release alarm pheromones from the skin that elicit escape responses in other members of a school. Similarly, under conditions of stress many types of ants broadcast alarm substances that induce fellow ants to become aggressive. Probably best known are the sex pheromones, by which individuals of either sex evoke reproductive behavior in potential mates. Mate attractants are known in numerous species, and in at least one instance, nature herself has performed an evolutionary experiment that reveals the effect of such chemical cues. Several species of orchids are known that not only resemble bees and wasps structurally but also secrete chemicals similar to the sex attractants normally released by female bees and wasps. As a result, males of these insects will try to mate with the flowers and in the process will pollinate them.

Synthetic pheromones eventually may be used to control the population size of many insects that often severely damage agricultural crops and other plants. Scientists already have succeeded in attracting specific species of insects to sites where artificial pheromones are released. Such techniques eventually may be used routinely to attract and kill insects selectively instead of using "broad-spectrum" insecticides that kill many species of insects indiscriminately.

Apart from functioning as attractants, sex pheromones also can have more subtle effects. For example, a group of caged female mice will become synchronized in their reproductive cycles if the animals are exposed to the scent of a male mouse. Moreover, a pregnant mouse can be induced to abort by exposing her to the odor of a strange male (even if the normal male mate is present). In many animals pheromonal cues also play important roles in the development of parent-young relationships, in recognition of species members, in establishing appropriate spatial distributions among the individuals of a social group, and indeed in influencing most behavioral interactions in the species.

Releasers and communication Clearly then, releasers as a whole represent various forms of *communication.* Moreover, it need hardly be pointed out that signs are particularly significant in human behavior. Human beings actually respond to more kinds and more complex kinds of signs than any other animal. Our entire language is a sign system, and this language includes not only words but also postural and facial expressions, as well as visual, olfactory, and tactile cues. Not every such communication evokes stereotyped responses, to be sure, but many certainly do. For example, the behavioral group response to the sound of the national anthem is quite specific. So to a considerable extent is the individual response to, for example, the smell of acrid smoke or the sight of well-developed contours in members of the opposite sex. Indeed, the wide occurrence of releasers of this sort is underscored even by common phrases such as "authority symbol," "danger sign," "friendship token," or "sex symbol."

Imprinting A particularly dramatic demonstration of the importance of releasers is provided by the phenomenon of *imprinting.* Newly hatched chickens, geese, ducks, and other birds develop a strong bond of kinship with their female parent, manifested primarily through a standardized "following" response: the young run behind their mother (Fig. 20.9). It has been found that this response develops during a specific period soon after hatching, the so-called critical period, and that it depends on certain releaser stimuli emanating from the mother bird: her overall size, certain aspects of her shape and coloring, the sounds she produces, and her movement away from the young. If such stimuli become "imprinted" in the young during the critical period, the offspring will henceforth accept the adult as their mother and will acknowledge this acceptance by the "following" response. It has also been found that imprinting normally provides the recognition signs which in later life prompt selection and acceptance of appropriate mates; a mate must have the same stimulus attributes as the parent (which presumably ensures that the mate will be of the right species).

Newly hatched ducklings at first will follow any duck, and a specific attachment to the mother develops only somewhat later. It appears, therefore, than an originally imprinted stimulus pattern can be refined later by experience and can thereby become individual-specific. Note in this connection that imprinting itself probably represents a special kind of learning. It differs from other kinds in that its occurrence is limited to a brief period in life and that it remains permanent thereafter.

Experiments show clearly that imprinting can still occur if the actual mother is dispensed with. All that is required is another stimulus source that will produce the necessary signs during the critical period. The best-known example of this phenomenon stems from an experiment performed by the Austrian behaviorist Konrad Lorenz (Fig. 20.10). He began by separating into two groups a clutch of eggs laid by a greylag goose. The mother greylag was the first living organism seen by goslings hatched from one group; Lorenz was the first seen by goslings hatched from the second group of eggs. The first group of young birds trailed behind the mother goose, but newly hatched goslings of the second group followed Lorenz as if he were their parent. The goslings recognized and followed their respective "parent" even after they had been mixed together in a large box and held there for a time.

Similar experiments have demonstrated that many other varieties of birds will readily accept foster mothers of the same species, adults of another species, or even mechanical models or inanimate objects having the requisite stimulus properties. The fixation on such surrogate mothers becomes just as strong and permanent as on a natural parent. Indeed, birds raised with surrogates may flee from their real parents; and at maturity such birds sometimes reject potential mates of their own species but will try to mate with the surrogates, even if they are inanimate objects (see Fig. 20.10).

Internal releasers Releaser stimuli also can originate inside the animal body. One of the best examples is hunger in mammals, which, as pointed out in Chap. 11, is probably induced when a low

A

Fig. 20.9 Imprinting. (A) The following response, illustrated by the offspring of a Canada goose. (B) The colored band indicates the critical period for establishment of a following response in ducklings.

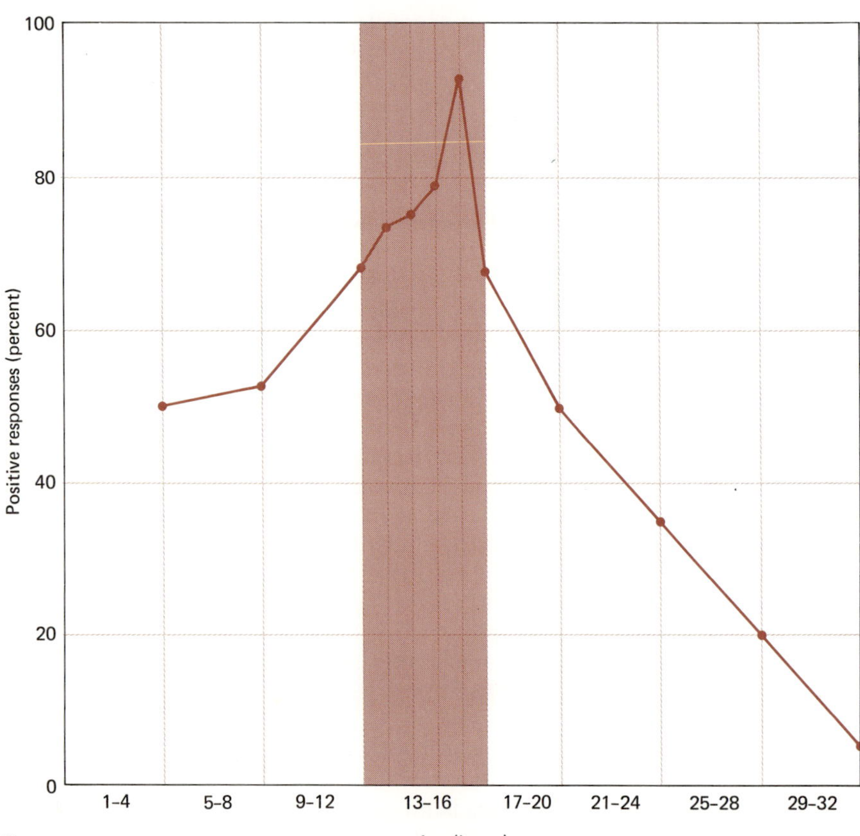

B

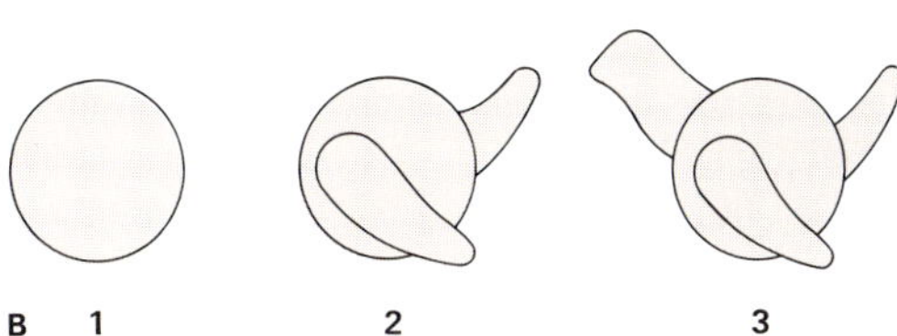

Fig. 20.10 Imprinting and surrogate mothers. (A) Young geese following Konrad Lorenz, who imprinted the birds to himself. (B) Inanimate models such as shown here are effective in eliciting the following response in young chickens. A simple model as in (1) proves to be more effective than a more complex one as in (3). Also, blue models are more effective than red ones, and the latter are more effective than yellow ones. Effectiveness is measured by the relative distance a chick will follow a model. (*After E. H. Hess.*)

sugar concentration in blood stimulates the hunger center in the brain. The irrelevance of stimulus contexts is shown by the finding that an animal will eat whenever its hunger center is stimulated, regardless of the actual nutritional state of the body. More recently a thirst center has been located that is differentially sensitive to salt concentrations in the body. If this concentration exceeds a certain level, an animal will feel thirsty and will drink water. In an experiment on goats, a device was installed in the brain that dripped salt solution into the thirst center whenever the experimenter desired; and as long as this device remained activated, a test animal continued to drink.

Experiments on rats also have revealed the existence of pleasure and displeasure centers in the brain. Test rats were fitted with tiny permanent electrodes that reached to these centers, and such animals were allowed to activate these devices on their own by pressing appropriate control levers. After a rat has stimulated its displeasure center once, it avoided a repeat performance forever. But if such animals stimulated their pleasure centers, they continued this self-stimulation from then on without interruption, not even pausing to eat, until they dropped from exhaustion; and on recovery they promptly resumed the self-stimulation to the exclusion of any other activity.

Under normal conditions, however, responses evoked by sign stimuli are among the most valuable functionally and thus among the most adaptive in the behavioral repertoire of an animal.

Time Orientation: Biological Clocks

Much of the behavior of all organisms is regularly recurrent in cyclic fashion, and such behavioral rhythms often are synchronized with some cycle in the physical environment. For example, numerous behaviors in plants and animals have a 24-h *circadian* rhythm, geared to the solar cycle of day and night and the accompanying cycle of temperature. Most coastal organisms display behavioral periodicities synchronized with *tidal* cycles. Many aquatic and terrestrial animals exhibit *lunar* rhythms. And behavior in nearly all organisms also occurs in annual *seasonal* rhythms. Reproductive activity in particular tends to be seasonally cyclic, both in plants and in animals.

In an attempt to explain such behavioral rhythms, a first obvious hypothesis might be that the rhythms are causally related to the recurrent environmental conditions. If so, it should be readily possible to change a behavioral rhythm by experimentally changing the associated environmental cycle. For example, what would happen to a circadian (or other kind of) rhythm if an organism were maintained artificially under uninterruptedly *constant* conditions of lighting, temperature, humidity, and other relevant environmental variables. Numerous experiments of this sort actually have been carried out on a wide variety of organisms. The results obtained are exceedingly uniform and clear-cut: an original behavioral rhythm always tends to *persist,* despite constant environmental conditions (Fig. 20.11).

It is usually observed in such cases that the successive cycles gradually drift out of phase from an exact 24-h (or other) periodicity. The rhythm then stabilizes at some shorter or longer cycle interval, yet this new interval nevertheless remains fairly close to the original rhythm. Such results show clearly that rhythmic behavior can occur independently of environmental cycles. Organisms are therefore considered to have built-in *biological clocks,* according to which the timing of recurrent activities is programmed.

That such clocks have an inherited component can be shown experimentally. For example, if adult chickens are maintained in constant, unchanging environments and are allowed to produce fertilized eggs under such conditions, the offspring hatched from the eggs nevertheless exhibit clear-cut circadian behavior. Biological clocks also are subject to metabolic influences. In one experiment bees were trained to feed at a set time of day and were then chilled to near-freezing for 5 h. After the insects were brought back to normal temperature, their feeding time proved to be almost 5 h late. Like other metabolic processes, therefore, the biological clocks apparently were nearly stopped

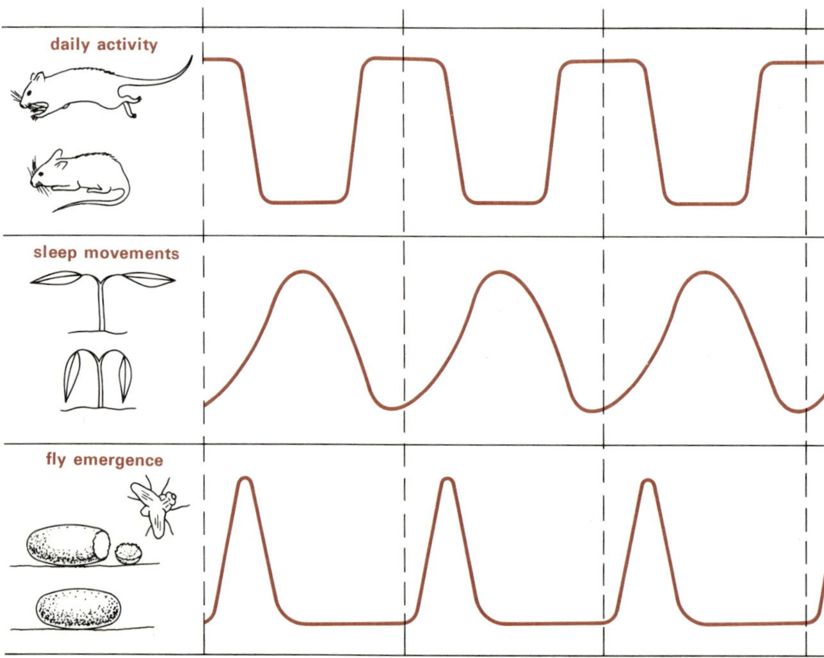

Fig. 20.11 Circadian rhythms. In these three examples, the (color) curves indicate the changing intensity of the activities symbolized in the column at left. Note the regular repeats during the 3-day-long intervals shown here. The daily activity curve applies specifically to rats but holds also for many other organisms. (*After F. A. Brown, Jr.*)

during the extreme cold treatment. However, less drastic temperature changes have remarkably little effect. A 10°F temperature difference, which alters the rate of most metabolic processes by a factor of 2 or 3, usually changes the running speed of biological clocks by no more than 15 to 30 min every 24 h. Biological clocks also are quite precise and keep correct time within 1 or 2 minutes per day. For example, caged mice or rats supplied with running wheels start their daily runs at a remarkably exact time each morning.

Much has been learned about the operation of biological clocks by experiments involving a geographic relocation of animals. Organisms are normally adapted to the geographic latitudes and longitudes at which they live, and their behavior follows the rhythm of local time. But it has been found that if organisms are transported to different geographic locations, their activities nevertheless continue in synchrony with the original local time. For example, Atlantic fiddler crabs flown in dark chambers to Pacific waters exhibit cyclic color changes according to the tides at their Atlantic point of origin. Bees trained in Paris to feed at a fixed time of day remain on Paris time after being airfreighted to New York. And fall-breeding sheep transported from the Northern to the Southern Hemisphere continue to reproduce at the time of the northern fall, when the Southern Hemisphere is in the spring season.

However, translocation experiments also show that, after some interval, biological clocks invariably do reset to new local times. Thus the crabs, bees, and sheep referred to above eventually synchronize behaviorally with their new longitudes and latitudes. Such gradual adjustment also is the common experience of people who take up residence in new time zones. In general, internally controlled rhythms are said to become *entrained* to local external cycles.

Entrainment proves to be possible only if a new periodicity imposed on an organism does not differ too greatly from that of a natural environmental cycle. In mice, for example, circadian rhythms can be entrained to artificial periodicities as short as 21 h or as long as 27 h. But entrainment cannot be readily achieved if an artificial cycle deviates by more than 3 h from the 24-h norm. Similarly, the sleeping-waking rhythm in people has repeatedly proved to be resistant to artificial night-day cycles that deviate substantially from 24-h periods. In general, cycles significantly shorter than 24 h tend to add together and those longer than 24 h tend to subdivide, with the result that the behavioral rhythms actually displayed by an organism follow a natural 24-h cycle as closely as the experimental conditions will allow.

In both circadian and seasonal rhythms, the most common stimuli by which organisms clock the passage of time appear to be light direction, light intensity, and light duration. For example, many animals tell daily time by the progressive change in the position of the sun (see next section). Plants as well as animals are sensitive to the daily and seasonal cycles of light intensity, and many of their rhythmic activities can be reset or modified by experimental alterations of such intensities. Moreover, as already shown in Chaps. 16 and 17, both plants and animals tell seasonal time most particularly by assessing changes in day lengths, or photoperiods.

In vertebrates, seasonal breeding rhythms are well known to be under neural and endocrine control: the external stimuli usually are changing photoperiods, and the critical regulating centers are the hypothalamus and the pituitary gland (see also Chap. 17). Among insects, similarly, the cycles of molting and reproduction are governed by specific neural and endocrine organs and their hormonal secretions (see Chap. 34). Clearly, however, neural or endocrine components are present neither in microorganisms nor in plants and certain animals, yet such organisms exhibit behavioral rhythms nevertheless. Also, any single organism exhibits numerous behavioral cycles simultaneously, all with their own specific periodicities. An organism therefore must be considered to possess many different biological clocks, with different rhythms, locations, and functional mechanisms.

Even so, the general conclusion is probably warranted that control of cyclic behavior is achieved by interaction of at least two sets of factors. One is internal and is represented by inherited biological clocks that, if left to themselves, keep their own intrinsic time. The other set is external and is represented by cycles in the physical environment. Within definite and relatively narrow limits, the settings of the internal clocks can become adjusted or readjusted until synchrony with the external cycles is established. In this way an organism interacts with its physical environment and can adapt its behavior to the cyclic time changes in its local habitat.

Space Orientation: Directional Motion

Just as biological clocks enable organisms to operate effectively in their time environment, so other behavioral mechanisms permit them to relate properly to their space environment.

The most basic orientational behaviors are kineses, taxes, and tropisms (see earlier section). Although comparatively primitive, such behaviors are exceedingly widespread and highly adaptive. Kineses and taxes, for example, are accompanied by locomotor activities that frequently distribute organisms to the optimal habitat zones available. Tropisms can maintain even sessile organisms in optimum positions relative to their immediate surroundings.

Many animals move well beyond their immediate home environments, and in the process they usually remain fully "aware" of their position and direction in space (Fig. 20.12). A particularly significant navigational aid is *sun-compass orientation,* ability to steer by the position of the sun and to compensate course directions according to the apparent motion of the sun across the sky. This process has been studied extensively in several migratory species of day-flying birds (Fig. 20.13). Starlings, for example, migrate semiannually in the spring and fall. At these times starlings maintained in outdoor aviaries become increasingly restless and on sunny days tend to fly in the direction of their migratory destination. However, no such orientation occurs on heavily overcast days.

These observations suggest that the birds use the positions of the sun as orienting cues. This hypothesis is supported by experiments in which the apparent position of the sun is shifted by mirrors placed outside a specially designed cage. When starlings are placed in such a cage during migratory seasons, the direction of their movements undergoes a shift that corresponds to the apparent displacement of the sun (see Fig. 20.13).

Sun-compass orientation is known to occur in honeybees, horseshoe crabs, certain ants, beetles, spiders, and in several other invertebrates. Among vertebrates the process also has been demonstrated

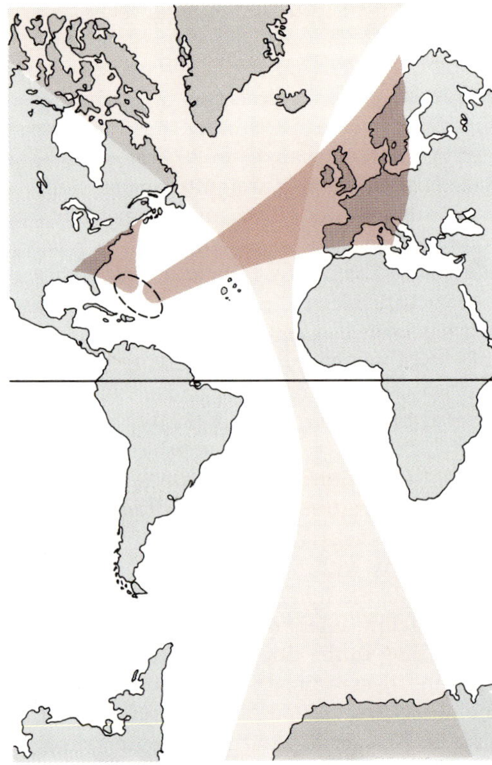

Fig. 20.12 Migrations. The migratory paths of Arctic terns are shown in light color, those of Atlantic eels in dark color. American and European eels spawn in the Sargasso Sea (indicated by a dashed line).

in some fishes and turtles. For example, certain sea turtles undertake annual migrations of several thousand miles to lay eggs at specific beaches. Correct navigation here appears to depend on the sun at least in part; as in many other vertebrates, location finding becomes confused or less precise if the sun is not visible.

Homing pigeons orient by the sun too. By entraining these birds to artificial photoperiods, it has been found that the flight directions taken in homing are adjusted to solar time and are correlated with a biological clock. However, homing pigeons usually orient as well under heavily overcast skies as they do on sunny days. The results of recently conducted experiments indicate that these birds can see patterns of ultraviolet light, which are invisible to people. The pigeons apparently can use such patterns to determine the position of the sun on extremely cloudy days. Other studies indicate that homing pigeons also can sense changes in barometric pressure, are sensitive to polarized light and to geographic changes in the magnetic field of the earth, and can detect infrasounds (high-frequency noises) in the atmosphere that cannot be heard by human beings. Such sounds can travel long distances and may enable a pigeon flying over Vermont, for example, to sense the impact of waves striking the New England shore.

These findings indicate (1) that homing pigeons perceive their environment in ways that are very different from ours and (2) that the navigational system of the pigeons is redundant. The birds use the position of the sun as a compass when it is available, but they can substitute information from other sources whenever the sun is obscured.

Some migratory animals normally navigate without aid of sun-compass orientation. For example, some birds that migrate more by night than by day seem to orient by star sightings. Indigo buntings appear to be one such species. If these birds are placed in a planetarium, they will orient themselves consistently according to the way the "stars" are projected overhead.

The methods of navigation by which migrant animals locate specific breeding grounds remain largely unclear. Although sun and star orientation might serve as navigational aids in certain cases, such mechanisms are insufficient to account for all aspects of migratory behavior. In aquatic organisms, for example, optical cues can only have limited significance at best. In some cases, as in salmon, navigation appears to be based on *chemotaxis,* that is, ability to distinguish different kinds of waters by relative oxygen content, amount of silting, and more subtle chemical characteristics that can be smelled or tasted. But for many other animals, eels, for example, the sensory basis of navigation is still obscure.

The eggs of both American and European eels hatch in the deep waters of the Sargasso Sea, an Atlantic area between and somewhat east of Bermuda and the Caribbean (see Fig. 20.12). The near-microscopic larvae are fishlike, transparent *elvers,* which migrate toward the coasts of North America and Europe. Larvae of the American species hatch farther west than those of the European species, and differences in the direction of the deep-ocean currents probably contribute to the initial separation of the two species. American elvers reach continental waters after about a year of travel, and European elvers, after about 3 years. In coastal estuaries the larvae metamorphose to elongated adults, and the males then remain in the estuaries. Females ascend rivers and settle in headwaters and in lakes. After 7 to 15 years the females migrate back to the estuaries and together with the males head out to the Atlantic. Reproductive organs mature during this migration, and on arrival in the Sargasso the eggs are spawned and fertilized. The adults then die.

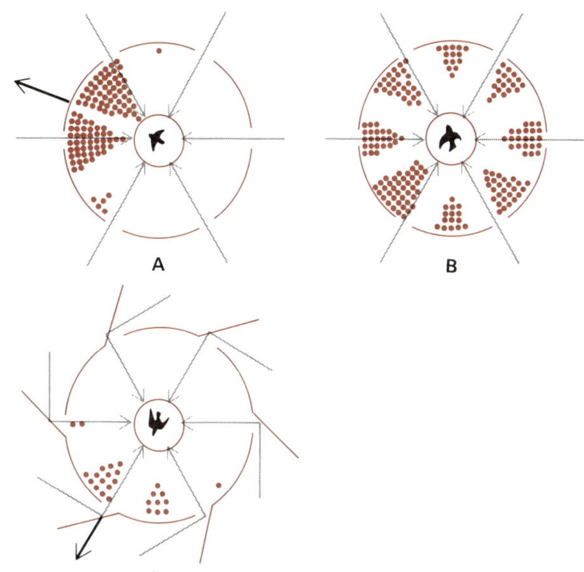

Fig. 20.13 Sun-compass orientation. Direction of spontaneous migratory activity of a starling placed in a covered circular cage illuminated by six windows (open spaces). Each dot represents a measured unit of activity aimed in the direction of the dot. Lighting conditions varied as follows: (A) clear sky and (B) heavily overcast sky. (C) The actual position of the sun here is the same as in (A), but its apparent position is shifted by mirrors (extended lines at windows). The mean direction of the bird's migratory activity (arrow) shifts accordingly.

How do the larvae find river mouths 1000 or 2000 miles away? And how do the adults find a specific area in a vast expanse of ocean? Both larvae and adults make their trip for the first and only time, and optical cues surely play little role in the depths of the ocean. Currents might be significant, but if so this has not been demonstrated. In line with the continental drift hypothesis (see Chap. 29), it has also been suggested that the migration routes might correspond to the courses of ancient river systems, obliterated when North America and Europe split off as separate continents from an originally single land mass. If so, however, it is not at all clear how a fixed "racial memory" could be of any value when the ancient geography has undergone drastic changes during millions of years—even assuming that an acquired trait such as a geographic memory could be inherited, which is not the case. Migratory behavior thus still represents one of the most enigmatic phenomena in all biology.

Review Questions

1 Defend the statement that behavior is basically adaptive and has a self-perpetuative function.

2 Review the general characteristics of reactive, active, and cognitive behavior and describe the kinds of learning that often are associated with each of these behavioral categories. Include specific examples of cognitive behavior in your discussion.

3 Contrast and compare short-term and long-term memory. What is memory consolidation? Review the possible mechanisms of long-term memory storage.

4 Illustrate the relationship between basic research on brain function and the treatment of human neural disorders.

5 Describe the general attributes of releaser stimuli and of sign-induced behavior. Give examples of visual and chemical stimuli that can act as releasers in particular animals. Include a description of pheromone-induced behavior and imprinting in your discussion.

6 Describe several different rhythmic behaviors. What kinds of experiments have suggested that organisms possess biological clocks? What is meant by entrainment, and to what extent can rhythmic behavior become entrained?

7 Describe behavioral mechanisms that permit specific organisms to orient their movements. Include a description of kineses and sun-compass orientation in your discussion.

8 What is the adaptive advantage of seasonal migrations? By what mechanisms do homing pigeons and other birds migrate? To what extent is previous experience important in seasonal migrations?

Collateral Readings

Alcock, J.: "Animal Behavior: An Evolutionary Approach," 2d ed., Sinauer, Stamford, Conn., 1979. An outstanding introduction to this field.

Binkley, S.: A Timekeeping Enzyme in the Pineal Gland, *Scientific American,* April 1979. The enzyme *N*-acetyltransferase provides a natural timing mechanism for certain behavioral patterns.

Brown, F. A., J. W. Hastings, and **J. D. Palmer:** "The Biological Clock: Two Views," Academic, New York, 1970. This paperback discusses two possible mechanisms for the regulation of biological rhythms.

Crews, D.: The Hormonal Control of Behavior in a Lizard, *Scientific American,* August 1979. This article examines how hormones and the brain interact in controlling the sexual behavior of the green anole, a lizard often mistakenly called a chameleon.

Emlen, S. T.: The Stellar-Orientation System of a Migratory Bird, *Scientific American,* August 1975. Reviews experiments demonstrating that indigo buntings can orient to the position of stars.

Fox, M. W.: "Concepts in Ethology," University of Minnesota Press, Minneapolis, 1974. A brief and highly readable book that includes a discussion of the practical applications of basic research on animal behavior.

Griffen, D. R.: "The Question of Animal Awareness," Rockefeller University Press, New York, 1976. The author challenges a long-held belief that only people can think and experience awareness.

Hess, E. H.: "Imprinting" in a Natural Laboratory, *Scientific American,* August 1972. Reviews experiments that have led to new discoveries about this behavior.

Julien, R. M.: "A Primer of Drug Action," Freeman, San Francisco, 1975. A well written, easy-to-understand discussion of many psychoactive drugs, including sedatives, stimulants, opiates, psychedelics, marijuana, alcohol, nicotine, and caffeine.

Lockley, R. M.: "The Private Life of the Rabbit," Macmillan, New York, 1974. The author's observations and experiments on rabbit behavior are described.

Manning, A.: "An Introduction to Animal Behavior," Addison-Wesley, Reading, Mass., 1979. This clearly written paperback introduces the basic principles of animal behavior.

Marler, P. R., and others: "The Marvels of Animal Behavior," National Geographic Society, Washington, 1972. A collection of National Geographic articles on animal behavior.

Olton, D. S.: Spatial memory, *Scientific American,* June 1977. The role of the hippocampus in memory storage is discussed.

Palmer, J. D.: Biological Clocks of the Tidal Zone, *Scientific American,* February 1975. This article examines organisms whose biological clocks are set to the rhythm of the lunar day.

Pengelley, E. T., and **S. J. Admundson:** Annual Biological Clocks, *Scientific American,* April 1971. Deals with organisms that have a yearly clock mechanism.

Pribram, K. H.: The Neurophysiology of Remembering, *Scientific American,* January 1969. Reviews evidence that memory is stored in many areas of the brain, not in one central site.

Saunders, D. S.: The Biological Clock of Insects, *Scientific American,* February 1976. Dormancy of some insects appears to be triggered by a biological clock.

Stein, D. G., and **J. J. Rosen** (eds.): "Learning and Memory," Macmillan, New York, 1974. Commentary by the editors helps guide the reader through an interesting series of articles.

Tinbergen, N.: The Curious Behavior of the Stickleback, *Scientific American,* December 1952. Discusses some of the behaviors illustrated in this chapter.

———: "The Herring Gull's World," Harper & Row, New York, 1971. The author, a Nobel laureate, describes his personal studies of herring gull behavior.

Todd, J. H.: The Chemical Language of Fishes, *Scientific American,* May 1971. Experiments with catfish demonstrate their extreme sensitivity to certain chemicals.

Wicksten, M. K.: Decorator Crabs, *Scientific American,* February 1980. Examines a certain group of crabs that decorate their shells with colored materials. This behavior is adaptive and serves to camouflage the animals.

Williams, T. C., and **J. M. Williams:** An Oceanic Mass Migration of Land Birds, *Scientific American,* October 1978. Describes how radar has been used to track the fall migrations of song- and shorebirds.

Wilson E. O.: Pheromones, *Scientific American,* May 1963. Contains several excellent examples of pheromone-induced behavior, particularly among insects.

Chapter 21 Behavioral Control: The Society

Learning Objectives

After reading this chapter you should be able to:

1. Name at least three characteristics that distinguish social from nonsocial animals; define biological communication, polymorphism, and altruism; list at least five adaptive advantages of social living among animals; differentiate between population and society.
2. Define, exemplify, and state the distinguishing characteristics of a motion group; define and give at least one example of a caste; name at least one organizational difference between insect and vertebrate societies and show how the relationship between individual and group differs in these two types of societies.
3. List the functional relationships between drones, workers, and queens in societies of honeybees; show how new honeybee societies are founded; define royal jelly; describe how honeybees gather nectar and produce honey; outline how the societies of at least three different kinds of insects differ from that of honeybees.
4. State the respective roles of individual aggression and social restraint in vertebrate societies; identify the behavioral relationship between threat display and combat; differentiate between redirected and displacement behavior; describe the relative importance of learning in the execution of aggressive and submissive behavior; identify at least two neuroendocrine mechanisms that regulate aggressive behavior in vertebrates; list the symptoms of the human stress syndrome.
5. Show how dominance hierarchies and territoriality restrict aggression among individuals in vertebrate societies.

Localized groupings of members of the same species are common throughout the living world, but true social populations are not. Individuals of a species group together when extraneous stimuli draw them to the same locale. Thus, plants, animals, and organisms of all kinds tend to aggregate in locations favorable to them, and organisms such as people aggregate temporarily at places of special interest. By contrast, the members of a population form a society only when they interact in a cooperative manner. The essential element leading to such cooperation is reciprocal communication. Social groups therefore occur only among animals.

PATTERNS OF SOCIAL ORGANIZATION

In all social animals the members of a group are interdependent and variously specialized in function. Cooperation between members of the group is achieved by one or more forms of *biological communication,* actions taken by one organism that alter the behavior of other animals in an adaptive fashion. Communication between organisms is achieved via a variety of signals, including pheromones and other kinds of chemicals, sounds, flashes of light, color changes, and gestures (see Chap. 20).

In addition to transmitting and receiving communication signals, most social animals also are *polymorphic,* or specialized structurally. Polymorphism is most pronounced in insect societies, which can include structurally different queens, soldiers, drones, and workers. Social vertebrates usually exhibit sexual dimorphism, or structural distinctions between males, females, and their young (see Figs. 21.3, 21.6, and 8.8).

Social living offers many adaptive advantages. Consider the capabilities of a nonsocial organism such as an oyster. If a single oyster can perform no more than a given number of functions, a group of oysters can do little more. By contrast, social behavior allows collections of organisms to accom-

Fig. 21.1 Motion groups. The defense response of a herd of musk oxen.

plish far more than can be performed by as many individuals of the group independently. Cooperating organisms often are more effective than separate individuals in obtaining food, in finding mates, and in protective and defensive activities. Indeed, a behavior unique to societies is individual self-sacrifice for the sake of the group, as among worker bees, which die after stinging, and among people, who are often prompted to give their lives for others. This kind of behavior, called *altruism*, is discussed more fully in Chap. 29.

Social behavior also can promote survival by ensuring optimum conditions for metabolism and growth, functions that often take place more effectively in a social milieu. In a slightly unfavorable environment, for example, goldfish and other aquatic animals survive better in social groups than as separate individuals, apparently because normal body secretions (mainly salts) neutralize toxic substances in the water and thereby condition the medium. Also, some secretions of social animals are known to have stimulating (or inhibiting) effects on growth, and the collective body heat generated by a compact group can reduce the level of metabolism each individual must maintain. Also, social living substantially facilitates learning and imitative behavior, an important factor in individual survival. Above all, by regulating and controlling the interactions between individuals, social life reduces aggression and competition, keeps conflict and combat on largely nonlethal levels, and in general provides standards of behavior that tend to promote survival of both the individual and the whole species.

Simple Societies

Cooperative interactions between the members of societies range from simple to complex. One kind of elementary society is the *motion group*, including schools of fish, flocks of birds, and herds of mammals. Communication within such assemblages is not extensive—just enough for maintenance of a close association between individuals as the group moves toward a new source of food, a breeding ground, or away from predators.

The most obvious adaptive advantage gained by motion groups is protection. Schools, flocks, and herds often contract into tight, closely packed formations in the presence of predators. When confronted by wolves, for example, adult musk oxen form a closed circle with their horned heads facing

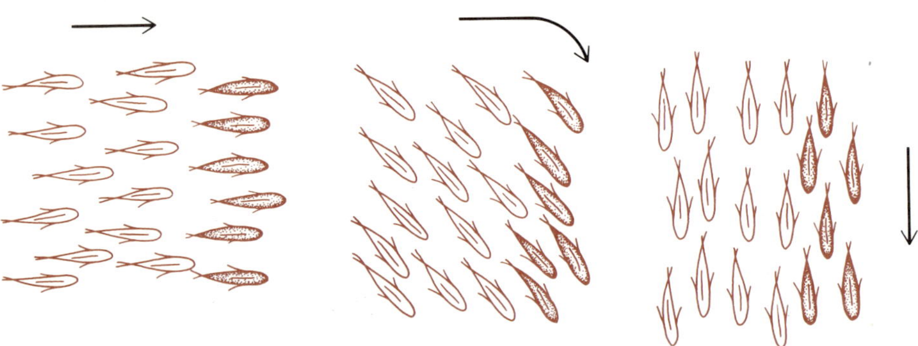

Fig. 21.2 Motion groups. Leadership of a school of fish changes whenever the school changes direction. After a school makes a 90° turn, for example, most of the former leaders will occupy flank positions (see also Color Fig. 22).

outward (Fig. 21.1). Young oxen gather at the center of the ring, where they are protected by the outer layer of adults. Although highly effective against the attack of wolves on open tundra, the native habitat of these animals, such behavior leaves musk oxen defenseless against gunfire. As a result, most herds of oxen have been exterminated over the past century in northern Canada and in Alaska.

In contrast to many advanced societies, the behavior of motion groups usually is not determined by one or more specific individuals who function as leaders. Schools of fish, for example, are led by individuals who by chance happen to be located at the forward edge of the group. New temporary "leaders" become established whenever the school changes direction (Fig. 21.2). Even "leadership" of a V-shaped flock of birds often is a shared responsibility, falling to different members of the flock at different times. The absence of permanent leaders does not mean that movements of motion groups are aimless, however. Indeed, such movements can be highly directional, as occurs when certain flocks of birds migrate hundreds or thousands of miles to specific breeding areas (see Chap. 20). Social behavior therefore does not always depend on establishment of permanent or long-term group leaders.

Complex Societies

Complex and highly structured societies occur most frequently in animals with advanced evolutionary status—insects and vertebrates. Social life has evolved quite independently in these two groups, and the organization of their societies also is quite different.

Relationships between individual members of insect societies are largely impersonal. Most insects have brief life-spans, a few days or weeks at most, and their colonies sometimes contain more than 1 million individuals. The remarkable complexity and efficiency of insect societies results from rigid divisions of labor between specialized *castes;* members of each caste are structurally and functionally adapted to carry out specific social functions. When the functions of each specialized subgroup are coordinated correctly, the entire colony can perform feats unachievable by any single caste. The essence of the caste system is that an individual is never free to seek its place in the society on its own, but that its place is already predetermined as soon as life begins. Intrasocial competition is thereby forestalled, and the responsibilities of the individual to the group and of the group to the individual remain fully defined at all times.

Vertebrate societies are organized quite differently in this respect. Most vertebrates devote considerable time to establishing and maintaining interpersonal relations with other members of the group. Moreover, behavior that depends on interpersonal recognition often contributes heavily to maintenance of order in vertebrate societies and to the perpetuation of vertebrate species. Examples of such behavior include parent-offspring relations, courtship, play among the young, and rituals establishing dominance hierarchies (see also Chap. 8). Although some divisions of labor frequently exist in vertebrate societies, individuals are rarely subdivided into castes and they are far less specialized than insects both structurally and functionally. Accordingly, each member of a vertebrate social group usually can produce responses that are far more variable and modifiable than those of insects.

Despite such great differences, it is interesting that certain external forms of their social behavior are nevertheless superficially rather parallel. Among all animals, only some social insects and some social vertebrates pursue agriculture, domesticate other organisms, practice slavery, engage in war, and commit suicide.

INSECT SOCIETIES

Honeybees

The best-known society of the four "social" insect groups—termites, ants, bees, and wasps—is that of the honeybees. A population of such bees contains three structurally distinct castes: a *queen*, tens or hundreds of male *drones*, and from 20,000 to 80,000 *workers*. The queen and the stingless drones are fertile, and their main functions are reproductive. The smaller-bodied workers are all sterile females. They build the nest, or *hive*, protect the colony from strange bees and enemies, collect food, feed the queen and the drones, and nurse the young (Fig. 21.3).

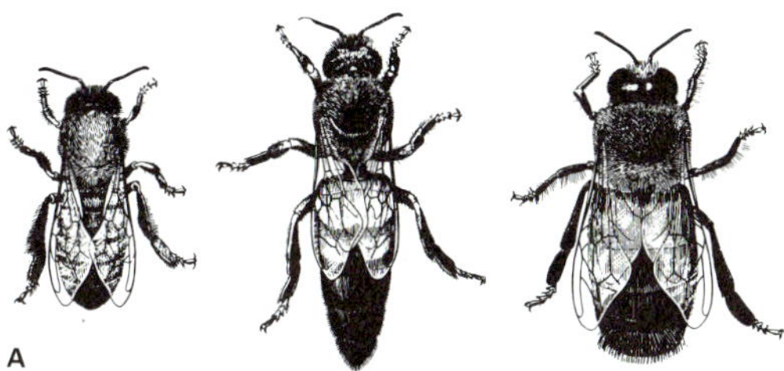
A

Fig. 21.3 Social insects. (A) Honeybees. Worker at left, queen in middle, drone at right. See also Fig. 21.5. (B) Nest of a wasp colony. (C) Nests of magnetic Australian ants. The edges of the anthills are oriented in precise compass directions.

B

C

Fig. 21.4 Honeybees. A swarm emigrated from a parental hive and searching for a new hive.

When a hive becomes overcrowded, the queen together with some drones and several thousand workers secedes from the colony. The emigrants swarm out and settle temporarily in a tree or other suitable place until a new hive is found (Fig. 21.4). In the old hive, the remaining workers then raise a few of the old queen's eggs in large, specially built honeycomb cells. These eggs develop as new queens. The first one to emerge from its cell immediately searches out the other queen cells and stings their occupants to death. If two new queens happen to emerge at the same time, they at once engage in mortal combat until one remains victorious. The young queen, her succession now undisputed, soon mates with one of the drones. In a nuptial flight high into the air she receives millions of sperms that are stored in a receptacle in her abdomen. The sperms from this single mating last through the entire egg-laying career of this queen.

Among the eggs laid individually into honeycomb cells, some escape fertilization even in a young queen. None is fertilized in an older queen once her sperm store is exhausted. Unfertilized eggs develop as drones. Fatherless development of this sort, or *natural parthenogenesis,* is widespread among social insects generally. Fertilized eggs develop either as queens or as workers, depending on the type of food the worker nurses supply to the larvae formed from the eggs. Larvae to be raised as workers are fed a "regular" diet of plant pollen and honey. Queens form when the larvae receive an especially rich *royal jelly,* containing pollen, honey, and comparatively huge amounts of certain vitamins (particularly pantothenic acid). But new queens are not raised while the original queen remains in the hive, healthy and fertile. If the queen produces eggs faster than honeycomb cells can be built, she receives less food from her attendants. Egg production then slows down. Conversely, if she is behind in her egg laying, she is fed more intensively (Fig. 21.5).

Other insects display similar patterns of reproductive behavior. Reproductive activity typically revolves around a single female, and the whole social population in effect consists of her own immediate family. All social institutions therefore rest on the genes of this one female, and her genes alone provide continuity from one generation to the next. This one-female lineage has important social consequences. Competition for mates is virtually nonexistent in the most complex insect societies, a circumstance that greatly reduces social conflict and concurrently promotes social order.

During the 6 weeks or so of its life, a worker bee carries out different duties at different ages. Housekeeping tasks are performed by young bees, food-collecting trips are made by older ones. On a food-collecting trip the bee gathers pollen, rich in protein, and nectar, a dilute sugar solution. Pollen is carried home in *pollen baskets* on the hind legs. Nectar is swallowed into the *honey crop,* a specialized part of the alimentary tract, where saliva partially digests the sugar of nectar. On arriving at the hive the bee first passes a security check on the way in, then unloads its pollen in one cell and regurgitates its nectar to another. Other bees pack the pollen tight and start converting nectar to honey. They rapidly beat their wings close to a nectar-filled cell until most of the water has evaporated. Then the honey cell is sealed up with wax.

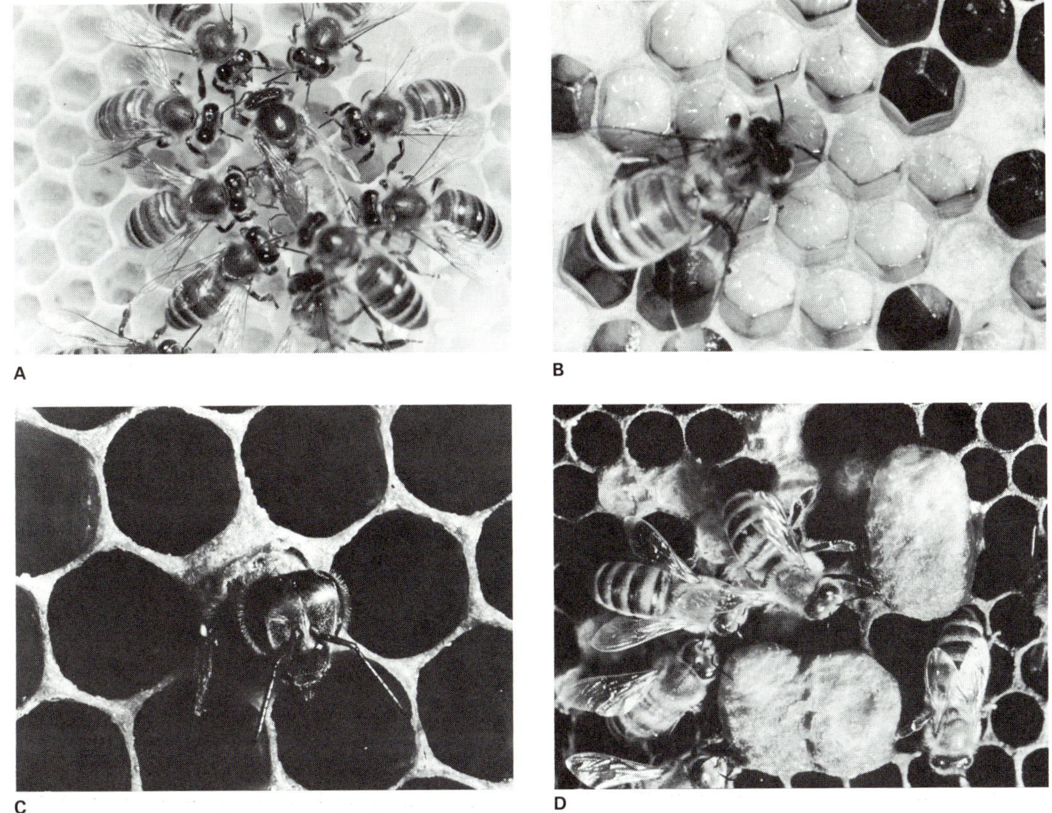

Fig. 21.5 Honeybees. (A) Queen bee laying eggs, surrounded by attendants. (B) Nurse bee feeds and cleans the larvae in the brood cells. (C) A worker bee just hatching out from its brood cell. (D) Two enlarged brood cells, capped over with wax, in which queen bees are being raised.

Honey is the main food during the winter, when pollen is unobtainable.

At the approach of winter all drones are expelled from the colony; males would merely use up irreplaceable food but would not contribute to the well-being of the population. The remaining bees cling together in compact masses, with animals in the center working their way out and those near the surface working their way in. A clump of bees thereby withstands freezing even at very low temperatures.

Termites and Ants

Among other social insects, polymorphic distinctions can be considerably more diversified. For example, many species of ants and termites include sterile wingless workers as well as sterile wingless *soldiers*. The latter are strong-jawed, heavily armored individuals that accompany work crews outside and keep order inside the nest. Soldiers in many cases cannot feed themselves and are cared for by workers. Besides a winged fertile queen and one or several winged fertile males (kings), ant and termite societies often maintain structurally distinct lesser "royalty." Such individuals probably develop when larvae are fed more than enough to produce workers but not enough to produce queens (Fig. 21.6).

Agricultural societies occur among both termites and ants. Populations of certain termite species make little garden plots of wood, excrement,

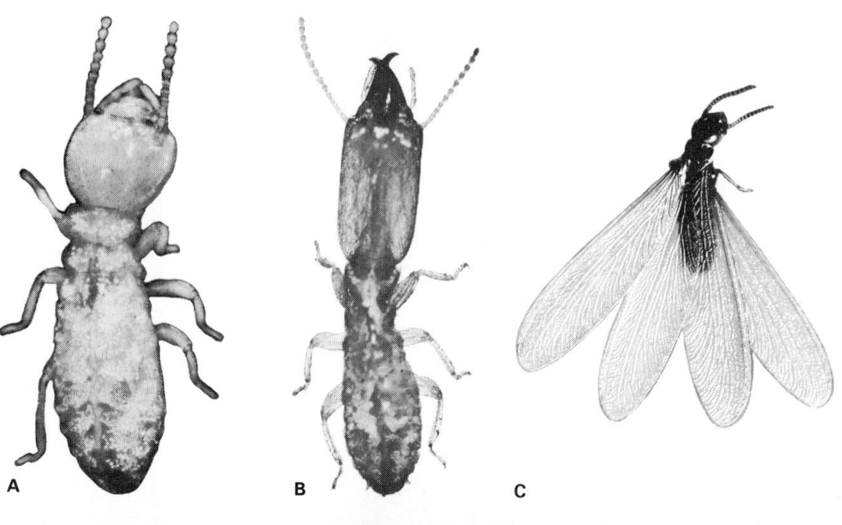

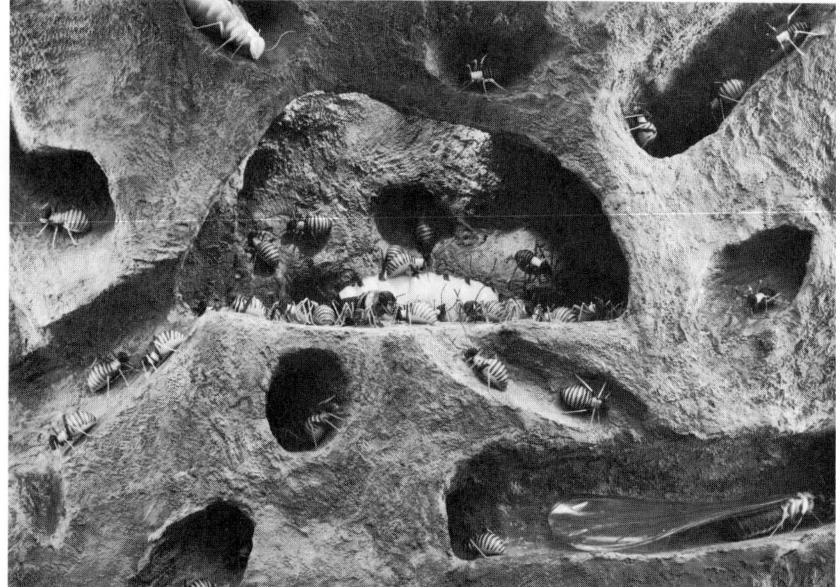

Fig. 21.6 Termites. (A) Worker. (B) Soldier. (C) Winged king. (D) Portion of nest. In central chamber note queen, her abdomen swollen with eggs, being cared for by workers. Winged king in lower right corner, larval queen in upper left corner. (*A, B, C, U.S. Department of Agriculture; D, Buffalo Museum of Science.*)

and dead termites. There they plant and rear fungi for food. *Leaf-cutting ants,* similarly, prepare pieces of leaves on which fungi are grown. The fungi are pruned systematically and cared for by gardening crews.

Dairy ants keep tiny green aphids (plant lice) as food suppliers. The aphids secrete honeydew, a mixture containing a sugar and protein, on which the ants depend. A common species of garden ant, for example, places "domesticated" plant lice on the roots of corn. The aphids feed there, and the ants thereafter milk these "ant cows" by gently stroking them (see Fig. 8.22). At the approach of winter the aphids are carried into the ant nest and put back on corn roots the following spring.

Slave-making ants can neither build nests, feed themselves, nor care for their larvae. They form workerless soldier societies capable only of making raids on populations of other ant species. These victims are robbed of their pupae. The captive pupae mature, and the emerging slaves then care for their masters, performing all the functions they would have carried out in their own nest.

Honeypot ants are desert forms that collect nectar from flowers and feed it to some of their fellow workers, which are kept inside the nest. These "living bottles" become greatly distended and serve as bacteria-free storage bins; during the dry season they dispense drops of honey to their thirsty mates.

Army ants in the tropics march cross-country in raiding expeditions. They travel in columns accompanied by larger-bodied "officer" ants. Everything living in the path of such columns is reduced to manageable pieces and carried off—even large animals if they cannot move away. It has been shown that the ants establish camps, or bivouacs, from which raids are launched; that chemical trails are laid and used on return trips; and that the timing of major raids coincides with the imminent maturation of large broods of offspring. The stereotyped nature of much of insect behavior is well displayed by these ants. If a column is made to travel in a circle, the ants will maintain the circle endlessly, each individual continuing to follow the one before it. Behavior evidently is so automatic that an ant is incapable of thinking itself out of an unproductive situation (see Fig. 20.1C).

VERTEBRATE SOCIETIES

Apart from the sexual dimorphism of males and females, the members of vertebrate populations are structurally more or less alike, at least during the early stages of life. Most important, *all* members of a vertebrate society are potential reproducers. Later specializations and social stratifications are largely functional and are based on differences resulting from various combinations of hereditary *and* acquired traits. The animals therefore come to differ in size, strength, intelligence, emotionality, skill, and in the comparative effectiveness with which they apply these and other attributes of individuality to the problems of living. The general result is that, unlike a social insect, a social vertebrate does have to seek a place in the society on its own, and it must usually do so in direct competition with the other members of the group. The competition revolves primarily around securing personal living space, food, and reproductive opportunity.

In effect, the vertebrate society is founded on a perpetual interaction of two opposing forces. On the one hand, each individual is equipped to function as a more or less effective competer, and thus is equipped to survive in a group, by being capable of *aggressive behavior.* On the other hand, the group is equipped to prevent its own disruption, and thus is equipped to survive as an adaptive unit, by controlling and limiting the aggressive behavior of its members through a number of powerful *social constraints.*

Aggressive Behavior

Aggressive behavior (technically also called *agonistic* behavior) is an activity through which an individual asserts its membership in the group generally and obtains its share of space, food, and mates specifically. The means of aggression include threat displays and actual fighting.

Aggressive displays follow more or less standardized patterns, and by variously warning, bluffing, or scaring a potential opponent they serve to forestall actual fighting. In many cases such displays are effective even against members of other species. For example, a prominent presentation of weapons, a fixed gaze leveled directly at an opponent, an evident muscular tensing, a slow wary stalk accompanied in some cases by fright-inducing sounds, or a size-increasing fluffing up or puffing up of the body—all are widely recognized among vertebrates as signs of threat. In most instances a series of exchanges of such displays between opponents suffices to elicit flight or submission by one (Fig. 21.7).

Aggressive (and also submissive) displays probably have evolved as symbolic offshoots of real fights; the actions and movements of displays often are quite similar to those of combat. However, they have become *ritualized,* by increases or decreases in the speeds, intensities, or durations of particular movements and by behavioral changes that exaggerate or draw attention to specific releaser signs of aggression or submission. Most probably, therefore, such displays represent stylized sham fights adaptively valuable as less dangerous substitutes for real fighting.

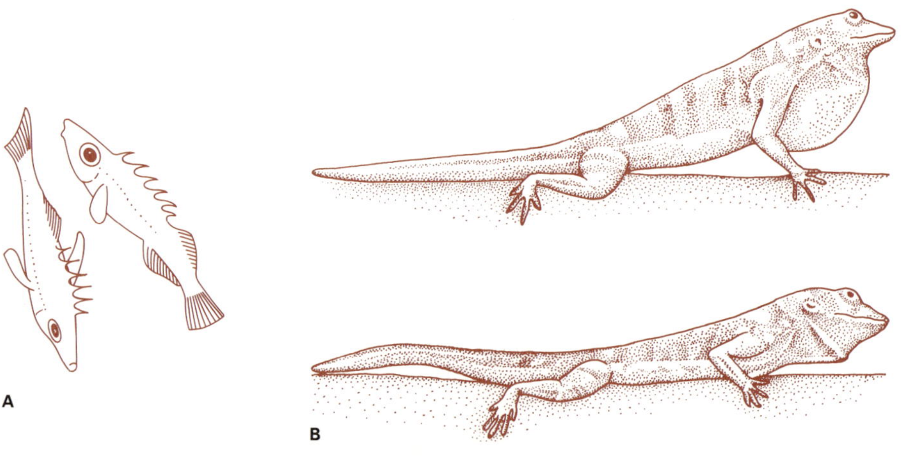

Fig. 21.7 Aggressive and submissive displays. (A) Sticklebacks assume a threatening stance by pointing the head downward (left), a submissive stance by lying in horizontal position or by pointing the head upward (right). (B) Aggressive male fence lizards stand as tall as possible and lower a throat structure called a dewlap, actions that enlarge their appearance when confronting rival males. Submissive lizards respond by flattening themselves. (C) In this confrontation between two baboons, the aggressive protagonist at left bares its teeth, points its ears up, stares at the opponent, raises its tail, and assumes a threat posture. The submissive animal meanwhile crouches down, lays its ears back, closes its mouth, lowers its tail, and carefully looks away from the opponent. (*C, Courtesy of Phyllis J. Dolhinow.*)

When an animal finds itself in a threatening social situation, the necessity of deciding on either fight or flight often creates psychological conflict—in many cases aggression or submission can be equally undesirable. In such circumstances the animal frequently can avoid becoming involved in either aggression or submission by minimizing the attention it creates; it might "freeze" to immobility or feign sleep. Sometimes psychological conflict can be resolved through *redirection:* directing an aggressive response not at the opponent but at an extraneous third entity—some nearby inanimate object, for example, or an "innocent bystander." Or the animal can carry out a *displacement* response, one not pertinent to the threat situation at all—excessive grooming, for example, or sudden preoccupation with some irrelevant feature of the environment. Responses of this sort are well known in human behavior and occur widely in other mammals and in birds (Fig. 21.8).

Outright combat occurs comparatively rarely, and indeed only when it cannot be avoided by other means—the cost could be death, injury, or at least exhaustion, while the gain could be zero. Also, notwithstanding some known exceptions (human beings, for example), very few animals seek out fights deliberately. In general, fighting tends to occur mainly when the living space, the food, the mates and the young, or the social status of animals is in jeopardy; or, more specifically, when the hazards of fighting become less significant than the motivation to compete for space, food, mates, or social status.

Thus it has been shown for most vertebrates studied that the frequency of fighting increases with rising population density. Similarly, many

A

B

Fig. 21.8 Redirection and displacement. (A) Male baboon in foreground is being threatened by male in background. However, avoiding both aggressive and submissive responses, the threatened male gives a redirected response instead: it focuses attention on uninvolved bystanders and walks over to the grooming couple nearby. (B) Under threat by male baboon at left, the male at right gives a displacement response: displaying neither aggressive nor submissive behavior, it carries out an activity not pertinent to the confrontation and grooms its mate instead.

animals require a free personal space immediately around them and will fight if this space is violated. For example, a nonbreeding male chaffinch will permit another male to approach no closer than about 8 in, and a female can approach to no more than about 4 in. A chicken permits a closer approach behind it than in front of it. And the size of a particular personal space tends to increase or decrease according to whether an approaching individual is familiar or not and displays signs of threat or submission (Fig. 21.9). Fighting also increases with progressive food scarcity and at the approach of the breeding season. A good many fights occur when an individual is prevented from completing a

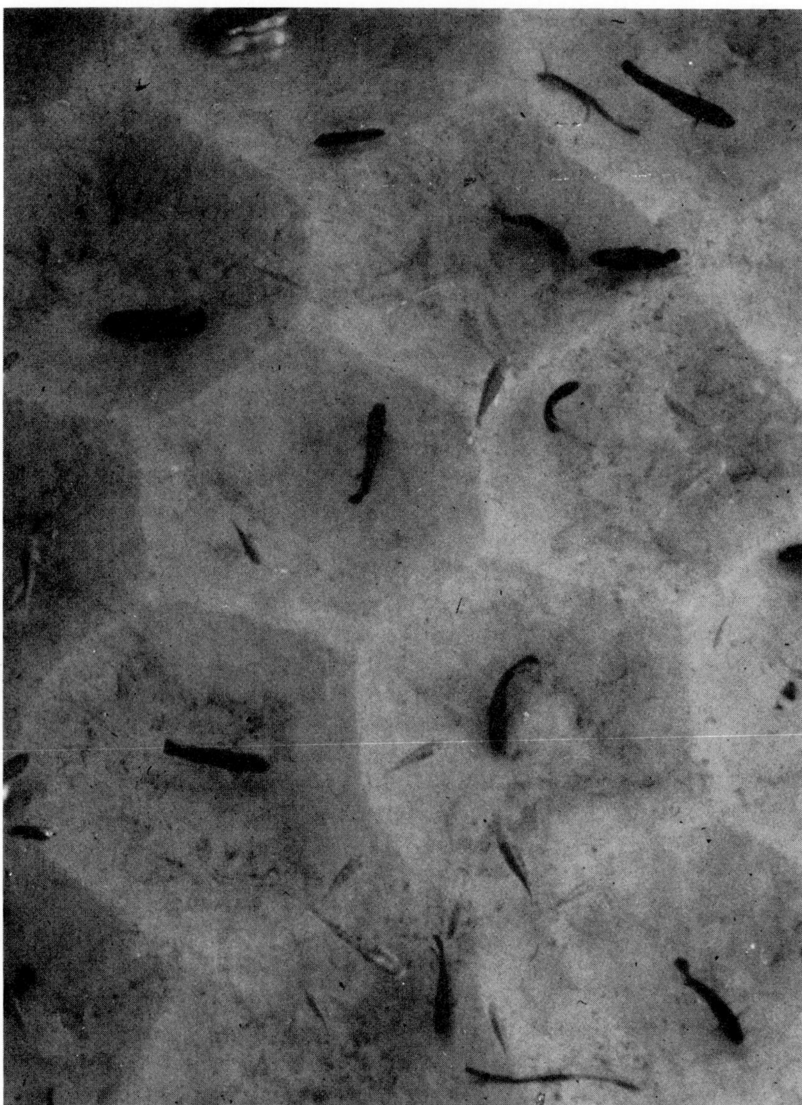

Fig. 21.9 Territoriality. Hexagonal pit nests of *Tilapia mossambica*, a species of mouthbreeding fish. Territory-holding males (the black fish) will attack male intruders entering their nest area. The gray fish, which do not defend territories, are females and juveniles.

goal-directed activity, a situation equivalent to frustration in people.

Whatever the provocation, vertebrates rarely fight to the death (people sometimes being a notable exception). If an exchange of aggressive displays does not establish the dominance of one of the opponents, such a dominance usually becomes apparent fairly quickly once combat has started. The fighting then terminates, and in most cases it terminates in any event as soon as one of the protagonists is wounded. The objective of animal combat is not destruction of an opponent but merely elimination of the threat his presence represents—at minimum cost of effort and risk to the threatened animal.

The capacity to behave aggressively or submissively is inherited, but the execution of such behavior is largely learned. Experience teaches not only the techniques of aggressive display and the tactics of combat but also the acceptable limits of the possible advantages and risks. Similarly significant is learning by imitation and, in predatory types, learning how to obtain food: predation and aggression involve many similar behavior patterns, even though killing is the objective in the first case. Notwithstanding the genetic variations among different individuals, early training to a large extent determines the threshold levels for aggressive responses and the intensities with which an individual will exhibit such responses. As has been shown for mice and as is well known for people, an individual can be *taught* to respond more or less readily and more or less intensely to a given provocation, and thus to be an aggressive or a submissive "type."

In vertebrates, aggressive behavior is under the control of at least two neural-endocrine mechanisms. In one of these, nerve impulses are relayed from the sense organs to the brain, which in turn stimulates the adrenal medulla. This gland then secretes increased amounts of epinephrine, a hormone that initiates a distinct fight or flight reaction (see Chap. 17). This reaction facilitates the sharply intensified activities that are required under most conditions of emotional or physical stress, including especially those calling for aggressive responses. Epinephrine specifically has been shown to promote more or less sudden and coordinated increases in blood pressure and in heart and breathing rates (manifested by red-faced anger in people); in blood sugar levels and blood-clotting rates; in muscle tension and resistance to fatigue; and in general alertness and responsiveness to stimuli.

In the second mechanism, sensory impulses are transmitted to the hypothalamus in the brain, and this region in turn transmits chemical signals to the pituitary gland. As a result, this gland secretes increased amounts of gonadotropic hormones that induce the reproductive organs to secrete larger quantities of male and female sex hormones (see Chaps. 17 and 25). The male hormones are specially potent in triggering aggressive behavior. Both sexes produce *both* male and female hormones, though in different relative quantities, and in either sex the male hormone promotes aggressive behavior. That this is so clearly shown by experimental hormone injections. Female hormones either are without significant effect or, in most (but not all) vertebrates, they reduce aggressiveness and correspondingly increase submissiveness. In effect, vertebrate aggressiveness waxes and wanes in synchrony with sexuality and the annual breeding cycle. Note, however, that aggressive behavior is not completely dependent on sex hormones; castrated animals do not become totally submissive, and in some cases castration reduces aggressiveness only very slightly.

Note also that actual reproductive capacity tends to be reduced by prolonged periods of heightened aggressiveness, even though sexual behavior can be intensified. The same stimuli that induce aggressiveness through effects on the pituitary also induce this gland to secrete increased amounts of ACTH (adrenocorticotropic hormone). This tropic hormone stimulates the adrenal cortex, and among the hormones then produced there in larger amounts are some that interfere with the proper maintenance of the sex organs. Persistent overstimulation of the adrenal cortex therefore can lead to a gradual structural decline of the sex organs and to lowered reproductive capacity. This effect often is observed in social groups in which the levels of aggressiveness are kept high by excessive population densities or by the repeated introduction of strange individuals. Under such conditions males produce fewer sperms, aggressive female birds such as chickens lay fewer eggs, and aggressive female mammals abort prematurely or cannot produce milk after pregnancy.

Chronic aggressiveness also has other, nonreproductive effects, all ultimately traceable to the endocrine and neural mechanisms just discussed. For example, growth often is inhibited and resistance to infections is lessened. People in particular also are subject to a distinct stress syndrome, characterized by an increase in allergic sensitivity, in the frequency of headaches and constipation, in the incidence of ulcers, and in other debilities typically associated with prolonged tension.

It is important to recognize, however, that notwithstanding the undesirable connotations of the idea of "aggression" in human affairs, occasional aggressive (or at least self-assertive) individual behavior is probably essential in vertebrate society, human society included. To be sure, a potential to behave aggressively might not even need to exist if every cause of competition and every source of frustration could be removed from all individuals in a social group. But competitive factors are known to play at least some role in all vertebrate groups, for the environmental supply of space and food is inherently limited. Moreover, it also has been pointed out by several investigators that loss of aggressive potentials in a species probably would lead to its destruction: the vertebrate mechanism for aggressive behavior is so intimately connected with other vital functions that abolition of one would amount to abolition of all. As noted, for example, reproduction, breeding cycles, learning through play and imitation, in some cases search for food and migratory behavior—all are based to greater or lesser degree on the same processes that also generate aggressive behavior. In addition, these same neural-endocrine processes regulate numerous internal metabolic reactions, as well as the social constraints against aggression (see below); and in people at least they contribute substantially to feelings of love and the drive to create, explore, control the environment, or be active in a very general sense. Without this constellation of capacities, aggressiveness necessarily included, a vertebrate would cease to be a functioning animal.

It is clear at the same time, however, that if aggressiveness—or submissiveness—is exaggerated unduly it ceases to be adaptive; like any other biological process, assertiveness or its lack becomes detrimental when carried to excess. In general, then, the *potential* of behaving aggressively can be regarded as an important safeguard for survival, evolved for the self-preservation of the individual under the massive—and not necessarily malicious—impact of the group. But if actual aggressiveness is misapplied and its use is mislearned, its survival function is lost and it becomes a destructive force instead.

Social Constraints

Every society operates within a framework of rules that serve to reduce individual aggression and thereby prevent disruption of the group. Like aggression, such constraining rules have a built-in, inherited basis, but their application is largely learned. Two kinds of constraints are characteristic of vertebrate societies in general, namely, *dominance* hierarchies and *territoriality*, phenomena already discussed in Chap. 8 (see Figs. 21.9, 8.27, and 8.28).

Because proportionately larger numbers of low-ranking individuals are unable to obtain food or acquire mates as population density increases, dominance hierarchies effectively limit the population growth of some species (see Chap. 8). But because each adult in these societies has an established social rank relative to every other adult of the same sex, dominance hierarchies also prevent competition and aggressive behavior from destroying the population. Once a hierarchical order has been established, aggression among individuals for resources and mates is restricted (Fig. 21.10).

The effectiveness of dominance hierarchies in reducing conflict depends greatly on easy rank identification: each individual must be able to recognize on sight the social rank of every other individual upon meeting (as in human military organizations). Dominance systems actually are most common in comparatively small social units, where every member can become a familiar "acquaintance" of all others. In such units communicative activities usually are important aids in intragroup recognition. For example, mutual grooming among primates serves not only a sanitary function but also maintains social familiarity. Similarly, play, vocalization, sniffing, and various forms of greeting help in enhancing familiarity. Recognition is aided further by the coloration patterns, which tend to be showy and quite individual-specific in their fine details. Also, sexual dimorphism generally is very pronounced. Males tend to be distinctly larger than females, and they usually have conspicuous and flashy display devices. Such males typically contribute little or nothing to the parental duties of building nests and caring for offspring. Because easy recognition and familiarity have great importance in social units of this type, the members tend to exhibit ingroup clannishness and considerable antagonism to outsiders.

The importance of dominance hierarchies in reducing social conflict can be demonstrated experimentally. For example, the peck order of a flock of hens (see Chap. 8) can be disrupted by periodically removing hens that have established a social rank in the flock and replacing them with hens from other flocks. The hens of the disrupted flock then will fight more, receive more injuries, and gain less weight than an undisrupted control flock that has established a stable dominance hierarchy.

Dominance hierarchies tend to limit extreme aggressiveness in yet another way, for there are built-in safeguards that make too high a status disadvantageous. In chickens, for example, the most dominant hens often are so aggressive that they dominate and reject even the rooster. And very dominant male mice often will fight each other so viciously that they make themselves impotent. Thus, most matings in many dominance hierarchies occur between subordinate males and subordinate

Fig. 21.10 Dominance hierarchies. Dominance relationships between members of a group of bicolor damselfish. Dominance is correlated with size and was measured by counting who chased whom. The largest fish, at the top, directed 36 per cent (286) of its chases at the one below it, 30 per cent (240) at the second below, and so on. The next largest fish directed only 1 per cent (6) of its chases to the largest fish but 12 per cent (73) to the fish below it, and so on. Note that aggressive behavior of most fish is directed at individuals occupying the next lower two or three positions in the hierarchy. Thus, aggressive behavior within dominance hierarchies is both constrained and limited.

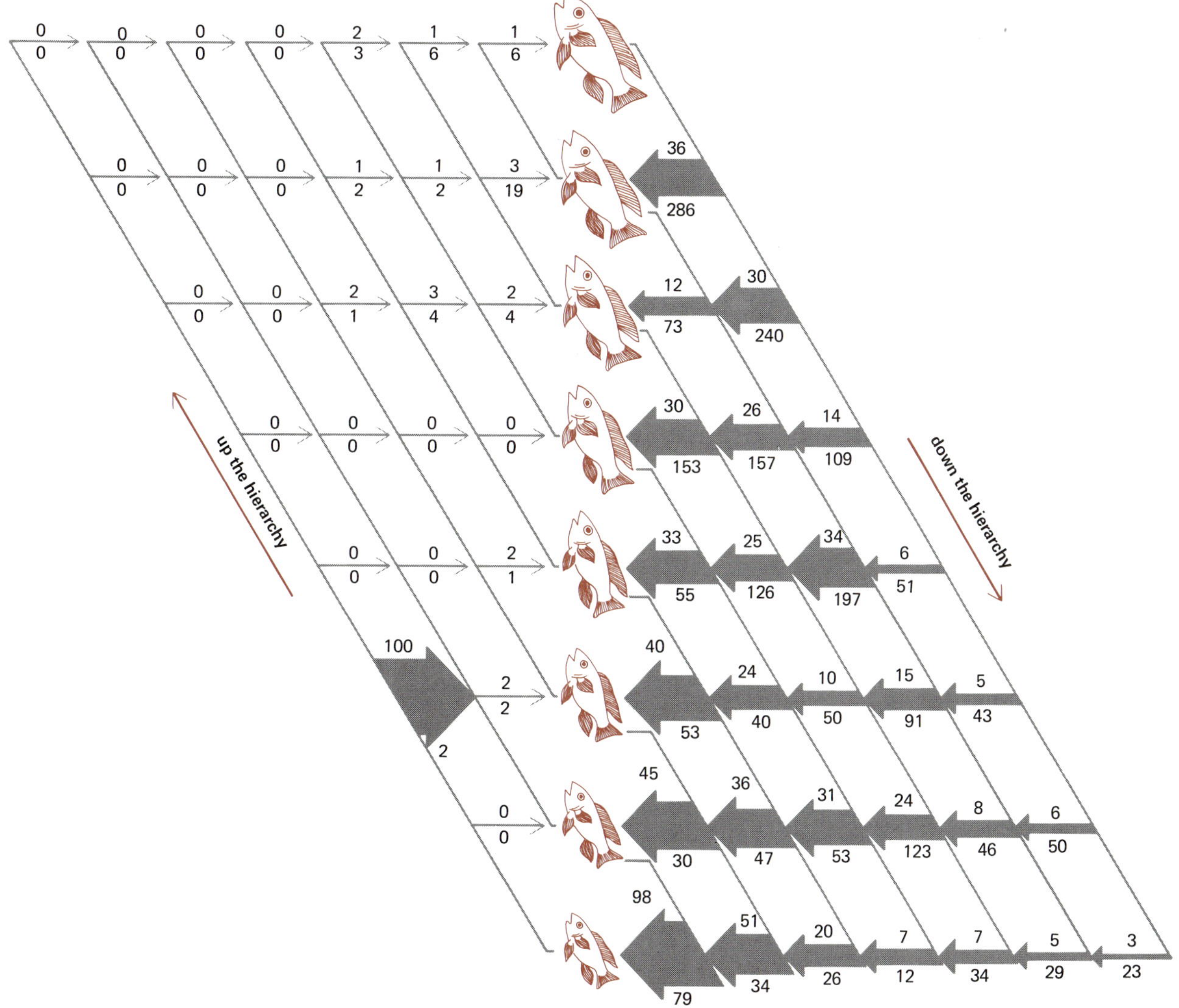

females, and their genetic contributions tend to maintain the average aggressive behavior of the next generation near the optimum for reproductive success of the total population.

By distributing individuals and subdividing resources on a spatial basis, territoriality not only limits the population growth of many species (see Chap. 8) but also aids in reducing social conflict. An invader of a well-established territory usually is driven away by the defender without bloodshed even when the invader is larger and stronger. Thus, for most species, territories tend to be "respected" once established. As a result, intraspecific conflicts between individuals occupying neighboring territories occur relatively infrequently.

A territorial organization also promotes propagation. Since males are spaced out and more or less bound to their domains, competition over females is lessened. Moreover, mating, nesting, and care of young are all facilitated in the comparatively undisturbed sanctuary of a domain. In contrast to a dominance system, a territorial system makes all adults effective reproducers; inasmuch as social ranks are absent, territoriality obviates the psychological castration often observed in dominance systems.

The fine structure of territorial organizations, like that of dominance systems, varies greatly not only for different species but also for a given species at different times. Moreover, changed conditions can lead to shifts from territoriality to dominance or the reverse. Further, a normally territorial group may shift to a dominance hierarchy altogether if its living space becomes too small. This is a common occurrence in domesticated animals, for example, and among caged groups in zoos and laboratories. Finally, a social group can be bound together by complex and simultaneous combinations of territoriality and dominance, as is illustrated particularly well in human society.

Review Questions

1 Describe some of the characteristics of social populations and some of the probable adaptive advantages of social living. Describe and contrast the organization of motion groups, insect societies, and vertebrate societies. Why is biological communication a universal characteristic among social animals?

2 What forms of polymorphism exist in insect societies? How do different polymorphic variants develop? How does the relation of individual to group differ between insect and vertebrate societies?

3 Review the roles of individual aggression and social restraint in vertebrate societies. Discuss the behavioral relations between threat display and combat.

4 Describe a personal example of a redirection response. Do the same for a displacement response. Under what circumstance did each occur?

5 Name and describe as many kinds of behavior as possible that are exhibited under the specific influence of sex-associated neural and endocrine mechanisms.

6 Describe the respective characteristics and adaptive advantages of dominance hierarchies and territorial organizations of social groups. Describe some aspects of human society in terms of aggression, dominance, and territoriality.

Collateral Readings

Bekoff, M., and **M. C. Wells:** The Social Ecology of Coyotes, *Scientific American,* April 1980. Contains a fascinating account of the social behavior of these animals.

Bertram, B. C. R.: The Social System of Lions, *Scientific American,* May 1975. The social interactions of these animals are examined.

Burgess, J. W.: Social Spiders, *Scientific American,* March 1976. Many spiders exhibit complex social behavior.

Eaton, G. G.: The Social Order of Japanese Macaques, *Scientific American,* October 1976. The author reports on a long-term observation of one troop of these monkeys.

Frisch, K. von: "Bees: Their Vision, Chemical Senses, and Language," rev. ed., Cornell University Press, Ithaca, N.Y., 1971. A fascinating short book summarizing many of the author's important experiments.

Hölldobler, B. K., and **E. O. Wilson:** Weaver Ants, *Scientific American,* December 1977. The behavior of the animals is coordinated by complex chemical stimuli.

Lore, R., and **K. Flannelly:** Rat Societies, *Scientific American,* May 1977. Highlights the social behavior of the remarkably intelligent Norway rat.

Milne, L. J., and **M. Milne:** The Social Behavior of Burying Beetles, *Scientific American,* August 1976. This delightful husband-and-wife team has spent many years watching the behavior of animals. This article focuses on one of their latest investigations.

Topoff, H. R.: The Social Behavior of Army Ants, *Scientific American,* November 1972. This article shows how the complex and permanent social organization of these insects is maintained by interactions between many individuals.

Watts, C. R., and **A. W. Stokes:** The Social Order of Turkeys, *Scientific American,* June 1971. The article describes the peculiar social organization of wild turkeys in Texas.

Part 5
The Operations of Life: Reproduction

Of all living functions, reproduction is among the most dramatic: now there is one, then there are two. To be sure, the significance of reproduction lies not in its dramatic nature but in its results. Just as an organism maintains steady states from the molecular level on up, so it also reproduces from the molecular level on up. And just as nucleic acids are the ultimate basis of steady states, so they are also the ultimate basis of reproduction; the reproductive properties of the first DNA molecules have been handed down in an unbroken succession from the first genes to all present genes. Accordingly, the first topics in this series of chapters deal with the reproductive *patterns* encountered on the various levels of the living hierarchy, particularly among molecules, cells, and whole organisms. Following this is a study of the specific reproductive *processes* that occur in plants and animals. The final two chapters of this part examine, first, the anatomical and regulatory aspects of human reproduction and, second, the developmental processes responsible for the aging and ultimate death of individual organisms.

A vervet mother, suckling her young. (*P. Whitten. Anthro Photo.*)

Chapter 22 Reproductive Patterns

Learning Objectives

After reading this chapter you should be able to:

1. Show how reproduction contributes to self-perpetuation.
2. Identify and describe four forms of molecular reproduction in cells and indicate how molecular reproduction contributes to organismic reproduction.
3. Differentiate between multiple fission, budding, and binary fission; distinguish between mitosis and cell division and show how cell division contributes to organismic reproduction.
4. Construct a diagram that depicts the three major periods of interphase and the four stages of mitosis; name the principal events that characterize each period and phase; indicate how mitosis differs in plant and animal cells; define chromatin, nucleosome, chromatid, kinetochore, centromere, centriole, aster, and spindle; list evidence suggesting a functional relation between histone H_1 and the condensation of chromosomes.
5. Define tissue culture; show how experiments with tissue cultures have contributed to a better understanding of cellular reproductive capacity; state how the G_1 period of interphase is related to the rate of cell division and the transformation of normal cells to cancer cells; define metastasis and malignancy.
6. Identify four general agents that can trigger conversion of normal cells to cancer cells; describe the evidence that has identified each as a cancer-causing agent and name at least one way in which each agent is thought to cause cancer; identify four methods of cancer treatment that are being used or developed; define cancer, RNA transcriptase, virus.
7. Distinguish between reproduction and development; define and describe at least three forms of vegetative reproduction; differentiate between vegetative and gametic reproduction.
8. List two general ways in which reproductive cells develop into adults; name the adaptive advantages and disadvantages of sporulation and gametic reproduction; differentiate between sex and reproduction and illustrate how meiosis counteracts the doubling effect of fertilization (use *Spirogyra* and *Chlamydomonas* as examples); define meiosis, state its basic function, and indicate where meiosis occurs; list the principal similarities and differences between meiosis and mitosis; define fertilization, zygote, gamete, haploid, diploid; state how many sets of chromosomes are found in a diploid cell.
9. Distinguish between isogamy, anisogamy, and oögamy. List at least one example of an organism that exhibits oögamy; distinguish between antheridia, archegonia, testes, and ovaries.
10. Define and list the chief adaptive advantages of haplontic, diplontic, and diplohaplontic life cycles: illustrate the principal differences between these cycles and state how the timing of meiosis is related to each of these differences; identify the major groups of organisms that reproduce by each cycle.
11. Outline a fundamental difference between the sexual and asexual patterns of development; differentiate between morphogenesis, determination, and differentiation; define and illustrate at least two subcomponent processes of morphogenesis; list at least two ways in which cellular differentiation appears to be regulated.

Reproduction can be defined broadly as the extension of living matter in space and time. The self-perpetuative importance of this process is clear, for the formation of new living units makes possible replacement and addition at every level of organization. Among molecules or cells, among whole organisms or species, replacement offsets death from normal wear and tear and from accident and disease. *Healing* and *regeneration* are two aspects of replacement. Apart from such maintenance functions, net addition of extra units results in four-dimensional *growth,* or increase in the amount of living matter.

The creation of new units requires raw materials, and reproduction at any level depends on ample nutrition. Duplication of a particular living unit also implies prior or simultaneous duplication of all smaller units within it. Reproduction therefore must occur on the molecular level before it can occur on any other.

MOLECULAR REPRODUCTION

The number of any kind of molecules in a cell can increase as the result of four different reproductive processes. The process employed depends on the nature of the molecule. All four are already familiar.

If water or another inorganic substance is to be reproduced, additional molecules or ions of such substances must be supplied ready-made by nutrition. Thus, *accumulation* is the simplest form of molecular "reproduction."

If a carbohydrate, a lipid, an amino acid, or any of their numerous derivatives is to be duplicated, it may have to be synthesized from accumulated raw materials with the aid of appropriate enzymes (so long as the enzymes of a cell remain the same, newly formed organic molecules will generally be duplicates of earlier ones). The second form of molecular reproduction therefore is *enzymatic synthesis.* It includes the first form, accumulation, as a component phase.

If a protein molecule is to be duplicated, enzymes must link amino acids together, and DNA and RNA must provide the information for the sequence of linking. The third form of molecular reproduction includes the first two forms but in addition is a directly *gene-dependent synthesis.*

Finally, if DNA is to be duplicated, it must control its own replication. This process depends on accumulation of phosphates, enzymatic synthesis of nitrogen bases and other required components, and DNA-dependent synthesis of the needed enzymes. But above all DNA duplication is a *self-duplication,* and this is the fourth form of molecular reproduction.

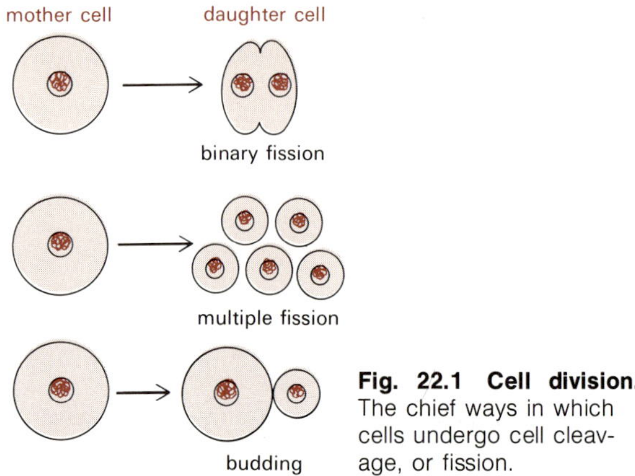

Fig. 22.1 Cell division. The chief ways in which cells undergo cell cleavage, or fission.

Molecular reproduction contributes either to normal replacements within cells or to internal net additions of molecules. A common result is *cell growth.* Increase in cell *size* then can be followed by an increase in cell *number,* or *cell division.*

CELLULAR REPRODUCTION

Few biological events are as central to life and as universally characteristic of it as cell division. It is the only means by which unicellular organisms multiply. It creates reproductive cells and transforms them to multicellular adults. It replaces dead cells and thereby offsets normal wear and tear. It heals wounds and regenerates body parts lost or destroyed. And cell division sometimes goes wild and produces tumors, cancers, and other abnormal overgrowths. Indeed, the life histories of organisms well can be described as changing dynamic equilibria between cell division and cell death.

In certain protists a cell divides into *several* offspring cells simultaneously, a process called *multiple fission.* In certain other protists a cell divides by *budding,* or formation of a much smaller offspring cell. In the vast majority of cases, however, cells divide by *binary fission;* one "mother" cell becomes two roughly equally large "daughter" cells. After a period of internal molecular reproduction and subsequent growth, the daughter cells in turn usually divide, and successive cell generations follow one another in this fashion (Fig. 22.1).

Cell division consists of at least two processes, cytoplasmic cleavage into two parts and gene duplication. All organisms except the Monera have nuclei with true chromosomes, and cell division here includes a mathematically precise doubling of the chromosomes and their genes. The two chromosome sets so produced then become separated and become part of two newly formed nuclei. This type of nuclear duplication represents *mitosis* (or *karyokinesis*); and if, as is usually the case, mitosis is accompanied by cytoplasmic cleavage (or *cytokinesis*), both processes together represent *mitotic cell division*. Clearly, "mitosis" is not another word for cell division but designates a particular kind of *nuclear* division. In Monera, cell division includes gene duplication but not mitosis, since nuclei are not present in prokaryotes.

Mitosis and Division

Interphase

The interval between two consecutive mitotic cell divisions is called *interphase*. Although under the microscope cells appear relatively quiescent at that time, their metabolic activity usually is greatest. For example, most DNA, RNA, and protein are manufactured during interphase. Chromosomal material is dispersed throughout the nuclei of inter-

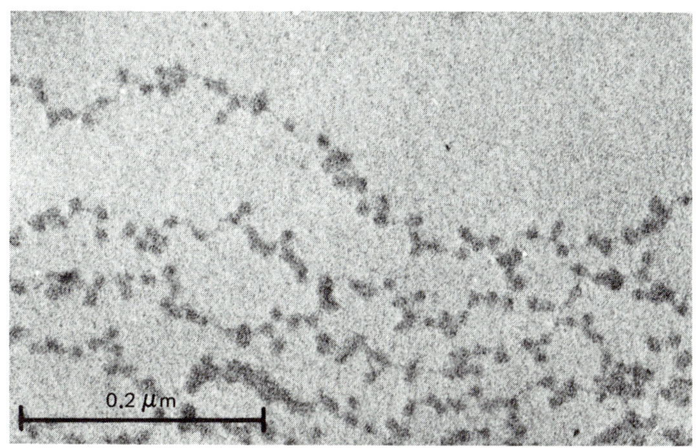

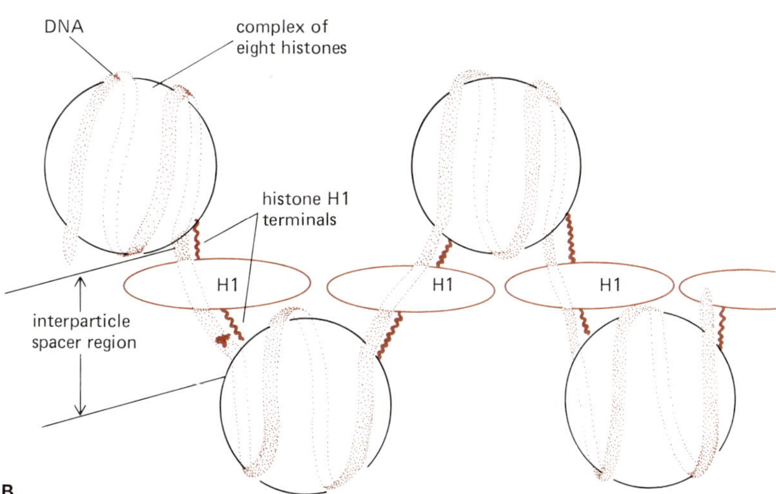

Fig. 22.2 Nucleosomes. (A) Electron micrograph of interphase chromatin. Each of the dense particles is a nucleosome. Note the thin strands interconnecting nucleosomes. (B) A model of the possible organization of DNA and histones in interphase chromatin. As noted in Chap. 15, histones are positively charged proteins that function as important structural components of chromatin. Current evidence suggests that each nucleosome consists of a core of histone molecules wrapped by DNA. Interparticle regions consist of DNA and (in most cells) a variety of histone called histone H1. The amount of histone H1 present in interparticle regions appears to increase substantially in most cells as chromatin shortens during the formation of chromosomes. Thus, histone H1 may play an important role in regulating the coiling of chromatin.

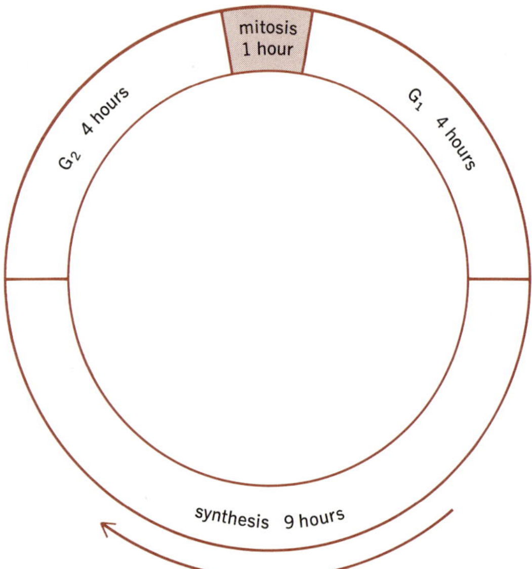

Fig. 22.3 The cell cycle. Hours indicate the amount of time an average mammalian cell might spend in each phase. Cycle proceeds in a clockwise direction.

phase cells. As stated in Chaps. 5 and 15, such dispersed nucleoprotein is called *chromatin.* The structural relationships between the nucleic acid and protein components of chromatin are not known with certainty, but these molecules appear to be organized as long sequences of small particles, called *nucleosomes,* interlinked by short strands, much like a string of beads (Fig. 22.2).

DNA and many other components of chromatin are duplicated during a subdivision of interphase called the S (synthesis) *period* (Fig. 22.3). The subdivision of interphase that extends from the end of a mitotic cell division to the beginning of the S period is designated the G_1 (G for gap) *period.* Similarly, the portion of interphase that extends from the end of the S period to the beginning of a mitotic cell division is called the G_2 *period.* RNA and protein synthesis continue throughout all periods of interphase. The visible events of mitosis begin at the end of the G_2 period. These consist of four successive, not sharply separated stages: *prophase, metaphase, anaphase,* and *telophase.*

Prophase

In the cells of all animals and many protists, the centriole, just outside the nucleus, has already duplicated by the time prophase begins (Fig. 22.4). During prophase, the centrioles then behave as if they repelled each other and migrate toward opposite sides of the cell nucleus. Concurrently, portions of the cytoplasm become organized as a highly organized system of microtubules, some of which radiate away from each centriole like the spokes of a wheel and form so-called *asters.* Other microtubules develop between the two centrioles and produce a *spindle,* with a *spindle pole* marked at each end by the centriole. In the cells of plants, centrioles are absent and asters do not form, but spindles do develop.

Next, the nuclear membrane usually dissolves, the nucleoli disappear, and distinct chromosomes become visible. Duplication of chromatin during interphase has produced a mathematically and genetically exact double, and this condition now becomes clearly apparent. Prophase chromosomes consist of two identical strands, called *chromatids,* that lie closely parallel (see Fig. 22.4). Each chromatid results from a coiling of chromatin fibers. The diameter of the chromatids continues to increase as coiling continues throughout prophase and early metaphase.

Mechanisms responsible for the coiling, or *condensation,* of chromatin fibers are not known, although cells about to enter prophase apparently produce substances that initiate this process. The existence of such substances has been deduced from experiments in which an interphase cell is fused either with a dividing cell or with a cell about to divide. Such *hybridized* cells initially contain a nucleus derived from the interphase cell and visible chromosomes from the mitotic cell. Shortly after fusion, however, the envelope of the interphase nucleus breaks down, and its dispersed chromatin begins to condense. If the nucleus was in the G_2 period of interphase, its chromatin condenses to chromosomes having two chromatids. If the nucleus was in the G_1 period of interphase, its chromatin condenses to chromosomes having one chromatid. And if the nucleus was in the S period, its chromatin condenses to chromosomes having one whole chromatid and partly duplicated fragments of a second chromatid (Fig. 22.5). Such experiments provide visual evidence that duplication of chromatin accompanies DNA replication during the S period of interphase.

A substance that may be at least partly respon-

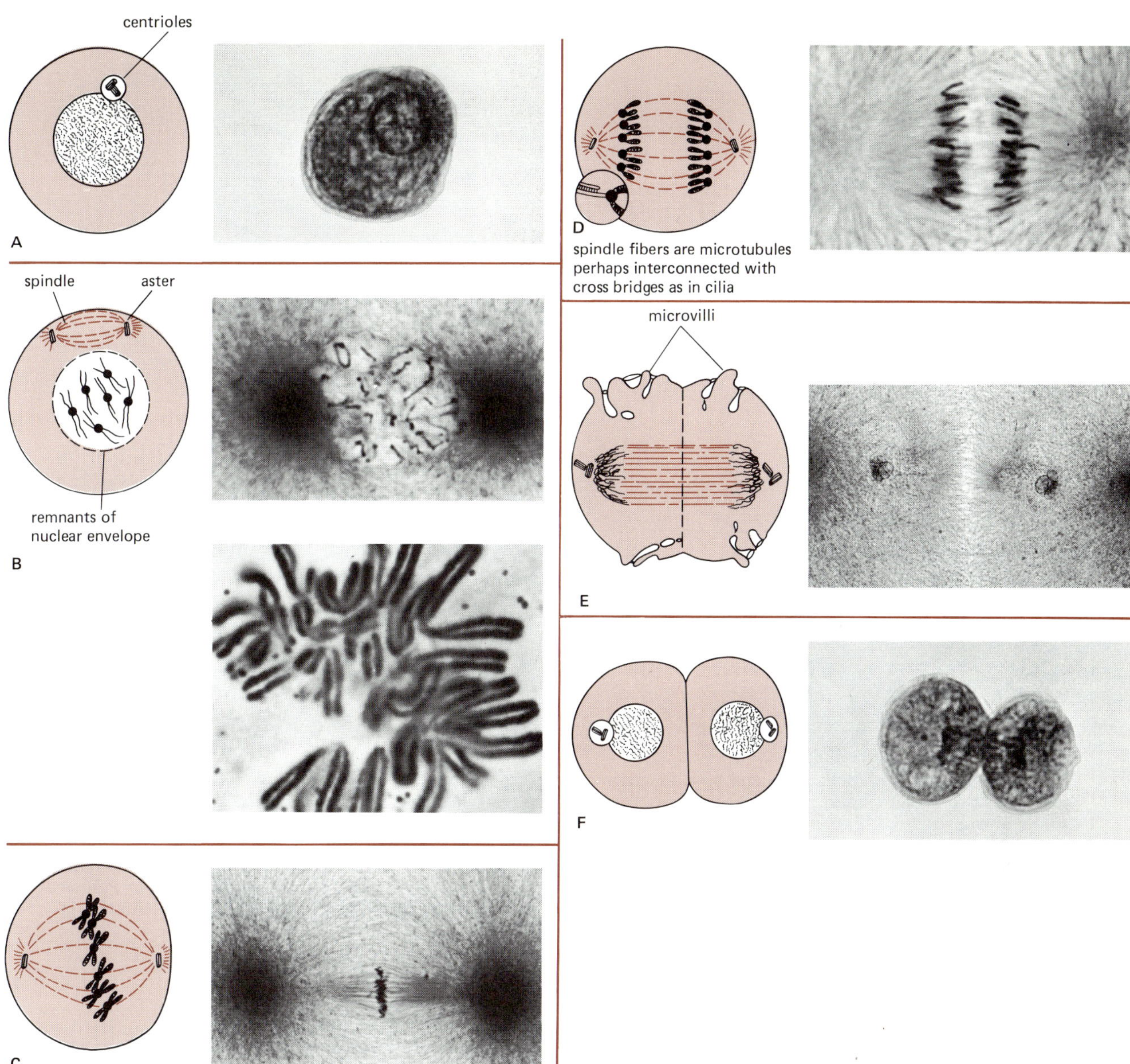

Fig. 22.4 Interphase and phases of mitosis in an animal cell. (A) Interphase. 1. Interphase cells contain complete nuclei. The centriole of this cell has already divided. 2. Light micrograph of an interphase cell. (B) Prophase. 1. The nuclear envelope and nucleolus have disappeared. Long, thin chromosomes have appeared, each composed of two chromatids. 2. Note the thin chromosomes of this prophase cell. To each side of the nuclear region is a darkly stained centriole area, from which aster fibrils are beginning to radiate out. 3. Closeup view of prophase chromosomes. Note the chromatids (arrows), which are held together at one point, the centromere. (C) Metaphase. 1. Chromosomes have moved to the equator (metaphase plate). Spindle fibers connect to dense kinetochores, located near centromeres. 2. Note asters, spindle, and metaphase plate, halfway along and at right angles to the spindle axis. (D) Anaphase. 1. Daughter chromosomes move toward the poles. A cleavage furrow has not yet formed. 2. Light micrograph of an anaphase cell, showing the two sets of chromosomes migrating toward the spindle poles. (E) Telophase. 1. Nuclear envelopes begin to reform around the elongating chromosomes, and a cleavage furrow becomes evident. Cytoplasmic projections at the cell surface are called microvilli (see also Fig. 22.6). 2. Note that the asters of this telophase cell are subsiding. Cytoplasmic cleavage occurs in the same plane as the earlier metaphase plate. (F) Daughter cells. 1. Nuclei have reformed. RNA transcription and translation is reestablished. 2. Light micrograph of daughter cells. Note presence of nuclei and nucleoli.

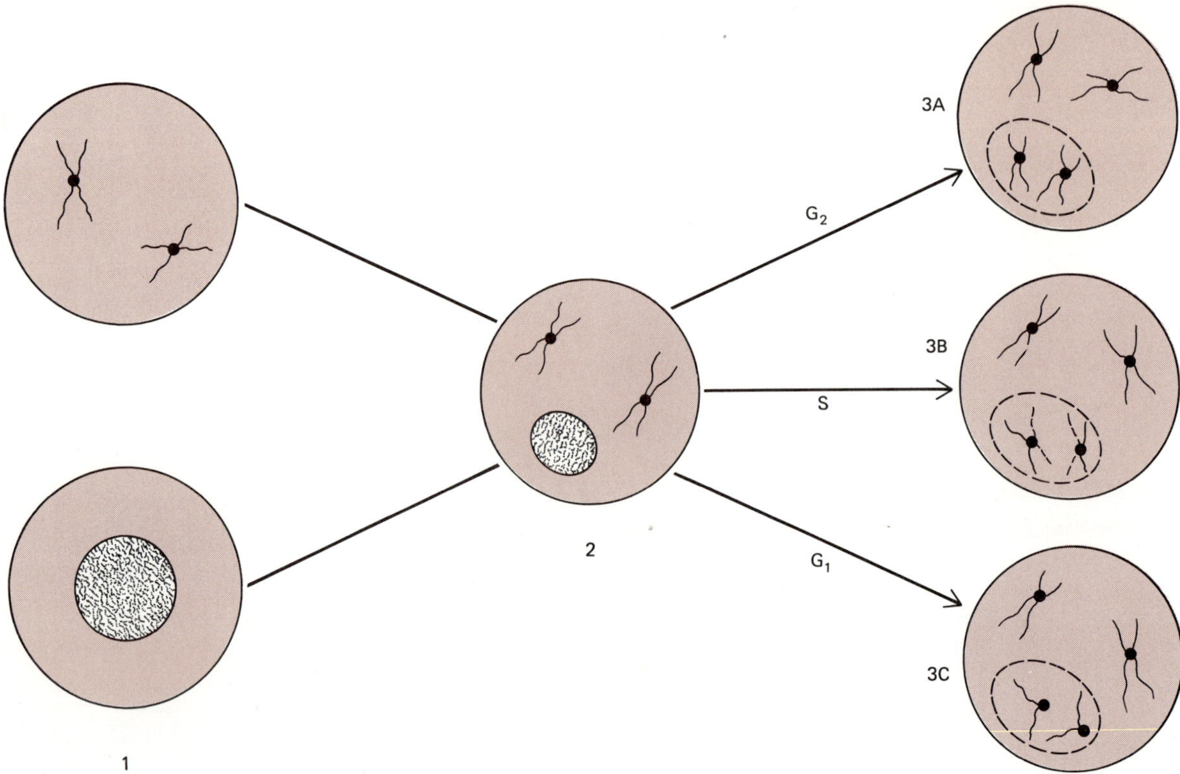

Fig. 22.5 Chromosome replication and condensation. The existence of substances that trigger condensation of chromosomes has been demonstrated through cell-hybridization techniques. An interphase and prophase cell are fused (1) , producing a hybridized cell (2) that contains an interphase nucleus (circle) and chromosomes from the prophase cell. The envelope of the interphase nucleus breaks down (dotted circles in 3A, 3B, and 3C) shortly after hybridization, and the chromatin of this nucleus begins to condense. If the interphase cell was in the G_1, S, and G_2 periods, respectively, its nuclear chromatin condenses to chromosomes containing one chromatid (3A), one whole chromatid and a partly replicated second chromatid (3B), and chromosomes containing two chromatids (3C). Such experiments suggest that chromatids and DNA are replicated simultaneously during the S period of interphase.

sible for chromosomal condensation is *histone H1* (see Fig. 22.2). As discussed in Chap. 15, histones are basic proteins bound to DNA in chromatin. Uncoiled chromatin of interphase cells contains little H1 histone, but this protein is highly concentrated in chromosomes. Concentrations of other histones in chromatin do not change appreciably during condensation.

The paired chromatids of condensing chromosomes are joined to each other at a single point called the *centromere* (see Fig. 22.4). Spindle microtubules become anchored to a dense granule, the *kinetochore,* located near the centromere (see also Chap. 5).

Metaphase, Anaphase, Telophase

Metaphase starts when the paired chromatids begin to migrate. If a line from one spindle pole to the other is considered to mark out a spindle axis, the chromatid pairs migrate to a plane at right angles to and midway along this axis. Here the chromatid pairs line up in a *metaphase plate* (see Fig. 22.4). At this stage (or sometimes earlier) the centromeres separate and the two chromatids of each pair thereby become unjoined *daughter chromosomes.* One set of daughter chromosomes migrates toward one spindle pole, and the identical twin set migrates toward the other. This period of chromosome movement represents the *anaphase* of mitosis.

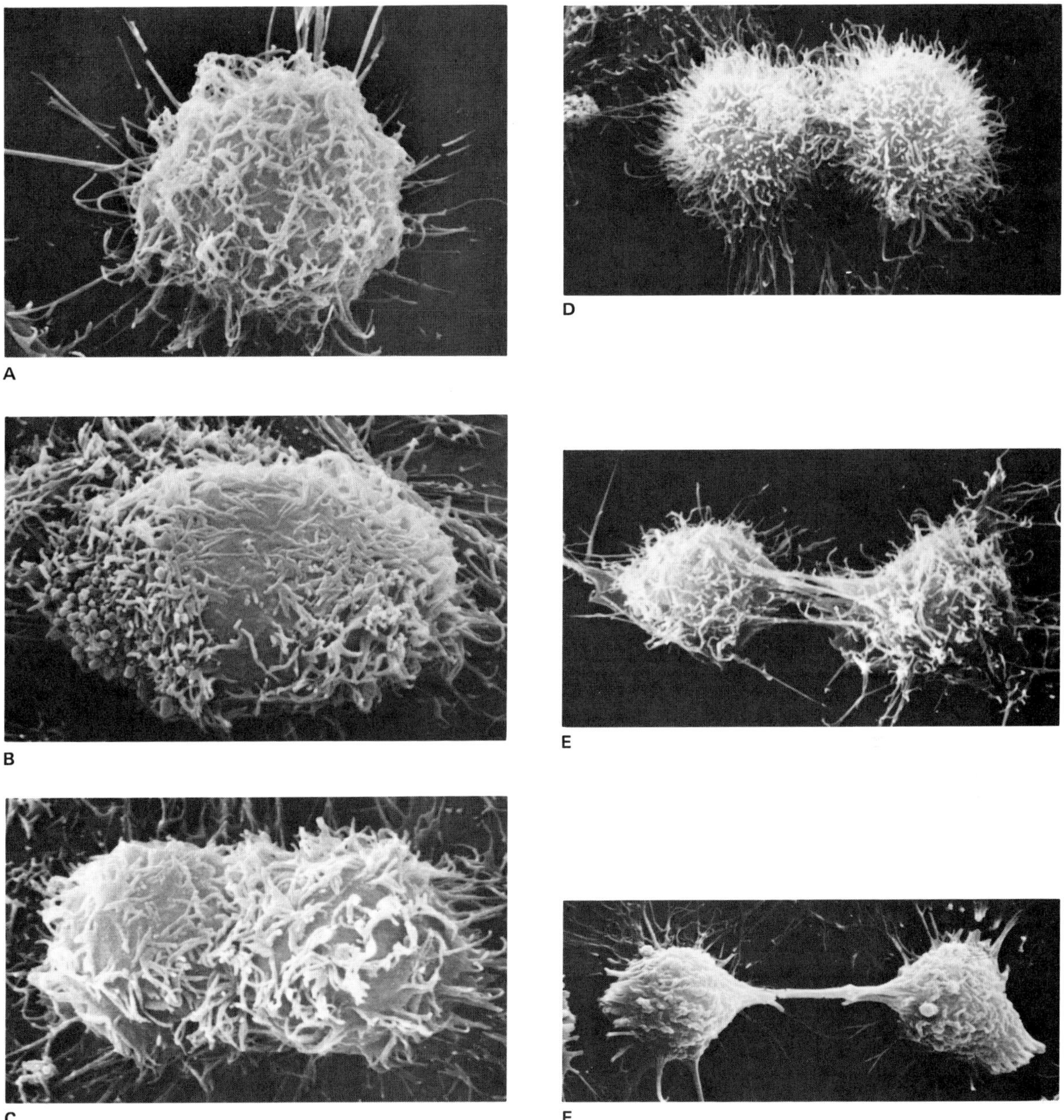

Fig. 22.6 Cleavage furrow. This sequence of scanning electron micrographs shows the division of a human cell into two daughter cells. The cleavage between the daughter cells deepens as the cells move apart. The hairlike projections on the cell surface are microvilli, extensions of the cytoplasm associated with cell movement.

As a set of daughter chromosomes now collects near each spindle pole, spindle fibers and asters disappear. A new nuclear envelope soon forms around each set of daughter chromosomes, and nucleoli appear in numbers characteristic of the particular cell type. Formation of new nuclear envelopes marks the beginning of *telophase.*

Division

In animal cells, cleavage begins with the appearance of a *cleavage furrow,* a gradually deepening surface groove that cuts through the spindle fibers and eventually constricts the cell into two daughters (Fig. 22.6). The plane of the cleavage furrow is clearly influenced by the position of the spindle apparatus, as shown by numerous experiments. In 1919, for example, E. G. Conklin found that the plane of division of a fertilized egg is altered when its spindle is displaced by centrifugation. Other biologists have induced new cleavage furrows in dividing cells by experimentally manipulating the position of the spindle. These and other procedures demonstrate that the spindle apparatus determines the location of cleavage furrows and establishes synchrony between mitosis and cytokinesis.

The spindle only initiates division, however. It normally is not responsible for the actual formation of a cleavage furrow. Indeed, once division has begun, the spindle apparatus can be excised or dissolved without altering division significantly (Fig. 22.7).

Constriction of cleavage furrows apparently is controlled by a dense ring of filaments arranged circumferentially around a cell much like a purse string. This aggregation of filaments, which is called the *contractile ring,* assembles when a cleavage furrow forms and disappears following division. Connected to the plasma membrane, the contractile ring functions by growing smaller, dragging the surface membrane with it until division is complete.

The composition of the contractile ring is not fully known, but it contains both actin and myosin filaments, the same proteins largely responsible for

Fig. 22.7 Cytokinesis without a spindle. (A) The spindle apparatus (clear area in center) of this sea urchin egg is dissolved by injecting less than 1 microliter of sucrose solution. The tip of the injecting instrument (a micropipette) can be seen at the left. The injection is made shortly after cleavage has begun. (B) Cytokinesis occurs on schedule. A cleavage furrow forms along the same plane that would have been established if the spindle had been left intact. The arrow in this picture indicates the position of the contractile ring, an aggregation of microfilaments too small to be seen with the light microscope.

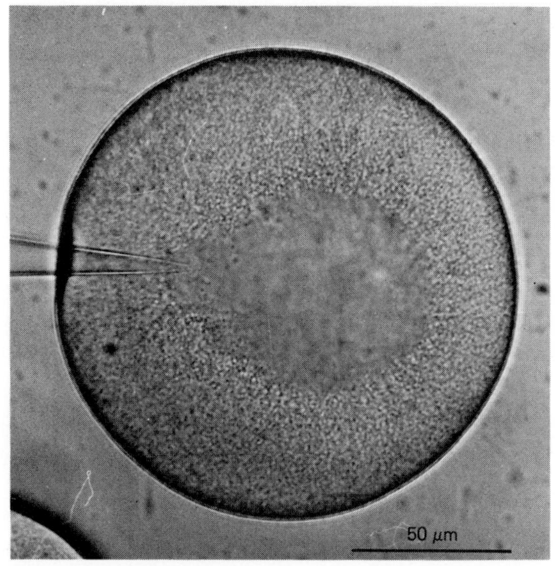

A

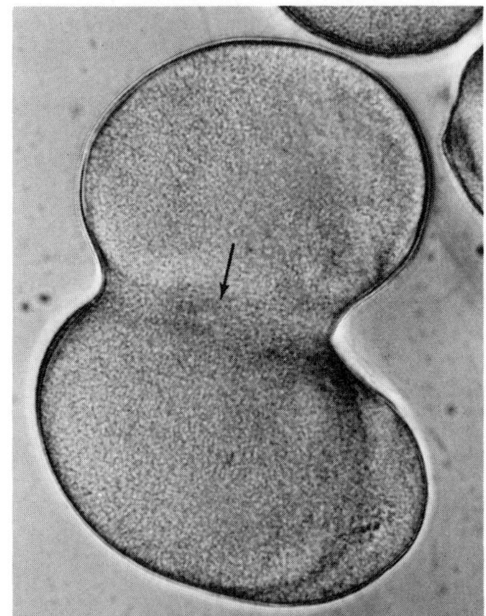

B

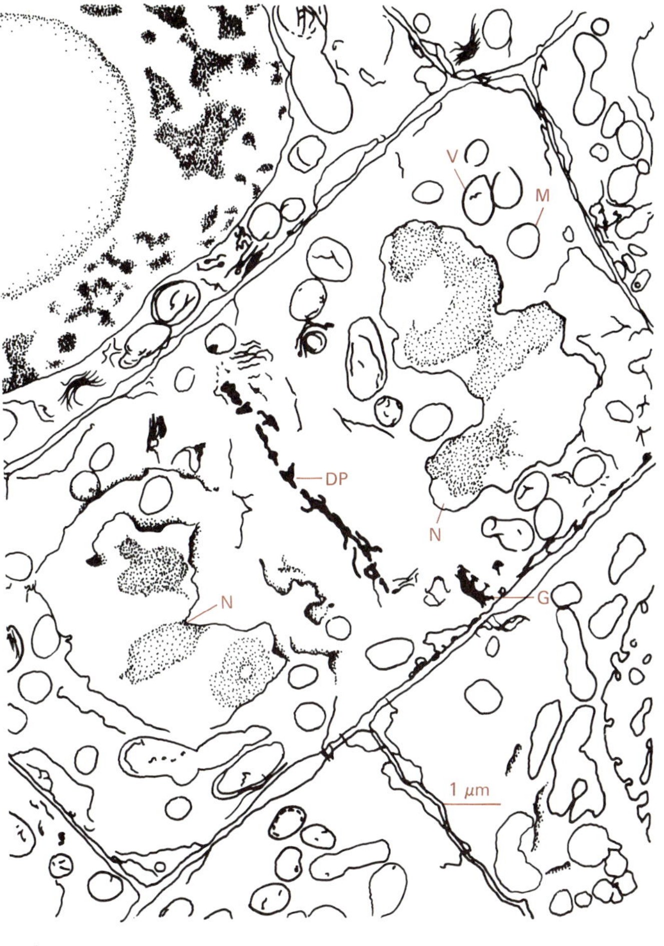

A

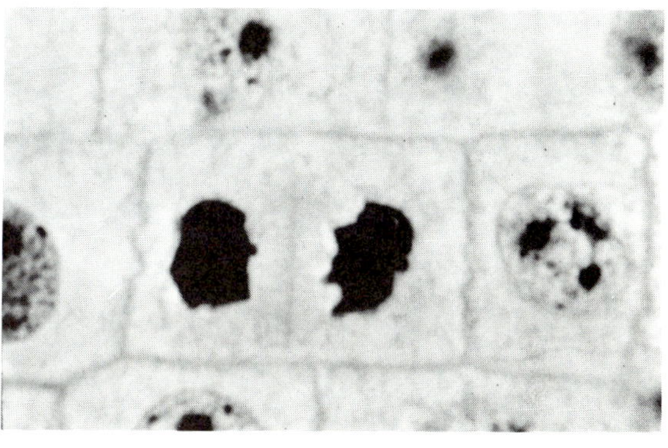

B

Fig. 22.8 Division plate. (A) Drawing (based on an electron micrograph) of a telophase cell sectioned from the root tip of a corn plant. A division plant (DP) is forming across the center of the cell. The disclike plate results from the fusion of many Golgi-derived vesicles. G, Golgi apparatus, N, nucleus; V, vacuole; M, mitochondrion. (B) Telophase of a plant cell. Note faint indications of division plate, midway between daughter nuclei and at right angles to the former spindle axis.

the contraction of muscle (see Chap. 19). Moreover, formation of cleavage furrows is influenced by calcium ions, like the contraction of skeletal muscle. Thus the contractile ring appears to be another example of a growing list of actin-myosin interactions.

Cleavage furrows do not form in plant cells, which instead are subdivided by formation of *division plates* (Fig. 22.8). Formation of such a plate, which is a partition of cellulose developed all along the plane of cleavage, begins during anaphase. At this time a collection of cytoplasmic vesicles (small vacuoles) accumulates around microtubules located at the middle of the cell. These vesicles, derived at least in part from the Golgi apparatus, fuse and form a disk, which in turn eventually fuses with the plasma membrane.

At this point the fused vesicular membranes of the disk have become inward extensions of the plasma membrane, and two daughter cells have been produced by the subdivision. Contents of the vesicles become trapped between the daughter cells. Some of the substances contained in the vesicles contribute to the formation of new cell walls. Following division of a plant or animal cell, genes in each daughter nucleus resume control of RNA transcription and a new growth cycle then can follow.

Biology Highlight Cancer: Wayward Cells

Cancer cells are unresponsive to controls that normally inhibit cell reproduction. As a result, they divide continually, often function abnormally, and interfere increasingly with the activities of normal cells. Most cancer cells lack at least some of the specialized features that characterize their normal counterparts. Cancerous endocrine cells of the pancreas, for example, usually appear less specialized than normal pancreatic cells but often continue to secrete hormones. The abnormally high concentrations of hormones that result from the rapid proliferation of these cancerous endocrine cells can produce gross functional aberrations in many normal cells. Some cancer cells synthesize substances normally produced by completely different types of cells. Such secretions also can disrupt the functions of normal cells.

Cancer cells often are transported by blood and lymph from their points of origin to other parts of the body. Once settled in such new locations, they reproduce rapidly and form secondary cancerous growths called *metastases*. Each of these growths can "seed" additional sites, and the entire body soon can become riddled with cancer. Because their uncontrolled reproduction and metastatic growth produces a steadily worsening condition, cancer cells often are termed *malignant*.

Cancer is second only to cardiovascular diseases as the leading cause of death in the United States (Table 1). Over 300,000 Americans die each year from cancer, and it is estimated that 25 per cent of all Americans now living eventually will develop this disease. Its financial burden is more than 20 billion dollars annually, or about 25 per cent of the national cost for all health care.

When a cell becomes cancerous, its rate of reproduction sometimes increases. However, it seldom reproduces at rates characteristic of the

TABLE 1

Leading Causes of Death in United States for Men and Women per 100,000 Population per Year

Cause of death	Male	Female
heart disease	383.5	293.4
cancer	196.6	156.0
stroke	77.1	98.0
accidents	67.3	27.7
pneumonia, flu	31.1	26.6
cirrhosis of the liver	19.8	9.8
suicide	18.7	6.7
diabetes	13.8	18.6
early infancy diseases	13.6	9.6

SOURCE: Statistical Abstract of the United States, 1978.

most rapidly dividing cells in an organism. As indicated earlier, bone marrow cells divide very rapidly—about once every 12 hours in human beings. Few human cancer cells reproduce at this rate. In certain kinds of *leukemia*, for example, cancerous white blood cells divide about every 24 hours. In some cancers of the liver, called *hepatomas*, cells divide only once every several days. Moreover, the amount of time required for most cancer cells to pass through the S, G_2, and division phases of their reproductive cycles is approximately the same as for normal cells; only the G_1 period appears to be shortened substantially.

Evidently, cells become cancerous when controls that normally retain them in G_1 periods become defective. Furthermore, the results of several experiments suggest that the rate at which a cancer cell reproduces depends in part on the severity of the defect to these controls. Although the nature of such controls has not been determined, much is known about four general kinds of factors that often trigger conversion of normal cells to cancer cells. These are *heredity*, certain *chemicals, radiation,* and some *viruses*.

A few forms of cancer are related strongly to heredity. One such example is *retinoblastoma,* a cancer affecting the retina of eyes. There is at least a 50 per cent chance that a child of an afflicted parent will develop the disease. Fortunately, this highly malignant cancer is quite rare. If found early, the cancer can be stopped by the removal of the cancerous eye or eyes.

In most cases of heredity-influenced cancer, the disease itself is not inherited. Instead, there exists a tendency to develop certain types of cancer if environmental agents responsible for triggering the disease are encountered. For example, people who have inherited "fair" skin complexions develop skin cancer more frequently than individuals having heavily pigmented skin. But the higher incidence of skin cancer does not result from the inheritance of specific skin cancer genes. People with fair complexions have less pigment to protect skin cells from the cancer-producing effects of solar radiation.

A large number of chemicals are known to cause cancer in experimental animals. Examples include certain *hydrocarbons,* such as those found in cigarette smoke, some oils, tars, plastics, and numerous petroleum products (Table 2). These chemicals apparently produce cancer in at least three different ways. Some appear to induce mutations of genes essential to the regulation of cell reproduction. Others probably alter the function of gene products. For example, some chemicals can alter the catalytic properties of enzymes by inducing changes in their three-dimensional configurations. Still other chemicals activate previously dormant viruses, which then multiply and disrupt controls regulating the reproductive cycles of their host cells. Chemicals injected into mice, for example, have been shown to trigger rapid proliferation of leukemia-causing viruses.

Evidence that certain types of radiation can cause cancer is incontestable. Among these are x-rays, ultraviolet light, and radiation produced by radioactive atoms. An abnormally high incidence of skin cancer exists among farmers, fishermen, and other people who frequently expose their skin to the sun for long periods. Moreover, an extraordinarily high incidence of cancer (primarily leukemia) developed among survivors of the atomic bomb explosions in Japan at the end of World War II.

TABLE 2

A Partial List of Chemicals that Can Cause Cancer (Chemical Carcinogens)

2-acetylaminofluorene	cycasin (from cycad nuts)
aflatoxin B_1	epoxides
aminobiphenyl	ethionine
anthracene	ethyl carbamate
arsenic	lead
asbestos	naphthylamine
azo dyes	nickel compounds
benzidine	nitrosamines
beryllium	oil of sassafras
cadmium	petroleum products
carbon tetrachloride	polycyclic aromatic hydrocarbons
chromium compounds	pyrrolizidine alkaloids
cigarette smoke	soots
cobalt	tars
creosote	

SOURCE: D. M. Prescott, "Cancer: The Misguided Cell," Pegasus, New York, 1973.

Radiation is thought to cause cancer through mutation. For example, the cells of animals exposed to large doses of radiation often contain structurally deformed chromosomes. Many of these cells eventually become cancerous. Furthermore, a piece of one of the smallest human chromosomes (chromosome 22) often is missing from cells of patients suffering from *chronic myelogenous leukemia,* a malignancy originating in bone marrow. This type of cancer appears frequently among people exposed to high doses of radiation.

Viruses trigger several types of cancer in laboratory animals and probably also in people. The milk of nursing human mothers afflicted with breast cancer frequently contains large numbers of viruses that closely resemble those known to cause breast cancer in hamsters and other experimental animals. Viruses also have been linked to certain kinds of leukemia in people.

Viruses are exceedingly small parasites incapable of reproducing outside a living cell (see also Chap. 30). They consist of an inner core of DNA or RNA surrounded by an outer coat composed largely of protein (Fig. 1). Viruses enter cells either as whole units or by injecting their nucleic acid cores through host cell membranes. Many viruses known to cause cancer are of the RNA type. These contain a unique enzyme called *RNA-directed DNA polymerase*. The enzyme is better known by its less formal name, *reverse transcriptase*. When viruses containing reverse transcriptase enter cells, the enzyme produces several DNA copies of the viral RNA by the reverse of the normal transcription process. Most of the DNA then is used as a template in the manufacture of many copies of viral RNA. These eventually become nucleic acid cores of new RNA viruses. However, the viral DNA molecules also can become incorporated into the chromosomes of the host cell. Directly or indirectly, these viral genes disrupt control mechanisms that regulate cell reproduction. As a result, such infected cells often become cancerous and produce large malignant growths. Cancer also can be induced in other ways by certain DNA viruses.

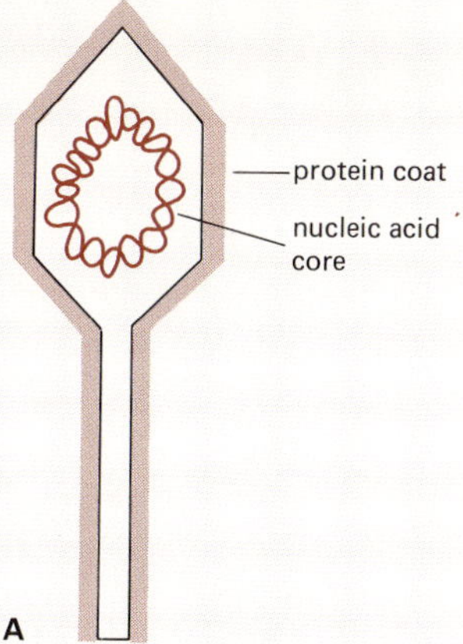

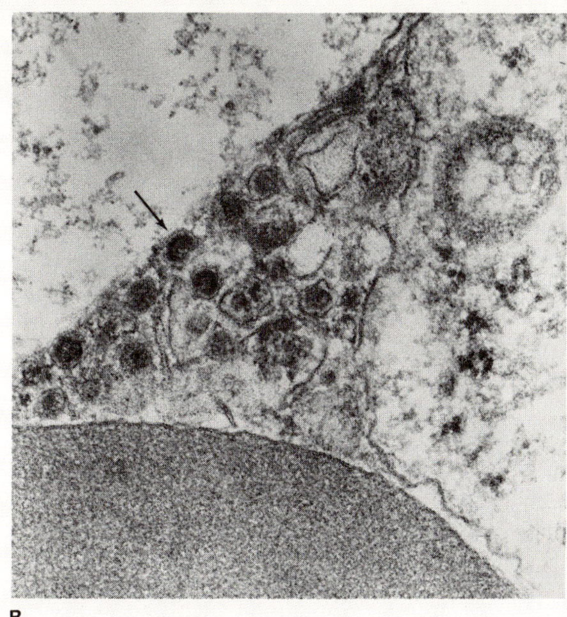

Fig. 1 Viruses and cancer. (A) Viruses largely consist of a nucleic acid "core" surrounded by an outer protein coat (see also Fig. 30.19). Not all viruses have the shape illustrated here, and only a few viruses appear to cause cancer. (B) The dark, circular structure (arrow) is one of several RNA tumor viruses visible in this photograph. Note that all of the viruses are in the cytoplasm of this gibbon spleen cell; none appears in the nucleus (foreground).

Three general methods of treating cancer are now used routinely, often in combination. If cancer cells remain localized, it is frequently possible to remove them all by *surgery,* but if even a single cancer cell remains in the body following surgery, it can soon give rise to large numbers of cells and thus perpetuate the malignancy. Surgery therefore is less effective when a cancer has progressed to a metastatic condition.

Drugs that inhibit DNA synthesis also have been used to treat cancer patients. This form of treatment, called *chemotherapy,* takes advantage of the higher than normal reproductive rate of cancer cells. Most of these drugs selectively kill cells that are reproducing without permanently injuring non-reproducing cells. Unfortunately, none of the drugs discovered kills all cancer cells or discriminates absolutely between cancer cells and normal cells undergoing mitosis.

Cancer also is treatable by *radiation therapy*. Rapidly reproducing cells are more sensitive to radiation-induced damage than cells reproducing slowly or not at all. Radiation is most effective when cancer cells are localized. If such cells are distributed generally throughout the body, radiation therapy usually cannot be used because of the many normal cells that would be destroyed by the treatment.

A fourth method of attacking cancer, *immunotherapy,* is now being developed, improved, and tested. Through their immune response, lymphocytes and certain other cells of the body cooperate in the isolation and destruction of foreign matter, diseased cells included (see Chap. 18). Some experimental evidence indicates that most cancer cells developing in organisms are destroyed rapidly by this "immune system." However, a few cancer cells occasionally escape immunological destruction and proliferate rapidly. Several researchers currently are seeking ways of "teaching" the immune system to be more effective in its attack on cancer cells. If such research efforts are successful, a significant additional step will have been taken in the attempt to control and cure cancer.

Rates of Cell Division

The time required to complete an S period, G_2 period, and a mitotic cell division is approximately the same for all cells of any given organism. For example, most actively reproducing mammalian cells spend about 9 h in the S period, 4 h in the G_2 period, and 1 h in cell division. However, the amount of time cells spend in a G_1 period varies considerably and is influenced by several factors, including nutrition, as noted, and cell specialization. Unspecialized cells generally have fairly rapid rates of cell division. Bone marrow cells, for example, normally divide very rapidly and often spend less than 3 h in G_1. By contrast, mature liver cells reproduce relatively slowly and frequently spend several months in G_1. Moreover, mature nerve cells appear to be "held" in G_1 permanently and do not divide. Destroyed neurons cannot be replaced. Thus, rates of cell division appear to be determined largely by controls that regulate the length of the G_1 period. In general, the more highly specialized a cell, the longer it is "held" in G_1, and vice versa.

The highest rates of cell division normally occur in embryonic stages, the lowest in old age. With few exceptions, cellular reproductive capacity in the adult remains *potentially* as great as in the embryo. This is shown, for example, by the high rates of cell division in wound healing, in regeneration, in cancers and other tumors (see accompanying Biology Highlight), and in *tissue cultures* (Fig. 22.9). Such cultures are prepared by separating groups of cells from an organism and growing them in artificial nutrient solutions. Isolated cells or cell groups then are found to reproduce faster than if they had remained within an organism. Conceivably, therefore, cell reproduction in intact organisms may be slower mainly because the cells are *not* isolated as in a tissue culture. Instead, they are part of a larger organization in which their reproductive potential is held in check.

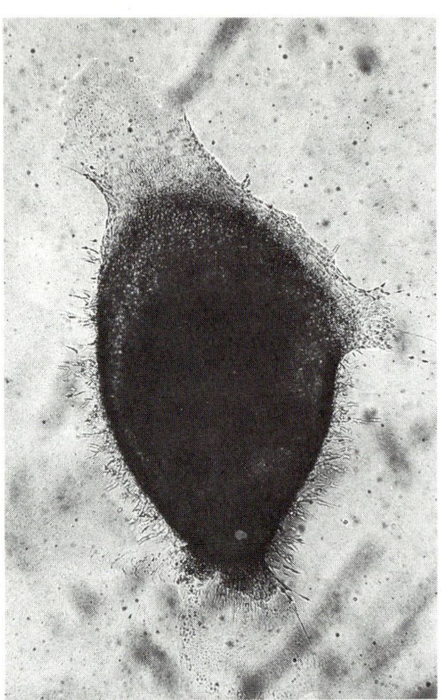

Fig. 22.9 Tissue culture. Embryonic mouse tissue produces epithelial masses at higher growth rates than it would have in the intact embryo. (*Courtesy of Clifford Grobstein: "13th Growth Symposium," Princeton, Princeton, N.J., 1954.*)

ORGANISMIC REPRODUCTION

The net result of cell division is the formation of two cells that match each other and the parent cell precisely in their gene contents and that contain approximately equal amounts and types of all other components. In unicellular organisms, cell division is equivalent to reproduction of the whole organism (see Chaps. 30 and 31). Daughter cells generally separate, but in some forms they continue to stick together and form *colonies* (see Chap. 31).

In multicellular types, cell division either contributes to *cell replacement,* as in regeneration and wound healing, or adds to *cell number.* The result is the growth of tissues and organs. A multicellular organism can therefore grow either by molecular reproduction and increase in cell size, or by cellular reproduction and increase in cell number, or both. After periods of growth by molecular and cellular reproduction, the whole multicellular organism may reproduce. This process generally includes at least two steps. First, a *reproductive unit* separates from the parent organism. Second, a duplicate organism forms from the reproductive unit through *development.*

Vegetative Reproduction

In all cases of *vegetative reproduction,* the reproductive unit consists of the whole or a substantial portion of the parent organism. In unicellular types, for example, the whole adult cell is the reproductive unit, and reproduction is accomplished by cell division.

Among multicellular organisms, the reproductive unit is a fairly large part of the parent, and it usually arises from parental regions that are not specialized for reproduction; almost *any* portion of the parent may cease its usual functions and become part of a vegetative reproductive unit. For example, multicellular forms often propagate by *budding*, the outgrowth of one or more offspring from the surface of a parent organism (Fig. 22.10). This process is exemplified by many plants and by animals such as sponges and hydras. In other cases, multiplication may take place by *fragmentation*, a spontaneous splitting or breaking of a parent organism into two or more parts (Fig. 22.11). This occurs, for example, in many filamentous algae, in some bryophytes, and in animals such as sea anemones and numerous types of worms. Each separated part of the parent then develops as a whole adult.

Quite similar to fragmentation is *regenerative*

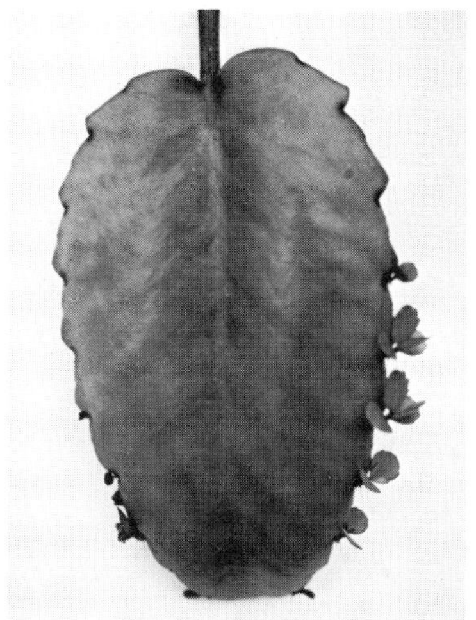

A

B

C

Fig. 22.10 Vegetative reproduction. (A) Budding. A leaf of *Kalanchoë,* with small budded plants developing along the leaf margins. (B) Fragmentation. A sea anemone fragments lengthwise as two offspring organisms. (C) Regenerative reproduction. An arm of a starfish regenerates all missing parts and becomes a whole animal.

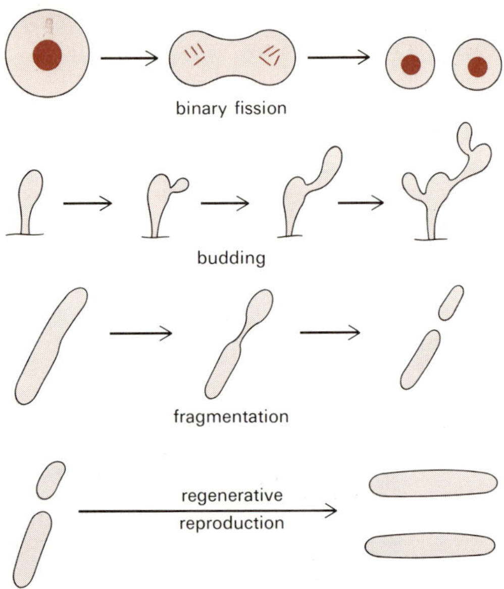

Fig. 22.11 **Vegetative reproduction.** Summary of the main variants.

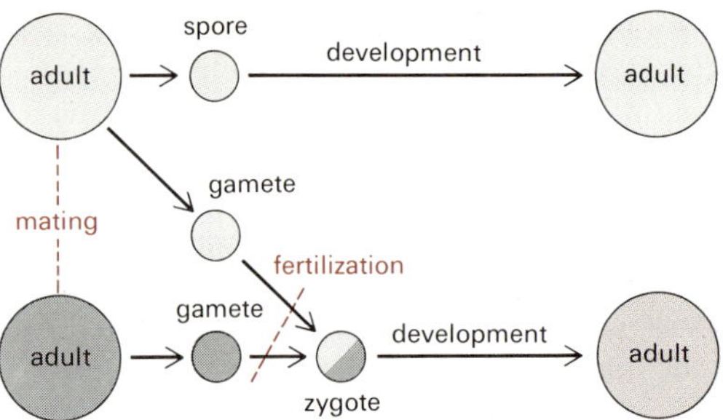

Fig. 22.12 Reproductive cells. (Top) Many organisms produce spores, reproductive cells capable of developing by themselves. (Bottom) Almost all organisms also produce sex cells, or gametes, that must fuse in fertilization and form a zygote before development can occur.

reproduction, in which a parent organism splits, not spontaneously, but as a result of injury by external agents (see Fig. 22.11). For example, almost any piece of a plant, a few segments of an earthworm, an arm of a starfish, a chunk of tissue from a hydra or a sponge, each is an effective reproductive unit that develops as a whole offspring. The parent organisms that lose such sections of their bodies often regenerate the missing parts.

The main adaptive advantage of vegetative reproduction is that the process can be carried out whenever environmental conditions are favorable and food supplies are ample. Moreover, special manufacturing processes are not required for the formation of reproductive units. Such processes must accompany manufacture of the *specialized* reproductive units considered next.

Reproductive Cells

The smallest parental unit that possesses the genetic information and the operating equipment representative of the whole organism is a single cell. Accordingly, the minimum unit for the construction of such an organism should be one cell. This is actually the universal case. Regardless of whether or not it can also reproduce vegetatively, every multicellular organism is capable of reproducing through single *reproductive cells.* All such cells are more or less specialized for reproduction, and in most cases they are formed in specialized parental reproductive tissues or organs.

Spores

According to their later fate, reproductive cells are of two general types (Fig. 22.12). One includes cells which, like vegetative reproductive units, can develop into adults *directly*. Such cells are *spores.* Their chief advantage is that they represent an excellent device for geographic dispersal. In water, a spore cell may be equipped with flagella and may swim to new territories. On land, spores may be protected against drying out by thick walls and can be distributed widely by wind and animals. As might be expected, therefore, spores are formed mainly by organisms that cannot disperse by locomotion—primarily plants and stationary protists.

Gametes

Reproductive cells of the second general type *cannot* develop as adults directly. Instead they must first undergo a *sexual process,* in which two of them fuse. Such cells are *sex cells,* or *gametes.* In most cases male gametes are distinct *sperms,* and female gametes are distinct *eggs.* A *mating* process makes possible the pairwise fusion, or *fertilization,* and the fusion product is a *zygote.* Development of gametes into adults cannot normally occur until fertilization has taken place. This form of reproduction can be termed *gametic reproduction.*

Gametic reproduction entails serious disadvantages. The process depends on chance, for gametes must meet and often they simply do not. Meeting requires locomotion, moreover, but neither eggs nor many organisms can move. Above all, gametic reproduction requires a water medium. In air, gametes would dry out quickly unless they had evaporation-resistant shells. But if two gametes were so encapsulated, they could then not fuse together. As will become apparent, terrestrial organisms actually can circumvent this dilemma only by means of special adaptations.

However, all these various disadvantages are relatively minor compared to the one vital advantage offered by gametes. This advantage is a result of sex.

SEX

Sex and reproduction are distinct processes. As already noted, sex involves fusion of male and female gametes. As a result of this fusion, the genes of two individuals are combined within the nucleus of a single cell, the zygote. Reproduction occurs when reproductive units develop as adults. This distinction is revealed most clearly in many Protista and some algal plants, where sex and reproduction do not occur together. A good example is *Spirogyra,* a filamentous green alga forming dense growths in freshwater ponds. Throughout spring, summer, and early fall, the cells reproduce vegetatively by mitotic division and add to the length of the filament. Pieces of the alga can break off and form new individuals elsewhere. Later in the fall two cells from two filaments lying side by side may mate through *conjugation;* an interconnecting bridge develops between the two cells. The contents of one cell then move in amoeboid fashion through the bridge to the other cell, and the two cells fuse (Fig. 22.13).

Such cellular fusion, or *syngamy,* is a sexual process. All unmated nonconjugated cells die when autumn temperatures fall, but the fused double cell, or zygote, secretes a heavy wall and lives through the winter. When temperatures begin to rise again the following spring, the cyst wall breaks open and a new *Spirogyra* filament develops from the surviving zygote.

Thus, the sexual process is fundamentally quite distinct from reproduction—*Spirogyra* does not increase in numbers through sex. In all other organisms sex and reproduction are equally distinct, even though in most cases the two processes do occur together. Moreover, sexual activity tends to take place particulary during periods of environmental stress.

Just how are sexual processes effective against conditions of stress? Events in *Spirogyra* supply the general answer: every cell resulting from the sexual process possesses the genes of *both* parental cells. Basically, therefore, sex may be defined as the accumulation within a single cell of genes derived from two relatively unrelated cells. One method of achieving this is cell fusion, as in *Spirogyra* and indeed in most organisms.

Sex evidently counteracts stress conditions on the principle of "two are better than one." If the self-perpetuating powers of two relatively unrelated parent organisms are joined through union of their genes, the offspring produced later may acquire a greater survival potential than that of either parent alone (Fig. 22.14). Moreover, a sexual pooling of genes often leads to a still poorly understood "rejuvenation" in the offspring, on a biochemical, metabolic level. For example, if in certain protozoa or fungi sex is experimentally prevented during many successive vegetative generations, the vigor of the line eventually declines. The organisms ultimately die, even under optimal environmental conditions. Genetic malfunctions and imbalances have been found to accumulate in many aged vegetative generations, and only a genetic restoration through sex can then save the line from dying out.

Vegetative reproduction thus is a "conservative" process, which faithfully passes on parental characteristics unchanged. As long as the external and internal environments remain favorable, succeeding generations survive as well as preceding ones. Gametic reproduction by contrast, is a "liberalizing" process, which can make possible survival under new or changed conditions. By combining the genes of two parents sex introduces *genetic change* in the later offspring. And to the extent that such change is advantageous for survival in new environments or under new conditions, sex has *adaptive* value. That is the key point. Sex is one of the chief processes of adaptation; it is *not* a process of reproduction.

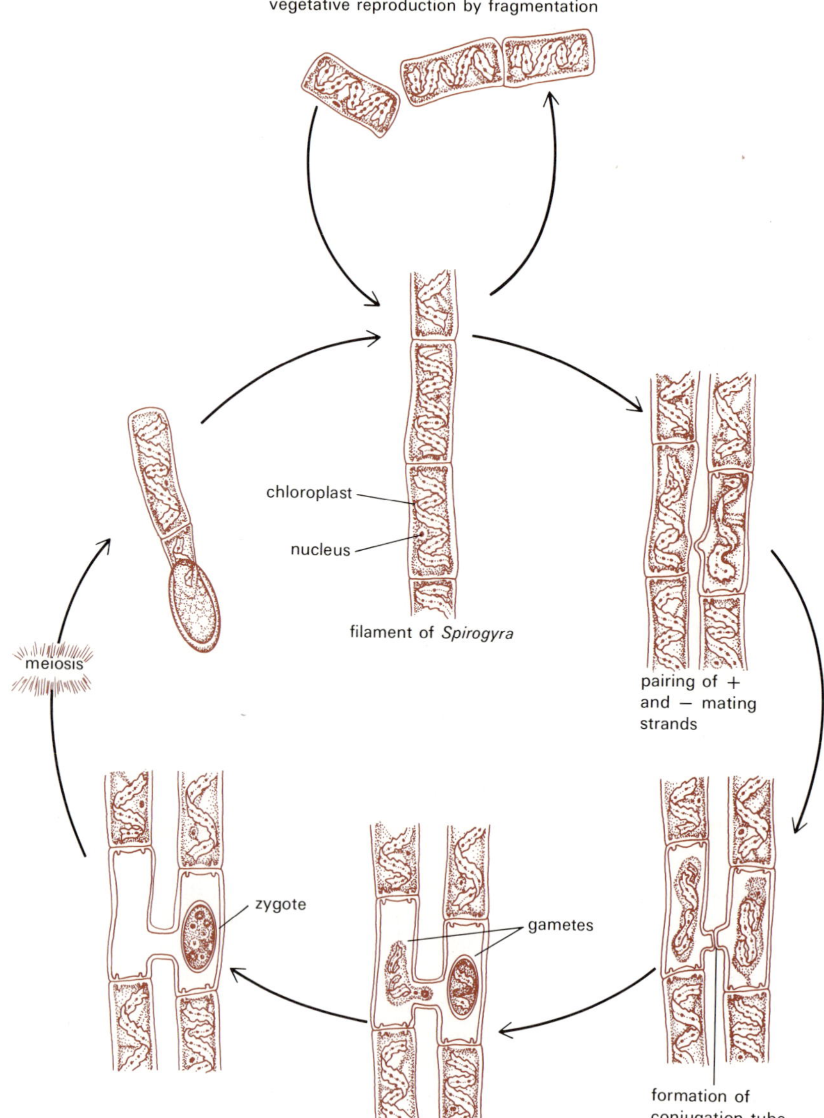

Fig. 22.13 Spirogyra life cycle. The green alga *Spirogyra* consists of filamentous strands of rectangular cells (see also Fig. 22.16). The alga can reproduce vegetatively by fragmentation or gametically by conjugation. Mature *Spirogyra* cells arise from zygotes through meiosis, a sequence of special nuclear divisions described in this chapter.

In *Spirogyra* and numerous other protists, all gametes, though functionally of two different types, are structurally alike (*isogamy*). In another group of protists, the gametes of a species are visibly of two different types; one kind is distinctly smaller than the other, but in other structural respects they are again alike (*anisogamy*). Still other protists, as well as all plants and animals, exhibit *oögamy*, a special form of anisogamy: one gamete type is flagellate and small, the other is nonmotile (or amoeboid) and large. The small types are *sperms*, the large types, *eggs* (Fig. 22.15).

If the two gamete types are produced in different individuals, as is the case in many protists, numerous plants, and most animals, the sexes are said to be *separate*. If such separately sexed organisms exhibit isogamy or anisogamy, the terms "male" and "female" are not strictly applicable.

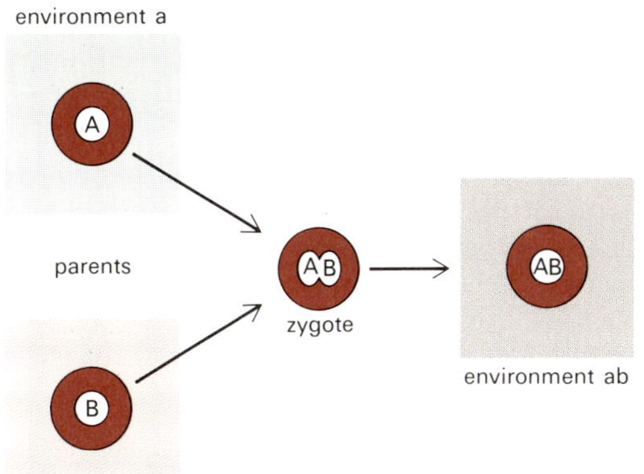

Fig. 22.14 Sex and stress. a and b represent two different environments containing two genetically different parents. A and B symbolize their genes. Through sex, the offspring (right) acquires the genes of both parents, hence, also the ability to live in either environment a or b.

Thus, filaments of *Spirogyra,* which are isogamous, are neither male nor female. Instead the two sex types, or *mating types,* are customarily identified by distinguishing symbols such as + and − (Fig. 22.16 and see Fig. 22.13).

True male and female sexes are recognized only in cases of oögamy, where distinct sperms and eggs are produced. Such organisms often exhibit a variety of other sex differences, too. For example, sperms and eggs are usually produced in differently constructed sex organs. Among plants, sperms are formed in *antheridia,* eggs in *archegonia.* Among animals, sperms arise in *testes,* eggs in *ovaries.* Male and female sex organs frequently are part of differently structured reproductive systems, and numerous secondary sex characteristics often provide external distinctions as well. Thus where the sexes are separate the degrees of sex distinction can vary considerably. At one extreme are the isogamous protists, where visible differences between sex types are zero. At the other extreme are the advanced plants and animals, in which nearly every part of the body, even every cell, can exhibit characteristics of maleness or femaleness.

In numerous organisms both gamete types are produced in the same individual. Known as *hermaphroditism,* this condition is believed to be more primitive than that of separate sexes; hermaphroditism could have evolved to separate sexuality by suppression of either the male or the female potential in different individuals. For example, all vertebrates have both potentials in the embryonic state, but only one potential is realized in a given individual.

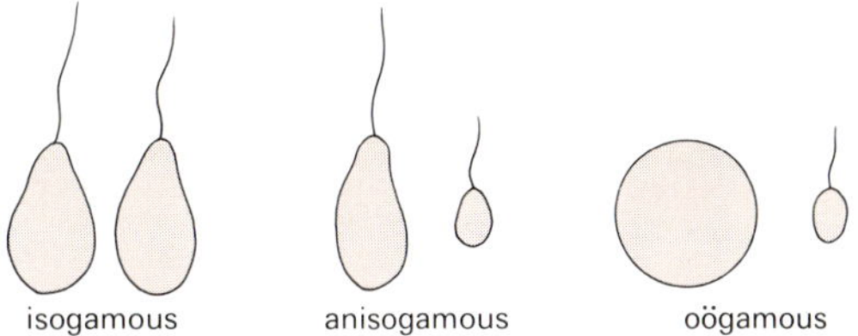

Fig. 22.15 Gamete types. In the isogamous and anisogamous pattern, both gamete types are motile. In the oögamous pattern, the large gamete is a nonmotile egg, the small gamete, a motile sperm.

In most cases hermaphroditism appears to be a direct adaptation to ways of life that offer only limited opportunities for geographic dispersal, as in sluggish, sessile, and parasitic forms. Since every hermaphrodite can function both as a "male" and a "female," a mating of two individuals often is not

Fig. 22.16 Mating types. In the Spirogyra filaments shown, all cells in one filament have the same sexual properties; they are either migrating sexual partners or stationary partners that receive cells from a neighboring filament (and thus form oval encased zygotes, as shown).

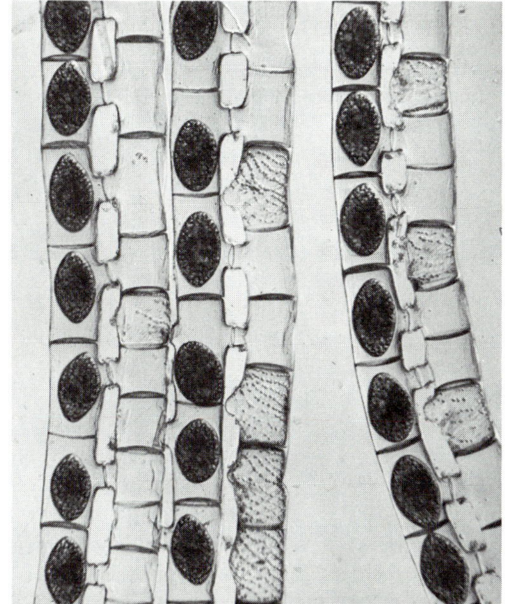

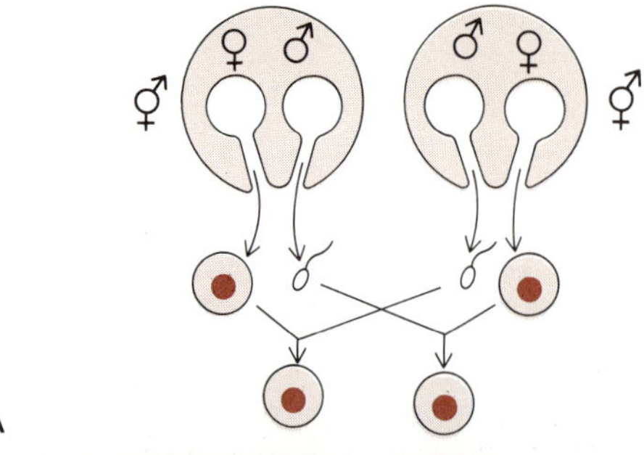

A

B

Fig. 22.17 Hermaphrodites. (A) The symbols ♀ and ♂ identify female and male reproductive systems, respectively. The symbols ⚥ identify whole hermaphroditic organisms. The figure illustrates the fertilization pattern in cross-fertilizing hermaphrodites. If sperms fertilize eggs from the same organism, the pattern is self-fertilizing. (B) Copulation of the land snails *Helix,* which are cross-fertilizing hermaphrodites.

even required and *self-fertilization* can take place. But most hermaphrodites carry out mutual *cross-fertilization,* such that two mating partners fertilize each other (Fig. 22.17).

The general adaptive advantage of hermaphroditism is that potentially fewer reproductive cells are wasted: sperms from one individual can meet eggs in *any* other individual, for every hermaphrodite produces eggs. In separately sexed types, by contrast, many sperms are wasted through chance misdistribution to the wrong sex. Similarly, if cross-fertilizing hermaphrodites are capable of some locomotion, like land snails or earthworms, fertilization becomes possible whenever *any* two individuals meet. Sluggish individuals do not meet very often, yet every such meeting can result in fertilization.

In any organism, separately sexed or hermaphroditic, it often happens that gametes fail to find compatible partners. Most of such unsuccessful gametes disintegrate very soon, but in exceptional cases single gametes can begin to develop and form normal adults. This phenomenon is *parthenogenesis,* "virginal development" of a gamete *without* fertilization. In many protists a gamete of either type can develop parthenogenetically. In oögamous organisms only eggs are sometimes capable of developing in this way. Thus, *natural* parthenogenesis occurs in, for example, rotifers, bees and other social insects (see Chap. 21), and sporadically also in birds such as turkeys and chickens. In some species *artificial* parthenogenesis can be induced by experimental means. For example, a frog egg can be made to develop before it has become fertilized by pricking its surface with a needle (in conjunction with other treatments). The puncture simulates the entrance of a sperm, and development then begins. It may be noted that a parthenogenetic gamete is functionally indistinguishable from a *spore;* both are single reproductive cells able to develop directly into adults.

MEIOSIS AND LIFE CYCLES

Meiosis

One consequence of every sexual process is that a zygote formed from two gametes has twice as many chromosomes as a single gamete. An adult organism developing from such a zygote would consist of cells having a doubled chromosome number. If the next generation is again produced sexually, the chromosome number would quadruple, and this process of progressive doubling would continue indefinitely through successive generations.

Such events do not happen, and chromosome numbers stay constant from one life cycle to the next. The constancy is maintained by a series of special nuclear divisions known as *meiosis.* This process occurs in every life cycle that includes sex—in other words, more or less universally. In many cases meiosis is accompanied by cytoplasmic divisions, and both events are then referred to col-

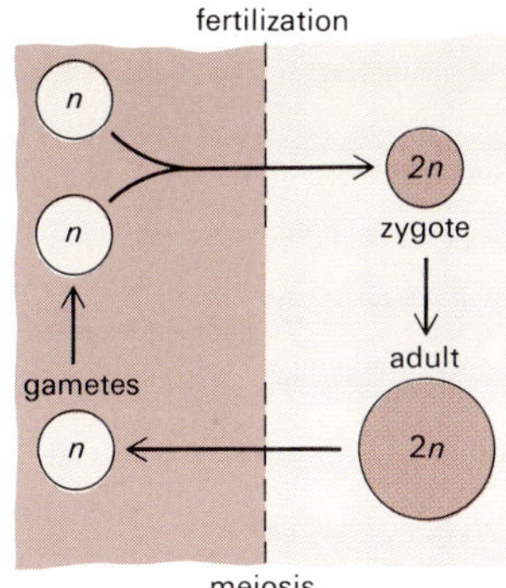

Fig. 22.18 Meiosis, fertilization, and chromosome numbers. Fertilization produces cells that each contain a double (2n) set of chromosomes; meiosis yields cells that each contain a single (n) set of chromosomes.

lectively as *meiotic cell divisions.* It is the function of meiosis to counteract the chromosome-doubling effect of fertilization by reducing a doubled chromosome number to half. The unreduced doubled chromosome number, before meiosis, is called the *diploid* number, symbolized as $2n$; the reduced number, after meiosis, is the *haploid* number, symbolized as n (Fig. 22.18).

This fundamental relationship between fertilization and meiosis is also illustrated in Fig. 22.19A, depicting movements of chromosomes during the first meiotic division. The diploid cell at the top of the figure contains four chromosomes, each composed of two chromatids joined at a centromere. This cell is entering the initial stages of meiosis. Note that the four chromosomes consist of two structurally identical pairs, exemplifying a universal feature of diploid cells: they all contain two *homologous* sets of chromosomes.

Meiosis has many features in common with mitosis. For example, each meiotic division passes through prophase, metaphase, anaphase, and telophase, as in mitosis. Moreover, spindles form and other nonchromosomal events are as in mitotic divisions. The critical difference between meiosis and mitosis occurs during prophase of the *first* meiotic division. In mitosis, all chromosomes, each composed of two chromatids, migrate to the metaphase plate, where all the centromeres line up in the same plane. In the first meiotic division, homologous chromosomes physically associate as pairs during prophase. The paired chromosomes then migrate to the metaphase plate, and each set of chromosomes assembles along an identical plane. As a result, every chromosome positioned along one plane lies parallel to its homolog (see Fig. 22.19). The metaphase plate is therefore made up of paired homologous chromosomes lying side by side.

During anaphase, each set of homologs migrates to a spindle pole—one set to one pole, the other to the opposite pole. The first meiotic division thus produces two cells, each with a single haploid set of chromosomes. In the metaphase of the second meiotic division, the haploid set of chromosomes lines up in the same plane. Each of these chromosomes contains two chromatids, which split and migrate as daughter chromosomes to each of the spindle poles during anaphase. Thus, movements of chromosomes during the second meiotic division are virtually identical to those occurring during mitosis.

At the end of meiosis as a whole, therefore, four cells are therefore present, each with a haploid set of daughter chromosomes. In many species, as for example in all animals, these cells mature as gametes. Zygotes formed from the union of two gametes inherit two sets of chromosomes, one from each gamete. In this way, fertilization produces a zygote with a diploid chromosome number (Fig. 22.20 and see Fig. 22.18). Each of the single daughter chromosomes then becomes duplicated in the zygote during the S period of interphase. Once this occurs, the zygotes of some species divide mitotically, producing two diploid cells that may divide again and again. Multicellular diploid organisms result from such divisions. Among other species, the zygote immediately undergoes meiosis, producing haploid cells. Thus, organisms differ according to when and where meiosis occurs in the life cycle.

In the unicellular alga *Chlamydomonas,* for example, meiosis takes place right after fertilization (Fig. 22.21). This organism, which can also reproduce vegetatively, leads a solitary existence except when it undergoes gametic reproduction. At this time, cells of different mating strains fuse with each other. Individuals of both mating types are identical in size and structure and therefore are designated simply as plus and minus strains, as in *Spirogyra.* Because each unicellular organism is haploid, the fused cell constitutes a diploid zygote. After losing its flagella and sinking to the bottom of

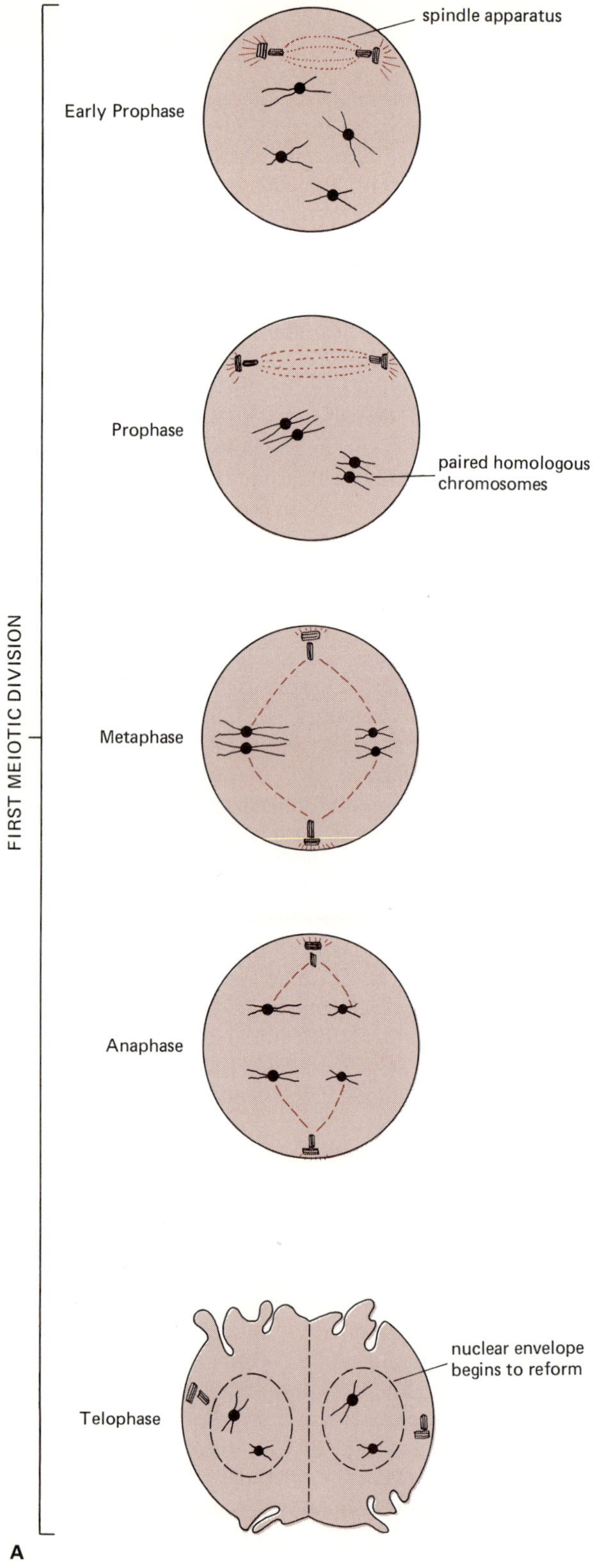

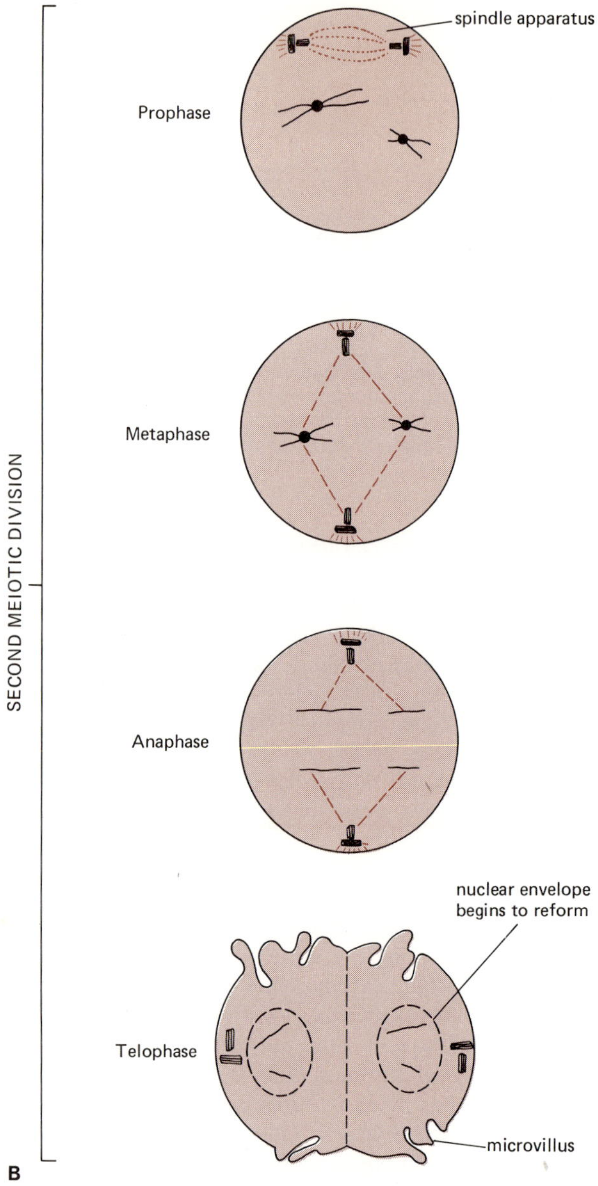

FIRST MEIOTIC DIVISION

spindle apparatus

Early Prophase

Prophase

paired homologous chromosomes

Metaphase

Anaphase

Telophase

nuclear envelope begins to reform

A

SECOND MEIOTIC DIVISION

spindle apparatus

Prophase

Metaphase

Anaphase

nuclear envelope begins to reform

Telophase

microvillus

B

Fig. 22.19 Meiosis. (A) Meiosis I. During the first meiotic division, the total number of chromosomes is reduced by one-half. Each of the daughter cells produced by this division contains one set of chromosomes. (B) Meiosis II. The fate of one of the daughter cells produced in (A) is illustrated. During prophase, each chromosome of the single set migrates to the metaphase plate. Separation of the chromatids marks the onset of anaphase. Each of the daughter cells resulting from this division develops as a gamete.

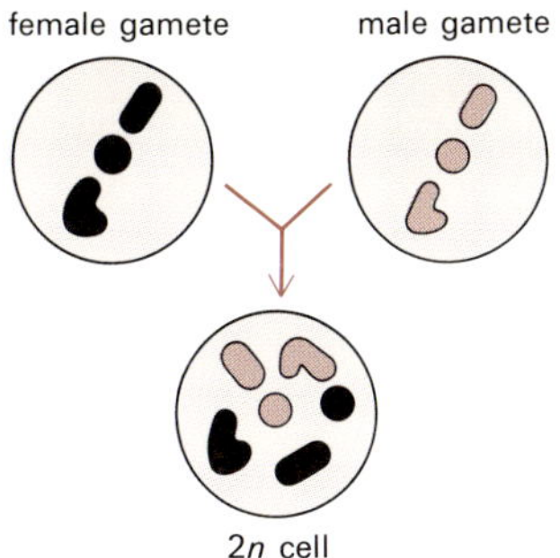

Fig. 22.20 Genetic effects of fertilization. A diploid cell contains a double (2n) set of chromosomes; one set derived from the male gamete, the other from the female gamete.

its freshwater habitat, the zygote develops a thick outer coat that protects the cell, particularly during periods of drought or cold. Meiosis occurs inside the protective coat, eventually giving rise to four haploid cells. Each of the cells may divide mitotically, producing many new haploid *Chlamydomonas* cells, or each may enter a new sexual cycle.

Life Cycles

In *Chlamydomonas*, the four haploid cells resulting from meiosis are four new adult organisms. All available evidence suggests that such a life cycle, in which the adults are haploid, represents a primitive condition. It is reasonable to suppose that very early ancestral cells were similarly haploid, each possessing only a single complete set of genes. Whenever a sexual process took place, a diploid zygote resulted from fertilization, and meiosis then must have been a likely ensuing event: the chromosome-doubling process of fertilization must have been a stimulus to which the chromosome-reducing process of meiosis was the rapidly following response.

A life cycle characterized in this way by haploid adults and meiosis in the zygote stage (or "zygotic" meiosis), is known as a *haplontic* life cycle (Fig. 22.22). It occurs in all Monera (insofar as sex is known among these organisms), in all primitive and many advanced groups of algae, and in many fungi. Many of these haplontic groups are capable of producing spores, and such cells are formed at

Fig. 22.21 Chlamydomonas life cycle. Haploid adult cells are of two mating strains, + and −. Zygotes result when cells of opposite mating types fuse. Zygotes undergo meiosis, producing new mature haploid cells. Note the similarity of this life cycle with that of *Spirogyra* (Fig. 22.13). Both organisms exhibit haplontic life cycles (Fig. 22.22).

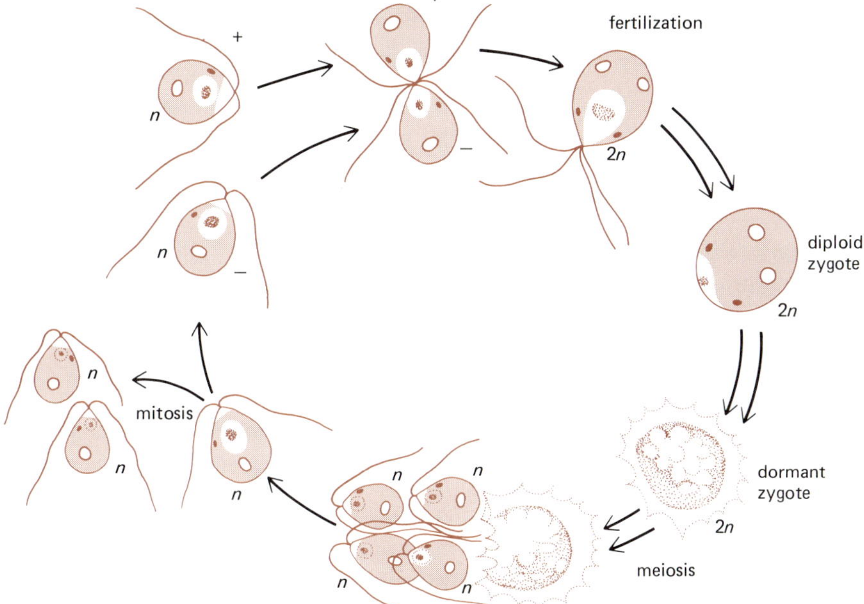

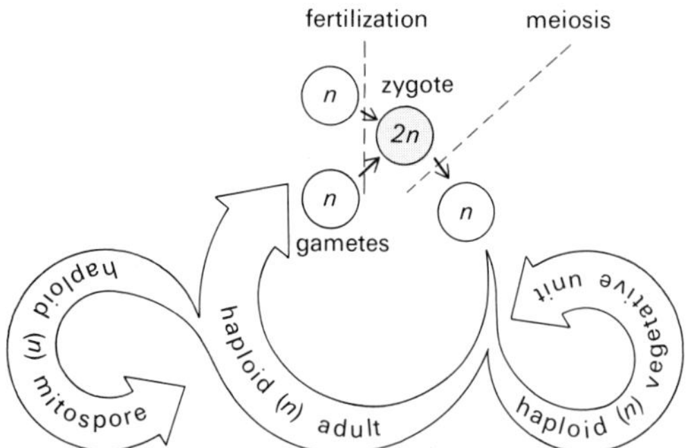

Fig. 22.22 **The haplontic life cycle.** The zygote is the only diploid stage. Since spores are formed mitotically, they can be called mitospores.

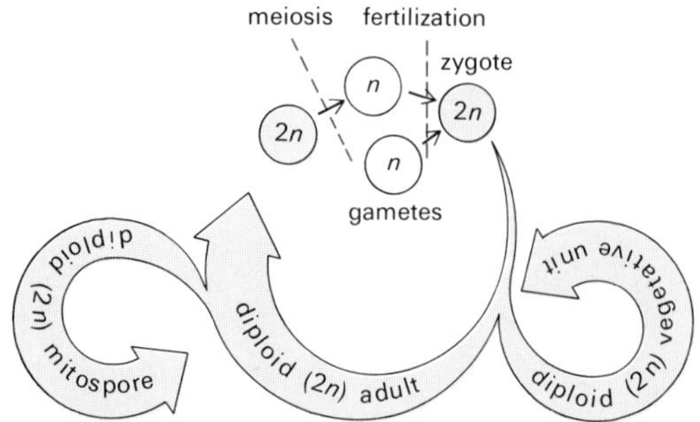

Fig. 22.23 **The diplontic life cycle.** Mature gametes represent the only haploid stage.

some point in the life cycle between one fertilization and the next. The method of spore formation is mitotic division and, like the adults that produce them, the spores are haploid (*mitospores*).

Haplontic patterns have probably given rise to all other types of life cycle. With regard to the timing of meiosis, the points at which the process possibly *could* occur can be guessed readily. Like sex, meiosis is a cellular process, and it can therefore take place only at a stage when the life cycle passes through a unicellular phase. The zygote represents such a phase. But even a multicellular organism can pass through unicellular stages on two other occasions, at the stage of the *gamete* and at the stage of the *spore.* Meiosis therefore might occur at either of these points, and in many organisms it does.

In human beings, for example, meiosis takes place during the formation of gametes. Within the sex organs of the adult, diploid gamete-producing cells mature as sperms and eggs. Meiosis occurs as part of this maturation process, and mature gametes thus are haploid, each with 23 chromosomes. These gametes then give rise to a diploid zygote. But now, as the zygote divides and develops as a mature human being, the cells *remain* diploid. The whole human adult becomes diploid in this fashion, including the sex organs it eventually forms. Gamete-producing cells therefore are diploid as well, and meiosis occurs again during their maturation.

Such a cycle, characterized by diploid adults and meiosis during gamete formation, is called a *diplontic* life cycle (Fig. 22.23). The only haploid stage in it is the mature gamete itself; the pattern here is almost the reverse of a haplontic cycle. Diplontic cycles occur not only in people but also in all other animals, in various advanced groups of algae, in some fungi, and in most protozoa. Some of these organisms form spores, and such cells are produced by the diploid adult. The method of spore formation is again mitotic division; hence mature spores are diploid as well.

The evolutionary transition from haplontic to diplontic cycles probably took place through a postponement of meiosis. Thus, diploid adults will form if meiosis is delayed from the zygote stage, the very start of the life cycle, to the gamete-forming stage, the very end of the life cycle. Such a postponement is advantageous adaptively, for in a diploid adult each gene in each cell is represented not just once but twice. As a result, the genetic stability of the organism is increased. For even if one gene of a pair changes—by mutation, for example—the other gene still preserves the original genetic code. Evidently, this stabilizing effect of the diploid state has been of sufficient adaptive significance to make diplontic life cycles exceedingly common.

The third possible time of meiosis is the stage of spore production. In this case fertilization produces a diploid zygote, and the developing adult remains diploid. In due course the adult develops a spore-forming structure in which diploid cells give rise to spores. Meiosis occurs during this process, and mature spores are therefore haploid. Since their production includes meiosis, they are called *meiospores*. A haploid meiospore eventually develops into a new *haploid* adult. This adult later manufactures haploid gametes, and these participate in fertilization. A new life cycle then begins with the resulting diploid zygote.

Because meiosis here occurs during spore formation, such a life cycle is split up into two generations, each represented by a separate adult. The diploid zygote gives rise to a diploid adult, and since this adult later produces meiospores it is called the *sporophyte generation*. The haploid meiospore then gives rise to a haploid adult, and since this adult later produces gametes, it is called the *gametophyte generation*.

Cycles of this sort, characterized by meiosis during spore formation and by an *alternation of generations*, are known as *diplohaplontic* life cycles (Fig. 22.24). They are exceedingly widespread, occurring in numerous algae, many fungi, all slime molds, and in all plants. Such cycles again are derived from the haplontic type by a postponement of meiosis, in this case from the zygote to the spore-producing stage. As might be expected, diplohaplontic cycles combine the adaptive advantages of haplontic and diplontic ones. The diploid sporophytes are genetically relatively stable, but the haploid gametophytes are genetically quite plastic; traits of gametophytes change fairly readily by mutation, hence they may evolve and adapt to changing environments comparatively rapidly.

Fig. 22.24 The diplohaplontic life cycle. Diploid sporophyte and haploid gametophyte adults form alternating generations in a single life cycle. Spores produced by the sporophyte have undergone meiosis, hence they are often called meiospores. In many cases mitospores are formed as well, diploid ones by sporophytes, haploid ones by gametophytes.

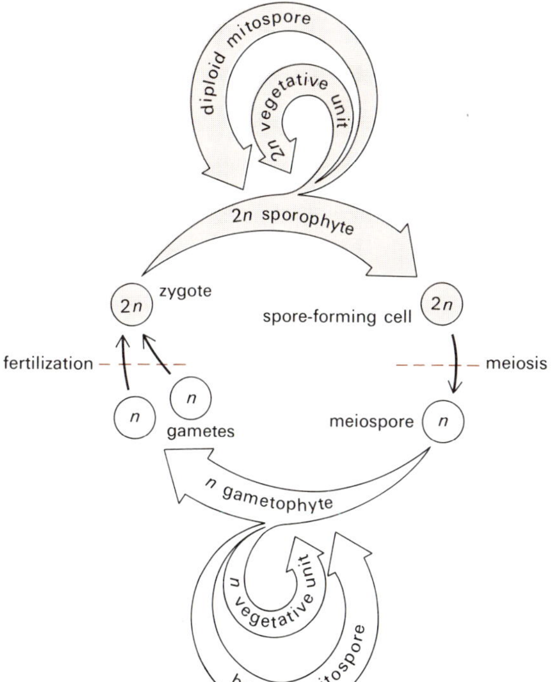

Many diplohaplontic organisms produce not only meiospores but also other spore types during either the sporophyte or the gametophyte generation or both. These and other spore types are formed by mitotic division. If a sporophyte manufactures such spores, they will be diploid *mitospores*, which grow into new diploid sporophyte adults. Numerous repeat generations of sporophytes can develop in this way, and the diploid phase of the life cycle ends only when haploid meiospores are formed. If a gametophyte manufactures spores, they will be haploid mitospores and will grow into new gametophyte adults. Here again many repeat generations can succeed one another, and the haploid part of the life cycle will terminate only with gamete formation and subsequent fertilization.

DEVELOPMENTAL PROCESSES

Development comprises all events that form single whole organisms and their parts. The course of development varies considerably according to whether the starting point is a zygote or some other unit—spore, vegetative body, or regenerating fragment. As already indicated earlier, zygotic development usually passes through several distinct phases: fertilization, embryonic period, in animals typically also a larval period, and then adulthood (see also Chap. 24). In sharp contrast, all other forms of development are exceedingly direct. In the development of spores or vegetative units of any type there is no sex, hence no fertilization or embryo. Instead, the reproductive unit becomes an adult in a smoothly continuous, single developmental sequence (Fig. 22.25).

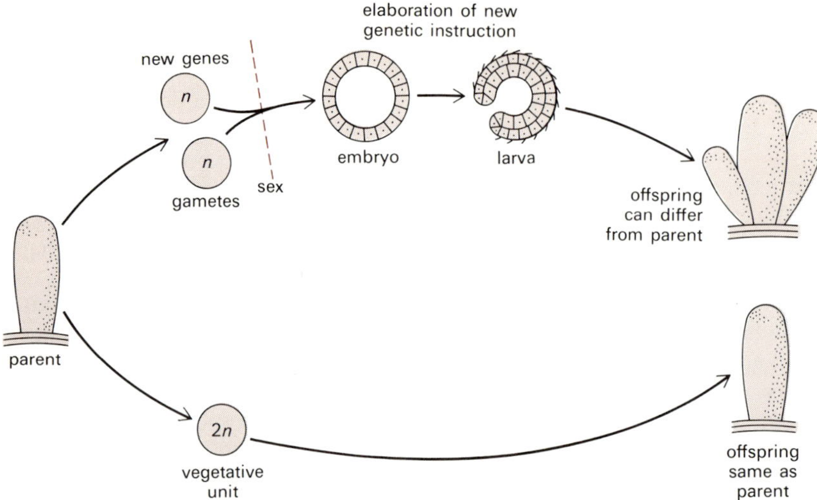

Fig. 22.25 Sexual and asexual development. In sexual development (top) new genetic instructions are introduced in the zygote by the gametes, and later these instructions are elaborated in the embryo and the larva. Hence the mature offspring can differ to greater or lesser extent from the parent. In asexual development (bottom) new genetic instructions are not introduced, and the offspring therefore resembles the parent fully.

This marked difference between sexual and asexual patterns of development is undoubtedly a result of the presence or absence of the sexual process itself. Unlike a spore or a vegetative body, a zygote is more than simply a reproductive unit; it is also the product of sex and therefore an *adaptive* device. Through fertilization the zygote acquires new genes, which often endow the future offspring with new, better-adapted traits. However, before any new traits can actually be displayed they must be *developed* during the transition from zygote to adult. Embryonic and larval periods appear to be the outcome. These stages provide the means and the necessary time for translating genetic instructions acquired sexually by the zygote into adaptively improved traits of the adult. Vegetative units do not acquire new genetic instructions through sex, and equivalent developmental processes for executing such instructions are therefore not needed. Correspondingly, embryos are absent here.

Moreover, to the extent that the genetic instructions contained in a zygote are different from those received by earlier generations of zygotes, embryos permit introduction of *evolutionary* changes into developmental histories. Indeed, evolutionary change is achieved not by alteration of already developed, fully differentiated adults, but primarily by modifications of zygotes and embryos. These incompletely developed stages are still plastic and unformed enough to be capable of executing new genetic instructions.

Transformation of a vegetative unit, spore, or zygote into a complex multicellular organism is brought about by three broad groups of integrated processes, *morphogenesis, determination,* and *differentiation.*

Morphogenesis

The process through which adult body form is attained during development is called *morphogenesis.* Two subcomponent processes contribute to morphogenesis. The first is increase in size, or *growth.* It can occur through an increase in the number of parts, the size of parts, the spacing between parts, or any combination of these. Molecular synthesis is the basic prerequisite for growth at any other level; organisms grow from their molecules on up. On the cellular level, the most significant growth process is usually increase in cell number by mitotic division. Fully grown organisms differ from undeveloped ones mostly in cell number, not in cell size or spacing.

Growth of any kind generally does not proceed randomly in all directions. How does it happen, for example, that net growth stops just when the nose, the brain, the root, the leaf, and all other body parts are of the "right" proportional size and shape? Or that the different parts of the fully grown adult *retain* correct proportions and shapes? Or that, when the limb of a salamander is cut off, regenerative growth stops just when the new limb has the size and the shape of the original one? Thus, apart from growth as such, *establishment of body form* is a second component of morphogenesis.

The main aspects of form are *polarity* and *symmetry*. If they are given, a great deal about the general appearance of an object is already specified. A structure is polarized if one of its three dimensions of space is in some way dominant. For example, the head-tail axis in most animals is longer than the other two. This is the chief axis around which the whole animal is organized, and such organisms are said to be polarized longitudinally. Symmetry indicates the degree of mirror-image regularity. A structure can be symmetrical in three, two, one, or in no dimensions and thus it can be spherical, radial, bilateral, or asymmetrical.

Each organism exhibits a certain polarity and a certain symmetry. These features are the earliest and most permanent expressions of form that appear during the development of any plant or animal. Many traits of an organism can be changed by experimental means, but its original polarity and symmetry can rarely be changed.

One form-producing process is *differential growth*. Here the amounts and rates of growth are unequal in different body parts, or they differ in different directions (Fig. 22.26). The lens of the vertebrate eye, for example, results from a patch of epidermal cells whose rate of division exceeds that of surrounding cells. Because of this unequal growth, a central mound of tissue is produced toward the interior, which later specializes as a lens (see also Chap. 24).

Another form-producing process is *form-regulating movement*, which produces shifts and outright migrations of growing parts relative to one another. Such sculpturings do not stem directly

Fig. 22.26 Differential growth. The right claw of this crab has been lost and is regenerating. The new claw grows differentially at a far faster rate than the rest of the animal, for in the time the regenerated claw takes to reach the size of the left claw the rest of the body does not increase in size appreciably. (*Carolina Biological Supply Company.*)

from the addition of new cells or the subtraction of old ones. For example, the thickening of certain neural tissues in vertebrate embryos results from the narrowing and lengthening of cylindrical cells (Fig. 22.27). This cellular reshaping is caused by the contraction of microfilaments. Because the microfilaments of these cells are interconnected, narrowing one cell pulls the other cells toward it, thereby causing the tissue to mound up. Other examples of form-regulating movements include splitting a sheet of cells into two or more layers, hollowing out a solid mass of cells, and inward and outward migrations of cells that produce new pockets of tissues (see Fig. 22.27).

Through these processes the form of a body part or a whole organism is first blocked out in the rough, through establishment of polarity and symmetry, and then it becomes progressively more refined in regional detail. Thus the organ system is delineated ahead of its organs; the tissue acquires definitive shape in advance of its cells; and the molecules are last to assume final form. Evidently, form develops as in a sculpture, from the coarse to the fine. Whereas an organism grows from its molecules on up, it forms from gross shape on down.

The net result of growth, differential growth, and form-regulating movements is the emergence of an appropriately shaped and sized anatomy. These processes of morphogenesis thus represent an organizational, architectural component of development.

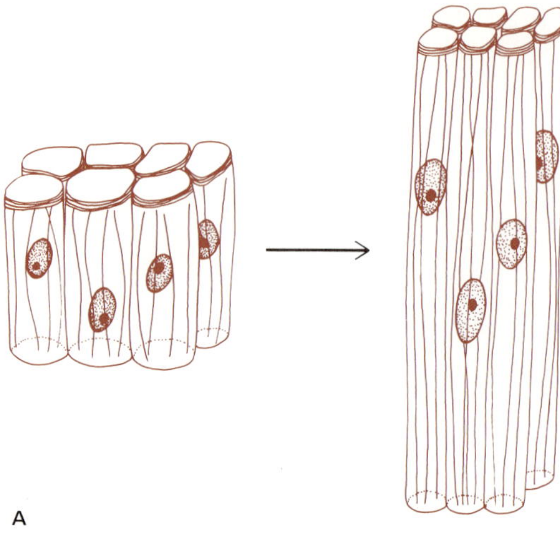

Fig. 22.27 Form-regulating movements. (A) Some tissues are shaped by the lengthening and shrinking of cells. Squat, cylindrical cells of a flat tissue mass (left), for example, can lengthen, producing a mounded column of narrow cells (right). (B) Pockets can be formed in tissues through the inward migration of cells. This surface view of a young frog embryo shows the inrolling of cells on each side of an elongated groove. The groove marks the entrance to an internal balloonlike pocket.

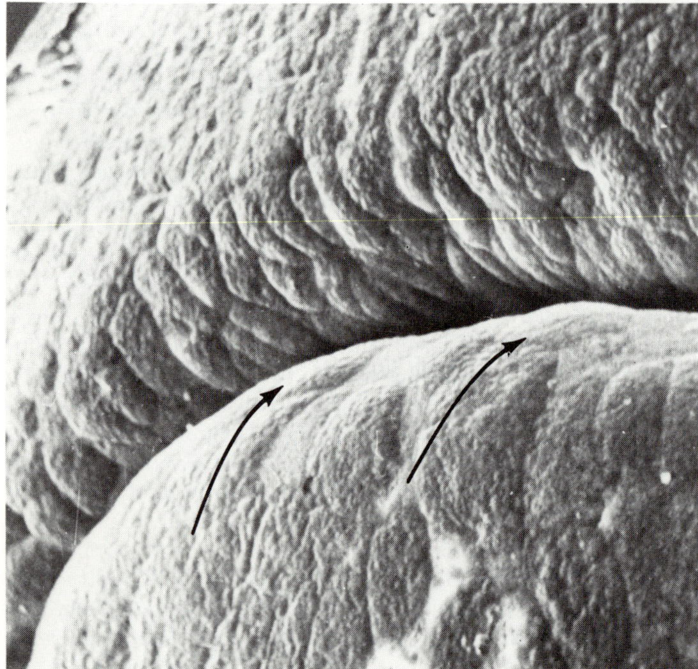

Determination and Differentiation

Determination and differentiation are operational, functional processes. Development does not produce simply a collection of many identical cells but a series of widely different cells; for example, some become nerve cells, some liver cells, some skin cells. Yet all arise from the same zygote, and all inherit the same genes from this zygote. Nevertheless, a multitude of differently specialized cells is formed (Fig. 22.28).

The process by which the developmental fate of unspecialized cells is established is called *deter-*

mination. This gene-mediated process restricts embryonic cells to specific developmental pathways before such cells actually develop specialized features. The process by which cells become different from one another and perform different functions is called *differentiation.* Since each of these differences result directly or indirectly from the synthesis of specific enzymes, cellular differentiation often is defined as the production of unique enzyme patterns. Thus, determination specifies the patterns of enzymes that can be established in a cell during development, and differentiation is the process through which these patterns are actually produced.

To be differentiation, operational changes must have a certain degree of permanence. We can make an animal vitamin-deficient, for example, and many of its cells will then behave differently. But if we now add the missing vitamin to the diet, normal cell functions probably will be resumed very promptly. Here cellular capacities have not been changed in any fundamental way. Only their expression has changed temporarily in response to particular conditions. Such easily alterable, reversible changes are *modulations.* By contrast, differentiation implies a more or less fundamental, relatively lasting alteration of operational potentials. For example, a vitamin-deficient cell that *maintained* its altered characteristics after addition of the missing vitamin would have differentiated.

Cellular differentiation appears to be regulated in several ways. For example, developing differences among cells could result from progressive changes in gene action. In a given cell some genes might become active at certain developmental stages, whereas others might become inactive. Indeed, different patterns of mRNA transcription have been observed among cells undergoing different patterns of differentiation.

In other cases mechanisms controlling RNA transcription might remain unchanged, but those influencing posttranscriptional, translational, or posttranslational processes could become altered (see Chap. 15). For example, some molecules of mRNA are translated preferentially as they enter the cytoplasm of many cells, while those produced by other genes are "stored" for variable periods. Following translation, some molecules of mRNA are destroyed more rapidly than others and thus produce fewer proteins. Moreover, many proteins are

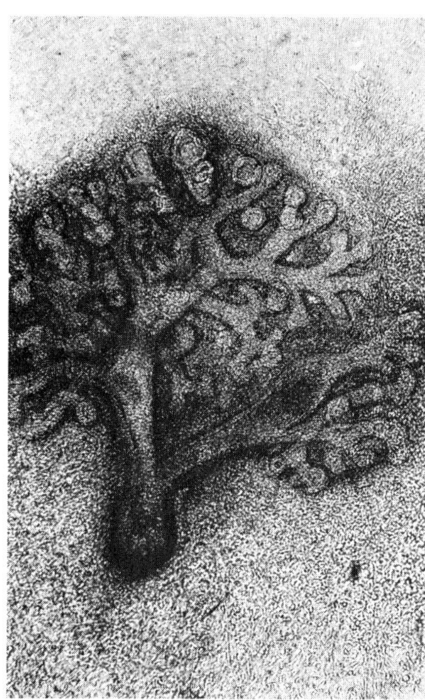

Fig. 22.28 Differentiation. Future lung tissue of an 11-day-old mouse embryo was placed in a tissue culture. After 6 days of growth in the culture, the well-formed lung shown in this photo had differentiated. Note ducts, branches, and alveoli. (*Clifford Grobstein and "13th Growth Symposium," Princeton, Princeton, N.J., 1954.*)

manufactured in an inactive form. The three-dimensional structure of insulin, for example, must be altered substantially following its production before it can function as a hormone. The rates at which such dormant molecules are activated by cytoplasmic controls appears to be an important means of regulating the differentiation of some cells. Thus, gene expression is controlled in several ways at several different sites within a cell. Differentiation probably results from sequences of interdependent actions and responses among such diverse intracellular controls.

The following chapters will show how the various reproductive processes, life cycles, and developmental sequences manifest themselves in different groups of specific organisms.

Review Questions

1 Review how reproduction contributes to self-perpetuation. Describe the basic forms of molecular reproduction and the relationship between molecular and organismic reproduction.

2 Describe how cell division contributes to organismic reproduction. What molecular events in cells precede the microscopically visible phases of division? Review the events that occur during mitosis.

3 Discuss how basic research on the periods of interphase has contributed to an understanding of mechanisms that trigger conversion of normal cells to cancer cells. Review the various factors known to cause cancer. Illustrate each of these factors with specific examples. What methods of cancer treatment are now in use or are being developed? Discuss the advantages and disadvantages of each method.

4 Review the fundamental differences and relationships between sex, reproduction, and development. Do the same for sporulation, gametic reproduction, and vegetative reproduction. Describe and give examples of the major variants of vegetative reproduction.

5 What are the most basic events of every sexual process? In what way is sex of adaptive value, and under what conditions do sexual processes tend to occur?

6 Review the major steps of meiosis and describe the principal similarities and differences between meiosis and mitosis.

7 Compare and contrast haplontic, diplontic, and diplohaplontic life cycles. Which of these types of life cycles is probably primitive, and how may it have given rise to the other types?

8 How many *pairs* of chromosomes does a diploid cell contain? Of these, which and how many are maternal, and which and how many are paternal?

9 Review the functional relations between morphogenesis, determination, and differentiation. Through what types of growth process does an organism enlarge in size? Explain the meaning of the phrase "organisms grow from their molecules on up."

10 What different symmetries are exhibited by living units? In what ways do polarity and symmetry circumscribe the form of an organism? What are the roles of differential growth and form-regulating movements in morphogenesis? What are the fundamental differences between asexual and sexual developmental patterns, and what accounts for such differences?

Collateral Readings

Bryant, P. J., S. V. Bryant, and **V. French:** Biological Regeneration and Pattern Formation, *Scientific American,* July 1977. This article illustrates how research on limb regeneration is providing much information about the fundamental principles of animal growth.

Cairns, J.: The Cancer Problem, *Scientific American,* November 1975. The incidence, causes, and kinds of cancer are discussed.

———: "Cancer: Science and Society," Freeman, San Francisco, 1978. The author reviews what is known about cancer, the current status of cancer research, and the prospects for finding cures for various forms of this disease.

Dyson, R. D.: "Cell Biology: A Molecular Approach," Allyn and Bacon, Boston, 1978. Good coverage of the molecular and ultrastructural aspects of cell reproduction.

Karp, G.: "Cell Biology," McGraw-Hill, New York, 1979. Chapters 14 and 15 deal with the growth and division of cells.

Mazia, D.: The Cell Cycle, *Scientific American,* January 1974. This article describes mitosis and focuses on the cellular events that occur during interphase.

Nicolson, G. L.: Cancer Metastasis, *Scientific American,* March 1979. Describes the circumstances in which certain malignant cells travel through the body and establish new tumors.

Old, L. J.: Cancer Immunology, *Scientific American,* May 1977. Discusses efforts to learn why cancer cells can escape destruction by the immune system.

Prescott, D. M.: "Cancer: The Misguided Cell," Pegasus, New York, 1973. This paperback discusses the nature and causes of cancer. It also contrasts the reproductive cycles of normal cells and cancer cells.

Rafferty, K. A.: Herpes Viruses and Cancer, *Scientific American,* October 1973. Describes a category of viruses that may cause cancers in human beings.

Richards, V.: "Cancer: The Wayward Cell," 2d ed., University of California Press, 1978. A good general introduction to the types, causes, and treatment of this disease.

Swanson, C. P., and **P. L. Webster:** "The Cell," 4th eds., Prentice-Hall, Englewood Cliffs, N.J., 1977. A short book covering many aspects of cell biology. Less detailed than the Karp or Dyson books.

Weier, T. E., C. R. Stocking, and **M. G. Barbour:** "Botany: An Introduction to Plant Biology," 5th ed., Wiley, New York, 1974. Chapter 6 contains a well-written and well-illustrated account of reproduction among plant cells.

Wolfe, S.: "Biology of the Cell," 2d ed., Wadsworth, Belmont, California, 1977. This excellent text contains a comprehensive discussion of mitosis and meiosis.

Chapter 23 Reproduction: The Plant Pattern

Learning Objectives

After reading this chapter you should be able to:

1. Identify the general features that characterize the life cycles of all plants; differentiate between antheridia and archegonia and between spores, spore mother cells, and sporangia.
2. Illustrate vegetative and gametic reproduction in bryophytes using *Marchantia* as an example.
3. Name the principal differences between the life cycles of bryophytes and tracheophytes; construct a diagram or table that identifies and compares the terrestrial adaptations of bryophytes, ferns, gymnosperms, and angiosperms.
4. List the principal differences between primitive and seed-forming patterns of reproduction among tracheophytes, as exemplified by the life cycles of ferns, gymnosperms, and angiosperms; construct a diagram that depicts the structural components of a flower and indicate a function for each; specify the adaptive significance of flowers.
5. Distinguish between monoecious and dioecious patterns of spore formation in seed plants.
6. Define the following terms and indicate how each is related to the life cycles of bryophytes, ferns, gymnosperms, or angiosperms:
   - **a.** homosporous
   - **b.** heterosporous
   - **c.** microsporangium
   - **d.** megaspore
   - **e.** ovule
   - **f.** pollination
   - **g.** fertilization
   - **h.** seed
   - **i.** ovary
   - **j.** double fertilization
   - **k.** endosperm
   - **l.** fruit
   - **m.** strobili
   - **n.** sperm nuclei
   - **o.** polar nuclei
7. Construct a diagram of a bean and corn seed that depicts the following structures (note that not all structures are present in both types of seeds):
   - **a.** cotyledon(s)
   - **b.** embryo
   - **c.** seed coat
   - **d.** hypocotyl
   - **e.** plumule
   - **f.** radicle
   - **g.** endosperm
   - **h.** scutellum
   - **i.** coleoptile

   Label each of these structures and list at least one function of each.
8. Name at least two structural adaptations of fruits that promote species dispersal of angiosperms; write a paragraph that explains the principal differences between seedling development in most dicots and monocots (e.g., beans and corn).
9. List at least three ways in which reproduction in angiosperms differs from that of all other plants.
10. Identify at least two circumstances that make Wilhelm Hofmeister's contributions to plant science so noteworthy; state two contributions of Matthias Schleiden to the modern science of biology; state why Hofmeister's description of the "alternation of generations" life cycle revolutionized botanical science; define cryptogam and state the historical significance of this term.

Plant reproduction is characterized by *diplohaplontic* life cycles with dissimilar gametophyte and sporophyte generations. The accompanying Biology Highlight describes the discovery of this pattern of development. Most plants have multicellular sex organs, *antheridia* and *archegonia*, which develop as parts of gametophytes and produce sperms and eggs, respectively. Zygotes typically pass through distinct embryonic stages as they develop into mature sporophytes (see Fig. 22.24).

BRYOPHYTES

Gametophytes are physically larger than sporophytes in virtually all species of bryophytes, and an unqualified reference to a moss or a liverwort generally is a reference to the haploid, gamete-producing plant. These gametophytes are well known for their vegetative means of propagation. In the liverwort *Marchantia*, for example, older parts of a thallus often die off, leaving younger branch thalli as separate plants. In addition to such fragmentation by *posterior decay*, many liverworts form *gemma cups* on the surfaces of their thalli. Within these cups develop successive sets of buds called *gemmae*, each an upright spindle-shaped cell group attached by a tiny stalk. Gemmae are readily dislodged by raindrops, and if the water carries them to suitable ground, they develop as new plants (Fig. 23.1).

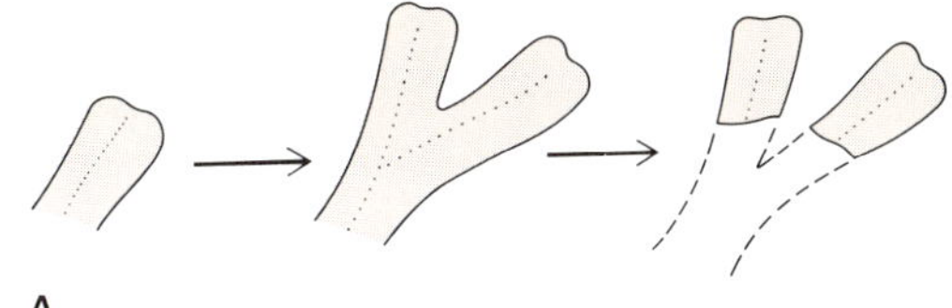

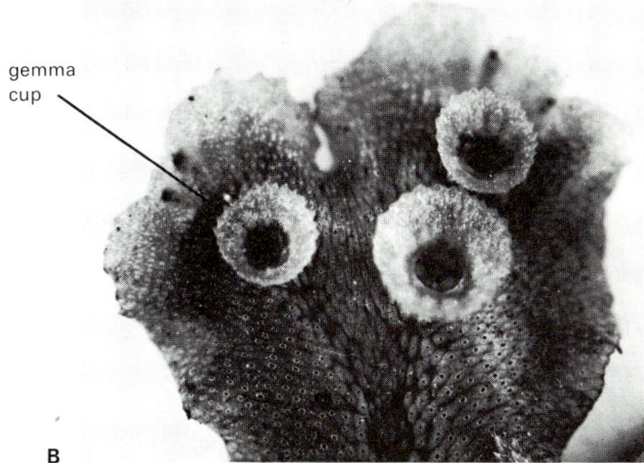

Fig. 23.1 Bryophyte vegetative reproduction. (A) Branching growth and posterior decay can lead to the formation of two separate individuals from one parent organism. (B) Gemma cups of *Marchantia.* (*Courtesy of Melvin S. Fuller.*)

The sex organs develop in different regions in different bryophyte groups. Mosses typically form such organs at the tips of their leafy shoots. In liverworts the sex organs arise in some cases directly on the surface of a thallus, in others in receptacles formed on stalks that grow up from the thallus (Fig. 23.2). Regardless of the location, a male organ, or antheridium, consists of an external protective layer and internal sperm-forming cells. Each such cell matures as a biflagellate sperm. In the female organ, or archegonium, a large egg lies in the expanded part (*venter*) of a flask-shaped protective layer. The narrow neck of this organ provides a sperm path to the egg. Many bryophytes are hermaphroditic, others are separately sexed.

Fertilization requires free water; continuous films of water must be present between nearby sex organs, or fluid droplets must carry sperms to archegonia. Consequently, most bryophytes are restricted to damp, moist habitats (see Chap. 6). After sperms enter an archegonium, one fertilizes the egg. The zygote then grows into a diploid few-celled embryo that later matures as an adult sporophyte, still attached to the gametophyte. Such a sporophyte consists of a basal *foot* anchored in the archegonium, a *stalk* of different lengths in different bryophyte groups, and a terminal *sporangium* (Fig. 23.3). The cells of developing sporophytes are photosynthetic, but in all except those of hornworts the chlorophyll is lost as sporophytes become mature. Such sporophytes therefore are nutritionally dependent on the green gametophytes to which they remain attached.

In a sporangium, generating cells called *spore mother cells* undergo meiosis and give rise to haploid spores. Each of these secretes a heavy wall around itself. The sporangia of liverworts and hornworts also produce *elaters*, hygroscopic cellular filaments with spirally thickened inner walls. Interspersed among the spores, elaters twist and coil as they dry out. These jerky motions aid in flipping the spores out of a mature sporangium that has become brittle and has broken open. After its spores have been shed, a sporophyte dies off. This phase of the bryophyte life cycle is therefore short-lived compared with the gametophyte phase. On suitable ground, spores germinate and develop as new gametophytes (Fig. 23.4).

Biology Highlight

Wilhelm Hofmeister and the Plant Reproduction Puzzle: Joining the Pieces

Some historians trace the origin of the modern science of botany to a single publication, *On the Germination, Development, and Fructification of the Higher Cryptogamia, and on the Fructification of the Coniferae.*[1] As implied by its title, it is a highly technical book, definitely not bedtime reading for most, yet it created an immediate sensation among botanists when it first appeared in 1851—and with good reason.

Its author was Wilhelm Friedrich Benedikt Hofmeister, a short, dark, extremely vivacious and stubborn German, whose knowledge of botany was almost exclusively self-taught. In his book Hofmeister not only established the basic theme of most subsequent publications dealing with plant reproduction, but also documented basic principles which today underlie many major subdisciplines of botany, including the applied sciences of agriculture and horticulture. Hofmeister was the first scientist to present evidence revealing a common "alternation of generations" life cycle among all major groups of plants. He also clearly illustrated both the process of fertilization in plants and the development of plant embryos from fertilized eggs. Never before had these events been described and depicted so accurately.

At least two circumstances make Hofmeister's contributions particulary noteworthy. The first concerns the status of botany during the first four decades of the nineteenth century. In some respects the science of botany was not a science at all. Botanists of the day typically expended most of their energies cataloging purely descriptive information pertaining to the anatomical features of plants—mostly angiosperms. Few botanists seemed interested in uncovering fundamental relationships between the structure and function of plant parts. Botany textbooks of the period were crammed with superfluous terminology related to differences in stem, leaf, and flower anatomy. The books contained few, if any, important principles.

Needed were botanists who could arrange known facts within whole concepts. Hofmeister was such an individual, but his contributions probably would not have been so great had he not been influenced by Matthias Schleiden. Together with Theodor Schwann, Schleiden is best remembered as a founder of the modern cell theory (see Chap. 5).

Schleiden was a rebel botanist, dissatisified with the mere collection of anatomical data. His greatest contribution was a radically different, comprehensive textbook of botany, which first appeared in 1842. Unlike most texts published before or since, Schleiden's began with a 131-page formal essay on the use of inductive reasoning in scientific investigation (see Chap. 1 for a discussion of inductive logic). Schleiden implored students to examine the structure of plant parts in the light of their possible functions; to determine how specific facts were related to overriding principles; to analyze how

[1]This is the English edition of an original German publication, *"Vergleichende Untersuchungen höherer Kryptogamen."*

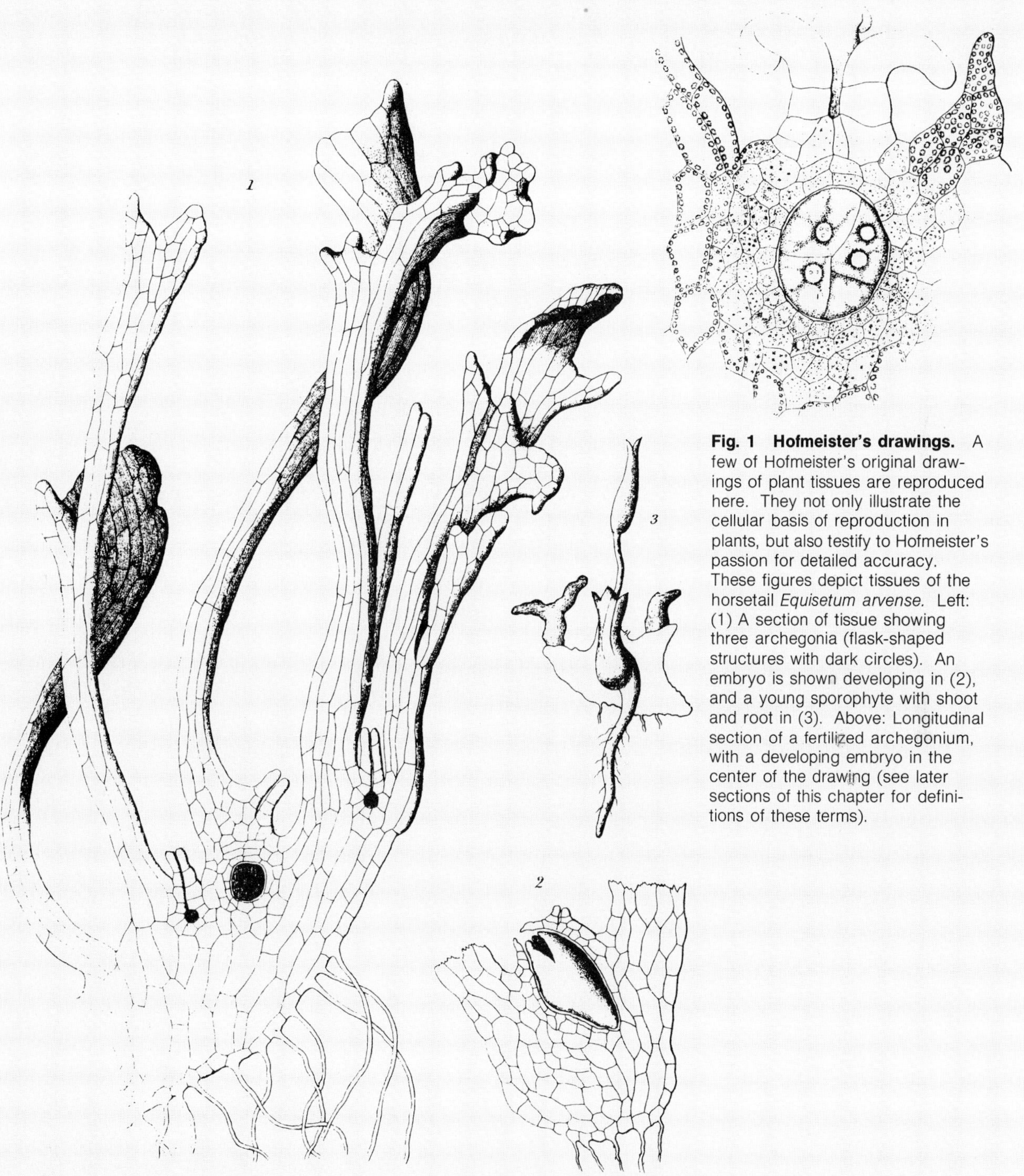

Fig. 1 Hofmeister's drawings. A few of Hofmeister's original drawings of plant tissues are reproduced here. They not only illustrate the cellular basis of reproduction in plants, but also testify to Hofmeister's passion for detailed accuracy. These figures depict tissues of the horsetail *Equisetum arvense.* Left: (1) A section of tissue showing three archegonia (flask-shaped structures with dark circles). An embryo is shown developing in (2), and a young sporophyte with shoot and root in (3). Above: Longitudinal section of a fertilized archegonium, with a developing embryo in the center of the drawing (see later sections of this chapter for definitions of these terms).

structures related to the development and life histories of plants—not only for angiosperms but also for less studied forms such as mosses, liverworts, and ferns.

The pages of Schleiden's textbook included praise for fellow workers who examined such relationships and condemnation for those who did not. He also urged botanists to examine more closely the fundamental relationships between *cells,* the basic units of life, and not be content with a mere examination of gross anatomy. Since the cell was the starting point in plant development, why not make the cell the principal focus for the study of plant development, form, and function?

Hofmeister, greatly impressed by Schleiden's arguments, began to examine from a cellular point of view the processes of fertilization and development in a wide variety of plants. He did not have any formal training in these fields of study, a second reason why Hofmeister's work is considered so noteworthy. His secondary schooling, although excellent, was not intended as preparation for an academic career. On finishing high school in 1839, Hofmeister served as apprentice to a family friend who owned a music shop in Hamburg.

In 1841, Hofmeister returned to his native Leipzig and took over a major part of his father's businesses, which included a bookshop and a music publishing house. The bookshop contained a large number of botany books and illustrations of plant anatomy. Friedrich Hofmeister, Wilhelm's father, was an amateur naturalist, whose passion for botany eventually passed to his son. For the next decade, Wilhelm combined a full-time career as a music publisher with that of a research botanist.

To find time for his research, Hofmeister rose daily at 5 A.M., spending the first hours of the day preparing plant tissues for microscopic examination. He became exceptionally skilled at making such preparations and at drawing what he observed beneath the lenses of his microscope. His ability to perform exceedingly delicate manipulations of plant tissues stemmed in part, ironically, from his poor eyesight. Hofmeister was extremely myopic. Yet, true to his character, he stubbornly refused to wear eyeglasses. He would bring his face very close to the specimens he was preparing and directly performed manipulations better-sighted people carried out indirectly using a dissecting microscope.

As the months and years of study passed, Hofmeister began to see a common pattern in the life histories of plants. Whether moss, fern, conifer, or angiosperm, all plants pass *twice* through a single-cell stage in the course of development. Moreover, each single-cell stage marks the starting point of a new phase of development. One of the cells, the spore, produces a plant body (the gametophyte) that bears reproductive organs. The female organs of this plant produces eggs, and the male organs produce sperms. A fertilized egg, the second single-cell stage, forms when a sperm and egg fuse. The fertilized egg then divides repeatedly, forming a second plant body (the sporophyte), which produces spores. In this way, all plants pass through two generations in the course of development, each generation produced from a single cell.

When Hofmeister announced these findings in his now famous 1851 publication, most of his contempories were stunned but impressed. Hofmeister's evidence and precise illustrations immediately overturned much of what previously had been assumed about plant development (Fig. 1). For example, most botanists erroneously believed that all plants produced flowers and seeds. Some, the angiosperms, obviously produced such structures. It was assumed that nonflowering plants produced them too, but that they somehow were concealed within vegetative organs. Consequently, nonflowering plants were called *cryptogams* (Greek, "hidden marriage"), a term occasionally found in the botanical literature even today.

Hofmeister's evidence also corrected an erroneous interpretation strongly endorsed by Schleiden, namely, that the angiosperm embryo arises from the tip of the pollen tube. Hofmeister clearly demonstrated that the pollen tube is a "male" component and that the embryo arises in the embryo sac of the ovule.

In place of these and other incorrect concepts, Hofmeister's book firmly established the true relationships between the pieces of the plant-reproduction puzzle, the "alternation of generations" life cycle. Botanists at once could see the plant world as a whole. Many of the details of plant anatomy that were scattered almost haphazardly through textbooks of the day now could be tied to a unifying conceptual framework. Equally important, the common alternation-of-generations pattern of development provided an evolutionary more correct means of classifying plants, which previously had been based almost exclusively on similiarities in the gross anatomy of mature plant parts.

Between 1852 and 1862, Hofmeister published a series of supplemental papers, all of which were incorporated in a second edition of his book, published only in English (see Collateral Readings at the end of this chapter). In 1863, Hofmeister was appointed Professor of Botany at the University of Heidelberg. The appointment was extraordinary and almost unprecedented, considering Hofmeister's lack of any previous association with a university. He held the Heidelberg professorship until 1872, when he accepted a similar position at the Universtity of Tübingen.

Hofmeister enjoyed mixed success as a teacher. He had little patience with beginning students; many of his lectures went hopelessly over their heads. But he was a superb teacher in the laboratory, greatly admired by most of his graduate students. Throughout much of his professorial career, Hofmeister continued his business as a music publisher. He refused to limit his responsibilities, working long hours, incessantly, to the eventual damage of his health. The first of several cerebral hemorrhages came on his fifty-second birthday in 1876. He died less than a year later in Lindenau, a few miles from his Leipzig birthplace.

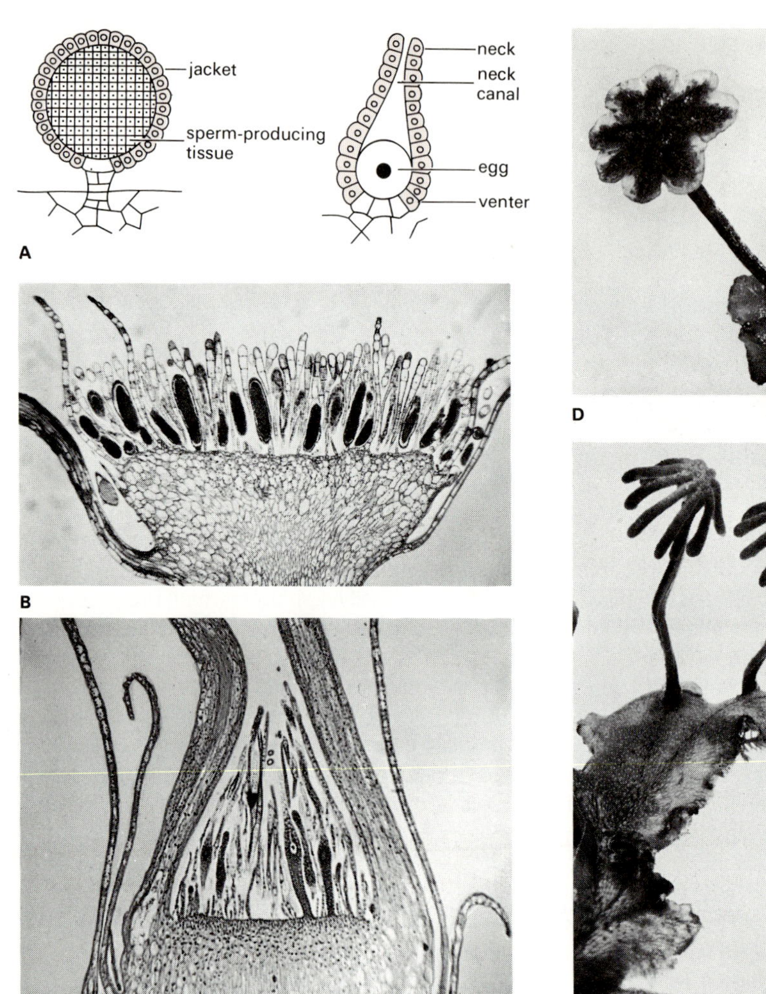

Fig. 23.2 Bryophyte sex organs. (A) Structure of antheridium (left) and archegonium (right). (B, C) Sections through the apical tips of moss shoots, showing the position of an antheridial head (B) and an archegonial head (C). Note the numerous sex organs on each head. (D, E) Sex-organ-bearing stalks in *Marchantia*. (D) Structure containing male sex organs. (E) Stalk bearing fingerlike processes in which female sex organs are located. *(B, C, Courtesy of Melvin S. Fuller; D, E, Carolina Biological Supply Company.)*

TRACHEOPHYTES

Primitive Pattern

Regardless of how well adapted to land the gametophyte generation of bryophytes may be in other respects, it can never be really well adapted in its reproduction; gametic reproduction requires free external water for the swimming sperms, but ample water is not always available in a terrestrial environment. As noted, bryophytes "make do" by gearing their sperm release to wet periods.

Although primitive tracheophytes actually cannot do much better, the emphasis in their life cycles is on the diploid sporophyte, not the gametophyte. The sporophyte produces encapsulated spores, excellently adapted to terrestrial conditions. But the gametophyte is reduced to microscopic dimensions and to a generally short-lived existence. This deemphasis of the gametophyte reduces the water problem correspondingly.

The pattern is well illustrated in primitive tracheophytes such as club mosses, horsetails, and ferns. In most of these plants, the sporophyte and

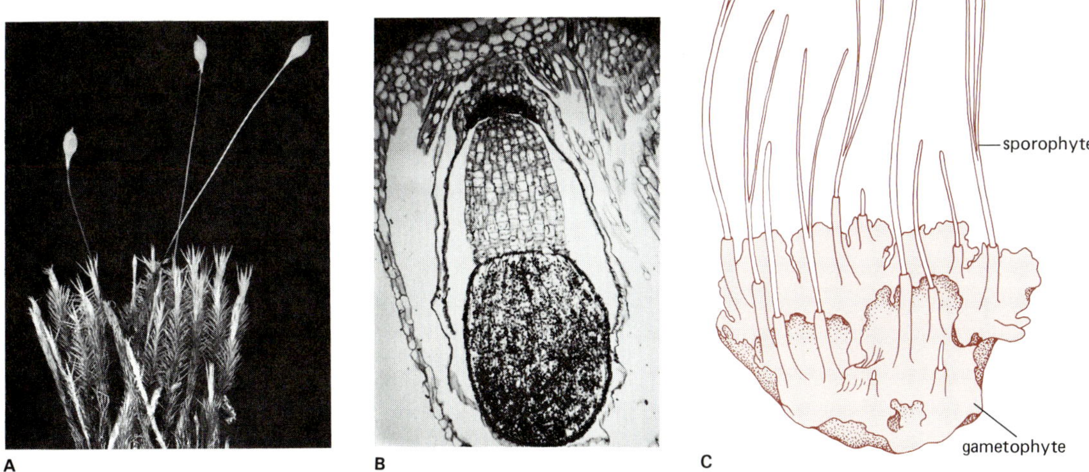

Fig. 23.3 Bryophyte sporophytes. (A) Moss gametophytes bearing attached sporophytes on top. (B) The sporophyte of the liverwort *Marchantia.* (C) Hornwort gametophyte with elongated sporophytes growing from it. Spores are produced inside the whole length of a sporophyte.

gametophyte generations are separate green organisms living in soil independently. And the gametophytes are exceedingly tiny, often near-microscopic ground-hugging plantlets. They usually live only just long enough to produce sperms and eggs. By contrast, the sporophytes are large and generally perennial. Many grew to tree size in past ages; some ferns still do today. The life cycle of ferns exemplifies the reproductive pattern typical for this entire group of plants.

Fig. 23.4 Bryophyte life cycles. A moss cycle is summarized.

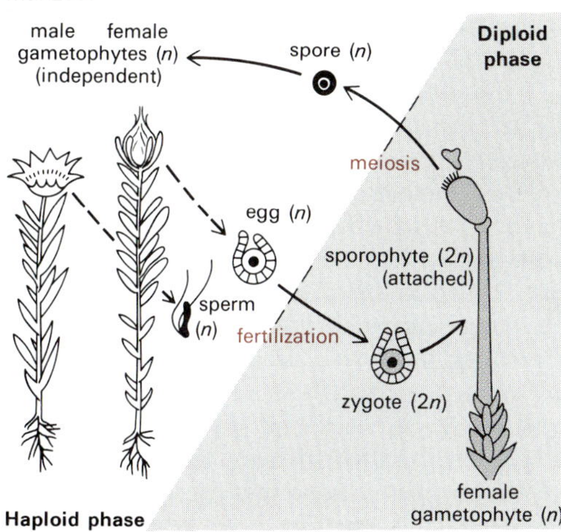

The plant commonly called a "fern" is actually the dominant sporophyte. It is large, leafy, green and it may persist the year round. At certain seasons cells on the underside of fern leaves give rise to stalked, lens-shaped sporangia. Several sporangia usually develop in the same area of a leaf. Such a group, called a *sorus,* is often covered by an *indusium,* a single-layered, sometimes pigmented shield of tissue (Fig. 23.5). In many cases sori form in regular double rows, one row on each side of a main leaf vein. Internally a sporangium contains spore mother cells that undergo meiosis and give rise to encapsulated haploid spores.

Sporangia eventually dry out and rupture, and in the process the spores are forcefully catapulted out. Such spores later develop into haploid gametophytes. Each of these is a green plantlet consisting mainly of a heart-shaped, flat plate of tissue that lies on moist, shaded ground and measures not more than about $\frac{1}{4}$ inch across (Fig. 23.6). Rhizoids that project from the underside into the soil serve an absorptive function. In size, way of life, and function, this inconspicuous gametophyte greatly resembles a gametophyte of, for example, liverworts.

On the lower side of the gametophyte develop the sex organs. In hermaphroditic ferns the antheridia usually form near the tip of the heart-shaped plant, archegonia near the notch. The locations of

Fig. 23.5 Sori. Each of the whitish structures on the undersurface of these woodfern (*Dryopteris marginalis*) leaves, is an indusium, a sorus-covering, protective shield of tissue. Each of the darker, pebblelike structures projecting from beneath each indusium is a spore-producing sporangium (compare with Fig. 23.6A and see Color Fig. 9).

these organs are similar also in separately sexed species. As in bryophytes, groundwater must be present if the flagellate swimming sperms are to reach eggs. After fertilization the zygote is retained in the archegonium and develops into a small, diploid, sporophyte embryo. Four organ zones become recognizable in it: a *foot,* which anchors the whole embryo to the base of the archegonium; the *embryonic root;* the *embryonic stem;* and an *embryonic leaf* (Fig. 23.7). At this stage the embryo is still without chlorophyll and depends on food supplied by the gametophyte. But soon the root and stem penetrate through the archegonial tissues and the leaf becomes green. Thereafter the gametophyte shrivels and degenerates, leaving the young sporophyte as a separate, independent plant (Fig. 23.8).

Evidently, the primitive vascular plants and the ferns do not differ greatly in their gametophytes from those of bryophytes. And although these various vascular plants have highly developed sporophytes, well adapted to the general lack of free water on land, their gametophytes still must cope with a fundamental difficulty, the water requirement in fertilization. Only the seed plants have fully circumvented this problem.

Seed-Forming Pattern

Ferns and virtually all other primitive tracheophytes are *homosporous;* the spores produced by all sporophytes of a given species are indistinguishable, and one cannot tell ahead of time whether a given spore will become a male gametophyte, a female gametophyte, or a hermaphrodite. By contrast, seed plants are *heterosporous;* each sporophyte produces two kinds of spores. Small *microspores* are formed in *microsporangia,* and such spores give rise to male *microgametophytes;* larger *megaspores* develop in *megasporangia* and become female *megagametophytes.* This heterosporous condition has evolved independently in several ancestral tracheophyte groups, and in one of these the capacity of forming two spore types has prepared the way for the later evolution of seeds.

The life cycle of a seed plant thus begins with diploid sporophytes that develop microsporangia and megasporangia (Fig. 23.9). Some species form the two types of sporangium in the same plant (*monoecious condition*), others, in different plants (*dioecious condition*). Spore mother cells in the sporangia then undergo meiosis, and the haploid products become microspores and megaspores, respectively.

A microspore gives rise to a male gametophyte that consists of a few cells only and remains enclosed by the wall of the microspore. Such a walled microgametophyte is a *pollen grain.* In comparable fashion, a megaspore develops into a few-celled female gametophyte that is retained in the megasporangium in which it is produced. Megasporangia are also called *ovules.*

Next, pollen grains are dispersed from the microsporangia and are carried by wind or animals to ovules. This dispersion, leading eventually to contact between pollen grains and ovules, is called *pollination.*

Thereafter, the male gametophyte in a pollen grain develops a *pollen tube* that carries sperms or sperm nuclei at the tip. This tube digests a path to the female gametophyte in which an egg has matured by this time. The tip of the pollen tube makes contact with the egg, and a sperm nucleus then enters and brings about *fertilization*. Pollination and fertilization clearly are distinct and separate events; in some cases several months may intervene between them. And it is the pollen tube that circumvents the requirement of free water in fertilization. The success of seed plants rests in large measure on the evolutionary development of such tubes.

The fertilized egg, the female gametophyte, the surrounding wall of the megaspore, and the covering layers of the ovule, all together now develop as a *seed*. Within it, the zygote develops into a new sporophyte embryo. Through later dispersion from the parent plant and through seed germination, an independent young sporophyte finally becomes established. In effect, the gametophyte generation remains hidden throughout, and the *visible* reproductive pattern of a seed plant is sporophyte ⟶ seed ⟶ sporophyte.

Seeds germinate only under appropriate environmental conditions and will remain dormant if sufficient oxygen or water is not available or if the temperature is unfavorable. In addition, the seeds of many species germinate only if induced to do so by appropriate amounts and types of light. This requirement often exists in species such as lettuce and in many weeds that produce small seeds. Germination here will occur only if the seeds are covered with a layer of soil thin enough to let some light through. In the absence of such a triggering action by light, deeply buried seeds will remain dormant, and will germinate only when brought to the surface by some disturbance in the soil. Thus, weeds often tend to persist despite efforts to eliminate them by tilling the soil.

Seeds can remain dormant for variously long periods, even centuries in some cases. Such dor-

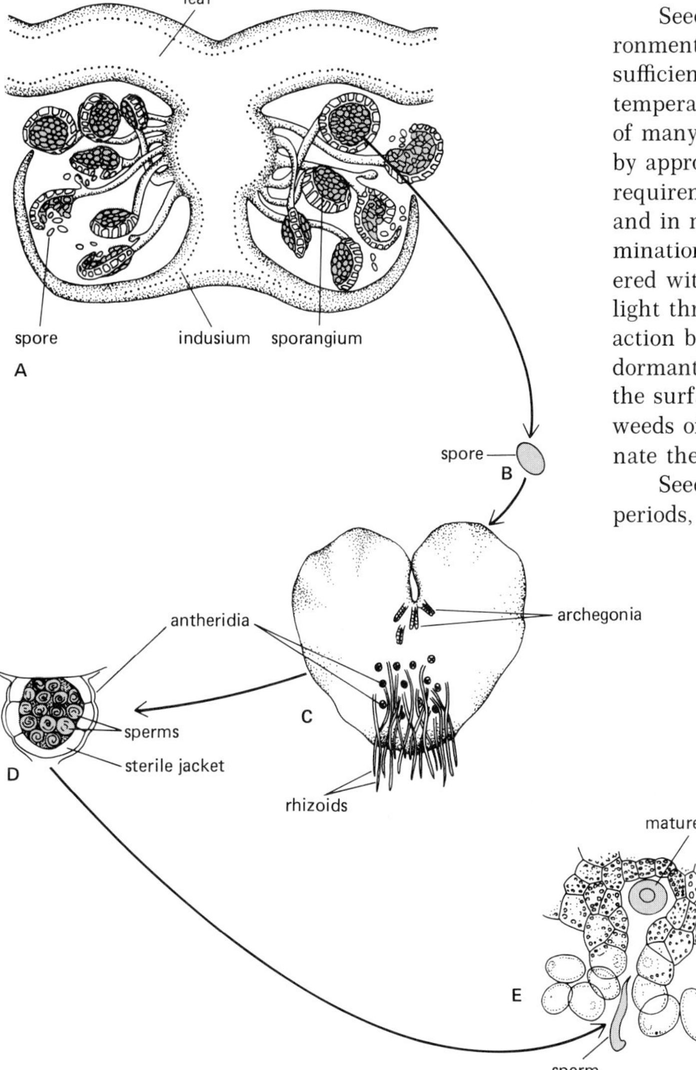

Fig. 23.6 Stages in the life cycle of a fern. (A) Section through a sorus, showing indusium, sporangia, and spores. (B) Spore. (C) Gametophyte, showing rhizoids and locations of antheridia and archegonia. (D) Section through an antheridium showing sperm. (E) Archegonium with mature egg about to be fertilized by a sperm.

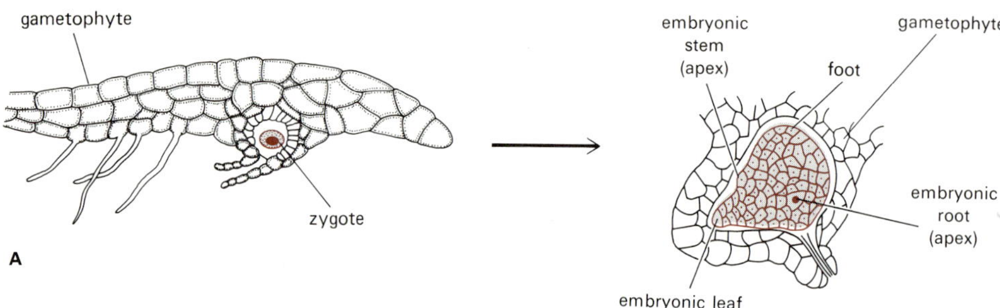

Fig. 23.7 Fern reproduction. (A) A zygote undergoes cell division inside an archegonium (left), producing a sporophyte embryo with four distinct organ zones (right). (B) Gametophyte with developing sporophyte still attached. Note sporophyte root and leaf.

mancy is adaptively advantageous, for it lengthens the time available for seed dispersal and thereby improves the chance that germination will occur in a suitable environment (see also Chap. 16).

The dormant condition is in some respects similar to the state of hibernation encountered in various mammals; the rate of respiration and of metabolism in general is exceptionally low, and reserve foods are used up exceedingly slowly.

Gymnosperms (Cone-Bearing Plants)

In almost all gymnosperms the reproductive structures form in cones, or *strobili.* In a pine, for example, small microstrobili develop in clusters on the ends of tree branches (Fig. 23.10). In such a cone the underside of each cone leaf (*microsporophyll*) bears a microsporangium. In it, microspore mother cells undergo meiosis and give rise to microspores (Fig. 23.11) Each such spore has a two-layered wall. The outer one will later inflate partially and form two conspicuous "wings." The inner one encloses the microspore cell, which divides and produces one small and one large cell. The small cell divides once more and forms two *prothalial cells,* which represent the whole vegetative portion of the male gametophyte. They eventually disintegrate and play no further role. The

Fig. 23.8 Fern life cycle, summary.

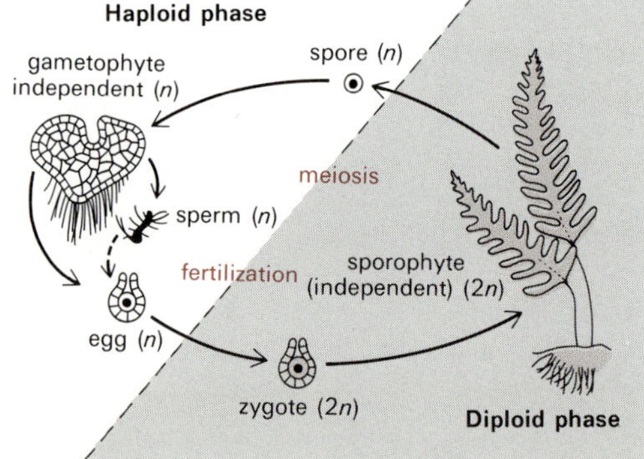

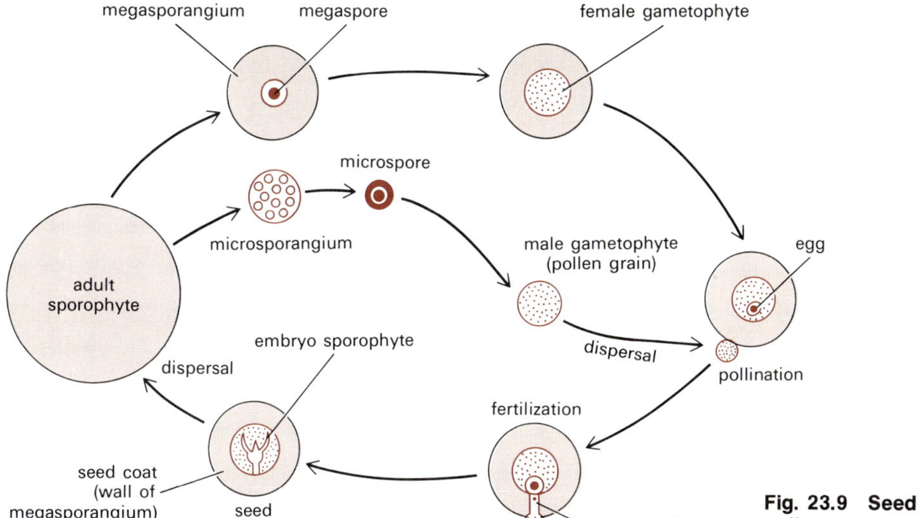

Fig. 23.9 Seed plant reproduction, basic pattern.

larger cell also divides, producing a smaller *generative cell* and a larger *tube cell.* At such a stage of development a pollen grain is mature and is shed from the microsporangium.

Fig. 23.10 Pine reproduction: cones. A megastrobilus (left) and microstrobilus (right) of jack pine. Note the size difference (see also Color Fig. 10).

Pines also bear larger *megastrobili,* in which woody cone scales carry paired ovules (see Figs. 23.10 and 23.11). An ovule is bounded on the outside by an *integument,* a tissue layer extended on one side as two flaps, the *micropylar arms.* Between these arms is a narrow canal, the *micropyle,* which leads to the main part of the ovule. Deep in this part a single megaspore mother cell undergoes meiosis. Three of the four haploid cells so produced degenerate, and the remaining one is the functional megaspore.

When pollination occurs, some pollen grains usually fall into the space between the micropylar arms. In this region the ovule secetes a *pollination fluid,* which traps pollen grains and permits them to sink deep into the micropyle. In this manner pollen grains come to make contact with the inner tissues of the ovule. After pollination the outer tips of the cone scales press against each other, and the whole cone thereby becomes sealed off from the environment.

The following events in a pine ovule occur exceedingly slowly; about a year elapses between pollination and fertilization. During this time the whole cone and its contents increase in size and each megaspore enlarges and elongates. Also, the megaspore nucleus divides repeatedly until some 2000 haploid nuclei are present. Cell walls are then laid down betwen these nuclei, and in this way the megaspore is transformed into a multicel-

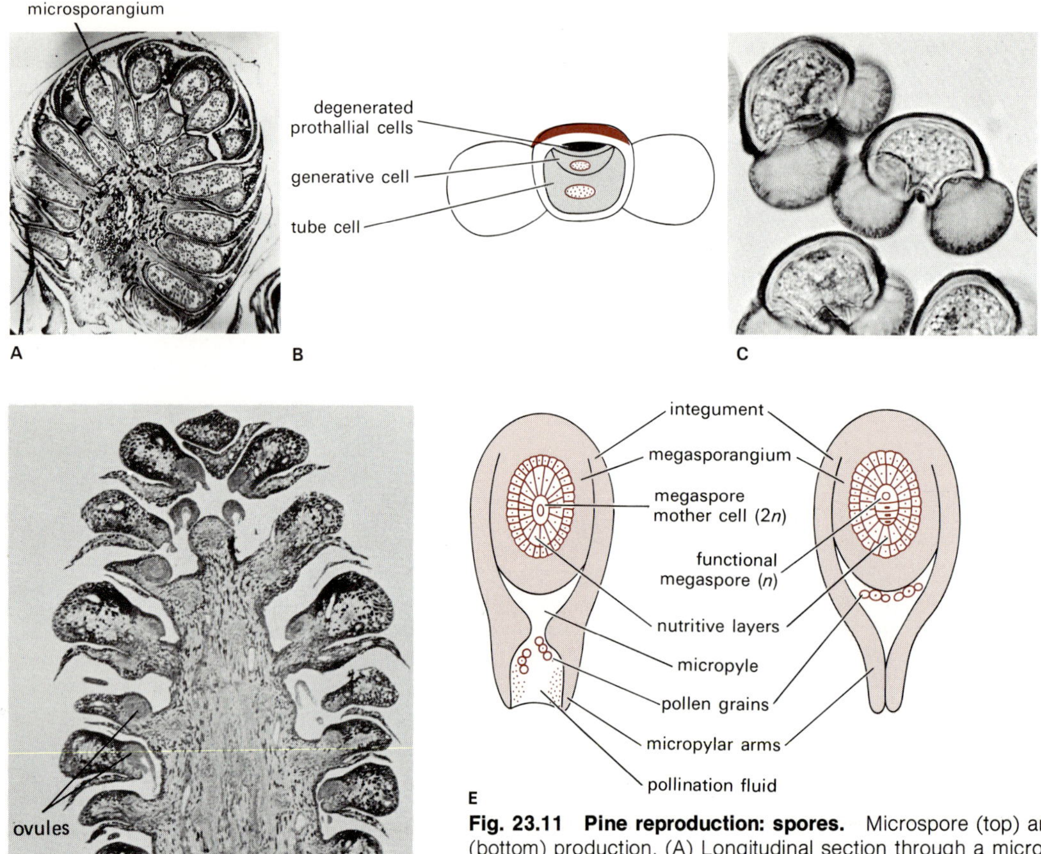

Fig. 23.11 Pine reproduction: spores. Microspore (top) and megaspore (bottom) production. (A) Longitudinal section through a microstrobilus. Microspores are produced in microsporangia. (B), (C) mature microspores, or pollen grains. (D) Longitudinal section through a pine megastrobilus. Note position of ovules. (E) The early development of a megasporangium within an ovule: (left) before meiosis; (right) after meiosis.

lular female gametophyte. On the side of the micropyle a few highly reduced sex organs develop, each with an egg (Fig. 23.12).

In the meantime, the pollen grain resting against the ovule develops too (Fig. 23.13). The tube cell of each pollen grain elongates slowly and produces a pollen tube, which secretes enzymes that digest a path through ovule tissue. The generative cell of the male gametophyte divides, and the two resulting cells (*stalk cell* and *body cell*) migrate toward the tip of the pollen tube, where the tube-cell nucleus is already present. The nucleus of the body cell later divides once again, forming two *sperm nuclei.* Fertilization occurs when a pollen tube penetrates into an egg and discharges all or most of the four nuclei at the tip into the egg cytoplasm. All except one sperm nucleus degenerates, and that nucleus fuses with the egg nucleus. The resulting diploid zygote represents the beginning of a new sporophyte generation.

Several or all the eggs present in a female gametophyte can become fertilized independently, but in pines only one zygote usually develops much further. It soon forms 16 cells arranged as four groups of four, one quartet below the other. The four cells of the uppermost quartet are *embryo initials;* each begins to produce an embryo (see Fig. 23.13). One usually develops faster than the oth-

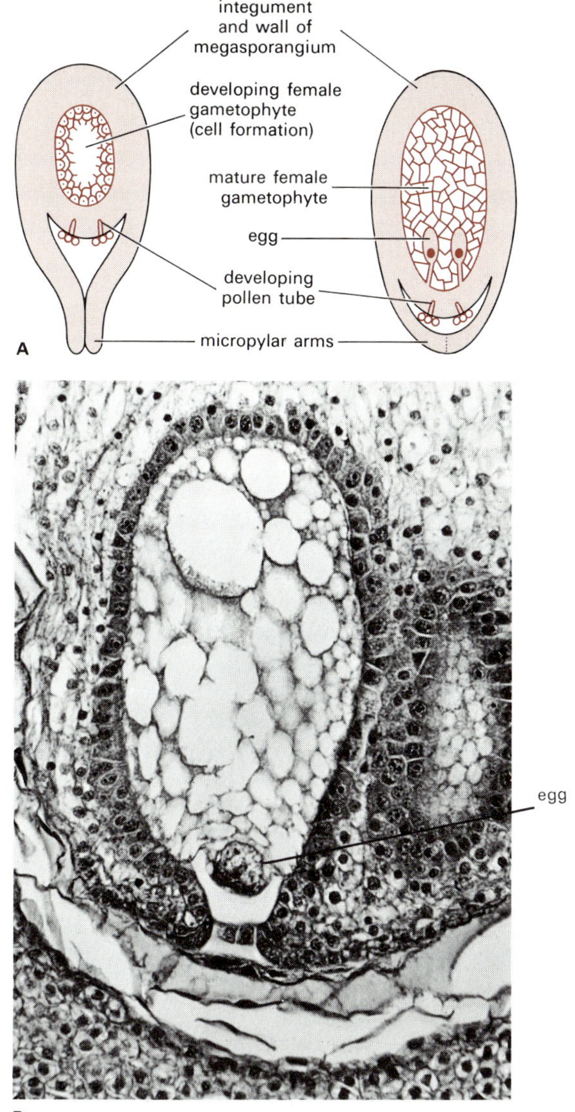

Fig. 23.12 Pine reproduction: the female gametophyte. (A) Cell formation in the developing female gametophyte. (B) The mature female gametophyte with egg (near bottom). Megasporangial tissue surrounds the gametophyte.

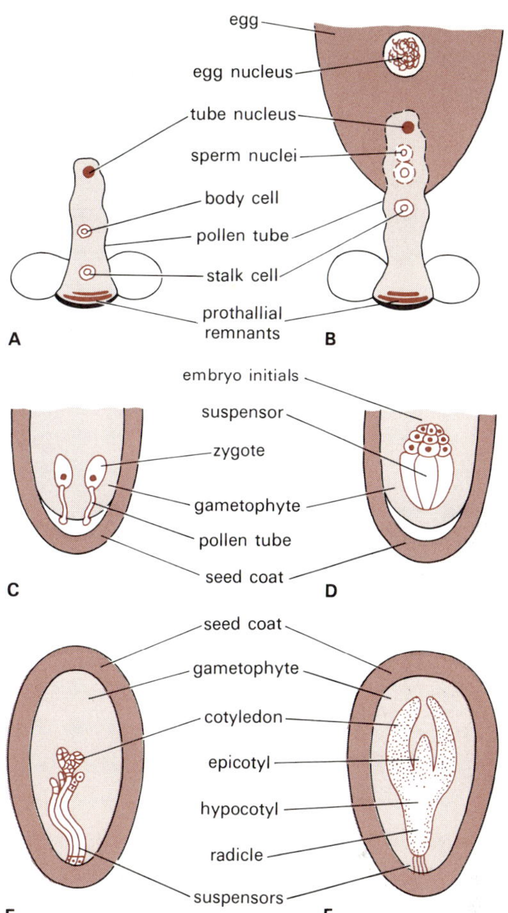

Fig. 23.13 Pine reproduction: fertilization and development. (A) Pollen-tube growth. (B) Fertilization. Sperm nuclei have formed from the body cell; all four nuclei at the tip of the pollen tube are discharged into the egg. (C) The zygote has formed from one of the sperm nuclei and the egg nucleus. (D) Division of the zygote has given rise to tiers of cells, of which the upper will form the embryo, the rest the suspensor. (E) The seed coat has hardened, and the embryo initials have proliferated and given rise to an early embryo. (F) Later embryo, with embryonic leaves (cotyledons), stem apex (epicotyl), and embryonic stem and root (hypocotyl and radicle).

ers, and eventually only that one develops further; the other three degenerate. The next lower quartet of cells elongates as a *suspensor* that attaches the embryo to the gametophyte tissues and pushes it deep into these tissues.

Repeated divisions of the surviving embryo initial soon transform it to a distinct embryo with young root, stem, and two or more embryonic leaves (*cotyledons*). The whole embryo is embedded in the remains of the female gametophyte, which in turn is surrounded by the remains of the ovule and the external integument. The latter has hardened by this time into a *seed coat*, and a portion of the cone scale extending away from the seed coat has matured as the *wing* of the seed (Fig. 23.14).

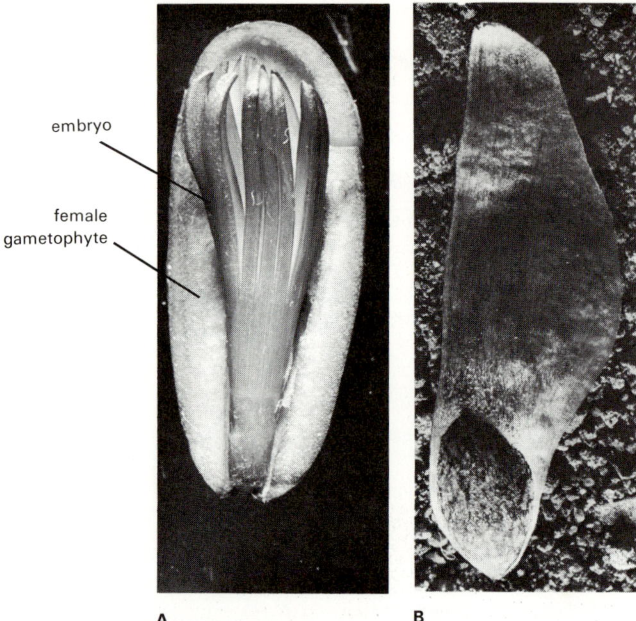

Fig. 23.14 Pine seeds. (A) Dissected seed showing embryo and surrounding female gametophyte. (B) The mature winged seed at time of dispersal. *(Courtesy of R. H. Noailles.)*

Pine seeds are ripe several months after fertilization. At that time the cone scales become brittle and spread open, and the seeds then can become dispersed. The name "gymnosperm" indicates that these plants form naked, exposed seeds. Not all gymnosperms require 2 or 3 years for seed formation, like pines, with pollination occurring one year and fertilization not until the next. In spruces, for example, the interval between pollination and fertilization is only a few weeks. Such time variations notwithstanding, the reproductive processes themselves are basically the same in all gymnosperms.

Angiosperms (Flowering Plants)

In this group of plants the equivalents of gymnosperm cones are *flowers* (Fig. 23.15). Whereas cone leaves are attached around a more or less elongated central stem, flower leaves grow out from a highly shortened and flattened stem terminal, the *receptacle.* From this receptacle arise four whorls of modified leaves: *sepals, petals, stamens,* and one or more *carpels.* Sepals enclose the other flower parts in the bud, and these outermost modified leaves generally are green. Taken together, all sepals collectively constitute the *calyx.* The petals, which collectively make up the *corolla,* usually are the conspicuously colored flower parts. Each stamen is composed of a stalk and a terminal *anther,* in which microsporangia develop.

The carpel, or carpels, constitute the central whorl of modified leaves. Some flowers have only one carpel, but others have several, which are often fused. Carpels are composed of a terminal *stigma,* a middle stalklike *style,* and an expanded basal *ovary,* which contains the ovules. Pollen grains are deposited on the stigma (see Fig. 23.15).

Flowers can be with or without calyx or corolla. Where these leaves are present, they may or may not be pigmented (other than green) and they may or may not produce scents. Pigments and scents are familiar adaptations that attract various pollen-dispersing animals (bees, wasps, butterflies, moths, sometimes small birds, and people; see Color Fig. 11). Plants depending on animals for pollination generally also secrete abundant nectar (sugar water) in their flowers. Many ingenious structural devices have evolved through which only particular animal types can have access to the nectar of a particular flower type. Potential "robbers" either cannot enter the flower or cannot reach the nectar stores. But qualified animals such as bees often find landing platforms, colored guide marks on petals, and other conveniences. As such animals reach for nectar, they pick up new pollen on their body surfaces or deposit pollen from other flowers visited earlier.

Some species of angiosperms are regularly *self-pollinating;* pollen grains fall on the stigma of the same flower and develop normally thereafter. However, most angiosperms depend on *cross-pollination,* where pollen grains from one flower are transferred to the stigma of other flowers of the same species.

Meiosis occurs in anthers and leads to the formation of haploid microspores (Fig. 23.16). The microspore nucleus then divides once, producing a *generative nucleus* and a *tube nucleus.* The generative nucleus soon divides once more and forms two *sperm nuclei.* The whole male gametophyte then consists of a single cell with three nuclei.

A comparably condensed development occurs in

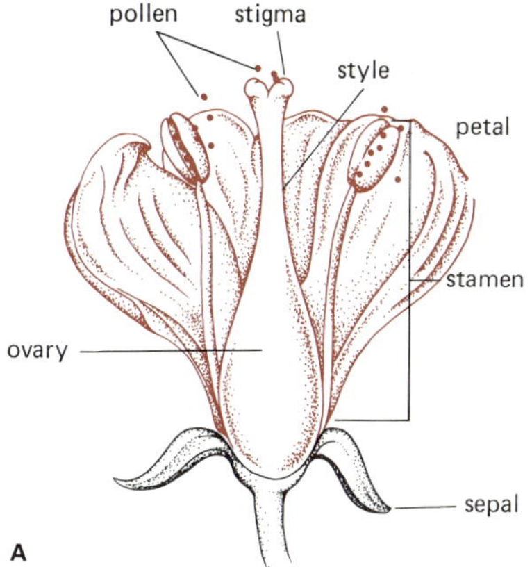

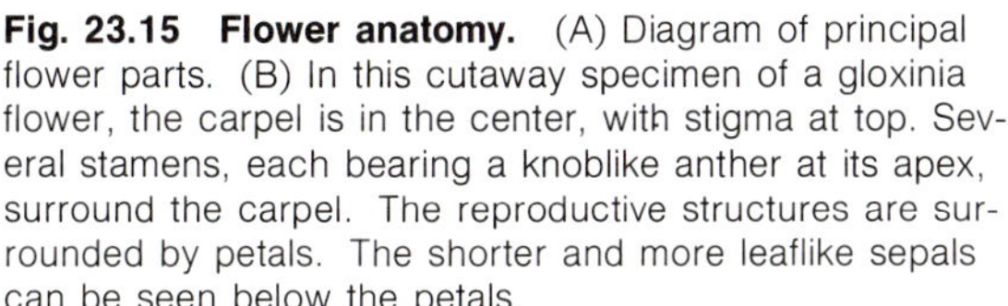
Fig. 23.15 Flower anatomy. (A) Diagram of principal flower parts. (B) In this cutaway specimen of a gloxinia flower, the carpel is in the center, with stigma at top. Several stamens, each bearing a knoblike anther at its apex, surround the carpel. The reproductive structures are surrounded by petals. The shorter and more leaflike sepals can be seen below the petals.

the ovary, which contains one or more ovules (Fig. 23.17). As in gymnosperms, a micropyle in each ovule leads past one or more integuments to the inner tissues. A single deep-lying megaspore mother cell there undergoes meiosis, and of the four resulting haploid cells one persists as a functional megaspore. The nucleus of this spore cell divides mitotically three time in succession. Four of the resulting eight haploid nuclei come to lie at one end of the spore cell, four at the other. Three of each group of four soon become partitioned off as independent cells, and the remaining two, called

Fig. 23.16 Pollen grains. (A) Cross section through the anther of a lily. Note the two spore sacs, the openings in these sacs, and the microspores (pollen grains). (B) Development of a microspore.

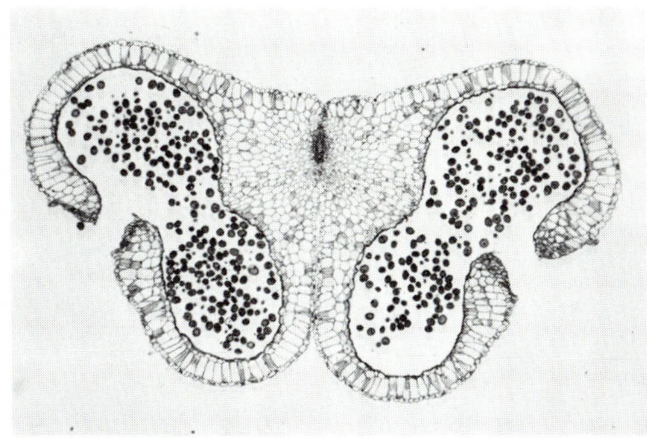

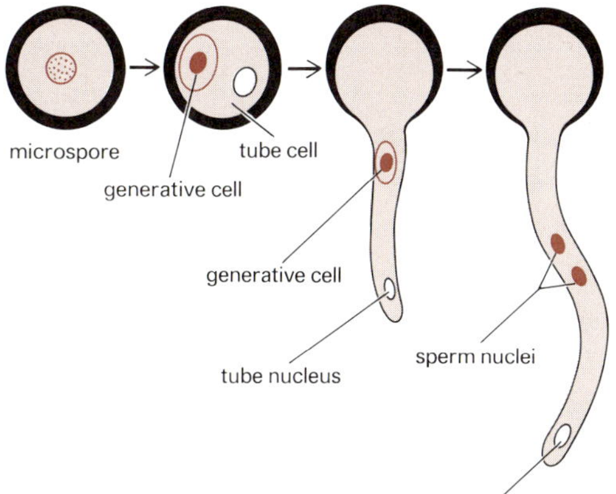

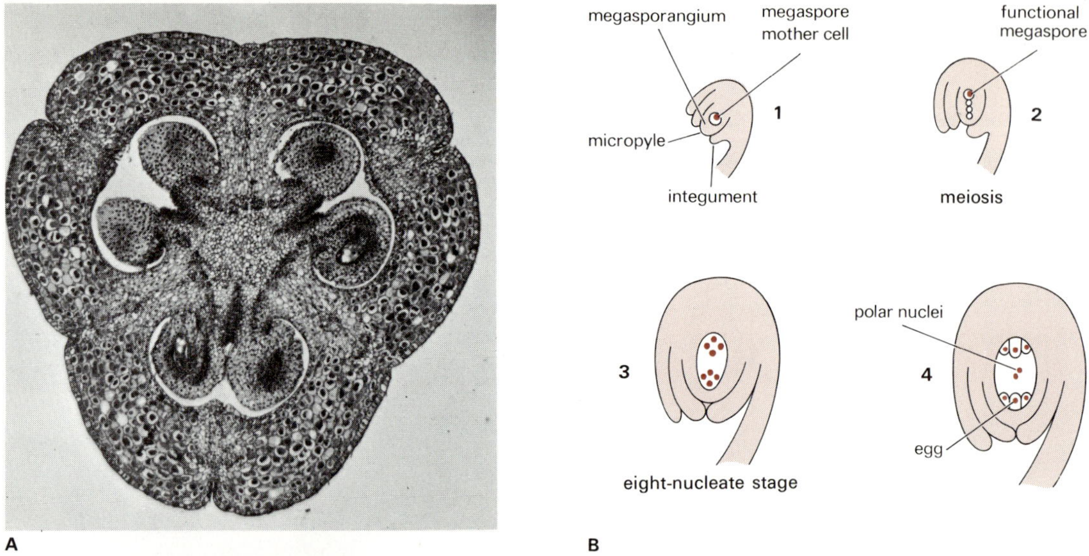

Fig. 23.17 The female gametophyte. (A) Cross section through the ovary of a lily. Note the ovary wall (which will eventually give rise to the "meat" of a fruit) and the three pairs of ovules containing female gametophytes. (B) The basic pattern of the development of a female gametophyte in angiosperms. (1) The megasporangium, (2) meiosis and functional megaspore, (3) eight-nucleate stage of gametophyte; (4) egg formation and polar nuclei. *(A, Ward's Natural Science Establishment, Inc.)*

polar nuclei, migrate to the center of what is now a seventh large cell. These seven cells represent the entire female gametophyte. Sex organs are not formed at all. Instead, of the three gametophyte cells near the micropyle, one becomes an egg directly.

The pollen of some angiosperms is dispersed by wind; that of others by insects and animals. Numerous pollen grains become trapped on the sticky stigma of a pistil (Fig. 23.18). Each grain then produces one pollen tube, which grows between the cells of the style toward the ovary. Such a tube generally enters an ovule through the micropyle and digests a path through the ovule tissues. The

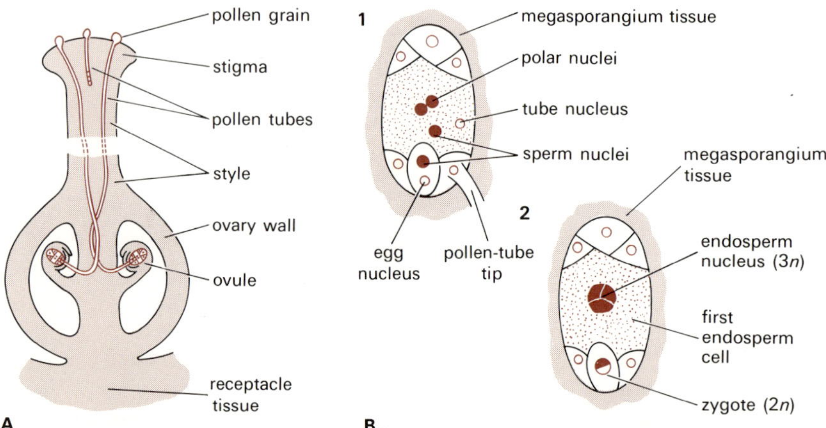

Fig. 23.18 Pollen tubes and fertilization. (A) Growth of pollen tubes after pollination. (B) Fertilization. (1) Double fertilization. One sperm nucleus fuses with the egg nucleus, and the other sperm nucleus combines with the two polar nuclei. (2) The triploid endosperm nucleus and the diploid zygote.

tip of the tube contains the two sperm nuclei, both of which are eventually discharged into the female gametophyte.

The next event is *double fertilization,* unique to the angiosperms (see Fig. 23.18). One of the sperm nuclei enters the egg and fertilizes it. The other sperm nucleus migrates to the two polar nuclei in the large central cell of the female gametophyte, and all three of these nuclei fuse together as a so-called *endosperm nucleus.* Being formed from three haploid nuclei, the endosperm nucleus is *triploid,* with three sets of chromosomes. This nucleus then divides repeatedly, cell walls are usually laid down, and the tissue so formed is the *endosperm.* It soon fills up the space formerly occupied by the female gametophyte. Endosperm cells accumulate food substances from the parent sporophyte.

While the endosperm develops, the zygote divides and gives rise to a sporophyte embryo (Fig. 23.19), in which seed leaves, or *cotyledons,* develop. Monocot angiosperms contain one cotyledon; dicots contain two (see also Chap. 6). In addition to seed leaves, sporophyte embryos contain three other major parts, a *plumule,* a *hypocotyl,* and an *embryonic root,* or *radicle* (Fig. 23.20).

In some plants, the plumule consists solely of an embryonic shoot apex composed of a few rapidly dividing cells; in others, the plumule also contains one or more embryonic leaves. The hypocotyl is the embryonic stem and lies between the cotyledons and the radicle. In the embryos of some seeds, the hypocotyl is very short, particularly in corn and other monocots.

The whole embryo is embedded in endosperm, and this tissue gradually contributes more or less of its food to the developing sporophyte. In a mature seed, therefore, endosperm may or may not be used up. Where the endosperm has been used up, its substance has become incorporated in the cotyledons, which are likely to be massive, as in peanuts or peas. But if the endosperm is still extensive, the cotyledons are likely to be small, leafy, and without significant amounts of nutrient. In monocots such as rice, wheat, barley, and corn, the cotyledon has undergone considerable evolutionary modification and consists of two main parts: the *scutellum,* which absorbs nutrients for other embryonic structures from the endosperm; and the *coleoptile,* which protects the plumule as it grows upward through the soil following germination (see Fig. 23.20).

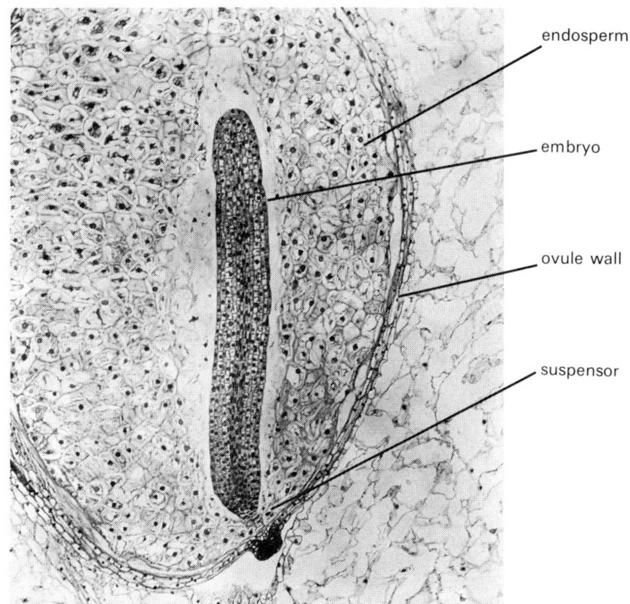

Fig. 23.19 Early angiosperm development. Embryo of lily surrounded by endosperm. The embryo is attached to the ovule wall by a short suspensor.

The seeds in an ovary soon develop hardened seed coats, and much of the flower then withers. On the other hand, the ovary and in some cases also parts of the receptacle enlarge rapidly and mature as a *fruit.* This structure can become *dry* or *fleshy,* and it hides the seeds inside it. The name "angiosperm" indicates that these plants produce encased seeds, embedded in fruits (Fig. 23.21).

The evolution of fruits has contributed greatly to the dispersal of angiosperm species; for if fleshy fruits are eaten by animals, seeds are usually spit out or egested in new locations. Dry fruits such as nuts may be carried about by squirrels, for example, and often are left in some forgotten hiding place. Fruits with burrs, hooks, or wing blades are distributed widely by animals and wind (Fig. 23.22). And fruits that simply fall to the ground eventually decay and thereby aid seed development indirectly by enriching a patch of soil.

When conditions for germination become favorable, hydrolytic enzymes are released into the nutrient storage areas of the seeds; these enyzmes convert starch to sugar, lipids to glycerol, and fatty

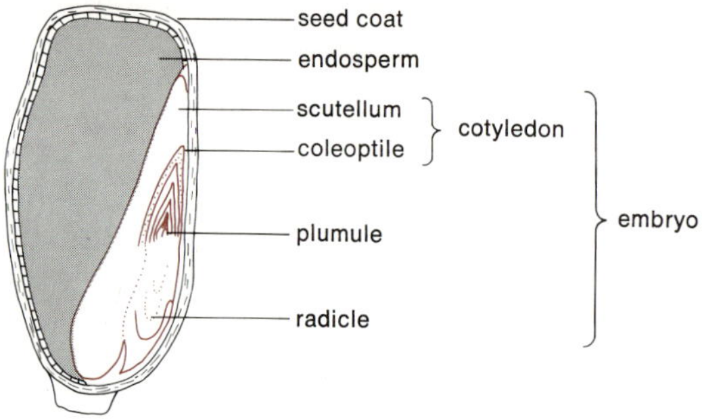

Fig. 23.20 Seeds. (A) Longitudinal section of a corn seed. (B) Section through a corn seed (kernel) showing embryo at right and endosperm tissue filling rest of seed. The single seed leaf, or cotyledon, is small in this case. (C) Longitudinal section of a bean seed, showing one of the two cotyledons. (D) Dissected bean seed showing the two large endosperm-filled cotyledons and the small embryo.

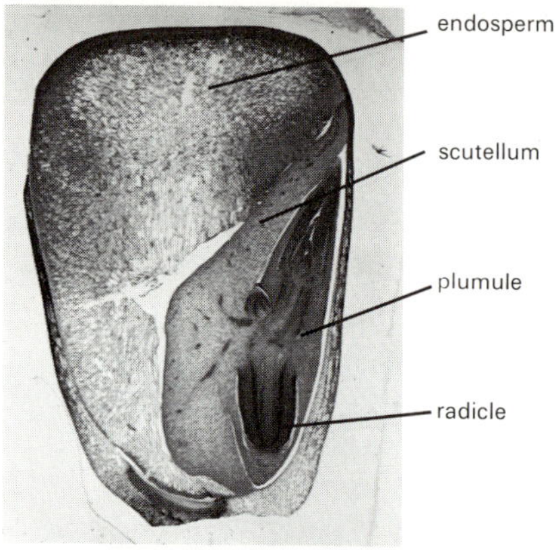

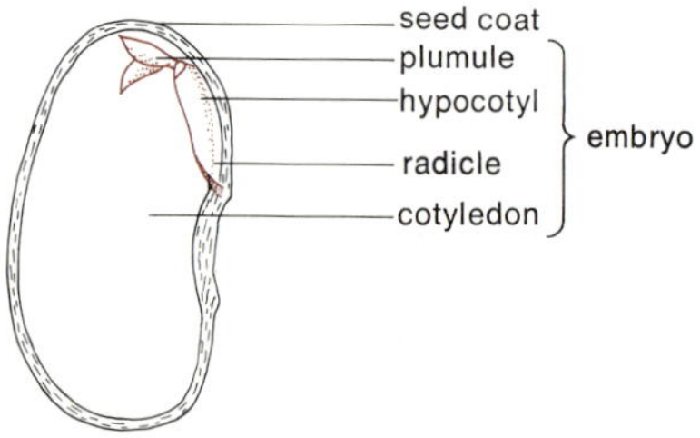

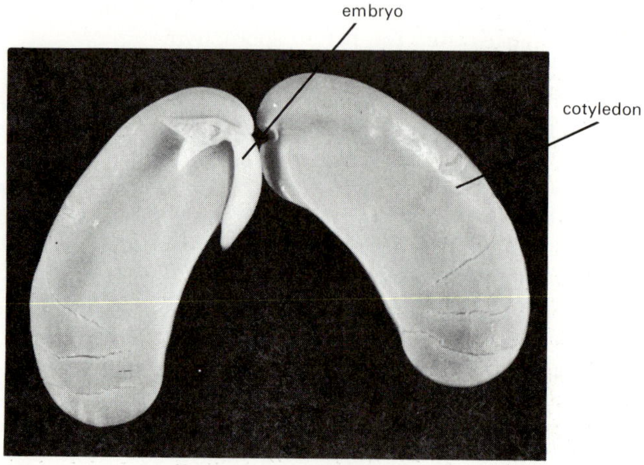

Fig. 23.21 Fruit structure. Equatorial section through an apple, showing the ovary, composed of five seed chambers (ovules) with seeds, and the expanded ovary wall, which makes up much of the "meat" of this fruit.

acids, and stored proteins to amino acids. These building blocks are transported to all parts of the embryo and support its growth until it has broken ground, produced leaves, and begun to nourish itself through photosynthesis.

In most seeds, the radicle is the first part of the embryo to break through the seed coat; it then grows downward to form the *primary root* (Fig. 23.23). This earlier outgrowth permits the young plant, or *seedling*, to become anchored in the soil before other parts of the embryo begin to grow. How the seedling develops further and emerges from the ground varies considerably for different species, but two basic patterns exist: one common to many dicots such as beans or peas; the other common to monocots such as corn, onions, and coconuts.

Fig. 23.22 Dry fruits. (A) Following pollination and fertilization, a dandelion flower develops as a "puff ball." Each of the featherlike structures making up the puff ball is an individual fruit, diagrammed in (B). The seed is located at the base of the fruit. The feathery tuft at the top functions in wind dispersal (see also Color Fig. 18).

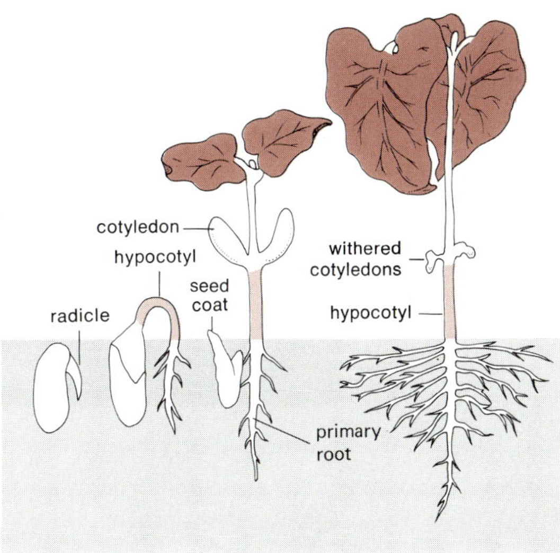

Fig. 23.23 Dicot pattern of germination. Stages in the germination of a garden bean. (*After C. L. Wilson, W. E. Loomis, and T. A. Steeves, "Botany," 5th ed., Holt, New York, 1971.*)

The dicot pattern is exemplified by the bean plant (see Fig. 23.23). Following emergence of the radicle, the hypocotyl arches upward and becomes the first part of the bean seedling to appear above the ground. As the hypocotyl continues to grow, it pulls the cotyledons up into the air. The cotyledons move apart, exposing the growing plumule, and steadily decrease in size as their supply of stored nutrients is diminished and eventually exhausted. Cotyledons often disappear completely about the time chloroplasts become established fully in the developing stems and leaves.

In the monocot pattern, illustrated by corn in Fig. 23.24, emergence of the seedling often occurs by elongation of the coleoptile. The plumule remains encased in the coleoptile until the coleoptile tip breaks through the soil, whereupon the plumule emerges and develops elongated leaves.

Thus the reproduction of angiosperms is characterized by three major features not found in gymnosperms: the *flower* itself; double fertilization, resulting in the inclusion of *endosperm* tissue in seeds; and the *fruit,* which contains a number of seeds. Each of these evolutionary innovations is of pronounced adaptive value. The flower often promotes pollination by attracting insects. The endosperm nourishes the embryo. And, as stated earlier, the fruit promotes seed dispersal and seed germination.

It can be concluded that the solution to the problem of terrestrial reproduction is rather similar in seed plants and terrestrial animals. As the next chapter will show, most terrestrial animals circumvent the requirement of external water by copula-

Fig. 23.24 Monocot pattern of germination. In corn, roots develop from the radicle and from the base of the stem. Because they develop at an atypical location, the latter are called adventitious roots. (*After C. L. Wilson, W. E. Loomis, and T. A. Steeves, "Botany," 5th ed., Holt, New York, 1971.*)

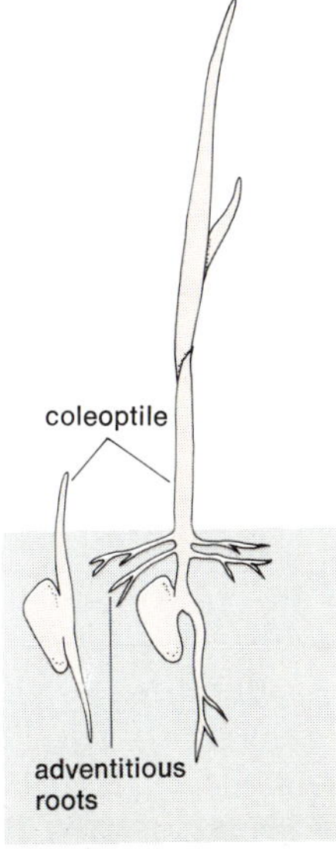

tion and *internal* fertilization: a male deposits sperms directly into a female containing mature eggs. In seed plants internal fertilization in a sense takes place as well. A sporophyte produces microspores and, through them, sperm nuclei. Another sporophyte produces megaspores and, through them, eggs. The sperm nuclei then reach the eggs by means of pollen tubes, which are the plant equivalents of the copulating organs of animals.

Review Questions

1 What features characterize the reproduction of all Metaphyta? Describe the structure of the sex organs in primitive plants. Describe the detailed life cycle of a bryophyte. In what respects is it well adapted to terrestrial life? Poorly adapted?

2 Define homosporous, heterosporous, microsporangium, megasporophyll, megaspore mother cell. Describe the reproduction and life cycles of primitive tracheophytes. Indicate where gametes and spores are formed.

3 Describe the life cycle of a fern. Compare it with that of bryophytes; what is similar and what is different? What are the adaptive advantages of a dominant diploid phase?

4 Review the general reproductive processes among seed plants. What are monoecious and dioecious conditions? Distinguish between pollination and fertilization. In what ways are seeds particularly advantageous in a terrestrial life?

5 Outline the specific life cycle of a pine. Define seed, pollen tube, self-pollination, ovule, microgametophyte.

6 Describe the structure and adaptive significance of a flower and the detailed life cycle of angiosperms. Define ovary, double fertilization, endosperm, fruit. What is the adaptive significance of endosperms and fruits?

7 Review Hofmeister's contributions to plant science. What role did Matthias Schleiden play in Hofmeister's discovery of the "alternation of generations" life cycle? How did Schleiden and Hofmeister change the ways in which botanists studied plants?

Collateral Readings

Arditti, J.: Orchids, *Scientific American,* January 1966. A case study of adaptations in flower structure.

Bold, H. C.: "Morphology of Plants and Fungi," 4th ed., Harper & Row, New York, 1980. This basic text contains excellent coverage of plant reproduction.

Delevoryas, T.: "Plant Diversification," 2d ed., Holt, New York, 1972. A good treatment of plant life cycles.

Echlin, P.: Pollen, *Scientific American,* April 1968. An electron-microscope study of these reproductive bodies is described.

Galston, A. W.: "Life of the Green Plant," 3d ed., Prentice-Hall, Englewood Cliffs, N.J., 1980. This short paperback contains a concise summary of plant growth and development.

Grant, V.: The Fertilization of Flowers, *Scientific American,* June 1951. The article discusses the adaptive features of flowers and the related adaptations of pollinating animals.

Hofmeister, W.: "On the Germination, Development, and Fructification of the Higher Cryptogamia and on the Fructification of the Coniferae," trans. F. Currey, Ray Society, London, 1862. The English translation of Hofmeister's most famous publication.

Ray, P. M.: "The Living Plant," 2d ed., Holt, New York, 1972. This paperback contains a good description of plant reproduction.

Sacks, J. von: "History of Botany 1530–1860," Russell and Russell, New York, 1967. Chapter 5 contains a good account of Hofmeister's contributions.

Salisbury, F. B., and **R. V. Parke:** "Vascular Plants: Form and Function," 2d ed., Wadsworth, Belmont, Calif., 1970. A paperback with very good coverage of reproduction in tracheophytes.

Torrey, J. G.: "Development in Flowering Plants," Macmillan, New York, 1967. A paperback emphasizing the functional mechanisms underlying the development of angiosperms.

Weier, T. E., C. R. Stocking, and **M. G. Barbour:** "Botany: An Introduction to Plant Biology," 5th ed., J Wiley, New York, 1974. Contains several sections pertaining to the topics of this chapter.

Wilson, C. L., W. E. Loomis, and **T. A. Steeves:** "Botany," 5th ed., Holt, New York, 1971. A classic text in the field of botany. Contains chapters on the reproduction of plants.

Chapter 24 Reproduction: The Animal Pattern

Learning Objectives

After reading this chapter you should be able to:

1. Explain how one egg and four sperms result from two successive meiotic cell divisions in female and male gonads, respectively; differentiate between first and second polar bodies; describe the general structure of a mature sperm and a mature egg.
2. Distinguish between external and internal fertilization and state the relative importance of water for each process; show why sporulation is not adaptively advantageous for most animals.
3. Distinguish between oviparous, ovoviviparous, and viviparous patterns of reproduction; name at least one type of animal that reproduces by each of these patterns.
4. Describe the structure, function, and embryonic origin of the testis and ovary in vertebrates; identify and describe the function of all other major male and female reproductive structures that facilitate fertilization and embryonic development in animals; define and indicate the function of primordial germ cells; show how an immature vertebrate gonad develops into either an ovary or a testis.
5. Show how hormones can influence reproductive behavior of animals; list at least one example of how reproductive behavior influences group sociality among animals.
6. Outline the interdependent roles played by the hypothalamus, pituitary, and gonads in promoting:
   - **a.** development of secondary sex characteristics
   - **b.** ovulation
   - **c.** development and maintenance of a thickened uterine lining
   - **d.** menstruation
7. Distinguish between puberty and menopause, and between sperm and semen; indicate which animal groups have menstrual cycles.
8. Define activation of eggs, and list at least three events that are triggered by this process in eggs.
9. Differentiate between blastula, blastodisc, and blastocoel.
10. Distinguish between mosaic and regulative eggs; show how egg size, cleavage rate, and the amount and distribution of yolk can influence embryonic development; state how identical twins can develop; describe the principal structural and functional events that occur during cleavage and gastrulation.
11. Name the three primary germ layers of a gastrula, describing at least one way in which these layers originate, and listing the major organs and tissues produced by each layer.
12. Define embryonic induction and illustrate how this process contributes to an orderly sequence of developmental events in embryos.
13. List two functions of larvae, and describe at least two different patterns of morphogenesis; differentiate between hatching and metamorphosis.
14. Describe the position and function of extraembryonic membranes within the shelled eggs of reptiles and birds.

Vegetative reproduction by fragmentation or budding occurs regularly in some animal groups as a normal process of propagation. Regenerative reproduction after injury is widespread, but in most groups the ability to regenerate is severely restricted. Sporulation does not occur and indeed is superfluous, since species dispersal can be achieved by locomotion in adult or preadult stages.

Whatever other forms of reproduction may or may not be exhibited, gametic reproduction occurs in all cases. The sexes typically are separate, but hermaphroditism is common, particularly in sessile and sluggish animals. Reproductive systems contain testes or ovaries, or *gonads* collectively, and generally also ducts that lead to the outside of the body. Gamete formation is accompanied by meiosis; sperms and eggs represent the only haploid phase in the diplontic life cycle. Fertilized eggs develop into embryos that become either adults directly or, more typically, *larvae* first and then adults.

PATTERNS

Reproductive Cells

Gametes are formed from special groups of diploid generative cells in the gonads. Such cells become sperms or eggs by maturation processes that affect both the cell nucleus and the cytoplasm.

The nuclear phase of gamete maturation is meiosis (Fig. 24.1). In a male, a diploid generative cell in a testis undergoes both meiotic divisions in fairly rapid succession, and all four resulting haploid cells are functional sperms. In a female, a generative cell in the ovary undergoes a first meiotic division and produces two cells. Of these one is small and soon degenerates; called the *first polar body,* it remains attached to the other cell. When this cell passes through the second meiotic division, one of the two resulting cells becomes the egg, and the other again is small and degenerates. It forms the *second polar body,* which also remains attached to the egg. Each original generative cell thus gives rise to only one functional egg. In vertebrates and numerous other groups, eggs are ready for fertilization as soon as the first meiotic division has occurred. Such eggs remain in a state of meiotic arrest until a sperm enters, which provides the stimulus for the completion of meiosis.

In parallel with the nuclear maturation of gametes, cytoplasmic maturation takes place. In sperm-forming cells, much of the cytoplasm degenerates. The nucleus enlarges as an oval *sperm head,* and the mature sperm retains only three structures having a cytoplasmic origin: a long posterior *sperm tail,* which serves as locomotor flagellum; a *middle piece,* which contains energy-supplying mitochondria; and an *acrosome,* a large vacuole at the forward end of the sperm head (Fig. 24.2). The acrosome contains substances that dissolve the

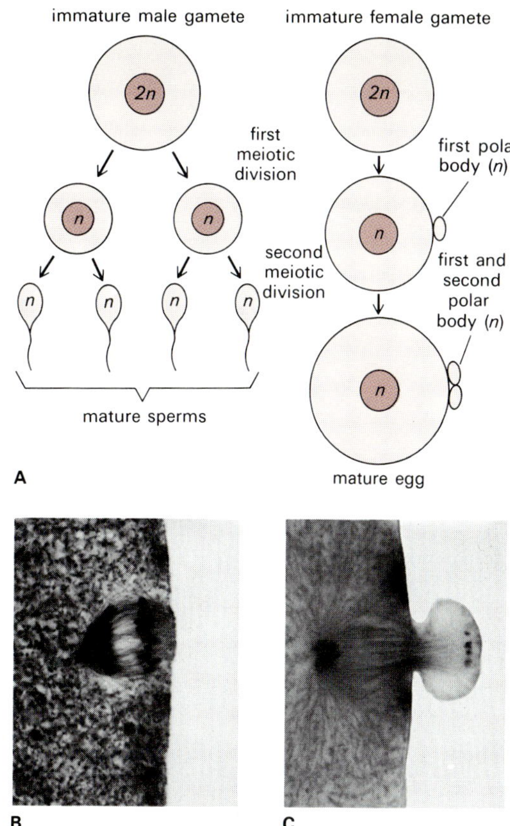

Fig. 24.1 Meiosis. (A) In males all four haploid cells formed become functional sperms. In females one cell formed by the first meiotic division is small and degenerates and becomes the first polar body. Also, one cell formed by the second meiotic division becomes the second polar body. Thus only one cell matures as a functional egg. (B), (C) Polar-body formation. (B) Section through the edge of an immature whitefish egg, showing the extremely eccentric position of the spindle and the chromosomes during a meiotic division. Chromosomes are in anaphase. Cleavage will occur at right angles to the spindle axis and will therefore produce an extremely large and an extremely small cell. (C) Cytoplasmic cleavage under way. The small cell formed will degenerate, and its remnant will be a polar body.

surface membrane of an egg during fertilization. Having lost most of the cytoplasm, mature sperms are among the smallest cells in the body. But mature eggs are among the largest; the eggs of many species accumulate large amounts of yolk, a complex mixture of substances that contain most of the raw materials required for the construction of embryos.

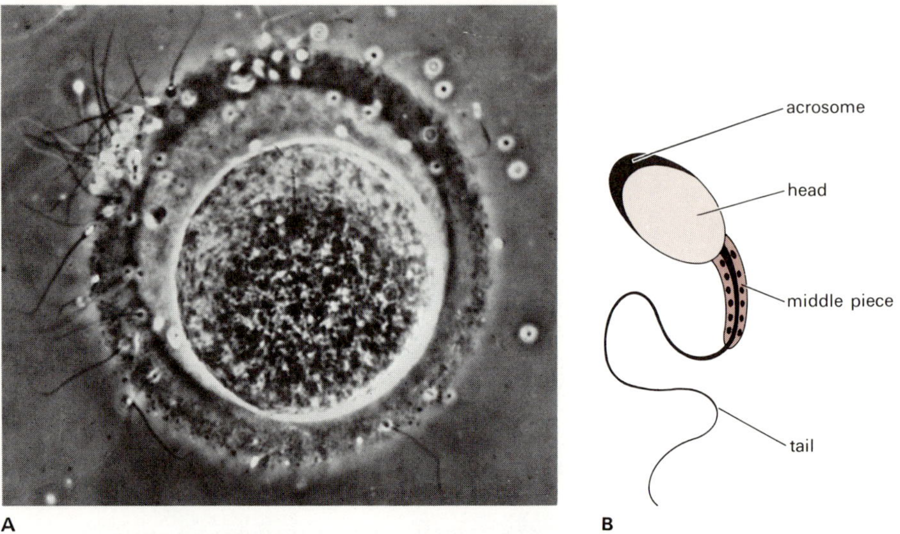

Fig. 24.2 Sperms. (A) Fertilization of a human egg. Several sperms (note flagellated tails) cover the surface of this egg. One sperm has penetrated the cytoplasm of the egg, triggering a chemical change in a thick membrane (zona pelucida) that surrounds the egg. The chemically altered membrane is impermeable to other sperms. As a result, the egg cannot be fertilized by more than one sperm (x1000). (B) Sperm structure.

Fertilization

As in plants, sperms must fuse with eggs in an aqueous environment. This water requirement has led to the elaboration of two basic animal mating patterns (Fig. 24.3). In *external fertilization,* mating partners are or come close to each other in natural bodies of water and both simultaneously *spawn;* they release sperms and eggs directly into the water, where many fertilizations then take place. This pattern is characteristic of most aquatic animals and also of terrestrial types such as certain insects and amphibia, which migrate to permanent bodies of water for reproduction.

The second pattern is *internal fertilization.* Mating partners here come into physical contact, and by various means the male transfers sperms directly to the reproductive system of the female. The internal tissues of the female here provide moisture for the sperms, and the need for external water is thereby circumvented. Internal fertilization is characteristic of most terrestrial animals, but the process occurs also in numerous aquatic groups (for example, in many fishes).

In most cases internal fertilization is achieved by *copulation,* a process in which sperms leave from the exit of the male reproductive system and enter the female reproductive system directly through its exterior opening. Copulatory organs of various kinds often assist in this transfer. If such organs are lacking, as in birds (see Chap. 35), the mating partners bring their bodies together so that the two reproductive openings touch. In many groups the males shed not loose sperms but compact sperm packets (*spermatophores*). Squids use their tentacles to transfer such packets into females, some amphibia use their mouths, and some animals transfer sperms into females by a process akin to hypodermic injection, through any part of the skin.

Development

In all cases of external and also in some of internal fertilization, development of zygotes into adults takes place externally, in natural bodies of water. Such animals, in which eggs are shed to the

Fig. 24.3 Fertilization. (A) External fertilization. Eggs just spawned by the female are about to be fertilized by the male (see also Color Fig. 14). (B) Internal fertilization. A copulating pair of land snails, suspended by mucus cord. See also Fig. 34.22. (C) Female katydid carrying spermatophore. Formed by many different kinds of animals, such sperm packets are transferred by various means into the reproductive systems of females.

outside either in an unfertilized or a fertilized state, are said to be *oviparous* (Fig. 24.4). Among vertebrates, for example, many fishes are oviparous and externally fertilizing, whereas all birds are oviparous and internally fertilizing. The developing eggs eventually *hatch*, as larvae or as miniature, immature adults. If development takes place in water, the zygotes often have coats of jelly around them (for example, frog eggs) but are otherwise protected very little. Zygotes developing on land usually are protected against evaporation by cocoons or shells (see Color Fig. 15).

Most animals are oviparous as above. Among the rest, one group is *ovoviviparous*. Fertilization here is internal, and the zygotes are retained inside the female reproductive system. Development then occurs there. However, beyond providing a substantial measure of protection, the female body does not otherwise contribute to zygote development; as in oviparous types, food is supplied by the yolk stored in each egg. Ultimately the young are *born* rather than hatched, and the females release fully formed animals, not eggs. Among vertebrates some of the fishes, amphibia, and reptiles are ovoviviparous.

A third group of animals comprises *viviparous* types. Here fertilization again is internal, zygotes are retained inside the female, and the young are born as developed animals. However, the female body now provides not merely protection but also food, and it contributes to offspring metabolism in other vital ways. The females in such cases are said to be *pregnant*. Viviparous vertebrates include, for example, some fishes, some snakes, and most mammals (see Fig. 24.4).

Reproductive Systems

In vertebrates, gonads arise as a pair of pouches growing into the body cavity just posterior

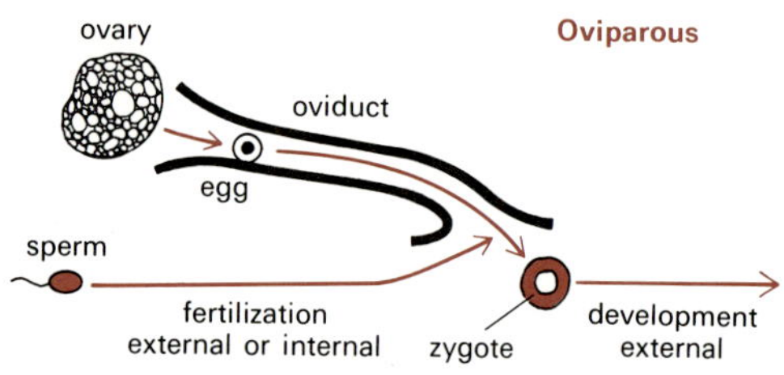

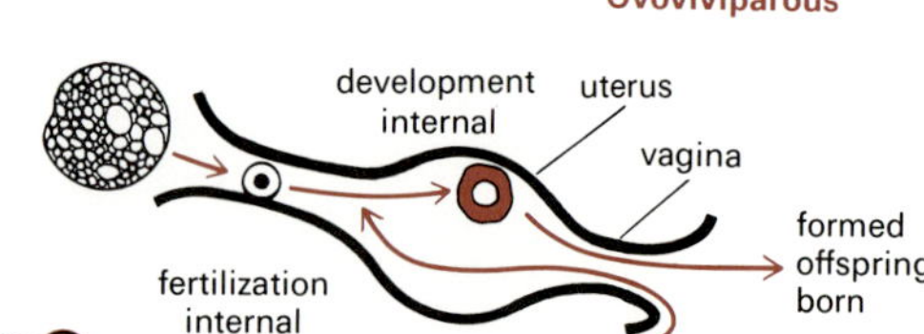

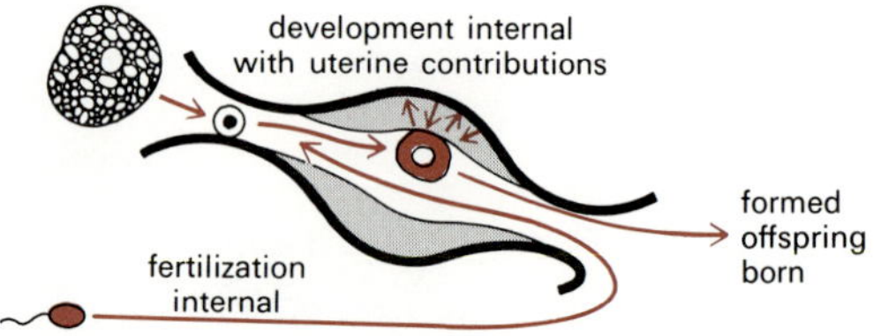

Fig. 24.4 Development. The three basic patterns of fertilization and development in animals.

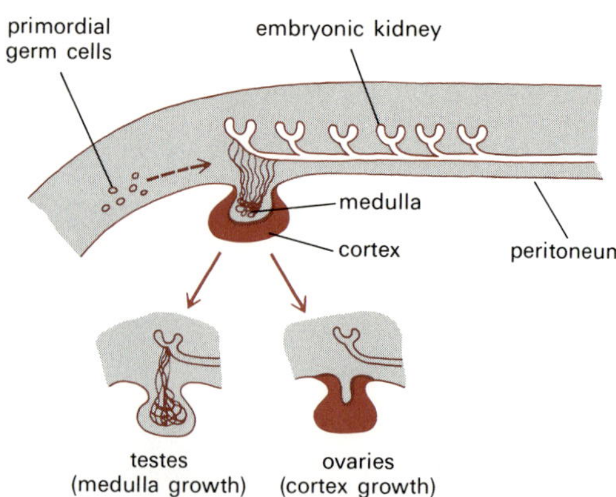

Fig. 24.5 Gonad development. Top, sectional side view of part of vertebrate embryo, indicating place of origin of primordial germ cells in head region in relation to developing gonad, embryonic kidney, and body cavity. Bottom, differential growth fo the medullary (kidney-derived) tissue results in testes, and differential growth of the cortical (peritoneum-derived) tissue results in ovaries.

to the embryonic kidneys. Each pouch enlarges and fills with tissue. The outer layers of the gonad then form a *cortex,* and the interior tissue represents a *medulla.* Gamete-producing cells, called *primordial germ cells,* arise not in the developing gonad itself but in anterior regions of the embryo. From such regions the cells migrate to the embryonic gonad and disperse inside it. At this stage the gonad still is sexually undetermined and can develop in either a male or a female direction (Fig. 24.5).

If the gonad becomes a testis, the cortex develops very little more but the medulla proliferates and becomes the bulk of the mature testis. But if the immature gonad develops as an ovary, it is the medulla that undergoes little further growth, whereas the cortex enlarges greatly.

In mammals such as opossums, bats, and whales, testes remain at their original locations permanently. In a second group, which includes elephants and many rodents, the testes leave their original positions when the breeding season begins and migrate to a *scrotum,* a skin sac between the hind legs. After sperms cease to be produced at the end of the breeding season, the testes migrate back to their original positions. In a third group, exemplified by rodents such as mice and rats, the testes descend to a scrotum when the animals reach sexual maturity, and from then on the gonads remain there permanently. And in a fourth group, of which human beings are members, the testes are internal only during embryonic stages; the organs migrate to a scrotum just before birth and then remain in this sac throughout life.

It is known that the temperature in a scrotum is up to 7°C lower than inside the trunk. It is also known that lower temperatures tend to promote and higher temperatures to inhibit sperm production. Temperature, testis location, and continuity of sperm manufacture therefore appear to be related.

The interior of the testis contains interconnected sperm chambers, or *seminiferous tubules* (Fig. 24.6). Viewed in cross section, each tubule consists of a lining of sperm-producing cells and a central passageway through which sperms leave the testis. The most immature sperm-producing cells

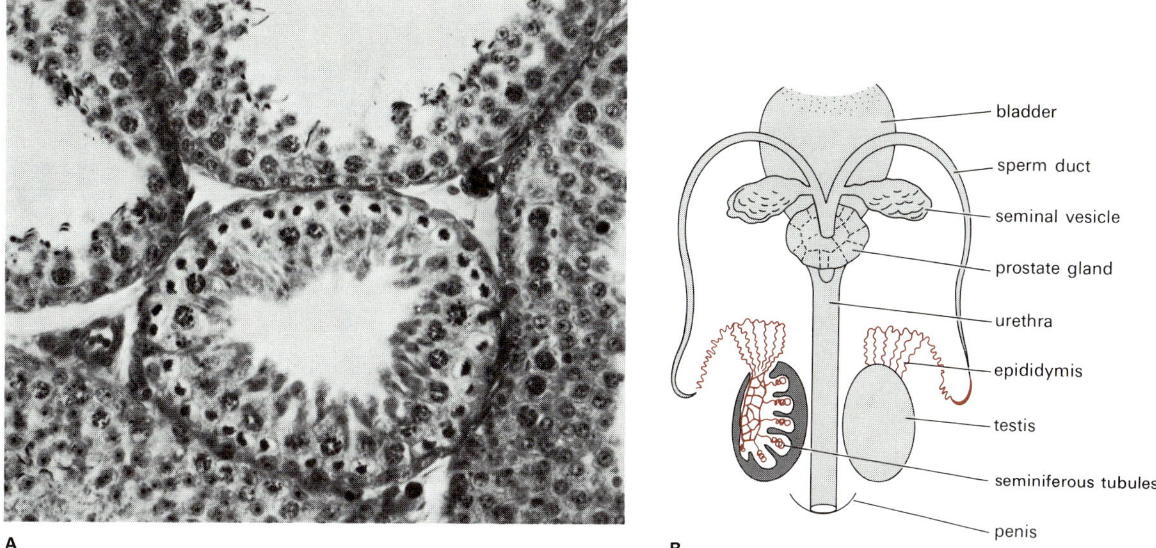

Fig. 24.6 Male reproductive systems. (A) Section through a testis. In the tubular chambers (seminiferous tubules) sperms accumulate in the spaces in the tubules. The tissue between the seminiferous tubules contains endocrine cells that manufacture androgens, the male sex hormones, under the stimulus of LH from the pituitary (see also Chap. 17). (B) The system in human males, left testis in section.

are located at the outer boundary of a tubule. These diploid cells produce daughter cells that move inward toward the center of the tubule. During this migration the daughter cells undergo meiosis. The resulting ripe sperms move along the central passageway of each tubule and collect in *sperm ducts.*

Various accessory organs generally are associated with such ducts. Thus, sperm ducts often pass through or past *sperm sacs,* chambers that store sperms before discharge. In men, sperms are stored in the *epididymis,* a highly coiled portion of the sperm duct just outside the testis. Collected sperms are expelled when nerve impulses bring about contraction of the walls in the storage regions. Also connected with sperm ducts may be *prostate glands* and *seminal vesicles,* which secrete *seminal fluids.* Together with sperms these fluids make up *semen.* In many viviparous animals, men included, sperms constitute only 1 percent of the semen expelled during *ejaculation.* The remainder is composed of seminal fluids, which contain activating substances that induce the previously quiescent sperms to lash their tails.

Many animals possess *copulatory organs* at or near the exterior termination of the sperm ducts, and semen may or may not leave the body through such an organ. If it does, as in men, the copulatory organ is a *penis* (see also Chap. 25). The sperm channel in the penis of mammals is the *urethra,* which connects with both the sperm ducts and the excretory channel from the urinary bladder. Simultaneous discharges of semen and urine are prevented by nervous reflexes that bring about closure of one channel when the other is in operation.

In female vertebrates, the primordial germ cells give rise to an egg-producing epithelium on the surface of an ovary (Fig. 24.7). This layer forms successive batches of new cells, but in each batch usually only one undergoes meiosis and matures as a reproductive cell. The surrounding cells are inhibited in some unknown way from also becoming eggs. Instead these cells form a *follicle,* a ball of tissue that soon acquires an enlarging central cavity. The egg is located eccentrically in such a follicle, in a thickened region of the follicular wall. An embryonic ovary of a human female is estimated to contain some 400,000 primordial germ

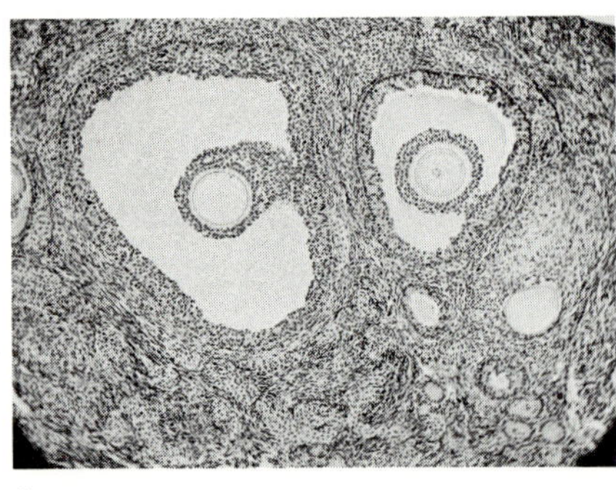

A

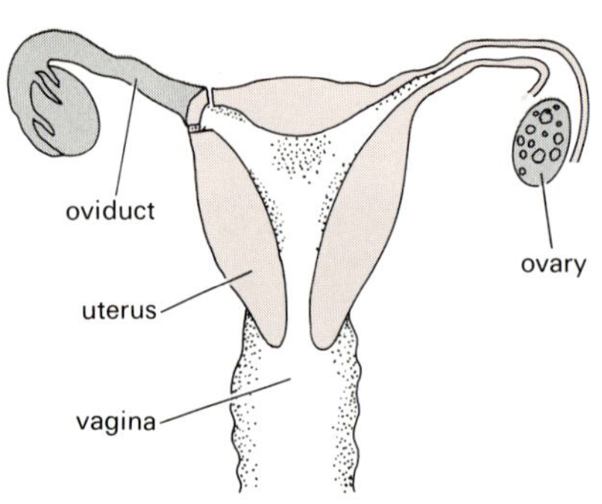

B

Fig. 24.7 Female reproductive systems. (A) Section through an ovary. Note the two large follicles, the follicular cavities, and the large egg cell in each follicle embedded in a mass of cells along the follicular wall. Endocrine cells secrete estrogens into the follicular cavity. When the eggs are mature, ovulation will occur and the eggs will escape by rupture of follicle and ovary walls. (B) The system in human females. *(A, Ward's Natural Science Establishment, Inc.)*

cells; but only about 400 functional eggs are actually formed during adult life.

As it matures, a follicle moves toward the surface of an ovary where it produces a blisterlike elevation. *Ovulation* occurs when such a follicle bursts and releases its egg into the funnel-shaped opening of an elongated reproductive tube called an *oviduct;* one oviduct leads from each ovary (see Fig. 24.7). Along the oviducts of certain animals (but not women) are *seminal receptacles,* pouches that store sperms after mating and before fertilization, as well as *yolk glands, shell glands,* and other glands producing nutritive or protective layers around fertilized eggs.

In some animals each oviduct enlarges near its external terminal and forms a *uterus,* in which egg development occurs. Both oviducts unite and form a single uterus in human females and several other mammals. In copulating animals, the terminal section of the uterus that receives the male copulatory organ during mating is called a *vagina.* The uterus narrows at the *cervix* before opening into the vagina of human females (see Chap. 25). Also, in contrast to the arrangement in human males, the reproductive tract of human females has an independent exit separate from that of the urinary pore.

REPRODUCTIVE BEHAVIOR

Like plants, most animals produce gametes only during specific *breeding seasons.* Such seasons are largely annual, most occurring in spring or fall. But many animals have two or more breeding seasons per year; for example, there are two in dogs. In some cases breeding seasons last only a single day (or night, as in clamworms and many other marine invertebrates); but in others, as in monkeys, apes, and people, reproduction can occur the year round. Breeding seasons tend to be continuous also where environmental conditions remain uniformly favorable throughout the year, as in domesticated cattle, chickens, and rabbits, and in laboratory mice and rats. Even in such cases, however, fertility is usually greatest during the spring.

As shown in Chap. 20, breeding cycles tend to be synchronized with seasonal rhythms in day lengths and temperatures. Thus breeding seasons in vertebrates usually are initiated after the animals have been exposed to a certain total amount of illumination, counted from the winter solstice in spring breeders and the summer solstice in fall breeders. Such photoperiodic stimuli affect the reproductive system through the eyes and the neuroendocrine mechanism outlined in Figs. 24.8 and 17.12. The anterior lobe of the pituitary thereby becomes stimulated to secrete increasing amounts of gonadotropic hormones (see Chap. 17), and all parts of the reproductive system increase in size as a result and become functional. The higher concentrations of sex hormones then produced by the gonads elicit not only reproductive behavior and sexuality, but also enhanced aggressiveness and closer social interrelations based on dominance and territoriality. After a breeding season, the hormone output of the anterior pituitary declines again and the reproductive system becomes quiescent and reduced in size.

The behavioral and social aspects of vertebrate reproduction appear to be just as significant as the internal functional ones. For example, if mature pigeons or mice are prevented from having social

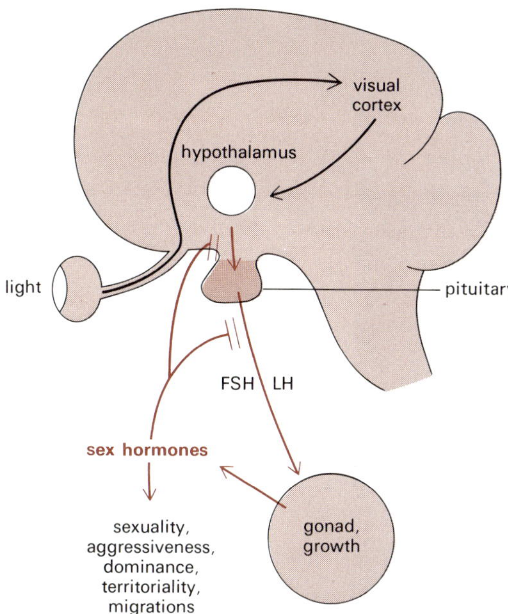

Fig. 24.8 Neuroendocrine control of reproductive functions. Light (and many other external) stimuli, as well as internal psychological states, are communicated to the hypothalamus over neural pathways (black arrows). Releasing factors (see also Chap. 17) then stimulate the pituitary, which (superimposed on an intrinsic rhythm of activity) secretes gonadotropic hormones (FSH, LH). These induce gonad growth and sex-hormone production. The hormones in turn bring about the onset of breeding seasons and all associated reproductive functions, as well as various sex-associated behaviors. When sex-hormone concentrations exceed certain levels, they inhibit the hypothalamus and pituitary (double bars), and the reproductive and associated activities then decline.

contact with other members of the species, they usually fail to come into breeding condition, even at the right season. However, pigeons can be induced to lay eggs if they are at least permitted to see themselves in a mirror, and female mice come into heat when exposed at least to the smell given off by males. In many zoo animals reproduction will not occur even when a male and a female are allowed to live together. Such animals evidently require considerably more elaborate social settings if their neural and endocrine controls of reproductive processes are to function normally.

Furthermore, mating in most vertebrates and many invertebrates is functionally dependent on preliminary *courtship.* Consisting of a series of more or less precisely programmed displays and movements, courtship serves to advertise the presence of sexually receptive individuals and to forestall or inhibit aggression by a prospective mate. The last is particularly necessary if the mate is a predator, a high-ranking member of a dominance hierarchy, or the owner of a territory.

For example, male bowerbirds and prairie chickens prance, strut, and posture within fixed territories while females look on. The females eventually indicate their choice by entering the territory of a strutting male. This courtship behavior not only indicates sexual interest on the part of males, but it also signals the conditions under which a male will tolerate crossing of its boundaries. Finches of the Galapogos Islands recognize each other by the shape of their beaks. Courtship behavior among these birds involves passing food from the beak of a male to that of a female. In short, courtship by either sex usually includes token or actual submissive behavior, prominent display of sex recognition signs, or other signals indicating nonaggressive intent (Fig. 24.9).

Most important, courtship often is required to bring both mating partners to reproductive readiness simultaneously. In some vertebrates, for example, the internal reproductive mechanism does not become operational unless visual, olfactory, or other stimuli from a mate provide a trigger. Often a whole sequence of successive triggers is needed to initiate a corresponding sequence of internal hormonal processes. For example, courtship by male ring doves elicits production of sex hormones in females, which then are induced by the hormones to build nests. This activity in turn is the specific stimulus for mate acceptance and egg laying. In female canaries, similarly, a progressive sequence of hormonal changes and a succession of steps of nest construction have been found to be reciprocally necessary stimuli. In some instances, as among cats and rabbits, male-female coordination through courtship dovetails so finely that eggs are not released from the ovary until a mating pair is actually copulating.

Like displays of threat and submission, courtship too probably has evolved as a highly ritualized version of combat. In both sexes courtship usually includes behavioral elements that are very similar to those of attack and flight, and that in some instances involve real attack and flight. In sticklebacks and gulls, for example, intermittent bursts of male attack and female flight continue right up to mating. In finches it is the female who attacks the

Fig. 24.9 Courtship. The tail display of male peacocks is one of the most familiar courtship behaviors (see also Color Fig. 17).

male with increasing vigor until copulation actually takes place. In most cases, however, the ritual elements of courtship appear to differentiate reproductive intent from real hostility. Males use aggressive displays for actual threats but ritualized versions of them to attract females; and whereas females are submissive to discourage real attack, their stylized submission in courtship is used to invite attention from males.

Mating normally terminates when sperms and eggs have been shed. In many vertebrates sexual activity ceases not primarily because the male has released sperms, but because he may be inhibited from further activity by the sight of shed eggs (as in certain fishes) or because he may have become habituated to a particular female. In guinea pigs and cattle, for example, a female is normally inseminated several times in succession during a single mating sequence. The sequence ends when male interest wanes. However, a male that has become inactive with one female will readily and repeatedly copulate with a succession of other females. In the case of bulls this prolonged copulatory capability has become commercially important: prize bulls can be induced to deliver maximal amounts of semen (for use in artificial inseminations) by presenting them with a series of dummy cows.

The mating structure of a social group varies considerably for different species. Most fishes, mammals such as rodents, and numerous other vertebrates mate promiscuously, and in such animals distinct family organizations tend to be absent. Where families are distinguishable, the units are often solitary or they can be parts of larger herds or herdlike groups. In either case a mating unit can be polygamous, like chickens, or monogamous, like parrots or bears. Also, such a unit may stay together either for a single season or for life. For example, bears and wolves typically mate for life.

Whatever the mating structure, reproductive behavior usually contributes to group sociality well beyond the breeding season. Thus, many vertebrates guard and tend eggs at least until hatching, and many also nourish, care for, and train their young after hatching or birth. Such parental behavior is induced partly by the sex hormones and specifically by *prolactin*, one of the three pituitary gonadotropic hormones (see Chap. 17 and Table 17.1).

Parental behavior does not have an exclusively endocrine basis, however, but is subject also to complex psychological controls. In mammals, for example, development of the emotional bond between mother and offspring, normally firmly established within an hour or two after birth, depends in large part on maternal licking, cleaning, and handling of offspring. If a just-born offspring is cleaned by an experimenter or is handled by another animal, the mother often will refuse to acknowledge this offspring as her own. Similarly, many female mammals will retrieve young that have rolled out of the nest, and since this activity is undertaken even by nonbreeding animals it, too, appears to be independent of hormonal states. Continued milk secretion likewise requires not merely hormonal but also external stimuli, particularly tactile stimulation of the nipples and withdrawal of already accumulated milk by sucking. Moreover, as shown in Chap. 21, adequate social settings and social behavior learned during young stages are essential for normal parental behavior and establishment of proper parent-young relations.

REPRODUCTIVE CONTROL

In male vertebrates, control over reproduction and reproductive behavior is exercised mainly through three gonadotropic hormones secreted by the pituitary gland: *FSH*, *prolactin*, and *LH* (see Table 17.1). The production of each hormone is controlled by a specific hypothalamic releasing factor (see also Chap. 17). FSH promotes sperm production in seminiferous tubules, and prolactin is known to control paternal behavior (for example, protective attitudes toward mate and offspring). Pituitary LH is the specific hormone that stimulates the testis to produce *androgens*, the male sex hormones. These are manufactured by cells in the tissue partitions between the seminiferous tubules of a testis (see Fig. 24.6).

In animals that mate only at certain times of the year, the concentration of the most potent androgen, *testosterone*, rises sharply at the start of a breeding season under the influence of LH. Sperms are then produced actively, sex urge increases, and secondary sex traits such as mating colors in skin and plumage become pronounced (Fig. 24.10). If it is present in excessive amounts, testosterone has an inhibitory effect on the hypothalamus. This structure responds to high concentrations of testosterone in blood by reducing its output of *LH-releasing factor*, the neurosecretion that stimulates production of LH by the pituitary. This reduced output results in a corresponding decrease in LH production, and testosterone secretions therefore decline as well. Through such feedback control, androgen concentrations remain at fairly steady levels during breeding seasons. Human beings can reproduce at any time of the year. Here the production of androgens and sperms begins at sexual maturity, or *puberty*, and may continue for life.

Females produce one or several successive batches of eggs during a breeding season. Periods of egg maturation are called *estrus cycles* in mammals, and female dogs, for example, come into estrus just once per breeding season (*monoestrous*

Fig. 24.10 Secondary sex traits. (A) Swordtail male at top, female at bottom. (B) Male pintail duck at left, female at right. Note sexual dimorphism in both examples. See also Fig. 8.8.

A

B

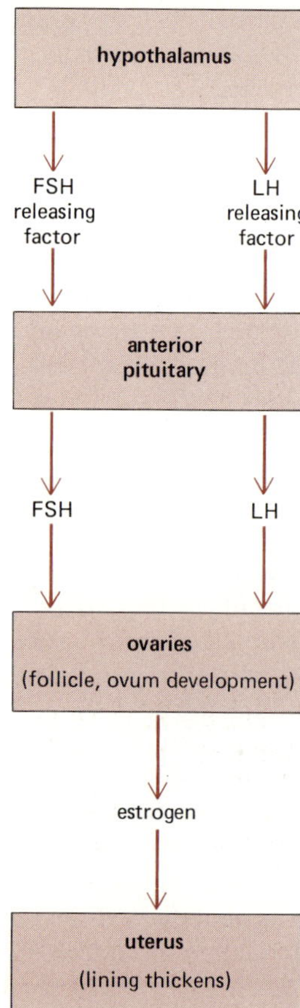

Fig. 24.11 Follicle and ovum development. Summary of hormonal control of estrogen secretion and of ovum and follicle development. In human beings estrogens play a major role in stimulating proliferation of the uterine lining following menstruation.

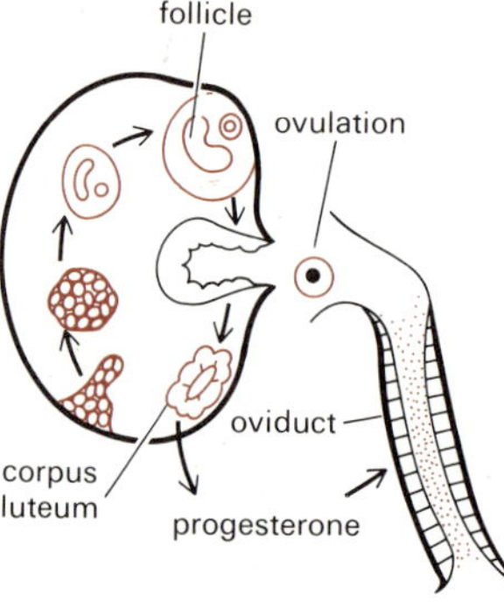

Fig. 24.12 Egg growth in oviparous vertebrates. Progesterone induces the oviduct to secrete jelly coats or shell-forming substances around eggs.

types). Horses and sheep are among *polyestrous* types, which produce several batches of eggs. However, egg manufacture ceases after one batch is fertilized.

The hormonal controls of egg production in vertebrates parallel those of sperm production. At the onset of the breeding season, the pituitary secretes prolactin and FSH. Prolactin induces maternal behavior and broodiness, and FSH, the *f*ollicle-*s*timulating *h*ormone, influences ovarian activity. More specifically, the follicle cells around an egg are stimulated to produce *estrogens,* the female sex hormones (Fig. 24.11). Corresponding functionally to the male hormones, they promote growth of the follicle, pronounced development of secondary sex traits, and an increase in sex urge.

In human beings and all viviparous mammals, estrogens induce proliferation of cells and blood vessels in the uterine lining. Moreover, certain amounts of estrogens accumulate in the fluid-filled cavity of a follicle and stimulate its enlargement and maturation. As the follicle matures under the influence of FSH, the hypothalamus stimulates release of steadily increasing amounts of LH from the pituitary. This increasing concentration of LH causes the wall of the maturing follicle to weaken. The wall ruptures as the concentration of LH reaches a peak, and the egg escapes into the oviduct. The release of the egg from the follicle is called *ovulation.*

An immediate consequence of ovulation is that the ruptured and eggless follicle remaining in the ovary loses its fluid and collapses. Under the influence of continued release of LH from the pituitary, the follicular remains transform into a yellowish body, the *corpus luteum* (LH stands for "luteinizing hormone"). The corpus luteum secretes estrogens in large amounts and also secretes a second hormone, *progesterone.* This hormone stimulates the oviducts of oviparous vertebrates to secrete jelly coats or shells around the eggs passing through (Fig. 24.12).

In viviparous mammals, progesterone and estrogen combine to cause further development of the uterine lining. The wall of the uterus thickens greatly and develops numerous glandular pockets and extra blood vessels, thereby preparing the organ to receive a fertilized egg. An egg normally is fertilized in an oviduct of these animals, human beings included, where embryonic development begins. Upon reaching the uterus, the developing embryo embeds in the thick uterine wall. The maternal blood in this wall then supplies the embryo with nourishment and oxygen. But if the egg is not fertilized in the oviduct it soon disintegrates, and the uterus will have been prepared for nothing.

PHOTO ESSAY 2: REPRODUCTION

Reproduction is essential for the perpetuation of all species. However, the patterns and processes of reproduction vary considerably among different organisms, as exemplified by the following sequence of photographs.

Plants

Color Fig. 9. Ferns. Underside of a fern leaf with sori. Indusia are absent in this type. *(R. H. Noailles.)*

Color Fig. 10. Gymnosperms. A cluster of microstrobili (male cones) at tip of a branch of red pine. Male gametophytes (pollen grains) are produced in these small cones. *(Barbara K. Deans, DPI.)*

Color Fig. 11. Angiosperms. The life cycles of many insects and flowering plants are interdependent. The movements of this honeybee are insuring pollination of the asters. Note the yellow pollen adhering to the body of the bee. *(© 1978 Harry Rogers, DPI.)*

Invertebrates

Color Fig. 12. Egg deposition. Many egg-producing animals, such as this land snail, lay eggs in underground chambers, hidden from potential predators. *(© Hans Pfletschinger, Peter Arnold, Inc.)*

Color Fig. 13. Molting. Many developing insects shed their inflexible exoskeletons as they grow. Shown here is a dragonfly emerging from its nymphal case. A new, larger exoskeleton already is forming about the growing insect. *(© Hans Pfletschinger, Peter Arnold, Inc.)*

Color Fig. 14. Frog amplexus. The eggs of frogs and most amphibians are shed into water and then fertilized. The shedding (note dark eggs) is triggered when a male frog grasps an egg-laden female from behind. The male responds by releasing sperms over the eggs as they are shed. This reproductive behavior is termed amplexus. *(© Hans Pfletschinger, Peter Arnold, Inc.)*

Color Fig. 15. Reptile development. Many reptiles, such as these sand lizards, hatch from eggs. The evolution of shelled eggs contributed greatly to the adaptive radiation of terrestrial vertebrates. *(© Hans Pfletschinger, Peter Arnold, Inc.)*

B

A

Color Fig. 16. Care and protection of young. Offspring are cared for in diverse ways. (A) A young Jackson's chameleon rests on one of the horns of its male parent. (B) A hungry herring gull pecks at the red patch on its parent's bill, an action that induces the parent to regurgitate food it has recently caught and swallowed before returning to the nest. *(A, R. Andrew Odum, © Peter Arnold, Inc.; B, From "The Gull's Way" by Louis Darling, with drawings by the author. William Morrow, 1965.)*

Color Fig. 17. Courtship display. Most animals are sexually active only during specific seasons of the year. At such times, the males and females of some species engage in elaborate courtship behavior. Here a male frigate displays its brightly colored breast. The display encourages sexual receptivity among female frigates. *(Leonard Lee Rue III, DPI.)*

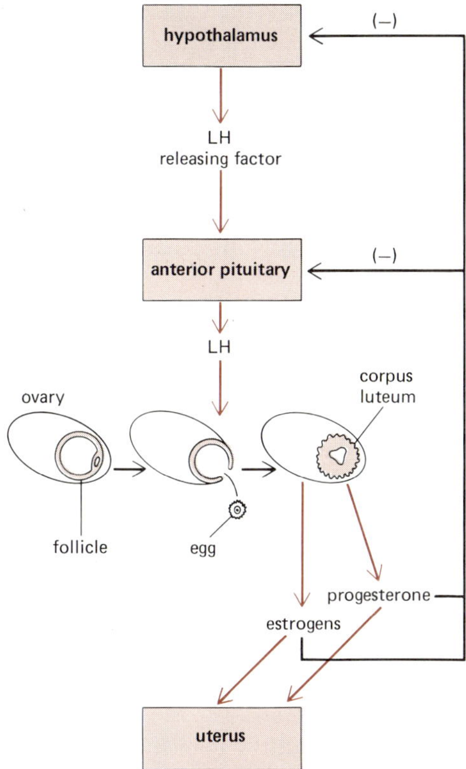

Fig. 24.13 Corpus luteum. Summary of the effects of LH on ovulation and corpus luteum development. A surge in LH released from the pituitary triggers ovulation. The gonadotropin then promotes transformation of the eggless follicle into a corpus luteum, or "yellow body." The corpus luteum continues to secrete estrogens and also produces a second sex hormone, progesterone. The two sex hormones promote increased thickening of the uterine lining. After a time, the high concentrations of estrogens and progesterone exert a negative effect on release of LH from the pituitary (indicated by the negative symbols). As a result, the corpus luteum degenerates, causing a sharp reduction in the production of estrogens and progesterone. Reduced concentrations of these sex hormones brings about a sloughing of the uterine lining.

In this case, the thickened uterine lining will not be maintained indefinitely. The high concentrations of progesterone and estrogens produced by the corpus luteum increasingly inhibit the release of LH- and FSH-releasing factors from the hypothalamus. In addition, progesterone and estrogens probably also directly inhibit release of LH and FSH from the pituitary (Fig. 24.13 and see Fig. 24.8). Because the corpus luteum cannot be maintained in the absence of these gonadotropins, it degenerates and ceases its production of estrogens and progesterone. Without these sex hormones the ready condition of the uterus cannot be maintained, and its lining reverts to normal thickness.

In some monkeys, all apes, and women, the preparations for pregnancy in the uterus are so extensive that if fertilization does not occur and progesterone and estrogen production ceases, the lining of the uterus actually disintegrates. Tissue fragments separate away, and some blood escapes from torn vessels. Over a period of a few days, all this debris is expelled through the vagina to the outside. This process is *menstruation.*

A *menstrual cycle* in such animals lasts about 28 days. Follicle maturation occurs during the first 10 to 14 days under the control of FSH and estrogen, and this *follicular phase* of the cycle terminates with ovulation. During the next 14 to 18 days, the uterus grows in preparation for pregnancy under the influence of LH, estrogens, and progesterone. If pregnancy does not begin during this *luteal phase,* menstruation takes place in the course of the first few days of the next menstrual cycle. As a result of the sharply reduced concentrations of estrogens and progesterone that follow degeneration of the corpus luteum, the hypothalamus is released from its inhibition. The flow of FSH-releasing factor to the pituitary is reinitiated, and the cycle begins anew (Fig. 24.14). In human females, menstrual cycles begin to occur at puberty and continue to the time of *menopause* in middle age, when the sex-hormone control system ceases to operate.

Estrogen is not absent altogether during the luteal phase, nor is progesterone completely absent during the follicular phase of a menstrual cycle. The hormones merely attain definite peak concentrations at particular times (see Fig. 24.14). These fluctuations have important consequences. Under the influence of progesterone, for example, which promotes growth of the duct system in the mammary glands, a slight swelling of these glands generally occurs during the luteal phase. Body temperature increases somewhat during the follicular phase, then falls during the luteal phase. Sex drive is likely to be more pronounced during the follicular phase, since estrogen maintains it. And inasmuch as estrogens, like androgens in males, affect many aspects of behavior, monthly hormonal and behavioral fluctuations in some cases tend to be correlated.

The production of sperms and eggs sets the stage for fertilization. Regardless of whether this

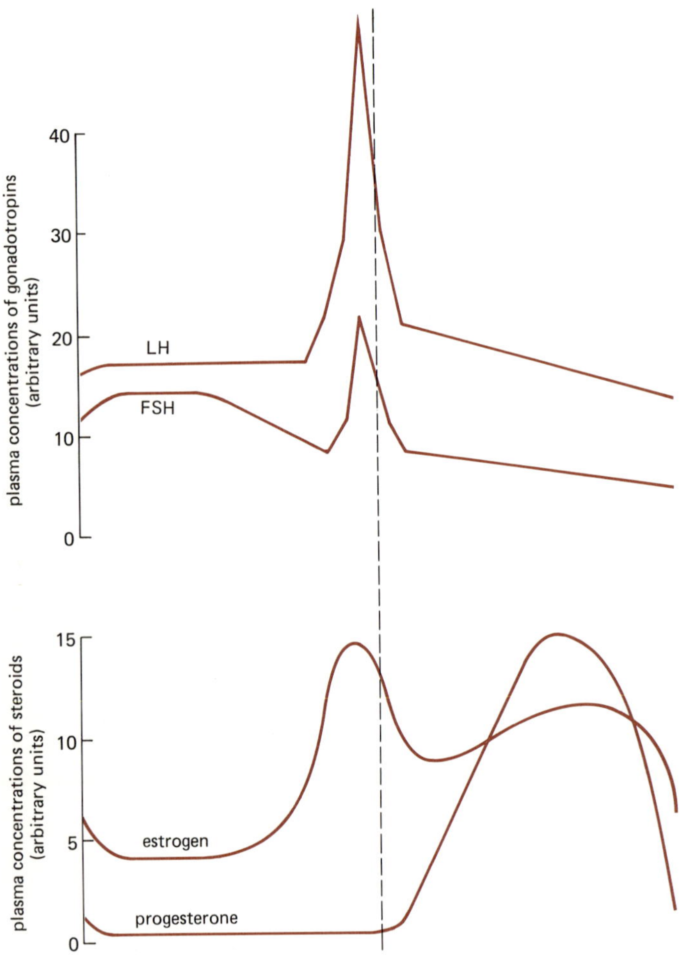

process occurs in free water after spawning or within the oviduct after copulation, the first step always is the entrance of a sperm into an egg, usually through a fusion of the cell membranes of the sperm and the egg.

This fusion triggers a sequence of events called *activation* of the egg. First, the egg surface undergoes metabolic changes that make it unreceptive to additional sperms (see Fig. 24.2). In many animals, these changes appear to involve fusion of many membrane-bound vacuoles, called *cortical granules,* with the surface membrane. The contents of cortical granules are thereby released to the exterior, where they evidently "sperm-proof" the egg surface. In certain aquatic invertebrates, a *fertilization membrane* that has formed during egg maturation lifts away from the egg surface after a sperm has made contact. This membrane serves as a barrier to additional sperms (Fig. 24.15).

Second, activation often triggers a dramatic increase in the metabolism of eggs; the rates of respiration, protein synthesis, and other metabolic processes increase sharply. Third, activation stimulates movement of various substances and particles, or *inclusions,* throughout the cytoplasm of the egg. Such inclusions play important roles in embryonic development (see next section). Finally, most eggs are fertilized before they have completed meiosis, and activation stimulates resumption of this process. Upon its completion, the sperm nucleus within the egg migrates toward the egg nucleus. The union of the two haploid nuclei completes fertilization. The nuclear envelopes dissolve, the now diploid chromosomes line up in a metaphase plate, and the zygote undergoes a first mitotic division. Embryonic development is launched in this manner.

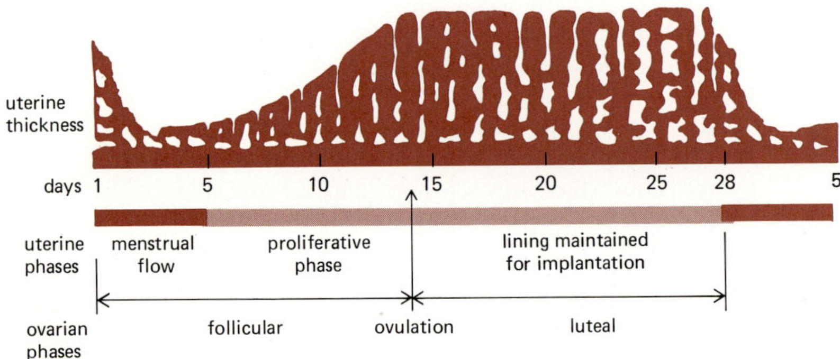

Fig. 24.14 Menstrual cycles. Summary of hormone concentrations in blood and of uterine changes during the human menstrual cycle.

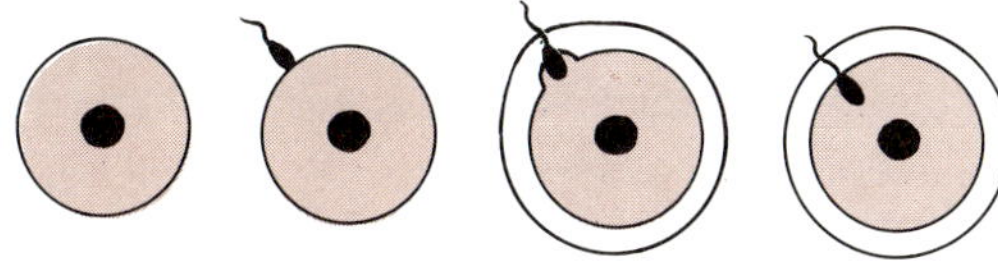

Fig. 24.15 Fertilization, as in aquatic invertebrates. A fertilization membrane lifts off the egg surface after a sperm has made contact, preventing additional sperms from entering (C, D). The sperm tail is left at the egg surface, and the sperm head (nucleus) alone migrates into the egg cytoplasm, where it fuses with the egg nucleus. An egg is fertilized only after sperm and egg nuclei have fused.

THE EMBRYO

An embryo represents a first developmental phase in which all basic structures and functions of an animal become elaborated in at least rough detail. Such elaborations are codirected by *morphogenesis, determination,* and *differentiation,* three integrated processes discussed in Chap. 22. The embryonic period begins with *cleavage,* the subdivision of the fertilized egg.

Cleavage and Blastula

Eggs typically are the largest cells produced by organisms. A frog egg, for example, is almost 100,000 times larger than the average size of differentiated frog cells. Large amounts of stored cytoplasmic nutrients, or *yolk,* account for much of the volume of many eggs. Mitotic *cleavage* divisions cut an egg into progressively smaller cells called *blastomeres* (Fig. 24.16). Very little new RNA is produced by the nuclei of blastomeres during early cleavage, and most of the metabolic activities of these cells is controlled by large amounts of stored mRNA that had been produced during maturation of the egg. Evidently, translation of these stored messengers is triggered by egg activation. Cleavage typically continues until the blastomeres have attained the size of adult cells.

Cleavage also segregates cytoplasmic inclusions of eggs that often function in cellular determination. The cytoplasm of eggs rarely is homogeneous. Eggs usually contain localized aggregations of substances that become part of the cytoplasm of individual blastomeres during cleavage. In many invertebrates, these substances apparently influence early egg differentiation. For example, the head-tail, dorsal-ventral, and left-right axes already are firmly established in the zygote. After cleavage in such *mosaic* (or *determined*) eggs, it is possible to separate the cells from each other experimentally. Each isolated blastomere then develops as a *partial* embryo; it produces the same portion of the embryo it would have produced if the cleaving egg had been left intact (Fig. 24.17).

By contrast, the eggs of vertebrates and certain other animals are of the *regulative* (or *undetermined*) variety. In these the fate of various egg portions becomes fixed much later, usually not until three cleavages have produced eight cells. If blastomeres are isolated before that time, each develops as a *whole* embryo, not as a partial one. Formation of two or more whole animals from separated blastomeres is equivalent to the production of identical *twins,* triplets, quadruplets, or larger sets. Natural production of identical twins undoubtedly occurs through similar separations, but the forces or accidents that actually isolate blastomeres in nature are not understood. If the blastomeres are separated incompletely, Siamese twins result. And if separation occurs after the time of developmental determination, each blastomere forms only a partial embryo, like a part of a mosaic.

Apart from the mosaic or regulative characteristics of an egg, three additional properties influence development greatly: egg *size,* cleavage *rate,*

Fig. 24.16 Cleavage and organ-forming zones. (A) Egg, four-cell, and later cleavage stage in frogs. (B) Organ-forming zones. The main egg axis is marked by so-called animal and vegetal poles at opposite areas of the egg. As cleavage progresses, a given zone of the egg becomes segregated in progressively smaller but more numerous blastomeres. (*Roberts Rugh and Burgess Publishing Company.*)

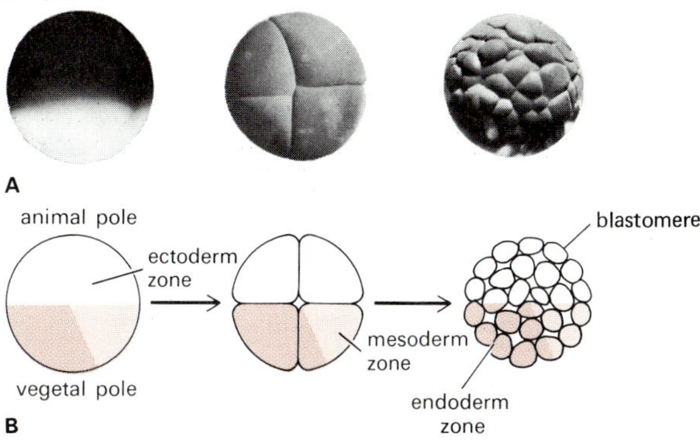

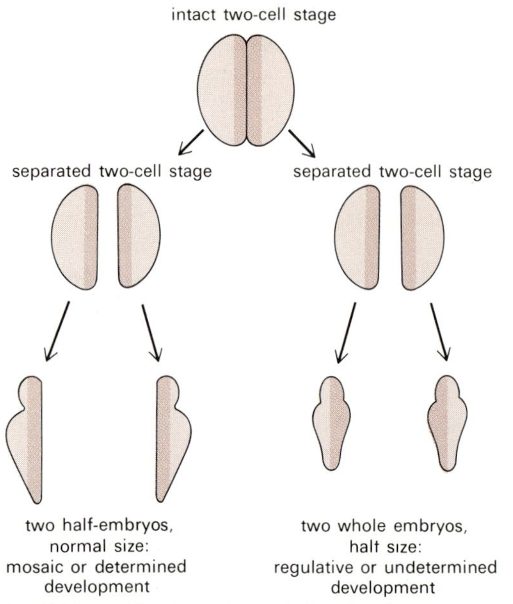

Fig. 24.17 Mosaic and regulative development. If the cells of early cleavage stages of mosaic eggs are isolated experimentally (left), each cell develops as it would have in any case. The inference is that the fates of cytoplasmic regions in such eggs (dark central parts) are determined very early. But if the cells of early cleaving regulative eggs are isolated (right), each cell develops as a smaller whole animal. The inference here is that the fate of the cytoplasm is still undetermined. Thus if the two-cell-stage blastomeres are separated, the central cytoplasm, which normally would form central body parts, actually forms left structures in one case, right structures in the other.

and amount and distribution of *yolk.* Depending on the original size of an egg, cleavage will continue for a longer or a shorter period until the cells are considerably smaller; and starting from a given egg size, a particular rate of cleavage will produce such final cell sizes more or less quickly. Thus, both egg size and cleavage rate govern the number and size of the blastomeres that will be present at the end of cleavage. In their turn, the number and size of the cellular building blocks will influence the later architectural development of the embryo (see below).

With respect to yolk, some eggs, those of mammals included, contain very little. In others the amount of yolk is large, and it is accumulated either in the center of an egg, as in insects, spiders, and other arthropods, or eccentrically in one egg half, as in frogs, salamanders, and other amphibians (Fig. 24.18). The eggs of birds and squids are among those with so much yolk that the nonyolky part of the cell forms a mere microscopic spot, or *blastodisc,* on top of the yolk mass. Yolk is a mechanically inert material which, when present in large quantities, interferes physically with the subdivision of an egg during cleavage. Thus, yolky eggs generally divide more slowly and form larger blastomeres than nonyolky ones. In extremely yolky eggs, as in birds, the yolk does not even become part of the dividing blastomeres; cleaving yolkless cells come to lie on top of the uncleaved yolk mass.

The general result of cleavage is the formation of an embryonic stage called a *blastula.* In most cases this stage has the form of a solid or hollow ball of cells. Solid blastulas usually are filled with more or less yolky cells or with undivided yolk, and in hollow blastulas the size of the internal space, or *blastocoel,* varies according to the size and number of cells that enclose it (see Fig. 24.18).

Gastrula and Induction

After a blastula has developed, the next major event is the formation of three *primary germ layers.* The outermost of these is the *ectoderm* ("outer skin"). The nervous system, skin, and the derivatives of the skin such as feathers, scales, hair, and nails are produced by this layer. The innermost germ layer, or *endoderm* ("inner skin"), gives rise to the alimentary tract and its associated digestive organs, such as the pancreas and liver in vertebrates. The middle germ layer is the *mesoderm* ("middle skin"). It gives rise to several different structures, including muscle, bone, blood, blood vessels, and the heart. Some organs, such as the pituitary and adrenal glands, are composites of tissues derived from more than one germ layer.

The processes that transform a blastula into an embryo composed of three germ layers are collectively called *gastrulation,* and the resulting embryo itself is a *gastrula.* There are almost as many different methods of gastrulation as there are animal types. In most animals, so-called *organ-forming zones* on the original egg surface already mark out the prospective regions that will produce the three germ layers (see Fig. 24.16). Gastrulation therefore

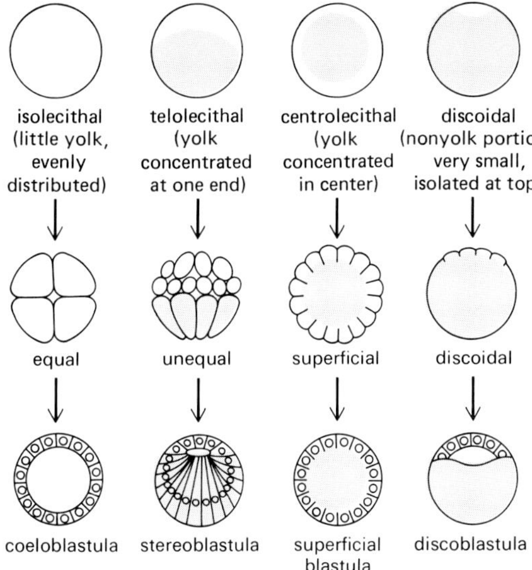

Fig. 24.18 Eggs, cleavage, and blastulas. Top row, egg types, named according to yolk content and distribution (indicated by colored areas). Center row, cleavage patterns. Note that yolk influences the nature of a given pattern. Bottom row, blastula types. Any free space in a blastula is a blastocoel.

involves an *interiorization* of the endoderm- and mesoderm-forming zones of the blastula. The prospective endoderm usually is brought into the interior first, generally through one of two processes: *epiboly,* or overgrowth of the ectoderm-forming regions around the endoderm-forming ones; and *emboly,* or ingrowth of the endoderm-forming regions under the ectoderm-forming ones (Fig. 24.19).

The first significant experiments elucidating the movements of cells during gastrulation were conducted between 1925 and 1929 by Walter Vogt. The principal experimental tool he used was small chips of agar stained with different colored dyes. Vogt placed these chips on the surface of amphibian blastulas, thereby imparting the dyes to different groups of blastomeres. By observing how the dyed cells moved, Vogt was able to map which groups of cells produced each of the primary germ layers.

Using this and other experimental methods, biologists have determined that most animals gastrulate by epiboly, emboly, or some combination of them. If a blastula is composed of but a few, large cells, embolic ingrowth may be difficult or impossible mechanically, and epibolic overgrowth is more likely to occur. By contrast, emboly readily will be possible in a blastula with many small cells and a large blastocoel. The form of emboly usually encountered in such cases is *invagination,* an indenting as when a balloon is pushed in at one side.

The common result of all methods of gastrulation is a basically two-layered gastrula having ectoderm on the outside, endoderm on the inside, a central cavity surrounded by endoderm, and an opening leading from this cavity to the outside. The cavity is the *archenteron,* the future alimentary space. The opening from it, called the *blastopore,* becomes the single alimentary opening of radiate animals and flatworms, the mouth of most invertebrates, and the anus of all vertebrates, human beings included. A second alimentary opening arises later as a perforation at the opposite side of the embryo.

Development of the third germ layer, the mesoderm, takes place in various ways. Depending on the species, mesoderm-forming cells become established before, with, or after production of the endoderm. In all instances at least some mesoderm-forming cells become established between ectoderm and endoderm by the end of gastrulation. At this time the future front and hind ends of the animal are already marked out and the body cavities are foreshadowed. In effect, the fundamental architecture of the future animal has become elaborated in rough outline (see Fig. 24.19).

All later development consists essentially of *morphogenesis,* the sculpturing of well-defined body parts. In general, such transformations occur by outfolding or infolding, outpouching or inpouching, of portions of the three layers of gastrula. For example, the nervous system of vertebrates forms by an infolding of a tube of ectoderm along the dorsal midline of the embryo (Fig. 24.20). Limbs arise by combined outpouchings from ectoderm and mesoderm. Lungs and digestive glands develop as outpouchings from various levels of the endoderm. All other body parts develop in similar fashion. The ultimate result of these processes of morphogenesis and differentiation is a fully formed embryo, clearly recognizable as a young stage of a particular species.

Experiments have shown how these orderly sequences of development are controlled. Eye de-

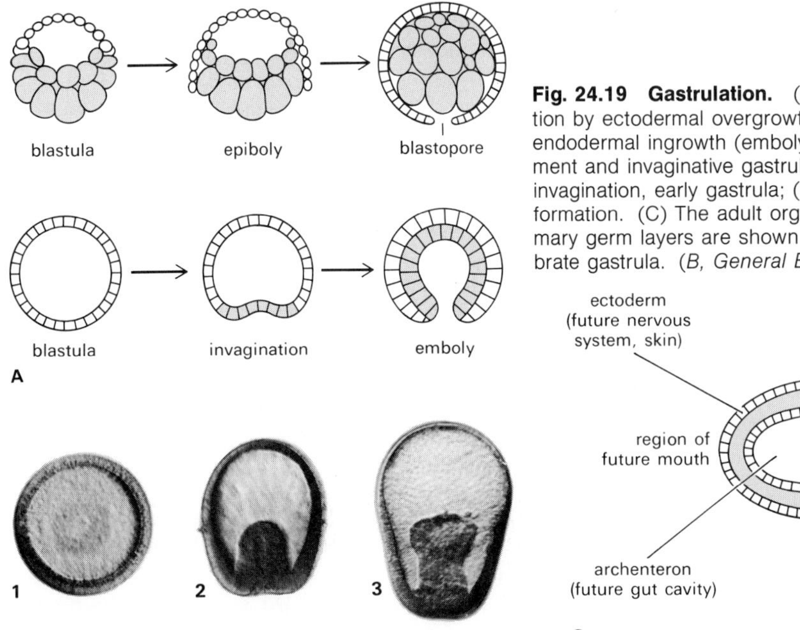

Fig. 24.19 Gastrulation. (A) Transverse sections. (Top) Gastrulation by ectodermal overgrowth (epiboly). (Bottom) Gastrulation by endodermal ingrowth (emboly, or invagination). (B) Early development and invaginative gastrulation in starfish: (1) blastula; (2) embolic invagination, early gastrula; (3) late gastrula, beginning of mesoderm formation. (C) The adult organ systems formed by each of the primary germ layers are shown in this sectional side view of a vertebrate gastrula. (*B, General Biological Supply House, Inc.*)

velopment in vertebrates provides a particularly striking example. An eye begins to form when a pocket grows out from the side of the future brain (Fig. 24.21). This pocket has a bulbous tip that eventually invaginates into a double-layered eyecup, the future eyeball. The bulbous tip of brain tissue soon comes into contact with the outer, skin-forming ectoderm of the body. Just where the tip of brain tissue rests against it, this skin ectoderm begins to thicken as a ball of cells, and the ball is then nipped off toward the inside. It fits neatly into the developing eyecup and represents the future lens. The lens cells and the overlying skin ectoderm later become transparent, and in this manner the basic structure of the eye is established.

In experiments on amphibian embryos, the bulbous tip of brain tissue can be cut off before it has grown very far and can be transplanted, for example, into a region just under the belly ectoderm of another embryo. Under such conditions the patch of belly ectoderm overlying the transplanted brain tissue soon thickens, a ball of cells is nipped off toward the inside, and a lens differentiates. Moreover, lens and overlying skin become transparent. In effect, the transplanted brain tissue has caused the formation of a structurally normal eye in a highly abnormal location (Fig. 24.22).

A common conclusion emerges from this and many similar types of experiments. One embryonic tissue interacts with an adjacent one, and the latter

Fig. 24.20 Early development of vertebrate nervous system. (A) Left to right, dorsal views of progressive stages in neural-tube formation in frogs. The anterior ends of the embryos are toward the right. (B) Diagrammatic cross sections corresponding to the stages shown in (A).

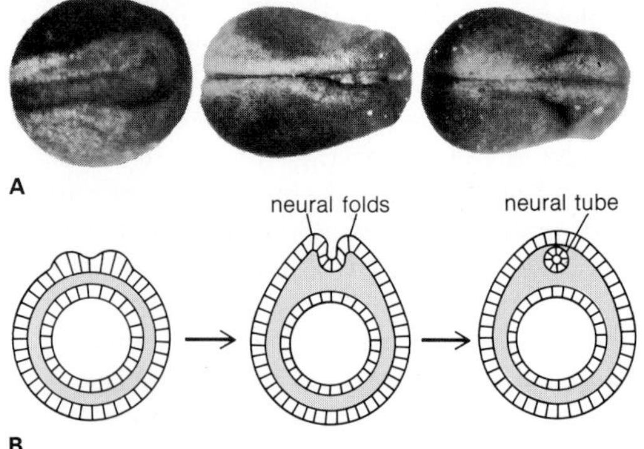

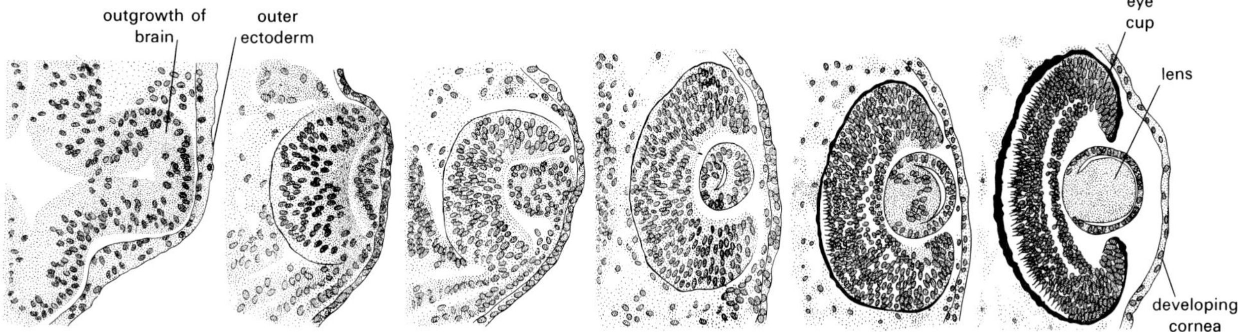

Fig. 24.21 Vertebrate (amphibian) eye development. This series of diagrams shows the successive outgrowth of a pocket from the brain, contact of this pocket with the outer body ectoderm, formation of an eyecup, gradual formation of a lens from the outer ectoderm, and development of the pigmented and other tissue layers of the eyeball. *(From D. Bodenstein, Journal of Experimental Zoology, vol. 108, 1948, pp. 96–97.)*

is thereby induced to differentiate, to grow, to develop in a particular way. This developed tissue then interacts with another one in turn and induces it to develop. In such fashion, one tissue provides the stimulus for the development of the next. Hundreds of such *embryonic inductions* have been identified in many different developing tissues, and these interactions appear to account for the orderly sequence in which many body parts normally are elaborated.

The nature of the inductive stimulus and its mode of transmission have been subjects of intensive research. Most experimental evidence indicates that inducers are chemicals. Filters, porous to molecules but not to cells, have been placed between inducing and responding tissues of several developing vertebrate organs. Normal induction occurs in virtually all cases. However, barriers that block flow of all substances between the tissues almost always prevent induction.

Several classes of chemicals can produce inductions, often in the same tissue. These include such diverse substances as inorganic ions, proteins, nucleoproteins, and steroids. Moreover, several of these substances have been shown to induce responses in tissues of different species. For example, frog skin responds to inducers derived from salamander tissue and vice versa. Such evidence supports the hypothesis that most inducers act as nonspecific triggers of responses already "programmed" in the cells of reacting tissues. Indeed, some evidence suggests that inducers activate blocks of coordinated genes in responding cells. Most of this evidence is inconclusive, however, and the nature of inductive processes remains one of the fundamental unsolved problems of modern biology.

Fig. 24.22 Eye transplantation. If embryonic brain tissue destined to form an eyecup is excised from a donor embryo and transplanted to an abnormal location in a host embryo, a structurally perfect eye can develop at that abnormal location. The photo shows a larva of a salamander (*Amblystoma*) with two supernumerary eyes grafted to abnormal locations. The picture was taken 43 days after the transplant operation.

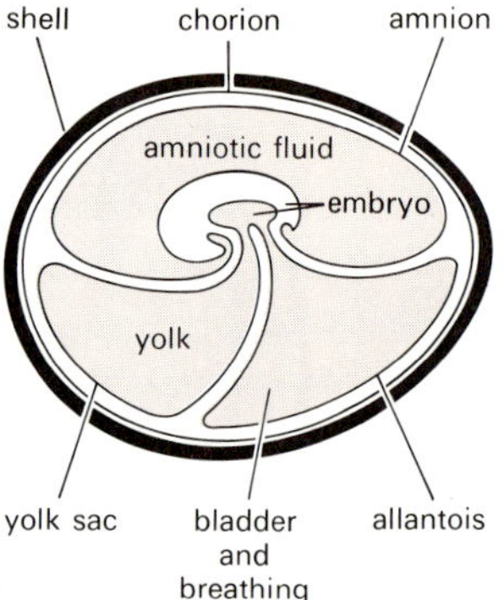

Fig. 24.23 Extraembryonic membranes in reptile and bird eggs.

LARVAE

The embryonic phase of development typically terminates with a process of *hatching*, in which an embryo escapes from its external protective coats and becomes a free-living *larva*. Larvae occur in virtually all phyla, but some of the subgroups within a phylum often are without them. In most cases, animals with larvae tend to be the comparatively primitive members of a phylum, those without larvae, the more advanced or specialized members.

Larvae serve mainly in one or both of two capacities. In many animals, immobile ones in particular, the larvae are the chief agents for geographic distribution of the species. In some cases, such species-dispersers still are without fully formed alimentary systems, but locomotor structures are always well developed. For example, the tadpole larvae of frogs and other vertebrates possess strongly muscled tails, and the swimming larvae of many invertebrates have greatly folded and ciliated surfaces, with bands and tufts of extra-long cilia in given regions. In many other animals, the larvae can disperse geographically far less well than the adults (insect caterpillars, for example). The primary function of larvae here appears to be nutritional; the larvae are transitional feeding stages that accumulate food reserves required for the construction of an adult. Several insect larvae are such voracious feeders that they can severely damage agricultural crops. Among these are various "grubs" and caterpillars.

Some types of larvae exist for only a few hours, others for months or years. The larval period ends with *metamorphosis*, transformation into an adult. In this process of reorganization, three kinds of changes usually take place: body parts having purely larval functions atrophy or disintegrate; body parts having purely adult functions undergo exceedingly rapid development; and all other body parts are carried over from larva to adult with relatively little reorganization. In a frog tadpole, for example the tail is of purely larval significance, and it atrophies at the time of metamorphosis. The legs play a purely adult role, and metamorphosis accelerates their growth. And the brain, among body parts that serve both the larva and the adult, undergoes comparatively less metamorphic change (see Fig. 17.11). As might be expected, metamorphic reorganization tends to be relatively slight where a larva resembles the adult greatly. In such cases metamorphosis usually is a more or less gradual process, as among fishes or grasshoppers, for example. By contrast, reorganization is drastic where larva and adult are quite unlike each other. Metamorphosis then tends to be a fairly sudden, sharply defined event, as when an insect caterpillar becomes a pupa which, in turn, becomes an adult moth or butterfly (see also Chap. 34).

In animals without free-living larvae, the developmental events that elsewhere take place in a larva are either omitted or are compressed into the embryonic phase. The embryo then emerges as a miniature adult directly. Good examples among vertebrates are reptiles, birds, and mammals, in which free larval life has been replaced by a long-lasting embryonic phase within egg shells or inside a uterus.

Ancestral reptiles were the first vertebrates without free-swimming aquatic larvae. They evolved not only shelled eggs that could be laid on land, but also special adaptations within the eggs that facilitated egg survival on land. A particularly important adaptation involves a special group of cells that came to surround the embryo after gastrulation and formed four so-called *extraembryonic membranes*. All modern reptiles have inherited these membranes, as have two other groups of descendants of ancestral reptiles—birds and mammals (see Chap. 35).

One of these membranes, the *chorion*, lies just

inside the shell of a reptile or bird egg and prevents excessive evaporation of water through the shell (Fig. 24.23). A second membrane, the *amnion*, surrounds the developing embryo everywhere except on its ventral side. This membrane holds lymph-like *amniotic fluid*, which bathes the embryo in a "private pond." The fluid represents the substitute of the actual ponds in which the larvae of ancestral land vertebrates developed. Because reptiles, birds, and mammals all have an amnion, these animals are called *amniotes* (and all other vertebrates are *anamniotes*).

Two other extraembryonic membranes pouch out ventrally from the alimentary tract of the embryo. One of these is the *allantois*, which lies against the egg shell just inside the chorion. This membrane is the breathing structure of the embryo; gas exchange occurs between the numerous blood vessels in the allantois and the air outside the shell. Also, the allantois serves as an embryonic urinary bladder in which metabolic wastes are stored up to the time of hatching. The second membrane on the ventral side is the *yolk sac*, which gets smaller gradually as yolk is used up during the growth of the embryo.

Mammals include some primitive types that still lay shelled eggs like reptiles and birds, but most become pregnant and the eggs develop in the uterus. The ways in which extraembryonic membranes function here is illustrated by the embryonic development of human beings, a subject discussed in the next chapter.

Review Questions

1 Review the events that result in the production of sperms and eggs in vertebrates. Compare and contrast the oviparous, ovoviviparous, and viviparous patterns of reproduction. In which vertebrates does each pattern occur?

2 Describe the structure of the reproductive system in male and female vertebrates. Review the function of each structure.

3 How are vertebrate breeding seasons initiated, maintained, and terminated? Show in what ways reproductive behavior is under hormonal control, and describe such reproductive behavior.

4 Describe the hormonal controls and the process of follicle growth in women up to the time of ovulation. What events take place during ovulation? After ovulation, what happens to the egg? The follicle? Describe the hormonal controls of the menstrual cycle and the events in the uterus up to the time of menstruation. What happens during menstruation in the ovary and the uterus?

5 Describe fertilization, cleavage, blastula formation, and gastrulation. How does the yolk content of eggs affect cleavage and gastrulation? Show how the three primary germ layers develop in vertebrates.

6 By what general processes of morphogenesis do the primary germ layers develop into adult structures? Illustrate this in the development of the human eye. What role does induction play in such transformations?

7 What are the functions of larvae, and what kinds of processes take place during metamorphosis? Describe the location and function of the extraembryonic membranes in reptiles and birds.

8 Write an essay illustrating how the solution to the problem of terrestrial reproduction is similar in seed plants and land-adapted animals.

Collateral Readings

Balinsky, B. I.: "An Introduction to Embryology," 4th ed., Saunders, Philadelphia, 1975. A classic, excellent introduction to basic principles.

Brachet, J.: "Introduction to Molecular Embryology," Springer, Heidelberg, 1974. This short book, available in paperback, is a clearly written account of the molecular basis of development.

Bryant, P. J., S. V. Bryant and **V. French:** Biological Regeneration and Pattern Formation, *Scientific American*, July 1977. This article describes how regeneration experiments in insects and vertebrates have contributed to our understanding of embryonic differentiation.

Gierer, A.: Hydra as a Model for the Development of Biological Form, *Scientific American*, December 1974. This article describes mechanisms that may control patterns of morphogenesis.

Gordon, R., and **A. G. Jacobson:** The Shaping of Tissues in Embryos, *Scientific American,* June 1978. The authors show how computers can be used to study how embryos develop.

Grant, P.: "Biology of Developing Systems," Holt, New York, 1978. The emphasis of this well-illustrated textbook is on the molecular aspects of development.

Gray, G. W.: The Organizer, *Scientific American,* November 1957. Experiments that led to the discovery of embryonic induction are described.

Lehrman, D. S.: The Reproductive Behavior of Ring Doves, *Scientific American,* November 1964. External stimuli, the behavior of the mating partner, and hormones form a sequence of triggers that initiate successive steps of reproductive activity.

Lein, A.: "The Cycling Female: Her Menstrual Rhythm," Freeman, San Francisco, 1979. This well-written book, available in paperback, describes the hormonal control of the human female menstrual cycle and shows how disturbances in the cycle can affect the physical and emotional responses of women.

Levine, S.: Sex Differences in the Brain, *Scientific American,* April 1966. Masculine behavior in both males and females appears to be a consequence of the effect of testosterone on the brain of the newborn.

Marx, J. L.: The Mating Game: What Happens When Sperm Meets Egg, *Science,* vol. 200, pp. 1256–1259, June 16, 1978. An excellent account of fertilization, including a description of several recent experiments that have provided much new information about egg activation.

Oppenheimer, S. B.: "Introduction to Embryonic Development," Allyn and Bacon, Boston, 1980. This concise textbook includes a chapter on cancer and embryology.

Patten, B. M., and **B. M. Carlson:** "Foundations of Embryology," 3d ed., McGraw-Hill, New York, 1974. A well-illustrated, basic embryology textbook. Contains more information on the later stages of embryological development than the Grant text.

Phillips, J. B.: "Development of Vertebrate Anatomy," Mosby, St. Louis, 1975. A basic textbook on animal development.

Taylor, T. G.: How an Eggshell Is Made, *Scientific American,* March 1970. The process of eggshell formation in chickens is discussed.

Wessells, N. K.: "Tissue Interactions and Development," Benjamin, Menlo Park, Calif., 1977. An excellent account of mechanisms controlling later stages of embryonic development.

Wolpert, L.: "The Development of Pattern and Form in Animals," Oxford University Press, New York, 1974. Interactions between cells and tissues during development constitute the principal focus of this well-illustrated book.

Chapter 25 Human Reproduction

Learning Objectives

After reading this chapter you should be able to:

1. Describe the principal interactions that usually occur during human courtship; define precopulatory activity, coitus, and orgasm.
2. Identify at least one function for each of the major structures that make up the human male and female reproductive systems.
3. List the structures of the female reproductive tract that sperms must pass through to reach a fertilized egg; list at least seven causes of human infertility; define in vitro fertilization and show how it can be used to overcome some causes of infertility in women.
4. Specify the anatomical relations between the yolk sac, allantois, and umbilical cord; describe how the placenta is formed; indicate the major functions of the placenta and amnion.
5. Define human chorionic gonadotropin and describe the hormonal influence of the placenta on the pituitary, corpus luteum, and uterus.
6. Describe the human embryo at the time of its implantation in the uterus and after 8 weeks of development; list the principal changes in the normal movements and intrauterine position of a human fetus during the last 7 months of pregnancy.
7. Indicate how relaxin, estrogens, oxytocin, and prostaglandins influence childbirth; define the three phases of childbirth and identify the chief events that occur during each phase.
8. Indicate at least three changes that occur in the circulatory and breathing systems of infants following childbirth.
9. Define cesarean section, and explain why this procedure is sometimes used to avoid breech deliveries.
10. Define colostrum, specify where and when it is produced, and list three ways in which infants benefit from this secretion.
11. Distinguish between milk production and milk letdown; describe the endocrine and neural mechanisms that trigger each process.
12. List the modern methods of birth control; describe how each method prevents fertilization or birth and state the comparative effectiveness, advantages, and disadvantages of each method; define thrombophlebitis and outline statistics linking increased incidence of this disease to use of oral contraceptives; list at least three circumstances under which use of oral contraceptive constitutes a significant health risk.
13. Distinguish between surgical curettage and suction curettage; describe at least three new methods of birth control currently being researched.

The pattern of human reproduction parallels that of terrestrial animals in general and viviparous mammals in particular. Close contact between specialized reproductive organs facilitates internal fertilization; nutrients are transferred to a developing embryo through an interdigitation of uterine and embryonic tissues called the placenta; and the uterus, corpus luteum, and extraembryonic membranes perform the same functions during pregnancy in people as they do in all other placental mammals.

Despite these similarities, human sexual behavior and reproduction are characterized by several unique features. For example, courtship behavior in human beings is remarkably prolonged in comparison with general animal standards. Following puberty, men and women often are sexually responsive throughout their lives, even during pregnancy or on other occasions when fertilization is unlikely or impossible. By contrast, most animals are sexually responsive only at times when mating is likely to result in reproduction. Above all, only people are able to exercise significant control over fertilization and reproduction.

Knowledge of these similarities and differences greatly influences our personalities, interpersonal relations, attitudes, and actions. Individuals can readily determine whether or when they will reproduce. Women can now terminate pregnancies by abortion safely and legally in many countries throughout the world. At no other time in history have societies been better equipped to influence the rate of human population growth. Yet many people have less than a rudimentary understanding of their own sexual behavior and reproduction. This is both unfortunate and potentially dangerous, for each of us repeatedly faces questions that involve human sexual behavior and reproduction. When and under what conditions shall we produce offspring? Should abortion legislation be amended? What are the safest and most effective birth control techniques? Should governments influence the rate of human population growth and determine who shall reproduce? We shall be better able to provide answers to such questions if we first examine our sexual behavior and embryonic development from a biological perspective.

SEXUAL BEHAVIOR

Human sexual behavior is characterized by three phases: courtship, precopulatory activity, and copulation, or *coitus.*

Courtship

As in many animals, the first courtship responses between men and women usually are tentative and ambivalent, but the hesitancy produced by conflicting emotions of fear, aggression, and sexual attraction gradually disappears if mutual courtship signals are sufficiently strong. Such signals include complex facial expression, gestures, body positions, and vocalizations. The "sweet nothings" murmured between courting individuals are one example.

These visual and vocal signals then may be followed by tentative body contacts. The first of these usually are hand-to-hand and arm-to-arm. They are then followed by mouth-to-face and mouth-to-mouth contacts. Displays of this type often occur in public, but most couples seek privacy for the precopulatory behavior that follows courtship.

Precopulatory Behavior

Couples sometimes adopt side-to-side positions at the start of precopulatory phase, but these almost always give way to face-to-face contacts. As in many monkeys, apes, and a few other vertebrates, mutual use of the lips and tongue to increase sexual responsiveness occurs most frequently at this stage. Most couples engage in prolonged mouth-to-mouth contact. Often the mouth is also used to stimulate many other areas of the partner's body.

One result of precopulatory activity in males is erection of the penis. This organ contains three elongated bodies of spongy tissue; two *corpora cavernosa,* which lie next to each other along the upper side of the penis, and a single *corpus spongiosum* (Fig. 25.1). The latter is situated along the bottom portion of the penis and contains the urethra. It also expands at the tip of the penis and forms the mushroom-shaped *glans penis,* which contains large numbers of mechanoreceptors. Transmission of nerve impulses from these receptors to the brain is responsible for many of the pleasurable sensations that accompany sexual stimulation. A fold of tissue, called the *foreskin,* covers the glans penis. This tissue often is removed surgically at birth by *circumcision.* Unlike the penis of most mammals, that of human males does not contain supporting bone or cartilage. When a male becomes sexually excited, blood vessels that lead to the penis dilate and fill the cavities of the spongy corpora with blood. The penis hardens and erects, often doubling in length, thereby facilitating its penetration into the vagina of the female.

Similar changes accompany sexual arousal in women. The walls of the vagina are flaccid prior to arousal and lie close together. During sexual stimulation, however, the walls of the inner two-thirds of the vagina separate and form an enlarged vaginal barrel (Fig. 25.2). The outer third undergoes a similar expansion as sexual tension increases. A second primary sexual response of women is the secretion of a mucuslike fluid from the walls of the vagina. Like drops of sweat, this lubricating fluid exudes through pores in the vaginal walls. Vaginal expansion and the "sweating phenomenon" facilitate insertion of the penis. Both responses are involuntary reactions triggered by autonomic motor neurons.

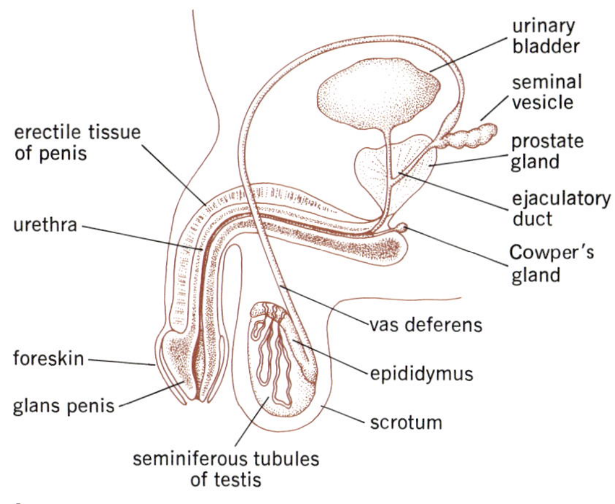

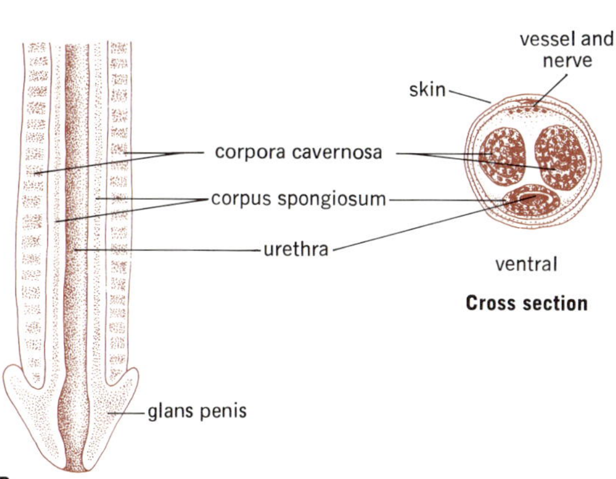

Fig. 25.1 Reproductive system of the human male. (A) Basic anatomy. Sperms, produced in the seminiferous tubules of the testes, are stored in the epididymis prior to ejaculation through vas deferens and urethra. The prostate gland, Cowper's gland, and the seminal vesicle produce fluids that constitute the main volume of semen. (B) Principal structures of the human penis shown in longitudinal and cross section.

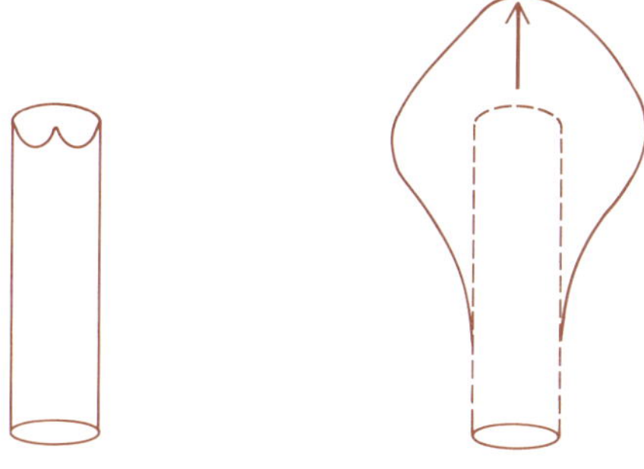

Fig. 25.2 Sexual response of human females. The walls of the vagina, normally flaccid in a sexually quiescent state, balloon outward when women are stimulated sexually.

The external parts of the female reproductive system also undergo changes in response to sexual stimulation (Fig. 25.3). The outer vaginal lips, or *labia majora,* flatten back during sexual arousal, exposing the vagina for insertion of the penis. Concurrently, the inner vaginal lips, or *labia minora,* become engorged with blood and double or triple in diameter. As a result, the labia minora protrude outward past the folded-back labia majora. The *clitoris,* a structure homologous to the male penis, responds to sexual stimulation by enlarging. Much smaller than its male counterpart, the clitoris is highly innervated and is composed of spongy tissue that hardens when engorged with blood. Many of the pleasurable sensations derived from sexual stimulation result from nervous impulses transmitted from the clitoris to the brain.

Coitus

Coitus begins when the penis is inserted into the vagina. During coitus, the penis is stimulated by the friction that results from its rhythmic thrusting in the vagina. By contrast, the clitoris withdraws into its protective foreskin prior to coitus and is not stimulated directly by the penis. Indeed, direct touching of the clitoris is irritating to many women at this time. The rhythmic motion of the penis stimulates the clitoral area indirectly by its push-pull stretching of the vaginal lips.

Marked increases in pulse rate, blood pressure, and breathing accompany increased sexual arousal in both sexes, and each of these rates peaks at the sexual climax, or *orgasm.* For example, the normal pulse rate of 70 or 80 beats per minute usually increases to about 130 during coitus and 170 at sexual climax. Orgasm in males is accompanied by contractions of pelvic muscles that force semen through the urethra and into the female reproduc-

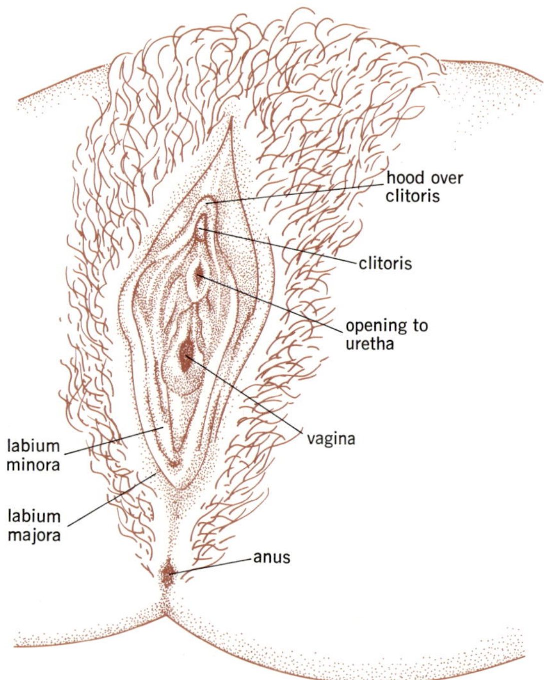

Fig. 25.3 Reproductive system of the human female, external anatomy.

tive tract, a process termed *ejaculation.* Orgasm in women is preceded by an intense clitoral-pelvic awareness. This is followed by a series of four to eight muscular contractions localized primarily in the outer third of the vagina. In most individuals, all the changes that occur during precopulatory activity and coitus are rapidly reversed following orgasm; blood pressure and pulse rate usually return to normal within 10 minutes.

FERTILIZATION AND PREGNANCY

Approximately 300 to 500 million sperms are deposited into the vagina following ejaculation. If fertilization is to occur, at least one of these cells must enter the oviducts and penetrate the surface of a fertilizable egg. This is not accomplished easily, for sperms encounter several anatomical and chemical "barriers" that restrict their movement through the female genital tract (Fig. 25.4). Moreover, eggs are present and fertilizable in an oviduct for only a limited time following ovulation. Thus, sperms that overcome all transport barriers often reach an unfertilizable egg or no egg at all.

Vaginal secretions constitute a first barrier to sperm transport. Many sperms are killed or inactivated by the acidity of these fluids. The cervix is a second obstacle to sperm transport, for two principal reasons: (1) the cervix is very narrow compared with the vagina, and many sperms never negotiate this anatomical barrier; and (2) the opening of the cervix normally is bathed by an alkaline mucus produced by secretory cells of the cervical lining. This mucus can be quite viscous, and sperms often become trapped in it. Near the time of ovulation, however, the mucus usually becomes less viscous and more easily penetrable by sperms. Also, the alkalinity of cervical mucus usually reaches a peak at ovulation. This increase of pH probably facilitates sperm transport further by reducing the acidity of vaginal fluids.

Sperms entering the uterus are transported into and along oviducts by a complex group of processes that include muscular contractions, fluid currents, and ciliary movements. These processes greatly increase the speed of sperm transport, for sperms swim at an average rate of only 0.5 cm/min. Such processes also reduce the continued loss of viable sperms that occurs after their entrance into the uterus. If sperms were propelled only by their own motility, virtually all of them would be engulfed by white blood cells that line the surfaces of the uterus and oviducts long before sperms could reach an egg. A few sperms, however, usually overcome all these obstacles and enter the upper third of the oviducts. Fertilization occurs most frequently when sperms reach this region within a period extending from about 48 h before to about 12 h after ovulation.

Many causes of infertility in women involve an almost total restriction of sperm transport at one or more points below the upper third of the oviducts. For example, the vaginal secretions of some women constitute particularly hostile environments for sperms. In some cases, almost all sperms are killed when they contact such fluids. Other factors that

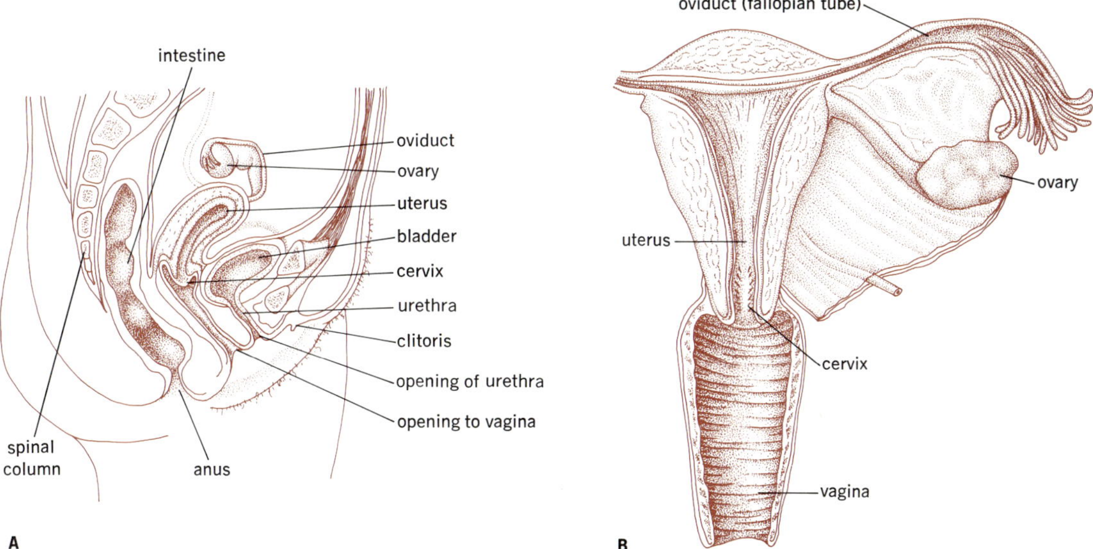

Fig. 25.4 Reproductive system of the human female, internal anatomy. (A) Longitudinal section through the pelvic region. Note position of the reproductive organs in relation to the bladder and large intestine. (B) Longitudinal section of the reproductive organs. Note narrow opening of the cervix.

can block sperm transport are anatomical deformities of the cervix, a production of cervical mucus hostile to sperms, malformations of the uterus, and constriction of one or both oviducts.

Such causes of infertility sometimes can be overcome by *in vitro fertilization* (in vitro, occurring "in a glass," as in a test tube). This technique involves surgical removal of ripe eggs from ovaries of an infertile woman, fertilizing the eggs in a laboratory dish, nurturing a resulting embryo in special culture solutions, and then placing the embryo in the uterus of the woman. The embryo continues development inside the uterus until birth.

The inability of a couple to produce offspring is not always caused by structural or functional abnormalities of the female reproductive system. For example, sperm production by males may be insufficient to overcome the many normal barriers encountered by sperms following their release into the female genital tract. Infertility also can be caused by a man producing a high proportion of deformed sperms that cannot fertilize an egg.

Most men produce more than enough normal sperms to ensure fertilization of a mature ovum. A fertilized egg immediately begins to divide within the oviduct and reaches the uterus as an embryo just beyond the gastrula stage. Such an embryo then *implants* in the uterus wall, which, as noted in Chap. 24, has already become prepared for pregnancy under the influence of progesterone and estrogens (Fig. 25.5). The first extraembryonic membrane, the chorion, next develops as an enclosure around the embryo, in direct contact with the tissue of the uterus. In one region the chorion produces numerous branching, fingerlike outgrowths that erode paths through the uterus wall. In this manner the tissues of chorion and uterus become attached to each other firmly. These interfingering and interlacing tissues represent the *placenta*. When fully formed, the placenta functions both as a mechanical and a metabolic connection between the embryo and the maternal body (Fig. 25.6).

The developing allantois still serves as in reptiles and birds as an embryonic lung (see Chap. 24), except that now gas exchange occurs in the placenta, between the blood vessels of the allantois and the maternal blood vessels of the uterus. The embryonic and maternal bloods normally do not mix in the placenta; the chorion separates the two circulations. Maternal blood also carries off embry-

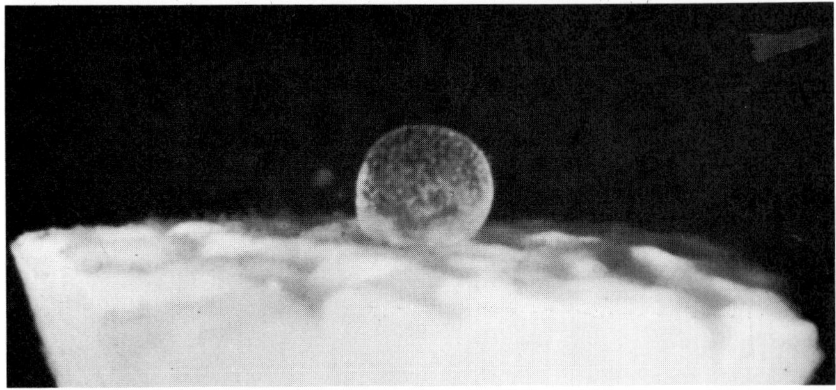

Fig. 25.5 Implantation. Early monkey embryo just arrived in the uterus and beginning to implant in the uterus wall.

onic wastes and supplies food; hence the allantois no longer functions as urinary bladder, and the yolk sac no longer contains yolk. Both these membranes are collapsed, empty sacs. They later become enveloped by connective tissue and skin, the whole representing the *umbilical cord.* This lifeline between placenta and embryo leaves a permanent mark in the offspring, in the form of the navel. The fluid of the amnion still serves as in reptiles and birds as a "private pond." It is this enlarging amnion more than the embryo itself that produces the bulging abdomen of pregnant women.

The presence of placenta and embryo usually inhibits further egg production (and menstruation) during the period of pregnancy. The placenta produces a protein hormone, *chorionic gonadotropin,* that maintains the corpus luteum during the first stages of pregnancy. In women this hormone usually is called *human chorionic gonadotropin* (HCG). As a result of HCG production by the placenta, the corpus luteum continues to secrete estrogens and progesterone, thereby preventing a breakdown of the uterine lining that would terminate pregnancy. Moreover, the placenta itself soon specializes as an endocrine organ. It manufactures slowly increasing amounts of estrogens and progesterone, and the progesterone output eventually becomes far greater than that of the corpus luteum. The production of HCG by the placenta declines as its manufacture of steroid hormone increases. Without the stimulatory effects of HCG, the corpus luteum degenerates, usually about the twelfth week

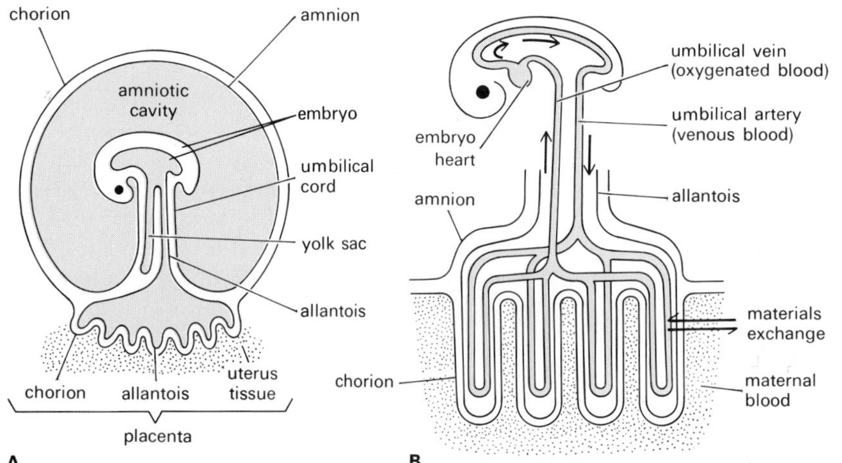

Fig. 25.6 Placenta and embryo. (A) The yolk sack is rudimentary and collapsed. The allantois functions as a breathing organ, via blood vessels it carries from placenta to embryo. The amnion and chorion are ectodermal; the yolk sac and allantois are endodermal; and the white areas correspond to mesodermal regions. (B) The embryonic blood circulation in the placenta. Embryonic and maternal bloods do not mix, being separated by the chorionic and allantoic membranes.

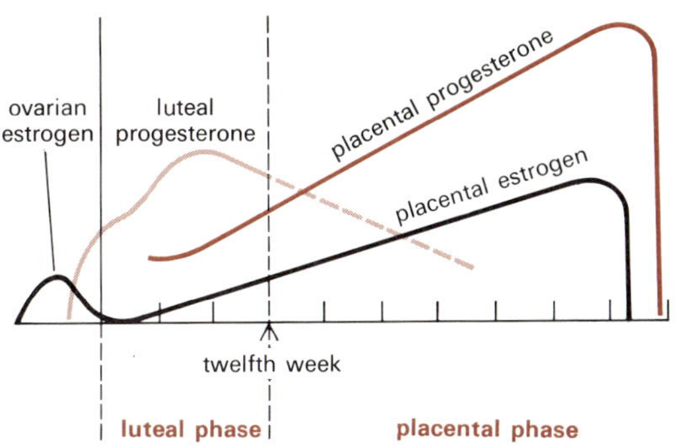

Fig. 25.7 Hormones in pregnancy. Curves indicate the amounts and sources of sex hormones during pregnancy in human females.

of pregnancy. From this time on, the placenta provides the main hormonal control of pregnancy (Fig. 25.7).

A human embryo often is called a *fetus* after the second month of development. Most organs have attained their permanent form by this time. Eyes, ears, nose, and mouth are present, the arms and legs have a full complement of fingers and toes, and the fetus is unquestionably human (Fig. 25.8). By the ninth week of development, a normal fetus weighs about 1 g and measures 2 to 3 cm in length. During the remainder of its intrauterine development, it becomes about 3000 times heavier and as much as 25 times longer. The rapid intrauterine growth of a fetus slows substantially during the ninth month of pregnancy; growth slows even further immediately after birth. If the average intrauterine growth rate of a fetus continued after

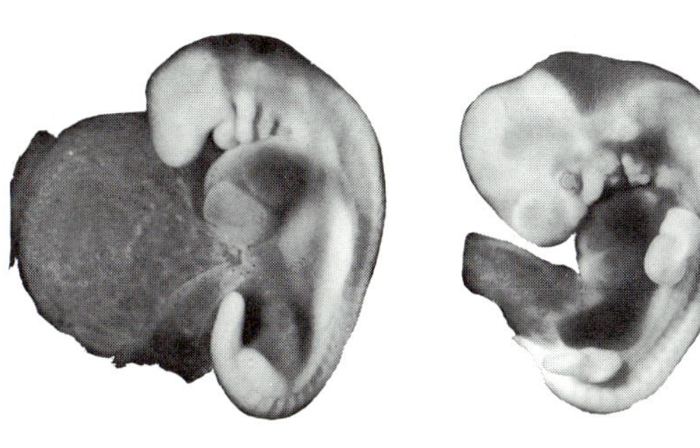

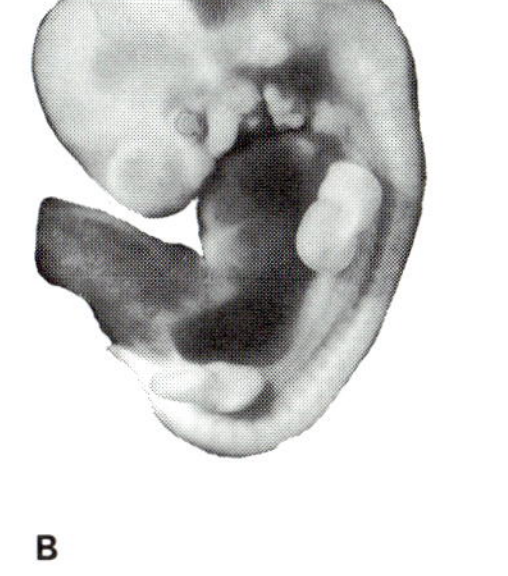

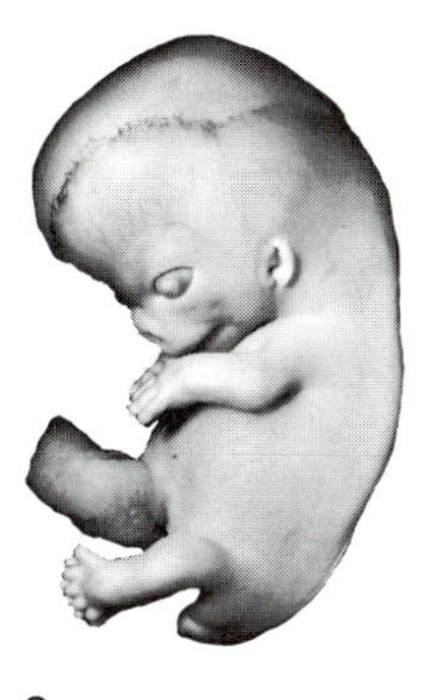

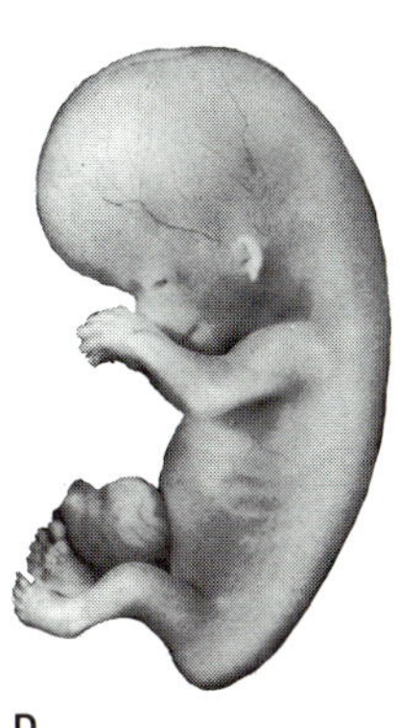

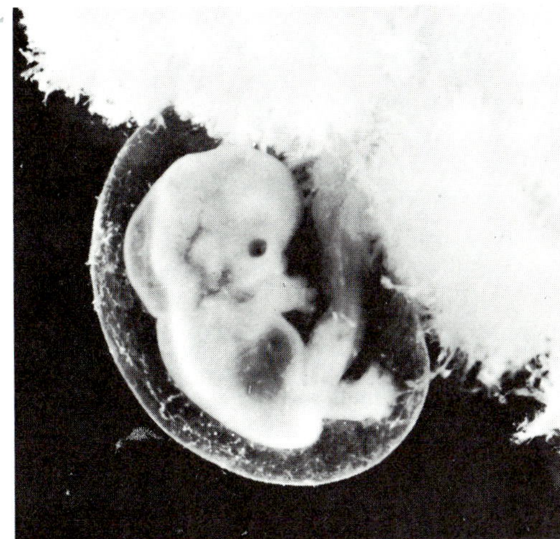

Fig. 25.8 The human embryo and extraembryonic membranes. (A to D) Four successive stages of embryonic growth: 25 days, 33 days, 6 weeks, and 8 weeks after fertilization, respectively. The series indicates that chordate features arise first, e.g., dorsal skeletal supports, gill pouches, as in (A); that vertebrate features develop next, e.g., anteroposterior segments, paired limb buds, tail, as in (B); that mammalian traits appear later, e.g., four legs, umbilical cord, as in (C); and that distinctly human traits appear last, e.g., arm-leg differences, flat face, individualized facial expression, as in (D). (E) Embryo about 8 weeks after fertilization, obtained after surgical removal of portions of the reproductive system of a female patient. The chorion is pushed to the side, revealing the amniotic sac. Note umbilical cord. *(A–D, Courtesy of G. W. Corner and Carnegie Institution of Washington; E, from A. Gesell, "The Embryology of Behavior." Harper, New York.)*

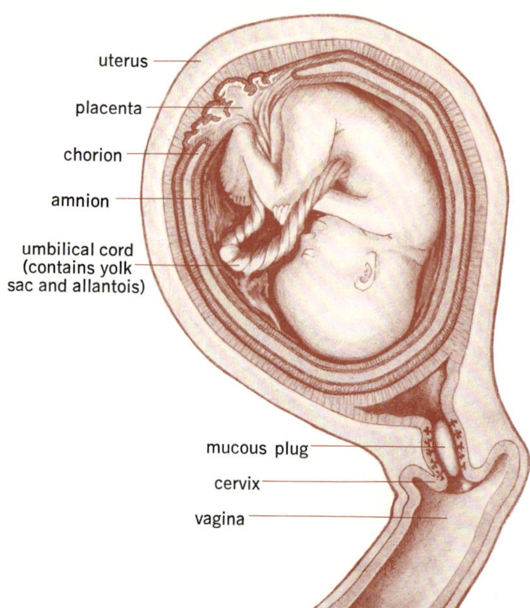

Fig. 25.9 Normal position of fetus during terminal stages of pregnancy. Note extraembryonic membranes, placenta, and umbilical cord. *(From T. Steyaert, "Biology: A Contemporary View," © 1975 by McGraw-Hill, Inc., New York.)*

birth, most children would weigh almost 200 lb by their first birthday.

A fetus usually can voluntarily stretch its arms and legs and respond to external stimuli by the end of the fourth month of pregnancy. Pregnant women often feel the first movements of the fetus at this time. These movements increase in frequency and force throughout the fifth month. Although the fetus appears fully formed by the sixth month of development, it cannot survive on its own outside the uterus. The youngest premature infant known to survive was born at 25 weeks and weighed 650 g (about 23 oz). The survival rate for premature infants rises after this time and is approximately 10 per cent during the seventh month of pregnancy, 70 per cent in the eighth month, and 95 per cent in the ninth month.

A fetus often becomes less active during the ninth month of pregnancy, largely because of its confinement in a uterus that now provides little space for movement (Fig. 25.9). A few weeks before birth, the fetus descends to a lower position in the uterus. The head usually becomes positioned nearest the cervix. By the time of birth, the uterus has stretched 60 times its normal size, and the placenta already has begun to degenerate.

CHILDBIRTH

The termination of pregnancy that normally occurs about 266 days after the initiation of intrauterine development is called *childbirth*, or *labor*. This process involves the forceful expulsion of amniotic fluid, fetus, and placenta from the uterus by contractions of smooth muscles in the uterine lining.

Mechanisms responsible for childbirth are poorly understood, but several hormones apparently play important roles. One of them is *relaxin*, a peptide produced by the corpus luteum and the placenta during pregnancy. This hormone makes the cervix more pliable and relaxes connective tissues that join the bones of the pelvis. Both actions facilitate childbirth by enlarging the birth canal. Estrogens stimulate contraction of uterine muscles, and secretion of these hormones by the placenta increases sharply just before the onset of labor.

Estrogens probably do not act alone, however, for oxytocin stimulates uterine contraction as well, and circumstantial evidence suggests that increased amounts of this pituitary hormone may be released during childbirth. Moreover, labor also can be induced by injecting *prostaglandins* into pregnant women. The precise functional roles of these lipid-soluble hormones have not been established fully, but prostaglandins have been shown to influence the activities of nerves, liver, adipose tissue, blood vessels, and reproductive organs. Originally discovered in semen, prostaglandins now are known to be present in several tissues of male and female animals. The hormones appear to induce labor by triggering contraction of smooth muscles in the uterus.

Childbirth usually takes several hours to complete and occurs in three steps. The first of these, *dilation*, requires the most time. It often lasts from 8 to 12 h in women experiencing childbirth for the first time (less in women who have given birth before). Dilation begins with the first contractions of uterine muscles and ends with full expansion of the cervical opening. The first contractions of the uterus last for less than 1 min and are repeated

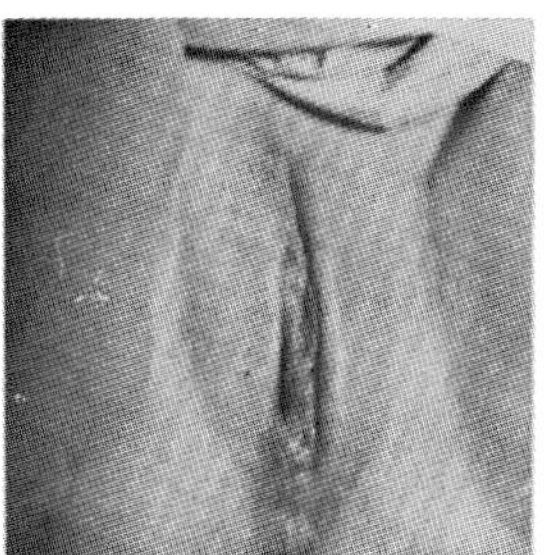
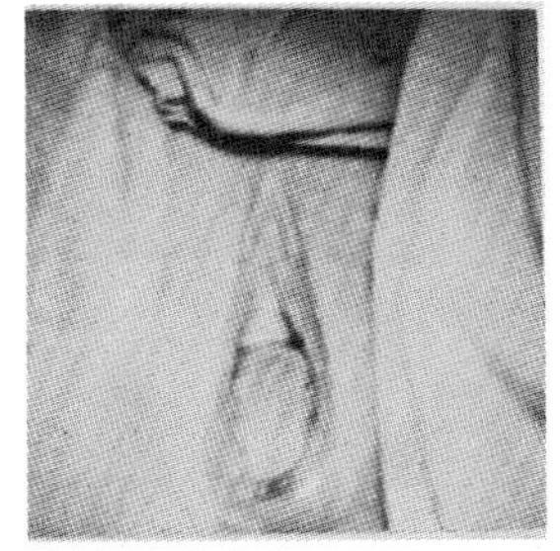
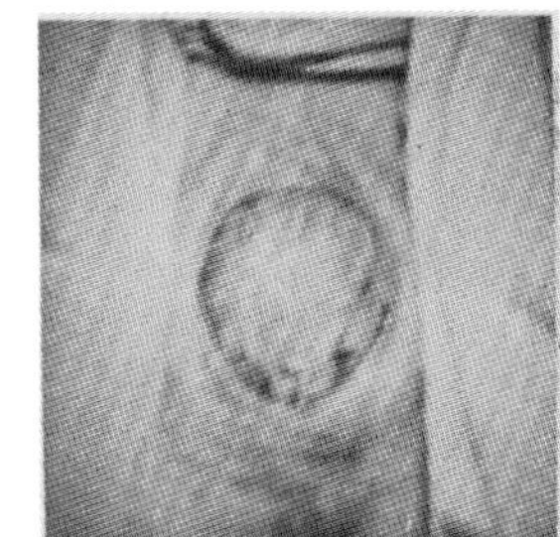
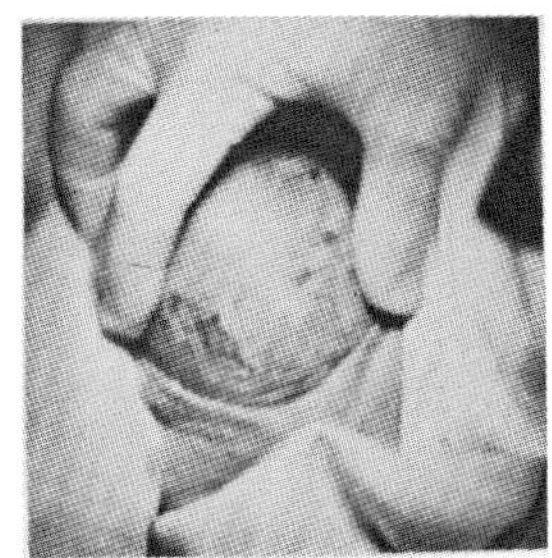
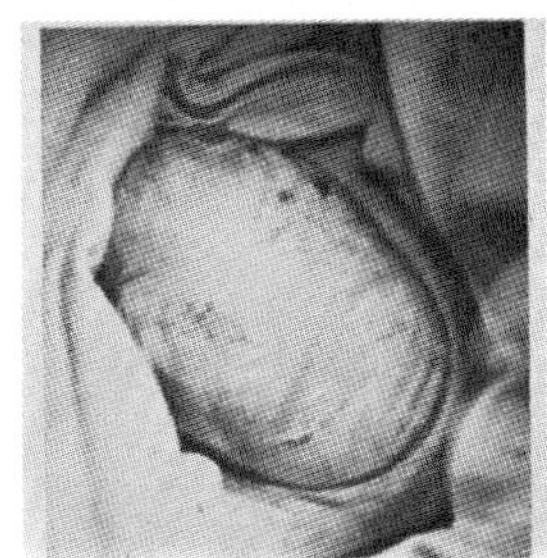
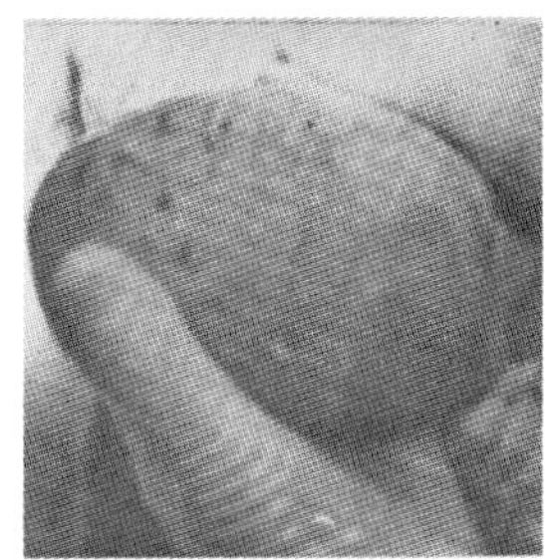
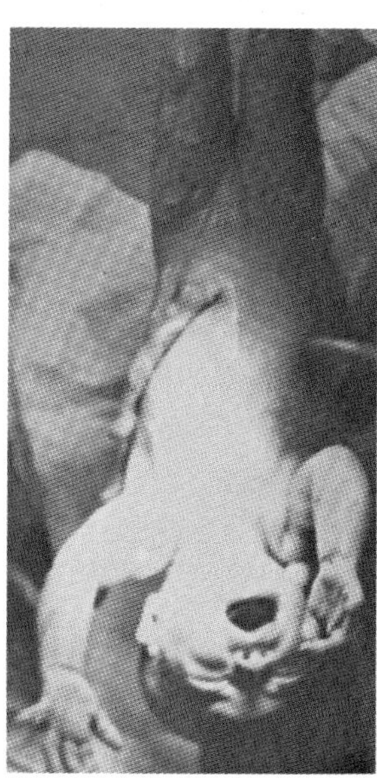

Fig. 25.10 Fetal expulsion. *(From R. Rugh and L. B. Shettles, "From Conception to Birth; The Drama of Life's Beginnings," Harper & Row, New York, 1971.)*

approximately every 15 to 20 min. As labor continues the contractions become more intense, more frequent, and of longer duration. By the end of dilation, contractions often occur every 2 min or less.

The second stage, *fetal expulsion*, lasts from 2 to 60 min. The head of the child usually emerges from the vaginal opening first (Fig. 25.10). Obstetricians often facilitate emergence of the head by making an incision beginning at the posterior end of the vaginal opening and extending toward the anus. This operation, called an *episiotomy*, prevents excessive tearing of tissue during childbirth. Also, this single incision usually heals far more rapidly than the lacerations that could occur if an episiotomy were not performed.

Once the child has completely emerged from the vagina, the umbilical cord is cut, thereby severing all connection to the degenerating placenta and causing the CO_2 concentration of blood to rise rapidly in the child. This increase stimulates the respiratory center in the brain and triggers contraction of the diaphragm and other muscles that coordinate breathing. The infant expands its lungs, issues its first cry, and starts breathing on its own.

In conjunction with this switchover from placental to lung breathing, a structural change occurs in the heart (Fig. 25.11). Before birth the dividing wall between the right and left atria is incomplete, and a movable flap of tissue provides a passage be-

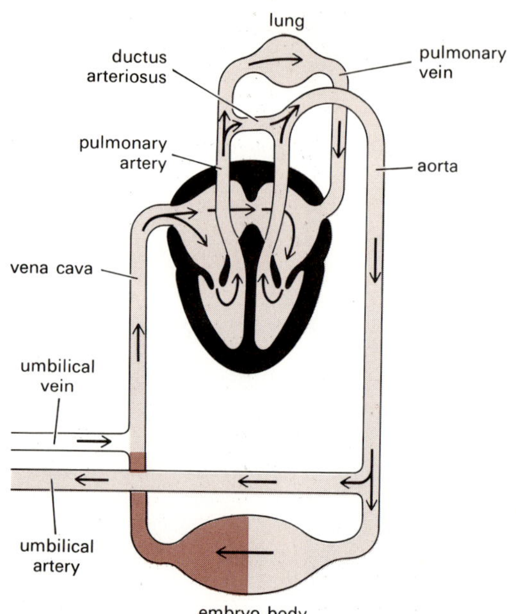

Fig. 25.11 The embryonic circulation in mammals. Oxygenated blood, white (only in umbilical vein, from placenta); venous blood, dark color (from embryo body to vena cava); mixed blood, light color (in vena cava, heart, lung, and aorta). The embryo lung is nonfunctional as a breathing organ, and blood may pass directly from the pulmonary artery via the ductus arteriosus to the aorta. Note also the open passage between the two atria. Determine the effect if the umbilical vessels, the ductus, and the atrial passage all disappear and the lungs become functional, as at birth. Compare with adult circulation, Figs. 18.16 and 18.17.

tween these chambers. Once lung breathing is initiated the blood-pressure pattern in the heart changes and the tissue flap is pressed over the opening between the atria. The flap eventually grows in place, and the left and right sides of the heart then are separated permanently. Another structural change involves an embryonic blood vessel (*ductus arteriosus,* see Fig. 25.11), which before birth leads from the pulmonary artery to the aorta and thus shunts blood around the nonfunctional lung. At birth a specially developed muscle in this vessel constricts and never relaxes thereafter. Blood thereby is forced to pass through the lungs. The muscle degenerates to scar tissue, and the blood vessel as a whole degenerates soon after birth.

Immediately following hospital births, newborn infants are given a series of tests to evaluate their breathing, muscle tone, reflexes, heart rate, and several other functions. Drops of silver nitrate are placed in the eyes of infants at this time to protect against infection.

The uterus begins to contract and return to its nonpregnant size within minutes after birth. However, the placenta cannot contract and soon is dislodged and expelled from the uterus along with the remains of fetal membranes, some fluid, and a small quantity of blood. This third and final stage of childbirth is called *placental expulsion.*

Although all women experience some pain during labor, most childbirths do not endanger the health of mother or child and usually require little assistance from a physician. Some deliveries, however, are both difficult and dangerous. For example, the posterior end of the fetus occasionally emerges first through the cervix. The incidence of infant mortality that results from such *breech* deliveries is much higher than for normal births, largely because of difficulties in delivering the head of the infant. Approximately 3.5 per cent of all childbirths are breech deliveries. Because of the risks accompanying breech births, physicians sometimes deliver an abnormally positioned fetus by removing it surgically from the uterus through an incision in the abdomen of the mother. Called a *cesarean section,* this surgical procedure is also used whenever the head of the fetus is too large to pass through the opening of the pelvis.

During the 6 weeks that follow childbirth, functional changes that have accompanied pregnancy are largely reversed. The uterus returns to its normal, nonpregnant weight, lacerations of vaginal tissue heal, and the hypothalamus responds to the decreased concentration of estrogens and progesterone that follow placental expulsion by stimulating the pituitary to secrete FSH. Unless the mother is breast feeding, a normal menstrual period resumes within 6 to 8 weeks following childbirth.

Milk production by the breasts, or *mammary glands,* begins early in this 6-week recovery period. A precursor of milk, called *colostrum,* is produced by mammary glands during the last $4\frac{1}{2}$ months of pregnancy and constitutes the major nutrient of a mother's breasts for the first 2 days after birth. In addition to its high concentration of protein, colostrum appears to contain substances that protect

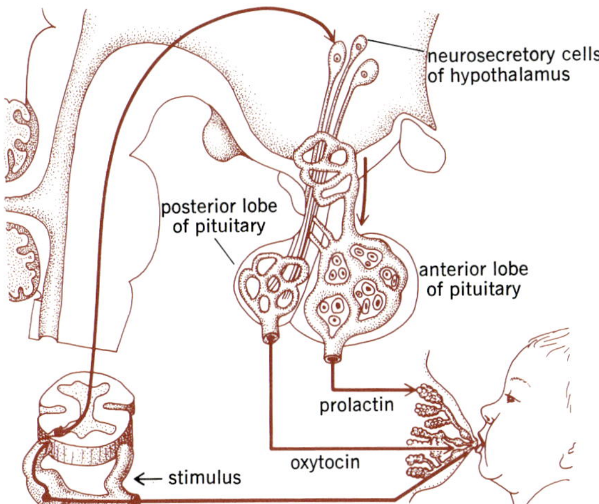

Fig. 25.12 Milk production and milk letdown. Release of prolactin from the anterior lobe of the pituitary stimulates milk production in specialized cells of the breasts. Milk letdown is triggered when the infant stimulates nerve receptors in the nipple of a breast. A nerve impulse is transmitted from the receptors to the hypothalamus, which responds by secreting oxytocin from the terminals of neurosecretory cells in the posterior lobe of the pituitary. Oxytocin stimulates contraction of small breast muscles that force milk through nipples. *(Modified from T. Steyaert, "Biology: A Contemporary View," © 1975 by McGraw-Hill, Inc., New York.)*

against diarrhea in newborn infants. Moreover, colostrum also contains maternal antibodies that provide some protection against foreign antigens. Production of milk is stimulated by the hormone prolactin. Because release of this hormone from the pituitary is inhibited by high concentrations of estrogens and progesterone, the concentration of prolactin is very low during pregnancy. Following expulsion of the placenta, however, the concentration of these steroid hormones drops, and the production of prolactin increases correspondingly. Specialized cells in the breasts respond to this increase by producing milk (Fig. 25.12).

The release of milk from breasts requires physical stimulation of the nipples. When a nipple is put in the mouth of an infant, the baby responds by sucking. This action triggers a nervous impulse from the nipple to the brain that results in a rapid release of oxytocin from the posterior lobe of the pituitary (see Fig. 25.12). The hormone circulates through the blood to the breasts, where it stimulates *milk letdown.* Milk production continues as long as the breasts are drained of milk, but breasts "dry up" quickly if they are not drained. For women who choose to bottle-feed their infants, the drying up period can be shortened by administration of synthetic steroid hormones that inhibit the production of prolactin.

BIRTH CONTROL

The search for a convenient and foolproof method of preventing unwanted pregnancies began centuries ago and continues unabated to the present day. About 1850 B.C., for example, some Egyptian women placed a mixture of honey and crocodile dung in their vaginas before coitus. Although far from foolproof, the honey in this thick paste probably trapped and killed significant numbers of sperms, and thus actually reduced the risk of pregnancy. In spite of the subsequent development of more reliable and esthetically pleasing contraceptive methods, none has yet proved completely effective. Moreover, all modern methods of birth control have inherent disadvantages that limit or prevent their use by some people. A summary of the comparative effectiveness of these methods is presented in Table 25.1.

The most reliable method of contraception is *sterilization,* and the procedure used most often to sterilize males is called *vasectomy.* It is a relatively simple surgical procedure usually performed under local anesthesia in the office of a qualified physician. An incision is made along each scrotal sac, and the major sperm duct, or *vas deferens,* that leads from each testis is cut and tied off (Fig. 25.13). As a result, the passage of sperms from testes to urethra is blocked. Vasectomy does not interfere with secretion of testosterone by the testes and does not block the flow of seminal fluids to the urethra. This operation, therefore, does not alter male secondary sex characteristics or significantly reduce the volume of semen expelled during ejaculation.

A similar sterilization procedure, *tubal ligation,* can be performed on females. Here both oviducts are cut and tied off, thereby preventing transport of eggs to the uterus. Like vasectomy, tubal ligation does not affect the ability of women to en-

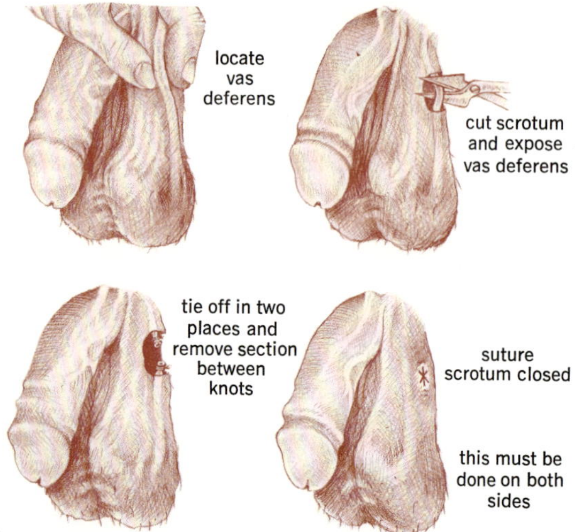

Fig. 25.13 Vasectomy. This procedure prevents sperms from mixing with seminal fluid released by the prostate gland and other secretory structures of the male reproductive system. Compare with Fig. 25.1. *(From T. Steyaert, "Biology: A Contemporary View," © 1975 by McGraw-Hill, Inc., New York.)*

gage in coitus and experience orgasm. Until recently, tubal ligation was a far more complex surgical procedure than vasectomy, usually requiring hospitalization for at least a few days. Simpler techniques have been developed, however, and tubal ligations now can be performed under local anesthesia in a physician's office or clinic. Patients frequently return home 4 to 6 h after surgery.

The cut ends of a vas deferens or oviduct sometimes reunite and reestablish transport of gametes to the urethra or uterus. But this occurs rarely. It is estimated that severed ducts reunite in less than 1 per cent of individuals sterilized by these procedures. In spite of their effectiveness, both vasectomy and tubal ligation share the disadvantage of being largely irreversible, and thus are not a practical means of contraception for people who wish to produce offspring at a later time.

Oral contraceptives, collectively called "the pill," are the next most effective contraceptive method. The pregnancy rate for women who use birth control pills is less than 1 per cent. Oral contraceptives contain synthetic steroids that mimic the biological actions of estrogens and progesterone. Most birth control pills are taken at a rate of one per day for 20 to 21 days beginning on the fifth day of menstruation. The synthetic estrogens of these pills appear to inhibit secretion of FSH from the hypothalamus. Consequently, little FSH is released from the pituitary, follicles do not develop in an ovary, an egg is not produced, and ovulation does not occur. However, the lining of the uterus does undergo a normal thickening in response to the synthetic steroids contained in the pills. The concentration of these hormones decreases rapidly when use of the pills is discontinued on the

TABLE 25.1
Effectiveness of Contraceptive Methods

Method or device	How it works	Approximate failure rate*
sterilization	Permanently blocks passage of eggs or sperms	0.003
oral contraceptives	Prevents ovulation	0.5–1.0
IUD	Thought to prevent implantation of egg, spermicidal	3–4
diaphragm with jelly	Barrier to sperms	10–12
condom	Blocks sperm entrance to vagina	15
spermicides	Barrier to sperms, spermicidal	20
rhythm	Abstinence during fertile period	25
withdrawal	Ejaculation outside of vagina	30
douche	Flushing sperms from vagina, spermicidal	40
No. of women, per 100, who become pregnant using no contraceptive device or method		75–100

*Pregnancies per 100 women per year.
SOURCE: D. S. Luciano, A. J. Vander, and J. H. Sherman, McGraw-Hill, New York, 1978.

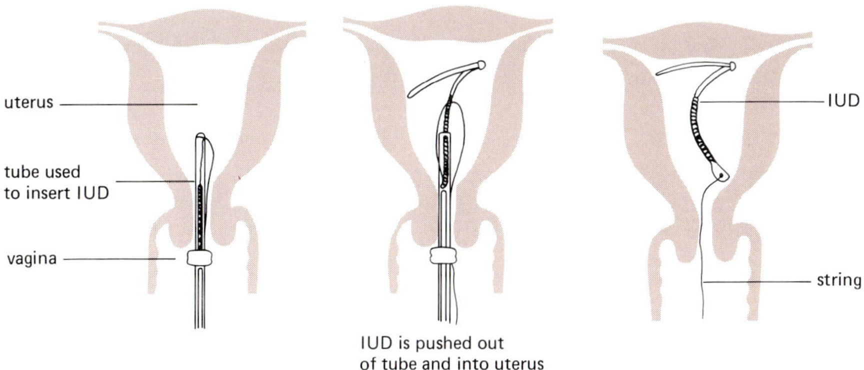

Fig. 25.14 The IUD. Intrauterine devices are flexible loops or coils. They usually prevent pregnancy when inserted into the uterus.

twenty-first or twenty-second day, and a normal menstruation begins about 1 to 3 days later.

In addition to preventing ovulation, birth control pills "regularize" menstrual cycles and greatly alleviate menstrual cramps in many women. Nevertheless, the side effects that sometimes accompany use of oral contraceptives are not always beneficial. Some women experience nausea, tender breasts, weight gain, and a bloated feeling while using birth control pills. These symptoms often disappear after the pills have been taken for 1 or 2 months.

A substantial amount of evidence suggests that use of oral contraceptives increases the occurrence of blood clots in the circulatory system. Women using birth control pills are as much as 6 times more likely to develop *thrombophlebitis* than women who do not use oral contraceptives. This potentially serious inflammation occurs when one or more blood clots develop along the walls of a vein. Severe illness or death can result if such clots break free, are transported through the circulatory system, and become lodged in the coronary artery or in a large oxygen-carrying blood vessel of the lung or brain (see also Chap. 18).

Results of many studies suggest that estrogens in oral contraceptives significantly elevate concentrations of clot-promoting substances in blood. Furthermore, the incidence of thrombophlebitis in women has been shown to be directly related to the dosage of estrogens in birth control pills. The appearance of thrombophlebitis among women using oral contraceptives containing 0.05 mg of estrogens is about 80 per 100,000 women annually; the rate for women using pills containing more than this dosage is about 110 per 100,000 annually.

These studies also demonstrate an increased incidence of heart attacks among women who use birth control pills. For example, users of oral contraceptives between 30 and 39 years of age have been shown to be almost 3 times more likely to suffer heart attack than nonusers; women between the ages of 40 and 44 who use birth control pills experience 5 times as many heart attacks as nonusers. Investigators also have found that smoking, obesity, diabetes, and high blood pressure interact synergistically with the estrogens of birth control pills, greatly increasing the risk of heart attack.

Further, estrogens in oral contraceptives can produce high blood pressure. This problem develops in approximately 5 to 7 per cent of all women who use birth control pills. In addition, some studies correlate use of oral contraceptives with an increased incidence of other maladies, such as certain liver disorders, certain forms of cancer, and diabetes. Despite such risks, birth control pills remain popular, largely because of their convenience and high reliability in preventing pregnancy. Moreover, the dangers of taking the pill must be weighed against the health risks inherent in pregnancy. But for some women, including those with a history of heart disease, diabetes, and high blood pressure, the risks of using birth control pills can be significant. All women, therefore, should avoid taking birth control pills that have not been prescribed by a qualified physician.

Slightly less effective than the pill are a group of variously shaped plastic coils and loops known collectively as *intrauterine devices* (IUDs). They are inserted by a physician into the uterus through the vagina and cervix (Fig. 25.14). Most IUDs have a nylon "tail" that protrudes from the cervix into the vagina. The length of tail extending through the cervical opening can be used to detect movement of the IUD from its proper position; the tail also provides a means by which IUDs can be removed.

How an IUD prevents pregnancy is not known and has been a subject of great controversy for several years. Some evidence indicates that IUDs prevent normal implantation of a developing embryo. A large body of opposing evidence suggests that IUDs produce a minor inflammation of the uterine lining. It is well known that phagocytic leukocytes migrate to inflammed tissue in large numbers (see Chap. 18), and it has been suggested that such leukocytes kill all sperms before they reach the oviducts. Several IUDs are coated with copper, a substance that probably enhances the inflammatory response. Copper also may inhibit sperm transport by chemically reacting with certain enzymes produced by uterine tissue.

Although an IUD can be installed quickly and simply, it can be expelled unnoticed from the uterus. Moreover, it can irritate or puncture the uterus if inserted improperly, producing bleeding and cramping. Accordingly, IUDs should not be worn by women who have a uterine tumor or an abnormally shaped uterus.

Less reliable than IUDs are a variety of barriers to sperm transport. In order of their effectiveness as contraceptives, these include the diaphragm, the condom, diverse spermicidal foams and jellies, and postcoital douches. The *diaphragm* is a flat, spherical rubber membrane that contains a metal spring around its perimeter. The device is folded and inserted into the vagina before coitus. When tension on the spring is released in the vagina, the diaphragm unfolds, covering the opening of the cervix and blocking passage of sperms into the uterus (Fig. 25.15). The contraceptive effectiveness of the diaphragm can be increased by placing a spermicidal cream or jelly around its outer edge. When properly fitted and used conscientiously, the diaphragm affords excellent protection against pregnancy.

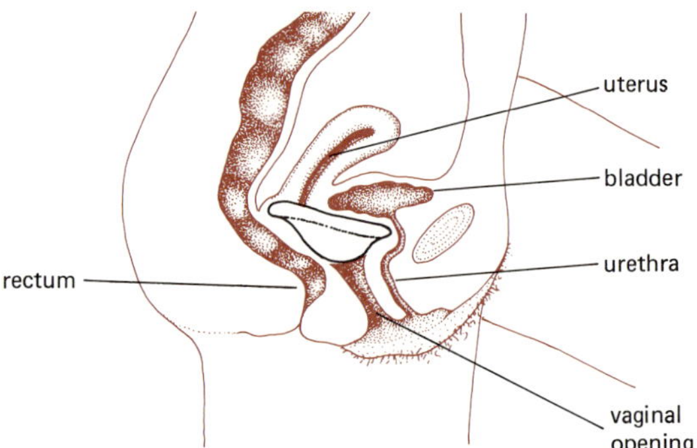

Fig. 25.15 Insertion of a diaphragm. Diaphragm is folded and inserted into the vagina. It is then pressed upward, covering the opening of the cervix. Properly positioned, the diaphragm blocks sperms from entering the uterus and oviducts.

Condoms are rubber sheaths that fit over the penis and trap semen. Although they are used more often than any other barrier to sperm transport, condoms can dull the pleasurable sensations that accompany coitus and can also develop leaks. Spermicidal foams, creams, jellies, and tablets are less effective than the contraceptive methods already discussed, largely because of their short-lived potency. Most of these spermicidal products can be obtained without prescription and are generally ineffective unless introduced into the vagina immediately before coitus. Spermicidal substances usually also are present in commercial vaginal douches. However, the practice of douching after coitus is an extremely ineffective contraceptive procedure, for sperm cells often are present in the oviducts before a douche can be sprayed into the vagina.

Two similarly unreliable forms of birth control are *withdrawal,* or *coitus interruptus,* and the *rhythm method.* Withdrawing the penis from the vagina just before ejaculation is one of the simplest and oldest methods of contraception. It requires considerable self-control on the part of the male and can result in pregnancy even when performed successfully, since small numbers of active sperms can be present in the seminal fluid that oozes from the penis before ejaculation. Furthermore, a man must concentrate on removing his penis before the onset of ejaculation and therefore cannot attend fully to his sexual pleasure or that of his partner.

People who use the rhythm method abstain

from coitus during the middle of the menstrual cycle. Ovulation usually occurs near this time, and human eggs are fertilizable for approximately 48 h thereafter. For the average 28-day menstrual cycle, ovulation occurs on the twelfth day following the onset of menstruation. Thus, pregnancy should result from coitus that occurs only on the thirteenth or fourteenth days of the cycle. However, very few women have such regular menstrual cycles. The cycles of many women are unpredictably irregular in length. Indeed, the timing of ovulation can vary considerably even among women who consistently have cycles of uniform length. Moreover, sperms remain viable in the oviducts of different women for variable periods. For reasons such as these, the contraceptive effectiveness of the rhythm method depends in part on luck.

In contrast to contraceptive birth control methods, *abortion* prevents the birth of a child by removal of an implanted embyro or fetus. Use of this most controversial method of birth control has increased in America since 1973. In that year, the United States Supreme Court ruled that states cannot prevent women from obtaining an abortion during the first 12 weeks of pregnancy. Before 1973, abortions could not be obtained legally in most states except for certain circumstances, such as when pregnancy jeopardized the life of a woman. Some people believe that abortions should not be performed under any circumstances, and the 1973 Supreme Court decision has inflamed the debate over abortion legislation.

The question of whether or under what circumstances abortions are to be permitted is a moral and social issue, not a scientific one. It cannot be argued, however, that recent technological advances in medicine have produced increasingly safe, reliable, and convenient abortion techniques. One of these is *dilation and curettage* (D and C). This is a two-part procedure in which the opening of the cervix first is expanded by a graduated series of mechanical dilators. Once it is expanded sufficiently, a scraping tool, or *curette,* is inserted into the uterus and used to dislodge and remove the developing embryo or fetus along with the placenta and extraembryonic membranes. The surgical curette has been replaced in many hospitals by an aspirator that removes the embryonic contents of the uterus by suction. This technique, called *suction curettage,* is faster than surgical curettage and results in fewer postoperative complications. In contrast to illegal abortions, the incidence of postoperative complications from abortions performed legally by skilled surgeons working under sterile conditions is less than 1 per 100 operations.

Because of the wish of many people to prevent or terminate pregnancy and the increasing political and social tensions that stem from human overpopulation, the search continues for even safer, more convenient, and more reliable methods of birth control. For example, research biologists are developing packets of hormonal concentrates that can be injected under the skin of women. The synthetic hormones of these packets are to be absorbed slowly in amounts sufficient to prevent ovulation for several months. Other biologists are experimenting with once-a-month pills that could be taken by a woman after coitus to abort an embryo that might be developing. In addition, several researchers are attempting to develop oral contraceptives for men that would inhibit the production of sperms, and some biologists are seeking ways of intensifying the immune response of women to sperms. Nevertheless, it is unlikely that any of these new methods will be ideal for all people and all circumstances. In spite of their drawbacks, most people in prosperous countries already can choose between several methods of birth control that are effective, safe, and convenient. In these societies, the means of eliminating unwanted pregnancies already exists.

Review Questions

1 Describe the events that characterize human courtship, precopulatory activity, coitus, and orgasm. What are the structural components of the human male and female reproductive systems? What are the functions of these structures?

2 Review the anatomical and chemical barriers to sperm transport through the reproductive system of human females. What are some of the causes of human infertility? Can infertility be overcome? How?

3 What happens to a human fertilized egg after it arrives in the uterus? When and how is a placenta formed and what are its functions? Describe the hormonal controls of reproduction during the placental phase of pregnancy.

4 Review the structure of the human placenta, with attention to embryonic and maternal blood circulation through it. What changes take place in the blood circulation of infants at birth?

5 Describe the appearance and relative size of the human embryo and fetus during various stages of pregnancy. Describe the three stages of childbirth. What events characterize each of these stages?

6 How is milk production initiated and maintained? Describe the neuroendocrine control of milk letdown.

7 Review the modern methods of birth control. Which methods and devices are most effective? Least effective? How does each of these methods or devices prevent fertilization? Discuss circumstances under which use of oral contraceptives should be avoided.

8 What is abortion? What is a D and C, and how does this abortion technique differ from suction curettage? Describe new methods of birth control currently being researched.

Collateral Readings

Beaconsfield, P., G. Birdwood, and **R. Beaconsfield:** The Placenta, *Scientific American,* July 1980. The structure and function of this mammalian embryonic structure is described.

Epel, D.: The Program of Fertilization, *Scientific American,* November 1977. This article describes how contact between sperm and egg triggers development of the embryo and initiates changes that prevent fertilization of eggs by more than one sperm.

Golanty, E.: "Human Reproduction," Holt, New York, 1975. An excellent and highly readable introduction to human sexual behavior, pregnancy, birth, and contraception. Available in paperback.

Grobstein, C.: External Human Fertilization, *Scientific American,* June 1979. Describes how human eggs are fertilized in glass containers and considers ethical issues surrounding use of such procedures in the development of human beings.

Hardin, G.: "Birth Control," Pegasus, New York, 1970. An informative and sometimes controversial paperback on the history and current methods of contraception.

Masters, W. H., and **V. E. Johnson:** "Human Sexual Response," Little, Brown, Boston, 1966. This classic work describes the sexual response of men and women in clinical terms.

McCary, J. L.: "Human Sexuality," 2d ed., Van Nostrand, Princeton, N.J., 1973. Less clinical than the previous reference; the author also discusses psychological and sociological factors that influence human sexuality.

Nilsson, L.: "Behold Man," Little, Brown, Boston, 1974. This book contains some of the most remarkable photographs of developing human embryos ever produced. It also includes numerous scanning electron micrographs of adult human tissues and organs.

Pengelley, E. T.: "Sex and Human Life," Addison-Wesley, Reading, Mass., 1974. Another excellent paperback on human sexuality.

Rugh, R., and **L. B. Shettles:** "From Conception to Birth: The Drama of Life's Beginnings," Harper & Row, New York, 1971. Remarkable color photographs of the human fetus are included in this excellent account of human development.

Shapiro, H. I.: "The Birth Control Book," St. Martin's, New York, 1977. An excellent description of the various contraceptive methods available today, including discussions of the pros and cons of each.

Swanson, H. D.: "Human Reproduction: Biological and Social Change," Oxford, New York, 1974. The basic processes of reproduction are described in this paperback.

Tietze, C., and **S. Lewit:** Legal Abortion, *Scientific American,* January 1977. An interesting discussion of the sociological effects of legalized abortion.

Chapter 26 Aging, Death

Learning Objectives

After reading this chapter you should be able to:

1. Give a biological definition of aging and show how the rates of aging vary between species of animals.
2. Distinguish between average and maximum life expectancies; write a paragraph demonstrating how improvements in living conditions often can increase average life-spans of animals; illustrate the effects of such improvements on maximum life expectancy.
3. List at least five manifestations of aging in cells; define lipofuscin granules and subculturing; describe the significance of cell culture experiments performed by Leonard Hayflick and his associates; outline evidence suggesting a relationship between the mean life-span of an animal species and the number of population doublings of its cells.
4. Define HeLa cells and describe their origin; list at least three characteristics of cellular aging that do not occur in cancer cell lines.
5. List at least three manifestations of aging in tissues; describe the mechanisms responsible for the shortened stature, increased "stiffness," and "leathery" skin of older people; distinguish between collagen and tropocollagen.
6. List at least five factors that influence the rate of aging in animals; outline experiments that suggest positive correlations between four of the factors you have listed and the rates at which animals age; name the principal symptoms of progeria.
7. Identify and describe at least two transcription-translation theories of aging; define somatic mutation and list evidence refuting the concept that aging is caused by a gradual accumulation of such mutations; illustrate how certain mutations could accelerate aging more than others.
8. Define and state evidence for the immunological theory of aging; define thymosin and state how deterioration of the thymus gland might promote aging in vertebrates.
9. Define free radical and indicate how these molecular fragments could produce symptoms of aging; list at least three observations consistent with the free-radical theory of aging.
10. Write a paragraph describing the programmed death theory of aging; list evidence that supports and refutes this theory.
11. Outline a possible relationship between thyroxine and aging; list evidence that supports the death-hormone theory of aging.
12. Describe at least three ways in which scientists are attempting to increase maximum human life expectancy; define liposome and show how this structure might be used to retard aging; discuss at least three ways in which dramatic increases in maximum human longevity could affect human social behavior and human social institutions.

Development continues throughout life: New tissues continually replace those which become defective, damaged, or lost. Indeed, whole parts of some organisms can be regenerated if lost (see Chap. 22). However, development does not always yield more efficient, viable, and therefore "young" structures. Components gradually deteriorate, and steady-state controls eventually become too disrupted to sustain life even in organisms maintained in optimal environments. This progressive deterioration of structures and functions is a manifestation of *aging*, a natural process of development. Thus, aging does not reflect an inherent defect in living systems, as some erroneously suppose. By providing living space for new generations, aging and death represent important evolutionary adaptations (see Chap. 29).

Most plants, some protists, and even Monera display signs of aging. However, the manifestations of aging occurring in most of these organisms are not strictly comparable to those of human beings or of animals generally. Consequently, the discussion that follows is almost entirely limited to aging in animals. Those wishing information about aging in nonanimal species are urged to consult specific references in the Collateral Readings for this chapter.

THE AGING PROCESS

The outward signs of aging often are obvious, but its underlying causes are poorly understood. It is clear, however, that aging is not the result of purely physical or chemical events that affect all organisms equally. Aging has a genetic basis that somehow establishes different life-spans for different species (Table 26.1). Mice, for example, live an average of $2\frac{1}{2}$ years, while the average life-spans of domestic sheep, pigs, shorthorn cattle, and donkeys are 12, 16, 20, and 40 years, respectively.

The importance of this genetic basis becomes even more apparent when maximum life-spans are considered. Habitat can greatly affect average life-spans, but living conditions have little bearing on maximum life expectancy. For example, the average life-span of lions is about 10 years in native habitats and can be increased to 15 years or more when the animals are maintained in zoos. But the maximum life-span of lions is about 35 years in both environments.

Improved living conditions, better nutrition, development of modern medicine, and other technological innovations have increased *average* human life expectancy from about 22 years in the fifth century B.C. to about 70 years today (Fig. 26.1). Further increases appear likely. For example, bioengineers already have created artificial human heart valves, blood vessels, joints, and limbs (Fig. 26.2). Artificial eyes, kidneys, gonads, and other organs now are being tested and soon will become available as replacement parts. Research aimed at the eradication of cancer, diabetes mellitus, and cardiovascular disease also should result in increased human life expectancy over the next few decades.

TABLE 26.1
Average Lifespans for Males and Females of Some Animals

	Days	
	Male	**Female**
fruit fly	31	33
beetle	60	111
spider	100	271
rat	750	900

SOURCE: Daniel Hershey, "Lifespan and Factors Affecting It," table VI, p. 26, Thomas, Springfield, Ill., 1974.

But these accomplishments will have little impact either on the general shape of the typical survival curve for human populations or on *maximum* life expectancy (Fig. 26.3). It is estimated that complete elimination of cancer and heart disease would increase average human life expectancy by only 10 to 12 years and would have almost no effect on maximum life expectancy. Even the accumulated benefits of biomedical research over the past two centuries have done little to increase maximum longevity. Today, greater numbers of people survive to the age of 70 than ever before, but the number of people who live to the age of 100 has not changed appreciably over the centuries. It can be concluded, therefore, that further improvements of human living conditions will not significantly increase maximum life-span. If such an increase is to occur, it will stem from a better understanding of the aging process itself.

Aging occurs at all levels of biological organization. The visible signs of aging that appear in whole animals often reflect less obvious changes in cells, tissues, and organs. For example, the number of degenerative changes found in neurons and other nondividing cells increases steadily with age. The nuclear chromatin of such cells typically undergoes progressive fragmentation and dissolution. The total number of mitochondria gradually diminishes in aging cells, while the number of abnormally shaped mitochondria gradually increases. In addition, the Golgi bodies of aging cells usually are far more fragmented than those of younger cells.

Another common manifestation of cellular aging is the progressive accumulation of pigmented granules in cytoplasm. Most of these "aging pigments" are thought to be degenerative waste products produced in lysosomes. Such pigments are sometimes called *lipofuscin granules,* particularly in heart muscle and nerve cells, where they accumulate

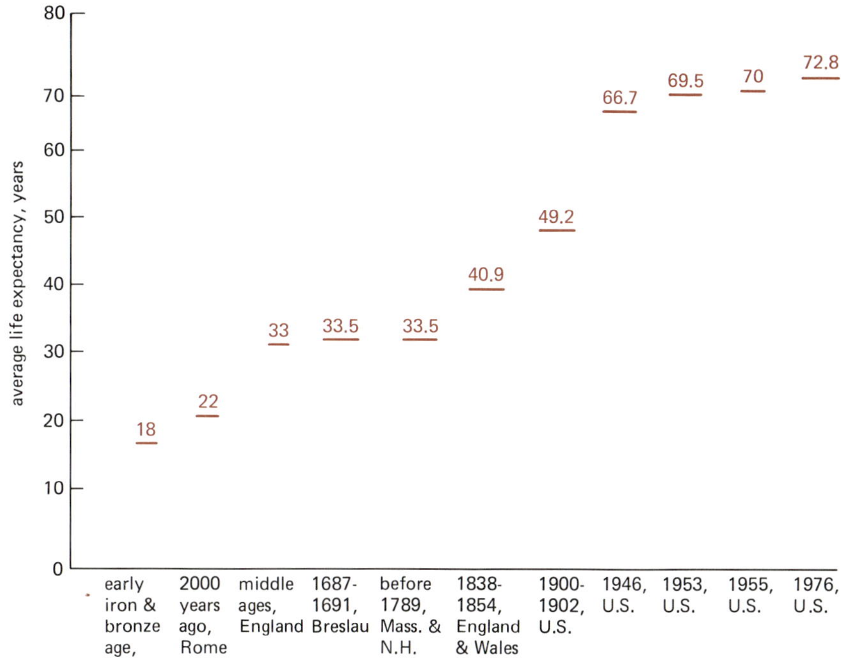

Fig. 26.1 Living conditions and average human life expectancy. Note the substantial increase in average human life expectancy that has occurred during the twentieth century.

steadily. Indeed, the age of an animal can be estimated by determining the concentration of lipofuscin in muscle or nerve tissue. For example, the amount of aging pigment in the cardiac muscle of an 80-year-old person is approximately 5 per cent of all substances making up the heart (Fig. 26.4).

Some of the most intriguing evidence demonstrating aging of individual cells has been obtained

Fig. 26.2 "Bionic" body parts. Artificial limbs have been developed that are regulated by neural impulses emanating from the brain. In this demonstration, the man at the left has lifted his arm upward. Nerve impulses coordinating this movement are picked up by electronic sensors in his skin and transmitted to the artificial arm held by the man at right. As a result, the artificial arm has duplicated the movement of the real arm.

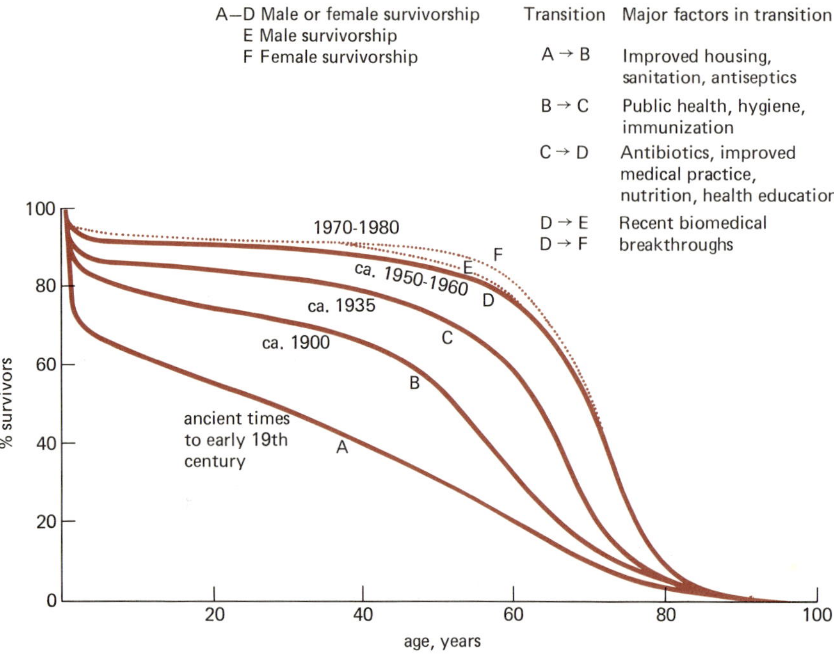

Fig. 26.3 Human survivorship curves from ancient times to the present. Inset at upper right lists factors chiefly responsible for the changing shapes of human survivorship curves over the past several centuries. Note that improved living standards have produced little change in maximum life expectancy. Also note that life expectancy for men has not changed appreciably since 1950 in the 50+ age group but that female longevity has increased during this period. One factor responsible for this difference is improved detection and treatment of cancers of the female reproductive system.

Fig. 26.4 Aging pigment. (A) Dense lipofuscin granules (arrows) in cells of an adrenal gland of a macaque. (B) Accumulation of lipofuscin in human heart muscle with age.

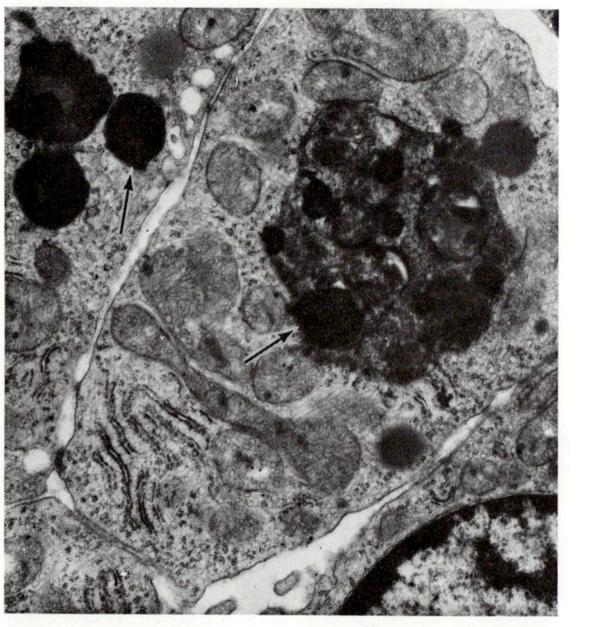

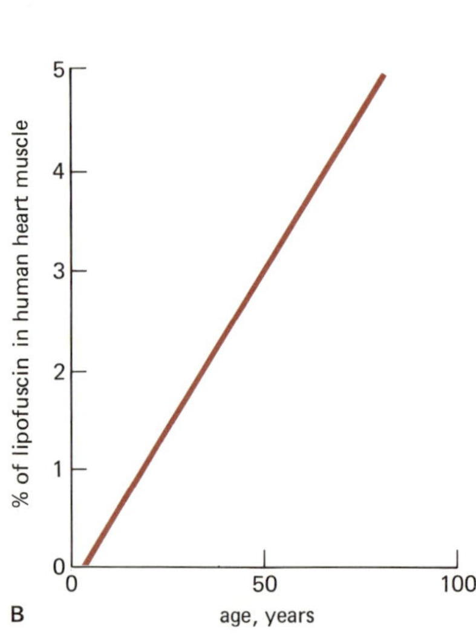

from cell-culture experiments. In these procedures a small piece of tissue is removed from skin, a lung, or similar organ (Fig. 26.5). After the cells of the tissue have been separated, a small mass of cells is transferred to a culture dish containing a nutrient-rich medium. The cells attach to the glass surface of the dish and begin to divide. After several divisions the density of cells in the dish becomes too great for normal growth; at this point the cell population is removed and temporarily suspended in a solution. A few of these suspended cells then are used to innoculate a second culture dish. After several more reproductive cycles, the cells are resuspended and a few of them are used to innoculate still another culture dish. If this process, called *subculturing,* is repeated several times, a point is usually reached where the cells cease dividing and die.

Results of experiments conducted by Leonard Hayflick, a long-time student of cellular aging, indicate that the number of divisions a group of cells passes through before dying out is inversely related to the age of the donor. Fibroblasts from the lung of a human fetus, for example, divide about 50 times before dying out. By contrast, fibroblasts taken from the lungs of a young adult can divide only about 30 times, and those from lungs of older people typically undergo even fewer divisions in cell culture.

Similar experiments demonstrate that this diminishing reproductive potential of cells is related directly to the number of times the cells have divided, not simply the passage of time. For example, Hayflick has placed cells in "suspended animation" by freezing them in liquid nitrogen for variable periods of time. Fetal cells frozen at the twentieth population doubling pass through approximately 30 more doublings after rethawing. Cells frozen after the tenth doubling undergo about 40 more doublings when rethawed. In other words, the total number of doublings before and after thawing always equals about 50. These results suggest that cells have a built-in "clock" that somehow measures the number of divisions in a time-independent manner.

Hayflick's experiments further indicate that cell death is not due to the gradual poisoning of the cultures by wastes or to the depletion of an essential nutrient. This last conclusion is not universally accepted by other scientists, however. Some biologists report that the number of divisions a group of cells passes through is greatly influenced by environmental conditions in the culture vessels, and that addition of certain kinds of growth factors can significantly increase the expected number of population doublings. Other biologists suggest that factors limiting the life-spans of *cultured* cell lines may not exist in the natural environment of the body. Thus, even if Hayflick's interpretations are correct, the gradual aging of cells in culture may not represent a fundamental cause of aging in whole, multicellular organisms. Resolution of this controversial issue requires additional research.

Less controversial are results of experiments showing the reproductive potential of cultured cells to be directly proportional to the mean life-span of

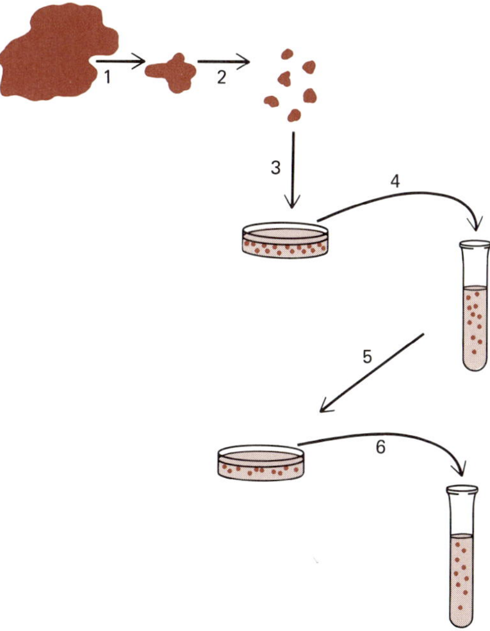

Fig. 26.5 Cell cultures. Successive generations of cells can be produced in special culture media. A piece of tissue is first excised (1) and broken up (2). Cells are separated from the bits of tissue and grown in culture dishes (3). After several divisions the culture dish can no longer support the large mass of cells. At this point some cells are removed from the dish and suspended (4). A few of the suspended cells are used to inoculate a second culture dish (5). After several more divisions the transfer process, called subculturing, is repeated (6). This technique has proved invaluable in measuring the longevity of a wide variety of cells.

TABLE 26.2
Life-spans of Cultured Human and Animal Fibroblast Cells

Species	Range of population doublings for cultured fibroblasts	Mean maximum life-span, years
Galapagos tortoise	90–125	175?
human beings	40–60	110
mink	30–34	10
chicken	15–35	30
mouse	14–28	3.5

SOURCE: G. J. Thorbecke (ed.), "Biology of Aging and Development," table 1, p. 12, Plenum, New York, 1975.

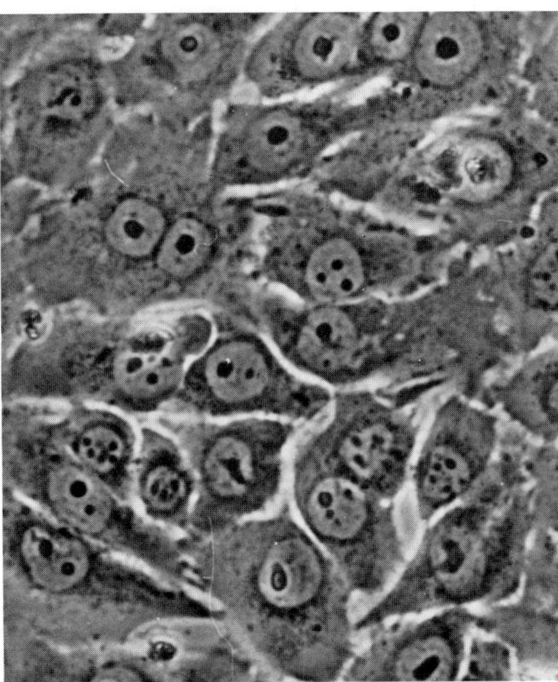

Fig. 26.6 HeLa cells. Note the variable number of nucleoli (dark dots) within the nuclei of these cancer cells, which are derived from malignant uterine tissue. Nuclei derived from cells of noncancerous animal tissues usually contain specific, fixed numbers of nucleoli (approx. × 350).

the species (Table 26.2). In other words, cell lines of long-lived species generally have greater reproductive potentials than those of short-lived species. Chickens, for example, have a maximum life expectancy only one-third that of human beings. Accordingly, fibroblasts removed from chicken embryos die out after about 20 doublings in cell culture compared with the 50 or so doublings of human fibroblasts.

Malignant cells represent a significant exception to these general rules: they continue to divide indefinitely. One line of malignant cells, *HeLa cells,* has been maintained in continuous culture by cancer researchers for over 30 years (Fig. 26.6). The original cells were obtained from the uterus of Henrietta Lacks, a young black woman who died of cancer in 1951. Like many malignant cells, the HeLa line contains an abnormal number of chromosomes, anywhere from 50 to about 350 per cell. Occasionally cells derived from normal donors continue to divide indefinitely instead of dying after several reproductive cycles. When such cells are examined, they often contain atypical numbers of chromosomes. Evidently, abnormalities in the genetic constitution of cells can interfere with at least some of the mechanisms responsible for normal aging.

Processes of cellular aging undoubtedly are related to the progressive structural and functional deterioration of aging tissues, organs, and organ systems, but the exact nature of the relationship remains obscure (Fig. 26.7). It is known that the number of neurons in the brain and other parts of the nervous system gradually declines as animals age. A similar deterioration takes place in muscle. These changes appear to be at least partly responsible for the decreased ability of old people to respond effectively to stress. Aging skin becomes progressively more wrinkled and "leathery," and people complain more of stiffness and general soreness as they get older. Moreover, old people are shorter than when they were younger; by the age of 60 we are about $\frac{1}{2}$ inch shorter than we were at 25.

These characteristics of "old age" largely stem from a deterioration of connective tissues, which become less distensible with age (Fig. 26.8). The shortened stature of older people mainly results from a gradual loss of cartilage between bones. But many other structural signs of aging result from changes in the properties of collagen. This fibrous glycoprotein, present in most connective tissues (see Chap. 7), accounts for up to 40 per cent of all body proteins. In contrast to most other biochemicals, collagen is largely nonrenewable. Thus, much of

structure or function	percent
weight of brain	56
blood supply to brain	80
output of heart at rest	70
number of glomeruli in kidney	56
glomerular filtration rate	69
speed of return to normal pH of blood after displacement	17
number of taste buds	36
vital capacity	56
strength of hand grip	55
maximum O_2 uptake during exercise	40
number of axons in spinal nerve	63
velocity of nerve impulse	90
body weight in males	88

Fig. 26.7 Structural and functional losses during aging. Percentages represent fractions of a specific structure or function remaining in an average 75-year-old man compared with that of an average 30-year-old man. Values for the 30-year-old are arbitrarily set as 100 percent.

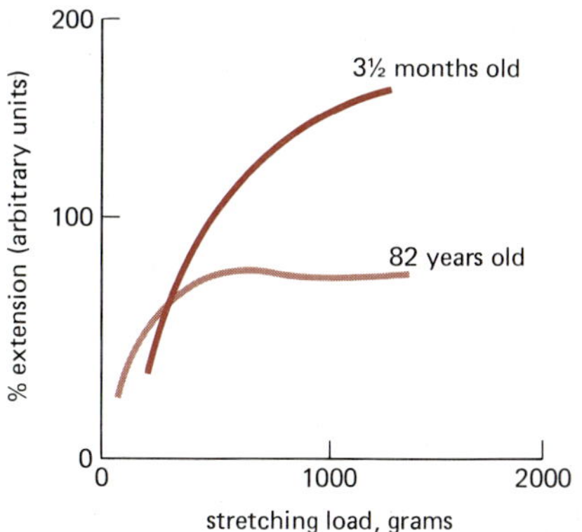

Fig. 26.8 Distensibility of abdominal skin. The skin of children is far more distensible than that of older people.

the collagen produced during childhood remains in the body for life.

Collagen is a polymer of *tropocollagen* subunits, each subunit composed of three polypeptide chains (Fig. 26.9). The chains are held together by noncovalent bonds in newly synthesized molecules of tropocollagen. Because these bonds are weaker and provide less rigidity than the covalent variety, newly manufactured collagen is moderately flexible. As collagen matures, however, increasing numbers of covalent bonds become established between the three polypeptides and between tropocollagen subunits. This cross-linking steadily increases the rigidity and "toughness" of collagen, a phenomenon readily appreciated by anyone who has eaten beefsteak derived from old cattle.

Cross-linking also occurs between the fibers of aging *elastin,* a second kind of connective tissue fiber. These highly distensible fibers are concentrated in skin, the walls of arteries, and other parts of the body that undergo frequent stretching. Cross-linking between elastin fibers reduces their distensible properties and, together with the greater rigidity of collagen, is a principal reason for increasing complaints of stiffness among older people. Not surprisingly, increased cross-linking between the fibers of connective tissues can be correlated with expected life-span. Accordingly, the collagen of a $2\frac{1}{2}$-year-old mouse is heavily cross-linked; that of a $2\frac{1}{2}$-year-old child is not.

Increased cross-linking of connective-tissue fibers, decreased metabolic efficiency, and a diminishing ability to respond to stress are characteristics of aging that apply generally to most animals. But studies that compare processes of aging in different individuals and different species also demonstrate that organs and organ systems age at different rates and to varying degrees. Such findings continue to frustrate those who seek a fundamental cause of aging in all organisms. Indeed, as will become apparent shortly, the view that aging stems from a single cause may be too simplistic; perhaps aging results from the cumulative effect of many factors operating at many different levels of organization within organisms.

FACTORS INFLUENCING LIFE-SPAN

Organisms die when steady-state control systems become inadequate to sustain living functions. Death can occur suddenly, as in an automobile accident, when steady-state controls are disrupted violently, or more slowly, as when the poisons of a deadly pathogen interfere with normal control processes (see Chap. 30). But even if an animal escapes death from accident or pathogens, it is sure to succumb from "old age," for the deterioration of steady-state and metabolic processes are *built-in* attributes of living systems.

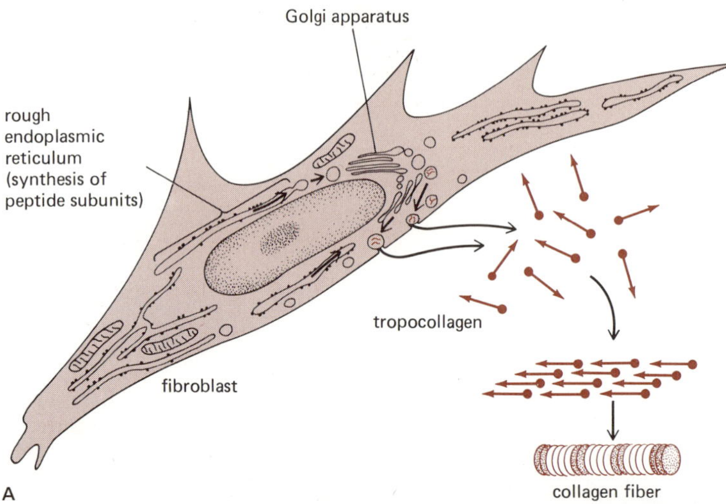

Fig. 26.9 Collagen. (A) Tropocollagen, the structural subunit of collagen, is produced along the rough endoplasmic reticulum of fibroblasts, packaged in the Golgi apparatus, and secreted to the extracellular environment. Tropocollagen subunits then become organized in a staggered parallel arrangement, which is manifested as bands within collagen fibers. (B) This low-magnification electron micrograph shows the banded appearance of collagen fibers.

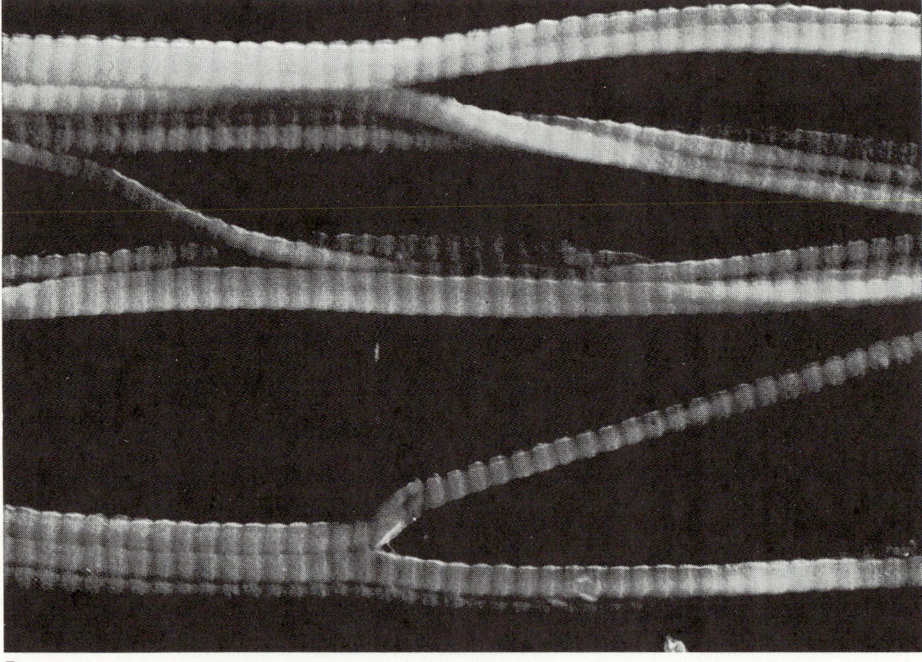

A host of factors influences the rate of this deterioration, but not to the same degree in all animals. For example, several experiments have shown that cold-blooded organisms have a rate of aging that is significantly influenced by temperature. In experiments with rotifers, microscopic animals that inhabit many freshwater lakes and ponds, a 10°C reduction in water temperature has prolonged life-span about 4 times. Similarly, water fleas have been shown to live almost 4 times longer at 15°C than at 5°C or at 33°C (Table 26.3). Corresponding results have been obtained in experiments with fish. By contrast, warm-blooded animals (birds and mammals) have a relatively

TABLE 26.3

Temperature Effect on Life-span for Water Fleas

Temperature, °C	Life-span, days
5	4.2
9	11.1
15	14.3
21	9.2
27	6.5
33	4.7

SOURCE: Daniel Hershey, "Life-span and Factors Affecting It," table IV, p. 13, Thomas, Springfield, 1974.

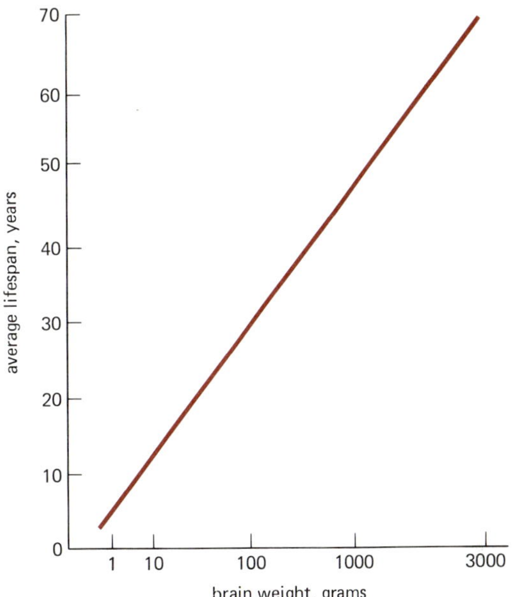

Fig. 26.10 Life-span and brain weight. This graph illustrates data collected from 63 species of animals.

constant body temperature. Experiments with these organisms show little, if any, relationship between environmental temperature and longevity.

The rate of aging in some animals is related statistically to nutrition. Underfed fish live longer than usual, and one strain of male rats starved every third or fourth day show a 20 per cent increase in life-span (females displayed only a 15 per cent increase).

Gender can also influence longevity. Most people are aware that women have a longer life expectancy than men, but few people are aware that this pattern holds generally for many animals. Reasons for this difference remain obscure. Some have speculated that the longer life expectancy of females may result from the differential inheritance of sex chromosomes. Females of many species, human beings included, inherit a pair of X chromosomes; their male counterparts inherit only one (see Chap. 27). For some animals the opposite holds true. Among birds, for example, males inherit two identical sex chromosomes, yet females still exhibit longer life-spans.

Some diseases influence life-span by seemingly accelerating the aging process. *Progeria,* for example, is a rare but particularly tragic disease that transforms children into old-appearing people in less than a decade. Indeed, many progeric children begin to look old and frail at the age of 4. Ten-year-old progeric children usually have wrinkled skin, may be bald, and frequently suffer from atherosclerosis, elevated levels of blood cholesterol, high blood pressure, and heart disease. Most of these children succumb to heart attack, usually less than 12 years after birth. Whether the effects of progeria are truly mimicking the natural aging process remains in doubt.

Several additional factors are correlated with average life expectancy. In some species, for example, the life expectancy of offspring is influenced by parental age. Rotifers produced from older parents usually have shorter life-spans than progeny of younger parents. Metabolic rate and the ratio of brain weight to body weight also are related to average life-span. Animals with comparatively large brains and those with low rates of metabolism generally live longer than animals having opposite characteristics (Fig. 26.10).

But how significant are these relationships and statistical correlations? Do any of these factors cause aging, or are they merely symptomatic of other underlying causes? How many of these correlations are simply coincidental? Scientists have been grappling with these questions for several years and, not surprisingly, have constructed almost as many theories of aging as there are factors influencing the process.

THEORIES OF AGING

Transcription-Translation Theories

Several theories propose that aging results from accumulating defects in the transcription and translation of nucleic acids. Flaws do develop in the complex and highly integrated processes of transcription and translation. Some, for example, result from *somatic mutations,* changes in the genetic constitution of body cells. As discussed more extensively in Chap. 27, the nitrogen base sequence of DNA can become altered in cells. Because they sometimes result in the continual production of erroneous RNA, such alterations can seriously disrupt normal cell functions.

Mutations occur infrequently and more or less randomly. But they do occur continually, and therefore over many years they could produce a gradual increase in the number of defective genes. The *somatic-mutation theory* of aging assumes (1) that the number of mutant, defective genes increases steadily over the life-span of an animal; and (2) that the manifestations of aging result from these mutations. This theory has undergone considerable experimental testing over the past several years. Many of these experiments have evaluated the following prediction of the theory: factors promoting increased rates of mutation in animals should always increase rates of aging.

Several agents, called *mutagens,* can significantly increase the number of mutations in cells (see also Chap. 27). These include x-radiation and a diverse array of chemicals. Many of these agents can decrease life expectancy, and some of them even produce physical changes in animals that mimic the effects of aging (Fig. 26.11). But do x-rays and other mutagens actually accelerate normal aging processes? Most research indicates that they do not. For example, Bernard Strehler of the University of Southern California has shown that at least one kind of mutagen can *increase* the life expectancy of some animals. In one of his experiments, the average life-span of fruit flies exposed to x-radiation was a few days longer than that of nonirradiated flies.

Another line of experimentation provides additional evidence that somatic mutations are not the cause of normal aging in animals. These studies used a species of wasp in which some males are haploid and some diploid. The double set of genes in diploid individuals provides a kind of "back up" genetic system lacking in the haploid males (see also Chap. 27). The mutation of, say, 10 genes in a cell of a haploid individual reduces the total number of normal genes by a much greater amount than in a corresponding cell of a diploid male. According to the somatic-mutation theory, the life expectancy of haploid males should be less than that of diploid individuals. Yet experiments clearly indicate that haploid and diploid males of this species have identical life-spans.

Experiments such as these have generally discredited the somatic-mutation theory. They also strongly suggest that the debilitating effects of radiation are not the result of an acceleration of normal aging processes.

A second transcription-translation theory of aging is the *error-catastrophe theory,* proposed independently by S. A. Medvedev and L. E. Orgel in the early 1960s. Certain kinds of errors in cells are likely to produce a great number of subsequent errors, and this fact is central to the error-catastrophe concept. Some proteins play important roles in the transcription and translation of nucleic acids. Examples include DNA polymerase, RNA polymerase, and a recently discovered group of enzymes that repair mistakes in the linear base sequences of DNA. A defect in any of these enzymes probably would disrupt cell function far more extensively than, say, a flaw in a structural protein found only in desmosomes. In other words, mutations of some genes can cause problems, but mutations of certain key genes can produce catastrophes (Fig. 26.12).

Despite its apparent logic, the error-catastrophe theory is refuted by a number of observations. For example, experiments have been conducted in which abnormal amino acids were added to the diets of animals. Abnormal amino acids that became incorporated in key sites of enzymes and other proteins sometimes destroyed the normal functioning of these larger molecules, but their incorporation did not significantly affect the average life-span of the animals. Because some of the abnormal amino acids should be incorporated in enzymes involved in transcription and translation, the absence of a life-shortening effect is inconsistent with the error-catastrophe theory of aging.

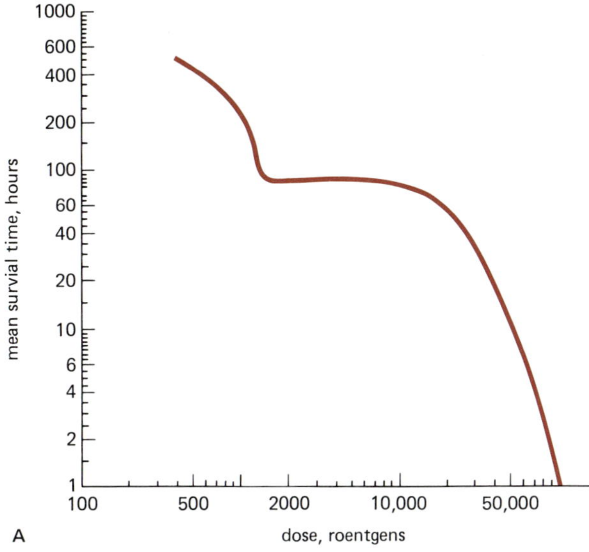

Fig. 26.11 Radiation and life-span. (A) Average survival time of mammals as a function of dosage following exposure of animals to whole-body radiation. Increments of dosage are roentgens, international units used in measuring radiation. (B) Visible effects of radiation. The mice in these two photographs are siblings (brothers and sisters). Mice on the left are control animals, those on the right received a large but nonlethal dose of radiation. Only three of the irradiated mice remain alive, and they have a far more "aged" appearance than the controls. However, the life-shortening effects of radiation do not appear to result from an acceleration of normal aging processes. Moreover, radiation does not decrease the life-span of all animals.

B

In their present form, neither the somatic-mutation nor the error-catastrophe theory adequately accounts for the effects of aging in whole organisms, and biologists increasingly are turning their attention to testing alternative explanations.

Immunological Theory

The *immunological theory* of aging provides a possible explanation of how aging cells might trigger aging of tissues, organs, and organ systems in vertebrates. Proponents of this theory contend that the structure primarily responsible for aging is the thymus gland. Since this organ is not present in invertebrates, the immunological theory is directed chiefly at aging in human beings and most other vertebrates. As noted in Chap. 18, the thymus gland is comparatively large in children but slowly atrophies and virtually disappears in late middle age.

The thymus appears to be a true endocrine organ, secreting *thymosin,* a hormone that transforms certain immature cells into T lymphocytes. Because they kill malignant and pathogenic mi-

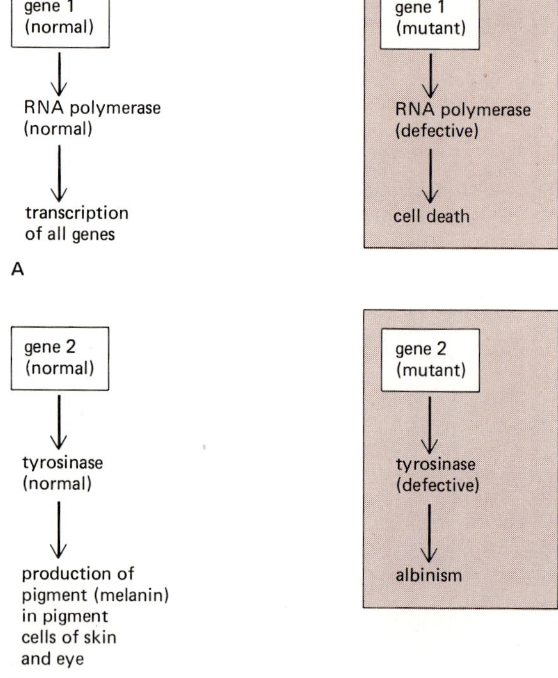

Fig. 26.12 Error catastrophe. (A) RNA polymerase influences transcription of all genes (left). Consequently, mutation of a gene coding for RNA polymerase could disrupt transcription of all other genes, bringing about cell death (right, color). (B) The enzyme tyrosinase influences production of melanin in pigment cells of the skin and eye (left). Because the effects of this enzyme are more limited than those of RNA polymerase, mutation of a gene coding for tyrosinase does not lead to cell death. Animals lacking normal tyrosinase produce viable pigment cells but cannot manufacture melanin (right, color). Such individuals are called albinos; see also Fig. 27.13.

crobes and destroy foreign tissues, T lymphocytes constitute a major part of the vertebrate immune surveillance system (see Chap. 18). Supporters of the immunological theory suggest that the progressive atrophy of the thymus reduces the efficiency of the cellular immune response in older people, increasing their susceptibility to infectious disease. This view is consistent with results of studies demonstrating a gradual reduction in the efficiency of the immune response in older people. These studies also reveal higher mortality rates in those groups of people having the least efficient immune responses.

Results of similar studies demonstrate other kinds of immunological breakdowns in older people. For example, the immune surveillance systems of aging individuals are less able to distinguish between "self" and "nonself" antigens than those of younger people. As a result, the incidence of autoimmune responses increases as people age. Rheumatoid arthritis, pernicious anemia, systemic lupus erythematosis, and other suspected autoimmune diseases develop far more frequently in older people than in younger ones. Moreover, biologists have been able to extend the life-spans of mice and other vertebrates by administering high doses of immunosuppressive drugs. It is not yet clear, however, whether these drugs increase life expectancy by inhibiting development of autoimmune responses generally or by some other means.

Aging in vertebrates, therefore, may be caused by two interrelated processes: (1) atrophy of the thymus may be responsible for a progressively less efficient destruction of malignant, pathogenic, and other "foreign" cells; and (2) lymphocytes become less able to discriminate accurately between foreign and self antigens. As a result, the immune response system begins to attack both normal and abnormal cells of the body. It is as if the armed forces of a community gradually became increasingly careless in protecting its citizenry from enemy attack and simultaneously began to destroy enemy soldiers and citizens indiscriminately.

Free-Radical Theory

Free radicals are fragments of larger molecules. Each fragment contains an unpaired electron, obtained when a covalent bond of the larger molecule is broken (Fig. 26.13). Free radicals are highly unstable.

Some free radicals participate in smog-producing photochemical reactions, others promote drying of linseed oil paints, and still others are responsible for reactions that produce rancid butter. Free radicals also are produced in living systems, and some of them enter organisms from the external environment. Regardless of their source, most free radicals interfere with normal cell functions. These fragments can knock pieces out of molecules and accelerate production of lipofuscin. Some free radicals react with DNA, producing unstable intermediate

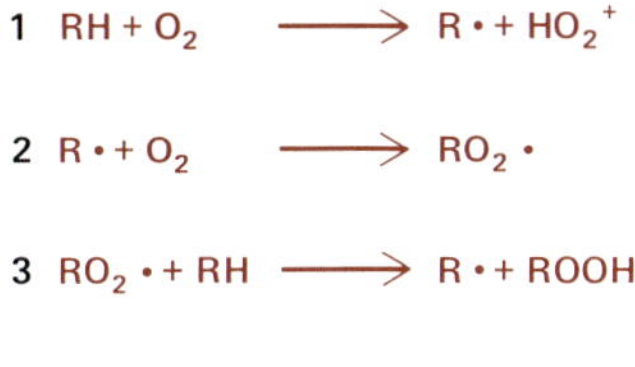

Fig. 26.13 Free radicals. This sequence of reactions illustrates how free radicals can fragment normal compounds in cells and produce abnormal substances. (1) Free radicals form when a covalent bond of a larger compound is broken (R of RH symbolizes any one of several possible atomic groupings). In this case, a hydrogen ion broken from RH unites with molecular oxygen, forming an ionic compound. The reaction also produces R·, a free radical (the dot in R· symbolizes an unpaired electron). R· triggers a sequence of reactions (2, 3, and 4), which produces several other free radicals and a potentially dangerous substance (R:R) that otherwise might never be produced in cells.

products and interfering with replication and transcription. By interacting with lipids, free radicals may be responsible for deleterious changes in membrane permeability, and they also can inhibit essential metabolic reactions by combining with enzymes.

Supporters of the free-radical theory of aging argue that damage caused by these molecular fragments gradually accumulates, weakening animals and eventually causing their death. Evidence supporting this concept does exist, but it is inconclusive and largely circumstantial. For example, animals fed diets deficient in vitamin E accumulate lipofuscin in heart muscle at faster than normal rates. Like certain other substances, vitamin E is a good free-radical scavenger. Thus, by combining with free radicals and yielding less damaging products, vitamin E may function in part as a natural age-retarding substance.

If a deficiency of vitamin E accelerates certain signs of aging, perhaps average life-span can be increased by supplementing diets with this and other free-radical scavengers. Several free-radical inhibitors have been tested, and some of them were reported to increase the life expectancy of certain strains of mice. As previously noted, however, reduced food consumption also can increase life span, and it is possible that mice fed diets containing certain free-radical scavengers may have consumed less food than control animals. Most evidence indicates that consumption of large amounts of vitamin E provides no protection against the accumulation of lipofuscin and does not extend animal longevity.

Nevertheless, several formulations of free-radical inhibitors are now being tested for human consumption. Unfortunately, some of the compounds contained in these dietary additives are extremely toxic in large doses and can act as poisons. Thus even if such formulations can prolong life expectancy, their widespread use poses significant health problems. Scientists are similarly concerned about the possible misuse of vitamins. Some of these compounds can neutralize free radicals, but large doses of some vitamins can produce harmful side effects. Excessive consumption of vitamin A, for example, can produce nausea, vomiting, headaches, and red, swollen skin.

Programmed-Death Theories

As noted earlier, most nonmalignant cells undergo a limited number of divisions in culture media before dying out. This observation has prompted some biologists to propose that cellular aging and death are programmed genetically. According to this view, specific groups of genes trigger degeneration and death after cells have passed through a set number of divisions, or after they have reached a certain stage of development. Different cells are presumed to contain different "death" programs, a circumstance that would explain why certain types of cells in an organism have shorter average life-spans than others and why different cells are affected by free radicals and other physical agents to varying degrees.

There is ample evidence for the concept of programmed cell death. Indeed, the scheduled death of some cell types is a necessary part of embryonic development. The human hand and foot, for example, develop initially as paddlelike structures. Separation of fingers and toes occurs when cells die in selected regions of the paddle (Fig. 26.14).

Similarly, the wings of birds are shaped by the death of selected cells. Recent studies show that the time of death of these wing cells is established at a given point during embryonic development. Location of the cells in the wing influences time of death. If cells destined for early death are transplanted to other parts of the embryo before a certain stage of development, the cells often survive

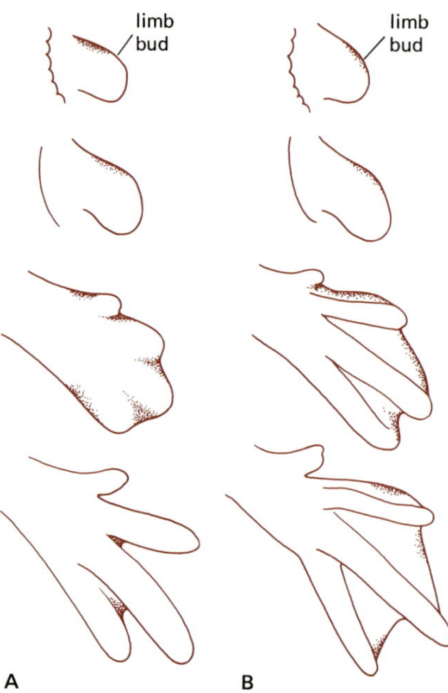

Fig. 26.14 **Programmed cell death.** Patterns of cell death in the development of chicken (A) and duck (B) appendages. The legs of birds and all other vertebrates arise as paddlelike outgrowths of tissues (limb buds). Cells in colored areas die before hatching. Separation of digits in the legs of chickens occurs when selected cells die during development. By contrast, cells between the digits of ducks are programmed differently and do not die. Instead, such cells form the "webbing" of the adult foot.

much longer than those left at the original site. But if the cells are transplanted after a given stage of development, they always die according to the schedule established for cells left at the original site. Such results suggest that the slow decline in the efficiency of bodily functions during aging might be due to a built-in rate of cell death.

Not all experimental results are consistent with programmed death theories of aging. For example, a recent study found no significant differences in the life-spans of cultured cells removed from 3-, 13-, and 19-month-old mice. As noted earlier, similar experiments conducted by Leonard Hayflick and his associates provide contrasting evidence. Consequently, programmed death theories of aging, although intriguing, are still tentative.

Death-Hormone Theory

Mention has already been made of the possible effects of thymosin on aging. Even if it truly influences longevity, this substance may not be the only or even primary aging hormone. Some biologists suspect that thyroxine affects the rate of aging in vertebrates through its control of metabolic processes. Cells of younger people, for example, are much more responsive to thyroxine than those of older ones, even though concentrations of the hormone in blood do not change appreciably with age.

Fig. 26.15 **Death-hormone theory.** Secretion of a "death hormone" by the pituitary is postulated. Proponents of the theory envision increased secretion of the hormone as individuals age. Blockage of thyroxine receptors on a wide variety of cells (double bar, right) could influence a host of age-promoting factors.

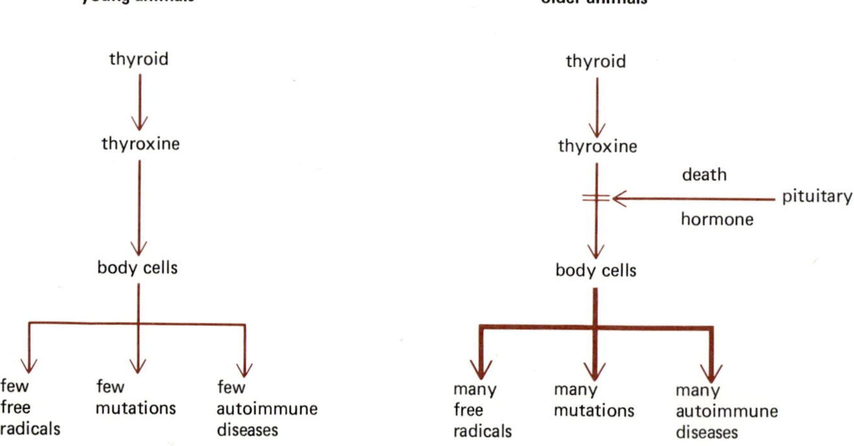

Results of some experiments indicate that at puberty the pituitary gland begins to release hormonelike substances which block thyroxine receptors on cell membranes. It has been suggested that release of these antithyroid substances, colorfully termed *death hormones,* increases with age. By interfering with thyroxine, these pituitary secretions could trigger a number of functional imbalances which in turn could bring about structural deterioration of the body and death. Diminished responsiveness of cells to thyroxine might increase the number of biochemcial oxidations, which might generate more free radicals, thus more crosslinkages, more mutations, and more error catastrophes. Lymphocytes also might become less efficient, sometimes attacking cells indescriminately and increasing the incidence of autoimmune reactions (Fig. 26.15).

W. Donner Denckla, a chief proponent of the death-hormone theory of aging, has been able to restore certain cardiovascular and immunological functions in aging rats by removing their pituitary glands and injecting them with thyroxine. This procedure also greatly increased concentrations of RNA polymerase in the livers of treated rats. Production of this enzyme normally decreases about fourfold in aging rats. It is possible, therefore, that aging pacemakers are released from the pituitary along with other hormones (see Chap. 17). Nevertheless, it must be emphasized that the existence of such aging hormones has not been demonstrated conclusively.

Our current understanding of the aging process thus is clouded by inconclusive experiments, conflicting results, and a large number of theories. This seemingly chaotic state of affairs actually is perfectly normal for any developing science. In describing the current status of aging research, V. V. Frolkis, a well-known Russian biologist, expressed a basic axiom of science when he stated that "the number of hypotheses is generally inversely proportional to the clarity of the problem." Except for the somatic-mutation theory, too few facts are known about the aging process to eliminate any of the proposed explanations of aging described in this chapter. Moreover, all these theories have been valuable, for each has led to experiments yielding new information about aging. As more facts become known, the fewer will be the number of theories that can explain all the facts.

HUMAN AND SOCIAL IMPLICATIONS OF AGING RESEARCH

When will it be possible to extend maximum human life expectancy significantly? It is impossible to establish timetables for biomedical "breakthroughs," which are almost totally dependent on

Fig. 26.16 Anti-free-radical drugs and life-span. (A) Addition of 1 percent 2-MEA hydrochloride, an anti-free-radical drug, to a commercial diet increased the average life-span of a certain strain of male mice. The drug had no effect on maximum life-span. (B) By contrast, addition of 0.5 percent BHT, another free-radical scavenger, to a synthetic diet increased both average and maximum life-spans of the same strain of male mice.

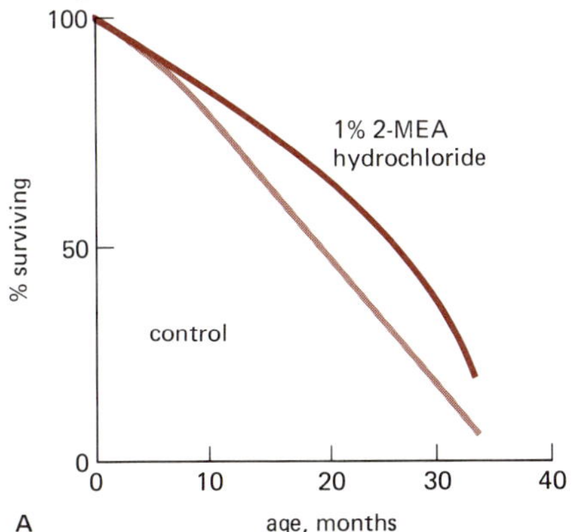

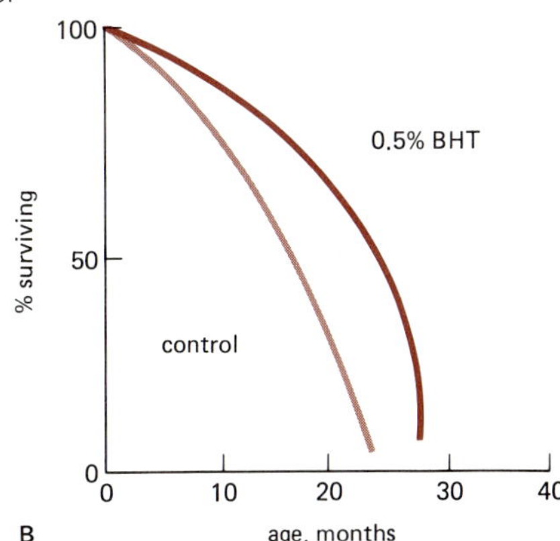

the acquisition of new knowledge. The rate at which such knowledge becomes available is influenced by many factors, including the availability of funds, the creative abilities of scientists, the number of unforeseen obstacles, and pure luck.

Nevertheless, some efforts to increase natural life-spans are already being made. As noted earlier, the age-prolonging effects of several drugs are being evaluated (Fig. 26.16). One of them, *centrophenoxine,* has improved the impaired mental capacities of some senile people. In addition, this drug has been shown to decrease concentrations of lipofuscin in aging human cells. The antiaging properties of thymosin also are being tested. Can this hormone prolong youth by decreasing autoimmune reactions? An answer to this question should be forthcoming soon.

At least some of the debilitating effects of aging probably result from a gradual decrease in enzyme efficiency. Biologists have compared the catalytic properties of several enzymes isolated from young and aged tissues. In many cases, enzymes isolated from younger tissues are more efficient than those produced by older cells. Other studies demonstrate a gradual loss of key enzymes during aging (Fig. 26.17). Conversely, concentrations of a few enzymes increase with age, and these high levels also may contribute to the aging process. Enzyme-replacement techniques are now being developed that could someday provide a means of inhibiting production of certain enzymes in cells while simultaneously augmenting intracellular concentrations of others. One of the newest and most promising techniques employs *liposomes* as transport vehicles for laboratory-derived enzymes and enzyme-inhibitor substances.

Fig. 26.17 Enzymes and aging. Changing concentrations of lactic dehydrogenase in the brain, heart, and skeletal muscle of aging rats. Lactic dehydrogenase is an important respiratory enzyme. Concentrations of certain other enzymes increase with age.

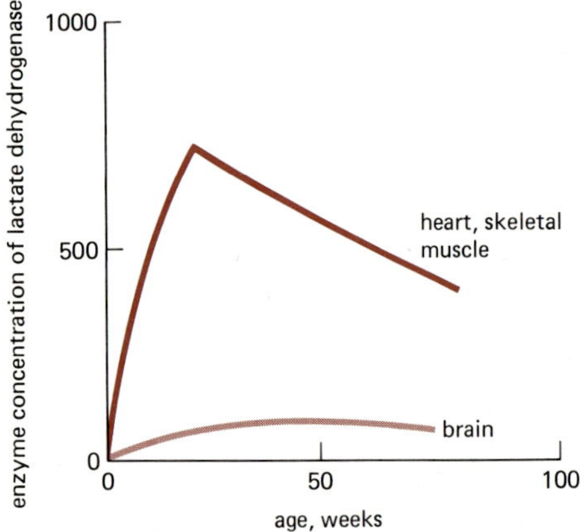

Consisting of several concentric layers of lipids, liposomes are small biodegradable spheres that can be manufactured in laboratories in large quantities (Fig. 26.18). Enzymes, drugs, and other therapeutic substances can be incorporated into liposomes and injected into the bloodstream. Because they are sequestered inside layers of lipid, substances housed in liposomes do not elicit an immune response and are protected from degradation during transport in body fluids. Although comparatively inert in such fluids, liposomes are readily phagocytized and digested by many kinds of cells. Eventually it may be possible to induce uptake of specially prepared liposomes by specific cells, thereby delivering "cargos" of replacement enzymes and other potentially age-retarding substances to target tissues.

Not all these techniques will slow aging processes and keep people fully functional until the very end of their lives, but at least a few successful methods are sure to be developed. It will then be possible to extend the human life-span. Many people would gladly accept "fountain of youth" treatments that might keep them alive and healthy for 150, 200, even 300 years or more. But other people neither desire nor condone earthly immortality. Some, for example, question the ethics of tampering with "natural" processes. Other individuals, some scientists included, argue that keeping people alive longer will aggravate the already serious problems of pollution, overpopulation, and diminishing natural resources.

Increased human longevity does have important social consequences. Sharp increases in human population growth could result from the widespread use of effective antiaging techniques. Decreased death rates could be counterbalanced by further reductions in the human birth rate, but how would such lowered rates affect family structure? Suppose many people lived to see the birth of their great-great-grandchildren. How would such polygenerational families affect human social institutions? Political and military leaders sometimes acquire considerable wealth and social influence.

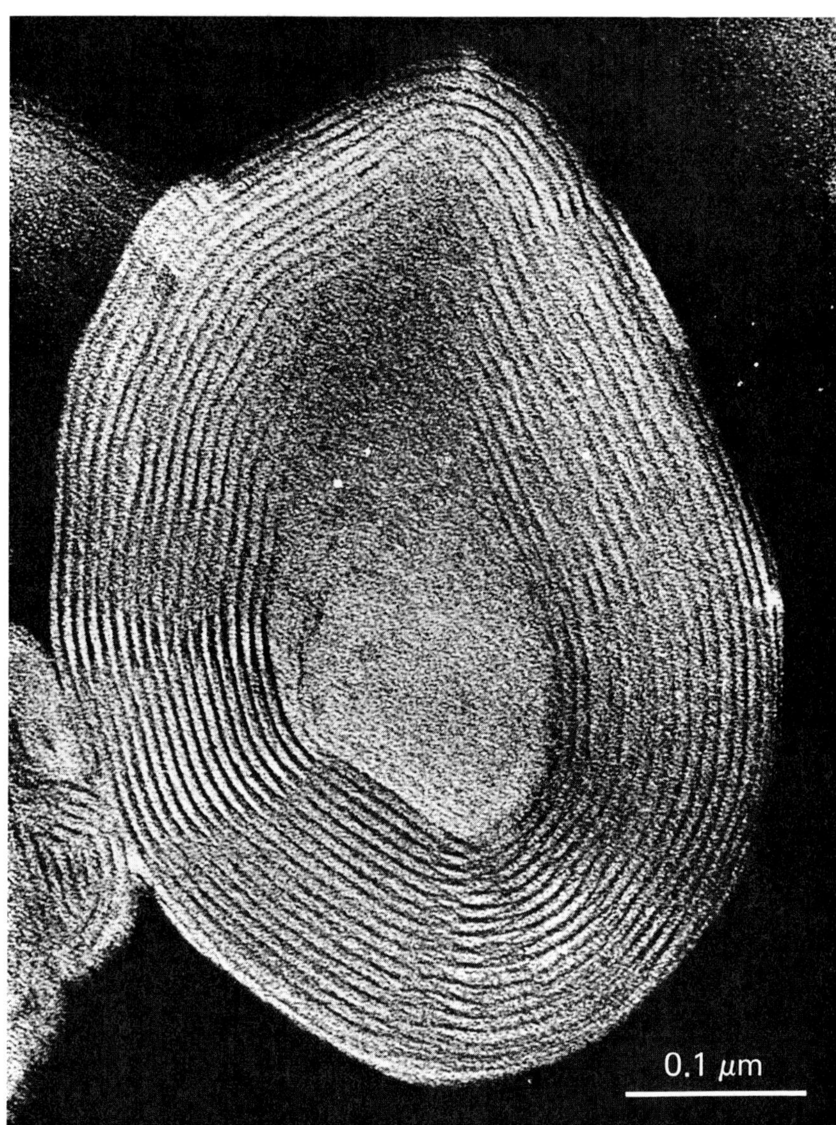

Fig. 26.18 Liposomes. Concentric layers of lipid-soluble molecules are visible in this electron micrograph of a liposome.

Suppose such people maintained their positions of power for 100 years or more? Would the innovations of youth be smothered by longer-lived social and political establishments? Will increased longevity cause social inflexibility?

Longer life-spans also could affect human behavior patterns. Some authors of science fiction have developed scenarios in which our longer-lived descendants become so concerned about dying from an accident early in life that they lose their sense of adventure and willingness to take risks. Fearing the unforeseen, such people live out their lives in protective suits and shelters. Will longer-lived people become less adventuresome?

There are no firm answers to such questions, but many people believe that the potential benefits of a longer life are well worth increased funding for aging research. They argue that attempts to increase human longevity will afford new methods of improving the health and vitality of old people, reducing the suffering, cost, and loneliness that often accompany old age. Above all, longer-lived people will have time to accomplish many more goals—time to visit and revisit favorite places; time to learn new skills, new languages, new musical instruments; time to pursue a variety of careers and a multiplicity of new interpersonal relationships; time to consolidate and integrate experiences in ways that could lead to wholly new philosophies, cultures, and patterns of social organization.

Because they are invented and controlled by people, technological innovations are subject to a variety of possible uses. The skills needed to retard human aging will almost certainly be developed, and with them will come new opportunities that we can either exploit or squander.

Review Questions

1 Define aging and death from a biological perspective. Do all animals age at the same rate? Illustrate.

2 How have improved living conditions affected human survival curves? Can you suggest why better living standards have not increased maximum human life expectancy significantly?

3 Provide evidence that cells and cell lines age. Are cancer cells potentially ageless? Give evidence to support your conclusion.

4 How do older tissues differ from younger ones? Why do athletes become progressively less mobile as they age?

5 Suggest at least four ways in which you might attempt to increase the rate of aging in animals. Show why you would expect each of your methods to accelerate aging.

6 Identify and describe at least five current theories of aging. Present evidence supporting or refuting each theory you describe. Why do scientists propose hypotheses such as these? You may wish to reread portions of Chap. 1 before answering this last question.

7 How are scientists attempting to increase maximum human life-spans? Have their attempts been successful? Evaluate the social impact of significantly increased human life expectancies. Would you like to live for 200 or 250 years? Why or why not?

Collateral Readings

Belinke, J. A., C. E., Finch, and **G. B. Moment:** "The Biology of Aging," Plenum, New York, 1978. A compendium of papers on various aspects of aging, including articles on aging in plants.

Berrill, N. J., and **G. Karp:** "Development," McGraw-Hill, New York, 1976. Chapter 21 contains a good discussion of cellular and extracellular aging.

Comfort, A.: "The Biology of Senescence," 3d ed., Elsevier–North Holland, New York, 1979. An excellent reference source, this book contains information on aging in protozoa.

Finch, C. E., and **L. Hayflick** (eds.): "Handbook of the Biology of Aging," Van Nostrand, New York, 1977. A collection of reports.

Hayflick, L.: The Cell Biology of Human Aging, *Scientific American,* January 1980. Processes limiting the life-span of cultured human cells are examined in this intriguing article.

Hershey, D.: "Lifespan and Factors Affecting It: Aging Theories in Gerontology," Thomas, Springfield, Ill., 1974. Although somewhat dated, this is a particularly well-written presentation.

Karp, G.: "Cell Biology," McGraw-Hill, New York, 1979. Part of Chap. 19 discusses processes of aging at the cellular and extracellular levels of organization.

Kohn, R. R.: "Principles of Mammalian Aging, 2d ed., Prentice-Hall, Englewood Cliffs, N.J., 1978. Considers all the topics of this chapter. Also discusses aging from an evolutionary perspective.

Rosenfeld, A.: "Prolongevity," Knopf, New York, 1976. Written for the nonscientist, this well-researched book contains an excellent account of all major theories of aging and presents interesting character sketches of scientists engaged in aging research.

Strehler, B. L.: "Time, Cells, and Aging," 2d ed., Academic, New York, 1977. Perhaps the most authoritative book on the biology of aging. Contains information of aging among moneran and protistan cells. Also considers the evolution of aging.

Thornebeck, G. J. (ed.)**:** "Biology of Aging and Development," Plenum, New York, 1975. A collection of research papers on specific aspects of aging. A good reference source for advanced students.

Part 6
The Operations of Life: Adaptation

On the molecular as on the organismic level, in structure as in function, every organism is *adapted* to its environment. For example, among thousands of different shapes that a fish *might* possess, its actual shape is well suited for rapid locomotion in water. A bird is cast in a form eminently suited for aerial life, yet its ancestry traces to fish. Particular adaptations of organisms change in response to new environments, and this property makes organisms potentially immortal as a group. Based on steady-state control and reproduction, adaptation is achieved through *sex, heredity,* and *evolution*. The adaptive role of sex has already been discussed, and this series of chapters, therefore, concentrates on the roles of heredity and evolution.

Marabu storks roosting in Queen Elizabeth Park, Uganda. The long legs and bills of these birds are well adapted for preying on several species of smaller animals that inhabit shallow marshes and swamps. Marabu and certain other varieties of storks frequently nest on roofs and chimneys, man-made environments that afford considerable protection for the birds and their young. (© *Tom Pix, Peter Arnold, Inc.*)

Chapter 27 Heredity

Learning Objectives

After reading this chapter you should be able to:

1. Describe at least one experiment that disproves the concept of "blending inheritance;" state the chromosomes theory of heredity; list evidence that genes actually are contained in chromosomes.
2. Define and illustrate each of the following: wild type, hybrid, true-breeding traits, phenotype, genotype, allele, dominant gene, recessive gene, homozygous, and heterozygous.
3. In your own words state the laws of segregation and independent assortment; describe breeding experiments that illustrate each of these laws; interpret each of these laws in terms of the movements of chromosomes during meiosis.
4. Numerically illustrate why every newborn human being probably is genetically unique.
5. Define linkage; show why inheritance of linked genes does not obey Mendel's law of independent assortment; define crossing-over and list the observations that led to Morgan's discovery of this phenomenon: indicate how knowledge of the frequency of crossing-over can be used to construct gene maps; define the law of the linear order of genes and illustrate the relation between crossing-over and genetic variability.
6. Describe how Beadle and Tatum, Watson and Crick, and Jacob and Monod each contributed to our current knowledge of the relation between genes and proteins; illustrate the experimental procedure, first used by Beadle and Tatum, which documented a functional interrelation between genes and enzymes.
7. Define and describe at least one experiment that demonstrates pleiotropy; define and state the symptoms of phyenylketonuria; differentiate between multiple alleles and polygenic interactions and illustrate how each influences phenotype.
8. Distinguish between sex chromosomes and autosomes; show how sex determination is brought about in human beings.
9. Define sex-linkage; describe at least one experiment that demonstrates the existence of sex-linked alleles; list at least two sex-linked diseases of human beings; explain why more men than women suffer from sex-linked diseases.
10. Define and indicate the origin of Barr bodies; list at least two examples of traits caused by X-chromosome inactivation; illustrate the mechanism responsible for such traits and show why these characteristics rarely appear in males.
11. Give at least two examples that demonstrate the influence of environmental factors on gene expression.
12. Define mutation; differentiate between chromosome and point mutation; name at least one way in which mutations can be induced.
13. Distinguish between somatic and germ mutations; define and illustrate chromosomal nondisjunction, translocation, deletion, and inversion; show how each of these mutations contributes to genetic variability.
14. List the symptoms of Kleinfelter's, Down's, and Turner's syndromes, and describe the mutations that produce each of these conditions; differentiate between nondisjunction and translocation forms of Down's syndrome; indicate the symptoms and genetic cause of "cri du chat" syndrome.
15. Identify the functional role of hemoglobin, and explain the structural and functional relations between the polypeptide chains that make up a molecule of hemoglobin; name the genetic cause of sickle-cell anemia and the sickle-cell trait; construct a hypothesis to explain observed differences in the incidence of the sickle-cell trait between black Americans and white Americans.
16. Illustrate how mutations sometimes result in unobservable changes in phenotype.

Life probably began after the first nucleic acids had originated. The creation of the first living units took billions of years, since it had to occur by physical and chemical chance; there was no blueprint to follow. But after nucleic acids were in existence, the appearance of new life forms probably occurred very rapidly. Today it takes only 20 min to produce a new bacterium, only 22 months to produce a new elephant.

This great acceleration is made possible by genes, the modern descendants of the first nucleic acids. Organisms now produce offspring according to instructions provided by genes, and through the inheritance of genes by successive generations construction of new life becomes a nonrandom, controlled process. What an organism inherits in large measure also determines its survival potential; heredity therefore has adaptive significance.

But organisms do *not* inherit strong muscles, green leaves, red blood, or any other trait. Organisms inherit the genes and all the other contents of reproductive cells. Visible traits then *develop* in an offspring, under the control of the inherited genes. The result of such heredity is a unique adult organism, which exhibits *likeness* to its parents in certain major respects and *variation* from parents in many minor respects. If the variations are not lethal or do not cause infertility, the organism can survive and pass on its genes to following generations.

Modern studies of heredity were begun in the last half of the nineteenth century by the Austrian monk Gregor Mendel. He discovered two basic rules that laid the foundation for all later advances in *genetics,* the biological subscience dealing with inheritance. Accordingly, this discussion begins with an examination of the rules of *Mendelian inheritance.*

MENDELIAN INHERITANCE

The Chromosome Theory

Most traits of organisms occur in two or more variant forms: some traits are exhibited in more or less sharp alternatives, like the different eye colors in people, while others form graded series between extremes, like body height in people. By studying

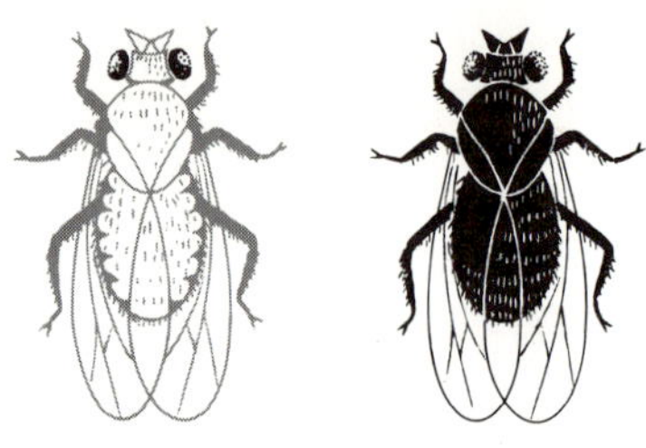

Fig. 27.1 Traits of fruit flies. Female gray-bodied wild type on left, ebony-bodied fly on right.

the offspring from matings between such variant organisms, the patterns of trait inheritance often can be determined. For example, in the fruit fly *Drosophila,* one of the most widely used organisms in genetic research, the trait of body pigmentation is expressed in at least two alternative forms. In one the general coloration of the animal is gray and the abdomen bears thin transverse bands of black melanin pigment. A gray body represents the *wild type,* or predominant form of coloration in nature. By contrast, some flies are pigmented black uniformly all over the skin, a coloration pattern referred to as the *ebony* trait (Fig. 27.1).

If two gray-bodied wild-type flies are mated, all offspring produced also are gray-bodied. Indeed, all later generations again develop only wild-type colorations. Similarly, a mating of two ebony flies yields ebony offspring in all later generations. Gray and ebony body colors here are said to be *true-breeding* traits (Fig. 27.2).

In Mendel's time it was generally supposed that if organisms having different forms of a trait are cross-bred, a *blending* of the traits would result. Thus if gray and black were mixed together, like paints, a dark-gray color should be produced. And if blending really occurred, dark-gray should be true-breeding as well; for mixed traits, like mixed paints, should be incapable of "unblending." In reality, however, the results of cross-breeding are strikingly different. When a wild type and an ebony fly are mated (parental generation, P), all offspring (first filial generation, F_1) are gray-bodied, exactly like the wild-type parent (Fig. 27.3). And when two such gray-bodied F_1 flies are then mated in turn, some of the offspring obtained are gray-bodied, others are ebony; color mixtures do

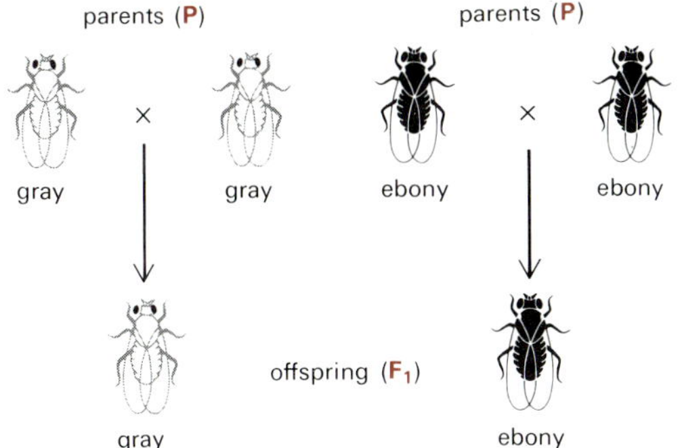

Fig. 27.2 True-breeding in *Drosophila*. If two gray-bodied (wild-type) flies are mated, all offspring will be gray-bodied (left); and if two ebony flies are mated, all offspring will be ebony (right).

not occur. Numerically, some 75 per cent of the second generation (F_2) are gray-bodied, like their parents and one of their grandparents; and the remaining 25 per cent are ebony, unlike their parents but like the other grandparent.

Evidently, the color traits of the offspring do not breed true; from gray-bodied flies in the F_1 can arise ebony flies in the F_2. Large numbers of tests of this kind have clearly established that, quite generally for any trait, blending inheritance does not occur and traits remain distinct and intact. They can become joined together in one generation, but they can then again become separated, or *segregated,* in a subsequent generation. Mendel was the first to reach such a conclusion from studies on plants. Moreover, he not only negated the old idea of blending but postulated a new interpretation.

He realized that traits trace back to the gametes that produce an organism, and he suspected that some "factors" in the gametes control the later development of traits. For any given trait, he argued, an organism must inherit at least one factor from the sperm and one from the egg. The offspring must then possess at least two factors for each trait. When that offspring becomes an adult and produces gametes in its turn, each gamete must similarly contribute one factor to the next generation. Hence, before gametes are mature, two factors must be reduced to one. Mendel therefore postulated the existence of a factor-reducing process.

With this he in effect predicted meiosis. Near the end of the nineteenth century meiosis was actually discovered, and it was later recognized that chromosome reduction during meiosis corresponded precisely to Mendel's postulated factor reduction. Chromosomes then came to be regarded as the carriers of the factors, and the *chromosome theory of heredity* thus emerged. This theory has since received complete confirmation, and Mendel's factors became the genes of today.

Segregation

On the basis of the chromosome theory the fruit-fly data above can be interpreted as follows. A true-breeding wild-type fly contains a pair of gray-color-producing genes on some pair of homologous chromosomes in each cell. These genes can be symbolized by the letters *EE.* Thus the gene content, or *genotype,* is *EE,* and the visible appearance, or *phenotype,* is gray. When such an animal produces gametes, meiosis occurs. Mature gametes therefore contain only one of the two homologous chromosomes, hence only one of the two genes (Fig. 27.4).

Fig. 27.3 Evidence disproving the "blending" hypothesis. If a gray-bodied fly is mated with an ebony fly (P generation), all offspring will be gray-bodied (F_1 generation). And if two of the F_1 flies are then mated in turn, the offspring (F_2 generation) will be gray-bodied and ebony in the ratio shown.

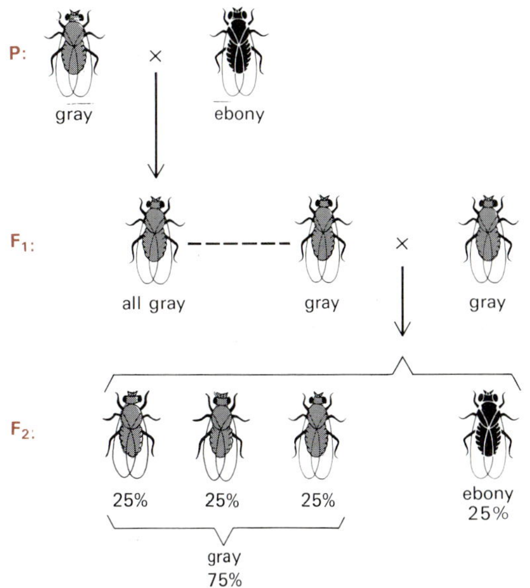

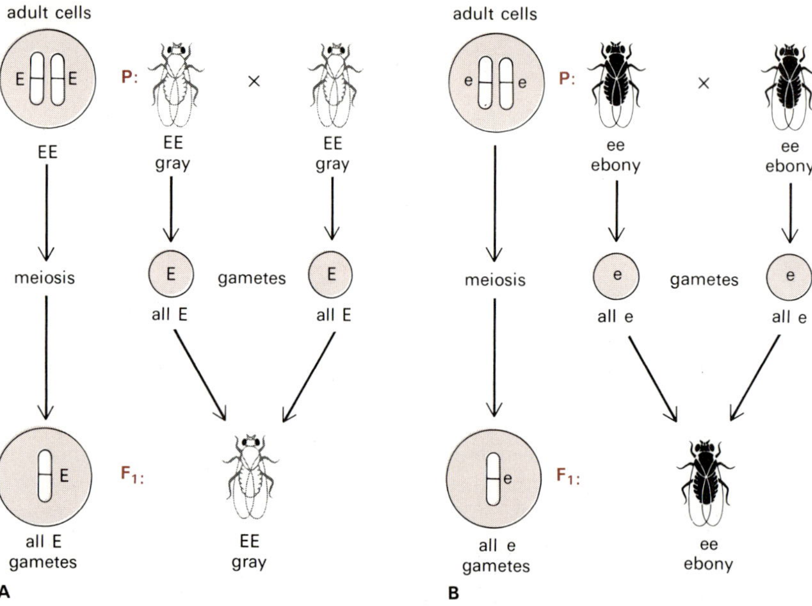

Fig. 27.4 Genetic effects of meiosis. (A and B, left) Because of meiotic chromosome reduction, gene pairs in adult cells become reduced to single genes in the gametes. (A and B, right) Gray-bodied wild type flies and ebony flies, respectively, breed true because in each case all offspring receive the same kind of gray-body-controlling or ebony-controlling genes from each of the two parents.

It is entirely a matter of chance which of the two adult chromosomes will become incorporated in a particular gamete. Since both adult chromomes here carry the same color gene, all gametes will be genetically alike in this respect. That is why *EE* animals are true-breeding and why a mating of *EE* × *EE* will produce only gray-bodied offspring. In similar fashion, the genotype of a true-breeding ebony fly can be symbolized as *ee.* A mating of two such flies will yield only black-bodied offspring (see Fig. 27.4).

If now a wild type and an ebony fly are mated, all offspring will be gray-bodied (Fig. 27.5). In such offspring the *E* and *e* genes are present together, yet the effect of the *e* gene evidently is overridden or masked completely. The single gene *E* by itself exerts the same effect as two *E* genes. By contrast, the single gene *e* by itself is without visible effect; a double dose, *ee,* is required if a visible result is to be produced. Genes that exert a maximum effect in a single dose, like *E,* are said to produce *dominant* traits. Such genes mask more or less completely the effect of corresponding genes such as *e,* which are said to produce *recessive* traits.

Genes that affect the same trait in different ways and that occur at equivalent (homologous) locations in a chromosome pair are called *allelic* genes, or *alleles.* Genes such as *E* and *e* are alleles, and pairs such as *EE, ee,* and *Ee* are different allelic pairs. If both alleles of a pair are the same, as in *EE* or *ee,* the combination is said to be *homozygous.* The combination *EE* is *homozygous dominant,* the combination *ee, homozygous recessive.* A combination of different alleles, such as *Ee,* is said to be *heterozygous.*

Thus the F_1 resulting from a mating of a wild type and an ebony fly as above is heterozygous, and this F_1 reveals that the wild-type trait is dominant over the ebony trait. That the heterozygous F_1 condition is not true-breeding now is shown if two F_1 flies are mated (Fig. 27.6). After meiosis, each fly will produce two types of gametes. Of the genes *Ee,* either the *E* gene or the *e* gene could by chance become incorporated in any one gamete. Approximately 50 per cent of the gametes therefore will carry the *E* gene, and the other 50 per cent the *e* gene.

In almost all organisms, genetically different male and female gametes fuse randomly; a sperm carrying the *E* allele, for example, does not have a better chance of fertilizing an egg than a sperm carrying the *e* allele. If many fertilizations occur simultaneously, as is usually the case, then all possibilities will be realized with appropriate frequency. The result is that approximately three-

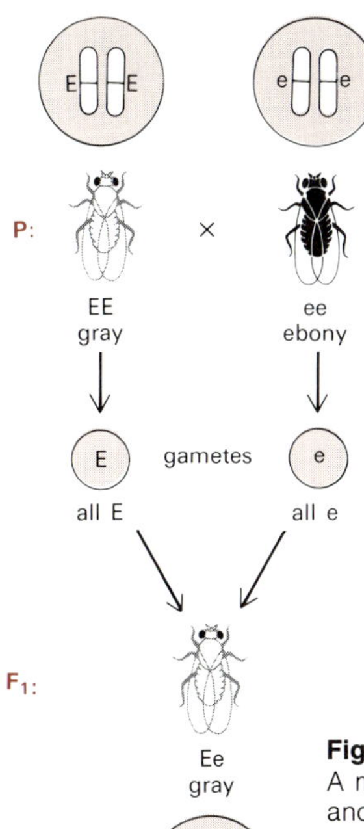

Fig. 27.5 Genetic dominance. A mating between a gray-bodied and an ebony fly yields all gray-bodied offspring, indicating that the gray-body trait is dominant and masks the recessive ebony trait.

quarters of the offspring are gray-bodied and resemble their parents in this respect. Approximately one-quarter is ebony, and these offspring resemble one of their grandparents. The result can be explained fully on the basis of nonblending, freely segregating genes and the operation of chance. Offspring in ratios of $\frac{3}{4}:\frac{1}{4}$ (or 3:1) usually are characteristic for matings of heterozygous organisms as above.

Not all genes produce sharply dominant and sharply recessive forms of a trait. Many allelic genes give rise to traits that are neither dominant nor recessive. In such cases, *each* allele in a heterozygous combination such as *Aa* exerts a definite effect, and the result usually is a visible trait intermediate between those produced by *AA* and *aa* combinations. For example, snapdragon plants occur in true-breeding red-flowered (*AA*) and true-breeding white-flowered (*aa*) forms. If two such plants are cross-bred, all offspring (*Aa*) are *pink*-flowered; neither gene in the *Aa* combination is fully dominant, and neither is fully recessive. However, the intermediate result again is not produced by color blending, for the pink-flowered condition is not true-breeding. A mating of two pink-flowered plants segregates red *and* pink *and* white offspring, in a characteristic phenotype ratio of $\frac{1}{4}:\frac{1}{2}:\frac{1}{4}$ (or 1:2:1). The inheritance pattern of the genotypes here is precisely the same as where genes have sharply dominant and recessive effects, and only the phenotype ratios are different (Fig. 27.7).

In modern terminology, Mendel's first law, the *law of segregation*, now can be stated as follows—*Genes do not blend, but behave as independent units. They pass intact from one generation to the next, where they may or may not produce visible traits, depending on their dominance characteristics. And genes segregate at random, thereby producing predictable ratios of traits in the offspring.*

Fig. 27.6 Dominance and segregation. If two heterozygous gray-bodied (F_1) flies are mated, the offspring (F_2) will be 25 percent gray-bodied and homozygous like one of their grandparents (P in Fig. 27.5), 50 percent gray-bodied and heterozygous like their parents, and 25 percent ebony and homozygous like their ebony grandparent (P in Fig. 27.5).

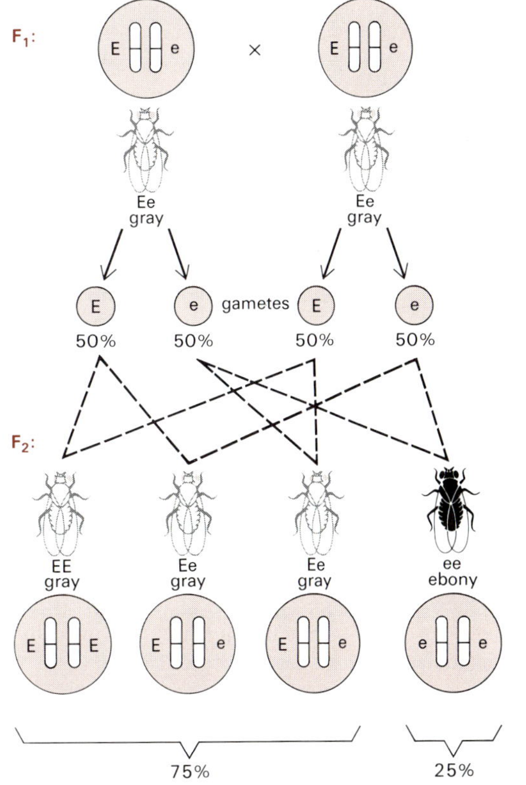

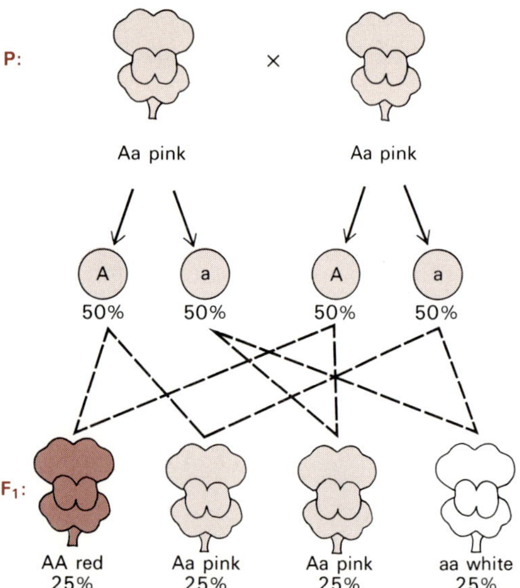

Fig. 27.7 Partial dominance. Allelic genes (*A* and *a*) can each have their own definite effect on phenotype, and neither thus produces completely dominant or recessive traits. This is the case in snapdragons, where gene *A* produces red flowers, gene *a* produces white flowers, and the gene combination *Aa* yields pink flowers. If two such pink-flowered adults are mated, the F_1 will have phenotypes and genotypes in the ratios shown. In this F_1 only 50 percent of the offspring are like the parents, the other 50 percent resembling their grandparents (verify this).

Implied in this law are chromosome reduction by meiosis and the operation of chance in the transmission of genes.

Independent Assortment

Organisms do not inherit genes one at a time, but all are inherited together. Therefore, given certain parents, what will the offspring be like with respect to two or more traits?

Mendel discovered a fundamental rule here. Phrased in modern terms, this *law of independent assortment* states—*The inheritance of a gene pair located on a given pair of homologous chromosomes is unaffected by the simultaneous inheritance of other gene pairs located on other pairs of homologous chromosomes.*

In other words, two or more traits produced by genes located on two or more different pairs of homologous chromosomes "assort independently"; each trait is expressed independently, as if no other traits were present.

The meaning of the law emerges if the inheritance of two traits of fruit flies is examined simultaneously—*body color* and *wing shape.* As already noted, body color can be either wild type gray or recessive ebony. Wing shape can be either normal or *vestigial,* i.e., the wings are reduced in size to such an extent that the animal cannot fly. Such stunted wings can be shown to develop whenever a recessive gene *vg* is present in homozygous condition, *vgvg.* Normal wings represent the dominant wild type, produced by either *VgVg* or *Vgvg* gene combinations. The body-color and wing-shape genes are located in different pairs of homologous chromosomes in *Drosophila,* and the wing genes, like the color genes, obey the law of segregation.

What will now be the results of a mating between two *EeVgvg* flies, individuals that are heterozygous for both traits simultaneously? After meiosis, each gamete will contain only *one* color gene and only *one* wing gene. But which of each pair—the dominant or the recessive gene? This is a matter of chance. Thus, a gamete might contain the genes *E* and *Vg,* or *E* and *vg,* or *e* and *Vg,* or *e* and *vg.* Many gametes are actually produced, and all four combinations therefore will occur with roughly equal frequency (Fig. 27.8)

Fertilization is also governed by chance. Consequently, *any* one of the 4 sperm types might fertilize *any* one of the 4 egg types. Hence there are 16 different combinations that can occur in fertilization. If large numbers of fertilizations take place simultaneously, all 16 combinations will occur with roughly equal frequency. These 16 combinations can be determined from a grid in which the gametes of one parent are put along a horizontal edge and the gametes of the other parent along a vertical edge (Fig. 27.9).

Among the 16 offspring types now formed, some individuals contain *both* dominant genes at least once, some contain one *or* the other of the dominant genes at least once, and some contain none of the dominant genes. A count reveals gray-normal, gray-vestigial, ebony-normal, and ebony-vestigial to be present in a ratio of 9:3:3:1.

This result proves the law of independent assortment. For if body color is considered *alone,* there are 9 plus 3—12 animals out of every 16 that are gray, and 3 plus 1—4 that are ebony. But 12:4 is a 3:1 ratio. Similarly, if wing shape is considered *alone,* again 12 out of every 16 animals have

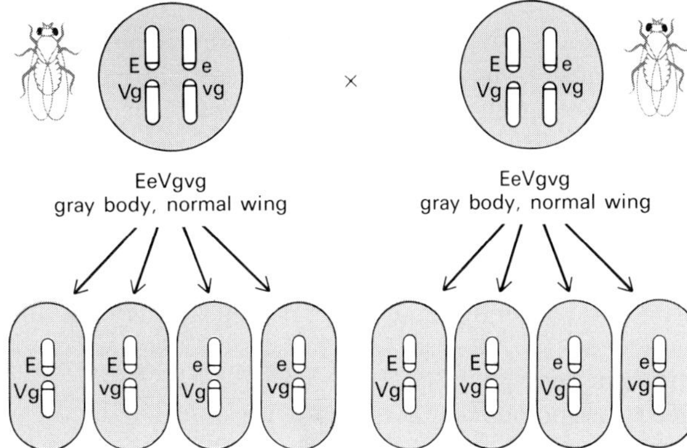

Fig. 27.8 Double heterozygotes (dihybrids). If two flies heterozygous (hybrid) for both body color and wing shape are mated (top), each fly will produce gametes as shown.

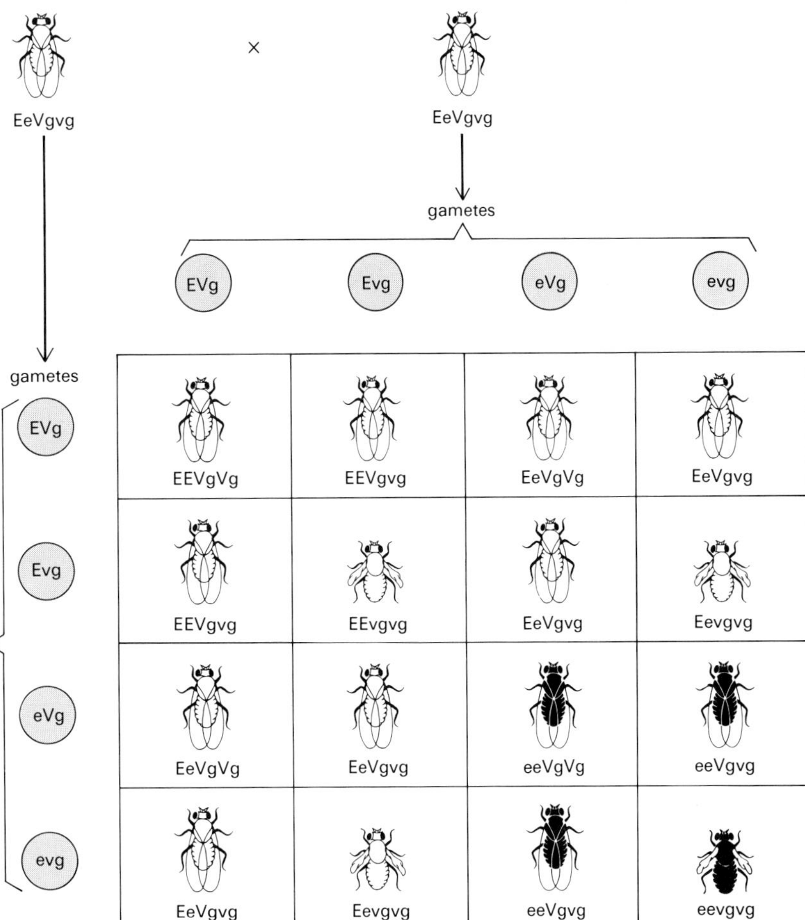

Fig. 27.9 The Punnett square. Gametes produced by flies as in Fig. 27.8 and at top of this figure can combine in the 16 combinations shown inside the square. The offspring then have a 9:3:3:1 phenotype ratio.

normal wings and 4 have vestigial wings; here, too, the ratio is 3:1. Evidently, although the color and wing traits are inherited simultaneously and yield a 9:3:3:1 offspring ratio overall, each trait considered *separately* nevertheless gives a 3:1 ratio of offspring. Each trait therefore is inherited as if the other trait were not present; or, in Mendel's phrase, the traits assort independently.

Mendel's second law applies specifically to gene pairs located on different pairs of homologous chromosomes. The law will therefore hold for as many different gene pairs as there are pairs of homologous chromosomes in each cell of an organism. Suppose we considered the inheritance of *three* different gene pairs, each located on a different pair of homologous chromosomes, in a mating of two triple heterozygotes *AaBbCc* × *AaBbCc*.

As shown above, a double heterozygote *AaBb* produces *four* different gamete types. Applying the same principles, it can be verified readily that a triple heterozygote produces *eight* different gamete types: *ABC, ABc, AbC, Abc, aBC, aBc, abC,* and *abc*. To determine all posssible genotypes of the offspring, we can use a grid 8 squares by 8 squares and place the 8 gamete types of each parent along the edges, as above. The result will be 64 offspring types, of which 27 will express all the three traits in dominant form. The complete phenotype ratio easily can be verified as 27:9:9:9:3:3:3:1.

Two quadruple heterozygotes, *AaBbCcDd* would manufacture 16 gamete types each, and we would need a grid 16 by 16 to represent the 256 different genotype combinations. The possibilities rapidly become astronomical once more than a few traits are considered simultaneously.

Organisms heterozygous for a large number of gene pairs are called *hybrids*, and one, two, or three heterozygous gene pairs can be referred to as monohybrids, dihybrids, or trihybrids, respectively. In people there are 23 pairs of chromosomes per cell. Mendel's second law therefore will apply to any 23 traits controlled by genes located on different pairs of homologous chromosomes. What then would be the genotypes resulting from a mating of, for example, two 23-fold hybrids: *AaBb* · · · *Ww* × *AaBb* · · · *Ww*? We know that:

a monohybrid yields $2^1 = 2$ gamete types
a dihybrid yields $2^2 = 4$ gamete types
a trihybrid yield $2^3 = 8$ gamete types
a quadruple hybrid yields $2^4 = 16$ gamete types

Carrying this progression further, a 23-fold hybrid can be shown to produce 2^{23}, or over 8 million genetically different gamete types. Hence in considering just 23 gene pairs on different pairs of homologous chromosomes, a grid of 8 million by 8 million would be required to represent the over 64 trillion possible genotypes. This number is far larger than the totality of human beings ever produced, and a good many millions or billions of these genotypes therefore have probably never yet arisen during the entire history of the human race.

Accordingly, chances are great that every newborn human being differs from every other one, past or present, in at least some genes controlling just 23 traits. And the genetic differences for *all* traits must be enormous indeed. Here is one major reason for the universal generalization that no two organisms produced by separate fertilizations are precisely identical.

A chromosome contains not just one gene but anywhere from a few hundred to a few thousand. What is the inheritance pattern of two or more gene pairs located on the *same* pair of homologous chromosomes? This question leads beyond Mendel's two laws.

Linkage

Genes located on the same chromosome are said to be *linked;* as the chromosome is inherited, so are all its genes inherited. Such genes clearly do not assort independently but are transmitted together in a block. The traits controlled by linked genes are similarly expressed in a block. In fruit flies, for example, the same pair of homologous chromosomes that carries the wing-shape genes also carries one of the many known pairs of eye-color genes: a dominant allele *Pr* produces red, wild-type eyes, and a recessive allele *pr* in homozygous condition produces distinctly purple eyes. If now a normal-winged, red-eyed heterozygous fly *VgvgPrpr* produces gametes, only two types should be expected, *VgPr* and *vgpr*, 50 per cent of each. In actuality, however, four gamete types are produced, in proportions as in Fig. 27.10.

If these four types occurred in approximately equal numbers, i.e., if they represented about 25 per cent of the total population each, the result could be regarded simply as a case without linkage, governed by Mendel's second law. But the actual results include significantly *more* than 25 per cent

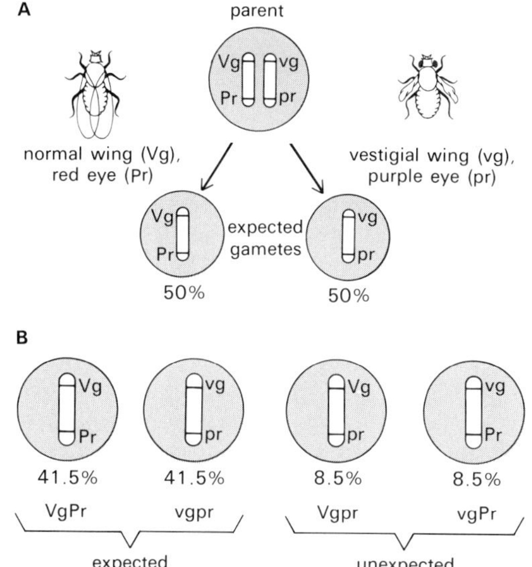

Fig. 27.10 Linkage. (A, left and right) The phenotypes of wing shape and eye color in *Drosophila*, two traits controlled by linked genes. (Center) The expected gametes of a heterozygous fly *VgvgPrpr*. (B) The proportions of the actual gamete types obtained. Expected types appear in smaller numbers than predicted, and considerable numbers of wholly unexpected types appear as well.

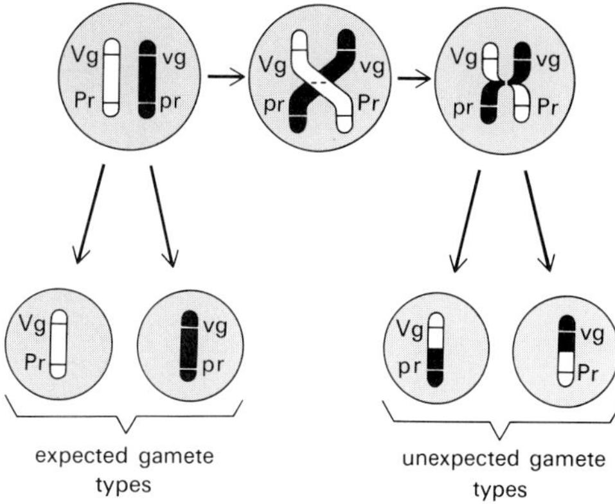

Fig. 27.11 Crossing-over. If during meiosis homologous chromosomes twist, break, and fuse again at the break points in the wrong order, unexpected gamete types will appear.

each of the expected gamete types, and significantly *fewer* than 25 per cent of the unexpected types.

To explain odd results of this sort, T. H. Morgan, a renowned American biologist of the early twentieth century, proposed a new hypothesis. He postulated that, during meiosis, paired homologous chromosomes in some cases might twist around each other and might break where they are twisted. The broken pieces might then fuse again in the "wrong" order (Fig. 27.11). This would account for the large percentage of expected and the small percentage of unexpected gamete types. The hypothesis was tested by microscopic examination of cells undergoing meiosis, and the occurrence of chromosomal *crossing-over* could actually be verified. Crossing-over now has been shown to involve the breaking of DNA chains and subsequent synthesis of new connections between these chains.

The implications of crossing-over have proved to be far-reaching. It has been reasoned that the frequency of crossovers should be an index of the *distance* between two genes. If two genes on a chromosome are located near each other, the chances should be relatively small that a twist will occur between these close points. But if two genes are relatively far apart, twists between them should be rather frequent. In general, the frequency of crossovers should be proportional to the distance between two genes (Fig. 27.12). Inasmuch as the crossover percentage of two genes can be determined by breeding experiments, it should be possible to construct *gene maps* showing the actual location of given genes on a chromosome. Indeed, since Morgan's time the exact positions of a few hundred genes have been mapped in the fruit fly. Large numbers of genes have similarly been located in corn plants, mice, and various other organisms.

A second implication of crossing-over is that genes on a chromosome must be lined up single file. Only if this is the case can linkage and crossing over occur as it actually does. This generalization has become known as the *law of the linear order of genes.* It represents the third major rule that governs Mendelian inheritance.

Third, crossing over makes meiosis a *source of genetic variations.* For example, when a diploid cell in a testis undergoes meiosis and produces four haploid sperms, these four do not contain merely the same whole chromosomes as the original cell. Because of crossing-over, the chromosomes in each sperm will be quiltworks composed of various joined pieces of the original chromosomes; and the four sperms are almost certain to be genetically different not only from each other but also from the

Biology Highlight

Big Value from Little Packages: The Emergence of Microbial Genetics

ENGLAND: 1910

It had been a frightening experience for the parents. The wet diapers of their newborn infant were streaked with a dark, almost black stain. Something must be terribly wrong with their child. After examining the infant, Dr. Archibald Garrod quietly reassured the worried parents. The child was affected with *alkaptonuria,* a harmless condition caused by high concentrations of "alkapton" in urine. This substance darkens appreciably when exposed to air, causing wet diapers of affected infants to turn black.

Garrod was quite familiar with alkaptonuria. He had already discovered that the amount of alkapton present in the urine of affected individuals is influenced by diet. Consumption of large amounts of the amino acids phenylalanine and tyrosine produce higher concentrations of alkapton, and vice versa. Unaffected individuals do not have alkapton in their urine, regardless of the amounts of phenylalanine and tyrosine consumed.

In his book, "Inborn Errors of Metabolism," published a year earlier, Garrod had hypothesized that alkapton is produced whenever excess concentrations of phenylalanine and tyrosine exist in the body, but that alkapton normally is broken down further into other products. Affected individuals, he theorized, do not contain a functional enzyme for this further conversion and therefore excrete large amounts of alkapton. Significantly, Garrod also suggested that the postulated alkapton enzyme was produced by alleles that were defective in infants exhibiting alkaptonuria.

Garrod was one of the first scientists to postulate correctly how genes produce visible traits. But over 30 years would pass before biologists would clearly demonstrate that enzymes and other proteins are the principal products of gene expression.

STANFORD UNIVERSITY: 1940

Like many biologists of the period, George Beadle, a geneticist, and Edward Tatum, a biochemist, were exploring the mechanics of gene expression using *Drosophila* as an experimental organism. Their investigations likewise suggested that genes are involved in the production of enzymes, but the two biologists had been unable to demonstrate the relationship conclusively.

Beadle and Tatum realized that the easiest way to trace an enzyme to an allele is through a metabolic malfunction. As Garrod and others had observed earlier, breakdowns of this sort often produce unusual traits that indicate possible interactions between genes and enzymes. But obtaining data from *Drosophila* documenting such interactions had proved exceedingly difficult. The genetic system of fruit flies was too complex. *Drosophila* is a diploid organism, whose recessive alleles for defective enzymes frequently are masked by dominant alleles. Moreover, collecting sufficient samples of enzymes and other substances for biochemical analysis often required very large numbers of genetically identical organisms.

To satisfy these and other experimental conditions, Beadle and Tatum turned to microorganisms. Most microbes are haploid; their recessive al-

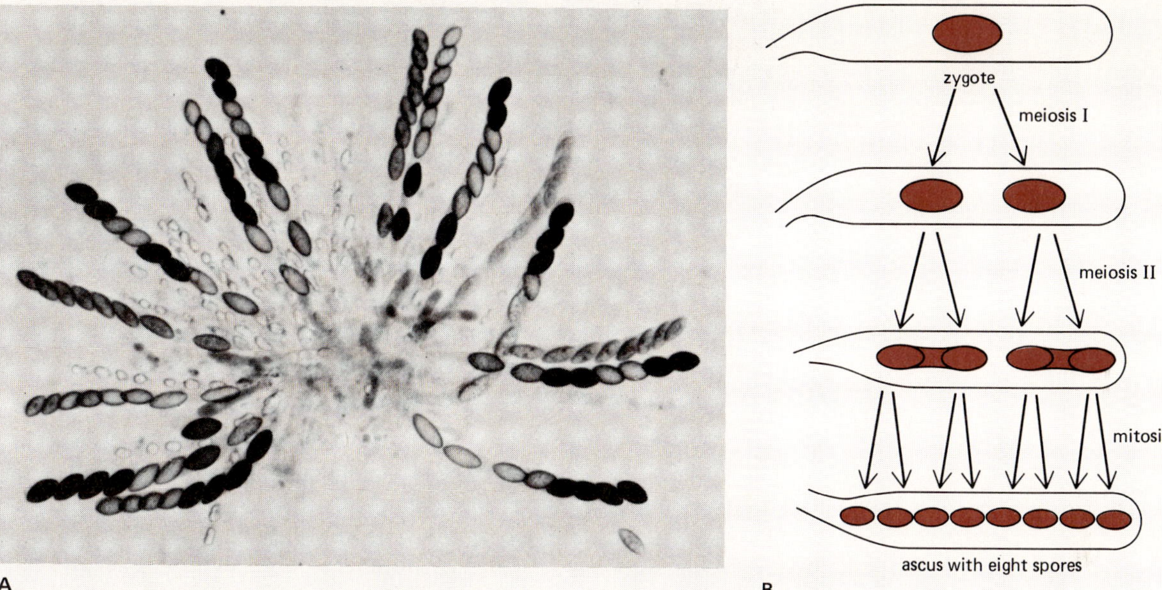

Fig. 1 ***Neurospora* fruiting bodies and spore formation.** (A) A squashed fruiting body. Note the sets of eight spores, each set contained within a saclike ascus (not visible). Most of the asci of this fruiting body contain four light- and four dark-colored spores. The appearance of an intact fruiting body is shown in Fig. 2. (B) The eight spores of an ascus result from two meiotic and one mitotic division.

leles are almost never masked. Also, obtaining large cultures of genetically identical cells is not a major obstacle. Several kinds of microorganisms can be induced to reproduce rapidly and vegetatively. Beadle and Tatum finally settled on the red bread mold *Neurospora crassa* as the organism they would use in an attempt to resolve the question: are enzymes produced by genes? In answering this question, the two scientists established a new experimental approach to the study of gene behavior that would become a model for generations of geneticists to come.

A considerable amount of research on the nutritional requirements of microorganisms had been conducted throughout the 1930s, and Beadle and Tatum used the knowledge gained from these studies as background for their investigations. Indeed, the existence of this knowledge constituted yet another reason for their choice of *Neurospora* as an experimental organism. The two biologists reasoned that it should be possible to find genetic strains of *Neurospora* that were unable to produce a particular vitamin, amino acid, or some other nutrient essential for growth. If such strains also lacked the enzymes necessary for production of the missing nutrient, a direct relationship between genes and enzymes would be established.

Beadle and Tatum began by exposing cultures of *Neurospora* to ultraviolet light. Although whole cultures were subjected to the radiation, spores were the important targets. These cells are produced in reproductive *fruiting bodies,* which in turn are made up of many elongated sacs called *asci* (see Chap. 31). At maturity each ascus contains eight spores, all derived via meiosis from a single zygote (Fig. 1).

Like certain other physical and chemical agents, ultraviolet light induces *mutations,* changes in the nitrogen base sequences of DNA (see final section of this chapter). Consequently, the likelihood of finding *Neurospora* having defective genes for the production of an essential nutrient is greater among those germinated from ultraviolet-treated spores than among those derived from untreated spores.

Beadle and Tatum next removed spores from irradiated *Neurospora* and germinated them on a complete culture medium (one containing all essential nutrients required for growth). Because the medium contained a full complement of essential nutrients, virtually all spores germinated and produced colonies, including mutants unable to produce all essential nutrients on their own (Fig. 2). Once sufficiently large colonies had been established, a small portion of each was transferred to a minimal medium, i.e., one lacking most essential nutrients for growth. This step distinguished normal from mutant colonies. Those able to produce all essential nutrients grew on the minimal medium; mutants lacking normal genes for the production of one or more essential nutrients did not grow.

When the mutant strains had been identified, the two biologists attempted to determine which essential nutrient a particular mutant could not produce. They devised a simple, although somewhat laborious way of finding out. To narrow the possibilities, Beadle and Tatum first prepared three new culture media: one containing all essential nutrients except amino acids, a second containing all nutrients except known vitamins, the third a minimal medium containing alternative carbon sources (such as glucose instead of sucrose).

A small portion of a particular mutant colony was then transferred to each of the three new media. If the mutant sample proved unable to grow on, say, the medium lacking essential amino acids, but was able to grow on the other two media, the experiment would have demonstrated that the missing essential nutrient was an amino acid (see Fig. 2).

Once this initial screening was carried out, the biologists attempted to reduce the possibilities to a single nutrient. For example, portions of a mutant colony unable to produce an essential amino acid could be transferred to a series of media, each complete except for a single essential amino acid. If the mutant grew only on the medium containing proline, for example, the missing nutrient clearly was proline.

Using such procedures, Beadle and Tatum isolated a large number of different *Neurospora* mutants. In every case where a mutant was unable to produce a specific essential nutrient, the biologists confirmed that the mutant also lacked an enzyme required for the production of that nutrient. Garrod's hypothetical relationship between genes and enzymes was finally established.

The experimental results obtained by Beadle and Tatum, although admittedly important, are not as significant as the experimental procedures themselves. Biologists now had a way of examining the biochemical mechanics of gene expression. This newly discovered field of microbial genetics offered a means of deducing how genes were controlled—indeed, of determining how genetic information was stored. Beginning in the mid- to late 1940s, increasing numbers of scientists began using, modifying, and extending the techniques of Beadle and Tatum, to study the molecular biology of gene expression in *Neurospora, E. coli,* viruses, and several other types of microbes. What began as a series of comparatively simple experiments on bits of red bread mold slowly was becoming transformed into one of the most fundamental subsciences of modern biology.

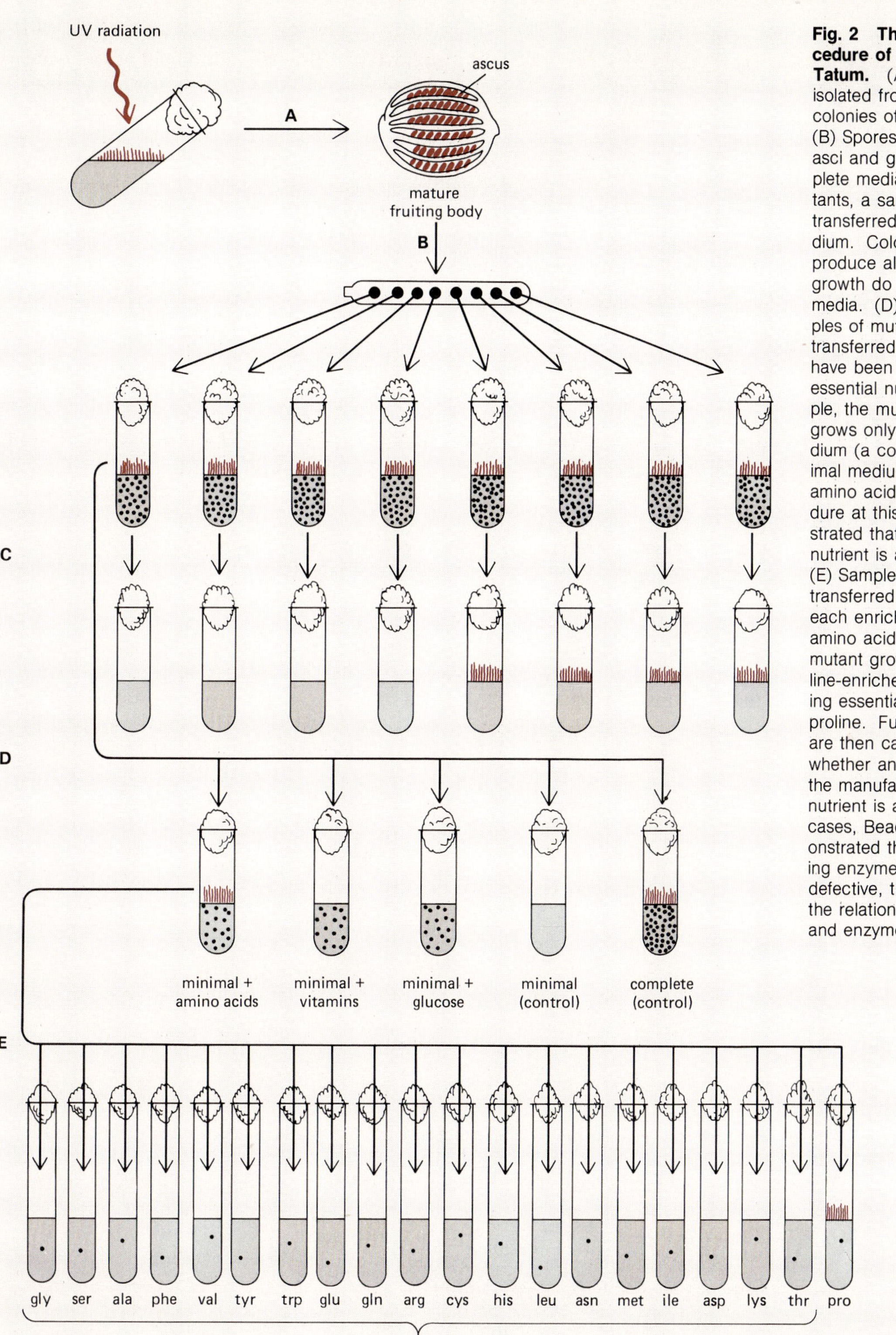

Fig. 2 The experimental procedure of Beadle and Tatum. (A) Fruiting bodies are isolated from ultraviolet-irradiated colonies of *Neurospora*. (B) Spores are removed from asci and germinated on complete media. (C) To identify mutants, a sample of each colony is transferred to a minimal medium. Colonies unable to produce all nutrients essential for growth do not grow on minimal media. (D) Once identified, samples of mutant colonies are transferred to minimal media that have been enriched with certain essential nutrients. In this example, the mutant being tested grows only on a complete medium (a control tube) and a minimal medium enriched with amino acids. Thus, the procedure at this point has demonstrated that the missing essential nutrient is an amino acid. (E) Samples of the mutant are transferred to minimal media, each enriched with a single amino acid. In this case, the mutant grows only on the proline-enriched medium. The missing essential nutrient is therefore proline. Further investigations are then carried out to determine whether an enzyme required for the manufacture of the missing nutrient is also absent. In all cases, Beadle and Tatum demonstrated that such corresponding enzymes were missing or defective, thereby demonstrating the relationship between genes and enzyme production.

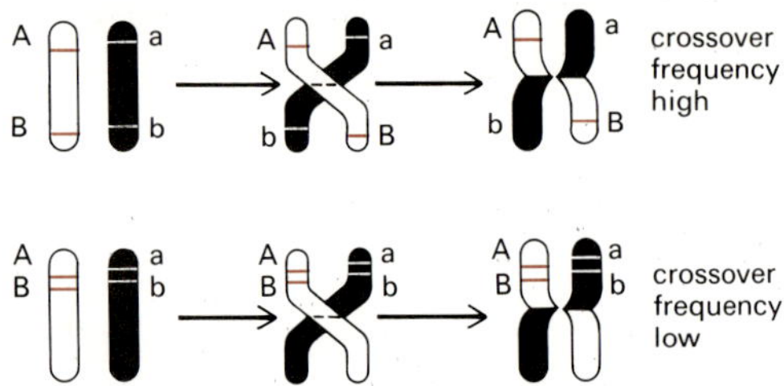

Fig. 27.12 Crossing-over and gene distances. If two genes are far apart, crossing-over between them is likely to occur fairly frequently (top). But, if genes are close together, crossing-over between them is less likely (bottom). In general, the farther apart given genes are on a chromosome, the more frequent crossing-over will be.

original diploid cell. Moreover, any two genetically identical diploid cells are almost certain to give rise to two genetically different quartets of sperms. Genetic variations thus are produced by both phases of sex: through fertilization, which doubles chromosome numbers, and through meiosis, which halves the number of chromosomes and also shuffles genes through crossing-over.

The three rules of heredity here outlined describe and predict the consequences of *sexual recombination,* i.e., the various results possible when different sets of genes become joined through fertilization and are pooled in the zygote. In other words, sexual recombination of genes leads to Mendelian inheritance.

As stated at the outset of this chapter, genes are merely storehouses of information, blueprints for specific traits, not traits themselves. Genes exert their influence only when expressed, a topic considered next.

GENE EXPRESSION

Morgan's interest in discerning the arrangement of genes on chromosomes and discovering how genes segregate and recombine was shared by most geneticists between 1910 and 1930. During the early 1930s, several biologists also became increasingly interested in determining how genes actually produce visible traits. The research efforts of these biologists generally proved unfruitful for almost a decade. Success first came in 1941, when George Beadle and Edward Tatum conducted a series of experiments with several strains of the red bread mold, *Neurospora crassa* (see accompanying Biology Highlight). Each strain produced a defective enzyme, and Beadle, Tatum, and others demonstrated that each of these enzymes corresponds to a specific gene. On the basis of such results, Beadle and Tatum proposed the *one gene–one enzyme* concept. This hypothesis suggested that the basic function of a gene is to control the synthesis of a specific enzyme. Later, genes were discovered that function in the production of proteins other than enzymes. Indeed, it is now known that some proteins are composed of two or more polypeptides produced by separate genes. Thus, the original hypothesis has now been restated as the *one gene–one polypeptide* concept.

The nature of the link between genes and polypeptides remained unresolved until the mid-1960s. During the years immediately following Beadle and Tatum's initial experiments with *Neurospora,* many biologists hypothesized that genes themselves were proteins and that chromosomes contained "master copies" of all proteins required by cells. Among biologists favoring alternate hypotheses were James Watson and Francis Crick who, in 1953, proposed that genes consisted of double-stranded DNA.

Confirmation of this proposal prompted many biologists to study the relation between DNA and proteins. If DNA contained coded information specifying the sequence of amino acids in proteins, how is this information transmitted and translated? A possible solution to this perplexing problem was proposed in 1961 by the French scientists François Jacob and Jacques Monod. They postulated that molecules of RNA, the other principal nucleic acid of cells, function as messengers in carrying copies of the genetic code from genes to areas of cells where the code is translated into protein. This hypothesis was confirmed within the next 2 years, and the chemical link between genes and proteins was resolved—DNA made RNA and RNA made protein (see Chap. 14).

The production of visible traits, therefore, depends first on the inherited sequences of nitrogen bases contained in genes, and second, on the manner in which the products of genes interact with other molecules. In a few cases, traits result more or less directly from proteins produced by single pairs of alleles. Such proteins can be important structural components of tissues or enzymes that catalyze specific chemical reactions. For example, *albinism* results from the inheritance of a pair of alleles that produce defective copies of the enzyme

Fig. 27.13 Albinism. A normally pigmented adult deer (left) and an albino fawn.

tyrosinase. Without this enzyme, albinos cannot convert the amino acid tyrosine to *melanin,* the principal pigment of skin, hair, and eyes. Consequently, albinos have extremely light skin complexions and unpigmented white hair (Fig. 27.13).

More often, traits result from many different substances produced simultaneously or sequentially by interactions between several, often widely separated pairs of alleles. Indeed, some highly composite traits result from the combined interactions of thousands of genes located on one or more chromosomes. The following examples illustrate some of the principal ways in which such interactions determine phenotype.

Allelic Interactions

Multiple Effects (Pleiotropy)

The inheritance of *phenylketonuria* (PKU), a metabolic disorder occurring in human beings and other mammals, illustrates how single pairs of alleles determine phenotype. The alleles involved in this disease code for *phenylalanine hydroxylase,* an enzyme that catalyzes conversion of phenylalanine to tyrosine. The latter compounds are amino acids commonly found in living systems.

Normal individuals have at least one allele that produces functional copies of phenylalanine hydroxylase. Individuals who suffer from PKU, however, have inherited a pair of defective alleles that both code for a nonfunctional enzyme. If A represents a normal allele and a represents a defective one, it can be seen that individuals who develop PKU have inherited a pair of recessive alleles. Normal individuals have the genotype AA or Aa; afflicted individuals are aa. Evidently, one normal allele produces sufficient functional copies of the enzyme to permit normal metabolism of phenylalanine.

About 1 child in every 40,000 born is homozygous for these defective alleles. Unless such children are treated, the complete absence of normal phenylalanine hydroxylase leads to an excessive accumulation of phenylalanine in their bodies. This accumulation disrupts other metabolic pathways and can result in progressive brain damage and mental retardation. Fortunately, this hereditary disease can be detected readily by directly or indirectly measuring the concentration of phenylalanine in the blood of infants. If the disease is detected, it can be treated by prescribing a diet containing reduced concentrations of phenylalanine. Because of the severe effects of the disease and the ease with which it can be detected, most states now require that all newborn infants be tested for phenylketonuria.

Untreated individuals who inherit genes for PKU frequently have blond hair and "fair" skin. These traits are another result of the genes that produce PKU. The absence of functional phenylalanine hydroxylase not only leads to an excessive accumulation of phenylalanine but also reduces synthesis of tyrosine, the raw material for the manufacture of melanin. Thus, single pairs of alleles sometimes determine more than one phenotypic trait. Genes that produce two or more phenotypic traits are said to be *pleiotropic.*

Multiple Alleles

As noted earlier, interaction between alleles does not always produce sharply dominant or recessive effects. As in the determination of flower color in snapdragons, alleles sometimes combine to produce "intermediate" phenotypes. The inheritance of an A, B, AB, or O blood type in human beings illustrates how such phenotypes can be produced.

Each of these four blood types is determined by a single pair of alleles (Table 27.1). Three such alleles exist in the population as a whole. These alleles, which can be represented as i, I^A, and I^B, constitute a series of *multiple alleles.* This term is used whenever more than two alleles exist in a population. Red blood cells that contain the I^A allele produce proteins called *A antigens,* and cells

TABLE 27.1
ABO Blood Groups in Human Beings

Blood group	Genotype	Antigen on red blood cells	Antibodies in serum of blood	Blood groups acceptable for transfusion
O	ii	neither A nor B	anti-A and anti-B	O (universal donor)
A	I^AI^A, I^Ai	A	anti-B	A, O
B	I^BI^B, I^Bi	B	anti-A	B, O
AB	I^AI^B	A, B	none	all (universal recipient)

that contain the I^B allele produce different proteins called *B antigens.* Most of these molecules coat the outer surfaces of red blood cells. The i allele produces neither antigen. As indicated in Chap. 18, antigens are substances that can elicit production of antibodies by lymphocytes.

Red blood cells of individuals who have type AB blood have both A and B antigens on their surface membranes. Thus, the genotype of such individuals is I^AI^B. Red blood cells of type O individuals have neither type of antigen on their surfaces, and their genotype is ii. Similarly, the genotype of individuals who have type A blood can be I^Ai or I^AI^A; the genotype of type B individuals is either I^Bi or I^BI^B.

Because the I^A and I^B alleles are both expressed when they interact as an allelic pair, neither functions as a dominant allele in AB individuals. The i allele, however, produces neither A nor B antigens and functions as a Mendelian recessive when paired with either I^A or I^B. Dominance, therefore, is not an absolute quality retained by certain alleles in all circumstances, nor does dominance usually result from a simple inhibition of one allele by its partner. Study of the molecular biology of gene expression reveals far more complex relations. The actual traits that develop from a single pair of alleles depend on how the alleles affect each other and how their products affect cell function generally.

The antigenic differences of red blood cells prohibit indiscriminate transfusions of blood from one person to another. For example, people with type A blood cannot accept transfusions of type B blood. Type A individuals do not produce B antigens, and the lymphocytes of such people respond to B antigens by secreting B antibodies. Because antibodies produce immune agglutinates by interlocking with foreign antigens (see Chap. 18), B antibodies quickly cause B type red blood cells to clump together. Formation of such agglutinates can block blood flow and severely disrupt most functions of the circulatory system.

Examination of the reciprocal relations between antigens and antibodies for A, B, AB, and O blood types in Table 27.1 reveals why type O individuals sometimes are termed *universal donors* and type AB individuals often are called *universal recipients.* Because red blood cells of type O individuals contain neither A nor B antigen, blood derived from these individuals can be transfused into persons who have type A, B, AB, or O blood. Conversely, the A *and* B antigens of AB red blood cells will elicit an immune response from lymphocytes of people who have A, B, or O blood.

Knowledge of how blood type is inherited sometimes is used to resolve cases of disputed paternity when it is possible to prove that a particular male could *not* be the father of a child. Suppose a mother who has type O blood gives birth to a child having type A blood. Further assume that the blood type of the alleged father is B. Since the mother's genotype is ii and the alleged father's is either I^BI^B or I^Bi, a child having a genotype of I^AI^A or I^Ai could not be produced by this couple. The man could not be the father of the child.

Polygenic Interactions

Most genes do not act alone in determining traits. Instead, allelic pairs usually interact with other, nonallelic genes located elsewhere on the same chromosome or on different chromosomes. One example of such *polygenic interactions* is the inheritance of skin color in human beings. The amount of melanin produced in skin is determined by the combined effects of more than one pair of alleles. Such alleles appear to be of two basic types. One type produces substances that lead to a heavy deposition of melanin in skin, the other generates compounds that lead to a light deposition of the pigment. Lightly pigmented individuals have inherited many "light" alleles and few "dark" alleles. The reverse is true for heavily pigmented people.

Children born to a heavily and lightly pigmented pair of parents inherit dark and light alleles in roughly equal numbers. Because none of these alleles is strictly dominant, such children will have a *mulatto* skin color intermediate between that of their parents. A child born to parents who both have mulatto skin complexions can have any one of a range of skin colors from very dark to very light. Figure 27.14 illustrates how such varied skin colors arise. This figure is based on the assumption that the quantity of melanin deposited in skin is influenced by two pairs of nonlinked alleles. Since each pair of the alleles segregates independently and none of the alleles is dominant, there are five different skin colors possible for a child born to parents who both have an *AaBb* genotype. The probability that such a child will be very dark, dark, mulatto, light, or very light is $\frac{1}{16}$, $\frac{4}{16}$, $\frac{6}{16}$, $\frac{4}{16}$, and $\frac{1}{16}$, respectively.

Results of recent studies suggest that alleles influencing the amount of melanin deposition in human skin do segregate and recombine as illustrated by Fig. 27.14. However, these results also indicate that the number of such alleles is at least 3, and that not all of these alleles are equally potent. Certain alleles appear to exert a greater influence than others in promoting or inhibiting melanin deposition. How several pairs of alleles interact to produce such varied effects is largely unknown. Indeed, discovering the biochemical mechanisms of polygenic inheritance is one of the most challenging problems currently confronting geneticists.

Chromosomal Interactions

Sex Determination

A few traits are influenced by the combined actions of hundreds or even thousands of genes. One of the best illustrations is the trait of sexuality, which in numerous organisms is controlled by whole chromosomes acting as functionally integrated units. Each organism is believed to possess genes for the production of male traits as well as genes for development of female traits. Such genes are not usually specialized "sex genes," but are of a type that, among other effects, also happen to influence sexual development.

In some organisms, people included, sexuality is influenced greatly by genes located on a pair of *sex chromosomes*, which differ in size and shape from all other chromosomes, or *autosomes*.

Sex chromosomes are of two kinds, X and Y, and a pair of sex chromosomes can consist either of one X and one Y or of two X chromosomes. For example, in mammals and fruit flies, cells of adult *males* contain an XY pair, and cells of *females*, an XX pair. Femaleness in these animals is controlled by the genes of the X chromosome. Maleness is determined by the autosomes in fruit flies but to a large extent by the Y chromosomes in mammals (Fig. 27.15).

Fig. 27.14 Polygenic inheritance. This illustration assumes that human skin color is determined by two pairs of alleles that assort independently. The *A* and *B* alleles promote pigment production in skin; the *a* and *b* alleles promote little deposition of pigment. None of these alleles is dominant or recessive. Thus, the skin of an *AaBb* individual will have an intermediate light-brown color, and the skin color of offspring produced by two such individuals can be light-brown, dark, light, very dark, or very light.

gametes produced by AaBb (light-brown) male

gametes produced by AaBb (light-brown) female	AB	Ab	aB	ab
AB	AABB (very dark)	AABb (dark)	AaBB (dark)	AaBb (light-brown)
Ab	AABb (dark)	AAbb (light-brown)	AaBb (light-brown)	Aabb (light)
aB	AaBB (dark)	AaBb (light-brown)	aaBB (light-brown)	aaBb (light)
ab	AaBb (light-brown)	Aabb (light)	aaBb (light)	aabb (very light)

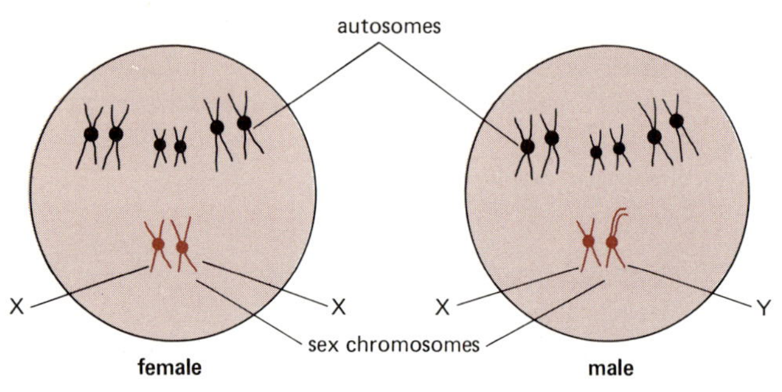

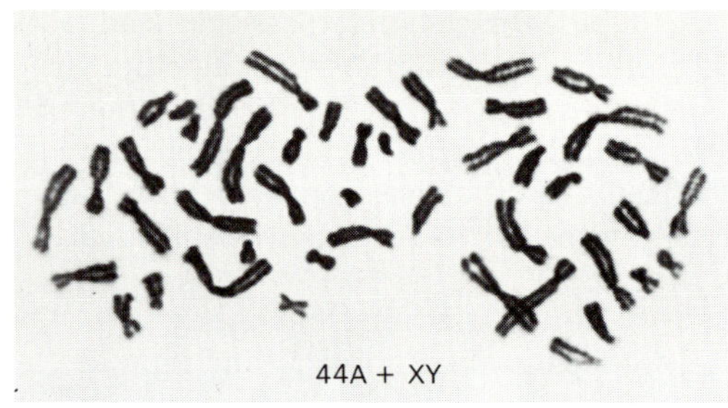

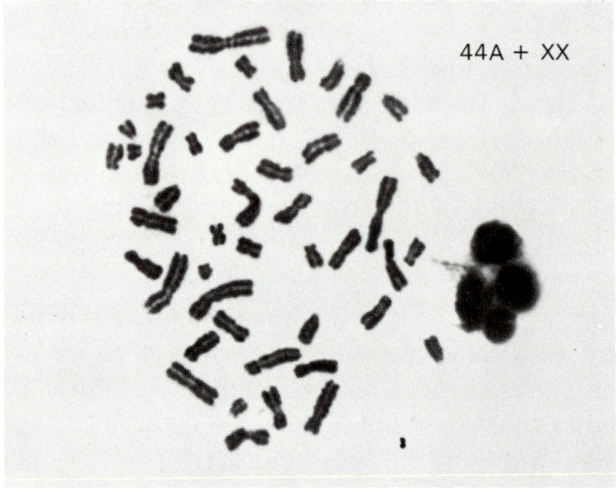

Fig. 27.15 Sex chromosomes and autosomes. (A) Chromosome types and numbers in the fruit fly, where $2n = 8$. Note that each chromosome consists of two chromatids. Homologous chromosomes are shown paired, as they would appear in prophase of a first meiotic division (see Chap. 22). Also note the structural dissimilarity between X and Y chromosomes. (B), (C), isolated chromosomes from cells of a human male and female, respectively. In both cases 46 pairs of chromosomes are present; each chromosome consists of two chromatids. (*B, C, Carolina Biological Supply Company.*)

In human beings, for example, each adult cell contains 22 pairs of autosomes plus either an XY or an XX pair. Female cells, 44A + XX, thus possess two female-determining chromosomes, whereas male cells, 44A + XY, contain one female-determining and one male-determining chromosome. This difference of one whole chromosome lies at the root of sexual differences between males and females. More specifically, genes of the Y chromosome cause the medulla of embryonic human gonads to differentiate as testes (see Chap. 24). These genes, together with others located on autosomes, eventually trigger testicular production of sperms and male sex hormones. Individuals inheriting a pair of X chromosomes lack the genes necessary for testicular development. As a result, the feminizing influence of the X chromosomes outweighs the masculinizing effects of certain autosomal genes, and ovaries develop from the cortical tissues of embryonic gonads.

That the sexual nature of an individual does indeed depend on a particular ratio, or *balance*, of chromosomes has been demonstrated by experiments in fruit flies. In these animals, in which maleness in controlled by the autosomes, it is possible to vary the number of X chromosomes and autosomes normally present in sperms and eggs. One can then obtain offspring with normal paired sets of autosomes but with three X chromosomes instead of two. Such individuals become so-called *superfemales;* all sexual traits are accentuated in the direction of femaleness. Other chromosome balances give rise to *supermales* and *intersexes*, the latter with sexual traits intermediate between those of normal males and females (Fig. 27.16). Paradoxically, supersexes and also intersexes generally are sterile; for as a result of the abnormal chromosome numbers meiosis occurs abnormally, and the sperms and eggs then produced are defective.

In the light of such balances, the normal mechanism of sex determination at the time of fertilization becomes clear. For example, human females produce eggs each of which contains 22A + X after meiosis (Fig. 27.17). Males produce two kinds of sperms, 22A + X and 22A + Y, in roughly equal numbers. Fertilization now occurs at random, and a sperm of either type may unite with an egg. Therefore, in about 50 per cent of the cases, the result will be 44A + XX, or female-producing zygotes; and in the remaining 50 per cent, the zygotes will be 44A + XY, or prospectively male.

Thus it is the paternal parent who, at the

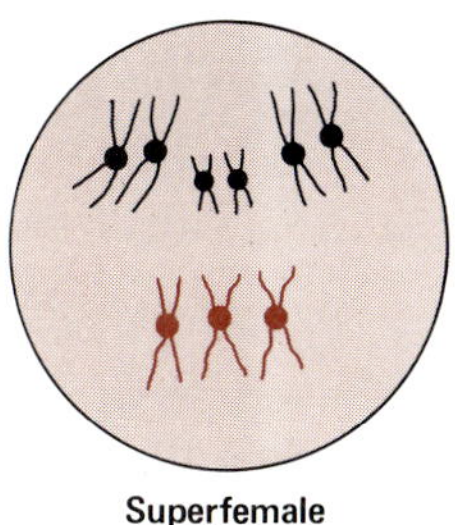

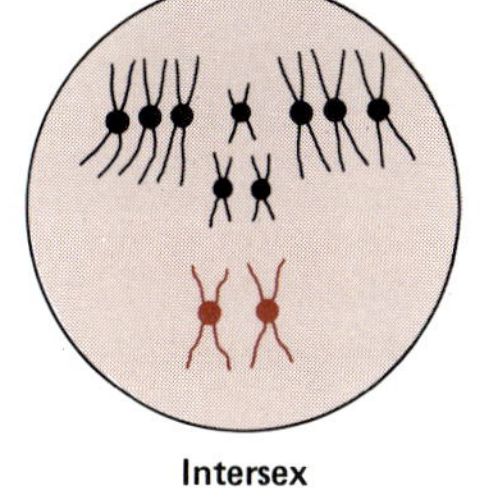

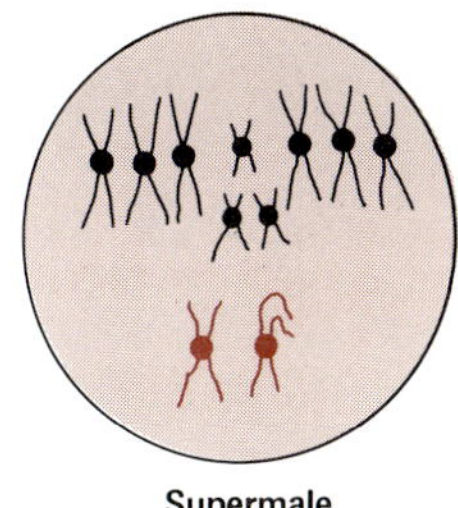

Fig. 27.16 Chromosome balances. The sexual character of a fruit fly is determined by the specific balances of autosomes and X chromosomes, as shown.

moment of fertilization, determines the sex of the offspring. When only a single offspring is produced, a 50:50 chance exists of its being a son or a daughter. When many offspring are produced, the number of males will generally equal the number of females.

Sex Linkage

Genes located on sex chromosomes are termed *sex-linked genes,* and the traits they produce are termed *sex-linked traits.* Morgan identified the first sex-linked alleles in 1910. One of these is responsible for white eye color in *Drosophila* (Fig. 27.18). Fruit flies normally have red eyes, but those inheriting genes for white eyes lack eye pigments. A cross between a white-eyed male and a female homozygous for red eyes will produce F_1 offspring that all have red eyes. When an F_1 female is mated to an F_1 male, all F_2 females develop red eyes, whereas approximately half of the males develop white eyes and half develop red eyes. These results were first obtained by Morgan, and they were not what he had expected. According to Mendel's law of segregation, F_1 flies heterozygous for eye color should produce a 3:1 ratio of red- to white-eyed offspring irrespective of gender.

To explain these unexpected results, Morgan hypothesized that alleles for eye color are expressed only when located on an X chromosome. Results of experiments conducted since Morgan's discovery of these alleles are fully consistent with this hypothesis. F_1 females produced from a cross between a red-eyed female and a white-eyed male have a dominant allele (R) on one X chromosome and a recessive allele (r) on the other. A sufficient amount of eye pigment is produced by R to give these flies a normal red-eyed phenotype. An F_1 male produced from this cross also has a dominant R allele on its X chromosome but it lacks an allele for eye color on its Y chromosome. Since only the R allele is expressed, such a male also has red eyes.

F_2 females produced by interbreeding F_1 flies have a genotype RR or Rr, and therefore they all are red-eyed. The genotype of F_2 males, however, is either $R\upharpoonleft$ or $r\upharpoonleft$. The symbol $\upharpoonleft$ represents the Y chromosome, genetically inert for these alleles. $R\upharpoonleft$ flies are red-eyed like their parents; $r\upharpoonleft$ flies are white-eyed like their paternal grandparents. Since 1910, many sex-linked genes have been discovered in *Drosophila* and numerous other organisms, people included. The pattern of sex-linked inheritance is similar in all cases, and it is now known that the Y chromosomes of these organisms are genetically inert for most alleles located at equivalent sites on X chromosomes.

An example of sex-linked inheritance in human beings is *hemophilia,* one form of "bleeders' disease." Afflicted individuals lack one of the plasma proteins required for normal clotting of blood. Cuts sustained by such individuals often bleed profusely, sometimes for 2 hours or more. Because hemo-

Fig. 27.17 Sex determination in human beings. Males produce two genetically different sperm types, roughly 50 percent of each. Offspring will then be male and female in a 1:1 ratio.

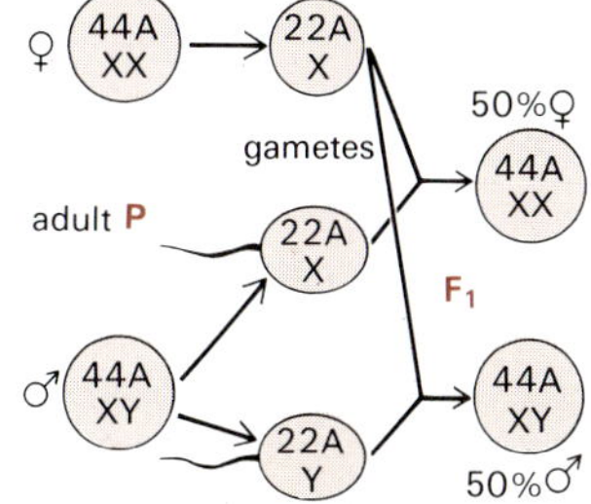

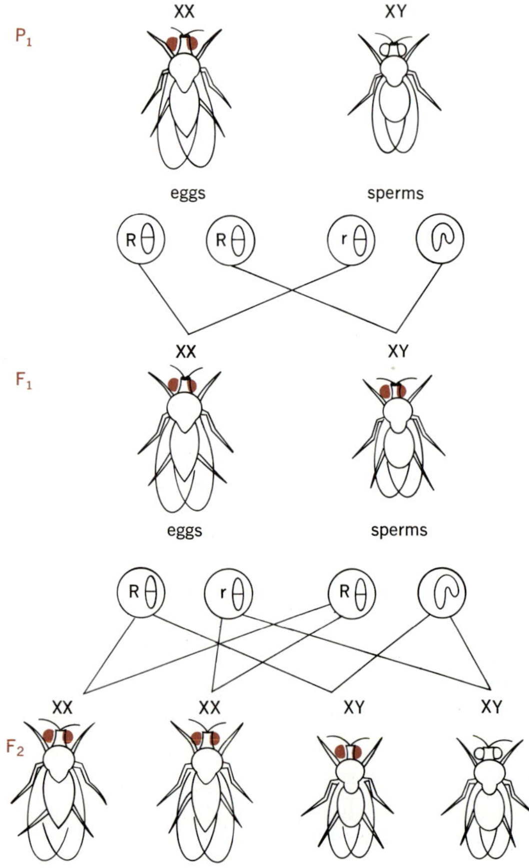

Fig. 27.18 Sex linkage. Approximately half of the F_2 males that result from this sequence of crosses will have an X chromosome that contains the dominant *R* allele for red eyes; the other half will have an X chromosome that contains the recessive *r* allele for white eyes. Because alleles for eye color linked to Y chromosomes are not expressed, the eye color of male *Drosophila* is determined solely by the allele linked to the X chromosome.

philia is caused by a recessive sex-linked allele, the disease is more prevalent in males than in females. In females, hemophilia occurs only if the recessive allele *h* is inherited on both X chromosomes. The plasma proteins produced by this defective allele are nonfunctional. *HH* or *Hh* females are normal because they have at least one allele producing functional copies of the plasma protein required for clotting. Since the Y chromosome is genetically inert for these alleles, all males who inherit an X chromosome containing an *h* allele develop hemophilia. Thus, all daughters born to an *H*↾ father and an *Hh* mother will be normal, but there is a 50 per cent chance that sons born to these parents will be hemophiliacs.

The hemophilia gene played an indirect but significant role in triggering the Russian revolution of 1917. Alexandra, wife of Czar Nicholas II, inherited an *h* allele on one of her X chromosomes. This allele had been carried originally by Queen Victoria of England. Four normal daughters and one hemophiliac son, Alexis, were born to Nicholas and Alexandra. During one incident of severe bleeding, an unscrupulous monk named Rasputin seemed "miraculously" to heal a wound Alexis had sustained. As a result, Alexandra developed a superstitious admiration for Rasputin, who capitalized on this relationship to gain considerable political power. Many historians believed that his abuse of this power to oppress the Russian people contributed greatly to the subsequent communist uprising and the assassination of the Russian royal family.

About 80 other sex-linked traits occur in human beings. Two of the most common are red-green color blindness and pseudohypertrophic muscular dystrophy (Fig. 27.19).

X Chromosome Inactivation

Certain sex-linked traits of mammals develop almost exclusively in females. For example, virtually all *calico cats* (also called tortoise-shell cats) are females; males rarely inherit the patches of black and orange-yellow fur that characterize this trait (Fig. 27.20). One form of anhydrotic *ectodermal dysplasia* normally occurs only in women. These people have patches of normal skin interspersed among patches containing very few sweat glands.

The mechanism producing such traits is different from the one responsible for hemophilia, red-green color blindness, white eye color in *Drosophila,* and other sex-linked phenotypes just described. Early in development one of the two X chromosomes of each embryonic cell becomes genetically inert. Which X chromosome becomes inactive appears to be a matter of chance for most mammals. However, all descendants of each *X-inactivated* embryonic cell have the same X chromosome in the inactive state. Because most of these descendant cells will take up adjoining positions in adult tissues, female mammals are patchwork mosaics of two cell types, the first having one

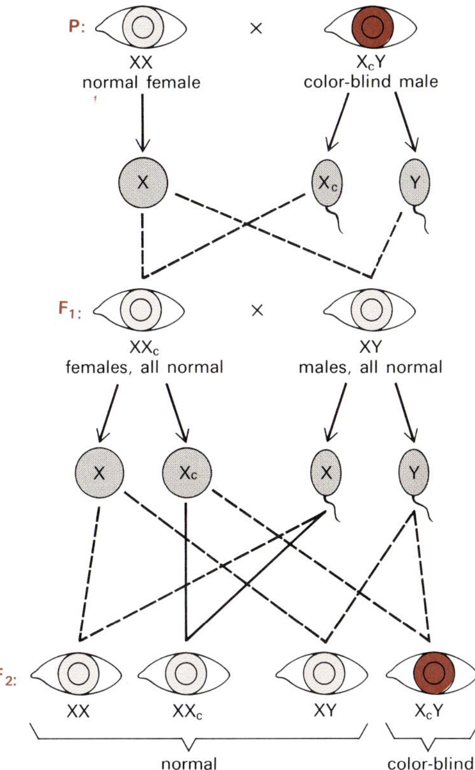

Fig. 27.19 Sex linkage: color blindness. Note that a color-blind male (P) transmits the sex-linked recessive gene X_c to all his daughters, who have normal vision, however. Such females then transmit the gene to half their sons, who are color-blind.

of the two X chromosomes active, the second have the reciprocal arrangement (see Fig. 27.20).

Inactive X chromosomes can be identified easily in nuclei of many interphase cells. The are tightly coiled, compact masses of nucleoprotein that stain far more intensely than diffuse chromatin. Called *Barr bodies* after their discoverer, inactive X chromosomes provide a convenient means of determining whether individual cells are derived from male or female mammals (Fig. 27.21).

The random pattern of X-chromosome inactivation explains why certain sex-linked traits appear only in females. In cats, for example, the alleles for black or yellow coat color are carried on the X chromosome; calico cats are heterozygous for these alleles. Descendants of embryonic pigment cells having a black allele on an active X chromosome will take up neighboring positions in a region of

Fig. 27.20 X-chromosome inactivation. (A) Calico cats, which have black-and-yellow coats, are almost always female. (B) Early in embryonic life, one or the other X chromosome becomes tightly coiled and genetically inactive. The inactive X chromosome is shown as circular, the active one as rod-shaped. Alleles for yellow and black cat color are sex-linked. Patches of cells that contain an active X chromosome bearing an allele for black coat color, *B*, produce black fur. Patches of cells that contain an active X chromosome bearing an allele for yellow coat color, *b*, produce yellow fur.

A

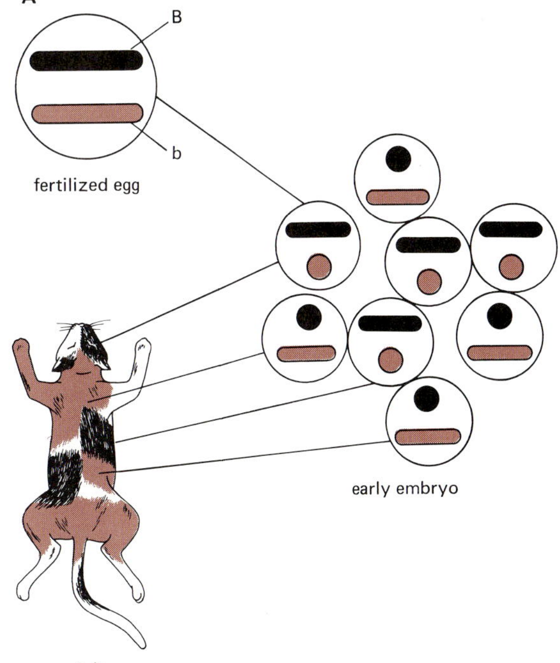

B

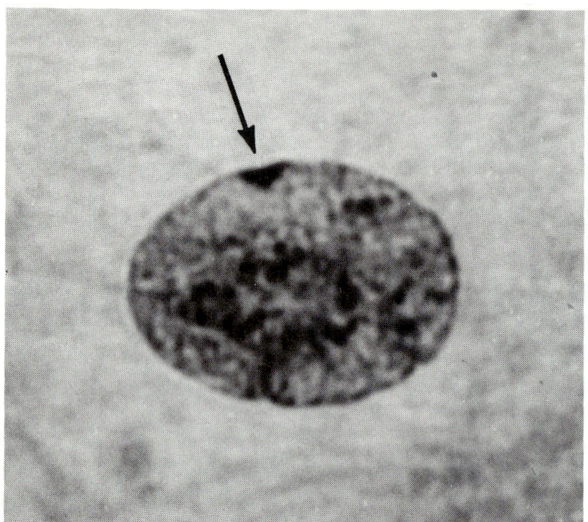

Fig. 27.21 Barr bodies. The dark structure (arrow) adjacent to the nuclear envelope of this nucleus is an inactivated X chromosome, or Barr body.

skin and produce a patch of black fur. Descendants of cells having a yellow allele on an active X chromosome will produce a patch of yellow-orange fur (see Fig. 27.20). Because alleles for coat color are inert on Y chromosomes, male cats of this variety have an all-black or all-yellow-orange appearance. Male calicos develop occasionally, but most if not all have two or more X chromosomes in addition to a Y chromosome (how organisms can inherit abnormal numbers of chromosomes is explained later in this chapter).

Gene-Environment Interactions

Genes not only interact with each other; their operation and effects also can be greatly influenced by the environments in which they reside. Indeed, if this were not the case, cellular differentiation could not occur and organisms could not develop. For example, *all* cells of a flowering plant possess flower-color genes, but only cells in the petals produce the colors (Fig. 27.22): *all* cells of a human being possess eye-color genes, but only iris cells actually develop the color.

Some of the ways genes interact with substances in their environment now are understood for relatively simple organisms such as bacteria. For example, many operons of bacteria are regulated by substances that repress or induce operator genes (see Chap. 15). Much less is known about the mechanisms that regulate gene expression in more complex organisms. The chromosomes of these organisms are significantly different from those of bacteria, and few, if any, of their genes appear to be organized as operons. As pointed out in Chap. 14, nonhistone proteins are associated with the chromosomal DNA of complex organisms, and some of them appear to play a role in controlling gene expression. Much current research is being aimed at determining the nature of this control.

The nongenetic regulation of sex determination illustrates the degree to which gene expression can be influenced by environmental factors. Unlike *Drosophila,* human beings, other animals, and many plants, many organisms do not inherit whole specialized sex chromosomes. Instead, these organisms inherit masculinizing and feminizing genes distributed generally on many or all chromosomes. The genetic influences of these two types of genes are matched exactly in "strength." In the absence of specific nongenetic influences, such organisms develop as *hermaphrodites* and produce both male and female gametes.

However, in many of these organisms environmental factors do tip the balanced strength of mas-

Fig. 27.22 Gene expression. Although all cells of an organism have the same kinds of genes, gene action is influenced differently by different cells. The result is a differential expression of traits. Thus all cells of a plant can have pigment-producing genes, but an actual pigmentation (other than green) might develop only in the cells of flower petals.

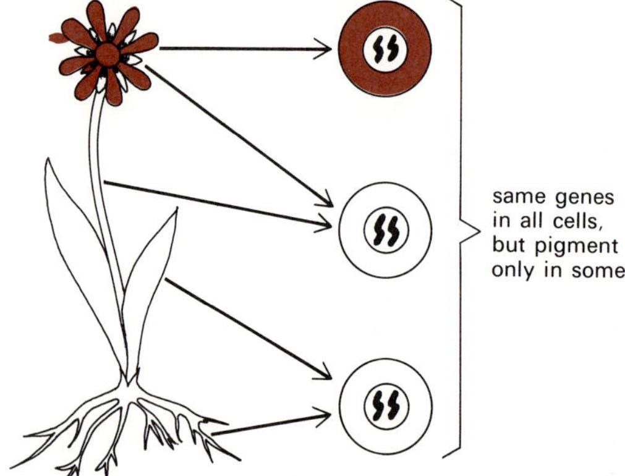

culinizing and feminizing genes in a male or female direction. In at least one case, namely the marine worm *Bonellia* (see Fig. 34.5), the sex-determining factor is known to be environmental CO_2. The relatively low concentrations of CO_2 in sea water allow free-swimming larvae of this worm to develop as females. But if a sexually indifferent larva happens to come in contact with an adult female or with a larva already determined as a female, the added respiratory CO_2 produced by the female causes the indifferent larva to be determined as a male; it becomes a small, sperm-producing, and structurally quite distinct parasitic animal, permanently attached inside the body of the female.

Although the effects of environment on phenotype are not always as dramatic as in *Bonellia*, most visible traits of an organism are the product of at least some interaction between heredity *and* environment. Thus, whereas the pre-Mendelians thought that traits were inherited, and whereas the Mendelian era advanced the concept that individual factors, or genes, were inherited, the modern post-Mendelian era recognizes that hereditary units are not independent genes as such but whole chromosome sets that contain coordinated complexes of genes. These subtly interacting *genetic systems* never lose their functional integration with the rest of the living material, and it is biologically almost meaningless to consider genes separately from their immediate or even more distant environment. Ultimately, therefore, the smallest real unit of inheritance is one whole cell.

MUTATIONS

Most of the traits discussed thus far in this chapter result from interactions between environments and sets of genes produced through sexual recombination. However, a great many hereditary events do not obey the rules of Mendelian inheritance. Some, such as bacterial transduction and transformation, have strictly limited significance. These events are discussed in Chap. 30. Far more important, and universally significant in all organisms, are *mutations*. Any stable, inheritable change in the genetic material of a cell is a mutation. Two major types of mutations exist: those resulting from changes in the structure or number of chromosomes, or *chromosome mutations;* and those resulting from changes of individual genes, or *point mutations*.

Both types of mutations can be induced by high-energy radiation such as x-rays, and the frequency of mutation has been found to be directly proportional to the amount of radiation a cell receives. Some naturally occurring mutations probably are produced by cosmic rays and other space radiation and by radioactive elements in the earth. But this unavoidable natural radiation is not sufficiently intense to account for the mutation frequency characteristic of genes generally, about one per million replications of a given gene. Most of these mutations probably represent errors in gene reproduction. Others undoubtedly are caused by artificial radiation, which adds to and increases the natural "background" radiation. Mutations also can be produced experimentally by physical agents other than radiation, and by various chemical agents.

Mutations occur entirely at random. Any gene can mutate at any time, in unpredictable ways. It may mutate several times in rapid succession, then not at all for considerable periods. It may mutate in one way, then back to its original state or in another way. Every gene existing today undoubtedly is a *mutant* that has undergone many mutations during its past history.

Most chromosome and some point mutations affect major traits in a radical, drastic manner. Others exert little or no effect. Some mutations have dominant effects and produce immediate alterations of traits. Others have recessive effects, and in diploid cells they remain masked by normal dominant alleles.

Gene changes that occur in body cells generally are *somatic mutations* (see also Chap. 26). They affect the heredity of the cell descendants—a patch of tissue at most. For example, "beauty spots" probably develop in this manner. Unless the effects of such mutations are lethal, as is sometimes the case in haploid organisms particularly, somatic mutations will have little direct bearing on the heredity of the whole individual. An entire offspring is likely to be affected only by *germ mutations,* stable genetic changes in immature and mature reproductive cells. Such mutations will be transmitted to all cells that ultimately compose the offspring. To the extent that germ mutations are recessive and masked by normal dominants, the traits of the offspring will not be altered. But if the offspring is haploid, or is diploid but homozygous recessive for a mutation, or if a mutation is dominant, then a particular trait may be expressed in altered form. Provided such a new trait is not lethal or does not cause sterility, it will persist and can affect the adaptation of an individual as much as the sexual recombination of genes.

Chromosome Mutations

Changes in Chromosome Number

As pointed out in Chap. 3, the exact number of chromosomes in each cell nucleus is a species-specific trait. Occasionally, however, some or all cells of an organism have abnormal numbers of chromosomes. Such aberrations usually result from abnormal separations of chromosomes during mitosis or meiosis. Chromosomes that normally move away from each other to opposite poles during a mitotic or meiotic anaphase sometimes move instead to the same pole and become incorporated in the same daughter nucleus. Sometimes only one pair of chromatids or chromosomes fails to separate during a mitotic or meiotic division. But occasionally cell division is so abnormal that all chromosomes move to the same pole and thereby become incorporated in a daughter cell that contains twice the normal number of chromosomes.

The effects of such chromosome *nondisjunctions* can be drastic, particularly if they occur during the first few cleavages of embryonic development. For example, diploid gametes can result from nondisjunction of all chromosomes during the first division of meiosis (Fig. 27.23). If such an abnormal gamete unites with a normal haploid gamete during fertilization, a *triploid* zygote with three sets of chromosomes will result. Similarly, a union of two diploid gametes produces a *tetraploid* zygote containing four sets of chromosomes.

Cells and organisms that have more than a double set of chromosomes are said to be *polyploid.* Many species of plants are naturally polyploid, and most of these probably arose from meiotic nondisjunctions that occurred in diploid ancestors. Indeed, horticulturalists have developed many new strains of polyploid plants during the past few decades by chemically inducing meiotic nondisjunctions of chromosomes in established varieties. By contrast, polyploid animal cells usually are not viable. Loss or addition of even a single chromosome often is lethal for most animal cells. When such cells are able to reproduce, the resulting tissues, organs, or organisms are almost always malformed or functionally defective.

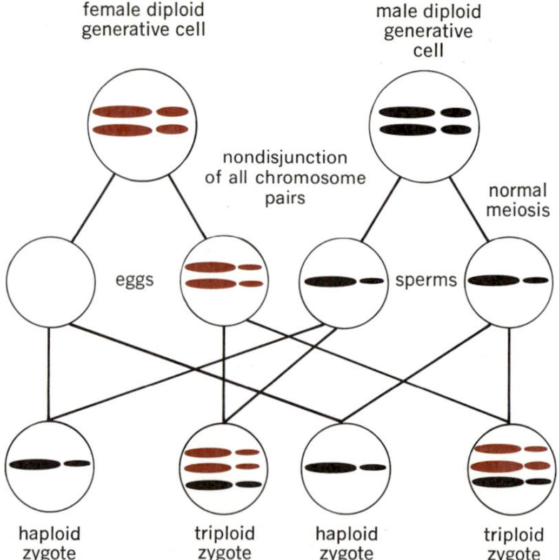

Fig. 27.23 Nondisjunction. Nondisjunction of all pairs of homologous chromosomes during meiosis produces diploid gametes and gametes that do not contain chromosomes. Fertilization of such cells with normal haploid gametes yields haploid and triploid zygotes. Nondisjunctions of this type often involve only one or two pairs of homologous chromosomes and can occur during the production of male or female gametes.

Several types of human genetic diseases are caused by chromosome nondisjunctions. Among these are *Down's, Kleinfelter's* and *Turner's syndromes.* Individuals who inherit Down's syndrome typically have round, slightly flattened faces with small slanting eyes (Fig. 27.24). Because these features superficially resemble Mongolian populations, Down's syndrome sometimes is inappropriately called "mongolism." The disease usually is caused by a nondisjunction of the No. 21 pair of chromosomes (see Fig. 27.24). Union of a normal gamete with a gamete haploid for all chromosomes except No. 21 can produce a *trisomic* zygote that contains 47 chromosomes. Such zygotes contain a normal diploid set of 22 chromosomes and three No. 21

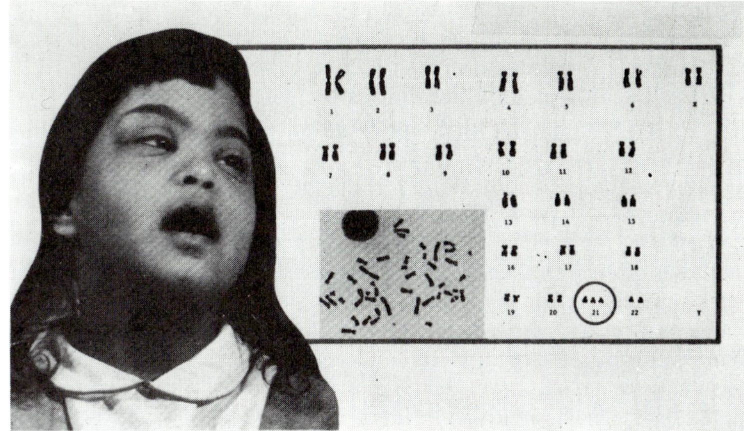

Fig. 27.24 **Down's syndrome.** Note the wide, rounded face and habitually open mouth of this child, two of several symptoms of Down's syndrome. This type of Down's syndrome results from the inheritance of three No. 21 chromosomes (circle).

chromosomes. The extra No. 21 chromosome is replicated during mitosis and passed on to all cells. Because genes are not expressed normally in many of these cells, children who inherit Down's syndrome are mentally retarded, and many of them suffer from heart and respiratory ailments.

The probability that pairs of No. 21 chromosomes will not disjoin during meiosis is greater for women than for men. Moreover, this probability increases as women grow older. The average incidence of Down's syndrome in the United States is about 1 in 700 births, but only 1 in 1500 for women who are in their twenties; the incidence for women 40 years of age or older is 1 in 80 births.

Kleinfelter's and Turner's syndromes both result from meiotic nondisjunctions of sex chromosomes. In females, such nondisjunctions can lead to the production of eggs that contain two X chromosomes or none at all. Fertilization of these eggs by normal sperms yields four types of zygotes, each of which contains an abnormal number of chromosomes (Fig. 27.25). If an egg without X chromosomes is fertilized by a Y sperm, the resulting OY zygote begins development but soon degenerates. Human development cannot occur in the absence of genes linked to the X chromosome (recall that most of the Y chromosome is genetically inert).

If an egg containing two X chromosomes is fertilized by a Y sperm, the resulting XXY zygote develops as a male afflicted with Kleinfelter's syndrome. Such individuals have underdeveloped testes that do not produce sperms, and they usually have a number of typically female characteristics such as a high-pitched voice, absence of facial hair, and some development of breasts. Evidently, the influence of the male-determining Y chromosome is

Fig. 27.25 Nondisjunction of human sex chromosomes. Nondisjunctions of sex chromosomes occur occasionally during the production of eggs and sperms. In this example, a nondisjunction produces an egg with two X chromosomes and an egg with none. Fertilizations by normal sperms can result in Turner's syndrome, a zygote without an X chromosome that fails to develop beyond a few cleavages, or a triple X superfemale, or a male afflicted with Kleinfelter's syndrome.

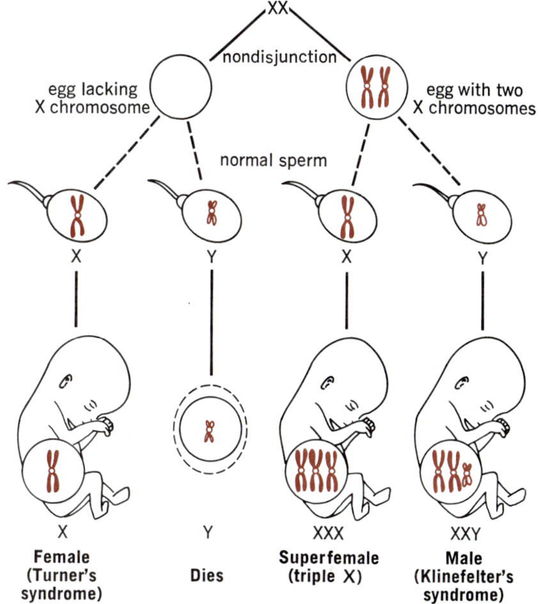

partly imbalanced by the combined effects of two X chromosomes.

When an egg without any sex chromosomes is fertilized by an X sperm, the resulting zygote contains 44 autosomes and one X chromosome. This combination produces an offspring with Turner's syndrome. Such individuals are female, but their sex organs do not mature. Many of these children are mentally retarded. Evidently, inheritance of a single set of genes linked to an X chromosome provides sufficient information for the development of female sex organs, but a double set of such genes is required to trigger production of sufficient female hormones for sexual maturation. If an egg containing two sex chromosomes is fertilized by an X sperm, an XXX zygote results. Persons developing from such zygotes are called *superfemales* (see also earlier section) and have few, if any, abnormalities. Indeed, many XXX females are unaware that their cells contain an extra sex chromosome.

Meiotic nondisjunctions also can occur during the production of sperms. If they occur during the first division of meiosis, the sperms that are produced can contain both X and Y chromosomes. Others can lack sex chromosomes. Kleinfelter's or Turner's syndromes result from the fertilization of normal eggs by such abnormal sperms.

Nondisjunctions of chromosomes similarly can occur during the second division of meiosis. In males, for example, such nondisjunctions occasionally produce sperms that contain two X or two Y chromosomes. Fertilizations of normal eggs by these abnormal sperms produce XXX or XYY zygotes. The latter develop as seemingly normal males, although the results of some studies suggest, inconclusively, that the XYY condition sometimes may promote abnormally aggressive behavior.

Changes in Chromosome Structure

Other mutations involve changes in the structure of chromosomes. All such mutations alter the nucleotide sequences of DNA and thus the genetic messages transmitted to RNA. One example of this type of chromosome mutation is *translocation* (Fig. 27.26). This occurs when two or more chromosomes break and then rejoin in a different combination. One translocation known to occur in human beings involves an unequal exchange of chromosome fragments between a No. 21 chromosome and a No. 15 chromosome (Fig. 27.27). The exchange produces a large chromosome that comprises the greater parts of both chromosomes 15 and 21, and a very small chromosome that comprises the smaller fragments of the original chromosomes. The larger chromosome is designated as the *15/21 chromosome;* the smaller contains few genes and almost always is lost from cells.

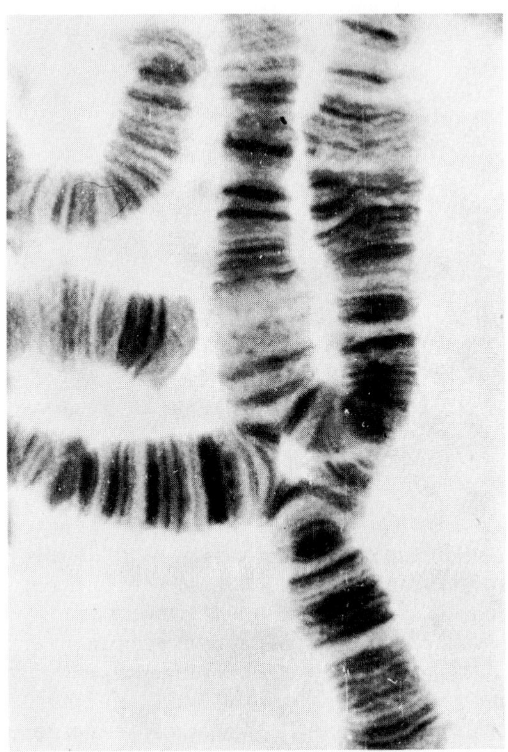

Fig. 27.26 Chromosome translocations. The U-shaped portion in the upper part of this photograph is a normal (stained) salivary-gland chromosome of a midge (a small gnatlike insect). The branches leading away from the bottom of the U are parts of other chromosomes that have become translocated and attached here. These translocations have been induced by irradiation with x-rays.

Figure 27.28 illustrates the four types of eggs that can result when a 15/21 translocation occurs during meiosis in a human female. If fertilized by normal sperms, each of these eggs will encounter different fates: (1) Normal eggs, without translocated chromosomes, will develop as normal children. (2) Eggs that contain a normal No. 15 chromosome but not a No. 21 chromosome will undergo only partial development and then degenerate. (3) Eggs that contain a 15/21 chromosome and a

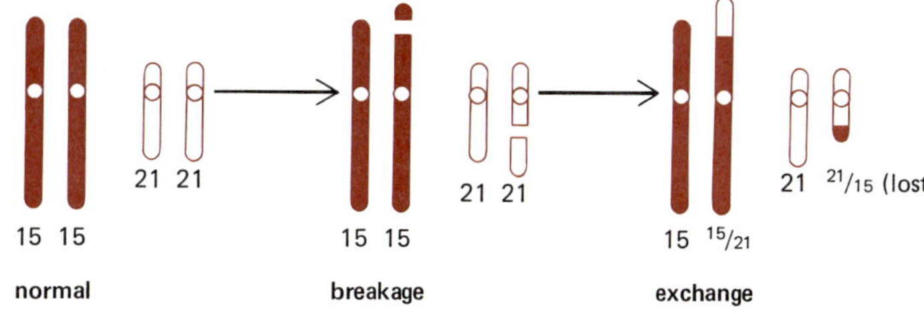

Fig. 27.27 Translocation 15/21. Down's syndrome can result from a translocation between chromosomes 15 and 21, in which a section of chromosome 21 is translocated to chromosome 15. A segment of chromosome 15 is sometimes also translocated to a piece of chromosome 21, but the two small fragments usually are lost.

No. 21 chromosome will develop as individuals whose cells contain *three* No. 21 chromosomes, one of them fused to a No. 15 chromosome. Such individuals will exhibit Down's syndrome. (4) Eggs that contain a 15/21 chromosome but not a No. 15 chromosome will develop as normal children. However, the diploid cells of such individuals will have only one normal No. 21 chromosome, one normal No. 15 chromosome, and a 15/21 chromosome. These individuals will produce the same four types of gametes generated by their mother. Such people are "carriers" of Down's syndrome; the probability that their children will inherit the genetic condition is 1 in 3. Moreover, there is a 50 per cent probability that normal children produced by such a carrier will themselves be carriers of Down's syndrome. Thus, unlike nondisjunction Down's syndrome, the translocation form of the disease tends to "run" in families.

Deletions are a second type of structural mutation of chromosomes. Here portions of chromosomes break away and are lost from cells. The effects of a deletion depend largely on which genes are lost. Deletions that occur in zygotes usually are lethal. The few organisms that develop from such zygotes are almost always abnormal.

The *cri du chat* ("cry of the cat") *syndrome* of human beings, for example, results from a deletion in a No. 5 chromosome. Infants afflicted with this genetic disease have a rounded moonlike face and remain both physically and mentally retarded throughout their lives. Because their vocal cords fail to develop normally, afflicted infants utter a feeble cry that is similar to the mewing of a cat. Fortunately, this syndrome occurs infrequently. Approximately 100 cases have been reported by physicians throughout the world since the discovery of this disease by a French physician in 1963.

Other structural changes of chromosomes produce several other genetic diseases. Some are caused by *inversions,* which occur when a piece of a chromosome breaks away, inverts, and fuses back into its original position with its ends reversed. Some genetic traits result from *duplications,* or the doubling of a limited part of a chromosome.

Most of such chromosome mutations usually disrupt normal development or otherwise upset normal biological functions. But an exceedingly small number of them undoubtedly establish new traits of increased survival value. As will be noted in Chap.

Fig. 27.28 Translocation Down's syndrome. This illustration assumes that a woman is a carrier of a 15/21 chromosome and that the male is not a carrier. The chances that a child born to this pair of individuals will have Down's syndrome is 1 in 3. See text for a full explanation.

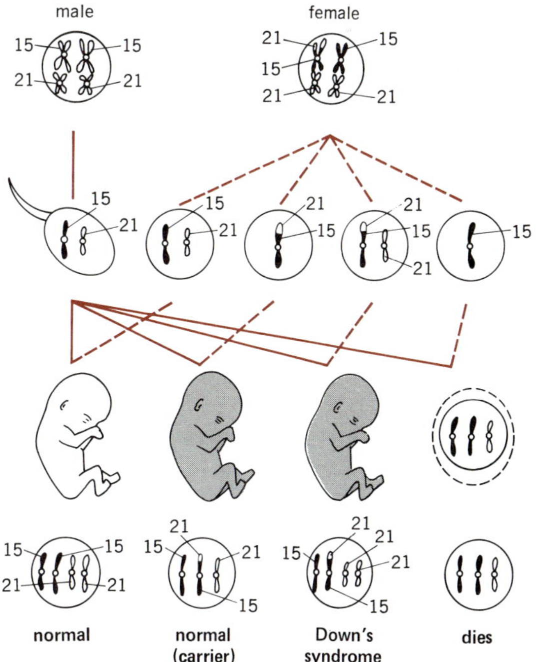

29, this small minority plays a major role in evolution.

Point Mutations

Whereas chromosome mutations involve gross changes in the organization of genetic material, point mutations usually involve a stable change of only one of two nucleotides in DNA. Point mutations can affect biological systems drastically, moderately, or not at all. And, like chromosome mutations, a small minority of point mutations establish new traits of substantial adaptive value. This diversity of effects can be illustrated by different point mutations of genes that code for *hemoglobin,* the oxygen-carrying pigment of red blood cells (see also Chap. 18).

Hemoglobin consists of four polypeptide chains: two α (alpha) chains and two β (beta) chains (Fig. 27.29). The structure of the α chains is determined by the α gene, the structure of the β chains by the β gene. Once produced, the four chains interlock as a whole hemoglobin molecule. The ability of hemoglobin to bind, transport, and release oxygen depends on subtle interactions between the α and β chains. These interactions can be disrupted by alterations in the amino acid sequences of the chains.

Fig. 27.29 Hemoglobin. The molecule consists of four subunits: two alpha chains (light blocks) and two beta chains (colored blocks). Each sequence of blocks represents a polypeptide. The alpha chains are produced by one pair of alleles, the beta chains by a second pair. Each chain enfolds a heme group (colored disk), an iron-containing compound that binds oxygen. *(From M. J. Sienko and R. A. Plane, "Chemistry," 5th ed., © 1976 by McGraw-Hill, Inc., New York.)*

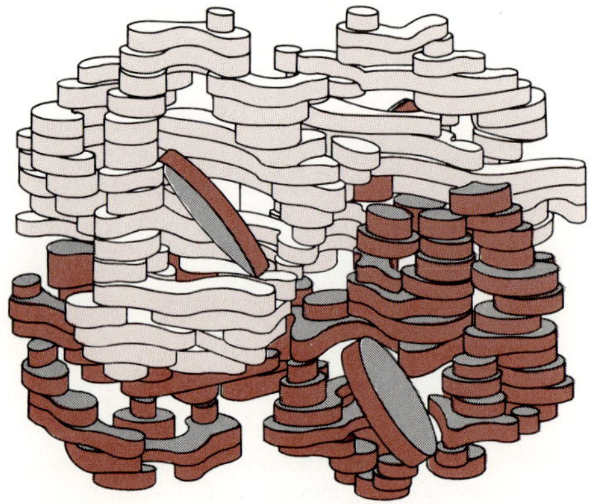

Individuals afflicted with *sickle-cell anemia,* for example, are homozygous for the mutant beta allele β^s. The genotype of these individuals is $\alpha\alpha\beta^s\beta^s$; both α alleles produce normal alpha chains and both β^s alleles produce abnormal beta chains. When the red blood cells of these individuals are fully loaded with oxygen, the aberrant β^s chains of hemoglobin interact normally with each other and with the α chains. But as oxygen is released from red blood cells in body tissues, the defective β^s chains adhere to each other abnormally. Such chains stack together in bunches and cause red blood cells to adopt a deformed crescentlike sickle shape (Fig. 27.30). The abnormally shaped cells clog capillaries, interfere with blood flow, and deprive body tissues of oxygen. This painful condition greatly reduces both the life expectancy and the mobility of afflicted individuals.

Individuals can be heterozygous for the β^s allele. The genotype of such individuals is $\alpha\alpha\beta\beta^s$, and their red cells produce both β and β^s chains. As a result, some of their hemoglobin is normal and some is abnormal. Although such heterozygous individuals have the *sickle-cell trait,* they are able to lead relatively normal lives. They occasionally suffer mild reactions, particularly when the oxygen content of their blood falls to low levels. Thus, people who have the sickle-cell trait usually cannot exercise strenuously and often experience difficulty in adjusting to high altitudes.

β^s chains differ from normal β chains in only one amino acid. The sixth amino acid of β chains is glutamic acid; β^s chains contain valine in this position. Although these amino acids share many common characteristics, they have dissimilar electric charges, and this difference is largely responsible for the abnormal interactions between α and β^s chains.

The substitution of valine for glutamic acid is caused by a change of one nitrogen base in the β gene. As a result of this point mutation, the RNA codon that specifies insertion of glutamic acid as the sixth amino acid in beta chains is altered. Figure 27.31 illustrates the effects of this alteration. One of the RNA codons for glutamic acid is GAA, and the corresponding triplet of DNA is CTT. If this DNA triplet mutates to CAT, the codon GAA in mRNA will be replaced by the codon GUA. This

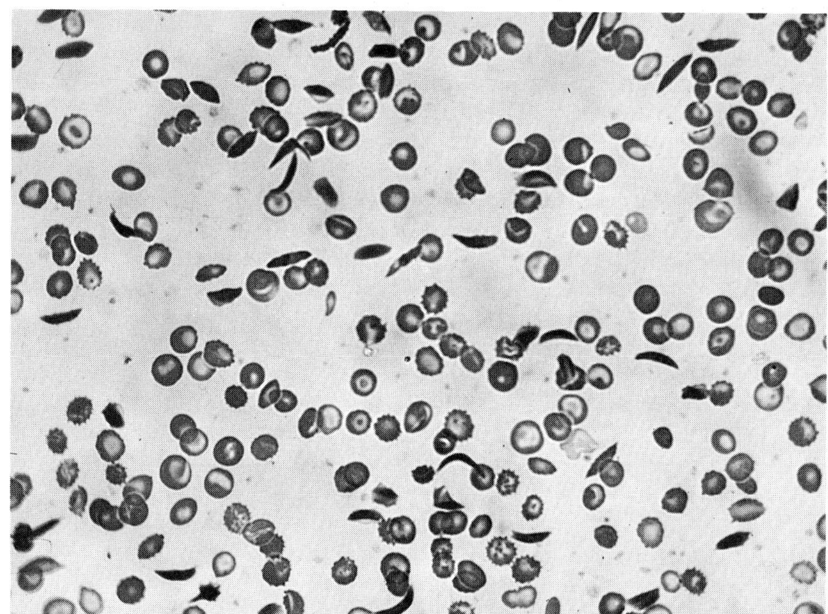

Fig. 27.30 Sickle-cell trait. The red blood cells of an individual who has inherited the sickle-cell trait change shape when the concentration of oxygen is lowered. Note the many sickle-shaped cells in this blood smear. (*Carolina Biological Supply Company.*)

seemingly minor change has great significance, for GUA is a codon for valine, not glutamic acid. Individuals who inherit DNA that contains such a point mutation from both parents are homozygous for the β^s allele and are afflicted with sickle-cell anemia. Inheritance of a "double dose" of this mutant gene is severely debilitating. By contrast, the consequences of inheriting a "single dose" of the mutant gene are comparatively mild.

Other mutations do not produce a change of phenotype. For example, the fifth amino acid of a normal beta hemoglobin chain is *proline.* This amino acid is specified by any one of the four codons CCU, CCC, CCA, or CCG. If a point mutation of a gene resulted in the substitution of CCA for CCU in its messenger RNA, the mutation does not have a phenotypic effect; proline is specified by both codons. In other cases, substitutions of amino acids do not affect the function of proteins. For example, the function of an enzyme usually is not affected by changes in amino acid sequences that do not alter its three-dimensional structure.

Fig. 27.31 Point mutations. Changes of individual nitrogen bases in DNA can alter RNA codons and produce substitutions of amino acids in proteins.

DNA triplet	RNA codon	amino acid
CTT	GAA	glutamic acid
CAT	GUA	valine

Still other mutations produce traits that increase chances of survival for the organisms that inherit them. Individuals who inherit the sickle-cell trait, for example, almost never die from *malaria.* This disease is caused by a protozoan parasite that spends part of its life cycle in the red blood cells of a host organism. During their infection of these cells, the parasites use up oxygen carried by hemoglobin. In people who have the sickle-cell trait, this depletion of oxygen causes infected red blood cells to "sickle." Such deformed cells then are engulfed by white blood cells, which destroy both the sickled cells and their resident parasites. As a result, the population of parasites in the blood of these individuals either is destroyed or maintained at a low level.

The β^s gene therefore can be both detrimental and beneficial. In a homozygous state, the β^s gene is severely debilitating. In a heterozygous state, however, the gene affords considerable protection against death from malaria. Consequently, the incidence of the β^s allele is higher among people who live in tropical areas where malaria is a common cause of death. In some African communities, for example, the sickle-cell trait appears in 40 per cent of the population.

Most black Americans are descendants of African ancestors and therefore have a higher incidence of the sickle-cell trait than Americans whose ethnic heritage stems from nontropical environments. Compared with African people, however, black Americans have a relatively low incidence of the sickle-cell trait (about 8 per cent). This lower incidence is a direct result of the sharply different environments in these two parts of the world. Malaria is a rare cause of death in the United States, and the continual loss of the β^s gene that results from the early death of people who inherit sickle-cell anemia is not counterbalanced by any beneficial effect of the gene in a heterozygous state. As a result, the incidence of sickle-cell anemia and the sickle-cell trait among black Americans is decreasing slowly. Thus, whether a mutation is "good," "bad," or "neutral" depends entirely on how the mutation affects the ability of an organism to survive in a particular environment. The same mutations that are disadvantageous in some environments can be advantageous in others.

Knowledge of how genes are inherited is being used to reduce the occurrence of deleterious mutations in many organisms. Eventually, it may even be possible to "repair" such mutations after they have been inherited, or to replace them with purely "synthetic" genes that yield new traits. Coupled with birth control, the emerging technology of *genetic intervention* is steadily increasing our ability to determine both the quantity and quality of our descendants. The methods, uses, and social impact of this technology are considered next.

Review Questions

1 What was meant by "blending inheritance?" Describe breeding tests showing that blending inheritance does not occur. What hypothesis did Mendel substitute for the blending concept?

2 Review the breeding tests on the inheritance of gray and ebony body colors in fruit flies and explain them on the basis of genes and chromosomes.

3 What are the quantitative results of the mating Aa × Aa if

- **a.** *A* is dominant over *a*?
- **b.** Neither gene is dominant over the other?

4 Interpret the laws of segregation and independent assortment on the basis of genes, meiosis, and gametes. By what kinds of breeding experiments and by what reasoning did Mendel come to discover these laws?

5 If *A* is dominant over *a*, what phenotype ratios of offspring are obtained from the following matings:

- **a.** *Aa* × *aa*?
- **b.** *AA* × *aa*?
- **c.** *Aa* × *Aa*?
- **d.** *Aa* × *AA*?

6 How many genetically different gamete types will be produced by an organism heterozygous for 10 gene pairs? If two such organisms were mated, how many genetically different offspring types could result?

7 How does the inheritance of linked alleles differ from that of nonlinked alleles? What were Morgan's observations that led him to the hypothesis of crossing-over? Describe this hypothesis. Show how crossing-over can be a source of genetic variations.

8 Describe how more than one phenotype can result from the inheritance of a single pair of alleles. Illustrate how traits can be influenced by multiple alleles and by polygenic interactions.

9 What is the significance of a given numerical balance between autosomes and sex chromosomes? Review the patterns of sex determination based on:

- **a.** Nongenetic mechanisms.
- **b.** Genetic mechanisms.

10 What are sex-linked genes? Review the kinds of disease that are caused by sex linkage. Why do more human males than females suffer from sex-linked diseases?

11 What traits result from X-chromosome inactivation in female mammals? Explain why males rarely exhibit such traits.

12 What are mutations? What are the characteristics of mutations from the standpoint of:

a. Predictability?
b. Effects on traits?
c. Relative advantage to the organism?

13 Review the major kinds of chromosome mutations, and describe the human genetic diseases that can result from them. Describe how Down's syndrome can be produced by at least two different kinds of mutations.

14 Review the nature of point mutations. What is sickle-cell anemia? Describe the symptoms and genetic cause of this disease. What is the sickle-cell trait? Why are the symptoms of the sickle-cell trait less severe than those of sickle-cell anemia? Explain why the incidence of the sickle-cell trait is greater among people who live in tropical regions of the world than among people who reside elsewhere.

15 Are mutations always harmful? Explain.

16 Review how Beadle and Tatum demonstrated a functional relationship between genes and enzymes. Why does the experimental procedure used by Beadle and Tatum represent a milestone in the history of genetic research?

Collateral Readings

Ayala, F. J., and **J. A. Kiger, Jr.:** "Modern Genetics," Benjamin/Cummings, Menlo Park, Calif., 1980. A fine, basic genetics textbook with special emphasis on population genetics.

Beadle, G. W.: Genes and Chemical Reactions in Neurospora, and **E. L. Tatum:** A Case History in Biological Research, "Nobel Lectures, Physiology or Medicine, 1942–1962," Elsevier, Amsterdam, 1964. Beadle and Tatum provide highly personal accounts of their Nobel Prize-winning work with *Neurospora crassa.*

Cerami, A., and **C. M. Peterson:** Cyanate and Sickle-Cell Disease, *Scientific American,* April 1975. Attempts to alleviate the symptoms of sickle-cell disease are discussed.

Goodenough, U.: "Genetics," 2d ed., Holt, New York, 1978. An excellent, well-written introductory textbook.

Harrison, D.: "Problems in Genetics with Notes and Examples," Addison-Wesley, Reading, Mass., 1970. A useful resource and practice book.

Jenkins, J. B.: "Genetics," 2d ed., Houghton Mifflin, Boston, 1979. A comprehensive introductory genetics text with a good balance between Mendelian and molecular genetics.

Mange, A. P., and **E. J. Mange:** "Genetics: Human Aspects," Saunders, Philadelphia, 1980. An outstanding introduction to human genetics. The book contains chapters devoted to many of the topics contained in this and the next chapter.

Mendel, G.: "Experiments in Plant Hybridisation," Oliver & Boyd, Edinburgh, 1965. This English translation of Mendel's original paper also gives a short biography of this famous scientist.

Mittwoch, U.: Sex Differences in Cells, *Scientific American,* July 1963. Differences in sex chromosomes and other cellular traits of males and females are examined.

Peters, J. A. (ed.): "Classic Papers in Genetics," Prentice-Hall, Englewood Cliffs, N.J., 1959. This book, available in paperback, contains papers written by some of the most important contributors to the field of genetics: Mendel, Morgan, Sutton, Beadle and Tatum, Watson and Crick, etc.

Ruddle, F. H., and **R. S. Kucherlapati:** Hybrid Cells and Human Genes, *Scientific American,* July 1974. A discussion of cell hybridization and how this technique has contributed to the localization of genes in human chromosomes.

Saxen, L., and **J. Rapola:** "Congenital Defects," Holt, New York, 1969. Genetic and other birth defects of human beings are described in this well-written book.

Stent, G. S., and **R. Calendar:** "Molecular Genetics: An Introductory Narrative," 2d ed., Freeman, San Francisco, 1978. This crisply written narrative provides an excellent introduction to the whole field of molecular genetics. Highly recommended for the serious student.

Volpe, E. P.: "Human Heredity and Birth Defects," Pegasus, New York, 1971. An excellent introduction to human reproduction and genetic diseases.

Wagner, R. P., B. H. Judd, B. G. Sanders, and **R. H. Richardson:** "Introduction to Modern Genetics," Wiley, New York, 1980. A well-illustrated and easily read introductory genetics text. Recommended.

Chapter 28 Genetic Intervention

Learning Objectives

After reading this chapter you should be able to:

1. Define genetic counseling, selective abortion, and amniocentesis; state how amniocentesis can be used to detect chromosome mutations in the cells of human fetuses.
2. Define artificial gestation and clone; describe at least one technique that can be used to produce clones of animals; name at least one practical application of cloning and at least one reason why some people might wish to produce children by artificial gestation or cloning.
3. Define recombinant DNA; define DNA ligases, restriction endonucleases, plasmids, and bacteriophages, and show how they can be used to produce organisms containing genes of different species; illustrate the relationship between palindromes and restriction enzymes; illustrate the general life cycle of bacteriophages.
4. Name at least two potential benefits and two possible hazards of recombinant DNA technology.
5. List at least three human proteins that have been produced by bacteria through use of recombinant DNA technology.
6. Define bacterial transformation and indicate its relevance to arguments concerning potential hazards of recombinant DNA technology.
7. Define and illustrate cell hybridization; show how cell-hybridization techniques eventually might be used to treat human genetic disorders; cite at least one other use of this technology.
8. Define tissue transplantation, and show how this technique might be used to treat inheritable diseases.

Knowledge of the basic principles of inheritance is steadily increasing our ability to control the genetic traits of many organisms, people included. The prospect of "artificially" regulating the genetic traits of human beings is openly feared and opposed by many people. Some argue that any interference with the normal processes of fertilization and intrauterine development kindles disrespect for human life, is immoral, and therefore should not be tolerated under any circumstances.

Other people oppose the use of genetic technology on human beings for less subjective reasons. Some fear that dictatorships might use this technology to create a slave labor class of individuals who would be programmed genetically to "enjoy" serving a "master race." This concept appears to be inspired at least in part by Aldous Huxley's classic novel, "*Brave New World.*" Others fear that certain governments might use genetic technology in more subtle ways to discriminate for or against certain racial groups.

Some people object to further development of genetic technology because of its potential use in the production of new and insidious forms of biological weaponry. What if new species of pesticide-resistant parasites were produced by governments to thrive on species of grain-producing plants that grow exclusively in certain regions of the world? Could such parasites be used as political blackmail? What if genetic technology were used to produce species of bacteria that would be immune to all existing kinds of antibiotics? Without rigid precautions, such bacteria might escape from laboratories and infect millions of people with diseases that physicians would be unable to treat.

Most people who favor the use and further development of genetic technology agree that knowledge of basic genetic principles could be used for tyrannical purposes. They point out, however, that the antidote for tyranny stems from humane politics, not from a paralysis of science and technology. They argue that attempts to prevent governments from developing and using genetic technology are both futile and impractical. This technology will be developed somewhere, either openly or in secret.

Proponents of genetic technology also are concerned about the accidental escape of potentially dangerous organisms that are genetically altered in laboratories. But most of these people believe that strict use of safer containment procedures and policies provide adequate safeguards against such accidents. They point out that continued development of genetic technology offers the best hope of reducing the number of children who are born each year with genetic defects, approximately 250,000 annually in the United States alone. This number undoubtedly will increase, for medical science is facilitating the spread of deleterious mutations. Children who previously would have succumbed to genetic diseases now are being saved by medical treatment and are surviving to adulthood. As a result, the number of deleterious mutant genes that are passed on to each succeeding generation is increasing.

For example, the genetic disorder *pyloric stenosis* is increasing at a rate of 10 per cent per generation of Americans. The gene responsible for this affliction produces a deformity of the stomach that blocks passage of food into the small intestine. Fortunately, the deformity can be remedied by surgery. Unfortunately, the gene that causes this defect cannot be eliminated and often is passed on to the next generation. An increasing number of people favor use of genetic technology to impede proliferation of such mutant genes and to reduce the steadily increasing cost of treating and supporting people who have inherited them.

Thus, different people provide different answers to ethical questions that surround the varied uses of genetic technology. Such questions undoubtedly will increase in number and complexity, for techniques now being used to determine the traits of organisms will be supplemented by others in the near future. The nature and objectives of these techniques are presented to help you establish an informed opinion about the potential applications of genetic technology.

GENETIC COUNSELING AND SELECTIVE ABORTION

Most *genetic counseling* programs perform two principal functions: they screen individuals for deleterious mutations, and they forewarn prospective parents about the chances of their children inheriting a genetic disorder. Increasingly, these dual functions of genetic counseling are combining to reduce the numbers of human beings born with genetic diseases. For example, some married couples who discover that they both carry the same recessive allele for a genetic disorder decide to adopt a child or remain childless rather than run the risk of producing an abnormal individual.

In other cases, couples decide to risk pregnancy and then abort the fetus should it be abnormal. The practice of *selective abortion* normally is practicable only in cases where a genetic disorder of a fetus can be detected during the first months of pregnancy. The genetic status of many fetuses can be checked by *amniocentesis*, a process in which a thin tube is inserted into the amniotic fluid that surrounds a fetus (Fig. 28.1). The tube is passed into the amnion either through the vagina or abdo-

Fig. 28.1 Amniocentesis. Amniotic fluid contains fetal cells that can be withdrawn by a device that operates much like a hypodermic syringe. The fetal cells can then be examined for genetic abnormalities. *(From P. Ehrlich et al., "Biology and Society,"* © 1976 *by McGraw-Hill, Inc., New York.)*

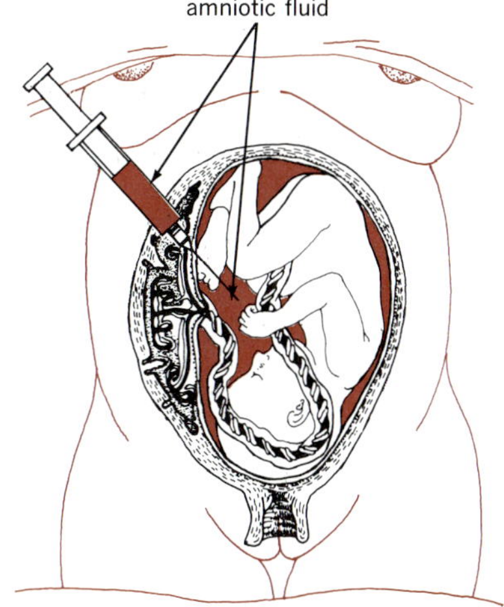

men of a pregnant woman, and a sample of the fluid is withdrawn. The sample invariably contains a few cells of the fetus, most of which are *fibroblasts.* These cells produce *collagen,* fiber-forming molecules that physically interconnect certain types of animal tissues (see Chap. 26). Fibroblasts can be examined for certain types of chromosome mutations. If such mutations are found, the prospective parents can choose to abort the abnormal fetus.

Many physicians recommend amniocentesis to older women who become pregnant. Although women over 40 years of age have only 2 per cent of all pregnancies, they produce 22 per cent of the children born with genetic disorders. Several of these disorders, such as Down's syndrome (see Chap. 27), are caused by chromosome mutations that can be detected by amniocentesis.

ARTIFICIAL GESTATION

As noted in Chap. 25, it has become possible to remove ova from women, fertilize such eggs with human sperms in glass containers, and implant one of the resulting embryos into the uterus of a woman. Such embryos can develop normally, producing children for apparently sterile couples. A related process, *artificial gestation,* someday may be used to spare many women the often psychologically traumatic experience of aborting a genetically defective fetus. The first steps of this hypothetical process will be similar to those used for intrauterine transplantation of a developing embryo. However, children produced by artificial gestation will pass through the embryonic period of development entirely within mechanical "wombs." Under these conditions, embryos could be watched and examined for genetic defects. Embryos that inherit genetic defects could be destroyed; those that develop normally could be maintained in the artificial "womb" until "birth." Such techniques probably will be accepted readily by some couples where both partners carry recessive genes for genetic disorders, by some women who have difficulty in "carrying" a fetus to term, and by women who wish to produce children but who do not wish to become pregnant.

It is difficult to predict when artificial gestation for human beings will become feasible. Normal development of mammalian embryos now can be maintained for several days in glass "wombs" that contain synthetic amniotic fluids. The greatest obstacle yet to be overcome is the manufacture of an effective artificial placenta. Until this occurs, it probably will not be possible to accommodate the normal exchange of substances that must flow into and out of a fetus during development.

CLONING

It may eventually be possible to predetermine the characteristics of human offspring by *cloning.* A *clone* is a group of organisms that have been produced from a single parent by vegetative reproduction. Unless mutations occur during the development of such cells, the resulting organisms of a clone are genetically identical to each other and to the original parent. For example, the circular group of sumac plants in Fig. 28.2 is a clone. Each of these plants originated as an outgrowth from the underground stems of a single, centrally located plant.

Although many organisms reproduce naturally by cloning, this form of vegetative reproduction occurs rarely or not at all among vertebrates. Nevertheless, the nuclei of all body cells of an organism are genetically identical to the zygote nucleus that produced them, and the genes of such nuclei theoretically should be able to direct development of a whole organism. Frogs and mice already have been used to test this hypothesis. The nuclei of frog eggs, for example, can be removed and replaced with diploid nuclei transplanted from intestinal cells of a single donor tadpole (Fig. 28.3) Of the reconstituted cells that undergo repeated divisions, many develop normally and differentiate as a clone of genetically identical frogs.

Several practical applications of cloning may become a reality in the next decade or two. The cloning of certain "select" cows, chickens, horses, and other animals may become economically more advantageous than selective breeding. Cloning also could be used to reduce the number of genetic disorders among human beings. Suppose, for example, that a husband and wife both carry a recessive gene for a genetic disease. Further assume that they do not want to produce a child through coitus because of the high probability that the child will

Fig. 28.2 Clones. Note the circular arrangement of this clone of sumac (lower foreground). Most of these plants have developed vegetatively from the underground stems of a single parent plant located at the center of the clone. All such plants are genetically identical. (*Courtesy of Hans-Erik Wennberg, Rhode Island College Audio Visual Department.*)

be abnormal. If cloning were a practical alternative, the woman could have a nucleus transplanted from one of her body cells (or from a body cell of her husband) to an enucleated human egg. The resulting diploid "zygote" then could be implanted in her uterus. Barring mutations, the child produced in this manner would be identical genetically to the parent who donated the nucleus.

There are other reasons why couples or individuals might choose to produce children by cloning. The technique could be used by sterile individuals, by those who wish to predetermine the sex of their children, and by individuals who wish to preserve a family likeness. Moreover, individuals of a clone would be able to donate organs to each other without fear of eliciting an immune response. It may even become possible to "disassemble" individual members of a clone when they die, freeze their healthy organs, and thus have a ready supply of "spare parts" should they be needed by any living members of the clone. Such possibilities raise a host of legal and ethical issues that must be examined before the technology required for human cloning is fully developed.

MANIPULATION OF GENES

Recombinant DNA

Certain methods of genetic control can be used to alter, delete, substitute, or replace specific genes or specific groups of genes in cells. The most controversial and most widely publicized of these techniques involves splicing together segments of DNA derived from cells of two or more species. Such hybridized DNA is termed *recombinant DNA*.

The ability to synthesize recombinant DNA largely grew out of the discovery of two kinds of enzymes, *DNA ligases* and *restriction endonucleases*. Discovered almost simultaneously in five labo-

Fig. 28.3 Experimental cloning of frogs. The nuclei of three genetically different frog eggs can be removed (as in 1) and replaced with nuclei obtained from the cells of a single young frog embryo (as in 2). Because the nuclei of the frog embryo are all genetically identical, so are the tadpoles that result from the nuclear transplants.

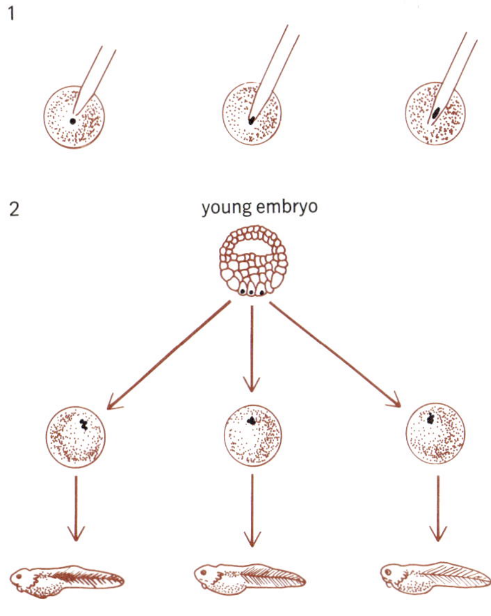

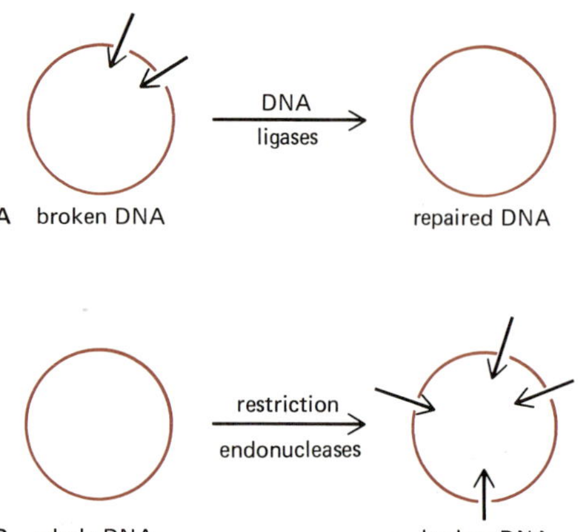

Fig. 28.4 DNA ligases and restriction endonucleases. (A) DNA ligases repair breaks (arrows) in DNA strands. The DNA of bacteria and many viruses is arranged in continuous loops, as shown. (B) Restriction endonucleases create breaks (arrows) in DNA by cleaving chemical bonds at specific sites in the nucleic acid strands.

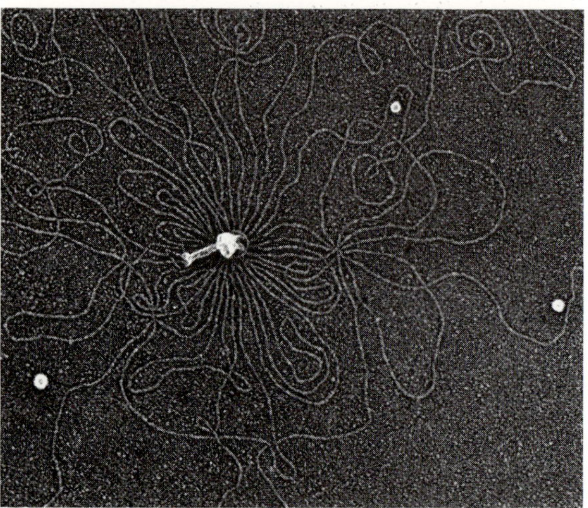

Fig. 28.5 Bacteriophages. (A) Structure. This phage (center) has been "shocked" by immersion in a solution that triggered release of its DNA (the long filament looped around the phage coat). Note the enormous amount of DNA normally packed into the phage head. A schematic representation of this type of phage structure is depicted in Fig. 1 of the Biology Highlight in Chap. 22. (B) The general life cycle of many phages is illustrated here. The DNA of some phages, such as phage lambda, can become incorporated into the circular DNA strand of the host bacterium. In such cases, phage DNA is replicated along with bacterial DNA. After a variable number of replications, the phage DNA can detach from the circular bacterial DNA and replicate independently. Phage DNA then causes formation of mRNA with genetic messages of the virus, and some of these messages cause formation of enzymes that destroy the circular DNA of the bacterial cell. The DNA of other phages does not become integrated with bacterial DNA. Instead, phage DNA replicates immediately and manufactures mRNA. Some of the mRNA produce enzymes that destroy the bacterial DNA. Other molecules of mRNA direct synthesis of new phages, which eventually burst through the wall of the host cell. (C) Phage infection of a bacterial cell. Several phages (dark particles) are in the bacterium. (D) The remnants of a bacterial cell after attack by bacteriophages. The viruses are small rodlets with knobby ends.

ratories in 1967, DNA ligases are enzymes that repair breaks in DNA. By contrast, restriction endonucleases, often simply called *restriction enzymes,* produce breaks at specific points in DNA strands (Fig. 28.4). These latter enzymes were discovered by microbiologists studying the life cycles of *bacteriophages,* a group of viruses that infect bacteria (Fig. 28.5).

Bacteriophages, or more simply *phages,* propagate by injecting their DNA into bacterial cells. The viral nucleic acid replicates repeatedly inside a host bacterium, producing multiple copies of DNA that become the genetic material of new viruses. Freshly produced phages then escape from the host cell, often destroying it as they leave, and repeat the life cycle by infecting other bacteria (see Fig. 28.5).

Investigators studying life cycles of viruses have noted that phages grown on certain strains of *E. coli* often display decreased ability to infect subsequent strains. This restricted growth on secondary strains was found to result from a group of *E. coli* enzymes that "recognize" specific sites on "foreign" DNA and cleave the molecule at these sites. Such enzymes, now called restriction endonucleases, inhibit subsequent infections of phages by breaking chemical bonds at internal sites in viral nucleic acids. Similar enzymes that remove terminal nucleotides from nucleic acids are called *exonucleases* (*endo-* = within, *exo-* = without; see Section A of Glossary).

Over 150 restriction enzymes have been found in many species of bacteria. The enzymes are highly specific for foreign DNA. They do not cleave the DNA of the parent bacterium. Such "self" DNA is protected from endonuclease attack

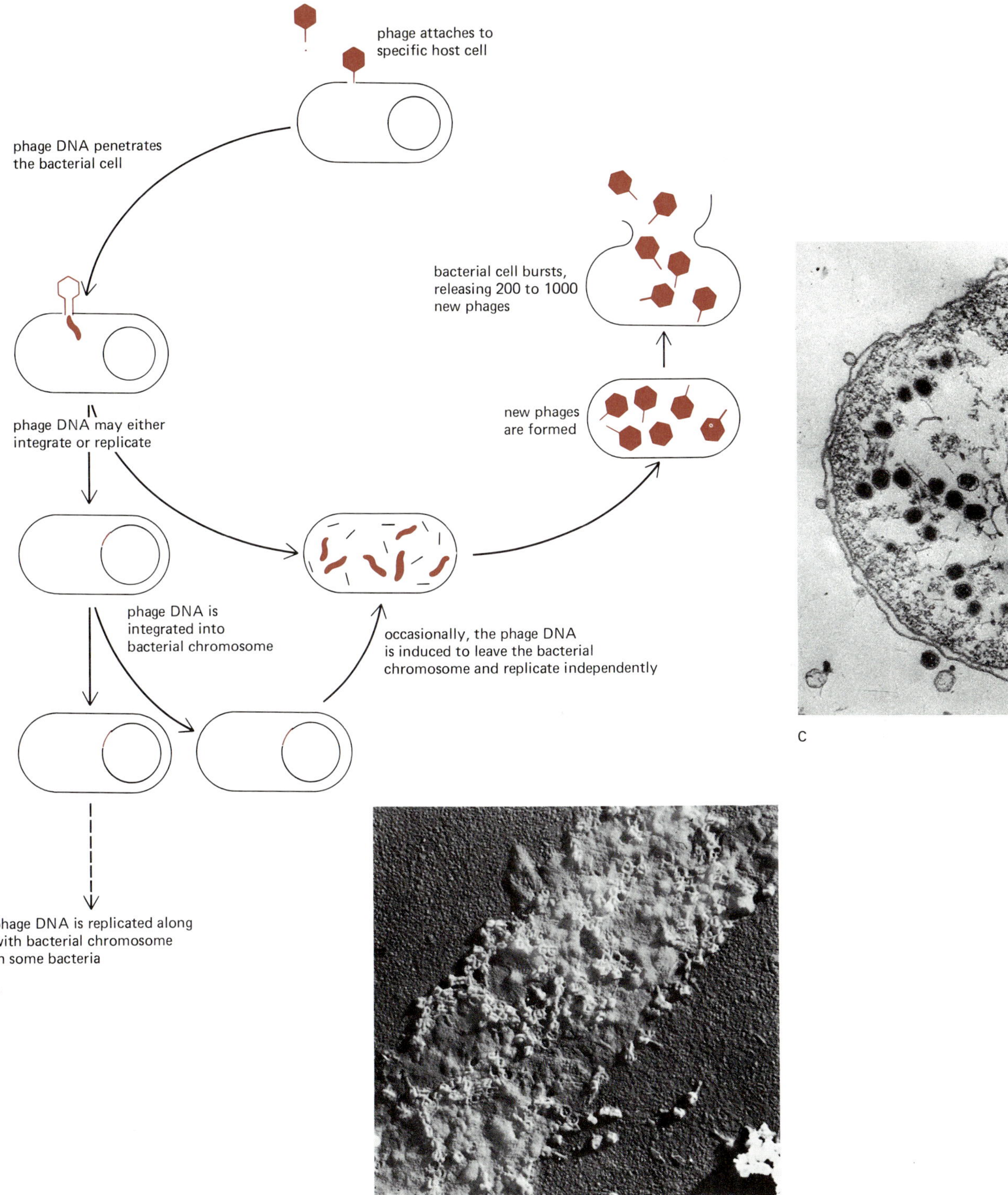
phage attaches to specific host cell
phage DNA penetrates the bacterial cell
bacterial cell bursts, releasing 200 to 1000 new phages
phage DNA may either integrate or replicate
new phages are formed
phage DNA is integrated into bacterial chromosome
occasionally, the phage DNA is induced to leave the bacterial chromosome and replicate independently
phage DNA is replicated along with bacterial chromosome in some bacteria

B

C

D

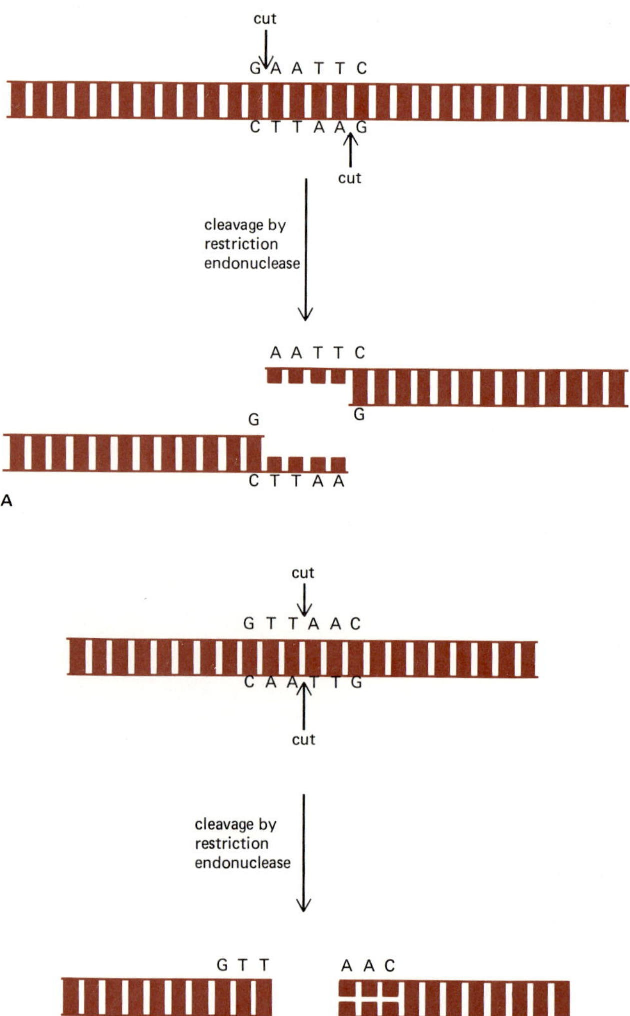

Fig. 28.6 Restriction endonucleases. (A) Cleavage of DNA by restriction endonuclease Eco R1. This enzyme recognizes the palindrome $\frac{\text{GAATTC}}{\text{CTTAAG}}$ and cleaves between G and A (arrows). The resulting cuts are staggered; i.e., they are single-stranded ends with complementary base-pair sequences. (B) Cleavage of DNA by restriction endonuclease Hpa 1. Note that this enzyme cuts the palindrome between T and A, producing an even break.

by methyl (CH_3—) groups, which project from nucleotides and which are recognition sites for restriction enzymes. Methyl groups are not present on nucleotides of viral DNA.

Recognition sites for most (perhaps all) restriction enzymes are *palindromes,* segments of DNA in which identical nucleotide base sequences run in opposite directions (Fig. 28.6) Some restriction enzymes create breaks at identical points in each DNA strand, producing so-called *even breaks.* Others produce breaks in the two strands that are separated by several nucleotides. Because of the symmetrical palindromic arrangement of nucleotides in the recognition site, these restriction enzymes yield fragments of DNA that end as short, single-stranded projections. Moreover, the two projections created by these endonucleases consist of complementary nitrogen base sequences (see Fig. 28.6). Pieces of DNA containing such *staggered breaks* can be rejoined by DNA ligases, but these segments also can interlock with pieces of DNA obtained from any cell. Cleavage of DNA by restriction enzymes depends only on the presence of specific recognition sites.

Thus, all fragments of DNA produced by a given endonuclease have the same self-complementary ends regardless of source. DNA from a variety of species therefore can be broken into a large number of pieces by restriction enzymes and then interjoined by DNA ligases in virtually any order.

By 1973, several investigators were using these enzymes to cut and rejoin segments of DNA, and this represented a major step in the development of artificial methods of manipulating genes in living systems. But because genes normally cannot be propagated or expressed outside living cells, some sort of "carrier" was needed to insert laboratory-produced recombinant DNA into cells. *Plasmids* seemed well suited for this purpose.

Plasmids are small circular strands of DNA that replicate independently of the main bacterial chromosome. Plasmid sizes vary considerably; some carry only one to three genes, others are up to 30 per cent as large as the main chromosome. One category of plasmids contains genes that confer antibiotic resistance. Bacteria having such genes often cannot be killed by ampicillin, streptomycin, or other antibiotics.

Use of plasmids as vehicles for the insertion of recombinant DNA into bacteria is best explained through a specific example. In the early 1970s, Stanley Cohen and his colleagues at Stanford University isolated a small plasmid of *E. coli* that could be cleaved at one point by a restriction en-

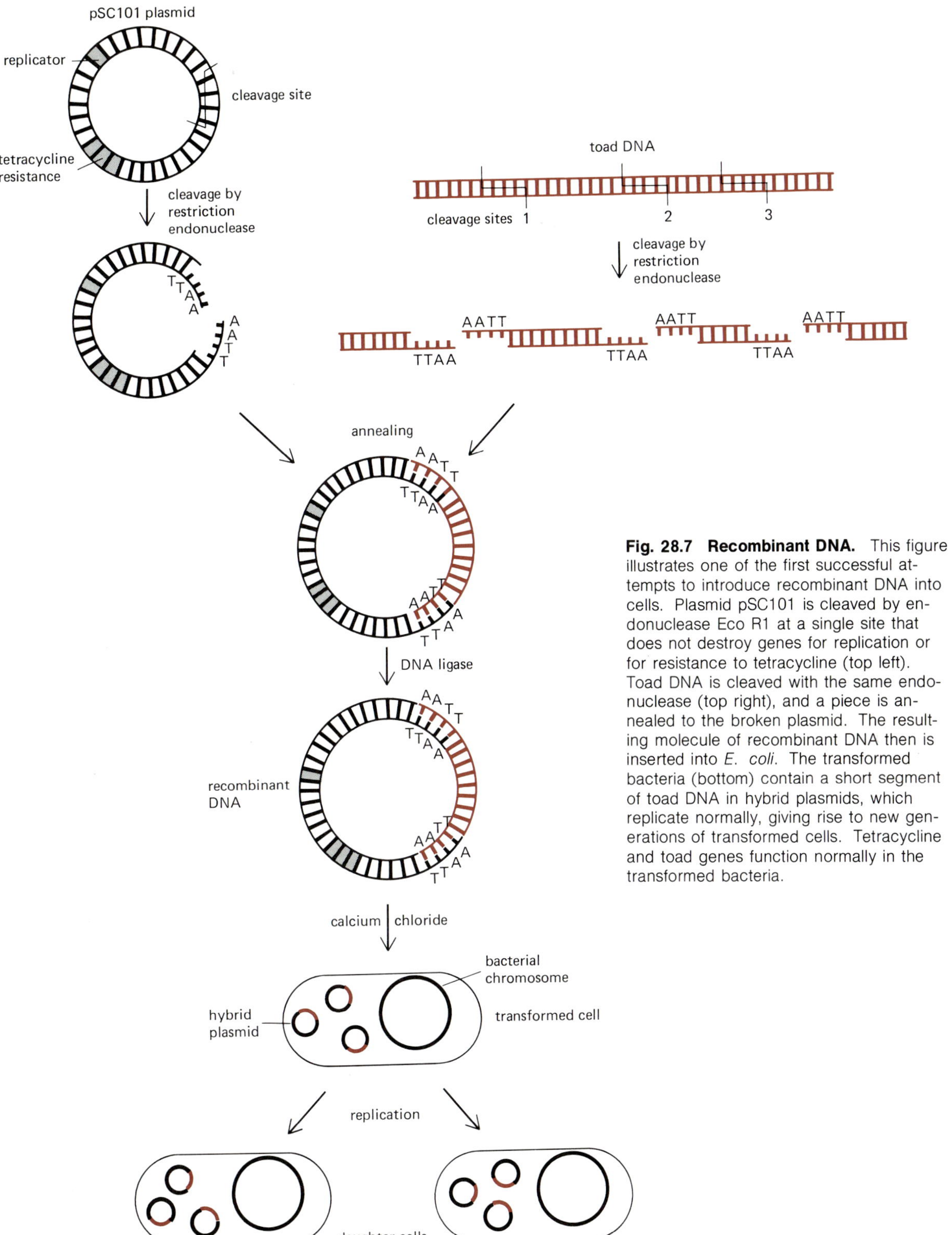

Fig. 28.7 Recombinant DNA. This figure illustrates one of the first successful attempts to introduce recombinant DNA into cells. Plasmid pSC101 is cleaved by endonuclease Eco R1 at a single site that does not destroy genes for replication or for resistance to tetracycline (top left). Toad DNA is cleaved with the same endonuclease (top right), and a piece is annealed to the broken plasmid. The resulting molecule of recombinant DNA then is inserted into *E. coli*. The transformed bacteria (bottom) contain a short segment of toad DNA in hybrid plasmids, which replicate normally, giving rise to new generations of transformed cells. Tetracycline and toad genes function normally in the transformed bacteria.

zyme. The cleavage yielded a linear plasmid with self-complementary staggered breaks at each end (Fig. 28.7). The plasmid, called pSC101, contains genes conferring resistance to the antibiotic *tetracycline.* Cohen next used the same restriction enzyme to isolate segments of DNA from the cells of African toads. Some of these segments contained genes that code for certain ribosomal proteins. DNA ligases then were used to attach segments of toad DNA to pSC101 plasmids (see Fig. 28.7).

The final step, inserting the recombinant DNA into bacterial cells, was accomplished by treating *E. coli* with a solution containing calcium chloride. The solution alters the permeability of bacterial cell membranes, permitting transfer of plasmids from the extracellular environment into the cells. When analyzed, the treated bacteria were found to be tetracycline-resistant *and* to contain genes producing toad ribosomal proteins. This experiment was one of the first to demonstrate that animal genes can be introduced into bacteria as components of recombinant DNA and that such genes can function normally in nonanimal cells.

Plasmids are not the only structures capable of inserting recombinant DNA into cells. Certain viruses, such as the well-studied bacteriophage *lambda* (λ), also can serve as carriers. These viruses do not always multiply after entering a host cell. Instead, the small, circular viral chromsome becomes inserted in a specific section of a host chromosome. In such instances, the viral chromosome becomes an integral part of the host chromosome and is replicated simultaneously with host genes (see Fig. 28.5). As a result, descendants of the originally infected cell often contain identical copies of viral genes. Viral chromosomes do not always remain permanently fused to host chromosomes, however. The segment of virus DNA can detach and replicate repeatedly. Each copy of viral nucleic acid becomes part of a new virus, which usually breaks through the plasma membrane of the host, ready to infect another cell.

Most viral genes appear to remain in a quiescent, repressed state while part of a host chromosome, but some viral genes can be expressed under these conditions, and a few viruses have been used to insert viable molecules of recombinant DNA into bacterial cells. For example, genes coding for ribosomal RNA of mouse cells have been spliced into the viral chromosome of phage lambda. Investigators can then insert the mouse genes into *E. coli* chromosomes by infecting the bacteria with the treated phage. Phages have even been used to insert artificial, wholly laboratory-synthesized genes into bacteria.

Other viruses can be used to insert recombinant DNA into nonbacterial cells. Indeed, it was a proposal for a series of gene-transfer experiments using *SV40 tumor viruses* that first triggered widespread concern over the possible hazards of recombinant-DNA research. SV40 viruses, first discovered in cultures of rhesus monkey kidney cells, have been shown to produce cancerous tumors in hamsters (Fig. 28.8). The viruses can also be used to transfer recombinant DNA into mammalian cells, human cells included.

Although insertion of artificial genes into cells and the splicing together of genes from different species at first may seem nothing more than fancy biochemical manipulations having little practical significance, many people believe recombinant DNA techniques have at least as much potential for good—or harm—as the earlier development of atomic nuclear technology.

Pessimists have put forth many worst-case scenarios. What if genes for smallpox, typhoid, diptheria, polio, or cancer were inserted into *E. coli,* bacteria found in the intestines of all human beings? Could recombinant-DNA technology be used to trigger worldwide epidemics? Could genetically altered organisms provide new tools for terrorists? Could organisms be artificially modified to give

Fig. 28.8 Tumor viruses. A large, viral-induced tumor (fibrosarcoma) projects from the left hip of this rhesus monkey fetus.

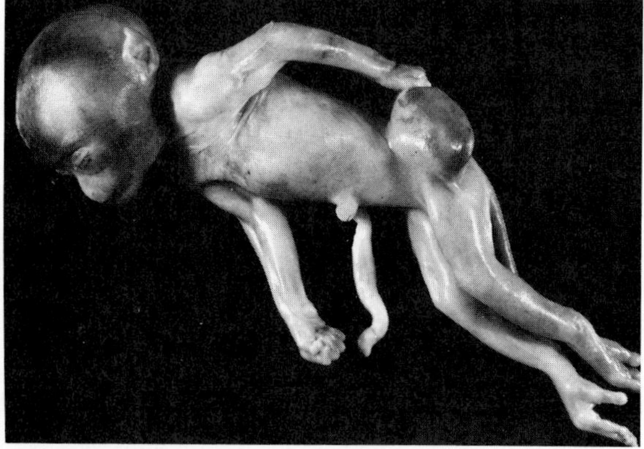

them a competitive advantage over other species, and could this competitive edge produce catastrophic ecological imbalances? Could genes be modified to manipulate human behavior?

The potential for harm is sufficiently alarming to warrant caution. Indeed, scientists throughout the world instituted a self-imposed moratorium on certain kinds of recombinant-DNA research in 1974. Formal discussions concerned with the potential hazards of recombinant-DNA research were held during the moratorium. Scientists, political leaders, health officials, and citizens participated in the discussions, which eventually led to a series of American guidelines regulating federally funded recombinant-DNA research projects. Many of these guidelines, first established in 1976 by the National Institutes of Health (NIH), have been adopted by governments of other countries.

The NIH guidelines balance the estimated risk of a given experiment with specific measures designed to contain the risk. Most recombinant-DNA experiments using *E. coli,* for example, must employ a genetically altered strain that can survive only in an artificial environment found exclusively in specially prepared culture media.

Happily, none of the worst-case scenarios has become a reality, and it may not be possible to create ugly monsters that crawl from test tubes and head for town, as depicted in horror movies of the 1950s. There are several reasons why scientists are now convinced that some of their worst fears are unfounded. For example, genes of eukaryotes appear to be organized so differently from those of prokaryotes that significant functional interactions between the two kinds of genes probably can occur only under conditions controlled by researchers.

Moreover, scientists now suspect that ample opportunities always have existed for exchange of DNA between prokaryotes and between pro- and eukaryotes. Bacteria can absorb naked DNA released from dead or decaying cells, a process called *transformation,* and such "foreign" DNA can become part of bacterial chromosomes (see Fig. 30.16). Thus, prokaryotes might routinely incorporate animal genes as they contribute to the decay of dead organisms. Human genes similarly might enter *E. coli* from dead cells that slough off the walls of the intestine. If so, many natural recombinant-DNA "experiments" have already occurred, without producing new viable strains of "superbugs."

By contrast, some of the best-case scenarios are becoming realities far more quickly than most scientists had anticipated. For example, the process of obtaining insulin from slaughterhouse animals is both time-consuming and costly. Moreover, there are increasing difficulties in meeting the rising demand for insulin. Plentiful supplies of insulin might be produced more cheaply by inserting insulin genes of mammals into *E. coli.*

During the mid-1970s, several knowledgeable scientists stated that at least a decade would be required to develop the technology for bacterial production of insulin, but by 1980 teams of biologists had already synthesized fragments of the insulin genes, assembled the pieces, and inserted the fragments into *E. coli* plasmids. To provide regulatory control, the scientists also inserted an operator and a promotor region (see Chap. 15) alongside the insulin genes. When the treated plasmids were placed into *E. coli,* the genetic components responded and began manufacturing insulin along with normal bacterial products.

Moreover, genetic engineers have inserted into *E. coli* genes that code for human *interferon,* an antiviral substance (see Chap. 30). Mass production of interferon undoubtedly will provide new methods for treating many viral diseases, including influenza and the common cold. In addition, growth hormone, a secretion of the anterior pituitary (see Chap. 17), is being manufactured by genetically altered bacteria, and bacterial manufacture of other mammalian proteins seems certain.

Recombinant-DNA techniques might also provide a means of transferring genes responsible for the nitrogen-fixing properties of certain microbes to chromosomes of wheat, rice, and other agriculturally useful plants (see Chap. 8 for a discussion of the nitrogen cycle). Such transfers might increase food production, while simultaneously decreasing the need for expensive inorganic fertilizers (see Chap. 11). It may even become possible to create enzymes that can react with inorganic compounds and sunlight in the direct production of food, commercial fuels, and other valuable organic substances.

Further, use of enzymes to cleave DNA and to splice genes together in different combinations is a tool of unprecedented value in identifying positions of genes on chromosomes and studying gene expression. In addition, recombinant-DNA technology already has provided substantial information about why certain genes cause cancer and why others produce abnormalities during embryonic development. Such information will almost certainly speed development of many new therapeutic procedures.

Despite such progress, the debate over the safety and suitability of recombinant-DNA research continues, largely because of disagreements over "estimated risks." What appears to be a low or moderate risk to some people is viewed by others as a much greater risk. The problem of evaluating estimated risks becomes especially difficult whenever specific issues involve large-scale value judgments. For example, should corporations have the right (as they do now) to patent genetically engineered forms of life? Questions such as these clearly involve considerations that extend far beyond the realm of science alone.

Cell Hybridization and Tissue Transplantation

A less widely publicized method of genetic manipulation is *cell hybridization,* a technique that involves fusing together animal cells of different species.

The fusion process can be carried out with surprising ease. Cells from two different animals, mice and human beings, for example, are mixed in a laboratory dish. After several hours, some mouse and human cells will fuse spontaneously, forming hybrid cells that contain genetic information from both species. Fusion can be enhanced by adding agents such as *Sendai virus* to the culture dish. This virus triggers formation of cytoplasmic bridges between closely adjacent cells.

The cultured cells then are placed in special selective solutions that simultaneously provide a favorable environment for rapid proliferation of fused cells and an unfavorable environment for reproduction of unfused cells. As a result, large colonies of hybrid cells form in the special culture media, each colony resulting from proliferation of a single fused cell (Fig. 28.9).

Much of the genetic material from one of the two original cell types usually is lost as the hybrid cells divide. For example, hybrids of mouse and human cells might be expected to contain 86 chromosomes, 40 donated by the mouse cell and 46 by the human cell. But the hybrids always have fewer than 86, the usual number being anywhere from 41 to 55 chromosomes. All 40 mouse chromosomes typically are present in the hybrid cells; most human chromosomes are lost. The loss of individual human chromosomes is random, however, and hybrid cells therefore contain different combinations of functional mouse and human chromosomes. Moreover, the two groups of chromosomes can be distinguished from each other, as can the products of their respective genes.

Genes normally inactive in a specific cell type sometimes begin to be transcribed when present in hybrid cells. The blood-plasma protein *albumin,* for example, is produced by liver cells but not by white blood cells. However, when mouse liver cells and human white blood cells are fused, some of the hybrids produce *human* albumin (Fig. 28.10).

The ability to trigger expression of normally repressed genes has great practical value. Such techniques provide yet another method of studying how eukaryotic genes are turned on and off during the normal differentiation of cells, and they could establish a means of detecting hereditary diseases in developing human embryos. Prenatal detection of human genetic diseases is now largely confined to diseases involving gross abnormalities of chromosomes, which can be observed in fibroblasts extracted from amniotic fluid, or to diseases involving enzymes normally produced by fibroblasts. Genetic diseases involving defective enzymes of the brain, liver, and most other organs cannot be evaluated through amniocentesis; the cells of these organs are not present in amniotic fluid, and they cannot be obtained safely through alternative procedures. However, it may become possible to hybridize fibroblasts of human embryos with cells of other species to "force" expression of genes not normally active in fibroblasts, thereby revealing enzymes produced in a wide variety of cell types.

Cell-hybridization techniques may prove valuable in still other ways. DNA from one species occasionally becomes attached permanently to a chromosome of the other species in fused cells. Thus, at least in principle, cell hybridization could be used to replace a defective gene of one individual with a normal gene from a second individual. For example, it eventually may be possible to remove genetically defective cells from a human being, place the cells in culture media, transfer normal genes to them by cell hybridization, and then

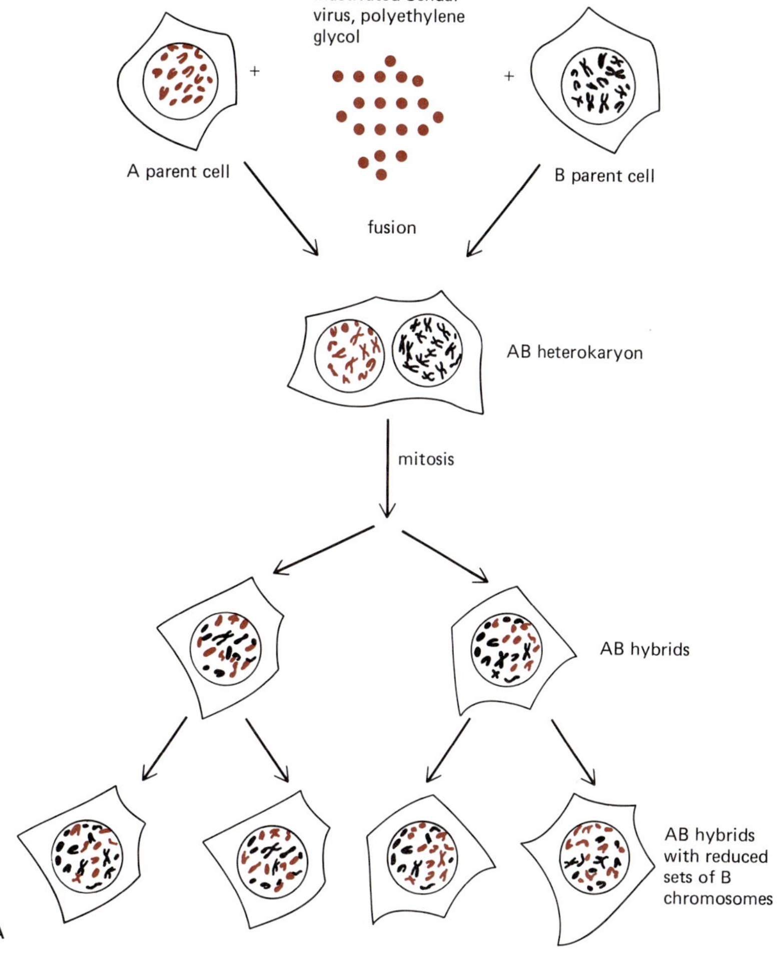

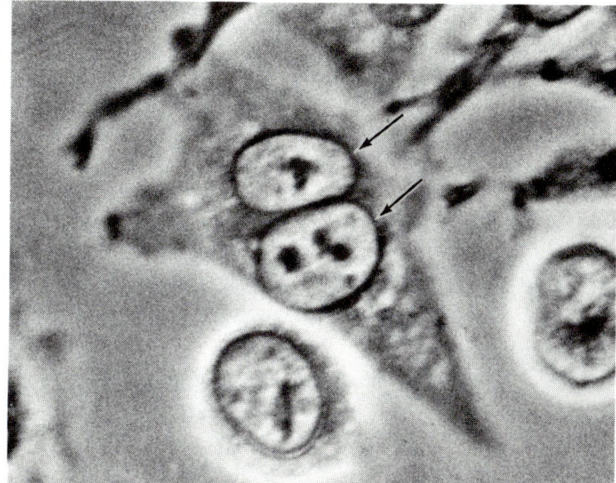

Fig. 28.9 Cell hybridization. (A) Cells from different species can be induced to fuse through use of agents such as Sendai virus or the chemical polyethylene glycol. The immediate result of fusion is a so-called heterokaryon, a single cell containing nuclei derived from cells of different species. The heterokaryon then divides, giving rise to two mononucleate hybrid cells. As the hybrids continue to divide, most of the chromosomes from one of the parent cells are lost. (B) A heterokaryon, derived from a mouse fibroblast and a rat myoblast (embryonic muscle cell), is visible in the center of this photograph. Note the two nuclei, indicated by the arrows. The fibroblast nucleus is below that of the rat myoblast. Parental cell types are also visible in the photograph. A mouse fibroblast is located just below the heterokaryon.

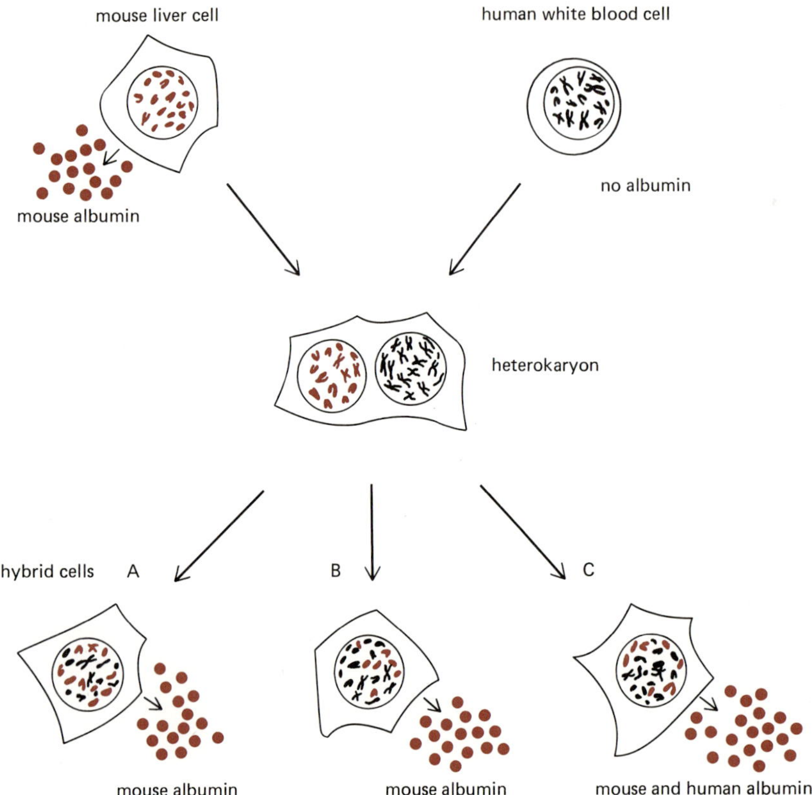

Fig. 28.10 Gene activation. The technology of cell hybridization has proved useful in elucidating mechanisms of gene control in eukaryotes. Heterokaryons can be formed through fusion of mouse liver cells and human white blood cells. Some of the resulting hybrid cells produce human albumin. Genes for this protein, normally repressed in white blood cells, have been activated as a result of hybridization.

transplant the "repaired" cells into the afflicted individual.

Other methods of gene manipulation are being developed as well. A few scientists are attempting to improve the function of genetically defective human tissues through *tissue transplantation.* These techniques involve transplantation of normal tissues from healthy donors to individuals who have inherited genetic disorders of corresponding tissues. Such techniques have met with limited success, largely because of immunogenic incompatibilities between donor and host. Despite these setbacks, some biologists predict that tissue transplantation may become the most successful method of alleviating genetic diseases of blood, such as hemophilia and sickle-cell anemia.

Unlike selective abortion, artificial gestation, and cloning, the objectives of gene manipulation techniques are aimed chiefly at determining the location of genes on chromosomes and understanding how gene expression is regulated. But, as we have seen, the knowledge gained from this research will be used to treat people who have inherited genetic abnormalities. The ability to repair mutant genes will not develop quickly. The controlled replacement of even single-gene defects probably is still many years away, and replacement of large numbers of genes will be impossible for several more decades at the very least. Unfortunately, like most genetic traits, most genetic disorders result from the combined actions of many genes.

Nevertheless, many of the techniques discussed in this chapter will be refined, producing even more powerful tools with which to study and control gene expression. How such tools should be used remains an open question, a problem that reflects one of the greatest challenges facing human society. The issue is stated particularly well by biologist Clifford Grobstein:

> *The policy challenge we face, refracted in the exquisite structure and potential of the double helix, is whether we can create institutions able to transform the fruits of an age of reason into the achievements of an age of intervention.*

Review Questions

1 Describe the objectives of genetic counseling. What is amniocentesis, and how is this technique used in genetic counseling?

2 What is artificial gestation? What is the major technological obstacle that must be overcome if artificial gestation is to be practicable for human beings?

3 What is a clone? Describe a technique that has been used to clone amphibians. Do such techniques have any practical applications?

4 Describe methods used to produce organisms containing genes of different species. Of what use are DNA ligases, restriction endonucleases, plasmids, and phages in producing such organisms?

5 Stage a debate concerning the potential hazards of recombinant-DNA technology. Present arguments for or against best- and worst-case scenarios that relate to continued use of recombinant-DNA technology.

6 Generally describe how biologists fuse together cells of different species. Evaluate the practical and scientific benefits of research involving cell hybridization and tissue transplantation.

7 Should people be permitted to produce children by artificial gestation or cloning? Should development of genetic technology be discontinued? Controlled? Should genetic technology be used to control the characteristics of human offspring? If so, how or under what conditions? Evaluate your attitudes toward the ethics of genetic control. Should the right of scientific inquiry sometimes be limited in the interests of society? If so, under what circumstances?

Collateral Readings

Abelson, J.: Recombinant DNA: Examples of Present-Day Research, *Science,* vol. 196, p. 159, Apr. 8, 1977. This entire issue of *Science* is devoted to recombinant-DNA research. Abelson's summary article provides background for the series of papers that follow. For the advanced student.

Cohen, S. N.: The Manipulation of Genes, *Scientific American,* July 1975. This article contains a description of some of the most recent attempts to manipulate genes. The article also discusses possible future uses of such techniques.

——— and **J. A. Shapiro:** Transposable Genetic Elements, *Scientific American,* February 1980. Evidence is presented suggesting that genes naturally pass between bacteria, viruses, and the chromosomes of eukaryotes. The evolutionary significance of such gene exchanges is discussed.

Fletcher, J.: "The Ethics of Genetic Control," Anchor Books, Garden City, N.Y., 1974. The techniques and ethics of genetic control are discussed.

Friedmann, T.: Prenatal Diagnosis of Genetic Disease, *Scientific American,* November 1971. Describes techniques that can detect hereditary disease of human embryos early in pregnancy. The author also speculates on the future use of such techniques. Recommended.

Fuchs, F.: Genetic Amniocentesis, *Scientific American,* June 1980. Describes how and why this procedure is performed.

Goodfield, J.: "Playing God: Genetic Engineering and the Manipulation of Life," Random House, New York, 1977. Perhaps the best-written of the many popular books on development and potential uses of recombinant-DNA technology.

Grobstein, C.: The Recombinant DNA Debate, *Scientific American,* July 1977. A noted scientist analyzes the controversy surrounding the applications of this new technology.

———**:** "A Double Image of the Double Helix: The Recombinant DNA Debate," Freeman, San Francisco, 1979. The background, course, and significance of the controversy over recombinant-DNA research is described in much greater detail.

Scientific American, September 1981. The entire issue is concerned with the industrial applications of genetic technology.

Sigurbjörnsson, B.: Induced Mutations in Plants, *Scientific American,* January 1971. A discussion of how new varieties of plants have been produced by exposing seeds to agents that induce mutations. The practical applications of such techniques are described.

Chapter 29 Evolution

Learning Objectives

After reading this chapter you should be able to:

1. State the concepts of spontaneous generation and immutability of species; show how Francesco Redi obtained evidence against the concept of spontaneous generation.
2. Differentiate between the evolutionary theories of Lamarck and of Darwin and Wallace; describe an experiment that provided evidence against Lamarck's theory of evolution.
3. Name the three main observations and the two conclusions drawn from these observations that constitute the basis of the Darwin-Wallace theory of natural selection; explain why the expressions "survival of the fittest" or "elimination of the unfit" should not be used to sum up the essence of the theory of natural selection.
4. Define the modern meaning of the theory of evolution; show how sexual recombination, mutation, and differential reproduction influence evolution; define natural selection and illustrate how this process influences the traits of organisms within populations; explain why natural selection tends to result in improved adaptation.
5. State the Hardy-Weinberg law; list and illustrate three conditions that disturb a Hardy-Weinberg equilibrium; explain how recessive genes can spread through a population; define and give an example of genetic drift.
6. Define species in genetic terms, and illustrate the process of speciation; differentiate between geographic and biological barriers to interbreeding and give an example of each; define, illustrate, and list biological evidence for the theory of continental drift; explain how new species can be produced artificially.
7. Indicate how rates of evolution are related to environmental stability; construct a diagram that depicts the general evolutionary relations between organisms; show why it is incorrect to speak of an evolutionary "ladder" or "scale"; define and illustrate adaptive radiation.
8. Define extinction; identify the general cause of all extinctions.
9. Define evolutionary replacement; differentiate between evolutionary divergence and convergence, and give at least one example of each.
10. Define random opportunism and state its evolutionary significance.
11. Identify and describe at least two experiments which demonstrate that behavior can be gene-influenced.
12. Define sociobiology; give an example of altruism and provide a biological definition of this term; define kin selection, list evidence supporting this theory, and show how sociobiologists use the theory of kin selection to explain the evolution of altruism; distinguish between personal and inclusive fitness.
13. State the central theorem of sociobiology and show how it has been used to increase our understanding of animal behavior.
14. Distinguish between biological and environmental determinists and describe the respective positions of these two groups in the debate over the influence of genes on human behavior; define the nature-vs.-nurture controversy and specify its historical relationship to current debates relating to human sociobiology.

In individual organisms, the interplay between sex, heredity, and environment results in various degrees of individual adaptation. In the long reproductive succession of organisms, this same interplay results in *evolution*—the origin of new species from preexisting species.

That evolution really occurs did not become definitely established till the nineteenth century. Some of the forces that drive and guide evolutional processes are now understood quite thoroughly, and evolution on a small scale can actually be brought about in the laboratory. Accordingly, the latter sections of this chapter deal with the *forces* of evolution as understood today and with the *nature* of evolution as determined by the underlying forces.

BACKGROUND

Early Concepts

The earliest written discussion of organic creation is contained in the Old Testament: God made the world and its living inhabitants in 6 days, people coming last. Later ideas included those of *spontaneous generation* and of *immutability of species*, which largely held sway until the eighteenth and nineteenth centuries. Each species was considered to have been created spontaneously, completely developed, from dust, dirt, and other nonliving sources. And once created, a species was held to be fixed and immutable, unable to change its characteristics.

In the sixth to fourth centuries B.C., Anaximander, Empedocles, and Aristotle independently considered the possibility that living forms might represent a *succession* rather than unrelated, randomly created types. However, the succession was thought of in an essentially philosophical way, as a progression from "less nearly perfect" to "more nearly perfect" forms. The historical nature of succession and the continuity of life were not yet recognized.

Francesco Redi, an Italian physician of the seventeenth century, was the first to obtain evidence against the idea of spontaneous generation, by showing experimentally that organisms could not arise from nonliving sources. Contrary to notions held at the time and earlier, Redi demonstrated that maggots would not form spontaneously in meat if flies were prevented from laying their eggs on the meat. But old beliefs die slowly, and it was not until the nineteenth century, chiefly through the work of Louis Pasteur on bacteria, that the notion of spontaneous generation finally ceased to be influential.

Evolution: The Lamarckian Concept

By this time, the idea of continuity and historical succession, or *evolution*, had occurred to a number of thinkers. An important theory of evolution was that of the French biologist Lamarck, published in 1809. To explain how evolution occurred, Lamarck proposed the two ideas of *use and disuse of parts* and of *inheritance of acquired characteristics*. He had observed that if a body part of an organism was used extensively, such a part would enlarge and become more efficient; but that if a structure was not fully employed, it would degenerate and atrophy. Therefore, by differential use and disuse of various body parts during its lifetime, an organism would change to some extent and would acquire certain traits. Lamarck then thought that such acquired traits were inheritable and could be transmitted to offspring.

According to this Lamarckian scheme, evolution would come about somewhat as follows. Suppose a given short-necked ancestral animal feeds on tree leaves. As it clears off the lower levels of a tree, it stretches its neck to reach farther up. During a lifetime of stretching the neck becomes a little longer, and a slightly longer neck is then inherited by the offspring. These in turn feed on tree leaves and keep on stretching their necks; and so on, for many generations. In time a very long-necked animal is formed, something like a modern giraffe.

This theory was exceedingly successful and did much to spread the idea of evolution. But Lamarck's views ultimately proved to be untenable. That use and disuse do lead to acquired traits is quite correct. For example, it is common knowledge that much exercise builds powerful muscles. However, Lamarck was mistaken in assuming that such (nongenetic) acquired variations were inheritable. Acquired traits are *not* inheritable, since they are effects produced by environment and development, not by genes. Only *genetic* traits are inheritable, and then only if such traits are controlled by the genes present in the reproductive cells. What happens to cells other than gametes through use and disuse, or in any other way for that matter, does not affect the genes of the gametes. Accordingly, although Lamarck observed some of the effects of use and disuse correctly in some cases, such effects cannot play a role in evolution.

One famous attempt at experimental refutation of Lamarckism was carried out by Weismann, an eminent biologist of the nineteenth century. The tails of mice were cut off for very many successive generations. According to Lamarck, such enforced disuse of tails should eventually have led to tailless mice. Yet mice in the last generation of the experiment still grew tails as long as those of their ancestors.

Evolution: The Darwin-Wallace Concept

The year in which Lamarck published his theory, 1809, was also the year in which Charles Darwin was born. In 1831, at the age of 22, Darwin sailed aboard the H.M.S. *Beagle* on a 5-year circumglobal voyage. The ship was under orders to complete a survey of the coasts of South America, which the crews of the *Beagle* and the H.M.S. *Adventure* had begun in earlier voyages. Throughout the expedition Darwin made innumerable observations and collected a large number of different plants and animals.

After returning home, Darwin spent nearly 20 years sifting and studying the collected data. In the course of his work, he found evidence for certain generalizations. Another biologist, Alfred Russel Wallace, independently had been led to substantially the same generalizations, which he communicated to Darwin. In 1858 Darwin and Wallace together announced a new theory of evolution, which was to supplant that of Lamarck. Darwin also elaborated the new theory in book form. This famous work, entitled "On the Origin of Species by Means of Natural Selection, or the Preservation of Favored Races in the Struggle for Life," was published in 1859.

In essence, the Darwin-Wallace *theory of natural selection* is based on three observations and on two conclusions drawn from these observations.

Observation Without environmental resistance, every species tends to multiply in geometric progression (see also Chap. 8).

In other words, a population doubling its number in a first year possesses a sufficient reproductive potential to quadruple its number in a second year, to increase eightfold in a third year, etc.

Observation But under field conditions, although fluctuations occur frequently, the size of a population remains remarkably constant over long periods of time.

Conclusion Evidently, not all eggs and sperms will become zygotes; not all zygotes will become adults; and not all adults will survive and reproduce. Consequently, there must be a "struggle for existence."

Observation Not all members of a species are alike; considerable individual variation is in evidence.

Conclusion In the struggle for existence, therefore, individuals exhibiting favorable variations will enjoy a competitive advantage over others. They will both survive and produce offspring in proportionately greater numbers.

Darwin and Wallace thus identified the *environment* as the principal cause of natural selection; the environment gradually would weed out organisms with unfavorable variations but preserve those with favorable variations. Over a long succession of generations, and under the continued selective influence of the environment, a group of organisms eventually would have accumulated so many new, favorable variations that in effect a new species would have arisen from the ancestral stock.

Nonbiologists often are under the impression that this Darwin-Wallace hypothesis is *the* modern explanation of evolution. This is not the case. Indeed, Darwinism was challenged even during Darwin's lifetime. What, it was asked, is the source of the all-important individual variations? How do individual variations arise? Here Darwin actually could do no better than fall back on the Lamarckian idea of inheritance of acquired characteristics. Ironically, the correct answer regarding variations began to be formulated just 6 years after Darwin published his *Origin*, when Mendel announced his rules of inheritance. But Mendel's work remained obscure and unappreciated for more than 30 years, and progress in understanding evolutionary mechanisms was retarded correspondingly.

Another objection to Darwinism concerned natural selection itself. If this process simply preserves or weeds out what already exists, it was asked, how can it ever create anything new? As will soon become apparent, natural selection actually does create novelty. The earlier criticism arose in part because the meaning of Darwin's theory was—and still is—widely misinterpreted. Social philosophers of the time and other "press agents" and disseminators of scientific information, not biologists, thought that the essence of natural selection was described by the phrase "struggle for ex-

PHOTO ESSAY 3: ADAPTATION

Biological adaptations take many forms—some biochemical, others structural, still others behavioral. All categories of adaptation are illustrated in this book (see discussion of C_4 plants in Chap. 13 for a particularly striking example of a biochemical adaptation to hot, dry environments). The following photographs highlight a few particularly noteworthy examples of structural and behavioral adaptations.

Structural Adaptations

A

B

Color Fig. 18. Fruit dispersal. (A) Each feathery tuft of this thistle is an individual fruit, well-adapted for wind dispersal. (B) Each bur of a cocklebur is an individual fruit, containing many surface "hooks" that facilitate attachment to the body of a passing animal. Still other fruits constitute important sources of nutrients for a wide variety of foraging animals (see Color Fig. 44). The seeds of such fruits usually resist digestion and germinate following their release in animal feces. *(A, J. R. McGregor, © Peter Arnold, Inc.; B, W. H. Hodge, © Peter Arnold, Inc.)*

Color Fig. 19. Mimicry. Some organisms resemble other objects. This and other forms of mimicry can greatly increase chances of escaping predators. Shown here is a Central American species of moth that bears a close resemblance to a wet feather. *(Peter Ward, Bruce Coleman, Inc.)*

Color Fig. 20. Adaptations to cold, dry environments. Gray-green lichen surrounds a colorful bloom of Lapland rosebay, *Diapensia,* and alpine azalea near the summit of Mount Washington, New Hampshire. Alpine tundra is too dry and cold to support large plants with an extensive foliage. Nevertheless, small species such as those shown here are well adapted to this often harsh environment. *(Clyde H. Smith, © Peter Arnold, Inc.)*

Color Fig. 21. Adaptations to hot, dry environments. The thick stems of many cacti are adapted for water storage, enabling these plants to withstand long periods of drought. Needlelike spines cover the stem surface, discouraging foraging by water-seeking animals. *(W. H. Hodge, © Peter Arnold, Inc.)*

Color Fig. 22. Schooling. The schooling behavior of fish provides considerable group protection, enabling many more individuals to survive than if each fish pursued an independent course. *(© Jeff Rotman.)*

Color Fig. 23. Aphid-herding ants. Some ants protect "herds" of aphids from predator attack. The aphids provide nutrients for the ants, releasing a sugar-rich "milk" when stroked by the larger insects. This form of symbiosis, where both species benefit from the association, is termed mutualism. *(Michael Ederegger, © Peter Arnold, Inc.)*

Color Fig. 24. Nest-building behavior. Nests are vital for the perpetuation of many animals, including the two lovebirds pictured here. Transporting strips of paper and other nest-building materials among tail feathers is unique to lovebirds and the related hanging parakeets. As discussed in Chap. 29, biologists have determined that heredity contributes heavily to successful nest-building behavior in lovebirds. *(William Vandivert, courtesy of Scientific American.)*

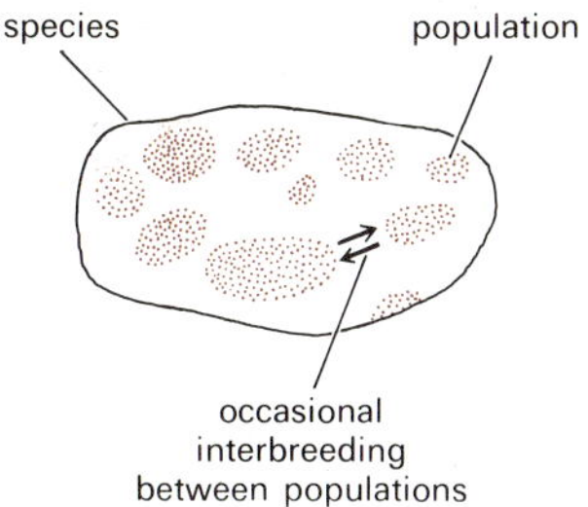

Fig. 29.1 The gene pool. In a species genes flow in and between populations. The total gene content of the species thus represents a gene pool to which all members of the species have access. Genes normally cannot flow between the gene pools of two different species.

istence." They then coined alternative slogans like "survival of the fittest" and "elimination of the unfit." Natural selection thus came to be viewed almost exclusively as a negative, destructive force. This had two unfortunate results. First, a major implication of Darwin's theory—the creative role of natural selection—was generally overlooked; and second, the wrong emphasis often was accepted in popular thinking as the last word on evolution.

Such thinking proceeded in high gear even in Darwin's day. Many people thought that evolution implied "man descended from the apes," and man's sense of superiority was duly outraged. Also, because evolutionary views denied the special creation of people, they were widely held to be antireligious. Actually, the idea of evolution is not any more or less antireligious than the idea of spontaneous generation. Neither really strengthens, weakens, or otherwise affects belief in God; to the religious person only the way God operates, not God as such, is in question.

Moreover, under the banner of phrases like "survival of the fittest," evolution was interpreted to prove an essential cruelty of nature; and human behavior, personal and national, often came to be guided by the ethic of "jungle law," "might is right," "every man for himself." Only in that way, it was thought, could the "fittest" prevail. Even today, unfortunately, evolution is still commonly—and erroneously—thought to be a matter of "survival of the fittest."

By now, a full century after Darwin and Wallace, it has become clear that natural selection is preeminently a peaceful process that has little to do with "struggle," "weeding out," or "the fittest." Also, natural selection is recognized to represent only a part of the evolutionary mechanism since, like Lamarck, Darwin was unsuccessful in identifying the genetic causes of evolutionary change. In short, Darwin (and Wallace) supplied an incomplete plete explanation; but as far as it went theirs was the first to point in the right direction.

The current modern theory of evolution is not the work of any one man, though it is the spiritual offspring of Mendel and of Darwin. It evolved slowly during the first half of the current century, and many biologists of various specializations contributed to its formulation.

FORCES OF EVOLUTION

The Evolutionary Process

Genetic Variations

As now understood, the mechanism of evolution can be described as *natural selection acting on the genetic variations that appear among the members of a population.*

Recall from Chap. 8 that a population is a geographically localized group of individuals of the same species, in which the members interbreed preferentially with one another and also occasionally with members of neighboring sister populations. The result of this close sexual communication in a population is a *free flow of genes.* Hereditary material present in some portion of a population can in time spread to the whole population, through the gene-pooling and gene-combining effects of sex. Moreover, interbreeding also can interconnect the *gene pools* of sister populations, and the total genetic content of a whole species can to some extent become shuffled and reshuffled among the member organisms (Fig. 29.1).

Chapter 27 has shown that genetic variations in a gene pool can arise by *sexual recombination,* by *mutation,* or both. In each generation some individuals appear that possess new, variant traits as a result of either recombinational or mutational processes. If such variant organisms survive and have offspring of their own, then their new genetic characteristics will persist in the gene pool of the population. And in the course of successive generations, the genetic novelty can spread to many or all members of the population.

Differential Reproduction

Whether or not such spreading actually takes place depends on natural selection. The real meaning of this term is *differential reproduction:* some members of a population leave more offspring than others. Those having more offspring will contribute a proportionately greater percentage of genes to the gene pool of the next generation than those having fewer offspring. Therefore, if differential reproduction continues in the same manner over many generations, the abundant reproducers will contribute a progressively larger number of individuals to the whole population. And as a result, *their* genes will become preponderant in the gene pool of the population (Fig. 29.2).

Which individuals leave more offspring than others? Usually (but not necessarily) those that are best adapted to the environment. Well-adapted animals, for example, generally are healthier and better fed, can find mates more readily, can defend themselves better, and can care for their offspring more appropriately than poorly adapted individuals. Yet what counts here is not how well or poorly an organism copes with its environment, but only how many offspring it manages to leave. The more there are, the greater the role that the parental genes will play in the total gene pool of the population. By and large the well-adapted organism contributes most to the gene pool.

It can happen, therefore, that a new trait originating in one organism spreads by differential reproduction and in time becomes a standard feature of the whole population. A particularly well-documented example of natural selection concerns the dramatic increase on the number of dark, or *melanic,* peppered moths (*Biston betularia*) that occurred in certain regions of Great Britain following the industrial revolution. Around Manchester, for example, the melanic variety made up a maximum of 1 per cent of the peppered moth population in 1848, shortly before industrialization. But by 1898, the melanic form made up more than 99 per cent of the population.

The spread of the dark peppered moths in the woods surrounding Manchester and many other cities of England clearly resulted from the pollution of trees with industrial soot. In unpolluted environments, light peppered moths are camouflaged by lichen growing on soot-free trees (Fig. 29.3). Melanic moths, which are more clearly visible on such trees, are more likely to be seen and eaten by birds and other predators. The situation is reversed in polluted regions, however, where the light moths are more visible on dark, soot-covered trees. Thus, light-colored moths are strongly favored in unpolluted environments, whereas natural selection favors the dark variety in heavily industrialized areas.

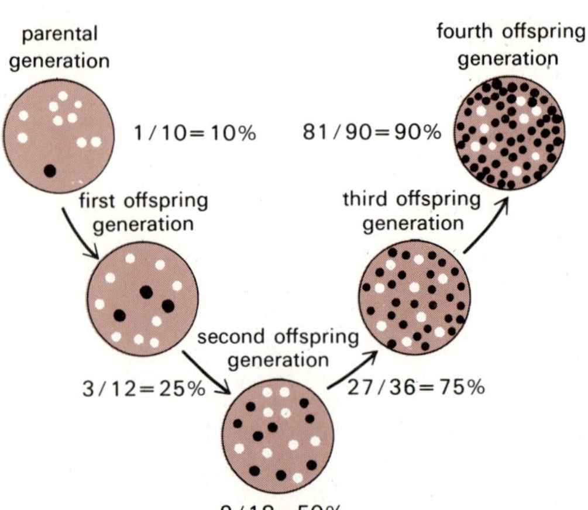

Fig. 29.2 Differential reproduction, or natural selection. Assume that a variation arises in one individual of a parental generation (black dot) and that the variant organism is able to leave three offspring. Each nonvariant organism (white dots) on the other hand only manages to leave one offspring. The complexion of the population will then change as shown during subsequent generations; the variant type will represent a progressively larger fraction of the numerical total. Such spreading of variations, brought about by differential reproduction, constitutes natural selection.

Although markedly different in outward appearance, light and melanic peppered moths share a sufficient number of genes to be members of the same species. Many traits usually must change before organisms are altered enough in structure or function to be recognizable as distinct species.

Evolution: The Two-Step Process

In any event, evolution operates through this basic two-step process:

1. Appearance of genetic variations by sexual recombination and mutation

A

B

Fig. 29.3 Industrial melanism. (A) Two peppered moths, one light and the other melanic, resting on an unpolluted, lichen-covered tree trunk. The light moth is almost invisible at the lower right. (B) A light and melanic moth resting on a soot-covered tree trunk. Because they are more visible on the polluted trees, light moths are more likely to be eaten by predators than the dark variety.

2. Spreading of these variations through a population by differential reproduction in successive generations

Note that this two-step process refutes two common misinterpretations of the evolutionary process. First, *populations* evolve, *not* individual organisms. The genetic traits of individuals are largely fixed and do not change appreciably over a lifetime. But because of differential reproduction, the characteristics of succeeding generations of populations change in response to changing environmental conditions.

Second, evolution *does not* progress in fixed or predetermined directions. Genetic variations appear *at random.* Therefore, evolutionary innovations similarly appear *at random.* However, this does not mean that evolution is without an overall guiding force. Because the best reproducers generally are the best adapted, evolution as a whole is directed by adaptation and is oriented toward continued or improved adaptation.

In this modern view of evolution, natural selection is fundamentally a *creative force,* one that spreads genetic novelty. And while it eliminates the reproductively "unfit," it does not necessarily eliminate the behaviorally or socially "unfit." The mightiest and grandest organism in the population could be exceedingly "fit" in a behavioral sense, but if it happened to be sterile it would be quite unfit in a reproductive and thus an evolutionary sense. Conversely, a sickly weakling might be behaviorally or socially unfit yet have numerous offspring. Natural selection therefore operates basically through reproduction, not through struggle for survival. Such struggles do occur, to be sure, often in a very physical sense, and indirectly they also may affect the reproductive success of organisms. To that extent such factors can have evolutionary consequences. But the important issue is neither "struggle" nor "elimination" nor even individual "survival"; all that finally matters is comparative reproductive success.

The Genetic Basis

From the preceding discussion, evolution can be described as a *progressive change of gene frequencies;* in the course of successive generations the proportion of some genes in a population increases and the proportion of others decreases. Clearly, the *rates* with which gene frequencies change will be a measure of the *speed* of evolution. What determines such rates?

Suppose we consider a large population made up of individuals of three genetic categories, *AA*, *Aa*, and *aa*, in the following numerical proportions:

AA	*Aa*	*aa*
36%	48%	16%

Assuming further that the choice of sexual mates is entirely random, that all individuals produce roughly equal numbers of gametes, and that the genes *A* and *a* do not mutate, we then can ask how the frequency of the genes *A* and *a* will change from one generation to the next.

Since *AA* individuals make up 36 per cent of the population, they will contribute approximately 36 per cent of all the gametes formed in the population. These gametes will all contain one *A* gene. Similarly, *aa* individuals will produce 16 per cent of all gametes in the population, and each will contain one *a* gene. The gametes of *Aa* individuals will be of two types, *A* and *a*, in equal numbers. Since their total amounts to 48 per cent, 24 per cent will be *A* and 24 per cent will be *a*. The overall gamete output of the population therefore will be:

parents		*gametes*	*parents*		*gametes*
36% *AA*	⟶	36% *A*	16% *aa*	⟶	16% *a*
48% *Aa*	⟶	24% *A*	48% *Aa*	⟶	24% *a*
		60% *A*			40% *a*

Fertilization now occurs in four possible ways: two *A* gametes join; two *a* gametes join; an *A* sperm joins an *a* egg; and an *a* sperm joins an *A* egg. Each of these possibilities will occur with a frequency dictated by the relative abundance of the *A* and *a* gametes. The ratio of sperms carrying allele *A* to sperms carrying allele *a* is 60:40; that is, 60 per cent of the sperms carry allele *A* and 40 per cent carry allele *a*. Similarly, the ratio of eggs carrying allele *a* is 60:40. This information can be used to create a Punnett square similar to those used for crosses between two individuals (Table 29.1 and see Figs. 27.9 and 27.14).

Note that the only difference between this Punnett square and those of Chap. 27 is that here the sperms and eggs are the product of *all* males and females in a population, not those produced by a *single* male and a *single* female. Numbers in the square indicate that the frequency of genotypes, *AA*, *Aa*, and *aa* in the new generation will be 36, 48, and 16 per cent, respectively, precisely the same proportions present originally. The gene frequencies have not changed.

The Hardy-Weinberg Law

By experiment and calculation it can be shown that such a result is obtained regardless of the

TABLE 29.1

	sperms	
eggs	***A*** **0.60**	***a*** **0.40**
A **0.60**	*AA* 0.36	*Aa* 0.24
a **0.40**	*Aa* 0.24	*aa* 0.16

numbers and the types of gene pairs considered simultaneously. The important conclusion is that, *if mating is random, if mutations do not occur, and if the population is large, then gene frequencies in a population remain constant from generation to generation.* This generalization is known as the *Hardy-Weinberg law.* It has somewhat the same central significance to the theory of evolution as Mendel's laws have to the theory of heredity.

The Hardy-Weinberg law indicates that, when a population is in genetic equilibrium and gene frequencies do not change, the rate of evolution is zero. Genes then continue to be reshuffled by sexual recombination and, as a result, genetic variations continue to originate from this source. But the overall gene frequencies do not change. Of themselves, therefore, the variations are not being propagated differentially, and evolution consequently does not occur. What does make evolution occur are deviations from the "ifs" specified in the Hardy-Weinberg law.

First, mating is decidedly *not* random in most natural situations. For example, it happens often that all genetic types in a population do not reach reproductive age in proportionate measure. Suppose that, in the sample population of *AA*, *Aa*, and *aa* individuals above, the *AA* genes cause death in one-third of the embryos of the population. Under such conditions 36 per cent of all zygotes will be *AA*, but only two-thirds of their number will reach reproductive age. The *Aa* and *aa* individuals will then form a proportionately larger fraction of the reproducing population, and will contribute proportionately more to the total gamete output. The ultimate result over successive generations will be a progressive decrease in the frequency of the *A* gene and a progressive increase of the *a* gene. Hence the *effective* mating population correspondingly will become more and more nonrandom.

In an effective mating population, moreover, mating pairs usually are formed on the basis of nonrandom criteria such as health, strength, mentality, external appearance, sexual attraction, or simply availability and geographic proximity of particular males and females. Mating thus becomes even more nonrandom, and the overall result is an uneven, nonrandom shuffling of genes—in effect, a form of natural selection. As some genes then spread more than others, gene frequencies become altered, and a Hardy-Weinberg equilibrium is not

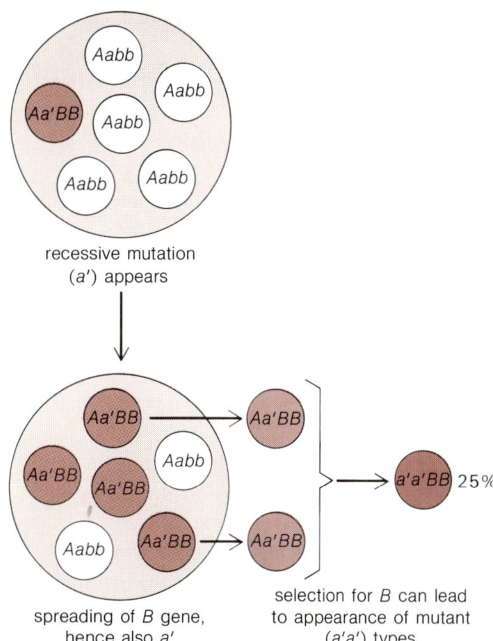

Fig. 29.4 Gene spreading. If a recessive mutation *a'* appears in an organism, and if that organism also carries a gene *B* that is strongly selected for, then both *B* and *a'* can spread through a population together. The appearance of mutant phenotypes *a'a'* then becomes rather likely.

maintained. This represents evolutionary change. Through nonrandom mating a certain *intensity* of natural selection, or *selection pressure,* operates for or against most genes, and in time even a very slight selection pressure substantially affects the genetic makeup of a population.

Second, mutations do occur among individuals of populations, and Hardy-Weinberg equilibria change for this reason also. Depending on whether a mutation has a beneficial or harmful effect on a trait, selection will operate for or against the mutated gene. In either case gene frequencies will change, for the mutated gene will either increase or decrease in abundance. Note, however, that the effect of selection on mutations will vary according to whether the trait changes produced are dominant or recessive. A newly originated mutation with dominant effect will influence traits immediately, and selection for or against the mutation will take place at once. But if in a diploid organism a mutation has a recessive effect, it does not influence traits immediately. Natural selection then will not influence the mutation immediately either. This is the case with most mutations, since, as noted earlier, most mutations in diploid organisms produce recessive effects.

A recessive mutant gene nevertheless can spread through a population if it happens to be closely linked to another gene that produces a dominant, adaptively desirable trait. Both genes are then inherited and propagated together. The recessive mutant here simply remains in the gene pool without effect, until two individuals carrying the same mutation happen to mate. Then one-fourth of their offspring will be homozygous recessive; if the mutant gene is a', then a mating of $Aa' \times Aa'$ will yield 25 per cent $a'a'$ offspring. These will exhibit altered visible traits, and natural selection now will affect the frequency of the mutation directly (Fig. 29.4).

The evolutionary role of mutations varies according to how greatly a given mutation influences a given trait. A "large" mutation that affects a vital trait in major ways is likely to be exceedingly harmful and usually will be lethal. But a "small" mutation that has only a minor effect on a trait can persist far more readily. Evolutionary alterations actually occur almost exclusively through accumulations of *many, small* changes in traits, not through single, large changes.

Genetic Drift

The third condition affecting Hardy-Weinberg equilibria is population size. If a population is large, regional imbalances of gene frequencies that might arise by chance are quickly smoothed out by the many random matings among the many individuals. The underlying principle here applies to statistical systems generally. In a coin-flipping experiment, for example, heads and tails will each come up 50 per cent of the time, but only if the number of throws is large. If only three or four throws are made, it is quite possible that *all* will come up heads by chance alone. Similarly, gene combinations attain Hardy-Weinberg equilibria only if a population is large. In small groups (less than about 100 individuals), chance alone can lead to *genetic drift,* a random establishment of genetic types that are numerically not in accordance with Hardy-Weinberg equilibria. For example, if *AA, Aa,* and *aa* individuals are expected in certain proportions, chance alone could result in the formation of many more *AA* and many fewer *aa* individuals if the population is small.

Because genetic drift is governed by chance, natural selection plays little role. Genes are being propagated not for their adaptive value but because they happen to be spread by chance. The result is that, in very small populations, nonadaptive and often bizarre traits can become established. These actually may be harmful to the population and may promote its becoming even smaller. Or, genetic drift may by chance happen to adapt a small population rather well to a given environment, and such a population later might evolve through natural selection and eventually give rise to a new species. Genetic drift is believed to be a significant factor in the evolution of organisms on islands and in small, reproductively isolated groups generally.

For example, the *Dunkers* are a small population of people in eastern Pennsylvania. They are descendants of the Old German Baptist Brethren who immigrated to the United States in the early eighteenth century. Because of strict religious principles, Dunkers intermarry only with each other. Consequently, they represent a small, genetically isolated group. Significant differences exist between the frequencies of certain genes in the Dunker population and the frequencies of the same genes in the general population of the United States or the general population of West Germany. For example, the A blood type is much more common among Dunkers. By contrast, B and AB blood types are extremely rare among Dunkers. Evidently, such atypical gene frequencies are the result of genetic drift (Table 29.2).

TABLE 29.2

Comparison of ABO Blood Groups in Dunkers, Rhineland Germans, and Residents of Pennsylvania

	percentage of ABO blood groups			
population	**O**	**A**	**B**	**AB**
Dunkers	35.5	59.3	3.1	2.2
Rhineland Germans	40.7	44.6	10.0	4.7
Americans (Pennsylvania)	45.2	39.5	11.2	4.2

SOURCE: A. M. Winchester, "Human Genetics," Merrill, Columbus, Ohio, 1971.

EFFECTS OF EVOLUTION

Speciation

The key process to be explained is how evolutionary changes in a population eventually culminate in the establishment of new species. As pointed out in Chap. 8, a species can be defined as a reproductive unit in which the member organisms interbreed with each other but not usually with members of other species. In other words, a reproductive barrier isolates one species from another. A more or less free gene flow therefore is maintained within a species but not normally between species. Thus, the problem of speciation is to show how reproductive barriers arise.

Continental Drift

Primary barriers usually appear through *geographic* changes, as when water comes to intrude into land or vice versa, or when a forest belt grows through a prairie or vice versa, or when mountains or new climatic conditions become interposed across a region. Some of these barriers result from *continental drift.* The continents of the earth are not fixed, as supposed until recently. Instead, continents drift slowly on a semiplastic underlayer.

The driving force for this movement comes from upwellings of molten rock that continuously add new land along certain geographic boundaries. South America and Africa, for example, are slowly drifting apart, because of an ascending current of molten lava deposited along the suboceanic chain of mountains located approximately halfway between the continents. The two land masses are forced farther and farther apart by the addition of new sea floor on both sides of this mountain chain, the *Mid-Atlantic ridge* (Fig. 29.5).

These movements also can jam continents together along other boundaries. For example, the eastern edge of the Pacific sea floor is being forced downward under western South America (see Fig. 29.5). Slippage of the two land masses along this boundary evidently accounts for the high incidence of earthquakes in these regions.

It recently has become possible to determine rates of continental drift. The Atlantic Ocean, for example, appears to be expanding at the rate of 1 to 2 inches/year, while the sea floor along the west coast of South America probably is moving almost

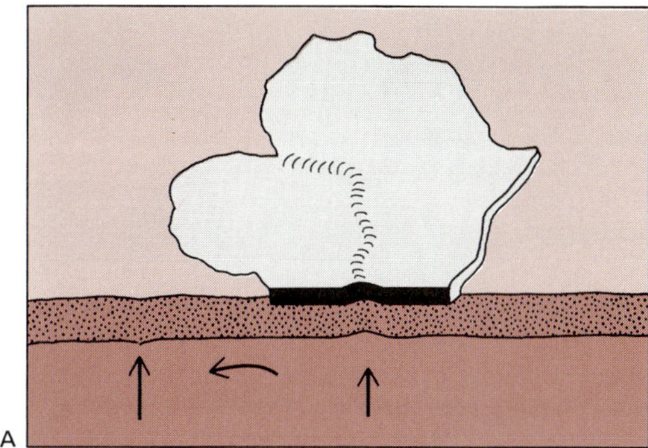

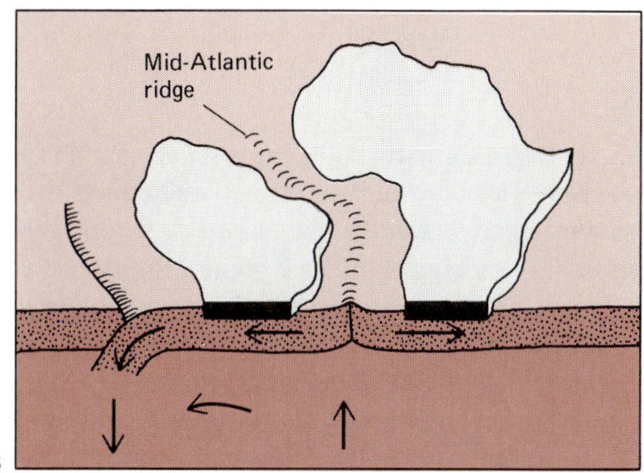

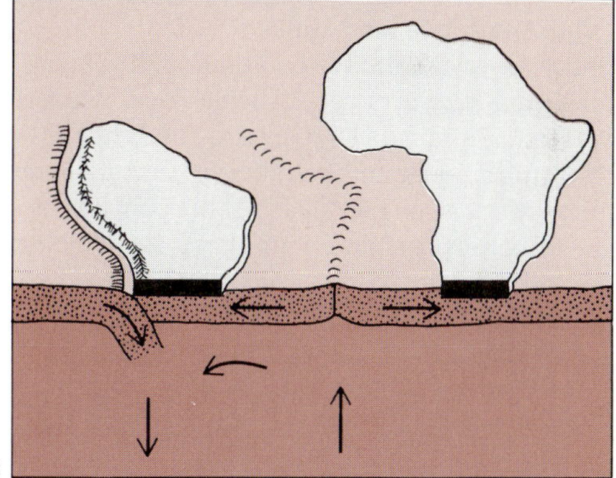

Fig. 29.5 Continental drift. (A) South America and Africa were once parts of an ancestral "supercontinent." Arrows indicate convection currents of molten rock deep within the earth. An ascending current appeared under the supercontinent and a descending current existed to the west of the land mass. (B) The ascending current split the supercontinent about 125 million years ago, creating the South Atlantic Ocean. Continued addition of molten rock to the sea floor under the mid-Atlantic ridge caused the African and South American continents to drift apart. The western edge of the South American continent was forced downward. (C) South America has drifted westward to the edge of the trench, its present location. Today, the downward current receives material from the west. The eastward-moving sea floor disappearing under the west coast of South America probably is responsible for the elevation of the Andes.

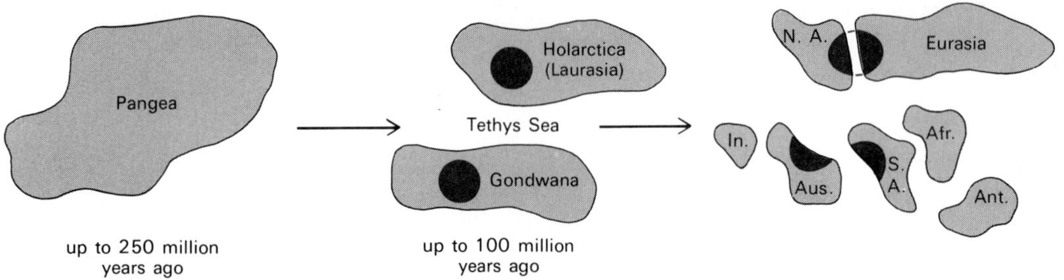

Fig. 29.6 Formation of continents. Continental areas at right, identified by abbreviations, are assumed to have drifted to their present positions during the last 200 million years. Color areas in Holarctica and at right indicate how the distribution of eels in North America and Europe might be accounted for. See also Fig. 20.12. Color areas in Gondwana and at right similarly suggest an explanation for the distribution of marsupials.

4 times as fast. By extrapolating back it can be deduced that the continents formed a single giant land mass, called *Pangaea* ("all lands"), about 200 million years ago (Fig. 29.6). Pangaea then split, forming a northern *Laurasia* and a southern *Gondwana*. These two land areas became totally separated by the *Tethys Sea* about 165 million years ago. Laurasia consisted of what is now North America, Europe, and Asia; Gondwana contained the present land masses of South America, Africa, Australia, Antarctica, and India.

South America and Africa began sliding apart about 125 million years ago. Then Africa, Antarctica, Australia, and India separated, the latter moving 5000 miles north and colliding with Asia about 40 million years ago (Fig. 29.7). This collision is thought to be responsible for uplifting the Tibetan plateau and the Himalayas. North America separated from Europe about 165 million years ago, somewhat earlier than the split between South America and Africa. Thus, like their biological counterparts, geological systems are in a continual state of flux.

Together with other less extensive geographic changes, continental drift has played a major role in the evolution of new species. Geographic barriers can separate sister populations of the same species, thereby eliminating reproductive contact between the two groups. In other instances, populations become isolated geographically simply by distance. As a species in time occupies a progressively larger territory, two populations at opposite ends of this territory eventually will be too far apart to permit direct interbreeding (Fig. 29.8).

Regardless of how isolation is actually brought about, an interruption of gene flow between sister populations will be followed by independent natural selection in each population. In the course of many generations, numerous genetic differences will appear, and these are likely to include *biological* barriers to interbreeding. For example, reproductive organs might change anatomically, gametes might become incompatible through altered protein specificities, or the times of the annual breeding seasons might shift. In effect, two sister populations of the same species will, in time, become two separate, new species.

At first, newly formed sister species tend to be rather similar structurally and functionally, and in some cases interbreeding might still take place if the species were not isolated geographically. Thus it sometimes happens that, when members of two similar species are brought together under artificial conditions, they can interbreed readily. Evidently, the circumstance that two different species *do not* interbreed in nature does not always mean that they cannot interbreed (Fig. 29.9). But after two sister species have been separated for long periods, interbreeding eventually may become impossible even if contact is provided artificially; the differences sooner or later can be pronounced enough to preclude interbreeding.

For example, two remarkably similar kinds of now extinct freshwater fishes once inhabited the lakes of South Africa and Australia. The fishes, *Cleithropepidina* from South Africa and *Cleithrolepis* from Australia, are so similar that they almost certainly evolved from a common ancestor living

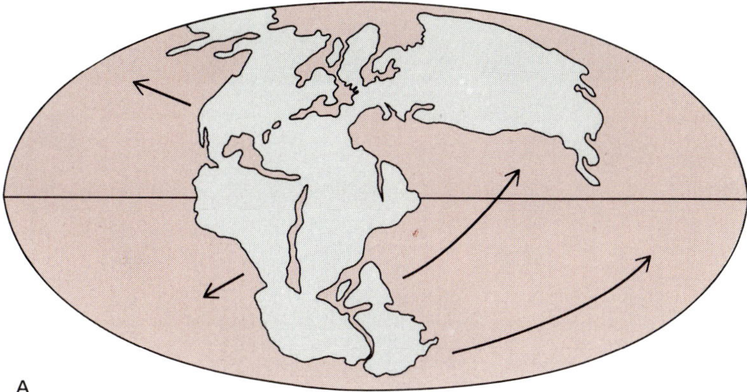

A

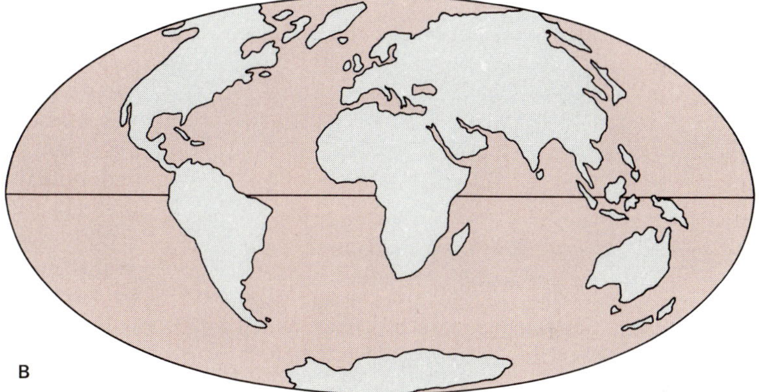

B

Fig. 29.7 Movements of the continents during the past 135 million years. (A) Position of continents about 135 million years ago. Arrows indicate direction of continental drift. (B) Position of continents today.

when Africa and Australia were part of Gondwana (Fig. 29.10). Because these fishes were freshwater organisms and probably could not live in marine environments, sister populations of the ancestral fish became isolated by the Indian Ocean. The environments of the once attached regions gradually changed as the two continents drifted to different latitudes, leading to somewhat different traits in the isolated populations.

Continental drift probably also explains certain curious migration patterns, such as those of eels. American and European species of eels apparently evolved from a common ancestor that once inhabited rivers in Laurasia. These ancestors may have spawned in a common central Laurasian river system. If so, this could explain why their descendants migrate from both American and European rivers and travel to the same ancestral spawning area, which now happens to lie in the middle of an ocean (see Figs. 20.12 and 29.6).

Polyploidy

Geographical barriers are not the only factors that establish reproductive isolation. *Polyploidy,* the exact multiplication of the chromosomes in cells, probably is responsible for the origin of almost half of all species of plants. Polyploid individuals result, for example, when meiotic nondisjunctions (see Chap. 27) produce diploid male and female gametes. Zygotes produced by the fusion of such gametes are *tetraploid,* having twice the normal diploid number of chromosomes. Similar mutations can yield offspring with other abnormal numbers of chromosomes.

Polyploid animals are extremely rare, but some polyploid plants are fertile. Meiosis occurs nor-

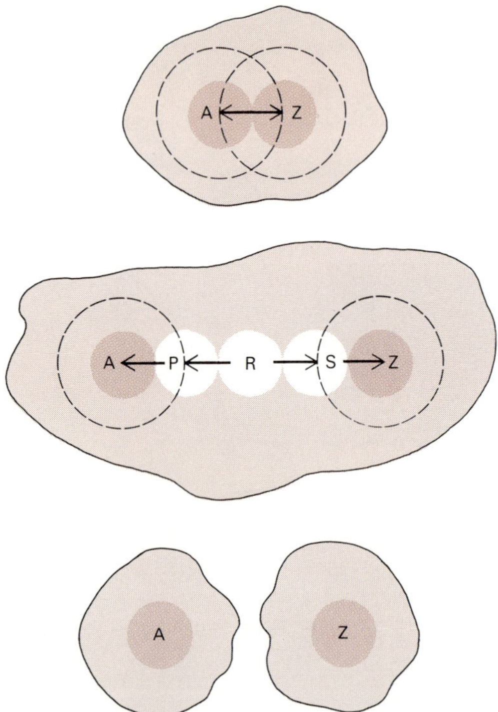

Fig. 29.8 Speciation. Top: two populations (A, Z) in a parent species have overlapping reproductive ranges (dashed circles); hence gene flow can be direct. Center: after population growth and territorial expansion the reproductive ranges of A and Z no longer overlap, and gene flow between them must now be indirect, via intervening populations (P, R, S). Bottom: if gene flow between A and Z ceases altogether, the two populations will have become reproductively isolated and will be independent offspring species.

mally in such plants, producing new generations of polyploid individuals. But because gametes of polyploid and diploid plants usually cannot unite in the production of fertile offspring, the polyploid individuals become reproductively isolated from diploid parental strains. In this way, entirely new species of polyploid plants can be formed in a single generation.

Artificial Selection

Nevertheless, geographical barriers probably trigger evolution of more new species than any other single factor. Thus most new species develop slowly, usually over a period of 1 million years or more. Consciously or unconsciously making use of this principle of reproductive isolation, people contribute to the evolution of many other organisms. The most ancient evolution-directing effort of people is our successful *domestication* of various plants and animals. Darwin was the first to recognize the theoretical significance of domestication, and indeed it was this that led him to his concept of natural selection. He reasoned that if human beings, by *artificial* selection and isolation, can transform wild varieties of given plants and animals into domesticated forms, then perhaps *natural* selection

Fig. 29.9 Interbreeding. Platyfish female at top, swordtail male at bottom. These animals belong to different species, and in nature they do not interbreed, but they can and do interbreed in the laboratory.

Fig. 29.10 Biological evidence of continental drift. Drawings made from fossil remains of *Cleithrolepidina* (A) and *Cleithrolepsis* (B), two extinct freshwater fish that lived in Gondwana over 165 million years ago.

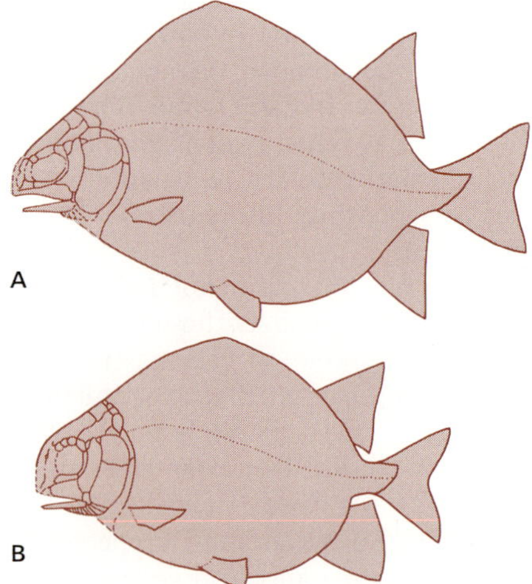

A

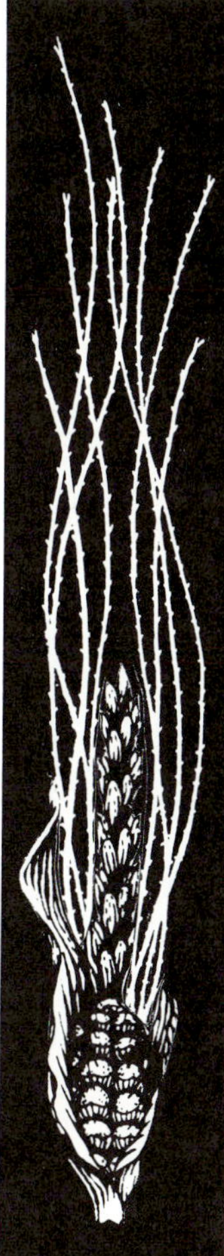

B

Fig. 29.11 Artificial selection. (A) Red jungle fowl, an example of a wild organism from which people have bred domesticated varieties. (B) Reconstruction of the most primitive known archeological corn plant (from the remains of Tehuacan, Mexico), a form clearly different from but in the ancestry of modern domesticated corn.

and isolation, acting for far longer periods, can produce even greater evolutionary transformations in nature. The domesticating process actually does involve all the elements of natural evolution: deliberate isolation of a wild population by people, followed by carefully controlled, differential reproduction of those member organisms that have traits considered desirable by people. The result is the creation of new strains, subspecies, and even species (Fig. 29.11).

During the last few decades, furthermore, rather rapid evolution caused by human intervention has taken place among certain viruses, bacteria, insects, various parasites, and other pests. These live now in an environment in which antibiotics and numerous pest-killing drugs have become distinct hazards. And the organisms have evolved, and are still evolving, increasing resistance to such drugs.

Clearly then, these examples offer direct proof that evolution actually occurs and is observable, and that it can be made to occur under conditions based on the postulated modern mechanism of evolution.

Diversification

Rates of Change

As already noted, evolution usually is an exceedingly slow process. Large numbers of very small variations must accumulate before a significant alteration of organisms can occur. Moreover, since genetic variations arise at random, organisms must *await* the appearance of adaptively useful changes. But there is no guarantee that useful variations will appear in successive generations or that they will appear at all. Thus, even though evolution may occur, it could occur too slowly to permit successful adaptation to changed environments.

As a rule, the actual *rates* of evolution have been proportional to the instability of the environment. Terrestrial organisms by and large have evolved faster than marine types, land being a less stable environment than the sea. Also, evolution generally has been fairly rapid in times of major geologic change, as during ice ages or periods of mountain formation. By contrast, the rate of evolution has been practically zero for millions of years in a few marine groups. For example, the structure of the horseshoe crab *Limulus* has remained essentially unaltered for the past 200 million years (see Chap. 34). The specific environment of such "living fossils" evidently has remained stable enough to make the ancient way of life still possible.

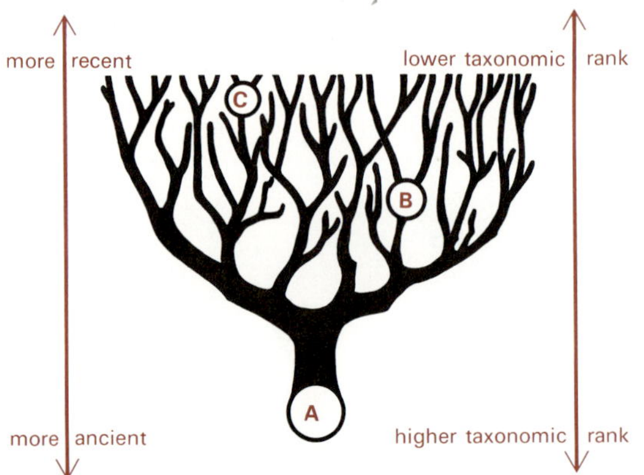

Fig. 29.12 The bush pattern of evolution. The uppermost tips of the branches represent currently living forms, all at the same time level, the present. Branches terminating below the top represent extinct forms. Fork points such as (B) and (C) are ancestral types. (B) is more ancient and of higher taxonomic rank than (C). (A) represents the archancestor of all living types.

Adaptive Radiations

Apart from variations in rates, evolution has tended to occur through successive *adaptive radiations.* Just as a parent species can give rise simultaneously to two or more descendant species, so a similar pattern of bushlike *branching* descent characterizes evolution on all levels; a newly evolved type becomes a potential ancestor for many different simultaneous lines of descendants. For example, the ancestral mammalian type has given rise simultaneously to several lines of modern grazing plains animals (horses, cattle, goats), to burrowing animals (moles), to flying animals (bats), to several lines of aquatic animals (whales, seals, sea cows), to animals living in trees (monkeys), to carnivorous predators (dogs, cats), and to many others. Each such line of descent has become specialized for a different way of life, and the sum of all these branch lines leading away from the common ancestral type represents an adaptive radiation.

Thus, the lines of interrelations among organisms have the form of a greatly branching bush (Fig. 29.12). All presently living organisms are *contemporaries,* appearing at the uppermost branch tips of the bush. Ancestral types appear lower down, where branches join. For example, an ancestral type of tree-living mammals has given rise simultaneously to modern animals as varied as lemurs, tarsiers, monkeys, apes, and people. Each such line of descent has exploited a different way of life, and each line also has branched out into its own sets of sublines. The sum of all these branches leading away from the common ancestral type represents an adaptive radiation. Thus, people did not descend from apes, but both have had a common ancestor and are contemporary members of the same adaptive radiation. All such radiations generally exhibit *divergence,* or development of more or less dissimilar traits in groups descended from a common ancestor.

Evidently, contrary to an erroneous assumption in vogue several decades ago, it is no longer possible to speak of an evolutionary "ladder" or "scale," implying a straight-line progression from one type of organism directly to the next. A scale simply does not exist, and only a bush pattern corresponds to the actual evidence. Also, we know that people, for example, did not descend "from amoebas." Instead, people, amoebas, and all other organisms now living are modern contemporaries that have evolved coequally, and along entirely separate paths, from some ancient, long-extinct ancestors. There is no evidence whatsoever that any contemporary species evolved from any other contemporary species. Moreover, there are no "higher" and "lower" organisms, since all types now in existence occur at the same time level of the evolutionary bush, namely, the present. There are only *different* organisms, with different histories and different characteristics.

Extinction and Replacement

Not all the branches on a bush lead right to the top, but some terminate abruptly at various intermediate points. In evolution, similarly, *extinction* has been a general feature. In many cases of extinction, the specific causes may never be known. However, in line with the nature of the evolutionary mechanism, the general cause of all extinctions is an inability of organisms to adapt rapidly enough to environmental changes (Fig. 29.13)

In conjunction with extinction, *replacement* has been another common occurrence in evolution. Replacement occurs when, after one group of organisms has become extinct, another group evolves that adopts the vacated environment and way of life. For example, pouched *marsupial mammals* were very abundant in the Americas a few million years ago, but with the exception of forms like the oppossum they were replaced in the Western Hemisphere by the competing *placental mammals.* In this case replacement was more or less immediate, but on occasion millions of years can elapse before a new group evolves into a previously occupied environmental niche. Such *delayed* replacement took place, for example, in the case of the ichthyosaurs. These fishlike marine reptiles became extinct some 100 million years ago. Their particular mode of living then remained unused for about 40 million years, when a newly evolved mammalian group, the whales and dolphins, replaced the ichthyosaurs. Similarly delayed replacement occurred between the flying reptilian pterosaurs and the later mammalian bats (Fig. 29.14).

A

B

Fig. 29.13 Recent extinctions. (A) Sabertooth cat. (B) Woolly mammoths. Mammoths and sabertooths became extinct some 20,000 years ago. (*A, American Museum of Natural History; B, Chicago Natural History Museum.*)

Convergent and Parallel Evolution

Replacing organisms usually exhibit some degree of evolutionary *convergence,* or *parallelism;* they resemble each other in one or more ways even though they need not be related particularly closely. For example, the development of finlike appendages in both ichthyosaurs and dolphins illustrates evolutionary convergence in replacing types. Since both groups have adapted to the same type of environment and way of life, their evolution has been oriented in the same direction; and the appearance of similar, or convergent, traits therefore is not surprising. But convergence occurs also in nonreplacing types. For example, the eyes of squids and of fish are remarkably alike. Squids and fish are not related directly and neither replaces the other. However, both types of animals are large, fast swimmers, and good eyes of a particular construction are a distinct advantage in the ways of life of both. Selection evidently has promoted variations that have led to eyes of similar structure, and the observed convergence is the result (Fig. 29.15).

Although the eyes of squids and fish are strikingly alike, they are by no means identical. Convergence leads to *similarity,* never to identity. Moreover, neither squids nor fish possess a theoretically "best" eye structure for fast swimmers. Similarly, none of the various animal groups that fly possesses a theoretically "best" wing design. In a way of life based on flying, wings of *some* sort are clearly essential. The various animal wings repre-

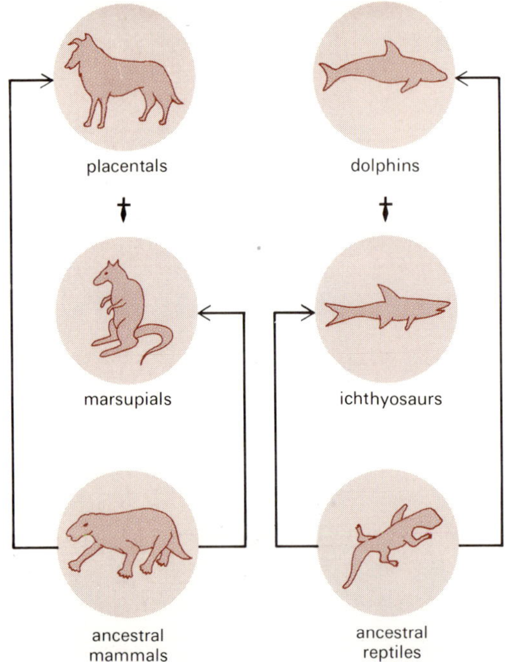

Fig. 29.14 Replacement. (Left) Immediate replacement: very soon after placental mammals evolved they replaced the earlier marsupials virtually everywhere, except in Australia. (Right) Delayed replacement: dolphins replaced the ichthyosaurs many millions of years after the latter had become extinct.

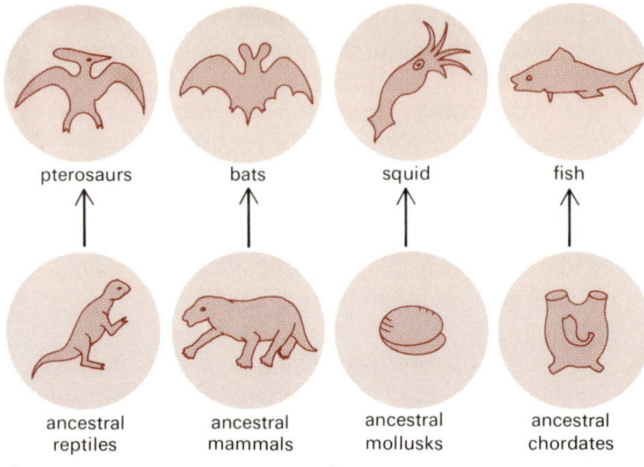

Fig. 29.15 Convergence. Relatively unrelated ancestors give rise to descendants whose ways of life and even superficial appearance are similar in many respects. In (A) the convergence is replacing: bats now occupy the same kinds of niches that pterosaurs did many millions of years ago. In (B) the convergence is nonreplacing: squids and fishes coexist today, each group occupying its own niche.

sent *multiple* solutions of the same problem, each evolved from a different starting point and each functioning in a different way.

Random Opportunism

This consideration focuses attention on one of the most important characteristics of evolution, that of *random opportunism.* Evolution has produced not what is theoretically desirable or best, but what is practically possible. Although it might have been adaptively exceedingly useful for terrestrial plants to grow legs or for terrestrial animals to grow wheels, neither development occurred because it could not occur; the ancestors simply did not possess the necessary structural and functional potential. However, they did possess the potential to evolve adequate, workable, alternative solutions. Among plants, already existing spores could become encapsulated and distributed by wind; and among animals, already existing fins could be reshaped as walking legs.

Evidently, evolution can only remodel and build on what already exists, in small, successive steps. Since, given a long enough time span, every feature of every organism undergoes random variations in many different directions, opportunities for diverse evolutionary changes have been and still are very numerous. In effect, every organism represents a patchwork of good opportunities seized by natural selection at the right time. In people, for example, the bones of the middle ear have arisen opportunistically from pieces of earlier vertebrate jawbones. The musculature of the lower face has evolved from the gill muscles of ancestral fish. The larynx has developed from the gill skeleton of ancient fish (Fig. 29.16). Such instances of evolutionary opportunism are legion. Clearly, organisms are not the result of any planned, goal-directed, or predetermined course of creation. They are the result of a cumulative, opportunistic process of piece-by-piece building, based on existing organisms and governed entirely by natural selection acting on random variations.

Animal Behavior

Natural selection clearly influences the structural characteristics of organisms. Birds have

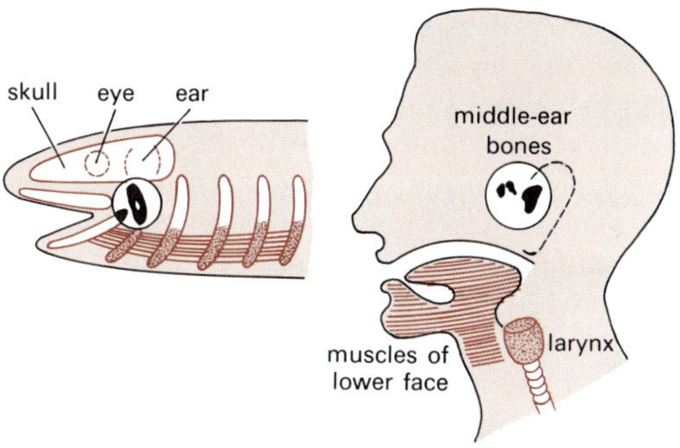

Fig. 29.16 Evolutionary opportunism. Parts of the lower jaw and the upper bone of the next bony gill arch of ancestral fishes have been the evolutionary sources of the middle-ear bones of people (black). Similarly, parts of the other gill supports of fishes have evolved as the cartilages of the mammalian larynx (dark color), and the gill musculature of fishes has contributed to the muscles of the lower part of the face of mammals (hatched areas).

feathers and lions have hair because they have inherited genes for these traits, genes that have been selected by environmental pressures over many millennia. But to what extent are the courtship rituals of birds and the hunting behavior of lions determined by genes? To what degree is natural selection responsible for the behavior of animals?

Behavioral Genetics

Unfortunately, little is known about the effects of genes on behavior; the field of *behavioral genetics* is a comparatively new, rapidly developing discipline. Consequently, there is considerable uncertainty about the impact of natural selection on the evolution of behavioral traits, especially those of people. It is clear, however, that genes can influence behavior. Reactive and active behaviors, for example, are largely unmodifiable and highly "programmed" genetically (see Chap. 20). But even relatively complex patterns of behavior can be gene-influenced, as evidenced by the nesting behavior of certain African parrots, more commonly known as lovebirds.

Two species of lovebirds have been found to differ in the way they carry nest-building materials. Members of one species carry grass, straw, pieces of paper, and other materials in their beaks. Members of the second species transport such materials by tucking them into their rump feathers (Color Fig. 24). The influence of genes on this behavior has been tested by crossing members of the two species and producing hybrid offspring. The hybrids appear hopelessly befuddled when they attempt to transport building materials to nest sites. Such offspring make vain attempts to carry the materials both in their beaks and tail feathers but are unable to perform either task adequately. They drop pieces of grass and paper before the materials are properly inserted into tail feathers. Or they insert nesting materials properly, only to remove and drop them immediately afterward. As a result, hybrid birds are unable to build satisfactory nests to rear the young. The maladaptive behavior of the hybrids apparently results from the inheritance of a genotype intermediate between that of the parent birds.

Other studies similarly suggest a strong genetic basis for many behaviors. For example, biologists have been able to alter distributions of behavioral traits in populations of animals. Under laboratory conditions, investigators have been able to increase or decrease the percentage of fruit flies displaying a tendency to move toward or away from gravity. Flies showing a particular tendency can be either preferentially killed or cultured. Offspring of the survivors usually display the tendency of their parents, thereby altering the distribution of this behavior in the population as a whole (Fig. 29.17).

Artificial selection of behaviors also has been demonstrated for aggressiveness in domestic fowl, mating speed in fruit flies, exploratory behavior in mice, and several other activities of animals. All these studies imply that many kinds of behavior, both individual and social, have a genetic basis and that natural selection probably plays a key role in determining and modifying the behaviors of animals.

Sociobiology

Like behavioral genetics, the application of evolutionary theory to the study of group behavior has developed only recently. Indeed, biologists who use the theory of natural selection as a tool in studying the social behavior of animals have coined a name for their new discipline, *sociobiology*. By definition, sociobiology is the systematic study of the *biological* basis of all forms of social behavior. One of the fundamental objectives of this new science is to elucidate general principles regarding the role of

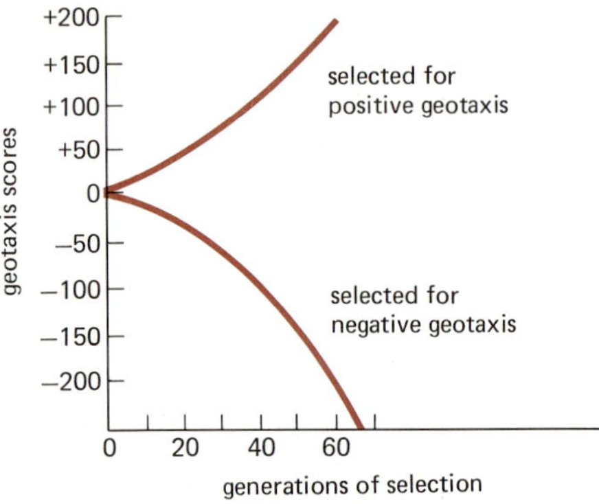

Fig. 29.17 Artificial selection of behavioral traits. Fruit flies displaying a tendency to fly upward (negative geotaxis i.e., movement away from the force of gravity) or downward (positive geotaxis) can be bred preferentially, gradually altering the behavioral characteristics of the population as a whole.

natural selection in the evolution of social behavior. Sociobiologists already have made progress toward this goal, particularly in regard to the evolution of a kind of cooperative behavior called *altruism.*

Altruism. Biologically, altruism is defined as self-destructive behavior for the benefit of others. Organisms exhibiting such behavior reduce their own chance of survival while increasing that of others. Worker honeybees, for example, protect other bees in the hive by stinging intruders. Since the sting is anchored firmly to the bee's abdomen, part of the abdomen is torn off as the attacking bee flies away. This altruistic behavior, although beneficial to neighboring bees, is lethal for the attacking worker bee.

Altruism is common among invertebrates, and it is widespread among vertebrates and even human beings. A prairie dog, for example, utters a loud alarm call when it sees a coyote approaching the colony of burrows in which prairie dogs live (Fig. 29.18). The loud call from one of these burrowing rodents undoubtedly draws the coyote's attention, increasing the probability that the one to sound the alarm will be captured by the intruder.

Why do organisms exhibit altruistic behavior? Would natural selection not favor a more selfish strategy, one in which prairie dogs or worker bees simply "sneak away," leaving unsuspecting colleagues to fend for themselves? Assume that alarm calling in prairie dogs is "programmed" by a set of genes *C* and that an alternate set *c*, establishes selfish, silent behavior. Prairie dogs inheriting gene set *C* are more likely to be eaten by coyotes and other predators than individuals inheriting gene set *c*. Thus, gene set *C*, establishing alarm calling, should eventually disappear, gene set *c* being clearly favored by natural selection. Yet this has not occurred, either for prairie dogs, worker bees, or the many other animals exhibiting altruistic behavior. How, then, did altruism evolve?

The answer generally accepted by biologists involves a special form of natural selection called *kin selection.* Gene set *C* would persist and even increase in frequency if its *ultimate* effect is to maintain or increase the total number of copies of gene set *C* in the next generation. In other words, alarm calling could be selected for if the caller alerted a sufficient number of *relatives* who also contained genes of set *C*. Thus, if the alarm call uttered by a prairie dog carrying gene set *C* increased the "fitness" of other prairie dogs which likewise carry gene set *C*, then this set of genes would be selected for, even though they reduce the personal "fitness" of the alarmer.

Note that prairie dogs do not utter alarm calls for individuals of other species, and that worker bees do not protect the hives of wasps or other so-

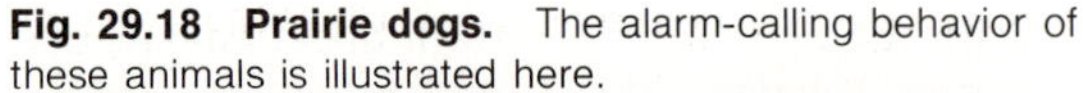

Fig. 29.18 Prairie dogs. The alarm-calling behavior of these animals is illustrated here.

cial insects. They do so only for individuals related to themselves, individuals likely to share genes responsible for the altruistic behavior.

Theoretically, the more distant the relative, the less intense the altruistic behavior should be. Brothers and sisters, for example, share about one-half of their genes, but the fraction of genes shared by first cousins is only about one in eight. Thus, if altruistic genes are to be favored, a sister would have to produce more than twice as many offspring to make up for a self-sacrificing act of her brother. By contrast, the self-sacrifice of one first cousin for another would require an eightfold increase in offspring for favorable selection of altruistic genes.

Biologists have tested this prediction of kin selection theory and generally have found corroborating evidence. Social animals do tend to group such that relatives are closely allied, regardless of whether exact relationships are recognized by the animals themselves. For example, adult zebras, who live in close-knit family groups, defend calves against predators. By contrast, wildebeests do not protect their young from predation. Significantly, wildebeest calves are not reared in family groups. The young tend to be scattered randomly in the herd, making it unlikely that adult wildebeests are closely related to neighboring calves.

Some of the best evidence supporting the kin selection concept comes from studies of *eusocial insects* (*eu-* means "true" or "proper"; see Section A of Glossary), species having a specialized nonreproductive worker caste, such as ants, wasps, and honeybees (see Chap. 21). The sterile female workers of such societies are highly altruistic, leaving no offspring of their own and devoting most of their energy to protecting the hive and ensuring reproductive success of their mother, the queen. Workers spend considerable time caring for the brood cells that constitute incubation chambers for the development of a new generation of insects. Because the queen continues to lay eggs well past the time when her first daughters reach maturity, many of the developing embryos in the brood cells are *sisters* of the workers monitoring their development.

The high degree of altruism in eusocial insects apparently stems from the inheritance of an unequal number of genes in males and females. Except for termites, all eusocial insects are *haplodiploid:* males are haploid, developing from unfertilized eggs and therefore having only one set of chromosomes per cell; females develop from fertilized eggs, inherit two sets of chromosomes, and therefore are diploid (Fig. 29.19).

This dichotomous arrangement of genes has significant evolutionary and behavioral consequences. Males, with only one set of chromosomes, contribute the same genetic material to each of their offspring. Females, like most diploid organisms, contribute either chromosome of a homologous pair to their young. Offspring receiving the same kind of chromosome from their mother are genetically identical with respect to that chromosome. But even if they receive different maternal chromosomes, they still share one-half their genes, i.e., those received from their father. Consequently, a few female offspring will be genetically identical and a few will share only one half of their genes, but most sisters will share an intermediate number of genes. On the average, female offspring share three-fourths of their genes.

Significantly, workers would share only one half of their genes with their offspring if worker bees were fertile. Thus, a daughter (worker) perpetuates more of her own genes by staying with her mother and caring for cells containing her sisters than if she left the hive and produced offspring of her own. In this way, the genetic makeup of most eusocial insects appears to predispose them toward evolution of a caste system in which sterile workers monitor and care for development of their younger siblings.

Additional evidence supports application of the kin-selection theory to the altruistic behavior of eusocial insects. Because males are haploid, they share only one-fourth of their genes with their sisters (see Fig. 29.19). If the kin-selection theory is correct, workers should favor their sisters (other workers) more than their brothers (drones). Robert Trivers and H. Hare of Harvard University have shown this to be the case for a number of activities. For example, worker bees provide about 3 times as much food for their sisters as for their brothers, a ratio consistent with their three-quarter one-quarter genetic relationship.

This discussion of kinship selection, which may account for all incidences of altruistic behavior, illustrates two important contributions already provided by the emerging discipline of sociobiology. The first is a more precise definition of biolog-

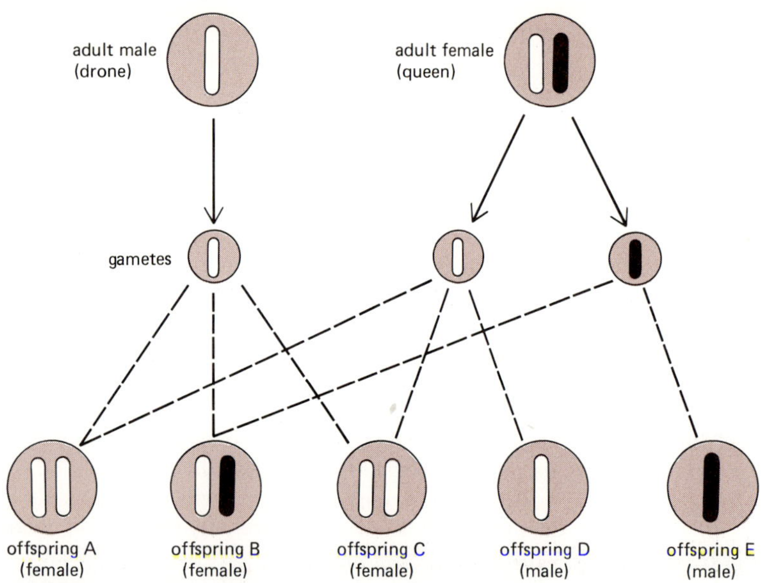

Fig. 29.19 Genetic consequences of haplodiploidy in eusocial insects. The inheritance of a single pair of chromosomes (symbols in circles) in bees is shown. Females are diploid, having both chromosomes of the pair; males, being haploid, have only one of the two chromosomes. Males, therefore, contribute the same genetic information to each of their offspring, and all such offspring are female (offspring A, B, and C). Consequently, all female offspring share *at least* one-half of their genes. By contrast, queens contribute either chromosomes of the pair to their offspring. Individuals receiving the same chromosome from their mother are genetically identical with respect to that pair of chromosomes (offspring A and C). Offspring receiving different maternal chromosomes still share one-half of their genes (offspring A and B). Because bees have more than a single pair of chromosomes, female offspring share *on the average* three-fourths of their genes. Note that a queen shares only half of her genes with her offspring, the same percentage that workers would share with their offspring *if* workers were fertile. Workers, therefore, share greater numbers of genes with their sisters than if workers left the hive and raised offspring. Males (drones) develop parthenogenically from unfertilized eggs. Some brothers will share one-half of their genes with their sisters (offspring B and E). Others will not share any genes (offspring A and E). Because many chromosomes are involved, brothers will share *on the average* one-quarter of their genes with their sisters. According to kin-selection theory, workers should favor their younger sisters more than their younger brothers. This prediction has been corroborated for several activities of honeybees.

ical "fitness." The Darwinian view is that fit individuals leave more offspring than less fit organisms. In doing so, fit individuals contribute a greater percentage of their genes to the population gene pool than less fit individuals, thereby altering the distribution characteristics of the gene frequencies in the new generation.

The kin-selection theory presents an expanded view of fitness by taking into account the impact of individuals *and* their relatives on the frequency of genes in populations. *Inclusive fitness* is the term coined to reflect the summed consequences of personal fitness (via offspring) *and* fitness derived through the representation of genes in relatives.

The central theorem of sociobiology This expanded view of fitness is the basis of a central hypothesis that underlies all of sociobiology. This so-called central theorem of sociobiology states that *when any behavior reflects an underlying genetic basis, animals should behave in a manner maximizing their inclusive fitness.* By this view, all behavior, whether altruistic or not, will evolve only if mediated by genes whose effect is to *increase* the inclusive fitness of the bearer. That is, environments should consistently select for behaviors maximizing production of offspring that live to reproductive maturity, whether or not such behavior maximizes the personal fitness of the parents.

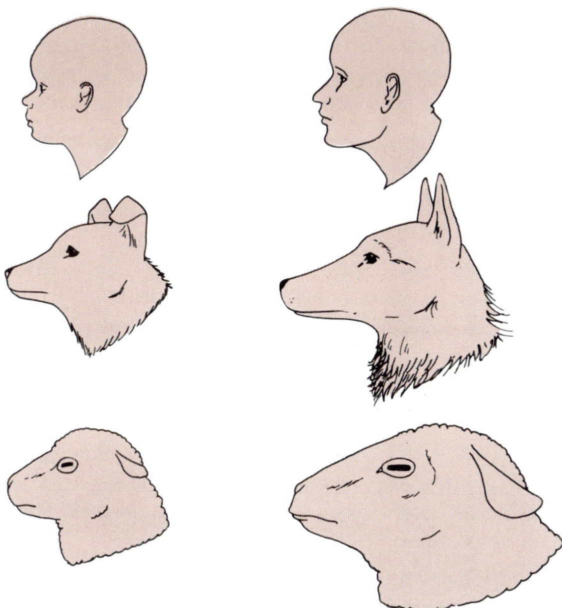

Fig. 29.20 Human response to babyish features. Most people feel more inclined to cuddle and care for individuals having blunt anatomical features and relatively large eyes (left) than for individuals with small eyes and sharply pointed features (right).

This fundamental postulate has led to a second important contribution of sociobiology. Like other unifying theories of science, the central theorem provides a predictive and therefore experimental approach to the study of all social animals. A diversity of experiments can be designed to test the predictions inherent in the central theorem. Results of such experiments will either support or undermine the central theorem as presently written.

For example, the prediction that altruism should be more common among closely related than among distantly related individuals has already been mentioned. Results of field studies with zebras and wildebeests, noted previously, and with other social animals tend to confirm the prediction. The central theorem also predicts that altruism should be more common among species which live in dense populations. Individuals of such species are more likely to share kinship ties with their neighbors than species comprising individuals scattered widely over large areas. Several field studies have corroborated this prediction, providing additional support for the central theorem.

Do human beings tend to behave so as to maximize their inclusive fitness? Do genes influence our tendencies to discriminate against "outsiders," our inclination to select mates having certain physical and behavioral attributes, or our tendency to cuddle and care for objects having the same physical traits that characterize human infants (Fig. 29.20)? Are genes in any way responsible for racist or sexist attitudes, or the development of human social institutions?

Such questions have triggered an intense, emotional, and often bitter debate between so-called *biological* and *environmental determinists.* In many respects, this confrontation is an extension of the *nature-vs.-nurture* controversy, debated intensively throughout the first half of this century. The nature-vs.-nurture dispute raged over the relative importance of inheritance and learning in animal behavior. Some psychologists denied that inheritance plays any significant role in determining the behavior of animals. Many biologists took the opposite position, claiming that inheritance determines all aspects of even the most complex patterns of animal behavior.

We now realize that both views are too extreme; behavioral traits of animals are determined by the interaction of genes *and* environment (see Chap. 27). But the *relative* importance of these two factors in determining *human* social behavior remains unresolved. Many environmental determinists, like former proponents of the nurture philosophy, state that genes have little or no influence in determining human social behavior. Indeed, some of these people even deny the legitimacy of human behavioral genetics and human sociobiology. By contrast, some biological determinists, some of whom are sociobiologists, minimize the role of learning as a determinant of human social traits.

Most scientists, including most sociobiologists, advocate neither view. People are not automatons whose every mannerism, attitude, and social institution result entirely from genetic programming. It is equally inconceivable that human beings are unique among animals in having no biological components influencing social behavior. Genes certainly do not control human behavior, but they undoubtedly influence it.

Thus, our social behavior, including our prevailing social attitudes and institutions, almost surely derive from a complex interaction of heredity and experience, and much can be gained by studying this interaction. For example, we might be able to use the results of such studies to decrease conflicts between people, to prevent and treat mental illnesses, and to improve education by building on the diversity of individual learning patterns. We are not yet sure that a biological examination of human social behavior will afford such benefits, but the approach is worth trying, for sociobiology could well provide a more complete understanding of why we behave as we do.

Review Questions

1 Describe the concept of spontaneous generation and the essential points of the evolutionary theories of Lamarck and of Darwin and Wallace. How could the evolution of giraffes from short-necked ancestors be explained in terms of these three theories? What are the strengths and weaknesses of each theory?

2 What different kinds of inheritable variations arise in organisms? Do such variations appear randomly or are they oriented toward usefulness?

3 Review the modern meaning of natural selection. Show how natural selection basically has little to do with "survival of the fittest" or "struggle" or "weeding out" and how it is a creative force.

4 What is the Hardy-Weinberg law, and what conditions disturb Hardy-Weinberg equilibria? Show how such equilibria are disturbed and how evolution is thereby affected. If a Hardy-Weinberg equilibrium exists in a population, what are the rate and amount of evolution?

5 Illustrate the process of speciation. What are some common geographic isolating conditions, and what is their effect on gene pools? How do reproductive barriers arise between populations? Describe and illustrate the theory of continental drift. Show how movements of continents over the past 165 million years help to explain the geographic distributions of certain organisms.

6 Review some actual evidence for evolution. How have rates of evolution varied?

7 Review the characteristics of evolution. Include a description of adaptive radiation, evolutionary replacement, evolutionary divergence and convergence, and the general cause of extinction in your discussion.

8 Criticize and correct the following statement: In the evolutionary scale, higher animals such as vertebrates have descended from lower animals such as protozoa.

9 In what way is evolution randomly opportunistic? List five structural or functional features of human beings and show for each:

- **a.** How it has evolved opportunistically.
- **b.** That it cannot be labeled as being theoretically best.

10 Do genes influence behavior? Support your answer with experimental evidence.

11 Explain how the theory of kin selection accounts for the evolution of altruism. Cite evidence supporting this explanation. How does the genetic makeup of eusocial insects appear to predispose them toward evolution of a caste system in which sterile workers spend their lives monitoring and caring for younger siblings?

12 What is the central theorem of sociobiology? Has the theorem proved to be a useful scientific tool? How?

13 Some sociobiologists postulate that many human attitudes and social predispositions are gene-determined. Are you offended or troubled by such suggestions? Why or why not?

Collateral Readings

Barash, D. P.: "Sociobiology and Behavior," Elsevier, New York, 1977. An excellent introduction to most aspects of sociobiology. Shorter and more elementary than Wilson's book, cited below.

Benzer, S.: Genetic Dissection of Behavior, *Scientific American,* December 1973. The author describes experiments with fruit flies that made it possible to identify the genetic components of behavior and locate the sites from which they operate.

Bishop, J. A., and **L. M. Cook:** Moths, Melanism, and Clean Air, *Scientific American,* January 1975. Describes how the natural selection of moth pigmentation has been influenced by clean and polluted air.

Calder, N.: "The Life Game," Viking, New York, 1974. A popularly written account of the modern theory of evolution.

Clarke, B.: The Causes of Biological Diversity, *Scientific American,* August 1975. Describes how the biological diversity of organisms is maintained.

Darwin, C.: "On the Origin of Species," Cambridge University Press, New York, 1975. This is one of the most recent reprintings of Darwin's famous treatise.

——**:** "The Voyage of the Beagle," Natural History Press, Garden City, N.Y., 1962. Darwin kept a journal of his findings and experiences on board the *Beagle.* This is the complete version of that journal.

Dickerson, R. E.: Cytochrome C and the Evolution of Energy Metabolism, *Scientific American,* March 1980. This article illustrates how certain biochemicals can be used to trace evolutionary interrelations between a wide variety of organisms.

Dobzhansky, T., F. J. Ayala, G. L. Stebbins, and **J. W. Valentine:** "Evolution," Freeman, San Francisco, 1977. One of the best advanced textbooks on evolution, written by four outstanding scientists.

Ehrlich, P. R., R. W. Holm, and **D. R. Parnell:** "The Process of Evolution," McGraw-Hill, New York, 1974. A good introduction to evolutionary theory. Shorter and somewhat less advanced than the Dobzhansky text.

Eiseley, L. C.: Charles Darwin, *Scientific American,* February 1956. A biographical article.

Glass, H. B.: The Genetics of the Dunkers, *Scientific American,* August 1953. Evidence for genetic drift within a human population is presented in this fascinating article.

Gould, S. J.: "Ever since Darwin: Reflections in Natural History," Norton, New York, 1977. A series of exceptionally well-written essays on Darwin and other topics related to the natural history of the earth and its organisms.

Grant, V.: "Organic Evolution," Freeman, San Francisco, 1977. This comprehensive textbook contains a particularly well-developed treatment of speciation.

Hunt, J. H. (ed.)**:** "Selected Readings in Sociobiology," McGraw-Hill, New York, 1980. This series of short articles, written by some of the world's foremost sociobiologists, contains a well-developed section on the controversial applications of sociobiological theory to human behavior.

Lack, D.: Darwin's Finches, *Scientific American,* April 1953. An examination of the famous Galapagos birds on which Darwin based much of his theory.

Mayer, E.: Evolution, *Scientific American,* September 1978. This article describes the historical development and essential elements of the modern theory of evolution. It also introduces all other articles in this issue of *Scientific American,* which is devoted exclusively to the topic of evolution.

Moorehead, A.: "Darwin and the Beagle," Harper & Row, New York, 1969. This lavishly illustrated book recounts the experiences that altered Darwin's perceptions of natural history.

Pasteur, L.: Examination of the Doctrine of Spontaneous Generation, in "Great Experiments in Biology," Prentice-Hall, Englewood Cliffs, N.J., 1955. A translation of the famous 1862 original.

Smith, J. M.: "The Theory of Evolution," 3d ed., Penguin, Baltimore, 1975. This paperback, written for nonscientists, contains many excellent examples of evolutionary changes among organisms.

White, M.: "Modes of Speciation," Freeman, San Francisco, 1977. Includes almost every aspect of this topic. For the advanced student.

Wilson, E. O.: "Sociobiology: The New Synthesis," Belknap, Cambridge, Mass., 1975. The classic treatment of this subject, more extensive and detailed than the Barash book. The author, well known for his studies on the social behavior of insects, triggered a storm of controversy by treating human beings just like other animals in describing the origins of behavior patterns.

Part 7
The World of Life

This part consists of an examination of the probable beginning of life on earth and of the evolutionary ancestry and biological characteristics of all major groups of organisms living today. The main objective of these chapters is to provide an appreciation of the vast diversity of living creatures. For it is this diversity that shows clearly that workable, successful adaptations have occurred countless times and under exceedingly varied environmental circumstances.

Providing solitary vertical dimension to an otherwise flat Kenyan plain, a giraffe pauses in the shade of an umbrella tree. (*L. Nielsen, © Peter Arnold, Inc.*)

Chapter 30

The Earliest Organisms

Learning Objectives

After reading this chapter you should be able to:

1. Indicate at least two possible origins for the first living cells on earth; name at least three gases that probably were present in the early atmosphere on the earth; list evidence in support of the hypothesis that biologically important organic molecules formed spontaneously through chemical interactions of these gases; name at least three such organic molecules; state a possible role in the origin of life of:
   - **a.** temperature
   - **b.** water
   - **c.** organic compounds
   - **d.** enzymes
2. Outline the physical characteristics of the earth:
   - **a.** at the time it was formed
   - **b.** before living systems originated
   - **c.** after living systems originated

   Estimate how many years ago the earth originated and life originated on earth; differentiate between biological and chemical evolution; explain why the critical events in the creation of cells probably did not occur in the open sea, and list a more likely location for these events; define microspheres and suggest the possible evolutionary significance of these structures.
3. Differentiate between prokaryotes and eukaryotes and between moneran and protistan cells; describe how membranous organelles of eukaryotic cells may have evolved; state the symbiotic theory of mitochondrial and chloroplast origins, and list at least five pieces of evidence that are consistent with the theory; state at least three arguments that tend to refute the symbiotic theory.
4. Name the major groups of organisms that are classified as Monera; describe and define the nutritional patterns of moneran and protistan organisms and show how such patterns may have evolved.
5. Describe the events and consequences of the oxygen revolution.
6. Name the characteristics of Protista, Fungi, Plantae, and Animalia and list characteristics that distinguish these kingdoms from Monera.
7. Identify and describe the three major kinds of bacteria; define endospore and name the function of this structure; define and describe the principal mode of bacterial reproduction; define and illustrate bacterial conjugation, transformation, and transduction, and indicate how each of these processes promotes genetic variability; cite the principal source of genetic variation in bacteria and show how bacteria can adapt rapidly to changing environments without sex.
8. List at least three ways in which bacteria are environmentally or economically beneficial; list at least five diseases caused by bacteria; identify at least three "lines of defense" that protect the human body against the invasion and proliferation of pathogenic microorganisms; differentiate between bacterial exotoxins and endotoxins; define immunization, vaccine, and antiserum; distinguish between active and passive immunity.
9. Distinguish between legionellosis, Legionnaires' disease, and Pontiac fever; describe the circumstances surrounding the discovery of *Legionella pneumonphila;* construct diagrams illustrating how this microorganism was first isolated and how it was demonstrated to be the cause of Legionnaires' disease. Identify nutritional patterns that occur among bacteria and blue-green algae; illustrate the environmental and economic importance of blue-green algae; name at least one feature that distinguishes bacteria from blue-green algae.
10. List identifying characteristics of viruses and rickettsias; name at least five diseases caused by viruses and one disease caused by rickettsias; define and state the function of interferon; cite at least two hypotheses that have been proposed to explain the evolutionary origin of viruses and rickettsias.

Living creatures on earth are a direct product of the earth. There is every reason to believe that living things owe their origin entirely to certain physical and chemical properties of the ancient earth. Nothing supernatural appears to have been involved—only time and natural physical and chemical laws operating within the peculiarly suitable earthy environment. Given such an environment, life probably *had* to happen; once the earth had formed, with particular chemical and physical properties, it was then virtually inevitable that life would later originate on it also. Similarly, if other solar systems contain planets where chemical and physical conditions resemble those of the ancient earth, life would originate on these other planets as well. It is now believed strongly that life occurs not only on earth but probably widely throughout the universe.

Fig. 30.1 The planet Jupiter. Some scientists suspect that environmental conditions in one or more layers of Jupiter's atmosphere resembles those present on the early earth. If so, further study of Jupiter may help clarify how life originated on earth.

THE ORIGIN OF LIFE

The beginning phases of life can be envisaged somewhat more clearly than many of the later ones. The first steps must have taken place on a purely chemical level, and it is now possible to simulate the simplest of these in the test tube. Even so, vast uncertainties still remain.

Chemical Evolution

According to the most widely accepted hypothesis, the solar system started out some 10 or more billion years ago as a hot, rotating ball of atomic gases. In it, hydrogen atoms probably were the most abundant, and other, heavier kinds of atoms were present in lesser quantities. The sun was formed when most of these gases gravitated toward the center of the ball. Even today the sun is composed largely of hydrogen atoms. A swirling belt of gases remained outside the new sun. In time this belt broke up into a few smaller gas clouds; these spinning masses of fiery gases were the early planets.

The earth probably began, about 4.6 billion years ago, as a glowing mass of free hydrogen and other elements. These eventually became sorted out according to weight. Heavy ones such as iron and nickel sank toward the center of the earth, where they are still present today. Lighter atoms such as silicon and aluminum formed a middle shell. The very lightest, such as hydrogen, nitrogen, oxygen, and carbon, collected in the outermost layers. In time the temperature of these surface gases became low enough to permit the formation of compounds, and free atoms then largely disappeared.

On the basis of the known chemical properties and the presumed relative abundance of hydrogen, carbon, oxygen, and nitrogen, the surface gases should have given rise to some half-dozen different combinations: water (H_2O); methane (CH_4); ammonia (NH_3); carbon dioxide (CO_2); hydrogen cyanide (HCN); and hydrogen molecules (H_2). We have evidence that at least the first three of these compounds actually came into being not only on the early earth but on Jupiter and other planets as well (Fig. 30.1). On the hot, primitive earth all of these compounds would have remained gaseous and could have given rise to new compounds later.

Temperatures in the outer layers of the earth eventually became low enough to allow some of the gases to liquefy and some of the liquids in turn to

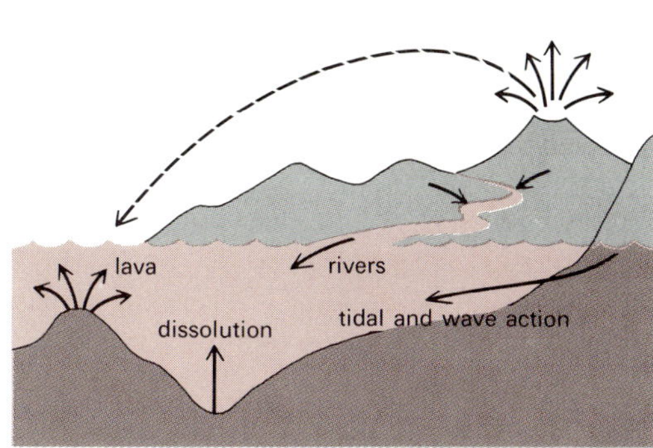

Fig. 30.2 Sources of ocean salt. Some came from volcanoes, both submarine and terrestrial; some was dissolved out of the sea bottom; some resulted from tidal action, which crumbled and dissolved the shorelines; and some originated on the land surface, leached out by rain and rivers.

solidify. Thus although to this day the earth contains a hot, thickly flowing center, the middle shell of lighter substances became a solid, gradually thickening crust. And as this crust thickened and cooled, it wrinkled and folded and gave rise to the first mountain ranges. Overlying the crust was the outer atmospheric mantle, which remained gaseous.

When the crust had cooled below the boiling point of water, most of the water in the atmosphere must have fallen as rain and formed oceans. Dissolved in them must have been some of the atmospheric methane and ammonia, as well as salts and minerals that leached out slowly from the solid crust of the earth and that spewed forth from numerous volcanoes. The oceans apparently acquired their saltiness relatively early, and to a small extent they became saltier still during succeeding ages (Fig. 30.2).

The earth finally was cool enough to support life. But where did the first organisms come from? Could life have developed spontaneously from the atoms and molecules present on the primitive planet? Results of several experiments suggest that this is just what happened. In 1953, for example, Stanley Miller, then a graduate student at the University of Chicago, demonstrated that *organic* compounds can arise spontaneously from simple inorganic substances (Fig. 30.3). Miller first prepared flasks containing mixtures of water, methane, ammonia, and other substances presumed to have been present in the surface environment of the early earth. Electricity was then discharged

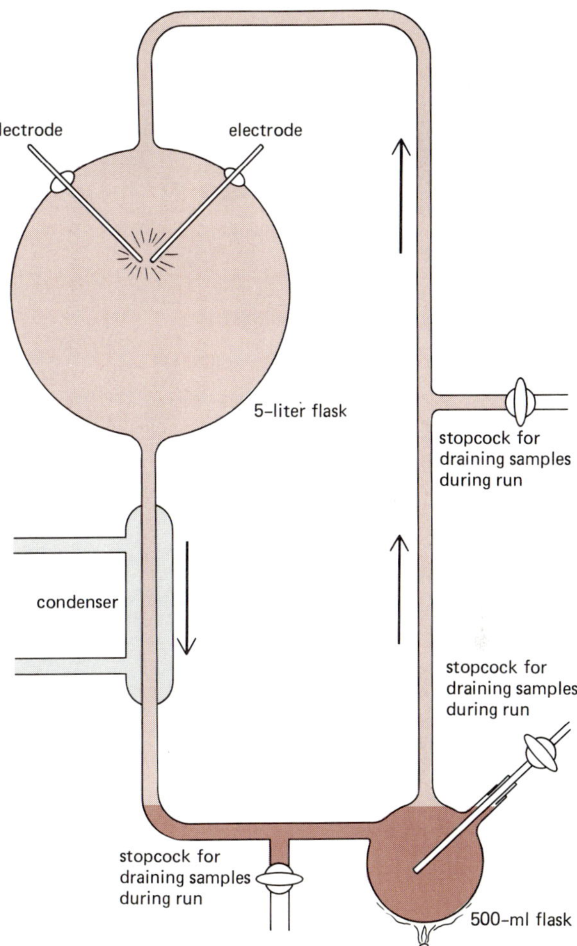

Fig. 30.3 Spontaneous generation of organic compounds. Schematized representation of an apparatus designed in the early 1950s by Stanley L. Miller and Harold C. Urey to test the hypothesis that organic compounds can be produced spontaneously from inorganic substances presumed to be present in the primitive atmosphere of the earth. Solutions of inorganic materials are heated (lower right), driving gases through a closed loop. Arrows indicate direction of gas flow. The heated gases are subjected to electric sparks (upper left), simulating discharges of lightning, also presumed to have been present in the earth's early atmosphere. Hot gases are cooled for reboiling by a condenser. Samples of circulating materials can be removed for analysis through stopcocks.

through these mixtures for several days, to stimulate the lightning discharges of the early earth. When the contents of the flask were examined, many amino acids, fatty acids, sugars, and other simple organic compounds were found to be present.

Thus there is excellent reason to think that, with energy from lightning and also from solar ra-

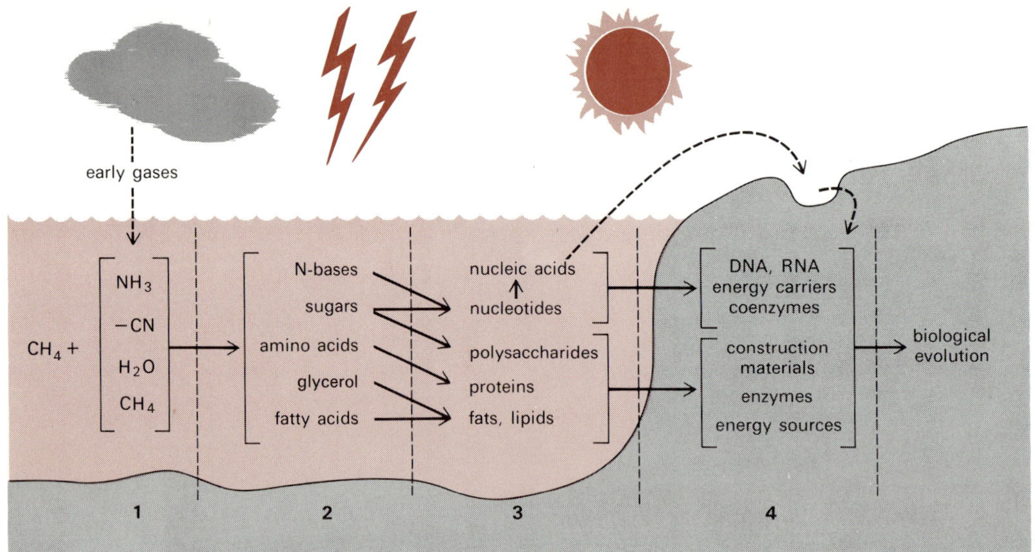

Fig. 30.4 Chemical evolution: summary of probable early synthesis reactions. At least three or four successive phases appear to have been involved. The original gaseous raw materials came from the early atmosphere (1), and, with the aid of energy from lightning and the sun, key biological compounds were synthesized progressively in the ocean (2, 3). The later, more complex synthesis reactions perhaps took place in sand pockets along the shore, where required ingredients could become highly concentrated by evaporation of water (4). The outcome was the origin of the first living units, and further biological evolution then followed.

diation, simple inorganic materials could give rise to a variety of organic compounds that accumulated in the ancient seas. Such compounds would have represented the chemical "staples" out of which more complex organic materials could be synthesized later (Fig. 30.4). At some point in the course of this *chemical* evolution, *biological* evolution could have begun: formation of the very complex chemicals so characteristic of life, and development of cells, the first actual living units.

Biological Evolution

If life on earth originated in this way, it is physically and chemically most plausible to assume that the critical events in the creation of cells took place not in the open sea, where the necessary ingredients would not have remained together, but along the shores of the early ocean. The sand and clay particles there would have provided surfaces to which oceanic molecules could have adhered, and evaporation of water would have increased the concentrations of such molecules. Indeed, microscopic sand pockets containing highly concentrated, nearly dry accumulations of simple organic materials well could have been the birthplaces of cells. This surmise again is reinforced by experimental data. For example, if concentrated mixtures of amino acids are heated under nearly dry conditions, proteinlike complexes are formed. Moreover, if mixtures of simple starting compounds such as ammonia and certain amino acids are heated under almost dry conditions, products appear that have the characteristics of nitrogen bases.

Furthermore, when complexes of proteins are heated in a concentrated aqueous solution at 130 to 180°C, the complexes aggregate spontaneously as small droplets called *microspheres* (Fig. 30.5). Many of the droplets have a two-layered outer boundary, suggestive of the double-layered plasma membrane of living cells. Under suitable conditions, the microspheres grow when they absorb dissolved organic molecules, and they even divide, producing smaller "daughter" microspheres. Such structures are not alive, but their spontaneous development illustrates the extent to which lifelike behavior is based on purely chemical and physical attributes.

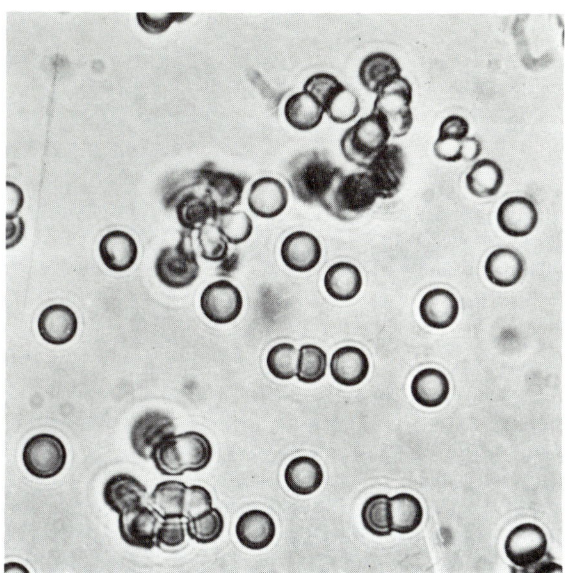

Fig. 30.5 Microspheres. Some of these nonliving, spherical structures are dividing, forming "daughter" microspheres.

Furthermore, it is possible that, inside minute membrane-bounded droplets along the shore, some of the proteinlike materials formed at the time could have been active enzymatically. These could then have triggered development of nucleotides by promoting chemical reactions between nitrogen bases, simple sugars, and phosphates. And nucleotides are only a simple chemical step away from energy carriers such as ATP. Once enzymes and ATP are available, a few additional chemical steps can lead to nucleotide derivatives such as coenzymes and to nucleic acids such as genetically active DNA and RNA. In their turn, the DNA molecules in the droplets could have controlled the formation of particular, *specific* proteins, just as they are known to do today.

In the laboratory it is now possible to create DNA, RNA, and specific proteins artificially from simpler organic precursors, and by steps that virtually duplicate those taking place in a living cell (see also Chap. 14). Thus there exists important experimental support for the hypothesis that progressive synthesis reactions, roughly as outlined above, must have been the critical steps in the original development of living matter. In effect, the droplets on the ocean shore would have been distinctly individual units marked off from the surrounding ocean water, and they would have remained individualized even if they absorbed more water and were later washed back to the open ocean. Such units would have been precursors of living cells (Fig. 30.6).

It therefore appears possible that the first cells on earth developed spontaneously from materials present on or near the planet's surface (Fig. 30.7). But did the first cells originate on earth? Some scientists speculate that life originated elsewhere and subsequently came to colonize earth once the primitive planet had cooled sufficiently. Some circumstantial evidence supports this conclusion. For example, amino acids and other organic molecules have been identified in several extraterrestrial objects and environments, including comets and interstellar gas clouds. Although no one is yet certain, sequences of life-generating synthesis reactions similar or identical to those already described may also occur deep in space.

Regardless of their origin, the first cells evolved as new forms of life, and here is perhaps the most dramatic illustratation that small beginnings can have surprisingly large endings. Evolution has been the hallmark of life ever since, and life today still is unceasingly forming and molding. Indeed it will never be finally "finished" until its last spark is extinguished.

Premonera

Early Groups

For present purposes the earliest cells can collectively be called *Premonera,* or organisms that preceded the Monera (see Chap. 2 for information on how organisms are classified).

Like modern *heterotrophs,* survival of the first premoneran cells undoubtedly depended on a continual supply of organic nutrients. Such nutrients probably were most readily available in the early ocean, in the form of methane and other simple organic molecules. Heterotrophs that can subsist solely on chemicals such as these are *chemoheterotrophs,* as already discussed in Chap. 11.

A few chemoheterotrophs survive today. All are microbes, such as certain of the methane-producing bacteria, or *methanogens.* These organisms commonly inhabit airless environments: stagnant swamps, sewage-treatment tanks, and the intestinal tract of some animals, people included. As their

Fig. 30.6 A possible origin of the first cells. Appropriate chemical ingredients might have accumulated by adsorption in microscopic pockets along the seashore (1), and these ingredients could have become concentrated progressively (2). Under relatively dry conditions and perhaps with the aid of ATP, which might have been present, nucleic acids and proteins could have formed (3). Some of the proteins then could have made possible enzymatically accelerated reactions and formation of structural membranes and internal fibrils (4). Finally, primitive cellular compartments might have been washed out to sea (5).

name suggests, methanogens produce methane as a metabolic by-product (because of its release from methanogens in swamps, methane is also called marsh gas).

Methanogens are among the simplest bacteria. Recent studies have shown the ribosomes, cell walls, and other cellular components of methanogens to be much less complex and very different from the corresponding structures of other bacteria. Indeed, the considerable differences between methanogens and other Monera have prompted some biologists to propose that methane-producing bacteria be classified in a kingdom separate from all other organisms. This reclassification may not occur, but it is possible that modern methanogens resemble ancient Premonera more closely than any other group of living organisms.

Later Groups

In later ages, premoneran cells must have become diversified as numerous new cell types in response to a powerful environmental stimulus: the gradual disappearance of free organic molecules from the ocean. For as more and more such molecules were used as food by an ever-increasing multitude of reproducing cells, the global rate of food consumption eventually must have become greater than the rate of food formation from organic substances. In time, therefore, the ocean became a largely inorganic medium, as it still is today. Unless the early cells then could have evolved new ways of obtaining food, they soon would have nourished themselves into extinction. Evidently they did not.

One of the first evolutionary responses to dwindling food supplies probably was the development of *symbiosis* (see also Chap. 8). If foods could not be obtained from the open ocean, they still could be obtained inside the bodies of living cells. Methods by which smaller cells could enter larger ones probably evolved almost as soon as cells themselves had originated. Even nonliving microspheres, described earlier, are able to unite, forming larger, more complex units. In some cases the united cells undoubt-

Fig. 30.7 Early cells. This series of photographs shows fossilized cells found in 3.5-billion-year-old rocks in South Africa. The cells resemble certain modern photosynthetic bacteria (cyanobacteria). Some of the fossilized cells appear to be undergoing cell division.

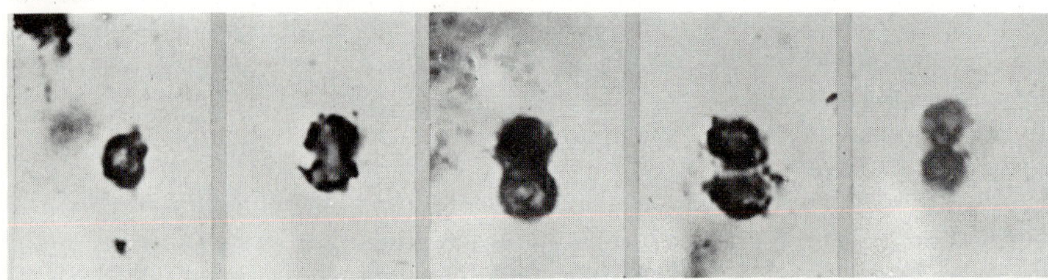

edly became mutually interdependent, but in many other instances the smaller cells probably became parasites of the larger hosts, and parasitism must have been an effective new way of life for many of the early cells (Fig. 30.8).

Another new way that required relatively little evolutionary adjustment was *saprotrophism*. Here a cell drew food molecules from the bodies of dead cells or disintegrated cellular material. Organic *decay* of such material was a result and has occurred ever since. Saprotrophic types are so abundant today in all environments that practically every organic substance begins to decay almost immediately after exposure.

A third new process that permitted survival despite dwindling food supplies was *holotrophism*, "eating" other living cells whole. This method of feeding presumably originated through phagocytosis, the general capacity of a cell to engulf microscopic particles (see Chap. 5). Amoeboid pseudopodia and permanent cellular mouths (*gullets*) must have been later elaborations.

But all three of these new heterotrophic food-gathering procedures were ultimately as self-limiting as chemoheterotrophism. All these forms of nutrition merely redistributed organic materials already in existence. If totally new food sources had not been obtained, life would have had to cease sooner or later.

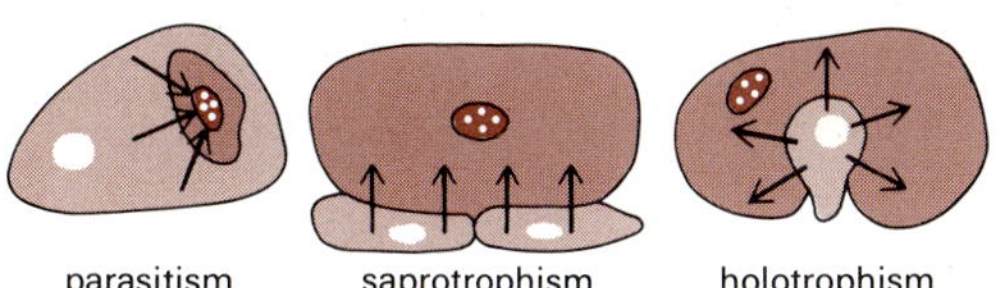

Fig. 30.8 Heterotrophic nutrition. In parasitism one organism obtains food from another living one (a small parasitic cell is shown inside a larger host cell). In saprotrophism food is obtained from dead organisms. And in holotrophism one organism eats another in whole or in part. These three methods are noncreative; they merely redistribute already existing foods and do not generate new supplies.

Autotrophism and the Oxygen Revolution

The raw materials for new foods were still present in abundance. Water was in inexhaustible supply and, in addition to methane, an even better source of carbon now existed directly inside cells in the form of respiratory carbon dioxide. With CO_2 and water available, organic molecules could be manufactured by cells, provided that new external sources of energy could be found. Internal energy was still obtainable from ATP, to be sure, but ATP was itself among the very organic molecules that were in danger of disappearing.

We know by hindsight that some Premonera actually did evolve means of using new external sources of energy. One group included cell types that could absorb sulfur, iron, nitrogen, or one of a number of other mineral materials obtainable in the environment. Such inorganic substances could be made to undergo various energy-yielding reactions in the cells, and chemical energy so obtained could then serve in transforming internal CO_2 and water into organic food molecules. Nutrition by such a process of *chemosynthesis* still occurs today in some of the bacteria (Fig. 30.9).

Fig. 30.9 Autotrophic nutrition. In chemosynthesis (1) energy is obtained from inorganic raw materials, and with the aid of this energy the organism creates organic materials out of carbon dioxide and water. Various inorganic by-products result as well. In photosynthesis (2) energy is obtained from the sun by means of energy-trapping molecules such as chlorophyll. The organism then again creates organic nutrients out of carbon dioxide and water. Oxygen is a by-product here (derived from water, which is split into separate hydrogen and oxygen fractions).

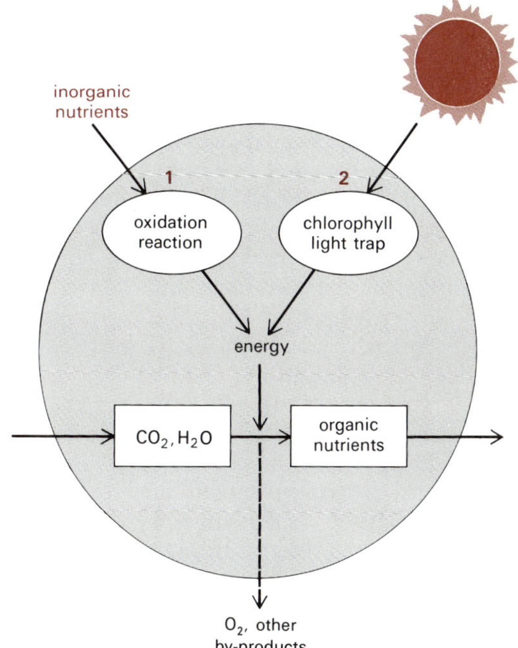

$CH_4 + 2\ O_2 \longrightarrow CO_2 + 2\ H_2O$

$4\ NH_3 + 3\ O_2 \longrightarrow 2\ N_2 + 6\ H_2O$

$O_2 + 2O_2 \longrightarrow 2O_3$, ozone

metals, minerals + $O_2 \longrightarrow$ ores, rocks

organisms + $O_2 \longrightarrow$ aerobic respiration

Fig. 30.10 The oxygen revolution. Oxygen from photosynthesis reacted with other materials. A major result was the establishment of a new, modern atmosphere containing N_2, CO_2, and H_2O, in addition to O_2 itself.

However, chemosynthesis was probably far less widespread right from the start than another new nutritional process, *photosynthesis*, evolved by other groups of Premonera. In photosynthesis the external energy source is light, and with the aid of the green photosensitive compound *chlorophyll* the energy of light is used to transform elements of CO_2 and water into foods. Collectively, chemosynthesis and photosynthesis represent the *autotrophic* forms of nutrition, exhibited by organisms that can survive in an exclusively inorganic environment and that therefore do not depend on other organisms.

Thus, once the autotrophic production of new organic compounds was assured, it did not matter that the supply of free molecular foods in the ocean finally became inadequate. Photosynthetic cells could make foods for themselves; holotrophic forms could swallow such cells as well as one another; parasites could invade photosynthesizers or holotrophs; and saprotrophs could find foods in the dead bodies of any of these. Today photosynthesis still supports all living creatures except the chemosynthesizers.

As photosynthesis occurred on an ever-increasing scale, it brought about far-reaching changes in the physical environment. A by-product of photosynthesis is free molecular oxygen (O_2), a gas that combines readily with other substances. The gas escaped from photosynthetic cells into the ocean and from there to the atmosphere, and it must have reacted promptly with everything it could. A slow, profound "oxygen revolution" then occurred. In the course of it the ancient atmosphere was transformed into the modern one, which no longer contains methane, ammonia, and cyanide. Instead it consists mainly of water vapor, carbon dioxide, and molecular nitrogen, plus large quantities of free molecular oxygen itself (Fig. 30.10).

Moreover, under the impact of x-rays and other high-energy radiation from space, oxygen molecules several miles up in the new atmosphere combined with each other and formed a layer of *ozone* (O_3). This layer became an excellent screen against high-energy rays, and ever since it has protected living organisms from excessive amounts of such space radiation. Free oxygen also reacted with the solid crust of the earth and converted most metals and minerals to *oxides*, the familiar ores and rocks now making up much of the land surface. Finally, free oxygen made possible a new form of respiration. The earliest cells respired *anaerobically*, without oxygen, and to a small extent all living organisms still do so (see Chap. 12). But when environmental oxygen became available in quantity, organisms newly evolving at the time developed means of using this gas. Since then the far more efficient oxygen-requiring, or *aerobic*, form of respiration has been perpetuated.

Evidently, the activities of the early organisms greatly altered the physical character of the earth and also the biological character of the organisms themselves. So has it been ever since: the physical earth creates and influences the development of the biological earth, and the biological earth then reciprocates by influencing the development of the physical earth.

In parallel with the nutritional evolution of the Premonera, an internal structural evolution must have taken place as well. At first, the gene-forming DNA molecules probably were suspended free within the cell substance. Occasionally such nucleic acid molecules could have escaped from a cell into the open ocean and by accident could have encountered other cells and entered them. Such transferable nucleic acids conceivably may have been ancestral to the viruses. As noted in Chap. 28 and in a later section of this chapter, modern viruses have similarly transferable nucleic acids, and it is possible that ancestral viruses perhaps were little more than naked nucleic acid molecules. If so, introduction of such molecules from one early cell into another must have had important consequences. For the transferred acids were cellular genes, and as they became shuffled among cells, so did the activities that such genes controlled. Exchanges of nucleic acids thus would have altered the genetic constitution of cells, and this process would have promoted the evolution of a great variety of new cell types.

Prokaryotes and Eukaryotes

Judging from the results today, we know that two of the new structural cell types came to have particular significance in later evolution. In one line of descent, the originally freely suspended nucleic acids later must have aggregated in threadlike filaments that formed loose clumps. Such clumps remained embedded in, and in direct contact with, the rest of the cell substance. The organisms exhibiting this type of internal cellular arrangement collectively form the *Monera*, represented today by the *bacteria* and the *blue-green algae*. These organisms are also called *prokaryotes* (*pro-*, "before"; *karyon;* "kernel" or "nut"; see section A of Glossary), a term that denotes their distinction from *eukaryotes* (*eu-*, "true"), species whose cells contain distinct nuclei. All organisms except Monera and viruses are eukaryotes. As a group, Monera exhibit four of the five methods of nutrition. Bacteria are variously photosynthetic, chemosynthetic, parasitic, or saprotrophic; blue-green algae are largely photosynthetic. Evidently all methods except holotrophic eating occur.

In a second major line of descent, the gene-forming nucleic acids in each cell again condensed as threadlike filaments. However, proteins became an integral structural part of such filaments, and these nucleoprotein organelles represented *chromosomes*. Furthermore, a double membrane formed around the chromosomes in a cell, setting off a distinct *nuclear* region from a surrounding *cytoplasmic* region. How the double membrane, or *nuclear envelope*, originated is not known; some biologists speculate that it may have evolved through an infolding and pinching off of the plasma membrane. All the cytoplasmic organelles now found in modern eukaryotic cells then evolved. Many membraneous structures, such as the endoplasmic reticulum, chloroplasts, and mitochondria also may have developed from infoldings of the plasma membrane. However, certain biologists have proposed a symbiotic origin for the latter two types of organelles.

According to this theory, chloroplasts are derived from ancestral blue-green algae that once lived symbiotically inside larger nongreen cells. Mitochondria are assumed to have originated through an analogous symbiotic relationship between ancestral bacteria and larger host cells. Proponents of the symbiotic theory provide the following supporting evidence:

1. Like Monera, but unlike other organelles, chloroplasts and mitochondria possess DNA.

2. The structural organization of mitochondrial and chloroplast DNA is very similar to that of moneran chromosomes.

3. The size of mitochondria and chloroplasts is similar to that of most moneran cells.

4. Many modern eukaryotic cells house symbiotic bacteria or blue-green algae in their cytoplasm.

5. Enzymes for the synthesis of DNA, RNA, and proteins in chloroplasts and mitochondria are similar to those of prokaryotes and unlike those in the rest of the cell.

6. Ribosomes of chloroplasts and mitochondria resemble ribosomes of Monera more than those of eukaryotic cells.

7. Certain drugs that inhibit RNA or protein synthesis in prokaryotes do not affect those processes in eukaryotic cells, and vice versa. In almost every case, mitochondria and chloroplasts react to the drugs in a manner identical to prokaryotes.

Despite these arguments, many biologists remain skeptical of the symbiotic theory. Here are a few of their counterarguments:

1. If mitochondria and chloroplasts arose by infoldings of the plasma membrane of prokaryote ancestors, these newly evolved organelles naturally would parallel prokaryotes in traits such as drug sensitivity, ribosome characteristics, and enzyme types.

2. Functions carried out by mitochondria and chloroplasts are largely performed by the plasma membrane of prokaryotes. This evidence is consistent with the hypothesis that the two organelles originated from infoldings of the plasma membrane.

3. DNA and the protein synthesis machinery of chloroplasts, mitochondria, *and* eukaryotic cells probably all evolved from prokaryotes. Nuclear DNA and its associated protein synthesis machinery presumably underwent greater evolutionary change than that of either mitochondria or chloroplasts, thereby accounting for the differences between the two in modern eukaryotic cells.

4. DNA of chloroplasts and mitochondria contain only a few of the genes required for the functioning of these organelles. All other genes are housed in nuclear DNA, including many required

TABLE 30.1
Modes of Nutrition of Modern Protists

Category	Modes of nutrition
algae (3 phyla)	most exclusively photosynthetic; a few unicellular forms both photosynthetic and holotrophic
slime molds	most holotrophic and/or saprotrophic; some parasitic on flowering plants
protozoa	most holotrophic; a few parasitic

for reproduction of chloroplasts and mitochondria. If the two organelles arose symbiotically, their ancestors originally must have had all the instructions required for self-perpetuation. Subsequently, many of these genes must have been transferred to the nucleus of the host cell. Yet there is no evidence that any such massive transfer of genes ever occurred, nor has anyone come up with a reasonable explanation of how such a transfer could have taken place.

Arguments concerning the symbiotic theory of mitochondrial and chloroplasts origins are likely to continue, with little hope of resolution. Evidence irrefutably establishing the origin of these or other organelles of eukaryotic cells may have been obliterated by the passage of time.

Their evolutionary origins notwithstanding, most modern organisms are eukaryotes. Unicellular and other comparatively simple eukaryotes collectively constitute the *Protista*. A major part of the living world today is made up of three groups descended from early protists: *slime molds, protozoa,* and three phyla of *algae* (see Chap. 2). Collectively they exhibit all nutritional methods except chemosynthesis—photosynthesis, holotrophism, saprotrophism, and parasitism (Table 30.1). Certain groups of protists, notably some primitive algae, actually can carry out two or more of these methods simultaneously. Thus a given individual of this type might either photosynthesize or eat holotrophically or do both together.

Monera and Protista probably were the only organisms in existence for long ages (Fig. 30.11). Eventually, various Protista gave rise to three new groups of organisms: *Fungi, Animalia,* and *Plantae.* Fungi, which include yeasts, toadstools, mushrooms, rusts, smuts, and many other organisms, are exclusively saprotrophic or parasitic. Like animals, fungi ultimately depend on photosynthetic organisms for supplies of organic nutrients. In many other respects fungi resemble plants, absorbing nutrients, for example, molecule by molecule through cell walls.

Animalia, or animals, evolved about $\frac{3}{4}$ billion years ago. Some taxonomists classify animals as *Metazoa.* Neither the date when animals first evolved nor the exact evolutionary source of the new group can be pinpointed well. But it is clear that these organisms must have lost all nutritional methods except holotrophism and parasitism, that they were multicellular, and that they attained new levels of structural complexity: they possessed *organs* and later also *organ systems,* and their individual development passed through distinct *embryonic* and *larval* phases.

Much later, about 350 million years ago, ancient Protista also gave rise to another basically new group (see Fig. 30.11). In this case the date is somewhat more certain, and the specific ancestors appear to have been some of the multicellular green algae then in existence. The new group, like their algal ancestors, had lost all nutritional methods except photosynthesis, and the structural complexity again reached the organ and organ-system levels. Moreover, the organisms characteristically also passed through embryonic phases of development. This group, the *Plantae,* or *Metaphyta,* comprised the *plants.*

Today the living world is a collection of Monera, Protista, Fungi, Animalia, and Plantae (see Fig. 2.14). Viruses are not cells and cannot reproduce outside a living host. Indeed, they display only some of the characteristics common to cells and organisms. Consequently, viruses represent a unique group of exclusively parasitic particles that exist in the "twilight zone" between the living and the inanimate. For this reason viruses are not included in the taxonomic chart below although they are discussed in this chapter.

The taxonomic chart below lists all five kingdoms, one in color type and four in black type. Monera and its subdivisions (color type) are discussed in the present chapter. The taxa in black type are not discussed in the present chapter but

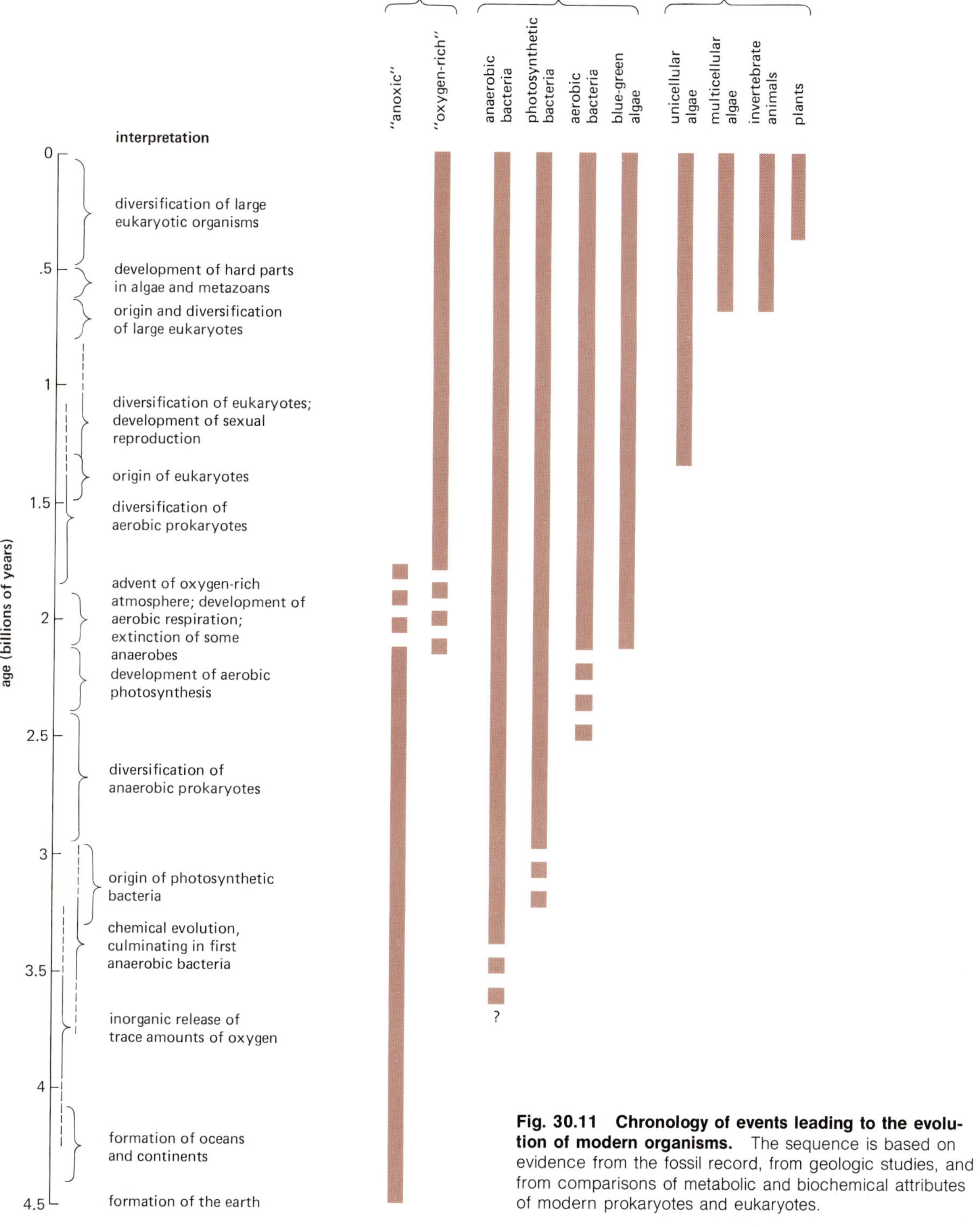

Fig. 30.11 Chronology of events leading to the evolution of modern organisms. The sequence is based on evidence from the fossil record, from geologic studies, and from comparisons of metabolic and biochemical attributes of modern prokaryotes and eukaryotes.

are included to give a clear picture of the relative position of the groups discussed in the overall taxonomic scheme. This convention is followed in the taxonomic charts of Chaps. 31 through 35.

Kingdom	Phylum	Subphylum	Class
Monera	Schizophyta (bacteria)		
	Cyanophyta (blue-green algae)		
Protista			
Fungi			
Plantae (Metaphyta)			
Animalia (Metazoa)			

MONERA

We cannot be sure whether Monera arose from just one group of premoneran cells or from two or more such groups, but we are sure that Monera appear to be more primitive than Protista in virtually all their characteristics.

As might be expected in view of their presumed evolutionary antiquity, Monera are distinguished largely by negative characteristics (Fig. 30.12). For example, a moneran cell does *not* possess an organized nucleus with a distinct surrounding membrane. Experiments indicate that the genetic DNA does form filamentous organelles, but the structure of these organelles does *not* correspond to that of chromosomes of the type found in other organisms. Instead, the moneran genetic material appears microscopically as one or more clumps exposed directly to the surrounding cytoplasm.

The cytoplasm itself does *not* appear to contain vacuoles, and it can*not* be observed to undergo the streaming movements typical of other cell types. Many Monera are photosynthetic, and these do *not* have complexly organized chloroplasts like those found in all other photosynthetic cells. Instead the structural unit of photosynthesis is a *chromatophore,* a protein disk that greatly resembles a single layer of a granum of a true chloroplast. Many such chromatophores normally are present. Monera also

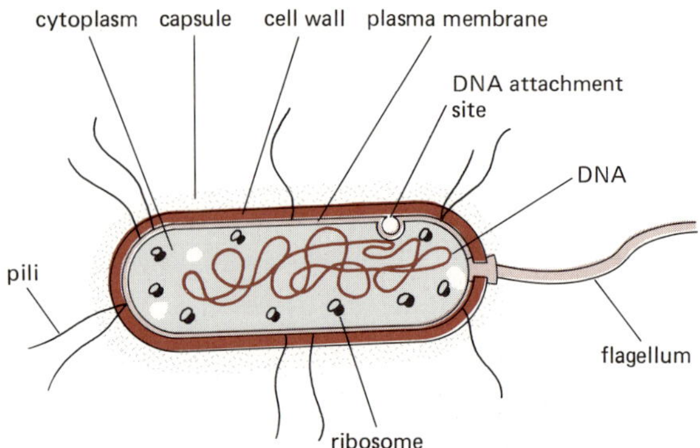

Fig. 30.12 The moneran cell, diagrammatic. Common features of moneran cells. The highly coiled, circular DNA of Monera is looped throughout the center of the cell; the hereditary material is not bounded by a nuclear envelope. The plasma membrane is infolded at various points, often where it attaches to a loop of DNA. Food and waste storage granules are interspersed between ribosomes throughout the cell interior. A rigid cell wall usually forms the outer boundary. Blue-green algae and some bacteria have a less rigid slime sheath, or capsule, around the cell wall. Some bacteria have one or more flagella, which propel the organism through watery environments. In addition, some bacteria have hairlike pili extending from the cell surface. Many of these proteinaceous filaments function as attachment structures, holding a bacterium to another cell or to other objects.

are without endoplasmic reticula, mitochondria, or Golgi bodies, but they do contain an abundance of ribosomes, the only organelles present that appear to be functionally equivalent to those of other cell types. These many features of nonpossession clearly suggest that, at the time the Monera arose, the internal elaboration and specialization of cellular structure had not progressed very far.

Within the moneran category, the bacteria form the phylum *Schizophyta,* and the blue-green algae, the phylum *Cyanophyta.* The exact evolutionary relation of one phylum to the other is still relatively obscure.

BACTERIA

Phylum Schizophyta (2000 species) In terms of numbers of individuals, bacteria probably outnumber all other organisms. They occur wherever life on earth is possible at all, and they are present in numerous places where other organisms cannot exist. They are the smallest cells known, averaging about 1 to 3 μm in length as compared with about 10 μm for most kinds of cells of other organisms. Bacteria usually have a cell wall, made of polysaccharides, proteins, and frequently also lipids. Often this wall in turn is surrounded by a gelatinous *capsule,* composed of mixtures of carbohydrates and amino acids. Frequently it is the presence or absence of a capsule that determines whether or not a bacterium will be disease-producing.

Bacteria are basically unicelluar, but many grow in colonies and form chains, disks, or compact aggregates. Many also possess fine surface flagella that endow them with a certain amount of locomotor capacity (Fig. 30.13). Such flagella are structurally unique. Each consists of just a single fibril, chemically different from the flagellar fibrils of other cell types (see Chap. 5).

Bacteria as a whole have come to be of major significance to all other life on earth. Three general groups are of particular ecological importance: the saprotrophic *decay-causing* types in soil and water; the chemosynthetic *nitrogen-using* types (nitrifiers, denitrifiers, and nitrogen fixers), which contribute to the maintenance of the global nitrogen cycle; and the parasitic *pathogenic* bacteria, which produce disease. Table 30.2 lists the names of the main groups of bacteria (each equivalent in taxonomic rank to an order) and some of the characteristics of each group. On the basis of shape, three kinds of bacteria can be distinguished: a *coc-*

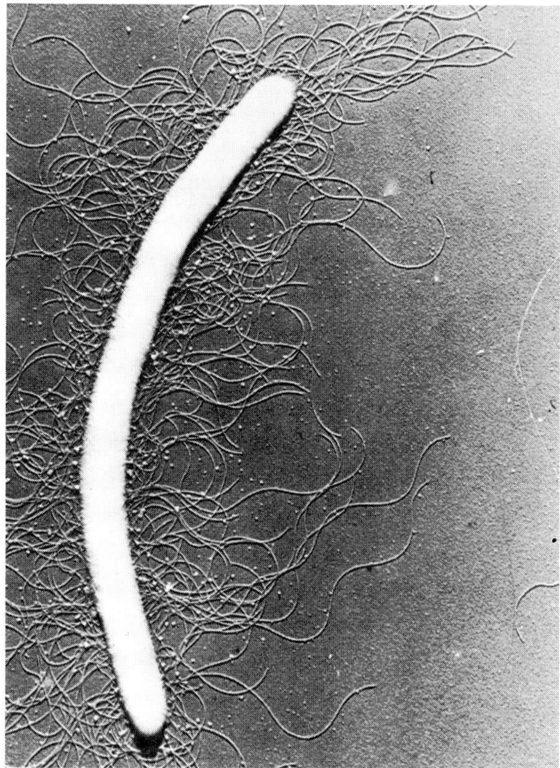

Fig. 30.13 Bacterial flagella. Electron micrograph of *Proteus vulgaris.* Note the large number of surface flagella. Only comparatively few bacterial types have such locomotor organelles.

TABLE 30.2
The Main Groups of Bacteria and Some of Their Characteristics

Group	Chief characteristics
Pseudomonadales, pseudomonads	most primitive group; generally flagellate; chemosynthetic, photosynthetic, and heterotrophic
Eubacteriales, true bacteria	largest group; some flagellate; all kinds of heterotrophism and symbiosis; many pathogenic; example: *Escherichia coli,* commensal in human gut
Actinomycetales, branching bacteria	in branching, filamentous colonies; antibiotic producers (streptomycin, aureomycin, etc.)
Spirochaetales, spiral bacteria	large spiral cells; whirling and spinning aids propulsion; example: *Treponema pallidum,* syphilis-causing parasite
Myxobacteriales, gliding slime bacteria	secrete slime track on which cells creep and glide; collect in masses and form "fruiting bodies" superficially like those of slime molds
Beggiatoales, gliding bacteria	in filamentous colonies; propulsion by jerky, oscillating movements; great resemblance to certain blue-green algae, except nonphotosynthetic

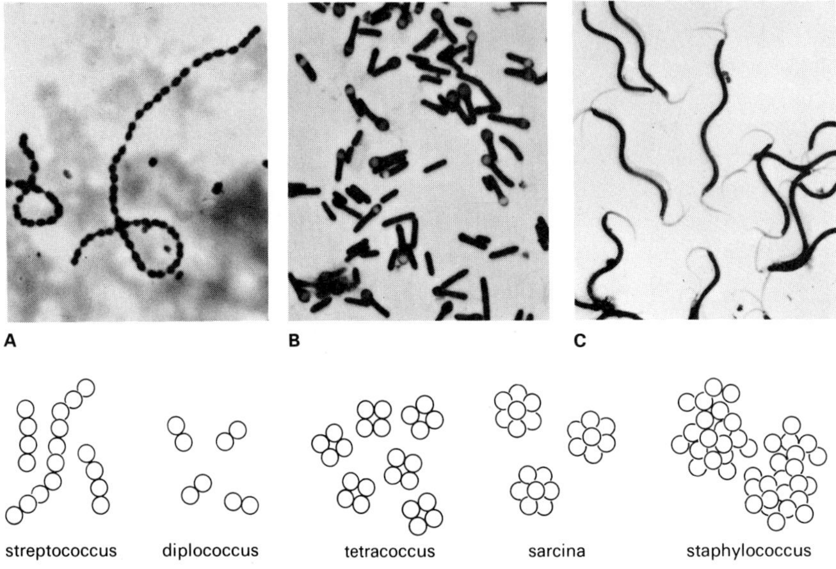

Fig. 30.14 Bacterial cells and colonies. (A) Cocci in chains. (B) Bacilli. (C) Spirilla. (D) Some of the types of colonies formed by cocci; the nature and designation of a colony varies according to whether cell divisions occur in one, two, or more numerous planes. *(A–C, General Biological Supply House, Inc.)*

cus is spherical, a *bacillus* rod-shaped, and a *spirillum* coiled (Fig. 30.14).

Some bacteria, many bacilli in particular, form specialized "resting cells" called *endospores* when environmental conditions become unfavorable. At such times the outer coat of an endospore develops inside a bacterial cell. The endospore coat encapsulates the DNA of the cell along with a small amount of cytoplasm (Fig. 30.15). The outer coat is highly protective and preserves the vital contents of the endospore until environmental conditions again become favorable. Endospores then germinate and produce new bacterial cells. Some endospores can survive an hour or more of boiling, decades of freezing, and perhaps even centuries of extremely dry conditions. Fortunately, endospores are produced by only a few pathogenic bacteria. Among this small group are *Clostridium tetani* and *C. botulinum,* causative agents of tetanus (lockjaw) and botulism, respectively.

With the exception of animal-like eating, all possible forms of food procurement occur among the bacteria. Some species are chemosynthesizers or photosynthesizers that produce their own food. The photosynthetic types contain unique varieties of chlorophyll all given the general name *bacteriochlorophyll,* located on the chromatophores. Bacterial photosynthesis also is chemically unique in that it never produces oxygen as a by-product.

Most bacteria are heterotrophs that depend on other organisms for food. Of these, some are free-living saprotrophs in terrestrial and aquatic environments, and the rest are parasitic, commensalistic, or mutualistic symbionts. Also, some bacteria must have oxygen for respiration, others can do without it, and still others can survive both with and without oxygen. In most of these types reserve foods are stored in the form of the polysaccharide glycogen.

The reproductive potential of bacteria is enormous. The interval between successive cell divisions can be as short as 20 min for some bacteria. Thus, if sufficient nutrients and space were availa-

Fig. 30.15 Thick-walled endospores have formed in bacilli. *(From C. F. Robinow, "The Cell," J. Brachet and A. E. Mirsky, eds., vol. 4, Academic, New York, 1960.)*

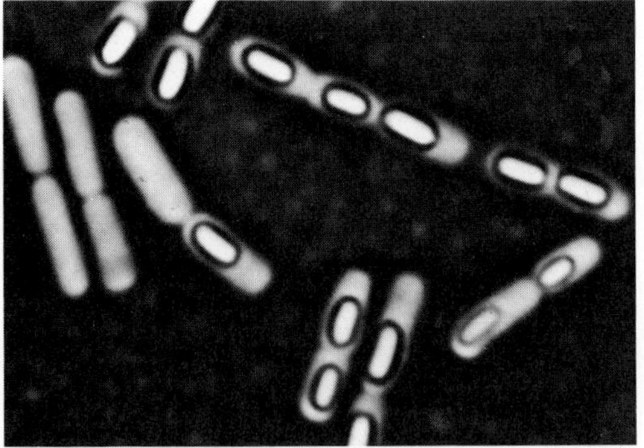

ble, a single bacterial cell could produce a mass of offspring equal to the mass of the earth in less than 2 days. Environmental conditions are rarely ideal, however, and bacteria do not grow at such rates for any length of time.

Most bacteria reproduce by *binary fission,* a type of nonmitotic cell division in which a parent cell divides across its midsection into two equal daughter cells. The DNA of the parent cell replicates prior to binary fission, and the daughter molecules then separate and become attached to the cell membrane of the parent cell at different sites. The subsequent division of the parent cell produces two cells that each contain one of the daughter molecules of DNA.

Binary fission produces offspring cells that are genetic copies of parent cells. New genotypes are introduced into bacterial populations by three types of genetic recombination—*conjugation, transformation,* and *transduction* (Fig. 30.16). During conjugation, a cytoplasmic bridge forms between specific types of mating cells, and a piece of DNA from one cell moves across the bridge into the other cell. The donated DNA often links together with the DNA of the recipient cell. As a result, new combinations of genes are established in recipient cells. In bacterial transformation, DNA extracted from one strain can be put in a medium that contains another strain of bacteria. These organisms then absorb some of the foreign DNA, incorporate it in their DNA, and thereby acquire some of the genetic traits of the original DNA donors. Similar in principle is bacterial transduction, in which viruses, not human experimenters, accomplish a transfer of DNA from one bacterial type to another. When a virus reproduces within an infected bacterium, pieces of bacterial DNA on occasion may be incorporated in the offspring viruses. If one of these offspring then infects a new bacterial host, additional bacterial genes are introduced into that host (see also Chap. 28). When a normally haploid bacterial cell receives extra DNA by one of these processes, it becomes partly diploid. This condition is only temporary, for a kind of gene-reduction process equivalent to meiosis takes place almost immediately.

Conjugation, transformation, and transduction promote genetic variability, but they occur too rarely to account for the rapid adaptation of bacteria to altered environments. However, rapid vegetative reproduction also facilitates rapid evolution,

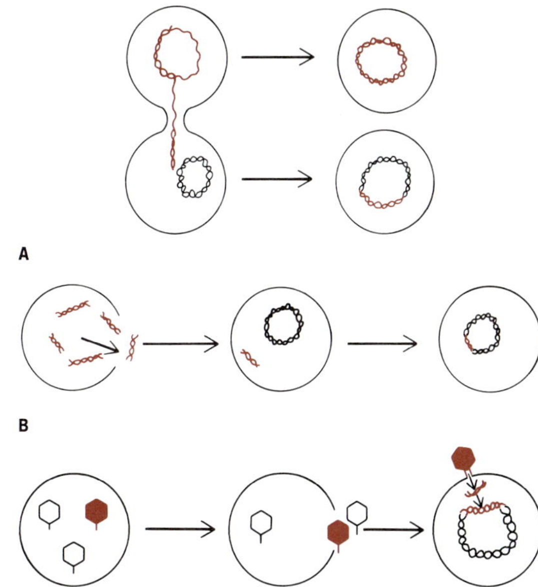

Fig. 30.16 Bacterial conjugation, transformation, and transduction. (A) Conjugation. Part of one strand of DNA is transferred from a donor cell to a recipient cell through a cytoplasmic bridge. Conjugation usually is interrupted before the entire strand is transferred. The donor strand is replicated as it enters the recipient cell, and the resulting double-stranded segment of donor DNA then usually replaces some DNA of the recipient cell. The portion of the DNA strand retained in the donor cell is replicated after conjugation is completed. (B) Transformation. Pieces of DNA released from fragmenting bacterial cells sometimes enter recipient bacteria. These pieces can replace some of the DNA of the recipient cells and thus alter their genetic characteristics. (C) Transduction. (Left) Newly forming bacteriophage viruses incorporate in their own structure some of the DNA of the host bacterium (color). (Center and right) When such viruses infect a new bacterial host, this host acquires additional bacterial genes.

particularly through mutations. Since Monera are haploid, each mutated gene immediately produces changes in traits. Therefore, even if millions or billions of bacteria succumb to one environment, a single survivor with appropriate mutations can within a few hours produce millions or billions of readapted organisms. Monera evidently rely on safety through numbers, and they generally do very well without sex.

Human beings benefit directly from bacteria in many ways. Some bacteria in the human intestine promote digestion of certain foods and synthesize vitamins that are absorbed by the body. Other species of saprotrophic bacteria play important roles in the decomposition of organic matter in sewage-treatment plants. Moreover, the metabolic by-products of bacteria are essential for the industrial manufacture of vinegar, acetone, butanol, lactic acid, rubber, cotton thread, leather goods, tobacco products, linen, and rope. Bacteria also participate in the production of many types of foods such as butter, cheese, coffee, cocoa, and sauerkraut. Scientists now are experimenting with a bacterial species that can convert cellulose to sucrose. At least one industry hopes to use this species in the production of livestock feed from waste paper. Ironically, scientists now use the metabolic by-products of certain beneficial bacteria to produce several antibiotic drugs that destroy many types of pathogenic bacteria. Such drugs include streptomycin, neomycin, Aureomycin, and Terramycin.

Compared with the large number of bacteria that directly or indirectly benefit mankind, the number of pathogenic types that infect human beings is very small. Nevertheless, the personal, economic, and social impact of these few species can be devastating (see accompanying Biology Highlight). Bubonic plague, for example, killed 25 million Europeans during the fourteenth century. Other diseases caused by bacteria include cholera, diphtheria, meningitis, bacterial pneumonia, scarlet fever, tuberculosis, typhoid fever, and leprosy.

The human body has several "lines of defense" against the invasion and proliferation of pathogenic microorganisms. Skin constitutes the first line of defense; it prevents most microorganisms from penetrating into internal tissues. Most viruses and bacteria enter these tissues either through lesions in skin or through natural body openings such as the mouth, nose, ears, anus, or genitals. Microorganisms are often then destroyed by the phagocytic activities of white bood cells or the immune response of lymphocytes (see Chap. 18). However, when an individual is exposed to the antigens of a microorganism for the first time, production of antibodies is a relatively slow process, requiring several days or weeks. Many pathogenic bacteria overcome the protective effects of phagocytic white cells during this interval and reproduce in great numbers.

Disease symptoms that appear in individuals at such times often result from the destruction of human tissue by rapidly growing populations of bacteria. Some bacteria, for example, produce poisons called *toxins.* Some of these are *exotoxins*, or poisons secreted by living bacterial cells into host tissues. In other cases, poisons are retained inside bacteria (*endotoxins*) and are released only when the cells die and disintegrate. Other pathogenic bacteria do not produce toxins but reproduce so rapidly that their immense population alone is sufficient to disrupt the normal functions of host tissues. Death of infected individuals can result if the normal functions of such tissues are impaired too severely.

In most cases, enough antibodies eventually are produced to destroy the pathogenic organisms. Depending on the nature of the immune response, human beings may then be immune to a second invasion of the microbes. For some diseases, such as whooping cough, the immunity is long-lasting. In other cases, such as most respiratory infections, the immunity lasts only for a few weeks or months. In still other cases, there is virtually no immunity to a second infection.

Severe infections by some pathogenic microorganisms can be prevented through *immunization.* Here individuals who have not contracted an infectious disease are inoculated with a *vaccine* or an *antiserum.* Vaccines are substances that contain antigens of specific pathogenic microbes. Such antigens can consist of dead microorganisms, of live microorganisms that have been treated in ways that prevent their rapid proliferation in host tissues, of small amounts of active bacterial toxins, or of treated, inactive toxins called *toxoids.* Tetanus "shots," for example, contain toxoids derived from the bacterium that causes tetanus. Regardless of their source, the antigens of vaccines produce *active immunity* by stimulating the production of antibodies in human beings.

Antiserums contain antibodies against the antigens of specific types of pathogenic microorganisms. Such antibodies are produced by injecting vaccines into animals, usually horses. Blood serum containing antibodies against the antigens of the vaccine is then removed from the animals and used to prepare antiserums. Because they contain presynthesized antibodies, antiserums provide almost immediate *passive immunity,* but this immunity is relatively short-lived.

Biology Highlight

Legionellosis: Discovery of a New (Old) Species of Pathogenic Bacteria

Although no one noticed, the spectre of tragedy had been apparent even before the gavel sounded final adjournment. The 58th Annual Convention of the Pennsylvania Department of the American Legion seemed to have gone off in typical style. There had been lots of partying, parades, meetings, elections of officers, and patriotic speeches. It had been a joyful celebration for most of the 4400 delegates and their families—but not for all.

By July 23, 1976, the third and next-to-last day of the convention, Sam Morris, a veteran of World War II and the Korean War, began to feel feverish. He felt so low, in fact, that he skipped dinner and spent the entire evening watching TV in his hotel room. Early the next day, Saturday, he began having stomach cramps and decided to leave the convention early. He drove from Philadelphia, the convention site, to his home in Lime Ridge. Upon arrival, he took a couple of aspirins and went to bed. When he awoke on Sunday he felt even worse. By Monday his fever had not subsided and he could not swallow without difficulty.

Believing he might have contracted food poisoning at the convention, Morris called his physician, Dr. Ernest Campbell, who quickly sent Morris to a nearby hospital in Bloomsburg. As Dr. Campbell was ordering a series of diagnostic tests for his patient, he learned that two of Morris's fellow conventioneers also had been admitted to the hospital suffering from similar symptoms. Campbell immediately suggested that the results of diagnostic tests performed on the three patients be compared. Although inconclusive, the data suggested that all three Legionnaires were suffering from typhoid fever.

Could these three cases signal the onset of a widespread epidemic? Dr. Campbell telephoned his concern to the Bloomsburg State Health Center. A few hours later, one of the three patients, 82-year-old William Baird, was dead.

Baird was not the first to die of the affliction, nor would he be the last. People who had attended the American Legion convention were showing up in hospitals throughout Pennsylvania. All displayed similar symptoms, chills, coughing, and fevers that ranged from 104 to 107°F. By Monday morning, August 2, evidence of an ongoing epidemic was undeniable. Several people had died of the feverish, pneumonialike illness; all were or recently had been in Philadelphia. The Pennsylvania Department of Health responded by declaring a statewide health alert. Scores of public health workers began organizing a systematic search for the cause of the illness.

There was much to do. The first step involved determining the characteristics of the illness, establishing who had become ill, and confirming when and where the affliction had been contracted. Finding a common denominator was the second step: what was unique about the people who had come down with the illness? How was their behavior different from companions who remained healthy? Such information might help establish how the disease-causing agent was contracted. And if that could be determined, the source and nature of the agent also might be identified.

To help gather and correlate data, the Center for Disease Control (CDC) of the U.S. Public Health Service dispersed 23 members of its staff throughout Pennsylvania. Located in a squat complex of red brick buildings in suburban Atlanta, Georgia, the CDC is the "family physician" of the American citizenry. It is the largest epidemiology center in the world, staffed by several hundred public health officials, laboratory technicians, and other medical personnel. The activities of the CDC take many forms, some statistical, others educational. But the most celebrated branch of this federal agency is the Epidemic Intelligence Service (EIS), a team of medical sleuths specially trained to identify, seek out, and destroy microbes, chemicals, or other agents that might trigger or perpetuate an epidemic.

The 23 representatives of the CDC dispatched to Pennsylvania during the week of August 2 all were members of the EIS. Upon arrival, they learned that 149 conventioneers already had developed disease symptoms. More would be stricken over the next several days. Eventually, 221 people would come down with the disease, and 34 would die.

The CDC investigators soon discovered that the illness was not confined to Legionnaires. Several of those afflicted had not attended the convention, but all had been in or near the Bellevue-Stratford Hotel, one of the facilities used to accommodate the conventioneers. Moreover, people who had stayed overnight at the Bellevue-Stratford displayed a higher incidence of illness than those who had roomed elsewhere. A first common denominator had been found.

Health officials then made another important and most gratifying discovery. All the relatives of Legionnaires who were stricken with the illness had attended the convention. This meant that the pathogenic agent was not transmitted from one person to another. How, then, did people contract the disease? Probably not through food or drink. People who ate at certain restaurants or attended particular dinner functions proved no more likely to come down with the illness than other conventioneers. However, certain observations suggested that the agent was transmitted through the air. People who had spent more time in the lobby of the Bellevue-Stratford or

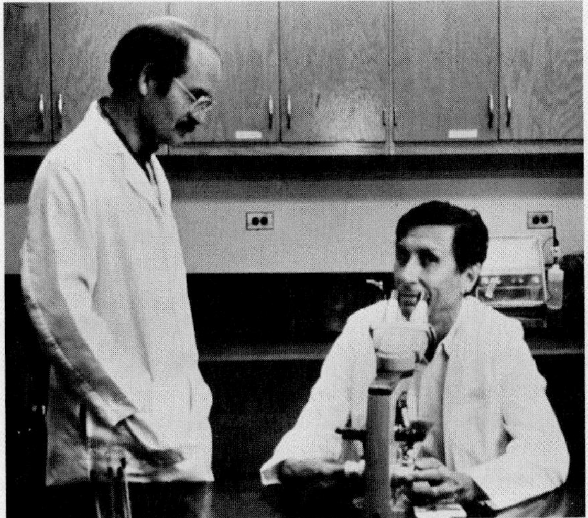

Fig. 1 Joseph McDade (standing) with Charles Shepard. These two scientists designed the experiment that identified the causative agent of Legionnaires' disease.

who had waited outside the doors of the hotel displayed a greater tendency to become ill than others. Perhaps the pathogenic agent had contaminated the air of the hotel. Perhaps this air subsequently passed through the hotel doors and into the lungs of people waiting on the sidewalk.

The pneumonialike symptoms of the disease could have been caused by a wide variety of airborne agents—toxic inorganic or organic chemicals, heavy metals, bacteria, viruses, or other infectious entities. CDC and Pennsylvania-based laboratories began to examine tissues of ill and deceased patients for signs of these agents. Results were negative in all cases.

Weeks passed, and the investigation began to wind down ingloriously. Public criticism of the CDC and the Pennsylvania Department of Health had increased steadily, peaked in the early fall, and then subsided somewhat as disease survivors recovered and follow-up reports of the incident passed to the back pages of newspapers.

Ironically, the organism responsible for the affliction, colloquially dubbed Legionnaires' disease, was first observed shortly after laboratory testing of suspected agents had begun. At that time, Joseph McDade of CDC's Leprosy and Rickettsia Branch, noted small, rod-shaped organisms in tissues of guinea pigs that had been inoculated with specimens from ill patients (Fig. 1). The short rods bore a superficial resemblance to certain varieties of rickettsias, but the guinea pigs McDade innoculated became ill far too quickly to be victims of such microorganisms, which have a long incubation period.

In an attempt to enhance the growth of the rod-shaped organisms, McDade prepared an inoculum from the spleens of infected guinea pigs and injected the preparation into a batch of eggs containing embryonic chickens. The eggs had been specially treated with a wide range of antibiotics that destroy bacteria but not rickettsias. Thus, if the chicken embryos died, McDade would have evidence that the disease agent was a rickettsia with an extremely short incubation period. The embryos did not die. McDade also attempted to infect other guinea pigs with the same spleen preparation. Again, the results were negative; the guinea pigs did not get sick. Finally, to determine if the rod-shaped organisms were pathogenic bacteria, McDade smeared the guinea pig spleen preparations onto several kinds of culture media known to support bacterial growth. None of the media provided a favorable environment for growth of the rod-shaped microbes. McDade logically concluded that the rodlike organisms were not the cause of Legionnaires' disease. But McDade had made an erroneous assumption.

Shortly after Christmas, 1976, McDade's attention again became focused on the rodlike microbes. He decided to make another attempt to cultivate the organisms, but this time he tried an alternate method. McDade thawed some of the guinea pig spleen preparation he had saved from his earlier experiments and injected it into eggs containing embryonic chickens; this time the eggs had *not* been protected by pretreatment with antibiotics. Within a few days, the embryos began to die. Upon examination, the embryo remains were found to be riddled with the rodlike organism (Fig. 2).

At this point, McDade called the head of his branch, Dr. Charles Shepard. The two scientists devised an experiment to test whether the microbes, intermediate in size between rickettsias and bacteria, were responsible for the pneumonia that had killed more than a score of conventioneers.

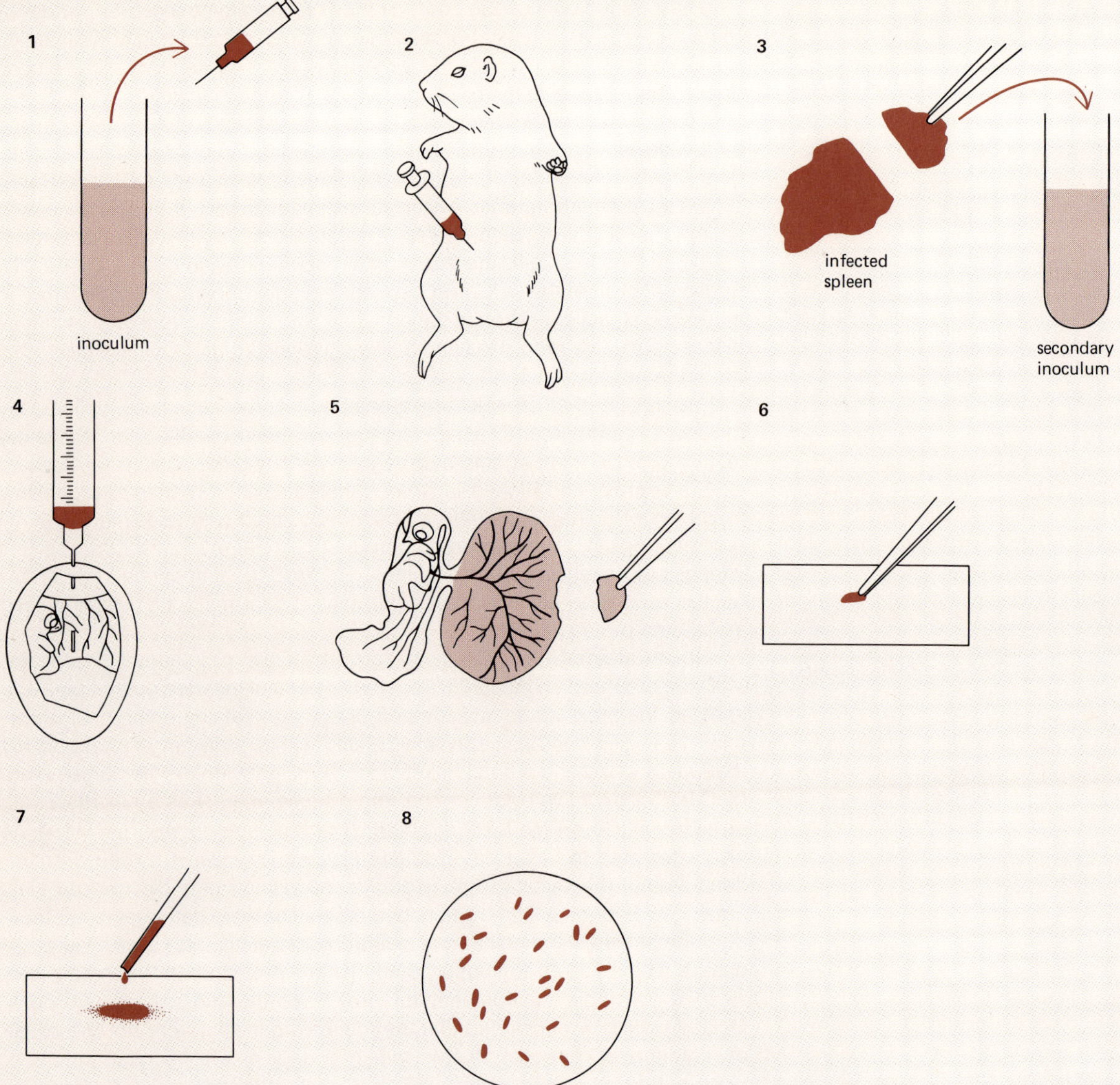

Fig. 2 How *L. pneumophila* was first isolated. Ironically, the bacillus was first isolated through techniques normally used to identify rickettsias. An inoculum, prepared from a small piece of infected human lung (1), was injected into a guinea pig (2). The animal was autopsied after becoming diseased, and a piece of spleen was used to make a secondary inoculum (3). The spleen preparation was then injected into eggs containing embryonic chicks (4). This second step typically is used to enhance the growth of rickettsias and other microorganisms that usually grow only in living tissue and not on synthetic culture media. The embryos died 3 to 4 days after inoculation. Pieces of the embryonic yolk sacs (5) were smeared on a slide (6) and stained by a method normally used to detect rickettsias (7). In this instance, thousands of small bacilli, *L. pneumophilia,* were visible under the microscope (8).

The scientists first obtained samples of blood serum from victims of Legionnaires' disease. Antigens on the surfaces of the suspected pathogen would have triggered production of antibodies in afflicted individuals, and these antibodies should be present in their serums (see also Chap. 18). Using an indirect fluorescent-antibody test,[1] the scientists demonstrated that the serums of people who had contracted Legionnaires' disease contained antibodies that became bound specifically to the rod-shaped microbes (Fig. 3). Moreover, samples of serums taken from disease victims over a period of time generally showed a steady rise in the concentration of such antibodies. Serums of individuals who remained free of the disease almost always showed no trace of the antibodies. The causative agent of Legionnaires' disease had been found.

Why had McDade's earlier work with the microbe, now named *Legionella pneumophila,* not been successful in identifying this organism as the disease-causing agent? Largely because McDade's task was to determine if rickettsias were present in tissues of diseased people. Thus his initial attempts to cultivate the rod-shaped organisms included use of antibiotics that would prevent bacterial growth without affecting rickettsias, whereas his subsequent attempts were carried out without antibiotics. When the microbe was finally isolated, electron microscopy revealed that it actually resembled a small bacillus more closely than a rickettsia (Fig. 4). This surprised most microbiologists, since *L. pneumophila* had not grown on culture media normally conducive to bacterial growth. Further, the organism could not be stained by procedures normally used in examining diseased tissues. Methods of staining and culturing the bacterium have now been worked out, but when McDade began his investigation, all attempts to detect a bacterial cause of the disease in infected human lungs had proved fruitless. In retrospect, McDade's initial failure to identify the microbe as the causative agent of Legionnaires' disease is quite understandable. No known bacterium either looked or behaved quite like *L. pneumophila,* and this is the principal reason why its isolation took so long.

In some respects, however, *L. pneumophila,* turned out to be not such a new organism after all. In fact, evidence now shows that the bacterium was responsible for several earlier outbreaks of respiratory disease. Perhaps the most notable is the "Pontiac fever" incident, which occurred during the summer of 1968. On July 2 of that year, almost all the 100 workers in a building of the Oakland County Health Department in Pontiac, Michigan suddenly became feverish and experienced headaches, nausea, and chest pains. None of the workers developed pneumonia, however, and all survived the illness, which lasted 3 to 4 days.

The CDC sent a team of investigators to examine the building in which the workers had become ill. Guinea pigs developed pneumonia after being placed in the building, and several CDC investigators developed the same symptoms suffered by the workers. Guinea pigs placed in control buildings remained healthy.

[1]A fluorescent-antibody test has now been developed in which labeled rabbit antibody attaches directly to the bacterial antigens. This is a significant advance, since the direct test can permit detection of *L. pneumophila* within a few hours after a patient has contracted pneumonia. The indirect method cannot be used to diagnose legionellosis until at least the end of the second week of illness. Still newer procedures, involving biochemical identification of bacterial antigens, may make future diagnosis of the disease even easier.

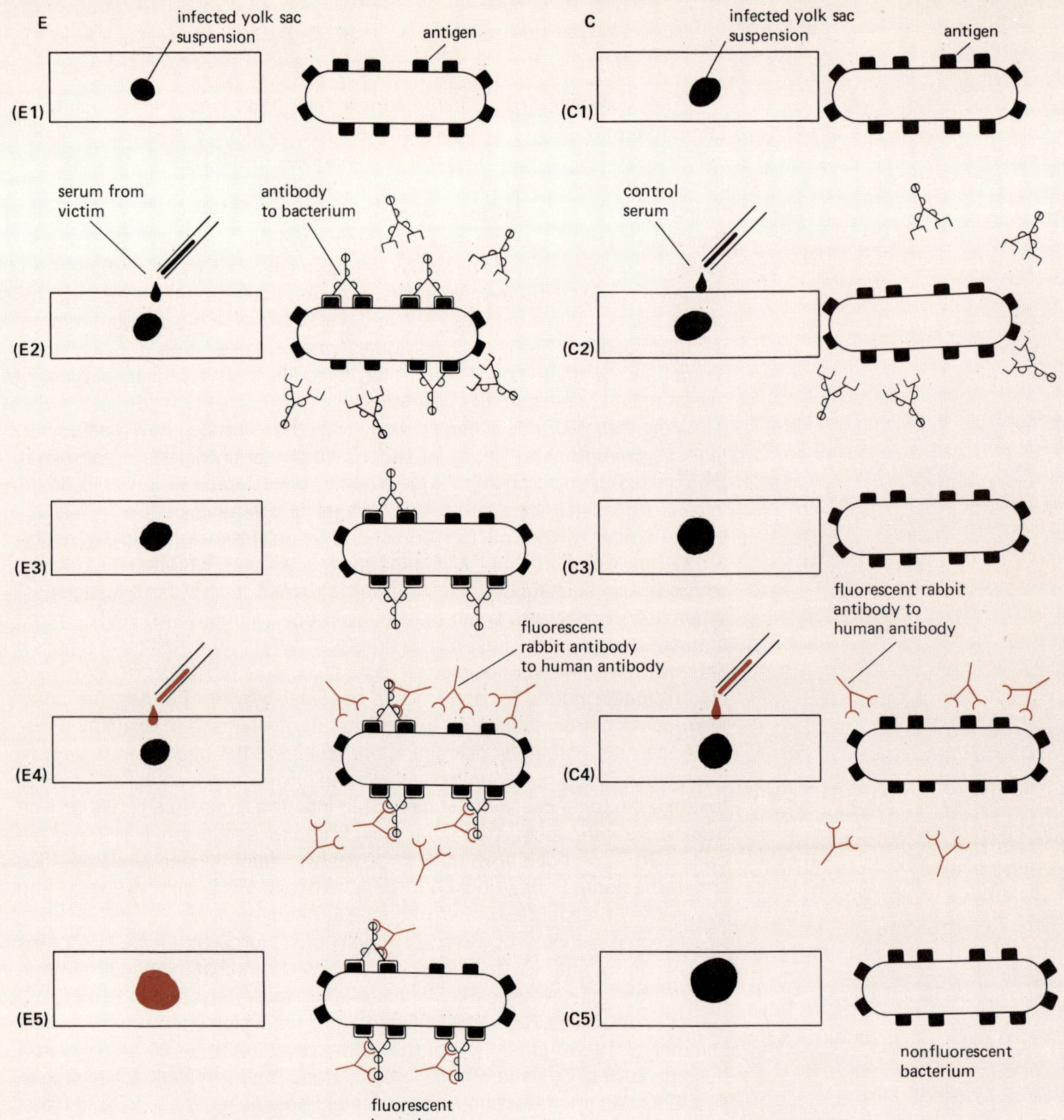

Fig. 3 Indirect fluorescent-antibody test. Both the experimental (E) and control (C) aspects of the technique are illustrated here. Each step of the procedure is depicted along the left; the molecular-cellular consequences of each step are illustrated along the right. A drop of suspension from the yolk sac of an infected chick embryo is placed on an experimental (E1) and a control (C1) slide. The rod-shaped microbe at the right of each slide represents the thousands of bacilli present in a drop of the infected suspension. On its surface each bacillus carries several highly specific antigens. A drop of serum prepared from the blood of a victim of Legionnaires' disease is mixed with the yolk sac suspension (E2). Any antibodies (Y-shaped structures) in the serum that have been produced in response to an invasion of the bacillus will attach to corresponding antigens projecting from the surfaces of the microbes (E2, right). Serum taken from a person who has not been exposed to the bacillus should not contain such antibodies (C2, left). Therefore, there are no antibodies to *L. pneumophila* contained in the control serum that could attach to the bacteria (C2, right). The slides are then washed, removing any unbound antibody (E3 and C3). In a separate procedure (not shown), rabbits are exposed to human antibodies. The immune response systems of the rabbits respond by producing antibodies to the foreign human antibodies. The rabbit antibodies are then isolated and labeled

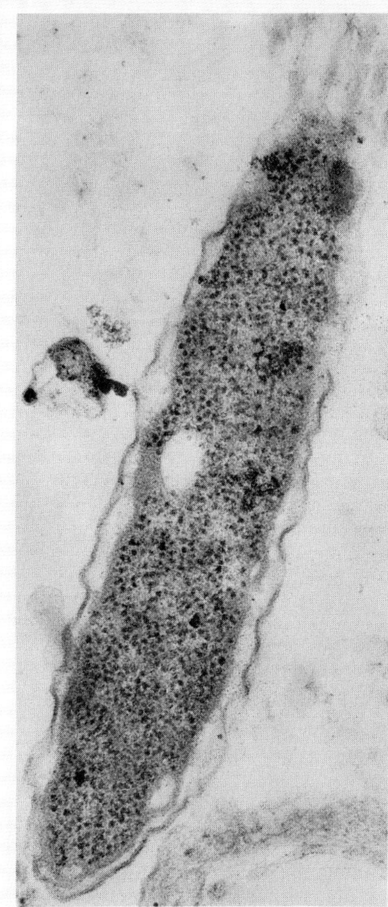

Fig. 4 ***Legionella pneumophila.*** Note the rodlike shape of this microbe (approx. 119,500×).

Interviews with the workers revealed that the only people escaping the illness were those who had been in the building when the air-conditioning system was turned off. The system was examined, and a seemingly minor defect was uncovered. Holes in an exhaust and fresh-air vent had allowed mist from the evaporative condenser to pool in the fresh-air intake duct. Guinea pigs sprayed with an aerosol of the condensation puddle all developed pneumonia, but at the time the disease-causing agent could not be isolated. Fortunately, the CDC had stored samples of blood serum from the people who had contracted Pontiac fever. Nine years later, in 1977, an indirect fluorescent-antibody test demonstrated that the causative agent of Pontiac fever was *L. pneumophila*.

A related investigation showed that the organism also had been responsible for an outbreak of pneumonia at St. Elizabeth's Hospital in Washington, D.C. during the summer of 1965. In that incident, 14 people died from symptoms identical to Legionnaires' disease. Antibodies in stored blood serums of the St. Elizabeth's victims readily attached to the small, rod-shaped bacterium. Still another investigation revealed the bacillus had been responsible for the death of a victim of a respiratory infection in 1947. Thus, the bacillus responsible for Legionnaires' disease and Pontiac fever is new only in terms of its recent discovery. The bacterium apparently has been triggering certain kinds of pneumonia and other respiratory illnesses for several decades at least. In fact, some CDC health officers suspect that the bacillus may be responsible for over 25,000 cases of respiratory disease in the United States each year. Because of its variable effects, all infections produced by the bacterium now are collectively termed *legionellosis*.

Where does the bacterium come from? Why does it produce severe damage and even death in some instances (Legionnaires' disease) and not in others (Pontiac fever). Answers to these and related questions are not known with certainty. Scientists suspect that the microorganism normally lives in water, but that it also can survive in environments that are only moist, such as air-conditioning systems, as demonstrated by the incident at Pontiac, Michigan. Indeed, it seems likely that the microbe entered the air of the Bellevue-Stratford Hotel as it passed through contaminated air-conditioning cooling towers. Perhaps certain environments are more conducive to the development of a bacterium having a more virulent character, while other environments promote growth of a less dangerous strain. No one really knows, but additional research should provide the answers.

The existence of *L. pneumophila,* despite its virulence and potentially tragic impact, should prove encouraging to aspiring biologists worried over the prospects of being left without new forms of life to discover. As this and an upcoming Biology Highlight suggest, there probably are many interesting, even startling organisms on earth whose identity remains unknown.

Fig. 3 (*Continued*)
with a fluorescent stain that glows when irradiated with ultraviolet light. A suspension of the labeled rabbit antibodies is added to the slides (E4 and C4). The rabbit antibodies become attached to any human antibodies exposed on the surfaces of the bacilli (E4, right). Such attachments do not occur on control slides, which after washing no longer contain human antibodies (C4, right). Experimental and control slides are washed once again, removing any unattached labeled rabbit antibody (E5 and C5). Bacilli supporting labeled rabbit antibody emit a yellow-green glow when viewed under an ultraviolet microscope (E5, right), showing that the person whose blood serum was being tested had been infected with the microbe. A positive result for *L. pneumophila* is almost always obtained when the serum being tested is derived from a victim of Legionnaires' disease or Pontiac fever.

BLUE-GREEN ALGAE

Phylum Cyanophyta (1500 species) This phylum name is somewhat misleading, since many cyanophytes are not actually blue-green but are red, yellow, green, blue, black, and various intermediate shades. These colors are produced by several pigments. The characteristic redness of the Red Sea, for example, is due largely to blue-green algae that contain considerable quantities of a red pigment.

The cells of cyanophytes are equipped with walls containing *cellulose* and, like bacterial cells, they lack a nuclear membrane. As in photosynthetic bacteria, the chlorophyll molecules are in granules dispersed through the cytoplasm. Again like certain bacteria, many cyanophytes can fix atmospheric nitrogen, and many are bioluminescent. Food is stored in the form of a unique type of starch called *cyanophycean starch*. Many blue-greens grow as single cells, and numerous others are multicellular. The latter usually form filaments or colonies of more complex shapes. Such types are often embedded in gelatinous masses secreted by the cells (Fig. 30.17).

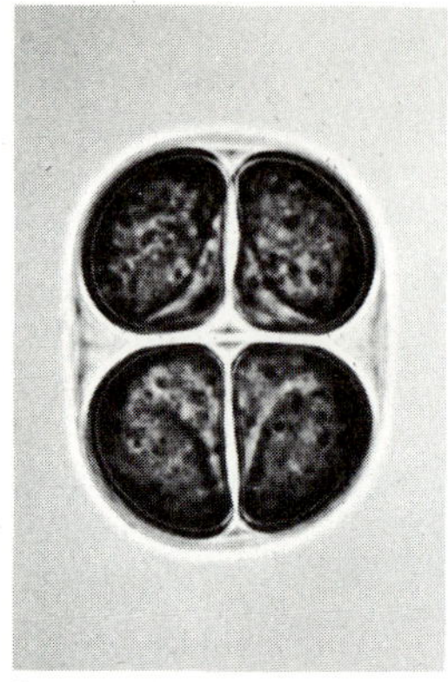
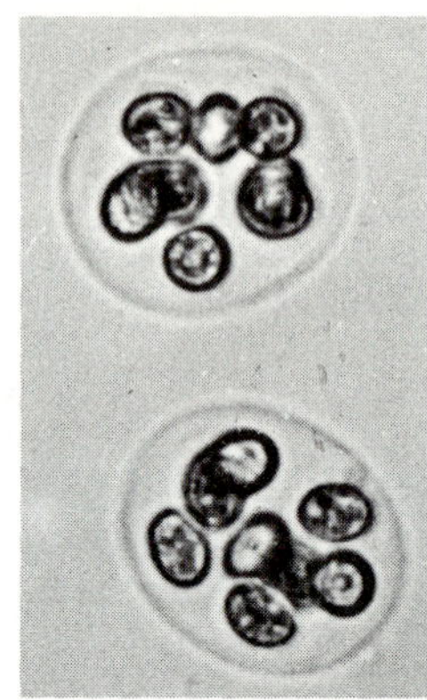

A B
Fig. 30.17 Blue-green algae. (A) A four-celled growth stage of *Chroococcus*. (B) Two colonies of *Gloeocapsa*. Note the gelatinous capsules (see also Color Fig. 25).

Cyanophytes occur in virtually all environments containing water, and in oceans and lakes they often form part of the plankton. Extensive growths also can occur in intermittently wetted regions, among them stream banks, tree bark, or rocks sprayed by seawater. The "blooms" of green scum that frequently cover the surfaces of polluted ponds and streams usually consist of huge populations of blue-green algae. Some of these cyanophytes produce toxic compounds that can poison other aquatic organisms or livestock that drink the water. Such blooms are often responsible for the objectionable odor of polluted water, and they frequently clog filters of water-supply machinery. Other blue-greens live in the icy waters of glaciers, and still others in hot springs where temperatures reach 85°C or more.

The phylum contains three subgroups (orders): *Chroococcales, Chamaeosiphonales,* and *Hormogonales.* The first two include solitary and colonial species (see Fig. 30.17), and the Hormogonales are distinctly filamentous. In such filaments groups of adjacent cells (*hormogones*) often are enclosed by a common wall, and two neighboring hormogones are joined by a unit called a *heterocyst* (Fig. 30.18). This structure appears to be a transparent cell with a double wall. A filament can break readily at these heterocysts, which function mainly as sites of nitrogen fixation (see Chap. 8). The separated hormogones then can settle elsewhere and grow as new filaments. In contrast with the other two groups, the Hormogonales are motile and display a jerky, rolling type of motion.

Two common representatives of the Hormogonales are *Oscillatoria,* so named after its characteristic motion, and *Nostoc.* The latter is found in clear fresh water, where it forms gelatinous balls of up to 2 feet in diameter. Such balls contain numerous filaments and their surrounding sheaths (see Color Fig. 25). *Nostoc* colonies can enter a dormant state and survive the winter in this condition. The organisms also occur as mutualistic symbionts in many lichens.

VIRUSES AND RICKETTSIAS

A virus is a stripped-down biological entity composed solely of an inner nucleic acid core and an outer coat constructed largely of protein (see Fig. 1 of the Biology Highlight in Chap. 22). The nucleic acid core consists of a single molecule of DNA or RNA. Viruses are without nucleus, cytoplasm, ribosomes, ATP, or any metabolic machinery of their own. Outside a host cell, these simplest of parasites are inert, no more alive than a bottle of chemicals on a laboratory bench (Fig. 30.19).

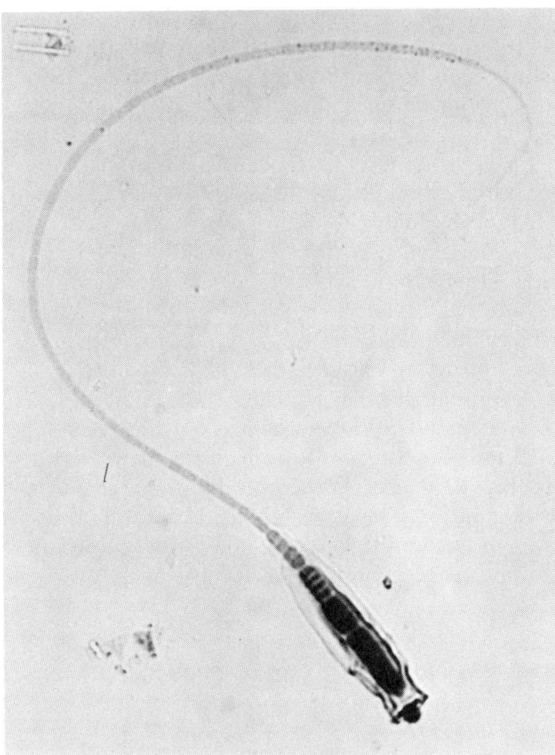

Fig. 30.18 Heterocysts. The large "head" of this chain of blue-green algal cells is a heterocyst. Recent research has shown that these specialized regions are sites of nitrogen fixation.

When a virus attaches to a host cell, however, its nucleic acid invades the cell and provides the genetic information for the synthesis of new viral nucleic acid and protein. The metabolic machinery of the host cell is used in the synthesis of these viral molecules (see Fig. 28.5). Thus, viruses provide only the genetic information for the reproduction of new viruses; living cells are required for the synthesis and assembly of viral components. Newly synthesized viruses eventually leave the host cells, usually killing them in the process, and they then may repeat their reproductive cycle by infecting neighboring cells.

Because of their interference with normal cell functions, viruses cause many diseases in other organisms. Human diseases caused by viruses include mumps, measles, yellow fever, rabies, viral pneumonia, shingles, infectious hepatitis, many types of respiratory infections, "colds," and influenza. Moreover, viruses cause some types of cancer

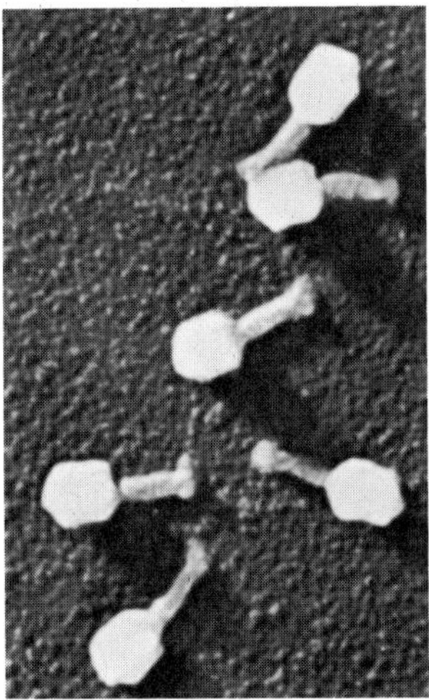

Fig. 30.19 Viruses. The protein mantles of viruses are shown in this electron micrograph. Nucleic acids are inside the expanded hexagonal parts. In an infection the nucleic acids are squeezed through the elongated necklike end into a host cell, and the protein mantle remains outside (×75,000). (*R. M. Herriott and J. L. Barlow, Journal of General Physiology, vol. 36, p. 17, 1953.*)

in animals and probably also in people (see Chap. 22).

Viruses generally are unaffected by penicillin and other antibiotics that effectively control most bacterial infections, but some viral diseases such as smallpox, measles, and polio now can be prevented by vaccines. A most important "retaliatory" response of some animal cells to virus infections is the production of a group of proteins collectively called *interferon.* These proteins, which also are secreted by many virus-infected cells of human beings, induce resistance to viral infections in neighboring uninfected cells. Unfortunately interferons largely are species-specific; an interferon produced by cells of one species usually does not block viral infections of cells in another species. Thus it appears unlikely that "viral antiserums" can be produced to treat virus infections of human beings. However, genes responsible for the production of human interferon have been "spliced" into bacteria through recombinant-DNA technology. The genetically altered bacteria have responded by producing human antiviral proteins. Use of this technology soon may provide an inexpensive way of producing large quantities of human interferon (see also Chap. 28).

The so-called *rickettsias* appear to be related to viruses and also to bacteria (Fig. 30.20). Their spherical or rodlike body is far smaller than that of even small bacteria, and like viruses they are obligate intracellular parasites, unable to carry out living functions outside the cells of specific hosts. Such hosts are ticks and lice. One rickettsial spe-

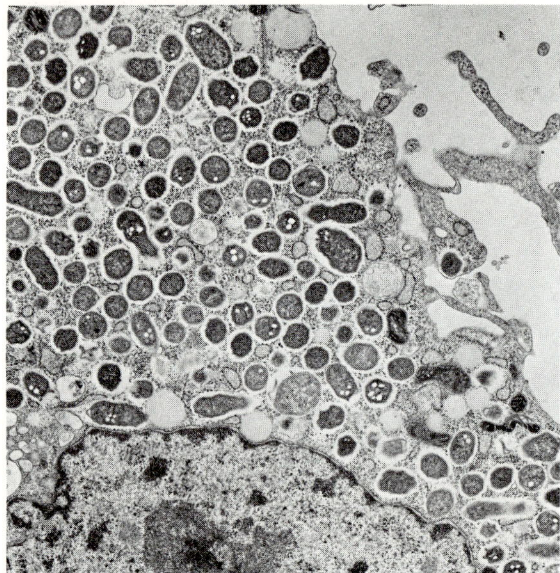

Fig. 30.20 Rickettsias. The many irregularly shaped dark particles in the cytoplasm of this chicken fibroblast cell are rickettsias. This species is *Rickettsia prowazekii*, the causative agent of epidemic typhus. Note that the rickettsias are not present in the nucleus (bottom) of the fibroblast (approx. 15,750×).

cies is the causative agent of Rocky Mountain spotted fever, and another of epidemic typhus fever, both human diseases. Ticks in the first case and body lice in the second transfer the rickettsias to people.

Viruses and rickettsias are an evolutionary enigma. Some biologists hypothesize that these parasites evolved from the same noncellular "ancestors" that gave rise to the first living cells on earth. But most biologists favor the hypothesis that viruses and rickettsias both evolved from free-living moneran or protistan ancestors. They argue that loss of structure has occurred frequently during the evolution of other parasites. According to this view, viruses and rickettsias evolved from one or more groups of intracellular parasites that eventually lost all structures except those required for infection and reproduction. If this hypothesis is correct, viruses and rickettsias should be regarded as evolutionary remnants of highly degenerated cells.

Review Questions

1 Review the probable chemical composition of the earth's early atmosphere. Which gases in the early atmosphere of the earth may have contributed to the formation of biologically important compounds? What were some of these compounds, and what evidence do we have that they could actually have formed?

2 Review the synthesis reactions through which compounds required for the origin of living systems might have occurred. Describe experiments duplicating some of these reactions. How are the first cells believed to have evolved?

3 Describe the physical character of the earth before and after living systems originated. Review the evolutionary significance of the oxygen revolution.

4 Through what processes of evolution may moneran nutritional patterns have arisen? What processes probably necessitated and promoted such nutritional evolution?

5 Describe how membraneous organelles of eukaryotic cells may have originated. Review the symbiotic theory of mitochondrial and chloroplast origins. Present arguments for and against this theory.

6 What features have been used to distinguish between Monera, Protista, Fungi, Plantae, and Animalia?

7 Review the characteristics that distinguish viruses from Monera; Monera from Protista. What are the major groups of bacteria? What features distinguish these groups from each other? What features distinguish bacteria from blue-green algae?

8 Suppose you had to determine the cause of an epidemic that suddenly developed in your community. Describe how you might begin to establish the cause of the illness. Describe how the causative agent of Legionnaires' disease was first isolated. Review how scientists determined that *L. pneumophila* is the cause of Legionnaires' disease and Pontiac fever.

9 Review mechanisms that promote genetic variability in bacteria. Discuss the relative importance of these mechanisms in promoting rapid adaptation of bacteria to changing environments.

10 What nutritional patterns occur among Monera? What roles do Monera play in the general ecology of the earth? Which groups of Monera and Protista are economically important? Give several examples.

11 Review the characteristics of pathogenic bacteria. What diseases are caused by bacteria? By viruses? By rickettsias? Describe steps that can be taken to prevent proliferation of specific microorganisms in the human body. What is a vaccine? An antiserum? Distinguish between passive and active immunity.

Collateral Readings

Adler, J.: The Sensing of Chemicals by Bacteria, *Scientific American*, April 1976. Movements of flagellated bacteria toward and away from different environments are described.

Barghoorn, E. S.: The Oldest Fossils, *Scientific American*, May 1971. The remains of ancient bacteria and algae provide evidence of the earliest stages of evolution.

Berg, H. C.: How Bacteria Swim, *Scientific American*, August 1975. Highlights the structure and function of bacterial flagella.

Bogorod, L.: Evolution of Organelles and the Eukaryotic Genomes, *Science*, vol. 188, pp. 891–898, May 30, 1975. An alternative to the symbiotic theory of the origin of eukaryotic organelles. For the advanced student.

Braude, A. I.: Bacterial Endotoxins, *Scientific American*, March 1964. The nature of endotoxins and their role in disease is the focus of this article.

Butler, P. J. G., and **A. Klug:** The Assembly of a Virus, *Scientific American*, November 1978. Describes how the protein and nucleic acid components of the tobacco-mosaic virus are integrated.

Campbell, A. M.: How Viruses Insert Their DNA into the DNA of the Host Cell, *Scientific American*, December 1976. A well-illustrated presentation.

Costerton, J. W., G. G. Geesey, and **K.-J. Cheng:** How Bacteria Stick, *Scientific American*, January 1978. Describes surface molecules of bacteria that enable these microbes to attach to host cells. The article also illustrates how antibiotics might be developed to attack such surface molecules.

Dickerson, R. E.: Chemical Evolution and the Origin of Cells, *Scientific American*, September 1978. Reviews evidence supporting the belief that cells evolved within 1 billion years after the earth had formed.

Durden-Smith, J.: The Disease Detectives, *Quest/80*, January 1980. A popular article describing the history and purpose of the Center for Disease Control in Atlanta, Georgia.

Echlin, P.: The Blue-Green Algae, *Scientific American*, June 1966. On the biology of these organisms and their importance to human beings.

Fogg, G. E., et al.: "The Blue-Green Algae," Academic, New York, 1973. A well-written book that includes discussions of the economic importance of blue-green algae.

Fraser, D. W., and **J. E. McDade:** Legionellosis, *Scientific American*, October 1979. Two members of the Center for Disease Control describe how the causative agent of Legionnaires' disease and Pontiac fever was discovered.

Henle, W., G. Henle, and **E. T. Lennette:** The Epstein-Barr Virus, *Scientific American*, July 1979. This well-studied virus is the cause of infectious mononucleosis and is linked with two kinds of human cancer. The article provides an excellent description of what some believe to be the most common human virus.

Luria, S. E., J. E. Darnell, D. Baltimore, and **A. Campbell:** "General Virology," 3d ed., Wiley, New York, 1978. An excellent textbook on all aspects of this topic.

Margulis, L.: "Origin of Eukaryotic Cells," Yale University Press, New Haven, Conn., 1970. A fascinating but highly controversial proposal describing how mitochondria and chloroplasts might have evolved symbiotically.

———: Symbiosis and Evolution, *Scientific American,* August 1971. Somewhat less technical than the preceding reference.

Marx, J. L.: Interferon, I: On the Threshold of Clinical Application; II: Learning How It Works, *Science,* vol. 204, no. 4398, pp. 1183–1186, June 15, 1979; no. 4399, pp. 1293–1295, June 22, 1979. The first of these two articles on interferon focuses on the potential clinical uses of these antiviral proteins. The second deals with progress in understanding how interferon works.

Miller, S. L., and **L. Orgel:** "The Origin of Life on Earth," Prentice-Hall, Englewood Cliffs, N.J., 1974. Emphasizes the molecular and biophysical aspects of the topic. Recommended for serious students of this subject.

Nester, E. W., C. E. Roberts, N. N. Pearsoll, and **B. J. McCarthy:** "Microbiology," 2d ed., Holt, New York, 1978. A good treatment of all aspects of this topic; bacteria are covered especially well.

Oparin, A. I.: "Genesis and Evolutionary Development of Life," Academic, New York, 1969. An excellent summary by one of the founding fathers of this discipline.

Schopf, J. W.: The Evolution of the Earliest Cells, *Scientific American,* September 1978. Part of an issue devoted exclusively to evolution.

Sharon, N.: The Bacterial Cell Wall, *Scientific American,* May 1969. Describes the structure of the bacterial cell wall. Also illustrates how penicillin and other antibiotics interfere with synthesis of new cell walls.

Spector, D. H., and **D. Baltimore:** The Molecular Biology of Poliovirus, *Scientific American,* May 1975. Describes how this once-dreaded agent of disease now is being used to study viral reproduction.

Stanier, R. Y., et al.: "The Microbial World," 4th ed., Prentice-Hall, Englewood Cliffs, N.J., 1976. An excellent introduction to the biology of microorganisms. One of the best general texts available.

Uzzel, T., and **C. Spolsky:** Mitochondria and Plastids as Endosymbionts? *American Scientist,* vol. 62, pp. 334–343, 1974. A critique of the symbiotic theory and an alternative proposal for the origins of eukaryotic organelles.

Walsby, A. E.: The Gas Vacuoles of Blue-Green Algae, *Scientific American,* August 1977. Describes how blue-green algae regulate their buoyancy.

Woese, C. R., and **G. E. Fox:** Phylogenetic Structure of the Prokaryotic Domain: The Primary Kingdoms, *Proc. Natl. Acad. Sci.,* vol. 74, no. 11, pp. 5088–5090, November 1977. The first significant proposal that methanogens be classified together in a kingdom separate from all other organisms. Provides a good view of how biologists debate the classification of organisms. A technical paper but not beyond the ability of many beginning students.

Chapter 31 Protists and Fungi

Learning Objectives

After reading this chapter you should be able to:

1. Name the unifying traits of the Protista and Fungi and describe the probable ancestral type from which these organisms are believed to have evolved; differentiate between coccine, sporine, amoeboid, and flagellate states of existence and indicate at least one example of each; name the evolutionary significance of these four states of existence among protists.
2. List the general characteristics of algal protists; name the three main groups of such algae and cite the identifying characteristics of each; illustrate the economic importance of golden and fire algae; outline the probable evolutionary significance of pairs of algae where one is photosynthetic and the other is not.
3. List the identifying characteristics of slime molds and illustrate the nutritional patterns of these protists; differentiate between plasmodium and pseudoplasmodium; construct a diagram that illustrates the life cycle of slime molds.
4. Describe the general characteristics and illustrate the nutritional patterns of protozoa; identify the four major subphyla of protozoa; state the identifying characteristics and list a representative organism of each subphylum; describe the life cycle of the malarial parasite *Plasmodium;* distinguish structurally and functionally between the macronuclei and micronuclei of ciliates; define and indicate the function of contractile vacuoles, gullets, trichocysts, and pseudopodia.
5. List the general characteristics and nutritional patterns of fungi; identify the major groups of fungi and give an example of each; define and name the structural relations between hyphae and mycelia; illustrate the economic importance of at least six kinds of fungi; construct diagrams illustrating the life cycles of *Rhizopus,* an ascomycete fungus, and a basidiomycete fungus; distinguish between plasmogamy and karyogamy.

Kingdom	Phylum	Subphylum	Class
Monera			
	Euglenophyta		
	Chrysophyta		Xanthophyceae (yellow-green algae)
			Chysophyceae (golden algae)
			Bacillariophyceae (diatoms)
	Pyrrophyta		Cryptophyceae (cryptoflagellates)
			Dinophyceae (dinoflagellates)
Protista	Gymnomycota		Myxomycetes (plasmodial slime molds)
			Acrasiomycetes (cellular slime molds)
			Protostelidomycetes
	Protozoa		Mastigophora (flagellated protozoa)
			Sarcodina (amoeboid protozoa)
			Sporozoa (spore-forming protozoa)
			Ciliophora (ciliated protozoa)
Fungi	Mycota		Chytridiomycetes (chytrids)
			Oomycetes (water molds, white rusts, downy mildews)
			Zygomycetes (bread mold, fly fungi, animal-trapping fungi)
			Ascomycetes (sac fungi)
			Basidiomycetes (club fungi)
			Deuteromycetes ("imperfect" fungi)
Plantae (Metaphyta)			
Animalia (Metazoa)			

Of the protistan phyla now in existence, the unicellular and colonial algae probably include descendants of the most ancient protists. Primitive living algae actually are thought to resemble the original protistan ancestors to a considerable degree, and from such primitive types we can infer what the first protists might have been like. Fungi, like modern slime molds and protozoa, probably arose from one or more groups of ancient heterotrophic protists, but fungi include forms far more complex than the vast majority of protists.

GENERAL CHARACTERISTICS

In the course of probably millions of years, the cell type we now recognize as protistan gradually must have evolved all the specialized organelles examined in Chap. 5. Thus, a definite membrane-bounded nucleus must have come to include nucleoli and filamentous nucleoprotein chromosomes. The cytoplasm must have become equipped with endoplasmic reticulum, mitochondria, Golgi bodies, chloroplasts, centrioles, and kinetosomes, as well as flagella, cilia, and the capacity to form pseudopods. Ribosomes must have been inherited from earlier premoneran ancestors, but protistan cells in addition evolved various kinds of vacuoles, granules, and fibrils (Fig. 31.1).

Fig. 31.1 Protistan cell structure: basic components. Not all of the structures found in protistan cells are shown.

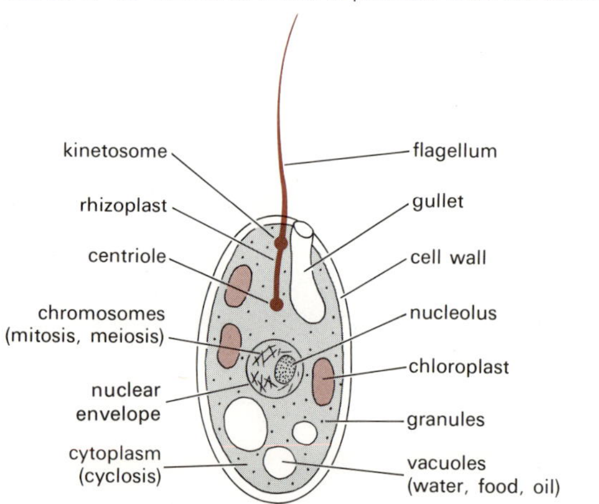

Further, judging from primitive algal types today, early protists must have had the capacity to obtain food by two or more methods simultaneously. For example, it must have been quite common for a protist to engulf or absorb preexisting food from the external environment *as well as* photosynthesize new food internally. In this respect the ancient protists probably were both plantlike and animal-like at once, as some of their algal descendants are today.

In conjunction with these alternative forms of nutrition and again judging from living types, ancient protists also must have been capable of existing in four alternative states, two of them locomotor and two nonmotile (Fig. 31.2). The locomotor states are *flagellate* and *amoeboid*, and these are readily interconvertible. An amoeboid state can arise when a flagellate cell casts off its flagellum (but retains the kinetosome) and then moves by means of pseudopodia. Later the amoeboid activity may cease and a new flagellum can grow out.

The two nonmotile states similarly develop by temporary or permanent loss of flagella. One, the *coccine* condition, is a special type of multinucleate state. The nucleus of a nonmotile cell here continues to divide, but the cytoplasm does not. The result is a progressively more multinucleate but still unicellular organism. Cytoplasmic division occurs only at the time of reproduction, when *multiple fission* takes place: the cell becomes partitioned into numerous offspring cells simultaneously, each containing a nucleus. Such new cells (*spores*) then either become temporarily flagellate or amoeboid or grow as new nonmotile multinucleates directly. In the second nonmotile condition, the *sporine* state, a cell does divide regularly during its vegetative life. The resulting nonmotile daughter cells then often remain attached to each other and form a multicellular aggregate. At any time, however, any of the cells can develop flagella or become amoeboid and disengage from the aggregate.

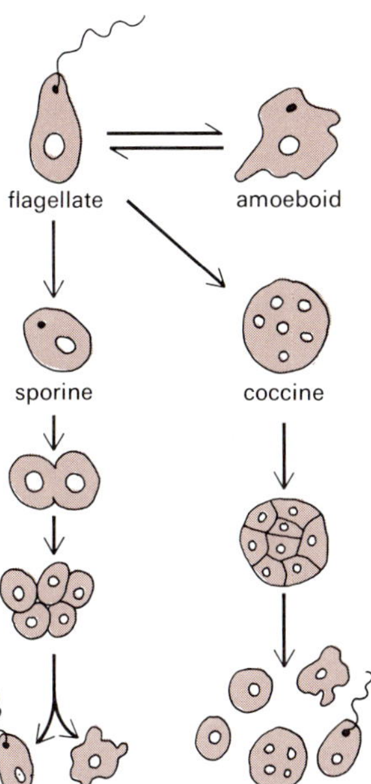

Fig. 31.2 Interconversion of protistan states. A flagellate cell can become amoeboid, and later that same cell or any of its offspring can revert to a flagellate state. Loss of flagella and development of multinuclearity leads to the nonmotile coccine state, in which, after cell-boundary formation during reproduction, the offspring cells can either remain coccine or resume flagellate or amoeboid existence. Loss of flagella and successive vegetative divisions produce the sporine state. The resulting cells can also assume the flagellate or the amoeboid condition.

Of these four different states of vegetative existence, the flagellate condition occurs in the most primitive protists known and is therefore believed to be basic; all other states might be derived from it. The adaptive advantage of such multiple alternative states must have been great, particularly in conjunction with the multiple means of nutrition. Thus, by permitting cellular locomotion, the two motile states must have made possible heterotrophic nutrition generally and holotrophic feeding specifically. At night or on the dimly lit bottoms of natural waters, an ancestral protist could actively hunt for food. But in the presence of ample light in the daytime, photosynthesis could occur and locomotor energy could be reduced to zero by assumption of one of the nonmotile states.

Among some modern Protists given individuals still can exist in two or more of these four alternative states, and certain species of unicellular algae can both photosynthesize and feed heterotrophically. However, most living protists and all fungi exhibit just one particular vegetative state and one method of nutrition more or less permanently. It can be inferred, therefore, that ancestral groups gave rise to modern ones by partial losses of function. Certain ancestral protists could have lost the heterotrophic capacity and evolved as more nearly plantlike forms, or they could have lost the photosynthetic capacity and evolved as more nearly animal-like forms. Similarly, different ancestral groups could have become specialized to exist in but one of the four vegetative states and lost the capacity to exist in the others. That such differential losses of function actually can occur is demonstrable in the laboratory. For example, primitive living algae with multiple means of nutrition can

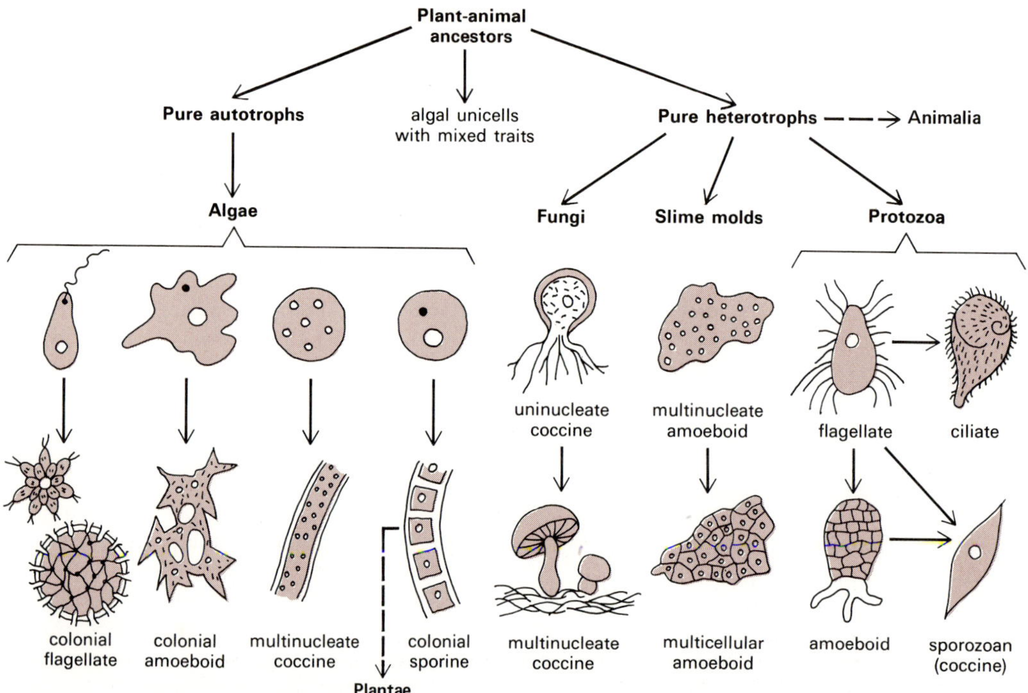

Fig. 31.3 Evolution of protists and fungi. Ancestral protists (top) probably were both autotrophic and heterotrophic simultaneously. From such stocks with joint plantlike and animal-like traits appear to have evolved purely autotrophic and purely heterotrophic types, represented today by the groups indicated. Also in existence are a few types that still retain mixed traits. In the algal groups, the colonial flagellates shown are *Synura* (top) and *Volvox* (bottom). Colonial sporine types also include branched filaments, sheets, and three-dimensional aggregates. Note that the heterotrophic groups do not include any sporine types—they might never have evolved or, if they did, have all become extinct.

be converted by various experimental procedures to either purely photosynthetic or purely heterotrophic organisms. Similarly, experimental removal of, for example, kinetosomes can convert flagellate cells to permanently nonmotile ones.

If we therefore regard specialization in photosynthetic and heterotrophic nutrition as two possible directions of evolution, and if each of these two could at the same time evolve four different vegetative states of existence, there must have been at least eight possible evolutionary pathways ancient protists could have followed.

These eight lines of descent are represented today by the modern Prostista and Fungi (Fig. 31.3). Some unicellular algae now living still display the ancestral traits of being both plantlike and animallike simultaneously. All other algae are exclusively photosynthetic. They are variously flagellate, amoeboid, coccine, and sporine, and each of these lines includes both unicellular and often quite complex multicellular members. The remaining Protista represent the exclusively heterotrophic lines of descent. Fungi exemplify a culmination of the coccine state; all fungi are or become multinucleate organisms that form distinct uninucleate cells only at the time of reproduction. Slime molds exemplify a culmination of the amoeboid state. These largely saprotrophic organisms are creeping multicellular or multinucleate amoeboid masses without permanent shape. Protozoa are holotrophic, parasitic, and in some cases saprotrophic, and the cells are mostly flagellate or amoeboid, though a few groups are coccine. The multicellular condition has developed to only a limited degree, but protozoa appear to have exploited the unicellular way of life perhaps more fully than any other group of protists.

It may be noted that protists and fungi which remain in one vegetative state permanently usually

TABLE 31.1
Distinguishing Characteristics of Algal Protists

Characteristic	Euglenophyta (euglenoids)	Chrysophyta ("golden" algae, mostly diatoms)	Pyrrophyta ("fire" algae, mostly dinoflagellates)
number of species	450	about 10,000	1100
photosynthetic pigments	chlorophylls *a*, *b*, carotenoids	chlorophylls *a*, *c*, carotenoids, fucoxanthin	chlorophylls *a*, *c*, fucoxanthin
storage food	paramylum*	oils, leucosin*	starch, oils
flagella (9 + 2) structure	1, 2, or 3 at one end	1 or 2, at one end	2, lateral
cell wall	none; protein pellicle	pectic compounds; often impregnated with silicon	cellulose
sexual processes	unknown	rare	rare
distribution	mostly freshwater	marine, freshwater, soil	marine, freshwater

*A polysaccharide.

still reveal at the time of reproduction the ancestral potential of developing other states. Thus even where the organisms are nonmotile, the reproductive cells generally are flagellate or amoeboid. Indeed, cells of both kinds are often formed at the same time; flagellate cells become sperms, amoeboid cells become eggs.

ALGAL PROTISTA

Three phyla of primarily unicellular algae are classified as protists: Euglenophyta, Chrysophyta, and Pyrrophyta. Like other eukaryotic algae, classified as Plantae, all algal protists have a variety of chlorophyll called *chlorophyll a*. In addition, representatives of each phylum of algae, whether protistan or plant, have at least one other type of chlorophyll which, in conjunction with other pigments, produces the characteristic green, yellow, brown, or red colors of each algal group. The characteristic photosynthetic pigments of the three phyla of algal protists are included in Table 31.1.

EUGLENOIDS

Phylum Euglenophyta (450 species)

Most of the predominantly unicellular euglenoids live in lakes, ponds, and other freshwater habitats. The chloroplasts of these organisms contain chlorophylls *a* and *b*, like those of all Plantae, but euglenoids are distinct in several respects. For example, these protists lack rigid cell walls. As a result, euglenoids are very pliable and deformable.

Fig. 31.4 Green algae. A, B, the euglenoid *Euglena* (photo approx. ×25,000). The genus *Astasia* is entirely similar to *Euglena* except that chloroplasts are lacking.

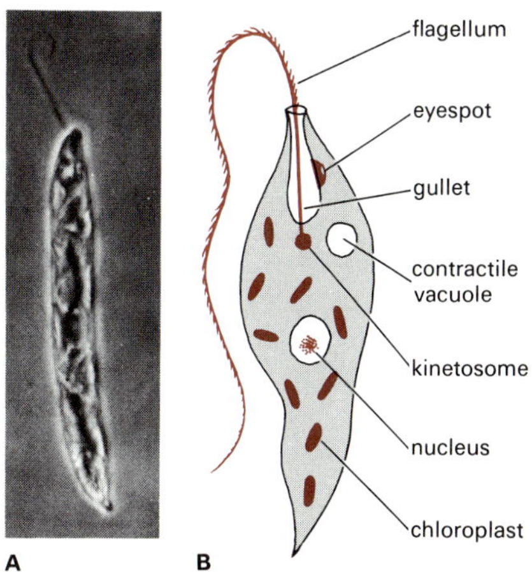

Indeed, the ability to change shape appears to be an important adaptation among mud-dwelling forms. Also, food is stored not as starch but partly as fatty material and partly as *paramylum,* a unique polysaccharide not found in any other group of organisms.

Euglena, a common representative of the group, can both engulf food through a *gullet* and manufacture nutrients via photosynthesis. This flagellated organism is able to orient with respect to light, normally exposing its chloroplasts to maximum amounts of illumination. The positive phototropic response of *Euglena* is mediated by a light-sensitive pigment contained in a *stigma,* or eyespot, at the anterior (forward) end of the organism (Fig. 31.4).

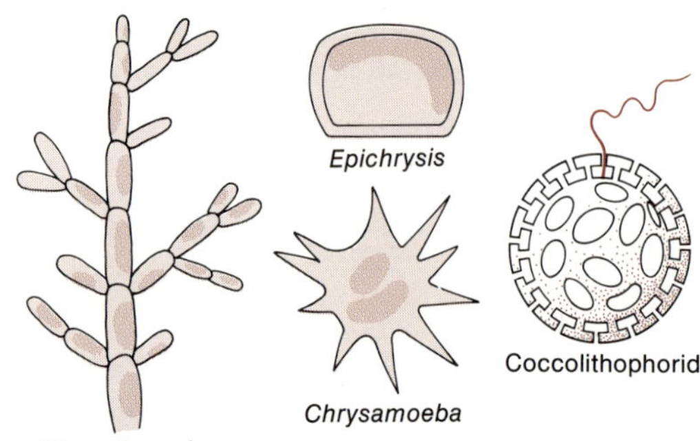

Fig. 31.5 Golden-brown algae. Chrysophyceans. The coccolithophorid is flagellate, *Chrysamoeba* is amoeboid, *Epichrysis* is coccine, and *Phaeothamnion* is sporine. Diatoms are shown in Fig. 9.14.

GOLDEN-BROWN ALGAE

Phylum Chrysophyta (17,000 species)

CLASS CHRYSOPHYCEAE golden algae

CLASS XANTHOPHYCEAE yellow-green algae

CLASS BACILLARIOPHYCEAE diatoms

This phylum encompasses more different structural types than any other algal group. Chrysophytes are identified by chlorophylls *a* and *c* (*e* in some cases) and by various carotene and xanthophyll pigments. The xanthophylls include the conspicuous yellow-brown *fucoxanthin.* Foods are stored not as starch but partly as *oils,* and partly as the polysaccharide *leucosin.* Cell walls can be absent or present. Where present, the wall is in two halves, the rim of one half tightly overlapping the rim of the other. Such walls usually are made of glassy silica.

The first two classes listed above are exceedingly diversified. Each includes flagellate, amoeboid, coccine, and sporine lines, and each of these contains unicellular and multicellular members (Fig. 31.5). Paired photosynthetic and colorless forms are common in each of the two classes, and some of these colorless types well could have been ancestors of other Protista. For example, a colorless chrysophycean amoeba is virtually indistinguishable from a protozoan amoeba.

In contrast to the first two classes, the diatoms are mainly sporine, unicellular, and occasionally colonial. As noted in Chap. 9, diatoms are the most abundant single group of plankton organisms, and as such they support much of the life in the sea and in fresh water. The silica shells of dead diatoms make up large tracts of the ocean floor. Geologically uplifted parts of this floor are the source of *diatomaceous earth,* mined for its abrasive and various other properties. For example, it is a common component of toothpaste. Moreover, much of the petroleum used in industry today probably is derived from the oils synthesized and stored by diatoms of past ages.

FIRE ALGAE

Phylum Pyrrophyta (1000 species)

CLASS CRYPTOPHYCEAE cryptoflagellates

CLASS DINOPHYCEAE dinoflagellates

The Cryptophyceae are mostly unicellular flagellates. Among them, paired photosynthetic and colorless types are well known. Most of the dinoflagellates possess cellulose walls in the form of distinct interlocking "armor" plates, as in *Peridinium* or *Ceratium* (Fig. 31.6). Two flagella are present, one directed backward in swimming, the other undulating in a transverse groove formed by the armor. Different nutritional variants are common. For example, *Ceratium* is photosynthetic, *Blasto-*

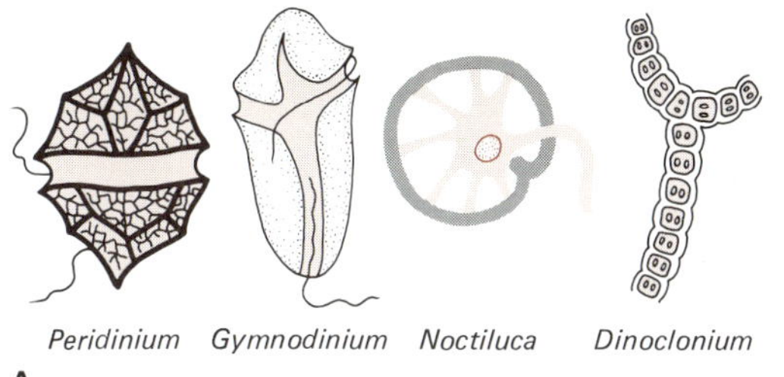

B

Fig. 31.6 Dinoflagellates. A, *Peridinium* and *Gymnodinium* are armor-plated dinoflagellates. *Noctiluca* is a bioluminescent dinoflagellate. *Dinoclonium* is a multicellular sporine type with flagellate sex cells. B, *Ceratium*, a dinoflagellate common in plankton.

dinium is a colorless parasite in animals, and *Noctiluca* either photosynthesizes or feeds holotrophically. Paired photosynthetic and colorless types are known as well. Many marine dinoflagellates are bioluminescent (*Noctiluca*, for example). On occasion, some dinoflagellates proliferate locally in fantastic numbers. For example, reddish species of the genus *Gonyaulax* occasionally produce so-called red tides (hence the name of the phylum). These species also produce neurotoxins that can kill fish, other aquatic animals, and even human beings. Such human deaths usually result from eating clams, oysters, or other shellfish that have subsisted on large numbers of toxic dinoflagellates.

SLIME MOLDS

Phylum Gymnomycota (500+ species)

CLASS MYXOMYCETES plasmodial slime molds

CLASS ACRASIOMYCETES cellular slime molds

These interesting organisms represent the evolutionary culmination of the colonial *amoeboid* state; the body of a slime mold is a naked, creeping, amoeboid mass, in some cases as much as 1 foot in diameter (Fig. 31.7). A few slime molds are parasitic, but most are saprotrophs, subsisting on fallen trees, dead leaves, or other sources of decaying organic matter (see Color Fig. 26). Most of these organisms live in moist, cool environments, such as wooded or otherwise shaded habitats.

Fig. 31.7 Slime molds. A plasmodium of *Physarella* is shown.

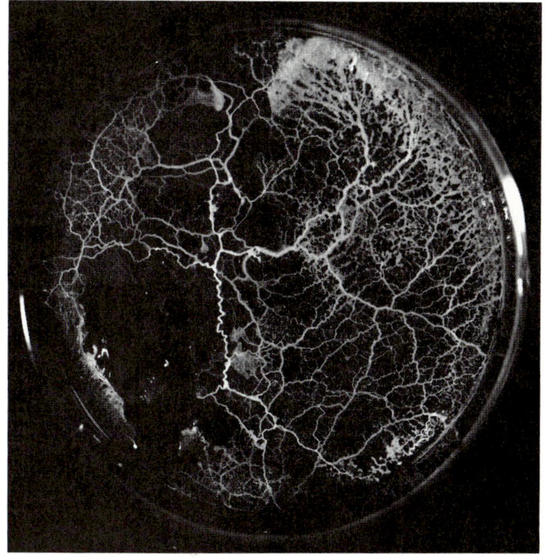

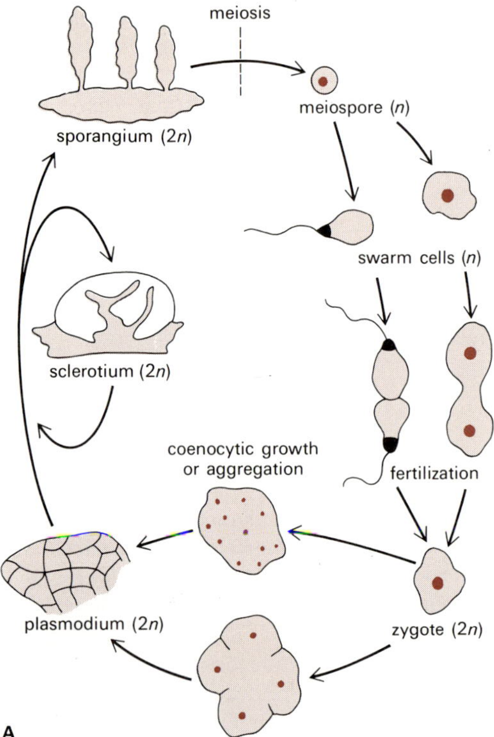

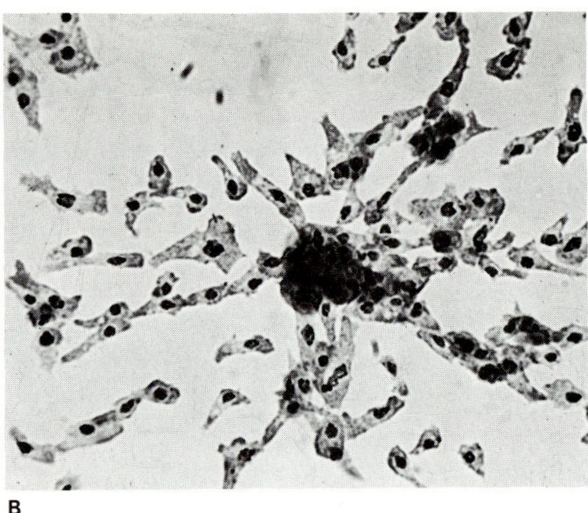

Fig. 31.8 Slime mold reproduction. (A) The life cycle. A sclerotium is an encapsulated resting stage formed from a plasmodium and germinating again as a plasmodium. Swarm cells derived from the meiospore can alternate between amoeboid and flagellate states. Coenocytic growth is the development of a multinucleate mass in which cell boundaries do not exist. (B) Amoeboid swarm cells migrating together (after a sexual process) and forming an adult pseudoplasmodium. In this type the cell boundaries are retained; hence the adult is multicellular.

Two major classes of slime molds have been identified: the *plasmodial slime molds* (Myxomycetes) and the *cellular slime molds* (Acrasiomycetes). The adult Myxomycetes is a *plasmodium,* an amoeboid sheet containing hundreds or thousands of nuclei. Internal cell boundaries are absent, however, and the whole organism is a continuous living mass. The Acrasiomycetes are superficially similar, but the adult form is a *pseudoplasmodium,* a true cellular colony composed of hundreds or thousands of uninucleate amoeboid cells that do not lose their cell boundaries.

The life cycle of slime molds is fundamentally diplohaplontic (see Chap. 22). An adult plasmodium or pseudoplasmodium represents the diploid sporophyte generation. From it develops a stalked fruiting body, or *sporangium,* in which meiosis occurs during spore formation. The spores give rise to haploid flagellate or amoeboid swarm cells. Successive vegetative generations of such swarmers represent the gametophyte generation, which thus consists not of a multicellular body but of a population of separate single cells. Eventually some of these cells function as gametes, and fertilization reestablishes the diploid condition. Diploid zygotic cells later grow into (or collect together as) plasmodial sporophytes (Fig. 31.8).

PROTOZOANS

Phylum Protozoa (15,000+ species)

CLASS MASTIGOPHORA **flagellate protozoa**

CLASS SARCODINA **amoeboid protozoa**

CLASS SPOROZOA **spore-forming protozoa**

CLASS CILIOPHORA **ciliate protozoa**

As algae are the most nearly plantlike protists, so protozoa are the most nearly animal-like. These largely unicellular organisms are classified according to their principal mode of locomotion. Thus, protozoa with flagella are grouped as Mastigophora, those with cilia as Ciliophora, and those producing pseudopodia as Sarcodina; sporozoans are nonmotile and largely parasitic. It is difficult to pinpoint the exact ancestry of protozoa, but there is little doubt that they are descended from several different ancestral groups among other Protista. By loss of chlorophyll, primitive algae in particular could have given rise to protozoa early and directly, or later and indirectly via other protistan types. There is fairly general agreement that flagellate and amoeboid protozoa are closely interrelated (they are often classified as a single group); that flagellate ancestors probably have also given rise to the ciliate group; and that the origin of the spore-forming group is obscure. Sporine states of existence are not represented in the phylum, and colonial types are comparatively rare; most protozoa are unicellular.

Protozoa are components of all ecosystems in all aquatic environments, in soils, and generally in any environments containing some moisture. Most types are free-living and holotrophic. So-called "herbivorous" protozoa subsist largely on bacteria and microscopic algae, and "carnivorous" forms feed on minute animals such as rotifers or on other protozoa (including fellow members of their own species in cannibalistic types). Some protozoa are saprotrophic; all the Sporozoa and certain subgroups of the other subphyla are parasitic. Many animals harbor at least one parasitic protozoan type, which means that protozoan species could well number in the hundreds of thousands. Thus although only some 15,000 species have been described to date, at least 100,000 species may actually be presumed to exist on a conservative estimate.

The protozoan cell is either naked or surrounded by a nonrigid *pellicle*, a cuticle composed of a variety of horny substances. Cellulose is not present. In many cases shells of various inorganic compounds are secreted as external covers. Foods are stored as glycogen and fats. In free-living flagellate and ciliate types, gullets usually are well developed. Amoeboid protozoa use pseudopodia for feeding.

The intracellular organization of protoza can be remarkably complex. Organelles such as *neurofibrils* (impulse conducting elements), *myofibrils* (filamentous contractile elements), and *contractile vacuoles* often lie below the cell surface. These last structures occur in nearly all freshwater forms as well as in a few marine and parasitic types. Where present, such vacuoles excrete excess water drawn into the cell osmotically (see also Chap. 18). Protozoa are largely uninucleate, but all ciliates and many amoeboid types are multinucleate, often highly so. Sporozoa become multinucleate at particular life-cycle stages.

Various protozoa "taste" food and refuse to ingest unsuitable materials; they give distinct avoidance responses to unsuitable temperatures, light, electric charges, pH, mechanical stimuli, and chemicals in the water; they seek out optimum environments by trial-and-error behavior; and some of them have been trained through conditioning to give "learned" responses to particular stimuli.

Mastigophora

The most primitive members of the Mastigophora, or *zooflagellates*, are generally free-living and holotrophic, and they greatly resemble colorless flagellate algae (Fig. 31.9). For example, the *collar flagellates* resemble certain flagellate golden-brown algae. The flagellum of collar flagellates creates a current that sweeps food toward the cell, where it is trapped in the collar and then engulfed. Some of these organisms are stalked and solitary; others form colonies. In many of the free-living zooflagellates the flagella can be lost temporarily and the organisms then become amoeboid.

Early free-living zooflagellates undoubtedly gave rise to the many symbiotic forms living today. For example, different species of *Trypanosoma* live parasitically in lymph and blood cells of various vertebrates. One such species produces sleeping sickness in people. Other symbiotic zooflagellates include *Trichomonas*, a commensal in the human gut and that of other vertebrates, and *Trichonympha*, a wood-digesting symbiont in the gut of termites.

Sarcodina

The Sarcodina move and feed by means of pseudopods. In one group each pseudopod is supported internally by a straight, rigid spike that resembles a flagellum structurally. To this group belong the largely freshwater *Heliozoa*, in which numerous permanent pseudopods radiate out from

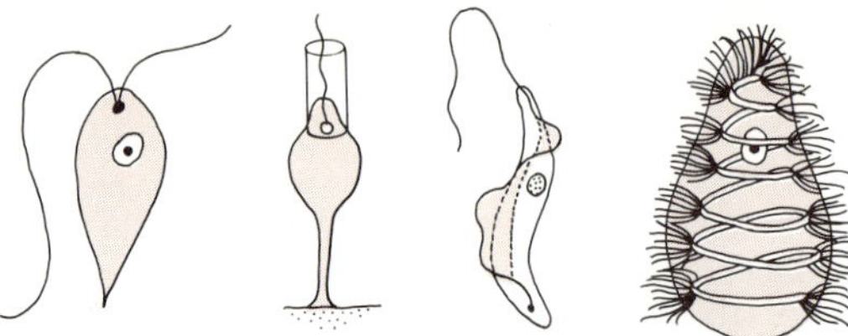

Fig. 31.9 Zooflagellates. The first two are free-living types. Note the collar in the attached collar flagellate *Codosiga*. The remaining two types are symbiotic. In *Trypanosoma* note the posterior kinetosome and the undulating membrane. *Macronspironympha* contains a spiral, ribbon-like kinetosome and hundreds of flagella emanating from it.

the cell like sun rays. The marine, planktonic *Radiolaria* have a similar appearance (see Color Fig. 2). Some Heliozoa and all Radiolaria have beautifully sculptured, latticelike silica shells, with pseudopodia protruding through the spaces in such lattices. Some 5 per cent of the area of the world's ocean floor consists of "radiolarian ooze," composed of the skeletons of these organisms. Compressed into rock, these bottom deposits form *flint* and *chert.*

In another group of Sarcodina the pseudopods are unsupported internally, and they therefore flow and change their contours freely (Fig. 31.10). The most familiar member of this group is the common amoeba, *Amoeba proteus* (see Fig. 5.18). Closely related is the parasitic *Entamoeba histolytica,* which causes human amoebic dysentery, and *Pelomyxa,* a large, free-living, highly multinucleate amoeba (see Fig. 31.10). Other such types encase their bodies in various kinds of shells. Most widespread are the *Foraminifera,* planktonic marine organisms that possess spiraled and coiled calcareous shells of many different forms (see Fig. 31.10). Pseudopods are extruded through holes in these shells, hence the name of the group (signifying "hole bearers"). Shells of dead organisms cover some 30 to 40 per cent of the world's ocean floor as "foraminiferan ooze." The rocky products here are *limestone* and *chalk.* Uplifted geologically, they form limestone mountain ranges and chalk cliffs such as those along the coast of the English Channel.

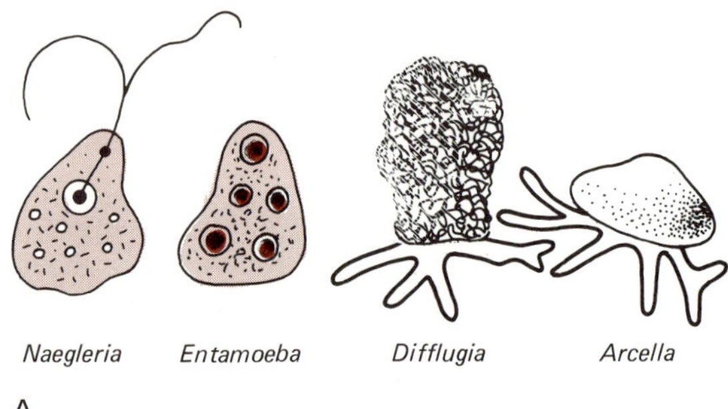

A

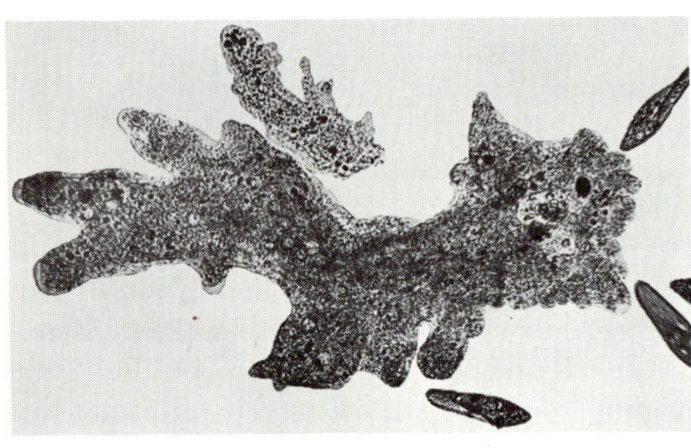

B

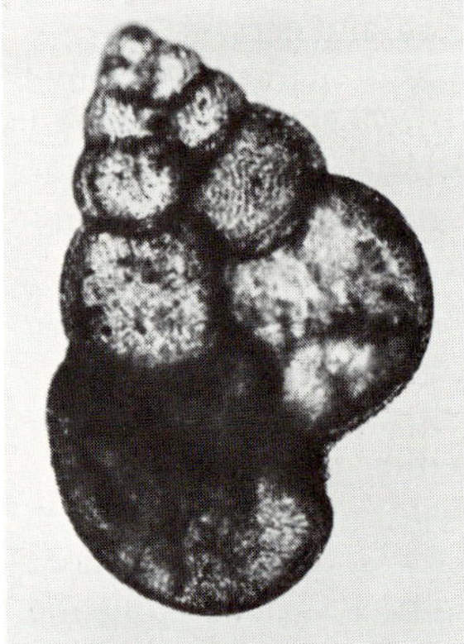

C

Fig. 31.10 "Shelled"' and "shell-less" sarcodines. (A) *Naegleria* is an amoeboid type that also has flagella. *Entamoeba histolytica* is shown with ingested blood corpuscles in food vacuoles. The shell of *Difflugia* is made of sand grains, that of *Arcella,* of chitinous substances. (B) *Pelomyxa,* one of the naked, multinucleate amoeboid types (with paramecia around it) and *Amoeba proteus* near top, for comparison (approx. ×70). An amoeba is also shown in Fig. 5.18. (C) The spiraled shell of a foraminiferan.

Sporozoa

The parasitic Sporozoa pass through complex life cycles that, as indicated by the name of the group, include spore-forming stages; a single-celled sporozoan can undergo *multiple fission* and divide into numerous smaller cells simultaneously. Each of the resulting cells is a spore with a single nucleus, and after such a cell has become established in a given host as a mature parasite, it eventually becomes multinucleate in preparation for another multiple fission.

The best-known sporozoan is *Plasmodium,* various species of which produce malaria in mammals and birds (Fig. 31.11). People are subject to infection by four species, each responsible for a different type of malaria. Repeated cycles of multiple fission and spore release from red blood corpuscles result in successive attacks of fever, the time interval between attacks being a main distinction between the four types of malaria. The specific intermediate host in human malaria is the *Anopheles* mosquito, where the parasites mature in the intestine and the salivary glands. From these glands the parasites reach the blood of new human hosts through mosquito bites.

Ciliophora

The Ciliophora are the most complexly elaborated protozoa and also represent the most diversely specialized of all known cell types (Fig. 31.12). The organisms move and feed by means of their cilia, which in most cases are arranged in orderly rows. Most ciliates, such as the well known *Paramecium,* possess permanent cellular mouths, or *gullets.* Food vacuoles migrate over a more or less definite path in the ciliate body, and digestive remains are cast out at a fixed point often located in or near the gullet. Contractile vacuoles occur at fixed positions near the body surface, and in many cases definite cytoplasmic channels form an internal drainage system leading to these vacuoles. Just under the body surface lies a complex system of

Fig. 31.11 Malaria: life cycle of the sporozoan parasite *Plasmodium vivax.* Mature parasitic cells invading human red blood corpuscles (top left) undergo multiple fission (schizogony) either inside the corpuscles, as shown, or outside them. Offspring cells (merozoites) destroy corpuscles and cause an attack of fever. They also reinfect new corpuscles and then lead to repetition of a 48-hour fever cycle. Merozoites entering red corpuscles also function as gamete producers, and if human blood is sucked by an *Anopheles* mosquito, the gamete producers break free in the mosquito stomach, transform into male and female sex cells, and bring about fertilization. The fertilization product then encysts in the stomach wall and undergoes multiple fission (sporogony). The resulting free spore cells later migrate through the body cavities and organs of the insect, including the salivary glands. From there the spores are injected into the human circulation when the mosquito bites a person. Spores mature in human liver cells, and fully formed parasites then begin a new life cycle.

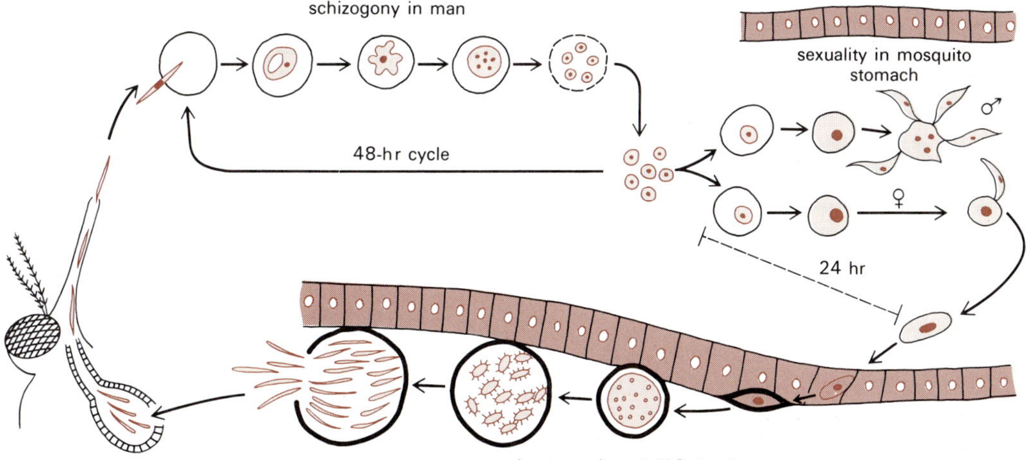

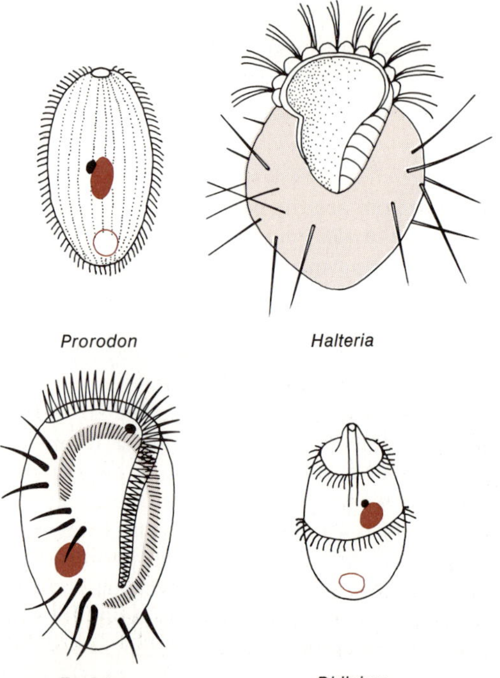

Fig. 31.12 Ciliate types. *Prorodon* is a relatively primitive form with uniform body cilia and a simple mouth. In *Didinium* the mouth is at the tip of a proboscis; in addition to the rings of cilia shown here, an otherwise uniform body ciliation is also present (but not indicated). *Halteria* and *Euplotes* are advanced types; simple cilia are absent, but various kinds of tufts of fused cilia are situated in specific regions.

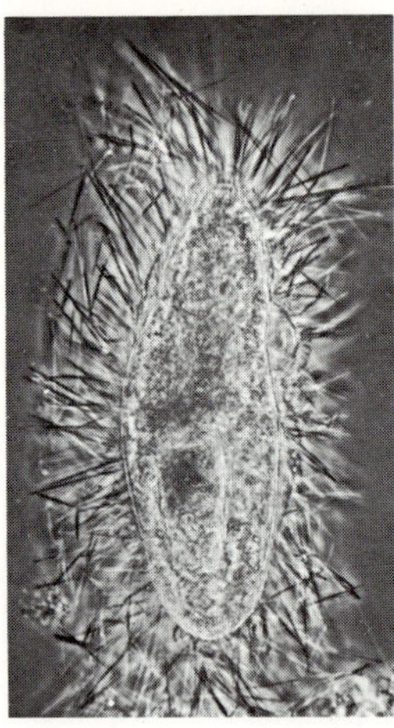

Fig. 31.13 *Paramecium discharging its trichocysts.*

coordinating neurofibrils, and in many species contractile myofibrils are also present. Rows of dischargeable and presumably protective or food-entangling *trichocysts* can be found under the surface of certain ciliates (Fig. 31.13).

Ciliates are multinucleate. They have at least one and often many (up to several hundred) *micronuclei,* and at least one or often many (up to several dozen) *macronuclei* (Fig. 31.14). Micronuclei produce the macronuclei and exert long-range control over them, and the micronuclei are also the chief controllers of sexual processes (see below). Macronuclei govern metabolic and developmental functions, and they are directly responsible for the maintenance of the visible traits of the organism.

A good many ciliates are symbiotic, and most free-living types are motile. The comparatively few sessile forms include, for example, *Vorticella,* a type attached by a contractile stalk (Fig. 31.15). Similarly sessile are the interesting *suctorians,* which trap microscopic food organisms by means of tentacles and suck the contents of such prey into their bodies. Immature suctorians swim about with the help of cilia, but when the organisms become attached adults, the cilia are lost.

Vegetative reproduction in protozoa takes place through binary fission in most cases (Fig. 31.16). Sexual processes occur universally among all protozoan groups, but some individual types are without sex (for example, *Amoeba*). Fertilization is achieved either by cellular fusion, as in zooflagellates, or by exchange of gamete nuclei, as in ciliates. Ciliate protozoa are hermaphroditic, each individual producing a gamete nucleus of each sex type. These gamete nuclei form from the micronuclei, and the macronuclei degenerate during conjugation (see Fig. 31.16). Ordinarily conjugation leads to cross-fertilization, or exchange of gamete nuclei between mating partners. Under certain circumstances, however, the two gamete nuclei of a single individual can fuse together and bring about self-fertilization.

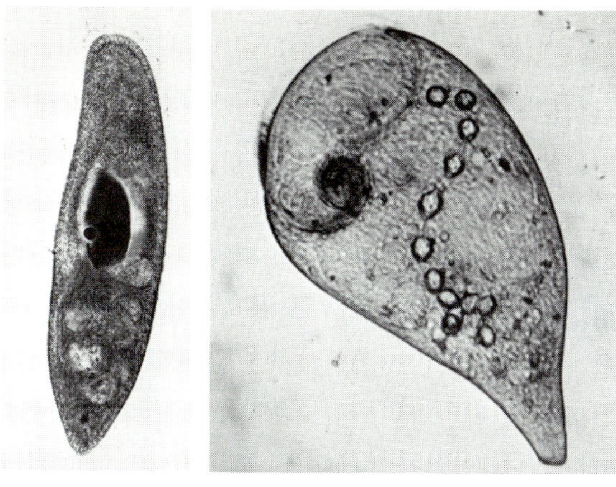

A B

Fig. 31.14 Ciliate nuclei. (A) *Paramecium caudatum* stained to reveal the macronucleus (large, dark central body) and the smaller micronucleus, which partly overlaps it on one side (approx. ×600). (B) *Stentor coeruleus,* from life. Note macronuclear chain. Faint rows of body cilia are also visible (approx. ×200). (*A, Carolina Biological Supply Company; B, courtesy of Roman Vishniac.*)

A

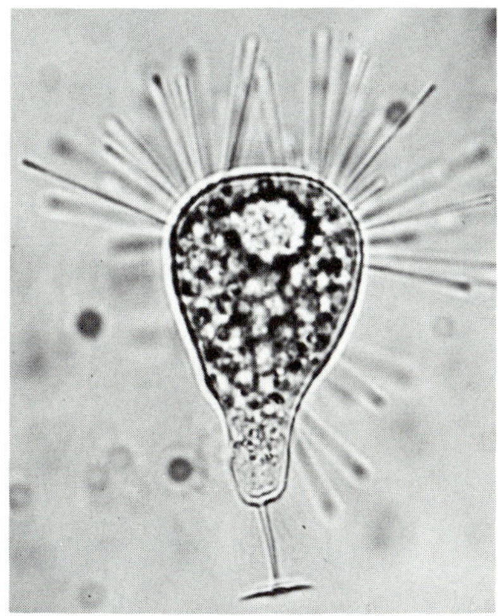

B

Fig. 31.15 Sessile ciliates. (A) A group of *Vorticella*. Each individual is attached by a stalk. In the contracted state the stalk is coiled, as in most individuals in the photo (×800). (B) A suctorian. The tentacles radiating out from the attached cell body suck up the juices of trapped prey (×400). (*A, courtesy Carolina Biological Supply Company.*)

FUNGI

Phylum Mycota (*90,000 species*)

CLASS CHYTRIDIOMYCETES chytrids

CLASS OOMYCETES water molds, white rusts, downy mildews

CLASS ZYGOMYCETES bread mold, fly fungi, animal-trapping fungi

CLASS ASCOMYCETES sac fungi

CLASS BASIDIOMYCETES club fungi

CLASS DEUTEROMYCETES "imperfect" fungi

General Characteristics

Fungi have many characteristics in common with plants and protists. Indeed, fungi are sometimes classified with these organisms. But in many ways fungi are so unlike all other organisms that most biologists assign them to a separate kingdom.

Fungi are highly successful. They exist in almost every available habitat on earth, and many are of major economic or medical significance. All fungi are heterotrophs; most are free-living saprotrophs, but many others live as parasites or in other kinds of symbiotic relationships. Together with

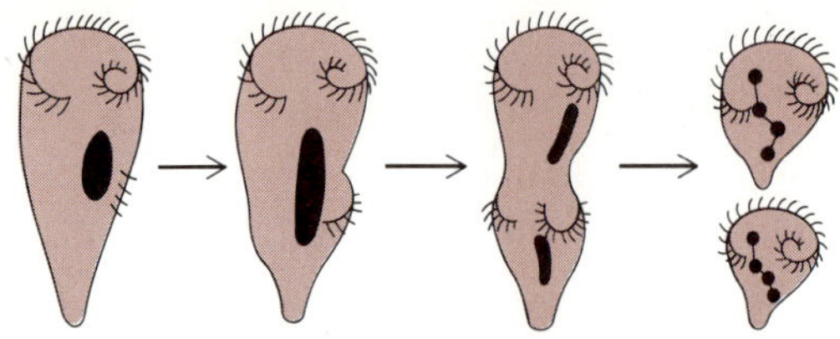

A

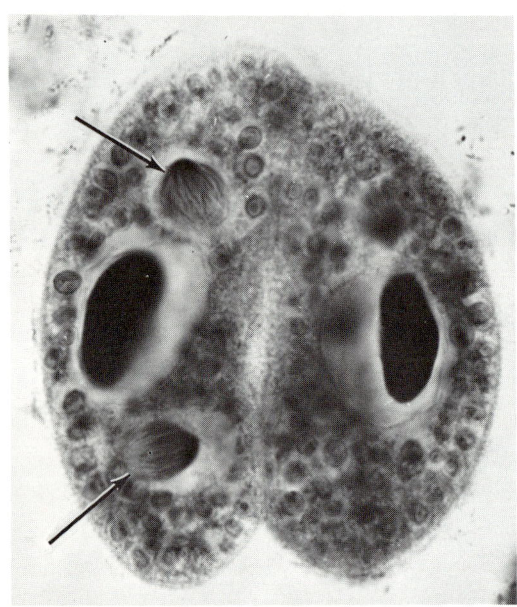

B

Fig. 31.16 Protozoan reproduction and sex. (A) Vegetative reproduction. Transverse fission in the ciliate *Stentor*. The macronucleus (black) condenses to a compact mass and then re-elongates as each micronucleus divides mitotically. Concurrently the future anterior offspring inherits the original set of mouth organelles, while the future posterior one develops a new set. After the two offspring separate, the macronuclear portion inherited by each recondenses. (B) and (C) Gametic reproduction. (B) A conjugating pair of *Paramecium*. Note spindles of dividing micronuclei in left individual (arrows). (C) In ciliates, gametic reproduction occurs through conjugation, or exchange and fusion of gamete nuclei. Conjugation in *Paramecium* is illustrated here. (1) Meiosis in each conjugating partner, followed by degeneration of macronucleus and of three haploid micronuclei resulting from meiosis. (2) Mitotic division of remaining haploid nucleus, yielding one stationary and one migratory gamete nucleus. (3), (4) Nuclear exchange and formation of diploid zygote nucleus. (3a), (4a) Autogamy, or self-fertilization (fusion of haploid gamete nuclei within same individual). (5), (5a) Three mitotic nuclear divisions, resulting in eight diploid nuclei. (6) Four of the eight become macronuclei, three degenerate, and one becomes a micronucleus. (7), (8) Cell and micronuclear divisions and parceling out of macronuclei, until each exconjugant has its normal nuclear complement.

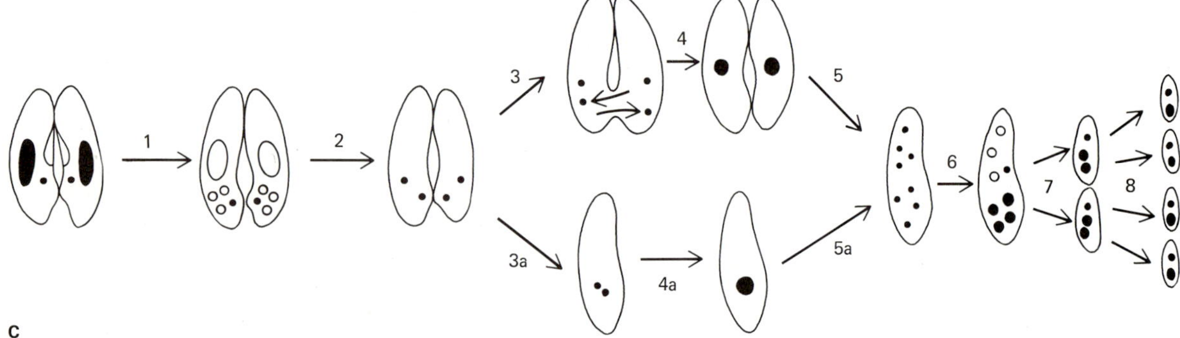

C

bacteria, fungi are the principal decomposer organisms of the living world.

As a group fungi can be regarded as a culmination of the coccine state in protistan evolution. The body of a fungus is multinucleate and without internal cell boundaries, though incomplete partitions do occur in the sac and club fungi (Fig. 31.17). Thus, a fungus is a continuous living mass that can grow in size and in the number of nuclei. True cells, with complete individual boundaries and one nucleus each, are formed only during reproduction.

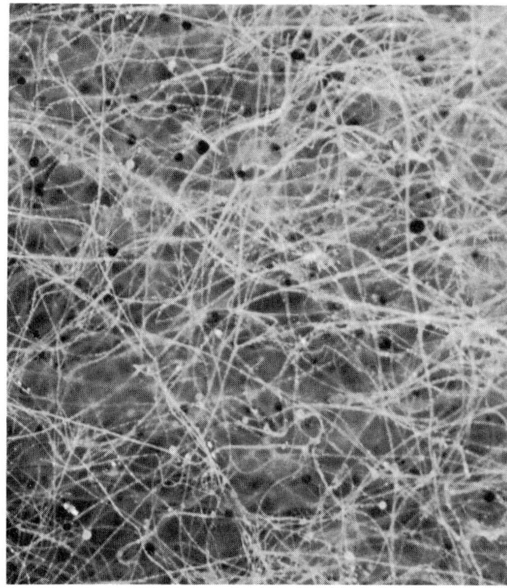

A

B

Fig. 31.17 Hyphae and mycelia. (A) The "body," or mycelium, of a fungus is composed of a tangled mass of threadlike hyphae. The hyphae of *Rhizopus,* a bread mold, are shown here. The small black structures are spore-containing sporangia. See Fig. 31.23 for an illustration of the *Rhizopus* life cycle. (B) The mycelium of a mold is shown growing in a culture dish. (C) Section through a hypha of the ascomycete *Neurospora,* showing one of the incomplete internal partitions. Note the continuity of the cytoplasm through the pore in the cross partition (approx. $\times 4000$).

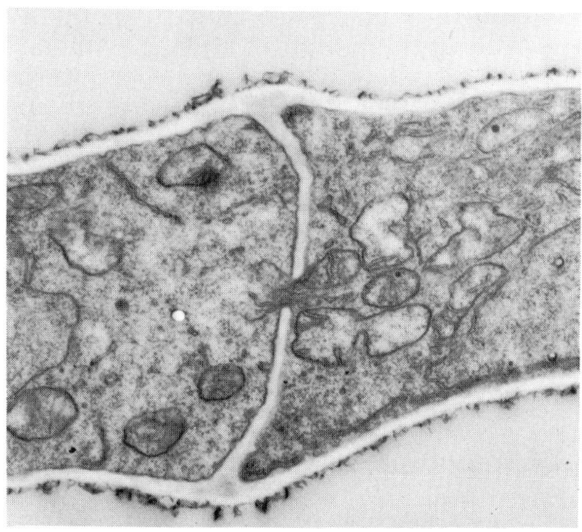

C

A fungus is covered by a rigid wall composed of cellulose in primitive types but of another complex polysaccharide, *chitin,* in most advanced forms. The latter substance is not produced by any of the Plantae but is a chief component of the hard outer covering of lobsters, insects, and other arthropods (see Chap. 34).

The basic unit of the fungus body generally is a *hypha,* a tubular, often branched filament. As it grows, it extends in length and can branch increasingly. Numerous hyphae usually are intermeshed as an irregular network, a so-called *mycelium* (see Fig. 31.17). Hyphae also can pack together in more orderly patterns and produce, for example, bodies structured like mushrooms.

Chytridiomycetes, Oomycetes, Zygomycetes

These three classes of fungi probably are the most primitive. Some members are entirely aquatic and often microscopic in size (Fig. 31.18). Other, larger forms are amphibious, able to live under both aquatic and terrestrial conditions. For example, *Saprolegnia* is a common saprotrophic water mold that can live both in calm fresh water and in irrigated soil. The most advanced members are strictly terrestrial; to this group belongs the familiar mold *Rhizopus,* which grows on stale bread (see Fig. 31.17). The mycelium of this fungus on and in bread is visible externally as a fuzzy whitish growth.

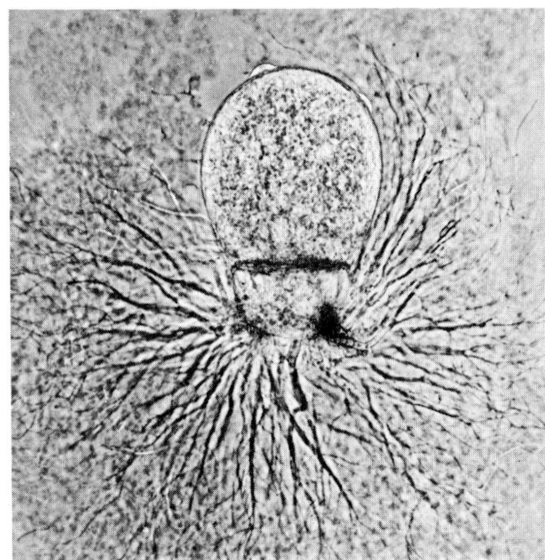

Fig. 31.18 Aquatic fungi. *Karlingia,* a simply constructed aquatic type. Note the two cellular compartments. From the lower one absorptive extensions (rhizoids) radiate away. The upper one is spore-producing.

A

B

Fig. 31.19 Oomycetes. (A) Potato blight. The potato on the right is infected with a blight-producing fungus. A blight-resistant potato, recently developed by plant scientists, is pictured on the left. (B) Downy mildew (whitish spots) on the upper surface of a grape leaf.

Other members of these classes have played major roles in shaping human economic, social, and political relationships. *Phytophthora infestans,* for example, a species of Oomycetes, is responsible for a series of potato blights in Ireland over the eighteenth and nineteenth centuries. The most devastating blights occurred between 1845 and 1847, when many Irish families were almost totally dependent on potatoes as a source of food. Fungal destruction of potato crops directly resulted in the starvation deaths of over 1 million people during this 3-year period and the emigration of another million Irish, mostly to the United States. Another species of Oomycetes, *Plasmopara viticola,* causes downy mildew of grapes. This fungus inflicted severe economic damage on the French wine industry during the latter part of the nineteenth century (Fig. 31.19).

Ascomycetes

The Ascomycetes, or sac fungi, are so called because their principal spores are manufactured in elongated sacs, or *asci.* Among these mostly terrestrial fungi are the largely unicellular *yeasts* and the fleshy, edible *morels* and *truffles* (Fig. 31.20). The class also includes *Penicillium,* one species of which is the source of the disease-curing antibiotic penicillin. Various ascomycete molds produce the characteristic flavors of Roquefort, Camembert, and other cheeses. Parasitic forms include types responsible for Dutch elm disease, scabs, rot, and mildewing of numerous fruits, and ergot disease in rye. The latter is dangerous. Even a small amount of the ergot-causing fungus, *Claviceps purpurea,* is

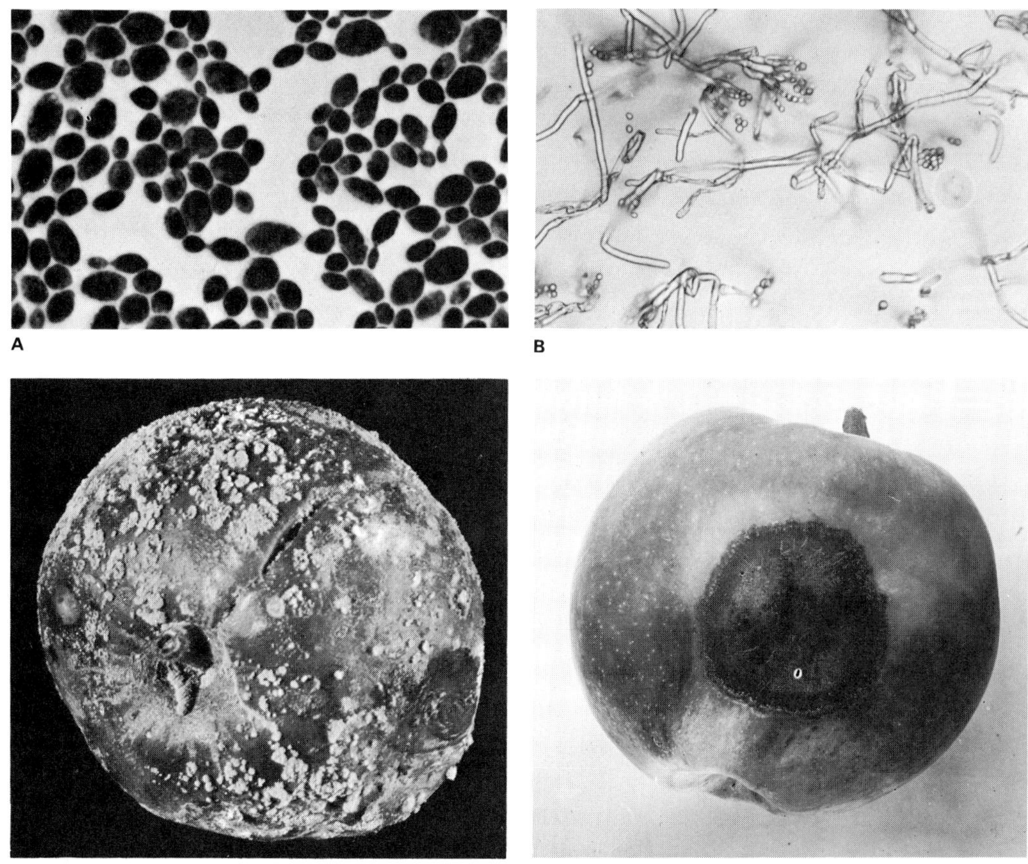

Fig. 31.20 Ascomycetes. (A) Yeasts. Note budding cells. (B) *Penicillium*. Note chains of spores (conidia) at ends of hyphae. (C) *Monolinia* producing brown rot on peach. (D) *Venturia inequalis,* causing mildewing of apple.

enough to cause sickness in animals that eat infected grain, or in people who eat bread made with contaminated flour. The sickness, called St. Anthony's Fire in the Middle Ages, often is accompanied by convulsions, delusions, and gangrene. This dangerous fungus is also the primary source of *lysergic acid diethylamide* (LSD), a psychedelic drug.

Ascomycetes are the most common fungal members of lichens. The algal members of these symbiotic associations usually are blue-green and coccine green algae. The fungus forms a mycelial framework in which the algae are held and supported. Lichens can be crustlike (*crustose*), leaflike (*foliose*), or branching (*fruticose*, Fig. 31.21). They often are found on trees (see Fig. 29.3), but more commonly they live independently on rock, where they aid in fragmenting the stone surfaces and thus contribute to the formation of soil (see Chap. 9).

Deuteromycetes

Ascomycetes also appear to make up most of the Deuteromycetes, or *Fungi imperfecti.* Fungi in this class undergo various forms of vegetative reproduction. Sexual processes undoubtedly occur as well, but as yet they remain undiscovered, thus the designation "imperfect." Species for which sexual stages are discovered are assigned to one of the other fungal classes. In this way the class Ascomycetes has enlarged most, and the membership of the *Fungi imperfecti* is decreasing.

Basidiomycetes

Early ascomycete ancestors probably have given rise to the class Basidiomycetes, identified by

Fig. 31.21 Lichens. (A) A leaf-like (foliose) type. (B) A branching (fruticose) type. See also Color Fig. 29.

hyphae with spore-producing terminal units called *basidia.* In some cases basidium-bearing hyphae are combined as large, stalked structures familiarly called *mushrooms* (Fig. 31.22).

Commercial fresh mushrooms are *Agaricus campestris,* the only species that has been cultivated commercially in the United States. Also known as the common field mushroom, this species can be harvested from its native habitats. But it is inadvisable for most people to eat wild mushrooms, for many are poisonous. Perhaps the most deadly is *Amanita phalloides;* one bite of the "death angel" can prove fatal. This species contains *phalloidine,* an extremely potent toxin that produces rapid degeneration of the kidneys, liver, and heart.

Not all Basidiomycetes form mushrooms, however. Among those that do not are the *jelly fungi,* saprotrophic on dead tree branches and decaying logs; and the *bracket fungi,* parasitic on living trees. Of great economic importance are the *rusts* and *smuts,* destructive parasites of plants such as wheat and corn. Saprotrophic types also include *bird's-nest fungi, stinkhorns,* and *puffballs,* some of the last attaining diameters of about 5 yards. Such giant puffballs probably have the distinction of being the most prolific of all living organisms. A single one can manufacture as many as 100 *trillion* spores; if each of these were to grow into a mature fungus, a mass of living matter nearly 1000 times the size of the earth would be produced.

Life Cycles

Vegetative reproduction in fungi occurs through mitotic nuclear divisions and cytoplasmic growth of the hyphae. Fragmentation of a mycelium can give rise to pieces that settle elsewhere and grow as new mycelia.

In the first three classes listed above, the spores of aquatic types are flagellate. Such spores form when a cell subdivides internally and releases numerous small spore cells. Terrestrial forms produce encapsulated spores. In the breadmold *Rhizopus,* for example, upright branch hyphae with expanded tips grow from many places in the mycelium (Fig. 31.23). The tips are *sporangia,* fruiting

A

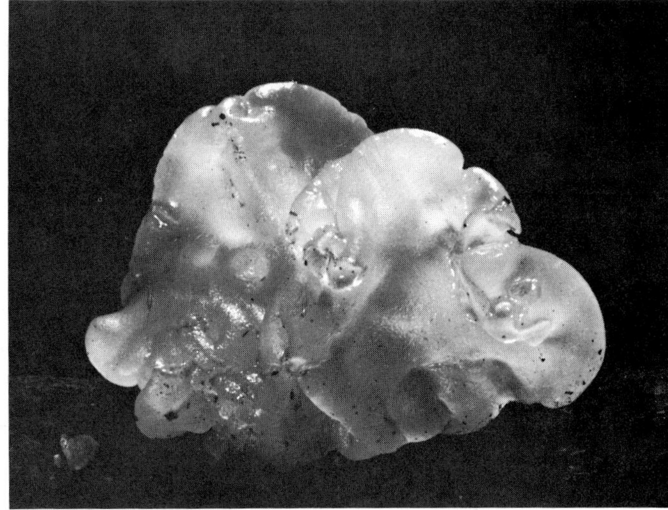
B

C

Fig. 31.22 Basidiomycetes. (A) A mushroom; note gills on underside of cap. (B) Jelly fungus. (C) A bracket fungus on a tree branch. See also Color Figs. 27 and 28.

bodies in which spores are formed. Each such spore is encapsulated in a wall that turns black as the spore matures. After the spores are dispersed, they germinate as new mycelia.

The mycelia, sporangia, and spores of *Rhizopus* are all haploid; the life cycle of the breadmold is haplontic. A sexual process can occur when two mycelia live in close proximity. Each then can develop a short *suspensor* hypha, one growing toward the other. The tip of such a hypha becomes partitioned off as a multinucleate gametelike compartment. When two of these compartments meet, they fuse and a cyst wall is secreted around the fusion mass (see Fig. 31.23). In the interior the nuclei pair off, one from each compartment joining one from the other. Such nuclear pairs fuse and form diploid zygote nuclei. Unpaired nuclei degenerate. When the cyst later germinates, its contents grow directly into an upright hypha with a terminal sporangium. The zygote nuclei divide in the process, and the first two divisions are meiotic. Numerous haploid nuclei are thereby formed, and some of them participate in spore formation in the sporangium. Mature spores are then released and grow as new vegetative mycelia.

Most Ascomycetes and many Basidiomycetes have life cycles basically equivalent to diplohaplontic ones (Fig. 31.24 and see Fig. 22.24). The ga-

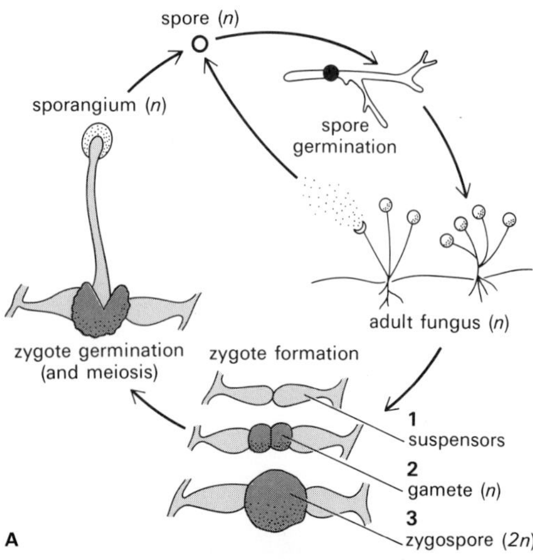

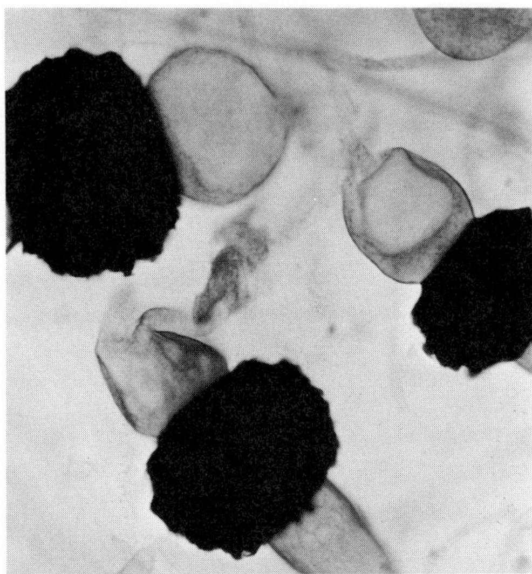
B

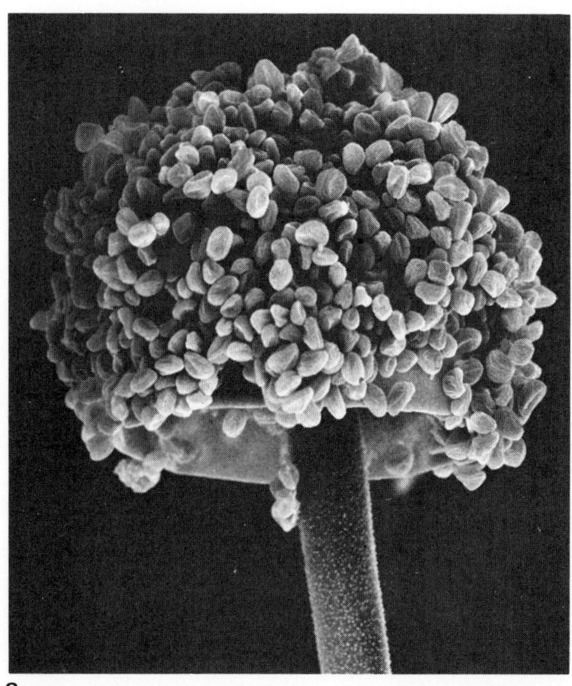
C

D

Fig. 31.23 Bread mold reproduction. (A) The *Rhizopus* life cycle. Bread mold zygotes become encased within a cyst wall. Such encysted zygotes are called zygospores, the dark structures shown in (B). (C) Scanning electron micrograph of a sporangium of *Rhizopus stolonifer* (approx. ×700). The particles covering the surface of this sporangium are spores that have been released by nearby sporangia. The spores are shown at higher magnification (approx. ×2800) in (D).

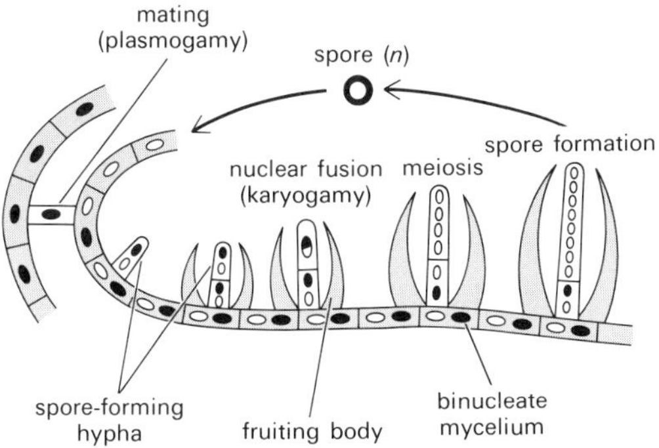

Fig. 31.24 The life cycle in Ascomycetes and Basidiomycetes. Read the diagram counterclockwise, beginning at left. If two uninucleate, haploid (gametophytelike) mycelia grow side by side, mating may occur by migration of a nucleus from one mycelium into the other through a cytoplasmic bridge (left). A binucleate (sporophytelike) mycelium arises. From it then grow special spore-forming hyphae, which are usually surrounded by packed hyphae forming a fruiting body. In terminal cells of the spore-forming hyphae nuclear fusion occurs, meiosis takes place, and haploid spores are eventually produced. The cell containing such spores is either an ascus or a basidium, depending on the fungal class. Liberated ascospores or basidiospores then germinate and form new uninucleate mycelia.

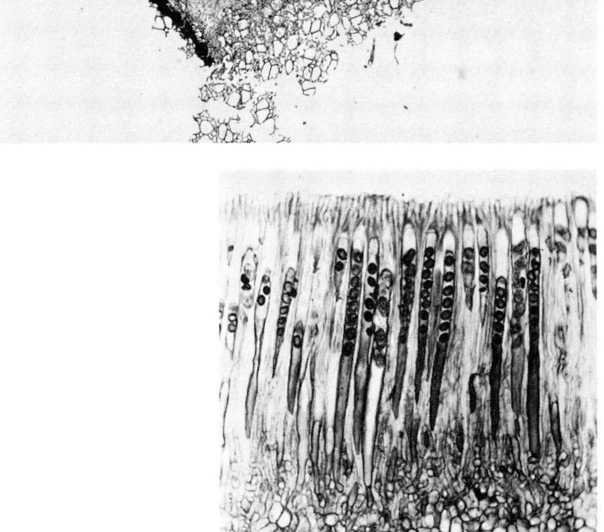

A

B

Fig. 31.25 Fungus fruiting bodies. (A) Section through the cup of a cup fungus, showing the layer of asci lining the cavity of the cup. (B) Higher magnification of a portion of the ascus layer. Note spores in elongated asci. (C) Section through the cap of a mushroom, showing gill arrangement. (D) Section of a gill, showing mycelial meshwork in the interior and basidiospores (attached to basidia) projecting from the surface. *(A, B, Carolina Biological Supply Company.)*

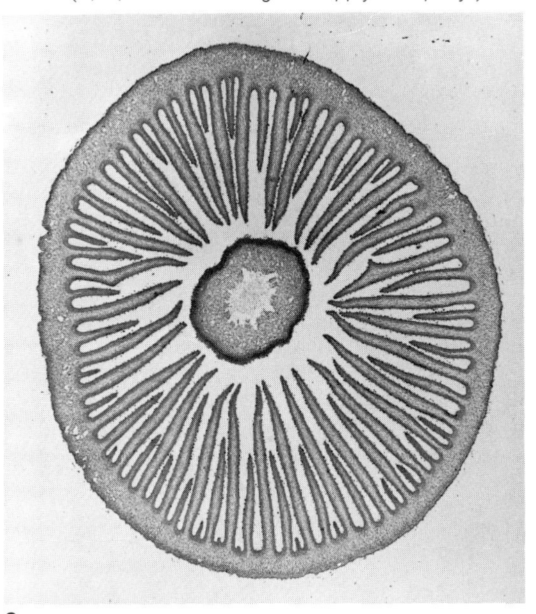

C

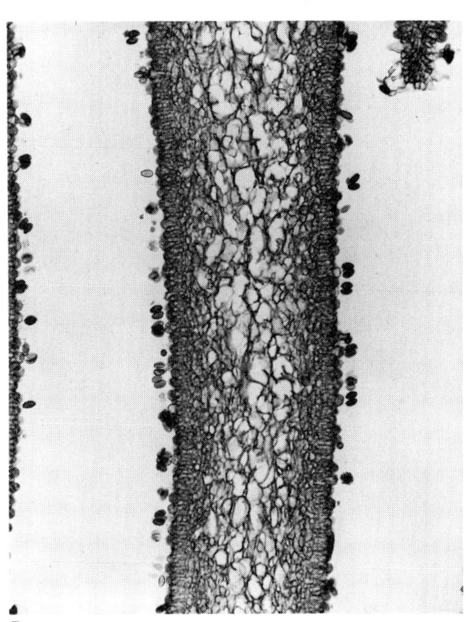

D

mete-producing generation of these fungi is represented by mycelia containing haploid nuclei. If two mycelia of this type live side by side, a cytoplasmic connecting bridge may grow between them and nuclei from one mycelium may migrate through the bridge into the other. This is a mating process. The nuclei represent gamete nuclei, and their coming together in one hypha is called *plasmogamy*. Such a hypha with nuclei from both parental mycelia is roughly equivalent to a diploid stage and represents the beginning of the spore-producing generation. It grows into a more or less extensive mycelium, in which each of the two gamete nuclei multiplies numerous times. Before long this mycelium also produces special spore-forming hyphae. Around such hyphae usually develop others that collectively form a conspicuous fruiting body of a particular shape. For example, a mushroom is a stalked fruiting body growing upright from a mycelium embedded in soil. The gill plates on the underside of the cap of the mushroom contain the ends of the special spore-forming hyphae (Fig. 31.25).

At the ends of these hyphae arise cells that become sporangia—saclike asci in Ascomycetes, club-shaped basidia in Basidiomycetes. A sporangium at first contains two haploid nuclei, derived from the two original gamete nuclei that participated in plasmogamy. These two sporangial nuclei fuse, a process equivalent to fertilization and called *karyogamy* (see Fig. 31.24). The resulting single diploid nucleus then undergoes meiosis, and haploid spore nuclei are thereby formed. Also, the cytoplasm surrounding each such nucleus becomes walled off, and distinct spore cells arise in this fashion—ascospores in an ascus, basidiospores in a basidium. The spores eventually scatter from the fruiting body; after they germinate they grow as new gamete-producing mycelia with haploid nuclei.

These fungi are unique in that mating, or plasmogamy, is not followed immediately by fusion of gamete nuclei, or karyogamy. In contrast to events in all other organisms, the two processes are separated here by a substantial time interval, and during this interval the original gamete nuclei can divide mitotically many times. As a result, a single mating can be followed by hundreds or thousands of nuclear fusions. Indeed in many cases it is known that a single mating may continue to have sexual results for years.

Most yeasts are unicellular and thus display patterns of reproduction somewhat different from those of multicellular fungi. Yeasts can reproduce vegetatively by budding (see Fig. 31.20), and individual yeast cells also can function as gametes. Diploid zygotes then produce populations of sporophytic cells, which eventually serve as spore-producing asci. Spore cells give rise to new populations of haploid gametic cells.

It should now be evident that both Protista and Fungi are far from "simple." Many of these organisms have remained unicellular and microscopic in size, yet in this very smallness lies perhaps their most remarkable characteristic: despite being limited to the dimensions of single cells they are as diverse, varied, and complex in the microsphere of life as only very few groups of far larger organisms can be in the macrosphere.

Review Questions

1 Review the unifying traits of Protista and Fungi. Why should these organisms no longer be classified simply as "plants" and "animals"? What states of existence did early protists and fungi probably exhibit? Define each of these states and give specific examples of each.

2 Describe the group characteristics of algal protists. Identify the major phyla of algal protists and describe the distinguishing characteristics of each.

3 What traits identify the slime molds? What justifies inclusion of these organisms in the Protista? Describe the life cycle of slime molds.

4 Distinguish between protozoa and other protists. What states of existence are exhibited by

- **a** Fungi?
- **b** Slime molds?
- **c** Protozoa?

5 Describe the general structural characteristics of protozoan cells. What cytoplasmic and nuclear organelles are typical of such cells?

6 Describe the general characteristics of the various fungal classes. What are lichens?

7 Review the life cycles of *Rhizopus*, Ascomycetes, and Basidiomycetes. What are basidia and how are they formed? What is the reproductive function of a mushroom? In what ways is the reproduction of terrestrial fungi well adapted to the absence of locomotion among the organisms and to the general lack of free environmental water?

8 Illustrate the economic and medical importance of protists and fungi.

Collateral Readings

Bold, H. C., and **M. J. Wynne:** "Introduction to the Algae," Prentice-Hall, Englewood Cliffs, N.J., 1978. A technical but comprehensive text.

Boney, A. D.: "A Biology of Marine Algae," Hutchinson Educational, New York, 1966. An excellent treatment. Algal ecology is also covered.

Bonner, J. T.: "The Cellular Slime Molds," 2d ed., Princeton University Press, Princeton, N.J., 1968. The biology of one of the most fascinating groups of organisms is discussed. Recommended.

______: Hormones in Social Amoebae and Mammals, *Scientific American,* June 1969. This interesting article outlines how cyclic AMP facilitates communication between amoebae of the cellular slime molds.

Cooke, R. C.: "Fungi, Man and His Environment," Longman, London, 1978. A short, readable treatment of fungi, including how these organisms affect human beings.

Curtis, H.: "The Marvelous Animals," Natural History Press, Garden City, N.Y., 1968. An introduction to protozoans.

Grell, K. G.: "Protozoology," 2d ed., Springer, Heidelberg, 1973. An outstanding treatment of protozoa.

Jackson, D. F. (ed.)**:** "Algae and Man," Plenum, New York, 1964. Contains several articles concerning relationships between algae and human health.

Litten, W.: The Most Poisonous Mushrooms, *Scientific American,* March 1975. The poisons of the *Amanita* fungi are described. This article also discusses the biological effects of these poisons on human beings.

Nisizaiva, K. (ed.)**:** *Proceedings of the Seventh International Seaweed Symposium,* University of Tokyo Press, Tokyo, 1971. The diversity, ecology, and economics of algae are highlighted.

Ramsbottom, J.: "Mushrooms and Toadstools," Collins, London, 1953. A delightful, highly readable account of mushroom biology. Written for the novice, the book contains many historical anecdotes about mushrooms and toadstools.

Round, F. E.: "The Biology of the Algae," Arnold, London, 1965. A short, interesting book on the biology of algae. The ecology and physiology of these organisms are emphasized.

Sleigh, M.: "The Biology of Protozoa," Arnold, London, 1973. A well-illustrated introduction, this textbook contains chapters on the structure, reproduction, ecology, and metabolism of protozoa.

Smith, A. H.: "The Mushroom Hunter's Field Guide," 2d ed., University of Michigan Press, Ann Arbor, Mich., 1966. A concise guide to the edible mushrooms. The author provides excellent advice and informative warnings for those seriously contemplating eating wild mushrooms.

Webster, J.: "Introduction to Fungi," Cambridge University Press, New York, 1977. Technical treatment of these organisms. For the serious student.

Chapter 32 Plants

Learning Objectives

After reading this chapter you should be able to:

1. List the three phyla of algal plants and state at least one characteristic that distinguishes these algae from photosynthetic protists; name at least one representative and two identifying characteristics of each phylum of algal plants; illustrate the economic importance of brown and red algae.
2. Using at least three different genera of algae, draw diagrams that distinguish between haplontic, diplontic, and diplohaplontic life cycles of algal plants.
3. List at least three characteristics that distinguish bryophytes and tracheophytes from algae; give evidence in support of the hypothesis that bryophytes and tracheophytes have evolved from green algae.
4. Identify the three major kinds of bryophytes; list at least four adaptations to terrestrial environments that have evolved in bryophytes; give at least two reasons why bryophytes are comparatively small plants that have adapted only to relatively moist terrestrial environments.
5. Identify the five subphyla of tracheophytes, and name a representative organism of each; identify two subclasses of gymnosperms and the two subclasses of angiosperms, and name a representative organism of each subclass; list the identifying characteristics of tracheophytes.
6. Define paleontology and fossil; show how fossils embedded in successive earth layers can provide a time picture of evolution; give the names and dates of the geologic eras; state criteria used to determine beginning and terminal dates for geologic eras; identify the geologic periods in which the major classes of terrestrial plants have evolved.
7. State the Lignier hypothesis; identify the probable evolutionary relations of tracheophyte subphyla.
8. List the general characteristics of psilopsids, lycopsids, and sphenopsids.
9. Identify at least one living and one extinct lycopsid; do the same for sphenopsids.
10. Outline the distinguishing characteristics and probable evolutionary origin of ferns; define circinate vernation; show how ferns are only slightly better adapted for life on land than bryophytes and primitive tracheophytes.
11. Distinguish between seed ferns, fossil conifers, and fossil cycads; name the geologic eras in which these plants were most abundant and illustrate the evolutionary significance of the three groups; name at least one living cycad and one modern ginkgo.
12. Name the probable evolutionary ancestor of gymnosperms; identify at least three ways in which conifers are better adapted to terrestrial environments than ferns, lycopsids, or sphenopsids; state the geologic era in which conifers were most abundant.
13. List at least two terrestrial adaptations of angiosperms that are not found in gymnosperms; name the geologic era in which angiosperms became the dominant form of plant life on earth.
14. Describe the principal architectural adaptations of tracheophytes to land; define rhizome, tuber, bulb, corm, runners, twining stems, fibrous roots, taproots, adventitious roots, prop roots, and aerial roots, and state the adaptive significance of each.
15. Illustrate how tracheophytes conserve water and how they protect against heat or cold; define perennial, biennial, and annual, and describe or illustrate the life cycles of such plants; show how these life cycles represent adaptations to terrestrial environments.

Kingdom	Phylum	Subphylum	Class	Subclass
Monera				
Protista				
Fungi				
Plantae	Phaeophyta (brown algae)			
	Rhodophyta (red algae)			
	Chlorophyta (green algae)			
	Bryophyta (moss plants)		Bryopsida (mosses)	
			Hepaticopsida (liverworts)	
			Anthoceropsida (hornworts)	
	Tracheophyta (vascular plants)	Psilopsida (psilopsids)		
		Lycopsida (club mosses)		
		Sphenopsida (horsetails)		
		Pteropsida (ferns)		
		Spermopsida (seed plants)	Gymnospermae (gymnosperms)	Cycadophytae (cycads)
				Coniferophytae (conifers)
			Angiospermae (angiosperms)	Dicotyledoneae (dicots)
				Monocotyledoneae (monocots)
Animalia				

Viewed through the porthole of a hypothetical spaceship traveling through our solar system 1 billion years ago, the land masses of the earth would have appeared as barren and bare as the surface of the moon appears today. Photosynthetic aquatic organisms had not yet adapted to harsher terrestrial habitats; fossil evidence indicates that evolution of land plants began less than 500 million years ago. Voyagers aboard this hypothetical spaceship would have observed a few signs of semiterrestrial life, however. Narrow bands of green or brown undoubtedly would have colored the shores of oceans and freshwater lakes. These hues would have been caused by masses of ancestral protistan algae, discussed in the previous chapter, and ancient representatives of three additional phyla of algae, *Phaeophyta*, *Rhodophyta*, and *Chlorophyta;* the brown, red, and green algae, respectively.

Each of these phyla includes unicellular or colonial species, but each also includes complex, multicellular forms. Some of the larger algae consist of several layers or regions of diversely specialized tissues. For example, certain of these algae have attachment structures, or *holdfasts,* which anchor the plants to rocks in intertidal zones, where sunlight and nutrients usually are plentiful. The upper surfaces of some multicellular algae have evolved as thinner and more expanded structures, exposing greater numbers of photosynthetic cells to sunlight.

Brown, green, and red algae gave rise to most modern seaweeds and the comparatively fewer species of large freshwater algae. Because they include many multicellular representatives, these three kinds of algae are classified as Plantae (Metaphyta). The organization, economic importance, and life cycles of these algae will be discussed in the first portion of this chapter. Remaining sections will deal with the even larger and terrestrially better adapted bryophytes and tracheophytes.

ALGAL PLANTS

General Characteristics

Brown Algae

Phylum Phaeophyta (1000 species)

Nearly all brown algae are marine. They are filamentous and generally have a more complex, tissue-level organization than most other algae. Indeed, there are no modern unicellular brown algae.

Many "seaweeds" are brown algae. The most familiar of these is probably the rockweed *Fucus*, found along many shores, and the most spectacular are the giant kelps (Fig. 32.1). For example, the kelp *Macrocystis* along the Pacific coast of North America sometimes attains lengths of more than 100 yards. *Laminaria*, the commonest of the kelps, is of worldwide distribution. Torn pieces of it can often be found washed up on beaches along with other algae. Another brown alga, *Sargassum natans*, makes up much of the giant floating mass of seaweed that fills the *Sargasso Sea*, an area of 2 million square miles extending from the Azores to the Bahamas (Fig. 32.2).

Among the identifying pigments of brown algae are chlorophyll *a* and *c* and the brown fucoxanthin (Table 32.1). The last occurs in amounts sufficient to mask all other pigments. Foods are stored partly as *laminarin*, a unique polysaccharide, partly as *mannitol*, a complex alcohol. The cell walls are composed of cellulose and *algin*, an organic material unique to the phylum. Most brown algae live in shallow water, attached to rocky bottoms by holdfasts (see Color Fig. 30). Ebb tides may expose the organisms to air for several hours, but their algin coating retains considerable amounts of water and protects the organisms from drying out.

Brown algae are the source of several useful substances. For example, the algae contain high concentrations of iodine, and algin is used to provide structure and consistency for such diverse products as ice cream, lipstick, cake frostings, insecticides, and salad dressings.

TABLE 32.1
Identifying Characteristics of Algal Plants

Characteristic	Phaeophyta (brown algae)	Rhodophyta (red algae)	Chlorophyta (green algae)
number of species	1100	4000	7000
photosynthetic pigments	chlorophylls *a*, *c*, carotenoids (especially fucoxanthin)	chlorophylls *a*, *d*, carotenoids, phycoerythrin	chlorophylls *a*, *b*, carotenoids (especially beta-carotene), xanthophyll
food reserve	laminarin, mannitol	floridean starch	starch
flagella	2, lateral; in reproductive cells only	none (amoeboid reproductive cells)	2 (or more), apical
cell-wall components	cellulose, algin	cellulose, pectin, algin	cellulose, pectin
distribution	almost all marine, mostly temperate	mostly marine, but some freshwater; many species tropical	mostly freshwater, but some marine

A

B

C

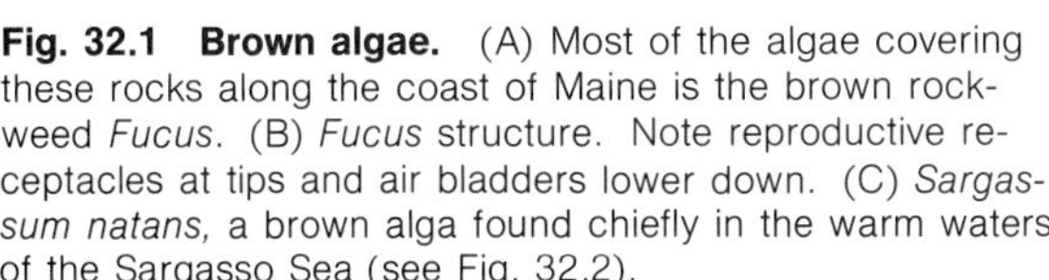

Fig. 32.1 Brown algae. (A) Most of the algae covering these rocks along the coast of Maine is the brown rockweed *Fucus*. (B) *Fucus* structure. Note reproductive receptacles at tips and air bladders lower down. (C) *Sargassum natans*, a brown alga found chiefly in the warm waters of the Sargasso Sea (see Fig. 32.2).

Fig. 32.2 Algae of the Sargasso Sea. Several species of *Sargassum* contribute to the dense masses of largely brown algae that float in this marine environment.

Red Algae

Phylum Rhodophyta (4000 species)

Red algae are almost exclusively multicellular, and almost all are marine. They make up much of the "seaweed" found in warm, tropical waters, although a few species thrive in temperate and polar seas (Fig. 32.3). Red algae live in somewhat deeper water than their brown counterparts, and their red pigment *phycoerythrin* appears to be an adaptation to their dimmer environment (see Table 32.1). This pigment absorbs blue light particularly well, and the blue wavelengths of sunlight actually penetrate deeper into water than red wavelengths. Indeed, phycoerythrin has been found to play an important auxiliary role in the photosynthesis of these algae. Red algae are lacier and more delicate than the sturdy brown algae. The latter are adapted to withstand pounding surf, but in deeper water the red algae are not so subject to wave action.

Some of the red algae are used commercially. The genus *Gelidium* is the source of agar jelly, used as a medium for culturing microorganisms, and *Porphyra*, *Rhodymenia*, and *Chondrus crispus*, the Irish moss, are among several types eaten as vegetables in various parts of the world.

Green Algae

Phylum Chlorophyta (7000 species)

Apart from chlorophylls *a* and *b*, green algae are identified also by red *carotene* and yellow *xanthophyll* pigments, by comparatively rigid cell walls containing cellulose, by reserve foods stored in most cases as starch, and by flagellate cells or stages that bear two (or rarely four or more) equally long anterior flagella (see Table 32.1). These characteristics occur in precisely this combination only in the green algae and the Plantae. Early chlorophyte stocks are therefore believed to have been the specific ancestors of plants.

More diverse than any other algal phylum, green algae are largely aquatic, although several species exist as symbionts in lichens and many other organisms, as green patches on the bark of trees, and even on the melting surfaces of glaciers. Some categories of green algae are exclusively marine, but most aquatic types are found in fresh water.

Chlorophytes include a flagellate, a coccine, and a sporine line (see Chap. 31). Each is represented by both unicellular and colonial forms. Flagellate algae are exemplified by single-celled types such as *Chlamydomonas* (Fig. 32.4). Very closely related is *Polytoma*, a genus nearly identical to *Chlamydomonas* except that it is colorless and nonphotosynthetic; it lives as a saprotroph.

As already noted, type pairs of this sort are also encountered in some of the other algal phyla. Undoubtedly such paired photosynthetic and colorless forms represent branch lines descended from a relatively recent common ancestor, one line having retained and the other having lost the photosynthetic method of nutrition. In certain cases such evolutionary processes have been duplicated experimentally.

Cells rather like *Chlamydomonas* form flagellate colonies, usually composed of fixed numbers of cells—4, 8, 16, 32, 64, or larger multiples. If there are relatively few cells, they form disks or cup-shaped colonies; if the cell number is comparatively large, the colony is usually a hollow sphere, as in *Volvox*. In this organism a network of presumably impulse-conducting fibrils joins the kinetosomes of all cells, and the flagella beat in a highly coordinated, locomotion-producing pattern (see Color Fig. 3).

Chlorophytes in the coccine line of evolution include *Chlorella*, used extensively in research on photosynthesis, and the large alga *Acetabularia* (Fig. 32.5 and see Fig. 1 in the Biology Highlight in Chap. 5). This marine organism, up to 2 or 3 inches long, consists of a stalk, an umbrellalike cap

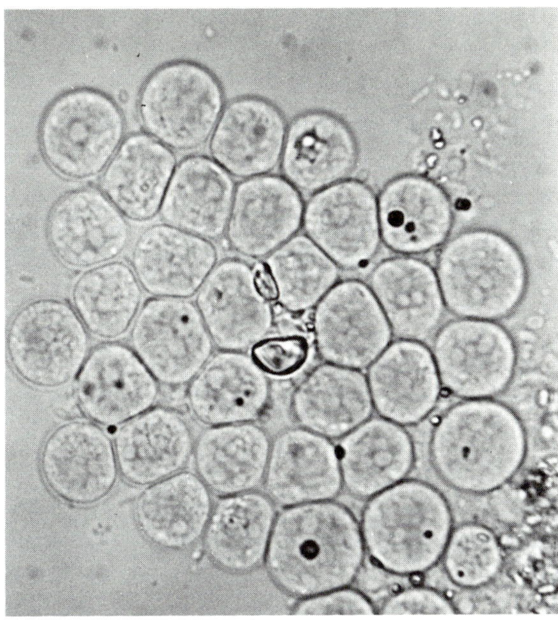

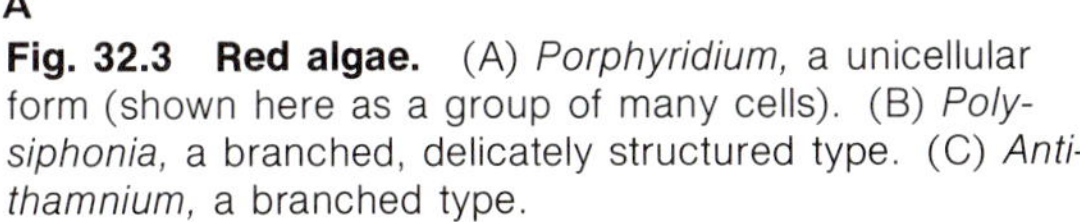
Fig. 32.3 Red algae. (A) *Porphyridium,* a unicellular form (shown here as a group of many cells). (B) *Polysiphonia,* a branched, delicately structured type. (C) *Antithamnium,* a branched type.

at the top, and fine outgrowths at the bottom of the stalk that anchor the organism on the sea floor. The whole organism is a single cell, the nucleus being situated in the base of the stalk.

The sporine line is the most diversified of the chlorophytes (Fig. 32.6). Unicellular types include the common *Protococcus,* which usually grows on moist tree bark in the form of loose colonies. More complexly organized are the filamentous green algae, among them *Spirogyra, Ulothrix,* and *Oedogonium,* freshwater forms commonly used in laboratories. Cell division extends the filaments of such organisms in length. The most complex green algae are types in which cell division produces extensive sheets of cells, as in the sea lettuce *Ulva,* or compact three-dimensional bodies composed of several layers of cells, as in *Schizomeris.* Such algae may be considered to have attained the tissue level of organization.

Reproduction

As a group, algae exhibit the whole range of possible reproductive methods, all types of life cycles,

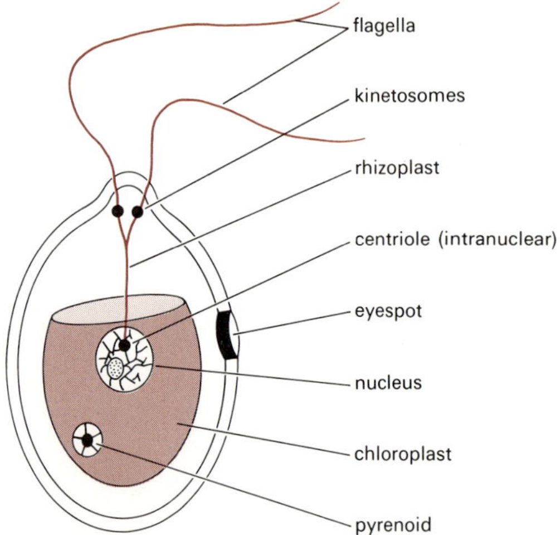

Fig. 32.4 Unicellular green algae: *Chlamydomonas* structure. The chloroplast is cup-shaped. On it, the pyrenoid is a refractile, presumably light-concentrating organelle, around which starch deposits accumulate. This organism is very similar to *Polytoma,* a nonphotosynthetic type in which chloroplast and pyrenoid are lacking.

and all basic variations in the degrees of maleness and femaleness. Vegetative reproduction by cell division occurs in all algae that are not coccine. This process increases the number of unicellular types and the size of multicellular algae. Multicellular forms commonly also propagate by fragmentation and by regeneration.

Algal plants exhibit a wide variety of haplontic, diplontic, and diplohaplontic life cycles, introduced in Chap. 22. For example, the life cycles of the green algae *Chlamydomonas* (Fig. 32.7 and see Fig. 22.21) and *Ulothrix* are haplontic. The life cycle of the latter alga, which resembles *Spirogyra* superficially, is illustrated in Fig. 32.8. *Ulothrix* is a filamentous alga, consisting of chains of predominantly haploid cells. In many species, any of these cells can function as a *gametangium.* Division occurs repeatedly in such structures, giving rise to many smaller cells. These develop flagella, escape through an opening in the original cell wall, and function as gametes. After fertilization, the resulting zygote swims about for a time and then undergoes meiosis. The four haploid cells formed eventually settle and undergo repeated mitotic divisions, giving rise to four haploid multicellular adults.

Ulothrix (and virtually all other green algae) also produces spores (see Fig. 32.8). Given cells of the organisms divide a number of times within the original cell wall. Each small cell so produced then secretes its own wall and matures as a flagellate spore. An opening later develops in the wall of the original cell, and the spores escape through it.

Haplontic life cycles occur commonly among many other algae, including *Spirogyra*, *Oedogonium*, and *Volvox* (Fig. 32.9). Spirogyra is unusual in that the gametes are not flagellate but amoeboid, moving directly from one filament to another through a conjugation tube. Moreover, of the four cells formed by meiosis in the zygote, three degen-

Fig. 32.5 Coccine green algae. (A) *Chlorella*. (B) *Acetabularia*. (C) *Bryopsis*.

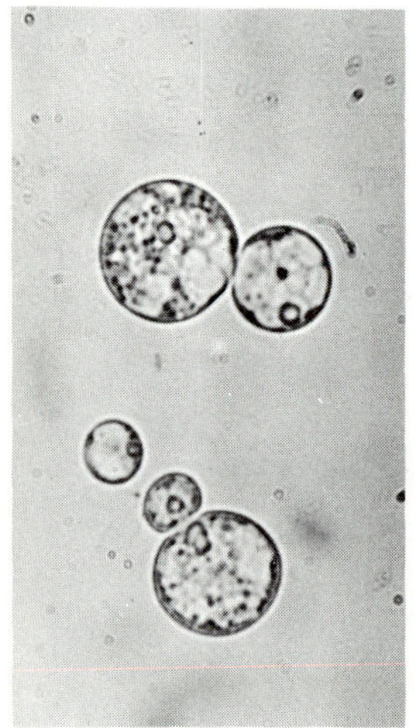
A

B

C

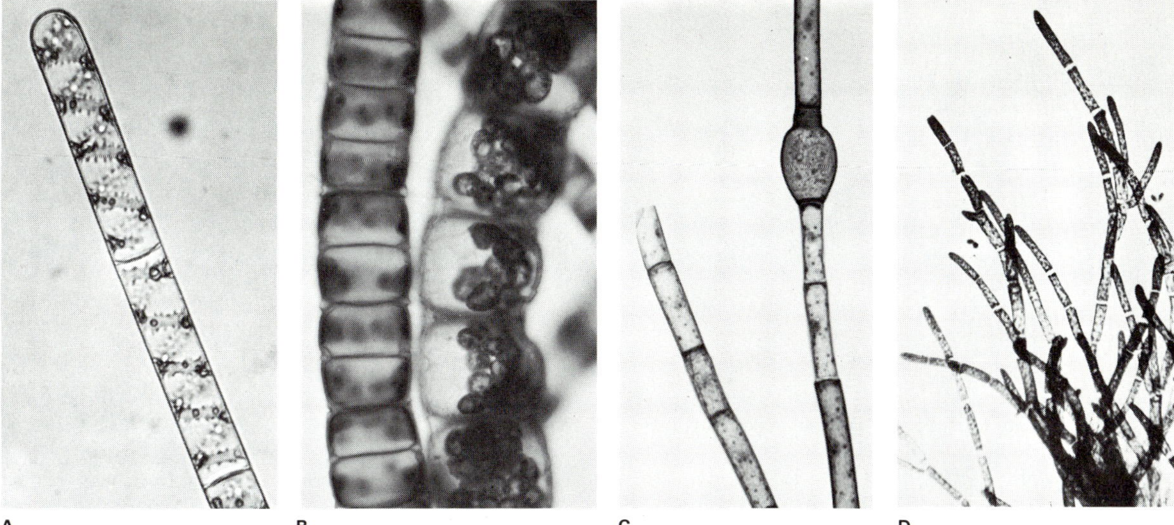

Fig. 32.6 Sporine green algae. (A) *Spirogyra*. Terminal cells of a filament. Note the spiraled chloroplasts in each elongated cell. (B) *Ulothrix*. In each cell of the filament at right the cell substance has become subdivided into many smaller sex cells. (C) *Oedogonium*. The enlarged cell is an egg. (D) *Cladophora,* a branching chlorophyte.

erate and only one gives rise to a new adult (see Chap. 22).

Among diplontic types are the green algae *Acetabularia* and *Bryopsis*, and the brown alga *Fucus* (Fig. 32.10). At the branch terminals of the latter two algal types are gamete-forming structures. In the rockweed *Fucus* these take the form of gelatinous swellings, or *receptacles*, that contain numerous gamete-producing cavities called *conceptacles* (Fig. 32.11). The lining layers of some concepta-

Fig. 32.8 Reproduction and sex in *Ulothrix*. Haploid vegetative cells give rise to haploid spores that grow into new adult filaments (top). Given cells also produce gametes that fertilize each other and form diploid zygotes (bottom). Germination of the zygotes includes meiosis, and new haploid adults arise thereafter. Thus the life cycle of this green alga is haplontic. Gamete formation is illustrated also in Fig. 32.7.

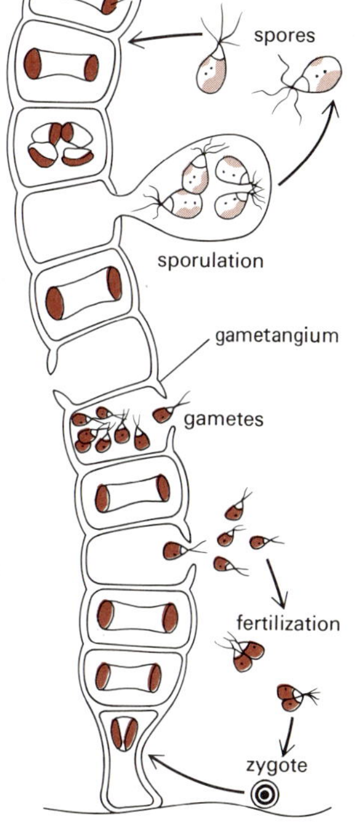

Fig. 32.7 Haplontic algae. Sex and the life cycle of *Chlamydomonas* are illustrated. Haploid vegetative cells give rise to haploid gametes of opposite mating types. The gametes fuse, forming zygospores (encased zygotes). Meiosis occurs in zygospores, yielding a new generation of haploid vegetative cells. A similar illustration of the *Chlamydomonas* life cycle is presented in Fig. 22.21.

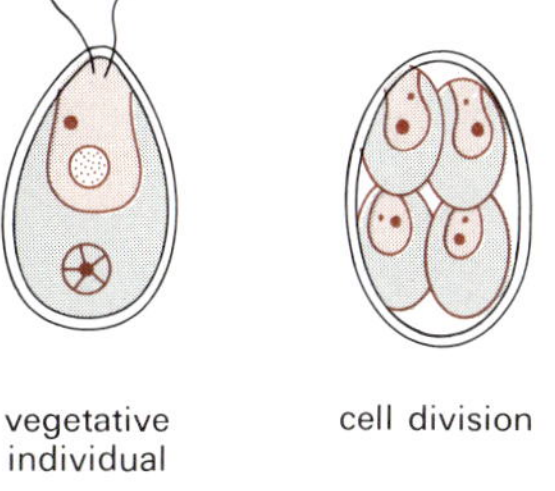

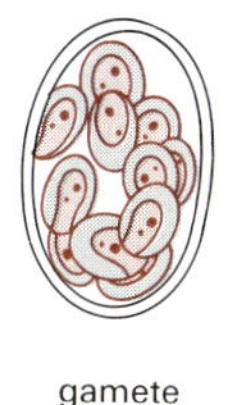

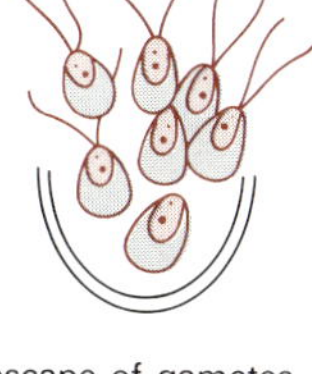

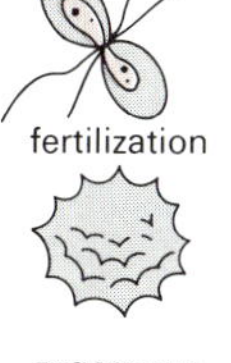

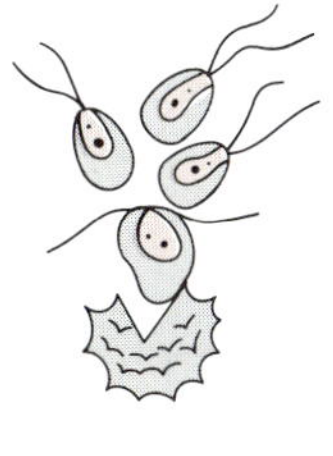

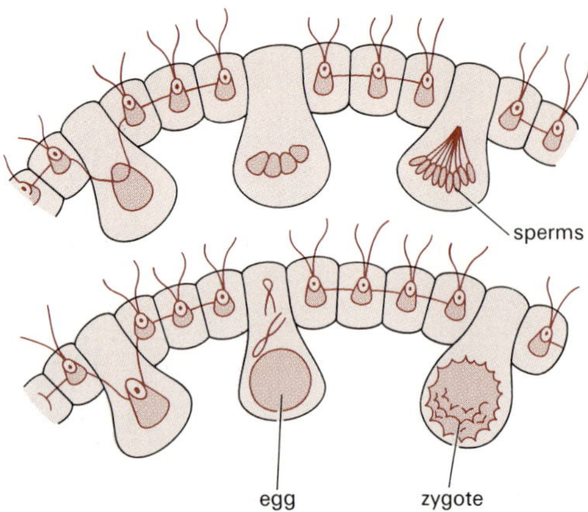

Fig. 32.9 Gamete formation in *Volvox.* Eggs and sperms are formed in separate colonies. See also Fig. 32.6 for eggs in *Oedogonium*.

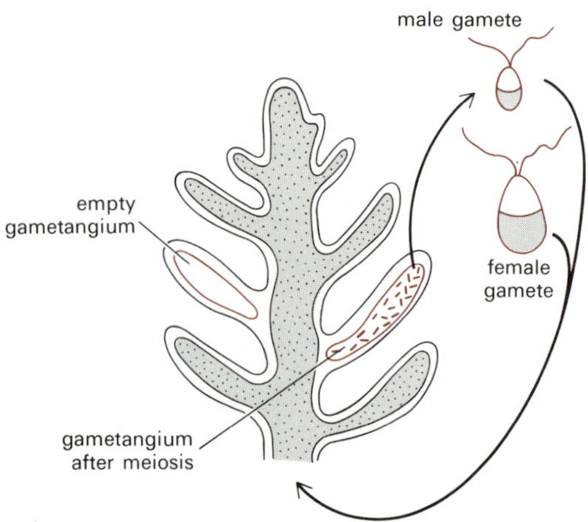

Fig. 32.10 Diplontic algae. Detail of a terminal branch of *Bryopsis,* showing gamete-forming side branches (gametangia) and the appearance of male and female gametes. See Fig. 32.5 for a photograph of this alga.

cles give rise to distinct sperms, those of others, to distinct eggs. Mature gametes escape through conceptacle openings along the surface of a receptable. After fertilization in open water a zygote encysts, settles on a rock, and eventually germinates as a new diploid adult.

Many algae are diplohaplontic, including the green sea lettuce *Ulva* and numerous brown and red algae. Among these organisms the spore-producing and gamete-producing generations often are structurally alike, and external appearance alone does not reveal whether a given individual is a diploid sporophyte or a haploid gametophyte (Fig. 32.12).

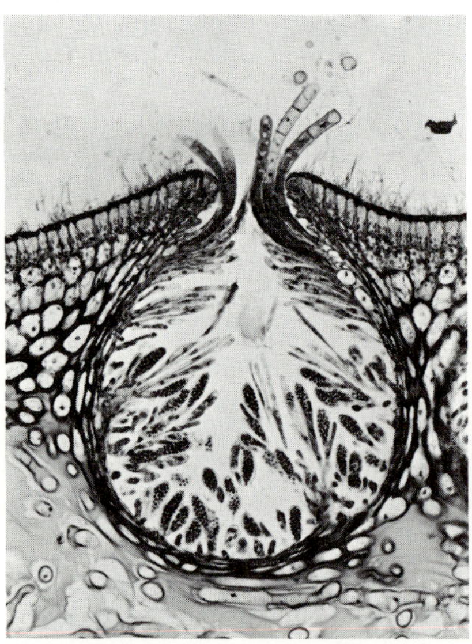

A

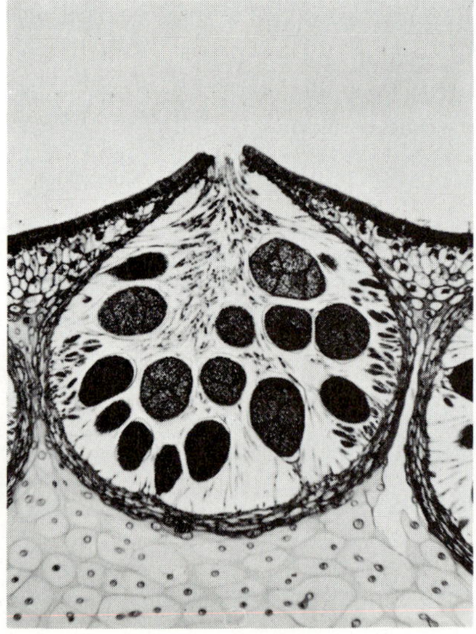

B

Fig. 32.11 Gametes in *Fucus.* (A) Sperm-forming conceptacle. (B) Egg-forming conceptacle. The lining layer in (A) bears branches that produce the sperms. Note the sterile hairs (paraphyses) that project through the conceptacle opening. In (B) the lining layer bears egg-forming branches. A mature branch of this type contains eight eggs. Conceptacles are located in so-called receptacles, enlarged terminals of branches of this brown alga. Such receptacles are illustrated in Fig. 32.1.

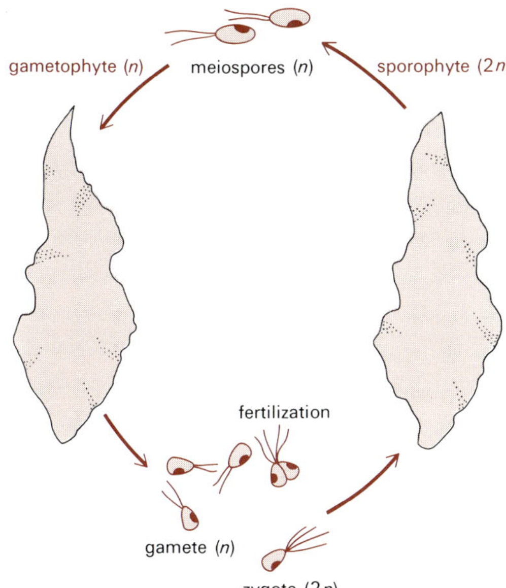

Fig. 32.12 Diplohaplontic algae. The life cycle of the sea lettuce *Ulva* is illustrated. Note that the gametophyte and sporophyte generations look alike, though one is haploid and the other diploid.

LAND PLANTS: BRYOPHYTES AND TRACHEOPHYTES

About 420 million years ago, the barren continents of earth began a slow transformation to the lush, green landscapes that typify much of the planet today. The transformation was triggered by the evolution of plants that gradually became strikingly different from aquatic algae. These new plants, descended from ancestral stocks of green algae, evolved adaptations that afforded protection against desiccation, wind, wide-ranging changes of temperatures and humidity, and other harsh conditions common to terrestrial environments.

Fossils provide some insight into the nature of these adaptations, but even without this evidence it is easy to imagine the qualities that must have distinguished the first truly terrestrial plants from their algal ancestors. For example, all truly terrestrial organisms must have some means of preventing excessive evaporation of water from body tissues. However, the surfaces of terrestrial plants cannot be sealed completely. There must be enough moist surface areas for exchange of gases between plant tissues and the surrounding air. Thus, a balance must be struck between the requirements of waterproofing and gas exchange. Terrestrial plants also must have ways of procuring and transporting water to aerial tissues. Moreover, they must have a means of transporting organic nutrients to specialized tissues that do not contain photosynthetic cells.

Most aquatic organisms are supported in large measure by the buoyancy of water. Since air provides almost no buoyancy, large terrestrial plants require "skeletal" tissues to support their weight. Also, the union of algal gametes and the development of adult algal tissues requires substantial amounts of water (see Chap. 22). Consequently, several major reproductive adaptations had to occur in the evolution of land plants.

The spread of terrestrially better adapted plants across once barren landscapes was followed rapidly by a radiation of land-adapted heterotrophs. Complex terrestrial food chains developed, each made possible by the earlier establishment of land-adapted plants. These descendants of green algae eventually became structurally far more complex than their aquatic ancestors. They slowly evolved organs; most later species evolved organ systems. Also unlike algae, primitive land plants typically passed through distinct embryonic stages during development, as their descendants do today.

Such structures and diverse adaptations for terrestrial life have evolved in all existing land plants, which consist of two phyla—the moss plants, or Bryophyta, and the vascular plants, or Tracheophyta. The basic nature and structural organization of both phyla were introduced in Chap. 6. The reproductive patterns of bryophytes and tracheophytes were introduced in Chap. 23. The remaining sections of this chapter deal with the evolution of these plants and with their adaptations to various kinds of terrestrial environments.

Bryophytes (Moss Plants)

Phylum Bryophyta (24,000 species)

CLASS BRYOPSIDA mosses

CLASS HEPATICOPSIDA liverworts

CLASS ANTHOCEROPSIDA hornworts

Mosses, liverworts, and hornworts may have evolved independently from different green algal ancestors. Mosses may be the most primitive members of the phylum. Indeed, the embryonic moss protonema closely resembles a strand of green algae (see Fig. 6.6). During the early stages of bryophyte evolution, some 350 million years ago, both the gametophyte and sporophyte generations probably existed as independent green plants. Based on fossil evidence, the two generations were structurally very similar at that time, except that sporophytes produced spores and gametophytes produced structurally identical gametes. Sporophytes later became attached to gametophytes and now often develop as small, nongreen parasites on larger gametophytes (see Fig. 23.3).

Several terrestrial adaptations have evolved in most species of bryophytes. For example, the surfaces of bryophytes are covered by a waxy substance called *cutin*, which waterproofs the epidermis and greatly reduces water loss. In addition, the spores and gametes of bryophytes are protected from desiccation by a layer of tough *jacket cells*, which cover the surfaces of sporangia, antheridia, and archegonia (see Fig. 23.2). Stomata cover the body surfaces of most gametophytes and even some sporophytes of bryophytes. These pores provide passages for the exchange of gases between bryophyte tissues and the surrounding atmosphere (see Fig. 6.7).

Egg cells of algae typically are fertilized after they have been released into water, but the eggs of bryophytes are fertilized in archegonia (see Fig. 23.2). Moreover, the initial stages of embryonic development also take place in these female organs, and bryophyte embryos obtain considerable amounts of water and nutrients from archegonial cells. Thus, the early stages of bryophyte development, which are most susceptible to desiccation, take place in a moist enclosed environment (see also Chap. 23). All these adaptations have also evolved in tracheophytes.

Despite these adaptations, bryophytes are comparatively small plants that have adapted only to relatively moist terrestrial environments. There are two principal reasons for this limitation. First, bryophytes lack vascular tissues. The absence of xylem, which functions as a major supporting tissue in tracheophytes, greatly restricts substantial vertical growth in bryophytes. And without vascular tissues, water and nutrients must be transported among the cells of bryophytes by diffusion. This relatively inefficient method of transport limits the size of bryophytes. Second, bryophytes have flagellated sperms similar to those of algae. These cells require moisture to move from antheridia to eggs in archegonia. Bryophytes therefore must live where water is plentiful. Some bryophytes can survive periods of drought, but only by becoming dormant and ceasing growth.

Tracheophytes (Vascular Plants)

Phylum Tracheophyta (*260,000+ species*)

Subphylum Psilopsida (*extinct*) psilopsids

Subphylum Lycopsida (*900 species*) club mosses

Subphylum Sphenopsida (*25 species*) horsetails

Subphylum Pteropsida (*10,000 species*) ferns

Subphylum Spermopsida (*seed plants*)

CLASS GYMNOSPERMAE
Subclass Cycadophytae (*100 species*) cycads
Subclass Coniferophytae (*600 species*) conifers

CLASS ANGIOSPERMAE
Subclass Dicotyledoneae (*200,000 species*) dicots
Subclass Monocotyledoneae (*50,000 species*) monocots

Tracheophytes are more numerous and generally better adapted to terrestrial environments than bryophytes. With respect to numbers of species, vascular plants represent the largest group of photosynthetic organisms and, after the arthropods, the second largest group of all organisms. As already discussed in Chap. 6, the phylum as a whole is identified by the presence of two highly specialized vascular tissues, xylem and phloem. Also, the body of tracheophytes typically is subdivided into roots, stems, and leaves.

Tracheophyte Evolution: The Fossil Record

Vascular plants probably arose independently from green algal ancestors at least 50 million years earlier than bryophytes. One of the main lines of investigation revealing the evolutionary relationships between vascular plants, and indeed between many other groups of organisms, is *paleontology*, the study of fossils. Representing the remains of formerly living individuals, fossils provide the most direct evidence of the kinds of organisms in existence at various earlier times.

Fig. 32.13 Fossils. (A) A sassafras leaf fossilized in rock. (B) Rock layers of different ages are often exposed to view. Generally speaking, the deeper a layer in the earth's crust, the older it is.

A

Any long-preserved remains of organisms are fossils (Fig. 32.13). They may be skeletons or shells, footprints later petrified, impressions left by body parts on solidifying rocks, or the remnants of organisms trapped in amber, gravel pits, swamps, and other places. Whenever a buried organism or any part of it becomes preserved in some way before it decays, it will be a fossil. Fossils embedded in successive earth layers provide a time picture of evolution. Deep-lying fossils are normally not accessible, but on occasion a canyon-cutting river or an earthquake fracture exposes a cross section through rock strata. Moreover, erosion gradually wears away top layers and exposes deeper rock (see Fig. 32.13).

The age of a rock layer can be determined by "clocks" in the earth's crust: radioactive substances. For example, a given quantity of radium is known to decay to lead in a certain span of time. When radium and lead are found together in one mass in a rock, the whole mass presumably had been radium originally, when the rock was formed. From the relative quantities of radium and lead present today, one can then calculate the time required for that much lead to form. A similar principle is used in potassium-argon dating and radiocarbon dating. In the first process one measures

B

TABLE 32.2
Evolution and the Geologic Time Table*

Era*	Period*	Epoch	Aquatic life	Terrestrial life
Cenozoic 63 ± 2	*Quaternary;* periodic glaciation 0.5–3	Recent, Pleistocene		human beings in the new world first human beings
	Tertiary 63 ± 2	Pliocene Miocene Oligocene Eocene Paleocene	all modern groups present	hominids and pongids; monkeys and ancestors of apes adaptive radiation of birds; modern mammals and herbaceous angiosperms
Mesozoic 230 ± 10	*Cretaceous;* mountain building (e.g., Rockies, Andes) at end of period 135 ± 5		modern bony fishes; extinction of plesiosaurs, ichthyosaurs	extinction of dinosaurs, pterosaurs; rise of woody angiosperms, snakes
	Jurassic; inland seas 180 ± 5		plesiosaurs, ichthyosaurs abundant; skates, rays, and bony fishes abundant	dinosaurs dominant; first lizards; insects abundant; first mammals, first angiosperms
	Triassic; warm climate, many deserts 230 ± 10		first plesiosaurs, ichthyosaurs; rise of bony fishes	adaptive radiation of reptiles (thecodonts, therapsids, turtles, crocodiles, first dinosaurs, rhynchocephalians)
Paleozoic 600 ± 50	*Permian;* Appalachian Mountains formed, periodic glaciation and arid climate 280 ± 10		extinction of trilobites, placoderms	reptiles abundant; (cotylosaurs, pelycosaurs); cycads and conifers; gingkos
	Upper Carboniferous (*Pennsylvanian*) warm humid climate 310 ± 10		evolution of bony fishes	first insects, centipedes; first reptiles; coal swamps
	Lower Carboniferous (*Mississippian*) warm humid climate 345 ± 10		adaptive radiation of sharks	forests of club mosses and seed ferns; amphibians abundant, land snails

Era*	Period*	Epoch	Aquatic life	Terrestrial life
Paleozoic (cont.)	*Devonian;* periodic aridity 405 ± 10		placoderms, cartilaginous and bony fishes	forests of club mosses and ferns, first gymnosperms; millipedes, spiders, first amphibians
	Silurian; extensive inland seas 425 ± 10		adaptive radiation of ostracoderms	first land plants; arachnids (e.g., scorpions)
	Ordovician; mild climate, inland seas 500 ± 10		first vertebrates (ostracoderms); mollusks; trilobites abundant	none
	Cambrian; mild climate, inland seas 600 ± 50		trilobites dominant; first crustaceans; mollusks, echinoderms; sponges, cnidarians, annelids; tunicates	none
Precambrian; periodic glaciation 4600			fossils rare but many protistan and invertebrate phyla present; first bacteria and blue-green algae	none

*With approximate starting dates in millions of years ago.

how much of a naturally occurring unstable form of potassium has decayed to argon. Radiocarbon dating involves measurement of how much of an unstable form of carbon is still present in a rock or fossil sample. The potassium-argon method can be used for dating fossils many millions of years old, but the carbon method is accurate only for fossils formed within the last 50,000 years. Fossils themselves often help in fixing the age of a rock layer. If such a layer contains a fossil known to be of a definite age (*index fossil*), the whole layer, including all other fossils in it, is likely to be of the same general age.

Relying on the data obtained from radioactive and fossil clocks, geologists have constructed a *geologic time table* that indicates the age of successive earth layers and provides a calendar of the earth's past history. This calendar consists of five successive main divisions, or *eras.* The last three in turn are subdivided into a number of successive *periods* (Table 32.2). The beginning and terminal dates of the eras and periods have not been chosen arbitrarily but have been made to coincide with major geologic events known to have occurred at those times. For example, the transition from the Paleozoic to the Mesozoic dates the *Appalachian revolution,* during which the mountain range of that name was built up. Similarly, the transition between the Mesozoic and the Cenozoic was marked by the *Laramide revolution,* which produced the Himalayas, the Rockies, the Andes, and the Alps.

The Paleozoic

Psilopsids The first truly terrestrial organisms appear in the fossil record of the Ordovician and Silurian Periods (Fig. 32.14 and see Table 32.2).

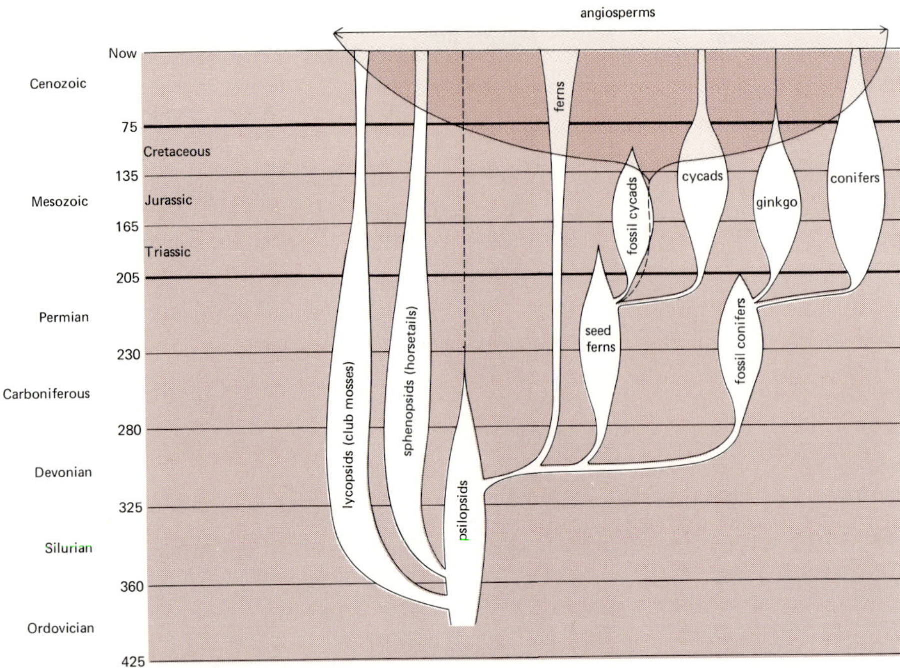

Fig. 32.14 The fossil record of vascular plants. Numbers at left indicate past time in millions of years. The varying width of the graph for each plant group approximates the changing abundance of the group in the course of time.

These were psilopsids. How these primitive tracheophytes arose from ancestral green algae is not known with certainty, but an intriguing and possibly correct hypothesis was first proposed in 1903 by Lignier, a French botanist. He suggested that the ancestors of terrestrial tracheophytes were green algae with a branching, rather *Fucus*-like structure. Such an ancestral stock was postulated to have become terrestrial by development of an epidermis with cuticles and stomata; by gradual straightening of some of the branches, leading to the formation of a main stem with smaller lateral branches; by growth of some of the lowest branches into the ground as roots; by development of vascular tissue in the interior; and by restriction of reproductive capacity to the terminals of stems. Lignier considered that the evolution of algae to tracheophytes might have occurred along sea or freshwater shores, where intermittent terrestrial conditions would have promoted the development of adaptations to land life (Fig. 32.15).

Later evidence has supported this hypothesis amply, and it is now widely accepted. Numerous psilopsid fossils have been discovered that were structured more or less exactly as postulated by Lignier's hypothesis. A case in point is *Rhynia*, a Silurian fossil psilopsid with rhizoids, forked upright branches about 1 foot high, and terminal sporangia. Leaves were absent (Fig. 32.16). All psilopsids are extinct. Until recently, two genera, *Psilotum* and *Tmesipteris*, were considered living representatives of psilopsids, but recent research has provided evidence linking these organisms to ferns.

Fig. 32.15 The Lignier hypothesis. Branching algae as in (A) may have evolved via stages as in (B) into primitive, rhizome-possessing tracheophytes as in (C).

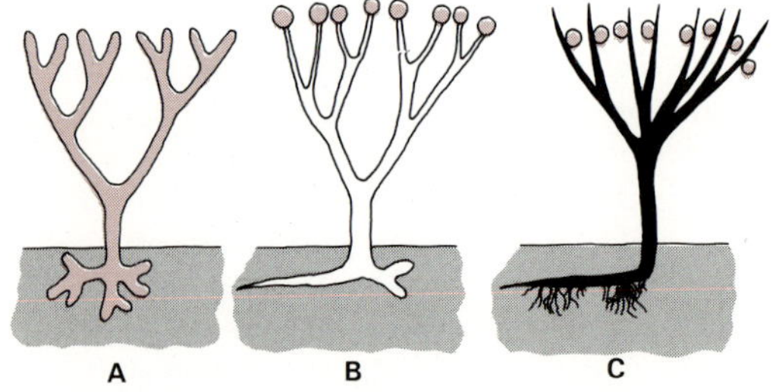

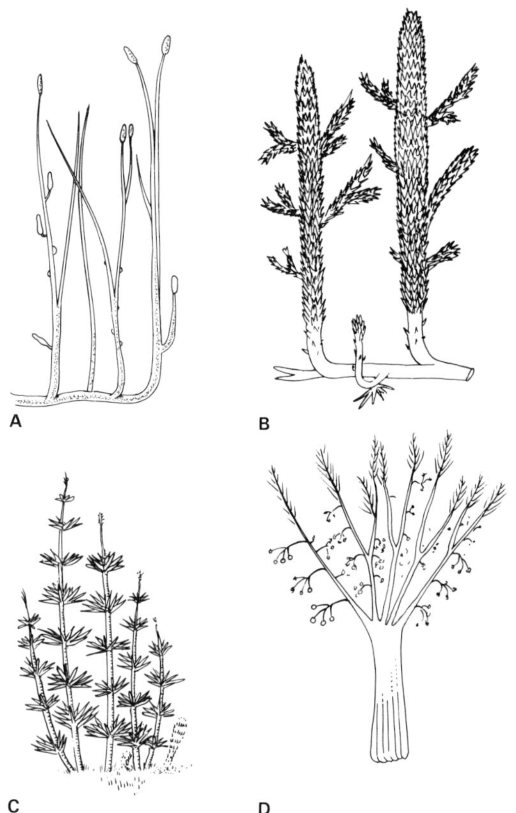

Fig. 32.16 Fossil psilopsids. (A) Model of the psilopsid *Rhynia,* one of the most ancient tracheophytes, that lived some 350 million years ago. (B) *Asteroxylon,* a psilopsid with lycopsidlike traits. (C) *Hyenia,* suggesting a sphenopsid direction of evolution. (D) *Pseudoporochnus,* a psilopsid with pteropsidlike characteristics.

***Lycopsids* (*Club Mosses*)** The earliest lycopsids evolved more than 400 million years ago, probably from one or more groups of ancestral psilopsids. Fossil remains of *Asteroxylon* indicate that this extinct psilopsid exhibited rootlike branches and several other traits suggesting evolutionary trends in the lycopsid direction. Lycopsids existed in large numbers between 345 and 280 million years ago. Many were huge trees up to 120 feet tall, with active secondary growth and leaves some 20 inches long. Among the largest were the *lepidodendrids,* the giant club mosses. Of these, the "scale tree" *Lepidodendron* became particularly abundant, as did *Sigillaria,* the "seal tree." The 60-foot-high stem of this tree bore leaves in a terminal tuft that gave the plant the general appearance of a giant paintbrush (Fig. 32.17).

The few lycopsids that still survive are all small and nonwoody. The ground pine *Lycopodium* in particular is relatively common and often used in Christmas decorations (Fig. 32.18). The plants of this subphylum possess true roots; stems that are partly horizontal and underground, partly upright and aerial; and small, spirally arranged leaves on the aerial stems. Another surviving lycopsid is *Selaginella.* Commonly called spike mosses and resurrection plants, *Selaginella* lives largely in damp, shady places in the tropics (see Fig. 32.18).

Quillworts are the only surviving lycopsids that by virtue of a special cortical cambium are still capable of secondary growth. They do not become woody, however. Part of the English name of these plants derives from dense clusters of erect leaves that project from underground stems. The clusters also give the plants a superficial resemblance to patches of lawn grass (see Fig. 32.18).

***Sphenopsids* (*Horsetails*)** Sphenopsids first appeared in the fossil record about 370 million years ago. These plants probably also arose from ancestral psilopsids. The structural features of *Hyenia* (see Fig. 32.16), a fossil psilopsid, closely resemble those of modern sphenopsids, or *horsetails.* All surviving sphenopsids are members of the genus *Equisetum* (Fig. 32.19). These plants range from the tropics to the temperate zone. They are identifiable by aerial stem parts that have nodes and by narrow, scalelike leaves that grow out in whorls at these nodes. The stems are usually ribbed lengthwise, strengthened with silica deposits, and hollow. Portions of the stem system are again underground and horizontal, and true roots grow from it in places. Like ancestral lycopsids, many Devonian sphenopsids were giant trees often up to 100 feet tall (Fig. 32.20).

***Pteropsids* (*Ferns*), *Spermopsids* (*Seed Plants*)** Several fossil psilopsids, among them *Pseudosporochnus,* point to the pteropsid direction of evolution (see Fig. 32.16). In these 9-foot treelike plants the leaves were flattened and quite large, with a webbing that could have foreshadowed the characteristic structure of fern fronds.

Fig. 32.17 Fossil lycopsids. (A) Reconstruction of *Lepidodendron*. (B) Reconstruction of *Sigillaria*.

Fig. 32.18 Lycopsids. (A) Upper portion of the ground pine *Lycopodium* (with spore-forming cone at top). (B) Aerial portion of *Selaginella*. (C) Aerial parts of the quillwort *Isoetes*.

Fig. 32.19 Sphenopsids. Portion of aerial stem of a horsetail, *Equisetum*. Note whorled arrangement of leaves (microphylls).

The first pteropsids appear to have originated about 340 million years ago, and they have greatly increased in numbers during the next 100 million years. Living species of ferns are most conspicuous in tropical rain forests, where many attain heights of 50 to 60 feet, with leaves 10 to 15 feet long (Fig. 32.21). Even so, such tree ferns are not woody. In the far smaller ferns of temperate regions, the stems are largely horizontal and underground. Roots project downward and the large, complexly shaped leaves point upward. A good many fern types grow on tree trunks, especially in the tropics, and a few species are secondarily aquatic.

Fig. 32.20 Fossil sphenopsids. (A) *Calamophyton*. (B) *Sphenophyllum*. (C) *Calamites*.

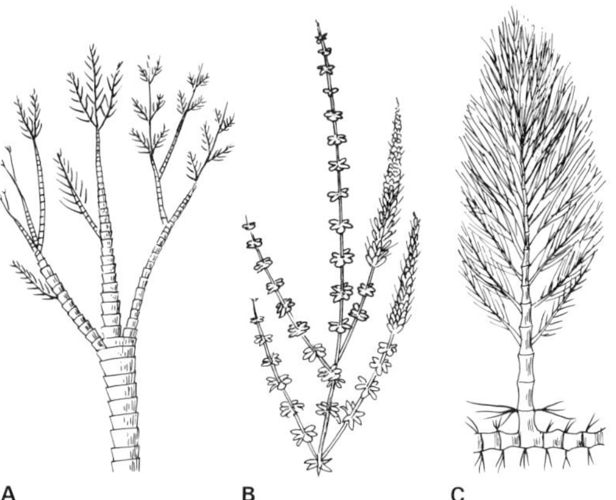

The stems of the plants are largely underground rhizomes, often covered with fibrous remnants of leaf bases that give stems a somewhat "hairy" appearance. Internally a fern stem has a thick sclerenchymatous cortex that gives strength like wood and permits some ferns to attain the size of trees (see Color Fig. 32). Leaves growing from rhizomes are large, upright, and complexly shaped. They are regrown every year in most species of the temperate zone; in other cases they last several seasons. Fern leaves are interesting in that they have functional apical meristems unlike leaves of other plants; thus they can grow continuously. These leaves also commonly exhibit *circinate vernation;* young leaves form tight coils, and as they grow they unroll and straighten up (see Fig. 32.21).

As in all tracheophytes, the fern sporophyte has evolved as the dominant generation (see Fig. 23.8). It is well adapted to terrestrial environments and is considerably larger and more complex than the diminutive heart-shaped gametophyte. The spores of ferns can be distributed by wind over wide areas. Indeed, ferns were among the first plants to become established on certain newly formed tropical islands that originated as the result of recent volcanic eruptions. By contrast, the fern gametophyte is greatly dependent on moisture for its delicate tissues and for fertilization of eggs by flagellated sperms. Because fern sporophytes develop directly from such moisture-dependent gametophytes, ferns are only slightly better adapted for life on land than bryophytes, lycopsids, and horsetails.

The first seed plants to evolve were the *seed ferns*, direct descendants of ancestral ferns. Seed ferns probably arose about 300 million years ago and are now extinct. They flourished during the Carboniferous and Permian Periods, some 280 to 205 million years ago. Indeed, the Carboniferous Period is often called the "age of seed ferns" (Fig. 32.22). All these ancient plants produced seeds but had bodies closely resembling true ferns.

Seed ferns have considerable evolutionary significance; they appear to have given rise to other

A

B

C

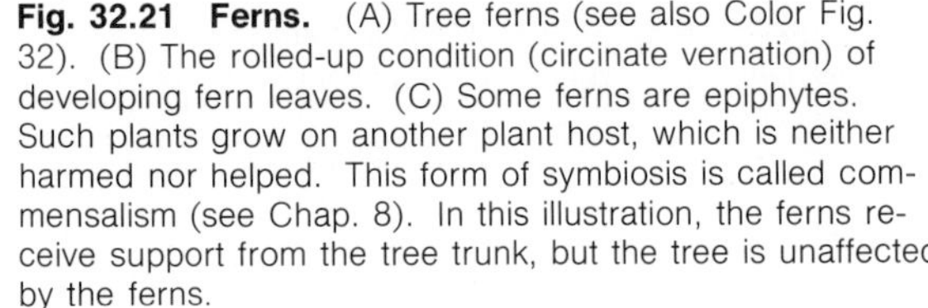

Fig. 32.21 Ferns. (A) Tree ferns (see also Color Fig. 32). (B) The rolled-up condition (circinate vernation) of developing fern leaves. (C) Some ferns are epiphytes. Such plants grow on another plant host, which is neither harmed nor helped. This form of symbiosis is called commensalism (see Chap. 8). In this illustration, the ferns receive support from the tree trunk, but the tree is unaffected by the ferns.

categories of plants (see Fig. 32.14). Like seed ferns themselves, two of these categories of plants qualify as gymnosperms, the now extinct *fossil conifers* and *fossil cycads* (Fig. 32.23). Fossil conifers were abundant during the Carboniferous Period; the trees grew up to 100 feet tall and had parallel-veined leaves that often grew 3 feet long.

Fossil cycads evolved somewhat later and did not become abundant until the Mesozoic (see Fig. 32.14). Most cycads are extinct, but a few continue to thrive in tropical and subtropical environments (Fig. 32.24). Only one genus, *Zamia*, is native to the United States, and it is found only in Florida. These usually small trees have large palmlike leaves and an extensive pith, which is surrounded by a relatively narrow, slowly developing band of xylem.

During the later part of the Carboniferous many regions became so wet that they were transformed to vast tracts of swamps and marshes. In these, much of the woody flora of the time died. Later geologic changes converted the bodies of the plants to coal, hence the name of the whole period, "coal-bearing." The rich coal beds of Pennsylvania and West Virginia came into being at that time, and the coal itself represents the remains of forests of lycopsids, sphenopsids, tree ferns, seed ferns, and fossil conifers.

As already noted, some of these plants survived to the Permian. They were joined then by the

Fig. 32.22 The "age of seed ferns." (A) Reconstruction of the seed fern, *Medullosa noei*. (B) Reconstruction of a Carboniferous swamp. Seed ferns, such as those clumped in the middle of the picture, dominated these landscapes throughout most of the latter half of the Carboniferous Period.

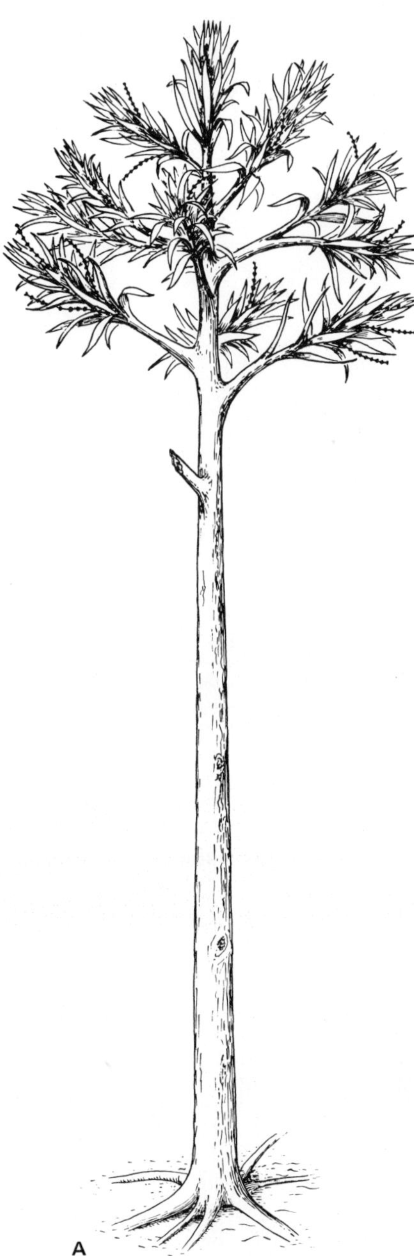

newly evolved *ginkgos,* descendants of fossil conifers. Ginkgos constitute one subclass of *coniferous,* or cone-bearing, gymnosperms. *Ginkgo biloba,* the *maidenhair tree,* is the only surviving member of this once flourishing group. Maidenhair trees are large, up to 100 feet tall, and in temperate regions they are commonly planted as shade trees (Fig. 32.25).

The direct ancestors of the maidenhair tree evolved late in the Paleozoic, which eventually terminated with the geologic upheavals of the Appalachian revolution. This in turn precipitated a so-called *Permo-Triassic crisis* among living organisms. This unstable time of transition was marked by widespread extinction of archaic forms and later replacement with rapidly evolving new types. Also, the total amount of life decreased temporarily, both in the sea and on land. Many groups of land plants became extinct—virtually all the psilopsids, lepidodendrids, and early sphenopsids, as well as many of the ancient ferns, seed ferns, and fossil conifers. Only remnant groups of psilopsids, lycopsids, and sphenopsids managed to survive. But the surviving groups of ferns and gymnosperms soon began to flourish anew and became the ancestors of the expanding flora of the new Mesozoic Era (see Fig. 32.14).

Fig. 32.23 Reconstructions of fossil conifers and fossil cycads. (A) A member of Chordaitales, 30- to 100-foot-tall fossil conifers. (B) A representative of Bennettitales, fossil cycads. This species was about 3 feet tall.

PHOTO ESSAY 4: THE WORLD OF LIFE

Biologists have subdivided the living world into five kingdoms: Monera, Protista, Fungi, Plantae, and Animalia. Representatives of each kingdom are depicted in this last photo essay.

Monera and Protista

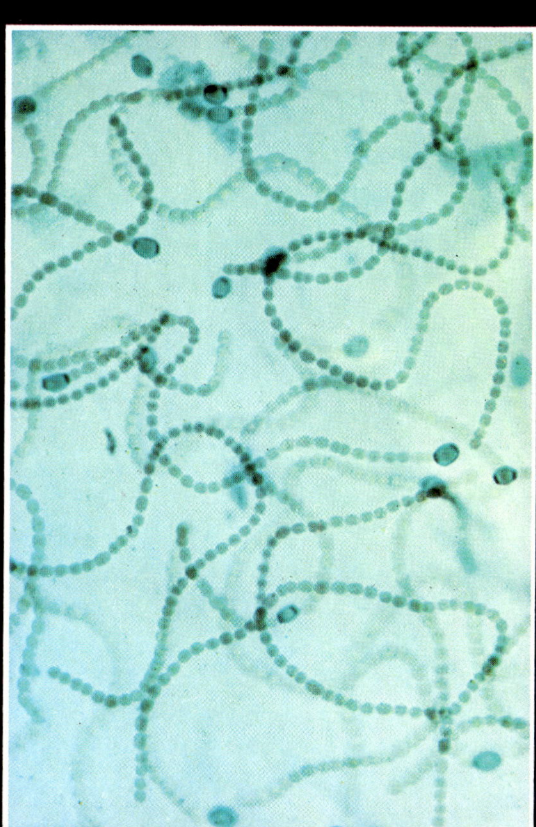

Color Fig. 25. Monera. *Nostoc*, a colonial blue-green alga: The cellular filaments are embedded in gelatinous sheaths. The enlarged cells are heterocysts, specialized for nitrogen fixation. *(Carolina Biological Supply Company.)*

Color Fig. 26. Protista. Slime molds consist of aggregations of amoeboid cells. This red slime mold is subsisting on a decomposing tree limb. *(Stephen J. Krasemann, © Peter Arnold, Inc.)*

Color Fig. 27. "Shaggy Mane" fungus. Like all mushrooms, this edible variety is a basidiomycete (club fungus). Spores are produced along gills on the undersurface of the domelike caps. *(W. H. Hodge, © Peter Arnold, Inc.)*

Color Fig. 28. Netted Stinkhorn, another basidiomycete. *(W. H. Hodge, © Peter Arnold, Inc.)*

Color Fig. 29. Lichens. A foliose (gray and brown) and a fruticose (yellow) lichen growing on a dead limb in one of the jack pine forests of eastern Oregon. Lichens consist of a mutualistic association of fungal and algal populations. *(James R. Leard, DPI.)*

Color Fig. 30. Algae. Red, brown, and green algae are classified as Plantae; other groups of algae, which largely consist of unicellular forms, are classified as Protista. Pictured here is feather boa kelp, a large brown alga, photographed in waters near Santa Cruz Island, off the coast of southern California. These algae produce air-filled structures that function as floats, often causing the nonanchored portions of the plant to arc toward the ocean surface. *(Bob Evans, © Peter Arnold, Inc.)*

Color Fig. 31. Indian pipe. Some species of this colorless angiosperm are saprotrophic, but at least one species is parasitic, subsisting on nutrients produced by a living host plant. During early stages of growth (shown here) the plant bears a superficial resemblance to a white pipe. Some tribes of American Indians once used the plant for medicinal purposes. *(Barbara K. Deans, DPI.)*

Color Fig. 32. Tree ferns. Part of a Mexican cloud forest, these largest of modern ferns once populated extensive areas of the earth's surface. *(W. H. Hodge, © Peter Arnold, Inc.)*

Color Fig. 33. Flowering plants. Indian paint brush, native to southwestern portions of the United States, is an angiosperm, the most colorful and most successful class of modern terrestrial plants. *(Cal Harbert, DPI.)*

Color Fig. 34. Sponges. The red, fingerlike projections are colonies of sponges, growing along the wall of a reef in the Red Sea. *(© Jeff Rotman.)*

Color Fig. 35. Coral. (A) Hard coral feeding at night. Note the yellow tentacles surrounding the orange opening into the gastrovascular cavity. (B) Bioluminescent solitary corals of the Great Barrier Reef. The bioluminescence produced by the many individual corals making up each of the glowing colonies probably attracts smaller organisms, which become entrapped by the tentacles of these coelenterates and are then eaten. *(A, © Jeff Rotman; B, Kjell B. Sandvred, Photoresearchers, Inc.)*

A

B

Color Fig. 36. Sea anemones. This white, almost transparent anemone was photographed off the coast of New England. Note the tentacles, used in trapping and paralyzing prey. *(© Jeff Rotman.)*

A

B

Color Fig. 37. Naked, free-swimming snails. (A) Nudibranchs. Note the orange antennae projecting from the dorsoanterior surface of this marine snail. A breathing rosette projects from the dorsoposterior surface. Shells are absent in nudibranchs. The red structure beneath the snail is a portion of a sponge, also shown in Color Fig. 34. (B) Sea butterflies. This free-swimming gastropod, photographed off the New England coast, spends its entire life swimming near the ocean surface feeding on marine plankton. Some sea butterflies have reduced, light shells; in other species shells are absent. *(A, B, © Jeff Rotman.)*

Color Fig. 38. Arthropods. A water (diving) spider, building a diving bell along the surface of a freshwater aquatic plant. When threatened, such spiders retreat to these underwater structures, breathing air trapped within the bell. Strands of spun webbing form the outer surface of the bell. *(© Hans Pfletschinger, Peter Arnold, Inc.)*

Color Fig. 39. Reptiles. Like certain insects (see Color Fig. 13), many reptiles periodically outgrow their outer coverings. This common grass snake is shedding the outermost layers of its skin, which are being replaced by underlying layers. *(© Hans Pfletschinger, Peter Arnold, Inc.)*

Color Fig. 40. Flightless birds. A greater rhea, native to South America. Like the ostrich and other flightless birds, rheas probably evolved from ancestors that were

Color Fig. 41. Flying birds. An immature male Rufous hummingbird approaching a flower. Hummingbirds do not land on flowers, but hover in front of them while sucking nectar. Note that the long beak of the bird is particularly well adapted for this feeding behavior. Some flowering plants are pollinated almost exclusively by hummingbirds. *(Charles G. Summers, Jr., DPI.)*

Color Fig. 42. Marsupials. A koala bear. Because of their highly specialized diet, consisting of leaves produced by a few species of smooth-barked eucalyptus trees, these pouched mammals are found only in certain wooded areas of southeastern Australia where eucalyptus thrive. *(Rob Chabot, DPI.)*

Color Fig. 43. Insectivores. Bats have sonarlike transmitting and receptor organs that allow them to locate and prey on flying insects. This fruit bat, hanging upside down in its natural resting position, inhabits the New Hebrides. Except for the natives of these islands, who consider bat meat a delicacy, fruit bats have few natural enemies. *(Jack Fields, Photoresearchers, Inc.)*

Color Fig. 44. Rodents. A dormouse perched on the limb of an apple tree. These squirrellike rodents are found exclusively in the Old World, including parts of Africa, Europe, and Asia. Prolific climbers, dormice frequently inhabit trees, shrubs, and rock outcrops. *(© Hans Pfletschinger, Peter Arnold, Inc.)*

Fig. 32.24 Cycads. One of the approximately 100 species of surviving cycads. These plants, which form comparatively little wood, are known as "sago palms."

Fig. 32.25 ***Ginkgo biloba,*** **the maidenhair tree.**

The Mesozoic and Cenozoic

The Mesozoic as a whole is often called the "age of gymnosperms" in plant evolution. Fossil cycads came to form extensive forests during the Jurassic. Trees like *Bennettitales* were some 10 feet tall, with terminal leaves almost as long as the tree trunk (see Fig. 32.23). These plants died out during the Cretaceous (and their ample remains can still be found in, for example, the Fossil Cycad National Monument in the Black Hills of South Dakota). The group was replaced on a reduced scale by the true cycads.

The ginkgos reached their peak during the Jurassic and early Cretaceous. Concurrently, new groups of coniferous gymnosperms related to the earlier *Cordaitales* came into ascendancy. They dominated the whole later part of the Mesozoic and included many of the presently living conifers, among them cypresses, yews, redwoods, and pines.

But the forests formed by these large trees had to share space with the flowering plants, which had undergone a first extensive proliferation at that time. Fragmentary fossils of angiosperms date back to the Jurassic, and the first ample finds occur in Cretaceous layers. As will become apparent in Chap. 36, the late Mesozoic expansion of angiosperms coincided with a similarly extensive radiation of insects. Most of the Mesozoic angiosperms were woody. They included many of the tree-forming types still living today, such as elms, oaks, maples, magnolias, and palms. Forests of these were already flourishing in the closing phases of the Mesozoic, when they began to rival the forests of conifers.

If the Mesozoic was the age of gymnosperms, the Cenozoic was unquestionably the "age of angiosperms" in plant evolution (see Fig. 32.14). The increasing dominance of the angiosperms and the corresponding decline of the gymnosperms was in large measure a consequence of the Laramide revolution, which terminated the Mesozoic.

Before the Cenozoic, much of the earth, polar regions included, was tropical and subtropical and permitted uninterrupted year-round growth. Fossil trees from the Mesozoic and early Cenozoic actually are without annual rings, a sure indication that climates were uniformly warm. But after the Laramide revolution had produced the high mountain ranges of today, cooler climates developed gradually at higher latitudes. Thus, the east-west barrier of the Himalayas in Asia and of the Alps in Europe prevented warm south winds from reaching the northern portions of Eurasia. These regions then became colder. In effect, the Laramide revolution eventually led to the establishment of distinct tropical, temperate, and polar zones on earth.

Consequently, seed plants already living in the tropics could remain tropical, but species in other regions could not. Such plants would have had to become extinct unless they could migrate to the tropics or could readapt right where they lived to the yearly succession of winter and summer. Many groups actually did migrate to warmer regions, but among those that did not many came to have reduced significance or died out altogether. The decline of gymnosperms traces to this time. Today only some 700 species are left, and those living in regions with cold seasons are protected against the low temperatures through processes of winter-hardening (see next section). Similarly, many woody angiosperms in temperate and northern regions now survive winter conditions by shedding their leaves. Even so, the luxuriant forests of coniferous and flowering plants once characteristic of northern regions thinned out and became less extensive. Fossil trees from the late Cenozoic do show annual rings, like trees today, indicating clearly that uninterrupted year-round growth was no longer possible.

Furthermore, some of the angiosperms of temperate and northern regions evolved a new way of coping with the cool seasons by becoming nonwoody herbaceous biennials and annuals. Winter then could not harm them, for during the winter they simply died and ceased to exist as mature plants. For the rest of the year their primary growth gave them only a minimum body, just barely large enough to permit them to reproduce.

Thus the long-range consequences of the Laramide revolution were, first, a decreased abundance of the woody seed plants in all regions except the tropics, and second, the gradual emergence of modern small-bodied flowering herbs in northern and arctic zones. Today these areas are characterized particularly by large populations of herbaceous angiosperms, whereas the tropics are inhabited by large populations of woody angiosperms.

As will become apparent shortly, the reduction of forest during the middle and late Cenozoic also was to prove highly significant for animal evolution, human evolution in particular.

Tracheophyte Adaptations: Patterns of Life

As Chaps. 6 and 23 demonstrate, most general features of tracheophytes, such as radial symmetry, production of pollen, and an internally developed gametophyte, represent significant adaptations to terrestrial life. In addition to these basic attributes, found in virtually all tracheophytes, many less ubiquitous adaptations have evolved only in particular kinds of land plants.

For example, many tracheophytes have highly modified body parts specifically adapted for food storage, extra water absorption, additional mechanical support, and the like. The modifications can be highly variable, such as those of stems. Some of the main types of modified stems (Fig. 32.26) are *rhizomes,* horizontal underground stems common particularly in primitive tracheophytes; *tubers,* expanded portions of underground stems usually adapted for food storage, as in potatoes; *bulbs,* shortened underground stems to which thickened storage leaves are attached, as in onions; *corms,* shortened bulky underground storage stems that resemble bulbs superficially but have scalelike leaves on the outer surfaces, as in gladioli; *runners,* horizontal stems flat on the ground, as in strawberries; and *twining stems,* which wind around other objects and obtain support from them, as in beans.

The structure of roots is equally diverse. Some roots are adapted for strong anchorage. These include *fibrous roots,* in which numerous branch roots lead off from the stem base into soil in all directions, as in grasses. *Taproots* are modified for food storage. They are thick vertical roots from which small branch roots lead off, as in carrots. *Adventitious roots,* which sprout from any region of the plant (except a root), can provide increased absorption of water and dissolved nutrients. *Prop roots* are adventitious roots specially adapted for mechanical support, as in banyan trees and older corn plants. *Aerial roots* absorb water from sources available above ground. Such roots, well developed in orchids, for example, have a many-layered epidermis in which the cells die and the remaining walls then serve in water storage (Fig. 32.27).

A suitable body construction is only one requirement for a successful nonmotile way of terres-

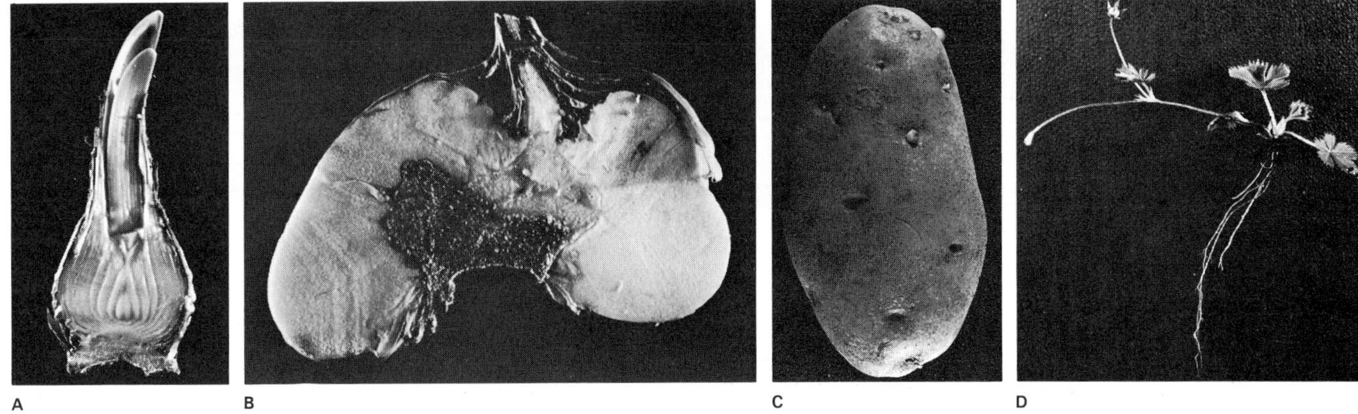

Fig. 32.26 Stem types. (A) A bulb. The central vertical stem is surrounded by leaves, which form the bulk of the bulb. (B) A corm. Leaves are borne at the top. (C) A tuber (potato). (D) A runner extends to the left of a strawberry plant. Note that the runner has already sprouted leaves. Once established, new plants develop from runners and often establish runners of their own, thereby propagating the species over a wide area.

trial life. Another is adaptability to potentially lethal changes in local weather, since a plant rooted to the ground cannot escape extremes of temperature; it can only protect against them. Water poses the key problem here. In summer heat and in deserts the plant is in danger of having too little internal water; and in winter or at high latitudes and altitudes there is often too much, for if internal water freezes, it can damage and kill cells.

The heat problem is one of internal *water conservation,* and it affects the exposed stems and leaves far more than the underground roots. Tracheophytes living in dry, warm or hot climates, so-called *xerophytes,* are protected in various ways against excessive evaporation of internal water (Fig. 32.28). For example, waxy cuticles over exposed surfaces are greatly thickened, sometimes becoming even thicker than the epidermal cells that secrete

Fig. 32.27 Root types. (A) Fibrous roots. (B) Taproots. (C) Prop roots.

A B

Fig. 32.28 Xerophytes. (A) Saguaro cactus and (B) creosote bush. Both xerophytes are widespread in deserts of the southwestern United States.

them (see Fig. 5.20). Stomata in stem and leaves are often reduced in number, and in leaves they can be located mostly or entirely on the underside, away from direct sunlight and settling dust. Or they are sunk deep in microscopic epidermal pits, which provide shade except when the sun shines straight into them (Fig. 32.29).

The stomata of many cacti and certain other desert *succulents* (plants having juicy or watery tissues) are uniquely adapted to dry conditions in yet another respect; they open only at night when daily temperatures normally are lowest. This arrangement obviously limits water loss, but it might seem to restrict photosynthesis severely. Stomata are not simply avenues for transpiration. They also function as points of entry for CO_2, a raw material for photosynthesis, and this fundamental food-manufacturing process occurs mostly in daylight, not at night.

This disadvantage is more apparent than real, however, for most desert succulents share a second important adaptation to day environments. At night, when stomata are open, the concentration of organic acids in these plants rises rapidly. Malic acid ($C_4H_6O_5$) is among the most important of these organic substances, which largely accumulate in the vacuoles of green cells. Part of the structure of malic acid is derived from the nighttime absorption of CO_2. This acid breaks down during the day, releasing CO_2 to the cytoplasm. In many desert succulents, the released CO_2 enters the Calvin cycle and becomes incorporated as sugar, probably through attachment to ribulose diphosphate (see Chap. 13). This metabolic adaptation thus complements the daytime closure of stomata. As a result, sufficient CO_2 is made available for photosynthesis during the day even though stomata are not open.

Despite such complementary adaptations, rates of transpiration may still be too high. However, water vaporization will be lessened if the area of exposed parts is reduced in proportion to their volume. Thus, xerophytic plants often have but a few leaves or small scalelike or needle-shaped leaves. In the extreme case, well exemplified by cacti, leaves do not develop at all, and the function of food manufacture is taken over largely by massive green stems (see Color Fig. 21). In contrast, some desert succulents have extremely thick leaves that

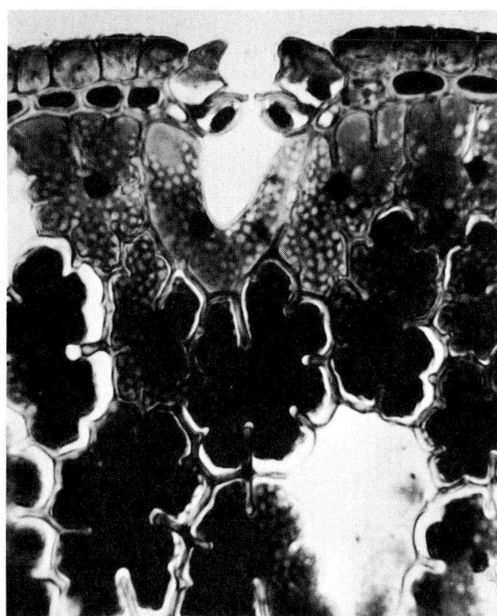

Fig. 32.29 Adaptations to dry conditions. Section of a pine leaf showing sunken stoma (top center) and lobed parenchyma cells in interior. See also Fig. 5.20 for thick, waxy cuticle over epidermis. (*Courtesy of Melvin S. Fuller.*)

serve as water-storage organs (another function of the large stems of cacti). Water is released from such tissues to other plant parts during the long intervals between rain showers in desert environments.

Desiccation can also be reduced if much of the plant is underground, and underground organs actually are particularly common in xerophytes. Still other xerophytes have extremely short reproductive cycles and are able to go from seed germination through flowering and seed production in about 2 weeks following a rainfall. Through such diverse adaptations, some tracheophytes are able to survive even in the hottest, driest regions, provided that at least *some* water is available at *some* time. Quite a number of tracheophytes have overcome the water-conservation problem altogether by adapting secondarily to an aquatic habitat and living as *hydrophytes* (see Fig. 9.4).

Where water supplies are neither too abundant nor too sparse, as in much of the temperate zone, the plants are *mesophytes.* Such plants must still cope with considerable fluctuations in climatic conditions. For example, a summer day might be excessively hot and dry, and the mesophytic tracheophyte then will droop and begin to wilt. But if water becomes available within a few days, conditions in the plant are soon restored to normal. In winter, by contrast, frost for even an hour is likely to kill; below the freezing point water that is not part of colloidal gels is transformed into ice crystals, which can tear the structural framework of cells. This is why very low temperatures are potentially lethal.

Probably in response to yearly cold seasons or outright winters, tracheophytes have evolved major adaptations profoundly affecting their whole way of life. On the basis of these adaptations three groups of vascular plants can be distinguished, *perennials, biennials,* and *annuals* (Fig. 32.30).

In perennials, major or all portions of the plant body last through many successive winters. Although such plants do not live indefinitely, their individual life-spans in many cases are far longer than those of any other organisms. At the approach of winter perennials usually manufacture large quantities of colloidal materials that convert the interior of cells to a gel state. Little water then remains free inside cells, and ice formation is forestalled. In *evergreen* plant groups, such *winter hardening* is particularly effective. Even leaves can be retained, as in most conifers, and vital processes can continue as in summer though at a slower pace.

Other perennials, the *deciduous* plants, cannot protect their foilage against the cold, and they shed leaves in the fall. But the rest of the plant lives on. Buds and embryonic leaves have developed during the preceding summer, and they sprout the next spring as new foliage. In the absence of mature leaves during the cold season little or no food can be produced. However, such plants accumulate food reserves at other seasons and store them in roots and stems. Flowering trees living in the temperate zone are familiar examples of deciduous perennials.

Still other perennials are soft-bodied and *herbaceous.* In such plants, exemplified by asparagus or dandelions, the leaves as well as the aerial parts of the stem die off in the fall. But the roots and a short underground piece of stem survive. Reserve foods in these underground body parts last through

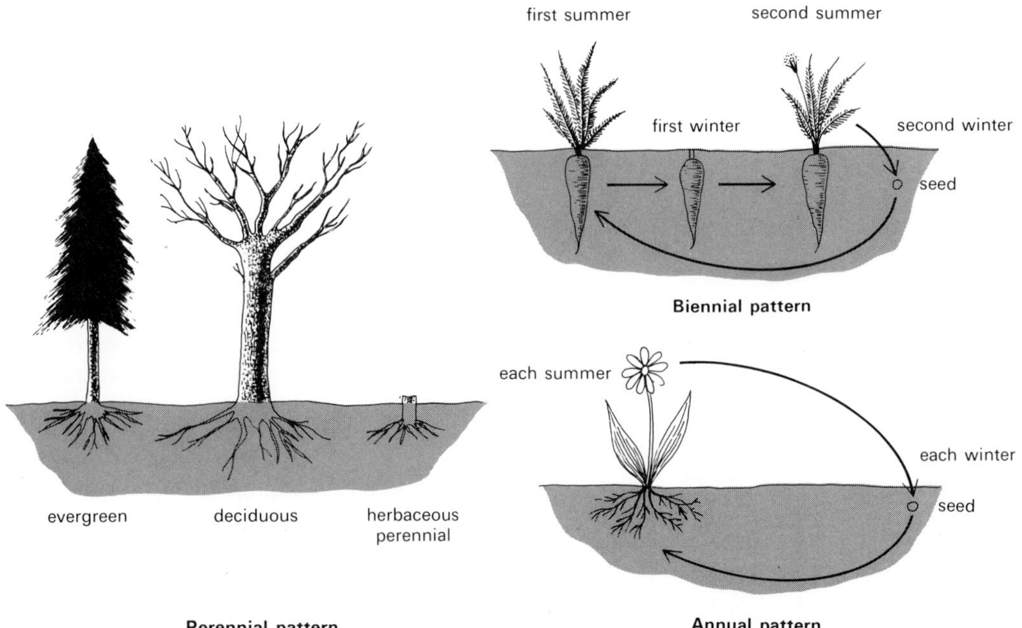

Fig. 32.30 Survival patterns in plants. In perennials such as conifers, the whole plant survives the winter. In deciduous perennials foliage is shed in the cold season, but the rest of the plant survives. In herbaceous perennials only the roots and a small piece of stem survive the winter. Biennial plants retain only the roots and a small piece of stem during a first winter, and only seeds survive the second winter. In an annual the whole plant dies every year and is perpetuated only by seeds.

the winter and suffice in spring for the development of a new aerial shoot. Leaves and a mature stem then grow from this shoot. Since the aerial portions of such plants live only during a relatively brief growing season, they never become very extensive; bulky wood is neither required nor formed, and the plants remain nonwoody herbs. For many perennials it is evidently more advantageous to retrench when life becomes difficult than to maintain elaborate aerial structures against heavy odds.

Winter retrenchment goes even further in biennial and annual herbaceous plants. In biennials, well exemplified by carrots, food reserves are stored in the bulky taproots and the leaves then die off at the approach of winter. The roots and portions of the shoot survive that winter, and from them develops a new plant the following spring. This second-year plant flowers and forms seeds. At the approach of the second winter the entire plant dies, roots included. Only the seeds survive, and they later begin a new 2-year cycle. An annual plant such as wheat flowers and produces seeds every year. The whole plant dies in the fall, and its seeds give rise to a new generation the following spring (see Fig. 32.30).

Evidently, vascular plants have found several workable solutions to the problem of cold. They can winterproof the whole body or some part of the body, or they can rely entirely and most economically on the handful of hardy cells that make up seeds. These often contain as little as 5 per cent water and are therefore excellently adapted to withstand the rigors of winter. Thus, tracheophytes make the most of their difficult terrestrial habitat. Actually there are only two types of land environment in which a tracheophyte cannot live: the glacial regions at very high altitudes and latitudes, and the permanently arid deserts. But most other organisms cannot live there either.

Review Questions

1 What characteristics distinguish algal plants from photosynthetic protists? Identify the principal phyla of algal plants and illustrate the economic importance of these organisms.

2 Review the reproductive patterns of algal plants. Which organisms display a haplontic pattern? Diplontic? Diplohaplontic? Describe the structure and function of sex organs in these algae.

3 What characteristics distinguish bryophytes and tracheophytes from all other photosynthetic organisms? What characteristics distinguish bryophytes from tracheophytes? What are the classes of bryophytes, the subphyla of tracheophytes, and the subclasses of gymnosperms and angiosperms? Name representative organisms of each of these taxonomic categories.

4 Review some of the identifying characteristics of psilopsids, lycopsids, sphenopsids, and pteropsids.

5 What is a fossil? How can the age of a fossil be determined? Review the names and dates of the geologic eras and periods. What were the Appalachian and Laramide revolutions?

6 Review the probable evolutionary relationships among the major subgroups of tracheophytes. Review Lignier's hypothesis regarding the origin of tracheophytes.

7 Describe the key events of plant evolution during the Silurian and the Devonian Periods. Cite fossil evidence in support of the view that psilopsids were ancestral to all other vascular plants. What were the characteristics of lepidodendrids?

8 Name and describe fossil sphenopsids. Which pteropsid groups were in existence by the end of the Devonian? Describe the key events of plant evolution during the Carboniferous and Permian Periods.

9 What were the seed ferns? Which other plant groups are they believed to have given rise to? Describe the causes and events of the Permo-Triassic crisis. At what date did it take place? When did bryophytes first leave fossils?

10 Review the key events of plant evolution during the Mesozoic Era and the Cenozoic Era. Describe the time and the events of the Laramide revolution. What were the consequences of the Laramide revolution on plants?

11 Contrast and compare the terrestrial adaptations of bryophytes, psilopsids, lycopsids, sphenopsids, ferns, gymnosperms, and angiosperms; review fully.

12 What are the architectural adaptations of tracheophytes to life on land? Name different modifications of stems and roots, and state the adaptive roles of such modifications.

13 What mechanisms conserve water within tracheophytes? What mechanisms protect tracheophytes against heat and cold?

14 Review the life cycles of annuals, biennials, and perennials and describe the adaptive features of each.

Collateral Readings

Baker, H.: "Plants and Civilization," 2d ed., Wadsworth, Belmont, Calif., 1970. Describes how plants have influenced the development of human culture.

Banks, H. P.: "Evolution and Plants of the Past," Wadsworth, Belmont, Calif., 1970. An outstanding and lively short book on fossil plants. Evolutionary relationships between tracheophytes are stressed.

Beadle, G. W.: The Ancestry of Corn, *Scientific American,* January 1980. Written by a gifted and extremely productive biologist (see Biology Highlight in Chap. 27), this article presents evidence suggesting that modern corn has evolved from the wild grass teosinite.

Bold, H. C., and **M. J. Wynne:** "Introduction to the Algae," Prentice-Hall, Englewood Cliffs, N.J., 1978. A thorough, technical treatment of all algal groups.

Chapman, V. J., and **D. J. Chapman:** "The Algae," 2d ed., Macmillan, New York, 1973. All major kinds of algae are reviewed in this comprehensive textbook. Includes chapters on the diversity, distribution, and ecology of these organisms.

Corner, E. J. H.: "The Life of Plants," Mentor Books, New York, 1968. This book emphasizes the evolution and adaptations of terrestrial plants.

Coulter, M. C.: "The Story of the Plant Kingdom," 3d ed., rev. H. Dittmer, University of Chicago Press, Chicago, 1964. A highly readable account of plant evolution.

Daubennire, R. E.: "Plants and Environment," 3d ed., Wiley, New York, 1974. Describes how soil, water, light, temperature, and other environmental factors have influenced the evolution of plants in diverse habitats.

Delevoryas, T.: "Plant Diversification," Holt, New York, 1966. A short paperback emphasizing the evolutionary development of plants.

Goin, C. J., and **O. B. Goin:** "Journey onto Land," Macmillan, New York, 1974. This short paperback contains a chapter on the evolution and terrestrial adaptations of seed plants.

Gottlieb, J. E.: "Plants: Adaptation through Evolution," Reinhold, New York, 1968. A good paperback on the evolution and basic characteristics of bryophytes and tracheophytes.

Heslop-Harrison, Y.: Carnivorous Plants, *Scientific American,* February 1978. Describes how the carnivorous behavior of certain plants enables them to survive in habitats where few other plants can live.

Pickett-Heaps, J. D.: "Green Algae: Structure, Reproduction, and Evolution in Selected Genera," Sivaner, Sunderland, Mass., 1975. Beautifully illustrated, this book contains a wealth of information on structure and function of green algal cells.

Regal, P. J.: Ecology and Evolution of Flowering Plant Dominance, *Science,* May 6, 1977, p. 622. Outlines the compelling hypothesis that the extremely rapid radiation of angiosperms was due in large part to particular interactions with animals.

Rick, C. M.: The Tomato, *Scientific American,* August 1978. Describes how new production technologies and genetic modifications have increased both the quality and quantities of tomatoes grown throughout the world.

Valentine, J. W.: The Evolution of Multicellular Plants and Animals, *Scientific American,* September 1978. Part of an issue devoted entirely to evolution.

Von Reis, A. S.: Exploring the Herbarium, *Scientific American,* May 1977. Illustrates the wealth of knowledge that can be gained by inspecting plants maintained in various botanical collections throughout the world.

Weier, T. E., C. R. Stocking, and **M. G. Barbour:** "Botany: An Introduction to Plant Biology," 5th ed., Wiley, New York, 1974. One of the best illustrated introductions to the biology of plants.

Wilson, C. L., W. E. Loomis, and **T. A. Steeves:** "Botany," 5th ed., Holt, New York, 1971. Chapters of this textbook provide an exceptionally clear, concise introduction to the evolution of plants.

Chapter 33 Animals: Noncoelomates

Learning Objectives

After reading this chapter you should be able to:

1. Cite at least one characteristic of Metaphyta and Metazoa not shared by Monera and Protista; list at least three characteristics that distinguish Metazoa from Metaphyta.
2. Differentiate between Parazoa and Eumetazoa and between Radiata and Bilateria. Differentiate between Acoelomata, Pseudocoelomata, and Coelomata; Protostomia and Deuterostomia; schizocoelomates, enterocoelomates, and lophophorates; state the criteria that define each of these taxonomic categories; construct a diagram that depicts the presumed evolutionary relations among the main animal groups; distinguish between peritoneum, mesenteries, and coelom.
3. Construct a diagram that depicts at least one architectural variant of sponges; list at least three kinds of cells found in sponges and name the function of each; state at least two ways in which sponges reproduce vegetatively; list at least two ways in which sponges are economically and ecologically important.
4. Name the identifying characteristics of the Radiata; list the two phyla that are classified as Radiata.
5. List the classes and identifying characteristics of coelenterates and name a representative organism of each class; differentiate between polyp and medusa and construct a diagram that depicts the structural features of each; list the three layers that typically make up the body of a polyp or medusa; outline the roles played by polyp and medusa in the life cycle of *Obelia*.
6. Differentiate between cnidocyte and nematocyst; define planula and state its role in the life cycle of coelenterates; state the possible evolutionary significance of an ancestral planulalike organism.
7. List the phyla that are classified as acoelomates; list the classes of flatworms and name a representative organism of each class; describe four variants of alimentary systems among free-living flatworms.
8. Construct a diagram that depicts the anatomical relations between components of the digestive, nervous, and excretory systems of planarians, and list a function for each structure you identify; construct a diagram that depicts the structural features of a fluke and a tapeworm; illustrate and describe the life cycle of the beef tapeworm.
9. Characterize nemertineans, listing at least two distinguishing characteristics of these animals; state the probable evolutionary origins of proboscis worms; describe the structural and functional relationships between proboscis, rhychocoel, and stylet; state taxonomic definitions of pseudocoelomates generally and aschelminths specifically; construct a diagram that depicts the general body organization of a rotifer and a nematode; identify at least two nematodes that can parasitize human beings, name the diseases they can produce and describe the symptoms of each disease you identify; define parthenogenesis and state an example of this phenomenon among sac worms.
10. Name at least one habitat in which each of the following organisms commonly resides:
    - **a.** sponges
    - **b.** coelenterates
    - **c.** planarians
    - **d.** nematodes

Kingdom	Branch	Grade	Subgrade	Phylum	Class
Monera					
Protista					
Fungi					
Plantae (Metaphyta)					
Animalia (Metazoa)	Parazoa			Porifera	Calcarea
					Hexactinellida
					Demospongiae
	Eumetazoa	Radiata		Cnidaria	Hydrozoa
					Scyphozoa
					Anthozoa
				Ctenophora	
		Bilateria	Acoelomata	Platyhelminthes	Turbellaria
					Trematoda
					Cestoda
				Nemertinea	
			Pseudocoelomata	Aschelminthes	Rotifera
					Gastrotricha
					Kinorhyncha
					Priapulida
					Nematoda
					Nematomorpha
				Acanthocephala	
				Entoprocta	
			Coelomata		

The evolutionary origin of animals is obscure. That they arose from ancestral Protista is hardly in doubt, but it is impossible at present to be sure exactly which protistan group was directly ancestral. According to early hypotheses, animals are assumed to have evolved from protozoa; but there is actually very little evidence for such a view. *Any* of the early protistan stocks could have given rise to animals, and indeed long before protozoa as such had originated. Moreover, *numerous* early protistan types could have contributed independently and at different times to animal evolution.

Like most Plantae, most animals exhibit a complex multicellular construction encompassing the organ and organ-system levels of organization. Animals differ from plants in that their cells typically possess centrioles and that cells not in direct contact with the external environment are naked, without walls or cuticles. Further, animals pass not only through embryonic stages during development, but typically through larval stages as well. Most obviously, animals are exclusively heterotrophic and nearly all are holotrophic; they ingest bulk foods, digest them thereafter, and then egest unusable remains. This collective function of *alimentation* is an almost universal animal characteristic, the counterpart of photosynthesis in plants.

ANIMAL TAXONOMY: AN OVERVIEW

The most general trait of animals, and the first to appear during development, is their *level of organization.* All animals typically begin life as single cells, and some then develop to a tissue level of complexity. But others pass beyond this level and become more complex. Accordingly, animals (Metazoa) are considered to include two taxonomic *branches.* In the branch *Parazoa,* the highest level of organization is the tissue. This branch happens to encompass just one phylum, the *sponges.* All other animals belong to the branch *Eumetazoa,* characterized by the presence of organs and organ systems (Fig. 33.1).

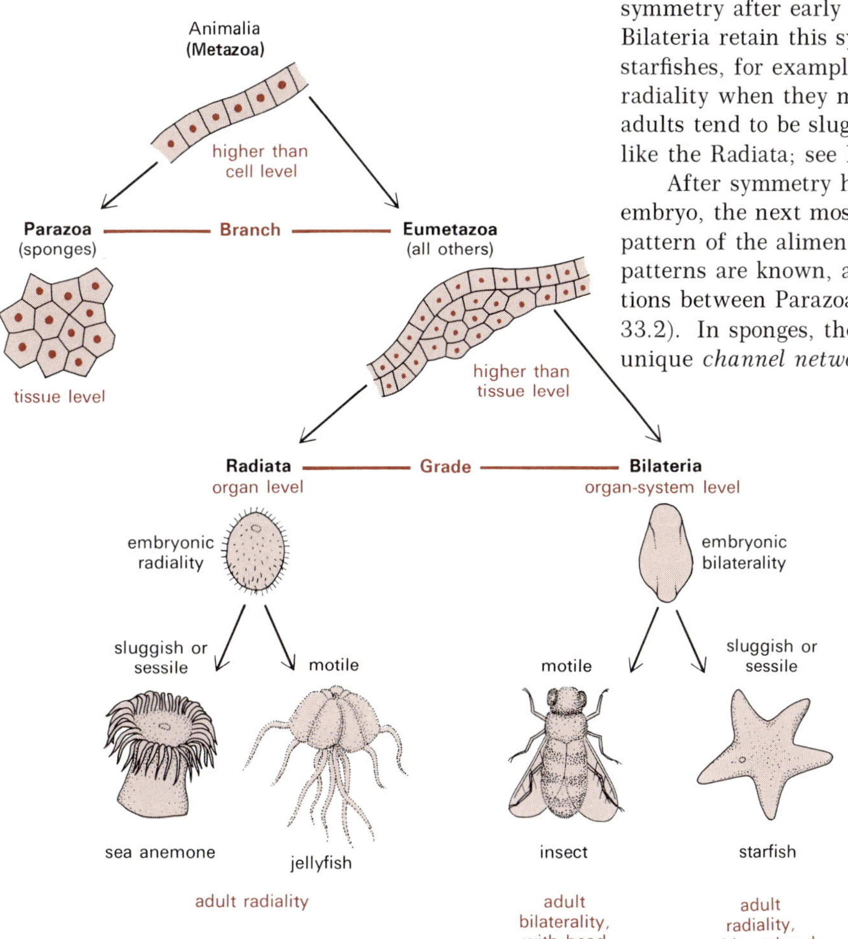

Fig. 33.1 Taxonomy, level of organization, and symmetry. Radiates have embryonic as well as adult radial symmetry. Bilateria have a primary embryonic bilateral symmetry. Adults are bilateral if they are motile but often secondarily radial if they are sessile.

After level of organization, the next most general trait to appear in animal development is that of *symmetry.* At first all animal embryos are radially symmetrical; they are solid or hollow balls composed of a few cells. Some animal groups then retain this radiality right to the adult stage, but in others the embryos soon become bilateral and the later larval and adult stages usually remain bilateral as well. On this basis the branch Eumetazoa can be subclassified into two *grades,* the *Radiata* and the *Bilateria.* Radiates are identified by a basic radial symmetry throughout life and also by a structural organization in which the organ is the highest level. The grade contains two phyla, the cnidarians (coelenterates) and the comb jellies. All other animals belong to the Bilateria, characterized by the presence of organ systems and by bilateral symmetry after early embryonic stages. (Most Bilateria retain this symmetry, but a few groups—starfishes, for example—acquire a secondary radiality when they metamorphose into adults; such adults tend to be sluggish or sessile and headless like the Radiata; see Fig. 33.1).

After symmetry has been established in the embryo, the next most general trait to appear is the pattern of the alimentary structures. Three major patterns are known, and they add to the distinctions between Parazoa, Radiata, and Bilateria (Fig. 33.2). In sponges, the alimentary structures are unique *channel networks:* food-bearing water flows

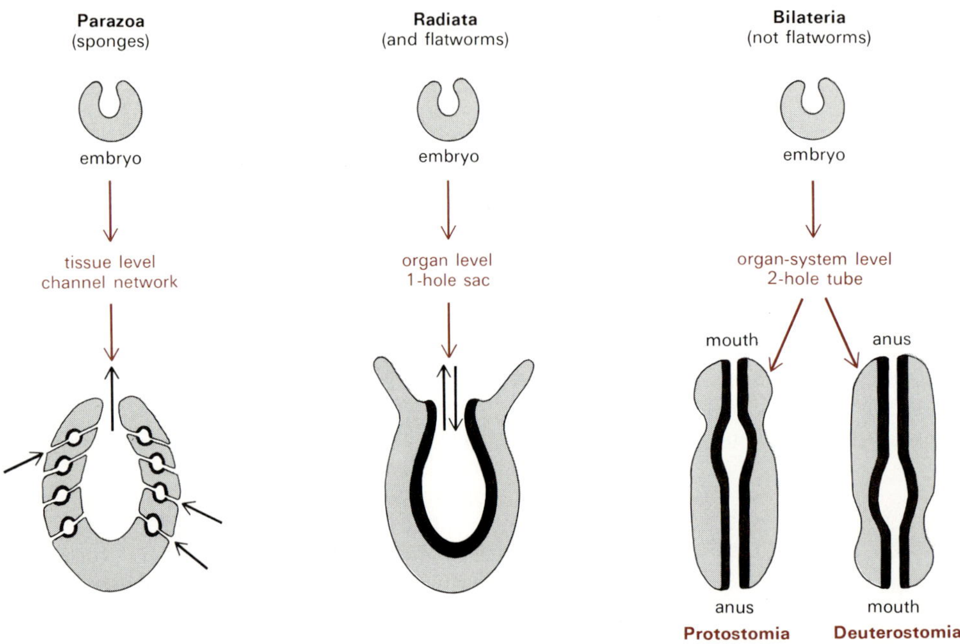

Fig. 33.2 Alimentary patterns. The position of the alimentary cells is shown as dark layers (endoderm in Radiata and Bilateria). Specialized flagellated cells line the water-filled channels of the sponge body and engulf suspended food. In radiates the single alimentary opening of the embryo becomes a joint mouth-anus in the adult. In bilaterial types the embryonic alimentary opening becomes the mouth in Protostomia, the anus in Deuterostomia. In each case a second alimentary opening develops later at the opposite end.

through systems of channels that branch throughout the body. In Radiata and one phylum of Bilateria (flatworms), the alimentary pattern is a *one-hole sac*. A single opening in the sac serves as both mouth and anus, and the layer of cells that forms the sac represents the endoderm, one of the primary germ layers (see Fig. 7.7). In all other Bilateria the alimentary structures form a *two-hole tube*. Such a tube develops in the embryo from a sac that later acquires a second opening, typically opposite the first one. One opening then specializes as a mouth, the other as an anus, and the tube interconnecting them becomes the alimentary tract in which food passes only one way, from mouth to anus. In one group of Bilateria (*Protostomia*) the first opening becomes the mouth, the second the anus; in another group (*Deuterostomia*), the first opening forms the anus and the second the mouth.

Taken together, the level of organization, the symmetry, and the alimentary pattern provide a broad outline of the fundamental body form of any animal. Alimentary pattern and symmetry specify the basic interior and exterior architecture, respectively, and the organizational level specifies the complexity of the architectural building blocks. Thus, at a comparatively early stage of development an embryo is already clearly recognizable as, for example, a bilateral type, and in it at least two of the three primary germ layers are already present: integumentary ectoderm outside and alimentary endoderm inside. Between these two the mesoderm now develops, from cells produced by ectoderm, endoderm, or both layers as in most cases. The pattern of mesoderm formation is an important criterion that can be used to divide the grade Bilateria into *subgrades*.

Acoelomata

In one bilaterial subgrade, mesoderm comes to fill completely the available space between ectoderm and endoderm. Animals so constructed lack an internal body cavity; they form the subgrade *Acoelomata*, and they are exemplified by, for example, flatworms. In all other Bilateria mesoderm comes to occupy only part of the space between ectoderm and endoderm, and the remainder later becomes a fluid-filled *principal body cavity*. The presence of such a cavity makes the motions of the alimentary tract independent of those of the body wall and the animal as a whole. Moreover the cavity permits an animal to attain considerable size, for the fluid in the cavity can provide internal support as a hydraulic "skeleton." It can also aid in transporting food and wastes, a necessary function that in a large animal could not be accomplished by direct diffusion between surface and deep-lying parts alone.

Pseudocoelomata

One group of Bilateria has a body cavity bounded on the outside directly by the body wall and on the inside directly by the alimentary system. The mesoderm here consists of cells and tissues that accumulate in certain restricted regions only. Animals with body cavities of this type make up the subgrade *Pseudocoelomata*. It is exemplified by rotifers and roundworms.

Coelomata

In all remaining Bilateria one portion of the developing mesoderm is situated along the inner surface of the ectoderm and another portion forms around the alimentary tract. Most of the free space left between these mesodermal layers typically comes to be enclosed by a mesodermal membrane, the *peritoneum*. The vertical portions of this membrane represent *mesenteries*, which suspend the alimentary tract from the body wall.

Any space or body cavity enclosed completely by mesodermal tissues, and especially by a peritoneal membrane, is known as a *coelom*. Accordingly, animals with a coelom are said to belong to the subgrade *Coelomata*. The terms "acoelomate" and "pseudocoelomate" now become clear. Acoelomates are animals without a coelom and indeed without a body cavity of any kind. Pseudocoelomates have a *pseudocoel*, or "false" coelom, a body cavity lined directly by ectoderm and endoderm, not by a peritoneum. Such a cavity resembles a true coelom superficially (Fig. 33.3).

Kinds of Coeloms

Schizocoels Among coelomate Bilateria in turn, subgroups can be distinguished according to how the coelomic cavities develop (Fig. 33.4). In one subgroup, exemplified by mollusks, annelids, and arthropods, all adult mesoderm arises from two endoderm-derived cells, one on each side of the future gut. Each of these so-called *teloblast cells* then forms a *teloblastic band* of tissue. This band later splits into an outer mesodermal layer that lies along the ectoderm and an inner layer that surrounds the

Fig. 33.3 Mesoderm and coelom in Bilateria. The main body cavity is a pseudocoel in the Pseudocoelomata and a peritoneum-lined coelom in the Coelomata. In coelomates a dorsal and ventral mesentery (formed by two mesodermal layers) supports the alimentary tract.

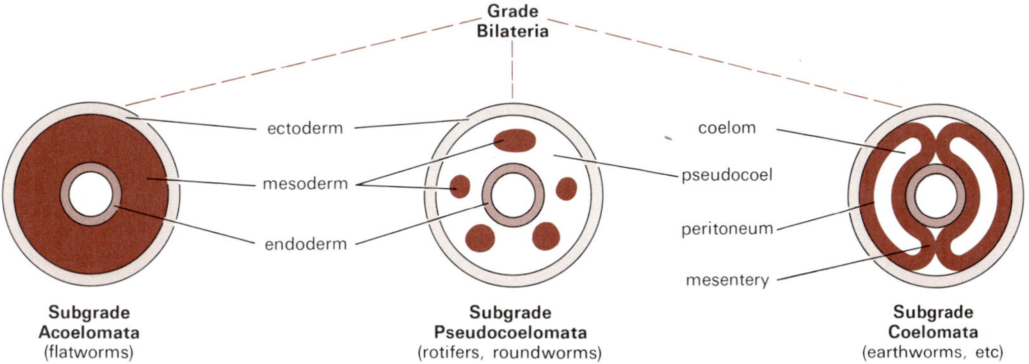

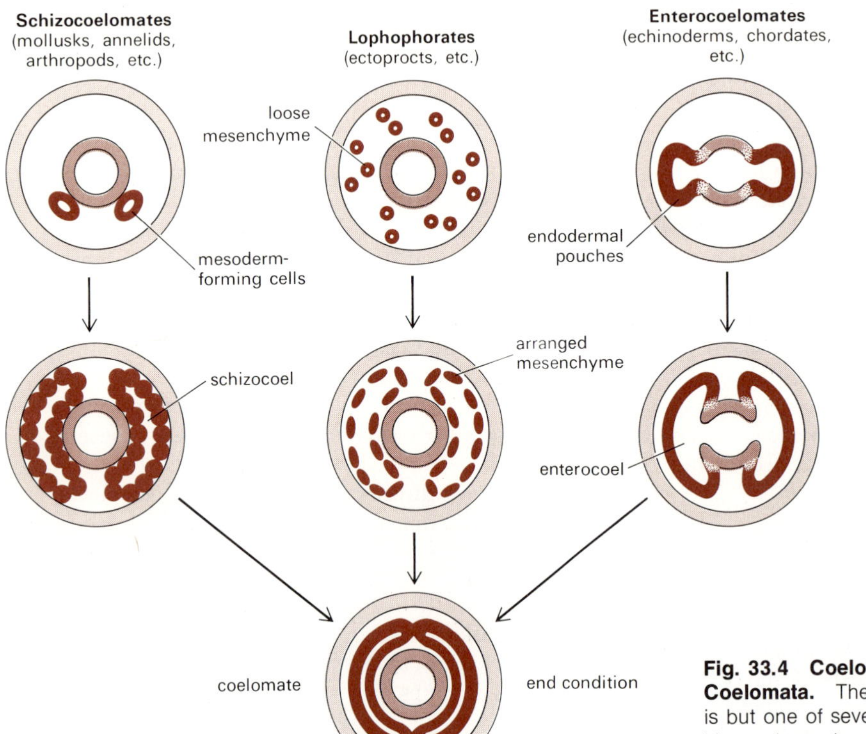

Fig. 33.4 Coelom formation in the subgrade Coelomata. The pattern shown for lophophorates is but one of several known to occur in that group. Mesenchyme is a group of unspecialized mesodermally derived cells.

endoderm. Because the coelom here forms by a splitting process, it is called a *schizocoel;* and animals with coelomic body cavities of this type make up the *schizocoelomates,* an assemblage roughly equivalent to a superphylum.

Enterocoels In another such superphylum, represented mainly by echinoderms and chordates, the mesoderm arises as a pair of lateral pouches that grow out from the endoderm. These pouches later separate away from the endoderm as closed sacs, but their inner portions still remain adjacent to the alimentary system and their outer portions come to lie along the body wall. The final condition is quite similar to that in schizocoelomates. But since the mesoderm and the coelom here are derived from the future gut ("enteron"), the body cavity is called an *enterocoel;* and animals with such cavities are known as *enterocoelomates.*

Lophophorates In a third subgroup or superphylum, various other, largely unique patterns of coelom formation occur. In one, for example, loose mesoderm cells migrate and eventually arrange themselves as a continuous peritoneal layer (see Fig. 33.4). Coeloms developed in this and various similar ways have not been given any special technical names. The animals in this group include brachiopods (lamp shells) and other so-called *lophophorates.* The ancestors of this group might have been among the most ancient coelomate animals, from which both the schizocoelomate and the enterocoelomate superphyla later evolved.

Partly on the basis of the developmental patterns just outlined, a number of presumed, tentative evolutionary interrelations among the main animal groups have been inferred. These inferences are summarized diagrammatically in Fig. 33.5.

BRANCH PARAZOA

Animals at or below tissue level of organization; body tissues not homologous to primary germ layers of other animals; *Porifera.*

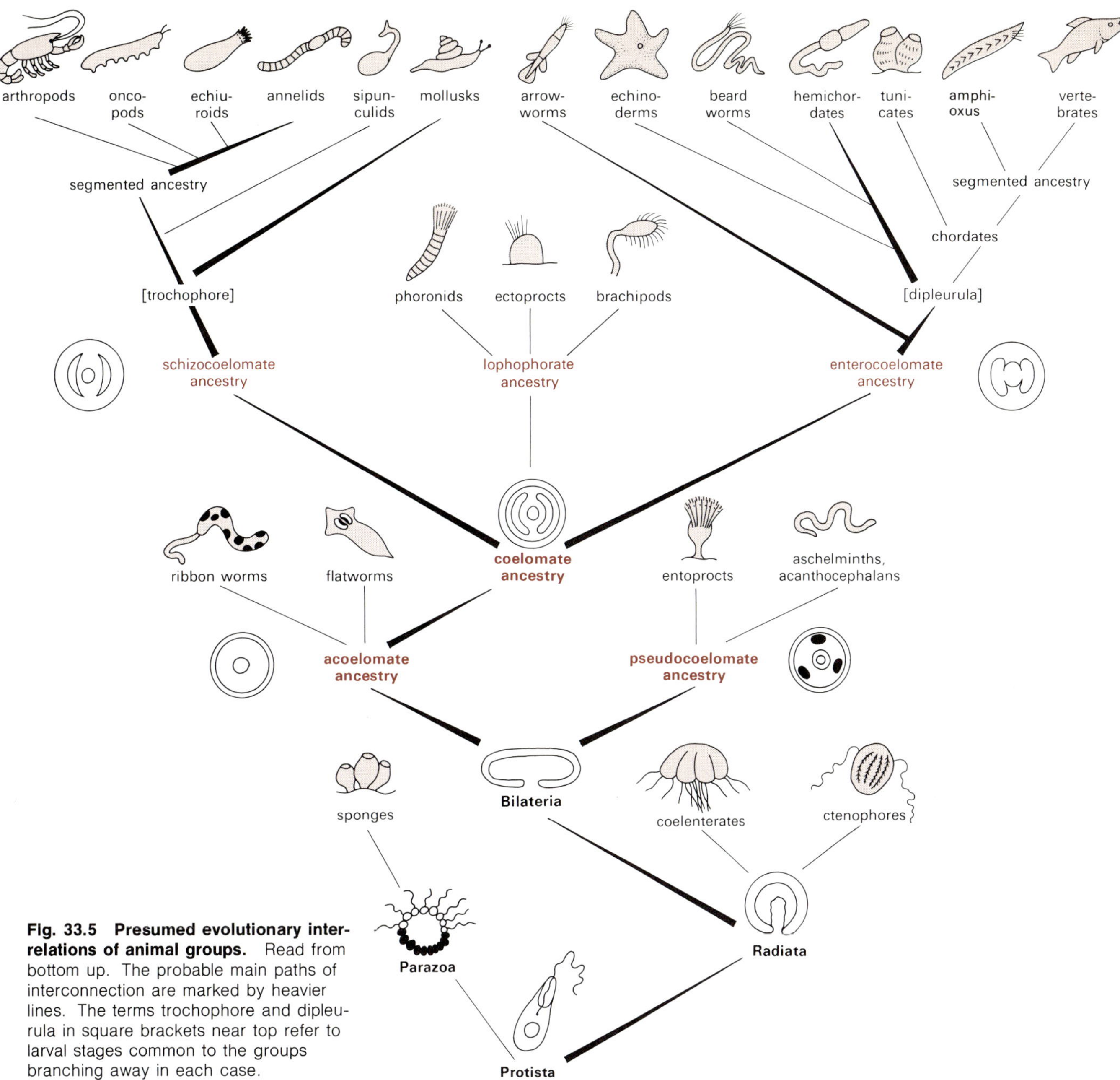

Fig. 33.5 Presumed evolutionary interrelations of animal groups. Read from bottom up. The probable main paths of interconnection are marked by heavier lines. The terms trochophore and dipleurula in square brackets near top refer to larval stages common to the groups branching away in each case.

Sponges

Phylum Porifera "pore-bearing" animals; mostly marine, some in fresh water; adults sessile, often in colonies; alimentation by means of channel system with flagellate collar cells; without nerve cells; 5000 species

CLASS CALCAREA chalk sponges

CLASS HEXACTINELLIDA glass sponges

CLASS DEMOSPONGIAE horny sponges

The larvae of sponges are globular, flagellate, free-swimming organisms composed of two cell lay-

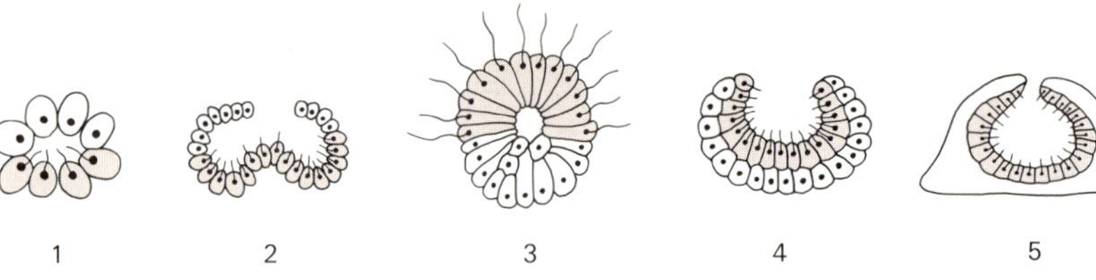

Fig. 33.6 Sponge development. 1, Blastulalike embryo; 2, inversion (embryo turns inside out through opening in nonflagellated half, resulting in exteriorized flagella); 3, amphiblastula larva; 4, invagination of flagellated half into nonflagellated half; 5, larva settles and becomes adult sponge.

ers. When they settle and metamorphose, they undergo a curious inversion: the flagellate cells of the outer layer move to the interior, and the cells of the originally interior layer move to the outside (Fig. 33.6). Jelly-secreting cells later come to lie between the outer and inner layers; hence an adult sponge basically has a three-layered construction. However, because of the earlier inversion, the three layers are not equivalent to ectoderm, mesoderm, and endoderm. This circumstance is one of the main reasons why sponges are regarded as representing a whole separate taxonomic branch, distinct from all other animals.

The outer layer of a sponge typically forms a covering epithelium (Fig. 33.7). At numerous places in this epithelium are small pores (*ostia*) that lead to the interior of the body and admit food-bearing water. The middle layer contains not only jelly-secreting cells but also others that form, for example, reproductive cells and skeletal *spicules.* These needlelike secretions have a variety of shapes, and their composition is the basis of sponge classification; spicules consist of calcium salts in chalk sponges, of silica in glass sponges, and of organic substances in horny sponges.

The inner layer of a sponge contains flagellate *collar cells* (or *choanocytes*), remarkably similar to the protozoan collar flagellates. The flagella are directed into the central cavity of the sponge, which communicates with the pores on the surface. Water is drawn through the pores into the cavity by the beat of the flagella, and a common

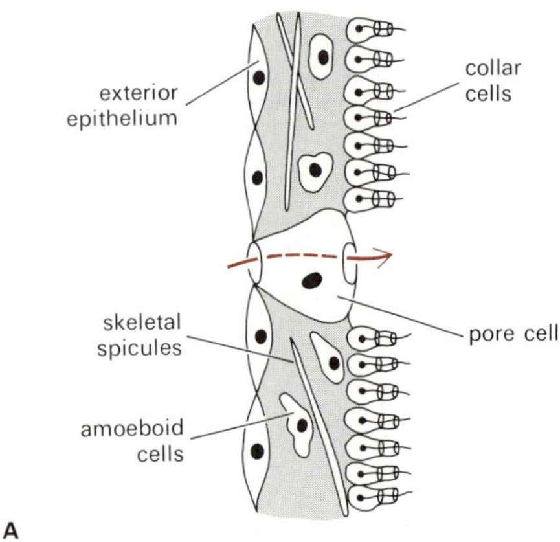

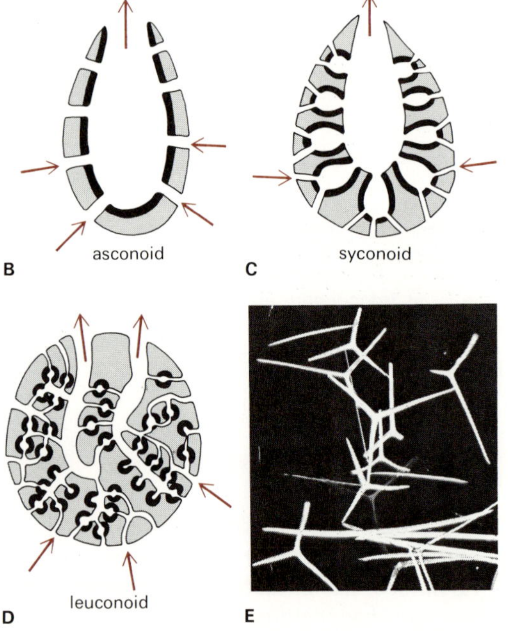

Fig. 33.7 Sponge structure. (A) Composition of the body wall of a sponge such as that shown in (B). (B) to (D) The three levels of structural complexity of sponges. The black layers indicate the position of the collar cells. Arrows show direction of water flow. Openings where water enters sponge are ostia, and the exits where water leaves are oscula. (E) Isolated skeletal spicules of a calcareous sponge. (*Carolina Biological Supply Company.*)

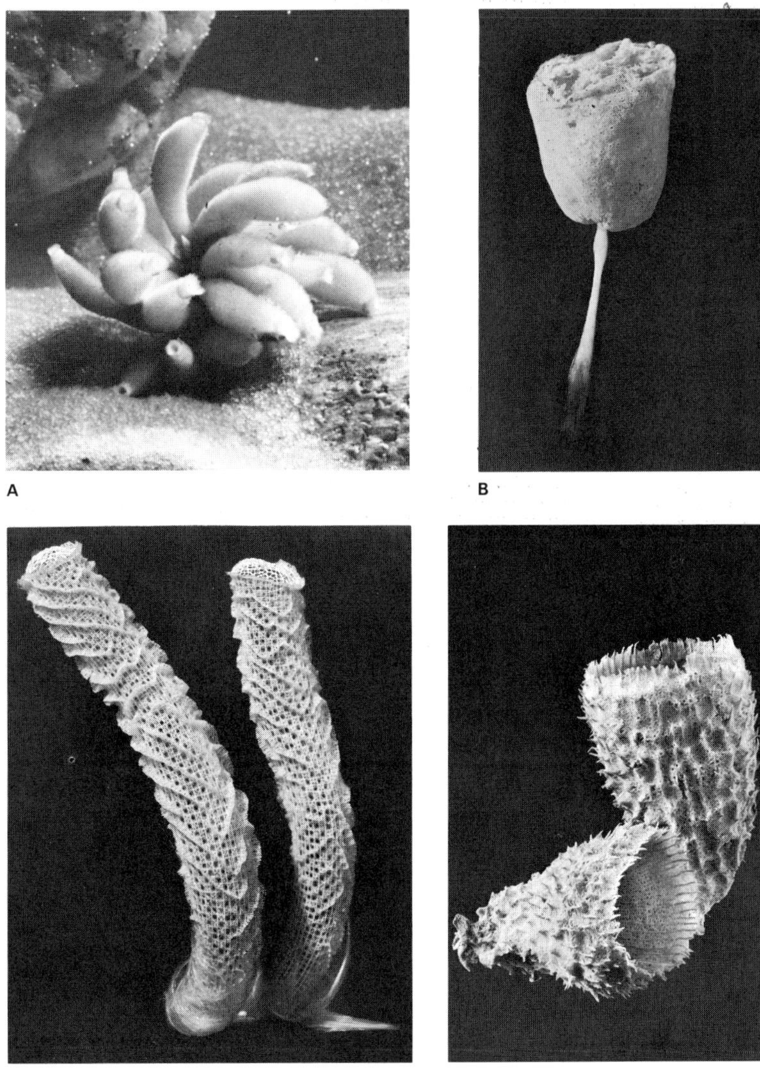

Fig. 33.8 Sponge types. (A) A cluster of *Scypha* (*Grantia*), a freshwater sponge. Each fingerlike projection is an individual sponge. (B) A glass sponge. The ropy tuft anchors the animal to the sea floor. (C) Venus flower basket, one of the glass sponges. (D) A horny sponge. To this group also belong the bath sponges. See also Color Fig. 34.

stream of water then leaves the sponge through an *osculum*, a larger opening from the inner cavity. Food present in water that flows past the collar cells is trapped by them and digested in food vacuoles.

In the simplest (or *asconoid*) sponges, the inner cavity is a wide, straight-walled chamber, with collar cells lining the entire wall. In more complex (or *syconoid*) types the central cavity is extended into numerous deep side chambers, and only these contain collar cells. The most complex (or *leuconoid*) sponges have a highly branched network of narrow channels throughout the body. Collar cells here occur only in small chambers spaced out along the channels (see Fig. 33.7). Calcareous sponges include all three of these structural types; glass and horny sponges are largely leuconoid (Fig. 33.8).

Apart from propagating through sex cells, sponges can reproduce by *budding*, and freshwater species can form *gemmules* under unfavorable conditions. A gemmule is an encapsulated group of cells that can form a new sponge when circumstances are again appropriate. Sponges can also be fragmented, and each piece usually regenerates as a complete individual. Indeed, a sponge can be decomposed into a suspension of loose cells, which then migrate together and rebuild themselves as an intact whole.

Because of their unusual developmental patterns, their alimentary water channels, and their primitive level of organization, sponges are regarded almost universally as an independent line of metazoan evolution. The animals well might be descendants of protozoan or more broadly protistan ancestors.

BRANCH EUMETAZOA

Animals above tissue level of organization; adult body formed from embryonic ectoderm, mesoderm, and endoderm; *Radiata, Bilateria.*

Radiate Forms

Grade Radiata animals attaining organ level of complexity; typically with adult radial symmetry

Phylum Cnidaria coelenterates; mostly marine, some in fresh water; tentacle-bearing radiates with *cnidoblasts* containing *nematocysts;* body saclike, with single alimentary opening serving as mouth and anus; polymorphic, with medusas and/or polyps; with *planula* larvae; 10,000 species

Phylum Ctenophora comb jellies (Fig. 33.9 and Color Fig. 5); all marine; medusalike construction; locomotion by eight meridian *comb plates;* tentacles if present with adhesive cells; 100 species

Fig. 33.9 Ctenophores. The animal shown is *Pleurobrachia,* photographed from life. Note locomotor comb plates in rows on globular body; fringed (adhesive-cell-containing) tentacles; and position of sensory balancing organ at top of animal.

Of these two phyla of radiate animals, the first is of major evolutionary and ecological significance. Early coelenterates might have been the ancestors of all other eumetazoan animals, comb jellies included; and coelenterates living today, particularly the builders of coral reefs and atolls, are important members of the marine environment.

COELENTERATES

Phylum Cnidaria

CLASS HYDROZOA *Obelia, Hydra, Physalia*

CLASS SCYPHOZOA jellyfishes

CLASS ANTHOZOA sea anemones, corals

The phylum name is derived from the stinging cells, or *cnidocytes,* found around the mouth, on the tentacles, and elsewhere in these carnivorous animals. Each cnidocyte contains a horny *nematocyst,* a stinging capsule with a coiled, hollow filament inside (Fig. 33.10). Appropriate stimuli cause explosive discharge of the nematocyst, a process in which the filament turns inside out and entangles prey. Some types of nematocysts also secrete a paralyzing toxin.

Coelenterates occur in two basic structural forms, *polyps* and *medusas* (Fig. 33.11). In polyps the main body axis is long in relation to the diameter, and in the umbrella- or bell-shaped medusas the main axis is short. Polyps are sessile; medusas are free-swimming and sexual. Both types or either one only can occur in a given life cycle.

The body of any coelenterate, whether polyp or medusa, typically consists of three layers (see Fig. 33.11). The outside layer is an ectodermal *epidermis,* which in many polyps secretes an exoskeleton. Such secretions are often little more than thin, transparent layers of chitin, but they can also be

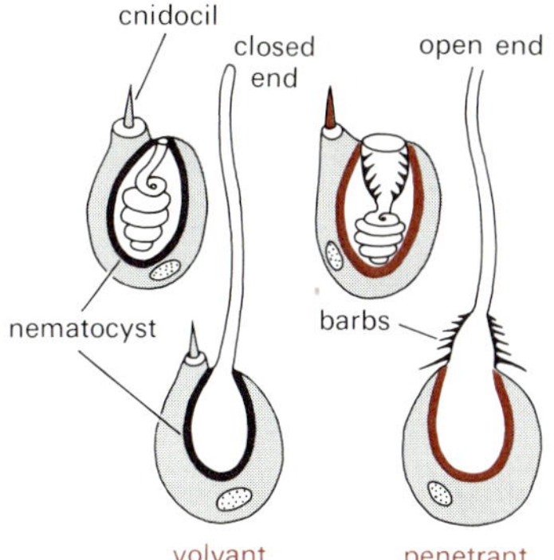

Fig. 33.10 Cnidocytes, undischarged and discharged. Numerous variants of each of the two basic types shown here are known. When touched, the cnidocil triggers release of the nematocyst.

massive accumulations of calcareous stone, as in reef-forming corals. The inside layer is an endodermal *gastrodermis,* which lines the alimentary cavity and contains flagellate and amoeboid digestive cells. Between epidermis and gastrodermis is a mesodermal *mesogloea,* a layer containing jelly-secreting cells and varying amounts of connective tissue fibers. In polyps the amount of jelly is generally small; it is absent altogether in *Hydra.* But in medusas the jelly becomes extensive and forms the bulk of the animal. Embedded in the mesogloea is a simple nerve net that innervates both the epidermis and the gastrodermis. Scyphozoa and Anthozoa also have distinct muscle cells. Hydrozoa are without them, but most of their epidermal and gastrodermal cells contain contractile fibrils.

Coelenterate development typically includes an oval, two-layered *planula* larva (Fig. 33.12). This ciliated, free-swimming form eventually settles and gives rise to the polyp phase of a life cycle. Some biologists hypothesize that all radiates evolved from animals now extinct that closely resembled the planula of modern coelenterates. In many Hydrozoa the planula grows into a highly branched colony of polyps that contains a continuous, interconnecting alimentary cavity (Fig. 33.13). Most of these polyps are feeding individuals, or *gastrozooids.* Each of them terminates in a *hydranth,* a flower-shaped body part in which a wreath of tentacles surrounds the alimentary opening. At various locations in such a colony develop reproductive polyps, or *gonozooids,* which give rise to medusas by budding. The medusas swim free, and at maturity they develop sex organs. Fertilized eggs then become new planula larvae.

In Hydrozoa such as *Obelia,* the polyp and medusa phases play roughly equally important roles. In other hydrozoan groups one or the other

Fig. 33.11 Coelenterate structure. (A) The oral (mouth side)-aboral (nonmouth side) axis is long compared with the body diameter in a polyp, whereas the reverse holds true in a medusa. Both polyp and medusa are variants of a single common body pattern. (B) Some cell types in the three body layers, as in jellyfishes and sea anemones. In these animals the inner ends of the epidermal and gastrodermal cells are pseudopodial, as shown, but in Hydrozoa the bases of these cells are T-shaped and contain contractile myofibrils. Correspondingly, Hydrozoa are without separate muscle cells. Cells in the mesogloea secrete jelly, considerable amounts of it in medusas. Nerve cells are part of the epidermis, gastrodermis, or both.

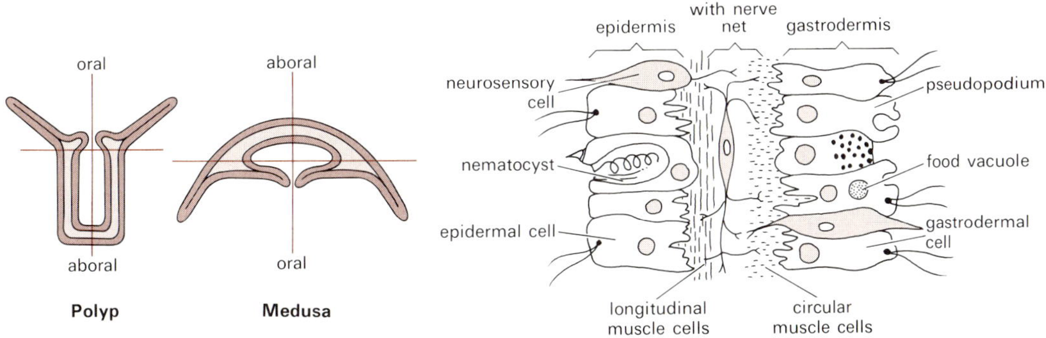

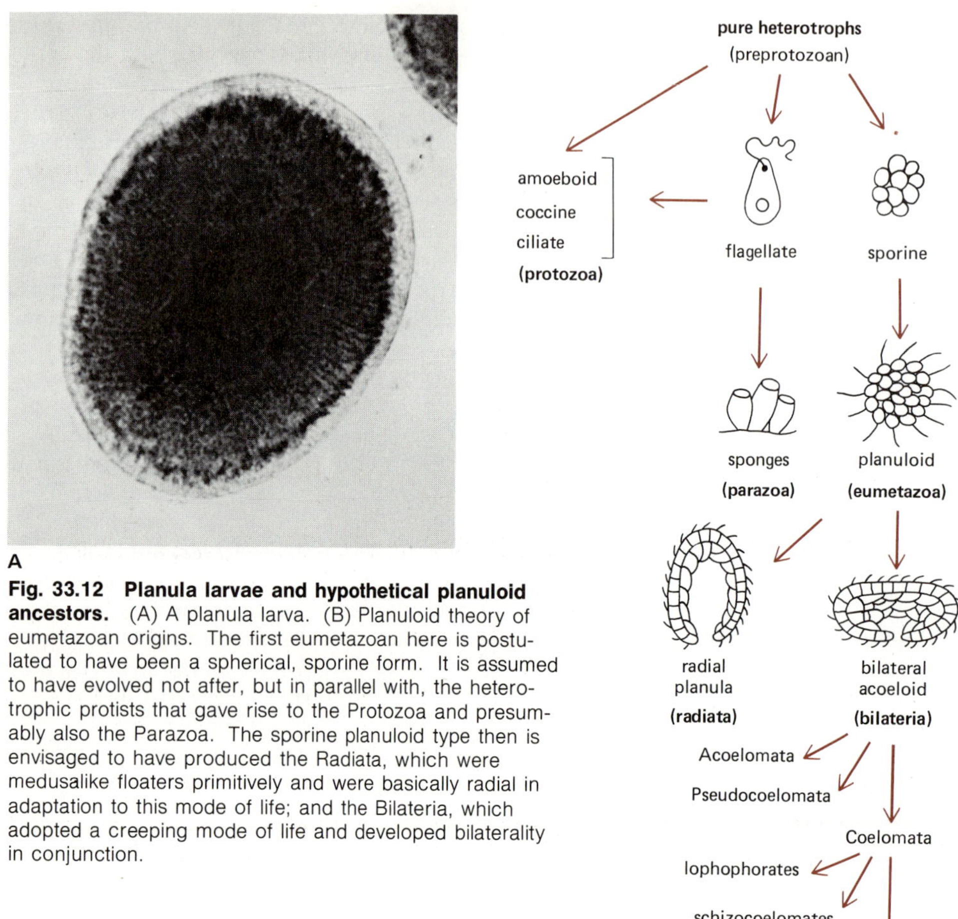

Fig. 33.12 Planula larvae and hypothetical planuloid ancestors. (A) A planula larva. (B) Planuloid theory of eumetazoan origins. The first eumetazoan here is postulated to have been a spherical, sporine form. It is assumed to have evolved not after, but in parallel with, the heterotrophic protists that gave rise to the Protozoa and presumably also the Parazoa. The sporine planuloid type then is envisaged to have produced the Radiata, which were medusalike floaters primitively and were basically radial in adaptation to this mode of life; and the Bilateria, which adopted a creeping mode of life and developed bilaterality in conjunction.

phase is reduced or omitted altogether. For example, in *Gonionemus* the only polyplike stage is a larval form (called *actinula*) that develops from the planula and does not become attached (Fig. 33.14). Later it transforms directly into a free-swimming medusa, which represents the entire adult phase of the life cycle. By contrast, the life cycle of the freshwater *Hydra* does not include a medusa phase. Instead the solitary parent polyp develops sex organs itself and gives rise to new polyps directly. Polyps are similarly dominant in the Portuguese man-of-war *Physalia*, in which several polymorphic types of polyps collectively form a floating colony (see Fig. 8.8).

In the class Scyphozoa, the planula settles and forms a *scyphistoma*, a solitary attached reproductive polyp (Fig. 33.15). From the free end of this polyp are then budded off a series of medusas; these jellyfishes later acquire sex organs and represent the dominant phase of the life cycle. Jellyfishes are structurally similar to hydrozoan medusas. Among several differences, however, an easily recognizable one is that the margin of the "umbrella" is straight in Hydrozoa but scalloped in Scyphozoa.

In Anthozoa it is the medusa phase that is absent. The sessile adult is a feeding polyp with sex organs, and planula larvae grow directly into new polyps. Such polyps are structurally quite com-

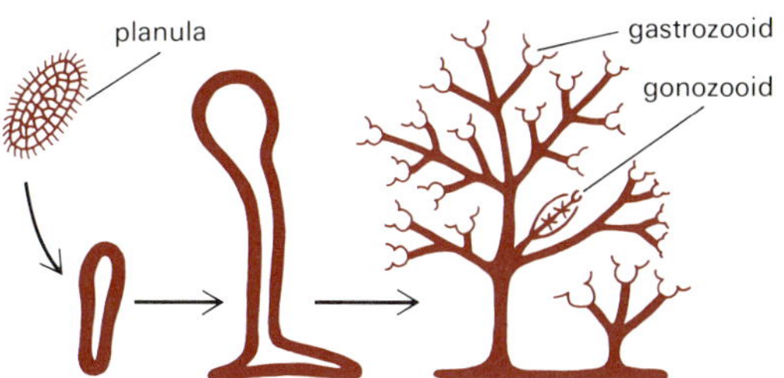

Fig. 33.13 Hydrozoan polyps. (A) A planula larva settles and grows into the stem of a polyp. Branching growth from both upright stems and stems along the ground then produces a colony. Most of the polyps are feeding individuals (gastrozooids) with a ring of tentacles around a mouth-containing terminal part (hydranth). Some polyps are gonozooids, from which medusas develop. (B) Detail of a polyp colony with gastrozooids and gonozooids. The exterior layer is a transparent chitinous exoskeleton. In gastrozooids note the tentacled hydranths, and in gonozooids, the medusas at various developmental stages under the chitin cover.

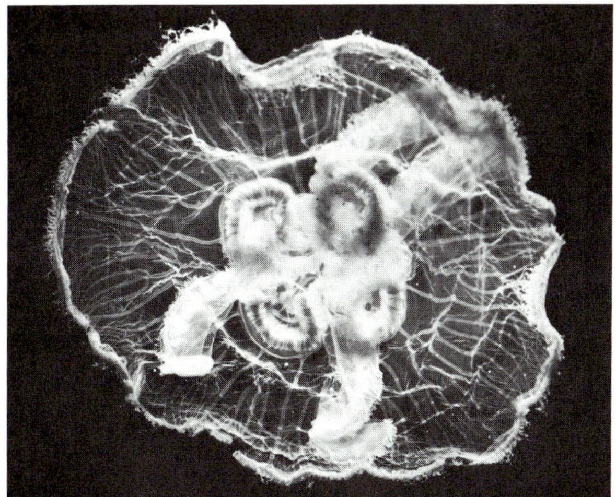

Fig. 33.14 Medusas and polyps. (A) *Gonionemus*, from life, a hydrozoan in which polyps are lacking from the life cycle. (B) The typical medusa body organization is also evident in the common jellyfish *Aurelia*. Note the tentacles around the bell margin, the four horseshoe-shaped gonads near the center, and the mouth-bearing manubrium, curving from center to lower left. (C) A freshwater *Hydra,* from life, with two budded offspring individuals still attached to the parent. Hydras are without medusas.

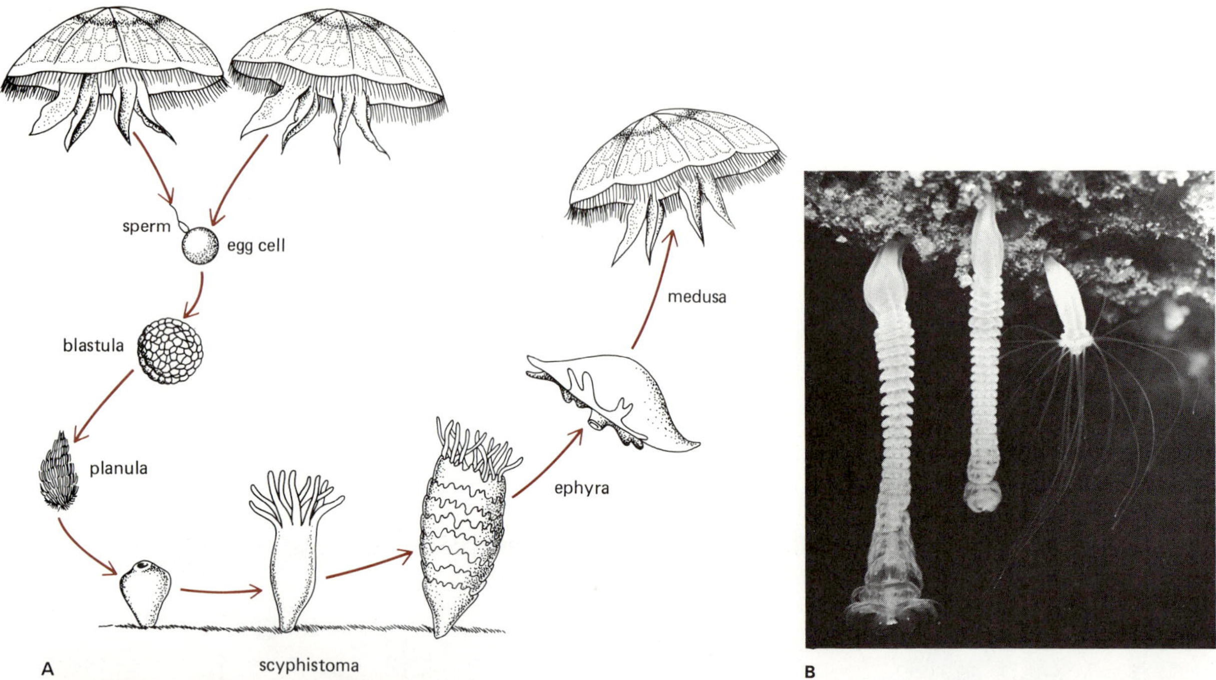

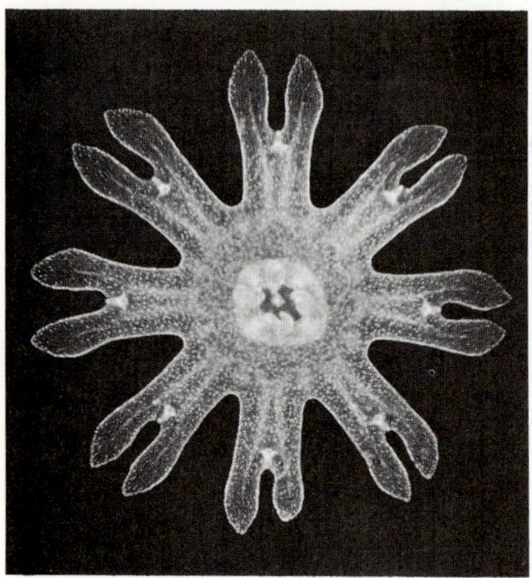

Fig. 33.15 Scyphozoan life cycle. (A) Life cycle of the common jellyfish *Aurelia*. Sperms and eggs are released from adult medusas into the water, where the gametes unite. The resulting zygote develops as a hollow blastula, which then transforms into a planula larva (see also Fig. 33.12A). The planula settles to the bottom and develops as a reproductive polyp, or scyphistoma. Individual larvae, called *ephyra,* bud from the reproductive polyp, each ephyra becoming a mature jellyfish. (B) Scyphistomas of *Aurelia* hanging from the underside of a rock. At right is a young larva; at center and left are older ones in the process of cutting off young medusas successively. A nearly liberated ephyra is seen in lower left corner. (C) Individual free ephyra larva of *Aurelia,* seen from underneath. The *Aurelia* medusa is pictured in Fig. 33.14.

plex. For example, the mesogloea is a true connective tissue that contains very little jelly, and the digestive surface of the alimentary cavity is enlarged by the presence of tissue folds (Fig. 33.16). Some Anthozoa are solitary (like sea anemones); most are colonial and include the majority of the builders of coral reefs and atolls (Fig. 33.17).

Coelenterates as a whole are widely believed to represent the most primitive Eumetazoa. If this view is correct, the Bilateria would all be descended from ancestral coelenterates. An alternative possibility is that coelenterates, and Radiata generally, are an independent line of eumetazoan evolution and that Bilateria evolved separately from an early protistan source. This issue cannot be resolved from the data now available.

A

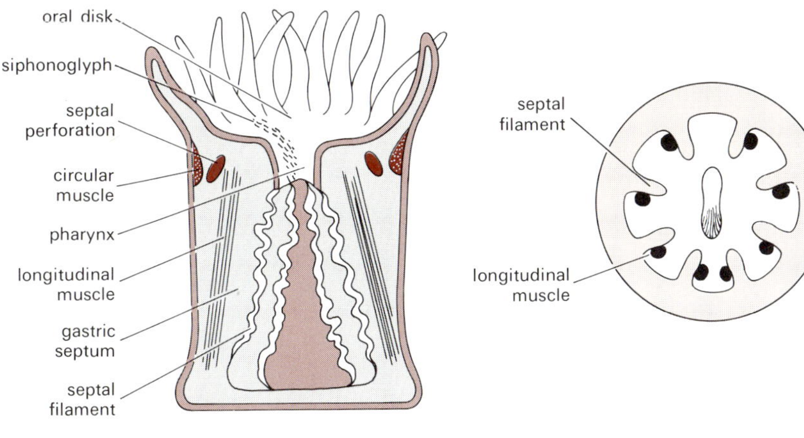

Fig. 33.16 Anthozoa: sea anemones. (A) *Metridium,* a sea anemone. Note the cnidocyte-containing tentacles, which surround the mouth. (B) Cutaway section through a sea anemone. The siphonoglyph is a band of flagella that aids in circulating water into and out of the gastrovascular cavity. Note the partitions (gastric septa) in this cavity. The septal filament contains batteries of stinging cells. (C) Cross section through a sea anemone. Note bilateral arrangement of the longitudinal muscles and the central mouth opening (with position of siphonoglyph indicated). See also Color Figs. 7 and 36.

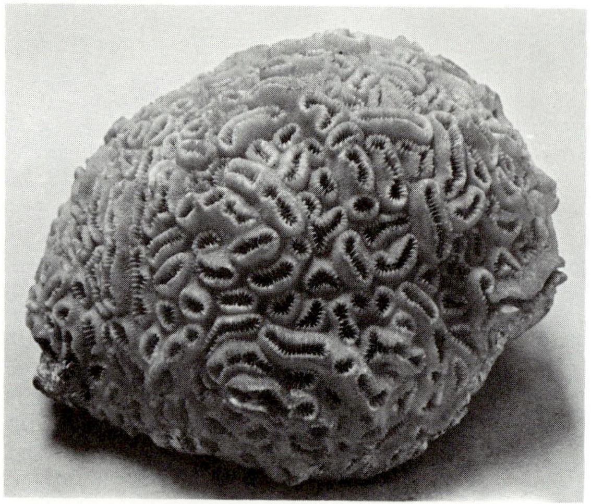
A

B

Fig. 33.17 Anthozoa: corals. (A) Skeletal remains of a colony of brain coral. Note the resemblance to the human cerebrum. (B) A closer view of the skeleton, showing the partitioned, groovelike compartments formerly occupied by the living polyps. See also Color Fig. 35.

BILATERAL FORMS

Grade Bilateria animals attaining an organ-system level of complexity; typically with adult bilateral symmetry; *Acoelomata, Pseudocoelomata, Coelomata*

Acoelomates

SUBGRADE ACOELOMATA animals without internal body cavities; protostomial (first embryonic opening of alimentary cavity becomes mouth); skeletal or breathing systems absent; nervous system basically a nerve net with localized thickenings

Phylum Platyhelminthes flatworms; freshwater and marine, some terrestrial; alimentary system with single opening; vascular system absent; 10,000 species

Phylum Nemertinea (Rhynchocoela) proboscis worms, ribbon worms, largely marine, some freshwater, a few terrestrial; alimentary system with separate mouth and anus; vascular system present; 600 species

As a group, flatworms are believed to represent the most primitive Bilateria. Thus, early stocks of flatworms might have been ancestral to the proboscis worms and, directly or indirectly, to all other bilaterial phyla as well.

FLATWORMS

Phylum Platyhelminthes

CLASS TURBELLARIA planarians; free-living

CLASS TREMATODA flukes; bulk-feeding parasites

CLASS CESTODA tapeworms; fluid-feeding parasites

Among the free-living flatworms, the members of the order Acoela are generally believed to be the most primitive (and thus the closest link to the ancestors of all Bilateria). An acoel worm is often no more than $\frac{1}{2}$ mm long; it consists of a single-layered epidermis and an inner mass of mesoderm and endoderm cells (Fig. 33.18). A single opening in the epidermis on the underside of the flattened body is the sole component of an alimentary sys-

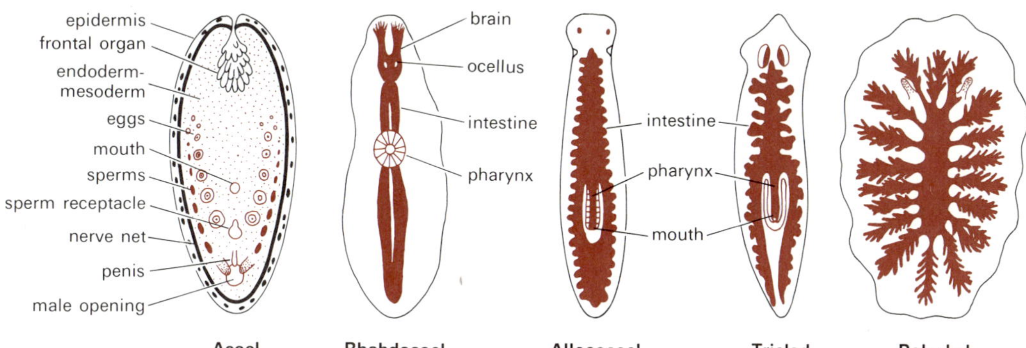

Fig. 33.18 Free-living flatworms. The major orders are illustrated. Note variations in the structure of the alimentary system.

tem; the interior endoderm cells digest food intracellularly. All other free-living orders possess a definite alimentary system composed of mouth, pharynx, and blind-ended intestine. These organs form a straight saclike tube in one order (*rhabdocoels*), a straight tube with lateral pouches in another (*alloeocoels*), a three-branched system with lateral pouches in a third (*triclads*), and a many-branched system in a fourth (*polyclads*).

The triclad planarians are the most familiar. Such a worm is up to $\frac{1}{2}$ inch long and has a roughly triangular head end with a pair of conspicuous dorsal eyes (Fig. 33.19). The epidermis is ciliated ventrally and secretes a slime track on which the cilia

Fig. 33.19 Planarian structure. (A) The free-living planarian *Dugesia*. (B) The ladder-type nervous system. (C) The excretory system. Flame bulbs are cup-shaped cells with flagella inside the cups. They filter the body fluids, and urine passes through a system of ducts that opens to the outside at several excretory pores. (D) The reproductive system. Each worm contains both a male and a female system.

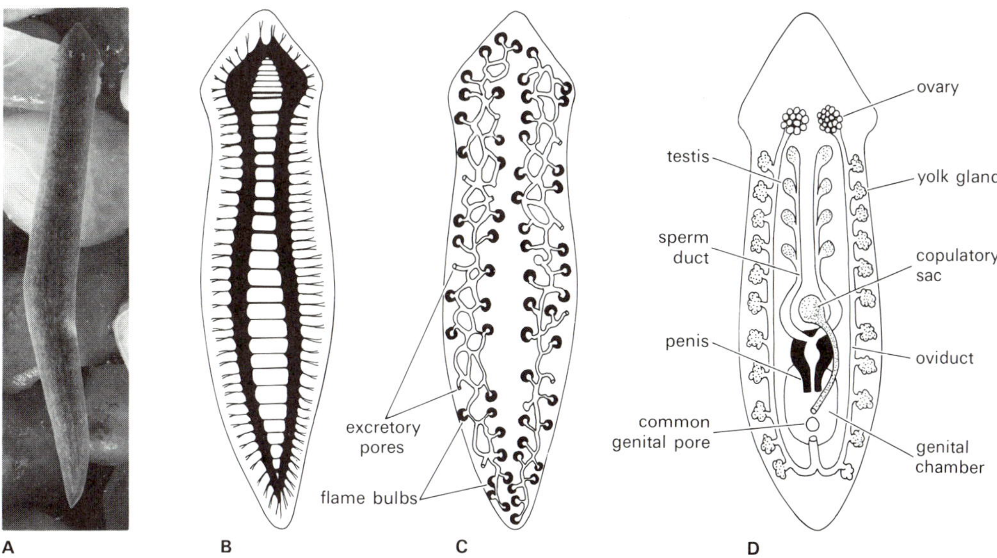

propel the animal in a gliding form of locomotion. Muscle layers underneath the epidermis also permit the worm to swim by undulations of its body. The nervous system contains a concentration of nervous tissue in the head, called the *brain ganglion.* A pair of ventral *nerve cords* leads from this ganglion posteriorly. Transverse nerve connections between the cords give the system a ladderlike appearance.

The mouth-anus opening is at the tip of a midventral tubular pharynx that can be protruded and retracted. The pharynx leads to three interconnected intestinal pouches, one pointing anteriorly and the other two posteriorly. The lining of these pouches contains flagellate and amoeboid cells; food is digested intracellularly, as in coelenterates. The space between the body wall and the intestine is filled solidly with connective tissue, in which the excretory and reproductive systems are embedded.

Excretion is accomplished by a so-called *flame-bulb* system (see Fig. 33.19). A flame bulb is a single cup-shaped cell with a tuft of flagella pointing into the cavity of the cup. On its outside surface the cell filters the body fluids, and the filtrate is then propelled by the flagella into a duct with which the flame bulb connects. The ducts of numerous flame bulbs join and lead to the exterior through several excretory pores. The reproductive structures include both male and female systems in the same worm. Each system consists of numerous pairs of sex organs and of ducts leading to a genital chamber. In mating each partner inserts a copulatory organ into the genital chamber of the other. Sperms are stored temporarily in a copulatory sac (see Fig. 33.19). Fertilized eggs are shed, and in triclads the eggs develop directly into miniature worms; in the marine acoels and polyclads, ciliated swimming larvae are formed first.

The exclusively parasitic flukes are structurally like free-living flatworms in most respects, but they exhibit three traits that appear to be direct adaptations to their parasitic way of life (Fig. 33.20). First, flukes lack an epidermis, the exterior layer being a tough and resistant horny cuticle secreted by mesenchyme cells. Second, eyes and other sense organs are reduced or lacking. And third, flukes have one or more muscular suckers, hooks, or other adhesive devices with which they hang on to host tissues. The life cycles are complex and usually require one or more intermediate hosts.

The tapeworms are intestinal parasites lacking an alimentary system of their own; they absorb molecular nutrients directly through their body surfaces. These worms likewise have an exterior cuticle instead of an epidermis. The body consists of a head equipped with hooks and suckers, a neck, and an up to 50-foot-long series of sex-organ-containing *proglottids* that are formed continuously behind the neck. Life histories again usually involve intermediate hosts (Fig. 33.21).

Both flukes and tapeworms are believed to have evolved from ancestral rhabdocoel turbellarians.

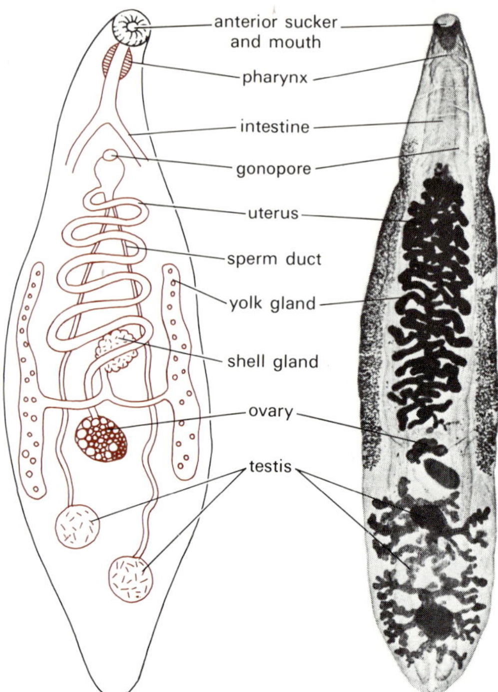

Fig. 33.20 Trematodes. The structure of *Clonorchis sinensis,* the Chinese liver fluke. Structures visible in the photograph are diagrammed at left.

Proboscis Worms

Phylum Nemertinea (Rhynchocoela)

These animals, often also called "ribbon worms," range in length from less than 1 inch to under 2 feet, but one species of *Lineus* can attain a length of some 100 feet (Fig. 33.22). Most nemertineans are marine, living at the bottom of shallow seas beneath shells and stones or in mud and sand. A few of the burrowing proboscis worms line their underwater dwellings with mucus, and some even construct distinct tubes.

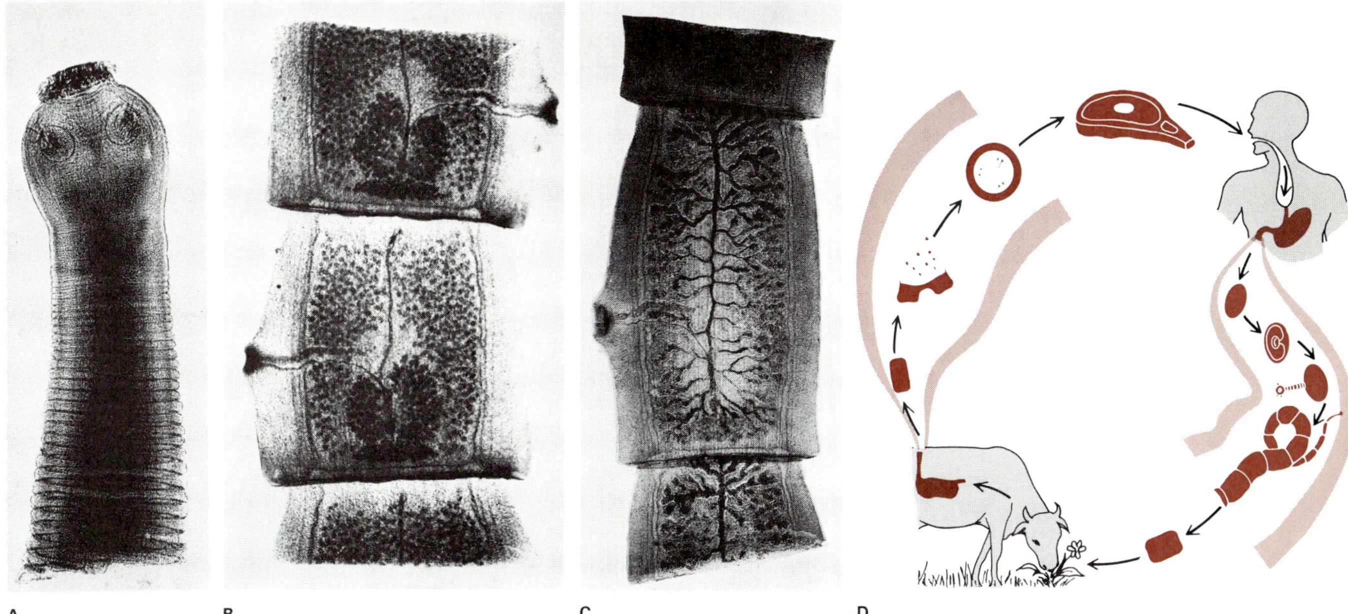

Fig. 33.21 Tapeworms. (A) Head, or scolex, with hooks and suckers. (B) Segmental sections, or proglottids, near middle of body. (C) Proglottids near hind end of body. Tree-shaped structures in (B) and (C) are reproductive organs. Note testes filling proglottids in (B) and genital pores opening on the sides. In (C) the uterus filled with eggs is conspicuous. (D) Beef tapeworm life cycle. Ripe sections of the worm pass with the feces from the human gut. Eggs are released from these sections in the gut of cattle. Walled, hook-bearing tapeworm embryos then encapsulate in beef muscle, and the embryos become adults in the human intestine. The head (scolex) of the worm is invaginated at first, but it soon everts, and with the hooks and newly developed suckers it attaches to intestinal tissues.

Nemertineans probably evolved from ancestral flatworms, but the body organization of proboscis worms is more complex than that of modern platyhelminths. The Nemertinea are the first phylum having an alimentary system with a one-way tube construction (see Fig. 33.22). Mouth, foregut, intestine, and anus are the principal components. The wall of the system is a single layer of ciliated cells, and digestion occurs *extracellularly,* i.e., right in the space of the alimentary tract. In this respect nemertineans are again different from all previous phyla. Food is moved through the tract by the muscular contractions of the body wall, and a solution of nutrient molecules in water is absorbed into the tract lining.

The nemertineans are also the first phylum having a circulatory system with blood. The system lies in the mesenchyme and consists basically of two lateral vessels joined anteriorly and posteriorly. In many cases a dorsal vessel or cross-connecting transverse vessels are also present. The blood of most nemertineans is colorless, but in some forms it contains hemoglobin in blood cells. Excretion is accomplished by a flame-bulb system similar to that of flatworms. Also similar is the nervous system, which contains anterior brain ganglia and a pair of lateral nerve cords in the body wall.

The most distinctive trait of a nemertinean is its *proboscis,* an anterior muscular tube which in the rest state lies in a chamber, the *rhynchocoel,* dorsal to the intestine (see Fig. 33.22). The tip of the proboscis is attached by a retractor muscle to the wall of the rhynchocoel. Muscular contraction of this wall exerts pressure on the fluid within the chamber, resulting in an explosive eversion of the proboscis to the exterior. This organ is used in locomotion, burrowing, and, principally, trapping food animals, which are encoiled by the proboscis. Often the tip of the proboscis is armed with a *stylet,* a sharp-pointed spike, and glands which secrete poison into a wound made by the stylet.

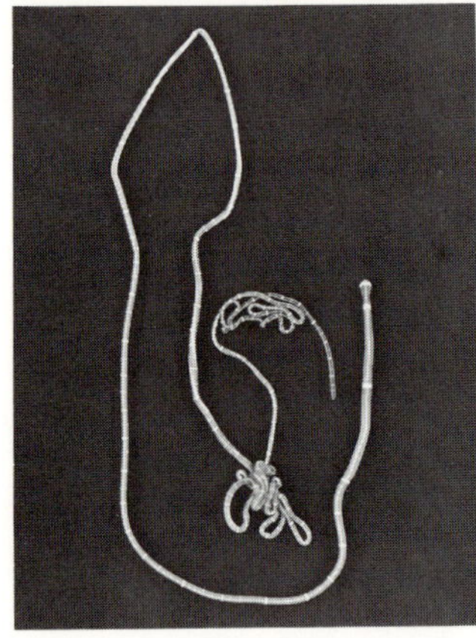

A

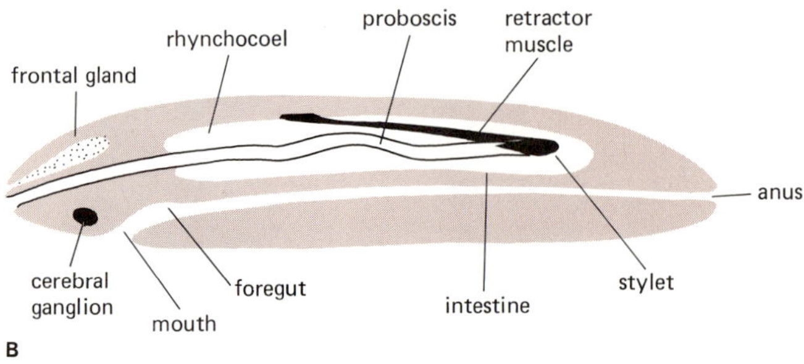

Fig. 33.22 Nemertineans. (A) The proboscis worm *Tubulanus*. The thicker, anterior end of the worm points upward at the right. (B) Nemertinean structure. This diagram depicts the position of the rhynchocoel and proboscis in rest condition. Note the one-way tube construction of the alimentary canal.

Pseudocoelomates

SUBGRADE PSEUDOCOELOMATA animals with mesoderm locally accumulated in a body cavity that is bounded by ectoderm and mesoderm; protostomial (first embryonic opening of alimentary cavity becomes mouth); skeletal, vascular, or breathing systems absent

Phylum Aschelminthes sac worms; marine, freshwater, and terrestrial; body often segmented superficially; cells or nuclei constant in number and arrangement for each species; musculature typically not in layers; pharynx elaborate; 15,000+ species

Phylum Acanthocephala spiny-headed worms; parasitic in vertebrates; with hook-bearing proboscis; alimentary system absent; with flame bulbs or excretory system absent; nuclear constancy in adult; 600 species

Phylum Entoprocta entoprocts; very largely marine; stalked and sessile, solitary and colonial; with mouth and anus inside a circlet of ciliated tentacles; 60 species

The sac worms and spiny-headed worms have vague evolutionary affinities to each other, and both phyla could be related very distantly to flatworms (Fig. 33.23). These animals are syncytial, the boundaries between cells disappearing during development. Moreover, each member of a given species is constructed from exactly the same number of embryonic cells. Thus all adults in a species are structurally identical, and their architecture can be mapped out precisely, nucleus for nucleus. Many of these animals also exhibit a superficial exterior segmentation that permits a telescoping of the body.

Entoprocts are the only pseudocoelomates that are not wormlike. They are microscopic and sessile, often colonial, each with a circlet of tentacles used in straining minute food particles out of water.

Sac Worms

Phylum Aschelminthes

CLASS ROTIFERA rotifers; 1500 species

CLASS GASTROTRICHA gastrotrichs; 200 species

CLASS KINORHYNCHA kinorhynchs; 100 species

CLASS PRIAPULIDA priapulids; 5 species

CLASS NEMATODA roundworms; 12,000+ species

CLASS NEMATOMORPHA hairworms; 80 species

This phylum encompasses a heterogeneous collection of types which are usually grouped into classes as above but which could be regarded

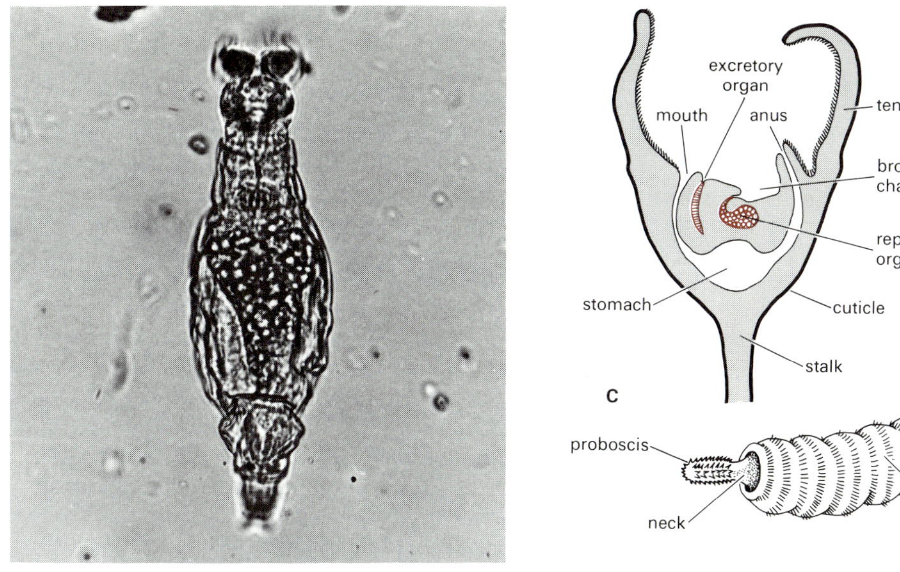

Fig. 33.23 Pseudocoelomates. (A) A rotifer, representative of the phylum Aschelminthes. (B) External features of a member of the Acanthocephala; the proboscis is shown extended in these parasitic worms. (C) Sectional view of an individual of the Entoprocta. The stalked cup-shaped body has a wreath of ciliated tentacles, a U-shaped alimentary system, and an anus that opens inside the tentacle ring. The animals also typically form colonies.

equally well as separate phyla. Only the rotifers and roundworms are sufficiently abundant to warrant consideration here.

The body of a rotifer is usually organized into a *head*, a *trunk*, and a tapered *foot* (Fig. 33.24 and see Fig. 33.23). The head bears an anterior *wheel organ*, a wreath of cilia used in swimming locomotion and in the creation of food-bearing water currents. At the end of the foot are two *toes*, each with a *cement gland*. The alimentary tract begins at the mouth ventral to the wheel organ and leads to a *mastax*, a complex muscular pharynx that contains horny jaws studded with teeth. The remainder of the tract is ciliated internally and terminates in the region between the toes.

From a brain ganglion dorsal to the pharynx lead two main ventral nerve cords. Most rotifers contain an eyespot, or *ocellus*, directly on the dorsal surface of the brain ganglion. Particularly characteristic of these animals is a *dorsal antenna*, a small surface projection dorsal to the brain ganglion. The precise function of this innervated and ciliated organ is obscure. The excretory system consists of a single pair of flame bulb clusters in the body cavity, with ducts opening in the hind part of the intestine.

During spring and summer, female rotifers produce eggs that develop into new females without being fertilized. These females in turn reproduce without fertilization, and many generations of females succeed each other in this manner (see Fig. 33.24). In the fall the females lay some eggs that are smaller than the rest. These hatch as small males, structurally simplified individuals lacking digestive systems but capable of producing sperms. Fertilization can then occur. The resulting eggs have thick hard shells and can resist unfavorable environments for months or years. Under suitably favorable conditions, as in the following spring, the shelled eggs develop into females. In some types of rotifers males are unknown altogether, the species being propagated exclusively by unfertilized eggs.

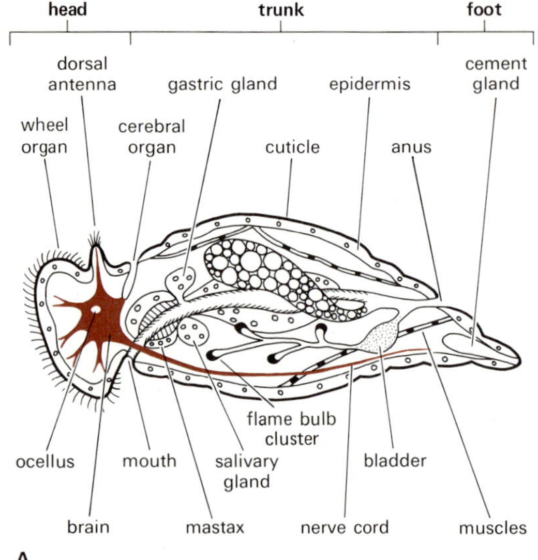

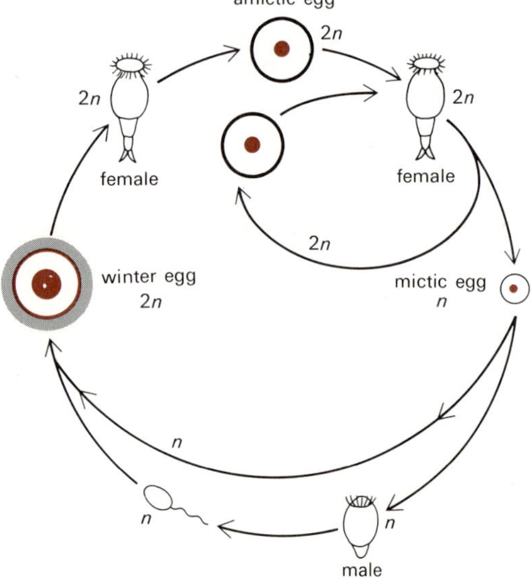

Fig. 33.24 Rotifer structure and development. (A) Diagram of animal seen from the side. (B) The life cycle. Amictic eggs are produced in spring and summer and develop without fertilization into new generations of females. Smaller mictic eggs are formed in fall and develop without fertilization into simplified males. If these males then fertilize mictic eggs, encysted winter eggs result. The latter develop into new females the following spring. The symbols *n* and 2*n* signify the presence of one or of two sets of chromosomes per cell, respectively.

This phenomenon of egg development without fertilization, or *parthenogenesis,* occurs also in other animal groups (for example, social insects; see Chap. 21).

Roundworms are possibly among the most abundant of all animals, both in numbers of individuals and in numbers of species. New species are being described at an average rate of one per day. Vast numbers of plants and nearly all animals harbor at least one and often more than one type of parasitic nematode, and these parasites are usually implicated when an animal is said to suffer from "worms." Moreover, free-living types are so abundant that a spade-full of garden earth is likely to contain up to a million tiny worms. Although slightly more than 12,000 species of nematodes have been classified, the actual number of existing groups undoubtedly is much higher. Some taxonomists suspect that about 500,000 species currently exist, an estimate that would make this class of organisms the second largest after the insects.

The mouth and anus of a nematode are at the tapered ends of the cylindrical body (Fig. 33.25). A resistant exterior cuticle is produced by a syncytial epidermis, which is thickened on its inner surface as four longitudinal *chords,* one dorsal, one ventral, and one on each side of the body. The two lateral chords are marked externally as faint lines. Longitudinal muscle cells lie in each body quadrant between the chords. The nervous system includes a nerve ring around the pharynx and a series of nerve cords connecting with this ring. The well-developed pharynx is a long muscular tube, often expanded along its length as one or more bulbous enlargements. The interior canal of the pharynx has a highly characteristic, three-cornered cross section. The excretory structures are unique. They consist of a pair of large cells, the *ventral glands,* situated under the pharynx. The necks of these cells lead forward to excretory pores.

Male nematodes are usually smaller than female ones and have curled posterior ends. During their larval development nematodes typically molt their cuticles, and enlargement of the larvae takes place at these molting stages. In the free-living types the larvae develop directly as new free-living adults. In parasitic types an infective stage is reached at a given point in development or during the adult phase. Up to that point the worms are free-living, and when they become infective they

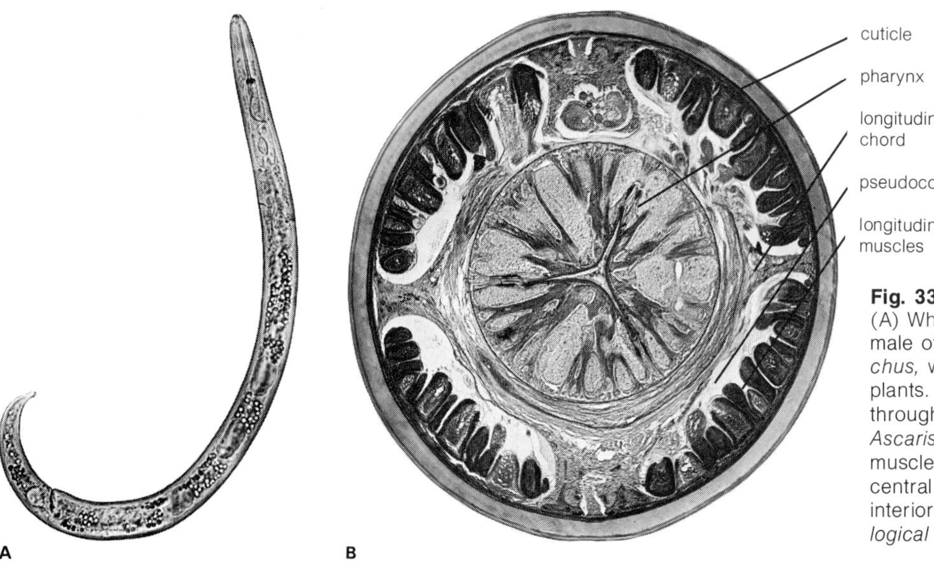

Fig. 33.25 Nematodes. (A) Whole view of a mature female of the nematode *Paratylenchus,* which causes disease in plants. (B) Cross section through the pharyngeal region of *Ascaris.* Note exterior cuticle, muscle quadrants, and thick central pharynx with triangular interior canal. (*B, Carolina Biological Supply Company.*)

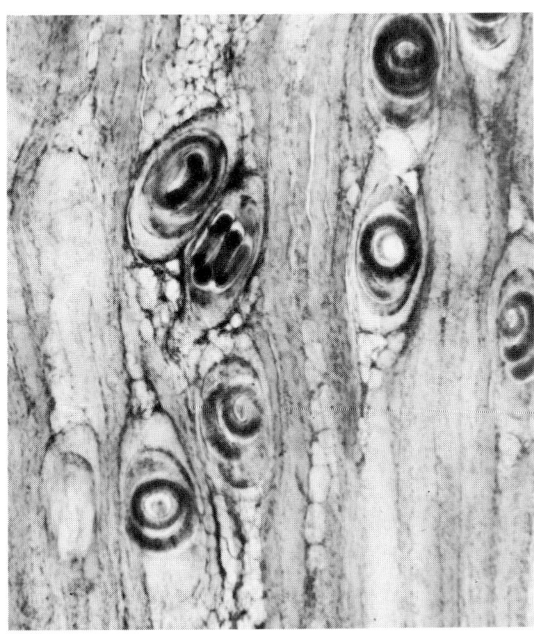

A

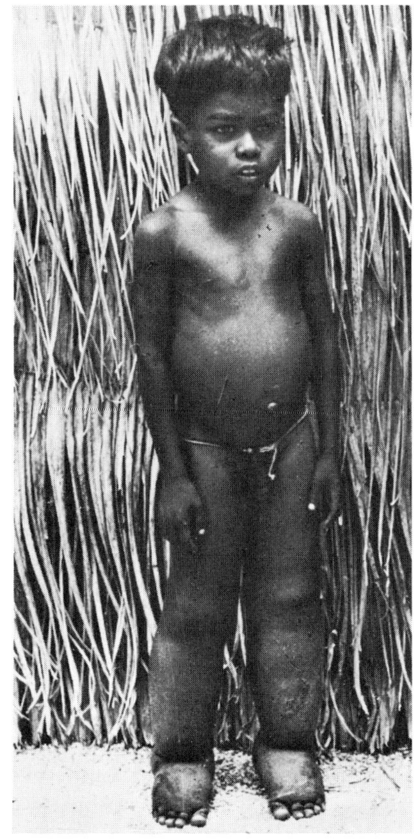

B

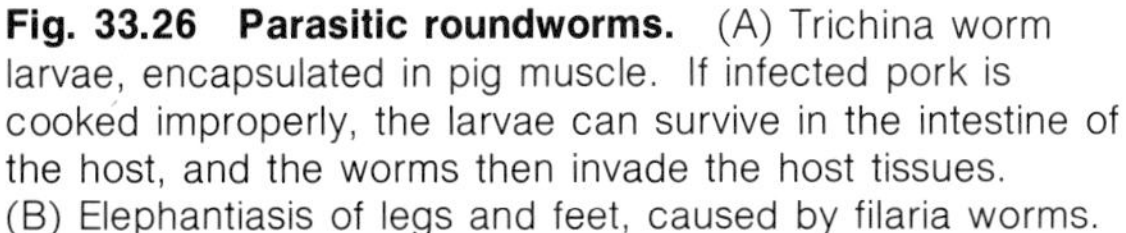

Fig. 33.26 Parasitic roundworms. (A) Trichina worm larvae, encapsulated in pig muscle. If infected pork is cooked improperly, the larvae can survive in the intestine of the host, and the worms then invade the host tissues. (B) Elephantiasis of legs and feet, caused by filaria worms.

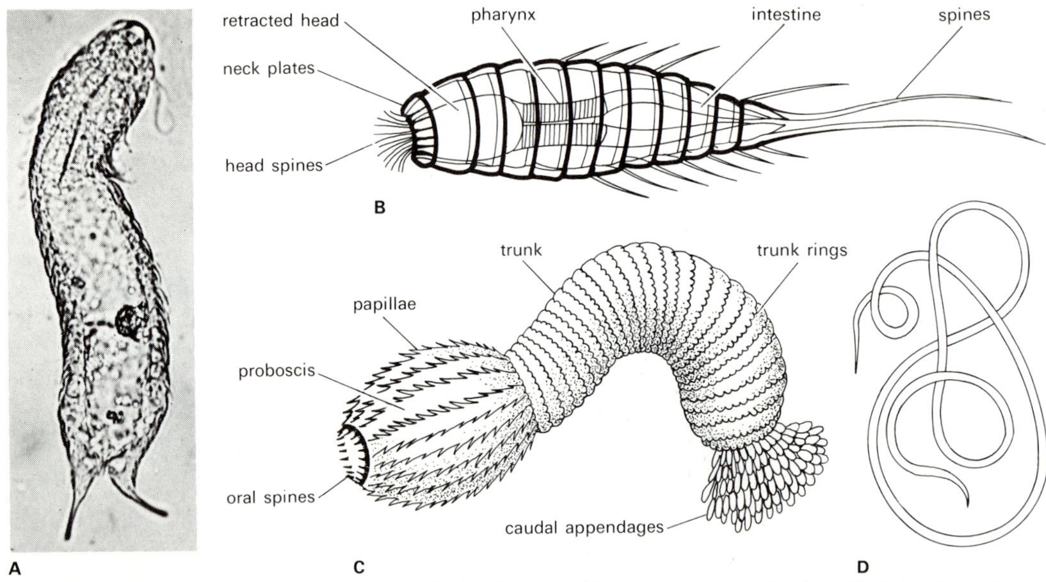

Fig. 33.27 Sac worms. (A) Gastrotrich. (B) Kinorhynch, with some structural details. (C) Priapulid, external features. (D) Hairworm outline. (*A, Carolina Biological Supply Company.*)

must enter a specific plant or animal host within a short time or perish. Numerous nematodes require one or more intermediate hosts.

Human beings are hosts of some 50 species of roundworms. Most of these, including for example the common intestinal nematode *Ascaris,* are fairly harmless. Those that are not include the *trichina worms,* introduced into the human body through ingestion of insufficiently cooked pork (Fig. 33.26); the *hookworms,* which live in soil and infect people by boring through their skin (see Fig. 8.25); the *guinea worms,* which form ulcerating blisters in human skin and from which the larvae of the next generation are released; and the *filaria worms,* which are transmitted by mosquitoes, block up lymph vessels, and cause the immense swellings of the disease *elephantiasis* (see Fig. 33.26).

The remaining groups of sac worms have many features that occur also in rotifers, nematodes, or both (Fig. 33.27). Gastrotrichs resemble rotifers in the organization of the body wall, and the exceedingly elongated hairworms are generally like nematodes. Gastrotrichs and kinorhynchs contain rotiferlike flame bulb systems, and in both classes, as well as in the priapulids, the pharynx is structured remarkably like that of nematodes. Kinorhynchs further have roundwormlike epidermal chords, they molt their larval cuticles, and they contain an adult nervous system nearly identical with that of priapulids. But each group also exhibits its own special traits; for example, surface spines and bristles in gastrotrichs, conspicuous superficial segmentation in kinorhynchs, a body having a bulbous, warty forward region in priapulids, and a reduced or absent alimentary system in the parasitic adults of hairworms. The shared traits thus suggest a reasonably close interrelation of these groups, but the unshared traits also suggest that the interrelation is probably not too close.

Review Questions

1 Review the distinguishing characteristics of Metazoa. Give definitions of coelomates, protostomial coelomates, deuterostomial coelomates, lophophorates, and schizocoelomates. Which phyla are included in each of these groups? What is a lophophore? How does a lophophorate animal feed?

2 Name the branches, grades, and subgrades of animals. What criteria define each of these ranks? What animals are included in each? Review the presumed evolutionary relationships of all major animal groups.

3 Show how Bilateria are subdivided taxonomically according to different patterns of mesoderm and coelom formation. What is the adaptive advantage of a coelom? Does a pseudocoel offer equivalent advantages?

4 What are the distinguishing characteristics of sponges? Describe some of the cell and tissue types of sponges, and indicate the function of each within the sponge body. Describe the three architectural variants of sponges. Review how sponges obtain nutrients.

5 Which phyla are included among the Radiata, and what diagnostic features distinguish these phyla? What are the distinguishing characteristics of coelenterates? Name the classes of coelenterates and describe the life cycle characteristic of each. Describe the structure of a polyp and a medusa.

6 Which phyla are included among acoelomates? Name the classes of flatworms and describe the structural features of planarians. Which flatworms are parasitic? How do they differ from free-living flatworms? Describe the life cycle of a parasitic flatworm.

7 Review the structural characteristics of proboscis worms (be sure to identify all distinguishing features of these animals). Where do nemertineans live, and how do they acquire food?

8 Give taxonomic definitions of pseudocoelomates generally and aschelminths specifically. Name the classes of aschelminths. Name a few representative examples of aschelminths.

9 Describe the structure and life cycle of a rotifer. Describe the structure of a nematode. Which nematodes can parasitize human beings? What diseases are caused by parasitic nematodes, and what are the symptoms of these diseases?

10 Describe the habitats of the animal phyla studied in this chapter.

Collateral Readings

Barnes, R. D.: "Invertebrate Zoology," 4th ed., Saunders, Philadelphia, 1980. An excellent up-to-date treatment of this topic.

Brien, P.: The Fresh Water Hydra, *American Scientist*, vol. 48, 1960. A detailed examination of this common but atypical coelenterate.

Buchsbaum, R.: "Animals without Backbones," University of Chicago Press, Chicago, 1948. A beautifully illustrated introductory account of invertebrates, including types studied in the present chapter.

Chitwood, B. G.: Nematoda, in "McGraw-Hill Encyclopedia of Science and Technology," rev. ed., vol. 9, 1966. A concise, informative article by one of the foremost students of roundworms.

Fingerman, M.: "Animal Diversity," Holt, New York, 1969. An excellent survey of animals, with emphasis on major evolutionary relations between animal groups. A good treatment of the invertebrates discussed in this chapter can be found in this paperback.

Goreau, T. F., N. I. Goreau, and **T. J. Goreau:** Corals and Coral Reefs, *Scientific American*, August 1979. Describes one of the richest and most beautiful ecosystems on earth, the huge limestone reefs built by coral polyps.

Hanson, E. D.: "The Origin and Early Evolution of Animals," Western University Press, Middletown, Conn., 1977. An excellent introduction to how biologists determine evolutionary interrelationships between animals.

Highman, C. P.: "Biology of the Invertebrates," 2d ed., Mosby, St. Louis, 1973. A good general textbook.

Hyman, L.: "The Invertebrates," vol. 1 (1940), chaps. 4, 6 to 8; vol. 2 (1951), chaps. 10 and 11; vol. 3 (1951), chaps. 12 to 14; McGraw-Hill, New York. Detailed accounts of the phyla discussed in this chapter.

Russell-Hunter, W. D.: "A Life of Invertebrates," Macmillan, New York, 1979. Another excellent introduction to animals discussed in this and following chapters.

Valentine, J. W.: The Evolution of Multicellular Plants and Animals, *Scientific American*, September 1978. One of several articles in this issue devoted entirely to evolution.

Chapter 34 Coelomates: Protostomes

Learning Objectives

After reading this chapter you should be able to:

1. Define coelomates; differentiate between lophophorates, schizocoelomates, and enterocoelomates, and list the phyla in each of these groups; define lophophore structurally and functionally.
2. State a taxonomic definition of the phylum Mollusca; name the classes of mollusks and name a representative organism of each; construct a diagram that depicts the structural traits of the hypothetical molluscan ancestor and illustrate the degree to which each class of living mollusks still exhibits the ancestral body construction.
3. Construct a diagram that depicts the principal structural features of a chiton, snail, tusk shell, clam, and squid, and state a function for each structure you identify; explain how the body organization of each mollusk listed in this objective is adapted to a particular way of life.
4. Define blood sinus and differentiate between open and closed circulatory systems; differentiate between trochophores, veligers, and glochidias; distinguish between torsion and detorsion and state the possible adaptive significance of torsion; define radula and mantle.
5. Give a taxonomic definition of the phylum Annelida; name the classes of annelids and list a representative of each; construct a diagram that depicts the external anatomy of polychaetes; construct a similar diagram that illustrates the structural organization of the digestive, nervous, and circulatory systems of polychaetes and earthworms, and state a function for each structure drawn; name the principal difference between polychaetes, earthworms, and leeches; define hirudin; specify the ecological and economic importance of at least one annelid.
6. State a taxonomic definition of the phylum Arthropoda; list the subphyla and classes of arthropods and list a representative organism of each class; construct a diagram that depicts the basic exterior structure of the arthropod body and the general organization of at least five organ systems; differentiate between simple and compound eyes; distinguish between gills, book gills, book lungs, tracheal systems, and spiracles.
7. Define and state the taxonomic significance of chelicerae, mandibles, and cephalothorax; construct a diagram that depicts the major external and internal structural differences between an insect, a crustacean, and a chelicerate arthropod and specify a function for each structure you identify.
8. Identify at least three different ways in which spiders capture prey; identify and state the function of at least three specialized appendages of spiders and scorpions; name and state the functions of at least five different appendages of a lobster; state the structural and functional relations between the X and Y organs of crustaceans; define nauplius; name at least two kinds of microscopic crustaceans; differentiate between millipedes and centipedes.
9. Define carapace, Malpighian tubules, and ovipositor; cite the two subclasses of insects, and list a representative organism of each; name and differentiate between the three superorders of winged insects; state at least three ways in which the mouthparts of insects have been modified for nutrient procurement.
10. Construct a diagram that depicts at least two kinds of insect metamorphosis; distinguish between imaginal disk, larva, nymph, and pupa; state the structural and functional relationships between endocrine structures that regulate molting in insects; outline one or more experiments whose results would demonstrate the effects of ecdysone and juvenile hormone on insect metamorphosis; give at least two examples of how arthropods benefit people and at least four examples of how arthropods can be harmful.

Kingdom	Branch	Grade	Subgrade	Phylum	Subphylum	Class
Monera						
Protista						
Fungi						
Plantae (Metaphyta)						
	Parazoa					
		Radiata				
Animalia (Metazoa)			Acoelomata			
			Pseudocoelomata			
				Phoronida		
				Ectoprocta		
	Eumetazoa			Brachiopoda		
						Amphineura
						Gastropoda
				Mollusca		Scaphopoda
						Pelecypoda
		Bilateria				Cephalopoda
				Sipunculida		
						Polychaeta
				Annelida		Oligochaeta
						Hirudinea
				Echiuroida		
				Oncopoda		
						Xiphosurida
					Chelicerata	Pantopoda
			Coelomata			Arachnida
				Arthropoda		
						Crustacea
					Mandibulata	Chilopoda
						Diplopoda
						Insecta
				Chaetognatha		
				Pogonophora		
				Hemichordata		
				Echinodermata		
				Chordata		

Grade Bilateria

SUBGRADE COELOMATA animals with true coelom, formed in various ways as a body cavity lined entirely by mesoderm

As pointed out in the preceding chapter, three groups of coelomates can be distinguished (see Fig. 33.4). In one, probably the most primitive, coeloms develop in largely unique ways, and the animals also possess a characteristic food-catching structure, namely, a lophophore. These types form the *lophophorates.* In a second group, the coelom arises by a splitting of mesoderm into outer and inner portions. Animals having such *schizocoelic* body cavities compose the *schizocoelomates.* In a last group, the coelom appears in the form of cavities within mesoderm pouches that grow out from the endoderm. These animals are said to possess *enterocoelic* body cavities, and they represent the *enterocoelomates.*

LOPHOPHORATES

Phylum Phoronida phoronids; marine; wormlike tube dwellers; 16 species (Fig. 34.1)

Phylum Ectoprocta moss animals; marine and freshwater; microscopic, colonial; 4000 species (Fig. 34.2)

Phylum Brachiopoda lamp shells; marine; often clamlike in appearance; 300 species (Fig. 34.3)

All the animals in these three phyla are sessile or sedentary *filter feeders;* they strain microscopic food organisms from their aquatic environment by means of ciliated tentacles. The latter are components of a *lophophore,* a body part in which the mouth is located. The alimentary tract is U-shaped, as is common in sedentary animals, and the anus opens outside the lophophore region. None of these animals has a clearly distinct head region. The body is simply marked into a lophophore-bearing forepart and a trunk, each enclosing a portion of the coelom (see Fig. 34.1).

Phoronids live in upright parchmentlike tubes, with the lophophore projecting from these housings. Ectoprocts (also called *Bryozoa*) have a superficial resemblance to entoprocts. Marine types secrete boxlike calcareous exoskeletons and grow in extensive colonies on seaweeds, wharf pilings, and other solid objects. Freshwater ectoprocts secrete massive gelatinous housings. Lamp shells resemble clams superficially (but the two shells are dorsal and ventral, not lateral as in clams). The present brachiopod genus *Lingula* (see Fig. 34.3) goes back 400 million years and represents the most ancient of the known "living fossils."

Each of the lophophorate phyla appears to represent a distinct evolutionary line, not obviously or closely related to any other coelomates.

SCHIZOCOELOMATES

Phylum Mollusca mollusks; marine, freshwater, and terrestrial; 50,000 species

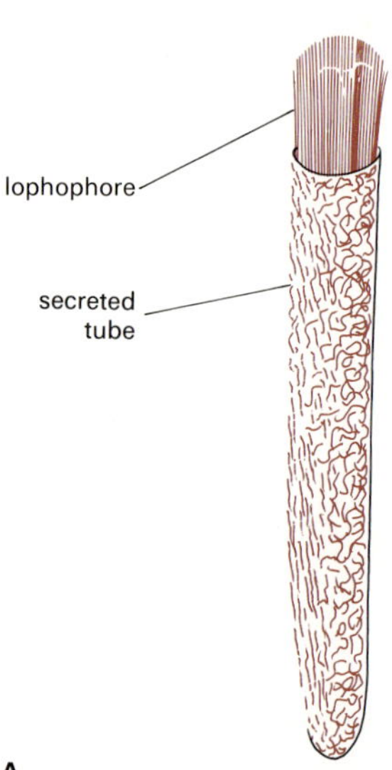

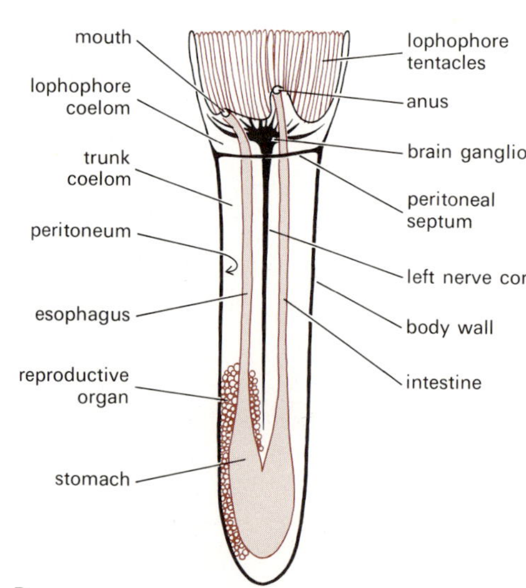

Fig. 34.1 Phoronids. (A) The secreted tube of a phoronid, with the lophophore projecting at top. (B) Sagittal section through a worm, simplified. Note the two parts of the coelom separated by the peritoneal septum.

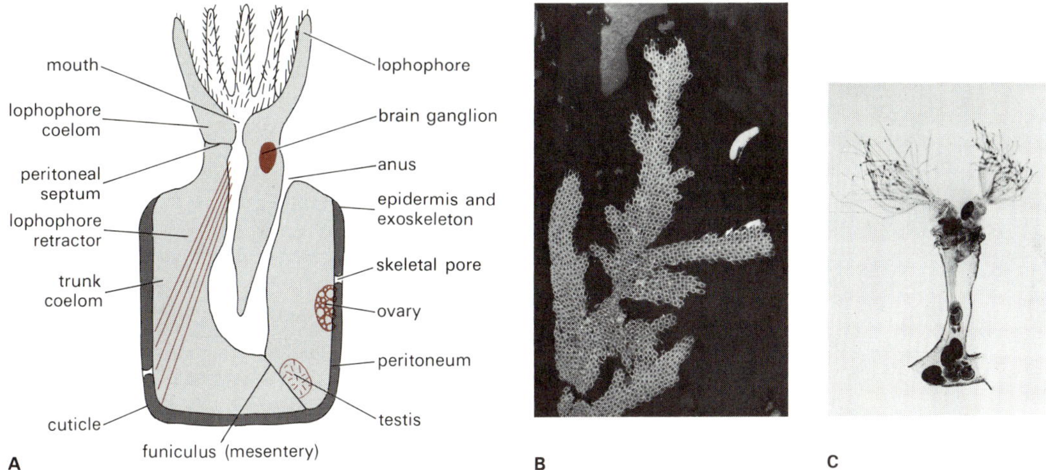

Fig. 34.2 Ectoprocts. (A) Diagrammatic section through a marine ectoproct with extended lophophore. The exoskeleton is calcareous. Note anus opening outside tentacle ring of lophophore. (B) A colony of marine ectoprocts on algae. Each small oval represents a single individual as in (A). (C) A freshwater ectoproct. The exoskeleton is gelatinous. Note lophophore at top. The black oval bodies are statoblasts, reproductive cysts capable of developing into new individuals.

Phylum Sipunculida peanut worms; marine, 250 species

Phylum Annelida segmented worms; marine, freshwater, and terrestrial; 9000 species

Phylum Echiuroida spoon worms; marine; 100 species

Phylum Oncopoda segmented claw-bearing animals; mostly terrestrial; 500 species

Fig. 34.3 Brachiopods. (A) A specimen of *Lingula*. The stalk is normally buried vertically in sandy sea bottoms. The lophophore is under the shell (valve). (B) Sagittal section through a brachiopod.

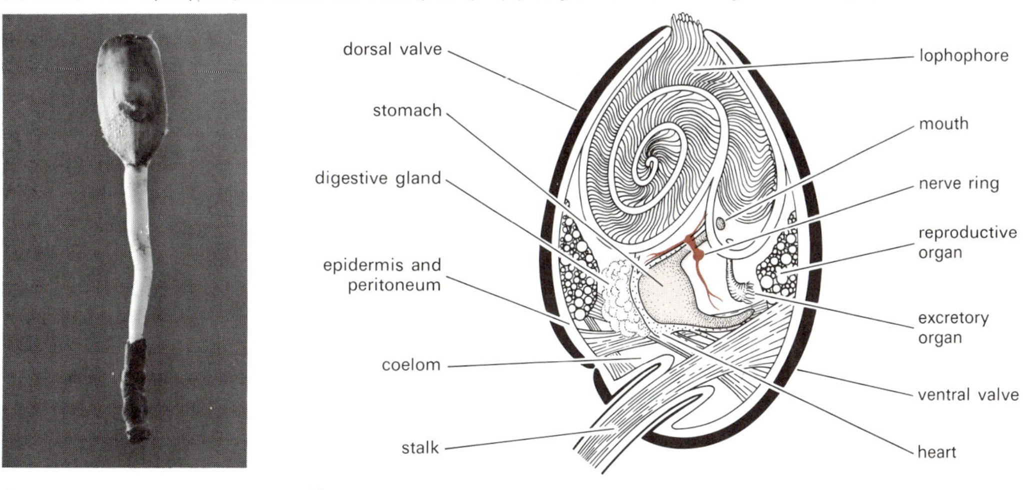

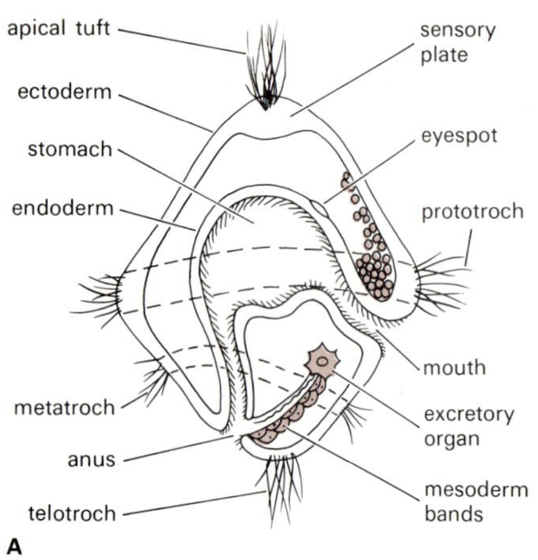

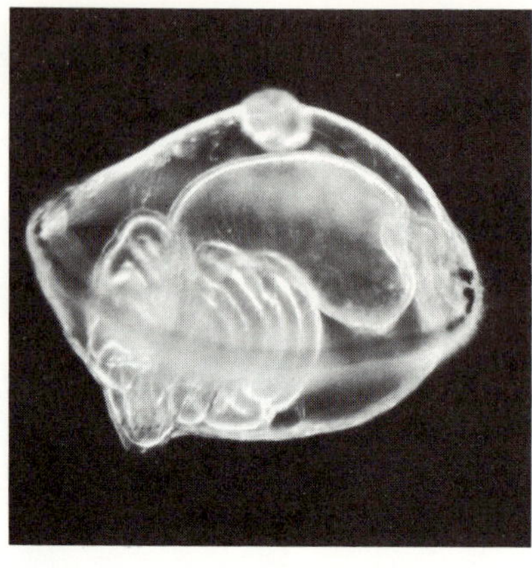

Fig. 34.4 The trochophore larva. Sagittal section. Mesodermal structures in color. The prototroch and metatroch are circlets of long cilia (indicated by broken lines). A metatroch or telotroch is not necessarily present in all types of trochophores. (B) Late trochophore, from life; the mouth is toward the right.

Phylum Arthropoda jointed-legged animals; marine, freshwater, and terrestrial; 1,000,000+ species

Although they include adult types as different as clams, earthworms, and houseflies, the schizocoelomates exhibit basically very similar patterns of development. Thus, the embryonic mesoderm splits into an outer layer along the body wall and an inner layer surrounding the alimentary tract, and a schizocoelic body cavity is formed in this manner. Moreover, the basic larval phase in all groups is a *trochophore* (Fig. 34.4). This form can occur as a ciliated, free-swimming larva or as a late stage in the development of the embryo. In many cases, other larval forms succeed the trochophore phase before the adult is produced.

Two main series of schizocoelomates appear to have evolved. An earlier one remained unsegmented and is represented by the first two phyla listed above. In a later series, represented by the last four phyla, body segmentation became more or less highly elaborated. The mollusks of the first series and the annelids and arthropods of the second are today among the most successful of all groups of living organisms (Fig. 34.5).

Mollusks

Phylum Mollusca soft-bodied animals

CLASS AMPHINEURA chitons; marine; head reduced, without eyes or tentacles; 700 species

CLASS GASTROPODA snails; marine, freshwater, and terrestrial; visceral hump typically coiled, with torsion or various degrees of detorsion; usually with shell; head with eyes and one or two pairs of tentacles; 35,000 species

CLASS SCAPHOPODA tusk shells; marine; shell tubular, open at both ends; foot a burrowing organ; 200 species

CLASS PELECYPODA clams; marine and freshwater; laterally compressed, with dorsally hinged shells; head rudimentary, food usually tongue-shaped and burrowing; radula absent; gills usually expanded to ciliary feeding organs; 12,000 species

CLASS CEPHALOPODA squids, octopuses; marine; head with tentacles; shell either external and chambered or internal and reduced; nervous system exceedingly well developed; with cartilaginous endoskeleton; 500 species

Ancestral mollusks that gave rise to the groups now in existence can be hypothesized to have had the following characteristics (Fig. 34.6).

The body consisted of a *head,* which may have borne a pair of sensory tentacles; a broad, ventral, muscular *foot,* functioning in a creeping form of locomotion; and a dome-shaped, dorsal *visceral hump,* which contained most of the organ systems. The body wall of the visceral hump was a *mantle* that secreted a protective layer of calcareous spicules along its outer surface. The mantle extended

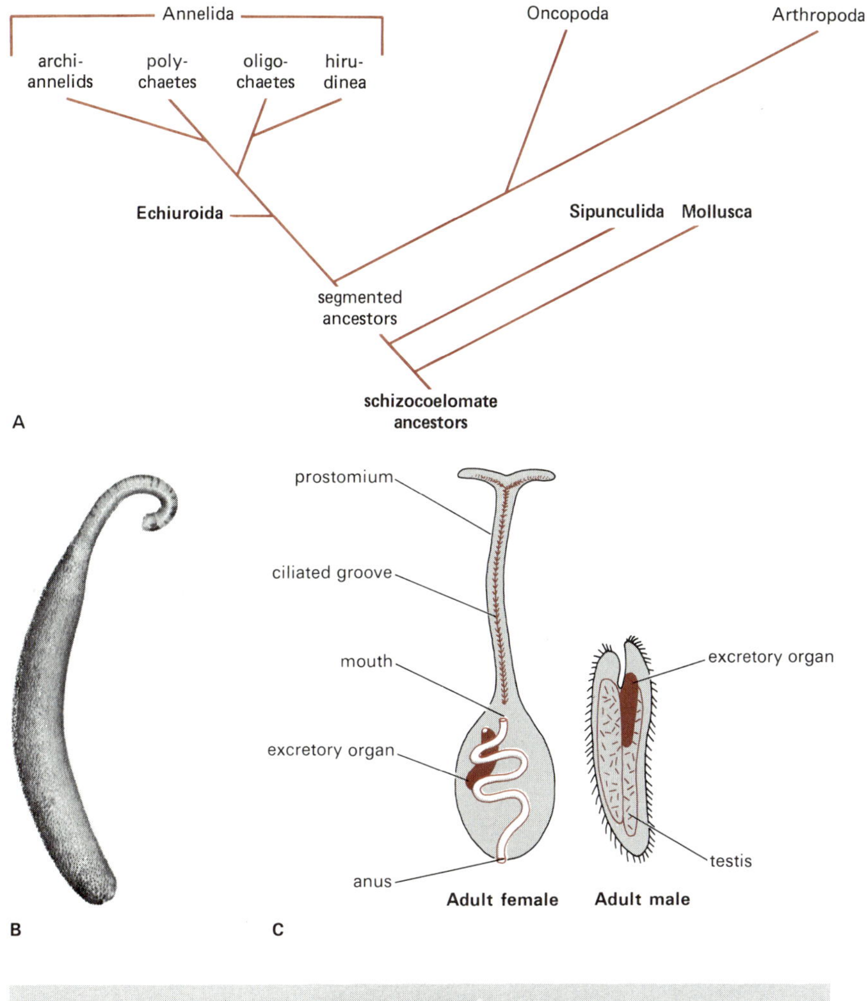

Fig. 34.5 Schizocoelomates. (A) Presumed evolutionary interrelations. Examples of some less common schizocoelomates follow. (B) A peanut worm, phylum Sipunculida. The mouth is at the tip of the curved tubular portion of the animal. (C) The spoonworm *Bonellia*, phylum Echiuroida. In the female the prostomium is a proboscislike food-catching extension. Note the simplified structure of the parasitic male. It lives permanently inside the excretory organ of the female. (D) *Peripatus*, of the phylum Oncopoda. The traits of this animal are transitional between those of annelids and those of arthropods (see later section of this chapter).

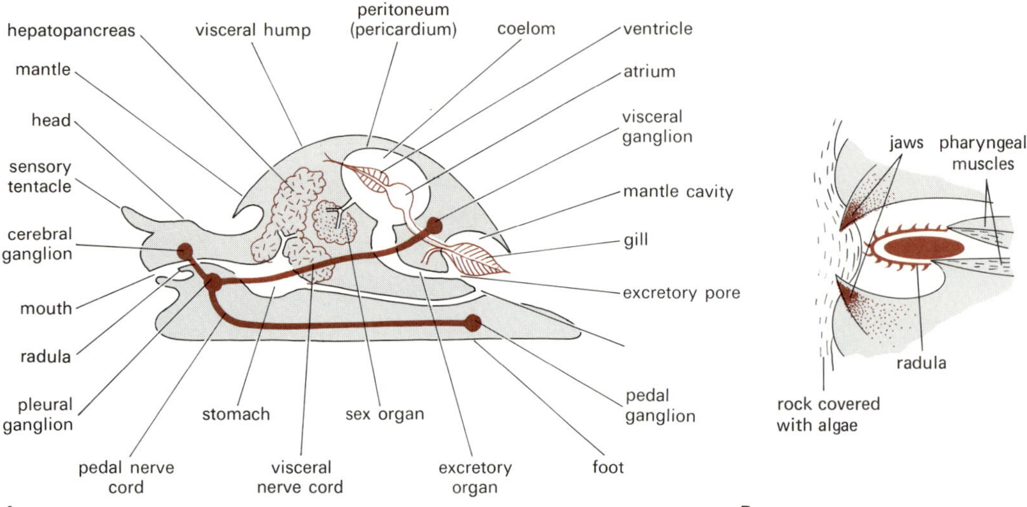

Fig. 34.6 Mollusks: structural characteristics. (A) Presumed structure of hypothetical ancestral mollusk in sagittal section. Of paired organs, only those on one side are indicated. Arteries from the ventricle lead to the blood sinuses in all parts of the body, and blood from there returns to the heart via the two excretory organs, the two gills, and the two atria of the heart. (B) The molluscan radula, as in a squid. The radula is a horny band with teeth and is moved back and forth by muscles around a cartilaginous supporting prop (dark oval). Unlike most mollusks, a squid also has horny jaws, as shown here.

as an overhanging rim around the sides of the body, particularly at the posterior end. The space under this posterior rim represented a *mantle cavity*. Projecting into it were a pair of feathery or leaflike *gills*. The mouth led into a pharynx equipped with a *radula*, a horny band studded with teeth. Muscles moved this band back and forth over a cartilaginous supporting rod in the pharynx. Protruded through the mouth, the radular apparatus served in rasping pieces of tissue from plant or animal food organisms. From the pharynx, food passed through an esophagus into a stomach, which connected with a conspicuous digestive gland, or *hepatopancreas*. The intestine opened posteriorly into the mantle cavity.

The nervous system consisted of a nerve ring around the esophagus, thickened in places as *ganglia*. From this ring emanated two pairs of nerve cords, one pair into the foot, another into the dorsal hump. Ganglia were present also at the ends of these cords. The ancestral mollusk probably possessed a circulatory system containing a heart with one ventricle and two posterior atria, as well as vessels from and to the gills. Additional vessels passed into all other body regions and opened into free spaces, or *blood sinuses*, that permeated all organs. Such a system was an *open* circulation, blood here flowing in great part outside vessels. The coelom was largely reduced to a *pericardial cavity* around the heart. Leading into this coelomic space were the ducts of the sex organs, located anteriorly, and passing posteriorly were a pair of excretory tubules. These led from the pericardial coelom to excretory pores in the mantle cavity near the anus. Sex cells reached the outside through the excretory ducts.

This ancestral organization is still preserved to varying degrees in the mollusks now in existence.

Chitons

CLASS AMPHINEURA

Chitons have deviated least from the ancestral construction. The head has become reduced, and tentacles and eyes are absent (Fig. 34.7). Eight overlapping shell plates secreted by the mantle form an exoskeleton. A narrow groove circling the animal under the mantle rim represents the mantle cavity, and into it project many pairs of small

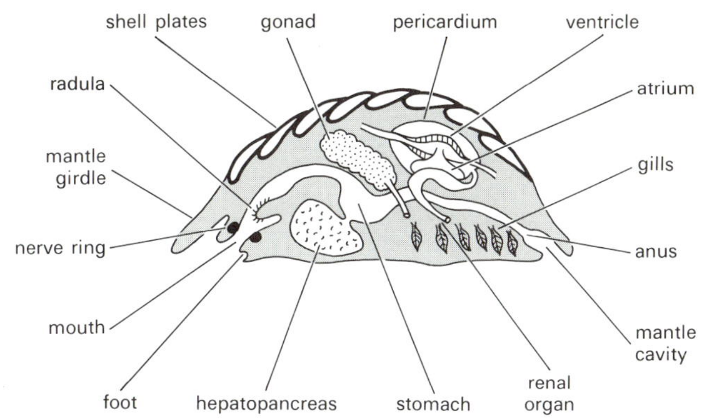

A B

Fig. 34.7 Chitons. (A) Dorsal view. Note the eight shell plates in the mantle. (B) Sagittal section showing some of the internal structures.

gills. In conjunction with the head reduction the nervous system has become simplified, and the only other notable deviation from the ancestral pattern is the presence of separate reproductive ducts to the outside. This condition is characteristic also of all other mollusks, as is the elaboration of the excretory ducts as complex *renal organs.*

Chitons live on rocky seashores, usually on exposed rocks or in shallow water. They cling tightly to rocks, their soft bodies protected by shell plates, and they subsist largely on marine algae. Chitons are exceedingly sluggish; they sometimes move only a few inches over a period of several weeks.

Snails

CLASS GASTROPODA

In snails the ancestral construction is again largely preserved, but two innovations have evolved in the larval stages that give a snail its characteristic organization.

First, the trochophore develops into a *veliger,* a larval form equipped with an elaborate ciliary girdle used as a swimming organ (Fig. 34.8). The dorsal side of the veliger eventually enlarges pronouncedly, and the developing visceral hump thus pushes up in a dorsal direction. However, this upward growth occurs unequally on the left and right sides, resulting in a spiral coiling of the visceral hump and the shell covering it. The upward growth also has the effect of pulling the alimentary tract into a U shape, until the anus comes to lie quite close to the mouth.

The second innovation is *torsion:* the whole visceral hump of the veliger rotates 180° relative to the rest of the body, usually in a counterclockwise direction (Fig. 34.9). As a result, the mantle cavity comes to lie anteriorly above the head; the gills are anterior; the anus, excretory pores, and reproduc-

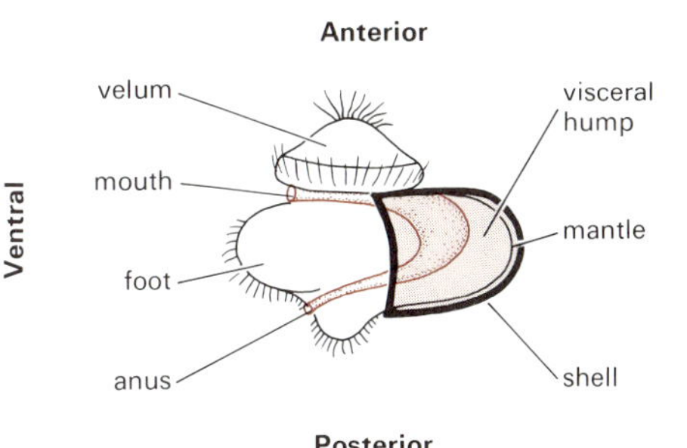

A B

Fig. 34.8 The veliger larva. (A) A mature veliger. Remnants of the earlier trochophore stage are still discernible anteriorly. The dorsal visceral hump has enlarged greatly, producing a U loop in the alimentary tract. (B) Veliger of a marine snail, from life. The view is from the anterior end, with the velum nearest and the dorsal visceral hump behind.

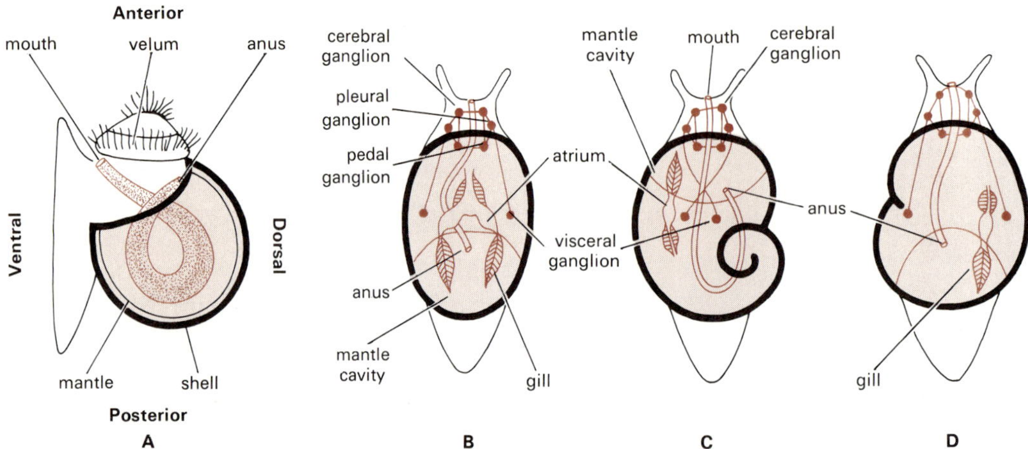

Fig. 34.9 Torsion and detorsion. (A) Sagittal view of veliger after torsion. The alimentary tract is now coiled, with the anus shifted to same (anterior) side as mouth; compare with Fig. 34.8A. (B) to (D), Top views. (B) Original condition before torsion. Paired organs present, anus posterior. (C) After torsion comparable to (A). Only right members of paired organs present (on left side), anus anterior, visceral cords form figure eight. (D) 180° detorsion. Pattern resembles (A), but only right members of paired organs are present.

tive openings all are anterior, in the mantle cavity; the alimentary tract is twisted from a U shape into a loop; and the heart is turned around.

The evolution of torsion undoubtedly is an adaptation to the adult way of life. Snails protect themselves by withdrawing into their shells, and inasmuch as a shell has only one opening, it is advantageous that both mouth and anus should open there, the mouth closer to the ground. Also, torsion places the heaviest part of the shell out of the way, over the posterior part of the body. As a result, the center of gravity is shifted in a manner that facilitates movement of shelled gastropods (Fig. 34.10).

In some snails, notably the land and sea slugs, shells are reduced or absent altogether (Fig. 34.11 and Color Fig. 37). Development here includes a *detorsion* that brings the visceral hump back partly or wholly to its original larval position (see Fig. 34.9). To avoid desiccation, land slugs must live in moist environments (under rocks, boards, or in holes). Land slugs usually emerge at night and feed on vegetation. Indeed, slugs can severely damage garden vegetables.

The mantle cavity of all land snails is modified from a gill chamber to a lung chamber, and such snails breathe air. Some of these have adapted secondarily to aquatic life but are still lungbreathers and must surface periodically for air.

Tusk Shells

CLASS SCAPHOPODA

This small class comprises some 350 species of sand-burrowing mollusks. The animals are elongated in a dorsal direction and are covered by tapered, tubular shells, which give them the appearance of canine teeth or tusks (Fig. 34.12). From the wider, ventral end of a shell projects the muscular, conical foot that serves as a digging organ. Also protruding at the ventral end is a reduced, proboscislike head, to which are attached numerous grasping tentacles. Although of minor biological importance, tusk shells are used as money in some primitive human societies.

Clams

CLASS PELECYPODA

In clams the ancestral body has become flattened from side to side, the head has disappeared, and the gills have expanded into ciliary food-collecting organs that also retain a breathing function (Fig. 34.13).

The two shells, or *valves,* of a clam are secreted by the paired lobes of the mantle, which lie on each side of the visceral mass. Pearls are formed when foreign objects lodge between valves

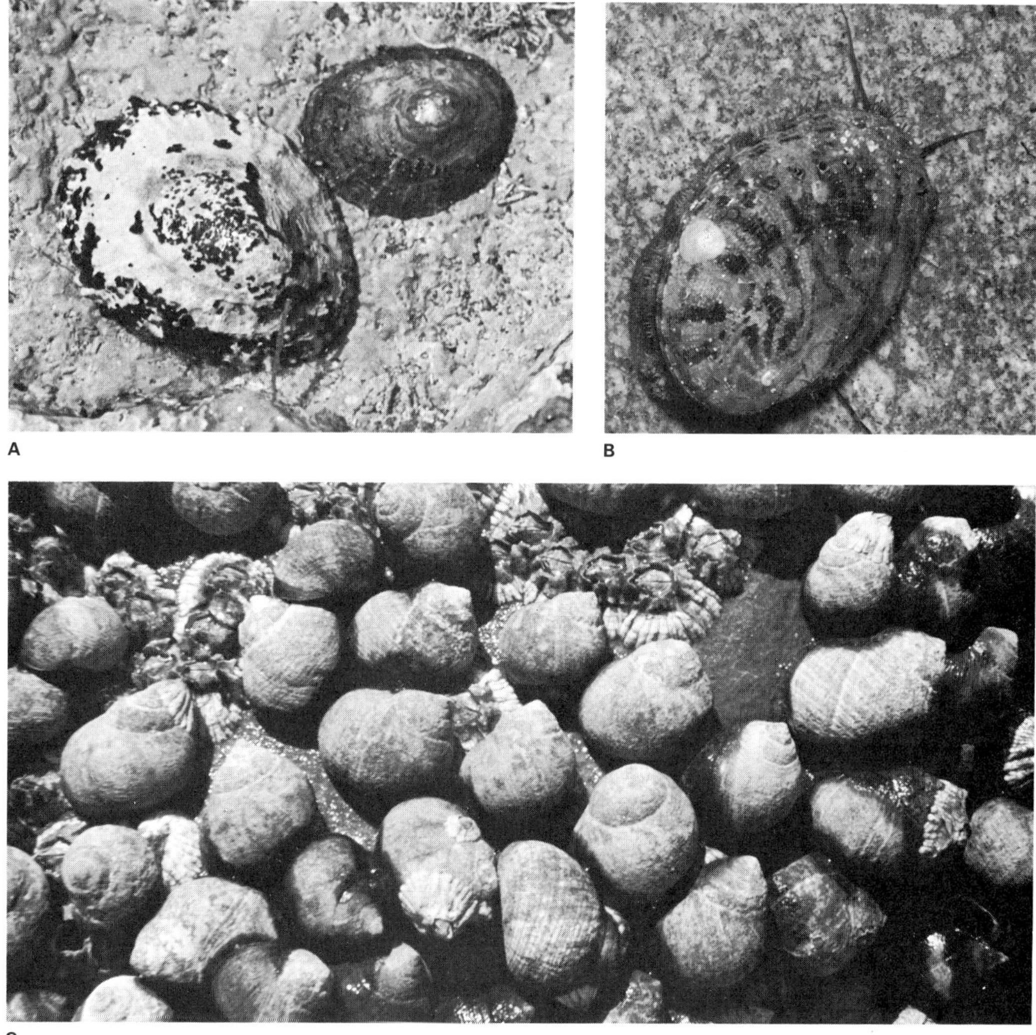

Fig. 34.10 Snails. (A) Limpets. The shell is hardly coiled. (B) Abalone. Shell coiling slight. Note row of shell perforations for excurrent water. (C) Periwinkles. Shell coiling pronounced. These snails live in tidal zones.

and mantle lobes. Such objects then become enveloped by successive layers of a crystalline substance secreted by the mantle. Some pearls are produced by freshwater clams, but the most valuable kinds come from marine oysters of the Persian Gulf and elsewhere in Asia.

The visceral mass of a clam is suspended from the dorsal midline. Continuous ventrally with the visceral mass is the foot. Many clams can protrude the foot between the shells and use it for digging and for a slow, push-pull form of locomotion.

Projecting into the mantle cavity are two pairs of large, platelike gills. They continue posteriorly as a horizontal partition that divides the hind region of the mantle cavity into a dorsal compartment and a ventral main compartment. Both open to the outside along the posterior shell edges, the dorsal chamber forming an *excurrent siphon,* the

A

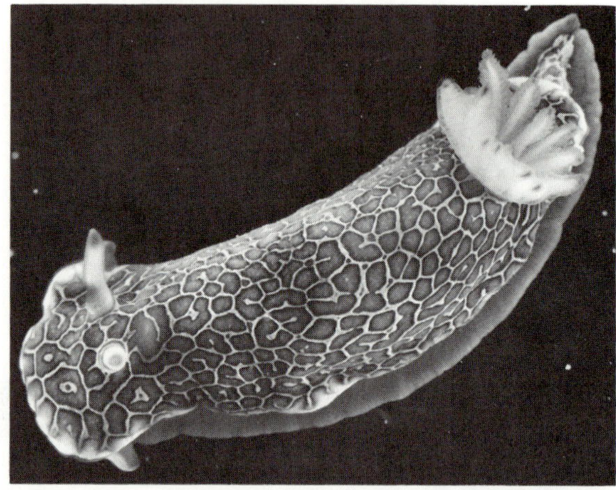

B

Fig. 34.11 Slugs. (A) Spotted garden slug, *Limax maximus,* on a tomato. (B) A nudibranch sea slug. Note the breathing rosette at the posterior of the animal (upper right of photo).

Fig. 34.12 Scaphopods. A tusk shell, as positioned in a sand burrow. Note tusklike shell, open at both ends. From the lower end projects a bulbous burrowing foot and a small head that bears grasping tentacles.

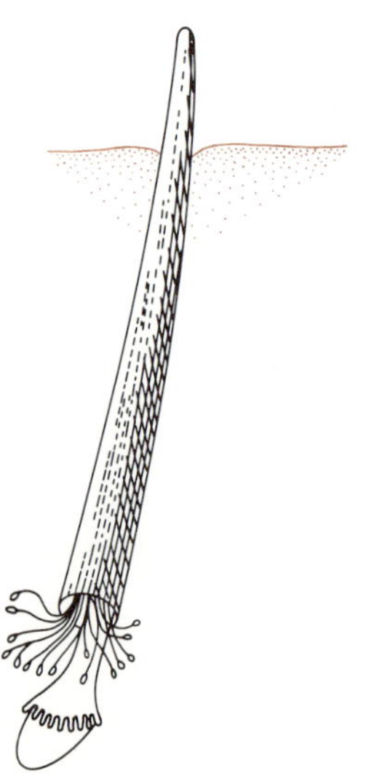

ventral one, an *incurrent siphon.* In some clams these siphons are extended as long retractile tubes projecting beyond the valves.

Cilia on the gills draw food-bearing water through the incurrent siphon. Food caught up in mucus on the gills then passes forward to *labial palps,* tissue flaps that conduct food into the mouth. Water passes into the gills through *gill pores* and leaves via the excurrent siphon (see Fig. 34.13C). Clams are without a radula, a superfluous structure in a filter-feeding animal. The alimentary tract passes through the pericardial coelom, coils through the visceral mass, and opens into the excurrent siphon. In conjunction with the reduction of the head, the nervous system is also reduced to some extent.

Marine clams develop via free-swimming trochophore and veliger larvae. Freshwater types produce highly modified veligers called *glochidia* (Fig. 34.14). These larvae perish unless they can attach themselves within a short time to fish gills or fins, where they live parasitically until they become independent adults. Most clams are semisedentary, partly or wholly buried in mud, with the siphon protruding up into clear water. Some are permanently attached, as for example oysters and also

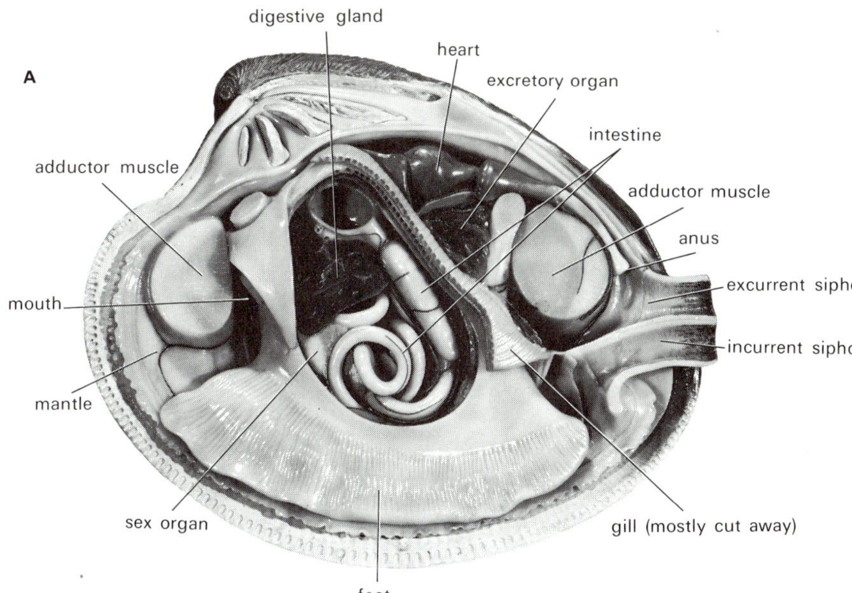

Fig. 34.13 Clam Structure. (A) Cutaway model indicating general anatomy. (B) Some of the internal organs in sagittal view. Products of the excretory and reproductive organs exit through the excurrent siphon. (C) Food and water paths. A pair of gill plates on one side of the clam are depicted, the outer gill plate shown cut away. A second pair of gill plates (obscured by visceral mass) is located on the opposite side of the clam. Arrows indicated ciliary paths of food particles toward mouth and water through the gill pores and into the excurrent siphon via the dorsal gill passage.

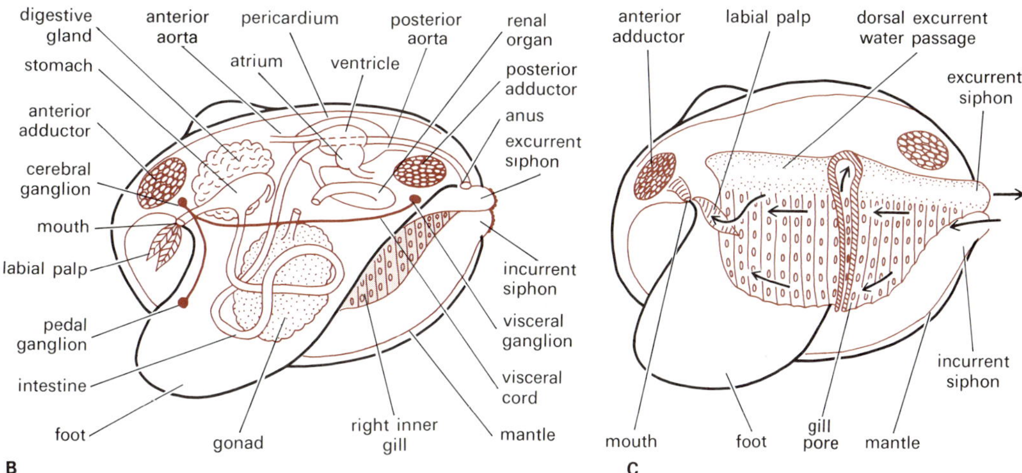

giant clams, which may be 2 yards wide and weigh $\frac{1}{4}$ ton.

Noteworthy for their destructiveness are the wood-boring clams. For example, the "shipworm" *Teredo* uses its reduced, roughened valves to bore tunnels in ship bottoms and wharf pilings, leaving nothing but sawdust, which the clams use for food. They secrete *cellulase,* a unique digestive enzyme among animals (even termites do not digest wood on their own but depend on flagellate protozoa).

Squids, Octopuses

CLASS CEPHALOPODA

These animals exhibit the most pronounced departures from the ancestral construction. Early cephalopods elongated in a dorsal direction (like snails), but growth remained equal on both sides

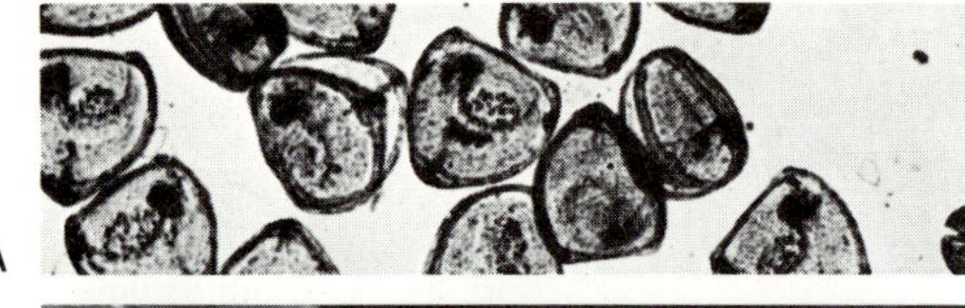

Fig. 34.14 Clams. (A) Glochidia larvae of a freshwater mussel. (B) An adult freshwater clam. Note conspicuous burrowing foot.

and the visceral hump therefore formed a flat coil. Also, the covering shell became partitioned into progressively larger compartments as the animal grew, and only the last, largest compartment was occupied by the animal. All earlier compartments were filled with air (Fig. 34.15). Cephalopods thus had considerable buoyancy, which permitted them to adopt a free-swimming existence. In conjunction with this new mode of life the foot became modified partly to muscular prehensile tentacles, which also equipped the animals as predatory carnivores. The chambered nautilus today still exemplifies this early stage of cephalopod evolution. In other evolutionary lines the shells became reduced greatly or were lost altogether, and the nervous and sensory systems became highly developed in conjunction with rapid, swimming locomotion. The result was the emergence of modern squids and octopuses.

In a squid, a thick muscular mantle surrounds the visceral mass (Fig. 34.16). Under this mantle on the upper side lies a horny, leaf-shaped *pen*, the remnant of the shell. The forward edge of the mantle, or *collar*, fits over a midventral tubular *funnel* that leads to the mantle cavity. On contraction of the mantle muscles the collar clamps tightly around the funnel, and water is forced from the mantle cavity out through the funnel tube. In this manner a squid jet-propels in the opposite direction.

A squid has 10 tentacles. One long pair catches prey, and the others hold the prey while powerful horny *jaws* in the mouth bite chunks out of it. A radula is also present. The alimentary tract is U-shaped and includes a stomach, to which a large digestive gland is connected. The anus opens anteriorly into the mantle cavity. An *ink sac* discharges into the mantle cavity via the anus. Expelled through the funnel, a cloud of ink probably distracts an enemy while the squid makes its escape.

Fig. 34.15 The chambered nautilus. (A) Sectional view showing position of some of the organs. Note double circlet of tentacles and absence of ink sac. Gills shown on one side only. (B) Section through shell. Note partitioned compartments and the siphuncle, a gas-filled channel.

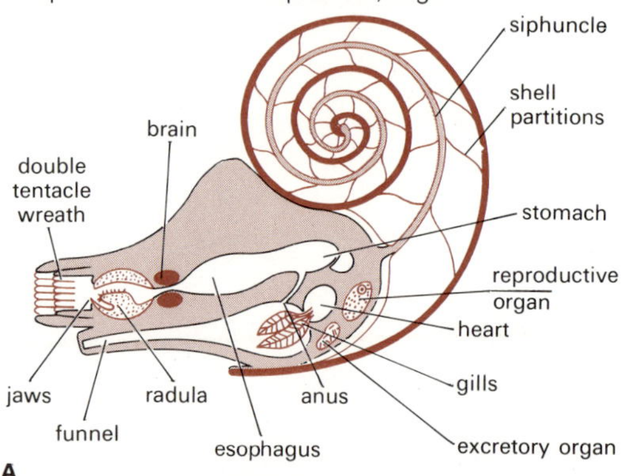

A

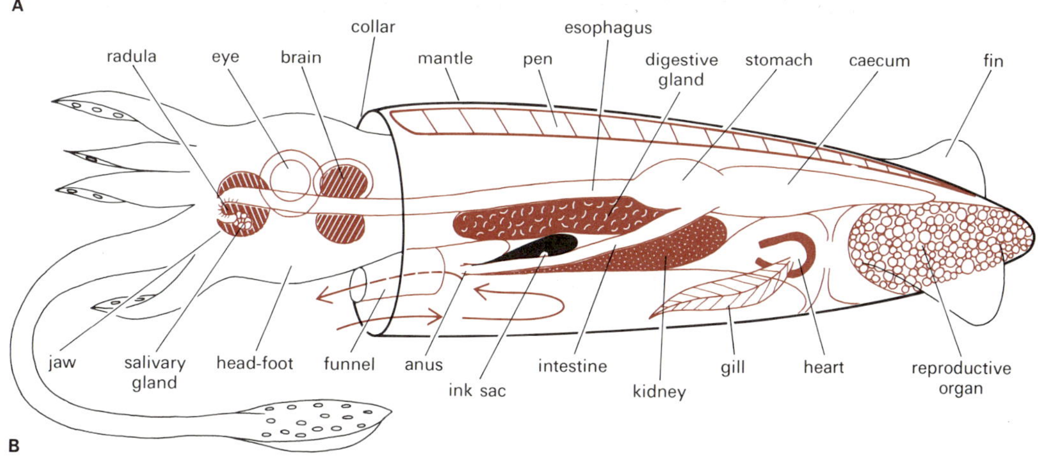

B

Fig. 34.16 Squids. (A) A cuttlefish, a squidlike cephalopod. (B) Squid structure. Tentacles are shown on left side only. Arrows indicate path of water into and out of mantle cavity, resulting in jet propulsion backward. Note that the head-foot end is anatomically ventral, the hind end, dorsal; the side where the pen is located is anterior, the opposite side, posterior.

In the highly developed nervous system, several fused pairs of ganglia form a complex brain, which is surrounded by a cartilage capsule. Located between the eyes, the brain represents the dorsal part of a nerve ring that encircles the esophagus. From the ring elaborate tracts of nerves lead throughout the body. The eyes of squids are as complex as those of vertebrates. Breathing is accomplished by a pair of feathery gills in the mantle cavity. The circulation is closed—blood flows entirely inside vessels. A heart ventricle pumps blood throughout the body, and returning blood passes first through the kidneys, then through *gill hearts* to the gills. Oxygenated blood circulates from the gills back to the main heart. The coelom is spacious, occupying the hind part of the visceral mass. A single sex organ and a pair of kidneys in the coelom open through separate ducts into the mantle cavity.

Fig. 34.17 An octopus.

Cephalopods are without larvae, the eggs developing directly into miniature adults. Squids are all active swimmers, and giant squids up to 60 feet long are the largest invertebrate animals. Giant squids inhabit the deep ocean, where they are preyed on by large fishes and particularly by toothed killer and sperm whales. Octopuses, many of which lack an internal shell entirely, lead a semisedentary life in dark cavities and coral reefs (Fig. 34.17). Most are quite small, but the largest have an arm spread of about 30 feet and can be dangerous to people.

Annelids

Phylum Annelida segmented worms

CLASS POLYCHAETA clamworms, tube worms; largely marine; with segmental parapodia, numerous bristles; with trochophore larvae

CLASS OLIGOCHAETA earthworms; terrestrial and freshwater; head reduced; parapodia absent, few bristles; without larvae

CLASS HIRUDINEA leeches, mostly freshwater parasites; parapodia and bristles absent; number of segments fixed; without larvae

The segmentation of the annelid body affects all organ systems except the alimentary tract, and the coelom too is partitioned segmentally by peritoneal membranes (*septa*). Best seen in polychaetes, the most primitive annelids, segmental development begins with a marked posterior elongation of the trochophore larva (Fig. 34.18). This extension is accompanied by a forward growth of the mesodermal teloblast band on each side. The bands produce a series of paired cell clusters (*somites*), which later hollow out and become segmental coelom sacs. Segments mature in anteroposterior succession, the anterior segments being the oldest. In each larval segment ventral ingrowths from the ectoderm give rise to segmental portions of the nervous system and to excretory organs called *metanephridia*. Laterally the ectoderm and mesoderm fold out as a *parapodium,* a flap of body wall on each side. Stiff chitinous bristles (*setae*) later develop on the parapodia. Blood vessels, muscles, and sex organs form from parts of the peritoneal mesoderm.

apical tuft
1
2
3
4
proto-
nephridium
teloblasts
mesodermal
somites
A

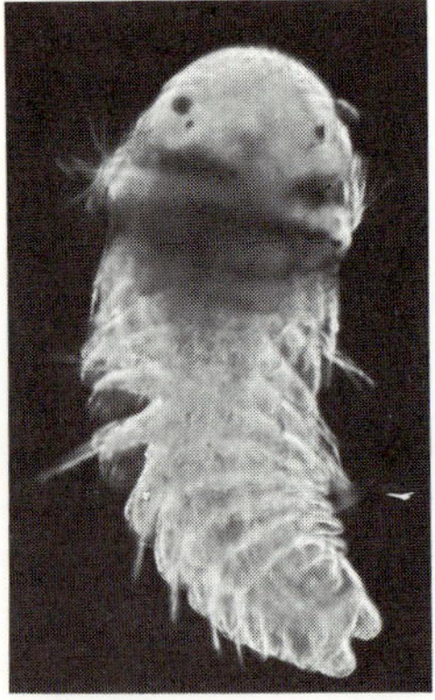
B

Fig. 34.18 Annelid development. (A) 1, Trochophore; 2, posterior elongation, proliferation of teloblastic mesoderm bands; 3, mesodermal somites forming; 4, later stage in segmental development, reduction of larval head structures. (B) Larva of marine annelid, corresponding roughly to stage 3 in (A).

A

B

Fig. 34.19 *Nereis,* the clamworm, external features. (A) Whole animal. (B) Head region, dorsal view, pharynx retracted and not visible. Palps are feelerlike appendages that function as mechano- and chemoreceptors.

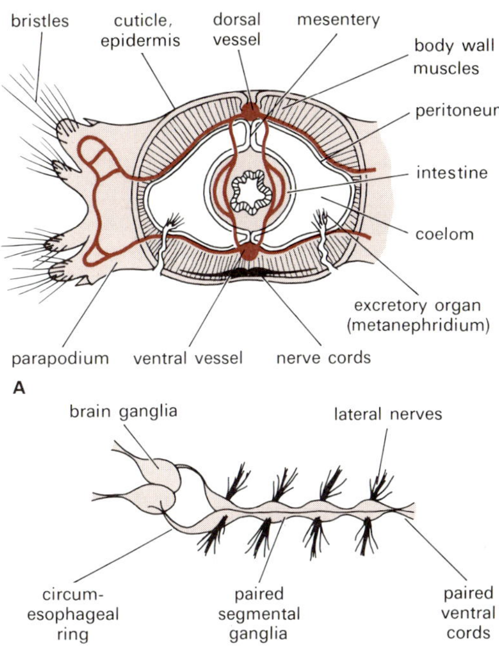

Fig. 34.20 Polychaete structure. (A) Schematic cross section through trunk segment. Parapodium shown only on one side. Note the blood-vessel pattern, with capillary beds in the parapodia and the intestine. Blood flows from the dorsal to the ventral vessel in the anterior segments, in the reverse direction in the posterior segments. (B) Scheme of the anterior portion of the (ladder-type) nervous system.

Polychaetes

In an adult polychaete such as *Nereis,* the common clamworm, the first segment is the head, or *prostomium,* which bears eyes (oscelli) and paired sensory tentacles (Fig. 34.19). The second segment is a *peristomium,* which contains the mouth and often additional sensory tentacles. The mouth leads to an eversible pharynx, armed with chitinous jaws. Behind the pharynx an esophagus with digestive glands continues as an intestine, and the tract terminates at the anus in the last segment of the body.

With the exception of the head and anal segments, all others are more or less alike (Fig. 34.20). Each bears a pair of parapodia, and the bristles on these fleshy lobes serve mainly as locomotor levers and holdfast spikes. Internally, the nervous system is ladderlike. A nerve ring around the pharynx is thickened dorsally as brain ganglia, and ventrally a pair of longitudinal cords passes to the hind end of the body. The cords have lateral branches and thickened ganglia in each segment. In the blood circulation, a longitudinal dorsal and ventral vessel are interconnected in each segment by transverse systems that include capillary nets in the alimentary tract, the parapodia, and the other segmental organs. Blood flows forward dorsally by wavelike contractions of the dorsal vessel, backward ventrally. Breathing occurs through the epidermis, particularly in the parapodia, which move back and forth and thereby circulate water around the body.

Polychaetes generally spend most of their time in sand or mud burrows, or they live in secreted tubes (Fig. 34.21). During the breeding season in many of these worms, the hind portions of the animals develop enlarged parapodia and long swimming bristles, and the coeloms in these segments fill with sperms or eggs. On certain fixed nights, determined in part by environmental factors such as the amount of moonlight in a particular month of the year, the posterior sexual parts of the worms become detached and swarm to the surface of the

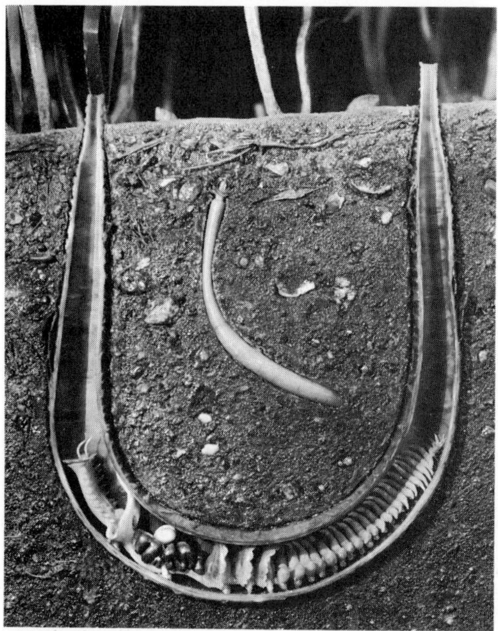

Fig. 34.21 Tube-secreting polychaetes. A model of a section through the tube of the parchment worm *Chaetopterus*. The head of the animal is at left. Note the greatly elaborated parapodia. Between the arms of the U tube is a sipunculid.

sea. There they burst, and the released sex cells bring about fertilization. The nonswarming body parts soon regenerate the lost regions.

Reef-dwelling palolo worms swarm precisely at one or two predictable nights of the year—during the last quarter of the October–November moon in a South Pacific type (*Eunice*), and the third quarter of the June–July moon in a West Indies type (*Leodice*). These nights are anticipated eagerly by the local islanders, who gather up the swarming palolos and eat them broiled.

Oligochaetes

Ancestral stocks of polychaetes appear to have given rise to the earthworms (Fig. 34.22). These burrowing, detritus-feeding animals are without eyes, head, appendages, or parapodia, and the segmental bristles are reduced to four pairs (Fig. 34.23). In the alimentary tract, an esophagus behind the pharynx carries paired *lime glands,* which regulate the calcium balance between swallowed earth and blood. Behind the esophagus is an earth-storing *crop,* and behind it a muscular *gizzard* grinds swallowed earth. In the intestine a dorsal fold (*typhlosole*) increases the nutrient-absorbing area. The blood circulation is maintained by five pairs of contractile vessels (''hearts'') that join the dorsal and ventral main vessels (in segments 7 to 11). In addition to segmental metanephridia, earthworms also contain excretory *chloragogue* cells in the peritoneum and the coelomic fluid. Such cells are carried to the body wall, where the excretion products are deposited as pigments.

Unlike polychaetes, each earthworm contains both male and female reproductive systems, and the animals mate by copulation. Shed sperms and eggs become encased in a mucus cocoon secreted by the *clitellum,* a thickened glandular band in the epidermis of each animal (in segments 31 to 37). Fertilized eggs in such cocoons then develop without free larval stages directly into new worms (see Fig. 34.22).

Charles Darwin was the first scientist to demonstrate the great ecological importance of earthworms. He calculated that 1 acre of land often contains over 50,000 earthworms. The feces of these worms, which consist of mixed soil and organic matter, are deposited on the ground as small black mounds called *castings.* Darwin demonstrated that more than 18 tons of castings may be released on 1 acre of ground in a single year. By releasing castings and creating multitudes of crisscrossing channels in the ground, earthworms generate substantial amounts of humus and help maintain the porosity of soil.

Hirudineans

Leeches are probably evolutionary offshoots of ancestral earthworms. In most leeches bristles are absent entirely, suckers are typically present at both ends of the body, and the number of internal segments is fixed at 34. Externally the body surface exhibits ringlike creases that are more numerous than the true internal segments and do not correspond to them. Most leeches are blood suckers of fishes and other vertebrates. The alimentary tract of these parasites contains numerous side branches that can hold up to 10 times as much blood as the weight of the leech itself, and permit the animal to survive as long as 9 months from a single feeding.

A

B

C

Fig. 34.22 Earthworms. (A) Note unsegmented clitellum at roughly one-third the length from the anterior end. During mating the clitellum secretes mucus, which comes to surround fertilized eggs as an egg cocoon. (B) Two earthworms in copulation. (C) Cocoons of earthworms.

Fig. 34.23 Earthworm structure. (A) Cutaway diagram of anterior body region, segments numbered. Segment 12 and all segments behind it contain on each side a transverse vessel (shown in cutaway view) that interconnects the dorsal and subneural longitudinal blood vessels. (B) Cross section through an earthworm. Note the epidermis, the body wall muscles, the intestine with the deep, dorsal typhlosole fold, the dorsal blood vessel just above it and the ventral vessel below it, and portions of the metanephridial (excretory) tubes in the coelom to each side of the intestine. Metanephridia transport wastes from body fluids to openings in the body wall.

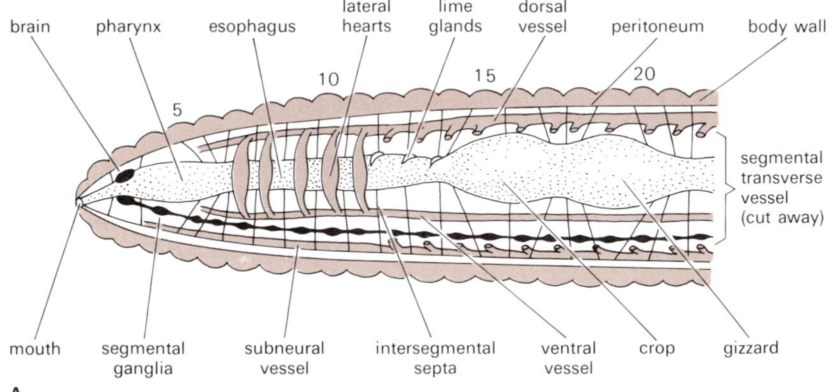

A

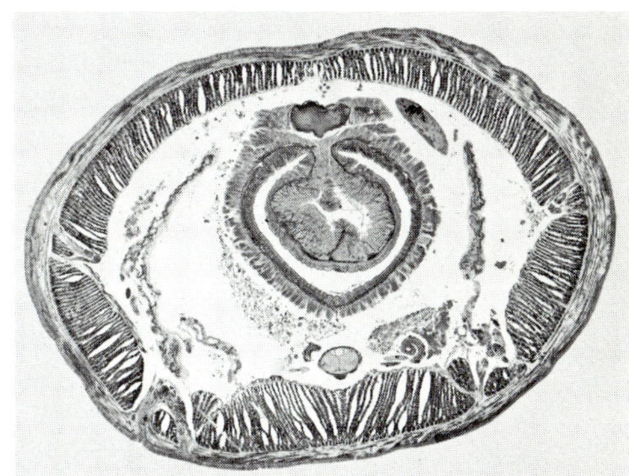
B

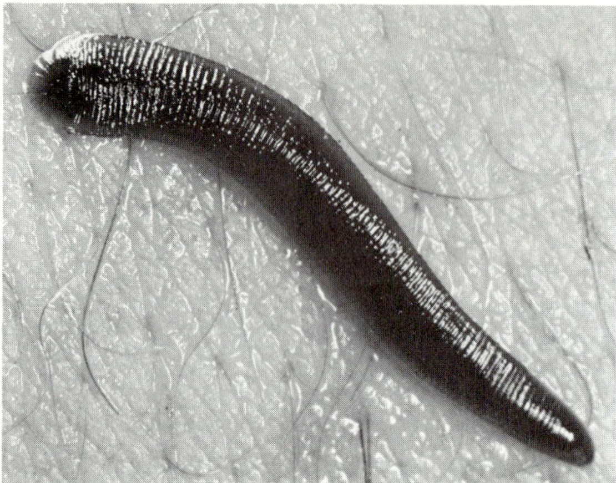

Fig. 34.24 A leech. The so-called medicinal leech, *Hirudo medicinalis,* sucking blood from the arm of a man. Most leeches have anterior (forward) and posterior (rear) suckers that firmly attach the worms to hosts.

The worms feed by cutting through host skin with sawlike mouth structures. As blood is then ingested, *hirudin* is secreted into the wound, and this anticoagulant prevents blood from clotting. The "medicinal" leech, *Hirudo medicinalis,* was widely used in earlier times for "blood letting," then thought to be beneficial (Fig. 34.24).

Oncopods

Phylum Oncopoda claw-bearing animals, segmented; usually with unjointed legs; sexes separate, development various

These animals represent a "phylum of convenience," an assemblage of three small groups perhaps interrelated very distantly. They have two features in common: claws of a type characteristic of arthropods, and various other traits that are more or less intermediate between those of polychaetes and arthropods.

Each of the three groups has been and still is classified in widely different ways, either as a separate phylum or as a subphylum or class with arthropod affinities. The present grouping of all three in one phylum follows a recent proposal and appears to be justified on at least structural grounds. Apart from their classification, the Oncopoda probably represent surviving remnants of three separate and independent lines, all offshoots of a main line that led from annelid ancestors to arthropod descendants (see Fig. 34.5).

Of all oncopods, *Peripatus* and its relatives are most clearly intermediate between annelids and arthropods. In fact, their very existence provides one of the best proofs that annelids and arthropods are closely related. These animals are distributed widely in humid environments, mostly in tropical and subtropical regions of the world. About 2 to 3 inches long, *Peripatus* lives in damp, leafy places on the ground and feeds mainly on insects (see Fig. 34.5).

The caterpillarlike body of these "walking worms" is covered with a nonchitinous velvet-textured cuticle. Along the trunk, the stumpy paired legs carry two recurved claws apiece (undoubtedly evolved from polychaete parapodia and setae). The legs mark the position of internal segments and segmentally arranged organs. The nervous and excretory systems of *Peripatus* most closely resemble those of annelids, but the breathing and circulatory systems are much more arthropodlike. Moreover, the coelom of these animals is small, as in arthropods.

Arthropods

Phylum Arthropoda jointed-legged animals

Subphylum Chelicerata body with cephalothorax, generally unsegmented, and abdomen, either segmented or not; cephalothorax typically with six pairs of appendages; first pair *cheliceras,* second pair *pedipalps,* last four pairs *walking legs;* jaws or antennae not present; *horseshoe crabs, sea spiders, arachnids*

Subphylum Mandibulata body with cephalothorax and abdomen, or head, thorax, and abdomen, or head and trunk; cephalothorax or head unsegmented externally; thorax, abdomen, or trunk segmented; head with one or two pairs of *antennae,* one pair of jaws (*mandibles*), two pairs of *maxillae; crustaceans, centipedes, millipedes, insects*

This is the largest phylum not only among animals but all living organisms. Since some 1 million

Fig. 34.25 Arthropod structure. Lateral view of a wasp showing general segmental structure. Head is externally unsegmented and bears antennae, eyes, and mouth parts. The thorax, consisting of three segments in insects, bears three pairs of legs (one per segment) and two pairs of wings (on the second and third thoracic segments). The abdomen in insects typically consists of 11 segments and is without appendages. Numbers of segments and types of appendages vary considerably for different arthropod groups, but sets of mutually different segments are present in all.

species have been described to date, more arthropod types are known than all other living types combined, plants included. About 75 per cent of the described species are insects, but according to one estimate, some 10 million insect species actually may exist. One of the orders of insects, the beetles, alone includes 300,000 species, which makes this order larger than any whole *phylum* of other organisms.

Arthropod sizes range from microscopic mites at one extreme to 5-foot giant crabs with 12-foot leg spans at the other. The animals are more widely and more densely distributed throughout the world than any others, and they occur in all environments and ecological niches, including many not open to other forms. Arthropods are also the main group that other animals must compete with, people included. The chief competitors of arthropods are arthropods themselves, bacteria, and vertebrates.

The unrivaled success of the phylum is a consequence of the basic arthropod construction, of which the essential features are the segmental organization and the chitinous exoskeleton. In all probability the ancestors of arthropods were early stocks of polychaete annelids, and during their evolution in the arthropod direction the segments of different body regions became elaborately specialized in different ways (Fig. 34.25). The arthropod body now consists of a *head,* a *thorax,* and an *abdomen,* and in many cases head and thorax are fused as a *cephalothorax.* The whole is covered by a chitinous armor that is molted periodically during larval growth or throughout life. The ancestral parapodia became distinct *segmental appendages* of a wide variety of forms and functions, the chitin cover here providing rigidity as well as joint connections.

Chitin also contributed to the development of the unique *compound eyes,* in which numerous complete visual units are grouped together as large composite structures. Each visual unit contains its own chitinous lens and light-sensitive cells. Arthropods in addition have *simple eyes,* in each of which a single lens covers a group of light-sensitive cells (Fig. 34.26).

Internally, the alimentary tract consists of foregut, midgut, and hindgut (Fig. 34.27). The first and last portions have a chitin lining continuous with the exoskeleton, and only the midgut functions digestively. Large digestive glands usually open to the midgut. Breathing is accomplished by *gills, book gills, book lungs,* or *tracheal systems,* all chitinous and segmentally arranged outgrowths or ingrowths from the body surface. Gills, characteristic of crustaceans, are feathery extensions from legs and other segmental appendages. Book gills of horseshoe crabs and book lungs of spiders and scorpions are chambers containing chitinous breathing plates resembling the pages of a book, the gills operating in water, the lungs in air. And tracheal systems, as in centipedes and insects, are interconnecting air ducts that lead from the body surface to all interior body parts (see below).

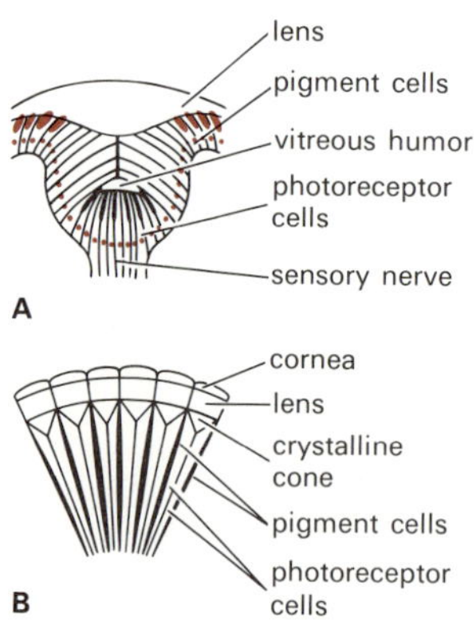

Fig. 34.26 Arthropod eyes. (A) Schematic section of a simple eye. (B) Several visual units (ommatidia) of a compound eye. One of these units is labeled; hundreds of them are usually present in a whole compound eye, as shown in (C).

Like mollusks, arthropods have an open circulatory system in which blood flows partly through blood vessels and partly through blood sinuses; a dorsal tubular and open-ended heart is the main and often the only vessel. Excretion takes place primarily through two kinds of organs. Aquatic arthropods excrete through variously named tubular organs that open at the bases of given segmental appendages—for example, at the antennal bases in lobsters. Terrestrial types, notably insects, have *Malpighian tubules* attached to and opening into the hindgut. The nervous system is basically of the ladder type and annelidlike. Arthropods also possess endocrine systems, consisting of hormone-secreting cells in the brain and a number of glands near the eyes and in the thorax. The hormones play a major role in, for example, control of molting and development. Arthropod embryos typically pass through annelidlike, wormlike phases, and in some cases even larvae (caterpillars) or adults (centipedes) are still wormlike. Other groups produce larvae of a variety of types.

Two main evolutionary lines of arthropods are in existence today, each with aquatic and terrestrial representatives. One line, the subphylum Chelicerata, includes the aquatic horseshoe crabs and sea spiders and the terrestrial arachnids. The second line, the subphylum Mandibulata, comprises the aquatic crustaceans and the terrestrial centipedes, millipedes, and insects. (A third and most ancient evolutionary line, the aquatic trilobites, has been extinct for 200 million years; see Chap. 36).

Chelicerates

Subphylum Chelicerata

CLASS XIPHOSURIDA (MEROSTOMATA) horseshoe crabs; marine; cephalothorax with carapace hinged to fused abdomen; telson a spine; breathing by book gills; with compound eyes; development with larvae; 5 species

CLASS PANTOPODA (PYCNOGONIDA) sea spiders, head and thorax with long, thin legs; abdomen reduced; compound eyes absent; egg-carrying legs on head of both sexes; 500 species

CLASS ARACHNIDA scorpions, spiders, ticks, mites; terrestrial, some secondarily aquatic; usually carnivorous, predatory; compound eyes absent; breathing by book lungs, tracheae, or both; 35,000 species

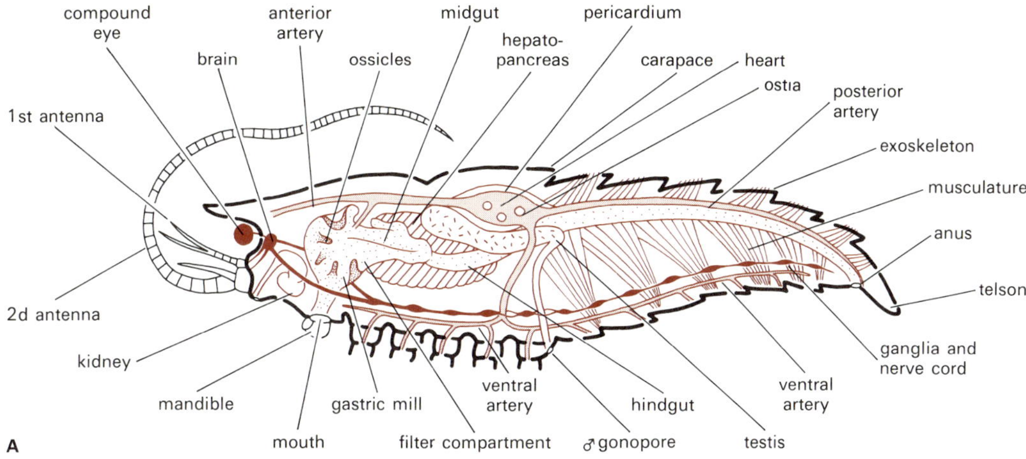

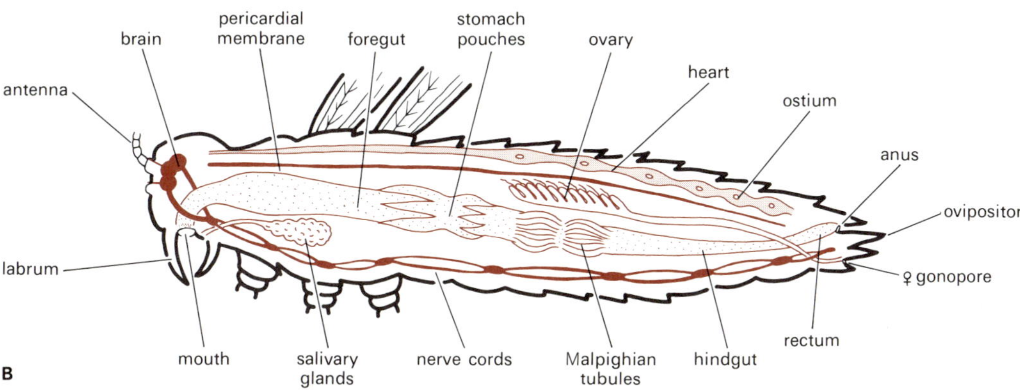

Fig. 34.27 Internal arthropod structure. (A) Lobster. (B) Grasshopper. In the lobster stomach, chitinous teeth in the gastric mill grind coarse food. A filter compartment then passes finely divided food through the short midgut into the digestive gland (hepatopancreas) for absorption. The midgut of the grasshopper extends from the region of the stomach pouches to that part of alimentary canal covered by the posteriormost extensions of the Malpighian tubules. The functions of several structures labeled in this diagram are described in later sections of this chapter.

The structure of representative chelicerates is indicated in Table 34.1 and Fig. 34.28. The head and thorax form a fused cephalothorax developed from eight segments, and the body frequently bears a *telson*, a terminal piece behind the abdomen. On the cephalothorax the appendages include *chelicer-as* and *pedipalps*, which are food-handling and sensory structures, as well as four pairs of walking legs. The ends of these appendages either are pincer-equipped (*chelate*) or they terminate in claws (Fig. 34.29). In the absence of jaws, chelicerates chew food with the spiny bases of their anterior appendages and generally suck up the fluid contents. With the exception of horseshoe crabs chelicerates lack compound eyes; spiders have up to eight simple eyes and some scorpions are eyeless.

On the abdomen the first segment of horseshoe crabs bears an *operculum*, a flat movable plate that covers and protects the plates of the book gills behind. The reproductive ducts open on the operculum (*gonopores*). A small operculum is present in scorpions, but spiders lack such a structure. Scorpions also have a pair of *pectines*, comblike appendages that brush over the ground and serve as important

TABLE 34.1
Segments and Appendages in Chelicerate Arthropods

	Horseshoe crab	Scorpion	Spider
cephalothorax			
1	embryo only	embryo only	embryo only
2	chelicerae (chelate)	chelicerae (small)	chelicerae (fangs)
3	pedipalps (chelate)	pedipalps (large)	pedipalps (tactile)
4	walking legs (chelate)	walking legs (clawed)	walking legs (clawed)
5	walking legs (chelate)	walking legs (clawed)	walking legs (clawed)
6	walking legs (chelate)	walking legs (clawed)	walking legs (clawed)
7	walking legs (chelate)	walking legs (clawed)	walking legs (clawed)
8	chilaria	embryo only	embryo only
abdomen			
9	operculum, gonopores	operculum, gonopores	embryo only
10	gill books	pectines	lung books/tracheae
11	gill books	lung books	lung books/tracheae
12	gill books	lung books	spinnerets
13	gill books	lung books	spinnerets
14	gill books	lung books	14–18, embryo only
	telson	15–20, "tail" without appendages	
		telson	

touch organs in these largely nocturnal animals. Four segments behind the pectines bear paired spiracles, slits that lead to chambers in which the book lungs are located. The most posterior abdominal segments of a scorpion form a narrow "tail," and at the end of it the telson is a poison sting. In horseshoe crabs the telson is represented by a long spine hinged to the abdomen.

Spiders lack a telson, but these animals have *spinnerets,* appendages that provide outlets for *silk glands* in the abdomen (Fig. 34.30). All spiders produce silk, but not all construct webs. Silk is also used, for example, to make egg cocoons, burrow linings, hinged trap-doors over burrows, binding thread for prey, draglines, and free-floating gossamer on which a spider rides air currents. The cheliceras of spiders are fangs, with poison glands opening at the tips. Food animals (mostly insects) are killed with the poison fangs, are chewed and torn with the spiny bases of the pedipalps, and are predigested externally for an hour or more by saliva. The food juices are then sucked up, suction being produced by the stomach. Amazonian tarantulas, 3 inches long and with leg spans of 10 inches are the largest spiders. The most dangerous are the black widows and the brown recluse spider, whose poisons can be fatal to human beings.

The few surviving species of horseshoe crabs, structurally unchanged for 200 million years, are "living fossils" found along sandy ocean shores, where they lead a burrowing, semisedentary existence. The exceedingly long-legged sea spiders are largely deepwater bottom forms. True spiders are the most abundant members of the arachnid class of chelicerates, and in addition to scorpions, this class also includes a variety of spiderlike groups (daddy longlegs, for example) as well as mites and ticks (Fig. 34.31).

Some of the blood-sucking mites and ticks complete their entire life cycle on one host, relinquishing their attachment only temporarily at the time of molting. Other forms fall off the host at each molt and must seek a new host thereafter. Larvae can survive for many months on a single blood meal, and adults often live for years from one feeding. Mites and ticks are notorious carriers of dis-

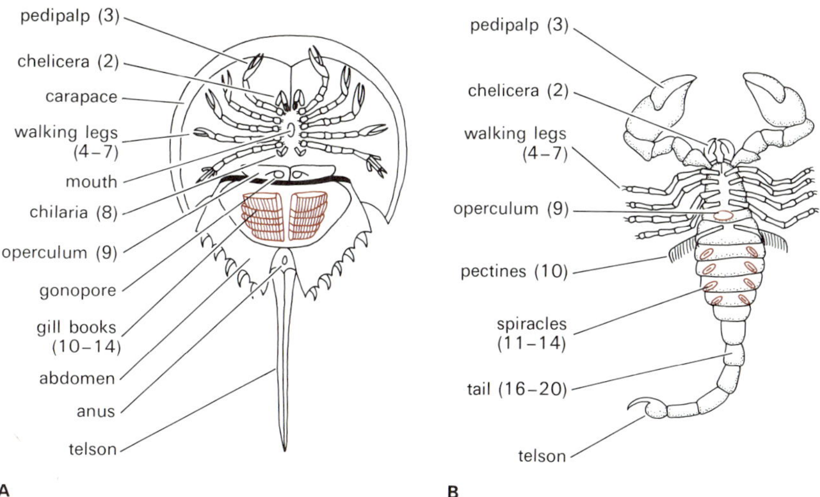

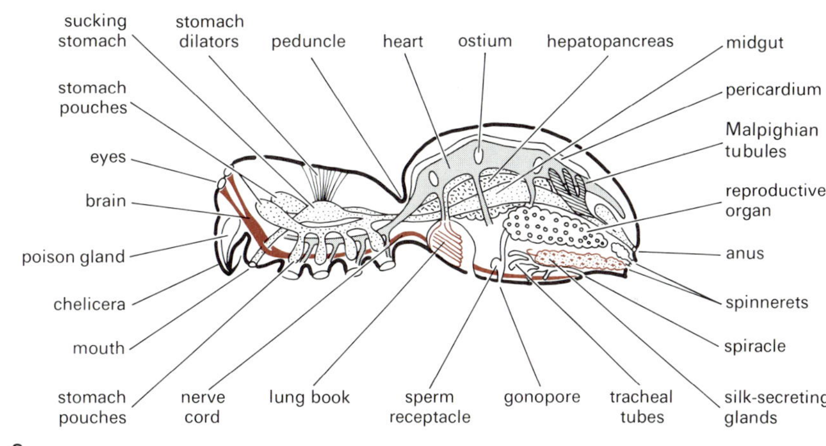

Fig. 34.28 Structure of chelicerates. The functions of some labeled structures are given later in this chapter. (A) Ventral view of the horseshoe crab *Limulus*. Segments numbered according to sequence in embryo. The operculum is drawn turned forward to show the reproductive openings (gonopores) on its underside and to expose the book gills. (B) Ventral view of a scorpion. Segments are numbered according to sequence in embryo. (C) Sagittal section showing the internal structure of a spider. The peduncle is the "waist" between cephalothorax and abdomen.

ease organisms that affect vertebrates—mammals and human beings in particular. For example, these arthropods are the exclusive carriers of the viruslike *rickettsial* parasites, responsible for Rocky Mountain spotted fever in people.

Mandibulates

Subphylum Mandibulata

CLASS CRUSTACEA crustaceans; marine and freshwater, some terrestrial; head and thorax or cephalothorax, often with carapace; two pairs of antennae; usually with compound eyes; breathing through gills; excretion through antennal or maxillary glands; typically with *nauplius* and other free larval stages; 30,000 species

CLASS CHILOPODA centipedes; carnivorous, predatory; trunk with one pair of poison-claw-containing prehensors and 15 or more pairs of walking legs; eyes compound or simple or absent; 3000 species

CLASS DIPLOPODA millipedes; herbivorous, scavenging; first four trunk segments single, rest double and fused; eyes simple; 10,000 species

Fig. 34.29 Chelicerae. Front view of head of a wolf spider. Note chelicerae with fangs and large and small eyes.

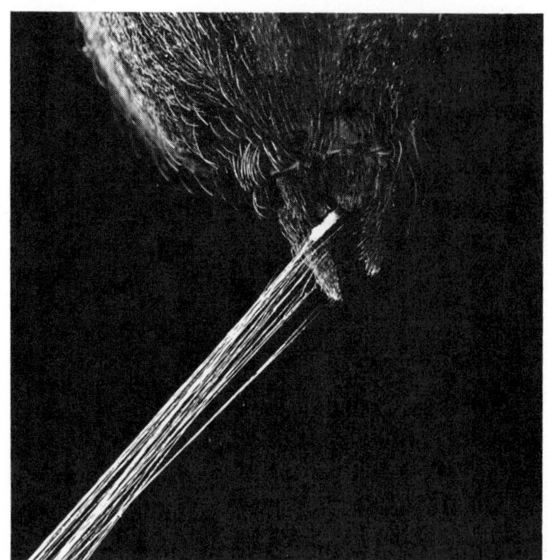

Fig. 34.30 Spinnerets. Abdomen of house spider in process of spinning silk from spinnerets.

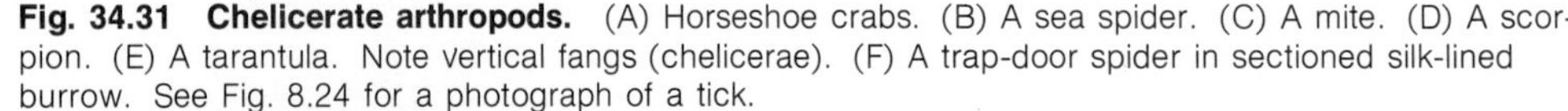

Fig. 34.31 Chelicerate arthropods. (A) Horseshoe crabs. (B) A sea spider. (C) A mite. (D) A scorpion. (E) A tarantula. Note vertical fangs (chelicerae). (F) A trap-door spider in sectioned silk-lined burrow. See Fig. 8.24 for a photograph of a tick.

A

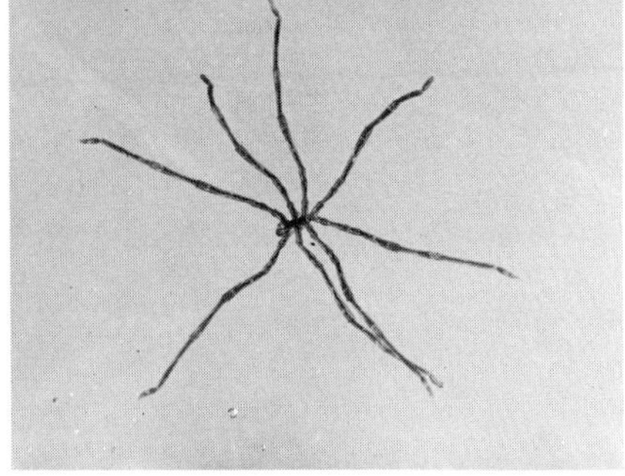

B

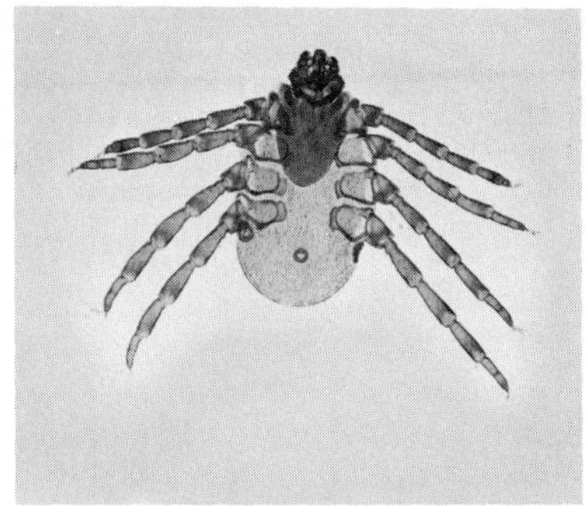

C

D

E

F

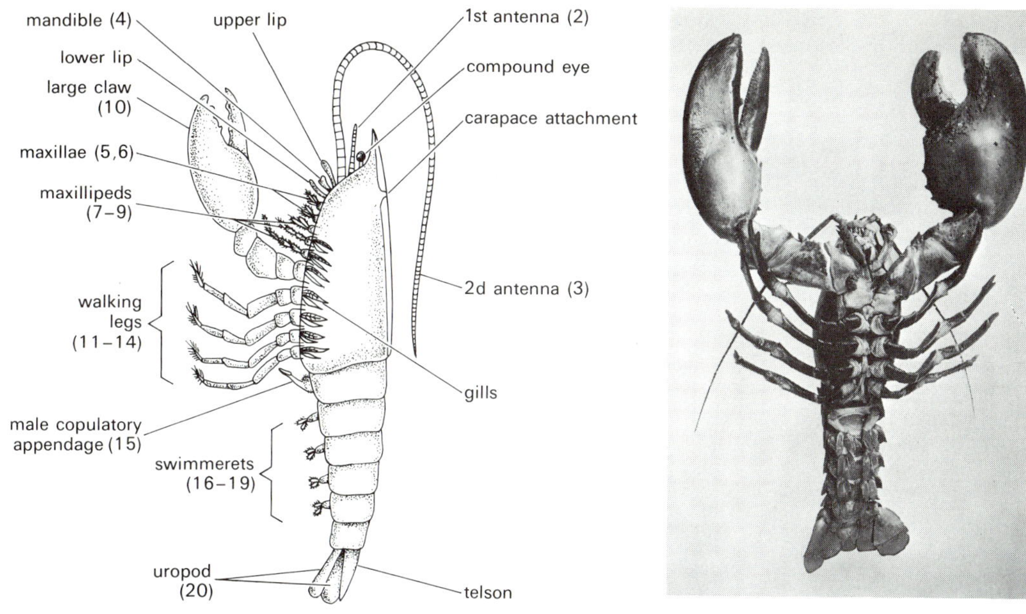

Fig. 34.32 Lobster appendages. (A) Segmental appendages are numbered according to sequence in embryo. The diagram also shows which of the thoracic appendages bear gills. The carapace is attached at the third head segment (which also bears the second antennae ventrally). Note that the eyes and the upper and lower lips are not segmental appendages but extensions of the body wall. (B) *Homarus,* a genus native to waters of the northeastern coast of the United States.

CLASS INSECTA (HEXAPODA) insects; terrestrial, some secondarily aquatic; head six segments; thorax three segments, typically with three pairs of legs, two pairs of wings; abdomen typically eleven segments, without locomotor appendages; eyes compound and simple; 800,000+ species

Crustaceans

CLASS CRUSTACEA

General characteristics The characteristics of this highly diversified class are well exemplified by a lobster (Fig. 34.32 and Table 34.2). The head and thorax are covered dorsally and along the sides by a *carapace,* an exoskeletal shield. As in all mandibulate arthropods, the head itself consists of six fused segments. On it are a median simple eye (reduced in lobsters) and a pair of compound eyes (stalked in lobsters). At the bases of the short first antennae are balancing organs, and at the bases of the long second antennae are the excretory openings of lobsters. The mandibles on the third segment are the chewing jaws, which lead into the mouth. Two pairs of maxillary appendages on the head pass bits of food toward the mouth.

In the eight segments of the thorax, the first three carry *maxillipeds,* appendages that aid in macerating food and in passing it to the mouth. At the bases of the second and third maxillipeds are feathery gills. The remaining five segments bear legs, of which the first pair is large and terminates in crushing and cutting pincers. At each leg base is a gill, normally hidden from view by the covering carapace.

In the abdomen, the reduced appendages of the first segment have functions associated with mating, and in many female crustacea they are fashioned into brood pouches or other egg-holding structures. Lobsters possess egg-holding *swimmerets* on the second to fifth abdominal segments. The last abdominal appendages are flat, platelike *uropods,* which together with a terminal telson form a tailfan.

TABLE 34.2
Segments and Appendages in Mandibulate Arthropods

	Lobster	Centipede	Insect
1			
2	antennae	antennae	antennae
3	antennae		
4	mandibles	mandibles	mandibles
5	maxillae	maxillae	maxillae
6	maxillae	labium (maxillae)	labium (maxillae)
7	maxillipeds	prehensors	legs
8	maxillipeds	legs	legs, wings (spiracles)
9	maxillipeds	legs	legs, wings (spiracles)
10	chelate legs	legs	(spiracles)
11	legs	legs	(spiracles)
12	legs (female gonopore)	legs	(spiracles)
13	legs	legs	(spiracles)
14	legs (male gonopore)	legs	(spiracles)
15	reproductive	legs	(spiracles)
16	swimmerets	legs	(spiracles)
17	swimmerets	legs	(spiracles), female ovipositor,
18	swimmerets	legs	male copulatory organ
19	swimmerets	legs	(anus)
20	uropods	legs	(anal cerci)
21	telson	legs	
22		legs (gonopores)	
		telson	

Lobsters are scavenging animals, and their stomach has two compartments well adapted to handle the great variety of ingested foods (see Fig. 34.27). An anterior "gastric mill," equipped with chitinous teeth and other hard outgrowths, grinds coarse food. A posterior filter compartment then sorts food: coarse particles are returned to the gastric mill; fine particles pass to the intestine; and liquefied food is conducted to a hepatopancreas ("liver") of the midgut, where the bulk of digestion and absorption occurs. In other respects the internal structure of the animals is typically arthropod. A few large, open-ended blood vessels lead away from the heart to various body regions, and blood reenters the heart through three pairs of openings in its wall (*ostia*). In other crustacea the heart is often more distinctly tubular and contains a pair of ostia in each segmental portion.

Crustacea have a well-developed endocrine system. Its components include *X organs,* located in each eyestalk, and a *sinus gland* near the base of each eyestalk (Fig. 34.33). Another endocrine component is a *Y organ* situated in the head. Hormones of the X organ can be shown to influence several functions, including regulation of epidermal pigment cells and control over some secretions of the Y organ.

Molting Interaction between X and Y organs has been demonstrated most convincingly in experiments dealing with the regulation of *molting,* the periodic shedding and replacement of exoskeletons. The softer body parts of growing crustaceans, insects, and certain other arthropods eventually exert considerable pressure against the inner surface of the rigid exoskeleton. At such times, the covering falls away and is replaced by a new larger one.

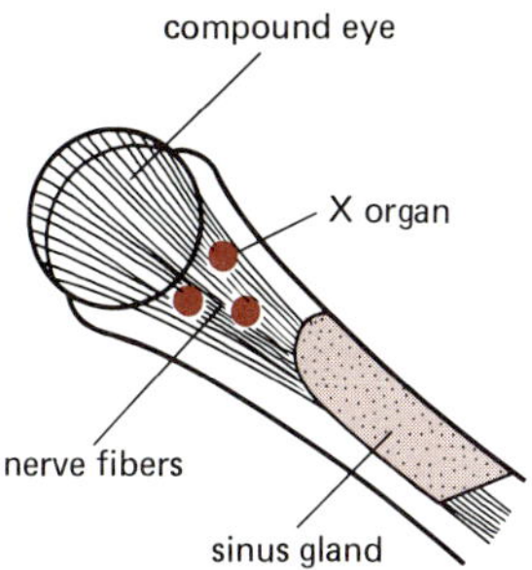

Fig. 34.33 X organs and sinus glands. X organs, represented by the colored circles, are clusters of neurosecretory cells that lie within the eyestalks of crustaceans. The sinus gland is composed of the swollen endings of nerve fibers that originate in the X organs. A molt-inhibiting hormone, produced in the X organs, is transported to the sinus gland, where the hormone is stored until release.

Lobsters and many other crustaceans molt throughout life, growing steadily larger. But some crustaceans, such as the crab *Carcinus maenas,* cease molting at maturity. Surgical removal of X organs and sinus glands stimulates continued molting in adult crabs, but injecting extracts of homogenized sinus glands into such surgically treated crabs prevents molting. These results suggest that the X organ and sinus gland secrete a molt-inhibiting hormone. But does this hormone act alone, inhibiting molting directly, or is the process more complex?

Results of other experiments provide a partial answer to this question. Surgical removal of the Y organ from young or medium-sized crabs prevents further molting, but if they are then injected with extracts of homogenized Y organs, the surgically treated crabs begin molting again. Injections of Y-organ extracts can even trigger molting in adult crabs. Surgical removal of the eyestalks and Y organs of young crabs always inhibits molting, further demonstrating that a hormone produced by the Y organ is necessary for molting. Biochemical analysis shows the molt-promoting hormone to be *ecdysone,* the same steroid that induces molting among insects (see below).

The overall hormonal interactions between X organ, sinus gland, and Y organ have now been established (see Fig. 34.46). Molt-inhibiting hormones, produced in an X organ, are stored in an associated sinus gland. Release of the inhibiting hormone is influenced by a number of internal and external factors, including the age of the animal, environmental temperature, and relative amounts of light and darkness. The amount of ecdysone released by the Y organ is largely influenced by concentrations of molt-inhibiting hormone; high concentrations reduce the output of ecdysone from the Y organ, thereby preventing molting; low concentrations have the opposite effect.

Reproduction The characteristic larval form of crustacea is the *nauplius,* which as yet contains only some of the head appendages and is still unsegmented (Fig. 34.34). Segments then develop in anteroposterior succession during the course of later larval stages, often distinct enough to have special names (*metanauplius, zoaea*). In many crustacea some or all of these later stages are part of the embryonic phase, and free larval phases are reduced or absent. Lobsters, for example, hatch in nearly adult form.

Diversity Crustacea are predominantly microscopic, and many, particularly *copepods* and *krill,* are important members of the marine plankton (Fig. 34.35). Copepods are also abundant in fresh water, as are water fleas (*daphnias*). Barnacles are sessile types, and quite a few crustacea live in fairly unusual environments, including subterranean wells, hot springs, glacial waters, salt lakes, and others. Sow bugs, slaters, and woodlice are terrestrial forms that breathe air through the thin areas on their abdominal appendages. The class also includes a number of parasitic types, including *Sacculina,* which infects crabs and spreads through such hosts like a malignant tumor.

Centipedes and Millipedes

CLASS CHILOPODA

CLASS DIPLOPODA

The head and the internal structure of these animals is generally like that of insects, but the exterior of the trunk is clearly wormlike (Fig. 34.36 and see Table 34.2). Millipedes lack compound eyes; centipedes may or may not have them. The first trunk segment of centipedes bears poison-gland-containing, fanglike *prehensors.* Each leg-bearing segment usually contains a pair of *spiracles,* openings leading to the tracheal breathing tubes.

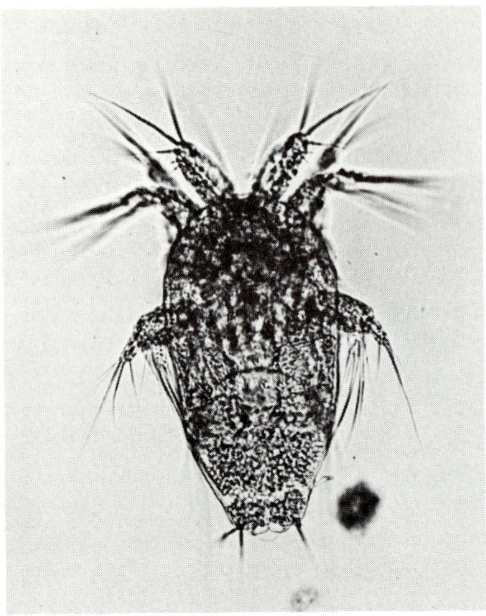

A

B

Fig. 34.34 Crustacean larvae. (A) A nauplius of a copepod. (B) A zoaea of a shore crab.

The animals are predators and rapid runners. During the day they shun exposure, and at night they leave their crevices and crannies in search for earthworms, insects, and snails. Millipedes carry *two* pairs of legs on most trunk segments, each of which is actually a fused double segment. But these animals are poor runners despite their large number of legs. They are herbivores, and rapid locomotion is not essential. They too are retiring in habit, and when exposed they tend to roll up as a ball.

Insects

CLASS INSECTA

Subclass Apterygota (*Ametabola*) primitively wingless: without metamorphosis

ORDER PROTURA piercing mouth parts concealed in head; without antennae; eyeless; with and without tracheae; abdomen 12 segments; first 3 small appendages; in moist places; 100 species

ORDER DIPLURA biting mouth parts deep in head; with long antennae; eyeless; with tracheae, without Malpighian tubules; abdomen 11 segments with cerci or forceps; in moist, rotting places; 400 species

ORDER COLLEMBOLA spring tails; biting mouth parts hidden in head; without compound eyes; six abdominal segments with three pairs of appendages (not legs), modified for jumping and adhesion; without tracheae or Malpighian tubules; in moist, rotting places; 2000 species

ORDER THYSANURA bristle tails; biting mouth parts, exposed; antennae long; 11 abdominal segments and two or three cerci; in buildings, nooks and crannies, book bindings; 750 species, *Lepisma,* silverfish

Subclass Pterygota (*Metabola*) with wings and metamorphosis

SUPERORDER EXOPTERYGOTA (HEMIMETABOLA) wing growth external on larval body; metamorphosis gradual; larvae *nymphs* if terrestrial, *naiads* if aquatic; compound eyes already in larvae

ORDER ORTHOPTERA grasshopper, locusts, crickets, praying mantises, katydids, walking-stick insects, cockroaches; biting mouth parts; forewings narrow, leathery; hind wings membranous, folding under forewings; many wingless, typically with cerci; herbivorous; 25,000 species

ORDER DERMAPTERA earwigs; biting mouth parts; forewings short, leathery; hind wings large, membranous; many wingless; cerci form terminal forceps; in dark places, nocturnal; 1200 species

ORDER PLECOPTERA stone flies; mouth parts biting or vestigial; wings pleated, hind wings larger

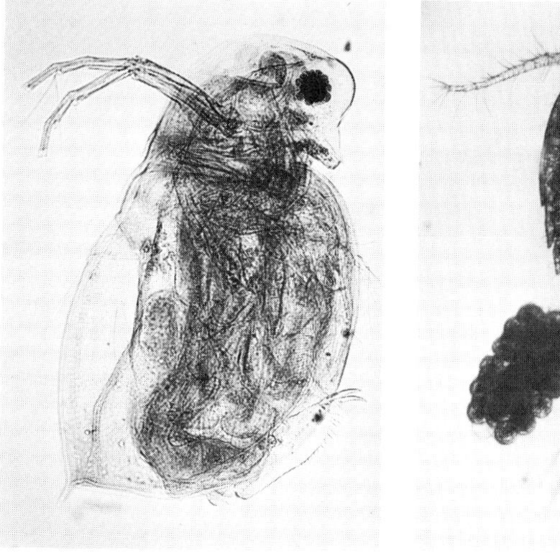

A

B

C

D

Fig. 34.35 Small crustacea. (A) *Daphnia,* a water flea. A carapace (with posterior spine) covers most of the body, and locomotion is carried out by the second antennae. The abdomen is reduced to a conical, claw-bearing structure near the hind end. (B) *Cyclops,* a freshwater copepod. Note the brood pouches. (C) *Balanus,* the rock barnacle. The legs are modified for food gathering. (D) *Ligia,* a slater, one of a number of terrestrial crustaceans. Some of their posterior appendages have thin surface areas where air breathing takes place. (E) *Leander,* a prawn. Eggs are carried in brood pouches.

E

Fig. 34.36 Centipedes and millipedes. (A) The centipede *Lithobius.* The head of the animal is to the right. (B) A millipede. Note two pairs of legs in most trunk segments.

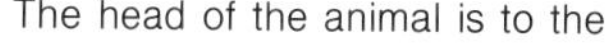

A

B

and hidden under forewings; weak fliers; with cerci; naiad larvae with tracheal gill tufts behind each leg; 1500 species

ORDER ISOPTERA termites; biting mouth parts; wings similar, membranous; social and polymorphic, largely tropical; 2000 species

ORDER EMBIOPTERA embiids, web-spinners; body flattened, elongate; in males wings similar, females wingless; cerci two-jointed, asymmetric in males; colonial, in tunnel networks of secreted silk; mainly tropical; 1000 species

ORDER ODONATA dragonflies, damsel flies; biting mouth parts; wings similar, net-veined; dragonfly wings do not fold back, damsel fly wings fold up at rest; compound eyes conspicuous; abdomen elongate and slender; predatory, legs catch insects in flight; naiads with tracheal gills; 5000 species

ORDER EPHEMERIDA mayflies; biting mouth parts vestigial; wings membranous, folded up at rest, hind wings small; long cerci; naiads with multiple paired tracheal gills, biting mouth parts, long-lived; adults nonfeeding, often live less than 24 hours; 1500 species

ORDER MALLOPHAGA biting lice; biting mouth parts; body flattened; wingless; eyes reduced or absent; two claws per leg for clinging; ectoparasitic on birds, some mammals, feeding on skin, feather, and hair fragments; 3000 species

ORDER ANOPLURA sucking lice, human body lice; piercing-sucking mouth parts, retractable; body flattened; wingless; thorax fused; without eyes; one claw per leg for clinging; ectoparasitic blood suckers on hair of mammals, transmitters of typhus fever, trench fever, and other diseases; 500 species

ORDER PSOCOPTERA book lice, bark lice; biting mouth parts; wings usually without crossveins or absent; 1300 species

ORDER ZORAPTERA biting mouth parts; often wingless, eyeless; in warm, dark, rotting places; 21 species

ORDER HEMIPTERA bugs, water striders; piercing-sucking mouth parts; forewings thickened basally, membranous terminally, crossed flat on body at rest; hind wings membranous, folded under forewings; herbivorous, predatory, and ectoparasitic; some viviparous; 40,000 species

ORDER HOMOPTERA plant lice, scale insects, 17-year locusts, cicadas, leaf hoppers; piercing-sucking mouth parts; wings tentlike at rest, forewings thickened or membranous; sapfeeders; 30,000 species

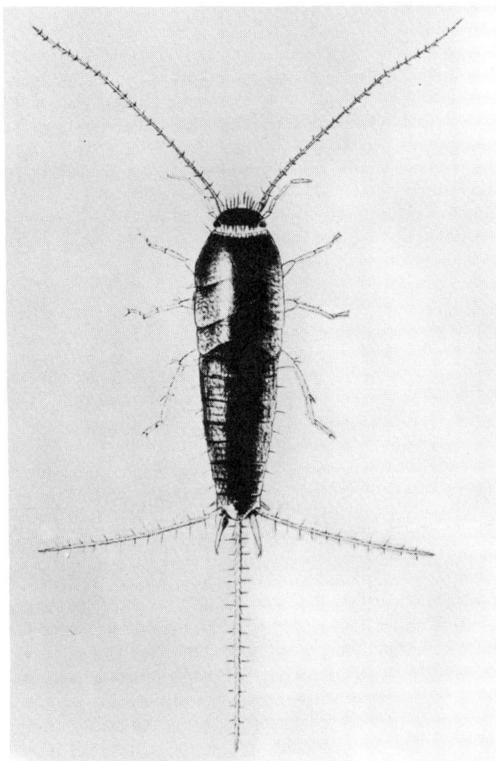

Fig. 34.37 Silverfish. A primitively flightless apterygote insect (order Thysanura).

ORDER THYSANOPTERA thrips; sucking mouth parts; wings similar, fringed with bristles, veins few or absent; some parthenogenetic; mostly herbivorous on fruit and grasses; 3500 species

SUPERORDER ENDOPTERYGOTA (HOLOMETABOLA) wing growth internal in larval body; metamorphosis abrupt; immature stages are larvae and pupae; larvae without compound eyes

ORDER MECOPTERA scorpion flies; biting mouth parts on turned-down beak; wings similar, with rhomboid venation, roofed over body at rest; 500 species

ORDER NEUROPTERA dobson flies, alder flies, ant lions, lacewings; biting mouth parts; wings similar, roofed over body at rest; larvae with biting or sucking mouth parts; abdominal gills; carnivorous insect feeders and mite feeders; 5000 species

ORDER TRICHOPTERA caddis flies; vestigial biting mouth parts; wings roofed over body at rest; wings and body hairy or scaly; larvae aquatic and carnivorous, with biting mouth parts; 7000 species

ORDER LEPIDOPTERA moths, butterflies, silkworms; sucking mouth parts, with proboscis, wings membranous, scaly; larvae with biting mouth parts; moths, wings horizontal at rest, antennae feathery or filamentous; butterflies, wings folded up at rest, antennae club-shaped or knobbed; 125,000 species

ORDER DIPTERA flies, gnats, mosquitoes, midges; piercing-sucking biting mouth parts in proboscis; hind wings reduced to *halteres;* 100,000 species

ORDER SIPHONAPTERA fleas; piercing-sucking mouth parts; wingless; laterally compressed; ectoparasitic blood suckers; 1500 species

ORDER COLEOPTERA beetles, weevils, meal worms, glow worms; biting mouth parts; forewings horny *elytra,* hind wings folded under forewings; 300,000 species

ORDER STREPSIPTERA aberrant coleopteran derivatives; biting mouth parts reduced to halteres, hind wings membranous; females larvalike, wingless, eyeless; legless; larvae and females parasitic in insects, permanently in body of host; 300 species

ORDER HYMENOPTERA bees, ants, wasps, sawflies; biting, sucking, and lapping mouth parts; hind wings smaller than forewings; first abdominal segment fused to thorax, waist behind it; ovipositor for piercing, stinging, or sawing, often long and looped forward and downward; social and polymorphic, parthenogenesis common; pupae typically in cocoons; 110,000 species.

Levels of specialization Insect evolution has produced three levels of specialization. In the primitive Apterygota the hatched young are miniature wingless adults, and larvae and metamorphosis

Fig. 34-38 Exopterygote insects. (A) Praying mantis (order Orthoptera). (B) Human body louse (order Anopleura). (C) Damsel fly (order Odonata). (D) Mayfly (order Ephemeroptera). (E) Bedbug (order Hemiptera). (F) A 17-year locust (order Homoptera). (*A, Carolina Biological Supply Company.*)

A

B

C

D

E

F

are essentially absent. Springtails and bristletails ("silverfish") are included in this smallest group (Fig. 34.37). A second level is represented by the Exopterygota, in which the larvae resemble the adults. Early larvae still lack wings, however, and wing buds on the outside of the body grow progressively larger in a series of molting steps until winged adults are formed (see below). Included in this group are grasshoppers, termites, lice, dragonflies, mayflies, bugs, locusts, aphids, and many others (Fig. 34.38).

The third and most specialized level constitutes the Endopterygota, in which the larvae are caterpillars or caterpillarlike. After a series of molts a caterpillar transforms to a *pupa*, in which the wings and other adult structures develop from internal buds (see below). To this largest group belong moths, butterflies, flies, mosquitoes, fleas, beetles, ants, wasps, and numerous others (Fig. 34.39).

Structural characteristics The head of an insect consists of six fused segments, of which four bear appendages (Fig. 34.40 and see Table 34.2). The mandibles and first maxillae lie lateral to the mouth, and an upper lip, or *labrum*, protects the mouth anteriorly. The second maxillae form an underlip, or *labium*. Primitively, labrum, mandibles, maxillae, and labium function as *biting-and-chewing* mouth parts. Most Exopterygota have oral structures of this type. More advanced forms are variously equipped with *sucking*, *licking*, or *piercing-and-sucking* mouth parts. In a butterfly, for example, the maxillae are drawn out as elongated sucking tubes. These are rolled up at rest but can be extended deep into a flower for nectar. Flies, mosquitoes, bees, and many other Endopterygota likewise have mouth parts modified and adapted in special ways.

Each of three segments of the thorax carries a pair of legs and the second and third each typically also bears a pair of wings. A wing is a flattened fold of the chitinous exoskeleton, with air-filled, tubular spaces forming supporting veins (Fig. 34.41). Either pair of wings may be modified. For

A B C

D

E

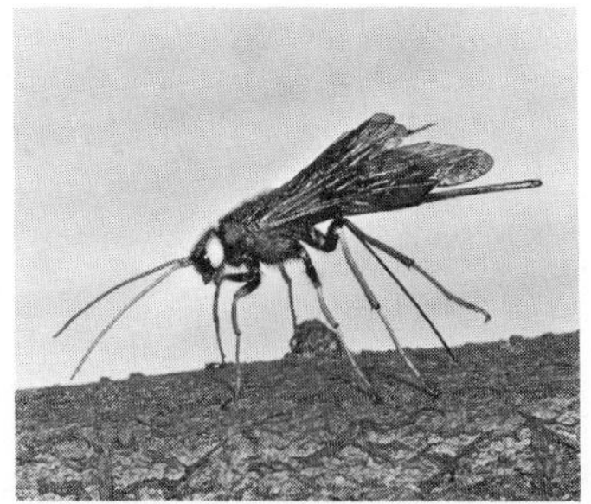

F

Fig. 34.39 Endopterygote insects. (A) Flea (order Siphonaptera). (B) Hercules beetle (order Coleoptera). (C) *Saturnia* moth (order Lepidoptera). (D) Larvae and one pupa of mosquito suspended from water surface (order Diptera). (E) Tropical fire ant (order Hymenoptera). (F) Wood wasp, with ovipositor (dark rod between hind legs) serving as wood borer (order Hymenoptera).

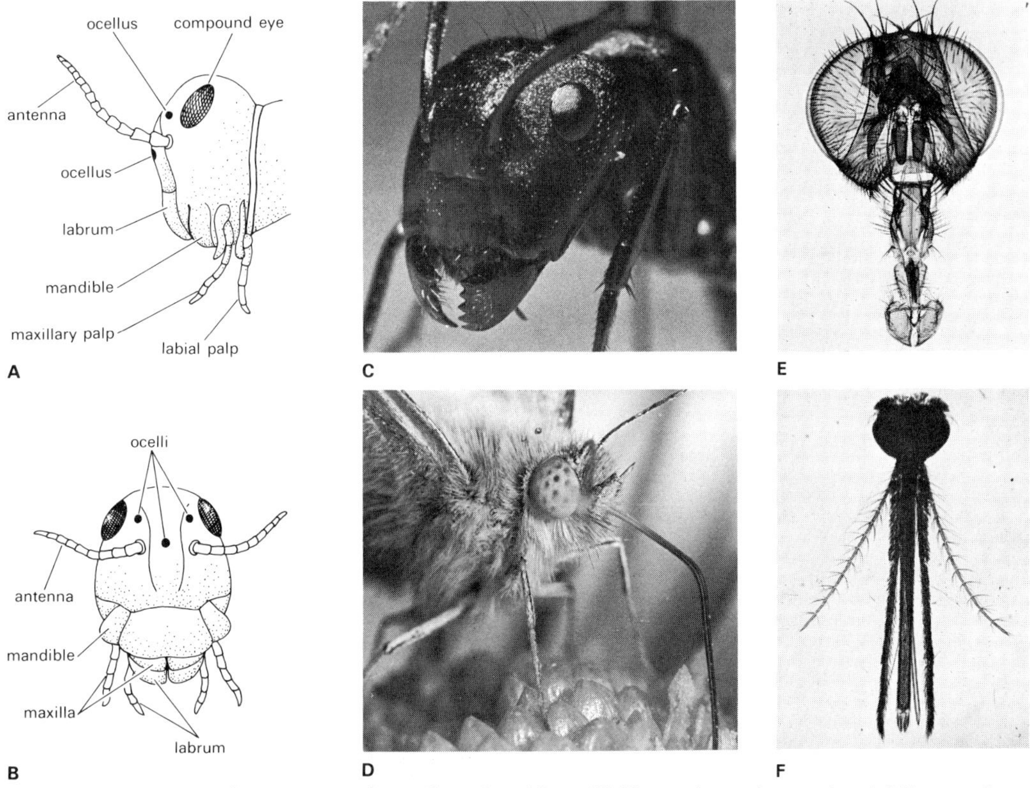

Fig. 34.40 Insect head structure and mouth parts. (A) to (C) Views of grasshopper head, biting mouth parts. See Fig. 34.19 for the function of palps. Note mandibles in (C). (D) Head of cabbage butterfly, showing sucking proboscis extended. The proboscis is a double tube formed from the pair of maxillae. It rolls up toward the head when not in use. (E) Front view of the proboscis apparatus of a housefly. Here the proboscis is a highly elaborate underlip (labium). (F) Head and sucking structures of a female mosquito. The sucking tube in the center is formed by long extensions of the upper lip (labrum) and the floor of the mouth. The dark bristly structures along each side of the central tube are the mandibles, and the shorter extensions on the outside are maxillae.

example, the hind wings are reduced to knobbed stumps, or *halteres,* in flies and mosquitoes (and the vibrations of halteres during flight produce the buzzing sounds made by these insects). The forewings are hardened into protective covers in grasshoppers, earwigs, and beetles. In fleas and many members of other groups, both pairs of wings are secondarily absent.

In the abdomen, the first seven segments lack appendages (see Fig. 34.27). The eighth and ninth segments of most female insects bear *ovipositors,* appendages modified to aid in egg laying (but formed into stings in bees and into saws and piercers in related groups). The appendages of the ninth segment in males form copulatory organs, and the anus is in the tenth segment in most cases. In these posterior segments are also the openings of the reproductive system. The eleventh segment, if present, is often extended as *anal cerci,* projections that form the "forceps" of earwigs, for example.

The last two thoracic and the first eight abdominal segments typically bear paired *spiracles* that lead to the tracheal breathing system. Such a

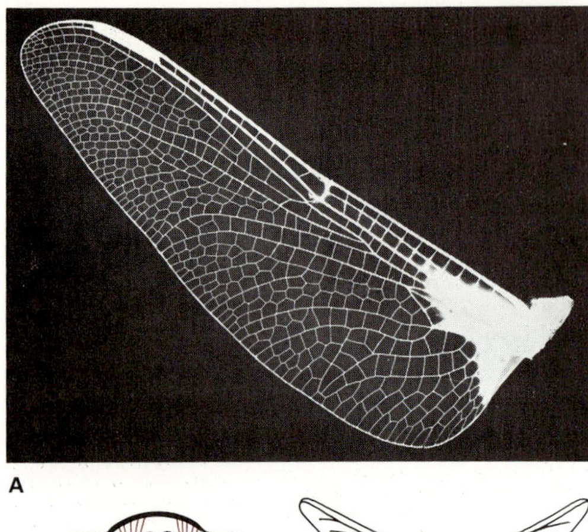

A

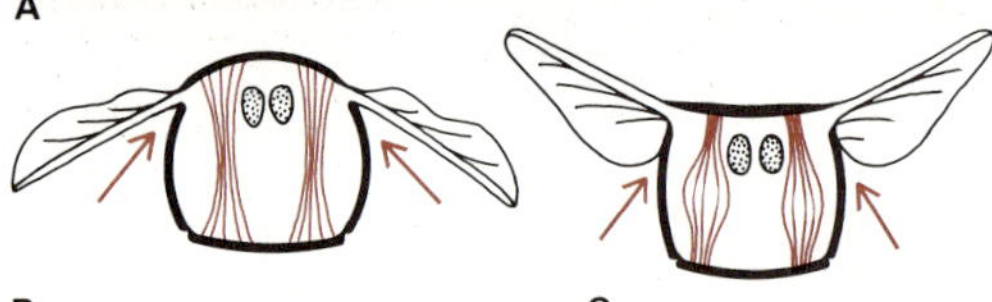

B C

Fig. 34.41 Insect flight. (A) A dragonfly wing, showing veins. (B) and (C) indicate the indirect, flight-producing wing musculature in the thorax. Arrows point to the fulcrums of the wings. In (B) the vertical muscles are relaxed, the longitudinal muscles are contracted, and the wings move down. In (C) the converse, with wings moved up.

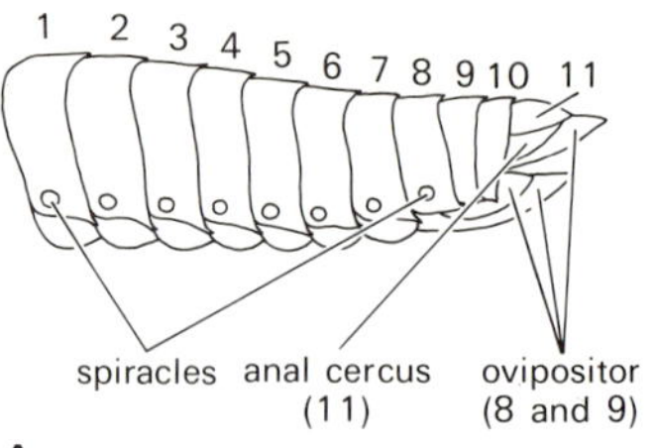

A

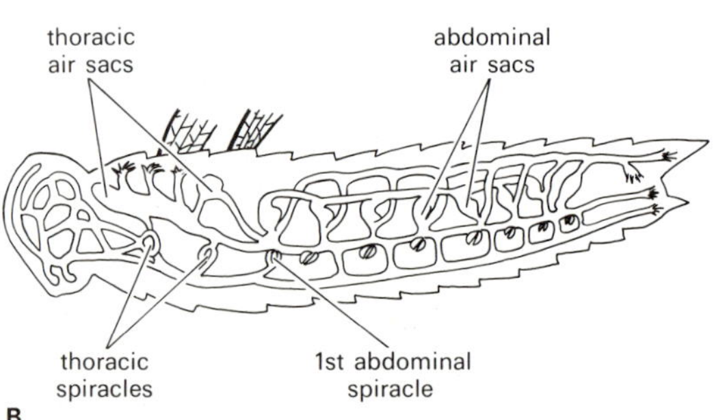

B

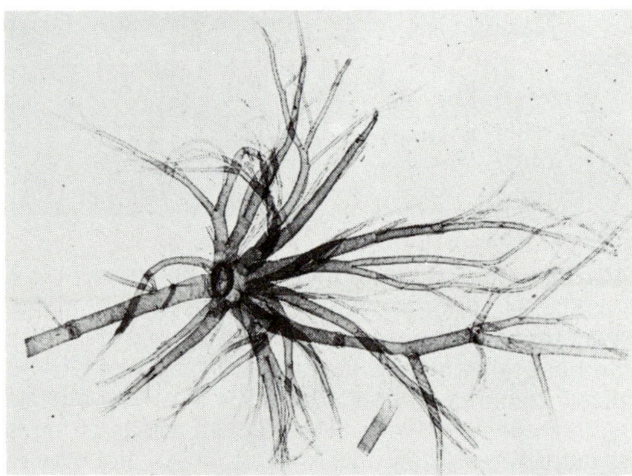

C

Fig. 34.42 Insect abdomen and breathing. (A) Side view of abdomen as in grasshopper; numbers refer to segment. (B) The main tracheal tubes and air sacs in the breathing system of a grasshopper. (C) A spiracle (center) and the systems of the tracheal tubes leading away from it.

system consists of interconnecting longitudinal tubes, air sacs, and branching air ducts (*tracheae;* Fig. 34.42). Contraction of muscles attached to the dorsal and ventral skeletal plates of the body produces exhalation, and relaxation of these muscles permits recoil of the skeletal plates and thus inhalation. Such breathing motions of the abdomen can be observed readily in a quiescent fly.

Internally, the nervous system is basically of the ladder type, but in many insects (as also in many other arthropods) various numbers of ventral ganglia are concentrated in single units. The elongated heart has paired ostia (see Fig. 34.28), and it lies dorsal to a usually well-developed pericardial membrane. Excretion occurs through Malpighian tubules that open to the hindgut.

Reproduction With very few exceptions fertilization takes place by copulation, and the fertilized eggs are laid (with the assistance of the ovipositors). In the embryos, appendage buds arise in anteroposterior succession (Fig. 34.43). In Apterygota and Exopterygota, such buds develop as adult appendages. Thus, when apterygotes hatch they are essentially miniature adults; and when exopterygotes hatch they are larvae (often called *nymphs*) that resemble adults greatly though the wings are still lacking. Exopterygote larvae then develop wings in the course of successive molting steps, during which external wing buds form from folds of chitin and become progressively larger (Fig. 34.44).

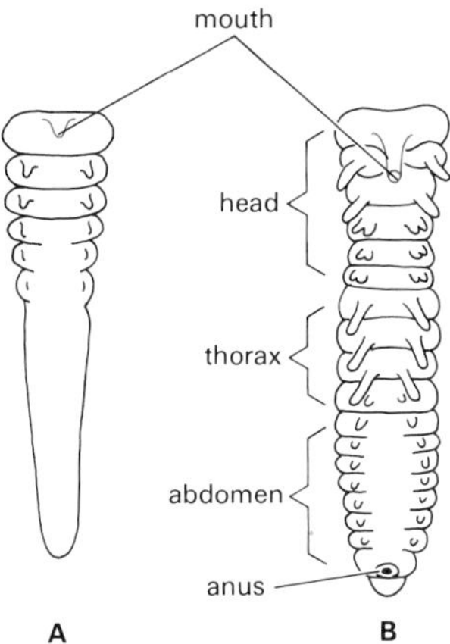

Fig. 34.43 Early insect development. (A), (B) Ventral views of two embryonic stages showing gradual anteroposterior formation of segments and segmental appendages. Note movement of mouth backward. Note also general annelidlike structure.

In Endopterygota the embryos hatch in a less fully developed condition, as annelidlike caterpillars. They undergo sucessive molts and grow, and eventually pockets arise in the body wall in which *imaginal disks* begin to develop. These disks are internal buds from which adult appendages such as wings, legs, and new mouth parts will later form. The transformation of caterpillar to adult occurs in the *pupa*. At this stage the pockets that contain the imaginal disks open out, and the adult appendages then make their first external appearance (Fig. 34.45).

Hormonal regulation of molting and metamorphosis The nymphal molts of exopterygotes and the larval and pupal molts of endopterygotes are regulated by a hormonal system quite similar to that of crustaceans (see above). Our present understanding of this system stems from experiments conducted in the 1920s and 1930s, the first of which provided results suggesting that a molt-inducing hormone is produced at the anterior end of an insect. Thread tied tightly around the body of an insect larva often prevented molting posterior to the ligature; the anterior end molted normally.

Such early experiments were greatly refined by the English biologist V. B. Wigglesworth. Most of his research was conducted on *Rhodnius*, a bloodsucking bug native to South America. This insect passes through five nymphal molts before undergoing metamorphosis into an adult. Each molt is preceded by a blood meal, which engorges the alimen-

Fig. 34.44 Exopterygote development. (A) Hatching. Emergence of a cicada larva (nymph) from an exoskeleton that has become too small for the growing insect. An already newly formed exoskeleton will harden quickly about the nymph. The cicada will be an adult when its wings are fully formed. (B) A grasshopper nymph, with wings at early growth stages. See also Color Fig. 13.

A

B

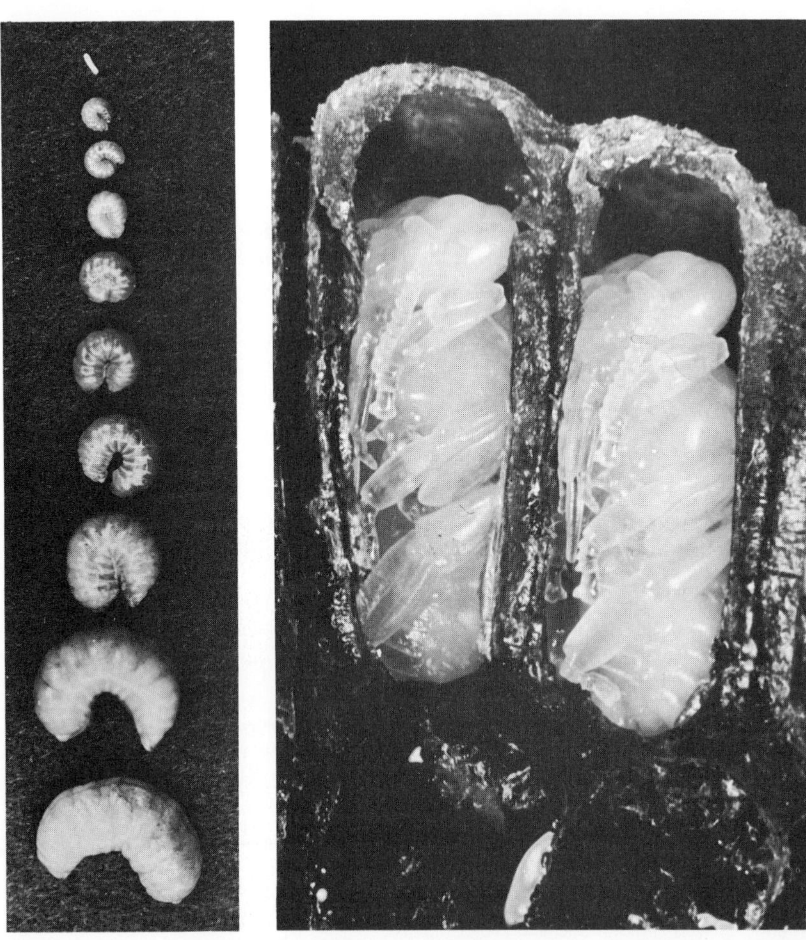

A B

Fig. 34.45 Endopterygote development. (A), (B) Honeybee. (A) Egg and series of larvae, each one day older than the previous one. (B) Pupae developing in (cutaway) brood cells of honeycomb. Legs already well formed. (C) to (F) Silkworm moth. (C) Caterpillar spinning pupation cocoon. (D) Fully formed cocoon, with pupa seen inside by translucent illumination. (E) Emergence of adult, wings still uninflated. (F) Some minutes later, wings attaining mature size.

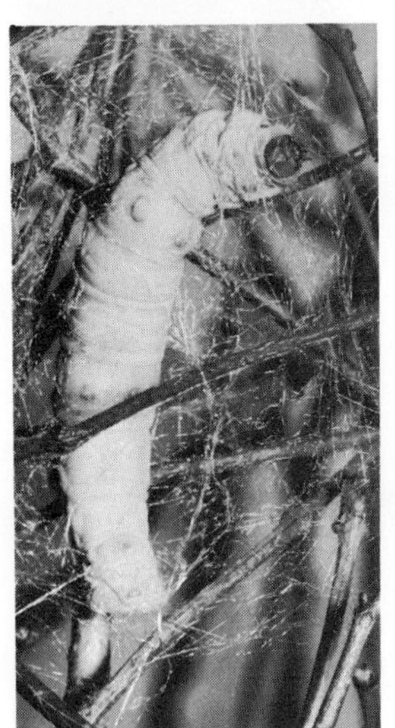

C

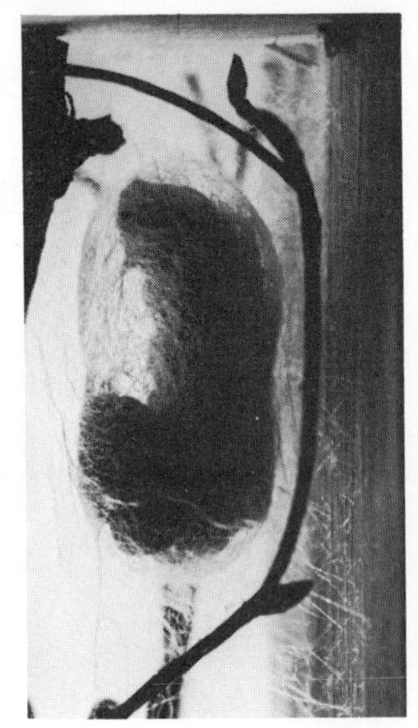

D

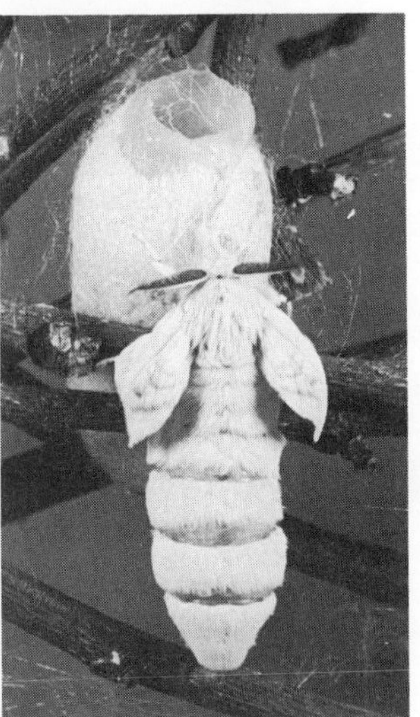

E

F

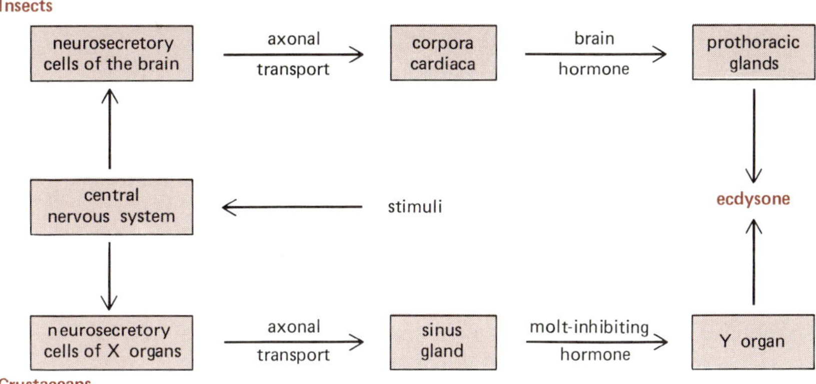

Fig. 34.46 Hormonal control of molting in crustaceans and insects. The prothoracic glands of insects and the Y organ of crustaceans are analogous structures. Both secrete ecdysone, but brain hormone of insects, produced in neurosecretory cells and released from the corpora cardiaca, stimulates secretion of ecdysone; the corresponding hormone released from the sinus gland of crustaceans inhibits release of ecdysone.

tary tract and stretches the abdomen. Wigglesworth determined that this distension was an essential trigger for a subsequent molt.

The last molt, from the fifth nymphal stage to adult, normally occurs about 28 days after a blood meal. Wigglesworth decapitated a group of the bugs during this 28-day interval to test for a molt-inducing hormone emanating from the anterior portion of the body. Nymphs decapitated more than 8 days after the blood meal almost always molted, becoming headless adults, but those decapitated earlier did not molt (headless *Rhodnius* nymphs often live for several months).

Wigglesworth also joined the circulatory systems of two headless nymphs surgically, one decapitated more than 8 days after its meal, the other decapitated earlier. Both nymphs underwent metamorphosis. These results clearly demonstrate passage of a bloodborne, molt-inducing hormone from the anterior region of the body to other body parts. Secretion of the hormone evidently begins about 8 days after the blood meal.

Later research showed the molt-inducing *brain hormone* of insects to be produced in neurosecretory cells of the brain. The hormone travels along the axons of these cells and becomes stored in the *corpora cardiaca*, a pair of glandular bodies located in the brain. Upon release, the brain hormone stimulates glands in the *prothorax*, a part of the body immediately posterior to the head (the first pair of legs connects to the prothorax). Stimulated by brain hormone, the *prothoracic glands* secrete ecdysone, the same molt-inducing hormone produced by the Y organ of crustaceans (Fig. 34.46).

Fig. 34.47 *Rhodnius prolixus.* Metamorphosis can be prevented by artificially raising the levels of juvenile hormone in an immature bug during its last nymphal stage. When treated individuals molt, they become giant nymphs instead of winged adults.

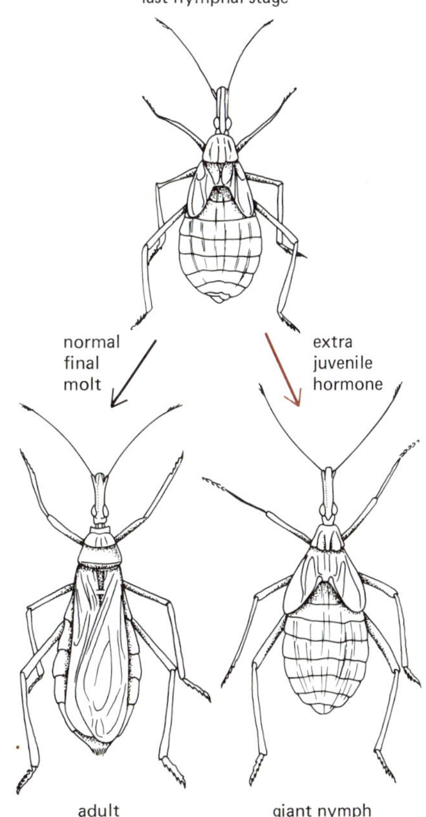

This steroid affects the genes of many cells, including those responsible for production of a new exoskeleton.

Wigglesworth's experiments also explained why metamorphosis in *Rhodnius* occurs only on the final molt. The British scientist injected blood from an adult bug into a young nymph. Shortly thereafter, the nymph underwent partial metamorphosis. Wigglesworth correctly hypothesized that the blood of nymphs normally contains a hormone which inhibits metamorphosis during early molts but whose secretion stops before the final molt.

The treated nymph underwent partial metamorphosis because Wigglesworth had *diluted* its blood, containing a high concentration of the molt-inducing hormone, with the blood of an adult. Mature insects do not secrete significant amounts of this *juvenile hormone,* now known to be secreted by a pair of glands (the *corpora allata*) located just behind the brain.

In addition to identifying where juvenile hormone is produced, biologists have validated yet another of Wigglesworth's suspicions. Metamorphosis accompanies specific molts in insects because of shifts in the relative concentrations of ecdysone and juvenile hormone. When sufficiently high concentrations of juvenile hormone are present at the time of molting, metamorphosis does not occur. But when production of juvenile hormone decreases enough, as occurs during the final molt of *Rhodnius,* the comparatively high concentrations of ecdysone triggers both a molt *and* metamorphosis. Indeed, metamorphisis can be prevented by artificially raising the level of juvenile hormone in *Rhodnius* nymphs about to undergo a final molt. Such nymphs molt normally, but they retain their immature characteristics and do not become winged adults (Fig. 34.47).

The larval and pupal metamorphoses of endopterygotes are similarly controlled. Larvae become transformed into pupae when the production of juvenile hormone decreases suffcently; metamorphosis from pupa into adult occurs when production of juvenile hormone virtually ceases (Fig. 34.48).

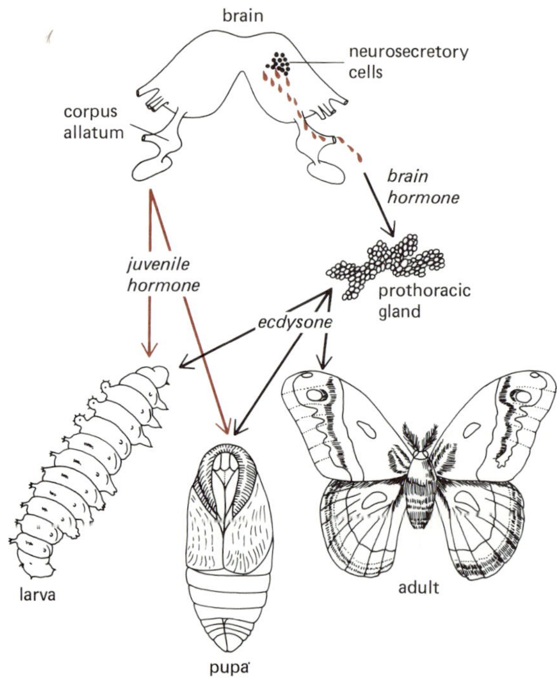

Fig. 34.48 Hormonal control of metamorphosis in endopterygotes. Larvae molt to another larval stage when concentrations of juvenile hormone are high. Metamorphosis into the pupal stage occurs when the concentration of juvenile hormone drops to low levels. When little or no juvenile hormone is present, pupae molt to the adult state.

Diversity The class of insects as a whole contains some two dozen orders, many of them representing a wide range of ways of life. For example, the order of beetles includes parasites, commensals, carnivores, herbivores (including wood-, wool-, and glue-eaters), omnivores (including rock borers), aquatic types, subterranean types, arboreal types, diurnal and nocturnal types, and dozens of others, each adapted to a particular, often highly specialized mode of existence.

Some insects are beneficial, but many others are harmful. Beneficial insects include silkworms, bees that produce honey, and a small group of "lac" insects that secrete a valuable waxy substance used in making shellac. Other insects benefit human beings by preying on disease-causing and other highly injurious organisms. The Australian lady bird beetle, for example, was introduced into California because it was known to prey on the fluted scale, a type of insect that can severely damage orange and lemon trees. Other injurious insects include potato beetles, Japanese beetles, European corn borers, cotton boll weevils, chinch bugs, aphids, and white grubs. These and other insect pests inflict over 4 billion dollars damage annually to agricultural crops grown in the United States. Some insects, such as the blood-sucking horn fly, can seriously injure livestock, and several insects carry disease-causing organisms. Indeed, insects are chiefly responsible for the spread of typhus, malaria, yellow fever, African sleeping sickness, bubonic plague, and many other diseases afflicting human beings.

Review Questions

1 Give definitions of coelomates, protostomial coelomates, lophophorates, and schizocoelomates. Which phyla are included in each of these groups? What is a lophophore?

2 What are the identifying characteristics of Mollusca? Annelida? Arthropoda?

3 Review the identifying characteristics of each class of mollusks and name a few representative organisms that are included in each class. In what ways do each of these classes still exhibit the body organization of the hypothetical ancestral mollusk?

4 Give taxonomic definitions of annelids and of each of the annelid classes. Describe the development of a segmented body organization from a trochophore larva. Then describe the segmental structure of an adult polychaete.

5 Compare and contrast the basic external structures of a squid, an annelid, an arthropod. Name and indicate a function for the principal external structures of each.

6 Describe the structure of an earthworm and contrast it with that of *Nereis*. Show how mating and fertilization occur in earthworms. Contrast the structure of a leech with that of an earthworm.

7 Characterize the phylum Arthropoda taxonomically and name the subphyla and classes. How are these subgroups presumably interrelated historically? Compare the species numbers of the various groups.

8 How have the chitinous exoskeleton and the body segmentation contributed to the broad diversification of the arthropod phylum? Describe the basic exterior structure of the arthropod body and the general organization of the 10 organ systems. Review the structure of arthropod eyes.

9 Review the segmental structure of the chelicerate cephalothorax and the structure and function of the appendages of that body division. Describe the structure of a horseshoe crab, a scorpion, a spider.

10 Distinguish between the chelicerate and mandibulate subphyla. Describe the segmental structure of the crustacean head, thorax, and abdomen. Where is the sinus gland located, and what is its function?

11 Name and state the functions of the appendages of a lobster. Describe the internal anatomy of a lobster. In the process review the organization of every organ system.

12 Review the nature of the larval stages of crustacea. Name crustacea:

- **a.** That live on land, in fresh water, and in the ocean
- **b.** That are parasitic
- **c.** That are sessile
- **d.** That are planktonic

13 Describe the segmental structure of centipedes and millipedes and contrast the external anatomy of these animals. What features are similar to those of insects?

14 Define insects taxonomically. Describe the segmental structure and the internal anatomy of an insect. Review the structure of insect mouth parts. What is the structure of an insect wing? How do insects breathe?

15 Show how insect development differs according to the subclass or superorder. What are imaginal disks? What developmental events occur in a pupa?

16 How have biologists demonstrated that specific hormones influence molting in insects and crustaceans? How have they shown hormones to be involved in the control of insect metamorphosis? Cite examples of specific experiments and experimental results. How is the hormonal control of molting similar in insects and crustaceans? How is it different?

17 Discuss the ecological and economic importance of several kinds of protostomes.

Collateral Readings

Barnes, R. D.: "Invertebrate Zoology," 4th ed., Saunders, Philadelphia, 1980. This modern treatment includes all invertebrate phyla, including those discussed in this chapter.

Borrer, D. J., D. M. DeLong, and **C. A. Triplehorn:** "An Introduction to the Study of Insects," 4th ed., Holt, New York, 1976. Thorough coverage of all major orders of insects.

Buchsbaum, R.: 'Animals without Backbones," University of Chicago, Chicago, 1948. All invertebrate groups are examined in elementary fashion, including those discussed in this chapter; well-illustrated.

Chapman, R. E.: "The Insects: Structure and Function," American Elsevier, New York, 1969. A thorough treatment of the anatomy and physiology of insects.

Chauvin, R.: "The World of an Insect," McGraw-Hill, New York, 1967. A well-illustrated account of these arthropods can be found in this paperback.

Daly, H. V., J. T. Doyen, and **P. R. Ehrlich:** "Introduction to Insect Biology and Diversity," McGraw-Hill, New York, 1978. An excellent introduction to these fascinating animals.

Horridge, G. A.: The Compound Eye of Insects, *Scientific American,* July 1977. Describes the many adaptive features of this complex sense organ.

Jones, J. C.: The Sexual Life of a Mosquito, *Scientific American,* April 1968. An account on the reproduction of the mosquito that transmits yellow fever.

Klots, A. B., and **E. B. Klots:** "Living Insects of the World," Doubleday, Garden City, N.Y., 1962. Written for the layperson, this informative book contains spectacular photographs.

Morton J. E.: "Molluscs," 4th ed., Hutchinson, London, 1967. Covers all aspects of molluscan biology.

Nicholls, J. G., and **D. V. Essen:** The Nervous System of the Leech, *Scientific American,* January 1974. The comparatively simple central nervous system of this annelid is described.

Purchon, R. D.: "The Biology of the Mollusca," Pergamon, New York, 1968. A general introduction to this phylum.

Russell-Hunter, W. D.: "A Life of Invertebrates," Macmillan, New York, 1979. A comprehensive coverage of all major invertebrate groups.

Schneider, D.: The Sex-Attractant Receptor of Moths, *Scientific American,* July 1974. Describes the mechanism whereby the sex pheromone of female silk moths is detected by male moths.

Wright R. H.: Why Mosquito Repellents Repel, *Scientific American,* July 1975. The interaction between insect repellents and mosquito receptor structures is discussed.

Chapter 35 Coelomates: Deuterostomes

Learning Objectives

After reading this chapter you should be able to:

1. Name five phyla of Enterocoelomates and list the distinguishing characteristics of each; define deuterostome and dipleurula.
2. State a taxonomic definition of the phylum Echinodermata; list the classes of echinoderms and a representative organism of each; construct a diagram that depicts the external anatomy of a starfish; construct a similar diagram that illustrates the structural organization of the digestive, reproductive, nervous, and water vascular systems of a starfish.
3. State the functional relationships between the madreporite, stone canal, ring canal, radial canals, ampullae, and tube feet of a starfish; explain how starfish are able to open clams and oysters; construct a diagram that depicts the principal structural features of a sea lily, sea cucumber, sea urchin, and sand dollar and name a function for each structure you identify.
4. Give a taxonomic definition of the phylum Chordata; name the three subphyla of chordates, and state a taxonomic definition of each; cite a representative organism of each chordate subphylum; define notochord, pharyngeal gill slits, and tadpole.
5. Construct a diagram that depicts the development and metamorphosis of an adult tunicate; state the possible evolutionary significance of the tunicate tadpole; construct a diagram that depicts the main structural features of an adult tunicate; explain how an adult tunicate obtains nutrients.
6. Identify the structural traits of a cephalochordate.
7. Name the classes of vertebrates and a repreresentative organism of each; list the changes in vertebrate anatomy that were associated with the change from ancestral filter feeding to bulk feeding by mouth; state the principal changes in surface anatomy and in the circulatory, breathing, reproductive, and excretory systems that occurred during the evolution of terrestrial vertebrates from aquatic ancestors; differentiate between pro-, meso-, and metanephros and describe the evolutionary relationships between these three structures.
8. Differentiate between how ammocoete larvae and lampreys obtain nutrients; illustrate the general structure of a lamprey; define pineal eye.
9. Differentiate between ostracoderms and placoderms and state the presumed evolutionary relationships between ostracoderms and fishes; differentiate between cartilage fishes and bony fishes; illustrate the general structural traits of sharks.
10. State the evolutionary significance of paleoniscoid fishes; differentiate between flesh-finned and ray-finned bony fishes and give an example of each; differentiate between clupeiform and perciform teleost fishes and give an example of each.
11. Name the presumed evolutionary ancestors of amphibians; state in what respects amphibia are basically aquatic and in what respects they are terrestrial; list at least two ways in which amphibians benefit people.
12. List the principal characteristics of reptiles, birds, and mammals and explain how these characteristics are adaptive to specific environments; construct a diagram contrasting the flow of blood through the heart of an amphibian, reptile, and bird or mammal; differentiate between egg-laying, marsupial, and placental mammals, and name a representative organism of each.
13. Identify the four main evolutionary lines of Eutherian mammals and list representative organisms of each line; name at least two adaptive trends that have occurred randomly in two or more of these evolutionary lines and postulate why such parallel trends have occurred.

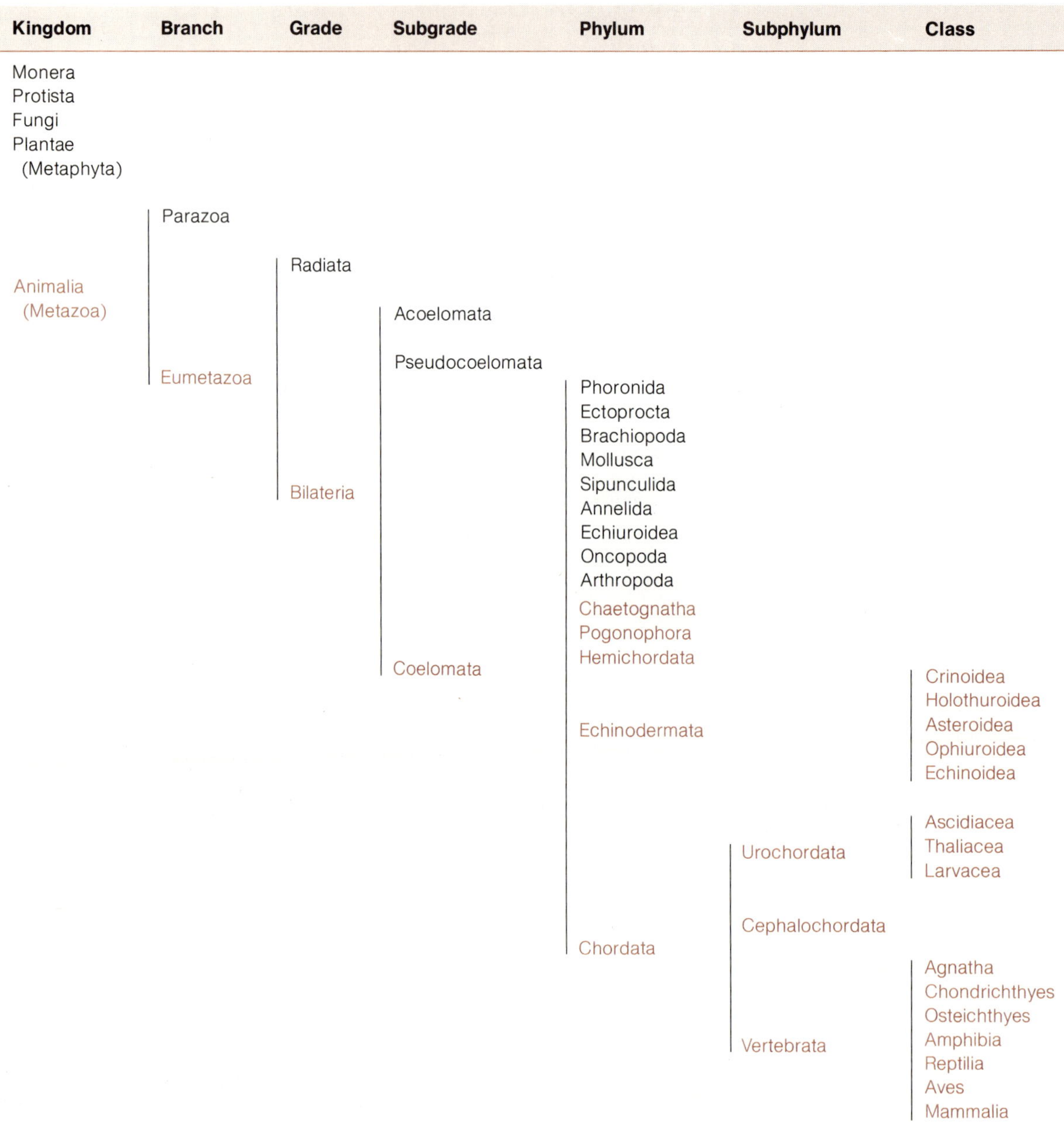

Kingdom	Branch	Grade	Subgrade	Phylum	Subphylum	Class
Monera						
Protista						
Fungi						
Plantae (Metaphyta)						
	Parazoa					
		Radiata				
Animalia (Metazoa)						
			Acoelomata			
			Pseudocoelomata			
	Eumetazoa					
				Phoronida		
				Ectoprocta		
				Brachiopoda		
				Mollusca		
		Bilateria				
				Sipunculida		
				Annelida		
				Echiuroidea		
				Oncopoda		
				Arthropoda		
				Chaetognatha		
				Pogonophora		
				Hemichordata		
			Coelomata			
						Crinoidea
						Holothuroidea
				Echinodermata		Asteroidea
						Ophiuroidea
						Echinoidea
						Ascidiacea
					Urochordata	Thaliacea
						Larvacea
					Cephalochordata	
				Chordata		
						Agnatha
						Chondrichthyes
						Osteichthyes
					Vertebrata	Amphibia
						Reptilia
						Aves
						Mammalia

As noted in Chap. 33, deuterostomial animals are those in which the first opening of the embryonic alimentary cavity becomes the anus, and the later second opening forms the mouth (see Fig. 33.2). Deuterostomes also happen to be enterocoelomates; their coeloms arise as cavities in mesoderm sacs that grow out from the gut- (or "enteron-") producing endoderm (see Fig. 33.4).

ENTEROCOELOMATES

Phylum Chaetognatha arrowworms; marine, planktonic; head with chitinous grasping spines and covering hood; trunk with lateral and tail fins; coelom subdivided into three compartments; without circulatory, breathing, or excretory systems; development without larvae; 50 species

Phylum Pogonophora beard worms; deep-sea, tube-dwelling; with anterior tentacles; alimentary system absent; circulatory system closed; without breathing system; body marked into three parts (*protosome, mesosome, metasome*) and coelom correspondingly divided (*protocoel, mesocoel, metacoel*); 25 species (see accompanying Biology Highlight)

Phylum Hemichordata acorn worms; marine; colonial in secreted housings or solitary in sand burrows; body marked into three parts (*protosome, mesosome, metasome*), and coelom correspondingly divided (*protocoel, mesocoel, metacoel*); mostly with gill slits; typically with larvae; 100 species

Phylum Echinodermata spiny-skinned animals; marine; larvae bilateral, with protocoel, mesocoel, and metacoel in early stages; adult pentaradial; with calcareous endoskeletons and coelomic water-vascular system; 6000 species

Phylum Chordata chordates; all environments; with notochord, pharyngeal gill slits, and dorsal hollow nerve cord in preadult stages or throughout life; with tailed *tadpoles* or without larvae; 50,000 species

Developmental and structural evidence suggests that arrowworms probably are not related very closely to the other enterocoelomates. Also, the presence of chitin in this phylum is unique for enterocoelomates. The other phyla do appear to represent a more or less broadly interrelated group. Hemichordates could be closest to an ancestral enterocoelomate line, and beard worms, echinoderms, and chordates could have evolved from it as branch lines (Fig. 35.1 and see Fig. 33.5).

Among unifying features exhibited with varying degrees of similarity in the last four phyla are, for example, the tendency to secrete a celluloselike compound (*tunicin*) as a body covering; the tendency of passing through a so-called *dipleurula* stage

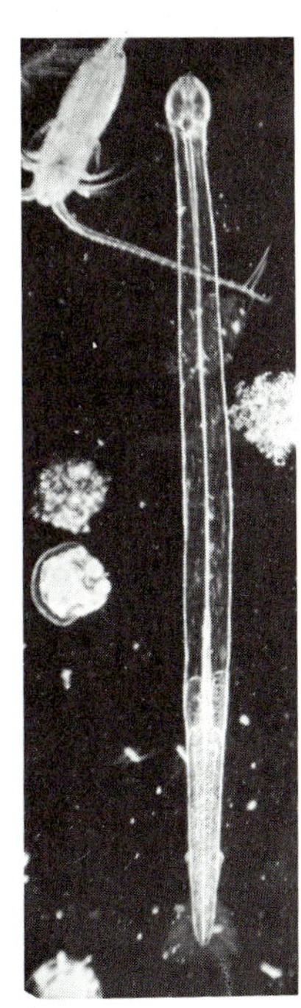

A

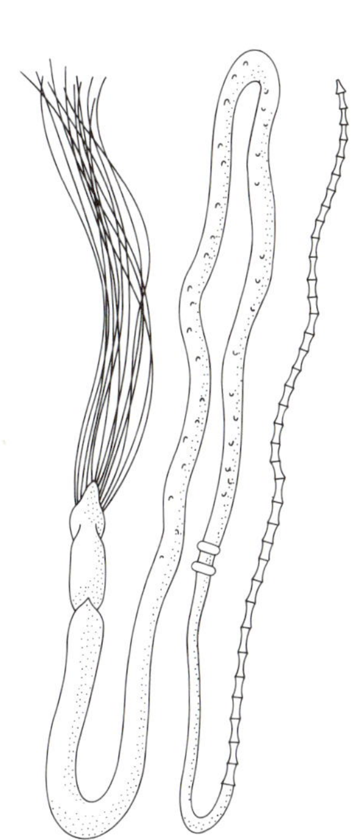

B

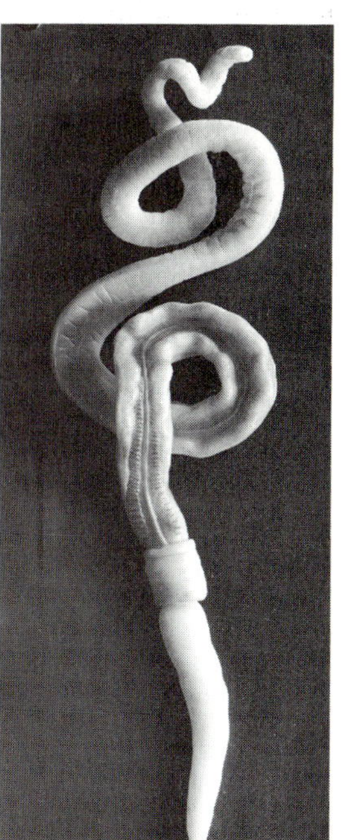

C

Fig. 35.1 Enterocoelomates. (A) An arrowworm. (B) External features of a beard worm. The tentacles emanate from a short head region. Behind this region is a collar section, and the rest of the body represents the trunk. (C) Model of an acorn worm, dorsal view. Note proboscis, conspicuous collar, and row of paired gill slits along anterior portion of trunk. (*A, Courtesy of Douglas P. Wilson; C, American Museum of Natural History.*)

Biology Highlight Benthic Oases, Giant Worms

The Galapagos Rift, East Pacific Ocean, February 1979

The three scientists have been descending for almost $1\frac{1}{2}$ hours. They are now almost 8000 feet below the ocean surface, inside the deep-sea submarine *Alvin*. Someone once jokingly described the 5-billion-dollar research vessel as an elaborate metal coffin. At this moment the description seems quite humorless; gauges indicate that water pressure on the submarine's hull is almost 38,000 tons per square inch.

Fred Grassle, a marine scientist from the Woods Hole Oceanographic Institution and the only biologist aboard, stares intently through one of the observation ports. There is nothing to see. The tiny sub has been cloaked in darkness since it passed below the 2000-foot mark. But the scientists are nearing the ocean bottom. *Alvin's* lights will soon reveal rock formations and perhaps what the three scientists are really looking for, the milky blue shimmer of a *hydrothermal vent,* a place where columns of mineral-laden hot water pour forth through fissures in the earth's oceanic crust.

The existence of hydrothermal vents had been confirmed a few years before. The volcanic activity that produces eruptions of molten lava in terrestrial environments triggers similar events along the ocean floor. The heat of the lava and the vibrations accompanying its movements produce fissures in the sea floor. Cold water seeps downward through cracks surrounding rising columns of lava, becomes heated, and eventually is forced upward, returning through vents (Fig. 1). Water surrounding the vents may be as much as 40°F warmer than the near freezing temperatures normally found in deep-sea habitats.

Considerable amounts of lava are forced upward along deep-ocean *rifts,* regions where the molten upwellings add new sea floor and contribute to continental drift (see Chap. 29). It therefore was not surprising when a series of hydrothermal vents was found in 1977 by a team of scientists exploring the Galapagos Rift off the coast of South America aboard the research ship *Knorr*. But when the vents were examined visually using a suspended movie camera, the scientists were stunned. The ocean floor immediately surrounding the vents was littered with hundreds of clams, some with shells over 12 inches long, strange dandelionlike creatures moored to rocks by long threads and, most interestingly of all, colonies of huge blood-red worms housed in white tubes that looked like plastic. It was as if the scientists aboard *Knorr* were receiving images from another planet. They had never seen anything like it (Fig. 2).

The ocean bottom at 8000-foot depths usually is comparatively barren. The amount of organic matter reaching such depths from the photic zone above is far too meager to support the wealth of biomass observed in and near the vents (see Chap. 9). What source of energy supported these benthic oases of life? The answer was provided by the rotten-egg smell of sulfur that emanated from containers of water retrieved from the vents; the

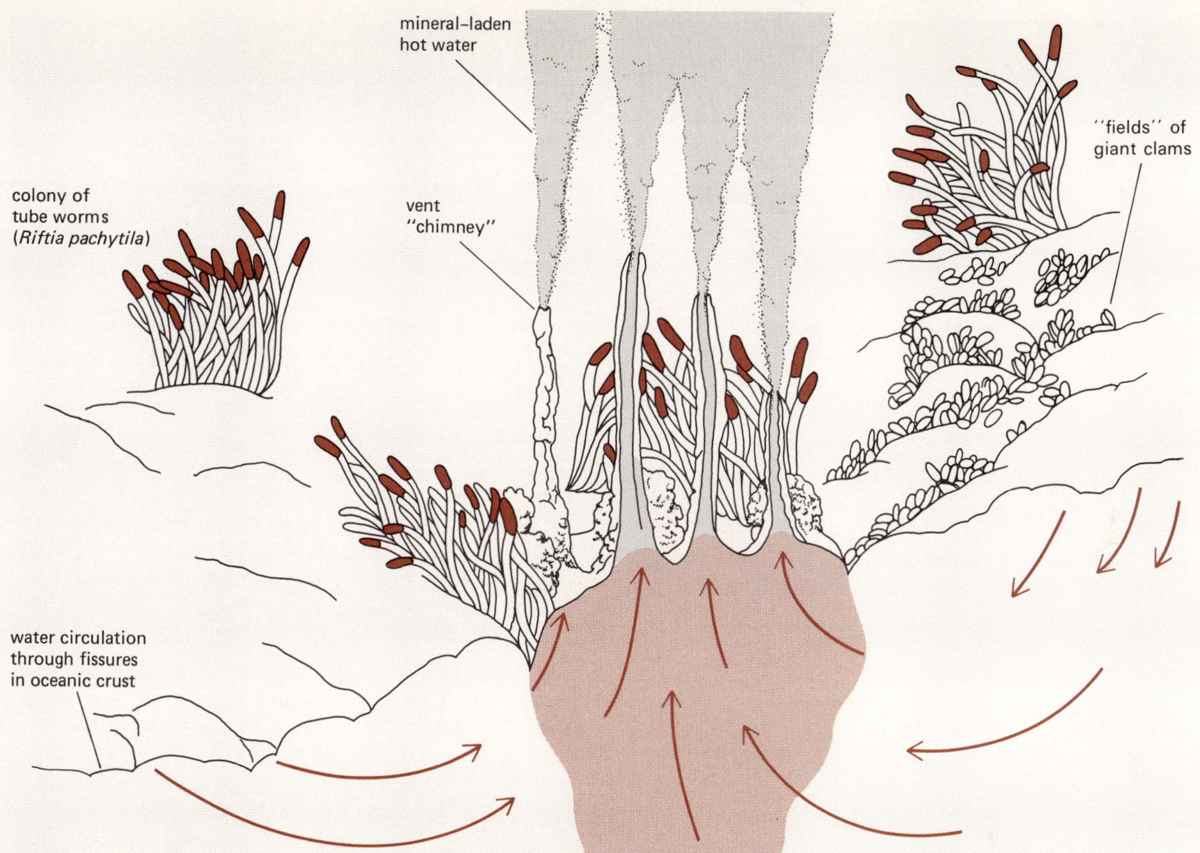

Fig. 1 Hydrothermal vents. A composite drawing of two hydrothermal vent areas; one off the coast of California, the other off the Galapagos Islands in the East Pacific. Cold (2°C) water seeps downward through the earth's crust around the periphery of the vents. The water, which is heated by upwellings of molten lava that underlie the sea floor, is forced upward through the vents. In hydrothermal vents off the coast of California, rocklike chimneys called "black smokers" have been formed from minerals in the rising streams of hot (350°C) water. The warm water surrounding the vents supports a rich diversity of animal life (see Fig. 2).

water samples teemed with chemoautotrophic sulfur bacteria (see Chap. 11).

The high sulfur content of seawater near vents was not unexpected. Large amounts of hydrogen sulfide (H_2S) become dissolved in water making the circuitous loop down through porous rock and fissures, and up through vents. Hydrogen sulfide is a prime source of energy for certain chemoautrotropic sulfur bacteria. When these microbes oxidize hydrogen sulfide, energy is released and used in the manufacture of organic foods (see Chap. 11). The sulfur bacteria apparently constitute the principal and probably sole producers for vent ecosystems, which are independent of sunlight. Moreover, the bacteria are extremely prolific. Samples of water analyzed aboard *Knorr* revealed concentrations of suspended food 300 to 500 times greater than that just outside vent areas and about 4 times greater than that of most coastal waters.

Fig. 2 Animals of hydrothermal vents. (A) Mats of acorn worms, nicknamed "spaghetti," cover rocks near a vent (see also Fig. 35.1C). (B) These fragile yellow-colored organisms, dubbed "dandelions" by scientists of the Galapagos Rift expedition, appear to be colonies of coelenterates (see Chap. 33). Each one-to-two-inch colony is attached to the sea floor by weblike fibers. (C) This photograph, taken by *Alvin's* exterior camera, shows a cluster of giant tube worms. The blood-red anterior portion of the worms can be seen projecting from the white tubes. (D) Geologist Robert Ballard of Woods Hole Oceanographic Institution examines a giant tube worm recovered during the Galapagos Rift expedition.

Fred Grassle had not been a member of the *Knorr* crew during its 1977 expedition, but now, 2 years later, he would be the first biologist to conduct an on-site examination of vents along the Galapagos Rift. Grassle's exploration proved to be exciting, satisfying, and most productive. Using *Alvin's* many instruments, including an extendable claw, Grassle and his colleagues were able to carry several organisms from the vents to the surface. After preservation, the organisms or their parts were distributed to a wide variety of scientists for classification and further study.

The Smithsonian Institution, Washington, D.C.

Of all the animals found in the vents, Meredith Jones was most interested in the giant tube worms. An invertebrate zoologist at the National Museum of Natural History, Jones had spent many productive years investigating the anatomical, taxonomic, and evolutionary relationships between a wide variety of worms—organisms many people shudder even to think about, much less look at. But to Jones, the opportunity to coordinate a first-hand investigation of the huge vent worms was a real treat.

Jones began by studying the gross anatomy of the worms. He prepared virtually all parts of an animal for microscopic examination, and then undertook the painstaking process of determining how all its tissues fit together as a composite whole. Eventually, he compared the fine and gross structures of the vent specimens with those of other species in order to determine how the giant worms should be classified.

The first studies confirmed what preliminary dissections had already revealed. The giant worms most closely resembled the Pogonophora, a phylum of almost exclusively deep-water organisms colloquially called *beard worms*. Pogonophorans were unknown before the twentieth century; the first beard worm was dredged from waters off the coast of Indonesia in 1900. More than 80 additional species have been discovered since then, all far smaller than the species discovered along the Galapagos Rift.

Like other pogonophorans, the vent worms have four body regions. The most anterior, the *plume,* consists of a semisolid core covered by a series of overlapping flaps, or *lamellae* (Fig. 3). An extensive array of tiny tentacles projects from the base of each lamella. Behind the tentacle-bearing plume is a short body part (the *vestimentum* in Fig. 3A) containing glands that produce tube-forming secretions. The *trunk,* the third and longest body part, is followed by the short *opisthosome,* a terminal segmented structure that bears chitinous bristles and probably functions in anchoring the worm in its tube. The structure of this most posterior body part suggests that pogonophorans might not be enterocoelomates, as indicated by other criteria (see Fig. 33.4), but instead might be related to annelids.

As the anatomical studies progressed, it became increasingly apparent that the giant vent worms were most like *Lamellibrachia barhami,* a species of beard worms collected in 1966 off the coast of California. *Lamellibrachia* were so different from other beard worms known at the time that they were categorized as a new class, the Afrenulata. The vent specimens exhibited the same structural features as the new class. Jones' studies also showed that the giant tube worms should be classified as Vestimentifera, the order that included *Lamellibrachia*.

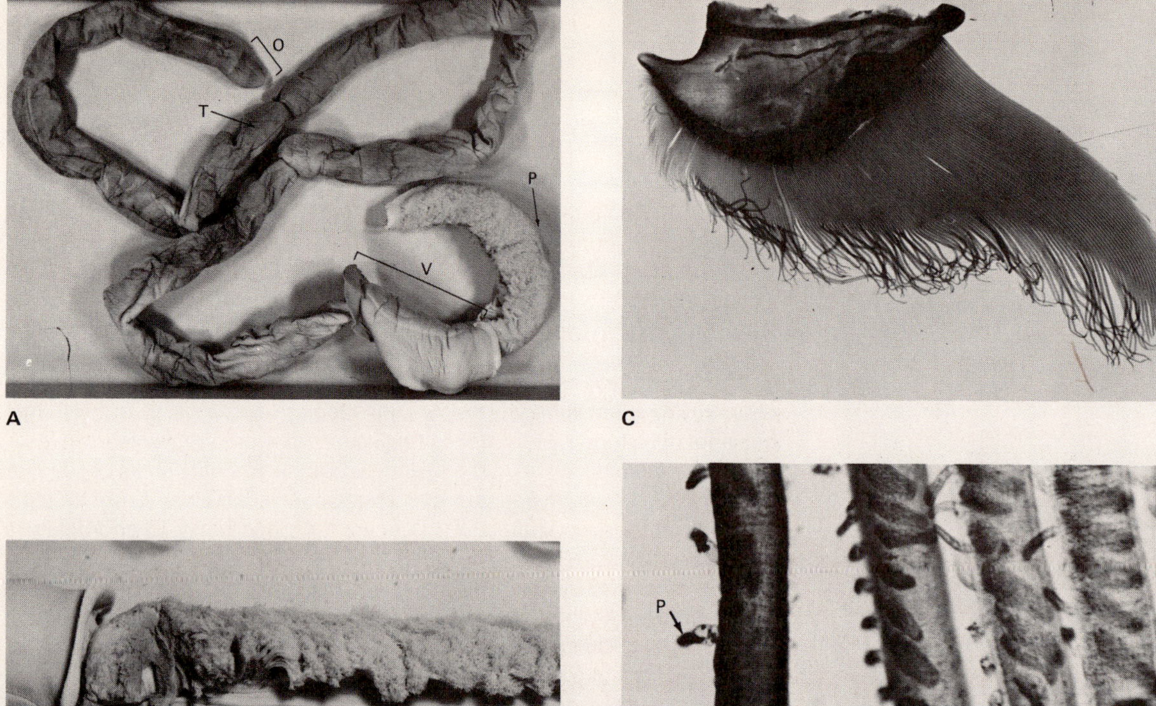

Fig. 3 Tube worms: external anatomy. (A) A preserved tube worm showing the four body regions. P, plume; V, vestimentum; O, opisthosome. The trunk (T) is the longest body part, extending from the posterior of the vestimentum to the anterior of the opisthosome. (B) Ventral surface of the plume. Note the many overlapping lamellae that cover the gelatinous core of the plume. (C) An individual lamella. The base of the lamella is at the top. Note the tentacles, which project outward from the base. The tentacles are fused along most of their length, and are free to move as individual units only at their tips. (D) Pinnules. The free ends of tentacles bear surface projections called pinnules (P). These structures each contain a vascular loop that greatly increases the surface area of blood vessels in the plume.

In many respects, however, the vent worms were significantly different from *Lamellibrachia* and from all other known pogonophorans. The relative size of the plume, the angle at which the lamellae projected, the orientation of the excretory ducts—structural details such as these convinced Jones that the vent worms should constitute a new family of Pogonophora. He set to work describing the characteristics that henceforth would be used to define this new family. Jones designated them as Riftiidae, a reference to the rift habitat in which the worms were discovered. He next selected structural attributes most appropriate for genus and species subdivisions. The name *Riftia* seemed a good choice for genus, another reference to the organism's habitat. Jones chose *pachytila* (*pachy* = thick, *ptilon* = feather) for the species name. One of the most striking features of the animal was its thick lamellae-bearing anterior plume.

In addition to establishing taxonomic criteria, Jones documented several of the worm's specialized adaptations to the unusual environmental conditions existing near deep-sea vents. In its native habitat, *Riftia* is almost constantly bathed by streams of warm water emanating from vents. Although they contain much organic matter, sufficient to support colonies of organisms as large as *Riftia,* these warm streams do not contain oxygen. *Riftia* apparently receives all its oxygen from currents of cold water that sweep in periodically from the surrounding environment. It seems logical, therefore, that that the worms must have a highly efficient method of absorbing oxygen and transporting it to all tissues of the body. Perhaps *Riftia* has a highly evolved blood and an elaborate system of blood vessels.

This hypothesis is supported chiefly by two observations. First, Alissa Arp, working in James Childress' laboratory at the Marine Science Institute at the University of California at Santa Barbara, has found that the blood of *Riftia* contains a high concentration of hemoglobin. Moreover, the affinity of the hemoglobin for oxygen also is extraordinarily high for an invertebrate.

Second, Jones' anatomical studies demonstrated that *Riftia* has an extremely extensive and intricate circulatory system, particularly in the tentacle-covered plume, the principal oxygen-absorbing organ of the worm. The heart, a large dorsal vessel, is located in the trunk. Blood travels toward the plume through the main branch of this dorsal vessel, which in turn gives rise to smaller branches. The more than 600 lamellae of the plume receive blood from these smaller branches. A pair of tiny blood vessels is housed inside each tentacle of a lamella, and since each of these flaplike structures contains as many as 340 tentacles, the total surface area of blood vessels in the plume is truly amazing. Yet this still is not the whole story, for each tentacle usually bears a number of minute projections called *pinnules* (Fig. 3D). Each pinnule, which arises as an extension of a number of epithelial cells, contains a vascular loop communicating with the blood vessels that traverse the length of the tentacle.

Certain accessory structures probably increase the absorbing potential of the plume even further. For example, tracts of cilia run the length of each tentacle. The cilia appear to be oriented so that their coordinated beat continually sweeps water and dissolved substances across the pinnules. Also, a series of U-shaped ring muscles is contained in the walls of each tentacular blood vessel. Selected contraction of these muscles could restrict blood flow to certain groups of tentacles or even to portions of individual tentacles, regulating the flow of blood throughout the plume and perhaps increasing oxygen-absorbing efficiency.

Is *Riftia* adapted to its unusual habitat in other ways? Do even more bizarre organisms await discovery near other deep-sea vents? Like most scientific investigations, the discoveries of the Galapagos Rift expedition have produced more questions than answers. But that is what makes science such an exciting and never-ending enterprise. There always remains much to answer and to explore.

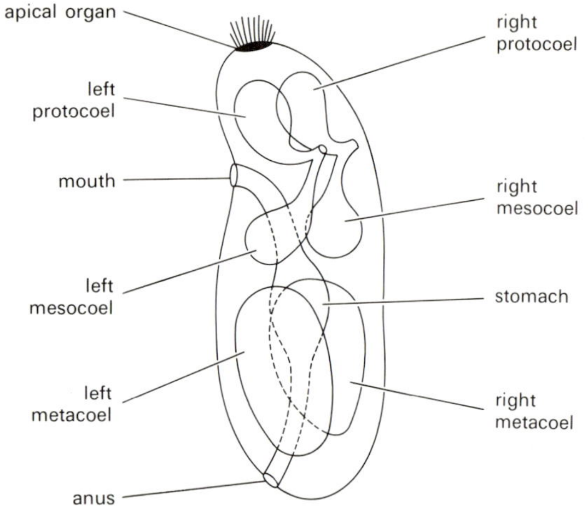

Fig. 35.2 The dipleurula. This hypothetical ancestor of deuterostomes resembles certain actual embryonic and larval stages of hemichordates and echinoderms.

during the embryonic or larval phase (Fig. 35.2); the tendency of the coelom to form three paired subdivisions (*protocoel, mesocoel, metacoel*), with corresponding anatomic divisions of the body as a whole (*protosome, mesosome, metasome*); and, at least in hemichordates and chordates, the formation of endodermal pharyngeal gill pouches that develop as gill slits.

The most familiar enterocoelomates are the echinoderms and the chordates, each probably related more to the hemichordates than to each other. Chordates of course are also of special interest, for they include vertebrates and people. Enterocoelomates arose as unsegmented animals, but segmentation did evolve later in two of the three chordate subphyla.

ECHINODERMS

Phylum Echinodermata spiny-skinned animals

CLASS CRINOIDEA sea lilies, feather stars; body cup-shaped, free or attached; endoskeleton limited to aboral side, oral side membranous; arms branched, with open ambulacral grooves; tube feet food-catching

CLASS HOLOTHUROIDEA sea cucumbers; secondarily bilateral; mouth region with tentacles; ambulacral grooves closed; endoskeleton reduced to ossicles; oral-aboral axis horizontal

CLASS ASTEROIDEA starfishes, sea stars; star-shaped; ambulacral grooves open; tube feet locomotor and projecting between endoskeletal plates

CLASS OPHIUROIDEA brittle stars, basket stars; star-shaped, with long, highly flexible arms; ambulacral grooves closed, tube feet reduced; madreporite on oral side; without intestine or anus

CLASS ECHINOIDEA sea urchins, sand dollars; spherical to disk-shaped, without arms; ambulacral grooves closed; endoskeleton fused, nonflexible, with pores for tube feet and with movable spines

Echinoderms develop bilateral, free-swimming (dipleurulalike) larvae, and fossils show that the earliest echinoderms were bilateral also as adults. Later descendants retained the bilateral larvae but became sessile and secondarily radial as adults. They evolved a starlike shape, with arms that could serve as feeding tentacles. Moreover, the entire body became clothed with endoskeletal plates that could protect the attached, vulnerable animal. However, such an endoskeleton must have restricted the mobility and food-catching capacity of the arms. This problem could be solved by the evolution of a *water-vascular* system that contained small, mobile branch tentacles, or *tube feet*, on the armor-plated arms. Also, furrows between rows of tube feet along the arms, so-called *ambulacral grooves*, could serve in passing food from the tube feet to the mouth, located in the center of the star-shaped body (Fig. 35.3). The unique water-vascular system of echinoderms thus may be interpreted as a modified tentacular system, evolved in response to a sessile way of life and a skeleton-induced body rigidity. Crinoids, the most primitive living echinoderms, still exhibit these ancient characteristics in large measure.

Once a tube-foot system for feeding had evolved, it could become modified also for locomotion. Some of the early echinoderm groups relinquished the stalked, attached mode of life and became motile, with the oral side directed downward. Tube feet, and in some cases also endoskeletal spines and the arms themselves, could

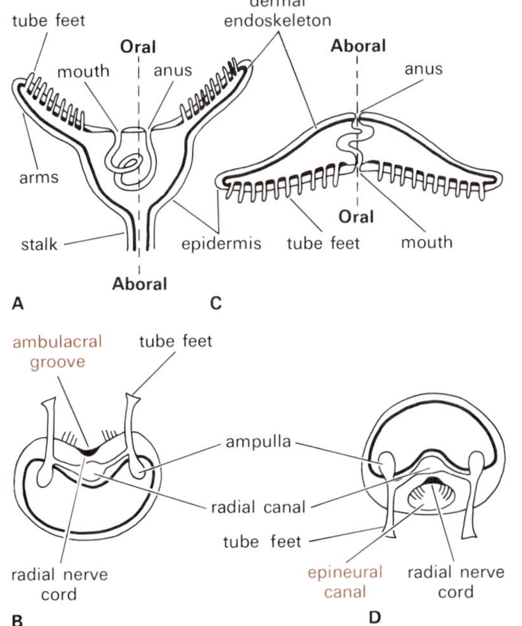

Fig. 35.3 Echinoderm body plans. (A) The crinoid pattern, with vertical oral-aboral axis, mouth and tube feet pointing up. (B) Cross section through an arm of a crinoid. Note open ambulacral groove. (C) The ophiuroid-echinoid pattern, with mouth and tube feet pointing down, and with ambulacral groove closed in as an epineural canal (D). Asteroids correspond to pattern C, but they have open ambulacral grooves.

function in propulsion. The animals thus could move to food actively, use the mouth directly, and no longer needed to depend on what the arms could strain out of water. The ambulacral grooves then largely ceased to be of importance, and they are actually closed over by folds of the body wall in all living echinoderms except the crinoids and asteroids.

Starfish

The basic traits of echinoderms as a whole are well illustrated by a common starfish (Figs. 35.4 and 35.5). The body of such an animal consists of a central disk and, typically, five *arms.* In given genera as many as 20 or more arms may be present. Under the epidermis is an endoskeleton, composed of knobby calcareous plates that are held together by connective tissue and muscle. In numerous places the body wall is folded out in microscopic fingerlike projections, the *skin gills.* The spaces in these breathing organs are extensions of the body coelom passing between adjacent skeletal plates. Also on the body surface are microscopic *pedicellariae,* muscle-operated pincers that protect the skin gills and the epidermis generally.

The water-vascular system operates through a series of coelomic sea-water-filled ducts and serves in locomotion and feeding. The system communicates with external sea water through a reddish *madreporite,* a sieve plate on the upper, or *aboral,* side of the animal, near the angle between two of the arms. From the madreporite a calcified *stone canal* conducts water to a *ring canal* within the body, and from this channel in turn emanate five *radial canals,* one into each arm. There each radial canal gives off short lateral branches, and each of these bifurcates into a saclike *ampulla* within the arm and a muscular *tube foot* protruding from the underside of the arm. Stiffened by water pressed into them from the ampullae, tube feet can be used as tiny walking legs. They also serve as suction disks when pressed against a solid surface and their end plates are lifted away. By such means the tube feet of a starfish can exert enough steady pull on the shells of a clam to tire the clam and force its shells open. Consequently, starfish are very destructive to oyster and clam beds; a single starfish has been observed to eat up to 10 oysters in a day.

The tube feet along each arm are arranged in rows that border an ambulacral groove, a furrow leading to the mouth in the center of the underside, or *oral* surface. The mouth connects via a short esophagus to a large stomach that can be everted through the mouth into the soft tissues of a clam. Small food particles and fluid foods pass into a short intestine and then into five pairs of large digestive glands, one pair occupying most of the free space within each arm (see Fig. 35.5). The alimentary system terminates at a small anal pore in the center of the aboral surface. Encircling the esophagus and situated close to the ring canal is a *nerve ring,* from which emanate five *radial nerves,* one into each arm. These nerves run along the bottom of the ambulacral grooves, and they terminate at an eye spot at the tip of each arm. The circulatory system consists of a series of coelomic blood channels, some of them contractile. Moreover, the fluid filling the coelom carries out a significant amount of internal transport, too. Excretion is achieved partly by diffusion through the body sur-

Fig. 35.4 Starfishes. (A) The aboral side of *Asterias*. The anus lies at the exact center of the disk but is too small to be visible. The buttonlike madreporite is seen eccentrically on the disk between the two lower arms. (B) The oral side. The mouth is at the center of the disk, and a tube-foot-lined ambulacral groove passes along each of the five arms to the mouth. (C) A many-armed starfish, aboral view. (D) Oral view of starfish eating a blue mussel. Note tube feet. (*A, B, Carolina Biological Supply Company*.)

face, partly by amoeboid cells present in the coelomic fluid. These cells absorb excretory waste and carry it to the exterior through the skin gills.

Starfishes have five pairs of sex organs, one pair per arm. In most cases fertilization occurs in open water, and development includes a free-swimming, bilateral *bipinnaria* larva (Fig. 35.6). This larva eventually undergoes a very complex metamorphosis into a young radial adult. Such a developmental pattern generally is typical also in the other echinoderm classes, though the larvae differ slightly in appearance and are named differently.

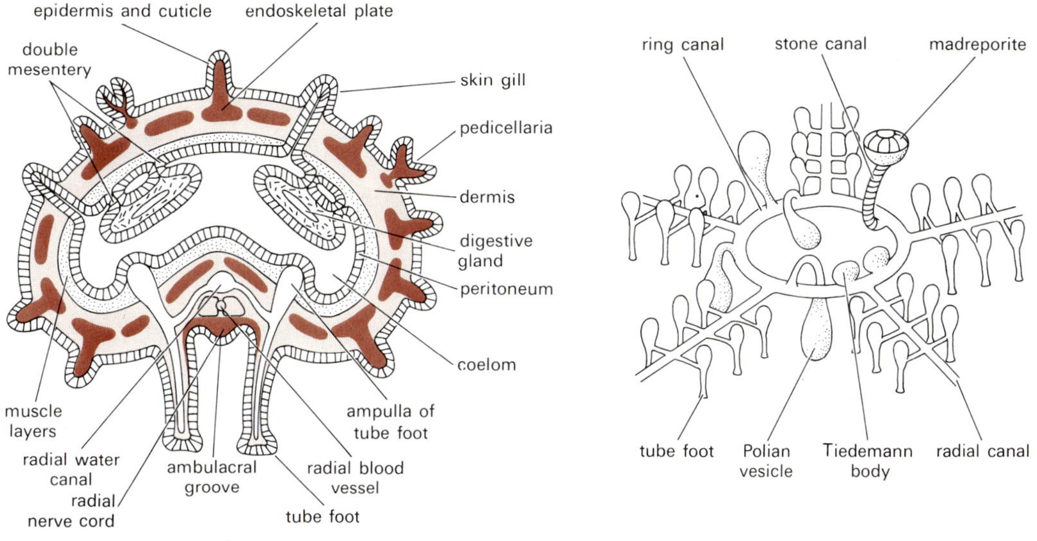

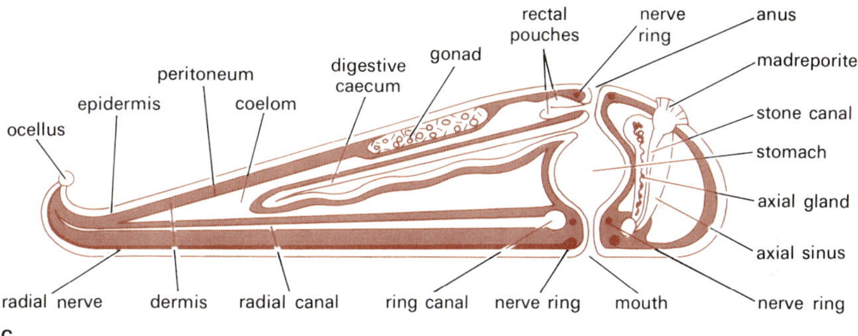

Fig. 35.5 Starfish structure. (A) Cross section of an arm. (B) The water-vascular system. Polian vesicles, which probably serve as water reservoirs, are absent in the common starfish *Asterias*. The specific function of a Tiedemann body is unknown. (C) Section through the disk and one arm, simplified. Note that much of the coelomic cavity of an arm is filled with a pair of digestive glands (digestive caeca). The axial gland and sinus function in blood circulation.

Other Echinoderms

The crinoid class comprises the stalked, sessile sea lilies and the unstalked, gracefully swimming feather stars. The bodies of these animals are cup-shaped, the greatly branched arms being attached to the rim of the cup. Sea cucumbers have a horizontal oral-aboral axis, retractile branched tentacles around the mouth, and a leathery body wall containing microscopic endoskeletal components. The water-vascular system is simplified, and in many cases functional tube feet are absent. Sea cucumbers are a delicacy in the Orient, where they are dried for use in soup (Fig. 35.7).

Brittle stars resemble starfishes to a certain extent, but their long, slender arms are marked off sharply from the central disk and are highly mobile in serpentine fashion. Functional tube feet are again absent, and the animals also lack an intestine or an anus, the stomach being a blind sac. The mouth is armed with five muscle-operated toothlike jaws that serve well in a primarily carnivorous way of life (Fig. 35.8).

Sea urchins are identified readily by their long, movable spines, which are outgrowths from the endoskeleton. This skeleton is fused together as a rigid, globular shell, with rows of pores through which the tube feet protrude. Sea urchins are scavenging omnivores, and they too have a toothed mouth as well as a highly complex chewing organ that operates the teeth. Sand dollars have a greatly flattened body and movable spines that are quite

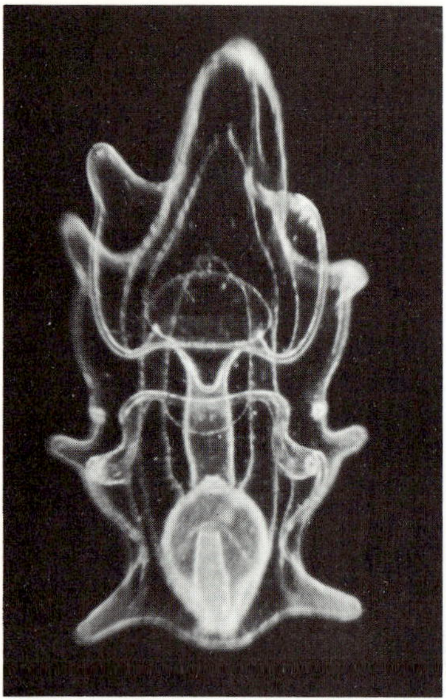

Fig. 35.6 Bipinnaria larva of a starfish. Note alimentary tract internally and lobes with ciliary bands externally. The larva as a whole resembles a dipleurula. Sea cucumbers have similar larvae.

short, but in most other respects these animals are similar to sea urchins (Fig. 35.9).

A

B

Fig. 35.8 Brittle stars. (A) A whole animal. (B) Close-up of the disk of *Ophiothrix*.

CHORDATES

Phylum Chordata notochord-possessing animals

Subphylum Urochordata tunicates, sea squirts; marine, sessile or free-swimming, often colonial through budding; with secreted external cellulose envelope (*tunic*); unsegmented; gill slits used in breathing and ciliary filter feeding; circulatory system open; 2000 species

Subphylum Cephalochordata amphioxus, lancelets; marine, in sand; notochord and dorsal nerve cord throughout life; head or brain absent; segmented; filter-feeding, with numerous gill slits; circulation open, without heart; 30 species

Subphylum Vertebrata vertebrates; segmented, with head, trunk, and tail; endoskeleton with skull enclosing brain; embryo with notochord, adult with notochord and/or vertebral column; with pharyngeal gills or lungs; circulation

A

B

Fig. 35.7 Sea cucumbers. (A) *Cucumaria,* a sea cucumber in which tube feet are arranged in five distinct double rows (two of them visible here). (B) *Thyone,* a sea cucumber in which tube feet are not arranged in any orderly pattern. (*Carolina Biological Supply Company*.)

A

B

C

Fig. 35.9 Echinoids. (A) *Psammechinus,* a sea urchin. Note the many spines protruding from the body surface. (B) Sand dollars, aboral (left) and oral (right) views. (C) Fused endoskeletal shell of a sea urchin, oral view, showing the five teeth around the mouth.

closed, with heart; blood with white blood cells and hemoglobin in red blood cells; with lymph system; liver present; endocrine system elaborate; 50,000 species

Since this phylum includes human beings and the animals most directly important to people, it is unquestionably the most interesting from almost any standpoint.

Chordates are so named because all have a *notochord,* a flexible skeletal supporting rod formed in the embryo from dorsal mesoderm (Fig. 35.10). In vertebrates this rod later becomes surrounded by vertebral components of cartilage or bone, and in most cases the notochord then degenerates. Chordates are identified also by a dorsal hollow nerve cord and paired gill slits, either or both of which are sometimes present during early life-cycle stages only. Gill slits are passages between the pharynx and the sides of the body. The slits serve in breathing; water entering the mouth returns to the outside through the gill slits, where oxygen is absorbed into the blood circulation. In tunicates and amphioxus the slits also have a feeding function. Microscopic food in the water is strained out by cilia around the slits and is passed to the esophagus and stomach. Vertebrates ingest bulkier food, and in fishes the gill slits still serve in breathing but no longer in feeding. In lung-breathing vertebrates, people included, the gill apparatus begins to form in the embryo but it does not develop very far and never becomes functional.

Tunicates

Subphylum Urochordata

CLASS ASCIDIACEA sea squirts, ascidians; larvae if present are nonfeeding tadpoles, with notochord and dorsal nerve cord in tail; adults

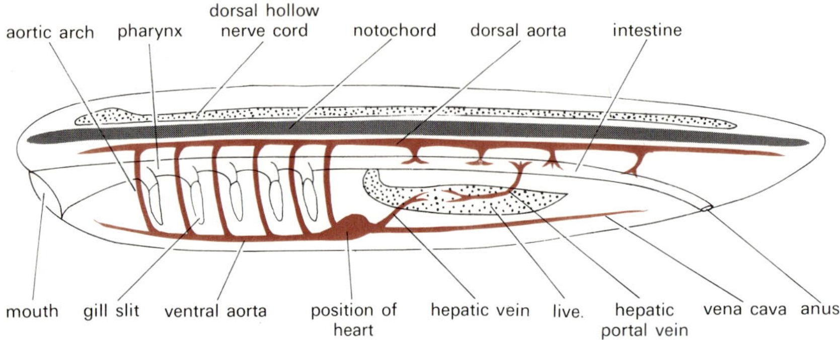

Fig. 35.10 Chordate characteristics, particularly as exemplifed in vertebrates. Dorsal nerve cord, notochord, and pharyngeal gill slits are diagnostic of all chordates. In the circulatory pattern (color), blood flows forward through the ventral aorta, up through the aortic arches where oxygenation takes place, and backward through the dorsal aorta. Intestinal blood passes to the liver through the hepatic portal vein and from the liver back to the general circulation through the hepatic vein. The vena cava collects blood from all other hind regions of the body. The gill slits are primitively ciliated and strain food particles from water that flows through mouth, pharynx, and out via the gill passages. Such food then reaches the intestine.

without tail, sessile, colonial through budding or solitary; gill slits numerous; alimentary tract U-shaped

CLASS THALIACEA chain tunicates; larvae if present with notochord and dorsal nerve cord in tail; adults without tail but free-swimming, locomotion by "jet" propulsion; gill slits few to numerous; polymorphic, with colonial stages budded in chains

CLASS LARVACEA appendicularians; tail with notochord and nerve cord permanent throughout life; adults larvalike, free-swimming; tunic forms complex housing used with tail in feeding; one pair of gill slits

Adult ascidians are not obviously recognizable as chordates, but their tadpole larvae are. Indeed it is believed that tadpoles of ancestral tunicate stocks have given rise to all other chordates. A tunicate tadpole has a conspicuous muscular *tail* supported by a notochord (Fig. 35.11). Above the notochord lies a hollow nerve cord, which extends forward and widens to a brain. A roughly U-shaped alimentary system is present, and both the gill slits and the anus open into an *atrium,* a chamber that surrounds the pharynx and leads to the outside at an excurrent *atrial siphon.* However, this opening as well as the mouth are covered over by the cellulose tunic that envelops the whole larva. Thus the tadpoles cannot feed. Usually within a few hours after being formed such tadpoles attach to a solid surface at their front ends and transform into adults.

During this metamorphosis the entire tail degenerates, the notochord and dorsal nerve cord disappear, and the brain is reduced to a single ganglion. Also, the alimentary system becomes shifted until both mouth and atrial siphon point away from the attached front end of the larva. The tunic over these openings is resorbed, and the animal then begins its sessile adult existence. In many species the adults remain solitary; in others colonies are formed through budding (Fig. 35.12).

Tunicates in the two other classes do not become sessile, but their larvae metamorphose into more or less elongated, still fairly tadpolelike, free-swimming adults (Fig. 35.13.) Chain tunicates are barrel-shaped, and the alimentary system is straight, not U-like. Cilia in the gill apparatus propel water through the body from one end of the "barrel" to the other, and the animal thereby jets in the opposite direction. Long chains of linked individuals form by budding. In the class of appendicularians the larval tail persists permanently. The animal is enclosed in a complex "house" developed from the tunic, and the long tail is tucked under the body of the animal along the floor of this house. Undulations of the tail draw food-bearing water through the house and also propel the animal.

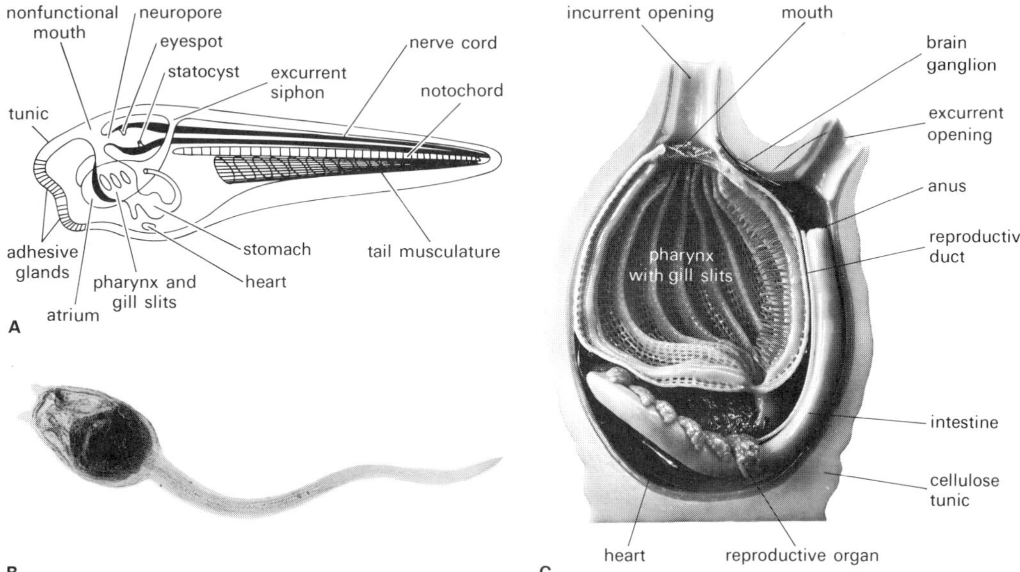

Fig. 35.11 Tunicate structure. (A) Section through a tadpole. (B) A whole tadpole. (C) Cutaway model of adult. Food-bearing water is drawn into the pharynx through the incurrent opening (siphon). Food passes to the U-shaped alimentary tract, and water flows to the outside through gill slits and excurrent opening (siphon).

Fig. 35.12 Ascidians. (A) *Ciona,* a solitary type. The incurrent siphon is at top, fully open. (B) *Ascidia,* a colonial type.

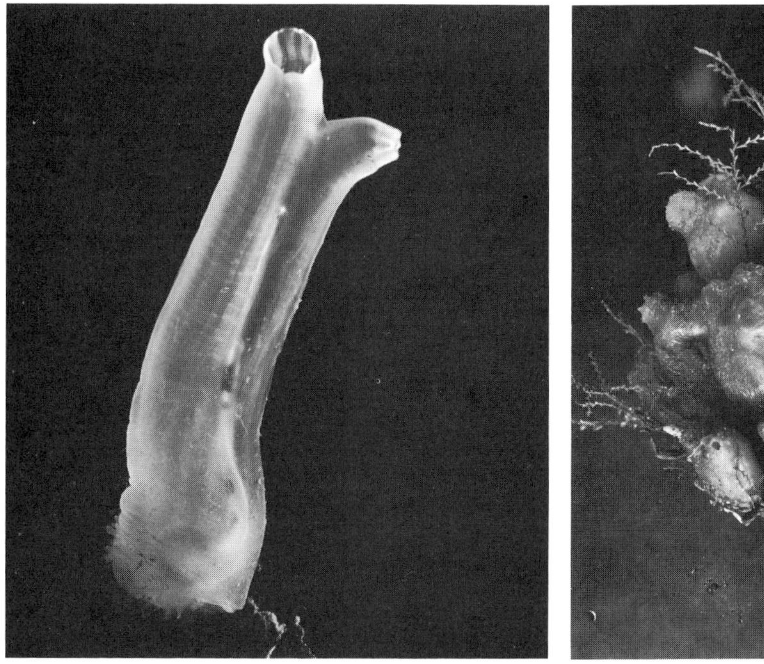

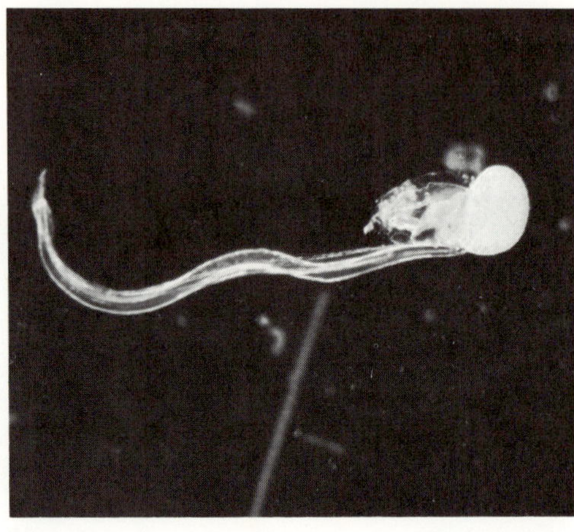

A B

Fig. 35.13 Tunicates. (A) *Doliolum,* a member of the class Thaliacea, in plankton, from life. Note muscle hoops around barrel-shaped body, siphons at opposite ends of body, and gill baskets inside. (B) *Oikopleura,* a member of the class Larvacea, in plankton, from life. Note long undulating tail, cellulose "house" at base of tail.

It is believed that, like chain tunicates and appendicularians, cephalochordates and vertebrates too could have evolved through retention of larval, tadpolelike features to the adult stage.

Amphioxus

Subphylum Cephalochordata

Amphioxus is slender, laterally compressed, and pointed at both ends (Fig. 35.14). It lies in sand of shallow coastal waters, only its anterior end sticking out of its burrow. The animal has a permanent notochord and nerve cord, both extending over the whole length of the body. But there is no brain or head. The mouth leads into a long ciliated pharynx with from 60 to more than 100 pairs of lateral sloping gill slits. Water passing through these emerges into a ventral atrium, which opens to the outside at a posterior pore.

Amphioxus is a segmented animal. Thus, the body musculature is formed into lateral V-shaped segmental bundles, and as in vertebrates these are innervated by paired segmental nerves from the nerve cord. Excretory and reproductive organs likewise have a segmental arrangement. Although a heart is not present and the blood vessels are open-ended, the anatomic pattern of the circulation greatly resembles that of vertebrates. A contractile ventral aorta below the pharynx pumps blood forward and then up through *aortic arches* between the gill slits (see Fig. 35.10). Blood collects above the pharynx in a dorsal aorta, which passes backward and gives off branches to the tissues. Veins from the tissues return blood to the beginning of the ventral aorta, where the heart would be located in a vertebrate. Amphioxus is specialized in many respects, but it does suggest in a rather distant way what ancient vertebrates might have been like.

Vertebrates

Subphylum Vertebrata

CLASS AGNATHA jawless fishes: lampreys, hagfishes; freshwater and marine; with notochord throughout life and cartilage skeleton; sucking mouth; paired fins absent; heart two-chambered; excretion pronephric in larva, mesonephric in adult; 50 species

CLASS CHONDRICHTHYES cartilage fishes: sharks, rays, skates; marine; notochord is reduced but persists in adult; skin with dermal denticles; heart two-chambered; excretion mesonephric; 600 species

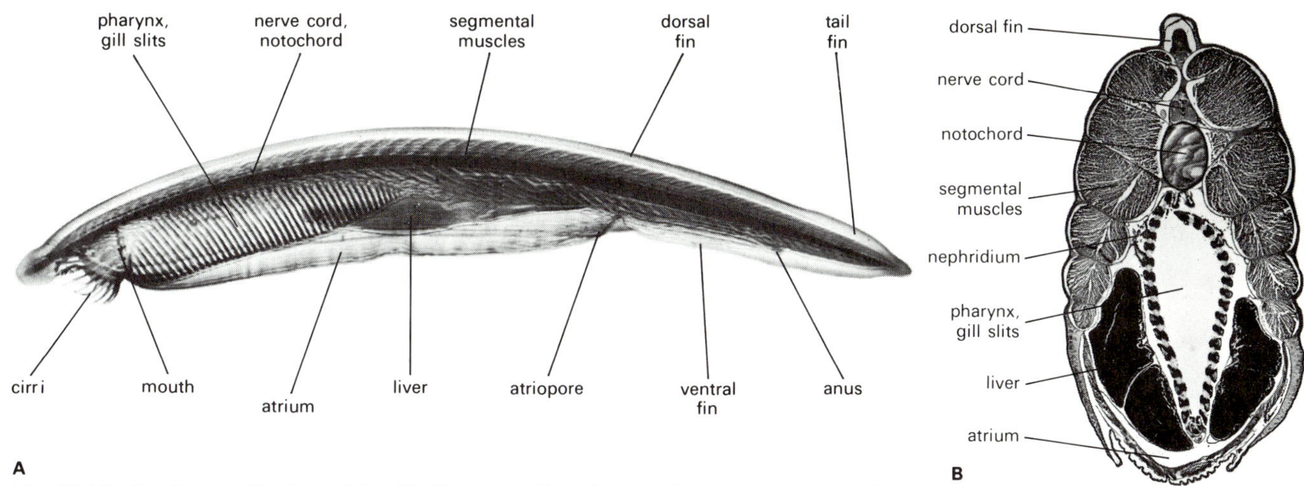

Fig. 35.14 Amphioxus, the lancelet. (A) Side view. Notochord and nerve cord are not visible separately in this picture; cirri are tentaclelike sensory structures that encircle the mouth. (B) Cross section near hind end of pharynx. Note segmental nephridia ("kidneys"). (*Carolina Biological Supply Company*.)

CLASS OSTEICHTHYES bony fishes; freshwater and marine; notochord does not persist in most; skin with dermal scales; with lung or swim bladder; heart two-chambered; excretion mesonephric; 25,000 species

CLASS AMPHIBIA amphibians: salamanders, newts, toads, frogs; freshwater and terrestrial; paired appendages with legs; skin without scales; breathing via gills, lungs, skin, and mouth cavity; heart three-chambered; 10 pairs of cranial nerves; fertilization mostly external, development mostly via tadpole larvae; 3000 species

CLASS REPTILIA reptiles: turtles, lizards, snakes, aligators; terrestrial and secondarily aquatic; skin with epidermal scales; breathing by lung; heart four-chambered; 12 pairs of cranial nerves; excretion metanephric; fertilization internal, eggs with shells, larvae absent; 6000 species

CLASS AVES birds; skin with feathers; forelimbs are wings; with horny beak, teeth absent; heart four-chambered; body temperature constant; 12 pairs of cranial nerves; excretion metanephric; fertilization internal, eggs with shells, larvae absent; 10,000 species

CLASS MAMMALIA mammals; skin with hair; teeth in sockets, heart four-chambered; red blood cells without nuclei; coelom divided by diaphragm; body temperature constant; 12 pairs of cranial nerves; excretion metanephric; fertilization internal, development in uterus in most cases, born young nourished by milk from mammary glands; 5000 species

Ancestral vertebrates probably invaded the freshwater rivers as segmented, tailed derivatives of tunicate antecedents. Their tadpole larvae had strongly muscled tails that could propel them upriver, and their adults must have been pharyngeal filter feeders like their marine forebears. Also, they evolved a new kind of kidney that could eliminate the large amounts of water drawn into the body osmotically.

This kidney, still formed today in fish larvae, was a *pronephros* (Fig. 35.15). In each of the anterior body segments developed a *nephron*, composed of a double-layered cup (*nephric capsule*) and a ball of blood capillaries (*glomerulus*) that projected into the capsule. Water filtered from glomerular blood into the capsule, and a (*Wolffian*) duct from there joined other such ducts from nephrons in neighboring segments and led to the exterior near the anus. In later vertebrates many more nephron units developed in the segments of the middle and hind regions of the body, and the original anterior neph-

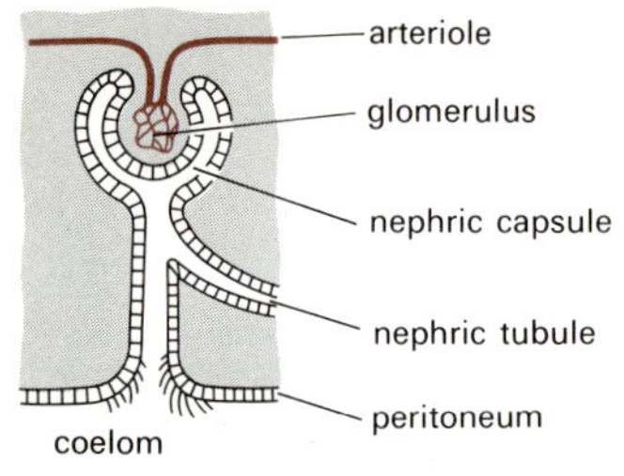

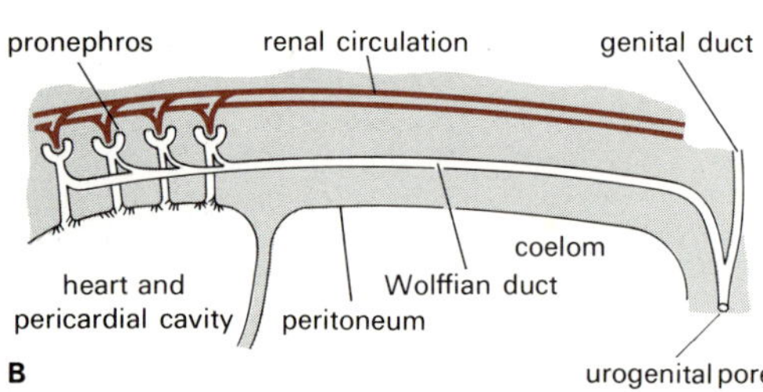

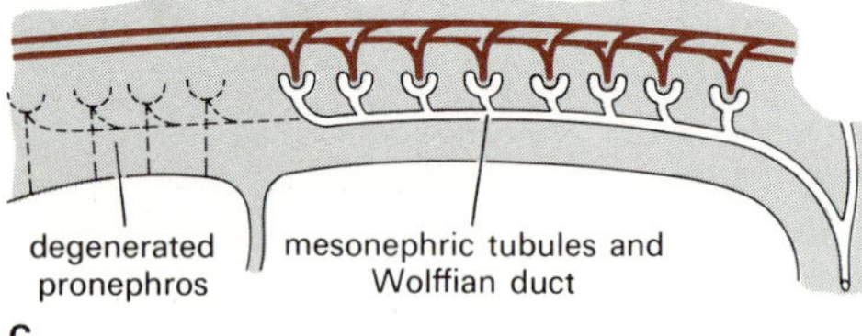

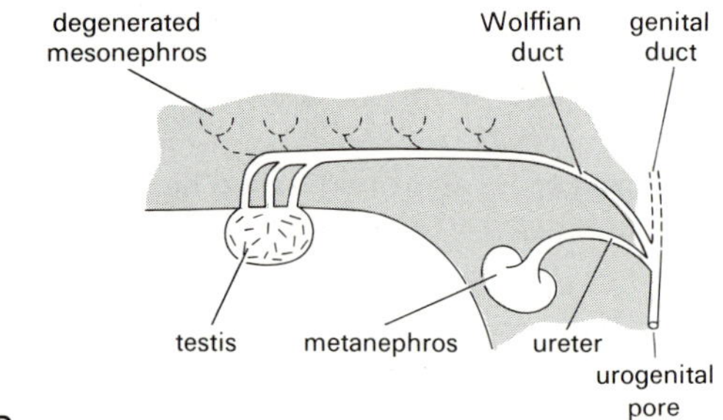

Fig. 35.15 The vertebrate kidney. (A) A primitive nephron unit. Note ciliated funnel opening to coelom. Cilia sweep waste-containing fluids into the nephric capsule and tubule, where wastes are removed. Such ciliated openings to the coelom do not occur in meso- and metanephric kidneys. In such advanced kidneys, waste removal occurs exclusively via filtration of blood. (B) The pronephric kidney. Note ciliated openings into the pericardial (coelomic) cavity. More nephron units actually occur than sketched here. (C) The mesonephric kidney. The pronephros has degenerated, and new nephrons have developed along the Wolffian duct. (D) The metanephric kidney. Mesonephric nephrons have degenerated, and a new large collection of nephrons has developed from the hind part of the Wolffian duct. In males this duct also makes new connections with the testes and becomes the sperm duct. In females the Wolffian duct degenerates, too, but the old genital duct becomes the egg channel from the ovaries to the outside.

rons actually degenerated. Such a kidney is a *mesonephros;* it occurs today in the adults of all fishes and in amphibia.

Like their ancestors, the most primitive living vertebrates still are pharyngeal filter feeders; in the larvae of Agnatha the cilia of the pharynx suck in water with small food particles through a round, jawless mouth (Fig. 35.16). Even in adult lampreys, food consists of body fluids and tiny tissue fragments rasped off the host. In all other evolutionary lines of vertebrates, however, the main food-collecting organ is no longer the pharynx but the mouth itself, which has become equipped with jaws and true teeth. The nature of the food has changed concurrently to bulk nutrients, and the ancestral method of filter feeding has ceased. This change has left the gill slits primarily as breathing structures; and since therefore tiny particles no longer needed to be strained out of water, the number of gill slits could become reduced.

Indeed, such a reduction has accompanied jaw development; the skeletal supports of the most anterior gills came to be remodeled as jaw supports (Fig. 35.17). But even though fewer gill slits then remained, these became highly efficient oxygenators; for the circulation became a closed network with extensive beds of capillaries in all body parts, gills included, and a newly evolved two-chambered heart moved blood rapidly through this circuit of vessels.

The freshwater environment continued to orient also the later stages of vertebrate evolution. Air sacs that pouched out from the pharynx appear to have been an original trait of bony fishes, in adaptation to occasional periods of drought. Such sacs still function as lungs in the most primitive bony fishes now living, but in most others they have become swim bladders (see Fig. 35.17). From early lung-possessing types then evolved vertebrates with additional adaptations to at first temporary and later permanent terrestrial life: fleshy fins with internal bones, elongated subsequently to legs; very yolky eggs first laid in water but later equipped with shells, laid on land, and developing without larval stages; three and then four chambers in the heart, permitting efficient separation of arterial and venous blood and thus providing enough oxygen for the increased energy requirements on land (see Chap. 18); a distinct energy-saving neck, with a swivel joint for the head; controls for maintenance

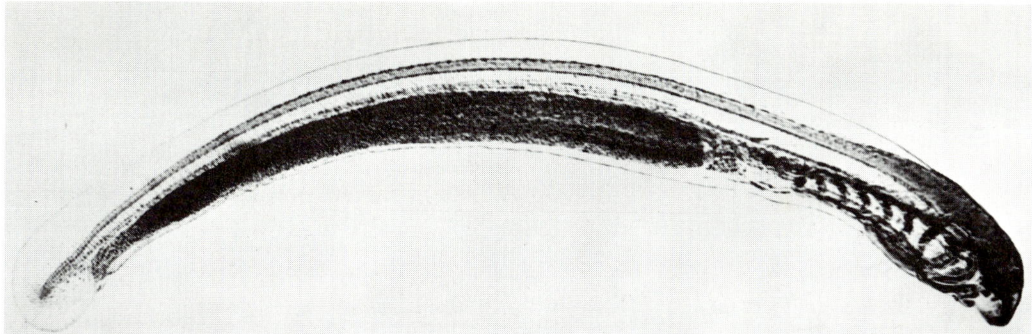

Fig. 35.16 Ammocoete larva of jawless fishes. Note gill slits, nerve cord and brain, and position of notochord just underneath nerve cord. This larva is a pharyngeal filter feeder like the ancestors of vertebrates.

of constant body temperature in birds and mammals, including insulating surface layers of fat, feathers, and fur; improved breathing and circulatory machinery in mammals, including a diaphragm and highly specialized blood cells; and a new mammalian reproductive mechanism, in which the laying of shelled eggs was replaced by egg development in the uterus of the female, and in which milk was secreted for the newborn.

Furthermore, terrestrial living by reptiles, birds, and mammals came to depend on a new, land-adapted kidney, in which the earlier water-

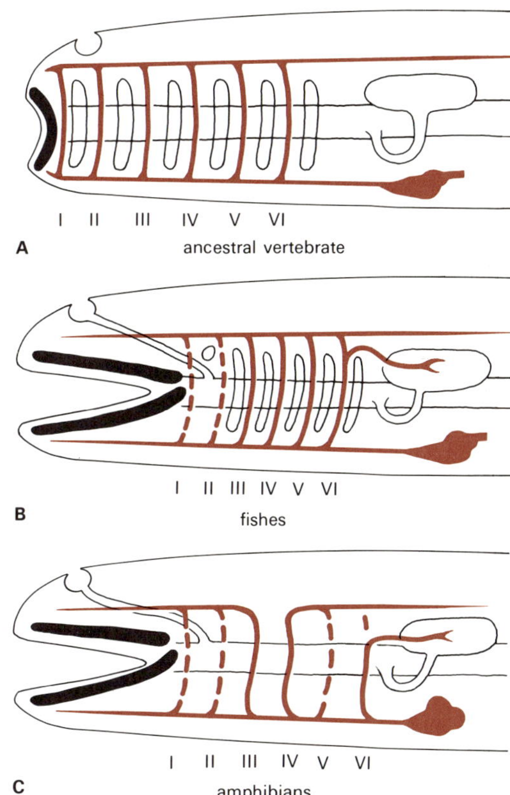

Fig. 35.17 Vertebrate jaws, gills, and lungs. (A) Ancestral vertebrates had six gill slits, six aortic arches (roman numerals), and six skeletal gill supports (the first indicated in black). Also present was a nasal organ and an air sac with a duct from the pharynx. (B) Development of jaws from the first gill supports was accompanied by a reduction of the first gill slit to a small opening called a spiracle (and even that disappeared in later bony fishes), and by a degeneration of the first two aortic arches. The air sac received blood from the sixth aortic arch, and the sac came to function as a lung in lobe-finned fishes and lungfishes but as a swim bladder in all other bony fishes. Swim bladders function as ballast tanks, readily permitting fish to rise or sink in water. Note that the nasal organ has acquired a connection with the pharynx. (C) Lobe-finned fishes were the ancestors of amphibia and the later land vertebrates, in which gill slits are absent in the adults and breathing occurs through lungs. Of the aortic arches remaining in these animals, the third forms the carotid artery to the head, the fourth represents part of the aorta to the body, and the lower portion of the sixth is part of the pulmonary artery to the lungs. The heart is three-chambered in amphibians, two-chambered in all earlier vertebrates.

A

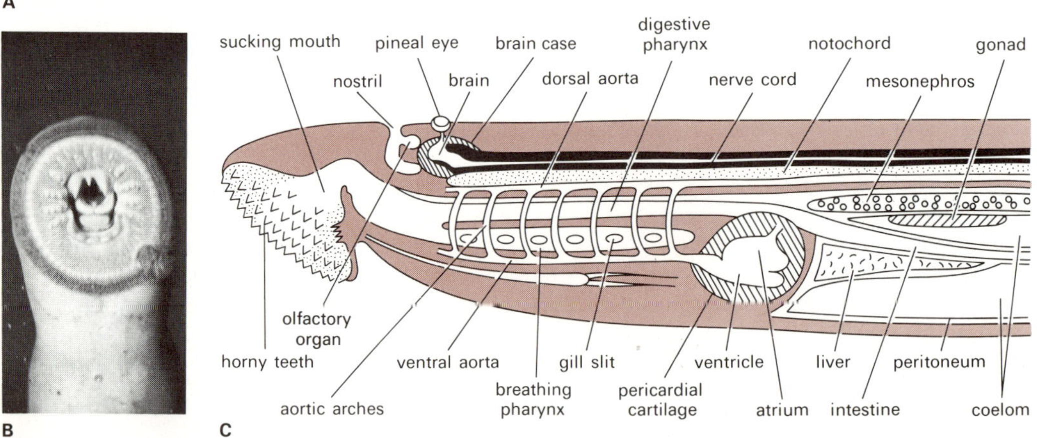

Fig. 35.18 Lampreys. (A) Side view. Note gill slits, fins. (B) The sucker mouth, showing the horny epidermal teeth. (C) Sagittal section of anterior part of body. (*A, B, Carolina Biological Supply Company.*)

excreting function became reversed to a water-saving function. This new kidney, the *metanephros*, developed as an outgrowth from the hind region of the earlier mesonephros (see Fig. 35.15). Reptiles, birds, and mammals still have a mesonephros as embryos, but in later stages the metanephros arises. Its important new feature in each of the nephrons is a highly elongated, coiled tubule specialized to reabsorb water from urine flowing through it, hence to retain as much water as possible in the body (see Chap. 18). Thus whereas the aquatic vertebrates excrete a dilute, watery urine, the fully terrestrial groups have adapted to the water scarcity on land by excreting a highly concentrated, salty urine.

Jawless Fishes

CLASS AGNATHA

In these roughly eel-shaped animals, the front end of the body is a round funnel-like sucker, equipped with epidermal teeth and a rasping tongue that can be protruded through the central mouth (Fig. 35.18). The skin is smooth and scaleless. Folds of it that extend dorsally and around the tail form low median fins. Paired pectoral or pelvic fins are absent. In lampreys a single dorsal nostril leads to a closed nasal sac. Just behind it lies a functional *pineal eye*, connected with the brain by a nerve as in the lateral eyes. Internally, the persisting notochord is stiffened by incompletely developed segmental cartilage supports, and cartilage also forms the brain case and a capsule around the heart. The pharyngeal gill chamber, ventral to the esophagus, opens to the exterior of a lamprey through seven pairs of gill slits.

A stomach is absent, and the esophagus continues directly as the intestine. The circulation is typically vertebrate, and, as in all fishes, the heart contains one atrium and one ventricle. A single sex organ discharges reproductive cells into the well-developed coelom. Such cells reach the outside through a genital pore in the mesonephric excretory duct, which opens just behind the anus.

All lampreys spawn in rivers. Eggs develop into long-lived *ammocoete* larvae, which filter-feed along river bottoms in the ancestral manner (see Fig. 35.16). After metamorphosis young sea lampreys migrate to the ocean, where they lead a mature life as bloodsuckers attached to fish. Adult brook lampreys remain in rivers. They do not feed but spawn within a few days and die. Hagfishes are marine jawless types that develop without larval stages.

Cartilage Fishes

CLASS CHONDRICHTHYES

In a shark (Fig. 35.19) the skin is studded with pointed *denticles* that correspond structurally to vertebrate teeth (those of mammals included). In addition to median fins, paired fins are present and are jointed to pectoral and pelvic girdles. As a result of the evolution of jaws, the first of the ancestral gill slits has become reduced in sharks to a small opening, the *spiracle* (see Figs. 35.17 and 35.19). Five fully developed gill slits are behind a spiracle. The notochord persists and is constricted where the vertebrae surround it. All skeletal components are permanently cartilaginous.

The mouth contains several rows of teeth structured like the surface denticles. The alimentary tract includes a stomach and, opening into the intestine, a large liver and a separate pancreas. In the intestine is a *spiral valve*, a tissue fold that increases the absorptive surface. Separate reproductive and excretory ducts open in a *cloaca*, the terminal part of the hindgut. A salt-secreting *rectal gland* is also attached to the cloaca. Males typically

Fig. 35.19 Sharks. (A) A dogfishlike type, from life. (B) High-power view of skin, showing the toothlike denticles. (C) Sagittal section of main part of body. (D) Spiral valve.

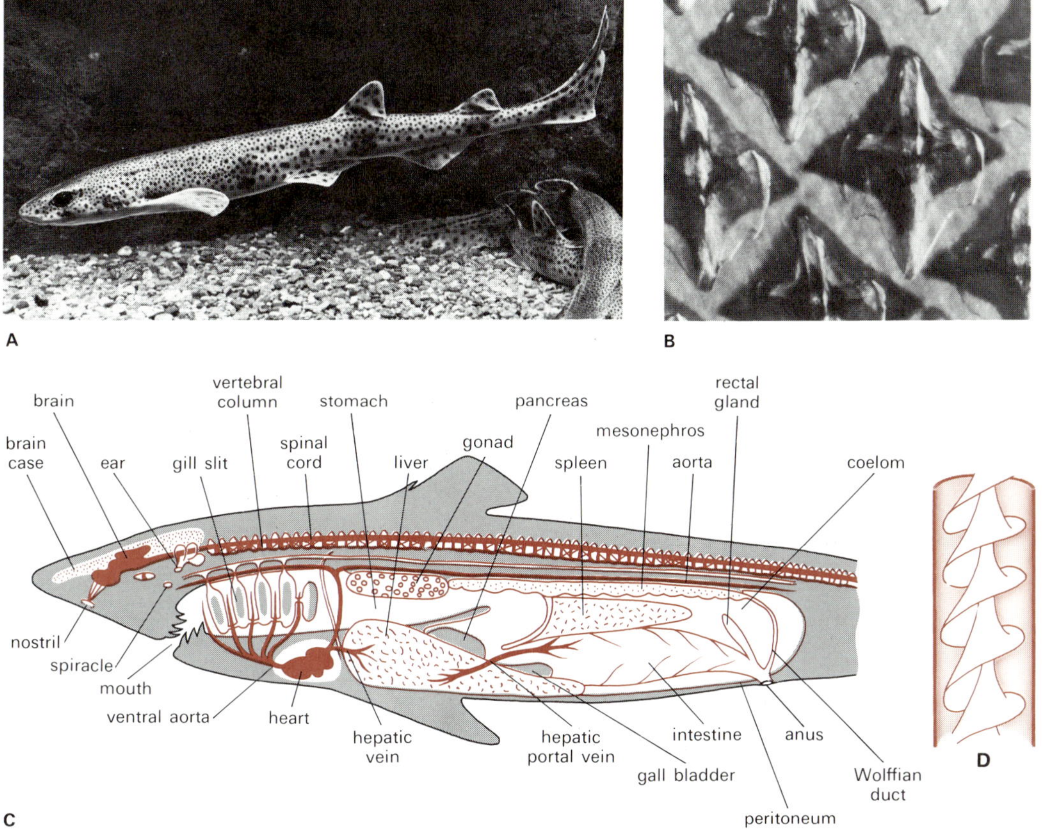

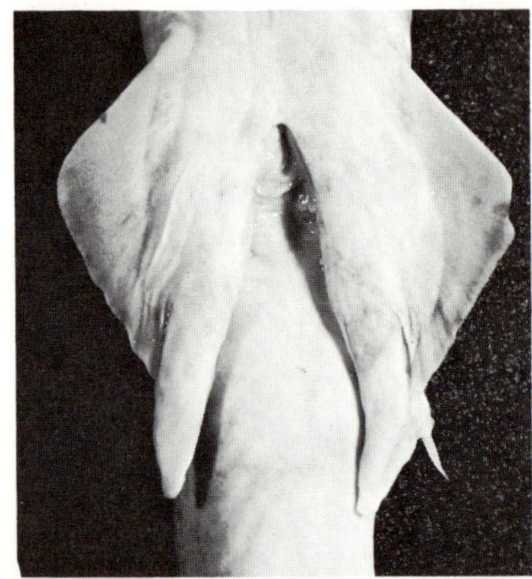
A

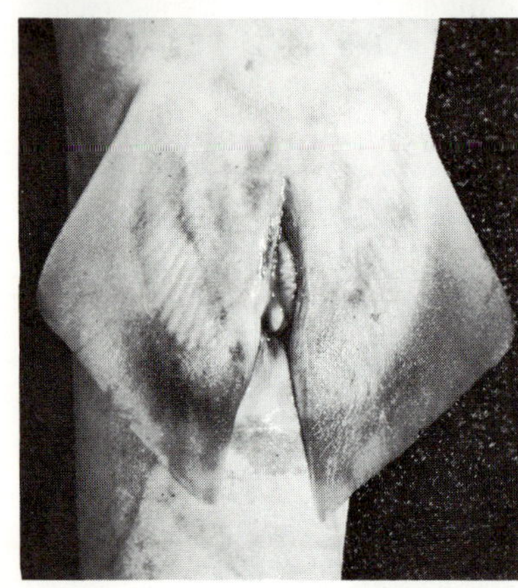
B

Fig. 35.20 Fin claspers. (A), (B) Ventral views of cloacal region of male and female shark, respectively, showing presence of pointed fin claspers in male and their relation to the pelvic fins.

have a pair of copulatory organs (*fin claspers*) between the pelvic fins (Fig. 35.20).

Most sharks are fiercely carnivorous, but the whale and basking sharks are plankton feeders. Basking sharks are the largest of all fishes, attaining lengths of over 50 ft. Many rays and skates exhibit interesting offensive and protective adaptations, among them snouts extended as "saws" in the sawfishes, poison spines at the end of the tail in stingrays, and electric organs lateral to the eyes in the torpedo rays (Fig. 35.21).

Bony Fishes

CLASS OSTEICHTHYES

This largest vertebrate class comprises two subclasses. In the primitive *flesh-finned* fishes, the pectoral and pelvic fins contain internal bones that correspond substantially to the limb bones of terrestrial vertebrates. Also, the pharyngeal air sac functions as a lung. These fishes are represented today by only four surviving genera, one of *lobe-finned fishes* (*coelacanths*) and three of *lungfishes* (Fig. 35.22). In the *ray-finned* subclass, by contrast, the paired fins are supported by needlelike body rays, and the air sac is usually a swim bladder (Fig. 35.23).

In both groups, connective tissue in the dermis of the skin gives rise to overlapping bony scales; which are overlain in turn by the epidermis. Gills are usually reduced in number to four pairs, and on each side of the head they are covered by an *operculum*, a bony plate hinged to the skeletal supports behind the jaws. Each gill is a double plate composed of highly vascularized *gill filaments*, and a skeletal arch supports the gill tissue. The inner edges of the gills are often expanded as fingerlike *gill rakers*, which prevent food from passing through the gill slits. Spiracles are absent in most cases (Fig. 35.24).

The largest group of bony fishes comprises the so-called *teleosts*, a superorder of some two dozen orders in the ray-finned subclass. Teleosts exhibit two general structural patterns (Fig. 35.25). In the *clupeiform* pattern, exemplified by fishes such as trout, salmon, and herring, the fin rays are soft, the scales are smooth (*cycloid*), the swim bladder remains connected to the pharynx by a duct, and the pelvic fins are in a primitive abdominal, posterior position. In the *perciform* pattern, exemplified by types such as perch, tuna, and bass, the fin rays are hard and spiny, the scales are rough-textured (*ctenoid*), the swim bladder lacks a duct, and the pelvic fins lie forward, often actually in the head region in front of the pectoral fins. These two patterns are not always sharply distinct, and many teleost groups exhibit mixed and intergrading characteristics.

Amphibians

CLASS AMPHIBIA

The most notable traits of amphibians are those that adapt the animals to an at least partly terrestrial life; and most of these traits trace their origin to ancestral lobe-finned fishes, from which amphibia evolved. The paired appendages are legs, each with five (or fewer) toes. Primitive amphibia

A

B

Fig. 35.21 Cartilage fishes. (A) A ray. (B) A sawfish.

still live entirely in water, but the majority are air breathers with lungs (Fig. 35.26). Gills still occur in the tadpole larvae and in exceptional cases also in some of the adults. In conjunction with the air-breathing habit, nasal passages open in the pharynx and make breathing possible while the mouth remains closed. The skin is thin and scaleless and serves as an accessory breathing organ. Also adaptive in air breathing is the three-chambered heart, capable to some extent of preventing a mixing of oxygen-rich arterial blood and oxygen-poor venous blood. The two bloods do come together in the single ventricle, but not so much as they do in a two-chambered heart. Thus, with a lobe-finned starting point, the terrestrial amphibian descendant walks and breathes air on a permanent basis. Yet even the most land-adapted amphibian still requires a moist environment, and reproductive and developmental processes actually retain the ancestral fish-like characteristics. Thus, eggs typically must be laid in water, fertilization takes place externally after egg-laying as in fishes, and the tadpoles are clearly fishlike even where the adults are terrestrial (see Fig. 24.23 and Color Fig. 14).

Newts and salamanders are tailed throughout life; frogs and toads are tailless as adults. Most of these are lung-breathers, and most frogs and toads also have eyelids, another adaptation to life out of water. In frogs and toads the hind legs are far longer and stronger than the forelegs, and in conjunction with this specialization as jumpers the animals are squat, foreshortened, and without neck. The tongue can be hurled out of the mouth

A

B

Fig. 35.22 Flesh-finned bony fishes. (A) A coelacanth, a rare flesh-finned fish still surviving today. The pectoral and pelvic fins of these lung-breathers have internal bony skeletons. Note the operculum, a bony plate covering the gills. Note also the diamond-shaped enamel-covered (ganoid) scales. (B) A lungfish (*Protopterus*), found today in West Africa.

at an insect, posterior end first. Toads are toothless; frogs have teeth on the upper jaw and the roof of the mouth.

Frogs, toads, and other amphibians benefit us by eating large numbers of potentially injurious insects. Some gardeners even buy toads to restrict local populations of insects. More than 3 million pounds of frogs' legs are consumed annually in the United States alone. Partly because they are collected for use as food and as experimental research

Fig. 35.23 Ray-finned bony fishes. (A) A pike. Note soft-rayed, smooth-contoured fins. (B) A perch. Note hard-rayed, spiky fins. See also Fig. 35.25.

A

B

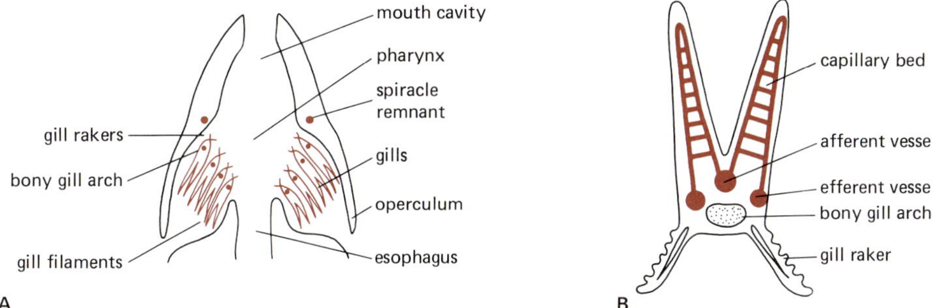

Fig. 35.24 Gills. (A) Horizontal section through fish head, showing position of the four pairs of gills. (B) Horizontal section through a gill. An afferent vessel brings blood to the two capillary beds of a gill filament; an efferent vessel drains each bed.

animals, the population of frogs in the United States has declined dramatically in the last decade or two. Unfortunately, artificial rearing of frogs, or "frog farming" has not proved sufficiently practicable to offset the dwindling number of native frogs.

Reptiles

CLASS REPTILIA

Representing the first fully terrestrial vertebrates, reptiles have a dry, impervious skin covered with epidermal scales (which are developmentally equivalent to feathers and hair). The limbs raise the body off the ground more than in amphibians. The breathing system contains a trachea (windpipe) and bronchial tubes to the lungs, as in birds and mammals. Also as in birds and mammals, the heart is four-chambered, completely so in crocodiles, nearly so in the other reptiles; it keeps arterial and venous blood separated. And the adult excretory system is metanephric, capable of producing a highly hypertonic, water-conserving urine.

The single most essential adaptation to land life is the shelled egg (see also Chap. 24). All rep-

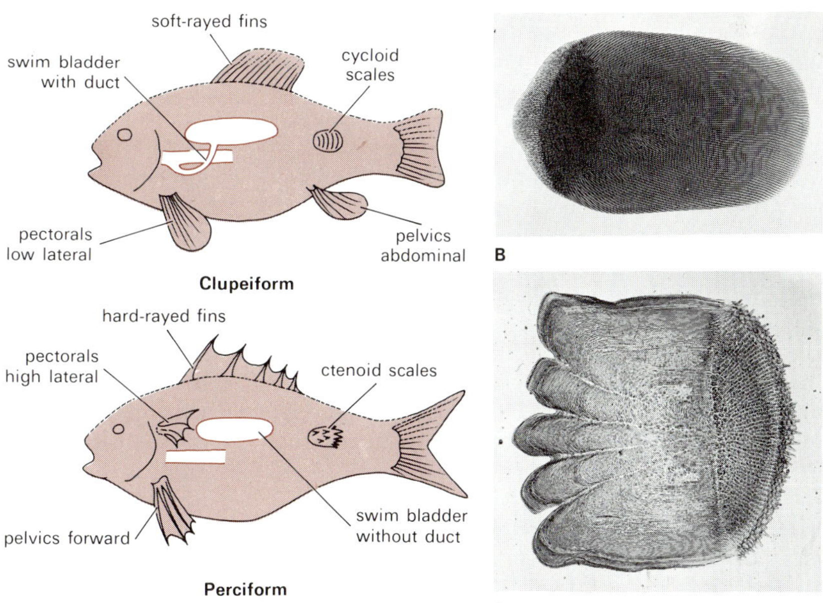

Fig. 35.25 Teleost traits. (A) The clupeiform pattern occurs in, for example, pike, herring, goldfishes, or guppies, and the perciform pattern in, for example, perches, basses, or tunas. See Fig. 35.23 for illustrations of fishes exhibiting these two patterns. Many teleosts exhibit a mixture of clupeiform and perciform traits. (B) Cycloid scales, smooth-textured. (C) Ctenoid scales, spiny or rough-textured. (*B, C, Carolina Biological Supply Company.*)

A

Fig. 35.26 Amphibia. (A) *Amphiuma,* the conger eel, a permanently aquatic type. Note reduced appendages. (B) A fire salamander. (C) *Hyla,* a tree frog.

B

C

tiles lay eggs on land, even if the adults are secondarily aquatic. And fertilization is always internal; it occurs by copulation as in mammals and birds.

In turtles the body is protected by a bony dome (*carapace*) formed from broadened, fused ribs, and by a lower plate (*plastron*) formed from the bones of the pectoral and pelvic girdles (Fig. 35.27). The whole bony casing is covered by skin, which in many cases develops an epidermal shell of hard horn. In sea turtles the legs are modified as flippers.

Some 95 per cent of reptile species now living comprise lizards and snakes. Though specialized in many ways, snakes could be characterized as limbless lizards. In snakes the left and right halves of the lower jaws are not fused together but are joined by ligaments. As a result the mouth can be distended greatly; a snake can ingest an animal several times wider than its own diameter. Snakes lack external ear openings, but they "hear" vibrations transmitted from the ground through the skeleton. Eyes are lidless but can be covered by a transparent (*nictitating*) membrane. Vertebrae often number up to 400. Limb girdles and limbs are generally absent, though vestigial remains of pelvic girdles persist in pythons and related types (see Fig. 35.27 and Color Fig. 39).

The tuatara of New Zealand is a lizardlike evolutionary relic with a functional pineal eye like a lamprey (Fig. 35.28). Crocodiles and alligators are the closest living relatives of dinosaurs on the one hand and of birds on the other. Among adaptations of these reptiles to a semiaquatic existence are closable nostrils; webbed hindfeet; ear openings that can be covered by flaps of skin; a long palate that separates the mouth and nasal cavities and permits breathing even when the mouth is submerged; and a powerful tail that serves in swimming as well as in offense and defense. Crocodiles and gavials have narrow jaws, and the fourth pair of teeth on the lower jaw remains exposed when the mouth is closed. Alligator and caiman jaws are broader and rounded anteriorly, and teeth are not exposed after mouth closure.

Birds

CLASS AVES

The earliest birds could fly and had feathers; flightless birds such as ostriches and kiwis today are descendants of flying ancestors (Fig. 35.29).

Flying birds consume much food to provide the energy and high operating temperature for flight. Feathers are the important heat regulators and also the means of flight. They are horny outgrowths from the epidermis, corresponding to the hairs of mammals. Flight feathers on the wings (and the tail) are maintained in overlapping position when a wing moves down (Fig. 35.30). On the upstroke the feathers are slanted like venetian blinds, letting air pass through with minimum drag. The short, heat-regulating down feathers retain a layer of insulating dead air between the skin and the environment. The same muscles that produce "gooseflesh" in people can erect the down feathers and permit cooling of the body.

Fig. 35.27 Skeletons of reptiles. (A) The turtle skeleton. The ventral part (plastron) is cut away and hinged back, showing the limb girdles underneath the dorsal part (carapace) formed by the rib cage. (B) The snake skeleton. Note numerous vertebrae and absence of limbs, limb girdles, and breastbone. *(A, Carolina Biological Supply Company.)*

The flight-adapted skeleton is light and delicate, the head is rounded and streamlined, and the skull bones are fused (see Fig. 35.30). Jaws form a toothless bill or beak and are covered with a layer of epidermal horn. Eardrums are recessed deeply, and the animals are without external earlobes or other projections that might disrupt smooth airflow over the head. The neck vertebrae provide extreme head mobility, but these vertebrae lock to one another firmly during flight. In flying birds, the prominent keel of the breastbone serves as attachment surface for the powerful flight muscles. A remarkable breathing system provides the large quantities of oxygen needed in flying. From the lungs extend several large air sacs that occupy much of the space between the internal organs of the body. Some of the sacs extend forward to the neck, where they often play an added role in distending the neck during courtship activities (Fig. 35.31 and see Color Fig. 17).

The reproductive pattern too is adjusted to the condition of flying. External genitals are absent (except in male ostriches, which have a penis). This lack, perhaps another adaptation for maintenance of smooth body contours, necessitates strong cooperation during mating, for the cloaca of the male must be apposed precisely against that of the female. Exercise of such cooperation is prepared for by courtship rituals, based at least in part on colorful display plumage and color vision (see Chap. 24). Thus color vision in birds and absence of a penis in males in a sense appear to go together.

The largest group of birds comprises the perching birds, in which a system of tendons in the legs assures that body weight alone can keep the toes curled tightly around a tree branch. The attention required for perching therefore is minimal. Perching birds include all the songbirds, which typically build elaborate nests. Song and brilliant mating plumage are usually characteristic of males only.

A

B

C

Fig. 35.28 Reptiles. (A) *Sphenodon,* the lizard-like tuatara of New Zealand. (B) The lizard *Chamaeleon,* catching grasshopper with tongue. (C) The green sea turtle *Chelonia*. See also Color Fig. 39.

Mammals

CLASS MAMMALIA

Subclass Prototheria egg-laying mammals; adults with horny bill; testes in abdomen; nipples absent, numerous ducts of mammary glands open individually

Subclass Metatheria pouched, marsupial mammals; nipples in ventral abdominal pouch (*marsupium*), where immature young complete development, attached to nipples

Subclass Eutheria placental mammals; in male, ducts from bladder and testes join and form single duct through penis, opening at common

A

B

C

Fig. 35.29 Birds. (A) An emu, one of the flightless types. (B) An Australian lyre bird. (C) A shoebill stork. See also Color Figs. 40 and 41.

urogenital orifice; in females, urethra and vagina open at separate urinary and reproductive orifices; young develop in uterus, attached to and nourished through placenta

The primitive platypuses and spiny anteaters (*Prototheria*, Fig. 35.32) lay shelled eggs like the reptilian ancestors, but in all other mammals the offspring develop inside the female parent. In marsupials such as kangaroos and opossums (*Metatheria*, Fig. 35.33) the young are born in an immature condition and complete development in a skin pouch on the abdomen of the female. In all other mammals (*Eutheria*) the offspring are born fully developed. These placental mammals comprise 16 orders representing four parallel evolutionary series (Fig. 35.34). One includes insectivores (shrews, moles), bats, anteaters, and armadillos, and particularly primates (lemurs, tarsiers, monkeys, apes, and people). A second series comprises rabbits and all rodents. The third is exemplified by whales, dolphins, and porpoises. And the fourth includes all carnivores such as dogs and cats, as well as elephants and all hoofed, or *ungulate,* mammals: horses, pigs, cattle, sheep, and many others.

Evolution in each of these series has been marked by rather similar adaptive trends. First, body size has tended to increase, an advantage in searching for food and in avoiding becoming food. Second, the number of teeth has tended to decrease; and instead of all teeth remaining alike, as in the reptilian ancestors, the fewer teeth have become different in parallel with specializations in the types of food eaten. Third, the legs have tended to become longer and stronger, the body and often also the heels being lifted off the ground more and more. As a result, locomotion has not only improved but also diversified, in line with the alimentary specializations. Fourth, in conjunction with new modes of locomotion, diverse environments and ecological niches could be occupied. And finally, partly as a result of the increase in body size, partly in conjunction with the improved motility, the size of the brain has increased; in the course of evolutionary time mammals of all kinds have become more intelligent.

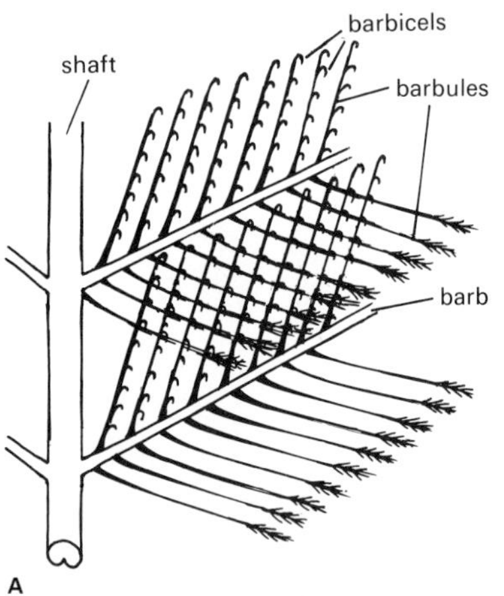

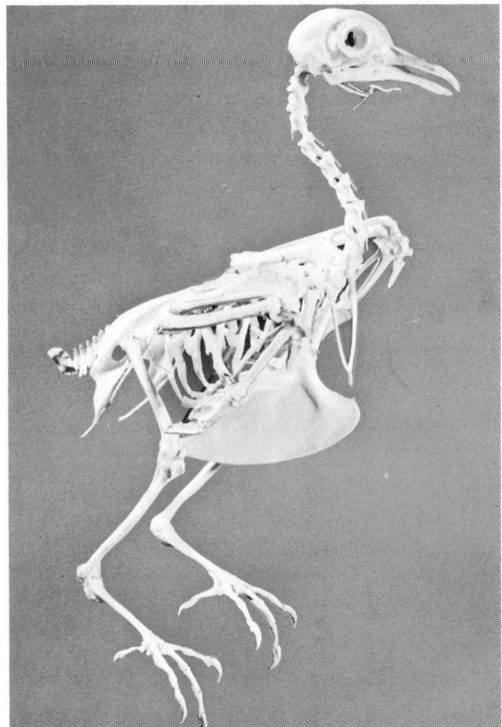

Fig. 35.30 Avian flight adaptations. (A) Diagram of part of a flight feather showing position of barbs, barbules, and barbicels, primary, secondary, and tertiary structures that interlock and maintain overlapping of feather parts. (B) Skeleton of a pigeon. Note large keel, for attachment of wing musculature, and ring of sclerotic plates around the eye, for minimizing wind pressure during flight.

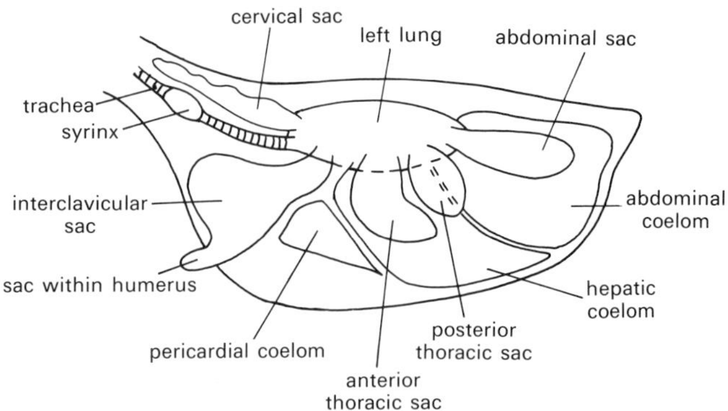

Fig. 35.31 Internal structure of birds. The position of the lungs, air sacs, and coelomic spaces are indicated. Five (paired) air sacs pouch from the lungs. The interclavicular sac projects between the clavicles, or collarbones. The humerus is a large wing bone. The syrinx, or voice box, contains vocal muscles.

Fig. 35.32 Egg-laying mammals (Prototheria). (A) Duck-billed platypus. (B) An echidna, or spiny anteater.

Fig. 35.33 Pouched, marsupial mammals (Metatheria). (A) Opossum, the only marsupial surviving in North America. (B) Koala bear, native to Australia. See also Color Fig. 42.

Thus the insectivore-primate group (Fig. 35.35) now actually includes the most intelligent of all animals, and locomotor diversifications to flying (as in bats) and bipedal walking (as in human beings) are in evidence as well. Moreover, primates are comparatively very large animals; and a person has only 32 teeth, of several types, whereas a mole, for example, has 44. The rabbit-rodent group is characterized particularly by its adaptation to a wide variety of habitats and again by high intelligence (as in rats) and by locomotor and dental specializations (for example, leaping and continuously growing incisors, as in rabbits). In the whale series body sizes have increased more than anywhere else, a drastic change to swimming locomotion and marine existence has occurred, and tooth reduction is

Fig. 35.34 The orders of mammals, arranged according to their main evolutionary groupings. Read from bottom up. A representative type is indicated for each order. The four eutherian series represent the placental mammals.

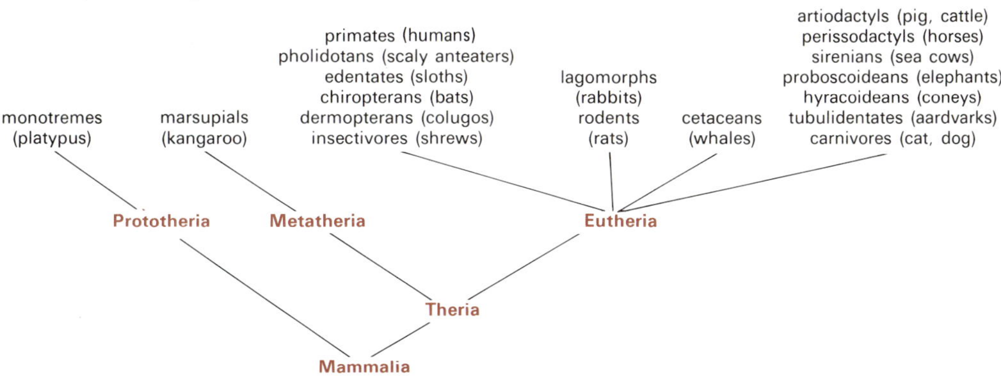

A

B

C

Fig. 35.35 Placental mammals (Eutheria). (A) A bat, an insectivore. (B) A woodrat, a rodent. (C) A killer whale, a cetacean. (D) A giraffe, an ungulate. See also Color Figs. 43 and 44 and see Chap. 36 for illustrations of primates.

maximal in whalebone whales, where baleen plates replace teeth altogether. Moreover, the remarkable mental prowess of types such as porpoises is well known (see Fig. 35.35).

In the carnivore-ungulate series, a running way of life on the plains has been exploited most. In several subseries within the group, the heel has lifted off the ground, the foot has elongated, and the animal walks on its toes, like cats and gazelles. Concurrently the toes have become increasingly hoofed, and the number of toes has become reduced. For example, carnivores are five-toed and still nonungulate; elephants have small nail-like hoofs on each toe; and a fully ungulate condition (with variously reduced toe numbers) is found in

D

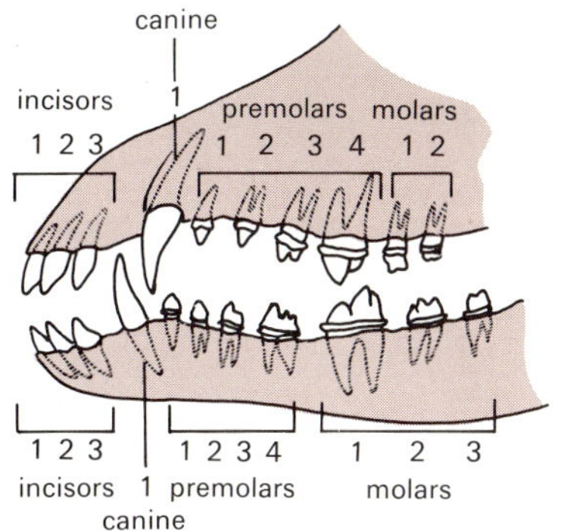

Fig. 35.36 Mammalian teeth. The dentition of a dog in one half of the head. These teeth are carnassial (pointed), as in carnivores generally.

the horse group and the deer-cattle group. With regard to tooth specializations, teeth are pointed and adapted for tearing in carnivores, and the canines form long fangs (Fig. 35.36). But in herbivorous ungulates, incisors are adapted for cutting, molars are adapted for grinding, and canines are often absent. Body size has increased independently several times—bears, horses, elephants, and cattle all have evolved from far smaller ancestors. And intelligence likewise has reached high levels more than once; types like bears, dogs, and elephants clearly are brainy animals.

Such fairly parallel results show well that if ecological opportunities are similar, organisms similar in many respects can evolve several times independently. At the root of these evolutionary trends in mammals actually have been just two basic and related adaptive forces: feeding and the requirement of finding food. Indeed these are the very same that have also shaped the nature of all other organisms since the first primeval cell types appeared in the ocean.

Review Questions

1 Give taxonomic definitions of deuterostomial coelomates as a whole and of each of the phyla. Discuss the possible evolutionary interrelations of the phyla and the evidence from which such possibilities are deduced.

2 What traits characterize the echinoderm phylum, and what are the classes? What adaptive factors appear to have led to the evolution of water-vascular systems in echinoderms?

3 Review the structure of a starfish and the organization of every organ system. What is the function of the water-vascular system, and how are such functions performed? How and on what does a starfish feed? What is the general course of echinoderm development?

4 Give taxonomic definitions and structural characteristics of the phylum Chordata and the three subphyla. Indicate the known species number of each of these groups, and name the five largest animal phyla in terms of species numbers.

5 Describe the structure of an ascidian and show how the adult emerges during metamorphosis. What is the probable evolutionary significance of the tunicate tadpole?

6 Compare and contrast the processes of nutrient and oxygen procurement, digestion, intercellular transport, excretion, and reproduction in a starfish and a tunicate. For each organism, name the principal structures that are associated with these processes.

7 Describe the structure of amphioxus and outline the organization of every organ system.

8 Show how most of the basic vertebrate traits are direct adaptations to a life in fresh water. What changes in vertebrate anatomy were associated with the change from ancestral filter feeding to bulk feeding by mouth?

9 What were the main steps in the evolution of the vertebrate breathing system, circulatory system, and excretory system? Characterize each vertebrate class taxonomically.

10 Describe the general structure and way of life of a lamprey and a bony fish. What are ammocoetes? Outline the structure of a fish gill.

11 Distinguish between flesh-finned and ray-finned fishes. What are clupeiform and perciform fishes? Contrast the structure of their fins and scales. Which group of fishes was probably ancestral to the amphibia?

12 Show in what respects amphibia are basically aquatic and in what respects they are terrestrial.

What prevents amphibia from being fully terrestrial?

13 Review the biological characteristics of reptiles, birds, and mammals. Name some of the adaptive specializations of snakes and crocodiles. Show how birds are adapted to flying.

14 List the evolutionary groups of mammals and of placental mammals and describe the specializations characteristic of each.

Collateral Readings

Alldredge, A.: Appendicularians, *Scientific American,* July 1976. An interesting account of those obscure urochordates.

Barrington, E. J. W.: "The Biology of the Hemichordates and Protochordata," Oliver & Boyd, Edinburgh, 1965. A good introduction to the nonvertebrate chordates.

Bellairs, A.: "The Life of Reptiles," Weidenfeld & Nicolson, London, 1969. A text on the structure, physiology, and evolution of reptiles.

Calder, W. A.: The Kiwi, *Scientific American,* July 1978. Examines the evolution and ecology of this flightless New Zealand bird.

Cochran, D. M.: "Living Amphibians of the World," Doubleday, Garden City, N.Y., 1961. A well-illustrated introduction to the amphibians; written for the nonscientist. The books by Gilliard, Herald, Schmidt and Inger, listed below, are part of the same series.

Dawson, T. G.: Kangaroos, *Scientific American,* August 1977. Focuses on ungulatelike adaptations of these fascinating mammals.

Gilliard, E. T.: "Living Birds of the World," Doubleday, Garden City, N.Y., 1958.

Herald, E. S.: "Living Fishes of the World," Doubleday, Garden City, N.Y., 1961.

Johansen, K.: Air-Breathing Fishes, *Scientific American,* October 1968. Introduces the modern descendants of an ancient group of fishes that also gave rise to other air-breathing vertebrates.

Marshall, N. B.: "The Life of Fishes," World, Cleveland, 1966. A general account of the biology of fishes.

McFarland, W. N., et al.: "Vertebrate Life," Macmillan, N.Y., 1979. A comprehensive, general introduction.

Neill, W. T.: "Reptiles and Amphibians in the Service of Man," Pegasus, New York, 1974. A nontechnical paperback on the biology of these animals and their interactions with human beings.

Nichols, D.: "Echinoderms," 4th ed., Hutchinson, London, 1969. An authoritative, readable introduction to these animals.

Orr, R. T.: "Vertebrate Biology," 4th ed., Saunders, Philadelphia, 1976. A good reference text for additional information about vertebrates.

Pooley, A. C., and **C. Gans:** The Nile Crocodile, *Scientific American,* April 1976. The anatomy, physiology, and behavior of this remarkable animal is described.

Schmidt, K. P., and **R. F. Inger:** "Living Reptiles of the World," Doubleday, Garden City, N.Y., 1957.

Weis-Fogh, T.: Unusual Mechanisms for the Generation of Lift in Flying Animals, *Scientific American,* November 1975. The aerodynamics of flying in birds and insects is discussed.

Welty, J. C.: "The Life of Birds," 2d ed., Saunders, Philadelphia, 1975. A highly readable account of the biology of birds.

Young, Y. Z.: "The Life of Mammals," 2d ed., Clarendon Press, Oxford, 1975. One of the best introductions to mammalian biology.

Chapter 36 Animals and People: Evolutionary Perspectives

Learning Objectives

After reading this chapter you should be able to:

1. Differentiate between ontogeny and phylogeny; write a short essay describing the evolutionary theories of Ernst Haeckel and explaining why his views are no longer considered valid by modern biologists; define and state examples of developmental divergence and neoteny.
2. Construct a diagram that shows the various periods of the Paleozoic Era and illustrates the approximate dates at which various classes of vertebrates arose; construct similar diagrams for the Mesozoic and Cenozoic Eras; among other organisms your diagrams should include at least one reference to each of the following:
   - **a.** ostracoderms
   - **b.** placoderms
   - **c.** cartilage and bony fishes
   - **d.** amphibians
   - **e.** labyrinthodonts
   - **f.** cotylosaurs
   - **g.** thecodonts
   - **h.** pterosaurs
   - **i.** dinosaurs
   - **j.** turtles
   - **k.** ichtyosaurs
   - **l.** plesiosaurs
   - **m.** therapsids
   - **n.** insectivores
   - **o.** primates
3. For each of the vertebrate types listed in Objective 2, state the general appearance of at least one representative.
4. List at least three kinds of animals that either became extinct or declined in numbers during the Paleozoic; do the same for the Mesozoic. Write a paragraph identifying one possible cause of the dramatic extinctions of dinosaurs and other prominent Mesozoic organisms, and describe supporting evidence for this hypothesis.
5. List at least six specialized adaptations that came into existence during the evolution of mammals.
6. Name the evolutionary line that gave rise to primates; construct a diagram that depicts the major features and time pattern of the primate radiation; name the five surviving sublines of primates and a representative organism of each.
7. State the general appearance of the first primates and list reasons for the extensive adaptive radiation of these mammals during the first 30 million years of their existence.
8. List the adaptations of lemurs, tarsiers, monkeys, and apes to arboreal life; list the characteristics of hominoids that distinguish them from other primates; state at least one way in which the evolution of pongids differs from that of hominids; identify the regions of the world where monkeys and apes probably first evolved; indicate the probable evolutionary origins of New World monkeys and name one extinct common ancestor of both apes and human beings.
9. Postulate why the primate ancestors of most apes and all species of human beings abandoned arboreal life to a greater or lesser degree; cite evidence in support of your hypothesis.
10. List at least three reasons for the limited amount of information pertaining to the evolution of our own species; illustrate how at least four factors have greatly facilitated the acquisition of knowledge about human evolution over the past two decades; define biochemical taxonomy.
11. State the general characteristics and probable evolutionary significance of dryopithecine apes: give the approximate date and site of origin of these extinct primates; name at least one difference between the dentition of hominids and pongids and show how this difference is related to the kinds of food eaten by these two groups of hominoids.
12. Name at least three structural, functional, or behavioral features of human beings that trace

back specifically to the arboreal way of life of primate ancestors; state the probable structural and behavioral characteristics of *Ramapithecus,* two forms of *Australopithecus, Homo erectus,* Neanderthal man, and Cro-Magnon man.

13. Construct a diagram contrasting the toolmaking and cultural attributes of homonids listed in Objective 12; cite changes in cranial capacity and brain structure that occurred during the evolution of modern man from ancestral hominids.

14. State the approximate date of the origin of *Homo sapiens;* list characteristics that human beings share with all other:

a. hominids
b. hominoids
c. primates
d. mammals

Since most animal phyla already appear to have been in existence 500 million years ago, when abundant fossil formation first began, the various basic animal types must have evolved earlier during the Precambrian (see Chap. 32 for definitions and descriptions of geologic eras and periods). The early evolution of animals consequently cannot be documented by fossils but must be inferred from the nature of animals now living.

This chapter describes several methods by which biologists attempt to deduce evolutionary lineages in different animal groups. The probable origins and evolutionary relationships between all phyla of animals, introduced in Chaps. 33 to 35, are described in sections that immediately follow. Later sections of this chapter examine possible paths of descent of our own species.

ANIMAL EVOLUTION

Ontogeny and Phylogeny

One of the notable attempts at inferring the course of animal evolution from existing forms was made by Ernst Haeckel, a German biologist of the late nineteenth century. Most of his views are now largely discredited, but they were once so influential that many of them still persist today under various guises. For this reason it may be of some value to review them briefly.

Haeckel recognized, as others did before him, that animal development typically passes through certain common embryonic stages—zygote, blastula, gastrula, and mesoderm formation. Haeckel thought that this succession of embryonic stages mirrored a succession of past evolutionary stages (Fig. 36.1). Thus the zygote would represent the unicellular protistan stage of evolution. The blastula would correspond to an evolutionary stage when animals were, according to Haeckel, hollow one-layered spheres. Haeckel coined the term *blastea* for such hypothetical adult animals, and he thought that his ancestral blasteas might have been quite similar to currently living green algae such as *Volvox* (see Chap. 32). The gastrula stage would correspond to a hypothetical ancestral adult type that Haeckel called a *gastrea.* He believed that gastreas were still represented by the living coelenterates, which in some respects do resemble early gastrulas—the body consists chiefly of two layers and the single alimentary opening is reminiscent of the blastopore of a gastrula.

On such grounds Haeckel considered the gastrea to have been the common ancestor of all Eumetazoa. He assumed the two-layered gastrealike condition to represent a *diploblastic* stage in animal evolution, attained by radiates such as the coelenterates. Further evolution then added mesoderm to the gastrealike radiates and so produced a three-layered *triploblastic* condition, as in flatworms and all other Bilateria. By extension the hypothesis also implied that, for example, a caterpillar larva represented an annelid stage in insect evolution, that a frog tadpole represented a fish stage in frog evolution, and that a human embryo, which exhibits its rudimentary gill structures at certain periods, represented a fish stage in human evolution.

Haeckel condensed his views into a *law of recapitulation,* the essence of which is described by two phrases: "ontogeny recapitulates phylogeny" and "phylogeny causes ontogeny." The first state-

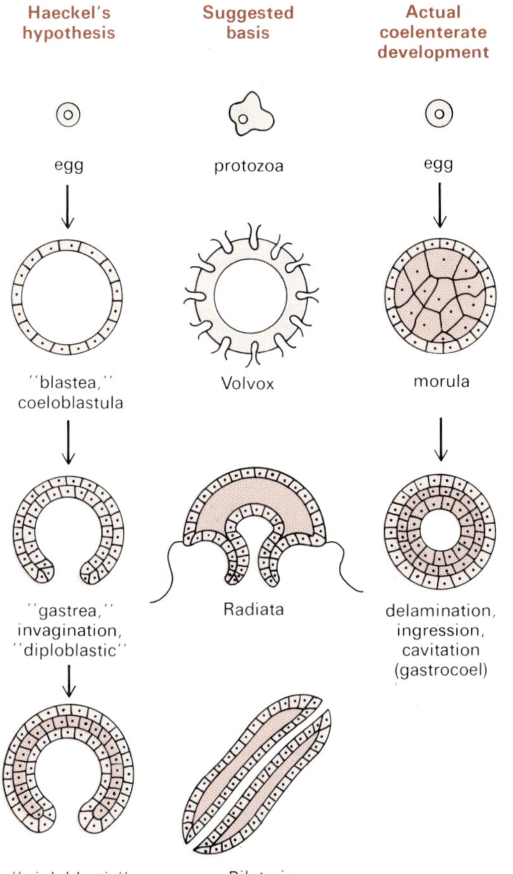

Fig. 36.1 Haeckel's "gastrea" hypothesis. Based primarily on coelenterate development, the hypothesis is at variance with the actual developmental patterns typical of most coelenterates (as at right). Thus, most coelenterates have solid, not hollow, blastulas; most do not gastrulate by invagination but by a variety of other processes, as indicated. Moreover, again contrary to Haeckel's hypothesis, the presence of mesoderm in coelenterates makes not only the Bilateria but also the Radiata (hence all Eumetazoa) "triploblastic," or formed from three primary germ layers.

ment means that the embryonic development of an egg (ontogeny) repeats the evolutionary development of the phyla (phylogeny); and the second, that *because* animals have evolved one phylum after another, their embryos still pass through this same succession of evolutionary stages.

Therefore, to determine the course of animal evolution, one need only study the course of embryonic development. For, according to Haeckel, evolution occurs by the addition of extra embryonic stages to the end of a given sequence of development. If to a protozoon is added cleavage, the protozoon becomes a zygote and the new adult is a blastea. If to a blastea is added gastrulation, the blastea becomes a blastula and the new adult is a gastrea. Similarly, if to a fish are added lungs and four legs, the fish represents a tadpole and the new adult is a frog. And if to such an amphibian are added a four-chambered heart, a diaphragm, a larger brain, an upright posture, and a few other features, then the frog is a human embryo and the new adult is a person.

We can attribute to the lingering influence of Haeckel, not to Darwin, this erroneous idea of an evolutionary "ladder" or "scale," proceeding from "simple amoeba" to "complex human being," with more and more rungs added on top of the ladder as time proceeds (see also Chap. 29). All such notions are invalid because Haeckel's basic thesis is invalid. Indeed, Haeckel's arguments were shown to be unsound even in his own day, but his generalizations were so neat and they seemed to explain so much so simply that the fundamental difficulties were ignored by many.

For example, it was already well known in Haeckel's time that, apart from exceptional forms, the radiate animals do not really have two-layered bodies but distinctly three-layered ones, with a mesoderm often highly developed (as in sea anemones, for example). Two-layered animals in effect do not exist, and a distinction between diploblastic and triploblastic types cannot be justified. Thus the conceptual foundation on which the recapitulatory law was based was never valid.

Moreover, new types are not known to evolve by addition of extra stages to ancestral adults. Instead, new evolution occurs for the most part through *developmental divergence;* a new path of embryonic or larval development branches away from some point along a preexisting ancestral path of development (Fig. 36.2). The best example is evolution by larval *neoteny,* a common process by which numerous new groups are believed to have arisen from the *larvae* of ancestral groups. An ancestral larva here does not metamorphose into the customary adult, but instead develops sex organs precociously and becomes established in this larval form as a new type of adult animal.

As pointed out earlier, for example, tunicates have tadpole larvae that develop into sessile adults.

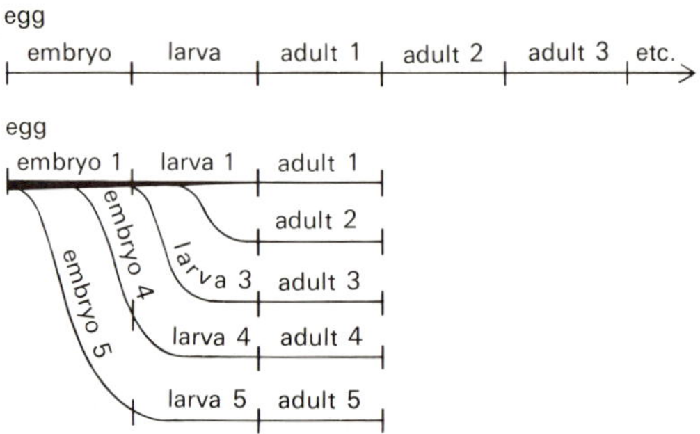

Fig. 36.2 Developmental divergence. Top, the pattern of evolution according to Haeckel, by addition of extra stages to a preexisting ancestral path of development. Bottom, the actual pattern of evolution, by divergence of new developmental paths (2, 3, 4, 5) from various points of a preexisting ancestral path (1). Thus if divergence occurs comparatively late, as in adult 2, its embryonic and most of its larval development can be very similar to that of adult 1. But if divergence takes place early, as in adult 5, then almost the whole developmental pattern will be quite dissimilar from that of adult 1. Adults 1 and 5 then might represent different phyla, whereas adults 1 and 2 might belong to the same class or order.

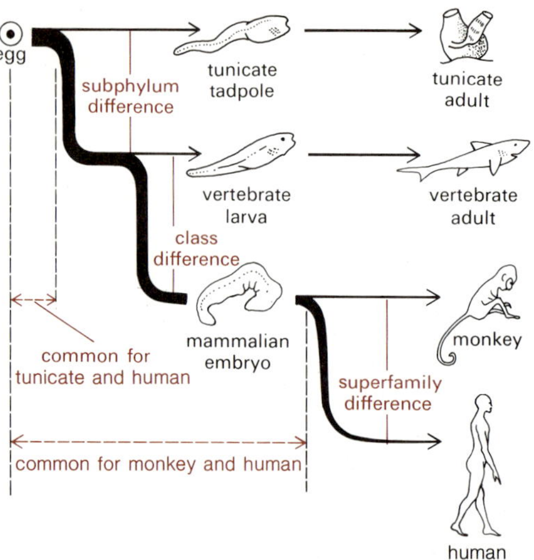

Fig. 36.3 Developmental divergence in chordate evolution. Tailed, tadpolelike early stages are characteristic of all chordates, and the earlier the developmental paths diverge from the ancestral one, the more different will be the adults and the taxonomic results. Thus the developmental paths of tunicates and people diverge early, and the adult differences are at the level of subphyla. But monkeys and people develop similarly for far longer periods, and the adult differences here are only at the level of superfamilies. To be sure, chordate eggs are not all the same but are merely similar. Also, "common" developmental stages of two animals are merely similar, not identical.

It is now considered most probable that vertebrates represent neotenous tunicate tadpoles. The tadpoles of certain tunicate ancestors are believed to have retained their tails, with notochord and dorsal hollow nerve cord intact, and to have become reproductively mature in such a larval condition. These permanent larvae then came to represent a new chordate subphylum, the vertebrates (Fig. 36.3).

Numerous other instances of evolution by neoteny are known, the evolution of human beings included. In all these cases the new developmental path branches away sooner or later along the course of the old path. The sooner two such paths do diverge, the more dissimilar will be the two types of resulting adult. For example, embryos of humans and of apes resemble each other till relatively late in development, and the developmental paths diverge only then. The embryos of humans and of tunicates are similar for considerably shorter periods; their developmental paths correspondingly diverge much sooner (see Fig. 36.3).

Such developmental correlations were clearly recognized before Haeckel and even before Darwin. They do have evolutionary meaning, but not in the Haeckelian sense. It is quite natural that related animals descended from a common ancestor should resemble each other in some of their developmental features. Thus, human embryos resemble those of fish and frogs in certain respects not because a human egg becomes a fish embryo first, a frog embryo next, and a human embryo last. The similarities arise instead from the common ancestry of all these three animal types, including their common developmental histories up to certain stages. Beyond these stages each type has modified its developmental processes in its own way.

Moreover, it can be shown that the formation of a particular structure in one type of organism often depends on the existence of an anatomical precursor that had evolved in an ancestral type of organism. Some of the evolutionary opportunisms discussed in Chap. 29 illustrate this generalization. As noted, for example, the human larynx has evolved opportunistically as a derivative of skeletal gill supports of ancestral fishes. An important point here is that, from an architectural standpoint, a larynx cannot be put together unless gill-derived skeletal components are available in the human embryo as structural raw materials. In other words, human embryos today still form rudimen-

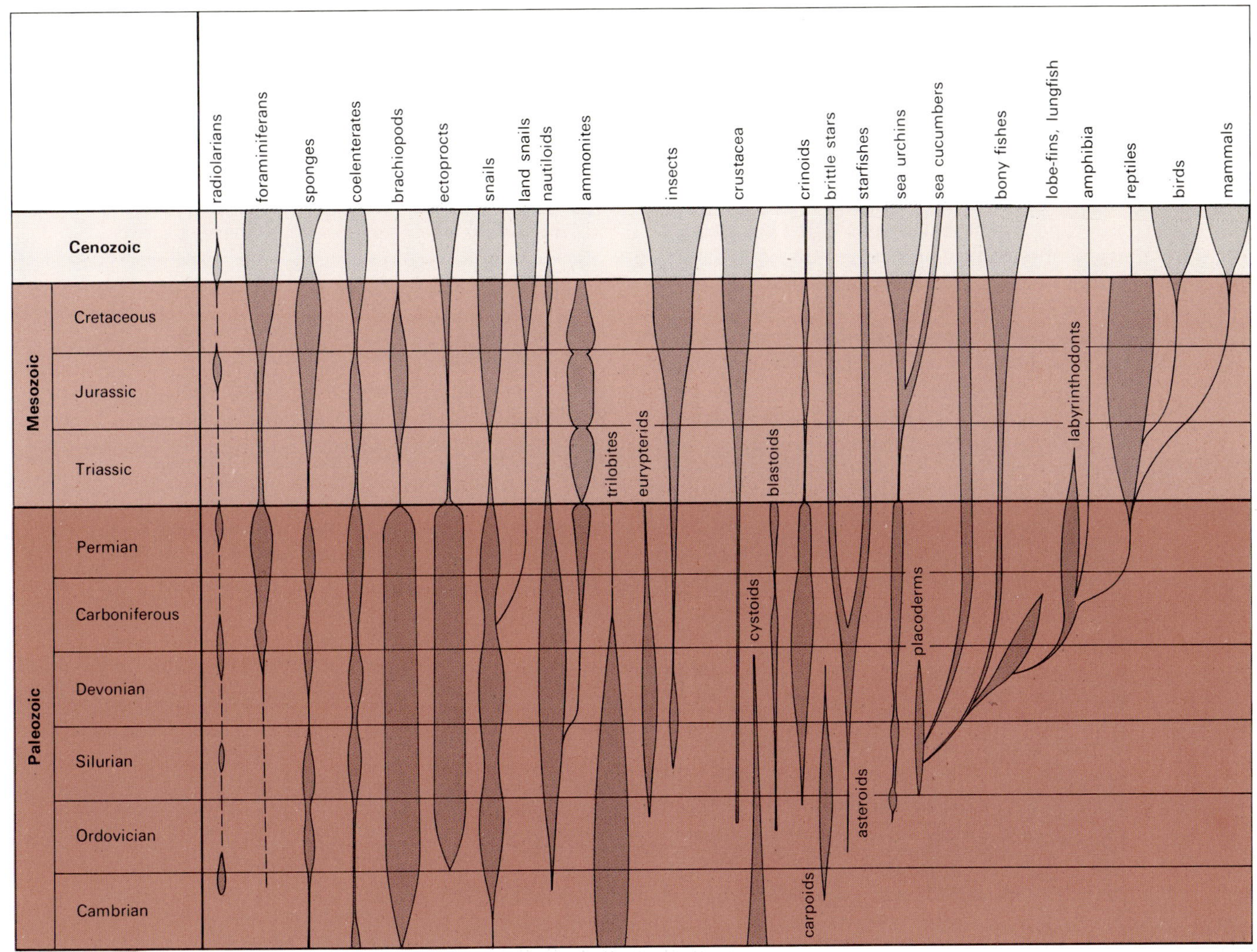

Fig. 36.4 The fossil record of animals. The varying width of each graph approximates the changing abundance of a given group in the course of time. Such widths are directly comparable only for different times within a group, not between groups. For example, the absolute Cenozoic abundance of insects would equal or exceed that of all other groups combined. The graphs clearly show the major decline that took place at the end of each era, particularly during the Permo-Triassic transition and on a smaller scale during the Mesozoic-Cenozoic transition.

tary, nonfunctioning gills, not because they "recapitulate" fish evolution as Haeckel supposed, but because gill rudiments must serve as necessary intermediate steps in the building process that leads to larynx construction. Similarly, gill rudiments are still required in human development as intermediate structural steps in the elaboration of the face musculature. In like fashion also, most other supposed instances of "recapitulation" turn out to involve precursor stages still necessary today for the development of other structures.

It should be pointed out, furthermore, that a branching pattern of developmental divergence is fully in line with the known bushlike pattern of evolution, whereas ladderlike end addition is not. It is quite obvious also that mammalian development, for example, does not really represent a successive transformation of an actual protozoan to an actual coelenterate, flatworm, tunicate, fish, etc. Indeed it is hardly conceivable that the billion or more years of animal evolution could be crowded into the few weeks or months of animal development. The common stages in animal development thus give evidence of general similarities only, not of specific identities.

For these various reasons the Haeckelian idea of recapitulation is not tenable; the embryonic stages of animals do not repeat the adult stages of earlier animals. Moreover, phylum evolution also cannot be the "cause" of the progressive stages in animal development. If anything, just the reverse probably holds; as pointed out above, developmental stages provide the sources from which new groups can evolve. What is acceptable today—as it was even before Haeckel—is the generalization that the embryonic development of different animals tends to be similar if the animals are related historically, and that the embryonic similarity generally lasts longer the closer the relationship. Indeed, as has become apparent in Chap. 33, developmental resemblances are important aids in both classifying animals and elucidating phylogenies—the "family trees" of animal groups before fossils were left. Figure 33.5 can serve as a summary of current views on this subject.

The Paleozoic

All animal phyla in existence 500 million years ago still survive today, but most subgroups in these phyla have since become replaced; all the ancient

A

B

Fig. 36.5 Paleozoic fossils, restorations. (A) Cambrian seas. Various algae, trilobites (in center foreground), eurypterids (in center background), sponges, jellyfishes, brachiopods, and different types of worms are the most prominent organisms shown. (B) Ordovician seas. The large animal in foreground is a straight-shelled nautiloid.

Fig. 36.6 Paleozoic echinoderms. (A) A cystoid. (B) A blastoid. (C) A crinoid. See Fig. 36.4 for history of first two.

species and genera have become extinct long ago. During the very long Cambrian and Ordovician Periods, life in the sea was already abundant. A large variety of protists probably existed long before the Cambrian, and fossil algae, foraminiferans, and radiolarians are known from earliest Cambrian time onward (Fig. 36.4). The fossil history of animals begins with Cambrian sponges and jellyfishes and Ordovician corals and sea anemones. A variety of tube-forming worms is known from these and even earlier periods, and stalked brachiopods already existed in the Cambrian. The Ordovician marks the beginning of a rich record of entoprocts and ectoprocts (Fig. 36.5).

Echinoderms were amply represented by six archaic groups. Three of these (*cystoids, carpoids, blastoids*) have since become extinct, but the stalked sessile *crinoids* and the ancient *asteroids* and *echinoids* gave rise to the present-day echinoderms (Fig. 36.6 and see Fig. 36.4). Mollusks included archaic clams and snails, as well as *nautiloids,* a group closely related to squids and octopuses and still represented today by the chambered nautilus. Early nautiloids had both coiled and uncoiled shells, and the uncoiled forms probably were the largest animals of the time; their shells were up to 5 or 6 yards long (see Fig. 36.5).

The most ancient arthropod types were the *trilobites,* believed to have been ancestral to all other arthropod groups (Fig. 36.7). Their body was marked into three lobes by two longitudinal furrows, hence the name "trilobites." These animals were already exceedingly abundant when the Cambrian began, and they are among the most plentiful of all fossil forms. A somewhat later group of arthropods comprised the *eurypterids,* large animals that well may have been ancestral to all chelicerate arthropods (horseshoe crabs, sea spiders, and arachnids).

A

B

Fig. 36.7 Paleozoic arthropods. (A) Trilobites. (B) A eurypterid.

Vertebrate history begins late in the Ordovician (Fig. 36.8). The marine tunicate ancestors probably were already present at or near the start of the Paleozoic, and the vertebrates evolved from them as freshwater forms. The first fossil vertebrates are *ostracoderms,* bone-plated members of the class of jawless fishes. Most of them became extinct near the end of the Devonian, and their only surviving descendants are the lampreys and hagfishes. All traces of external bone have been lost in these animals (Fig. 36.9).

The Silurian was the period during which the first tracheophytes evolved, and these land plants were soon followed by land animals: late Silurian land scorpions, probably evolved from earlier sea scorpions, are the earliest known terrestrial animals. Other groups of arthropods invaded the land during the latter part of the Silurian and the beginning of the Devonian. The first spiders, mites, centipedes, and insects appeared during these times. In the sea the nautiloids gave rise to a new molluscan group, the shelled *ammonites,* which were to flourish for long ages (see Fig. 36.9). Among echinoderms the ancient asteroids branched into two descendant groups, the brittle stars and starfishes. And among vertebrates a major adaptive radiation occurred during the Silurian and Devonian (see Fig. 36.8).

During the early Silurian some of the jawless ostracoderms gave rise to a new vertebrate class, the *placoderms.* Bone-plated like their ancestors, these fishes were generally small, but some reached lengths of 12 yards or more. Most placoderms used their jaws in a carnivorous mode of life (see Fig. 2.7). In time the placoderms replaced the ancestral ostraderms as the dominant animals, and late in the Silurian they produced two descendant lines of fishes that in turn came to replace the placoderms themselves; by the end of the Paleozoic the placoderms had disappeared completely, the only vertebrate class (and one of the few animal classes in general) that has become extinct.

The two new groups of fishes evolved from placoderms were the *cartilage fishes* and the *bony fishes,* each representing a separate class. Both groups arose in fresh water, but the cartilage fishes rapidly adopted the marine habit that sharks and rays still display today. The bony fishes at first remained in fresh water, where they soon radiated into three main subgroups: the *paleoniscoid fishes,* the *lungfishes,* and the *lobe-finned fishes.* During the Devonian, often called the "age of fishes," the

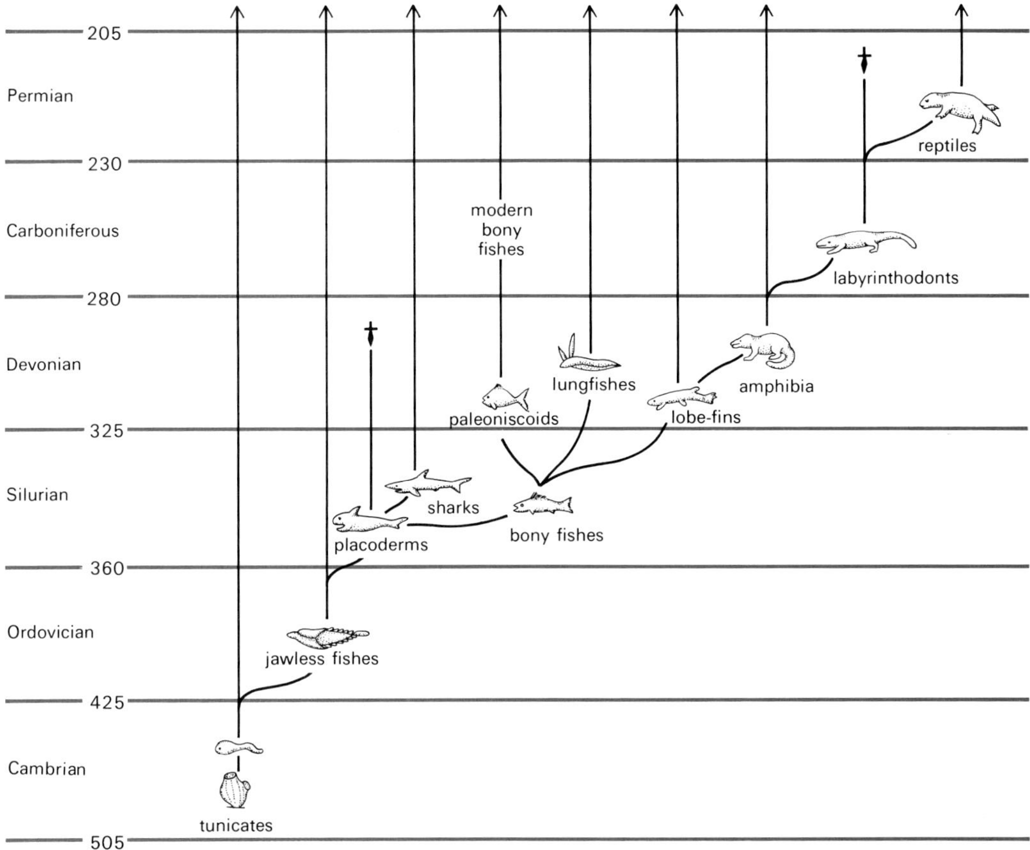

Fig. 36.8 Paleozoic vertebrates. The name of each group is shown roughly at the time level at which this group first appears in the fossil record. Daggers indicate extinction of a group.

paleoniscoids spread to the ocean and became the ancestors of practically all present bony fishes, both freshwater and marine. The lungfishes declined in later Paleozoic time, and only three genera survive today. The lobe-fins similarly now are almost extinct (Fig. 36.10 and see Fig. 36.8).

But the Devonian representatives of the lobe-fins included the ancestors of the *amphibia*, the first land vertebrates. Lobe-fins probably lived in fresh waters that dried out periodically, and their air sacs and fleshy fins presumably enabled them to crawl overland to other bodies of water or to embed themselves in mud and breathe air through the mouth. It appears likely, therefore, that terrestrial vertebrates arose not because certain fish preferred the land, but because they had to become terrestrial if they were to survive as fish.

Thus when the Devonian came to a close sharks were dominant in the ocean and bony fishes in fresh water. On land, terrestrial arthropods had become abundant and the first amphibia had made their appearance. Many of these land animals could shelter in the lycopsid and sphenopsid forests then already in existence.

During the Carboniferous and Permian Periods the first crablike and crayfishlike animals and the first land snails appeared, and insects produced extensive adaptive radiations. Some of these ancient insect types had wingspreads of close to a yard. Among vertebrates the early amphibia gave rise to more or less clumsy, often bizarre forms, the *labyrinthodonts* (see Fig. 36.10). These became the ancestors of two groups, the modern amphibia and the *reptiles*. This new class was represented at first

A

Fig. 36.9 Paleozoic fossils. (A) Ostracoderm, an ancient jawless fish. Note bony armor. A placoderm is illustrated in Fig. 2.7. (B) An ammonite, a cephalopod mollusk related to the chambered nautilus (see Fig. 34.15).

B

by the stem reptiles, or *cotylosaurs*, the first vertebrates that laid eggs on land. Cotylosaurs produced a major reptilian radiation during the Permian, which brought about the decline of the labyrinthodonts and also set the stage for an "age of reptiles" during the Mesozoic Era (Fig. 36.11).

The Paleozoic Era terminated with the Appalachian revolution, as noted in Chap. 32, and, as among plants, this geologically unstable time precipitated a Permo-Triassic crisis in the animal world. Archaic forms became extinct and were replaced by rapidly evolving new groups, and the total amount of animal life—particularly in the sea—decreased temporarily (see Fig. 36.4). Brachiopods and ectoprocts became almost extinct. All mollusks passed through a major decline; nautiloids became extinct with one exception, and ammonites were reduced to a small group. Trilobites and eurypterids disappeared altogether. Only a few crinoid types and a single echinoid type survived into the Triassic. Placoderms died out, and extensive replacements occurred among the cartilage and bony fishes. Land animals were less affected on the whole, though their numbers did decline temporarily. Labyrinthodonts lingered on to the Triassic, but soon they, too, became extinct. The reptiles on the contrary survived the crisis well, and when the new Mesozoic Era opened, they were already dominant.

The Mesozoic

The era as a whole was characterized by a reexpansion of nearly all groups that survived the Permo-Triassic crisis and by extensive replacements within groups (see Fig. 36.4). Sponges and coelenterates underwent major adaptive radiations during the Jurassic, with the result that these animals exist today in greater numbers than ever before. Ectoprocts and brachiopods similarly increased in abundance, but the latter became virtually extinct again at the end of the Mesozoic. Clams and snails diversified greatly and became the predominant mollusks from then on. The ammonites also reexpanded during the late Mesozoic, yet not a single one survived beyond the end of the era. The crinoids managed to linger on as relics, and the more abundant brittle stars and starfishes held their own. But one echinoid group underwent an explosive expansion during the late Mesozoic. In the course of it the modern sea urchins and sea cucumbers evolved. Crustacea gained slowly and steadily in numbers and types. Insects diversified explosively in parallel with the rise of flowering plants, and the present importance of insects traces to this

A B

Fig. 36.10 Devonian and Permian vertebrates. (A) Restoration of fossil lobe-finned fishes. See Fig. 35.22 for photograph of modern lungfish. (B) Reconstruction of *Diplovertebron,* a labyrinthodont amphibian.

Mesozoic expansion. An extensive radiation occurred also among the bony fishes, which became the dominant animals of the aquatic world from the Cretaceous on.

Reptiles, Birds, and Mammals

The most spectacular Mesozoic event was the expansion of the reptiles. They not only evolved as numerous terrestrial types but also invaded the water and the air. As a group they reigned supreme on earth for 130 million years, longer than any other animal group before or since. When their dominance was eventually broken, they were replaced by two new groups they themselves had given rise to, the birds and the mammals.

At the beginning of the Mesozoic five major

Fig. 36.11 Reptile evolution. (A) Reconstruction of *Seymouria,* a transitional amphibian type probably related to the stock from which reptiles appear to have evolved. (B) Reconstruction of *Labidosaurus,* one of the cotylosaurian stem reptiles.

A B

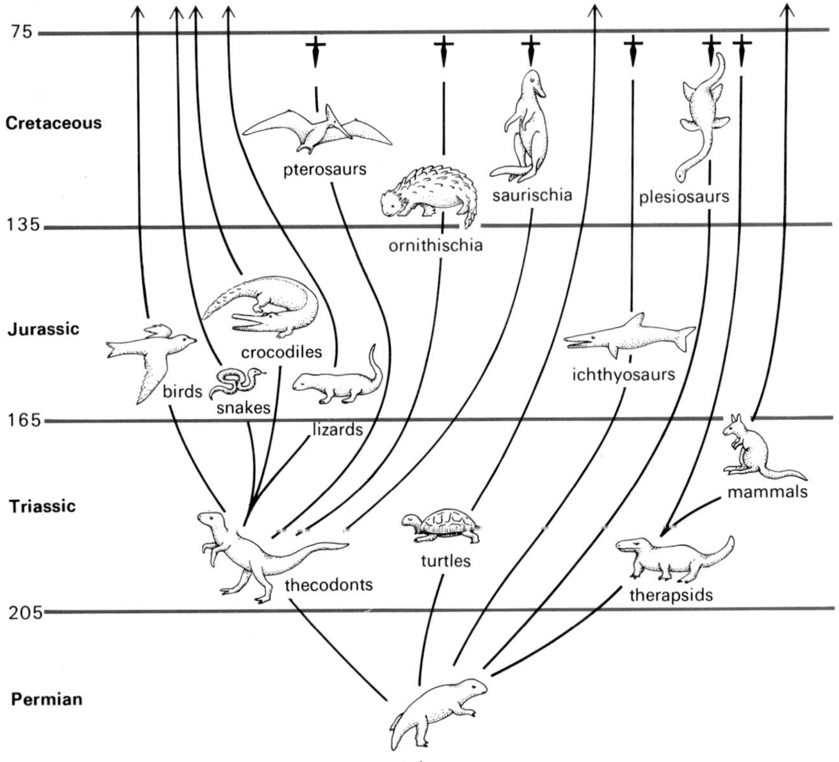

Fig. 36.12 Mesozoic reptiles. Placement of groups corresponds roughly with the time of their greatest abundance. Numbers at left indicate past time in millions of years. Daggers indicate extinction of a group.

reptilian groups were in existence, all evolved from the Permian stem reptiles (Fig. 36.12). One group, the *thecodonts,* reradiated extensively during the Triassic and gave rise to the following types: the ancestral *birds;* the ancestors of the modern *crocodiles, lizards,* and *snakes;* the flying *pterosaurs;* and two other groups collectively called *dinosaurs.* A second group was ancestral to the modern *turtles.* A third and fourth produced two kinds of marine reptile, the porpoise-like *ichthyosaurs* and the long-necked *plesiosaurs* (see Fig. 36.14). The fifth group comprised the *therapsids,* which included the ancestors of the mammals.

These various reptilian types did not all flourish at the same time. The Triassic was dominated largely by early therapsids and thecodonts. The former were four-footed walkers, but thecodonts were rather birdlike, with large hind limbs for walking, an enormous supporting tail, and diminutive forelimbs. During the Jurassic, ichthyosaurs became abundant in the ocean, and one of the thecodont lines evolved into birds. This transition is documented beautifully by the famous fossil animal *Archeopteryx* (Fig. 36.13). The reptile had teeth and a lizardlike tail, but it was also equipped with feathers and wings and presumably flew.

Like mammals, birds remained inconspicuous during the whole remaining Mesozoic. They were overshadowed particularly by their thecodont kin, the flying pterosaurs. These animals had their heyday during the Cretaceous, when reptiles as a whole attained their greatest abundance and variety. The unique, long-necked plesiosaurs were then common in the ocean, and the dinosaurs gained undisputed dominance on land. Not all dinosaurs were large, but some were enormous. The group included, for example, *Brontosaurus,* the largest land animal of all time, and *Tyrannosaurus,* probably the fiercest land carnivore of all time (Fig. 36.14).

Mammals arose from therapsids during the late Triassic (Fig. 36.15). Some of the factors that probably promoted this mammalian evolution can be deduced. The ancestors of mammals among therapsid reptiles generally were small, in the size range of mice, and this smallness must have entailed perpetual danger in a world dominated by far larger animals. Survival must have depended on ability to escape danger, mainly by running. But the running capacity of early reptiles was probably as limited as that of their modern descendants. Reptilian lungs hold only moderate amounts of air, and breathing movements are fairly shallow. Also, the oxygen-holding capacity of blood is comparable to that of fish and amphibian blood, which suffices for high levels of metabolic activity in water. On land, however, such capacities cannot support sustained body activity; most living reptiles actually are active only in brief bursts and are otherwise relatively slow and sluggish.

Living mammals give clear evidence that the evolution of the group from reptiles involved a pronounced elevation of metabolic levels. A newly developed diaphragm increased breathing efficiency; red blood corpuscles became nonnucleated and maximally specialized for oxygen transport; new chemical variants of hemoglobin permitted blood to carry almost three times as much oxygen as before. Equally important, temperature-control mechanisms came into being that permitted maintenance of a constant, uniformly high body temperature. As a result, "warm-blooded" animals could remain active in many environments and circumstances too warm or too cool for "cold-blooded" species.

All modern reptiles are cold-blooded, but some recent research suggests that mechanisms maintaining a uniform body temperature may have existed in certain dinosaurs. Fossilized dinosaur bones sometimes show evidence of an extensive blood vascular system, a trait found only among modern warm-blooded animals, birds and mammals. Moreover, some dinosaurs may have possessed heat-retaining body coverings. For example, dinosaurs that appear to be the direct ancestors of birds were at least partially covered by feathers. Nevertheless, other evidence seemingly contradicts arguments that such dinosaurs were warm-blooded, and additional research is needed to settle this intriguing issue.

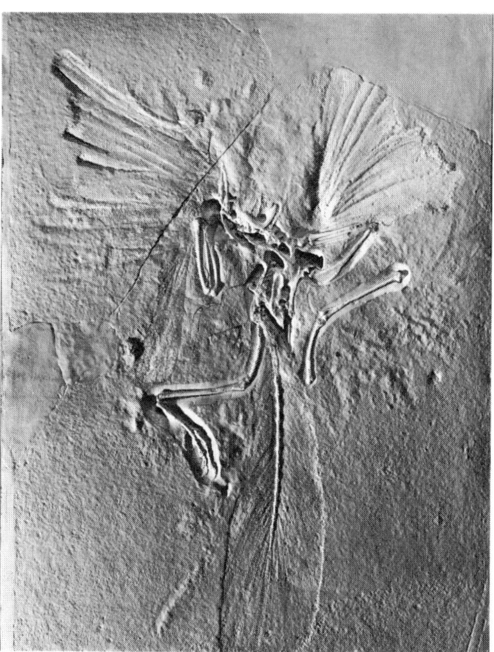

Fig. 36.13 Bird evolution. Plaster cast of *Archeopteryx*. Note feathered tail, wings. The head is bent back, and the tooth-bearing mouth is not easily visible here.

There is no doubt, however, that early mammals and birds were both warm-blooded and far more active than their reptilian ancestors. (Despite these similarities, the metabolic adaptations of birds are not identical to those of mammals. Birds did not evolve a diaphragm, the oxygen capacity of their blood is only twice that of reptiles, and their red blood cells remain nucleated. Yet body temperature is maintained at an even higher level than in mammals.)

As early mammals adapted to a life of running, they must have sought safety in the forests. They became primarily nocturnal and furtive, with a distinct preference for hiding in darkness. Their sense of sight was of limited value in such an existence and, like almost all mammals today, they were colorblind. The sense of smell became dominant instead, and the basic orientation to the environment came to depend on odor cues from the forest floor. Furthermore, in an active life of running and hiding it is unsafe merely to lay eggs and leave them in reptilian fashion. The first mammals probably did just that, and the primitive egg-laying mammals today still do likewise. Later mammals evolved means to carry the fertilized eggs with

A

B

Fig. 36.14 Prehistoric reptiles. (A) Dinosaurs. Left, *Triceratops*, a Cretaceous horned herbivore; right, *Tyrannosaurus*, a giant Cretaceous carnivore. (B) Reconstruction of plesiosaurs (left) and ichthyosaurs (right).

them, inside the females; they became viviparous. The pouched marsupial mammals and the placental mammals are their modern descendants.

The Late Cretaceous Extinctions

After mammals had originated late in the Triassic, they remained inconspicous for the rest of the Mesozoic, a period of about 80 million years. But as the Cretaceous came to a close, most of the reptilian multitude became extinct. The extraordinarily rapid demise of these vertebrates has both fascinated and puzzled scientists for decades. Why should dinosaurs, certain invertebrates, several species of aquatic microbes, and many other

A

B

Fig. 36.15 Mammalian evolution. (A) A Triassic therapsid, a mammal-like reptile. (B) A reconstruction of four mammal-like reptiles. The animal in the midforeground is a herbivorous therapsid (*Kannemeyeria*), which is under attack by a group of carnivorous types (*Cynognathus*).

organisms all become extinct at about the same time? And why should other organisms, including crocodiles, snakes, mammals, many invertebrates, and most terrestrial plants continue to flourish?

Several hypotheses have been proposed to explain this paradox. One of the most intriguing postulates that the late Cretaceous extinctions were caused by a collision between the earth and a large asteroid. Most of the asteroid would disintegrate on impact, disseminating huge quantities of dust into the upper atmosphere. If the blanket of dust was sufficiently dense, it could have prevented sunlight from reaching the surface of the planet for several years. Such a temporary absence of sunlight would suppress or obliterate photosynthesis, triggering the collapse of most food chains.

The fossil record of the late Cretaceous reveals a pattern of extinctions generally in accord with what biologists would expect if sunlight were temporarily "shut off." Microscopic organisms constitute the majority of producers in marine environments (see Chap. 9), and many of them became extinct at this time. Because they are largely dependent on photosynthetic plankton for nutrients, the asteroid-impact hypothesis predicts that marine animals would also die out. The fossil record confirms that many of these animals did become extinct, but several did not. This last finding does not rule out the hypothesis, however. It is possible that some invertebrates survived on a temporary food chain supported by the decay of terrestrial organisms. Nutrients produced by this decay would drain into rivers and flow to coastal salt-water habitats.

The loss of sunlight would kill virtually all land plants, but most would regenerate from seeds, spores, and root systems after the dust had settled and sunlight had returned. Darkness for several years would eliminate almost all large terrestrial herbivores and carnivores, but many small animals, including ancestors of mammals, might have survived by feeding on foraging insects and decaying vegetation.

Chemical evidence provides the strongest evidence for the asteroid impact hypothesis. Studies of sediments deposited in the earth's crust during the late Cretaceous reveal concentrations of iridium up to 160 times greater than average levels. It is likely that most or all of this iridium is derived from one or more extraterrestrial objects; little if any iridium is produced naturally in the earth's crust. Further analysis indicates that the iridium found in the late Cretaceous sediments originated from within our solar system and is not derived from an external source, such as a large exploding star (supernova).

TABLE 36.1
Epochs and Periods of the Cenozoic Era*

Period	Epoch	Duration, years	Beginning date, B.C.
Quaternary	Recent	20,000	20,000
	Pleistocene	1	1
Tertiary	Pliocene	11	12
	Miocene	16	28
	Oligocene	11	39
	Eocene	19	58
	Paleocene	17	65

*Number for Recent Epoch is years; all other numbers are millions of years.

Scientists are likely to continue debating the precise causes of the late Cretaceous extinctions for some time. Regardless of the final outcome, one fact is clear: extinctions of the Mesozoic reptiles cleared the way for a great Cenozoic expansion of mammals and birds.

The Cenozoic

The progressively cooler climates after the Laramide revolution culminated in the ice ages of the Pleistocene Epoch, a subdivision of the Quaternary Period of the Cenozoic (Table 36.1). Four ice ages occurred during the last 600,000 years. In each, ice sheets spread from both poles to the temperate zones and then receded. Warm interglacial periods intervened between the successive glaciations. The last recession began less than 20,000 years ago, at the beginning of the Recent Epoch, and it is still in progress; polar regions are still covered with ice. Cenozoic climates played a major role in plant evolution, as noted earlier, and animal evolution was greatly affected as well. Pleistocene ice in particular influenced human history, modern man in a sense being one of the products of the ice ages.

The adaptive radiations of mammals and birds were the main evolutionary events of the Cenozoic,

Fig. 36.16 Horse evolution, Cenozoic. This reconstructed sequence begins at left, with the fossil horse *Eohippus,* and proceeds via *Mesohippus, Hypohippus,* and *Neohipparion* to *Equus,* the modern horse at right. The drawings are to scale and show how the average sizes and shapes of horses have changed. Progressive reduction in the number of toes took place, as well as changes in dentition. Note, however, that the animals shown represent a highly selected series, and it should not be inferred that horse evolution followed a straight-line pattern. Here, as elsewhere, a bush pattern is evident.

the "age of mammals." Terrestrial mammals replaced the dinosaurs; aquatic mammals eventually took the place of the former ichthyosaurs and plesiosaurs; and bats, but more especially birds, gained the air left free by the pterosaurs. A total of some two dozen independent mammalian lines came into existence, each ranked as an order (see Fig. 35.34). The fossil record is fairly extensive for nearly all these groups, and it is extremely good for a few, horses and elephants in particular (Fig. 36.16).

Each mammalian line exploited either a new way of life available at the time or one left free after the extinction of the Mesozoic reptiles. One mammalian line is of particular interest, for it eventually led to human beings. The members of this line still made their home in the forests, like many earlier mammalian groups, but they adapted to an *arboreal* (tree-dwelling) life. Fossils show that such arboreal mammals of the early Paleocene were the ancestors of two orders, the *Insectivora* and the *Primates.* Some of the shrews now living still have the joint traits of primitive insect eaters and primitive primates, but the later members of the two groups became very different; insectivores now also include moles and hedgehogs, and primates include human beings.

Nevertheless, there can be little doubt that the distant mammalian ancestors of people were shrewlike, 2 to 3 inches long, with a long snout and a bushy tail (Fig. 36.17). They lived in trees and, like modern shrews, they were probably furtive, quick, color-blind and given to hiding in dark places, as well as ferocious and voracious; they ate anything eatable of appropriate size, insects particularly, and they ate nearly continuously, consuming their own weight every 3 hours or so: a highly active but small body requires comparatively very large amounts of fuel.

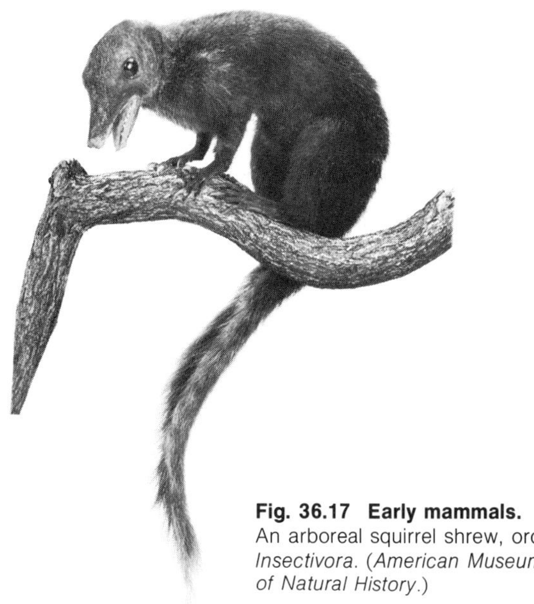

Fig. 36.17 Early mammals. An arboreal squirrel shrew, order *Insectivora. (American Museum of Natural History.)*

These primates, which appear to have evolved during the Paleocene epoch, about 65 million years ago, underwent an extensive adaptive radiation throughout the first 30 million years of their existence. Primitive primates apparently were well suited to the generally warmer environments that prevailed in much of the world at this time. Tropical forests covered extensive areas of both Northern

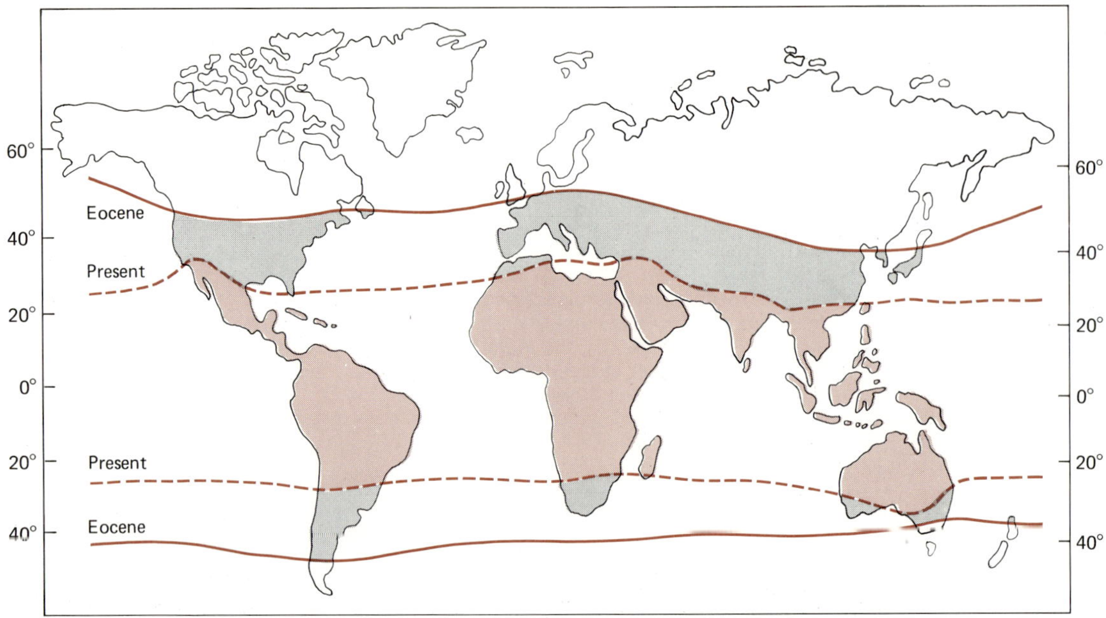

Fig. 36.18 Eocene forests. Limits of tropical and subtropical forests for Eocene (heavy lines) and modern times (dotted lines) are compared. Climates of the Eocene generally were warmer than those of today. Higher temperatures promoted a wider distribution of tropical and subtropical forests, environments to which early primates were well suited.

and Southern Hemispheres (Fig. 36.18). Regions surrounding what is now Seattle, London, and Paris had an annual mean temperature of approximately 21°C (70°F), about that of Mexico City today. Fossilized remains of Eocene primates have been found widely distributed in North America and Eurasia, an indication that these animals probably migrated between the continents via a land bridge which then crossed the present Bering Strait.

Before beginning a gradual but steady decline in numbers about 36 million years ago, primitive shrewlike primates gave rise to several sublines, of which five still survive: *lemuroids, tarsioids, ceboids, cercopithecoids,* and *hominoids* (Fig. 36.19).

Lemuroids include the *aye-ayes, lorises,* and *lemurs,* now found largely on the island of Madagascar (Fig. 36.20). These animals still have long snouts and tails, but instead of claws and paws they have strong flat nails, a general characteristic of all modern primates. Long nails are probably more useful than claws in anchoring the body on a tree branch.

In a tree, moreover, smelling is less important than seeing, and in lemuroids an important visual adaptation has evolved: each of the eyes can be directed forward independently, which permits better perception of branch configurations than if the eyes were fixed on the side of the head (as in shrews).

Tarsioids are represented today by the *tarsiers* of Southern Asia and Indonesia. In these animals the ancestral "smell brain" has become a "sight brain;" the olfactory lobes have become small, but the optic lobes have increased in size. Reduction of the olfactory lobes has also led to shortening of the snout, hence to the appearance of a fairly well-defined face. Indeed the eyes have moved into the face and, although they move independently, both can be focused on the same point. As a result, tarsiers are endowed with stereoscopic vision and efficient depth perception, traits that all other primates also share. Such traits are of considerable adaptive value if balance is to be maintained in a tree. Tarsiers have independently movable fingers and toes, with a branch-gripping pad at the

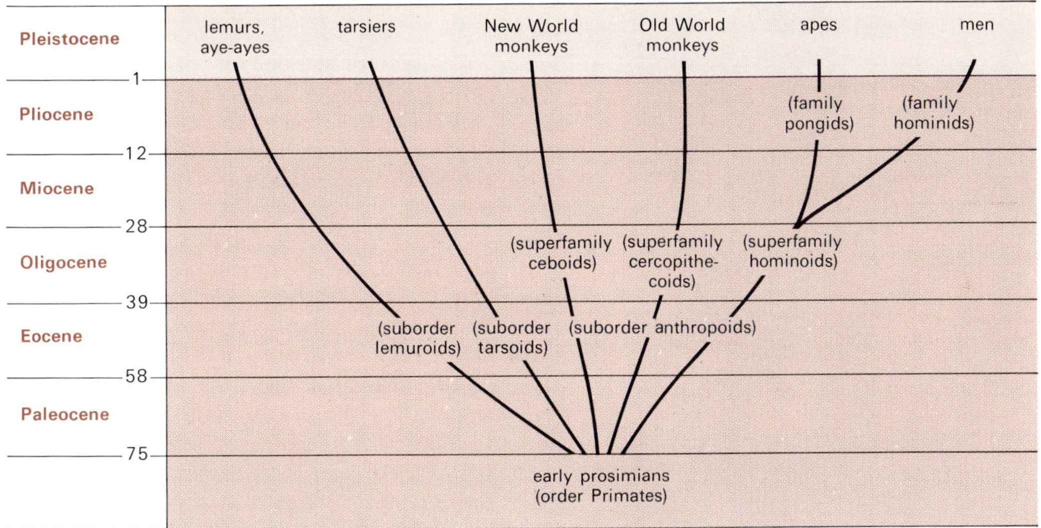

Fig. 36.19 The primate radiation. Numbers at left indicate past time in millions of years.

end of each. Moreover, whereas most mammals produce litters of several to many offspring, tarsiers have a single offspring at a time, a safer reproductive pattern in the branches of a tree.

Ceboids comprise the *New World monkeys,* confined today to South and Central America. Some of these animals have long strong tails used as fifth limbs (Fig. 36.21). Cercopithecoids are the *Old World monkeys,* found in Africa and Asia (Fig. 36.22). None of the Old World monkeys displays a prehensile tail; this trait has evolved only in New World monkeys. In both groups adaptations to arboreal life have developed a good deal further than in the earlier primates. Together with apes and the family of man, Old and New World monkeys are sometimes classified as *anthropoids* (see Fig. 36.19).

The oldest known fossils of monkeys date to Oligocene deposits, formed about 35 million years ago. Only a few such fossils have been found in South America, but over 200 have been uncovered in the Fayun Desert near Cairo, Egypt. This region was a dense tropical rain forest in Oligocene times. How monkeys evolved from more primitive primates is not known, but it is likely that anthropoids first evolved in Africa. New World monkeys may have descended from early cercopithecoids car-

Fig. 36.20 Primitive primates. (A) A lemur from Madagascar. (B) A tarsier from Indonesia. Both these groups are arboreal.

A

B

Fig. 36.21 New World monkeys. (A) Spider monkey. Note prehensile (grasping) tail. (B) Howler monkey.

ried from the African mainland on natural rafts of floating trees, when distances separating Africa and South America were markedly less than they are today (see Fig. 29.7).

If tarsoids have a "sight brain," monkeys can be said to have a "space brain." The eyes are synchronized like our eyes, and each also contains a fovea centralis, a retinal area of most acute vision (see Fig. 19.21). Moreover, monkeys are endowed with color vision, the only mammals other than the hominoids so characterized. Color is actually there to be seen: flowers, foliage, sky, and sun provide an arboreal environment of light and space, far different from the dark forest floor that forced the ancestral mammals literally to keep their noses to the ground. Indeed, the smelling capacity of monkeys is as poor as their sight is excellent. Correspondingly, the cerebrum is greatly enlarged and contains extensive vision-memory areas; monkeys store visual memories of shape and color as we do.

Monkeys also adopt a predominantly *sitting* position at rest, a posture that in a tree is probably safer than lying and that also relieves the forelimbs of locomotor functions. As a direct consequence, monkeys have a new freedom to use hands for touch exploration (see Figs. 36.21 and 36.22). Evolution of ability to *feel* out the environment and one's own body has led to a new self-awareness and to curiosity. Ability to touch offspring and fellow inhabitants of the tree has contributed to new patterns of communication and social life, reinforced greatly by good vision, by voice, and by varied facial expressions. Touch-control areas of the brain and centers controlling hand movements are extensive, and the brain as a whole has enlarged in parallel with the new patterns of living. The mind has quickened as a result, and the level of intelligence has increased well above the earlier primate average. A ground mammal such as a dog still sniffs its environment, but monkeys and the later primates explore it by sight and by touch. Evolution of intelligence has been associated specifically with improved coordination between eye and hand. Fundamentally, we note, primate intelligence is an adaptation to the arboreal way of life.

Tree life also provides a basically secure existence. Actually only two kinds of situations represent significant dangers, the hazard of falling off a branch and the hazard of snakes. The first is minimized by opposable thumbs, independently movable

A

B

Fig. 36.22 Old World monkeys. (A) Rhesus monkey. (B) Vervet monkey.

fingers on all limbs, and precocious gripping ability in general (displayed also in newborn human babies). The second is countered by the strength of the body, which is larger than in earlier primates. Perhaps partly because of this emancipation from perpetual fear, the life-span is lengthened considerably; monkeys live up to four decades, whereas shrews have a life expectancy of a single year. Furthermore, absence of danger and continuously warm climates make feasible a breeding season spanning the whole year, and in Old World monkeys this year-round breeding potential is accompanied by menstrual cycles.

As in monkeys, the adaptive radiation of the fifth primate line, the hominoids, can be traced to the Oligocene deposits of Egypt. Two main lines of hominoids evolved. One led to the *pongids*, the family of apes, the other to the *hominids*, the family of human beings (see Fig. 36.19). Hominoids evolved important locomotor modifications over and above those achieved by monkeys. Primitive apes developed universal limb sockets and a fully upright posture, and by hand-over-hand locomotion between two levels of branches they became tree *walkers* more than tree sitters; even a monkey cannot match the acrobatic tree-swinging of hominoids. Moreover, only hominoids can swivel their hips, and only they have long, strong collar bones and chests that are broader than they are deep. Hominoid locomotion has also become facilitated by a shortening of the tail and its interiorization under the skin between the hindlimbs. In this position the tail skeleton helps in counteracting the internal sag produced by gravity acting on an upright body.

Biologists now generally agree that the extinct primate *Aegyptopithecus* represents a common ancestor of both apes and man (Fig. 36.23). This monkeylike animal, whose fossilized bones were first uncovered in Egypt in 1965, roamed Africa about 30 million years ago. Fossils of certain other extinct primates show characteristics similar to those of modern apes, but *Aegyptopithecus* is the first to show features shared by both apes and man.

Apes are represented today by four genera, gibbons, orangutans, chimpanzees, and gorillas (Fig. 36.24). Gibbons are survivors of an early branch of ape evolution, characterized by comparatively small, light bodies and retention of a fully arboreal way of life. Indeed the gibbon is undoubtedly the most perfectly adapted arboreal primate.

But the other three types of apes, representing later and heavier pongid lines, have abandoned life in the trees to greater or lesser extent. It appears that these later apes ceased to be completely arboreal after their bodies had become so large and heavy that trees could no longer support them aloft. The feet of these apes give ample evidence of

Fig. 36.23 Aegyptopithecus. This mockup shows the probable appearance of a common ancestor of apes and man.

the weight they have to support; foot bones are highly foreshortened and stubby, as if crushed by heavy loads. Correspondingly, the agile grace of the arboreal gibbon is not preserved in the ground apes. These do not actually walk, but they *scamper* along in a crouching shuffle gait.

HUMAN EVOLUTION

The Science of Human Evolution: Development and Status

The fossil evidence of the hominid group is tantalizingly scant; we can trace the recent evolution of many mammals far better than our own. Moreover, the exact path of descent of our own species remains undiscovered as yet.

There are several reasons for the paucity of information about our own evolution. With the exception of the line leading to ourselves, all other lines of the hominid radiation became extinct at various times during the last 30 million years. As a result, knowledge of species that may have been ancestral to our own has come largely from fossils, and such objects have been extremely difficult to find. Until the middle of this century, most discoveries of hominid fossils were purely accidental, such as the finding of fossil human teeth in a Chinese drug store. Students of human evolution simply did not know where to look for evidence of extinct hominids. The first major discovery of the remains of a pre-*Homo sapiens* hominid did not occur until 1891, and the next two important such finds took place over 30 years later.

This slow pace of discovery also stemmed from a lack of sufficient investigators. Until recently, only a small number of scientists were interested in spending months or years digging through tons of stone debris in an often vain attempt to uncover a few fragments of prehistoric man (Fig. 36.25). In addition, students of human evolution working before the middle of this century had only one major investigative tool, comparative anatomy. This is not to suggest that comparative anatomy is valueless as a means of establishing evolutionary proximity between species. On the contrary, this subscience of biology has led to many important conclusions about ancestral relationships between primates.

For example, the ball-and-socket joints shared by all hominoids are far more efficient for climbing than the less flexible skeletal arrangement of monkey limbs. This observation strongly suggests that people are more closely related to apes than to monkeys, and that primitive hominoids were better adapted to life in trees than monkeys. Both conclusions have been substantiated by more recent methods of analyzing evolutionary lineages among primates. Moreover, discovery of a single fossilized fragment of a skull, for example, often provides enough evidence for a comparative anatomist to

Fig. 36.24 Apes. (A) A gibbon from Malaya. (B) A mountain gorilla from Africa. (C) Chimpanzees, African apes. (D) An orangutan from Sumatra.

Fig. 36.25 In search of prehistoric man. Students and faculty of Chadron State College research the Hudson-Meng site, near Crawford, Nebraska, where prehistoric American Indians killed scores of bison. Layers of bison bones can be seen in the left foreground.

deduce the overall structure of a prehistoric animal and to estimate its relative evolutionary status (see Fig. 36.38).

Nevertheless, comparative anatomy is not without limitations. As late as 1972, for example, the shape of one human tooth, the lower first premolar, was cited as evidence that human beings never went through an apelike stage during their evolutionary development. This tooth is anatomically quite different in apes and people. Yet despite such differences, the conclusion that our hominid ancestors never passed through apelike stages is undoubtedly incorrect. Several hominid fossil skulls recently have been found whose lower first premolars show characteristics intermediate between those of modern apes and people.

All anatomical evidence must be interpreted to have evolutionary significance, and such interpretations, however logical, are not always correct, especially when they are based on small amounts of evidence. Also, comparative anatomy offers little insight into the dramatic social and cultural changes that have occurred during the last million years of human evolution, for these profound changes have not been accompanied by any extensive modifications of human anatomy.

Compared with their earlier counterparts, modern students of human evolution face far fewer impediments to progress, thanks largely to a series of interrelated factors that have transformed the science of human evolution over the past 20 years. One factor is the accumulation of information about sites where fossil hominids are likely to be found. Indeed, systematic searches are now being conducted at several localities, and such investigations are turning up fossil specimens fairly routinely.

The science of human evolution has also benefited from several new disciplines and technologies that can be used in combination with comparative anatomy. One such discipline, the rapidly expanding science of *plate tectonics* (see Chap. 29), has established that continents are not stationary but are moving slowly on an underlayer of rock having a semiplastic consistency.

Combined with data from radioactive-isotope dating techniques (see Chap. 32), our understanding of continental drift has fundamentally changed our perspectives of evolutionary relationships between many organisms, primates included. For example, most scientists recently believed that New World monkeys were unrelated to Old World stocks, and that New World monkeys had evolved independently from primitive primates that once flourished in North America. Africa and South America seemed too far apart for any direct kinship between New and Old World lines. But plate-tectonic studies now clearly indicate that the two continents were once close together and, as indicated earlier, most scientists now suspect that New World monkeys are direct descendants of primitive cercopithecoids.

Plate tectonics also demonstrates that most continents formerly lay at latitudes very different from their present ones. Similarly, some continents now separated by oceans were once joined. These facts clarify why fossilized ancestors of tropical species, for example, can be found in lands now situated in temperate or even polar regions (see Chap. 29). They also explain why fossils of several almost identical species of Old World primates can be found in parts of Europe and Africa presently separated by the Mediterranean Sea (Fig. 36.26).

Several biochemical techniques have played a role in transforming the science of human evolution over the past few years. For example, it is now possible to compare the relative similarity of amino acid sequences in proteins taken from people, apes, monkeys, and most other vertebrates. Nucleotide sequences in DNA can also be compared. In short, it has become possible to compare genetic similarities of different species and thereby measure evolutionary interrelationships between organisms. Presumably, the greater number of genes shared by two species, the more recent their evolutionary divergence from a common ancestor.

Fig. 36.26 The Mediterranean "Sea" 5 Million Years ago. At this time only a few lakes (color) separated Africa and Europe, and Old World primates were free to move between the two continents. The Mediterranean basin (outlined in black) has since filled with water, separating the continents.

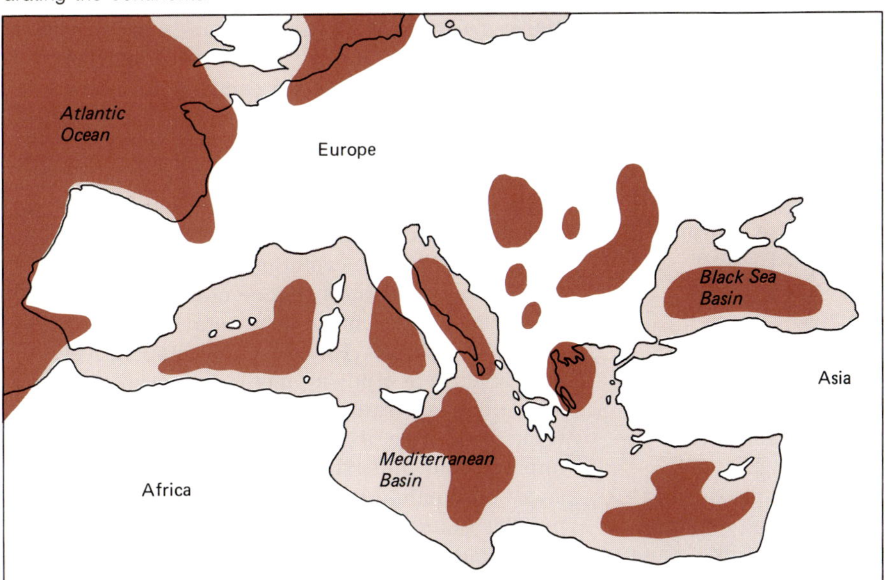

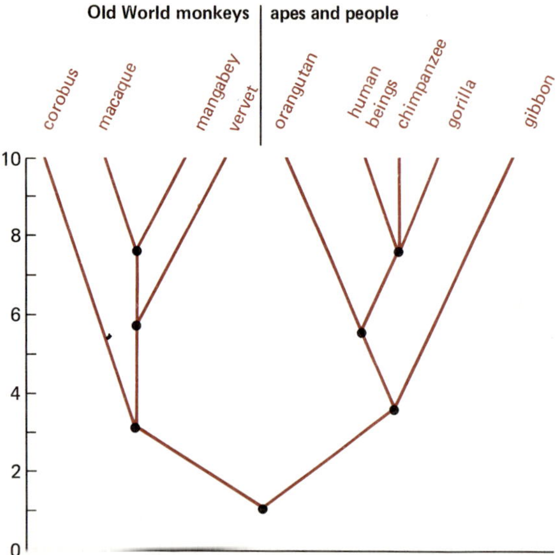

Fig. 36.27 Genetic relationships among Old World monkeys, apes, and people. Comparisons of genetic relationships among animals can be made through DNA hybridization experiments. Double-stranded DNA from two species is first separated. Formation of hybrid molecules occurs when single strands of DNA from one species are mixed with single strands from a second species. The extent to which the different strands are complementary is a measure of genetic similarity. Strands that are highly complementary bond together more tightly, and therefore are more stable, than strands displaying less complementarity. The stability of hybrid DNA is a function of temperature; the greater the stability, the greater the temperature needed to separate the hybrid. Consequently, the resistance of hybrid DNA to the disruptive effects of temperature can be used to measure genetic interrelatedness, as illustrated by the accompanying chart. Numbers at the left indicate degrees Celsius (see also Appendix B). Note that DNA hybrids formed from people and chimps, or from people and gorillas, separate about 2°C higher than a hybrid made from human and orangutan DNA. The chart also indicates that hybrids formed from human and gibbon DNA separate about 4°C lower than human and chimp DNA, or human and gorilla DNA. Such results suggest that people are more closely related to African than to Asian apes.

Fig. 36.28 Field studies of behavior. Studies of primate behavior under natural conditions have greatly increased our understanding of these animals.

This technology of *biochemical taxonomy* appears to yield data that are more objective and precise than some of the information obtained from the fossil record or from comparative anatomy. The latter two approaches variously suggest that our closest relatives among modern primates could be tarsiers, certain monkeys, certain apes, chimpanzees, or gorillas. Nor do data from these approaches clearly establish when our ancestors diverged from evolutionary lines leading to modern nonhuman primates.

By contrast, biochemical studies demonstrate a close genetic similarity between people and African apes—chimpanzees and gorillas (Fig. 36.27). For example, if the genetic difference between Old and New World monkeys is given an arbitrary value of 1 and other differences are expressed as fractions of 1, the difference between people and Old World monkeys is slightly more than 0.50, the difference between the Asian orangutan and people is about 0.25, and the difference between people and chimpanzees is about 0.13. Such numbers may also constitute measurements of the relative time when these species diverged from common ancestors, although this last conclusion remains a subject of considerable debate.

Together with comparative anatomy, the technologies of radioactive isotopes, plate tectonics, and biochemical taxonomy have greatly increased our ability to determine evolutionary lineages among long-extinct species. But none of these methods sheds much light on the behavioral characteristics of extinct animals. However, the comparatively new practice of studying monkeys and apes in their native habitats, rather than in zoos where animal behavior is often abnormal and erratic, has greatly improved our understanding of both modern and ancestral hominid behavior (Fig. 36.28).

For example, when fossils of early man were first found, scientists concluded that our hominid ancestors were far too primitive to have used stone

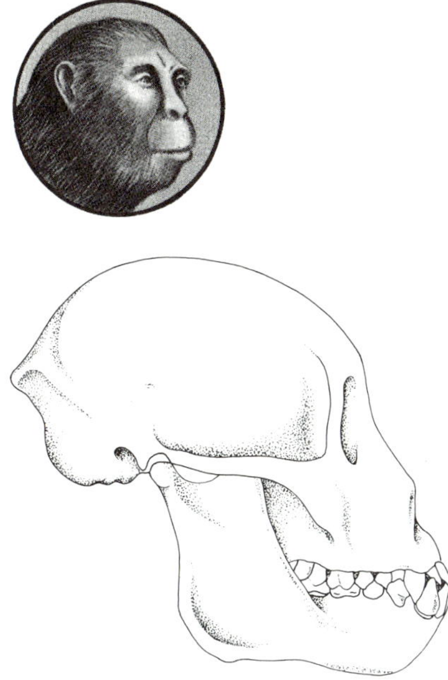

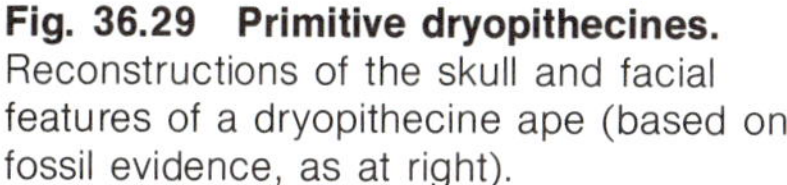

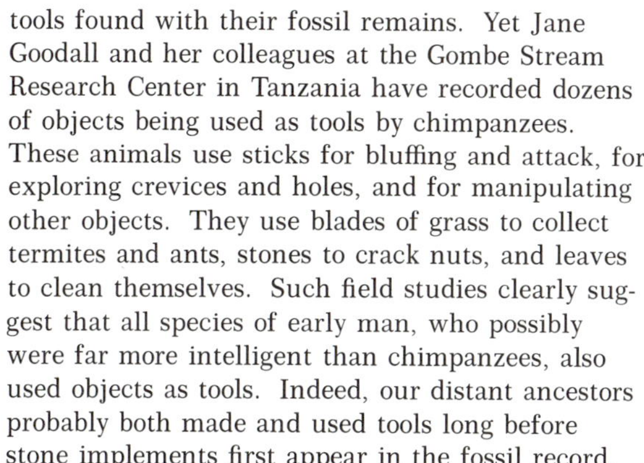

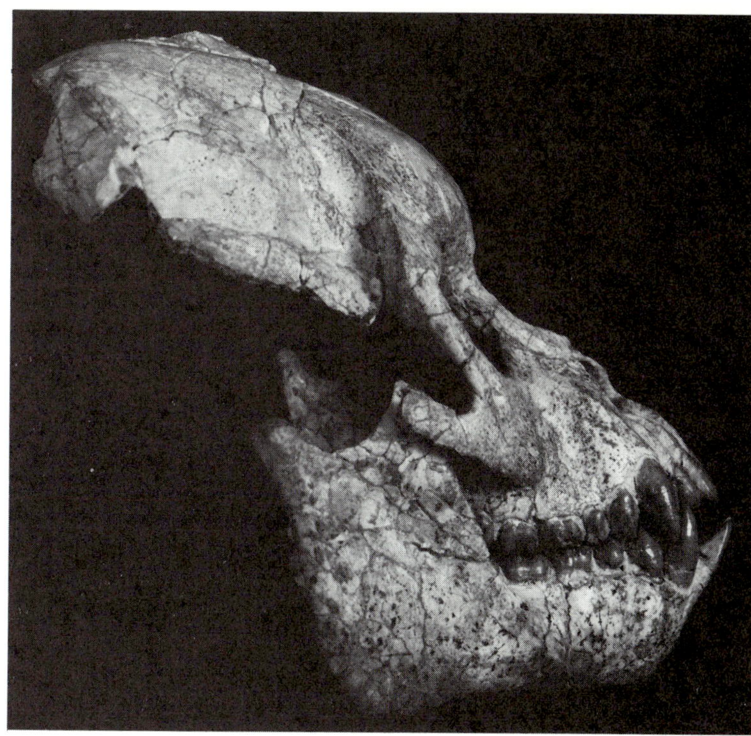

Fig. 36.29 Primitive dryopithecines. Reconstructions of the skull and facial features of a dryopithecine ape (based on fossil evidence, as at right).

tools found with their fossil remains. Yet Jane Goodall and her colleagues at the Gombe Stream Research Center in Tanzania have recorded dozens of objects being used as tools by chimpanzees. These animals use sticks for bluffing and attack, for exploring crevices and holes, and for manipulating other objects. They use blades of grass to collect termites and ants, stones to crack nuts, and leaves to clean themselves. Such field studies clearly suggest that all species of early man, who possibly were far more intelligent than chimpanzees, also used objects as tools. Indeed, our distant ancestors probably both made and used tools long before stone implements first appear in the fossil record.

Our understanding of how early man used tools is not limited to inferences from field studies. Recent development of a technique known as *microwear analysis* now permits scientists to determine precise uses of tools found with fossil hominids. It has been determined, for example, that early man used some tools to bore holes in wood, others to scrape hides, and still others to cut meat.

The ability to ascertain precise uses of archaic tools has greatly increased our knowledge and appreciation of how human cultures evolved. Moreover, development of such modern methods of analysis and the establishment of successful systematic searches for hominid fossils and artifacts has attracted growing numbers of students to the now rapidly advancing science of human evolution. Involvement of diverse scientists in this discipline has increased more than tenfold in the past 20 years. What follows is a current account of how human beings may have evolved.

Prehistoric Man

Dryopithecines

Some clues about the common ancestors of pongids and hominids are provided not only by Aegyptopithecus, but also by a subfamily of fossil apes called *dryopithecines* (pithecus = ape; see Section A of glossary). Remains of a number of dryopithecine apes have been found distributed widely throughout the Old World, including Africa, Europe, the Near East, India, China, and Russia. African dryopithecines have been found in rock deposits formed about 23 to 16 million years ago.

By contrast, Eurasian species have been discovered mainly in younger deposits ranging from 18 to 12 million years old. The older age of the African finds suggests that dryopithecines originated there and subsequently migrated to Europe and Asia.

Primitive dryopithecines generally were smaller and more monkeylike than most modern apes (Fig. 36.29). They probably spent most of their lives in trees, subsisting largely on fruits. Most of these extinct primates ranged in weight from 14 to 23 kg (30 to 50 lb), but some were larger and one species was probably bigger than modern gorillas. Ball-and-socket joints undoubtedly allowed graceful movement through trees, at least for smaller dryopithecines, but when these apes ventured onto the forest floor they were unquestionably *quadrupedal,* moving with much less grace on all four limbs.

Some dryopithecine species appear to have gradually increased in size while in trees and to have begun spending increasing amounts of time on the ground. This probably occurred in the three lines of dryopithecines that appear to have led to modern chimpanzees, gorillas, and orangutans.

A remote ancestor of chimpanzees may have been *Dryopithecus africanus,* a species that resembled chimps in many respects. *Dryopithecus major* was a much larger species whose jaw, lumbar vertebrae, and ankle bones were very similar to those of gorillas. Moreover, most fossils of *D. major* have been found high on the slopes of East African volcanoes, mountains that were covered with tropical rain forests during much of the Miocene Epoch. Gorillas inhabit similar environments today, strengthening the view that *D. major* is a direct ancestor of the largest modern ape. The dryopithecine ancestor of orangutans has not been clearly established, and it is likely that gibbons, the fourth major kind of modern ape, evolved from nondryopithecine ancestors.

The First Hominids

Early hominids probably evolved from dryopithecine types. It is not known which dryopithecines led to the first humanlike organisms, but it is likely that both they and their hominid descendants spent as much and perhaps even more time on the ground as in trees. Why should this be? Was this descent from trees prompted by an increase in body weight, as in the case of large apes? Probably not. Recall that ground apes scamper rather than walk.

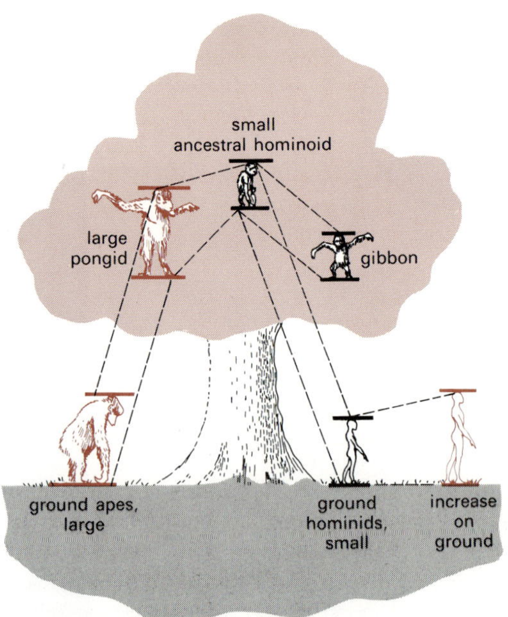

Fig. 36.30 Size evolution in hominoids. One group of apes probably developed to a large size in the trees, and modern descendants such as gorillas therefore were already heavy when they adopted life on the ground. Another group, exemplified by the gibbons, remained light and arboreal. Early hominids likewise probably remained light and small. They presumably left the trees as small types and their evolutionary size increase then occurred on the ground.

If the tree-dwelling dryopithecine ancestors of hominids were as large as those that gave rise to modern apes, then the human foot should resemble that of ground apes and people should scamper rather than walk.

In actuality the human gait is unique among ground forms, and as a gibbon swings in a tree so a person literally swings on the ground. It is likely, therefore, that the hominid line left the trees when its evolution had progressed to a gibbonlike level and when the body was still comparatively small and light. The walking grace perfected in the trees could then persist on the ground. Early hominids thus appear to have been small, perhaps only 3 to 4 feet tall, and in contrast to the later apes their size probably increased only *after* they had come out of the trees (Fig. 36.30).

But if not body weight what other conditions could have forced hominids to the ground? The chief cause appears to have been the progressively cooler climate, which led to a thinning out of forests in many regions. Our prehuman ancestors thus may have been forced to travel on the ground if they wished to move from one stand of trees to another. Such forced excursions often must have been fraught with considerable danger, however, for saber-toothed carnivores and other large mammals dominated the ground at those times (see Fig. 29.13). Ability to dash quickly across open spaces would then have had great selective value, and such conditions probably promoted the evolution of *running* feet. Also, strong muscles would be required to move the hindlimbs in new ways. Indeed, a unique trait of the hominid line is the presence of such muscles in the form of curving calves, thighs, and buttocks. In conjunction with this muscular change the hips have become broad and the waist narrow, and in these respects, too, people differ from apes.

These and other features that now distinguish people and apes came to be superimposed on the traits of the earlier arboreal primates. Clearly then, the modern human type could not have evolved if the ancestral type had not first been specialized for life in trees.

The earliest hominid known today is *Ramapithecus*, an apelike organism whose fossil remains vary in age from 15 to 10 million years old. Like dryopithecines, *Ramapithecus* probably originated in Africa and subsequently migrated to Eurasia. Its fossils have been recovered in East Africa, Germany, West Pakistan, northwestern India, and southeastern China.

Standing 90 to 110 cm (3 to $3\frac{1}{2}$ feet) tall, *Ramapithecus* may have looked much like modern pigmy chimpanzees (Fig. 36.31). The dentition of this hominid suggests that it lived largely on tough bits of food, such as seeds, blades of grass, roots, and probably also raw meat and bones. The canines and incisors of *Ramapithecus* are small, while the premolars and molars are large, broad, closely spaced, and covered with a thick layer of enamel. Such teeth, particularly the absence of long, fang-like canines, permit lateral chewing movements and the grinding of tough plant foods. The canines of all more advanced hominids, people included, are similarly incisorlike, rather than fang-like, providing a sharp cutting surface and therefore well adapted for meat eating as well as lateral grinding (Fig. 36.32).

Fig. 36.31 Pygmy chimpanzees. An adult male is shown here.

Ramapithecus appears to have lived at the edges of forests, around lakes, and along rivers and streams. The animal probably fed by day and retreated to the branches of trees at night. It probably was quadrupedal on the ground, but may have walked bipedally at times, much like chimpanzees. Although *Ramapithecus* may have fashioned a few simple tools out of twigs and grass, tools have not been found with its fossil remains.

Almost nothing is known about hominids that lived between 6 and 9 million years ago (see Fig. 36.41). Few fossils have been found dating to this period, and most of them have proved uniformative. It is known that grasslands expanded during this interval as dryer conditions forced shrinkage of forests. Descendants of *Ramapithecus* probably continued to move out of dwindling forested regions at this time, increasingly adopting a hunter-gatherer mode of life.

As noted earlier, the decrease of forest cover was an important factor influencing the change from a quadrupedal to a bipedal existence. Hands, no longer involved in locomotion, became free to

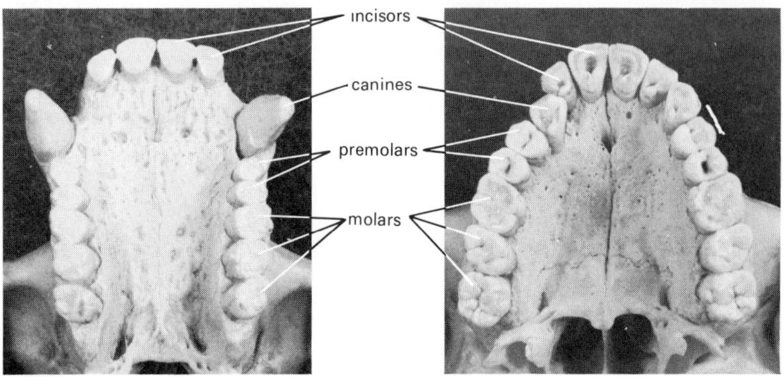

Fig. 36.32 Anthropoid dentition. Upper jaw dentition of a chimpanzee (left) and a human being (right). Note the pronounced difference in the canines, which are incisorlike in all hominids.

carry, transport, throw objects and, more importantly, to make tools. Tools could be used as weapons to kill prey, or as weapons to defend against other hominids. Even more food—and more defense—could be obtained if individuals worked harmoniously in groups, carrying out coordinated, planned maneuvers.

An evolutionary trend was being established. Advanced hominids were to become hunters, gradually evolving sufficient intelligence to survive on open grasslands in competition with quadrupedal predators and bipedal challengers (Fig. 36.33). Success was enhanced by the construction of tools, whose effectiveness was increased when used in a well-ordered social framework. Note that all of this was triggered by the evolution of bipedalism and an upright posture. Thus, bipedal locomotion is not simply another human anatomical adaptation; it is the most fundamental one.

Australopithecus

Of all hominids known, *Australopithecus* was the first to walk predominately on two limbs. These organisms lived in Africa. Their fossils range in age from 5.5 to 2 million years old. The oldest fossils have been found in East Africa, the youngest in South Africa.

Australopithecus appears to have inhabited open grasslands and often lived near lakes and streams. Its likely that they hunted lizards, rodents, rabbits, young antelope, and other game. They probably also scooped fish from nearby waterways. Tools of stone and bone have been discovered with *Australopithecus* fossils. Some tools appear to be fashioned as choppers, some as scraping instruments, others as chisels (Fig. 36.34).

Two major groups of *Australopithecus* appear in the fossil record, a *gracile* form and a *robust* form. One or both of these groups may have evolved from a recently discovered species called *Australopithecus afarensis.* This species, which appears to be older than other australopiths, may be a direct ancestor of modern man, but its evolutionary significance remains controversial.

Gracile and robust australopiths coexisted for many thousands of years. The two groups differed in several ways. Gracile species, exemplified by *A. africanus,* were smaller. They weighed approximately 25 to 35 kg (60 to 80 lb) and stood about 120 and 140 cm (4 to $4\frac{1}{2}$ feet) tall. Robust species, exemplified by *A. robustus* and *A. boisei,* were about 30 cm (1 foot) taller and 35 to 55 kilograms (75 to 120 lb) heavier. Robust individuals had flatter faces than gracile types, and many bones of robust skulls had a heavier construction (Fig. 36.35).

The cranial capacity of australopiths ranged from about 430 to 530 cm^3, considerably larger than *Ramapithecus* and approximately the volume of modern gorilla skulls (Table 36.2). The parietal region of the *Australopithecus* brain shows proportionately greater enlargement than other areas. This region includes neurons thought to be associated with language development. Moreover, *A. africanus* skulls reveal that jaw muscles were attached in a way facilitating speech.

Fig. 36.33 Hominids as hunters. Reconstruction of a hypothetical encounter between a band of early hominids and hyenas, jackals, vultures, and other scavengers. The hominids are fighting off the scavengers, who are competing for remains of a horned sivathere, an extinct relative of the giraffe.

Fig. 36.34 Australopithecine tools. Chopping tool (left) and primitive "hand ax" (right). Sometimes called pebble tools, artifacts like these were used by Australopithecine hominids between 1 and $2\frac{1}{2}$ or more million years ago.

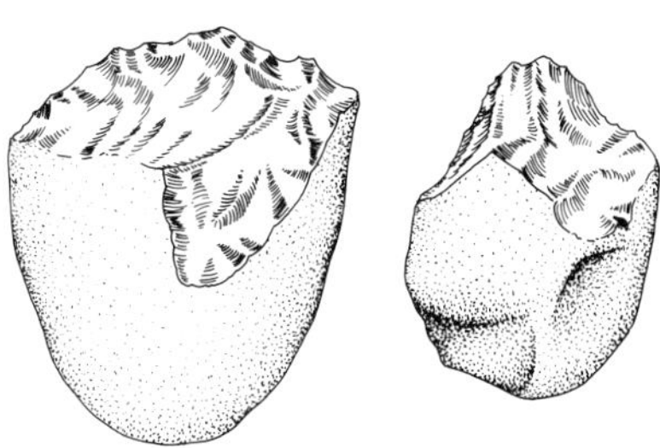

TABLE 36.2
Estimated Average Cranial Capacities and Body Weight of Selected Extinct Hominids

Hominid species	Approximate age, millions of years	Estimated average brain volume, cm^3	Estimated total body weight, kg
Ramapithecus	15	300?	25–35
H. africanus	5	450	25–35
H. erectus	0.5	1000	55–60
H. sapiens (Swanscombe-Steinheim)	0.2	1260	55–60

SOURCE: R. M. Tullar, "The Human Species," fig. 7-9 (modified), McGraw-Hill, 1977.

HOMO ERECTUS

Some species of *Australopithecus* may have given rise to the genus *Homo*. Scientists are divided on the issue of which australopith, if any, is ancestral early man. It is possible that the true ancestor of our genus has not yet been discovered.

The earliest known species of *Homo* is *H. erectus* (originally called *Pithecanthropus*), which lived until about 300,000 years ago (Fig. 36.36). The time of its origin is not known, but *H. erectus* probably evolved between 2 and 1 million years ago. The first members of the species likely were contemporaries of late representatives of *Australopithecus* (see Fig. 36.41).

H. erectus came to have a wide distribution, with subspecies known from southeastern Asia ("Java man"), China ("Peking man"), Europe ("Heidelberg man"), as well as various regions of Africa. Most individuals stood 150 to 170 cm (5 to 5½ feet) tall. The anatomy of fossil pelvic bones suggests that *H. erectus* was a true strider. The structure of its fossil skull indicates a cranial capacity of

Fig. 36.35 ***Australopithecus.*** (A) Skull cast of *A. africanus*, a gracile type, and a reconstruction of the probable facial features of this hominid. (B) Skull of *A. robustus* and a reconstruction of the likely features of this species. Note the more prominent bony crests and buttresses about the cheeks, eyes, and jaws of the robust form.

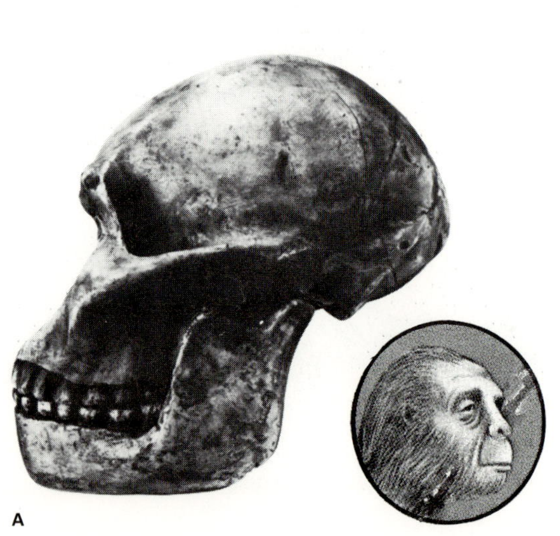

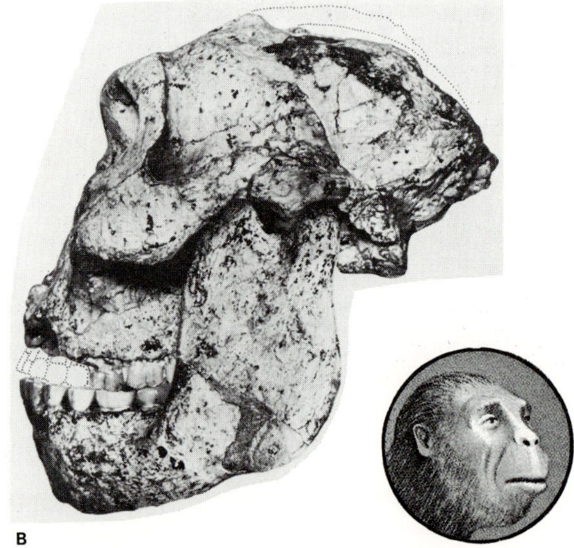

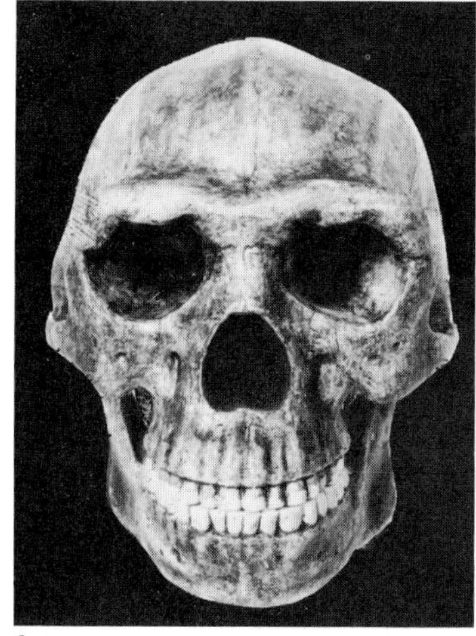

A

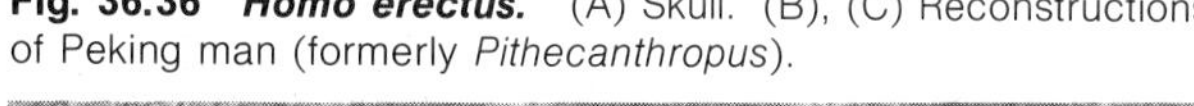

Fig. 36.36 ***Homo erectus.*** (A) Skull. (B), (C) Reconstructions of Peking man (formerly *Pithecanthropus*).

B

C

1000 cm^3, about 350 cm^3 smaller than that of modern man, but nearly double that of *Australopithecus.* Such skulls have a flat, sloping forehead and thick eyebrow ridges; the massive protruding jaw is virtually chinless.

Some groups of *H. erectus* appear to have lived in caves, but others evidently constructed more substantial dwellings. The latter often consisted of an oval outer boundary wall of stones. Interior portions of such dwellings presumably were covered by branches or hides supported on poles. These oval "homes" measured about 4.5 m (15 feet) in width and 9 m (30 feet) in length (Fig. 36.37).

Hearths have been found in such dwellings and also in caves used by *H. erectus.* For example, traces of charcoal, ash, and fire-cracked stones have been discovered in two caves in southern France once used as a home base by this species. The hearths of these caves appear to have been used for warmth and for cooking meat. It is likely that *H. erectus* also used fire to drive large carnivores out of caves before claiming them for personal use. In addition, this species of man probably used fire to stampede big game animals over cliffs or into swamps. Once immobilized, the game fell easy prey to the human hunters.

Tools found with fossils of *H. erectus* have a more sophisticated appearance than those of ancestral species. Some tools were large and heavy, such as wedge-shaped cleavers that could easily kill even moderately sized prey. Other tools were smaller and more delicate. Some of these were used for skinning animals and slicing meat, and some may have been used to fashion spears, digging sticks, and other instruments. The reason this species has been designated as human should now be apparent. *Homo erectus* was the first hominid having the capacity to modify physical and biological environments in a significant and purposeful manner.

Homo Sapiens

Some 500,000 to 250,000 years ago *H. erectus* appears to have given rise to our own species, *Homo sapiens.* The place of this event is again unknown, and if it indeed occurred in just one place *H. sapiens* must have rapidly spread from there to most parts of the world; early subspecies of *H. sapiens* are known from, for example, Africa ("Rhodesia man"), Java ("Solo man"), England ("Swanscombe man"), and Germany ("Steinheim man"). The latter two representatives appear to provide particularly good documentation of an ancestor-descendant relationship between *H. erectus* and early *H. sapiens.* Evidence for "Swanscombe" and "Steinheim" individuals is derived from two fossil skulls, one (Swanscombe) found in a gravel deposit in southeastern England, and the other (Steinheim) found near Stuttgart in southern West Germany (Fig. 36.38).

The Swanscombe skull, which is about 250,000 years old, consists only of an occipital bone and two parietal bones. Except for a crushed left side, the 200,000-year-old Steinheim skull is essentially complete. The Steinheim specimen has a cranial capacity of about 1200 cm^3, some 150 cm^3 less than modern man but 200 cm^3 larger than *H. erectus* (see Table 36.2). The cranial capacity of the Swanscombe skull is 1300 cm^3, substantially the same as our own. Moreover, both skulls are anatomically intermediate between *H. erectus* and modern *H. sapiens* in almost all other respects, supporting the view that the fossils belonged to an archaic form of *H. sapiens.* In fact, computer analysis of data obtained from skull measurements indicate that the Swanscombe and Steinheim specimens are very similar to the skulls of *Neanderthal man,* the best known prehistoric human being.

The Neanderthal subspecies, *Homo sapiens neanderthalis,* probably arose about 100,000 years ago or even earlier. The subspecies derives its name from the Neander Valley in West Germany, where the first fossils of these people were found in 1856. Neanderthal fossils have since been found throughout Europe and in many parts of Asia (Fig. 36.39).

Some anatomical differences distinguish Neanderthal man from *H. erectus,* but the principal distinctions are technological and cultural. Neanderthal man fashioned a variety of weapons, tools, hunting axes, clubs, and "household" equipment markedly more sophisticated than those of *H. erectus.* Culturally the Neanderthalers were nomadic cave people of the Upper Pleistocene epoch (see Fig. 36.41). Their home sites indicate that these people practiced elaborate religious or other rituals and apparently believed in life after death.

For example, a shallow grave was discovered in a Neanderthal cave located in the Dordogne Valley

Fig. 36.37 Dwellings of *H. erectus*. Some members of this species lived in oval huts. Interior (top) and exterior (bottom) of such dwellings are depicted, the latter showing entrance and chimney (depression near center of hut).

of France. The grave contained the fossil skeleton of an approximately 15-year-old boy whose body had been placed on its right side with its head positioned on its right forearm. Chips of flint lay about the head and a hand axe had been placed next to the body. Charred cattle bones were also found in the grave. Cooked meat presumably had been placed there to provide sustenance for the youth's journey to the hereafter. The skeleton of another Neanderthal youth was found with six pairs of wild goat horns encircling the head.

Like *H. erectus,* Neanderthal man undoubtedly practiced cannibalism. Fossil remains of both species include skull caps separated cleanly from the rest of the skeleton; sheer accident does not appear to have caused such neat separations. Because of an increased intelligence, Neanderthal man probably was a better and more effective killer than *H. erectus.* Over 500 human bone fragments belonging to at least a dozen individuals were found in the hearth of one Neanderthal cave. Many of the long bones were burned and split along their length in an apparent attempt to expose the marrow.

Late groups of Neanderthalers were contemporaries of early representatives of our own subspecies, *Homo sapiens sapiens.* Some scientists favor the hypothesis that our subspecies evolved

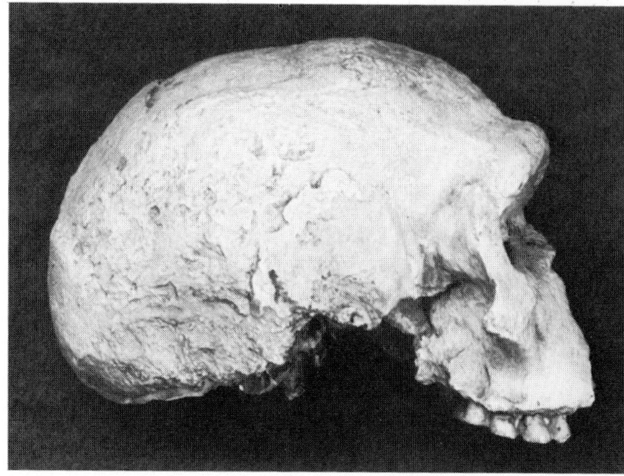

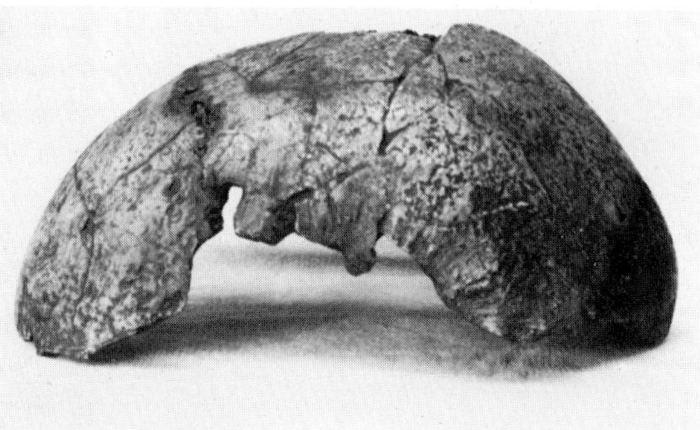

A

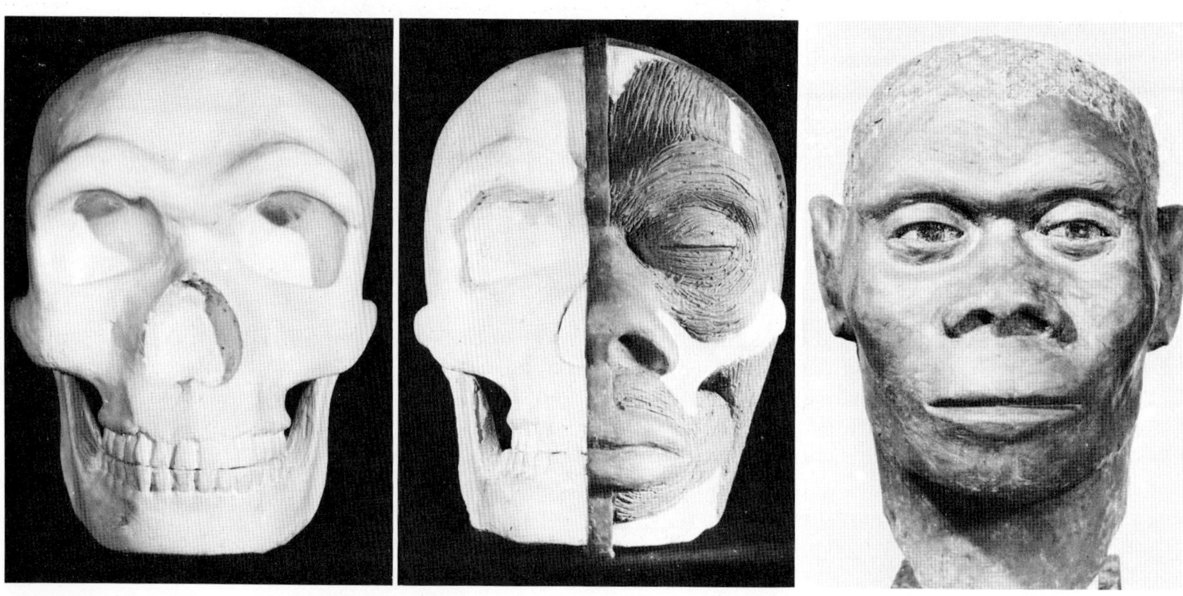

B

Fig. 36.38 Early *Homo sapiens.* (A) Steinheim (left) and Swanscombe (right) skulls. (B) Steps in the reconstruction of facial features of early *H. sapiens* based on Steinheim skull. Left, cast of whole skull is reconstructed. Middle, parts of skull to which muscles attach serve as guide for reconstruction of facial muscles. Right, completed bust.

A

B

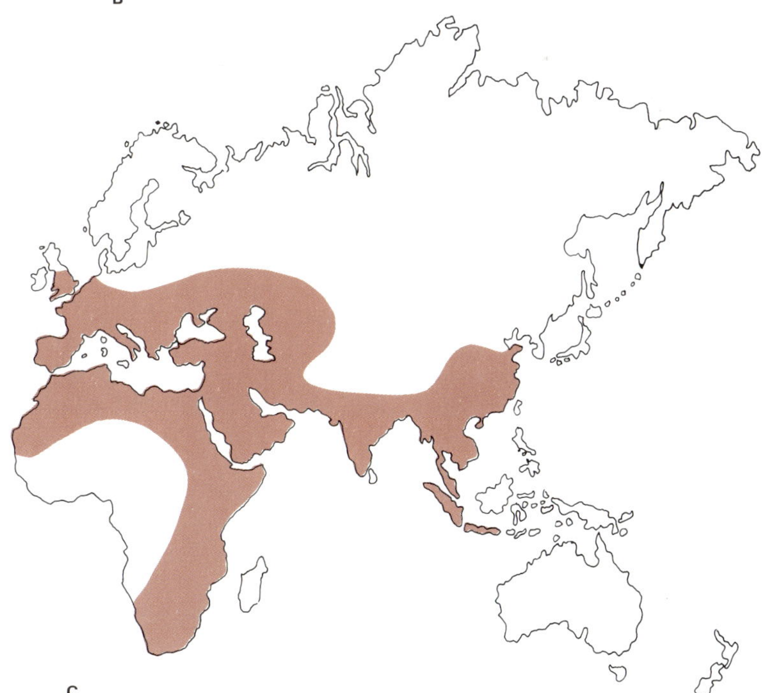

C

Fig. 36.39 ***Homo sapiens neanderthalis.*** (A), (B) Reconstructions of Neanderthal man. (C) Distribution of Neanderthal man based on skeletal and cultural remains.

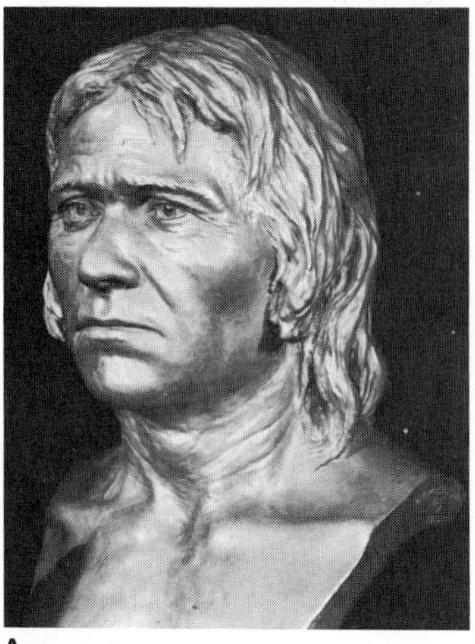

A

B

Fig. 36.40 Cro-Magnon man. Two reconstructions are shown.

independently of Neanderthal man, but a growing body of evidence suggests that we are descendants of one or more groups of Neanderthalers.

One early representative of our subspecies was *Cro-Magnon man,* who lived in Europe from about 40,000 to 25,000 years ago. Cro-Magnon males were 6 feet tall on the average, with a brain volume of about 1700 cm^3 (Fig. 36.40). In addition to stone implements these people used bone needles for sewing animal skins into crude garments. Bones, including antlers and ivory tusks, were also employed as tent poles, whistles, clothes fasteners, carved figurines, and perhaps even lunar calendars.

Cro-Magnon man domesticated the wild dog and created a diversity of art objects, including a wealth of painted murals on cave walls (see Fig. 36.40). The art of these people has provided considerable information regarding their culture. For example, paintings and sculptured figurines indicate that Cro-Magnon man practiced many religious rituals, most of them centering around a hunting theme. The distribution of certain cave murals also suggests that parts of home sites were considered sacred. As late as the 1960s, the Aborigines of northern Australia prepared for hunts by painting in sacred locations images of animals they sought.

The social organization of Cro-Magnon man also appears to be more advanced than that of Neanderthalers. Cro-Magnon people lived in larger communities where collaborative, group-oriented behavior takes on increased importance.

Cro-Magnon man was a contemporary of other populations of *H. sapiens sapiens* in different parts of the world. Through evolution, migration, and interbreeding, these groups gradually developed the present populations found around the globe. By the time the Pleistocene came to a close, some 20,000 or 25,000 years ago, our subspecies was the only human group in existence. For the next 10,000 years or more our ancestors were culturally in the *Middle Stone Age,* characterized chiefly by great improvements in stone tools. People were still nomadic hunters, however. The *New Stone Age* began about 7000 to 10,000 years ago, about the time Abraham settled in Canaan (Fig. 36.41). A great cultural revolution took place then. People learned to fashion pottery, they developed agriculture, and they were able to domesticate animals. From that period on, modern civilization developed very rapidly. By 3000 B.C. our ancestors entered the *Bronze Age.* Some 2000 years later the *Iron Age* began. And not very long after that people

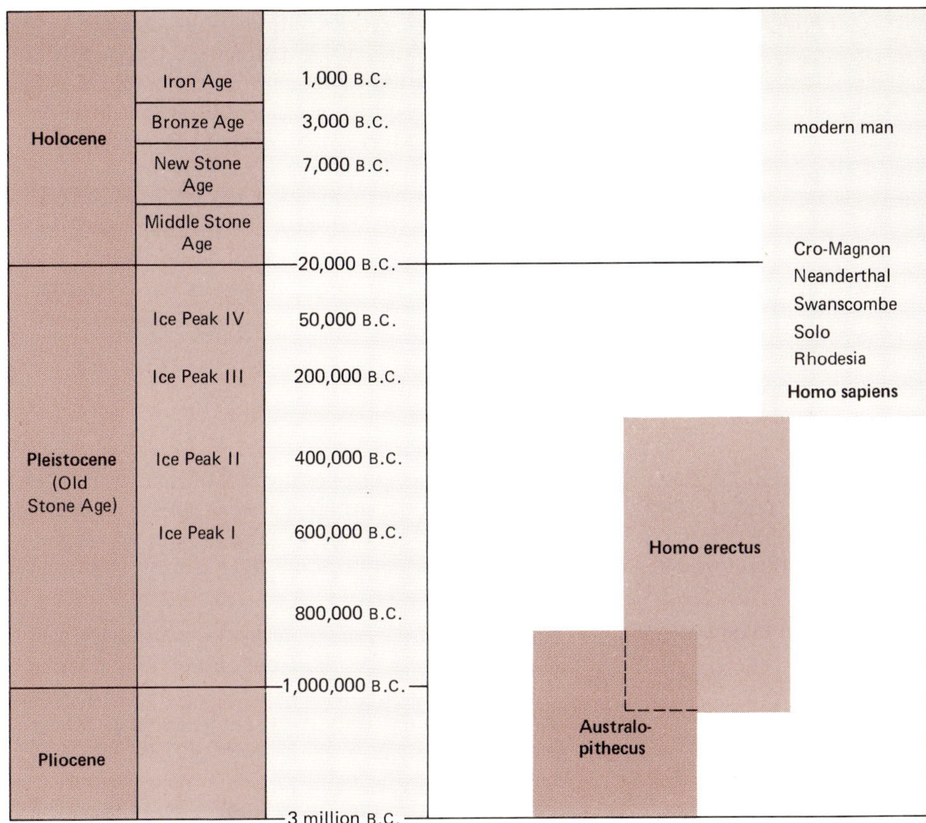

Gap in the Fossil Record

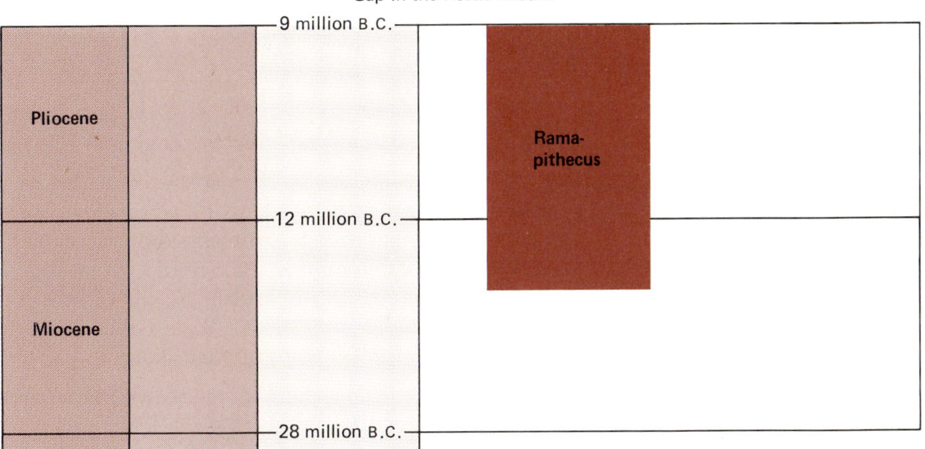

Fig. 36.41 The hominid radiation. Each main hominid group (in color boxes) is shown roughly at a time level at which it is known to have existed. Within each such group several more subgroups than indicated are known. In most cases the exact period at which the subgroups have lived is not certain.

discovered steam, electricity, and now the atom and outer space.

In retrospect, tracing the origins of mankind has proved exceedingly difficult, and we are not yet confident that the foregoing account of our evolutionary heritage is accurate in all respects. Nonetheless, we often appear to know far more about where we have come from than where we are going.

What will happen to modern man? Will *Homo sapiens sapiens* survive indefinitely? Will our subspecies become extinct, either before or after giving rise to a new kind of human being? Our future is uncertain and unpredictable. It is certain only that people today are just as subject to evolutionary forces as prehistoric man, with the important difference that we create many of these forces ourselves—and we usually are unaware where they might lead. Unlike all other organisms, therefore, we shall decide our fate largely on our own, under the impetus of our own reasoned or unreasoned purposes.

Review Questions

1 Review the recapitulatory hypotheses of Haeckel and show why they are not tenable. Does comparative animal embryology give any clues about the probable course of early animal evolution? Discuss.

2 Describe the key events of animal evolution during the:

a. Cambrian-Ordovician

b. Silurian-Devonian

c. Carboniferous-Permian

Review the course of vertebrate evolution during the entire Paleozoic.

3 Review the evolutionary happenings during the Mesozoic among groups other than reptiles. Make a similar review for reptile evolution. Which reptilian groups exist today, and what ancient groups did they derive from? What factors could have triggered the dramatic extinctions of dinosaurs and other prominent mesozoic organisms?

4 What group was ancestral to mammals? What factors probably promoted the evolution of mammals from reptiles? What factors appear to have promoted the evolution of birds from reptiles, and in what ways has the direction of bird evolution been different from that of mammals?

5 Describe the main features of the Cenozoic mammalian radiation, with special attention to the origin of primates. Describe the major features and the time pattern of the primate radiation, and name living animals representing each of the main lines.

6 Describe the various adaptations of each of the primate groups to arboreal life. Which structural, functional, and behavioral traits of man trace back specifically to the arboreal way of life of his ancestors? How do hominoids differ from other primates? How does the hominid line differ from the pongid line?

7 Review the status of human evolutionary science. In contrast to other organisms, why does so little information exist about the evolution of *Homo sapiens*? Describe the investigatory tools of the modern student of human evolution. Which of these methods and technologies have contributed to the great transformation of human evolutionary science over the past 20 years? Describe the nature of this transformation.

8 Describe the structural and probable behavioral characteristics of dryopithicine apes. When and where did dryopithicines live? What modern hominids appear to have evolved from these apes?

9 Describe some of the characteristics of *Ramapithecus, Australopithecus,* and *Homo erectus.* Describe the comparative tool-making and tool-using abilities of these hominids. When and where did they live? Were they human beings? Roughly when did *Homo sapiens* arise? What traits distinguish Neanderthalers from modern men?

10 Review the biological characteristics that *Homo sapiens* shares with all other:

a. hominids

b. hominoids

c. primates

d. mammals

Review some of the traits that distinguish man uniquely from all other animals.

Collateral Readings

Alvarez, L. W., et al.: Extraterrestrial Cause for the Cretaceous Tertiary Extinction, *Science,* June 6, 1980, vol. 208, pp. 1095–1108. An authoriatative, detailed introduction to the asteroid-impact hypothesis.

Bakker, R. T.: Dinosaur Renaissance, *Scientific American,* April 1975. States reasons why some biologists propose that dinosaurs were warm-blooded; also discusses the evolution of birds from dinosaur ancestors.

Bryant, V. M., and **G. Williams-Dean:** The Coprolites of Man, *Scientific American,* January 1975. Fossil human feces are providing new information on the diet and behavior of prehistoric man.

Colbert, E. H.: "Evolution of the Vertebrates," 2d ed., Wiley, New York, 1969. A detailed description of vertebrate evolution. For the serious student of this subject.

deCamp, L. Sprague, and **C. C. deCamp:** "The Day of the Dinosaur," Doubleday, Garden City, N.Y., 1968. Written for the nonscientist, this popular book focuses on the work of scientists who search for the fossilized remains of these Mesozoic reptiles.

Desmond, A.: "Hot-Blooded Dinosaurs: A Revolution in Paleontology," Dial, New York, 1976. A sometimes controversial argument that dinosaurs were warm-blooded. Interesting and provocative.

Klein, R. G.: Ice-Age Hunters of the Ukraine, *Scientific American,* June 1974. The discovery of ancient human camp sites provides considerable insight into the hunting behavior of our ancestors.

Langstrom, W.: Pterosaurs, *Scientific American,* February 1981. Highlights the anatomy and lifestyle of these extinct flying reptiles.

Leakey, R. E., and **R. Lewin:** "Origins," Dutton, New York, 1977. Leakey discovered several of the fossils discussed in this sometimes. controversial account of human evolution.

———: The Hominids of East Turkana, *Scientific American,* August 1978. Describes some recently discovered human fossils and speculates on their anthropological significance.

Pfeiffer, J. E.: "The Emergence of Man," 2d ed., Harper & Row, 1972. This highly readable book describes the evolution of hominids during the Pleistocene epoch.

Romer, A. S.: "The Vertebrate Body," 5th ed., Saunders, Philadelphia, 1977. A standard reference text on the comparative anatomy of both living and extinct vertebrates.

Simons, E. L.: Ramapithecus, *Scientific American,* May 1977. Describes how many newly discovered fossils have helped clarify the place of *Ramapithecus* in human evolution.

Teleki, G.: The Omnivorous Chimpanzee, *Scientific American,* January 1973. Relates how scientists discovered that chimpanzees, once thought exclusively herbivorous, sometimes hunt, kill, and eat other mammals.

Trinkhaus, E., and **W. W. Howells:** The Neanderthalers, *Scientific American,* 1979. The authors describe recent evidence suggesting that differences between the Neanderthals and our immediate ancestors are not so great as once thought.

Tullar, R. M.: "The Human Species: Its Nature, Evolution, and Ecology," McGraw-Hill, New York, 1977. A clearly written summary of human evolution.

Washburn, S. L.: The Evolution of Man, *Scientific American,* September 1978. An excellent summary article; part of an issue devoted exclusively to evolution.

——— and **R. Moore:** "Ape Into Human: A Study of Human Evolution," Little, Brown, Boston, 1980. This short, highly readable paperback provides a solid introduction to human evolution.

Appendix A Metric Conversion Table

	Metric to metric conversion	Metric to English conversion	English to metric conversion
Length			
	1 kilometer (km) = 1000 (10^3) meters	1 km = 0.62 mile	1 mile = 1.609 km
	1 meter (m) = 100 centimeters	1 m = 1.09 yards	1 yard = 0.914 m
		1 m = 3.28 feet	1 foot = 0.305 m
	1 centimeter (cm) = 0.01 (10^{-2}) meter	1 cm = 0.394 inch	1 foot = 30.5 cm
	1 millimeter (mm) = 0.001 (10^{-3}) meter	1 mm = 0.039 inch	1 inch = 2.54 cm
	1 micrometer (μm) = 0.000001 (10^{-6}) meter		
	1 nanometer (nm) = 0.000000001 (10^{-9}) meter		
	1 angstrom (Å) = 0.0000000001 (10^{-10}) meter		
Area			
	1 square kilometer (km^2) = 100 hectares	1 km^2 = 0.3861 square mile	1 square mile = 2.590 km^2
	1 hectare (ha) = 10,000 square meters	1 ha = 2.471 acres	1 acre = 0.4047 ha
	1 square meter (m^2) = 10,000 square centimeters	1 m^2 = 1.1960 square yards	1 square yard = 0.8361 m^2
		1 m^2 = 10.764 square feet	1 square foot = 0.0929 m^2
	1 square centimeter (cm^2) = 100 square millimeters	1 cm^2 = 0.155 square inch	1 square inch = 6.4516 cm^2
Mass			
	1 metric ton (t) = 1000 kilograms	1 t = 0.9842 ton	1 ton = 1.0160 t
	1 metric ton (t) = 1,000,000 grams	1 kg = 2.205 pounds	1 pound = 0.4536 kg
	1 kilogram (kg) = 1000 grams	1 g = 0.0353 ounce	1 ounce = 28.35 g
	1 gram (g) = 1000 milligrams		
	1 milligram (mg) = 0.001 gram		
	1 microgram (μg) = 0.000001 gram		
Volume (solids)			
	1 cubic centimeter (cm^3) = 1000 cubic millimeters	1 m^3 = 1.3080 cubic yards	1 cubic yard = 0.7646 m^3
		1 m^3 = 35.315 cubic feet	1 cubic foot = 0.0283 m^3
	1 cubic centimeter (cm^3) = 1000 cubic millimeters	1 cm^3 = 0.0610 cubic inch	1 cubic inch = 16.387 cm^3
Volume (liquids)			
	1 kiloliter (kl) = 1000 liters	1 kl = 264.17 gallons	1 gallon = 3.785 l
	1 liter (l) = 1000 milliliters	1 l = 1.06 quarts	1 quart = 0.94 l
	1 milliliter (ml) = 0.001 liter	1 ml = 0.034 fluid ounce	1 pint = 0.47 l
	1 microliter (μl) = 0.000001 liter		1 fluid ounce = 29.57 ml
Time			
	1 second (sec) = 1000 milliseconds		
	1 millisecond (msec) = 0.001 second		
	1 microsecond (μsec) = 0.000001 second		

Appendix B Temperature Conversion Scale

Several different temperature scales exist, but the centigrade scale is the one used most commonly by biologists. The temperature conversion diagram shown here can be used to interconvert Fahrenheit and centigrade temperatures. The two temperature scales also can be interconverted through use of the following formulas:

$$°C = \tfrac{5}{9}°F - 32$$

$$°F = \tfrac{9}{5}°C + 32$$

A third temperature scale frequently found in scientific literature is the Celsius scale. For all practical purposes, the Celsius and centigrade scales are interchangeable; any temperature read on the Celsius scale is the same as on the centigrade scale. Nevertheless the two scales are not identical. The zero point on the Celsius scale is fixed by a much more accurate method than on the centigrade scale. This makes Celsius measurements more accurate than centigrade readings. However, the accuracy of the centigrade scale is more than sufficient for most biological experiments.

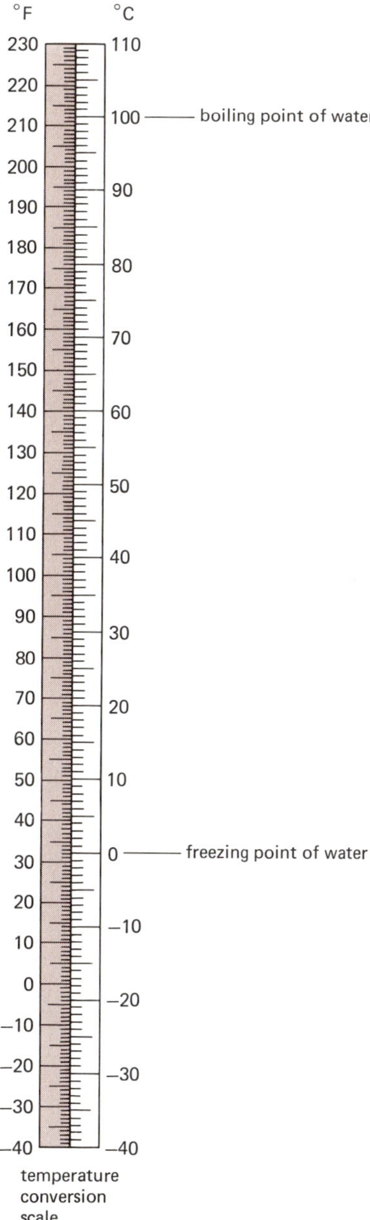

temperature conversion scale

Appendix C The Electromagnetic Spectrum, Including Action and Absorption Spectra for *Ulva taeniata*

This diagram illustrates the position occupied by visible light in the electromagnetic spectrum. Numbers indicate wavelength in nanometers [(nm), see Appendix A]. Note that visible light constitutes only a small portion of the whole spectrum. Moreover, chlorophyll absorbs different wavelengths of light to varying degrees, as evidenced by the action and absorption spectra of the green alga *Ulva taeniata*.

The absorption spectrum measures the amount of light of a given wavelength that is absorbed by the alga. Chlorophyll accounts for almost all of this absorption. This pigment absorbs violet-blue and red wavelengths more strongly than any other part of the visible spectrum; green wavelengths are largely reflected, accounting for the green color of chlorophyll-containing cells. The action spectrum indicates which wavelengths are most effective in actually bringing about photosynthesis. The close correlation of the two curves provides convincing evidence of the direct involvement of chlorophyll in photosynthesis.

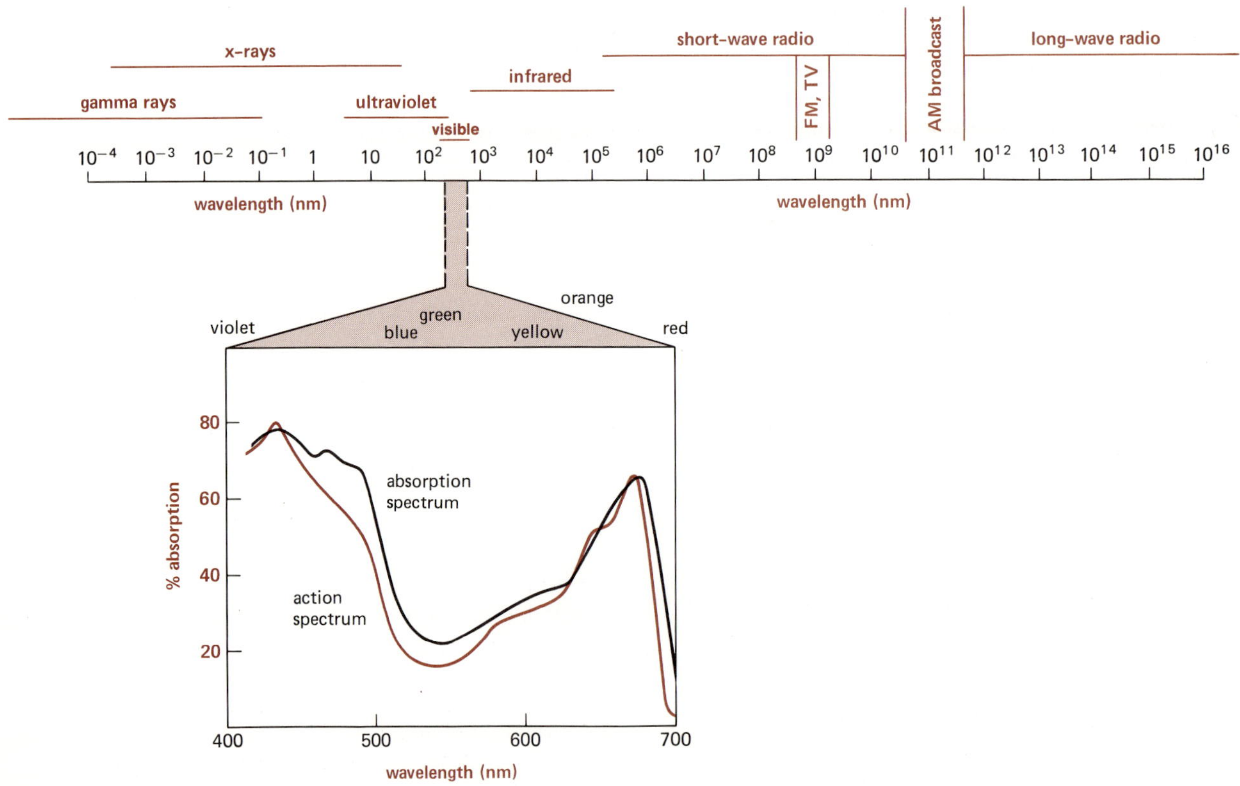

Glossary

SECTION A

COMMON PREFIXES, SUFFIXES, AND ANATOMICAL TERMS IN BIOLOGICAL USAGE*

The meaning of many terms not listed in Section B, below, can be ascertained from Section A. For example, certain fishes are known as the *Actinopterygii.* The parts of this term are the prefix *actino-* and the suffix *-pterygii;* the list below indicates the meanings of these word parts as "ray" and "fin," respectively. Hence the whole term denotes "ray-finned." A large number of technical designations can be translated into English equivalents by separating the words into parts and consulting this first section of the glossary.

a- [Gr. not]: negates succeeding part of word; e.g., *acoel,* without coelom.

ab- [L. away, off]: opposite of *ad;* e.g., *aboral,* away from mouth.

acro- (ăk′rō̆) [Gr. *akros,* outermost]: e.g., *acrosome,* body at tip of animal sperm.

actino- (ăk′tĭ·nō̆) [Gr. *aktis,* ray]: e.g., *actinopodial,* ray-footed.

ad- [L. toward, to]: opposite of *ab-;* e.g., *adrenal,* at (near) the kidney.

afferent (ăf′ẽr·ĕnt) [L. *ad* + *ferre,* to carry]: to lead or carry toward given position, opposite of efferent; e.g., afferent nerve, afferent blood vessel.

amphi- (ăm′fĭ) [Gr. on both sides]: e.g., *amphioxus,* pointed at both ends.

an- [Gr. not]: like *a-,* used before vowel or "h"; e.g., *anhydride,* compound without hydrogen.

ana- [Gr. up, throughout, again, back]: e.g., *analogy,* likeness, resemblance; *analysis,* thorough separation; *anatomy,* cutting apart.

andro- (ăn′drō̆) [Gr. *aner,* man, male]: e.g., *androgen,* male-producing hormone.

anterior, antero- (ăntē′rĭ·ẽr, ăn′tẽr·ō̆) [L. *ante,* before, in front of]: at, near, or toward front end.

antho- (ăn′thō̆) [Gr. *anthos,* flower]: e.g., *Anthozoa,* flowerlike (coelenterate) animals; *anther,* part of flower.

anthropo- (ăn′thrō̆·pō̆) [Gr. *anthrōpos,* man, human]: e.g., *anthropocentric,* man-centered.

apical (ăp′ĭ·kăl) [L. *apex,* tip]: belonging to an apex, being at or near the tip; as in apical meristem, the embryonic plant tissue at the tip of root or stem.

*NOTE: The system of indicating pronunciation is used by permission of the publishers of Webster's New Collegiate Dictionary. Copyright 1949, 1951, 1953, 1956, 1958 by G. & C. Merriam Co.

arch-, archeo- (ärch, är′kē̆·ō̆) [Gr. *archos,* chief]: first, main, earliest; e.g., *archenteron,* first embryonic gut.

arthro- (är′thrō̆) [Gr. *arthron,* joint]: e.g., *arthropod,* jointed-legged; *arthritis,* joint inflammation.

asc-, asco- (ās′kō̆-) [Gr. *askos,* sac]: e.g., *aschelminth,* sac worm; *ascomycete,* sac-forming fungus.

-ase (ās, āz): suffix added to root name of a chemical to denote an enzyme specific for that chemical; e.g., *maltase,* an enzyme catalyzing reactions of maltose.

aster-, -aster (ăs′tẽr) [Gr. star]: e.g., *asteroid,* star-shaped.

auto- (ô′tō̆) [Gr. same, self]: e.g., *autogamy,* self-fertilization; *autotroph,* self-feeding organism.

axo- (ăk′sō̆) [fr. Gr. *axine,* axis]: pertaining to an axis; e.g., *axoneme,* axial filament.

bi- (bī) [L. *bis,* twice, double, two]: e.g., *bilateral; bicuspid,* having two points.

bio- (bī′ō̆) [Gr. *bios,* life]: pertaining to life; e.g., *biology; amphibia,* living in water and on land.

-blast, blast-, blasto- (blăst, blăst′ō̆) [Gr. *blastos,* embryo]: pertaining to embryo; e.g., *blastopore,* embryonic opening.

brachio- (brā′kĭ·ō̆) [L. *brachium,* arm]: e.g., *brachiopod,* arm-footed animal.

-branch, branchio- (brăng′kĭ·ō̆) [Gr. *branchia,* gills]: e.g., *branchial* sac, breathing sac.

cardio- (kär′dĭ·ō̆) [Gr. *kardia,* heart]: e.g., *pericardial,* around the heart.

caudal (kô′dăl) [L. *caudo,* tail]: at, near, or toward the tail.

cephalo- (sĕf′ȧ·lō̆) [Gr. *kephalē,* head]: e.g., *cephalopod,* head-footed animal.

cerci, cerco- (sûr′sĭ, sûr·kō̆) [Gr. *kērkos,* tail]: per-

taining to tail: e.g., *anal cerci,* tail-like appendages, near anus.
cervical (sûr′vĭ·kăl) [L. *cervix,* neck]: at, near, or toward the neck region.
chaeto- (kē′tō̂) [Gr. *chaitē, bristle, hair*]: e.g., *chaetognath,* bristle-jawed animal.
chloro- (klō′rō̂) [Gr. *chloros,* green]: e.g., *chlorophyte,* green alga.
choano- (kō′ă·nō̂) [Gr. *choanē,* funnel]: e.g., *choanocyte,* funnel-bearing cell.
chondro- (kŏn′drō̂) [Gr. *chondros,* cartilage]: e.g., *Chondrichthyes,* cartilage fishes.
-chord, chorda- (kôrd, kôr′dă) [L. *chorda,* cord, string]: e.g., *notochord,* cord along back.
-chrome, chromo-, chroma- (krōm, krō′mō̂) [Gr. *chroma,* color]: for example, *cytochrome,* cell pigment; *chromosome,* stainable body (in cell nucleus).
-clad, clado- (klăd, klă′dō̂) [Gr. *klādos,* branch, sprout]: e.g., *triclad,* three-branched.
cocco-, cocci- (kŏkō̂, kŏk′sĭ- [Gr. *kokkos,* grain]: e.g., *coccine,* grainlike; *coccus,* grain-like (spherical) bacterium.
-coel, coela-, coelo- (sēl) [Gr. *koilos,* hollow, cavity]: e.g., *pseudocoel,* false coelomic cavity; *coelenterate,* having "gut cavity."
coeno- (sē′nō̂-) [Gr. *koinos,* common]: refers to aggregated or colonial groupings; e.g., *coenocyte,* multinuclear cell.
cten-, cteno- (tĕn) [Gr. *kteis,* comb]: e.g., *Ctenophora,* comb-bearing animals.
cyano- (sī·ȧ′nō̂-) [Gr. *kyanos,* dark-blue]: e.g., *cyanophyte,* blue-green alga.
-cyst (sĭst) [Gr. *kystis,* bladder, pouch, sac]: e.g., *sporocyst,* spore-containing cyst.
-cyte, cyto- (sīt) [Gr. *kytos,* vessel, container]: pertaining to cell; e.g., *cytoplasm,* cell substance; *fibrocyte,* fiber-forming cell.

de- (dē) [L. away, from, off]: like Gr. *apo-;* e.g., *dehydration,* removal of water.
-dent, denti- (dĕnt) [L. *dens,* tooth]: like Gr. *-dont;* e.g., *denticle,* little tooth.
dermis, -derm (dûr′mĭs) [Gr. *derma,* skin]: e.g., *ectoderm,* outer skin tissue; *epidermis,* exterior layer.
di- (dī) [Gr. twice, double, two]: like L. *bi-,* e.g., *disect,* to cut in two (distinct from *dis-,* see below).
dia- (dī′ȧ) [Gr. through, across, thorough]: e.g., *diaphragm,* across the midriff.
dino- (dī′nō̂-) [Gr. *dinos,* whirling]: e.g., *dinoflagellate;* dinosaur, "whirling lizard."
diplo- (dĭ′plō̂) [Gr. *diploos,* twofold]: e.g., *diploid,* with two chromosome sets.
dis- [L. apart, away]: e.g., *dissect,* cut apart (distinct from *di-,* see above).
distal (dĭs′tăl): situated away from or far from point of reference (usually the main part of body); opposite of *proximal.*
-dont (dŏnt) [Gr. *odontos,* tooth]: e.g., *thecodont,* having encased (socketed) teeth.
dorsal (dôr′săl) [L. *dorsum,* back]: at, near, or toward the back; opposite of *ventral.*

echino- (ê·kī′nō̂) [Gr. *echinos,* spiny, bristly]: e.g., *echinoderm,* spiny-skinned.
eco- (ēkŏ) [Gr. *oikos,* house, home]: e.g., *ecology,* study of relationships between organisms and their home territory.
ecto- (ĕk′tō̂) [Gr. *ektos,* outside]: e.g., *ectoproct,* outside-anus (that is, exterior to tentacle ring).
-ectomy (ĕk′tō̂mĭ) [Gr. *ek,* out of, + *tomein,* to cut]: excision; e.g., *thyroidectomy,* excision of thyroid gland.
efferent (ĕf′ĕr·ĕnt) [L. *ex,* out, away + *ferre,* to carry]: to lead or carry away from given position; opposite of *afferent;* e.g., efferent nerve, efferent blood vessel.
endo- (ĕn′dō̂) [Gr. *endon,* within]: e.g., *endoderm,* inner tissue layer.
entero-, -enteron (ĕn′tĕrō̂) [Gr. *enteron,* intestine]: e.g., *enterocoel,* coelom formed from intestine; *archenteron,* first intestine.
ento- (ĕn′tō̂) [Gr. var. of *endo-,* within]: e.g., *entoproct,* inside-anus (that is, inside tentacle ring).
epi- (ĕp′ĭ) [Gr. to, on, over, against]: e.g., *epidermis,* outer skin.
erythro- (ê·rĭth′rō̂) [Gr. *erythros,* red]: e.g., *erythrocyte,* red (blood) cell.
eu- (ū) [Gr. good, well, proper]: e.g., *Eumetazoa,* metazoa proper.
ex-, exo-, extero- (ĕks, ĕk′sō, ĕks′tĕr·ō̂) [L. out, from, exterior]: e.g., *exopterygote,* exterior-winged.

-fer, -fera (fĕr, fê′rȧ) [L. *ferre,* to carry]: like Gr. *-phore;* e.g., *foraminiferan,* hole-carrier; *rotifer,* wheel-carrier; *Porifera,* pore-carrying animals (sponges).
flori- (flō′rĭ-) [L. *flos,* flower]: pertaining to flowers; e.g., *florigen,* flower-producing (hormone).
-form, -formes (fôrm, fôr′mēz) [L. *-formis,* having the form of]: e.g., *perciform,* perchlike.

frontal [L. *front, frons,* forehead]: in a horizontal plane separating dorsal from ventral half.

gamo-, -gamy (găʹmō) [Gr. *gamein,* to marry]: pertaining to gametes or fertilization; e.g., *autogamy,* self-fertilization.
gastro- (găsʹtrō) [Gr. *gaster,* stomach]: e.g., *gastrozooid,* feeding individual.
-gen, -genic, geno- [Gr. *genēs,* born, created]: e.g., *hydrogen,* water-producing; *genotype,* genetic constitution.
geo- (jē·ŏ-) [Gr. *gē,* earth]: e.g., *geotropic,* growing toward center of earth.
-gest, gest- (jĕst) [L. *gestare,* to carry]: e.g., *ingest,* to carry in (food).
gluco-, glyco- (glo͞oʹkō-, glīʹkō-) [Gr. *gleukos,* sweet]: pertaining to sugars; e.g., *glucogenic,* sugar-producing; *glycolysis,* breakdown of sugar.
gnatho-, -gnath (nāʹthō) [Gr. *gnathos,* jaw]: e.g., *agnath,* jawless.
gon-, gono-, -gonium (gŏnʹō) [Gr. *gonòs,* seed, generation]: pertaining to reproduction; e.g., *gonopore,* reproductive opening.
gymno- (jĭmʹnō) [Gr. *gymnos,* naked]: e.g., *gymnosperm,* naked-seed former.
gyn-, -gyne, gyno- (jīnʹnō) [Gr. *gynē,* woman, female]: opposite of *andro-; e.g., gynogenic,* female-producing.

haem-: see *hem-*
haplo- (hăpʹlō) [Gr. *haploos,* single]: e.g., *haploid,* with one chromosome set.
-helminth (hĕlʹmĭnth) [Gr. *helminthos,* worm]: e.g., *platyhelminth,* flatworm.
hem-, hemo-, hemato- (hēm, hēʹmō, hĕmʹȧ tō) [Gr. *haima,* blood]: var. of *haem-;* e.g., *hemoglobin,* red blood pigment.
hemi- (hĕmʹĭ) [Gr. half]: like *semi-;* e.g., *hemichordate,* similar to chordate.
hepato- (hē·pătʹō-) [Gr. *hēpar,* liver]: pertaining to the liver; e.g., *hepatopancreas,* liverlike digestive gland.
hetero- (hĕtʹẽr·ō) [Gr. *heteros,* other, different]: opposite of *homo-,* e.g., *heterotrophic,* feeding on other living things.
hex-, hexa- (hĕks, hĕkʹsȧ) [Gr. six]: e.g., *hexapod,* six-legged; *hexose,* six-carbon sugar.
holo- (hŏlʹō) [Gr. *holos,* whole, entire]: e.g., *holotrophic,* eating whole (bulk) food.
homo-, homeo-, homoio- (hōʹmē,·ō, hō·moiʹō) [Gr. similar]: e.g., *homeostatic,* remaining similar in state; *homoiothermic,* possessing constant temperature.
hydro- (hīʹdrō) [Gr. *hydōr,* water]: e.g., *hydrolysis,* dissolution by water.
hyper- (hīʹpẽr) [Gr. above, over]: opposite of *hypo-;* e.g., *hypertrophy,* overgrowth.
hypo- hīʹpō) [Gr. under, less]: opposite of *hyper-;* e.g., *hypotonic,* less concentrated (than reference system).

ichthyo- (ĭkʹthĭ·ō) [Gr. *ichthyos,* fish]: e.g., *Osteichthyes,* bony fishes; *ichthyosaur,* fishlike reptile.
inter- (ĭnʹtẽr) [L. between, among]: e.g., *intercellular,* between cells.
intra- (ĭnʹtrȧ) [L. within]: e.g., *intracellular,* in cells.
iso- (īsō) [Gr. *isos,* equal]: like *homo;* e.g., *isolecithal,* having evenly distributed yolk.

leuko- (lūʹkō) [Gr. leukos, white]: e.g., *leukocyte,* white (blood) cell.
lip-, lipo- (lĭp-, lĭʹpō-) [Gr. *lipos,* fat]: pertaining to fats and fatty substances; e.g., *lipase,* fat-digesting enzyme.
-logy (lōʹjĭ) [Gr. *logos,* discourse, study]: e.g., *biology,* study of living things.
lumbar (lŭmʹbẽr) [L. *lumbus,* loin]: at, near, or toward loin region.
-lysis, -lytic, -lyte [Gr. *lysis,* a loosening]: pertaining to dissolving; e.g., *electrolytic,* dissolution by electricity.

macro- (măʹkrō) [Gr. *makros,* long]: opposite of *micro-;* e.g., *macromere,* large embryo cell.
mastigo- (măsʹtĭ·gō) [Gr. *mastix,* whip]: e.g., *Mastigophora,* flagellum-bearing (protozoa).
mega- (mĕgʹȧ-) [Gr. *megas,* large]: opposite of *micro-;* e.g., *megaspore,* large spore; used like *macro-.*
meri-, mero-, -mere, -mer (mĕrʹĭ, mēʹrō, mẹr, mĕr) [Gr. *meros,* part]: e.g., *blastomere,* embryo part (cell); *polymer,* chemical of many (similar) parts; *meristem,* dividing region.
meso- (mĕsʹō) [Gr. *mesos,* middle]: e.g., *mesophyll,* middle of leaf.
meta- (mĕtʹȧ) [Gr. after, behind]: e.g., *Metazoa,* later (advanced) animals.
micro- (mīʹkrō) [Gr. *mikros,* small]: e.g., micromere, small embryo cell.

mono- (mŏn′ō̇) [Gr. *monos,* single]: e.g., *monosaccharide,* single sugar (unit).
-morph, morpho- (mŏrf, mŏr′fō̇) [Gr. *morphē,* form]: e.g., *morphology,* study of form (structure); *metamorphosis,* process of acquiring later (adult) structure.
myc-, myco- (mīk-, mī′kō̇) [Gr. *mykēs,* mushroom]: pertaining to fungi; for example, *mycelium,* fungus filaments; *Mycophyta,* the phylum of fungi.
myo- (mī′ō̇) [Gr. *mys,* muscle]: e.g., *myofibril,* contractile fibril.
myx-, myxo-, (mĭks-, mĭk·sō̇-) [Gr. *myxa,* slime]: e.g., *myxophyte,* slime mold.

-neme, nemato- (nē′mĕ, nĕm′ȧ·tō̇) [Gr. *nema,* thread]: e.g., *nematode,* threadlike worm; *protonema,* first filament (in moss).
nephro- (nĕf′rō̇-) [Gr. *nephros,* kidney]: e.g., *nephric tubule,* excretory tubule.
neuro- (nū′rō̇) [Gr. *neuron,* nerve]: e.g., *neurofibril,* impulse-conducting fibril.
noto- (nō′tō̇) [Gr. *nōton,* the back]: e.g., *notochord,* cord along back.

octo- [Gr. *okto,* eight]: e.g., *octopus,* eight-"legged" animal.
-oid, -oida, -oidea (oid, oid′ȧ, oi′dē̇·ȧ) [Gr. *eidos,* form]: having the form of; like L. *-form;* e.g., *echinoid,* like *Echinus* (sea urchin).
oligo- (ŏl′ĭ·gō̇) [Gr. *oligos,* few, small]: e.g., *oligochaete, having few bristles.*
omni- (ŏm-nĭ-) [L. *omnis,* all]: e.g., *omnivore,* animal eating all kinds of foods.
onto- (ŏn′tŏ) [Gr. *on,* being]: e.g., *paleontology,* study of ancient (fossil) beings.
oö- (ō′ō̇) [Gr. *ōion,* egg]: e.g., *oöcyte,* egg cell; *oögonium,* egg-forming structure.
oral (ō′răl) [L. *or-, os,* mouth]: at, near, or toward mouth.
-ose (ōs, ōz): suffix denoting a sugar; e.g., *fructose,* fruit sugar.
osteo- (ŏs′tē̇·ō̇) [Gr. *osteon,* bone]: e.g., *osteoblast,* bone-forming cell; *periosteum,* tissue layer covering a bone.
ostraco- (ŏs′trȧ·kō̇) [Gr. *ostrakon,* shell]: pertaining to a skeletal cover or shield; e.g., *ostracoderm,* armor-skinned.
oto-, otic (ō′tō̇, ŏ′tĭk) [Gr. *ous,* ear]: e.g., *otolith,* ear stone.
ovi-, ovo- (ō′vĭ, ō′vō̇) [L. *ovum,* egg]: e.g., *oviduct; ovary,* egg-producing organ.

paleo- (pā′lē̇·ō̇-) [Gr. *palaios,* old]: e.g., *paleontology,* study of ancient (fossil) life.
para- (păr′ȧ) [Gr., beside]: e.g., *parapodium,* side foot; *Parazoa,* animals on side branch of evolution (sponges).
pectin- (pĕk′tĭn) [L. *pecten,* comb]: e.g., *pectine,* comblike organ.
pectoral (pĕk′tō̇·răl) [L. *pectorale,* breastplate]: at, near, or toward chest or shoulder region.
-ped, -pedia, pedi- (pĕd, pĕd′ĭ·ȧ, pĕd′ĭ) [L. *pes,* foot]: like Gr. *-pod;* e.g., *bipedal,* two-footed; *pedipalp,* leglike appendage.
pelvic (pĕl′vĭk) [L. *pelvis,* basin]: at, near, or toward hip region.
pent-, penta- (pĕnt, pĕn′tȧ) [Gr. *pente,* five]: e.g., *pentose,* five-carbon sugar.
peri- (pĕr′ĭ) [Gr. around]: e.g., *peristalsis,* wavelike compression around tubular organ (like gut).
phago-, -phage (făg′ō̇, fāj) [Gr. eating]: e.g., *phagocyte,* cell eater; *bacteriophage,* bacterium eater (virus).
phello- (fĕl′ō̇-) [Gr. *phellos,* cork]: pertaining to cork region of bark; e.g., *phellogen,* cork-producing tissue (cambium).
phono-, -phone (fōn′ō̇, fōn) [Gr. *phonē,* sound]: e.g., *phonoreceptor,* sound-sensitive sense organ.
phoro-, -phore (fŏr′ō̇, fōr) [Gr. *phoros,* bearing, carrying]: like L. *-fer;* for example, *trochophore,* "wheel"-bearing (larva).
photo-, photic (fō′tō̇, fō′tĭk) [Gr. *photos,* light]: e.g., *photosynthesis,* synthesis with aid of light.
-phragm (frăm) [Gr. barrier]: e.g., *diaphragm.*
phyco- (fī′kō̇-) [Gr. *phykos,* seaweed]: refers to aquatic protists; e.g., *phycomycete,* primitive (often aquatic) fungus; *phycoerythrin,* red pigment in blue-green and red algae.
phyllo-, -phyll (fĭl′ō̇, fĭl) [Gr. *phyllon,* leaf]: e.g., *chlorophyll,* green pigment in leaf.
phyto-, -phyte (fī′tō̇, fīt) [Gr. *phyton,* plant]: e.g., *Metaphyta,* later (advanced) plants.
-pithecus (-pĭ·thē′cūs) [Gr. *pithēkos,* ape]: e.g., *Australopithecus,* southern ape.
placo- (plă′kō̇) [Gr. *plax,* tablet, plate]: e.g., *placoderm,* plate-skinned.
-plasm, plasmo-, -plast (plăz′m, plăz′mō̇, plăst) [Gr. *plasma,* form, mold]: e.g., *protoplasm,* first-

molded (living matter); *chloroplast,* green-formed (body).
-pleur, pleuro- (ploor, ploor′ō) [Gr. *pleuron,* side, rib]: e.g., *pleura,* membrane lining rib cage.
-ploid [Gr. *-ploos,* -fold]: number of chromosome sets per cell; e.g., *haploid, diploid.*
poly- (pŏl′ĭ) [Gr. *polys,* many]: e.g., *polymorphic,* many-shaped; *polychaete,* many-bristled.
post-, postero-, posterior (pōst, pŏs′tẽr·ō) [L. behind, after]: opposite of *pre-, antero-;* at, near, or toward hind end or part.
pre- (prē) [L. before, in front of]: opposite of *post-;* e.g., *preoral,* in front of mouth.
pro- (prō) [Gr. before, in front of]: like L. *pre-;* e.g., *prostomial,* in front of mouth.
-proct, procto- (prŏkt, prŏk′tō) [Gr. *proctos,* anus]: e.g., *ectoproct,* having anus outside of ring of tentacles.
proto- (prō′tō) [Gr. *prōtos,* first]: e.g., *Protozoa,* first animals.
proximal (prŏk′sĭ·măl) [L. *proximus,* near]: situated near to point of reference (usually the main part of body); opposite of distal.
pseudo- (sū′dō) [Gr. *pseudēs,* false]: e.g., *pseudocoel,* false coelom; *pseudopodium,* false foot.
ptero-, -ptera, -ptery (tĕr′ō, tĕr′ȧ, tĕr′ĭ) [Gr. *pteron,* wing, fin]: e.g., *exopterygote,* exterior-winged.

renal (rē′năl) [L. *renes,* kidneys]: pertaining to kidney.
rhabdo- (răb′dō) [Gr. *rhabdos,* rod]: e.g., *rhabdocoel,* flatworm possessing straight (rod-like) intestine.
rhizo- (rī′zō) [Gr. *rhiza,* root]: e.g., *rhizopod,* having rootlike feet; *rhizoid,* rootlike hair.
-rhynch, rhyncho- (rĭngk, rĭng′kō) [Gr. *rhynchos,* snout]: e.g., *kinorhynch,* having movable snout.

sagittal (săj′ĭ·tăl) [L. *sagitta,* arrow]: at, near, or toward plane bisecting left and right halves; in median plane.
sarco-, -sarc (sär′kō, särk) [Gr. *sarx,* flesh]: e.g., *coenosarc,* common flesh (living portions).
saur-, -saur (sôr) [Gr. *sauros,* lizard]: e.g., *pterosaur,* flying reptile.
schizo- (skĭz′ō) [Gr. *schizein,* to split, part]: e.g., *schizocoel,* coelom formed by splitting of tissue layer; *schizophyte,* fission "plant" (bacterium).
sclero- (sklẹ̄r′ō) [Gr. *sklēros,* hard]: e.g., *scleroprotein,* hard (horny) protein; *sclereid,* hard-walled cell.
scypho- (sī′fō) [Gr. *skyphos,* cup]: e.g., *Scyphozoa,* cup-shaped animals (jellyfish).
semi- (sĕ′mĭ-) [L. half]: e.g., *semiherbaceous,* intermediate between herbaceous and woody.
sipho-, siphono- (sī′fō-) [Gr. *siphōn,* a pipe]: e.g., *siphonaceous,* tubular.
-soma, -some, somato- (sō′mȧ, sōm, sō′mȧ·tō) [Gr. *sōma,* body]: e.g., *chromosome,* stainable body.
-sperm, spermo-, sperma-, spermato- (spûrm, spûr′mō, spûr′mȧ, spûr′mȧ·tō) [Gr. *sperma,* seed]: e.g., *endosperm,* interior (region of) seed.
spora-, sporo- (spō′rȧ, spō′rō) [Gr. *sporā,* seed]: e.g., *Sporozoa,* spore-forming (protozoa); *sporophyte,* spore-forming plant.
stato- (stăt′ō) [Gr. *statos,* standing stationary, positioned]: e.g., *statolith,* position (-indicating) stone.
stereo- (stĕr′ē·ō) [Gr. *stereos,* solid]: e.g., *stereoblastula,* solid blastula.
-stome, -stoma, -stomato-, (stōm, stōm′ȧ, stŏm′ȧ·tō) [Gr. *stoma,* mouth]: *peristomial,* around the mouth.
sub-, sus- (sŭb-, sŭs-) [L. under, below]: e.g., *subepidermal,* underneath the epidermis; *suspensor,* suspending structure.
sym-, syn-, (sĭm, sĭn) [Gr. *syn,* together, with]: like L. *con-;* e.g., *syngamy,* coming together of gametes; *synapse,* looping together (of neurons); *synthesis,* construction, putting together; *symbiosis,* living together.

taxo-, taxi-, -taxis (tăksō, tăksĭ, tăks′ĭs) [Gr. *taxis,* arrangement]: e.g., *taxonomy,* "arrangement" laws; *taxidermy,* skin arrangement.
tel-, tele-, teleo- (tĕl, tĕl′ē, tĕl′ē·ō) [Gr. *telos,* end]: e.g., *telophase,* end phase; *teleost,* (fish with) bony end (adult) state; *teleology,* knowledge of end conditions.
tetra- (tĕr′rȧ) [Gr. four]: e.g., *tetrapod,* four-footed.
thallo- (thăl′ō-) [Gr. *thallos,* young shoot]: e.g., *prothallium,* precursor of definitive plant (fern gametophyte); *thallophyte,* old term for plantlike protists (those without leaf, stem, or root).
theco-, -theca (thē′kō, thē′kȧ) [Gr. *thēkē,* case, capsule]: e.g., *thecodont,* having socketed teeth.
thigmo- (thĭg′mō) [Gr. *thigma,* touch]: e.g., *thigmotropy,* movement due to touch.

thoracic (thô·răs′ĭk) [L. *thorax,* chest]: at, near, or toward chest region, or region between head and abdomen.
-tome, -tomy (tōm, tô′mĭ) [Gr. *tomē,* section, a cutting apart]: e.g., *anatomy,* study of structure based on dissection.
trans- [L. across]: e.g., *transpiration,* water evaporation from exposed plant parts.
transverse (trăns′vûrs) [L. *transversare,* to cross]: at, near, or toward plane separating anterior and posterior; cross-sectional.
tri- (trī) [L. *tria,* three]: e.g., *triclad,* three-branched (digestive tract).
-trich, tricho- (trĭk, trĭk′ô) [Gr. *trichos,* hair]: e.g., *trichocyst,* hair-containing sac.
-troch, trocho- (trŏk, trŏk′ô) [Gr. *trochos,* wheel]: e.g., *trochophore,* (larva) bearing wheel (of cilia).
-troph, tropho- (trŏf, trŏ′fô) [Gr. *trophos,* feeder]: e.g., *autotrophic,* self-nourishing.

uro-, ura (ū′rô, ūrȧ) [Gr. *oura,* tail]: e.g., *uropod;* tail foot; *urochordate,* tailed chordate.

ventral (vĕn′trăl) [L. *venter,* belly]: opposite to *dorsal;* at, near, or toward the belly or underside.

xantho- (zăn′thô-) [Gr. *xanthos,* yellow]: e.g., *xanthophyll,* yellow pigment (of leaf).
xero- (zē′rô-) [Gr. *xēros,* dry]: e.g., *xerophyte,* dry-climate plant.

zoo-, -zoa, -zoon (zō′ô, zōȧ, zō′ŏn) [Gr. *zōion,* animal]: e.g., *protozoon,* first animal; *zooid,* individual animal (in colony).
zygo- (zī′gô) [Gr. *zygon,* yoke, pair]: e.g., *zygote,* fertilized egg.

SECTION B
GENERAL LISTING OF TECHNICAL TERMS

Where derivations of particular word parts are not given in this section, such parts and their derivations can in many cases be found in Section A, above.

abdomen (ab′dŏ·mĕn) [L]: region of animal body posterior to thorax or chest.
abiotic (ā·bī·ŏt′ĭk) [Gr. *a,* without + *bios,* life]: inorganic; nonliving.
abscission (ăb·sĭzh′ŭn) [L. *abscindere,* to cut off]: separation of a body part from a plant, particularly after a special layer of cells weakens and dies.
Acanthocephala (ȧ·kăn′thô·sĕf′ă·lȧ) [Gr. *akantho,* thorn]: spiny-headed worms, a phylum of pseudocoelomate parasites.
acetylcholine (ȧ·sē′tĭl′kō′lēn): a neurotransmitter released at autonomic nerve endings.
acid (ăs′ĭd) [L. *acidus,* sour]: a substance that releases hydrogen ions in water; having a pH of less than 7.
acoel, acoelomate (ā·sēl′): (1) without coelom; (2) an animal without coelom; flatworms, nemertine worms.
acromegaly (ăk′rô·mĕg′ȧ·lĭ): skeletal overgrowths, particularly in the extremities, produced by excessive growth-hormone secretion from the pituitary.
acrosome (ăk′rô·sōm): structure at tip of head (nucleus) of animal sperm, which makes contact with egg during fertilization.
actin (ăk′tĭn): a filamentous muscle protein; together with myosin produces muscular contraction.
actinostele (ăk·tĭn′ô·stēl) [Gr. *stēlē,* upright post]: a type of stele in roots, in which the cross-sectional arrangement of vascular tissues has the form of a star with various numbers of points.
activation energy (ăk·tĭ·vā′shŭn ĕn′ẽr·jĭ): external energy required to produce significant rates in a reaction system; the energy needed to bring a reacting system over an energy barrier that otherwise prevents a reaction from occurring.
adaptation (ăd·ăp·tā′shŭn): process or state of adjustment to environmental conditions, particularly in a long-term, evolutionary sense.
adenine (ăd′ê·nēn): a purine component of nucleotides and nucleic acids.
adenosine (di-, tri-) phosphate (*ADP, ATP*) (ȧ·dĕn′ô·sēn): adenine-ribose-phosphates functioning in energy transfers in cells.
adenylic acid: equivalent to adenosine monophosphate, or AMP.
adipose (ăd′ĭ·pōs) [L. *adipis,* fat]: fat, fatty; fat-storing tissue.
ADP: abbreviation of adenosine diphosphate.

adrenal, adrenaline (ăd·rē′năl, ăd·rĕn′ăll·ĭn) [L. *renalis,* kidney]: (1) endocrine gland; (2) the hormone produced by the adrenal medulla; epinephrine.
adrenergic (ăd′rĕn·ûr′jĭk): applied to nerve fibers that release epinephrine from their axon terminals when impulses are transmitted across synapses.
adventitious (ăd′vĕn·tĭsh′ŭs): appearing not in usual place; as an adventitious root, which can sprout from anywhere on a stem.
aerobe, aerobic (ā′ẽr·ōb, -ō′bĭk) [Gr. *aeros,* air]: (1) oxygen-requiring organism; (2) pertaining to oxygen-dependent form of respiration.
Agnatha (ăg′nȧ·thȧ); jawless fishes, a class of vertebrates including lampreys and hagfishes.
albinism (ăl′bĭ·nĭz′m) [L. *albus,* white]: deficiency or absence of pigmentation.
albumin (ăl·bū′mĭn): water-soluble protein in blood plasma, egg white, and other substances.
aldehyde (ăl′dē̇·hīd) [L. abbr. for *alcohol-dehydrogenatum,* dehydrogenated alcohol]: organic compound with —CHO grouping.
aldosterone (ăl·dŏs′tẽr·ōn): a steroid hormone of the adrenal cortex; regulates salt and water balance.
alga (ăl′gȧ), pl. *algae* (-jē): any member of a largely photosynthetic superphylum of protists.
alimentation (ăl′ĭ·mĕn·tā′shŭn) [L. *alimentum,* food, nourishment]: the process of nutrition.
alkaline (ăl′kȧ·lĭn): pertaining to substances that release hydroxyl ions in water; having a pH greater than 7.
allantois (ă·lăn′tō̇·ĭs) [Gr. *allantoeides,* sausage-shaped]: one of the extraembryonic membranes in reptiles, birds, and mammals; functions as embryonic urinary bladder or as carrier of blood vessels to and from placenta.
allele (ă·lēl′) [Gr. *allēlōn,* of one another]: one of a group of alternative genes that can occupy a given locus on a chromosome; a dominant and its associated recessive are allelic genes.
allosteric site (ăl′ō̇·stĕr′ĭk): region in an enzyme other than the active site.
altruism (ăl′troo·ĭz′m) [L. *alter,* other]: unselfish devotion to welfare of others.
alveolus (ăl·vē′ō̇l·ŭs), pl. *alveoli* (-lī) [L; dim. of *alveus,* a hollow]: a small cavity or pit; for example, a microscopic air sac of lungs.
ambulacrum, ambulacral (ăm′bū̇·lā′krŭm, -ăl) [L. walk, avenue]: (1) tube-feet-lined ciliated groove leading over arm to mouth in certain echinoderms; conducts food to mouth; (2) adjective.
amino, amino acid (ă·mē′nō̇): (1) —NH_2 group; (2) acid-containing amino group, constituent of protein.
ammocoete (ăm′ō̇·sēt) [Gr. *ammons,* sand]: lamprey larva.
ammonites (ăm′ō̇·nīts): extinct cephalopods with flat, spiralled shells, abundant during the Mesozoic.
amniocentesis (ăm′nĭ·ō̇·sĕn·tē′sĭs) [L. *centesis,* puncture]: insertion of needle through abdominal and uterine walls of pregnant female to obtain amniotic fluid (with suspended fetal cells) for study of fetal chromosomes, e.g., to determine sex or chromosomal abnormalities.
amnion, amniote, amniotic (ăm′nĭ ŏn) [Gr. dim. of *amnos,* lamb]: (1) one of the extraembryonic membranes in reptiles, birds, and mammals that forms a sac around the embryo; (2) any reptile, bird, or mammal, that is, any animal with an amnion during the embryonic state; (3) pertaining to the amnion, as in *amniotic fluid.*
amphetamines (ăm·fĕt′ȧ·mēnz): stimulants of the central nervous system.
Amphineura (ăm′fĭ·nū′rȧ): a class of mollusks, including the chitons.
ampulla (ăm·pŭl′ä) [L. vessel]: enlarged saclike portion of a duct, as in ampullas of semicircular canals in mammalian ear, or in ampullas of echinoderm tube feet.
amylase (ăm′ĭ·lās) [L. *amylum,* starch]: an enzyme that promotes the decomposition of polysaccharides into smaller carbohydrate units.
amyloplast (ăm′ĭ·lō̇·plăst′): a starch-storing, nonpigmented plastid; a type of leucoplast.
amylose (ăm′ĭ·lōs): a polysaccharide composed of glucose units, a usual component of starch.
anabolism (ăn·ăb′ō̇·lĭz′m) [Gr. *ana,* up + bolē, change]: synthesis, or constructive, metabolism.
anaerobe, anaerobic (ăn·ā′ẽr·ob, -ō′bĭk): (1) an oxygen-independent organism; (2) pertaining to an oxygen-independent form of respiration.
anamniote (ăn·ăm′nĭ·ōt); any vertebrate other than a reptile, bird, or mammal, that is, one in which an amnion does not form during the embryonic phase.
anaphase (ăn′ȧ·fāz): a stage in mitotic division characterized by the migration of chromosome sets toward the spindle poles.
anatomy (ȧ·năt′ō̇·mĭ): the gross structure of an

organism, or the science that deals with gross structure; a branch of the science of morphology.
androgen (ăn′drȏ · jĕn): one of a group of male sex hormones.
anemia (ȧ · nē′mĭ · ȧ) [Gr. bloodlessness]: a blood deficiency of red cells, hemoglobin, or total volume.
angiosperm (ăn′jĭ · ȏ · spûrm′) [Gr. *angeion,* a vessel]: a member of a class of tracheophytic plants, characterized by flowers and fruits; a flowering plant.
anhydride (ăn · hī′drīd): compound from which hydrogen or water has been removed.
Animalia (ăn · ĭ · māl′yȧ): the kingdom of animals.
anion (ăn′ī · ŏn): an ion that migrates to the anode in an electrolyte solution; a negatively charged ion.
anisogamy (ăn · ī′sŏg′ȧm · ī): sexual fusion in which the gametes of opposite sex types are unequal in size.
Annelida (ăn′ĕ · lĭd · ȧ) [L. *anellus,* a ring]: the phylum of segmented worms.
anther (an′thẽr): the microsporangia in a stamen of flowering plants.
antheridium (ăn′thẽr · ĭd′ĭ · ŭm) [Gr. *antheros,* flowery]: the sperm-producing organ of plants.
anthocyanin (ăn′thȏ · sī′ȧ · nĭn): a water-soluble pigment in plants that produces red, purple, and blue colors.
anthropoids (ăn′thrȏ · poidz): general name for Anthropoidea, a primate suborder comprising monkeys, apes, and human beings.
antibody (ăn′tĭ · bŏd′ī): a protein that combines and renders harmless an antigen, that is, a foreign protein introduced into an organism by infectious processes.
anticodon (ăn′tĭ · kō′dŏn): nucleotide triplet in tRNA that binds specifically to complementary codon in mRNA.
antidiuretic (ăn′tĭ · dī · ûr · ĕt′ĭk): relating to inhibition of urine excretion; a substance with such inhibitory effect.
antigen (ăn′tĭ · jĕn): a foreign substance, usually protein in nature, which elicits the formation of specific antibodies in an organism.
anus (ā′nŭs) [L.]: posterior opening of alimentary tract.
aphotic (ā · fōt′ĭk) [Gr. *phōs,* light]: without light, e.g., *aphotic zone,* light-free region of deep ocean.
appendix (ȧ · pĕn′dĭks) [L., appendage]: outgrowth; e.g., saclike or fingerlike section at beginning of the human large intestine.
aorta (ā · ôr′tȧ) [fr. Gr., to lift]: the main artery leaving the left ventricle of the vertebrate heart and carrying blood through its branches to all body parts.
Arachnida (ȧ · răk′nĭd · d · ȧ) [Gr. *arachnē,* spider]: a class of chelicerate arthropods, including spiders, scorpions, mites, and ticks.
archegonium (ȧr′kȇ · gō′nĭ · ŭm) [Gr. *archegonos,* first of a race]: the egg-producing organ of plants.
archenteron (ȧr · kĕn′tẽr · ŏn): the central cavity of a gastrula, lined by endoderm and representing the future digestive cavity of the adult.
artery (är′tẽr · ĭ): a blood vessel carrying blood away from the heart.
Arthropoda (är · thrȏ′pŏd · ȧ): the phylum of jointed-legged invertebrates.
Aschelminthes (ăs · kĕl · mĭn′thēs): sac (bladderlike) worms; a pseudocoelomate phylum including rotifers, roundworms, and other groups.
asconoid (ă′skŏn · oid): saclike; refers specifically to a type of sponge architecture.
ascus (ăs′kŭs): the tubular spore sac of a class of fungi.
atactostele (ă · tăkt′ȏ · stēl) [Gr. *tassein,* to arrange]: type of stele in which vascular bundles are scattered throughout stem, as in monocots.
atherosclerosis (ăth′ẽr · ȏ · sklẽr · ō′sĭs): a form of arteriosclerosis; deposition of lipid substances (including cholesterol) along the inner surfaces of arterial walls.
atom (ăt′ŭm) [Gr. *atomos,* indivisible]: the smallest whole unit of a chemical element; composed of protons, neutron, and other particles, which form an atomic nucleus, and of electrons, which orbit around the nucleus.
ATP: abbreviation of adenosine triphosphate.
atrium, atrial (ā′trĭ · ŭm, -ăl) [L. yard, court, hall]: entrance or exit cavity; for example, entrance chamber to heart, exit chamber from chordate gill region.
auricle (ô′rĭ · k′l) [L. dim. of *auris,* ear]: ear-shaped structure or lobelike appendage; for example, atrium in mammalian heart, lateral flap near eyes in planarian worms.
autosome (ô′tȏ · sōm): a chromosome other than a sex chromosome.
autotroph, autotrophism (ô′tȏ · trŏf′, -ĭz′m): (1) an organism that manufactures organic nutrients from inorganic raw materials; (2) a form of nutrition in

which only inorganic substances are required as raw materials.
auxin (ôk′sĭn) [Gr. *auxein,* to increase]: a plant hormone promoting cell elongation, hence growth.
axil, axillary (ăk′sĭl) [L. *axilla,* armpit]: (1) the angle between a branch or leaf and the stem from which it arises; (2) adjective.
axon (ăk′sŏn): an outgrowth of a nerve cell that conducts impulses away from the cell body; a type of nerve fiber.

bacillus (bȧ·sĭl′ŭs) [L. dim. of *baculum,* rod]: any rod-shaped bacterium.
bacteriophage (băk·tē̜r′ĭ·ō̇·fāj) [*bacterium* + Gr. *phagein,* to eat]: one of a group of viruses that infect, parasitize, and eventually kill bacteria.
bacterium (băk·tē̜r′ĭ·ŭm) [Gr. dim. of *baktron,* a staff]: a small, typically unicellular organism characterized by the absence of a formed nucleus; genetic material is dispersed in clumps through the cytoplasm.
basidium (bȧ·sĭd′ĭ·ŭm) [Gr. dim. of *basis,* base]: a spore-bearing structure of a class of fungi.
basilar membrane (băs′ĭ·lẽr mĕm′brān): in the mammalian inner ear, a membrane that supports the organ of Corti.
benthos, benthonic (bĕn′thŏs) [Gr. depth of the sea]: (1) collective term for organisms living along the bottoms of oceans and lakes; (2) adjective.
beriberi (bĕr′ĭ·bĕr′ĭ) [Singhalese *beri,* weakness]: disease produced by deficiency of vitamin B_1 (thiamine).
bicuspid (bī·kŭs′pĭd) [L. *cuspis,* point]: ending in two points or flaps, as in bicuspid heart valve; syn. *mitral.*
biennial (bī·ĕn′ĭ·ăl) [L. *annus,* year]: occurring once in two years; as in biennial plant, which flowers and forms seeds the second year.
Bilateria (bī·lă·tēr′ĭ·ȧ): a taxonomic grade of Eumetazoa, comprising all basically bilateral animals, i.e., all but the Radiata.
binary fission (bī′nȧ·rĭ fĭsh′ŭn): the common form of cell reproduction, in which a parent cell divides into two more or less equal daughter cells.
bioluminescence (bī′ō̇·lū′mĭ·nĕs′ĕns) [L. *lumen,* light]: emission of light by living organisms.
biomass (bī′ō̇·măs): the amount of living matter, as in an ecosystem or other ecological unit.
biome (bī′ōm): habitat zone; for example, desert, grassland, tundra.
biosphere (bī′ō̇·sfēr): the sum total of all ecosystems on earth, i.e., all living matter on earth together with the physical environment in which the living matter exists.
biota, biotic (bī·ō′tă, -ŏt′ĭk): (1) the community of organisms of a given region; (2) adjective.
biotic potential: the inherent quantitative capacity of an organism or species to reproduce.
biotin (bī′ō̇·tĭn): a vitamin of the B complex.
bipinnaria (bī′pĭn·ărĭ·ȧ) [L. *pinna,* feather, fin]: larva of asteroid echinoderms, with ciliated bands suggesting two wings.
blastea (blăs·tē′ȧ): a hypothetical blastulalike organism postulated by Haeckel to have been ancestral to Metazoa; a theoretical conception no longer accepted today.
blastodisc (blăs′tō̇·dĭsk): the embryo-forming portion of a reptile or bird egg, i.e., the microscopic cell group representing the embryo on top of the yolk mass.
blastopore (blăs′tō̇·pōr): opening connecting archenteron of gastrula with outside; represents future mouth in some animals, future anus in others.
blastula (blăs′tů·lȧ): stage in early animal development, when embryo is a hollow or solid sphere of cells.
botulism (bŏt′yoo·lĭz′m): food poisoning caused by botulin, a toxin released by the spore-forming bacterium *Clostridium botulinum.*
brachiopod, Brachiopoda (brā′kĭ·ō̇·pŏd, brā·kĭ·ŏp′ō̇·dȧ): (1) a sessile, enterocoelomate, marine animal with a pair of shells (valves) and a lophophore; (2) phylum name.
bronchus, bronchiole (brŏng′kŭs, brŏng′kĭ·ōl) [Gr. *bronchos,* windpipe]: (1) a main branch of the trachea in air-breathing vertebrates; (2) a smaller branch of a bronchus.
bryophyte, Bryophyta (brī′ō̇·fīt) [Gr. *byron,* moss]: (1) a moss, liverwort, or hornwort; any metaphyte that is not tracheophytic; (2) phylum name.
budding (bŭd′ĭng): (1) form of cell reproduction in which a parent cell divides into two or more unequally large daughter cells; (2) form of organismic vegetative reproduction in which one or more small offspring organisms develop from somatic cell groups or tissues on a parent organism.
buffer (bŭf′ẽr): a substance that prevents appreciable changes of pH in solutions to which small amounts of acids or bases are added.

bulb (bŭlb): an underground stem with thickened leaves adapted for food storage.

bundle of His (bŭn'dl ŭv hĭss): a strand of vertebrate heart muscle modified for impulse conduction, branching out from the AV node throughout the muscles of both ventricles.

caecum (sē'kŭm) [L. *caecus,* blind]: cavity open at one end; for example, the blind pouch at the beginning of the large intestine, connecting at one side with the small intestine.

callus (kăl'ŭs) [L., hardened skin]: a tissue consisting of parenchymalike cells and formed as a tumorous overgrowth or over a wound or in tissue culture.

calorie (kăl'ō·rĭ) [L. *calor,* heat]: unit of heat, measuring 4.184 joules; a *large,* or *dietary, calorie* (kilocalorie) is a thousand of the units above.

calyx (kā'lĭks) [Gr. *kalyx*]: the outermost whorl of leaves (sepals) in a flower.

cambium (kăm'bĭ·ŭm) [L. exchange]: embryonic tissue in roots and stems of tracheophytes that gives rise to secondary xylem and phloem.

capillary (kăp'ĭ·lĕr·ĭ) [L. *capillus,* hair]: a microscopic blood vessel connecting an arteriole to a venule; composed of a single layer of cells (*endothelium*) and functioning in metabolic exchanges between blood and tissues.

carapace (kăr'ȧ·pās) [Sp. *carapacho*]: a hard case or shield covering the back of certain animals.

carbohydrate, carbohydrase (kär'bō·hī'drāt): (1) an organic compound consisting of a chain of carbon atoms to which hydrogen and oxygen, present in a 2:1 ratio, are attached; (2) an enzyme promoting the synthesis or decomposition of a carbohydrate.

carboxyl (kär·bŏk'sĭl): a —COOH group.

carnivore, Carnivora (kärnĭv'ō·rȧ) [L. *carnivorus,* flesh-eating]: (1) any holotrophic animal subsisting on other animals or parts of animals; (2) an order of mammals; includes cats, dogs, seals, walruses.

carotene, carotenoids (kăr'ō·tēn, kȧ·rŏt'ē·noid) [L. *carota,* carrot]: (1) a pigment producing cream-yellow to carrot-orange colors; a precursor of vitamin A; (2) a class of pigments of which carotene is one.

catabolism (kȧ·tăb'ō·lĭz'm) [Gr. *cata-,* down + *bolē,* change]: destructive, especially respiratory, metabolism.

catalysis, catalyst (kȧ·tăl'ĭ·sĭs) [Gr. *katalysis,* dissolution]: (1) acceleration of a chemical reaction by a substance that does not become part of the end product; (2) a substance accelerating a reaction as above.

cation (kăt'ī·ŭn): an ion that migrates to the cathode in an electrolyte solution; a positively charged ion.

causalism (kôs'ȧ·lĭz'm): a form of mechanistic philosophy, holding that each natural event is conditioned and made possible by a preceding natural event; opposed to *teleology.*

ceboid (sē'boid): a New World monkey; uses its tail as a fifth limb.

cell (sĕl) [L. *cella,* small room]: the smallest unit of living matter potentially capable of carrying out all processes of metabolism and self-perpetuation on its own.

cellulose (sĕl'yoo·lōs): a polysaccharide composed of glucose units.

Cenozoic (sē'nō·zō'ĭk) [Gr. *kainos,* recent]: geologic era after the Mesozoic, dating approximately from 75 million years ago to present.

centriole (sĕn'trĭ·ōl): cytoplasmic organelle forming spindle pole during mitosis and meiosis.

centrolecithal (sĕn'trō·lĕs'ĭ·thăl): pertaining to eggs with yolk accumulated in center of cell, as in arthropods.

centromere (sĕn'trō·mēr): region on chromosome at which spindle fibril is attached during mitosis and meiosis.

Cephalochordata, Cephalopoda, cephalothorax (sĕf'ȧ·lō-): (1) a subphylum of chordates; the lancelets or amphioxus; (2) a class of mollusks; squids, octopuses, nautiluses; (3) the fused head and thorax in certain arthropods.

cercaria (sûr·kā'rĭ·ȧ): a larval stage in the life cycle of flukes; produced by a redia and infects fish, where it encysts.

cercopithecoid (sûr'kō·pĭ·thē'koid): Old World monkey; its tail is not used as limb.

cerebellum (sĕr'ē·bĕl'ŭm) [L. dim. of *cerebrum*]: a part of the vertebrate brain; controls muscular coordination.

cerebrum (sĕr'ē·brŭm) [L. brain]: a part of the vertebrate brain; controls many voluntary functions and is seat of higher mental capacities.

Chaetognatha (kē'tŏg·năth·ä): a phylum of wormlike enterocoelomates; animals with curved bristles on each side of mouth.

chapparal(shăp·*ȧ*·răl′): a semiarid biome characterized by dense thickets of evergreen shrubs, as in certain regions of southern California.

chelate(kē′lāt) [Gr. *chēlē,* claw]: claw-possessing, esp. a limb or appendage.

chelicera(kê·lĭ′sēr·*ȧ*): a pincerlike appendage in a subphylum of arthropods (chelicerates).

chemolithotroph(kĕm′ô·lĭth′ô·trōf) [Gr. *lithos,* stone]: an organism that manufactures food with the aid of energy obtained from chemicals and with inorganic raw materials.

chemoorganotroph(kĕm′ô·ôr·găn′ô·trōf): an organism that manufactures food with the aid of energy obtained from chemicals and with organic raw materials.

chemosynthesis(kĕm′ô·sĭn′thê·sĭs): a form of autotrophic nutrition in certain bacteria, in which energy for the manufacture of carbohydrates is obtained from inorganic raw materials.

chemotaxis(kĕm′ô·tăk·sĭs): a movement oriented by chemical stimuli.

chemotherapy(kē′mô·thĕr′*ȧ*·pĭ): use of chemicals in treatment or control of disease.

chemotropism(kê·mŏt′rô·pĭz′m): orientation of organisms or their parts in relation to chemical stimuli.

chitin(kī′tĭn): a horny organic substance forming the exoskeleton or epidermal cuticle of many invertebrates (arthropods particularly,) and the cell walls of most fungi.

chloragogue(klô′ră·gŏg) [Gr. *agōgos,* leader]: excretory cell in annelids and some other invertebrates; leads wastes from body fluids to epidermis.

chlorocruorin(klô′rŏ·kro͞o′ôr·ĭn) [L. *cruor,* blood, gore]: green blood pigment in plasma of certain annelids.

chloroplast, chlorophyll, chlorophyte(klō′rô-): (1) chlorophyll-containing plastid; (2) green light-trapping pigment essential as electron donor in photosynthesis; (3) a green alga, member of the phylum Chlorophyta.

choanocyte(kō·ăn′ô·sīt) [Gr. *choanē,* funnel]: collar cell, a type of flagellate cell found in sponges.

cholesterol(kō·lĕs′tĕr·ôl): a steroid compond present as a normal constituent in animal cells and body fluids.

choline(kō′lēn): a vitamin of the B complex.

cholinergic(kō′lĭn·ûrjik): refers to a type of nerve fiber that releases acetylcholine from the axon terminal when impulses are transmitted across synapses.

Chondrichthyes(kŏn·drĭk′thĭ·ēz): fishes with cartilage skeleton, a class of vertebrates comprising sharks, skates, rays, and related types.

Chordata(kôr·dā′t*ȧ*): animal phylum in which all members have notochord, dorsal nerve cord, and pharyngeal gill slits at some stage of life cycle.

chorion(kō′rĭ·ŏn) [Gr.]: one of the extraembryonic membranes in reptiles, birds, and mammals; forms outer cover around embryo and all other membranes and in mammals contributes to structure of placenta.

choroid(kō′roid): pigmented mid-layer in wall of vertebrate eyeball, between retina and sclera; also blood vessel-carrying membranes in vertebrate brain.

chromatid(krō′m*ȧ*·tĭd): a newly formed chromosome in mitosis and meiosis.

chromatin(krō′m*ȧ*·tĭn): the nucleoprotein of a cell nucleus as it appears in stained preparations during nondividing stages.

chromatophore(krō′m*ȧ*·tô·fōr′): pigment-containing body; refers specifically to chlorophyll-bearing granules in bacteria and to pigment cells in animals.

chromoplast(krō′mô·plăst): a pigmented plastid without chlorophyll but usually containing carotenoids.

chromosome(krō′mô·sōm): gene-containing filament in cell nucleus, becoming conspicuous during mitosis and meiosis.

Chrysophyta(krĭs′ô·fīt ä): [Gr. *chrysos,* gold]: phylum of golden-brown algae.

chymotrypsin(kī′mŏ·trĭp′sĭn): enzyme promoting protein digestion; acts in small intestine, produced in pancreas as inactive chymotrypsinogen.

Ciliophora(sĭl′ĭ·ôf′ôr*ȧ*) [L. *cilium,* eyelid]: a protozoan subphylum in which member organisms have cilia on body surface.

cilium(sĭl′ĭ·*ŭ*m): microscopic bristlelike variant of a flagellum; functions in cellular locomotion and in creation of currents in water.

circadian(sûr·kā′dĭ·*ȧ*n) [L. *circa,* about + *dies,* day]: relating to a periodicity of approximately 24 hours.

circinate(sûr′sĭ·nāt) [Gr. *kirkinos,* circle]: rolled up along an axis, as in young fern leaves.

cirrus(sĭr′*ŭ*s) [L. tuft, fringe]: a movable tuft or fingerlike projection from a cell or a body surface.

cline (klīn): a graded series of differences exhibited by members of a species along a line of geographic transition.
clitellum (klī·tĕl′ŭm) [L., packsaddle]: thickened glandular section of body wall in some annelid worms, secreting cocoon that holds fertilized eggs.
clitoris (klĭt′ô·rĭs) [Gr. *kleitoris*]: female homolog of penis, a small organ in anterior part of vulva.
cloaca (klô ā′kȧ) [L. sewer]: exit chamber from alimentary system; also serves as exit for excretory and/or reproductive system.
clone (klōn): the aggregate progeny of a cell or organism produced without sexual processes.
clupeiform (klū·pē′ĭ·fôrm) [L. *clupea*, a small river fish]: anatomical pattern among teleost fishes, characterized by soft-rayed fins, swim bladders with ducts, cycloid scales, and other traits.
Cnidaria (nī·dā′rĭ·ȧ) [Gr. *knidē*, nettle]: coelenterates; the phylum of cnidoblast-possessing animals.
cnidoblast (nī′dô·blăst): stinging cell characteristic of coelenterates; contains nematocyst.
cnidocil (nī′dô·sĭl): spike of hair trigger on cnidoblast serving in nematocyst discharge.
coccine (kŏk′sēn) [Gr. *kokkos*, grain]: pertaining to sessile protistan state of existence in which reproduction does not take place during vegetative condition.
coccus (kŏk′ŭs), pl. ***cocci*** (kŏk′sī): any spherical bacterium.
cochlea (kŏk′lê·ȧ) [Gr. *kochlias*, snail]: part of the inner ear of mammals, coiled like a snail shell.
coelacanth (sē′lȧ·kănth): a type of lobe-finned fish, nearly extinct.
coelenterate (sê·lĕn′tẽr·ât): an invertebrate animal having a single alimentary opening and tentacles with sting cells; for example, jellyfish, corals, sea anemones, hydroids.
coelom (sē′lŏm): body cavity lined entirely by mesoderm, especially by peritoneum.
coenocyte (sē′nô·sīt): a multinucleate cell, particularly among algae.
coenzyme (kō·ĕn′zīm): one of a group of organic substances required in conjunction with many enzymes; usually carries and transfers parts of molecules.
cofactor (kō′făk·tẽr): a specific substance required for the functioning of a particular enzyme; e.g., a *coenzyme*.
coitus (kō·ī′tŭs) [L. *coire*, to come together]: mating, copulation, sexual intercourse.
coleoptile (kō·lē·ŏp′tĭl): the first leaf of a monocot that forms a protective sheath around the plumule.
collagen (kŏl′ȧ·jĕn): a water-insoluble fibrous protein, chief constituent of a major type of fiber in connective tissue.
collenchyma (kŏ·lĕng′kĭ·mȧ) [Gr. *kolla*, glue]: a type of plant cell with somewhat thickened walls, especially at the angles; frequently present as support in maturing plant tissues.
colloid (kŏl′oid): a substance divided into fine particles, where each particle is larger than one of a true solution but smaller than one in a coarse suspension.
colon (kō′lŏn): the large intestine of mammals; portion of alimentary tract between caecum and rectum.
colostrum (kô·lŏs′trŭm): the first, lymphlike secretion of the mammary glands of pregnant mammals.
columella (kŏl′û·mĕl′ȧ) [L. little column]: an axial shaft; for example, in a sporangium.
commensal, commensalism (kŏ·mĕn′săl, ĭz′m) [L. *cum*, with, + *mensa*, table]: (1) an organism that lives symbiotically with a host, where the host neither benefits nor suffers from the association; (2) noun.
community (kŏm·yoo′nĭ·tĭ): the living components of an ecosystem, usually comprising populations of many different species.
compound (kŏm′pound) [L. *componere*, to put together]: a combination of atoms or ions in definite ratios, held together by chemical bonds.
conceptacle (kŏn·sĕp′tȧ·k′l) [L. *conceptaculum*, container]: a cavity containing gamete-forming structures, as in *Fucus*.
conidium, conidiophore (kô·nĭd′ĭ·ŭm, -ô·fōr′) [Gr. *konis*, dust]: (1) one of a linear series of spores formed on a conidiophore; (2) a spore-producing branch or body part in bacteria and fungi.
coniferous (kô·nĭf′ẽr·ŭs): cone-bearing.
conjugation (kŏn·joo·gă′shŭn) [L. *conjugare*, to unite]: a mating process characterized by temporary fusion of the mating partners.
convergence (kŏn·vûr′jĕns) [L. *convergere*, to turn together]: the evolution of similar characteristics in organisms of widely different ancestry.
Copepoda (kō′pê·pŏd·ȧ) [Gr. *kope*, oar]: a subclass of crustaceans.
copulation (kŏp·yoo·lā′shŭn) [L. *copulare*, to join]: mating by means of a copulatory organ.

corm (kôrm) [Gr. *kormos,* tree trunk]: an axially shortened and enlarged underground stem.
cornea (kôr'nē·ȧ) [L. *corneus,* horny]: the anterior, transparent portion of the outermost layer of the eyeball.
corolla (kō̂·rōl'ȧ) [L. little crown]: the whorl of petals in a flower.
corona (kō̂·rō'nȧ) [L. garland, crown]: any wreath or circlet of cilia, tentacles, or cells.
corpus allatum (kôr'pŭs ă·lā'tŭm) pl. ***corpora allata*** [L. added body]: endocrine gland in insect head behind brain; secretes hormone inducing larval molt.
corpus callosum (kôr'pŭs kă·lō'sŭm) pl. ***corpora callosa*** [L. hard body]: broad tract of transverse nerve fibers that unites cerebral hemispheres in mammals.
corpuscle (kôr'pŭs'l) [L. dim. of *corpus,* body]: a small, rounded structure, cell, or body.
corpus luteum (kôr'pŭs lū'tē̂·ŭm) pl. ***corpora lutea*** [L. yellow body]: progesterone-secreting bodies in vertebrate ovaries, formed from remnants of follicles after ovulation.
cortex (kôr'tĕks) pl. ***cortices*** [L. bark]: the outer layers of an organ or body part; for example, adrenal cortex, cerebral cortex, stem cortex.
cotyledon (kŏt'ĭ·lē'dŭn) [Gr. *kotylēlōn,* a cup shape]: the first leaf of a seed plant, developed by embryo in seed.
cotylosaur (kŏt'ĭ·lō̂ sôr') [Gr. *kotylē,* something hollow]: a member of a group of Permian fossil reptiles, evolved from labyrinthodont amphibian stock and ancestral to all other reptiles.
covalence (kō·vā'lĕnts): electron sharing between two or more atoms.
cretinism (krē'tĭn·ĭz'm) [fr. L. *christianus,* a Christian]: an abnormal condition in man resulting from underactivity of the thyroid in the young.
crinoid (krī'noid) [Gr. *krinoeides,* lilylike]: a member of a class of echinoderms; a sea lily or feather star.
Crustacea (krŭs·tā'shē ȧ) [L. *crusta,* shell, rind]: a class of mandibulate arthropods; crustaceans.
Cryptophyceae (krĭp'tō̂·fī'sē̂·ē) [Gr. *kryptos,* hidden]: a class of algae, vaguely related to dinoflagellates.
crystalloid (krĭs'tăl·oid) [Gr. *krystallos,* ice]: a system of particles in a medium, able to form crystals under appropriate conditions; a substance that forms a true solution.
ctenoid (tĕn'oid) [Gr. *ktenoeides,* comb]: a type of fish scale with toothed margins.
Ctenophora (tē̂·nŏf'ō̂·rä): a phylum of radiate animals characterized by comb plates; the comb jellies.
CTP: abbreviation of cytidine triphosphate.
cutaneous (kū̂·tā'nē̂·ŭs) [L. *cutis,* skin]: pertaining to the skin; for example, cutaneous sense organ.
Cyanophyta (sī·ă·nŏf'·ĭtä): the phylum of blue-green algae.
cycloid (sī'kloid) [Gr. *kyklos,* circle]: a type of fish scale, smooth, round, and with concentric rings of growth.
cyclosis (sī·klō'sĭs) [Gr. *kyklos,* circle]: circular streaming and eddying of cytoplasm.
cytidine (di-, tri-) phosphates (sī'tĭ·dēn): cytosine-ribose-phosphates (CDP, CTP).
cytidylic acid: equivalent to cytosine monophosphate (CMP).
cytochrome (sī'tō̂·krōm): one of a group of iron-containing hydrogen or electron carriers in cell metabolism.
cytokinin (sī'tō̂·kī'nĭn): one of a group of adenine derivatives functioning as growth hormones in plants.
cytolysis (sī·tŏl'ĭ·sĭs): dissolution or disintegration of a cell.
cyton (sī'tŏn): the nucleus-containing main portion (cell body) of a neuron.
cytoplasm (sī'tō̂·plăz'm): the substance of a cell between cell membrane and nucleus.
cytosine (sī'tō̂·sēn): a nitrogen base in nucleotides and nucleic acids.

deamination (dē·ămĭ·nā'shŭn): removal of an amino group, especially from an amino acid.
decapod (dĕk'ä·pŏd) [Gr. *deka,* ten]: 10-footed animal, specifically decapod crustacean (for example, lobster), decapod mollusk (for example, squid).
decarboxylation (dē·kär·bŏk'sĭ·lā'shŭn): removal of a carboxyl group (—COOH).
deciduous (dē̂·sĭd'ū̂·ŭs) [L. *decidere,* to fall off]: to fall off at maturity, as in trees that shed foliage in autumn.
dedifferentiation (dē'dĭf·ĕr·ĕn'shĭ·ā'shŭn): a regressive change toward a more primitive, embryonic, or earlier state; for example, a process changing a highly specialized cell to a less specialized cell.
degrowth (dē'grōth): negative growth; becoming smaller.

dehydrogenase (dḗ·hī'drŏ·jĕn·ās): an enzyme promoting dehydrogenation.
dehydrogenation (dē'hī·drŏj'ĕ·nā'shŭn): removal of hydrogen from a compound.
denaturation (dē·nā'tûr·ā'shŭn): physical disruption of the three-dimensional structure of a protein molecule.
dendrite (dĕn'drīt) [Gr. *dendron,* tree]: filamentous outgrowth of a nerve cell; conducts nerve impulses from free end toward the cell body.
denitrify, denitrification (dē·nī'trĭ·fī): (1) to convert nitrates to ammonia and molecular nitrogen, as by denitrifying bacteria; (2) noun.
denticle (dĕn'tĭ·k'l) [L. *denticulus,* small tooth]: small toothlike scale, as on shark skin.
deoxyribose (dĕ·ŏk'sĭ·rī'bōs): a 5-carbon sugar having one oxygen atom less than parent–sugar ribose; component of deoxyribose nucleic acid (DNA).
dermis (dûr'mĭs): the inner, mesodermal layer of skin; overlain by *epidermis.*
detorsion (dē·tôr'shŭn): reversal of torsion, as in certain snails, where developmental detorsion produces an uncoiled shell.
Deuterostomia (dū'tĕr·ŏ·stō'mē·ȧ) [Gr. *deuteros,* second]: animals in which blastopore becomes anus; mouth forms as second embryonic opening opposite blastopore.
diabetes (dī'ȧ·bē'tēz) [Gr. *diabainein,* to pass through]: abnormal condition marked by insufficiency of insulin, sugar excretion in urine, high blood-glucose levels.
diaphragm (dī'ȧ·frăm) [Gr. *diaphrassein,* to barricade]: muscular partition separating thoracic and abdominal cavities in mammals.
diastole (dī·ăs'tŏ·lē) [Gr. *diastolē,* moved apart]: phase of relaxation of atria or ventricles, during which they fill with blood; preceded and succeeded by contraction, or systole.
diastrophism (dī·ăs'trŏ·fĭz'm) [Gr. *diastrophē,* distortion]: geologic deformation of the earth's crust, leading to rise of land masses.
diatom (dī'ȧ·tŏm) [Gr. *diatomos,* cut in half]: any of a class of golden-brown algae.
dichotomy (dī·kŏt'ŏ mĭ) [Gr. *dicha,* in two + *temnein,* to cut]: a repeatedly bifurcating pattern of branching.
dicotyledon (dī·kŏt'ĭ·lēdŭn) [Gr. *kotylēdōn,* a cup shape]: a plant having two seed leaves or cotyledons; often abbreviated as dicot.
dictyostele (dĭk'tĭ·ŏ·stē'lē): a type of stele in which the vascular tissue is arranged in circularly placed bundles.
diencephalon (dī'ĕn·sĕf'*a*·lŏn) [Gr. *enkephalos,* brain]: hind portion of the vertebrate forebrain.
differentiation (dĭf'ĕr·ĕn'shĭ·ā'shŭn): a progressive change toward a permanently more mature, advanced, or specialized state.
diffusion (dĭ·fū'zhŭn) [L. *diffundere,* to pour out]: migration of particles from a more concentrated to a less concentrated region, leading to equalization of concentrations.
dimorphism (dī·môr'fĭz'm): difference of form between two members of a species, as between males and females; a special instance of polymorphism.
Dinophyceae (dĭ'nŏ·fī'sē·ē): a class of Pyrrophyta.
dioecious (dī·ē'shŭs) [Gr. *oikos,* house]: megaspores and microspores are produced in different individuals of a heterosporous plant species.
dipeptide (dī·pĕp'tīd): a compound formed by the union of two amino acid molecules via a peptide bond.
dipleurula (dī·ploor'ŭ·lȧ): hypothetical ancestral form of most enterocoelomate animals, resembling developmental stage of hemichordates and echinoderms.
diplohaplontic (dĭp'lŏ·hăp·lŏn'tĭk): designating a life cycle with alternation of diploid and haploid generations.
diploid (dĭp'loid): a chromosome number twice that characteristic of a gamete in a particular species.
diplontic (dĭp·lŏn'tĭk): designating a life cycle with gametogenic meiosis and diploid adults.
disaccharide (dī·săk'ă rĭd) [Gr. *sakcharon,* sugar]: a sugar composed of two monosaccharides; usually refers to 12-carbon sugars.
dissociation (dĭ·sō'sĭ·ā'shŭn) [L. *dissociare,* to dissociate]: the breakup of a covalent compound in water; results in formation of free ions.
disulfide bond (dī·sŭl'fīd): —S—S—, a bond formed by union of two sulfur atoms.
diurnal (dī·ûr'năl) [L. *diurnalis,* daily]: for example, as in daily up and down migration of plankton in response to absence or presence of sunlight.
divergence (dī·vûr'jĕns) [L. *divergere,* to incline apart]: evolutionary development of dissimilar characteristics in two or more lines descended from the same ancestral stock.
DNA: abbreviation of deoxyribose nucleic acid.
dominance: a functional attribute of genes; the

dominant effect of a gene masks the recessive effect of its allelic partner.

ductus arteriosus (dŭk′tŭs är·tē′rĭ·ō′sŭs): an artery in the embryo and fetus of mammals that conducts blood from the pulmonary artery to the aorta; shrivels at birth, when lungs become functional.

duodenum (dū′ô·dē′nŭm) [L. *duodeni,* twelve each]: most anterior portion of the small intestine of vertebrates.

ecdysone (ĕk′dĭ·sōn) [Gr. *ekdysis,* getting out]: insect hormone produced in prothoracic gland, triggers molting and metamorphosis.

Echinodermata (ê·kī′nô·dûr′mȧ·tȧ): the phylum of spiny-skinned animals; includes starfishes, sea urchins.

Echiuroida (ê·kĭ′ûr·oi′dȧ): a phylum of wormlike, schizocoelomate animals, characterized by spines at hind end.

ecology (ē·kŏl′ô·jĭ) [Gr. *oikos,* house]: subscience of biology dealing with interrelations of organisms and their environment.

ecosystem (ē′kô·sĭs·tĕm): an ecological unit consisting of a community and its environment.

ectoderm (ĕk′tô-): outer tissue layer of an animal embryo.

Ectoprocta (ĕk′tô·prŏk·tȧ): a phylum of sessile coelomate animals in which the anus opens outside the lophophore.

effector (ê·fĕk′tẽr): in steady-state control, the component that carries out the response; e.g., muscles, glands.

egestion (ê·jĕs′chŭn) [L. *egerere,* to discharge]: elimination of unusable and undigested material from the alimentary system.

elasmobranch (ê·lăs′mô·brăngk) [Gr. *elasmos,* plate]: a member of a subclass of cartilage fishes (sharks and rays); also used as adjective.

elater (ĕl′ȧ·tẽr) [Gr. *elatēr,* driver]: a hygroscopic filament in the sporangium of, for example, certain bryophyte groups; functions in spore dispersal.

electrolyte (ê·lĕk′trô·līt) [Gr. *ēlektron,* amber]: a substance that dissociates as ions in aqueous solution; permits conduction of electric current through the solution.

electron (ê·lĕk′trŏn): a subatomic particle that carries a unit of negative electric charge; orbits around atomic nucleus.

electrovalence (ê·lĕk′trô·vā′lĕns): electron transfer between two or more atoms.

element (ĕl′ê·mĕnt): one of 105 distinct types of matter, which, singly or in combination, compose all materials of the universe; an atom is the smallest representative unit of an element.

emboly (ĕm′bô·lĭ): invaginative gastrulation.

embryo (ĕm′brĭ·ō) [Gr. *en* in, + *bryein,* to swell]: an early developmental stage of an organism following fertilization.

emulsion (ê·mŭl′shŭn) [L. *emulgere,* to milk out]: a colloidal system in which both the dispersed and the continuous phase are liquid.

endemic (ĕn·dĕm′ĭk) [Gr. belonging to a district]: pertaining to or occurring in a limited locality; opposite of cosmopolitan.

endergonic (ĕn′dẽr·gŏ·nĭk): energy-requiring, as in a chemical reaction.

endocrine (ĕn′·dô·krīn) [Gr. *krinein,* to separate]: applied to type of gland that releases secretion not through a duct but directly into blood or lymph; equivalent to hormone-producing.

endocytosis (ĕn′dô·sī·tō′sĭs): intake of fluid (*pinocytosis*) or particulates (*phagocytosis*) into a cell by engulfment.

endoderm, endodermis (ĕn′dô·dûrm): (1) innermost tissue layer of an embryo; (2) single layer of tissue in a root or stem separating cortex from stele.

endoplasm, endoplasmic (ĕn′dô·plăz′m): (1) the portion of cellular cytoplasm immediately surrounding the nucleus; contrasts with ectoplasm or cortex, the portion of cytoplasm immediately under the cell surface; (2) adjective.

endorphin (ĕn·dôr′fĭn): one of a group of pain-suppressing hormones found in the brain and pituitary of vertebrates.

endosperm (ĕn′dô·spûrm): triploid, often nutritive tissue in seed, formed by union of one sperm nucleus with two polar nuclei of female gametophyte.

endospore (ĕn′dô·spōr): a dormant cell commonly formed in bacteria.

endothermic (ĕn′dô·thûrm′ĭk): heat-requiring, as in a chemical reaction.

energy (ĕn′ẽr·jĭ) [Gr. *energos,* active]: capacity to do work; the time rate of doing work is called power.

enkephalin (ĕn·kĕf′ȧ·lĭn): a pain-suppressing hormone of the vertebrate brain; functions similarly to endorphin.

enterocoel, enterocoelomate (ĕn′tẽr·ô·sēl′): (1) a coelom formed by outpouching of a mesodermal sac from endoderm; (2) an animal having an enterocoel.

enterokinase (ĕn′tĕr·ô·kē′nā) [Gr. *kinētos,* moving]: an enzyme in intestinal juice that converts trypsinogen to trypsin.

enthalpy (ĕn′thăl·pĭ) [Gr. *enthalpein,* to warm in]: a measure of the amount of energy in a reacting system.

Entoprocta (ĕn′tô·prŏk′tȧ): a phylum of sessile pseudocoelomate animals in which the anus opens inside a ring of ciliated tentacles.

entrainment (ĕn·trān′mĕnt): synchronization of a rhythmic behavior and rhythmic environmental stimuli.

entropy (ĕn′trô·pĭ) [Gr. *entropia,* transformation]: a measure of the distribution of energy in a reacting system.

enzyme (ĕn′zīm) [Gr. *en,* in + *zymē,* leaven]: a protein capable of accelerating a particular chemical reaction; a type of catalyst.

ephyra (ĕf′ĭr·ȧ): attached polyplike larval stage in development of jellyfishes (Scyphozoa).

epiboly (ê·pĭb′ô·lĭ) [Gr. *epibolē,* throwing over]: gastrulation by overgrowth of animal upper region over vegetal lower region of blastula.

epidermis (ĕp′ĭ·dûr′mĭs): the outermost surface tissue of an organism.

epididymis (ĕp′ĭ·dĭd′ĭ mĭs) [Gr. *didymos,* testicle]: the coiled portion of the sperm duct adjacent to the mammalian testis.

epiglottis (ĕp′ĭ·glŏt′ĭs) [Gr. *glōssa,* tongue]: a flap of tissue above the mammalian glottis; covers the glottis in swallowing and thereby closes the air passage to the lungs.

epilimnion (ĕp′ĭ·lĭm′nĭ·ŏn) [Gr. *limne,* lake]: water layer overlying the thermocline in a lake.

epinasty (ĕp′ĭ·năs′tĭ) [Gr. *nastos,* pressed together]: faster growth on the upper or inner surface of a leaf or other flattened plant part, leading to outfolding.

epinephrine (ĕp′ĭ·nĕf′rĭn) [Gr. *epi* + *nephros,* kidney]: one of the neurotransmitter hormones, also called *adrenaline;* mediates synaptic transmission of impulses in parasympathetic nervous system; also secreted by adrenal medulla.

epiphyte (ĕ′pĭ·fīt): a plant that lives as a commensal on another plant.

episiotomy (ê·pĭz′ĭ·ŏt′ô·mĭ) [Gr. *epision,* pubic region]: surgical incision of vulvar region to prevent laceration during childbirth.

epitheca (ĕp′ĭ·thē′kȧ): the larger half of a diatom shell.

epithelium (ĕp′ĭ·thē′lĭ·ŭm) [Gr. *thēlē,* nipple]: animal tissue type in which cells are packed tightly together, leaving little intercellular space.

esophagus (ê·sŏf′ȧ·gŭs) [Gr. *oisō,* I shall carry]: part of alimentary tract that connects pharynx and stomach.

estrogen (ĕs′trô·jĕn) [Gr. *oistros,* frenzy]: one of a group of female sex hormones of vertebrates.

estrus (ĕs′trŭs) [L. *oestrus,* gadfly]: egg production and fertilizability in mammals; for example, estrus cycle, monestrous, polystrous.

etiolation (ē′tĭ·ô·lā′shŭn) [F. *étioler,* to blanch]: pathological condition in plants produced by prolonged absence of light; characterized by whitened leaves, excessively long, weak stems.

eukaryote (yoo·kăr′ē·ōt) [Gr. *eu-,* true + *karyon,* nucleus]: any of a group of organisms in which cells have membrane-bounded nuclei and nucleoprotein chromosomes.

Eumetazoa (yoo·mĕt·ȧ·zō′ȧ): a taxonomic branch of Metazoa, comprising all animals except the Parazoa (sponges).

eurypterid (ū·rĭp′tĕr·ĭd) [Gr. *eurys,* wide]: extinct Paleozoic chelicerate arthropod.

eustachian (û·stā′shŭn): applied to canal connecting middle-ear cavity and pharynx of mammals.

eutrophic (yoo·trō′fĭk) [Gr. *eutrophos,* well-nourished]: relating to a body of water rich in dissolved nutrients, e.g., phosphates, nitrates.

exergonic (ĕk′sĕr·gŏ·nĭk): energy-yielding, as in a chemical reaction.

exocrine (ĕk′sô·krīn): applied to type of gland that releases secretion through a duct.

exocytosis (ĕk′sô·sī·tō′sĭs): expulsion of fluid or particulate matter from a cell.

exteroceptor (ĕk′stĕr·ô·sĕp′tĕr): a sense organ receptive to stimuli from external environment.

FAD: abbreviation of flavin adenine dinucleotide.

feces (fē′sēz) [L. *faeces,* dregs]: waste matter discharged from the alimentary system through the anus.

feedback (fēd′băk): in steady-state control, the return to the receptor of part of the response of an effector, resulting in a new stimulus-response sequence.

fermentation (fûr′mĕn·tā′shŭn): synonym for anaerobic respiration; fuel combustion in the absence of oxygen.

fertilization (fûr′tĭl·ĭ·zā′shŭn): the merging of gamete nuclei, resulting in a zygote nucleus.

fetus (fē′tŭs) [L. offspring]: prenatal stage of mammalian development following the embryonic stage; in humans, roughly from third month of pregnancy to birth.

fiber (fī′bẽr) [L. *fibra,* thread]: a strand or filament produced by cells but located outside cells; also a type of sclerenchyma cell.

fibril (fī′brĭl) [L. dim. of *fibra*]: a strand of filament produced by cells and located inside cells.

fibrin, fibrinogen (fī′brĭn, fī·brĭn′ô·jĕn): (1) coagulated blood protein forming the bulk of a blood clot in vertebrates; (2) a blood protein which on coagulation forms a clot.

fibroblast (fī′brô·blăst): a type of mesenchyme cell, representing a major cell type in connective tissue.

flagellate, flagellum (flăj′ĕ·lāt, -ŭm) [L. whip]: (1) equipped with one or more flagella; an organism or cell with flagella; (2) a microscopic, whiplike filament serving as locomotor structure in flagellate cells.

flame bulb (flām bŭlb): a cup-shaped cell with a tuft of flagella at the bottom of the cup, serving as filtering component in excretory systems of many invertebrates.

flavin: multiple-ring compound forming component of riboflavin and hydrogen carriers such as FAD and FMN.

floridean (flô·rĭd′ê·ăn): pertaining to red algae.

florigen (flō′rĭ·jĕn): flowering stimulus believed to be produced as a result of appropriate photoperiodic treatment of plants.

fluorescence (flo͞o′ô·rĕs′ĕns) [L. *fluere,* to flow]: emission of radiation (light) by a substance that has absorbed radiation from another source.

folic acid (fŏl′ĭk): a vitamin of the B complex.

follicle (fŏl′ĭ·k′l) [L. *folliculus,* small ball]: ball of cells; as in egg-containing balls in ovaries of many animals, or cellular balls at base of hair of feather.

food (fūd): an organic nutrient.

Foraminifera (fŏ·răm̂ĭ·nĭf′ẽr·ȧ) [L. *foramen,* hole]: sarcodine protozoa characterized by calcareous shells with holes through which pseudopods are extruded.

fossil (fŏs′ĭl): any remnant or trace of an organism of past ages preserved in some way in the earth's crust.

fovea centralis (fō′vê·ȧ sĕn·trā′lĭs) [L. central pit]: small area in optic center of mammalian retina; only cone cells are present here and stimulation leads to most acute vision.

fucoxanthin (fū′kô·zăn′thĭn): a brownish pigment found in diatoms, brown algae, and dinoflagellates.

galactose (gȧ·lăk′tōs) [L. *galact-,* milk]: a 6-carbon sugar.

gametangium (găm′ê·tăn′jĭ·ŭm): cell, tissue, or organ in which gametes are formed, particularly in protists and plants.

gamete (găm′ēt): reproductive cell that must fuse with another before it can develop; sex cell.

gametophyte (găm·ē′tô·fīt): a gamete-producing plant; phase of life cycle in diplohaplontic organisms that alternates with a sporophyte phase.

ganglion (găng′glĭ·ŭn) [Gr. a swelling]: a localized collection of cell bodies of neurons, typically less complex than a brain.

ganoid (găn′oid) [Gr. *ganos,* brightness]: pertaining to shiny, enamel-covered type of fish scale.

gastrea (găs′trê·ȧ): a hypothetical gastrulalike organism postulated by Haeckel to have been ancestral to Eumetazoa; a theoretical conception no longer accepted today.

gastrin (găs′trĭn): a hormone produced by the stomach wall of mammals when food makes contact with the wall; stimulates other parts of the wall to secrete gastric juice.

gastrodermis (găs′trô·dûrm′ĭs): the inner, digestive tissue layer in coelenterates.

Gastropoda (găs·trŏp′ô·dȧ) a class of mollusks; comprises snails and slugs.

Gastrotricha (găs′trŏt′rĭ·kȧ): a class of minute, aquatic, pseudocoelomate animals, members of the phylum Aschelminthes.

gastrozooid (găs′trŏ·zōóid): a feeding individual in a polymorphic colony.

gastrula, gastrulation (găs′troo·lȧ, -lā′shŭn): (1) a two-layered and later three-layered stage in the embryonic development of animals; (2) the process of gastrula formation.

gel (jĕl) [L. *gelare,* to freeze]: quasi-solid state of a colloidal system, where the solid particles form the continuous phase and the liquid is the dispersed phase.

gemma (jĕm′ȧ) [L. a bud]: vegetative bud in cup-shaped growth on bryophyte body, capable of developing into whole plant.

gemmule (jĕm′ūl): vegetative, multicellular bud of (largely freshwater) sponges.

gene (jēn) a segment of a chromosome, definable in operational terms as a unit of biochemical action; repository of genetic information.

genetic code (jĕ·nĕt′ĭk kōd′): universal biochemical basis of heredity, consisting of a sequence of DNA triplets (codons) that determines the specific amino acid sequence in proteins.

genome (jēn′ōm): the totality of genes in a haploid set of chromosomes, hence the sum of all different genes in a cell.

genotype (jĕn′ô·tīp): the particular set of genes in an organism and its cells; the genetic constitution.

genus (jē′nŭs) [L. race]: a rank category in taxonomic classification between species and family; a group of closely related species.

geotropism (jē·ŏt′rō·pĭz′m) [Gr. *tropē*, a turning]: behavior governed and oriented by gravity; e.g., growth of roots toward center of the earth.

gestation (jĕs·tā′shŭn): process or period of carrying offspring in uterus.

gibberellin (jĭb·ĕr·ĕl′ĭn): one of a group of growth hormones in plants; promotes elongation of internodes in shoots and stems.

globin (glō′bĭn): a protein; in combination with heme it forms hemoglobin.

globulin (glŏb′ū·lĭn): one of a class of proteins in blood plasma of vertebrates; can function as antibody.

glochidia (glô·kĭd′ĭă) [Gr. *glochis*, arrow point]: pincer-equipped bivalve larvae of freshwater clams, parasitic on fish.

glomerulus (glô·mĕr′ū·lŭs) [L. dim. of *glomus*, ball]: small meshwork of blood capillaries or channels, as in a vertebrate nephron.

glottis (glŏt′ĭs) [Gr. *glōssa*, tongue]: slitlike opening in mammalian larynx formed by vocal cords.

glucagon (gloo′kȧ·gŏn) [Gr. *glyk-*, sweet + *agon*, driving]: a pancreatic protein hormone, secreted from the islets of Langerhans; promotes conversion of glycogen to glucose and thus is antagonistic to action of insulin.

glucogenic (glōo′kô·jĕn′ĭk): glucose-producing, esp. amino acids which, after deamination, metabolize like carbohydrates.

glucose (gloo′kōs): a 6-carbon sugar; main form in which carbohydrates are transported from cell to cell.

glycerol (glĭs′ĕr·ôl): an organic compound with a 3-carbon skeleton; can unite with fatty acids and form a fat; syn. *glycerin*.

glycine (glī′sēn): the structurally simplest amino acid.

glycocalyx (glī′kô·kā′lĭks): a coating around the plasma membrane of many types of animal cells, formed from glycoproteins and glycolipids.

glycogen (glī′kô·jĕn): a polysaccharide composed of glucose units; a main storage form of carbohydrates.

glycolysis (glī·kŏl′ĭ·sĭ): respiratory breakdown of carbohydrates to pyruvic acid.

glyoxysome (glī·ŏk′sĭ·sōm): a type of microbody, a cytoplasmic vesicular organelle containing catalases, oxidases, and other enzymes, particularly in plant cells.

goiter (goi′tĕr) [L. *guttur*, throat]: an enlargement of the thyroid gland.

Golgi apparatus (body) (gôl′jê): a cytoplasmic organelle playing a role in the manufacture of cell secretions.

gonad (gōn′ăd) [Gr. *gonē*, generator]: animal reproductive organ; collective term for testes and ovaries.

gonadotropin (gō·năd·ô·trō′pĭn): one of a group of hormones stimulating growth of gonads; secreted by anterior lobe of the pituitary.

gonopore (gŏn′ô·pôr): the exterior opening of a reproductive system.

gonozooid (gōn′ŏ·zō′oid): a reproductive individual in a polymorphic colony.

gradation (grâ·dā′shŭn) [L. *gradus*, step]: leveling of land by geologic effects of erosion.

granum (grăn′ŭm) [L. grain]: a functional unit of a chloroplast; smallest particle capable of carrying out photosynthesis.

guanine (gŭ′â·nēn): purine component of nucleotides and nucleic acids.

guanosine (di-, tri-) phosphates (gū·â′nô·sēn): guanine-ribose-phosphates (GDP, GTP).

guanylic acid: equivalent to guanosine monophosphate, or GMP.

guttation (gŭ·tā′shūn) [L. *gutta*, drop]: extrusion of water droplets from leaf pores by root pressure.

gymnosperms (jĭm′nô·spûrm): a plant belonging to a class of seed plants in which the seeds are not enclosed in an ovary; includes the conifers.

habitat (hăb′ĭ·tăt) [L. *habitare,* to inhabit]: the geographic region where an organism or a collection of organisms normally lives.

habituation (hȧ·bĭt′yoo·ā′shŭn): a primitive form of learning, based on repetition of the same stimulus.

haltere (häl′tēr) [Gr. *haltēr,* leaping]: one of a pair of club-shaped organs in the insect order Diptera, representing the modified second pair of wings and functioning as sensory instruments in flight.

haploid (hăp′loid): a chromosome number characteristic of a mature gamete of a given species.

haplontic (hăp·lŏn′tĭk): designating a life cycle with zygotic meiosis and haploid adults.

helix (hē′liks) [L. a spiral]: spiral shape; e.g., polypeptide chain, snail shell.

heme (hēm): an iron-containing red blood pigment.

Hemichordata (hĕm′ĭ·kŏr dă′tȧ): a phylum of enterocoelomate animals.

hemoglobin (hē′mô·glō′bĭn) [L. *globus,* globe]: oxygen-carrying constituent of blood; consists of red pigment heme and protein globin.

hemophilia (hē′mô fĭl′ĭȧ) [Gr. *philos,* loving]: hereditary disease in man characterized by excessive bleeding from even minor wounds; clotting mechanism is impaired by failure of blood platelets to rupture.

hepatoma (hĕp′ȧ·tō′mȧ): a liver tumor.

herbaceous (hēr·bā′shŭs): herblike; without wood.

herbivore (hûr′bĭ·vōr) [L. *herba,* herb + *vorare,* to devour]: a plant-eating animal.

hermaphrodite (hûr·măf′rô·dīt) [fr. Gr. *Hermes* + *Aphrodite*]: an organism that contains both male and female reproductive structures.

heterocyst (hĕt′ĕr·ô·sĭst′): colorless cell in filamentous blue-green algae; functions as center for nitrogen fixation.

heterosporous (hĕt′ĕr·ŏs′pô·rŭs): producing two different types of spores, microspores and megaspores; microspores give rise to male gametophytes, megaspores to female gametophytes.

heterotroph, heterotrophism (hĕt′ĕr·ô·trŏf): (1) an organism dependent on both inorganic and organic raw materials from the environment; (2) form of nutrition characteristic of heterotrophs.

heterozygote (hĕt′ĕr·ô·zī′gōt): an organism in which a pair of alleles for a given trait consists of different (for example, dominant and recessive) kinds of genes.

hexose (hĕk′sōs): group name for any 6-carbon monosaccharide.

hippocampus (hĭp·ô·kăm′pŭs) [Gr., seahorse]: a broad nerve tract in the brain that connects the left and right cerebral hemispheres.

histamine (hĭss′tȧ·mēn): a nitrogenous compound that increases permeability of blood vessels and plays a major role in allergic reactions.

histone (hĭss′tōn): one of a group of proteins containing a high proportion of basic amino acids; associated with DNA in nucleoprotein.

holothuroid (hŏl·ô·thū′·roid) [L. *holothuria,* water polyp]: a member of a class of echinoderms; a sea cucumber.

holotroph, holotrophism (hō′lô·trŏf): (1) a bulk-feeding organism; nutrition usually includes alimentation; (2) form of nutrition characteristic of holotrophs.

homeostasis (hō′mē·ô·stā′sĭs) [Gr. *homos,* same + *stasis,* state]: a dynamic equilibrium, or steady state, which tends to maintain itself despite external or internal stresses.

hominid (hŏm′ĭ·nĭd) [L. *homo,* man]: a living or extinct man or manlike type; the family of man or pertaining to this family.

hominoid (hŏm′ĭ·noid): superfamily including hominids, the family of man, and pongids, the family of apes.

homology (hô·mŏl′ô·jĭ) [Gr. *homologia,* agreement]: similarity in embryonic development and adult structure, indicative of common evolutionary ancestry.

homosporous (hô·mŏs′pô·rŭs): producing spores of the same size or form; each gives rise either to a male or to a female gametophyte.

homozygote (hō′mô·zī′gōt): an organism in which a pair of alleles for a given trait consists of the same (e.g., either dominant or recessive, but not both) kinds of genes.

hormogone (hôr′mô·gōn): a section of a filament of blue-green algae, located between two consecutive heterocysts.

hormone (hôr′mōn) [Gr. *hormaein,* to excite]: a secretion produced in an organism and affecting another part of that organism.

humoral (hū′mĕr·ăl) [L. *humor,* moisture, liquid]: pertaining to body fluids, esp. biologically active chemical agents carried in body fluids; e.g., hormones or similar substances.

humus (hū'mŭs) [L. soil]: the organic portion of soil.

hybrid (hī'brĭd) [L. *hibrida,* offspring of tame sow and wild boar]: an organism heterozygous for one or more (usually many) gene pairs.

hydathode (hī'dȧ·thōd) [Gr. *hydatis,* water vesicle]: channel or gland in leaf for water excretion.

hydranth (hī'drănth): flowerlike terminal part of coelenterate polyp, containing mouth and tentacles; a feeding polyp.

hydrolysis (hī·drŏl'ĭ·sĭs): dissolution through the agency of water; esp. decomposition of a chemical by addition of water.

hydrophyte (hī'drō̍·fīt): a water plant, or one living in water-rich areas.

hydroponics (hī'drō̍·pŏn'ĭks)[Gr. *ponos,* labor]: plant culture without soil by immersing the roots in a nutrient-rich water medium.

hyperopia (hī·pēr·ō'pĭ·ȧ): farsightedness; visual images focus behind the retina.

hyperparasitism (hī'pēr-): infection of a parasite by one or more other parasites.

hypertonic (hī'pēr·tŏn'ĭk): exerting greater osmotic pull than the medium on the other side of a semipermeable membrane; hence having a greater concentration of particles and acquiring water during osmosis.

hypha (hī'fȧ) [Gr. *hyphē,* a web]: a filamentous structural unit of a fungus; a meshwork of hyphae forms a mycelium.

hypocotyl (hī'pō̍·kŏt'l): the part of a plant embryo or seedling below the cotyledon.

hypolimnion (hī·pō̍·lĭm'nĭ·ŏn) [Gr. *limnē,* lake]: the water below the thermocline in a lake.

hyponasty (hī'pō̍·năs'tĭ) [Gr. *nastos,* pressed together]: faster growth on the lower or outer surface of a leaf or other flattened plant part, leading to infolding.

hypothalamus: forebrain region containing various centers of the autonomic nervous system.

hypotheca (hī'pō̍·thē'kȧ): the smaller half of a diatom shell.

hypothesis (hī·pŏth'ē̍·sĭs) [Gr. *tithenai,* to put]: a guessed solution of a scientific problem; must be tested by experimentation.

hypotonic (hī'pō̍·tŏn'ĭk): exerting lesser osmotic pull than the medium on the other side of a semipermeable membrane; hence having a lesser concentration of particles and losing water during osmosis.

ichthyosaur (ĭk'thĭ·ō̍·sôr): extinct marine Mesozoic reptile, with fish-shaped body and porpoiselike snout.

imago, imaginal (ĭ·mā'gō, ĭ·măj'ĭ·nȧl) [L. image]: (1) an adult insect; (2) adjective.

immunoglobulin (ĭm'yoo·nō̍·glŏb'yoo·lĭn): a protein that functions as an antibody; formed in response to an antigen.

imprinting (ĭm·prĭn'tĭng): a special form of learning that occurs soon after hatching in many social vertebrates; involves recognition and identification of, and fixation on, traits of the parent organisms (or experimental surrogates).

induction (ĭn·dŭk'shŭn) [L. *inducere,* to induce]: process in animal embryo in which one tissue or body part causes the differentiation of another.

indusium (ĭn·dū'zĭŭm) [L. undergarment]: tissue covering sori in ferns.

ingestion (ĭn·jĕs'chŭn) [L. *ingerere,* to put in]: intake of food from the environment into the alimentary system.

insulin (ĭn'sū̍·lĭn) [L. *insula,* island]: hormone produced in the pancreas; promotes conversion of blood glucose to tissue glycogen.

integument (ĭn·tĕg'ū̍·mĕnt) [L. *integere,* to cover]: covering; external coat; skin.

interferon (ĭn·tēr·fēr'ŏn): one of a group of proteins produced by cells after invasion of viruses; tends to prevent or inhibit viral infections.

intermedin (ĭn·tēr·mē'dĭn): hormone produced by the mid-portion of the pituitary gland.

internode (ĭn'tēr·nōd): section of a plant stem between two successive nodes.

interoceptor (ĭn'tēr·ō̍·sĕp'tēr): a sense organ receptive to stimuli generated in the interior of an organism.

interstitial (ĭn·tēr·stĭsh'ŭl) [L. *intersistere,* to stand still in the middle]: relating to a space between closely positioned units, e.g., cells.

invagination (ĭn·vaj'ĭ·nā'shŭn) [L. *in,* + vagina, sheath]: local infolding of a layer of tissue, leading to formation of pouch or sac; as in invagination during a type of embolic gastrulation.

invertase (ĭn·vûr'tās) [L. *invertere,* to invert]: enzyme promoting a splitting of sucrose into glucose and fructose.

ion, ionization (ī'ŏn, -ĭ·zā'shŭn) [Gr. *ienai,* to go]: (1) electrically charged atom or group of atoms; (2) addition or removal of electrons from atoms.

isogamy (ī·sŏg′*ȧ*·mĭ): sexual fusion in which the gametes of opposite sex types are structurally alike.
isolecithal (ī·sȯ·lĕs′ĭ·thăl): pertaining to animal eggs with yolk evenly distributed throughout egg cytoplasm.
isomer (ī′sȯ·mẽr): one of a group of compounds identical in atomic composition but differing in structural arrangement.
isotonic (ī′sȯ·tŏn′ĭk): exerting same osmotic pull as medium or other side of a semipermeable membrane, hence having the same concentration of particles; net gain or loss of water during osmosis is zero.
isotope (ī′sȯ·tōp) [Gr. *topos,* place]: one of several possible forms of a chemical element differing from other forms in atomic weight but not in chemical properties.

karyogamy (kăr′ĭ·ŏg′·*ȧ*·mĭ) [Gr. *karyon,* nut]: fusion of nuclei during fertilization.
karyokinesis (kăr′ĭ·ȯ·kĭ·nē′sĭs): alternative name for mitotic nuclear division.
keratin (kĕr′*ȧ*·tĭn) [Gr. *keratos,* horn]: a protective protein formed by the epidermis of vertebrate skin.
ketogenic, ketone (kē′tȯ·jĕn′ĭk, -tōn): (1) keto-acid-producing, esp. amino acids which after deamination metabolize like fatty acids; (2) organic compound with a —CO— group.
kilocalorie: see *calorie.*
kinesis (kĭ·nē′sĭs): locomotor movement that changes in intensity in direct proportion with the intensity of a stimulus.
kinetochore (kĭ·nĕt′ȯ·kôr) [Gr. *kinetos,* moving + *choros,* place]: place of attachment of spindle fibril on a chromosome.
kinetosome (kĭ·nĕt′ȯ·sōm) [Gr. *kinētos,* moving]: granule at base of flagellum, presumably motion-controlling.
kinin (kī′nĭn, kĭn′ĭn) [Gr. *kinein,* to stimulate]: one of a group of plant growth hormones.
Kinorhyncha (kĭn′ȯ·rĭng′k*ȧ*): a class of pseudocoelomate animals in the phylum Aschelminthes.

labium, labial (lā′bĭ·ŭm, -ăl) [L. lip]: (1) any liplike structure, esp. underlip in insect head; (2) adjective.
labrum (lā′brŭm) [L. lip]: a liplike structure; esp. upper lip in arthropod head.
labyrinthodont (lăb′ĭ rĭn′thȯ·dŏnt) [Gr. *labyrinthos,* labyrinth]: extinct, late-Paleozoic fossil amphibian.
lacteal (lăk′tē·*ȧ*l) [L. *lactis,* milk]: lymph vessel in a villus of intestinal wall of mammals.
lactogenic (lăk′tȯ jĕn′ĭk): milk-producing; as in lactogenic hormone, secreted by vertebrate pituitary.
lamella (l*ȧ*·mĕl′*ȧ*) [L. small plate]: layer cementing adjacent plant cells in a tissue; usually called middle lamella.
lamina (lăm′ĭ·n*ȧ*) [L. thin plate]: the blade of a leaf.
larva (lär′vä) pl. ***larvae*** (-vē) [L. mask]: period in development history of animals between hatching and metamorphosis.
larynx (lăr′ĭngks) [Gr.]: voice box; sound-producing organ in mammals.
lenticel (lĕn′tĭ·sĕl) [F. *lenticelle,* little lentil]: porous region on surface of woody stem, aiding gas exchange.
leukemia (lū·kē′mĭ·*ȧ*) [Gr. *leukos,* white]: a type of cancer characterized by production of excessive amounts of leukocytes.
leukocyte (lū′kȯ·sīt): a type of white blood cell in vertebrates characterized by a beaded, elongated nucleus; formed in bone marrow.
leukoplast (lū′kȯ·plăst): an unpigmented plastid; see also *amyloplast.*
lichen (lī′kĕn) [Gr. *leichēn*]: mutualistic association of algal and fungal types.
ligament (lĭg′*ȧ*·mĕnt) [L. *ligare,* to tie, bind]: a type of connective tissue, with tough and elastic fibers arranged irregularly.
lignin (lĭg′nĭn) [L. *lignum,* wood]: a complex substance present in substantial quantities in wood.
lipase (lī′pās): enzyme promoting conversion of fat to fatty acids and glycerin or reverse.
lipid (lĭp′ĭd): fat, fatty, pertaining to fat; syn. *lipoid.*
lithosphere (lĭth′ȯ·sfēr) [Gr. *lithos,* stone]: collective term for the solid, rocky components of the earth's surface layers.
littoral (lĭt′ȯ·răl) [L. *litus,* seashore]: the sea floor from the shore to the edge of the continental shelf.
lophophore (lō′fȯ·fōr) [Gr. *lophos,* crest]: tentacle-bearing food-trapping arm in anterior region of certain coelomates (lophophorate animals).
luciferse, luciferin (lū·sĭf′ẽr·ās, -ĭn) [L. *lux,* light]: (1) enzyme contributing to production of light in organisms; (2) a group of various sub-

stances essential in the production of bioluminescence.

lutein (lū′tē·ĭn) [L. *luteus,* yellow]: a yellow xanthophyll pigment.

lycopsid (lī·kŏp′sid) [Gr. *lykos,* wolf]: a member of a subphylum of tracheophytes; the club mosses.

lymph (lĭmf) [L. *lympha,* goddess of moisture]: the body fluid outside the blood circulation.

lymphocyte (lĭm′fō·sīt): a type of white blood cell of vertebrates characterized by a rounded or kidney-shaped nucleus; formed in lymphatic tissues.

lysosome (lī′sō·sōm): a cytoplasmic vesicular organelle containing various hydrolytic enzymes.

macromolecule (măk′rō-): a molecule of very high molecular weight; refers specifically to proteins, nucleic acids, polysaccharides, and complexes of these.

macronucleus (măk′rō·nū′klē·ŭs): a large type of nucleus found in ciliate protozoa; controls all but sexual functions.

madreporite (măd′rē·pō·rīt) [It. *madre,* mother + *poro,* passage]: a sievelike opening on the surface of echinoderms; connects the water-vascular system with the outside.

malaria (mȧ·lăr′ĭ·ȧ) [It. *mala aria,* bad air]: disease produced by the protozoon *Plasmodium,* transmitted by bites of the mosquito *Anopheles,* and characterized by recurrent attacks of fever.

maltose (môl′tōs): a 12-carbon sugar formed by the union of two glucose units.

mandible (măn′dĭ·b′l) [L. *mandibula,* jaw]: in arthropods, one of a pair of mouth appendages, basically biting jaws; in vertebrates, the main support of the lower jaw.

marsupial (mär·sū′pĭ·ăl) [Gr. *marsypion,* little bag]: a pouched mammal, member of the mammalian subclass Metatheria.

mastax (măs′tăks) [L. *masticare,* to chew]: horny, toothed chewing apparatus in pharynx of rotifers.

Mastigophora (măs′tĭ gŏfôrä): the subphylum of flagellate protozoa; zooflagellates.

matrix (mā′trĭks) [L., womb]: an intercellular substance; a material in which something is embedded or enclosed.

maxilla (măk·sĭl′ȧ) [L.]: in arthropods, one of the head appendages; in vertebrates, one of the upper jawbones.

maxilliped (măk·sĭl′ĭ·pĕd): one of three pairs of segmental appendages in lobsters, located posterior to the maxillae.

medulla (mē·dŭl′ȧ) [L.]: the inner layers of an organ or body part; for example, adrenal medulla; the *medulla oblongata* is a region of the vertebrate hindbrain that connects with the spinal cord.

medusa (mē·dū′sȧ): free-swimming stage in the life cycle of coelenterates; a jellyfish.

megagametophyte (mĕg′ȧ·gȧ·mē′tō·fīt): the gametophyte produced by a megaspore; the female gametophyte.

megaphyll (mĕg′ȧ·fĭl): a leaf with numerous vascular bundles in a vein; it leaves a leaf gap in the stele of the stem.

megasporangium (mĕg′ȧ·spō·răn′jĭ·ŭm): a sporangium that produces megaspores; an ovule.

megaspore (mĕg′ȧ·spōr′): a meiospore formed in a megasporangium and developing into a megagametophyte.

megastrobilus (mĕg′ȧ·strŏ′bĭ·lŭs) [Gr. *strobilos,* a pine cone]: a megasporangium-bearing cone.

meiosis (mī·ō′sĭs) [Gr. *meioun,* to make smaller]: nuclear division in which the chromosome number is reduced by half; compensates for the chromosome-doubling effect of fertilization.

meiospore (mī′ō·spōr): a spore produced by meiosis.

melanin (mĕl′ȧ·nĭn) [Gr. *melas,* black]: black pigment in organisms.

melanophore (mĕl′ȧ·nō·fôr): a cell containing granules of melanin pigment.

menopause (mĕn′ō·pôz) [Gr. *menos,* month + *pauein,* to cause to cease]: the time at the end of the reproductive period of (human) females when menstrual cycles cease to occur.

menstruation (mĕn′stroo·ā′shŭn) [L. *mensis,* month]: discharge of uterine tissue and blood from the vagina in women and female apes at the end of a menstrual cycle in which fertilization has not occurred.

meristem (mĕr′ĭ·stĕm): embryonic tissue in plants, capable of giving rise to additional tissues.

mesencephalon (mĕs′ĕn·sĕf′ȧ·lŏn) [Gr. *enkephalos,* brain]: the vertebrate midbrain.

mesenchyme (mĕs′ĕng·kĭm) [Gr. *enchyma,* infusion]: mesodermal connective tissue cells; often jelly-secreting.

mesentery (mĕs′ĕn·tĕr·ĭ) [Gr. *mes.* middle + *enteron,* gut]: in coelomate animals, the median (dorsoventral) part of the peritoneum that suspends and supports the intestine.

mesocoel (mĕs′ô·sēl): middle coelom sac in animal embryos (e.g., enterocoelomates), located between anterior protocoel and posterior metacoel.
mesoderm (mĕs′ô·dûrm): the middle primary germ layer of animal embryos, between ectoderm and endoderm.
mesogloea (mĕs′ô·glē′*ȧ*) [Gr. *gloisos,* glutinous substance]: the often jelly-containing layer between ectoderm and endoderm of coelenterates and comb jellies.
mesonephros (mĕs′ô·nĕf′rŏs): a type of vertebrate excretory system, present in the adults of fishes and amphibia and in the embryos of reptiles, birds, and mammals.
mesophyll (mĕs′ô·fĭl): tissue in interior of leaves composed of chlorophyll-containing cells arranged either as compact layers (palisade mesophyll) or as loose aggregations (spongy mesophyll).
mesophyte (mĕs′ô·fīt): a plant adapted to live in regions with intermediate amounts of water supply.
metabolism (mĕ·tăb′ô·lĭz′m) [Gr. *metabolē,* change]: a group of life-sustaining processes including mainly nutrition, respiration, and synthesis of more living substance.
metabolite (mĕ·tăb′ô·līt): any chemical participating in metabolism; a nutrient.
metacoel (mĕt′*ȧ*·sēl): posterior coelom sac in animal embryos, e.g., enterocoelomates.
metal (mĕt′*ȧ*l): any element that ionizes by loss of electrons and thus forms cations.
metamorphosis (mĕt′*ȧ* môr′fô·sĭs) [Gr. *metamorphoun,* to transform]: transformation of a larva to an adult.
metanephros (mĕt′*ȧ*·nĕf′rŏs): a type of vertebrate excretory system present in adult reptiles, birds, and mammals.
metaphase (mĕt′ä·fāz): a stage during mitotic division in which the chromosomes line up in a plane at right angles to the spindle axis.
Metaphyta (mê·tăf′ĭ·t*ȧ*): a major category of living organisms comprising the phyla Bryophyta and Tracheophyta; plants.
metastasis (mĕ·tăs′t*ȧ*·sĭs) [Gr. *methistanai,* to change]: internal transfer of a disease-producing agency (e.g., tumor cells) from one part of the body to another (e.g., by bloodstream).
Metazoa (mĕt′*ȧ*·zō*ȧ*): a major category of living organisms comprising all animals.
metencephalon (mĕt′ĕn·sĕf′*ȧ*·lŏn) [Gr. *enkephalos,* brain]: anterior portion of vertebrate hindbrain.
microgametophyte (mī′krô-): the gametophyte produced by a microspore; the male gametophyte.
micron (mī′krŏn) pl. ***microns, micra:*** one-thousandth part of a millimeter, a unit of microscopic length; a micrometer.
micronucleus (mī′krô·nū′klê·*ŭ*s): a small type of nucleus found in ciliate protozoa; controls reproductive functions and macronucleus.
microphyll (mī′krô·fĭl): a leaf with a vein consisting of a single vascular bundle; it does not leave a leaf gap in the stele of the stem.
micropyle (mī′krô·pīl) [Gr. *pilē,* gate]: an opening in the integument of an ovule; permits entry of a pollen grain or pollen tube.
microsporangium (mī′krô·spô·răn′jĭ·*ŭ*m): a sporangium that produces microspores.
microspore (mī′krô·spōr): a meiospore formed in a microsporangium and developing into a microgametophyte; in seed plants, equivalent to pollen grain.
microstrobilus (mī′krô·strŏ′bĭ·l*ŭ*s): a microsporangium-bearing cone.
microvillus (mī′krô·vĭl′*ŭ*s): a fingerlike microscopic projection from a cell surface.
mictic (mĭk′tĭk) [Gr. *mixis,* act of mixing]: pertaining to fall and winter eggs of rotifers, which if fertilized produce males and if not fertilized produce females.
mimicry (mĭm′ĭk·rĭ) [Gr. *mimos,* mime]: the superficial resemblance of certain animals, particularly insects, to other more powerful or more protected ones, or to leaves and other plant parts.
mineral (mĭn′ẽr·*ă*l) [L. *minera,* ore]: an inorganic material.
miracidium (mī′r*ă* sĭd′ĭ·*ŭ*m): larval stage in the life cycle of flukes; develops from an egg and gives rise to a sporocyst larva.
mitochondrion (mī′tô·kŏn′drĭ·ŏn) [Gr. *mitos,* thread, + *chondros,* grain]: a cytoplasmic organelle serving as site of respiration.
mitosis (mī·tō′sĭs): nuclear division characterized by complex chromosome movements and exact chromosome duplication.
mitospore (mī′tô·spōr): a spore produced by mitosis.
mitral (mī′tr*ă*l) [fr. *miter*]: applied to valve between left atrium and ventricle of mammalian heart; syn. *bicuspid.*
modulator (mŏd′yoo·lā·tẽr): in steady-state control, a component that receives and interprets in-

coming sensory signals and releases outgoing motor signals.

mole (mōl) [L. *moles,* mass]: the gram-molecular weight of a substance; its weight in grams equal to its molecular weight.

molecule (mŏl'ĕ·kūl) [L. *moles,* mass]: a compound in which the atoms are held together by covalent bonds.

Mollusca, mollusk (mŏ·lŭs'kȧ, mŏl'ŭsk) [L. *molluscus,* soft]: (1) a phylum of nonsegmented schizocoelomate animals; (2) a member of the phylum Mollusca.

Monera (mŏn·ē'rȧ) [Gr. *monos,* alone]: a major category of living organism comprising bacteria and blue-green algae.

monestrous (mŏn·ĕs'trŭs) [Gr. *oistros,* frenzy]: having a single estrus (egg-producing) cycle during a given breeding season.

monocotyledon (mŏn'ō·kŏt'ĭ·lē'dŭn): a plant having a single seed leaf or cotyledon; often abbreviated as monocot.

monoecious (mō·nē'shŭs) [Gr. *oikos,* house]: megaspores and microspores are produced in same individual of a heterosporous plant species.

monoestrous (mŏn·ō·es'trŭs): having a single estrus cycle during a breeding season.

monophyletic (mŏn'ō·fī·lĕt'ĭk) [Gr. *phylon,* tribe]: developed from a single ancestral type; contrasts with polyphletic.

monosaccharide (mŏn'ō·săk'ȧ·rīd) [Gr. *sakcharon,* sugar]: a simple sugar, such as 5- and 6-carbon sugars.

morphogenesis (môr'fō·jĕn'ĕ·sĭs): development of size, form, and other architectural features of organisms.

morphology (môr·fŏl'ō·jĭ): the study or science of structure, at any level of organization; e.g., cytology, study of cell structure; histology, study of tissue structure; anatomy, study of gross structure.

morula (mŏr'ū·lȧ) [L. little mulberry]: solid ball of cells resulting from cleavage of egg; a solid blastula.

mucosa (mū·kō'sȧ) [L. *mucosus,* mucus]: a mucus-secreting membrane; e.g., the inner lining of the intestine.

mutagen (mū'tȧ·jĕn) a substance or agent that increases the rate or incidence of mutations.

mutation (mū·tā'shŭn) [L. *mutare,* to change]: a stable change of a gene or gene part (muton); the changed condition is inherited by offspring cells.

mutualism (mū'tū·ȧl·ĭz'm): a form of symbiosis in which both partners benefit in some way from their association.

mycelium (mī·sē'lĭ·ŭm): the vegetative portion of a fungus, consisting of a meshwork of hyphae.

Mycophyta (mī'kō·fī'tȧ): the phylum of fungi.

myelencephalon (mī'ĕ·lĕn·sĕf'ȧlŏn) [Gr. *myelos,* marrow]: the most posterior part of the vertebrate hindbrain, confluent with the spinal cord; the medulla oblongata.

myelin (mī'ĕ·lĭn): a fatty material surrounding the axons of nerve cells in the central nervous system of vertebrates.

myofibril (mīō·fī'brĭl): a contractile filament inside a cell.

myopia (mī·ō'pĭ·ȧ): nearsightedness; visual images form in front of the retina.

myosin (mī'ō·sĭn): a muscle protein

myxedema (mĭk'sē·dē'mȧ) [Gr. *oidēma,* a swelling]: a disease resulting from thyroid deficiency in the adult characterized by local swellings in and under the skin.

myxomycete (mĭk'sō·mī·sēt'): a slime mold, member of a class of Myxophyta.

Myxophyta (mīks·ŏf'ī·tȧ): the phylum of slime molds.

NAD: abbreviation of nicotinamide-adenine-dinucleotide.

NADP: abbreviation of nicotinamide-adenine-dinucleotide-phosphate.

naloxone (năl·ŏk'sōn): an antagonist of morphine and allied narcotics.

nastic (năs'tĭk): pertaining to a change in position, as in nastic growth movement; see *epinasty, hyponasty.*

nauplius (nô'plĭ·ŭs) [L. shellfish]: first in a series of larval phases in crustacea.

nekton (nĕk'tŏn) [Gr. *nēktos,* swimming]: collective term for the actively swimming animals in the ocean.

nematocyst (nĕm'ȧ·tō·sĭst) [Gr. *nēma,* thread]: in coelenterates, a stinging capsule with eversible stinging filament, contained within stinging cell (cnidoblast).

Nematoda (nĕm'ä tō'dȧ): the class of roundworms in the phylum Aschelminthes.

Nematomorpha (nĕm'ä tō·môr'fä): the class of hairworms in the phylum Aschelminthes.

Nemertina (nĕm·ẽr tīn'ä): ribbon or proboscis

worms, an acoelomate phylum (also called Rhynchocoela).

neoteny (nê·ŏt′ē·nĭ) [Gr. *neo,* new + *tenein,* extend]: retention of larval or youthful traits as permanent adult features.

nephric, nephron (nĕf′rik, -rŏn): (1) pertaining to a nephron or excretory system generally; (2) a functional unit of the vertebrate kidney.

neuroglia (nū·rŏg′lĭ·*ȧ*) [Gr. *glia,* glue]: supporting cells that along with neurons form brain tissue.

neuron (nū′rŏn) [Gr. nerve]: nerve cell.

neurotransmitter (nū′rô·trăns·mĭt′ẽr): one of a variety of hormonal substances normally secreted by axon terminals in synapses; transmits a nerve impulse across a synapse to dendrite terminals of adjacent neurons.

neutron (nū′trŏn): a subatomic particle with a unit of mass; it is uncharged and occurs in an atomic nucleus.

nicotinamide: a derivative of nicotinic acid (niacin, one of the B vitamins), a component of the hydrogen carriers NAD and NADP.

nictitating membrane (nĭk′tĭ·tā·tĭng) [L. *nictare,* to wink]: a more or less transparent membrane under the lower eyelid of many vertebrates; can be extended across eyeball ("third eyelid").

nitrify, nitrification (nī′trĭ·fī, -fĭ·kā′shŭn): (1) to convert ammonia and nitrite to nitrate; (2) noun.

node (nōd) [L. *nodus,* knot]: place where branches and leaves are joined to a stem.

nonmetal (nŏn′mĕt′ŭl): any element that ionizes by gain of electrons and thus forms anions.

norepinephrine (nôr·ĕp′ĭ·nef′rĭn): one of the neurotransmitter hormones, also called *noradrenalin;* mediates synaptic transmission of impulses in sympathetic nervous system.

notochord (nō′tô·kôrd): longitudinal elastic rod serving as internal skeleton in the embryos of all chordates and in the adults of some.

nucleic acid (nû·klē′ik): one of a class of molecules composed of joined nucleotides; DNA or RNA.

nucleolus (nû·klē′ô·lŭs): an RNA-containing body in the nucleus of a cell; a derivative of chromosomes.

nucleoprotein (nū′klê·ô-): a molecular complex composed of nucleic acid and protein.

nucleosome (nū′klē·ô·sōm): chromosomal nucleoprotein unit consisting of a segment of DNA spirally wound around a set of histone molecules.

nucleotide (nū′klê·ô·tīd): a molecule consisting of a phosphate, a 5-carbon sugar (ribose or deoxyribose), and a nitrogen base (adenine, guanine, uracil, thymine, or cytosine).

nucleus (nū′klê·ŭs) [L. a kernel]: an organelle in all cell types except those of the Monera; consists of external nuclear membrane, interior nuclear sap, and chromosomes and nucleoli suspended in the sap; also the central body of an atom.

nutation (nû·tā′shŭn) [L. *nutare,* to nod]: a slow, nodding growth movement in plants, more or less rhythmic and produced by internal stimuli.

nutrient (nū′trĭ·ĕnt) [L. *nutrire,* to nourish]: a substance usable in metabolism; a metabolite; includes inorganic materials and foods.

nymph (nĭmf) [Gr. *nymphē,* bride]: general designation for any larva of heterometabolous insects.

ocellus (ô·sĕl′ŭs) [L. dim. of *oculus,* eye]: eye or eyespot, of various degrees of structural and functional complexity; in arthropods, a simple eye, as distinct from a compound eye.

oidiospore (ô·ĭd′ĭ·ô·spōr) [Gr. *eidos,* form]: a spore formed by partitioning of a body part or filament.

olfaction, olfactory (ŏl·făk′shŭn, -tô·rĭ) [L. *olfacere,* to smell]: (1) the process of smelling; (2) pertaining to smell.

oligotrophic (ŏl′ĭ·gô·trō′fĭk): relating to a body of water deficient in dissolved nutrients but with adequate oxygen.

ommatidium (ŏm′ȧ tĭd′ĭ·ŭm) [Gr. *omma,* eye]: single visual unit in compound eye of arthropods.

omnivore (ŏm′nĭ·vōr) [L. *omnis,* all]: an animal living on plant foods, animal foods, or both.

Oncopoda (ŏn·kŏ′pô·dȧ) [Gr. *onkos,* bulk]: a small phylum comprising schizocoelomate animals related to arthropods.

ontogeny (ŏn·tŏj′ĕ·nĭ) [Gr. *ont-,* being]: individual development, or embryology.

Onychophora (ŏnĭ·kŏ′fŏr·*ȧ*) [Gr. *onych,* claw]: a subphylum of Oncopoda, comprising *Peripatus* and related types.

oögamy (ô·ŏg′*ȧ*·mĭ): sexual fusion in which the gametes of opposite sex type are unequal, the female gamete being a nonmotile egg; the male gamete, a motile sperm.

oögonium (ō′·ŏ·gō′nĭ·ŭm): the female gametangium of oögamous fungi and other Protista; contains one or more eggs.

operator (ŏp′ẽr·ā·tẽr): a gene regulating the activity of the structural genes with which it is associated in an operon.

operon (ŏp′ẽr·ŏn): a closely linked combination of genes on a chromosome; includes an operator gene and one or more structural genes regulated by the operator.

operculum (ȯ·pûr′kū·lŭm) [L. a lid]: a lidlike structure.

opisthosome (ȯ·pĭs′thȯ·sōm): a posterior body part or cell.

ophiuroid (ŏf′ĭ·ū·roid) [Gr. *ophis,* snake]: a member of a class of echinoderms; a brittle star.

organ (ôr′găn) [Gr. *organon,* tool, instrument]: a group of different tissues joined structurally and cooperating functionally to perform a composite task.

organelle (ôr·găn·el′): a structure or body in a cell.

organic (ôr·găn′ĭk): pertaining to compounds of carbon of nonmineral origin.

organism (ôr′găn·ĭz′m): an individual living creature, either unicellular or multicellular.

orgasm (ôr′găz′m) [Gr. *orgasmos*]: the climax of sexual excitement during coitus.

ornithine (ôr′nĭ·thēn) [Gr. *ornithos,* bird]: an amino acid which, in the liver of vertebrates, contributes to the conversion of ammonia and carbon dioxide to urea.

osculum (ŏs′kū·lŭm) [L., little mouth]: an excurrent siphon in sponges.

osmosis (ŏs·mō′sĭs) [Gr. *ōsmos,* impulse]: the process in which water migrates through a semipermeable membrane, from the side containing a lesser to the side containing a greater concentration of particles; migration continues until concentrations are equal on both sides.

ossicle (ŏs′ĭ·k′l) [L. dim. of *ossis,* bone]: a small bone or hard bonelike supporting structure.

Osteichthyes (ŏs·tȇ·ĭk′thĭ·ēz): the vertebrate class of bony fishes.

ostium (ŏs′tĭ·ŭm) [L. door]: orifice or small opening; for example, one of several pairs of lateral pores in an arthropod heart, pore for entry of water in certain sponges.

ovary (ō′vȧrĭ): the egg-producing organ of animals; the ovule- (megasporangium-) containing organ of flowering plants.

oviparity, oviparous (ō′vĭ·păr′ĭ·tĭ, ȯ·vĭp′ȧrŭs) [L. *parere,* to bring forth]: (1) animal reproductive pattern in which eggs are released by the female and offspring development occurs outside the maternal body; (2) adjective.

ovipositor (ō·vĭ·pŏz′ĭ·tẽr): a specialized organ for depositing eggs, e.g., in insects.

ovoviviparity, ovoviviparous (ō′vȯ·vīv′ĭ·păr′ĭ·tĭ, ō′vȯ·vī vĭp′ȧ·rŭs): (1) animal reproductive pattern in which eggs develop inside the maternal body, but without nutritive or other metabolic aid by the female parent; offspring are born as miniature adults; (2) adjective.

ovulation (ō′vū·lā′shŭn): explusion of an animal egg from ovary and deposition of egg in oviduct.

ovule (ō′vūl): the integument-covered megasporangium of a seed plant.

oxidation (ŏk′sĭ·dā′shŭn): one half of an oxidation-reduction (redox) process; the process is exergonic and the endproducts are more stable than the starting materials; often takes the form of removal of hydrogen (or electrons) from a compound.

paleoniscoid (pā′lȇ·ȯ·nĭs′koid): extinct Devonian bony fish, ancestral to modern bony fishes, lungfishes, and lobe-fin fishes.

paleontology (pā′lȇ·ŏn·tŏl′ȯ·jĭ): study of past geologic times by means of fossils.

Paleozoic (pā′lȇ·ȯ·zō′ĭk): geologic era between the Precambrian and the Mesozoic, dating approximately from 500 to 200 million years ago.

palp (pălp) [L. *palpus,* feeler]: a feelerlike appendage.

Pantopoda (păn·tŏ′pȯdȧ) [Gr. *pantos,* all]: a subphylum of Oncopoda.

papilla (pȧ·pĭl′ȧ) [L. nipple]: any small nipplelike projection.

paramylum (pȧ·răm′ĭ·lŭm) [L. *par,* equal, + Gr. *amylon,* fine meal]: starchlike food-storage compound in Euglenophyta.

paraphysis (pȧ·răf′ĭ·sĭs) [Gr. *physis,* nature]: one of the sterile filaments in the reproductive organs of many organisms (e.g., *Fucus*).

parapodia (păr′ȧ·pō′dĭ·ȧ): fleshy segmental appendages in polychaete worms; serve in breathing, locomotion, and creation of water currents.

parasite (păr′ȧ·sīt) [Gr. *sitos,* food]: an organism living symbiotically on or in a host organism, more or less detrimental to the host.

parasympathetic (păr′ä·sĭm′pȧ·thĕt′ĭk): applied to a subdivision of the autonomic nervous system of vertebrates; centers are located in brain and most anterior part of spinal cord.

parathyroid (păr′*ȧ*·thī′roid): an endocrine gland of vertebrates, usually paired, located near or in the thyroid.

parenchyma (pä·rĕng′kĭ·m*ȧ*) [Gr. *para* + *en,* in + *chein,* to pour]: a thin-walled cell type of plants, relatively little specialized but often with chlorophyll; can function in food storage and is a component of many other tissue types.

parthenogenesis (pär′thē·nō·jĕn′ē·sĭs) [Gr. *parthenos,* virgin]: development of an egg without fertilization; occurs naturally in some animals (e.g., rotifers) and can be induced artificially in others (e.g., frogs).

pathogenic (păth′ōjĕn′ĭk) [Gr. *pathos,* suffering]: disease-producing.

pectin (pĕk′tĭn) [Gk. *pektos,* curdled]: one of a group of compounds frequently present in cell walls of plants.

pectine (pĕk′tīn) [L. *pecten,* comb]: one of a pair of comblike segmental appendages on scorpion abdomen, tactile in function.

pedicellaria (pĕd′ĭ·sĕl ā′rĭ·*ȧ*) [L. *pedicellus,* little stalk]: a pincerlike structure on the surface of echinoderms; protects skin gills.

pedipalp (pĕd′ĭ·pălp): one of a pair of head appendages in chelicerate arthropods.

pelagic (pē·lăj′ĭk) [Gr. *pelagos,* ocean]: oceanic habitat zone comprising the open water of an ocean basin.

Pelecypoda (pĕ′lē·sĭp′ō·d*ȧ*): a class of the phylum Mollusca, comprising clams, mussels, oysters.

pellagra (pĕ·lăg′r*ȧ*) [L. *pellis,* skin]: a disease resulting from vitamin B (niacin) deficiency.

pellicle (pĕl′ĭ·k′l) [L. dim. of *pellis,* skin]: a thin, membranous surface coat, as on many protozoa.

pentose (pĕn′tōs): any 5-carbon sugar.

pepsin (pĕp′sĭn) [Gr. *peptein,* to digest]: a protein-digesting enzyme in gastric juice of vertebrates.

peptidase (pĕp′tĭ·dās): an enzyme promoting the liberation of individual amino acids from a whole or partially digested protein.

peptide (pĕp′tīd): the type of bond formed when two amino acid units are joined.

perciform (pûr′sĭ·fôrm) [L. *perca,* perch]: anatomical pattern among teleost fishes, characterized by hard-rayed fins, swim bladders without ducts, ctenoid scales, and other traits.

perennial (pĕr·ĕn′ĭ·*ȧ*l) [L. *perennis,* throughout a year]: a plant that lives continuously from year to year.

pericycle (pĕr′ĭ·sī′k′l) [Gr. *perikyklos,* spherical]: a tissue layer composed of parenchymatous or sclerenchymatous cells surrounding the vascular tissues of the stele; often reduced or absent in stems.

periderm (per′i·dûrm): a collective term for cork cambium and its products (cork and phelloderm).

peristalsis (pĕr′ĭ·stăl′sĭs) [Gr. *peristaltikos,* compressing]: successive contraction and relaxation of tubular organs such as the alimentary tract, resulting in a wavelike propagation of a transverse constriction.

peristomium (pĕr·ĭ·stō′mĭ·*ŭ*m): the region around the mouth in various invertebrates.

peritoneum (pē·rĭ′tō·nē′*ŭ*m) [Gr. *peritonos,* stretched over]: a mesodermal membrane lining the coelom.

permafrost (pûr′m*ȧ*·frôst): in subpolar and polar regions, the permanently frozen layer at various depths below the ground surface.

permeability (pûr′mē·*ȧ*·bĭl′ĭ·tĭ) [L. *permeare,* to pass through]: penetrability, as in membranes that let substances pass through.

permease (pûr′mē·ās): an enzyme catalyzing the transfer of a substrate through a cell membrane.

peroxisome (pĕr·ŏk′sĭ·sōm): a type of microbody, a cytoplasmic vesicular organelle containing peroxidases and other enzymes.

petal (pĕt′′l) [Gr. *petalos,* outspread]: one of the leaves of the corolla in a flower.

petiole (pĕt′ĭ·ōl) [L. *petiolus,* little foot]: leafstalk; the slender stem by which a leaf blade is attached to a branch or a stem.

pH: a symbol denoting the relative concentration of hydrogen ions in a solution; pH values normally run from 0 to 14, and the lower the value, the more acid is a solution.

Phaeophyta (fē′ō·fī′t·*ȧ*): the phylum of brown algae.

phage (fāj): short for *bacteriophage,* a type of virus that infects and kills bacteria.

phagocytosis (făg′ō·sī·tō′sĭs) [Gr. *phagos,* eater]: engulfing of particulate matter by a cell (*phagocyte*), by a process akin to amoeboid engulfment.

pharynx (făr′ĭngks): [Gr.]: the part of the alimentary tract between mouth cavity and esophagus.

phellem (fĕl′ĕm) [Gr. *phellos,* cork]: cork, the exterior product of cork cambium.

phelloderm (fĕl′ō·dûrm): the interior, parenchymatous tissue formed by the cork cambium; becomes part of cortex.

phellogen (fĕl′ô·jĕn): cork cambium.
phenotype (fē′nô·tīp) [Gr. *phainein,* to show]: the physical appearance of an organism resulting from its genetic constitution (genotype).
phenylketonuria (fĕn′ĭl·kē′tōn·yoo′rĭ·ȧ): a human genetic disease characterized by inability to metabolize phenylalanine and severe mental retardation.
pheromone (fĕr′ô·mōn) [Gr. *pherein,* to carry]: a chemical released by an animal and functioning as a stimulus to other members of the species, leading to particular behavioral responses; e.g., a sex attractant.
phloem (flō′ĕm) [Gr. *phloos,* bark]: one of the vascular tissues in tracheophytic plants; consists of sieve tubes and companion cells and transports organic nutrients both up and down.
Phoronida (fô·rŏn′ĭ·dȧ): a phylum of wormlike lophophore-possessing animals.
phosphagen (fŏs′fă·jĕn): collective term for compounds such as creatine-phosphate, which store and may be sources of high-energy phosphates.
phosphorylation (fŏs′fô·rĭ·lā′shŭn): the addition of a phosphate group (—O—H_2PO_3) to a compound.
photic (fōt′ĭk): with light, e.g., *photic zone,* the sunlit water in ocean and lake.
photolithotroph (fō′tô·lĭth′ô·trōf) [Gr. *lithos,* stone]: an organism that manufactures food with the aid of light energy and with inorganic raw materials.
photolysis (fô·tŏl′ĭ·sĭs): a phase of photosynthesis in which water is decomposed and the hydrogen is joined to NADP under the indirect influence of solar energy.
photoorganotroph (fō′tô·ôr·găn′ô·trōf): an organism that manufactures food with the aid of light energy and with organic raw materials.
photoperiod, photoperiodism (fō′tô·pēr′ĭ·ŭd, -ĭz′m): (1) day length, (2) the responses of plants to different day lengths.
photosynthesis (fō′tô·sĭn′thê·sĭs) [Gr. *tithenai,* to place]: process in which light energy and chlorophyll are used to manufacture carbohydrates out of carbon dioxide and water.
phototropism (fô·tŏt′rô·pĭz′m) [Gr. *tropē,* a turning]: behavior oriented by light; e.g., growth of plant stems toward light source.
phrenic (frĕn′ĭk) [Gr. *phrenos,* diaphragm]: pertaining to the diaphragm; e.g., phrenic nerve, which innervates the diaphragm.
phycocyanin, phycoerythrin (fī′kô·sī′ă·nĭn, fī′kô·ê·rĭth′rĭn): blue and red pigments found in blue-green and red algae.
phyllotaxy (fĭl′ô·tăk′sĭ): the geometric arrangement of leaves on a stem.
phylogeny (fī·lŏj′ê·nĭ) [Gr. *phylon,* race, tribe]: the study of evolutionary descent and interrelations of groups of organisms.
phylum (fī′lŭm), pl. ***phyla:*** a category of taxonomic classification, ranked above class.
physiology (fĭz′ĭ·ŏl′ô·jĭ) [Gr. *physis,* nature]: study of living processes, activities, and functions in general; contrasts with morphology, the study of structure.
phytochromes (fī′tô·krōmz): pigmented compounds in plant cells serving as receptors of different wavelengths of light; mediate red–far-red growth responses of plants.
phytoplankton (fī′tô·plăngk′tŏn) [Gr. *planktos,* wandering]: collective term for the plants and plantlike organisms in plankton; contrasts with zooplankton.
pineal (pĭn′ê·ăl) [L. *pinea,* pine cone]: a structure in the brain of vertebrates; functions as a median dorsal eye in lampreys and tuataras.
pinocytosis (pĭ′nō·sī·tō′sĭs) [Gr. *pinein,* to drink]: intake of fluid droplets through cell surface.
pistil (pĭs′til) [L. *pistulus,* a pestle]: the megaspore-producing organ of a flower; consists of stigma, style, and ovary.
pituitary (pĭ·tū′ĭ·tĕrĭ) [L. *pituita,* phlegm]: a composite vertebrate endocrine gland ventral to the brain; composed of anterior, intermediate, and posterior lobes, each a functionally separate gland.
placenta (plȧ·sĕn′tȧ) [L. cake]: a mammalian tissue complex formed from the inner lining of the uterus and the chorion of the embryo; serves as mechanical, metabolic, and endocrine connection between adult female and embryo during pregnancy.
placoderm (plăk′ô·dûrm) [Gr. *plakos,* flat plate]: a member of an extinct class of Devonian fishes.
planarian (plȧ·nâr′ĭ·ăn) [L. *planarius,* level]: any member of the class of free-living flatworms.
plankton (plăngk′tŏn) [Gr. *planktos,* wandering]: collective term for the largely microscopic, passively floating or drifting flora and fauna of a body of water.
planula (plăn′ü·lȧ) [L. dim. of *planus,* flat]: basic larval form characteristic of coelenterates.

plasma (plăz′mȧ): the fluid, cell-free fraction of blood.

plaque (plăk) [Fr., plate, patch]: a cholesterol-containing deposit on the inner surface of an arterial wall, characteristic of atherosclerosis.

Plantae (plăn′tē): the kingdom of plants.

plasmodesma (plăz′mô·dĕz′mȧ), pl. ***plasmodesmata*** [Gr. *desmos*, chain]: fine cytoplasmic strand interconnecting adjacent cells in many plant tissues.

plasmodium (plăz·mō′dĭ·ŭm): multinucleate amoeboid mass representing aggregated diploid phase in certain slime molds.

plasmogamy (plăz·mŏ′gă·mĭ): mating union of cytoplasms, a component of fertilization.

plastid (plăs′tĭd): a cytoplasmic organelle with or without pigments; chlorophyll-containing plastids are chloroplasts, sites of photosynthesis.

plastron (plăs′trŏn) [It. *piastrone*, breastplate]: a ventral shell part, as in turtles.

plastoquinone (plăs′tô·kwĭn′ōn): a fat-soluble ring compound functioning as electron carrier in photolysis; associated with photosystem II.

platelets (plāt′lĕts): cell fragments in blood, produced in bone marrow and containing thrombokinase which, when released by platelet rupture, initiates blood clotting.

Platyhelminthes (plăt′ĭ·hĕl·mĭn′thēz) [Gr. *platys*, flat]: flatworms, a phylum of acoelomate animals; comprises planarians, flukes, and tapeworms.

pleiotropic (plī′ô·trŏp′ĭk) [Gr. *plēion*, more]: producing more than one genic effect; having multiple phenotypic expressions.

plesiosaur (plē′sĭ·ô·sôr) [Gr. *plesios*, near]: a long-necked, marine, extinct Mesozoic reptile.

pleural (ploor′ȧl) [L. *pleura*, side, lateral]: relating to membranes lining the chest cavity of mammals and covering the lungs.

plexus (plĕk′sŭs) [L. braid]: a network, esp. nerves or blood vessels.

plumule (ploom′yool) [L. *pluma*, feather]: primary bud of a plant embryo, at the apex of the hypocotyl.

pluteus (ploot′ē·ŭs) [Gr. *plein*, to sail, float, flow]: the larva of echinoids and ophiuroids; also called echinopluteus and ophiopluteus, respectively.

Pogonophora (pō·gŏ′nô·fōr′ȧ) [Gr. *pōgōn*, beard]: beard worms, a phylum of enterocoelomate deep-sea animals.

poikilothermic (poi′kĭ·lô·thûr′mĭk) [Gr. *poikilos*, multicolored]: pertaining to animals without internal temperature controls; "cold-blooded."

pollen (pŏl′ĕn) [L. fine dust]: microspore of seed plants.

pollination (pŏl′ĭ·nā′shŭn): transfer of pollen to the micropyle or a receptive surface associated with an ovule (e.g., a stigma).

polyclad (pŏl′ĭ·klăd): a member of an order of free-living flatworms, characterized by a digestive cavity with many branch pouches.

polyestrous (pŏl′ĭ·ĕs′trŭs): having several estrus (egg-producing) cycles during a given breeding season.

polymer (pŏl′ĭ·mĕr): a large molecule composed of many like molecular subunits.

polymorphism (pŏl′ĭ·môr′fĭz′m): differences of form among the members of a species; individual variations affecting form and structure.

polyp (pŏl′ĭp) [L. *polypus*, many-footed]: the usually sessile stage in the life cycle of coelenterates.

polypeptide (pŏl′ĭ·pĕp′tīd): a polymeric chain of amino acids, linked together by peptide bonds.

polyphyletic (pŏl′ĭ·fī·lĕt′ĭk) [Gr. *phylon*, tribe]: derived from more than one ancestral type; contrasts with monophyletic.

polyploid (pŏl′ĭ ploid): having many complete chromosome sets per cell.

polysaccharide (pŏl′ĭ·săk′*a*·rīd): a carbohydrate composed of many joined monosaccharide units; e.g., glycogen, starch, cellulose, all formed out of glucose units.

population (pŏp·yoo·lā′shŭn): [L. *populus*, people]: a group of organisms of the same species, occupying a particular territory.

Porifera (pô·rĭf′ĕr·ȧ): the phylum of sponges.

Premonera (prē·mō·nĭr′ȧ): organisms in existence before the origin of Monera; the earliest cells.

Priapulida (prī′ȧ·pū′·lĭ·dȧ): a class in the phylum Aschelminthes.

primordium (prī′·môr′dĭ·ŭm) [L. beginning]: the earliest developmental stage in the formation of an organ or body part.

proboscis (prô·bŏs′ĭs) [L.]: any tubular process or prolongation of the head or snout.

progesterone (prô·jĕs′tĕr·ōn): hormone secreted by the vertebrate corpus luteum and the mammalian placenta; functions as pregnancy hormone in mammals.

proglottid (prô·glŏ′ĭd): a segment of a tapeworm.

prokaryote (prō·kăr′ē·ōt) [Gr. *pro*, before +

karyon, nucleus]: any of a group of organisms (bacteria and blue-green algae) in which the cells lack nuclear membranes and the DNA is in the form of naked filaments surrounded directly by cytoplasm.

prolactin (prō·lăk′tĭn): a protein hormone secreted by the anterior lobe of the pituitary; induces lactation in mammals, among other effects.

pronephros (prō·nĕf′rŏs): a type of vertebrate excretory system, present in the embryos of fishes.

prostaglandin (prŏs′tȧ·glăn′dĭn): any of a number of cyclic, lipid-derived substances having a variety of hormonelike effects.

prophase (prō′fāz′): a stage during mitotic division in which the chromosomes become distinct and a spindle forms.

proprioceptor (prō·′prĭ·ȏ·sĕp′·tẽr) [L. *proprius,* one's own]: sensory receptor of stimuli originating in internal organs; a stretch receptor.

prostomium (prō·stō′mĭ·ŭm) [Gr. *pro* + *stoma,* mouth]: the portion of the head in annelids and other worms situated in front of the mouth.

protein (prō′tȇ·ĭn): [Gr. *prōteios,* primary]: one of a class of organic compounds composed of many joined amino acids.

proteinase (prō′tȇ·ĭn·ās): an enzyme promoting the conversion of protein to amino acids or the reverse; also called *protease.*

prothallial cells (prō·thăl′ĭ·ŭl) the vegetative portion of the male gametophyte in gymnosperms.

prothorax (prō·thôr′ăks): the first thoracic segment in insects.

prothrombin (prȏ·thrŏm′bĭn) [Gr. *thrombos,* clot]: a clotting factor in vertebrate blood plasma; converted to thrombin by thrombokinase.

Protista (prȏ·tĭs′tȧ) [Gr. *prōtistos,* first]: a major category of living organisms, including algae (except blue-greens), slime molds, and protozoa.

protocoel (prō′tȏ·sēl): anterior coelom sac in animal embryos, e.g., enterocoelomates.

proton (prō′tŏn): a subatomic particle with a unit of positive electric charge and a mass of 1; a component of an atomic nucleus.

protonema (prō′tȏ·nē′mȧ): the first-formed, often filamentous portion of a moss gametophyte.

protoplasm (prō′tȏ·plăz′m): synonym for living matter, living material, or living substance.

protostele (prō′tȏ·stēl′) [Gr. *stēlē,* upright post]: a general type of stele in which the vascular tissues form a solid central aggregation in the stem or root, phloem being outside the xylem; the main variants are haplosteles and actinosteles.

Protostomia (prō′tȏ·stō′mē·ȧ): animals in which blastopore becomes mouth; anus forms as second embryonic opening opposite blastopore.

protozoon (prō′tȏ·zō′ŏn): a member of either of four subphyla (Mastigophora, Sarcodina, Ciliophora, Sporozoa) of a protistan phylum.

pseudocoel, pseudocoelomate (sū′dȏ·sēl, -ȏ·māt): (1) an internal body cavity lined by ectoderm and endoderm; (2) an animal having a pseudocoel.

pseudoplasmodium (sū′dȏ·plăz·mō′dĭ·ŭm): multicellular amoeboid mass representing diploid phase in certain slime molds.

pseudopodium (sū′dȏ·pō′dĭ·ŭm): a cytoplasmic protrusion from an amoeboid cell; functions in locomotion and feeding.

Psilopsida (sī·lŏp′sĭ·dȧ) [Gr. *psilos,* bare]: a subphylum of tracheophytes; includes the earliest representatives of the vascular plants.

Pteropsida (tȇ·rŏp′sĭ·dȧ) [Gr. *pteridos,* fern]: a subphylum of tracheophytes; includes large-leafed vascular plants (ferns and all seed plants).

pterosaur (tĕr′ȏ·sôr): extinct Mesozoic flying reptile.

puberty (pū′bẽr·tĭ) [L. *puber,* pubescent]: stage of human development characterized by attainment of sexual maturity.

pulmonary (pŭl′mȏ·nĕr′ĭ) [L. *pulmonis,* lung]: pertaining to the lungs.

pupa (pū′pȧ) [L. doll]: a developmental stage, usually encapsulated or in cocoon, between larva and adult in holometabolous insects.

purine (pŭ′rēn): a nitrogen base such as adenine or guanine; a component of nucleotides and nucleic acids.

pylorus (pı·lō′rŭs) [Gr. *pylōros,* gatekeeper]: the opening from stomach to intestine.

pyrenoid (pī′rē·noid) [Gr. *pyrēn,* fruit stone]: a starch-containing granular body on or near a chloroplast in many Protista.

pyrimidine (pĭ·rĭ′mĭ·dēn): a nitrogen base such as cytosine, thymine, or uracil; a component of nucleotides and nucleic acids.

Pyrrophyta (pĭ·rŏf′ĭ·tȧ) [Gr. *pyrros,* fiery]: a phylum of algae; includes dinoflagellates and possibly also Cryptophyceae.

pyruvic acid (pī·roo′vĭk): a 3-carbon keto acid, the usual end product of glycolysis.

Radiata (rā·dĭ·ă′tȧ) [L. *radius,* ray]: a taxonomic grade within the Eumetazoa, comprising coelenterates and ctenophores.
radicle (răd′ĭ·k′l): the rootlet of a plant embryo or seedling.
Radiolaria (rā′dĭ·ō·lâr′ĭ·ȧ): sarcodine protozoa characterized by silicon-containing shells.
radula (răd′ū·lȧ) [L. *radere,* to scrape]: a horny rasping organ in the mouth of many mollusks.
receptacle (rē·sĕp′tȧk′l) [L. *receptaculum,* receiver]: (1) conceptacle-containing thallus tip in *Fucus;* (2) modified branch of thallus bearing sex organs in *Marchantia;* (3) expanded terminal of stalk bearing the components of a flower.
receptor (rē·sĕp′tẽr): in steady-state control, a component that receives stimuli and as a result sends out sensory signals to a modulator.
recessive (rē·sĕs′ĭv) [L. *recedere,* to recede]: a functional attribute of genes; the recessive effect of a gene is masked if the allelic gene has a dominant effect.
rectum (rĕk′tŭm) [L. *rectus,* straight]: a terminal nonabsorptive portion of the alimentary tract in many animals; opens via the anus.
redia (rē′dĭ·ȧ): a larval stage in the life cycle of flukes; produced by a sporocyst larva and gives rise to many cercarias.
reduction (rē·dŭk′shŭn) [L. *reducere,* to lead back]: one half of an oxidation-reduction (redox) process; the phase that yields the net energy gain; often takes the form of addition of hydrogen (or electrons) to a compound.
reflex (rē′flĕks) [L. *reflectere,* to bend back]: the unit action of the nervous system; consists of stimulation of a receptor, interpretation and emission of nerve impulses by a neural center, and execution of a response by an effector.
renal (rē′năl) [L. *renes,* kidneys]: pertaining to the kidney.
rennin (rĕn′ĭn) [Middle Engl. *rennen,* to run]: an enzyme in the gastric juice of ruminant mammals; promotes coagulation of milk.
reproduction (rē·prō·dŭk′shŭn): formation of new living units, at any level in the hierarchial organization of living matter.
respiration (rĕs′pĭ·rā′shŭn) [L. *respirare,* to breathe]: liberation of metabolically useful energy from fuel molecules in cells; can occur anaerobically or aerobically.
reticulum (rē·tĭk′ū·lŭm) [L. little net]: a network or mesh of fibrils, fibers, filaments, or membranes, as in *endoplasmic reticulum.*
retina (rĕt′ĭ·nȧ) [L. *rete,* a net]: the innermost tissue layer of the eyeball; contains the photoreceptor cells.
rhabdocoel (răb′dō·sēl) [Gr. *rhabdos,* rod]: member of a group of free-living flatworms having a straight, unbranched digestive cavity.
rhizoid (rī′zoid) [Gr. *rhiza,* root]: a rootlike absorptive filament.
rhizome (rī′zōm) [Gr. *rhizōme,* mass of roots]: an underground stem.
rhizoplast (rī′zō·plăst): a microtubular connection between a kinetosome and a centriole.
Rhodophyta (rō′dŏf′ĭ·tȧ) [Gr. *rhodon,* red]: the phylum of red algae.
rhodopsin (rō·dŏp′sĭn) [Gr. *rhodon* + *opsis,* sight]: red photosensitive pigment in rod cells of retina; also called *visual purple.*
riboflavin (rī·bō·flā′vĭn): a vitamin of the B complex also known as vitamin B_2.
ribose (rī′bōs): one of the 5-carbon sugars.
ribosome (rī′bō·sōm): an RNA-containing cytoplasmic organelle; the site of protein synthesis.
ribotide (rī′bō·tīd): a nucleotide in which the sugar component is ribose.
rickettsia (rĭk·ĕt′sĭ·ȧ) [after H. T. Ricketts, American pathologist]: a type of microorganism intermediate in nature between a virus and a bacterium, parasitic in cells of insects and ticks.
RNA: abbreviation of ribonucleic acid.
Rotifera (rō·tĭf′ĕrȧ) [L. *rota,* wheel]: a class of microscopic animals in the phylum Aschelminthes.
rudimentary (roo′dĭ·mĕn′tȧ·rĭ) [L. *rudis,* unformed]: pertaining to an incompletely developed body part.

saccule (săc′ūl) [L. *sacculus,* little sac]: portion of the inner ear of vertebrates containing the receptors for the sense of static balance.
salt (sôlt): the result of interaction of an acid and an alkali.
saprotroph (săp′rō·trōf) [Gr. *sapros,* rotten]: an organism subsisting on dead or decaying matter.
Sarcodina (sär′kō·dī′nȧ): a subphylum of protozoa; amoeboid protozoa.
sarcomere (sär′kō·mĭr): one of the repeating structural units of a striated muscle fibril.

Scaphopoda (skă·fŏp′ŏ·dȧ) [Gr. *skaphē,* boat]: tooth shells, a class of the phylum Mollusca.

schizocoel, schizocoelomate (skĭ′ō·sēl): (1) coelom formed by splitting of embryonic mesoderm; (2) an animal having a schizocoel.

Schizophyta (skī·zŏf′ĭ·tȧ): the phylum of bacteria.

sclera (sklē′rȧ): the outermost coat of the eyeball, continuous with the cornea.

sclereid (sklę′ēr·ĭd): a type of sclerenchyma cell.

sclerenchyma (sklē·rĕng′kĭ·mȧ) [Gr. *en,* in, + *chein,* to pour]: plant cells with greatly thickened and lignified walls, and without living substance when mature; two variants are fibers and sclereids.

scolex (skō′lĕks) [L. worm, grub]: the head of a tapeworm.

scrotum (skrō′tŭm) [L.]: external skin pouch containing the testes in most mammals.

sebaceous (sē·ba′shŭs) [L. *sebum,* tallow, grease]: pertaining to sebum, an oil secreted from skin glands near the hair bases of mammals.

seminal (sĕm′ĭ·nȧl) [L. *semen,* seed]: pertaining to semen or sperm-carrying fluid.

sepal (sēp′ȧl) [L. *sepa-,* covering]: one of the leaves of a calyx.

septum, septate (sĕp′tŭm), -tāt) [L. enclosure]: (1) a complete or incomplete partition; (2) adjective.

sere (sēr) [fr. L. *series,* series]: an ecological succession of communities, from the virginal condition to a stable climax community.

serosa (sē·rō′sȧ): the outermost tissue membrane of many organs, e.g., intestinal serosa, which is continuous with the mesentery.

serotonin (sĕr·ō·tō′nĭn): one of the neurotransmitters in vertebrate nervous systems; also present in blood platelets, inducing vasoconstriction upon release.

serum (sę′rŭm) [L.]: the fluid remaining after removal of fibrinogen from vertebrate blood plasma.

sex (sĕks): union of DNA from two usually unrelated cellular sources; generally takes the form of syngamy (cell fusion) or conjugation (nuclear exchange and fusion).

siliceous (sĭ·lĭsh′ŭs): relating to or containing silica or silicates.

sinus (sī′nŭs) [L. a curve]: a cavity, recess, space or depression.

siphon (sī′fŏn): tubular structure for drawing in or ejecting fluids.

siphonaceous (sī′fŏn·ā′shŭs): tubular; applied specifically to coccine, elongate Protista.

siphonoglyph (sī·fŏn′ō·glĭf) [Gr. *glyphein,* to carve]: flagellated groove in pharynx of sea anemones; creates water current to gastrovascular cavity.

Sipunculida (sī′pŭng·kū′lĭ·dȧ): a phylum of wormlike schizocoelomate animals.

sol (sŏl): quasi-liquid state of a colloidal system, where water forms the continuous phase and solid particles the dispersed phase.

somatic (sō·măt′ĭk): pertaining to the animal body generally.

somite (sō′mīt): one of the longitudinal series of segments in segmented animals, esp. an incompletely developed embryonic segment or a part thereof.

sorus (sō′rŭs) [Gr. *soros,* heap]: a cluster of sporangia on a fern leaf.

species (spē′shĭz), pl. ***species*** (spē′shēz) [L. kind sort]: a category of taxonomic classification, below genus rank, defined by breeding potential or gene flow; interbreeding and gene flow occur among the members of a species but not between members of difference species.

specificity (spĕs′ĭ·fĭs′ĭ·tĭ): uniqueness, esp. of proteins and genes in a given organism and of enzymes in given reactions.

spectrum (spĕk′trŭm) [L. image]: a series of radiations arranged in the order of wavelengths; e.g., solar spectrum, visible spectrum.

spermatangium (spûr′mȧ·tăn′jĭ·ŭm): sperm-producing structure; male gametangium.

spermatogenous (spûr′mȧ·tŏj′ē·nŭs): sperm-producing.

spermatophore (spûr·măt′ō·fôr): compact sperm packet formed by many animals in lieu of fluid semen.

Sphenopsida (sfē·nŏp′sĭ·dȧ) [Gr. *sphēn,* a wedge]: a subphylum of tracheophytes; includes the horsetails.

spicule (spĭk′ūl) [L. *spiculum,* little dart]: a slender, often needle-shaped secretion of sponge cells; serves as skeletal support.

spiracle (spī′rȧ·k′l) [L. *spirare,* to breathe]: reduced evolutionary remnant of first gill slit in fishes; also surface opening of breathing system in terrestrial arthropods.

spirillum (spī·rĭl′ŭm) [L. *spirilla,* little coil]: any bacterium having a wavy, coiled, or spiral shape.

sporangiospore (spō·răn′jĭ·ō·spōr′): a spore produced in a sporangium (as distinct from conidia and oidiospores).

sporangium (spô·răn′jĭ·ŭm): a spore-producing structure.

spore (spōr): a reproductive cell capable of developing into an adult directly.

sporine (spō′rēn): pertaining to a sessile state of protistan existence in which cell division can occur during the vegetative condition.

sporocyst (spō′rô·sĭst): a larval stage in the life cycle of flukes; produced by a miracidium larva and gives rise to many redias.

sporogenous (spô·rŏj′ê·nŭs): spore-producing.

sporophyll (spō′rô·fĭl): a sporangium-bearing leaf.

sporophyte (spōr′ô·fīt): a spore-producing organism; phase of diplohaplontic life cycle that alternates with a gametophyte phase.

Sporozoa (spō′rô·zō′ȧ): a subphylum of parasitic protozoa.

squamous (skwā′mŭs) [L. *squama,* scale]: scalelike, especially flattened cells forming squamous epithelium.

stamen (stā′mĕn) [L. a thread]: the microspore-producing organ of a flower; consists of stalk and anther.

stele (stēl) [Gr. *stēlē,* upright post]: collective term for those portions of stem and root that contain vascular tissues and, where present, pericycle and pith.

sternum (stûr′nŭm) [Gr. *sternon,* chest]: vertebrate breastbone, articulating with ventral ends of ribs on each side.

sterol, steroid (stĕr′ōl, stĕr′oid): one of a class of organic compounds containing a molecular skeleton of four fused carbon rings; includes cholesterol, sex hormones, adrenocortical hormones, and vitamin D.

stigma (stĭg′mȧ) [Gr. the mark of a pointed instrument]: the uppermost part of a pistil, serving as receptive surface for pollen grains.

stimulus (stĭm′û·lŭs) [L. goad, incentive]: any internal or external environmental change that activates a receptor structure.

stipule (stĭp′ūl) [L. *stipula,* stalk]: one of a pair of appendages at the base of the petiole in many plants.

stoma (stō′mȧ) pl. ***stomata*** [Gr. a mouth]: a microscopic opening in the epidermis of a leaf, formed by a pair of guard cells.

streptococcus (strĕp′tô·kŏk′ŭs) [Gr. *streptos,* curved]: member of a type of colony of bacterial cocci in which the cells divide in one plane only, forming chains.

strobilus (strŏb′ĭ·lŭs): a cone or conelike aggregation of (usually modified) leaves.

stroma (strō′mȧ) [Gr. couch, bed]: the connective tissue network supporting the epithelial portions of animal organ.

style, stylet (stīl, stī′lĕt) [Gr. *stylos,* pillar]: a stalklike or elongated body part, often pointed at one end.

suberin (sū′bĕr·ĭn) [L. *suber,* cork tree]: a waterproofing material secreted by cork and endodermal cells.

substrate (sŭb′strāt) [L. *substratus,* strewn under]: a substance that is acted on by an enzyme.

suspensor (sŭs·pĕn′sĕr) [L. *suspensus,* suspended]: an elongated strand connecting a plant embryo to the surrounding tissue layers.

symbiont, symbiosis (sĭm′bī·ŏnt, sĭm′bī·ō′sĭs): (1) an organism living in symbiotic association with another; (2) the intimate living together of two organisms of different species, for mutual or one-sided benefit; the main variants are mutualism, commensalism, and parasitism.

sympathetic (sĭm′pȧ·thĕt′ĭk): applied to a subdivision of the autonomic nervous system; centers are located in the mid-portion of the spinal cord.

synapse (sĭ·năps′): the microscopic space between the axon terminal of one neuron and the dendrite terminal of an adjacent one.

syncytium (sĭn·sĭ′shĭ·ŭm): a multinucleate animal tissue without internal cell boundaries.

syngamy (sĭng′gȧ·mĭ): a sexual process in which two gamete cells and their nuclei fuse.

syngen (sĭn′jĕn): a mating group (or variety) within a protozoan species; mating can occur in a syngen but not usually between syngens; a functional (as distinct from taxonomic) "species."

synthesis (sĭn′thê·sĭs) [Gr. *tithenai,* to place]: the joining of two or more molecules resulting in a single larger molecule.

systole (sĭs′tô·lē) [Gr. *stellein,* to place]: the contraction of atria or ventricles of a heart.

taiga (tī′gȧ) [Russ.]: terrestrial habitat zone characterized by large tracts of coniferous forests, long, cold winters, and short summers; found particularly in Canada, northern Europe, and Siberia.

tardigrade (tär′dĭ·grād) [L. *tardigradus,* a slow stepper]: a member of a subphylum of Oncopoda; water bears.

taxis (tăk′sĭs) [Gr. arrangement, order]: pl. ***taxes:*** orientational movement by an organism in response to a specific stimulus.

taxon (tăks′ŏn) pl. ***taxa:*** the actual organisms in a taxonomic rank.

taxonomy (tăks·ŏn′ō·mĭ) [Gr. *nomos,* law]: classification of organisms, based as far as possible on natural relationships.

tectorial membrane (tĕk·tō′rĭ·ȧl) [L. cover, covering]: component of the organ of Corti in cochlea of mammalian ear.

telencephalon (tĕl′ĕn·sĕf′ȧ·lŏn) [Gr. *enkephalos,* brain]: the vertebrate forebrain.

telolecithal (tĕl′ō·lĕs′ĭ·thăl): pertaining to eggs with large amounts of yolk accumulated in the vegetal (lower) half; e.g., as in frog eggs.

telophase (tĕl′ō·fāz): a stage in mitotic division during which two nuclei form; usually accompanied by partitioning of cytoplasm.

telson (tĕl′sŭn) [Gr. boundary, limit]: terminal body part of an arthropod (not counted as a segment).

template (tĕm′plĭt): a pattern or mold guiding the formation of a duplicate.

temporal lobe (tĕm′pō·rȧl) [L. *tempora,* the temples]: a part of the vertebrate cerebrum; contains centers for speech and hearing.

tentacle (tĕnt′ȧ·k′l) [L. *tentare,* to feel]: any of a variety of elongated, flexible, often retractile processes around or near the mouth of many animal types.

testis, pl. ***testes*** (tĕs′tĭs, -tēs) [L.]: sperm-producing organ in animals.

tetracycline (tĕt′rȧ·sī′klēn): an antibiotic produced by the bacterium *Streptomyces;* inhibits protein synthesis.

tetrad (tĕt′răd): a pair of chromosome pairs during the first metaphase of meiosis.

tetrapyrrol (tĕt′rȧ·pī′rŏl): a molecule consisting of four joined rings of carbon and nitrogen; heme and chlorophyll pigments are of this type.

tetrose (tĕt′rōs): any 4-carbon sugar.

thalamus (thăl′ȧ·mŭs) [Gr. *thalamos,* chamber]: a lateral region of the diencephalic portion of the vertebrate forebrain.

thallus (thăl′ŭs) [Gr. *thallos,* young shoot]: a plant or plantlike body without differentiation into root, stem, and leaf.

theory (thē′ō·rĭ) [Gr. *theōrein,* to look at]: a scientific statement based on experiments that verify a hypothesis; the usual last step in scientific procedure.

therapsid (thē·răp′sĭd) [Gr. *thērion,* beast]: extinct Mesozoic mammal-like reptile.

thermocline (thûr′mō·klīn): a layer in a body of water separating an upper warmer zone from a lower colder one; prevents substantial vertical mixing of the two zones.

thiamine (thī′ȧ·mĭn): a vitamin of the B complex; also known as vitamin B_1.

thigmotropism (thĭg·mŏt′rō·pĭz′m) [Gr. *thigma,* touch]: growth of organisms toward or away from contact stimuli.

thorax (thō′răks) [L.]: part of animal body between neck or head and abdomen; chest.

thrombin (thrŏm′bĭn) [Gr. *thrombos,* clot]: a clotting factor in vertebrate blood; formed from prothrombin and in turn converts fibrinogen to fibrin.

thrombokinase (thrŏm′bō·kĭn′ās): enzyme released from vertebrate blood platelets during clotting; transforms prothrombin to thrombin; also called thromboplastin.

thymidine (di, tri-) phosphates (thī′mĭ·dēn): thymine-deoxyribose-phosphate (TDP, TTP).

thymidylic acid (thī·mĭ·dĭ′lĭk): equivalent to thymine monophosphate (TMP).

thymine (thī′mēn): a pyrimidine component of nucleotides and nucleic acids.

thymosin (thī′mō·sĭn): hormone produced by thymus glands; participates in conversion of immature lymphocytes to T cells.

thymus (thī′mŭs) [Gr.]: a lymphatic gland in most young and many adult vertebrates; disappears in man at puberty; located in lower part of throat and upper part of thorax.

thyroxin (thī·rŏk′sĭn): the hormone secreted by the thyroid gland.

tissue (tĭsh′ū) [L. *texere,* to weave]: a group of cells of similar structure performing similar functions.

torus (tôr′ŭs) [L., bulge, protruberance]: a thickening in a pit membrane of tracheids.

toxin (tŏk′sĭn): any substance poisonous to living matter.

trachea, tracheal (trā′kē·ȧ) [Gr. *trachys,* rough]: (1) air-conducting tube, as in windpipe of mammals and breathing system of terrestrial arthropods; (2) adjective.

tracheid (trā′kē·ĭd): plant cell type specialized for water conduction; component of xylem.

tracheophyte, Tracheophyta (trā′kē·ō·fīt): (1) a vascular plant (one with xylem and phloem); (2) phylum name.

transamination (trăns·ăm·ĭ·nā′shŭn): transfer (usually enzymatic) of an amino group from an amino acid (or other —NH_2-containing compound) to a keto acid (or other amino group acceptor).

transduction (trăns·dŭk′shŭn): transfer of genetic material from one bacterium to another through the agency of a virus.

translocation (trăns·lō·kā′shŭn): transport of organic substances in phloem.

transpiration (trăns′spĭ·rā′shŭn) [L. *spirare,* to breathe]: evaporation of water from leaves or other exposed plant surfaces.

triclad (trī′klăd): a member of a group of free-living flatworms, characterized by a digestive cavity with three branch pouches; a planarian.

tricuspid (trī·kŭs′pĭd) [L. *cuspis,* a point]: ending in three points or flaps, as in tricuspid valve of mammalian heart.

trilobite (trī′lō·bīt): an extinct marine Paleozoic arthropod, marked by two dorsal longitudinal furrows into three parts or lobes.

triose (trī′ōs): any 3-carbon sugar.

triploid (trĭp′loid) [Gr. *triploos,* triple]: having three complete chromosome sets per cell.

trochophore (trŏk′ō·fōr): a free-swimming ciliated marine larva, characteristic of schizocoelomate animals.

trophic level (trō′fĭk): in a food chain, producers represent the lowest (first) feeding level, and the sequence of consumers that subsist on the producers and on one another represent successively higher feeding (trophic) levels.

tropic, tropism (trŏp′ĭk) [Gr. *tropē,* a turning]: (1) pertaining to behavior or action brought about by specific stimuli; for example, phototropic (light-oriented) motion, gonadotropic (stimulating the gonads); (2) noun.

trypsin (trĭp′sĭn) [Gr. *tryein,* to wear down]: enzyme promoting protein digestion; acts in small intestine, produced in pancreas as inactive trypsinogen.

tuber (tū′bẽr) [L. knob]: a short, fleshy, underground stem; e.g., potato.

tumor (tū′mẽr) [L. *tumere,* to swell]: a noninflammatory overgrowth.

tundra (to͞on′drȧ) [Russ.]: terrestrial habitat zone between taiga and polar region, characterized by absence of trees, short growing season, and frozen ground during much of the year.

Turbellaria (tûr′bĕ·lâr′ĭ·ȧ) [L. *turba,* disturbance]: the class of free-living flatworms; planarians.

turgor (tûr′gŏr): [L. *turgere,* to swell]: the distension of a cell by its fluid content.

typhlosole (tĭf′lō·sōl) [Gr. *typhlos,* blind]: dorsal fold of intestinal wall projecting into gut cavity in oligochaete annelids (earthworms).

umbilicus (ŭm·bĭl′ĭ·kŭs) [L.]: the navel of mammals; during pregnancy, an umbilical cord connects the placenta with the offspring, and the point of connection with the offspring later becomes the navel.

ungulate (ŭng′gū·lāt) [L. *ungula,* hoof]: hoofed, as in certain orders of mammals.

uracil (ū′rȧ·sĭl): a pyrimidine component of nucleotides and nucleic acids.

urea (ū·rē′ä) [Gr. *ouron,* urine]: compound formed in the mammalian liver out of ammonia and carbon dioxide and excreted by the kidneys.

ureter (ū·rē′tẽr) [Gr.]: duct carrying urine from a mammalian kidney to the urinary bladder.

urethra (ū·rē′thrȧ) [Gr.]: duct carrying urine from the urinary bladder to the outside of the body; in the males of most mammals the urethra also leads sperms to the outside during copulation.

uric acid (ūr′ĭk): end product of nitrogen metabolism in birds, insects, and certain other terrestrial animals.

uridine (di-, tri-) phosphates (ū′rĭ·dēn-): uracil-ribose-phosphates (UDP, UTP).

uridylic acid (ū·rĭ·dĭ′lĭk): equivalent to uridine monophosphate (UMP).

Urochordata (ū′rō·kôr·dā′tȧ): a subphylum of chordates; comprises the tunicates.

uropod (ū′rō·pŏd): an abdominal appendage in lobsters and other crustaceans.

uterus (ū′tẽr·ŭs) [L. womb]: enlarged region of a female reproductive duct in which animal embryo undergoes all or part of its development.

utricle (ū′trĭ·k′l) [L. *utriculus,* little bag]: portion of the vertebrate inner ear containing the receptors for dynamic body balance; the semicircular canals lead from and to the utricle.

vacuole (văk′ů·ōl) [L. *vacuus,* empty]: a small, usually spherical space in a cell, bounded by a membrane and containing fluid, solid matter, or both.
vagina (vȧ·jī′nȧ) [L. sheath]: the terminal, penis-receiving portion of a female reproductive system.
vagus (vā′gŭs) [L. wandering]: the 10th cranial nerve in vertebrates.
valence (vā′lĕns) [L. *valere,* to have power]: a measure of the bonding capacity of an atom; bonds can be electrovalent, formed through electron transfer, or covalent, formed through electron sharing.
vas deferens (văs′ dĕf′ẽr·ĕnz) sperm duct, leading from testis to genital opening.
vasectomy (vȧ·sĕk′tȯ·mĭ): surgical transsection of the vas deferens, to induce sterility.
vasomotion (văs′ȯ·mō′shŭn) [L. *vasum,* vessel]: collective term for the constriction (vasoconstriction) and dilation (vasodilation) of blood vessels.
vegetative (vĕj·ĕ·tā′tĭv): relating to nonreproductive structures or functions.
veliger (vēl′ĭ·jĕr) [L. *velum,* veil]: posttrochophoral larval stage in many mollusks.
venous (vē′nŭs) [L. *vena,* vein]: pertaining to veins; also applied to oxygen-poor, carbon dioxide-rich blood.
ventricle (vĕn′trĭ·k′l) [L. *ventriculus,* the stomach]: a heart chamber that receives blood from an atrium and pumps out blood from the heart.
vernalization (vûr′năl·ĭ·zā′shŭn) [L. *vernalis,* spring]: induction of flowering by cold (or heat) treatment of seeds or later developmental stages.
vertebrate (vûr′tĕ·brāt): possessing a vertebral column; a member of the Vertebrata, a subphylum of chordates characterized by presence of a vertebral column.
vestigial (vĕs·tĭj′ĭ·ȧl) [L. *vestigium,* footprint]: degenerate or incompletely developed, but more fully developed at an earlier stage or during the evolutionary past.
villus (vĭl′ŭs) pl. ***villi*** [L. a tuft of hair]: a microscopic fingerlike projection from the intestinal lining (mucosa) into the cavity of the mammalian gut.
virus (vī′rŭs) [L. slimy liquid, poison]: a submicroscopic noncellular particle, composed of a nucleic acid core and a protein shell; parasitic inside host cell.
viscera (vĭs′ẽr·ȧ), sing. ***viscus*** [L.]: collective term for the internal organs of an animal.
vitamin (vī tȧ·mĭn) [L. *vita,* life]: one of a class of growth factors contributing to the formation of coenzymes.
vitreous (vĭt′rē·ŭs) [L. *vitrum,* glass]: glassy; as in vitreous body, the clear transparent jelly filling the posterior part of the vertebrate eyeball.
viviparity, viviparous (vĭv′ĭ·păr′ĭ·tĭ, vī·vĭp′ȧ·rŭs) [L. *vivus,* living + *parere,* to bring forth]: (1) animal reproductive pattern in which eggs develop inside female body with nutritional and other metabolic aid of maternal parent; offspring are born as miniature adults; (2) adjective.

xanthophyll (zăn′thȯ·fĭl): one of a group of yellow pigments, members of the carotenoid group.
xerophyte (zē′rȯ·fīt): a plant adapted to live under dry or desert conditions.
Xiphosurida (zĭf′ȯ·sū′r·ĭ·dȧ) [Gr. *xiphos,* sword]: a class of chelicerate arthropods; the horseshoe crabs (*Limulus*).
xylem (zī′lĕm) [Gr. *xylon,* wood]: plant tissue that conducts water from roots upward; consists of tracheids, vessels, and other cell types; in bulk represents wood.

zoaea (zō·ē′ä) pl. ***zoaeae:*** a larval form of crustaceans.
zooid (zō′oid): an individual animal in a colony; often physically joined with fellow zooids and can be a polymorphic variant.
zooplankton (zō′ȯ·plăngk′tŏn): collective term for the nonphotosynthetic organisms in plankton; contrasts with phytoplankton.
zoospore (sō′ȯ·spōr): a motile, flagellate spore.
zygospore (zī′gȯ·spōr): an encysted zygote, as in *Spirogyra.*
zygote (zī′gōt) [Gr. *zygōtos,* paired together]: the cell resulting from sexual fusion of two gametes; a fertilized egg.

Illustration Credits

1.1 Copyright © 1979 Anne Beaman, Anthro-Photo.
BH 1 Copyright © 1951 Reader's Digest Association, Inc.

2.2 Anthro-Photo.
2.7 *A,* American Museum of Natural History: *B,* R. H. Noailles.
2.10 Richard N. Keogh, Rhode Island College.
2.11 *A,* Hal H. Harrison, Monkmeyer Press Photo Service; *B,* Hrdy, Anthro-Photo.
2.12 E. B. Small and D. S. Marszalek, from G. A. Antipa.
2.14 Adapted from D. L. Kirk, "Biology Today," fig. 2.10, p. 39, Random House, Inc., New York, 1980.
2.13 *A, B,* San Diego Zoological Society; *C,* Grant Heilman.

4.10 Adapted from C. F. Herreid, "Biology," p. 655. Copyright © 1977 Macmillan Publishing Co., Inc., New York. Used with permission of Macmillan Publishing Co., Inc.

5.2 *A,* from D. S. Luciano et al., "Human Function and Structure," p. 3, fig. 1.1. Copyright © 1978 McGraw-Hill, Inc., New York. Used with permission of McGraw-Hill Book Company.
5.3 Grant Heilman.
5.4 From W. Bloom and D. W. Fawcett, "A Textbook of Histology," 10th ed., W. B. Saunders Co., Philadelphia, 1975.
5.9, 5.10, 5.11A, 5.16 Figures by B. Tagawa from S. J. Singer, Architecture and Topography of Biologic Membranes, in G. Weissmann and R. Claiborne, eds., "Cell Membranes: Biochemistry, Cell Biology, and Pathology," pp. 37, 44, 38, 43, HP Publishing Co., Inc., New York, 1975. Used with permission.
5.11 *B,* Daniel Branton.
5.17 Omikron, Photo Researchers, Inc.
5.18 *A,* Carolina Biological Supply Company; *B,* Eric V. Gravé.
5.19 *A,* Robert Brenner, Oregon Regional Primate Research Center.
5.21 Martin M. Rotker, Taurus Photos.
5.22 *A,* adapted from E. D. DeRobertis et al., "Cell Biology," 6th ed., fig. 8.9, p. 159, W. B. Saunders, Co, Philadelphia, 1975; *B,* from D. Fawcett, "An Atlas of Ultrastructure," W. B. Saunders, Co., Philadelphia, 1966; *C,* D. S. Friend.
5.23 *B,* Dorothy R. Pitelka, University of California, Berkeley; *C,* G. A. Antipa.
5.24 *A,* Robert Brenner, Oregon Regional Primate Research Center; *B,* Martin M. Rotker, Taurus Photos.
5.25 W. G. Whaley, University of Texas.
5.26 Adapted from C. P. Swanson and P. L. Webster, "The Cell," 4th ed., p. 128. Copyright © 1977 Prentice-Hall, Inc., Englewood Cliffs, N.J. Used with permission of Prentice-Hall, Inc.
5.29 *A,* Grant Heilman; *B,* A. J. Hodge, *J. Biophys. Biochem. Cytol.,* vol. 1, p. 605.
5.31 S. E. Frederick and E. H. Newcomb, *J. Cell Biol.,* vol. 43, p. 350, 1969; *B,* Richard N. Trelease.
BH 1 *A,* Genthe, Taurus Photos.

6.8 *A, B, E,* Grant Heilman; *C,* Richard Gross; *D,* Hal. H. Harrison, Monkmeyer Press Photo Service; *F,* Leonard L. Rue, Monkmeyer Press Photo Service.
6.9 R. H. Noailles.
6.14 C. L. Curry, Pennsylvania State University.
6.18 Melvin S. Fuller, University of Georgia.
6.20 *C,* John Troughton; *D,* C. J. Hillson, Pennsylvania State University.
6.21 *C,* General Biological Supply House, Inc.
6.22 *B,* C. J. Hillson, Pennsylvania State University.
6.26 *A,* G. H. Conant, Triarch Products, Inc.; *B,* C. J. Limbach, Ripon Microslides, Inc.
6.33 *A,* Ward's Natural Science Establishment, Inc.; *B,* Gary T. Breckon.
6.41 *B,* Melvin S. Fuller, University of Georgia.

7.3 *A,* Carolina Biological Supply Company; *B, U.S.* Department of Agriculture; *C,* Ward's Natural Science Establishment, Inc.
7.9 *B,* Robert Brenner, Oregon Regional Primate Research Center.
7.10 *A,* General Biological Supply House, Inc.; *B, C,* B. J. Serber; *D,* copyright © 1980 Victor B. Eichler.
7.12 Richard N. Keogh, Rhode Island College.
7.14 Robert Brenner, Oregon Regional Primate Research Center.
7.15 *A,* Ward's Natural Science Establishment, Inc.; *B, C,* Carolina Biological Supply Company.
7.16 *A,* Mac E. Hadley, University of Arizona; *B,* R. H. Noailles; *C,* M. C. Noailles.
7.17 *A,* Carolina Biological Supply Company; *B,* from E. P. Solomon and P. W. Davis, "Understanding Human Anatomy and Physiology," fig. 8.2b, p. 211. Copyright © 1978 McGraw-Hill, Inc., New York. Used with permission of McGraw-Hill Book Company.

8.2 From E. O. Wilson et al., "Life On Earth," 2d ed., p. 674, Sinauer Associates, Inc., Stamford Conn., 1978.
8.3 *A, B,* New York Zoological Society.
8.4 American Museum of Natural History.
8.5 *A,* Standard Oil Company, New Jersey; *B,* Jeanne White, from National Audubon Society.
8.6 From E. O. Wilson et al., "Life On Earth," 2d ed., p. 687, Sinauer Associates, Inc., Stamford, Conn., 1978.
8.7 From J. M. Savage, "Evolution," 2d ed., fig. 8.2, p. 94. Copyright © 1969 Holt, Rinehart and Winston, New York. Used with permission of Holt, Rinehart and Winston.
8.18 Adapted from E. Kormondy, "Concepts in Ecology," 2d ed., Prentice-Hall, Englewood Cliffs, N.J., 1973. Data from H. T. Odum, *Ecological Monographs,* vol. 27, pp. 55–112, 1957.
8.19 Adapted from E. Kormondy, "Concepts in Ecology," 2d ed., Prentice-Hall, Englewood Cliffs, N.J., 1973. Data from R. Lindeman, *Ecology,* vol. 23, pp. 399–418, 1942.
8.21 From G. F. Gause, "The Struggle for Existence," Williams and Wilkins Company, Baltimore, 1934.
8.22 From E. O. Wilson et al., "Life On Earth," 2d ed., p. 730, Sinauer Associates, Inc., Stamford, Conn., 1978.
8.26 From D. A. MacLulich, *University of Toronto Studies,* Biological Series No. 43, 1937.
8.27 Popp, Anthro-Press.
8.28 *A,* Jeanne White, from National Audubon Society, Photo Researchers, Inc.; *B,* from E. O. Wilson et al., "Life On Earth," 2d ed., p. 489, Sinauer Associates, Inc., Stamford, Conn., 1978.
8.29 *A, B,* United Nations (FAO).
8.31 Elinor S. Beckwith.
8.33 From E. O. Wilson et al., "Life On Earth," 2d ed., p. 715, Sinauer Associates, Inc., Stamford, Conn., 1978.
8.35 *A,* from E. O. Wilson et al., "Life On Earth," 2d ed., p. 703, Sinauer Associates, Inc., Stamford, Conn., 1978; *B,* adapted from R. Ricklefs, "Ecology," fig. 43.6, p. 711, Chiron Press, Newton, Mass., 1973.
8.36 From Eugene P. Odum, "Ecology," fig. 5.8, p. 143. Copyright © 1975 Holt, Rinehart and Winston, New York. Used with permission of Holt, Rinehart and Winston.

9.4 *A,* U.S. Department of Interior—U.S. Fish and Wildlife Service; *B,* R. H. Noailles; *C,* Clay-Adams Company, Inc.
9.5 *A,* from H. Lepp, "Dynamic Earth," fig. 10.15, p. 250. Copyright © 1973 McGraw-Hill, Inc., New York. Used with permission of McGraw-Hill Book Company; *B,* Canadian Government Travel Bureau; *C,* from Weedsport quadrangle, New York, U.S. Geological Survey; *D,* David A. Rahm, "Slides for Geology," no. 250. Copyright ©

1971 McGraw-Hill, Inc., New York. Used with permission of McGraw-Hill Book Company.
9.6 John McConnell, U.S. Department of Agriculture—Soil Conservation Service.
9.7 Alan A. Amen, U.S. Department of Agriculture—Soil Conservation Service.
9.10 U.S. Forest Service.
9.11 Robert Perron, Photo Researchers, Inc.
9.14 *A*, D. P. Wilson; *B*, Boris Gueft.
9.15 General Biological Supply House, Inc.
9.17 *A, B*, Jean Carel and Larousse Publishing Company; *C, D*, D. P. Wilson.
9.18 *A–D*, American Museum of Natural History.
9.19 John S. Shelton.
9.20 Adapted from E. P. Odum, "Fundamentals of Ecology," W. B. Saunders Company, Philadelphia, 1959.
9.25 *A*, U.S. Forest Service; *B*, E. R. Kalmbach, U.S. Department of Interior—U.S. Fish and Wildlife Service.

10.9 World Health Organization, United Nations.
10.12 Date from Ratcliffe, *Nature*, vol. 215, pp. 208–210, 1967.
10.13 Adapted from J. M. Moran et al., "An Introduction to Environmental Sciences," fig. 11.12, p. 278, Little, Brown, and Company, Boston, 1973.
10.14 Adapted from D. M. Gates, "Man and His Environment: Climate," Harper & Row, New York, 1972.
10.15 *A*, U.S. Geological Survey WRD/EROS; *B*, adapted from *National Geographic*, vol. 159, no. 1, pp. 54 and 55, Jan. 1981.
10.18 F. M. Stone, U.S. Department of Agriculture—Soil Conservation Service.
10.19 D. Mason, United Nations (FAO).
10.22 U.S. Department of Agriculture.
10.24 From Baldwin and Sealfield, Great Lakes Fisheries Commission, Technical Report #3, 1962, plus supplement, 1966.
10.25 U.S. Department of Agriculture—Soil Conservation Service.
10.26 Edward B. Trovillion, U.S. Department of Agriculture—Soil Conservation Service.
10.27 *B*, Carolina Biological Supply Company.
10.28 *B*, Murray Lemon, U.S. Department of Agriculture; *C*, from Kenneth A. Wagner, Paul C. Bailey, and Glenn H. Campbell, "Under Seige; Man, Men, and Earth," fig. 9.12, p. 205 (based on tabular data from A. H. Baumhover et al., *J. Econ. Entomol.*, vol. 48, pp. 462–466, 1955). Copyright © 1973 Harper & Row, Publishers, Inc., New York. Used with permission of Harper & Row, Publishers, Inc.
BH 1 From *Chem. Eng. News*, p. 43, Nov. 22, 1976. Copyright © 1976 American Chemical Society. Used with permission of *Chem. Eng. News*.
BH 2 *A*, adapted from Anne Bastile, The Deadly Toll of Acid Rain: All of Nature Is Suffering, *Science Digest*, p. 61, Oct. 1979; *B*, from Mark Taylor, The Rain that Kills, *Wildlife in North Carolina*, p. 15, Wildlife Resources Commission of North Carolina, Nov. 1979.
BH 3 From Mark Taylor, The Rain That Kills, *Wildlife in North Carolina*, p. 12, Wildlife Resources Commission of North Carolina, Nov. 1979.
BH 4 Environmental Protection Agency.
BH 5 *A*, George Raimondi, New York City Parks, Recreation, and Cultural Administration; *B*, Elinor S. Beckwith.

11.2 *A*, E. B. Small, G. A. Antipa, and D. S. Marszalek, *Acta Protozool.*, vol. 9, pp. 275–282, 1972; *B*, H. S. Wessenberg and G. A. Antipa, *J. Protozool.*, vol. 17, pp. 250–270, 1970; *C, D*, G. A. Antipa.
11.3 Grant Heilman.
11.4 *A, B*, adapted from T. E. Weier et al., "Botany: An Introduction to Plant Science," 5th ed., figs, 9.10 and 9.11, p. 158. Copyright © 1974 John Wiley & Sons, Inc., New York. Used with permission of John Wiley & Sons, Inc.
11.7 K. Esau, from "Plant Anatomy," John Wiley & Sons, Inc., New York, 1953.
11.13 Ward's Natural Science Establishment, Inc., from model by J. F. Mueller.
BH 4 *A*, Omikron; *B*, World Health Organization, United Nations.
BH 5 From P. R. Ehrlich et al., "Ecoscience: Population, Resources, Environment," fig. 7.11, p. 310. Copyright © 1977 W. H. Freeman and Company, San Francisco.
BH 6 *A*, from P. R. Ehrlich et al., "Ecoscience: Population, Resources, Environment," fig. 7.12, p. 314. Copyright © 1977 W. H. Freeman and Company, San Francisco; *B*, from L. R. Brown, Population and Affluence: Growing Pressures on World Food Resources, *Popul. Bull.*, vol. 29, no. 2, 1973. Used with permission of the Population Reference Bureau, Inc., Washington, D.C.
BH 7 Data from J. S. Steinhart and C. E. Steinhart, *Science*, vol. 184, p. 312, April 19, 1974.
BH 8 From C. Ward, Better Diets Possible by Shifting Food Expenditure Pattern, *Family Econ. Rev.*, p. 13, Dec. 1970. Used by permission of U.S. Department of Agriculture, Consumer and Food Economic Research Division.
BH 9 From P. R. Ehrlich et al., "Ecoscience: Population, Resources, Environment," box 7.3, p. 353. Copyright © 1977 W. H. Freeman & Company, San Francisco.

12.7 H. Fernandez-Moran, *J. Cell Biol.*, vol. 22, 1964.
BH 1 Joseph Schlitz Brewing Company.
BH 3 Adapted from diagram from Falstaff Brewing Company.
BH 4 Wide World Photos.
BH 5 Anheuser-Busch Brewing Company.
BH 6 Anheuser-Busch Brewing Company.
BH 7 Anheuser-Busch Brewing Company.

13.2 *A*, adapted from Stephen L. Wolfe, "Biology of the Cell," 1st ed., fig. 7.2. Copyright © 1972 by Wadsworth Publishing Company, Inc., Belmont, Calif. Used with permission of Wadsworth Publishing Company, Inc.; *B*, from T. E. Weier, C. R. Stocking, and L. K. Shamway, *Brookhaven Symp. Biol.*, vol. 19, p. 371, 1961.
13.6 *A*, H. T. Horner, Jr.
13.13 *A, B*, from William T. Keeton, "Biological Science," 3d ed., fig. 4.15, p. 157. Copyright © 1980 W. W. Norton & Company, Inc., New York. Used with permission of W. W. Norton & Company, Inc. Illustrated by Paula DiSanto Bensadoun.

14.4 Adapted from J. Watson, "Molecular Biology of the Gene," 3d ed., fig. 9.27, p. 235, Benjamin/Cummings Publishing Company, Inc., Menlo Park, Calif., 1976.
14.5 *A*, adapted from J. A. Huberman and A. Riggs, *J. Mol. Biol.*, vol. 32, p. 340; *B*, C. S. Newton.
14.7 Adapted from J. Watson, "Molecular Biology of the Gene," 3d ed., fig. 11.16, p. 299, Benjamin/Cummings Publishing Company, Inc., Menlo Park, Calif., 1976.
14.8 O. L. Miller, Jr.
14.10 *B*, adapted from W. DeWitt, "Biology of the Cell: An Evolutionary Approach," W. B. Saunders Company, Philadelphia, 1977.

15.11 O. L. Miller, Jr.
15.13 *A*, O. L. Miller, Jr., B. H. Hamkalb, and C. A. Thomas, Jr., *Science*, vol. 169, pp. 392–395, 1970.
15.14 *A*, Lester V. Bergman & Associates, Inc.; *B*, G. W. F. Engler, from G. F. Bahr.
15.16 *A*, W. Beerman.
15.21 *A–E*, Bureau of Human Nutrition and Home Economics.

16.5 C. H. Muller.
16.7 Boyce Thompson Institute for Plant Research.
16.11 Melvin S. Fuller, University of Georgia.
16.12 *A*, Carolina Biological Supply Company; *B, C*, General Biological Supply House, Inc.
16.14 *A*, K. Esau, "Plant Anatomy," John Wiley & Sons, Inc., New York, 1953.
16.22 Boyce Thompson Institute for Plant Research.
16.23 Monsanto Chemical Company.

17.2 After J. Morgan.
17.5 Adapted from R. Eckert and D. Randell, "Animal Physiology," fig. 11.47, p. 387. Copyright © 1978 W. H. Freeman and Company.
17.6 Ward's Natural Science Establishment, Inc.

17.7 *A*, Ward's Natural Science Establishment, Inc.
17.8 *A, B*, Mac E. Hadley.
17.10 *A*, Fuad A. Ashkar; *B*, Martin M. Rotker, Taurus Photo.
17.11 L. E. Perkins, Natural History Photographic Agency.
BH 1 *A*, Roger Guillemin; *B*, A. V. Schally.

18.3 From Emil Bernstein, *Science*, vol. 173, cover, Aug. 24, 1971. Copyright © 1971 Association for the Advancement of Science.
18.6 From R. J. Dubos, Rockerfeller Institute, and R. J. Dubos and J. G. Hirsch, "Bacterial and Mycotic Infections of Man," 4th ed., J. B. Lippincott Company, Philadelphia, 1965.
18.13 *B*, B. J. Serber.
18.16 *A*, Rhode Island Hospital Photographic Department; *B*, Boris Gueft.
18.14 From D. S. Luciano et al., "Human Function and Structure," fig. 2.2, p. 44. Copyright © 1978 McGraw-Hill, Inc., New York. Used with permission of McGraw-Hill Book Company.
18.21 *A–C*(1), American Heart Association; *A–C*(2), from P. W. Davis and E. P. Solomon, "The World of Biology," fig. 6.9, p. 132. Copyright © 1974 McGraw-Hill, Inc., New York. Used with permission of McGraw-Hill Book Company.
18.22 From "McGraw-Hill Encyclopedia of Science and Technology," 3d ed. Copyright © 1971 McGraw-Hill Inc., New York. Used with permission of McGraw-Hill Book Company.
18.24 *A*, Ward's Natural Science Establishment, Inc.; *B, C*, from D. S. Luciano et al., "Human Function and Structure," figs., 17.1, 17.9 pp. 462, 468. Copyright © 1978 McGraw-Hill, Inc., New York. Used with permission of McGraw-Hill Book Company.
18.25 Bell Telephone Laboratories, Inc.
BH 1 Rohlich et al., *J. Cell Biol.*, vol. 51, pp. 465–483, fig. 3, 1971.
BH 2 *A*, Rohlich et al., *J. Cell Biol.*, vol. 51, pp. 465–483, fig. 5, 1971; *B*, adapted from R. D. Dyson, "Cell Biology: A Molecular Approach," 2d ed., fig. 10.39, p. 479, Allyn and Bacon, Inc., Boston, 1978.

19.1 *B*, Ward's Natural Science Establishment, Inc.; *D*, Jan Cammermeyer, *Z. Anat. Entwickl.*, vol. 124, pp. 543–561, 1965.
19.4 *C*, from D. S. Luciano et al., "Human Function and Structure," fig. 8.10, p. 252. Copyright © 1978 McGraw-Hill, Inc., New York. Used by Permission of McGraw-Hill Book Company.
19.11 *A*, from D. S. Luciano et al., "Human Function and Structure," fig. 4.23A, p. 108. Copyright © 1978 McGraw-Hill, Inc., New York. Used with permission of McGraw-Hill Book Company; *B*, from W. F. Windle, "Textbook of Histology," 5th ed. Copyright © 1976 McGraw-Hill, Inc., New York. Used with permission of McGraw-Hill Book Company.
19.12 From D. S. Luciano et al., "Human Function and Structure," fig. 8.17, p. 260. Copyright © 1978 McGraw-Hill, Inc., New York. Used with permission of McGraw-Hill Book Company.
19.16 *A*, Carolina Biological Supply Company; *B*, William Montagna, Oregon Regional Primate Research Center.
19.18 *B*, Ward's Natural Science Establishment, Inc., *C*, J. E. Hawkins, Jr., Kresge Hearing Research Institute, University of Michigan Medical School.
19.19 *A*, General Biological Supply House, Inc.
19.21, 19.22 Adapted from D. S. Luciano et al., "Human Function and Structure," figs. 9.16, 9.17, pp. 287 and 288. Copyright © 1978 McGraw-Hill, Inc., New York. Used with permission of McGraw-Hill Book Company.
19.25 Ward's Natural Science Establishment, Inc.
19.30 Adapted from D. S. Luciano et al., "Human Function and Structure," fig. 5.5, p. 117. Copyright © 1978 McGraw-Hill, Inc., New York. Used with permission of McGraw-Hill Book Company.
19.33 Adapted from W. Bloom and D. W. Fawcett, "Textbook of Histology," 10th ed., W. B. Saunders Co., Philadelphia, 1975.
19.34 Adapted from L. D. Peachey, "Muscle and Motility, Biocore Unit XVIII," fig. 26, p. 24. Copyright © 1974 McGraw-Hill, Inc., New York. Used with permission of McGraw-Hill Book Company.
BH 1 *A, B*, adapted from D. S. Luciano et al., "Human Function and Structure," figs. 11.3, 8.11A, pp. 331 and 254. Copyright © 1978 McGraw-Hill, Inc., New York. Used with permission of McGraw-Hill Book Company.
BH 2 Herkenham and Pert, *Proc. Nat. Academy of Science*, in press.
BH 4 Wide World Photos.

20.1 *B*, from C. A. Oviatt, *Behaviour*, vol. 33, no. 1–2, pp. 52–57, 1969; *C*, American Museum of Natural History.
20.2 Ringling Bros. and Barnum & Bailey Circus photo.
20.3 *B*, adapted from E. O. Wilson et al., "Life On Earth," 1st ed., fig. 2, p. 582, Sinauer Associates, Inc., Stamford, Conn., 1973.
20.5 Andrew Lewis Botwick, Monkmeyer Press Photo.
20.6 N. Tinbergen.
20.7 *A–C*, after N. Tinbergen; *D*, from W. Wickler, "Mimicry in Plants and Animals," paperback ed. Copyright © 1968 McGraw-Hill, Inc., New York. Used with permission of McGraw-Hill Book Company.
20.8 *A*, from G. W. Barlow, Ethology, in "McGraw-Hill Yearbook of Science and Technology." Copyright © 1968 McGraw-Hill, Inc., New York. Used with permission of McGraw-Hill Book Company; *B*, from E. O. Wilson et al., "Life on Earth," 2d ed. fig. 4, p. 456, Sinauer Associates, Inc., Stamford, Conn., 1978.
20.9 *A*, Leonard L. Rue, from National Audubon Society; *B*, From E. Hess, Imprinting in Animals, *Sci. Am.*, March 1958, p. 81. Copyright © 1958 Scientific American, Inc. Used with permission.
20.10 *A*, H. Kacher.
20.13 Adapted from K. Hoffman, "Experimental Manipulation of the Orientation Clock in Birds, *Cold Spring Harbor Laboratory Quantitative Biology*, vol. 25, pp. 379–387, 1960.

21.1 Leonard L. Rue, DPI.
21.2 From E. O. Wilson et al., "Life On Earth," 1st ed., fig. 9, p. 481, Sinauer Associates, Inc., Stamford, Conn., 1973.
21.3 *A*, U.S. Department of Agriculture; *B*, R. H. Noailles; *C*, Australian News and Information Bureau.
21.4 U.S. Department of Agriculture.
21.5 *A–D*, copyright © Walt Disney Productions.
21.7 *B*, from G. W. Barlow, Animal Behaviour II, "Biocore Unit XX," fig. 6, p. 8. Copyright © 1974 McGraw-Hill Inc., New York. Used with permission of McGraw-Hill Book Company; *C*, Phyllis J. Dolhinow.
21.8 Irven DeVore.
21.9 G. W. Barlow, *Anim. Behav.*, vol. 22, p. 876ff, 1974.
21.10 A. A. Myrberg, Jr., *Behaviour*, vol. 41, pts 3, 4, pp. 207–231, fig. 3, 1972.

22.2 *A*, Ada L. Olins, *Science*, vol. 183, pp. 330–332, Jan. 25, 1974; *B*, after an illustration by B. Ramsay Shaw presented in 1976.
22.4 *A, F*, Copyright © 1980 Victor B. Eichler; *B–E*, General Biological Supply House, Inc.
22.6 *A–F*, R. G. Kessel and G. Shih.
22.7 *A, B*, Yukio Hiramoto.
22.8 *A*, after a photograph by H. Mollenhauer; *B*, Carolina Biological Supply Company.
22.10 *A*, Melvin S. Fuller, University of Georgia; *B, C*, D. P. Wilson.
22.13 From P. Abramoff and R. G. Thompson, "Laboratory Studies in Biology," 872, fig. 27.2, p. 4. Copyright © 1972 W. H. Freeman and Company, San Francisco.
22.16 General Biological Supply House, Inc.
22.17 R. H. Noailles.
22.27 *B*, David Tarin.
BH 1 *B*, National Cancer Institute, N.I.H.

23.3 *A*, Carolina Biological Supply Company; *B*, Melvin S. Fuller, University of Georgia.
23.5 Runk/Schoenberger, Grant Heilman.
23.6 Adapted from T. E. Weier et al., "Botany: An Introduction to Plant Science," 5th ed., fig. 27.29, p.

568. Copyright © 1974 John Wiley & Sons, Inc., New York. Used with permission of John Wiley & Sons, Inc.
23.10 Len West, Rhode Island College.
23.11 *A, D,* Melvin S. Fuller, University of Georgia; *C,* Ward's Natural Science Establishment, Inc.
23.12 *B,* Melvin S. Fuller.
23.15 *B,* Hans-Erik Wennberg, Rhode Island College.
23.16 *A,* Ward's Natural Science Establishment, Inc.
23.19 J. Limbach, Ripon Microslides, Inc.
23.20 *B, D,* Melvin S. Fuller, University of Georgia.
23.21 Sid Carson, McGraw-Hill Book Company.
23.22 *A,* Elinor S. Beckwith.
BH 1 From W. Hofmeister (translated by Frederick Currey), "On the Germination, Development, and Fructification of the Higher Cryptogamia and on the Fructification of the Coniferae," published for the Ray Society by Robert Hardwicke, London, 1862. Courtesy The New York Public Library.

24.1 *B, C,* General Biological Supply House, Inc.
24.2 *A,* Landrum B. Shettles, M.D.
24.3 *A,* Ruda Zukal, TFH Photo; *B,* Lynwood M. Chace; *C,* David Rentz, Academy of Natural Sciences, Philadelphia.
24.6 *A,* G. Karp and N. J. Berrill, "Development," 2d ed., fig. 4.1, p. 101. Copyright © 1980 McGraw-Hill, Inc., New York. Used with permission of McGraw-Hill Book Company.
24.9 J. VanWormer.
24.11, 24.12, 24.14 Adapted from D. S. Luciano et al., "Human Function and Structure," figs. 21.14, 21.15, and 21.13, pp. 634, 633. Copyright © 1978 McGraw-Hill, Inc., New York. Used with permission of McGraw-Hill Book Company.
24.20 Roberts Rugh, "Experimental Embryology," Harcourt, Brace & World, Inc.
24.22 S. R. Detwiler and R. H. Van Dyke, *J. Exp. Zool.,* vol. 69, p. 157, fig. 16.

25.5 Carnegie Institution of Washington.

26.1 Adapted from D. Hershey, "Lifespan and Factors Affecting It," fig. 15, p. 27, 1974. Used with permission of Charles C Thomas, Publisher, Springfield, Ill.
26.2 Wide World Photos.
26.3 From G. J. Thornbecke, ed., "Biology of Aging and Development," fig. 1, p. 5, FASEB, 1975. Used with permission.
26.4 *A,* Robert Brenner, Oregon Regional Primate Research Center; *B,* from D. Hershey, "Lifespan and Factors Affecting It," fig. 34, p. 56, 1974. Used with permission of Charles C Thomas, Publisher, Springfield, Ill.
26.6 Robert J. Hay, American Type Culture Collection.
26.7 From J. Kimball, "Biology," 4th ed., fig. 23.9, p. 407, Addison-Wesley Publishing Company, Inc., Reading, Mass., 1978.
26.8 From D. Hershey, "Lifespan and Factors Affecting It," fig. 31, p. 43, 1974. Used with permission of Charles C Thomas, Publisher, Springfield, Ill.
26.9 *A,* adapted from W. Bloom and D. W. Fawcett, "A Textbook of Histology," 10th ed., W. B. Saunders Co., Philadelphia, 1975; *B,* R. O. Greep and L. Weiss, "Histology," 4th ed., fig. 3.12. Copyright © 1977 McGraw-Hill, Inc., New York. Used with permission of McGraw-Hill Book Company.
26.10 From D. Hershey, "Lifespan and Factors Affecting It," fig. 13, p. 21, 1974. Used with permission of Charles C Thomas, Publisher, Springfield, Ill.
26.11 *A,* from Special Publications and Editing Division, U.S. Department of Energy, Technical Information center; *B,* H. J. Curtis.
26.14 *A, B,* after J. W. Saunders and J. F. Fallon, *25th Symp. Soc. Dev. Biol.,* p. 293, 1966.
26.16 *A, B,* From D. Hershey, "Lifespan and Factors Affecting It," figs. 41, 42, p. 95, 1974. Used with permission of Charles C Thomas, Publisher, Springfield, Ill.
26.17 From D. Hershey, "Lifespan and Factors Affecting It," fig. 43, p. 105, 1974. Used with permission of Charles C Thomas, Publisher, Springfield, Ill.
26.18 G. Gregoriadis, *New Eng. J. Med.,* vol. 295, p. 704, 1976.

27.13 Richard C. Finke, from National Audubon Society, Photo Researchers, Inc.
27.20 *A,* Emily Harste.
27.21 Carolina Biological Supply Company.
27.24 March of Dimes.
27.29 From M. F. Perutz, "The Hemoglobin Molecule," *Sci. Am.,* vol. 211, no. 5, Nov. 1964. Copyright © 1964 Scientific American, Inc. Used with permission.
BH 1 *A,* R. L. Phillips and A. M. Irb, *Can. J. Genet. Cytol.,* vol. 9, pp. 766–775, 1967.

28.5 *A,* A. K. Kleinschmidt et al., *Biochim. Biophys. Acta,* vol. 16, pp. 857–864, 1962; *C,* William Margaretten and Councilman Morgan; *D,* R. W. G. Wyckoff, "Electron Microscopy," Interscience Publishers, Inc., New York, 1949.
28.8 Robert M. Brenner, Oregon Regional Primate Research Center.
28.10 *B,* John Coleman, Division of Biological and Medical Sciences, Brown University.

29.3 *A, B,* American Museum of Natural History.
29.5 From W. D. Stansfield, "The Science of Evolution," fig. 4.12, p. 87. Copyright © 1977 W. D. Stansfield. Used with permission of Macmillan Publishing Co., Inc., New York.
29.9 New York Zoological Society.
29.11 *A,* New York Zoological Society; *B,* W. C. Galinat, University of Massachusetts, and *Mass. Agric. Exp. Stn. Bull.,* 577, 1969.
29.17 From D. P. Barash, "Sociobiology and Behaviour," fig. 3.3A, p. 46, Elsevier-NDU, Amsterdam, Netherlands, 1977. Used with permission.
29.18 Joy Spurr.
29.20 From D. P. Barash, "Sociobiology and Behaviour," fig. 10.1, p. 285, Elsevier-NDU, Amsterdam, Netherlands, 1977. Used with permission.

30.1 National Aeronautics and Space Administration.
30.5 Sidney W. Fox.
30.7 E. S. Barghoorn.
30.11 Adapted from J. W. Schopf, "The Evolution of Earliest Cells," *Sci. Am.,* Sept. 1978. Copyright © 1978 Scientific American, Inc. Used with permission.
30.13 C. F. Robinow and J. Hiller and Society of American Bacteriologists.
30.17 *A, B,* Melvin S. Fuller, University of Georgia.
30.18 Copyright © 1980 Victor B. Eichler.
30.20 David Silverman.
BH 1 J. E. McDade, Center for Disease Control.
BH 2, BH 3 Modified from D. W. Fraser and J. E. McDade, *Sci. Am.,* Oct., 1979, pp. 88, 89.
BH 4 J. E. McDade, Center for Disease Control.

31.4 *A,* Melvin S. Fuller, University of Georgia.
31.6 *B,* Runk/Schoenberger, Grant Heilman.
31.7 Melvin S. Fuller, University of Georgia.
31.8 *B,* John T. Bonner, *J. Exp. Zool.,* vol. 106, p. 7.
31.10 *B,* Carolina Biological Supply Company; *C,* Copyright © 1980 Victor B. Eichler.
31.13 Eric V. Gravé.
31.15 *A,* Carolina Biological Supply Company; *B,* Maria A. Rudzinska, *J. Gerontol.,* vol. 16, p. 213, 1961.
31.16 *B,* Carolina Biological Supply Company.
31.17 *A,* Charles L. Curry, Pennsylvania State University; *B,* Melvin S. Fuller, University of Georgia; *C,* A. J. Shatkin and E. L. Tatum, *J. Biophys. Biochem. Cytol.,* vol. 6, p. 423.
31.18 R. Emerson, University of California, Berkeley and *Mycologia,* vol. 50, p. 589.
31.19 *A, B,* U.S. Department of Agriculture.
31.20 *A, B,* General Biological Supply House, Inc.; *C, D,* C. L. Fergus, Pennsylvania State University.
31.21 *A,* Jean Carel; *B,* Melvin S. Fuller, University of Georgia.
31.22 *A, C,* Melvin S. Fuller, University of Georgia, *B,* C. M. Christensen, University of Minnesota, and University of Minnesota Press.
31.23 *B,* Ward's Natural Science Establishment, Inc.; *C, D,* R. A. Samson.
31.25 *A, B,* Carolina Biological Supply Company; *C, D,* General Biological Supply House, Inc.

32.1 *A*, Tunk, Maine Publicity Bureau; *B*, General Biological Supply House, Inc.; *C*, Grant Heilman.
32.2 Ray, Photo Researchers, Inc.
32.3 *A*, Melvin S. Fuller, University of Georgia; *B*, General Biological Supply House, Inc.; *C*, Carolina Biological Supply Company.
32.5 *A*, *C*, Melvin S. Fuller, University of Georgia; *B*, General Biological Supply House, Inc.
32.6 *A*, *C*, *D*, Melvin S. Fuller, University of Georgia; *B*, General Biological Supply House, Inc.
32.13 *A*, Runk/Schoenberger, Grant Heilman; *B*, American Museum of Natural History.
32.16 *A*, Chicago Natural History Museum.
32.17 *A*, *B*, Chicago Natural History Museum.
32.18 *A*, Melvin S. Fuller, University of Georgia; *B*, Jean Carel and Larousse Publishing Company; *C*, R. H. Mohlenbrock, *Amer. Fern J.*, vol. 50, p. 181.
32.19 Jean Carel and Larousse Publishing Company.
32.21 *A*, Walter H. Hodge; *B*, Melvin S. Fuller, University of Georgia; *C*, Paul Popper, Ltd.
32.22 *A*, from W. Stewart and T. Delevoryas, The Medullosan Pteridosperms, *Bot. Rev.*, vol. 22, no. 1, pp. 44–80, Jan. 1956; *B*, American Museum of Natural History.
32.23 *A*, *B*, from T. E. Weier et al., "Botany: An Introduction to Plant Biology," 5th ed., fig. 30.20, p. 629. Copyright © 1974 John Wiley & Sons, Inc., Publishers, New York. After A. S. Foster and E. M. Gifford, "Comparative Morphology of Vascular Plants," 1st ed., W. H. Freeman and Company, San Francisco, and D. H. Scott, "Studies in Fossil Botany," Adam and Charles Black, London, 1920.
32.24 Walter H. Hodge.
32.25 New York Botanical Garden.
32.26 *A–D*, Melvin S. Fuller, University of Georgia.
32.27 *A*, *B*, U.S. Department of Agriculture; *C*, Brooklyn Botanical Garden.
32.28 *A*, Allan D. Cruickshank, from National Audubon Society, Photo researchers, Inc.

33.8 *A*, Runk/Schoenberger, Grant Heilman; *B*, *C*, American Museum of Natural History.
33.9 D. P. Wilson.
33.12 Copyright © 1980 Victor B. Eichler.
33.13 *B*, M. C. Noailles.
33.14 *A*, D. P. Wilson; *B*, Carolina Biological Supply Company; *C*, Roman Vishniac.
33.15 *B*, *C*, D. P. Wilson.
33.16 *A*, Runk/Shoenberger, Grant Heilman.
33.17 Richard N. Keogh, Rhode Island College.
33.19 *A*, Runk/Schoenberger, Grant Heilman.
33.20 Ward's Natural Science Establishment, Inc.
33.21 *A–C*, General Biological Supply House, Inc.
33.22 *A*, D. P. Wilson.
33.23 *A*, M. C. Noailles.
33.25 *A*, W. F. Mai, Cornell University; *B*, Carolina Biological Supply Company.
33.26 *A*, Ward's Natural Science Establishment, Inc.; *B*, United Nations.

34.2 *B*, R. H. Noailles; *C*, General Biological Supply House, Inc.
34.3 *A*, General Biological Supply House, Inc.
34.4 *B*, D. P. Wilson.
34.5 *B*, Carolina Biological Supply Company; *C*, Australian News and Information Bureau.
34.7 *A*, American Museum of Natural History.
34.8 *B*, D. P. Wilson.
34.10 *A*, *B*, R. H. Noailles; *C*, D. P. Wilson.
34.11 *A*, *B*, Runk/Schoenberger, Grant Heilman.
34.13 *A*, American Museum of Natural History.
34.14 *A*, Carolina Biological Supply Company; *B*, R. H. Noailles.
34.15 *B*, American Museum of Natural History.
34.16 *A*, R. H. Noailles.
34.17 American Museum of Natural History.
34.18 *B*, D. P. Wilson.
34.19 *A*, R. H. Noailles.
34.21 American Museum of Natural History.
34.22 *A*, Lynwood M. Chace; *B*, General Biological Supply House, Inc.; *C*, Carolina Biological Supply Company.
34.23 *B*, Ward's Natural Science Establishment, Inc.
34.24 Grant Heilman.
34.25 U.S. Department of Agriculture.
34.26 *C*, Paul Popper, Ltd.
34.29 Lynwood M. Chace.
34.30 Dalton, Natural History Photographic Agency.
34.31 *A*, Leonard L. Rue; *B*, R. H. Noailles; *C*, Ward's Natural Science Establishment, Inc.; *E*, General Biological Supply House, Inc.; *F*, *G*, Lynwood M. Chace.
34.32 *B*, American Museum of Natural History.
34.34 *A*, M. C. Noailles; *B*, D. P. Wilson.
35.35 *A*, R. H. Noailles; *B*, Hal H. Harri- *C*, American Museum of Natural History; *D*, U.S. Department of Agriculture; *E*, R. H. Noailles.
34.36 *A*, R. H. Noailles; *B*, Carolina Biological Supply Company.
34.37 U.S. Department of Agriculture.
34.38 *A*, Carolina Biological Supply Company; *B*, Eric V. Gravé; *C*, *F*, Leonard L. Rue and J. Focht; *D*, R. H. Noailles; *E*, U.S. Department of Agriculture.
34.39 *A*, M. C. Noailles; *B*, Lynwood M. Chace; *C*, *D*, R. H. Noailles; *E*, U.S. Department of Agriculture; *F*, Natural History Photographic Agency.
34.40 *C*, John L. Schumacher; *D*, R. H. Noailles; *E*, *F*, Carolina Biological Supply Company.
34.41 *A*, Lynwood M. Chace.
34.42 *C*, Ward's Natural Science Establishment, Inc.
34.44 *A*, Carolina Biological Supply Company; *B*, U.S. Department of Agriculture.
34.45 *A*, U.S. Department of Agriculture; *B*, Lynwood M. Chace; *C*, *D*, R. H. Noailles.
34.47 From Karen Arms and Pamela S. Camp, "Biology," fig. 30.24, p. 502. Copyright © 1979 Holt, Rinehart and Winston, New York. Used with permission of Holt, Rinehart and Winston.
34.48 Adapted from H. A. Schneiderman and L. I. Gilbert, *Science*, vol. 143, pp. 325–333, 1964. Copyright © 1964 American Association for the Advancement of Science.

35.4 *A*, *B*, Carolina Biological Supply Company; *C*, U.S. Fish and Wildlife Service; *D*, Runk/Schoenberger, Grant Heilman.
35.6 D. P. Wilson.
35.8 *A*, American Museum of Natural History; *B*, R. H. Noailles.
35.9 *A*, *C*, American Museum of Natural History; *B*, Paul B. Green.
35.11 *B*, General Biological Supply House, Inc.; *C*, American Museum of Natural History.
35.12 *A*, D. P. Wilson; *B*, Natural History Photographic Agency.
35.13 *A*, *B*, D. P. Wilson.
35.16 William Montagna, Oregon Regional Primate Research Center.
35.19 *A*, R. H. Noailles; *B*, General Biological Supply House, Inc.
35.20 *A*, *B*, Carolina Biological Supply Company.
35.21 *A*, Robert C. Hermes, from National Audubon Society. Photo Researchers, Inc.; *B*, Karl H. Maslowski, Photo researchers, Inc.
35.22 *A*, *B*, American Museum of Natural History.
35.23 *A*, R. H. Noailles; *B*, Natural History Photographic Agency.
35.26 *A*, *B*, Carolina Biological Supply Company; *C*, Lynwood M. Chace.
35.27 *A*, Carolina Biological Supply Company; *C*, Ward's Natural Science Establishment, Inc.
35.28 *A*, American Museum of Natural History; *B*, Paul Popper, Ltd; *C*, M. Woodbridge Williams.
35.29 *A*, *B*, Australian News and Information Bureau; *C*, Lynwood M. Chace.
35.30 *B*, Ward's Natural Science Establishment, Inc.
35.32 *A*, *B*, Australian News and Information Bureau.
35.33 *A*, *B*, American Museum of Natural History.
35.35 *A*, R. H. Noailles; *B*, Hal H. Harrison, Grant Heilman; *C*, Copyright © Paolo Koch, Photo Researchers, Inc.; *D*, Grant Heilman.
BH 1 Adapted from *National Geographic*, vol. 156, p. 686, Nov. 1979.
BH 2 *A*, Jim Childress, University of California, Santa Barbara, Woods Hole Oceanographic Institution; *B*, Jon Corliss, Oregon State University, Woods Hole Oceanographic Institution; *C*, Woods Hole Oceanographic Institution; *D*, Jack Donnelly, Woods Hole Oceanographic Institution.
BH 3 M. L. Jones, National Museum of Natural History, Woods Hole Oceanographic Institution.

36.5 *A,* American Museum of Natural History; *B,* Chicago Natural History Museum.
36.6 *A, B,* Chicago Natural History Museum; *C,* American Museum of Natural History.
36.7 *A, B,* American Museum of Natural History.
36.9 *A, B,* American Museum of Natural History.
36.10 *A, B,* American Museum of Natural History.
36.11 *A,* American Museum of Natural History; *B,* Chicago Natural History Museum.
36.13 American Museum of Natural History.
36.14 *A, B,* Chicago Natural History Museum.
36.15 *A,* American Museum of Natural History; *B,* General Biological Supply House, Inc.
36.16 American Museum of Natural History.
36.17 American Museum of Natural History.
36.18 After John Napier, "The Roots of Mankind," Smithsonian Institution Press, 1970.
36.20 *A, B,* American Museum of Natural History.
36.21 *A,* D. J. Chivers, Anthro-Photo; *B,* Paul Popper, Ltd.
36.22 *A,* Lynwood M. Chace; *B,* Irven DeVore, Anthro-Photo.
36.23 Copyright © 1980 The New York Times Company. Used with permission.
36.24 *A,* W. Sushitsky; *B,* American Museum of Natural History; *C,* Richard Wrangham, Anthro-Photo; *D,* D. J. Chivers, Anthro-Photo.
36.25 Tom McHugh, Photo Researchers, Inc.
36.26 From Sherwood L. Washburn, The Evolution of Man, *Sci. Am.*, p. 204, Sept. 1978. Copyright © 1978 Scientific American, Inc. Used with permission.
36.28 Hrdy, Anthro-Photo.
36.29 Left top, from Exploring Man's Past, *Newsweek,* p. 60, May 21, 1979; left bottom, from R. M. Tullar, "The Human Species," fig. 6.12A, p. 169. Copyright © 1977 McGraw-Hill Inc., New York. Used with permission of McGraw-Hill Book Company; right, British Museum (Natural History).
36.31 Tom McHugh, Photo Researchers, Inc.
36.32 From R. M. Tullar, "The Human Species," fig. 1.12, p. 23. Copyright © 1977 McGraw-Hill Inc. Used with permission of McGraw-Hill Book Company.
36.33 From R. M. Tullar, "The Human Species," fig. 6.21, p. 183. Copyright © 1977 McGraw-Hill Inc., New York. Used with permission of McGraw-Hill Book Company.
36.34 After F. Bordes, "The Old Stone Age." Copyright © 1968 McGraw-Hill Inc., New York. Used with permission of McGraw-Hill Book Company.
36.35 *A* (left), from R. M. Tullar, "The Human Species," fig. 6.18, p. 180. Copyright © 1977 McGraw-Hill Inc., New York. Used with permission of McGraw-Hill Book Company; *A* (right), from Exploring Man's Past, *Newsweek,* p. 60, May 21, 1979; *B* (left), E. L. Simons; *B* (right) from Human Evolution, *Newsweek,* p. 60, May 21, 1979.
36.36 *A–C,* American Museum of Natural History.
36.37 From Henry de Lumley, Muséum National d'Histoire Naturelle.
36.38 *A,* from R. M. Tullar, "The Human Species," fig. 7.6, p. 197. Copyright © McGraw-Hill Inc., New York. Used with permission of McGraw-Hill Book Company; *B,* Zbigniew Rajchel.
36.39 *A, B,* American Museum of Natural History; *C,* from R. M. Tullar, "The Human Species," fig. 7.11, p. 204. Copyright © 1977 McGraw-Hill Inc., New York. Used with permission of McGraw-Hill Book Company.
36.40 *A,* American Museum of Natural History; *B,* Chicago Natural History Museum.

Index

Boldface page numbers refer to illustrations or tables.